ISTEP+ Pacing

Glencoe/McGraw-Hill's ***Indiana Math Connects,*** Course 2 Student Edition has a 3-part organization that is front-loaded for the ISTEP+.

1. **Start Smart** gets students ready for grade 7 with a review of key Indiana Academic Standards from grade 6 that are prerequisites for grade 7.
2. **Chapters 1–12** Each chapter has coherent groups of lessons focused on related grade 7 Indiana Academic Standards.
3. **Get Ready for the ISTEP+** provides students with practice of standards-based multiple-choice, gridded-response, constructed-response, and extended-response questions.

The organization and pacing of ***Indiana Math Connects*** helps ensure in-depth coverage of all grade 7 standards, success on the ISTEP+, and a good start for grade 8. Refer to the pacing guide on pages xii–xv for more information regarding the pacing of ***Indiana Math Connects,*** Course 2.

The School Year

About 135 School Days

Teach **Start Smart** and core lessons from **Chapters 1–12**. Use **Get Ready for the ISTEP+** to prepare students for success on the ISTEP+.

ISTEP+

About 30 School Days

Teach Optional Lessons and **Unit Projects.**

Pacing Guide

Each chapter includes multiple days for review and assessment.

Start Smart	optional
Chapter 1	15 days
Chapter 2	10 days
Chapter 3	11 days
Chapter 4	12 days
Chapter 5	7 days
Chapter 6	16 days
Chapter 7	11 days
Chapter 8	17 days
Chapter 9	11 days
Chapter 10	9 days
Chapter 11	9 days
Chapter 12	7 days
Total	135 days
ISTEP+	
Optional Lessons	25 days
Unit Projects	5 days

Authors

Roger Day, Ph.D.
Mathematics Department Chair
Pontiac Township High School
Pontiac, Illinois

Patricia Frey, Ed.D.
Math Coordinator at Westminster Community Charter School
Buffalo, New York

Arthur C. Howard
Mathematics Teacher
Houston Christian High School
Houston, Texas

Deborah A. Hutchens, Ed.D.
Principal
Chesapeake, Virginia

Beatrice Luchin
Mathematics Consultant
League City, Texas

Kay McClain, Ed.D.
Assistant Professor
Vanderbilt University
Nashville, Tennessee

IN Math Online Meet the Authors at glencoe.com

Contents in Brief

About the Cover

Nothing beats the thrill of a giant waterslide! Next time you are at a water park, think about math. The waterslide is exciting because there is a big vertical drop in a small horizontal distance. In math, that is expressed as a ratio $\frac{\text{rise}}{\text{run}}$, which is called slope.

You'll learn more about slope in Chapter 6.

Cover image photographed on location courtesy Busch Gardens/Adventure Island, Tampa, Florida. Credit Richard Hutchings.

About the Graphics

Twisted torus. Created with *Mathematica.*
A torus with a rose-shaped cross section is constructed. Then the cross section is rotated around its center as it moves along a circle to form a twisted torus. For more information, and for programs to construct such graphics, see: www.wolfram.com/r/textbook.

The McGraw-Hill Companies

Glencoe

Send all inquiries to:
Glencoe/McGraw-Hill
8787 Orion Place
Columbus, OH 43240-4027

ISBN: 978-0-07-892338-8 *(Student Edition)*
MHID: 0-07-892338-7 *(Student Edition)*
ISBN: 978-0-07-892342-5 *(Teacher Edition, Vol. 1)*
MHID: 0-07-892342-5 *(Teacher Edition, Vol. 1)*
ISBN: 978-0-07-892343-2 *(Teacher Edition, Vol. 2)*
MHID: 0-07-892343-3 *(Teacher Edition, Vol. 2)*

Printed in the United States of America.

2 3 4 5 6 7 8 9 10 11 MER 18 17 16 15 14 13 12 11 10

Authors

Rhonda J. Molix-Bailey
Mathematics Consultant
Mathematics by Design
DeSoto, Texas

Jack M. Ott, Ph.D.
Distinguished Professor of Secondary Education Emeritus
University of South Carolina
Columbia, South Carolina

Ronald Pelfrey, Ed.D.
Mathematics Specialist
Appalachian Rural Systemic Initiative and Mathematics Consultant
Lexington, Kentucky

Jack Price, Ed.D.
Professor Emeritus
California State Polytechnic University
Pomona, California

Kathleen Vielhaber
Mathematics Consultant
St. Louis, Missouri

Teri Willard, Ed.D.
Assistant Professor
Department of Mathematics
Central Washington University
Ellensburg, Washington

Contributing Author

FOLDABLES™ **Dinah Zike**
Educational Consultant
Dinah-Might Activities, Inc.
San Antonio, Texas

Indiana Advisory Board

Glencoe/McGraw-Hill wishes to thank the following professionals for their invaluable feedback during the development of the program. They reviewed a variety of instructional materials at different stages of development.

John Collins
6th Grade Math/Science Teacher
Perry Meridian 6th Grade Academy
Indianapolis, IN

Sarah E. Collins
Math Teacher
Perry Meridian High School
Indianapolis, IN

Ms. Dunn
8th Grade Math and Algebra 1 Teacher
Tipton Middle School
Tipton, IN

Kathie J. Freed
Math Teacher
Carmel High School
Carmel, IN

Patricia A. Hufford
Mathematics Teacher
West Lafayette Jr./Sr. High School
West Lafayette, IN

Dr. Sherri L. Mitchell
Director Curriculum K–12
School Town of Highland
Highland, IN

Indiana Advisory Board

Angela S. Moreman
Mathematics Department Chair
Creekside Middle School
Carmel, IN

Richard R. Soendlin
Teacher; Former Math
Department Head
Araenal Technical H.S.
Indianapolis, IN

Cindy Yoder
7th Grade Math Teacher
Center Grove Middle School
Central
Greenwood, IN

Consultants

Glencoe/McGraw-Hill wishes to thank the following professionals for their feedback. They were instrumental in providing valuable input toward the development of this program in these specific areas.

Mathematical Content

Viken Hovsepian
Professor of Mathematics
Rio Hondo College
Whittier, California

Grant A. Fraser, Ph.D.
Professor of Mathematics
California State University, Los Angeles
Los Angeles, California

Arthur K. Wayman, Ph.D.
Professor of Mathematics Emeritus
California State University, Long Beach
Long Beach, California

Marguerite Hart
Mathematics Consultant
Indianapolis, Indiana

English Language Learners

Josefina V. Tinajero, Ph.D.
Dean, College of Education
The University of Texas at El Paso
El Paso, Texas

Gifted and Talented

Ed Zaccaro
Author and Consultant
Bellevue, Iowa

Graphing Calculator

Ruth M. Casey
National Mathematics Consultant
National Instructor, Teachers Teaching with Technology
Frankfort, Kentucky

Learning Disabilities

Kate Garnett, Ph.D.
Chairperson, Coordinator Learning Disabilities
School of Education
Department of Special Education
Hunter College, CUNY
New York, New York

Mathematical Fluency

Jason Mutford
Mathematics Instructor
Coxsackie-Athens Central School District
Coxsackie, New York

Pre-AP

Dixie Ross
Mathematics Teacher
Pflugerville High School
Pflugerville, Texas

Reading and Vocabulary

Douglas Fisher, Ph.D.
Professor of Language and Literacy Education
San Diego State University
San Diego, California

Lynn T. Havens
Director of Project CRISS
Kalispell, Montana

Reviewers

Each reviewer reviewed at least two chapters of the Student Edition, giving feedback and suggestions for improving the effectiveness of the mathematics instruction.

Sheila J. Allen
Mathematics Teacher
A.I. Root Middle School
Medina, Ohio

Paula Barnes
Mathematics Teacher
Minisink Valley CSD
Slate Hill, New York

Deborah Barnett
Mathematics Consultant
Lake Shore Public Schools
St. Clair Shores, Michigan

Laurel W. Blackburn
Teacher/Mathematics Department Chair
Hillcrest Middle School
Simpsonville, South Carolina

Drista Bowser
Mathematics Teacher
New Windsor Middle School
New Windsor, Maryland

Matthew Bowser
Teacher
Oil City Middle School
Oil City, Pennsylvania

Susan M. Brewer
Mathematics Teacher
Brunswick Middle School
Brunswick, Maryland

Patricia A. Bruzek
Mathematics Teacher
Glenn Westlake Middle School
Lombard, Illinois

Luanne Budd
Supervisor of Mathematics
Randolph Township
Randolph, New Jersey

Ella Violet Burch
Mathematics Teacher
Penns Grove High School
Carneys Point, New Jersey

Hailey Caldwell
7th Grade Mathematics Teacher
Greenville Middle Academy of Traditional Studies
Greenville, South Carolina

Linda K. Chandler
7th Grade Mathematics Teacher
Willard Middle School
Willard, Ohio

Debra M. Cline
7th Grade Mathematics Teacher
Thomas Jefferson Middle School
Winston-Salem, North Carolina

Randall G. Crites
Principal
Bunker R-3
Bunker, Missouri

Rose Dickinson
Science and Mathematics Teacher
Seneca Middle School
Clinton Township, Michigan

Joyce Wolfe Dodd
6th Grade Mathematics Teacher
Bryson Middle School
Simpsonville, South Carolina

John G. Doyle
Middle School Chairperson/Mathematics Teacher
Wyoming Valley West School District
Kingston, Pennsylvania

Katie England
Secondary Mathematics Resource Teacher
Carroll County Public Schools
Westminster, Maryland

Carol A. Fincannon
6th Grade Mathematics Teacher
Southwood Middle School
Anderson, South Carolina

Sally J. Fulmer
7th Grade Mathematics Teacher/Department Chair
C.E. Williams Middle School
Charleston, South Carolina

Marian K. Geist
Mathematics Teacher/Leadership Team
Baker Prairie Middle School
Canby, Oregon

Becky Gorniack
Middle School Mathematics Teacher
Fremont Middle School
Mundelein, Illinois

Donna Tutterow Hamilton
Curriculum Facilitator
Corriher Lipe Middle School
Landis, North Carolina

Danny Liebertz
8th Grade Mathematics Instructor
Fowler Middle School
Tigard, Oregon

Marie Merkel
Learning Support
North Pocono School District
Scranton, Pennsylvania

Tonda North
Algebra 1/8th Grade Mathematics Teacher
Indian Valley Middle School
Enon, Ohio

Natasha L.M. Nuttbrock
7th Grade Mathematics Teacher
Ferguson Middle School
Beavercreek, Ohio

Paul Penn
Curriculum Team Leader, Mathematics
Lima City Schools
Lima, Ohio

Casey Condran Plackett
7th Grade Mathematics Teacher
Kennedy Junior High School
Lisle, Illinois

E. Elaine Rafferty
Mathematics Consultant
Summerville, South Carolina

Edward M. Repko
Mathematics Teacher
Kilbourne Middle School
Worthington, Ohio

Alfreda Reynolds
Teacher
Charlotte-Mecklenburg School System
Charlotte, North Carolina

Alice Roberts
Mathematics Teacher
Oakdale Middle School
Ijamsville, Maryland

Jennifer L. Rodriguez
Mathematics Teacher
Glen Crest Middle School
Glen Ellyn, Illinois

Natalie Rohaley
6th Grade Mathematics
Riverside Middle School
Greer, South Carolina

Annika Lee Schilling
Mathematics and Science Teacher
Duniway Middle School
McMinnville, Oregon

Sherry Scott
Mathematics Teacher
E.A. Tighe School
Margate, New Jersey

Eli Shaheen
Mathematics Teacher/Department Chair
Plum Senior High School
Pittsburgh, Pennsylvania

Kelly Eady Shaw
7th Grade Mathematics Teacher
Rawlinson Road Middle School
Rock Hill, South Carolina

Evan J. Silver
Mathematics Teacher
Walkersville Middle School
Frederick, Maryland

Charlotte A. Thore
6th/7th Grade Mathematics Teacher
Northwest School of the Arts
Charlotte, North Carolina

Gene A. Tournoux
Mathematics Department Head
Shaker Heights High School
Shaker Heights, Ohio

Pamela J. Trainer
Mathematics Teacher
Roland-Grise Middle School
Wilmington, North Carolina

David A. Trez
Mathematics Teacher
Bloomfield Middle School
Bloomfield, New Jersey

Pauline D. Von Hoffer
Mathematics Teacher
Wentzville School District
Wentzville, Missouri

Kentucky Consultants

Jenn Crase
8th Grade Mathematics Teacher/Department Chair
South Oldham Middle School
Crestwood, Kentucky

Max DeBoer Lux
8th Grade Mathematics
Summit View Middle School
Independence, Kentucky

Jennifer Wells Phipps
Middle School Mathematics Teacher
Corbin Middle School
Corbin, Kentucky

Bea Torrence
Teacher/Mathematics Content Leader
Camp Ernst Middle School
Burlington, Kentucky

J. Ron Vanover
Advanced Placement Calculus
Boone County High School
Florence, Kentucky

TEACHER HANDBOOK

Indiana Teacher Handbook

Table of Contents

PreK–12 Mathematics: Focus on Grade 7

Welcome to Math Connects

Concepts • Skills • Problem Solving

The only true vertically aligned PreK–12 Mathematics Curriculum

Math Connects offers three dimensions of vertical alignment.

❶ Content Design

Vertical content alignment is a process that ensures you and your students experience an articulated, coherent sequence of content from grade level to grade level. This provides you with the assurance that content is introduced, reinforced, and assessed at appropriate times in the series, eliminating gaps and unnecessary duplication. You are able to target your instruction to student needs because you are not teaching content intended to be covered later or that students have previously mastered.

❷ Instructional Design

Our strong vertical alignment in instructional approach from PreKindergarten through Algebra 2 provides a smooth transition for students from elementary to middle school to high school. Our common vocabulary, technology, manipulatives, lesson planning, and Data-Driven Decision Making reduces the confusion students often encounter when transitioning between grade levels without this built-in articulation.

❸ Visual Design

The student pages of ***Math Connects*** have a consistent visual design from grade to grade. This aids students' transition from elementary school to middle school and from middle school to Algebra 1. Students are more likely to succeed when they are already familiar with how to navigate student pages.

PreK-2 3–5

5 Keys to Success

1 Backmapping

According to College Board research, about 80% of students who successfully complete Algebra 1 and Geometry by 10th grade attend and succeed in college. (Changing the Odds: Factors Increasing Access to College, 1990) ***Math Connects*** was conceived and developed by backmapping with the final result in mind–student success in Algebra 1 and beyond.

2 Balanced, In-Depth Content

Math Connects was developed to specifically target the skills and topics that give students the most difficulty, such as Problem Solving, in each grade span.

Grades K–2	Grades 3–5
1. Problem Solving 2. Money 3. Time 4. Measurement 5. Fractions 6. Computation	1. Problem Solving 2. Fractions 3. Measurement 4. Decimals 5. Time 6. Algebra
Grades 6–8	**Grades 9–12**
1. Fractions 2. Problem Solving 3. Measurement 4. Algebra 5. Computation	1. Problem Solving 2. Fractions 3. Algebra 4. Geometry 5. Computation 6. Probability

– *K-12 Math Market Analysis Survey,* Open Book Publishing, 2006

3 Ongoing Assessment

Math Connects includes diagnostic, formative, and summative assessment; data-driven instruction; intervention options; and performance tracking, as well as remediation, acceleration, and enrichment tools throughout the program.

4 Intervention and Differentiated Instruction

A three-tiered Response to Intervention (RtI) is provided.

TIER 1 **Daily Intervention** Options for Differentiated Instruction in the Teacher Edition address concepts for different modalities or learning styles.

TIER 2 **Strategic Intervention** Teachers can use the myriad of intervention tips and ancillary materials, such as the Strategic Intervention Guide (1–5) and Study Guide and Intervention (6–8).

TIER 3 **Intensive Intervention** For students who are two or more years below grade level, ***Math Triumphs*** provides step-by-step instruction, vocabulary support, and data-driven decision making to help students succeed.

5 Professional Development

Math Connects includes many opportunities for teacher professional development. Additional learning opportunities in various formats–video, online, and on-site instruction–are fully aligned and articulated from Kindergarten through Algebra 2.

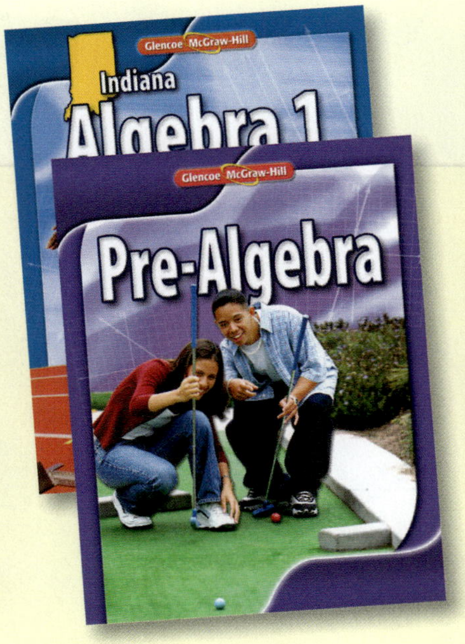

6–8 | Pre-Algebra and Algebra 1 | Geometry and Algebra 2

The Research Base

Continuous research with teachers, students, academician, and leading experts helps to build a solid foundation for ***Math Connects.***

1 Program Development Research

- Evaluating state and local standards
- Qualitative market research
- Academic content research

For more detailed information about our classroom research results, please consult the ***Math Connects*** *Program Efficacy Research Report.*

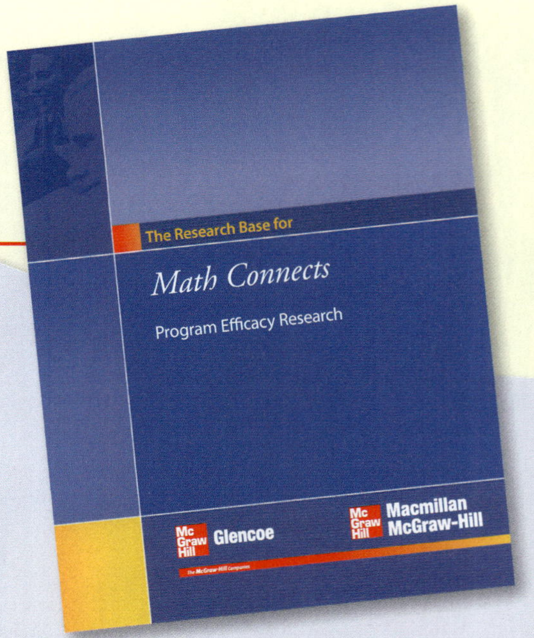

for *Math Connects*

2 Formative Research

- Pedagogical research base
- Classroom field tests
- Teacher advisory boards
- Academic consultants and reviewers

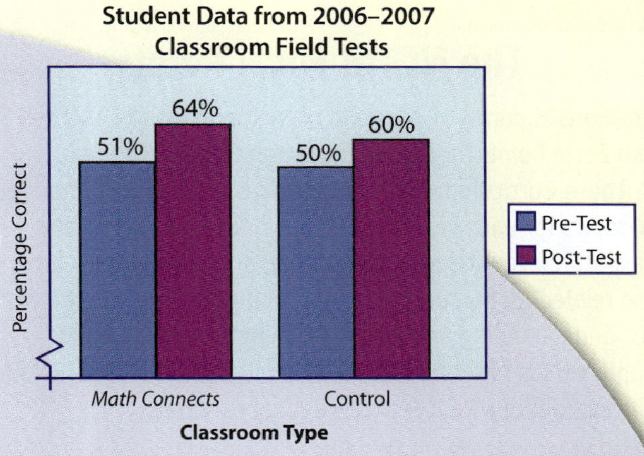

Students using a field test of the ***Math Connects*** program (**experimental group**) had ***higher*** pre-test to post-test gains than students using other textbook programs (**control group**).

3 Summative Research

- Evidence of increased test scores
- Quasi-experimental program efficacy research
- Longitudinal studies
- Qualitative program evaluations

Access all ***Math Connects*** research at glencoe.com.

NCTM Focal Points

The NCTM Focal Points

In 2006, the National Council of Teachers of Mathematics (NCTM) released the Curriculum Focal Points for Pre-Kindergarten through Grade 8 Mathematics. These Curriculum Focal Points focus on the most important mathematical topics for each grade level. The concepts are vertically aligned and expect a level of depth, complexity, and rigor at each level. They comprise related ideas, concepts, skills, and procedures that form the foundation for understanding and lasting learning. The Focal Points emphasize depth versus breadth. The Focal Points will be addressed and highlighted throughout our PreK-8 and Pre-Algebra series.

What is the benefit to you in your classroom?

These Focal Points identify content for each grade level that should be mastered in order for your students to have true mathematical understanding–being able to not only calculate the answer, but to explain the answer and how to apply the calculation. The NCTM Focal Points were used as the basis in the development of ***Math Connects.*** The authors have incorporated the Focal Points into the content to assist you in building depth of understanding.

NCTM Focal Points for Grade 7	Supporting Chapters in *Math Connects*
Number and Operations and *Algebra* and *Geometry*	Chapters 6, 7, 12
Measurement and *Geometry* and *Algebra*	Chapters 10, 11
Number and Operations and *Algebra*	Chapters 1, 2, 3, 4, 5
Connections to the Focal Points	
Measurement and *Geometry*	Chapter 11
Number and Operations	Chapter 4
Data Analysis	Chapter 8
Probability	Chapter 9

KEY

G7-FP1 Grade 7 Focal Point 1	**G7-FP5C** Grade 7 Focal Point 5 Connection
G7-FP2 Grade 7 Focal Point 2	**G7-FP6C** Grade 7 Focal Point 6 Connection
G7-FP3 Grade 7 Focal Point 3	**G7-FP7C** Grade 7 Focal Point 7 Connection
G7-FP4C Grade 7 Focal Point 4 Connection	

The Curriculum Focal Points identify key mathematical ideas for this grade. They are not discrete topics or a checklist to be mastered; rather, they provide a framework for the majority of instruction at a particular grade level and the foundation for future mathematics study. The complete document may be viewed at www.nctm.org/focalpoints.

G7-FP1 ***Number and Operations*** and ***Algebra*** and ***Geometry:*** **Developing an understanding of and applying proportionality, including similarity**

Students extend their work with ratios to develop an understanding of proportionality that they apply to solve single and multistep problems in numerous contexts. They use ratio and proportionality to solve a wide variety of percent problems, including problems involving discounts, interest, taxes, tips, and percent increase or decrease. They also solve problems about similar objects (including figures) by using scale factors that relate corresponding lengths of the objects or by using the fact that relationships of lengths within an object are preserved in similar objects. Students graph proportional relationships and identify the unit rate as the slope of the related line. They distinguish proportional relationships $\left(\frac{y}{x} = k, \text{ or } y = kx\right)$ from other relationships, including inverse proportionality $\left(xy = k, \text{ or } y = \frac{k}{x}\right)$.

G7-FP2 ***Measurement*** and ***Geometry*** and ***Algebra:*** **Developing an understanding of and using formulas to determine surface areas and volumes of three-dimensional shapes**

By decomposing two- and three-dimensional shapes into smaller, component shapes, students find surface areas and develop and justify formulas for the surface areas and volumes of prisms and cylinders. As students decompose prisms and cylinders by slicing them, they develop and understand formulas for their volumes (*Volume* = *Area of base* × *Height*). They apply these formulas in problem solving to determine volumes of prisms and cylinders. Students see that the formula for the area of a circle is plausible by decomposing a circle into a number of wedges and rearranging them into a shape that approximates a parallelogram. They select appropriate two- and three dimensional shapes to model real-world situations and solve a variety of problems (including multistep problems) involving surface areas, areas and circumferences of circles, and volumes of prisms and cylinders.

G7-FP3 ***Number and Operations*** and ***Algebra:*** **Developing an understanding of operations on all rational numbers and solving linear equations**

Students extend understandings of addition, subtraction, multiplication, and division, together with their properties, to all rational numbers, including negative integers. By applying properties of arithmetic and considering negative numbers in everyday contexts (e.g., situations of owing money or measuring elevations above and below sea level), students explain why the rules for adding, subtracting, multiplying, and dividing with negative numbers make sense. They use the arithmetic of rational numbers as they formulate and solve linear equations in one variable and use these equations to solve problems. Students make strategic choices of procedures to solve linear equations in one variable and implement them efficiently, understanding that when they use the properties of equality to express an equation in a new way, solutions that they obtain for the new equation also solve the original equation.

Connections to the Focal Points

G7-FP4C ***Measurement*** and ***Geometry:*** Students connect their work on proportionality with their work on area and volume by investigating similar objects. They understand that if a scale factor describes how corresponding lengths in two similar objects are related, then the square of the scale factor describes how corresponding areas are related, and the cube of the scale factor describes how corresponding volumes are related. Students apply their work on proportionality to measurement in different contexts, including converting among different units of measurement to solve problems involving rates such as motion at a constant speed. They also apply proportionality when they work with the circumference, radius, and diameter of a circle; when they find the area of a sector of a circle; and when they make scale drawings.

G7-FP5C ***Number and Operations:*** In grade 4, students used equivalent fractions to determine the decimal representations of fractions that they could represent with terminating decimals. Students now use division to express any fraction as a decimal, including fractions that they must represent with infinite decimals. They find this method useful when working with proportions, especially those involving percents. Students connect their work with dividing fractions to solving equations of the form $ax = b$, where a and b are fractions. Students continue to develop their understanding of multiplication and division and the structure of numbers by determining if a counting number greater than 1 is a prime, and if it is not, by factoring it into a product of primes.

G7-FP6C ***Data Analysis:*** Students use proportions to make estimates relating to a population on the basis of a sample. They apply percentages to make and interpret histograms and circle graphs.

G7-FP7C ***Probability:*** Students understand that when all outcomes of an experiment are equally likely, the theoretical probability of an event is the fraction of outcomes in which the event occurs. Students use theoretical probability and proportions to make approximate predictions.

Program Philosophy

Balanced Instruction, Vertically-Aligned from Grades PreK through Algebra 1

The vertical alignment of ***Math Connects*** PreK-8 and ***Algebra 1*** incorporates a balance of instruction throughout. These programs provide students a balanced approach to mathematics by:

- investigating concepts and building conceptual understanding.
- developing, reinforcing, and mastering computational and procedural skills.
- applying mathematics to problem-solving situations.

This sequence of Student Edition pages illustrates the vertically-aligned development of the conceptual understanding and corresponding computational and procedural skills for an important algebra topic.

Primary Students use two-color counters to model addition sentences. This activity forms a basis for future understanding of and success in solving algebraic equations.

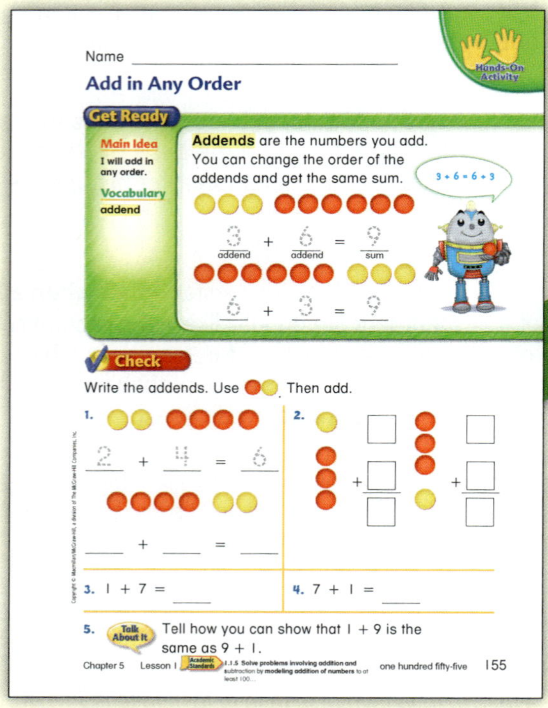
Name ______________________

Add in Any Order

Hands-On Activity

Get Ready

Main Idea
I will add in any order.

Vocabulary
addend

Addends are the numbers you add. You can change the order of the addends and get the same sum.

3 + 6 = 9 (addend, addend, sum)

6 + 3 = 9

Check

Write the addends. Use counters. Then add.

1. 2 + 4 = 6

___ + ___ = ___

2.

3. 1 + 7 = ___

4. 7 + 1 = ___

5. Talk About It: Tell how you can show that 1 + 9 is the same as 9 + 1.

Chapter 5 Lesson 1 one hundred fifty-five 155

Math Connects, Grade 1, Student Edition, page 155

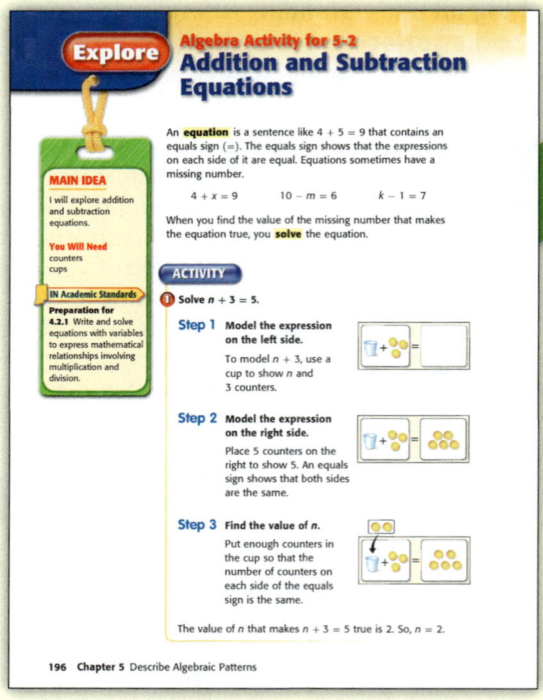
Explore

Algebra Activity for 5-2

Addition and Subtraction Equations

MAIN IDEA
I will explore addition and subtraction equations.

You Will Need
counters
cups

IN Academic Standards
Preparation for 4.2.1 Write and solve equations with variables to express mathematical relationships involving multiplication and division.

An **equation** is a sentence like 4 + 5 = 9 that contains an equals sign (=). The equals sign shows that the expressions on each side of it are equal. Equations sometimes have a missing number.

$4 + x = 9$ $10 - m = 6$ $k - 1 = 7$

When you find the value of the missing number that makes the equation true, you **solve** the equation.

ACTIVITY

1 Solve $n + 3 = 5$.

Step 1 Model the expression on the left side. To model $n + 3$, use a cup to show n and 3 counters.

Step 2 Model the expression on the right side. Place 5 counters on the right to show 5. An equals sign shows that both sides are the same.

Step 3 Find the value of n. Put enough counters in the cup so that the number of counters on each side of the equals sign is the same.

The value of n that makes $n + 3 = 5$ true is 2. So, $n = 2$.

196 Chapter 5 Describe Algebraic Patterns

Math Connects, Grade 4, Student Edition, page 196

Intermediate Students build on their experience with counters to using cups and counters to model and solve addition and subtraction equations. The exercises are designed to help students bridge the gap from using cups and counters to solving equations symbolically.

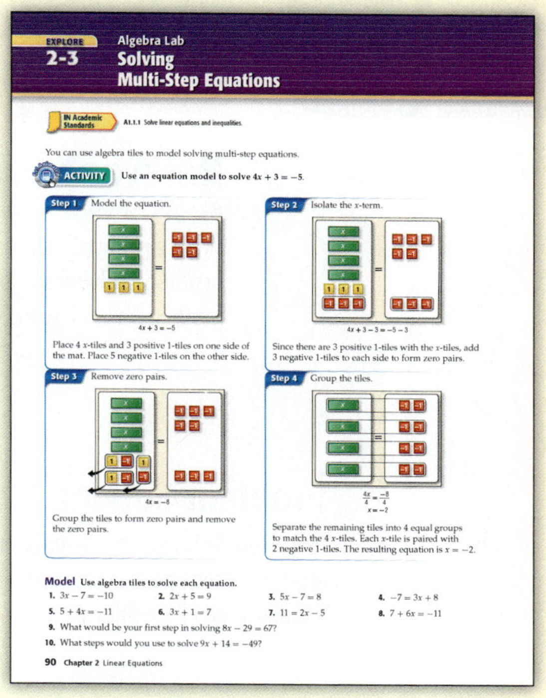

EXPLORE 2-3 Algebra Lab
Solving Multi-Step Equations

IN Academic Standards A1.1.1 Solve linear equations and inequalities.

You can use algebra tiles to model solving multi-step equations.

ACTIVITY Use an equation model to solve $4x + 3 = -5$.

Step 1 Model the equation.

$4x + 3 = -5$

Place 4 x-tiles and 3 positive 1-tiles on one side of the mat. Place 5 negative 1-tiles on the other side.

Step 2 Isolate the x-term.

$4x + 3 - 3 = -5 - 3$

Since there are 3 positive 1-tiles with the x-tiles, add 3 negative 1-tiles to each side to form zero pairs.

Step 3 Remove zero pairs.

$4x = -8$

Group the tiles to form zero pairs and remove the zero pairs.

Step 4 Group the tiles.

$\frac{4x}{4} = \frac{-8}{4}$

$x = -2$

Separate the remaining tiles into 4 equal groups to match the 4 x-tiles. Each x-tile is paired with 2 negative 1-tiles. The resulting equation is $x = -2$.

Model Use algebra tiles to solve each equation.

1. $3x - 7 = -10$
2. $2x + 5 = 9$
3. $5x - 7 = 8$
4. $-7 = 3x + 8$
5. $5 + 4x = -11$
6. $3x + 1 = 7$
7. $11 = 2x - 5$
8. $7 + 6x = -11$
9. What would be your first step in solving $8x - 29 = 67$?
10. What steps would you use to solve $9x + 14 = -49$?

90 Chapter 2 Linear Equations

Glencoe Algebra 1,
Student Edition, page 90

Algebra 1 Students continue the use of algebra tiles to investigate solving multi-step equations. In the next lesson, students apply the procedure developed in the Algebra Lab to a symbolic approach.

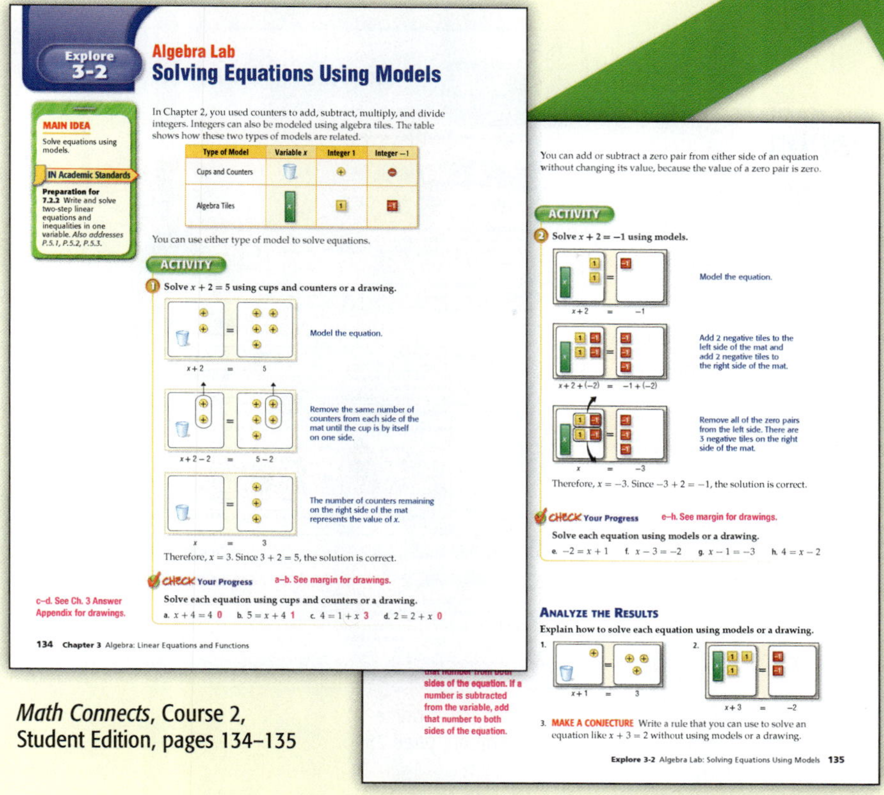

Explore 3-2 Algebra Lab
Solving Equations Using Models

MAIN IDEA
Solve equations using models.

IN Academic Standards
Preparation for 7.2.2 Write and solve two-step linear equations and inequalities in one variable. *Also addresses P.5.1, P.5.2, P.5.3.*

In Chapter 2, you used counters to add, subtract, multiply, and divide integers. Integers can also be modeled using algebra tiles. The table shows how these two types of models are related.

Type of Model	Variable x	Integer 1	Integer −1
Cups and Counters			
Algebra Tiles			

You can use either type of model to solve equations.

ACTIVITY

1 Solve $x + 2 = 5$ using cups and counters or a drawing.

$x + 2 = 5$ Model the equation.

$x + 2 - 2 = 5 - 2$ Remove the same number of counters from each side of the mat until the cup is by itself on one side.

$x = 3$ The number of counters remaining on the right side of the mat represents the value of x.

Therefore, $x = 3$. Since $3 + 2 = 5$, the solution is correct.

CHECK Your Progress a–b. See margin for drawings.

Solve each equation using cups and counters or a drawing.

a. $x + 4 = 4$ 0 b. $5 = x + 4$ 1 c. $4 = 1 + x$ 3 d. $2 = 2 + x$ 0

c–d. See Ch. 3 Answer Appendix for drawings.

134 Chapter 3 Algebra: Linear Equations and Functions

You can add or subtract a zero pair from either side of an equation without changing its value, because the value of a zero pair is zero.

ACTIVITY

2 Solve $x + 2 = -1$ using models.

$x + 2 = -1$ Model the equation.

$x + 2 + (-2) = -1 + (-2)$ Add 2 negative tiles to the left side of the mat and add 2 negative tiles to the right side of the mat.

$x = -3$ Remove all of the zero pairs from the left side. There are 3 negative tiles on the right side of the mat.

Therefore, $x = -3$. Since $-3 + 2 = -1$, the solution is correct.

CHECK Your Progress e–h. See margin for drawings.

Solve each equation using models or a drawing.

e. $-2 = x + 1$ f. $x - 3 = -2$ g. $x - 1 = -3$ h. $4 = x - 2$

ANALYZE THE RESULTS

Explain how to solve each equation using models or a drawing.

1. $x + 1 = 3$
2. $x + 3 = -2$
3. MAKE A CONJECTURE Write a rule that you can use to solve an equation like $x + 3 = 2$ without using models or a drawing.

sides of the equation. If a number is subtracted from the variable, add that number to both sides of the equation.

Explore 3-2 Algebra Lab: Solving Equations Using Models 135

Math Connects, Course 2,
Student Edition, pages 134–135

Middle School Students represent the variable *x* as a cup, as a counter, or as a written *x*. In this Algebra Lab, students make the transition from cups and counters to the more abstract algebra tiles. In the next lesson, students solve simple equations symbolically.

Continuity of Instruction The instructional sequence described demonstrates the power of backward mapping from the desired result, success in Algebra 1. This process of development avoids gaps and overlaps between grade levels and ensures that at each grade level the concepts and skills are built on the strong foundation developed in previous grades. The same approach was used across all strands throughout the entire PreK-12 series.

Program Philosophy Balance of Instruction

Relevant Problem Solving

Math Connects provides students with the appropriate development of problem-solving strategies, skills, and applications from PreK through grade 5. In grades 6–8, students continue to learn and apply problem-solving skills and strategies. Students are provided with ongoing opportunities to apply their math skills and solve problems using visual thinking, logical reasoning, number sense, and algebra.

Problem-Solving Investigations

Problem-Solving Investigations help students learn different problem-solving strategies for attacking word problems.

5-2 Problem-Solving Investigation

MAIN IDEA: Solve problems by acting them out.

Academic Standards P.1.3 Apply and adapt a variety of appropriate strategies to solve problems *Also addresses P.1.1, P.1.4.*

P.S.I. TEAM +

e-Mail: ACT IT OUT

BETHANY: Tonya, Liseli, Meghan, and I want to ride the new ride Teradactyl at the amusement park. Each car on the ride has two rows with two seats in each row.

YOUR MISSION: Act it out to find how many different ways the four friends can sit in a car on the ride so that Tonya and Meghan sit next to each other.

Understand	You know that each car on the ride has two rows of seats. There are two seats in each row. Tonya and Meghan want to sit next to each other.
Plan	You can arrange student desks to model the amusement park ride. Place four desks in two rows with two desks in each row. Have four students act out possible arrangements and record each one. Use B for Bethany, T for Tonya, L for Liseli, and M for Meghan.
Solve	Meghan and Tonya can either sit in the front row or the back row. There are 8 possible ways for the friends to sit in the car on the ride.
Check	In each row, there are four ways for the friends to sit. So, having 8 possible ways makes sense.

Analyze The Strategy

1. Explain how this strategy could help determine the reasonableness of your answer after the calculations were completed.
2. WRITING IN MATH Write a problem that could be solved by using the *act it out* strategy. Then explain how you would act it out.

254 Chapter 5 Operations with Fractions

Math Connects, Course 1
Student Edition, page 254

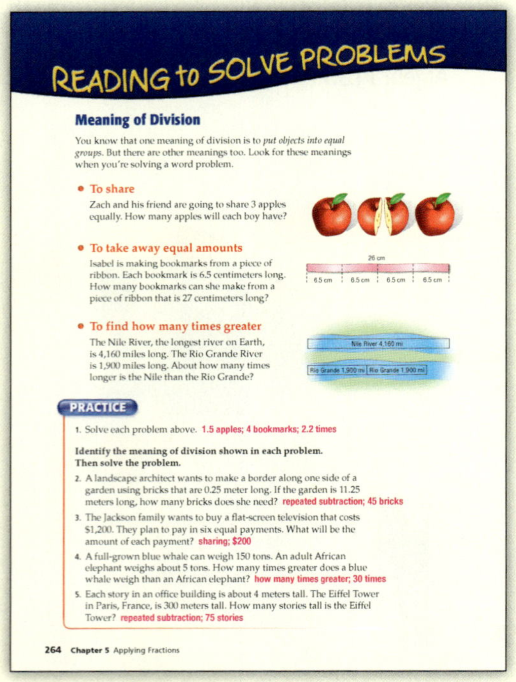

READING to SOLVE PROBLEMS

Meaning of Division

You know that one meaning of division is to *put objects into equal groups*. But there are other meanings too. Look for these meanings when you're solving a word problem.

- **To share**
  Zach and his friend are going to share 3 apples equally. How many apples will each boy have?
- **To take away equal amounts**
  Isabel is making bookmarks from a piece of ribbon. Each bookmark is 6.5 centimeters long. How many bookmarks can she make from a piece of ribbon that is 27 centimeters long?
  26 cm; 6.5 cm 6.5 cm 6.5 cm 6.5 cm
- **To find how many times greater**
  The Nile River, the longest river on Earth, is 4,160 miles long. The Rio Grande River is 1,900 miles long. About how many times longer is the Nile than the Rio Grande?
  Nile River 4,160 mi; Rio Grande 1,900 mi Rio Grande 1,900 mi

PRACTICE

1. Solve each problem above. 1.5 apples; 4 bookmarks; 2.2 times

Identify the meaning of division shown in each problem. Then solve the problem.

2. A landscape architect wants to make a border along one side of a garden using bricks that are 0.25 meter long. If the garden is 11.25 meters long, how many bricks does she need? repeated subtraction; 45 bricks
3. The Jackson family wants to buy a flat-screen television that costs $1,200. They plan to pay in six equal payments. What will be the amount of each payment? sharing; $200
4. A full-grown blue whale can weigh 150 tons. An adult African elephant weighs about 5 tons. How many times greater does a blue whale weigh than an African elephant? how many times greater; 30 times
5. Each story in an office building is about 4 meters tall. The Eiffel Tower in Paris, France, is 300 meters tall. How many stories tall is the Eiffel Tower? repeated subtraction; 75 stories

264 Chapter 5 Applying Fractions

Math Connects, Course 2
Student Edition, page 264

Reading to Solve Problems

Reading to Solve Problems helps students understand and interpret mathematical language.

Real-World Problem-Solving Graphic Novels

Motivating, teen-relevant problem solving in graphic novel format provides practice with Number Sense, Algebraic Thinking, Geometry, Measurement, Statistics and Probability, and Mathematical Reasoning.

Hands-On Labs

Some labs act as an introduction to a mathematical topic, while others extend the topic just presented. **Algebra, Geometry, Measurement, Statistics,** and **Probability** labs use models to bridge the gap between concrete understanding and mathematical symbolism.

Concepts in Motion

Concepts in Motion are online illustrations of key concepts through animations, Interactive Labs, and BrainPOPs®.

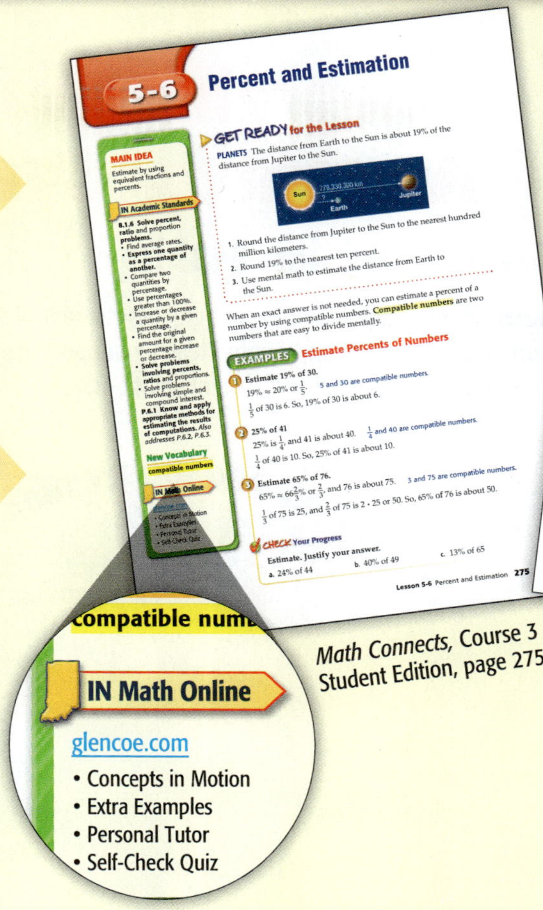

Math Connects, Course 3
Student Edition, page 275

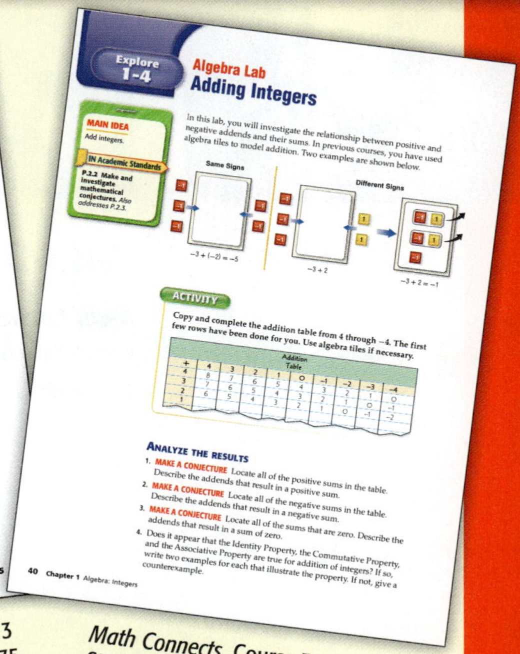

Math Connects, Course 3
Student Edition, page 40

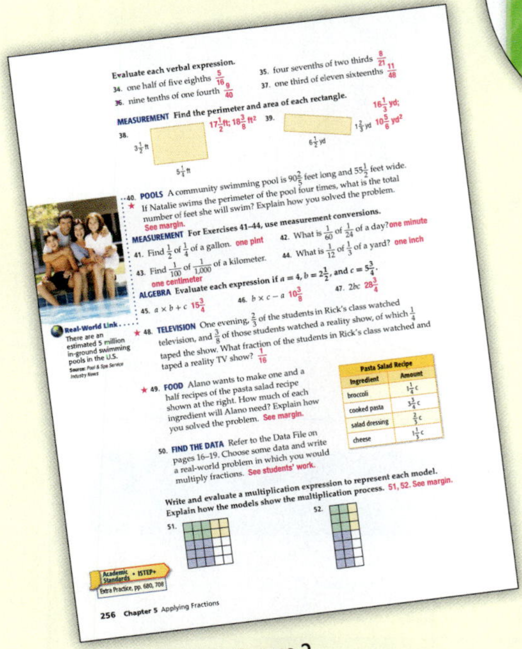

Math Connects, Course 2
Student Edition, page 256

Multi-Step Word Problems

Multi-step word problems are not simple computation problems using the numbers given. Students must analyze exactly what the problem is asking and how to use the information given. These problems are starred in the Teacher Edition.

H.O.T. Problems

H.O.T. Problems require students to use **Higher Order Thinking** skills to solve problems.

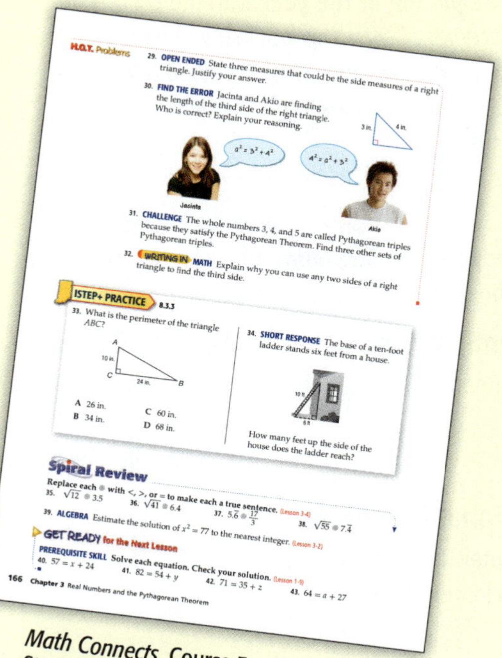

Math Connects, Course 3
Student Edition, page 166

Comprehensive Assessment System

Data-Driven Decision Making

Math Connects offers frequent and meaningful assessment of student progress within the curriculum structure and printed teacher support materials.
See pages T22 and T23 for digital assessment solutions.

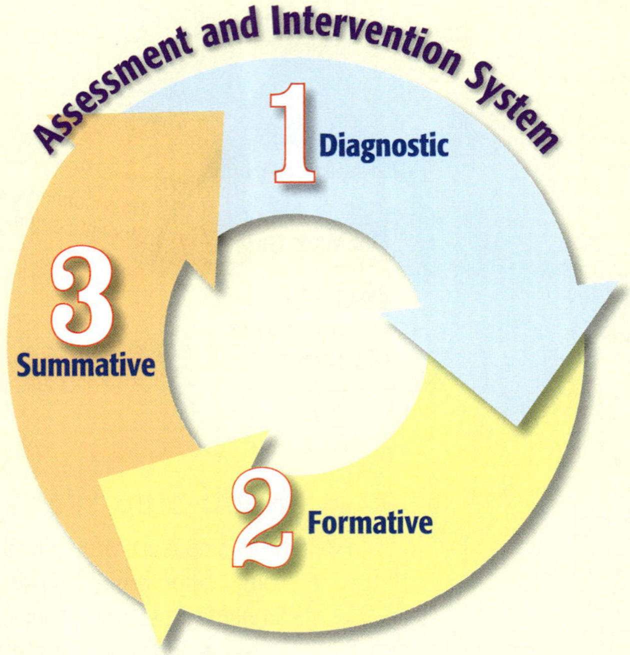

1 Diagnostic

Initial Assessment Assess students' knowledge **at the beginning of the year** with the *Diagnostic and Placement Tests*. This booklet will help you determine whether your students need additional materials and resources to meet grade-level standards.

Entry–Level Assessment Assess students' prior knowledge **at the beginning of a chapter or lesson** with one of the following options.

Student Edition

- Get Ready

Teacher Edition

- Options for Differentiated Instruction
- 5-Minute Check

Additional Resources

- Chapter Resource Masters, Anticipation Guide

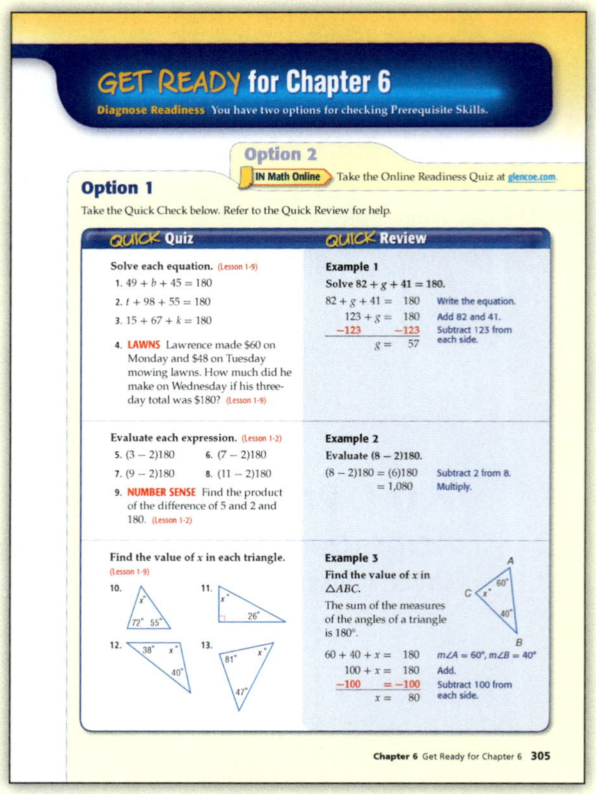

GET READY for Chapter 6

Diagnose Readiness You have two options for checking Prerequisite Skills.

Option 2

IN Math Online Take the Online Readiness Quiz at glencoe.com.

Option 1

Take the Quick Check below. Refer to the Quick Review for help.

QUICK Quiz

Solve each equation. (Lesson 1-9)

1. $49 + b + 45 = 180$
2. $t + 98 + 55 = 180$
3. $15 + 67 + k = 180$
4. LAWNS Lawrence made $60 on Monday and $48 on Tuesday mowing lawns. How much did he make on Wednesday if his three-day total was $180? (Lesson 1-9)

Evaluate each expression. (Lesson 1-2)

5. $(3 - 2)180$
6. $(7 - 2)180$
7. $(9 - 2)180$
8. $(11 - 2)180$
9. NUMBER SENSE Find the product of the difference of 5 and 2 and 180. (Lesson 1-2)

Find the value of x in each triangle. (Lesson 1-9)

10. 11. 12. 13.

QUICK Review

Example 1

Solve $82 + g + 41 = 180$.

$82 + g + 41 = 180$ Write the equation.
$123 + g = 180$ Add 82 and 41.
$-123 \quad -123$ Subtract 123 from each side.
$g = 57$

Example 2

Evaluate $(8 - 2)180$.

$(8 - 2)180 = (6)180$ Subtract 2 from 8.
$= 1{,}080$ Multiply.

Example 3

Find the value of x in $\triangle ABC$.

The sum of the measures of the angles of a triangle is 180°.

$60 + 40 + x = 180$ $m\angle A = 60°, m\angle B = 40°$
$100 + x = 180$ Add.
$-100 = -100$ Subtract 100 from each side.
$x = 80$

Chapter 6 Get Ready for Chapter 6 305

Math Connects, Course 3
Student Edition, page 305

2 Formative

Progress Monitoring Determine if students are progressing adequately as you teach each lesson. Use the assessments to differentiate lesson instruction and practice.

Student Edition

- Mid-Chapter Quiz
- Find the Error
- Check Your Understanding
- Writing in Math
- Study Guide and Review
- Foldables™

Teacher Edition

- Options for Differentiated Instruction
- Step 4 (Assess) of the Teaching Plan
- Data-Driven Decision Making

Additional Resources

Chapter Resource Masters

- Mid-Chapter Test
- 4 Quizzes
- Standardized Test Practice

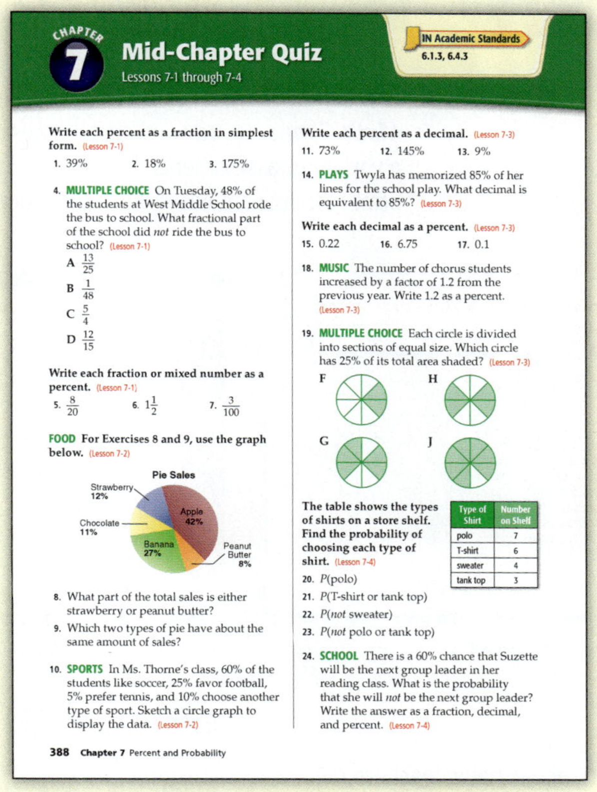

CHAPTER 7 Mid-Chapter Quiz
Lessons 7-1 through 7-4
IN Academic Standards 6.1.3, 6.4.3

Write each percent as a fraction in simplest form. (Lesson 7-1)
1. 39% 2. 18% 3. 175%

4. MULTIPLE CHOICE On Tuesday, 48% of the students at West Middle School rode the bus to school. What fractional part of the school did *not* ride the bus to school? (Lesson 7-1)
A $\frac{13}{25}$
B $\frac{1}{48}$
C $\frac{5}{4}$
D $\frac{12}{15}$

Write each fraction or mixed number as a percent. (Lesson 7-1)
5. $\frac{8}{20}$ 6. $1\frac{1}{2}$ 7. $\frac{3}{100}$

FOOD For Exercises 8 and 9, use the graph below. (Lesson 7-2)

8. What part of the total sales is either strawberry or peanut butter?
9. Which two types of pie have about the same amount of sales?

10. SPORTS In Ms. Thorne's class, 60% of the students like soccer, 25% favor football, 5% prefer tennis, and 10% choose another type of sport. Sketch a circle graph to display the data. (Lesson 7-2)

Write each percent as a decimal. (Lesson 7-3)
11. 73% 12. 145% 13. 9%

14. PLAYS Twyla has memorized 85% of her lines for the school play. What decimal is equivalent to 85%? (Lesson 7-3)

Write each decimal as a percent. (Lesson 7-3)
15. 0.22 16. 6.75 17. 0.1

18. MUSIC The number of chorus students increased by a factor of 1.2 from the previous year. Write 1.2 as a percent. (Lesson 7-3)

19. MULTIPLE CHOICE Each circle is divided into sections of equal size. Which circle has 25% of its total area shaded? (Lesson 7-3)
F H G J

The table shows the types of shirts on a store shelf. Find the probability of choosing each type of shirt. (Lesson 7-4)

Type of Shirt	Number on Shelf
polo	7
T-shirt	6
sweater	4
tank top	3

20. *P*(polo)
21. *P*(T-shirt or tank top)
22. *P*(*not* sweater)
23. *P*(*not* polo or tank top)

24. SCHOOL There is a 60% chance that Suzette will be the next group leader in her reading class. What is the probability that she will *not* be the next group leader? Write the answer as a fraction, decimal, and percent. (Lesson 7-4)

388 Chapter 7 Percent and Probability

Math Connects, Course 1
Student Edition, page 388

3 Summative

Summative Evaluation Assess student success in learning the concepts in each chapter.

Student Edition

- Chapter Test
- Test Practice
- Foldables™

Teacher Edition

- Data-Driven Decision Making

Additional Resources

Chapter Resource Masters

- Vocabulary Test
- 6 Leveled Chapter Tests
- Extended Response Test

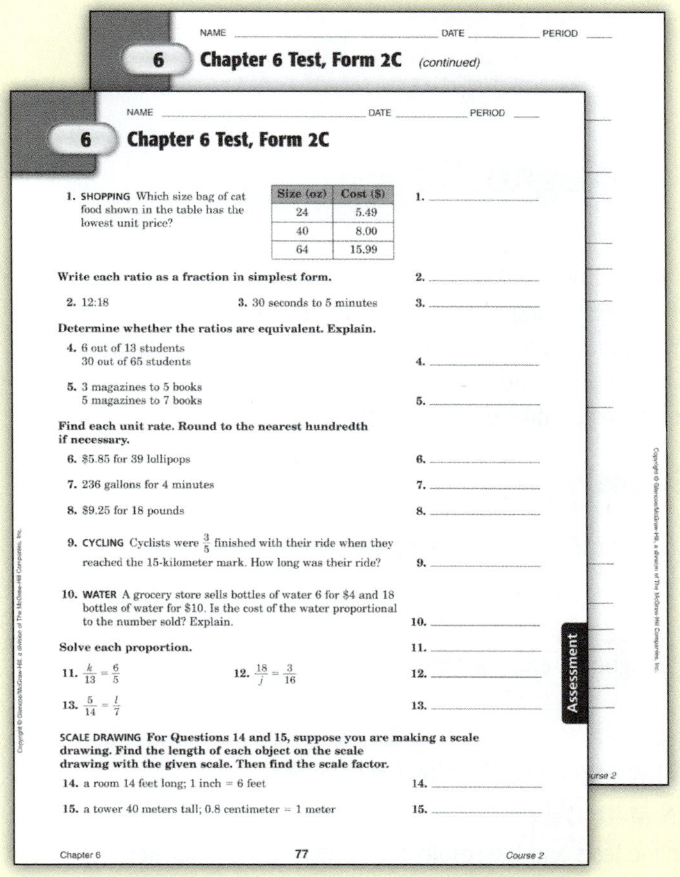

NAME ______ DATE ______ PERIOD ______
6 Chapter 6 Test, Form 2C (continued)

NAME ______ DATE ______ PERIOD ______
6 Chapter 6 Test, Form 2C

1. SHOPPING Which size bag of cat food shown in the table has the lowest unit price?

Size (oz)	Cost ($)
24	5.49
40	8.00
64	15.99

Write each ratio as a fraction in simplest form.
2. 12:18 3. 30 seconds to 5 minutes

Determine whether the ratios are equivalent. Explain.
4. 6 out of 13 students
30 out of 65 students
5. 3 magazines to 5 books
5 magazines to 7 books

Find each unit rate. Round to the nearest hundredth if necessary.
6. $5.85 for 39 lollipops
7. 236 gallons for 4 minutes
8. $9.25 for 18 pounds

9. CYCLING Cyclists were $\frac{3}{5}$ finished with their ride when they reached the 15-kilometer mark. How long was their ride?

10. WATER A grocery store sells bottles of water 6 for $4 and 18 bottles of water for $10. Is the cost of the water proportional to the number sold? Explain.

Solve each proportion.
11. $\frac{k}{13} = \frac{6}{5}$ 12. $\frac{18}{j} = \frac{3}{16}$
13. $\frac{5}{14} = \frac{l}{7}$

SCALE DRAWING For Questions 14 and 15, suppose you are making a scale drawing. Find the length of each object on the scale drawing with the given scale. Then find the scale factor.
14. a room 14 feet long; 1 inch = 6 feet
15. a tower 40 meters tall; 0.8 centimeter = 1 meter

Assessment

Chapter 6 77 Course 2

Math Connects, Course 2
Chapter 6 Resource Masters, pages 77–78

Comprehensive Assessment System

DIGITAL SOLUTIONS

Data-Driven Decision Making

Math Connects provides digital assessment options to create, customize, administer, and instantly score a variety of assessments. These digital solutions offer the same quality assessments and reporting as the print resources in easy-to-use technology tools.

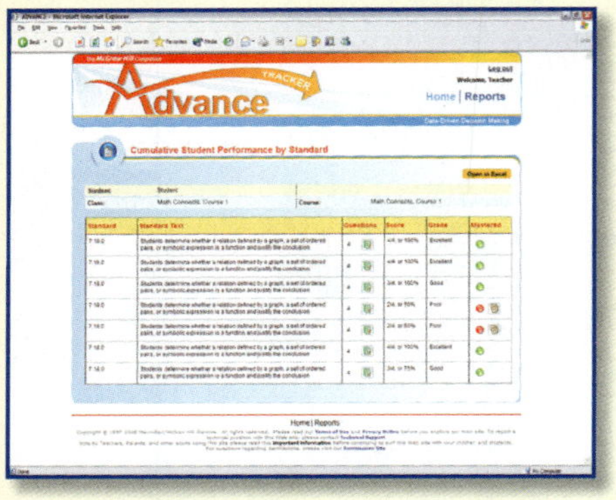

Math Connects, Course 1

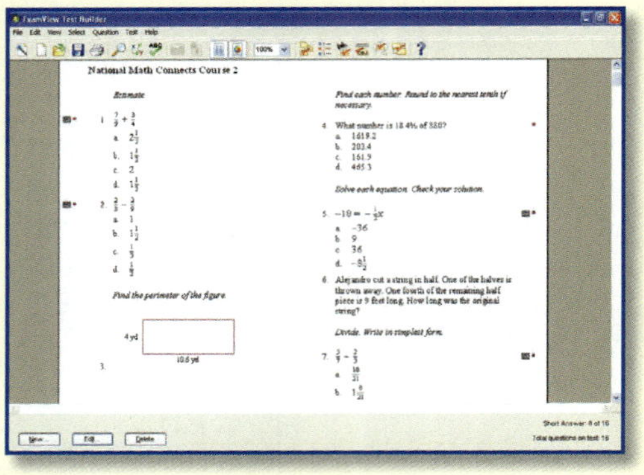

Math Connects, Course 2

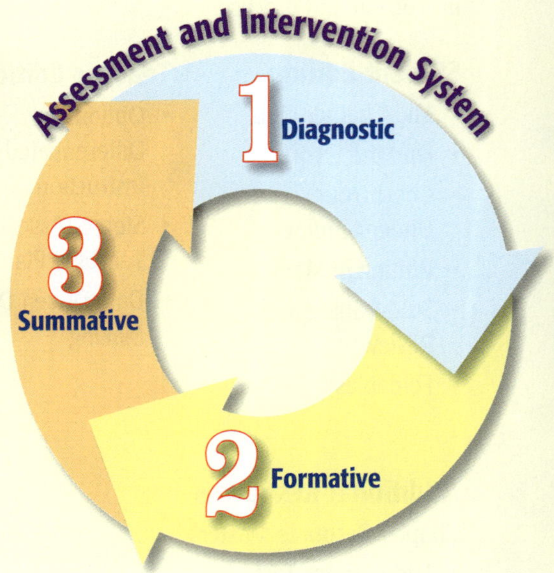

Advance Tracker helps teachers administer online tests, diagnose student achievement, and create prescriptive reports for a student or class.

Exam*View*® Assessment Suite allows teachers to create and customize their own assessment and assignments. Print in one or two columns to match the state test.

1 Diagnostic

Initial Assessment Assess students' knowledge **at the beginning of the year** with the *Diagnostic and Placement Tests.* These assessments will help you determine whether your students need additional materials and resources to meet grade-level standards.

ExamView Assessment Suite

- Diagnostic and Placement Tests

Advance Tracker

- Diagnostic and Placement Tests

Entry-Level Assessment Assess students' prior knowledge **at the beginning of a chapter or lesson.**

IN Math Online glencoe.com Students can complete online tests and the results are e-mailed to the teacher.

- Chapter Readiness

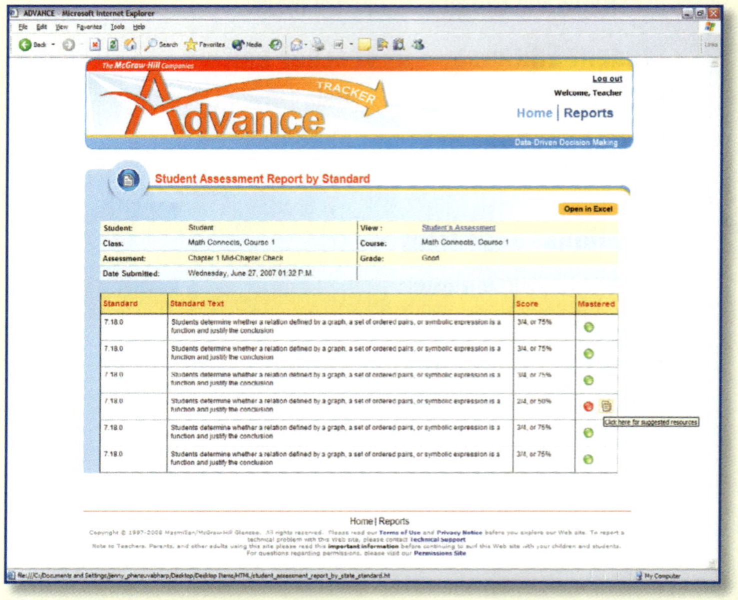

Math Connects, Course 1 Advance Tracker

2 Formative

Progress Monitoring Determine if students are progressing adequately as you teach each lesson. Use the assessments to differentiate lesson instruction and practice.

ExamView® Assessment Suite

Advance Tracker

- Mid-Chapter Test
- Study Guide and Review

MindJogger, Super DVD

IN Math Online glencoe.com

- Self-Check Quizzes

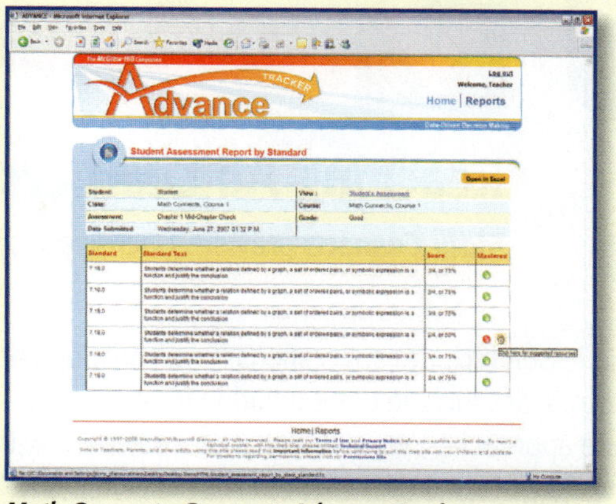

Math Connects, Course 1, Advance Tracker

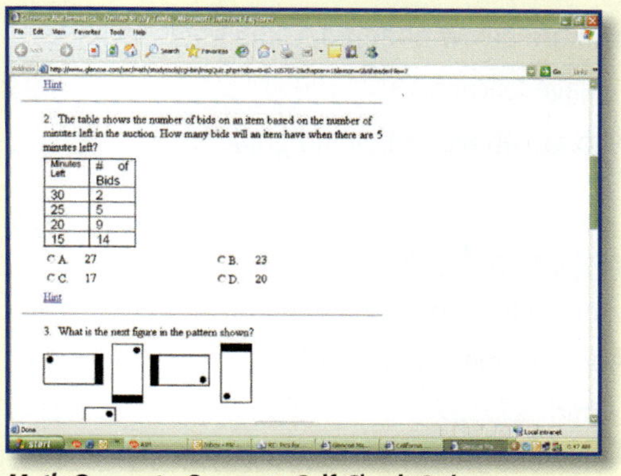

Math Connects, Course 3, Self-Check Quiz

3 Summative

Summative Evaluation Assess students' success in learning the concepts in each chapter.

ExamView® Assessment Suite

- Chapter Tests
- Cumulative Standardized Test Practice

Advance Tracker

- Chapter Tests
- Cumulative Standardized Test Practice

IN Math Online glencoe.com

- Chapter Tests

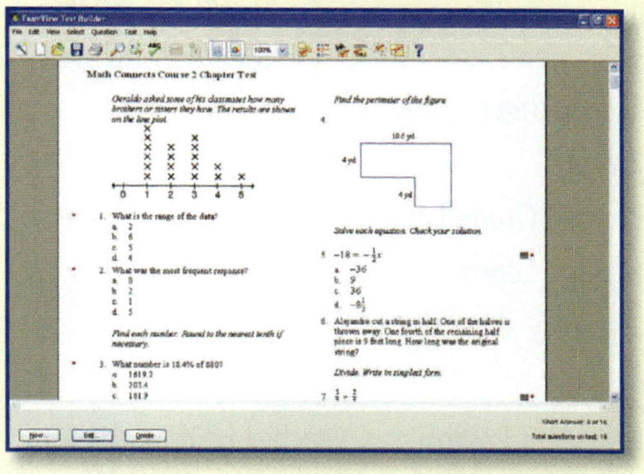

Math Connects, Course 2, Exam*View*® Assessment Suite

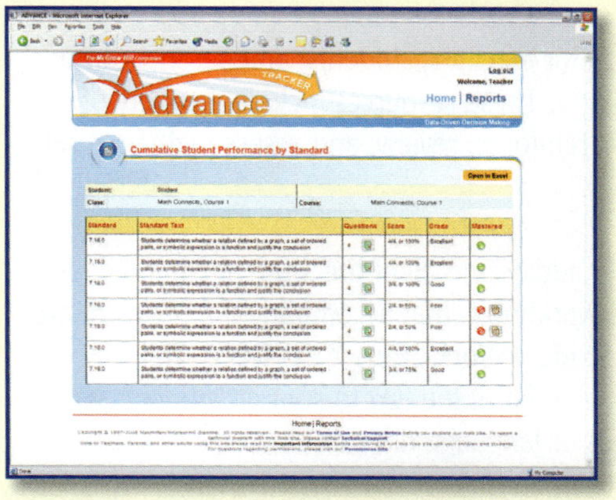

Math Connects, Course 1, Advance Tracker

TEACHER HANDBOOK

Differentiated Instruction

Reaching All Learners

Math Connects provides extensive support for reaching all learners.

Every chapter and lesson includes suggestions for identifying and meeting your students' needs. Strategies include differentiation in pacing and student grouping, alternate approaches, ways to enhance instruction with manipulatives, questions to promote higher-order thinking, and language hints.

Personalize instruction for:

- BL Students who are below or approaching grade level
- ELL English language learners
- AL Students who are above or beyond grade level

Leveled Exercise Sets

The assignments for each lesson are leveled for students.

- BL Below or Approaching Grade Level
- OL On Grade Level
- AL Above or Beyond Grade Level

Leveled Resources

All of the blackline masters and transparencies that accompany the program, as well as all of the Teacher Edition pages, are available on the **TeacherWorks Plus™ CD-ROM**. Resources and assignments are leveled for students who are:

- BL Below or Approaching Grade Level
- OL On Grade Level
- AL Above or Beyond Grade Level
- ELL English Language Learners

Technology

In addition to the Student Edition and Teacher Edition, ***Math Connects*** includes extensive resources online, on CD-ROM, and on DVD.

Online Resources for teachers, students, and parents can be found at glencoe.com. These resources include a variety of activities to teach, reinforce, review, and assess mathematical concepts.

CD-ROM/DVD In addition to all of the Student Edition pages, all of the student workbooks that accompany the program are available on the **StudentWorks Plus™ CD-ROM**. This resource offers full audio of the text to support students with hearing challenges or language difficulty.

Additional tools for class presentations and assessment are available on a variety of CD-ROMs and DVDs.

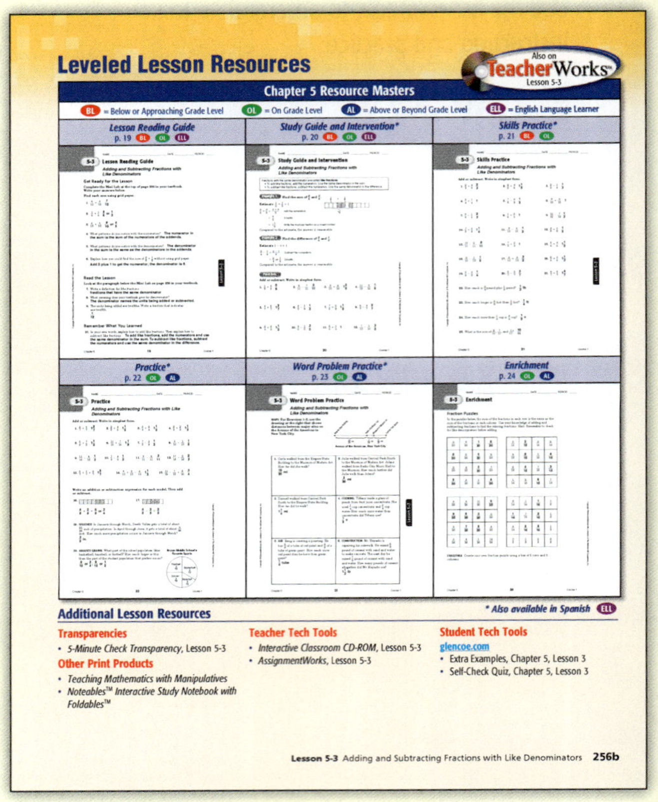

Leveled Lesson Resources

Also on TeacherWorks™ Lesson 5-3

Chapter 5 Resource Masters

BL = Below or Approaching Grade Level · OL = On Grade Level · AL = Above or Beyond Grade Level · ELL = English Language Learner

Lesson Reading Guide p. 19 BL OL ELL · Study Guide and Intervention* p. 20 BL OL ELL · Skills Practice* p. 21 BL OL

Practice* p. 22 OL AL · Word Problem Practice* p. 23 OL AL · Enrichment p. 24 OL AL

Additional Lesson Resources

* Also available in Spanish ELL

Transparencies
- *5-Minute Check Transparency*, Lesson 5-3

Other Print Products
- *Teaching Mathematics with Manipulatives*
- *Noteables™ Interactive Study Notebook with Foldables™*

Teacher Tech Tools
- *Interactive Classroom CD-ROM*, Lesson 5-3
- *AssignmentWorks*, Lesson 5-3

Student Tech Tools

glencoe.com
- Extra Examples, Chapter 5, Lesson 3
- Self-Check Quiz, Chapter 5, Lesson 3

Lesson 5-3 Adding and Subtracting Fractions with Like Denominators 256b

Math Connects, Course 1
Teacher Edition, page 256b

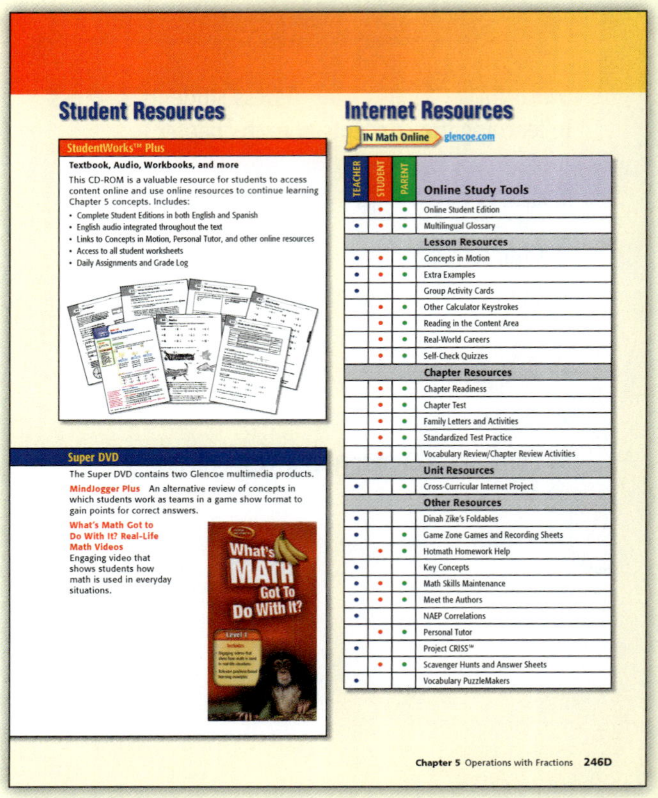

Student Resources

StudentWorks™ Plus

Textbook, Audio, Workbooks, and more

This CD-ROM is a valuable resource for students to access content online and use online resources to continue learning Chapter 5 concepts. Includes:
- Complete Student Editions in both English and Spanish
- English audio integrated throughout the text
- Links to Concepts in Motion, Personal Tutor, and other online resources
- Access to all student worksheets
- Daily Assignments and Grade Log

Super DVD

The Super DVD contains two Glencoe multimedia products.

MindJogger Plus An alternative review of concepts in which students work as teams in a game show format to gain points for correct answers.

What's Math Got to Do With It? Real-Life Math Videos Engaging video that shows students how math is used in everyday situations.

Internet Resources

IN Math Online glencoe.com

TEACHER	STUDENT	PARENT	Online Study Tools
	•	•	Online Student Edition
•	•	•	Multilingual Glossary
			Lesson Resources
•	•	•	Concepts in Motion
•	•	•	Extra Examples
•			Group Activity Cards
	•	•	Other Calculator Keystrokes
	•	•	Reading in the Content Area
	•	•	Real-World Careers
	•	•	Self-Check Quizzes
			Chapter Resources
	•	•	Chapter Readiness
	•	•	Chapter Test
	•	•	Family Letters and Activities
	•	•	Standardized Test Practice
	•	•	Vocabulary Review/Chapter Review Activities
			Unit Resources
•		•	Cross-Curricular Internet Project
			Other Resources
•			Dinah Zike's Foldables
•		•	Game Zone Games and Recording Sheets
	•	•	Hotmath Homework Help
•			Key Concepts
•	•	•	Math Skills Maintenance
•	•	•	Meet the Authors
•			NAEP Correlations
	•	•	Personal Tutor
•			Project CRISS℠
	•	•	Scavenger Hunts and Answer Sheets
•			Vocabulary PuzzleMakers

Chapter 5 Operations with Fractions 246D

Math Connects, Course 1
Teacher Edition, page 246D

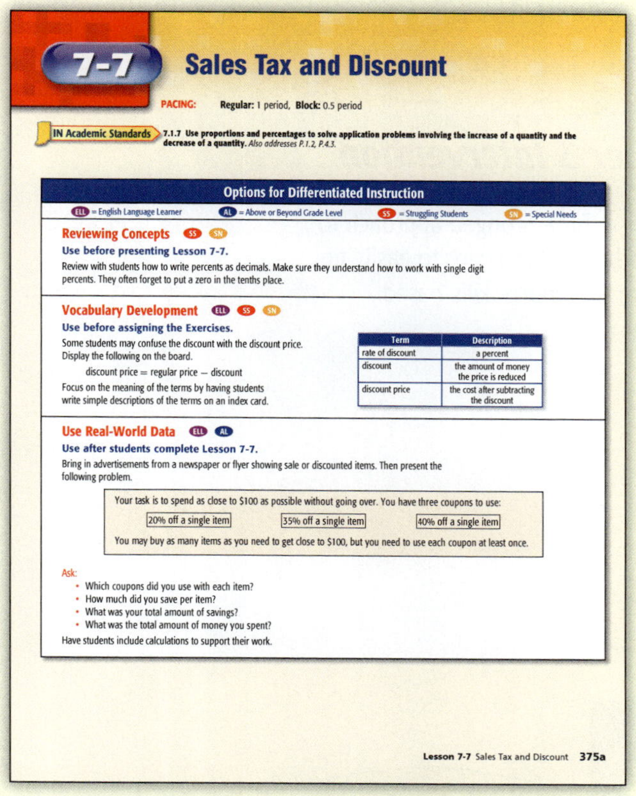

7-7 Sales Tax and Discount

PACING: **Regular:** 1 period, **Block:** 0.5 period

IN Academic Standards **7.1.7 Use proportions and percentages to solve application problems involving the increase of a quantity and the decrease of a quantity.** *Also addresses P.1.2, P.4.3.*

Options for Differentiated Instruction

ELL = English Language Learner   AL = Above or Beyond Grade Level   SS = Struggling Students   SN = Special Needs

Reviewing Concepts SS SN

Use before presenting Lesson 7-7.

Review with students how to write percents as decimals. Make sure they understand how to work with single digit percents. They often forget to put a zero in the tenths place.

Vocabulary Development ELL SS SN

Use before assigning the Exercises.

Some students may confuse the discount with the discount price. Display the following on the board.

discount price = regular price − discount

Focus on the meaning of the terms by having students write simple descriptions of the terms on an index card.

Term	Description
rate of discount	a percent
discount	the amount of money the price is reduced
discount price	the cost after subtracting the discount

Use Real-World Data ELL AL

Use after students complete Lesson 7-7.

Bring in advertisements from a newspaper or flyer showing sale or discounted items. Then present the following problem.

Your task is to spend as close to $100 as possible without going over. You have three coupons to use:

20% off a single item   35% off a single item   40% off a single item

You may buy as many items as you need to get close to $100, but you need to use each coupon at least once.

Ask:

- Which coupons did you use with each item?
- How much did you save per item?
- What was your total amount of savings?
- What was the total amount of money you spent?

Have students include calculations to support their work.

Lesson 7-7 Sales Tax and Discount **375a**

Math Connects, Course 2,
Teacher Edition, page 375a

Meeting Students' Needs

Diagnostic Teaching Every chapter and lesson includes suggestions for identifying and meeting your students' needs. Strategies include differentiation in pacing and student grouping, alternate approaches, ways to enhance instruction with manipulatives, questions to promote higher order thinking, and language hints.

Personalize instruction for:

- Struggling students
- English language learners
- Students with special needs
- Students who are above or beyond grade level in their comprehension of mathematics

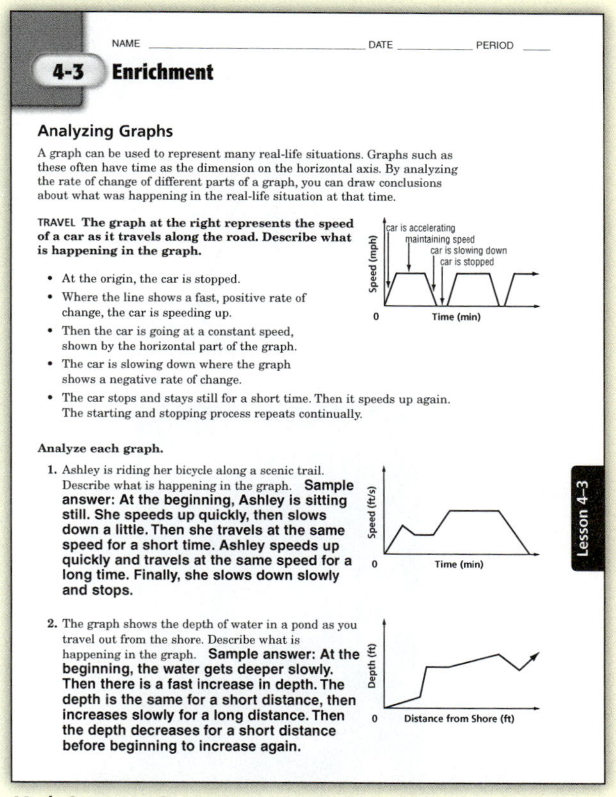

NAME ______________ DATE ________ PERIOD ____

4-3 Enrichment

Analyzing Graphs

A graph can be used to represent many real-life situations. Graphs such as these often have time as the dimension on the horizontal axis. By analyzing the rate of change of different parts of a graph, you can draw conclusions about what was happening in the real-life situation at that time.

TRAVEL **The graph at the right represents the speed of a car as it travels along the road. Describe what is happening in the graph.**

- At the origin, the car is stopped.
- Where the line shows a fast, positive rate of change, the car is speeding up.
- Then the car is going at a constant speed, shown by the horizontal part of the graph.
- The car is slowing down where the graph shows a negative rate of change.
- The car stops and stays still for a short time. Then it speeds up again. The starting and stopping process repeats continually.

car is accelerating
maintaining speed
car is slowing down
car is stopped
Speed (mph)
0
Time (min)

Analyze each graph.

1. Ashley is riding her bicycle along a scenic trail. Describe what is happening in the graph. **Sample answer: At the beginning, Ashley is sitting still. She speeds up quickly, then slows down a little. Then she travels at the same speed for a short time. Ashley speeds up quickly and travels at the same speed for a long time. Finally, she slows down slowly and stops.**

Speed (ft/s)
0
Time (min)

2. The graph shows the depth of water in a pond as you travel out from the shore. Describe what is happening in the graph. **Sample answer: At the beginning, the water gets deeper slowly. Then there is a fast increase in depth. The depth is the same for a short distance, then increases slowly for a long distance. Then the depth decreases for a short distance before beginning to increase again.**

Depth (ft)
0
Distance from Shore (ft)

Lesson 4-3

Math Connects, Course 3,
Chapter 4 Resource Masters, page 27

Advanced Learners

Acceleration and Enrichment Resources and assignments that are coded for students who are above or beyond level may be used with advanced learners. In particular, the **Enrichment Masters** may provide students with valuable opportunities for extending your lessons. **Pre-AP Activities** in the Teacher Edition provide additional opportunities for extension.

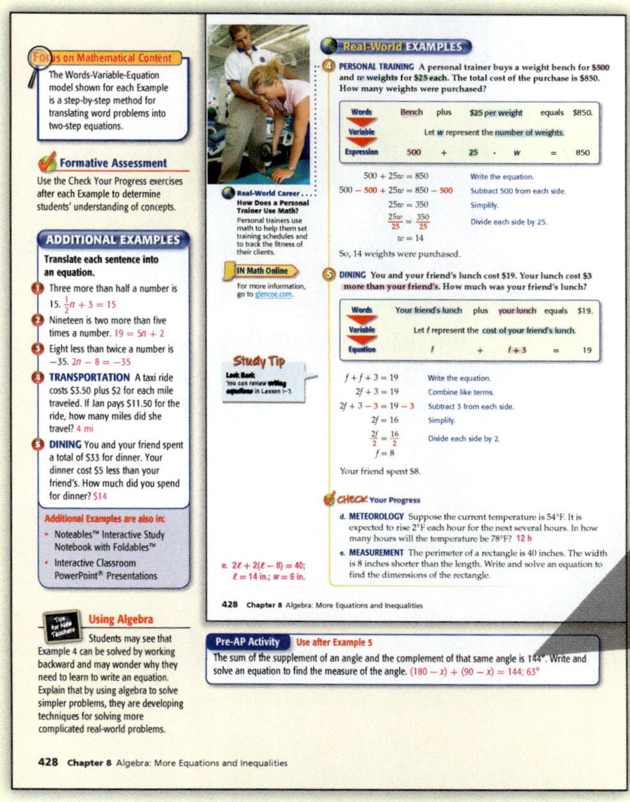

Focus on Mathematical Content

The Words-Variable-Equation model shown for each Example is a step-by-step method for translating word problems into two-step equations.

Formative Assessment

Use the Check Your Progress exercises after each Example to determine students' understanding of concepts.

ADDITIONAL EXAMPLES

Translate each sentence into an equation.

1. Three more than half a number is 15. $\frac{1}{2}n + 3 = 15$
2. Nineteen is two more than five times a number. $19 = 5n + 2$
3. Eight less than twice a number is −35. $2n - 8 = -35$
4. **TRANSPORTATION** A taxi ride costs $3.50 plus $2 for each mile traveled. If Jan pays $11.50 for the ride, how many miles did she travel? 4 mi
5. **DINING** You and your friend spent a total of $33 for dinner. Your dinner cost $5 less than your friend's. How much did you spend for dinner? $14

Additional Examples are also in:

- Noteables™ Interactive Study Notebook with Foldables™
- Interactive Classroom PowerPoint® Presentations

Real-World Career . . . How Does a Personal Trainer Use Math? Personal trainers use math to help them set training schedules and to track the fitness of their clients.

IN Math Online For more information, go to glencoe.com.

Study Tip Look Back You can review writing equations in Lesson 1-7.

Real-World EXAMPLES

4 **PERSONAL TRAINING** **A personal trainer buys a weight bench for $500 and w weights for $25 each. The total cost of the purchase is $850. How many weights were purchased?**

Words	Bench	plus	$25 per weight		equals	$850.
Variable	Let w represent the number of weights.					
Expression	500	+	25	· w	=	850

$500 + 25w = 850$ Write the equation.

$500 - 500 + 25w = 850 - 500$ Subtract 500 from each side.

$25w = 350$ Simplify.

$\frac{25w}{25} = \frac{350}{25}$ Divide each side by 25.

$w = 14$

So, 14 weights were purchased.

5 **DINING** **You and your friend's lunch cost $19. Your lunch cost $3 more than your friend's. How much was your friend's lunch?**

Words	Your friend's lunch	plus	your lunch	equals	$19.
Variable	Let f represent the cost of your friend's lunch.				
Equation	f	+	$f + 3$	=	19

$f + f + 3 = 19$ Write the equation.

$2f + 3 = 19$ Combine like terms.

$2f + 3 - 3 = 19 - 3$ Subtract 3 from each side.

$2f = 16$ Simplify.

$\frac{2f}{2} = \frac{16}{2}$ Divide each side by 2.

$f = 8$

Your friend spent $8.

CHECK Your Progress

d. **METEOROLOGY** Suppose the current temperature is 54°F. It is expected to rise 2°F each hour for the next several hours. In how many hours will the temperature be 78°F? 12 h

e. **MEASUREMENT** The perimeter of a rectangle is 40 inches. The width is 8 inches shorter than the length. Write and solve an equation to find the dimensions of the rectangle.

e. $2\ell + 2(\ell - 8) = 40$; $\ell = 14$ in.; $w = 6$ in.

428 **Chapter 8** Algebra: More Equations and Inequalities

Using Algebra (Tips for New Teachers) Students may see that Example 4 can be solved by working backward and may wonder why they need to learn to write an equation. Explain that by using algebra to solve simpler problems, they are developing techniques for solving more complicated real-world problems.

Pre-AP Activity Use after Example 5

The sum of the supplement of an angle and the complement of that same angle is 144°. Write and solve an equation to find the measure of the angle. $(180 - x) + (90 - x) = 144$; 63°

428 **Chapter 8** Algebra: More Equations and Inequalities

Math Connects, Course 3,
Teacher Edition, page 428

Pre-AP Activity Use after Example 5

The sum of the supplement of an angle and the complement of that same angle is 144°. Write and solve an equation to find the measure of the angle. $(180 - x) + (90 - x) = 144$; 63°

TEACHER HANDBOOK

Blending Your Instruction

Basal – NSF-Funded – Tier 3 Intervention

Math Connects, MathScape, and ***Math Triumphs*** provide a three-pronged approach to mathematics instruction. This unique combination provides built-in strategies to easily tip the balance of instruction to a more conceptual approach or to a more skills-based approach, depending on the needs of your students.

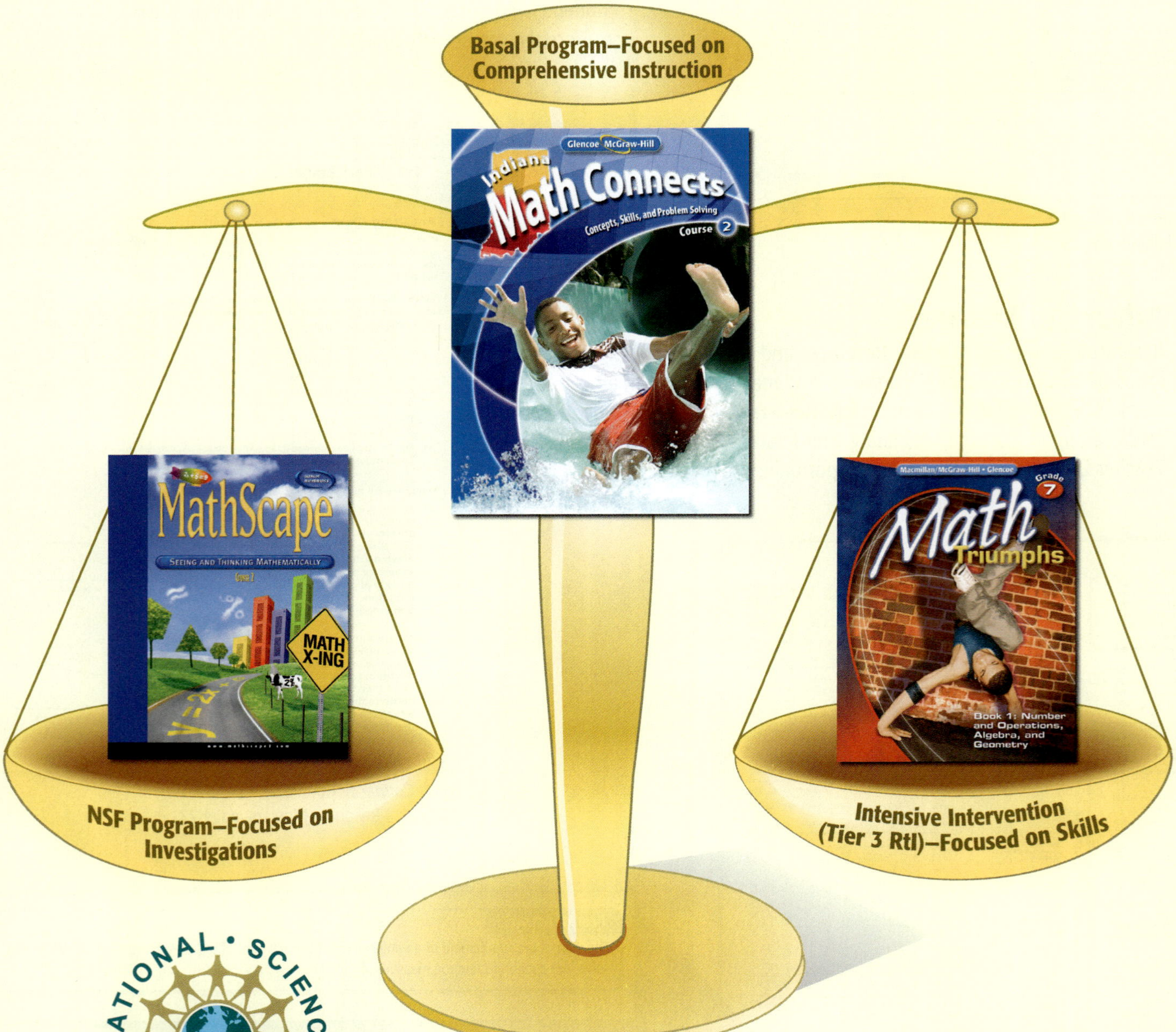

NATIONAL • SCIENCE • FOUNDATION

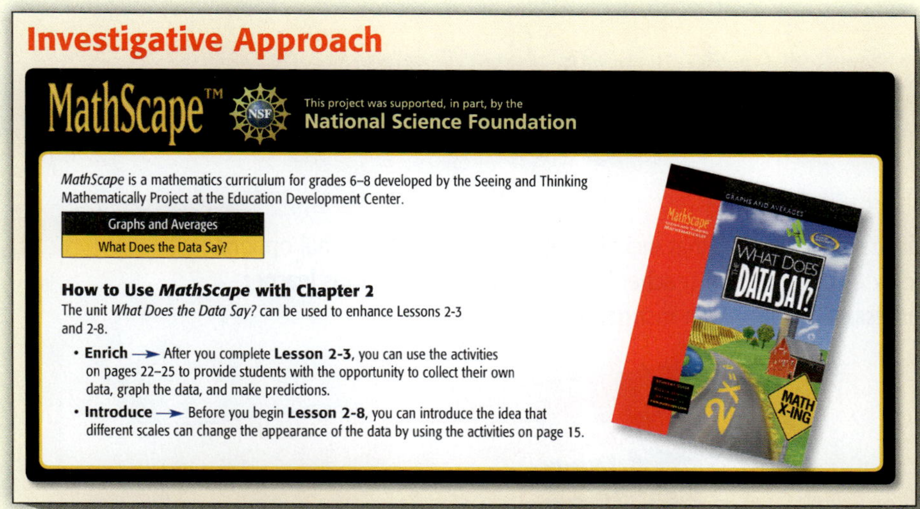
Investigative Approach

MathScape™ This project was supported, in part, by the **National Science Foundation**

MathScape is a mathematics curriculum for grades 6–8 developed by the Seeing and Thinking Mathematically Project at the Education Development Center.

Graphs and Averages
What Does the Data Say?

How to Use *MathScape* with Chapter 2
The unit *What Does the Data Say?* can be used to enhance Lessons 2-3 and 2-8.

- **Enrich** → After you complete **Lesson 2-3**, you can use the activities on pages 22–25 to provide students with the opportunity to collect their own data, graph the data, and make predictions.
- **Introduce** → Before you begin **Lesson 2-8**, you can introduce the idea that different scales can change the appearance of the data by using the activities on page 15.

Investigative Approach

The Chapter Planner, in the Teacher Edition of ***Math Connects,*** references alternative lessons found in ***MathScape.*** These lessons provide opportunities for investigative instruction with hands-on explorations.

RtI (Response to Intervention)

In the ***Math Connects*** Teacher Editions, the Data-Driven Decision Making chart provides a comprehensive RtI (Response to Intervention) beginning with diagnostic review and continuing with prescriptions at all three RtI tiers.

- **Tier 1** – Leveled exercise sets and leveled resources
- **Tier 2** – Strategic Intervention Guide (1–5), Study Guide and Intervention (6–8)
- **Tier 3** – Intensive Intervention, ***Math Triumphs***

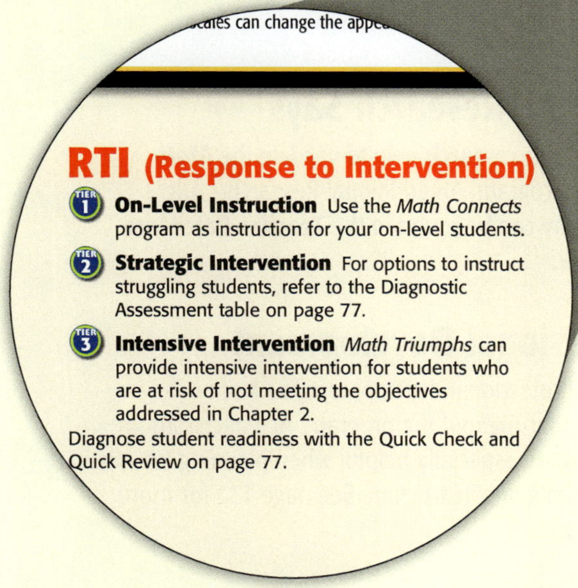

...cales can change the appe...

RTI (Response to Intervention)

On-Level Instruction Use the *Math Connects* program as instruction for your on-level students.

Strategic Intervention For options to instruct struggling students, refer to the Diagnostic Assessment table on page 77.

Intensive Intervention *Math Triumphs* can provide intensive intervention for students who are at risk of not meeting the objectives addressed in Chapter 2.

Diagnose student readiness with the Quick Check and Quick Review on page 77.

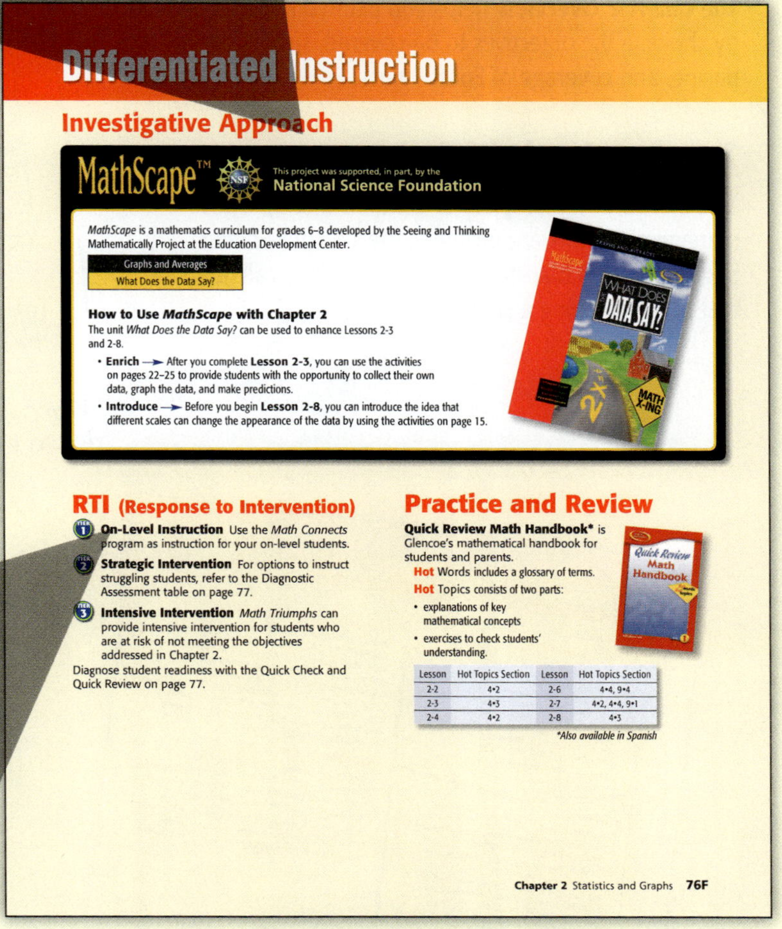
Differentiated Instruction

Investigative Approach

MathScape™ This project was supported, in part, by the **National Science Foundation**

MathScape is a mathematics curriculum for grades 6–8 developed by the Seeing and Thinking Mathematically Project at the Education Development Center.

Graphs and Averages
What Does the Data Say?

How to Use *MathScape* with Chapter 2
The unit *What Does the Data Say?* can be used to enhance Lessons 2-3 and 2-8.

- **Enrich** → After you complete **Lesson 2-3**, you can use the activities on pages 22–25 to provide students with the opportunity to collect their own data, graph the data, and make predictions.
- **Introduce** → Before you begin **Lesson 2-8**, you can introduce the idea that different scales can change the appearance of the data by using the activities on page 15.

RTI (Response to Intervention)

On-Level Instruction Use the *Math Connects* program as instruction for your on-level students.

Strategic Intervention For options to instruct struggling students, refer to the Diagnostic Assessment table on page 77.

Intensive Intervention *Math Triumphs* can provide intensive intervention for students who are at risk of not meeting the objectives addressed in Chapter 2.

Diagnose student readiness with the Quick Check and Quick Review on page 77.

Practice and Review

Quick Review Math Handbook* is Glencoe's mathematical handbook for students and parents.

Hot Words includes a glossary of terms.

Hot Topics consists of two parts:

- explanations of key mathematical concepts
- exercises to check students' understanding.

Lesson	Hot Topics Section	Lesson	Hot Topics Section
2-2	4•2	2-6	4•4, 9•4
2-3	4•3	2-7	4•2, 4•4, 9•1
2-4	4•2	2-8	4•3

*Also available in Spanish

Chapter 2 Statistics and Graphs **76F**

Math Connects, Course 1
Teacher Edition, page 76F

Planning for Success

Ease of Use

Math Connects has a strong instructional model that includes differentiated instructional options, reteaching, reinforcement, and extension options, Teacher Tips to help address various learners, Pre-AP/Advanced items, and assessment linked with instruction.

Convenient Lesson Planning at Your Fingertips

The **Chapter Overview** helps you plan your instruction by showing the objectives to be covered, suggested pacing, and coverage of Focal Points.

TeacherWorks™ Plus

This electronic lesson planner contains multi-purpose management software including the Teacher Edition pages, program blackline masters, and daily calendars that make planning a snap.

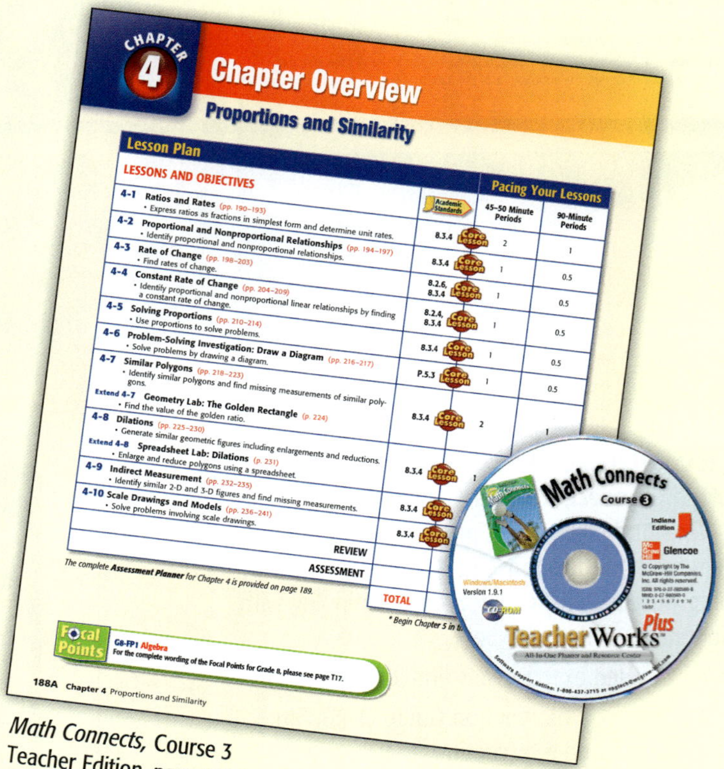

Chapter 4

Chapter Overview

Proportions and Similarity

Lesson Plan

LESSONS AND OBJECTIVES	Academic Standards	Pacing Your Lessons: 45–50 Minute Periods	90-Minute Periods
4-1 Ratios and Rates (pp. 190–193) • Express ratios as fractions in simplest form and determine unit rates.	8.3.4 Core Lesson	2	1
4-2 Proportional and Nonproportional Relationships (pp. 194–197) • Identify proportional and nonproportional relationships.	8.3.4 Core Lesson	1	0.5
4-3 Rate of Change (pp. 198–203) • Find rates of change.	8.2.6, 8.3.4 Core Lesson	1	0.5
4-4 Constant Rate of Change (pp. 204–209) • Identify proportional and nonproportional linear relationships by finding a constant rate of change.	8.2.4, 8.3.4 Core Lesson	1	0.5
4-5 Solving Proportions (pp. 210–214) • Use proportions to solve problems.	8.3.4 Core Lesson	1	0.5
4-6 Problem-Solving Investigation: Draw a Diagram (pp. 216–217) • Solve problems by drawing a diagram.	P.5.3 Core Lesson	1	0.5
4-7 Similar Polygons (pp. 218–223) • Identify similar polygons and find missing measurements of similar polygons. **Extend 4-7 Geometry Lab: The Golden Rectangle** (p. 224) • Find the value of the golden ratio.	8.3.4 Core Lesson	2	1
4-8 Dilations (pp. 225–230) • Generate similar geometric figures including enlargements and reductions. **Extend 4-8 Spreadsheet Lab: Dilations** (p. 231) • Enlarge and reduce polygons using a spreadsheet.	8.3.4 Core Lesson	1	
4-9 Indirect Measurement (pp. 232–235) • Identify similar 2-D and 3-D figures and find missing measurements.	8.3.4 Core Lesson		
4-10 Scale Drawings and Models (pp. 236–241) • Solve problems involving scale drawings.	8.3.4 Core Lesson		
REVIEW			
ASSESSMENT			
TOTAL			

The complete ***Assessment Planner*** for Chapter 4 is provided on page 189.

* Begin Chapter 5 in t

Focal Points **G8-FP1 Algebra** For the complete wording of the Focal Points for Grade 8, please see page T17.

188A **Chapter 4** Proportions and Similarity

Math Connects, Course 3
Teacher Edition, page 188A

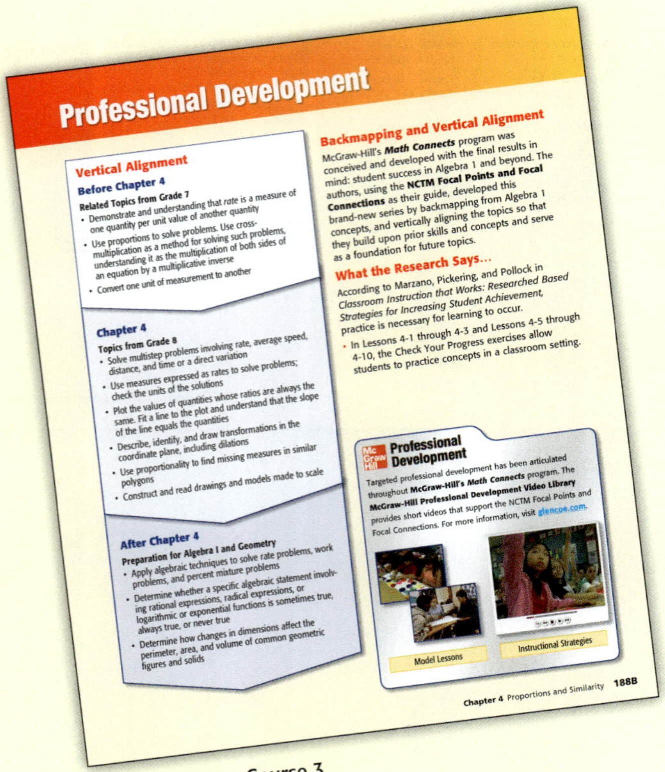

Professional Development

Vertical Alignment

Before Chapter 4

Related Topics from Grade 7
- Demonstrate and understanding that *rate* is a measure of one quantity per unit value of another quantity
- Use proportions to solve problems. Use cross-multiplication as a method for solving such problems, understanding it as the multiplication of both sides of an equation by a multiplicative inverse
- Convert one unit of measurement to another

Chapter 4

Topics from Grade 8
- Solve multistep problems involving rate, average speed, distance, and time or a direct variation
- Use measures expressed as rates to solve problems; check the units of the solutions
- Plot the values of quantities whose ratios are always the same. Fit a line to the plot and understand that the slope of the line equals the quantities
- Describe, identify, and draw transformations in the coordinate plane, including dilations
- Use proportionality to find missing measures in similar polygons
- Construct and read drawings and models made to scale

After Chapter 4

Preparation for Algebra I and Geometry
- Apply algebraic techniques to solve rate problems, work problems, and percent mixture problems
- Determine whether a specific algebraic statement involving rational expressions, radical expressions, or logarithmic or exponential functions is sometimes true, always true, or never true
- Determine how changes in dimensions affect the perimeter, area, and volume of common geometric figures and solids

Backmapping and Vertical Alignment

McGraw-Hill's ***Math Connects*** program was conceived and developed with the final results in mind: student success in Algebra 1 and beyond. The authors, using the **NCTM Focal Points and Focal Connections** as their guide, developed this brand-new series by backmapping from Algebra 1 concepts, and vertically aligning the topics so that they build upon prior skills and concepts and serve as a foundation for future topics.

What the Research Says...

According to Marzano, Pickering, and Pollock in *Classroom Instruction that Works: Researched Based Strategies for Increasing Student Achievement,* practice is necessary for learning to occur.
- In Lessons 4-1 through 4-3 and Lessons 4-5 through 4-10, the Check Your Progress exercises allow students to practice concepts in a classroom setting.

Professional Development

Targeted professional development has been articulated throughout McGraw-Hill's ***Math Connects*** program. The **McGraw-Hill Professional Development Video Library** provides short videos that support the NCTM Focal Points and Focal Connections. For more information, visit glencoe.com.

Model Lessons

Instructional Strategies

Chapter 4 Proportions and Similarity 188B

Math Connects, Course 3
Teacher Edition, page 188B

Vertical Alignment

Topics are presented to build upon prior grade level skills and concepts and to serve as a foundation for future topics.

What the Research Says

Citations from **research** help to validate the ***Math Connects*** program. An additional Research Bibliography can be found in the **Teacher Reference Handbook.**

Professional Development

Targeted professional development has been articulated throughout the program. Actual classroom video clips are especially helpful when planning lessons and differentiating instruction. See page T32 for more information.

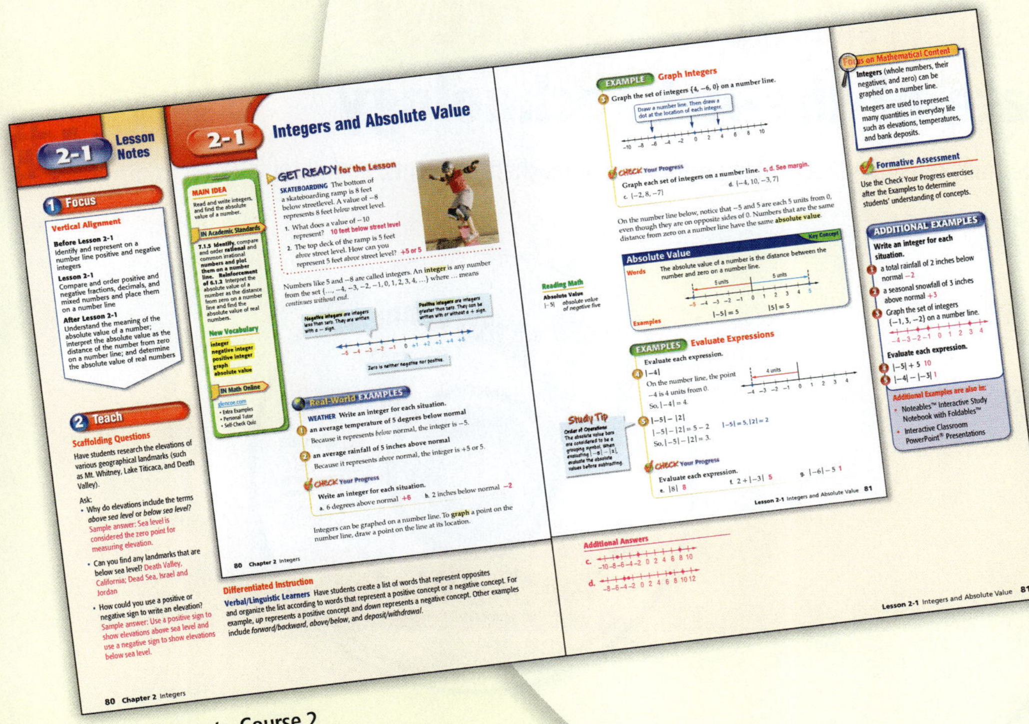

Math Connects, Course 2
Teacher Edition, pages 80–81

Four-Step Teaching Plan

This organizes your instruction as you **Focus** and **Teach** and help your students **Practice** and **Assess** what they've learned.

Vertical Alignment

Vertical Alignment at the beginning of each lesson shows the objectives that lead into and follow the current lesson's content for a coherent PreK–12 scope and sequence.

Scaffolding Questions

Each lesson contains **Scaffolding Questions** for you to use to help students investigate and understand the main ideas of the lesson.

Additional Examples

Each **Additional Example** mirrors the example in the Student Edition. The Additional Examples are also available as a PowerPoint® presentation on the **Interactive Classroom** CD-ROM.

Differentiated Homework Options

Because most classrooms include students at a wide range of ability levels, **Differentiated Homework Options** allow you to customize your assignments.

Assessment Activities

Formative Assessment activities provide alternate ways to determine student comprehension at the end of each lesson.

- **Ticket Out the Door** Students must answer the given question and hand it to the teacher as they leave the classroom.
- **Yesterday's News** Students connect what they learned today to yesterday's lesson.
- **Crystal Ball** Students predict how today's lesson will relate to the next lesson.
- **Name the Math** Students tell what mathematics are used in a problem.

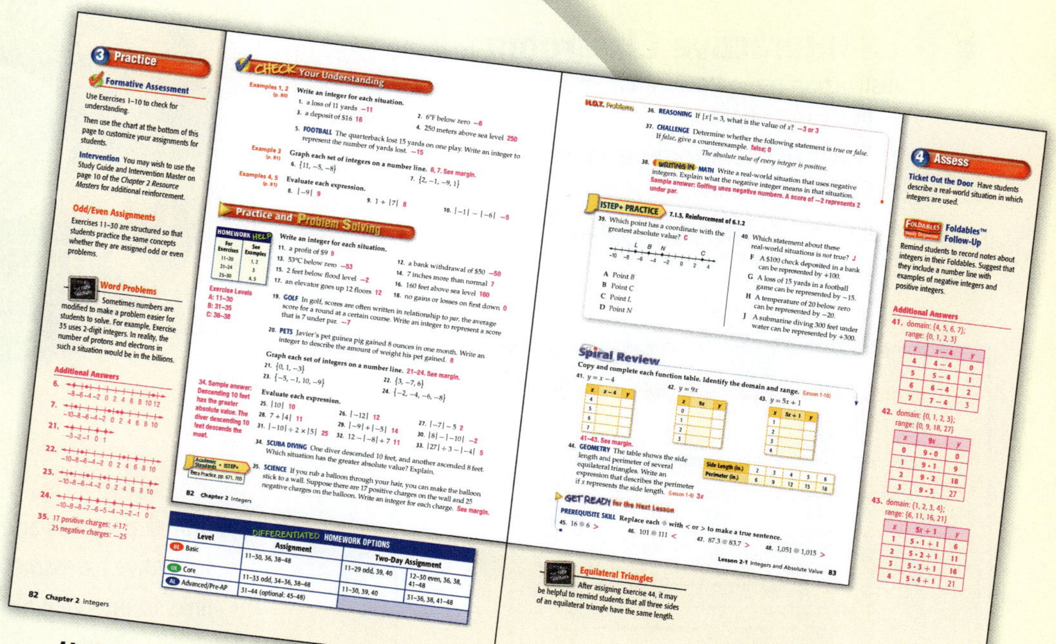

Math Connects, Course 2
Teacher Edition, pages 82–83

Planning for Success
State-of-the-Art Technology

Math Connects provides fully integrated technology resources for teachers, students, and parents.

For Teachers

TeacherWorks™ Plus is your all-in-one planner and resource center.

- entire Teacher Edition
- all print ancillaries
- electronic lesson planner

ExamView® Assessment Suite allows teachers to create and customize their own assessment and assignments.

New features:

- correlated to state standards
- online content update
- one- or two-column formatting

Use **Interactive Classroom** to guide instruction using PowerPoint™

- In-Class Examples
- 5-Minute Check Transparencies
- Concepts in Motion
- links to **IN Math Online**

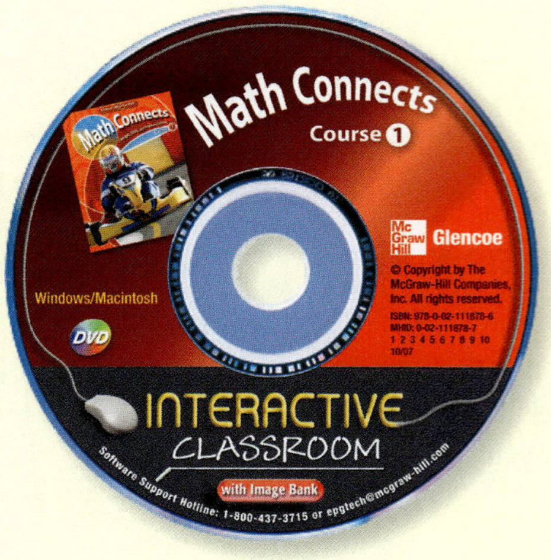

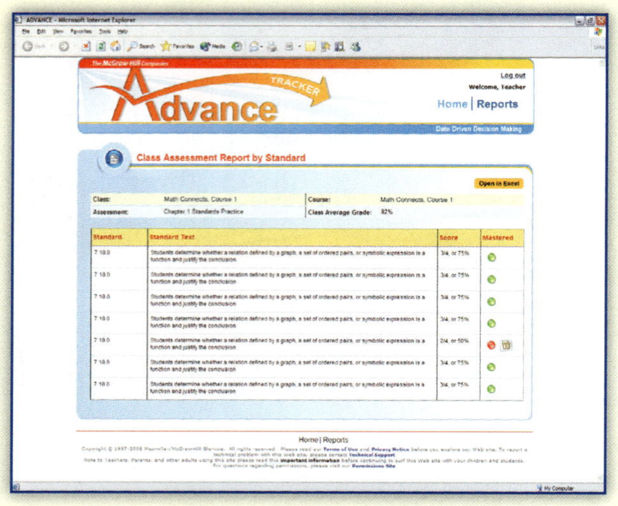

Math Connects, Course 1

Advance Tracker Learner Management System helps you track progress and differentiate your instruction.

- formative assessments aligned to standards
- links to intervention help

For Students

StudentWorks™ Plus is your students' backpack solution.

- entire Student Edition
- all student worksheets
- links to **IN Math Online**

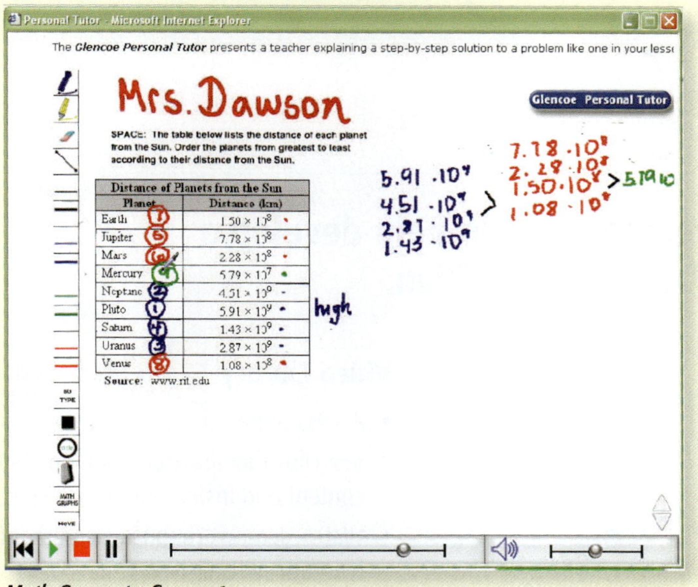

Math Connects, Course 1
Web site, Personal Tutor

IN Math Online provides a wealth of resources convenient for students and parents!

- Self-Check Quizzes
- Personal Tutor
- Concepts in Motion
- eGlossary (14 languages)
- And much, much more!

IN Math Online *Math Connect's* **eBook** is easy to use, easy to read, and packed with features.

- links to online study tools and resources right from the page
- includes audio

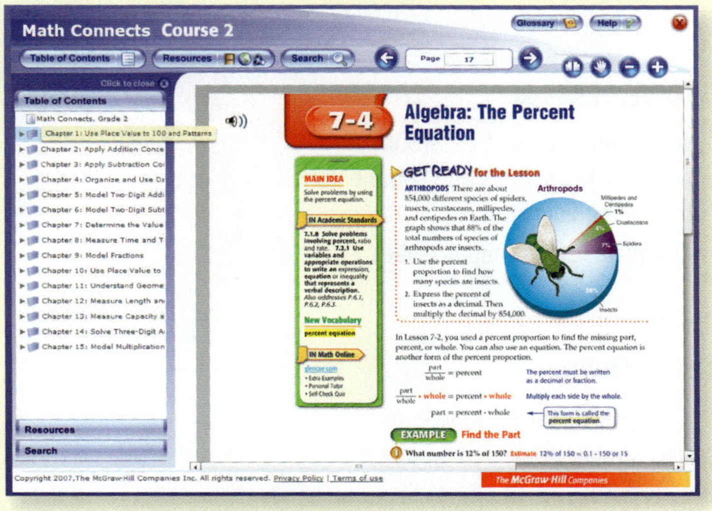

Math Connects, Course 2
eBook, page 361

PreK-12 Data-Driven Professional Development

McGraw-Hill Professional Development (MHPD) provides a comprehensive plan for mathematics that is fully aligned and articulated with ***Math Connects K–8*** and the ***Glencoe Mathematics*** high school series.

Professional Development Needs	Online Courses	DVD Workshops	Video Library	Teach-Use-Succeed	Ready-Access Math
Has immediate classroom application	✓	✓	✓	✓	✓
Builds content knowledge	✓	✓			✓
Promotes best teaching practices		✓	✓		
Supports new and experienced teachers	✓	✓	✓	✓	✓
Allows customization of courses	✓	✓			✓
Can be self-paced	✓	✓		✓	✓
Adaptable for various timeframes	✓	✓	✓	✓	✓
Is grade-level specific			✓	✓	✓
Promotes a learning community	✓	✓			✓
Provides vertically-aligned content	✓	✓	✓		✓
Helps with RtI (Response to Intervention), Tiers 1–3	✓	✓	✓		✓

Use students' mathematics achievement data to help develop a targeted Professional Development Plan.

Accredited Online Courses

(available for purchase)

- Watch video clips of math classrooms, complete interactive exercises, and develop electronic portfolios.
- Complete each 3- to 5-hour online module one segment at a time.
- Earn university credit (additional tuition charge)

DVD Workshops

- Watch video clips of classroom mathematics lessons and commentaries by leading educators.
- Complete lessons and activities.

MHPD Online

- Access this online Professional Development resource for K–12 educators.
- Link to relevant Web sites.
- Download grade-level student resources.

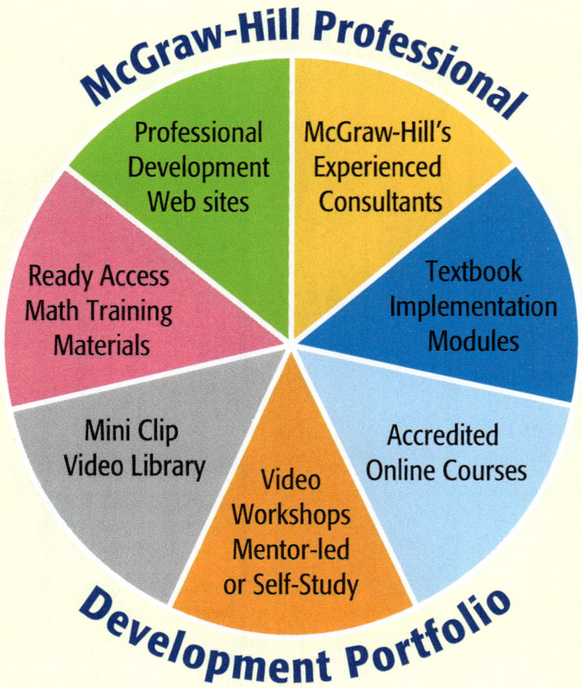

Video Library

IN Math Online

- Access hundreds of K–12 video clips.
- See clips that illustrate mathematics content and instructional strategies.
- Watch demonstrations or commentaries by math specialists.

Teach-Use-Succeed Textbook Implementation Modules

- Watch an experienced teacher demonstrate the *Math Connects* K–8 Student Editions, Teacher Editions, and program ancillaries
- Online or DVD

Ready-Access Math, Personalized Professional Development

- Access training materials for nearly 300 mathematics professional development lessons.
- Create a customized sequence of professional development sessions.
- Deliver 45–60 minute after-school professional development sessions.

Program Components

	Grade K	Grade 1	Grade 2	Grade 3	Grade 4	Grade 5	Grade 6	Grade 7
Chapter Resource Masters	●	●	●	●	●	●	●	●
Daily Reteach Transparencies	●	●	●	●	●	●		
5-Minute Check Transparencies		●	●	●	●	●	●	●
Noteables Interactive Notebook							●	●
Hands-On Activity Tools and Resources	●	●	●	●	●	●		
Teaching Math with Manipulatives							●	●
ELL Guide	●	●	●	●	●	●	●	
Strategic Intervention Guide		●	●	●	●	●		
Problem of the Day/Week	●	●	●	●	●	●	●	●
Learning Station Cards	●	●	●	●	●	●		
Math Routines on the Go	●	●	●					
Quick Review Math Handbook							●	●
Visual Vocabulary Cards	●	●	●	●	●	●		
Transition Blackline Masters				●				
Math Skills Maintenance							●	●
Real-World Problem Solving Readers	●	●	●	●	●	●		
Graphic Novels							●	●
Dinah Zike's Teaching with Foldables	●	●	●	●	●	●	●	●
Diagnostic and Placement Tests	●	●	●	●	●	●	●	●
StudentWorks Plus CD-ROM	●	●	●	●	●	●	●	●
TeacherWorks Plus DVD	●	●	●	●	●	●	●	●
ExamView CD-ROM	●	●	●	●	●	●	●	●
Interactive Classroom PowerPoint™				●	●	●	●	●
Math Adventures with Dot and Ray CD-ROM	●	●	●	●	●	●	●	
Classroom Games CD-ROM	●	●	●	●	●	●		
AssignmentWorks CD-ROM							●	●
Math Songs CD-ROM	●	●	●	●	●	●		
Individual Manipulative Kit	●	●	●	●	●	●	●	●
Classroom Manipulative Kit	●	●	●	●	●	●	●	●
Overhead Manipulative Kit	●	●	●	●	●	●	●	●
Teacher Tool Kit	●	●	●	●	●	●		
Magnetic Manipulative Kit	●	●	●	●	●	●		
Student Edition Flip Book	●							
Activity Flip Chart	●							
Robot Puppet	●	●	●					
WorkMats	●	●	●	●	●	●		
Professional Development	●	●	●	●	●	●	●	●

Program Manipulatives

Manipulative	Suggested Alternative	PreK	Grade K	Grade 1	Grade 2	Grade 3	Grade 4	Grade 5	Grade 6	Grade 7	Grade 8
Attribute Buttons	real buttons, pasta	●	●								
Color Tiles	blocks, buttons	●	●								
Graphing Mats	posterboard	●	●								
Attribute Blocks	pasta, buttons	●	●	●	●						
Student Clock	paper plate, brads		●	●	●	●	●	●			
Demonstration Clock	paper plate, brads		●	●	●	●	●	●			
Connecting Cubes	paper clips	●	●	●	●	●	●	●			
Number Cubes	spinner, cards	●	●	●	●	●	●	●	●	●	●
Spinners	construction paper, paper clip, pencil	●	●	●	●	●	●	●	●	●	●
Two-Colored Counters	buttons, coins, beans	●	●	●	●	●	●	●	●	●	●
Pattern Blocks	construction paper	●	●	●	●	●	●	●	●	●	
Geometric Solids/ Models	cans, boxes, balls	●	●	●	●	●	●	●			
Bucket Balance	ruler, paper cups, string	●	●	●	●	●	●	●			
Base-Ten Blocks	grid paper			●	●	●	●	●	●	●	
Money	real money, construction paper			●	●	●	●	●			
Ruler	straightedge, book			●	●	●	●	●	●	●	●
Fraction Circles	construction paper			●	●	●	●	●			
Fraction Models						●	●	●			
Geoboards	dot paper			●	●	●	●	●	●	●	●
Compass	paper clip					●	●	●	●	●	●
Protractor						●	●	●	●	●	●
Plastic Cups	paper cups					●	●	●	●	●	●
Algebra Tiles	blocks, buttons, coins								●	●	●
Centimeter Cubes	blocks								●	●	●
Equation Mats	construction paper								●	●	●
Stopwatch	clock, watch								●	●	
Measuring Cups	paper cups								●	●	
Geomirrors	mirror								●	●	
Tangrams	construction paper								●	●	

Teacher Edition

Glencoe McGraw-Hill

Indiana Math Connects

Concepts, Skills, and Problem Solving

Course 2

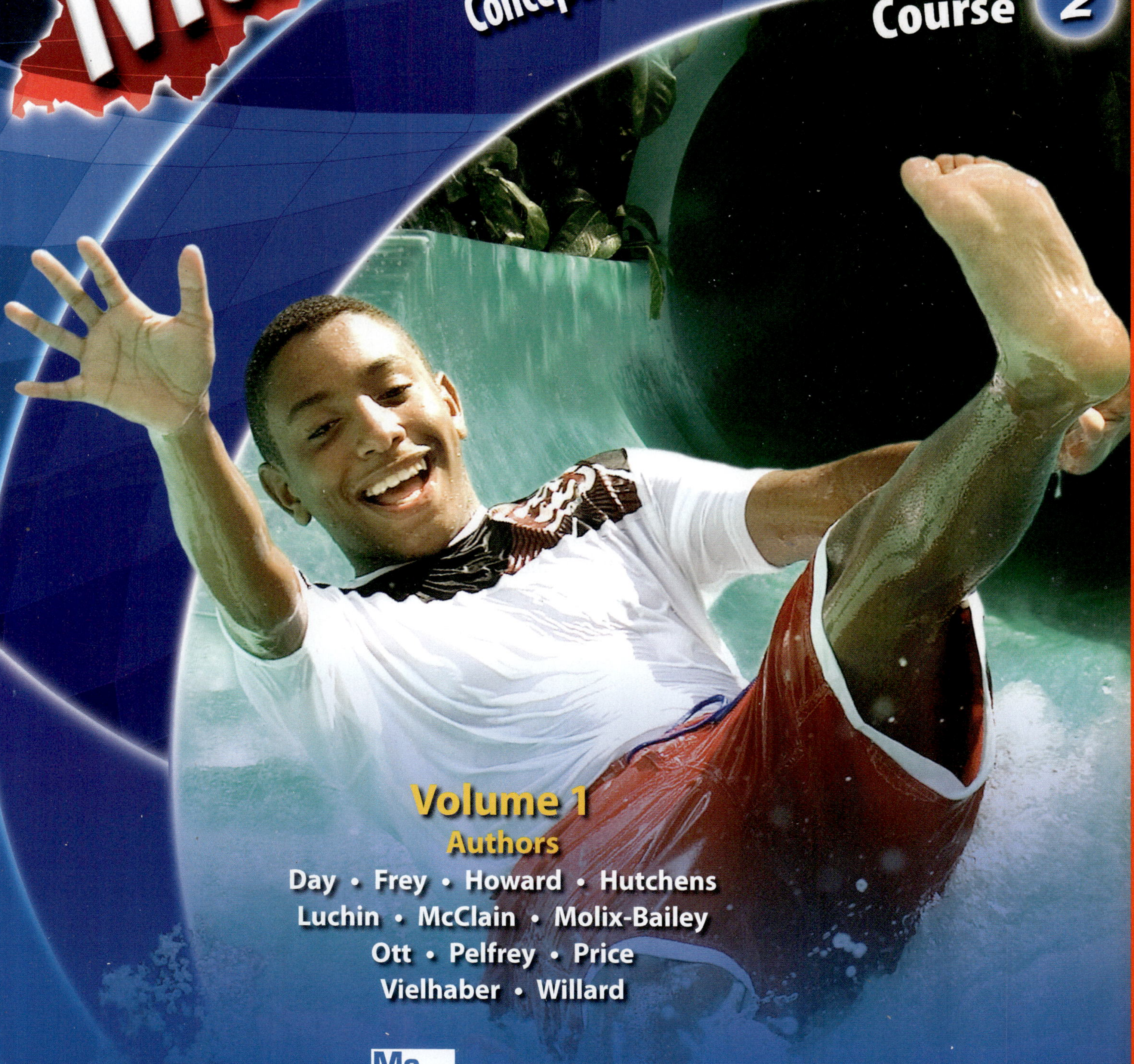

Volume 1

Authors

Day • Frey • Howard • Hutchens
Luchin • McClain • Molix-Bailey
Ott • Pelfrey • Price
Vielhaber • Willard

Mc Graw Hill Glencoe

Welcome to *Indiana Math Connects*

WELCOME TO

Indiana Math Connects

COURSE 2

Master Indiana's Academic Standards in 3 Easy Steps

1 Practice the Standards throughout the Lessons

- The lessons address the October 2008 draft of Indiana's Academic Standards for Mathematics. Look for the Indiana Academic Standards logo throughout the lessons.

IN Academic Standards

7.3.3 Identify, describe and construct similarity relationships and solve problems involving similarity by using proportional reasoning.

New Vocabulary

- Your textbook also contains more lessons for Indiana. Look for the Focus on Indiana section after the Table of Contents.

- Lessons contain ISTEP+ practice questions that are aligned to the October 2008 draft of Indiana's Academic Standards. These questions are like those on ISTEP+ and they will provide you with ongoing opportunities to sharpen your test-taking skills.

ISTEP+ PRACTICE

Indiana Reviewers

Each Indiana Reviewer gave feedback and suggestions for improving the effectiveness of the PreK–8 *Indiana Math Connects* program.

Stacy Arnold
Mathematics Teacher
Clay Middle School
Carmel, IN

Marilyn Elleman
Mathematics Department Chairperson
Union County Middle School
Liberty, IN

Larry Hart
Department Chairperson
St. Malachy School
Brownsburg, IN

Chad Hartmann
Mathematics Teacher
Helfrich Park Middle School
Evansville, IN

Patricia Hufford
Mathematics Teacher
West Lafayette Junior/Senior High School
West Lafayette, IN

Nathan Keith
Mathematics Teacher and Department Chairperson
Westlane Middle School
Indianapolis, IN

Jane Mahan
Math Coach
Lincoln Elementary
Evansville, Indiana

Kathleen Rieke
Coordinator of Mathematics, Science, and Title I MSD
Washington Township Schools
Indianapolis, IN

Paul E. Smith
Principal
Glenwood Middle School
Evansville, IN

2 Practice the Standards throughout the Chapter

- Every chapter contains two full pages of ISTEP+ Test Practice. The ISTEP+ Test Practice gives you a chance to put your math skills to use.

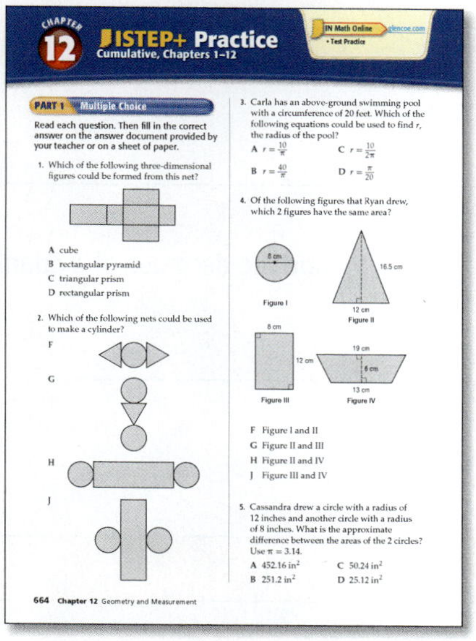

CHAPTER 12 ISTEP+ Practice
Cumulative, Chapters 1–12

IN Math Online glencoe.com
• Test Practice

PART 1 Multiple Choice

Read each question. Then fill in the correct answer on the answer document provided by your teacher or on a sheet of paper.

1. Which of the following three-dimensional figures could be formed from this net?

A cube
B rectangular pyramid
C triangular prism
D rectangular prism

2. Which of the following nets could be used to make a cylinder?

F
G
H
J

3. Carla has an above-ground swimming pool with a circumference of 20 feet. Which of the following equations could be used to find r, the radius of the pool?

A $r = \frac{10}{\pi}$ C $r = \frac{10}{2\pi}$
B $r = \frac{40}{\pi}$ D $r = \frac{\pi}{20}$

4. Of the following figures that Ryan drew, which 2 figures have the same area?

F Figure I and II
G Figure II and III
H Figure II and IV
J Figure III and IV

5. Cassandra drew a circle with a radius of 12 inches and another circle with a radius of 8 inches. What is the approximate difference between the areas of the 2 circles? Use $\pi = 3.14$.

A $452.16\ in^2$ C $50.24\ in^2$
B $251.2\ in^2$ D $25.12\ in^2$

664 Chapter 12 Geometry and Measurement

3 Practice the Standards Before the Test

- If you've followed steps 1 and 2, you should be more than ready for the ISTEP+ test. But just in case you want to make sure, use the *Get Ready for the ISTEP+* section at the end of your book to practice questions that are organized by strand. Lesson references are included for you should you need a little refresher.

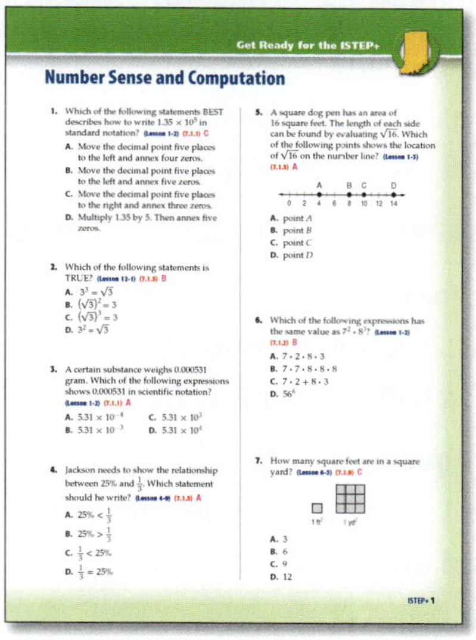

Get Ready for the ISTEP+

Number Sense and Computation

1. Which of the following statements BEST describes how to write 1.35×10^5 in standard notation? (Lesson 1-2) (7.1.1) C
A. Move the decimal point five places to the left and annex four zeros.
B. Move the decimal point five places to the left and annex five zeros.
C. Move the decimal point five places to the right and annex three zeros.
D. Multiply 1.35 by 5. Then annex five zeros.

2. Which of the following statements is TRUE? (Lesson 12-1) (7.1.5) B
A. $3^3 = \sqrt{3}$
B. $(\sqrt{3})^2 = 3$
C. $(\sqrt{3})^3 = 3$
D. $3^2 = \sqrt{3}$

3. A certain substance weighs 0.000531 gram. Which of the following expressions shows 0.000531 in scientific notation? (Lesson 1-2) (7.1.1) A
A. 5.31×10^{-4} C. 5.31×10^3
B. 5.31×10^{-3} D. 5.31×10^4

4. Jackson needs to show the relationship between 25% and $\frac{1}{3}$. Which statement should he write? (Lesson 4-9) (7.1.5) A
A. $25\% < \frac{1}{3}$
B. $25\% > \frac{1}{3}$
C. $\frac{1}{3} < 25\%$
D. $\frac{1}{3} = 25\%$

5. A square dog pen has an area of 16 square feet. The length of each side can be found by evaluating $\sqrt{16}$. Which of the following points shows the location of $\sqrt{16}$ on the number line? (Lesson 1-5) (7.1.5) A

A. point A
B. point B
C. point C
D. point D

6. Which of the following expressions has the same value as $7^2 \cdot 8^3$? (Lesson 1-2) (7.1.2) B
A. $7 \cdot 2 \cdot 8 \cdot 3$
B. $7 \cdot 7 \cdot 8 \cdot 8 \cdot 8$
C. $7 \cdot 2 + 8 \cdot 3$
D. 56^6

7. How many square feet are in a square yard? (Lesson 6-3) (7.1.9) C

A. 3
B. 6
C. 9
D. 12

ISTEP+ 1

Pink Peonies

Indiana's Core Standards, Grade 7, Correlated to *Indiana Math Connects*, Course 2

See pages vi-xi for standard indicators and their correlations.

Core Standard 1 Number Sense and Computation
Exponents Use whole number exponents for repeated multiplication. Use scientific notation for large numbers. **Standard Indicators: 7.1.1, 7.1.2, 7.1.3**
Proportions and Percentages Use proportions and percentages to solve application problems involving the increase of a quantity and the decrease of a quantity. Solve problems involving percent, ratio, rate and similar triangles. **Standard Indicators: 7.1.8, 7.1.9**
Multiplication and Division with Fractions and Decimals Understand and perform multiplication and division with negative decimals and fractions. **Standard Indicator: 7.1.7**
Core Standard 2 Geometry and Measurement
Transformations Identify and use the following transformations: translations, rotations and reflections. **Standard Indicator: 7.3.2**
Core Standard 3 Algebra and Functions
Expressions Evaluate numerical expressions and simplify algebraic expressions involving rational and irrational numbers. **Standard Indicators: 7.2.1, 7.2.3**
Linear Equations Write and solve two-step equations and inequalities in one variable. **Standard Indicators: 7.2.1, 7.2.2**
Graphs of Lines Find the slope of a line from its graph and relate the slope of a line to similar triangles. Draw the graph of a line given its slope and one point on the line or two points on the line. Graph proportional relationships and identify the unit rate as the slope of the related line. **Standard Indicators: 7.2.5, 7.2.6, 7.2.7**

Core Standard 4 Data Analysis and Probability
Making Estimates and Data Displays Use proportions to make estimates about a population based on a sample. Create, analyze and interpret data sets in multiple ways using bar graphs, frequency tables, line plots, histograms and circle graphs. **Standard Indicators: 7.4.1, 7.4.2, 7.4.3, 7.4.4**
Theoretical Probability Understand that when all outcomes of an experiment are equally likely, the theoretical probability of an event is the fraction of outcomes in which the event occurs. Use theoretical probability and proportions to make predictions. **Standard Indicators: 7.4.5**

RSP = Reading to Solve Problems; For the Additional Lessons, see the *Focus on Indiana* section (IN0-IN57).

Indiana's Academic Standards, Grade 7, Correlated to *Indiana Math Connects*, Course 2

Boldfaced standards indicate the standard(s) that are the main focus of the lesson.

Academic Standards		Lesson(s)	Page Number(s)
Standard 1	**Number Sense and Computation**		
7.1.1	Read, write, compare and solve problems using whole numbers in scientific notation.	**Indiana Additional Lesson 1**	**IN2–IN5**
7.1.2	Recognize and compute whole number powers of positive integers.	**1-2,** 1-3, 1-4, 1-6, 4-2, 4-8, 12-2	**30–33,** 34–37, 38–41, 44–47, 186–189, 211–214, 640–645
7.1.3	Recognize the prime factors of a number and find the prime factorization of whole numbers and write the results using exponents.	**4-1,** 4-2, 4-8	**181–184,** 186–189, 211–214
7.1.4	Recognize or use prime and composite numbers to solve problems.	**4-1,** 4-2	**181–184,** 186–189
7.1.5	Recognize and use the inverse relationship between squaring and finding the square root of a perfect square integer.	**1-3, 12-1,** 12-2	**34–37, 636–639,** 640–645
7.1.6	Identify, write, rename, compare and order rational and common irrational numbers and plot them on a number line.	**2-1, 2-2, 4-4, 4-5, 4-6, 4-7, 4-9,** 6-9, **12-1** **Indiana Additional Lesson 13**	**80–83, 84–87, 192–195, 196–200, 202–205, 206–210, 215–220,** 328–332, **636–639** **IN54–IN57**
7.1.7	Solve problems that involve multiplication and division with integers, fractions, decimals and combinations of the four operations.	**1-4, 1-8, 2-6, 2-8, 5-1, Explore 5-5, 5-5, 5-6, 5-7** **Indiana Additional Lesson 4**	**38–41, 53–56, 107–111, 114–118, 230–235, 250–251, 252–257, 258–263, 265–270** **IN14–IN17**
7.1.8	Solve problems involving percents. • Find the whole given a part and the percentage • Find percentage increase or decrease.	Ch. 7 RSP, **7-2, 7-4, 7-6, 7-7**	349, **350–354, 361–365, 369–374, 375–378**

	Academic Standards	Lesson(s)	Page Number(s)
7.1.9	Solve problems involving ratios and proportions. • Express one quantity as a fraction of another, given their ratio, and vice versa. • Find how many times one quantity is as large as another, given their ratio, and vice versa. • Express one quantity as a fraction of another given the two quantities. • Find the whole, or one part, when a whole is divided into parts in a given ration. • Solve problems involving two pairs of equivalent ratios.	**6-1, 6-2, 6-3, 6-6, 7-2**	**282–286, 287–292, 293–297, 310–315, 350–354**
Standard 2	**Algebra and Functions**		
7.2.1	Use variables and appropriate operations to write an expression, equation or inequality that represents a verbal description.	**1-6, 1-9, 1-10, Extend 1-10, 3-1,** 3-2, **3-3, Explore 3-7,** 6-6, **7-4, Extend 11-10**	**44–47, 57–61, 63–67, 68–69, 128–133,** 136–141, **142–146, 162,** 310–315, **361–365, 624–625**
7.2.2	Write and solve two-step linear equations and inequalities in one variable.	**3-5,** 6-6 **Indiana Additional Lesson 2**	**151–155,** 310–315 **IN6–IN9**
7.2.3	Evaluate numerical expressions and simplify algebraic expressions involving rational and irrational numbers.	**1-4, 1-8,** 12-1 **Indiana Additional Lesson 13**	**38–41, 53–56,** 636–639 **IN54–IN57**
7.2.4	Solve an equation or formula with two variables for a particular variable.	**3-6** **Indiana Additional Lesson 3**	**156–161** **IN10–IN13**
7.2.5	Find the slope of a line from its graph and relate the slope of a line to similar triangles.	**6-3** **Indiana Additional Lesson 5**	**293–297** **IN18–IN23**
7.2.6	Draw the graph of a line given its slope and one point on the line or two points on the line.	**6-3** **Indiana Additional Lesson 6**	**293–297** **IN24–IN28**
7.2.7	Identify situations that involve proportional relationships, draw graphs representing these situations and recognize that these situations are described by a linear function in the form $y = mx$ where the unit rate m is the slope of the line.	**6-6, Extend 6-6** **Indiana Additional Lesson 7**	**310–315, 316** **IN29–IN33**
Standard 3	**Geometry and Measurement**		
7.3.1	Identify and use basic properties of angles formed by transversals intersecting pairs of parallel lines.	**Indiana Additional Lesson 10**	**IN42–IN45**

RSP = Reading to Solve Problems; For the Additional Lessons, see the *Focus on Indiana* section (IN0–IN57).

	Academic Standards	Lesson(s)	Page Number(s)
7.3.2	Identify, describe, and use transformations (translations, rotations, reflections and simple compositions of these transformations) to solve problems.	**10-9, 10-10** **Indiana Additional Lesson 11**	**553–557, 558–562** **IN46–IN49**
7.3.3	Draw two-dimensional patterns (nets) for three-dimensional objects, such as right prisms, pyramids, cylinders and cones.	**Extend 11-6** **Indiana Additional Lesson 12**	**600–601** **IN50–IN53**
7.3.4	Recognize, describe, or extend geometric patterns using tables, graphs, words, or symbols.	**1-1,** 1-5, 1-6, **1-9, Extend 1-9,** 2-7, 3-4, Explore 3-7, 5-4, 10-8, **Extend 11-10**	**25–29,** 42–43, 44–47, **57–61, 62,** 112–113, 148–149, 162, 248–249, 546–551, **624–625**
7.3.5	Identify, describe and construct similarity relationships and solve problems involving similarity (including similar triangles) and scale drawings by using proportional reasoning.	**6-8, Extend 6-8, 10-7, Extend 12-4**	**320–326, 327, 540–545, 654–655**
7.3.6	Solve simple problems involving distance, speed and time. • Understand concepts of speed and average speed. • Understand the relationship between distance, time and speed. • Find speed, distance or time given the other two quantities. • Solve simple problems involving speed and average speed.	**6-2,** 6-4, 6-5 **Indiana Additional Lesson 3**	**287–292,** 298–303, 304–309 **IN10–IN13**
Standard 4	**Data Analysis and Probability**		
7.4.1	Create, analyze and interpret data sets in multiple ways using bar graphs, frequency tables, line plots, histograms and circle graphs. Justify the choice of data display.	**8-1, 8-4, Extend 8-4, 8-5,** 8-6, **Extend 8-6, 10-3** **Indiana Additional Lesson 8**	**396–401, 415–421, 422, 424–425,** 426–431, **432–433, 518–523** **IN34–IN38**
7.4.2	Make predictions from statistical data and use proportions to make estimates about a population based on a sample.	**Extend 8-2, 8-5, 8-6, 8-7, 8-8**	**409, 424–425, 426–431, 434–437, 438–443**
7.4.3	Describe how additional data, particularly outliers, added to a data set may affect the mean, median and mode.	**8-2, 8-3**	**402–408, 410–414**
7.4.4	Analyze data displays, including ways that they can be misleading. Analyze ways in which the wording of questions can influence survey results.	**8-8, 8-9** **Indiana Additional Lesson 9**	**438–443, 444–449** **IN39–IN41**
7.4.5	Understand that when all outcomes of an experiment are equally likely, the theoretical probability of an event is the fraction of outcomes in which the event occurs. Use theoretical probability and proportions to make approximate predictions.	**9-1,** 9-2, 9-3, 9-4, 9-5, **9-7, Extend 9-7,** 9-8	**460–464,** 465–470, 471–474, 475–478, 480–483, **486–490, 491,** 492–497

The process standards code was devised by the publisher for easy reference in the book.
The code P.1.1 represents Process Standard 1, Objective 1.

PROCESS STANDARDS			
Process Standard 1 Problem Solving *Indiana Math Connects Course 2 addresses problem solving throughout the text and in Problem-Solving Strategy lessons, Problem-Solving Investigation lessons, and Cross-Curricular features.*			
P.1.1	Build new mathematical knowledge through problem solving.	Throughout the text; for example, 1-1, Extend 6-6, Explore 10-6, Extend 12-4	Throughout the text; for example, 25–29, 316, 532, 654–655
P.1.2	Solve problems that arise in mathematics and in other contexts.	Throughout the text; for example, 6-8, Extend 6-8, 7-7, 7-8	Throughout the text; for example, 320–326, 327, 375–378, 379–382
P.1.3	Apply and adapt a variety of appropriate strategies to solve problems.	Throughout the text; for example, 2-7, 6-7, 9-6, 11-5	Throughout the text; for example, 112–113, 318–319, 484–485, 594–595
P.1.4	Monitor and reflect on the process of mathematical problem solving.	Throughout the text; for example, 1-5, 2-7, 3-4, Explore 10-6	Throughout the text; for example, 42–43, 112–113, 148–149, 532
Process Standard 2 Reasoning and Proof *Indiana Math Connects Course 2 addresses reasoning and proof throughout the text and in H.O.T. Problems: Challenge, Find the Error, Number Sense, Open Ended, Reasoning, and Which One Doesn't Belong.*			
P.2.1	Recognize reasoning and proof as fundamental aspects of mathematics.	Throughout the text; for example, 1-5, 5-4, 7-5, 10-5	Throughout the text; for example, 42–43, 248–249, 366–367, 530–531
P.2.2	Make and investigate mathematical conjectures.	Throughout the text; for example, Explore 2-4, Explore 2-5, 7-5, 10-5	Throughout the text; for example, 93–94, 101–102, 366–367, 530–531
P.2.3	Develop and evaluate mathematical arguments and proofs.	Throughout the text; for example, 7-5, 10-5, Explore 10-6, Extend 12-4	Throughout the text; for example, 366–367, 530–531, 532, 654–655
P.2.4	Select and use various types of reasoning and methods of proof.	Throughout the text; for example, 1-5, 5-4, 7-5, 10-5	Throughout the text; for example, 42–43, 248–249, 366–367, 530–531
Process Standard 3 Communication *Indiana Math Connects Course 2 addresses communication in every lesson. See H.O.T. Problems: Challenge, Find the Error, Number Sense, Open Ended, Reasoning, and Which One Doesn't Belong.*			
P.3.1	Organize and consolidate their mathematical thinking through communication.	Throughout the text; for example, 9-6, Extend 9-7, Explore 10-6, 10-8	Throughout the text; for example, 484–485, 491, 532, 546–551
P.3.2	Communicate their mathematical thinking coherently and clearly to peers, teachers, and others.	Throughout the text; for example, Extend 1-10, 8-8, 9-6, Explore 10-6	Throughout the text; for example, 68–69, 438–443, 484–485, 532

RSP = Reading to Solve Problems; For the Additional Lessons, see the *Focus on Indiana* section (IN0–IN57).

PROCESS STANDARDS			
P.3.3	Analyze and evaluate the mathematical thinking and strategies of others.	Throughout the text; for example, 8-8, 8-9, 11-3, 11-4	Throughout the text; for example, 438–443, 444–449, 587, 592
P.3.4	Use the language of mathematics to express mathematical ideas precisely.	Throughout the text; for example, 1-8, Ch. 4 RSP, 9-7, 10-6	Throughout the text; for example, 53–56, 185, 486–490, 533–538
Process Standard 4 Connections *Indiana Math Connects Course 2 addresses connections throughout the text by including real-world application problems in every lesson. Cross-curricular features are found in each chapter.*			
P.4.1	Recognize and use connections among mathematical ideas.	Throughout the text; for example, 1-10, Extend 1-10, 3-7, Extend 3-7	Throughout the text; for example, 63–67, 68–69, 163–167, 168
P.4.2	Understand how mathematical ideas interconnect and build on one another to produce a coherent whole.	Throughout the text; for example, Ch. 3 RSP, 4-5, 6-9, 11-5	Throughout the text; for example, 150, 196–200, 328–332, 594–595
P.4.3	Recognize and apply mathematics in contexts outside of mathematics.	Throughout the text; for example, 6-8, Extend 6-8, 7-7, 7-8	Throughout the text; for example, 320–326, 327, 375–378, 379–382
Process Standard 5 Representation *Indiana Math Connects Course 2 addresses multiple representations throughout the text by incorporating manipulatives, diagrams, charts, tables, symbols, and graphs.*			
P.5.1	Create and use representations to organize, record, and communicate mathematical ideas.	Throughout the text; for example, Extend 1-9, 6-7, 9-6, 12-3	Throughout the text; for example, 62, 318–319, 484–485, 646–647
P.5.2	Select, apply, and translate among mathematical representations to solve problems.	Throughout the text; for example, Extend 1-10, 5-4, Explore 5-5, 5-5	Throughout the text; for example, 68–69, 248–249, 250–251, 252–257
P.5.3	Use representations to model and interpret physical, social, and mathematical phenomena.	Throughout the text; for example, 2-8, 8-6, 8-7, 8-8	Throughout the text; for example, 114–118, 426–431, 434–437, 438–443
Process Standard 6 Estimation and Mental Computation			
P.6.1	Know and apply appropriate methods for estimating the results of computations.	Throughout the text; for example, 5-1, 7-3, 7-4, 12-1	Throughout the text; for example, 230–235, 355–360, 361–365, 636–639
P.6.2	Use estimation to decide whether answers are reasonable.	Throughout the text; for example, 5-5, 5-7, 7-3, 7-4	Throughout the text; for example, 252–257, 355–360, 361–365
P.6.3	Decide when estimation is an appropriate strategy for solving a problem.	Throughout the text; for example, 5-1, 7-3, 7-4, 12-1	Throughout the text; for example, 230–235, 355–360, 361–365, 636–639
P.6.4	Determine appropriate accuracy and precision of measurement in problem solving situations.	Throughout the text; for example, 6-4, 6-5, 11-3, 11-4	Throughout the text; for example, 298–303, 304–309, 584–588, 589–593

PROCESS STANDARDS			
P.6.5	Use properties of numbers and operations to perform mental computation.	Throughout the text; for example, 1-7, 2-4, 2-6, 2-8	Throughout the text; for example, 49–52, 95–99, 107–112, 114–118
P.6.6	Recognize when the numbers involved in a computation allow for a mental computation strategy.	Throughout the text; for example, 1-7, 2-4, 2-6, 2-8	Throughout the text; for example, 49–52, 95–99, 107–112, 114–118
Process Standard 7 Technology *Indiana Math Connects Course 2 addresses technology in Graphing Calculator and Spreadsheet Labs.*			

P.7.1	• Technology should be used as a tool in mathematics education to support and extend the mathematics curriculum.
	• Technology can contribute to concept development, simulation, representation, communication, and problem solving.
	• The challenge is to ensure that technology supports – but is not a substitute for – the development of skills with basic operations, quantitative reasoning, and problem-solving skills.
	  ◦ Graphing calculators should be used to enhance middle school and high school students' understanding and skills.
	  ◦ The focus must be on learning mathematics, using technology as a tool rather than as an end in itself.
		Throughout the text; for example, Extend 1-10, Extend 3-7, Extend 6-8, Extend 7-8, Extend 8-2, Extend 8-4, Extend 8-6, Extend 11-10	Throughout the text; for example, 68–69, 168, 327, 383, 409, 422, 432–433, 624–625

RSP = Reading to Solve Problems; For the Additional Lessons, see the *Focus on Indiana* section (IN0-IN57).

Evansville, Indiana

Pacing Guide for *Indiana Math Connects*

The organization and pacing of *Indiana Math Connects,* Course 2 is front-loaded for the ISTEP+. Following this pacing guide helps ensure in-depth coverage of all Grade 7 academic standards and success on the ISTEP+.

Boldfaced standards indicate the academic standard(s) that are the main focus of the lesson.

Chapter 1 Introduction to Algebra and Functions		**15 Days**
1-1	A Plan for Problem Solving	**7.3.4,** P.1.1
1-2	Powers and Exponents	**7.1.2**
IN 1	Scientific Notation	**7.1.1**
1-3	Squares and Square Roots	7.1.2, **7.1.4**
1-4	Order of Operations	7.1.2, **7.1.7, 7.2.3**
1-5	**PSI:** Guess and Check	7.3.4, P.1.4, P.2.1, P.2.4
1-6	**Algebra:** Variables and Expressions	7.3.4, 7.1.2, **7.2.1**
1-7	**Algebra:** Equations	P.6.5, P.6.6
1-8	**Algebra:** Properties	**7.1.7, 7.2.3,** P.3.4
1-9	**Algebra:** Arithmetic Sequences	**7.2.1, 7.3.4**
Extend 1-9	**Algebra Lab:** Exploring Sequences	**7.3.4,** P.5.1
1-10	**Algebra:** Equations and Functions	**7.2.1,** P.4.1
Extend 1-10	**Graphing Calculator Lab:** Functions and Tables	**7.2.1,** P.3.2, P.4.1, P.5.2, P.7.1
Chapter 2 Integers		**10 Days**
2-1	Integers and Absolute Value	**7.1.6**
2-2	Comparing and Ordering Integers	**7.1.6**
Explore 2-4	**Algebra Lab:** Adding Integers	P.2.2
2-4	Adding Integers	P.6.5, P.6.6
Explore 2-5	**Algebra Lab:** Subtracting Integers	P.2.2
2-6	Multiplying Integers	**7.1.7,** P.6.5, P.6.6
2-7	**PSI:** Look for a Pattern	7.3.4, P.1.3, P.1.4
2-8	Dividing Integers	**7.1.7,** P.5.3, P.6.5, P.6.6
Chapter 3 Algebra: Linear Equations and Functions		**11 Days**
3-1	Writing Expressions and Equations	**7.2.1**
3-2	Solving Addition and Subtraction Equations	7.2.1
3-3	Solving Multiplication Equations	**7.2.1**
3-4	**PSI:** Work Backward	7.3.4, P.1.3, P.1.4
3-5	Solving Two-Step Equations	**7.2.2**
IN 2	Linear Inequalities	**7.2.2**
3-6	**Measurement:** Perimeter and Area	**7.2.4**
IN 3	Literal Equations	**7.2.4, 7.3.6**
Explore 3-7	**Measurement Lab:** Representing Relationships	**7.2.1**
Chapter 4 Fractions, Decimals, and Percents		**12 Days**
4-1	Prime Factorization	**7.1.3, 7.1.4**
4-2	Greatest Common Factor	7.1.2, 7.1.3, 7.1.4
4-3	**PSI:** Make an Organized List	P.1.3
4-4	Simplifying Fractions	**7.1.7**
4-5	Fractions and Decimals	**7.1.7**
4-6	Fractions and Percents	**7.1.7**
4-7	Percents and Decimals	**7.1.7**
4-8	Least Common Multiple	7.1.2, 7.1.3
4-9	Comparing and Ordering Rational Numbers	**7.1.7**

IN4	Operations with Decimals	**7.1.7**
Chapter 5 Applying Fractions		**7 Days**
5-1	Estimating with Fractions	**7.1.7**, P.6.1, P.6.3
5-4	**PSI:** Eliminate the Possibilities	7.3.4, P.1.3, P.2.1, P.2.4, P.5.2
Explore 5-5	**Math Lab:** Multiplying Fractions	**7.1.7**, P.5.2
5-5	Multiplying Fractions and Mixed Numbers	**7.1.7**, P.5.2, P.6.2
5-7	Dividing Fractions and Mixed Numbers	**7.1.7**, P.6.2
Chapter 6 Ratios and Proportions		**16 Days**
6-1	Ratios	**7.1.9**
6-2	Rates	**7.1.9, 7.3.6**
6-3	Rate of Change and Slope	**7.1.9, 7.2.5, 7.2.6**
6-4	**Measurement:** Changing Customary Units	7.3.6, P.6.4
6-5	**Measurement:** Changing Metric Units	7.3.6, P.6.4
IN5	Slope and Similar Triangles	**7.2.5**
IN6	Graphs of Linear Equations	**7.2.6**
IN7	Direct Variation	**7.2.7**
6-6	**Algebra:** Solving Proportions	**7.1.9, 7.2.1,** 7.2.2, **7.2.7**
Extend 6-6	**Math Lab:** Inverse Proportionality	**7.2.7,** P.1.1
6-7	**PSI:** Draw a Diagram	P.1.3, P.5.1
6-8	Scale Drawings	**7.3.5,** P.1.2, P.4.3
Extend 6-8	**Spreadsheet Lab:** Scale Drawings	**7.3.5,** P.1.2, P.4.3, P.7.1
6-9	Fractions, Decimals, and Percents	**7.1.7**
Chapter 7 Applying Percents		**11 Days**
RSP	**Reading to Solve Problems:** Meaning of Percent	7.1.8
7-2	The Percent Proportion	**7.1.8, 7.1.9**
7-3	Percents and Estimation	**7.1.8,** P.6.1, P.6.2, P.6.3
7-4	**Algebra:** The Percent Equation	**7.1.8, 7.2.1,** P.6.1, P.6.2, P.6.3
7-5	**PSI:** Determine Reasonable Answers	P.2.1, P.2.2, P.2.3, P.2.4
7-6	Percent of Change	**7.1.8**
7-7	Sales Tax and Discount	**7.1.8,** P.1.2, P.4.3
7-8	Simple Interest	P.1.2, P.4.3
Extend 7-8	**Spreadsheet Lab:** Simple Interest	P.7.1
Chapter 8 Statistics: Analyzing Data		**17 Days**
8-1	Line Plots	**7.4.1**
8-2	Measures of Central Tendency and Range	**7.4.3**
Extend 8-2	**Graphing Calculator Lab:** Mean and Median	**7.4.2,** P.7.1
8-3	Stem-and-Leaf Plots	**7.4.3**
8-4	Bar Graphs and Histograms	**7.4.1**
Extend 8-4	**Spreadsheet Lab:** Circle Graphs	**7.4.1,** P.7.1
8-5	**PSI:** Use a Graph	**7.4.1, 7.4.2**
8-6	Using Graphs to Predict	7.4.1, **7.4.2,** P.5.3
Extend 8-6	**Spreadsheet Lab:** Multiple-Line and -Bar Graphs	**7.4.1,** P.7.1
8-7	Using Data to Predict	**7.4.2,** P.5.3
8-8	Using Sampling to Predict	**7.4.2, 7.4.4,** P.3.2, P.3.3, P.5.3
8-9	Misleading Statistics	**7.4.4,** P.3.3
IN8	Choose an Appropriate Display	**7.4.1**
IN9	Analyze Questions in Surveys	**7.4.4**
Chapter 9 Probability		**11 Days**
9-1	Simple Events	**7.4.5**
9-2	Sample Spaces	7.4.5
9-3	The Fundamental Counting Principle	7.4.5
9-4	Permutations	7.4.5
9-5	Combinations	7.4.5

9-6	**PSI:** Act it Out	P.1.3, P.3.1, P.3.2, P.5.1
9-7	Theoretical and Experimental Probability	**7.4.5,** P.3.4
Extend 9-7	**Probability Lab:** Simulations	**7.4.5,** P.3.1
9-8	Compound Events	7.4.5
Chapter 10 Geometry: Polygons		**9 Days**
IN10	Parallel Lines and Transversals	**7.3.1**
10-3	**Statistics:** Display Data in a Circle Graph	**7.4.1**
10-5	**PSI:** Use Logical Reasoning	P.2.1, P.2.2, P.2.3, P.2.4
10-7	Similar Figures	**7.3.5**
10-9	Translations	**7.3.2**
10-10	Reflections	**7.3.2**
IN11	Rotations	**7.3.2**

Chapter 11 Measurement: Two- and Three-Dimensional Figures		**9 Days**
11-3	Circles and Circumference	P.3.3, P.6.4
11-4	Area of Circles	P.3.3, P.6.4
11-5	**PSI:** Solve a Simpler Problem	P.1.3, P.4.2
IN12	Nets of Cylinders and Cones	**7.3.3**
Extend 11-6	**Measurement Lab:** Nets and Surface Area	**7.3.3**
11-10	Volume of Cylinders	**7.3.4**
Extend 11-10	**Graphing Calculator Lab:** Graphing Geometric Relationships	**7.2.1,** P.7.1
Chapter 12 Geometry and Measurement		**7 Days**
12-1	Estimating Square Roots	**7.1.4,** 7.1.6, 7.2.3, P.6.1, P.6.3
IN13	Irrational Numbers	**7.1.6,** 7.2.3
12-2	The Pythagorean Theorem	7.1.2, 7.1.5
12-3	**PSI:** Make a Model	P.5.1
Extend 12-4	**Measurement Lab:** Changes in Scale	**7.3.5,** P.1.1, P.2.3

Indiana State Museum

Optional Lessons	
2-3	The Coordinate Plane
2-5	Subtracting Integers
Explore 3-2	**Algebra Lab:** Solving Equations Using Models
3-7	Functions and Graphs
Extend 3-7	**Graphing Calculator Lab:** Graphing Relationships
Explore 4-1	**Math Lab:** Exploring Factors
5-2	Adding and Subtracting Fractions
5-3	Adding and Subtracting Mixed Numbers
5-6	**Algebra:** Solving Equations
Explore 7-1	**Math Lab:** Percent of a Number
7-1	Percent of a Number
10-1	Angle Relationships
10-2	Complementary and Supplementary Angles
10-4	Triangles

Explore 10-6	**Geometry Lab:** Investigating Quadrilaterals
10-6	Quadrilaterals
10-8	Polygons and Tessellations
Extend 10-8	**Geometry Lab:** Tessellations
11-1	Area of Parallelograms
Explore 11-2	**Measurement Lab:** Triangles and Trapezoids
11-2	Area of Triangles and Trapezoids
Explore 11-3	**Measurement Lab:** Circumference of Circles
11-6	Area of Complex Figures
11-7	Three-Dimensional Figures
Explore 11-8	**Geometry Lab:** Three-Dimensional Figures
11-8	Drawing Three-Dimensional Figures
11-9	Volume of Prisms
12-4	Surface Area of Rectangular Prisms
12-5	Surface Area of Cylinders

RSP = Reading to Solve Problems; IN = Indiana Additional Lessons (see *Focus on Indiana*)

Contents

Start Smart

Unit 1

Algebra and Functions

Chapter 1 Introduction to Algebra and Functions

Academic Standards

ISTEP+ Practice

H.O.T. Problems
Higher Order Thinking

Focal Points and Connections
See page T17 for key.

G7-FP3 Number and Operations and Algebra

CHAPTER 2 Integers

Academic Standards

ISTEP+ Practice

H.O.T. Problems
Higher Order Thinking

Focal Points and Connections
See page T17 for key.

G7-FP3 Number and Operations and Algebra

CHAPTER 3

Algebra: Linear Equations and Functions

Academic Standards

ISTEP+ Practice

- Extended Response 175
- Multiple Choice 126, 131, 133, 141, 147, 155, 161, 167
- Short Response/Grid In 146, 175
- Worked Out Example 130

H.O.T. Problems

Higher Order Thinking

- Challenge 132, 141, 146, 155, 160, 161, 167
- Find the Error 132, 146
- Number Sense 160
- Open Ended 132, 160, 167
- Select the Operation 149
- Select a Technique 155
- Which One Doesn't Belong? 141

Focal Points and Connections

See page T17 for key.

G7-FP3 **Number and Operations and Algebra**

Unit 2

Number Sense: Fractions

CHAPTER 4 Fractions, Decimals, and Percents

ISTEP+ Practice

H.O.T. Problems
Higher Order Thinking

Focal Points and Connections
See page T17 for key.

G7-FP3 Number and Operations and Algebra
G7-FP5C Number and Operations

CHAPTER 5

Applying Fractions

Academic Standards

ASSESSMENT

ISTEP+ Practice

H.O.T. Problems
Higher Order Thinking

Focal Points and Connections
See page T17 for key.

G7-FP3 Number and Operations and Algebra

Unit 3

Algebra and Number Sense: Proportions and Percents

Chapter 6 Ratios and Proportions

ISTEP+ Practice

- Extended Response 339
- Multiple Choice 286, 289, 292, 297, 303, 309, 315, 326, 332
- Short Response/Grid In 297, 339
- Worked Out Example 288

H.O.T. Problems
Higher Order Thinking

- Challenge 286, 292, 302, 308, 314, 325
- Find the Error 286, 308
- Number Sense 292
- Open Ended 292, 297, 302, 305, 325
- Reasoning 302, 325
- Select a Technique 315
- Select a Tool 61
- Which One Doesn't Belong? 314

Focal Points and Connections
See page T17 for key.

G7-FP1 Number and Operations and Algebra and Geometry

CHAPTER 7

Applying Percents

Academic Standards

ISTEP+ Practice

H.O.T. Problems
Higher Order Thinking

Focal Points and Connections
See page T17 for key.

G7-FP1 Number and Operations and Algebra and Geometry

Table of Contents

Unit 4

Statistics, Data Analysis, and Probability

CHAPTER 8 Statistics: Analyzing Data

Academic Standards

ISTEP+ Practice

H.O.T. Problems

Higher Order Thinking

Focal Points and Connections

See page T17 for key.

G7-FP6C Data Analysis

CHAPTER 9 Probability

Academic Standards

ISTEP+ Practice

H.O.T. Problems
Higher Order Thinking

Focal Points and Connections
See page T17 for key.

G7-FP7C Probability

Unit 5

Geometry and Measurement

Chapter 10 Geometry: Polygons

Academic Standards

ISTEP+ Practice

- Extended Response 569
- Multiple Choice 513, 517, 523, 529, 537, 545, 551, 557, 5627
- Short Response/Grid In 551, 569
- Worked Out Example 527

H.O.T. Problems
Higher Order Thinking

- Challenge 513, 517, 523, 529, 537, 545, 550, 556, 562
- Collect the Data 523
- Find the Error 537
- Open Ended 529, 550, 562
- Reasoning 529, 537, 550, 556
- Which One Doesn't Belong? 552

Focal Points and Connections
See page T17 for key.

G7-FP2 Measurement and Geometry and Algebra

CHAPTER 11

Measurement: Two- and Three-Dimensional Figures

Academic Standards

ASSESSMENT

ISTEP+ Practice

- Extended Response 633
- Multiple Choice 576, 582, 588, 593, 599, 606, 612, 618, 623
- Short Response/Grid In 582, 633
- Worked Out Example 590

H.O.T. Problems
Higher Order Thinking

- Challenge 576, 582, 588, 592, 599, 606, 611, 618, 622
- Find the Error 587, 592
- Number Sense 622
- Open Ended 576, 587, 606, 611, 622
- Reasoning 582, 606, 618
- Which One Doesn't Belong? 611

Focal Points and Connections
See page T17 for key.

G7-FP2 Measurement and Geometry and Algebra

G7-FP4C Measurement and Geometry

CHAPTER 12

Geometry and Measurement

Academic Standards

ISTEP+ Practice

- Extended Response 665
- Multiple Choice 639, 645, 653, 659
- Short Response/Grid In 639, 665
- Worked Out Example 651

H.O.T. Problems
Higher Order Thinking

- Challenge 639, 645, 653, 658
- Find the Error 645
- Number Sense 639
- Open Ended 639, 645
- Reasoning 653, 658
- Which One Doesn't Belong? 638

Focal Points and Connections
See page T17 for key.

G7-FP1 Number and Operations and Algebra and Geometry

Student Handbook

Built-In Workbooks

Reference

FOCUS ON

Indiana

GRADE 7

Focus on Indiana includes additional lessons which address Indiana's Academic Standards.

The Table of Contents on the next page directs you where to use these lessons in *Indiana Math Connects,* Course 2 and informs you of the Indiana Academic Standard that is covered by each lesson.

Farm in Northern Indiana

Contents

IN1

1 Lesson Notes

Lesson Planner

Use this lesson after Lesson 1-2 to address standard 7.1.1.

Objective

Read, write, compare, and solve problems using scientific notation.

Vocabulary

scientific notation

IN Academic Standards

7.1.1 Read, write, compare and solve problems using whole numbers in scientific notation.

1 Focus

- Review exponents by having students simplify 3^4, 8^3, and 30^1. 81, 512, 30
- Review powers of 10 by having students simplify 10^4, 10^3, 10^2, and 10^1. 10,000, 1,000, 100, 10

1 Scientific Notation

MAIN IDEA

Read, write, compare, and solve problems using scientific notation.

IN Academic Standards

7.1.1 Read, write, compare and solve problems using whole numbers in scientific notation.

New Vocabulary

scientific notation

IN Math Online

glencoe.com

GET READY for the Lesson

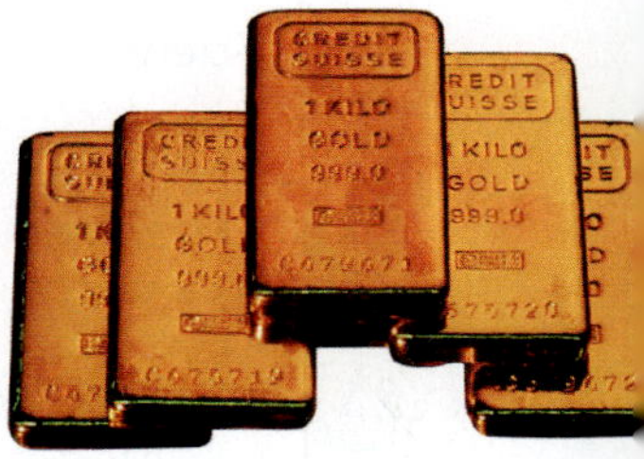

More than 425 million pounds of gold has been discovered in the world. If all this gold were in one place, it would form a cube seven stories on each side.

1. Write 425 million in standard form.
2. Complete: $4.25 \times$ __?__ = 425 million.
3. Write your answer to Exercise 2 as a power of 10.

1. 425,000,000 2. 100,000,000 3. 10^8

When you deal with very large numbers like 425,000,000, it can be difficult to keep track of the zeros. You can express numbers such as this in **scientific notation** by writing the number as the product of a factor and a power of 10.

Scientific Notation — Key Concept

Words	A number is expressed in scientific notation when it is written as the product of a factor and a power of 10. The factor must be greater than or equal to 1 and less than 10.
Symbols	$a \times 10^n$, where $1 \leq a < 10$ and n is an integer
Example	$425{,}000{,}000 = 4.25 \times 10^8$

EXAMPLE Express Large Numbers in Standard Form

1 Express 2.16×10^5 in standard form.

$2.16 \times 10^5 = 2.16 \times 100{,}000$ $10^5 = 100{,}000$

$= 216{,}000$ Move the decimal point 5 places to the right.

In standard form, 2.16×10^5 is 216,000.

Scientific notation is also used to express very small numbers. Study the pattern of products at the right. Notice that multiplying by a negative power of 10 moves the decimal point to the left the same number of places as the absolute value of the exponent. For example, the number 1.25×10^{-2} has an exponent with an absolute value of 2. The decimal point in 1.25 will be moved to the left two places to become 0.0125.

$1.25 \times 10^3 = 1{,}250$
$1.25 \times 10^2 = 125$
$1.25 \times 10^1 = 12.5$
$1.25 \times 10^0 = 1.25$
$1.25 \times 10^{-1} = 0.125$
$1.25 \times 10^{-2} = 0.0125$
$1.25 \times 10^{-3} = 0.00125$

Study Tip

Move the Decimal Point
The exponent tells you how many places to move the decimal point.

- If the exponent is positive, move the decimal point to the right.
- If the exponent is negative, move the decimal point to the left.

EXAMPLE Express Small Numbers in Standard Form

2 **Express 5.8×10^{-3} in standard form.**

$5.8 \times 10^{-3} = 5.8 \times 0.001$ $10^{-3} = 0.001$

$= 0.0058$ Move the decimal point 3 places to the left.

In standard form, 5.8×10^{-3} is 0.0058.

To write a number in scientific notation, place the decimal point after the first nonzero digit. Then find the power of 10.

EXAMPLES Express Numbers in Scientific Notation

Express each number in scientific notation.

3 **1,457,000**

$1{,}457{,}000 = 1.457 \times 1{,}000{,}000$ The decimal point moves 6 places to the left.

$= 1.457 \times 10^6$ The exponent is positive.

4 **0.00063**

$0.00063 = 6.3 \times 0.0001$ The decimal point moves 4 places to the right.

$= 6.3 \times 10^{-4}$ The exponent is negative.

To compare numbers in scientific notation, first compare the exponents. With positive numbers, any number with a greater exponent is greater. If the exponents are the same, compare the factors.

Real-World Link At the deepest point in the ocean, the pressure is greater than 8 tons per square inch and the temperature is only a few degrees above freezing.
Source: Ocean Planet Smithsonian

Real-World EXAMPLES Compare Numbers in Scientific Notation

Refer to the table at the right which gives the approximate area in square kilometers of Earth's oceans.

Earth's Oceans

Ocean	Approximate Area (km^2)
Arctic	1.41×10^7
Atlantic	7.68×10^7
Indian	6.86×10^7
Pacific	1.56×10^8
Southern	2.03×10^7

5 **OCEANS Which ocean has the greater area, the Arctic or the Southern?**

Since both exponents are the same, compare the factors.

$1.41 < 2.03 \rightarrow 1.41 \times 10^7 < 2.03 \times 10^7$

So, the Southern Ocean has the greater area.

6 **Which ocean has the greater area, the Arctic or the Pacific?**

Compare the exponents.

$8 > 7 \rightarrow 1.56 \times 10^8 > 1.41 \times 10^7$

So, the Pacific Ocean has the greater area.

2 Teach

Scaffolding Questions

Have students explore how a change in the power of 10 affects the value of a number written in scientific notation.

Present students with the following scenario: A recent study showed that the number of people in the world who speak Japanese is 1.25×10^7.

Ask:

- What is this expression in standard form? How did you get your answer? 12,500,000; moved the decimal point seven places to the right
- How would *increasing* the exponent by one affect the value of the expression? Then increase the value of the exponent by one and write the new expression in standard form. Sample answer: The value would be 10 times the value of the original expression; 125,000,000.
- How would *decreasing* the exponent by one affect the value of the expression? Then decrease the value of the exponent by one and write the new value in standard form. Sample answer: The value would be $\frac{1}{10}$ times the value of the original expression; 1,250,000.

Lesson IN 1 Scientific Notation **IN3**

3 Practice

Use Exercises 1–12 to check for understanding.

Exercises 13–49 are structured so that students practice the same concepts they learned in the lesson.

Have students discuss and complete the Higher Order Thinking problems.

WRITING IN MATH Have students complete Exercise 47 in their Math Journals. You may choose to use this exercise as an optional formative assessment.

Additional Answers

46. Sample answer: The distance between Earth and the Sun is 1.55×10^8 km or 155,000,000 km.

47. Sample answer: Numbers that are greater than 1 can be expressed as the product of a factor and a positive power of 10. So, these numbers are written in scientific notation using positive exponents. Numbers between 0 and 1 cannot be expressed as the product of a factor and a whole number power of 10, so they are written in scientific notation using negative exponents.

CHECK Your Understanding

Examples 1, 2 (pp. IN2–IN3)

Express each number in standard form.

1. 3.754×10^5 **375,400**
2. 8.34×10^6 **8,340,000**
3. 1.5×10^{-4} **0.00015**
4. 2.68×10^{-3} **0.00268**

Examples 3, 4 (p. IN3)

Express each number in scientific notation.

5. 4,510,000 **4.51×10^6**
6. 0.00673 **6.73×10^{-3}**
7. 0.000092 **9.2×10^{-5}**
8. 11,620,000 **1.162×10^7**
9. **PHYSICAL SCIENCE** Light travels 300,000 kilometers per second. Write this number in scientific notation. **3.0×10^5**

Example 5 (p. IN3)

10. **TECHNOLOGY** The distance between tracks on a CD and DVD are shown in the table. Which disc has the greater distance between tracks? **CD**

Disc	Distance (mm)
CD	1.6×10^{-3}
DVD	7.4×10^{-4}

Replace each ● with <, >, or = to make a true sentence.

11. 2.3×10^5 ● 1.7×10^5 **>**
12. 0.012 ● 1.4×10^{-1} **<**

Practice and Problem Solving

HOMEWORK HELP

For Exercises	See Examples
13–22	1, 2
23–32	3, 4
33–39	5

Express each number in standard form.

13. 6.1×10^4
14. 5.72×10^6
15. 3.3×10^{-1}
16. 5.68×10^{-3}
17. 9.014×10^{-2} **0.09014**
18. 1.399×10^5 **139,900**
19. 2.505×10^3 **2,505**
20. 7.4×10^{-5} **0.000074**
21. **SPIDERS** The diameter of a spider's thread is 1.0×10^{-3} inch. Write this number in standard form. **0.001**

22. **DINOSAURS** The *Gigantosaurus* dinosaur weighed about 1.4×10^4 pounds. Write this number in standard form. **14,000**

13. 61,000
14. 5,720,000
15. 0.33
16. 0.00568

Express each number in scientific notation.

23. 499,000
24. 2,000,000
25. 0.006
26. 0.0125
27. 50,000,000 **5.0×10^7**
28. 39,560 **3.956×10^4**
29. 0.000078 **7.8×10^{-5}**
30. 0.000425 **4.25×10^{-4}**
31. **CHESS** The number of possible ways that a player can play the first four moves in a chess game is 3 billion. Write this number in scientific notation. **3.0×10^9**
32. **SCIENCE** A particular parasite is approximately 0.025 inch long. Write this number in scientific notation. **2.5×10^{-2}**

23. 4.99×10^5
24. 2.0×10^6
25. 6.0×10^{-3}
26. 1.25×10^{-2}

Find each of the following. Write in standard form.

33. $(8 \times 10^0) + (4 \times 10^{-3}) + (3 \times 10^{-5})$ **8.00403**
34. $(4 \times 10^4) + (8 \times 10^3) + (3 \times 10^2) + (9 \times 10^1) + (6 \times 10^0)$ **48,396**

SPORTS For Exercises 35 and 36, use the table. Determine which category in each pair had a greater amount of sales.

Category	Sales ($)
Camping	1.547×10^9
Golf	3.243×10^9
Tennis	3.73×10^8

Source: National Sporting Goods Assoc.

35. golf or tennis **golf**

36. camping or golf **golf**

Replace each ● with <, >, or = to make a true sentence.

37. 1.8×10^3 ● 1.9×10^{-1} **>**

38. 5.2×10^2 ● 5000 **<**

39. 0.00701 ● 7.1×10^{-3} **<**

40. 6.49×10^4 ● 649×10^2 **=**

Metric Measures	
Prefix	**Meaning**
atto	10^{-18}
giga	10^9
kilo	10^3
nano	10^{-9}
peta	10^{15}
pico	10^{-12}

41. **MEASUREMENT** The table at the right shows the values of different prefixes that are used in the metric system. Write the units attometer, gigameter, kilometer, nanometer, petameter, and picometer in order from greatest to least measure. **petameter, gigameter, kilometer, nanometer, picometer, attometer**

42. **NUMBER SENSE** Write the product of 0.00004 and 0.0008 in scientific notation. **3.2×10^{-8}**

43. **NUMBER SENSE** Order 6.1×10^4, 6100, 6.1×10^{-5}, 0.0061, and 6.1×10^{-2} from least to greatest. **6.1×10^{-5}, 0.0061, 6.1×10^{-2}, 6100, 6.1×10^4**

H.O.T. Problems

44. **REASONING** Which is a better estimate for the number of times per year that a person blinks, 6.25×10^{-2} times or 6.2×10^6? Explain your reasoning. **6.25×10^6 times; Sample answer: $6.25 \times 10^{-2} < 1$ and a person blinks multiple times per day.**

45. **CHALLENGE** Convert the numbers in each expression to scientific notation. Then evaluate the expression. Express in scientific notation and in decimal notation.

a. $\frac{(420,000)(0.015)}{0.025}$ **2.52×10^5; 252,000**

b. $\frac{(0.078)(8.5)}{0.16(250,000)}$ **1.6575×10^{-5}; 0.000016575**

46. **OPEN ENDED** Describe a real-life value or measure using numbers in scientific notation and in standard form. **See margin.**

47. **WRITING IN MATH** Explain the relationship between a number in standard form and the sign of the exponent when the number is written in scientific notation. **See margin.**

ISTEP+ PRACTICE 7.1.1

48. Which of the following expressions is the GREATEST: 3.2×10^4, 9.8×10^{-1}, 5.6×10^2, or 1.7×10^5? **A**

A 1.7×10^5

B 3.2×10^4

C 5.6×10^2

D 9.8×10^{-1}

49. Which of the following expressions is equivalent to 4.01×10^3? **H**

F 0.00401

G 40.1

H 4,010

J 40,100

4 Assess

Ticket Out the Door Have students explain how to write a number between 0 and 1 in scientific notation. Students should support their answer with an example. Sample answer: To write 0.41 in scientific notation, place the decimal point between 4 and 1. Then count the number of places the decimal point has been moved. This will be the exponent for the power of 10. Since the decimal point would have to be moved to the left to write the standard form of the number in scientific notation, the exponent is negative. $0.41 = 4.1 \times 10^{-1}$

2 Lesson Notes

Lesson Planner

Use this lesson after Lesson 3-5 to address standard 7.2.2.

Objective

Write and solve two-step linear inequalities.

IN Academic Standards

7.2.2 Write and solve two-step linear equations and **inequalities in one variable.**

1 Focus

- Have students name the inverse operations of addition and division. subtraction, multiplication
- Model how to solve the two-step linear equations $3x + 1 = -14$ and $4 + \frac{d}{5} = 10$. Emphasize when inverse operations are used in isolating the variable. -5; 30
- Then have students solve the two-step linear equations $6 = 2a - 4$, $\frac{p}{10} + 2 = 6$, and $-3 = \frac{(5 + w)}{6}$. 5; 40; -23

2 Linear Inequalities

MAIN IDEA

Write and solve two-step linear inequalities.

IN Academic Standards

7.2.2 Write and solve two-step linear equations and **inequalities in one variable.**

IN Math Online

glencoe.com

GET READY for the Lesson

MEASUREMENT The perimeter of a rectangle is less than 34 centimeters. The inequality $2\ell + 2w < 34$ represents this situation.

$P < 34$ cm

1. The length of the rectangle is 12 centimeters. Write the inequality by replacing ℓ with 12. **$2(12) + 2w < 34$ or $24 + 2w < 34$**
2. What operations are used in the inequality you wrote in Exercise 1? **addition and multiplication**
3. Describe how you would solve the equation $24 + 2w = 34$.
4. List three different possible widths w that would result in a perimeter less than 34 centimeters if the length is 12 centimeters.

3. Sample answer: Subtract 24 from each side. Then divide both sides by 2.

4. Sample answer: 3 cm, 4 cm, 4.5 cm

You learned how to solve a two-step linear equation in Lesson 3-5. Recall that to solve a two-step linear equation, undo the addition or subtraction first. Then undo the multiplication or division.

You can use a similar method to solve a two-step linear inequality. You already learned how to solve a one-step linear inequality in *Indiana Math Connects*, Course 1.

EXAMPLE Solve Two-Step Inequalities

1 **MEASUREMENT The perimeter of a rectangle is less than 34 centimeters. The length of the rectangle is 12 centimeters. Solve the two-step linear inequality $24 + 2w < 34$ to find an expression that gives the width of the rectangle. Check your solution.**

$24 + 2w < 34$	Write the inequality.
$-24 \quad\quad -24$	Subtract 24 from each side.
$\frac{2w}{2} < \frac{10}{2}$	Divide each side by 2.
$w < 5$	Simplify.

Check

$24 + 2w < 34$	Write the inequality.
$24 + 2(4) \overset{?}{<} 34$	Replace w with a number less than 5, such as 4.
$32 < 34$ ✓	Simplify. This statement is true.

The solution is $w < 5$.
So, the width of the rectangle must be less than 5 centimeters.

Recall from *Indiana Math Connects,* Course 1, that the direction of the inequality symbol is reversed when multiplying or dividing each side by a negative number. This is demonstrated below using the inequality $-3x \geq 12$.

$-3x \geq 12$	Write the inequality.
$\frac{-3x}{-3} \leq \frac{12}{-3}$	Divide each side by −3. Reverse the direction of the inequality symbol.
$x \leq -4$	Simplify.

EXAMPLES Solve Two-Step Inequalities

Solve each two-step linear inequality. Check your solution.

2 $\frac{y}{-5} + 3 > -7$

$\frac{y}{-5} + 3 > -7$	Write the inequality.
$-3 \quad -3$	Subtract 3 from each side.
$\frac{y}{-5} > -10$	Simplify.
$(-5)\frac{y}{-5} < (-5)(-10)$	Multiply both sides by −5. Reverse the direction of the inequality symbol.
$y < 50$	Simplify.
Check $\frac{y}{-5} + 3 > -7$	Write the inequality.
$\frac{40}{-5} + 3 \stackrel{?}{>} -7$	Replace *y* with a number less than 50, such as 40.
$-5 > -7$ ✓	Simplify. This statement is true.

The solution is $y < 50$.

Study Tip

Solving Inequalities Remember to reverse the direction of the inequality only when you are multiplying or dividing by a negative number.

In the inequality $3x < -9$, you would not reverse the direction of the inequality even though there is a negative number, −9. You are dividing both sides by a positive number, 3.

3 $8 - 4a \leq 24$

$8 - 4a \leq 24$	Write the inequality.
$-8 \quad -8$	Subtract 8 from each side.
$-4a \leq 16$	Simplify.
$\frac{-4a}{-4} \geq \frac{16}{-4}$	Divide each side by −4. Reverse the direction of the inequality symbol.
$a \geq -4$	Simplify.
Check $8 - 4a \leq 24$	Write the inequality.
$8 - 4(0) \stackrel{?}{\leq} 24$	Replace *a* with a number less than 24, such as 0.
$8 \leq 24$ ✓	Simplify. This statement is true.

The solution is $a \geq -4$.

2 Teach

Scaffolding Questions

Display the inequality $4 < 5$.

Ask:

- If you add 2 to each side of the inequality, what is the resulting inequality? $6 < 7$
- If you subtract 2 from each side of the inequality, what is the resulting inequality? $2 < 3$
- If you multiply both sides of the inequality by 2, what is the resulting inequality? $8 < 10$
- If you divide both sides of the inequality by 10, what is the resulting inequality? $0.4 < 0.5$
- If you multiply both sides of the inequality by −2, what is the resulting inequality? Explain your answer. $-8 > -10$; Sample answer: Reverse the inequality symbol to get a true statement. $-8 < -10$ is not true, but $-8 > -10$ is true.

3 Practice

Use Exercises 1–7 to check for understanding.

Exercises 8–29 are structured so that students practice the same concepts they learned in the lesson.

Have students discuss and complete the Higher Order Thinking problems.

WRITING IN MATH Have students complete Exercise 26 in their Math Journals. You may choose to use this exercise as an optional formative assessment.

Additional Answer

26. Sample answer: In solving both the equation and the inequality, you would first subtract 4 from each side. Then you would divide each side by –5. However, in solving the inequality, you would have to reverse the direction of the inequality symbol because you are dividing by a negative number. In the equation, the value of x is -3. In the inequality, the value of x is less than or equal to -3.

Real-World Link In a recent year, snowboarding was the fastest growing sport in the United States, with over 7.2 million participants.

Real-World EXAMPLE

4 **SNOWBOARDING** Three friends went snowboarding. The admission price was \$5 each. Two of the friends rented boards. If they spent a total of at least \$19, write and solve an inequality to find the dollar amount that each board rental could cost.

Words	The cost of two rentals	and three admissions	is at least \$19.
Variable	Let s = cost for snowboard rental.		
Inequality	Two rentals at \$$s$ each	plus admission	is at least \$19.
	$2s$	$+\ 3(5)$	≥ 19

$2s + 15 \geq 19$	Write the inequality.
$-15 \quad -15$	Subtract 15 from each side.
$2s \geq 4$	Simplify.
$\frac{2s}{2} \geq \frac{4}{2}$	Divide each side by 2.
$s \geq 2$	Simplify.

So, one snowboard rental is at least \$2.

CHECK Your Understanding

Examples 1–3 (pp. IN6–IN7)

Solve each two-step linear inequality. Check your solution.

1. $2a + 5 < 13$ **$a < 4$**
2. $7 + 3p \leq -14$ **$p \leq -7$**
3. $-4m - 1 \geq 11$ **$m \leq -3$**
4. $\frac{k}{8} + 1 > 5$ **$k > 32$**
5. $-4 + \frac{y}{-3} < 6$ **$y > -30$**
6. $\frac{h}{-9} + 6 \leq 5$ **$h \geq 9$**

Example 4 (p. IN8)

7. **ZOOS** Jenna visited the zoo with both of her parents. They paid a total of at least \$24 and Jenna's admission cost \$6. Each parent paid the same adult admission amount. Write and solve an inequality to find the dollar amount that each adult admission could cost. **$6 + 2a \geq 24$; $a \geq 9$**

Practice and Problem Solving

HOMEWORK HELP

For Exercises	See Examples
8–19	1–3
20–23	4

Solve each two-step linear inequality. Check your solution.

8. $6d + 1 < 19$ **$d < 3$**
9. $-n - 5 \geq 7$ **$n \leq -12$**
10. $3 + 2q \leq -9$ **$q \leq -6$**
11. $-10y - 4 \geq 56$ **$y \leq -6$**
12. $11c + 2 < 35$ **$c < 3$**
13. $1 + 8x \leq -39$ **$x \leq -5$**
14. $\frac{g}{7} + 3 > 6$ **$g > 21$**
15. $-1 + \frac{p}{-4} < 2$ **$p > -12$**
16. $\frac{t}{5} + 3 > 12$ **$t > 45$**
17. $\frac{z}{9} - 2 \geq 9$ **$z \geq 99$**
18. $\frac{w}{4} + 6 \leq 4$ **$w \leq -8$**
19. $8 + \frac{j}{-6} > 11$ **$j < -18$**

20. $4p + 6 \le 7$; $p \le \frac{1}{4}$

22. $\frac{p}{3} + 2 \le 7$; $p \le 15$

23. $\frac{x}{5} - 4 > 20$; $x > 120$

20. **GROCERIES** Carter bought 6 pounds of fruit and four potatoes that each weighed the same amount. If the total weight of the items he bought was no more than 7 pounds, write and solve an inequality to find the number of pounds that each potato could weigh.

21. **TENNIS** On Saturday, Danielle played tennis at the local community center. Racket rental was $7 and court time cost $27 per hour. If the total cost was less than $88, write and solve an inequality to find the number of hours Danielle could have spent playing tennis. $27h + 7 < 88$; $h < 3$

22. **PIZZA** Three friends shared the cost of an extra-large pizza. In addition, each friend spent $2 on a beverage. If each friend paid no more than $7, write and solve an inequality to find the dollar amount that the pizza could cost.

23. **ALGEBRA** The mean of five numbers less four is greater than 20. Write and solve an inequality to find how large the sum of these numbers could be.

H.O.T. Problems

24. **CHALLENGE** Use what you know about the Distributive Property and solving two-step linear inequalities to solve the inequality $2(n - 9) > -4$. $n > 7$

25. **OPEN ENDED** Write a two-step inequality involving division and addition. Solve your inequality. **See students' work.**

26. **WRITING IN MATH** Explain the similarities and differences in the methods used to solve the equation $19 = -5x + 4$ and the inequality $19 \le -5x + 4$. **See margin.**

ISTEP+ PRACTICE 7.2.2

27. Felisa solved the linear inequality $\frac{b}{-2} - 1 \le 3$ by first adding 1 to each side and then by multiplying both sides by −2. Her result was $b \le -8$. Which of the following BEST describes her error? **D**

    A She added 1 to each side when she should have multiplied each side by −1.

    B She multiplied both sides by −2 when she should have divided both sides by −2.

    C She added 1 to each side when she should have subtracted 1 from each side.

    D She did not reverse the direction of the inequality symbol.

28. Which of the following is the correct FIRST step in solving the linear inequality $3x - 9 > 12$? **H**

    F Divide both sides by 3.

    G Multiply both sides by 3.

    H Add 9 to each side.

    J Subtract 9 from each side.

29. Hakim bought 3 DVDs. Each DVD was the same price. He also spent $15 on a CD. He spent less than $45 altogether. Which of the following inequalities represents this situation? **B**

    A $3x - 15 < 45$

    B $3x + 15 < 45$

    C $3x + 15 \le 45$

    D $3x + 15 > 45$

4 Assess

Ticket Out the Door Ask students to describe the similarities and differences between solving equations and solving inequalities. Sample answer: Solving equations and inequalities requires adding, subtracting, multiplying, or dividing both sides by the same number. When solving both, the goal is to isolate the variable in order to determine its value. However, when solving an inequality, the inequality symbol is reversed when multiplying or dividing each side by a negative number.

Lesson IN 2 Linear Inequalities IN9

3 Lesson Notes

Lesson Planner

Use this lesson after Lesson 3-6 to address standard 7.2.4.

Objective

Solve equations and formulas with two variables for a particular variable.

Vocabulary

literal equation

IN Academic Standards

7.2.4 Solve an equation or formula with two variables for a particular variable. *Also addresses 7.3.6.*

1 Focus

- Review the meaning of *formula* by asking students to recall formulas they have used previously. Sample answers: area of a rectangle: $A = \ell w$; simple interest formula: $I = prt$
- Have students explain how they use the formulas to determine missing values.
- Then have students evaluate $5n + 2$ if n equals 6, 35, and -10. 32; 177; -48
- Have students solve $\frac{b}{3} = 7$ and $3x + 1 = 12$. 21, $\frac{11}{3}$ or $3\frac{2}{3}$
- Next, have students explain the difference between one- and two-step equations.

3 Literal Equations

MAIN IDEA

Solve equations and formulas with two variables for a particular variable.

IN Academic Standards

7.2.4 Solve an equation or formula with two variables for a particular variable. *Also addresses 7.3.6.*

New Vocabulary

literal equation

IN Math Online

glencoe.com

GET READY for the Lesson

TORNADOES Most tornadoes travel at an average speed of 30 miles per hour. The formula $d = rt$ gives the distance d traveled given a rate r and a time t.

1. An F5 tornado is traveling at a speed of 30 miles per hour. Write the equation that gives the distance d traveled by this tornado for a time of t hours. $d = 30t$
2. If the tornado in Exercise 1 covers a distance of 5.4 miles, write the equation that gives the distance traveled by this tornado for a time of t hours. $5.4 = 30t$
3. Solve the equation you wrote in Exercise 2 for t. What operation(s) did you perform to solve the equation?

3. $t = 0.18$ h or 10.8 min; Sample answer: Divide both sides of the equation by 30.

Common Literal Equations	
Area of a Rectangle	$A = \ell w$
Area of a Triangle	$A = \frac{1}{2}bh$
Distance, Rate, and Time	$d = rt$
Perimeter of a Rectangle	$P = 2\ell + 2w$

The formula $d = rt$ represents a literal equation. A **literal equation** is an equation or formula that contains more than one variable. Some common literal equations are shown in the table.

Often, you may need to solve a literal equation for a particular variable when the other variables still remain unknown. This process is called *solving a literal equation*. You can solve a literal equation using the same methods you have been using to solve one- and two-step equations.

EXAMPLE Solve Literal Equations

1 TORNADOES Solve the literal equation $d = rt$ for t. Then use the equation to find the time t that it takes an F2 tornado traveling at 25 miles per hour to cover a distance of 2.7 miles.

Solve the literal equation $d = rt$ for t.

$d = rt$	Write the equation.
$\frac{d}{r} = \frac{\cancel{r}t}{\cancel{r}}$	To solve for t, divide both sides of the equation by r.
$\frac{d}{r} = t$	Since the variables remain unknown, you cannot simplify $\frac{d}{r}$.

The literal equation $d = rt$ solved for t is $\frac{d}{r} = t$ or $t = \frac{d}{r}$.

IN10 Focus on Indiana

Use this equation to find the time t that it takes an F2-tornado traveling at 25 miles per hour to cover a distance of 2.7 miles.

$t = \frac{d}{r}$ Write the equation.

$t = \frac{2.7}{25}$ Replace d with 2.7 and r with 25.

$t = 0.108$ Divide.

It takes the tornado 0.108 hour, or 6.48 minutes, to travel a distance of 2.7 miles.

EXAMPLES Solve Multi-Step Literal Equations

Solve each literal equation for the indicated variable.

2 $P = 2\ell + 2w$, **for** w

$P = 2\ell + 2w$ Write the equation.

$-2\ell \quad -2\ell$ Subtract 2ℓ from each side.

$P - 2\ell = 2w$ You cannot simplify $P - 2\ell$.

$\frac{P - 2\ell}{2} = \frac{2w}{2}$ Divide both sides by 2.

$\frac{P - 2\ell}{2} = w$ You cannot simplify $\frac{P-2\ell}{2}$.

The literal equation solved for w is $\frac{P - 2\ell}{2} = w$, or $w = \frac{P - 2\ell}{2}$.

3 $A = \frac{1}{2}bh$, **for** b

$A = \frac{1}{2}bh$ Write the equation.

$(2)A = (2)\frac{1}{2}bh$ Dividing both sides by $\frac{1}{2}$ is the same as multiplying both sides by 2.

$2A = bh$ Simplify.

$\frac{2A}{h} = \frac{bh}{h}$ Divide both sides by h.

$\frac{2A}{h} = b$ You cannot simplify $\frac{2A}{h}$.

The literal equation solved for b is $\frac{2A}{h} = b$, or $b = \frac{2A}{h}$.

Check You can check the answer by substituting values for b, h, and A. For example, if the base of a triangle is 6 units and the height is 4 units, then the area is $\frac{1}{2}(6)(4)$, or 12 square units.

$b = \frac{2A}{h}$ Write the answer.

$6 \stackrel{?}{=} \frac{2(12)}{4}$ Replace b with 6, h with 4, and A with 12.

$6 \stackrel{?}{=} \frac{24}{4}$ Multiply.

$6 = 6$ ✓ Divide. This statement is true.

2 Teach

Scaffolding Questions

Have students refer to the paragraph about tornadoes at the top of page IN10. On the board, display the formula $d = rt$.

Ask:

- What do the variables represent? What does the formula state? d = distance, r = rate, t = time; The formula states that the rate multiplied by the time equals the distance.
- Suppose $d = 240$ and $r = 30$. What is the value of t? 8 h
- Suppose $d = 240$ and $r = 40$. What is the value of t? 6 h
- Suppose $d = 240$ and $r = 60$. What is the value of t? 4 h
- In each situation, how did you solve for t? Divide each side of the equation by r.
- How can you rewrite the formula to solve for t? $\frac{d}{r} = t$

Additional Answers

1. $a = \frac{F}{m}$
2. $F = PA$
3. $w = 4(x - z)$
4. $y = \frac{12 - 4x}{3}$

Real-World EXAMPLES

SCIENCE **The *momentum* of a moving object can be described as the level of energy carried by the object. It is the product of an object's mass and velocity. The formula for the momentum M of a moving object with a mass m and a velocity v is given by $M = mv$.**

4 **Solve the equation $M = mv$ for v.**

$M = mv$ — Write the equation.

$\frac{M}{m} = \frac{mv}{m}$ — Divide both sides by m.

$\frac{M}{m} = v$ — You cannot simplify $\frac{M}{m}$ because they are different variables.

The literal equation solved for v is $\frac{M}{m} = v$, or $v = \frac{M}{m}$.

5 **Use the equation to find the velocity of a black bear whose mass is 185 kilograms and whose momentum is 1,517 kilograms-kilometers per hour.**

$v = \frac{M}{m}$ — Write the equation.

$v = \frac{1{,}517}{185}$ — Replace M with 1,517 and m with 185.

$v = 8.2$ — Divide.

The velocity of the black bear is 8.2 kilometers per hour.

Check

$M = mv$ — Write the original equation.

$1{,}517 \stackrel{?}{=} 185(8.2)$ — Replace M with 1,517, m with 185, and v with 8.2.

$1{,}517 \stackrel{?}{=} 1{,}517$ ✓ — Multiply. This statement is true.

CHECK Your Understanding

Examples 1–4 (pp. IN10–IN12)

Solve each literal equation for the indicated variable. **1–4. See margin.**

1. $F = ma$, for a
2. $P = \frac{F}{A}$, for F
3. $x = \frac{1}{4}w + z$, for w
4. $4x + 3y = 12$, for y

Examples 1, 4, 5 (pp. IN10, IN12)

SCIENCE **The amount of work W done on an object is given by the formula $W = Fd$, where F is the force applied to an object and d is the distance the object moved. The amount of work W is measured in joules. The amount of force applied on the object is measured in newtons.**

5. Solve the equation $W = Fd$ for F. **$F = \frac{W}{d}$**
6. Find the amount of force applied on an object if the distance the object moved was 2.1 meters and the work done on the object was 19.53 joules. **9.3 newtons**

Practice and Problem Solving

HOMEWORK HELP	
For Exercises	See Examples
7–14	1–3
15–18	4, 5

Solve each literal equation for the indicated variable. 7–14. See margin.

7. $A = lw$, for w
8. $V = Bh$, for h
9. $I = \frac{V}{R}$, for V
10. $P = \frac{w}{t}$, for w
11. $3T = 5r - s$, for r
12. $d = 3b + \frac{1}{3}a$, for a
13. $-3x + 5y = 15$, for x
14. $-2A + 6B = C$, for B

SCIENCE **The density D of an object is the amount of mass m is contained in one unit of volume v. The density of an object is given by the formula $D = \frac{m}{v}$. Solve this literal equation for m.**

15. Solve the equation $D = \frac{m}{v}$ for m. $m = Dv$
16. Find the mass of 800 cubic centimeters of steel if steel has a density of 7.80 grams per cubic centimeter. (*Hint:* The volume is measured in cubic centimeters.) 6,240 g

SCIENCE **The acceleration a of a moving object is given by the formula $a = \frac{f - o}{t}$, where f is the final speed of an object, o is the original speed of the object, and t is the time.**

17. Solve the equation $a = \frac{f - o}{t}$ for f. $f = at + o$
18. Find the final speed of a car with an original speed of 30 miles per hour, an acceleration rate of 2 miles per hour per second, and a time of 10 seconds. 50 mph

H.O.T. Problems

19. **CHALLENGE** To convert a temperature in degrees Celsius C to a temperature in degrees Fahrenheit F, you can use the formula $F = \frac{9}{5}C + 32$. Solve this literal equation for C and use your equation to find the temperature in degrees Celsius if the temperature in degrees Fahrenheit is 80. Round to the nearest tenth of a degree if necessary. $C = \frac{5}{9}(F - 32)$; 26.7°C
20. **WRITING IN MATH** Explain the steps you would take to solve the literal equation $3x + 2y = 6$ for y. Then explain the steps you would use to solve the equation $3x + 2y = 6$ for x. Your answer should include both literal equations solved for each variable. See margin.

ISTEP+ PRACTICE 7.2.4

21. A rectangle with a length of 8.4 yards has a perimeter of P yards. Which equation could be used to find the width w of the rectangle? D

    A $w = P - 8.4$

    B $w = 2P - 8.4$

    C $w = \frac{P}{2} - 16.8$

    D $w = \frac{P - 16.8}{2}$

22. Which of the following equations is NOT equivalent to the formula for the volume of a rectangular prism $V = \ell wh$? G

    F $\ell = \frac{V}{wh}$

    G $h = V - \ell w$

    H $w = \frac{V}{\ell h}$

    J $h = \frac{V}{\ell w}$

3 Practice

Use Exercises 1–6 to check for understanding.

Exercises 7–22 are structured so that students practice the same concepts they learned in the lesson.

Have students discuss and complete the Higher Order Thinking problems.

WRITING IN MATH Have students complete Exercise 20 in their Math Journals. You may choose to use this exercise as an optional formative assessment.

4 Assess

Ticket Out the Door Ask students to explain when it would be helpful to solve a literal equation for a specified variable. Sample answer: It would be helpful to solve for a specified variable when you have several different unknown values.

Additional Answers

7. $w = \frac{A}{\ell}$
8. $h = \frac{V}{B}$
9. $V = IR$
10. $w = Pt$
11. $r = \frac{3T + s}{5}$
12. $a = 3d - 9b$
13. $x = \frac{15 - 5y}{-3}$
14. $B = \frac{C + 2A}{6}$
20. Sample answer: To solve $3x + 2y = 6$ for y, subtract $3x$ and divide by 2. To solve $3x + 2y = 6$ for x, subtract $2y$ and divide by 3. $y = \frac{6 - 3x}{2}$; $x = \frac{6 - 2y}{3}$

4 Lesson Notes

Lesson Planner

Use this lesson after Lesson 4-9 to address standard 7.1.6.

Objective

Solve problems that involve operations with decimals.

IN Academic Standards

7.1.6 Solve problems that involve multiplication and division with integers, fractions, **decimals, and combinations of the four operations.**

1 Focus

- Have students review multiplication and division of whole numbers by finding each product or quotient.

  15×8 120 $\qquad 23 \times 45$ 1,035

  $3\overline{)912}$ 304 $\qquad 21\overline{)336}$ 16

- In small groups, have students write the steps for multiplying and dividing whole numbers. Have each group share their steps with the class.

4 Operations with Decimals

MAIN IDEA

Solve problems that involve operations with decimals.

IN Academic Standards

7.1.7 Solve problems that involve multiplication and division with integers, fractions, **decimals and combinations of the four operations.**

IN Math Online

glencoe.com

GET READY for the Lesson

NUTS Nina is buying bags of nuts. The nuts costs \$1.25 for each pound. The average weight of each bag is 2.6 pounds.

1. The expression 1.25×2.6 can be used to find the total price of each bag. Estimate the product of 1.25 and 2.6. **Sample answer: $1 \times 3 = 3$**
2. Multiply 125 by 26. **3,250**
3. **MAKE A CONJECTURE** about how you can use your answers from Exercises 1 and 2 to find the product of 1.25 and 2.6.
4. What is the total cost of one bag? **\$3.25**
5. Use your conjecture from Exercise 3 to find 5.2×2.7. Explain each step.

3. Sample answer: The digits are the same. The decimal points are in different positions.

5. The estimate is $5 \times 3 = 15$; $52 \times 27 = 1{,}404$; $15 \approx 14.04$, so the product of 5.2 and 2.7 is 14.04.

To multiply by a decimal, multiply as with whole numbers. To decide where to place the decimal point, count the number of decimal places in each factor. The product has the same number of decimal places.

EXAMPLES Multiply Decimals

Multiply.

1 **1.3×0.9** Estimate $1 \times 1 = 1$

$$\begin{array}{r} 1.3 \\ \times\ 0.9 \\ \hline 1.17 \end{array}$$

1.3 ← 1 decimal place
0.9 ← 1 decimal place
1.17 ← 2 decimal places

Compare to the estimate. Since $1.17 \approx 1$, the answer is reasonable.

2 **0.054×1.6** Estimate $0 \times 2 = 0$

$$\begin{array}{r} 0.054 \\ \times\ 1.6 \\ \hline 324 \\ 540 \\ \hline 0.0864 \end{array}$$

0.054 ← 3 decimal places
1.6 ← 1 decimal place
0.0864: Annex a zero on the left so the answer has four decimal places.

Compare to the estimate. Since $0.0864 \approx 0$, the answer is reasonable.

When dividing by decimals, change the divisor into a whole number. To do this, multiply both the divisor and the dividend by the same power of 10. Then divide as with whole numbers.

EXAMPLES Divide Decimals

Divide.

3 **25.8 ÷ 2** **Estimate** 26 ÷ 2 = 13

The divisor, 2, is already a whole number, so you do not need to move the decimal point. Divide as with whole numbers.

```
   12.9
2)25.8     Place the decimal point in the quotient directly above
 - 2       the decimal point in the dividend.
   5
 - 4
   18
 - 18
    0      Compare to the estimate. Since 12.9 ≈ 13, the answer is reasonable.
```

4 **199.68 ÷ 9.6** **Estimate** 200 ÷ 10 = 20

```
      20.8
9.6)199.68    Move each decimal point one place to the right.
  - 192
      768
    - 768
        0     Compare to the estimate. Since 20.8 ≈ 20, the answer is reasonable.
```

EXAMPLE Evaluate an Expression

5 **ALGEBRA** **Evaluate $3.5x$ if $x = 4.5$.**

$3.5x = 3.5 \times 4.5$ Replace x with 4.5.

```
    3.5   ← one decimal place
  × 4.5   ← one decimal place
    175
 + 1400
  15.75   The product has two decimal places.
```

CHECK Your Understanding

Examples 1, 2 (p. IN14)

Multiply or divide.

1. 0.3×0.9 **0.27**
2. 0.45×0.12 **0.054**
3. 0.003×4.82 **0.01446**
4. 3.06×0.9 **2.754**

Examples 3, 4 (p. IN15)

5. $0.3\overline{)9.81}$ **32.7**
6. $3.2\overline{)5.76}$ **1.8**
7. $0.34 \div 0.2$ **1.7**
8. $14.4 \div 0.12$ **120**

ALGEBRA **Evaluate each expression if $a = 2.41$.**

Example 5 (p. IN15)

9. $0.6a - 1.016$ **0.43**
10. $3.8 + 5.3a$ **16.573**
11. $\frac{10a}{0.5}$ **48.2**
12. $a \div 0.02 - 35.4$ **85.1**
13. **JOBS** Antonia earns $10.75 per hour. What are her total weekly earnings if she works 34.5 hours? Round to the nearest cent. **$370.88**

2 Teach

Scaffolding Questions

Write 0.537 on the board.

Ask:

- What is the place value of 5? tenths
- What is the place value of 3? hundredths
- What is the place value of 7? thousandths
- How many decimal places are in the number? three
- Suppose you moved the decimal point one place to left. How many decimal places would the number have? four

3 Practice

Use Exercises 1–13 to check for understanding.

Exercises 14–56 are structured so that students practice the same concepts they learned in the lesson.

Have students discuss and complete the Higher Order Thinking problems.

WRITING IN MATH Have students complete Exercise 54 in their Math Journals. You may choose to use this exercise as an optional formative assessment.

Additional Answers

51. Sample answer: $0.2 \div 0.8 = 0.25$, which is less than 1 and would make the statement true. $0.8 \div 0.2 = 4$, which is greater than 1 and would make the statement false.

53. 0.41308852; Sample answer: There are 4 decimal places in each number, so the product will have 8 decimal places. Starting from the right, move the decimal place 8 places to the left.

54. Sample answer: Michael has 162.4 feet of wood to make birdhouses. If each birdhouse uses 1.4 feet of wood, how many birdhouses can he make? 116 birdhouses

Practice and Problem Solving

HOMEWORK HELP

For Exercises	See Examples
14–29	1–4
30–37	5

19. 1,114.53
20. 0.0901
21. 4.4165
22. 0.06
23. 0.21
27. 82.5
28. 12.8
29. 88.92

Multiply or divide.

14. 1.8×4.3 **7.74**
15. 1.21×0.35 **0.4235**
16. 0.0023×0.28 **0.000644**
17. 6.007×1.48 **8.89036**
18. 0.44×0.5 **0.22**
19. 38.3×29.1
20. 0.017×5.3
21. 6.05×0.73
22. $0.22\overline{)0.0132}$
23. $0.04\overline{)0.0084}$
24. $3.18\overline{)0.636}$ **0.2**
25. $19.2\overline{)4.416}$ **0.23**
26. $20.24 \div 2.3$ **8.8**
27. $2.475 \div 0.03$
28. $4.6848 \div 0.366$
29. $97.812 \div 1.1$

ALGEBRA **Evaluate each expression if $x = 1.07$, $y = 3.1$, and $z = 0.4$. Round to the nearest tenth.** **31. 6.0**

30. $xy + z$ **3.7**
31. $x \times 6.023 - z$
32. $3.25y + x$ **11.1**
33. xyz **1.3**
34. $\frac{xy}{z}$ **8.3**
35. $\frac{yz}{x}$ **1.2**
36. $\frac{x + y}{z}$ **10.4**
37. $\frac{x + y - z}{z}$ **9.4**

38. **MEASUREMENT** Neal bought 6.75 yards of fleece fabric to make blankets for a charity. He needs 1.35 yards of fabric for each blanket. How many blankets can Neal make with the fabric he bought? **5 blankets**

39. **MEASUREMENT** A meter is approximately equal to about 39.37 inches. How many inches are in 3.3 meters? Round to the nearest tenth. **129.9 in.**

COMMUNICATION **For Exercises 40–42, use the table that shows the most used method to communicate with friends.**

Most Used Method To Communicate

Communication Method	Portion of Responses
cell phone	0.27
E-mail	0.12
between class	0.11
text message	0.3
web site	0.1
other	0.05
home phone	0.03
mail	0.02

40. How many times more respondents use cell phones rather than E-mail? Round to the nearest tenth. **2.3**

41. How many times more respondents communicate between classes than by home phone? Round to the nearest tenth. **3.7**

42. How many times more respondents use either cell phones or text messages than Web sites? Round to the nearest tenth. **5.7**

43. **OLYMPICS** In the 2008 Olympics, LaShawn Merritt of the U.S. ran the 400-meter run in 43.75 seconds. To the nearest hundredth, find his speed in meters per second. **9.14 meters per second**

44. **GROCERY SHOPPING** Potatoes cost \$1.47 per pound, and carrots cost \$1.99 per pound. Mrs. Rolloson bought 4.65 pounds of potatoes and 1.7 pounds of carrots. How much did she pay for the potatoes and carrots? Round to the nearest hundredth. **\$10.22**

45. Sample answer: Separate the figure into two rectangles. One rectangle has a length of 7.6 in. and a width of 3.2 in. The other rectangle has a length of 3.4 in. and a width of 2.6 in. You can also separate the figure into a rectangle with length 5.8 in. and width 3.4 in. and a rectangle with length 4.2 in. and width 3.2 in.

MEASUREMENT Refer to the figure shown at the right.

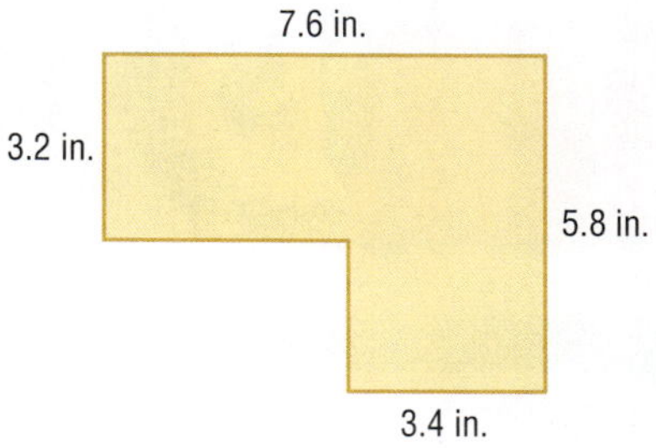

45. Describe two different methods you could use to find the area of the figure.

46. Find the area of the figure using each method. What do you notice? **33.16 in^2; Sample answer: They are the same.**

STATISTICS Find the mean for each set of data.

47. 12.8, 14.6, 15.1, 16.7 **14.8**

48. 4.06, 5.17, 4.87, 5.11, 5.09 **4.86**

49. **MOUNTAINS** Find the average height of the mountains shown in the table. **5.346 mi**

World's Tallest Mountains (mi)				
5.49	5.35	5.33	5.29	5.27

50. **MEASUREMENT** The thickness of each type of coin is shown in the table. How much thicker is a stack of a dollar's worth of nickels than a dollar's worth of quarters? **32 mm; $20 \times 1.95 = 39$; 4×1.75; $39 - 7 = 32$**

Coin	Thickness (mm)
penny	1.55
nickel	1.95
dime	1.35
quarter	1.75

H.O.T. Problems

51. **CHALLENGE** Find two positive decimals x and y that make the following statement true. Then find two positive decimals x and y that make the statement false. **See margin.**

If $x < 1$ and $y < 1$, then $x \div y < 1$.

52. **OPEN ENDED** Write a multiplication problem in which the product is between 0.05 and 0.5. **Sample answer: $0.25 \times 0.5 = 0.125$**

53. **NUMBER SENSE** Place the decimal point in the answer to make it correct. Explain your reasoning. **See margin.**

$0.0458 \times 9.0194 = 41308852$

54. **WRITING IN MATH** Write a real-world problem that involves dividing a decimal by a decimal. **See margin.**

ISTEP+ PRACTICE 7.1.7

55. What is the area of the rectangle? **C**

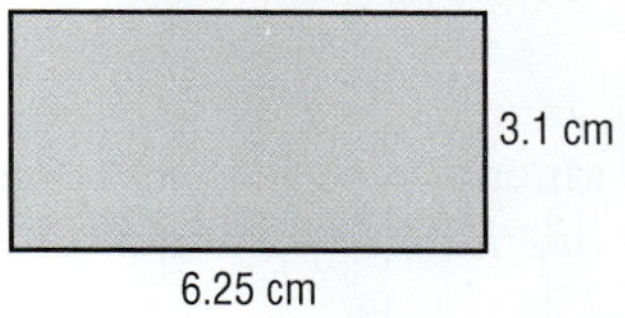

A 9.35 cm^2

B 18.7 cm^2

C 19.375 cm^2

D 193.75 cm^2

56. Callie is 4.05 feet tall. Her brother, Lance, is 5.67 feet tall. How many times as tall as Callie is Lance? **H**

F 0.7

G 1.2

H 1.4

J 2.8

4 Assess

Ticket Out the Door Ask students to evaluate the expression $3.24 \times \frac{1.8}{k}$ if $k = 0.3$. Students should include the steps they followed to determine the value of k. **19.44; Sample answer: First I replaced the variable k with 0.3. Next, I divided 1.8 by 0.3 and got 6. Then I multiplied 3.24 by 6 to get 19.44.**

5 Lesson Notes

Lesson Planner

Use this lesson after Lesson 6-3 to address standard 7.2.5.

Objective

Relate the slope of a line to similar triangles.

Vocabulary

congruent triangles, **similar triangles**

IN Academic Standards

7.2.5 Find the slope of a line from its graph and relate the slope of a line to similar triangles.

1 Focus

- Have students review the concepts of congruency and similarity. Draw a square on the board and then have a student volunteer draw a congruent and similar square on the board. Repeat this process with other geometric figures, including triangles and circles.
- Next, have students describe the characteristics of right triangles. Be sure students' descriptions include that there is 1 right angle and 2 acute angles and that the side opposite of the right angle is always the longest side.

5 Slope and Similar Triangles

MAIN IDEA

Relate the slope of a line to similar triangles.

IN Academic Standards

7.2.5 Find the slope of a line from its graph and relate the slope of a line to similar triangles.

New Vocabulary

congruent triangles
similar triangles

IN Math Online

glencoe.com

GET READY for the Lesson

Refer to the graph at the right.

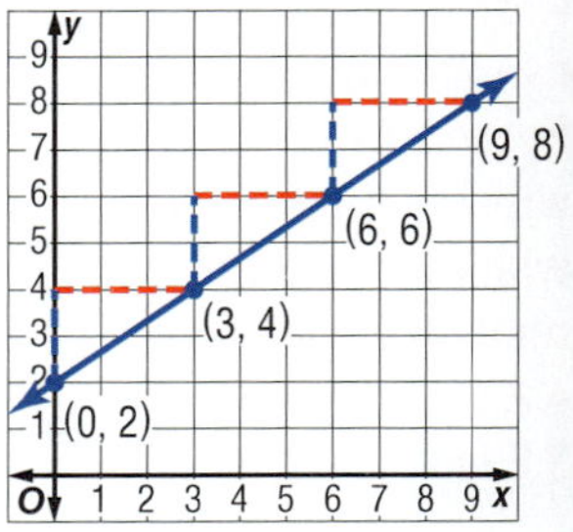

1. Find the slope of the line. $\frac{2}{3}$
2. What geometric figure is formed by connecting the vertices (0, 2), (0, 4), and (3, 4)? **right triangle**
3. What geometric figure is formed by connecting the vertices (6, 6), (6, 8), and (9, 8)? **right triangle**
4. How do the two figures you identified in Exercises 3 and 4 relate to each other? **They have the same shape and the same size.**
5. What geometric figure is formed by connecting the vertices (0, 2), (0, 6), and (6, 6)? **right triangle**
6. How do the two figures you identified in Exercises 3 and 5 relate to each other?

6. They have the same shape but the triangle in Exercise 5 is larger than the triangle in Exercise 3.

In Lesson 6–3, you learned to find the slope of a line from its graph. In this lesson, you will extend this concept to study the triangles that can be formed in relationship to the slope of a line.

The triangles you identified in Exercises 3 and 4 above are congruent triangles. **Congruent triangles** have the same size and the same shape. The corresponding side lengths of congruent triangles are equal.

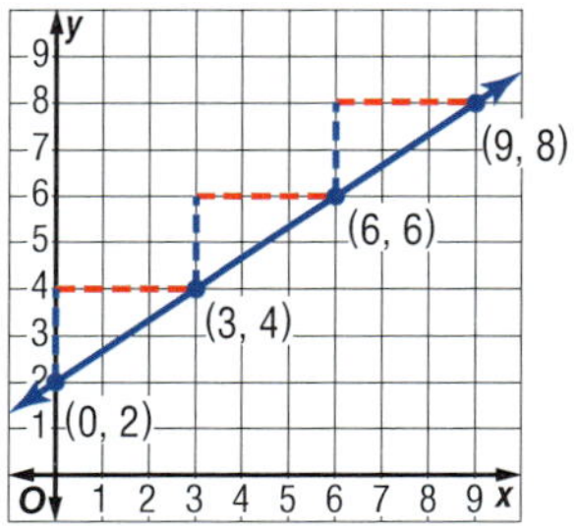

Each triangle has a vertical side length of 2 units and a horizontal side length of 3 units.

In addition, the slanted line segments between each point have equivalent lengths. You can confirm this by using a ruler.

The slope of the line above is $\frac{2}{3}$. Note that the ratio of the vertical side length to the horizontal side length of each triangle is also $\frac{2}{3}$. This demonstrates the Key Concept at the top of the next page.

IN18 Focus on Indiana

Slope and Congruent Triangles

Key Concept

Words

The simplified ratio of the vertical side length to the horizontal side length of each congruent triangle formed by the slope of a line is equivalent to the absolute value of the slope.

Example

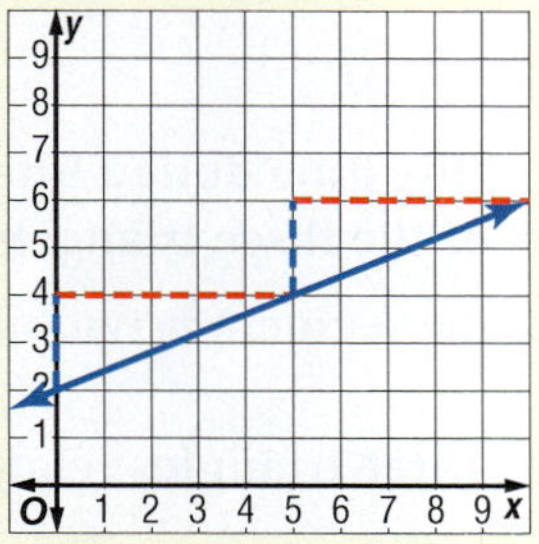

ratio: $\frac{\text{vertical side length}}{\text{horizontal side length}} = \frac{2}{5}$

slope $= \frac{2}{5}$

Note that the ratio of the side lengths is equivalent to the absolute value of the slope. Recall that the *absolute value* of a number is the distance the number is from zero. In the Key Concept box above, both the slope and the ratio were positive.

The slope of a line can sometimes be positive or negative. However, the side lengths of each triangle formed are always positive. When a line has a negative slope, the ratio of the side lengths of the triangles formed remains positive and is equal to the absolute value of the slope.

Refer to the graph below.

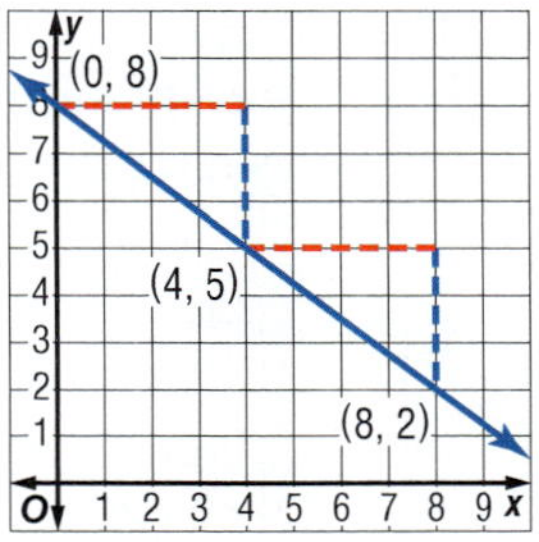

The slope of the line is $-\frac{3}{4}$.

The lengths of the horizontal red dotted line segments are each 4 units.

The lengths of the vertical blue dotted line segments are each 3 units.

The ratio of the vertical side length to the horizontal side length of each triangle is $\frac{3}{4}$.

Note that the ratio of the side lengths is positive. However, the slope is negative.

Since $\left|-\frac{3}{4}\right| = \frac{3}{4}$, the ratio is equivalent to the absolute value of the slope.

You can use the information from the Key Concept box above to analyze the congruent triangles formed by the slope of the line.

2 Teach

Scaffolding Questions

Have students draw various figures on grid paper using specific coordinates.

Ask:

- What type of figure can be created by connecting the coordinates (1, 1), (1, 4), (4, 4), (5, 1), and then (1, 1) again, in that order? trapezoid
- What type of figure can be created by connecting the coordinates (7, 1), (8, 3), (7, 4), (6, 2), and then (7, 1) again, in that order? parallelogram
- What type of figure can be created by connecting the coordinates (4, 9), (2, 7), (2, 4), (4, 2), (7, 2), (9, 4), (9, 7), (7, 9), and (4, 9) again, in that order? octagon

Have students practice finding the slope of a line. Draw and label the following lines on a grid: line A $\left(\text{slope} = 2\right)$, line B $\left(\text{slope} = -\frac{1}{3}\right)$, and line C $\left(\text{slope} = -1\right)$.

Ask:

- What is the slope of line A? 2
- What is the slope of line B? $-\frac{1}{3}$
- What is the slope of line C? -1

EXAMPLES Analyze Congruent Triangles

Refer to the graph at the right.

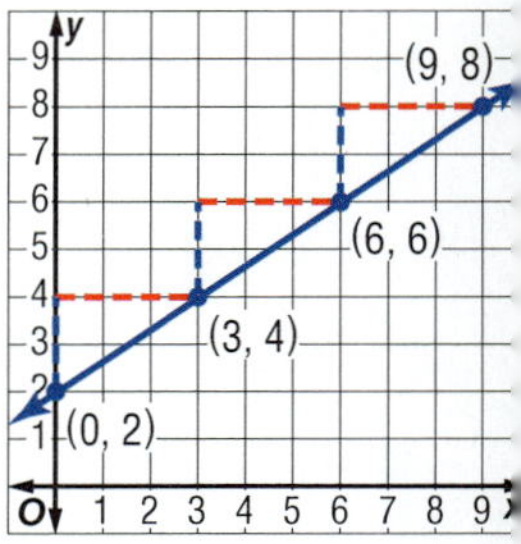

1 Find the length of the red dotted line segments in each of the three triangles formed.

Each red dotted line segment is three units long.

2 Find the length of the blue dotted line segments in each of the three triangles formed.

Each blue dotted line segment is two units long.

3 Describe how the three triangles relate to each other.

The three triangles are congruent. They have the same shape and the same size.

4 Describe how the side lengths of each triangle relate to the slope of the line.

The slope of the line is $\frac{2}{3}$. The ratio of the vertical side length to the horizontal side length of each triangle is equivalent to the absolute value of the slope.

The triangles you identified in Exercises 3 and 5 at the beginning of the lesson are similar triangles. Those triangles are shown below. **Similar triangles** have the same shape but not necessarily the same size.

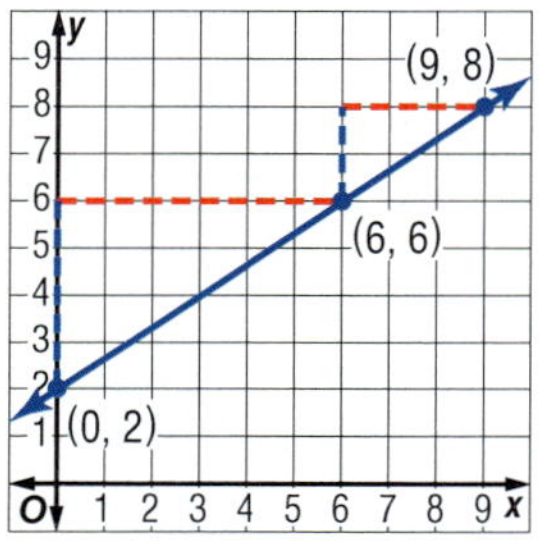

The ratio of the vertical side length to the horizontal side length of the larger triangle is 4 to 6, or $\frac{2}{3}$.

The ratio of the vertical side length to the horizontal side length of the smaller triangle is 2 to 3, or $\frac{2}{3}$.

The corresponding side lengths of similar triangles are *proportional.* Recall from Lesson 6-6 that two quantities are proportional if they have the same ratio. The side lengths of the similar triangles above have the same simplified ratio, $\frac{2}{3}$. Note that the slope of the line is also $\frac{2}{3}$.

Both the slope and the simplified ratio of the side lengths of the graph above are positive. When a line has a negative slope, the simplified ratio will still be positive.

IN20 Focus on Indiana

The relationship between the slope of a line and the side lengths of the similar triangles formed is the same as the relationship between the slope of a line and the side lengths of the congruent triangles formed.

Slope and Similar Triangles

Key Concept

Words

The simplified ratio of the vertical side length to the horizontal side length of each congruent triangle formed by the slope of a line is equivalent to the absolute value of the slope.

Example

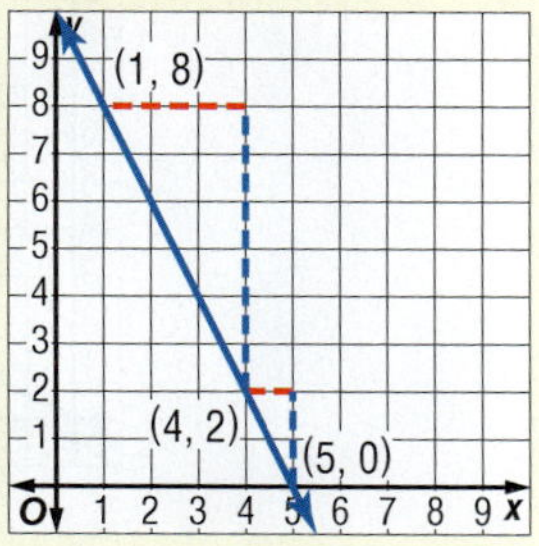

slope $= \frac{-2}{1}$, or -2

Larger Triangle

ratio: $\frac{\text{vertical side length}}{\text{horizontal side length}} = \frac{6}{3}$, or 2

Smaller Triangle

ratio: $\frac{\text{vertical side length}}{\text{horizontal side length}} = \frac{2}{1}$, or 2

You can use the information from the Key Concept box above to analyze the similar triangles formed by the slope of the line.

EXAMPLES Analyze Similar Triangles

Refer to the graph of the line at the right.

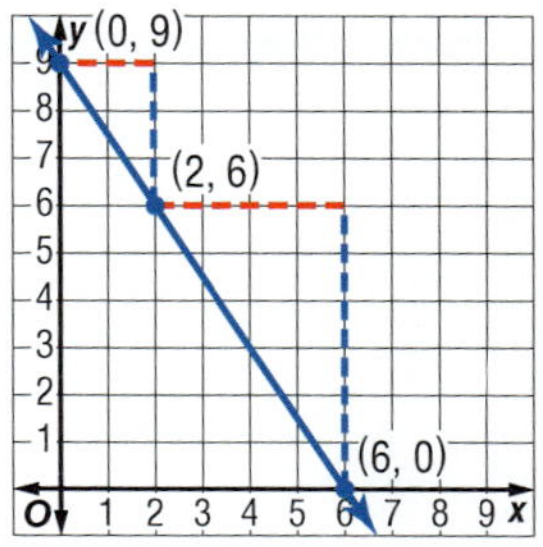

5 Find the length of the red dotted line segments in each triangle formed.

In the smaller triangle, the length of the red dotted line segment is two units. In the larger triangle, the length of the red dotted line segment is four units.

6 Find the length of the blue dotted line segments in each triangle formed.

In the smaller triangle, the length of the blue dotted line segment is three units. In the larger triangle, the length of the blue dotted line segment is six units.

7 Describe how the triangles relate to each other.

The two triangles are similar. They have the same shape but not the same size.

8 Describe how each triangle relates to the slope of the line.

The slope of the line is $-\frac{3}{2}$. The simplified ratio of the vertical side length to the horizontal side length of each triangle is $\frac{3}{2}$, which is equivalent to the absolute value of the slope.

Lesson IN 5 Slope and Similar Triangles **IN21**

3 Practice

Use Exercises 1 and 2 to check for understanding.

Exercises 3–13 are structured so that students practice the same concepts they learned in the lesson.

Have students discuss and complete the Higher Order Thinking problems.

WRITING IN MATH Have students complete Exercise 11 in their Math Journals. You may choose to use this exercise as an optional formative assessment.

Additional Answers

1a. $-\frac{4}{3}$

1b. 4 units, 3 units

1c. $\frac{4}{3}$; It is equivalent to the absolute value of the slope.

2a. $\frac{1}{2}$

2b. 1 unit, 2 units

2c. $\frac{1}{2}$; It is equivalent to the absolute value of the slope.

3a. $\frac{2}{3}$

3b. 2 units, 3 units

3c. $\frac{2}{3}$; It is equivalent to the absolute value of the slope.

4a. $-\frac{3}{2}$

4b. 3 units, 2 units

4c. $\frac{3}{2}$; It is equivalent to the absolute value of the slope.

5a. $-\frac{5}{3}$

5b. 5 units, 3 units

5c. $\frac{5}{3}$; It is equivalent to the absolute value of the slope.

6a. $\frac{2}{3}$

6b. 2 units, 3 units

6c. $\frac{2}{3}$; It is equivalent to the absolute value of the slope.

11. Sample answer: The ratio of the vertical side length to the horizontal side length of each congruent triangle formed by the slope of a line is equivalent to the absolute value of the slope.

CHECK Your Understanding

1, 2. See margin.

Examples 1–8 (pp. IN20–IN21)

For each graph,

a. Find the slope of each line.

b. Find the length of the vertical and horizontal side lengths of each triangle shown.

c. Find the simplified ratio of the vertical side length to the horizontal side length and explain how this ratio relates to the slope of the line.

1.

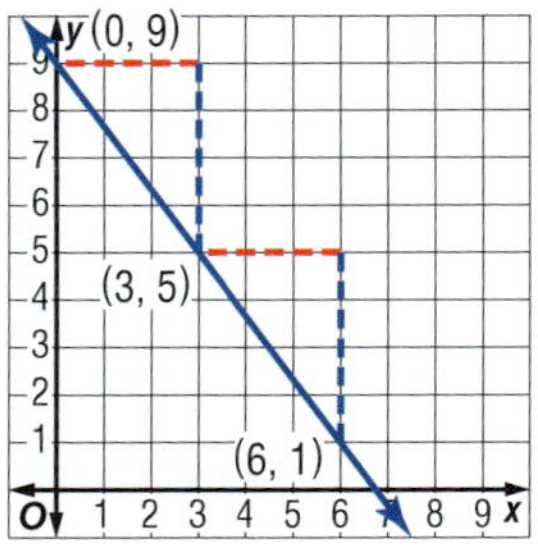

2.

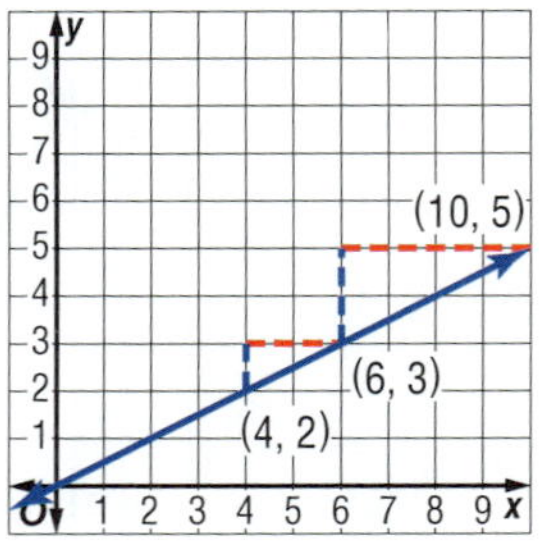

Practice and Problem Solving

3–6. See margin.

HOMEWORK HELP	
For Exercises	See Examples
3–6	1–8

For each graph,

a. Find the slope of each line.

b. Find the length of the vertical and horizontal side lengths of each triangle shown.

c. Find the simplified ratio of the vertical side length to the horizontal side length and explain how this ratio relates to the slope of the line.

3.

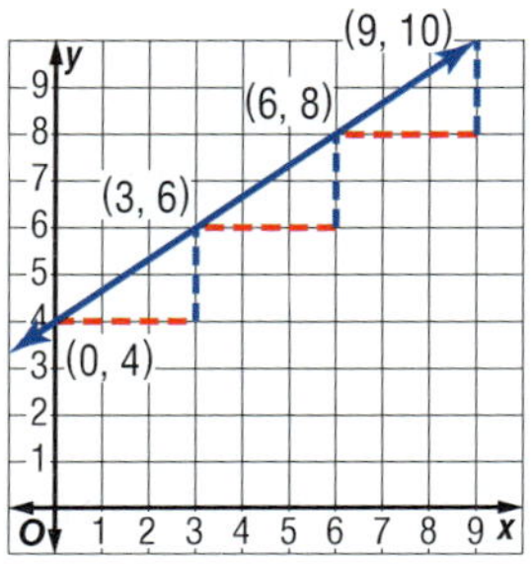

4.

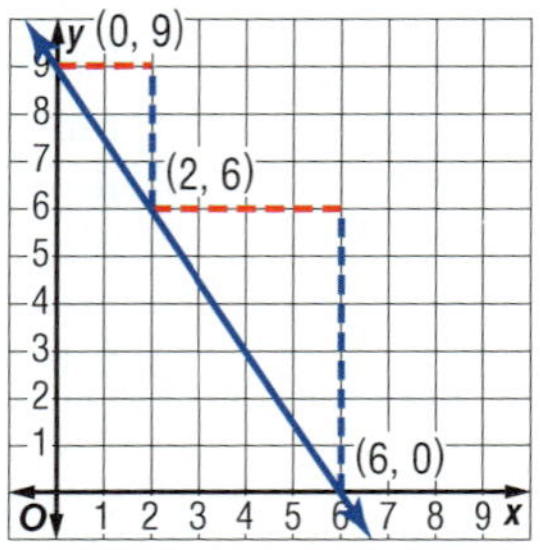

5.

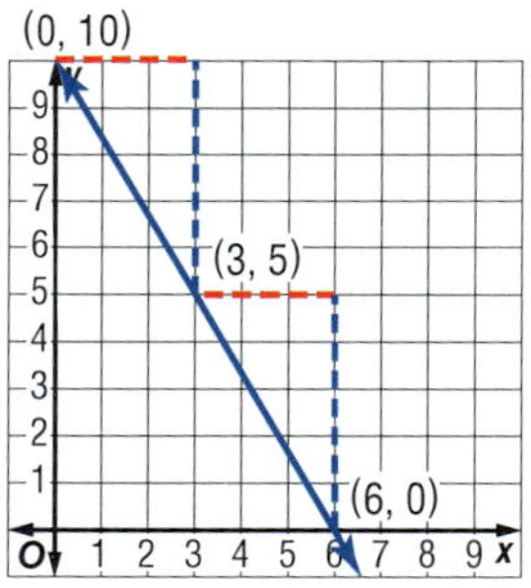

6.

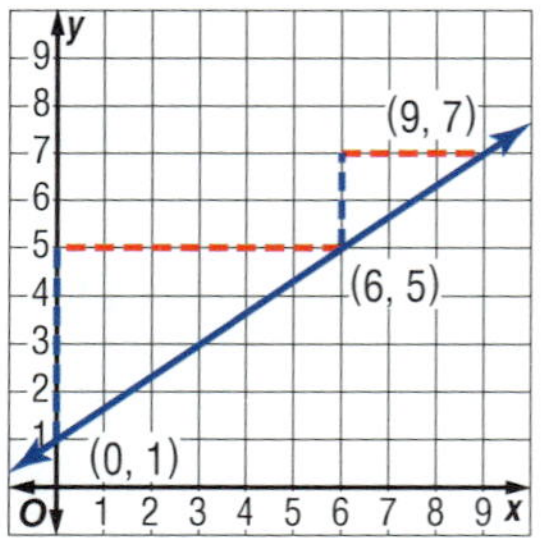

IN22 Focus on Indiana

H.O.T. Problems

8. $\frac{1}{5}$, $-\frac{1}{5}$; Sample answer: The absolute value of $\frac{1}{5}$ is $\frac{1}{5}$ and the absolute value of $-\frac{1}{5}$ is $\frac{1}{5}$.

9. no; Sample answer: Line b could have a slope of $\frac{3}{2}$, not $\frac{-3}{2}$.

10. $\frac{7}{2}$; Sample answer: The ratio is equivalent to the absolute value of the slope, 3.5. As an improper fraction, 3.5 is equal to $\frac{7}{2}$.

7. **OPEN ENDED** Draw the graph of a line with a positive slope. Then draw the triangles formed by the slope of the line and demonstrate that the simplified ratio of the vertical side length to the horizontal side length of each triangle is equivalent to the slope. **See students' work.**

8. **REASONING** The ratio of the vertical side length to the horizontal side length of each triangle formed by the slope of a line is $\frac{1}{5}$. Find two possible slopes for the line. Justify your response.

9. **REASONING** If two lines have the same slope, then they are parallel. The graph of line a has a slope of $\frac{-3}{2}$. For line b, the ratio of the vertical side length to the horizontal side length of each triangle formed by the slope is $\frac{3}{2}$. Does this automatically imply that lines a and b are parallel? Explain.

10. **CHALLENGE** The slope of a line is -3.5. What is the simplified ratio of the vertical side length to the horizontal side length of each triangle formed? Justify your response.

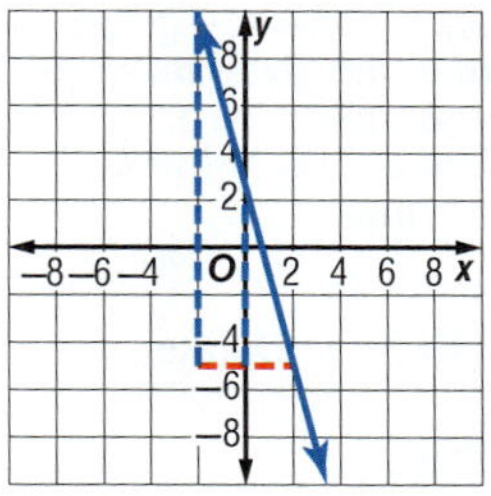

11. **WRITING IN MATH** Write a few sentences explaining how the slope of a line is related to similar triangles. **See margin.**

ISTEP+ PRACTICE 7.2.5

12. Which of the following statements is NOT true concerning the graph below? **B**

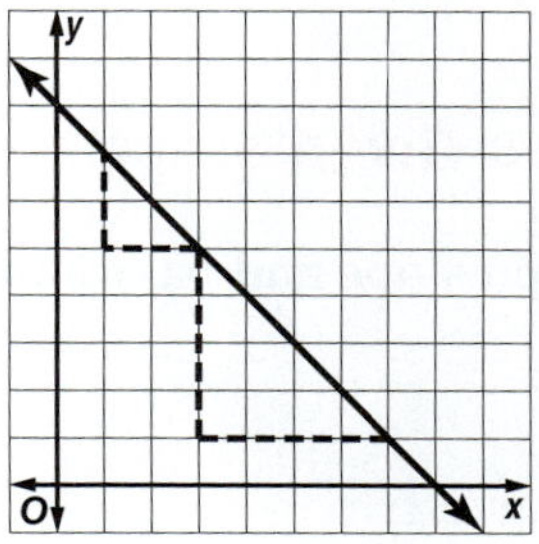

A The simplified ratio of the vertical side length to the horizontal side length of each triangle is 1.

B The slope of the line is 1.

C The slope of the line is -1.

D The smaller triangle and the larger triangle shown are similar.

13. Which statement is TRUE concerning the slope of the line below? **F**

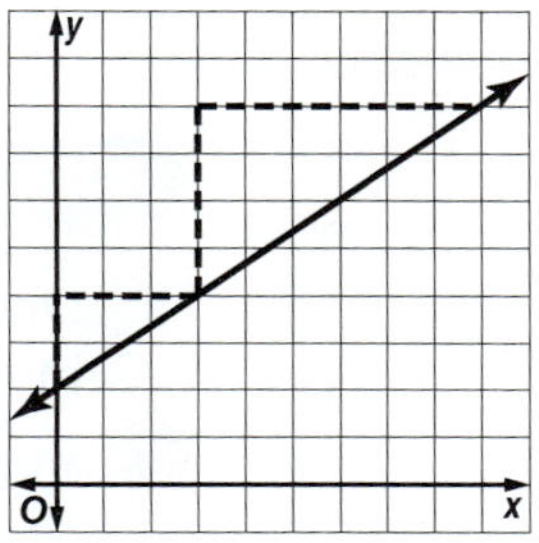

F It is equivalent to the simplified ratio of the vertical side length to the horizontal side length of each triangle shown.

G It is equivalent to $\frac{3}{2}$.

H It is equivalent to the simplified ratio of the horizontal side length to the vertical side length of each triangle shown.

J It is equivalent to $-\frac{2}{3}$.

4 Assess

Ticket Out the Door Have students graph and connect the following coordinates: (0, 1), (5, 4), and (10, 7). Ask students to determine the slope. Then, have students use the slope and the coordinates given to draw a congruent right triangle on the grid. Finally, have students create a triangle that is similar to the two triangles they just drew. slope $= \frac{3}{5}$

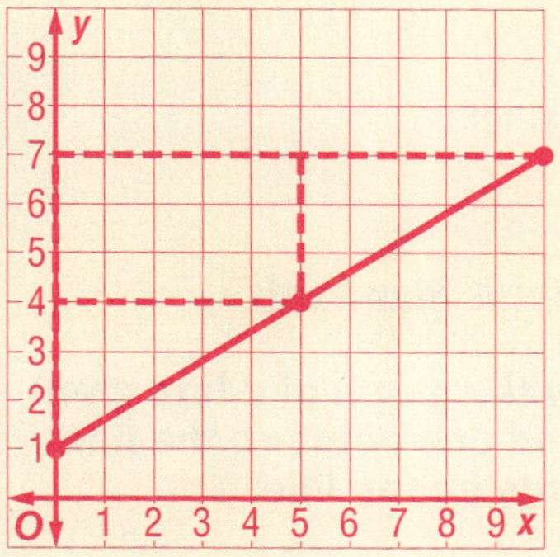

Lesson IN 5 Slope and Similar Triangles **IN23**

6 Lesson Notes

Lesson Planner

Use this lesson after Lesson 6-3 and Indiana Lesson 5 to address standard 7.2.6.

Objective

Draw a line given its slope and one point on the line or two points on the line.

Materials

grid paper, rulers

IN Academic Standards

7.2.6 Draw the graph of a line given its slope and one point on the line or two points on the line.

1 Focus

Have students practice plotting points on a coordinate grid. Include points in all four quadrants. Next, have students draw various lines on a grid and then locate and record points on the line. Ensure that students understand that the numerator of a given slope relates to vertical movement on the grid and the denominator relates to horizontal movement on the grid.

6 Graphs of Linear Equations

MAIN IDEA

Draw a line given its slope and one point on the line or two points on the line.

IN Academic Standards

7.2.6 Draw the graph of a line given its slope and one point on the line or two points on the line.

IN Math Online

glencoe.com

GET READY for the Lesson

Refer to the graph at the right.

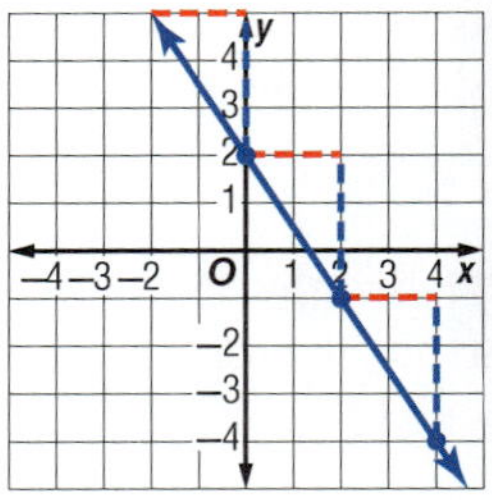

1. Find the slope of the line. $-\frac{3}{2}$
2. Complete the statement below by filling in the blanks with whole numbers.

   From the point (0, 2), count ____ units down and ____ units to the right to arrive at the point (2, −1). **3; 2**
3. How do the numbers you found in Exercise 2 relate to the slope of the line you found in Exercise 1?
4. To arrive at the point (2, −1) from the point (0, 2), you need to count *down* and to the right. How is counting *down* represented in the value of the slope?

3. The numerator of the slope represents the number of vertical units counted. The denominator of the slope represents the number of horizontal units counted.
4. The slope is negative.

In Lesson 6-3, you found the slope of a line from a table of values and from a graph. In this lesson, you will extend this concept to graph a line given its slope and a point on the line. Begin by graphing the point. Then use the slope to find additional points on the line. Connect the points with a solid line.

EXAMPLES Draw Lines Given Slope and Point

Draw a line that has the given slope and passes through the indicated point.

1 slope: $\frac{3}{2}$, point: (−3, −4)

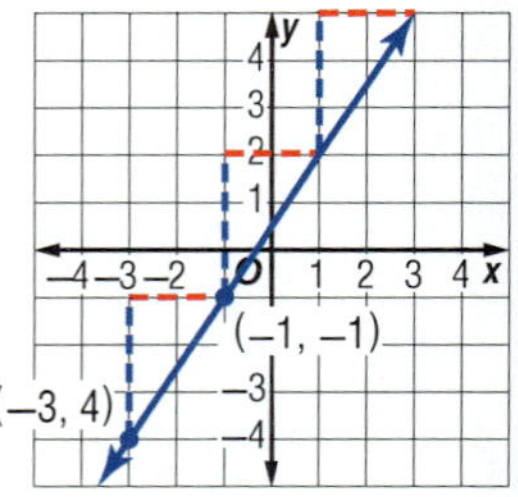

STEP 1 Graph the point (−3, −4).

STEP 2 Use the slope to find a second point on the line. The slope is $\frac{3}{2}$. The numerator 3 represents the vertical change. The denominator 2 represents the horizontal change. So, from (−3, −4), count 3 units up and 2 units to the right. Graph the point (−1, −1).

STEP 3 From (−1, −1), count 3 units up and 2 units to the right. Graph the point (1, 2).

STEP 4 Continue this process to find additional points on the line. Connect the points with a solid line.

IN24 Focus on Indiana

2 **slope: −2, point: (−5, 5)**

STEP 1 Graph the point (−5, 5).

STEP 2 Use the slope to find a second point on the line. The slope is −2. As a fraction, this is $\frac{-2}{1}$. The numerator −2 represents the vertical change. The denominator 1 represents the horizontal change. So, from (−5, 5), count 2 units down and 1 unit to the right. Graph the point (−4, 3).

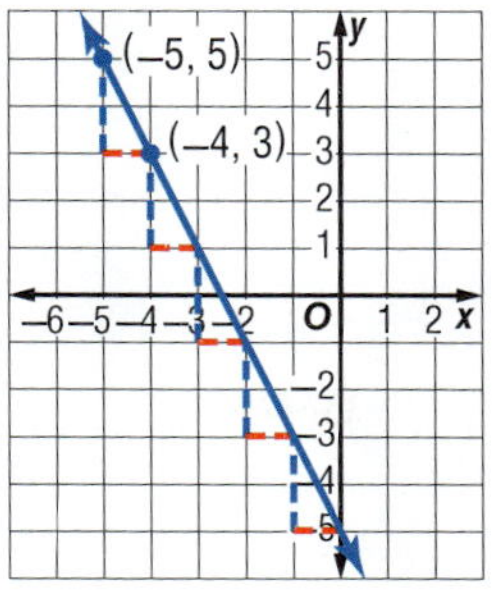

STEP 3 From (−4, 3), count 2 units down and 1 unit to the right. Graph the point (−3, 1).

STEP 4 Continue this process to find additional points on the line. Connect the points with a solid line.

You can also draw a line given two points on the line by graphing each point and then drawing a line that connects the points.

EXAMPLE Draw a Line Given Two Points

3 **Draw a line that passes through the points (−1, 3) and (2, −2). Then find the slope of the line as a ratio in simplest form.**

Graph each point. Using a straightedge, connect the two points with a solid line.

Find the slope of the line.

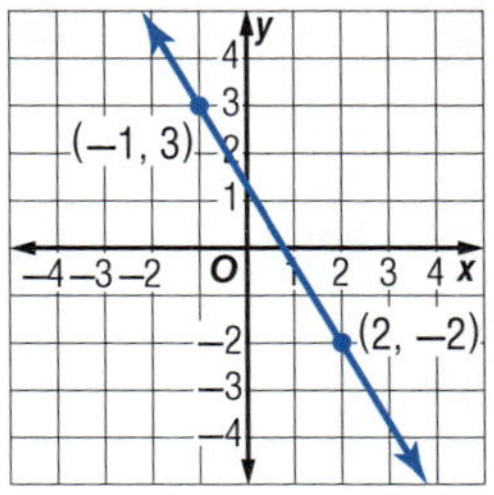

$\text{slope} = \frac{\text{change in } y}{\text{change in } x}$

$= \frac{-2-3}{2-(-1)}$ Use (−1, 3) and (2, −2).

$= \frac{-5}{3}$, or $-\frac{5}{3}$ Simplify. The slope is $-\frac{5}{3}$.

You can also use an equation to find one or more points on a line and the slope of a line.

EXAMPLE Find Points and Slope

4 **ALGEBRA** **Find a point on the line $y = 4x - 1$. Then find the slope of the line.**

$y = 4x - 1$ Write the equation.

$y = 4(1) - 1$ Replace x with any value, such as 1.

$y = 3$ Simplify. The y-value is 3.

One point on the line is (1, 3).

To find the slope, find another point on the line using the same method as above. Another point on the line is (2, 7).

The slope between the points (1, 3) and (2, 7) is $\frac{7-3}{2-1}$, or 4.

2 Teach

Scaffolding Questions

Display a grid showing the following lines: line T passing through points (0, 3) and (3, −3), line U passing through points (1, 4) and (5, 4), line V passing through points (4, 4) and (0, 3), and line W passing through points (1, 1) and (2, −1).

Ask:

- What is the slope of line W? −2
- What is the slope of line U? 0
- Which line passes through point (0, 3) and has a slope of $\frac{1}{4}$? line V
- Which line passes through point (0, 3) and has a slope of −2? line T
- Which line passes through point (1, 4) and has a slope of 0? line U

Lesson IN 6 Graphs of Linear Equations **IN25**

Additional Answers

1.

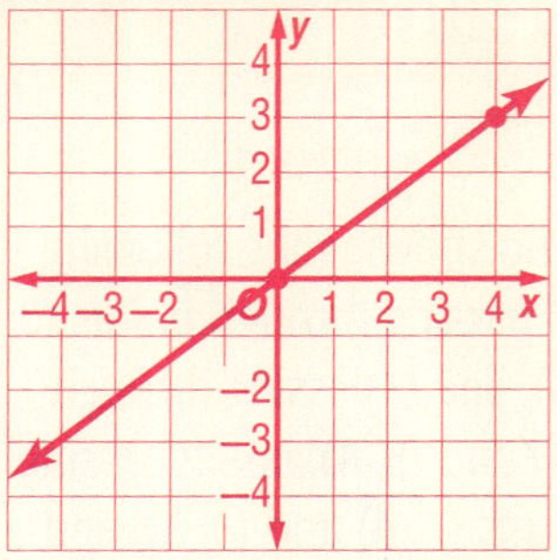

2.

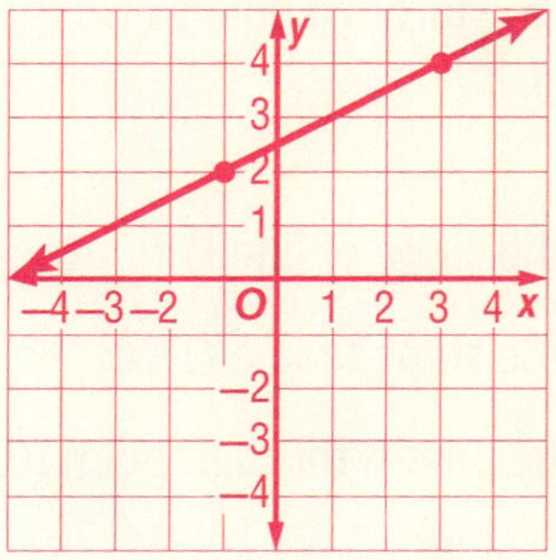

3.

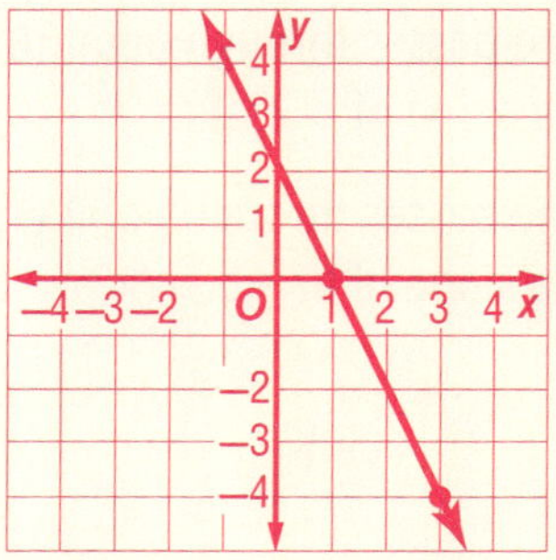

4. $\frac{4}{5}$

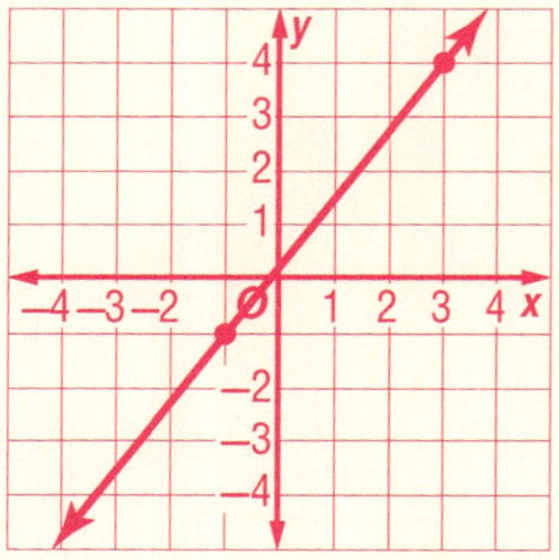

5. $\frac{2}{3}$

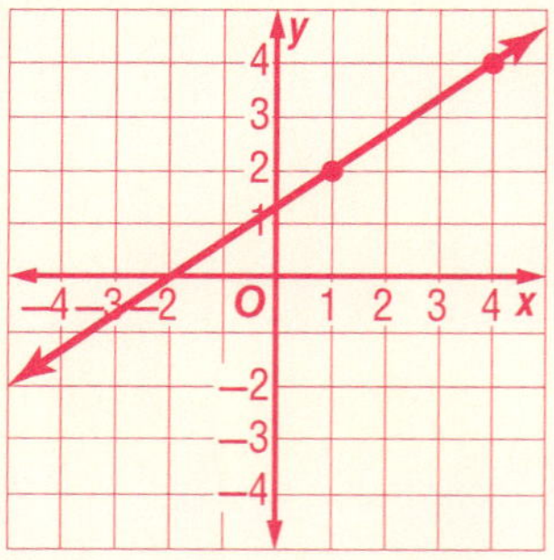

6. $-\frac{6}{5}$

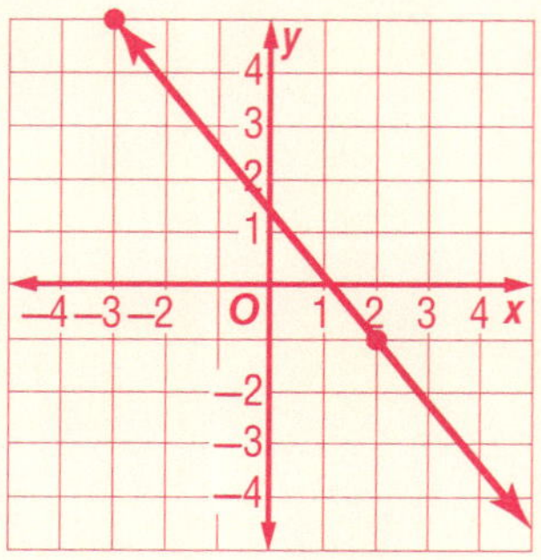

Real-World EXAMPLE

5 RUNNING **Alexa is training for a race. She ran 2 miles on the second day of training. She ran 3 miles on the fourth day of training. The points (2, 2) and (4, 3) represent this situation where each x-coordinate represents the number of days of training and each y-coordinate represents the number of miles ran. Graph the line that passes through these points. Then use your line to find the number of miles Alexa will run on the sixth day of training if this pattern continues.**

Graph each point. Using a straightedge, connect the two points with a solid line as shown.

Find the point on the line that has an x-coordinate of 6. The point is (6, 4).

So, on the sixth day of training, Alexa will run 4 miles.

Alexa's Race Training

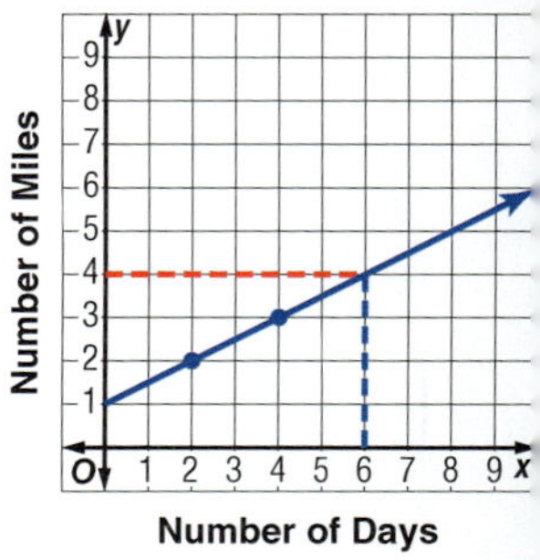

CHECK Your Understanding

1–6. See margin.

Examples 1, 2 (pp. IN24–IN25)

Draw a line that has the given slope and passes through the indicated point.

1. slope: $\frac{3}{4}$, point (0, 0)
2. slope: $\frac{1}{2}$, point (−1, 2)
3. slope: −2, point (3, −4

Example 3 (p. IN25)

Draw a line that has passes through each pair of points. Then find the slope of the line as a ratio in simplest form.

4. (3, 4) and (−1, −1)
5. (1, 2) and (4, 4)
6. (−3, 5) and (2, −1)

Example 4 (p. IN25)

ALGEBRA **For each equation, find a point on the line. Then find the slope of the line.** 7–9. Sample points are given.

7. $y = x + 1$ 1; (0, 1)
8. $y = \frac{1}{4}x + 3$ $\frac{1}{4}$; (0, 3)
9. $y = -\frac{2}{3}x - 2$ $-\frac{2}{3}$; (0, −2)

10–12. Sample points are given.

ALGEBRA **For each equation, find two points on the line.**

10. $y = x - 5$ (0, −5); (1, −4)
11. $y = \frac{3}{4}x + 1$ (0, 1); (4, 4)
12. $y = -\frac{4}{5}x$ (0, 0), (5, −4)

Example 5 (p. IN26)

13. **JOBS** During the summer, Harrison mows lawns in the neighborhood. In the third week of the summer, he mowed 2 lawns. In the sixth week of the summer, he mowed 4 lawns. The points (3, 2) and (6, 4) represent this situation where each x-coordinate represents the number of weeks and each y-coordinate represents the number of lawns mowed. Graph the line that passes through these points. Then use your line to find the number of lawns Harrison will mow during the ninth week of the summer if this pattern continues. See margin.

13. 6 lawns

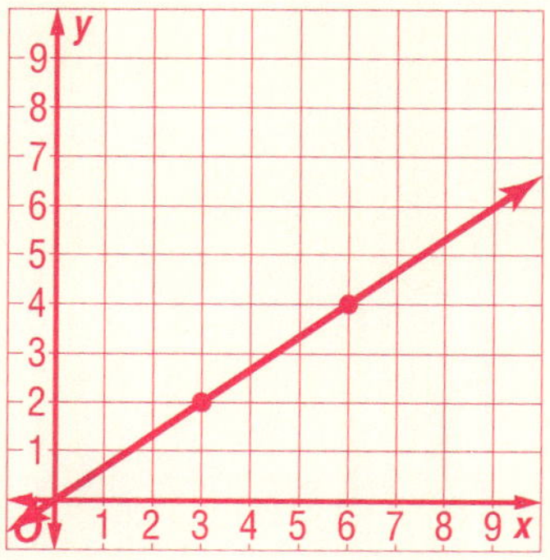

Practice and Problem Solving

14–29. See margin.

HOMEWORK HELP	
For Exercises	See Examples
14–21	1, 2
22–29	3
32–43	4
30, 31	5

Draw a line that has the given slope and passes through the indicated point.

14. slope: 3, point (1, 4)
15. slope: $-\frac{3}{2}$, point (−3, 2)
16. slope: $\frac{1}{4}$, point (0, −1)
17. slope: −2, point (0, 0)
18. slope: 1, point (2, −3)
19. slope: $-\frac{3}{2}$, point (0, 8)
20. slope: $\frac{2}{5}$, point (−2, −9)
21. slope: −1, point (−3, 4)

Draw a line that passes through each pair of points. Then find the slope of the line as a ratio in simplest form.

22. (0, 1) and (−3, −1)
23. (2, −5) and (0, 0)
24. (2, 2) and (4, 0)
25. (−1, 4) and (3, −2)
26. (−1, 1) and (3, 2)
27. (0, 0) and (2, 1)
28. (−2, −1) and (2, 0)
29. (0, 3) and (3, −4)

30. **SCHOOL** Elisa is selling bracelets to raise funds for the German Club. On the second day, she sold 5 bracelets. On the fourth day, she sold ten bracelets. The points (2, 5) and (4, 10) represent this situation where each x-coordinate represents the number of days and each y-coordinate represents the number of bracelets sold. Graph the line that passes through these points. Then use your line to find the number of bracelets Elisa will sell on the 8th day if this pattern continues. **See margin.**

31. **TEXT MESSAGES** Prim sent 5 text messages for $1. Later, he sent 10 text messages for $2. The points (5, 1) and (10, 2) represent this situation where each x-coordinate represents the number of text messages and each y-coordinate represents the cost in dollars. Graph the line that passes through these points. Then use your line to find the cost in dollars if Prim sends 20 text messages. **See margin.**

ALGEBRA For each equation, find a point on the line and the slope of the line. **32–37. Sample points are given.**

32. $y = 2x + 1$ **2; (0, 1)**
33. $y = \frac{3}{4}x$ **$\frac{3}{4}$; (0, 0)**
34. $y = -\frac{1}{2}x + 2$ **$-\frac{1}{2}$; (2, 1)**
35. $y = x$ **1; (0, 0)**
36. $y = 3x$ **3; (0, 0)**
37. $y = \frac{1}{3}x + 1$ **$\frac{1}{3}$; (0, 1)**

38–43. Sample points are given.

42. (0, −1); (1, 2)

ALGEBRA For each equation, find two points on the line.

38. $y = 4x$ **(0, 0); (1, 4)**
39. $y = \frac{1}{2}x + 5$ **(0, 5); (2, 6)**
40. $y = -x + 4$ **(0, 4); (1, 3)**
41. $y = \frac{2}{3}x$ **(0, 0); (3, 2)**
42. $y = 3x - 1$
43. $y = 2x$ **(0, 0); (1, 2)**

3 Practice

Use Exercises 1–13 to check for understanding.

Exercises 14–50 are structured so that students practice the same concepts they learned in the lesson.

Have students discuss and complete the Higher Order Thinking problems.

WRITING IN MATH Have students complete Exercise 48 in their Math Journals. You may choose to use this exercise as a formative assessment.

Additional Answers

20–31. See the Focus on Indiana Answer Appendix.

14.

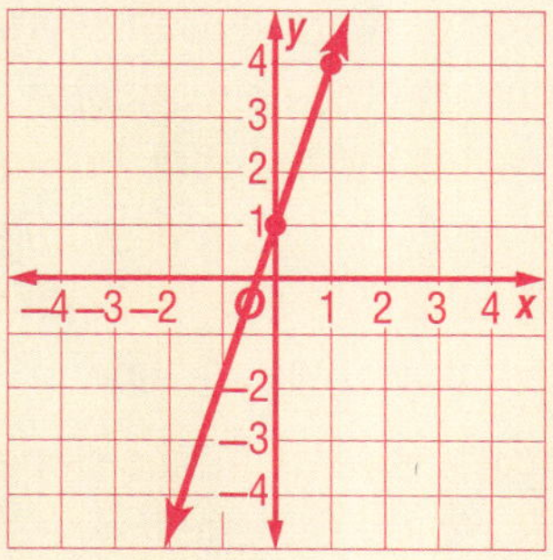

15.

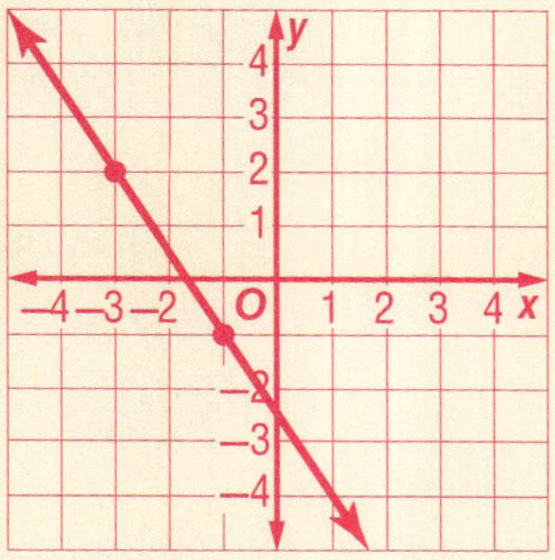

16.

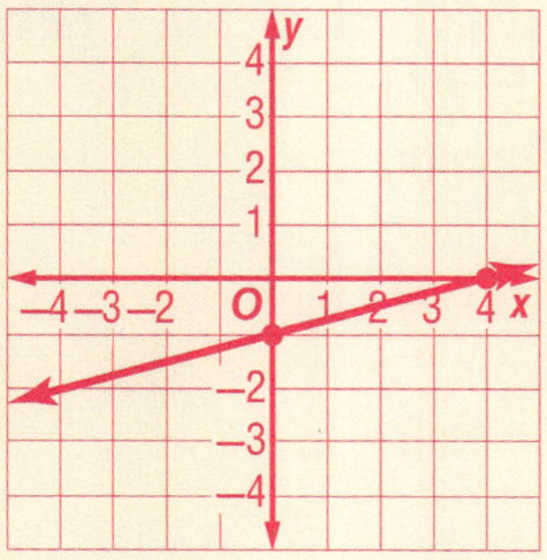

17.

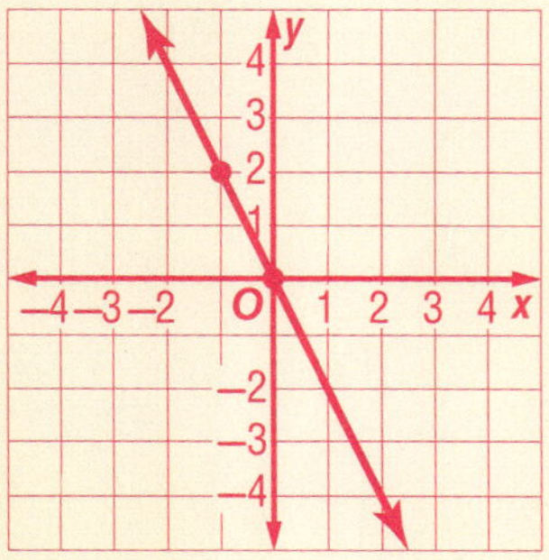

18.

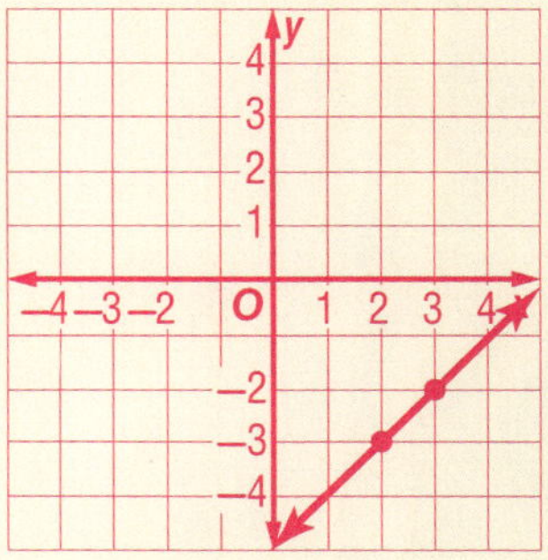

19.

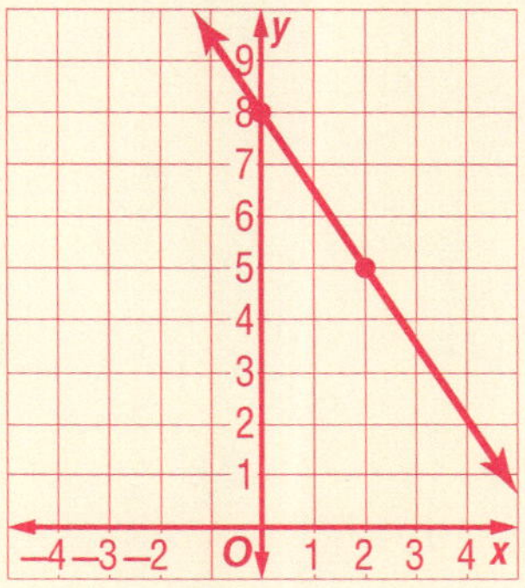

Lesson IN 6 Graphs of Linear Equations **IN27**

4 Assess

Ticket Out the Door Is it possible for a line to contain the coordinates (1, 3) and (2, 5) and have a slope of −2? Explain your thinking and support your answer with a graph. Sample answer: no; From the point (1, 3), you would move 2 units up and 1 unit to the right to get to the next point on the line. So, the slope for the line mentioned is 2, not −2. See students' graphs.

Additional Answers

46. Sample answer: Graph the point (−3, 1). Use the slope to find a second point on the line. The slope is 1.5. As a fraction, this is $\frac{3}{2}$. The numerator represents the vertical change and the denominator represents the horizontal change. So, from (−3, 1), count 3 units up and 2 units to the right. Connect the points with a solid line.

47. Sample answer: Find the slope of the line using the graph. The slope is $-\frac{5}{8}$. Half of the vertical distance between the points is $\frac{1}{2}(5)$, or $2\frac{1}{2}$. Half of the horizontal distance between the points is $\frac{1}{2}(8)$, or 4. Count $2\frac{1}{2}$ units down from (−4, 3) and 4 units to the right. The result is (0, 0.5).

48. Sample answer: Graph the coordinates given first. Then use the slope to determine the second point on the line. Change the slope to a fraction or improper fraction to determine the vertical and horizontal change. Connect the points with a solid line.

H.O.T. Problems

46–48. See margin.

44. **OPEN ENDED** A line passes through the points (−3, 1) and (2, 4). Find three other points on this line. **Sample answer: (7, 7), (12, 10), (17, 13)**

45. **ALGEBRA** A line passes through the points (a, b) and $(a + 3, b + 2)$. What is the slope of this line? $\frac{2}{3}$

46. **REASONING** A line has a slope of 1.5 and passes through the point (−3, 1). Describe the steps you would take to graph this line beginning at the point (−3, 1).

47. **CHALLENGE** The *midpoint* of a line segment is the point on the line that marks the halfway point between the segment's two endpoints. The line segment at the right has endpoints (4, −2) and (−4, 3). Use the slope of this line segment to find the midpoint of this line segment. Explain your method.

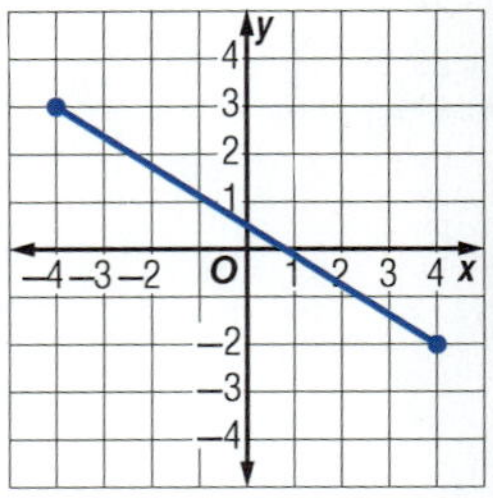

48. **WRITING IN MATH** Write a few sentences explaining how to draw the graph of a line given its slope and a point on the line.

ISTEP+ PRACTICE 7.2.6

49. A line has a slope of 3 and passes through the point (3, 5). Which of the following is the correct graph of the line? **B**

A

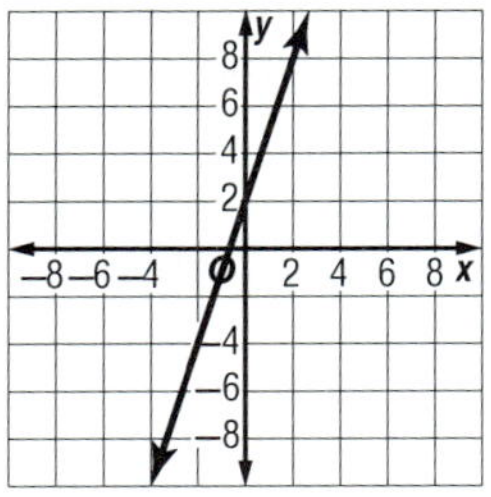

C

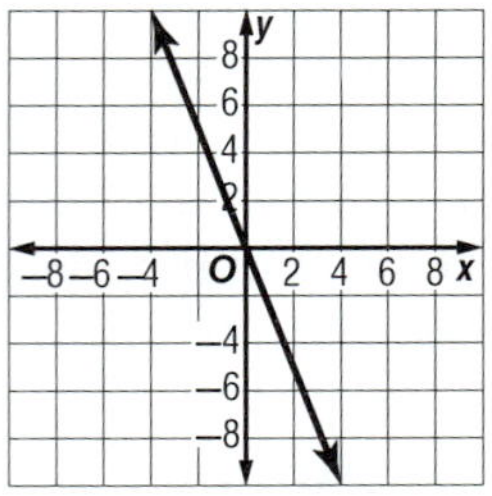

B

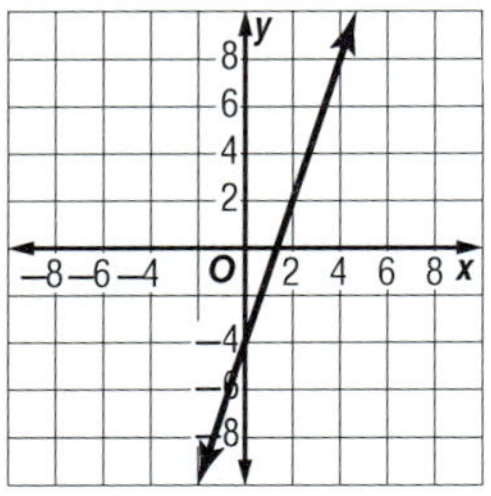

D

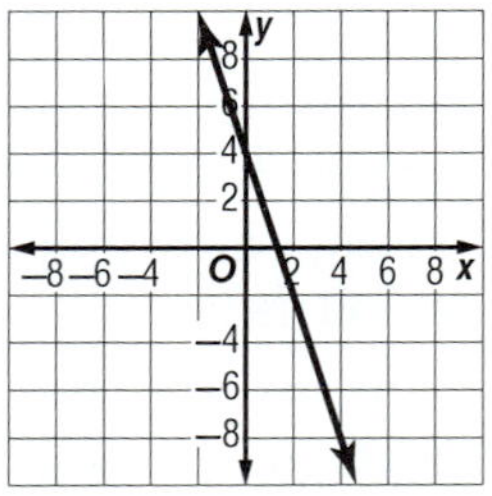

50. What is the correct FIRST step in graphing the line that passes through the point (−1, 4) and that has a slope of $\frac{2}{3}$? **H**

F Graph the point (0, 0).

G Graph a point that is 2 units up and 3 units to the right of the origin.

H Graph the point (−1, 4).

J Graph a point that is 3 units up and 2 units to the right of the point (−1, 4).

IN28 Focus on Indiana

7 Direct Variation

MAIN IDEA

Solve problems that involve direct variation.

IN Academic Standards

7.2.7 Identify situations that involve proportional relationships, draw graphs representing these situations and recognize that these situations are described by a linear function in the form $y = mx$ where the unit rate m is the slope of the line.

New Vocabulary

direct variation
constant of variation

IN Math Online

glencoe.com

The y-value is twice the x-value.

GET READY for the Lesson

CATS The graph at the right shows the average number of heartbeats for an adult housecat.

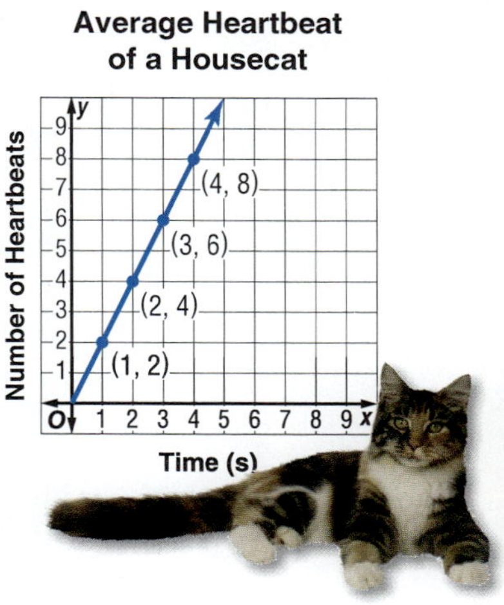

1. Find the slope of the line. $\frac{2}{1}$ or 2
2. Describe the relationship between the x-value and the y-value of each point on the line.
3. Write an equation that gives the value of y for each value of x on the line. $y = 2x$
4. How does the equation you wrote in Exercise 2 show the slope of the line? The slope, 2, is the coefficient of x.
5. What is the value of y when the x-value is zero? 0

The graph above demonstrates a proportional relationship. Recall that two quantities are *proportional* if they have a constant rate or ratio. In the graph above, the constant rate is the slope of the line, 2.

When two quantities are proportional, their relationship is a **direct variation**. The graph of a direct variation is a straight line that passes through the origin.

Direct Variation — Key Concept

Words
A direct variation is a relationship in which the ratio of y to x is a constant, k. We say y varies directly with x.

Symbols
$y = kx$, where $k \neq 0$

Example
$y = \frac{2}{3}x$

Graph

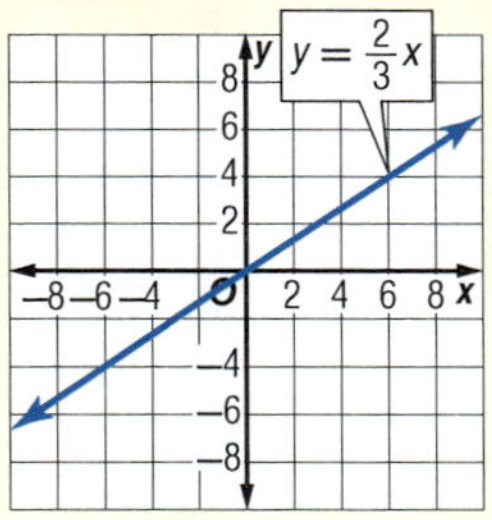

In the equation $y = kx$, k is called the **constant of variation**. Note that k is the slope of the line. Often, the slope of a line is noted by the variable m. So, $y = mx$ and $y = kx$ each represent a direct variation relationship.

7 Lesson Notes

Lesson Planner

Use this lesson after Lesson 6-3 and Indiana Lessons 5 and 6 to address standard 7.2.7.

Objective

Solve problems that involve direct variation.

Vocabulary

direct variation, **constant of variation**

Materials

grid paper

IN Academic Standards

7.2.7 Identify situations that involve proportional relationships, draw graphs representing these situations, and recognize that these situations are described by a linear function in the form $y = mx$ where the unit rate m is the slope of the line.

1 Focus

Display a coordinate plane. Review with students how to find the slope of a line. Remind students that the vertical distance serves as the numerator of the slope whereas the horizontal distance serves as the denominator of the slope. A negative slope signifies that the line slants to the left rather than to the right.

Next, to prepare students for working with the constant of variation, write several coordinate points on the plane and have students determine which are x-values and which are y-values.

2 Teach

Scaffolding Questions

Ask:

- What formula is used to determine the slope of a line? slope $= \frac{\text{change in } y}{\text{change in } x}$
- A line contains the points (10, 6) and (9, 3). What is the slope of the line? $\frac{3}{1}$, or 3
- A line contains the points (14, 10) and (7, 8). What is the slope of the line? $\frac{2}{7}$
- A line contains the points (4, 0) and (−1, −1). What is the slope of the line? $\frac{1}{5}$

Not all relationships with a constant rate of change are proportional. Likewise, not all linear functions are direct variations.

EXAMPLES Identify Direct Variation

Find the slope of each linear function. Then determine whether each linear function is a direct variation. If so, state the constant of variation and write the direct variation equation. If not, explain why not.

1

Miles, *x*	25	50	75	100
Gallons, *y*	1	2	3	4

Find the slope.

$$\text{slope} = \frac{\text{change in } y}{\text{change in } x} = \frac{2-1}{50-25} = \frac{1}{25}$$

Use two points, such as (25, 1) and (50, 2).

The slope is $\frac{1}{25}$.

Determine if the linear function is a direct variation. Each y-value is obtained by multiplying each x-value by $\frac{1}{25}$. The linear function is a direct variation since the ratio of each y-value to each x-value is constant, $\frac{1}{25}$.

The constant of variation is $\frac{1}{25}$. So, the direct variation equation is $y = \frac{1}{25}x$. The slope is also $\frac{1}{25}$.

Check your answer by graphing the line through the points in the table.

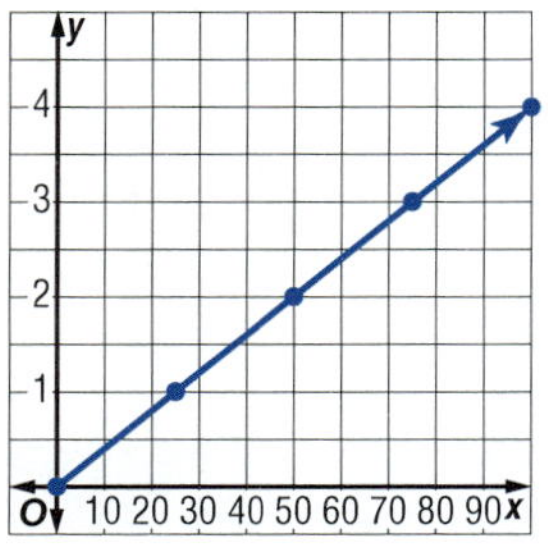

The graph is a straight line with a slope of $\frac{1}{25}$.

The graph passes through the origin.

So, the graph is a direct variation with equation $y = \frac{1}{25}x$. The answer is correct.

2

Hours, *x*	2	4	6	8
Earnings, *y*	36	52	68	84

Find the slope.

$$\text{slope} = \frac{\text{change in } y}{\text{change in } x} = \frac{52-36}{4-2} = \frac{16}{2} = 8$$

Use two points, such as (2, 36) and (4, 52).

The slope is 8.

Determine if the linear function is a direct variation. Check to see if the two quantities are proportional.

$$\frac{\text{earnings, } y}{\text{hours, } x} \longrightarrow \frac{36}{2}, \text{ or } 18 \quad \frac{52}{4}, \text{ or } 13 \quad \frac{68}{6}, \text{ or } 11\frac{1}{3} \quad \frac{84}{8}, \text{ or } 10\frac{1}{2}$$

The ratios are not the same, so the function is not a direct variation.

Note that the rate of change, or slope, of the linear function in Example 2 is constant. But since the ratio of each y-value to each x-value is not constant, the relationship is not a direct variation. In a direct variation, as in Example 1, the slope of the line is the same as the constant of variation.

You can draw the graph of a direct variation. Recall from Indiana Additional Lesson 6 that you can graph a line given its slope and a point on the line. The graph of a direct variation passes through the origin, (0, 0). You can use (0, 0) as a point on the line. Then use the slope to find a second point on the line.

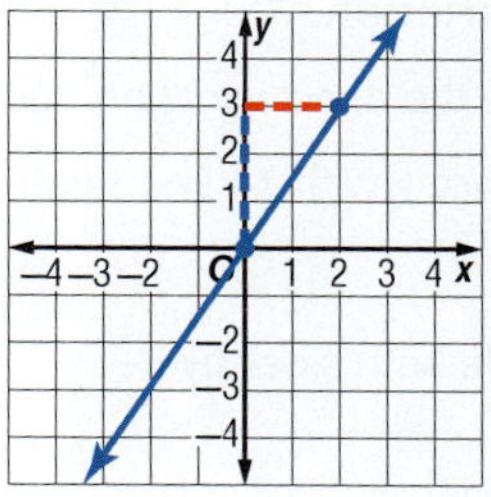

Consider the direct variation equation $y = \frac{3}{2}x$.

The graph passes through (0, 0). Graph the point (0, 0).

The slope is $\frac{3}{2}$.

From (0, 0), count up 3 units and 2 units to the right. Graph the point (2, 3).

Connect the points with a solid line.

EXAMPLE Graph a Direct Variation

3 Graph the direct variation function $y = -\frac{3}{5}x$.

The slope of the line is $-\frac{3}{5}$. Because the function is a direct variation, it passes through the origin, (0, 0). Use the point (0, 0) as a point on the line.

STEP 1 Graph the point (0, 0).

STEP 2 Use the slope to find a second point on the line.

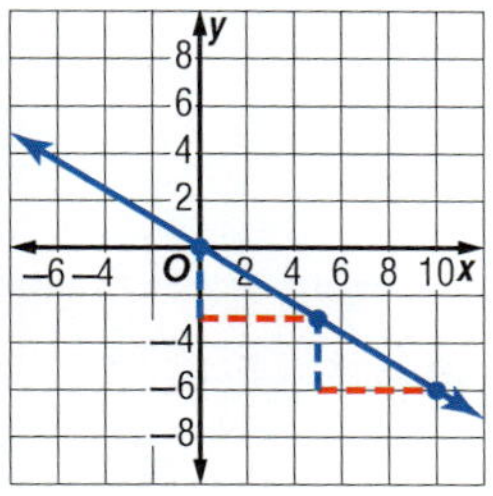

The slope is $-\frac{3}{5}$. The numerator −3 represents the vertical change.

The denominator 5 represents the horizontal change.

So, from (0, 0), count 3 units down and 5 units to the right. Graph the point (−3, −5).

STEP 3 From (−3, −5), count 3 units down and 5 units to the right. Graph the point (10, −6).

STEP 4 Continue this process to find additional points on the line. Connect the points with a solid line.

Lesson IN 7 Direct Variation **IN31**

3 Practice

Use Exercises 1–5 to check for understanding.

Exercises 6–19 are structured so that students practice the same concepts they learned in the lesson.

Have students discuss and complete the Higher Order Thinking problems.

WRITING IN MATH Have students complete Exercise 18 in their Math Journals. You may choose to use this exercise as an optional formative assessment.

Additional Answers

1. $\frac{12.5}{5}$; The linear function is a direct variation; $y = 2.5x$.

2. 2; The linear function is not a direct variation.

3. -2

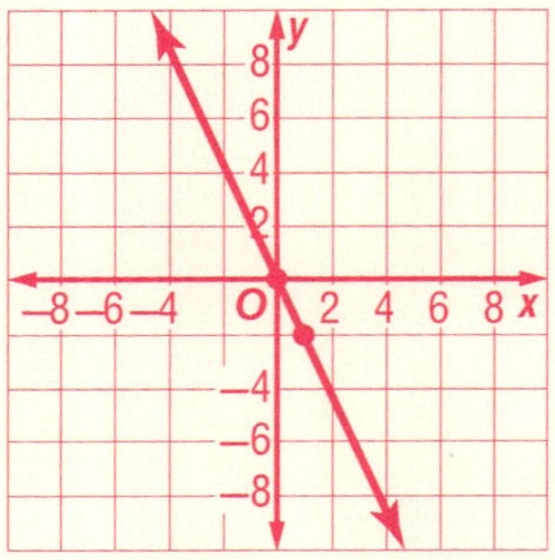

4. $\frac{2}{3}$

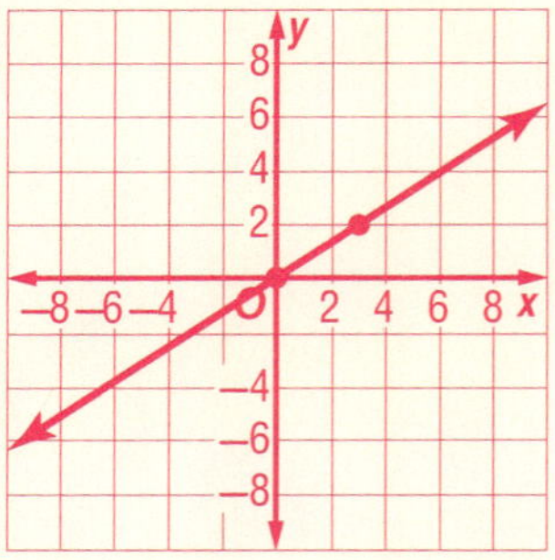

Real-World EXAMPLE — Write the Direct Variation

4 **BAKING** **The recipe at the right requires $3\frac{1}{2}$ cups of flour and makes 14 servings of turtle cake. The relationship of number of servings to number of cups of flour is directly proportional. Find the constant of variation and write the direct variation equation that gives the number of servings y for x cups of flour.**

Find the constant of variation.

$y = kx$	Write the direct variation equation.
$14 = k\left(3\frac{1}{2}\right)$	Replace y with 14 and x with $3\frac{1}{2}$.
$\frac{14}{3\frac{1}{2}} = \frac{k\left(3\frac{1}{2}\right)}{3\frac{1}{2}}$	Divide both sides by $3\frac{1}{2}$.
$4 = k$	Simplify.

The constant of variation is 4.

Write the direct variation equation.

$y = kx$	Write the direct variation equation.
$y = 4x$	Replace k with 4.

The direct variation equation is $y = 4x$.

Check $y = kx$	Write the direct variation equation.
$y = 4\left(3\frac{1}{2}\right)$	Replace k with 4 and x with $3\frac{1}{2}$.
$y = 14$	Multiply.

Since 14 is the correct number of servings that can be made from $3\frac{1}{2}$ cups of flour, the equation $y = 4x$ is correct. ✓

CHECK Your Understanding

Examples 1, 2 (p. IN30)

Find the slope of each linear function. Then determine whether each linear function is a direct variation. If so, state the constant of variation and write the direct variation equation. **1, 2. See margin.**

1.

Days, x	5	10	15	20
Height, y	12.5	25	37.5	50

2.

Time, x	4	6	8	10
Distance, y	12	16	20	24

Example 3 (p. IN31)

Graph each direct variation function. State the constant of variation.

3. $y = -2x$ **See margin.**

4. $y = \frac{2}{3}x$ **See margin.**

Example 4 (p. IN32)

5. **GROCERIES** A grocery store sells 6 oranges for $2. The relationship of cost to number of oranges is directly proportional. Find the constant of variation and write the direct variation equation that gives the cost y of x number of oranges. **3; $y = 3x$**

IN32 Focus on Indiana

Practice and Problem Solving

OMEWORK HELP	
For xercises	See Examples
6–9	1, 2
10–13	3
14, 15	4

Find the slope of each linear function. Then determine whether each linear function is a direct variation. If so, state the constant of variation and write the direct variation equation. If not, explain why not. **6–9. See margin.**

6.

Hours, x	2	3	4	5
Miles, y	116	174	232	290

7.

Price ($), x	10	15	20	25
Tax ($), y	0.70	1.05	1.40	1.75

8.

Minutes, x	200	400	600	800
Cost ($), y	65	115	165	215

9.

Pictures, x	5	6	7	8
Profile, y	20	24	28	32

)–13. See margin.

Graph each direct variation function. State the constant of variation.

10. $y = -\frac{3}{4}x$ 11. $y = \frac{2}{3}x$ 12. $y = \frac{1}{3}x$ 13. $y = -x$

14. **ELECTRONICS** The width of a wide-screen television screen is directly proportional to its height. The width of a screen is 57.6 centimeters and its height is 32 centimeters. Find the constant of variation and write the direct variation equation that gives the width y given the height x. **1.8; $y = 1.8x$**

15. **MEASUREMENT** An object that weighs 70 pounds on Mars weighs 210 pounds on Earth. The relationship of weight on Mars to weight on Earth is directly proportional. Find the constant of variation and write the direct variation equation that gives the weight on Mars y given the weight on Earth x. **$\frac{1}{3}$; $y = \frac{1}{3}x$**

.O.T. Problems

16. **OPEN ENDED** Write a linear equation that represents a direct variation. Identify the constant of variation and state three points that satisfy your equation. **See students' work.**

17. **REASONING** The formula $d = rt$ gives the distance d traveled by an object with a rate r for a time t. Suppose a car is traveling at a rate of 50 miles per hour. Explain how the equation $d = 50t$ represents a direct variation relationship. **See margin.**

18. **WRITING IN MATH** Determine whether the statement below is *always*, *sometimes*, or *never* true. Explain your reasoning. **See margin.**

A relationship that has a constant rate of change is a proportional relationship.

ISTEP+ PRACTICE 7.2.7

19. Which equation represents the relationship shown at the right? **B**

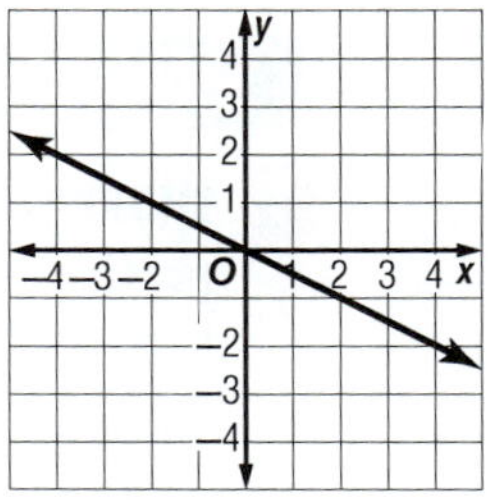

A $y = -2x$ C $y = -\frac{1}{2}x + 1$

B $y = -\frac{1}{2}x$ D $y = 2x$

4 Assess

Ticket Out the Door Given the point (0, 0), have students produce at least two other points and create a linear function that can be classified as a direct variation. Have students graph the linear function and then determine the slope and the constant of variation. See students' work.

Additional Answers

6. 58; The linear function is a direct variation; $y = 58x$.

7. 0.07; The linear function is a direct variation; $y = 0.07x$.

8. 0.25; The linear function is not a direct variation.

9. 4; The linear function is a direct variation; $y = 4x$.

10. $-\frac{3}{4}$

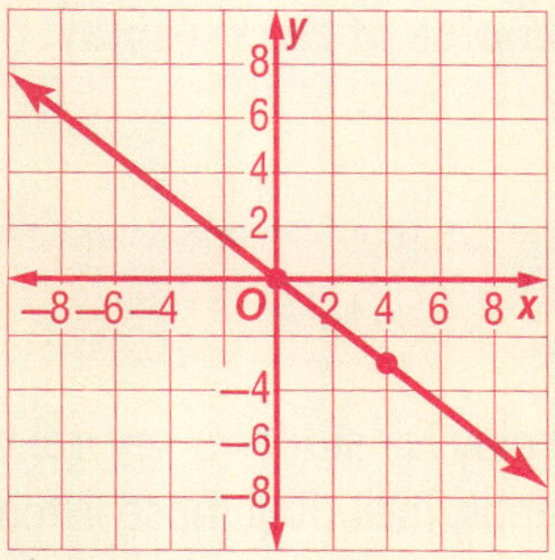

11. $\frac{2}{3}$

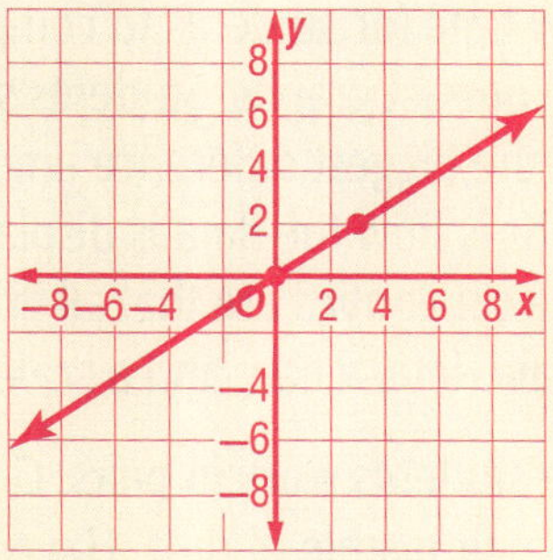

12. $\frac{1}{3}$

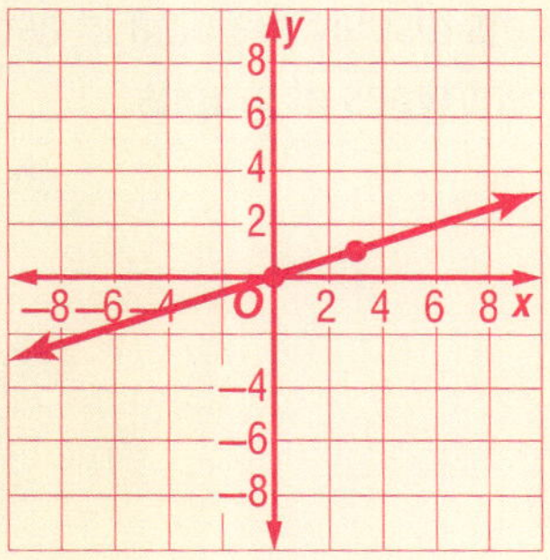

13. −1

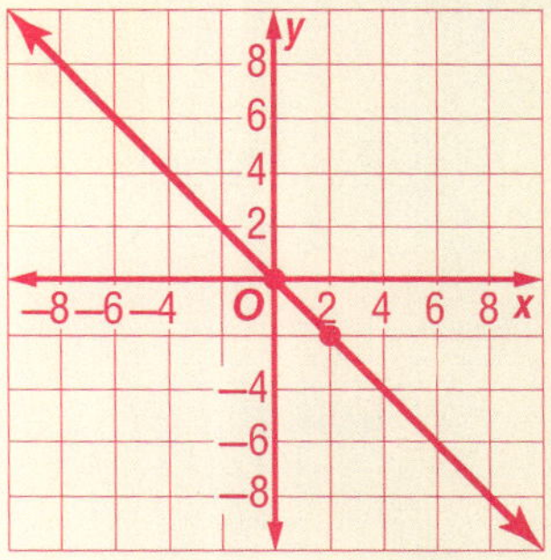

17. Sample answer: Since the rate is a constant rate of 50 miles per hour that does not change, the relationship will be a direct variation and the ratio of y to x will be proportional.

18. Sometimes; The relationship $y = 2x + 5$ has a constant rate of change, 2. However, the relationship between x and y is not proportional.

Lesson Notes

Lesson Planner

Use this lesson after Lesson 8-9 to address standard 7.4.1.

Objective

Choose the most appropriate display for a situation and justify the choice.

Materials

real-world examples of statistical displays

IN Academic Standards

7.4.1 Create, analyze and interpret data sets in multiple ways using bar graphs, frequency tables, line plots, histograms and circle graphs. Justify the choice of data display.

1 Focus

- Display for students several types of graphs, including those listed in the Statistical Displays table on page IN34. Allow time for students to compare and contrast graphs. Students should note the biggest difference among the graphs is how the data is displayed. Some similarities are that all graphs contain data, a title, and a scale.
- Have students work in pairs. Give each pair a table of data. Have students display the data in two different types of graphs.

Choose an Appropriate Display

MAIN IDEA

Choose the most appropriate display for a situation and justify the choice.

IN Academic Standards

7.4.1 Create, analyze and interpret data sets in multiple ways using bar graphs, frequency tables, line plots, histograms and circle graphs. Justify the choice of data display.

IN Math Online

glencoe.com

GET READY for the Lesson

TYPING The displays show the typing speed of eight students in Mr. Terrell's typing class.

Typing Speed of Students (words per minute)

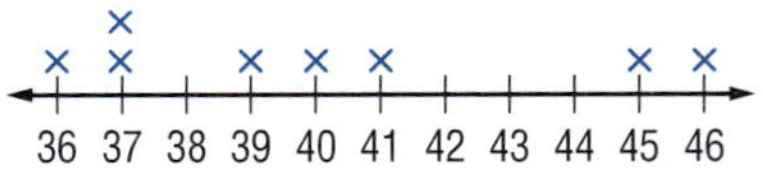

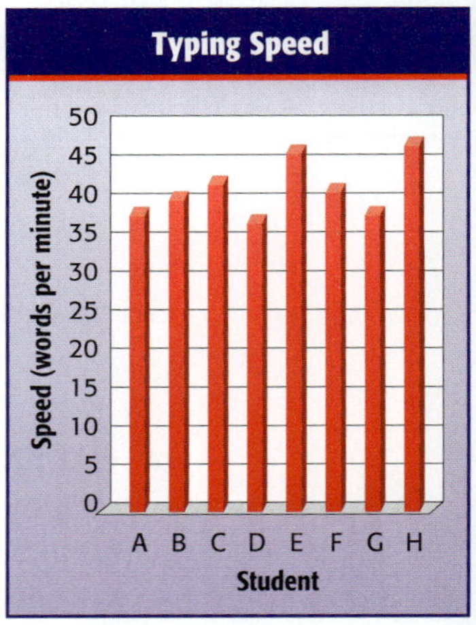

1. Which display allows you to find student A's typing speed? Justify your choice.
2. In which display is it easier to find the number of students that type 45 words per minute? Justify your choice.

1. bar graph; Sample answer: The line plot just lists the data and not which speed correlates with which student.
2. line plot; Sample answer: In the bar graph, you have to search for the value of 45 instead of going to 45 on the number line and counting the Xs.

Data can often be displayed in several different ways. The display you choose depends on your data and what you want to show.

Statistical Displays — Concept Summary

Type of Display	Best Used to
Bar Graph	show the number of items in specific categories
Circle Graph	compare parts of the data to the whole
Histogram	show frequency of data divided into equal intervals
Line Graph	show change over a period of time
Line Plot	show how many times each number occurs in the data

EXAMPLE Choose an Appropriate Display

1. **SHOPPING Choose an appropriate display to show the sales of a particular brand of clothing compared to the total sales of all brands sold at the store. Justify your choice.**

Since the display will show the parts of a whole, a circle graph would be an appropriate display to represent this data.

Real-World EXAMPLE Choose an Appropriate Display

2 **TIME** **Which display allows you to easily estimate the number of hours that Chi-Wei typically spends on each activity throughout the day? Justify your choice.**

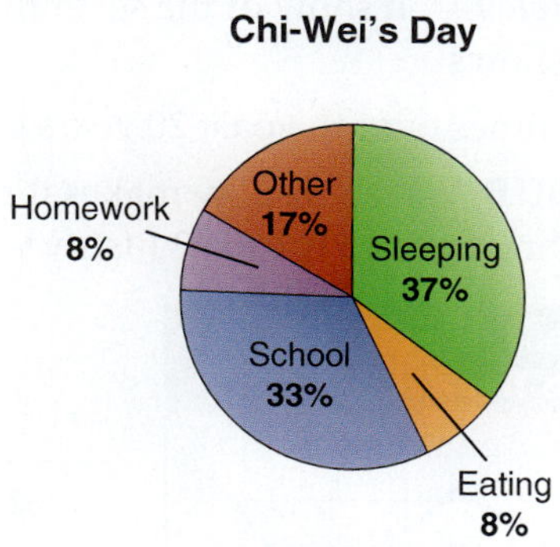

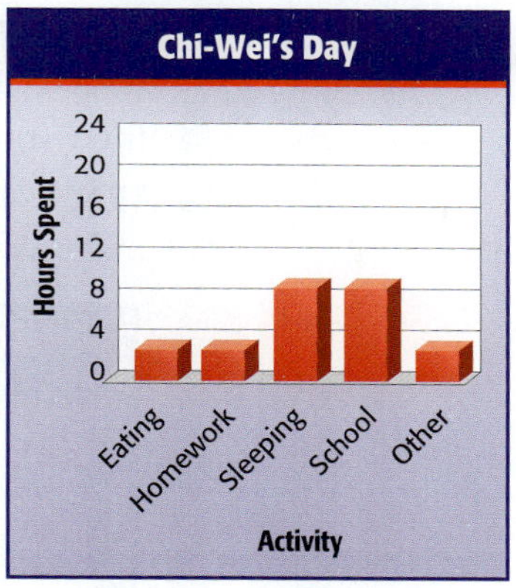

The bar graph allows you to estimate the number of hours that Chi-Wei typically spends on each activity. The circle graph gives you the percentage of the entire day that Chi-Wei spends on each activity.

Because you know that there are 24 hours in a day, you can use the circle graph to determine the number of hours spent, but this is not *easily* determined from the display itself.

EXAMPLE Construct an Appropriate Display

3 **MARKETING** **A market researcher conducted a survey to compare different brands of soap. The table shows the number of first-choice responses for each brand. Construct an appropriate type of display to compare the number of responses for each brand of soap. Justify your choice.**

Favorite Soap Survey			
Brand	**Responses**	**Brand**	**Responses**
A	24	D	13
B	11	E	7
C	31	F	6

These data show the number of responses for each brand. So, a bar graph would be the best display to compare the responses.

STEP 1 Draw and label horizontal and vertical axes. Add a title.

STEP 2 Draw a bar to represent the number of responses for each brand.

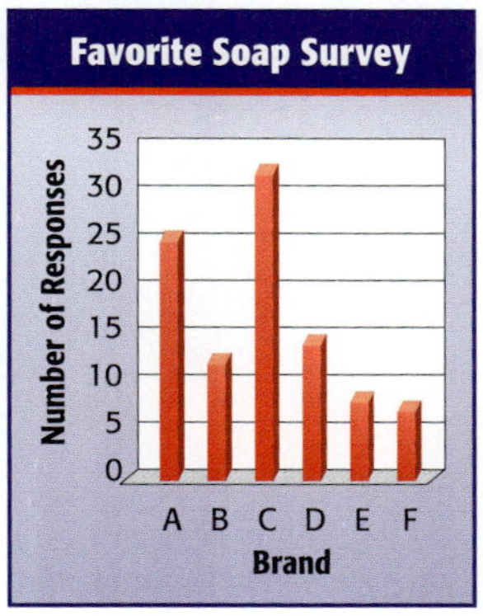

Study Tip

Appropriate Displays A circle graph could also be used to display the data. A circle graph would show the portion of responses of the whole, 92 responses, but it would not show the number of responses for each brand.

2 Teach

Scaffolding Questions

Display a bar graph, a circle graph, a histogram, a line graph, and a line plot.

Ask:

- Which type(s) of display can be used to show a change over a period of time? line graph
- Which type(s) of display can be used to quickly determine the frequency of a value? histogram, line plot
- Which type(s) of display can be used to compare two or more values? bar graph
- Which type(s) of display can be used to quickly compare one value to the whole? circle graph

3 Practice

Use Exercises 1–4 to check for understanding.

Exercises 5–22 are structured so that students practice the same concepts they learned in the lesson.

Have students discuss and complete the Higher Order Thinking problems.

WRITING IN MATH Have students complete Exercise 21 in their Math Journals. You may choose to use this exercise as an optional formative assessment.

Additional Answers

1. bar graph; Sample answer: A bar graph would show the number of students that like each specific TV show.
2. line graph; Sample answer: A line graph would show how the winning times have changed over the time period of the data.
3. line plot; Sample answer: A line plot would show how many times each number occurs in the data. So, one can quickly count the number of times the discus was thrown over 101 feet.
4. Sample answer: histogram; A teacher could easily identify the number of scores by intervals.

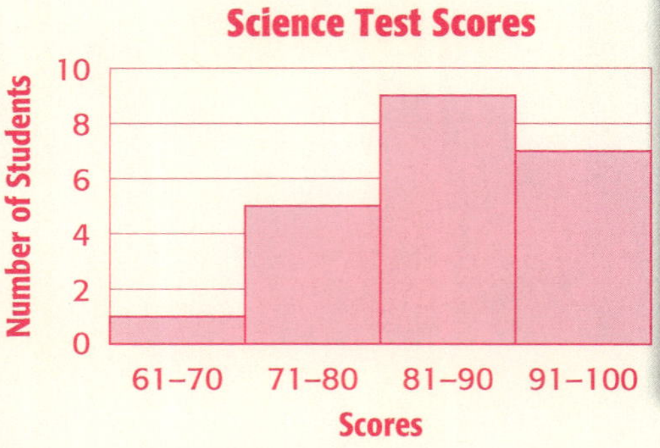

5. Sample answer: A line graph would show the change over a period of time.
6. Sample answer: A bar graph would show the different shoes and the specific price for those shoes.
7. Sample answer: A line graph would show Juliana's height change over the years.
8. Sample answer: A circle graph would allow you to compare parts of the day to the whole day.
9. Sample answer: The line graph shows the change in games won from season to season, revealing some declines in the number of wins.

CHECK Your Understanding

Example 1 (p. IN34)

Choose an appropriate type of display for data gathered about each situation. Justify your choice. 1, 2. See margin.

1. the favorite television show of the seventh-grade students from a list of 5 television shows

Example 2 (p. IN35)

2. the winning times over the past 20 years of the Boston marathon
3. **TRACK AND FIELD** Which display makes it easier to see how many times the discus was thrown over 101 feet? Justify your choice. See margin.

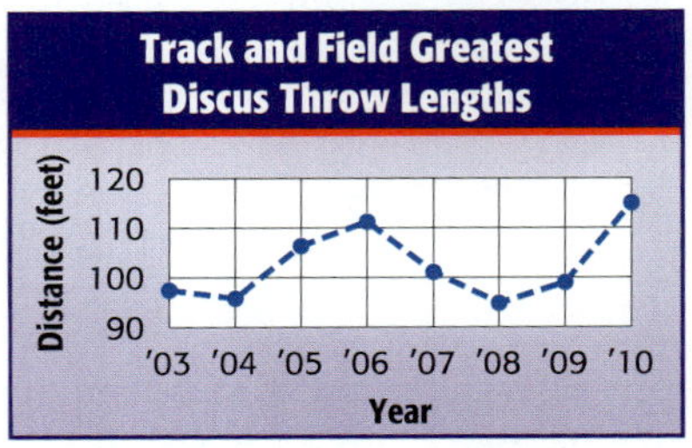

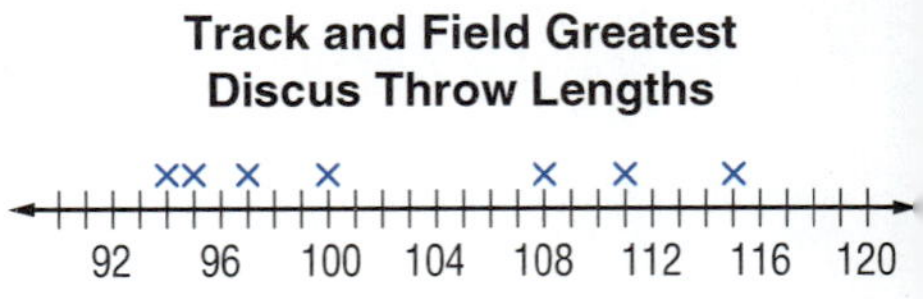

Example 3 (p. IN35)

4. **TESTS** Choose and construct an appropriate display for the data in the table below. Justify your choice. See margin.

Science Test Scores

78	89	94	75	87	91	93	86	97	97	92
65	98	86	72	85	90	83	74	88	81	77

Practice and Problem Solving

HOMEWORK HELP

For Exercises	See Examples
5–8	1
9, 10	2
11, 12	3

Choose an appropriate type of display for data gathered about each situation. Justify your choice. 5–8. See margin.

5. the number of cell phone subscribers for the past 10 years
6. the prices of six different brands of athletic shoes
7. Juliana's height on January 1st of each year for the past 5 years
8. the portion of your day spent doing various activities
9. **SOCCER** Which display allows you to see whether the team's record of wins has steadily improved since 2002? Justify your choice. See margin.

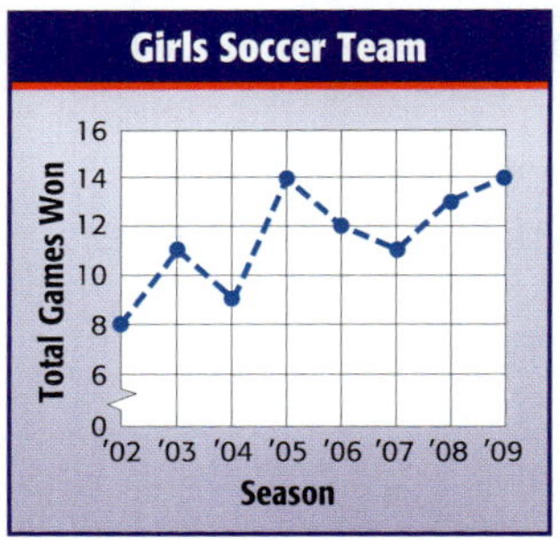

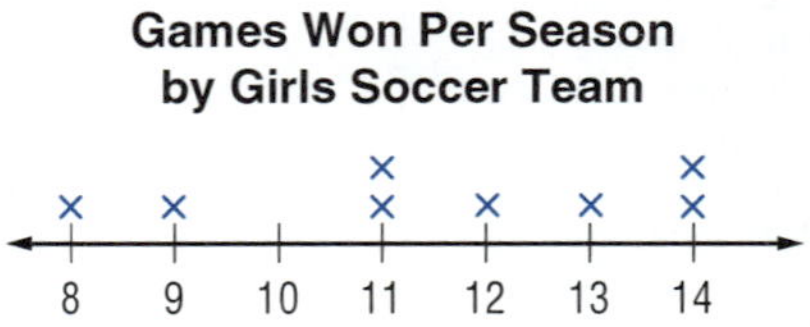

IN36 Focus on Indiana

10. **OLYMPICS** Which display makes it easier to see how many times the winning distance of the javelin throw was 90 meters? Explain. **See margin.**

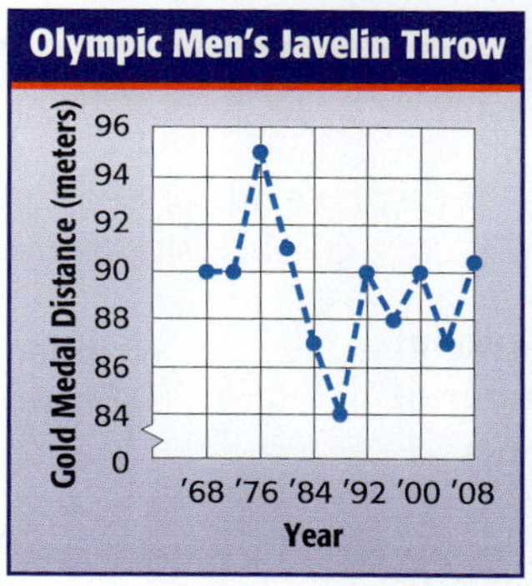

Olympic Men's Javelin Throw
Gold Medal Distance (m) 1968–2008

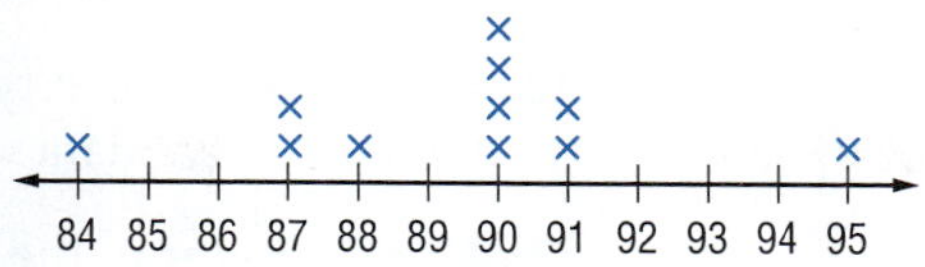

11, 12. See margin.

Choose and construct an appropriate type of display for each situation.

11.

Ocean Areas	
Ocean	**Area (sq. mi)**
Arctic	5,427,000
Atlantic	29,637,900
Indian	26,469,900
Pacific	60,060,700
Southern	7,848,300

12.

Average Height of Females	
Age (yr)	**Height (in.)**
10	56.4
11	59.6
12	61.4
13	62.6
14	63.7
15	63.8

13. **GEOGRAPHY** Display the data in the bar graph using another type of display. Compare the advantages of each display. **See margin.**

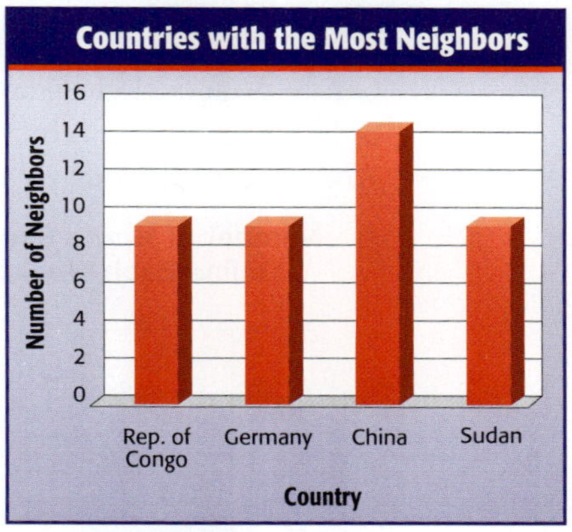

Source: *Top 10 of Everything*

14. **RESEARCH** Use the Internet or another source to find a set of data that is displayed in a bar graph, line graph, stem-and-leaf plot, or line plot. Was the most appropriate type of display used? What other ways might these same data be displayed? **See students' work.**

15. See margin.

15. **MUSIC** Which display is most appropriate to determine the number of students who like only country music? Justify your response.

8th Grade Music Preference

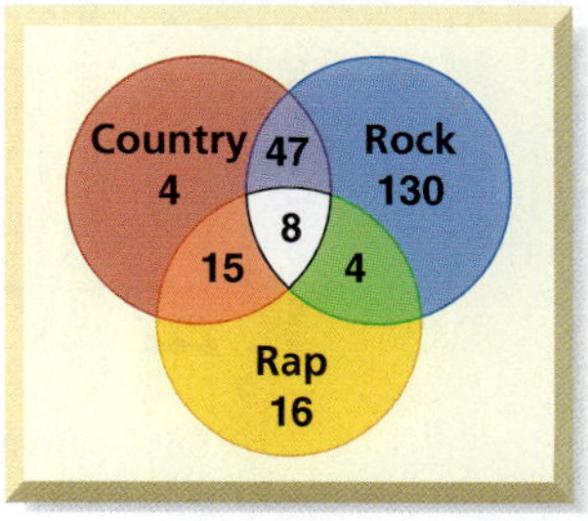

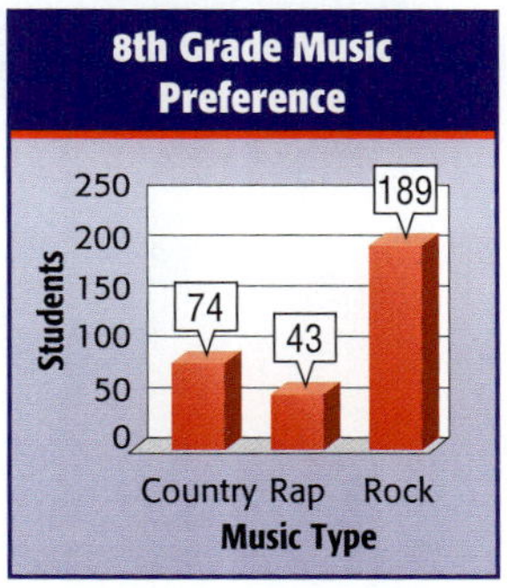

Additional Answers

10. Sample answer: The line plot allows you to count the amount of throws that were 90 meters.

11. Sample answer: A circle graph allows you to compare parts of the ocean to the entire ocean;

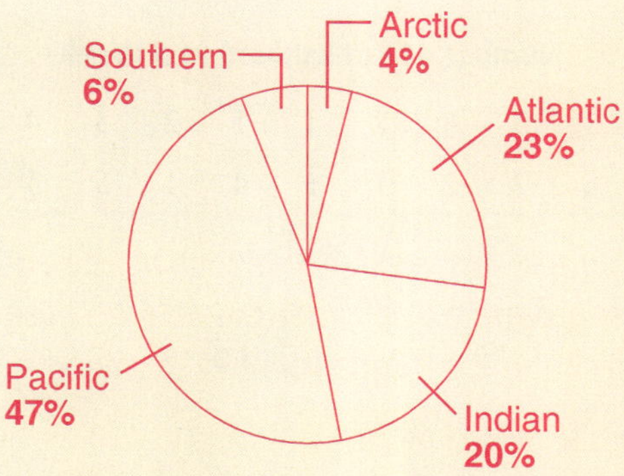

12. Sample answer: A line graph would be most appropriate because it shows the change over time;

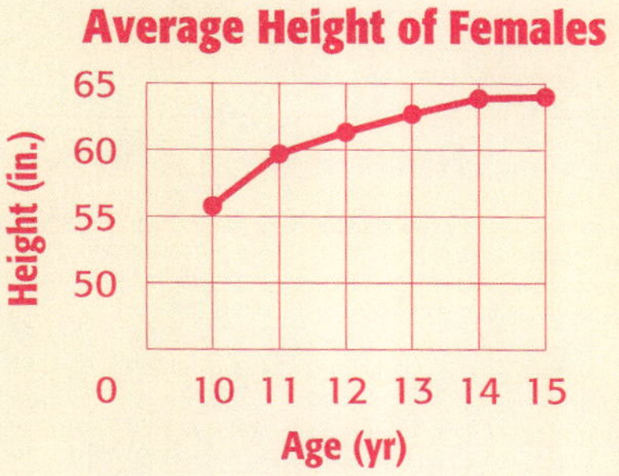

13. Sample answer: From the bar graph, it is easy to see how many neighbors each country has. The line plot does not show country name.

15. Sample answer: The Venn diagram allows you to see which students like only country rather than country and another genre.

4 Assess

Ticket Out the Door Have students analyze the data contained within the table. Then, have students choose an appropriate type of display. Students should create the display and justify their choice.

Number of Books Read in a Week								
3	3	4	2	1	1	2	3	4
5	2	2	1	3	4	1	5	3

Sample answer: A line plot would be an appropriate display for the data because it shows the frequency of each value.

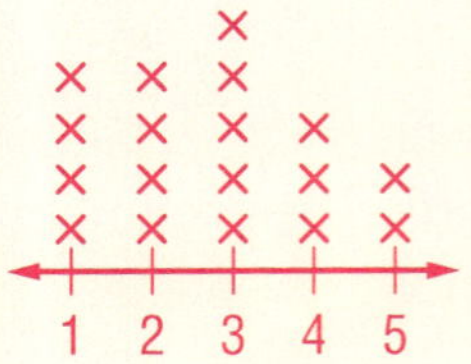

Additional Answers

19. Number of Text Messages Received on Saturday

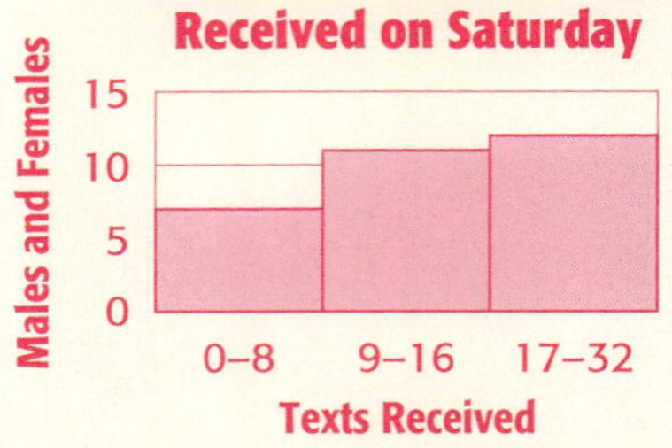

20. Sample answer: The line plot allows you to easily see the number of text messages received on Saturday by males and females. The histogram gives you the amount of males and females that received a range of text messages. The disadvantage of the line plot is that there is no easy way to find the total number of people that received text messages. The histogram does not allow you to determine how many females received 0-8 text messages or even how many males.

H.O.T. Problems

17. line plot or bar graph; Sample answer: The mode is the data value that corresponds with the most number of ×'s in a line plot or the highest bar in a bar graph.

16. **OPEN ENDED** Give an example of data that could be represented using a histogram. **See students' work.**

17. **REASONING** Which type(s) of display allows you to easily find the mode of the data? Explain your reasoning.

18. **REASONING** Which type(s) of displays addressed in this lesson do *not* show the individual data values? **circle graph, histogram**

CHALLENGE Refer to the line plot at the right that shows the number of text messages selected students received on Saturday.

Number of Text Messages Received on Saturday

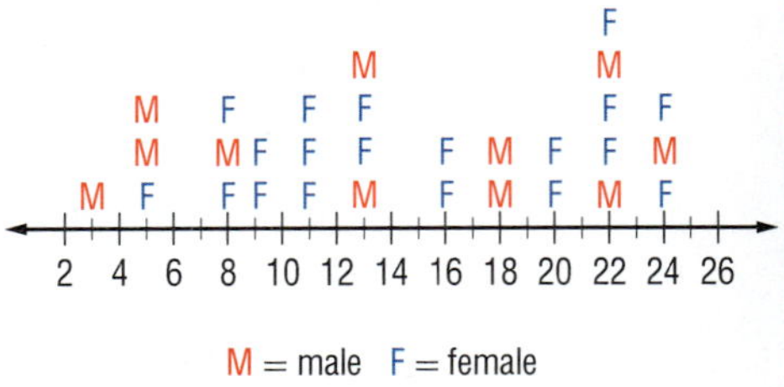

19. Display the data in another type of display. **See margin.**

20. Write a paragraph comparing and contrasting the advantages and disadvantages of each type of display. **See margin.**

21. **WRITING IN MATH** Write a paragraph explaining when it is best to use each of the following types of displays: bar graph, line graph, circle graph, line plot, and histogram. **See margin.**

ISTEP+ PRACTICE 7.4.1

22. Guido polled 24 classmates to find out the average number of hours each spends online each week. Which of the following displays is appropriate for this situation AND shows the individual student responses? **B**

A Number of Hours Spent Online Each Week

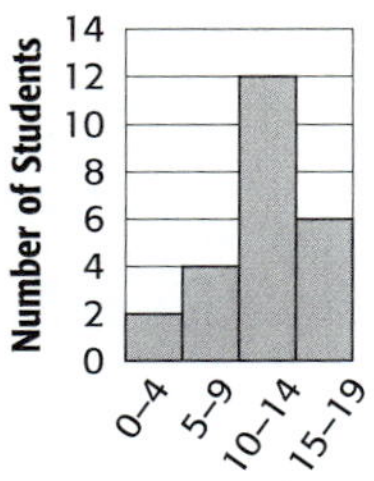

C Number of Hours Spent Online Each Week

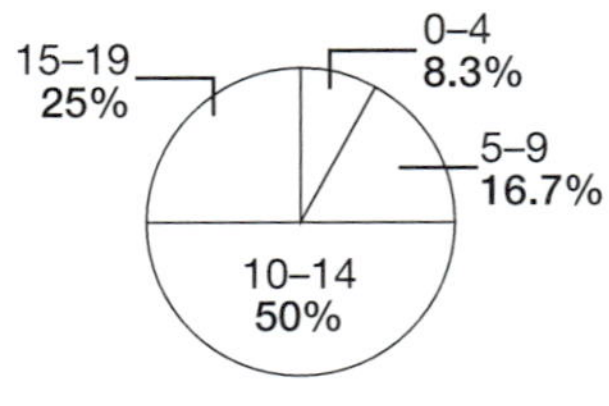

B Number of Hours Spent Online Each Week

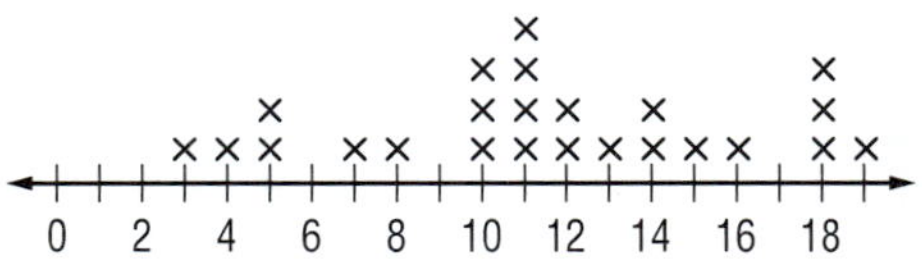

D Number of Hours Spent Online Each Week

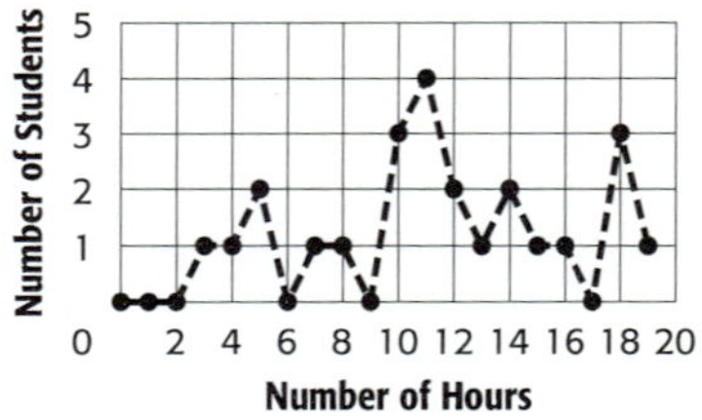

21. Sample answer: It is best to use a bar graph when you need to show the number of items in specific categories, such as the number of students whose favorite color is red. A line graph is best used to show change over a period of time, such as the change in height over a 10-year time period. A circle graph is best used to compare the parts of the data to the whole, such as the amount of time throughout the day spent studying. A line plot is best used to show how many times each number occurs in the data, such as if more than one student gets the same score on a test. A histogram is best used to show the frequency of the data divided into equal intervals, such as the ages of people that shop at a local store.

9 Analyze Questions in Surveys

MAIN IDEA

Analyze ways in which the wording of questions can influence survey results.

IN Academic Standards

7.4.4 Analyze data displays, including ways that they can be misleading. Analyze ways in which the wording of questions can influence survey results.

New Vocabulary

valid survey results

IN Math Online

glencoe.com

2. Sample answer: Those four students could like a type of pet that is not listed in the table, such as a hamster.

3. Sample answer: She could have listed more pets in the table and had an entry for *other.*

GET READY for the Lesson

SURVEYS Mary Anne wanted to determine the favorite type of pet of the students in her science class. Mary Anne asked the students in her class to choose one of the pet types listed in the table as their favorite. Of the 24 students surveyed, 8 responded that their favorite pet is a dog. Six students preferred a cat, four preferred a reptile, and two preferred a rabbit.

What is Your Favorite Type of Pet?
cat
dog
reptile
rabbit

1. How many students did not choose any of the pets listed in the table? **4**
2. Mary Anne stated that those students who did not choose any of the pets listed in the table did not like pets. What is wrong with her statement?
3. How could Mary Anne have reworded her question to determine the pet preferences of everyone in the class?

The way that questions are worded in surveys can often influence the actual survey results. This can happen when a survey question includes information that describes how others feel about the question being asked.

EXAMPLES Analyze Wording of Survey Questions

Analyze each of the following survey questions. Describe how the wording of the question can influence the survey results.

1 Do you prefer thrilling action movies or boring documentaries?

Action movies are described as thrilling which could influence responses to prefer them over documentaries which are described as boring.

The question also limits the responses to only two choices. The question does not lend itself to responses from people who do not like either type of movie or who prefer another type of movie.

2 Most employees working at Sam's Supply Store love their jobs. How do you feel about working at Sam's Supply Store?

By stating that most employees love their jobs, the question does not encourage other responses. An employee who is not satisfied with their job may not be honest with their response.

9 Lesson Notes

Lesson Planner

Use this lesson after Lesson 8-9 and Indiana Lesson 8 to address standard 7.4.4.

Objective

Analyze ways in which the wording of questions can influence survey results.

Vocabulary

valid survey results

IN Academic Standards

7.4.4 Analyze data displays, including ways that they can be misleading. Analyze ways in which the wording of questions can influence survey results.

1 Focus

Have students find an advertisement from a newspaper or another source that contains misleading information. Have students share their advertisements in small groups. Allow time for groups to analyze the advertisements.

2 Teach

Scaffolding Questions

Introduce students to language within questions that can influence their answers. Ask students to think of their answers in their heads rather than share them aloud.

Ask:

- Would you rather watch an exciting television program or a boring television program?
- Most students like reading magazines better than reading comic books. Which do you like better?
- Don't you think flying is the best way to travel?

Present the following questions to students and have them classify each as either closed-ended or open-ended.

Ask:

- Which day of the week is your favorite? open-ended
- Do you prefer lemonade or orange juice? closed-ended
- Would you rather visit a rainforest or a desert? closed-ended
- What is your favorite flavor of ice cream? open-ended
- Would you rather spend your money on music or clothes? closed-ended

Valid survey results occur when they are not influenced by other factors, such as the wording of the survey questions.

EXAMPLES Rewrite a Survey Question

3 **Rewrite the survey question from Example 1 so that the survey results might be more valid.**

Do you prefer thrilling action movies or boring documentaries?

The survey question "Do you like movies? If so, what kind of movies do you enjoy?" does not influence the survey results. People who do not enjoy movies can answer the question. People who do enjoy movies can also answer the question with their preferred type(s) of movie(s).

4 **Rewrite the survey question from Example 2 so that the survey results might be more valid.**

Most employees working at Sam's Supply Store love their jobs. How do you feel about working at Sam's Supply Store?

You could rewrite the survey question by simply deleting the first sentence. The question "How do you feel about working at Sam's Supply Store?" does not influence the survey results. It is an open-ended question.

Another possible question could be "Do you enjoy working at Sam's Supply Store?" This second question encourages responses of *yes* or *no*, which is more of a closed-ended question.

Either question is appropriate.

Study Tip

Open-Ended vs. Closed-Ended Questions Open-ended questions typically do not have one definite answer. Closed-ended questions have a certain number of answer choices. One of the choices may be "Other."

CHECK Your Understanding

1–4. See margin.

Examples 1, 2 (p. IN39)

Analyze each of the following survey questions. Describe how the wording of the question could influence the survey results.

1. Which is your favorite season: summer or fall?
2. Didn't you think that the book was too long?
3. Most students prefer to text message than e-mail. How do you prefer to communicate?
4. Do you play a sport or work an after-school job?

Examples 3, 4 (p. IN40)

Rewrite each of the following survey questions so that the survey results might be more valid. 5–7. Sample answers are given.

5. My favorite subject in school is French. What is your favorite subject?
6. Most of the students at Jefferson Middle School prefer pepperoni pizza. Do you like pepperoni pizza? **What is your favorite pizza topping?**
7. Would you rather travel to Italy or Germany?

5. What is your favorite subject?
7. To which place would you like to travel?

Additional Answers

1. Sample answer: By only giving two options, the results will suggest that no one likes spring or winter.
2. Sample answer: The statement influences you to believe that the book is too long.
3. Sample answer: By stating that most students prefer to send texts, the question does not encourage other responses. A student who uses another method to communicate might not be honest about how they communicate.
4. Sample answer: The question only allows two different responses, which does not allow people that do not play sports or work to respond with what they do.

Practice and Problem Solving

8–13. See margin.

HOMEWORK HELP

For Exercises	See Examples
8–13	1, 2
14–19	3, 4

Analyze each of the following survey questions. Describe how the wording of the question could influence the survey results.

8. Do you walk or ride your bicycle to school?
9. Most Americans think that we should recycle more. Do you think that we should recycle more?
10. Would you rather join the Debate Team or the Drama Club?
11. Most students at Winslow High School plan to go to college. Do you?
12. Would you rather go downhill skiing or cross-country skiing?
13. Don't you think that cats make better pets than dogs?

Rewrite each of the following survey questions so that the survey results might be more valid. 14–19. Sample answers are given.

14. I like the color yellow. Don't you? What is your favorite color?
15. Do you prefer basketball or football? What is your favorite sport?
16. Aren't roses the prettiest of flowers? Which kind of flower do you think is the prettiest?
17. Do you prefer roller coasters or water rides?
18. Most teenagers like to listen to rock music. Do you like to listen to rock music?
19. Would you rather go camping or swimming during your summer vacation? What do you like to do during your summer vacation?

17. Do you like amusement parks? If so, what is your favorite amusement park ride?
18. What kind of music do you like to listen to?

H.O.T. Problems

20. See students' work.

20. **CHALLENGE** Write an open-ended survey question. Then write a closed-ended survey question about the same topic. Describe the similarities and differences in the kinds of responses you might get from each question.
21. **WRITING IN MATH** Write a survey question that is worded to specifically influence a survey's results. Then explain how your question might affect the survey results. See students' work.

ISTEP+ PRACTICE 7.4.4

22. Mei-Ling asked the survey question: *Do you prefer vanilla or chocolate ice cream?* All of the following are possible reasons for why the survey results might not be valid EXCEPT for which one? D
    - A Some people may not like ice cream.
    - B Some people might like vanilla and chocolate ice cream equally.
    - C Some people might like strawberry ice cream the best.
    - D Most people prefer chocolate ice cream.

23. How could the following survey question be reworded so that the results would be more valid? G

    Didn't you think the new comedy movie was hilarious?

    - F I laughed through the whole movie. Didn't you?
    - G Did you think the new comedy movie was funny?
    - H Wasn't the new comedy movie funnier than the last one?
    - J I thought the new comedy movie was hilarious. Did you?

3 Practice

Use Exercises 1–7 to check for understanding.

Exercises 8–23 are structured so that students practice the same concepts they learned in the lesson.

Have students discuss and complete the Higher Order Thinking problems.

WRITING IN MATH Have students complete Exercise 21 in their Math Journals. You may choose to use this exercise as an optional formative assessment.

4 Assess

Ticket Out the Door Have students analyze the question below and explain how its wording could influence survey results. Then, have students rewrite the question so that it would produce more valid survey results.

Most of my friends love to go to the movies. Do you? Sample answer: The person answering the question might say yes just because he or she wants to be considered a friend of the person who asked the question. The question might produce more valid survey results if it were rewritten in this way: What do you like to do in your free time?

Additional Answers

8. Sample answer: Doesn't allow people to give other methods of getting to school.
9. Sample answer: By stating that most Americans prefer to recycle, the question does not encourage other responses. An American who does not recycle might not be honest in their response.
10. Sample answer: The question only allows you to choose between the two clubs and not other clubs.
11. Sample answer: By stating that most students plan to go to college, the question does not encourage other responses. A student who does not plan to go to college might not be honest in their response.
12. Sample answer: The question only asks about skiing and no other activities that a person may be interested in.
13. Sample answer: By stating that cats make better pets, the question does not encourage other responses. A person who likes dogs might not be honest in their response.

10

Lesson Notes

Lesson Planner

Use this lesson after Lesson 10-1 to address standard 7.3.1.

Objective

Analyze the relationships of angles formed by two parallel lines and a transversal.

Vocabulary

parallel lines
transversal
alternate interior angles
alternate exterior angles
corresponding angles

IN Academic Standards

7.3.1 Identify and use basic properties of angles formed by transversals intersecting pairs of parallel lines.

1 Focus

- Review complementary and supplementary angles by having students give a complement and supplement of a 30° angle. 60°; 150°
- Review vertical and adjacent angles by having students draw an example of two vertical angles and two adjacent angles. See students' work.

10

Parallel Lines and Transversals

MAIN IDEA

Analyze the relationships of angles formed by two parallel lines and a transversal.

IN Academic Standards

7.3.1 Identify and use basic properties of angles formed by transversals intersecting pairs of parallel lines.

New Vocabulary

parallel lines
transversal
alternate interior angles
alternate exterior angles
corresponding angles

IN Math Online

glencoe.com

- Personal Tutor
- Self-Check Quiz
- Extra Examples

GET READY for the Lesson

In the United States, the standard distance between rails on a railroad track is 4 feet 8.5 inches. The diagram at the right shows a road crossing over railroad tracks.

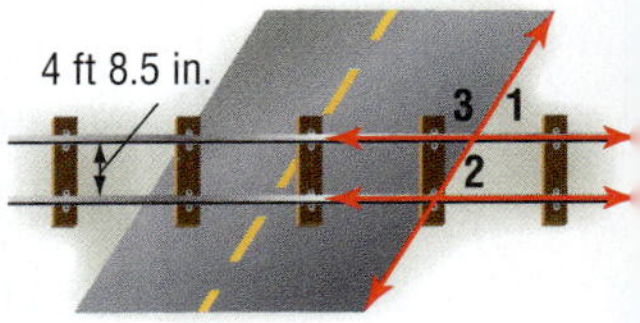

1. Measure angles 1 and 2. Record the measures. 52°; 52°
2. Make a conjecture about the measure of angle 3. Then measure the angle to verify your conjecture. The angle has a measure of 128°.

Lines in a plane that never intersect are **parallel lines**. When two or more parallel lines are intersected by a third line, this line is called a **transversal**. Angles formed when two parallel lines are intersected by a transversal have special relationships. Those relationships are described below.

Special Relationships

Key Concept

If a pair of parallel lines is intersected by a transversal, the following pairs of angles are congruent.

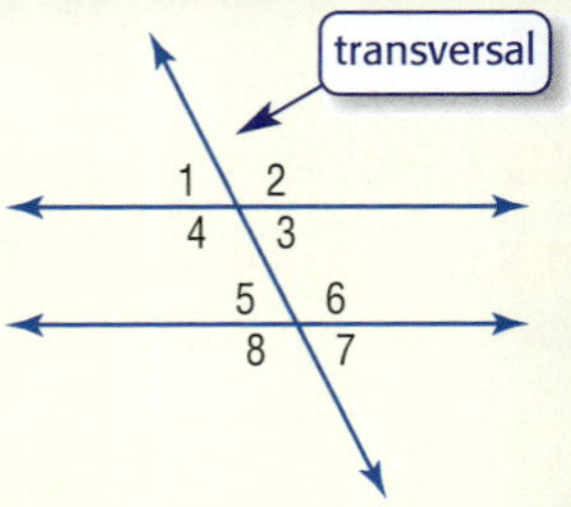

Alternate interior angles are on opposite sides of the transversal and inside the parallel lines.

$\angle 3 \cong \angle 5$, $\angle 4 \cong \angle 6$

Alternate exterior angles are on opposite sides of the transversal and outside the parallel lines.

$\angle 1 \cong \angle 7$, $\angle 2 \cong \angle 8$

Corresponding angles are in the same position on the parallel lines in relation to the transversal.

$\angle 1 \cong \angle 5$, $\angle 2 \cong \angle 6$, $\angle 3 \cong \angle 7$, $\angle 4 \cong \angle 8$

You can use these special relationships to find measures of angles.

EXAMPLE Find Measures of Angles

1 **In the figure at the right, $p \parallel q$ and $m\angle 3 = 95°$. Find $m\angle 7$.**

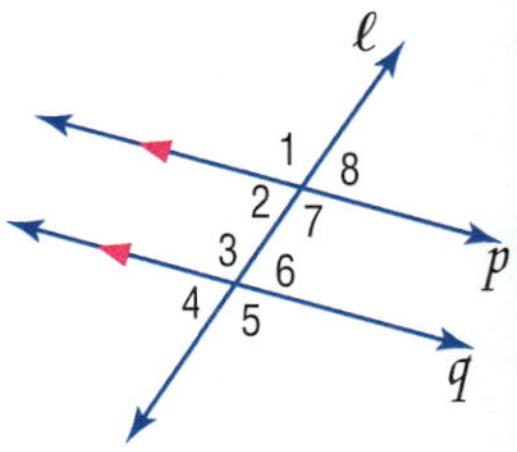

$m\angle 7$

$\angle 3$ and $\angle 7$ are alternate interior angles.

Alternate interior angles are congruent, so $m\angle 7 = m\angle 3 = 95°$.

Vertical Angles and Adjacent Angles

Key Concept

Vertical angles are opposite angles formed by the intersection of two lines. Vertical angles are congruent.

$\angle 1 \cong \angle 3$, $\angle 2 \cong \angle 4$

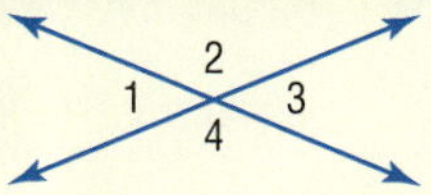

Two angles that have the same vertex, share a common side, and do not overlap are *adjacent angles*. Adjacent angles are supplementary.

$\angle 1$ and $\angle 2$, $\angle 2$ and $\angle 3$, $\angle 3$ and $\angle 4$, $\angle 4$ and $\angle 1$

Reading Math

Congruent Angles

- Angle 1 *is congruent to* angle 2: $\angle 1 \cong \angle 2$.
- The measure of $\angle 1$ *is equal to* the measure of $\angle 2$: $m\angle 1 = m\angle 2$.

EXAMPLES Use Vertical Angles and Adjacent Angles

In the figure at the right, $m\angle 1 = 70°$. Find each measure.

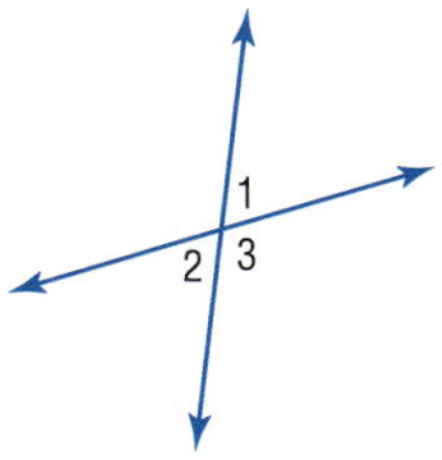

2 $m\angle 2$

$\angle 1$ and $\angle 2$ are vertical angles, so they are congruent.

$m\angle 2 = m\angle 1 = 70°$

3 $m\angle 3$

$\angle 1$ and $\angle 3$ are adjacent angles, so they are supplementary.

$m\angle 1 + m\angle 3 = 180$	Definition of supplementary angles
$70 + m\angle 3 = 180$	Replace $m\angle 1$ with 70.
$m\angle 3 = 110°$	Subtract 70 from each side.

EXAMPLES Use Angle Relationships

ALGEBRA In the figure at the right, $r \parallel s$.

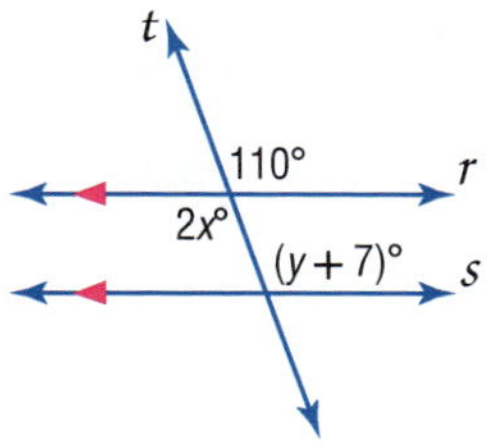

4 Find the value of x.

The angles with measures $2x°$ and $110°$ are vertical angles, so they are congruent.

$2x = 110$	Congruent angles have equal measures.
$\frac{2x}{2} = \frac{110}{2}$	Divide each side by 2.
$x = 55$	Simplify.

5 Find the value of y.

The angles with measures $2x°$ and $(y + 7)°$ are alternate interior angles, so they are congruent.

$2x = y + 7$	Congruent angles have equal measures.
$2(55) = y + 7$	Replace x with 55.
$110 = y + 7$	Multiply.
$110 - 7 = y + 7 - 7$	Subtract 7 from each side.
$103 = y$	Simplify.

2 Teach

Scaffolding Questions

Select a rectangular wall in the classroom. State the distance between the top and the bottom edges at one end.

Ask:

- How is the distance at the other end related to the distance at one end? They are the same.
- Why are the distances the same? The floor and the ceiling are parallel and therefore always the same distance apart.

3 Practice

Use Exercises 1–10 to check for understanding.

Exercises 11–37 are structured so that students practice the same concepts they learned in the lesson.

Have students discuss and complete the Higher Order Thinking problems.

WRITING IN MATH Have students complete Exercise 35 in their Math Journals. You may choose to use this exercise as an optional formative assessment.

Additional Answers

34. Sample answer:

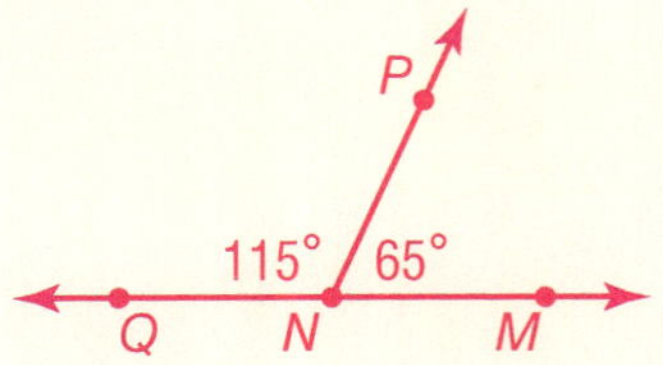

35. Sample answer: When two parallel lines are cut by a transversal, the following special angle pairs are formed: alternate interior, alternate exterior, corresponding, vertical, and adjacent. The angles in each of these pairs are congruent, except for the adjacent angles, which are supplementary.

CHECK Your Understanding

Examples 1–3 (pp. IN42–IN43)

In the figure at the right, $\ell \parallel m$ and k is a transversal. If $m\angle 1 = 56°$, find each measure.

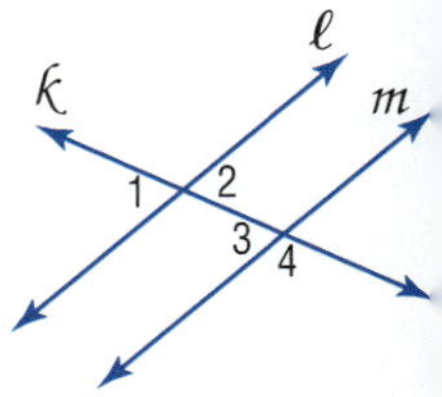

1. $m\angle 2$ **56°**
2. $m\angle 3$ **56°**
3. $m\angle 4$ **124°**

4. **GEOMETRY** Refer to the figure above. Classify angles 1 and 3 as *alternate interior angles, alternate exterior angles,* or *corresponding angles.* **corresponding angles**

In the figure at the right, p ∥ q and ℓ is a transversal. If $m\angle 8 = 120°$, find each measure.

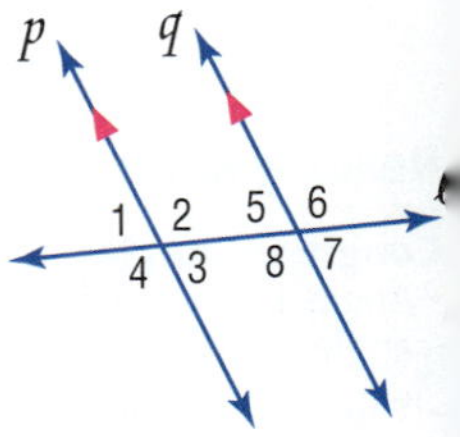

5. $m\angle 1$ **60°**
6. $m\angle 3$ **60°**
7. $m\angle 5$ **60°**

8. **GEOMETRY** Refer to the figure for Exercises 5–7. Classify angles 4 and 6 as *alternate interior angles, alternate exterior angles,* or *corresponding angles.* **alternate exterior angles**

Example 4 (p. IN43)

9. **SWIMMING** A swimmer crosses the lanes in a pool and swims from point A to point B, as shown in the figure. What is the value of x? **16**

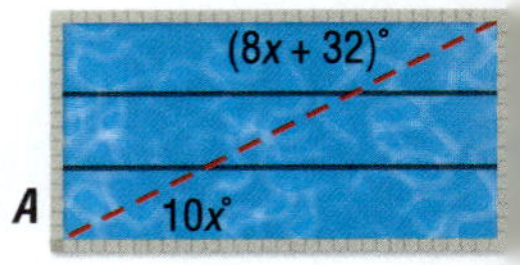

10. **ALGEBRA** Find the value of x in the figure at the right. **4**

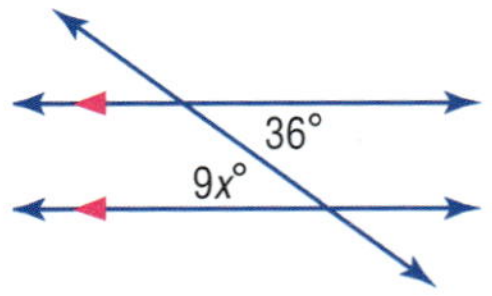

Practice and Problem Solving

HOMEWORK HELP

For Exercises	See Examples
11–18	1–3
19–26	4

In the figure at the right, if $m\angle 5 = 108°$, find each measure.

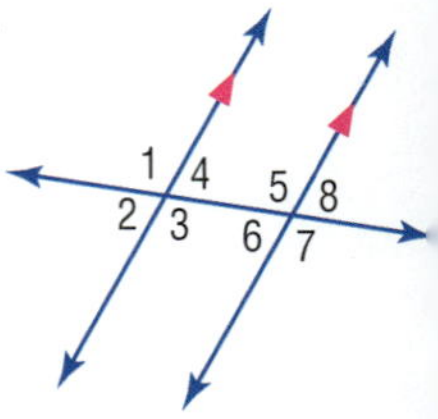

11. $m\angle 1$ **108°**
12. $m\angle 3$ **108°**
13. $m\angle 6$ **72°**
14. $m\angle 7$ **108°**

In the figure at the right, if $m\angle 2 = 74°$, find each measure.

15. $m\angle 8$ **74°**
16. $m\angle 6$ **74°**
17. $m\angle 4$ **74°**
18. $m\angle 1$ **106°**

FURNITURE For Exercises 19–21, refer to the chair at the right where $m\angle 4 = 106°$.

19. Find $m\angle 6$ and $m\angle 3$. **74°; 106°**
20. Find $m\angle 1$ and $m\angle 2$. **106°**
21. Find $m\angle 5$ and $m\angle 4$. **74°; 106°**

22. **DRIVING** Ambulances can't safely make turns of less than 70°. The angle at the southeast corner of Delavan and Elmwood is 108°. Can an ambulance safely turn the northeast corner of Bidwell and Elmwood? Explain your reasoning.

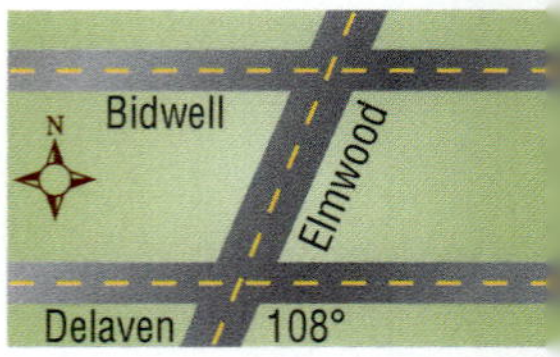

22. Yes; the two corners at the intersection have measures of 108° and 72°. Therefore, it is just within the safety limits.

In the figure at the right, $m\angle 7 = 96°$. Find each measure.

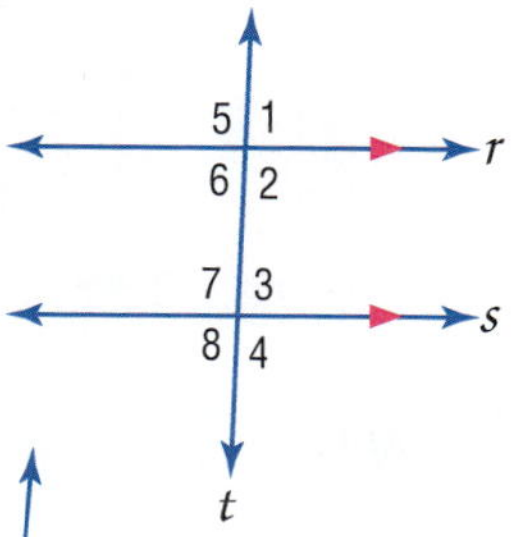

23. $m\angle 2$ **96°**
24. $m\angle 5$ **96°**
25. $m\angle 4$ **96°**
26. $m\angle 8$ **84°**

ALGEBRA Find the value of x in each figure.

27. **20**

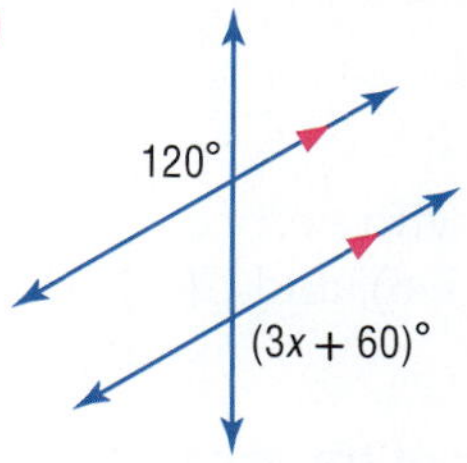

28. **39**

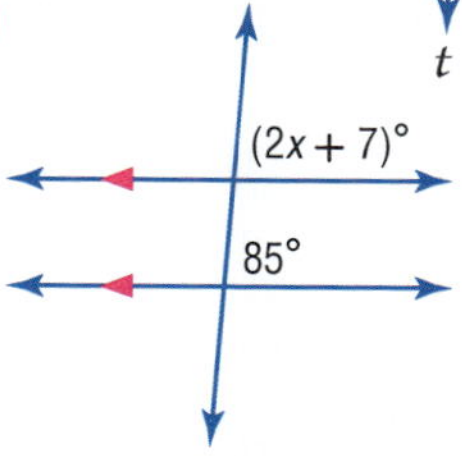

ALGEBRA In the figure at the right, $m \parallel \ell$ and t is a transversal. Find the value of x for each of the following.

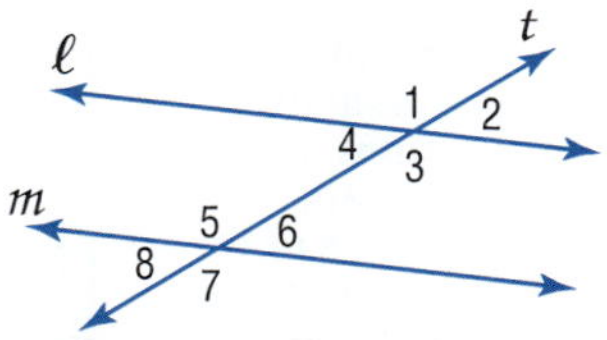

29. $m\angle 2 = 2x + 3$ and $m\angle 4 = 4x - 7$ **5**
30. $m\angle 8 = 4x - 32$ and $m\angle 5 = 5x + 50$ **18**

Real-World Link

The area of Bosnia is 19,741 square miles. Until 1992, this country was a part of Yugoslavia.

Source: *Time for Kids Almanac*

31. **FLAGS** The flag at the right is the national flag of Bosnia. If $m\angle 1 = 135°$, what is $m\angle 2$? Explain how you found your answer.

31. 45°; $m\angle 2 + m\angle 3 = m\angle 1$; $m\angle 3 = 90$; $m\angle 2 = 135 - 90$, or 45

32. **ALGEBRA** A transversal intersects two parallel lines and forms adjacent angles 5 and 6. If $m\angle 5 = (7x - 11)°$ and $m\angle 6 = (3x + 1)°$, find the measures of the angles. **$m\angle 5 = 122°$; $m\angle 6 = 58°$**

H.O.T. Problems

33. They are supplementary.
35. See margin.

33. **CHALLENGE** Suppose two parallel lines are cut by a transversal. How are the interior angles on the same side of the transversal related?
34. **OPEN ENDED** Draw a pair of adjacent, supplementary angles. Label the angle measures. **See margin.**
35. **WRITING IN MATH** Summarize the angle relationships that are formed by parallel lines and a transversal. Describe which angles are congruent.

ISTEP+ PRACTICE 7.3.1

36. **CONSTRUCTED RESPONSE** In the figure below, $a \parallel b \parallel c$ and d is a transversal.

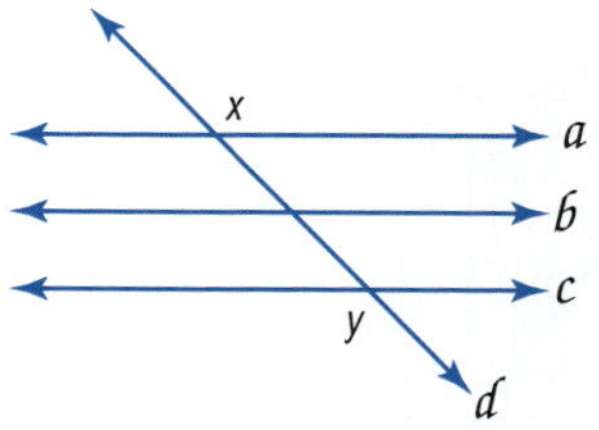

What is the value of angle y if $m\angle x$ is 135°? **135°**

37. A transversal intersects two parallel lines and forms adjacent angles 1 and 2. If $m\angle 1$ is $(2x + 5)°$ and $m\angle 2$ is $3x°$, what is the measure of angle 1? **B**

A 35°
B 75°
C 105°
D 135°

4 Assess

Ticket Out the Door Ask students to answer the following questions:

If two lines intersect and the measure of one of the four angles formed is 27°, what is the measure of the angle opposite this angle? **27°**

What are the measures of the other two angles formed? **153° and 153°**

11 Lesson Notes

Lesson Planner

Use this lesson after Lesson 10-10 to address standard 7.3.1.

Objective

Identify and graph rotations on a coordinate plane.

IN Academic Standards

7.3.1 Identify, describe and use transformations (translations, rotations, reflections and simple compositions of these transformations) to solve problems.

1 Focus

- Review transformations such as translations and reflections with students. Provide students with examples of each type of transformation.
- Review line symmetry. Remind students that the figure must match itself exactly in order to have symmetry.

11 Rotations

MAIN IDEA

Identify and graph rotations on a coordinate plane.

IN Academic Standards

7.3.1 Identify, describe and use transformations (translations, rotations, reflections and simple compositions of these transformations) to solve problems.

New Vocabulary

rotation
rotational symmetry
angle of rotation

IN Math Online

glencoe.com

1. Sample answer: The triangle was turned, or rotated, about the origin.

MINI Lab

STEP 1 Draw and label triangle *ABC* with vertices $A(-5, 1)$, $B(-5, 6)$, and $C(-1, 1)$.

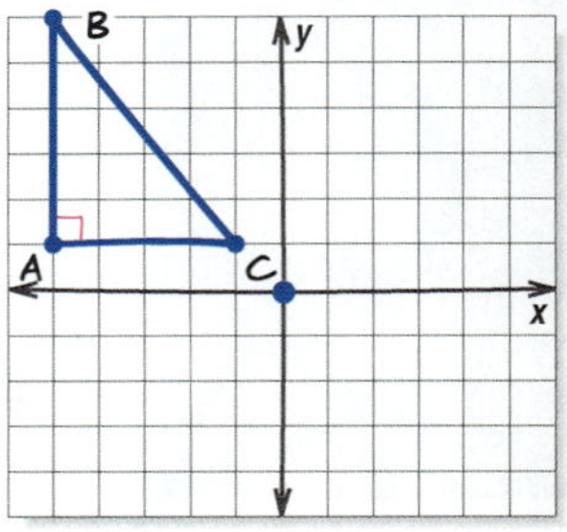

STEP 2 Attach a piece of tracing paper to the coordinate plane with a fastener. Then trace the triangle and the *x*- and *y*-axis.

STEP 3 Turn the tracing paper clockwise so that the original *y*-axis is on top of the original *x*-axis.

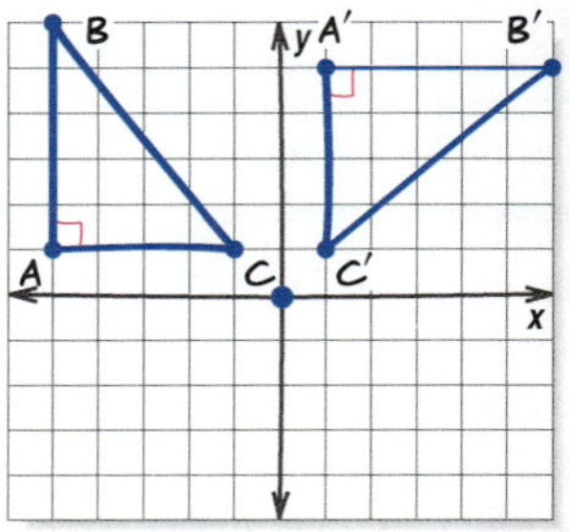

1. Describe the transformation that occurred from triangle *ABC* to triangle *A′B′C′*.
2. What are the coordinates of triangle *A′B′C′*? **A′(1, 5), B′(6, 5), C′(1, 1)**
3. Measure the line segment connecting point *C* and the origin. Then measure the segment connecting point *C′* and the origin. What do you notice? **The segments are congruent.**
4. Measure the angle formed by the segments in Exercise 3. What is this angle measure? **90°**

A **rotation** occurs when a figure is rotated around a point, such as the origin. A rotation does not change the size or shape of the figure. The three different rotations shown below are clockwise around the origin.

90° Rotation

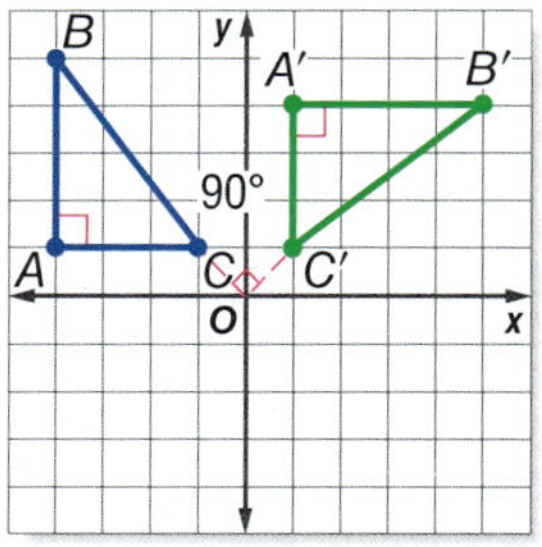

180° Rotation

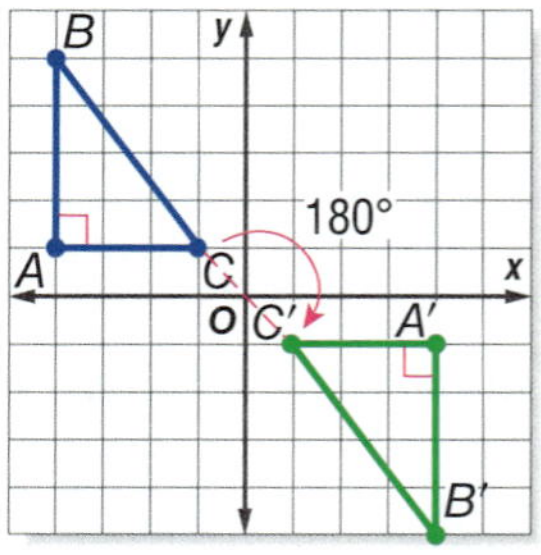

270° Rotation

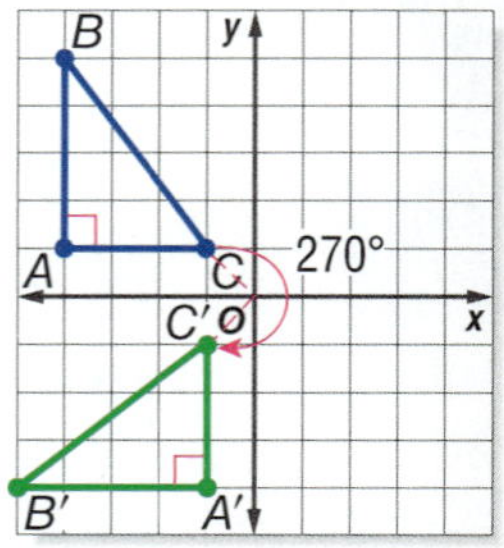

EXAMPLE Rotate a Figure About the Origin

1 **Triangle *ABC* has vertices *A*(–4, 4), *B*(–1, 2), and *C*(–3, 1). Graph the figure and its rotated image after a clockwise rotation of 90° about the origin. Then give the coordinates of the vertices for △*A′B′C′*.**

STEP 1 Graph △*ABC* on a coordinate plane.

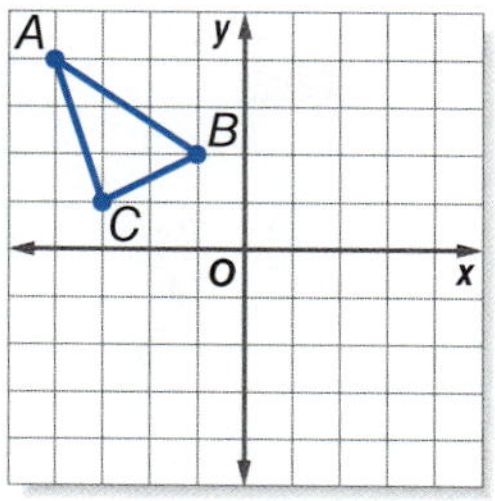

STEP 2 Sketch segment $\overline{BO}$ connecting point *B* to the origin. Sketch another segment, $\overline{B'O}$ so that the angle between point *B*, *O*, and *B′* measures 90° and the segment is congruent to $\overline{BO}$.

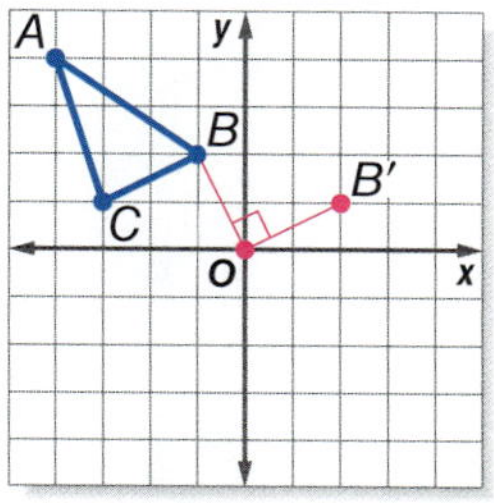

STEP 3 Repeat Step 2 for points *A* and *C*. Then connect the vertices to form △*A′B′C′*.

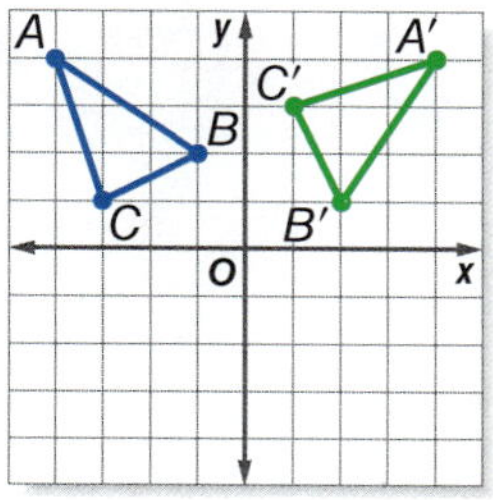

So, the coordinates of the vertices of △*A′B′C′* are *A′*(4, 4), *B′*(2, 1), and *C′*(1, 3).

EXAMPLE Rotate a Figure About a Point

2 **Triangle *LMN* has vertices *L*(5, 4), M(5, 7), and *N*(8, 7). Graph the figure and its rotated image after a counterclockwise rotation of 180° about vertex *L*. Then give the coordinates of the vertices for △*L′M′N′*.**

STEP 1 Graph the original triangle.

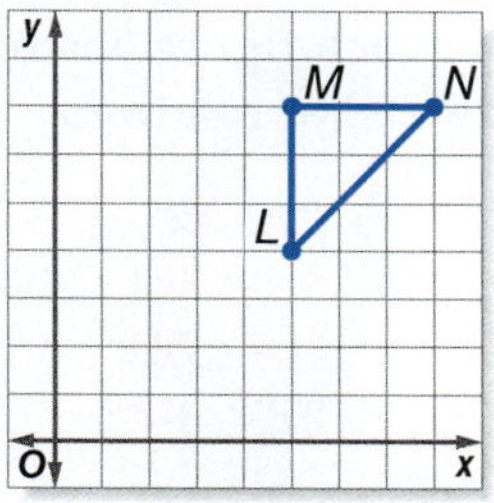

STEP 2 Graph the rotated image.

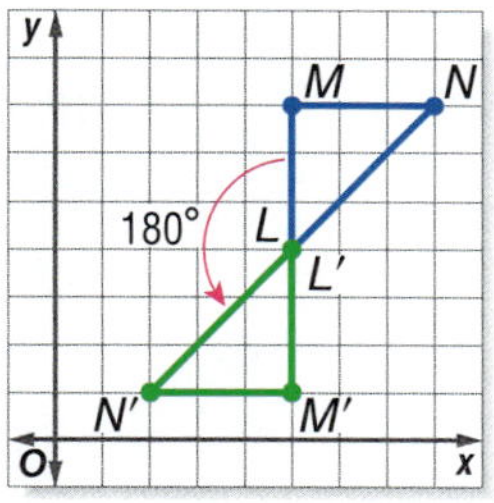

So, the coordinates of the vertices of △*L′M′N′* are *L′*(5, 4), *M′*(5, 1), and *N′*(2, 1).

Reading Math

Segment Notation $\overline{BO}$ means the line segment connecting points *B* and *O*.

2 Teach

Scaffolding Questions

Help students make a connection between rotations and what they already know about them.

Ask:

- What does it mean for an object to rotate? turn
- If an object turns or rotates, does the size of the object change? No.
- If an object turns or rotates, does the shape of the object change? No.
- Where have you seen examples of rotations? Sample answer: clock hands rotate around the center, tires, mixing bowl, Ferris wheel

3 Practice

Use Exercises 1–8 to check for understanding.

Exercises 9–22 are structured so that students practice the same concepts they learned in the lesson.

Have students discuss and complete the Higher Order Thinking problems.

WRITING IN MATH Have students complete Exercise 20 in their Math Journals. You may choose to use this exercise as an optional formative assessment.

Additional Answers

1.

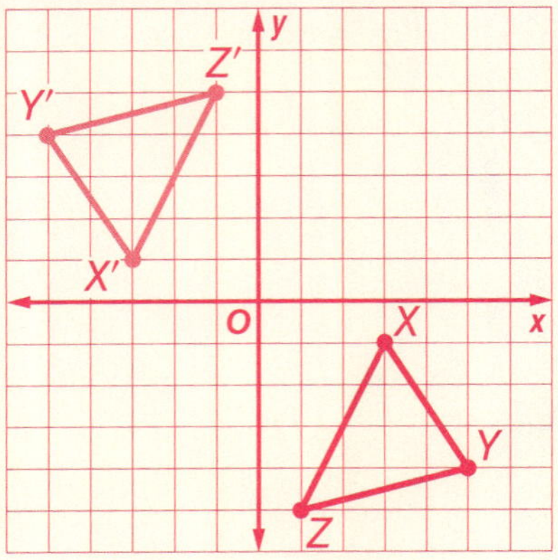

$X'(-3, 1)$, $Y'(-5, 4)$, and $Z'(-1, -5)$

2.

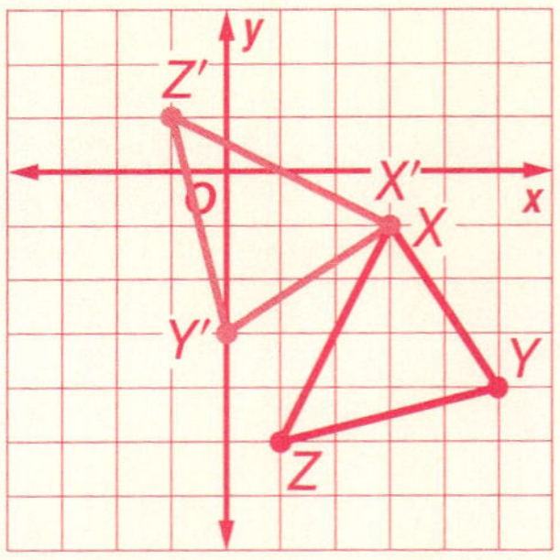

$X'(3, -1)$, $Y'(0, -3)$, and $Z'(-1, 1)$

3.

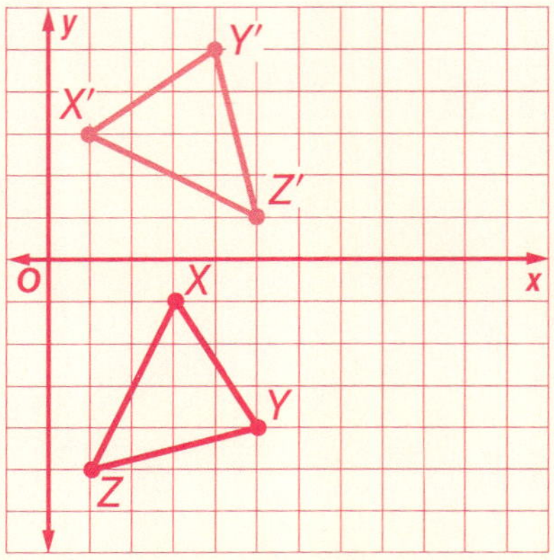

$X'(1, 3)$, $Y'(4, 5)$, and $Z'(5, 1)$

A figure can have **rotational symmetry** if the figure can be rotated a certain number of degrees about its center and still look like the original. The **angle of rotation** is the degree measure of the angle through which the figure is rotated.

Real-World EXAMPLE — Determine Rotational Symmetry

3 SNOW Determine whether the snowflake has rotational symmetry. Write *yes* or *no*. If *yes*, name its angle(s) of rotation.

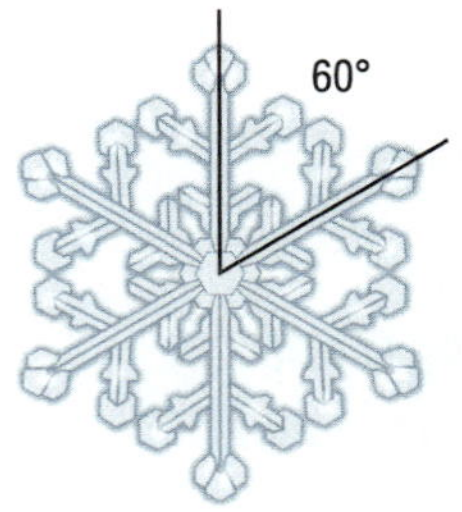

Since the snowflake can be rotated and still look like it does in its original position, the snowflake has rotational symmetry. The snowflake will match itself after being rotated 60°, 120°, 180°, 240°, 300°, and 360°.

CHECK Your Understanding

Examples 1–2 (p. IN46)

Graph $\triangle XYZ$ and its rotated image after each rotation. Then give the coordinates of the vertices for $\triangle X'Y'Z'$. 1–6. See margin.

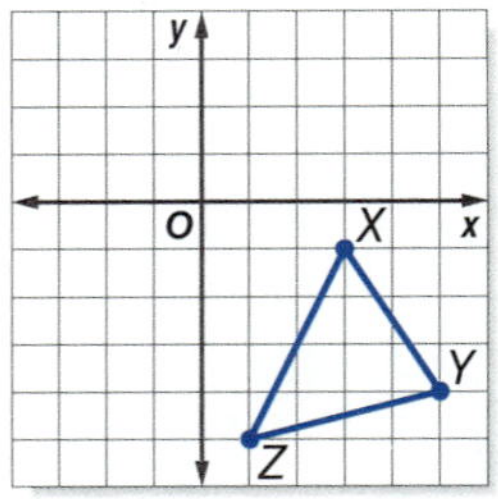

1. 180° clockwise about the origin
2. 270° counterclockwise about vertex X
3. 90° counterclockwise about the origin
4. 270° clockwise about vertex Y
5. 180° counterclockwise about vertex Z
6. 90° clockwise about the origin

Example 3 (p. IN48)

Determine whether each figure has rotational symmetry. Write *yes* or *no*. If *yes*, name its angle(s) of rotation.

7.

yes; 45°, 90°, 135°, 180°, 225°, 270°, 315°, 360°

8.

yes; 72°, 144°, 216°, 288°, 360°

IN48 Focus on Indiana

4.

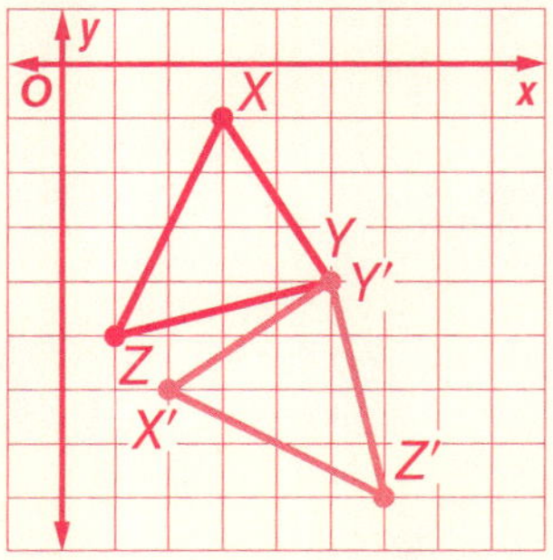

$X'(2, -6)$, $Y'(5, -4)$, and $Z'(6, -8)$,

5.

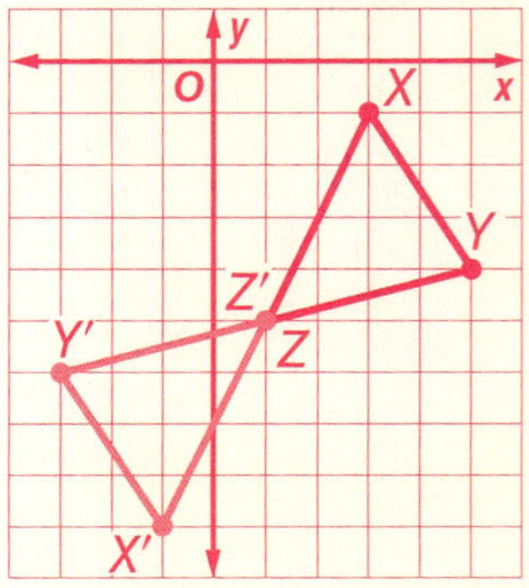

$X'(-1, -9)$, $Y'(-3, -6)$, and $Z'(1, -5)$

6.

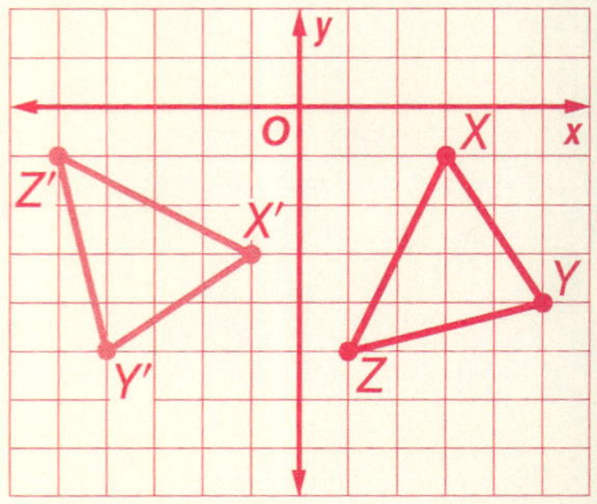

$X'(-1, -3)$, $Y'(-4, -5)$, and $Z'(-5, -1)$

Practice and Problem Solving

HOMEWORK HELP	
For Exercises	See Examples
9–14	1–2
15–18	3

Graph quadrilateral *ABCD* and its rotated image after each rotation. Then give the coordinates of the vertices for quadrilateral *A′B′C′D′*. 9–14. See margin.

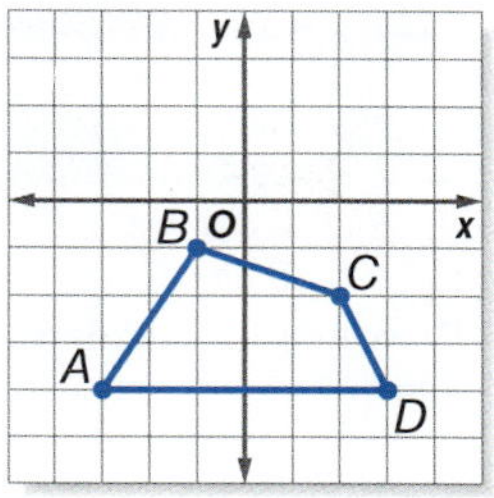

9. 90° counterclockwise about the origin
10. 90° clockwise about vertex *A*
11. 180° counterclockwise about vertex *D*
12. 270° clockwise about the origin
13. 90° clockwise about the origin
14. 180° clockwise about vertex *B*

Determine whether each figure has rotational symmetry. Write *yes* or *no*. If *yes*, name its angle(s) of rotation.

15. no
16. yes; 45°, 90°, 135°, 180°, 225°, 270°, 315°, 360°
17. yes; 90°, 180°, 270°, 360°
18. yes; 120°, 240°, 360°

15.

16.

17.

18.

H.O.T. Problems

19. **OPEN ENDED** Sketch a figure that has rotational symmetry. Describe the angle(s) of rotation. See students' work.
20. **WRITING IN MATH** Describe what information is needed to rotate a figure. See margin.

ISTEP+ PRACTICE 7.3.2

21. Which figure shows the letter F after a rotation of 270° clockwise? **A**

A 
C 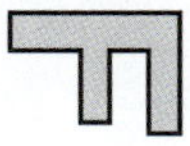
B 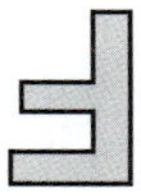
D 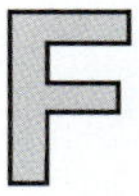

22. Triangle *XYZ* has vertices $X(2, -2)$, $Y(5, 0)$, and $Z(3, -4)$. What are the coordinates of point Y' after a rotation of 180°? **G**

F $(0, -5)$ H $(0, 5)$
G $(-5, 0)$ J $(5, 0)$

4 Assess

Ticket Out the Door Have students list the effects of 90°, 180°, and 270° rotations on the ordered pairs of an original figure. Ask students to show their work. See students' work.

Additional Answers

9.

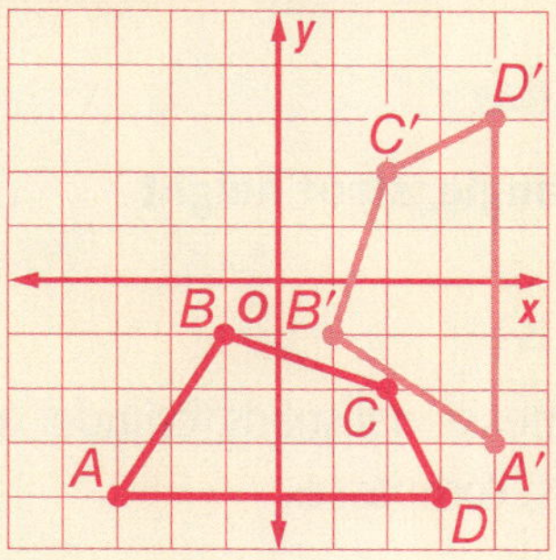

$A'(4, -3)$, $B'(1, -1)$, $C'(2, 2)$, and $D'(4, 3)$

10.

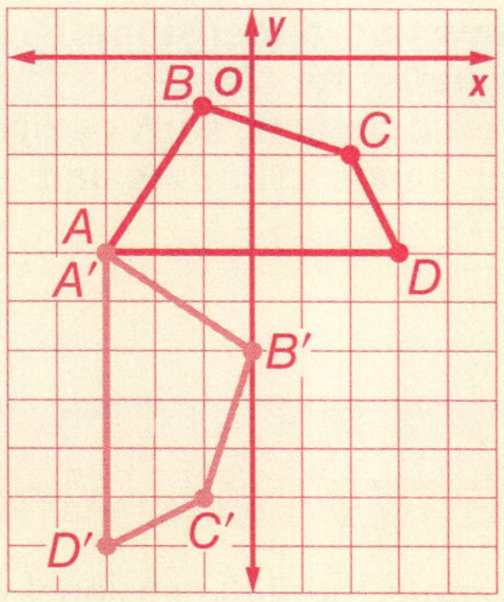

$A'(-3, -4)$, $B'(0, -6)$, $C'(-1, -9)$, and $D'(-3, -10)$

11.

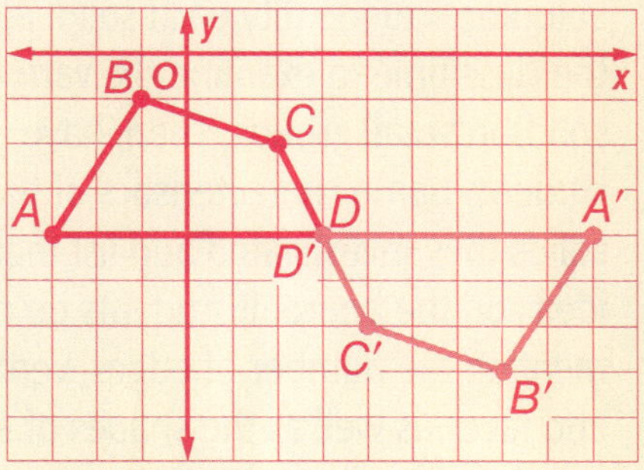

$A'(9, -4)$, $B'(7, -7)$, $C'(4, -6)$, and $D'(3, -4)$

12.

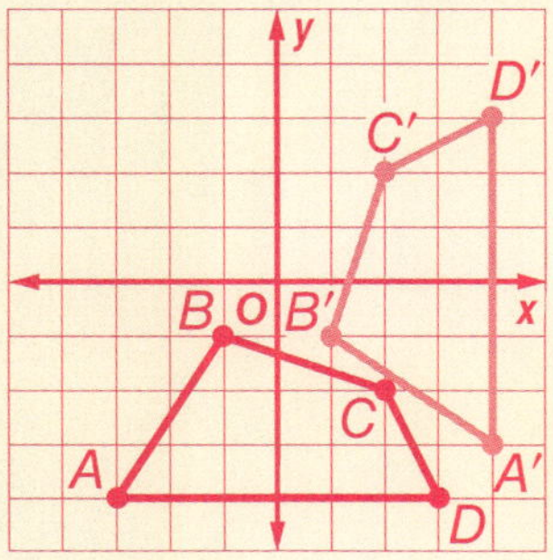

$A'(4, -3)$, $B'(1, -1)$, $C'(2, 2)$, and $D'(4, 3)$

13.

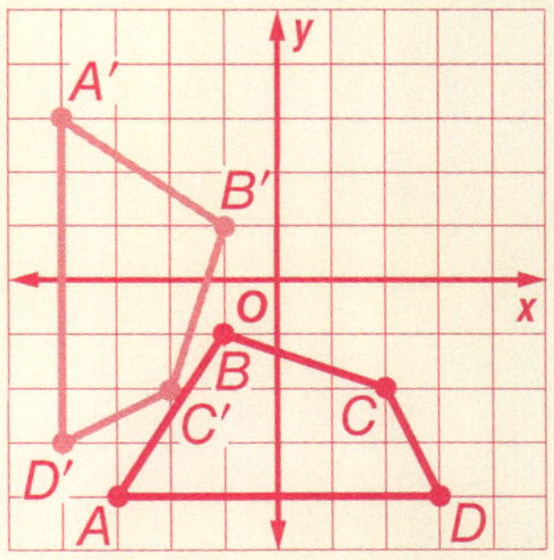

$A'(-4, 3)$, $B'(-1, 1)$, $C'(-2, -2)$, and $D'(-4, -3)$

14.

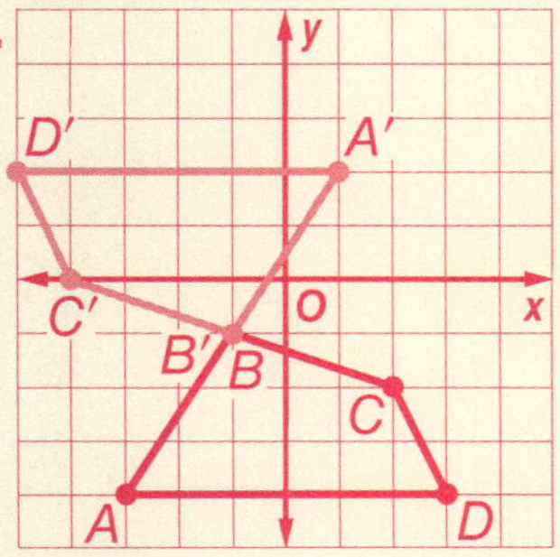

$A'(1, 2)$, $B'(-1, -1)$, $C'(-4, 0)$, and $D'(-5, 2)$

20. Sample answer: To rotate a figure, you need to know the number of degrees it is going to be rotated, the direction of rotation, and what point the figure is being rotated about.

Lesson IN 11 Rotations IN49

12 Lesson Notes

Lesson Planner

Use this lesson after Extend 11-6 to address standard 7.3.2.

Objective

Draw nets for cylinders and cones.

Vocabulary

central angle, **slant height**

Materials

three-dimensional solids, cylinder and cone nets, compasses

IN Academic Standards

7.3.2 Draw two-dimensional patterns (nets) for three-dimensional objects, such as right prisms, pyramids, **cylinders and cones.**

1 Focus

Display various three-dimensional solids such as prisms, pyramids, cylinders, and cones to the class and call upon volunteers to identify each solid. Allow the class time to examine the various solids in small groups. Then, have students name characteristics of the solids they investigated and list their ideas on the board. If students do not mention the number of edges, vertices, and faces as well as the shapes of each solid's faces, elicit this information so that it may be included in the data written on the board.

12 Nets of Cylinders and Cones

MAIN IDEA

Draw nets for cylinders and cones.

IN Academic Standards

7.3.2 Draw two-dimensional patterns (nets) for three-dimensional objects, such as right prisms, pyramids, **cylinders and cones.**

New Vocabulary

central angle
slant height

IN Math Online

glencoe.com

GET READY for the Lesson

Refer to the figures at the right.

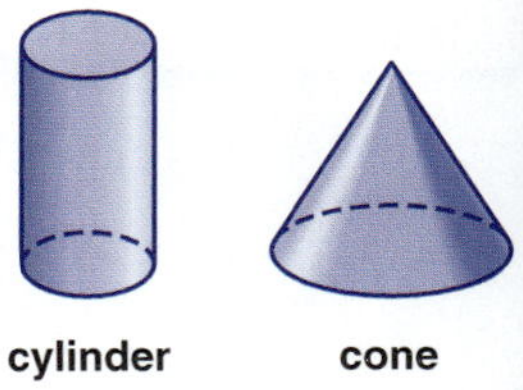

1. How many bases does a cylinder have? **2**
2. Describe the shape of the base(s) of a cylinder. **Sample answer: They are congruent circles.**
3. How many bases does a cone have? **1**
4. Describe the shape of the base(s) of a cone. **Sample answer: It is a circle.**

In Extend 11-6, you drew nets for three-dimensional figures such as prisms and pyramids. Recall that a net is a two-dimensional figure that helps you see the faces that make up the surface of a figure. In this activity, you will draw nets for cylinders and cones.

You can use a cylindrical container with a lid to help you draw the net of a cylinder.

EXAMPLE Draw a Net of a Cylinder

1 **Draw a net of a cylinder using a cylindrical container with a lid.**

STEP 1 Use an empty cylinder-shaped container that has a lid. Measure and record the height of the container.

STEP 2 Then label the lid and bottom face using a blue marker. Label the curved side using a red marker.

STEP 3 Take off the lid of the container and make 2 cuts as shown. Next, cut off the sides of the lid. Finally, lay the lid, the curved side, and the bottom flat to form the net of the container.

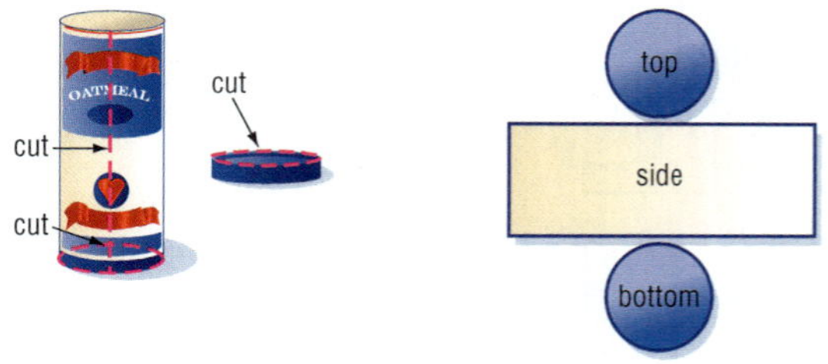

To draw a net of a cone, you will need a compass. The base of a cone is a circle. The lateral surface of a cone is part of a larger circle. So that the edges match, the circumference of the base is equal to part of the circumference of the larger circle.

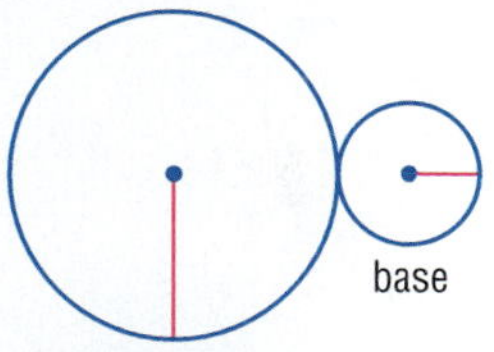

To draw the lateral surface of the cone from its partial circumference, you need to know the measure of its central angle. A **central angle** of a circle is an angle whose vertex is the center of the circle.

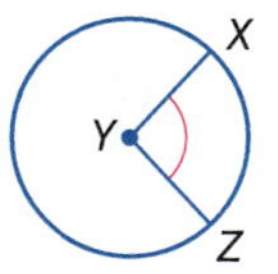

The activity below shows you how to draw the net of a cone given its radius and slant height. The **slant height** of a cone is the height of the cone's lateral surface. The slant height is also the radius of the larger circle.

EXAMPLE 2 Draw a Net of a Cone

Draw a net of a cone with a radius of 8 centimeters and a slant height of 17 centimeters.

STEP 1 Use a compass to draw two circles slightly touching, one with a radius of 17 centimeters and one with a radius of 8 centimeters.

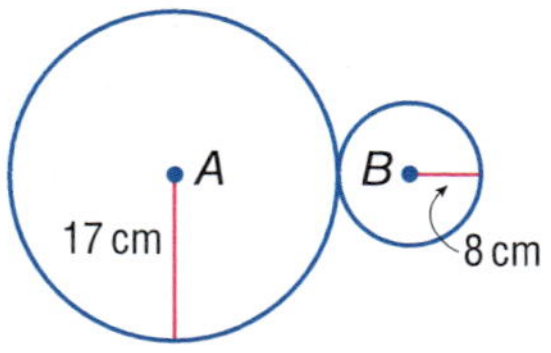

STEP 2 Think: What is the ratio of the circumference of B to the circumference of A? Let x represent this ratio.

$x = \frac{16\pi}{34\pi}$ The circumference of B is 16π. The circumference of A is 34π.

$x = \frac{16\cancel{\pi}}{34\cancel{\pi}}$ Cancel the common factor π.

$x \approx 0.47$ Simplify.

You need 0.47 of the circumference of A.

STEP 3 Find the size of the central angle to be cut from A.

$0.47 \cdot 360° \approx 170°$

Cut a central angle of 170° from circle A.

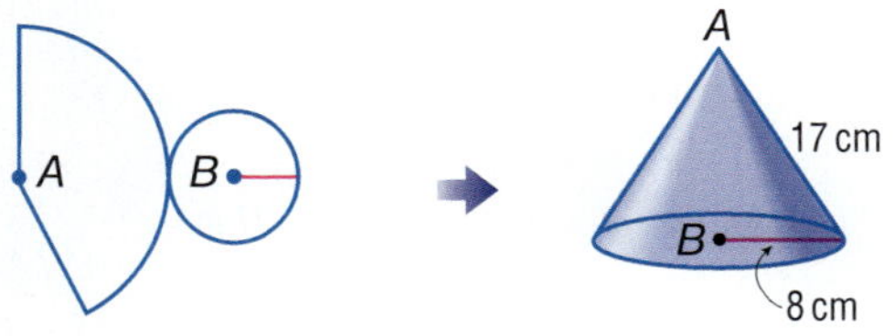

2 Teach

Scaffolding Questions

Ask:

- Name the different parts of a circle. center, radius, diameter, chord, circumference, and arc
- How can you determine the radius of a circle? Sample answer: You can measure the distance from its center to any point on its circumference.
- How can you determine the circumference of a circle? Sample answer: Use the formula $C = \pi d$.
- What is the length of the circumference of a circle with a diameter of 6? of 14? of 5.9? 18.84; 43.96; 18.526

Lesson IN 12 Nets of Cylinders and Cones **IN51**

3 Practice

Use Exercises 1–4 to check for understanding.

Exercises 5–22 are structured so that students practice the same concepts they learned in the lesson.

Have students discuss and complete the Higher Order Thinking problems.

WRITING IN MATH Have students complete Exercise 20 in their Math Journals. You may choose to use this exercise as an optional formative assessment.

Additional Answers

1.

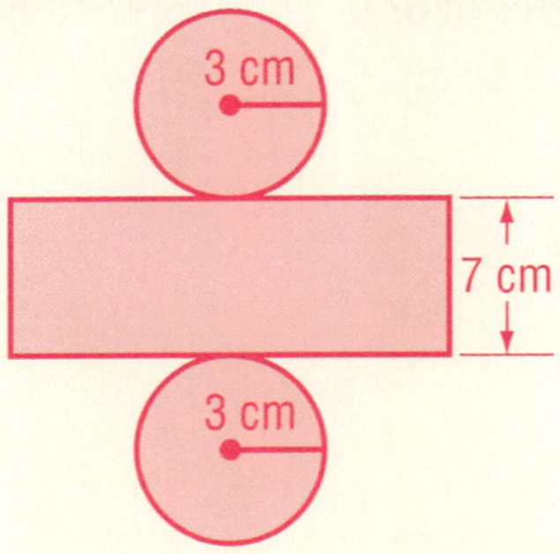

2.

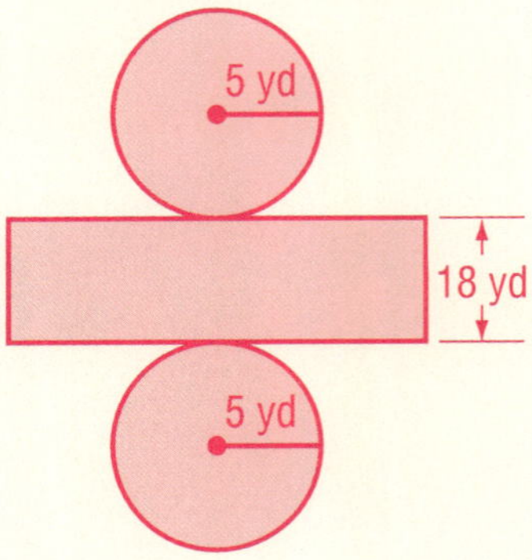

3.

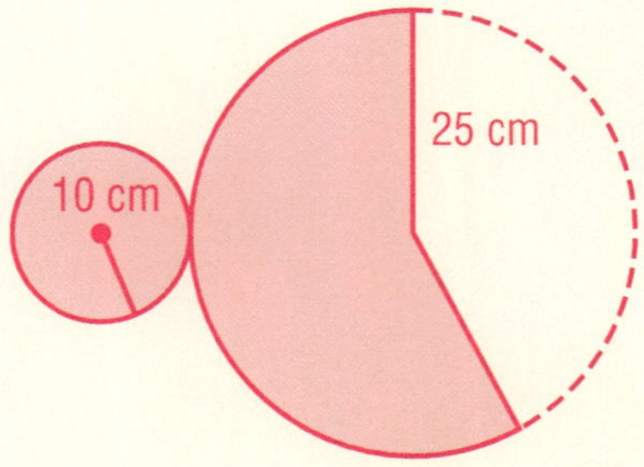

4.

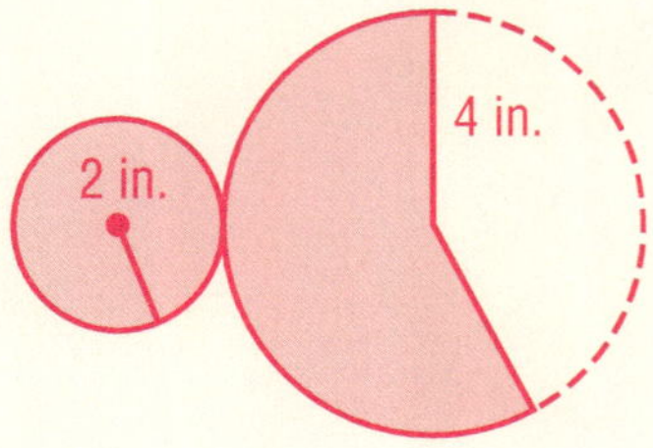

CHECK Your Understanding

1–4. See margin.

Example 1 (p. IN50) Draw the net for each cylinder. Label the dimensions on the net.

1.

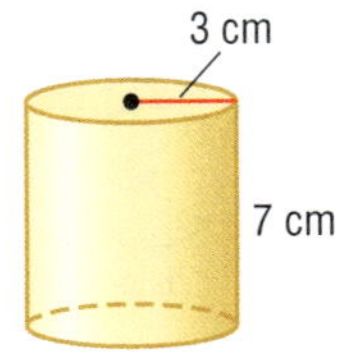

2.

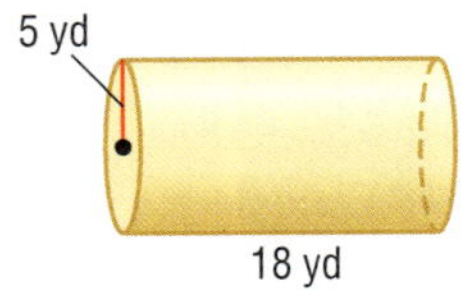

Example 2 (p. IN51) Find the central angle of each cone. Then draw the net of the cone. Label the dimensions on the net.

3.

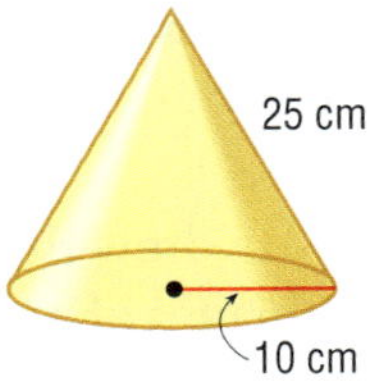

4.

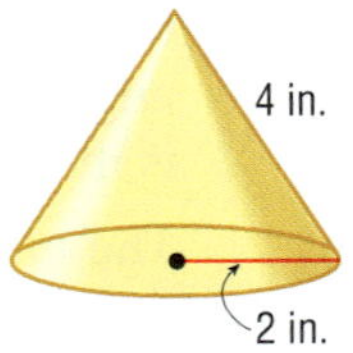

Practice and Problem Solving

5–12. See margin.

HOMEWORK HELP	
For Exercises	See Examples
5–8	1
9–12	2

Draw the net for each cylinder. Label the dimensions on the net.

5.

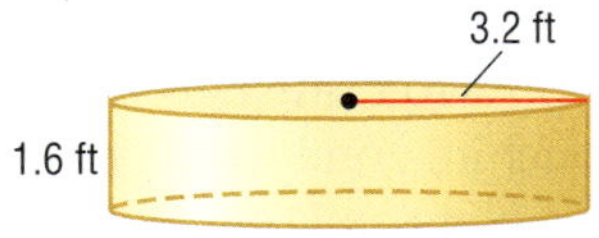

6.

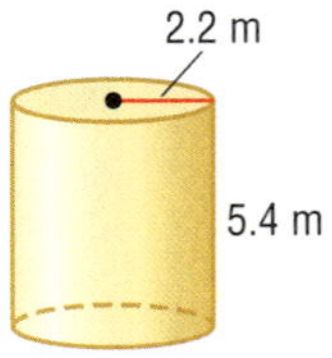

7.

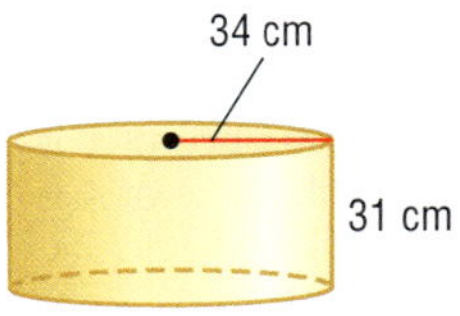

8.

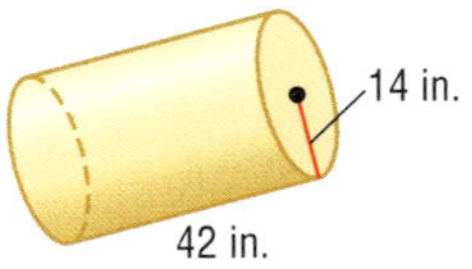

Find the central angle of each cone. Then draw the net of the cone. Label the dimensions on the net.

9.

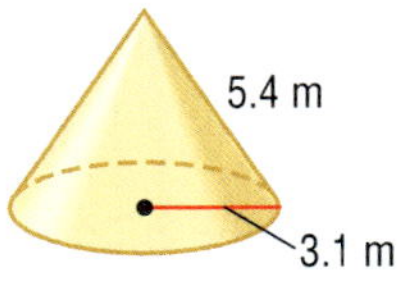

10.

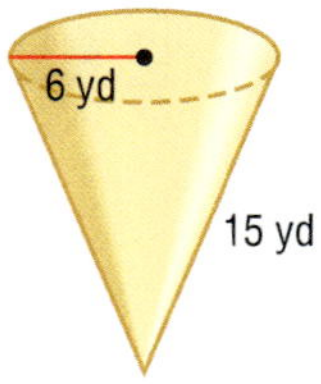

11.

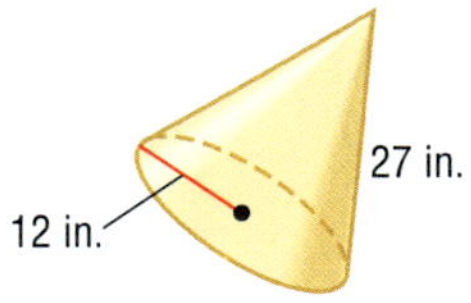

12.

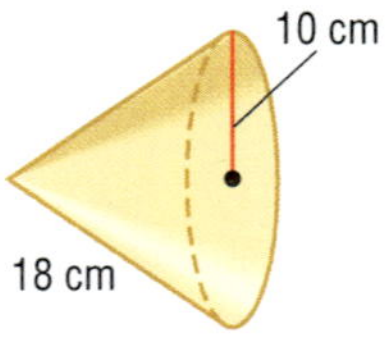

5.

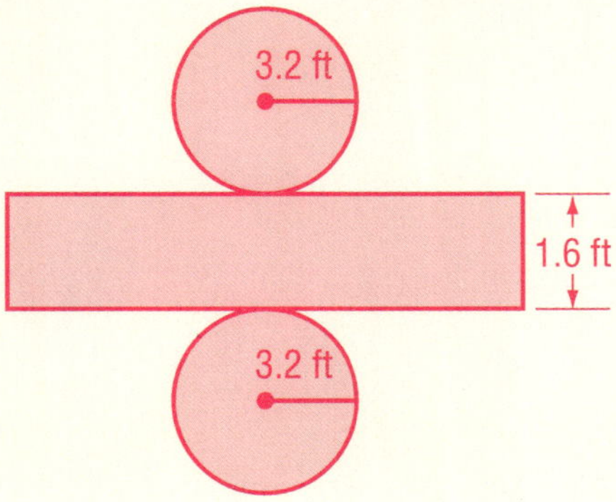

6.

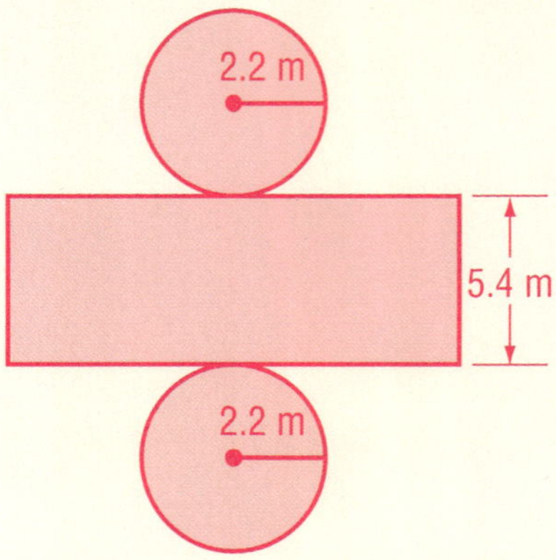

CONTAINERS For Exercises 13–15, refer to the cylindrical can of vegetables shown at the right.

13. Draw the net of this cylinder. Label the dimensions on the net. **See Focus on Indiana Answer Appendix.**

14. Find the area of each circular base. Then find the area of the lateral surface. Use 3.14 for π. Round to the nearest hundredth, if necessary. **9.62 in^2; 54.95 in^2**

15. What is the total area, including both circular bases and the lateral surface, of the cylinder? **74.19 in^2**

PARTY HATS For Exercises 16–18, refer to the conical party hat shown at the right.

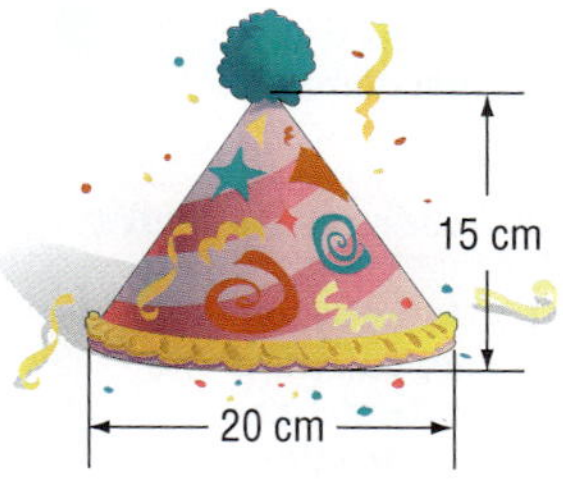

16. See Focus on Indiana Answer Appendix.

16. Draw the net of this cone. Label the dimensions on the net.

17. What is the central angle of the cone? **240°**

18. Find the area of the lateral surface by setting up and solving the following proportion, where r is the slant height, y is the central angle, and x is the area of the lateral surface of the cone. Use 3.14 for π. Round to the nearest hundredth, if necessary. **471 cm^2**

$$\frac{\text{area of the lateral surface } (x)}{\text{area of whole circle } (\pi r^2)} = \frac{\text{central angle of cone } (y)}{\text{number of degrees in whole circle } (360)}$$

H.O.T. Problems

19, 20. See Focus on Indiana Answer Appendix.

19. **CHALLENGE** The radius of a cone is tripled. The height of the cone remains unchanged. Describe how the net of the cone is affected.

20. **WRITING IN MATH** Describe the similarities and differences between the net of a rectangular prism and the net of a cylinder.

ISTEP+ PRACTICE 7.3.3

21. Which of the following is the correct net of a cone? **C**

A 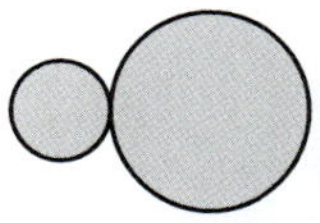

C 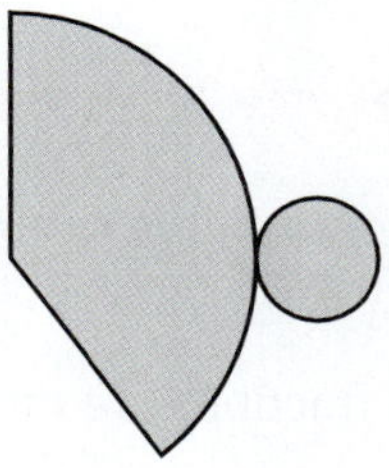

B 

D 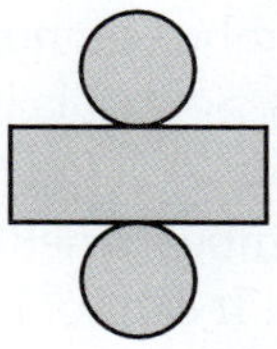

22. Which of the following BEST describes the two-dimensional figures that make up the net of a cylinder with radius r and height h? **J**

F a square with a side length of r units

G one rectangle with a width of h units and a length of $r\pi$ units

H two congruent circles each with a radius of r units

J one rectangle with a width of h units and a length of $2r\pi$ units and two congruent circles each with a radius of r units

4 Assess

Ticket Out the Door Have students design and create a net for a cone with a lateral height that is twice the diameter of its base. Ask students to create a table that includes the following information: the cone's lateral height, the diameter of the cone's base, and the size of the central angle. **See students' work.**

7.

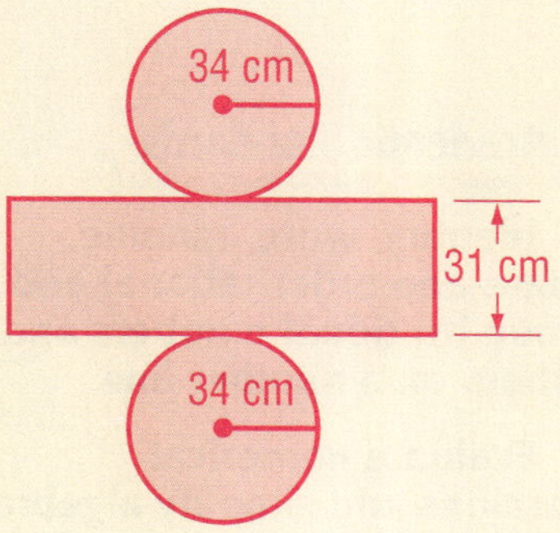

8.

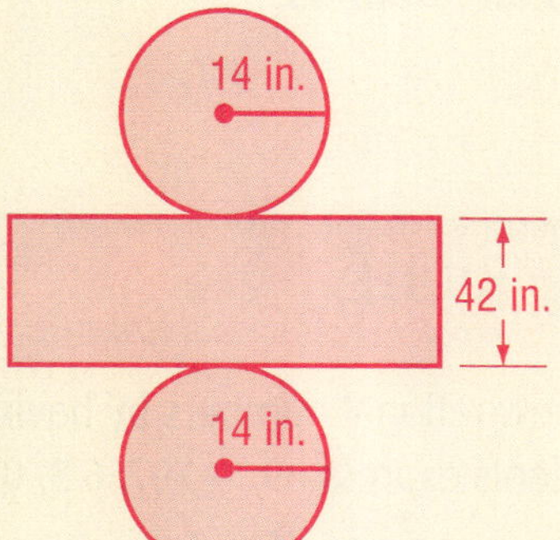

9.

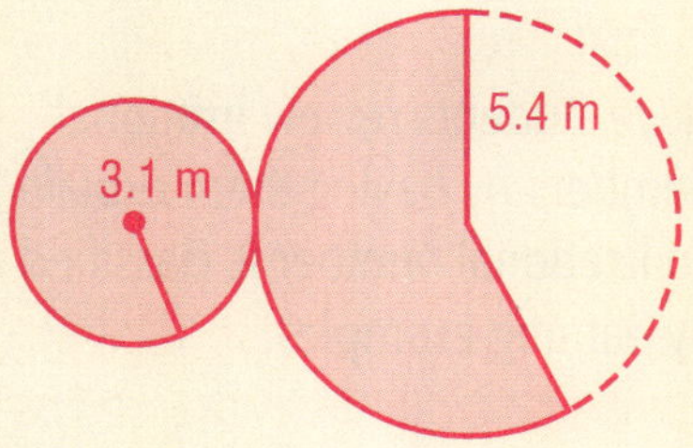

10.

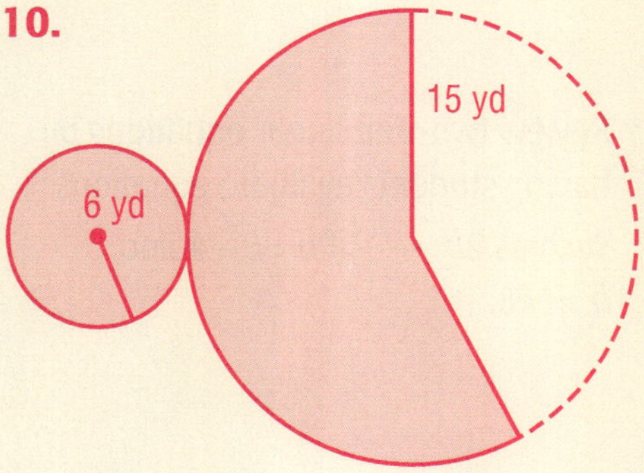

11.

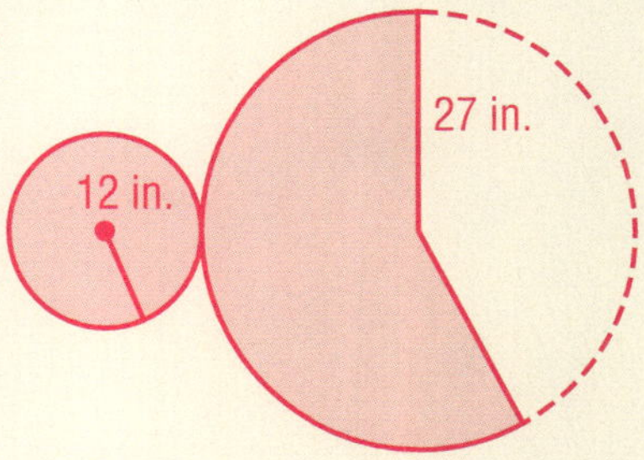

12.

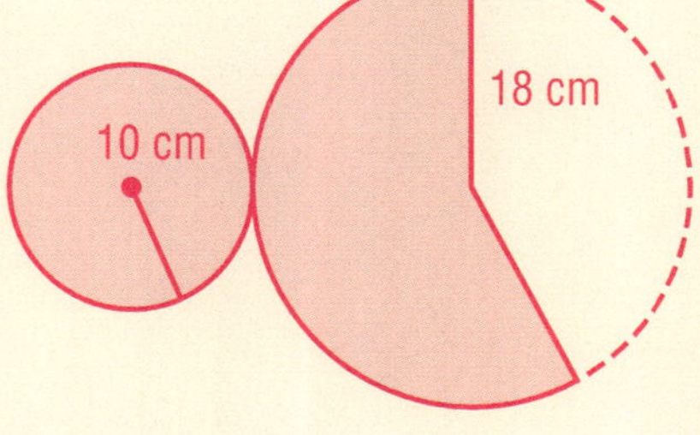

Lesson IN 12 Nets of Cylinders and Cones IN53

13 Lesson Notes

Lesson Planner

Use this lesson after Lesson 12-1 to address standards 7.1.6 and 7.2.3.

Objective

Identify, compare, and order irrational numbers. Evaluate expressions with irrational numbers.

IN Academic Standards

7.1.6 Identify, write, rename, compare and order rational and common irrational numbers and plot them on a number line.

7.2.3 Evaluate numerical expressions and simplify algebraic expressions involving rational and irrational numbers.

1 Focus

- Review rational numbers by having students express 89, −107, 6.3, 0.008, 72%, and $0.1\overline{6}$ as fractions. $\frac{89}{1}$, $-\frac{107}{1}$, $6\frac{3}{10}$, $\frac{8}{1{,}000}$, $\frac{72}{100}$, $\frac{1}{6}$
- Have students review irrational numbers by having them explain how an irrational number is classified and by naming examples. Irrational numbers cannot be expressed as fractions; $\sqrt{3}$, $\sqrt{7}$, π, 0.12122122212…
- Review two-step linear equations by having students evaluate equations such as $2b - \frac{h}{12}$ if $b = -4$ and $h = 48$. −12

13 Irrational Numbers

MAIN IDEA

Identify, compare, and order irrational numbers. Evaluate expressions with irrational numbers.

IN Academic Standards

7.1.6 Identify, write, rename, compare and order rational and common irrational numbers and plot them on a number line.
7.2.3 Evaluate numerical expressions and simplify algebraic expressions involving rational and irrational numbers.

IN Math Online

glencoe.com

GET READY for the Lesson

NUMBER SENSE Consider the two sets of numbers in the table at the right.

Set A	Set B
5.87	$\sqrt{2}$
$\frac{3}{4}$	π
22%	4.58369…
−1	$\sqrt{5}$
$0.\overline{4}$	1.39142…

1. How does the decimal 5.87 in Set A compare with the decimal 1.39142… in Set B?
2. How does the decimal $0.\overline{4}$ in Set A compare with the decimal 1.39142… in Set B?
3. Can any of the numbers in Set A be written as fractions? Justify your response.
4. Can any of the numbers in Set B be written as fractions? Justify your response.

1. Sample answer: The decimal in Set A is a terminating decimal. The decimal in Set B does not terminate.
2. Sample answer: The decimal in Set A is a repeating decimal. The decimal in Set B does not repeat.
3. All of the numbers in Set A can be written as fractions.
4. None of the numbers in Set B can be written as fractions.

Recall from Lesson 4-9 that a *rational number* is a number that can be expressed as a fraction. Fractions, terminating and repeating decimals, percents, and integers are all rational numbers. The numbers in Set A above are all examples of rational numbers.

Recall from Lesson 12-2 that an *irrational number* cannot be expressed as the quotient of two integers. A fraction is the quotient of two integers. In other words, an irrational number cannot be expressed as a fraction where the numerator and denominator are both integers. The numbers in Set B above are all examples of irrational numbers.

EXAMPLES Identify Numbers

State whether each number is *rational* or *irrational*. Justify your response.

1. $\frac{7}{9}$ — All fractions are rational numbers. So, $\frac{7}{9}$ is rational.
2. $\sqrt{3}$ — This number cannot be written as the quotient of two integers. So, $\sqrt{3}$ is irrational.
3. 0.787787778… — This number is neither a terminating nor a repeating decimal. It cannot be written as the quotient of two integers. So, 0.787787778…is irrational.

You can compare and order rational and irrational numbers by plotting the numbers on a number line or by writing each number as a decimal.

EXAMPLES Compare and Order Numbers

Study Tip

Irrational Numbers Even though $\sqrt{15}$ is not a terminating decimal, you can still approximate its graph on a number line.

4 **Replace ● with <, >, or = to make $3\frac{1}{3}$ ● $\sqrt{15}$ a true sentence.**

Express each number as a decimal. Then compare the decimals.

$3\frac{1}{3} = 3.\overline{3}$, or 3.3333333...

$\sqrt{15} \approx 3.872983346$

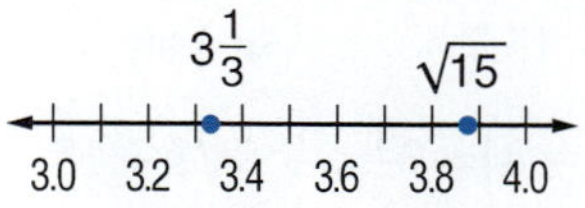

Since $3.\overline{3} < 3.872983346...$, $3\frac{1}{3} < \sqrt{15}$.

5 **Order $8\frac{4}{5}$, $\sqrt{64}$, $8.\overline{3}$, $\sqrt{76}$ from least to greatest.**

Express each number as a decimal. Then order the decimals.

$8\frac{4}{5} = 8.8$

$\sqrt{64} = 8$

$8.\overline{3} = 8.333333333...$

$\sqrt{76} \approx 8.717797887$

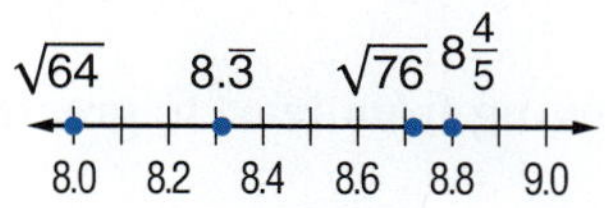

From least to greatest, the order is $\sqrt{64}$, $8.\overline{3}$, $\sqrt{76}$, and $8\frac{4}{5}$.

You can evaluate expressions involving rational and irrational numbers.

EXAMPLE Evaluate Expressions

6 **Evaluate the expression $4y + 3\sqrt{x}$ if $x = 20$ and $y = 0.\overline{5}$. Round any irrational numbers to the nearest hundredth.**

$4y + 3\sqrt{x}$	Write the expression.
$= 4(0.\overline{5}) + 3\sqrt{20}$	Replace x with 20 and y with $0.\overline{5}$.
$= 2.22 + 3\sqrt{20}$	Multiply. Round to the nearest hundredth.
$\approx 2.22 + 3(4.47)$	The square root of 20 is about 4.47.
$\approx 2.22 + 13.41$	Multiply.
≈ 15.63	Add.

2 Teach

Scaffolding Questions

Help students gain practice with comparing and ordering rational numbers before they attempt to do the same with irrational numbers. Model for students how to convert the numbers to decimals before comparing them.

Ask:

- Which is greater, $\frac{5}{2}$ or $\frac{9}{7}$? $\frac{4}{13}$ or $0.\overline{3}$? 56,000 or 5.6×10^3? $\frac{5}{2}$, $0.\overline{3}$, 56,000
- How would you list 13%, 68%, 1.3, and 0.64 in order from least to greatest? 13%, 0.64, 68%, 1.3
- How would you list $\frac{9}{20}$, 2.1×10^{-2}, and $\frac{10}{7}$ in order from greatest to least? $\frac{10}{7}$, $\frac{9}{20}$, 2.1×10^{-2}
- How would you list $\frac{3}{8}$, 4.17×10^{-1}, $\sqrt{9}$, and 30.2 in order from least to greatest? $\frac{3}{8}$, 4.17×10^{-1}, $\sqrt{9}$, 30.2

3 Practice

Use Exercises 1–14 to check for understanding.

Exercises 15–59 are structured so that students practice the same concepts they learned in the lesson.

Have students discuss and complete the Higher Order Thinking problems.

WRITING IN MATH Have students complete Exercise 57 in their Math Journals. You may choose to use this exercise as an optional formative assessment.

Additional Answers

1–4, 15–26. See students' justifications.

1. rational
2. irrational
3. rational
4. rational
15. rational
16. rational
17. irrational
18. rational
19. irrational
20. rational
21. rational
22. irrational
23. rational
24. irrational
25. rational
26. irrational
53. irrational; the product is 5π
54. irrational; the addend is neither a terminating nor a repeating decimal
55. rational; the product is a whole number
56. rational; the quotient is a whole number
57. Sometimes; Sample answer: $\sqrt{25}$ equals 5 which is a rational number but $\sqrt{24}$ equals 4.898979486… which is an irrational number.

You can simplify algebraic expressions involving rational and irrational numbers. Recall the Distributive Property from Lesson 1-8.

Study Tip

Multiplying a Whole Number by a Square Root The product of 5 and $\sqrt{b}$ can be written as $5 \times \sqrt{b}$, $5 \cdot \sqrt{b}$, or $5\sqrt{b}$.

EXAMPLE Simplify Expressions

7 Simplify the algebraic expression $5\left(\frac{2}{3}a + \sqrt{b} - \pi\right)$.

$5\left(\frac{2}{3}a + \sqrt{b} - \pi\right)$	Write the expression.
$= 5\left(\frac{2}{3}a\right) + 5(\sqrt{b}) - 5(\pi)$	Distributive Property
$\approx \frac{10}{3}a + 5\sqrt{b} - 15.7$	Multiply. Round π to 3.14.
$\approx 3\frac{1}{3}a + 5\sqrt{b} - 15.7$	Simplify.

So, $5\left(\frac{2}{3}a + \sqrt{b} - 4\right) \approx 3\frac{1}{3}a + 5\sqrt{b} - 15.7$.

CHECK Your Understanding

1–4. See margin.

Examples 1–3 (p. IN49)

State whether each number is *rational* or *irrational*. Justify your response.

1. -39.2
2. $\sqrt{14}$
3. $-\frac{4}{15}$
4. $\sqrt{81}$

Example 4 (p. IN55)

Replace each ● with <, >, or = to make a true statement. Use a number line if necessary.

5. π ● $3\frac{1}{3}$ **<**
6. $1\frac{1}{4}$ ● $\sqrt{2}$ **<**
7. $\sqrt{40}$ ● 6.25 **>**
8. $7\frac{3}{8}$ ● 7.375 **=**

Example 5 (p. IN55)

Order each of the following from least to greatest. Use a number line if necessary.

9. $\frac{1}{7}, \sqrt{7}, -1.7, \frac{7}{10}$ **$-1.7, \frac{1}{7}, \frac{7}{10}, \sqrt{7}$**
10. $0.\overline{5}, \sqrt{5}, \frac{2}{3}, \frac{3}{5}$ **$0.\overline{5}, \frac{3}{5}, \frac{2}{3}, \sqrt{5}$**

Example 6 (p. IN55)

Evaluate each expression if $a = 4$ and $b = \pi$. Round any irrational numbers to the nearest hundredth.

11. $-6b + \sqrt{a}$ **−16.84**
12. $b\sqrt{7} - 2a$ **0.32**

Example 7 (p. IN56)

Simplify each algebraic expression.

13. $10(r + \sqrt{s} + t)$ **$10r + 10\sqrt{s} + 10t$**
14. $j(k + \sqrt{7})$ **$jk + j\sqrt{7}$**

Practice and Problem Solving

15–26. See margin.

HOMEWORK HELP

For Exercises	See Examples
15–26	1–3
27–38	4, 5
39–46	6, 7

State whether each number is rational or irrational. Justify your response.

15. $\sqrt{9}$
16. -1.05
17. $\sqrt{41}$
18. 42.875
19. $\sqrt{27}$
20. $\sqrt{25}$
21. $23.44444\ldots$
22. $3.910742382\ldots$
23. $6.\overline{71}$
24. $\sqrt{30}$
25. $\sqrt{144}$
26. π

Replace each ● with <, >, or = to make a true statement. Use a number line if necessary. **27. > 28. > 29. = 30. > 31. <**

27. $6\frac{1}{6}$ ● 6.16
28. $4\frac{1}{4}$ ● $\sqrt{15}$
29. $\sqrt{121}$ ● 11
30. $5\frac{2}{9}$ ● 5.22
31. $\sqrt{48}$ ● $7\frac{2}{3}$
32. π ● $\sqrt{\pi}$ **>**
33. $3\frac{3}{4}$ ● $\sqrt{13}$ **>**
34. $\sqrt{400}$ ● 20 **=**

Order each of the following from least to greatest. Use a number line if necessary.

35. $\frac{1}{10}, \sqrt{10}, 0.15, \frac{1}{15}$ **35. $\frac{1}{15}, \frac{1}{10}, 0.15, \sqrt{10}$**
36. $0.\overline{4}, \sqrt{4}, \frac{3}{4}, \frac{1}{4}$ **$\frac{1}{4}, 0.\overline{4}, \frac{3}{4}, \sqrt{4}$**
37. $\frac{1}{6}, \sqrt{6}, 5.6, \frac{5}{6}$ **37. $\frac{1}{6}, \frac{5}{6}, \sqrt{6}, 5.6$**
38. $0.\overline{9}, \sqrt{8}, \frac{4}{5}, \frac{8}{9}$ **$\frac{4}{5}, \frac{8}{9}, 0.\overline{9}, \sqrt{8}$**

Evaluate each expression if $g = \sqrt{2}$ and $h = -1.5$. Round any irrational numbers to the nearest hundredth.

39. $7h - g$ **−11.91**
40. $2g + 3h$ **−1.67**
41. $\sqrt{3} \times h + g$ **−1.18**
42. $g \times h$ **−2.12**
43. $5g - h$ **8.57**
44. g^2 **2**

Simplify each algebraic expression.

45. $\sqrt{2}\,(w + y - z)$ **45. $\sqrt{2}w + \sqrt{2}y - \sqrt{2}z$**
46. $\frac{1}{4}\left(\frac{3}{5}m + \sqrt{n}\right)$ **46. $\frac{3}{20}m + \frac{1}{4}\sqrt{n}$**
47. $-7(c + \sqrt{d} + 1)$ **47. $-7c - 7\sqrt{d} - 7$**
48. $\pi(p + q)$ **$\pi p + \pi q$**
49. $\sqrt{x}(\sqrt{x} + 1)$ **$x + \sqrt{x}$**
50. $\frac{2}{3}(\sqrt{a} + b)$ **$\frac{2}{3}\sqrt{a} + \frac{2}{3}b$**

H.O.T. Problems

51. **OPEN ENDED** Find a rational number and an irrational number that are each between 4 and 5. Include the decimal approximation of the irrational number to the nearest hundredth. **51. Sample answer: 4.5 and $\sqrt{17} \approx 4.12$**

52. **REASONING** The area of a square is 40 square meters. Is the length of a side of the square a rational or irrational number? Explain. **Irrational; Sample answer: The number $\sqrt{40}$ cannot be written as the quotient of two integers.**

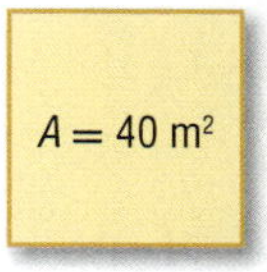

CHALLENGE Tell whether each of the following is a rational or irrational number. Justify your response. **53–56. See margin.**

53. $5 \times \pi$
54. $\sqrt{8} + \sqrt{8}$
55. $\sqrt{50} \times \sqrt{50}$
56. $\sqrt{6} \div \sqrt{6}$

57. **WRITING IN MATH** Determine whether the following statement is *always*, *sometimes*, or *never* true. Explain. **See margin.**
All square roots are irrational numbers.

ISTEP+ PRACTICE 7.1.6, 7.2.3

58. Which of the following expressions is the GREATEST: $\sqrt{35}$, $5\frac{4}{5}$, 5.92, or $\sqrt{36}$? **A**
A $\sqrt{36}$
B $\sqrt{35}$
C 5.92
D $5\frac{4}{5}$

59. Which of the following expressions is equivalent to $y\sqrt{x}$ if $x = 49$ and $y = \pi$? **G**
F $\sqrt{7}\pi$
G 7π
H 14π
J 49π

4 Assess

Ticket Out the Door Explain what it means to simplify an algebraic equation. Support your answer with an example of an equation that contains an irrational number. Sample answer: When simplifying an algebraic equation, you are trying to write the equation in the most compact way possible. Usually this involves collecting like terms, such as $2x$ and $-x$ or $5y^2$ and $2y^2$. The Distributive Property can be applied when simplifying equations, as you will see in the following example.

$\sqrt{8} + \pi(4g - 9g + 5.2) + g$

$= \sqrt{8} + \pi(4g) - \pi(9g) + \pi(5.2) + g$

$\approx \sqrt{8} + 12.56g - 28.26g + 16.33 + g$

$\approx \sqrt{8} - 14.7g + 16.33$

Page IN27, Lesson IN 6

20.

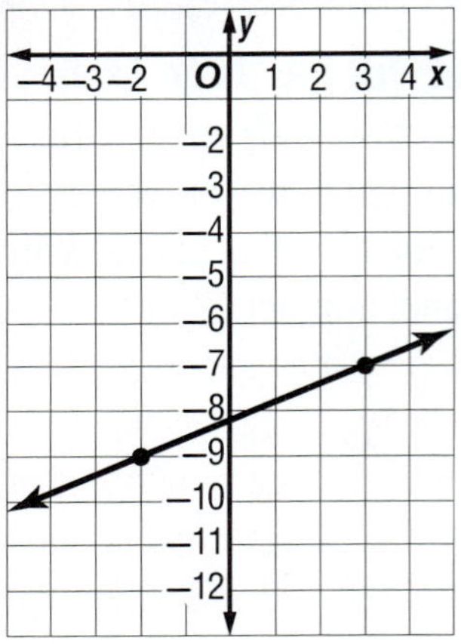

21.

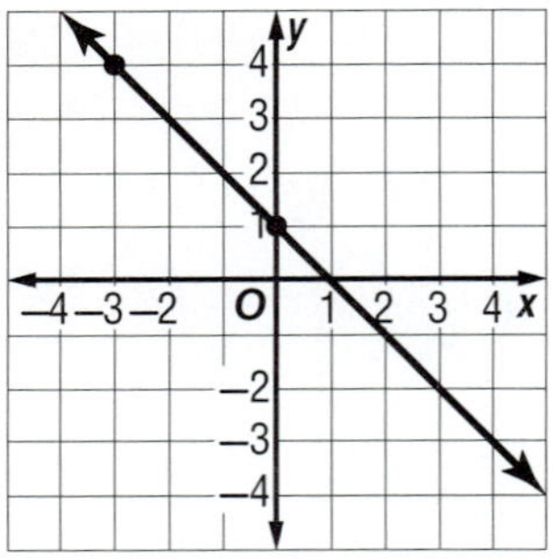

22. $\frac{2}{3}$

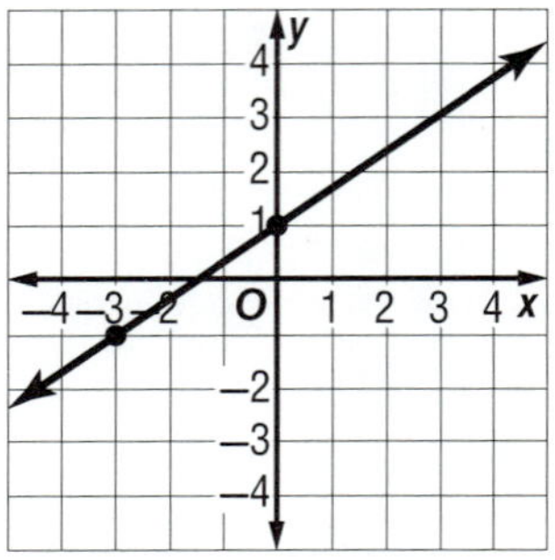

23. $-\frac{5}{2}$

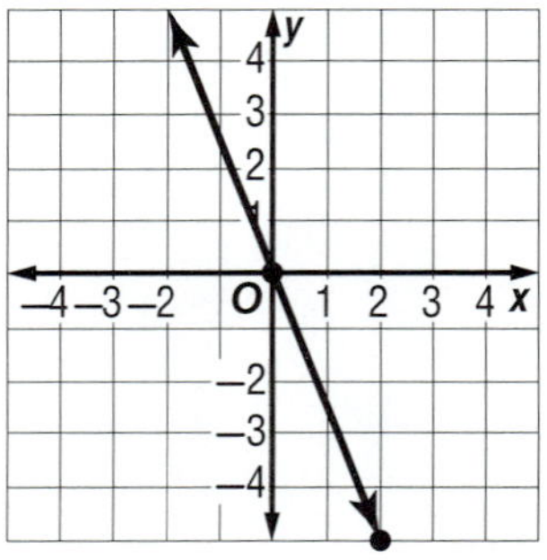

24. −1

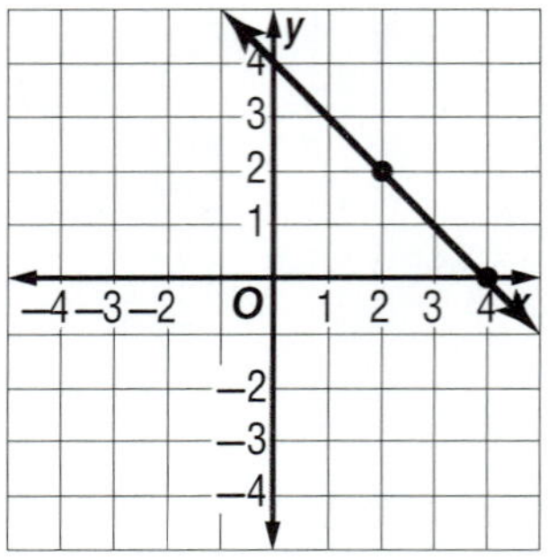

25. $-\frac{3}{2}$

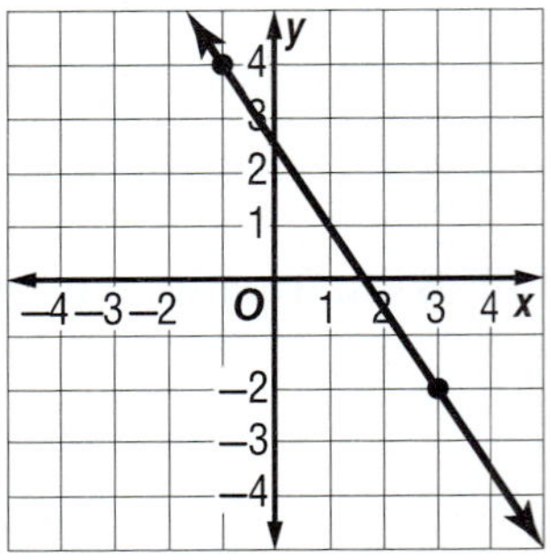

26. $\frac{1}{4}$

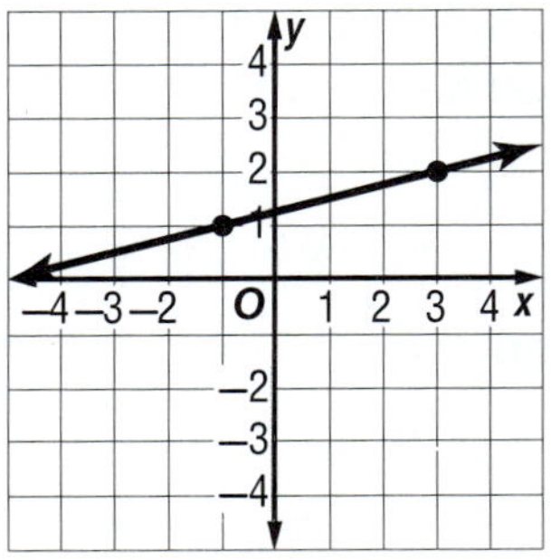

27. $\frac{1}{2}$

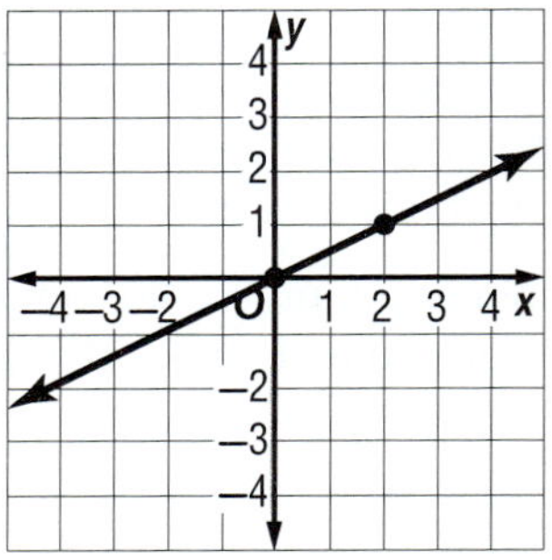

28. $\frac{1}{4}$

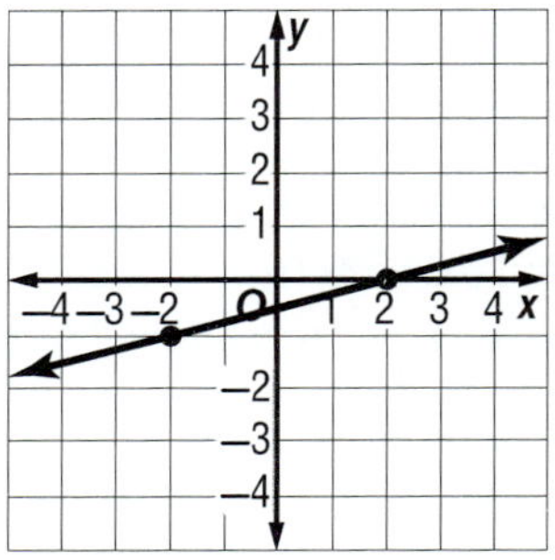

29. $-\frac{7}{3}$

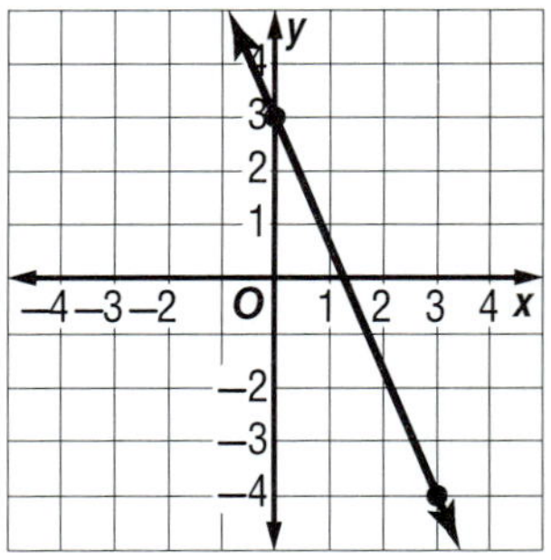

30. 20 bracelets

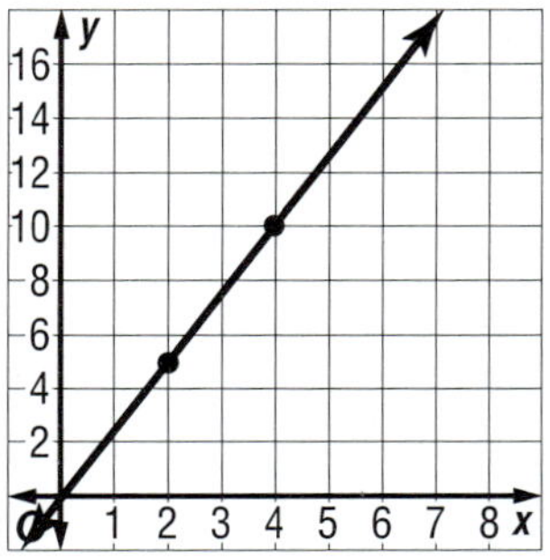

31. $4

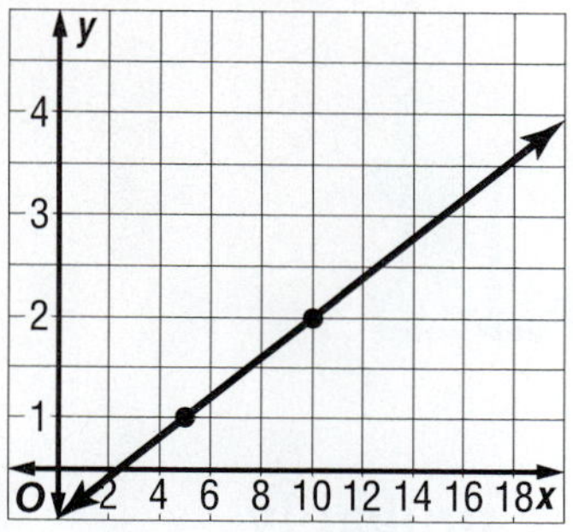

Page IN53, Lesson IN 12

13.

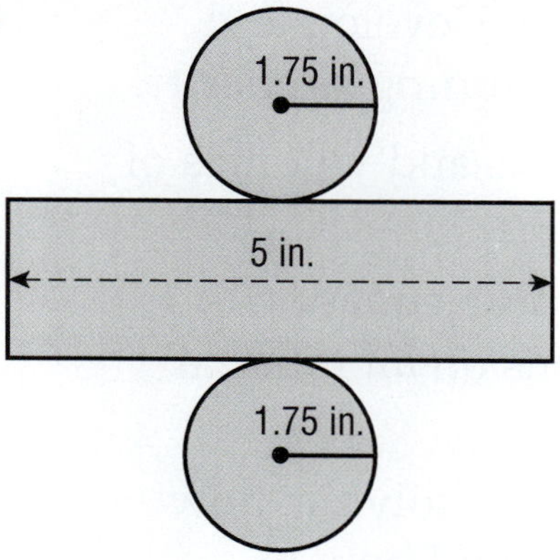

16.

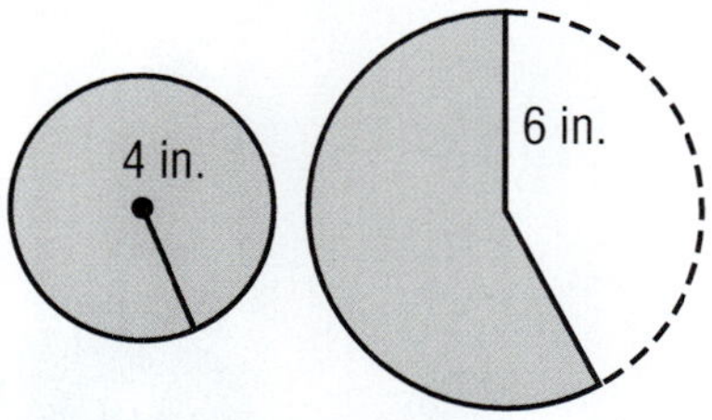

19. Sample answer: If the radius of a cone is tripled, the full circle will become three times larger. The circle that is used for the central angle will remain unchanged.

20. Sample answer: Both nets include two-dimensional figures that have rectangles as part of their nets. The difference between the two is that the rectangular prism has a base of a rectangle or square and the cylinder has a base of a circle.

To the Student

As you gear up to study mathematics, you are probably wondering, "What will I learn this year?" You will focus on these three areas.

- **Number and Operations, Algebra, and Geometry:** Develop and apply an understanding of proportions, including similarity.
- **Measurement and Geometry:** Find surface areas and volumes of three-dimensional shapes.
- **Number and Operations and Algebra:** Solve linear equations and deepen an understanding of operations on all rational numbers.

Along the way, you'll learn more about problem solving, how to use the tools and language of mathematics, and how to THINK mathematically.

How to Use Your Math Book

Have you ever been in class and not understood all of what was being presented? Or, you understood everything in class, but got stuck on how to solve some of the homework problems? Don't worry. You can find answers in your math book!

- **Read** the **MAIN IDEA** at the beginning of the lesson.
- **Find** the **New Vocabulary** words, **highlighted in yellow**, and read their definitions.
- **Review** the **EXAMPLE** problems, solved step-by-step, to remind you of the day's material.
- **Refer** to the **HOMEWORK HELP** boxes that show you which examples may help with your homework problems.
- **Go** to **IN Math Online** where you can find extra examples to coach you through difficult problems.
- **Review** the notes you've taken on your **FOLDABLES™**.
- **Find** the answers to odd-numbered problems in the back of the book. Use them to see if you are solving the problems correctly.

Scavenger Hunt

Let's Get Started

Use the Scavenger Hunt below to learn where things are located in each chapter.

1. What is the title of Chapter 1? **Introduction to Algebra and Functions**
2. How can you tell what you'll learn in Lesson 1-1? **the main idea**
3. Sometimes you may ask, "When am I ever going to use this?" Name a situation that uses the concepts from Lesson 1-2. **computing power in a computer chip**
4. In the margin of Lesson 1-2, there is a Vocabulary Link. What can you learn from that feature? **the everyday use of a word and its corresponding math use**
5. What is the key concept presented in Lesson 1-3? **squares and square roots**
6. How many examples are presented in Lesson 1-3? **5**
7. What is the title of the feature in Lesson 1-3 that tells you how to read square roots? **Reading Math**
8. What is the Web address where you could find extra examples? **www.glencoe.com**
9. Suppose you're doing your homework on page 40 and you get stuck on Exercise 18. Where could you find help? **Example 3**
10. What problem-solving strategy is presented in the Problem-Solving Investigation in Lesson 1-5? **guess and check**
11. List the new vocabulary words that are presented in Lesson 1-7. **equation, solution, solving an equation, defining the variable**
12. What is the web address that would allow you to take a self-check quiz to be sure you understand the lesson? **www.glencoe.com**
13. There is a Real-World Career mentioned in Lesson 1-10. What is it? **botanist**
14. On what pages will you find the Study Guide and Review for Chapter 1? **pages 70–74**
15. Suppose you can't figure out how to do Exercise 25 in the Study Guide and Review on page 72. Where could you find help? **pages 34–37**

Start Smart

Let's Review!

The Statue of Liberty
on the Fourth of July

Start Smart

Begin the year with the lessons found in the **Start Smart** section. These lessons help students get ready for the coming year by reviewing and reinforcing skills and concepts they learned in the previous grade. The **Start Smart** lessons also prepare students for skills and concepts they will need for success in the upcoming year.

START SMART 1

Lesson Notes

1 Focus

Identify and use the steps in the four-step problem-solving plan.

2 Teach

Read and discuss the introduction.

- Lead a discussion about farms and complete a 4-column table. The first column should contain information that is known. Label this column "U" for "understand."
- **What do we know about this problem? What do we need to find?** List students' responses in the "U" column.
- The second column should contain a plan for how to go about solving the problem. Label this column "P" for "plan."
- **What will we do to solve the problem? What operation or strategy will we use?** List students' responses in the "P" column.
- The third column should contain the information used to solve the problem. Label this column "S" for "solve."
- **How do we execute the plan? What is the answer?** List students' responses in the "S" column.
- The fourth column should give an explanation of why the solution is reasonable. Label this column "C" for "check."
- **Does our answer make sense? Do we need to solve the problem in a different way?** List students' responses in the "C" column.

Start Smart 1 A Plan for Problem Solving

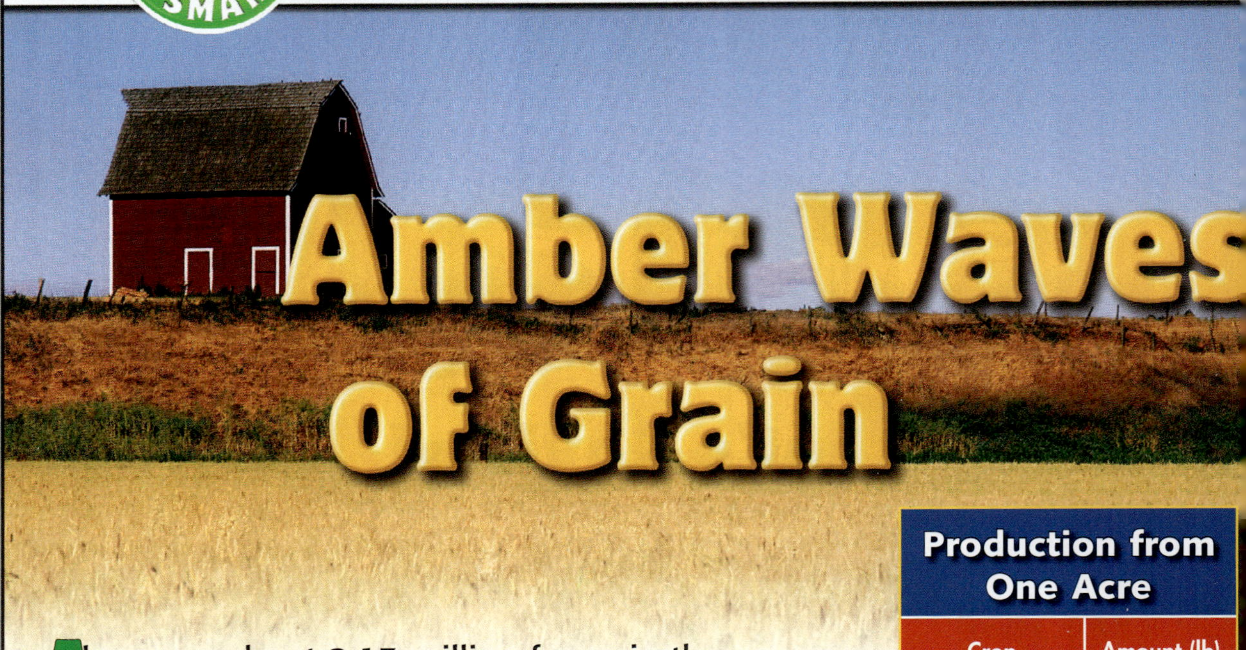

Amber Waves of Grain

There are about 2.13 million farms in the United States. The average size of each farm is about 440 acres. One acre is about the size of a football field, without the end zones. The table shows the number of pounds of each crop that one acre will produce in a season.

Production from One Acre

Crop	Amount (lb)
Cotton	725
Lettuce	35,000
Potatoes	36,700
Rice	5,500
Strawberries	42,800
Sweet Corn	11,600
Wheat	2,880

Source: American Farm Bureau

How many more pounds of rice can one acre produce in a season than wheat?

You can use the four-step problem-solving plan to solve many kinds of problems. The four steps are Understand, Plan, Solve, and Check.

Understand

- Read the problem carefully.
- What facts do you know?
- What do you need to find?

You know the number of pounds of rice and wheat produced by each acre. You need to find how many more pounds of rice the average farm produces in a season than wheat.

Plan

- **How do the facts relate to each other?**
- **Plan a strategy to solve the problem.**

One acre produces 5,500 pounds of rice or 2,880 pounds of wheat. Subtract 2,880 from 5,500.

Solve

- **Use your plan to solve the problem.**

$$\begin{array}{r} {}^{4}\,{}^{14}{}^{10} \\ \not{5},\not{5}\not{0}0 \\ -2,880 \\ \hline 2,620 \end{array}$$

In one season, one acre can produce 2,620 more pounds of rice than wheat.

Check

- **Look back at the problem.**
- **Does your answer make sense?**
- **If not, solve the problem another way.**

Estimate. Round 5,500 to 6,000 and 2,880 to 3,000.
6,000 – 3,000 = 3,000

Since 3,000 is close to 2,620, the answer is reasonable.

CHECK Your Understanding

1. One pound of wheat can make 0.98 pound of whole-wheat flour but only 0.74 pound of refined flour. How many more pounds of whole wheat flour could one acre of wheat make than refined flour? **691.2 lb flour**

2. WRITING IN MATH How many more pounds of rice can the average-size farm in the United States produce in one season than wheat? Explain. **1,152,800 pounds; You know that one acre can produce 2,620 more pounds than wheat. Multiply 2,620 by 440 to find the number of pounds the average-size farm can produce in one season.**

3 Practice

Using the Exercises

Exercise 1 Remind students that adding or subtracting decimals requires aligning the decimal.

Writing in Math Remind students that in a process, steps are done in order to complete a task. They should list and describe the four steps in the correct order.

4 Assess

Discuss the **More FUN Facts**. Have students work in groups and create their own word problems using the statistics given. Have groups trade problems and follow the four-step problem-solving plan to solve the problems.

More FUN Facts

- In 1935, the number of farms in the United States peaked with 7 million farms.
- As of 2006, there were approximately 2.1 million farms in the United States.
- The largest number of farms raise cattle for beef; 27% of all American farms are cattle ranches.
- The most prevalent crop is hay; 7.9% of all farms are hay farms.
- Corn is grown by 5.3% of the farms in our country.

Start Smart 5

Lesson Notes

1 Focus

Compare, order, and find sums and differences of decimals.

2 Teach

Adding and Subtracting Decimals

- Computing and estimating with decimals is an important life skill, as students will deal with money on a daily basis.

Scaffolding Questions

Use the information in the table on page 7 regarding lap speeds to answer the following questions.

Ask:

- Which year had the fastest lap speed: 2006 or 2007? 2007
- Which is the fastest lap speed on record at the Indianapolis 500? 229.188 mph
- How much faster is the fastest lap speed than the slowest lap speed in the recorded data? 10.787 mph

Reinforcement of 6.1.1 Compare, order, and represent on a number line positive and negative integers, fractions, decimals (to hundredths), and mixed numbers.

Number and Operations

Start Your Engines

The Indianapolis 500 consists of 200 laps covering a total distance of 500 miles. Each lap covers 2.5 miles. The table shows the winners of the Indianapolis 500 and their average speeds in miles per hour from 2000 to 2007.

Winners of the Indianapolis 500 2000–2007

Year	Winner	Average Speed (mph)
2000	Juan Montoya	167.607
2001	Helio Castroneves	153.601
2002	Helio Castroneves	166.499
2003	Gil de Ferran	156.291
2004	Buddy Rice	138.518
2005	Dan Wheldon	157.603
2006	Sam Hornish, Jr.	157.085
2007	Dario Franchitti	151.774

Source: ESPN

CHECK Your Understanding — Compare and Order Decimals

When comparing and ordering decimals, first line up the decimal points. Then compare the digits in each place to order the amounts.

Use the information in the table on page 6 to answer each question.

1. Which of the Indianapolis 500 winners listed in the table had the greatest average speed? the least? **Juan Montoya; Buddy Rice**
2. Between Dan Wheldon and Gil de Ferran, who had the lower average speed? **Gil de Ferran**
3. List the Indianapolis 500 winners in order from least to greatest average speed. **Buddy Rice, Dario Franchitti, Helio Castroneves (2001), Gil de Ferran, Sam Hornish Jr., Dan Wheldon, Helio Castroneves (2002), Juan Montoya**

CHECK Your Understanding — Subtract Decimals

When subtracting decimals, first line up the decimal points. Then subtract as with whole numbers and place the decimal point in the answer.

Use the table on page 6 to answer each question.

4. How much greater was the average speed in 2000 than in 2007? **15.833 mph**
5. How much greater was the average speed in 2007 than in 2004? **13.256 mph**
6. How much greater was the average speed in 2006 than in 2007? **5.311 mph**
7. **WRITING IN MATH** The table shows the fastest lap speeds on record for the Indianapolis 500 from 2002 to 2007. Use the information to write and solve a real-world problem about the fastest lap speeds. **Sample answer: How much greater was the fastest lap speed in 2003 than the fastest lap speed in 2007? 5.768 mph**

Year	Fastest Lap Speed (mph)
2002	226.499
2003	229.188
2004	218.401
2005	228.102
2006	221.251
2007	223.420

More FUN Facts

- The Indianapolis 500 held its inaugural race in 1911. The total purse winnings went to Ray Harroun's team for the amount of $27,550. Dario Franchitti's team won a total purse amount of $10,668,815 in 2007.
- The youngest driver to ever win the Indy 500 was Troy Ruttman at age 22 in 1952.
- The oldest driver to ever win the Indy 500 was Al Unser at age 47 in 1987.
- Janet Guthrie was the first woman to qualify for the race in 1977. Danica Patrick was the first woman to ever lead the race (for 19 laps), and held the highest female finish of 4th place in 2005.

3 Practice

Using the Exercises

Exercises 1 through 3 Remind students that when comparing and ordering decimals, they may have to inspect numerous place values.

Exercises 4 through 6 Emphasize the importance of properly aligning the decimal before performing the operation.

Writing in Math Have students work in groups to time themselves walking a measured distance. Students should determine the fastest and slowest time. Have them order their group times from least to greatest.

4 Assess

- Ask several questions using the data from fastest lap speeds on page 7. Invite volunteers to show on the board how to answer each question.
- Using the average speed data on page 6, have students figure average times for the entire race for each driver.
- Have students work in pairs to make up several word problems using the information in the **More FUN Facts**.

Lesson Notes

1 Focus

Write and evaluate algebraic expressions to represent data given in a table.

2 Teach

Writing Expressions

- Remind students that when writing an expression, a variable should be used to represent the unknown value.
- Encourage students to look for key words to indicate the operation to be represented in the expression. Common key words are "more than," "times," "less than," and "divided by."

Scaffolding Questions

Write the following on the board:

The wingspan of a Boeing F/A-18 Hornet is 16 feet less than its length.

Ask:

- What variable can be used to represent the length of the Boeing F/A-18 Hornet? ℓ
- Write an expression that could be used to represent the Boeing F/A-18 Hornet's wingspan. $\ell - 16$
- If the Boeing F/A-18 Hornet has a length of 56 feet, evaluate the expression to find its wingspan. 40 ft

Reinforcement of 6.2.1 Write and solve one-step linear equations and inequalities in one variable.

Start Smart 3 Algebra

The Sky's the Limit

Since 1946, the Blue Angels have represented the United States Navy in flight demonstrations around the country. There are six jets in the formation during each demonstration. The pilots perform approximately 30 maneuvers during a demonstration that lasts for approximately 1 hour 15 minutes. The table shows several speeds of the Boeing F/A-18 Hornet jets used in the demonstration.

Boeing F/A-18 Hornet	Speed (mph)
Slowest Cruising Speed	120
Sneak Pass Maneuver	700
Top Speed	1,400

CHECK Your Understanding

Variables and Equations

Use the table on page 8 to answer the following questions.

1. The average speed of the Boeing F/A-18 Hornet Jet is 200 miles per hour less than its top speed. If s represents its top speed, write an expression that represents its average speed. **$s - 200$**

2. Evaluate the expression you wrote in Exercise 1. What is the average speed of the Boeing F/A-18 Hornet jet? **1,200 miles per hour**

3. The equation $d = rt$ represents the distance d in miles that the jet can travel at its average speed of r miles per hour in h hours. Use your answer from Exercise 2 to find the distance the jet can travel in 2 hours. **2,400 miles**

4. The jets are transported by the C-130 Hercules aircraft *Fat Albert* which has an average speed 230 more miles per hour than the jet's slowest cruising speed. Write an equation that could be used to represent *Fat Albert's* average speed s. **$s = 230 + 120$**

5. Evaluate the expression you wrote in Exercise 4. What is *Fat Albert's* average speed? **$s = 350$ miles per hour**

For Exercises 6 and 7, use the table and the information below.

The table shows the heights of two of the most famous maneuvers of the Blue Angels.

6. The maximum rate of climb for the Boeing F/A-18 Hornet jet is 30,000 feet per minute. How long would it take the jet to climb 15,000 feet? **0.5 min**

7. WRITING IN MATH Write a real-world problem to represent the relationship between the heights of a Sneak Pass and a Vertical Roll. Then solve the equation. **Sample answer: How many times greater is the height of Vertical Roll than Sneak Pass? $50x = 15{,}000$; $x = 300$**

Maneuver	Height (ft)
Sneak Pass	50
Vertical Roll	15,000

3 Practice

Using the Exercises

Exercises 1 through 5 Emphasize the importance of paying close attention to the order in which the variable and constants should occur in the expression.

Exercise 6 Suggest students set up a proportion to solve this problem.

Writing in Math Consolidate all of the class's problems onto a worksheet and have the students complete it as an assignment.

4 Assess

- Ask several questions using the data from the maneuver table on page 9. For example, what expression can be used to represent the difference in heights? Invite volunteers to come to the front of the room and formulate questions to ask the students regarding the table.
- Have students work in pairs to make up several word problems using the information in **More FUN Facts**.

More FUN Facts

- The Blue Angels have been flying since 1946. As of 2007, they have performed for 427 million spectators.
- There have been eight different types of aircraft flown throughout the history of the Blue Angels.
- The fleet currently consists of 10 single-seat F/A–18 A Hornets and 2 two-seat F/A–18 B Hornets.
- Each plane in the fleet cost approximately $21,000,000.00.
- An F/A–18 weighs approximately 24,500 pounds, which is over 12 tons.

START SMART 4

Lesson Notes

1 Focus

Estimate angle measures and use a protractor to measure an angle precisely.

2 Teach

Scaffolding Questions

Have students observe the architecture of their classroom and objects around the room. Record the students' responses on the board.

Ask:

- Where might you observe a right angle in the classroom? See students' work.
- Do you see an angle that could be estimated at over 100°? Explain. See students' work.
- Can you think of some architectural buildings that would have a good display of common angles? See students' work.

Reinforcement of 6.3.1 Identify, draw and use the properties of vertical, adjacent, complementary, and supplementary angles, and properties of triangles and quadrilaterals, to solve problems involving a missing angle.

START SMART 4 Geometry

What's Your Angle?

Geometric angles are used in architectural design. The Seattle Central Library in Seattle, Washington, has many different geometric angles in its design. Several of those angles are outlined in different colors in the photo above.

CHECK Your Understanding **Estimate Angle Measures**

Use the photo of the Seattle Central Library to estimate the measure of each of the following angles.

1. the angle outlined in red Sample answer: 120°

2. the angle outlined in green Sample answer: 30°

3. the angle outlined in yellow Sample answer: 90°

4. the angle outlined in purple Sample answer: 60°

CHECK Your Understanding — Measure Angles

The photo below is of the interior of the Denver Art Museum in Denver, Colorado. Use a protractor to measure each of the following angles.

5. the angle outlined in blue **Sample answer: 60°**

6. the measure of the angle outlined in yellow **Sample answer: 120°**

7. the angle outlined in green **Sample answer: 120°**

8. the angle outlined in red **Sample answer: 75°**

9. Use the Internet or another source to find a photo that uses geometric angles in art or architecture. Estimate the measure of several angles in the photo. Then use a protractor to measure the angles. Compare to your estimates. **See students' work.**

10. WRITING IN MATH Write a few sentences explaining how to use a protractor to find the measure of an angle.
Sample answer: Place the center point of the protractor's base on the vertex of the angle. Align the straight side with the base of the angle so that the marker for 0° is on that side. Use the scale that begins with 0° on the angle's base. Read where the other side of the angle crosses this scale.

3 Teach

Using the Exercises

Exercises 1 through 4 Remind students that when they estimate the measure of an angle, they should use certain reference angles. Knowing what a 90° angle and a 180° straight angle look like will help narrow down a reasonable estimation.

Exercises 5 through 8 Review the rules for using a protractor. Students should be cautious to read the correct measurement line and line up the sides of the angle carefully.

Exercise 9 Have students print their examples and mark the angles with colored pencils or markers.

Writing in Math Have students pretend they are writing the instructions for using a protractor for a third-grade class. They should assume the students they are writing for have never seen a protractor.

4 Assess

- Ask several questions regarding the photo of the Denver Art Museum on p. 11. Allow students to play a game of "I Spy" and give clues to see if other students can see the same relationships.
- After discussing **More FUN Facts**, have students work with a partner to measure their height and the height of their navel. Students should divide their height by the height of their navel and compare to the Golden Ratio.

More FUN Facts

- Geometry has been in use in architectural buildings since the beginning of history. Pythagoras (560–480 B.C.) was especially interested in the Golden Ratio. (1.618... : 1).
- The Parthenon in Athens, Greece, is one of the best examples of a mathematical approach to building. The Golden Rectangle, which is a rectangle with a proportion of length to width equal to the Golden Ratio, is used throughout the Parthenon.
- Pythagoras proved that many human body parts are built upon the Golden Ratio. In general, a person's height compared to the height of their navel is very close to the Golden Ratio.

START SMART 5

Lesson Notes

1 Focus

Convert and determine reasonableness of measurements of length within the customary system

2 Teach

Converting Units

- Emphasize that when changing from a smaller unit to a larger unit, students should use division. When changing from a larger unit to a smaller unit, the students should use multiplication.
- Remind students to make sure they check to see if their solution is reasonable.

Scaffolding Questions

Use the table on page 12 for students to answer the following questions.

Ask:

- What unit of length is used in the table? feet
- What is the height of the head? 60 ft
- How many inches are in one foot? 12 in.
- To find the height of the head in inches, would you multiply or divide by 12? Explain. Multiply; to convert from a larger unit to a smaller unit, you need to multiply.
- What is the height of the head in inches? 720 in.

START SMART 5 Measurement

Dynamite Dimensions!

Mount Rushmore, located in the Black Hills of South Dakota, is a tribute to four American presidents: George Washington, Thomas Jefferson, Theodore Roosevelt, and Abraham Lincoln. More than 90% of the monument was carved by dynamite! The table gives the measurements of several of the facial features for one of the presidents.

Feature	Measurement (ft)
head	60 (height)
nose	20 (height)
mouth	18 (length)
eye	11 (length)

Source: Mount Rushmore National Monument

Standard units of measurement are most commonly used in the United States. They include *inch, foot, yard,* and *mile.*

✓ CHECK Your Understanding

Use Appropriate Units

1. How many inches are in one foot? How many feet are in one yard? **12 in.; 3 ft**

2. Which is a more reasonable estimate for the height in yards of each president's head on Mount Rushmore: 20 yards or 180 yards? Justify your response. **20 yd; Sample answer: Yards are a larger unit of measurement than feet. The number of yards in 60 feet will be smaller than 60.**

3. How tall or long is each presidential feature in yards? Round to the nearest tenth if necessary. **head: 20 yd; nose: 6.7 yd; mouth: 6 yd; eye: 3.7**

4. Which is a more reasonable estimate for the length in inches of each president's eye on Mount Rushmore: 1 inch or 120 inches? Justify your response. **120 in.; Sample answer: Inches are a smaller unit of measurement than feet. The number of inches in 11 feet will be larger than 11.**

5. How tall or long is each presidential feature in inches? Round to the nearest tenth if necessary. **head: 720 in.; nose: 240 in.; mouth: 216 in.; eye: 132 in.**

6. Mount Rushmore is about 6,000 feet above sea level. Which is a more reasonable estimate for this height: about 2,000 yards or about 18,000 yards? Justify your response. **about 2,000 yd; Sample answer: Yards are a larger unit of measurement than feet. The number of yards in 6,000 feet will be smaller than 6,000.**

7. **WRITING IN MATH** The photo below shows the Stone Mountain Confederate Memorial Carving in Atlanta, Georgia. The carving measures 90 feet by 190 feet. Explain how to find the carving's dimensions in yards. Then find the carving's dimensions in yards, rounding to the nearest tenth if necessary.
Sample answer: There are 3 feet in 1 yard. Divide 90 by 3 to get 30. Then divide 190 by 3 to get 63.3, rounded to the nearest tenth. The carving's dimensions in yards are 30 ft by 63.3 ft.

Start Smart 13

3 Practice

Using the Exercises

Exercise 1 You may want to have students investigate a yardstick to answer this question.

Exercises 2 through 6 Have students measure something large, such as the classroom door or a wall in inches to remind them to use reasonable units.

Writing in Math Have students create a table that has one column with dimensions in feet and the second column with dimensions in yards.

4 Assess

- Ask several questions regarding the photo of the carving on p. 13. Have students synthesize what type of carving they would like to create and what size it would be.
- Have students work in pairs to design a large carving of a common classroom object and give the new dimensions of the larger object.

More FUN Facts

- The Iwo Jima Memorial in Washington, D.C., is a bronze sculpture of a photograph taken after the Battle of Iwo Jima during World War II.
- Felix DeWeldon was so moved by the picture that within 72 hours he had a completed clay sculpture.
- Hundreds of artisans worked 8 years to create the Iwo Jima Memorial.
- Each figure is 32 feet high. The pole is 60 feet long.
- Standing on its pedestal, the monument stands 78 feet high, the tallest bronze statue in the world.

START SMART 6

Lesson Notes

1 Focus

Analyze data in a table and arrange the data in a pictograph.

2 Teach

Pictographs

- Emphasize to students that reading pictographs is not an exact science. Estimating a partial picture cannot be exact.

Scaffolding Questions

Make a table with 4 rows and 3 columns. Label the rows as 1–3, 4–6, 7–9, and more than 9. Label the columns as "number of vowels," "frequency," and "pictograph." Poll the students by asking them how many vowels they have in their full names (first, middle, and last). In the frequency column, use tally marks to represent each student that falls in the interval. Now allow a star to equal two students.

Ask:

- How many stars would we need for the third column for each interval? See students' work.
- If we did not choose a reasonable number to equal the star, how could this type of graph be misleading? See students' work.

START SMART 6

Data Analysis

Do You Hear What I Hear?

Bats have a much greater range of hearing than humans. They use this sense to locate food and prey. Many other animals also have a greater hearing range than humans. The frequency of a dog whistle is about 22,000 Hertz (Hz) which is greater than the maximum hearing frequency for humans. The table shows the minimum and maximum frequencies for hearing of ten animal species, including humans.

Hearing Ranges of Animal Species

Species	Minimum Frequency (Hz)	Maximum Frequency (Hz)
bat	2,000	110,000
Beluga whale	1,000	123,000
cat	45	64,000
dog	67	45,000
elephant	16	12,000
goldfish	20	3,000
horse	55	33,500
human	64	20,000
mouse	1,000	91,000
owl	200	12,000

Source: Louisiana State University

CHECK Your Understanding — Pictographs

1. Copy and complete the pictograph below using the data of the maximum hearing frequencies in the table on page 14.

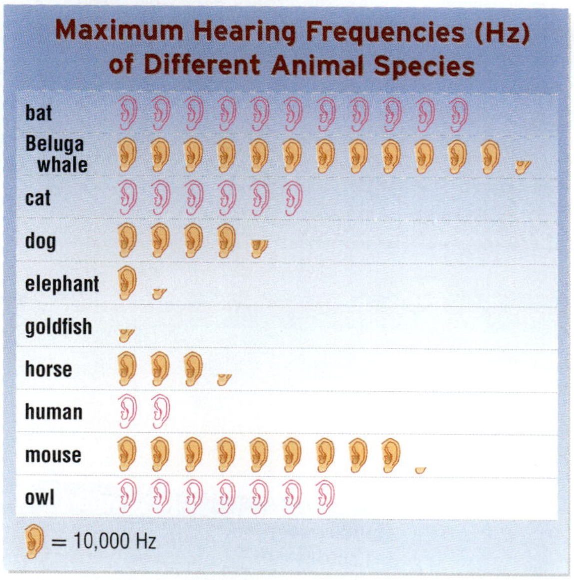

5. Sample answer: A lawn mower is twice as loud as normal speech. An alarm clock is twice as loud as a whisper.

2. Name two animals whose maximum hearing frequencies are about the same. **Sample answer: cat and dog**

3. About how many times greater is a Beluga whale's maximum hearing frequency than a cat's? **about 2 times greater**

4. The table gives the loudness of different sounds measured in decibels (dB). Construct a pictograph of the information. **See margin.**

Sound	Decibels (dB)
jet engine	140
chainsaw	120
lawn mower	100
alarm clock	80
normal speech	60
whisper	40

5. **WRITING IN MATH** Refer to pictograph you created in Exercise 4. Write one or two sentences describing the data.

3 Practice

Using the Exercises

Exercise 1 Encourage students to copy and complete the table in an organized, neat manner. Being able to interpret the data is dependent upon the presentation of the data.

Exercises 2 and 3 Emphasize the importance of carefully reading and interpreting the data. Careful analysis of the data ensures proper conclusions.

Exercise 4 You may want to explain that 20 decibels is 10 times louder than 10 decibels. Therefore, 30 decibels (20 decibels higher than 10) is 10^2 or 100 times louder than 10 decibels.

Writing in Math Discuss how the table could be misleading and how to accurately describe the data.

4 Assess

- After discussing **More FUN Facts**, have students do research on the Internet regarding animals' ability to smell. Have them make a pictograph with categories listed as "no smell," "some smell," "acute smell." They may want to start with a frequency table and then transfer the data to a pictograph.

Additional Answer

4.

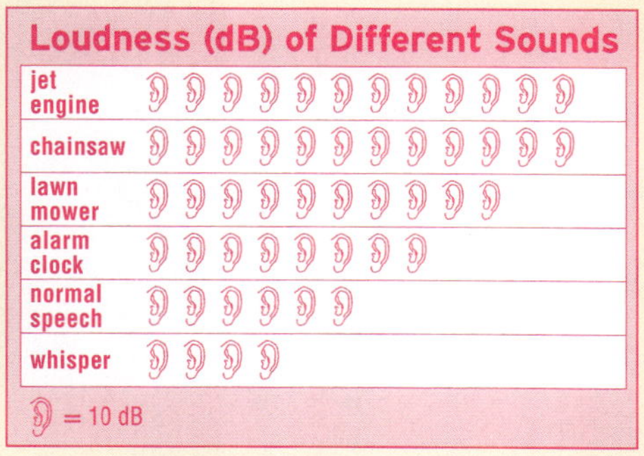

More FUN Facts

- Mammals' sense of smell is the most acute and discriminating of the five senses. Humans are the only mammal where this is not true.
- Most birds cannot smell.
- Smell is the only sense that cannot be measured.
- Smell is responsible for 80% of humans' taste.

Data File

Each chapter has a Find the Data exercise that asks students to write a real-world problem using the data on these pages.

Data File

The following pages contain data that you'll use throughout the book.

Temperature

Record Temperatures in New York State					
Record	°F	°C	Date	Location	Elevation (feet)
High	108	42.2	July 22, 1976	Troy	35
Low	−52	−46.7	February 18, 1979	Old Forge	1,720

Source: National Climatic Data Center

Vertical Velocity Roller Coaster

Amusement Park: Six Flags Great America, Illinois
Length: 2,700 feet
Height: 185 feet
Speed: 65 miles per hour
Duration: 1 minute
Vehicles: 1
Riders per vehicle: 28

Source: Coaster Buzz

Kentucky Stadiums

Stadium	Location	Capacity
Churchill Downs	Louisville	120,000
Commonwealth Stadium	Lexington	67,530
Kentucky Speedway	Sparta	66,089
Papa John's Cardinal Stadium	Louisville	42,000
Rupp Arena	Lexington	23,000
Roy Kidd Stadium	Richmond	20,000

Source: World Stadiums

Harker's Island, North Carolina

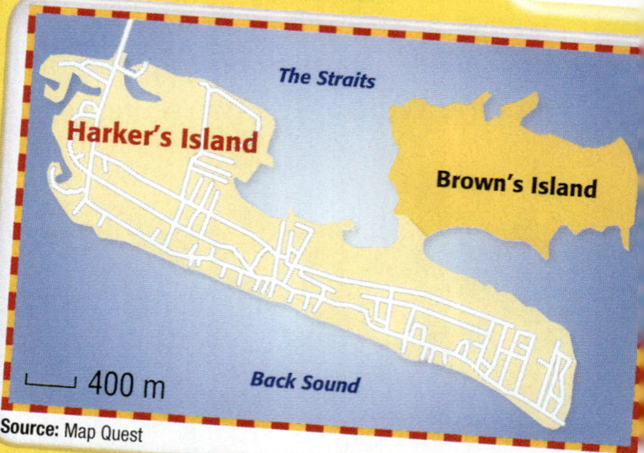

Source: Map Quest

Museum of Glass, Tacoma

WASHINGTON

Regular Ticket Prices

- $10 Adults
- $8 Seniors (age 62+), Military, and Students (age 13+)
- $4 Children (age 6–12)
- $30 Families (two adults and up to four children under age 18)
- Free: Museum of Glass Members, Children under age 6, and Third Thursday of each month (5-8 P.M.)

n Eagle

Source: National Geographic

ght: about 3 feet (91 cm)

gspan: 7 feet (213 cm)

itat: Usually found in high altitudes throughout the ntains of Arizona and along the Colorado River.

U.S. Bank Center, Milwaukee

WISCONSIN

Height: 183 meters

Floors: 42

Exterior: 66% glass

Windows: 5,000

Foundation: 500 steel H-piles capable of holding 640 tons each

Source: Emporis

Delicate Arch, Arches National Park

Source: Climb-Utah

UTAH Delicate Arch, located in Arches National Park, is found along a hiking trail that is 1.5 miles each way. The average time to hike the trail is $1\frac{1}{4}$ hours each way. The elevation of the arch is 4,800 feet, and the arch towers 80 feet above the average hiker. It is recommended that each person carries 2 liters of water for the hike.

Data File 17

Riverbanks Zoo and Garden, Columbia

SOUTH CAROLINA

Number of Animals: more than 2,000
Number of Animal Species: 350
Number of Plant Species: 4,200
Annual Attendance: about 900,000
Hours: 9 A.M.–5 P.M.
Admission: $9.75 for adults
$7.25 ages 3–12
Sea Lion Feedings: 10:30 A.M. and 3 P.M.
Penguin Feedings: 11 A.M. and 3:30 P.M.
Elephant Training: 11:30 A.M.

Source: Riverbanks Zoo and Garden

George S. Mickelson Trail

SOUTH DAKOTA Bicyclists of all ages and abilities can enjoy the George S. Mickelson Trail, in the Black Hills of South Dakota, which runs for a total of 114 miles. It tops out at 6,100 feet but never exceeds a 4% grade.

Source: Travel South Dakota

Boston Baked Beans

Boston Baked Beans

Ingredients

- 2 cups navy beans
- $\frac{1}{2}$ cup brown sugar
- $\frac{1}{4}$ cup molasses
- 1 cup bean liquid
- 1 teaspoon salt

Rock City

KANSAS Rock City is a tiny park, located 3.5 miles from Minneapolis, Kansas. It contains about 200 huge sandstone concretions. The rocks are up to 27 feet in diameter. There is no other place in the world where there are so many rocks of such giant size.

Source: Kansas Travel and Tourism

18 Data File

Montana Rivers

The longest and shortest rivers in the United States can be found in Montana. The Roe River is exclusively located in Montana and is also the shortest river in the world.

Source: Montana Kids

River	Total Length	Length in Montana
Missouri	2,540 mi (13,411,200 ft)	1,029 mi (5,433,120 ft)
Roe	$\frac{5}{132}$ mi (200 ft)	$\frac{5}{132}$ mi (200 ft)

Mackinac Island

MICHIGAN Mackinac Island is an island covering 3.8 square miles. There are 61 miles of roads and trails within Mackinac Island State Park, most of which are wooded inland trails for hikers, bikers, and horseback riders in spring, summer, and fall. Fort Holmes is at the island's highest point, 320 feet above lake level.

Source: Mackinac State Historic Parks

Baltimore Oriole

Habitat: Usually found in Maryland during the summer months and in the southern states during winter months. Male orioles have a bright orange color on their shoulders and underbelly. Females are light orange.

Size: 7 to $8\frac{1}{4}$ inches

Weight: $1\frac{1}{5}$ ounces

Source: National Geographic

iladelphia 76ers

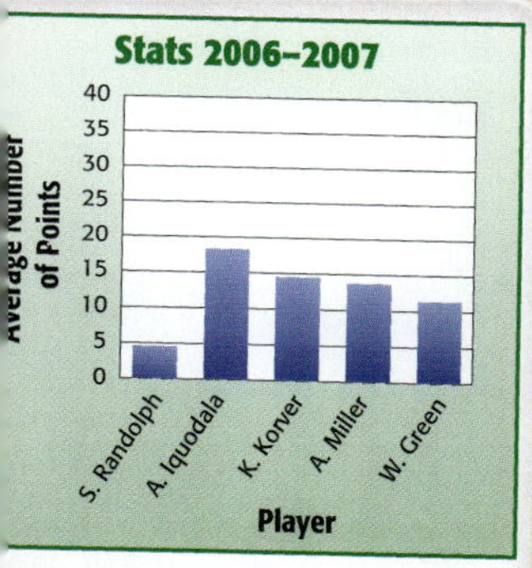

ce: National Basketball Association

Denver International Airport

COLORADO

Opening Date: February 28, 1995

Size: 34,000 acres, 53 square miles

Runways: 6 (five are 12,000 feet long, and the sixth is 16,000 feet long)

Concourses: 3

Gates: 89

Passenger Airlines: 23

Flight and baggage information display monitors: 1,500

Accommodation: 50 million passengers per year

Source: Denver International Airport

Data File 19

Unit 1
Notes

Introduction

In this unit, students will explore numbers and operations. They will learn how to solve problems using a four-step plan. They will examine powers, exponents, square roots, the order of operations, and sequences. In addition, they will use their knowledge of algebraic variables, expressions, and properties to solve equations and make function tables.

Students will find absolute values, compare and order integers, and add, subtract, multiply, and divide integers. Finally, they will apply their knowledge of operations to write and solve one- and two-step equations and graph linear equations.

Assessment Options

Unit 1 Test Pages 75–76 of the *Chapter 3 Resource Masters* may be used as a test or a review for Unit 1. This assessment contains both multiple-choice and short-response items.

ExamView Assessment Suite

Create additional customized Unit Tests and review worksheets for differentiated instruction.

Unit 1
Algebra and Functions

Focus
Use appropriate operations to solve problems and linear equations.

CHAPTER 1
Introduction to Algebra and Functions

BIG Idea Represent relationships in numerical, verbal, geometric and symbolic form.

CHAPTER 2
Integers

BIG Idea Know the properties of, and compute with, integers.

CHAPTER 3
Algebra: Linear Equations and Functions

BIG Idea Solve linear equations in one variable.

20

What's MATH Got To Do With It? DVD

Real-Life Math Videos engage students, showing them how math is used in everyday situations. Use Video 1 with this unit to discuss how linear equations are used in soccer, baseball, and horseback riding. (also available on one Super DVD combined with MindJogger Videoquizzes)

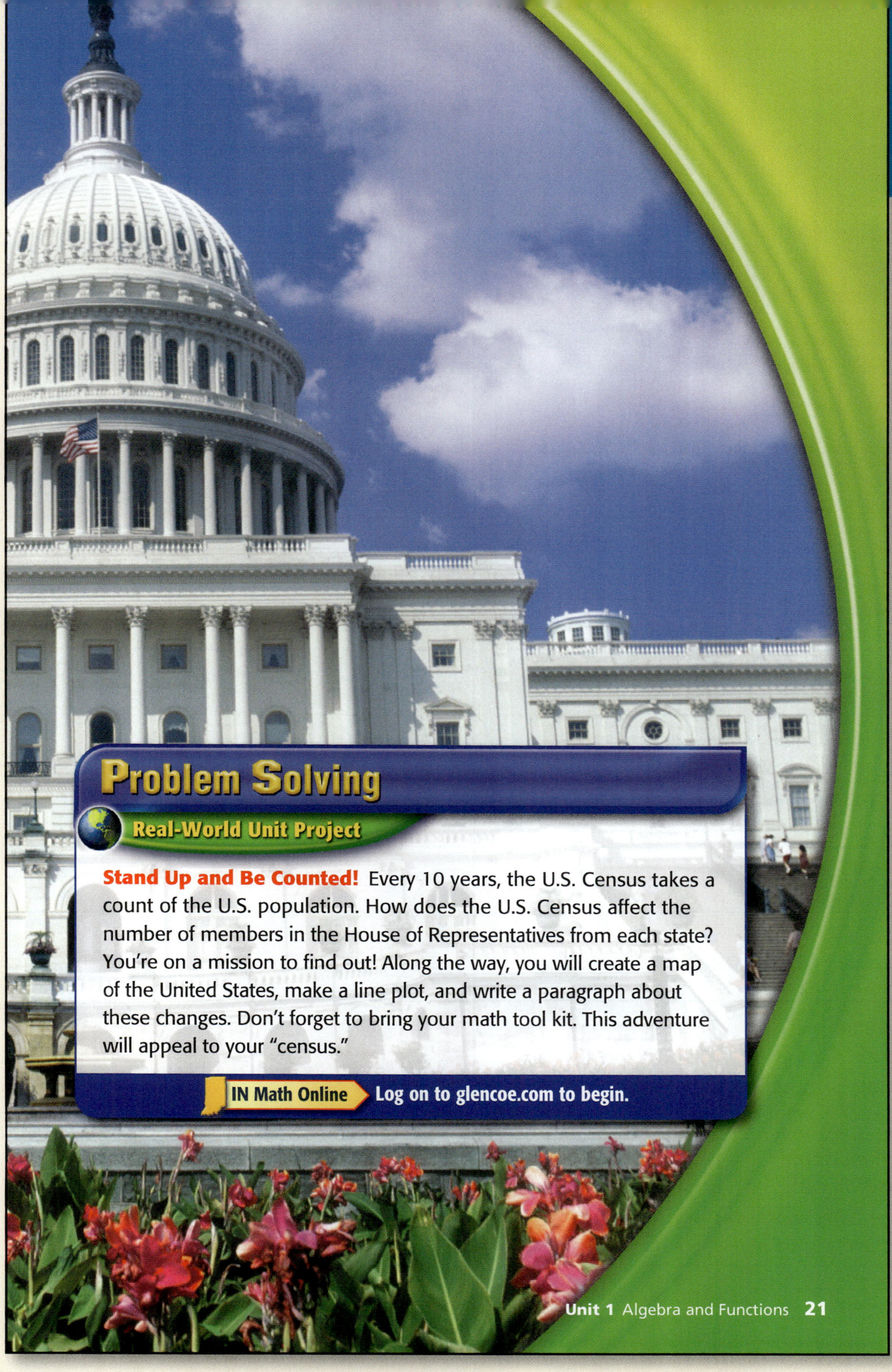

Problem Solving

Real-World Unit Project

Stand Up and Be Counted! Every 10 years, the U.S. Census takes a count of the U.S. population. How does the U.S. Census affect the number of members in the House of Representatives from each state? You're on a mission to find out! Along the way, you will create a map of the United States, make a line plot, and write a paragraph about these changes. Don't forget to bring your math tool kit. This adventure will appeal to your "census."

IN Math Online Log on to glencoe.com to begin.

Real-World Unit Project

Problem Solving in Social Studies

Stand Up and Be Counted

This cross-curricular project is a project in which students do research on the Internet, gather data, and make presentations using word processing, graphing, page-making, or presentation software. In each chapter, students advance to the next step in their project. At the end of Chapter 3, the project culminates with a presentation of their findings.

IN Math Online

glencoe.com Log on for teaching suggestions and sample answers for this project.

Team Teaching You can use this cross-curricular project with your students' social studies teacher to make the connection from mathematics to the social studies your students are studying.

*The **Real-World Unit Projects** send students to the Web to work on ongoing interdisciplinary projects.*

More Cross-Curricular Connections

You may wish to share these suggestions with your students' other teachers.

Math and Language Arts

Research the U.S. Census. Write an essay about an aspect of the U.S. Census. Why is the U.S. Census taken? How could the U.S. Census become more accurate? How are the results used?

Math and Science

Research the computer science behind polling and the U.S. Census. Have students come up with different ways the census could be taken, and investigate how the census works.

CHAPTER 1

Chapter Overview

Introduction to Algebra and Functions

Lesson Plan

LESSONS AND OBJECTIVES	Academic Standards		Pacing Your Lessons: 40-50 Minute Periods	Pacing Your Lessons: 90-Minute Periods
1-1 A Plan for Problem Solving (pp. 25–29) • Solve problems using the four-step plan.	7.3.4, P.1.1	Core Lesson	1	0.5
1-2 Powers and Exponents (pp. 30–33) • Use powers and exponents.	7.1.2	Core Lesson	1	0.5
1-3 Squares and Square Roots (pp. 34–37) • Find squares of numbers and square roots of perfect squares.	7.1.5	Core Lesson	1	0.5
1-4 Order of Operations (pp. 38–41) • Evaluate expressions using the order of operations.	7.1.7, 7.2.3	Core Lesson	1	0.5
1-5 Problem-Solving Investigation: Guess and Check (pp. 42–43) • Solve problems using the guess and check strategy.	P.1.3, P.1.4	Core Lesson	1	0.5
1-6 Algebra: Variables and Expressions (pp. 44–47) • Evaluate simple algebraic expressions.	7.2.1	Core Lesson	1	0.5
1-7 Algebra: Equations (pp. 49–52) • Solve equations using mental math.	P.6.6	Core Lesson	1	0.5
1-8 Algebra: Properties (pp. 53–56) • Use Commutative, Associative, Identity, and Distributive properties to solve problems.	7.1.7, 7.2.3	Core Lesson	1	0.5
1-9 Algebra: Arithmetic Sequences (pp. 57–61) • Describe the relationships and extend terms in arithmetic sequences. **Extend 1-9 Algebra Lab: Exploring Sequences** (p. 62) • Explore patterns in sequences of geometric figures.	7.2.1, 7.3.4, P.5.1	Core Lesson	1.5	0.5
1-10 Algebra: Equations and Functions (pp. 63–67) • Make function tables and write equations. **Extend 1-10 Graphing Calculator Lab: Functions and Tables** (pp. 68–69) • Use technology to represent and compare functions.	7.2.1	Core Lesson	1.5	1
REVIEW			1	0.5
ASSESSMENT			1	0.5*
	TOTAL		**13**	**6.5**

*The complete **Assessment Planner** for Chapter 1 is provided on page 23.*

** Begin Chapter 2 in the second half of the chapter.*

Focal Points

G7-FP3 Algebra
For the complete wording of the Focal Points for Grade 7, please see page T17.

Professional Development

Vertical Alignment

Before Chapter 1

Related Topics from Grade 6

- calculate with positive and negative integers
- use a letter to represent an unknown number; write and evaluate simple algebraic expressions in one variable by substitution
- solve problems involving linear functions with integer values and write the equation

Chapter 1

Topics from Grade 7

- analyze problems by identifying relationships, distinguishing relevant from irrelevant information, identifying missing information
- write and solve one-step linear equations in one variable
- solve problems manually by using the correct order of operations
- apply algebraic order of operations and properties and justify each step in the process
- use a variety of methods to explain mathematical reasoning

After Chapter 1

Preparation for Grade 8

- multiply and divide expressions involving exponents with a common base
- use variables and appropriate operations to write an expression, an equation, an inequality, or a system of equations or inequalities that represents a verbal
- use the correct order of operations to evaluate algebraic expressions
- multiply and divide monomials; extend the process of taking powers and extracting roots to monomials

Backmapping and Vertical Alignment

McGraw-Hill's ***Math Connects*** program was conceived and developed with the final results in mind: student success in Algebra 1 and beyond. The authors, using the **NCTM Focal Points and Focal Connections** as their guide, developed this brand-new series by backmapping from Algebra 1 concepts, and vertically aligning the topics so that they build upon prior skills and concepts and serve as a foundation for future topics.

What the Research Says...

According to Olson in "Up Close and Personal," which appeared in Education Week, classroom assessment that teachers use day in and day out provides one of the most powerful tools available for improving student achievement.

- Every lesson contains Standards-based questions, providing practice and ongoing assessment.
- The Study Guide and Review at the end of the chapter allows students to assess their understanding of each lesson's key concepts.

Professional Development

Targeted professional development has been articulated throughout **McGraw-Hill's *Math Connects*** program. The **McGraw-Hill Professional Development Video Library** provides short videos that support the NCTM Focal Points and Focal Connections. For more information, visit glencoe.com.

Model Lessons

Instructional Strategies

CHAPTER 1

Technology Solutions

Teacher Resources

TeacherWorks™ All-in-One Planner and Resource Center

All of the print materials from the Classroom Resource Masters are available on your TeacherWorks™ CD-ROM.

BL = Below or Approaching Grade Level   OL = On Grade Level   AL = Above or Beyond Grade Level   ELL = English Language Learner

				Chapter Resource Masters	1-1	1-2	1-3	1-4	1-5	1-6	1-7	1-8	1-9	1-10
BL	OL		ELL	Lesson Reading Guide	9	15	22	29		40	47	53	60	67
BL	OL		ELL	Study Guide and Intervention*	10	16	23	30	36	41	48	54	61	68
BL	OL			Skills Practice*	11	17	24	31	37	42	49	55	62	69
	OL	AL		Practice*	12	18	25	32	38	43	50	56	63	70
	OL	AL		Word Problem Practice*	13	19	26	33	39	44	51	57	64	71
	OL	AL		Enrichment	14	20	27	34		45	52	58	65	72
	OL	AL		Calculator and Spreadsheet Activities		21	28	35		46		59	66	73
	OL	AL		Chapter Assessments*	75–96									
BL	OL	AL		5-Minute Check Transparencies	✓	✓	✓	✓	✓	✓	✓	✓	✓	✓
BL	OL			Teaching Mathematics with Manipulatives		✓				✓			✓	
BL	OL	AL		Real-World Investigations for Differentiated Instruction	21–26									

Also available in Spanish.

Graphing Calculator Easy Files

- Timesaving Tech Tools for the TI-Navigator
- Quick Checks to diagnose student progress
- Deliver Differentiated Instruction with Ready Files
- Vocabulary Review

AssignmentWorks

Differentiated Assignments, Answers, and Solutions

- Print a customized assignment worksheet using the Student Edition exercises along with an answer key or worked-out solutions.
- Use default lesson assignments as outlined in the Differentiated Homework Options in the Teacher Edition.

Interactive Classroom

This CD-ROM is a customizable Microsoft® PowerPoint® presentation that includes:

- In-Class Examples
- Your Turn Exercises*
- 5-Minute Check Transparencies*
- Links to Online Study Tools
- Concepts in Motion

**compatible with response pad technology*

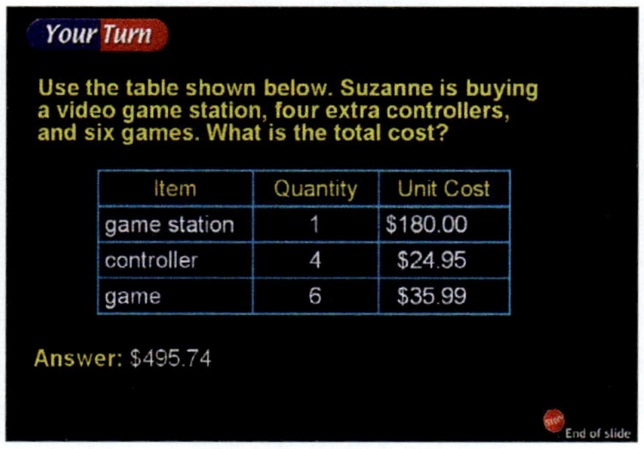

ExamView® Assessment Suite

ExamView® Assessment Suite

- Create, edit, and customize tests and worksheets using QuickTest Wizard
- Create multiple versions of tests and modify them for a desired level of difficulty
- Translate from English to Spanish and vice versa
- Build tests aligned with your state standards
- Track students' progress using the Teacher Management System

This program is supported by a wealth of **technology options** on CD-ROM, on DVD, and online.

Student Tools

StudentWorks™ Plus

Textbook, Audio, Workbooks, and more

This CD-ROM is a valuable resource for students to access content online and use online resources to continue learning Chapter 1 concepts. Includes:

- Complete Student Editions in both English and Spanish
- English audio integrated throughout the text
- Links to Concepts in Motion, Personal Tutor, and other online resources
- Access to all student worksheets
- Daily Assignments and Grade Log

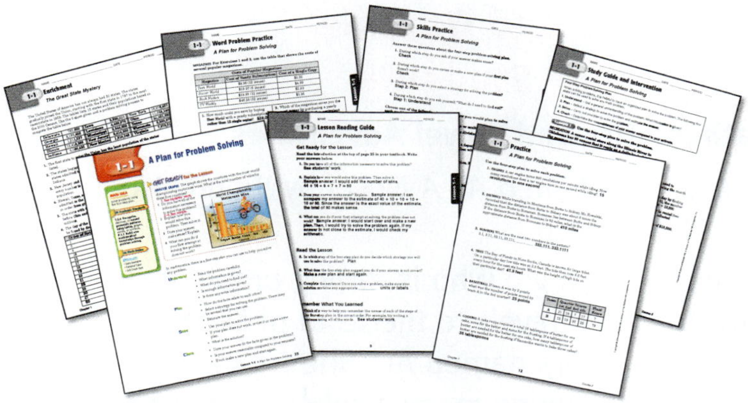

Super DVD

The Super DVD contains two Glencoe multimedia products.

MindJogger Plus An alternative review of concepts in which students work as teams in a game show format to gain points for correct answers.

What's Math Got to Do With It? Real-Life Math Videos
Engaging video that shows students how math is used in everyday situations.

Internet Resources

IN Math Online glencoe.com

TEACHER	STUDENT	PARENT	Online Study Tools
	●	●	Online Student Edition
●	●	●	Multilingual Glossary
			Lesson Resources
	●	●	BrainPOP®
●	●	●	Concepts in Motion
●	●	●	Extra Examples
●			Group Activity Cards
	●	●	Other Calculator Keystrokes
	●	●	Reading in the Content Area
	●	●	Real-World Careers
	●	●	Self-Check Quizzes
			Chapter Resources
	●	●	Chapter Readiness
	●	●	Chapter Test
	●	●	Family Letters and Activities
	●	●	Standardized Test Practice
	●	●	Vocabulary Review/Chapter Review Activities
			Unit Resources
●	●		Cross-Curricular Internet Project
			Other Resources
●			Dinah Zike's Foldables
●	●		Game Zone Games and Recording Sheets
	●	●	Hotmath Homework Help
●			Key Concepts
●	●	●	Math Skills Maintenance
●	●	●	Meet the Authors
●			NAEP Correlations
	●	●	Personal Tutor
●			Project CRISS℠
	●	●	Scavenger Hunts and Answer Sheets
●			Vocabulary PuzzleMakers

CHAPTER 1

Reading and Writing in Mathematics

Noteables™ Interactive Study Notebook with Foldables™

This workbook is a study organizer that provides helpful steps for students to follow to organize their notes for Chapter 1.

- Students use Noteables to record notes and to complete their Foldables as you present the material for each lesson.
- Noteables correspond to the Examples in the *Teacher Edition* and *Interactive Classroom CD-ROM.*

Real-World Problem Solving Graphic Novels

Mathematical problem solving is presented in a motivating, graphic novel format. The novels contain real-world problems for each of the following mathematical strands: Number Sense, Algebraic Thinking, Geometry, Measurement, Statistics and Probability, and Mathematical Reasoning.

READING in the Content Area

This online worksheet provides strategies for reading and analyzing Lesson 1-4, Order of Operations. Students are guided through questions about the main idea, subject matter, supporting details, conclusion, clarifying details, and vocabulary of the lesson.

glencoe.com

Recommended Outside Reading for Students

Mathematics and Travel Adventures

- *A Gebra Named Al: A Novel* by Wendy Isdell ©1993 [fiction]

The story of a girl who is having problems learning algebra. She travels to the Land of Mathematics and meets a "gebra named Al." She travels through the land encountering many algebraic concepts, finally finding the equation she needs to return home.

Project CRISS℠

STUDY SKILL

A problem-solution graphic structure can be used by students to develop a step-by-step plan for solving a problem. Students begin by writing details of the problem. Next, they write steps that are necessary to solve the problem. Finally, they solve the problem and write out their result. The graphic structure at the right applies the four-step plan presented in Chapter 1 to solving a problem containing an exponent. Have students develop a similar structure to help them solve sequence problems and other types of problems they encounter in this chapter.

Problem Evaluate the expression 4×6^3.		
	Step	**Result**
Steps to Solution	1. Explore	1. The exponent means the 6 is used as a factor 3 times.
	2. Plan	2. Write out all the factors and multiply.
	3. Solve	3. $4 \times 6^3 = 4 \times 6 \times 6 \times 6 = 864$
	4. Examine	4. $4 \times 6^3 = 864$ is a reasonable answer.
End Result $4 \times 6^3 = 864$		

CReating Independence through Student-owned Strategies

Differentiated Instruction

Investigative Approach

MathScape™ NSF

This project was supported, in part, by the
National Science Foundation

MathScape is a mathematics curriculum for grades 6–8 developed by the Seeing and Thinking Mathematically Project at the Education Development Center.

Writing and Solving Equations
Exploring the Unknown

How to Use *MathScape* with Chapter 1

The unit *Exploring the Unknown* can be used to enhance Lessons 1-6 and 1-9.

- **Enrich** → Before you complete **Lesson 1-6**, you can introduce Lab Gear Blocks and play "What's in the Bag" on page 184.
- **Reinforce** → Before you begin **Lesson 1-9**, you can help students who are still having difficulty with patterns by using the activities on pages 198–199.

RTI (Response to Intervention)

TIER 1 On-Level Instruction Use the *Math Connects* program as instruction for your on-level students.

TIER 2 Strategic Intervention For options to instruct struggling students, refer to the Diagnostic Assessment table on page 23.

TIER 3 Intensive Intervention *Math Triumphs* can provide intensive intervention for students who are at risk of not meeting the objectives addressed in Chapter 1.

Diagnose student readiness with the Quick Check and Quick Review on page 23. Then use *Math Triumphs* to accelerate their achievment.

Introduction to Algebra and Functions

Prerequisite Skill	*Math Triumphs*
Variables and Expressions	Chapter 4
Order of Operations	Chapter 9

Practice and Review

Quick Review Math Handbook* is Glencoe's mathematical handbook for students and parents.

Hot Words includes a glossary of terms.

Hot Topics consists of two parts:

- explanations of key mathematical concepts
- exercises to check students' understanding.

Lesson	Hot Topics Section	Lesson	Hot Topics Section
1-1	1•5	1-6	6•1
1-2	3•1	1-7	6•1
1-3	3•2	1-8	1•2
1-4	1•3	1-10	6•7, 6•8

*Also available in Spanish

CHAPTER 1 Notes

FOLDABLES™ Study Organizer — Dinah Zike's Foldables

Focus This Foldable is a study guide where students will write about algebra and functions.

Teach Students should use their Foldables to take notes, define terms, record key concepts, and write examples. Encourage students to record what they learn about the parts of each lesson that they find most difficult.

When to Use It At the end of each lesson, students should record their notes on the Foldable page with the appropriate tab.

A version of a completed Foldable is shown on p. 70.

Differentiated Instruction

CRM Student-Built Glossary, p. 1

Students complete the chart by providing a definition for each term and an example as they progress through Chapter 1.

This study tool can also be used to review for the chapter test.

Materials Needed for Chapter 1

- square tiles (Lesson 1-3)
- butcher block paper (Lesson 1-5)
- isometric dot paper (Lesson 1-6)
- index cards (Lessons 1-6, 1-7, 1-8)
- centimeter cubes and grid paper (Lesson 1-9)
- toothpicks (Extend 1-9)
- graphing calculator (Extend 1-10)

CHAPTER 1 Introduction to Algebra and Functions

Indiana Academic Standards

7.2.1 Use variables and appropriate operations to write an expression, equation or inequality that represents a verbal description.
7.2.3 Evaluate numerical expressions and simplify algebraic expressions involving rational and irrational numbers.

Key Vocabulary

algebra (p. 44)
defining the variable (p. 50)
evaluate (p. 31)
numerical expression (p. 38)

Real-World Link

PARKS Admission to the Kentucky Horse Park in Lexington, Kentucky, costs $15 for each adult and $8 for each child. You can use the four-step problem-solving plan to determine the cost of admission for a family of 2 adults and 3 children.

FOLDABLES® Study Organizer

Introduction to Algebra and Functions Make this Foldable to help you organize your notes. Begin with eleven sheets of notebook paper.

1. **Staple** the eleven sheets together to form a booklet.

2. **Cut** tabs. Make each one 2 lines longer than the one before it.

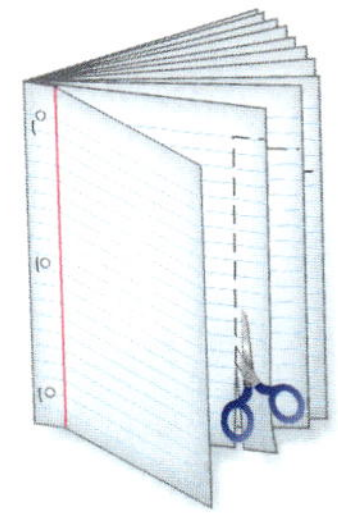

3. **Write** the chapter title on the cover and label each tab with the lesson number.

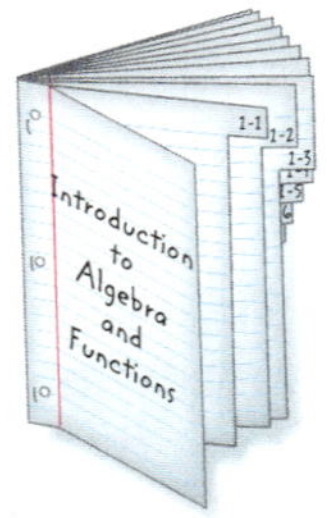

Foldables™ are a unique way to enhance students' study skills. Encourage students to add to their Foldable as they work through the chapter and to use it to review for their chapter test.

GET READY for Chapter 1

Diagnose Readiness You have two options for checking Prerequisite Skills.

Option 2

IN Math Online Take the Online Readiness Quiz at glencoe.com.

Option 1

Take the Quick Quiz below. Refer to the Quick Review for help.

QUICK Quiz

(Used in Lessons 1-1, 1-4 through 1-10)
Add. (Prior Grade)

1. 89.3 + 16.5 **105.8**
2. 7.9 + 32.45 **40.35**
3. 54.25 + 6.39 **60.64**
4. 10.8 + 2.6 **13.4**
5. **TECHNOLOGY** Patrick bought a personal electronic organizer for \$59.99 and a carrying case for \$12.95. What was his total cost, not including tax? (Prior Grade) **\$72.94**

(Used in Lessons 1-1, 1-4 through 1-10)
Subtract. (Prior Grade)

6. 24.6 − 13.3 **11.3**
7. 9.1 − 6.6 **2.5**
8. 30.55 − 2.86 **27.69**
9. 17.4 − 11.2 **6.2**

(Used in Lessons 1-1 through 1-10)
Multiply. (Prior Grade)

10. 4 × 7.7 **30.8**
11. 9.8 × 3 **29.4**
12. 2.7 × 6.3 **17.01**
13. 8.5 × 1.2 **10.2**

(Used in Lessons 1-1, 1-4 through 1-10)
Divide. (Prior Grade)

14. 37.49 ÷ 4.6 **8.15**
15. 14.31 ÷ 2.7 **5.3**
16. 6.16 ÷ 5.6 **1.1**
17. 11.15 ÷ 2.5 **4.46**
18. **PIZZA** Four friends decided to split the cost of a pizza evenly. The total cost was \$25.48. How much does each friend need to pay? (Prior Grade) **\$6.37**

QUICK Review

Example 1 Find 17.89 + 43.2.

```
  17.89    Line up the decimal points.
+ 43.20    Annex a zero.
  61.09
```

Example 2 Find 37.45 − 8.52.

```
  37.45    Line up the decimal points.
−  8.52
  28.93
```

Example 3 Find 1.7 × 3.5.

```
  1.7  ←   1 decimal place
× 3.5  ← + 1 decimal place
  5.95 ←   2 decimal places
```

Example 4 Find 24.6 ÷ 2.5.

2.5)24.6 → 25.)246. Multiply both numbers by the same power of 10.

```
       9.84
  25)246.00    Annex zeros.
    −225
      210      Divide as with
     −200      whole numbers.
      100
     −100
        0
```


The one-stop **Assessment Planner** organizes the resources available for diagnostic, formative, and summative assessment in this chapter.

Diagnostic Assessment

Exercises	Academic Standards	Intervention
1–5	7.1.7	*Math Skills Maintenance Masters* 17, 19, pp. 34–35, 38–40
6–9	7.1.5	*Math Skills Maintenance Masters* 18–19, pp. 36–40
10–13	7.2.1	*Math Skills Maintenance Masters* 20, pp. 41–42
14–18	7.1.7	*Math Skills Maintenance Masters* 21, pp. 43–44

ASSESSMENT PLANNER — CHAPTER 1

Formative Assessment

CRM Anticipation Guide, pp. 7–8
Spotting Preconceived Ideas
Students complete this survey to determine prior knowledge about ideas from Chapter 1. Revisit this worksheet after completing the chapter. Also see page 74.

TE Lesson Activities

- Ticket Out the Door, pp. 29, 52, 61
- Crystal Ball, pp. 33, 41
- Name the Math, pp. 37, 47, 56
- Yesterday's News, pp. 43, 67

Chapter Checkpoints

- SE Mid-Chapter Quiz, p. 48
- SE Study Guide and Review, pp. 70–74
- SE Test Practice, pp. 76–77
- CRM Quizzes, pp. 77–78
- CRM Standardized Test Practice, pp. 94–96

IN Math Online glencoe.com

- Self-Check Quizzes
- Practice Test
- Test Practice

Summative Assessment

- SE Chapter Practice Test, p. 75
- CRM Mid-Chapter Test, p. 79
- CRM Vocabulary Test, p. 80
- CRM Extended-Response Test, p. 93
- CRM Leveled Chapter Tests, pp. 81–92
- CD-ROM ExamView Pro® Assessment Suite

KEY
- CRM *Chapter 1 Resource Masters*
- SE Student Edition
- TE Teacher Edition
- CD-ROM

READING to SOLVE PROBLEMS

1 Focus

Sometimes students read word problems too quickly. As a result, they may plan an incorrect solution, performing the wrong operation(s). In this activity, students learn to check their work by asking whether their solutions make sense.

2 Teach

Make sure students realize that multiplication does not make sense because it would result in a greater distance, and the problem states that Miguel lives closer to school than Kelly does.

Encourage students to analyze the key terms of word problems, looking for clues about the operation(s) to use.

Before students begin the exercises, you might want to use a yardstick and a 1-foot ruler to model addition and subtraction. Point out that placing them end-to-end models an addition problem (3 ft + 1 ft), while placing them side-by-side models a subtraction problem (3 ft − 1 ft).

3 Assess

Tell students you made some cookies, which you want to distribute equally among 6 friends. Have students write which operation you should use to find the number of cookies to give each friend. division

READING to SOLVE PROBLEMS

Making Sense

Academic Standards **P.5.2 Select, apply, and translate among mathematical representations to solve problems.**

When you solve a word problem, the first thing to do is to read the problem carefully. The last thing to do is to see whether your answer makes sense. Sometimes a picture or diagram can help.

> Kelly lives 5 miles from school. This is 4 times as far as Miguel lives from school. How far does Miguel live from school?

If you look just at the key words in the problem, it might seem that 4 *times* 5 would give the solution.

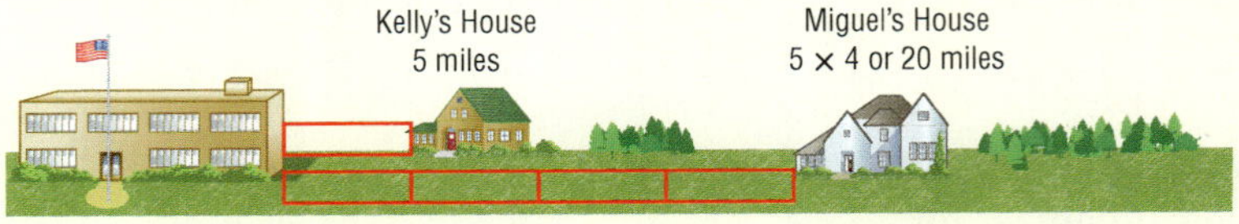

But the important question is, "Does this solution make sense?" In this case, the solution does *not* make sense because Kelly lives farther away. This problem is solved by dividing.

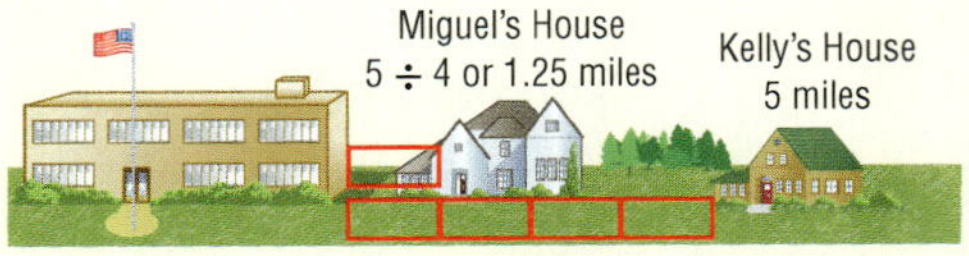

So, Miguel lives 1.25 miles away from school.

Reading to Solve Problems features help students learn and use the language of mathematics.

PRACTICE

For Exercises 1 and 2, choose the model that illustrates each problem. Explain your reasoning. Then solve.

1. Jennifer has saved $210 to purchase an MP3 player. She needs $299 to buy it. How much more money does she need? **See margin.**

Model A

Model B

2. The school cafeteria sold 465 lunches on Thursday. They expect to sell 75 more lunches on Friday because they serve pizza that day. How many lunches do they expect to sell on Friday? **See margin.**

Model C

Model D

Tips for New Teachers — Meaning of Multiplication

The correct use of the word *times* is to multiply 4 by the distance Miguel lives from school. This product is equal to the distance Kelly lives from school, which is five miles. So, Miguel's distance is 5 ÷ 4, or 1.25 miles.

Additional Answers

1. Model A; Even though the word *more* is in the problem, adding $210 to $299 does not make sense. The problem is solved by subtracting; $89.
2. Model D; In this case, *more* does mean to add, because number of lunches expected on Friday is in *addition* to the 465 lunches sold on Thursday; 540 lunches

1-1 A Plan for Problem Solving

PACING: **Regular:** 1 period, **Block:** 0.5 period

IN Academic Standards **7.3.4 Recognize,** describe, or **extend geometric patterns using tables,** graphs, words, or symbols. **P.1.1 Build new mathematical knowledge through problem solving.**

Options for Differentiated Instruction

ELL = English Language Learner AL = Above or Beyond Grade Level SS = Struggling Students SN = Special Needs

Brainstorming AL

Use before presenting Example 1.

Before students look at the list of problem-solving strategies on page 25, have them brainstorm a list of strategies that they have used in past courses.

Ask:

- Which strategies have you used before?
- Which strategies do you think work best for you and why?
- What type of problem might lend itself to a given problem-solving strategy?

Organizing Student Work and Thinking ELL SS

Use while presenting Example 1.

Create a template for the students to organize their work. A sample template can be found on page 33 of *Teaching Mathematics with Manipulatives.*

Understand Read the problem carefully. What facts do you know? What do you need to find out? Is enough information given? Is there extra information?	What is the question you need to answer?
Plan How are the facts related to each other? Plan a strategy for solving the problem. Estimate the answer.	What strategy will you use? Estimate:
Solve Use your plan to solve the problem. If your plan does not work, revise it or make a new plan. What is the solution?	Workspace Your answer:
Check Reread the problem. Does the answer fit the facts given in the problem? Is the answer close to my estimate? Does the answer make sense? If not, solve the problem in another way.	Does your answer make sense?

Working in Pairs ELL SS SN

Use with Exercises 1 and 2.

Use the think-pair-share technique to help students choose problem-solving strategies. Have students read Exercises 1 and 2. Then pair them up and have them discuss with their partners which strategy would work the best to solve the problems. The pair then presents their results and the problem-solving strategy that they used to the class. If time allows, regroup students into different pairs and have them repeat the process with a different exercise.

Leveled Lesson Resources

Also on TeacherWorks™ Lesson 1-1

Chapter 1 Resource Masters

BL = Below or Approaching Grade Level | OL = On Grade Level | AL = Above or Beyond Grade Level | ELL = English Language Learner

Lesson Reading Guide
p. 9 BL OL ELL

NAME ________ DATE ________ PERIOD ____

1-1 Lesson Reading Guide
A Plan for Problem Solving

Get Ready for the Lesson

Read the introduction at the top of page 25 in your textbook. Write your answers below.

1. Do you have all of the information necessary to solve this problem? See students' work.
2. Explain how you would solve this problem. Then solve it. Sample answer: I would add the number of wins. 44 + 14 + 8 + 7 + 7 = 80
3. Does your answer make sense? Explain. Sample answer: I can compare my answer to the estimate of 40 + 10 + 10 + 10 or 80. Since the answer is the exact value of the estimate, the total of 80 makes sense.
4. What can you do if your first attempt at solving the problem does not work? Sample answer: I would start over and make a new plan. Then, I would try to solve the problem again. If my answer is not close to the estimate, I would check my arithmetic.

Read the Lesson

5. In which step of the four-step plan do you decide which strategy you will use to solve the problem? Plan
6. What does the four-step plan suggest you do if your answer is not correct? Make a new plan and start again.
7. Complete the sentence: Once you solve a problem, make sure your solution contains any appropriate ________. units or labels

Remember What You Learned

8. Think of a way to help you remember the names of each of the steps of the four-step plan in the correct order. For example, try writing a sentence using all of the words. See students' work.

Chapter 1 9 Course 2

Study Guide and Intervention*
p. 10 BL OL ELL

NAME ________ DATE ________ PERIOD ____

1-1 Study Guide and Intervention
A Plan for Problem Solving

Four-Step Problem-Solving Plan

When solving problems, it is helpful to have an organized plan to solve the problem. The following four steps can be used to solve any math problem.

1. **Understand** – Get a general understanding of the problem. What information is given?
2. **Plan** – Select a strategy to solve the problem and estimate the answer.
3. **Solve** – Carry out your plan to solve the problem.
4. **Check** – Determine the reasonableness of your answer compared to your estimate.

Example 1 Use the four-step plan to solve the problem.

RECREATION **A canoe rental store along the Illinois River in Oklahoma has 30 canoes that it rents on a daily basis during the summer season. If canoes rent for $15 per day, how much money can the store collect for canoe rentals during the month of July?**

Understand — You know that they rent 30 canoes per day for $15 each. You need to determine the total amount of money that can be collected during the month of July.

Plan — First, find the total amount of money that can be collected each day by finding the product of 30 and 15. Next, multiply the previous result by 31, the number of days in July. You can estimate this result by 30. 30 × 15 × 30 → 13,500

Solve — Since 30 × $15 → $450, the canoe rental store can collect $450 in rental fees each day. This means the total amount of money that could be collected during the month of July is $450 × 31 or $13,950.

Check — Is your answer reasonable? The answer is close to the estimate of $13,500.

Exercises

Use the four-step plan to solve each problem.

1. MONEY Colin works for his dad during summer vacation. His dad pays him $5.20 per hour and he works 20 hours per week. How much will Colin earn during his 8-week summer vacation? $832.00
2. BOOKS A student assistant in the school library is asked to shelve 33 books. If he puts away 9 books the first hour and then 6 books each hour after that, how long will it take him to shelve all 33 books? 5 hours
3. SHOPPING Alicia bought a $48 sweater on sale for $25 and a $36 purse on sale for $22. How much did Alicia save? $37
4. MAIL It cost Ramon $3.73 to mail a package to his grandmother. The post office charged $2.38 for the first pound and 45 cents for each additional pound. How much did the package weigh? 4 pounds

Chapter 1 10 Course 2

Skills Practice*
p. 11 BL OL

NAME ________ DATE ________ PERIOD ____

1-1 Skills Practice
A Plan for Problem Solving

Answer these questions about the four-step problem-solving plan.

1. During which step do you ask if your answer makes sense? Check
2. During which step do you revise or make a new plan if your first plan doesn't work? Check
3. During which step do you select a strategy for solving the problem? Step 2: Plan
4. During which step do you ask yourself, "What do I need to find out?" Step 1: Understand

Choose one of the following to describe how you would plan to solve each problem. Do not solve the problems.

A. Use only one operation, such as addition or multiplication.
B. Use a combination of operations, such as division and addition.
C. Use a different strategy.

5. MONEY Julia opened a savings account with a deposit of $36. She then deposited $5 per week for one month. If she then withdrew $9.50, how much is left in her savings account? B
6. In how many different patterns can 3 rose bushes, 2 sunflowers, and 5 tulip plants be planted in a garden? C
7. Use the four-step plan to solve Exercise 5.
   A. Understand
   I need to find how much is left in the savings account. First, I need to find the total deposits.
   B. Plan
   Find the total deposits. Add them to the first deposit, then subtract the withdrawal.
   C. Solve
   Since there are 4 weeks in a month, the total deposits are 4 × 5 = 20. 36 + 20 = 56. Subtract $9.50. 56 − 9.50 = $46.50.
   D. Check
   The difference between the deposits and withdrawal is about $10. This means the account should be about $10 more than $36, so the answer is reasonable.

Chapter 1 11 Course 2

Practice*
p. 12 OL AL

NAME ________ DATE ________ PERIOD ____

1-1 Practice
A Plan for Problem Solving

Use the four-step plan to solve each problem.

1. ENGINES A car engine turns 900 revolutions per minute while idling. How many revolutions does a car engine turn in one second while idling? 15 revolutions in one second
2. DISTANCE While traveling in Montana from Butte to Sidney, Mr. Kowalski, recorded that the distance from Butte to Sidney was about 6 times the distance from Butte to Bozeman. Bozeman lies between Butte and Sidney. If the distance from Butte to Bozeman is 82 miles, what is the approximate distance from Bozeman to Sidney? 410 miles
3. NUMBERS What are the next two numbers in the pattern? 3.1, 3.11, 33.11, 33.111, ____, ____ 333.111, 333.1111
4. TIDES The Bay of Fundy in Nova Scotia, Canada is known for large tides. On a particular day low tide was at 2.3 feet. The tide then rose 6.6 feet every hour for the next six hours. What was the height of high tide on that particular day? 41.9 feet
5. BASKETBALL If team A won by 2 points what was the number of points scored by team A in the 3rd quarter? 25 points

Team	Quarter Scores 1st	2nd	3rd	4th	Final Score
A	21	18	?	17	?
B	15	19	20	25	79

6. COOKING A cake recipe requires a total 16 tablespoons of butter for one cake, some for the batter and some for the frosting. If 4 tablespoons of butter are needed for the batter for one cake, how many tablespoons of butter are needed for the frosting if Samantha wants to bake three cakes? 36 tablespoons

Chapter 1 12 Course 2

Word Problem Practice*
p. 13 OL AL

NAME ________ DATE ________ PERIOD ____

1-1 Word Problem Practice
A Plan for Problem Solving

MAGAZINES **For Exercises 1 and 2, use the table that shows the costs of several popular magazines.**

Costs of Popular Magazines

Magazine	Cost of Yearly Subscription	Cost of a Single Copy
Teen World	$9.98 (12 issues)	$3.25
Soccer World	$19.97 (6 issues)	$4.99
Book Nation	$19.98 (12 issues)	$2.99
TV Weekly	$46.28 (52 issues)	$1.95

1. How much could you save by buying *Teen World* with a yearly subscription rather than 12 single copies? $29.02
2. Which of the magazines saves you the most money by purchasing a yearly subscription instead of an equivalent number of single copies? How much will you save? TV Weekly; $55.12
3. BICYCLING Adriana can ride her bicycle 6 miles in one hour. How long will it take her to ride 15 miles? 2.5 h
4. BASKETBALL At Johnson Middle School an average of 500 people attended each of the 15 home basketball games. If admission was $3 per person, about how much money was collected in all? $22,500
5. THEATER A local theater has floor seating, balcony seating, and box seating. If the theater contains 2,500 seats with 425 seats in the balcony and 215 box seats, how many seats are on the floor? 1,860 seats
6. POPCORN Janelle plans to buy three boxes of popcorn at the movies for herself and two friends. If each box costs $1.95, how much change will she receive when she pays with a ten-dollar bill? $4.15

Chapter 1 13 Course 2

Enrichment
p. 14 OL AL

NAME ________ DATE ________ PERIOD ____

1-1 Enrichment
The Great State Mystery

The United States of America has not always had 50 states. The states gradually joined the Union, starting with the first state in 1787 to the most recent state in 1959. The tables lists 15 states and their populations based on the 2000 Census. Use the 6 clues given and a problem solving process to complete the table below.

Delaware	783,600	Iowa	2,926,324	New York	18,976,457
Georgia	8,186,453	Louisiana	4,468,976	Ohio	11,353,140
Hawaii	1,211,537	Mississippi	2,844,658	Texas	20,851,820
Illinois	12,419,293	New Jersey	8,414,350	Wisconsin	5,363,675
Indiana	6,080,485	New Mexico	1,819,046	Virginia	7,078,515

1. The first state to enter the Union has the least population of the states listed.
2. The states beginning with the letter 'I' were the 19th, 21st, and 29th states admitted to the Union. Iowa entered the Union 30 years after Indiana.
3. New Jersey and Georgia were among the original thirteen colonies. Their entry number is the same as the digit in the hundreds place of their population.
4. Hawaii, Texas, and Wisconsin were the 28th, 30th, and 50th states admitted to the Union, but not in that order. To find their order, put them in order from greatest to least population.
5. The state with the second largest population entered the Union 15 years before Ohio and 24 years before the state with a population in the 4 millions.
6. The day of the month that Mississippi was admitted into the Union can be found by dividing its order of entry by 2.

Order of Entry	State Name	Date of Entry
1	Delaware	December 7, 1787
3	New Jersey	December 18, 1787
4	Georgia	January 2, 1788
10	Virginia	June 25, 1788
11	New York	June 26, 1788
17	Ohio	March 1, 1803
18	Louisiana	April 30, 1812
19	Indiana	December 11, 1816
20	Mississippi	December 10, 1817
21	Illinois	December 3, 1818
28	Texas	December 29, 1845
29	Iowa	December 28, 1846
30	Wisconsin	May 29, 1848
47	New Mexico	January 6, 1912
50	Hawaii	August 21, 1959

Chapter 1 14 Course 2

*** Also available in Spanish** ELL

Additional Lesson Resources

Transparencies
- *5-Minute Check Transparency,* Lesson 1-1

Other Print Products
- *Noteables™ Interactive Study Notebook with Foldables™*

Teacher Tech Tools
- *Interactive Classroom CD-ROM,* Lesson 1-1
- *AssignmentWorks,* Lesson 1-1

Student Tech Tools
glencoe.com
- Extra Examples, Chapter 1, Lesson 1
- Self-Check Quiz, Chapter 1, Lesson 1

1-1 A Plan for Problem Solving

MAIN IDEA

Solve problems using the four-step plan.

IN Academic Standards

7.3.4 Recognize, describe, or **extend geometric patterns using tables,** graphs, words, or symbols.
P.1.1 Build new mathematical knowledge through problem solving.

IN Math Online

glencoe.com
- Extra Examples
- Personal Tutor
- Self-Check Quiz

GET READY for the Lesson

ANALYZE GRAPHS The graph shows the countries with the most world championship motocross wins. What is the total number of wins for these five countries?

1. See students' work.
2–4. See margin.

1. Do you have all of the information necessary to solve this problem?
2. Explain how you would solve this problem. Then solve it.
3. Does your answer make sense? Explain.
4. What can you do if your first attempt at solving the problem does not work?

In mathematics, there is a *four-step plan* you can use to help you solve any problem.

Understand
- Read the problem carefully.
- What information is given?
- What do you need to find out?
- Is enough information given?
- Is there any extra information?

Plan
- How do the facts relate to each other?
- Select a strategy for solving the problem. There may be several that you can use.
- Estimate the answer.

Solve
- Use your plan to solve the problem.
- If your plan does not work, revise it or make a new plan.
- What is the solution?

Check
- Does your answer fit the facts given in the problem?
- Is your answer reasonable compared to your estimate?
- If not, make a new plan and start again.

1-1 Lesson Notes

1 Focus

Vertical Alignment

Before Lesson 1-1
Analyze problems by identifying relationships and distinguishing relevant from irrelevant information

Lesson 1-1
Analyze problems by identifying relationships, distinguishing relevant from irrelevant information, identifying missing information

After Lesson 1-1
Analyze problems by identifying relationships and distinguishing relevant from irrelevant information

2 Teach

Scaffolding Questions

Before you begin the opening activity, present the class with the following scenario. Tell students that you want to determine the two months in which the most members of the class were born.

Ask:
- What question(s) do you need to ask? What month were you born?
- How could you gather the data? class survey
- What would be a good way to record the data? tally chart; table
- How might you organize and display the data? table; bar graph; circle graph

Additional Answers

2. Sample answer: I would add the number of wins. $44 + 14 + 8 + 7 + 7 = 80$
3. Sample answer: I can compare my answer to the estimate of $40 + 10 + 10 + 10 + 10$ or 80. Since the answer is the exact value of the estimate, the total of 80 makes sense.
4. Sample answer: I would start over and make a new plan. Then, I would try to solve the problem again. If my answer is not close to the estimate, I would check my arithmetic.

Tips for New Teachers

Draw a Picture

For some learners, it may be beneficial to actually draw a picture of the problem during the *"plan"* stage of the *four-step* problem solving plan.

Focus on Mathematical Content

Some problems look difficult at first, but students can solve most of them by following the **four-step plan**.

Problems can often be solved by using **different strategies**. Sometimes a problem can be solved more easily with one strategy than with another. Some students will find using one strategy easier than others.

Estimating is a good way to check answers (in the check step).

Formative Assessment

Use the Check Your Progress exercises after each Example to determine students' understanding of concepts.

ADDITIONAL EXAMPLE

1 **SPENDING** A can of soda holds 12 fluid ounces. A 2-liter bottle holds about 67 fluid ounces. If a pack of six cans costs the same as a 2-liter bottle, which is the better buy? pack of six cans

Additional Examples are also in:

- Noteables™ Interactive Study Notebook with Foldables™
- Interactive Classroom PowerPoint® Presentations

Real-World Link In a recent year, worldwide consumers purchased 8.8 million LCD (Liquid Crystal Display) TVs.
Source: DisplaySearch

EXAMPLE Use the Four-Step Plan

1 **TELEVISION** **There were about 268 million TVs in the U.S. in 2007. This amount increases by 4 million each year after 2007. In what year will there be at least 300 million TVs?**

Understand *What are you trying to find?*
In what year will there be at least 300 million TVs in the U.S.?

What information do you need to solve the problem?
You know how many TVs there were in 2007. Also, the number increases by 4 million each year.

Plan Find the number of TVs needed to reach 300 million. Then divide this number by 4 to find the number of years that will pass before the total reaches 300 million TVs.

Solve The change in the number of TVs from 268 million to 300 million is 300 − 268 or 32 million TVs. Dividing the difference by 4, you get 32 ÷ 4 or 8.

You can also use the *make a table* strategy.

Year	'07	'08	'09	'10	'11	'12	'13	'14	'15
Number (millions)	268	272	276	280	284	288	292	296	300

+4 +4 +4 +4 +4 +4 +4 +4

So, there will be at least 300 million TVs in the U.S. in the year 2015.

Check 8 years × 4 million = 32 million
268 million + 32 million = 300 million ✔

CHECK Your Progress a. about 8 pounds

a. **WHALES** A baby blue whale gains about 200 pounds each day. About how many pounds does a baby blue whale gain per hour?

Problems can be solved using different operations or strategies.

Problem-Solving Strategies — Concept Summary

guess and check	use a graph
look for a pattern	work backward
make an organized list	eliminate possibilities
draw a diagram	estimate reasonable answers
act it out	use logical reasoning
solve a simpler problem	make a model

26 Chapter 1 Introduction to Algebra and Functions

EXAMPLE Use a Strategy in the Four-Step Plan

2 **GEOMETRY** A *diagonal* connects two nonconsecutive vertices in a figure, as shown at the right. Find how many diagonals a figure with 7 sides would have.

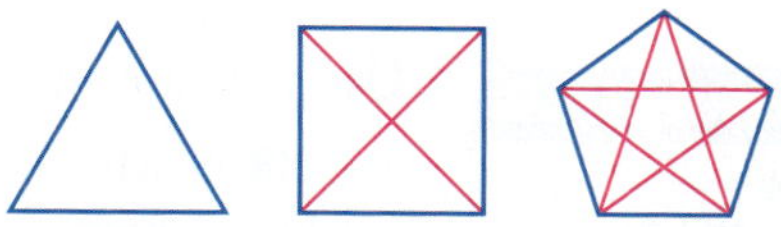

3 sides 0 diagonals | 4 sides 2 diagonals | 5 sides 5 diagonals

Understand You know the number of diagonals for figures with three, four, and five sides.

Plan You can look for a pattern by organizing the information in a table. Then continue the pattern until you find the diagonals for an object with 7 sides.

Solve

Sides	3	4	5	6	7
Diagonals	0	2	5	9	14

+2 +3 +4 +5

So, a 7-sided figure would have 14 diagonals.

Check Check your answer by making a drawing.

CHECK Your Progress

. 1, 3, 6, 10, 15, 21, 28, 6; Add 2 to the first erm, add 3 to the second erm, add 4 to the third erm, and so on.

b. **GEOMETRY** Numbers that can be represented by a triangular arrangement of dots are called *triangular numbers.* The first five triangular numbers are shown below. Write a sequence formed by the first eight triangular numbers. Write a rule for generating the sequence.

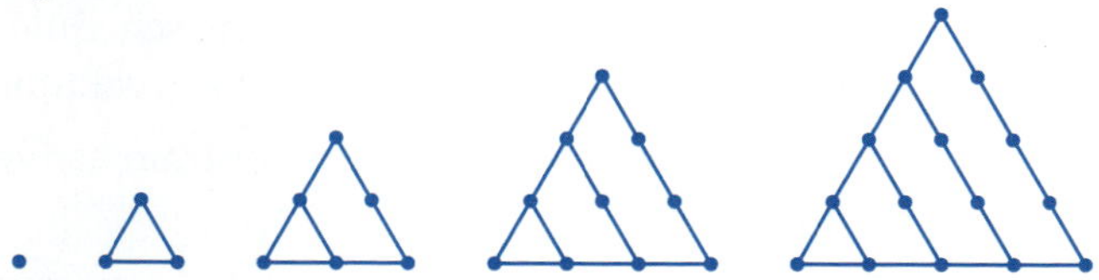

1 3 6 10 15

★ indicates multi-step problem

CHECK Your Understanding

Use the four-step plan to solve each problem.

Example 1 (p. 26)

1. **ANALYZE TABLES** The table lists the sizes of six of the largest lakes in North Carolina. About how many times as large is High Rock Lake than Hyco Lake?

Sample answer: 4 times; 6,000 ÷ 4,000 = 4

Lake	Size (acres)
Lake Mattamuskeet	40,000
Falls Lake	12,000
Hyco Lake	3,750
Lake Gaston	20,000
Lake James	6,500
High Rock Lake	15,000

Example 2 (p. 27)

2. **ALGEBRA** What are the next two numbers in the pattern below?

1, 1, 2, 6, 24, ■, ■ 120, 720

ADDITIONAL EXAMPLE

2 **POPULATION** For every 100,000 people in the United States, there are 5,750 radios. For every 100,000 people in Canada, there are 323 radios. Suppose Sheamus lives in Des Moines, Iowa, and Alex lives in Windsor, Ontario. Both cities have about 200,000 residents. About how many more radios are there in Sheamus' city than in Alex's city? 10,854 radios

3 Practice

Formative Assessment

Use Exercises 1–2 to check for understanding.

Then use the chart at the bottom of the next page to customize your assignments for students.

Intervention You may wish to use the Study Guide and Intervention Master on page 10 of the *Chapter 1 Resource Masters* for additional reinforcement.

Lesson 1-1 A Plan for Problem Solving 27

Odd/Even Assignments

Exercises 3–10 are structured so that students practice the same concepts whether they are assigned odd or even problems.

Differentiated Instruction

Interpersonal Learners After assigning Exercise 13, have students write their problems on index cards with the solution on the back. Then have students exchange index cards with each other and solve each others' problems.

Practice and Problem Solving

HOMEWORK HELP	
For Exercises	See Examples
3–6	1
7–10	2

Exercise Levels
A: 3–10
B: 11–15
C: 16–18

Use the four-step plan to solve each problem.

3. **BIRDS** Most hummingbirds flap their wings about 50 times a second. How many times can a hummingbird flap its wings in one minute? **3,000**

4. **PLANETS** Jupiter is about 3 times the size of Neptune. If the diameter of Jupiter is 88,736 miles, estimate the diameter of Neptune. **Sample answer: 30,000 miles; 90,000 ÷ 3 = 30,000**

5. **FIELD TRIPS** To attend a field trip to a museum, each student will have to pay $6.00 for transportation and $5.75 for admission. If there are 65 students attending the field trip, how much money will their teacher need to collect? **$763.75**

6. **CANOE RENTALS** A state park took in $12,000 in canoe rentals during March. June rentals are expected to double that amount. If canoes rent for $40, how many canoe rentals are expected in June? **600 canoe rentals**

7. **GEOMETRY** What are the next two figures in the pattern?

8. **ALGEBRA** What are the next two numbers in the pattern below?

9, 27, 81, 243, 729, ■, ■ **2,187 and 6,561**

ANALYZE TABLES For Exercises 9 and 10, use the commuter train schedule shown.

A commuter train departs from a train station and travels to the city each day. The schedule shows the first five departure and arrival times.

Commuter Train Schedule	
Departure	Arrival
6:30 A.M.	6:50 A.M.
7:15 A.M.	7:35 A.M.
8:00 A.M.	8:20 A.M.
8:45 A.M.	9:05 A.M.
9:30 A.M.	9:50 A.M.

9. How often does the commuter train arrive in the city? **every 45 minutes**

★ 10. What is the latest time that passengers can depart from the train station if they need to arrive in the city no later than noon? **11:00 A.M.**

11. **HOMEWORK** Angel has guitar practice at 7:00 P.M. He has homework in math, science, and history that will take him 30 minutes each to complete. He also has to allow 20 minutes for dinner. What is the latest time Angel can start his homework? **5:10 P.M.**

★ 12. **ESTIMATION** Terry opened a savings account in December with $132 and saved $27 each month beginning in January. Estimate the value of Terry's account in July. Then calculate the amount and evaluate the reasonableness of your estimate. **Sample answer: about $130 + $30 × 7 or $340; $132 + $27 × 7 = $321; The estimate is reasonable.**

13. **FIND THE DATA** Refer to the Data File on pages 16–19 of your book. Choose some data and write a real-world problem in which you would use the four-step plan to solve the problem. **See students' work.**

DIFFERENTIATED HOMEWORK OPTIONS

Level	Assignment	Two-Day Option	
BL Basic	3–10, 17–24	3–9 odd, 19–24	4–10 even, 17–18
OL Core	3–15, 17–24	3–10, 19–24	11–15, 17–18
AL Advanced/Pre-AP	11–20 (optional: 21–24)		

The **Differentiated Homework Options** provide suggestions for the exercises that are appropriate for basic, core, or advanced students. Many of the homework exercises are paired, so that students could do the odds one day and the evens the next day.

★ 14. **ANALYZE TABLES** The sizes of Earth's oceans in millions of square kilometers are shown in the table. If the combined size of Earth's oceans is 367 million square kilometers, what is the size of the Pacific Ocean? **156 million km^2**

Earth's Oceans	
Ocean	Size (million km^2)
Arctic	45
Atlantic	77
Indian	69
Pacific	▒
Southern	20

Source: *The World Factbook*

15. **MONEY** Meli wants to buy a pair of rollerblades that cost $140.75. So far, she has saved $56.25. If she saves $6.50 every week, in how many weeks will she be able to purchase the rollerblades? **13 weeks**

Academic Standards • ISTEP+

xtra Practice, pp. 668, 704

.O.T. Problems

16. **CHALLENGE** Use the digits 5, 6, 7, and 8 to form two 2-digit numbers so that their product is as great as possible. Use each digit only once. **85 × 76 = 6,460**

17. **OPEN ENDED** Create a real-world problem that can be solved by adding 79 and 42 and then multiplying the result by 3. **See margin.**

18. **WRITING IN MATH** Explain why it is important to plan before solving a problem.

8. Sample answer: helps to organize our thoughts and ocus on how to pproach solving e problem.

ISTEP+ PRACTICE P.1.1

19. Sheryl has $2 to spend at the school store. Based on the choices below, which three items from the table could Sheryl purchase? **C**

Item	Cost
Folder	$1.50
Pencil	$0.20
Pen	$0.50
Ruler	$1.75
Highlighter	$0.40

A folder, pencil, pen

B folder, highlighter, pencil

C pencil, pen, highlighter

D ruler, highlighter, pencil

20. Mr. Brooks went on a business trip. The trip was 380 miles, and the average price of gasoline was $3.15 per gallon. What information is needed to find the amount Mr. Brooks spent on gasoline for the trip? **G**

F Number of times Mr. Brooks stopped to fill his tank with gasoline

G Number of miles the car can travel using one gallon of gasoline

H Number of hours the trip took

J Average number of miles Mr. Brooks drove per day

GET READY for the Next Lesson

PREREQUISITE SKILL Multiply.

21. 10 × 10 **100**   22. 3 × 3 × 3 **27**   23. 5 × 5 × 5 × 5 **625**   24. 2 × 2 × 2 × 2 × 2 **32**

4 Assess

Tips for New Teachers

Writing

If students have difficulty with Exercise 17, have them first decide what objects or units the numbers represent. Encourage them to be creative. For example, if the numbers represent fish, what real-world situation might require finding the sum of 79 fish and 42 fish? And why would the sum be multiplied by 3?

Ticket Out the Door Read the following problem to students. Then tell them to write how they would follow the four-step plan to find the answer.

The seventh grade had a bake sale to raise money for a class trip. On Monday they made $30. On Tuesday they made $20. On Wednesday they made $50. School was closed on Thursday and Friday. How much money did they make that week?

FOLDABLES Study Organizer

Foldables™ Follow-Up

Remind students to note key concepts in their Foldables. For example, they might want to write the steps of the four-step plan and the names of the problem-solving strategies that they find most useful.

Additional Answer

17. Sample answer: For the school bake sale, Samantha bakes 79 cookies and 42 brownies. If two other students baked the same amount of cookies and brownies, how many items did they bake altogether?

1-2 Powers and Exponents

PACING: **Regular:** 1 period, **Block:** 0.5 period

IN Academic Standards **7.1.2 Recognize and compute whole number powers of positive integers.**

Options for Differentiated Instruction

ELL = English Language Learner AL = Above or Beyond Grade Level SS = Struggling Students SN = Special Needs

Vocabulary Development ELL SS SN

Use after introducing the term *power*.

Have students compare multiplying integers and evaluating powers. Suggest that they write out a short series of products and a short series of powers having the same base. An example is shown below. Have them explain how the terms increase in each case. Sample answer: In the first case, the terms increase by 3. In the second case, the terms increase by powers of 3.

Products
$3 \times 1 = 3$
$3 \times 2 = 6$
$3 \times 3 = 9$
$3 \times 6 = 18$

Powers	
3^1	$= 3$
$3^2 = 3 \times 3$	$= 9$
$3^3 = 3 \times 3 \times 3$	$= 27$
$3^6 = 3 \times 3 \times 3 \times 3 \times 3 \times 3 = 729$	

Graphic Organizers ELL SS SN

Use before presenting Examples 1 and 2.

It is easier for students to remember related terms if the terms are clustered around a natural heading or category. Having students create *vocabulary charts* is one way to do this. Distribute copies of the following vocabulary chart for this lesson. As a class, have students find examples for each term in the chart. Students can use this chart to create vocabulary charts for other lessons. Sample examples are given.

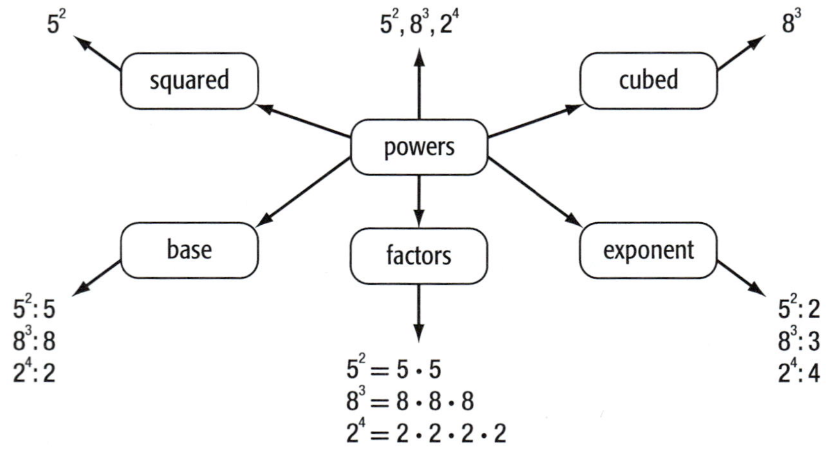

Each chapter includes ideas for **differentiating instruction** in your classroom. These hints are keyed for English learners, students above grade level, struggling students, and students with special needs.

Leveled Lesson Resources

Also on TeacherWorks™
Lesson 1-2

Chapter 1 Resource Masters

BL = Below or Approaching Grade Level OL = On Grade Level AL = Above or Beyond Grade Level ELL = English Language Learner

Lesson Reading Guide
p. 15 BL OL ELL

NAME ________ DATE ________ PERIOD ____

1-2 Lesson Reading Guide
Powers and Exponents

Get Ready for the Lesson

Read the introduction at the top of page 30 in your textbook. Write your answers below.

1. How is doubling shown in the table? **multiplying by 2**
2. How many text messages will be sent after 4 minutes? **16**
3. What is the relationship between the number of 2s and the number of minutes? **There is one 2 for every minute.**

Read the Lesson

4. What is the difference between a power and an exponent? **An exponent tells how many times the base is used as a factor, and a power is a number expressed using an exponent.**
5. Identify the exponent in each expression.
 a. 5^8 **8**
 b. 8^5 **5**
 c. 8^3 **3**
 d. 8 **1**
6. Complete the sentence: Numbers written with exponents are in ________ form, whereas numbers written without exponents are in ________ form. **exponential; standard**

Remember What You Learned

7. In the expression 6^7, circle the exponent in red. Then circle the power in another color. **See students' work.**

Chapter 1 15 Course 2

Study Guide and Intervention*
p. 16 BL OL ELL

NAME ________ DATE ________ PERIOD ____

1-2 Study Guide and Intervention
Powers and Exponents

$3^4 = \underbrace{3 \cdot 3 \cdot 3 \cdot 3}_{\text{common factors}} = 81$ (Exponent; Base)

The **exponent** tells you how many times the **base** is used as a factor.

Example 1 Write 6^3 as a product of the same factor.
The base is 6. The exponent 3 means that 6 is used as a factor 3 times.
$6^3 = 6 \cdot 6 \cdot 6$

Example 2 Evaluate 5^4.
$5^4 = 5 \cdot 5 \cdot 5 \cdot 5$
$= 625$

Example 3 Write $4 \cdot 4 \cdot 4 \cdot 4 \cdot 4$ in exponential form.
The base is 4. It is used as a factor 5 times, so the exponent is 5.
$4 \cdot 4 \cdot 4 \cdot 4 \cdot 4 = 4^5$

Exercises

Write each power as a product of the same factor.
1. 7^3 $7 \cdot 7 \cdot 7$ 2. 2^7 $2 \cdot 2 \cdot 2 \cdot 2 \cdot 2 \cdot 2 \cdot 2$ 3. 9^2 $9 \cdot 9$ 4. 15^4 $15 \cdot 15 \cdot 15 \cdot 15$

Evaluate each expression.
5. 3^5 243 6. 7^3 343 7. 8^4 4,096 8. 5^3 125

Write each product in exponential form.
9. $2 \cdot 2 \cdot 2 \cdot 2$ 2^4 10. $7 \cdot 7 \cdot 7 \cdot 7 \cdot 7 \cdot 7$ 7^6
11. $10 \cdot 10 \cdot 10$ 10^3 12. $9 \cdot 9 \cdot 9 \cdot 9 \cdot 9$ 9^5
13. $12 \cdot 12 \cdot 12$ 12^3 14. $5 \cdot 5 \cdot 5 \cdot 5$ 5^4
15. $6 \cdot 6 \cdot 6 \cdot 6 \cdot 6$ 6^5 16. $1 \cdot 1 \cdot 1 \cdot 1 \cdot 1 \cdot 1 \cdot 1 \cdot 1$ 1^8

Chapter 1 16 Course 2

Skills Practice*
p. 17 BL OL

NAME ________ DATE ________ PERIOD ____

1-2 Skills Practice
Powers and Exponents

Write each power as a product of the same factor.
1. 11^2 $11 \cdot 11$ 2. 3^4 $3 \cdot 3 \cdot 3 \cdot 3$
3. 2^5 $2 \cdot 2 \cdot 2 \cdot 2 \cdot 2$ 4. 9^3 $9 \cdot 9 \cdot 9$
5. 15^3 $15 \cdot 15 \cdot 15$ 6. 4^3 $4 \cdot 4 \cdot 4$
7. 1^6 $1 \cdot 1 \cdot 1 \cdot 1 \cdot 1 \cdot 1$ 8. 17^4 $17 \cdot 17 \cdot 17 \cdot 17$
9. 3^7 $3 \cdot 3 \cdot 3 \cdot 3 \cdot 3 \cdot 3 \cdot 3$ 10. 8^6 $8 \cdot 8 \cdot 8 \cdot 8 \cdot 8 \cdot 8$

Evaluate each expression.
11. 9^2 81 12. 8^2 64
13. 8^3 512 14. 2^4 16
15. 2^5 32 16. 6^3 216
17. 3^4 81 18. 3^5 243
19. 9^3 729 20. 11^2 121
21. 4^7 16,384 22. 12^3 1,728
23. 1^9 1 24. 10^4 10,000
25. 20^4 160,000 26. 2^6 64

Write each product in exponential form.
27. $12 \cdot 12$ 12^2 28. $10 \cdot 10 \cdot 10$ 10^3
29. $4 \cdot 4 \cdot 4 \cdot 4 \cdot 4$ 4^5 30. $9 \cdot 9 \cdot 9 \cdot 9$ 9^4
31. $15 \cdot 15 \cdot 15 \cdot 15 \cdot 15$ 15^5 32. $6 \cdot 6 \cdot 6 \cdot 6 \cdot 6 \cdot 6 \cdot 6 \cdot 6$ 6^8

Chapter 1 17 Course 2

Practice*
p. 18 OL AL

NAME ________ DATE ________ PERIOD ____

1-2 Practice
Powers and Exponents

Write each power as a product of the same factor.
1. 5^7 $5 \cdot 5 \cdot 5 \cdot 5 \cdot 5 \cdot 5 \cdot 5$ 2. 2^4 $2 \cdot 2 \cdot 2 \cdot 2$ 3. 7^2 $7 \cdot 7$
4. 10^5 $10 \cdot 10 \cdot 10 \cdot 10 \cdot 10$ 5. 3^3 $3 \cdot 3 \cdot 3$ 6. 6^8 $6 \cdot 6 \cdot 6 \cdot 6 \cdot 6 \cdot 6 \cdot 6 \cdot 6$
7. *four to the eighth power* $4 \cdot 4 \cdot 4 \cdot 4 \cdot 4 \cdot 4 \cdot 4 \cdot 4$ 8. *eight cubed* $8 \cdot 8 \cdot 8$ 9. *ten squared* $10 \cdot 10$

Write each product in exponential form.
10. $9 \cdot 9 \cdot 9 \cdot 9 \cdot 9 \cdot 9$ 9^6 11. $1 \cdot 1 \cdot 1 \cdot 1 \cdot 1$ 1^5 12. $2 \cdot 2 \cdot 2 \cdot 2 \cdot 2 \cdot 2 \cdot 2$ 2^7
13. $6 \cdot 6 \cdot 6 \cdot 6 \cdot 6 \cdot 6 \cdot 6 \cdot 6 \cdot 6$ 6^9 14. $5 \cdot 5$ 5^2 15. $4 \cdot 4 \cdot 3 \cdot 3 \cdot 3 \cdot 3 \cdot 3$ $4^2 \cdot 3^5$

Evaluate each expression.
16. 4^3 64 17. 1^{11} 1 18. 2^5 32
19. 10^3 1,000 20. 9^3 729 21. 8^1 8
22. *five to fourth power* 625 23. *7 squared* 49 24. *zero to the sixth power* 0

Use a calculator to determine whether each sentence is *true* or *false*.
25. $2^8 = 8^2$ false 26. $17^2 < 172$ false 27. $3^2 > 1^{19}$ true

Order the following powers from least to greatest.
28. $7^2, 5^3, 3^4, 2^5$ — $2^5, 7^2, 3^4, 5^3$ 29. $4^3, 1^{13}, 12^2, 8^3$ — $1^{13}, 4^3, 12^2, 8^3$ 30. $3^9, 5^7, 7^5, 9^3$ — $9^3, 7^5, 3^9, 5^7$

31. INTERACTIVE MAPS Mansi is using an interactive map on her computer that allows her to zoom in or zoom out. Each time she zooms out the scale of the map increases by a power of ten. If she zooms out four times the scale is 10^4 times greater. Write this number in standard form. $10^4 = 10{,}000$

32. BACTERIA A lab technician observed 5 bacteria growing in a lab dish. One hour later he observed 25 bacteria. Every hour he notices about 5 times as many as the hour before. After several hours of observation, he determined the lab dish had 5^9 bacteria. Use a calculator to find the number in standard form that represents the bacteria in the lab dish. $5^9 = 1{,}953{,}125$

Chapter 1 18 Course 2

Word Problem Practice*
p. 19 OL AL

NAME ________ DATE ________ PERIOD ____

1-2 Word Problem Practice
Powers and Exponents

1. SPACE SHUTTLE The cost of each flight of the Space Shuttle is about \$10,000,000. Write this amount in exponential form. 10^7 dollars

2. ANIMALS The African bush elephant is the largest land animal and weighs about 8 tons. Write this amount in exponential form. 2^3 tons

3. VOLUME To find the volume of a rectangular box you multiply the length times the width times the height. In a cube all sides are the same length. If the cube has length, width, and height of 6 inches, write the volume as a product. Then write it in exponential form. $6 \times 6 \times 6$; 6^3 in³

4. SCIENCE A certain type of cell doubles every hour. If you start with one cell, at the end of one hour you would have 2 cells, at the end of two hours you have 4 cells, and so on. The expression $2 \times 2 \times 2 \times 2 \times 2$ tells you how many cells you would have after five hours. Write this expression in exponential form; then evaluate it. 2^5 cells; 32 cells

5. MATH Write 625 using exponents in as many ways as you can. 5^4; 25^2

6. PREFIXES Many prefixes are used in mathematics and science. The prefix giga in gigameter represents 1,000,000,000 meters. Write this prefix as a power of ten. 10^9 meters

7. LIBRARY The school library contains 9^4 books. How many library books are in the school library? 6,561 books

8. HOT DOGS The concession stand at the county fair sold 6^3 hot dogs on the first day. How many hot dogs did they sell? 216 hot dogs

Chapter 1 19 Course 2

Enrichment
p. 20 OL AL

NAME ________ DATE ________ PERIOD ____

1-2 Enrichment
The Four-Digit Problem

Use the digits 1, 2, 3, and 4 to write expressions for the numbers 1 through 50. Each digit is used exactly once in each expression. (There might be more than one expression for a given number.)

You can use addition, subtraction, multiplication (not division), exponents, and parentheses in any way you wish. Also, you can use two digits to make one number, as in 34. A few expressions are given to get you started.

Sample answers given.

$1 = (3 \times 1) - (4 - 2)$	$18 = (2 \times 3) \times (4 - 1)$	$35 = 2^{(4-1)} + 3$
$2 = (4 - 3) + (2 - 1)$	$19 = 3(2 + 4) + 1$	$36 = 34 + (2 \times 1)$
$3 = (4 - 3) + (2 \times 1)$	$20 = 21 - (4 - 3)$	$37 = 31 + 4 + 2$
$4 = (4 - 2) + (3 - 1)$	$21 = (4 + 3) \times (2 + 1)$	$38 = 42 - (1 + 3)$
$5 = (4 - 2) + (3 \times 1)$	$22 = 21 + (4 - 3)$	$39 = 42 - (1 \times 3)$
$6 = 4 + 3 + 1 - 2$	$23 = 31 - (4 \times 2)$	$40 = 41 - (3 - 2)$
$7 = 3(4 - 1) - 2$	$24 = (4 + 2) \times (3 + 1)$	$41 = 43 - (2 \times 1)$
$8 = 4 + 3 + 2 - 1$	$25 = (2 + 3) \times (4 + 1)$	$42 = 43 - (2 - 1)$
$9 = 4 + 2 + (3 \times 1)$	$26 = 24 + (3 - 1)$	$43 = 42 + 1^3$
$10 = 4 + 3 + 2 + 1$	$27 = 3^2 \times (4 - 1)$	$44 = 43 + (2 - 1)$
$11 = (4 \times 3) - (2 - 1)$	$28 = 21 + 4 + 3$	$45 = 43 + (2 \times 1)$
$12 = (4 \times 3) \times (2 - 1)$	$29 = 2^{(4+1)} - 3$	$46 = 43 + (2 + 1)$
$13 = (4 \times 3) + (2 - 1)$	$30 = (2 \times 3) \times (4 + 1)$	$47 = 31 + 4^2$
$14 = (4 \times 3) + (2 \times 1)$	$31 = 34 - (2 + 1)$	$48 = 4^2 \times (3 \times 1)$
$15 = 2(3 + 4) + 1$	$32 = 4^2 \times (3 - 1)$	$49 = 41 + 2^3$
$16 = (4 \times 2) \times (3 - 1)$	$33 = 21 + (4 \times 3)$	$50 = 41 + 3^2$
$17 = 3(4 + 2) - 1$	$34 = 2 \times (14 + 3)$	

Chapter 1 20 Course 2

* Also available in Spanish ELL

Additional Lesson Resources

Transparencies
- *5-Minute Check Transparency,* Lesson 1-2

Other Print Products
- *Teaching Mathematics with Manipulatives*
- *Noteables™ Interactive Study Notebook with Foldables™*

Teacher Tech Tools
- *Interactive Classroom CD-ROM,* Lesson 1-2
- *AssignmentWorks,* Lesson 1-2

Student Tech Tools
glencoe.com
- Extra Examples, Chapter 1, Lesson 2
- Self-Check Quiz, Chapter 1, Lesson 2

1-2 Lesson Notes

1 Focus

Vertical Alignment

Before Lesson 1-2
Calculate with positive and negative integers

Lesson 1-2
Understand and compute positive integer powers of nonnegative integers; compute examples as repeated multiplication

After Lesson 1-2
Understand whole-number exponents. Multiply and divide expressions involving exponents with a common base

2 Teach

Scaffolding Questions

Give each pair of students ten unit cubes ($1 \times 1 \times 1$). Have students use the unit cubes to make squares.

Ask:

- How many unit cubes are in a square with sides of 1? 1
- How many unit cubes are in a square with sides of 2? 4
- How many unit cubes are in a square with sides of 3? 9
- How many unit cubes do you predict will be in a square with sides of 4? with sides of 5? 16; 25
- What is the relationship between the number of unit cubes needed to build a square and the number of units per side? The number of cubes needed to build a square equals the number of squares per side multiplied by the same number.

1-2 Powers and Exponents

MAIN IDEA

Use powers and exponents.

IN Academic Standards

7.1.2 Recognize and compute whole number powers of positive integers.

New Vocabulary

factors
exponent
base
powers
squared
cubed
evaluate
standard form
exponential form

IN Math Online

glencoe.com

- Extra Examples
- Personal Tutor
- Self-Check Quiz

GET READY for the Lesson

TEXT MESSAGING Suppose you text message one of your friends. That friend then text messages two friends after one minute. The pattern continues.

Minutes	Number of Text Messages	
0	1	= 1
1	1 × 2	= 2
2	2 × 2	= 4
3	2 × 2 × 2	= 8

1. How is doubling shown in the table? multiplying by 2
2. How many text messages will be sent after 4 minutes? 16
3. What is the relationship between the number of 2s and the number of minutes? There is one 2 for every minute.

Two or more numbers that are multiplied together to form a product a called **factors**. When the same factor is used, you may use an exponen to simplify the notation. The **exponent** tells how many times the base i used as a factor. The common factor is called the **base**.

$16 = 2 \cdot 2 \cdot 2 \cdot 2 = 2^4$ ← exponent; ↑ base

Numbers expressed using exponents are called **powers**.

Powers	Words
5^2	five to the second powe or five **squared**
4^3	four to the third power or four **cubed**
2^4	two to the fourth power

EXAMPLES Write Powers as Products

Write each power as a product of the same factor.

1 7^5

Seven is used as a factor five times.

$7^5 = 7 \cdot 7 \cdot 7 \cdot 7 \cdot 7$

2 3^2

Three is used as a factor twice.

$3^2 = 3 \cdot 3$

CHECK Your Progress

Write each power as a product of the same factor.

a. 6^4 $6 \cdot 6 \cdot 6 \cdot 6$ b. 1^3 $1 \cdot 1 \cdot 1$ c. 9^5 $9 \cdot 9 \cdot 9 \cdot 9 \cdot 9$

Scaffolding Questions give direction and momentum to the lesson, clarify its purpose, and keep students on task.

You can **evaluate**, or find the value of, powers by multiplying the factors. Numbers written without exponents are in **standard form**.

EXAMPLES Write Powers in Standard Form

Evaluate each expression.

Vocabulary Link **Evaluate**
Everyday Use to find what something is worth
Math Use find the value of

3 2^5

$2^5 = 2 \cdot 2 \cdot 2 \cdot 2 \cdot 2$ 2 is used as a factor 5 times.
$= 32$ Multiply.

4 4^3

$4^3 = 4 \cdot 4 \cdot 4$ 4 is used as a factor 3 times.
$= 64$ Multiply.

CHECK Your Progress

Evaluate each expression.

d. 10^2 **100** e. 7^3 **343** f. 5^4 **625**

Numbers written with exponents are in **exponential form**.

EXAMPLE Write Numbers in Exponential Form

5 **Write $3 \cdot 3 \cdot 3 \cdot 3$ in exponential form.**

3 is the base. It is used as a factor 4 times. So, the exponent is 4.
$3 \cdot 3 \cdot 3 \cdot 3 = 3^4$

CHECK Your Progress

Write each product in exponential form.

g. $5 \cdot 5 \cdot 5$ 5^3 h. $12 \cdot 12 \cdot 12 \cdot 12 \cdot 12 \cdot 12$ 12^6

★ indicates multi-step problem

CHECK Your Understanding

Examples 1, 2 (p. 30)
Write each power as a product of the same factor.

1. 9^3 $9 \cdot 9 \cdot 9$ 2. 3^4 $3 \cdot 3 \cdot 3 \cdot 3$ 3. 8^5 $8 \cdot 8 \cdot 8 \cdot 8 \cdot 8$

Examples 3, 4 (p. 31)
Evaluate each expression.

4. 2^4 **16** 5. 7^2 **49** 6. 10^3 **1,000**

7. **POPULATION** There are approximately 5^{10} people living in North Carolina. About how many people is this? **9,765,625 people**

Example 5 (p. 31)
Write each product in exponential form.

8. $5 \cdot 5 \cdot 5 \cdot 5 \cdot 5 \cdot 5$ 5^6 9. $1 \cdot 1 \cdot 1 \cdot 1$ 1^4 10. $4 \cdot 4 \cdot 4 \cdot 4 \cdot 4$ 4^5

Focus on Mathematical Content

A number written in **exponential form** has a base and an exponent.

To **evaluate** a number in exponential form, use the base as a factor and multiply it the number of times shown by the exponent.

Formative Assessment

Use the Check Your Progress exercises after each Example to determine students' understanding of concepts.

ADDITIONAL EXAMPLES

Write each power as a product of the same factor.

1 8^4 $8 \cdot 8 \cdot 8 \cdot 8$
2 4^6 $4 \cdot 4 \cdot 4 \cdot 4 \cdot 4 \cdot 4$

Evaluate each expression.

3 8^3 512
4 6^4 1,296
5 Write $9 \cdot 9 \cdot 9 \cdot 9 \cdot 9 \cdot 9$ in exponential form. 9^6

Additional Examples are also in:

- Noteables™ Interactive Study Notebook with Foldables™
- Interactive Classroom PowerPoint® Presentations

3 Practice

Formative Assessment

Use Exercises 1–10 to check for understanding.

Then use the chart at the bottom of the next page to customize your assignments for students.

Intervention You may wish to use the Study Guide and Intervention Master on page 16 of the *Chapter 1 Resource Masters* for additional reinforcement.

Odd/Even Assignments

Exercises 11–28 are structured so that students practice the same concepts whether they are assigned odd or even problems.

Practice and Problem Solving

HOMEWORK HELP

For Exercises	See Examples
11–16	1, 2
17–24	3, 4
25–28	5

Exercise Levels
A: 11–28
B: 29–39
C: 40–43

Write each power as a product of the same factor. **13. 3 • 3 • 3 • 3 • 3 • 3 • 3 •**

11. 1^5 **1 • 1 • 1 • 1 • 1** 12. 4^2 **4 • 4** 13. 3^8
14. 8^6 **8 • 8 • 8 • 8 • 8 • 8** 15. 9^3 **9 • 9 • 9** 16. 10^4 **10 • 10 • 10 • 10**

Evaluate each expression.

17. 2^6 **64** 18. 4^3 **64** 19. 7^4 **2,401**
20. 4^6 **4,096** 21. 1^{10} **1** 22. 10^1 **10**

23. **BIKING** In a recent year, the number of 12- to 17-year-olds that went off-road biking was 10^6. Write this number in standard form. **1,000,000**

24. **TRAINS** The Maglev train in China is the fastest passenger train in the worl Its average speed is 3^5 miles per hour. Write this speed in standard form. **243 mph**

Write each product in exponential form.

25. $3 \cdot 3$ **3^2** 26. $7 \cdot 7 \cdot 7 \cdot 7$ **7^4**
27. $1 \cdot 1 \cdot 1 \cdot 1 \cdot 1 \cdot 1 \cdot 1 \cdot 1$ **1^8** 28. $6 \cdot 6 \cdot 6 \cdot 6 \cdot 6$ **6^5**

Write each power as a product of the same factor.

29. *four to the fifth power* **4 • 4 • 4 • 4 • 4** 30. *nine squared* **9 • 9**

Evaluate each expression.

31. *six to the fourth power* **1,296** 32. *6 cubed* **216**

GEOMETRY **For Exercises 33 and 34, use the puzzle cube below.**

33. Suppose the puzzle cube is made entirely of unit cubes. Find the number of unit cubes in the puzzle. Write your answer using exponents. **3^3**

34. Why do you think the expression 3^3 is sometimes read as *3 cubed*?

34. Sample answer: A number taken to the third power is the same as the volume of a cube, or the amount of space inside a cube.

35. **NUMBERS** Write $5 \cdot 5 \cdot 5 \cdot 5 \cdot 4 \cdot 4 \cdot 4$ in exponential form. **$5^4 \cdot 4^3$**

★36. **COMPUTERS** A gigabyte is a measure of computer data storage capacity. One gigabyte stores 2^{30} bytes of data. Use a calculator to find the number in standard form that represents two gigabytes. **2,147,483,648**

Order the following powers from least to greatest.

★37. $6^5, 1^{14}, 4^{10}, 17^3$ **$1^{14}, 17^3, 6^5, 4^{10}$** ★38. $2^8, 15^2, 6^3, 3^5$ **$6^3, 15^2, 3^5, 2^8$** ★39. $5^3, 4^6, 2^{11}, 7^2$ **$7^2, 5^3, 2^{11}, 4^6$**

40. **OPEN ENDED** Select a number between 1,000 and 2,000 that can be expresse as a power. **Sample answer: $4^5 = 1,024$**

Academic Standards • ISTEP+

Extra Practice, pp. 668, 704

DIFFERENTIATED HOMEWORK OPTIONS

Level	Assignment	Two-Day Option	
BL Basic	11–28, 41–50	11–27 odd, 44	12–28 even, 41–43, 45–50
OL Core	11–21 odd, 23–24, 25–31 odd, 33–37, 39, 41–50	11–28, 44	29–39, 41–43, 45–50
AL Advanced/Pre-AP	29–46 (optional: 47–50)		

.O.T. Problems

41. **CHALLENGE** Write two different powers that have the same value. $8^2 = 64$ and $4^3 = 64$

42. **Which One Doesn't Belong?** Identify the number that does not belong with the other three. Explain your reasoning.

121	361	576	1,000

1,000; 1,000 cannot be expressed as a square: $11^2 = 121$, $19^2 = 361$, $24^2 = 576$

43. **WRITING IN MATH** Analyze the number pattern shown at the right. Then write a convincing argument as to the value of 2^0. Based on your argument, what do you think will be the value of 2^{-1}?

$2^4 = 16$
$2^3 = 8$
$2^2 = 4$
$2^1 = 2$
$2^0 = ?$

3. Sample answer: he pattern is that ach successive rm is $\frac{1}{2}$ of the revious one, so $^0 = 1$ and $^{-1} = \frac{1}{2}$.

ISTEP+ PRACTICE 7.1.2

44. Which model represents 6^3? **A**

A
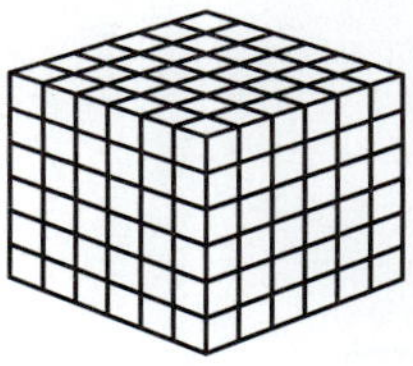

C
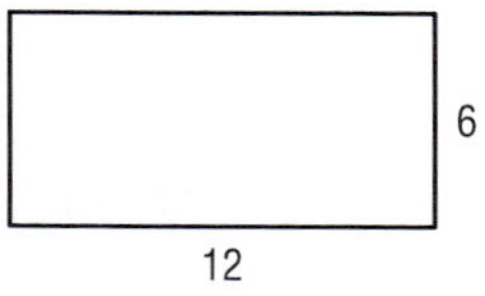

B
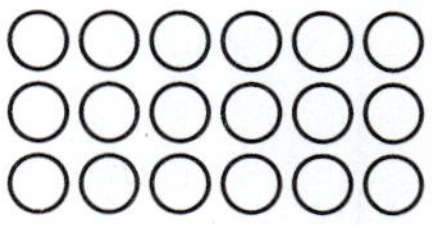

D
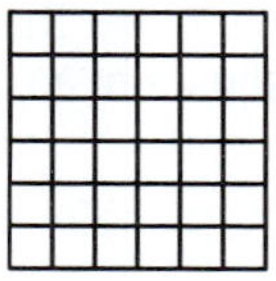

Spiral Review

45. **FOOTBALL** The graph shows the number of wins the Pittsburgh Steelers had from 2003–2006. How many more wins did the Steelers have in 2004 than 2006? (Lesson 1-1) **7 wins**

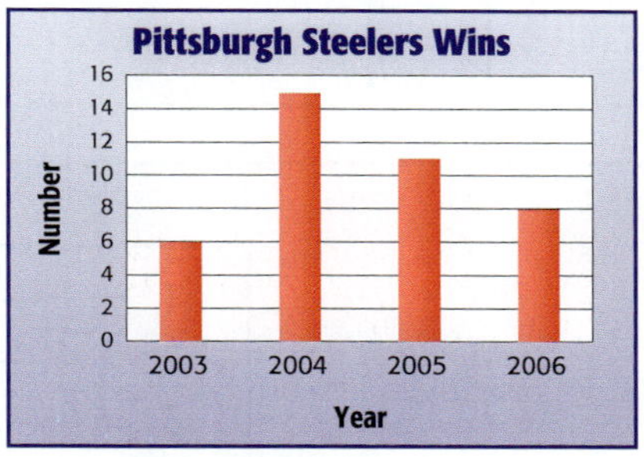

Source: National Football League

46. **COOKING** Ms. Jackson is serving fried turkey at 5:00 P.M. The 12-pound turkey has to cook 3 minutes for every pound, and then cool for at least 45 minutes. What is the latest time she can start frying? (Lesson 1-1) **3:39 P.M.**

GET READY for the Next Lesson

PREREQUISITE SKILL Multiply.

47. $2 \cdot 2$ **4**
48. $3 \cdot 3$ **9**
49. $5 \cdot 5$ **25**
50. $7 \cdot 7$ **49**

4 Assess

Crystal Ball Tell students that tomorrow's lesson is about squaring numbers and finding the square roots of numbers. Have students write how they think what they learned today will connect with tomorrow's lesson.

Pre-AP Activity — Use as an Extension

You might want to have students compare a standard multiplication series with an exponential series. Suggest that they write a series of products, such as $3 \times 1 = 3$, $3 \times 2 = 6$, $3 \times 3 = 9$, and so on. Then have them write a series of exponents using the same factor, such as $3^1 = 3$, $3^2 = 9$, $3^3 = 27$, and so on. Ask them to write a sentence that compares how the products of each series increase.

Pre-AP Activities help you cultivate skills that students will need to have success in higher mathematics.

1-3 Squares and Square Roots

PACING: **Regular:** 1 period, **Block:** 0.5 period

IN Academic Standards **7.1.5 Recognize and use the inverse relationship between squaring and finding the square root of a perfect square integer.** *Also addresses 7.1.2.*

Options for Differentiated Instruction

ELL = English Language Learner AL = Above or Beyond Grade Level SS = Struggling Students SN = Special Needs

Building Vocabulary ELL SN

Use while presenting the lesson.

Have students create visual vocabulary cards for the terms in Lesson 1-3. An example of a visual vocabulary card for *perfect square* is shown below.

Vocabulary word and definition	Picture or diagram
Example	A personal way to remember the term

Perfect Square A number that is the square of an integer.	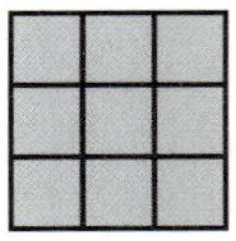 $3 \times 3 = 9$, so 9 is a perfect square.
25 is a perfect square because $25 = 5^2$.	A number to the second power means square. 4^2 is a 4×4 square, or 16.

Cooperative Groups ELL SS SN

Use before presenting Example 3.

Have students create a resource sheet listing the first ten perfect squares and their square roots.

$1^2 = 1 \rightarrow \sqrt{1} = 1$
$2^2 = 4 \rightarrow \sqrt{4} = 2$
$3^2 = 9 \rightarrow \sqrt{9} = 3$

$10^2 = 100 \rightarrow \sqrt{100} = 10$

Challenge Beyond the Lesson Content AL

Use after presenting the lesson.

Propose the following question to students.

If you double the sides of a square, will the area of the square *sometimes*, *always*, or *never* double? Explain your reasoning. Never; the area will be 2 • 2 or 4 times greater.

Leveled Lesson Resources

Also on TeacherWorks™ Lesson 1-3

Chapter 1 Resource Masters

BL = Below or Approaching Grade Level OL = On Grade Level AL = Above or Beyond Grade Level ELL = English Language Learner

Lesson Reading Guide
p. 22 BL OL ELL

NAME ______ DATE ______ PERIOD ____

1-3 Lesson Reading Guide

Squares and Square Roots

Get Ready for the Lesson

Complete the Mini Lab at the top of page 34 in your textbook. Write your answers below.

1. Using tiles, try to construct squares with areas 4, 9, and 16 square units. **See students' work.**
2. Try to construct squares with areas 12, 18, and 20 square units. **See students' work.**
3. Which of the areas form squares? **4, 9, and 16 square units**
4. What is the relationship between the lengths of the sides and the areas of these squares? **The length of the side squared equals the area.**
5. Using your square tiles, create a square that has an area of 49 square units. What are the lengths of the sides of the square? **7 units**

Read the Lesson 6a–c. Sample answers are given.

6. In this lesson, the word *square* is used in several different ways. Tell the meaning of the word as it is used in each phrase or sentence.
   a. Find the *square* of 3. **3 times 3**
   b. 9 units *squared* **9 square units; 9 squares with sides of 1 unit each**
   c. A boxing ring is a *square* with an area of 400 ft². **a rectangle with equal sides**

Remember What You Learned

7. Work with a partner. Use a calculator to find the squares of six numbers, some of them decimals. Then write only the squares in a list and exchange lists with your partner. Find the square roots of the squares in the list that you receive. Write your answers in the form $\sqrt{x} = y$. **See students' work.**

Chapter 1 22 Course 2

Study Guide and Intervention*
p. 23 BL OL ELL

NAME ______ DATE ______ PERIOD ____

1-3 Study Guide and Intervention

Squares and Square Roots

The product of a number and itself is the **square** of the number. Numbers like 4, 25, and 2.25 are called **perfect squares** because they are squares of rational numbers. The factors multiplied to form perfect squares are called **square roots**. Both 5 · 5 and (−5)(−5) equal 25. So, 25 has two square roots, 5 and −5. A **radical sign**, $\sqrt{\ }$, is the symbol used to indicate the *positive* square root of a number. So, $\sqrt{25} = 5$.

Examples

1. Find the square of 5. 5 · 5 = 25
2. Find the square of 16. 16 [x²] [ENTER] 256
3. Find $\sqrt{49}$. 7 · 7 = 49, so $\sqrt{49} = 7$.
4. Find $\sqrt{169}$. [2nd] [√] 169 [ENTER] 13. So, $\sqrt{169} = 13$.

Example 5 A square tile has an area of 144 square inches. What are the dimensions of the tile?

[2nd] [√] 144 [ENTER] 12 Find the square root of 144.

So, the tile measures 12 inches by 12 inches.

Exercises

Find the square of each number.

1. 2 **4** 2. 9 **81** 3. 14 **196**
4. 15 **225** 5. 21 **441** 6. 45 **2,025**

Find each square root.

7. $\sqrt{16}$ **4** 8. $\sqrt{36}$ **6** 9. $\sqrt{256}$ **16**
10. $\sqrt{1{,}024}$ **32** 11. $\sqrt{361}$ **19** 12. $\sqrt{484}$ **22**

Chapter 1 23 Course 2

Skills Practice*
p. 24 BL OL

NAME ______ DATE ______ PERIOD ____

1-3 Skills Practice

Squares and Square Roots

Find the square of each number.

1. 3 **9** 2. 22 **484**
3. 25 **625** 4. 24 **576**
5. 35 **1,225** 6. 26 **676**
7. 37 **1,369** 8. 50 **2,500**

Find each square root.

9. $\sqrt{25}$ **5** 10. $\sqrt{100}$ **10**
11. $\sqrt{441}$ **21** 12. $\sqrt{900}$ **30**
13. $\sqrt{961}$ **31** 14. $\sqrt{784}$ **28**
15. $\sqrt{3{,}600}$ **60** 16. $\sqrt{1{,}936}$ **44**
17. What is the square of −37? **1,369** 18. Find both square roots of 4,900. **70, −70**
19. Square 7.2. **51.84** 20. Square 4.5. **20.25**

Chapter 1 24 Course 2

Practice*
p. 25 OL AL

NAME ______ DATE ______ PERIOD ____

1-3 Practice

Squares and Square Roots

Find the square of each number.

1. 2 **4** 2. 8 **64** 3. 10 **100**
4. 11 **121** 5. 15 **225** 6. 25 **625**
7. What is the square of 5? **25** 8. Find the square of 16. **256** 9. Find the square of 21. **441**

Find each square root.

10. $\sqrt{64}$ **8** 11. $\sqrt{121}$ **11** 12. $\sqrt{169}$ **13**
13. $\sqrt{0}$ **0** 14. $\sqrt{81}$ **9** 15. $\sqrt{289}$ **17**
16. $\sqrt{900}$ **30** 17. $\sqrt{1}$ **1** 18. $\sqrt{484}$ **22**

PACKAGING An electronics company uses three different sizes of square labels to ship products to customers. The area of each type of label is shown in the table.

Labels	
Type	Area
Priority:	100 cm²
Caution:	225 cm²
Address:	144 cm²

19. If the length of a side of a square is the square root of the area, what is the length of a side for each label? **Priority: 10 cm; Caution: 15 cm; Address: 12 cm**
20. How much larger is the Caution label than the Address label? **81 cm²**
21. RECREATION A square hot tub is outlined by a 2-foot wide tile border. In an overhead view, the area of the hot tub and the border together is 144 square feet. What is the length of one side of the hot tub itself? **8 feet**

Chapter 1 25 Course 2

Word Problem Practice*
p. 26 OL AL

NAME ______ DATE ______ PERIOD ____

1-3 Word Problem Practice

Squares and Square Roots

1. FERTILIZER John bought a bag of lawn fertilizer that will cover 400 square feet. What are the dimensions of the largest square plot of lawn that the bag of fertilizer will cover? **20 ft by 20 ft**
2. GEOMETRY The area A of a circle in square feet with a radius r in feet is given approximately by the formula $A \approx 3.14r^2$. What is the approximate area of a circle with a radius of 3 feet? **28.26 ft²**
3. MOTION The time t in seconds for an object dropped from a height of h feet to hit the ground is given by the formula $t = \sqrt{\frac{2h}{32}}$. How long will it take an object dropped from a height of 500 feet to hit the ground? Round to the nearest tenth. **5.6 s**
4. PACKAGING A cardboard envelope for a compact disc is a square with an area of 171.61 square centimeters. What are the dimensions of the envelope? **13.1 cm by 13.1 cm**
5. GEOGRAPHY Refer to the squares below. They represent the approximate areas of California, Alabama, and Nebraska. Find the area of Alabama.

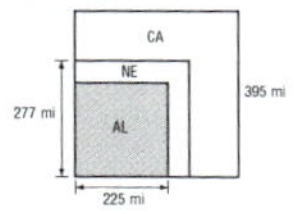

50,625 mi²

6. Use the figure in Exercise 5. How much larger is California than Nebraska? **79,296 mi²**

Chapter 1 26 Course 2

Enrichment
p. 27 OL AL

NAME ______ DATE ______ PERIOD ____

1-3 Enrichment

The Geometric Mean

The square root of the product of two numbers is called their **geometric mean**. The geometric mean of 12 and 48 is $\sqrt{12 \cdot 48} = \sqrt{576}$ or 24.

Find the geometric mean for each pair of numbers.

1. 2 and 8 **4** 2. 4 and 9 **6** 3. 9 and 16 **12**
4. 16 and 4 **8** 5. 16 and 36 **24** 6. 12 and 3 **6**
7. 18 and 8 **12** 8. 2 and 18 **6** 9. 27 and 12 **18**

Recall the definition of a **geometric sequence**. Each term is found by multiplying the previous term by the same number. A missing term in a geometric sequence equals the geometric mean of the two terms on either side.

Find the missing term in each geometric sequence.

10. 4, 12, [?], 108, 324 **36** 11. 10, [?], 62.5, 156.25, 390.625 **25**
12. 1, 0.4, [?], 0.064, 0.0256 **0.16** 13. 700, 70, 7, 0.7, [?], 0.007 **0.07**
14. 6, [?], 24 **12** 15. 18, [?], 32 **24**

Chapter 1 27 Course 2

* Also available in Spanish ELL

Additional Lesson Resources

Transparencies

- *5-Minute Check Transparency,* Lesson 1-3

Other Print Products

- *Noteables™ Interactive Study Notebook with Foldables™*

Teacher Tech Tools

- *Interactive Classroom CD-ROM,* Lesson 1-3
- *AssignmentWorks,* Lesson 1-3

Student Tech Tools

glencoe.com

- Extra Examples, Chapter 1, Lesson 3
- Self-Check Quiz, Chapter 1, Lesson 3

1-3 Lesson Notes

1 Focus

Vertical Alignment

Before Lesson 1-3
Understand and compute positive integer powers of nonnegative integers

Lesson 1-3
Use the inverse relationship between raising to a power and extracting the root of a perfect square

After Lesson 1-3
Multiply and divide monomials; extend the process of taking powers and extracting roots to monomials

2 Teach

Scaffolding Questions

Draw the following squares on the board: 1×1, 2×2, and 3×3.

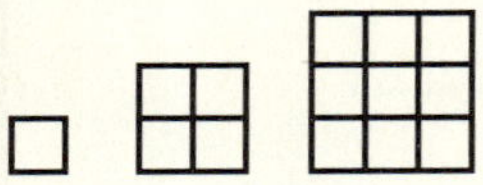

Ask:

- What is the area of the first square? 1 sq. unit
- What are two methods you could use to find the area of the second square? count the number of units or multiply length of the sides ($2 \times 2 = 4$)
- What is the area of the third square? 9 sq. units
- Could you make a square with an area of 6 square units? If not, what shape would you make that has an area of 6 square units? No; it is not possible to make a square, but you could make a rectangle.

1-3 Squares and Square Roots

MAIN IDEA

Find squares of numbers and square roots of perfect squares.

IN Academic Standards

7.1.5 Recognize and use the inverse relationship between squaring and finding the square root of a perfect square integer. *Also address 7.1.2.*

New Vocabulary

square
perfect squares
square root
radical sign

IN Math Online

glencoe.com

- Extra Examples
- Personal Tutor
- Self-Check Quiz

MINI Lab

A square with an area of 36 square units is shown.

1. Using tiles, try to construct squares with areas of 4, 9, and 16 square units. **1, 2. See students' work.**
2. Try to construct squares with areas 12, 18, and 20 square units.
3. Which of the areas form squares? **4, 9, and 16 square units**
4. What is the relationship between the lengths of the sides and the areas of these squares? **The length of the side squared equals the area**
5. Using your square tiles, create a square that has an area of 49 square units. What are the lengths of the sides of the square? **7 uni**

The area of the square at the right is $5 \cdot 5$ or 25 square units. The product of a number and itself is the **square** of that number. So, the square of 5 is 25.

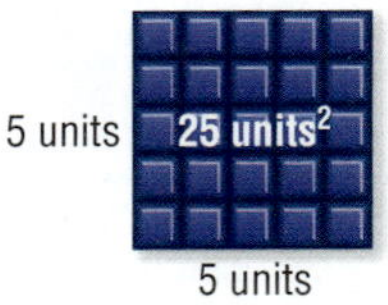

EXAMPLES Find Squares of Numbers

1 **Find the square of 3.**

$3 \cdot 3 = 9$ Multiply 3 by itself.

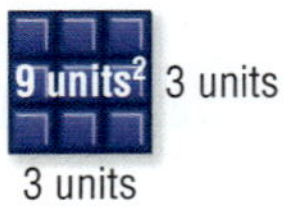

2 **Find the square of 28.**

METHOD 1 **Use paper and pencil.**

$$\begin{array}{r} 28 \\ \times\ 28 \\ \hline 224 \\ +\ 560 \\ \hline 784 \end{array}$$

Multiply 28 by itself.

Annex a zero.

METHOD 2 **Use a calculator.**

28 [x^2] [ENTER] 784

CHECK Your Progress

Find the square of each number.

a. 8 **64** b. 12 **144** c. 23 **529**

Numbers like 9, 16, and 225 are called square numbers or **perfect squares** because they are squares of whole numbers.

New Vocabulary is listed at the beginning of every lesson. Review Vocabulary is listed where appropriate. Some lessons also have a Vocabulary Link, which shows how mathematical words are related to everyday words.

The factors multiplied to form perfect squares are called **square roots**. A **radical sign**, $\sqrt{\ }$, is the symbol used to indicate a square root of a number.

eading Math

quare Roots Read $\sqrt{16} = 4$ as *the square* *ot of 16 is 4.*

Square Root — Key Concept

Words A square root of a number is one of its two equal factors.

Examples

Numbers	Algebra
$4 \cdot 4 = 16$, so $\sqrt{16} = 4$.	If $x \cdot x$ or $x^2 = y$, then $\sqrt{y} = x$.

EXAMPLES Find Square Roots

3 **Find $\sqrt{81}$.**

$9 \cdot 9 = 81$, so $\sqrt{81} = 9$. What number times itself is 81?

4 **Find $\sqrt{225}$.**

[2nd] [$\sqrt{\ }$] 225 [ENTER] 15

So, $\sqrt{225} = 15$.

CHECK Your Progress

Find each square root.

d. $\sqrt{64}$ 8

e. $\sqrt{289}$ 17

Real-World EXAMPLE

5 **SPORTS** **The infield of a baseball field is a square with an area of 8,100 square feet. What are the dimensions of the infield?**

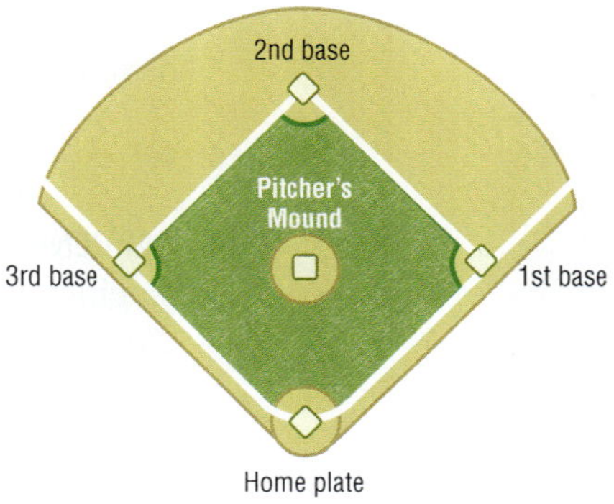

The infield is a square. By finding the square root of the area, 8,100, you find the length of one side of the infield.

$90 \cdot 90 = 8{,}100$, so $\sqrt{8{,}100} = 90$.

The length of one side of the infield is 90 feet. So, the dimensions of the infield are 90 feet by 90 feet.

Real-World Link The average lifespan of a major league baseball is 7 pitches.
Source: SuperKids

CHECK Your Progress

f. **SPORTS** The largest ring in amateur boxing is a square with an area of 400 square feet. What are the dimensions of the ring? 20 ft by 20 ft

Focus on Mathematical Content

Square Roots In Example 3, both $9 \cdot 9$ and $(-9)(-9)$ equal 81. So, 81 has two square roots, 9 and −9. The radical sign, $\sqrt{\ }$, indicates the *positive* square root of a number. Thus, the expression $\sqrt{81}$ indicates the positive square root of 81, or 9. To indicate the *negative* square root of 81, or −9, use the expression $-\sqrt{81}$. For any positive number x, we indicate the positive square root of x by $\sqrt{x}$ and the negative square root by $-\sqrt{x}$.

Formative Assessment

Use the Check Your Progress exercises after Examples to determine students' understanding of concepts.

ADDITIONAL EXAMPLES

1. Find the square of 5. 25
2. Find the square of 19. 361
3. Find $\sqrt{36}$. 6
4. Find $\sqrt{676}$. 26
5. **GAMES** A checkerboard is a square with an area of 1,225 square centimeters. What are the dimensions of the checkerboard? 35 cm × 35 cm

Additional Examples are also in:

- Noteables™ Interactive Study Notebook with Foldables™
- Interactive Classroom PowerPoint® Presentations

*Additional Examples, which are included for every example in the Student Edition, exactly parallel the examples in the text. Step-by-step solutions for these examples are included in **Interactive Classroom** and **Noteables: Interactive Study Notebook with Foldables™**.*

Tips for New Teachers — Square Roots

After presenting Example 3, you may wish to mention that every positive number has two square roots. The square roots of 81 are 9 and −9 since 9^2 is equal to 81 and $(-9)^2$ is equal to 81. The square roots of a positive number are always two numbers with the same absolute value and opposite signs, such as 9 and −9.

The square root of 0 is always 0. A negative number has no square roots, since the square of any number is at least 0.

3 Practice

Formative Assessment

Use Exercises 1–9 to check for understanding.

Then use the chart at the bottom of this page to customize your assignments for students.

Intervention You may wish to use the Study Guide and Intervention Master on page 23 of the *Chapter 1 Resource Masters* for additional reinforcement.

Odd/Even Assignments

Exercises 10–27 are structured so that students practice the same concepts whether they are assigned odd or even problems.

Differentiated Instruction

Visual/Spatial Learners If students are having difficulty visualizing the square root of a number in completing Exercises 5–8 and 18–25, have them draw square grids as geometric models. For example, in Exercise 18, have students draw a square grid containing 4 squares. Then ask them how many squares are on each side of the grid. This number represents the square root of 4.

Additional Answer

33.

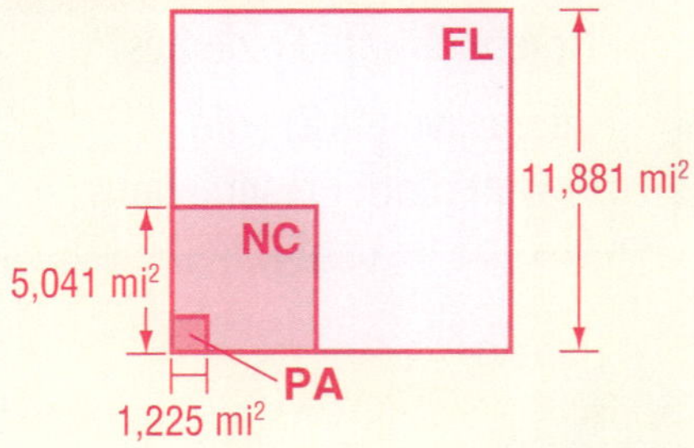

★ indicates multi-step problem

CHECK Your Understanding

Examples 1, 2 (p. 34) — **Find the square of each number.**

1. 6 **36**
2. 10 **100**
3. 17 **289**
4. 30 **900**

Examples 3, 4 (p. 35) — **Find each square root.**

5. $\sqrt{9}$ **3**
6. $\sqrt{36}$ **6**
7. $\sqrt{121}$ **11**
8. $\sqrt{169}$ **13**

Example 5 (p. 35)

9. **ROAD SIGNS** Historic Route 66 from Chicago to Los Angeles is known as the Main Street of America. If the area of a Route 66 sign measures 576 square inches and the sign is a square, what are the dimensions of the sign? **24 in. by 24 in.**

Practice and Problem Solving

HOMEWORK HELP	
For Exercises	See Examples
10–17	1, 2
18–25	3, 4
26–27	5

Exercise Levels
A: 10–27
B: 28–34
C: 35–39

Find the square of each number.

10. 4 **16**
11. 1 **1**
12. 7 **49**
13. 11 **121**
14. 16 **256**
15. 20 **400**
16. 18 **324**
17. 34 **1,156**

Find each square root.

18. $\sqrt{4}$ **2**
19. $\sqrt{16}$ **4**
20. $\sqrt{49}$ **7**
21. $\sqrt{100}$ **10**
22. $\sqrt{144}$ **12**
23. $\sqrt{256}$ **16**
24. $\sqrt{529}$ **23**
25. $\sqrt{625}$ **25**

26. **MEASUREMENT** Emma's bedroom is shaped like a square. What are the dimensions of the room if the area of the floor is 196 square feet? **14 ft by 14 ft**

27. **SPORTS** For the floor exercise, gymnasts perform their tumbling skills on a mat that has an area of 1,600 square feet. How much room does a gymnas have to run along one side of the mat? **40 ft**

28. What is the square of 12? **144**

29. Find the square of 19. **361**

★ 30. **GARDENING** A square garden has an area of 225 square feet. How much fencing will a gardener need to buy in order to place fencing around the garden? **60 ft**

GEOGRAPHY For Exercises 31–33, refer to the squares in the diagram. They represent the approximate areas of Florida, North Carolina, and Pennsylvania.

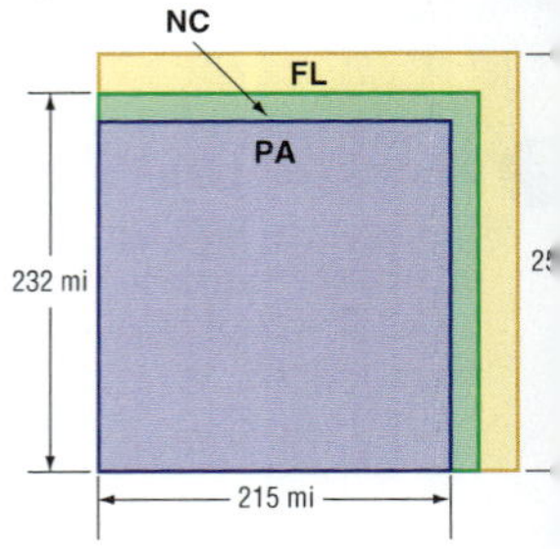

31. What is the area of North Carolina in square miles? **53, 824 mi²**

32. How much larger is Florida than Pennsylvania? **19,311 mi²**

33. The water areas of Florida, North Carolina, and Pennsylvania are 11,881 square miles; 5,041 square miles; and 1,225 square miles, respectively. Mal a similar diagram comparing the water areas of these states. **See margin.**

Academic Standards • ISTEP+

Extra Practice, pp. 668, 704

DIFFERENTIATED HOMEWORK OPTIONS

Level	Assignment	Two-Day Option	
BL Basic	10–27, 36, 39–50	11–27 odd, 40–41	10–26 even, 36, 39, 42–50
OL Core	11–25 odd, 26–34, 36, 39–50	10–27, 40–41	28–34, 36, 39, 42–50
AL Advanced/Pre-AP	28–46 (optional: 47–50)		

36 Chapter 1 Introduction to Algebra and Functions

★ 34. **MEASUREMENT** A chessboard has an area of 324 square inches. There is a 1-inch border around the 64 squares on the board. What is the length of one side of the region containing the small squares? **16 in.**

35. **MEASUREMENT** The area of a square that is 7 meters by 7 meters is how much greater than the area of a square containing 8 square meters? Explain.
41 m^2 greater; The area of a 7 by 7 square has an area of 49 m^2.

.O.T. Problems

36. **OPEN ENDED** Write a number whose square is between 100 and 150. **Sample answer: 12**

CHALLENGE For Exercises 37 and 38, use the diagram shown.

37. Could the area of the dog's pen be made larger using the same amount of fencing? Explain.

38. Describe the largest pen area possible using the same amount of fencing. How do the perimeter and area compare to the original pen?

7. Yes; For xample, a pen that easures 10 feet y 10 feet has the ame perimeter, ut its area is 100 quare feet, which greater than 84 quare feet.

8. See margin.

39. **WRITING IN MATH** Explain why raising a number to the second power is called *squaring* the number. **Sample answer: It is called squaring the number because the area of a square is found by multiplying the two side lengths together.**

ISTEP+ PRACTICE 7.1.5

40. Which model represents the square of 4? **D**

A 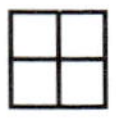

C 

B 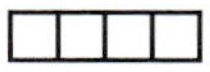

D 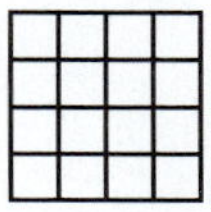

41. Which measure can be the area of a square if the measure of the side length is a whole number? **J**

F 836 sq ft

G 949 sq ft

H 1,100 sq ft

J 1,225 sq ft

Spiral Review

Write each power as a product of the same factor. (Lesson 1-2)

42. 3^4 **3 • 3 • 3 • 3**
43. 8^5 **8 • 8 • 8 • 8 • 8**
44. 7^2 **7 • 7**
45. 2^6 **2 • 2 • 2 • 2 • 2 • 2**

46. **SHIPPING** Jocelyn spent a total of $24 to ship 4 packages. If the packages are equal in size and weight, how much did it cost to ship each package? (Lesson 1-1) **$6**

GET READY for the Next Lesson

PREREQUISITE SKILL Add, subtract, multiply, or divide.

47. 13 + 8 **21**
48. 10 − 6 **4**
49. 5 × 6 **30**
50. 36 ÷ 4 **9**

4 Assess

Name the Math Have students describe a real-world problem that involves finding either the square or square root of a number. Make sure students identify the operation as "finding the square" or "finding the square root."

Formative Assessment

Check for student understanding of concepts in Lessons 1-1 through 1-3.

CRM Quiz 1, p. 77

Additional Answer

38. A square that measures 10 feet on each side; the perimeter is the same, and the area is 100 square feet, or 16 square feet greater than that of the original pen.

Pre-AP Activity **Use after Exercise 39.**

Ask students what they think the cube of a number is. Ask them what they think the cube root of a number is. Have them give examples and relate the concepts to squares and square roots.

1-4 Order of Operations

PACING: **Regular:** 1 period, **Block:** 0.5 period

IN Academic Standards **7.1.7 Solve problems that involve multiplication and division with integers,** fractions, decimals **and combinations of the four operations. 7.2.3 Evaluate numerical expressions and** simplify algebraic expressions **involving rational** and irrational **numbers.** *Also addresses 7.1.2.*

Options for Differentiated Instruction

ELL = English Language Learner AL = Above or Beyond Grade Level SS = Struggling Students SN = Special Needs

Assessing Students' Understanding SS SN

Use after presenting Examples 1 and 2.

A common misconception regarding the order of operations is that multiplication is always done before division instead of working left to right, and that addition is always done before subtraction instead of working left to right. To assess students' understanding of the order of operations, display the following expressions on the board or overhead and have students evaluate them.

$20 \div 2 \times 5$ 50 $7 - 3 + 4$ 8

Extensions and Challenges AL

Use after completing the lesson.

Insert the symbols $+$, $-$, $\times$, or $\div$ to make each sentence true. Sample answers are given.

2 2 2 2 = 0 $2 + 2 - 2 - 2 = 0$

2 2 2 2 = 1 $2 - 2 + 2 \div 2 = 1$

2 2 2 2 = 2 $2 \div 2 + 2 \div 2 = 2$

2 2 2 2 = 3 $2 \times 2 - 2 \div 2 = 3$

2 2 2 2 = 4 $2 \times 2 + 2 - 2 = 4$

2 2 2 2 = 5 $2 + 2 + 2 \div 2 = 5$

Creating Problems ELL AL

Use after completing the lesson.

Organize small groups of students with different learning abilities. Have them write problems that can be solved using the order of operations. Encourage them to include some real-life problems related to activities that interest them. Have groups trade problems and work through them.

After students complete each other's word problems, have the class share their work and discuss the different strategies they used to complete the problems.

Leveled Lesson Resources

Also on TeacherWorks™ Lesson 1-4

Chapter 1 Resource Masters

BL = Below or Approaching Grade Level   OL = On Grade Level   AL = Above or Beyond Grade Level   ELL = English Language Learner

Lesson Reading Guide
p. 29 BL OL ELL

NAME ______ DATE ______ PERIOD ____

1-4 Lesson Reading Guide
Order of Operations

Get Ready for the Lesson

Read the introduction at the top of page 38 in your textbook. Write your answers below.

1. List the differences between their calculations. **Megan multiplied 4 by 3 and then added 6. Dexter added 6 and 4, and then multiplied the result by 3.**
2. Whose calculations are correct? **Megan**
3. Make a conjecture about what should be the first step in simplifying 6 + 4 · 3. **Multiply 4 by 3.**

Read the Lesson

4. Why did mathematicians agree on an order of operations? **so that numerical expressions would have only one value**
5. What are three ways to indicate multiplication in a mathematical expression? **×, ·, and parentheses**

Remember What You Learned

6. In your own words, describe the order of operations that is used in finding the value of a mathematical expression. **1. Do all operations within grouping symbols first. 2. Evaluate all powers before other operations. 3. Multiply and divide in order from left to right. 4. Add and subtract in order from left to right.**

Chapter 1 29 Course 2

Study Guide and Intervention*
p. 30 BL OL ELL

1-4 Study Guide and Intervention
Order of Operations

Use the **order of operations** to evaluate numerical expressions.
1. Evaluate the expressions inside grouping symbols.
2. Evaluate all powers.
3. Multiply and divide in order from left to right.
4. Add and subtract in order from left to right.

Example 1 Evaluate $(10 - 2) - 4 \cdot 2$.

$(10 - 2) - 4 \cdot 2 = 8 - 4 \cdot 2$ Subtract first since 10 − 2 is in parentheses.
$= 8 - 8$ Multiply 4 and 2.
$= 0$ Subtract 8 from 8.

Example 2 Evaluate $8 + (1 + 5)^2 \div 4$.

$8 + (1 + 5)^2 \div 4 = 8 + 6^2 \div 4$ First, add 1 and 5 inside the parentheses.
$= 8 + 36 \div 4$ Find the value of 6^2.
$= 8 + 9$ Divide 36 by 4.
$= 17$ Add 8 and 9.

Exercises

Evaluate each expression.

1. $(1 + 7) \times 3$ **24**
2. $28 - 4 \cdot 7$ **0**
3. $5 + 4 \cdot 3$ **17**
4. $(40 \div 5) - 7 + 2$ **3**
5. $35 \div 7(2)$ **10**
6. 3×10^3 **3,000**
7. $45 \div 5 + 36 \div 4$ **18**
8. $42 \div 6 \times 2 - 9$ **5**
9. $2 \times 8 - 3^2 + 2$ **9**
10. $5 \times 2^2 + 32 \div 8$ **24**
11. $3 \times 6 - (9 - 8)^3$ **17**
12. 3.5×10^2 **350**

Chapter 1 30 Course 2

Skills Practice*
p. 31 BL OL

1-4 Skills Practice
Order of Operations

Evaluate each expression.

1. $9 - 3 + 4$ **10**
2. $8 + 6 - 5$ **9**
3. $12 \div 4 + 5$ **8**
4. $25 \times 2 - 7$ **43**
5. $36 \div 9(2)$ **8**
6. $6 + 3(7 - 2)$ **21**
7. $3 \times 6.2 + 5^2$ **43.6**
8. $(1 + 11)^2 \div 3$ **48**
9. $12 \div (2 + 8)$ **2**
10. $15 - 24 \div 4 \cdot 2$ **3**
11. $(4 + 2) \cdot (7 + 4)$ **66**
12. $(3 \cdot 18) \div (2 \cdot 9)$ **3**
13. $24 \div 6 + 4^2$ **20**
14. $3 \times 8 - (9 - 7)^3$ **16**
15. $9 + (9 - 8 + 3)^4$ **265**
16. $3 \times 2^2 + 24 \div 8$ **15**
17. $(15 \div 3)^2 + 9 \div 3$ **28**
18. $(52 \div 4) + 5^3$ **138**
19. 26×10^3 **26,000**
20. 7.2×10^2 **720**
21. $5 \times 4^2 - 3 \times 2$ **74**
22. $24 \div 6 \div 2$ **2**
23. $13 - (6 - 5)^5$ **12**
24. $(8 - 3 \times 2) \times 6$ **12**
25. $(11 \cdot 4 - 10) \div 2$ **17**
26. $10 \div 2 \times (4 - 3)$ **5**
27. 1.82×10^5 **182,000**
28. $35 \div 7 \times 2 - 4$ **6**
29. $2^5 + 7(9 - 1)$ **88**
30. $12 + 16 \div (3 + 1)$ **16**

Chapter 1 31 Course 2

Practice*
p. 32 OL AL

1-4 Practice
Order of Operations

Evaluate each expression.

1. $(2 + 9) \times 4$ **44**
2. $8 - (5 + 2)$ **1**
3. $(15 \div 3) + 7$ **12**
4. $(14 + 7) \div 7$ **3**
5. $5 \cdot 6 - 12 \div 4$ **27**
6. $8 \div 2 + 8 - 2$ **10**
7. $16 - 8 \div 2 + 5$ **17**
8. $15 - 3 \cdot 5 + 7$ **7**
9. 7×10^3 **7,000**
10. $2 \times 5^2 + 6$ **56**
11. $7 \cdot 2^3 - 9$ **47**
12. $27 \div 3 \times 2 + 4^2$ **34**
13. $6^2 - 12 \times 4 \cdot 3$ **72**
14. $(15 - 3) \div (8 + 4)$ **1**
15. $(9 - 4) \cdot (7 - 7)$ **0**
16. $8 + 3(5 + 2) - 7 \cdot 2$ **15**
17. $5(6 - 1) - 4 \cdot 6 \div 3$ **17**
18. $(5 + 7)^2 \div 12$ **12**
19. $12 + (8 - 6)^2$ **3**
20. $(7 + 2)^2 \div 3^2$ **9**
21. $(11 - 9)^2 \cdot (8 - 5)^2$ **36**
22. $64 \div 8 - 3(4 - 3) + 2$ **7**
23. $8 \times 5.1 - (4.1 + 1.4) + 7.1$ **42.4**

For Exercises 24 and 25, write an expression for each situation. Then evaluate the expression to find the solution.

24. LAWN AREA The Solomons need to find the area of their front and side yards since they want to reseed the lawn. Both side yards measure 3 meters by 10 meters, while the front yard is a square with a side of 9 meters. They do not need to reseed a portion of the front yard covering 16 square meters where a flower bed is located. What is the area of the yard that the Solomons want to reseed? **$2(3 \times 10) + 9^2 - 16 = 125$; The area is 125 m².**

25. COMMUNITY SERVICE Jariah volunteers at the hospital during the week. She volunteers 3 hours on Monday and Thursday, 4 hours on Saturday and Sunday, and 2 hours on Tuesday. How many hours does Jariah volunteer at the hospital during the week? **$2 \cdot 3 + 2 \cdot 4 + 2 = 16$; Jariah volunteers 16 hours a week.**

Chapter 1 32 Course 2

Word Problem Practice*
p. 33 OL AL

1-4 Word Problem Practice
Order of Operations

1. FOOTBALL The middle school team scored three field goals worth three points each and two touchdowns with extra points worth seven points each. Write a numerical expression to find the team's score. Then evaluate the expression. **3(3) + 2(7); 23 points**

2. BOOKS Juan goes to the school book fair where paperback books are $1.50 and hardback books are $3.00. Juan buys 5 paperback and 2 hardback books. Write a numerical expression to find how much Juan paid for the books. Then evaluate the expression. **5(1.5) + 2(3); $13.50**

3. GEOMETRY The perimeter of a hexagon is found by adding the lengths of all six sides of the hexagon. For the hexagon below write a numerical expression to find the perimeter. Then evaluate the expression. **4(5) + 2(8); 36**

4. MONEY Aisha bought school supplies consisting of 6 spiral notebooks costing $0.39 each, 2 packages of pencils at $0.79 each, and a 3-ring binder for $1.99. Write an expression to find the total amount Aisha spent on school supplies. Then evaluate the expression. **6 × 0.39 + 2 × 0.79 + 1.99; $5.91**

5. REASONING Use the order of operations and the digits 2, 4, 6, and 8 to create an expression with a value of 2. **Sample answer: $4^2 - (8 + 6)$**

6. NUMBER SENSE Without parentheses, the expression 8 + 30 ÷ 2 + 4 equals 27. Place parentheses in the expression so that it equals 13; then 23. **8 + 30 ÷ (2 + 4); (8 + 30) ÷ 2 + 4**

7. MONEY Tyrone bought 5 postcards at $0.55 each and a set of postcards for $1.20. Write an expression to find the total amount Tyrone spent on postcards. Then evaluate the expression. **5(0.55) + 1.2; $3.95**

8. DINING Mr. Firewalks took his family out to eat. They ordered 3 meals costing $8.99 each, 2 sodas at $1.50 each, and 1 glass of tea for $1.25. Write an expression to find the total amount the Firewalks family spent on dinner before taxes and tip. Then evaluate the expression. **3(8.99) + 2(1.5) + 1.25; $31.22**

Chapter 1 33 Course 2

Enrichment
p. 34 OL AL

1-4 Enrichment
Nested Expressions

Nested Expressions

Sometimes more than one set of parentheses are used to group the quantities in an expression. These expressions are said to have "nested" parentheses. The expression below has "nested" parentheses.

$(4 + (3 \cdot (2 + 3)) + 8) \div 9$

Expressions with several sets of grouping symbols are clearer if braces such as { } or brackets such as [ ] are used. Here is the same example written with brackets and braces.

$\{4 + [3 \cdot (2 + 3)] + 8\} \div 9$

To evaluate expressions of this type, work from the inside out.

$\{4 + [3 \cdot (2 + 3)] + 8\} \div 9 = \{4 + [3 \cdot 5] + 8\} \div 9 = \{4 + 15 + 8\} \div 9 = 27 \div 9 = 3$

Evaluate each expression.

1. $3 + [(24 \div 8) \cdot 7] - 20$ **4**
2. $[(16 - 7 + 5) \div 2] - 7$ **0**
3. $[2 \cdot (23 - 6) + 14] \div 6$ **8**
4. $50 - [3 \cdot (15 - 5)] + 25$ **45**
5. $12 + \{28 - [2 \cdot (11 - 7)] + 3\}$ **35**
6. $\{75 + 3 \cdot [(17 - 9) \div 2]\} \cdot 2$ **174**
7. $20 + \{3 \cdot [6 + (56 \div 8)]\}$ **59**
8. $\{4 + [5 \cdot (12 - 5)] + 15\} \cdot 10$ **540**
9. $\{15 \cdot [(38 - 26) \div 4]\} - 15$ **30**
10. $\{[(34 + (6 \cdot 5)] \div 8\} + 40$ **48**

Chapter 1 34 Course 2

* Also available in Spanish ELL

Additional Lesson Resources

Transparencies
- *5-Minute Check Transparency,* Lesson 1-4

Other Print Products
- *Noteables™ Interactive Study Notebook with Foldables™*

Teacher Tech Tools
- *Interactive Classroom CD-ROM,* Lesson 1-4
- *AssignmentWorks,* Lesson 1-4

Student Tech Tools
glencoe.com
- Extra Examples, Chapter 1, Lesson 4
- Self-Check Quiz, Chapter 1, Lesson 4

1-4 Lesson Notes

1 Focus

Vertical Alignment

Before Lesson 1-4
Understand and compute positive integer powers of nonnegative integers

Lesson 1-4
Apply algebraic order of operations to evaluate expressions. Solve problems manually by using the correct order of operations

After Lesson 1-4
Use the correct order of operations to evaluate algebraic expressions

2 Teach

Scaffolding Questions

Write the following expression on the board: $5 + 3 \times 4$.

Ask:

- What is the value of the expression if you add first? 32
- What is the value of the expression if you multiply first? 17
- How do you know which operation to perform first? order of operations

Additional Answers

1. Megan multiplied 4 by 3 and then added 6. Dexter added 6 and 4 and then multiplied the result by 3.

a. Sample answer: Add first, since $9 + 4$ is in parentheses. Then divide 39 by 13.

b. Sample answer: Divide first, because division comes before addition or subtraction. Then add 10 and subtract 6 in order from left to right.

1-4 Order of Operations

MAIN IDEA

Evaluate expressions using the order of operations.

IN Academic Standards

7.1.7 Solve problems that involve multiplication and division with integers, fractions, decimals **and combinations of the four operations.**
7.2.3 Evaluate numerical expressions and simplify algebraic expressions **involving rational** and irrational **numbers.** *Also addresses 7.1.2.*

New Vocabulary

numerical expression
order of operations

IN Math Online

glencoe.com

- Extra Examples
- Personal Tutor
- Self-Check Quiz
- Reading in the Content Area

GET READY for the Lesson

SPORTS The Kent City football team made one 6-point touchdown and four 3-point field goals in its last game. Megan and Dexter each use an expression to find the total number of points the team scored.

Megan	Dexter
$6 + 4 \cdot 3 = 6 + 12$	$(6 + 4) \cdot 3 = 10 \cdot 3$
$= 18$	$= 30$
The team scored 18 points.	The team scored 30 points.

1. List the differences between their calculations. **See margin.**
2. Whose calculations are correct? **Megan**
3. Make a conjecture about what should be the first step in simplifying $6 + 4 \cdot 3$. **Multiply 4 by 3.**

The expression $6 + 4 \cdot 3$ is a **numerical expression**. To evaluate expressions, use the **order of operations**. These rules ensure that numerical expressions have only one value.

Order of Operations — Key Concept

1. Evaluate the expressions inside grouping symbols.
2. Evaluate all powers.
3. Multiply and divide in order from left to right.
4. Add and subtract in order from left to right.

EXAMPLES Use Order of Operations

1 Evaluate $5 + (12 - 3)$. Justify each step.

$5 + (12 - 3) = 5 + 9$ — Subtract first, since $12 - 3$ is in parentheses.
$= 14$ — Add 5 and 9.

2 Evaluate $8 - 3 \cdot 2 + 7$. Justify each step.

$8 - 3 \cdot 2 + 7 = 8 - 6 + 7$ — Multiply 3 and 2.
$= 2 + 7$ — Subtract 6 from 8.
$= 9$ — Add 2 and 7.

CHECK Your Progress a–b. See margin for justification.

Evaluate each expression. Justify each step.

a. $39 \div (9 + 4)$ **3**

b. $10 + 8 \div 2 - 6$ **8**

Web addresses, or URLs, are provided to point students to online assets such as **Personal Tutor, Extra Examples, Self-Check Quizzes** and **Concepts in Motion.**

Study Tip

Scientific Calculators
'f you have a scientific :alculator, you can enter numbers and operations in order from left to right. The scientific calculator follows the order of operations.

EXAMPLE 3 Use Order of Operations

Evaluate $5 \cdot 3^2 - 7$. Justify each step.

$5 \cdot 3^2 - 7 = 5 \cdot 9 - 7$	Find the value of 3^2.
$= 45 - 7$	Multiply 5 and 9.
$= 38$	Subtract 7 from 45.

CHECK Your Progress c–d. See margin for justification.

c. 3×10^4 30,000

d. $(5 - 1)^3 \div 4$ 16

In addition to using the symbols × and •, multiplication can be indicated by using parentheses. For example, 2(3 + 5) means 2 × (3 + 5).

Subtract first, since – 1 is in parentheses. ext, multiply by 2 and ultiply by 3 in order om left to right. Finally, ubtract the product om 20.
Subtract first, since – 1 is in parentheses. ext, divide 8 by 2 and ultiply 2 by 2 in order om left to right. Finally, dd 6, 4, and 4.

EXAMPLE 4 Use Order of Operations

Evaluate $14 + 3(7 - 2)$. Justify each step.

$14 + 3(7 - 2) = 14 + 3(5)$	Subtract 2 from 7.
$= 14 + 15$	Multiply 3 and 5.
$= 29$	Add 14 and 15.

CHECK Your Progress

e. $20 - 2(4 - 1) \cdot 3$ 2

f. $6 + 8 \div 2 + 2(3 - 1)$ 14

e–f. See justification at left.

Real-World EXAMPLE 5

MONEY Julian orders 3 rolls of crepe paper, 4 boxes of balloons, and 2 boxes of favors for the school dance. What is the total cost?

Item	Unit Cost
crepe paper	$2
favors	$7
balloons	$5

Words	cost of 3 rolls of crepe paper	+	cost of 4 boxes of balloons	+	cost of 2 boxes of favors
Expression	3 × 2	+	4 × 5	+	2 × 7

$3 \times 2 + 4 \times 5 + 2 \times 7 = 6 + 20 + 14$	Multiply from left to right.
$= 40$	Add.

The total cost is $40.

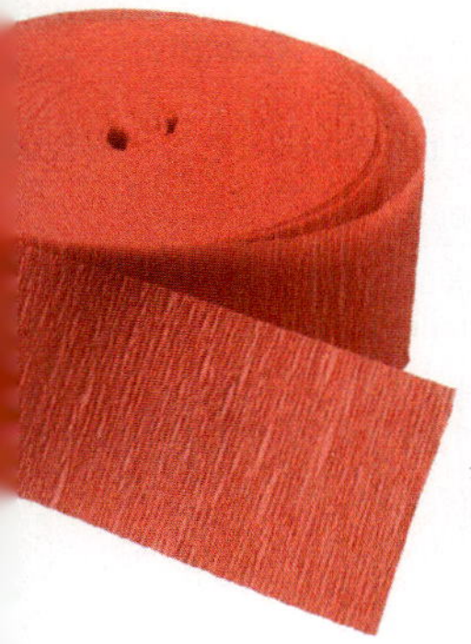

Real-World Link
Crepe paper originated in the late 1700s. It was critical to the invention of masking tape! The texture allows the tape to partially adhere to the surface, making it easily removable.
Source: Wilsonart International

CHECK Your Progress

g. What is the total cost of twelve rolls of crepe paper, three boxes of balloons, and three boxes of favors? $60

Focus on Mathematical Content

Order of Operations Sometimes it is necessary to evaluate powers before evaluating an expression inside grouping symbols. For example, when evaluating the expression $2(4^3 + 5)$, it is necessary to evaluate 4^3 before evaluating the expression inside the parentheses.

Formative Assessment

Use the Check Your Progress exercises after each Example to determine students' understanding of concepts.

ADDITIONAL EXAMPLES

1. Evaluate $27 - (18 + 2)$. 7
2. Evaluate $15 + 5 \cdot 3 - 2$. 28
3. Evaluate $12 \times 3 - 2^2$. 32
4. Evaluate $28 \div (3 - 1)^2$. 7
5. **VIDEO GAMES** Use the table shown in Example 5 in the Student Edition. Julian is buying one box of favors, one box of balloons, and three rolls of crepe paper. What is the total cost? $18

Additional Examples are also in:

- Noteables™ Interactive Study Notebook with Foldables™
- Interactive Classroom PowerPoint® Presentations

Additional Answers

c. Evaluate 10^4 first because it is a power. Then multiply by 3.

d. Subtract first, since 5 – 1 is in parentheses. Then evaluate the power. Finally, divide by 4.

3 Practice

Formative Assessment

Use Exercises 1–9 to check for understanding. Then use the chart at the bottom of this page to customize your assignments for students.

Intervention You may wish to use the Study Guide and Intervention Master on page 30 of the *Chapter 1 Resource Masters* for additional reinforcement.

Odd/Even Assignments

Exercises 10–29 are structured so that students practice the same concepts whether they are assigned odd or even problems.

Tips for New Teachers

Order of Operations

A common mnemonic for helping students remember the order of operations is, "Please excuse *my dear Aunt Sally*." The first letters of each word stand for *parentheses*, *exponents*, *multiply*, *divide*, *add*, and *subtract*. Stress to students that multiplication and division is *always* evaluated in the order that the expression is written. In the expression 15 ÷ 5 × 2, students *must* first divide before multiplying. The same is true for addition and subtraction. In the expression 10 − 7 + 3, students must subtract before adding.

Tips for New Teachers

Scientific Calculators

Scientific calculators are useful for evaluating expressions. Encourage students to become familiar with using a scientific calculator in some of the exercises, especially in understanding how to enter entries correctly.

Check Your Understanding exercises are intended to be completed in class. **Example references** show students where to look back for review. In the Exercises, **Homework Help** boxes function in the same way.

★ indicates multi-step problem

CHECK Your Understanding

Evaluate each expression. Justify each step. **1–8. See Ch. 1 Answer Appendix for justification.**

Examples 1, 2 (p. 38)

1. $8 + (5 - 2)$ **11**
2. $25 \div (9 - 4)$ **5**
3. $14 - 2 \cdot 6 + 9$ **11**
4. $8 \cdot 5 - 4 \cdot 3$ **28**

Examples 3, 4 (p. 39)

5. 4×10^2 **400**
6. $45 \div (4 - 1)^2$ **5**
7. $17 + 2(6 - 3) - 3 \times 4$ **11**
8. $22 - 3(8 - 2) + 12 \div 4$ **7**

Example 5 (p. 39)

★ 9. **COINS** Isabelle has 3 nickels, 2 quarters, 2 dimes, and 7 pennies. Write an expression that can be used to find how much money Isabelle has altogether. How much money does Isabelle have? **3(0.05) + 2(0.25) + 2(0.10) + 7(0.01); $0.92**

Practice and Problem Solving

HOMEWORK HELP	
For Exercises	See Examples
10–17	1, 2
18–23	3
24–27	4
28, 29	5

Exercise Levels
A: 10–29
B: 30–34
C: 35–37

Evaluate each expression. Justify each step. **10–27. See Ch. 1 Answer Appendix for justification.**

10. $(1 + 8) \times 3$ **27**
11. $10 - (3 + 4)$ **3**
12. $(25 \div 5) + 8$ **13**
13. $(11 - 2) \div 9$ **1**
14. $3 \cdot 2 + 14 \div 7$ **8**
15. $4 \div 2 - 1 + 7$ **8**
16. $12 + 6 \div 3 - 4$ **10**
17. $18 - 3 \cdot 6 + 5$ **5**
18. 6×10^2 **600**
19. 3×10^4 **30,000**
20. $5 \times 4^3 + 2$ **322**
21. $8 \times 7^2 - 6$ **386**
22. $8 \div 2 \times 6 + 6^2$ **60**
23. $9^2 - 14 \div 7 \cdot 3$ **75**
24. $(17 + 3) \div (4 + 1)$ **4**
25. $(6 + 5) \cdot (8 - 6)$ **22**
26. $6 + 2(4 - 1) + 4 \times 9$ **48**
27. $3(4 + 7) - 5 \cdot 4 \div 2$ **23**

For Exercises 28 and 29, write an expression for each situation. Then evaluate to find the solution.

28. **MP3 PLAYERS** Reina is buying an MP3 player, a case, three packs of batteries, and six songs. What is the total cost? **$254**

Item	Quantity	Unit Cost
MP3 player	1	$20
case	1	$3
pack of batteries	3	$4
songs	6	$2

29. **BOOKS** Ian goes to the library's used book sale. Paperback books are $0.25, and hardback books are $0.50. If Ian buys 3 paperback books and 5 hardback books, how much does he spend? **$3.25**

Evaluate each expression. Justify each step.

30–33. See Ch. 1 Answer Appendix for justification.

30. $(2 + 10)^2 \div 4$ **36**
31. $(3^3 + 8) - (10 - 6)^2$ **19**
32. $3 \cdot 4(5.2 + 3.8) + 2.7$ **110.7**
33. $7 \times 9 - (4 - 3.2) + 1.8$ **64**

★ 34. **MONEY** Suppose that your family orders 2 pizzas, 2 orders of garlic bread, and 1 order of BBQ wings from Mario's Pizza Shop. Write an expression to find the amount of change you would receive from $30. Then evaluate the expression. **30 − (2 × 8 + 2 × 2 + 4); $6**

Mario's Pizza Shop	
Item	Cost
14" pizza	$8
garlic bread	$2
BBQ wings	$4

Academic Standards • ISTEP+
Extra Practice, pp. 669, 704

DIFFERENTIATED HOMEWORK OPTIONS

Level	Assignment	Two-Day Option	
BL Basic	10–29, 35, 36, 38–45	11–29 odd, 38–40	10–28 even, 35, 36, 38, 41–45
OL Core	11–27 odd, 28, 29, 31, 33, 34–36, 38–45	10–29, 38–40	30–36, 41–45
AL Advanced/Pre-AP	30–44 (optional: 45)		

O.T. Problems

5. Peggy; the first
tep is to do the
ivision, 24 ÷ 6.
houng incorrectly
ultiplied 6 and
first.

35. **FIND THE ERROR** Phoung and Peggy are evaluating $16 - 24 \div 6 \cdot 2$. Who is correct? Explain your reasoning.

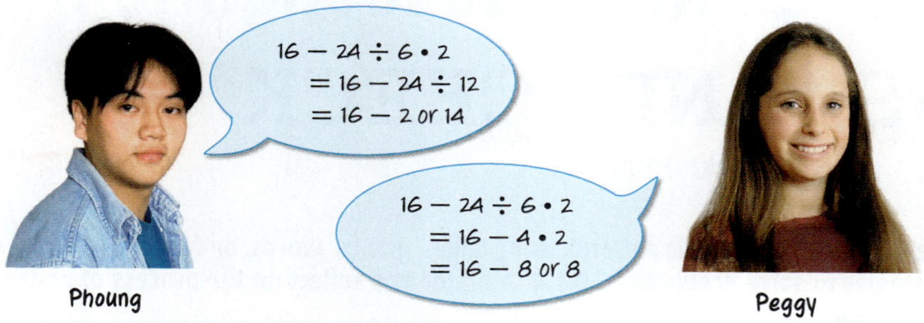

6. 72 ÷ (9 + 27) −
= 0

36. **CHALLENGE** Insert parentheses to make $72 \div 9 + 27 - 2 = 0$ a true statement.

37. **WRITING IN MATH** Write a real-world problem in which you would need to use the order of operations or a scientific calculator to solve it. **See students' work.**

ISTEP+ PRACTICE 7.1.7, 7.2.3

38. Simplify $3^2 + 9 \div 3 + 3$. **C**

A 3 C 15

B 9 D 18

39. Grace has 2 boxes that contain 24 straws each and 3 boxes that contain 15 cups each. Which expression *cannot* be used to find the total number of items she has? **H**

F $2(24) + 3(15)$

G $3 \times 15 + 2 \times 24$

H $5 \times (24 + 15)$

J $15 + 15 + 15 + 24 + 24$

40. The steps Alana took to evaluate the expression $4y + 4 \div 4$ when $y = 7$ are shown below.

$4y + 4 \div 4$ when $y = 7$
$4 \times 7 = 28$
$28 + 4 = 32$
$32 \div 4 = 8$

What should Alana have done differently in order to evaluate the expression correctly? **C**

A divided $(28 + 4)$ by (28×4)

B divided $(28 + 4)$ by $(28 + 4)$

C added $(4 \div 4)$ to 28

D added 4 to $(28 \div 4)$

Spiral Review

Find each square root. (Lesson 1-3)

41. $\sqrt{64}$ **8**

42. $\sqrt{2{,}025}$ **45**

43. $\sqrt{784}$ **28**

44. **INTERNET** Each day, Internet users perform 2^5 million searches using a popular search engine. How many searches is this? (Lesson 1-2) **32 million**

GET READY for the Next Lesson

45. **PREREQUISITE SKILL** A Chinese checkerboard has 121 holes. How many holes can be found on eight Chinese checkerboards? (Lesson 1-1) **968**

Exercise Alert!

Find the Error Exercise 35 illustrates that by not following the order of operations, Phoung found the wrong answer. Remind students to multiply and divide in order from left to right. Multiplication does not automatically come before division.

4 Assess

Crystal Ball Tell students that tomorrow's lesson is about using the guess and check strategy to solve word problems. Have students write how they think what they learned today will connect with tomorrow's lesson.

Foldables™ Follow-Up

Suggest to students that they summarize the order of operations in their Foldables for this chapter. They might include an example illustrating how to use the order of operations to evaluate expressions.

Lesson 1-4 Order of Operations **41**

1-5 Problem-Solving Investigation

GUESS AND CHECK

PACING: **Regular:** 1 period, **Block:** 0.5 period

IN Academic Standards **7.3.4 Recognize, describe, or extend geometric patterns using** tables, graphs, **words,** or symbols. **P.1.3 Apply and adapt a variety of appropriate strategies to solve problems. P.1.4 Monitor and reflect on the process of mathematical problem solving.** *Also addresses P.2.1, P.2.4.*

Options for Differentiated Instruction

ELL = English Language Learner AL = Above or Beyond Grade Level SS = Struggling Students SN = Special Needs

Visual Learners ELL SS SN

Use while presenting Lesson 1-5.

Have students hang butcher block paper or large packing paper on the wall. Use this paper to make a table to chart the *guess and check* strategy used on page 42.

Number of Cars	Number of SUVs	Total Cost ($)	Too High or Too Low?
5	5	$5(5) + 7(5) = \$60$	too high
5	4	$5(5) + 7(4) = \$49$	too low
6	4	$5(6) + 7(4) = \$58$	correct

Have students check reasonable answers rather than guess randomly.

Making Study Tools ELL SS

Use after presenting Lesson 1-5.

Have students create a personal problem-solving booklet. Have them include a description, examples, the best time to use, and advantages and disadvantages of the following problem-solving strategies.

- Use the four-step plan
- Guess and check

Have students add new strategies to the booklet as they are introduced.

Organizing Student Work and Thinking SS SN

Use with Exercise 3.

Students with learning disabilities often have difficulty organizing information.
Provide a table like the one below for students to organize their work as they solve Exercise 3.

Number of Adults	Number of Students	Total Cost ($)	Too High or Too Low?

Leveled Lesson Resources

Also on **TeacherWorks™**
Lesson 1-5

Chapter 1 Resource Masters

BL = Below or Approaching Grade Level

OL = On Grade Level

AL = Above or Beyond Grade Level

ELL = English Language Learner

*Study Guide and Intervention**
p. 36 BL OL ELL

NAME ______________________ DATE __________ PERIOD ____

1-5 Study Guide and Intervention

Problem-Solving Investigation: Guess and Check

When solving problems, one strategy that is helpful to use is guess and check. Based on the information in the problem, you can make a guess of the solution. Then use computations to check if your guess is correct. You can repeat this process until you find the correct solution.

You can use guess and check, along with the following four-step problem solving plan to solve a problem.

Understand • Read and get a general understanding of the problem.
Plan • Make a plan to solve the problem and estimate the solution.
Solve • Use your plan to solve the problem.
Check • Check the reasonableness of your solution.

Example

VETERINARY SCIENCE **Dr. Miller saw 40 birds and cats in one day. All together the pets he saw had 110 legs. How many of each type of animal did Dr. Miller see in one day?**

Understand You know that Dr. Miller saw 40 birds and cats total. You also know that there were 110 legs in all. You need to find out how many of each type of animal he saw in one day.

Plan Make a guess and check it. Adjust the guess until you get the correct answer.

Solve

Number of birds	Number of cats	Total number of feet
20	20	2(20) + 4(20) = 120
30	10	2(30) + 4(10) = 100
25	15	2(25) + 4(15) = 110

Check 25 birds have 50 feet. 15 cats have 60 feet. Since 50 + 60 is 110, the answer is correct.

Exercise

GEOMETRY In a math class of 26 students, each girl drew a triangle and each boy drew a square. If there were 89 sides in all, how many girls and how many boys were in the class?

15 girls, 11 boys

Chapter 1 36 *Course 2*

*Skills Practice**
p. 37 BL OL

NAME ______________________ DATE __________ PERIOD ____

1-5 Skills Practice

Problem-Solving Investigation: Guess and Check

Solve each problem using the guess and check problem-solving strategy.

1. SPORTS Susan made 2-point baskets and 3-point baskets in her last basketball game. All together she scored 9 points. How many of each type of basket did she make?

   3, 2-point baskets
   1, 3-point basket

2. ENTERTAINMENT Tickets to the local circus cost $3 for children and $5 for adults. There were three times as many children tickets sold as adult tickets. All together the circus made $700. How many children and how many adults bought tickets to the circus?

   150 children tickets
   50 adult tickets

3. NUMBERS What are the next two numbers in the following sequence?

   5, 13, 37, 109, 325, ___, ___

   973, 2917

4. MONEY Richard found $2.40 in change while cleaning his couch. He found the same number of quarters, dimes, and nickels. How many of each coin did he find?

   6 quarters
   6 dimes
   6 nickels

Lesson 1–5

Chapter 1 37 *Course 2*

*Practice**
p. 38 OL AL

NAME ______________________ DATE __________ PERIOD ____

1-5 Practice

Problem-Solving Investigation: Guess and Check

Mixed Problem Solving

For Exercises 1 and 2, choose the appropriate method of computation. Then use the method to solve the problem.

1. NUMBERS A number is multiplied by 7. Then 5 is added to the product. The result is 33. What is the number?

   The number is 4.

2. FOOD Mr. Jones paid $23 for food for his family of seven at the ballpark. Everyone had a drink and either one hot dog or one hamburger. How many hamburgers were ordered?

MENU	
ITEM	PRICE
Hot Dog	$2
Hamburger	$3
Drink	$1

   2 hamburgers

Use any strategy to solve Exercises 3–6. Some strategies are shown below.

PROBLEM-SOLVING STRATEGIES
- Guess and Check.
- Find a pattern.

3. PATTERNS What are the next two "words" in the pattern?

   ace, bdf, ceg, dfh, egi, ___ , ___

   fhj; gik

4. GEOMETRY The area of each square is twice the area of the next smaller square drawn in it. If the area of the smallest square is 3 square centimeters, what is the area of the largest square?

   24 cm²

5. ALGEBRA What are the next two numbers in the pattern?

   32, 28, 24, 20, **16** , **12**

6. MONEY Leeann received $60 for her birthday. The money came in $10 bills and $5 bills. If she received 8 bills, how many of each type did she receive?

   4 $10 bills and 4 $5 bills

7. MONEY Duane has four dimes, half as many nickels as dimes, and three times as many quarters as nickels. How much money does Duane have?

   $2.00

8. LIBRARY Mr. Shuck, the librarian, counted 157 books checked-in during the day. This number was 8 less than 3 times the number of books checked-out that same day. How many books were checked-out that day?

   55 books

Chapter 1 38 *Course 2*

*Word Problem Practice**
p. 39 OL AL

NAME ______________________ DATE __________ PERIOD ____

1-5 Word Problem Practice

Problem-Solving Investigation: Guess and Check

1. Joan and Amber have a combined age of 34. If Amber is 2 years less than twice Joan's age, how old is each person?

   Joan is 12

   Amber is 22

2. A number is divided by 3. Then 14 is added to the quotient. The result is 33. What is the original number?

   57

3. The key club made $192 at their candle sale. They sold round candles for $4 and square candles for $6. If they sold twice as many square candles as round ones, how many of each type of candle did the key club sell?

   12 round

   24 square

4. Landon has 37 baseball cards. If 4 cards can fit on one page, how many pages does Landon need to buy?

   10 pages

5. Rick earns $500 less than three times as much as Jim. If their combined salary is $49,500, how much do they each earn?

   Rick earns $37,000.00

   Jim earns $12,500.00

6. The square root of a number is subtracted from the sum of the number and 12. The result is 42. What is the original number?

   36

Lesson 1–5

Chapter 1 39 *Course 2*

** Also available in Spanish* ELL

Additional Lesson Resources

Transparencies

- *5-Minute Check Transparency,* Lesson 1-5

Other Print Products

- *Noteables™ Interactive Study Notebook with Foldables™*

Teacher Tech Tools

- *Interactive Classroom CD-ROM,* Lesson 1-5
- *AssignmentWorks,* Lesson 1-5

Student Tech Tools

glencoe.com

- Extra Examples, Chapter 1, Lesson 5
- Self-Check Quiz, Chapter 1, Lesson 5

1-5 Lesson Notes

1 Focus

Guess and Check Guess and check is an important strategy for problem solving, and is especially useful in taking multiple-choice tests. Sometimes, the easiest way to find a solution to a problem is to make an educated guess, check the answer for reasonableness, and then adjust the guess until the correct answer is found. When students take multiple-choice tests, they can use this strategy to choose a reasonable answer and check to see if that answer is correct.

2 Teach

Scaffolding Questions

Have students read the introduction to the lesson.

- How many of each type of vehicle do you guess were washed? Answers will vary.
- How could you check your guess? by writing a number sentence for the problem and substituting the values I guessed
- How would you know how to adjust your guess? If the total is too low, adjust the values up; if the total is too high, adjust the values down.

ADDITIONAL EXAMPLE

Solve. Use the *guess and check* strategy.

CONCESSIONS The concession stand at the school play sold lemonade for \$0.50 and cookies for \$0.25. They sold 7 more lemonades than cookies, and they made a total of \$39.50. How many lemonades and cookies were sold?
55 lemonades; 48 cookies

1-5 Problem-Solving Investigation

MAIN IDEA: Solve problems using the guess and check strategy.

Academic Standards **7.3.4 Recognize, describe, or extend geometric patterns using** tables, graphs, **words,** or symbols. **P.1.3 Apply and adapt a variety of appropriate strategies to solve problems. P.1.4 Monitor and reflect on the process of mathematical problem solving.** *Also addresses P.2.1, P.2.4.*

P.S.I. TEAM +

e-Mail: GUESS AND CHECK

TREVOR: My soccer team held a car wash to help pay for a trip to a tournament. We charged \$5 for a car and \$7 for an SUV. During the first hour, we washed 10 vehicles and earned \$58.

YOUR MISSION: Use guess and check to find how many of each type of vehicle were washed.

Understand	You know car washes are \$5 for cars and \$7 for SUVs. Ten vehicles were washed for \$58.
Plan	Make a guess and check it. Adjust the guess until you get the correct answer.
Solve	Make a guess. 5 cars and 5 SUVs $5(5) + 7(5) = \$60$ too high Adjust the number of SUVs downward. 5 cars and 4 SUVs $5(5) + 7(4) = \$53$ too low Adjust the number of cars upward. 6 cars and 4 SUVs $5(6) + 7(4) = \$58$ correct ✔ So, 6 cars and 4 SUVs were washed.
Check	Six cars cost \$30, and four SUVs cost \$28. Since $\$30 + \$28 = \$58$, the guess is correct.

Analyze The Strategy

1. Explain why you should keep a careful record of each of your guesses. See margin.
2. WRITING IN MATH Write a problem that could be solved by guess and check. Then write the steps you would take to find the solution to your problem. See Ch. 1 Answer Appendix.

Additional Examples are also in:

- Noteables™ Interactive Study Notebook with Foldables™
- Interactive Classroom PowerPoint® Presentations

Additional Answer

1. Sample answer: You need to keep track of what numbers you have already guessed, so that you do not make the same guess twice. You also need to know what numbers produce answers that are too large or too small, so you can make better guesses.

Mixed Problem Solving

★ indicates multi-step problem

Academic Standards • ISTEP+

Extra Practice, pp. 669, 704

Use the *guess and check* strategy to solve exercises 3–6.

3. **TICKET SALES** The total ticket sales for the school basketball game were $1,625. Adult tickets were $7, and student tickets were $3. Twice as many students bought tickets as adults. How many adult and student tickets were sold? ★
125 adult tickets and 250 student tickets

4. **NUMBERS** A number is multiplied by 6. Then 4 is added to the product. The result is 82. What is the number? **13** ★

5. **ANALYZE TABLES** Camila is transferring her home videos onto a DVD. Suppose the DVD holds 60 minutes. Which videos should Camila select to have the maximum time on the DVD without going over? ★

Video	Time
birthday	25 min 15 s
family picnic	18 min 10 s
holiday	15 min 20 s
vacation	19 min 20 s

birthday, holiday, and vacation

6. **MONEY** Susan has $1.60 in change in her purse. If she has an equal number of nickels, dimes, and quarters, how many of each does she have? ★
Susan has 4 nickels, 4 dimes, and 4 quarters.

Use any strategy to solve Exercises 7–13. Some strategies are shown below.

PROBLEM-SOLVING STRATEGIES
- Guess and check.
- Find a pattern.

7. **BRIDGES** The total length of wire used in the cables supporting the Golden Gate Bridge in San Francisco is about 80,000 miles. This is 5,300 miles longer than three times the distance around Earth at the Equator. What is the distance around Earth at the Equator? ★ **See margin.**

8. **GEOMETRY** What are the next two figures in the pattern? **See margin.**

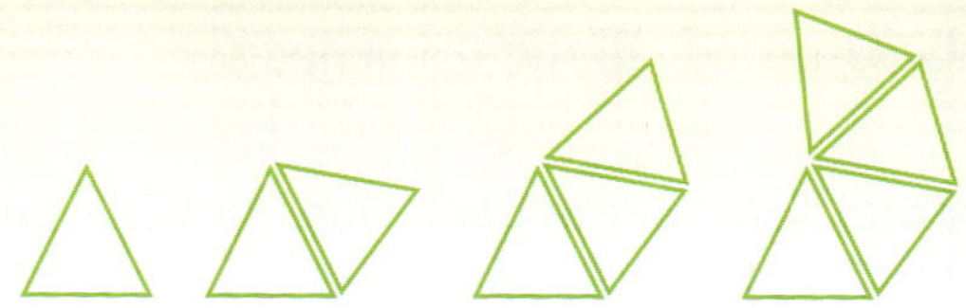

9. **ALGEBRA** What are the next two numbers in the pattern? **512 and 1,024**

16, 32, 64, 128, 256, ■, ■

10. **FRUIT** Mason places 4 apples and 3 oranges into each fruit basket he makes. If he has used 24 apples and 18 oranges, how many fruit baskets has he made? **6**

11. **ANALYZE TABLES** The table gives the average snowfall, in inches, for Valdez, Alaska, for the months of October through April. ★

Month	Snowfall
October	11.6
November	40.3
December	73.0
January	65.8
February	59.4
March	52.0
April	22.7

Source: National Climatic Data Center

How many inches total of snowfall could a resident of Valdez expect to receive from October to April? **324.8 in. of snow**

12. **ROLLER COASTERS** The Jackrabbit roller coaster can handle 1,056 passengers per hour. The coaster has 8 vehicles. If each vehicle carries 4 passengers, how many runs are made in one hour? ★ **See margin.**

13. **NUMBERS** Della is thinking of 3 numbers from 1 through 9 with a product of 36. Find the numbers. **2, 3, 6**

3 Practice

Using the Exercises

Exercises 1 and 2 can be used to check for understanding.

Exercises 3–6 require students to determine first whether they can compute mentally or need to use a pencil and paper.

Exercises 7–13 are structured so that students have the opportunity to practice many different problem-solving strategies. You may wish to review some of the strategies they have studied.

- Use the four-step plan p. 25
- Guess and check p. 42

4 Assess

Yesterday's News Remind students that yesterday's lesson was about the order of operations. Ask students to write how the order of operations helped them to solve today's problems.

Formative Assessment

Check for student understanding of concepts in Lessons 1-4 and 1-5.

CRM Quiz 2, p. 77

Problem-Solving Investigations help students learn different problem-solving strategies for attacking word problems.

Additional Answers

7. The circumference of the Earth is 24,900 miles long at the Equator.

8.

12. Thirty-three runs are made in one hour.

1-6 Algebra: Variables and Expressions

PACING: **Regular:** 1 period, **Block:** 0.5 period

IN Academic Standards **7.2.1 Use variables and appropriate operations to write an expression,** equation or inequality **that represents a verbal description.** *Also addresses 7.1.2, 7.3.4.*

Options for Differentiated Instruction

ELL = English Language Learner AL = Above or Beyond Grade Level SS = Struggling Students SN = Special Needs

Using Symbols ELL SS SN

Use after presenting Examples 1–4.

Make sure students understand that in word problems, there is nothing special about the letters that are used for variables. Point out that it is common to use letters signifying the object being replaced, such as using *a* for age. However, this is merely a convenience.

- Have students practice writing expressions with different variables to become accustomed to using a variety of letters.
- Have ELL students write the following words in their primary language and choose variables to represent the quantities: age, time, number.

Using Math Games ELL AL SS SN

Use before assigning the Exercises.

Write each of the numbers 1-15 on a separate index card and place the cards in a bag. Write ten different rules, each on a separate index card and place those cards in a different bag. Three examples of rules are shown below.

Find a number plus 2.	**Double a number, and then subtract 1.**	**Multiply a number by itself, and then add 3.**

Pick one card from each bag and ask students to use the number on the card and the mathematical rule to calculate the answer. The first person to raise his or her hand and give the correct answer gets a point. For each round, choose a new number for the same rule, choose a new rule for the same number, or choose both a new number and a new rule. The student with the most points after the predetermined time is the winner.

Make the connection that playing this game is the same as evaluating expressions. The rules above represent $n + 2$, $2n - 1$, and $n^2 + 3$, respectively.

Leveled Lesson Resources

Also on TeacherWorks™ Lesson 1-6

Chapter 1 Resource Masters

BL = Below or Approaching Grade Level OL = On Grade Level AL = Above or Beyond Grade Level ELL = English Language Learner

Lesson Reading Guide
p. 40 BL OL ELL

NAME ________ DATE ________ PERIOD ____

1-6 Lesson Reading Guide
Algebra: Variables and Expressions

Get Ready for the Lesson

Complete the Mini Lab at the top of page 44 in your textbook. Write your answers below.

1. Draw the next three figures in the pattern.
2. Find the number of squares in each figure and record your data in the table below. The first three are completed for you. **6, 7, 8**

Figure	1	2	3	4	5	6
Number of squares	3	4	5			

3. Without drawing the figure, determine how many squares would be in the 10th figure. Check by making a drawing. **12; See students' work.**
4. Find a relationship between the figure and its number of squares. **The number of squares is two more than the figure number.**

Read the Lesson

5. Match the description with the appropriate term.

The number 3 in the expression $3y + 2$. **c** a. variable
The entire expression $2v - 1$. **b** b. algebraic expression
The z in the expression $z^2 - 21$. **a** c. coefficient

Remember What You Learned

6. The expression $\frac{1}{3}\pi r \cdot r \cdot h$ represents the volume of a cone where r is the radius of the circular base and h is the height of the figure. Identify the coefficients, variables and constants. **$\frac{1}{3}$ is the coefficient, r and h are the variables. π (pi, pronounced "pie") is a constant. It represents the value 3.14159...**

Chapter 1 40 Course 2

Study Guide and Intervention*
p. 41 BL OL ELL

NAME ________ DATE ________ PERIOD ____

1-6 Study Guide and Intervention
Algebra: Variables and Expressions

To evaluate an algebraic expression you replace each variable with its numerical value, then use the order of operations to simplify.

Example 1 Evaluate $6x - 7$ if $x = 8$.

$6x - 7 = 6(8) - 7$ Replace x with 8.
$= 48 - 7$ Use the order of operations.
$= 41$ Subtract 7 from 48.

Example 2 Evaluate $5m - 3n$ if $m = 6$ and $n = 5$.

$5m - 3n = 5(6) - 3(5)$ Replace m with 6 and n with 5.
$= 30 - 15$ Use the order of operations.
$= 15$ Subtract 15 from 30.

Example 3 Evaluate $\frac{ab}{3}$ if $a = 7$ and $b = 6$.

$\frac{ab}{3} = \frac{(7)(6)}{3}$ Replace a with 7 and b with 6.
$= \frac{42}{3}$ The fraction bar is like a grouping symbol.
$= 14$ Divide.

Example 4 Evaluate $x^3 + 4$ if $x = 3$.

$x^3 + 4 = 3^3 + 4$ Replace x with 3.
$= 27 + 4$ Use the order of operations.
$= 31$ Add 27 and 4.

Exercises

Evaluate each expression if $a = 4$, $b = 2$, and $c = 7$.

1. $3ac$ **84** 2. $5b^3$ **40** 3. abc **56**
4. $5 + 6c$ **47** 5. $\frac{ab}{8}$ **1** 6. $2a - 3b$ **2**
7. $\frac{b^4}{4}$ **4** 8. $c - a$ **3** 9. $20 - bc$ **6**
10. $2bc$ **28** 11. $ac - 3b$ **22** 12. $6a^2$ **96**
13. $7c$ **49** 14. $6a - b$ **22** 15. $ab - c$ **1**

Chapter 1 41 Course 2

Skills Practice*
p. 42 BL OL

NAME ________ DATE ________ PERIOD ____

1-6 Skills Practice
Algebra: Variables and Expressions

Evaluate each expression if $w = 2$, $x = 3$, $y = 5$, and $z = 6$.

1. $2w$ **4** 2. $y + 5$ **10** 3. $9 - z$ **3**
4. $x + w$ **5** 5. $3 + 4z$ **27** 6. $6y - 5$ **25**
7. y^2 **25** 8. $y - x$ **2** 9. $\frac{z}{2}$ **3**

Evaluate each expression if $m = 3$, $n = 7$, and $p = 9$.

10. $m + n$ **10** 11. $12 - 3m$ **3** 12. $5p$ **45**
13. $3.3p$ **29.7** 14. $3.3p + 2$ **31.7** 15. $2p + 3.3$ **21.3**
16. $20 + 2n$ **34** 17. $20 - 2n$ **6** 18. $\frac{n}{7}$ **1**
19. n^2 **49** 20. $6m^2$ **54** 21. $\frac{p^2}{3}$ **27**
22. $1.1 + n$ **8.1** 23. $p - 8.1$ **0.9** 24. $3.6m$ **10.8**
25. $3n - 2m$ **15** 26. $3m - n$ **2** 27. $2.1n + p$ **23.7**
28. $\frac{m^2}{p}$ **1** 29. $\frac{2.5m + 2.5}{5}$ **2** 30. $\frac{(n + 2)^2}{3}$ **27**

Chapter 1 42 Course 2

Practice*
p. 43 OL AL

NAME ________ DATE ________ PERIOD ____

1-6 Practice
Algebra: Variables and Expressions

Evaluate each expression if $r = 5$, $s = 2$, $t = 7$, and $u = 1$.

1. $s + 7$ **9** 2. $9 - u$ **8** 3. $3t + 1$ **22**
4. $5r - 4$ **21** 5. $t - s$ **5** 6. $u + r$ **6**
7. $11t - 7$ **70** 8. $6 + 3u$ **9** 9. $4r - 10s$ **0**
10. $3u^2$ **3** 11. $2t^2 - 18$ **80** 12. $r^2 + 8$ **33**
13. $\frac{s}{2}$ **1** 14. $\frac{30}{r}$ **6** 15. $\frac{(3 + u)^2}{8}$ **2**

Evaluate each expression if $a = 4.1$, $b = 5.7$, and $c = 0.3$.

16. $a + b - c$ **9.5** 17. $10 - (a + b)$ **0.2** 18. $b - c + 2$ **7.4**

19. MOON The expression $\frac{w}{6}$ gives the weight of an object on the Moon in pounds with a weight of w pounds on Earth. What is the weight of a space suit on the Moon if the space suit weighs 178.2 pounds on Earth? **29.7 pounds**

20. **Complete the table.**

Pounds (p)	Ounces ($16p$)
1	16
2	32
3	**48**
4	**64**
5	**80**

Chapter 1 43 Course 2

Word Problem Practice*
p. 44 OL AL

NAME ________ DATE ________ PERIOD ____

1-6 Word Problem Practice
Algebra: Variables and Expressions

1. FIELD TRIP The seventh grade math classes are going on a field trip. The field trip will cost $7 per student. Write an expression to find the cost of the field trip for s students. What is the total cost if 26 students go on the trip? **7s; $182**

2. SOCCER Jason earns $20 per game as a referee in youth soccer games. Write an expression to find how much money Jason will earn for refereeing any number of games. Let n represent the number of games Jason has refereed. How much will he earn for refereeing 6 games? **20n; $120**

3. PROFIT The expressions $c - e$, where c stands for the money collected and e stands for the expenses, is used to find the profit from a basketball concession. If $500 was collected and expenses were $150, find the profit for the concession. **$350**

4. SAVINGS Kata has a savings account that contains $230. She decides to deposit $5 each month from her monthly earnings for baby-sitting after school. Write an expression to find how much money Kata will have in her savings account after x months. Let x represent the number of months. Then find out how much she will have in her account after 1 year. **5x + 230; $290**

5. MONEY Mr. Wilson has $2,500 in his savings account and m dollars in his checking account. Write an expression that describes the total amount that he has in both accounts. **2,500 + m**

6. ANIMALS Write an expression to represent the total number of legs on h horses and c chickens. How many legs are there in 5 horses and 6 chickens? **4h + 2c; 32 legs**

7. T-SHIRTS The band wants to order T-shirts. The T-shirts cost $15 each plus a shipping fee of $10. Write an expression to find the total cost of c T-shirts. **15c + 10**

8. TEMPERATURE The expression $\frac{9}{5}C + 32$, where C stands for temperature in degrees Celsius, is used to convert Celsius to Fahrenheit. If the temperature is 20 degrees Celsius, find the temperature in degrees Fahrenheit. **68°F**

Chapter 1 44 Course 2

Enrichment
p. 45 OL AL

NAME ________ DATE ________ PERIOD ____

1-6 Enrichment

The First Lady of Science

Chinese-American physicist Chien-Shiung Wu (1912–1997) was born in Shanghai, China. At the age of 24, she came to the United States to further her studies in science. She received her doctorate in physics from the University of California, Berkeley in 1940. Dr. Wu became the first female professor at Princeton University and worked on the Manhattan Project during World War II.

Dr. Wu paved the way for many female scientists. She received numerous awards and honors from American and Chinese universities and was the first woman president of the American Physical Society. She was also the first living scientist to have an asteroid named in her honor.

Evaluate each expression for $p = 9$, $q = 5$, $r = 7$, and $x = 8$. The problem letter and the solution form a key to decoding another fact about Dr. Wu shown below.

A. $r + 3$ **10** C. $10q$ **50** E. $q + r$ **12** G. $p + 5$ **14**
H. $6r - x$ **34** N. $6 + 4x$ **38** O. $3q + 5p$ **60** P. $70 - 2p$ **52**
R. $r^2 + 5$ **54** S. $4q^2 - 3$ **97** T. $2r^2$ **98** Y. $8r - 5$ **51**

In Chinese, *Chien-Shiung* means....

S	T	R	O	N	G		H	E	R	O
97	98	54	60	38	14		34	12	54	60

Chapter 1 45 Course 2

* Also available in Spanish ELL

Additional Lesson Resources

Transparencies
- *5-Minute Check Transparency*, Lesson 1-6

Other Print Products
- *Teaching Mathematics with Manipulatives*
- *Noteables™ Interactive Study Notebook with Foldables™*

Teacher Tech Tools
- *Interactive Classroom CD-ROM*, Lesson 1-6
- *AssignmentWorks*, Lesson 1-6

Student Tech Tools
glencoe.com
- Extra Examples, Chapter 1, Lesson 6
- Self-Check Quiz, Chapter 1, Lesson 6

1-6 Lesson Notes

1 Focus

Vertical Alignment

Before Lesson 1-6
Use a letter to represent an unknown number; write and evaluate simple algebraic expressions in one variable by substitution

Lesson 1-6
Evaluate an algebraic expression for a given situation. Solve problems manually by using the correct order of operations

After Lesson 1-6
Use variables and appropriate operations to write an expression, an equation, an inequality, or a system of equations or inequalities that represents a verbal description

2 Teach

MINI Lab

The purpose of the lab is to find a relationship between two series of numbers and to express that relationship algebraically.

Provide isometric dot paper for students to complete the drawing activity in the Mini Lab.

1-6 Algebra: Variables and Expressions

MAIN IDEA

Evaluate simple algebraic expressions.

IN Academic Standards

7.2.1 Use variables and appropriate operations to write an expression, equation or inequality **that represents a verbal description.** *Also addresses 7.1.2, 7.3.4.*

New Vocabulary

variable
algebra
algebraic expression
coefficient

IN Math Online

glencoe.com
- Concepts In Motion
- Extra Examples
- Personal Tutor
- Self-Check Quiz

MINI Lab

A pattern of squares is shown.

1. Draw the next three figures in the pattern.
2. Find the number of squares in each figure and record your data in a table like the one shown below. The first three are completed for you.

Figure	1	2	3	4	5	6
Number of Squares	3	4	5	6	7	8

3. Without drawing the figure, determine how many squares would be in the 10th figure. Check by making a drawing.
4. Find a relationship between the figure and its number of squares.

1, 3, and 4. See Ch. 1 Answer Appendix.

In the Mini Lab, you found that the number of squares in the figure is two more than the figure number. You can use a placeholder, or variable to represent the number of squares. A **variable** is a symbol that represents an unknown quantity.

figure number ⟶ $n + 2$
⟶ number of squares

The branch of mathematics that involves expressions with variables is called **algebra**. The expression $n + 2$ is called an **algebraic expression** because it contains variables, numbers, and at least one operation.

EXAMPLE Evaluate an Algebraic Expression

1. **Evaluate $n + 3$ if $n = 4$.**

$n + 3 = 4 + 3$ Replace n with 4.
$= 7$ Add 4 and 3.

CHECK Your Progress

Evaluate each expression if $c = 8$ and $d = 5$.

a. $c - 3$ **5** b. $15 - c$ **7** c. $c + d$ **13**

Scaffolding Questions

Ask:
- What does the word *variable* mean in an everyday context? subject to change
- What do you think *variable* means in math? a letter or symbol with no fixed quantitative value
- Why are *variables* important in math? They can be used whenever you do not know a number or when the number could change based on the situation.

Tips for New Teachers

Algebraic Expressions

Students may require additional practice reading and writing algebraic expressions. For example, the phrase *two less than m* can be written as $m - 2$. The expression $\frac{a}{2}$ can be read *a divided by 2*, *the quotient of a and 2*, or *half of a*.

In algebra, the multiplication sign is often omitted.

$6d$	$9st$	mn
↑	↑	↑
6 times d	9 times s times t	m times n

The numerical factor of a multiplication expression that contains a variable is called a **coefficient**. So, 6 is the coefficient of $6d$.

EXAMPLES Evaluate Expressions

2 **Evaluate $8w - 2v$ if $w = 5$ and $v = 3$.**

$8w - 2v = 8(5) - 2(3)$ Replace w with 5 and v with 3.

$= 40 - 6$ Do all multiplications first.

$= 34$ Subtract 6 from 40.

3 **Evaluate $4y^2 + 2$ if $y = 3$.**

$4y^2 + 2 = 4(3)^2 + 2$ Replace y with 3.

$= 4(9) + 2$ Evaluate the power.

$= 38$ Multiply, then add.

CHECK Your Progress

Evaluate each expression if $a = 4$ and $b = 3$.

d. $9a - 6b$ 18

e. $\frac{ab}{2}$ 6

f. $2a^2 + 5$ 37

The fraction bar is a grouping symbol. Evaluate the expressions in the numerator and denominator separately before dividing.

Real-World Link . . . . Athletic trainers use the formula $\frac{3(220 - a)}{5}$, where a is a person's age, to find their minimum training heart rate.

Source: CMPMedica Ltd.

Real-World EXAMPLE

4 **HEALTH** **Use the formula at the left to find Latrina's minimum training heart rate if she is 15 years old.**

$\frac{3(220 - a)}{5} = \frac{3(220 - 15)}{5}$ Replace a with 15.

$= \frac{3(205)}{5}$ Subtract 15 from 220.

$= \frac{615}{5}$ Multiply 3 and 205.

$= 123$ Divide 615 by 5.

Latrina's minimum training heart rate is 123 beats per minute.

CHECK Your Progress

g. **MEASUREMENT** To find the area of a triangle, you can use the formula $\frac{bh}{2}$, where h is the height and b is the base. What is the area in square inches of a triangle with a height of 6 inches and base of 8 inches? 24 in²

Focus on Mathematical Content

In an algebraic expression, a **variable** represents an unknown number or numbers. Make sure students understand there is nothing special about which letters are used for variables. It is common to use letters signifying the object being replaced, such as a for *age*. However, this is merely a convenience. Have students practice using expressions with different variables to become accustomed to using a variety of letters.

To evaluate an algebraic expression, replace the variables with their given values and follow the **order of operations**.

Formative Assessment

Use the Check Your Progress exercises after the Examples to determine students' understanding of concepts.

ADDITIONAL EXAMPLES

1. Evaluate $t - 4$ if $t = 6$. 2
2. Evaluate $5x + 3y$ if $x = 7$ and $y = 9$. 62
3. Evaluate $5 + a^2$ if $a = 5$. 30
4. **TEMPERATURE** The formula for rewriting a Fahrenheit temperature as a Celsius temperature is $\frac{5(F - 32)}{9}$, where F equals the temperature in degrees Fahrenheit. Find the Celsius equivalent of 99°F. about 37.2°C

Additional Examples are also in:

- Noteables™ Interactive Study Notebook with Foldables™
- Interactive Classroom PowerPoint® Presentations

3 Practice

Formative Assessment

Use Exercises 1–13 to check for understanding.

Then use the chart at the bottom of this page to customize your assignments for students.

Intervention You may wish to use the Study Guide and Intervention Master on page 41 of the *Chapter 1 Resource Masters* for additional reinforcement.

Odd/Even Assignments

Exercises 14–31 are structured so that students practice the same concepts whether they are assigned odd or even problems.

★ indicates multi-step problem

CHECK Your Understanding

Example 1 (p. 44)

Evaluate each expression if $a = 3$ and $b = 5$.

1. $a + 7$ **10**
2. $8 - b$ **3**
3. $b - a$ **2**
4. **HEALTH** The standard formula for finding your maximum heart rate is $220 - a$, where a represents a person's age in years. What is your maximu heart rate? **See students' work.**

Examples 2–4 (p. 45)

Evaluate each expression if $m = 2$, $n = 6$, and $p = 4$.

5. $6n - p$ **32**
6. $7m - 2n$ **2**
7. $3m + 4p$ **22**
8. $n^2 + 5$ **41**
9. $15 - m^3$ **7**
10. $3p^2 - n$ **42**
11. $\frac{mn}{4}$ **3**
12. $\frac{3n}{9}$ **2**
13. $\frac{5n + m}{8}$ **4**

Practice and Problem Solving

HOMEWORK HELP	
For Exercises	See Examples
14–29	1–3
30–31	4

Exercise Levels
A: 14–31
B: 32–38
C: 39–41

Evaluate each expression if $d = 8$, $e = 3$, $f = 4$, and $g = 1$.

14. $d + 9$ **17**
15. $10 - e$ **7**
16. $4f + 1$ **17**
17. $8g - 3$ **5**
18. $f - e$ **1**
19. $d + f$ **12**
20. $10g - 6$ **4**
21. $8 + 5d$ **48**
22. $\frac{d}{5}$ **1.6**
23. $\frac{16}{f}$ **4**
24. $\frac{5d - 25}{5}$ **3**
25. $\frac{(5 + g)^2}{2}$ **18**
26. $6f^2$ **96**
27. $4e^2$ **36**
28. $d^2 + 7$ **71**
29. $e^2 - 4$ **5**

★ 30. **BOWLING** The expression $5n + 2$ can be used to find the total cost in dolla of bowling where n is the number of games bowled. How much will it cos Vincent to bowl 3 games? **$17**

31. **HEALTH** The expression $\frac{w}{30}$, where w is a person's weight in pounds, is use to find the approximate number of quarts of blood in the person's body. Ho many quarts of blood does a 120-pound person have? **4 quarts**

Evaluate each expression if $x = 3.2$, $y = 6.1$, and $z = 0.2$.

32. $x + y - z$ **9.1**
33. $14.6 - (x + y + z)$ **5.1**
34. $xz + y^2$ **37.85**

35. **CAR RENTAL** A car rental company charges $19.99 per day and $0.17 per mile to rent a car. Write an expression that gives the total cost in dollars to rent a car for d days and m miles. **$19.99d + 0.17m$**

36. **MUSIC** A Web site charges $0.99 to download a song onto an MP3 player and $12.49 to download an entire album. Write an expression that gives th total cost in dollars to download a albums and s songs. **$12.49a + 0.99s$**

DIFFERENTIATED HOMEWORK OPTIONS

Level	Assignment	Two-Day Option	
BL Basic	14–31, 39, 41–52	15–31 odd, 42, 43	14–30 even, 39, 41, 44–52
OL Core	15–29 odd, 30, 31, 33, 35, 37–39, 41–52	14–31, 42, 43	32–39, 41, 44–52
AL Advanced/Pre-AP	32–49 (optional: 50–52)		

★ 37. **SCIENCE** The expression $\frac{32t^2}{2}$ gives the falling distance of an object in feet after t seconds. How far would a bungee jumper fall 2 seconds after jumping? **64 ft**

★ 38. **GEOMETRY** To find the total number of diagonals for any given polygon, you can use the expression $\frac{n(n-3)}{2}$, where n is the number of sides of the polygon. What is the total number of diagonals for a 10-sided polygon? **35**

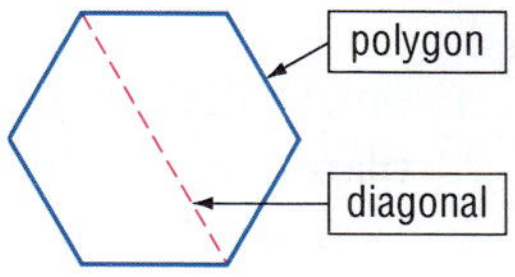

Academic Standards • ISTEP+

xtra Practice, pp. 669, 704

.O.T. Problems

39. **OPEN ENDED** Write an algebraic expression with the variable x that has a value of 3 when evaluated. **Sample answer: $5x - 37$ if $x = 8$**

40. **CHALLENGE** Name values of x and y so that the value of $5x + 3$ is greater than the value of $2y + 14$. **Sample answer: $x = 15$, $y = 30$**

41. **WRITING IN MATH** Tell whether the statement below is *sometimes*, *always*, or *never* true. Justify your reasoning.

The expressions $x - 3$ and $y - 3$ represent the same value.

Sometimes; Sample answer: $x - 3$ and $y - 3$ represent the same value only when $x = y$.

ISTEP+ PRACTICE 7.2.1

42. Which expression could be used to find the cost of buying b books at \$7.95 each and m magazines at \$4.95 each? **A**

A $7.95b + 4.95m$

B $7.95b - 4.95m$

C $12.9(b + m)$

D $12.9(bm)$

43. Tonya has x quarters, y dimes, and z nickels in her pocket. Which of the following expressions gives the total amount of change she has in her pocket? **G**

F $\$0.25x + \$0.05y + \$0.10z$

G $\$0.25x + \$0.10y + \$0.05z$

H $\$0.05x + \$0.25y + \$0.10z$

J $\$0.10x + \$0.05y + \$0.25z$

Spiral Review

44. **SHOPPING** A grocery store sells hot dog buns in packages of 8 and 12. How many 8-packs and 12-packs could you buy if you needed 44 hot dog buns? Use the *guess and check* strategy. (Lesson 1-5) **three 12-packs and one 8-pack, or four 8-packs and one 12-pack**

Evaluate each expression. (Lesson 1-4)

45. $6(5) - 2$ **28**
46. $9 + 9 \div 3$ **12**
47. $4 \cdot 2(8 - 1)$ **56**
48. $(17 + 3) \div 5$ **4**

49. Find $\sqrt{361}$. (Lesson 1-3) **19**

GET READY for the Next Lesson

PREREQUISITE SKILL **Determine whether each sentence is *true* or *false*.** (Lesson 1-4)

50. $15 - 2(3) = 9$ **true**
51. $20 \div 5 \times 4 = 1$ **false**
52. $4^2 + 6 \cdot 7 = 154$ **false**

4 Assess

Name the Math Have students describe a word problem with a variable (or variables). Make sure they identify the variable.

*The Four-step Teaching Plan shows you how to **Focus, Teach, Practice,** and **Assess** each lesson. Each lesson ends with a creative strategy for closing the lesson.*

Lesson 1-6 Algebra: Variables and Expressions **47**

Formative Assessment

Use the Mid-Chapter Quiz to assess students' progress in the first half of the chapter.

Have students review the lesson indicated for the problems they answered incorrectly.

Summative Assessment

CRM Mid-Chapter Test, p. 79

ExamView Assessment Suite — Customize and create multiple versions of your Mid-Chapter Test and their answer keys.

Foldables Study Organizer — **Dinah Zike's Foldables**

Before students complete the Mid-Chapter Quiz, encourage them to review the information on the first three pages of their Foldables.

*The **Mid-Chapter Quiz** reviews skills and concepts presented in previous lessons. Students' results on the quiz can be used for **Data-Driven Decision Making**.*

Chapter 1 Mid-Chapter Quiz

Lessons 1-1 through 1-6

IN Academic Standards 7.1.2, 7.2.3

1. **MULTIPLE CHOICE** A cycling club is planning an 1,800-mile trip. The cyclers average 15 miles per hour. What additional information is needed to determine the number of days it will take them to complete the trip? (Lesson 1-1) **C**

   A The number of cyclists in the club
   B The number of miles of rough terrain
   C The number of hours they plan to cycle each day
   D Their average speed per minute

Write each power as a product of the same factor. (Lesson 1-2)

2. 4^5 **$4 \cdot 4 \cdot 4 \cdot 4 \cdot 4$**
3. 9^6 **$9 \cdot 9 \cdot 9 \cdot 9 \cdot 9 \cdot 9$**

4. **OCEANS** The world's largest ocean, the Pacific Ocean, covers approximately 4^3 million square miles. Write this area in standard form. (Lesson 1-2) **64 million mi²**

5. **ZOOS** The Lincoln Park Zoo in Illinois is $2 \cdot 2 \cdot 2 \cdot 2 \cdot 2 \cdot 2 \cdot 2$ years old. Write this age in exponential form. (Lesson 1-2) **2^7 yr**

6. **MULTIPLE CHOICE** The model below represents $\sqrt{49} = 7$.

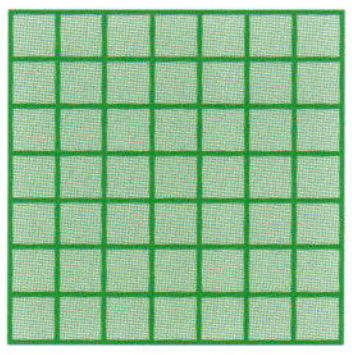

   Which arrangement of small squares can be used to model a large square that represents $\sqrt{324}$? (Lesson 1-3) **G**

   F 9 rows of 36 squares
   G 18 rows of 18 squares
   H 12 rows of 27 squares
   J 6 rows of 54 squares

Find the square of each number. (Lesson 1-3)

7. 4 **16**
8. 12 **144**

Find each square root. (Lesson 1-3)

9. $\sqrt{64}$ **8**
10. $\sqrt{289}$ **17**

11. **LANDSCAPING** A bag of lawn fertilizer cove[rs] 2,500 square feet. Describe the largest squa[re] that one bag of fertilizer could cover. (Lesson 1-3) **50 ft by 50 ft**

Evaluate each expression. (Lesson 1-4)

12. $25 - (3^2 + 2 \times 5)$ **6**
13. $\frac{2(7-3)}{2^2}$ **2**

14. ★ **MEASUREMENT** The perimeter of a rectangl[e] is 42 inches, and its area is 104 square inches. Find the dimensions of the rectang[le]. Use the *guess and check* strategy. (Lesson 1-5) **8 in. by 13 in.**

15. **MULTIPLE CHOICE** Ana buys some baseball bats at $35 each and some baseball gloves at $48 each. Which expression could be used to find the total cost of the sports items? (Lesson 1-6) **C**

   A $35b \cdot 48g$
   B $\frac{35b}{48g}$
   C $35b + 48g$
   D $48g - 35b$

Evaluate each expression if $x = 12$, $y = 4$, and $z = 8$. (Lesson 1-6)

16. $x - 5$ **7**
17. $3y + 10z$ **92**
18. $\frac{yz}{2}$ **16**
19. $\frac{(y+8)^2}{x}$ **12**

20. ★ **HEALTH** A nurse can use the expression $110 + \frac{A}{2}$, where A is a person's age, to estimate a person's normal systolic blood pressure. Estimate the normal systolic bloo[d] pressure for a 16-year-old. (Lesson 1-6) **118**

Data-Driven Decision Making

Diagnostic Teaching Based on the results of the Chapter 1 Mid-Chapter Quiz, use the following to review concepts that students continue to find challenging.

Exercises	Lesson	Academic Standards
1	1-1	P.1.1
2–5	1-2	7.1.2
6–11	1-3	7.1.5
12, 13	1-4	7.1.7
14	1-5	P.1.3, P.1.4
15–20	1-6	7.2.1

Resources for Review

CRM Study Guide and Intervention pp. 10, 16, 23, 30, 36, and 41

IN Math Online glencoe.com

- Extra Examples
- Personal Tutor
- Concepts in Motion

1-7 Algebra: Equations

PACING: **Regular:** 1 period, **Block:** 0.5 period

IN Academic Standards

Preparation for 7.2.2 Write and solve two-step linear equations and inequalities in one variable.
P.6.6 Recognize when the numbers involved in a computation allow for a mental computation strategy. *Also addresses P.6.5.*

Options for Differentiated Instruction

ELL = English Language Learner AL = Above or Beyond Grade Level SS = Struggling Students SN = Special Needs

Connections to Prior Knowledge SN SS

Use before presenting the lesson.

It is helpful if students are able to make connections between concepts with which they are familiar and algebra. Being able to do so can make new algebraic concepts seem less intimidating. Write the following equations on the board.

$\blacksquare + 3 = 7$

$\blacksquare - 2 = 6$

$\blacksquare \div 2 = 5$

$3 \times \blacksquare = 18$

Ask:

- What number can be written in each box to make the equation true? 4; 8; 10; 6
- Have you seen problems like this before? If so, when?

Building Vocabulary ELL SS SN

Use while presenting the lesson.

Have students use one index card for each new vocabulary term and create a *vocabulary index.* On each card, have students define or describe the term in their own words and give an example of the term. They should file all the cards alphabetically in their index. Have students keep their index on their desks so they have easy access to definitions.

Kinesthetic Learner ELL AL

Use before assigning the Exercises.

Have students work in groups of three. Have them write a simple equation such as $n + \$0.05 = \$0.10$. Then have them use actual coins to model the equation and solve for n.

Have students take turns writing an equation, modeling it, and solving for n. Encourage them to challenge each other with difficult equations.

Leveled Lesson Resources

Also on TeacherWorks™
Lesson 1-7

Chapter 1 Resource Masters

BL = Below or Approaching Grade Level   OL = On Grade Level   AL = Above or Beyond Grade Level   ELL = English Language Learner

Lesson Reading Guide
p. 47 BL OL ELL

NAME ______________ DATE ________ PERIOD ____

1-7 Lesson Reading Guide
Algebra: Equations

Get Ready for the Lesson

Read the introduction at the top of page 49 in your textbook. Write your answers below.

1. Suppose each team played 34 games. How many losses did each team have?

Women's College Volleyball		
Team	Wins	Losses
Bowling Green State University	28	**6**
Kent State University	13	**21**
Ohio University	28	**6**
University of Akron	7	**27**
University of Buffalo	14	**20**
Miami University	13	**21**

Source: Mid-American Conference

2. Write a rule to describe how you found the number of losses. **34 = wins + losses**
3. Let w represent the number of wins and ℓ represent the number of losses. Rewrite your rule using numbers, variables, and an equals sign. **Sample answer: $34 = w + \ell$**

Read the Lesson

4. Complete the sentence: An equation that contains a variable is neither true nor false until the variable is replaced with a ________. **number**
5. Describe what it means to model a problem. **Sample answer: Write an equation that represents the problem.**
6. What must you do before you write an equation using a variable when modeling a problem? **Define the variable.**

Remember What You Learned

7. Calculating change after buying lunch is a situation that can be modeled with a simple equation. What other daily activities require you to solve an equation? Write down three sample equations. **See students' work.**

Lesson 1-7

Chapter 1 47 Course 2

Study Guide and Intervention*
p. 48 BL OL ELL

NAME ______________ DATE ________ PERIOD ____

1-7 Study Guide and Intervention
Algebra: Equations

- An **equation** is a sentence in mathematics that contains an equals sign, =.
- The **solution** of an equation is the value that when substituted for the variable makes the equation true.

Example 1 **Solve 23 + y = 29 mentally.**

$23 + y = 29$ Write the equation.
$23 + 6 = 29$ You know that 23 + 6 is 29.
$29 = 29$ Simplify.
The solution is 6.

Example 2

TRAVEL On their annual family vacation, the Wilsons travel 790 miles in two days. If on the first day they travel 490 miles, how many miles must they drive on the second day to reach their destination?

The total distance to travel in two days is 790 miles.
Let m represent the distance to travel on day two.
$m + 490 = 790$

$m + 490 = 790$ Write the equation.
$300 + 490 = 790$ Replace m with 300 to make the equation true.
$790 = 790$ Simplify.

The number 300 is the solution. The distance the Wilsons must travel on day two is 300 miles.

Exercises

Solve each equation mentally.

1. $k + 7 = 15$ **8**
2. $g - 8 = 20$ **28**
3. $6y = 24$ **4**
4. $\frac{a}{3} = 9$ **27**
5. $\frac{x}{6} = 9$ **54**
6. $8 + r = 24$ **16**
7. $12 \cdot 8 = h$ **96**
8. $n \div 11 = 8$ **88**
9. $48 \div 12 = x$ **4**
10. $h - 12 = 24$ **36**
11. $19 + y = 28$ **9**
12. $9f = 90$ **10**

Define a variable. Then write and solve an equation.

13. MONEY Aaron wants to buy a video game. The game costs $15.50. He has $10.00 saved from his weekly allowance. How much money does he need to borrow from his mother in order to buy the video game? **M = the amount of money he needs to borrow; M + 10 = 15.5; $5.50**

Chapter 1 48 Course 2

Skills Practice*
p. 49 BL OL

NAME ______________ DATE ________ PERIOD ____

1-7 Skills Practice
Algebra: Equations

Solve each equation mentally.

1. $a + 7 = 16$ **9**
2. $12 + x = 21$ **9**
3. $4d = 60$ **15**
4. $15 = \frac{u}{3}$ **45**
5. $\frac{b}{7} = 12$ **84**
6. $13 \cdot 3 = y$ **39**
7. $8 + r = 17$ **9**
8. $27 - 12 = m$ **15**
9. $h - 22 = 67$ **89**
10. $27 + 15 = n$ **42**
11. $36 + a = 96$ **60**
12. $99 \div d = 3$ **33**
13. $6t = 66$ **11**
14. $25 = y \div 4$ **100**
15. $b - 25 = 120$ **145**
16. $n \div 5 = 10$ **50**
17. $4y = 48$ **12**
18. $5t = 40$ **8**
19. $50 \cdot d = 150$ **3**
20. $w + 61 = 65$ **4**
21. $88 \div k = 2$ **44**

Graph the solution of each equation on a number line.

22. $v - 6 = 30$ **36**
23. $3a = 27$ **9**
24. $n + 7 = 14$ **7**

See students' work for graphs.

Define a variable. Write an equation and solve.

25. BAKING Judy wants to buy some cookies for her birthday party. Cookies come in packages of 6. If she is inviting 24 friends to her party, how many packages of cookies does she need to buy so that each of her friends can have one cookie each?

P = the number of packages of cookies; 6p = 24; 4 packages

Lesson 1-7

Chapter 1 49 Course 2

Practice*
p. 50 OL AL

NAME ______________ DATE ________ PERIOD ____

1-7 Practice
Algebra: Equations

Solve each equation mentally.

1. $a + 5 = 14$ **9**
2. $7 + y = 24$ **17**
3. $t - 13 = 33$ **46**
4. $b - 17 = 11$ **28**
5. $12 - r = 0$ **12**
6. $x + 18 = 59$ **41**
7. $63 = 9g$ **7**
8. $8d = 96$ **12**
9. $n = \frac{42}{7}$ **6**
10. $9 = \frac{z}{7}$ **63**
11. $10 = h \div 4$ **40**
12. $55 \div m = 11$ **5**
13. $1.2 + k = 3.0$ **1.8**
14. $2.7 = f - 1.1$ **3.8**
15. $v - 0.5 = 0.2$ **0.7**
16. $12.6 - c = 7.0$ **5.6**
17. $8.8 + j = 18.7$ **9.9**
18. $w + 13.5 = 16.0$ **2.5**

19. WEATHER The temperature was 78°F. A cold front moved in, and the temperature dropped to 54°F. Solve the equation $78 - d = 54$ to find the drop in temperature.

24°F

20. HOBBIES Elissa can cut out the pieces of cloth to make four pillows in one hour. Solve the equation $4h = 20$ to find how many hours Elissa needs to cut cloth for 20 pillows.

5 hours

21. BOWLING Jean Conrad is an amateur bowler with an average score of 187. She recently bowled a perfect 300 score. Write an equation that can be used to find how much the perfect score was above her average score and then solve the equation.

$300 - n = 187$ or $n = 300 - 187$; $n = 113$
The perfect score of 300 is 113 above her average.

Chapter 1 50 Course 2

Word Problem Practice*
p. 51 OL AL

NAME ______________ DATE ________ PERIOD ____

1-7 Word Problem Practice
Algebra: Equations

1. GAS MILEAGE Mr. Moseley's car has a 20-gallon gas tank. It took 14 gallons of gas to fill his tank. Use the equation $14 + g = 20$ to find the number of gallons g that he had before he filled his tank with gas. **6 gal**
2. PAINTING Latisha earned $5 an hour painting for her dad. If she made $40 last week, use $5h = 40$ to find how many hours h she painted. **8 h**
3. LUMBER Mrs. Garcia had a piece of board that was 15 feet long. She cut off 6.5 feet. Use the equation $6.5 + \ell = 15$ to determine how much of the board ℓ she has left. **8.5 ft**
4. MAGAZINES Mahpee was selling magazine subscriptions. He earned $5 plus $0.50 for each subscription he sold. If Mahpee earned $25, use the equation $25 = 5 + 0.50n$ to find the number of subscriptions n he sold. **40 subscriptions**
5. TIRES The cost of a car tire is $45 plus $10 per order regardless of the number of tires purchased. If Mrs. Sato places an order for $190, use the equation $45t + 10 = 190$ to find the number of tires t she purchased. **4 tires**
6. AREA If the area of a rectangle is 30 square centimeters and the length is 6 centimeters, use the equation $30 = 6w$ to find the width w of the rectangle. **5 cm**
7. SUPPLIES The Jones Middle School had $4,000 to spend on office supplies. They had already spent $1,250. Use the equation $1,250 + d = 4,000$ to find how much money d the school had left for other supplies. **$2,750**
8. PENCILS Mi-Leng spent 90 cents on 6 pencils. Use the equation $90 = 6c$ to find the cost c of each pencil. **15 cents or $0.15**

Lesson 1-7

Chapter 1 51 Course 2

Enrichment
p. 52 OL AL

NAME ______________ DATE ________ PERIOD ____

1-7 Enrichment
Equations as Models

Equations as Models

When you write an equation that represents the information in a problem, the equation serves as a model for the problem. One equation can be a model for several different problems.

Each of Exercises 1–8 can be modeled by one of these equations.

$n + 2 = 10$ $n - 2 = 10$ $2n = 10$ $\frac{n}{2} = 10$

Choose the correct equation. Then solve the problem.

1. Chum earned $10 for working two hours. How much did he earn per hour? **$2n = 10$; $5**
2. Ana needs $2 more to buy a $10 scarf. How much money does she already have? **$n + 2 = 10$; $8**
3. Kathy and her brother won a contest and shared the prize equally. Each received $10. What was the amount of the prize? **$\frac{n}{2} = 10$; $20**
4. Jameel loaned two tapes to a friend. He has ten tapes left. How many tapes did Jameel originally have? **$n - 2 = 10$; 12 tapes**
5. In the figure below, the length of $\overline{AC}$ is 10 cm. The length of $\overline{BC}$ is 2 cm. What is the length of $\overline{AB}$?

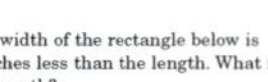

$n + 2 = 10$; 8 cm

6. Ray $\overrightarrow{AC}$ bisects $\angle BAD$. The measure of $\angle BAC$ is 10°. What is the measure of $\angle BAD$?

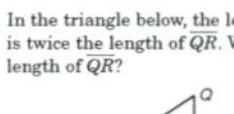

$\frac{n}{2} = 10$; 20°

7. The width of the rectangle below is 2 inches less than the length. What is the length?

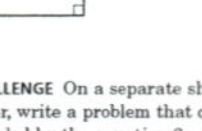

$n - 2 = 10$; 12 in.

8. In the triangle below, the length of $\overline{PQ}$ is twice the length of $\overline{QR}$. What is the length of $\overline{QR}$?

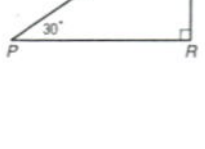

$2n = 10$; 5 cm

9. CHALLENGE On a separate sheet of paper, write a problem that can be modeled by the equation $3a + 5 = 29$. **Answers will vary.**

Chapter 1 52 Course 2

* Also available in Spanish ELL

Additional Lesson Resources

Transparencies

- *5-Minute Check Transparency*, Lesson 1-7

Other Print Products

- *Noteables™ Interactive Study Notebook with Foldables™*

Teacher Tech Tools

- *Interactive Classroom CD-ROM*, Lesson 1-7
- *AssignmentWorks*, Lesson 1-7

Student Tech Tools

glencoe.com

- Extra Examples, Chapter 1, Lesson 7
- Self-Check Quiz, Chapter 1, Lesson 7

1-7 Algebra: Equations

MAIN IDEA

Write and solve equations using mental math.

IN Academic Standards

Preparation for 7.2.2 Write and solve two-step linear equations and inequalities in one variable.
P.6.6 Recognize when the numbers involved in a computation allow for a mental computation strategy. *Also addresses P.6.5.*

New Vocabulary

- **equation**
- **solution**
- **solving an equation**
- **defining the variable**

IN Math Online

glencoe.com

- Extra Examples
- Personal Tutor
- Self-Check Quiz

GET READY for the Lesson

VOLLEYBALL The table shows the number of wins for six women's college volleyball teams.

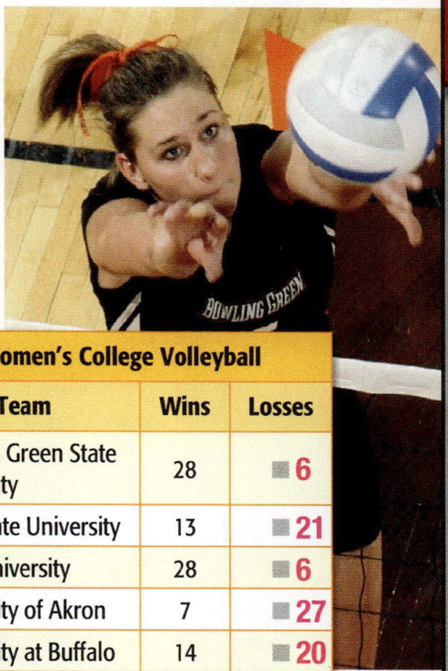

1. Suppose each team played 34 games. How many losses did each team have? **See table.**
2. Write a rule to describe how you found the number of losses. **34 = wins + losses**
3. Let w represent the number of wins and ℓ represent the number of losses. Rewrite your rule using numbers, variables, and an equals sign.

Women's College Volleyball

Team	Wins	Losses
Bowling Green State University	28	6
Kent State University	13	21
Ohio University	28	6
University of Akron	7	27
University at Buffalo	14	20
Miami University	13	21

Source: Mid-American Conference

3. $34 = w + \ell$

An **equation** is a sentence that contains two expressions separated by an equals sign, =. The equals sign tells you that the expression on the left is equivalent to the expression on the right.

$$7 = 8 - 1 \qquad 3(4) = 12 \qquad 17 = 13 + 2 + 2$$

An equation that contains a variable is neither true nor false until the variable is replaced with a number. A **solution** of an equation is a numerical value for the variable that makes the sentence true.

The process of finding a solution is called **solving an equation**. Some equations can be solved using mental math.

EXAMPLE Solve an Equation Mentally

1 **Solve $18 = 14 + t$ mentally.**

$18 = 14 + t$	Write the equation.
$18 = 14 + 4$	You know that 14 + 4 is 18.
$18 = 18$	Simplify.

So, $t = 4$. The solution is 4.

CHECK Your Progress

Solve each equation mentally.

a. $p - 5 = 20$ **25**   b. $8 = y \div 3$ **24**   c. $7h = 56$ **8**

Examples illustrate all of the lesson concepts taught in the lesson and closely mirror the exercises in the exercise sets. Check Your Progress exercises give students an opportunity to try a similar problem on their own.

1-7 Lesson Notes

1 Focus

Vertical Alignment

Before Lesson 1-7
Solve problems involving linear functions with integer values; write the equation; and graph the resulting ordered pairs of integers on a grid

Lesson 1-7
Write and solve one-step linear equations in one variable

After Lesson 1-7
Solve two-step linear equations and inequalities in one variable over the rational numbers and verify the reasonableness of the results

2 Teach

Scaffolding Questions

Tell the class that Emily received her $4 allowance and went to the ice cream store to buy a treat.

Ask:

- How much money would Emily have left if she bought a banana split for $3.25? $0.75
- How much money would she have left if she bought an ice cream cone for $1.50? $2.50
- What is the rule for finding how much money Emily will have left? allowance − cost of treat = amount left

ADDITIONAL EXAMPLE

1 Solve $p - 14 = 5$ mentally. 19

Focus on Mathematical Content

An algebraic **equation** includes an equals sign, while an algebraic **expression** does not.

Students should use **mental math** to solve the problems in this lesson.

Formative Assessment

Use the Check Your Progress exercises after each Example to determine students' understanding of concepts.

ADDITIONAL EXAMPLES

2 TEST EXAMPLE A store sells pumpkins for $2 per pound. Paul has $18. Use the equation $2x = 18$ to find how large a pumpkin Paul can buy with $18. D

A 6 lb
B 7 lb
C 8 lb
D 9 lb

3 ENTERTAINMENT An adult paid $18.50 for herself and two students to see a movie. If the student tickets cost $11 altogether, what is the cost of an adult ticket? $7.50

Additional Examples are also in:

- Noteables™ Interactive Study Notebook with Foldables™
- Interactive Classroom PowerPoint® Presentations

Test-Taking Tip

Backsolving To find which answer choice is the solution, you can also substitute each value for *x* to see which answer choice makes the left side of the equation equal to the right side.

ISTEP+ EXAMPLE

Preparation for 7.2.2, P.6.6

2 **Each day, Sierra cycles 3 miles on a bicycle trail. The equation $3d = 36$ represents how many days it will take her to cycle 36 miles. How many days d will it take her to cycle 36 miles?**

A 10 **B** 12 **C** 15 **D** 20

Read the Item

Solve $3d = 36$ to find how many days it will take to cycle 36 miles.

Solve the Item

$3d = 36$ Write the equation.

$3 \cdot 12 = 36$ You know that $3 \cdot 12$ is 36.

Therefore, $d = 12$. The answer is B.

CHECK Your Progress

d. Jordan has 16 video games. This is 3 less than the number Casey has. To find how many video games Casey has, the equation $v - 3 = 16$ can be used. How many video games v does Casey hav

F 13 **G** 15 **H** 18 **J** 19

Choosing a variable to represent an unknown quantity is called **defining the variable**.

Study Tip

Defining the Variable Although any symbol can be used, it is a good idea to use the first letter of the word you are defining as a variable. For example, *m* stands for the number of miles.

Real-World EXAMPLE

3 WHALES **Each winter, Humpback whales migrate 1,500 miles to th Indian Ocean. However, one whale migrated 5,000 miles in one season. How many miles farther than normal did this whale travel?**

Words	normal migration	+	miles farther	=	farthest migration
Variable	Let m represent the number of miles farther.				
Equation			$1{,}500 + m = 5{,}000$		

$1{,}500 + m = 5{,}000$ Write the equation.

$1{,}500 + 3{,}500 = 5{,}000$ Replace m with 3,500 to make the equation tru

So, $m = 3{,}500$. The whale went 3,500 miles farther than normal.

CHECK Your Progress

e. Aaron buys a movie rental, popcorn, and a soft drink for a total cost of $6.25. What is the cost of the popcorn if the movie rental and soft drink cost $4.70 together? **$1.55**

Differentiated Instruction

Kinesthetic Learners Separate students into groups of three. Have the students in each group take turns writing simple money equations such as $n + \$0.10 = \$0.25$, modeling the equation with coins, and then solving the equation. Encourage students to challenge each other with increasingly difficult equations.

Every chapter includes a worked-out **Test Example** that is similar to problems found on state assessments.

★ indicates multi-step problem

CHECK Your Understanding

Example 1 (p. 49)

Solve each equation mentally.

1. $75 = w + 72$ **3**
2. $y - 18 = 20$ **38**
3. $\frac{r}{9} = 6$ **54**

Example 2 (p. 50)

4. **MULTIPLE CHOICE** Daniel scored 7 points in a football game. Together, he and Judah scored 28 points. Solve the equation $7 + p = 28$ to find how many points p Judah scored. **B**

   A 14 B 21 C 23 D 35

Example 3 (p. 50)

5. **MONEY** Jessica buys a notebook and a pack of pencils for a total of \$3.50. What is the cost of the notebook if the pack of pencils costs \$1.25? **\$2.25**

Practice and Problem Solving

OMEWORK HELP

For xercises	See Examples
6–17	1
18–19, 33–34	2
20–21	3

xercise Levels
: 6–21
: 22–29
: 30–32

Solve each equation mentally.

6. $b + 7 = 13$ **6**
7. $8 + x = 15$ **7**
8. $y - 14 = 20$ **34**
9. $a - 18 = 10$ **28**
10. $25 - n = 19$ **6**
11. $x + 17 = 63$ **46**
12. $77 = 7t$ **11**
13. $3d = 99$ **33**
14. $n = \frac{30}{6}$ **5**
15. $16 = \frac{u}{4}$ **64**
16. $20 = y \div 5$ **100**
17. $84 \div z = 12$ **7**
18. **MONEY** Rosa charges \$9 per hour of babysitting. Solve the equation $9h = 63$ to find how many hours h Rosa needs to babysit to earn \$63. **7 hours**
19. **SNACKS** A box initially contained 25 snack bars. There are 14 snack bars remaining. Solve the equation $25 - x = 14$ to find how many snack bars x were eaten. **11**

For Exercises 20 and 21, define a variable. Then write and solve an equation.

★ 20. **BASKETBALL** During one game of his rookie year, LeBron James scored 41 of the Cleveland Cavaliers' 107 points. How many points did the rest of the team score? **Let p = the rest of the team's points; $41 + p = 107$; 66 points**

★ 21. **EXERCISE** On Monday and Tuesday, Derrick walked a total of 6.3 miles. If he walked 2.5 miles on Tuesday, how many miles did he walk on Monday? **Let m = the number of miles Derrick walked on Monday; $m + 2.5 = 6.3$; 3.8 miles**

Solve each equation mentally.

22. $1.5 + j = 10.0$ **8.5**
23. $1.2 = m - 4.2$ **5.4**
24. $n - 1.4 = 3.5$ **4.9**
25. $13.4 - h = 9.0$ **4.4**
26. $9.9 + r = 24.2$ **14.3**
27. $w + 15.8 = 17.0$ **1.2**

3. $275 + l = 372$; $= 97$

28. **CATS** The table shows the average weight of lions. Write and solve an addition equation to find how much more male lions weigh than female lions.

Lions	Weight (lb)
Female	275
Male	372

Academic Standards • ISTEP+

xtra Practice, pp. 670, 704

3 Practice

Formative Assessment

Use Exercises 1–5 to check for understanding.

Then use the chart at the bottom of this page to customize your assignments for students.

Intervention You may wish to use the Study Guide and Intervention Master on page 48 of the *Chapter 1 Resource Masters* for additional reinforcement.

Odd/Even Assignments

Exercises 6–21 are structured so that students practice the same concepts whether they are assigned odd or even problems.

DIFFERENTIATED HOMEWORK OPTIONS

Level	Assignment	Two-Day Option	
BL Basic	6–21, 31–44	7–21 odd, 33, 34	6–20 even, 31, 32, 36–44
OL Core	7–17 odd, 18–21, 23–27 odd, 28, 29, 31–44	6–21, 33, 34	22–29, 31, 32, 36–44
AL Advanced/Pre-AP	22–39 (optional: 41–44)		

Exercise Alert!

Find the Error In Exercise 31, Justin made an error by using the wrong operation (addition). Remind students to ask themselves which operation they need to perform to solve the equation.

4 Assess

Ticket Out the Door Write a simple algebraic equation (such as $35 = 2 + x$) on the board. Have each student write the solution to the equation on a small piece of paper.

29. **FOOD** The total cost of a chicken sandwich and a drink is \$6.25. The drink costs \$1.75. Write and solve an equation that can be used to find how muc the chicken sandwich is alone. **$1.75 + c = \$6.25; c = \$4.50$**

H.O.T. Problems

30. **CHALLENGE** Find the values of a and b if $0 \cdot a = b$. Explain your reasoning. **Sample answer: $b = 0$; a is any number.**

31. **FIND THE ERROR** Justin and Antonio each solved $w - 35 = 70$. Whose solution is correct? Explain your reasoning.

31. Antonio; $105 - 35 = 70$ is a true statement. $35 - 35 \neq 70$

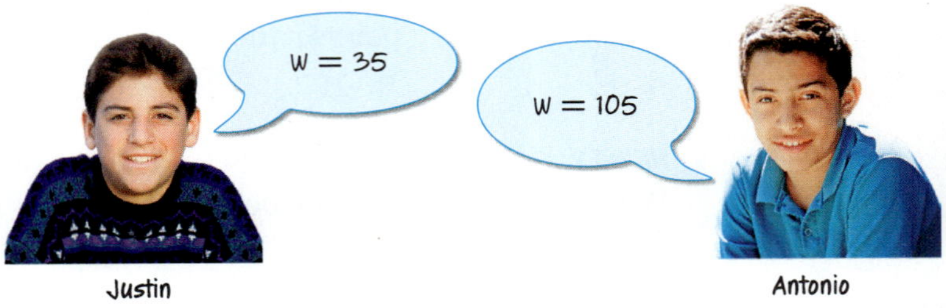

32. **WRITING IN MATH** Explain what it means to solve an equation. **Sample answer: Find the value of the variable that makes the equation true.**

ISTEP+ PRACTICE Preparation for 7.2.2, P.6.6

33. The diagram shows the distance from Madison to Hudson and from Lawrence to Hudson. Which equation can be used to find how many more miles x Lawrence is from Madison? **A**

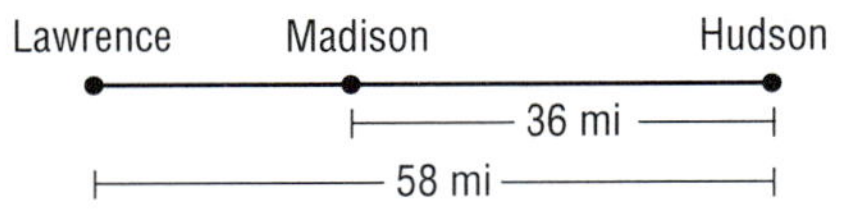

A $58 = x + 36$ **C** $36 \cdot 58 = x$

B $58 = \frac{x}{36}$ **D** $x - 36 = 58$

34. **SHORT RESPONSE** What value of h makes the following equation true? **12**

$$h \div 4 = 32$$

35. Solve $u + 8 = 15$. **J**

F 23 **H** 8

G 22 **J** 7

Spiral Review

36. **ALGEBRA** Evaluate $3a + b^2$ if $a = 2$ and $b = 3$. (Lesson 1-6) **15**

Evaluate each expression. (Lesson 1-4)

37. $11 \cdot 6 \div 3 + 9$ **31**
38. $5 \cdot 13 - 6^2$ **29**
39. $1 + 2(8 - 5)^2$ **19**

40. **FARMING** A farmer planted 389 acres of land with 78,967 corn plants. How many plants were planted per acre? (Lesson 1-1) **203 plants**

GET READY for the Next Lesson

PREREQUISITE SKILL **Multiply.** (Lesson 1-4)

41. $2 \cdot (4 + 10)$ **28**
42. $(9 \cdot 1) \cdot 8$ **72**
43. $(5 \cdot 3)(5 \cdot 2)$ **150**
44. $(6 + 8) \cdot 12$ **168**

52 **Chapter 1** Introduction to Algebra and Functions

1-8 Algebra: Properties

PACING: **Regular:** 1 period, **Block:** 0.5 period

IN Academic Standards **7.1.7 Solve problems that involve multiplication and division with integers,** fractions, decimals **and combinations of the four operations. 7.2.3 Evaluate numerical expressions and simplify algebraic expressions involving rational** and irrational **numbers.** *Also addresses P.3.4.*

Options for Differentiated Instruction

ELL = English Language Learner   AL = Above or Beyond Grade Level   SS = Struggling Students   SN = Special Needs

Conceptual Understanding SS SN

Use with Example 1.

Remind students of the relationship between multiplication and addition.

Multiplication	Meaning in Words	Addition
4×3	4 groups of 3	$3 + 3 + 3 + 3$
$5(3 + 2)$	5 groups of $(3 + 2)$	$(3 + 2) + (3 + 2) + (3 + 2) + (3 + 2) + (3 + 2)$

The second addition expression above shows 5 groups of 3 and 5 groups of 2, so it can be written as $5(3) + 5(2)$. Explain that in the same way, $3(x + 2)$ can be written as $(x + 2) + (x + 2) + (x + 2)$, which is $3x + 3(2)$, or $3x + 6$.

Study Helps ELL SS

Use after presenting the lesson.

Have students use an index card to explain each of the properties presented in Lesson 1-8.

- Distributive
- Commutative
- Associative
- Identity

Each card should include a definition, examples, and an indication of which of the four operations that it applies.

Commutative Property

The order in which numbers are added or multiplied does not matter.

Examples	
Addition	**Multiplication**
$2 + 3 = 3 + 2$	$2 \cdot 3 = 3 \cdot 2$

- The Commutative Property does not hold true for subtraction or division.

Peer Teaching ELL AL SS SN

Use after presenting the lesson.

Students who lack confidence tend to not participate in whole-class discussions. Working in small groups reduces the isolation of these students and allows them to share their ideas and knowledge in a more relaxed environment.

- Organize students into groups of four, grouping them heterogeneously according to ability, skills, background, and so on.
- Assign each student one of the properties in the lesson. Have them meet with the other students assigned the same property to coach/tutor each other on that property.

Have the students rejoin their original groups and teach the other students about the property they studied.

Leveled Lesson Resources

Also on TeacherWorks™ Lesson 1-8

Chapter 1 Resource Masters

BL = Below or Approaching Grade Level OL = On Grade Level AL = Above or Beyond Grade Level ELL = English Language Learner

Lesson Reading Guide*
p. 53 BL OL ELL

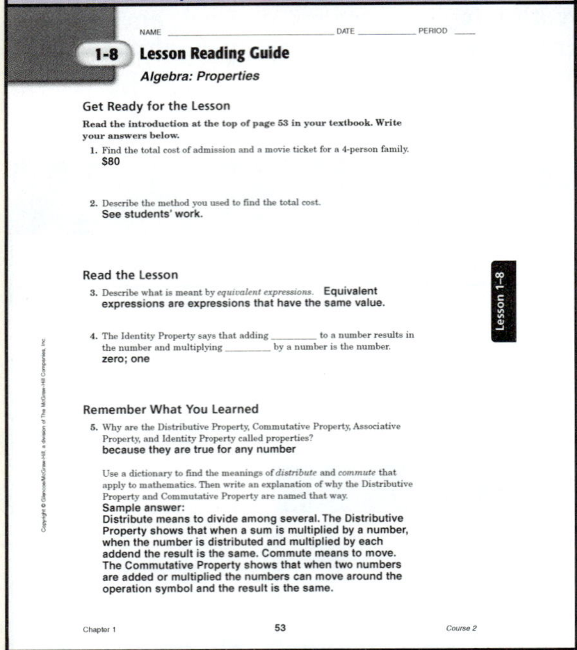

NAME ____ DATE ____ PERIOD ____

1-8 Lesson Reading Guide
Algebra: Properties

Get Ready for the Lesson

Read the introduction at the top of page 53 in your textbook. Write your answers below.

1. Find the total cost of admission and a movie ticket for a 4-person family. $80
2. Describe the method you used to find the total cost. See students' work.

Read the Lesson

3. Describe what is meant by *equivalent expressions*. Equivalent expressions are expressions that have the same value.
4. The Identity Property says that adding ____ to a number results in the number and multiplying ____ by a number is the number. zero; one

Remember What You Learned

5. Why are the Distributive Property, Commutative Property, Associative Property, and Identity Property called properties? because they are true for any number

Use a dictionary to find the meanings of *distribute* and *commute* that apply to mathematics. Then write an explanation of why the Distributive Property and Commutative Property are named that way. Sample answer: Distribute means to divide among several. The Distributive Property shows that when a sum is multiplied by a number, when the number is distributed and multiplied by each addend the result is the same. Commute means to move. The Commutative Property shows that when two numbers are added or multiplied the numbers can move around the operation symbol and the result is the same.

Chapter 1 53 Course 2

Study Guide and Intervention*
p. 54 BL OL ELL

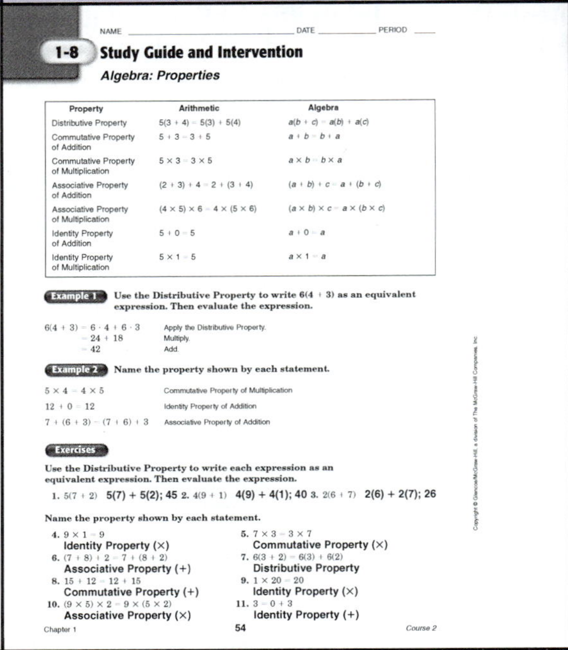

1-8 Study Guide and Intervention
Algebra: Properties

Property	Arithmetic	Algebra
Distributive Property	5(3 + 4) = 5(3) + 5(4)	a(b + c) = a(b) + a(c)
Commutative Property of Addition	5 + 3 = 3 + 5	a + b = b + a
Commutative Property of Multiplication	5 × 3 = 3 × 5	a × b = b × a
Associative Property of Addition	(2 + 3) + 4 = 2 + (3 + 4)	(a + b) + c = a + (b + c)
Associative Property of Multiplication	(4 × 5) × 6 = 4 × (5 × 6)	(a × b) × c = a × (b × c)
Identity Property of Addition	5 + 0 = 5	a + 0 = a
Identity Property of Multiplication	5 × 1 = 5	a × 1 = a

Example 1 Use the Distributive Property to write 6(4 + 3) as an equivalent expression. Then evaluate the expression.

6(4 + 3) = 6 · 4 + 6 · 3 Apply the Distributive Property.
= 24 + 18 Multiply.
= 42 Add.

Example 2 Name the property shown by each statement.

5 × 4 = 4 × 5 Commutative Property of Multiplication
12 + 0 = 12 Identity Property of Addition
7 + (6 + 3) = (7 + 6) + 3 Associative Property of Addition

Exercises

Use the Distributive Property to write each expression as an equivalent expression. Then evaluate the expression.

1. 5(7 + 2) 5(7) + 5(2); 45 2. 4(9 + 1) 4(9) + 4(1); 40 3. 2(6 + 7) 2(6) + 2(7); 26

Name the property shown by each statement.

4. 9 × 1 = 9 Identity Property (×)
5. 7 × 3 = 3 × 7 Commutative Property (×)
6. (7 + 8) + 2 = 7 + (8 + 2) Associative Property (+)
7. 6(3 + 2) = 6(3) + 6(2) Distributive Property
8. 15 + 12 = 12 + 15 Commutative Property (+)
9. 1 × 20 = 20 Identity Property (×)
10. (9 × 5) × 2 = 9 × (5 × 2) Associative Property (×)
11. 3 + 0 = 3 Identity Property (+)

Chapter 1 54 Course 2

Skills Practice*
p. 55 BL OL

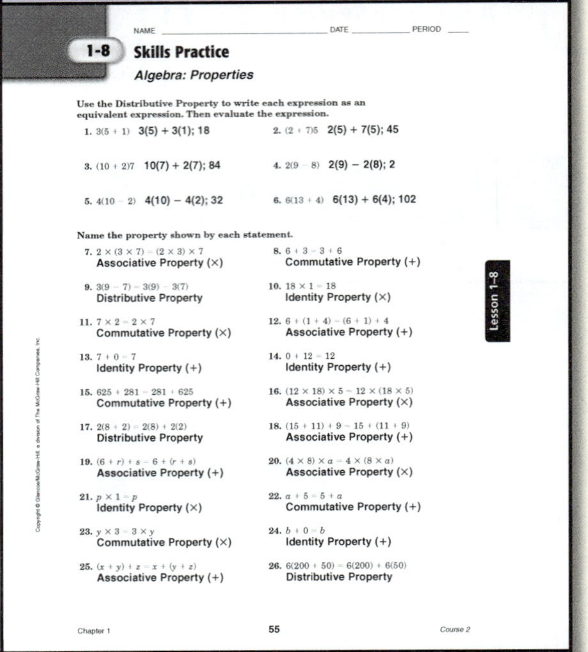

1-8 Skills Practice
Algebra: Properties

Use the Distributive Property to write each expression as an equivalent expression. Then evaluate the expression.

1. 3(5 + 1) 3(5) + 3(1); 18
2. (2 + 7)5 2(5) + 7(5); 45
3. (10 + 2)7 10(7) + 2(7); 84
4. 2(9 − 8) 2(9) − 2(8); 2
5. 4(10 − 2) 4(10) − 4(2); 32
6. 6(13 + 4) 6(13) + 6(4); 102

Name the property shown by each statement.

7. 2 × (3 × 7) = (2 × 3) × 7 Associative Property (×)
8. 6 + 3 = 3 + 6 Commutative Property (+)
9. 3(9 − 7) = 3(9) − 3(7) Distributive Property
10. 18 × 1 = 18 Identity Property (×)
11. 7 × 2 = 2 × 7 Commutative Property (×)
12. 6 + (1 + 4) = (6 + 1) + 4 Associative Property (+)
13. 7 + 0 = 7 Identity Property (+)
14. 0 + 12 = 12 Identity Property (+)
15. 625 + 281 = 281 + 625 Commutative Property (+)
16. (12 × 18) × 5 = 12 × (18 × 5) Associative Property (×)
17. 2(8 + 2) = 2(8) + 2(2) Distributive Property
18. (15 + 11) + 9 = 15 + (11 + 9) Associative Property (+)
19. (6 + r) + s = 6 + (r + s) Associative Property (+)
20. (4 × 8) × a = 4 × (8 × a) Associative Property (×)
21. p × 1 = p Identity Property (×)
22. a + 5 = 5 + a Commutative Property (+)
23. y × 3 = 3 × y Commutative Property (×)
24. b + 0 = b Identity Property (+)
25. (x + y) + z = x + (y + z) Associative Property (+)
26. 6(200 + 50) = 6(200) + 6(50) Distributive Property

Chapter 1 55 Course 2

Practice*
p. 56 OL AL

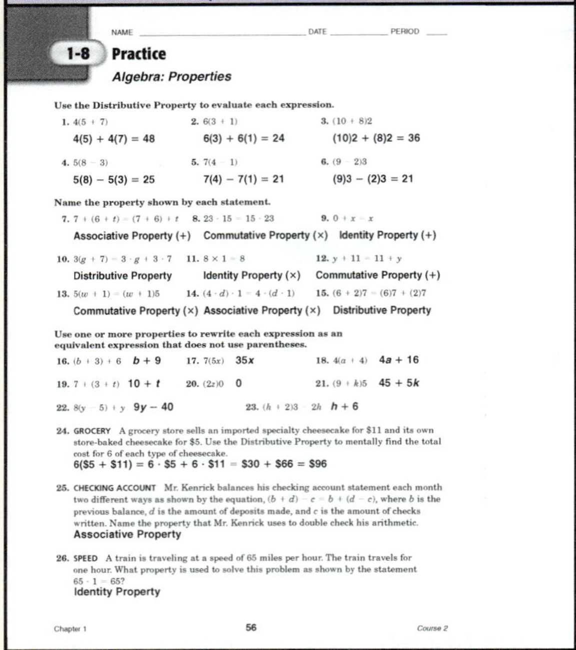

1-8 Practice
Algebra: Properties

Use the Distributive Property to evaluate each expression.

1. 4(5 + 7) 4(5) + 4(7) = 48
2. 6(3 + 1) 6(3) + 6(1) = 24
3. (10 + 8)2 (10)2 + (8)2 = 36
4. 5(8 − 3) 5(8) − 5(3) = 25
5. 7(4 − 1) 7(4) − 7(1) = 21
6. (9 − 2)3 (9)3 − (2)3 = 21

Name the property shown by each statement.

7. 7 + (6 + t) = (7 + 6) + t Associative Property (+)
8. 23 · 15 = 15 · 23 Commutative Property (×)
9. 0 + x = x Identity Property (+)
10. 3(g + 7) = 3 · g + 3 · 7 Distributive Property
11. 8 × 1 = 8 Identity Property (×)
12. y + 11 = 11 + y Commutative Property (+)
13. 5(w + 1) = (w + 1)5 Commutative Property (×)
14. (4 · d) · 1 = 4 · (d · 1) Associative Property (×)
15. (6 + 2)7 = (6)7 + (2)7 Distributive Property

Use one or more properties to rewrite each expression as an equivalent expression that does not use parentheses.

16. (b + 3) + 6 b + 9
17. 7(5x) 35x
18. 4(a + 4) 4a + 16
19. 7 + (3 + t) 10 + t
20. (2z)0 0
21. (9 + k)5 45 + 5k
22. 8(y − 5) + y 9y − 40
23. (h + 2)3 − 2h h + 6

24. GROCERY A grocery store sells an imported specialty cheesecake for $11 and its own store-baked cheesecake for $5. Use the Distributive Property to mentally find the total cost for 6 of each type of cheesecake. 6($5 + $11) = 6 · $5 + 6 · $11 = $30 + $66 = $96

25. CHECKING ACCOUNT Mr. Kenrick balances his checking account statement each month two different ways as shown by the equation, (b + d) − c = b + (d − c), where b is the previous balance, d is the amount of deposits made, and c is the amount of checks written. Name the property that Mr. Kenrick uses to double check his arithmetic. Associative Property

26. SPEED A train is traveling at a speed of 65 miles per hour. The train travels for one hour. What property is used to solve this problem as shown by the statement 65 · 1 = 65? Identity Property

Chapter 1 56 Course 2

Word Problem Practice*
p. 57 OL AL

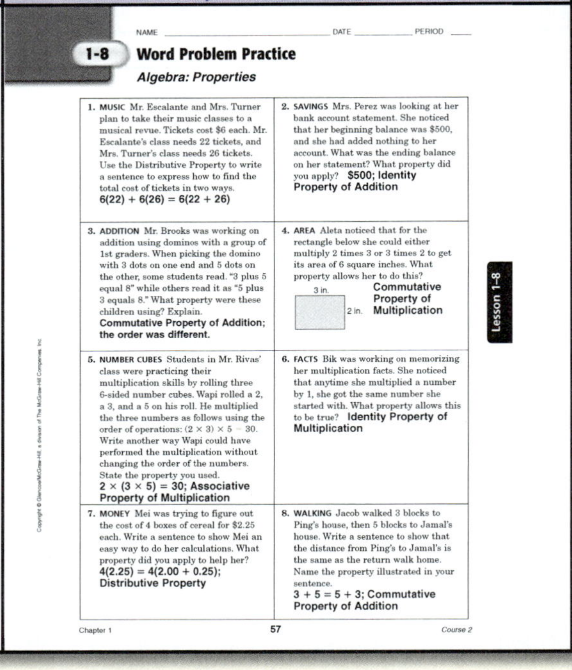

1-8 Word Problem Practice
Algebra: Properties

1. MUSIC Mr. Escalante and Mrs. Turner plan to take their music classes to a musical revue. Tickets cost $6 each. Mr. Escalante's class needs 22 tickets, and Mrs. Turner's class needs 26 tickets. Use the Distributive Property to write a sentence to express how to find the total cost of tickets in two ways. 6(22) + 6(26) = 6(22 + 26)

2. SAVINGS Mrs. Perez was looking at her bank account statement. She noticed that her beginning balance was $500, and she had added nothing to her account. What was the ending balance on her statement? What property did you apply? $500; Identity Property of Addition

3. ADDITION Mr. Brooks was working on addition using dominos with a group of 1st graders. When picking the domino with 3 dots on one end and 5 dots on the other, some students read, "3 plus 5 equal 8" while others read it as "5 plus 3 equals 8." What property were these children using? Explain. Commutative Property of Addition; the order was different.

4. AREA Aleta noticed that for the rectangle below she could either multiply 2 times 3 or 3 times 2 to get its area of 6 square inches. What property allows her to do this? Commutative Property of Multiplication

5. NUMBER CUBES Students in Mr. Rivas' class were practicing their multiplication skills by rolling three 6-sided number cubes. Wapi rolled a 2, a 3, and a 5 on his roll. He multiplied the three numbers as follows using the order of operations: (2 × 3) × 5 = 30. Write another way Wapi could have performed the multiplication without changing the order of the numbers. State the property you used. 2 × (3 × 5) = 30; Associative Property of Multiplication

6. FACTS Bik was working on memorizing her multiplication facts. She noticed that anytime she multiplied a number by 1, she got the number she started with. What property allows this to be true? Identity Property of Multiplication

7. MONEY Mei was trying to figure out the cost of 4 boxes of cereal for $2.25 each. Write a sentence to show Mei an easy way to do her calculations. What property did you apply to help her? 4(2.25) = 4(2.00 + 0.25); Distributive Property

8. WALKING Jacob walked 3 blocks to Ping's house, then 5 blocks to Jamal's house. Write a sentence to show that the distance from Ping's to Jamal's is the same as the return walk home. Name the property illustrated in your sentence. 3 + 5 = 5 + 3; Commutative Property of Addition

Chapter 1 57 Course 2

Enrichment
p. 58 OL AL

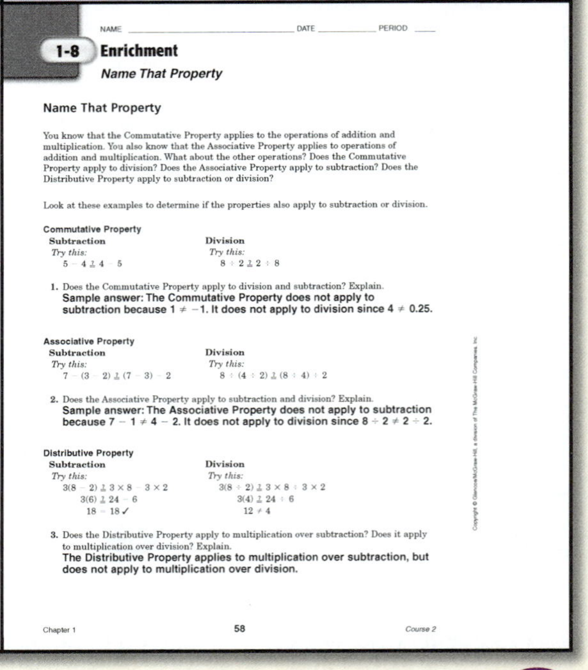

1-8 Enrichment
Name That Property

Name That Property

You know that the Commutative Property applies to the operations of addition and multiplication. You also know that the Associative Property applies to operations of addition and multiplication. What about the other operations? Does the Commutative Property apply to division? Does the Associative Property apply to subtraction? Does the Distributive Property apply to subtraction or division?

Look at these examples to determine if the properties also apply to subtraction or division.

1. Does the Commutative Property apply to division and subtraction? Explain. Sample answer: The Commutative Property does not apply to subtraction because 1 ≠ −1. It does not apply to division since 4 ≠ 0.25.

2. Does the Associative Property apply to subtraction and division? Explain. Sample answer: The Associative Property does not apply to subtraction because 7 − 1 ≠ 4 − 2. It does not apply to division since 8 ÷ 2 ≠ 2 ÷ 2.

3. Does the Distributive Property apply to multiplication over subtraction? Does it apply to multiplication over division? Explain. The Distributive Property applies to multiplication over subtraction, but does not apply to multiplication over division.

Chapter 1 58 Course 2

* Also available in Spanish ELL

Additional Lesson Resources

A Study Guide and Intervention, Skills Practice, Practice, Word Problem Practice, Lesson Reading Guide, and Enrichment Master is shown for every lesson in the Student Edition. These masters can be found in the Chapter Resource Masters.

Transparencies

- *5-Minute Check Transparency,* Lesson 1-8

Other Print Products

- *Noteables™ Interactive Study Notebook with Foldables™*

Teacher Tech Tools

- *Interactive Classroom CD-ROM,* Lesson 1-8
- *AssignmentWorks,* Lesson 1-8

Student Tech Tools

glencoe.com

- Extra Examples, Chapter 1, Lesson 8
- Self-Check Quiz, Chapter 1, Lesson 8

1-8 Algebra: Properties

MAIN IDEA

Use Commutative, Associative, Identity, and Distributive properties to solve problems.

IN Academic Standards

7.1.7 Solve problems that involve multiplication and division with integers, fractions, decimals **and combinations of the four operations.**
7.2.3 Evaluate numerical expressions and simplify algebraic expressions involving rational and irrational **numbers.** *Also addresses P.3.4.*

New Vocabulary

equivalent expressions
properties

IN Math Online

glencoe.com
- Extra Examples
- Personal Tutor
- Self-Check Quiz

GET READY for the Lesson

MUSEUMS The admission costs for the Louisville Science Center are shown.

Louisville Science Center Admission	
Admission	$12
IMAX Movie	$8

Source: Louisville Science Center

1. Find the total cost of admission and a movie ticket for a 4-person family. **$80**
2. Describe the method you used to find the total cost.

2. See students' work.

Here are two ways to find the total cost.

cost of 4 movies → 4($12) + 4($8) ← cost of 4 admissions

number of people → 4($12 + $8) ← 1 admission and 1 movie

The expressions 4($12) + 4($8) and 4($12 + $8) are **equivalent expressions** because they have the same value, $80. This shows how the **Distributive Property** combines addition and multiplication.

Distributive Property — Key Concept

Words To multiply a sum by a number, multiply each addend of the sum by the number outside the parentheses.

Examples

Numbers	Algebra
$3(4 + 6) = 3(4) + 3(6)$	$a(b + c) = a(b) + a(c)$
$5(7) + 5(3) = 5(7 + 3)$	$a(b) + a(c) = a(b + c)$

EXAMPLES Write Sentences as Equations

Use the Distributive Property to rewrite each expression. Then evaluate it.

1 5(3 + 2)

$5(3 + 2) = 5(3) + 5(2)$
$= 15 + 10$ Multiply.
$= 25$ Add.

2 3(7) + 3(4)

$3(7) + 3(4) = 3(7 + 4)$
$= 3(11)$ Add.
$= 33$ Multiply.

CHECK Your Progress

a. 6(1 + 4) **6 • 1 + 6 • 4; 30**

b. 6(9) + 6(3) **6(9 + 3); 72**

Key Concept boxes highlight definitions, formulas, and other important ideas. Multiple representations—words, symbols, examples, models—help students understand the concepts.

1-8 Lesson Notes

1 Focus

Vertical Alignment

Before Lesson 1-8
Know and use the distributive property in equations and expressions

Lesson 1-8
Apply algebraic order of operations and properties and justify each step in the process

After Lesson 1-8
Use the correct order of operations to evaluate algebraic expressions

2 Teach

Scaffolding Questions

Ask:
- What is the product of 9 × 8? 72
- What is the product of 8 × 9? 72
- Does changing the order of the factors change the product? no
- What is the sum of 3 + 2 + 5? 10
- What is the sum of 5 + 3 + 2? 10
- Does changing the order of the addends change the sum? no
- What is the product of $a \times 1$? a
- What is the sum of $b + 0$? b

ADDITIONAL EXAMPLES

Use the Distributive Property to rewrite each expression. Then evaluate it.

1 8(5 + 7) 96

2 6(9) + 6(2) 66

Tips for New Teachers: Distributive Property

You may want to show students that the Distributive Property can also be illustrated as: $(a + b)c = (a)c + (b)c$ and $(a)c + (b)c = (a + b)c$

Focus on Mathematical Content

The **Distributive Property** allows you to find the product of a sum and a number by multiplying each addend by the number and then adding the products.

The **Commutative Property** allows you to change the order in which two numbers are multiplied or added without changing the product or sum. For all numbers a and b, $a + b = b + a$ and $ab = ba$.

The **Associative Property** allows you to change the grouping of numbers being multiplied or added without changing the product or sum. For all numbers a, b, and c, $a + (b + c) = (a + b) + c$ and $a(bc) = (ab)c$.

The **Identity Property** allows you to add 0 to an addend without changing the addend and to multiply a factor by 1 without changing the factor. For all numbers a, $a + 0 = a$ and $a \cdot 1 = a$.

Formative Assessment

Use the Check Your Progress exercises after each Example to determine students' understanding of concepts.

ADDITIONAL EXAMPLES

3 **VACATIONS** Mr. Harmon has budgeted $150 per day for his hotel and meals during his vacation. If he plans to spend six days on vacation, how much money will he spend? $900

4 Find 5 • 13 • 20 mentally. Justify each step. 5 • 13 • 20 = 5 • 20 • 13 Comm. Prop. (×) = (5 • 20) • 13 Assoc. Prop. (×) = 100 • 13 or 1,300 Multiply 100 and 13 mentally.

Real-World Link American Lance Armstrong won the Tour de France seven times in a row from 1999 through 2005.

Source: Capital Sports Entertainment

Real-World EXAMPLE

3 **TOUR DE FRANCE** **The Tour de France is a cycling race through France that lasts 22 days. If a cyclist averages 90 miles per day, about how far does he travel?**

Use the Distributive Property to multiply 90 × 22 mentally.

$90(22) = 90(20 + 2)$	Rewrite 22 as 20 + 2.
$= 90(20) + 90(2)$	Distributive Property
$= 1{,}800 + 180$	Multiply.
$= 1{,}980$	Add.

The cyclist travels about 1,980 miles.

CHECK Your Progress

c. Jennifer saved $120 each month for five months. How much did she save in all? Explain your reasoning.

c. 5($100 + $20) = $600; The expression $100 + $20 represents the amount of money Jennifer saved each month. The expression 5($100 + $20) represents the amount of money she saved for five months. Since 5 × $100 = $500 and 5 × $20 = $100, find $500 + $100, or $600, to find the amount of money Jennifer saved for five months.

Properties are statements that are true for all numbers.

Real Number Properties — Concept Summary

Commutative Properties	The order in which two numbers are added or multiplied does not change their sum or product. $a + b = b + a$ $\quad a \cdot b = b \cdot a$
Associative Properties	The way in which three numbers are grouped when they are added or multiplied does not change their sum or product. $a + (b + c) = (a + b) + c$ $\quad a \cdot (b \cdot c) = (a \cdot b) \cdot c$
Identity Properties	The sum of an addend and 0 is the addend. The product of a factor and 1 is the factor. $a + 0 = a$ $\quad a \cdot 1 = a$

EXAMPLE Use Properties to Evaluate Expressions

4 **Find 4 • 12 • 25 mentally. Justify each step.**

$4 \cdot 12 \cdot 25 = 4 \cdot 25 \cdot 12$	Commutative Property of Multiplication
$= (4 \cdot 25) \cdot 12$	Associative Property of Multiplication
$= 100 \cdot 12$ or $1{,}200$	Multiply 100 and 12 mentally.

Study Tip

Mental Math Look for sums or products that end in zero. They are easy to compute mentally.

CHECK Your Progress d–e. See Ch. 1 Answer Appendix for justification.

Find each of the following. Justify each step.

d. $40 \cdot (7 \cdot 5)$ **1,400**

e. $(89 + 15) + 1$ **105**

Pre-AP Activity — Use after Example 4

Ask students whether there are Commutative and Associative Properties of Subtraction. Have them explain their reasoning and give examples. Repeat the question for division, again having students explain their reasoning and give examples.

★ indicates multi-step problem

CHECK Your Understanding

Examples 1, 2 (p. 53)

Use the Distributive Property to rewrite each expression. Then evaluate it.

1. 7(4 + 3) **7(4) + 7(3); 49**	2. 5(6 + 2) **5(6) + 5(2); 40**	3. 3(9) + 3(6) **3(9 + 6); 45**	4. 6(17) + 6(3) **6(17 + 3); 120**

Example 3 (p. 54)

★ 5. **MENTAL MATH** Admission to a baseball game is \$12, and a hot dog costs \$5. Use the Distributive Property to mentally find the total cost for 4 tickets and 4 hot dogs. Explain your reasoning. **4(12 + 5); \$68**

★ 6. **MENTAL MATH** A cheetah can run 65 miles per hour at maximum speed. At this rate, how far could a cheetah run in 2 hours? Use the Distributive Property to multiply mentally. Explain your reasoning. **2(60 + 5); 130 mph**

5–6. See Ch. 1 Answer Appendix for explanation.

Example 4 (p. 54)

Find each expression mentally. Justify each step.

7. 44 + (23 + 16) **83**

8. 50 • (33 • 2) **3,300**

7–8. See margin for justification.

Practice and Problem Solving

HOMEWORK HELP	
For Exercises	See Examples
9–12	1, 2
13–22	4
23, 24	3

xercise Levels
: 9–24
: 25–38
: 39–42

Use the Distributive Property to rewrite each expression. Then evaluate it.

9. 2(6 + 7) **2(6) + 2(7); 26**	10. 5(8 + 9) **5(8) + 5(9); 85**	11. 4(3) + 4(8) **4(3 + 8); 44**	12. 7(3) + 7(6) **7(3 + 6); 63**

Find each expression mentally. Justify each step.

13. (8 + 27) + 52 **87**

14. (13 + 31) + 17 **61**

15. 91 + (15 + 9) **115**

16. 85 + (46 + 15) **146**

17. (4 • 18) • 25 **1,800**

18. (5 • 3) • 8 **120**

19. 15 • (8 • 2) **240**

20. 2 • (16 • 50) **1,600**

21. 5 • (30 • 12) **1,800**

22. 20 • (48 • 5) **4,800**

13–22. See Ch. 1 Answer Appendix for justification.

MENTAL MATH For Exercises 23 and 24, use the Distributive Property to multiply mentally. Explain your reasoning.

3–24. See Ch. 1 nswer Appendix r explanation.

★ 23. **TRAVEL** Each year about 27 million people visit Paris, France. About how many people will visit Paris over a five-year period? **5(20 + 7); 135 million**

★ 24. **ROLLER COASTERS** One ride on a roller coaster lasts 108 seconds. How long will it take to ride this coaster three times? **3(100 + 8); 324 s**

The Distributive Property also can be applied to subtraction. Use the Distributive Property to rewrite each expression. Then evaluate it.

25. 7(9) − 7(3) **7(9 − 3); 42**	26. 12(8) − 12(6) **12(8 − 6); 24**	27. 9(7) − 9(3) **9(7 − 3); 36**	28. 6(12) − 6(5) **6(12 − 5); 42**

ALGEBRA Use one or more properties to rewrite each expression as an equivalent expression that does not use parentheses.

9. $y + 5$
0. $x + 6$
6. $5f + 12$

29. $(y + 1) + 4$ 30. $2 + (x + 4)$ 31. $4(8b)$ **$32b$** 32. $(3a)2$ **$6a$**

33. $2(x + 3)$ **$2x + 6$** 34. $4(2 + b)$ **$8 + 4b$** 35. $6(c + 1)$ **$6c + 6$** 36. $3(f + 4) + 2f$

3 Practice

Formative Assessment

Use Exercises 1–8 to check for understanding.

Then use the chart at the bottom of this page to customize your assignments for students.

Intervention You may wish to use the Study Guide and Intervention Master on page 54 of the *Chapter 1 Resource Masters* for additional reinforcement.

Odd/Even Assignments

Exercises 9–24 are structured so that students practice the same concepts whether they are assigned odd or even problems.

Additional Answers

7. Sample answer: Rewrite 44 + (23 + 16) as 44 + (16 + 23) using the Commutative Property of Addition. Rewrite 44 + (16 + 23) as (44 + 16) + 23 using the Associative Property of Addition. Find 44 + 16, or 60, mentally. Then find 60 + 23, or 83, mentally.

8. Sample answer: Rewrite 50 • (33 • 2) as 50 • (2 • 33) using the Commutative Property of Multiplication. Rewrite 50 • (2 • 33) as (50 • 2) • 33 using the Associative Property of Multiplication. Find 50 • 2, or 100 • 33, or 3,300, mentally.

DIFFERENTIATED HOMEWORK OPTIONS

Level	Assignment	Two-Day Option	
BL Basic	9–24, 39–40, 42–51	9–23 odd, 43, 44	10–24 even, 39, 40, 42, 45–51
OL Core	9–23 odd, 24, 25–35 odd, 37–40, 42–51	9–24, 43, 44	25–40, 42, 45–51
AL Advanced/Pre-AP	25–48 (optional: 49–51)		

Every effort is made to show answers on the reduced Student Edition page, or in the margin of the Teacher Edition. However, **answers** that do not fit in either of these places can be found in **Answer Appendix** pages at the end of each chapter.

4 Assess

Name the Math Have students name and describe one of the properties studied in this lesson.

Formative Assessment

Check for student understanding of concepts in Lessons 1-6 through 1-8.

CRM Quiz 3, p. 78

FOLDABLES Study Organizer Foldables™ Follow-Up

Remind students to record the properties they studied in this lesson in their Foldables. Encourage them to write the key idea of each property and also to give an example.

Additional Answers

40. false; $(11 + 18) \times 5 = 145$; $11 + 18 \times 5 = 101$

41. Sample answer: Since $24 \div (12 \div 2) = 4$ and $(24 \div 12) \div 2 = 1$, $24 \div (12 \div 2) \neq (24 \div 12) \div 2$.

MILEAGE **For Exercises 37 and 38, use the table that shows the driving distance between certain cities in Pennsylvania.**

From	To	Driving Distance (mi)
Pittsburgh	Johnstown	55
Johnstown	Allentown	184

37. ★ Write a sentence that compares the mileage from Pittsburgh to Johnstown to Allentown, and the mileage from Allentown to Johnstown to Pittsburgh. $55 + 184 = 184 + 55$

38. Name the property that is illustrated by this sentence. **Commutative Property of Addition**

Academic Standards • ISTEP+
Extra Practice, pp. 670, 704

H.O.T. Problems

39. **OPEN ENDED** Write an equation that illustrates the Associative Property of Addition. **Sample answer: $(5 + z) + 9 = 5 + (z + 9)$**

40. **NUMBER SENSE** Analyze the statement $(18 + 35) \times 4 = 18 + 35 \times 4$. Then tell whether the statement is *true* or *false*. Explain your reasoning. **See margin.**

41. **CHALLENGE** A *counterexample* is an example showing that a statement is n true. Provide a counterexample to the following statement. **See margin.**

Division of whole numbers is associative.

42. **WRITING IN MATH** Write about a real-world situation that can be solve using the Distributive Property. Then use it to solve the problem. **Answers will vary.**

ISTEP+ PRACTICE 7.1.7, 7.2.3

43. Which expression can be written as $6(9 + 8)$? **B**
   - A $8 \cdot 6 + 8 \cdot 9$
   - B $6 \cdot 9 + 6 \cdot 8$
   - C $6 \cdot 9 \cdot 6 \cdot 8$
   - D $6 + 9 \cdot 6 + 8$

44. Jared deposited \$5 into his savings account. Six months later, his accoun balance had doubled. If his old balar was b dollars, which of the following would be equivalent to his new balance of $2(b + 5)$ dollars? **J**
   - F $2b + 5$
   - G $2b + 7$
   - H $b + 10$
   - J $2b + 10$

Spiral Review

Name the number that is the solution of the given equation. (Lesson 1-7)

45. $7.3 = t - 4$; 10.3, 11.3, 12.3 **11.3**

46. $35.5 = 5n$; 5.1, 7.1, 9.1 **7.1**

47. **CATS** It is believed that a cat ages 5 human years for every calendar year. This situation can be represented by the expression $5y$ where y is the age of the cat in calendar years. Find the human age of a cat that has lived for 15 calendar years. (Lesson 1-6) **75 yr**

48. Evaluate $(14 - 9)^4$. (Lesson 1-4) **625**

GET READY for the Next Lesson

PREREQUISITE SKILL **Find the next number in each pattern.**

49. 2, 4, 6, 8, ■ **10**

50. 10, 21, 32, 43, ■ **54**

51. 1.4, 2.2, 3.0, 3.8, ■ **4.6**

1-9 Algebra: Arithmetic Sequences

PACING: **Regular:** 1.5 periods, **Block:** 0.5 period

IN Academic Standards **7.2.1 Use variables and appropriate operations to write an expression,** equation or inequality **that represents a verbal description. 7.3.4 Recognize, describe, or extend geometric patterns using tables,** graphs, **words, or symbols.** *Also addresses P.5.1, P.5.2.*

Options for Differentiated Instruction

ELL = English Language Learner AL = Above or Beyond Grade Level SS = Struggling Students SN = Special Needs

Visual Learners SS SN

Use after presenting the Mini Lab.

Have students build the following patterns with cubes.

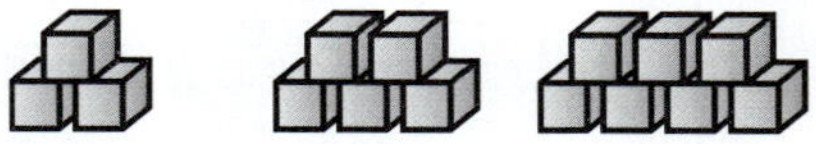

Figure 1 Figure 2 Figure 3

Ask:

- What pattern do you see? Describe it in words. Each figure increases by 2 blocks.
- Suppose this pattern continues. How many blocks would be in Figure 5? 11 blocks

Have students create two different visual patterns that represent the same arithmetic sequence. For example, they could create two different patterns that increase by 3 each term.

Visual Cues SS SN

Use with Example 1.

Have students use number lines drawn on grid paper to plot the sequence 8, 11, 14, 17, 20, … and the sequence given in Example 1.

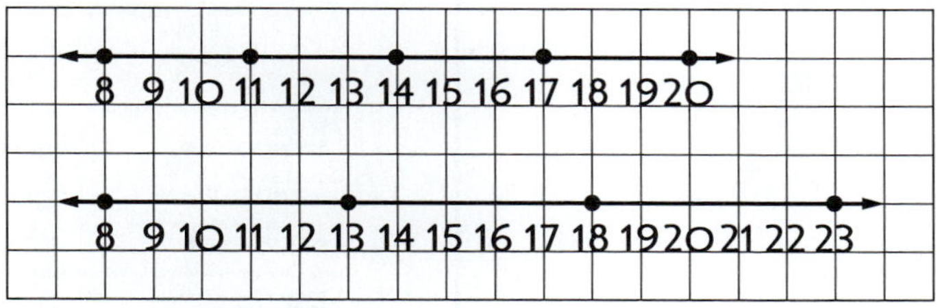

Then have them graph a non-arithmetic sequence such as 2, 4, 8, 16, … This will help students visualize the distinction between sequences that are arithmetic and those that are not.

Leveled Lesson Resources

Also on TeacherWorks™ Lesson 1-9

Chapter 1 Resource Masters

BL = Below or Approaching Grade Level OL = On Grade Level AL = Above or Beyond Grade Level ELL = English Language Learner

Lesson Reading Guide*
p. 60 BL OL ELL

NAME ________ DATE ________ PERIOD ____

1-9 Lesson Reading Guide
Algebra: Arithmetic Sequences

Get Ready for the Lesson

Complete the Mini Lab at the top of page 57 in your textbook. Write your answers below.

1. How many centimeter cubes are used to make each figure? **4, 8, 12**
2. What pattern do you see? Describe it in words. **Each time 4 more cubes are added.**
3. Suppose this pattern continues. Complete the table to find the number of cubes needed to make each figure.

Figure	1	2	3	4	5	6	7	8
Cubes Needed	4	8	12	16	20	24	28	32

4. How many cubes would you need to make the 10th figure? Explain your reasoning. **40; For the 9th figure, you need 32 + 4 or 36 cubes and for the 10th figure, you need 36 + 4 or 40 cubes.**

Read the Lesson

Complete each sentence.

5. In an arithmetic sequence, each term is found by ________ the same number to the previous term. **adding**
6. In a geometric sequence, each term is found by ________ the previous term by the same number. **multiplying**

What is the next term in each of the following sequences?

7. 1, 5, 25, ... **125** (×5 ×5)
8. 7, 10, 13, ... **16** (+3 +3)

Remember What You Learned

9. Write down the first four terms of two of your own sequences, an arithmetic sequence and a geometric sequence. Trade with a partner. Describe your partner's sequences. How did you identify the patterns? **See students' work.**

Chapter 1 60 Course 2

Study Guide and Intervention*
p. 61 BL OL ELL

NAME ________ DATE ________ PERIOD ____

1-9 Study Guide and Intervention
Algebra: Arithmetic Sequences

An **arithmetic sequence** is a list in which each term is found by adding the same number to the previous term. 1, 3, 5, 7, 9, ... (+2 +2 +2 +2)

Example 1 Describe the relationship between terms in the arithmetic sequence 17, 23, 29, 35, ... Then write the next three terms in the sequence.

17, 23, 29, 35, ... (+6 +6 +6) Each term is found by adding 6 to the previous term.
35 + 6 = 41 41 + 6 = 47 47 + 6 = 53

The next three terms are 41, 47, and 53.

Example 2

MONEY Brian's parents have decided to start giving him a monthly allowance for one year. Each month they will increase his allowance by $10. Suppose this pattern continues. What algebraic expression can be used to find Brian's allowance after any given number of months? How much money will Brian receive for allowance for the 10th month?

Make a table to display the sequence.

Position	Operation	Value of Term
1	1 · 10	10
2	2 · 10	20
3	3 · 10	30
n	n · 10	10n

Each term is 10 times its position number. So, the expression is 10n.
How much money will Brian earn after 10 months?
10n Write the expression.
10(10) = 100 Replace n with 10

So, for the 10th month Brian will receive $100.

Exercises

Describe the relationship between terms in the arithmetic sequences. Write the next three terms in the sequence.

1. 2, 4, 6, 8, ... **+2; 10, 12, 14**
2. 4, 7, 10, 13, ... **+3; 16, 19, 22**
3. 0.3, 0.6, 0.9, 1.2, ... **+0.3; 1.5, 1.8, 2.1**
4. 200, 212, 224, 236, ... **+12; 248, 260, 272**
5. 1.5, 2.0, 2.5, 3.0, ... **+0.5; 3.5, 4.0, 4.5**
6. 12, 19, 26, 33, ... **+7; 40, 47, 54**
7. SALES Mama's bakery just opened and is currently selling only two types of pastry. Each month, Mama's bakery will add two more types of pastry to their menu. Suppose this pattern continues. What algebraic expression can be used to find the number of pastries offered after any given number of months? How many pastries will be offered in one year? **2n; 24**

Chapter 1 61 Course 2

Skills Practice*
p. 62 BL OL

NAME ________ DATE ________ PERIOD ____

1-9 Skills Practice
Algebra: Arithmetic Sequences

Describe the relationship between the terms in each arithmetic sequence.

1. 3, 6, 9, 12... **+3**
2. 1, 3, 5, 7, ... **+2**
3. 1, 2, 3, 4, ... **+1**
4. 0, 7, 14, 21, ... **+7**
5. 2, 5, 8, 11, ... **+3**
6. 5, 10, 15, 20, ... **+5**
7. 0.3, 0.6, 0.9, 1.2, ... **+0.3**
8. 1, 10, 19, 28, ... **+9**
9. 6, 18, 24, 30, ... **+6**
10. 0.5, 2.5, 4.5, 6.5, ... **+2**
11. 3, 7, 11, 15, ... **+4**
12. 0, 4.5, 9, 13.5, ... **+4.5**
13. 11, 22, 33, 44, ... **+11**
14. 11, 22, 33, 44, ... **+11**

Give the next three terms in each sequence.

15. 3, 6, 9, 12, ... **15, 18, 21**
16. 18, 21, 24, 27, ... **30, 33, 36**
17. 7, 10, 13, 16, ... **19, 22, 25**
18. 4, 8, 12, 16, ... **20, 24, 28**
19. 0, 7, 14, 21, ... **28, 35, 42**
20. 7, 12, 17, 22, ... **27, 32, 37**
21. 5, 7, 9, 11, ... **13, 15, 17**
22. 5, 15, 25, 35, ... **45, 55, 65**
23. 21, 42, 63, 84, ... **105, 126, 147**
24. 1.1, 2.2, 3.3, 4.4, ... **5.5, 6.6, 7.7**
25. 0.5, 1.0, 1.5, 2.0, ... **2.5, 3.0, 3.5**
26. 1.7, 1.9, 2.1, 2.3, ... **2.5, 2.7, 2.9**
27. 0.5, 1.5, 2.5, 3.5, ... **4.5, 5.5, 6.5**
28. 0.1, 0.2, 0.3, 0.4, ... **0.5, 0.6, 0.7**

Chapter 1 62 Course 2

Practice*
p. 63 OL AL

NAME ________ DATE ________ PERIOD ____

1-9 Practice
Algebra: Arithmetic Sequences

Describe the relationship between the terms in each arithmetic sequence. Then write the next three terms in each sequence.

1. 0, 5, 10, 15, ... **5 is added to each term; 20, 25, 30**
2. 1, 3, 5, 7, ... **2 is added to each term; 9, 11, 13**
3. 18, 27, 36, 45, ... **9 is added to each term; 54, 63, 72**
4. 7, 19, 31, 43, ... **12 is added to each term; 55, 67, 79**
5. 8, 18, 28, 38, ... **10 is added to each term; 48, 58, 68**
6. 25, 26, 27, 28, ... **1 is added to each term; 29, 30, 31**
7. 0.4, 0.8, 1.2, 1.6, ... **0.4 is added to each term; 2.0, 2.4, 2.8**
8. 3.7, 3.7, 3.7, 3.7, ... **0 is added to each term; 3.7, 3.7, 3.7**
9. 5.1, 6.2, 7.3, 8.4, ... **1.1 is added to each term; 9.5, 10.6, 11.7**
10. 17, 31, 45, 59, ... **14 is added to each term; 73, 87, 101**
11. 30, 50, 70, 90, ... **20 is added to each term; 110, 130, 150**
12. 14, 41, 68, 95, ... **27 is added to each term; 122, 149, 176**

In a *geometric sequence*, each term is found by multiplying the previous term by the same number. Write the next three terms of each geometric sequence.

13. 5, 10, 20, 40, ... **80, 160, 320**
14. 3, 9, 27, 81, ... **243, 729, 2,187**
15. 2, 8, 32, 128, ... **512, 2,048, 8,192**

NUMBER SENSE **Find the 40th term in each arithmetic sequence.**

16. 4, 8, 12, 16, ... **160**
17. 13, 26, 39, 52, ... **520**
18. 6, 12, 18, 24, ... **240**

19. GEOMETRY The lengths of the sides of a 6-sided polygon are in arithmetic sequence. The length of the shortest side is 3 meters. If the length of the next longer side is 5 meters, what is the length of the longest side? **13 meters**

20. FREE FALLING OBJECT A free falling object increases speed by a little over 22 miles per hour each second. The arithmetic sequence 22, 44, 66, ..., represents the speed after each second, in miles per hour, of a dropped object. How fast is a rock falling after 8 seconds if it is dropped over the side of a cliff? **176 mph**

Chapter 1 63 Course 2

Word Problem Practice*
p. 64 OL AL

NAME ________ DATE ________ PERIOD ____

1-9 Word Problem Practice
Algebra: Arithmetic Sequences

1. NUMBERS The multiples of two form a sequence as follows: 2, 4, 6, 8, 10, 12, 14, 16, ... Describe the sequence you see? What about the multiples of three? Four? Five? **Arithmetic; the multiples of any number would result in an arithmetic sequence.**

2. OLYMPICS The summer Olympics occur every four years. If the last summer Olympics happened in 2004, when are the next three times that it will occur? Describe the sequence the Olympic years form? **2008, 2012, 2016; arithmetic**

3. BABY-SITTING Tonya charges $3.50 per hour to baby-sit. The sequence $3.50, $7.00, $10.50, $14.00, ... represents how much she charges for each subsequent hour. For example, $10.50 is the third term that represents how much she charges for 3 hours. What are the next three terms in the sequence? How much does she charge for 7 hours of baby-sitting? **$17.50, $21.00, $24.50; $24.50**

4. RECTANGLES Suppose you start with 1 rectangle and then divide it in half. You now have 2 rectangles. You divide each of these in half, and you have 4 rectangles. The sequence for this division is 1, 2, 4, 8, 16, . . . rectangles after each successive division. Describe the sequence that results? **geometric**

5. BACTERIA Three bacteria are in a dish. Each hour the number of bacteria multiplies by four. If at the end of the first hour there are 12 bacteria, how many bacteria are there at the end of the next three hours? Describe the sequence that results? **48, 192, 768; geometric**

6. ENROLLMENT The enrollment at Grove Middle School is expected to increase by 40 students each year for the next 5 years. If their current enrollment is 600 students, find their enrollment after each of the next 5 years. **640, 680, 720, 760, 800**

7. SALARY Mrs. Malone's current salary is $1,500. She expects it to increase $100 per year. Write the first 6 terms of a sequence that represents her salary. The first term should be her current salary. What does the sixth term represent? **$1,500, $1,600, $1,700, $1,800, $1,900, $2,000; her salary after 5 years or at the beginning of the sixth year**

8. FIBONACCI The Fibonacci sequence is named after Leonardo Fibonacci who first explored it. Look at the Fibonacci sequence below and describe its pattern. 1, 1, 2, 3, 5, 8, 13, 21, 34, ... **Each term is found by adding the two previous terms; it is neither arithmetic nor geometric.**

Chapter 1 64 Course 2

Enrichment
p. 65 OL AL

NAME ________ DATE ________ PERIOD ____

1-9 Enrichment

Other Sequences

When each term in a sequence decreases, it is described as a *declining sequence*. Either subtracting the same number from the previous term or dividing the previous term by the same number creates a declining sequence.

81, 27, 9, 3, ... (÷3 ÷3 ÷3) In this sequence, each term is found by dividing the previous term by 3.

Some sequences are formed by using two operations.

2, 5, 11, 23, 47, ... (×2+1 ×2+1 ×2+1 ×2+1) In this sequence, each term is found by multiplying the previous term by 2 and then adding 1.

Describe the rule in each sequence. Then write the next three terms.

1. 40, 38, 36, 34, ... **Subtract 2; 32, 30, 28**
2. 128, 64, 32, 16, ... **Divide by 2; 8, 4, 2**
3. 7.5, 6.4, 5.3, 4.2, ... **Subtract 1.1; 3.1, 2.0, 0.9**
4. 1, 4, 13, 40, ... **Multiply by 3 and add 1; 121, 364, 1093**
5. 1, 5, 13, 61, ... **Multiply by 2 and add 3; 125, 253, 509**
6. 1, 5, 21, 85, ... **Multiply by 4 and add 1; 341, 1365, 5461**

Create a five-term sequence using the rule stated. Start with the given number.

7. Subtract 8 from each term; 78. **78, 70, 62, 54, 46**
8. Divide each term by 10; 80. **80, 8, 0.8, 0.08, 0.008**
9. Subtract 11 from each term; 132. **132, 121, 110, 99, 88**
10. Multiply each term by 10 and subtract 9; 4. **4, 31, 301, 3001, 30,001**
11. Multiply each term by 7 and add 2; 1. **1, 9, 65, 457, 3201**
12. Multiply each term by 3 and subtract 2; 6. **6, 16, 46, 136, 406**

CHALLENGE For Exercises 13–15, use the sequence 589, 5,889, 58,889, 588,889, ...

13. Describe the rule of the sequence. **Multiply each term by 10 and subtract 1.**
14. Study the pattern in the sequence. Without extending the sequence, what is the sixth term of the sequence? What is the tenth term? **58,888,889; 588,888,888,889**
15. Describe how you can find any term of the sequence. **Sample answer: The nth term starts with 5, followed by n eights, and ends with 9.**

Chapter 1 65 Course 2

* Also available in Spanish ELL

Additional Lesson Resources

Transparencies

- *5-Minute Check Transparency*, Lesson 1-9

Other Print Products

- *Teaching Mathematics with Manipulatives*
- *Noteables™ Interactive Study Notebook with Foldables™*

Teacher Tech Tools

- *Interactive Classroom CD-ROM*, Lesson 1-9
- *AssignmentWorks*, Lesson 1-9

Student Tech Tools

glencoe.com

- Extra Examples, Chapter 1, Lesson 9
- Self-Check Quiz, Chapter 1, Lesson 9

1-9 Algebra: Arithmetic Sequences

1-9 Lesson Notes

MAIN IDEA

Describe the relationships and extend terms in arithmetic sequences.

IN Academic Standards

7.2.1 Use variables and appropriate operations to write an expression, equation or inequality **that represents a verbal description.**
7.3.4 Recognize, describe, or extend geometric patterns using tables, graphs, **words, or symbols.** *Also addresses P.5.1, P.5.2.*

New Vocabulary

sequence
term
arithmetic sequence

IN Math Online

glencoe.com

- Concepts In Motion
- Extra Examples
- Personal Tutor
- Self-Check Quiz

MINI Lab

Use centimeter cubes to make the three figures shown.

Figure 1 Figure 2 Figure 3

1. How many centimeter cubes are used to make each figure?
2. What pattern do you see? Describe it in words.
3. Suppose this pattern continues. Copy and complete the table to find the number of cubes needed to make each figure.

Figure	1	2	3	4	5	6	7	8
Cubes Needed	4	8	12	16	20	24	28	32

4. How many cubes would you need to make the 10th figure? Explain your reasoning. **1, 2, 4. See margin.**

A **sequence** is an ordered list of numbers. Each number in a sequence is called a **term**. In an **arithmetic sequence**, each term is found by adding the same number to the previous term. An example of an arithmetic sequence is shown.

8, 11, 14, 17, 20, ...
+3 +3 +3 +3

Each term is found by adding 3 to the previous term.

EXAMPLE Describe and Extend Sequences

1 **Describe the relationship between the terms in the arithmetic sequence 8, 13, 18, 23, ... Then write the next three terms in the sequence.**

8, 13, 18, 23, ...
+5 +5 +5

Each term is found by adding 5 to the previous term. Continue the pattern to find the next three terms.

$23 + 5 = 28$ $\quad$ $28 + 5 = 33$ $\quad$ $33 + 5 = 38$

The next three terms are 28, 33, and 38.

CHECK Your Progress

a. 13 is added to each term; 52, 65, 78
b. 3 is added to each term; 16, 19, 22

Describe the relationship between the terms in each arithmetic sequence. Then write the next three terms in the sequence.

a. 0, 13, 26, 39, ... $\quad$ b. 4, 7, 10, 13 ...

Additional Answers

1. 4, 8, 12
2. Each time, 4 more cubes are added.
4. 40; For the 9th figure, you need $32 + 4$ or 36 cubes, and for the 10th figure, you need $36 + 4$ or 40 cubes.

1 Focus

Vertical Alignment

Before Lesson 1-9
Use a letter to represent an unknown number; write and evaluate simple algebraic expressions in one variable by substitution

Lesson 1-9
Write and evaluate an algebraic expression for a given situation

After Lesson 1-9
Use variables and appropriate operations to write an expression, an equation, an inequality, or a system of equations or inequalities that represents a verbal description

2 Teach

MINI Lab

You might want to point out that each figure's number is the same as its height, so students can also multiply to find the total number of cubes in later figures.

Scaffolding Questions

Ask:

- What is the next number in the sequence 10, 12, 14, 16, . . . ? 18
- What is the next number in the sequence 25, 30, 35, 40, . . . ? 45
- What is the next number in the sequence 0, 3, 6, 9, . . . ? 12
- How did you find the next number in each sequence? by adding the difference between consecutive numbers to the last number in the sequence

Formative Assessment

Use the Check Your Progress exercises after each Example to determine students' understanding of concepts.

ADDITIONAL EXAMPLES

1. Describe the relationship between the terms in the arithmetic sequence 7, 11, 15, 19 . . . Then write the next three terms in the sequence. 4 is added to each term; 23, 27, 31
2. Describe the relationship between the terms in the arithmetic sequence 0.1, 0.5, 0.9, 1.3, . . . Then write the next three terms in the sequence. Each term is 0.4 greater than the previous term; 1.7, 2.1, 2.5

Additional Examples are also in:

- Noteables™ Interactive Study Notebook with Foldables™
- Interactive Classroom PowerPoint® Presentations

Focus on Mathematical Content

A **sequence** is a list of numbers in a certain order.

Each **term** in a sequence has a position (first, second, third, and so on).

In an **arithmetic sequence**, the same number is added to each term to get the following term. This is the relationship between consecutive terms.

*The **Focus on Mathematical Content** provides background information for each lesson. This information would be especially valuable to new teachers or those new to teaching mathematics.*

c. 0.3 is added to each term; 2.2, 2.5, 2.8
d. 0.5 is added to each term; 4.5, 5.0, 5.5

Arithmetic sequences can also involve decimals.

EXAMPLE Describe and Extend Sequences

2 **Describe the relationship between the terms in the arithmetic sequence 0.4, 0.6, 0.8, 1.0, ... Then write the next three terms in the sequence.**

0.4, 0.6, 0.8, 1.0, . . .
+0.2 +0.2 +0.2

Each term is found by adding 0.2 to the previous term. Continue the pattern to find the next three terms.

$1.0 + 0.2 = 1.2$ $\quad 1.2 + 0.2 = 1.4$ $\quad 1.4 + 0.2 = 1.6$

The next three terms are 1.2, 1.4, and 1.6.

CHECK Your Progress

Describe the relationship between the terms in each arithmetic sequence. Then write the next three terms in the sequence.

c. 1.0, 1.3, 1.6, 1.9, . . .
d. 2.5, 3.0, 3.5, 4.0, . . .

In a sequence, each term has a specific position within the sequence. Consider the sequence 2, 4, 6, 8, 10, . . .

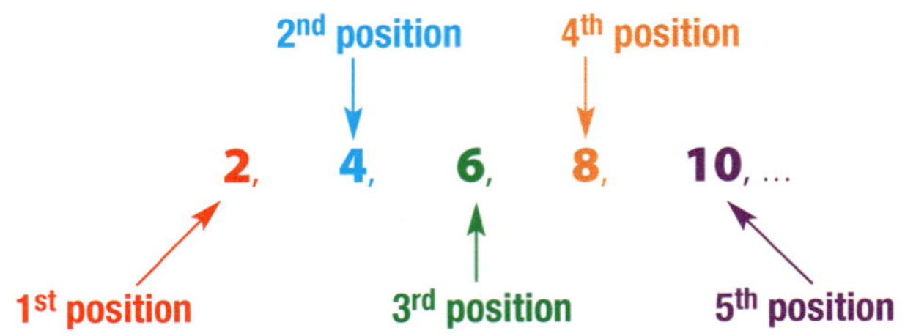

The table below shows the position of each term in this sequence. Notice that as the position number increases by 1, the value of the term increases by 2.

Position	Operation	Value of Term
1	$1 \cdot 2 = 2$	2
2	$2 \cdot 2 = 4$	4
3	$3 \cdot 2 = 6$	6
4	$4 \cdot 2 = 8$	8
5	$5 \cdot 2 = 10$	10

(Position: +1 between consecutive rows; Value of Term: +2 between consecutive rows)

You can also write an algebraic expression to represent the relationship between any term in a sequence and its position in the sequence. In this case, if n represents the position in the sequence, the value of the term is $2n$.

Real-World EXAMPLE

3 **GREETING CARDS** **The homemade greeting cards that Meredith makes are sold in boxes at a local gift store. Each week, the store sells five more boxes.**

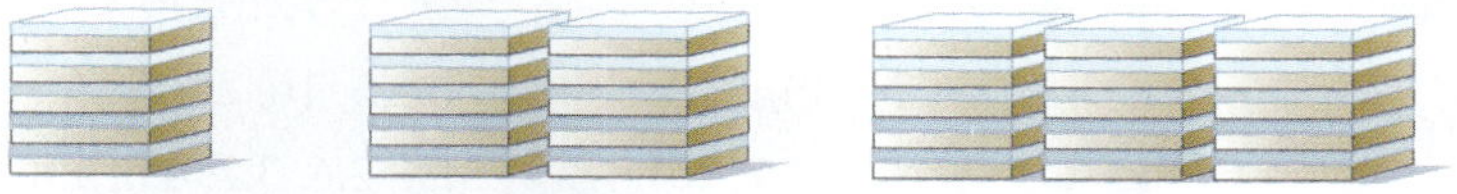

Week 1 Week 2 Week 3

If this pattern continues, what algebraic expression can be used to help her find the total number of boxes sold at the end of the 100th week? Use the expression to find the total.

Make a table to display the sequence.

Position	Operation	Value of Term
1	1 • 5	5
2	2 • 5	10
3	3 • 5	15
n	*n* • 5	5*n*

Each term is 5 times its position number. So, the expression is $5n$.

$5n$ Write the expression.

$5(100) = 500$ Replace *n* with 100.

So, at the end of 100 weeks, 500 boxes will have been sold.

CHECK Your Progress e. $3n$, 150

e. **GEOMETRY** If the pattern continues, what algebraic expression can be used to find the number of circles used in the 50th figure? How many circles will be in the 50th figure?

Figure 1 Figure 2 Figure 3

Study Tip

Arithmetic Sequences When looking for a pattern between the position number and each term in the sequence, it is often helpful to make a table.

★ indicates multi-step problem

CHECK Your Understanding

Examples 1, 2 (pp. 57–58)

Describe the relationship between the terms in each arithmetic sequence. Then write the next three terms in each sequence. 1–4. See margin.

1. 0, 9, 18, 27, …
2. 4, 9, 14, 19, …
3. 1, 1.1, 1.2, 1.3, …
4. 5, 5.4, 5.8, 6.2, …

Example 3 (p. 59)

5. **PLANTS** The table shows the height of a certain plant each month after being planted. If this pattern continues, what algebraic expression can be used to find the height of the plant at the end of twelve months? Find the plant's height after 12 months. $3n$, 36 in.

Month	Height (in.)
1	3
2	6
3	9
4	12

ADDITIONAL EXAMPLE

3 **EXERCISE** Mehmet started a new exercise routine. The first day, he did 2 sit-ups. Each day after that, he did 2 more sit-ups than the previous day. If he continues this pattern, what algebraic expression can be used to help find the total number of sit-ups on the tenth day? Use the expression to find the number. $2d$; 20

3 Practice

Formative Assessment

Use Exercises 1–5 to check for understanding.

Then use the chart at the bottom of the next page to customize your assignments for students.

Intervention You may wish to use the Study Guide and Intervention Master on page 61 of the *Chapter 1 Resource Masters* for additional reinforcement.

Additional Answers

1. 9 is added to each term; 36, 45, 54
2. 5 is added to each term; 24, 29, 34
3. 0.1 is added to each term; 1.4, 1.5, 1.6
4. 0.4 is added to each term; 6.6, 7.0, 7.4

Lesson 1-9 Algebra: Arithmetic Sequences **59**

Odd/Even Assignments

Exercises 6–19 are structured so that students practice the same concepts whether they are assigned odd or even problems.

⚠ Exercise Alert!

Use the Internet Exercise 31 requires students to use the Internet or another source to research the Fibonacci sequence.

Additional Answers

6. 7 is added to each term; 28, 35, 42
7. 6 is added to each term; 25, 31, 37
8. 8 is added to each term; 58, 66, 74
9. 12 is added to each term; 67, 79, 91
10. 10 is added to each term; 46, 56, 66
11. 5 is added to each term; 53, 58, 63
12. 0.3 is added to each term; 1.3, 1.6, 1.9
13. 0.8 is added to each term; 5.6, 6.4, 7.2
14. 1.1 is added to each term; 6.4, 7.5, 8.6
15. 1.5 is added to each term; 10.5, 12.0, 13.5
16. 2 is added to each term; 9.2, 11.2, 13.2
17. 4 is added to each term; 20.6, 24.6, 28.6
31. The Fibonacci sequence is 1, 1, 2, 3, 5, 8, 13, ... In this sequence, each term after the second term is the sum of the two terms before it. Fibonacci numbers occur in many areas of nature, including pine cones, shell spirals, and branching plants.

Practice and Problem Solving

HOMEWORK HELP

For Exercises	See Examples
6–11	1
12–17	2
18, 19	3

Exercise Levels
A: 6–19
B: 20–31
C: 32–36

Describe the relationship between the terms in each arithmetic sequence. Then write the next three terms in each sequence. 6–17. See margin.

6. 0, 7, 14, 21, …
7. 1, 7, 13, 19, …
8. 26, 34, 42, 50, …
9. 19, 31, 43, 55, …
10. 6, 16, 26, 36, …
11. 33, 38, 43, 48, …
12. 0.1, 0.4, 0.7, 1.0, …
13. 2.4, 3.2, 4.0, 4.8, …
14. 2.0, 3.1, 4.2, 5.3, …
15. 4.5, 6.0, 7.5, 9.0, …
16. 1.2, 3.2, 5.2, 7.2, …
17. 4.6, 8.6, 12.6, 16.6, …

18. **COLLECTIONS** Hannah is starting a doll collection. Each year, she buys 6 dolls. Suppose she continues this pattern. What algebraic expression can be used to find the number of dolls in her collection after any number of years? How many dolls will Hannah have after 25 years? $6n$, 150 dolls

19. **EXERCISE** The table shows the number of laps that Jorge swims each week. Jorge's goal is to continue this pace. What algebraic expression can be used to find the total number of laps he will swim after any given number of weeks? How many laps will Jorge swim after 6 weeks? $7n$; 42 laps

Week	Number of Laps
1	7
2	14
3	21
4	28

20. 15 is added to each term; 78, 93, 108
21. 25 is added to each term; 120, 145, 170
22. 23 is added to each term; 130, 153, 176

Describe the relationship between the terms in each arithmetic sequence. Then write the next three terms in each sequence.

20. 18, 33, 48, 63, …
21. 20, 45, 70, 95, …
22. 38, 61, 84, 107, …

In a *geometric sequence*, each term is found by multiplying the previous term by the same number. Write the next three terms of each geometric sequence.

23. 1, 4, 16, 64, … 256, 1,024, 4,096
24. 2, 6, 18, 54, … 162, 486, 1,458
25. 4, 12, 36, 108, … 324, 972, 2,916

★ 26. **GEOMETRY** Kendra is stacking boxes of tissues for a store display. Each minute, she stacks another layer of boxes. If the pattern continues, how many boxes will be displayed after 45 minutes? 135 boxes

NUMBER SENSE **Find the 100th number in each sequence.**

27. 12, 24, 36, 48, … 1,200
28. 14, 28, 42, 56, … 1,400
29. 0, 50, 100, 150, … 4,950
30. 0, 75, 150, 225, … 7,425

Academic Standards • ISTEP+
Extra Practice, pp. 670, 704

31. **RESEARCH** The Fibonacci sequence is one of the most well-known sequences in mathematics. Use the Internet or another source to write a paragraph about the Fibonacci sequence. See margin.

DIFFERENTIATED HOMEWORK OPTIONS

Level	Assignment	Two-Day Option	
BL Basic	6–19, 34–47	7–19 odd, 37, 38	6–18 even, 34–36, 39–47
OL Core	7–17 odd, 18, 19, 21–25 odd, 26, 27, 29, 31, 34–47	6–19, 37, 38	20–31, 34–36, 39–47
AL Advanced/Pre-AP	20–44 (optional: 45–47)		

H.O.T. Problems

CHALLENGE Not all sequences are arithmetic. But, there is still a pattern. Describe the relationship between the terms in each sequence. Then write the next three terms in the sequence.

32. 1, 2, 4, 7, 11, … $+1, +2, +3, +4, \ldots$; 16, 22, 29

33. 0, 2, 6, 12, 20, … $+2, +4, +6, +8, \ldots$; 30, 42, 56

34. **OPEN ENDED** Write five terms of an arithmetic sequence and describe the rule for finding the terms. Sample answer: 5, 6, 7, 8, …; $n + 4$

35. **SELECT A TOOL** Suppose you want to begin saving $15 each month. Which of the following tools would you use to determine the amount you will have saved after 2 years? Justify your selection(s). Then use the tool(s) to solve the problem. See margin.

paper/pencil | real object | technology

36. **WRITING IN MATH** Janice earns $6.50 per hour running errands for her neighbor. Explain how the hourly earnings form an arithmetic sequence. See margin.

ISTEP+ PRACTICE 7.2.1

37. Which sequence follows the rule $3n - 2$, where n represents the position of a term in the sequence? D

A 21, 18, 15, 12, 9, …

B 3, 6, 9, 12, 15, …

C 1, 7, 10, 13, 16, …

D 1, 4, 7, 10, 13, …

38. Which expression can be used to find the nth term in this sequence? F

Position	1	2	3	4	5	n^{th}
Value of Term	2	5	10	17	26	

F $n^2 + 1$

G $2n + 1$

H $n + 1$

J $2n^2 + 2$

Spiral Review

Find each expression mentally. Justify each step. (Lesson 1-8)

39. $(23 + 18) + 7$ 48

40. $5 \cdot (12 \cdot 20)$ 1,200

39–40. See margin for justification.

Solve each equation mentally. (Lesson 1-7)

41. $f - 26 = 3$ 29

42. $\frac{a}{4} = 8$ 32

43. $30 + y = 50$ 20

44. **SCIENCE** At normal temperatures, sound travels through water at a rate of $5 \cdot 10^3$ feet per second. Write this rate in standard form. (Lesson 1-2) 5,000 ft/s

GET READY for the Next Lesson

PREREQUISITE SKILL Find the value of each expression. (Lesson 1-6)

45. $2x$ if $x = 4$ 8

46. $d - 5$ if $d = 8$ 3

47. $3m - 3$ if $m = 2$ 3

H.O.T. Problems require students to use Higher Order Thinking skills to solve problems.

4 Assess

Ticket Out the Door Write an arithmetic sequence such as 8, 16, 24, 32, . . . on the board. Have students write a term of the sequence (for example, the 9th term) on a small piece of paper.

Additional Answers

35. Sample answer: paper/pencil; Write the equation that represents this situation, $15n$. Since 2 years = 24 months, evaluate the expression when n is 24. $15(24) = 360$. So, after 2 years, $360 will be saved.

36. Sample answer: The total amount earned forms the sequence 6.5, 13, 19.5 , 26, ... Since each term is 6.5 more than the previous term, the sequence is arithmetic.

39. Sample answer: Rewrite $(23 + 18) + 7$ as $(18 + 23) + 7$ using the Commutative Property of Addition. Rewrite $(18 + 23) + 7$ as $18 + (23 + 7)$ using the Associative Property of Addition. Find $23 + 7$, or 30, mentally. Then find $18 + 30$, or 48, mentally.

40. Sample answer: Rewrite $5 \cdot (12 \cdot 20)$ as $5 \cdot (20 \cdot 12)$ using the Commutative Property of multiplication. Rewrite $5 \cdot (20 \cdot 12)$ as $(5 \cdot 20) \cdot 12$ using the Associative Property of Multiplication. Find $5 \cdot 20$, or 100, mentally. Then find $100 \cdot 12$, or 1,200, mentally.

Pre-AP Activity Use after Exercise 38.

Explain that the first term of some arithmetic sequences isn't the number that is added to each term to get the following term. Write a sequence such as 3, 5, 7, 9, . . . on the board. Have students make a table showing the positions and terms of the sequence. Have them find the 5th and 6th terms and then write an expression to find the nth term. $2n + 1$

Position	1	2	3	4	5	6
Value of Term	3	5	7	9	11	13

Extend 1-9

Lesson Notes

1 Focus

Materials

- toothpicks

Teaching Tip

You may wish to have students work in pairs for this lab.

2 Teach

Working in Cooperative Groups You may wish for students to work in groups of two or three. Student 1 can build the figures, Student 2 can count the toothpicks, and Student 3 can record the results in the table.

Activity Some students will be able to perform the activity and analyze the results without toothpicks, either by visualizing the pattern or by drawing the figures.

3 Assess

Formative Assessment

Use Exercises 3 and 4 to determine whether students comprehend how to use toothpicks to create and analyze arithmetic sequences.

From Concrete to Abstract Use Exercise 5 to bridge the gap between using toothpicks to create arithmetic sequences and writing an expression to describe such a sequence.

*Algebra Labs use manipulatives and models to help students learn key concepts. There are teacher notes for every Algebra Lab in the Student Edition. Other labs include **Measurement, Geometry, Statistics,** and **Probability.***

Extend 1-9

Algebra Lab
Exploring Sequences

MAIN IDEA

Explore patterns in sequences of geometric figures.

IN Academic Standards

7.3.4 Recognize, describe, or **extend geometric patterns using tables,** graphs, words, or symbols.
P.5.1 Create and use representations to organize, record, and communicate mathematical ideas.
Also addresses P.5.2.

ACTIVITY

STEP 1 Use toothpicks to build the figures below.

Figure 1 Figure 2 Figure 3

STEP 2 Make a table like the one shown and record the figure number and number of toothpicks used in each figure.

Figure Number	Number of Toothpicks
1	4
2	7
3	10
■	■

STEP 3 Construct the next figure in this pattern. Record your results.

STEP 4 Repeat Step 3 until you have found the next four figures in the pattern.

Analyze the Results 1, 3, 4, 6, and 7. See Ch. 1 Answer Appendix.

1. How many additional toothpicks were used each time to form the next figure in the pattern? Where is this pattern found in the table?
2. Based on your answer to Exercise 1, how many toothpicks would be in Figure 0 of this pattern? 1
3. Remove one toothpick from your pattern so that Figure 1 is made up of just three toothpicks as shown. Then create a table showing the number of toothpicks that would be in the first 7 figures by continuing the same pattern as above.

Figure 1

4. How many toothpicks would there be in Figure n of this new patter
5. How could you adapt the expression you wrote in Exercise 4 to find the number of toothpicks in Figure n of the original pattern? $3n + 1$
6. **MAKE A PREDICTION** How many toothpicks would there be in Figure 10 of the original pattern? Explain your reasoning. Then check your answer by constructing the figure.
7. Find the number of toothpicks in Figure n of the pattern below, and predict the number of toothpicks in Figure 12. Justify your answer.

Figure 1 Figure 2 Figure 3

Extending the Concept Ask students to write an expression for the number of toothpicks in figure n of a sequence in which each figure is composed of equilateral triangles and an expression for the number of toothpicks in figure n of a sequence in which each figure is composed of regular pentagons. $2n + 1$; $4n + 1$

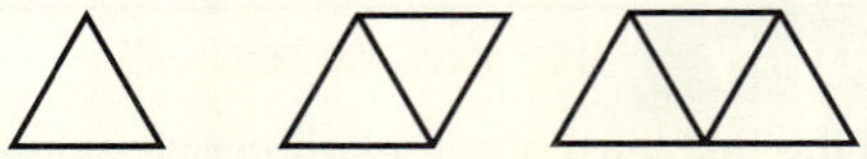

Fig. 1 Fig. 2 Fig. 3

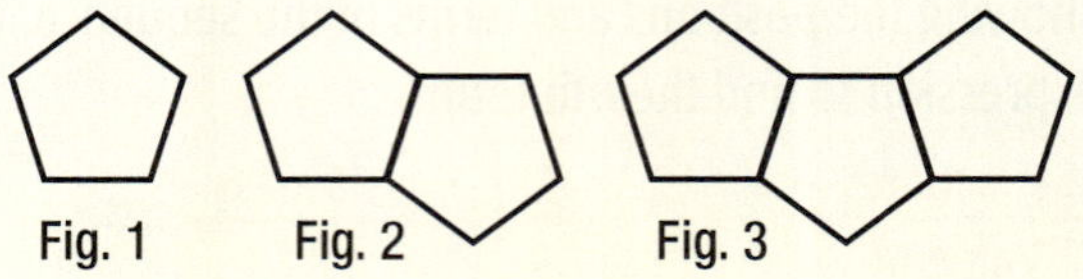

Fig. 1 Fig. 2 Fig. 3

1-10 Algebra: Equations and Functions

PACING: **Regular:** 1.5 periods, **Block:** 1 period

IN Academic Standards **7.2.1 Use variables and appropriate operations to write an** expression, **equation** or inequality **that represents a verbal description.** *Also addresses P.4.1, P.5.1, P.5.2.*

Options for Differentiated Instruction

ELL = English Language Learner AL = Above or Beyond Grade Level SS = Struggling Students SN = Special Needs

Auditory Learning ELL SS

Use while presenting Examples 1–3.

Some students take in information more easily through listening than through reading. Think aloud as you demonstrate the steps for completing a function table and writing and using an equation. Verbalize what you would normally perform automatically.

Organizing Student Work and Thinking SS SN

Use with the Exercises.

For students with organizational difficulties, it may be helpful to provide enlarged photocopies of the function tables in Exercises 1, 2, 6–8, and 15–18 so that they do not have to copy them. It may also be helpful to provide a template like the one shown below for the exercises that require students to make a function table.

Input	Function Rule	Output

Use for both homework and class work, making sure that they identify both the page number and the problem number as a reference.

Extensions and Challenges AL

Use with the H.O.T. Problems.

Remind students that a function rule can often have more then one operation.
Have them examine the following function tables and determine the function rule for each.

Input x	Output y
1	5
2	8
3	11
4	14

$y = 3x + 2$

Input x	Output y
1	0
2	2
3	4
4	6

$y = 2x - 2$

Input x	Output y
1	2
2	5
3	10
4	17

$y = x^2 + 1$

Leveled Lesson Resources

Also on TeacherWorks™ Lesson 1-10

Chapter 1 Resource Masters

BL = Below or Approaching Grade Level   OL = On Grade Level   AL = Above or Beyond Grade Level   ELL = English Language Learner

Lesson Reading Guide*
p. 67 BL OL ELL

NAME ______ DATE ______ PERIOD ____

1-10 Lesson Reading Guide

Algebra: Equations and Functions

Get Ready for the Lesson

Read the introduction at the top of page 63 in your textbook. Write your answers below.

1. Complete the table to find the cost of 2, 3, and 4 magazines.

Magazines		
Number	Multiply by 4	Cost($)
1	4 × 1	4
2	4 × 2	8
3	4 × 3	12
4	4 × 4	16

2. Describe the pattern in the table between the cost and the number of magazines.
The cost increases by 4 each time the number of magazines increases by 1.

Read the Lesson

3. Complete each function table. Then identify the domain and range.

a.

x	$2x - 1$	y
−1	2(−1) − 1	−3
0	2(0) − 1	−1
1	2(1) − 1	1

domain: {−1, 0, 1}
range: {−3, −1, 1}

b.

x	$4x$	y
−1	4(−1)	−4
0	4(0)	0
1	4(1)	4

domain: {−1, 0, 1}
range: {−4, 0, 4}

4. MONEY John earns $15 per lawn that he mows.
a. Write an equation in two variables showing the relationship between lawns mowed and the money John earns.
m = lawns mowed, d = dollars earned, $15m = d$
b. How much money does John earn after mowing 3, 5, and 10 lawns?
3, $45 5, $75 10, $150

Remember What You Learned

5. Draw a picture of a "machine" that shows how a function works. Your picture should illustrate input, a function rule, and output. **See students' work.**

Lesson 1-10

Study Guide and Intervention*
p. 68 BL OL ELL

NAME ______ DATE ______ PERIOD ____

1-10 Study Guide and Intervention

Algebra: Equations and Functions

The solution of an equation with two variables consists of two numbers, one for each variable that makes the equation true. When a relationship assigns exactly one output value for each input value, it is called a function. Function tables help to organize input numbers, output numbers, and function rules.

Example 1 **Complete a function table for $y = 5x$. Then state the domain and range.**

Choose four values for x. Substitute the values for x into the expression. Then evaluate to find the y value.

x	$5x$	y
0	5(0)	0
1	5(1)	5
2	5(2)	10
3	5(3)	15

The domain is {0, 1, 2, 3}. The range is {0, 5, 10, 15}.

Exercises

Complete the following function tables. Then state the domain and range.

1. $y = x + 4$

x	$x + 4$	y
0	0+4	4
1	1+4	5
2	2+4	6
3	3+4	7

domain: {0, 1, 2, 3}
range: {4, 5, 6, 7}

2. $y = 10x$

x	$10x$	y
1	10(1)	10
2	10(2)	20
3	10(3)	30
4	10(4)	40

domain: {1, 2, 3, 4}
range: {10, 20, 30, 40}

3. $y = x - 1$

x	$x - 1$	y
2	2−1	1
3	3−1	2
4	4−1	3
5	5−1	4

domain: {2, 3, 4, 5}
range: {1, 2, 3, 4}

4. $y = 3x$

x	$3x$	y
10	3(10)	30
11	3(11)	33
12	3(12)	36
13	3(13)	39

domain: {10, 11, 12, 13}
range: {30, 33, 36, 39}

Skills Practice*
p. 69 BL OL

NAME ______ DATE ______ PERIOD ____

1-10 Skills Practice

Algebra: Equations and Functions

Copy and complete each function table. Identify the domain and range.

1. $y = x - 1$

x	$x - 1$	y
1	1 − 1	0
2	2 − 1	1
3	3 − 1	2
4	4 − 1	3

domain: {1, 2, 3, 4}
range: {0, 1, 2, 3}

2. $y = x + 7$

x	$x + 7$	y
1	1 + 7	8
2	2 + 7	9
3	3 + 7	10
4	4 + 7	11

domain: {1, 2, 3, 4}
range: {8, 9, 10, 11}

3. $y = 3x$

x	$3x$	y
1	3(1)	3
2	3(2)	6
3	3(3)	9
4	3(4)	12

domain: {1, 2, 3, 4}
range: {3, 6, 9, 12}

4. $y = 4x$

x	$4x$	y
2	4(2)	8
3	4(3)	12
4	4(4)	16
5	4(5)	20

domain: {2, 3, 4, 5}
range: {8, 12, 16, 20}

5. $y = x - 0.5$

x	$x - 0.5$	y
1	1 − 0.5	0.5
2	2 − 0.5	1.5
3	3 − 0.5	2.5
4	4 − 0.5	3.5

domain: {1, 2, 3, 4}
range: {0.5, 1.5, 2.5, 3.5}

6. $y = 10x$

x	$10x$	y
0	10(0)	0
1	10(1)	10
2	10(2)	20
3	10(3)	30

domain: {0, 1, 2, 3}
range: {0, 10, 20, 30}

Solve each word problem.

For Exercises 7 and 8, use the following information.

TRAVEL **For every gallon of gas, a car can travel 30 miles.**

7. Write an equation using two variables to show the relationship between the distance the car travels and the gallons of gas it uses.
d = distance, g = gallons of gas, $30g = d$

8. If a car had 8 gallons of gas left in its tank, how many miles can it travel before the tank runs out?
240 miles

For Exercises 9 and 10, use the following information.

FARMING **Every row of corn in Mr. Jones' garden has 5 cornstalks.**

9. Write an equation using two variables to show the relationship between the number of rows and the number of cornstalks.
r = rows, s = stalks, $5r = s$

10. If Mr. Jones has 7 rows of corn, how many cornstalks will he need to harvest?
35 cornstalks

Lesson 1-10

Practice*
p. 70 OL AL

NAME ______ DATE ______ PERIOD ____

1-10 Practice

Algebra: Equations and Functions

Complete each function table. Then identify the domain and range.

1. $y = 5x$

x	$5x$	y
1	5 · 1	5
2	5 · 2	10
3	5 · 3	15
4	5 · 4	20

Domain: {1, 2, 3, 4}
Range: {5, 10, 15, 20}

2. $y = 8x$

x	$8x$	y
1	8 · 1	1
2	8 · 2	16
3	8 · 3	24
4	8 · 4	32

Domain: {1, 2, 3, 4}
Range: {1, 16, 24, 32}

3. $y = 7x$

x	$7x$	y
3	7 · 3	21
4	7 · 4	28
5	7 · 5	35
6	7 · 6	42

Domain: {3, 4, 5, 6}
Range: {21, 28, 35, 42}

4. $y = x - 2$

x	$x - 2$	y
2	2 − 2	0
3	3 − 2	1
4	4 − 2	2
5	5 − 2	3

Domain: {2, 3, 4, 5}
Range: {0, 1, 2, 3}

5. $y = x + 3$

x	$x + 3$	y
2	2 + 3	5
3	3 + 3	6
4	4 + 3	7
5	5 + 3	8

Domain: {2, 3, 4, 5}
Range: {5, 6, 7, 8}

6. $y = x + 0.75$

x	$x + 0.75$	y
0	0 + 0.75	0.75
1	1 + 0.75	1.75
2	2 + 0.75	2.75
3	3 + 0.75	3.75

Domain: {0, 1, 2, 3}
Range: {0.75, 1.75, 2.75, 3.75}

7. PRODUCTION A car manufacturer makes 15,000 hybrid cars a month. Using the function table, find the number of hybrid cars produced after 3, 6, 9, and 12 months.

m	$15{,}000m$	P
3	15,000 · 3	45,000
6	15,000 · 6	90,000
9	15,000 · 9	135,000
12	15,000 · 12	180,000

8. SUNSPOTS The changing activity of sunspots, which are cooler and darker areas of the sun, occur in 11-year cycles. Use the function $y = 11c$ to find the numbers of years necessary to complete 1, 2, 3, and 4 sunspot cycles.

11 years, 22 years, 33 years, and 44 years

Word Problem Practice*
p. 71 OL AL

NAME ______ DATE ______ PERIOD ____

1-10 Word Problem Practice

Algebra: Equations and Functions

1. TECHNOLOGY The fee for your pager service is $22 per month. Make a function table that shows your total charge for 1, 2, 3, and 4 months of service.

x, Months	y, Total Charge
1	22
2	44
3	66
4	88

2. MEASUREMENT Joe takes 2 steps for every one step that Kim takes. Write an equation in two variables showing the relationship between Joe's steps and Kim's steps. If Kim takes 15 steps, how many steps will Joe have to take to cover the same distance?
j = the number of steps Joe takes
k = the number of steps Kim takes, $2k = j$
30 steps

3. TRAINS Between Hiroshima and Kokura, Japan, the bullet train averages a speed of 164 miles per hour, which is the fastest scheduled train service in the world. Make a function table that shows the distance traveled at that speed in 1, 2, 3, and 4 hours.

x, Hours	y, Distance
1	164
2	328
3	492
4	656

4. BUSINESS Grant earns $5 for each magazine that he sells. Write an equation in two variables showing the relationship between the number of magazines sold and the amount of money made. If Grant sells 12 magazines, how much money will he make?
m = the number of magazines sold, d = Grant's earnings in dollars, $5m = d$
$60

5. GEOMETRY The formula for the volume of a rectangular prism whose base has an area of 8 square units is $V = 8h$, where V is the volume and h is the height. Make a function table that shows the volume of a rectangular prism with a height of 3, 4, 5, and 6 units.

h	$8h$	V
3	8(3)	24
4	8(4)	32
5	8(5)	40
6	8(6)	48

6. GEOMETRY The fastest insect in the world is the dragonfly with a top speed of 36 miles per hour. Write an equation in two variables describing the relationship between the length of the dragonfly's flight and the distance traveled. If a dragonfly flies for 3 hours, how far can he travel?
y = time, d = distance, $36t = d$
108 miles

Lesson 1-10

Enrichment
p. 72 OL AL

NAME ______ DATE ______ PERIOD ____

1-10 Enrichment

To solve equations containing two variables, find ordered pair solutions for the equation by selecting values for x and completing a table. Although any value can be selected for x, values usually selected include −2, −1, 0, 1, and 2.

For example, to solve the equation $y = 2x$ given below in Exercise 1, first select values for x, then complete a table.

Ordered pair solutions for the equation $y = 2x$ include (−2, −4), (−1, −2), (0, 0), (1, 2), and (2, 4).

Match each equation with the point whose coordinates are a solution of the equation. Then, at the bottom of the page, write the letter of the point on the line directly above the number of the equation *each time it appears*. (The first one has been done as an example.) If you have matched the equations and solutions correctly, the letters below will reveal a message.

1. $y = 2x$	$A(-3, 8)$	$N(-1, 0)$
2. $y = x - 3$	$B(0, 2)$	$O(3, 0)$
3. $y = -x + 1$	$C(-2, 1)$	$P(1, 5)$
4. $y = 3x - 2$	$D(0, -5)$	$Q(0, 6)$
5. $y = -2x - 4$	$E(-1, -5)$	$R(1, 6)$
6. $y = x + (-2)$	$F(1, 3)$	$S(2, 1)$
7. $y = -4x - 1$	$G(0, -4)$	$T(-2, 3)$
8. $y = \frac{1}{2}x$	$H(-1, 3)$	$U(1, 2)$
9. $y = x + 3$	$I(2, 0)$	$V(-3, 5)$
10. $y = 7x + 7$	$J(0, 4)$	$W(0, -7)$
11. $y = -2x - 6$	$K(-3, 1)$	$X(-3, -3)$
12. $y = -x + 5$	$L(-4, 2)$	$Y(1, 8)$
13. $y = -5x + 8$	$M(-2, 2)$	$Z(0, -8)$
14. $y = -x$		

M A T H E M A T I C S   I S   T H E
14 12 3 7 4 14 12 3 6 9 8   6 8   3 7 4

L A N G U A G E   O F   S C I E N C E
11 12 10 5 1 12 5 4   2 13   8 9 6 4 10 9 4

*** Also available in Spanish** ELL

Additional Lesson Resources

Transparencies

- *5-Minute Check Transparency,* Lesson 1-10

Other Print Products

- *Noteables™ Interactive Study Notebook with Foldables™*

Teacher Tech Tools

- *Interactive Classroom CD-ROM,* Lesson 1-10
- *AssignmentWorks,* Lesson 1-10

Student Tech Tools

glencoe.com

- Extra Examples, Chapter 1, Lesson 10
- Self-Check Quiz, Chapter 1, Lesson 10

1-10 Algebra: Equations and Functions

MAIN IDEA

Make function tables and write equations.

IN Academic Standards

7.2.1 Use variables and appropriate operations to write an expression, **equation** or inequality **that represents a verbal description.** *Also addresses P.4.1, P.5.1, P.5.2.*

New Vocabulary

function
function rule
function table
domain
range

IN Math Online

glencoe.com
- Concepts In Motion
- Extra Examples
- Personal Tutor
- Self-Check Quiz

GET READY for the Lesson

MAGAZINES Suppose you can buy magazines for $4 each.

1. Copy and complete the table to find the cost of 2, 3, and 4 magazines.
2. Describe the pattern in the table between the cost and the number of magazines.

Number	Multiply by 4	Cost ($)
1	4×1	4
2	4×2	8
3	4×3	12
4	4×4	16

2. The cost increases by 4 each time the number of magazines increases by 1.

A relationship that assigns exactly one *output* value for each *input* value is called a **function**. In a function, you start with an input number, perform one or more operations on it, and get an output number. The operation performed on the input is given by the **function rule**.

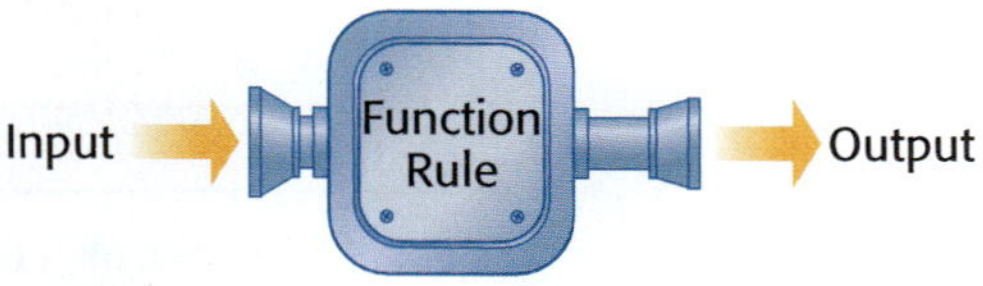

You can organize the input numbers, output numbers, and the function rule in a **function table**. The set of input values is called the **domain**, and the set of output values is called the **range**.

EXAMPLE Make a Function Table

1 **MONEY Javier saves $20 each month. Make a function table to show his savings after 1, 2, 3, and 4 months. Then identify the domain and range.**

Input	Function Rule	Output
Number of Months	Multiply by 20	Total Savings ($)
1	20×1	20
2	20×2	40
3	20×3	60
4	20×4	80

The domain is {1, 2, 3, 4}, and the range is {20, 40, 60, 80}.

CHECK Your Progress

a. See Ch. 1 Answer Appendix for table.

a. Suppose a student movie ticket costs $3. Make a function table that shows the total cost for 1, 2, 3, and 4 tickets. Then identify the domain and range. **domain: {1, 2, 3, 4}; range: {$3, $6, $9, $12}**

1-10 Lesson Notes

1 Focus

Vertical Alignment

Before Lesson 1-10
Solve problems involving linear functions with integer values and write the equation

Lesson 1-10
Write and evaluate an algebraic expression for a given situation, using up to three variables. Use a variety of methods to explain mathematical reasoning

After Lesson 1-10
Graph linear functions, noting that the vertical change per unit of horizontal change is always the same and know that the ratio is called the slope of a graph

2 Teach

Scaffolding Questions

Ask:
- If an insect has 6 legs, how many legs do 2 insects have altogether? 3 insects? 4 insects? 12, 18, 24
- If a zebra has 4 legs, how many legs do 2 zebras have altogether? 3 zebras? 4 zebras? 8, 12, 16
- If a camp stool has 3 legs, how many legs do 2 camp stools have altogether? 3 camp stools? 4 camp stools? 6, 9, 12

ADDITIONAL EXAMPLE

1 Asha earns $6.00 an hour working at a grocery store. Make a function table that shows Asha's total earnings for working 1, 2, 3, and 4 hours.

Tips for New Teachers

Braces

The symbols { and }, which are called braces, are used to list the elements in a set.

Additional Answer

1.

Number of Hours	Multiply by 6	Total Earnings ($)
1	6×1	6
2	6×2	12
3	6×3	18
4	6×4	24

Focus on Mathematical Content

A good way to explore functional relationships is to create a **function table**.

You can write a function as an **equation** with one variable representing the input number and a different variable representing the output number.

Formative Assessment

Use the Check Your Progress exercises after the Examples to determine students' understanding of concepts.

ADDITIONAL EXAMPLES

2 **READING** Melanie read 14 pages of a detective novel each hour. Write an equation using two variables to show how many pages p she read in h hours.
$p = 14h$

3 Use your equation to find how many pages Melanie read in 7 hours. 98 pages

Additional Examples are also in:

- Noteables™ Interactive Study Notebook with Foldables™
- Interactive Classroom PowerPoint® Presentations

Additional Answer

c. Sample answer: Replace h with 6 in the equation $g = 4h$ to find the growth in inches for this species of bamboo after 6 months.

Study Tip

Input and Output
When x and y are used in an equation, x usually represents the input, and y usually represents the output.

Functions are often written as equations with two variables—one to represent the input and one to represent the output. Here's an equation for the situation in Example 1.

$$20x = y$$

Function rule: multiply by 20
Input: number of months
Output: total savings

Study Tips offer students helpful information about the topics they are studying.

Real-World EXAMPLES

2 **ANIMALS** An armadillo sleeps 19 hours each day. Write an equation using two variables to show the relationship between the number of hours h an armadillo sleeps in d days.

Input	Function Rule	Output
Number of Days (d)	Multiply by 19	Number of Hours Slept (h)
1	1 × 19	19
2	2 × 19	38
3	3 × 19	57
d	d × 19	19d

Words: Number of hours slept equals number of days times 19 hours each day.

Variable: Let d represent the number of days. Let h represent the number of hours.

Equation: $h = 19d$

3 How many hours does an armadillo sleep in 4 days?

$h = 19d$ Write the equation.
$h = 19(4)$ Replace d with 4.
$h = 76$ Multiply.

An armadillo sleeps 76 hours in 4 days.

Real-World Career **How Does a Botanist Use Math?** A botanist gathers and studies plant statistics to solve problems and draw conclusions about various plants.

IN Math Online
For more information, go to glencoe.com.

CHECK Your Progress

BOTANIST A botanist discovers that a certain species of bamboo grows 4 inches each hour. b. $g = 4h$

b. Write an equation using two variables to show the relationship between the growth g in inches of this bamboo plant in h hours.

c. Use your equation to explain how to find the growth in inches of this species of bamboo after 6 hours. 24 in.; See margin for explanation.

★ indicates multi-step problem

CHECK Your Understanding

Example 1 (p. 63)

Copy and complete each function table. Then identify the domain and range.

1. $y = 3x$

x	3x	y
1	3 • 1	3
2	3 • 2	6
3	3 • 3	9
4	3 • 1	12

domain: {1, 2, 3, 4}; range: {3, 6, 9, 12}

2. $y = 4x$

x	4x	y
0	4 • 0	0
1	4 • 1	4
2	4 • 2	8
3	4 • 3	12

domain: {0, 1, 2, 3}; range: {0, 4, 8, 12}

★ 3. **MUSIC** Jonas downloads 8 songs each month onto his digital music player. Make a function table that shows the total number of songs downloaded after 1, 2, 3, and 4 months. Then identify the domain and range. **domain: {1, 2, 3, 4}; range: {8, 16, 24, 32}; See margin for table.**

Examples 2, 3 (p. 64)

SPORTS For Exercises 4 and 5, use the following information.

The top speed reached by a race car is 231 miles per hour.

4. Write an equation using two variables to show the relationship between the number of miles m that a race car can travel in h hours. $m = 231h$

5. Use your equation to explain how to find the distance in miles the race car will travel in 3 hours. **693 mi; See margin for explanation.**

Practice and Problem Solving

HOMEWORK HELP	
For Exercises	See Examples
6–10	1
11–14	2, 3

xercise Levels
: 6–14
: 15–23
: 24–28

. domain: {0, 1, 2, 3}; nge: {0, 2, 4, 6}
. domain: {1, 2, 3, 4}; nge: {6, 12, 18, 24}
. domain: {1, 2, 3, 4}; nge: {9, 18, 27, 36}

Copy and complete each function table. Then identify the domain and range.

6. $y = 2x$

x	2x	y
0	2 • 0	0
1	2 • 1	2
2	2 • 2	4
3	2 • 3	6

7. $y = 6x$

x	6x	y
1	6 • 1	6
2	6 • 2	12
3	6 • 3	18
4	6 • 4	24

8. $y = 9x$

x	9x	y
1	9 • 1	9
2	9 • 2	18
3	9 • 3	27
4	9 • 4	36

Make a function table for each situation. Then identify the domain and range. **9–10. See margin for tables.**

9. ★ **PIZZA** A pizza shops sells 25 pizzas each hour. Find the number of pizzas sold after 1, 2, 3, and 4 hours. **domain: {1, 2, 3, 4}; range: {25, 50, 75, 100}**

10. ★ **TYPING** Suppose you can type 60 words per minute. What is the total number of words typed after 5, 10, 15, and 20 minutes? **domain: {5, 10, 15, 20}; range: {300, 600, 900, 1,200}**

CELL PHONES For Exercises 11 and 12, use the following information.

A cell phone provider charges a customer $40 for each month of service.

11. Write an equation using two variables to show the relationship between the total amount charged c, after m months of cell phone service. $c = 40m$

12. Use your equation to explain how to find the total cost for 6 months of cell phone service. **$240; See margin for explanation.**

DIFFERENTIATED HOMEWORK OPTIONS

Level	Assignment	Two-Day Option	
BL Basic	6–14, 27–36	7–13 odd, 29, 30	6–10 even, 27, 28, 31–36
OL Core	7, 9–15, 17, 19–23, 27–36	6–14, 29, 30	15–23, 27, 28, 31–36
AL Advanced/Pre-AP	15–36		

3 Practice

Formative Assessment

Use Exercises 1–5 to check for understanding.

Then use the chart at the bottom of this page to customize your assignments for students.

Intervention You may wish to use the Study Guide and Intervention Master on page 68 of the *Chapter 1 Resource Masters* for additional reinforcement.

Odd/Even Assignments

Exercises 6–14 are structured so that students practice the same concepts whether they are assigned odd or even problems.

Additional Answers

3.

x	8x	y
1	8 • 1	8
2	8 • 2	16
3	8 • 3	24
4	8 • 4	32

5. Sample answer: Replace h with 3 in the equation $m = 231h$ to find the distance in miles the race car travels in 3 hours.

9.

x	25x	y
1	25 • 1	25
2	25 • 2	50
3	25 • 3	75
4	25 • 4	100

10.

x	60x	y
5	60 • 5	300
10	60 • 10	600
15	60 • 15	900
20	60 • 20	1,200

12. Sample answer: Replace m with 6 in the equation $c = 40m$ to find the total cost for 6 months of cell phone service.

Variables

Tips for New Teachers

You may wish to point out that mathematicians and scientists call *y* the *dependent variable* of a function because it depends on the input, or *independent variable*, *x*.

New teachers, or teachers new to teaching mathematics, may especially appreciate the **Tips for New Teachers**.

Additional Answers

14. Sample answer: Replace *m* with 15 in the equation $t = 35m$ to find the number of times a cricket will have chirped after 15 minutes at this temperature.

23. Sample answer: Replace *s* with 60 in the equation $m = 8s$ and in the equation $m = 19s$ to find the number of miles Jupiter travels in 1 minute and the number of miles Earth travels in 1 minute, respectively.

Real-World Link
Crickets are among the 800,000 different types of insects in the world.

INSECTS **For Exercises 13 and 14, use the following information.**

A cricket will chirp approximately 35 times per minute when the outside temperature is 72°F.

13. Write an equation using two variables to show the relationship between the total number of times a cricket will chirp *t*, after *m* minutes at this temperature. **$t = 35m$**

14. Use your equation to explain how to find the number of times a cricket will have chirped after 15 minutes at this temperature. **525 times; See margin for explanation.**

Copy and complete each function table. Then identify the domain and range.

15. domain: {1, 2, 3, 4}; range: {0, 1, 2, 3}
16. domain: {1, 2, 3, 4}; range: {6, 7, 8, 9}
17. domain: {0, 1, 2, 3}; range: {0.25, 1.25, 2.25, 3.25}
18. domain: {2, 3, 4, 5}; range: {0.5, 1.5, 2.5, 3.5}

15. $y = x - 1$

x	x − 1	y
1	1 − 1	0
2	2 − 1	1
3	3 − 1	2
4	4 − 1	3

16. $y = x + 5$

x	x + 5	y
1	1 + 5	6
2	2 + 5	7
3	3 + 5	8
4	4 + 5	9

17. $y = x + 0.25$

x	x + 0.25	y
0	0 + 0.25	0.25
1	1 + 0.25	1.25
2	2 + 0.25	2.25
3	3 + 0.25	3.25

18. $y = x - 1.5$

x	x − 1.5	y
2	2 − 1.5	0.5
3	3 − 1.5	1.5
4	4 − 1.5	2.5
5	5 − 1.5	3.5

MEASUREMENT **For Exercises 19 and 20, use the following information.**

The formula for the area of a rectangle with length 6 units is $A = 6w$.

19. Make a function table that shows the area in square units of a rectangle with a width of 2, 3, 4, and 5 units.

19.

w	6w	A
2	6 • 2	12
3	6 • 3	18
4	6 • 4	24
5	6 • 5	30

20. Study the pattern in your table. Explain how the area of a rectangle with a length of 6 units changes when the width is increased by 1 unit. **The area increases by 6 square units.**

ANALYZE TABLES **For Exercises 21–23, use the table that shows the approximate velocity of certain planets as they orbit the Sun.**

Orbital Velocity Around Sun	
Planet	Velocity (mi/s)
Mercury	30
Earth	19
Jupiter	8
Saturn	6
Neptune	5

21. Write an equation to show the relationship between the total number of miles *m* Jupiter travels in *s* seconds as it orbits the Sun. **$m = 8s$**

22. What equation can be used to show the total number of miles Earth travels? **$m = 19s$**

23. Use your equation to explain how to find the number of miles Jupiter and Earth each travel in 1 minute. **480 mi; 1,140 mi; See margin for explanation.**

Academic Standards • ISTEP+
Extra Practice, pp. 671, 704

66 **Chapter 1** Introduction to Algebra and Functions

H.O.T. Problems

CHALLENGE Write an equation for the function shown in each table.

24.

x	y
1	3
2	4
3	5
4	6

$y = x + 2$

25.

x	y
2	6
4	12
6	18
8	24

$y = 3x$

26.

x	y
1	3
2	5
3	7
4	9

$y = 2x + 1$

27. **OPEN ENDED** Write about a real-world situation that can be represented by the equation $y = 3x$. **See margin.**

28. **WRITING IN MATH** Explain the relationship among an *input*, an *output*, and a *function rule*. **You start with an input number, perform the operations in the function rule, and the result is the output number.**

ISTEP+ PRACTICE 7.2.1

29. The table shows the number of hand-painted T-shirts Mi-Ling can make after a given number of days.

Number of Days (x)	Total Number of T-Shirts (y)
1	6
2	12
3	18
4	24

Which function rule represents the data? **C**

A $y = 4x$
B $y = 5x$
C $y = 6x$
D $y = 12x$

30. Cristina needs to have 50 posters printed to advertise a community book fair. The printing company charges $3 to print each poster. Which table represents this situation? **G**

F

Posters	Cost ($)
3	3
6	6
9	9
p	p

H

Posters	Cost ($)
1	3
2	6
3	9
p	$3 + p$

G

Posters	Cost ($)
1	3
2	6
3	9
p	$3p$

J

Posters	Cost ($)
3	1
6	2
9	3
p	$p \div 3$

Spiral Review

31. **ALGEBRA** Write the next three terms of the sequence 27, 36, 45, 54, … (Lesson 1-9) **63, 72, 81**

Use the Distributive Property to rewrite each expression. Then evaluate it. (Lesson 1-8)

32. $5(9 + 7)$ **$5(9) + 5(7)$; 80**
33. $(12 + 4)4$ **$(12)4 + (4)4$; 64**
34. $8(7) - 8(2)$ **$8(7 - 2)$; 40**
35. $10(6) - 10(5)$ **$10(6 - 5)$; 10**

36. **ALLOWANCE** If Karen receives a weekly allowance of $8, about how much money in all will she receive in two years? (Lesson 1-1) **Sample answer: $8 × 50 × 2 or $800**

4 Assess

Yesterday's News Remind students that yesterday's lesson was about arithmetic sequences. Have students write how yesterday's concepts helped them with today's material.

Formative Assessment

Check for student understanding of concepts in Lessons 1-9 and 1-10.

CRM Quiz 4, p. 78

FOLDABLES Study Organizer Foldables™ Follow-Up

Suggest to students that they create a function table in their Foldables and label the domain, range, and rule.

Additional Answer

27. Sample answer: Sam charges $3 for each dog that he walks. In the equation $y = 3x$, x represents the number of dogs and y represents the total amount of money earned.

Extend 1-10 Lesson Notes

1 Focus

Materials

- graphing calculators

Teaching Tip

If your class does not have enough graphing calculators for every student, have students work in pairs or groups of three, sharing calculators.

2 Teach

Activity 1 If students have difficulty, have volunteers create a function table (such as in Lesson 1-10) on the chalkboard. Make sure everyone sees how the calculator performs the same work.

Additional Answer

1. 6 bottles; The table shows that 6 bottles will cost \$9.80 and 7 bottles will cost \$11.60. Since \$11.60 > \$10, you can only buy 6 bottles for \$10.

Extend 1-10

Graphing Calculator Lab
Functions and Tables

MAIN IDEA

Use technology to represent and compare functions.

IN Academic Standards

7.2.1 Use variables and appropriate operations to write an expression, **equation** or inequality **that represents a verbal description.** *Also addresses P.3.2, P.4.1, P.5.2, P.7.1.*

IN Math Online

glencoe.com

- Other Calculator Keystrokes

You can use a graphing calculator to represent functions.

ACTIVITY

1 **GROCERIES** **A grocery store has 12-ounce bottles of sports drink on sale for \$1.80 each, with no limit on how many you can buy. In addition, you can use a coupon for \$1 off one bottle. Make a table showing the cost for 3, 4, 5, 6, and 7 bottles of this drink.**

STEP 1 Write an equation to show the relationship between the number of bottles purchased x and their cost y.

Cost is \$1.80 per bottle less \$1.

$$y = 1.80x - 1$$

STEP 2 Press [Y=] on your calculator. Then enter the function into Y_1 by pressing 1.80 [X,T,θ,n] [–] 1 [ENTER].

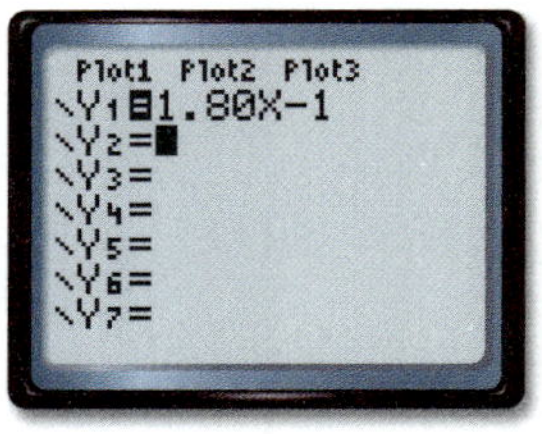

STEP 3 Next, set up a table of x- and y-values. Press [2nd] [TBLSET] to display the table setup screen. Then press [⇩] [⇩] [⇨] [ENTER] to highlight Indpnt: Ask.

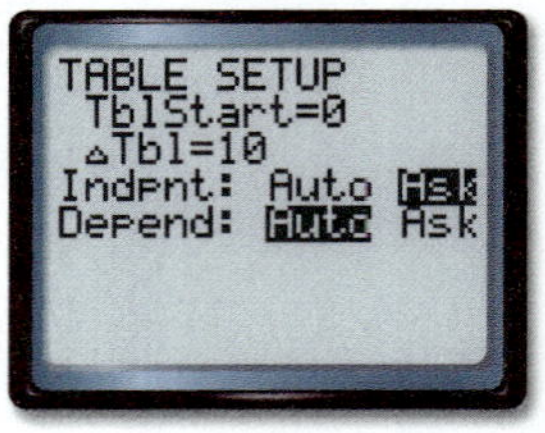

STEP 4 Access the table by pressing [2nd] [TABLE]. Then key in each number of bottles, pressing [ENTER] after each entry.

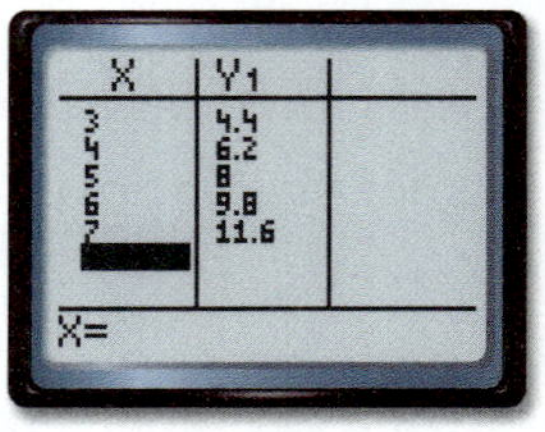

Analyze the Results

1. Analyze the table to determine how many bottles you can buy for \$10. Explain your reasoning. **See margin.**

2. **MAKE A CONJECTURE** Notice that you can purchase 5 bottles for the whole dollar amount of \$8. How many bottles will you be able to purchase for \$9, the next whole dollar amount? Use the calculator to test your conjecture. **5 bottles**

68 Chapter 1 Introduction to Algebra and Functions

eading Math

ne phrase $4.25 per person
eans $4.25 for each
erson.

ACTIVITY

2 **CAMPING** **Out-There Campground charges each group a camping fee of $20 plus $4.25 per person per night. Roughing-It Campground charges $6.25 per person per night. Make a table showing the one-night fee for 2, 3, 4, 5, and 6 people to camp at each campground.**

STEP 1 Write an equation to show the relationship between the number of people *x* and the one-night fee *y* for them to camp at each campground.

Out-There Campground

Fee is $20 plus $4.25 per person.

$$y = 20 + 4.25x$$

Roughing-It Campground

Fee is $6.25 per person.

$$y = 6.25x$$

STEP 2 Enter the function for the Out-There Campground into Y_1 and the function for the Roughing-It Campground into Y_2.

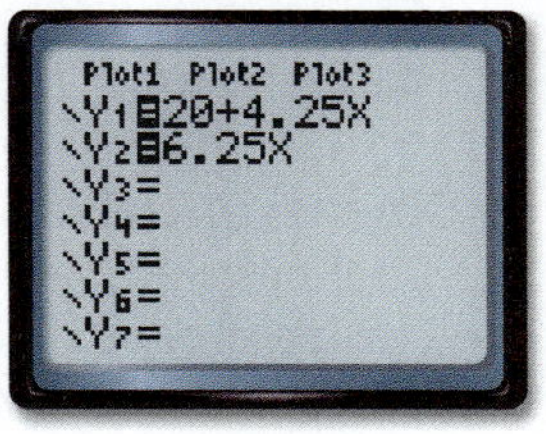

STEP 3 Next, set up a table of *x*- and *y*-values as in Activity 1.

STEP 4 Then access the table and key in each number of people. Notice that the calculator follows the order of operations multiplying each *x*-value by 4.25 first and then adding 20.

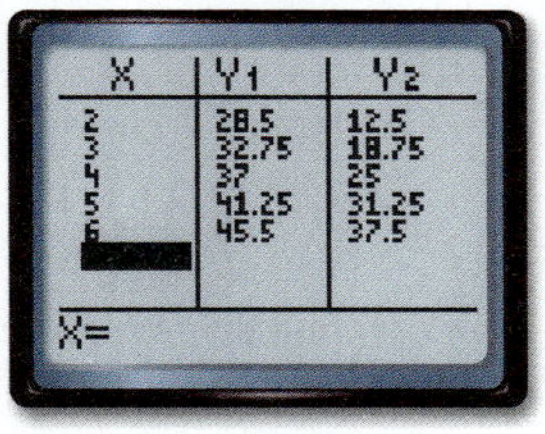

Analyze the Results

3. For 2, 3, 4, 5, and 6 people, which campground charges the greater total nightly cost to camp? **Out-There Campground**
4. **MAKE A CONJECTURE** Will the total nightly cost to camp at each campground ever be the same? If so, for what number of people?
5. Use the graphing calculator to test your conjecture from Exercise 4. Were you correct? If not, use the graphing calculator to guess and check until you find the correct number of people. **See students' work.**
6. If all other aspects of these two campgrounds are equal, write a recommendation as to which campground a group of *n* people should choose based on your cost analysis. **See margin.**

. **yes; 10 people**

Activity 2 Make sure students realize that the differences between each pair of fees (*y*-values) decrease as the number of people (*x*-values) increases.

3 Assess

Formative Assessment

Use Exercise 3 to determine whether students comprehend how to use a graphing calculator to write and compare functions.

From Concrete to Abstract
Use Exercise 4 to bridge the gap between using a graphing calculator to write functions and making conjectures about functions.

Extending the Concept Have students write their own word problems involving functions. Then have students exchange problems and use their graphing calculators to solve the problems.

Additional Answer

6. Sample answer: If *n* is less than 10, the Roughing-It Campground is cheaper. If *n* is greater than 10, the Out-There Campground is cheaper. If *n* equals 10, then both campgrounds charge the same fee, so it doesn't matter which campground the group chooses.

Extend 1-10 Graphing Calculator Lab: Functions and Tables **69**

Dinah Zike's Foldables

Foldables™ Study Organizer

Have students look through the chapter to make sure they have included notes in their Foldables for each lesson.

Encourage students to refer to their Foldables while completing the Study Guide and Review and while preparing for the Chapter Test.

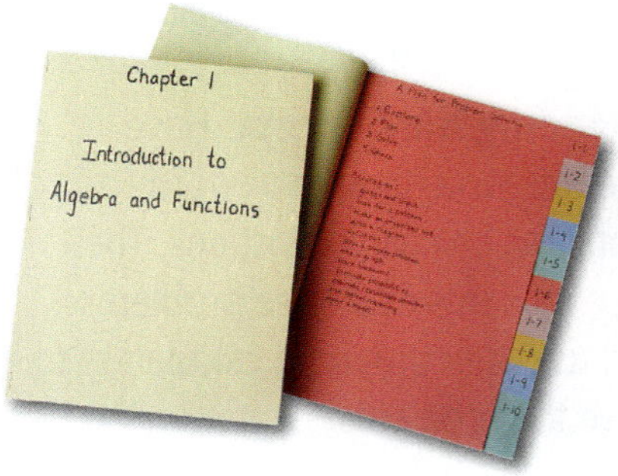

Formative Assessment

Key Vocabulary The page references after each word denote where that term was first introduced. If students have difficulty answering Exercises 1–7, remind them that they can use these page references to refresh their memories about the vocabulary terms.

IN Math Online glencoe.com

Vocabulary PuzzleMaker improves students' mathematics vocabulary using four puzzle formats–crossword, scramble, word search using a word list, and word search using clues. Students can work online or from a printed worksheet.

Summative Assessment

CRM Vocabulary Test, p. 80

Students can use the **Vocabulary Check** in the Study Guide and Review and the **Vocabulary PuzzleMaker** to review the vocabulary of the chapter.

Chapter 1 Study Guide and Review

IN Math Online glencoe.com
- STUDY TO GO
- Vocabulary Review

Foldables® Study Organizer — GET READY to Study

Be sure the following Big Ideas are noted in your Foldable.

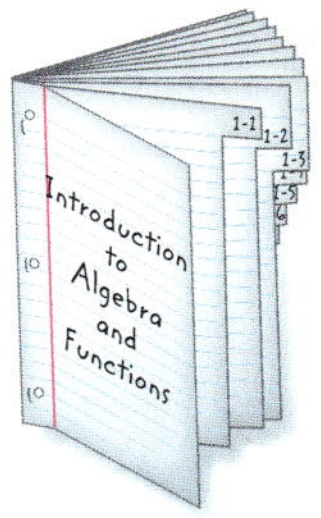

BIG Ideas

Squares and Square Roots (Lesson 1-3)
- The square of a number is the product of a number and itself.
- A square root of a number is one of its two equal factors.

Order of Operations (Lesson 1-4)
- Do all operations within grouping symbols first. Evaluate all powers before other operations. Multiply and divide in order from left to right. Add and subtract in order from left to right.

Properties (Lesson 1-8)
- Distributive Property
  $5(2 + 4) = 5 \cdot 2 + 5 \cdot 4$
  $(3 + 2)4 = 3 \cdot 4 + 2 \cdot 4$
- Commutative Property
  $3 + 2 = 2 + 3$
  $7 \cdot 4 = 4 \cdot 7$
- Associative Property
  $6 + (3 + 8) = (6 + 3) + 8$
  $5 \cdot (2 \cdot 3) = (5 \cdot 2) \cdot 3$
- Identity Property
  $4 + 0 = 4$
  $4 \cdot 1 = 4$

Functions (Lesson 1-10)
- A function is a relationship that assigns exactly one *output* value for each *input* value.
- In a function, the function rule gives the operation to perform on the input.

Key Vocabulary

- algebra (p. 44)
- algebraic expression (p. 44)
- arithmetic sequence (p. 57)
- base (p. 30)
- coefficient (p. 45)
- defining the variable (p. 50)
- domain (p. 63)
- equation (p. 49)
- equivalent expressions (p. 53)
- evaluate (p. 31)
- exponent (p. 30)
- factors (p. 30)
- function (p. 63)
- function rule (p. 63)
- numerical expression (p. 38)
- order of operations (p. 38)
- perfect square (p. 34)
- powers (p. 30)
- radical sign (p. 35)
- range (p. 63)
- sequence (p. 57)
- solution (p. 49)
- square (p. 34)
- square root (p. 35)
- term (p. 57)
- variable (p. 44)

Vocabulary Check

State whether each sentence is *true* or *false*. If *false*, replace the underlined word or number to make a true sentence.

1. Numerical expressions have the same value. **false; equivalent expressions**
2. Two or more numbers that are multiplied together are called powers. **false; factors**
3. The range of a function is the set of input values. **false; domain**
4. A function assigns exactly two *output* values for each *input* value. **false; one**
5. An equation is a sentence that contains an equals sign. **true**
6. A sequence is an ordered list of numbers. **tr**
7. The product of a number and itself is the square root of the number. **false; square**

Lesson-by-Lesson Review

1-1 A Plan for Problem Solving (pp. 25–29)

.1.1

Use the four-step plan to solve each problem.

8. **PHONE CALLS** When Tamik calls home from college, she talks ten minutes per call for 3 calls each week. How many minutes does she use in a 15-week semester? **450 min**

9. **RUNNING** Darren runs at a rate of 6 feet per second, and Kim runs at a rate of 7 feet per second. If they both start a race at the same time, how far apart are they after one minute? **60 ft**

10. **WORK** Alan was paid \$9 per hour and earned \$128.25. How many hours did he work? **14.25 h**

Example 1 **One quart of paint covers 40 square feet of wall space. Brock uses 5 quarts of paint to cover his walls. How many square feet did Brock paint?**

Understand Brock uses 5 quarts of paint, each covering 40 square feet.

Plan Multiply 40 by 5.

Solve $40 \cdot 5 = 200$
Brock painted 200 square feet.

Check $200 \div 5 = 40$, so the answer is reasonable.

1-2 Powers and Exponents (pp. 30–33)

.1.2

Write each power as a product of the same factor.

11. 3^4 **$3 \cdot 3 \cdot 3 \cdot 3$**
12. 9^6 **$9 \cdot 9 \cdot 9 \cdot 9 \cdot 9 \cdot 9$**
13. 5^1 **5**
14. 7^5 **$7 \cdot 7 \cdot 7 \cdot 7 \cdot 7$**
15. Write *5 to the fourth power* as a product of the same factor. **$5 \cdot 5 \cdot 5 \cdot 5$**

Evaluate each expression.

16. 3^5 **243**
17. 7^9 **40,353,607**
18. 2^8 **256**
19. 18^2 **324**
20. 10^4 **10,000**
21. 100^1 **100**
22. Write $15 \cdot 15 \cdot 15$ in exponential form. **15^3**
23. **PATHS** At the edge of a forest, there are two paths. At the end of each path, there are two additional paths. If at the end of each of those paths there are two more paths, how many paths are there at the end? **8**

Example 2 **Write 2^3 as a product of the same factor.**

The base is 2. The exponent 3 means that 2 is used as a factor 3 times.

$2^3 = 2 \cdot 2 \cdot 2$

Example 3 **Evaluate 4^5.**

The base is 4. The exponent 5 means that 4 is used as a factor 5 times.

$4^5 = 4 \cdot 4 \cdot 4 \cdot 4 \cdot 4$
$= 1,024$

Chapter 1 Study Guide and Review

Lesson-by-Lesson Review

Intervention If the given examples are not sufficient to review the topics covered by the questions, remind students that the page references tell them where to review that topic in their textbooks.

Two-Day Option Have students complete the Lesson-by-Lesson Review on pages 71–74. Then you can use ExamView® Assessment Suite to customize another review worksheet that practices all the objectives of this chapter or only the objectives on which your students need more help.

For more information on ExamView® Assessment Suite, see page 22C.

Differentiated Instruction

Super DVD: MindJogger Plus
Use this DVD as an alternative format of review for the test. For more information on this game show format, see page 22D.

Students can complete the exercises in the **Lesson-by-Lesson Review** as they prepare for the chapter test. If they need extra help, examples are provided.

CHAPTER 1 Study Guide and Review

1-3 Squares and Square Roots (pp. 34–37)

7.1.5

Find the square of each number.

24. 4 **16**
25. 13 **169**

Find each square root.

26. $\sqrt{81}$ **9**
27. $\sqrt{324}$ **18**

28. **MEASUREMENT** The area of a certain kind of ceramic tile is 25 square inches. What is the length of one side? **5 in.**

Example 4 **Find the square of 15.**

$15 \cdot 15 = 225$ Multiply 15 by itself.

Example 5 **Find the square root of 441.**

$21 \cdot 21 = 441$, so $\sqrt{441} = 21$.

1-4 Order of Operations (pp. 38–41)

7.1.7, 7.2.3

Evaluate each expression.

29. $24 - 8 + 3^2$ **25**
30. $48 \div 6 + 2 \cdot 5$ **18**
31. $9 + 3(7 - 5)^3$ **33**
32. $15 + 9 \div 3 - 7$ **11**

33. **SEATING** In planning for a ceremony, 36 guests need to be seated with 4 guests per table. An additional 12 guests need to be seated with 3 guests per table. Write an expression to determine how many tables are needed. Then evaluate the expression. **$36 \div 4 + 12 \div 3$; 13**

Example 6 **Evaluate $24 - (8 \div 4)^4$.**

$24 - (8 \div 4)^4 = 24 - 2^4$ Divide 8 by 4.

$= 24 - 16$ Find the value of 2^4.

$= 8$ Subtract.

1-5 PSI: Guess and Check (pp. 42–43)

P.1.3, P.1.4

Solve. Use the *guess and check* strategy.

34. **TRAVEL** Lucinda is driving away from Redding at 50 miles per hour. When she is 100 miles away, Tom leaves Redding, driving at 60 miles per hour in the same direction. After how many hours will Tom pass Lucinda? **10 h**

35. **FARMING** A farmer sells a bushel of soybeans for \$5 and a bushel of corn for \$3. If he hopes to earn \$164 and plans to sell 40 bushels in all, how many bushels of soybeans does he need to sell? **22**

Example 7 **Find two numbers with a product of 30 and a difference of 13.**

Make a guess, and check to see if it is correct. Then adjust the guess until it is correct.

5 and 6	$5 \cdot 6 = 30$ and $6 - 5 = 1$ incorrect
3 and 10	$3 \cdot 10 = 30$ and $10 - 3 = 7$ incorrect
2 and 15	$2 \cdot 15 = 30$ and $15 - 2 = 13$ correct

The two numbers are 2 and 15.

72 Chapter 1 Introduction to Algebra and Functions

Mixed Problem Solving
For mixed problem-solving practice, see page 704.

CHAPTER 1 Study Guide and Review

1-6 Algebra: Variables and Expressions (pp. 44–47)

.2.1

Evaluate each expression if $a = 10$, $b = 4$, and $c = 8$.

36. $(a - b)^2$ **36**
37. $ab \div c$ **5**
38. $3b^2 + c$ **56**
39. $\frac{(b + c)^2}{3}$ **48**
40. **CLOTHING** The cost of buying h hats and s shirts is given by the expression $\$5.75h + \$8.95s$. Find the cost of purchasing 3 hats and 5 shirts. **$62**

Example 8 Evaluate $2m^2 - 5n$ if $m = 4$ and $n = 3$.

$2m^2 - 5n = 2(4)^2 - 5(3)$ Replace m with 4 and n with 3.

$= 2(16) - 5(3)$ Find the value of 4^2.

$= 32 - 15$ Multiply.

$= 17$ Subtract.

1-7 Algebra: Equations (pp. 49–52)

.2.2, .6.6

Solve each equation mentally.

41. $h + 9 = 17$ **8**
42. $31 - y = 8$ **23**
43. $\frac{t}{9} = 12$ **108**
44. $100 = 20g$ **5**
45. **COUNTY FAIRS** Five friends wish to ride the Ferris wheel, which requires 3 tickets per person. The group has a total of 9 tickets. Write and solve an equation to find the number of additional tickets needed for everyone to ride the Ferris wheel. **$9 + x = 15$; 6 tickets**

Example 9 Solve $14 = 5 + x$ mentally.

$14 = 5 + x$ Write the equation.

$14 = 5 + 9$ You know that $5 + 9 = 14$.

$14 = 14$ Simplify.

The solution is 9.

1-8 Algebra: Properties (pp. 53–56)

.1.7, .2.3

Find each expression mentally. Justify each step. **46–48. See margin for justification.**

46. $(25 \cdot 15) \cdot 4$ **1,500**
47. $14 + (38 + 16)$ **68**
48. $8 \cdot (11 \cdot 5)$ **440**
49. **ROSES** Wesley sold roses in his neighborhood for $2 a rose. He sold 15 roses on Monday and 12 roses on Tuesday. Use the Distributive Property to mentally find the total amount Wesley earned. Explain your reasoning. **$2(15 + 12); $54 See margin for explanation.**

Example 10 Find $8 + (17 + 22)$ mentally. Justify each step.

$8 + (17 + 22)$

$= 8 + (22 + 17)$ Commutative Property of Addition

$= (8 + 22) + 17$ Associative Property of Addition

$= 30 + 17$ or 47 Add 30 and 17 mentally.

Additional Answers

46. Sample answer: Rewrite $(25 \cdot 15) \cdot 4$ as $(15 \cdot 25) \cdot 4$ using the Commutative Property of Multiplication. Rewrite $(15 \cdot 25) \cdot 4$ as $15 \cdot (25 \cdot 4)$ using the Associative Property of Multiplication. Find $25 \cdot 4$, or 100, mentally. Then find $15 \cdot 100$, or 1,500, mentally.

47. Sample answer: Rewrite $14 + (38 + 16)$ as $14 + (16 + 38)$ using the Commuative Property of Addition. Rewrite $14 + (16 + 38)$ as $(14 + 16) + 38$ using the Associative Property of Addition. Find $14 + 16$, or 30, mentally. Then find $30 + 38$, or 68, mentally.

48. Sample answer: Rewrite $8 \cdot (11 \cdot 5)$ as $8 \cdot (5 \cdot 11)$ using the Commutative Property of Multiplication. Rewrite $8 \cdot (5 \cdot 11)$ as $(8 \cdot 5) \cdot 11$ using the Associative Property of Multiplication. Find $8 \cdot 5$, or 40, mentally. Then find $40 \cdot 11$, or 440, mentally.

49. Sample answer: The expression $15 + 12$ represents the total number of roses Wesley sold. The expression $\$2(15 + 12)$ represents the total amount of money Wesley earned. Since $\$2 \times 15 = \$30$ and $\$2 \times 12 = \$24$, find $\$30 + \$24$, or $54, to find the total amount Wesley earned.

Problem Solving Review

For additional practice in problem solving for Chapter 1, see the Mixed Problem Solving Appendix, page 704 in the Student Handbook section.

Anticipation Guide

Have students complete the Chapter 1 Anticipation Guide and discuss how their responses have changed now that they have completed Chapter 1.

CRM Anticipation Guide, p. 7

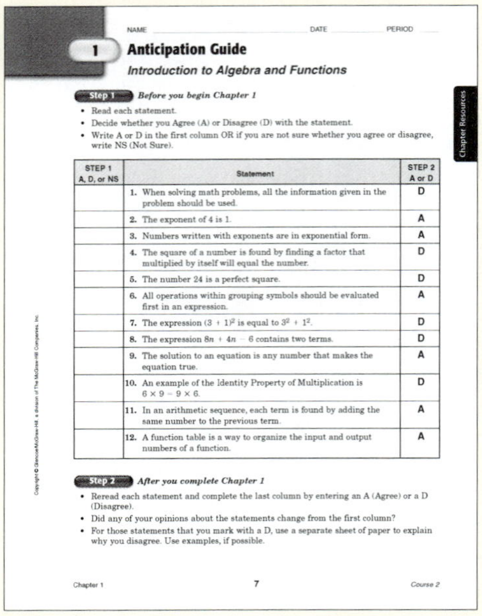

NAME ______ DATE ______ PERIOD ______

1 Anticipation Guide

Introduction to Algebra and Functions

Step 1 *Before you begin Chapter 1*

- Read each statement.
- Decide whether you Agree (A) or Disagree (D) with the statement.
- Write A or D in the first column OR if you are not sure whether you agree or disagree, write NS (Not Sure).

STEP 1 A, D, or NS	Statement	STEP 2 A or D
	1. When solving math problems, all the information given in the problem should be used.	D
	2. The exponent of 4 is 1.	A
	3. Numbers written with exponents are in exponential form.	A
	4. The square of a number is found by finding a factor that multiplied by itself will equal the number.	D
	5. The number 24 is a perfect square.	D
	6. All operations within grouping symbols should be evaluated first in an expression.	A
	7. The expression $(3 + 1)^2$ is equal to $3^2 + 1^2$.	D
	8. The expression $8n + 4n - 6$ contains two terms.	D
	9. The solution to an equation is any number that makes the equation true.	A
	10. An example of the Identity Property of Multiplication is $6 \times 9 = 9 \times 6$.	D
	11. In an arithmetic sequence, each term is found by adding the same number to the previous term.	A
	12. A function table is a way to organize the input and output numbers of a function.	A

Step 2 *After you complete Chapter 1*

- Reread each statement and complete the last column by entering an A (Agree) or a D (Disagree).
- Did any of your opinions about the statements change from the first column?
- For those statements that you mark with a D, use a separate sheet of paper to explain why you disagree. Use examples, if possible.

Chapter Resources

Chapter 1 7 Course 2

Additional Answers

50. Each term is found by adding 6 to the previous term; 33, 39, 45

51. Each term is found by adding 0.8 to the previous term; 6.6, 7.4, 8.2

52. Each term is found by adding 7 to the previous term; 35, 42, 49

56.

x	$32x$	y
3	32(3)	96
4	32(4)	128
5	32(5)	160
6	32(6)	192

CHAPTER 1 Study Guide and Review

1-9 Algebra: Arithmetic Sequences (pp. 57–61)

7.2.1

Describe the relationship between the terms in each arithmetic sequence. Then find the next three terms in each sequence. 50–52. See margin.

50. 3, 9, 15, 21, 27, ...

51. 2.6, 3.4, 4.2, 5, 5.8, ...

52. 0, 7, 14, 21, 28, ...

MONEY For Exercises 53 and 54, use the following information.

Tanya collected $4.50 for the first car washed at a band fund-raiser. After the second and third cars were washed, the donations totaled $9 and $13.50, respectively.

53. If this donation pattern continues, what algebraic expression can be used to find the amount of money earned for any number of cars washed? **$4.50n**

54. How much money will be collected after a total of 8 cars have been washed? **$36**

Example 11 **At the end of day 1, Sierra read 25 pages of a novel. By the end of days 2 and 3, she read a total of 50 and 75 pages, respectively. If the pattern continues, what expression will give the total number of pages read after any number of days?**

Make a table to display the sequence.

Position	Operation	Value of Term
1	1 • 25	25
2	2 • 25	50
3	3 • 25	75
n	n • 25	$25n$

Each term is 25 times its position number. So, the expression is $25n$.

1-10 Algebra: Equations and Functions (pp. 63–67)

7.2.1

Copy and complete the function table. Then identify the domain and range.

55. $y = 4x$

x	$4x$	y
5	4(5)	20
6	4(6)	24
7	4(7)	28
8	4(8)	32

The domain is {5, 6, 7, 8}. The range is {20, 24, 28, 32}.

56. **NAME TAGS** Charmaine can make 32 name tags per hour. Make a function table that shows the number of name tags she can make in 3, 4, 5, and 6 hours. **See margin.**

Example 12 **Create and complete a function table for $y = 3x$. Then identify the domain and range.**

Select any four values for the input x.

x	$3x$	y
3	3(3)	9
4	3(4)	12
5	3(5)	15
6	3(6)	18

The domain is {3, 4, 5, 6}. The range is {9, 12, 15, 18}.

*Six forms of **chapter tests**, a **Vocabulary Test**, and an **Extended-Response Test** are provided for each chapter. These are available in the Chapter Resource Masters.*

IN Math Online glencoe.com
• Chapter Test

1. **PIZZA** Ms. Carter manages a pizza parlor. The average daily cost is \$40, plus \$52 to pay each employee. It also costs \$2 to make each pizza. If 42 pizzas were made one day, requiring the work of 7 employees, what was her total cost that day? **\$488**

Write each power as a product of the same factor. Then evaluate the expression.

2. 3^5 **3 • 3 • 3 • 3 • 3; 243**

3. 15^4 **15 • 15 • 15 • 15; 50,625**

4. **MEASUREMENT** Gregory wants to stain the 15-foot-by-15-foot deck in his backyard. One can of stain covers 200 square feet of surface. Is one can of stain enough to cover his entire deck? Explain your reasoning. **No; 15 × 15 = 225. Since 225 > 200, one can is not enough.**

Find each square root.

5. $\sqrt{121}$ **11**

6. $\sqrt{900}$ **30**

7. **MULTIPLE CHOICE** What is the value of $8 + (12 \div 3)^3 - 5 \times 9$? **C**

A 603
B 135
C 27
D 19

8. **ANIMALS** Sally has 6 pets, some dogs and some birds. Her animals have a total of 16 legs. How many of each pet does Sally have? **4 birds and 2 dogs**

Evaluate each expression if $x = 12$, $y = 5$, and $z = 3$.

9. $x - 9$ **3**

10. $8y$ **40**

11. $(y - z)^3$ **8**

12. $\dfrac{xz}{y + 13}$ **2**

Solve each equation mentally.

13. $9 + m = 16$ **7**

14. $d - 14 = 37$ **51**

15. $32 = \dfrac{96}{t}$ **3**

16. $6x = 126$ **21**

17. **SAVINGS** Deb is saving \$54 per month to buy a new camera. Use the Distributive Property to mentally find how much she has saved after 7 months. Explain. **See margin.**

Find each expression mentally. Justify each step.

18. $13 + (34 + 17)$ **64**

19. $50 \cdot (17 \cdot 2)$ **1,700**

18–19. See Ch. 1 Answer Appendix for justification.

20. **MULTIPLE CHOICE** The table shows the number of hours Teodoro spent studying for his biology test over four days. If the pattern continues, how many hours will Teodoro study on Sunday? **H**

Day	Study Time (hours)
Monday	0.5
Tuesday	0.75
Wednesday	1.0
Thursday	1.25

F 1.5 hours
G 1.75 hours
H 2.0 hours
J 2.5 hours

Describe the relationship between the terms in each arithmetic sequence. Then write the next three terms in the sequence.

21. 7, 16, 25, 34, … **See margin.**

22. 59, 72, 85, 98, … **See margin.**

23. **TRAVEL** Beth drove at the rate of 65 miles per hour for several hours. Make a function table that shows her distance traveled after 2, 3, 4, and 5 hours. Then identify the domain and range. **domain: {2, 3, 4, 5}; range: {130, 195, 260, 325}; See margin for table.**

MONEY **For Exercises 24 and 25, use the following information.**

Anthony earns extra money after school doing yard work for his neighbors. He charges \$12 for each lawn he mows.

24. Write an equation using two variables to show the relationship between the number of lawns mowed m and number of dollars earned d. **$d = 12m$**

25. Then find the number of dollars earned if he mows 14 lawns. **\$168**

CHAPTER 1 Practice Test

Summative Assessment

Chapter 1 Resource Masters

Leveled Chapter 1 Tests			
Form	**Type**	**Level**	**Pages**
1	MC	BL	81–82
2A	MC	OL	83–84
2B	MC	OL	85–86
2C	FR	OL	87–88
2D	FR	OL	89–90
3	FR	AL	91–92

MC = multiple-choice questions
FR = free-response questions
BL = below or approaching grade level
OL = on grade level
AL = above or beyond grade level

- Vocabulary Test, p. 80
- Extended-Response Test, p. 93

ExamView Assessment Suite Customize and create multiple versions of your chapter test and their answer keys. All of the questions from the leveled chapter tests in the *Chapter 1 Resource Masters* are also available on ExamView Assessment Suite.

Additional Answers

17. The number 54 can be written as 50 + 4. You know that 7 • 50 = 350 and 7 • 4 = 28. Mentally adding 350 and 28 you get \$378.

21. Add 9 to each term; 43, 52, 61

22. Add 13 to each term; 111, 124, 137

23.

x	$65x$	y
2	65 • 2	130
3	65 • 3	195
4	65 • 4	260
5	65 • 5	325

Data-Driven Decision Making

Diagnostic Teaching Based on the results of the Chapter 1 Practice Test, use the following to review concepts that students continue to find challenging.

Exercises	Lesson	Academic Standards	Resources for Review
1–6	1-1, 1-2, 1-3	P.1.1, 7.1.2, 7.1.5	Study Guide and Intervention pp. 48, 54, 61, and 68
7–12	1-4, 1-5, 1-6	7.1.7, P.1.3, P.1.5, 7.2.1	IN Math Online glencoe.com
13–19	1-7, 1-8	P.6.6, 7.1.7, 7.2.3	• Extra Examples • Personal Tutor
20–25	1-9, 1-10	7.2.1	• Concepts in Motion

CHAPTER 1 ISTEP+ Practice

Formative Assessment

You can use these two pages to benchmark student progress.

Chapter 1 Resource Masters

- Standardized Test Practice, pp. 94–96

ExamView Assessment Suite Create practice worksheets or tests that align to your state's standards, as well as TIMSS and NAEP tests.

CHAPTER 1 ISTEP+ Practice

IN Math Online glencoe.cc

- Test Practice

PART 1 Multiple Choice

Read each question. Then fill in the correct answer on the answer document provided by your teacher or on a sheet of paper.

1. A store owner bought some paperback books and then sold them for $4.50 each. He sold 35 books on Monday and 52 books on Tuesday. What piece of information is needed to find the amount of profit made from sales on Monday and Tuesday? **D**

   A Number of books sold on Wednesday

   B Number of hardback books sold on Monday and Tuesday

   C Total number of paperback books sold

   D How much the owner paid for each of the paperback books

2. The table shows the number of milkshakes sold at an ice cream shop each day last week.

Day of Week	Number of Milkshakes
Sunday	31
Monday	9
Tuesday	11
Wednesday	15
Thursday	18
Friday	24
Saturday	28

   Which statement does *not* support the data? **H**

   F There were almost three times as many milkshakes sold on Sunday as on Tuesday.

   G There were half as many milkshakes sold on Monday as on Thursday.

   H There were 11 more milkshakes sold on Tuesday than on Saturday.

   J The total number of milkshakes sold during the week was 136.

3. Which description shows the relationship between the value of a term and n, its position in the sequence? **C**

Position	1	2	3	4	5	n
Value of Term	3	6	9	12	15	

   A Add 2 to n.

   B Divide n by 3.

   C Multiply n by 3.

   D Subtract n from 2

TEST-TAKING TIP

Question 3 Have students eliminate unlikely answer choices. Since the value of each term is greater than its position, eliminate answer choices B and D.

4. Andrew spent $\frac{1}{2}$ of his Saturday earnings o a pair of jeans and $\frac{1}{2}$ of the remaining amount on a DVD. After he spent $7.40 on lunch, he had $6.10 left. How much did Andrew earn on Saturday? **H**

   F $13.50

   G $27

   H $54

   J $108

5. Lemisha drove an average of 50 miles per hour on Sunday, 55 miles per hour on Monday, and 53 miles per hour on Tuesday. If s represents the number of hours she drove on Sunday, m represents the number of hours she drove on Monday, and t represents the number of hours she drove on Tuesday, which of the following expressions gives the total distance Lemish traveled? **C**

   A $50s + 53m + 55t$

   B $55s + 50m + 53t$

   C $50s + 55m + 53t$

   D $53s + 55m + 50t$

76 **Chapter 1** Introduction to Algebra and Functions

The items in the **Test Practice** give students an opportunity to practice the kinds of questions found on state assessments. The **Need Extra Help?** box allows students to diagnose and address weaknesses.

Preparing for ISTEP+

For test-taking strategies and practice, see pages 716–733.

Chapter 1 ISTEP+ Practice

6. Mrs. Albert drove 850 miles and the average price of gasoline was \$2.50 per gallon. What information is needed to find the amount Mrs. Albert spent on gasoline for the trip? **H**

F Number of hours the trip took

G Number of miles per hour traveled

H Average number of miles the car traveled per gallon of gasoline

J Average number of miles Mrs. Albert drove per day

7. Mr. Thompson wants to estimate the total amount he spends on insurance and fuel for his car each month. Insurance costs about \$300 per month, and he expects to drive an average of 150 miles per week. What else does he need to estimate his monthly expenses? **B**

A The cost of fuel and the one-way distance to work

B The cost of fuel and the number of miles per gallon his car gets

C The cost of fuel and his weekly pay

D The gallons of fuel needed per week

8. Jeremy bought 3 hamburgers at \$1.99 each, 2 orders of onion rings at \$0.89 each, and 4 soft drinks at \$1.25 each. He paid 6.75% tax on the whole order. What other information is necessary to find Jeremy's correct change? **J**

F Total cost of the order

G Amount he paid in tax

H Reason for buying the food

J Amount he gave the cashier

PART 2 Short Response/Grid In

Record your answers on the answer sheet provided by your teacher or on a sheet of paper.

9. Emily bought 2.5 pounds of salami for \$1.99 per pound. About how much did she pay? **between \$4.50 and \$5.50**

10. How do you correctly evaluate the expression $4 \times (5 + 4) - 27$? **Add first, since 5 + 4 is in parentheses.**

11. What value of t makes the following equation true? **288**

$$t \div 6 = 48$$

12. Use the Distributive Property to rewrite $4(3 + 5)$. **12 + 20**

PART 3 Extended Response

Record your answers on the answer sheet provided by your teacher or on a sheet of paper. Show your work.

13. **GEOMETRY** The first and fifth terms of a toothpick sequence are shown below.

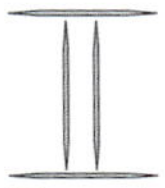

Term 1

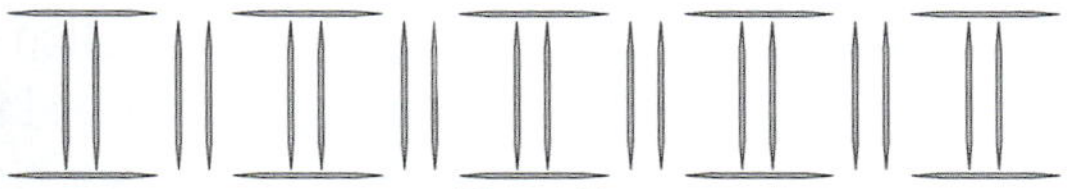

Term 5

a. What might the third term look like? **See margin.**

b. Write a rule that connects the term number and the number of toothpicks in your sequence. **$6x - 2$**

NEED EXTRA HELP?													
If You Missed Question...	1	2	3	4	5	6	7	8	9	10	11	12	13
Go to Lesson...	1-1	1-1	1-9	1-1	1-6	1-1	1-1	1-1	1-1	1-4	1-6	1-8	1-9
IN Academic Standards	P.1.1	P.1.1	7.2.1	P.1.1	7.2.1	P.1.1	P.1.1	P.1.1	P.1.1	7.2.3	7.2.1	7.2.3	7.2.1

Chapter 1 ISTEP+ Practice

Answer Sheet Practice

Have students simulate taking a standardized test by recording their answers on a practice recording sheet.

CRM Student Recording Sheet, p. 75

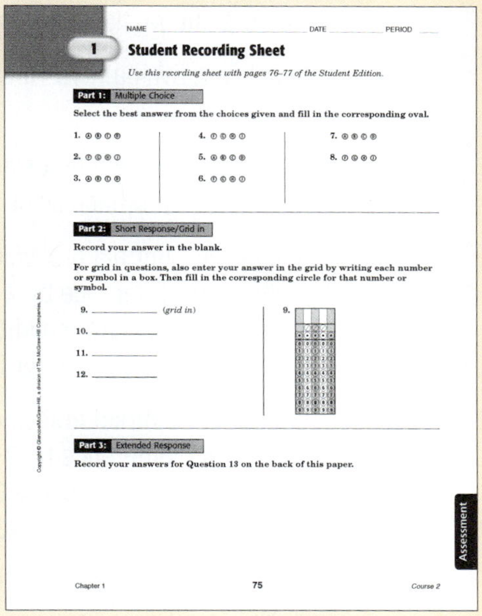
NAME DATE PERIOD

1 Student Recording Sheet

Use this recording sheet with pages 76–77 of the Student Edition.

Part 1: Multiple Choice

Select the best answer from the choices given and fill in the corresponding oval.

Part 2: Short Response/Grid In

Record your answer in the blank.

For grid in questions, also enter your answer in the grid by writing each number or symbol in a box. Then fill in the corresponding circle for that number or symbol.

Part 3: Extended Response

Record your answers for Question 13 on the back of this paper.

Chapter 1 75 Course 2

A Student Recording Sheet is provided for each chapter in the Chapter Resource Masters.

13a.

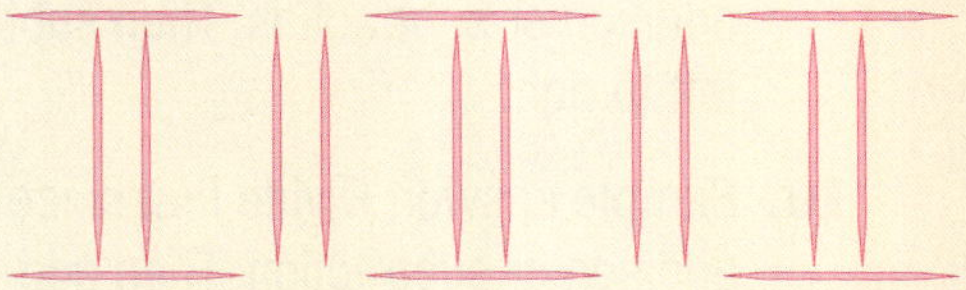

Page 40, Lesson 1-4

1. Sample answer: Subtract first since 5 − 2 is in parentheses. Then add 8.

2. Sample answer: Subtract first since 9 − 4 is in parentheses. Then divide 25 by 5.

3. Sample answer: Multiply 2 by 6 first since multiplication comes before addition or subtraction. Then subtract and add in order from left to right.

4. Sample answer: Multiply 8 by 5 and 4 by 3 since multiplication comes before subtraction. Then subtract.

5. Sample answer: Evaluate 10^2 first since it is a power. Then multiply by 4.

6. Sample answer: Subtract first since 4 − 1 is in parentheses. Next, square the difference since 2 is a power. Finally, divide.

7. Sample answer: Subtract first since 6 − 3 is in parentheses. Then multiply the difference by 2 and multiply 3 by 4 since multiplication comes before addition or subtraction. Finally, add 17 + 6 and subtract 12 in order from left to right.

8. Sample answer: Subtract first since 8 − 2 is in parentheses. Then multiply the difference by 3 and divide 12 by 4 since multiplication and division come before addition or subtraction. Finally, subtract 22 and 18 and add 3.

10. Sample answer: Add first since 1 + 8 is in parentheses. Then multiply by 3.

11. Sample answer: Add first since 3 + 4 is in parentheses. Then subtract.

12. Sample answer: Divide first since 25 ÷ 5 is in parentheses. Then add.

13. Sample answer: Subtract first since 11 − 2 is in parentheses. Then divide.

14. Sample answer: Multiply 3 by 2 first and then divide 14 by 7 since multiplication and division come before addition. Then add.

15. Sample answer: Divide first since division comes before addition or subtraction. Then subtract 1 and add 7 in order from left to right.

16. Sample answer: Divide first since division comes before addition or subtraction. Then add 12 and subtract 4.

17. Sample answer: Multiply first since multiplication comes before addition or subtraction. Then subtract the product from 118 and add 5.

18. Sample answer: Evaluate 10^2 first since it is a power. Then multiply by 6.

19. Sample answer: Evaluate 10^4 first since it is a power. Then multiply by 3.

20. Sample answer: Evaluate 4^3 first since it is a power. Then multiply by 5 since multiplication comes before addition. Finally, add.

21. Sample answer: Evaluate 7^2 first since it is a power. Then multiply by 8 since multiplication comes before subtraction. Finally, subtract.

22. Sample answer: Evaluate 6^2 first since it is a power. Then divide 8 by 2 and multiply the quotient by 6 since multiplication and division occur from left to right. Finally, add.

23. Sample answer: Evaluate 9^2 since it is a power. Then divide 14 by 7 and multiply the quotient by 3 since multiplication and division occur from left to right. Finally, subtract.

24. Sample answer: Add first since 17 + 3 and 4 + 1 are in parentheses. Then divide.

25. Sample answer: Add first since 6 + 5 is in parentheses. Then subtract 6 from 8 since 8 − 6 is in parentheses. Finally, multiply.

26. Sample answer: Subtract first since 4 − 1 is in parentheses. Then multiply the difference by 2 and multiply 4 by 9 since multiplication comes before addition. Finally, add.

27. Sample answer: Add first since 4 + 7 is in parentheses. Then multiply the sum by 3. Next, multiply 5 by 4 and divide the product by 2 since multiplication and division occur in order from left to right. Finally, subtract.

30. Sample answer: Add first since 2 + 10 is in parentheses. Next, square the sum since 2 is a power. Then divide by 4.

31. Sample answer: Evaluate 3^3 first since it is a power. Then add 8. Next subtract 6 from 10 since 10 − 6 is in parentheses. Then square the difference since the power is 2. Finally subtract 16 from 35.

32. Sample answer: Add first since 5.2 + 3.8 is in parentheses. Since multiplication and division occur from left to right, multiply 3 by 4 and then multiply the product, 12, by 9. Finally, add 2.7 since addition and subtraction occur from left to right.

33. Sample answer: Subtract first since 4 − 3.2 is in parentheses. Multiply 7 by 9 next since multiplication occurs from left to right. Then subtract 0.8 from the product, 63, and add 1.8 since addition and subtraction occur from left to right.

Page 42, Lesson 1-5

2. Sample answer: Julia scored 16 points in a basketball game. She missed 18 of her 28 attempts. All of her shots were either one- or two-point shots. How many one-and two point shots did Julia make?

Understand: We know how many points Julia scored and can find how many shots she made.

Plan: Let's make a guess until we get the correct answer.

Solve: Julia had 28 – 18 = 10 successful shots. Make a guess.
5 one-point and 5 two-point 5(1) + 5(2) = 15 *too low*
4 one-point and 6 two-point 4(1) + 6(2) = 16 *correct*
Julia had 4 one-point and 6 two-point shots.

Check: 4 one-point shots are 4 points, and 6 two-point shots are 12 points. Since 4 + 12 = 16 points and 4 + 6 + 18 = 28 attempts, the guess is correct.

Page 44, Lesson 1-6 (Mini Lab)

1.

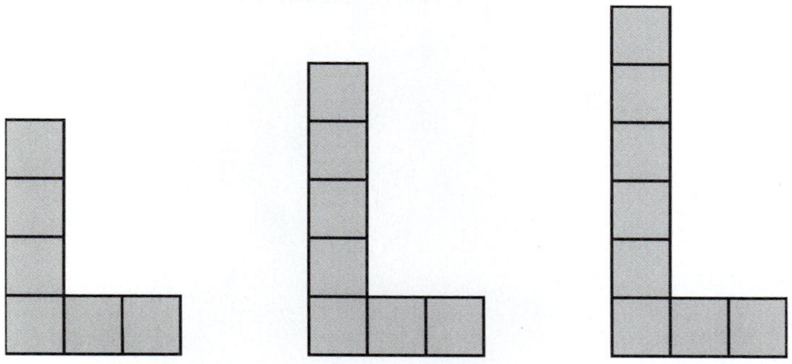

3. 12; See students' work.

4. The number of squares is two more than the figure number.

Page 54, Lesson 1-8

d. Sample answer: Rewrite 40 • (7 • 5) as 40 • (5 • 7) using the Commutative Property of Multiplication. Then rewrite 40 • (5 • 7) as (40 • 5) • 7 using the Associative Property of Multiplication. Find 40 • 5, or 200, mentally. Then find 200 • 7, or 1,400, mentally.

e. Sample answer: Rewrite (89 + 15) + 1 as (15 + 89) + 1 using the Commutative Property of Addition. Then rewrite (15 + 89) + 1 as 15 + (89 + 1) using the Associative Property of Addition. Find 89 + 1, or 90, mentally. Then find 15 + 90, or 105, mentally.

Page 55, Lesson 1-8

5. The expression 12 + 5 represents the cost of one ticket and one hot dog. The expression 4(12 + 5) represents the cost of four tickets and four hot dogs. Since 4 × 12 = 48 and 4 × 5 = 20, find 48 + 20, or 68, to find the total cost of four tickets and four hot dogs.

6. The expression 60 + 5 represents the cheetah's maximum speed. The expression 2(60 + 5) represents how far the cheetah could run in 2 hours at maximum speed. Since 2 × 60 = 120 and 2 × 5 = 10, find 120 + 10, or 130, to find the distance the cheetah could run in 2 hours.

13. Sample answer: Rewrite (8 + 27) + 52 as (27 + 8) + 52 using the Commutative Property of Addition. Rewrite (27 + 8) + 52 as 27 + (8 + 52) using the Associative Property of Addition. Find 8 + 52, or 60, mentally. Then find 60 + 27, or 87, mentally.

14. Sample answer: Rewrite (13 + 31) + 17 as (31 + 13) + 17 using the Commutative Property of Addition. Rewrite (31 + 13) + 17 as 31 + (13 + 17) using the Associative Property of Addition. Find 13 + 17, or 30, mentally. Then find 30 + 31, or 61, mentally.

15. Sample answer: Rewrite 91 + (15 + 9) as 91 + (9 + 15) using the Commutative Property of Addition. Rewrite 91 + (9 + 15) as (91 + 9) + 15 using the Associative Property of Addition. Find 91 + 9, or 100, mentally. Then find 100 + 15, or 115, mentally.

16. Sample answer: Rewrite 85 + (46 + 15) as 85 + (15 + 46) using the Commutative Property of Addition. Rewrite 85 + (15 + 46) as (85 + 15) + 46 using the Associative Property of Addition. Find 85 + 15, or 100, mentally. Then find 100 + 46, or 146, mentally.

17. Sample answer: Rewrite (4 • 18) • 25 as (18 • 4) • 25 using the Commutative Property of Multiplication. Rewrite (18 • 4) • 25 as 18 • (4 • 25) using the Associative Property of Multiplication. Find 4 • 25, or 100, mentally. Then find 100 • 18, or 1,800, mentally.

18. Sample answer: Rewrite (5 • 3) • 8 as (3 • 5) • 8 using the Commutative Property of Multiplication. Rewrite (3 • 5) • 8 as 3 • (5 • 8) using the Associative Property of Multiplication. Find 5 • 8, or 40, mentally. Then find 40 • 3, or 120, mentally.

19. Sample answer: Rewrite 15 • (8 • 2) as 15 • (2 • 8) using the Commutative Property of Multiplication. Rewrite 15 • (2 • 8) as (15 • 2) • 8 using the Associative Property of Multiplication. Find 15 • 2, or 30, mentally. Then find 30 • 8, or 240, mentally.

20. Sample answer: Rewrite 2 • (16 • 50) as 2 • (50 • 16) using the Commutative Property of Multiplication. Rewrite 2 • (50 • 16) as (2 • 50) • 16 using the Associative Property of Multiplication. Find 2 • 50, or 100, mentally. Then find 100 • 16, or 1,600, mentally.

21. Sample answer: Rewrite 5 • (30 • 12) as 5 • (12 • 30) using the Commutative Property of Multiplication. Rewrite 5 • (12 • 30) as (5 • 12) • 30 using the Associative Property of Multiplication. Find 5 • 12, or 60, mentally. Then find 60 • 30, or 1,800, mentally.

22. Sample answer: Rewrite 20 • (48 • 5) as 20 • (5 • 48) using the Commutative Property of Multiplication. Rewrite 20 • (5 • 48) as (20 • 5) • 48 using the Associative Property of Multiplication. Find 20 • 5, or 100, mentally. Then find 100 • 48, or 4,800, mentally.

23. Sample answer: The expression 20 + 7 represents the number of millions of people who visit Paris each year. The expression 5(20 + 7) represents the number of millions of people who visit Paris over a five-year period. Since 5 × 20 = 100 and 5 × 7 = 35, find 100 + 35, or 135, to find the number of millions of people who visit Paris over a five-year period.

24. Sample answer: The expression 100 + 8 represents the time, in seconds, to ride the roller coaster. The expression 3(100 + 8) represents the time, in seconds, to ride the roller coaster three times. Since 3 × 100 = 300 and 3 × 8 = 24, find 300 + 24, or 324 to find the time in seconds to ride the roller coaster three times.

Page 62, Extend 1-9

1. 3; add 3 to the previous row's number of toothpicks

3.

Figure Number	Number of Toothpicks
1	3
2	6
3	9
4	12
5	15
6	18
7	21

4. $3n$

6. 31; Evaluate the expression $3n + 1$ for $n = 10$. $3(10) + 1 = 31$.

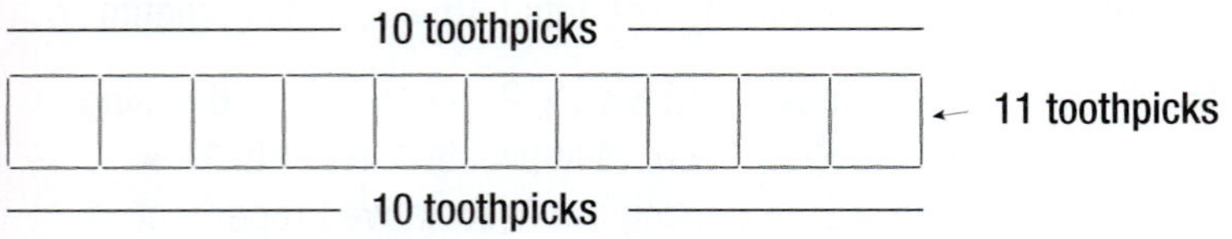

7. $2n + 2$; 26; Sample answer: The number of toothpicks on the top and bottom of each figure is always twice the figure number ($2n$), but there are always two toothpicks added on either side of the figure ($+2$), so Figure n will have $2n + 2$ toothpicks. Evaluating $2n + 2$ for $n = 12$ gives $2(12) + 2$ or 26.

Page 63, Lesson 1-10

a.

Number of Tickets	Multiply by 3	Total Cost ($)
1	1×3	3
2	2×3	6
3	3×3	9
4	4×3	12

Page 75, Chapter 1 Practice Test

18. Sample answer: Rewrite $13 + (34 + 17)$ as $13 + (17 + 34)$ using the Commutative Property of Addition. Rewrite $13 + (17 + 34)$ as $(13 + 17) + 34$ using the Associative Property of Addition. Find $13 + 17$, or 30, mentally. Then find $30 + 34$, or 68, mentally.

19. Sample answer: Rewrite $(50 \bullet 17) \bullet 2$ as $(17 \bullet 50) \bullet 2$ using the Commutative Property of Multiplication. Rewrite $(17 \bullet 50) \bullet 2$ as $17 \bullet (50 \bullet 2)$ using the Associative Property of Multiplication. Find $50 \bullet 2$, or 100, mentally. Then find $17 \bullet 100$, or 1,700, mentally.

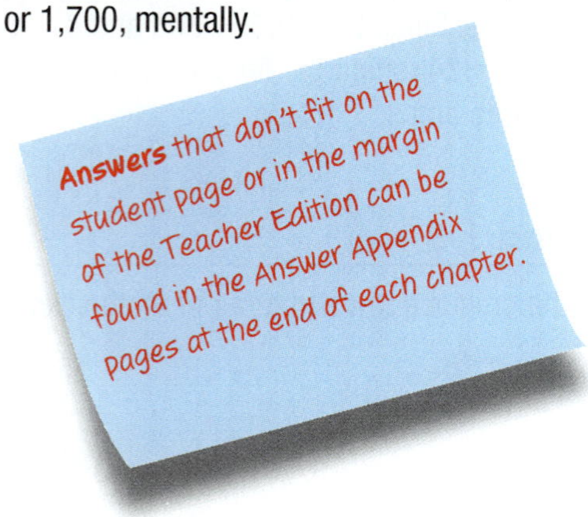

NOTES

CHAPTER 2

Chapter Overview

Integers

Lesson Plan		Pacing Your Lessons	
LESSONS AND OBJECTIVES	**Academic Standards**	**40–50 Minute Periods**	**90-Minute Periods**
2-1 Integers and Absolute Value (pp. 80–83) • Read and write integers, and find the absolute value of a number.	7.1.6 Core Lesson	1	0.5
2-2 Comparing and Ordering Integers (pp. 84–87) • Compare and order integers.	7.1.6 Core Lesson	1	0.5
2-3 The Coordinate Plane (pp. 88–92) • Graph points on a coordinate plane.	7.3.2	1	0.5
Explore 2-4 Algebra Lab: Adding Integers (pp. 93–94) • Use counters to model the addition of integers. **2-4 Adding Integers** (pp. 95–99) • Add integers.	6.1.5	1.5	0.5
Explore 2-5 Algebra Lab: Subtracting Integers (pp. 101–102) • Use counters to model the subtraction of integers. **2-5 Subtracting Integers** (pp. 103–106) • Subtract integers.	6.1.5	1.5	0.5
2-6 Multiplying Integers (pp. 107–111) • Multiply Integers.	7.1.7 Core Lesson	1	0.5
2-7 Problem-Solving Investigation: Look for a Pattern (pp. 112–113) • Solve problems by looking for a pattern.	P.1.3, P.1.4 Core Lesson	1	0.5
2-8 Dividing Integers (pp. 114–118) • Divide integers.	7.1.7 Core Lesson	1	0.5
REVIEW		1	0.5
ASSESSMENT		1	0.5*
	TOTAL	**11**	**5**

The complete ***Assessment Planner*** *for Chapter 2 is provided on page 79.*

** Begin Chapter 3 in the second half of the period.*

Focal Points

G7-FP3 Number and Operations
For the complete wording of the Focal Points for Grade 7, please see page T17.

Professional Development

Vertical Alignment

Before Chapter 2

Related Topics from Grade 6

- identify and represent on a number line positive and negative integers
- add with negative integers; subtract positive integers from negative integers

Chapter 2

Topics from Grade 7

- compare and order positive and negative fractions, decimals, and mixed numbers and place them on a number line
- use graphs to explain mathematical reasoning
- solve addition, subtraction, multiplication, and division problems, including those arising in concrete situations, that use positive and negative integers and combinations of these operations

After Chapter 2

Preparation for Grade 8

- understand the meaning of the absolute value of a number; interpret the absolute value as the distance of the number from zero on a number line; and determine the absolute value of real numbers
- read, write and compare rational numbers in scientific notation with approximate numbers using scientific notation
- graph linear functions, noting that the vertical change per unit of horizontal change is always the same and know that the ratio is called the slope of a graph
- add, subtract, multiply, and divide rational numbers and take positive rational numbers to whole-number powers

Backmapping and Vertical Alignment

McGraw-Hill's ***Math Connects*** was conceived and developed with the final results in mind: student success in Algebra 1 and beyond. The authors, using the **NCTM Focal Points and Focal Connections** as their guide, developed this brand-new series by backmapping from Algebra 1 concepts, and vertically aligning the topics so that they build upon prior skills and concepts and serve as a foundation for future topics.

What the Research Says...

According to Kalathil and Sherin in *Role of Students' Representations in the Mathematics Classroom,* student-created representations can help teachers understand individual student thinking and be instructional tools to illustrate various solution methods.

- In Lessons 2-1, 2-2, 2-4, and 2-5, students make number lines to represent integers and to add and subtract integers.

Professional Development

Targeted professional development has been articulated throughout **McGraw-Hill's *Math Connects*** program. The **McGraw-Hill Professional Development Video Library** provides short videos that support the NCTM Focal Points and Focal Connections. For more information, visit glencoe.com.

Model Lessons

Instructional Strategies

CHAPTER 2 Technology Solutions

Teacher Resources

TeacherWorks™ All-in-One Planner and Resource Center

All of the print materials from the Classroom Resource Masters are available on your TeacherWorks™ CD-ROM.

BL = Below or Approaching Grade Level OL = On Grade Level AL = Above or Beyond Grade Level ELL = English Language Learner

				Chapter Resource Masters	2-1	2-2	2-3	2-4	2-5	2-6	2-7	2-8
BL	OL		ELL	Lesson Reading Guide	9	16	22	29	36	42		52
BL	OL		ELL	Study Guide and Intervention*	10	17	23	30	37	43	48	53
BL	OL			Skills Practice*	11	18	24	31	38	44	49	54
	OL	AL		Practice*	12	19	25	32	39	45	50	55
	OL	AL		Word Problem Practice*	13	20	26	33	40	46	51	56
	OL	AL		Enrichment	14	21	27	34	41	47		57
	OL	AL		Calculator and Spreadsheet Activities	15		28	35				
	OL	AL		Chapter Assessments*	59–80							
BL	OL	AL		5-Minute Check Transparencies	✓	✓	✓	✓	✓	✓	✓	✓
BL	OL			Teaching Mathematics with Manipulatives			✓	✓	✓	✓		
BL	OL	AL		Real-World Investigations for Differentiated Instruction	27–29							

Also available in Spanish.

Graphing Calculator Easy Files

- Timesaving Tech Tools for the TI-Navigator:
- **Quick Checks** to diagnose student progress
- Motivate students with **Concept Launchers**
- Deliver differentiated instruction with **Ready Files**
- **Vocabulary Review**

AssignmentWorks

Differentiated Assignments, Answers, and Solutions

- Print a customized assignment worksheet using the Student Edition exercises along with an answer key or worked-out solutions.
- Use default lesson assignments as outlined in the Differentiated Homework Options in the Teacher Edition.

Interactive Classroom

This CD-ROM is a customizable Microsoft® PowerPoint® presentation that includes:

- In-Class Examples
- Your Turn Exercises*
- 5-Minute Check Transparencies*
- Links to Online Study Tools
- Concepts in Motion

compatible with response pad technology

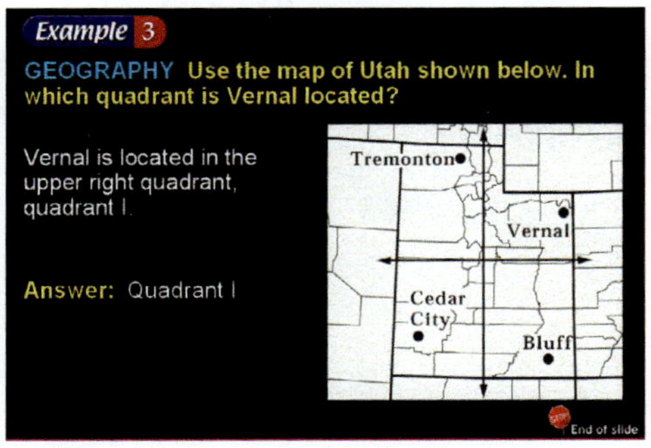

ExamView® Assessment Suite

ExamView® Assessment Suite

- Create, edit, and customize tests and worksheets using QuickTest Wizard
- Create multiple versions of tests and modify them for a desired level of difficulty
- Translate from English to Spanish and vice versa
- Build tests aligned with your state standards
- Track students' progress using the Teacher Management System

Professional Development

Vertical Alignment

Before Chapter 2

Related Topics from Grade 6

- identify and represent on a number line positive and negative integers
- add with negative integers; subtract positive integers from negative integers

Chapter 2

Topics from Grade 7

- compare and order positive and negative fractions, decimals, and mixed numbers and place them on a number line
- use graphs to explain mathematical reasoning
- solve addition, subtraction, multiplication, and division problems, including those arising in concrete situations, that use positive and negative integers and combinations of these operations

After Chapter 2

Preparation for Grade 8

- understand the meaning of the absolute value of a number; interpret the absolute value as the distance of the number from zero on a number line; and determine the absolute value of real numbers
- read, write and compare rational numbers in scientific notation with approximate numbers using scientific notation
- graph linear functions, noting that the vertical change per unit of horizontal change is always the same and know that the ratio is called the slope of a graph
- add, subtract, multiply, and divide rational numbers and take positive rational numbers to whole-number powers

Backmapping and Vertical Alignment

McGraw-Hill's ***Math Connects*** was conceived and developed with the final results in mind: student success in Algebra 1 and beyond. The authors, using the **NCTM Focal Points and Focal Connections** as their guide, developed this brand-new series by backmapping from Algebra 1 concepts, and vertically aligning the topics so that they build upon prior skills and concepts and serve as a foundation for future topics.

What the Research Says...

According to Kalathil and Sherin in *Role of Students' Representations in the Mathematics Classroom,* student-created representations can help teachers understand individual student thinking and be instructional tools to illustrate various solution methods.

- In Lessons 2-1, 2-2, 2-4, and 2-5, students make number lines to represent integers and to add and subtract integers.

Professional Development

Targeted professional development has been articulated throughout **McGraw-Hill's *Math Connects*** program. The **McGraw-Hill Professional Development Video Library** provides short videos that support the NCTM Focal Points and Focal Connections. For more information, visit glencoe.com.

Model Lessons

Instructional Strategies

Technology Solutions

Teacher Resources

TeacherWorks™ All-in-One Planner and Resource Center

All of the print materials from the Classroom Resource Masters are available on your TeacherWorks™ CD-ROM.

BL = Below or Approaching Grade Level OL = On Grade Level AL = Above or Beyond Grade Level ELL = English Language Learner

				Chapter Resource Masters	2-1	2-2	2-3	2-4	2-5	2-6	2-7	2-8
BL	OL		ELL	Lesson Reading Guide	9	16	22	29	36	42		52
BL	OL		ELL	Study Guide and Intervention*	10	17	23	30	37	43	48	53
BL	OL			Skills Practice*	11	18	24	31	38	44	49	54
	OL	AL		Practice*	12	19	25	32	39	45	50	55
	OL	AL		Word Problem Practice*	13	20	26	33	40	46	51	56
	OL	AL		Enrichment	14	21	27	34	41	47		57
	OL	AL		Calculator and Spreadsheet Activities	15		28	35				
	OL	AL		Chapter Assessments*	59–80							
BL	OL	AL		5-Minute Check Transparencies	✓	✓	✓	✓	✓	✓	✓	✓
BL	OL			Teaching Mathematics with Manipulatives			✓	✓	✓	✓		
BL	OL	AL		Real-World Investigations for Differentiated Instruction	27–29							

Also available in Spanish.

Graphing Calculator Easy Files

- Timesaving Tech Tools for the TI-Navigator:
- **Quick Checks** to diagnose student progress
- Motivate students with **Concept Launchers**
- Deliver differentiated instruction with **Ready Files**
- **Vocabulary Review**

AssignmentWorks

Differentiated Assignments, Answers, and Solutions

- Print a customized assignment worksheet using the Student Edition exercises along with an answer key or worked-out solutions.
- Use default lesson assignments as outlined in the Differentiated Homework Options in the Teacher Edition.

Interactive Classroom

This CD-ROM is a customizable Microsoft® PowerPoint® presentation that includes:

- In-Class Examples
- Your Turn Exercises*
- 5-Minute Check Transparencies*
- Links to Online Study Tools
- Concepts in Motion

compatible with response pad technology

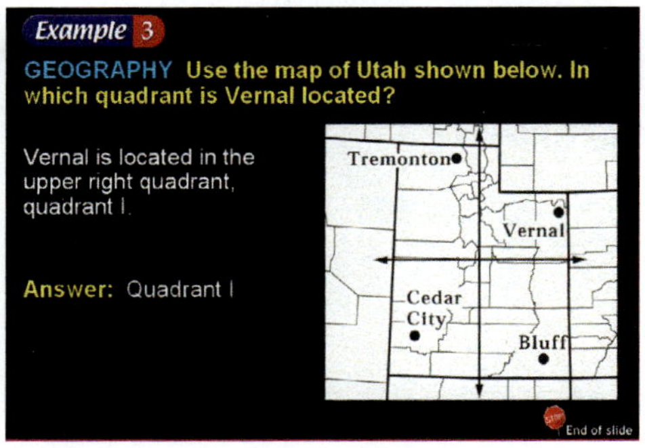

ExamView® Assessment Suite

ExamView® Assessment Suite

- Create, edit, and customize tests and worksheets using QuickTest Wizard
- Create multiple versions of tests and modify them for a desired level of difficulty
- Translate from English to Spanish and vice versa
- Build tests aligned with your state standards
- Track students' progress using the Teacher Management System

Student Tools

StudentWorks™ Plus

Textbook, Audio, Workbooks, and more

This CD-ROM is a valuable resource for students to access content online and use online resources to continue learning Chapter 2 concepts. Includes:

- Complete Student Editions in both English and Spanish
- English audio integrated throughout the text
- Links to Concepts in Motion, Personal Tutor, and other online resources
- Access to all student worksheets
- Daily Assignments and Grade Log

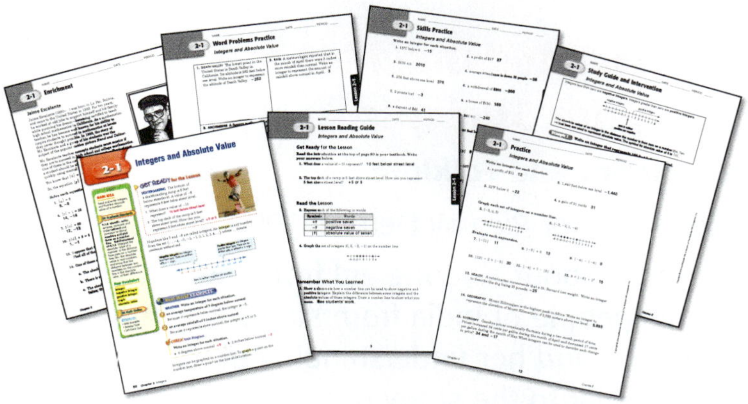

Super DVD

The Super DVD contains two Glencoe multimedia products.

MindJogger Plus An alternative review of concepts in which students work as teams in a game show format to gain points for correct answers.

What's Math Got to Do With It? Real-Life Math Videos
Engaging video that shows students how math is used in everyday situations.

Internet Resources

IN Math Online glencoe.com

TEACHER	STUDENT	PARENT	Online Study Tools
	•	•	Online Student Edition
•	•	•	Multilingual Glossary
			Lesson Resources
	•	•	Extra Examples
	•	•	BrainPOPS
	•	•	Self-Check Quizzes
•	•	•	Concepts in Motion
	•	•	Other Calculator Keystrokes
	•	•	Real-World Careers
	•	•	Reading in the Content Area
•			Group Activity Cards
			Chapter Resources
	•	•	Family Letters and Activities
	•		Chapter Readiness Quiz
	•	•	Vocabulary Review
	•	•	Chapter Test
	•	•	Standardized Test Practice
			Unit Resources
•	•		WebQuest Project
			Other Resources
	•		Personal Tutor
•			NAEP Correlations
•			Key Concepts
•	•	•	Meet the Authors
•	•		Game Zone
•	•	•	Math Skills Maintenance
•			National Resources (Professional Organizations)
•			State Resources
•			Vocabulary PuzzleMakers

CHAPTER 2 Reading and Writing in Mathematics

Noteables™ Interactive Study Notebook with Foldables™

This workbook is a study organizer that provides helpful steps for students to follow to organize their notes for Chapter 2.

- Students use Noteables to record notes and to complete their Foldables as you present the material for each lesson.
- Noteables correspond to the Examples in the *Teacher Edition* and *Interactive Classroom CD-ROM.*

Real-World Problem Solving Graphic Novels

Mathematical problem solving is presented in a motivating, graphic novel format. The novels contain real-world problems for each of the following mathematical strands: Number Sense, Algebraic Thinking, Geometry, Measurement, Statistics and Probability, and Mathematical Reasoning.

READING in the Content Area

This online worksheet provides strategies for reading and analyzing Lesson 2-2, Comparing and Ordering Integers. Students are guided through questions about the main idea, subject matter, supporting details, conclusion, clarifying details, and vocabulary of the lesson.

glencoe.com

Recommended Outside Reading for Students

Mathematics and Folklore

- *One Grain of Rice* by Demi ©1997 [fiction]

This book is about a young girl from India who saved the people of India from starvation through her cunningness and her understanding of math. The math is similar to the study of powers of numbers and patterns found in Chapter 1.

Project CRISS℠ STUDY SKILL

A pre-reading organizer can help students examine their background knowledge before they begin to study a new topic. The pre-reading organizer at the right shows the background a student might have for the lesson on integers and absolute value. Have students skim through a lesson and note any familiar concepts. Then have them complete a pre-reading organizer based on their individual experiences. Students can use their organizers as the basis for a discussion of the topics presented in the lesson.

Topic	What I Already Know
integers	• positive and negative numbers and zero • graphing points on number lines
absolute value	• always a nonnegative number • distances on number lines

CReating Independence through Student-owned Strategies

Differentiated Instruction

Investigative Approach

MathScape™

This project was supported, in part, by the
National Science Foundation

MathScape is a mathematics curriculum for grades 6–8 developed by the Seeing and Thinking Mathematically Project at the Education Development Center.

Writing and Solving Equations
Exploring the Unknown

How to Use *MathScape* with Chapter 2

The unit *Exploring the Unknown* can be used to enhance Lessons 2-4 and 2-5.

- **Enrich** ⟶ After you complete **Lessons 2-4 and 2-5**, you can use the activity on page 192 and 193 to reinforce operations with integers.

RTI (Response to Intervention)

TIER 1 **On-Level Instruction** Use the *Math Connects* program as instruction for your on-level students.

TIER 2 **Strategic Intervention** For options to instruct struggling students, refer to the Diagnostic Assessment table on page 79.

TIER 3 **Intensive Intervention** *Math Triumphs* can provide intensive intervention for students who are at risk of not meeting the objectives addressed in Chapter 1.

Diagnose student readiness with the Quick Check and Quick Review on page 79. Then use *Math Triumphs* to accelerate their achievement.

Integers

Prerequisite Skill	*Math Triumphs*
Whole Numbers and Integers	Chapter 8
Integer Operations	Chapter 9

Practice and Review

Quick Review Math Handbook* is Glencoe's mathematical handbook for students and parents.

Hot Words includes a glossary of terms.

Hot Topics consists of two parts:

- explanations of key mathematical concepts
- exercises to check students' understanding.

Lesson	Hot Topics Section	Lesson	Hot Topics Section
2-1	1•5	2-5	1•5
2-2	1•1, 1•5	2-7	1•5
2-3	6•7	2-8	1•5
2-4	1•5		

**Also available in Spanish*

CHAPTER 2

Notes

FOLDABLES™ Study Organizer

Dinah Zike's Foldables

Focus This Foldable is designed to help students organize the information they learn about integers.

Teach After students make their Foldables, have them label pages with the titles of the lessons of the chapter. Students should use their Foldables to take notes, define terms, record key concepts, write examples, and describe how the subject matter relates to everyday life. Encourage students to record what they learn about difficult parts of each lesson.

When to Use It As students study each lesson in the chapter, they should record their notes on the appropriate page of their Foldables.

A version of a completed Foldable is shown on p. 119.

Differentiated Instruction

CRM Student-Built Glossary, p. 1

Students complete the chart by providing a definition for each term and an example as they progress through Chapter 2.

This study tool can be used to review for the chapter test.

Materials Needed for Chapter 2

- graph paper (Lesson 2-3)
- integer counters (Explore 2-4 and 2-5 and Lessons 2-7 and 2-8)
- integer mat (Explore 2-4 and 2-5 and Lessons 2-7 and 2-8)

CHAPTER 2

Integers

Indiana Academic Standards

7.1.6 Identify, write, rename, compare and order rational and common irrational numbers and plot them on a number line.
7.1.7 Solve problems that involve multiplication and division with integers, fractions, decimals and combinations of the four operations.

Key Vocabulary

graph (p. 80)
integer (p. 80)
negative integer (p. 80)
positive integer (p. 80)

Real-World Link

Sports In miniature golf, a score above par can be written as a positive integer and a score below par can be written as a negative integer.

FOLDABLES® Study Organizer

Integers Make this Foldable to help you organize your notes. Begin with two sheets of $8\frac{1}{2}$" by 11" paper.

1. **Fold** one sheet in half from top to bottom. Cut along fold from edges to margin.

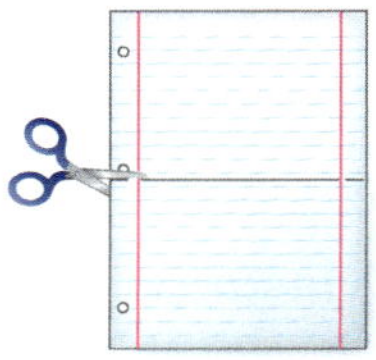

2. **Fold** the other sheet in half from top to bottom. Cut along fold between margins.

3. **Insert** first sheet through second sheet and align folds.

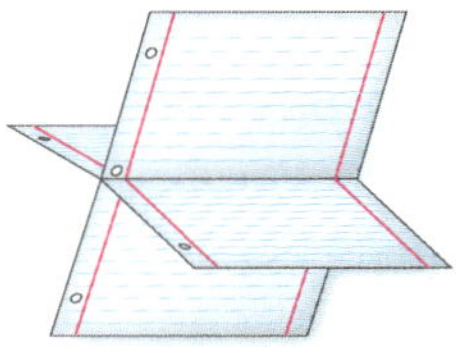

4. **Label** each inside page with a lesson number and title.

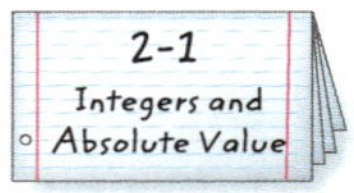

GET READY for Chapter 2

Diagnose Readiness You have two options for checking Prerequisite Skills.

Option 2

IN Math Online Take the Online Readiness Quiz at glencoe.com.

Option 1

Take the Quick Check below. Refer to the Quick Review for help.

QUICK Quiz

(Used in Lesson 2-2)

Replace each ● with < or > to make a true sentence. (Prior Grade)

1. 1,458 ● 1,548 <
2. 36 ● 34 >
3. 1.02 ● 1.20 <
4. 76.7 ● 77.6 <
5. **COINS** Philippe has $5.17 in coins and Garrett has $5.71 in coins. Who has the greater amount? (Prior Grade) **Garrett**

(Used in Lessons 2-4 and 2-5)

Evaluate each expression if $a = 7$, $b = 2$, and $c = 11$. (Prior Grade)

6. $a + 8$ **15**
7. $a + b + c$ **20**
8. $c - b$ **9**
9. $a - b + 4$ **9**
10. **TEMPERATURE** At 8 A.M., it was 63°F. By noon, the temperature had risen 9 degrees Fahrenheit. What was the temperature at noon? (Prior Grade) **72°F**

(Used in Lessons 2-6 and 2-8)

Evaluate each expression if $m = 9$ and $n = 4$. (Prior Grade)

11. $6mn$ **216**
12. $n \div 2 - 1$ **1**
13. $m + 5 \times n$ **29**
14. $m^2 \div (n + 5)$ **9**
15. **PLANES** The distance in miles that an airplane travels is given by rt where r is the rate of travel and t is the time. Find the distance an airplane traveled if $t = 4$ hours and $r = 475$ miles per hour. (Prior Grade) **1,900 mi**

QUICK Review

Example 1

Replace the ● with < or > to make a true sentence.

3.14 ● 3.41

3.14
3.41
↑

Line up the decimal points. Starting at the left, compare the digits in each place-value position.

The digits in the tenths place are not the same. Since 1 tenth < 4 tenths, 3.14 < 3.41.

Example 2

Evaluate the expression $11 - a + b$ if $a = 2$ and $b = 8$.

$11 - a + b = 11 - 2 + 8$ — Replace a with 2 and b with 8.

$= 9 + 8$ — Subtract 2 from 11.

$= 17$ — Add 9 and 8.

Example 3

Evaluate the expression $n^2 \div 16 + m$ if $m = 3$ and $n = 8$.

$n^2 \div 16 + m = 8^2 \div 16 + 3$ — Replace m with 3 and n with 8.

$= 64 \div 16 + 3$ — Evaluate 8^2.

$= 4 + 3$ — Divide 64 by 16.

$= 7$ — Add 4 and 3.

Diagnostic Assessment

Exercises	Academic Standards	Strategic Intervention
1–5	7.1.6	*Math Skills Maintenance Masters* pp. 2, 32–33
6–10	6.1.5	SE Review Lesson 1-6, pp. 44–47
11–15	7.1.7	SE Review Lesson 1-4, pp. 38–41

ASSESSMENT PLANNER

CHAPTER 2

Formative Assessment

CRM Anticipation Guide, pp. 7–8

Spotting Preconceived Ideas
Students complete this survey to determine prior knowledge about ideas from Chapter 2. Revisit the worksheet after completing the chapter. Also see page 122.

TE Lesson Activities

- Ticket Out the Door, p. 83
- Crystal Ball, pp. 87, 92, 111
- Name the Math, pp. 99, 113, 118
- Yesterday's News, p. 106

Chapter Checkpoints

- SE Mid-Chapter Quiz, p. 100
- SE Study Guide and Review, pp. 119–122
- SE Test Practice, pp. 124–125
- CRM Quizzes, pp. 61 and 62
- CRM Standardized Test Practice, pp. 78–80

IN Math Online glencoe.com

- Self-Check Quizzes
- Practice Test
- Test Practice

Summative Assessment

- SE Chapter Practice Test, p. 123
- CRM Mid-Chapter Test, p. 63
- CRM Vocabulary Test, p. 64
- CRM Extended-Response Test, p. 77
- CRM Leveled Chapter Tests, pp. 65–76
- CD-ROM ExamView® Assessment Suite

KEY

- CRM *Chapter 2 Resource Masters*
- SE Student Edition
- TE Teacher Edition
- CD-ROM

2-1 Integers and Absolute Value

PACING: **Regular:** 1 period, **Block:** 0.5 period

IN Academic Standards **7.1.6 Identify, write,** rename, compare and order **rational** and common irrational **numbers and plot them on a number line. Reinforcement of 6.1.2** Interpret the absolute value of a number as the distance from zero on a number line, find the absolute value of real numbers, and know that the distance between two numbers on the number line is the absolute value of their difference.

Options for Differentiated Instruction

ELL = English Language Learner AL = Above or Beyond Grade Level SS = Struggling Students SN = Special Needs

Making Real-World Connections ELL SS SN

Use after presenting Examples 1 and 2 on page 80.

Students do not learn as effectively if they are not interested in the topic being presented. Use as many different contexts for positive and negative numbers as possible to help students make connections between their own experiences and the study of integers. Some examples are shown below.

- temperature
- football yardage, gains and losses
- savings accounts, deposits and withdrawals
- elevators
- profit and losses in business

Kinesthetic Learning ELL SS

Use after presenting Absolute Value on page 81.

Many students think that the absolute value of a number is the opposite of that number. Make a number line on the floor using masking tape. Make sure the units for the number line are a comfortable stride length. Use index cards to label the number line. Then have students take turns finding the absolute value of various positive and negative integers by finding how many steps or units the number is from zero.

Simplifying Tasks ELL SS SN

Use before assigning the Exercises.

Create homework help sheets that have repeated entries like the one shown below.

Problem Number ______

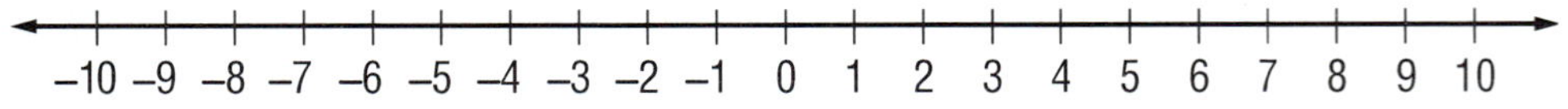

Have students use these to help them tackle the exercises in which they are asked to graph integers on a number line.

Leveled Lesson Resources

Also on **TeacherWorks**™ Lesson 2-1

Chapter 2 Resource Masters

BL = Below or Approaching Grade Level | OL = On Grade Level | AL = Above or Beyond Grade Level | ELL = English Language Learner

Lesson Reading Guide
p. 9 BL OL ELL

NAME ______ DATE ______ PERIOD ____

2-1 Lesson Reading Guide
Integers and Absolute Value

Get Ready for the Lesson

Read the introduction at the top of page 80 in your textbook. Write your answers below.

1. What does a value of −10 represent? **10 feet below street level**
2. The top deck of a ramp is 5 feet above street level. How can you represent 5 feet above street level? **+5 or 5**

Read the Lesson

3. Express each of the following in words.

Symbols	Words
+7	positive seven
−7	negative seven
|7|	absolute value of seven

4. Graph the set of integers {0, 3, −2, −1} on the number line.

Remember What You Learned

5. Show a classmate how a number line can be used to show negative and positive integers. Explain the difference between some integers and the absolute values of those integers. Draw a number line to show what you mean. **See students' work.**

Chapter 2 — 9 — Course 2

Study Guide and Intervention*
p. 10 BL OL ELL

NAME ______ DATE ______ PERIOD ____

2-1 Study Guide and Intervention
Integers and Absolute Value

Integers less than zero are **negative integers**. Integers greater than zero are **positive integers**.

(negative integers; positive integers; zero is neither positive nor negative)

The absolute value of an integer is the distance the number is from zero on a number line. Two vertical bars are used to represent absolute value. The symbol for absolute value of 3 is |3|.

Example 1 Write an integer that represents 160 feet below sea level.

Because it represents *below* sea level, the integer is −160.

Example 2 Evaluate |−2|.

On the number line, the graph of −2 is 2 units away from 0. So, |−2| = 2.

Exercises

Write an integer for each situation.

1. 12°C above 0 **12**
2. a loss of $24 **−24**
3. a gain of 20 pounds **20**
4. falling 6 feet **−6**

Evaluate each expression.

5. |12| **12**
6. |−150| **150**
7. |−8| **8**
8. |75| **75**
9. |−19| **19**
10. |84| **84**

Chapter 2 — 10 — Course 2

Skills Practice*
p. 11 BL OL

NAME ______ DATE ______ PERIOD ____

2-1 Skills Practice
Integers and Absolute Value

Write an integer for each situation.

1. 15°C below 0 **−15**
2. a profit of $27 **27**
3. 2010 A.D. **2010**
4. average attendance is down 38 people **−38**
5. 376 feet above sea level **376**
6. a withdrawal of $200 **−200**
7. 3 points lost **−3**
8. a bonus of $150 **150**
9. a deposit of $41 **41**
10. 240 B.C. **−240**
11. a wage increase of $120 **120**
12. 60 feet below sea level **−60**

Evaluate each expression.

13. |−1| **1**
14. |9| **9**
15. |23| **23**
16. |−107| **107**
17. |−45| **45**
18. |19| **19**
19. |0| **0**
20. |6| − |−2| **4**
21. |−8| + |4| **12**
22. |−12| − |12| **0**

Graph each set of integers on a number line.

23. {0, 2, −3}
24. {−4, −1, 3}

Chapter 2 — 11 — Course 2

Practice*
p. 12 OL AL

NAME ______ DATE ______ PERIOD ____

2-1 Practice
Integers and Absolute Value

Write an integer for each situation.

1. a profit of $12 **12**
2. 1,440 feet below sea level **−1,440**
3. 22°F below 0 **−22**
4. a gain of 31 yards **31**

Graph each set of integers on a number line.

5. {−5, 0, 5}
6. {−3, −2, 1, −4}

Evaluate each expression.

7. |−11| **11**
8. |−5| + 8 **13**
9. |−4| − |−4| **0**
10. |12| + 2 × |−5| **30**
11. |−4| + 7 − |3| **8**
12. 9 + |−6| + 1^2 **15**

13. HEALTH A veterinarian recommends that a St. Bernard lose weight. Write an integer to describe the dog losing 25 pounds. **−25**

14. GEOGRAPHY Mount Kilimanjaro is the highest peak in Africa. Write an integer to represent the elevation of Mount Kilimanjaro of 5,895 meters above sea level. **5,895**

15. ECONOMY Gasoline prices occasionally fluctuate during a two month period of time. Prices increased 34 cents per gallon during the month of April and decreased 17 cents per gallon during the month of May. What integers can be used to describe each change in price? **34 and −17**

Chapter 2 — 12 — Course 2

Word Problem Practice*
p. 13 OL AL

NAME ______ DATE ______ PERIOD ____

2-1 Word Problems Practice
Integers and Absolute Value

1. DEATH VALLEY The lowest point in the United States is Death Valley in California. Its altitude is 282 feet below sea level. Write an integer to represent the altitude of Death Valley. **−282**
2. RAIN A meteorologist reported that in the month of April there were 3 inches more rainfall than normal. Write an integer to represent the rainfall above normal in April. **3**
3. ARCHIMEDES A famous mathematician and physicist named Archimedes was born in 287 B.C. Write an integer to express the year of his birth. **−287**
4. TEMPERATURE In our world's tropical rain forests, the average temperature of every month is 64 degrees above zero or higher. Write an integer to express this temperature. **64**
5. STOCK MARKET A certain stock gained 5 points in one day and lost 4 points the next day. Write integers to represent the stock's gains and losses for the two days. **5; −4**
6. ALTITUDE An airplane pilot changed his altitude by 100 meters. Describe what this could mean. **either 100 or −100 meaning the plane is either 100 feet higher or 100 feet lower than its original position.**

Chapter 2 — 13 — Course 2

Enrichment
p. 14 OL AL

NAME ______ DATE ______ PERIOD ____

2-1 Enrichment

Jaime Escalante

Jaime Escalante (1930–) was born in La Paz, Bolivia, and came to the United States in 1963. For ten years, he worked at odd jobs to support himself and his family while pursuing his dream—becoming certified to teach high school mathematics in California. As a mathematics teacher, he has become well known for his ability to inspire students to succeed in mathematics at levels they never thought possible. In 1988, the story of Mr. Escalante and a group of his students was the subject of the popular motion picture *Stand and Deliver.*

Mr. Escalante teaches concepts students must master if they are to succeed in high school and college mathematics. One of these is the concept of absolute value. For instance, a student should be able to solve an equation like |y| = 6 quickly using mental math. Here's how.

You know that |6| = 6 and |−6| = 6.

So, the equation |y| = 6 has *two* solutions: 6 and −6.

Solve each equation. (*Hint:* One equation has no solution.)

1. |c| = 8 **8, −8**
2. |r| = 0 **0**
3. |j| = −3 **no solution**
4. |t| + 1 = 15 **14, −14**
5. 10 = |m| + 3 **7, −7**
6. |c| − 4 = 16 **20, −20**
7. 5|z| = 60 **12, −12**
8. 12 = |g| + 4 **3, −3**
9. 48 = 8|x| **6, −6**
10. 2|d| + 3 = 5 **1, −1**
11. 4|p| − 9 = 59 **17, −17**
12. 7|z| + 12 = 12 **0**

13. Suppose that the value of x can be selected from the set {−2, −1, 0, 1, 2}. Find all of the solutions of the equation |x| = x. **0, 1, 2**

14. One of these statements is false. Which one is it? Explain.
    a. The absolute value of every integer is positive.
    b. There is at least one integer whose absolute value is zero.
    c. The absolute value of an integer is never negative. **Statement a is false; the absolute value of 0 is 0, which is not positive.**

Chapter 2 — 14 — Course 2

* Also available in Spanish ELL

Additional Lesson Resources

Transparencies

- *5-Minute Check Transparency,* Lesson 2-1

Other Print Products

- *Noteables™ Interactive Study Notebook with Foldables™*

Teacher Tech Tools

- *Interactive Classroom CD-ROM,* Lesson 2-1
- *AssignmentWorks,* Lesson 2-1

Student Tech Tools

glencoe.com

- Extra Examples, Chapter 2, Lesson 1
- Self-Check Quiz, Chapter 2, Lesson 1

2-1 Lesson Notes

1 Focus

Vertical Alignment

Before Lesson 2-1
Identify and represent on a number line positive and negative integers

Lesson 2-1
Compare and order positive and negative fractions, decimals, and mixed numbers and place them on a number line

After Lesson 2-1
Understand the meaning of the absolute value of a number; interpret the absolute value as the distance of the number from zero on a number line; and determine the absolute value of real numbers

2 Teach

Scaffolding Questions

Have students research the elevations of various geographical landmarks (such as Mt. Whitney, Lake Titicaca, and Death Valley).

Ask:

- Why do elevations include the terms *above sea level* or *below sea level?* Sample answer: Sea level is considered the zero point for measuring elevation.
- Can you find any landmarks that are below sea level? Death Valley, California; Dead Sea, Israel and Jordan
- How could you use a positive or negative sign to write an elevation? Sample answer: Use a positive sign to show elevations above sea level and use a negative sign to show elevations below sea level.

2-1 Integers and Absolute Value

MAIN IDEA

Read and write integers, and find the absolute value of a number.

IN Academic Standards

7.1.6 Identify, **write**, rename, compare and order **rational** and common irrational **numbers and plot them on a number line.** **Reinforcement of 6.1.2** Interpret the absolute value of a number as the distance from zero on a number line, find the absolute value of real numbers, and know that the distance between two numbers on the number line is the absolute value of their difference.

New Vocabulary

integer
negative integer
positive integer
graph
absolute value

IN Math Online

glencoe.com
- Extra Examples
- Personal Tutor
- Self-Check Quiz

GET READY for the Lesson

SKATEBOARDING The bottom of a skateboarding ramp is 8 feet below streetlevel. A value of −8 represents 8 feet *below* street level.

1. What does a value of −10 represent? **10 feet below street level**
2. The top deck of the ramp is 5 feet *above* street level. How can you represent 5 feet *above* street level? **+5 or 5**

Numbers like 5 and −8 are called integers. An **integer** is any number from the set {…, −4, −3, −2, −1, 0, 1, 2, 3, 4, …} where … means *continues without end*.

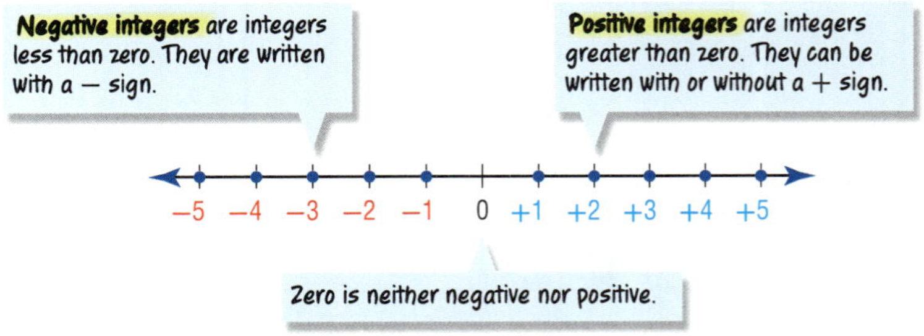

Real-World EXAMPLES

WEATHER Write an integer for each situation.

1 **an average temperature of 5 degrees below normal**

Because it represents *below* normal, the integer is −5.

2 **an average rainfall of 5 inches above normal**

Because it represents *above* normal, the integer is +5 or 5.

CHECK Your Progress

Write an integer for each situation.

a. 6 degrees above normal **+6** b. 2 inches below normal **−2**

Integers can be graphed on a number line. To **graph** a point on the number line, draw a point on the line at its location.

Differentiated Instruction

Verbal/Linguistic Learners Have students create a list of words that represent opposites and organize the list according to words that represent a positive concept or a negative concept. For example, *up* represents a positive concept and *down* represents a negative concept. Other examples include *forward/backward*, *above/below*, and *deposit/withdrawal*.

80 Chapter 2 Integers

EXAMPLE Graph Integers

3 **Graph the set of integers {4, −6, 0} on a number line.**

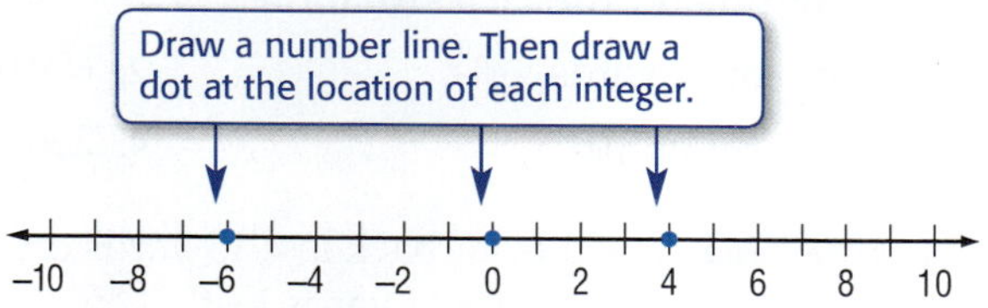

CHECK Your Progress

Graph each set of integers on a number line. **c, d. See margin.**

c. {−2, 8, −7} d. {−4, 10, −3, 7}

On the number line below, notice that −5 and 5 are each 5 units from 0, even though they are on opposite sides of 0. Numbers that are the same distance from zero on a number line have the same **absolute value**.

Absolute Value — Key Concept

Words The absolute value of a number is the distance between the number and zero on a number line.

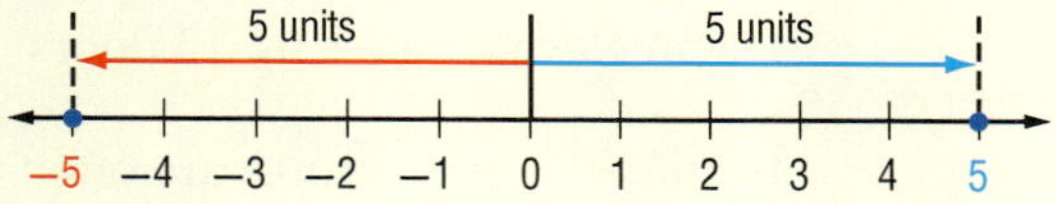

Examples |−5| = 5 |5| = 5

Reading Math

Absolute Value

|−5| *absolute value of negative five*

EXAMPLES Evaluate Expressions

Evaluate each expression.

4 **|−4|**

On the number line, the point −4 is 4 units from 0.

So, |−4| = 4.

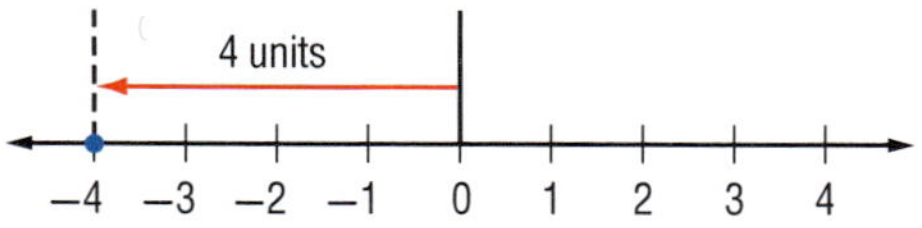

5 **|−5| − |2|**

|−5| − |2| = 5 − 2 |−5| = 5, |2| = 2

So, |−5| − |2| = 3.

Study Tip

Order of Operations The absolute value bars are considered to be a grouping symbol. When evaluating |−5| − |2|, evaluate the absolute values before subtracting.

CHECK Your Progress

Evaluate each expression.

e. |8| **8** f. 2 + |−3| **5** g. |−6| − 5 **1**

Focus on Mathematical Content

Integers (whole numbers, their negatives, and zero) can be graphed on a number line.

Integers are used to represent many quantities in everyday life such as elevations, temperatures, and bank deposits.

Formative Assessment

Use the Check Your Progress exercises after the Examples to determine students' understanding of concepts.

ADDITIONAL EXAMPLES

Write an integer for each situation.

1. a total rainfall of 2 inches below normal −2
2. a seasonal snowfall of 3 inches above normal +3
3. Graph the set of integers {−1, 3, −2} on a number line.

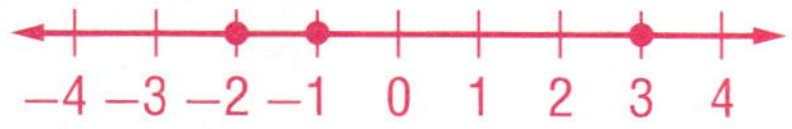

Evaluate each expression.

4. |−5| + 5 10
5. |−4| − |−3| 1

Additional Examples are also in:

- Noteables™ Interactive Study Notebook with Foldables™
- Interactive Classroom PowerPoint® Presentations

Additional Answers

c. 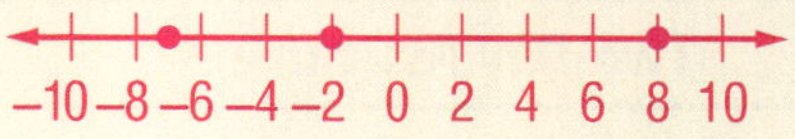

d. 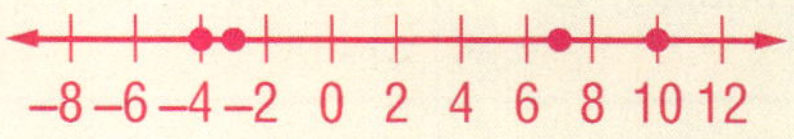

Lesson 2-1 Integers and Absolute Value **81**

3 Practice

Formative Assessment

Use Exercises 1–10 to check for understanding.

Then use the chart at the bottom of this page to customize your assignments for students.

Intervention You may wish to use the Study Guide and Intervention Master on page 10 of the *Chapter 2 Resource Masters* for additional reinforcement.

Odd/Even Assignments

Exercises 11–30 are structured so that students practice the same concepts whether they are assigned odd or even problems.

Tips for New Teachers: Word Problems

Sometimes numbers are modified to make a problem easier for students to solve. For example, Exercise 35 uses 2-digit integers. In reality, the number of protons and electrons in such a situation would be in the billions.

Additional Answers

6. 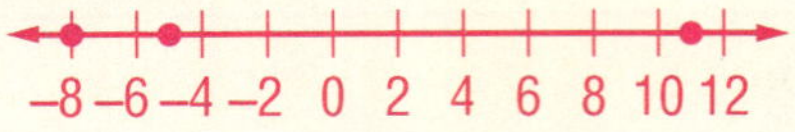

7. 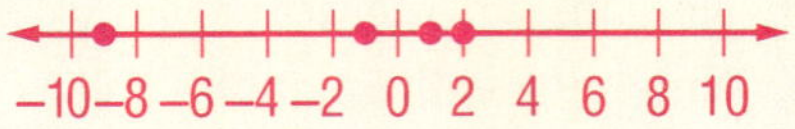

21. 

22. 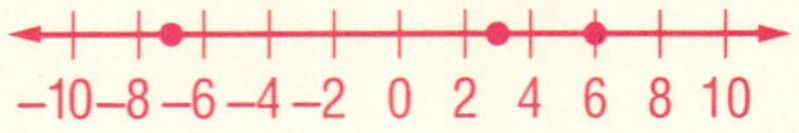

23. 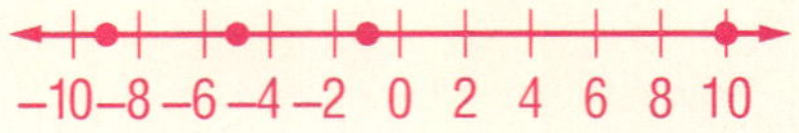

24. 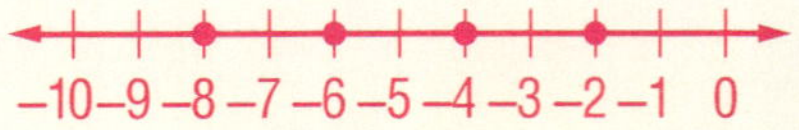

35. 17 positive charges: +17; 25 negative charges: −25

CHECK Your Understanding

Examples 1, 2 (p. 80)

Write an integer for each situation.

1. a loss of 11 yards **−11**
2. 6°F below zero **−6**
3. a deposit of $16 **16**
4. 250 meters above sea level **250**
5. **FOOTBALL** The quarterback lost 15 yards on one play. Write an integer to represent the number of yards lost. **−15**

Example 3 (p. 81)

Graph each set of integers on a number line. **6, 7. See margin.**

6. $\{11, -5, -8\}$
7. $\{2, -1, -9, 1\}$

Examples 4, 5 (p. 81)

Evaluate each expression.

8. $|-9|$ **9**
9. $1 + |7|$ **8**
10. $|-1| - |-6|$ **−5**

Practice and Problem Solving

HOMEWORK HELP	
For Exercises	See Examples
11–20	1, 2
21–24	3
25–30	4, 5

Exercise Levels
A: 11–30
B: 31–35
C: 36–38

Write an integer for each situation.

11. a profit of $9 **9**
12. a bank withdrawal of $50 **−50**
13. 53°C below zero **−53**
14. 7 inches more than normal **7**
15. 2 feet below flood level **−2**
16. 160 feet above sea level **160**
17. an elevator goes up 12 floors **12**
18. no gains or losses on first down **0**
19. **GOLF** In golf, scores are often written in relationship to *par,* the average score for a round at a certain course. Write an integer to represent a score that is 7 under par. **−7**
20. **PETS** Javier's pet guinea pig gained 8 ounces in one month. Write an integer to describe the amount of weight his pet gained. **8**

Graph each set of integers on a number line. **21–24. See margin.**

21. $\{0, 1, -3\}$
22. $\{3, -7, 6\}$
23. $\{-5, -1, 10, -9\}$
24. $\{-2, -4, -6, -8\}$

Evaluate each expression.

25. $|10|$ **10**
26. $|-12|$ **12**
27. $|-7| - 5$ **2**
28. $7 + |4|$ **11**
29. $|-9| + |-5|$ **14**
30. $|8| - |-10|$ **−2**
31. $|-10| \div 2 \times |5|$ **25**
32. $12 - |-8| + 7$ **11**
33. $|27| \div 3 - |-4|$ **5**
34. **SCUBA DIVING** One diver descended 10 feet, and another ascended 8 feet. Which situation has the greater absolute value? Explain.

34. Sample answer: Descending 10 feet has the greater absolute value. The diver descending 10 feet descends the most.

35. **SCIENCE** If you rub a balloon through your hair, you can make the balloon stick to a wall. Suppose there are 17 positive charges on the wall and 25 negative charges on the balloon. Write an integer for each charge. **See margin.**

Academic Standards • ISTEP+
Extra Practice, pp. 671, 705

DIFFERENTIATED HOMEWORK OPTIONS

Level	Assignment	Two-Day Assignment	
BL Basic	11–30, 36, 38–48	11–29 odd, 39, 40	12–30 even, 36, 38, 41–48
OL Core	11–33 odd, 34–36, 38–48	11–30, 39, 40	31–36, 38, 41–48
AL Advanced/Pre-AP	31–44 (optional: 45–48)		

H.O.T. Problems

36. **REASONING** If $|x| = 3$, what is the value of x? **−3 or 3**

37. **CHALLENGE** Determine whether the following statement is *true* or *false*. If *false*, give a counterexample. **false; 0**

The absolute value of every integer is positive.

38. **WRITING IN MATH** Write a real-world situation that uses negative integers. Explain what the negative integer means in that situation. **Sample answer: Golfing uses negative numbers. A score of −2 represents 2 under par.**

ISTEP+ PRACTICE 7.1.6, Reinforcement of 6.1.2

39. Which point has a coordinate with the greatest absolute value? **C**

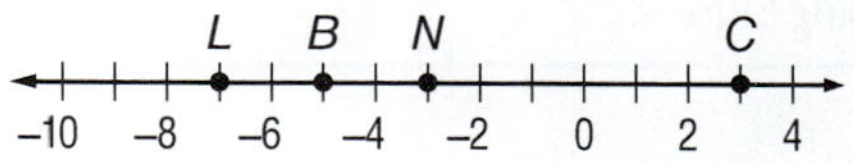

A Point *B*

B Point *C*

C Point *L*

D Point *N*

40. Which statement about these real-world situations is *not* true? **J**

F A \$100 check deposited in a bank can be represented by +100.

G A loss of 15 yards in a football game can be represented by −15.

H A temperature of 20 below zero can be represented by −20.

J A submarine diving 300 feet under water can be represented by +300.

Spiral Review

Copy and complete each function table. Identify the domain and range. (Lesson 1-10)

41. $y = x - 4$

x	x − 4	y
4		
5		
6		
7		

42. $y = 9x$

x	9x	y
0		
1		
2		
3		

43. $y = 5x + 1$

x	5x + 1	y
1		
2		
3		
4		

41–43. See margin.

44. **GEOMETRY** The table shows the side length and perimeter of several equilateral triangles. Write an expression that describes the perimeter if x represents the side length. (Lesson 1-9) **3x**

Side Length (in.)	2	3	4	5	6
Perimeter (in.)	6	9	12	15	18

GET READY for the Next Lesson

PREREQUISITE SKILL **Replace each ● with < or > to make a true sentence.**

45. 16 ● 6 **>**

46. 101 ● 111 **<**

47. 87.3 ● 83.7 **>**

48. 1,051 ● 1,015 **>**

4 Assess

Ticket Out the Door Have students describe a real-world situation in which integers are used.

FOLDABLES Study Organizer **Foldables™ Follow-Up**

Remind students to record notes about integers in their Foldables. Suggest that they include a number line with examples of negative integers and positive integers.

Additional Answers

41. domain: {4, 5, 6, 7}; range: {0, 1, 2, 3}

x	x − 4	y
4	4 − 4	0
5	5 − 4	1
6	6 − 4	2
7	7 − 4	3

42. domain: {0, 1, 2, 3}; range: {0, 9, 18, 27}

x	9x	y
0	9 • 0	0
1	9 • 1	9
2	9 • 2	18
3	9 • 3	27

43. domain: {1, 2, 3, 4}; range: {6, 11, 16, 21}

x	5x + 1	y
1	5 • 1 + 1	6
2	5 • 2 + 1	11
3	5 • 3 + 1	16
4	5 • 4 + 1	21

Tips for New Teachers

Equilateral Triangles

After assigning Exercise 44, it may be helpful to remind students that all three sides of an equilateral triangle have the same length.

Lesson 2-1 Integers and Absolute Value 83

2-2 Comparing and Ordering Integers

PACING: **Regular:** 1 period, **Block:** 0.5 period

IN Academic Standards **7.1.6 Identify, write, rename, compare and order rational** and common irrational **numbers and plot them on a number line.**

Options for Differentiated Instruction

ELL = English Language Learner AL = Above or Beyond Grade Level SS = Struggling Students SN = Special Needs

Visual Cues SS

Use before presenting Example 1.

On an index card, have students create a number line that includes both positive and negative integers. Have them include reminders for comparing and ordering integers like the ones in arrows shown below.

Have students provide examples of statements using the signs < and >.

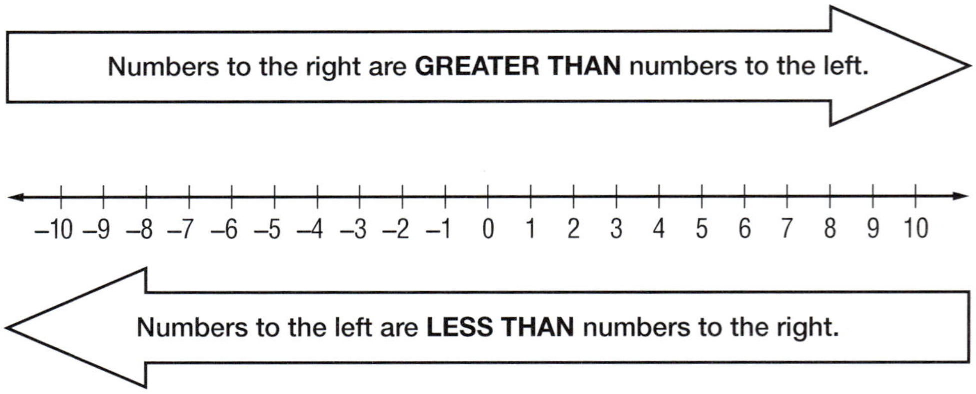

Have students provide examples of statements using the signs < and >.

Kinesthetic Learning ELL AL SS SN

Use before assigning the Exercises.

Choose any integers between −50 and 50 and write one number per student on a piece of card stock.

- Pass out a number to each student.
- Have students stand up. Ask them to line up as quickly as possible from least to greatest *without* talking to each other.
- After students have correctly lined up, have a class discussion about strategies that might make the process go faster next time.
- Shuffle the cards, pass out the numbers, and have students line up again.

Leveled Lesson Resources

Also on **TeacherWorks™** Lesson 2-2

Chapter 2 Resource Masters

BL = Below or Approaching Grade Level **OL** = On Grade Level **AL** = Above or Beyond Grade Level **ELL** = English Language Learner

Lesson Reading Guide
p. 16 BL OL ELL

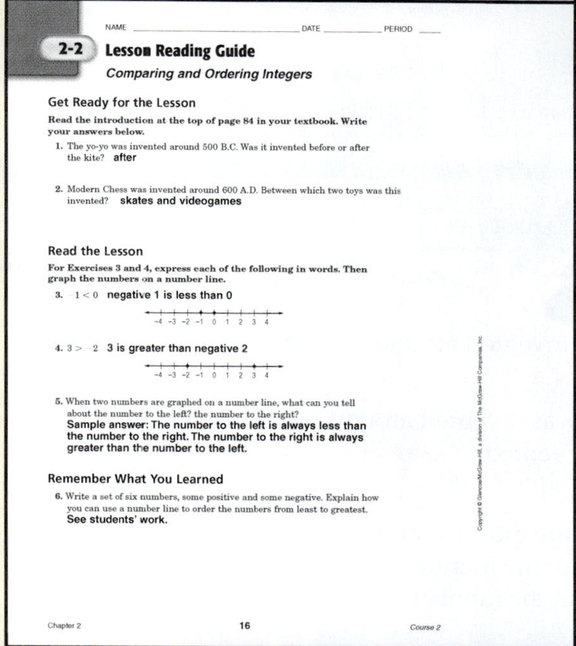

2-2 Lesson Reading Guide
Comparing and Ordering Integers

Get Ready for the Lesson
Read the introduction at the top of page 84 in your textbook. Write your answers below.
1. The yo-yo was invented around 500 B.C. Was it invented before or after the kite? after
2. Modern Chess was invented around 600 A.D. Between which two toys was this invented? skates and videogames

Read the Lesson
For Exercises 3 and 4, express each of the following in words. Then graph the numbers on a number line.
3. −1 < 0 negative 1 is less than 0
4. 3 > −2 3 is greater than negative 2
5. When two numbers are graphed on a number line, what can you tell about the number to the left? to the right? Sample answer: The number to the left is always less than the number to the right. The number to the right is always greater than the number to the left.

Remember What You Learned
6. Write a set of six numbers, some positive and some negative. Explain how you can use a number line to order the numbers from least to greatest. See students' work.

Chapter 2 16 Course 2

*Study Guide and Intervention**
p. 17 BL OL ELL

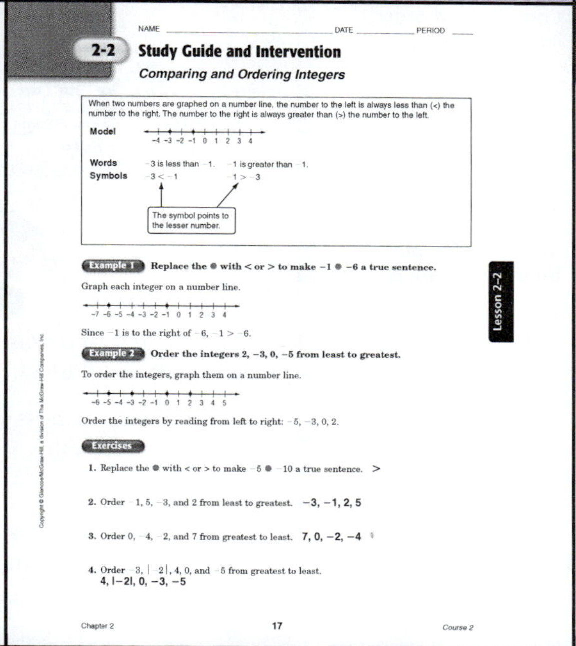

2-2 Study Guide and Intervention
Comparing and Ordering Integers

When two numbers are graphed on a number line, the number to the left is always less than (<) the number to the right. The number to the right is always greater than (>) the number to the left.

Example 1 Replace the ● with < or > to make −1 ● −6 a true sentence.
Since −1 is to the right of −6, −1 > −6.

Example 2 Order the integers 2, −3, 0, −5 from least to greatest.
Order the integers by reading from left to right: −5, −3, 0, 2.

Exercises
1. Replace the ● with < or > to make −5 ● −10 a true sentence. >
2. Order −1, 5, −3, and 2 from least to greatest. −3, −1, 2, 5
3. Order 0, −4, −2, and 7 from greatest to least. 7, 0, −2, −4
4. Order −3, |−2|, 4, 0, and −5 from greatest to least. 4, |−2|, 0, −3, −5

Chapter 2 17 Course 2

*Skills Practice**
p. 18 BL OL

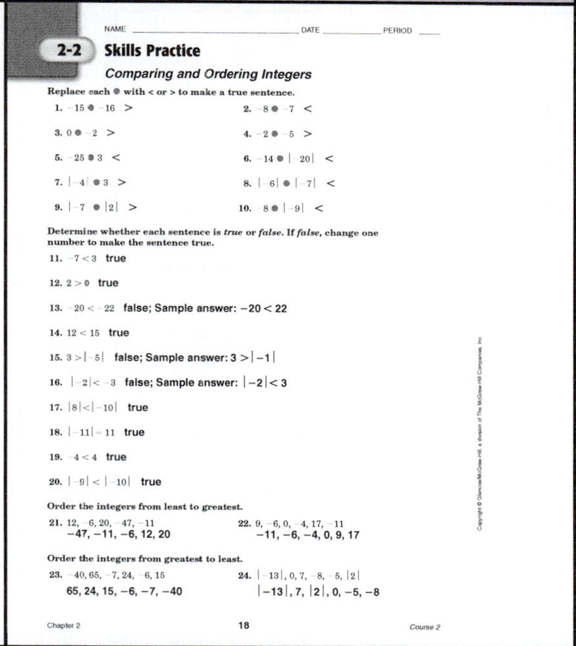

2-2 Skills Practice
Comparing and Ordering Integers

Chapter 2 18 Course 2

*Practice**
p. 19 OL AL

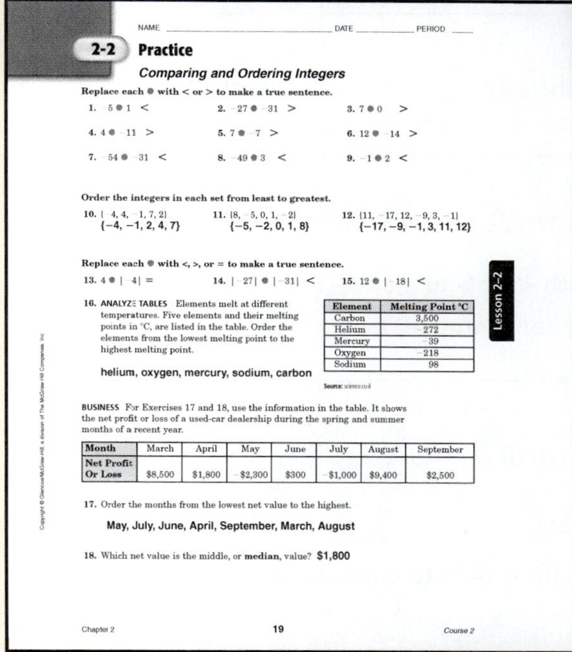

2-2 Practice
Comparing and Ordering Integers

Chapter 2 19 Course 2

*Word Problem Practice**
p. 20 OL AL

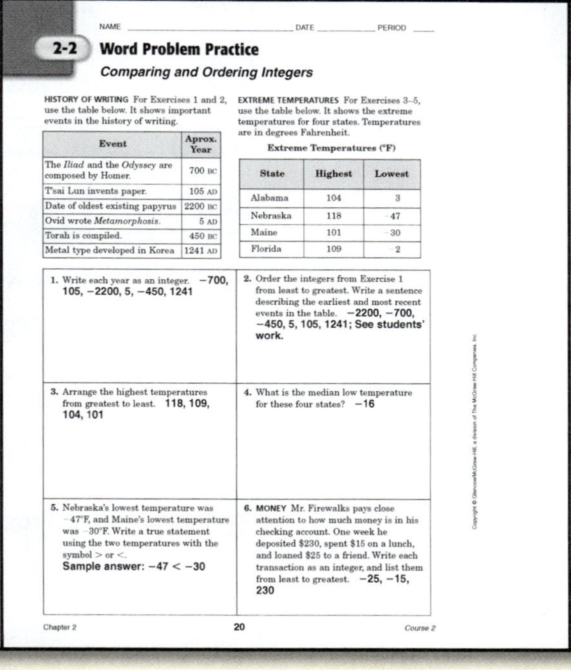

2-2 Word Problem Practice
Comparing and Ordering Integers

Chapter 2 20 Course 2

Enrichment
p. 21 OL AL

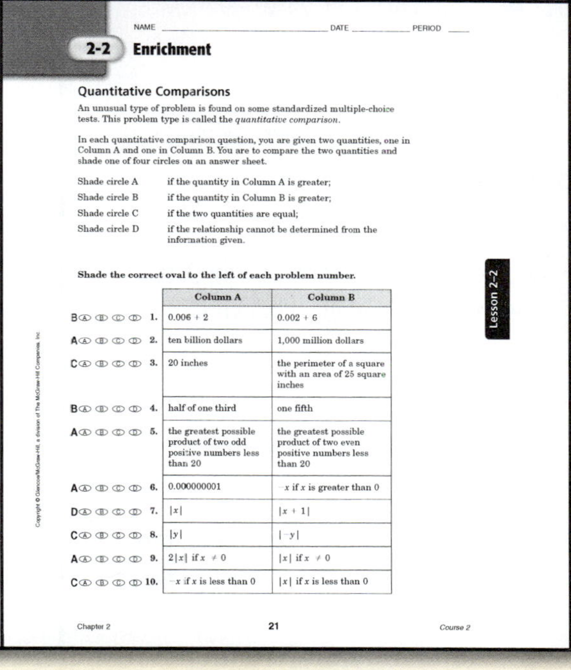

2-2 Enrichment
Quantitative Comparisons

Chapter 2 21 Course 2

** Also available in Spanish* ELL

Additional Lesson Resources

Transparencies
- *5-Minute Check Transparency,* Lesson 2-2

Other Print Products
- *Noteables™ Interactive Study Notebook with Foldables™*

Teacher Tech Tools
- *Interactive Classroom CD-ROM,* Lesson 2-2
- *AssignmentWorks,* Lesson 2-2

Student Tech Tools
glencoe.com
- Extra Examples, Chapter 2, Lesson 2
- Self-Check Quiz, Chapter 2, Lesson 2

2-2 Lesson Notes

1 Focus

Vertical Alignment

Before Lesson 2-2
Identify and represent on a number line positive and negative integers

Lesson 2-2
Compare and order positive and negative fractions, decimals, and mixed numbers and place them on a number line

After Lesson 2-2
Read, write and compare rational numbers in scientific notation with approximate numbers using scientific notation

2 Teach

Scaffolding Questions

Have students look at the Toys Timeline on the first page of the lesson.

Ask:

- According to the timeline, which toy was invented earliest: checkers or video games? checkers
- How many years were between the invention of checkers and the invention of the kite? 400 years
- Which is the correct way to read the timeline to determine earliest to most recent toy inventions? left to right

2-2 Comparing and Ordering Integers

MAIN IDEA

Compare and order integers.

IN Academic Standards

7.1.6 Identify, write, rename, **compare and order rational** and common irrational **numbers and plot them on a number line.**

IN Math Online

glencoe.com

- Concepts In Motion
- Extra Examples
- Personal Tutor
- Self-Check Quiz
- Reading in the Content Area

GET READY for the Lesson

TOYS The timeline shows when some toys were invented.

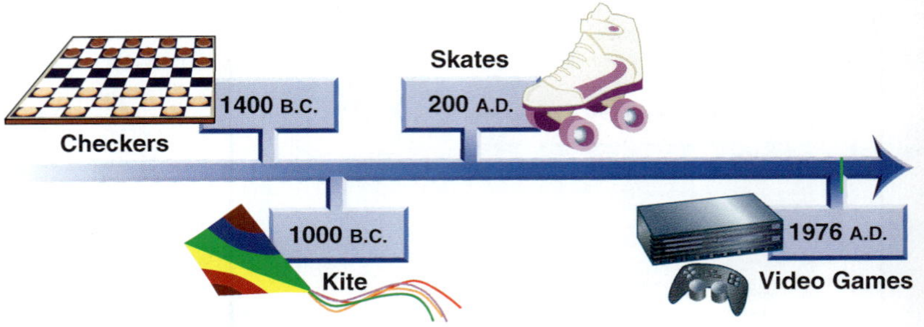

1. The yo-yo was invented around 500 B.C. Was it invented before or after the kite? **after**
2. Modern chess was invented around 600 A.D. Between which two toys was this invented? **skates and video games**

When two numbers are graphed on a number line, the number to the left is always less than the number to the right. The number to the right is always greater than the number to the left.

Compare Integers — Key Concept

Model

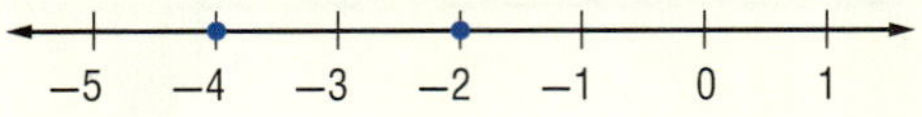

Words	−4 is less than −2.	−2 is greater than −4.
Examples	$-4 < -2$	$-2 > -4$

EXAMPLE Compare Two Integers

1 **Replace the ● with < or > to make −5 ● −3 a true sentence.**

Graph each integer on a number line.

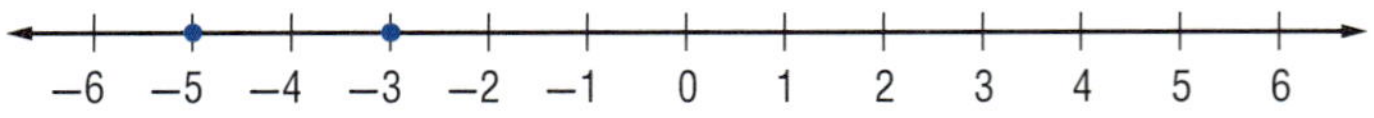

Since −5 is to the left of −3, $-5 < -3$.

CHECK Your Progress

Replace each ● with < or > to make a true sentence.

a. −8 ● −4 **<** b. 5 ● −1 **>** c. −10 ● −13 **>**

ADDITIONAL EXAMPLE

1 Replace the ● with < or > to make −9 ● −5 a true sentence. <

Tips for New Teachers — Inequality Symbols

If students are having trouble identifying the inequality symbols < and >, point out that the symbol itself points to the lesser number. In the statement $-5 < 3$, the inequality symbol is pointing towards −5 which is less than 3.

ISTEP+ EXAMPLE 7.1.6

2 **The elevations, in feet, for the lowest points in California, Oklahoma, Louisiana, and Kentucky are listed. Which list shows the elevation in order from highest to lowest?**

State	Elevation (ft)
California	−282
Oklahoma	289
Louisiana	−8
Kentucky	257

A 289, −282, 257, −8

B −8, 257, −282, 289

C −282, −8, 257, 289

D 289, 257, −8, −282

Test-Taking Tip

Eliminating Answer Choices
If you are unsure of the correct answer, eliminate the choices you know are incorrect. Then consider the remaining choices. You can eliminate choices B and C since those lists begin with a negative number.

Read the Item

To order the integers, graph them on a number line.

Solve the Item

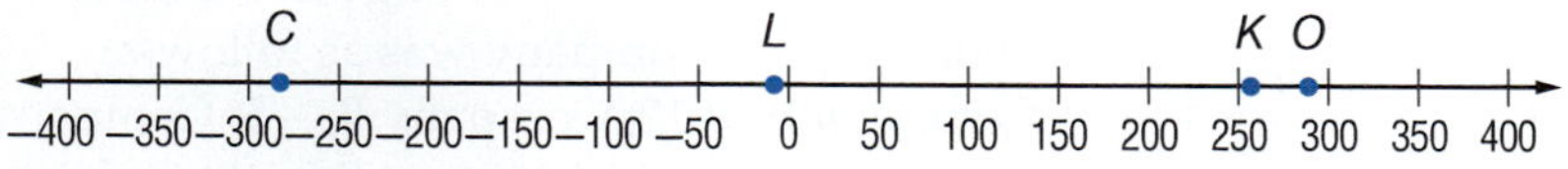

Order the integers by reading from right to left: 289, 257, −8, −282. So, the answer is D.

CHECK Your Progress

d. A newspaper reporter lists the third round scores of the top five finishers in a golf tournament. Which list shows these scores from least to greatest? **H**

F 5, 2, 0, −1, −3

G −1, −3, 0, 2, 5

H −3, −1, 0, 2, 5

J 0, −1, 2, −3, 5

CHECK Your Understanding

Example 1 (p. 84) **Replace each ● with < or > to make a true sentence.**

1. −4 ● −6 **>**
2. −2 ● 8 **<**
3. 0 ● −10 **>**

Example 2 (p. 85) **Order the integers in each set from least to greatest.**

4. {−13, 9, −2, 0, 4} **{−13, −2, 0, 4, 9}**
5. {12, −16, −10, 19, −18} **{−18, −16, −10, 12, 19}**
6. **MULTIPLE CHOICE** The lowest temperatures in Hawaii, Illinois, Minnesota, and South Carolina are listed. Which list shows these temperatures in order from coldest to warmest? **C**

A −19, −36, −60, 12

B 12, −19, −36, −60

C −60, −36, −19, 12

D −60, −19, 12, −36

Formative Assessment

Use the Check Your Progress exercises after each Example to determine students' understanding of concepts.

ADDITIONAL EXAMPLE

2 **TEST EXAMPLE** The lowest temperatures in Europe, Greenland, Oceania, and Antarctica are listed in the table.

Place	Record Low Temperature (°F)
Europe	−67
Greenland	−87
Oceania	14
Antarctica	−129

Which list shows the temperatures in order from coldest to warmest? **C**

A −67, −87, 14, −129

B 14, −67, −87, −129

C −129, −87, −67, 14

D −67, −87, −129, 14

Additional Examples are also in:

- Noteables™ Interactive Study Notebook with Foldables™
- Interactive Classroom PowerPoint® Presentations

3 Practice

Formative Assessment

Use Exercises 1–6 to check for understanding.

Then use the chart at the bottom of the next page to customize your assignments for students.

Intervention You may wish to use the Study Guide and Intervention Master on page 17 of the *Chapter 2 Resource Masters* for additional reinforcement.

Odd/Even Assignments

Exercises 7–20 are structured so that students practice the same concepts whether they are assigned odd or even problems.

Practice and Problem Solving

HOMEWORK HELP

For Exercises	See Examples
7–14	1
15–20	2
35–36	2

Exercise Levels
A: 7–20
B: 21–31
C: 32–34

Replace each ● with < or > to make a true sentence.

7. -7 ● -3 **<**
8. -21 ● -12 **<**
9. -6 ● -11 **>**
10. -15 ● -33 **>**
11. 17 ● -20 **>**
12. 4 ● -4 **>**
13. -5 ● 17 **<**
14. -12 ● 8 **<**

Order the integers in each set from least to greatest. **15. {−8, −5, −3, 6, 11}**

15. $\{-8, 11, 6, -5, -3\}$
16. $\{7, -2, 14, -9, 2\}$ **{−9, −2, 2, 7, 14}**
17. $\{5, -6, -7, -4, 1, 3\}$ **{−7, −6, −4, 1, 3, 5}**
18. $\{-12, 15, 8, -15, -23, 10\}$ **{−23, −15, −12, 8, 10, 15}**

19. **ANALYZE TABLES** The ocean floor is divided into five zones according to how deep sunlight penetrates. Order the zones from closest to the surface to nearest to the ocean floor. **Sunlight, Twilight, Midnight, Abyssal, Hadal**

Zone	Beginning Ocean Depth
Abyssal	−4,000 m
Hadal	−6,000 m
Midnight	−1,000 m
Sunlight	0 m
Twilight	−200 m

20. **STOCK MARKET** Kevin's dad owns stock in five companies. The change in the stock value for each company was as follows: Company A, +12; Company B, −5; Company C, −25; Company D, +18; Company E, −10. Order the companies from the worst performing to best performing. **Company C, Company E, Company B, Company A, Company D**

Replace each ● with <, >, or = to make a true sentence.

21. -13 ● $|-14|$ **<**
22. $|36|$ ● -37 **>**
23. -12 ● $|12|$ **<**
24. $|-29|$ ● $|92|$ **<**

FOOTBALL For Exercises 25 and 26, use the information at the right. It shows the yardage gained each play for five plays.

Play	1	2	3	4	5
Yardage	10	−2	5	−5	20

25. Order the yardage from least to greatest. **−5, −2, 5, 10, 20**
26. Which run is the middle, or *median*, yardage? **5**

27. **WEATHER** The wind chill index was invented in 1939 by Paul Siple, a polar explorer and authority on Antarctica. Wind chill causes the air to feel colder on human skin. Which feels colder: a temperature of 10° with a 15-mile-per-hour wind or a temperature of 5° with a 10 mile per hour wind? **5° with a 10-mile-per-hour wind**

WIND CHILL

Wind (mph)	Temperature (°F)				
	15	10	5	0	−5
5	7	1	−5	−11	−16
10	3	−4	−10	−16	−22
15	0	−7	−13	−19	−26
20	−2	−9	−15	−23	−29

Determine whether each sentence is *true* or *false*. If *false*, change one number to make the sentence true. **28, 30. Sample answers given.**

28. $-8 > 5$ **false; 8 > 5**
29. $-7 < 0$ **true**
30. $|5| < -6$ **false; |5| < 6**
31. $10 > |-8|$ **true**

Academic Standards • ISTEP+
Extra Practice, pp. 671, 705

DIFFERENTIATED HOMEWORK OPTIONS

Level	Assignment	Two-Day Assignment	
BL Basic	7–20, 32, 34–44	7–19 odd, 35, 36	8–20 even, 32, 34, 37–44
OL Core	7–25 odd, 26, 27, 29, 31, 32, 34–44	7–20, 35, 36	21–32, 34, 37–44
AL Advanced/Pre-AP	21–40 (optional: 41–44)		

86 Chapter 2 Integers

H.O.T. Problems

32. **NUMBER SENSE** If 0 is the greatest integer in a set of five integers, what can you conclude about the other four integers? **They are negative integers.**

33. **CHALLENGE** What is the greatest integer value of n such that $n < 0$? **−1**

34. **WRITING IN MATH** Develop a method for ordering a set of negative integers from least to greatest without the aid of a number line. Explain your method and use it to order the set {−5, −8, −1, −3}. **See margin.**

ISTEP+ PRACTICE 7.1.6

35. On a certain game show, contestants receive positive numbers of points for correct responses and negative numbers of points for incorrect responses. Which list gives the points a contestant received during one round of the game in order from highest to lowest? **C**

A −200, −400, −1000, 200, 600

B 600, −1000, −400, −200, 200

C 600, 200, −200, −400, −1000

D −1000, −400, −200, 600, 200

36. Which statement about the values shown is *not* true? **J**

State	Low Temperature (°F)
AR	−29
GA	−17
MS	−19
VA	−30
TX	−23

Source: *The World Almanac*

F Virginia's record low is less than the record low for Arkansas.

G Arkansas' record low is less than the record low for Georgia.

H Mississippi's record low is greater than the record low for Texas.

J Texas' record low is less than the record low for Arkansas.

Spiral Review

Write an integer for each situation. (Lesson 2-1)

37. 9°C below zero **−9**

38. a gain of 20 feet **20**

HOBBIES For Exercises 39 and 40, use the following information. (Lesson 1-10)

Sophia estimates that she knits 6 rows of an afghan each hour.

39. Write an equation using two variables to represent the total number of rows r completed by Sophia after time t. $r = 6t$

40. How many rows will Sophia have completed after 4 hours? **24**

GET READY for the Next Lesson

PREREQUISITE SKILL Graph each point on a vertical number line that goes from −10 on the bottom to 10 at the top. (Lesson 2-1) **41–44. See margin.**

41. −3

42. 0

43. 4

44. −7

4 Assess

Crystal Ball Tell students that tomorrow's lesson is about graphing points on a coordinate plane. Ask them to write how they think what they learned today will connect with tomorrow's lesson.

Formative Assessment

Check for student understanding of concepts in Lessons 2-1 and 2-2.

CRM Quiz 1, p. 61

Additional Answers

34. Sample answer: To order a set of negative integers from least to greatest, order the integers from greatest to least according to their absolute values. For example, to order the set {−5, −8, −1, −3}, first determine the absolute value of each integer. The set of absolute values is {5, 8, 1, 3}. Then, order these absolute values from greatest to least, {8, 5, 3, 1}. Replacing these absolute values with their original integers orders the original set integers from least to greatest, {−8, −5, −3, −1}.

41–44.

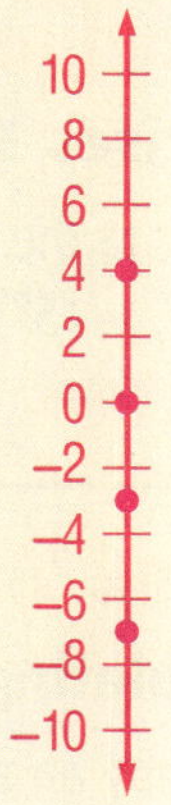

Differentiated Instruction

Logical Learners Have students work in groups to research how integers are used in journalism. Assign each group a different section of a print or online newspaper, including the following sections: Sports, Weather, News, and Business. Ask a volunteer from each group to describe how integers are used in their section of the newspaper and give examples.

Lesson 2-2 Comparing and Ordering Integers **87**

2-3 The Coordinate Plane

PACING: **Regular:** 1 period, **Block:** 0.5 period

IN Academic Standards **Preparation for 7.3.2** Identify, describe, and use transformations (translations, rotations, reflections, and simple compositions of these transformations) to solve problems.

Options for Differentiated Instruction

ELL = English Language Learner AL = Above or Beyond Grade Level SS = Struggling Students SN = Special Needs

Scaffolding the Lesson SS SN

Use before presenting Example 1.

To scaffold this lesson, begin by having students name points and graph ordered pairs in the first quadrant only. Examples of possible exercises are shown below.

Write the ordered pair for each point graphed below.

1. *A* (1, 5)
2. *B* (3, 2)
3. *C* (0, 1)
4. *D* (6, 7)

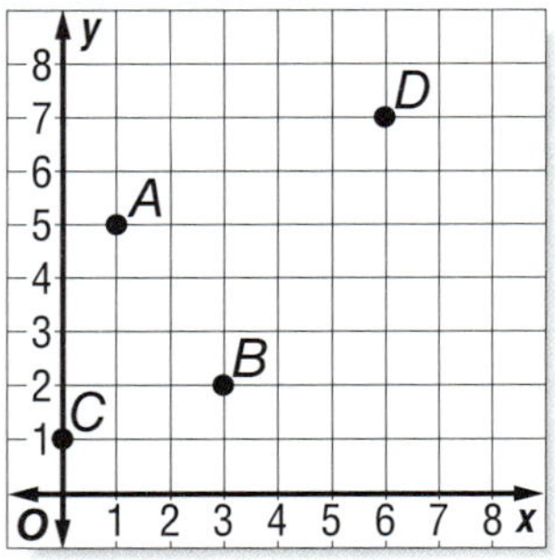

Graph and label each point below on the coordinate plane.

5. *L* (6, 5)
6. *M* (4, 0)
7. *N* (2, 4)
8. *P* (7, 2)

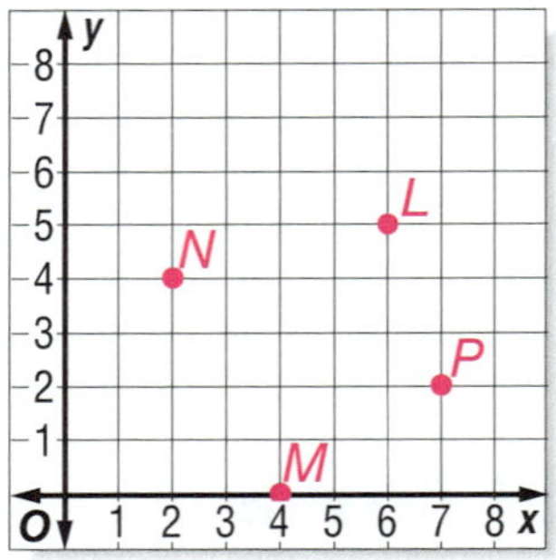

Once students are successful identifying the *x*- and *y*-coordinates of points and are able to plot points on a graph, expand to the four quadrants.

Verbal Explanations ELL AL SS

Use with Exercises 35–38.

Have students refer to the map in Exercises 35–38. Ask them to explain how they would determine what continent is located at (−90°, −15°). Sample answer: From the origin, move left to −90° and then down to −15° to find that the coordinate point (−90°, −15°) is located in South America.

Kinesthetic and Visual Learning ELL AL SS SN

Use after completing the lesson.

If possible, photocopy an aerial photo or schematic of the school grounds. Have students draw a grid on the photo and label where different features are located. Then take students outside and have them walk between landmarks to get a sense of the distance shown on the map. Have them plot their paths on their grids.

Leveled Lesson Resources

Also on TeacherWorks™ Lesson 2-3

Chapter 2 Resource Masters

BL = Below or Approaching Grade Level   OL = On Grade Level   AL = Above or Beyond Grade Level   ELL = English Language Learner

Lesson Reading Guide
p. 22 BL OL ELL

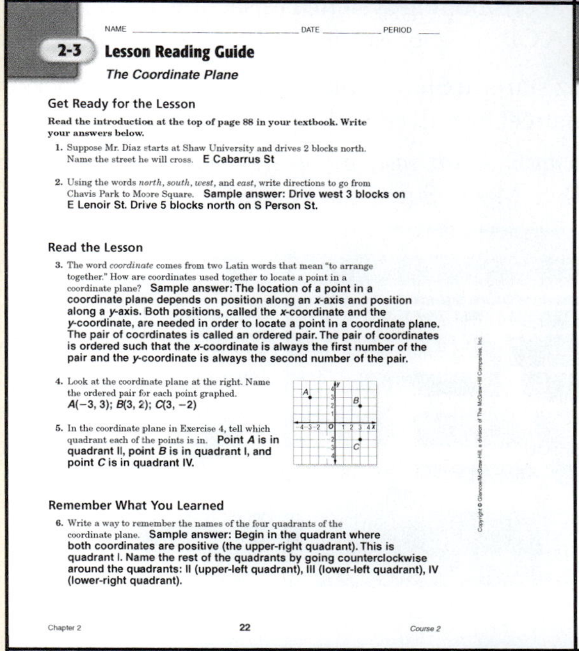

NAME ______ DATE ______ PERIOD ____

2-3 Lesson Reading Guide

The Coordinate Plane

Get Ready for the Lesson

Read the introduction at the top of page 88 in your textbook. Write your answers below.

1. Suppose Mr. Diaz starts at Shaw University and drives 2 blocks north. Name the street he will cross. **E Cabarrus St**
2. Using the words *north, south, west,* and *east,* write directions to go from Chavis Park to Moore Square. **Sample answer: Drive west 3 blocks on E Lenoir St. Drive 5 blocks north on S Person St.**

Read the Lesson

3. The word *coordinate* comes from two Latin words that mean "to arrange together." How are coordinates used together to locate a point in a coordinate plane? **Sample answer: The location of a point in a coordinate plane depends on position along an x-axis and position along a y-axis. Both positions, called the x-coordinate and the y-coordinate, are needed in order to locate a point in a coordinate plane. The pair of coordinates is called an ordered pair. The pair of coordinates is ordered such that the x-coordinate is always the first number of the pair and the y-coordinate is always the second number of the pair.**
4. Look at the coordinate plane at the right. Name the ordered pair for each point graphed. **A(−3, 3); B(3, 2); C(3, −2)**
5. In the coordinate plane in Exercise 4, tell which quadrant each of the points is in. **Point A is in quadrant II, point B is in quadrant I, and point C is in quadrant IV.**

Remember What You Learned

6. Write a way to remember the names of the four quadrants of the coordinate plane. **Sample answer: Begin in the quadrant where both coordinates are positive (the upper-right quadrant). This is quadrant I. Name the rest of the quadrants by going counterclockwise around the quadrants: II (upper-left quadrant), III (lower-left quadrant), IV (lower-right quadrant).**

Chapter 2 22 Course 2

Study Guide and Intervention*
p. 23 BL OL ELL

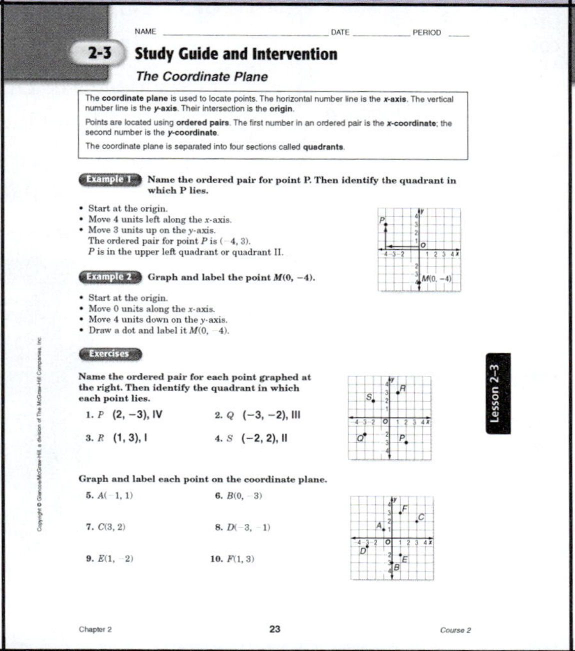

NAME ______ DATE ______ PERIOD ____

2-3 Study Guide and Intervention

The Coordinate Plane

The **coordinate plane** is used to locate points. The horizontal number line is the **x-axis**. The vertical number line is the **y-axis**. Their intersection is the **origin**.

Points are located using **ordered pairs**. The first number in an ordered pair is the **x-coordinate**; the second number is the **y-coordinate**.

The coordinate plane is separated into four sections called **quadrants**.

Example 1 Name the ordered pair for point P. Then identify the quadrant in which P lies.

- Start at the origin.
- Move 4 units left along the x-axis.
- Move 3 units up on the y-axis.

The ordered pair for point P is (−4, 3). P is in the upper left quadrant or quadrant II.

Example 2 Graph and label the point M(0, −4).

- Start at the origin.
- Move 0 units along the x-axis.
- Move 4 units down on the y-axis.
- Draw a dot and label it M(0, −4).

Exercises

Name the ordered pair for each point graphed at the right. Then identify the quadrant in which each point lies.

1. P **(2, −3), IV** 2. Q **(−3, −2), III**
3. R **(1, 3), I** 4. S **(−2, 2), II**

Graph and label each point on the coordinate plane.

5. A(−1, 1) 6. B(0, −3)
7. C(3, 2) 8. D(−3, −1)
9. E(1, −2) 10. F(1, 3)

Chapter 2 23 Course 2

Skills Practice*
p. 24 BL OL

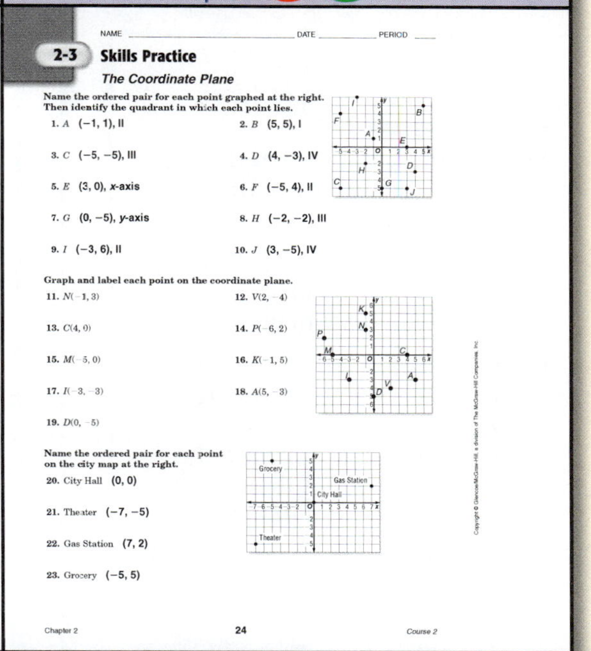

NAME ______ DATE ______ PERIOD ____

2-3 Skills Practice

The Coordinate Plane

Name the ordered pair for each point graphed at the right. Then identify the quadrant in which each point lies.

1. A **(−1, 1), II** 2. B **(5, 5), I**
3. C **(−5, −5), III** 4. D **(4, −3), IV**
5. E **(3, 0), x-axis** 6. F **(−5, 4), II**
7. G **(0, −5), y-axis** 8. H **(−2, −2), III**
9. I **(−3, 6), II** 10. J **(3, −5), IV**

Graph and label each point on the coordinate plane.

11. N(−1, 3) 12. V(2, −4)
13. C(4, 0) 14. P(−6, 2)
15. M(−5, 0) 16. K(−1, 5)
17. R(−3, −3) 18. A(5, −3)
19. D(0, −5)

Name the ordered pair for each point on the city map at the right.

20. City Hall **(0, 0)**
21. Theater **(−7, −5)**
22. Gas Station **(7, 2)**
23. Grocery **(−5, 5)**

Chapter 2 24 Course 2

Practice*
p. 25 OL AL

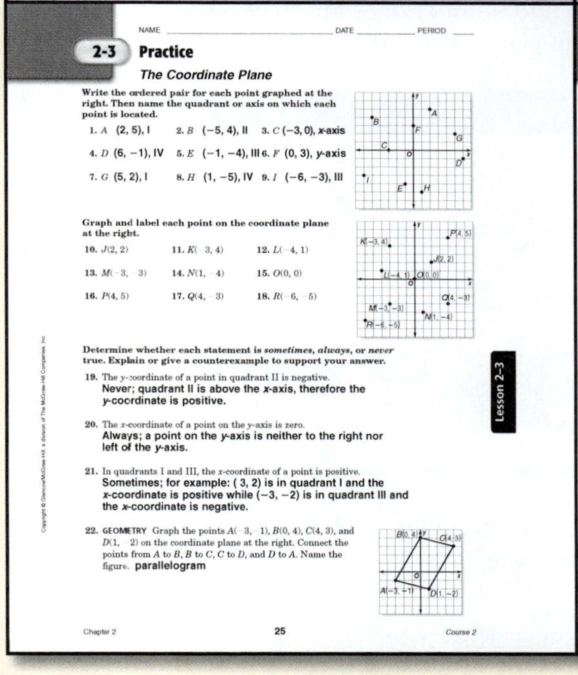

NAME ______ DATE ______ PERIOD ____

2-3 Practice

The Coordinate Plane

Write the ordered pair for each point graphed at the right. Then name the quadrant or axis on which each point is located.

1. A **(2, 5), I** 2. B **(−5, 4), II** 3. C **(−3, 0), x-axis**
4. D **(6, −1), IV** 5. E **(−1, −4), III** 6. F **(0, 3), y-axis**
7. G **(5, 2), I** 8. H **(1, −5), IV** 9. I **(−6, −3), III**

Graph and label each point on the coordinate plane at the right.

10. J(2, 2) 11. K(−3, 4) 12. L(−4, 1)
13. M(−3, −3) 14. N(1, −4) 15. O(0, 0)
16. P(4, 5) 17. Q(4, −3) 18. R(−6, −5)

Determine whether each statement is *sometimes, always,* or *never* true. Explain or give a counterexample to support your answer.

19. The y-coordinate of a point in quadrant II is negative. **Never; quadrant II is above the x-axis, therefore the y-coordinate is positive.**
20. The x-coordinate of a point on the y-axis is zero. **Always; a point on the y-axis is neither to the right nor left of the y-axis.**
21. In quadrants I and III, the x-coordinate of a point is positive. **Sometimes; for example: (3, 2) is in quadrant I and the x-coordinate is positive while (−3, −2) is in quadrant III and the x-coordinate is negative.**
22. GEOMETRY Graph the points A(−3, −1), B(0, 4), C(4, 3), and D(1, −2) on the coordinate plane at the right. Connect the points from A to B, B to C, C to D, and D to A. Name the figure. **parallelogram**

Chapter 2 25 Course 2

Word Problem Practice*
p. 26 OL AL

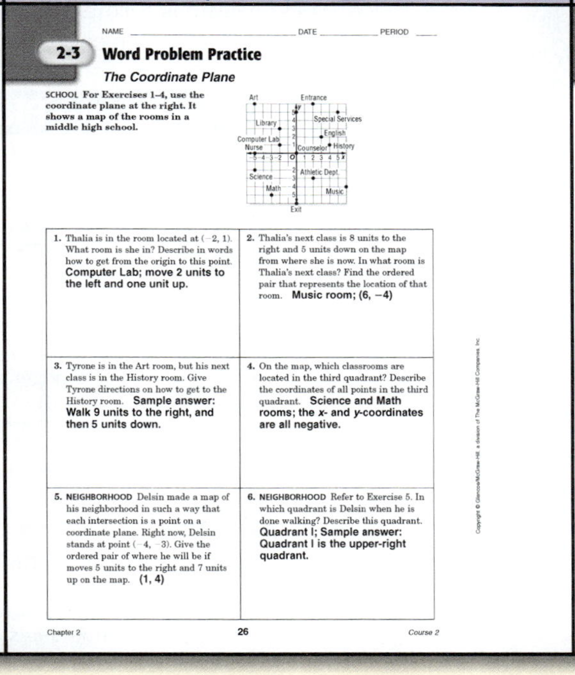

NAME ______ DATE ______ PERIOD ____

2-3 Word Problem Practice

The Coordinate Plane

SCHOOL For Exercises 1–4, use the coordinate plane at the right. It shows a map of the rooms in a middle high school.

1. Thalia is in the room located at (−2, 1). What room is she in? Describe in words how to get from the origin to this point. **Computer Lab; move 2 units to the left and one unit up.**
2. Thalia's next class is 8 units to the right and 5 units down on the map from where she is now. In what room is Thalia's next class? Find the ordered pair that represents the location of that room. **Music room; (6, −4)**
3. Tyrone is in the Art room, but his next class is in the History room. Give Tyrone directions on how to get to the History room. **Sample answer: Walk 9 units to the right, and then 5 units down.**
4. On the map, which classrooms are located in the third quadrant? Describe the coordinates of all points in the third quadrant. **Science and Math rooms; the x- and y-coordinates are all negative.**
5. NEIGHBORHOOD Delsin made a map of his neighborhood in such a way that each intersection is a point on a coordinate plane. Right now, Delsin stands at point (−4, −3). Give the ordered pair of where he will be if he moves 5 units to the right and 7 units up on the map. **(1, 4)**
6. NEIGHBORHOOD Refer to Exercise 5. In which quadrant is Delsin when he is done walking? Describe this quadrant. **Quadrant I; Sample answer: Quadrant I is the upper-right quadrant.**

Chapter 2 26 Course 2

Enrichment
p. 27 OL AL

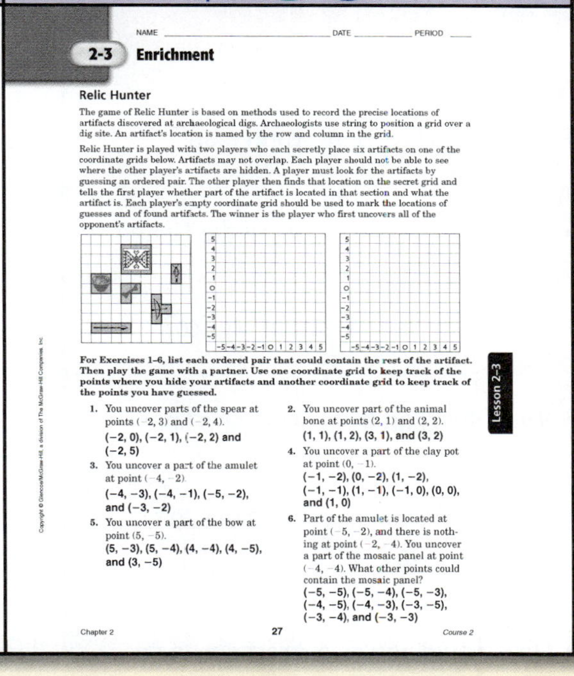

NAME ______ DATE ______ PERIOD ____

2-3 Enrichment

Relic Hunter

The game of Relic Hunter is based on methods used to record the precise locations of artifacts discovered at archaeological digs. Archaeologists use string to position a grid over a dig site. An artifact's location is named by the row and column in the grid.

Relic Hunter is played with two players who each secretly place six artifacts on one of the coordinate grids below. Artifacts may not overlap. Each player should not be able to see where the other player's artifacts are hidden. A player must look for the artifacts by guessing an ordered pair. The other player then finds that location on the secret grid and tells the first player whether part of the artifact is located in that section and what the artifact is. Each player's empty coordinate grid should be used to mark the locations of guesses and of found artifacts. The winner is the player who first uncovers all of the opponent's artifacts.

For Exercises 1–6, list each ordered pair that could contain the rest of the artifact. Then play the game with a partner. Use one coordinate grid to keep track of the points where you hide your artifacts and another coordinate grid to keep track of the points you have guessed.

1. You uncover parts of the spear at points (−2, 3) and (−2, 4). **(−2, 0), (−2, 1), (−2, 2) and (−2, 5)**
2. You uncover part of the animal bone at points (2, 1) and (2, 2). **(1, 1), (1, 2), (3, 1), and (3, 2)**
3. You uncover a part of the amulet at point (−4, −2). **(−4, −3), (−4, −1), (−5, −2), and (−3, −2)**
4. You uncover a part of the clay pot at point (0, −1). **(−1, −2), (0, −2), (1, −2), (−1, −1), (1, −1), (−1, 0), (0, 0), and (1, 0)**
5. You uncover a part of the bow at point (5, −5). **(5, −3), (5, −4), (4, −4), (4, −5), and (3, −5)**
6. Part of the amulet is located at point (−5, −2), and there is nothing at point (−2, −4). You uncover a part of the mosaic panel at point (−4, −4). What other points could contain the mosaic panel? **(−5, −5), (−5, −4), (−5, −3), (−4, −5), (−4, −3), (−3, −5), (−3, −4), and (−3, −3)**

Chapter 2 27 Course 2

** Also available in Spanish* ELL

Additional Lesson Resources

Transparencies

- *5-Minute Check Transparency,* Lesson 2-3

Other Print Products

- *Teaching Mathematics with Manipulatives*
- *Noteables™ Interactive Study Notebook with Foldables™*

Teacher Tech Tools

- *Interactive Classroom CD-ROM,* Lesson 2-3
- *AssignmentWorks,* Lesson 2-3

Student Tech Tools

glencoe.com

- Extra Examples, Chapter 2, Lesson 3
- Self-Check Quiz, Chapter 2, Lesson 3

2-3 Lesson Notes

1 Focus

Vertical Alignment

Before Lesson 2-3
Identify and graph ordered pairs in the four quadrants of the coordinate plane

Lesson 2-3
Use graphs to explain mathematical reasoning

After Lesson 2-3
Graph linear functions, noting that the vertical change per unit of horizontal change is always the same and know that the ratio is called the slope of a graph

2 Teach

Scaffolding Questions

Point to the classroom world map.

Ask:

- Is Mexico north or south of the United States? south
- Is Senegal west or east of Mexico? east
- What direction from Senegal is Spain? north
- How would you give directions to go from Spain to Peru? go west and south
- How would you give directions to go from Peru to Spain? go east and north

Additional Answer

2. Sample answer: Drive west 3 blocks on E Lenoir St. Drive 3 blocks north on S Person St.

2-3 The Coordinate Plane

MAIN IDEA

Graph points on a coordinate plane.

IN Academic Standards

Preparation for 7.3.2 Identify, describe, and use transformations (translations, rotations, reflections and simple compositions of these transformations) to solve problems.

New Vocabulary

coordinate plane
quadrant
x-axis
y-axis
origin
ordered pair
x-coordinate
y-coordinate

IN Math Online

glencoe.com

- Extra Examples
- Personal Tutor
- Self-Check Quiz

GET READY for the Lesson

GPS A GPS, or global positioning system, is a satellite based navigation system. A GPS map of Raleigh, North Carolina, is shown.

1. Suppose Mr. Diaz starts at Shaw University and drives 2 blocks north. Name the street he will cross. E. Lenoir
2. Using the words *north, south, east,* and *west,* write directions to go from Chavis Park to Moore Square. See margin.

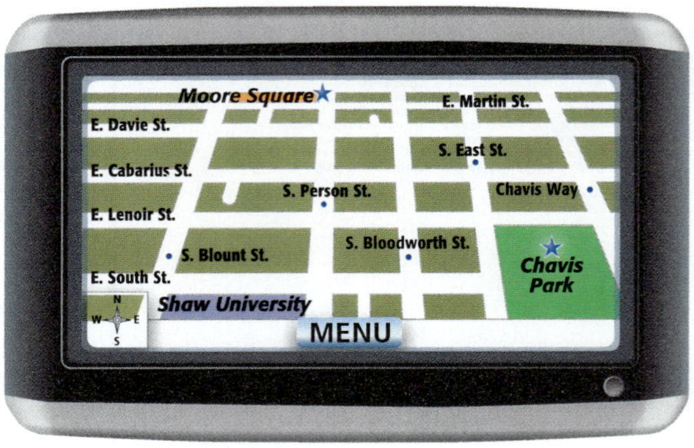

On a GPS, towns and streets are often located on a grid. In mathematics, we use a grid called a coordinate plane, to locate points. A **coordinate plane** is formed when two number lines intersect. The number lines separate the coordinate plane into four regions called **quadrants**.

Coordinate Plane — Key Concept

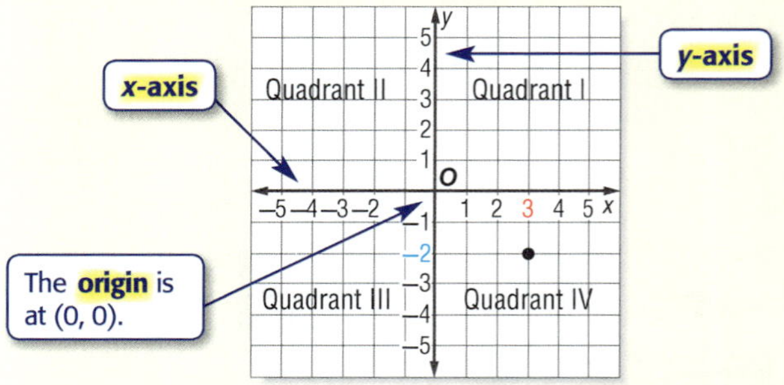

An **ordered pair** is a pair of numbers, such as (3, −2), used to locate a point in the coordinate plane.

***x*-coordinate** corresponds to a number on the *x*-axis. (3, −2) ***y*-coordinate** corresponds to a number on the *y*-axis.

When locating an ordered pair, moving *right* or *up* on a coordinate plane is in the *positive* direction. Moving *left* or *down* is in the *negative* direction.

EXAMPLE Naming Points Using Ordered Pairs

1 Write the ordered pair that corresponds to point D. Then state the quadrant in which the point is located.

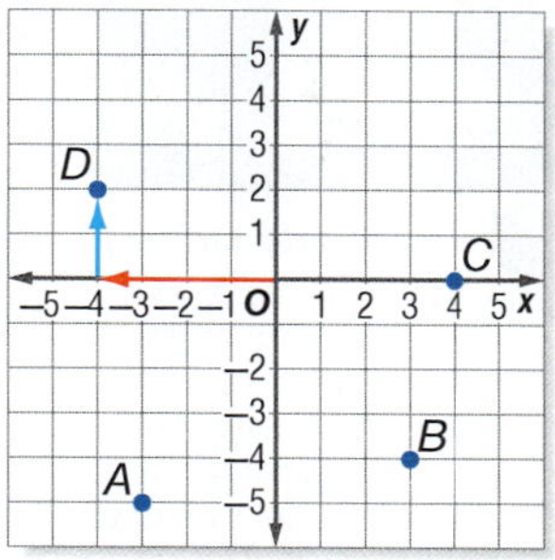

- Start at the origin.
- Move left on the x-axis to find the x-coordinate of point D, which is -4.
- Move up to find the y-coordinate, which is 2.

So, point D corresponds to the ordered pair $(-4, 2)$. Point D is located in Quadrant II.

CHECK Your Progress

Write the ordered pair that corresponds to each point. Then state the quadrant or axis on which the point is located.

a. A (–3, –5); III b. B (3, –4); IV c. C (4, 0); x-axis

EXAMPLE Graph an Ordered Pair

2 Graph and label point K at $(2, -5)$.

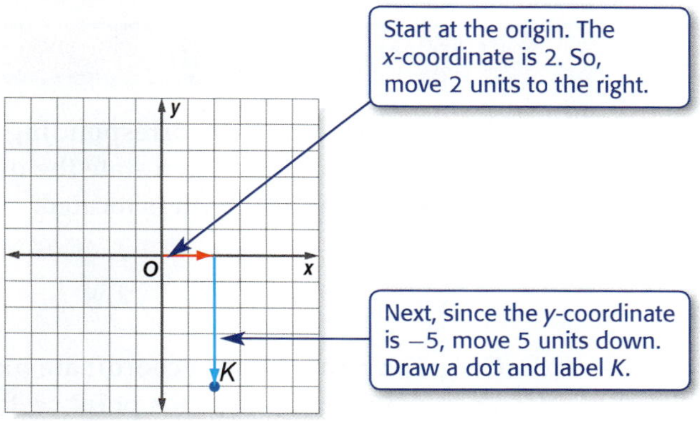

CHECK Your Progress

On graph paper, draw a coordinate plane. Then graph and label each point. d–f. See margin.

d. $L(-4, 2)$ e. $M(-5, -3)$ f. $N(0, 1)$

Focus on Mathematical Content

The first number of an ordered pair tells how far to move right or left along the **x-axis.** The second number of an ordered pair tells how far to move up or down along the **y-axis.**

Maps are a kind of coordinate plane.

Formative Assessment

Use the Check Your Progress exercises after each Example to determine students' understanding of concepts.

ADDITIONAL EXAMPLES

1 Write the ordered pair that corresponds to point R. Then state the quadrant in which the point is located.
(–2, 4); quadrant II

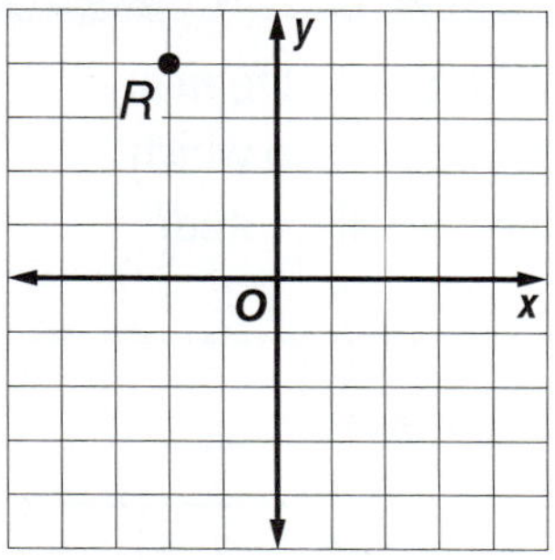

2 Graph and label point M at $(3, 5)$.

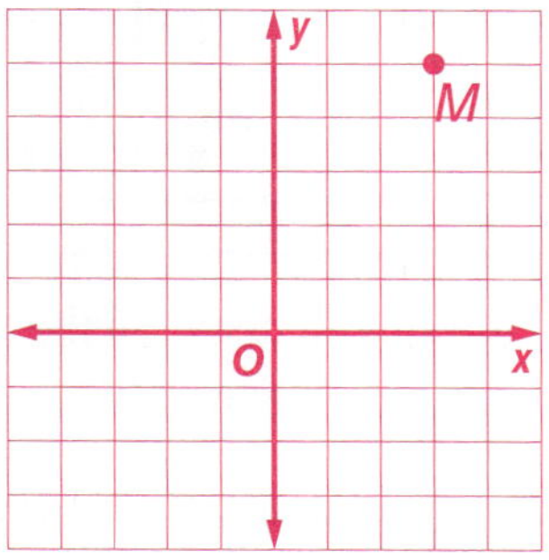

Additional Examples are also in:

- Noteables™ Interactive Study Notebook with Foldables™
- Interactive Classroom PowerPoint® Presentations

Reading Math

Scale When no numbers are shown on the x- or y-axis, you can assume that each square is 1 unit long on each side.

Additional Answers

d–f.

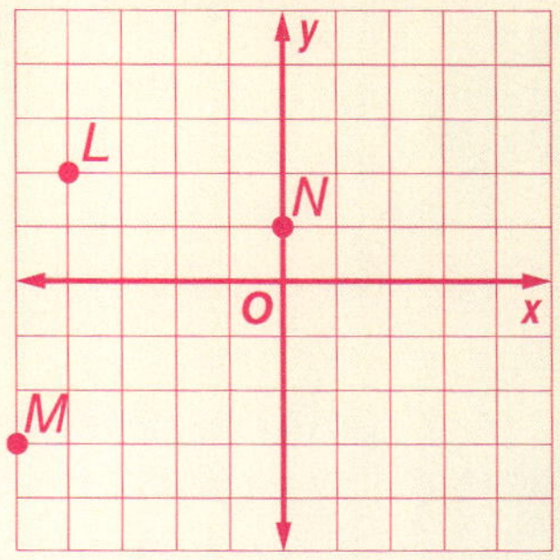

Lesson 2-3 The Coordinate Plane 89

3 Practice

Formative Assessment

Use Exercises 1–10 to check for understanding.

Then use the chart at the bottom of the next page to customize your assignments for students.

Intervention You may wish to use the Study Guide and Intervention Master on page 23 of the *Chapter 2 Resource Masters* for additional reinforcement.

Tips for New Teachers

Coordinate Planes

You may wish to point out that the quadrants of a coordinate plane are numbered in order, from I to IV, in a *counterclockwise* direction.

ADDITIONAL EXAMPLES

3 **GEOGRAPHY** Use the map of Utah shown below. In which quadrant is Vernal located? Quadrant 1

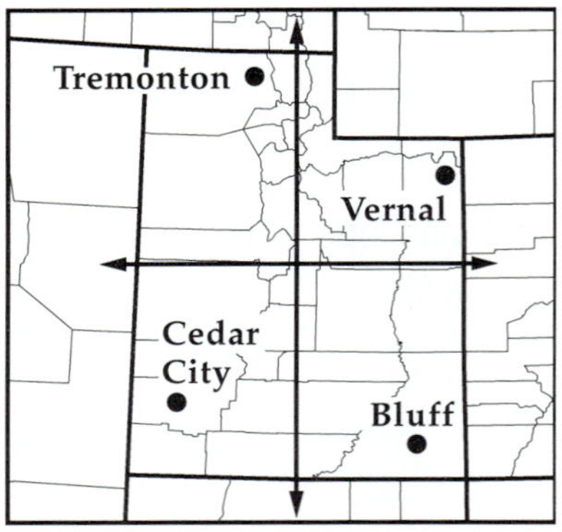

4 Which of the cities labeled on the map is located in Quadrant IV? Bluff

Additional Answers

5–8.

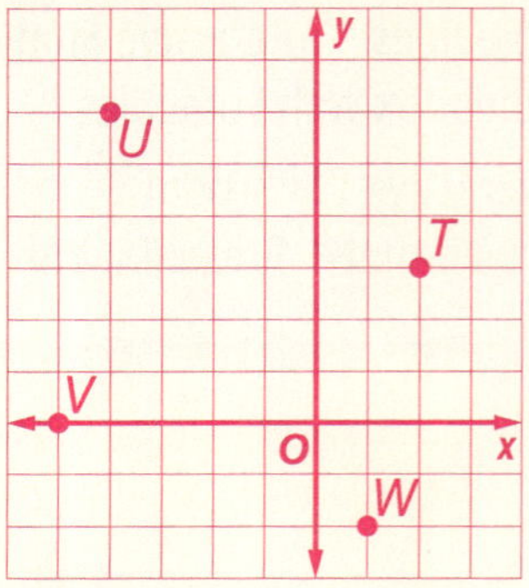

Real-World Link New York Aquarium has a marine mammal exhibit that includes sea otters. Large male sea otters can grow to be over 4 feet in length.

Real-World EXAMPLES

3 **AQUARIUMS** A map can be divided into a coordinate plane where the x-coordinate represents how far to move right or left and the y-coordinate represents how far to move up or down. What exhibit is located at (6, 5)?

New York Aquarium, Bronx, NY

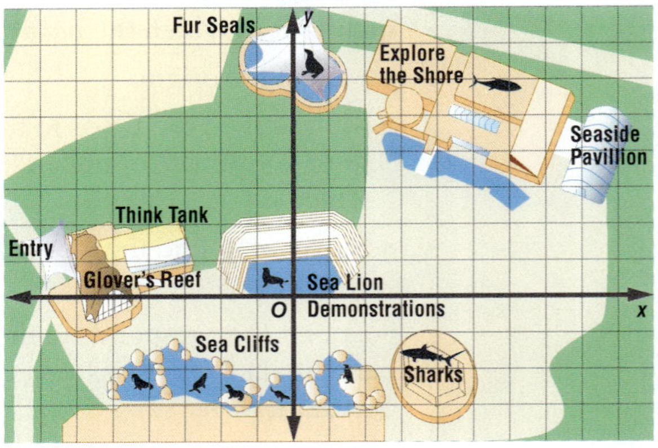

Start at the origin. Move 6 units to the right and then 5 units up. Explore the Shore is located at (6, 5).

4 **In which quadrant is the Shark Exhibit located?**

The Shark Exhibit is located in Quadrant IV.

CHECK Your Progress

For Exercises g and h, use the map above. g. (–4, 2)

g. Find the ordered pair that represents the location of the Think Tank.

h. What is located at the origin? Sea Lion Demonstrations

CHECK Your Understanding

Example 1 (p. 89)

Write the ordered pair corresponding to each point graphed at the right. Then state the quadrant or axis on which each point is located.

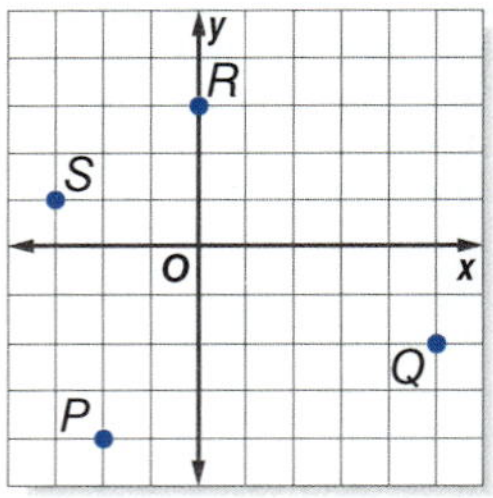

1. P (–2, –4); III
2. Q (5, –2); IV
3. R (0, 3); y-axis
4. S (–3, 1); II

Example 2 (p. 89)

On graph paper, draw a coordinate plane. Then graph and label each point. 5–8. See margin.

5. $T(2, 3)$
6. $U(-4, 6)$
7. $V(-5, 0)$
8. $W(1, -2)$

Examples 3, 4 (p. 90)

GEOGRAPHY **For Exercises 9 and 10, use the map in Example 3 above.**

9. What exhibit is located at (0, –3)? Sea Cliffs
10. In which quadrant is the Seaside Pavillion located? I

Practice and Problem Solving

HOMEWORK HELP

For Exercises	See Examples
11–22, 37	1
23–34, 38	2
35–36	3

Exercise Levels
A: 11–38
B: 39–46
C: 47–49

13. (−5, 0); *x*-axis
16. (−3, 5); II
19. (2, 2); I
22. (1, 0); *x*-axis

Write the ordered pair corresponding to each point graphed at the right. Then state the quadrant or axis on which each point is located.

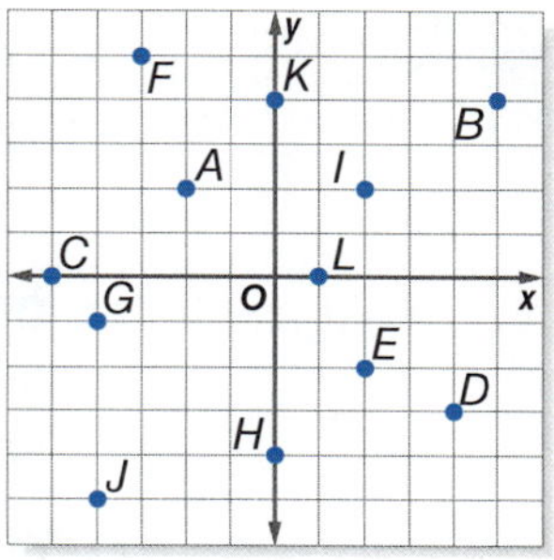

11. A (−2, 2); II
12. B (5, 4); I
13. C
14. D (4, −3); IV
15. E (2, −2); IV
16. F
17. G (−4, −1); III
18. H (0, −4); *y*-axis
19. I
20. J (−4, −5); III
21. K (0, 4); *y*-axis
22. L

On graph paper, draw a coordinate plane. Then graph and label each point. 23–34. See Ch. 2 Answer Appendix.

23. $M(5, 6)$
24. $N(-2, 10)$
25. $P(7, -8)$
26. $Q(3, 0)$
27. $R(-1, -7)$
28. $S(8, 1)$
29. $T(-3, 7)$
30. $U(5, -2)$
31. $V(0, 6)$
32. $W(-5, -7)$
33. $X(-4, 0)$
34. $Y(0, -5)$

GEOGRAPHY **For Exercises 35–38, use the world map.**

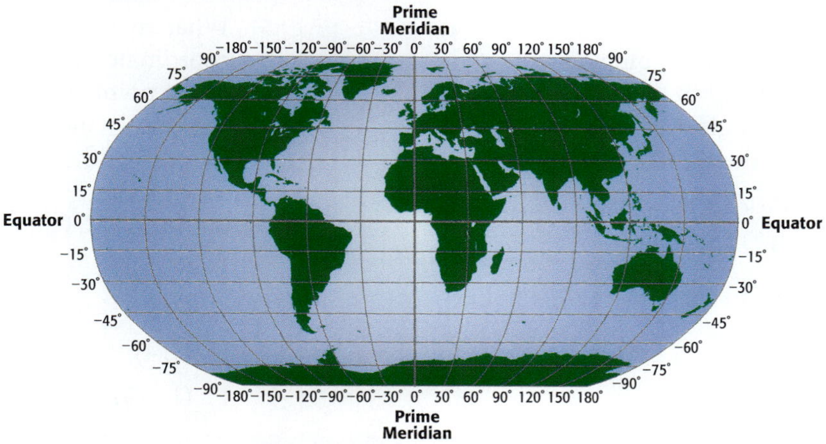

35. The world map can be divided into a coordinate plane where (x, y) represents (degrees longitude, degrees latitude). In what continent is the point (30° longitude, −15° latitude) located? Africa
36. Which of the continents is located entirely in Quadrant II? North America
37. In what continent is the point (−90° longitude, 0° latitude) located?
38. Name a continent on the map that is located entirely in Quadrant I. Asia

37. South America

On graph paper, draw a coordinate plane. Then graph and label each point.

39–41. See margin.

39. $X(1.5, 3.5)$
40. $Y\left(3\frac{1}{4}, 2\frac{1}{2}\right)$
41. $Z\left(2, 1\frac{2}{3}\right)$
42. **GEOMETRY** Graph four points on a coordinate plane so that they form a square when connected. Identify the ordered pairs. See margin for graph.
43. **RESEARCH** Use the Internet or other resources to explain why the coordinate plane is sometimes called the Cartesian plane. See margin.

Odd/Even Assignments

Exercises 11–38 are structured so that students practice the same concepts whether they are assigned odd or even problems.

Additional Answers

39–41.

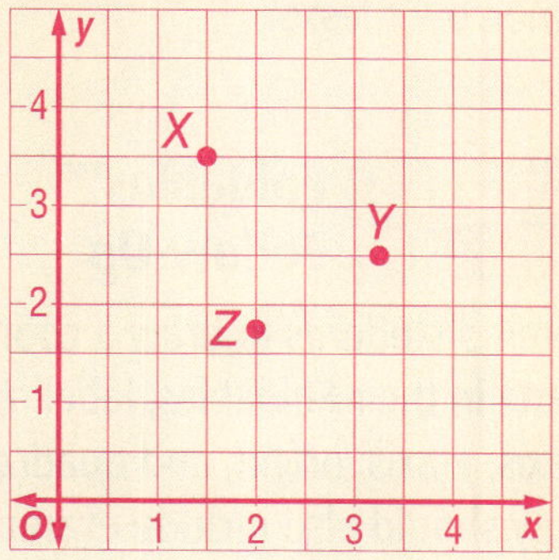

42.

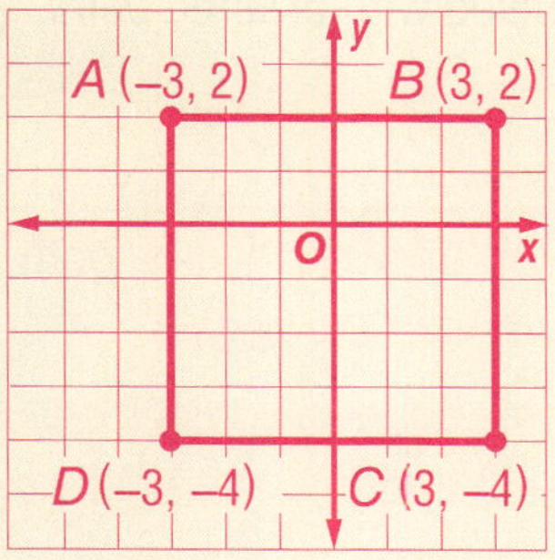

43. Sample answer: Rene Descartes is often credited with inventing the coordinate plane and so the coordinate plane is sometimes called the Cartesian plane, in his honor.

DIFFERENTIATED HOMEWORK OPTIONS

Level	Assignment	Two-Day Assignment	
BL Basic	11–38, 47, 49–61	11–37 odd, 50, 51	12–38 even, 47, 49, 52–61
OL Core	11–41 odd, 42–47, 49–61	11–38, 50, 51	39–47, 49, 52–61
AL Advanced /Pre-AP	39–57 (optional: 58–61)		

4 Assess

Crystal Ball Tell students that tomorrow's lesson is about finding the sums of integers, such −4 + 5. Ask students to write how they think what they learned today will connect with tomorrow's lesson.

FOLDABLES Study Organizer **Foldables™ Follow-Up**

Remind students to draw a coordinate plane in their Foldables, labeling the *x*-axis, *y*-axis, origin, and quadrants. They should also include examples of points labeled with ordered pairs.

Additional Answers

44. Sample answer: Always; both coordinates are negative.

45. Sample answer: Sometimes; both (0, −2) and (0, 2) lie on the *y*-axis.

47. Sample answer: Using the graphic, you can see that an ordered pair such as (−5, −4) is in Quadrant III.

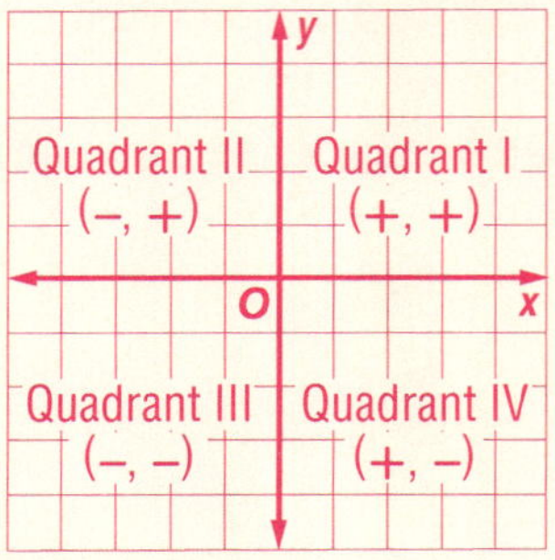

48. Quadrant I when both *x*- and *y*-coordinates are positive; Quadrant III when both *x*- and *y*-coordinates are negative; the origin when both *x*- and *y*-coordinates are 0.

49. Sample answer: Point *A* is 1 unit to the right and 2 units down from the origin, in quadrant IV. Point *B* is 2 units to the left and 1 unit up from the origin, in quadrant II.

Determine whether each statement is *sometimes, always,* or *never* true. Explain or give a counterexample to support your answer.

Academic Standards • ISTEP+
Extra Practice, pp. 672, 705

44. Both *x*- and *y*-coordinates of a point in Quadrant III are negative. **See margin.**

45. The *y*-coordinate of a point that lies on the *y*-axis is negative. **See margin.**

46. The *y*-coordinate of a point in Quadrant II is negative. **Sample answer: never; the *y*-coordinate is always positive in Quadrant II.**

H.O.T. Problems

47. **OPEN ENDED** Create a display that shows how to determine in what quadrant a point is located without graphing. Then provide an example that demonstrates how your graphic is used. **See margin.**

48. **CHALLENGE** Find the possible locations for any ordered pair with *x*- and *y*-coordinates always having the same sign. Explain. **See margin.**

49. **WRITING IN MATH** Explain why the location of point $A(1, -2)$ is different than the location of point $B(-2, 1)$. **See margin.**

ISTEP+ PRACTICE Preparation for 7.3.2

50. Which of the following points lie within the triangle graphed at the right? **C**

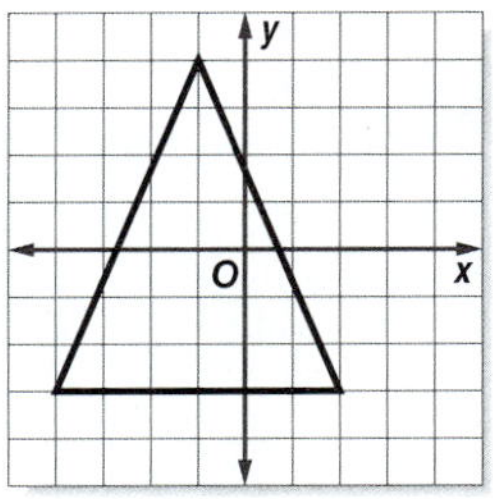

A $A(-4, -1)$
B $B(1, 3)$
C $C(-1, 2)$
D $D(2, -2)$

51. What are the coordinates of the point that shows the location of the lunch room on the map? **G**

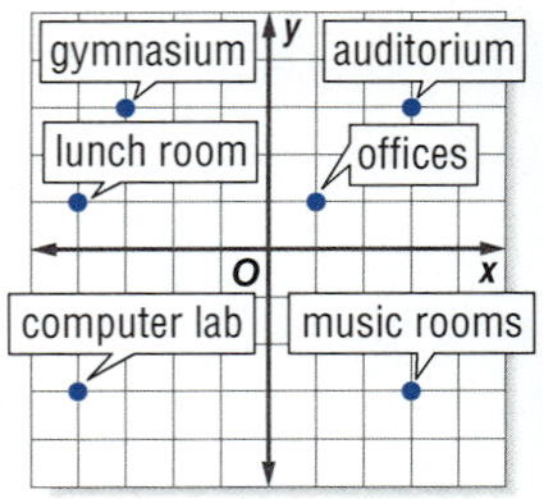

F (4, −1)
G (−4, 1)
H (1, 4)
J (1, −4)

Spiral Review

Replace each ● with <, >, or = to make a true sentence. (Lesson 2-2)

52. −8 ● −3 **<** 53. 26 ● −30 **>** 54. 14 ● |−15| **<** 55. −40 ● |40| **<**

56. Find the absolute value of −101. (Lesson 2-1) **101**

57. **RUNNING** Salvador is training for a marathon. He runs 5 miles each day on weekdays and 8 miles each day on the weekends. How many miles does Salvador run in one week? (Lesson 1-1) **41 miles**

GET READY for the Next Lesson

PREREQUISITE SKILL Add.

58. 138 + 246 **384** 59. 814 + 512 **1,326** 60. 2,653 + 4,817 **7,470** 61. 6,003 + 5,734 **11,737**

Explore 2-4

Algebra Lab
Adding Integers

MAIN IDEA

Use counters to model the addition of integers.

IN Academic Standards

Reinforcement of 6.1.5 Solve problems involving addition, subtraction, multiplication and division of integers and represent computation with integers on a number line. Describe the effect of operations with numbers less than zero. *Also addresses P.2.2, P.5.1, P.5.2, P.5.3.*

IN Math Online

glencoe.com

- Concepts In Motion

You can use positive and negative counters to model the addition of integers. The counter ⊕ represents 1, and the counter ⊖ represents −1. Remember that addition means *combining* two sets.

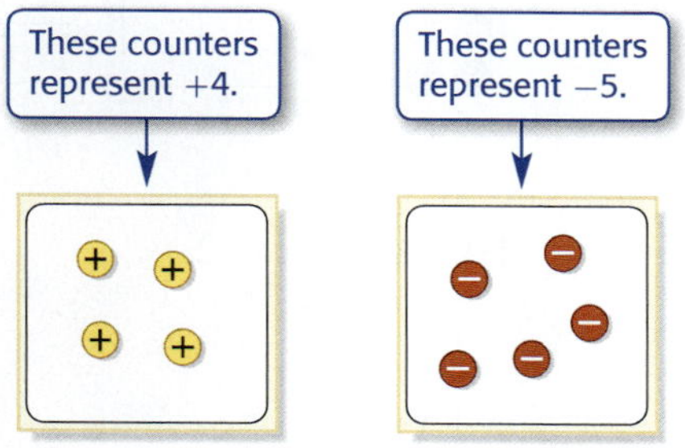

ACTIVITY

1 **Use counters to find −3 + (−6).**

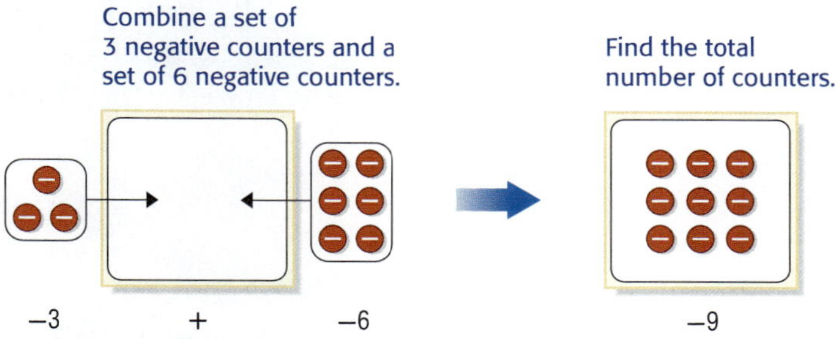

So, $-3 + (-6) = -9$.

CHECK Your Progress

Use counters or a drawing to find each sum. a–f. See margin.

a. $5 + 6$	b. $-3 + (-5)$	c. $-5 + (-4)$
d. $7 + 3$	e. $-2 + (-5)$	f. $-8 + (-6)$

The following two properties are important when modeling operations with integers.

- When one positive counter is paired with one negative counter, the result is called a **zero pair.** The value of a zero pair is 0.
- You can add or remove zero pairs from a mat because adding or removing zero does not change the value of the counters on the mat.

Explore 2-4

Lesson Notes

1 Focus

Materials

- positive and negative counters

Easy-to-Make Manipulatives

Teaching Mathematics with Manipulatives, templates for:

- integer counters, p. 7

2 Teach

Activity 1 Point out that when the second addend of an expression is a negative integer, it is enclosed by parentheses so that the negative symbol (−) is separated from the addition symbol (+).

Make sure students realize that Exercises a–f involve adding like integers—positive and positive, or negative and negative.

Additional Answers

a.

$5 + 6 = 11$

b.

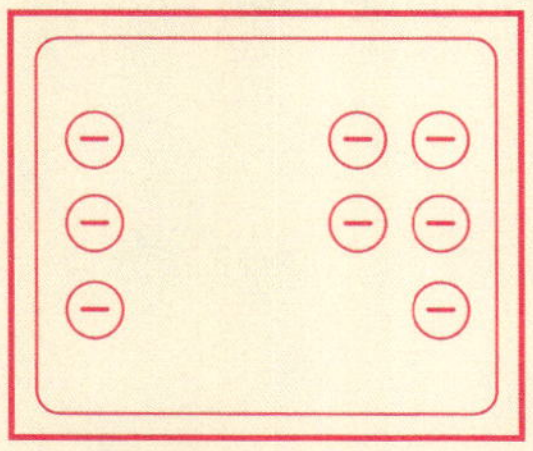

$-3 + (-5) = -8$

c.

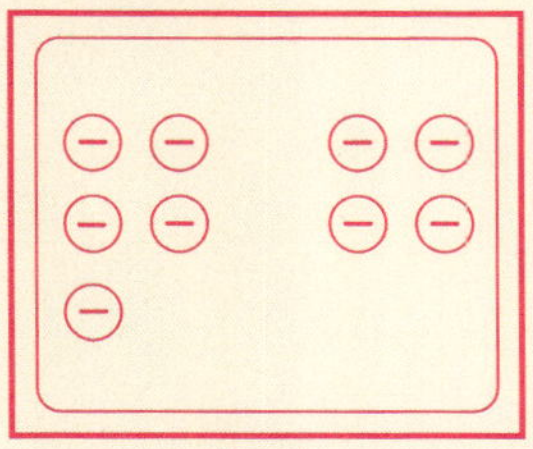

$-5 + (-4) = -9$

d.

$7 + 3 = 10$

e.

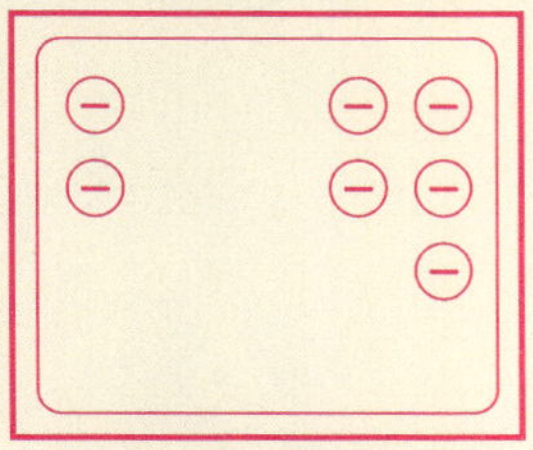

$-2 + (-5) = -7$

f.

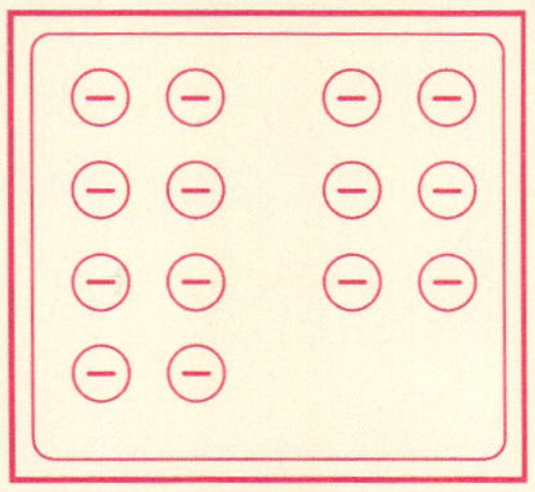

$-8 + (-6) = -14$

Activities 2 and 3 Make sure students realize that these problems involve adding unlike integers—positive and negative. Some students may realize that adding a negative integer is the same as subtracting the same number of positive counters.

3 Assess

Formative Assessment

Use Exercises g–l to determine whether students comprehend how to use counters to model the addition of integers.

From Concrete to Abstract Use Exercises 1 and 2 to bridge the gap between using counters to add integers and writing addition problems with given (positive or negative) results.

Extending the Concept You might want to have students use counters to model repeated addition problems, such as $-2 + (-2) + (-2) + (-2)$. Point out that such a problem can be written as a multiplication problem: $4 \times (-2)$. Have students use what they know about adding integers to write a rule for multiplying integers with different signs.

Tips for New Teachers

Addends and Sums

Remind students the numbers you add are called *addends*. The result is called the *sum*.

ACTIVITIES

Use counters to find each sum.

2 $-4 + 2$

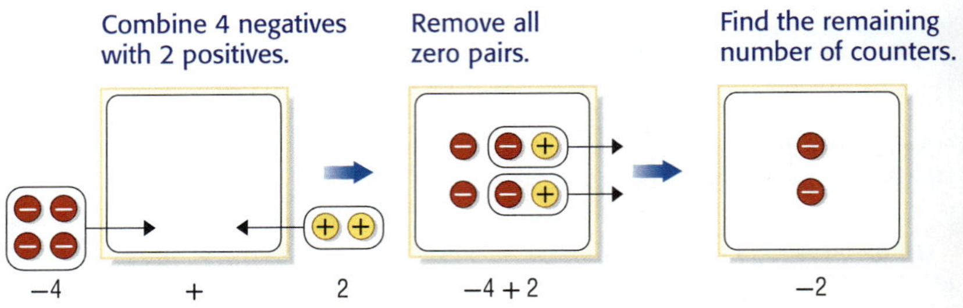

So, $-4 + 2 = -2$.

Study Tip

Adding Integers If there are more negatives than positives, the sum is negative.

3 $5 + (-3)$

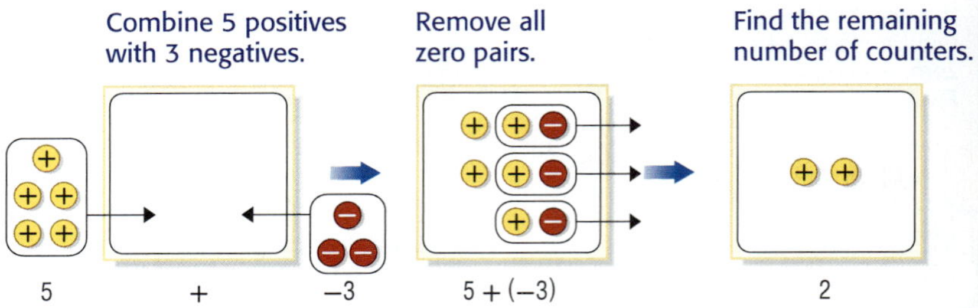

So, $5 + (-3) = 2$.

CHECK Your Progress

Use counters or a drawing to find each sum. **g–l. See Ch. 2 Answer Appendix.**

g. $-6 + 5$ h. $3 + (-6)$ i. $-2 + 7$

j. $8 + (-3)$ k. $-9 + 1$ l. $-4 + 10$

Analyze the Results

1. Write two addition sentences where the sum is positive. In each sentence, one addend should be positive and the other negative. **Sample answer: $-1 + 2 = 1$; $5 + (-4) = 1$**
2. Write two addition sentences where the sum is negative. In each sentence, one addend should be positive and the other negative. **Sample answer: $2 + (-7) = -5$; $-10 + 5 = -5$**
3. **MAKE A CONJECTURE** What is a rule you can use to determine how to find the sum of two integers with the same sign? two integers with different signs?

3. Sample answer: If two integers have the same sign, add and keep the sign. If two integers have different signs, subtract and keep the sign of the integer with the greater absolute value.

2-4 Adding Integers

PACING: **Regular:** 1.5 periods, **Block:** 0.5 period

IN Academic Standards **Reinforcement of 6.1.5** Solve problems involving addition, subtraction, multiplication, and division of integers and represent computation with integers on a number line. Describe the effect of operations with numbers less than zero. *Also addresses P.5.1, P.5.2, P.5.3, P.6.5, P.6.6.*

Options for Differentiated Instruction

ELL = English Language Learner AL = Above or Beyond Grade Level SS = Struggling Students SN = Special Needs

Using Manipulatives ELL SS SN

Use while presenting Examples 3 and 4.

Use positive and negative counters to model the addition of integers with different signs. Example 3 is shown at the right.

Remind students to remove all zero pairs. The remaining counters represent the solution. In this case, there are two positive counters remaining, so the answer is 2.

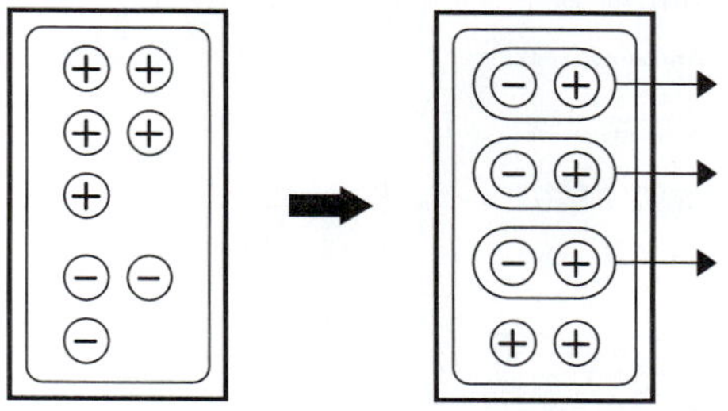

5 + (–3) 5 + (–3) = 2

Connections to Familiar Experiences ELL AL SS SN

Use after presenting Examples 1–8.

Engage students by providing the following application problem involving a video game.

The scoring system for a video game is shown in the table. Assume Dylan starts with zero points. What will be his score after he finds two treasure chests, captures a monster, and is knocked off three cliffs? +8

Action	Points
find treasure chest	+10
knocked off cliff	–5
capture monster	+3

Using Manipulatives SS

Use before assigning the Exercises.

Many students would benefit from having number lines to use as they do independent work. Provide number lines such as the ones shown below.

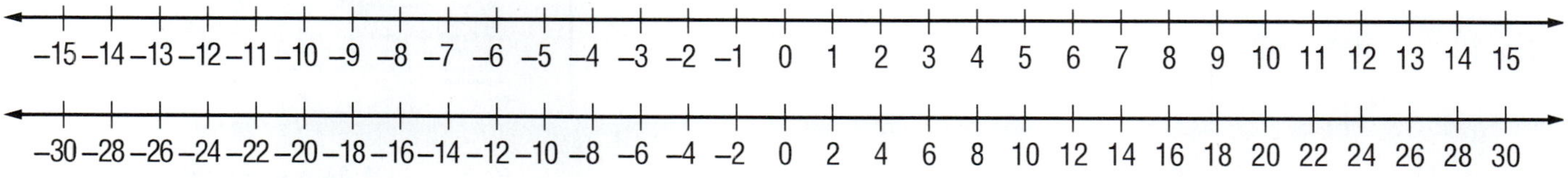

Give each student a copy of a number line sheet in a clear sheet protector so they can reuse the number lines with dry erase markers. Have students place the sheet in their three-ring binders so they can use it as a resource.

Leveled Lesson Resources

Also on TeacherWorks™ Lesson 2-4

Chapter 2 Resource Masters

BL = Below or Approaching Grade Level OL = On Grade Level AL = Above or Beyond Grade Level ELL = English Language Learner

Lesson Reading Guide
p. 29 BL OL ELL

NAME ________ DATE ________ PERIOD ____

2-4 Lesson Reading Guide
Adding Integers

Get Ready for the Lesson

Read the introduction at the top of page 95 in your textbook. Write your answers below.

1. Represent the number of electrons in an atom of helium with an integer. −2
2. Represent the number of protons in an atom of helium with an integer. 2
3. Each proton-electron pair has a value of 0. What is the total charge of an atom of helium? 0

Read the Lesson

For Exercises 4 and 5, tell how you would find each sum on a number line. Then add.

4. −7 + (−9) Starting at 0, move left 7 units, then move left another 9 units; −16.
5. −7 + 9 Starting at 0, move left 7 units, then move right 9 units; 2.
6. What property are you applying when you add a number and its opposite only to find that its result is zero? Additive Inverse Property
7. How many units away from 0 is the number 17? How many units away from 0 is the number −17? What are 17 and −17 called? 17; 17; opposites or additive inverses

Remember What You Learned

8. Work with a partner. Tell your partner how to use absolute values to add integers with different signs when the positive integer has the greater absolute value. Then have your partner explain to you how to use absolute values to add integers with different signs when the negative integer has the greater absolute value. See students' work.

Lesson 2-4

Study Guide and Intervention*
p. 30 BL OL ELL

NAME ________ DATE ________ PERIOD ____

2-4 Study Guide and Intervention
Adding Integers

For integers with the same sign:
- the sum of two positive integers is positive.
- the sum of two negative integers is negative.

For integers with different signs, subtract their absolute values. The sum is:
- positive if the positive integer has the greater absolute value.
- negative if the negative integer has the greater absolute value.

To add integers, it is helpful to use counters or a number line.

Example Find 4 + (−6).

Method 1 Use counters. Combine a set of 4 positive counters and a set of 6 negative counters on a mat.

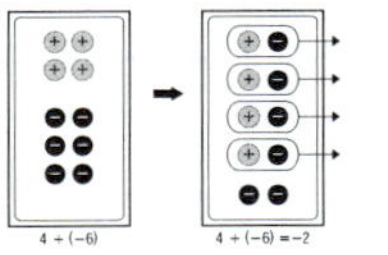

Method 2 Use a number line.
- Start at 0.
- Move 4 units right.
- Then move 6 units left.

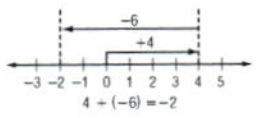

Exercises

Add.

1. −5 + (−2) −7
2. 8 + 1 9
3. −7 + 10 3
4. 16 + (−11) 5
5. −22 + (−7) −29
6. −50 + 50 0
7. −10 + (−10) −20
8. 100 + (−25) 75
9. −35 + −20 −55

Evaluate each expression if a = 8, b = −8, and c = 4.

10. a + 15 23
11. b + (−9) −17
12. a + b 0
13. b + c −4
14. −10 + c −6
15. 12 + b 4

Skills Practice*
p. 31 BL OL

NAME ________ DATE ________ PERIOD ____

2-4 Skills Practice
Adding Integers

Add.

1. 5 + (−8) −3
2. −3 + 3 0
3. −3 + (−8) −11
4. −7 + (−7) −14
5. −8 + 10 2
6. −7 + 13 6
7. 15 + (−10) 5
8. −11 + (−12) −23
9. 25 + (−12) 13
10. −14 + (−13) −27
11. 14 + (−27) −13
12. −28 + 16 −12

Evaluate each expression if a = −8, b = 12, and c = −4.

13. 5 + a −3
14. b + (−9) 3
15. c + (−5) −9
16. a + b 4
17. a + 0 −8
18. b + c 8
19. −12 + b 0
20. a + (−7) −15
21. 21 + c 17
22. a + c −12

Lesson 2-4

Practice*
p. 32 OL AL

NAME ________ DATE ________ PERIOD ____

2-4 Practice
Adding Integers

Add.

1. 34 + 22 56
2. −29 + 30 1
3. 9 + (−32) −23
4. −16 + (−28) −44
5. 4 + (−50) −46
6. −12 + (−63) −75
7. −42 + 42 0
8. −28 + 14 −14
9. 13 + 63 76
10. 18 + (−12) + 5 11
11. −22 + (−10) + 15 −17
12. −14 + 0 + 13 −1

Write an addition expression to describe each situation. Then find each sum and explain its meaning.

13. WEIGHT An actor gains 20 pounds for a part and then loses 15 pounds during the filming of a movie to go along with the story. 20 + (−15) or 5 pounds; the actor is 5 pounds above his/her original weight.

14. TEMPERATURE At 4:00 A.M., the outside temperature was −28°F. By 4:00 P.M. that same day, it rose 38 degrees. −28 + 38 or 10 degrees; the temperature at 4:00 P.M. was 10°F.

ALGEBRA **Evaluate each expression if a = 12, b = −15, and c = −10.**

15. a + (−12) 0
16. −20 + b −35
17. c + 23 13
18. b + c −25
19. a + c 2
20. a + b −3

21. ROLLER COASTERS The latest thrill ride at a popular theme park takes roller coaster fans on an exciting ride. In the first 20 seconds, it carries its passengers up a 100-meter hill, plunges them down 72 meters, and quickly takes them back up a 48-meter rise. How much higher or lower from the start of the ride are they after these 20 seconds? 76 meters higher

Word Problem Practice*
p. 33 OL AL

NAME ________ DATE ________ PERIOD ____

2-4 Word Problem Practice
Adding Integers

Write an addition expression to describe each situation. Then find each sum.

1. FOOTBALL A team gains 20 yards. Then they lose 7 yards. 20 + (−7); 13
2. MONEY Roger owes his mom \$5. He borrows another \$6 from her. (−5) + (−6); −11
3. GOLF Juanita's score was 5 over par on the first 9 holes. Her score was 4 under par on the second 9 holes. 5 + (−4); 1
4. HOT AIR BALLOON A balloon rises 340 feet into the air. Then it descends 130 feet. 340 + (−130); 210
5. CYCLING A cyclist travels downhill for 125 feet. Then she travels up a hill 50 feet. −125 + 50; −75
6. AIRPLANE A plane descends 1,200 feet. Then it descends another 500 feet. −1,200 + (−500); −1,700

Lesson 2-4

Enrichment
p. 34 OL AL

NAME ________ DATE ________ PERIOD ____

2-4 Enrichment

Adding a List of Integers

When you need to add a list of integers, sometimes it can be helpful to reorder the list of integers so you first add all the positive integers, and then all the negative integers.

Example

Marcy is studying weather conditions for her science fair project. During one 24-hour period, she recorded the changes in air temperature in the table at right. If the air temperature was 76°F at the start of her observations, what was the air temperature 24 hours later?

Time	Change in Temp. (°F)	Time	Change in Temp. (°F)
02:00	−1	14:00	−16
04:00	−2	16:00	+2
06:00	+2	18:00	+1
08:00	+4	20:00	+3
10:00	+4	22:00	−1
12:00	+3	00:00	−2

First add all the positive changes in air temperature and then all the negative changes in air temperature.

(+2) + (+4) + (+4) + (+3) + (+2) + (+1) + (+3) = +19

(−1) + (−2) + (−16) + (−1) + (−2) = −22

Next add the results to find the overall change and the new temperature.

+19 + (−22) = −3 76° + (−3°) = 73°F

Exercises

1. The passenger elevator in the Empire State Building registered the following journey log between 9:00 A.M. and 9:15 A.M. on a Monday morning. At which floor was the elevator at 9:15 A.M. if it started in the Lobby, which is Floor 1? On the 8th floor

Number of floors	↑17	↑21	↓16	↓3	↓4	↑11	↓19

2. A deep-sea diver attached to a safety cable was lowered into the water to a depth of 600 feet. During the next hour, the safety cable was let out 250 feet, pulled in 36 feet, pulled in 69 feet, let out 23 feet, pulled in 51 feet, let out 68 feet, and pulled in 24 feet to allow the diver to explore. At the end of the hour, what was the depth of the diver? 761 ft below the surface or −761 ft

3. The Franklin Wildcats football team was competing in the regional championship game. The offense had the ball at the 50-yard line as they tried to score to win the game. Their progress during each play was as follows.

gain 7, gain 2, lose 1, gain 4, lose 5, gain 27, gain 4, gain 5, gain 0, gain 3, lose 2, lose 1, gain 1, gain 2

On what yard line did the Wildcats end? On the 4-yard line

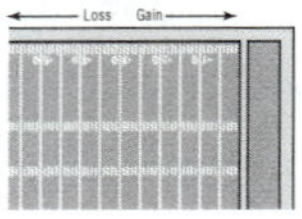

***Also available in Spanish** ELL

Additional Lesson Resources

Transparencies
- *5-Minute Check Transparency*, Lesson 2-4

Other Print Products
- *Teaching Mathematics with Manipulatives*
- *Noteables™ Interactive Study Notebook with Foldables™*

Teacher Tech Tools
- *Interactive Classroom CD-ROM*, Lesson 2-4
- *AssignmentWorks*, Lesson 2-4

Student Tech Tools
glencoe.com
- Extra Examples, Chapter 2, Lesson 4
- Self-Check Quiz, Chapter 2, Lesson 4

2-4 Adding Integers

MAIN IDEA

Add integers.

IN Academic Standards

Reinforcement of 6.1.5 Solve problems involving addition, subtraction, multiplication and division of integers and represent computation with integers on a number line. Describe the effect of operations with numbers less than zero. *Also addresses P.5.1, P.5.2, P.5.3, P.6.5, P.6.6.*

New Vocabulary

opposites
additive inverse

IN Math Online

glencoe.com

- Extra Examples
- Personal Tutor
- Self-Check Quiz

GET READY for the Lesson

SCIENCE Atoms are made of negative charges (electrons) and positive charges (protons). The helium atom shown has a total of 2 electrons and 2 protons.

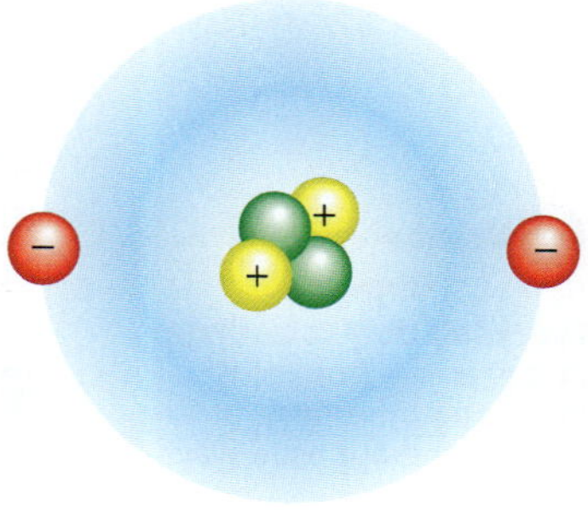

1. Represent the electrons in an atom of helium with an integer. **−2**
2. Represent the protons in an atom of helium with an integer. **2**
3. Each proton-electron pair has a value of 0. What is the total charge of an atom of helium? **0**

Combining protons and electrons in an atom is similar to adding integers.

EXAMPLE Add Integers with the Same Sign

1 **Find −3 + (−2).**

Use a number line.

- Start at 0.
- Move 3 units left to show −3.
- From there, move 2 units left to show −2.

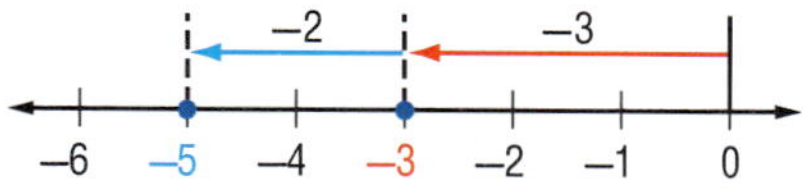

So, −3 + (−2) = −5.

CHECK Your Progress

a. −5 + (−7) **−12**

b. −10 + (−4) **−14**

These and other examples suggest the following rule.

Add Integers with the Same Sign — *Key Concept*

Words To add integers with the same sign, add their absolute values. The sum is:

- positive if both integers are positive.
- negative if both integers are negative.

Examples 7 + 4 = 11 −7 + (−4) = −11

2-4 Lesson Notes

1 Focus

Vertical Alignment

Before Lesson 2-4
Add with negative integers and subtract positive integers from negative integers

Lesson 2-4
Solve addition problems, including those arising in concrete situations, that use positive and negative integers

After Lesson 2-4
Add rational numbers and take positive rational numbers to whole-number powers

2 Teach

Scaffolding Questions

As you ask the following questions, take the appropriate numbers of steps in the appropriate directions.

Ask:

- If I walk 4 steps north and then 4 steps south, where am I relative to my starting point? at the starting point
- If I walk 5 steps west and then 5 steps east, where am I relative to my starting point? at the starting point
- If I walk 3 steps south and then 2 steps north, where am I relative to my starting point? 1 step south of the starting point
- If I walk 2 steps east and then 4 steps west, where am I relative to my starting point? 2 steps west of the starting point

ADDITIONAL EXAMPLE

1 Find −6 + (−3). −9

Lesson 2-4 Adding Integers **95**

EXAMPLE Add Integers with the Same Sign

2 **Find $-26 + (-17)$.**

$-26 + (-17) = -43$ Both integers are negative, so the sum is negative.

CHECK Your Progress

c. $-14 + (-16)$ **-30**

d. $23 + 38$ **61**

The integers 5 and -5 are called **opposites** because they are the same distance from 0, but on opposite sides of 0. Two integers that are opposites are also called **additive inverses**.

Vocabulary Link
Opposite
Everyday Use something that is across from or is facing the other way, as in running the opposite way
Math Use two numbers that are the same distance from 0, but on opposite sides of 0 on the number line

Additive Inverse Property — Key Concept

Words The sum of any number and its additive inverse is 0.

Examples $5 + (-5) = 0$

Number lines can also help you add integers with different signs.

EXAMPLES Add Integers with Different Signs

3 **Find $5 + (-3)$.**

Use a number line.

- Start at zero.
- Move 5 units right.
- Then move 3 units left.

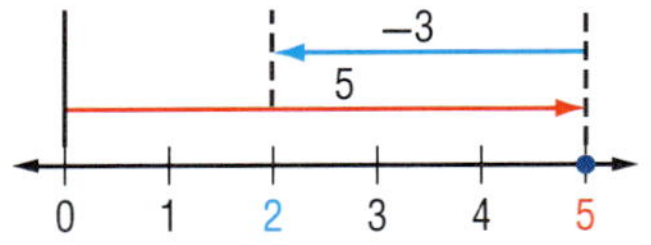

So, $5 + (-3) = 2$.

4 **Find $-3 + 2$.**

Use a number line.

- Start at zero.
- Move 3 units left.
- Then move 2 units right.

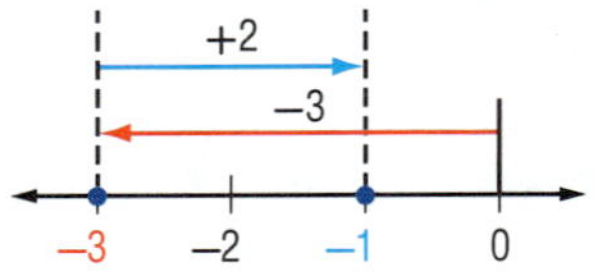

So, $-3 + 2 = -1$.

CHECK Your Progress

e. $6 + (-7)$ **-1**

f. $-15 + 19$ **4**

Study Tip
Look Back You can review **absolute value** in Lesson 2-1.

Add Integers with Different Signs — Key Concept

Words To add integers with different signs, subtract their absolute values. The sum is:

- positive if the positive integer's absolute value is greater.
- negative if the negative integer's absolute value is greater.

Examples $9 + (-4) = 5$ $-9 + 4 = -5$

Focus on Mathematical Content

The **Commutative Property of Addition** states that the order in which you add does not change the sum. $a + b = b + a$.

The **Identity Property of Addition** states that the sum of any number and zero is that number. $a + 0 = a$

Formative Assessment

Use the Check Your Progress exercises after the Examples to determine students' understanding of concepts.

ADDITIONAL EXAMPLES

2 Find $-34 + (-21)$. -55

3 Find $8 + (-7)$. 1

4 Find $-5 + 4$. -1

Additional Examples are also in:

- Noteables™ Interactive Study Notebook with Foldables™
- Interactive Classroom PowerPoint® Presentations

96 Chapter 2 Integers

EXAMPLES Add Integers with Different Signs

5 **Find $7 + (-1)$.**

$7 + (-1) = 6$ Subtract absolute values; $7 - 1 = 6$. Since 7 has the greater absolute value, the sum is positive.

6 **Find $-8 + 3$.**

$-8 + 3 = -5$ Subtract absolute values; $8 - 3 = 5$. Since -8 has the greater absolute value, the sum is negative.

Study Tip

Properties Using the Commutative, Associative, and Additive Inverse Properties allows the calculation to be as simple as possible.

7 **Find $2 + (-15) + (-2)$.**

$2 + (-15) + (-2) = 2 + (-2) + (-15)$ Commutative Property (+)

$= [2 + (-2)] + (-15)$ Associative Property (+)

$= 0 + (-15)$ Additive Inverse Property

$= -15$ Additive Identity Property

CHECK Your Progress

g. $10 + (-12)$ **-2** h. $-13 + 18$ **5** i. $(-14) + (-6) + 6$ **-14**

Real-World EXAMPLE

8 **ROLLER COASTERS** **The graphic shows the change in height at several points on a roller coaster. Write an addition sentence to find the height at point *D* in relation to point *A*.**

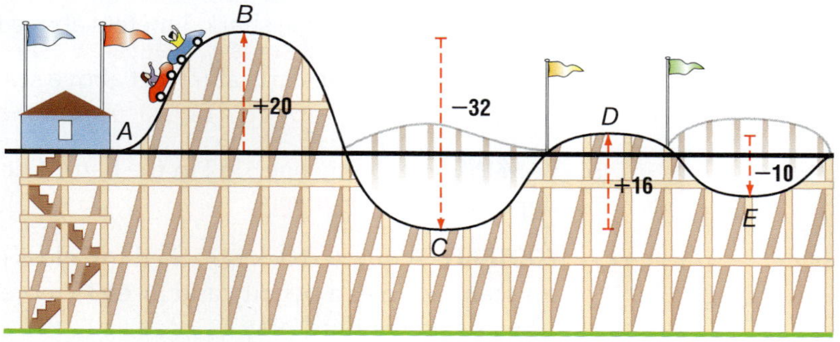

$20 + (-32) + 16 = 20 + 16 + (-32)$ Commutative Property (+)

$= 36 + (-32)$ $20 + 16 = 36$

$= 4$ Subtract absolute values. Since 36 has the greater absolute value, the sum is positive.

The result is a positive integer. So, point *D* is 4 feet higher than point *A*.

CHECK Your Progress

j. **WEATHER** The temperature is −3°F. An hour later, it drops 6° and 2 hours later, it rises 4°. Write an addition sentence to describe this situation. Then find the sum and explain its meaning.

j. $-3 + (-6) + 4$; -5; The new temperature is −5°F.

ADDITIONAL EXAMPLES

5 Find $2 + (-7)$. -5

6 Find $-9 + 6$. -3

7 Find $11 + (-4) + (-11)$. -4

8 **OCEANOGRAPHY** Oceanographers divide the ocean into three light zones. The deeper the water, the less light shines through. The middle zone is called the Twilight Zone. The lowest part of this zone is 1,000 meters below the surface of the water. The top of the zone lies 800 meters above the lowest zone. What is the depth of the top of the zone? Write an addition sentence to describe this situation. Then find the sum and explain its meaning.
$-1{,}000 + 800$; -200; The depth of the top of the middle zone is 200 meters below the surface of the water.

Tips for New Teachers: Adding Integers with Different Signs

Remind students that in adding integers with different signs, the larger absolute value does not always come first. For example, in adding $6 + (-11)$, the larger absolute value is 11, not 6.

Lesson 2-4 Adding Integers 97

3 Practice

Formative Assessment

Use Exercises 1–9 to check for understanding.

Then use the chart at the bottom of this page to customize your assignments for students.

Intervention You may wish to use the Study Guide and Intervention Master on page 30 of the *Chapter 2 Resource Masters* for additional reinforcement.

Odd/Even Assignments

Exercises 10–31 are structured so that students practice the same concepts whether they are assigned odd or even problems.

Differentiated Instruction

Kinesthetic Learners Separate students into pairs and give each pair 10 pennies (or 10 coin models). Determine which side (heads or tails) will represent –1 and which will represent 1. Have one student in each pair toss the 10 coins. The other student adds the negative and positive coins, removes the zero pairs, and writes the sum for that turn. Players take turns tossing and keeping score. The first player to reach an absolute value of 5 wins.

Additional Answers

30. $152 + (-20) + 84$; Stephanie now has $216 in the bank.

31. $-5 + (-15) + 12$; The team has lost a total of 8 yards.

CHECK Your Understanding

Examples 1–6 (pp. 95–97)

Add.

1. $-6 + (-8)$ **−14**
2. $4 + 5$ **9**
3. $-3 + 10$ **7**
4. $-15 + 8$ **−7**
5. $7 + (-11)$ **−4**
6. $14 + (-6)$ **8**

Example 7 (p. 97)

7. $-17 + 20 + (-3)$ **0**
8. $15 + 9 + (-9)$ **15**

Example 8 (p. 97)

9. **MONEY** Camilia owes her brother $25, so she gives her brother the $18 she earned dog-sitting for the neighbors. Write an addition sentence to describe this situation. Then find the sum and explain its meaning.
−$25 + $18; −$7; Camilia still owes her brother $7.

Practice and Problem Solving

HOMEWORK HELP	
For Exercises	See Examples
10–13	1, 2
14–21	3–6
22–27	7
28–31	8

Exercise Levels
A: 10–31
B: 32–37
C: 38–43

Add.

10. $-22 + (-16)$ **−38**
11. $-10 + (-15)$ **−25**
12. $6 + 10$ **16**
13. $17 + 11$ **28**
14. $18 + (-5)$ **13**
15. $13 + (-19)$ **−6**
16. $13 + (-7)$ **6**
17. $7 + (-20)$ **−13**
18. $-19 + 24$ **5**
19. $-12 + 10$ **−2**
20. $-30 + 16$ **−14**
21. $-9 + 11$ **2**
22. $21 + (-21) + (-4)$ **−4**
23. $-8 + (-4) + 12$ **0**
24. $-34 + 25 + (-25)$ **−34**
25. $-16 + 16 + 22$ **22**
26. $25 + 3 + (-25)$ **3**
27. $7 + (-19) + (-7)$ **−19**

Write an addition expression to describe each situation. Then find each sum and explain its meaning.

28. **SCUBA DIVING** Lena was scuba diving 14 meters below the surface of the water. She saw a nurse shark 3 meters above her.
−14 + 3;(−11); The shark is 11 feet below sea level.
29. **PELICANS** A pelican starts at 60 feet above sea level. It descends 60 feet to catch a fish. **60 + (−60); 0; The pelican is now at sea level.**
30. **BANKING** Stephanie has $152 in the bank. She withdraws $20. Then she deposits $84. **See margin.**
31. **FOOTBALL** A quarterback is sacked for a loss of 5 yards. On the next play, his team receives a penalty and loses 15 more yards. Then the team gains 12 yards on the third play.
See margin.
32. **MONEY** Josephine is saving money for a new bike and has already saved $17. Write the integers she should use to represent each entry.
+32, +19, +29, +25, +38

Deposit	Withdrawal	Balance
$15		■
	$13	■
$10		■
	$4	■
$13		■

ALGEBRA Evaluate each expression if $x = -10$, $y = 7$, and $z = -8$.

33. $x + 14$ **4**
34. $z + (-5)$ **−13**
35. $x + y$ **−3**
36. $x + z$ **−18**

DIFFERENTIATED HOMEWORK OPTIONS

Level	Assignment	Two-Day Assignment	
BL Basic	10–31, 38, 43–55	11–31 odd, 44–46	10–30 even, 38, 43, 47–55
OL Core	11–35 odd, 36, 37, 38, 43–55	10–31, 44–46	32–38, 43, 47–55
AL Advanced/Pre-AP	32–50 (optional: 51–55)		

98 Chapter 2 Integers

Academic Standards • ISTEP+

Extra Practice, pp. 672, 705

37. **FIND THE DATA** Refer to the Data File on pages 16–19 of your book. Choose some data and write a real-world problem in which you would add a positive and a negative integer. Then find the sum and explain its meaning. **See students' work.**

H.O.T. Problems

38. Beth; Jordan added correctly but did not give the sum the sign of the integer with the greater absolute value.

38. **FIND THE ERROR** Beth and Jordan are finding $-12 + 15$. Who is correct? Explain your reasoning.

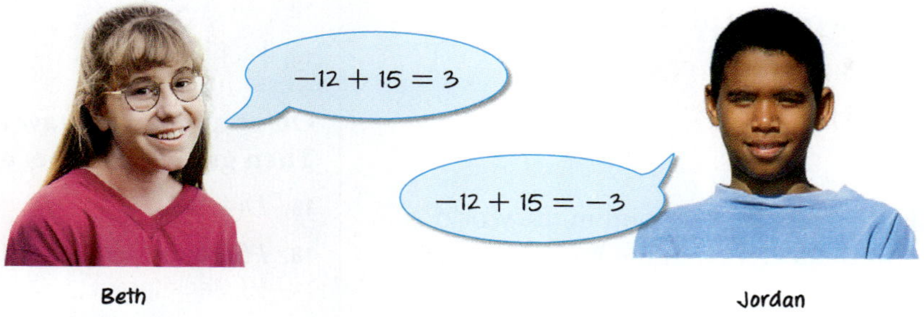

CHALLENGE Simplify.

39. $8 + (-8) + a$ **a**

40. $x + (-5) + 1$ **$x + (-4)$**

41. $-9 + m + (-6)$ **$m + (-15)$**

42. $-1 + n + 7$ **$n + 6$**

43. **WRITING IN MATH** Explain how you know whether a sum is positive, negative, or zero without actually adding. **See margin.**

ISTEP+ PRACTICE Reinforcement of 6.1.5

44. **SHORT RESPONSE** Find $-8 + (-11)$. **−19**

45. Find $-8 + 7 + (-3)$. **B**

A −18 C 2

B −4 D 18

46. At 8 A.M., the temperature was 3°F below zero. By 1 P.M., the temperature rose 14°F and by 10 P.M. dropped 12°F. What was the temperature at 10 P.M.? **J**

F 5°F above zero

G 5°F below zero

H 1°F above zero

J 1°F below zero

Spiral Review

Write the ordered pair for each point graphed at the right. Then name the quadrant or axis on which each point is located. (Lesson 2-3)

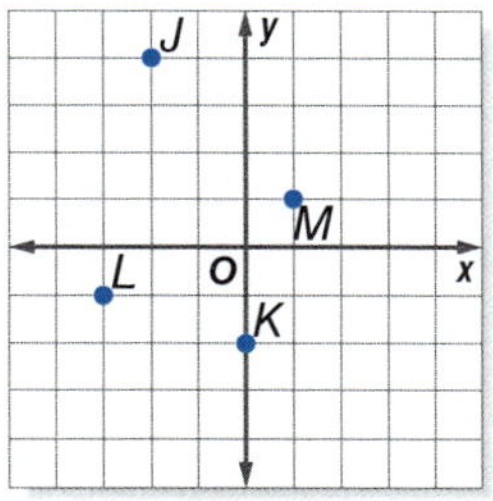

47. J **(−2, 4); II**

48. K **(0, −2); y-axis**

49. L **(−3, −1); III**

50. M **(1, 1); I**

51. Order 6, −3, 0, 4, −8, 1, and −4 from least to greatest. (Lesson 2-2) **−8, −4, −3, 0, 1, 4, 6**

GET READY for the Next Lesson

PREREQUISITE SKILL Subtract.

52. 287 − 125 **162**

53. 420 − 317 **103**

54. 5,684 − 2,419 **3,265**

55. 7,000 − 3,891 **3,109**

Exercise Alert!

Find the Error For Exercise 38, Jordan found the difference of the addends correctly, but he gave the sum the wrong sign. Remind students that the sum of integers with different signs will always have the sign of the addend with the greater absolute value.

4 Assess

Name the Math Have students tell what steps they followed to solve one of the exercises in the first skill set (Exercises 10–27).

Formative Assessment

Check for student understanding of concepts in Lessons 2-3 and 2-4.

CRM Quiz 2 , p. 61

FOLDABLES Study Organizer Foldables™ Follow-Up

Remind students to record the rules for adding integers in their Foldables. Encourage them to also note the Additive Inverse Property.

Additional Answer

43. Sample answer: Look at the signs. If the numbers being added are both positive, the sum is positive. If the numbers being added are both negative, the sum is negative. If the numbers being added have different signs, subtract their absolute values and give the sum the sign of the number with the greatest absolute value. If the numbers being added are opposites, the sum is zero.

Formative Assessment

Use the Mid-Chapter Quiz to assess students' progress in the first half of the chapter.

Have students review the lesson indicated for the problems they answered incorrectly.

Summative Assessment

CRM Mid-Chapter Test, p. 63

ExamView Assessment Suite Customize and create multiple versions of your Mid-Chapter Test and their answer keys.

Foldables Study Organizer Dinah Zike's Foldables

Before students complete the Mid-Chapter Quiz, encourage them to review the information on the first three pages of their Foldables.

Additional Answers

16–19.

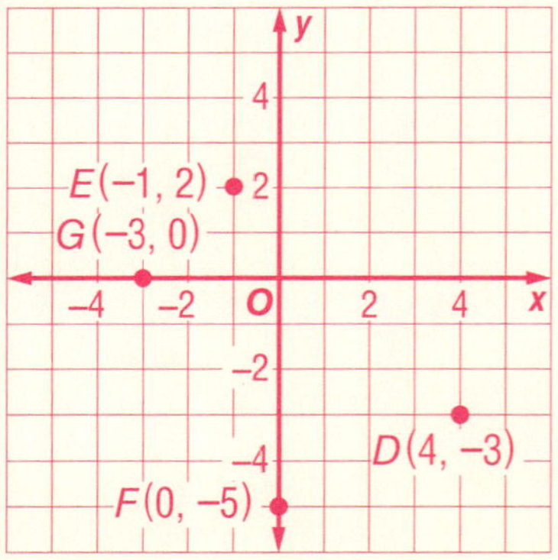

Chapter 2 Mid-Chapter Quiz

Lessons 2-1 through 2-4

IN Academic Standards 7.1.6, 6.1.5

Write an integer for each situation. (Lesson 2-1)

1. dropped 45 feet **−45**
2. a bank deposit of \$100 **100 or + 100**
3. gained 8 pounds **8 or + 8**
4. lost a \$5 bill **−5**

5. **OCEANS** The deepest point in the world is the Mariana Trench in the Western Pacific Ocean at a depth of 35,840 feet below sea level. Write this depth as an integer. (Lesson 2-1) **−35,840**

Evaluate each expression. (Lesson 2-1)

6. $|-16|$ **16**
7. $|24|$ **24**
8. $|-9| - |3|$ **6**
9. $|-13| + |-1|$ **14**

10. **ANALYZE TABLES** The table shows the record low temperatures for January and February in Lincoln, Nebraska.

Month	Temperature (°F)
January	−33
February	−27

Source: University of Nebraska, Lincoln

Which month had the coldest temperature? (Lesson 2-2) **January**

11. **MULTIPLE CHOICE** The local news records the following changes in average daily temperature for the past week: 4°, −7°, −3°, 2°, 9°, −8°, 1°. Which list shows the temperatures from least to greatest? (Lesson 2-2) **C**

A 9°, 4°, 2°, 1°, −3°, −7°, −8°

B −7°, −8°, 1°, −3°, 2°, 4°, 9°

C −8°, −7°, −3°, 1°, 2°, 4°, 9°

D −8°, −7°, 1°, 2°, 3°, 4°, 9°

Replace each ● with <, >, or = to make a true sentence. (Lesson 2-2)

12. -4 ● 4 **<**
13. -8 ● -11 **>**
14. $|-14|$ ● $|3|$ **>**
15. $|-12|$ ● $|12|$ **=**

On graph paper, draw a coordinate plane. Then graph and label each point. (Lesson 2-3)

16. $D(4, -3)$
17. $E(-1, 2)$
18. $F(0, -5)$
19. $G(-3, 0)$

16–19. See margin.

20. **MULTIPLE CHOICE** Which line contains the ordered pair (−1, 4)? (Lesson 2-3) **F**

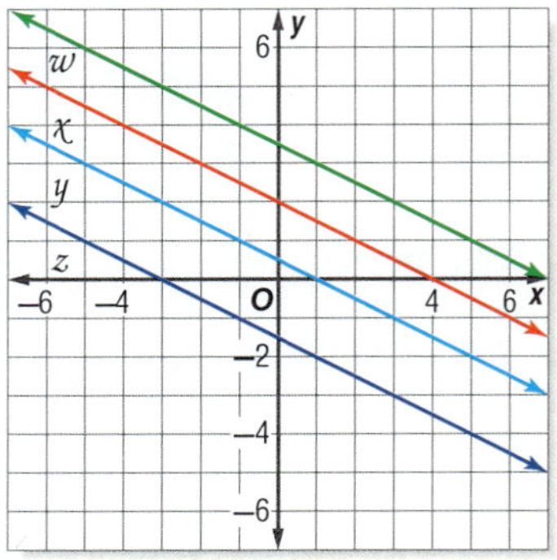

F line w H line y

G line x J line z

Add. (Lesson 2-4)

21. $3 + 4 + (-3)$ **4**
22. $7 + (-11)$ **−4**
23. $-5 + (-6)$ **−11**
24. $8 + (-1) + 1$ **8**

25. **MULTIPLE CHOICE** Kendra deposited \$78 into her savings account. Two weeks later, she deposited a check for \$50 into her account and withdrew \$27. Which of the following expressions represents the amount of money left in her account? (Lesson 2-4) **C**

A \$78 + (−\$50) + (−\$27)

B \$78 + (−\$50) + \$27

C \$78 + \$50 + (−\$27)

D \$78 + \$50 + \$27

Data-Driven Decision Making

Diagnostic Teaching Based on the results of the Chapter 2 Mid-Chapter Quiz, use the following to review concepts that students continue to find challenging.

Exercises	Lesson	Academic Standards
1–10	2-1	7.1.6
11–15	2-2	7.1.6
16–20	2-3	7.3.2
21–25	2-4	6.1.5

Resources for Review

CRM Study Guide and Intervention pp. 10, 17, 23, and 30

IN Math Online glencoe.com

- Extra Examples
- Personal Tutor
- Concepts in Motion

100 Chapter 2 Integers

Explore 2-5

Algebra Lab
Subtracting Integers

MAIN IDEA

Use counters to model the subtraction of integers.

IN Academic Standards

Reinforcement of 6.1.5 Solve problems involving addition, subtraction, multiplication and division of integers and represent computation with integers on a number line. Describe the effect of operations with numbers less than zero. *Also addresses P.2.2, P.5.1, P.5.2, P.5.3.*

You can also use counters to model subtraction of integers. Remember one meaning of subtraction is to *take away*.

ACTIVITY

Use counters to find each difference.

1 5 − 2

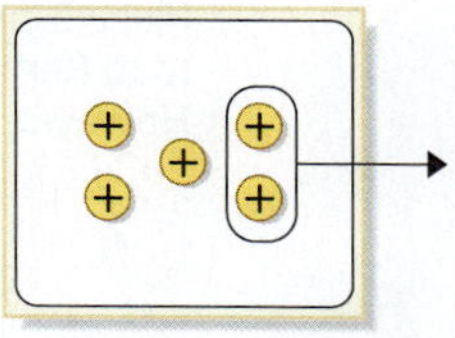

Place 5 positive counters on the mat. Remove 2 positive counters.

So, 5 − 2 = 3.

2 4 − (−3)

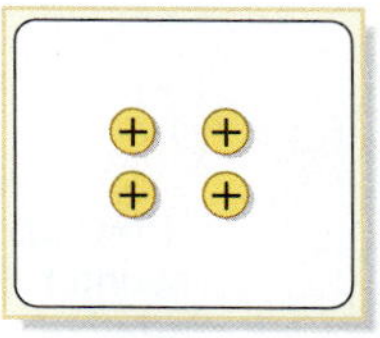

Place 4 positive counters on the mat. Remove 3 negative counters. However, there are 0 negative counters.

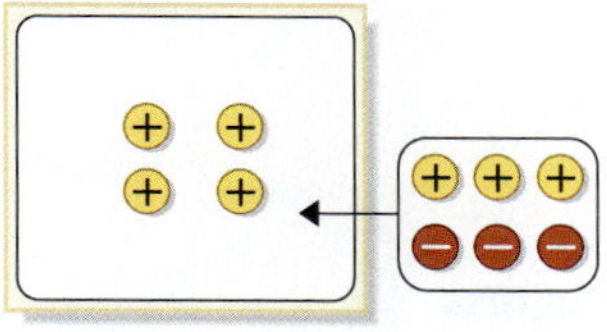

Add 3 zero pairs to the set.

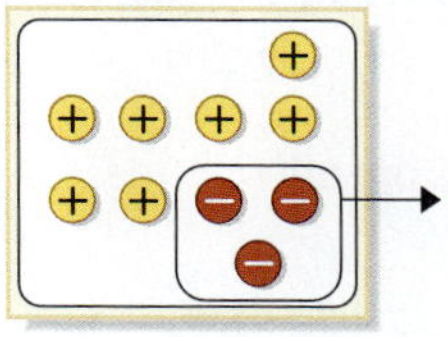

Now you can remove 3 negative counters. Find the remaining number of counters.

So, 4 − (−3) = 7.

CHECK Your Progress

Use counters or a drawing to find each difference. a. See margin.

a. 7 − 6 b. 5 − (−3) c. 6 − (−3) d. 5 − 8

b–d. See Ch. 2 Answer Appendix.

Explore 2-5

Lesson Notes

1 Focus

Materials

- positive and negative counters

Easy-to-Make Manipulatives

Teaching Mathematics with Manipulatives templates for:

- integer counters, p. 7

2 Teach

Activity 2 You may need to remind students that a zero pair–one positive counter and one negative counter–has a value of 0 and thus can be added to or subtracted from a set without changing the set's total value.

You may wish to point out that Exercises a–d involve positive minuends.

Additional Answer

a.

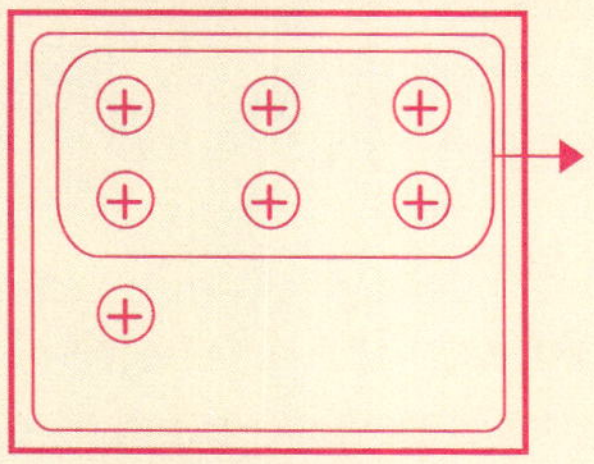

7 − 6 = 1

Explore 2-5 Algebra Lab: Subtracting Integers **101**

Activities 3 and 4 Point out that these problems have negative minuends. Some students may realize that subtracting a negative integer is the same as adding positive counters, and subtracting a positive integer is the same as adding negative counters.

3 Assess

Formative Assessment

Use Exercises e–g to determine whether students comprehend how to use counters to model the subtraction of integers.

From Concrete to Abstract Use Exercises 1 and 2 to bridge the gap between using counters to subtract integers and writing subtraction problems with given (positive or negative) results.

Additional Answers

e.

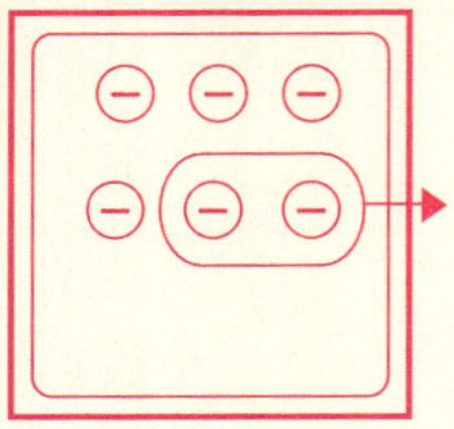

$-6 - (-2) = -4$

3. Sample answer: The difference of two integers is positive when the minuend is greater than the subtrahend. The difference of two integers is negative when the minuend is less than the subtrahend.

Reading Math

Minuends, Subtrahends, and Differences In the subtraction sentence $-5 - 1 = -6$, -5 is the *minuend*, 1 is the *subtrahend*, and -6 is the *difference*.

ACTIVITY

Use counters to find each difference.

3 $-6 - (-3)$

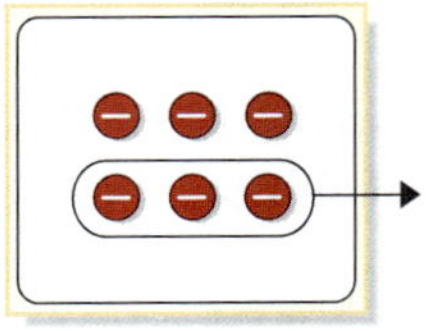

Place 6 negative counters on the mat. Remove 3 negative counters.

So, $-6 - (-3) = -3$.

4 $-5 - 1$

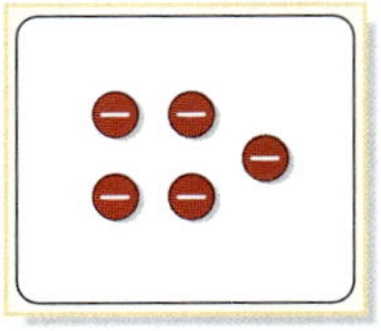

Place 5 negative counters on the mat. Remove 1 positive counter. However, there are 0 positive counters.

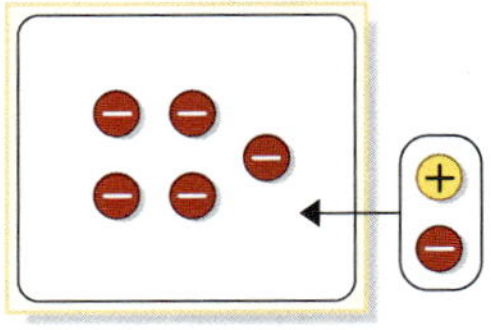

Add 1 zero pair to the set.

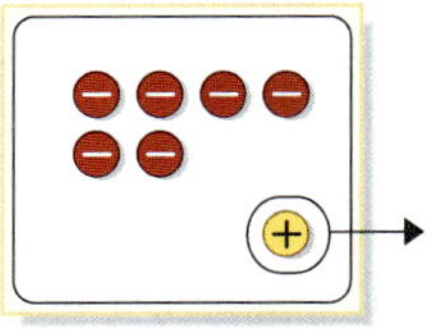

Now you can remove 1 positive counter. Find the remaining number of counters.

So, $-5 - 1 = -6$.

CHECK Your Progress

Use counters or a drawing to find each difference. **e. See margin.**

e. $-6 - (-2)$ f. $-7 - 3$ g. $-5 - (-7)$

f, g. See Ch. 2 Answer Appendix.

Analyze the Results

1. Write two subtraction sentences where the difference is positive. Use a combination of positive and negative integers.
2. Write two subtraction sentences where the difference is negative. Use a combination of positive and negative integers.
3. **MAKE A CONJECTURE** Write a rule that will help you determine the sign of the difference of two integers. **See margin.**

1. Sample answers:
$8 - 2 = 6$;
$7 - (-6) = 13$;
$-3 - (-6) = 3$

2. Sample answers:
$-5 - (-2) = -3$;
$-1 - 4 = -5$;
$2 - 3 = -1$

2-5 Subtracting Integers

PACING: **Regular:** 1.5 periods, **Block:** 0.5 period

IN Academic Standards **Reinforcement of 6.1.5** Solve problems involving addition, subtraction, multiplication, and division of integers and represent computation with integers on a number line. Describe the effect of operations with numbers less than zero. *Also addresses P.5.1, P.5.2, P.5.3.*

Options for Differentiated Instruction

ELL = English Language Learner AL = Above or Beyond Grade Level SS = Struggling Students SN = Special Needs

Visualizing the Concept SS SN

Use before presenting Examples 1 and 2.

To further show that subtracting integers is the same as adding the opposite, use counters to compare the subtraction 6 – 3 to the addition 6 + (–3).

The models show that 6 – 3 = 6 + (–3).

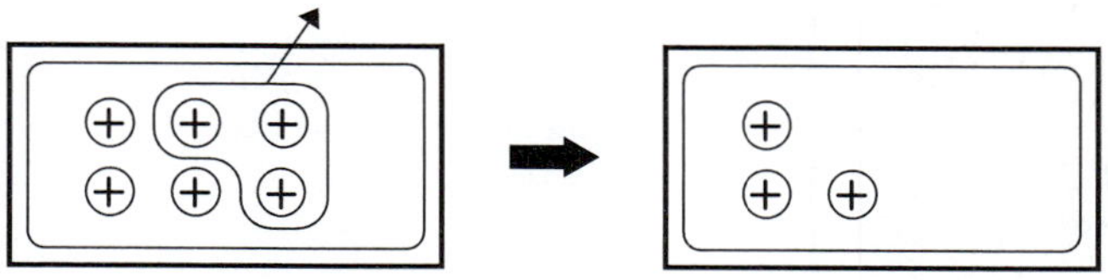

$6 - 3 = 3$

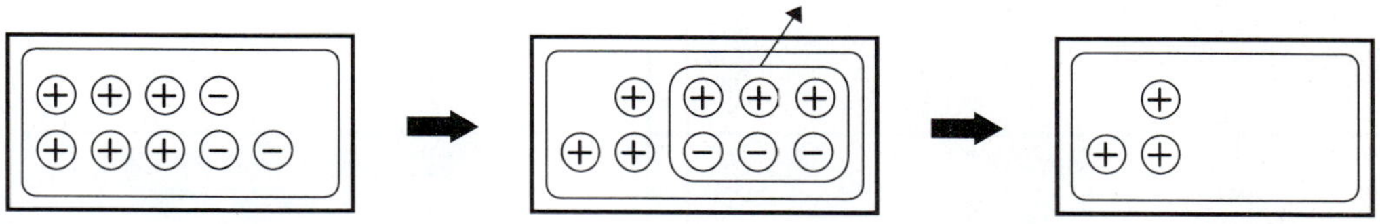

$6 + (-3) = 3$

Real-World Applications ELL AL

Use after presenting Examples 1–6.

The diagram below is a timeline showing the lives of three rulers of Rome. Present the diagram on the overhead or make a sketch of it on the board.

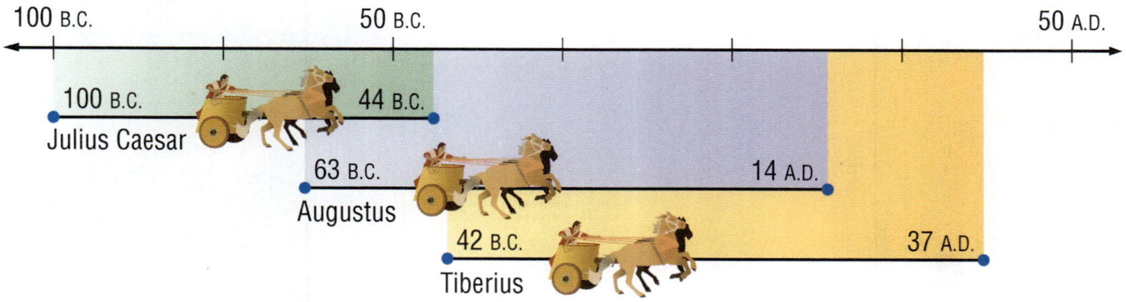

Ask:

- How old was Augustus when he died? 77 yr
- Which ruler lived the longest? How old was he when he died? Tiberius; 79 yr
- Find the number of years between Julius Caesar's birth and Augustus' birth. 37 yr
- How could you determine how long ago each of the three rulers were born? Explain. Add their birth year to the current year. This works because all three rulers were born in years B.C.

Leveled Lesson Resources

Also on TeacherWorks™ Lesson 2-5

Chapter 2 Resource Masters

BL = Below or Approaching Grade Level   OL = On Grade Level   AL = Above or Beyond Grade Level   ELL = English Language Learner

Lesson Reading Guide
p. 36 BL OL ELL

NAME ____________ DATE ________ PERIOD ____

2-5 Lesson Reading Guide
Subtracting Integers

Get Ready for the Lesson

Complete the Mini Lab at the top of page 103 in your textbook. Write your answers below.

1. Write a related addition sentence for the subtraction sentence. **Sample answer: −1 + 7 = 6**

Use a number line to find each difference. Write an equivalent addition sentence for each.

2. 1 − 5 **1 − 5 = −4; 1 + (−5) = −4**
3. −2 − 1 **−2 − 1 = −3; −2 + (−1) = −3**
4. −3 − 4 **−3 − 4 = −7; −3 + (−4) = −7**
5. 0 − 5 **0 − 5 = −5; 0 + (−5) = −5**

Read the Lesson

Tell how you would solve each of the following on a number line. Then solve.

6. −8 − (−6) **Sample answer: Change the subtraction sentence to an addition sentence. To subtract negative 6, add positive 6. Then, on a number line start at 0, move left 8 units, then move right 6 units; −2.**
7. 6 − 8 **Sample answer: Change the subtraction sentence to an addition sentence. To subtract 8, add negative 8. Then, on a number line start at 0, move right 6 units, then move left 8 units; −2.**

Remember What You Learned

8. Write the rule that tells how to subtract integers. Then give an example. **To subtract an integer, add its opposite. Sample answer: 12 − (−3) = 12 + 3 = 15**

Study Guide and Intervention*
p. 37 BL OL ELL

NAME ____________ DATE ________ PERIOD ____

2-5 Study Guide and Intervention
Subtracting Integers

To subtract an integer, add its opposite.

Example 1 Find 6 − 9.

6 − 9 = 6 + (−9)   To subtract 9, add −9.
= −3   Simplify.

Example 2 Find −10 − (−12).

−10 − (−12) = −10 + 12   To subtract −12, add 12.
= 2   Simplify.

Example 3 Evaluate $a - b$ if $a = -3$ and $b = 7$.

$a - b$ = −3 − 7   Replace *a* with −3 and *b* with 7.
= −3 + (−7)   To subtract 7, add −7.
= −10   Simplify.

Exercises

Subtract.

1. 7 − 9 **−2**
2. 20 − (−6) **26**
3. −10 − 4 **−14**
4. 0 − 12 **−12**
5. −7 − 8 **−15**
6. 13 − 18 **−5**
7. −20 − (−5) **−15**
8. −8 − (−6) **−2**
9. 25 − (−14) **39**
10. −75 − 50 **−125**
11. 15 − 65 **−50**
12. 19 − (−10) **29**

Evaluate each expression if $m = -2$, $n = 10$, and $p = 5$.

13. $m - 6$ **−8**
14. $9 - n$ **−1**
15. $p - (-8)$ **13**
16. $p - m$ **7**
17. $m - n$ **−12**
18. $-25 - p$ **−30**

Lesson 2–5

Skills Practice*
p. 38 BL OL

NAME ____________ DATE ________ PERIOD ____

2-5 Skills Practice
Subtracting Integers

Subtract.

1. 5 − 2 **3**
2. 6 − (−7) **13**
3. −3 − 2 **−5**
4. 8 − 13 **−5**
5. −7 − (−7) **0**
6. 6 − 12 **−6**
7. 15 − (−7) **22**
8. −15 − 6 **−21**
9. −3 − 8 **−11**
10. −10 − 12 **−22**
11. 13 − (−12) **25**
12. 14 − (−22) **36**
13. 10 − (−20) **30**
14. −16 − 14 **−30**
15. −25 − 25 **−50**
16. 6 − (−31) **37**
17. −18 − (−40) **22**
18. 15 − (−61) **76**

Evaluate each expression if $r = -4$, $s = 10$, and $t = -7$.

19. $r - 7$ **−11**
20. $t - s$ **−17**
21. $s - (-8)$ **18**
22. $t - r$ **−3**
23. $s - t$ **17**
24. $r - s$ **−14**

Practice*
p. 39 OL AL

NAME ____________ DATE ________ PERIOD ____

2-5 Practice
Subtracting Integers

Subtract.

1. 16 − 14 **2**
2. −4 − 2 **−6**
3. 9 − (−2) **11**
4. −6 − (−8) **2**
5. −20 − 10 **−30**
6. −28 − (−13) **−15**
7. −33 − 33 **−66**
8. 28 − 14 **14**
9. 13 − (−63) **76**
10. −18 − (−12) **−6**
11. 52 − (−30) **82**
12. −15 − 0 **−15**

13. WEATHER The highest and lowest recorded temperatures for the state of Texas are 120°F and −23°F. Find the difference in these extreme temperatures. **143°F**

ALGEBRA **Evaluate each expression if $x = -8$, $y = 7$, and $z = -11$.**

14. $x - 7$ **−15**
15. $-13 - y$ **−20**
16. $-11 - z$ **0**
17. $x - z$ **3**
18. $z - y$ **−18**
19. $y - x$ **15**
20. $x - (-z)$ **−19**
21. $|y - z|$ **18**
22. $x - z - y$ **−4**

ANALYZE TABLES In golf, scores are often stated as the number of strokes above or below par for the course. Four golfers played two rounds of golf during the weekend. The table lists their scores for each round in relation to par.

Golfer	Patrick	Diane	James	Juanita
Round 1	−6	+1	+2	−3
Round 2	−2	−4	+7	+6

For Exercises 23 and 24, use the information in the table.

23. Find the difference between James's Round 2 score and Diane's Round 2 score. **11**
24. Find the difference between Patrick's lower score and Juanita's higher score. **−12**

Lesson 2–5

Word Problem Practice*
p. 40 OL AL

NAME ____________ DATE ________ PERIOD ____

2-5 Word Problem Practice
Subtracting Integers

Subtract.

1. FOOTBALL A team gained 5 yards on their first play of the game. Then they lost 6 yards. Find the total change in yardage. **−1 yd**
2. CHECKING Your checking account is overdrawn by $50. You write a check for $20. What is the balance in your account? **−$70**
3. TEMPERATURE The average temperature in Calgary, Canada, is 22°C in July and −11°C in January. Find the range of the highest and lowest temperatures in Calgary. **33°C**
4. ROLLER COASTER A roller coaster begins at 90 feet above ground level. Then it descends 105 feet. Find the height of the coaster after the first descent. **−15 ft**
5. SAVINGS Sonia has $235 in her savings account. She withdraws $45. What is left in her savings account? **$190**
6. BEACH Wai and Kuri were digging in the sand at the beach. Wai dug a hole that was 15 inches below the surface, and Kuri dug a hole that was 9 inches below the surface. Find the difference in the depths of their holes. **6 in.**

Enrichment
p. 41 OL AL

NAME ____________ DATE ________ PERIOD ____

2-5 Enrichment

Distance on the Number Line

To find the distance between two points on a number line, subtract their coordinates. Then, take the absolute value of the difference.

−4 − 3 = −7
|−7| = 7

You can also find the distance by finding the absolute value of the difference of the coordinates.

|−4 − 3| = 7

Graph each pair of points. Then write an expression using absolute value to find the distance between the points.

1. *A* at −5 and *B* at 2 **|−5 − 2| = 7**

2. *C* at −7 and *D* at −1 **|−7 − (−1)| = 6**

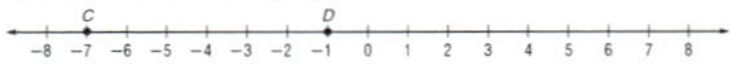

3. *E* at −5 and *F* at 5 **|−5 − 5| = 10**

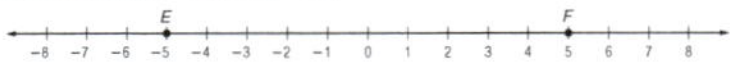

4. *W* at 0 and *X* at 6 **|0 − 6| = 6**

5. *Y* at −4 and *Z* at 0 **|−4 − 0| = 4**

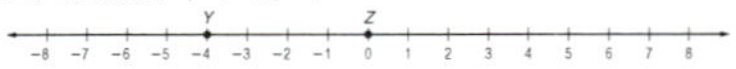

Lesson 2–5

** Also available in Spanish* ELL

Additional Lesson Resources

Transparencies

- *5-Minute Check Transparency,* Lesson 2-5

Other Print Products

- *Teaching Mathematics with Manipulatives*
- *Noteables™ Interactive Study Notebook with Foldables™*

Teacher Tech Tools

- *Interactive Classroom CD-ROM,* Lesson 2-5
- *AssignmentWorks,* Lesson 2-5

Student Tech Tools

glencoe.com

- Extra Examples, Chapter 2, Lesson 5
- Self-Check Quiz, Chapter 2, Lesson 5

2-5 Subtracting Integers

MAIN IDEA

Subtract integers.

IN Academic Standards

Reinforcement of 6.1.5 Solve problems involving addition, subtraction, multiplication and division of integers and represent computation with integers on a number line. Describe the effect of operations with numbers less than zero. *Also addresses P.5.1, P.5.2, P.5.3.*

IN Math Online

glencoe.com

- Concepts In Motion
- Extra Examples
- Personal Tutor
- Self-Check Quiz

MINI Lab

You can use a number line to model a subtraction problem.

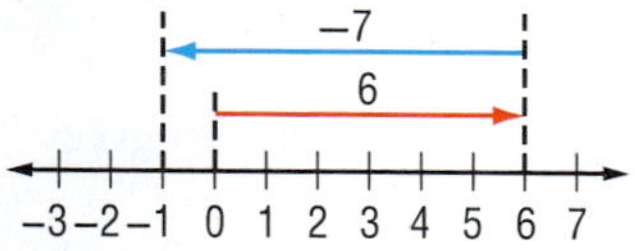

1. $6 + (-7) = -1$

1. Write a related addition sentence for the subtraction sentence.

Use a number line to find each difference. Write an equivalent addition sentence for each. 2–5. See Ch 2. Answer Appendix.

2. $1 - 5$ 3. $-2 - 1$ 4. $-3 - 4$ 5. $0 - 5$

When you subtract 7, the result is the same as adding its opposite, −7.

opposite

$$6 - 7 = -1 \qquad 6 + (-7) = -1$$

same result

This and other examples suggest the following rule.

Subtract Integers — Key Concept

Words	To subtract an integer, add its opposite.
Examples	$4 - 9 = 4 + (-9) = -5$ $7 - (-10) = 7 + (10) = 17$

EXAMPLES Subtract Positive Integers

1 **Find 8 − 13.**

$8 - 13 = 8 + (-13)$ To subtract 13, add −13.

$= -5$ Simplify.

2 **Find −10 − 7.**

$-10 - 7 = -10 + (-7)$ To subtract 7, add −7.

$= -17$ Simplify.

CHECK Your Progress

a. $6 - 12$ **−6** b. $-20 - 15$ **−35** c. $-22 - 26$ **−48**

2-5 Lesson Notes

1 Focus

Vertical Alignment

Before Lesson 2-5
Subtract positive integers from negative integers

Lesson 2-5
Solve subtraction problems, including those arising in concrete situations, that use positive and negative integers

After Lesson 2-5
Subtract rational numbers and take positive rational numbers to whole-number powers

2 Teach

MINI Lab

You might want to have students also model the related addition sentences on their number lines, thus "undoing" the original subtractions. For example, for the number done on the right, students could model $-1 - 4 = -5$ and then $-5 + 4 = -1$.

Scaffolding Questions

Draw a number line from −10 to 10 on the board. As you ask the following questions, move a pointer along the number line.

Ask:

- What direction do I move if I subtract 2 from 6? left
- What direction do I move if I subtract 1 from −6? left
- What direction do I move if I add −3 to 1? left
- What direction do I move if I add −9 to 0? left

Formative Assessment

Use the Check Your Progress exercises after the Examples to determine students' understanding of concepts.

ADDITIONAL EXAMPLES

1. Find $2 - 15$. -13
2. Find $-13 - 8$. -21
3. Find $12 - (-6)$. 18
4. Find $-21 - (-8)$. -13
5. **ALGEBRA** Evaluate $g - h$ if $g = -2$ and $h = -7$. 5
6. **GEOGRAPHY** In Mongolia, the temperature can fall to -45°C in January. The temperature in July may reach 40°C. What is the difference between these two temperatures in Mongolia? 85 °C

Additional Examples are also in:

- Noteables™ Interactive Study Notebook with Foldables™
- Interactive Classroom PowerPoint® Presentations

Tips for New Teachers — Subtracting Integers

Students can use a number line to check their results. First, have them change the subtraction sentence to an addition sentence. Then, they can draw a number line.

EXAMPLES Subtract Negative Integers

3 **Find $1 - (-2)$.**

$1 - (-2) = 1 + 2$ To subtract -2, add 2.

$= 3$ Simplify.

4 **Find $-10 - (-7)$.**

$-10 - (-7) = -10 + 7$ To subtract -7, add 7.

$= -3$ Simplify.

CHECK Your Progress

d. $4 - (-12)$ **16** e. $-15 - (-5)$ **-10** f. $18 - (-6)$ **24**

EXAMPLE Evaluate an Expression

5 **ALGEBRA** **Evaluate $x - y$ if $x = -6$ and $y = -5$.**

$x - y = -6 - (-5)$ Replace x with -6 and y with -5.

$= -6 + (5)$ To subtract -5, add 5.

$= -1$ Simplify.

CHECK Your Progress

Evaluate each expression if $a = 5$, $b = -8$, and $c = -9$.

g. $b - 10$ **-18** h. $a - b$ **13** i. $c - a$ **-14**

Real-World EXAMPLE

Real-World Link The mean surface temperature on the Moon during the day is 107°C.

Source: Views of the Solar System

6 **SPACE** **The temperatures on the Moon vary from -173°C to 127°C. Find the difference between the maximum and minimum temperatures.**

To find the difference in temperatures, subtract the lower temperature from the higher temperature.

Estimate $100 + 200 = 300$

$127 - (-173) = 127 + 173$ To subtract -173, add 173.

$= 300$ Simplify.

So, the difference between the temperatures is 300°C.

CHECK Your Progress

j. **GEOGRAPHY** The Dead Sea's deepest part is 799 meters below sea level. A plateau to the east of the Dead Sea rises to about 1,340 meters above sea level. What is the difference between the top of the plateau and the deepest part of the Dead Sea? **2,139 m**

104 Chapter 2 Integers

CHECK Your Understanding

Examples 1, 2 (p. 103)

Subtract.

1. $14 - 17$ **−3**
2. $10 - 30$ **−20**
3. $-4 - 8$ **−12**
4. $-2 - 23$ **−25**

Examples 3, 4 (p. 104)

5. $14 - (-10)$ **24**
6. $5 - (-16)$ **−21**
7. $-3 - (-1)$ **−2**
8. $-11 - (-9)$ **−2**

Example 5 (p. 104)

ALGEBRA Evaluate each expression if $p = 8$, $q = -14$, and $r = -6$.

9. $r - 15$ **−21**
10. $q - r$ **−8**
11. $p - q$ **22**

Example 6 (p. 104)

12. **EARTH SCIENCE** The sea-surface temperatures range from −2°C to 31°C. Find the difference between the maximum and minimum temperatures. **33°C**

Practice and Problem Solving

HOMEWORK HELP

For Exercises	See Examples
13–16, 21–24	1, 2
17–20, 25–28	3, 4
29–36	5
37–40	6

Exercise Levels
A: 13–40
B: 41–43
C: 44–47

Subtract.

13. $0 - 10$ **−10**
14. $13 - 17$ **−4**
15. $-9 - 5$ **−14**
16. $-8 - 9$ **−17**
17. $4 - (-19)$ **23**
18. $27 - (-8)$ **35**
19. $-11 - (-42)$ **31**
20. $-27 - (-19)$ **−8**
21. $12 - 26$ **−14**
22. $31 - 48$ **−17**
23. $-25 - 5$ **−30**
24. $-44 - 41$ **−85**
25. $52 - (-52)$ **104**
26. $15 - (-14)$ **29**
27. $-27 - (-33)$ **6**
28. $-18 - (-20)$ **2**

ALGEBRA Evaluate each expression if $f = -6$, $g = 7$, and $h = 9$.

29. $g - 7$ **0**
30. $f - 6$ **−12**
31. $-h - (-9)$ **0**
32. $f - g$ **−13**
33. $h - f$ **15**
34. $g - h$ **−2**
35. $5 - f$ **11**
36. $4 - (-g)$ **11**

ANALYZE TABLES For Exercises 37–40, use the information below.

State	California	Georgia	Louisiana	New Mexico	Texas
Lowest Elevation (ft)	−282	0	−8	2,842	0
Highest Elevation (ft)	14,494	4,784	535	13,161	8,749

37. What is the difference between the highest elevation in Texas and the lowest elevation in Louisiana? **8,757 ft**
38. Find the difference between the lowest elevation in New Mexico and the lowest elevation in California. **3,124 ft**
39. Find the difference between the highest elevation in Georgia and the lowest elevation in California. **5,066 ft**
40. What is the difference between the lowest elevations in Texas and Louisiana? **8 ft**

Academic Standards • ISTEP+
Extra Practice, pp. 672, 705

ALGEBRA Evaluate each expression if $h = -12$, $j = 4$, and $k = 15$.

41. $-j + h - k$ **−31**
42. $|h - j|$ **16**
43. $k - j - h$ **23**

3 Practice

Formative Assessment

Use Exercises 1–12 to check for understanding.

Then use the chart at the bottom of this page to customize your assignments for students.

Intervention You may wish to use the Study Guide and Intervention Master on page 37 of the *Chapter 2 Resource Masters* for additional reinforcement.

Odd/Even Assignments

Exercises 13–40 are structured so that students practice the same concepts whether they are assigned odd or even problems.

DIFFERENTIATED HOMEWORK OPTIONS

Level	Assignment	Two-Day Assignment	
BL Basic	13–40, 44, 45, 47–59	13–43 odd, 48, 49	14–42 even, 44, 45, 47, 50–56
OL Core	13–43 odd, 44, 45, 47–59	13–40, 48, 49	41–45, 47, 50–59
AL Advanced/Pre-AP	41–55 (optional: 56–59)		

⚠ Exercise Alert!

Find the Error For Exercise 45, Alicia knew that she could subtract the integer by adding its opposite, but she forgot to rewrite the integer as its opposite. Remind students to check the signs of the integers before they subtract or add.

4 Assess

Yesterday's News Remind students that yesterday's lesson was about adding integers. Have them write how yesterday's concepts helped them with today's material.

H.O.T. Problems

44. Sample answer: $-5 - 11 = -5 + (-11) = -16$; **Add 5 and 11 and keep the negative sign.**

44. **OPEN ENDED** Write a subtraction sentence using integers. Then, write the equivalent addition sentence, and explain how to find the sum.

45. **FIND THE ERROR** Alicia and Mei are finding $-15 - (-18)$. Who is correct? Explain your reasoning. **Mei; Alicia did not add the additive inverse of −18.**

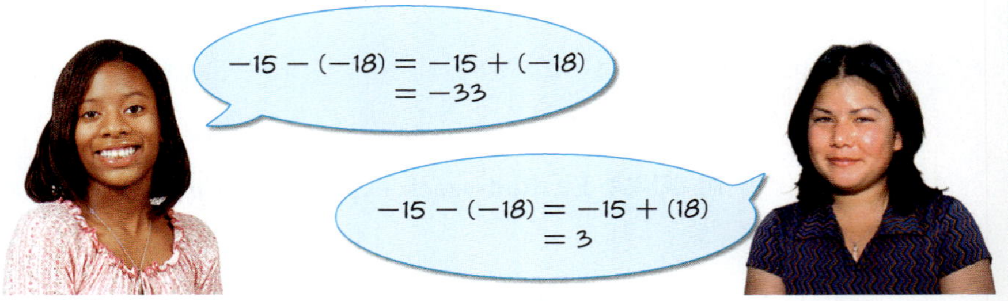

Alicia — Mei

46. **CHALLENGE** *True* or *False*? When n is a negative integer, $n - n = 0$. **true**

47. **WRITING IN MATH** Explain how additive inverses are used in subtraction. **Sample answer: To subtract an integer, add its additive inverse.**

ISTEP+ PRACTICE Reinforcement 6.1.5

48. Which sentence about integers is *not* always true? **A**
   - **A** positive − positive = positive
   - **B** positive + positive = positive
   - **C** negative + negative = negative
   - **D** positive − negative = positive

49. Morgan drove from Los Angeles (elevation 330 feet) to Death Valley (elevation −282 feet). What is the difference in elevation between Los Angeles and Death Valley? **J**
   - **F** 48 feet
   - **G** 148 feet
   - **H** 582 feet
   - **J** 612 feet

Spiral Review

Add. (Lesson 2-4)

50. $10 + (-3)$ **7**

51. $-2 + (-9)$ **−11**

52. $-7 + (-6)$ **−13**

53. $-18 + 4$ **−14**

54. In which quadrant does the ordered pair $(5, -6)$ lie? (Lesson 2-3) **quadrant IV**

55. **NUMBERS** A number times 2 is added to 7. The result is 23. What is the number? Use the *guess and check* strategy. (Lesson 1-5) **8**

GET READY for the Next Lesson

Add. (Lesson 2-4)

56. $-6 + (-6) + (-6) + (-6)$ **−24**

57. $-11 + (-11) + (-11)$ **−33**

58. $-2 + (-2) + (-2) + (-2)$ **−8**

59. $-8 + (-8) + (-8)$ **−24**

Pre-AP Activity — Use after Exercise 45.

Remind students that to subtract an integer they can add its opposite. Ask them whether when adding an integer they can subtract its opposite. Have them explain their reasoning and give examples.

106 Chapter 2 Integers

2-6 Multiplying Integers

PACING: **Regular:** 1 period, **Block:** 0.5 period

IN Academic Standards **7.1.7** **Solve problems that involve multiplication** and division **with integers**, fractions, decimals and combinations of the four operations. *Also addresses P.5.1, P.5.2, P.5.3, P.6.5, P.6.6.*

Options for Differentiated Instruction

ELL = English Language Learner AL = Above or Beyond Grade Level SS = Struggling Students SN = Special Needs

Find the Error AL

Use after presenting Examples 1–7.

Display the following two expressions on the board: $(-3)^{15}$ $(-5)^{10}$

Share with the class each of the statements shown below and have students determine whether John's or Sarah's statement is correct. Have them explain their reasoning.

John	Sarah
$(-3)^{15}$ is greater than $(-5)^{10}$ because the exponent is greater.	$(-5)^{10}$ is greater because it is positive and $(-3)^{15}$ is negative.

Sarah; a negative number raised to an even power is positive and a negative number raised to an odd power is negative. So, $(-5)^{10}$ is greater than $(-3)^{15}$.

Alternative Methods ELL SS SN

Use before assigning the Exercises.

Some students may mistakenly assign the wrong sign to a product that involves one or more negative integers. Suggest that students multiply first, disregarding the signs, and then use the rules provided to affix the correct sign to the product.

Visualizing Substitutions SS SN

Use with Exercises 30–37 and 40–43.

To help students identify which values should be substituted for variables in an expression, suggest that they use different color highlighters to organize the information. It may be helpful to provide an enlarged photocopy of these exercises so that students can use the highlighters directly on the homework problems.

ALGEBRA Evaluate each expression if $a = -6$, $b = -4$, $c = 3$, and $d = 9$.

40. $-3a^2$ **41.** $-cd^2$ **42.** $-2a + b$ **43.** $b^2 - 4ac$

Leveled Lesson Resources

Also on TeacherWorks™ Lesson 2-6

Chapter 2 Resource Masters

BL = Below or Approaching Grade Level OL = On Grade Level AL = Above or Beyond Grade Level ELL = English Language Learner

Lesson Reading Guide
p. 42 BL OL ELL

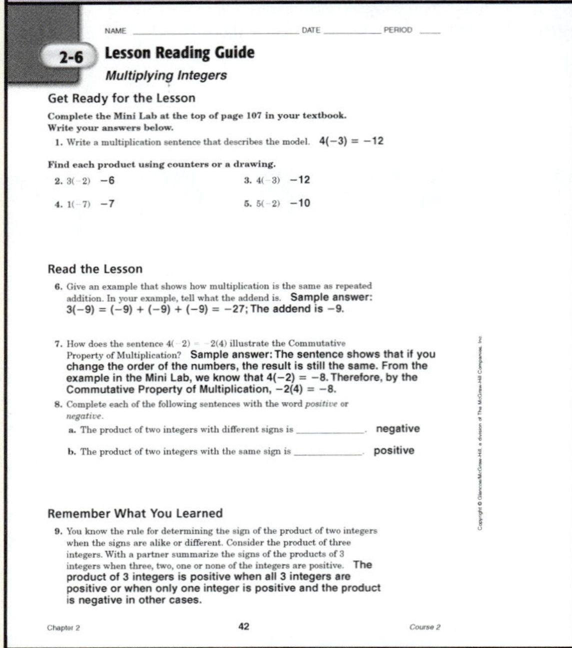
2-6 Lesson Reading Guide
Multiplying Integers
Get Ready for the Lesson
Complete the Mini Lab at the top of page 107 in your textbook. Write your answers below.
1. Write a multiplication sentence that describes the model. 4(−3) = −12
Find each product using counters or a drawing.
2. 3(−2) −6 3. 4(−3) −12
4. 1(−7) −7 5. 5(−2) −10
Read the Lesson
6. Give an example that shows how multiplication is the same as repeated addition. In your example, tell what the addend is. Sample answer: 3(−9) = (−9) + (−9) + (−9) = −27; The addend is −9.
7. How does the sentence 4(−2) = −2(4) illustrate the Commutative Property of Multiplication? Sample answer: The sentence shows that if you change the order of the numbers, the result is still the same. From the example in the Mini Lab, we know that 4(−2) = −8. Therefore, by the Commutative Property of Multiplication, −2(4) = −8.
8. Complete each of the following sentences with the word *positive* or *negative*.
a. The product of two integers with different signs is negative
b. The product of two integers with the same sign is positive
Remember What You Learned
9. You know the rule for determining the sign of the product of two integers when the signs are alike or different. Consider the product of three integers. With a partner summarize the signs of the products of 3 integers when three, two, one or none of the integers are positive. The product of 3 integers is positive when all 3 integers are positive or when only one integer is positive and the product is negative in other cases.
Chapter 2 42 Course 2

*Study Guide and Intervention**
p. 43 BL OL ELL

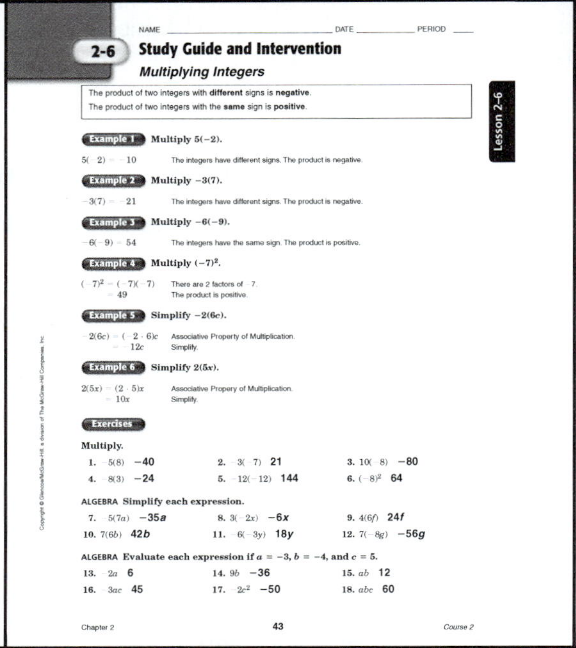
2-6 Study Guide and Intervention
Multiplying Integers
The product of two integers with different signs is negative.
The product of two integers with the same sign is positive.
Example 1 Multiply 5(−2).
Example 2 Multiply −3(7).
Example 3 Multiply −6(−9).
Example 4 Multiply (−7)².
Example 5 Simplify −2(6c).
Example 6 Simplify 2(5x).
Exercises
Multiply.
1. 5(8) −40 2. −3(−7) 21 3. 10(−8) −80
4. 8(3) −24 5. −12(−12) 144 6. (−8)² 64
ALGEBRA Simplify each expression.
7. 5(7a) −35a 8. 3(−2x) −6x 9. 4(6f) 24f
10. 7(6b) 42b 11. −6(−3y) 18y 12. 7(−8g) −56g
ALGEBRA Evaluate each expression if a = −3, b = −4, and c = 5.
13. −2a 6 14. 9b −36 15. ab 12
16. −3ac 45 17. −2c² −50 18. abc 60
Chapter 2 43 Course 2

*Skills Practice**
p. 44 BL OL

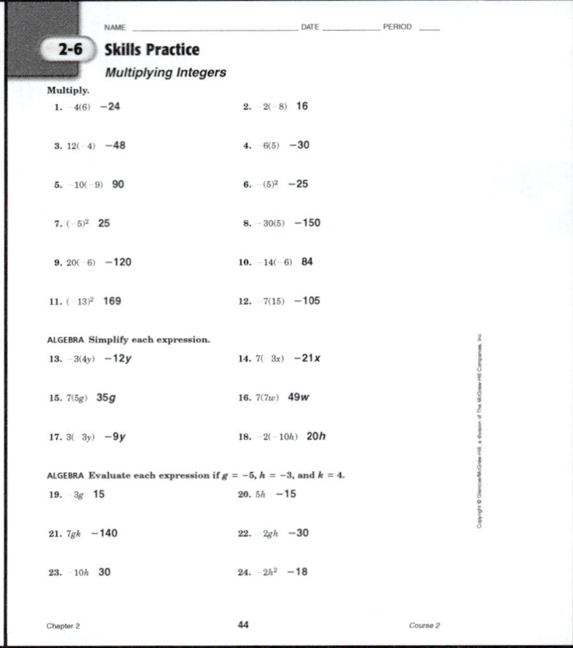
2-6 Skills Practice
Multiplying Integers
Multiply.
1. −4(6) −24 2. −2(−8) 16
3. 12(−4) −48 4. −6(5) −30
5. −10(−9) 90 6. −(5)² −25
7. (−5)² 25 8. −30(5) −150
9. 20(−6) −120 10. −14(−6) 84
11. (−13)² 169 12. −7(15) −105
ALGEBRA Simplify each expression.
13. −3(4y) −12y 14. 7(−3x) −21x
15. 7(5g) 35g 16. 7(7w) 49w
17. 3(−3y) −9y 18. −2(−10h) 20h
ALGEBRA Evaluate each expression if g = −5, h = −3, and k = 4.
19. −3g 15 20. 5h −15
21. 7gk −140 22. 2gh −30
23. −10h 30 24. −2h² −18
Chapter 2 44 Course 2

*Practice**
p. 45 OL AL

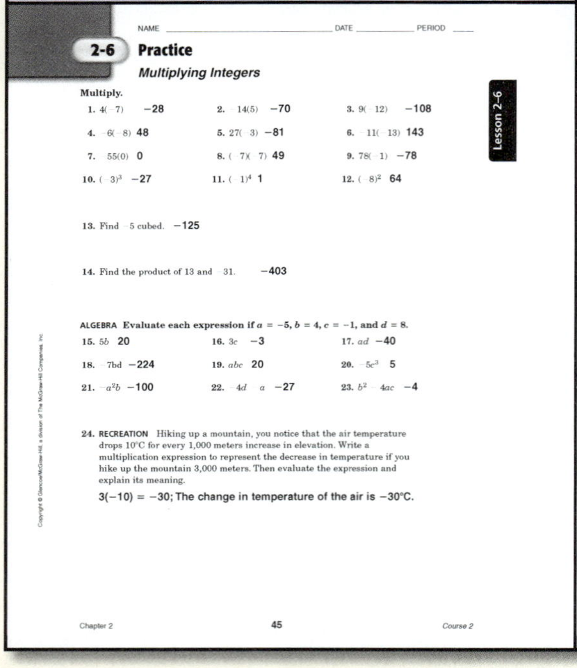
2-6 Practice
Multiplying Integers
Multiply.
1. 4(−7) −28 2. −14(5) −70 3. 9(−12) −108
4. −6(−8) 48 5. 27(−3) −81 6. −11(−13) 143
7. −55(0) 0 8. (−7)(−7) 49 9. 78(−1) −78
10. (−3)³ −27 11. (−1)⁴ 1 12. (−8)² 64
13. Find −5 cubed. −125
14. Find the product of 13 and −31. −403
ALGEBRA Evaluate each expression if a = −5, b = 4, c = −1, and d = 8.
15. 5b 20 16. 3c −3 17. ad −40
18. 7bd −224 19. abc 20 20. −5c³ 5
21. −a²b −100 22. −4d − a −27 23. b² − 4ac −4
24. RECREATION Hiking up a mountain, you notice that the air temperature drops 10°C for every 1,000 meters increase in elevation. Write a multiplication expression to represent the decrease in temperature if you hike up the mountain 3,000 meters. Then evaluate the expression and explain its meaning.
3(−10) = −30; The change in temperature of the air is −30°C.
Chapter 2 45 Course 2

*Word Problem Practice**
p. 46 OL AL

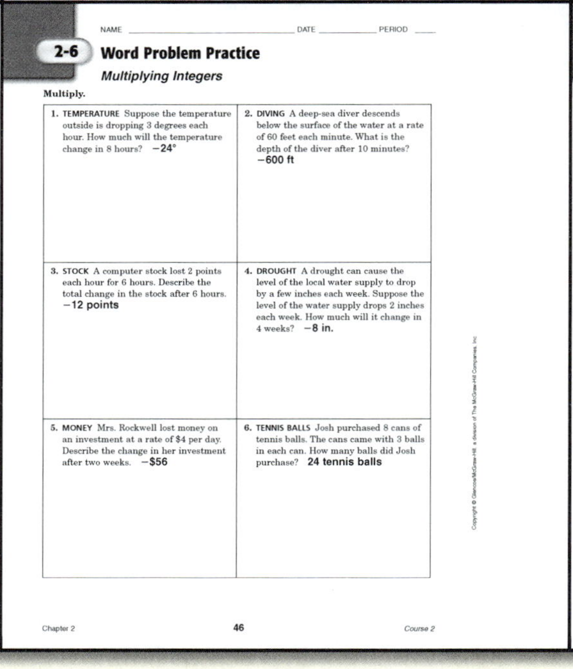
2-6 Word Problem Practice
Multiplying Integers
Multiply.
1. TEMPERATURE Suppose the temperature outside is dropping 3 degrees each hour. How much will the temperature change in 8 hours? −24°
2. DIVING A deep-sea diver descends below the surface of the water at a rate of 60 feet each minute. What is the depth of the diver after 10 minutes? −600 ft
3. STOCK A computer stock lost 2 points each hour for 6 hours. Describe the total change in the stock after 6 hours. −12 points
4. DROUGHT A drought can cause the level of the local water supply to drop by a few inches each week. Suppose the level of the water supply drops 2 inches each week. How much will it change in 4 weeks? −8 in.
5. MONEY Mrs. Rockwell lost money on an investment at a rate of $4 per day. Describe the change in her investment after two weeks. −$56
6. TENNIS BALLS Josh purchased 8 cans of tennis balls. The cans came with 3 balls in each can. How many balls did Josh purchase? 24 tennis balls
Chapter 2 46 Course 2

Enrichment
p. 47 OL AL

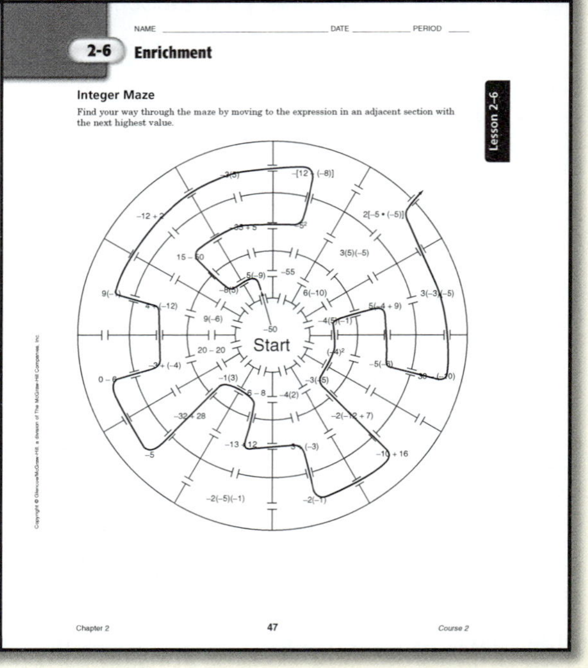
2-6 Enrichment
Integer Maze
Find your way through the maze by moving to the expression in an adjacent section with the next highest value.
Start
Chapter 2 47 Course 2

** Also available in Spanish* ELL

Additional Lesson Resources

Transparencies
- *5-Minute Check Transparency,* Lesson 2-6

Other Print Products
- *Teaching Mathematics with Manipulatives*
- *Noteables™ Interactive Study Notebook with Foldables™*

Teacher Tech Tools
- *Interactive Classroom CD-ROM,* Lesson 2-6
- *AssignmentWorks,* Lesson 2-6

Student Tech Tools
glencoe.com
- Extra Examples, Chapter 2, Lesson 6
- Self-Check Quiz, Chapter 2, Lesson 6

2-6 Multiplying Integers

MAIN IDEA

Multiply integers.

IN Academic Standards

7.1.7 Solve problems that involve multiplication and division **with integers**, fractions, decimals and combinations of the four operations. *Also addresses P.5.1, P.5.2, P.5.3, P.6.5, P.6.6.*

IN Math Online

glencoe.com

- Extra Examples
- Personal Tutor
- Self-Check Quiz

MINI Lab

Counters can be used to multiply integers.

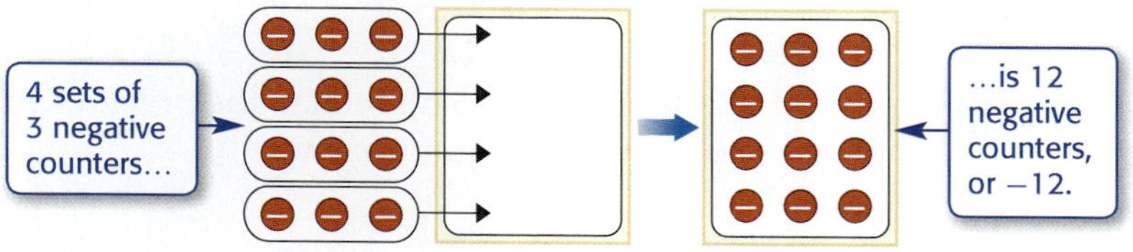

1. Write a multiplication sentence that describes the model above. $4(-3) = -12$

Find each product using counters or a drawing.

2. $3(-2)$ -6 3. $4(-3)$ -12 4. $1(-7)$ -7 5. $5(-2)$ -10

Remember that multiplication is the same as repeated addition.

$4(-3) = (-3) + (-3) + (-3) + (-3)$ −3 is used as an addend four times.

$= -12$

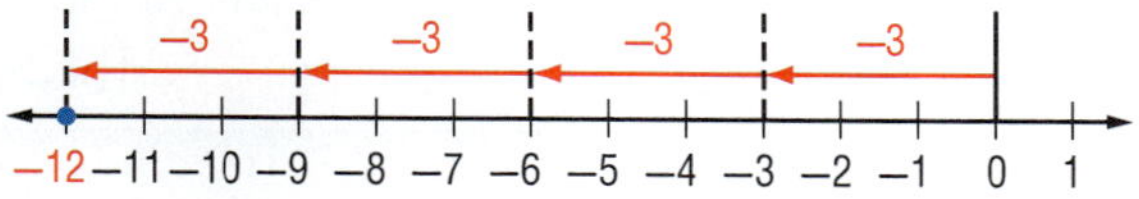

By the Commutative Property of Multiplication, $4(-3) = -3(4)$.

Multiply Integers with Different Signs — Key Concept

Words	The product of two integers with different signs is negative.
Examples	$6(-4) = -24$ $\quad -5(7) = -35$

EXAMPLES Multiply Integers with Different Signs

1 **Find $3(-5)$.**

$3(-5) = -15$ The integers have different signs. The product is negative.

2 **Find $-6(8)$.**

$-6(8) = -48$ The integers have different signs. The product is negative.

CHECK Your Progress

a. $9(-2)$ -18 b. $-7(4)$ -28

Tips for New Teachers

Multiplying Integers

Remind students that repeated addition can be used to check their work. For example, $3(-5) = (-5) + (-5) + (-5)$ or -15.

2-6 Lesson Notes

1 Focus

Vertical Alignment

Before Lesson 2-6
Add with negative integers; subtract positive integers from negative integers

Lesson 2-6
Solve multiplication problems, including those arising in concrete situations, that use positive and negative integers

After Lesson 2-6
Multiply rational numbers and take positive rational numbers to whole-number powers

2 Teach

MINI Lab

Remind students that two numbers separated only by a parenthesis (such as in Exercises 2–5) are to be multiplied.

Scaffolding Questions

As students answer the following questions, write the expressions on the board.

Ask:

- How can I write 3 + 3 + 3 + 3 as a multiplication problem? 4 • 3
- How can I write 7 + 7 + 7 as a multiplication problem? 3 • 7
- How can I write 1 + 1 + 1 + 1 + 1 + 1 as a multiplication problem? 6 • 1
- How can I write (−2) + (−2) + (−2) + (−2) as a multiplication problem? 4 • (−2)

Focus on Mathematical Content

Number lines are a good way to model multiplying integers.

Multiplication can be shown as **repeated addition.**

The **Commutative Property of Multiplication** is related to the Commutative Property of Addition. The order in which you multiply (or add) does not change the product (or sum).

Formative Assessment

Use the Check Your Progress exercises after the Examples to determine students' understanding of concepts.

ADDITIONAL EXAMPLES

1. Find $5(-4)$. -20
2. Find $-3(9)$. -27
3. Find $-6(-8)$. 48
4. Find $(-8)^2$. 64
5. Find $-2(-5)(-6)$. -60

Additional Examples are also in:

- Noteables™ Interactive Study Notebook with Foldables™
- Interactive Classroom PowerPoint® Presentations

The product of two positive integers is positive. You can use a pattern to find the sign of the product of two negative integers.

Study Tip

Multiplying by Zero The Multiplicative Property of Zero states that when any number is multiplied by zero, the product is zero.

positive × negative = negative

$(2)(-3) = -6$
$(1)(-3) = -3$ (+3)
$(0)(-3) = 0$ (+3)
$(-1)(-3) = 3$ (+3)
$(-2)(-3) = 6$ (+3)

negative × negative = positive

Each product is 3 more than the previous product. This pattern can also be shown on a number line.

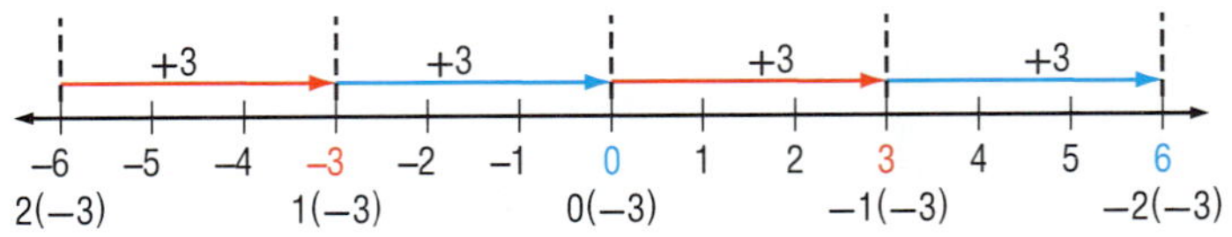

These and other examples suggest the following rule.

Multiply Integers with Same Sign — Key Concept

Words The product of two integers with the same sign is positive.

Examples $2(6) = 12$ $-10(-6) = 60$

EXAMPLES Multiply Integers with the Same Sign

3 **Find $-11(-9)$.**

$-11(-9) = 99$ The integers have the same sign. The product is positive.

Study Tip

Look Back You can review **exponents** in Lesson 1-2.

4 **Find $(-4)^2$.**

$(-4)^2 = (-4)(-4)$ There are two factors of -4.

$= 16$ The product is positive.

5 **Find $-3(-4)(-2)$.**

$-3(-4)(-2) = [-3(-4)](-2)$ Associative Property

$= 12(-2)$ $-3(-4) = 12$

$= -24$ $12(-2) = -24$

CHECK Your Progress

c. $-12(-4)$ 48 d. $(-5)^2$ 25 e. $-7(-5)(-3)$ -105

108 Chapter 2 Integers

Real-World Link The MIR submersible that explored the Titanic shipwreck was able to descend to −20,000 feet.
Source: Space Adventures

Real-World EXAMPLE

6 **SUBMERSIBLES** **A submersible is diving from the surface of the water at a rate of 90 feet per minute. What is the depth of the submersible after 7 minutes?**

If the submersible descends 90 feet per minute, then after 7 minutes, the vessel will be at 7(−90) or −630 feet. Thus, the submersible will descend to 630 feet below the surface.

CHECK Your Progress

f. **MONEY** Mr. Simon's bank automatically deducts a $4 monthly maintenance fee from his savings account. What integer represents a change in his savings account from one year of fees? **−48**

Negative numbers are often used when evaluating algebraic expressions.

EXAMPLE Evaluate Expressions

7 **ALGEBRA** **Evaluate pqr if $p = -3$, $q = 4$, and $r = -1$.**

$pqr = -3(4)(-1)$	Replace p with −3, q with 4, and r with −1.
$= (-12)(-1)$	Multiply −3 and 4.
$= 12$	Multiply −12 and −1.

CHECK Your Progress

g. Evaluate xyz if $x = -7$, $y = -4$, and $z = 2$. **56**

CHECK Your Understanding

Examples 1, 2 (p. 107)

Multiply.

1. 6(−10) **−60**
2. 11(−4) **−44**
3. −2(14) **−28**
4. −8(5) **−40**

Examples 3–5 (p. 108)

Multiply.

5. −15(−3) **45**
6. −7(−9) **63**
7. $(-8)^2$ **64**
8. $(-3)^3$ **−27**
9. −1(−3)(−4) **−12**
10. 2(4)(5) **40**

Example 6 (p. 109)

11. **MONEY** Tamera owns 100 shares of a certain stock. Suppose the price of the stock drops by $3 per share. Write a multiplication expression to find the change in Tamera's investment. Explain the answer. **See margin.**

Example 7 (p. 109)

ALGEBRA **Evaluate each expression if $f = -1$, $g = 7$, and $h = -10$.**

12. $5f$ **−5**
13. fgh **70**

ADDITIONAL EXAMPLES

6 **MINES** A mine elevator descends at a rate of 300 feet per minute. How far below the earth's surface will the elevator be after 5 minutes? −1,500 ft

7 **ALGEBRA** Evaluate abc if $a = -3$, $b = 5$, and $c = -8$. 120

3 Practice

Formative Assessment

Use Exercises 1–13 to check for understanding.

Then use the chart at the bottom of the next page to customize your assignments for students.

Intervention You may wish to use the Study Guide and Intervention Master on page 43 of the *Chapter 2 Resource Masters* for additional reinforcement.

Additional Answer

11. 100(−3) = −300; Tamera's investment is now worth $300 less than it was before the price of the stock dropped.

Differentiated Instruction

Visual/Spatial Learners If students are having difficulty completing the Exercises, have them use counters, drawings, or number lines to represent the multiplication of integers. For example, in Exercise 1, students could display 6 sets of 10 negative counters and count the total number of negative counters, or −60. Remind students to connect this representation with the rule that the product of two integers with different signs is negative.

Odd/Even Assignments

Exercises 14–39 are structured so that students practice the same concepts whether they are assigned odd or even problems.

Tips for New Teachers

Multiplication

When multiplying more than two integers, some students may find it easier to multiply first, ignoring the signs. Then they can apply the rules to find the product's sign. You may wish to point out that if the number of negative integers being multiplied is odd (1, 3, 5, and so on), the product will be negative.

Differentiated Instruction

Kinesthetic Learners If students are having difficulty, have them use algebra tiles or a drawing to model and find the product of a negative and a positive integer and the product of two negative integers.

Additional Answer

47.

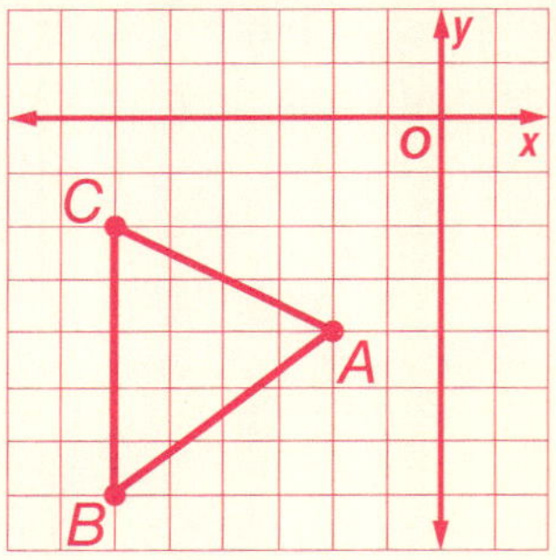

Sample answer: new triangle $A'B'C'$ is on the other side of the origin (in quadrant III) from original triangle *ABC* (which is in quadrant I).

Practice and Problem Solving

HOMEWORK HELP

For Exercises	See Examples
14–19, 28	1, 2
20–27, 29	3–5
30–37	7
38–39	6

Exercise Levels
A: 14–39
B: 40–48
C: 49–53

Multiply.

14. $8(-12)$ **−96**
15. $11(-20)$ **−220**
16. $-15(4)$ **−60**
17. $-7(10)$ **−70**
18. $-7(11)$ **−77**
19. $25(-2)$ **−50**
20. $-20(-8)$ **160**
21. $-16(-5)$ **80**
22. $(-6)^2$ **36**
23. $(-5)^3$ **−125**
24. $(-4)^3$ **−64**
25. $(-9)^2$ **81**
26. $-4(-2)(-8)$ **−64**
27. $-9(-1)(-5)$ **−45**
28. Find the product of 10 and −10. **−100**
29. Find −7 squared. **49**

ALGEBRA Evaluate each expression if $w = 4$, $x = -8$, $y = 5$, and $z = -3$.

30. $-4w$ **−16**
31. $3x$ **−24**
32. xy **−40**
33. xz **24**
34. $7wz$ **−84**
35. $-2wx$ **64**
36. xyz **120**
37. wyx **−160**

Write a multiplication expression to represent each situation. Then find each product and explain its meaning.

38. **ECOLOGY** Wave erosion causes a certain coastline to recede at a rate of 3 centimeters each year. This occurs uninterrupted for a period of 8 years.

38. $8(-3) = -24$; The coastline's new position is 24 centimeters farther inland than it was 8 years ago.

39. **EXERCISE** Ethan burns 650 Calories when he runs for 1 hour. Suppose he runs 5 hours in one week.
$5(-650) = -3{,}250$; Ethan burns 3,250 Calories each week.

ALGEBRA Evaluate each expression if $a = -6$, $b = -4$, $c = 3$, and $d = 9$.

40. $-3a^2$ **−108**
41. $-cd^2$ **−243**
42. $-2a + b$ **8**
43. $b^2 - 4ac$ **88**

44. **BANKING** Tamika's aunt writes a check for $150 each month for her car loan. She writes another check for $300 twice a year to pay for car insurance. Write an expression involving multiplication and addition to describe how these expenses affect her checking account balance on a yearly basis. Then evaluate the expression and explain its meaning.

44. $12(-150) + 2(-300) = -2{,}400$; A total of $2,400 is subtracted from her checking account each year for these expenses.

45. **FIND THE DATA** Refer to the Data File on pages 16–19 of your book. Choose some data and write a real-world problem in which you would multiply integers. **See students' work.**

GEOMETRY For Exercises 46–48, use the graph at the right.

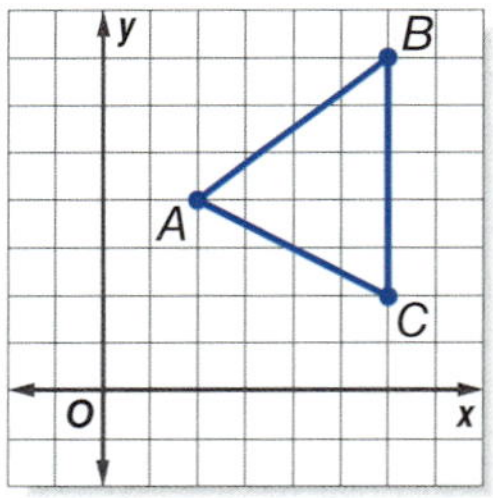

46. Name the ordered pairs for *A*, *B*, and *C*. Multiply each *x*- and *y*-coordinate by −1 to get three new ordered pairs.
47. Graph the ordered pairs and connect them to form a new triangle. Describe its position with respect to the original triangle. **See margin.**
48. In which quadrant would a new triangle lie if only the *y*-coordinates of the original triangle are multiplied by −1? **quadrant IV**

46. *A*(2, 4) is now (−2, −4); *B*(6, 7) is now (−6, −7); *C*(6, 2) is now (−6, −2).

Academic Standards • ISTEP+
Extra Practice, pp. 673, 705

DIFFERENTIATED HOMEWORK OPTIONS

Level	Assignment	Two-Day Assignment	
BL Basic	14–39, 49, 50, 52–66	15–39 odd, 54, 55	14–38 even, 49, 50, 52, 53, 56–66
OL Core	13–43 odd, 44–50, 52–66	14–39, 54, 55	40–50, 52, 53, 56–66
AL Advanced/Pre-AP	40–65 (optional: 66)		

110 Chapter 2 Integers

H.O.T. Problems

49. **OPEN ENDED** Write a multiplication sentence with a product of -18. **Sample answer: $-6 \times 3 = -18$**

50. **NUMBER SENSE** Explain how to evaluate each expression as simply as possible. **See margin.**

a. $(-9)(-6)(15)(-7+7)$ b. $(-15)(-26) + (-15)(25)$

51. **CHALLENGE** Evaluate $(-1)^{50}$. Explain your reasoning. **See margin.**

52. **SELECT A TECHNIQUE** Luis is trying to determine whether the product of three negative integers is negative or positive. Which of the following techniques might he use to determine the answer? Justify your selections. Then provide an example that illustrates the answer. **See margin.**

mental math | number sense | estimation

53. **WRITING IN MATH** Explain when the product of three integers is positive. **See margin.**

ISTEP+ PRACTICE 7.1.7

54. The temperature drops 2 degrees per hour for 3 hours. Which expression does *not* describe the change in temperature? **D**

A $-2(3)$ C $-2 - 2 - 2$
B $-2 + (-2) + (-2)$ D $2(3)$

55. Which of the following numbers is the 7th number in the sequence shown?

$1, -2, 4, -8, 16, \ldots$ **J**

F -64 H 32
G -32 J 64

Spiral Review

56. **TEMPERATURE** The highest and lowest recorded temperatures in Europe are 122°F and −67°F. Find the difference in these temperatures. (Lesson 2-5) **189°F**

Subtract. (Lesson 2-5)

57. $-25 - (-33)$ **8** 58. $-6 - 14$ **−20** 59. $9 - 30$ **−21** 60. $13 - (-12)$ **25**

ALGEBRA **Evaluate each expression if $x = -4$, $y = 6$, and $z = 1$.** (Lesson 2-4)

61. $x + (-2)$ **−6** 62. $-1 + z$ **0** 63. $-15 + y$ **−9** 64. $x + y$ **2**

65. **PENGUINS** The Emperor penguin's average height is 51 inches, and the Adelie's average height is 18 inches. Write and solve an addition equation to find how much taller Emperor penguins are than Adelie penguins. (Lesson 1-7) **$18 + x = 51$; $x = 33$**

GET READY for the Next Lesson

66. **NUMBERS** A number is multiplied by −4. Then 15 is added to the product, and the result is 3. What is the number? Use the *guess and check* strategy. (Lesson 1-5) **3**

4 Assess

Crystal Ball Tell students that tomorrow's lesson is about dividing integers. Ask them to write how they think what they learned today will connect with tomorrow's material.

Formative Assessment

Check for student understanding of concepts in Lessons 2-5 and 2-6.

CRM Quiz 3, p. 62

FOLDABLES Study Organizer — Foldables™ Follow-Up

Remind students to write what they learn about multiplying integers in their Foldables. Make sure they include examples of each case (negative × positive, positive × negative, negative × negative, and positive × positive).

Additional Answers

50a. Sample answer: Evaluate $-7 + 7$ first. Since $-7 + 7 = 0$, and any number times 0 is 0, the value of the expression is 0;

50b. Sample answer: First use the Distributive Property to rewrite the expression as $-15(-26 + 25)$. Then evaluate $-26 + 25$. Since $-26 + 25 = -1$ and $-15 \times -1 = 15$, the value of the expression is 15.

51. Sample answer: 1; $(-1)(-1) = 1$. Since there are $50 \div 2 = 25$ pairs of (-1) factors, $(-1)^{50} = 1^{25}$. One raised to any power is still 1.

52. Sample answer: number sense; A negative integer times a negative integer is positive. The resulting positive integer times the third negative number is negative. So, the product of three negative numbers is negative. For example, $-2 \times -5 \times -3 = 10 \times -3$ or -30

53. Sample answer: The product of three integers is positive when exactly two of the integers are negative or all three integers are positive.

2-7 Problem-Solving Investigation
LOOK FOR A PATTERN

PACING: **Regular:** 1 period, **Block:** 0.5 period

IN Academic Standards **7.3.4 Recognize, describe, or extend geometric patterns** using tables, graphs, words, or symbols. **P.1.3 Apply and adapt a variety of appropriate strategies to solve problems. P.1.4 Monitor and reflect on the process of problem solving.**

Options for Differentiated Instruction

ELL = English Language Learner AL = Above or Beyond Grade Level SS = Struggling Students SN = Special Needs

Using Pairs ELL SS SN

Use before assigning Exercises 4–6.

Use the think-pair-share technique of cooperative learning. Assign Exercise 4, 5, or 6. Let students read over it individually. Then pair them up and have them look for the pattern to solve the problem. Repeat with pairs rearranged.

Breaking Down the Problem SS SN

Use with Exercise 6.

Some students may be intimidated by seeing two columns of numbers. Encourage them to find the pattern in each column and then extend the pattern to find how many times per minute a cricket will chirp when the outside temperature is 60°F.

Outside Temperature (°F)	Chirps per Minute
85°F	180
80°F	160
75°F	140
70°F	120
65°F	100
60°F	80

Choosing the Best Strategy SS SN

Use before assigning Exercises 7–14.

Prior to assigning Exercises 7–14, read each exercise aloud and discuss with the class which strategy might be best to solve each problem. Possible discussion questions are listed below.

- What question do you need to answer?
- What information is given?
- Is this like any exercises you have done before?
- What strategy would be most effective to solve the problem?
- How could you check your answer to make sure it is reasonable?

Make sure that all students have chosen a strategy for each problem so that they can complete the assignment independently.

Leveled Lesson Resources

Also on TeacherWorks™
Lesson 2-7

Chapter 2 Resource Masters

BL = Below or Approaching Grade Level

OL = On Grade Level

AL = Above or Beyond Grade Level

ELL = English Language Learner

Study Guide and Intervention*
p. 48 BL OL ELL

NAME ________________ DATE ________ PERIOD ____

2-7 Study Guide and Intervention
Problem-Solving Investigation: Look for a Pattern

Looking for a pattern is one strategy that can help you when solving problems. You can use the four-step problem-solving plan along with looking for a pattern to solve problems.

Understand	• Determine what information is given in the problem and what you need to find.
Plan	• Select a strategy including a possible estimate.
Solve	• Solve the problem by carrying out your plan.
Check	• Examine your answer to see if it seems reasonable.

Example MEMBERSHIP The local tennis club started the year with 675 members. In one month they had 690 members. After two months they had 705 members. After three months they had 720 members. When the tennis club reaches 750 members they will close their enrollment. How many months will it take the club to reach their maximum enrollment if they continue adding new members at the same rate?

Understand The club began with 590 members and is adding new members every month. It needs to find out when it reaches its maximum enrollment of 750 members.

Plan Look for a pattern or rule that increases the membership each month. Then use the rule to extend the patter to find the solution.

Solve After the initial 575 members, 15 new members joined each month. Extend the pattern to find the solution.
675, 690, 705, 720, 735, 750
+15 +15 +15 +15 +15
They will have reached their maximum enrollment in 5 months.

Check They increased by 5 · 15 or 75 members in 5 months which when added to the original 675 members is 675 + 75 = 750. So, 5 months is a reasonable answer.

Exercises

1. PRODUCE A farmer has 42 apples sitting on his front porch. The next day there are only 36 apples left on the porch. After 2 days there are only 30 apples left on the porch and in 3 days 24 apples remain on the porch. After how many days will the 42 apples disappear from the porch if the same amount of apples are missing each day?
7 days

2. TELEPHONE A local phone company charges a standard rate of $3 per call. After one minute the charge is $4.50. In two minutes the charge is $6.00. If Susan only has $10.00, how long can her phone conversation be if the charges per minute stay constant?
4 minutes

Chapter 2 48 Course 2

Skills Practice*
p. 49 BL OL

NAME ________________ DATE ________ PERIOD ____

2-7 Skills Practice
Problem-Solving Investigation: Look for a Pattern

Look for a pattern to solve the problem.

1. NUMBERS What are the next two numbers in the pattern listed below?
7, 21, 63, 189, ...
567, 1701

2. POPULATION The Springfield Zoo is breeding gorillas. They have 3 gorillas, which can mate and give birth. After the first year there are 7 gorillas. After the second year there are 11 gorillas. If the gorillas continue to increase at the same rate, how long will it take for the Springfield Zoo to have 35 gorillas?
8 years

3. ALGEBRA Read the table below to find a pattern relating x and y. Then write an equation to describe the pattern in general.

x	y
1	5
2	8
3	11
4	14
5	17

y is two more than three times x. So, $y = 3x + 2$

4. SAVINGS Maria receives $50 for her birthday. She decides to put the money into a bank account and start saving her money from babysitting in order to buy a television that costs $200. After the first week she has $74. After the second week, she has $98. After the third week she has $122. How many weeks will she have to save at the same rate in order to buy the television?
7 weeks

Lesson 2-7

Chapter 2 49 Course 2

Practice*
p. 50 OL AL

NAME ________________ DATE ________ PERIOD ____

2-7 Practice
Problem-Solving Investigation: Look for a Pattern

Mixed Problem Solving

Use the look for a pattern strategy to solve Exercises 1 and 2.

1. NUMBERS What are the next two numbers in the pattern below?
3, 15, 75, 375, ...
1,875 and 9,375

2. QUILTING Mrs. Perez is a talented quilter. In the center of the design of her quilt are four identical red squares in the shape of a square. Surrounding these red squares is a border of 12 identical white squares. Surrounding these white squares is a border of 20 identical blue squares. How many squares are in the next border surrounding the 20 blue squares?
28 squares

B	B	B	B	B	B
B	W	W	W	W	B
B	W	R	R	W	B
B	W	R	R	W	B
B	W	W	W	W	B
B	B	B	B	B	B

Use any strategy to solve Exercises 3–6. Some strategies are shown below.

PROBLEM-SOLVING STRATEGIES
• Guess and Check.
• Look for a pattern.

3. TRANSPORTATION A college needs to transport the swim team to a state meet. The large van carries 15 people and each smaller van carries 9 people. How many smaller vans are needed to provide rides for 54 people if the large van is used?
5 smaller vans

4. ALPHABET What are the next three letters in each pattern shown?
D, H, L, P, ... **T and X**
C, F, I, L, ... **O and R**

5. POPULATION The land area of Ebeye, an island in the Pacific, is 90 acres. About 155 persons per acre live on this island. What is the population of Ebeye?
13,950 people

6. ASTRONOMY Earth is 93 million miles from the sun, while Mars is 142 million miles from the sun. Theoretically, what is the closest distance Mars could be to Earth?
49 million miles

Chapter 2 50 Course 2

Word Problem Practice*
p. 51 OL AL

NAME ________________ DATE ________ PERIOD ____

2-7 Word Problem Practice
Problem-Solving Investigation: Look for a Pattern

Solve each problem using any strategy you have learned.

1. COLLECTIONS Brittany received 8 silver dollars on her eighth birthday. After her next birthday she had 15 and after the next she had 22. After her eleventh birthday she had 29 silver dollars. How many silver dollars will she have after her 16th birthday if her collection increases at the same rate every year?
64 silver dollars

2. PATTERNS List the next three terms in the following sequence.
27, 39, 51, 63, ...
75, 87, 99

3. GEOMETRY There are 6 rows of squares stacked upon each other. The first three are shown. How many total squares are needed for the entire pattern?
42 Squares

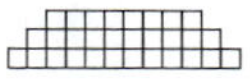

4. TICKET SALES Madison High School is putting on a school play. They decide to charge $11 for main floor seats and $7 for balcony seats. If the school sold twice as many main floor seats as balcony seats and made $870, how many of each type of seat did they sell?
60 main floor seats, 30 balcony seats

5. EXERCISE The table below shows the distance Katie ran each day this week. If Katie wants to run 30 a week. How many miles must she run on Sunday?
Katie must run 4 miles on Sunday.

Monday	4 miles
Tuesday	7 miles
Wednesday	5 miles
Thursday	5 miles
Friday	2 miles
Saturday	3 miles

6. AGE Brad is three years more than half of Brandon's age. If their combined age is 93 years, how old is each man?
**Brad, 33
Brandon, 60**

Lesson 2-7

Chapter 2 51 Course 2

** Also available in Spanish* ELL

Additional Lesson Resources

Transparencies
- *5-Minute Check Transparency*, Lesson 2-7

Other Print Products
- *Noteables™ Interactive Study Notebook with Foldables™*

Teacher Tech Tools
- *Interactive Classroom CD-ROM*, Lesson 2-7
- *AssignmentWorks*, Lesson 2-7

Student Tech Tools
glencoe.com
- Extra Examples, Chapter 2, Lesson 7
- Self-Check Quiz, Chapter 2, Lesson 7

2-7 Lesson Notes

1 Focus

Look for a Pattern The *look for a pattern* strategy is useful for solving many kinds of problems. Students will work with patterns involving numbers, letters, and geometric figures. It is usually easier to find a pattern if information is organized in a list or a table.

2 Teach

Scaffolding Questions

Tell students that you saw a digital camera on sale for $900.

Ask:

- If I save $100 each month, how many months will it take me to save enough money to buy the camera? 9
- If I save $150 each month, how many months will it take me to save enough money to buy the camera? 6
- If I save $300 each month, how many months will it take me to save enough money to buy the camera? 3

ADDITIONAL EXAMPLE

Solve. Use the *look for a pattern* strategy.

1 **HAIR** Lelani wants to grow an 11-inch ponytail. She has a 3-inch ponytail now, and her hair grows about one inch every two months. How long will it take for her ponytail to reach 11 inches? 16 months

Additional Examples are also in:

- Noteables™ Interactive Study Notebook with Foldables™
- Interactive Classroom PowerPoint® Presentations

2-7 Problem-Solving Investigation

MAIN IDEA: Solve problems by looking for a pattern.

Academic Standards **7.3.4 Recognize, describe, or extend geometric patterns** using tables, graphs, words, or symbols. **P.1.3 Apply and adapt a variety of appropriate strategies to solve problems. P.1.4 Monitor and reflect on the process of problem solving.**

P.S.I. TEAM +

e-Mail: LOOK FOR A PATTERN

LAURA: I've been practicing free throws every day after school to get ready for basketball tryouts. Now, I can make 3 free throws out of every 5 attempts I make.

YOUR MISSION: Look for a pattern to find the number of free throws Laura can make after 30 attempts.

Understand Laura can make an average of 3 free throws out of every 5 attempts. You need to find the number of free throws she can make after 30 attempts.

Plan Look for a pattern. Then extend the pattern to find the solution.

Solve Laura can make 3 free throws out of every 5 she attempts. Extend the pattern.

	+3	+3	+3	+3	+3
Free throws	3	6	9	12	15	18
Attempts	5	10	15	20	25	30

+5 +5 +5 +5 +5

She can make 18 free throws out of 30 attempts.

Check She makes free throws a little more than half the time. Since 18 is a little more than 15, the answer is reasonable. ✓

Analyze The Strategy

1–3. See margin.

1. Explain when you would use the *look for a pattern* strategy to solve a problem.
2. Describe how to solve a problem using the *look for a pattern* strategy.
3. WRITING IN MATH Write a problem that could be solved by looking for a pattern.

Additional Answers

1. Sample answer: Use the *look for a pattern* strategy when there is a data table, a series of numbers, or a geometric pattern as part of the problem.
2. Sample answer: Look for a rule or pattern in the data or number facts. Then use the rule to extend the pattern, and then find the solution to the problem.
3. Sample answer: Amanda has $2 in change in her bank. If she adds $0.50 each week for 7 weeks, how much money will be in her bank? $5.50

Mixed Problem Solving

Academic Standards • ISTEP+

Extra Practice, pp. 673, 705

Use the *look for a pattern* strategy to solve Exercises 4–6.

4. **DISPLAYS** A display of cereal boxes is stacked as shown below.

If the display contains 7 rows of boxes and the top three rows are shown, how many boxes are in the display? **70**

5. **MONEY** Peter is saving money to buy an MP3 player. After one month, he has \$50. After 2 months, he has \$85. After 3 months, he has \$120. After 4 months, he has \$155. He plans to keep saving at the same rate. How long will it take Peter to save enough money to buy an MP3 player that costs \$295? **8 months**

6. **INSECTS** The table shows how many times a cricket chirps at different temperatures. About how many times will a cricket chirp when the temperature is 60°F? **80 times**

Outside Temperature (°F)	Chirps per Minute
85°F	180
80°F	160
75°F	140
70°F	120

Use any strategy to solve Exercises 7–14. Some strategies are shown below.

PROBLEM-SOLVING STRATEGIES
- Guess and check
- Look for a pattern

7. **COINS** Adelina has six coins that total \$0.86. What are the coins? **See margin.**

8. **ELEVATION** The lowest point in Mexico is Laguna Salada with an elevation of −10 meters. The highest point in Mexico is Volcan Pico de Orizaba with an elevation of 5,700 meters. What is the difference in these elevations? **5,710 m**

9. **MONEY** While on vacation, Edmundo sent postcards and letters to his friends. He spent \$3.42 on postage. A stamp for a letter costs 41¢, and a stamp for a postcard costs 26¢. How many postcards and letters did he send? **2 letters and 10 postcards**

10. **GEOMETRY** What is the next figure in the pattern shown? **See margin.**

11. **POPULATION** The total land area of North Carolina is about 48,711 square miles. If an average of 183 persons were living in each square mile of North Carolina in 2007, what was the population of North Carolina in 2007? **8,914,113**

12. **GOLF** Allie's golf scores for the first five holes are given in the table. What is her total score after the first five holes? **+1 over par**

Hole	Score
1	0
2	1
3	−1
4	−2
5	3

13. **FLOWERS** A sunflower grows to be about 252 centimeters tall in 3 months. What is the average rate of growth per month? **84 cm**

14. **NUMBERS** Determine the next three numbers in the pattern below.

48, 42, 36, 30, 24, … **18, 12, 6**

3 Practice

Using the Exercises

Exercises 1–3 can be used to check for understanding.

Exercises 4–6 utilize the look for a pattern strategy.

Exercises 7–14 are structured so that students have the opportunity to practice many different problem solving strategies. You may wish to review some of the strategies they have studied.

- Use the four-step plan (p. 25)
- Guess and check (p. 42)
- Look for a pattern (p. 112)

Tips for New Teachers

Choosing Strategies

You may wish to separate students into pairs. Have the members of each pair work together to find the patterns, choose strategies, and solve the problems.

4 Assess

Name the Math Have students write or tell what mathematical procedure they used to solve one of the exercises.

Additional Answers

7. Sample answer: 3 quarters, 2 nickels, and 1 penny

10.

2-8 Dividing Integers

PACING: **Regular:** 1 period, **Block:** 0.5 period

IN Academic Standards **7.1.7 Solve problems that involve multiplication** and division **with integers**, fractions, decimals and combinations of the four operations. *Also addresses P.5.1, P.5.2, P.5.3, P.6.5, P.6.6.*

Options for Differentiated Instruction

ELL = English Language Learner AL = Above or Beyond Grade Level SS = Struggling Students SN = Special Needs

Scaffolding the Lesson ELL SS SN

Use before presenting Examples 1–5.

To scaffold this lesson, remind students the relationship between multiplication and division. Display the following example on the board.

Example: Write two multiplication problems related to the division problem $12 \div 6 = 2$.

Solution: $2 \times 6 = 12$ and $6 \times 2 = 12$

To help students see this relationship involving negative integers, have them solve several problems like the ones shown below.

Write two multiplication problems related to each division problem.

1. $8 \div 2 = 4$ $4 \times 2 = 8; 2 \times 4 = 8$
2. $15 \div 3 = 5$ $5 \times 3 = 15; 3 \times 5 = 15$
3. $8 \div (-2) = -4$ $-4 \times (-2) = 8; -2 \times (-4) = 8$
4. $-15 \div 3 = -5$ $-5 \times 3 = -15; 3 \times (-5) = -15$

Write two division problems related to each multiplication problem.

5. $5 \times 2 = 10$ $10 \div 2 = 5; 10 \div 5 = 2$
6. $3 \times 4 = 12$ $12 \div 4 = 3; 12 \div 3 = 4$
7. $5 \times (-2) = -10$ $-10 \div (-2) = 5; -10 \div 5 = -2$
8. $-3 \times (-4) = 12$ $12 \div (-4) = -3; 12 \div (-3) = -4$

Knowing how multiplication and division are related will also help students check their work.

Naturalistic Learning ELL AL SS SN

Use after presenting Example 5.

Have students work in pairs. Assign each pair an animal and have them find their estimated population for both today and 10 years ago. Have students use the expression in Example 5 to determine the average change in number for their animals. On poster board, make a table like the one shown below. Each pair of students should fill in the information on the animal they researched.

Animal	Population Today	Population 10 Years Ago	Average Change in Numbers

Leveled Lesson Resources

Also on TeacherWorks™ Lesson 2-8

Chapter 2 Resource Masters

BL = Below or Approaching Grade Level OL = On Grade Level AL = Above or Beyond Grade Level ELL = English Language Learner

Lesson Reading Guide
p. 52 BL OL ELL

NAME ______ DATE ______ PERIOD ____

2-8 Lesson Reading Guide
Dividing Integers

Get Ready for the Lesson

Complete the Mini Lab at the top of page 114 in your textbook. Write your answers below.

Find each quotient using counters or a drawing.

1. $-6 \div 2$ **−3**

2. $-12 \div 3$ **−4**

Read the Lesson

Write two division sentences related to each of the following multiplication sentences.

3. $-6(-3) = 18$ **18 ÷ (−3) = −6; 18 ÷ (−6) = −3**

4. $-21(-2) = 42$ **42 ÷ (−21) = −2; 42 ÷ (−2) = −21**

5. $-6(3) = -18$ **−18 ÷ 3 = −6; −18 ÷ (−6) = 3**

6. $2(-21) = -42$ **−42 ÷ (−21) = 2; −42 ÷ 2 = −21**

7. Complete each of the following sentences with the word *positive* or *negative*.
   a. The quotient of two integers with different signs is ______. **negative**
   b. The quotient of two integers with the same sign is ______. **positive**

8. In the division sentence $-72 \div 8 = -9$, identify the dividend, the divisor, and the quotient. **dividend: −72; divisor: 8; quotient: −9**

Remember What You Learned

9. Describe how the operations of multiplication and division are opposite of each other. Are these operations opposite in all cases? What is the one integer that cannot be a divisor? **Multiplication is the opposite of division in that the product of a quotient and divisor gives the dividend. Even though you can take the product of zero and a number, zero cannot be a divisor.**

Chapter 2 52 Course 2

Study Guide and Intervention*
p. 53 BL OL ELL

NAME ______ DATE ______ PERIOD ____

2-8 Study Guide and Intervention
Dividing Integers

The quotient of two integers with different signs is negative.
The quotient of two integers with the same sign is positive.

Example 1 Divide 30 ÷ (−5).

$30 \div (-5)$ The integers have different signs.
$30 \div (-5) = -6$ The quotient is negative.

Example 2 Divide −100 ÷ (−5).

$-100 \div (-5)$ The integers have the same sign.
$-100 \div (-5) = 20$ The quotient is positive.

Exercises

Divide.

1. $-12 \div 4$ **−3**
2. $-14 \div (-7)$ **2**
3. $\frac{18}{-2}$ **−9**
4. $-6 \div (-3)$ **2**
5. $-10 \div 10$ **−1**
6. $\frac{-80}{-20}$ **4**
7. $350 \div (-25)$ **−14**
8. $-420 \div (-3)$ **140**
9. $\frac{540}{-45}$ **12**
10. $\frac{-256}{16}$ **−16**

ALGEBRA Evaluate each expression if $d = -24$, $e = -4$, and $f = 8$.

11. $12 \div e$ **−3**
12. $40 \div f$ **5**
13. $d \div 6$ **−4**
14. $d \div e$ **6**
15. $f \div e$ **−2**
16. $e^2 \div f$ **2**
17. $\frac{d}{e}$ **−6**
18. $ef \div 2$ **−16**
19. $\frac{f^2}{e^2}$ **4**
20. $\frac{de}{f}$ **12**

Lesson 2-8

Chapter 2 53 Course 2

Skills Practice*
p. 54 BL OL

NAME ______ DATE ______ PERIOD ____

2-8 Skills Practice
Dividing Integers

Divide.

1. $-15 \div 3$ **−5**
2. $-24 \div (-8)$ **3**
3. $22 \div (-2)$ **−11**
4. $-49 \div (-7)$ **7**
5. $-8 \div (-8)$ **1**
6. $\frac{36}{-4}$ **−9**
7. $225 \div (-15)$ **−15**
8. $\frac{0}{-9}$ **0**
9. $-38 \div 2$ **−19**
10. $\frac{64}{4}$ **16**
11. $-500 \div (-50)$ **10**
12. $-189 \div (-21)$ **9**

ALGEBRA Evaluate each expression if $m = -32$, $n = 2$, and $p = -8$.

13. $m \div n$ **−16**
14. $p \div 4$ **−2**
15. $p^2 \div m$ **−2**
16. $m \div p$ **4**
17. $-\frac{p}{n}$ **4**
18. $p \div n^2$ **−2**
19. $\frac{p^2}{n^2}$ **16**
20. $\frac{18-n}{p}$ **−2**
21. $m \div (np)$ **2**
22. $\frac{m}{p} + n$ **6**

Chapter 2 54 Course 2

Practice*
p. 55 OL AL

NAME ______ DATE ______ PERIOD ____

2-8 Practice
Dividing Integers

Divide.

1. $42 \div (-7)$ **−6**
2. $45 \div (-5)$ **−9**
3. $-9 \div 3$ **−3**
4. $-64 \div (-8)$ **8**
5. $-39 \div (-13)$ **3**
6. $-121 \div 11$ **−11**
7. $\frac{-48}{12}$ **−4**
8. $\frac{-35}{7}$ **−5**
9. $\frac{-38}{-2}$ **19**
10. $\frac{32}{-16}$ **−2**
11. $\frac{55}{-5}$ **−11**
12. $(-8)^2$ **64**

13. Divide 75 by −25. **−3**
14. Find the quotient of −30 and −15. **2**

ALGEBRA Evaluate each expression if $f = -15$, $g = 5$, and $h = -45$.

15. $-20 \div g$ **−4**
16. $90 \div h$ **−2**
17. $h \div f$ **3**
18. $fg \div 25$ **−3**
19. $\frac{f-h}{10}$ **3**
20. $\frac{g-5}{1}$ **0**
21. $-f^2 \div g$ **−45**
22. $\frac{h-3g}{f}$ **4**
23. $\frac{f+h}{-g}$ **12**

ZOOLOGY The table below shows the weight in pounds of large adult males in the cat family.

Cat	Cheetah	Cougar	Leopard	Lion	Tiger
Weight	143	227	200	550	400

Source: www.umbergroove.org

For Exercises 24 and 25 use the information in the table.

24. What is the mean weight of these cats? **304 pounds**

25. What is the mean weight of the two largest cats? **475 pounds**

Lesson 2-8

Chapter 2 55 Course 2

Word Problem Practice*
p. 56 OL AL

NAME ______ DATE ______ PERIOD ____

2-8 Word Problem Practice
Dividing Integers

Divide.

1. STOCK MARKET During a 5-day workweek, the stock market decreased by 65 points. Find the average daily change in the market for the week. **−13 points**

2. MOTION Mr. Diaz decreased the speed of his car by 30 miles per hour over a period of 10 seconds. Find the average change in speed each second. **−3 mph per second**

3. WEATHER Over the past seven days, Mrs. Cho found that the temperature outside had dropped a total of 35 degrees. Find the average temperature change in temperature each day. **−5 degrees per day**

4. BASKETBALL The basketball team lost their last 6 games. They lost by a total of 48 points. Find their average number of points relative to their opponents. **−8 points per game**

5. POPULATION The enrollment at Davis Middle School dropped by 60 students over a 5-year period. What is the average yearly drop in enrollment? **−12 students annually**

6. SUBMARINE A submarine descends at a rate of 60 feet each minute. How long will it take it to descend to a depth of 660 feet below the surface? **11 min**

Chapter 2 56 Course 2

Enrichment
p. 57 OL AL

NAME ______ DATE ______ PERIOD ____

2-8 Enrichment

Division by Zero?

Some interesting things happen when you try to divide by zero. For example, look at these two equations.

$\frac{5}{0} = x$ $\frac{0}{0} = y$

If you can write the equations above, you can also write the two equations below.

$0 \cdot x = 5$ $0 \cdot y = 0$

However, there is no number that will make the left equation true. This equation has no solution. For the right equation, *every* number will make it true. The solutions for this equation are "all numbers."

Because division by zero leads to impossible situations, it is not a "legal" step in solving a problem. People say that division by zero is undefined, or not possible, or simply not allowed.

Describe the solution set for each equation.

1. $4x = 0$ **0**
2. $x \cdot 0 = 0$ **all numbers**
3. $x \cdot 0 = x$ **0**
4. $\frac{0}{x} = 0$ **all numbers but 0**
5. $\frac{0}{x} = x$ **no solution**
6. $\frac{0}{x} = 5$ **no solution**

What values for x must be excluded to prevent division by 0?

7. $\frac{1}{x^2}$ **0**
8. $\frac{1}{x-1}$ **1**
9. $\frac{1}{x+1}$ **−1**
10. $\frac{0}{2x}$ **0**
11. $\frac{1}{2x-2}$ **1**
12. $\frac{1}{3x+6}$ **−2**

Explain what is wrong with this "proof."

13. Step 1 $0 \cdot 1 = 0$ and $0 \cdot (-1) = 0$
Step 2 Therefore, $\frac{0}{0} = 1$ and $\frac{0}{0} = -1$. **Step 2 involves division by zero.**
Step 3 Therefore, $1 = -1$.

Lesson 2-8

Chapter 2 57 Course 2

* Also available in Spanish ELL

Additional Lesson Resources

Transparencies

- *5-Minute Check Transparency,* Lesson 2-8

Other Print Products

- *Noteables™ Interactive Study Notebook with Foldables™*

Teacher Tech Tools

- *Interactive Classroom CD-ROM,* Lesson 2-8
- *AssignmentWorks,* Lesson 2-8

Student Tech Tools

glencoe.com

- Extra Examples, Chapter 2, Lesson 8
- Self-Check Quiz, Chapter 2, Lesson 8

2-8 Lesson Notes

1 Focus

Vertical Alignment

Before Lesson 2-8
Add with negative integers; subtract positive integers from negative integers

Lesson 2-8
Solve division problems, including those arising in concrete situations, that use positive and negative integers

After Lesson 2-8
Divide rational numbers and take positive rational numbers to whole-number powers

2 Teach

MINI Lab

You may wish to have students practice evaluating more expressions, such as $-7 \div 1$ and $-15 \div 3$.

Scaffolding Questions

As students answer the following questions, write the expressions on the board.

Ask:

- How can I write a division problem to separate 15 apples into 3 equal groups? $15 \div 3$
- How can I write a division problem to separate 28 pennies into 7 equal groups? $28 \div 7$
- How can I write a division problem to separate 20 into 4 equal groups? $20 \div 4$
- How can I write a division problem to separate -18 into 6 equal groups? $-18 \div 6$

2-8 Dividing Integers

MAIN IDEA

Divide integers.

IN Academic Standards

7.1.7 Solve problems that involve multiplication and division **with integers**, fractions, decimals and combinations of the four operations. *Also addresses P.5.1, P.5.2, P.5.3, P.6.5, P.6.6.*

IN Math Online

glencoe.com

- Extra Examples
- Personal Tutor
- Self-Check Quiz

MINI Lab

You can use counters to model division of integers. Follow these steps to find $-8 \div 2$.

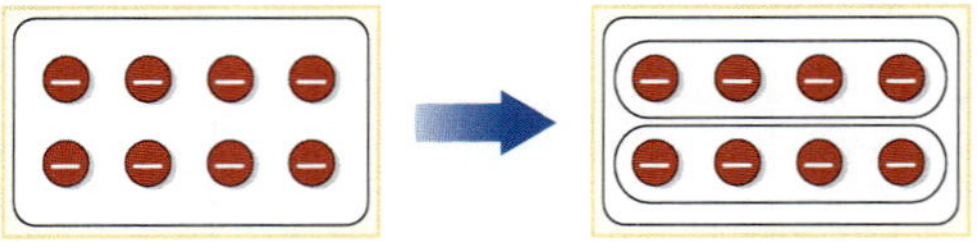

Place 8 negative counters on the mat.

Separate the counters into 2 equal groups.

There are 4 negative counters in each group. So, $-8 \div 2 = -4$.

Find each quotient using counters or a drawing.

1. $-6 \div 2$ -3
2. $-12 \div 3$ -4

Division of numbers is related to multiplication. When finding the quotient of two integers, you can use a related multiplication sentence.

The factor in the multiplication sentence …

$2(6) = 12 \rightarrow 12 \div 2 = 6$

$4(5) = 20 \rightarrow 20 \div 4 = 5$

… is the quotient in the division sentence.

Since multiplication and division sentences are related, you can use them to find the quotient of integers with different signs.

different signs

$2(-6) = -12 \rightarrow -12 \div 2 = -6$

$-2(-6) = 12 \rightarrow 12 \div (-2) = -6$

negative quotient

These related sentences lead to the following rule.

Dividing Integers with Different Signs — Key Concept

Words	The quotient of two integers with different signs is negative.
Examples	$33 \div (-11) = -3$ $\quad -64 \div 8 = -8$

EXAMPLES Dividing Integers with Different Signs

1 **Find $80 \div (-10)$.** The integers have different signs.

$80 \div (-10) = -8$ The quotient is negative.

2 **Find $\frac{-55}{11}$.** The integers have different signs.

$\frac{-55}{11} = -5$ The quotient is negative.

CHECK Your Progress

a. $20 \div (-4)$ **−5** b. $\frac{-81}{9}$ **−9** c. $-45 \div 9$ **−5**

Study Tip

Dividing Integers Dividing integers with same or different signs follow the same rules as the ones for multiplication.

You can also use multiplication and division sentences to find the quotient of integers with the same sign.

same signs

$4(5) = 20 \rightarrow 20 \div 4 = 5$

$-4(5) = -20 \rightarrow -20 \div (-4) = 5$

positive quotient

These related sentences lead to the following rule.

Divide Integers with the Same Sign — Key Concept

Words The quotient of two integers with the same sign is positive.

Examples $15 \div 5 = 3$ $-64 \div (-8) = 8$

EXAMPLES Dividing Integers with the Same Sign

3 **Find $-14 \div (-7)$.** The integers have the same sign.

$-14 \div (-7) = 2$ The quotient is positive.

4 **ALGEBRA Evaluate $-16 \div x$ if $x = -4$.**

$-16 \div x = -16 \div (-4)$ Replace x with −4.

$= 4$ Divide. The quotient is positive.

CHECK Your Progress

d. $-24 \div (-4)$ **6** e. $-9 \div (-3)$ **3** f. $\frac{-28}{-7}$ **4**

g. **ALGEBRA** Evaluate $a \div b$ if $a = -9$ and $b = -3$. **3**

Focus on Mathematical Content

Division is the **inverse operation** of multiplication. You can rewrite a division equation as a multiplication equation. The rules for dividing integers are related to the rules for multiplying integers.

Formative Assessment

Use the Check Your Progress exercises after the Examples to determine students' understanding of concepts.

ADDITIONAL EXAMPLES

1. Find $51 \div (-3)$. −17
2. Find $\frac{-121}{11}$. −11
3. Find $-12 \div (-2)$. 6
4. **ALGEBRA** Evaluate $-18 \div x$ if $x = -2$. 9

Additional Examples are also in:

- Noteables™ Interactive Study Notebook with Foldables™
- Interactive Classroom PowerPoint® Presentations

ADDITIONAL EXAMPLE

5 **PHYSICS** You can find an object's acceleration with the expression $\frac{S_f - S_s}{t}$, where S_f = final speed, S_s = starting speed, and t = time. If a car was traveling at 80 feet per second and, after 10 seconds, it was traveling at 40 feet per second, what was its acceleration? −4 ft/sec

3 Practice

Formative Assessment

Use Exercises 1–9 to check for understanding.

Then use the chart at the bottom of the next page to customize your assignments for students.

Intervention You may wish to use the Study Guide and Intervention Master on page 53 of the *Chapter 2 Resource Masters* for additional reinforcement.

Real-World Link
An adult koala is 25–30 inches long and weighs 15–30 pounds.
Source: Koala Express

Real-World EXAMPLE

5 **ANIMALS** **Ten years ago, the estimated Australian koala population was 1,000,000. Today there are about 100,000 koalas. Use the expression $\frac{N-P}{10}$, where N represents the new population and P the previous population to find the average change in the koala population per year for the 10-year period.**

$$\frac{N-P}{10} = \frac{100{,}000 - 1{,}000{,}000}{10}$$ Replace N with 100,000 and P with 1,000,000.

$$= \frac{-900{,}000}{10} \text{ or } -90{,}000$$ Divide.

The koala population has changed by −90,000 per year.

CHECK Your Progress

h. **WEATHER** The average temperature in January for North Pole, Alaska, is −24.4°C. Use the expression $\frac{9C + 160}{5}$, where C represents the number of degrees Celsius, to find this temperature in degrees Fahrenheit. **about −12°F**

Operations with Integers — Concept Summary

Operation	Rule
Add	**Same Sign:** Add absolute values. The sum has the same sign as the integers. **Different Signs:** Subtract absolute values. The sum has the sign of the integer with greater absolute value.
Subtract	To subtract an integer, add its opposite.
Multiply and Divide	**Same Signs:** The product or quotient is positive. **Different Signs:** The product or quotient is negative.

★ indicates multi-step problem

CHECK Your Understanding

Examples 1–3 (p. 115)

Divide.

1. $32 \div (-8)$ **−4**
2. $-16 \div 2$ **−8**
3. $\frac{42}{-7}$ **−6**
4. $-30 \div (-5)$ **6**
5. $55 \div 11$ **5**
6. $\frac{-16}{-4}$ **4**

Example 4 (p. 115)

ALGEBRA **Evaluate each expression if $x = 8$ and $y = -5$.**

7. $15 \div y$ **−3**
8. $xy \div (-10)$ **4**

Example 5 (p. 116)

9. **TEMPERATURE** The lowest recorded temperature in Wisconsin is −55°F on February 4, 1996. Use the expression $\frac{5(F-32)}{9}$ to find this temperature in degrees Celsius. Round to the nearest tenth. **−48.3°C**

Differentiated Instruction

Logical Learners Have each student pick a country and find the highest and lowest temperatures recorded in that country. Students can use the expression in Guided Practice h to rewrite Celsius temperatures in degrees Fahrenheit. Use the expression $\frac{5(F-32)}{9}$, where F represents the number of degrees Fahrenheit to find the temperature in Celsius. You might want to draw a thermometer on the chalkboard and have students write their countries' high and low temperatures on the thermometer.

Practice and Problem Solving

HOMEWORK HELP

For Exercises	See Examples
10–13, 16–19	1, 2
14–15, 20–23	3
24–31	4
32–33	5

Exercise Levels
A: 10–33
B: 34–39
C: 40–44

Divide.

10. $50 \div (-5)$ **−10**
11. $56 \div (-8)$ **−7**
12. $-18 \div 9$ **−2**
13. $-36 \div 4$ **−9**
14. $-15 \div (-3)$ **5**
15. $-100 \div (-10)$ **10**
16. $\frac{22}{-2}$ **−11**
17. $\frac{84}{-12}$ **−7**
18. $\frac{-26}{13}$ **−2**
19. $\frac{-27}{3}$ **−9**
20. $\frac{-21}{-7}$ **3**
21. $\frac{-54}{-6}$ **9**
22. Divide −200 by −100. **2**
23. Find the quotient of −65 and −13. **5**

ALGEBRA **Evaluate each expression if $r = 12$, $s = -4$, and $t = -6$.**

24. $-12 \div r$ **−1**
25. $72 \div t$ **−12**
26. $r \div s$ **−3**
27. $rs \div 16$ **−3**
28. $\frac{t-r}{3}$ **−6**
29. $\frac{8-r}{-2}$ **2**
30. $\frac{s+t}{5}$ **−2**
31. $\frac{t+9}{-3}$ **−1**

32. **MONEY** Last year, Mr. Engle's total income was \$52,000, while his total expenses were \$53,800. Use the expression $\frac{I-E}{12}$, where I represents total income and E represents total expenses, to find the average difference between his income and expenses each month. **−\$150 per month**

33. **SCIENCE** The boiling point of water is affected by changes in elevation. Use the expression $\frac{-2A}{1{,}000}$, where A represents the altitude in feet, to find the number of degrees Fahrenheit the boiling point of water changes at an altitude of 5,000 feet. **−10°F**

ALGEBRA **Evaluate each expression if $d = -9$, $f = 36$, and $g = -6$.**

34. $\frac{-f}{d}$ **4**
35. $\frac{12-(-f)}{-8}$ **8**
36. $\frac{f^2}{d^2}$ **16**
37. $g^2 \div f$ **1**

★ 38. **PLANETS** The temperature on Mars ranges widely from −207°F at the winter pole to almost 80°F on the dayside during the summer. Use the expression $\frac{-207+80}{2}$ to find the average of the temperature extremes on Mars. **−63.5°F**

★ 39. **ANALYZE GRAPHS** The *mean* of a set of data is the sum of the data divided by the number of items in the data set. The graph shows the approximate depths where certain fish are found in the Caribbean. What is the mean depth of the fish shown? **−53 ft**

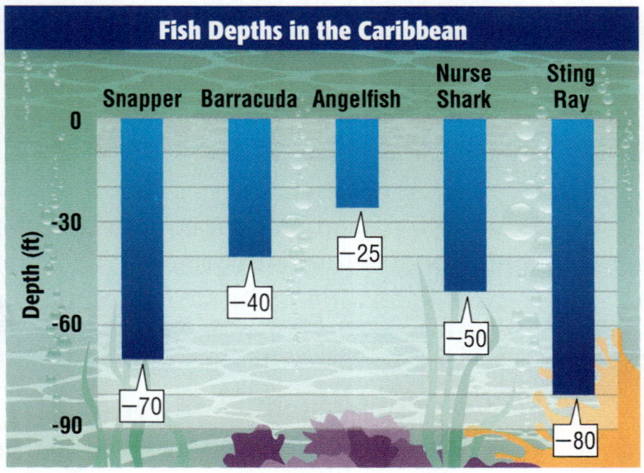

Academic Standards • ISTEP+
Extra Practice, pp. 673, 705

DIFFERENTIATED HOMEWORK OPTIONS

Level	Assignment	Two-Day Assignment	
BL Basic	10–33, 40–42, 44–56	11–33 odd, 45, 46	10–32 even, 40–42, 44, 47–56
OL Core	11–37 odd, 38–42, 44–56	10–33, 45, 46	34–42, 44, 47–56
AL Advanced/Pre-AP	34–56		

Odd/Even Assignments

Exercises 10–33 are structured so that students practice the same concepts whether they are assigned odd or even problems.

Differentiated Instruction

Visual/Spatial Learners If students are having difficulty completing the exercises, have them use counters, drawings, or number lines to represent the division of integers. For example, in Exercise 12, students could place 18 negative counters on the mat. Separate the counters into 9 equal groups and count the number of negative counters in each group, resulting in an answer of −2. Remind students to connect this representation with the rule that the quotient of two integers with different signs is negative.

4 Assess

Name the Math Have students tell what mathematical procedure they used to solve Exercise 42.

Formative Assessment

Check for student understanding of concepts in Lessons 2-7 and 2-8.

CRM Quiz 4, p. 62

FOLDABLES Study Organizer Foldables™ Follow-Up

Remind students to write what they learn about dividing integers in their Foldables. They may want to consult the Operations with Integers table on page 119 as they update their Foldables.

Additional Answers

44. First evaluate each 2^2 since they are powers. Rewrite the expression as $-2 \cdot (4 + 2) \div 4$. Then add since $4 + 2$ is in parentheses. Rewrite the expression as $-2 \cdot 6 \div 4$. Next, multiply and then divide since multiplication and division occur in order from left to right. Since $-2 \cdot 6 = -12$ and $-12 \div 4 = -3$, the value of the expression is -3.

47.

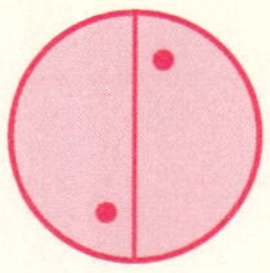

H.O.T. Problems

41. $-32 \div (-4)$ has a positive quotient; the others have negative quotients.

40. **OPEN ENDED** Write a division sentence with a quotient of -12. Sample answer: $36 \div (-3) = -12$

41. **Which One Doesn't Belong?** Identify the expression that does not belong with the other three. Explain your reasoning.

$-66 \div 11$	$-32 \div (-4)$	$16 \div (-4)$	$-48 \div 4$

42. **PATTERNS** Find the next two numbers in the pattern 729, -243, 81, -27, 9, … . Explain your reasoning. -3, 1; Divide the previous term by -3.

43. **CHALLENGE** Order from least to greatest all of the numbers by which -20 is divisible. $-20, -10, -5, -4, -2, -1, 1, 2, 4, 5, 10, 20$

44. **WRITING IN MATH** Evaluate $-2 \cdot (2^2 + 2) \div 2^2$. Justify each step in the process. See margin.

ISTEP+ PRACTICE 7.1.7

45. Find $18 \div (-3)$. A

 A -6

 B $\frac{-1}{6}$

 C 6

 D 15

46. On December 24, 1924, the temperature in Fairfield, Montana, fell from 63°F at noon to -21°F at midnight. What was the average temperature change per hour? G

 F -3.5°F

 G -7°F

 H -42°F

 J -84°F

Spiral Review

47. **GEOMETRY** What is the next figure in the pattern shown at the right? (Lesson 2-7) See margin.

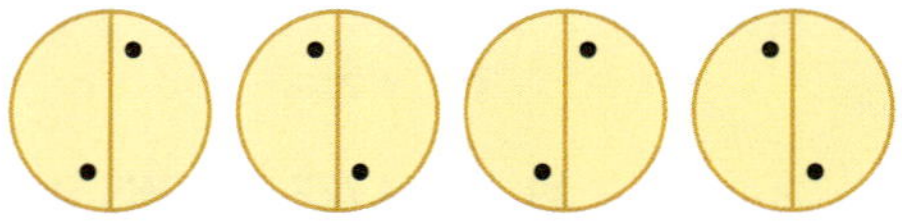

Multiply. (Lesson 2-6)

48. $14(-2)$ -28

49. $-20(-3)$ 60

50. $-5(7)$ -35

51. $(-9)^2$ 81

52. Find $6 - (-12)$. (Lesson 2-5) 18

53. **DIVING** Valentina jumped into 10 feet of water and touched the bottom of the pool before she surfaced. Write an integer to describe where Valentina was in relation to the surface of the water when she touched the bottom of the pool. (Lesson 2-1) -10

Find each square root. (Lesson 1-3)

54. $\sqrt{324}$ 18

55. $\sqrt{900}$ 30

56. $\sqrt{196}$ 14

Pre-AP Activity Use after Exercise 44

Write the following questions on the chalkboard: *Can a square number be negative? Can the square root of a number be negative?* Have students write their answers on a piece of paper. Encourage them to explain their reasoning and give examples.

CHAPTER 2 Study Guide and Review

IN Math Online glencoe.com
- STUDY TO GO
- Vocabulary Review

FOLDABLES Study Organizer GET READY to Study

Be sure the following Big Ideas are noted in your Foldable.

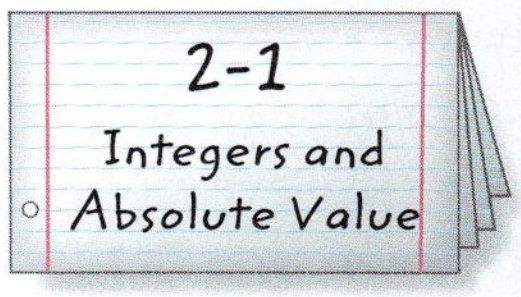

BIG Ideas

Absolute Value (Lesson 2-1)
- The absolute value of a number is the distance the number is from zero on a number line.

Comparing and Ordering Integers (Lesson 2-2)
- When two numbers are graphed on a number line, the number to the left is always less than the number to the right.

Graphing Points (Lesson 2-3)
- On a coordinate plane, the horizontal number line is the x-axis and the vertical number line is the y-axis. The origin is at (0, 0) and is the point where the number lines intersect. The x-axis and y-axis separate the plane into four quadrants.

Integer Operations (Lessons 2-4, 2-5, 2-6, 2-8)
- To add integers with the same sign, add their absolute value. The sum is positive if both integers are positive and negative if both integers are negative.
- The sum of any number and its additive inverse is 0.
- To add integers with different signs, subtract their absolute values. The sum is positive if the positive integer's absolute value is greater and negative if the negative integer's absolute value is greater.
- To subtract an integer, add its opposite.
- The product or quotient of two integers with different signs is negative.
- The product or quotient of two integers with the same sign is positive.

Key Vocabulary

absolute value (p. 81)
additive inverse (p. 96)
coordinate plane (p. 88)
graph (p. 80)
integer (p. 80)
negative integer (p. 80)
opposites (p. 96)
ordered pair (p. 88)
origin (p. 88)
positive integer (p. 80)
quadrant (p. 88)
x-axis (p. 88)
x-coordinate (p. 88)
y-axis (p. 88)
y-coordinate (p. 88)

Vocabulary Check

State whether each sentence is *true* or *false*. If *false*, replace the underlined word or number to make a true sentence.

1. Integers less than zero are positive integers. **false; negative**
2. The origin is the point where the x-axis and y-axis intersect. **true**
3. The absolute value of 7 is −7. **false; opposite**
4. The sum of two negative integers is positive. **false; negative**
5. The x-coordinate of the ordered pair (2, −3) is −3. **false; y-coordinate**
6. Two integers that are opposites are also called additive inverses. **true**
7. The product of a positive and a negative integer is negative. **true**
8. The x-axis and the y-axis separate the plane into four coordinates. **false; quadrants**
9. The quotient of two negative integers is negative. **false; positive**

Summative Assessment

Vocabulary Test, p. 64

CHAPTER 2 Study Guide and Review

FOLDABLES Study Organizer Dinah Zike's Foldables

Have students look through the chapter to make sure they have included notes, key concepts, and examples in their Foldables for each lesson.

Encourage students to refer to their Foldables while completing the Study Guide and Review and while preparing for the Chapter Test.

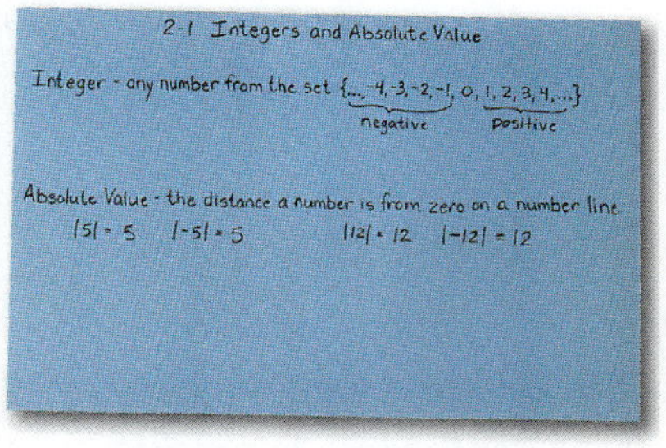

Formative Assessment

Key Vocabulary The page references after each word denote where that term was first introduced. If students have difficulty answering Exercises 1–9, remind them that they can use these page references to refresh their memories about the vocabulary terms.

IN Math Online glencoe.com

Vocabulary PuzzleMaker improves students' mathematics vocabulary using four puzzle formats–crossword, scramble, word search using a word list, and word search using clues. Students can work on a computer screen or from a printed handout.

StudiOhio

Lesson-by-Lesson Review

Intervention If the given examples are not sufficient to review the topics covered by the questions, remind students that the page references tell them where to review that topic in their textbooks.

Two-Day Option Have students complete the Lesson-by-Lesson Review on pages 120–122. Then you can use ExamView® Assessment Suite to customize another review worksheet that practices all the objectives of this chapter or only the objectives on which your students need more help.

For more information on ExamView® Assessment Suite, see page 78C.

Differentiated Instruction

Super DVD: MindJogger Plus
Use this DVD as an alternative format of review for the test. For more information on this game show format, see page 78D.

Additional Answer

25. {−32, −23, −21, 14, 19, 25}

Lesson-by-Lesson Review

2-1 Integers and Absolute Value (pp. 80–83)

7.1.6, 6.1.2

Write an integer for each situation.

10. a loss of $150 **−$150**
11. 350 feet above sea level **350 ft**
12. a gain of 8 yards **8 yd**
13. 12°F below 0 **−12°F**

Evaluate each expression.

14. $|100|$ **100**
15. $|-32|$ **32**
16. $|-16| + |9|$ **25**
17. **JUICE** Mavis drank 48 milliliters of apple juice before replacing the carton in the refrigerator. Write an integer that shows the change in the volume of juice in the carton. **−48 mL**

Example 1 Write an integer for 8 feet below sea level.

Since this situation represents an elevation *below* sea level, −8 represents the situation.

Example 2 Evaluate $|-10|$.

On the number line, the graph of −10 is 10 units from 0.

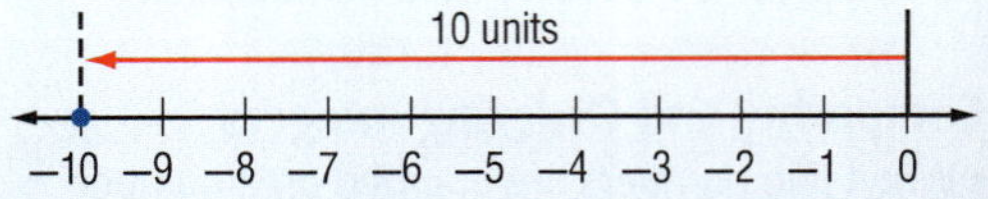

So, $|-10| = 10$.

2-2 Comparing and Ordering Integers (pp. 84–87)

7.1.6

Replace each ● with < or > to make a true sentence.

18. −3 ● −9 **>**
19. 8 ● −12 **>**
20. −3 ● 3 **<**
21. $|-10|$ ● $|-13|$ **<**
22. 25 ● $|8|$ **>**
23. 0 ● $|-4|$ **<**

Order each set of integers from least to greatest. 24. **{−12, −10, −3, 0, 5, 8, 9}**

24. {−3, 8, −10, 0, 5, −12, 9}
25. {−21, 19, −23, 14, −32, 25} **See margin.**
26. {−17, −18, 18, 15, −16, 16} **{−18, −17, −16, 15, 16, 18}**
27. **WEATHER** The high temperatures in degrees Celsius for ten cities were 0, 10, −5, 12, 25, −6, 20, −10, 5 and 2. Order these temperatures from least to greatest. **−10, −6, −5, 0, 2, 5, 10, 12, 20, 25**

Example 3 Replace ● with < or > to make −4 ● −7 a true sentence.

Graph each integer on a number line.

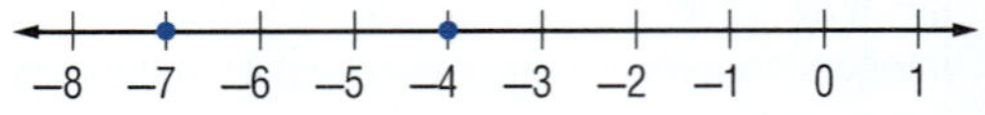

Since −4 is to the right of −7, −4 > −7.

Example 4 Order the integers −4, −3, 5, 3, 0, −2 from least to greatest.

Graph the integers on a number line.

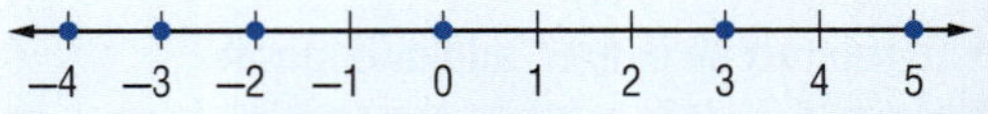

Order the integers by reading from left to right: −4, −3, −2, 0, 3, 5.

Mixed Problem Solving
For mixed problem-solving practice, see page 705.

2-3 The Coordinate Plane (pp. 88–92)

7.3.2

On graph paper, draw a coordinate plane. Then graph and label each point.

28. $E(1, -4)$ **28–31. See margin.**
29. $F(-4, 2)$
30. $G(-2, -3)$
31. $H(4, 0)$

32. **ROUTES** Starting at the school, Pilar walked 1 block east and 3 blocks south. From there, she walked 5 blocks west and 4 blocks north to the park. If the school represents the origin, what is the ordered pair for the park? **(−4, 1)**

Example 5 Graph and label the point $S(3, -1)$.

Draw a coordinate plane. Move 3 units to the right. Then move 1 unit down. Draw a dot and label it $S(3, -1)$.

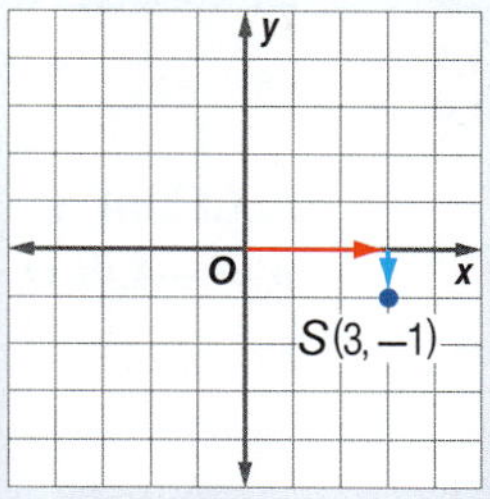

2-4 Adding Integers (pp. 95–99)

6.1.5

Add.

33. $-6 + 8$ **2**
34. $-4 + (-9)$ **−13**
35. $7 + (-12)$ **−5**
36. $-18 + 18$ **0**

37. **HIKING** Samuel hiked 75 feet up a mountain. He then hiked 22 feet higher. Then, he descended 8 feet, and finally climbed up another 34 feet. What is Samuel's final elevation? **123 feet**

Example 6 Find $-4 + 3$.

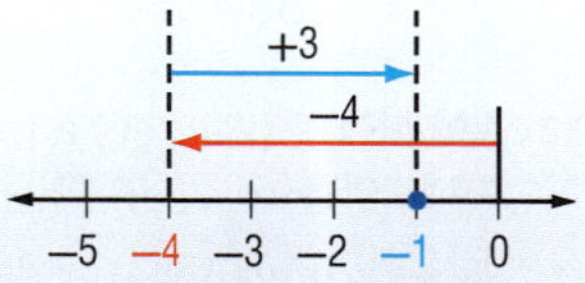

So, $-4 + 3 = -1$.

2-5 Subtracting Integers (pp. 103–106)

6.1.5

Subtract.

38. $-5 - 8$ **−13**
39. $3 - 6$ **−3**
40. $5 - (-2)$ **7**
41. $-4 - (-8)$ **4**

42. **GOLF** Owen shot 2 under par while his friend Nathan shot 3 above par. By how many shots was Owen's score better than Nathan's? **5**

Example 7 Find $-3 - 9$.

$-3 - 9 = -3 + (-9)$ To subtract 9, add −9.

$= -12$ Simplify.

Additional Answers

28–31.

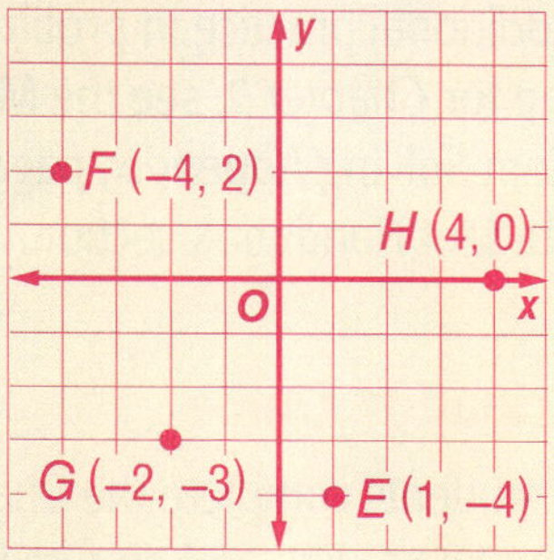

Chapter 2 Study Guide and Review 121

Problem Solving Review

For additional practice in problem solving for Chapter 2, see the Mixed Problem Solving Appendix, page 716 in the Student Handbook section.

Anticipation Guide

Have students complete the Chapter 2 Anticipation Guide and discuss how their responses have changed now that they have completed Chapter 2.

CRM Anticipation Guide, p. 7

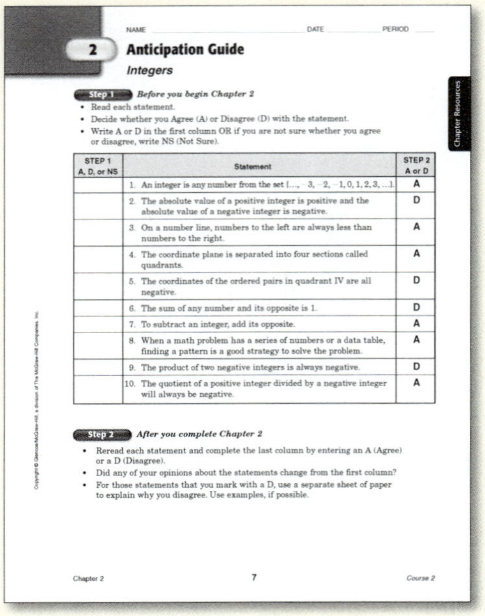

NAME ______ DATE ______ PERIOD ______

2 Anticipation Guide

Integers

Step 1 *Before you begin Chapter 2*

- Read each statement.
- Decide whether you Agree (A) or Disagree (D) with the statement.
- Write A or D in the first column OR if you are not sure whether you agree or disagree, write NS (Not Sure).

STEP 1 A, D, or NS	Statement	STEP 2 A or D
	1. An integer is any number from the set {..., −3, −2, −1, 0, 1, 2, 3, ...}.	A
	2. The absolute value of a positive integer is positive and the absolute value of a negative integer is negative.	D
	3. On a number line, numbers to the left are always less than numbers to the right.	A
	4. The coordinate plane is separated into four sections called quadrants.	A
	5. The coordinates of the ordered pairs in quadrant IV are all negative.	D
	6. The sum of any number and its opposite is 1.	D
	7. To subtract an integer, add its opposite.	A
	8. When a math problem has a series of numbers or a data table, finding a pattern is a good strategy to solve the problem.	A
	9. The product of two negative integers is always negative.	D
	10. The quotient of a positive integer divided by a negative integer will always be negative.	A

Step 2 *After you complete Chapter 2*

- Reread each statement and complete the last column by entering an A (Agree) or a D (Disagree).
- Did any of your opinions about the statements change from the first column?
- For those statements that you mark with a D, use a separate sheet of paper to explain why you disagree. Use examples, if possible.

Chapter Resources

Chapter 2 7 Course 2

Chapter 2 Study Guide and Review

2-6 Multiplying Integers (pp. 107–111)

P.1.3, P.1.4

Multiply.

43. $-4(3)$ **−12**
44. $8(-6)$ **−48**
45. $-5(-7)$ **35**
46. $-2(40)$ **−80**

ALGEBRA Evaluate each expression if $a = -4$, $b = -7$, and $c = 5$.

47. ab **28**
48. $-3c$ **−15**
49. bc **−35**
50. abc **140**

Example 8 Find $-5(3)$.

$-5(3) = -15$ The integers have different signs. The product is negative.

Example 9 Evaluate xyz if $x = -6$, $y = 11$, and $z = -10$.

xyz

$= (-6)(11)(-10)$ $x = -6, y = 11, z = -10.$

$= (-66)(-10)$ Multiply −6 and 11.

$= 660$ Multiply −66 and −10.

2-7 PSI: Look for a Pattern (pp. 112–113)

7.1.7

Solve. Look for a pattern.

51. **HEALTH** The average person blinks 12 times per minute. At this rate, how many times does the average person blink in one day? **17,280**

52. **SALARY** Suki gets a job that pays \$31,000 per year. She is promised a \$2,200 raise each year. At this rate, what will her salary be in 7 years? **\$46,400**

53. **DOGS** A kennel determined that they need 144 feet of fencing to board 2 dogs, 216 feet to board 3 dogs, and 288 feet to board 4 dogs. If this pattern continues, how many feet of fencing is needed to board 8 dogs? **576 ft**

Example 10 A theater has 18 seats in the first row, 24 seats in the second row, 30 seats in the third row, and so on. If this pattern continues, how many seats are in the sixth row?

Begin with 18 seats and add 6 seats for each additional row.

So, there are 48 seats in the sixth row.

Row	Number of Seats
1	18
2	24
3	30
4	36
5	42
6	48

2-8 Dividing Integers (pp. 114–118)

7.1.7

Divide.

54. $-45 \div (-9)$ **5**
55. $36 \div (-12)$ **−3**
56. $-12 \div 6$ **−2**
57. $-81 \div (-9)$ **9**

Example 11 Find $-72 \div (-9)$.

$-72 \div (-9) = 8$ The integers have the same sign. The quotient is positive.

Differentiated Instruction

Visual/Spatial Learners If students are having difficulty completing the Exercises, have them use counters, drawings, or number lines to represent the multiplication and division of integers. For example, in Exercise 46, students could display 2 sets of 40 negative counters and count the total number of negative counters, resulting in an answer of −80. Remind students to connect this representation with the rule that the product of two integers with different signs is negative. In Exercise 54, students could display 45 negative counters and then separate the counters into groups so that there are 9 negative counters in each group. Ask students to count the number of groups, resulting in an answer of 5.

122 Chapter 2 Integers

CHAPTER 2 Practice Test

IN Math Online glencoe.com
• Chapter Test

1. **WEATHER** Adam is recording the change in the outside air temperature for a science project. At 8:00 A.M., the high temperature was 42°F. By noon, the outside temperature had fallen 11°F. By mid-afternoon, the outside air temperature had fallen 12°F and by evening, it had fallen an additional 5°F. Write an integer that describes the final change in temperature. **−28**

Evaluate each expression.

2. $|-3|$ **3**
3. $|-18| - |6|$ **12**

Replace each ● with <, >, or = to make a true sentence.

4. −3 ● −9 **>**
5. $|9|$ ● $|-12|$ **<**
6. The Iowa Hawkeyes recorded the following yardage in six plays: 9, −2, 5, 0, 12, and −7. Order these integers from least to greatest. **−7, −2, 0, 5, 9, 12**
7. **MULTIPLE CHOICE** Which of the following coordinates lie within the rectangle graphed below? **D**

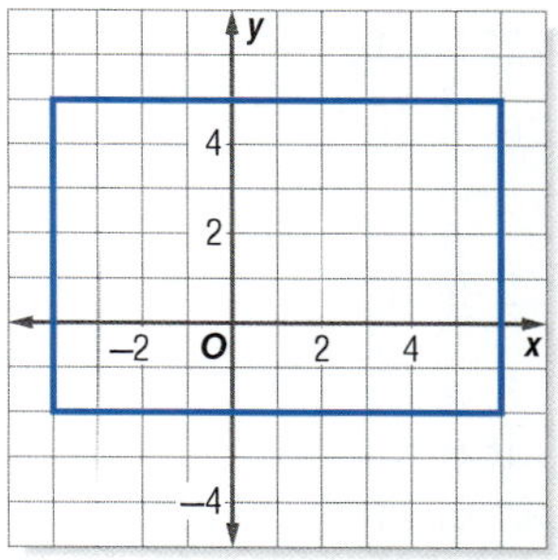

A (5, 6)
B (0, −3)
C (−5, 1)
D (−3, 0)

8. **DEBT** Amanda owes her brother $24. If she plans to pay him back an equal amount from her piggy bank each day for six days, describe the change in the amount of money in her piggy bank each day. **−$4**

Write the ordered pair for each point graphed. Then name the quadrant in which each point is located.

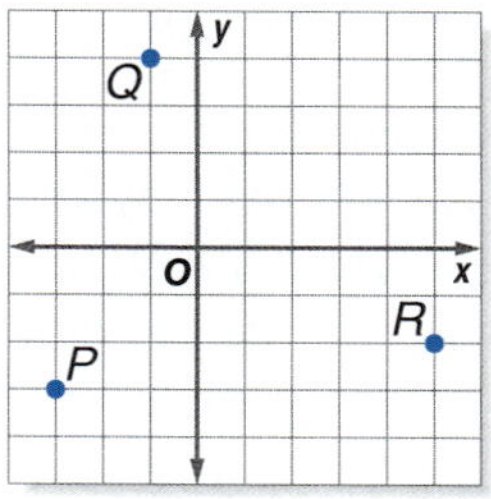

9. *P* **(−3, −3), III**
10. *Q* **(−1, 4), II**
11. *R* **(5, −2), IV**

Add, subtract, multiply, or divide.

12. 12 + (−9) **3**
13. −3 − 4 **−7**
14. −7 − (−20) **13**
15. −7(−3) **21**
16. 5(−11) **−55**
17. −36 ÷ (−9) **4**
18. −15 + (−7) **−22**
19. 8 + (−6) + (−4) **−2**
20. −9 − 7 **−16**
21. −13 + 7 **−6**

22. **MULTIPLE CHOICE** Kendrick created a 6-week schedule for practicing the piano. If the pattern continues, how many hours will he practice during the sixth week?

The table shows the number of hours he practiced in the first three weeks. **H**

Week	1	2	3
Hours	4	7	10

F 15 hours
G 18 hours
H 19 hours
J 22 hours

Evaluate each expression if $a = -5$, $b = 4$, and $c = -12$.

23. $ac \div b$ **15**
24. $\frac{a-b}{3}$ **−3**

25. −$24 or the stock decreased by $24

25. **STOCKS** The value of a stock decreased $4 each week for a period of six weeks. Describe the change in the value of the stock at the end of the six-week period.

CHAPTER 2 Practice Test

Summative Assessment

CRM *Chapter 2 Resource Masters*

Leveled Chapter 2 Tests			
Form	Type	Level	Pages
1	MC	BL	65–66
2A	MC	OL	67–68
2B	MC	OL	69–70
2C	FR	OL	71–72
2D	FR	OL	73–74
3	FR	AL	75–76

MC = *multiple-choice questions*
FR = *free-response questions*
BL = *below or approaching grade level*
OL = *on grade level*
AL = *above or beyond grade level*

- Vocabulary Test, p. 64
- Extended-Response Test, p. 77

ExamView Assessment Suite Customize and create multiple versions of your chapter test and their answer keys. All of the questions from the leveled chapter tests in the *Chapter 2 Resource Masters* are also available on ExamView Assessment Suite.

Data-Driven Decision Making

Diagnostic Teaching Based on the results of the Chapter 2 Practice Test, use the following to review concepts that students continue to find challenging.

Exercises	Lesson	Academic Standards	Resources for Review
1–11	2-1, 2-2, 2-3	7.1.6, 7.3.2	CRM Study Guide and Intervention pp. 37, 43, 48, and 53
12–21, 23–25	2-4, 2-5, 2-6, 2-8	6.1.5, 7.1.7	IN Math Online glencoe.com • Extra Examples • Personal Tutor • Concepts in Motion
22	2-7	P.1.3, P.1.4	

Chapter 2 ISTEP+ Practice

TEST-TAKING TIP

Exercise 5 Have students use mental math to eliminate answer choices. The lower end of Sue's projected spending can be estimated with 6 × \$200, or \$1,200, so answer choices A and B can be eliminated. Since the original factor (\$175) was rounded upward, the estimated product is an overestimate, so answer choice D can be eliminated.

Formative Assessment

You can use these two pages to benchmark student progress.

Chapter 2 Resource Masters

- Test Practice, pp. 78–80

ExamView Assessment Suite Create practice worksheets or tests that align to your state's standards, as well as TIMSS and NAEP tests.

Chapter 2 ISTEP+ Practice
Cumulative, Chapters 1–2

IN Math Online glencoe.com
- Test Practice

PART 1 Multiple Choice

Read each question. Then fill in the correct answer on the answer document provided by your teacher or on a sheet of paper.

1. The daily low temperatures for Cleveland, Ohio, over the last five days were 15°F, −2°F, 8°F, −6°F, and 5°F. Which expression can be used to find the average daily low temperature during the last five days? **C**

   A $(15 + 2 + 8 + 6 + 5) \div 5$

   B $15 + 2 + 8 + 6 + 5 \div 5$

   C $[15 + (-2) + 8 + (-6) + 5] \div 5$

   D $15 + (-2) + 8 + (-6) + 5 \div 5$

TEST-TAKING TIP

Question 1 Check every answer choice of a multiple-choice question. Each time you find an incorrect answer, cross it off so you remember that you've eliminated it.

2. Marcia runs r miles on Mondays, Tuesdays, and Thursdays. She bicycles for b miles on Wednesday and Saturdays. If she rests on Fridays and Sundays, which equation represents the total number of miles M she exercises each week? **F**

   F $M = 3r + 2b$

   G $M = r + b$

   H $M = 2r + 3b$

   J $M = 5(r + b)$

3. Simplify the expression below. **B**

$$3 + 6(10 - 7) - 3^2$$

   A 0

   B 12

   C 18

   D 74

4. At 8 A.M., the temperature was 13°F below zero. By 1 P.M., the temperature rose 22°F and by 6 P.M. dropped 14°F. What was the temperature at 6 P.M.? **G**

   F 5°F above zero

   G 5°F below zero

   H 21°F above zero

   J 21°F below zero

5. Sue typically spends between \$175 and \$250 each month on clothes. Which of the following is the best estimate for the amount she spends in 6 months? **C**

   A From \$600 to \$1,200

   B From \$900 to \$1,300

   C From \$1,050 to \$1,500

   D From \$1,200 to \$1,500

6. On their first play, a football team gained 17 yards. On their next play, they lost 22 yards. On their third play, they gained 14 yards. Which expression represents the total number of yards gained after the third play? **F**

   F $17 + (-22) + 14$

   G $17 + 22 + (-14)$

   H $-17 + (-22) + (-14)$

   J $-17 + 22 + 14$

7. The top four runners of a race were Alicia, Kyle, Drew, and Juanita. Drew finished before Juanita. Alicia finished after both boys, but before Juanita. What information is needed to determine the order of the runners from first to fourth? **A**

   A Did Kyle finish before or after Drew?

   B Did Alicia finish before or after Juanita?

   C Did Drew finish before or after Alicia?

   D Did Kyle finish before or after Alicia?

Preparing for ISTEP+
For test-taking strategies and practice, see pages 716–733.

8. The lowest point in Japan is Hachiro-gata (elevation −4 meters), and the highest point is Mount Fuji (elevation 3,776 meters). What is the difference in elevation between Mount Fuji and Hachiro-gata? **F**

F 3,780 meters

G 3,772 meters

H 3,080 meters

J 944 meters

9. Which of the following relationships is best represented by the data in the table? **D**

x	y
1	36
2	72
3	108
4	144
5	180

A Conversion of feet to inches

B Conversion of inches to yards

C Conversion of feet to yards

D Conversion of yards to inches

10. A storeowner has n employees and pays each employee $440 per week. If the owner also pays $$d$ weekly to rent the building and $$w$ for utilities, which equation below represents the total E of these weekly expenses? **H**

F $E = 440w + n + w$

G $E = 440n + dw$

H $E = 440n + d + w$

J $E = 440(n + d + w)$

PART 2 Short Response/Grid In

Record your answers on the answer sheet provided by your teacher or on a sheet of paper.

11. Nick spends a total of 75 hours per week at work and at the gym. He goes to the gym from 6:45 A.M. to 8:45 A.M., Monday through Friday. Write an equation that can be used to find t, the maximum number of hours Nick works at his job each week. **$t = 75 - (5 \times 2)$**

12. Find −8 − 17. **−25**

PART 3 Extended Response

Record your answers on the answer sheet provided by your teacher or a sheet of paper. Show your work.

13. A rectangle and a square are graphed on a coordinate plane. Use the graph below to answer the questions.

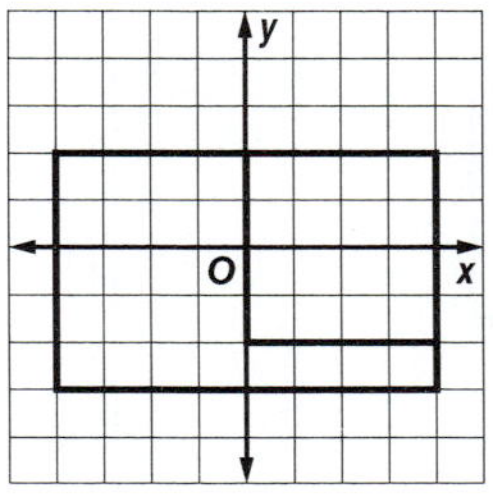

a. Pick an ordered pair both objects have in common. **Sample answer: (4, 2)**

b. Find an ordered pair that is inside the rectangle, but not the square. **Sample answer: (−2, 1)**

c. How could you increase the size of the square so that it still lies within the rectangle? What are the four coordinates?

d. Draw a graph with the new square inside the rectangle. **c., d. See margin.**

NEED EXTRA HELP?													
If You Missed Question...	1	2	3	4	5	6	7	8	9	10	11	12	13
Go to Lesson...	1-6	1-7	1-4	2-4	1-1	2-4	1-1	2-5	2-7	1-6	1-7	2-5	2-3
IN Academic Standards	7.2.1	P.6.6	7.2.3	6.1.5	P.1.1	6.1.5	P.1.1	6.1.5	7.1.7	7.2.1	P.6.6	6.1.5	6.2.4

Chapter 2 ISTEP+ Practice

Answer Sheet Practice

Have students simulate taking a standardized test by recording their answers on a practice recording sheet.

CRM Student Recording Sheet, p. 59

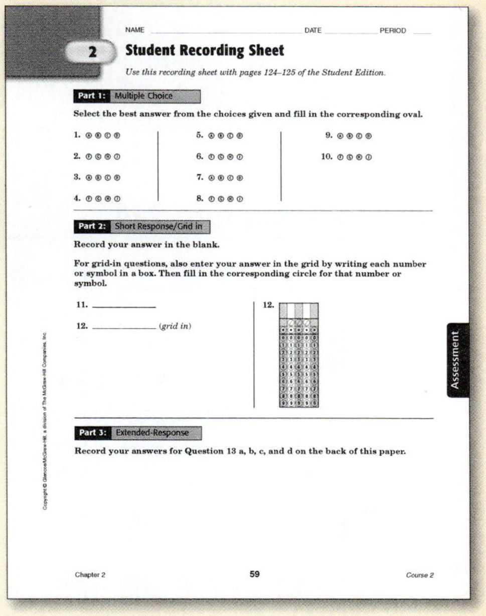
NAME DATE PERIOD

2 Student Recording Sheet

Use this recording sheet with pages 124–125 of the Student Edition.

Part 1: Multiple Choice

Select the best answer from the choices given and fill in the corresponding oval.

1.–10.

Part 2: Short Response/Grid In

Record your answer in the blank.

For grid-in questions, also enter your answer in the grid by writing each number or symbol in a box. Then fill in the corresponding circle for that number or symbol.

11. ______

12. ______ (grid in)

Part 3: Extended-Response

Record your answers for Question 13 a, b, c, and d on the back of this paper.

Chapter 2 59 Course 2

Additional Answers

13c. Make the square 5 × 5; (4, 2), (−1, 2), (−1, −3), and (4, −3).

13d.

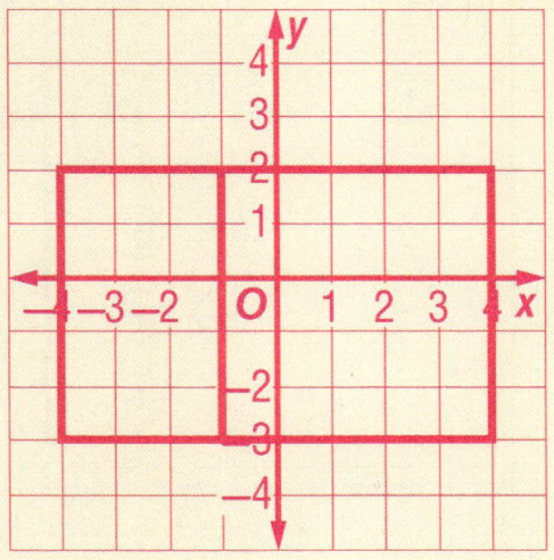

Page 91, Lesson 2-3

23–34.

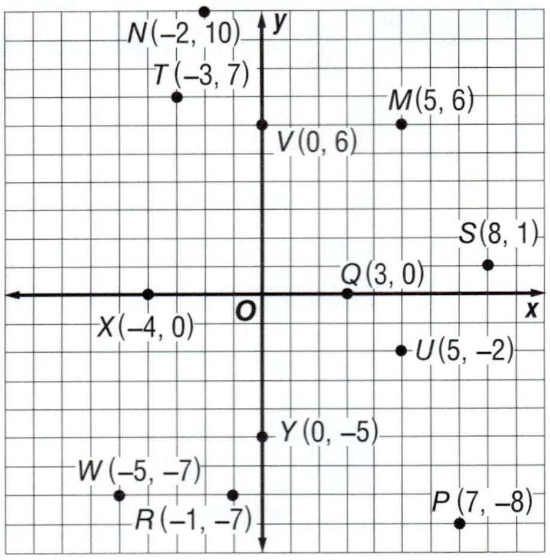

Page 94, Explore 2-4

g.

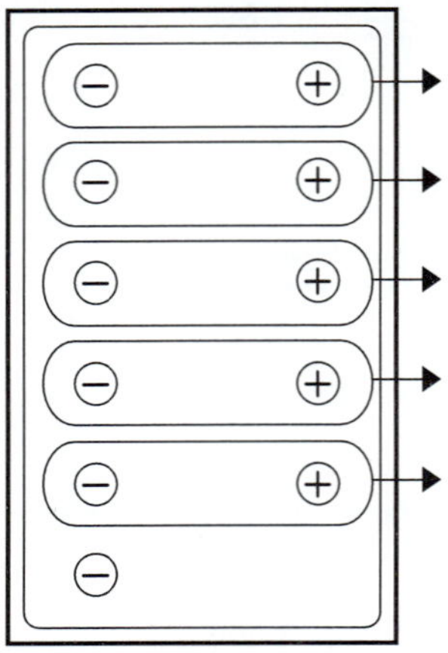

−6 + 5 = −1

h.

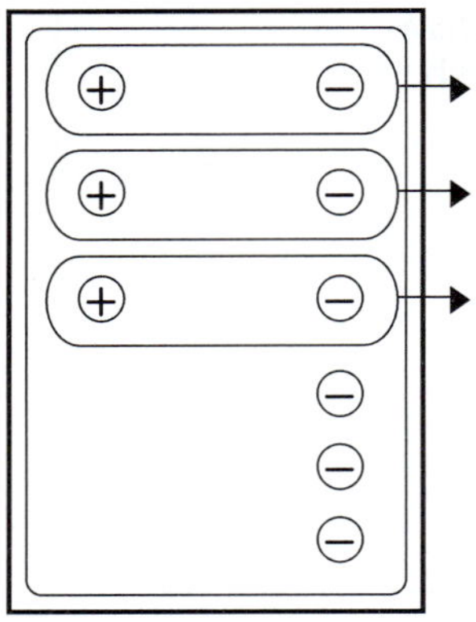

3 + (−6) = −3

i

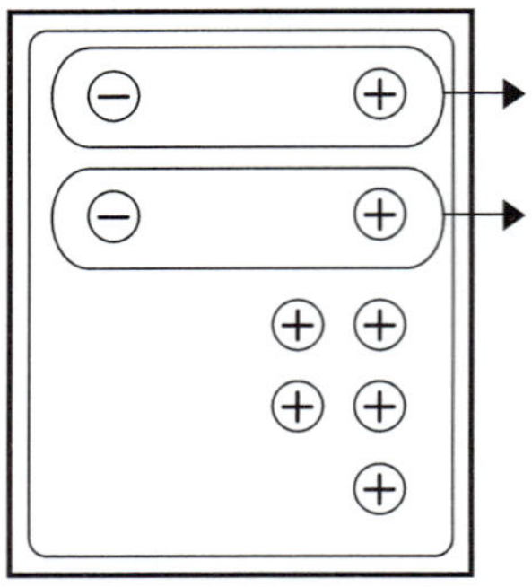

−2 + 7 = 5

j.

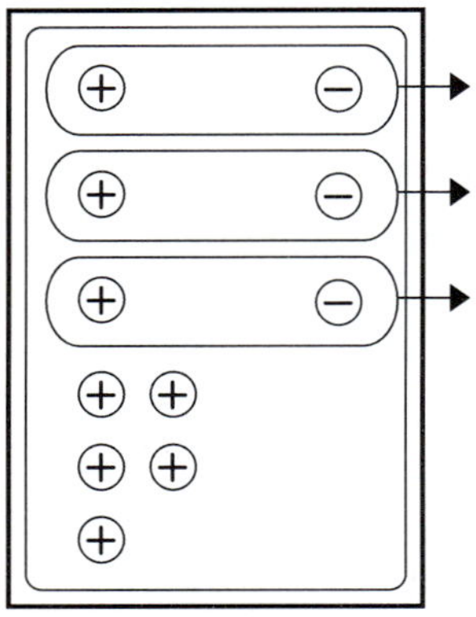

8 + (−3) = 5

k.

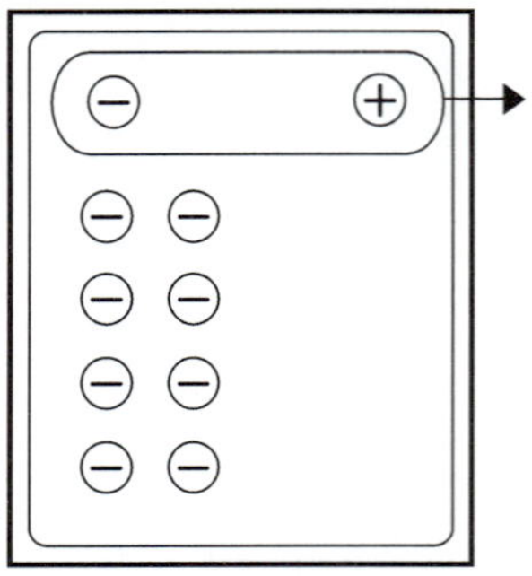

−9 + 1 = −8

l.

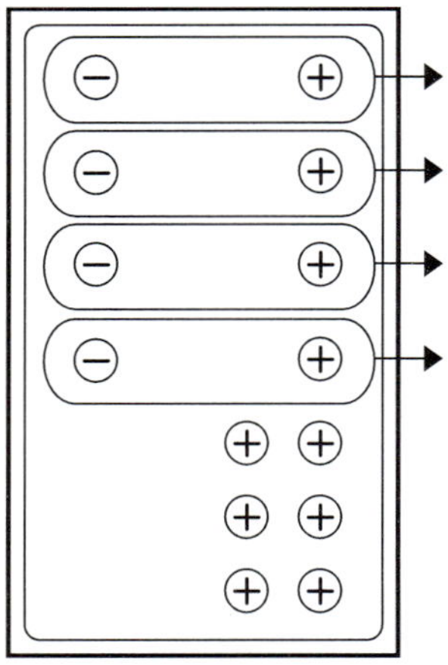

−4 + 10 = 6

Page 101, Explore 2-5

b.

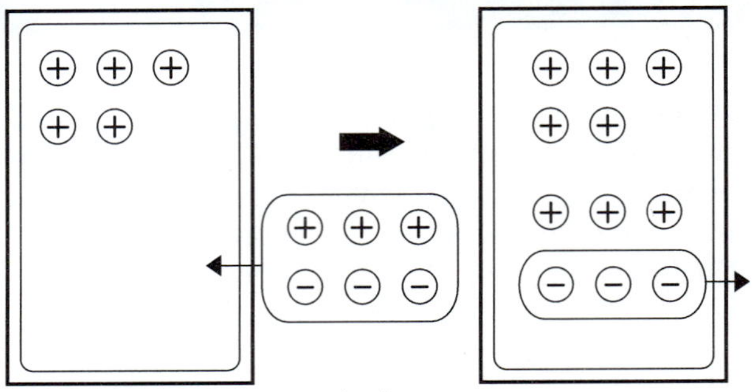

5 − (−3) = 8

c.

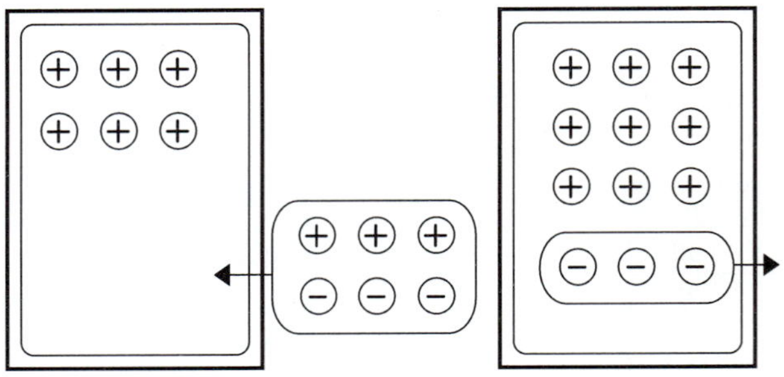

6 − (−3) = 9

d.

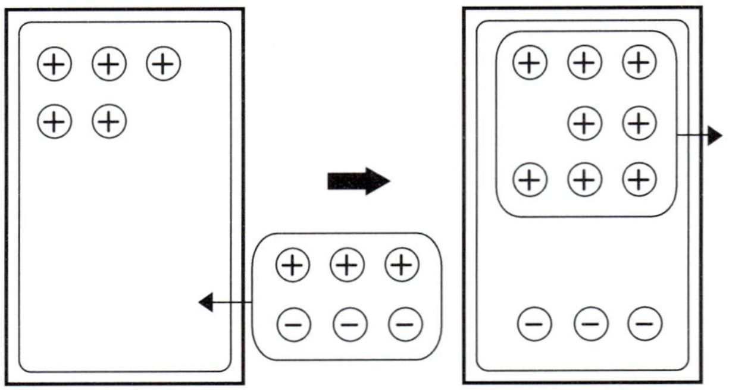

5 − 8 = −3

Page 102, Explore 2-5

f.

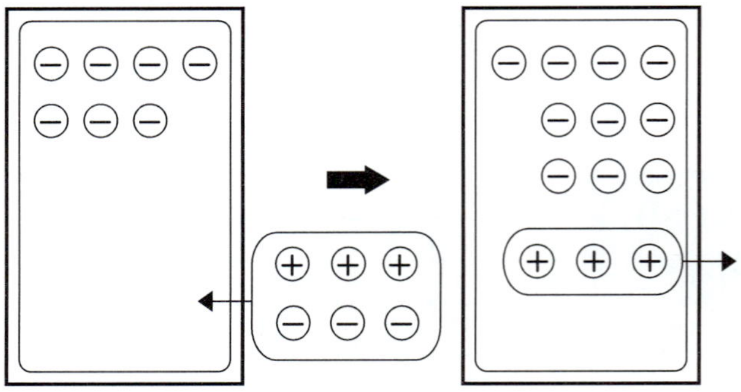

−7 − 3 = −10

g.

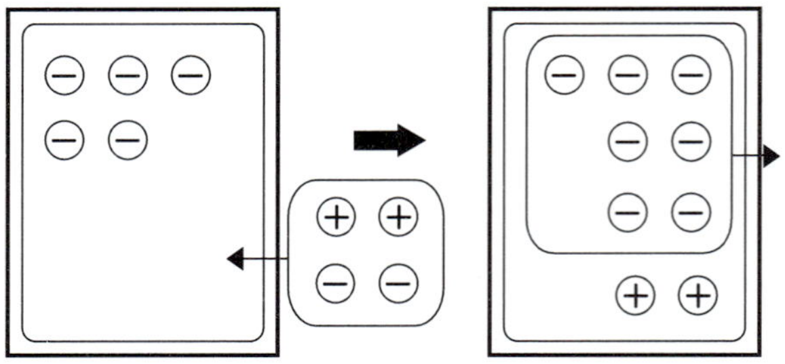

−5 − (−7) = 2

Page 103, Lesson 2-5 (Mini-Lab)

2.

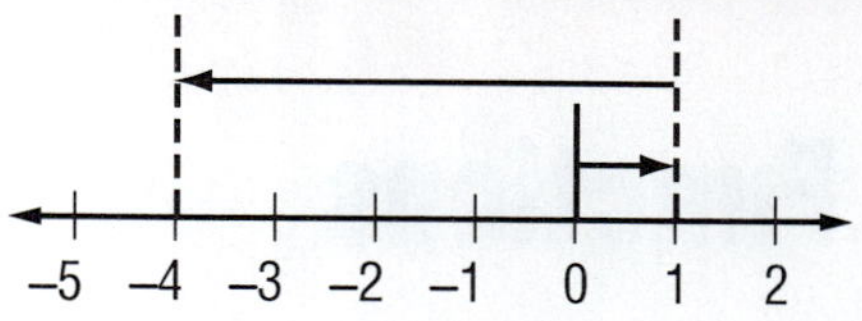

1 + (–5) = –4

3.

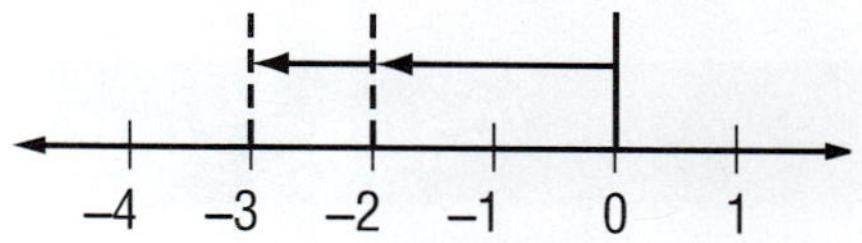

–2 + (–1) = –3

4.

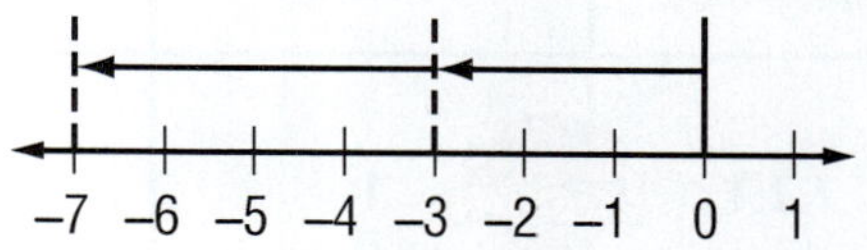

–3 + (–4) = –7

5.

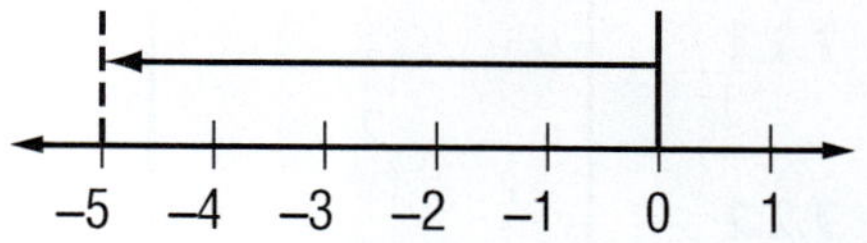

0 + (–5) = –5

CHAPTER 3

Chapter Overview

Algebra: Linear Equations and Functions

Lesson Plan — Pacing Your Lessons

LESSONS AND OBJECTIVES	Academic Standards		40–50 Minute Periods	90-Minute Periods
3-1 Writing Expressions and Equations (pp. 128–133) • Write verbal phrases and sentences as simple algebraic expressions and equations.	7.2.1	Core Lesson	1	0.5
Explore 3-2 Algebra Lab: Solving Equations Using Models (pp. 134–135) • Solve equations using models. **3-2 Solving Addition and Subtraction Equations** (pp. 136–141) • Solve addition and subtraction equations.	7.2.1 7.2.2		2	1
3-3 Solving Multiplication Equations (pp. 142–146) • Solve multiplication equations.	7.2.2		2	1
3-4 Problem-Solving Investigation: Work Backward (pp. 148–149) • Solve problems using the work backward strategy.	7.3.4, P.1.3	Core Lesson	1	0.5
3-5 Solving Two-Step Equations (pp. 151–155) • Solve two-step equations.	7.2.2	Core Lesson	1	0.5
3-6 Measurement: Perimeter and Area (pp. 156–161) • Find the perimeters and areas of figures.	7.2.4	Core Lesson	1	0.5
Explore 3-7 Measurement Lab: Representing Relationships (p. 162) • Graph data to demonstrate the relationship between the dimensions and the perimeter of a rectangle. **3-7 Functions and Graphs** (pp. 163–167) • Graph data to demonstrate relationships. **Extend 3-7 Graphing Calculator Lab: Graphing Relationships** (p. 168) • Use technology to graph relationships involving conversions of measurement.	7.2.1, 7.3.4, 8.2.4	Core Lesson	2	1
REVIEW			1	0.5
ASSESSMENT			1	0.5*
	TOTAL		**12**	**6**

*The complete **Assessment Planner** for Chapter 3 is provided on page 127.*

** Begin Chapter 4 in the second half of the period.*

Focal Points

G7-FP3 Algebra
For complete wording of the Focal Points for Grade 7, please see page T17.

Professional Development

Vertical Alignment

Before Chapter 3

Related Topics from Grade 6

- use a letter to represent an unknown number; write and evaluate simple algebraic expressions in one variable by substitution.
- differentiate between and use appropriate units of measures for two- and three-dimensional objects
- identify and graph ordered pairs in the four quadrants of the coordinate plane

Chapter 3

Topics from Grade 7

- write and solve one-step linear equations in one variable
- write an algebraic expression for a given situation, using up to three variables
- solve problems involving rates, average speed, distance, and time
- use variables in expressions describing the formulas for the perimeter of a rectangle

After Chapter 3

Preparation for Grade 8

- use variables and appropriate operations to write an expression, an equation, an inequality, or a system of equations
- solve two-step linear equations and inequalities in one variable over the rational numbers
- solve multistep problems involving rate, average speed, distance, and time or a direct variation
- plot the values of quantities whose ratios are always the same. Fit a line to the plot and understand that the slope of the line equals the ratio of the quantities

Backmapping and Vertical Alignment

McGraw-Hill's ***Math Connects*** program was conceived and developed with the final results in mind: student success in Algebra 1 and beyond. The authors, using the **NCTM Focal Points and Focal Connections** as their guide, developed this brand-new series by backmapping from Algebra 1 concepts and vertically aligning the topics so that they build upon prior skills and concepts and serve as a foundation for future topics.

What the Research Says...

According to the Rand Mathematics Study Panel, connecting algebra with arithmetic, geometry, and statistics helps build student understanding.

- In Lessons 3-2 and 3-3, the Addition, Subtraction, and Division Properties of Equality are shown using arithmetic and using algebra.
- In Lessons 3-2, 3-3, and 3-6, students use algebra to solve problems involving triangles, parallelograms, and area.

Professional Development

Targeted professional development has been articulated throughout **McGraw-Hill's *Math Connects*** program. The **McGraw-Hill Professional Development Video Library** provides short videos that support the NCTM Focal Points and Focal Connections. For more information, visit glencoe.com.

Model Lessons

Instructional Strategies

CHAPTER 3

Technology Solutions

Teacher Resources

TeacherWorks™ All-in-One Planner and Resource Center

All of the print materials from the Classroom Resource Masters are available on your TeacherWorks™ CD-ROM.

BL = Below or Approaching Grade Level OL = On Grade Level AL = Above or Beyond Grade Level ELL = English Language

				Chapter Resource Masters	3-1	3-2	3-3	3-4	3-5	3-6	3-7
BL	OL		ELL	Lesson Reading Guide	9	15	22		32	38	45
BL	OL		ELL	Study Guide and Intervention*	10	16	23	28	33	39	46
BL	OL			Skills Practice*	11	17	24	29	34	40	47
	OL	AL		Practice*	12	18	25	30	35	41	48
	OL	AL		Word Problem Practice*	13	19	26	31	36	42	49
	OL	AL		Enrichment	14	20	27		37	43	50
	OL	AL		Calculator and Spreadsheet Activities		21				44	51
	OL	AL		Chapter Assessments*	53–76						
BL	OL	AL		5-Minute Check Transparencies	✓	✓	✓	✓	✓	✓	✓
BL	OL			Teaching Mathematics with Manipulatives		✓	✓		✓	✓	✓
BL	OL	AL		Real-World Investigations for Differentiated Instruction	31–33, 35–36, 37–38, 61–62						

**Also available in Spanish.*

Graphing Calculator Easy Files

- Timesaving Tech Tools for the TI-Navigator:
- **Quick Checks** to diagnose student progress
- Motivate students with **Concept Launchers**
- Deliver differentiated instruction with **Ready Files**
- **Vocabulary Review**

AssignmentWorks

Differentiated Assignments, Answers, and Solutions

- Print a customized assignment worksheet using the Student Edition exercises along with an answer key or worked-out solutions.
- Use default lesson assignments as outlined in the Differentiated Homework Options in the Teacher Edition.

Interactive Classroom

This CD-ROM is a customizable Microsoft® PowerPoint® presentation that includes:

- In-Class Examples
- Your Turn Exercises*
- 5-Minute Check Transparencies*
- Links to Online Study Tools
- Concepts in Motion

**compatible with response pad technology*

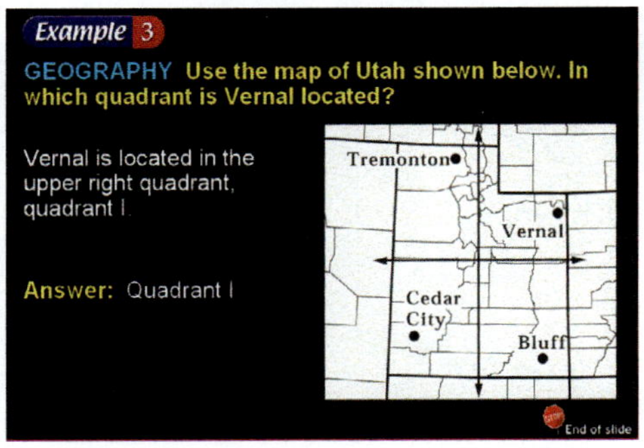

ExamView® Assessment Suite

ExamView® Assessment Suite

- Create, edit, and customize tests and worksheets using QuickTest Wizard.
- Create multiple versions of tests and modify them for a desired level of difficulty.
- Translate from English to Spanish and vice versa.
- Build tests aligned with your state standards.
- Track students' progress using the Teacher Management System.

Student Tools

StudentWorks™ Plus

Textbook, Audio, Workbooks, and more

This CD-ROM is a valuable resource for students to access content online and use online resources to continue learning Chapter 3 concepts. Includes:

- Complete Student Editions in both English and Spanish
- English audio integrated throughout the text
- Links to Concepts in Motion, Personal Tutor, and other online resources
- Access to all student worksheets
- Daily Assignments and Grade Log

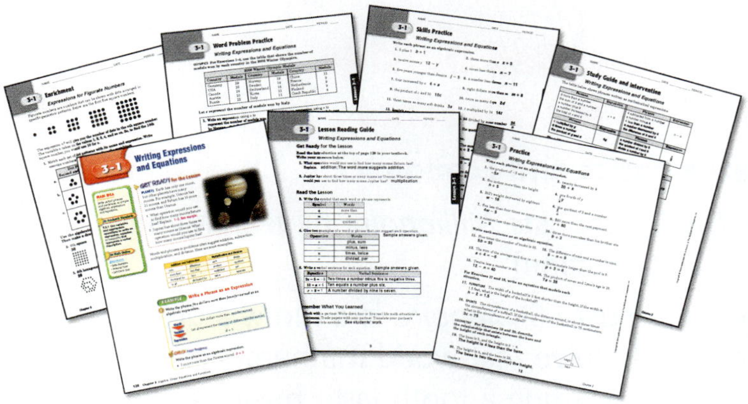

Super DVD

The Super DVD contains two Glencoe multimedia products.

MindJogger Plus An alternative review of concepts in which students work as teams in a game show format to gain points for correct answers.

What's Math Got to Do With It? Real-Life Math Videos Engaging video that shows students how math is used in everyday situations.

Internet Resources

IN Math Online glencoe.com

TEACHER	STUDENT	PARENT	**Online Study Tools**
	●	●	Online Student Edition
●	●	●	Multilingual Glossary
			Lesson Resources
	●	●	Extra Examples
	●	●	BrainPOPS
	●	●	Self-Check Quizzes
●	●	●	Concepts in Motion
	●	●	Other Calculator Keystrokes
	●	●	Real-World Careers
	●	●	Reading in the Content Area
●			Group Activity Cards
			Chapter Resources
	●	●	Family Letters and Activities
	●		Chapter Readiness Quiz
	●	●	Vocabulary Review
	●	●	Chapter Test
	●	●	Standardized Test Practice
			Unit Resources
●	●		WebQuest Project
			Other Resources
	●		Personal Tutor
●			NAEP Correlations
●			Key Concepts
●	●	●	Meet the Authors
●	●		Game Zone
●	●	●	Math Skills Maintenance
●			National Resources (Professional Organizations)
●			State Resources
●			Vocabulary PuzzleMakers

CHAPTER 3 Reading and Writing in Mathematics

Noteables™ Interactive Study Notebook with Foldables™

This workbook is a study organizer that provides helpful steps for students to follow to organize their notes for Chapter 3.

- Students use Noteables to record notes and to complete their Foldables as you present the material for each lesson.
- Noteables correspond to the Examples in the *Teacher Edition* and *Interactive Classroom CD-ROM.*

Real-World Problem Solving Graphic Novels

Mathematical problem solving is presented in a motivating, graphic novel format. The novels contain real-world problems for each of the following mathematical strands: Number Sense, Algebraic Thinking, Geometry, Measurement, Statistics and Probability, and Mathematical Reasoning.

READING in the Content Area

This online worksheet provides strategies for reading and analyzing Lesson 3-2, Solving Addition and Subtraction Equations. Students are guided through questions about the main idea, subject matter, supporting details, conclusion, clarifying details, and vocabulary of the lesson.

glencoe.com

Recommended Outside Reading for Students

Mathematics and Economics

- *The Toothpaste Millionaire* by Jean Merrill ©1974 [fiction]

The Toothpaste Millionaire is a funny story of how two friends solve real-world mathematics problems involved in starting a toothpaste business and making a profit. They use functions, which students will study in Lesson 3-7.

Project CRISS STUDY SKILL

A story frame can help students organize information contained in word problems. They can use story frames either to solve word problems or to help them develop word problems of their own. The sample story frame at the right describes the following word problem: *A car travels 74 miles less than a truck travels in one day. If the truck travels 252 miles, how far has the car traveled?* Have students use story frames to write equation word problems as they work through Chapter 3.

Things Involved:	truck, car
Setting:	truck travels 252 miles; car travels 74 miles less
Goal:	distance traveled by car:
Steps:	**1.** Write an equation relating the distance taveled by the car to the distance taveled by the truck ($t - 74 = c$) **2.** Insert t, the distance traveled by the truck, 252 miles. ($252 - 74 = c$) **3.** Solve for c, the distance traveled by the car.
Solution:	$c = 178$ miles
Check your solution:	Is it reasonable? Recheck calculations.

CReating Independence through Student-owned Strategies

Differentiated Instruction

Investigative Approach

MathScape™ This project was supported, in part, by the **National Science Foundation**

MathScape is a mathematics curriculum for grades 6–8 developed by the Seeing and Thinking Mathematically Project at the Education Development Center.

Equations, Tables, and Graphs
The Language of Algebra

How to Use MathScape with Chapter 3

The unit *The Language of Algebra* can be used to enhance Lessons 3-2 and 3-5.

- **Introduce** → Before you complete **Lesson 3-2**, you can introduce the idea of solving equations by using the activities on pages 204–205.
- **Enrich** → After you complete **Lesson 3-5**, you can use the activities on pages 206–207 to challenge students to solve both equations and inequalities.

RTI (Response to Intervention)

TIER 1 **On-Level Instruction** Use the *Math Connects* program as instruction for your on-level students.

TIER 2 **Strategic Intervention** For options to instruct struggling students, refer to the Diagnostic Assessment table on page 127.

TIER 3 **Intensive Intervention** *Math Triumphs* can provide intensive intervention for students who are at risk of not meeting the objectives addressed in Chapter 3.

Diagnose student readiness with the Quick Check and Quick Review on page 127. Then use *Math Triumphs* to accelerate their achievement.

Algebra: Linear Equations and Functions

Prerequisite Skill	*Math Triumphs*
Translating Verbal Expressions and Sentences	Ch. 4
Solving Equations	Ch. 10

Practice and Review

Quick Review Math Handbook* is Glencoe's mathematical handbook for students and parents.

Hot Words includes a glossary of terms.

Hot Topics consists of two parts:

- explanations of key mathematical concepts
- exercises to check students' understanding.

Lesson	Hot Topics Section	Lesson	Hot Topics Section
3-1	6•5	3-5	6•4
3-2	6•1, 6•4	3-6	7•4, 7•5, 8•3
3-3	6•4	3-7	6•7, 6•8

*Also available in Spanish

Chapter 3 Notes

FOLDABLES™ Study Organizer — Dinah Zike's Foldables

Focus Students write about expressions, equations, functions, and perimeter and area.

Teach After students make their Foldables, discuss note taking with them. Make sure they understand that they should listen or read for main ideas and then record those ideas in a simple form that makes sense to them.

When to Use It Under the tabs of their Foldables, students should take notes about what they learn about expressions, equations, perimeter and area, and functions. Encourage students to also write examples of each concept. *A version of a completed Foldable is shown on p. 169.*

Differentiated Instruction

CRM Student-Built Glossary, p. 1

Students complete the chart by providing the definition for each term and an example as they progress through Chapter 3.

This study tool can be used to review for the chapter test.

Materials Needed for Chapter 3

- cups and counters (Explore 3-2)
- algebra tiles (Explore 3-2, Lessons 3-3, 3-5)
- equation mats (Explore 3-2, Lessons 3-3, 3-5)
- graph paper (Explore 3-7)
- chenille stems or yarn (Explore 3-7)
- scissors (Explore 3-7)
- centimeter rules (Explore 3-7)
- graphing calculator (Extend 3-7)

Chapter 3 Algebra: Linear Equations and Functions

Indiana Academic Standards

7.2.1 Use variables and appropriate operations to write an expression, equation or inequality that represents a verbal description.
7.2.2 Write and solve two-step linear equations and inequalities in one variable.

Key Vocabulary

formula (p. 144)
linear equation (p. 164)
two-step equation (p. 151)
work backward strategy (p. 148)

Real-World Link

Segways The Segway's top speed is 12.5 miles per hour—two to three times faster than walking. You can use the equation $d = 12.5t$ to find the distance d you can travel in t hours.

FOLDABLES® Study Organizer

Algebra: Linear Equations and Functions Make this Foldable to help you organize your notes. Begin with a sheet of 11" by 17" paper.

1. **Fold** the short sides toward the middle.

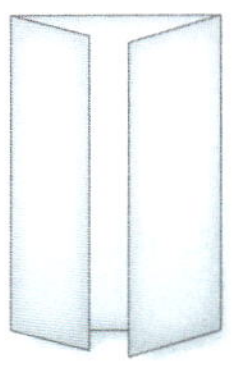

2. **Fold** the top to the bottom.

3. **Open.** Cut along the second fold to make four tabs.

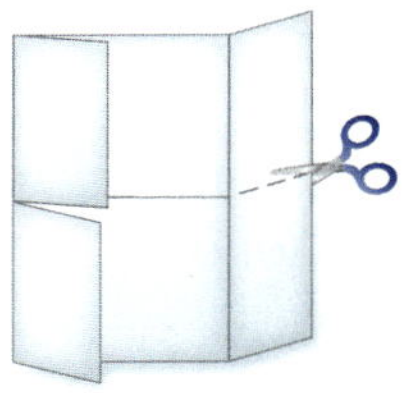

4. **Label** each of the tabs as shown.

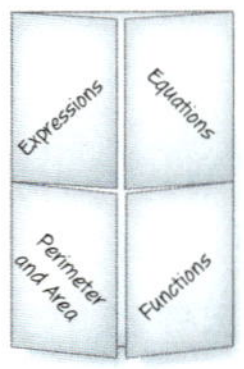

GET READY for Chapter 3

Diagnose Readiness You have two options for checking Prerequisite Skills.

Option 2

IN Math Online Take the Online Readiness Quiz at glencoe.com.

Option 1

Take the Quick Quiz below. Refer to the Quick Review for help.

QUICK Quiz

(Used in Lessons 3-2, 3-3, and 3-5)
Name the number that is the solution of the given equation. (Lesson 1-6)

1. $a + 15 = 19$; 4, 5, 6 **4**
2. $11k = 77$; 6, 7, 8 **7**
3. $x + 9 = -2$; 7, −11, 11 **−11**

QUICK Review

Example 1 Name the number that is the solution of $24 \div a = 3$; 7, 8, or 9.

$24 \div a = 3$	Write the equation.
$24 \div 7 = 3$? No.	Substitute $a = 7$.
$24 \div 8 = 3$? Yes.	Substitute $a = 8$.
$24 \div 9 = 3$? No.	Substitute $a = 9$.

(Used in Lesson 3-7)
Graph each point on a coordinate plane. (Lesson 2-3)

4. $(-4, 3)$
5. $(-2, -1)$

4–6. See Ch. 3 Answer Appendix.

6. **HIKING** Keith hiked 4 miles north and 2 miles west from the campground before he rested. If the origin represents the campground, graph Keith's resting point. (Lesson 2-3)

Example 2 Graph the point $(-1, 3)$ on a coordinate plane.

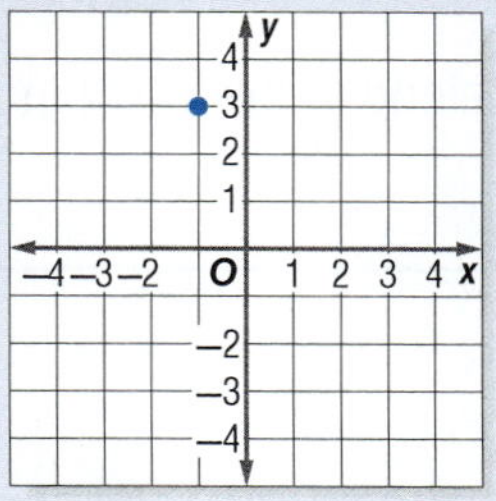

The first number in an ordered pair tells you to move left or right from the origin. The second number tells you to move up or down.

(Used in Lessons 3-2 and 3-5)
Add. (Lesson 2-4)

7. $-3 + (-5)$ **−8**
8. $-8 + 3$ **−5**
9. $9 + (-5)$ **4**
10. $-10 + 15$ **5**

Example 3 Find $-4 + (-2)$.

$-4 + (-2) = -6$ Since −4 and −2 are both negative, add their absolute values. The sum is negative also.

(Used in Lessons 3-2 through 3-5)
Subtract. (Lesson 2-5)

11. $-5 - 6$ **−11**
12. $8 - 10$ **−2**
13. $8 - (-6)$ **14**
14. $-3 - (-1)$ **−2**

Example 4 Find $9 - (-7)$.

$9 - (-7) = 9 + (7)$ Subtracting −7 is the same as adding 7.

$= 16$ Add.

(Used in Lessons 3-3 and 3-5)
Divide. (Lesson 2-8)

15. $-6 \div (-3)$ **2**
16. $-12 \div 3$ **−4**
17. $10 \div (-5)$ **−2**
18. $-24 \div (-4)$ **6**

Example 5 Find $-16 \div 2$.

$-16 \div 2 = -8$ Since −16 and 2 have opposite signs, their quotient is negative.

Diagnostic Assessment

Exercises	Academic Standards	Strategic Intervention
1–3	**7.2.2**	SE Review Lesson 1-7, pp. 49–52
4–6	**8.2.4**	SE Review Lesson 2-3, pp. 88–92
7–14	**7.2.2**	SE Review Lessons 2-4 and 2-5, pp. 95–99, 103–106
15–18	**7.2.2**	SE Review Lesson 2-8, pp. 114–118

ASSESSMENT PLANNER CHAPTER 3

Formative Assessment

CRM Anticipation Guide, pp. 7–8
Spotting Preconceived Ideas
Students complete this survey to determine prior knowledge about ideas from Chapter 3. Revisit this worksheet after completing the chapter. Also see page 172.

TE Lesson Activities

- Ticket Out the Door, pp. 133, 146, 167
- Crystal Ball, pp. 141, 149
- Name the Math, p. 155
- Yesterday's News, p. 161

Chapter Checkpoints

- SE Mid-Chapter Quiz, p. 147
- SE Study Guide and Review, pp. 169–172
- SE Test Practice, pp. 174–175
- CRM Quizzes, pp. 55 and 56
- CRM Standardized Test Practice, pp. 72–74

IN Math Online glencoe.com

- Self-Check Quizzes
- Practice Test
- Test Practice

Summative Assessment

- SE Chapter Practice Test, p. 173
- CRM Mid-Chapter Test, p. 57
- CRM Vocabulary Test, p. 58
- CRM Extended-Response Test, p. 71
- CRM Leveled Chapter Tests, pp. 59–70
- CD-ROM ExamView Pro® Assessment Suite

KEY

- CRM *Chapter 3 Resource Masters*
- SE Student Edition
- TE Teacher Edition
- CD-ROM

3-1 Writing Expressions and Equations

PACING: **Regular:** 1 period, **Block:** 0.5 period

IN Academic Standards **7.2.1 Use variables and appropriate operations to write an expression, equation** or inequality **that represents a verbal description.**

Options for Differentiated Instruction

ELL = English Language Learner AL = Above or Beyond Grade Level SS = Struggling Students SN = Special Needs

Review Vocabulary ELL SN

Use before presenting Lesson 3-1.

Have students review the following vocabulary terms and write their definitions on index cards.

- variable
- equation
- numerical expression
- algebraic expression

Being able to refer to the definitions quickly will allow students to follow along in the lesson more easily and participate in class discussions.

Use Brainstorming ELL SS SN

Use before presenting Lesson 3-1.

Brainstorm a list of words and phrases that indicate each of the four operations. As students make suggestions, write the words and phrases on the board. With help from ELL students, write translations in their primary languages.

Addition	Subtraction	Multiplication	Division
added - sumarlos	difference - diferencia	multiplied - multiplicarlos	quotient - cociente
plus - más		product - producto	
sum - suma			

Match the list that the class generates with the list on page 128.

Use Visual Clues ELL SS SN

Use before assigning the Exercises.

When students translate a verbal phrase into an algebraic expression, have them circle the clue words that indicate the operation and underline the phrase that represents the variable. Have students refer to the list of clue words on page 128.

Examples:

three (more) than <u>a number</u>   (four times) <u>the number of years</u>   <u>the length</u> (decreased) by six meters

Leveled Lesson Resources

Also on **TeacherWorks™** Lesson 3-1

Chapter 3 Resource Masters

BL = Below or Approaching Grade Level OL = On Grade Level AL = Above or Beyond Grade Level ELL = English Language Learner

Lesson Reading Guide
p. 9 BL OL ELL

NAME ____________ DATE ________ PERIOD ____

3-1 Lesson Reading Guide
Writing Expressions and Equations

Get Ready for the Lesson

Read the introduction at the top of page 128 in your textbook. Write your answers below.

1. What operation would you use to find how many moons Saturn has? Explain. **addition; The word *more* suggests addition.**
2. Jupiter has about three times as many moons as Uranus. What operation would you use to find how many moons Jupiter has? **multiplication**

Read the Lesson

3. Write the symbol that each word or phrase represents.

Symbol	Words
+	more than
=	is
÷	quotient

4. Give two examples of a word or phrase that can suggest each operation. **Sample answers given.**

Operation	Words
+	plus, sum
−	minus, less
×	times, twice
÷	divided, per

5. Write a verbal sentence for each equation. **Sample answers given.**

Equation	Verbal Sentence
$2x - 5 = -3$	Two times a number minus five is negative three.
$10 = a + 6$	Ten equals a number plus six.
$r \div 9 = 7$	A number divided by nine is seven.

Remember What You Learned

6. Work with a partner. Write down four or five real life math situations as sentences. Trade papers with your partner. Translate your partner's sentences into symbols. **See students' work.**

Chapter 3 9 Course 2

Study Guide and Intervention*
p. 10 BL OL ELL

NAME ____________ DATE ________ PERIOD ____

3-1 Study Guide and Intervention
Writing Expressions and Equations

The table below shows phrases written as mathematical expressions.

Phrases	Expression	Phrases	Expression
9 more than a number; the sum of 9 and a number; a number plus 9; a number increased by 9; the total of x and 9	$x + 9$	4 subtracted from a number; a number minus 4; 4 less than a number; a number decreased by 4; the difference of h and 4	$h - 4$
6 multiplied by g; 6 times a number; the product of g and 6	$6g$	a number divided by 5; the quotient of t and 5; divide a number by 5	$\frac{t}{5}$

The table below shows sentences written as an equation.

Sentences	Equation
Sixty less than three times the amount is \$59. Three times the amount less 60 is equal to 59. 59 is equal to 60 subtracted from three times a number. A number times three minus 60 equals 59.	$3n - 60 = 59$

Exercises

Write each phrase as an algebraic expression.

1. 7 less than m **$m - 7$**
2. the quotient of 3 and y **$\frac{3}{y}$**
3. the total of 5 and c **$5 + c$**
4. the difference of 6 and r **$6 - r$**
5. n divided by 2 **$\frac{n}{2}$**
6. the product of k and 9 **$9k$**

Write each sentence as an algebraic equation.

7. A number increased by 7 is 11. **$n + 7 = 11$**
8. The price decreased by \$4 is \$29. **$p - 4 = 29$**
9. Twice as many points as Bob would be 18 points. **$2b = 18$**
10. After dividing the money 5 ways, each person got \$67. **$\frac{m}{5} = 67$**
11. Three more than 8 times as many trees is 75 trees. **$8t + 3 = 75$**
12. Seven less than a number is 15. **$n - 7 = 15$**

Chapter 3 10 Course 2

Skills Practice*
p. 11 BL OL

NAME ____________ DATE ________ PERIOD ____

3-1 Skills Practice
Writing Expressions and Equations

Write each phrase as an algebraic expression.

1. b plus 1 **$b + 1$**
2. three more than x **$x + 3$**
3. twelve minus y **$12 - y$**
4. seven less than n **$n - 7$**
5. five years younger than Jessica **$j - 5$**
6. a number less eleven **$n - 11$**
7. four increased by a **$4 + a$**
8. eight dollars more than m **$m + 8$**
9. the product of c and 10 **$10c$**
10. twice as many days **$2d$**
11. three times as many soft drinks **$3s$**
12. t multiplied by 14 **$14t$**
13. Emily's age divided by 3 **$\frac{e}{3}$**
14. 24 divided by some number **$\frac{24}{n}$**
15. a number divided by 2 **$\frac{n}{2}$**
16. the quotient of −15 and w **$\frac{-15}{w}$**

Write each sentence as an algebraic equation.

17. A number plus three is 9. **$n + 3 = 9$**
18. The sum of x and 2 is 10. **$x + 2 = 10$**
19. Four cents more than the price is 93¢. **$p + 4 = 93$**
20. Fifteen minus y is 7. **$15 - y = 7$**
21. A number decreased by 5 is 12. **$n - 5 = 12$**
22. Five dollars less than Yumi's pay is \$124. **$y - 5 = 124$**
23. A number times four is 20. **$4n = 20$**
24. Twice the number of cars is 40. **$2c = 40$**
25. The product of z and 6 is 54. **$6z = 54$**
26. A number divided by 6 is 12. **$\frac{n}{6} = 12$**
27. 72 divided by y is −9. **$\frac{72}{y} = -9$**
28. 175 students separated into n classes is 25. **$\frac{175}{n} = 25$**
29. One more than twice as many CDs is 17. **$2c + 1 = 17$**
30. Four less than three times a number is 14. **$3n - 4 = 14$**

Chapter 3 11 Course 2

Practice*
p. 12 OL AL

NAME ____________ DATE ________ PERIOD ____

3-1 Practice
Writing Expressions and Equations

Write each phrase as an algebraic expression.

1. the product of −5 and x **$-5x$**
2. twenty increased by k **$20 + k$**
3. five inches more than the height **$h + 5$**
4. one fourth of y **$\frac{1}{4}y$**
5. Bill's weight decreased by eighteen **$w - 18$**
6. the quotient of 3 and a number **$\frac{3}{n}$**
7. five less than four times as many women **$4w - 5$**
8. \$60 more than the rent payment **$r + 60$**
9. 9 minutes less than Chang's time **$t - 9$**
10. three more pancakes than his brother ate **$b + 3$**

Write each sentence as an algebraic equation.

11. Five times the number of books is 95. **$5b = 95$**
12. The difference of nine and a number is nine. **$9 - n = 9$**
13. The sum of the average and four is −6. **$a + 4 = -6$**
14. Three meters longer than the pool is 8. **$p + 3 = 8$**
15. Twelve less a number is 40. **$12 - n = 40$**
16. The product of seven and Lynn's age is 28. **$7a = 28$**

For Exercises 17 and 18, write an equation that models each situation.

17. FURNITURE The width of a bookshelf is 2 feet shorter than the height. If the width is 1.5 feet, what is the height of the bookshelf? **$h - 2 = 1.5$**
18. SPORTS The circumference of a basketball, the distance around, is about three times the circumference of a softball. If the circumference of the basketball is 75 centimeters, what is the circumference of a softball? **$3c = 75$**

GEOMETRY **For Exercises 19 and 20, describe the relationship that exists between the base and the height of each triangle.**

19. The base is b, and the height is $b - 4$. **The height is 4 less than the base.**
20. The height is h, and the base is $2h$. **The base is two times (twice) the height.**

Chapter 3 12 Course 2

Word Problem Practice*
p. 13 OL AL

NAME ____________ DATE ________ PERIOD ____

3-1 Word Problem Practice
Writing Expressions and Equations

OLYMPICS **For Exercises 1–4, use the table that shows the number of medals won by each country in the 2006 Winter Olympics.**

2006 Winter Olympic Medals

Country	Medals	Country	Medals	Country	Medals
Germany	29	Norway	19	China	11
USA	25	Sweden	14	France	9
Canada	24	Switzerland	14	Netherlands	9
Austria	23	Korea	11	Finland	9
Russia	22	Italy	11	Czech Republic	4

Let x represent the number of medals won by Italy.

1. Write an expression using x to represent the number of medals won by Norway. **$x + 8$**
2. Write an expression using x to represent the number of medals won by the Czech Republic. **$x - 7$**
3. Which country's number of medals can be represented by $2x$? **Russia**
4. Which country's number of medals can be represented by $2x + 3$? **USA**
5. GEOGRAPHY The Virgin Islands were acquired by the United States in 1927. This is 29 years after Puerto Rico was acquired. Write an equation to model this situation. **$y + 29 = 1927$**
6. POPULATION According to the Census Bureau, the U.S. population grew from 281.4 million in April 2000 to 284.8 million in July 2001. Write an equation to model this situation. **$281.4 + x = 284.8$**

Chapter 3 13 Course 2

Enrichment
p. 14 OL AL

NAME ____________ DATE ________ PERIOD ____

3-1 Enrichment
Expressions for Figurate Numbers

Figurate numbers are numbers that can be shown with dots arranged in specific geometric patterns. Below are the first five square numbers.

The expression n^2 will give you the number of dots in the nth square number. The variable n takes on the values 1, 2, 3, 4, and so on. So, to find the 10th square number, you would use 10 for n.

1. Match each set of dot patterns with its name and expression. Write exercise numbers in the boxes to show the matchings.

	Dot Patterns for Second and Third Numbers	Name of Figurate Number	Expression
a.		pentagonal b	$\frac{n(2n-1)}{1}$ c
b.		hexagonal c	$\frac{n(n+1)}{2}$ a
c.		triangular a	$\frac{n(3n-1)}{2}$ b

Use the algebraic expressions on this page to compute each number. Then make a drawing of the number on a separate sheet of paper.

2. 6th square **36**
3. 4th triangular **10**
4. 4th pentagonal **22**
5. 4th hexagonal **28**
6. 5th triangular **15**
7. 5th pentagonal **35**

Chapter 3 14 Course 2

* Also available in Spanish ELL

Additional Lesson Resources

Transparencies

- *5-Minute Check Transparency,* Lesson 3-1

Other Print Products

- *Noteables™ Interactive Study Notebook with Foldables™*

Teacher Tech Tools

- *Interactive Classroom CD-ROM,* Lesson 3-1
- *AssignmentWorks,* Lesson 3-1

Student Tech Tools

glencoe.com

- Extra Examples, Chapter 3, Lesson 1
- Self-Check Quiz, Chapter 3, Lesson 1

3-1 Lesson Notes

1 Focus

Vertical Alignment

Before Lesson 3-1
Use a letter to represent an unknown number; write and evaluate simple algebraic expressions in one variable by substitution

From Lesson 3-1
Write an algebraic expression for a given situation, using up to three variables

After Lesson 3-1
Use variables and appropriate operations to write an expression, an equation, an inequality, or a system of equations or inequalities

2 Teach

Scaffolding Questions

Write the following expressions on the board.

a. $7 - 2$ **c.** 7×2
b. $7 + 2$ **d.** $7 \div 2$

Ask:

- Which expression represents the phrase *two more than seven?* b
- Which expression represents the phrase *the product of seven and two?* c
- Which expression represents the phrase *seven less two?* a
- Which expression represents the phrase *seven divided by two?* d
- What multiplication expression could you use to find the number of minutes in one day? 24×60

3-1 Writing Expressions and Equations

MAIN IDEA

Write verbal phrases and sentences as simple algebraic expressions and equations.

IN Academic Standards

7.2.1 Use variables and appropriate operations to write an expression, equation or inequality **that represents a verbal description.**

IN Math Online

glencoe.com
- Extra Examples
- Personal Tutor
- Self-Check Quiz

GET READY for the Lesson

PLANETS Earth has only one moon, but other planets have many moons. For example, Uranus has 21 moons, and Saturn has 10 more moons than Uranus.

1. What operation would you use to find how many moons Saturn has? Explain. **1–2. See margin.**
2. Jupiter has about three times as many moons as Uranus. What operation would you use to find how many moons Jupiter has?

Words and phrases in problems often suggest addition, subtraction, multiplication, and division. Here are some examples.

Addition and Subtraction		Multiplication and Division	
sum	difference	each	divide
more than	less than	product	quotient
increased by	less	multiplied	per
in all	decreased by	twice	separate

EXAMPLE Write a Phrase as an Expression

1 **Write the phrase** ***five dollars more than Jennifer earned*** **as an algebraic expression.**

Words	five dollars more than Jennifer earned.
Variable	Let d represent the number of dollars Jennifer earned.
Expression	$d + 5$

CHECK Your Progress

Write the phrase as an algebraic expression.

a. 3 more runs than the Pirates scored $p + 3$

ADDITIONAL EXAMPLE

1 Write the phrase *twenty dollars less the price of a movie ticket* as an algebraic expression. $20 - m$

Additional Answers

1. Addition; the word *more* suggests addition.
2. multiplication

Remember, an equation is a sentence in mathematics that contains an equals sign. When you write a verbal sentence as an equation, you can use the equals sign (=) for the words *equals* or *is*.

EXAMPLES Write Sentences as Equations

Write each sentence as an algebraic equation.

2 Six less than a number is 20.

Six less than a number is 20.

Let n represent the number.

$n - 6 = 20$

3 Three times Jack's age equals 12.

Three times Jack's age equals 12.

Let a represent Jack's age.

$3a = 12$

CHECK Your Progress

Write each sentence as an algebraic equation.

b. Seven more than a number is 15. $n + 7 = 15$

c. Five times the number of students is 250. $5s = 250$

Reading Math

Less Than You can write *six more than a number* as either $6 + n$ or $n + 6$. But *six less than a number* can only be written as $n - 6$.

Real-World EXAMPLE

4 WATERFALLS The tallest waterfall in the United States is Yosemite Falls in California with a height of about 739 meters. This height is 617 meters taller than Raven Cliff Falls. What is the height of Raven Cliff Falls? Write an equation that models this situation.

Words	*Yosemite Falls* is 617 meters taller than *Raven Cliff Falls.*
Variable	Let h represent the height of *Raven Cliff Falls.*
Equation	$739 = 617 + h$

The equation is $739 = 617 + h$.

Real-World Link The tallest waterfall in South Carolina is Raven Cliff Falls, located in Caesars Head State Park.

Source: South Carolina Department of Parks, Recreation, and Tourism

CHECK Your Progress d. $1.5c = 75$

d. **ANIMALS** North American cougars are about 1.5 times as long as cougars found in the tropical jungles of Central America. If North American cougars are about 75 inches long, how long is the tropical cougar? Write an equation that models this situation.

Focus on Mathematical Content

Word problems contain words or terms that tell which **operation** to use to solve the problem.

An **equation** is a number sentence. It includes an equals sign.

The unknown number in a word problem can be represented by a **variable** in an algebraic expression or equation.

Formative Assessment

Use the Check Your Progress exercises after each Example to determine students' understanding of concepts.

ADDITIONAL EXAMPLES

Write each sentence as an algebraic equation.

2 A number less 4 is 12. $n - 4 = 12$

3 Twice a number is 18. $2n = 18$

4 **FOOD** An average American adult drinks more soft drinks than any other beverage each year. Three times the number of gallons of soft drinks plus 27 is equal to the total 183 gallons of beverages consumed. Write an equation that models this situation. $3s + 27 = 183$

Additional Examples are also in:

- Noteables™ Interactive Study Notebook with Foldables™
- Interactive Classroom PowerPoint® Presentations

Tips for New Teachers — Language

Emphasize the importance of reading a problem carefully. A small change in wording can indicate a different expression. For example, *five less than a number* is $n - 5$, but *five less a number* is $5 - n$.

ADDITIONAL EXAMPLE

5 TEST EXAMPLE Which problem situation matches the equation $4.9y = 17.3$? D

A After giving away 4.9 kilograms of tomatoes, Harry had 17.3 kilograms left. What is y, the number of kilograms of tomatoes that Harry began with?

B The total length of two toy cars is 17.3 centimeters. One car is 4.9 centimeters long. What is y, the length of the other car?

C A chemist separated a solution into 4 equal quantities of 17.3 milliliters. What is y, the amount of solution she began with?

D Rodrigo spent $17.30 on fishing line. If each meter of line cost $4.90, what is y, the total length of the line?

Test-Taking Tip

Vocabulary Terms Before taking a standardized test, review the meaning of vocabulary terms such as *average*.

ISTEP+ EXAMPLE 7.2.1

5 Which problem situation matches the equation $x - 5.83 = 3.17$?

A Tyler ran 3.17 kilometers. His friend ran the same distance 5.83 seconds faster than Tyler. What is x, the time in seconds that Tyler ran?

B Lynn and Heather measured the length of worms in science class. Lynn's worm was 5.83 centimeters long, and Heather's worm was 3.17 centimeters long. What is x, the average length of the worms?

C Keisha's lunch cost $5.83. She received $3.17 in change when she paid the bill. What is x, the amount of money she gave the cashier?

D Mr. Carlos paid $3.17 for a notebook that originally cost $5.83. What is x, the amount of money that Mr. Carlos saved?

Read the Item

You need to find which problem situation matches the equation $x - 5.83 = 3.17$.

Solve the Item

- You can eliminate A because you cannot add or subtract different units of measure.
- You can eliminate B because to find an average you add and then divide.
- Act out C. If you gave the cashier x dollars and your lunch cost $5.83, you would subtract to find your change, $3.17. This is the correct answer.
- Check D, just to be sure. To find the amount Mr. Carlos saved, you would calculate $5.83 - 3.17$, not $x - 5.83$.

The solution is C.

CHECK Your Progress

e. **Which problem situation matches the equation $4y = 6.76$?** F

F Mrs. Thomas bought 4 gallons of gas. Her total cost was $6.76. What is y, the cost of one gallon of gas?

G Jordan bought 4 CDs that were on sale for $6.76 each. What is y, the total cost of the CDs?

H The width of a rectangle is 4 meters. The length is 6.76 meters more than the width. What is y, the length of the rectangle?

J The average yearly rainfall is 6.76 inches. What is y, the amount of rainfall you might expect in 4 years?

130 Chapter 3 Algebra: Linear Equations and Functions

CHECK Your Understanding

Example 1 (p. 128)

Write each phrase as an algebraic expression.

1. a number increased by eight $n + 8$
2. ten dollars more than Grace has $j + 10$

Examples 2, 3 (p. 129)

Write each sentence as an algebraic equation. 4. $s - 2 = 4$

3. Nine less than a number equals 24. 3. $n - 9 = 24$
4. Two points less than his score is 4.
5. Twice the number of miles is 18. $2m = 18$
6. One half the regular price is $13. $p \div 2 = 13$

Example 4 (p. 129)

7. **ALGEBRA** The median age of people living in Arizona is 1 year younger than the median age of people living in the United States. Use this information and the information at the right to write an equation to find the median age in the United States. $x - 1 = 34.3$

Example 5 (p. 130)

8. **MULTIPLE CHOICE** Which problem situation matches the equation $x - 15 = 46$? B

   A The original price of a jacket is $46. The sale price is $15 less. What is x, the sale price of the jacket?

   B Mark had several baseball cards. He sold 15 of the cards and had 46 left. What is x, the amount of cards Mark had to start with?

   C Sonja scored 46 points in last week's basketball game. Talisa scored 15 points less. What is x, the amount of points Talisa scored?

   D Katie earned $15 babysitting this week. Last week she earned $46. What is x, her average earnings for the two weeks?

Practice and Problem Solving

HOMEWORK HELP

For Exercises	See Examples
9–16	1
17–22	2, 3
23–24	4
41	5

Exercise Levels
A: 9–24
B: 25–36
C: 37–40

Write each phrase as an algebraic expression.

9. fifteen increased by t $15 + t$
10. five years older than Luis $y + 5$
11. a number decreased by ten $n - 10$
12. three feet less than the length $\ell - 3$
13. the product of r and 8 $8r$
14. twice as many oranges $2f$
15. Emily's age divided by 3 $\frac{a}{3}$
16. the quotient of a number and -12 $\frac{z}{-12}$

Write each sentence as an algebraic equation.

17. The sum of a number and four is equal to -8. $n + 4 = -8$
18. Two more than the number of frogs is 4. $c + 2 = 4$
19. The product of a number and five is -20. $5d = -20$
20. Ten times the number of students is 280. $10k = 280$
21. Ten inches less than her height is 26. $h - 10 = 26$
22. Five less than a number is 31. $n - 5 = 31$

3 Practice

Formative Assessment

Use Exercises 1–8 to check for understanding.

Then use the chart at the bottom of this page to customize your assignments for students.

Intervention You may wish to use the Study Guide and Intervention Master on page 10 of the *Chapter 3 Resource Masters* for additional reinforcement.

Odd/Even Assignments

Exercises 9–24 are structured so that students practice the same concepts whether they are assigned odd or even problems.

Tips for New Teachers: Writing Algebraic Expressions

After assigning Exercise 11, it may be helpful to have students distinguish between the phrases a number decreased by ten and ten decreased by a number. The first phrase can be represented by the expression $n - 10$, but the second phrase is represented by the expression $10 - n$.

DIFFERENTIATED HOMEWORK OPTIONS

Level	Assignment	Two-Day Option	
BL Basic	9–24, 37, 38, 40–56	9–23 odd, 41, 42	10–24 even, 37, 38, 40, 43–56
OL Core	9–21 odd, 23, 24, 25–33 odd, 35–38, 40–56	9–24, 41, 42	25–38, 40, 43–56
AL Advanced/Pre-AP	25–52 (optional: 53–56)		

⚠ Exercise Alert!

Find the Error For Exercise 38, Candace is correct. Sancho correctly determined the operation but confused the order of the terms because he ignored the word *than*. Remind students to analyze the wording of problems carefully.

Real-World Link A giraffe's heart can pump 16 gallons of blood in one minute.

Source: Woodland Park Zoo

For Exercises 23 and 24, write an equation that models each situation.

23. **ANIMALS** A giraffe is 3.5 meters taller than a camel. If a giraffe is 5.5 meters tall, how tall is a camel? $c + 3.5 = 5.5$

24. **FOOTBALL** Carson Palmer led the National Football League with 32 touchdown passes in a season. This was twice as many touchdown passes as Donovan McNabb had. Find the number of touchdown passes for McNabb. $2f = 32$

MEASUREMENT For Exercises 25–28, describe the relationship that exists between the length and width of each rectangle.

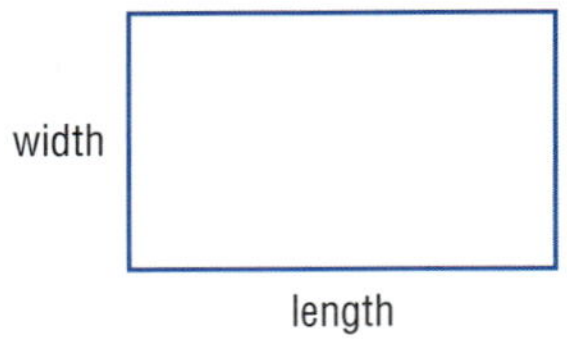

25. The width is x, and the length is $4x$.
26. The length is $x + 3$, and the width is x.
27. The length is x, and the width is $x - 5$.
28. The length is x, and the width is $0.5x$. the width is half the length

25. The length is 4 times the width.
26. The length is 3 more than the width.
27. The width is 5 less than the length.

Write each phrase as an algebraic expression.

29. 2 more than twice as many bikes $2b + 2$
30. nine CDs less than three times the number of CDs Margaret owns $3c - 9$
31. 43 dollars off the price of each admission, which is then multiplied by 3 admissions $3(a - 43)$
32. the quotient of a number w and (-8), which is then increased by 7 $\frac{w}{-8} + 7$
33. the square of a number k which is then multiplied by 13 $13k^2$
34. the sum of a number p and 0.4 which is then decreased by the fifth power of the same number $p + 0.4 - p^5$

ANALYZE TABLES For Exercises 35 and 36, use the table. 35. American toad

The table shows the average lifespan of several types of pets. Let y represent the average lifespan of a gerbil.

Pets	
Type	Lifespan (years)
American toad	15
cat	25
dog	22
gerbil	5
rabbit	9

35. Which lifespan can be represented by $3y$?
36. Write an expression to represent the lifespan of a cat. $5y$ or $y + 20$

Academic Standards • ISTEP+
Extra Practice, pp. 674, 706

H.O.T. Problems

37. **OPEN ENDED** Write a verbal sentence for the equation $n - 3 = 6$. Sample answer: 3 less than a number is 6.

38. **FIND THE ERROR** Sancho and Candace are writing an algebraic expression for the phrase *5 less than a number*. Who is correct? Explain.

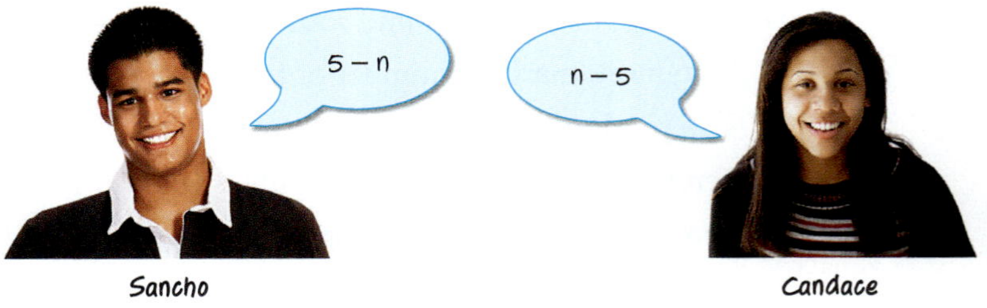

38. Candace; "five less than a number" indicates that 5 is subtracted from the variable

132 Chapter 3 Algebra: Linear Equations and Functions

39. **CHALLENGE** If x is an odd number, how would you represent the odd number immediately following it? preceding it? **$x + 2$; $x - 2$**

40. **WRITING IN MATH** Analyze the meaning of the expressions $a + 5$, $a - 3$, $2a$, and $\frac{a}{2}$ if a represents someone's age.
5 years more than someone's age, 3 years less than someone's age, twice someone's age, and half of someone's age

ISTEP+ PRACTICE 7.2.1

41. Asha had some change in her purse. After her brother gave her \$0.79, Asha had \$2.24 altogether. Which equation can she use to find the original amount of money m she had in her purse? **C**

A $2.24 = m - 0.79$

B $m = 2.24 \times 0.79$

C $m + 0.79 = 2.24$

D $m + 2.24 = 0.79$

42. Which algebraic equation best describes the total distance D traveled in miles after a 6-hour period, if r represents the rate of travel in miles per hour? **H**

F $D = 6 + r$

G $D = \frac{r}{6}$

H $D = 6r$

J $D = \frac{6}{r}$

Spiral Review

Divide (Lesson 2-8)

43. $-42 \div 6$ **−7**

44. $36 \div (-3)$ **−12**

45. $-45 \div (-3)$ **15**

46. **MONEY** Jordan withdraws \$14 per week from his savings account for a period of 7 weeks. Write a multiplication expression to represent this situation. Then find the product and explain its meaning. (Lesson 2-7)
−14(7); −98; Jordan withdraws \$98 over the 7 weeks.

Evaluate each expression. (Lesson 1-4)

47. $3 + 7 \cdot 4 - 6$ **25**

48. $8(16 - 5) - 6$ **82**

49. $75 \div 3 + 6(5 - 1)$ **49**

ANALYZE DATA For Exercises 50–52, use the table that shows the cost of two different plans for downloading music. (Lesson 1-1) **50. about \$1.33 per song**

50. Suppose you download 12 songs in one month. Find the cost per song using Plan B.

51. Which plan is less expensive for downloading 9 songs in one month? **Plan A**

52. When is it less expensive to use Plan B instead of Plan A?
when you download 17 or more songs each month

Music Downloads	
Plan A	\$0.99 per song
Plan B	\$15.99 per month for unlimited downloads

GET READY for the Next Lesson

PREREQUISITE SKILL Find each sum. (Lesson 2-4)

53. $-8 + (-3)$ **−11**

54. $-10 + 9$ **−1**

55. $12 + (-20)$ **−8**

56. $-15 + 15$ **0**

4 Assess

Ticket Out the Door Write a phrase such as *13 less pennies than 20 pennies times 4* on the board. Have students write what operations the phrase describes and which operation should be performed first.

FOLDABLES Study Organizer Foldables™ Follow-Up

Remind students to take notes about writing algebraic expressions and equations under the tabs of their Foldables. Make sure they describe the difference between an expression and an equation. Encourage them to give examples.

Explore 3-2 **Lesson Notes**

1 Focus

Materials

- algebra tiles (optional)

Easy-to-Make Manipulatives

Teaching Mathematics with Manipulatives, templates for:

- algebra tiles, pp. 10–11

2 Teach

Working in Cooperative Groups

You may wish for students to work in groups of 2 or 3. Student 1 can model the equation using algebra tiles. Student 2 can remove tiles from each side of the mat. Student 3 can count the remaining tiles to find the value of *x*.

Activity 1 Make sure students understand that they can represent the variable *x* with a cup, an *x* algebra tile, or a written *x*.

You might wish to emphasize that to solve for *x*, students need to isolate it, so that it is the only term remaining on the left side of the equals sign.

Explore 3-2

Algebra Lab
Solving Equations Using Models

MAIN IDEA

Solve equations using models.

IN Academic Standards

Preparation for 7.2.2 Write and solve two-step linear equations and inequalities in one variable. *Also addresses P.5.1, P.5.2, P.5.3.*

In Chapter 2, you used counters to add, subtract, multiply, and divide integers. Integers can also be modeled using algebra tiles. The table shows how these two types of models are related.

Type of Model	Variable *x*	Integer 1	Integer −1
Cups and Counters	cup	⊕	⊖
Algebra Tiles	x	1	−1

You can use either type of model to solve equations.

ACTIVITY

1 **Solve $x + 2 = 5$ using cups and counters or a drawing.**

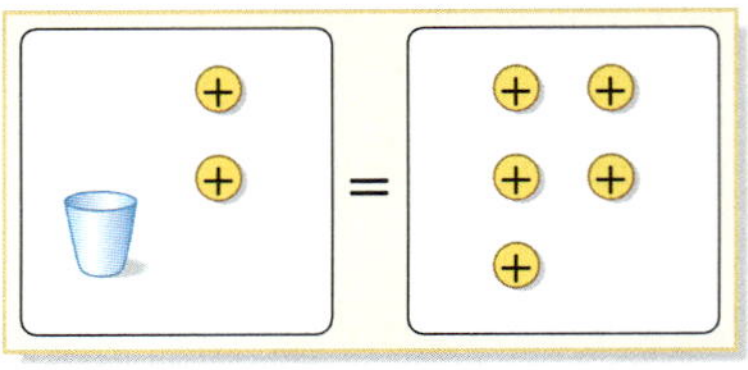

$x + 2 \quad = \quad 5$

Model the equation.

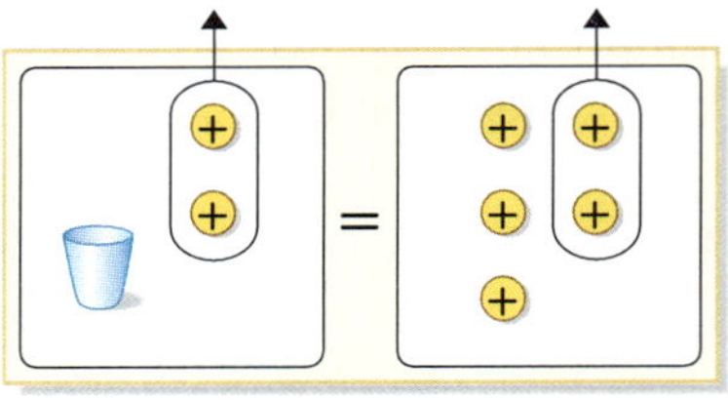

$x + 2 - 2 \quad = \quad 5 - 2$

Remove the same number of counters from each side of the mat until the cup is by itself on one side.

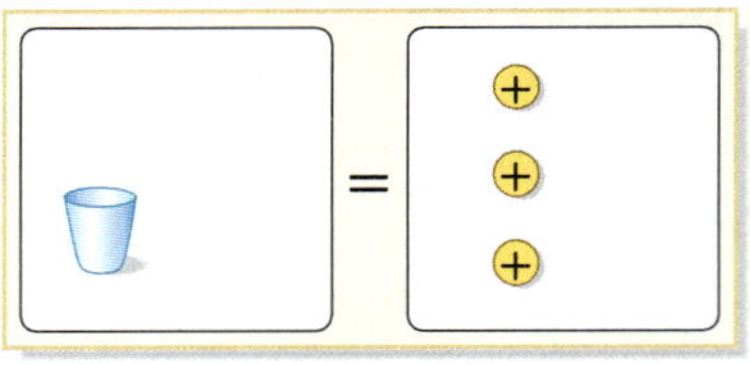

$x \quad = \quad 3$

The number of counters remaining on the right side of the mat represents the value of *x*.

Therefore, $x = 3$. Since $3 + 2 = 5$, the solution is correct.

CHECK Your Progress a–b. See margin for drawings.

Solve each equation using cups and counters or a drawing.

a. $x + 4 = 4$ **0** b. $5 = x + 4$ **1** c. $4 = 1 + x$ **3** d. $2 = 2 + x$ **0**

c–d. See Ch. 3 Answer Appendix for drawings.

Additional Answers

a.

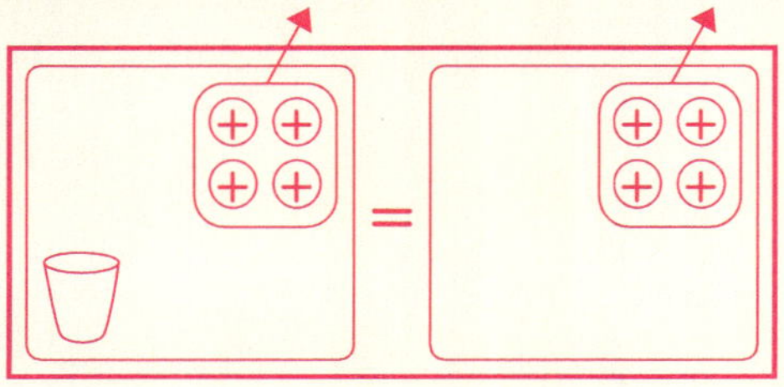

b.

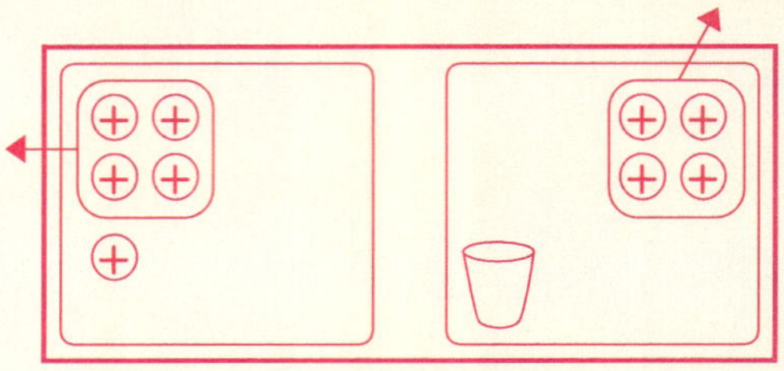

Review Vocabulary

zero pair a number paired with its opposite; Example: 2 and -2. (Explore 2-4)

You can add or subtract a zero pair from either side of an equation without changing its value, because the value of a zero pair is zero.

ACTIVITY

2 **Solve $x + 2 = -1$ using models.**

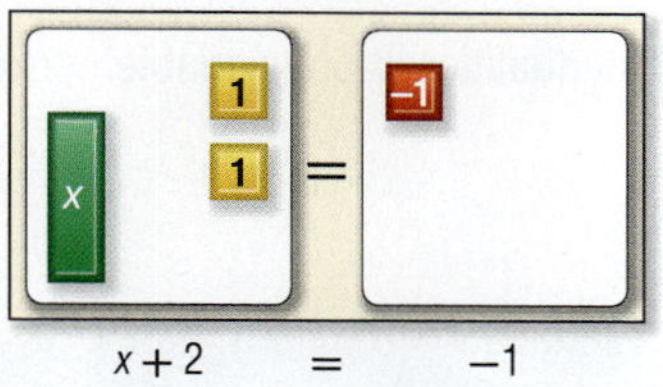

Model the equation.

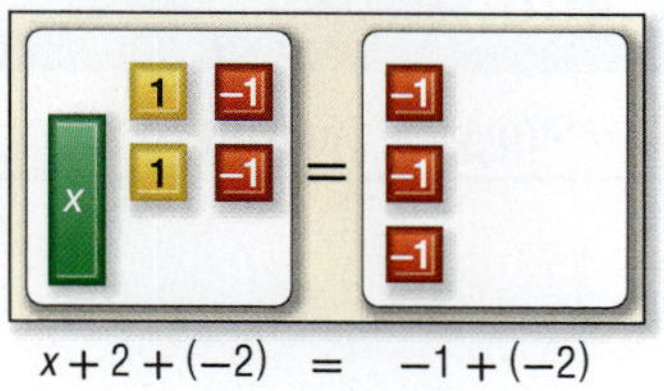

Add 2 negative tiles to the left side of the mat and add 2 negative tiles to the right side of the mat.

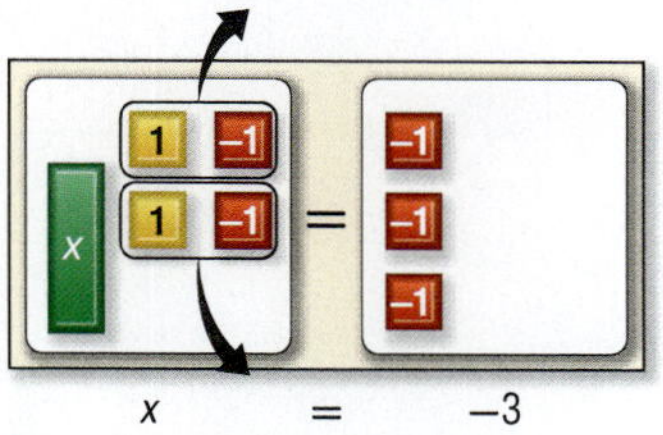

Remove all of the zero pairs from the left side. There are 3 negative tiles on the right side of the mat.

Therefore, $x = -3$. Since $-3 + 2 = -1$, the solution is correct.

CHECK Your Progress e–h. See margin for drawings.

Solve each equation using models or a drawing.

e. $-2 = x + 1$ f. $x - 3 = -2$ g. $x - 1 = -3$ h. $4 = x - 2$

e. -3 f. 1 g. -2 h. 6

ANALYZE THE RESULTS

Explain how to solve each equation using models or a drawing.

1.

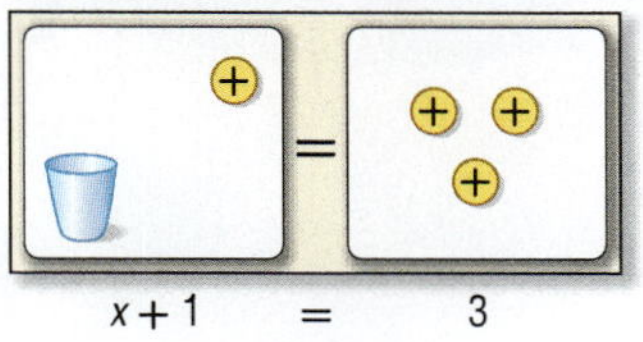

2.

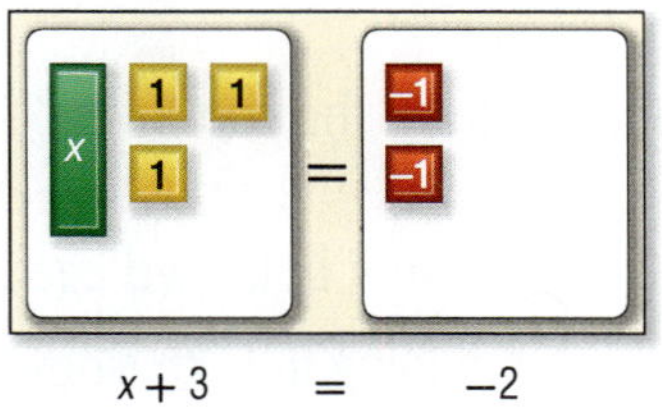

3. **MAKE A CONJECTURE** Write a rule that you can use to solve an equation like $x + 3 = 2$ without using models or a drawing.

1. Remove 1 counter from each side of the equation mat; $x = 2$.
2. Add 3 negative tiles to each side of the mat. Remove the zero pairs; $x = -5$.
3. If a number is added to the variable, subtract that number from both sides of the equation. If a number is subtracted from the variable, add that number to both sides of the equation.

Activity 2 Make sure students understand that they cannot simply subtract the two positive tiles from the left side of the equation, since the right side doesn't have any positive tiles to subtract. Remind students that if they add or subtract tiles to or from one side of the equation, they must add or subtract the same tiles to or from the other side (unless, of course, they are adding or subtracting zero pairs).

3 Assess

Formative Assessment

Use Exercises e–h to determine whether students comprehend how to use algebra tiles or drawings to solve equations.

From Concrete to Abstract Use Exercise 4 to bridge the gap between using algebra tiles to solve equations and using an algorithm.

g.

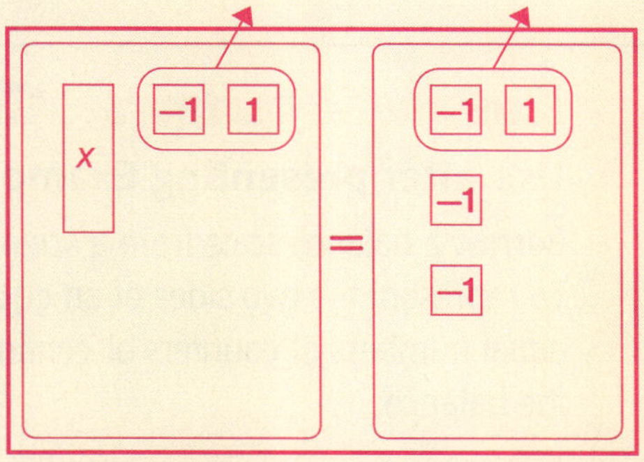

h.

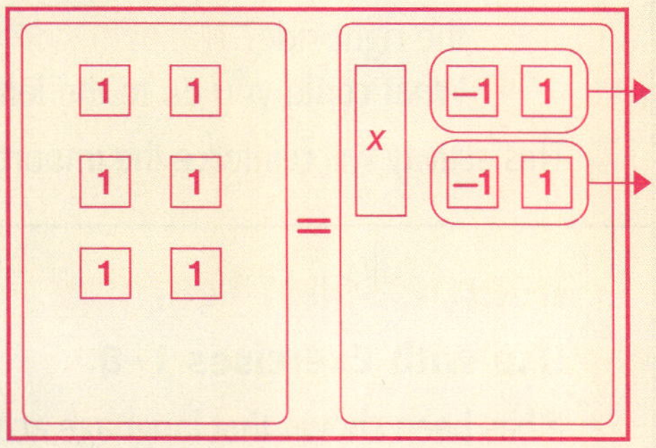

Additional Answers

e.

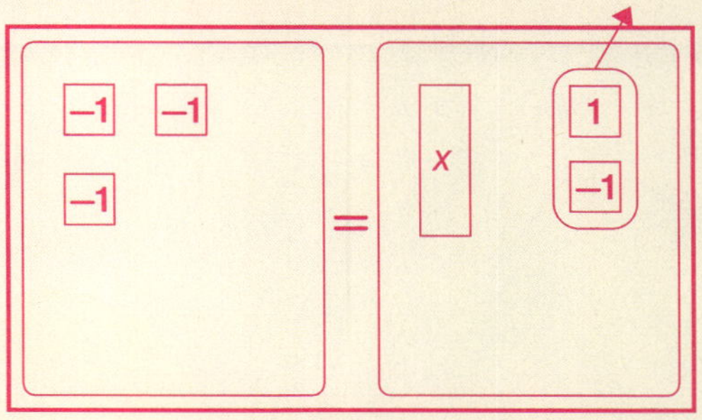

f.

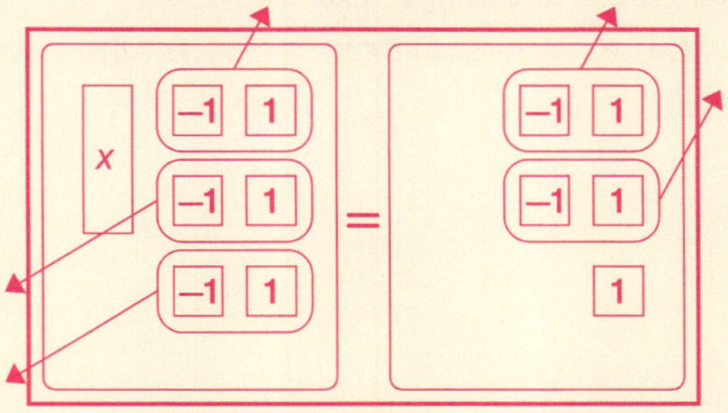

3-2 Solving Addition and Subtraction Equations

PACING: **Regular:** 2 periods, **Block:** 1 period

IN Academic Standards **Preparation for 7.2.2** Write and solve two-step linear equations and inequalities in one variable. *Also addresses 7.2.1, P.5.1, P.5.2, P.5.3.*

Options for Differentiated Instruction

ELL = English Language Learner AL = Above or Beyond Grade Level SS = Struggling Students SN = Special Needs

Using Mental Math SS SN

Use before presenting Example 1.

Ask students to use mental math to do the following:

1. Choose a number.
2. Add 4 to the number.
3. Subtract 4 from the answer.

Ask:

- What was your final answer? the original number
- Will the same thing happen if you start with a different number? Explain. Yes; subtracting 4 undoes the adding 4.

Kinesthetic Learners ELL SS SN

Use after presenting Examples 1–5.

Borrow a balance scale from a science teacher.
To represent the two sides of an equation, place cups containing equal numbers of counters or centimeter cubes on each side of the balance.

Ask:

- What would happen if you removed two counters from the cup on the right side? The right side of the balance would be higher than the left.
- What could you do to the left side of the scale to make it balanced again? Remove two counters.

This activity will reinforce the importance of doing the same thing to both sides of an equation.

Interpersonal Learning ELL

Use with Exercises 1–8.

It has been shown that language acquisition is a social activity and that ELL students develop the academic language they need by collaborating with other students. To give ELL students practice communicating their ideas orally, have students work in pairs or small groups to complete Exercises 1–8.

Leveled Lesson Resources

Also on **TeacherWorks™** Lesson 3-2

Chapter 3 Resource Masters

BL = Below or Approaching Grade Level OL = On Grade Level AL = Above or Beyond Grade Level ELL = English Language Learner

Lesson Reading Guide
p. 15 BL OL ELL

NAME ________ DATE ________ PERIOD ____

3-2 Lesson Reading Guide
Solving Addition and Subtraction Equations

Get Ready for the Lesson
Read the introduction at the top of page 136 in your textbook. Write your answers below.
1. What does x represent in the figure? number of games initially had
2. What addition equation is shown in the figure? $x + 2 = 6$
3. Explain how to solve the equation. Find the number that when added to 2 is 6.
4. How many games did Max have in the beginning? 4

Read the Lesson
5. Match the method of solving with the appropriate equation.

$x + 5 = 9$ c — a. add 2 to each side
$-2 + y = 1$ a — b. add 5 to each side
$5 = m - 1$ d — c. subtract 5 from each side
$r + 9 = 7$ e — d. add 1 to each side
$k - 5 = 2$ b — e. subtract 9 from each side

6. Explain in words how to solve each equation.
$a - 10 = 3$ Add ten to each side and simplify.
$4 + t = 12$ Subtract four from each side and simplify.
$18 = n - 7$ Add seven to each side and simplify.

7. Solve each equation.
a. $w + 23 = 11$ −34 b. $35 = z - 15$ 50 c. $42 + c = -9$ −51

Remember What You Learned
8. Take turns with a partner explaining the Addition and Subtraction Properties of Equality in your own words. Then each of you write two addition and two subtraction equations. Trade equations and solve. Check your work by explaining to each other the method you used to solve the equations.
See students' answers.

Chapter 3 15 Course 2

Study Guide and Intervention*
p. 16 BL OL ELL

NAME ________ DATE ________ PERIOD ____

3-2 Study Guide and Intervention
Solving Addition and Subtraction Equations

Remember, equations must always remain balanced. If you subtract the same number from each side of an equation, the two sides remain equal. Also, if you add the same number to each side of an equation, the two sides remain equal.

Example 1 Solve $x + 5 = 11$. Check your solution.

$x + 5 = 11$ Write the equation.
$-5 \; -5$ Subtract 5 from each side.
$x = 6$ Simplify.

Check $x + 5 = 11$ Write the equation.
$6 + 5 \stackrel{?}{=} 11$ Replace x with 6.
$11 = 11$ ✓ This sentence is true.

The solution is 6.

Example 2 Solve $15 = t - 12$. Check your solution.

$15 = t - 12$ Write the equation.
$+12 \; +12$ Add 12 to each side.
$27 = t$ Simplify.

Check $15 = t - 12$ Write the equation.
$15 \stackrel{?}{=} 27 - 12$ Replace t with 27.
$15 = 15$ ✓ This sentence is true.

The solution is 27.

Exercises
Solve each equation. Check your solution.
1. $h + 3 = 14$ 11 2. $m + 8 = 22$ 14 3. $p + 5 = 15$ 10 4. $17 = y + 8$ 9
5. $w + 4 = -1$ −5 6. $k + 5 = -3$ −8 7. $25 = 14 + r$ 11 8. $57 + z = 97$ 40
9. $b - 3 = 6$ 9 10. $7 = c - 5$ 12 11. $j - 12 = 18$ 30 12. $v - 4 = 18$ 22
13. $-9 = w - 12$ 3 14. $y - 8 = -12$ −4 15. $14 = f - 2$ 16 16. $23 = n - 12$ 35

Chapter 3 16 Course 2

Skills Practice*
p. 17 BL OL

NAME ________ DATE ________ PERIOD ____

3-2 Skills Practice
Solving Addition and Subtraction Equations

Solve each equation. Check your solution.
1. $x + 2 = 8$ 6 2. $y + 7 = 9$ 2 3. $a + 5 = 12$ 7
4. $16 = n + 6$ 10 5. $q + 10 = 22$ 12 6. $m + 9 = 17$ 8
7. $b - 4 = 9$ 13 8. $8 = c - 4$ 12 9. $11 = t - 7$ 18
10. $d - 10 = 8$ 18 11. $x - 11 = 9$ 20 12. $2 = z - 14$ 16
13. $72 = 24 + w$ 48 14. $86 + y = 99$ 13 15. $6 + y = -8$ −14
16. $-5 = m + 11$ −16 17. $n + 3.5 = 6.7$ 3.2 18. $x + 1.6 = 0.8$ −0.8
19. $98 = t - 18$ 116 20. $12 = g - 56$ 68 21. $x - 18 = -2$ 16
22. $p - 11 = -5$ 6 23. $a - 1.5 = 4.2$ 5.7 24. $7.4 = n - 2.6$ 10

Chapter 3 17 Course 2

Practice*
p. 18 OL AL

NAME ________ DATE ________ PERIOD ____

3-2 Practice
Solving Addition and Subtraction Equations

Solve each equation. Check your solution.
1. $a + 4 = 11$ $a = 7$ 2. $6 = g + 8$ $g = -2$ 3. $x - 3 = -2$ $x = 1$
4. $k + 8 = 3$ $k = -5$ 5. $j + 0 = 9$ $j = 9$ 6. $12 + y = 15$ $y = 3$
7. $h - 4 = 0$ $h = 4$ 8. $m - 7 = 1$ $m = 8$ 9. $w + 5 = 4$ $w = -1$
10. $b - 28 = 33$ $b = 61$ 11. $45 + f = 48$ $f = 3$ 12. $n + 7.1 = 8.6$ $n = 1.5$
13. $-14 + t = 26$ $t = 40$ 14. $d - 3.03 = 2$ $d = 5.03$ 15. $10 = z + 15$ $z = -5$
16. $c - 5.3 = -6.4$ $c = -1.1$ 17. $35 + p = 77$ $p = 42$ 18. $-15 = -15 + u$ $u = 0$

For Exercises 19 and 20, write an equation. Then solve the equation.
19. CAFFEINE A cup of brewed tea has 54 milligrams less caffeine than a cup of brewed coffee. If a cup of tea has 66 milligrams of caffeine, how much caffeine is in a cup of coffee?
$c - 54 = 66$; $c = 120$; A cup of coffee has 120 milligrams of caffeine.
20. GEOMETRY The sum of the measures of the angles of a trapezoid is 360°. Find the missing measure.
$d° + 100° + 110° + 80° = 360°$; $d° = 70°$

Chapter 3 18 Course 2

Word Problem Practice*
p. 19 OL AL

NAME ________ DATE ________ PERIOD ____

3-2 Word Problem Practice
Solving Addition and Subtraction Equations

ANIMALS For Exercises 1–4, use the table.
The average lifespans of several different types of animals are shown in the table.

Average Lifespans of Animals			
Animal	Lifespan (yr)	Animal	Lifespan (yr)
Black Bear	18	Guinea Pig	4
Dog	12	Puma	?
Giraffe	10	Tiger	16
Gray Squirrel	10	Zebra	?

1. The lifespan of a black bear is 3 years longer than the lifespan of a zebra. Write an addition equation that you could use to find the lifespan of a zebra.
$z + 3 = 18$
2. Solve the equation you wrote in Exercise 1. What is the lifespan of a zebra?
15 yr
3. The lifespan of a guinea pig is 8 years shorter than the lifespan of a puma. Write a subtraction equation that you could use to find the lifespan of a puma.
$p - 8 = 4$
4. Solve the equation you wrote in Exercise 3. What is the lifespan of a puma?
12 yr
5. TECHNOLOGY A survey of teens showed that teens in Pittsburgh aged 12-17 spend 15.8 hours per week online. Teens in Miami/Ft. Lauderdale spend 14.2 hours per week online. Write and solve an addition equation to find the difference in time spent online by teens in these cities. $14.2 + d = 15.8$; 1.6 hours per week
6. SPORTS Annika Sorenstam won the 2006 MasterCard Classic with a final score of 8 under par, or −8. Her scores for the first two of the three rounds were −5 and −1. What was Ms. Sorenstam's score for the third round?
−2

Chapter 3 19 Course 2

Enrichment
p. 20 OL AL

NAME ________ DATE ________ PERIOD ____

3-2 Enrichment
Equation Hexa-maze

This figure is called a *hexa-maze* because each cell has the shape of a hexagon, or six-sided figure.

To solve the maze, start with the number in the center. This number is the solution to the equation in one of the adjacent cells. Move to that cell. The number in the new cell will then be the solution to the equation in the next cell. At each move, you may only move to an adjacent cell. Each cell is used only once.

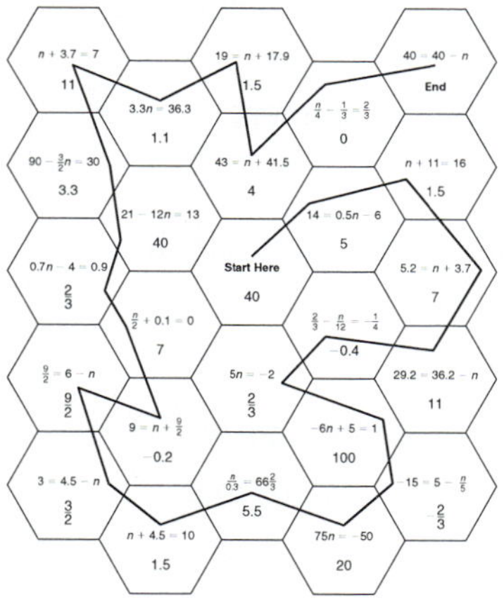

Chapter 3 20 Course 2

* Also available in Spanish ELL

Additional Lesson Resources

Transparencies
- *5-Minute Check Transparency,* Lesson 3-2

Other Print Products
- *Teaching Mathematics with Manipulatives*
- *Noteables™ Interactive Study Notebook with Foldables™*

Teacher Tech Tools
- *Interactive Classroom CD-ROM,* Lesson 3-2
- *AssignmentWorks,* Lesson 3-2

Student Tech Tools
glencoe.com
- Extra Examples, Chapter 3, Lesson 2
- Self-Check Quiz, Chapter 3, Lesson 2

3-2 Lesson Notes

1 Focus

Vertical Alignment

Before Lesson 3-2
Use a letter to represent an unknown number; write and evaluate simple algebraic expressions in one variable by substitution

Lesson 3-2
Write and solve one-step linear equations in one variable

After Lesson 3-2
Solve two-step linear equations and inequalities in one variable over the rational numbers

2 Teach

Scaffolding Questions

Either show a balance scale with 10 counters on each side or draw one on the board. As you ask the following questions, add or subtract the appropriate number of counters.

Ask:

- If I add 3 counters to the left side, how can I balance the scale? by adding 3 counters to the right side
- If I take away 5 counters from the right side, how can I balance the scale? by taking away 5 counters from the left side
- When the sides are in balance, how would you compare the number of counters on each side? The number of counters on the left equals the number of counters on the right.

3-2 Solving Addition and Subtraction Equations

MAIN IDEA

Solve addition and subtraction equations.

IN Academic Standards

Preparation for 7.2.2 Write and solve two-step linear equations and inequalities in one variable. *Also addresses 7.2.1, P.5.1, P.5.2, P.5.3.*

IN Math Online

glencoe.com

- Extra Examples
- Personal Tutor
- Self-Check Quiz
- Reading in the Content Area

GET READY for the Lesson

VIDEO GAMES Max had some video games, and then he bought two more games. Now he has six games.

1. What does x represent in the figure? number of games initially had
2. What addition equation is shown in the figure? $x + 2 = 6$
3. Explain how to solve the equation.
4. How many games did Max have in the beginning? 4

3. Find the number that when added to 2 is 6.

You can solve the equation $x + 2 = 6$ by *removing*, or subtracting, the same number of positive tiles from each side of the mat. You can also subtract 2 from each side of the equation. The variable is now by itself on one side of the equation.

Use Models

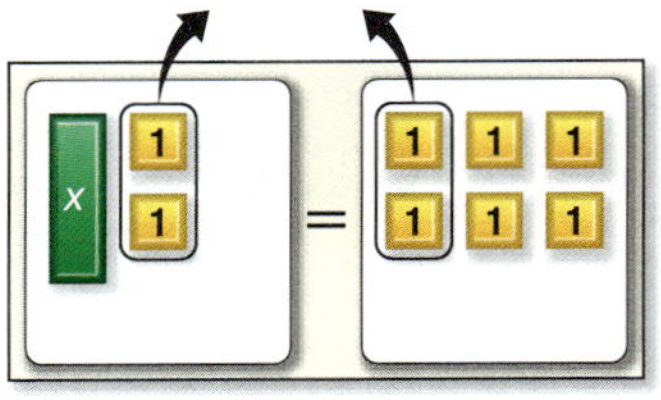

Use Symbols

$$\begin{aligned} x + 2 &= 6 \\ \underline{-2} &= \underline{-2} \\ x &= 4 \end{aligned}$$

Subtracting 2 from each side of an equation illustrates the Subtraction Property of Equality.

Subtraction Property of Equality — Key Concept

Words If you subtract the same number from each side of an equation, the two sides remain equal.

Symbols If $a = b$, then $a - c = b - c$.

Examples

Numbers	Algebra
$6 = 6$	$x + 2 = 6$
$-2 = -2$	$-2 = -2$
$4 = 4$	$x = 4$

Tips for New Teachers

Additive Inverses

When solving the addition equation $x + 2 = 6$, you can subtract 2 from each side of the equation. Subtracting 2 is the same as adding -2. Since 2 and -2 are additive inverses, the sum is 0 and the variable x is isolated on the left side of the equation.

EXAMPLES Solve Addition Equations

1 **Solve $x + 5 = 8$. Check your solution.**

$x + 5 = 8$	Write the equation.
$\underline{-5 = -5}$	Subtract 5 from each side.
$x = 3$	Simplify.

Check	$x + 5 = 8$	Write the original equation.
	$3 + 5 \stackrel{?}{=} 8$	Replace x with 3.
	$8 = 8$ ✓	The sentence is true.

The solution is 3.

2 **Solve $x + 6 = 4$. Check your solution.**

$x + 6 = 4$	Write the equation.
$\underline{-6 = -6}$	Subtract 6 from each side.
$x = -2$	Simplify.

The solution is -2. Check the solution.

Study Tip

Solutions Notice that your new equation, $x = 3$, has the same solution as the original equation, $x + 5 = 8$.

CHECK Your Progress

Solve each equation. Check your solution.

a. $y + 6 = 9$ **3** b. $x + 3 = 1$ **−2** c. $-3 = a + 4$ **−7**

Real-World EXAMPLE

3 **MARINE BIOLOGY** **Clownfish and angelfish are popular tropical fish. An angelfish can grow to be 12 inches long. If an angelfish is 8.5 inches longer than a clownfish, how long is a clownfish?**

Words	An angelfish	is	8.5 inches longer than		a clownfish.
Variable	Let c represent the length of the clownfish.				
Equation	12	=	8.5	+	c

$12 = 8.5 + c$	Write the equation.
$\underline{-8.5 = -8.5}$	Subtract 8.5 from each side.
$3.5 = c$	Simplify.

A clownfish is 3.5 inches long.

Real-World Career . . .
How Does a Marine Biologist Use Math?
A marine biologist uses math to analyze data about marine plants, animals, and organisms.

IN Math Online
For more information, go to: glencoe.com.

CHECK Your Progress

d. **WEATHER** The highest recorded temperature in Warsaw, Missouri, is 118°F. This is 158° greater than the lowest recorded temperature. Write and solve an equation to find the lowest recorded temperature. **$118 = 158 + t$; −40°F**

Focus on Mathematical Content

The **inverse operation** of addition is subtraction, and the inverse operation of subtraction is addition.

You can use inverse operations to **isolate the variable** in an algebraic equation, thus solving the equation.

Formative Assessment

Use the Check Your Progress exercises after each Example to determine students' understanding of concepts.

ADDITIONAL EXAMPLES

1. Solve $14 + y = 20$. Check your solution. 6
2. Solve $a + 7 = 6$. Check your solution. -1
3. **FRUIT** A grapefruit weighs 11 ounces, which is 6 ounces more than an apple. How much does the apple weigh? 5 ounces

Additional Examples are also in:

- Noteables™ Interactive Study Notebook with Foldables™
- Interactive Classroom PowerPoint® Presentations

Lesson 3-2 Solving Addition and Subtraction Equations **137**

ADDITIONAL EXAMPLES

4 Solve $12 = z - 8$. Check your solution. 20

5 **MUSIC** Vivian practiced the piano for 32 minutes. She practiced 11 minutes less than her brother did. How long did her brother practice the piano? 43 minutes

Similarly, you can use inverse operations and the Addition Property of Equality to solve equations like $x - 2 = 1$.

Vocabulary Link
Inverse
Everyday Use something that is opposite
Math Use undo

Addition Property of Equality

Key Concept

Words If you add the same number to each side of an equation, the two sides remain equal.

Symbols If $a = b$, then $a + c = b + c$.

Examples

Numbers	Algebra
$5 = 5$	$x - 2 = 4$
$+3 = +3$	$+2 = +2$
$8 = 8$	$x = 6$

EXAMPLE Solve a Subtraction Equation

4 **Solve $x - 2 = 1$. Check your solution.**

$x - 2 = 1$ Write the equation.
$+2 = +2$ Add 2 to each side.
$x = 3$ Simplify.

Check the solution. Since $3 - 2 = 1$, the solution is 3.

CHECK Your Progress

e. $y - 3 = 4$ **7** f. $r - 4 = -2$ **2** g. $q - 8 = -9$ **−1**

Real-World EXAMPLE

5 **SHOPPING** **A pair of shoes costs $25. This is $14 less than the cost of a pair of jeans. Find the cost of the jeans.**

Words	Shoes	are	$14 less than	jeans	
Variable	Let j represent the cost of jeans.				
Equation	25	=	j	−	14

$25 = j - 14$ Write the equation.
$+14 = +14$ Add 14 to each side.
$39 = j$ Simplify.

The jeans cost $39.

Study Tip
Check for Reasonableness Ask yourself which costs more: the shoes or the jeans. Then check your answer. Does it show that the jeans cost more than the shoes?

CHECK Your Progress

h. **ANIMALS** The average lifespan of a tiger is 22 years. This is 13 years less than a lion. Write and solve an equation to find the lifespan of a lion. $x - 13 = 22$; **35 years**

Pre-AP Activity Use after Example 5.

Remind students that subtracting an integer is the same as adding its opposite. For example, $2 - 5$ is the same as $2 + (-5)$. Have students use what they know about integers to compare the Subtraction and Addition Properties of Equality.

CHECK Your Understanding

Examples 1, 2 (p. 137)

Solve each equation. Check your solution.

1. $n + 6 = 8$ **2**
2. $7 = y + 2$ **5**
3. $m + 5 = 3$ **−2**
4. $-2 = a + 6$ **−8**

Example 3 (p. 137)

5. **FLYING** Orville and Wilbur Wright made the first airplane flights in 1903. Wilbur's flight was 364 feet. This was 120 feet longer than Orville's flight. Write and solve an equation to find the length of Orville's flight. **$d + 120 = 364$; 244 ft**

Example 4 (p. 138)

Solve each equation. Check your solution.

6. $x - 5 = 6$ **11**
7. $-1 = c - 6$ **5**

Example 5 (p. 138)

8. **PRESIDENTS** John F. Kennedy was the youngest president to be inaugurated. He was 43 years old. This was 26 years younger than the oldest president to be inaugurated—Ronald Reagan. Write and solve an equation to find how old Reagan was when he was inaugurated. **$43 = r - 26$; 69 years old**

Practice and Problem Solving

HOMEWORK HELP

For Exercises	See Examples
9–12	1
13–16	2
17–20	4
21–24	3, 5

Exercise Levels
A: 9–24
B: 25–45
C: 46–48

Solve each equation. Check your solution.

9. $a + 3 = 10$ **7**
10. $y + 5 = 11$ **6**
11. $9 = r + 2$ **7**
12. $14 = s + 7$ **7**
13. $x + 8 = 5$ **−3**
14. $y + 15 = 11$ **−4**
15. $r + 6 = -3$ **−9**
16. $k + 3 = -9$ **−12**
17. $s - 8 = 9$ **17**
18. $w - 7 = 11$ **18**
19. $-1 = q - 8$ **7**
20. $-2 = p - 13$ **11**

For Exercises 21–24, write an equation. Then solve the equation.

21. **MUSIC** Last week Tiffany practiced her bassoon a total of 7 hours. This was 2 hours more than she practiced the previous week. How many hours did Tiffany practice the previous week? **$7 = w + 2$; 5**

22. **CIVICS** In the 2004 presidential election, Ohio had 20 electoral votes. This is 14 votes less than Texas had. How many electoral votes did Texas have in 2004? **$20 = t - 14$; 34 votes**

23. **AGES** Zack is 15 years old. This is 3 years younger than his brother Tyler. How old is Tyler? **$15 = t - 3$; 18 years old**

24. **BASKETBALL** The Miami Heat scored 79 points in a recent game. This was 13 points less than the Chicago Bulls score. How many points did the Chicago Bulls score? **$x - 13 = 79$; $x = 92$**

3 Practice

Formative Assessment

Use Exercises 1–8 to check for understanding.

Then use the chart at the bottom of this page to customize your assignments for students.

Intervention You may wish to use the Study Guide and Intervention Master on page 16 of the *Chapter 3 Resource Masters* for additional reinforcement.

Odd/Even Assignments

Exercises 9–24 are structured so that students practice the same concepts whether they are assigned odd or even problems.

Differentiated Instruction

Kinesthetic Learners If students have difficulty, you may wish to have them model Exercises 9–20 with a balance and counters.

DIFFERENTIATED HOMEWORK OPTIONS

Level	Assignment	Two-Day Option	
BL Basic	9–24, 46, 48, 49–57	9–23 odd, 49, 50	10–24 even, 46, 48, 51–57
OL Core	9–19 odd, 21–24, 25–35 odd, 37–46, 48–57	9–24, 49, 50	25–46, 48, 51–57
AL Advanced/Pre-AP	25–53 (optional: 54–57)		

Solve each equation. Check your solution.

25. $34 + r = 95$ **61**
26. $64 + y = 84$ **20**
27. $-23 = x - 18$ **−5**
28. $-59 = m - 11$ **−48**
29. $-18 + c = -30$ **−12**
30. $-34 = t + 9$ **−43**
31. $a - 3.5 = 14.9$ **18.4**
32. $x - 2.8 = 9.5$ **12.3**
33. $r - 8.5 = -2.1$ **6.4**
34. $z - 9.4 = -3.6$ **5.8**
35. $n + 1.4 = 0.72$ **−0.68**
36. $b + 2.25 = 1$ **−1.25**

For Exercises 37–42, write an equation. Then solve the equation.

37. **MONEY** Suppose you have d dollars. After you pay your sister the $5 you owe her, you have $18 left. How much money did you have at the beginning? **$d - 5 = 18$; $23**

38. **MONEY** Suppose you have saved $38. How much more do you need to save to buy a small television that costs $65? **$38 + x = 65$; $27**

39. **GEOMETRY** The sum of the measures of the angles of a triangle is 180°. Find the missing measure.

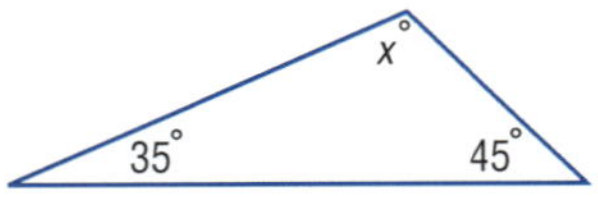

$35 + 45 + x = 180$; 100°

40. **VOLCANOES** Alaska, Hawaii, and Washington have active volcanoes. Alaska has 43, Hawaii has 5, and Washington has v. If they have 52 active volcanoes in all, how many volcanoes does Washington have? **$43 + 5 + v = 52$; 4 volcanoes**

41. **GOLF** The table shows Cristie Kerr's scores for four rounds of the 2007 U.S. Women's Open. Her total score was −5 (5 under par). What was her score for the third round? **$1 - 1 + s = -5$; −5**

Round	Score
First	0
Second	+1
Third	s
Fourth	−1

42. **BUSINESS** At the end of the day, the closing price of XYZ Stock was $62.87 per share. This was $0.62 less than the opening price. Find the opening price. **$62.87 = p - 0.62$; $63.49**

Real-World Link
Cristie Kerr donates $50.00 to breast cancer research for every birdie she makes.
Source: Birdies for Breast Cancer

ANALYZE TABLES **For Exercises 43–45, use the table.**

Tallest Wooden Roller Coasters	Height (feet)	Drop (feet)	Speed (mph)
Son of Beast	218	214	s
El Toro	181	176	70
The Rattler	180	d	65
Colossos	h	159	75
Voyage	163	154	67

Source: Coaster Grotto

43. The difference in speeds of Son of Beast and The Rattler is 13 miles per hour. If Son of Beast has the greater speed, write and solve a subtraction equation to find its speed. **$s - 65 = 13$; 78 mph.**

44. The Rattler has a drop that is 52 feet less than El Toro. Write and solve an addition equation to find the height of The Rattler. **$d + 52 = 176$; 124 ft**

45. Colossos is 13 feet taller than Voyage. Write and solve a subtraction equation to find the height of Colossos. **$h - 13 = 163$; 176 ft**

Academic Standards • ISTEP+
Extra Practice, pp. 674, 706

140 Chapter 3 Algebra: Linear Equations and Functions

H.O.T. Problems

46. $b + 5 = -8$; All of the other equations have solutions of -3. This solution is -13.

46. **Which One Doesn't Belong?** Identify the equation that does not have the same solution as the other three. Explain your reasoning.

$x - 1 = -4$	$b + 5 = -8$	$11 + y = 8$	$-6 + a = -9$

47. **CHALLENGE** Suppose $x + y = 11$ and the value of x increases by 2. If their sum remains the same, what must happen to the value of y? The value of y decreases by 2.

48. **WRITING IN MATH** Write a problem about a real-world situation that can be represented by the equation $p - 25 = 50$. See margin.

ISTEP+ PRACTICE

Preparation for 7.2.2, 7.21

49. The Oriental Pearl Tower in Shanghai, China, is 1,535 feet tall. It is 280 feet shorter than the Canadian National Tower in Toronto, Canada. Which equation can be used to find the height of the Canadian National Tower? C

A $1{,}535 + h = 280$

B $h = 1{,}535 - 280$

C $1{,}535 = h - 280$

D $280 - h = 1{,}535$

50. Which of the following statements is true concerning the equation $x + 3 = 7$? J

F To find the value of x, add 3 to each side.

G To find the value of x, add 7 to each side.

H To find the value of x, find the sum of 3 and 7.

J To find the value of x, subtract 3 from each side.

Spiral Review

51. **SCIENCE** The boiling point of water is 180° higher than its freezing point. If p represents the freezing point, write an expression that represents the boiling point of water. (Lesson 3-1) $p + 180$

52. **ALGEBRA** Evaluate the expression $xy \div (-4)$ if $x = 12$ and $y = -2$. (Lesson 2-8) 6

53. **ALGEBRA** The table shows the number of pages of a novel Ferguson read each hour. If the pattern continues, how many pages will Ferguson read during the 8th hour? (Lesson 2-7) 46 pages

Hour	Number of Pages Read
1	11
2	13
3	16
4	20
5	25

GET READY for the Next Lesson

PREREQUISITE SKILL Find each quotient.

54. $15.6 \div 13$ 1.2

55. $8.84 \div 3.4$ 2.6

56. $75.25 \div 0.25$ 301

57. $0.76 \div 0.5$ 1.52

4 Assess

Crystal Ball Tell students that tomorrow's lesson is about solving multiplication equations. Have students write how they think today's lesson will connect with tomorrow's.

Formative Assessment

Check for student understanding of concepts in Lessons 3-1 and 3-2.

CRM Quiz 1, p. 55

FOLDABLES Study Organizer Foldables™ Follow-Up

Remind students to take notes about today's lesson under the *Equations* tab of their Foldables. Encourage them to record the Addition and Subtraction Properties of Equality and give examples of how to use the properties to solve equations.

Additional Answer

48. Sample answer: An office building is 50 stories tall. Its height is 25 stories less than an apartment building. What is the height of the apartment building?

Lesson 3-2 Solving Addition and Subtraction Equations 141

3-3 Solving Multiplication Equations

PACING: **Regular:** 2 periods, **Block:** 1 period

IN Academic Standards **Preparation for 7.2.2** Write and solve two-step linear equations and inequalities in one variable. *Also addresses 7.2.1, P.5.1, P.5.2, P.5.3.*

Options for Differentiated Instruction

ELL = English Language Learner AL = Above or Beyond Grade Level SS = Struggling Students SN = Special Needs

Scaffolding the Lesson ELL SS SN

Use before presenting Lesson 3-3.

Scaffold this lesson by investigating the relationship between multiplication and division.

Ask:

- What is the relationship between multiplication and division? They are inverse operations.
- How is the relationship between multiplication and division like the relationship between addition and subtraction? Give some examples to help explain your reasoning. Like addition and subtraction, multiplication and division "undo" each other. For example, $8 \times 2 \div 2 = 8$ and $15 \div 3 \times 3 = 15$.
- How are addition and subtraction used to solve equations? How might multiplication and division be used to solve equations? To solve addition equations, you subtract; to solve subtraction equations, you add. Similarly, to solve multiplication equations, you divide; to solve division equations, you multiply.
- What division facts are related to the multiplication problem $3 \times 4 = 12$? $12 \div 3 = 4$ and $12 \div 4 = 3$

Students' Self-Monitoring SS

Use before presenting the Mini Lab.

Have students write the equation given in the beginning of the Mini Lab, $3x = 6$.

- Before beginning the activity, have students write down what they do not yet know about solving an equation like this one. For example, they may not know how to find the value of x.
- After completing the activity, have students look over what they wrote. Are there things they still need to learn?

Visual Clues SS SN

Use before assigning the Exercises.

When solving multiplication equations, have students circle the coefficient of the variable as a visual cue of what they will be dividing by. This will be particularly helpful when the variable is not the first term in the equation.

1. $(6)c = 18$ **2.** $15 = (3)z$ **3.** $(-8)x = 24$ **4.** $(-9)r = -36$

Leveled Lesson Resources

Also on TeacherWorks™ Lesson 3-3

Chapter 3 Resource Masters

BL = Below or Approaching Grade Level   OL = On Grade Level   AL = Above or Beyond Grade Level   ELL = English Language Learner

Lesson Reading Guide
p. 22 BL OL ELL

NAME ______ DATE ______ PERIOD ______

3-3 Lesson Reading Guide
Solving Multiplication Equations

Get Ready for the Lesson

Complete the Mini Lab at the top of page 142 in your textbook. Write your answers below.

Solve each equation using models or a drawing.
1-5. See students' models or drawings. Solutions are given.

1. $3x = 12$ **4** 2. $2x = -8$ **−4**

3. $4x = 20$ **5** 4. $8 = 2x$ **4** 5. $3x = -9$ **−3**

6. What operation did you use to find each solution? **division**

7. How can you use the coefficient of x to solve $8x = 40$? **Divide each side by 8.**

Read the Lesson

8. Complete each sentence.
   a. To solve $4x = 36$, divide each side by ______. **4**
   b. To solve $-27 = -3d$, divide each side by ______. **−3**
   c. To solve $15h = -75$, divide each side by ______. **15**
   d. To solve $-8a = 96$, divide each side by ______. **−8**

9. Write and solve two different equations that both require you to divide each side by −2 in order to solve. **Sample answer: $-2b = 14$, $b = -7$; $26 = -2y$, $y = -13$**

Remember What You Learned

10. In your own words, define the Division Property of Equality. Describe a real-life situation in which you may need to use the Division Property of Equality. **Sample answer: When you divide each side of an equation by the same nonzero number, the two sides remain equal. Suppose you have 25 pieces of candy to share amongst 4 friends. This is represented by the equation $5c = 25$ where $c = 5$, so you and your 4 friends get 5 pieces of candy each.**

Chapter 3 22 Course 2

Study Guide and Intervention*
p. 23 BL OL ELL

NAME ______ DATE ______ PERIOD ______

3-3 Study Guide and Intervention
Solving Multiplication Equations

If each side of an equation is divided by the same non-zero number, the resulting equation is equivalent to the given one. You can use this property to solve equations involving multiplication and division.

Example 1 Solve $45 = 5x$. Check your solution.

$45 = 5x$ Write the equation.
$\frac{45}{5} = \frac{5x}{5}$ Divide each side of the equation by 5.
$9 = x$ $45 \div 5 = 9$

Check $45 = 5x$ Write the original equation.
$45 \stackrel{?}{=} 5(9)$ Replace x with 9. Is this sentence true?
$45 = 45$ ✓

The solution is 9.

Example 2 Solve $-21 = -3y$. Check your solution.

$-21 = -3y$ Write the equation.
$\frac{-21}{-3} = \frac{-3y}{-3}$ Divide each side by −3.
$7 = y$ $-21 \div (-3) = 7$

Check $-21 = -3y$ Write the original equation.
$-21 \stackrel{?}{=} -3(7)$ Replace y with 7. Is this sentence true?
$-21 = -21$ ✓

The solution is 7.

Exercises

Solve each equation. Then check your solution.

1. $8q = 56$ **7** 2. $4p = 32$ **8** 3. $42 = 6m$ **7** 4. $104 = 13h$ **8**
5. $-6n = 30$ **−5** 6. $18x = 36$ **−2** 7. $48 = -8y$ **−6** 8. $72 = -3b$ **−24**
9. $-9a = -45$ **5** 10. $12m = -120$ **10** 11. $66 = -11t$ **6** 12. $-144 = -9r$ **16**
13. $3a = 4.5$ **1.5** 14. $2h = 3.8$ **1.9** 15. $4.9 = 0.7k$ **7** 16. $9.75 = 2.5z$ **3.9**

Chapter 3 23 Course 2

Skills Practice*
p. 24 BL OL

NAME ______ DATE ______ PERIOD ______

3-3 Skills Practice
Solving Multiplication Equations

Solve each equation. Check your solution.

1. $4c = 16$ **4** 2. $10x = 50$ **5** 3. $42 = 6s$ **7**
4. $9c = 45$ **5** 5. $49 = 7y$ **7** 6. $11t = 44$ **4**
7. $15a = 60$ **4** 8. $72 = 12c$ **6** 9. $18x = 162$ **9**
10. $14d = 154$ **11** 11. $24z = 288$ **12** 12. $16c = 256$ **16**
13. $-5b = 40$ **−8** 14. $32 = -2f$ **−16** 15. $-9x = -63$ **7**
16. $4g = -52$ **−13** 17. $-5x = -85$ **17** 18. $-63 = 7a$ **−9**
19. $0.6m = 1.8$ **3** 20. $1.5z = 6$ **4** 21. $0.6q = 3.6$ **6**
22. $1.8a = 0.9$ **0.5** 23. $1.2r = 4.8$ **4** 24. $2.4 = 0.2t$ **12**

Chapter 3 24 Course 2

Practice*
p. 25 OL AL

NAME ______ DATE ______ PERIOD ______

3-3 Practice
Solving Multiplication Equations

Solve each equation. Check your solution.

1. $8e = 32$ **$e = 4$** 2. $4v = -8$ **$v = -2$** 3. $7k = -7$ **$k = -1$**
4. $18 = 3y$ **$y = 6$** 5. $4j = 0$ **$j = 0$** 6. $-11x = -44$ **$x = 4$**
7. $5a = 5$ **$a = 1$** 8. $-1c = 8$ **$c = -8$** 9. $15 = 5b$ **$b = 3$**
10. $-2w = -14$ **$w = 7$** 11. $9f = 45$ **$f = 5$** 12. $13m = -26$ **$m = -2$**
13. $1.4t = 2.8$ **$t = 2$** 14. $0.9g = 5.4$ **$g = 6$** 15. $2.5 = 0.5h$ **$h = 5$**
16. $3.74 = 1.7d$ **$d = 2.2$** 17. $4.1z = 16.81$ **$z = 4.1$** 18. $5.2q = 3.64$ **$q = 0.7$**

For Exercises 19 and 20, write an equation. Then solve the equation.

19. TRAVEL A cheetah can travel at an amazing speed of 32 meters per second when chasing its prey. At that rate, how long would it take the cheetah to run 2,000 meters? **$2{,}000 = 32t$; $t = 62.5$; It would take the cheetah 62.5 seconds to run 2000 meters.**

20. AUTO LOAN Mrs. Kim borrowed $1,350 to buy a used automobile. If she repays $75 a month, how many months will it take to pay back the loan? **$75m = 1{,}350$; $m = 18$; It will take Mrs. Kim 18 months to repay the loan.**

Chapter 3 25 Course 2

Word Problem Practice*
p. 26 OL AL

NAME ______ DATE ______ PERIOD ______

3-3 Word Problem Practice
Solving Multiplication Equations

1. TRAVEL The speed limit on an Arizona highway is 75 miles per hour. Suppose a truck traveling at the speed limit drives 225 miles before the driver stops for a break. Write a multiplication equation to find the length of time the truck has traveled. **$75t = 225$**

2. TRAVEL Solve the equation you wrote in Exercise 1. How long did the truck travel? **3 h**

3. FLOWERS A gardening expert recommends that flower bulbs be planted to a depth of three times their height. Suppose Jenna determines that a certain bulb should be planted at a depth of 4.5 inches. Write a multiplication equation to find the height of the bulb. **$3h = 4.5$**

4. FLOWERS Solve the equation you wrote in Exercise 3. What is the height of the bulb? **1.5 in.**

5. EXERCISE A 125-pound person uses 4.4 Calories per minute when walking. Write a multiplication equation to find the number of minutes of walking it will take for a 125-pound person to use 198 Calories. **$4.4m = 198$**

6. EXERCISE Solve the equation you wrote in Exercise 5. How many minutes of walking it will take for a 125-pound person to use 198 Calories? **45 min**

7. ELECTRICITY The electric company charges $0.06 per kilowatt hour of electricity used. Write a multiplication equation to find the number of kilowatt hours of electricity for which the Estevez family was charged if their electric bill was $45.84. **$0.06k = 45.84$**

8. ELECTRICITY Solve the equation you wrote in Exercise 7. For how many kilowatt hours of electricity was the Estevez family charged? **764 kilowatt h**

Chapter 3 26 Course 2

Enrichment
p. 27 OL AL

NAME ______ DATE ______ PERIOD ______

3-3 Enrichment
Direct Variation

Equations of the form $y = ax$ and $y = x \div a$ can be used to show how one quantity varies with another. Here are two examples.

Driving at a speed of 50 miles per hour, the distance you travel d varies directly with the time you are on the road t. The longer you drive, the farther you get. $d = 50t$

It is also the case that the time t varies directly with the distance d. The farther you drive, the more time it takes. $t = \frac{d}{50}$

Complete the equation for each situation. Then describe the relationship in words.

1. If you go on a diet and lose 2 pounds a month, after a certain number of months m, you will have lost p pounds. **$p = 2m$; The longer you diet, the more weight you will lose.**

2. You and your family are deciding between two different places for your summer vacation. You plan to travel by car and estimate you will average 55 miles per hour. The distance traveled d will result in a travel time of t hours. **$t = \frac{d}{55}$; The farther you drive, the more time it will take.**

3. You find that you are spending more than you had planned on renting video movies. It costs $2.00 to rent each movie. You can use the total amount spent a to find the number of movies you have rented m. **$m = \frac{a}{2}$; The greater the amount spent, the more movies rented.**

4. You spend $30 a month to take the bus to school. After a certain number of months m, you will have spent a total of dollars d on transportation to school. **$d = 30m$; The longer you ride the bus, the more you will spend.**

5. You are saving money for some new athletic equipment and have 12 weeks before the season starts. The amount you need to save each week s will depend on the cost c of the equipment you want to buy. **$s = \frac{c}{12}$; The more expensive the equipment, the more money must be saved each week.**

Chapter 3 27 Course 2

Additional Lesson Resources

* Also available in Spanish ELL

Transparencies

- *5-Minute Check Transparency*, Lesson 3-3

Other Print Products

- *Teaching Mathematics with Manipulatives*
- *Noteables™ Interactive Study Notebook with Foldables™*

Teacher Tech Tools

- *Interactive Classroom CD-ROM*, Lesson 3-3
- *AssignmentWorks*, Lesson 3-3

Student Tech Tools

glencoe.com

- Extra Examples, Chapter 3, Lesson 3
- Self-Check Quiz, Chapter 3, Lesson 3

3-3 Lesson Notes

1 Focus

Vertical Alignment

Before Lesson 3-3
Write and solve one-step linear equations in one variable

Lesson 3-3
Write and solve one-step linear equations in one variable; solve problems involving rates, average speed, distance, and time

After Lesson 3-3
Solve two-step linear equations and inequalities in one variable over the rational numbers

2 Teach

MINI Lab

Make sure students understand how the model represents the equation $3x = 6$.

Scaffolding Questions

Remind students that yesterday's lesson involved inverse operations.

Ask:

- What is the inverse operation of addition? subtraction
- What is the inverse operation of subtraction? addition
- What is the inverse operation of multiplication? division
- How can you use division to solve a multiplication equation? Sample answer: Since division is the inverse operation of multiplication, you can undo multiplication by dividing.

3-3 Solving Multiplication Equations

MAIN IDEA

Solve multiplication equations.

IN Academic Standards

Preparation for 7.2.2 Write and solve two-step linear equations and inequalities in one variable. *Also addresses 7.2.1, P.5.1, P.5.2, P.5.3.*

New Vocabulary

formula

IN Math Online

glencoe.com

- Concepts In Motion
- Extra Examples
- Personal Tutor
- Self-Check Quiz

MINI Lab

MONEY Suppose three friends order an appetizer of nachos that costs \$6. They agree to split the cost equally. The figure below illustrates the multiplication equation $3x = 6$, where x represents the amount each friend pays.

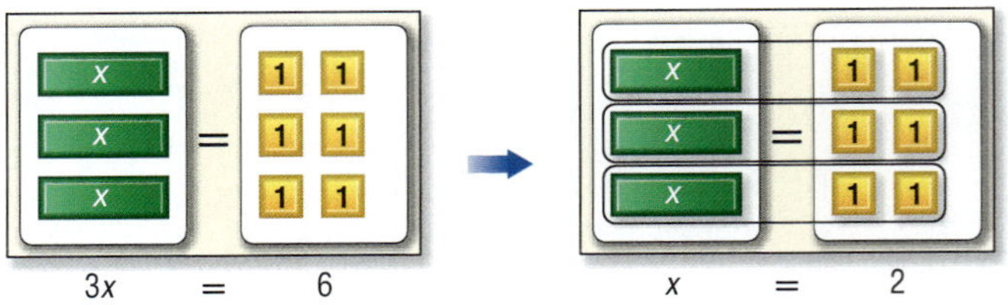

Each friend pays \$2. The solution of $3x = 6$ is 2.

Solve each equation using models or a drawing. 1–5. See Ch. 3 Answer Appendix.

1. 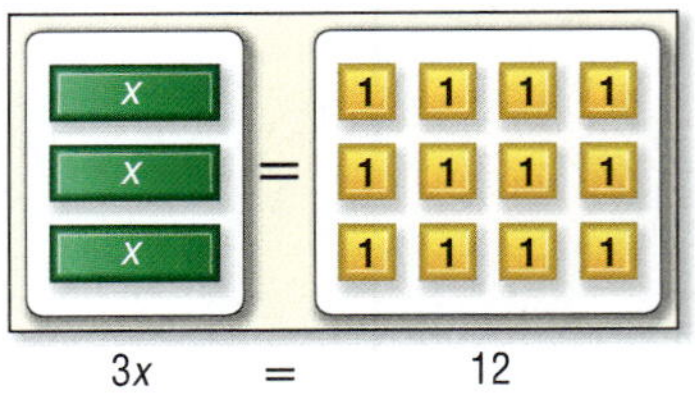

2. 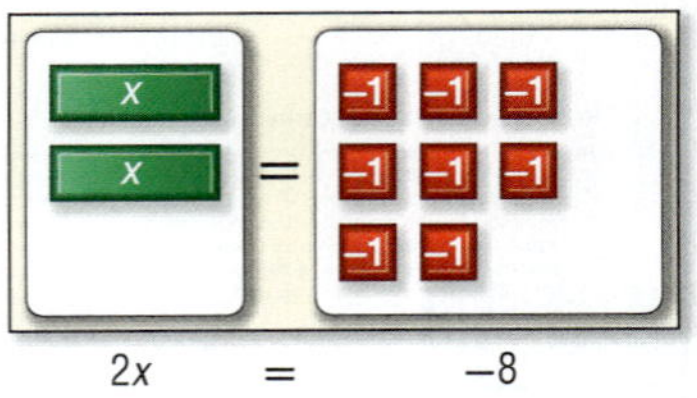

3. $4x = 20$
4. $8 = 2x$
5. $3x = -9$
6. What operation did you use to find each solution? division
7. How can you use the coefficient of x to solve $8x = 40$?

7. divide each side by 8

Equations like $3x = 6$ are called multiplication equations because the expression $3x$ means 3 *times the value of x*. So, you can use the Division Property of Equality to solve multiplication equations.

Division Property of Equality — Key Concept

Words If you divide each side of an equation by the same nonzero number, the two sides remain equal.

Symbols If $a = b$ and $c \neq 0$, then $\frac{a}{c} = \frac{b}{c}$.

Examples

Numbers	Algebra
$8 = 8$	$2x = -6$
$\frac{8}{2} = \frac{8}{2}$	$\frac{2x}{2} = \frac{-6}{2}$
$4 = 4$	$x = -3$

142 Chapter 3 Algebra: Linear Equations and Functions

Review Vocabulary

coefficient the numerical factor for a multiplication expression; Example: the coefficient of x in the expression $4x$ is 4. (Lesson 1-4)

EXAMPLES Solve Multiplication Equations

1 **Solve $20 = 4x$. Check your solution.**

$20 = 4x$	Write the equation.
$\frac{20}{4} = \frac{4x}{4}$	Divide each side of the equation by 4.
$5 = x$	$20 \div 4 = 5$
The solution is 5.	Check the solution.

2 **Solve $-8y = 24$. Check your solution.**

$-8y = 24$	Write the equation.
$\frac{-8y}{-8} = \frac{24}{-8}$	Divide each side by -8.
$y = -3$	$24 \div (-8) = -3$
The solution is -3.	Check the solution.

CHECK Your Progress

Solve each equation. Check your solution.

a. $30 = 6x$ **5** b. $-6a = 36$ **-6** c. $-9d = -72$ **8**

Many real-world situations increase at a constant rate. These can be represented by multiplication equations.

Real-World EXAMPLE

3 **TEXT MESSAGING** **It costs $0.10 to send a text message. You can spend a total of $5.00. How many text messages can you send?**

Words	Total	is equal to	cost of each message	times	number of messages.
Variable	Let m represent the number of messages you can send.				
Equation	5.00	=	0.10	•	m

$5.00 = 0.10m$	Write the equation.
$\frac{5.00}{0.10} = \frac{0.10m}{0.10}$	Divide each side by 0.10.
$50 = m$	$5.00 \div 0.10 = 50$

At $0.10 per message, you can send 50 text messages for $5.00.

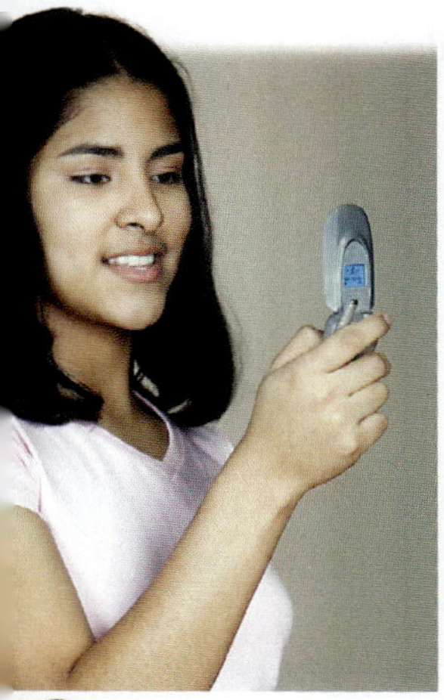

Real-World Link . . . . Over 60% of teenagers' text messages are sent from their homes—even when a landline is available.
Source: Xerox

CHECK Your Progress

d. **TRAVEL** Mrs. Acosta's car can travel an average of 24 miles on each gallon of gasoline. Write and solve an equation to find how many gallons of gasoline she will need for a trip of 348 miles.

d. $24x = 348$; 14.5 gal

Focus on Mathematical Content

Dividing each side of an equation by the same nonzero number maintains the equation.

Rate problems can be shown with multiplication equations.

Formative Assessment

Use the Check Your Progress exercises after each Example to determine students' understanding of concepts.

ADDITIONAL EXAMPLES

1 Solve $39 = 3y$. Check your solution. **13**

2 Solve $-4z = 60$. Check your solution. **-15**

3 **MAIL** Serena went to the post office to mail some party invitations. She had $6.15. If each invitation needed a $0.41 stamp, how many invitations could she mail? **15**

Additional Examples are also in:

- Noteables™ Interactive Study Notebook with Foldables™
- Interactive Classroom PowerPoint® Presentations

Tips for New Teachers — Solving Equations

Remind students that to solve an algebraic equation, they need to find a value for the variable that makes the equation true. That is, they need to isolate the variable on one side of the equals sign. They can do this by "undoing" any operation performed with the variable. When students "undo" multiplication by dividing each side of the equation by the same number, they are using the Division Property of Equality.

FOLDABLES Study Organizer — Foldables™ Follow-Up

Remind students to take notes about today's lesson under the *Equations* tab of their Foldables. Encourage them to record the Division Property of Equality and give examples of how to use the property to solve equations.

Lesson 3-3 Solving Multiplication Equations **143**

ADDITIONAL EXAMPLE

4 **SWIMMING** Ms. Wang swims at a speed of 0.6 mph. At this rate, how long will it take her to swim 3 miles? 5 hours

Tips for New Teachers

Choosing Your Method

Point out to students the benefit of choosing Method 2 in solving Example 4. By solving the equation for *t*, you can solve similar problems more quickly. Given a distance of 250 miles and a rate of 60 miles per hour, you can quickly substitute *d* and *r* into the equation $\frac{d}{r} = t$ to find *t*.

3 Practice

Formative Assessment

Use Exercises 1–6 to check for understanding.

Then use the chart at the bottom of the next page to customize your assignments for students.

Intervention You may wish to use the Study Guide and Intervention Master on page 23 of the *Chapter 3 Resource Masters* for additional reinforcement.

A **formula** is an equation that shows the relationship among certain quantities. One of the most common formulas is the equation $d = rt$, which gives the relationship among distance d, rate r, and time t.

Reading Math

Speed Another name for *rate* is *speed*.

Real-World EXAMPLE

4 **ANIMALS** **The tortoise is one of the slowest land animals, reaching an average top speed of about 0.25 mile per hour. At this speed, how long will it take a tortoise to travel 1.5 miles?**

You are asked to find the time t it will take to travel a distance d of 1.5 miles at a rate r of 0.25 mile per hour.

METHOD 1 **Substitute, then solve.**

$d = rt$ Write the equation.

$1.5 = 0.25t$ Replace d with 1.5 and r with 0.25.

$\frac{1.5}{0.25} = \frac{0.25t}{0.25}$ Divide each side by 0.25.

$6 = t$ $1.5 \div 0.25 = 6$

METHOD 2 **Solve, then substitute.**

$d = rt$ Write the equation.

$\frac{d}{r} = \frac{rt}{r}$ Divide each side by r to solve the equation for t.

$\frac{d}{r} = t$ Simplify.

$\frac{1.5}{0.25} = t$ Replace d with 1.5 and r with 0.25.

$6 = t$ $1.5 \div 0.25 = 6$

It would take a tortoise 6 hours to travel 1.5 miles.

CHOOSE Your Method

e. **SCIENCE** A sound wave travels a distance of 700 meters in 2.5 seconds. Find the average speed of the sound wave. **280 m/s**

★ indicates multi-step problem

CHECK Your Understanding

Examples 1, 2 (p. 143) **Solve each equation. Check your solution.**

1. $6c = 18$ **3**
2. $15 = 3z$ **5**
3. $-8x = 24$ **−3**
4. $-9r = -36$ **4**

Example 3 (p. 143)

5. **WORKING** Antonia earns $6 per hour helping her grandmother. How many hours does she need to work to earn $48? **8 h**

Example 4 (p. 144)

6. **SWIMMING** A shark can swim at an average speed of about 25 miles per hour. At this rate, how long will it take a shark to swim 60 miles? **2.4 hours**

144 Chapter 3 Algebra: Linear Equations and Functions

Practice and Problem Solving

HOMEWORK HELP	
For Exercises	See Examples
7–12	1
13–18	2
19–20	3
21–22	4

Exercise Levels
A: 7–22
B: 23–32
C: 33–37

Solve each equation. Check your solution.

7. $7a = 49$ **7**
8. $9e = 27$ **3**
9. $2x = -6$ **−3**
10. $3y = -21$ **−7**
11. $35 = 5v$ **7**
12. $72 = 12r$ **6**
13. $-4j = 36$ **−9**
14. $-12y = 60$ **−5**
15. $-4s = -16$ **4**
16. $-6z = -36$ **6**
17. $48 = -6r$ **−8**
18. $-28 = -7f$ **4**

For Exercises 19–22, write an equation. Then solve the equation.

19. **MONEY** Brandy wants to buy a digital camera that costs $300. If she saves $15 each week, in how many weeks will she have enough money for the camera? **$15w = 300$; 20 weeks**

20. **COMPUTERS** The width of a computer monitor is 1.25 times as long as its height. Find the height of the computer monitor at the right. **$1.25x = 15$; $x = 12$ in.**

21. **SPEED** A racecar can travel at a rate of 205 miles per hour. At this rate, how long would it take to travel 615 miles? **3 h**

22. **INSECTS** A dragonfly, the fastest insect, can fly a distance of 50 feet in about 2 seconds. Find a dragonfly's average speed in feet per second. **$50 = 2r$; 25 feet per second**

Solve each equation. Check your solution.

23. $0.4x = 9.2$ **23**
24. $0.9y = 13.5$ **15**
25. $5.4 = 0.3p$ **18**
26. $9.72 = 1.8a$ **5.4**
27. $3.9y = 18.33$ **4.7**
28. $2.6b = 2.08$ **0.8**

ANALYZE TABLES **For Exercises 29 and 30, use the following information.** The table shows women's championship record holders for several track events.

29. Without calculating explain whether Evelyn Ashford or Sanya Richards has the faster average speed.

30. Find the average speed of each athlete in meters per second. Round to the nearest hundredth.

Name	Race (m)	Time (s)
Evelyn Ashford	200	21.88
Sanya Richards	400	49.27

Source: USA Outdoor Track & Field

29. Sample answer: Evelyn Ashford has the faster average speed. Her race is half the distance as Sanya Richards', and it took her less than half the time as Sanya Richards to complete the race.

30. Evelyn Ashford 9.14 m/s; Sanya Richards 8.12 m/s

31. **HURRICANES** A category 3 hurricane reaches speeds up to 20.88 kilometers per hour. The distance from Cuba to Key West is 145 kilometers. Write and solve a multiplication equation to find how long it would take a category 3 hurricane to travel from Cuba to Key West. **$20.88h = 145$; $h \approx 6.94$**

32. ★ **WATER** A case of water bottles costs $9.48. If there are 12 water bottles in the case, find the cost per bottle. Then find the decrease in cost per bottle if the cost of a case is reduced to $8.64. **$0.79; $0.07**

Academic Standards • ISTEP+

Extra Practice, pp. 674, 706

Odd/Even Assignments

Exercises 7–22 are structured so that students practice the same concepts whether they are assigned odd or even problems.

DIFFERENTIATED HOMEWORK OPTIONS

Level	Assignment	Two-Day Option	
BL Basic	7–22, 33, 35–45	7–21 odd, 38–39	8–22 even, 33, 35–37, 40–45
OL Core	7–17 odd, 19–22, 23–27 odd, 29–33, 35–45	7–22, 38–39	23–33, 35–37, 40–45
AL Advanced/Pre-AP	23–44 (optional: 45)		

Exercise Alert!

Find the Error In Exercise 33, Steve is correct. Becky divided each side of the equation by 6 rather than by −6. Remind students to pay attention to the signs of coefficients when deciding how to solve an equation.

4 Assess

Ticket Out the Door Write the rate formula ($d = rt$) on the board. Have students write their own rate problem.

Additional Answers

35. Sample answer: Billie has twice as many cards as Tyree. If Billie has 16 cards, how many does Tyree have?

36. Sample answer: Three coins of the same value are worth 75 cents. How much is each coin worth?

37. Sample answer: If it takes a scuba diver 4 seconds to swim 8 meters below the surface of the water, what is the rate of descent?

45.

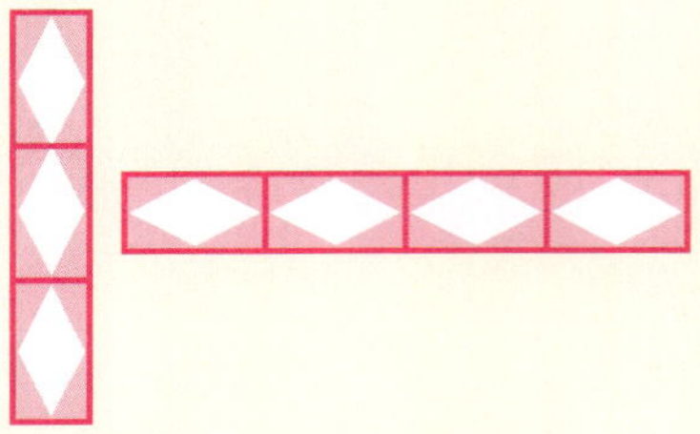

H.O.T. Problems

33. Steve; the variable is multiplied by −6. To solve for x, you need to divide each side of the equation by the entire coefficient, −6.

34. The absolute value of a positive or negative number is always positive. So, $x = 4$ or $x = -4$.

33. **FIND THE ERROR** Steve and Becky are solving $-6x = 72$. Who is correct? Explain.

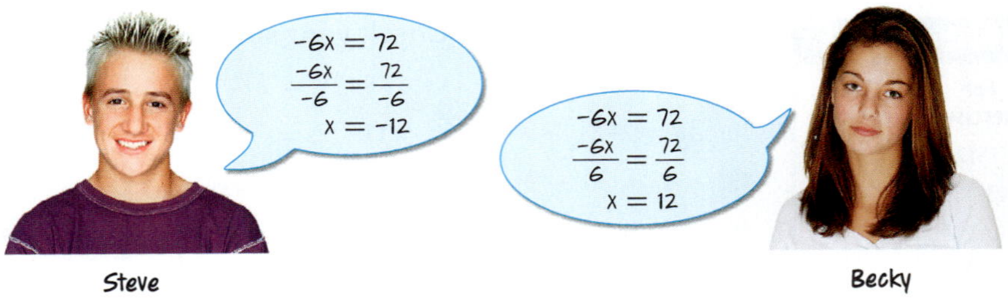

34. **CHALLENGE** Solve $3|x| = 12$. Explain your reasoning.

WRITING IN MATH Write a real-world problem that could be represented by each equation. 35–37. See margin.

35. $2x = 16$ 36. $3x = 75$ 37. $4x = -8$

ISTEP+ PRACTICE Preparation for 7.2.2, 7.2.1

38. A football player can run 20 yards in 3.4 seconds. Which equation could be used to find y, the number of yards the football player can run in a second? **C**

A $20y = 3.4$

B $3.4 - y = 20$

C $3.4y = 20$

D $20 + y = 3.4$

39. **SHORT RESPONSE** Use the formula $A = bh$ to find the base in inches of a rhombus with a height of 7 inches and an area of 56 square inches. **8**

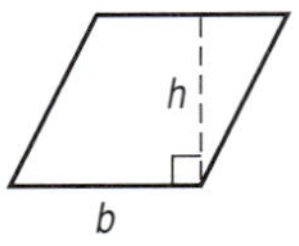

Spiral Review

ALGEBRA Solve each equation. Check your solution. (Lesson 3-2)

40. $y + 8 = -2$ **−10** 41. $x - 7 = -2$ **5** 42. $20 = z + 23$ **−3**

43. **ALGEBRA** Write an algebraic expression for the phrase *the product of −3 and y.* (Lesson 3-1) **$-3y$**

★ 44. **MONTHS** A lunar month, the time from one new moon to the next, is 29.5 days. How many days longer is our calendar year of 365 days than 12 lunar months? (Lesson 1-1) **11 days**

GET READY for the Next Lesson

PREREQUISITE SKILL Draw the next two figures in the pattern. (Lesson 2-7) See margin.

45.

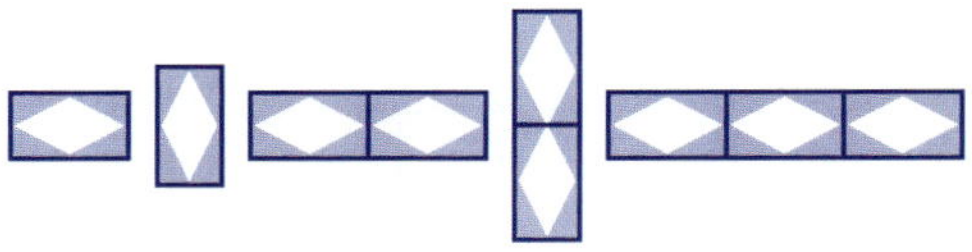

Pre-AP Activity Use after Exercise 37

Write a two-part equation such as $3x - 4 = 41$ on the board. Have students write what steps they would take to solve it.

146 Chapter 3 Algebra: Linear Equations and Functions

Mid-Chapter Quiz

Lessons 3-1 through 3-3

IN Academic Standards
7.2.1

Write each sentence as an algebraic equation. (Lesson 3-1)

1. The product of a number and 3 is -16. **1. $3n = -16$**
2. 10 less than a number is 45. **$n - 10 = 45$**

3. **CLIMBING** A rock climber is at an altitude of a feet before she climbs up another 80 feet. Write an expression for her new altitude. (Lesson 3-1) **$a + 80$**

4. **MULTIPLE CHOICE** Stephanie has 5 dollars more than Necie. If Necie has d dollars, which expression represents the number of dollars Stephanie has? (Lesson 3-1) **B**

   A $d - 5$ C $5 - d$

   B $d + 5$ D $5d$

Solve each equation. Check your solution. (Lesson 3-2)

5. $21 + m = 33$ **12**
6. $a - 5 = -12$ **-7**
7. $p + 1.7 = -9.8$ **-11.5**
8. $56 = k - (-33)$ **23**

9. **GEOMETRY** The sum of the measures of the angles of a triangle is 180°. Write and solve an equation to find the missing measure m. (Lesson 3-2) **$45 + 20 + m = 180$; 115°**

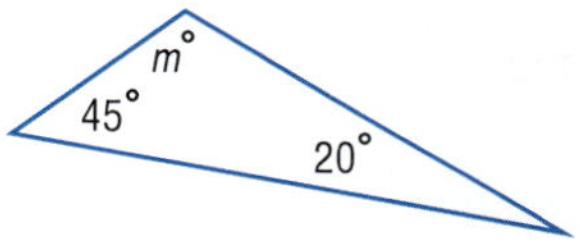

10. **MULTIPLE CHOICE** Trevor's test score was 5 points lower than Ursalina's test score. If Ursalina scored 85 on the test, which equation would give Trevor's score d when solved? (Lesson 3-2) **F**

    F $85 = d + 5$

    G $d - 5 = 85$

    H $80 = d + 5$

    J $d - 5 = 80$

11. **PETS** Cameron has 11 adult Fantail goldfish. This is 7 fewer Fantail goldfish than his friend Julia has. Write and solve a subtraction equation to determine the number of Fantail goldfish g that Julia has. (Lesson 3-2) **$11 = g - 7$; 18 Fantail goldfish**

12. **MEASUREMENT** The Grand Canyon has a maximum depth of almost 5,280 feet. An average four-story apartment building has a height of 66 feet. Write and solve a multiplication equation to determine the number of apartment buildings b, stacked on top of each other, that would fill the depth of the Grand Canyon. (Lesson 3-3) **$66b = 5{,}280$; $b = 80$**

Solve each equation. Check your solution. (Lesson 3-3)

13. $5f = -75$ **-15**
14. $-1.6w = 4.8$ **-3**
15. $63 = 7y$ **9**
16. $-28 = -2d$ **14**
17. $3.7g = -4.44$ **-1.2**
18. $2.25 = 1.5b$ **1.5**

19. **MULTIPLE CHOICE** Michelann drove 44 miles per hour and covered a distance of 154 miles. Which equation accurately describes this situation if h represents the number of hours Michelann drove? (Lesson 3-3) **B**

    A $154 = 44 + h$

    B $44h = 154$

    C $154 = 44 \div h$

    D $h - 44 = 154$

20. **LAWN SERVICE** Trey estimates he will earn \$470 next summer cutting lawns in his neighborhood. This amount is 2.5 times the amount a he earned this summer. Write and solve a multiplication equation to find how much Trey earned this summer. (Lesson 3-3) **$2.5a = 470$; \$188**

CHAPTER 3 Mid-Chapter Quiz

Formative Assessment

Use the Mid-Chapter Quiz to assess students' progress in the first half of the chapter.

Have students review the lesson indicated for the problems they answered incorrectly.

Summative Assessment

CRM Mid-Chapter Test, p. 57

ExamView Assessment Suite — Customize and create multiple versions of your Mid-Chapter Test and their answer keys.

FOLDABLES Study Organizer — **Dinah Zike's Foldables**

Before students complete the Mid-Chapter Quiz, encourage them to review the information on the first two pages of their Foldables.

Data-Driven Decision Making

Diagnostic Teaching Based on the results of the Chapter 3 Mid-Chapter Quiz, use the following to review concepts that students continue to find challenging.

Exercises	Lesson	Academic Standards	Resources for Review
1–4	3–1	7.2.1	CRM Study Guide and Intervention pp. 10, 16, and 23 IN Math Online glencoe.com • Extra Examples • Personal Tutor • Concepts in Motion
5–11	3–2	7.2.2	
12–20	3–3	7.2.2	

3-4 Problem-Solving Investigation
WORK BACKWARD

PACING: **Regular:** 1 period, **Block:** 0.5 period

IN Academic Standards **7.3.4 Recognize, describe, or extend geometric patterns** using tables, graphs, words, or symbols. **P.1.3 Apply and adapt a variety of appropriate strategies to solve problems.**

Options for Differentiated Instruction

ELL = English Language Learner   AL = Above or Beyond Grade Level   SS = Struggling Students   SN = Special Needs

Relating to Everyday Tasks ELL SS SN

Use before presenting Lesson 3-4.

Have students list the steps they would take to put on their socks and tennis shoes. Their steps might be similar to those shown to the right.

Step	Action
1	Put on my right sock.
2	Put on my left sock.
3	Put on my right tennis shoe.
4	Tie my right tennis shoe.
5	Put on my left tennis shoe.
6	Tie my left tennis shoe.

Ask:

- If you were to work backward to take off your socks and shoes, what would be the first step? List the remaining steps.
- Would it make sense for you to take off your socks before your tennis shoes?
- Would it make a difference if you untied both shoes before taking them off?
- When can the steps of working backward have flexibility and when can they not?

Organizing Student Work and Thinking ELL SS SN

Use before assigning the Exercises.

Have students add the work backward strategy to their problem-solving booklets. They should include the following about the strategy:

- a description of the strategy
- an explanation of the best time to use the strategy
- examples of problems that are solved using the strategy
- advantages and disadvantages of using the strategy

Analyzing Problems ELL SS

Use with Exercises 4–7.

Make sure that students correctly identify the order in which events occur in order to solve problems using the work backward strategy. Stress that they read the problems carefully, as steps are not always presented in order.

Leveled Lesson Resources

Also on TeacherWorks™
Lesson 3-4

Chapter 3 Resource Masters

BL = Below or Approaching Grade Level

OL = On Grade Level

AL = Above or Beyond Grade Level

ELL = English Language Learner

*Study Guide and Intervention** p. 28 BL OL ELL

NAME ____________________ DATE __________ PERIOD ____

3-4 Study Guide and Intervention

Problem-Solving Investigation: Work Backward

By working backward from where you end to where you began, you can solve problems. Use the four-step problem solving model to stay organized when working backward.

Example 1 **Jonah put half of his birthday money into his savings account. Then he paid back the $10 that he owed his brother for dance tickets. Lastly, he spent $3 on lunch at school. At the end of the day he was left with $12. How much money did Jonah receive for his birthday?**

Understand	You know that he had $12 left and the amounts he spent throughout the day. You need to find out how much money he received for his birthday.
Plan	Start with the amount of money he was left with and work backward.
Solve	He had $12 left. 12 Undo the $3 he spent on lunch. + 3 = 15 Undo the $10 he gave back to his brother. + 10 = 25 Undo the half put into his savings account. × 2 = 50 So, Jonah received $50 for his birthday.
Check	Assume that Jonah receive $50 for his birthday. After putting half into his savings account he had $50 ÷ 2 or $25. Then he gave $10 to his brother for dance tickets, so he had $25 − $10 or $15. Lastly, he spent $3 on lunch at school, so he had $15 − $3, or $12. So, our answer of $50 is correct.

Exercises

Solve each problem by using the work backward strategy.

1. On Monday everyone was present in Mr. Miller's class. At 12:00, 5 students left early for doctors' appointments. At 1:15, half of the remaining students went to an assembly. Finally, at 2:00, 6 more students left for a student council meeting. At the end of the day, there were only 5 students in the room. Assuming that no students returned after having left, how many students are in Mr. Miller's class?
27 students

2. Jordan was trading baseball cards with some friends. He gave 15 cards to Tommy and got 3 back. He gave two-thirds of his remaining cards to Elaine and kept the rest for himself. When he got home he counted that he had 25 cards. How many baseball cards did Jordan start with?
87 baseball cards

Chapter 3 28 *Course 2*

*Skills Practice** p. 29 BL OL

NAME ____________________ DATE __________ PERIOD ____

3-4 Skills Practice

Problem-Solving Investigation: Work Backward

Solve. Use the work backward strategy

1. GOVERNMENT There are 99 members in the Ohio House of Representatives. All of them were present when a vote was taken on a piece of legislation. If 6 of them did not vote, and 13 more voted "yes" than voted "no", how many "no" votes were there?
There were 40 "no" votes.

2. MONEY Jessie and Amar eat lunch at a restaurant and their bill is $21.65. Amar gives the cashier a coupon for $6 off their bill, and also hands the cashier two bills. If he receives $4.35 in change, what were the denominations of the two bills he gave the cashier?
They were both ten dollar bills.

3. AGE Justine is 13 years younger than her uncle Stewart. Stewart is 18 years older than Justine's sister, Julia. Julia's mother is 8 year older than Stewart, and 28 years older than her youngest child, Jared. If Jared is 12 years old, how old is Justine?
Justine is 19 years old.

4. NUMBER THEORY A number is divided by 6. Then 7 is added to the divisor. After dividing by 4, the result is 4. What is the number?
54

5. COMPACT DISCS Carmella borrowed half as many CDs from the library as her friend Ariel. Ariel borrowed 2 more than Juan, but four less than Sierra. Sierra borrowed 12 CDs. How many did each person borrow?
Ariel 8 CDs
Juan 6 CDs
Carmella 4 CDs

6. TIME Ashish needs to leave for the bus stop 15 minutes earlier than his friend Rami. Rami leaves five minutes later than Susan, but 10 minutes earlier than Raphael. If Raphael leaves for the bus stop at 8:15, what time does Ashish need to leave?
Ashish needs to leave at 7:50.

Lesson 3–4

Chapter 3 29 *Course 2*

*Practice** p. 30 OL AL

NAME ____________________ DATE __________ PERIOD ____

3-4 Practice

Problem-Solving Investigation: Work Backward

Mixed Problem Solving

Use the work backward strategy to solve Exercises 1 and 2.

1. NUMBER THEORY A number is divided by 5. Then 3 is added to the quotient. After subtracting 10, the result is 30. What is the number?
The number is 185.

2. COUPONS Kendra used 35 cents more in coupons at the store than Leanne. Leanne used 75 cents less than Teresa, who used 50 cents more than Jaclyn. Jaclyn used 40 cents in coupons. What was the value of the coupons Kendra used?
Kendra used 50 cents in coupons.

Use any strategy to solve Exercises 3–6. Some strategies are shown below.

PROBLEM-SOLVING STRATEGIES
• Look for a pattern • Guess and check. • Work backward

3. PATTERNS What are the next three numbers in the following pattern?
2, 3, 5, 9, 17, 33, . . .
65, 129, and 257

4. AGES Mr. Gilliam is 3 years younger than his wife. The sum of their ages is 95. How old is Mr. Gilliam?
Mr. Gilliam is 46 years old.

5. GRAND CANYON The elevation of the North Rim of the Grand Canyon is 2,438 meters above sea level. The South Rim averages 304 meters lower than the North Rim. What is the average elevation of the South Rim?
The South Rim averages 2,134 meters above sea level.

6. WATER BILL The water company charges a residential customer $41 for the first 3,000 gallons of water used and $1 for every 200 gallons used over 3,000 gallons. If the water bill was $58, how many gallons of water were used?
6,400 gallons

Chapter 3 30 *Course 2*

*Word Problem Practice** p. 31 OL AL

NAME ____________________ DATE __________ PERIOD ____

3-4 Word Problem Practice

Problem-Solving Investigation: Work Backward

For Exercises 1-3, use the information below.

WEATHER The temperature in Columbus, Ohio on Monday is 35 degrees warmer than it was on Sunday. Saturday's temperature was 7 degrees cooler than Sunday's. At 45 degrees, Friday's temperature was 22 degrees warmer than Saturday's.

For Exercises 4-6, refer to the table below.

MONEY Shelly needs to go to the grocery store to get some items for a dinner party she is hosting with her brother Preston.

Green Pepper	$1.79
Flank Steak	$8.54
Wild Rice	$3.29
Romaine Lettuce	$3.79
Cucumber	$0.99

1. What was the temperature on Monday? **65 degrees.**	2. Estimate the average temperature for the time period from Saturday to Monday. **The average temperature from Saturday to Monday is about 39 degrees.**
3. How many degrees cooler was the temperature on Friday than Monday? **20 degrees.**	4. How much money should she take to purchase the items contained in the table? **$18.40**
5. If Shelly has $24.00 in her purse before she goes to the store, how much will she have left after she shops? **$5.60**	6. If Preston pays Shelly for half the cost of the groceries, how much does he pay? **$9.20**
7. NUMBER THEORY How many different two-digit numbers can you make using the numbers 3, 7, 9, and 2 if no digit is repeated within a number? **12**	8. PATTERNS The following numbers follow a pattern: 2, 8, 32, 128. What would the fifth number in the pattern be? **512**

Lesson 3–4

Chapter 3 31 *Course 2*

**** Also available in Spanish*** ELL

Additional Lesson Resources

Transparencies

- *5-Minute Check Transparency,* Lesson 3-4

Other Print Products

- *Noteables™ Interactive Study Notebook with Foldables™*

Teacher Tech Tools

- *Interactive Classroom CD-ROM,* Lesson 3-4
- *AssignmentWorks,* Lesson 3-4

Student Tech Tools

glencoe.com

- Extra Examples, Chapter 3, Lesson 4
- Self-Check Quiz, Chapter 3, Lesson 4

3-4 Lesson Notes

1 Focus

Work Backward Working backward is not only useful in problem solving but has a strong link to solving equations. Students have used the reverse process when solving addition/subtraction and multiplication equations.

2 Teach

Scaffolding Questions

Write the steps for putting on your shoes on the board: 1) put on your socks, 2) put on your shoes, and 3) tie your shoes. Now tell students that you want to take your shoes off.

Ask:

- If I want to take my shoes off, which step must I undo first? third
- Which step must I undo second? second
- And which step must I undo third? first

ADDITIONAL EXAMPLE

SHOPPING Lucy and Elena went to the mall. Each girl bought a CD for $16.50, a popcorn for $3.50, and a drink for $2.50. Altogether, they had $5.00 left over. How much money did they take to the mall? $50

Additional Examples are also in:

- Noteables™ Interactive Study Notebook with Foldables™
- Interactive Classroom PowerPoint® Presentations

3-4 Problem-Solving Investigation

MAIN IDEA: Solve problems using the work backward strategy.

Academic Standards **7.3.4 Recognize, describe, or extend geometric patterns** using tables, graphs, words, or symbols. **P.1.3 Apply and adapt a variety of appropriate strategies to solve problems.**

P.S.I. TEAM +

e-Mail: WORK BACKWARD

MIGUEL: Yesterday, I earned extra money by doing yardwork for my neighbor. Then I spent $5.50 at the convenience store and four times that amount at the bookstore. Now I have $7.75 left.

YOUR MISSION: Work backward to find how much money Miguel had before he went to the convenience store and the bookstore.

Understand	You know he has $7.75 left. You need to find the amount he started with.	
Plan	Start with the end result and work backward.	
Solve	He has $7.75 left. **Undo** the four times $5.50 spent at the bookstore. Since $5.50 × 4 is $22, add $7.75 and $22. **Undo** the $5.50 spent at the convenience store. Add $5.50 and $29.75. So, Miguel had $35.25 to start with.	$7.75 + 22.00 $29.75 + $5.50 $35.25
Check	Assume Miguel started with $35.25. After going to the convenience store, he had $35.25 − $5.50 or $29.75. He spent four times the amount he spent at the convenience store at the bookstore. So, he had $29.75 − 4($5.50) or $7.75 left. So, $35.25 is correct. ✓	

Analyze The Strategy

1–3. See margin.

1. Explain when you would use the work backward strategy to solve a problem.
2. Describe how to solve a problem by working backward.
3. WRITING IN MATH Write a problem that could be solved by working backward. Then write the steps you would take to find the solution to your problem.

Additional Answers

1. When you are given the final result and asked to find an earlier amount.
2. Begin by taking the last value in the problem and perform opposite operations with each subsequent value until you arrive at the initial value.
3. Sample answer: In the first four games, Hannah scored a total of 83 points. In the fourth game she scored 19 points. In game three, she scored 27 points and in the second game she scored 22 points. How many points did she score in the first game? To solve, first subtract 19 from 83, which is 64. Then subtract 27 from 64 to get 37. Finally, subtract 22 from 37. So, Hannah scored 15 points in her first game.

Mixed Problem Solving

★ indicates multi-step problem

Academic Standards • ISTEP+

Extra Practice, pp. 674, 706

Use the *work backward* strategy to solve Exercises 4–7.

4. **MONEY** Marisa spent \$8 on a movie ticket. Then she spent \$5 on popcorn and one half of what was left on a drink. She has \$2 left. How much did she have initially? **\$17**

5. ★ **NUMBER THEORY** A number is multiplied by -3. Then 6 is subtracted from the product. After adding -7, the result is -25. What is the number? **4**

6. **TIME** Timothy's morning schedule is shown. At what time does Timothy wake up? **7:50 A.M.**

Timothy's Schedule

Activity	Time
Wakes up	■
Get ready for school – 45 min	■
Walk to school – 25 min	9:00 A.M.

7. **LOGIC** A small box has 4 tennis balls inside it. There are 6 of these small boxes inside a medium box. There are 8 medium boxes inside each large box, and there are 100 large boxes shipped in a large truck. How many tennis balls are on the truck? **19,200 tennis balls**

Use any strategy to solve Exercises 8–15. Some strategies are shown below.

PROBLEM-SOLVING STRATEGIES
- Guess and check.
- Look for a pattern.
- Work backward.

8. **GEOGRAPHY** The land area of North Dakota is 68,976 square miles. This is about 7 times the land area of Vermont. Estimate the land area of Vermont. **about 10,000 mi^2**

9. ★ **AGE** Brie is two years older than her sister Kiana. Kiana is 4 years older than their brother Jeron, who is 8 years younger than their brother Trey. Trey is 16 years old. How old is Brie? **Brie is 14 years old.**

10. ★ **ELEVATION** New Orleans, Lousiana, has an elevation of -8 feet related to sea level. Death Valley, California, is 274 feet lower than New Orleans. What is the elevation of Death Valley? **−282 ft**

11. ★ **GEOMETRY** Draw the sixth figure in the pattern shown. **See margin.**

12. ★ **WATERFALLS** Angel Falls in Venezuela, the highest waterfall in the world, is 3,212 feet high. It is 87 feet higher than 2.5 times the height of the Empire State Building. Find the height of the Empire State Building. **1,250 ft**

13. ★ **AIRCRAFT** An aircraft carrier travels about 6 inches per gallon of fuel. Raquel's car travels about 28 miles per gallon of fuel. If there are 5,280 feet in one mile, how many more inches per gallon would Raquel's car get than an aircraft carrier? **See margin.**

14. **SCHOOL SUPPLIES** Alexandra wishes to buy 5 pens, 1 ruler, and 7 folders to start the school year. The prices are shown in the table.

Item	Cost
Pens	\$2.09
Ruler	\$0.99
Folder	\$1.19

If there is no tax, is \$20 enough to pay for Alexandra's school supplies? Explain your reasoning. **See margin.**

15. **MONEY** Antonio has saved \$25 in cash to spend at the arcade. If he has 10 bills, how many of each kind of bill does he have? **1-\$10 bill, 2-\$5 bills, and 7-\$1 bills**

3 Practice

Using the Exercises

Exercises 1–3 can be used to check for understanding.

Exercises 4–7 can be used to check for understanding. Tell students to first determine which operations the problem describes. Then students can use the inverse operations to undo them, working backward.

Exercises 8–15 are structured so that students have the opportunity to practice many different problem-solving strategies. You may wish to review some of the strategies they have studied.
- use the four-step plan (p. 25)
- guess and check (p. 42)
- look for a pattern (p. 112)
- work backward (p. 148)

Intervention You may wish to use the Study Guide and Intervention master on p. 28 of the *Chapter 3 Resource Masters* for additional reinforcement.

Tips for New Teachers

Draw a Diagram

Point out that problems do not always present the steps in order. Some students may find it helpful to draw a diagram of the steps and number them.

4 Assess

Crystal Ball Tell students that tomorrow's lesson is about solving two-step equations such as $3x + 5 = 8$. Ask them to write how the work backward strategy might help them solve two-step equations.

Formative Assessment

Check for student understanding of concepts in Lessons 3-3 and 3-4.

CRM Quiz 2, p. 55

Additional Answers

11.

13. Raquel's car gets 1,774,074 more inches per gallon than an aircraft carrier.

14. Yes, the total purchase price would be \$19.77 which is less than \$20.

READING to SOLVE PROBLEMS

1 Focus

Word problems—like real-world math problems—often contain extra or unneeded information. This activity teaches students to simplify such problems by identifying and selecting the key terms and their relationships.

2 Teach

You may want to have students ask themselves questions such as the following:

- What information am I looking for?
- What information can I use?
- What information is extra?

Some students will be able to skip Step 2, and some may be able to write the problem as a number sentence.

Encourage students to rewrite the problem in as few words as possible, preferably in one sentence. You may also wish to encourage students to use numbers, operation symbols, and variables.

3 Assess

Have students tell what mathematical operations they described for Exercise 1. multiplication, addition

READING to SOLVE PROBLEMS

Simplify the Problem

Academic Standards **P.1.3 Apply and adapt a variety of appropriate strategies to solve proble[ms]** *Also addresses P.4.2.*

Have you ever tried to solve a long word problem and didn't know where to start? Try to rewrite the problem using only the most important words. Here's an example.

STEP 1 Read the problem and identify the important words and numbers.

CELL PHONES There is a wide range of cell phone plans available for students. With Janelle's plan, she pays $15 per month for 200 minutes, plus $0.10 per minute once she talks for more than 200 minutes. Suppose Janelle can spend $20 each month for her cell phone. How many minutes can she talk?

STEP 2 Simplify the problem. Keep all of the important words and numbers, but use fewer of them.

The total monthly cost is the $15 for 200 minutes plus $0.10 times the number of minutes over 200. How many minutes can she talk for $20?

STEP 3 Simplify it again. Use a variable for the unknown.

The cost of m minutes at $0.10 per minute plus $15 is $20.

1–4. Sample answers are given.
1. Saving $5 each week for x weeks plus $80 is $125.
3. 40° plus an increase of 5° for each of x hours is 60°.

PRACTICE

Use the method above to simplify each problem.

1. **MONEY** Akira is saving money to buy a scooter that costs $125. He has already saved $80 and plans to save an additional $5 each week. In how many weeks will he have enough money for the scooter?
2. **SHOPPING** Online shopping is a popular way to buy books. Cheryl wants to order several books that cost $7 each. In addition, she will pay a shipping fee of $8. How many books can she order with $43? **5 books**
3. **TEMPERATURE** The current temperature is 40°. It is expected to rise 5° each hour for the next several hours. In how many hours will the temperature be 60°?
4. **MONEY** Joaquin wants to buy some DVDs that are each on sale for $10 plus a CD that costs $15. How many DVDs can he buy if he has $75 to spend?

4. The total cost of x DVDs at $10 each plus $15 is $75.

150 Chapter 3 Algebra: Linear Equations and Functions

3-5 Solving Two-Step Equations

PACING: **Regular:** 1 period, **Block:** 0.5 period

IN Academic Standards 7.2.2 Write and solve two-step linear equations and inequalities in one variable.

Options for Differentiated Instruction

ELL = English Language Learner AL = Above or Beyond Grade Level SS = Struggling Students SN = Special Needs

Visual and Kinesthetic Learning SS SN

Use after presenting Examples 1–5.

Have students work in pairs to write and solve two-step equations. Give each pair an equation on a sheet of paper; for example, $x = 3$.

- Have the first person multiply both sides of the equation by an integer of his or her choice, such as 6.
- The other partner adds or subtracts a number of his or her choice, such as adding 2.
- Then have each pair exchange their final equations with another pair and reverse the steps to solve the equation that they receive.

Given:	$x = 3$
Partner 1:	$6x = 6(3)$
	$6x = 18$
Partner 2:	$6x + 2 = 18 + 2$
	$6x + 2 = 20$

Creating a Template SS SN

Use before assigning the Exercises.

Create a template for students to organize their work that provides a space for them to check their answers.

Page Number ______ Exercise Number ______	Check

Extending the Concept AL

Use after students complete Lesson 3-5.

Display the following equation on the board: $5x - 2 = 3x + 12$

Ask:

- Apply what you have learned about solving two-step equations to solve the equation. 7
- Describe the steps that you used and check your solution. Sample answer: Subtract $3x$ from each side. Add 2 to each side. Divide each side by 2.

Leveled Lesson Resources

Also on TeacherWorks™ Lesson 3-5

Chapter 3 Resource Masters

BL = Below or Approaching Grade Level OL = On Grade Level AL = Above or Beyond Grade Level ELL = English Language Learner

Lesson Reading Guide p. 32 BL OL ELL	Study Guide and Intervention* p. 33 BL OL ELL	Skills Practice* p. 34 BL OL
Practice* p. 35 OL AL	Word Problem Practice* p. 36 OL AL	Enrichment p. 37 OL AL

*Also available in Spanish ELL

Additional Lesson Resources

Transparencies

- *5-Minute Check Transparency*, Lesson 3-5

Other Print Products

- *Teaching Mathematics with Manipulatives*
- *Noteables™ Interactive Study Notebook with Foldables™*

Teacher Tech Tools

- *Interactive Classroom CD-ROM*, Lesson 3-5
- *AssignmentWorks*, Lesson 3-5

Student Tech Tools

glencoe.com

- Extra Examples, Chapter 3, Lesson 5
- Self-Check Quiz, Chapter 3, Lesson 5

3-5 Solving Two-Step Equations

MAIN IDEA

Solve two-step equations.

IN Academic Standards

7.2.2 Write and solve two-step linear equations and inequalities in one variable.

New Vocabulary

two-step equation

IN Math Online

glencoe.com

- Concepts In Motion
- Extra Examples
- Personal Tutor
- Self-Check Quiz

MINI Lab

MONEY A florist charges $2 for each balloon in an arrangement and a $3 delivery fee. You have $9 to spend. The model illustrates the equation $2x + 3 = 9$, where x represents the number of balloons.

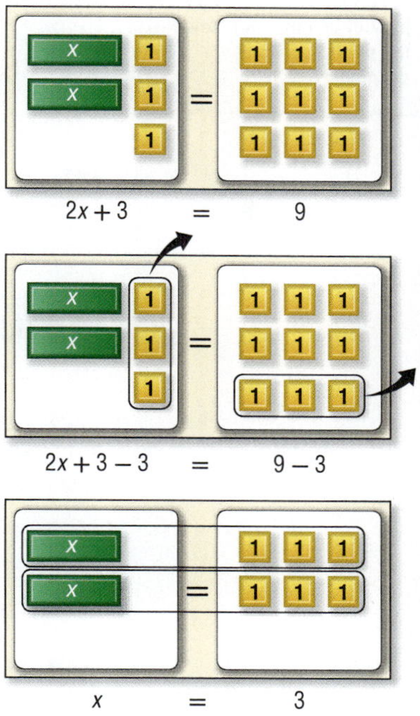

To solve $2x + 3 = 9$, remove three 1-tiles from each side of the mat. Then divide the remaining tiles into two equal groups. The solution of $2x + 3 = 9$ is 3.

Solve each equation by using models or a drawing.

1. $2x + 1 = 5$ **2**
2. $3x + 2 = 8$ **2**
3. $2 = 5x + 2$ **0**

1–3. See Ch. 3 Answer Appendix for models.

A **two-step equation** has two different operations. To solve a two-step equation, undo the operations in reverse order of the order of operations. You can review the order of operations in Lesson 1-4.

EXAMPLE Solve a Two-Step Equation

1 **Solve $2x + 3 = 9$. Check your solution.**

$2x + 3 = 9$	Write the equation.
$-3 = -3$	Undo the addition first by subtracting 3 from each side.
$2x = 6$	
$\frac{2x}{2} = \frac{6}{2}$	Next, undo the multiplication by dividing each side by 2.
$x = 3$	Simplify.

Check the solution. Since $2(3) + 3 = 9$, the solution is 3.

CHECK Your Progress

Solve each equation. Check your solution.

a. $2x + 4 = 10$ **3** b. $3x + 1 = 7$ **2** c. $5 = 2 + 3x$ **1**

3-5 Lesson Notes

1 Focus

Vertical Alignment

Before Lesson 3-5
Write and solve one-step linear equations in one variable

Lesson 3-5
Solve two-step linear equations and inequalities in one variable over the rational numbers

After Lesson 3-5
Solve multistep problems involving rate, average speed, distance, and time or a direct variation

2 Teach

MINI Lab

Make sure students understand how to solve one-step equations. Point out that this is just an extension of the modeling tools they already know.

Scaffolding Questions

Write the following expressions on the board: $7 + 3 \cdot (-2)$ and $11 - 10 \div 5$.

Ask:

- Look at the first expression. Which operation should I perform first? multiplication
- Look at the second expression. Which operation should I perform first? division

ADDITIONAL EXAMPLE

1 Solve $4x + 3 = 19$. Check your solution. 4

Tips for New Teachers: Undoing Operations

To solve a two-step equation, students reverse the order of operations. It may be helpful to remind students of the order of operations and to clarify what it means to "undo" an operation. For example, ask students to undo the operation in the expression $4x$. The expression involves the operation of multiplication of 4 by x. To undo this operation, divide the expression $4x$ by 4. In doing so, the expression becomes simply x.

Focus on Mathematical Content

Use the **work backward strategy** to solve two-step equations. Follow the **order of operations** in reverse order. Undo any **addition or subtraction** first. Then undo any **multiplication or division**.

Students should get in the habit of **checking their solutions**.

Formative Assessment

Use the Check Your Progress exercises after each Example to determine students' understanding of concepts.

ADDITIONAL EXAMPLES

2. Solve $6 + 5y = 26$. Check your solution. 4
3. Solve $-3c + 9 = 3$. Check your solution. 2
4. Solve $0 = 6 + 3t$. Check your solution. -2

Additional Examples are also in:

- Noteables™ Interactive Study Notebook with Foldables™
- Interactive Classroom PowerPoint® Presentations

Study Tip

Order of Operations Multiplication comes before addition in the order of operations. To undo these operations, reverse the order. So, undo the addition first by subtracting. Then, undo the multiplication by dividing.

EXAMPLES Solve Two-Step Equations

2 **Solve $3x + 2 = 23$. Check your solution.**

$3x + 2 = 23$	Write the equation.
$\underline{-2 = -2}$	Undo the addition first by subtracting 2 from each side.
$3x = 21$	
$\frac{3x}{3} = \frac{21}{3}$	Divide each side by 3.
$x = 7$	Simplify.
Check $3x + 2 = 23$	Write the original equation.
$3(7) + 2 \stackrel{?}{=} 23$	Replace x with 7.
$21 + 2 \stackrel{?}{=} 23$	Simplify.
$23 = 23$ ✓	The sentence is true.

The solution is 7.

3 **Solve $-2y - 7 = 3$. Check your solution.**

$-2y - 7 = 3$	Write the equation.
$\underline{+7 = +7}$	Undo the subtraction first by adding 7 to each side.
$-2y = 10$	
$\frac{-2y}{-2} = \frac{10}{-2}$	Divide each side by −2.
$y = -5$	Simplify.
The solution is −5.	Check the solution.

Study Tip

Equations Remember, solutions of the new equation are also solutions of the original equation.

4 **Solve $4 + 5r = -11$. Check your solution.**

$4 + 5r = -11$	Write the equation.
$\underline{-4 \quad = -4}$	Undo the addition of 4 first by subtracting 4 from each side.
$5r = -15$	
$\frac{5r}{5} = -\frac{15}{5}$	Divide each side by 5.
$r = -3$	Simplify.
The solution is −3.	Check the solution.

CHECK Your Progress

Solve each equation. Check your solution.

d. $4x + 5 = 13$ **2**   e. $8y + 15 = 71$ **7**   f. $-3n - 8 = 7$ **−5**

g. $-5s + 8 = -2$ **2**   h. $1 + 2y = -3$ **−2**   i. $-2 + 6w = 10$ **2**

Solving Two-Step Equations — Key Concept

To solve a two-step equation like $3x + 4 = 16$ or $2x - 1 = -3$:

Step 1 Undo the addition or subtraction first.

Step 2 Then undo the multiplication or division.

Tips for New Teachers: Solving Two-Step Equations

The guidelines presented in the Concept Summary box are generally valid, but there are exceptions. For example, when solving the equation $4(x + 7) = 26$, students should undo the multiplication prior to undoing the addition. When evaluating the expression $4(x + 7)$ using the order of operations, students should first add 7 to x and then multiply the result by 4. By stressing to students that they should reverse the order of operations when solving the equation $4(x + 7)$, it becomes clear that students should "undo" the multiplication and then undo the addition. Another example that illustrates this exception is the equation $\frac{x + 5}{3} = 8$. Students should undo the division prior to undoing the addition.

Some real-world situations start with a given amount and increase at a certain rate.

Real-World EXAMPLE

5 **MOVIES** **Aisha wants to have her birthday party at the movies. It costs $27 for pizza and $8.50 per friend for the movie tickets. Since it is Aisha's birthday, she does not have to pay for her movie ticket. How many friends can Aisha have at her party if she has $78 to spend?**

Real-World Link Most teenagers see more than 7 movies a year.
Source: Gallup News Service

Words	Cost of pizza	plus	cost of 1 friend	times	number of friends	equals $78.	
Variable	Let n represent the number of friends.						
Equation	27	+	8.50	·	n	=	78

$27 + 8.50n = 78$ — Write the equation.
$-27 \quad = -27$ — Subtract 27 from each side.
$8.50n = 51$
$\frac{8.50n}{8.50} = \frac{51}{8.50}$ — Divide each side by 8.50.
$n = 6$ — $51 \div 8.50 = 6$

Check
$27 + 8.50n = 78$ — Write the original equation.
$27 + 8.50(6) \stackrel{?}{=} 78$ — Replace n with 6.
$27 + 51 \stackrel{?}{=} 78$ — Simplify.
$78 = 78$ ✓ — The sentence is true.

Aisha can have 6 friends at her party.

CHECK Your Progress

j. **FITNESS** A fitness club is having a special offer where you pay $22 to join plus a $16 monthly fee. You have $150 to spend. Write and solve an equation to find how many months you can use the fitness club. **$22 + 16m = 150$; 8 months**

CHECK Your Understanding

Examples 1–4 (pp. 151–152)

Solve each equation. Check your solution.

1. $3x + 1 = 7$ **2**
2. $4h - 6 = 22$ **7**
3. $-6r + 1 = -17$ **3**
4. $-3y - 5 = 10$ **−5**
5. $13 = 1 + 4s$ **3**
6. $-7 = 1 + 2n$ **−4**

Example 5 (p. 153)

7. **MONEY** Syreeta wants to buy some CDs, each costing $14, and a DVD that cost $23. She has $65 to spend. Write and solve an equation to find how many CDs she can buy. **$14c + 23 = 65$; 3 CDs**

ADDITIONAL EXAMPLE

5 **PARKS** There are 76 thousand acres of state parkland in Georgia. This is 4 thousand acres more than three times the number of acres of state parkland in Mississippi. How many acres of state parkland are there in Mississippi? **24 thousand acres**

Tips for New Teachers — Negative Integers

Many problems in this lesson involve negative integers. You may wish to have students review the rules for adding, subtracting, multiplying, and dividing negative integers.

3 Practice

Formative Assessment

Use Exercises 1–7 to check for understanding.

Then use the chart at the bottom of the next page to customize your assignments for students.

Intervention You may wish to use the Study Guide and Intervention Master on page 33 of the *Chapter 3 Resource Masters* for additional reinforcement.

Odd/Even Assignments

Exercises 8–21 are structured so that students practice the same concepts whether they are assigned odd or even problems.

Practice and Problem Solving

HOMEWORK HELP

For Exercises	See Examples
8–11	1, 2
12–15	3
16–19	4
20–21	5

Exercise Levels
A: 8–21
B: 22–31
C: 32–35

Solve each equation. Check your solution.

8. $3x + 1 = 10$ **3**
9. $5x + 4 = 19$ **3**
10. $2t + 7 = -1$ **−4**
11. $6m + 1 = -23$ **−4**
12. $-4w - 4 = 8$ **−3**
13. $-7y + 3 = -25$ **4**
14. $-8s + 1 = 33$ **−4**
15. $-2x + 5 = -13$ **9**
16. $3 + 8n = -5$ **−1**
17. $5 + 4d = 37$ **8**
18. $14 + 2p = 8$ **−3**
19. $25 + 2y = 47$ **11**

For Exercises 20 and 21, write an equation. Then solve the equation.

20. **BICYCLES** Cristiano is saving money to buy a new bike that costs \$189. He has saved \$99 so far. He plans on saving \$10 each week. In how many weeks will Cristiano have enough money to buy a new bike? **$189 = 10x + 99$; 9 weeks**

21. **PETTING ZOOS** It cost \$10 to enter a petting zoo. Each cup of food to feed the animals is \$2. If you have \$14, how many cups of food can you buy? **$2c + 10 = 14$; 2 cups**

Solve each equation. Check your solution.

22. $2r - 3.1 = 1.7$ **2.4**
23. $4t + 3.5 = 12.5$ **2.25**
24. $16b - 6.5 = 9.5$ **1**
25. $5w + 9.2 = 19.7$ **2.1**
26. $16 = 0.5r - 8$ **48**
27. $0.2n + 3 = 8.6$ **28**

For Exercises 28 and 29, write an equation. Then solve the equation.

28. **CELL PHONES** A cell phone company charges a monthly fee of \$39.99 for unlimited *off-peak* minutes on the nights and weekends but \$0.45 for each *peak* minute during the weekday. If Brad's monthly cell phone bill was \$62.49, for how many *peak* minutes did he get charged? **$39.99 + 0.45m = 62.49$; 50 *peak* minutes**

29. **PLANTS** In ideal conditions, bamboo can grow 47.6 inches each day. At this rate, how many days will it take a bamboo shoot that is 8 inches tall to reach a height of 80 feet? **$8 + 47.6d = 960$; 20 days**

TEMPERATURE For Exercises 30 and 31, use the following information and the table.

Temperature is usually measured on the Fahrenheit scale (°F) or the Celsius scale (°C). Use the formula $F = 1.8C + 32$ to convert from one scale to the other.

Alaska Record Low Temperatures (°F) by Month	
January	−80
April	−50
July	16
October	−48

30. Convert the temperature for Alaska's record low in July to Celsius. Round to the nearest degree. **−9°C**

31. Hawaii's record low temperature is −11°C. Find the difference in degrees Fahrenheit between Hawaii's record low temperature and the record low temperature for Alaska in January. **92.2°F**

Academic Standards • ISTEP+
Extra Practice, pp. 675, 706

DIFFERENTIATED HOMEWORK OPTIONS

Level	Assignment	Two-Day Option	
BL Basic	8–21, 34–47	9–21 odd, 36, 37	8–20 even, 34, 35, 38–47
OL Core	9–19 odd, 20, 21, 23–27 odd, 28–31, 34–47	8–21, 33, 36, 37	22–31, 34, 35, 38–47
AL Advanced/Pre-AP	22–43 (optional: 44–47)		

H.O.T. Problems

33. $\frac{1}{2}(20x) - 18 = 200$; $x = 21.8$; they must sell at least 22 subscriptions

34. Estimation; Bianca doesn't need an exact answer. Sample answer: $50 − $20 = $30. $30 ÷ 0.25 = 120. Bianca can drive for about 120 mi.

32. **CHALLENGE** Refer to Exercises 30 and 31. Is there a temperature at which the number of Celsius degrees is the same as the number of Fahrenheit degrees? If so, find it. If not, explain why not. **No, none of the Fahrenheit temperatures convert to the same temperature in Celsius. Only −40°F = −40°C.**

33. **CHALLENGE** Suppose your school is selling magazine subscriptions. Each subscription costs $20. The company pays the school half of the total sales in dollars. The school must also pay a one-time fee of $18. What is the fewest number of subscriptions that can be sold to earn a profit of $200?

34. **SELECT A TECHNIQUE** Bianca rented a car for a flat fee of $19.99 plus $0.26 per mile. Which of the following techniques might she use to determine the approximate number of miles she can drive for $50? Justify your selection(s). Then use the technique(s) to solve the problem.

Mental Math | Number Sense | Estimation

35. **WRITING IN MATH** Write a real-world problem that would be represented by the equation $2x + 5 = 15$. **See margin.**

ISTEP+ PRACTICE 7.2.2

36. A rental car company charges $30 a day plus $0.05 a mile. Which expression could be used to find the cost of renting a car for m miles? **C**
A $30.05m$
B $30m + 0.05m$
C $30 + 0.05m$
D $30m + 0.05$

37. The Rodriguez family went on a vacation. They started with $1,875. If they spent $140 each day, which expression represents how much money they had after d days? **G**
F $1{,}735d$
G $1{,}875 - 140d$
H $140d$
J $1{,}875 + 140d$

Spiral Review

38. **SCHEDULES** Jaime needs to be at the bus stop by 7:10 A.M. If it takes her 7 minutes to walk to the bus stop and 40 minutes to get ready in the morning, what is the latest time that she can set her alarm in order to be at the bus stop 5 minutes earlier than she needs to be? (Lesson 3-4) **6:18 A.M.**

ALGEBRA Solve each equation. Check your solution. (Lessons 3-2 and 3-3)

39. $4f = 28$ **7**
40. $-3y = -15$ **5**
41. $p - 14 = 27$ **41**
42. $-11 = n + 2$ **−13**

43. **HIKING** Two people are hiking in the Grand Canyon. One is 987 feet below the rim and the other is 1,200 feet below the rim. Find the vertical distance between them (Lesson 2-5) **213 ft**

GET READY for the Next Lesson

PREREQUISITE SKILL Multiply or divide.

44. 2.5×20 **50**
45. 3.5×4 **14**
46. $4{,}200 \div 2.1$ **2,000**
47. $104 \div 6.5$ **16**

4 Assess

Name the Math Have students choose a problem from Exercises 8–19 or 22–27 and tell what procedures they used to solve it.

FOLDABLES Study Organizer

Foldables™ Follow-Up

Remind students to take notes about today's lesson under the *Equations* tab of their Foldables. Encourage them to include examples of how to solve two-step equations.

Additional Answer

35. Sample answer: A flower shop charges $2 for each flower in a vase and $5 for the vase. How many flowers can you place in a vase if you have $15 to spend?

Differentiated Instruction

Interpersonal Learners Separate students into pairs. Have each member of each pair write 3 or 4 two-step equations. Then have the members of each pair exchange equations and solve them.

3-6 Measurement: Perimeter and Area

PACING: **Regular:** 1 period, **Block:** 0.5 period

IN Academic Standards **7.2.4 Solve an equation or formula with two variables for a particular variable.**

Options for Differentiated Instruction

ELL = English Language Learner   AL = Above or Beyond Grade Level   SS = Struggling Students   SN = Special Needs

Scaffolding the Lesson SS SN

Use before presenting the Key Concept on page 156.

Scaffold this lesson by asking students to find the perimeter of rectangles like the one at the right, where the dimensions of all four sides are labeled. 16 cm

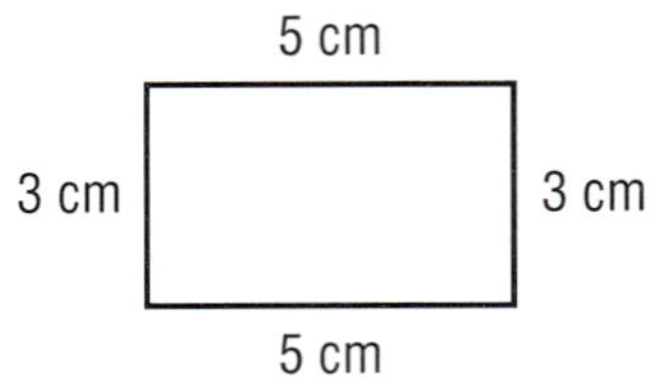

Next, have students find the perimeter of rectangles like the one at the right, where only one length and one width are labeled. 18 in.

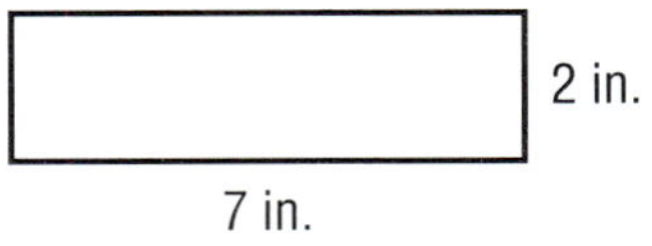

Finally, give students the perimeter and one dimension of a rectangle and ask them to find the other dimension. Once students are comfortable with this, then introduce the formula $P = 2\ell + 2w$.

Check for Understanding ELL AL SS

Use after presenting Examples 1–4.

Have each student draw and label a rectangle that has a perimeter of 36 centimeters. Have them calculate the area of the rectangle. Then gather the class data and record the information on the board in a table like the one shown below.

Rectangle	Length (cm)	Width (cm)	Area (cm^2)
1	15	3	45
2	10	8	80
3	9	9	81

Ask:

- Are there any other possible dimensions for a rectangle with a perimeter of 36 centimeters that aren't shown in the table?
- Which rectangle in the table has the greatest area? the least area?

Kinesthetic Learners ELL AL SS SN

Use after presenting Lesson 3-6.

Have students explore the school and grounds, measuring lengths. Suggestions include exterior walls, sidewalks, and sides of rectangular regions bounded by trees, rocks, and so forth. They should record their data, and then calculate perimeter and area for the buildings and regions measured.

Leveled Lesson Resources

Also on TeacherWorks™ Lesson 3-6

Chapter 3 Resource Masters

BL = Below or Approaching Grade Level | OL = On Grade Level | AL = Above or Beyond Grade Level | ELL = English Language Learner

Lesson Reading Guide
p. 38 BL OL ELL

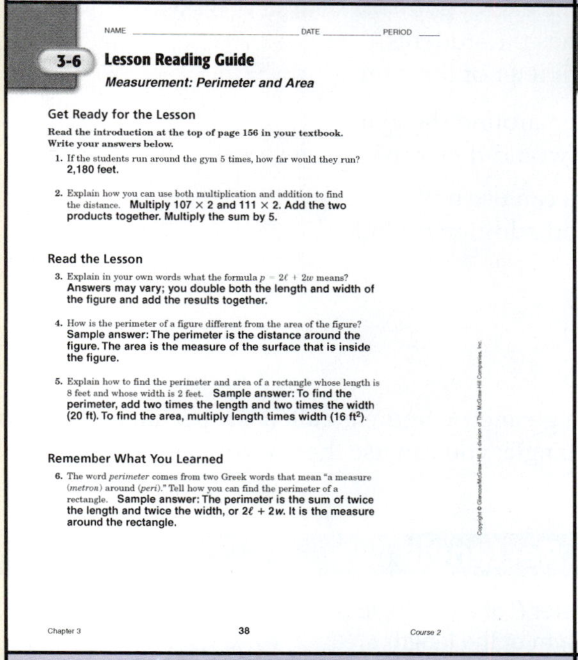
NAME ______ DATE ______ PERIOD ______

3-6 Lesson Reading Guide
Measurement: Perimeter and Area

Get Ready for the Lesson

Read the introduction at the top of page 156 in your textbook. Write your answers below.

1. If the students run around the gym 5 times, how far would they run? 2,180 feet.
2. Explain how you can use both multiplication and addition to find the distance. Multiply 107 × 2 and 111 × 2. Add the two products together. Multiply the sum by 5.

Read the Lesson

3. Explain in your own words what the formula $p = 2\ell + 2w$ means? Answers may vary; you double both the length and width of the figure and add the results together.
4. How is the perimeter of a figure different from the area of the figure? Sample answer: The perimeter is the distance around the figure. The area is the measure of the surface that is inside the figure.
5. Explain how to find the perimeter and area of a rectangle whose length is 8 feet and whose width is 2 feet. Sample answer: To find the perimeter, add two times the length and two times the width (20 ft). To find the area, multiply length times width (16 ft²).

Remember What You Learned

6. The word *perimeter* comes from two Greek words that mean "a measure (*metron*) around (*peri*)." Tell how you can find the perimeter of a rectangle. Sample answer: The perimeter is the sum of twice the length and twice the width, or $2\ell + 2w$. It is the measure around the rectangle.

Chapter 3 38 Course 2

Study Guide and Intervention*
p. 39 BL OL ELL

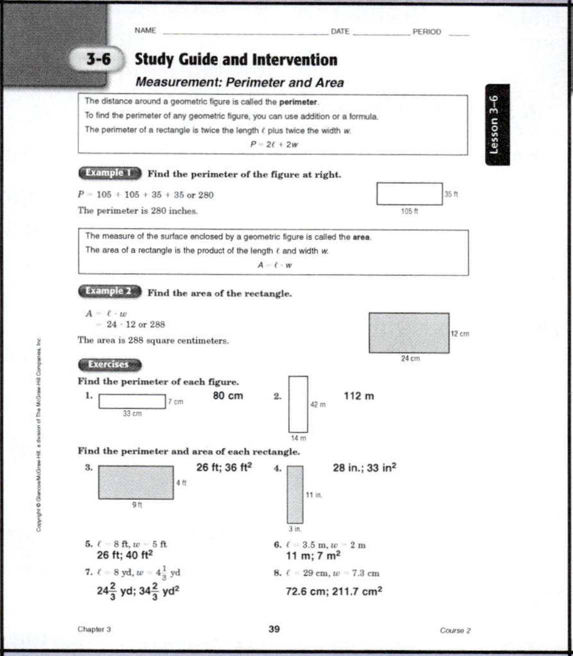
NAME ______ DATE ______ PERIOD ______

3-6 Study Guide and Intervention
Measurement: Perimeter and Area

The distance around a geometric figure is called the **perimeter**.
To find the perimeter of any geometric figure, you can use addition or a formula.
The perimeter of a rectangle is twice the length ℓ plus twice the width w.
$P = 2\ell + 2w$

Example 1 Find the perimeter of the figure at right.
$P = 105 + 105 + 35 + 35$ or 280
The perimeter is 280 inches.

The measure of the surface enclosed by a geometric figure is called the **area**.
The area of a rectangle is the product of the length ℓ and width w.
$A = \ell \cdot w$

Example 2 Find the area of the rectangle.
$A = \ell \cdot w$
$= 24 \cdot 12$ or 288
The area is 288 square centimeters.

Exercises

Find the perimeter of each figure.
1. 80 cm 2. 112 m

Find the perimeter and area of each rectangle.
3. 26 ft; 36 ft² 4. 28 in.; 33 in²
5. ℓ = 8 ft, w = 5 ft 26 ft; 40 ft² 6. ℓ = 3.5 m, w = 2 m 11 m; 7 m²
7. ℓ = 8 yd, w = $4\frac{1}{3}$ yd $24\frac{2}{3}$ yd; $34\frac{2}{3}$ yd² 8. ℓ = 29 cm, w = 7.3 cm 72.6 cm; 211.7 cm²

Chapter 3 39 Course 2

Skills Practice*
p. 40 BL OL

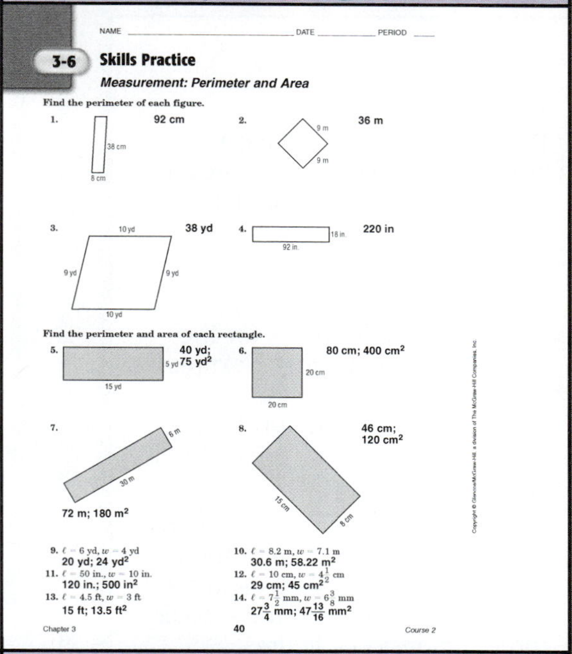
NAME ______ DATE ______ PERIOD ______

3-6 Skills Practice
Measurement: Perimeter and Area

Find the perimeter of each figure.
1. 92 cm 2. 36 m
3. 38 yd 4. 220 in

Find the perimeter and area of each rectangle.
5. 40 yd; 75 yd² 6. 80 cm; 400 cm²
7. 72 m; 180 m² 8. 46 cm; 120 cm²
9. ℓ = 6 yd, w = 4 yd 20 yd; 24 yd² 10. ℓ = 8.2 m, w = 7.1 m 30.6 m; 58.22 m²
11. ℓ = 50 in., w = 10 in. 120 in.; 500 in² 12. ℓ = 10 cm, w = $4\frac{1}{2}$ cm 29 cm; 45 cm²
13. ℓ = 4.5 ft, w = 3 ft 15 ft; 13.5 ft² 14. ℓ = $7\frac{1}{2}$ mm, w = $6\frac{3}{8}$ mm $27\frac{3}{4}$ mm; $47\frac{13}{16}$ mm²

Chapter 3 40 Course 2

Practice*
p. 41 OL AL

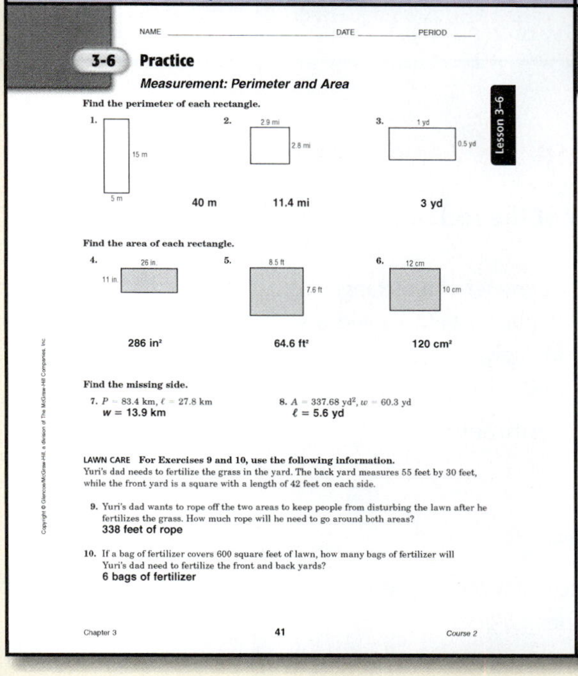
NAME ______ DATE ______ PERIOD ______

3-6 Practice
Measurement: Perimeter and Area

Find the perimeter of each rectangle.
1. 40 m 2. 11.4 mi 3. 3 yd

Find the area of each rectangle.
4. 286 in² 5. 64.6 ft² 6. 120 cm²

Find the missing side.
7. P = 83.4 km, ℓ = 27.8 km w = 13.9 km 8. A = 337.68 yd², w = 60.3 yd ℓ = 5.6 yd

LAWN CARE For Exercises 9 and 10, use the following information.
Yuri's dad needs to fertilize the grass in the yard. The back yard measures 55 feet by 30 feet, while the front yard is a square with a length of 42 feet on each side.

9. Yuri's dad wants to rope off the two areas to keep people from disturbing the lawn after he fertilizes the grass. How much rope will he need to go around both areas? 338 feet of rope
10. If a bag of fertilizer covers 600 square feet of lawn, how many bags of fertilizer will Yuri's dad need to fertilize the front and back yards? 6 bags of fertilizer

Chapter 3 41 Course 2

Word Problem Practice*
p. 42 OL AL

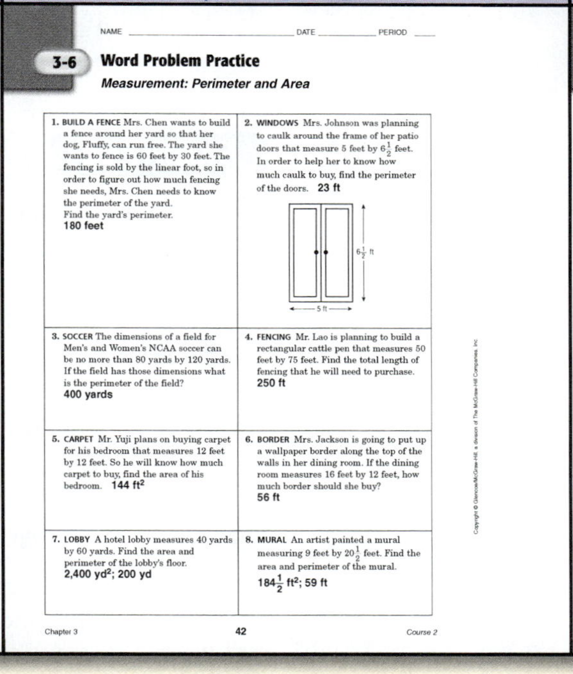
NAME ______ DATE ______ PERIOD ______

3-6 Word Problem Practice
Measurement: Perimeter and Area

1. BUILD A FENCE Mrs. Chen wants to build a fence around her yard so that her dog, Fluffy, can run free. The yard she wants to fence is 60 feet by 30 feet. The fencing is sold by the linear foot, so in order to figure out how much fencing she needs, Mrs. Chen needs to know the perimeter of the yard. Find the yard's perimeter. 180 feet
2. WINDOWS Mrs. Johnson was planning to caulk around the frame of her patio doors that measure 5 feet by $6\frac{1}{2}$ feet. In order to help her to know how much caulk to buy, find the perimeter of the doors. 23 ft
3. SOCCER The dimensions of a field for Men's and Women's NCAA soccer can be no more than 80 yards by 120 yards. If the field has those dimensions what is the perimeter of the field? 400 yards
4. FENCING Mr. Lao is planning to build a rectangular cattle pen that measures 50 feet by 75 feet. Find the total length of fencing that he will need to purchase. 250 ft
5. CARPET Mr. Yuji plans on buying carpet for his bedroom that measures 12 feet by 12 feet. So he will know how much carpet to buy, find the area of his bedroom. 144 ft²
6. BORDER Mrs. Jackson is going to put up a wallpaper border along the top of the walls in her dining room. If the dining room measures 16 feet by 12 feet, how much border should she buy? 56 ft
7. LOBBY A hotel lobby measures 40 yards by 60 yards. Find the area and perimeter of the lobby's floor. 2,400 yd²; 200 yd
8. MURAL An artist painted a mural measuring 9 feet by $20\frac{1}{2}$ feet. Find the area and perimeter of the mural. $184\frac{1}{2}$ ft²; 59 ft

Chapter 3 42 Course 2

Enrichment
p. 43 OL AL

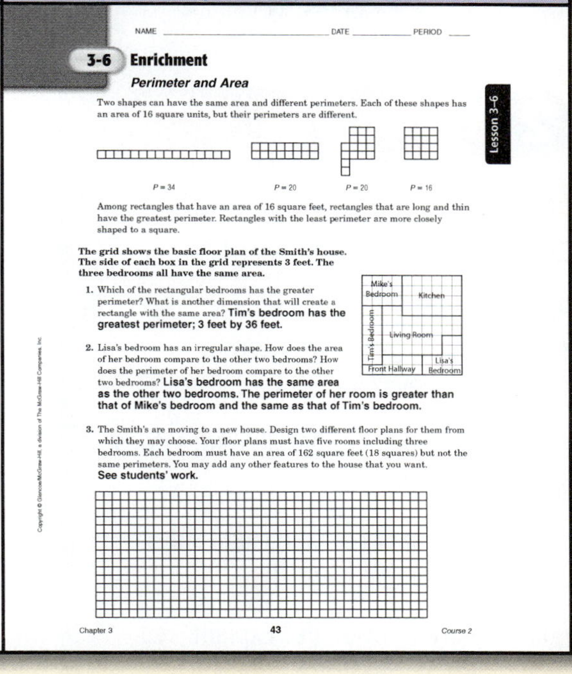
NAME ______ DATE ______ PERIOD ______

3-6 Enrichment
Perimeter and Area

Two shapes can have the same area and different perimeters. Each of these shapes has an area of 16 square units, but their perimeters are different.

P = 34 P = 20 P = 20 P = 16

Among rectangles that have an area of 16 square feet, rectangles that are long and thin have the greatest perimeter. Rectangles with the least perimeter are more closely shaped to a square.

The grid shows the basic floor plan of the Smith's house. The side of each box in the grid represents 3 feet. The three bedrooms all have the same area.

1. Which of the rectangular bedrooms has the greater perimeter? What is another dimension that will create a rectangle with the same area? Tim's bedroom has the greatest perimeter; 3 feet by 36 feet.
2. Lisa's bedroom has an irregular shape. How does the area of her bedroom compare to the other two bedrooms? How does the perimeter of her bedroom compare to the other two bedrooms? Lisa's bedroom has the same area as the other two bedrooms. The perimeter of her room is greater than that of Mike's bedroom and the same as that of Tim's bedroom.
3. The Smith's are moving to a new house. Design two different floor plans for them from which they may choose. Your floor plans must have five rooms including three bedrooms. Each bedroom must have an area of 162 square feet (18 squares) but not the same perimeters. You may add any other features to the house that you want. See students' work.

Chapter 3 43 Course 2

* Also available in Spanish ELL

Additional Lesson Resources

Transparencies
- *5-Minute Check Transparency,* Lesson 3-6

Other Print Products
- *Teaching Mathematics with Manipulatives*
- *Noteables™ Interactive Study Notebook with Foldables™*

Teacher Tech Tools
- *Interactive Classroom CD-ROM,* Lesson 3-6
- *AssignmentWorks,* Lesson 3-6

Student Tech Tools
glencoe.com
- Extra Examples, Chapter 3, Lesson 6
- Self-Check Quiz, Chapter 3, Lesson 6

3-6 Lesson Notes

1 Focus

Vertical Alignment

Before Lesson 3-6
Differentiate between and use appropriate units of measures for two- and three-dimensional objects

Lesson 3-6
Use variables in expressions describing the formulas for the perimeter of a rectangle; express in symbolic form simple relationships arising from geometry

After Lesson 3-6
Use formulas routinely for finding the perimeter and area of basic two-dimensional figures and the surface area and volume of basic three-dimensional figures

2 Teach

Scaffolding Questions

Draw a rectangle on the board.

Ask:

- How many right angles does a rectangle have? four
- How many pairs of parallel sides does a rectangle have? two
- How many pairs of congruent sides does a rectangle have? Two
- Is a square a rectangle? Explain. Yes. A square has 4 right angles, 2 pairs of parallel sides, and 2 pairs of congruent sides.

ADDITIONAL EXAMPLE

1 Find the perimeter of the rectangle. 40 ft

2 ft

18 ft

3-6 Measurement: Perimeter and Area

MAIN IDEA

Find the perimeters and areas of figures.

IN Academic Standards

7.2.4 Solve an equation or formula with two variables for a particular variable.

New Vocabulary

perimeter
area

IN Math Online

glencoe.com

- Extra Examples
- Personal Tutor
- Self-Check Quiz

GET READY for the Lesson

MEASUREMENT At the end of gym class, Mrs. Dalton has the students run around the perimeter of the gym.

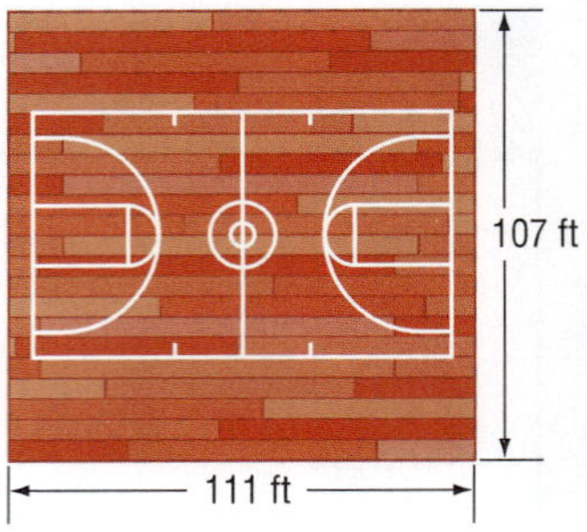

1. If the students run around the gym 5 times, how far would they run?
2. Explain how you can use both multiplication and addition to find the distance. See margin.

1. 2,180 feet

The distance around a geometric figure is called the **perimeter**. To find the perimeter of a rectangle, you can use these formulas.

Perimeter of a Rectangle — Key Concept

Words The perimeter P of a rectangle is twice the sum of the length ℓ and width w.

Symbols $P = \ell + \ell + w + w$

$P = 2\ell + 2w$ or $2(\ell + w)$

Model (rectangle with sides ℓ and w)

EXAMPLE Find the Perimeter of a Rectangle

1 **Find the perimeter of the rectangle shown at the right.**

4 cm

15 cm

$P = 2\ell + 2w$	Perimeter of a rectangle
$P = 2(15) + 2(4)$	Replace ℓ with 15 and w with 4.
$P = 30 + 8$	Multiply.
$P = 38$	Add.

The perimeter is 38 centimeters.

CHECK Your Progress

a. Find the perimeter of a rectangle whose length is 14.5 inches and width is 12.5 inches. 54 in.

Additional Answer

2. Multiply 107 × 2 and 111 × 2. Add the two products together. Multiply the sum by 5.

156 Chapter 3 Algebra: Linear Equations and Functions

Real-World EXAMPLE Find a Missing Side

2 **GARDENS** **Elan is designing a rectangular garden. He wants the width to be 8 feet. He also wants to put a fence around the garden. If he has 40 feet of fencing, what is the greatest length the garden can be?**

$P = 2\ell + 2w$	Perimeter of a rectangle
$40 = 2\ell + 2(8)$	Replace P with 40 and w with 8.
$40 = 2\ell + 16$	Multiply.
$-16 = \quad -16$	Subtract 16 from each side.
$24 = 2\ell$	Simplify.
$12 = \ell$	Divide each side by 2.

The greatest length the garden can be is 12 feet.

CHECK Your Progress

b. **FRAMES** Angela bought a frame for a photo of her friends. The width of the frame is 8 inches. If the distance around the frame is 36 inches, what is the length of the frame? **10 inches**

The distance *around* a rectangle is its perimeter. The measure of the surface *enclosed* by a rectangle is its **area**.

Area of a Rectangle — Key Concept

Words The area A of a rectangle is the product of the length ℓ and width w.

Model

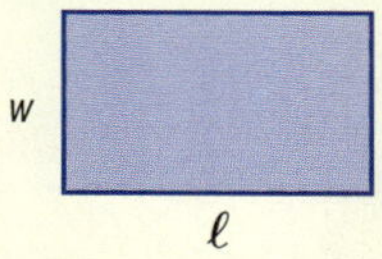

Symbols $A = \ell w$

EXAMPLE Find the Area of a Rectangle

3 **TOYS** **Find the area of the top of the wooden train table shown at the right.**

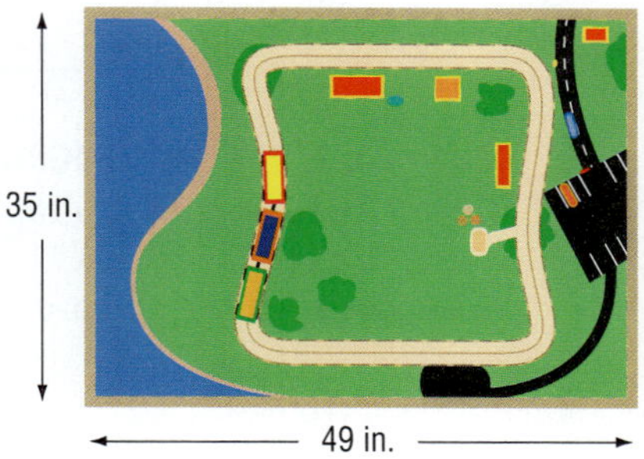

$A = \ell w$	Area of a rectangle
$A = 49 \cdot 35$	Replace ℓ with 49 and w with 35.
$A = 1{,}715$	Multiply.

The area is 1,715 square inches.

CHECK Your Progress

c. **VIDEO GAMES** Find the perimeter and area of the top of a video game console that measures 18 inches long and 15 inches wide.

c. 66 in.; 270 in^2

Study Tip

Area Units When finding area, the units are also multiplied. So, area is given in *square units*. Consider a rectangle 2 ft by 3 ft.

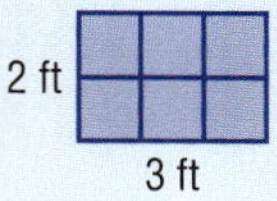

$A = 2 \text{ ft} \cdot 3 \text{ ft}$

$A = (2 \cdot 3)(\text{ft} \cdot \text{ft})$

$A = 6 \text{ ft}^2$

Focus on Mathematical Content

Students can use what they know about solving **two-step equations** to apply the formulas for the perimeter and area of rectangles.

Formative Assessment

Use the Check Your Progress exercises after each Example to determine students' understanding of concepts.

ADDITIONAL EXAMPLES

2 **ART** A painting has a perimeter of 68 inches. If the width of the painting is 13 inches, what is its length? 21 inches

3 **FRESHWATER** Find the area of the surface of the reservoir shown below. 2.5 mi^2

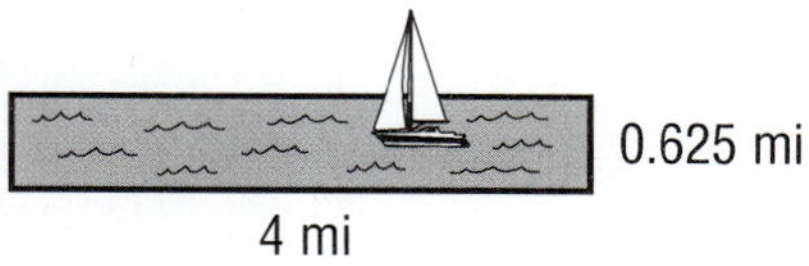

Additional Examples are also in:

- Noteables™ Interactive Study Notebook with Foldables™
- Interactive Classroom PowerPoint® Presentations

Lesson 3-6 Measurement: Perimeter and Area 157

ADDITIONAL EXAMPLE

4 A rectangle has an area of 34.2 square meters. If the length is 11.2 meters, find the width.
3.05 meters

3 Practice

Formative Assessment

Use Exercises 1–6 to check for understanding.

Then use the chart at the bottom of the next page to customize your assignments for students.

Intervention You may wish to use the Study Guide and Intervention Master on page 39 of the *Chapter 3 Resource Masters* for additional reinforcement.

EXAMPLE Use Area to Find a Missing Side

4 The area of a rectangle is 53.94 square feet. If the width is 8.7 feet, find the length.

METHOD 1 Substitute, then solve.

$A = \ell w$	Write the equation.
$53.94 = \ell(8.7)$	Replace *A* with 53.94 and *w* with 8.7.
$\frac{53.94}{8.7} = \frac{\ell(8.7)}{8.7}$	Divide each side by 8.7.
$\ell = 6.2$	Simplify.

METHOD 2 Solve, then substitute.

$A = \ell w$	Write the equation.
$\frac{A}{w} = \frac{\ell w}{w}$	Divide each side by *w*.
$\frac{A}{w} = \ell$	Simplify.
$\frac{53.94}{8.7} = \ell$	Replace *A* with 53.94 and *w* with 8.7.
$\ell = 6.2$	Simplify.

So, the length of the rectangle is 6.2 feet.

Study Tip

Check for Reasonableness You know that $53.94 \approx 54$ and that $8.7 \approx 9$. Since $54 \div 9 = 6$, the answer is reasonable.

CHOOSE Your Method

d. What is the width of a rectangle that has an area of 135 square meters and a length of 9 meters? **15 m**

★ indicates multi-step problem

CHECK Your Understanding

Example 1 (p. 156) **Find the perimeter of each rectangle.**

1.
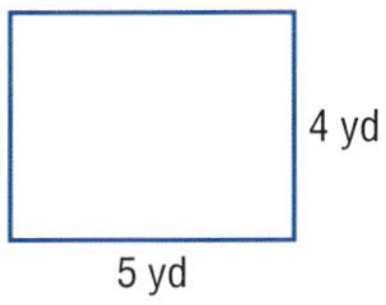

18 yd

2.
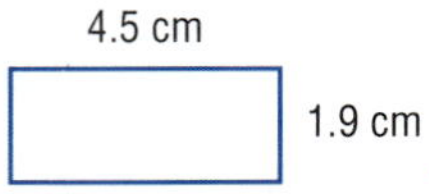

12.8 cm

Example 2 (p. 157)

3. **PHOTOGRAPHY** A photograph is 5 inches wide. The perimeter of the photograph is 24 inches. What is the length of the photograph? **7 in.**

Example 3 (p. 157) **Find the area of each rectangle.**

4.
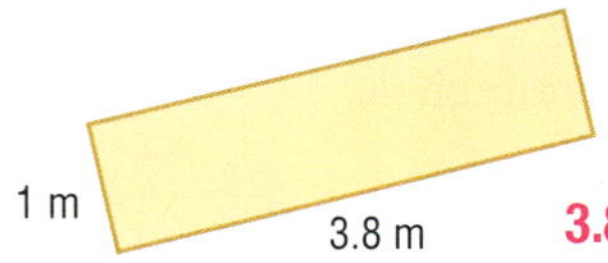

3.8 m²

5.
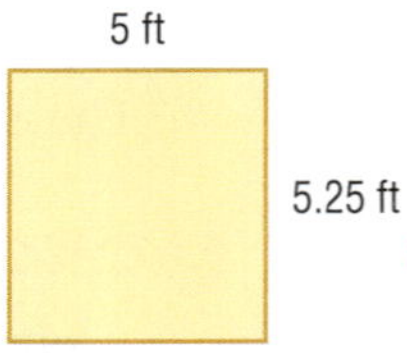

26.25 ft²

Example 4 (p. 158)

6. **MEASUREMENT** The area and length of a rectangle are 30 square feet and 6 feet, respectively. What is the width of the rectangle? **5 ft**

Differentiated Instruction

Kinesthetic Learners Separate students into teams of three or four. Have each team measure the length and width of a rectangular surface in the classroom (such as a desktop, chalkboard, book cover, or floor). Then have each team write a perimeter problem and an area problem, each with a missing dimension. Have teams exchange problems and solve them.

Practice and Problem Solving

HOMEWORK HELP	
For Exercises	See Examples
7–12	1
13–14	2
15–20	3
21–22	4

Exercise Levels
A: 7–22
B: 23–33
C: 34–42

Find the perimeter of each rectangle.

7. 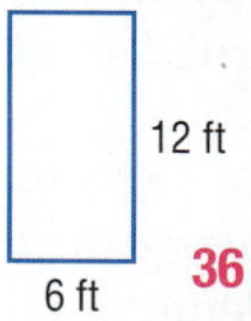

36 ft

8. 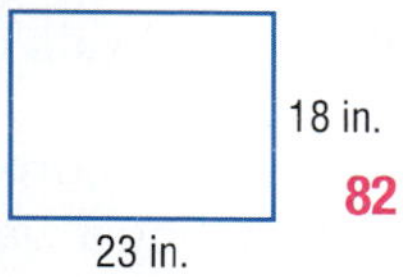

82 in.

9. 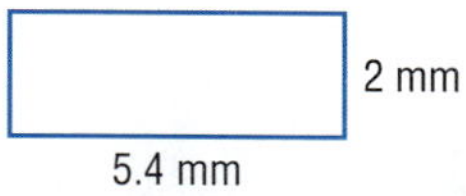

14.8 mm

10. 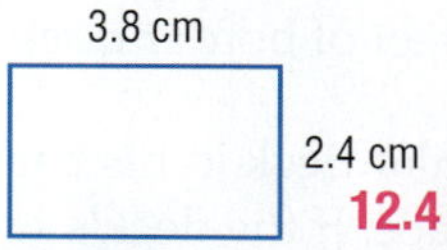

12.4 cm

11. $\ell = 1.5$ ft, $w = 4$ ft **11 ft**

12. $\ell = 5.75$ ft, $w = 8$ ft **27.5 ft**

13. **SEWING** The fringe used to outline a placemat is 60 inches. If the width of the placemat is 12 inches, what is the measure of its length? **18 in.**

14. **GAMES** Orlando marks off a rectangular section of grass to use as a playing field. He knows that he needs to mark off 111 feet around the border of the playing field. If the field is 25.5 feet long, what is its width? **30 ft**

Find the area of each rectangle.

15. 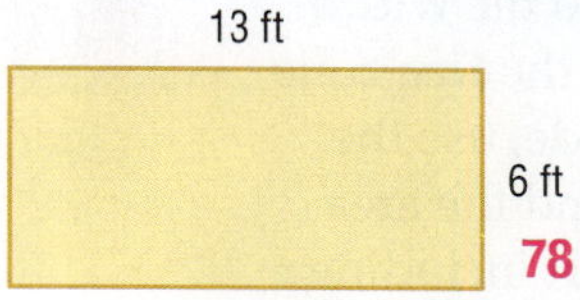

78 ft²

16. 

33 yd²

17. 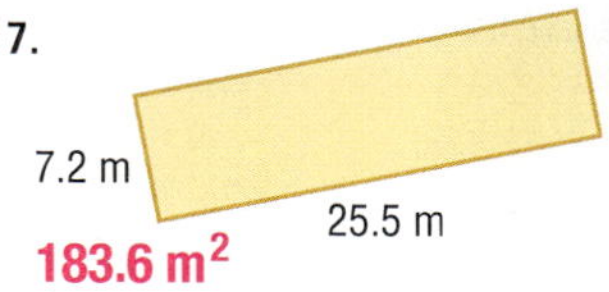

183.6 m²

18. 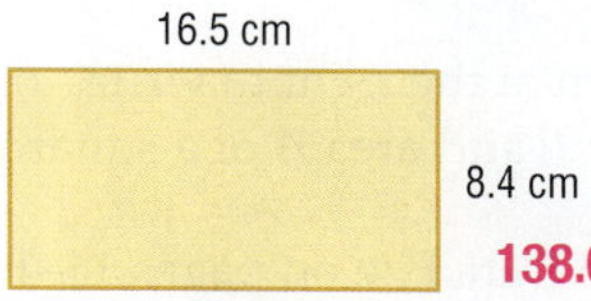

138.6 cm²

19. $\ell = 3.25$ in., $w = 2$ in. **6.5 in²**

20. $\ell = 4.5$ ft, $w = 10.6$ ft **47.7 ft²**

21. **QUILTING** Daniela's grandmother is making a quilt that is 7 squares wide. If she needs 35 squares total, how many squares long is the length? **5 squares**

22. **PAINTING** A rectangular mural is painted on a wall. If the mural is 12 feet wide and covers 86.4 square feet, what is the height of the mural? **7.2 feet**

Find the missing measure.

23. $P = 115.6$ ft, $w = 24.8$ ft **$\ell = 33$ ft**

24. $A = 189.28$ cm^2, $w = 16.9$ cm **$\ell = 11.2$ cm**

ANALYZE TABLES For Exercises 25 and 26, use the table shown.

Youth Soccer Fields		
Age (years)	Length (yards)	Width (yards)
10	70	40
12	80	50
14	100	60

25. How much greater is the area of a soccer field for a 14-year-old than for a 10-year-old? **3,200 yd²**

26. An *acre* equals 4,840 square yards. How many acres are there in a field for a 12-year-old? Round to the nearest hundredth. **0.83 acre**

Odd/Even Assignments

Exercises 7–22 are structured so that students practice the same concepts whether they are assigned odd or even problems.

Tips for New Teachers: Using Exponents

You may need to remind students that square units can be shown by the same small 2 used to show square numbers (^{2}). Thus, 1 square yard = 1 yd^2.

DIFFERENTIATED HOMEWORK OPTIONS

Level	Assignment	Two-Day Options	
BL Basic	7–22, 34, 39, 40, 42–57	7–21 odd, 43, 44	8–22 even, 34, 39, 40, 42, 45–57
OL Core	7–11 odd, 13, 14, 15–19 odd, 21–23, 25–34, 39, 40, 42–57	7–22, 43, 44	23–34, 39, 40, 42, 45–57
AL Advanced/Pre-AP	22–53 (optional: 54–57)		

For Exercises 27–30, determine whether the problem involves perimeter, area, or both. Then solve.

27. ★ **HIKING** Ramón walked along a rectangular hiking path. Initially, he walked 3 miles north before he turned east. If he walked a total of 14 miles, how many miles did he walk east before he turned south? **perimeter; 4 mi**

28. **BORDERS** Kaitlyn's bedroom is shaped like a rectangle with rectangular walls. She is putting a wallpaper border along the top of the two longer walls and one of the shorter walls. If the length of the room is 13 feet and the width is 9.8 feet, how many feet of border does she need? **perimeter; 35.8 feet**

29. **DECKS** Armando built a rectangular deck in his backyard. The deck takes up 168.75 square feet of space. If the deck's width is 12.8 feet, what is its approximate length? **area; 13 ft**

30. **FENCING** Kina plans to fence her rectangular backyard on three sides. Her backyard measures 48 feet in length. She will not fence one of the shorter sides. If the area of her backyard is 1,752 square feet, how many feet of fencing is required? **both; 132.5 feet**

Real-World Link Regulation volleyball courts are 18 meters long by 9 meters wide, not including the free zone.
Source: USA Volleyball

31. ★ **VOLLEYBALL** For safety, regulation courts have a "free zone" added to the width of each side of the court. If the free zone on each side is 3 meters wide, use the information to the left to find the area of the entire volleyball court including the free zone. **270 m^2**

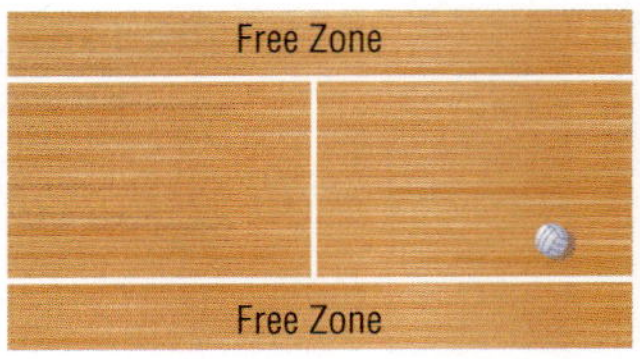

32. **GEOMETRY** Use the diagram at the right to write formulas for the perimeter P and area A of a square. $P = 4s$; $A = s^2$

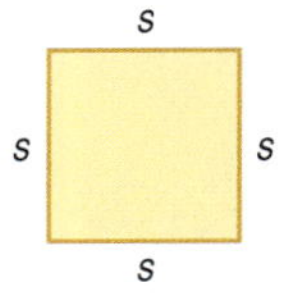

33. **FIND THE DATA** Refer to the Data File on pages 16–19. Choose some data and write a real-world problem in which you would find the perimeter and area of a rectangle. **See students' work.**

Academic Standards • ISTEP+
Extra Practice, pp. 675, 706

H.O.T. Problems

34. **OPEN ENDED** Draw and label three different rectangles that have an area of 24 square centimeters. **See Ch. 3 Answer Appendix.**

CHALLENGE For Exercises 35–38, find each equivalent measurement. Provide a diagram to justify your answers. The diagram for Exercise 35 is shown.

35. 1 yd^2 = ■ ft^2 **9**

36. 4 yd^2 = ■ ft^2 **36**

37. 1 ft^2 = ■ in^2 **144**

38. 2 ft^2 = ■ in^2 **288**

35–38. See Ch. 3 Answer Appendix for diagrams.

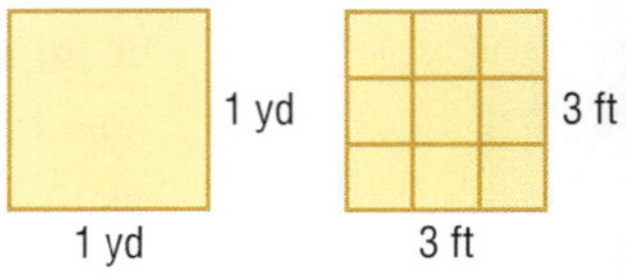

NUMBER SENSE For Exercises 39 and 40, describe the effect on the perimeter and area in each of the following situations.

39. The width of a rectangle is doubled. **See Ch. 3 Answer Appendix.**

40. The length of a side of a square is doubled.

40. When the length of a side of a square is doubled, the perimeter is doubled and the area is quadrupled.

160 Chapter 3 Algebra: Linear Equations and Functions

41. **CHALLENGE** A rectangle has width w. Its length is one unit more than 3 times its width. Write an expression that represents the perimeter of the rectangle. **$P = 2(3w + 1) + 2w$ or $P = 8w + 2$**

42. True; The closer a rectangle comes to being a square, the greater the area.

42. **WRITING IN MATH** Decide whether the statement is *true* or *false*. Explain your reasoning and provide examples.

Of all rectangles with a perimeter of 24 square inches, the one with the greatest area is a square.

ISTEP+ PRACTICE 7.2.4

43. Oakland Garden Center created a design plan for the Nelson family's rock garden. The shaded areas will hold flowers and the rest of the garden will be rock.

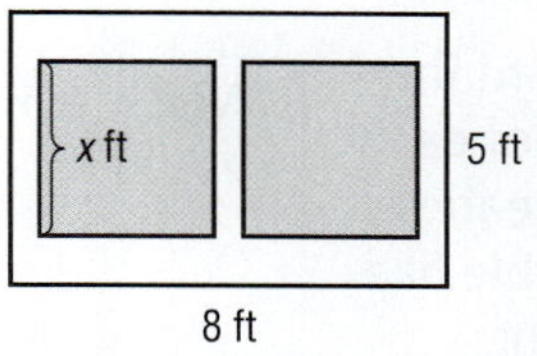

If each shaded area is a square, which expression represents the area of the garden that will be rock? **A**

A $(40 - 2x^2)$ ft^2
B $(40 - x)$ ft^2
C $(40 + x)$ ft^2
D $(40 + x^2)$ ft^2

44. The rectangle below has width 4.75 feet and perimeter P feet.

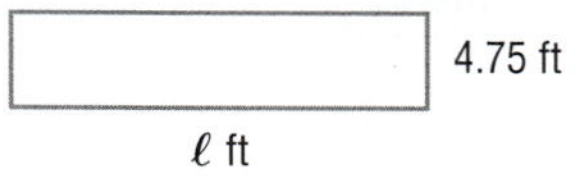

Which of the following could be used to find the length of the rectangle? **H**

F $P = 4.75 + \frac{\ell}{2}$
G $P = 4.75 - \ell$
H $P = 9.5 + 2\ell$
J $P = 9.5 - 2\ell$

Spiral Review

Solve each equation. Check your solution. (Lesson 3-5)

45. $5d + 12 = 2$ **−2**
46. $13 - f = 7$ **6**
47. $10 = 2g + 3$ **3.5**
48. $6 = 3 - 3h$ **−1**

49. **ALGEBRA** Anna was charged $11.25 for returning a DVD 5 days late. Write and solve an equation to find how much the video store charges per day for late fees. (Lesson 3-3) **$5x = 11.25$; $2.25**

Multiply. (Lesson 2-6)

50. $14(-5)$ **−70**
51. $(-3)^3$ **−27**
52. $-10(2)(-8)$ **160**

53. **AGE** The sum of Denise's and Javier's ages is 26 years. If Denise is 4 years older than Javier, find Javier's age. Use the *guess and check* strategy. (Lesson 1-5) **11 years old**

GET READY for the Next Lesson **54–57. See margin.**

PREREQUISITE SKILL Graph and label each point on a coordinate plane. (Lesson 2-3)

54. $(-4, 2)$
55. $(3, -1)$
56. $(-3, -4)$
57. $(2, 0)$

4 Assess

Yesterday's News Remind students that yesterday's lesson was about solving two-step equations. Have them write how yesterday's concepts helped them with today's material.

Formative Assessment

Check for student understanding of concepts in Lessons 3-5 and 3-6.

CRM Quiz 3, p. 56

Additional Answers

54.

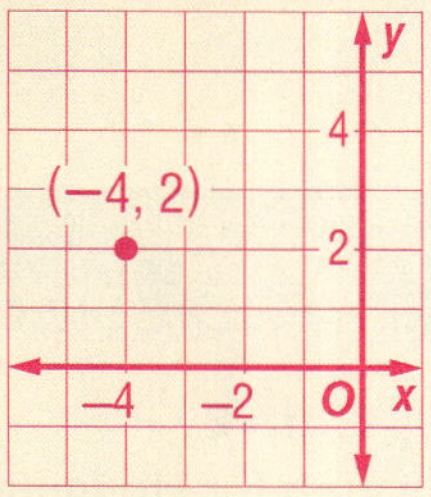

55.

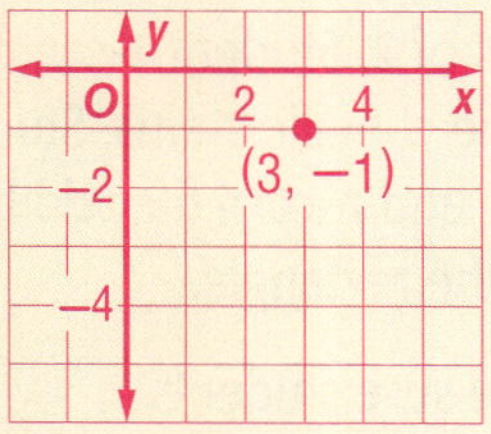

56.

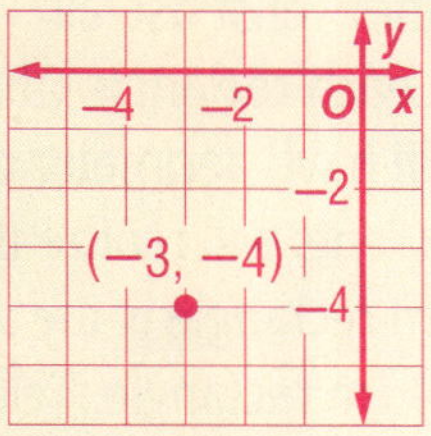

57.

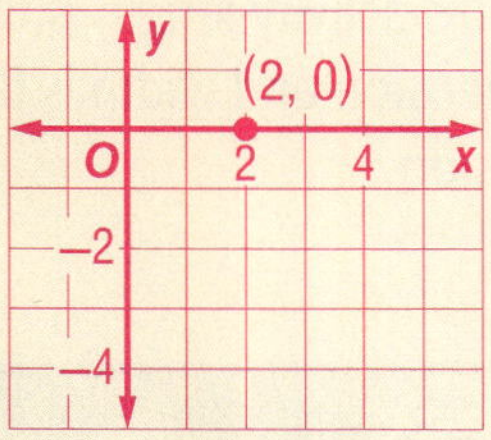

Explore 3-7 Lesson Notes

1 Focus

Materials

- chenille stems
- scissors
- centimeter rulers
- graph paper

Easy-to-Make Manipulatives

Teaching Mathematics with Manipulatives, templates for:

- quarter-inch grid, p. 14

2 Teach

Working in Cooperative Groups You may wish for students to work in groups of 2. Student 1 can cut and arrange the chenille stems. Student 2 can measure and record the width and length of the rectangle.

Activity Make sure students understand that they must use all 10 stems to form each rectangle (thus, each rectangle will have perimeter of 24 cm). Some students will realize that a 2.4 cm × 9.6 cm rectangle is the same as a 9.6 cm × 2.4 cm rectangle. Tell them that for this activity length is the horizontal dimension and width is the vertical dimension.

3 Assess

Formative Assessment

Use Exercises 1 and 2 to determine whether students understand the relationship between a rectangle's perimeter and its dimensions.

Explore 3-7 Measurement Lab
Representing Relationships

MAIN IDEA

Graph data to demonstrate the relationship between the dimensions and the perimeter of a rectangle.

IN Academic Standards

7.2.1 Use variables and appropriate operations to write an expression, equation or inequality **that represents a verbal description.**
7.3.4 Recognize, describe, or extend **geometric patterns using tables, graphs, words,** or symbols.

In this lab, you will investigate the relationships between the dimensions and the perimeter of a rectangle.

ACTIVITY

STEP 1 Use 10 chenille stems, 24 centimeters in length, to form 10 rectangles with different dimensions.

STEP 2 Measure and record the width and length of each rectangle to the nearest centimeter in a table like the one at the right.

Width (cm)	Length (cm)

Analyze the Results 1–7. See Ch. 3 Answer Appendix.

1. What rectangle measure does 24 centimeters represent?
2. Find the sum of the width and length for each of your rectangles. Write a sentence that describes the relationship between this sum and the measure of the length of the stem for each rectangle. Then write a rule that describes this relationship for a rectangle with a width w and length ℓ.
3. In this activity, if a rectangle has a length of 4.5 centimeters, what is its width? Explain your reasoning. Write a rule that can be used to find w when ℓ is known for any rectangle in this Activity.
4. **GRAPH THE DATA** Graph the data in your table on a coordinate plane like the one at the right.

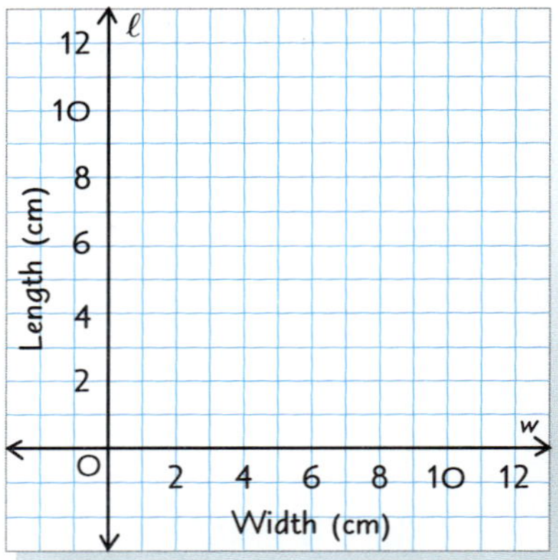

5. Describe what the ordered pair (w, ℓ) represents. Describe how these points appear on the graph.
6. Use your graph to find the width of a rectangle with a length of 7 centimeters. Explain your method.
7. **MAKE A CONJECTURE** If the length of each chenille stem was 20 centimeters, how would this affect the data in your table? the rule you wrote in Exercise 3? the appearance of your graph?

From Concrete to Abstract Use Exercise 7 to bridge the gap between using models of rectangles' dimensions to explore the relationship (between a rectangle's perimeter and its dimensions) and making predictions about other rectangles.

162 Chapter 3 Algebra: Linear Equations and Functions

3-7 Functions and Graphs

PACING: **Regular:** 2 periods, **Block:** 1 period

IN Academic Standards **Preparation for 8.2.4** Identify and graph linear functions and identify lines with positive and negative slope. *Also addresses P.4.1.*

Options for Differentiated Instruction

ELL = English Language Learner   AL = Above or Beyond Grade Level   SS = Struggling Students   SN = Special Needs

Reviewing Concepts SS SN

Use before presenting Lesson 3-7.

Review vocabulary terms related to the coordinate plane. Review how to graph points on a coordinate plane.

- *x*-axis
- *y*-axis
- origin
- *x*-coordinate
- *y*-coordinate

Creating a Template ELL SS SN

Use before assigning the Exercises.

Create a template that students can use to organize work, evaluate expressions, and determine the specific points to be plotted.

x	Evaluate Expression:	*y*	(*x*, *y*)

Extensions and Challenges AL

Use after students complete Lesson 3-7.

Display the pairs of lines shown on the board or overhead.

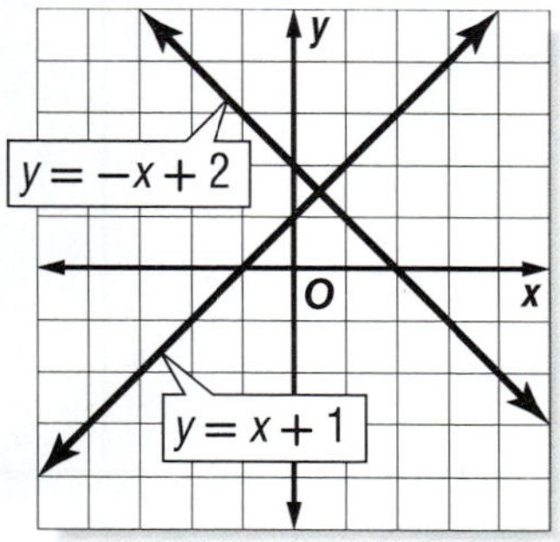

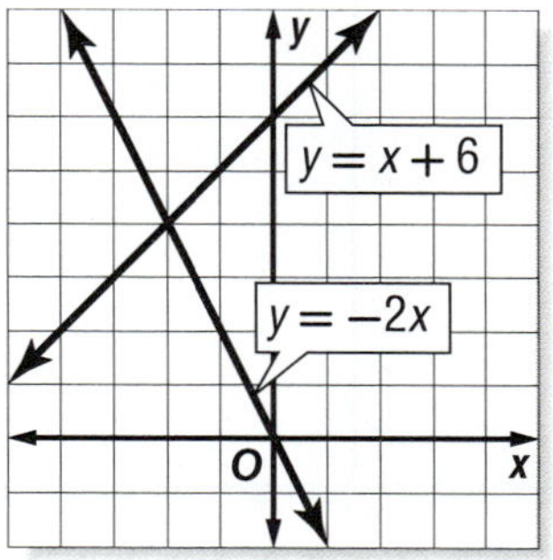

Ask:

- What can you conclude about the point of intersection for two lines? The point of intersection for two lines is a solution to the equations of each of the two lines.
- Test your hypothesis with two more equations. Were you correct? Explain your results. See students' work.

Leveled Lesson Resources

Also on TeacherWorks™ Lesson 3-7

Chapter 3 Resource Masters

BL = Below or Approaching Grade Level   OL = On Grade Level   AL = Above or Beyond Grade Level   ELL = English Language Learner

Lesson Reading Guide
p. 45 BL OL ELL

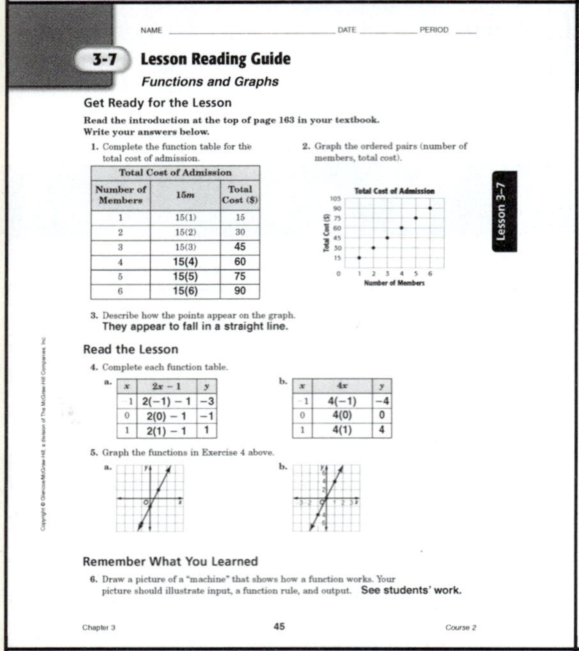

Study Guide and Intervention*
p. 46 BL OL ELL

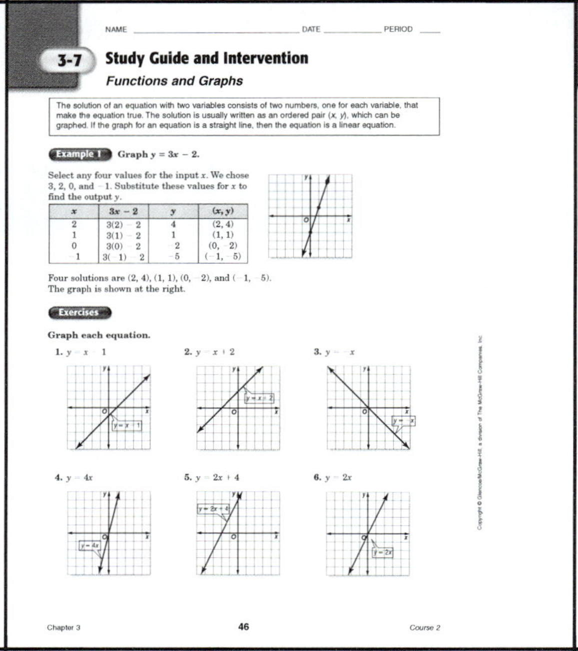

Skills Practice*
p. 47 BL OL

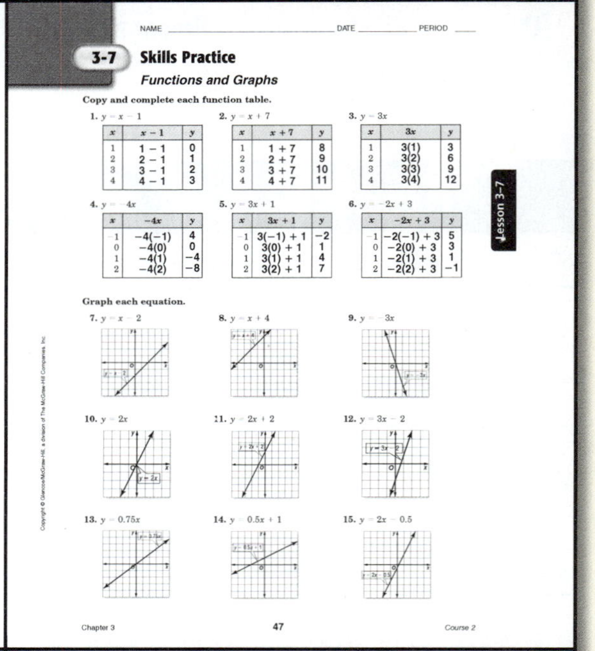

Practice*
p. 48 OL AL

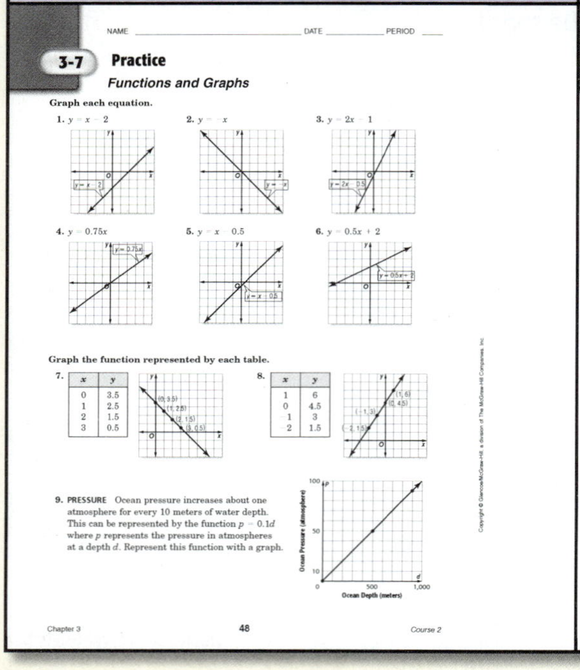

Word Problem Practice*
p. 49 OL AL

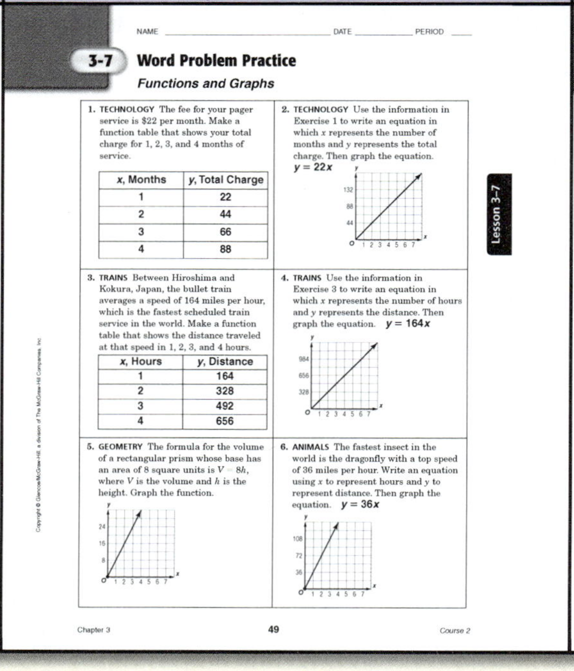

Enrichment
p. 50 OL AL

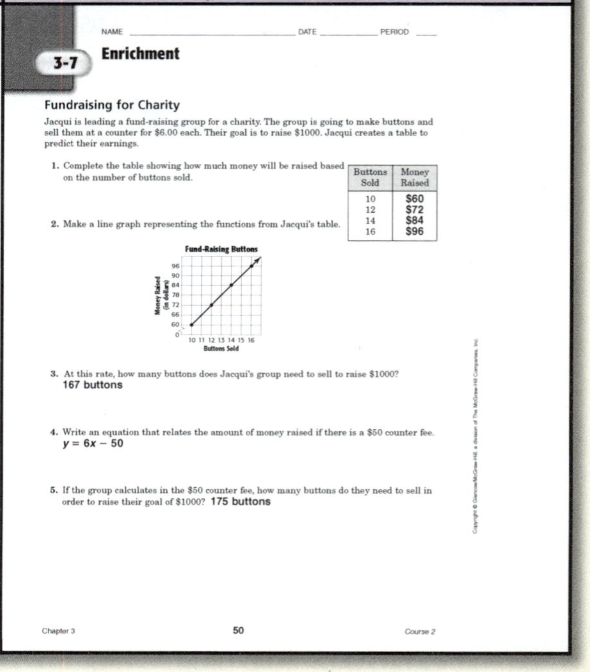

Additional Lesson Resources

* *Also available in Spanish* ELL

Transparencies

- *5-Minute Check Transparency,* Lesson 3-7

Other Print Products

- *Teaching Mathematics with Manipulatives*
- *Noteables™ Interactive Study Notebook with Foldables™*

Teacher Tech Tools

- *Interactive Classroom CD-ROM,* Lesson 3-7
- *AssignmentWorks,* Lesson 3-7

Student Tech Tools

glencoe.com

- Extra Examples, Chapter 3, Lesson 7
- Self-Check Quiz, Chapter 3, Lesson 7

3-7 Functions and Graphs

MAIN IDEA

Graph data to demonstrate relationships.

IN Academic Standards

Preparation for 8.2.4 Identify and graph linear functions and identify lines with positive and negative slope. *Also addresses P.4.1.*

New Vocabulary

linear equation

IN Math Online

glencoe.com

- Extra Examples
- Personal Tutor
- Self-Check Quiz

GET READY for the Lesson

MONEY The Westerville Marching Band is going on a year-end trip to an amusement park. Each band member must pay an admission price of $15. In the table, this is represented by $15m$.

Total Cost of Admission		
Number of Members	15*m*	Total Cost ($)
1	15(1)	15
2	15(2)	30
3	15(3)	45
4	15(4)	60
5	15(5)	75
6	15(6)	90

1. Copy and complete the function table for the total cost of admission.
2. Graph the ordered pairs (number of members, total cost). **See Ch. 3 Answer Appendix.**
3. Describe how the points appear on the graph.

3. They appear to fall in a straight line.

If you are given a function, ordered pairs in the form (input, output), or (x, y), provide useful information about that function. These ordered pairs can then be graphed on a coordinate plane and form part of the graph of the function. The graph of the function consists of the points in the coordinate plane that correspond to *all* the ordered pairs of the form (input, output).

Real-World EXAMPLE

1 TEMPERATURE The table shows temperatures in Celsius and the corresponding temperatures in Fahrenheit. Make a graph of the data to show the relationship between Celsius and Fahrenheit.

Celsius (input)	Fahrenheit (output)
5	41
10	50
15	59
20	68
25	77
30	86

The ordered pairs (5, 41), (10, 50), (15, 59), (20, 68), (25, 77), and (30, 86) represent this function. Graph the ordered pairs.

Celsius to Fahrenheit

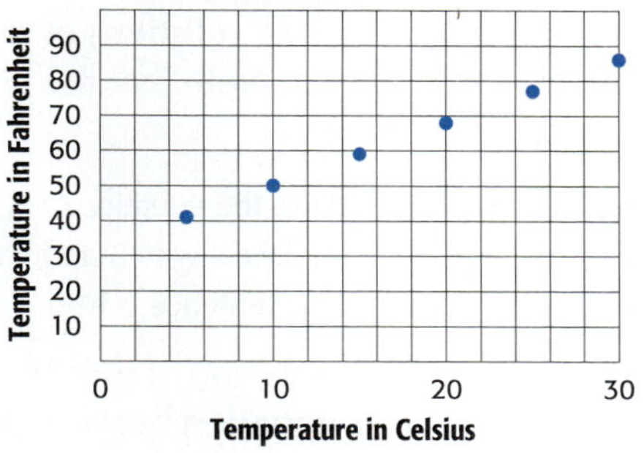

Focus on Mathematical Content

Discrete Functions Some of the functions described in this lesson are *not* continuous but are drawn with a line connecting the points. This is intentional to prepare students to make predictions from line and other graphs in Chapter 8.

3-7 Lesson Notes

1 Focus

Vertical Alignment

Before Lesson 3-7
Identify and graph ordered pairs in the four quadrants of the coordinate plane

Lesson 3-7
Solve problems involving rates, average speed, distance, and time; use a variety of methods, such as words, numbers, symbols, graphs, and tables to explain mathematical reasoning

After Lesson 3-7
Plot the values of quantities whose ratios are always the same; fit a line to the plot and understand that the slope of the line equals the ratio of the quantities

2 Teach

Scaffolding Questions

Tell students that a cheeseburger costs $2 at a local restaurant. After students answer each of the following questions, write an ordered pair (number of cheeseburgers, cost).

Ask:

- How much will 1 cheeseburger cost? (1, $2)
- How much will 2 cheeseburgers cost? (2, $4)
- How much will 3 cheeseburgers cost? (3, $6)
- How much will 4 cheeseburgers cost? (4, $8)
- How could you use this information to make a line graph? Sample answer: Show the number of cheeseburgers on the *x*-axis and the cost on the *y*-axis.

Lesson 3-7 Functions and Graphs 163

Review Vocabulary

function a relation in which each element of the input is paired with exactly one element of the output according to a specified rule (Lesson 1-10)

CHECK Your Progress

a. **MUSIC** The table shows the money remaining on a \$75 gift certificate after a certain number of CDs are bought. Make a graph to show how the number of CDs bought and the remaining balance are related.
See Ch. 3 Answer Appendix.

$75 Music Gift Certificate	
Number of CDs	Balance ($)
1	63
2	51
3	39
4	27
5	15

The solution of an equation with two variables consists of two numbers, one for each variable, that make the equation true. The solution is usually written as an ordered pair (x, y).

EXAMPLE Graph Solutions of Linear Equations

2 **Graph $y = 2x + 1$.**

Select any four values for the input x. We chose 2, 1, 0, and -1. Substitute these values for x to find the output y.

x	$2x + 1$	y	(x, y)
2	$2(2) + 1$	5	(2, 5)
1	$2(1) + 1$	3	(1, 3)
0	$2(0) + 1$	1	(0, 1)
-1	$2(-1) + 1$	-1	$(-1, -1)$

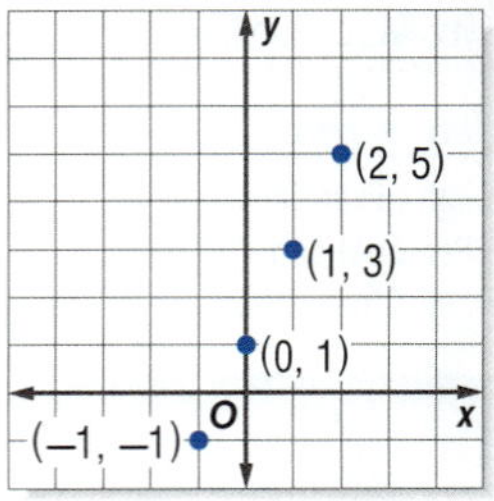

The four inputs correspond to the solutions (2, 5), (1, 3), (0, 1), and $(-1, -1)$. By graphing these ordered pairs, you can create the graph of $y = 2x + 1$.

CHECK Your Progress Graph each equation.
b–d. See Ch. 3 Answer Appendix.

b. $y = x - 3$ c. $y = -3x$ d. $y = -3x + 2$

Study Tip

Graphing Equations Only two points are needed to graph the line. However, graph more points to check accuracy.

Notice that all four points in the graph lie on the same straight line. Draw a line through the points to graph *all* solutions of the equation $y = 2x + 1$. Note that the point (3, 7) is also on this line.

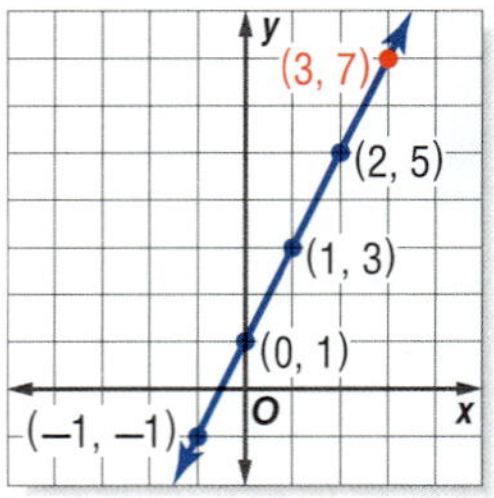

$y = 2x + 1$	Write the equation.
$7 \stackrel{?}{=} 2(3) + 1$	Replace x with 3 and y with 7.
$7 = 7$ ✓	This sentence is true.

So, (3, 7) is also a solution of $y = 2x + 1$. An equation like $y = 2x + 1$ is called a **linear equation** because its graph is a straight line.

Focus on Mathematical Content

Functions can be graphed on a **coordinate plane**.

To find **solutions** to a function, substitute values for the input variable, x, and then solve to get the corresponding values for the output variable, y. Each solution is an **ordered pair** (x, y).

To show a function on a coordinate plane, **graph several ordered pairs** that represent it, and then connect the points.

The graph of a **linear function** is a line.

Formative Assessment

Use the Check Your Progress exercises after each Example to determine students' understanding of concepts.

ADDITIONAL EXAMPLES

1 **WORK** The table shows the number of hours Abby worked and her corresponding earnings. Make a graph of the data to show the relationship between the number of hours Abby worked and her earnings.

Number of Hours	Earnings ($)
1	6
2	12
3	18
4	24

2 Graph $y = x + 3$.

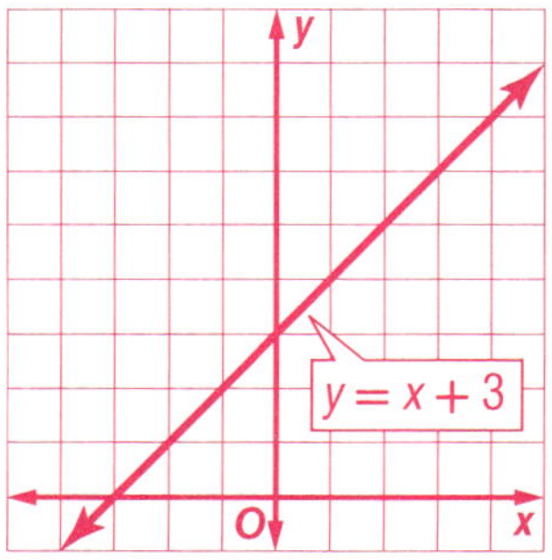

Real-World EXAMPLE

3 **SWIMMING** **Michael Phelps swims the 400-meter individual medley at an average speed of 100 meters per minute. The equation $d = 100t$ describes the distance d that he can swim in t minutes at this speed. Represent the function by a graph.**

Step 1 Select any four values for t. Select only positive numbers because t represents time. Make a function table.

t	$100t$	d	(t, d)
1	100(1)	100	(1, 100)
2	100(2)	200	(2, 200)
3	100(3)	300	(3, 300)
4	100(4)	400	(4, 400)

Step 2 Graph the ordered pairs and draw a line through the points.

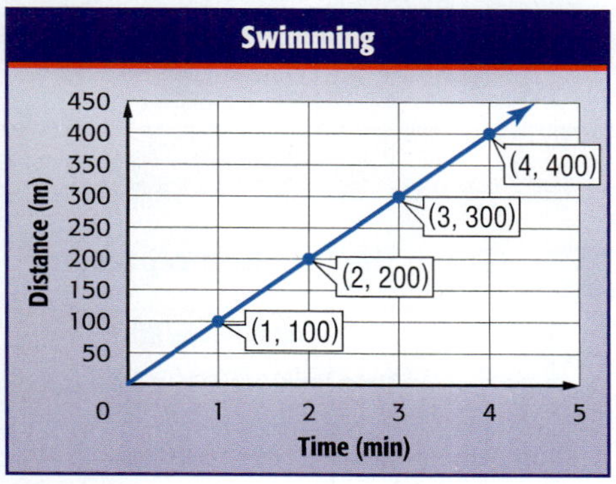

CHECK Your Progress

e. **JOBS** Sandi makes \$6 an hour babysitting. The equation $m = 6h$ describes how much money m she earns babysitting for h hours. Represent this function by a graph. **See Ch. 3 Answer Appendix.**

Representing Functions

Key Concept

Words There are 12 inches in one foot.

Table

Feet	Inches
1	12
2	24
3	36
4	48

Graph

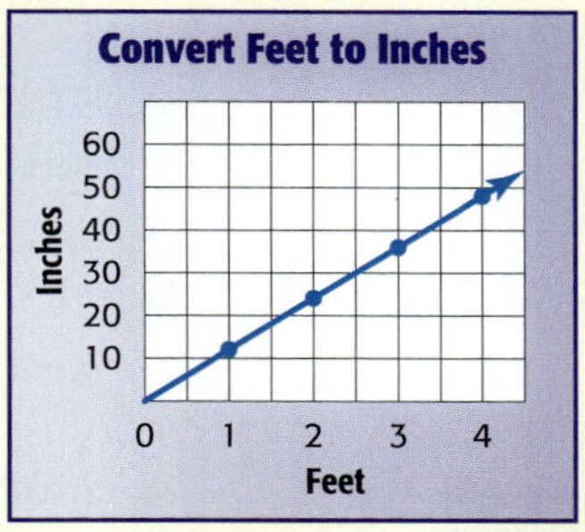

Equation $f = 12n$, where f represents the number of feet and n represents the number of inches.

ADDITIONAL EXAMPLE

3 **ANIMALS** Blue whales can reach a top speed of 30 miles per hour. The equation $d = 30t$ describes the distance d that a whale swimming at that speed can travel in time t. Assuming that a whale can maintain the speed, represent the function with a graph.

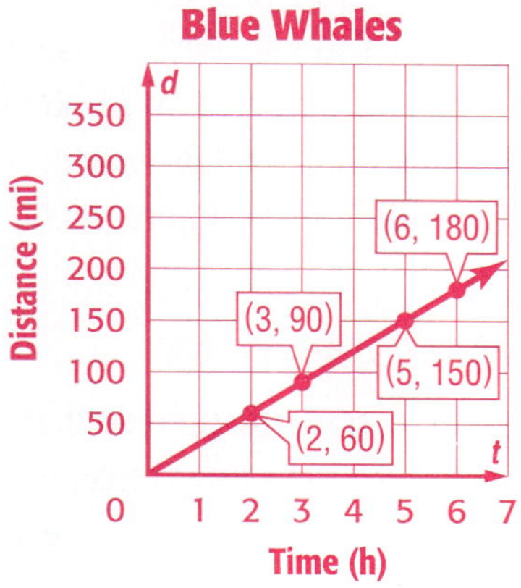

Additional Examples are also in:

- Noteables™ Interactive Study Notebook with Foldables™
- Interactive Classroom PowerPoint® Presentations

Lesson 3-7 Functions and Graphs **165**

3 Practice

Formative Assessment

Use Exercises 1–6 to check for understanding.

Then use the chart at the bottom of this page to customize your assignments for students.

Intervention You may wish to use the Study Guide and Intervention Master on page 46 of the *Chapter 3 Resource Masters* for additional reinforcement.

Odd/Even Assignments

Exercises 7–16 are structured so that students practice the same concepts whether they are assigned odd or even problems.

Tips for New Teachers: Graphs

Some students may wonder why some of the directions say to "graph the equation" while others say to "graph the function." Remind them that functions can be shown in tables and written as equations. You may wish to have students review Lesson 1-10 to see how functions can be written as equations.

CHECK Your Understanding

Example 1 (p. 163)

1–6. See Ch. 3 Answer Appendix.

Graph the function represented by each table.

1. Total Cost of Baseballs

Baseball	Total Cost ($)
1	4
2	8
3	12
4	16

2. Convert Minutes to Seconds

Minutes	Seconds
1	60
2	120
3	180
4	240

Example 2 (p. 164)

Graph each equation.

3. $y = x - 1$
4. $y = -1x$
5. $y = -2x + 3$

Example 3 (p. 165)

6. **MEASUREMENT** The perimeter of a square is 4 times greater than the length of one of its sides. The equation $p = 4s$ describes the perimeter p of a square with sides s units long. Represent this function by a graph.

Practice and Problem Solving

HOMEWORK HELP

For Exercises	See Examples
7–8	1
9–14	2
15–16	3

Exercise Levels
A: 7–16
B: 17–20
C: 21–24

Graph the function represented by each table. 7–20. See Ch. 3 Answer Appendix.

7. Total Phone Bill

Time (min)	Total (¢)
1	8
2	16
3	24
4	32

8. Calories in Fruit Cups

Servings	Total Calories
1	70
3	210
5	350
7	490

Graph each equation.

9. $y = x + 1$
10. $y = x + 3$
11. $y = x$
12. $y = -2x$
13. $y = 2x + 3$
14. $y = 3x - 1$

For Exercises 15 and 16, represent each function by a graph.

15. **CARS** A car averages 36 miles per gallon of gasoline. The function $m = 36g$ represents the miles m driven using g gallons of gasoline.

16. **FITNESS** A health club charges $35 a month for membership fees. The equation $c = 35m$ describes the total charge c for m months of membership.

Graph each equation.

17. $y = 0.25x$
18. $y = x + 0.5$
19. $y = 0.5x - 1$

Academic Standards • ISTEP+
Extra Practice, pp. 676, 706.

20. **SHOPPING** You buy a DVD for $14 and CDs for $9 each. The equation $t = 14 + 9c$ represents the total amount t that you spend if you buy 1 DVD and c CDs. Represent this function by a graph.

DIFFERENTIATED HOMEWORK OPTIONS

Level	Assignment	Two-Day Option	
BL Basic	7–16, 21, 24–31	7–15 odd, 25	8–16 even, 21, 24, 26–31
OL Core	7–13 odd, 15–17, 19–21, 24–31	7–16, 25	17–21, 24, 26–31
AL Advanced/Pre-AP	17–31		

H.O.T. Problems

21. **OPEN ENDED** Draw the graph of a linear function. Name three ordered pairs in the function. **See students' work.**

CHALLENGE For Exercises 22 and 23, let x represent the first number and let y represent the second number. Draw a graph of each function.

22. The second number is three more than the first number. **22–23. See margin.**
23. The second number is the product of -3 and the first number.

24. **WRITING IN MATH** Describe how you use a function table to create the graph of a function. **See Ch. 3 Answer Appendix.**

ISTEP+ PRACTICE Preparation for 8.2.4

25. The graph shows the relationship between the number of hours Jennifer spent jogging and the total number of miles she jogged. Which table best represents the data in the graph? **C**

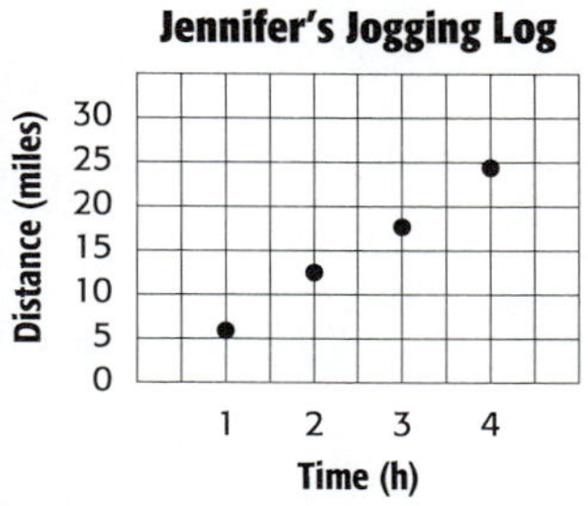

A

Time (h)	Distance (mi)
6	4
12	3
18	2
24	1

B

Time (h)	Distance (mi)
2	6
3	12
4	18
5	24

C

Time (h)	Distance (mi)
1	6
2	12
3	18
4	24

D

Time (h)	Distance (mi)
4	6
3	6
2	6
1	6

Spiral Review

26. **MEASUREMENT** The area and width of a rug are 323 square inches and 17 inches respectively. What is the perimeter of the rug? (Lesson 3-6) **72 in.**

Solve each equation. Check your solution. (Lesson 3-5)

27. $4y + 19 = 7$ **−3**
28. $10x + 2 = 32$ **3**
29. $48 - 8j = 16$ **4**
30. $14 = 2 - 6d$ **−2**

31. Evaluate $|5| + |-10|$. (Lesson 2-1) **15**

Problem Solving in Social Studies

Real-World Unit Project

Stand Up and Be Counted! It's time to complete your project. Use the data you have gathered about how the U.S. Census affects the House of Representatives to prepare a poster. Be sure to include a map, frequency table, and paragraph discussing the changes in the House of Representatives.

IN Math Online Unit Project at glencoe.com

Pre-AP Activity Use after Exercise 19

Have students describe the functions they graphed for Exercises 17–19. Do the lines slope upward or downward? How steep are the lines? Where do the lines intersect the y-axis?

4 Assess

Ticket Out the Door Have students describe the functions they graphed for one of the following exercises: 11, 12, or 19. Are the functions linear? Do the functions rise or fall?

Formative Assessment

Check for student understanding of concepts in Lesson 3-7.

CRM Quiz 4, p. 56

FOLDABLES Study Organizer Foldables™ Follow-Up

Remind students to take notes about today's lesson under the *Functions* tab of their Foldables. Encourage them to write a linear function from the lesson, complete a function table, and graph the function.

Additional Answers

22.

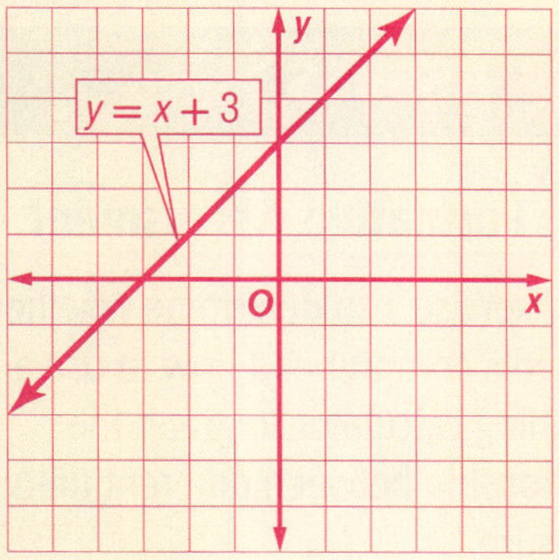

23.

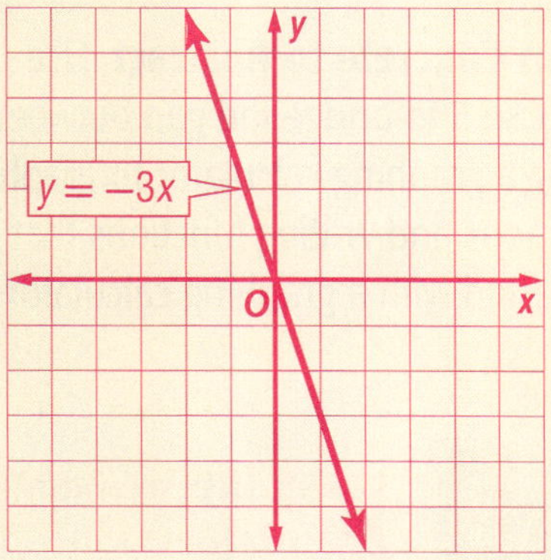

Extend 3-7 Lesson Notes

1 Focus

Materials

- graphing calculator

Teaching Tip

If your class does not have enough graphing calculators for every student, have students work in pairs or groups of three, sharing calculators.

2 Teach

Activity When typing fractions into the graphing calculator, place parentheses around the fraction and use the division button to denote the fraction bar. For example, type (1/3) to represent the fraction $\frac{1}{3}$.

3 Assess

Formative Assessment

Use Exercise 1 to determine whether students comprehend how to use a graphing calculator to graph the relationship between different units of measure.

From Concrete to Abstract Use Exercise 5 to bridge the gap between using a graphing calculator to graph functions and writing functions that can be tested with a graphing calculator.

Tips for New Teachers — Using the Graphing Calculator

The first function key under the MATH key is ▶Frac. Use this function key to convert a terminating decimal to a fraction. For example, to convert the decimal 0.356 to a fraction, enter 0.356 on your calculator. Press the MATH key and then press 1 (or ENTER). The screen displays the conversion of 0.356 as 89/250. You can also use this function key to convert a repeating decimal as a fraction as long as you type in several of the repeating digits.

Extend 3-7

Graphing Calculator Lab
Graphing Relationships

MAIN IDEA

Use technology to graph relationships involving conversions of measurement.

IN Academic Standards

Preparation for 8.2.4 Identify and graph linear functions and identify lines with positive and negative slope. *Also addresses P.4.1, P.7.1.*

You can use a graphing calculator to graph relationships.

ACTIVITY

1 MEASUREMENT **Use the table at the right to write a function that relates the number of yards x to the number of feet y. Then graph your function.**

Yards (x)	Feet (y)
1	3
2	6
3	9
4	12

STEP 1 By examining the table, you can see that the number of feet is 3 times the number of yards. Write a function.

The number of feet	is	3 times	the number of yards.
y	$=$	3	x

STEP 2 Press Y= and enter the function $y = 3x$ into Y_1.

STEP 3 Adjust your viewing window. Press WINDOW and change the values to reflect the range of values in the table.

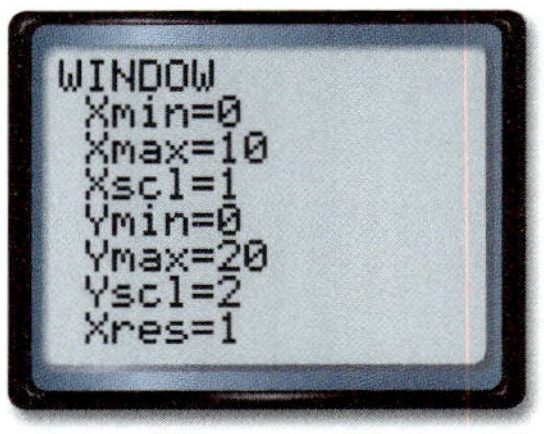

STEP 4 Finally, graph the function by pressing Graph.

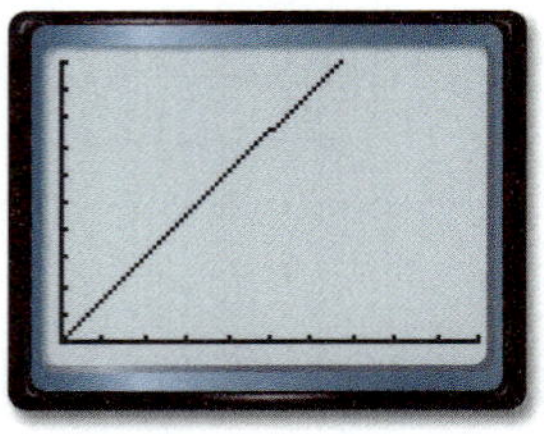

ANALYZE THE RESULTS 1–5. See Ch. 3 Answer Appendix.

1. Test the function above using one of the values from the table and the CALC feature on your calculator. Press 2nd [CALC] 1 and then enter an x-value of 3. What y-value is displayed? What do each of these values represent and how are they represented on the graph?
2. Use your graph to convert 7 yards into feet. Explain your method.
3. **MAKE A CONJECTURE** Write a function that could be used to convert feet into yards. What is an appropriate window for a graph of this function? Graph and test your function.
4. Use your function from Exercise 3 to convert 16 feet into yards.
5. Write a function that could be used to convert 36 ounces to pounds. Indicate an appropriate window, then use a graph of the function to convert 36 ounces to pounds. (*Hint*: 1 pound = 16 ounces)

168 Chapter 3 Algebra: Linear Equations and Functions

CHAPTER 3 Study Guide and Review

IN Math Online glencoe.com
- STUDY TO GO
- Vocabulary Review

FOLDABLES Study Organizer GET READY to Study

Be sure the following Big Ideas are noted in your Foldable.

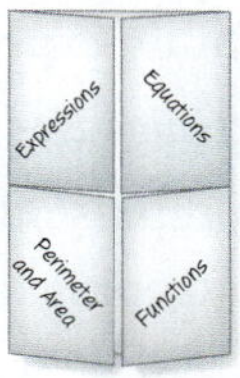

BIG Ideas

Solving Equations (Lessons 3-2, 3-3, and 3-5)
- If you add or subtract the same number from each side of an equation, the two sides remain equal.
- If you divide each side of an equation by the same nonzero number, the two sides remain equal.
- To solve a two-step equation like $3x + 4 = 19$ or $2x - 1 = -5$:

  Step 1 Undo the addition or subtraction first.

  Step 2 Then undo the multiplication or division.

Perimeter and Area Formulas (Lesson 3-6)
- The perimeter P of a rectangle is twice the sum of the length ℓ and width w.
- The area A of a rectangle is the product of the length ℓ and width w.

Linear Functions (Lesson 3-7)
- The graph of a linear function is a straight line. Ordered pairs in the form (x, y) can be used to represent a function and graphed on the coordinate plane as part of the graph of the function.

2. false; addition
7. False; subtract 3 from each side.
10. false; 5 times the value of x

Key Vocabulary

formula (p. 144)
linear equation (p. 164)
two-step equation (p. 151)
work backward strategy (p. 148)

Vocabulary Check

State whether each sentence is *true* or *false*. If *false*, replace the underlined word or number to make a true sentence.

1. The expression $\frac{1}{3}y$ means <u>one third of y</u>. **true**
2. The words *more than* sometimes suggest the operation of <u>multiplication</u>.
3. The formula <u>$d = rt$</u> gives the distance d traveled at a rate of r for t units of time. **true**
4. The algebraic expression representing the words *six less than m* is <u>$6 - m$</u>. **false; $m - 6$**
5. Use the <u>work backward</u> strategy when you are given a final result and asked to find an earlier amount. **true**
6. The word *each* sometimes suggests the operation of <u>division</u>. **false; multiplication**
7. In solving the equation $4x + 3 = 15$, first <u>divide each side by 4</u>.
8. The solution to the equation $p + 4.4 = 11.6$ is <u>7.2</u>. **true**
9. The process of solving a <u>two-step equation</u> uses the work backward strategy. **true**
10. The expression $5x$ means <u>5 more than x</u>.
11. To find the distance around a rectangle, use the formula for its <u>area</u>. **false; perimeter**
12. The word *per* sometimes suggests the operation of <u>subtraction</u>. **false; division**

CHAPTER 3 Study Guide and Review

FOLDABLES Study Organizer Dinah Zike's Foldables

Have students look through the chapter to make sure they have included notes, key concepts, and examples in their Foldables for each lesson.

Encourage students to refer to their Foldables while completing the Study Guide and Review and while preparing for the Chapter Test.

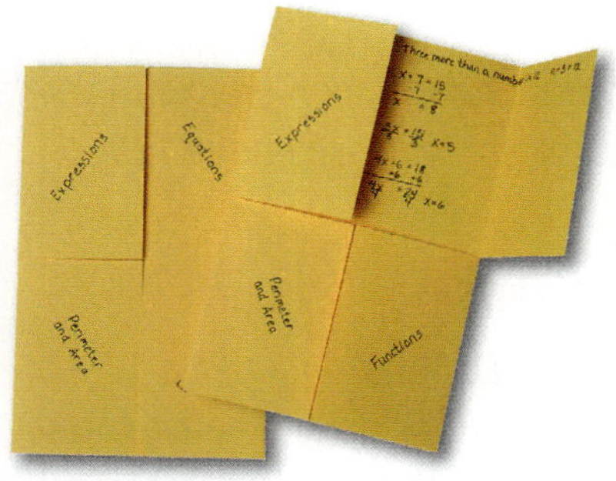

Formative Assessment

Key Vocabulary The page references after each word in the Key Vocabulary denote where that term was first introduced. If students have difficulty answering Exercises 1–12, remind them that they can use these page references to refresh their memories about the vocabulary terms.

IN Math Online glencoe.com

Vocabulary PuzzleMaker improves students' mathematics vocabulary using four puzzle formats—crossword, scramble, word search using a word list, and word search using clues. Students can work online or from a printed worksheet.

Summative Assessment

CRM Vocabulary Test, p. 58

CHAPTER 3 Study Guide and Review

Lesson-by-Lesson Review

Intervention If the given examples are not sufficient to review the topics covered by the questions, remind students that the page references tell them where to review that topic in their textbooks.

Two-Day Option Have students complete the Lesson-by-Lesson Review on pages 170–172. Then you can use ExamView® Assessment Suite to customize another review worksheet that practices all the objectives of this chapter or only the objectives on which your students need more help.

For more information on ExamView® Assessment Suite, see page 126C.

Differentiated Instruction

Super DVD: MindJogger Plus
Use this DVD as an alternative format of review for the test. For more information on this game show format, see page 126D.

CHAPTER 3 Study Guide and Review

Lesson-by-Lesson Review

3-1 Writing Expressions and Equations (pp. 128–133)

7.2.1

Write each phrase as an algebraic expression.

13. the sum of a number and 5 **$x + 5$**
14. six inches less than her height **$h - 6$**
15. twice as many apples **$2a$**

Write each sentence as an algebraic equation.

16. Ten years older than Theresa's age is 23. **$10 + t = 23$**
17. Four less than a number is 19. **$n - 4 = 19$**
18. The quotient of 56 and a number is 14. **$\frac{56}{n} = 14$**
19. **AMUSEMENT PARKS** This year, admission to a popular amusement park is $8.75 more than the previous year's admission fee. Write an expression describing the cost of this year's admission. **$f + \$8.75$**

Example 1 Write the phrase as an algebraic expression.

four times the price

Let p represent the price.

The algebraic expression is $4p$.

Example 2 Write the sentence as an algebraic equation.

Six less than the number of cookies is 24.

Let c represent the number of cookies.

The equation is $c - 6 = 24$.

3-2 Solving Addition and Subtraction Equations (pp. 136–141)

7.2.2

Solve each equation. Check your solution.

20. $x + 5 = 8$ **3**
21. $r + 8 = 2$ **−6**
22. $p + 9 = -4$ **−13**
23. $s - 8 = 15$ **23**
24. $n - 1 = -3$ **−2**
25. $w - 9 = 28$ **37**
26. **COOKIES** Marjorie baked some chocolate chip cookies for her and her sister. Her sister ate 6 of these cookies. If there were 18 cookies left, write and solve an equation to find how many cookies c Marjorie baked.

Example 3 Solve $x + 6 = 4$.

$$\begin{aligned} x + 6 &= 4 \\ -6 &= -6 \quad \text{Subtract 6 from each side.} \\ x &= -2 \end{aligned}$$

Example 4 Solve $y - 3 = -2$.

$$\begin{aligned} y - 3 &= -2 \\ +3 &= +3 \quad \text{Add 3 to each side.} \\ y &= 1 \end{aligned}$$

26. $c - 6 = 18$; 24 cookies

Mixed Problem Solving
For mixed problem-solving practice, see page 706.

CHAPTER 3 Study Guide and Review

3-3 Solving Multiplication Equations (pp. 142–146)

7.2.2

Solve each equation. Check your solution.

27. $7c = 28$ **4**
28. $-8w = 72$ **−9**
29. $10y = -90$ **−9**
30. $-12r = -36$ **3**
31. **MONEY** Matt borrowed \$98 from his father. He plans to repay his father at \$14 per week. Write and solve an equation to find the number of weeks w required to pay back his father.

31. $14w = 98$; 7 weeks

Example 5 Solve $-4b = 32$.

$$-4b = 32$$

$$\frac{-4b}{-4} = \frac{32}{-4} \quad \text{Divide each side by } -4.$$

$$b = -8$$

3-4 PSI: Work Backward (pp. 148–149)

P.1.3

Solve. Use the *work backward* strategy.

32. **BASEBALL** Last baseball season, Nelson had four less than twice the number of hits Marcus had. Nelson had 48 hits. How many hits did Marcus have last season? **26 hits**
33. **CREDIT CARDS** Alicia paid off \$119 of her credit card balance and made an additional \$62.75 in purchases. If she now owes \$90.45, what was her starting balance? **\$146.70**

Example 6 **A number is divided by 2. Then 4 is added to the quotient. After subtracting 3, the result is 18. What is the number?**

Start with the final value and work backward with each resulting value until you arrive at the starting value.

$18 + 3 = 21$ Undo subtracting 3.

$21 - 4 = 17$ Undo adding 4.

$17 \cdot 2 = 34$ Undo dividing by 2.

The number is 34.

3-5 Solving Two-Step Equations (pp. 151–155)

7.2.2

Solve each equation. Check your solution.

34. $3y - 12 = 6$ **6**
35. $6x - 4 = 20$ **4**
36. $2x + 5 = 3$ **−1**
37. $5m + 6 = -4$ **−2**
38. $10c - 8 = 90$ **9.8**
39. $3r - 20 = -5$ **5**
40. **ALGEBRA** Ten more than five times a number is 25. Find the number. **3**

Example 7 Solve $3p - 4 = 8$.

$$3p - 4 = 8$$

$$+4 = +4 \quad \text{Add 4 to each side.}$$

$$3p = 12$$

$$\frac{3p}{3} = \frac{12}{3} \quad \text{Divide each side by 3.}$$

$$p = 4$$

Chapter 3 Study Guide and Review 171

Problem Solving Review

For additional practice in problem solving for Chapter 3, see the Mixed Problem Solving Appendix, page 706 in the Student Handbook section.

Anticipation Guide

Have students complete the Chapter 3 Anticipation Guide and discuss how their responses have changed now that they have completed Chapter 3.

CRM Anticipation Guide, pp. 7–8

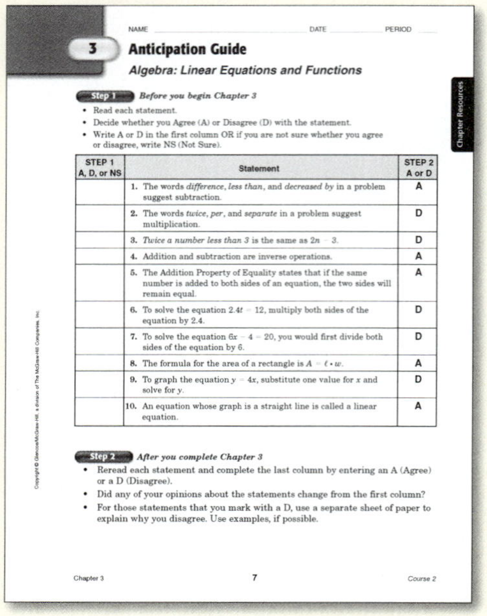
NAME ______ DATE ______ PERIOD ______

3 **Anticipation Guide**

Algebra: Linear Equations and Functions

Step 1 *Before you begin Chapter 3*

- Read each statement.
- Decide whether you Agree (A) or Disagree (D) with the statement.
- Write A or D in the first column OR if you are not sure whether you agree or disagree, write NS (Not Sure).

STEP 1 A, D, or NS	Statement	STEP 2 A or D
	1. The words *difference*, *less than*, and *decreased by* in a problem suggest subtraction.	A
	2. The words *twice*, *per*, and *separate* in a problem suggest multiplication.	D
	3. *Twice a number less than 3* is the same as $2n - 3$.	D
	4. Addition and subtraction are inverse operations.	A
	5. The Addition Property of Equality states that if the same number is added to both sides of an equation, the two sides will remain equal.	A
	6. To solve the equation $2.4t = 12$, multiply both sides of the equation by 2.4.	D
	7. To solve the equation $6x - 4 = 20$, you would first divide both sides of the equation by 6.	D
	8. The formula for the area of a rectangle is $A = \ell \cdot w$.	A
	9. To graph the equation $y = 4x$, substitute one value for x and solve for y.	D
	10. An equation whose graph is a straight line is called a linear equation.	A

Step 2 *After you complete Chapter 3*

- Reread each statement and complete the last column by entering an A (Agree) or a D (Disagree).
- Did any of your opinions about the statements change from the first column?
- For those statements that you mark with a D, use a separate sheet of paper to explain why you disagree. Use examples, if possible.

Chapter Resources

Chapter 3 7 Course 2

Additional Answers

48.

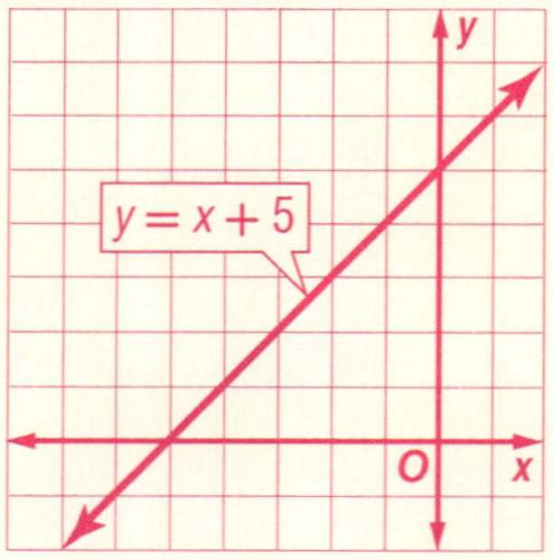

49.

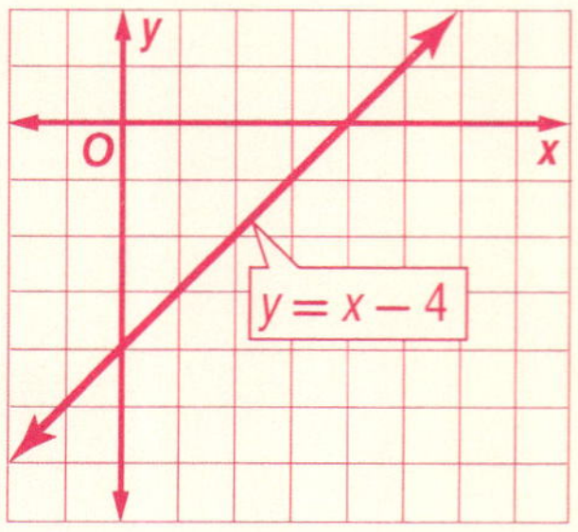

50.

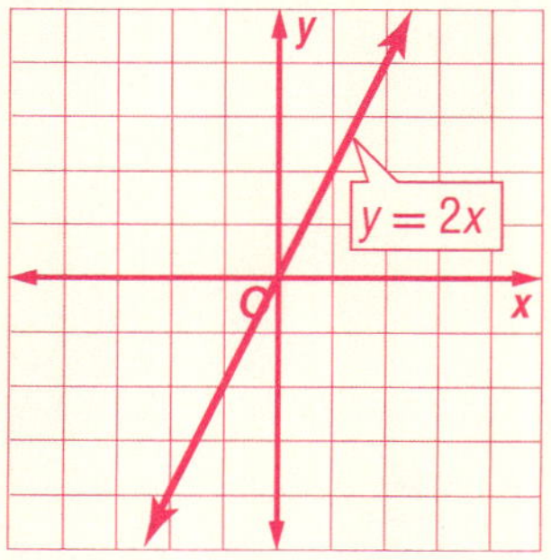

51.

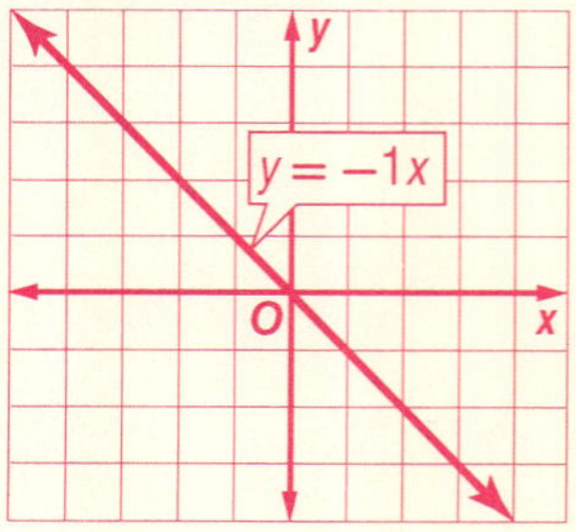

CHAPTER 3 Study Guide and Review

3-6 Measurement: Perimeter and Area (pp. 156–161)

7.2.4

Find the perimeter and area of each rectangle.

41.

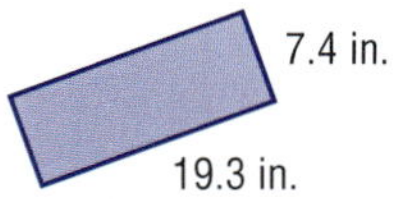

53.4 in.; 142.82 in²

42.

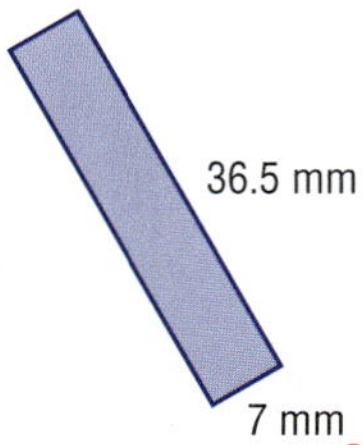

87 mm; 255.5 mm²

Find the missing measure.

43. $P = 56$ mi, $\ell = 21$ mi **7 mi**

44. $A = 10.26$ ft², $w = 2.7$ ft **3.8 ft**

45. $A = 272$ yd², $\ell = 17$ yd **16 yd**

46. $P = 14.2$ cm, $w = 2.6$ cm **4.5 cm**

47. **CARPET** In order to carpet her rectangular living room, Flora needs 192 square feet of carpet. If the length of her living room is 16 feet, find the width. **12 ft**

Example 8 The perimeter of a rectangle is 38 meters. If the length is 7 meters, find the width.

$P = 2\ell + 2w$	Perimeter formula
$38 = 2(7) + 2w$	Replace P with 38 and ℓ with 7.
$38 = 14 + 2w$	Simplify.
$24 = 2w$	Subtract 14 from each side.
$\frac{24}{2} = \frac{2w}{2}$	Divide each side by 2.
$12 = w$	Simplify.

The width is 12 meters.

Example 9 The area of a rectangle is 285 square inches. If the width is 15 inches, find the length.

$A = \ell w$	Area formula
$285 = \ell(15)$	Replace A with 285 and w with 15.
$\frac{285}{15} = \frac{15\ell}{15}$	Divide each side by 15.
$19 = \ell$	Simplify.

The length is 19 inches.

3-7 Functions and Graphs (pp. 163–167)

8.2.4

Graph each equation. **48–51. See margin.**

48. $y = x + 5$

49. $y = x - 4$

50. $y = 2x$

51. $y = -1x$

52. $y = 3x + 2$

53. $y = -2x + 3$

52–53. See Ch. 3 Answer Appendix.

MONEY For Exercises 54–56, use the following information.

Clara earns $9 per hour mowing lawns.

54. Make a table that shows her total earnings for 2, 4, 6, and 8 hours.

55. Write an equation in which x represents the number of hours and y represents Clara's total earnings. **$y = 9x$**

56. Graph the equation.

54, 56. See Ch. 3 Answer Appendix.

Example 10 Graph $y = x + 3$.

Select four values for x. Substitute these values for x to find values for y.

x	$x + 3$	y
−1	−1 + 3	2
0	0 + 3	3
1	1 + 3	4
2	2 + 3	5

Four solutions are (−1, 2), (0, 3), (1, 4), and (2, 5). The graph is shown below.

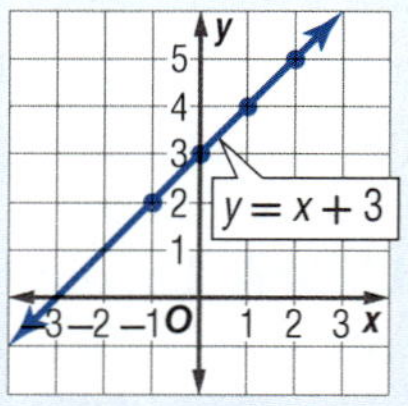

CHAPTER 3 Practice Test

IN Math Online glencoe.com
• Chapter Test

CHAPTER 3 Practice Test

Write each phrase as an algebraic expression or equation.

1. \$5 less than Tomasita has $t - 5$
2. 4 years older than Hana $h + 4$
3. 56 inches is 9 inches shorter than Jacob's height. $56 = j - 9$
4. Twice the distance from the park to the post office is 5 miles. $2d = 5$
5. **FLOWERS** The number of tulips in Paula's garden is 8 less than the number of marigolds. If there are 16 tulips, write and solve an equation to determine the number of marigolds m. $16 = m - 8$; 24
6. **MULTIPLE CHOICE** If you divide a number by 8 and subtract 11 from the result, the answer is 4. Which equation matches this relationship? B

   A $\frac{n - 11}{8} = 4$ **C** $\frac{n}{8} = 11 - 4$

   B $4 = \frac{n}{8} - 11$ **D** $4 = 11 - \frac{n}{8}$

ANALYZE TABLES **For Exercises 7–9, use the table below. It shows how Jared's age and his sister Emily's are related.** 7. $y = x + 6$

Jared's age (yr)	1	2	3	4	5
Emily's age (yr)	7	8	9	10	11

7. Write an equation in which x represents Jared's age, and y represents Emily's age.
8. Graph the equation. See margin.
9. Predict how old Emily will be when Jared is 10 years old. 16 yr

$x - 835 = 151$; 986 ft

10. **TOURISM** The Statue of Liberty is 151 feet tall. It is 835 feet shorter than the Eiffel Tower. Write and solve an equation to find the height of the Eiffel Tower.

Solve each equation. Check your solution.

11. $x + 5 = -8$ -13
12. $y - 11 = 15$ 26
13. $9z = -81$ -9
14. $-6k + 4 = -38$ 7
15. $3z - 7 = 17$ 8
16. $2g - 9 = -5$ 2

17. **PIZZA** Chris and Joe shared a pizza. Chris ate two more than twice as many pieces as Joe, who ate 3 pieces. If there were 3 pieces left, how many pieces were there initially? Use the *work backward* strategy. 14 pieces
18. **MULTIPLE CHOICE** A giant cake in the shape of and decorated as an American flag was 60 feet in length. If it took A square feet of icing to cover the top of the cake, which of the following would represent the cake's perimeter? F

    F $P = 120 + 2 \cdot \frac{A}{60}$ **H** $P = 60 + \frac{A}{60}$

    G $P = 120 + 2A$ **J** $P = 60 + 2A$

Find the perimeter and area of each rectangle.

19.
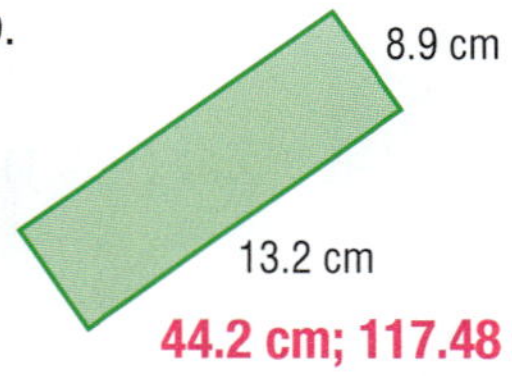

44.2 cm; 117.48 cm^2

20.
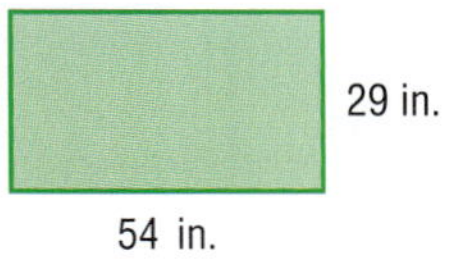

166 in.; 1,566 in^2

Graph each equation. 21–24. See Ch. 3 Answer Appendix.

21. $y = x + 1$
22. $y = 2x$
23. $y = 2x - 3$
24. $y = -x + 1$

25. See Ch. 3 Answer Appendix.

25. **MOVIES** A student ticket to the movies costs \$6. The equation $c = 6t$ describes the total cost c for t tickets. Make a function table that shows the total cost for 1, 2, 3, and 4 tickets and then graph the equation.

Summative Assessment

Chapter 3 Resource Masters

Leveled Chapter 3 Tests			
Form	Type	Level	Pages
1	MC	BL	59–60
2A	MC	OL	61–62
2B	MC	OL	63–64
2C	FR	OL	65–66
2D	FR	OL	67–68
3	FR	AL	69–70

MC = multiple-choice questions
FR = free-response questions
BL = below or approaching grade level
OL = on grade level
AL = above or beyond grade level

- Vocabulary Test, p. 58
- Extended-Response Test, p. 71
- Unit 1 Test, pp. 75–76

ExamView Assessment Suite Customize and create multiple versions of your chapter test and the answer key. All of the questions from the leveled chapter tests in the *Chapter 3 Resource Masters* are also available on ExamView® Assessment Suite.

Additional Answer

8.
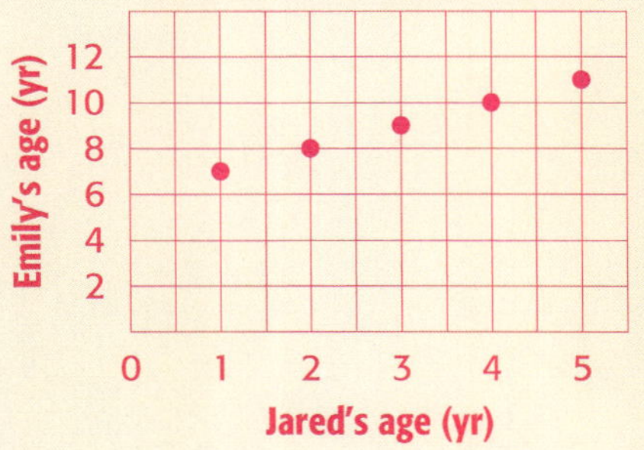

Data-Driven Decision Making

Diagnostic Teaching Based on the results of the Chapter 3 Practice Test, use the following to review concepts that students continue to find challenging.

Exercises	Lesson	Academic Standards
1–5, 10–12	3-1, 3-2	7.2.1, 7.2.2
6, 13, 17	3-3, 3-4	7.2.2, P.1.3
14–16, 18–20	3-5, 3-6	7.2.2, 7.2.4
7–9, 21–25	3-7	8.2.4

Resources for Review

Study Guide and Intervention
pp. 10, 16, 23, 28, 33, 39, and 46

IN Math Online
- Extra Examples
- Personal Tutor
- Concepts in Motion

CHAPTER 3 ISTEP+ Practice

TEST-TAKING TIP

Exercise 3 Remind students that they can eliminate incorrect answer choices by substituting one of the given positions, say 3, for *n* and using mental math to perform the described operations. Is the result 13? Using this procedure, students can eliminate answer choices A, B, and C.

Formative Assessment

You can use these two pages to benchmark student progress.

CRM *Chapter 3 Resource Masters*

- Standardized Test Practice, pp. 72–74

ExamView Assessment Suite Create practice worksheets or tests that align to your state's standards, as well as TIMSS and NAEP tests.

CHAPTER 3 ISTEP+ Practice
Cumulative, Chapters 1–3

IN Math Online glencoe.com
- Test Practice

PART 1 Multiple Choice

Read each question. Then fill in the correct answer on the answer sheet provided by your teacher or on a sheet of paper.

1. During a bike-a-thon, Shalonda cycled at a constant rate. The table shows the distance she covered in half-hour intervals.

Time (h)	Distance (mi)
$\frac{1}{2}$	6
1	12
$1\frac{1}{2}$	18
2	24

Which of the following equations represents the distance *d* Shalonda covered after *h* hours? **D**

A $d = 6 + h$

B $d = 6h$

C $d = 12 + h$

D $d = 12h$

2. Which line contains the ordered pair $(-2, 4)$? **H**

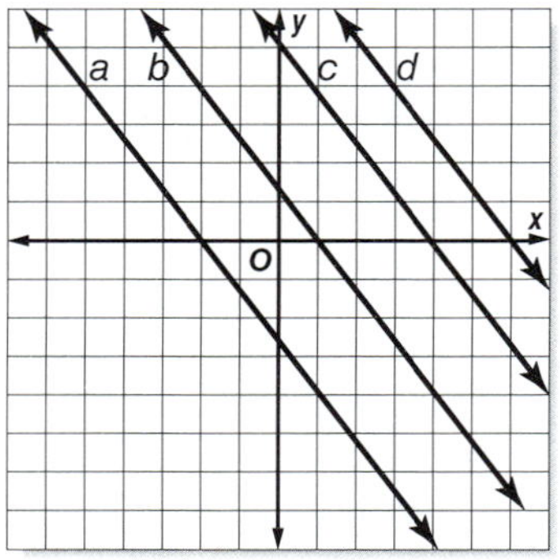

F line *a** **H** line *b*

G line *c* **J** line *d*

3. The table gives the value of several terms and their positions in a sequence.

Position	3	4	5	6	7	*n*
Value of Term	13	17	21	25	29	

Which description shows the relationship between a term and *n*, its position in the sequence? **D**

A Add 4 to *n*.

B Multiply *n* by 5 and add 1.

C Multiply *n* by 3 and add 2.

D Multiply *n* by 4 and add 1.

4. Mr. McDowell owes $1,750 on his car loan and pays off $185 each month towards the loan balance. Which expression represents how much money in dollars he still owes after *x* months? **J**

F $1{,}750x$

G $1{,}750x + 185$

H $1{,}750x - 185$

J $1{,}750 - 185x$

5. Which of the following problems can be solved by solving the equation $x - 9 = 15$? **A**

A Allison is nine years younger than her sister Pam. Allison is 15 years old. What is *x*, Pam's age?

B David's portion of the bill is $9 more than Sam's portion of the bill. If Sam pays $9, find *x*, the amount in dollars that David pays.

C The sum of two numbers is 15. If one of the numbers is 9, what is *x*, the other number?

D Pedro owns 15 CDs. If he gave 9 of them to a friend, what is *x*, the number of CDs he has left?

Preparing for ISTEP+
For test-taking strategies and practice, see pages 716–733.

CHAPTER 3 ISTEP+ Practice

6. The table below shows values for x and corresponding values for y.

x	y
18	2
27	3
9	1
36	4

Which of the following represents the relationship between x and y? **H**

F $y = x + 16$

G $y = 9x$

H $y = \frac{1}{9}x$

J $y = x + 9$

TEST-TAKING TIP

Question 7 Read the question carefully to check that you answered the question that was asked. In question 7, you are asked to pick which coordinates lie within the triangle, not to identify a vertex.

7. Which of the following coordinates lies within the triangle graphed below? **D**

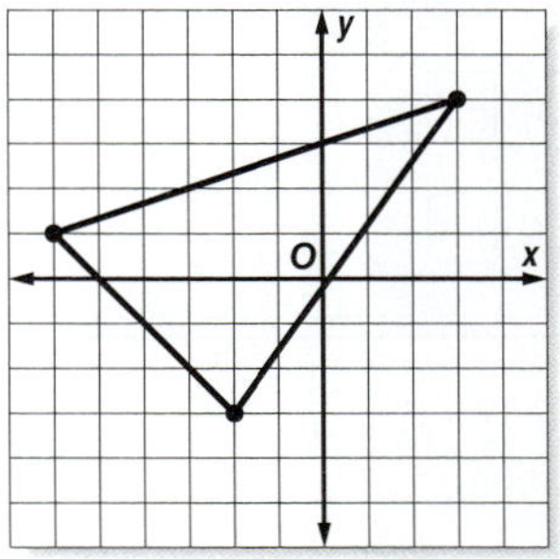

A (3, 4)

B (2, 0)

C (−3, 6)

D (−1, −1)

PART 2 Short Response/Grid In

Record your answers on the answer sheet provided by your teacher or on a sheet of paper.

8. Write an expression that can be used to find the maximum number of 3-foot pieces of lumber than can be cut from a 12-foot length of lumber. **12 ÷ 3**

9. Tonya bought p pounds of sand. Each pound of sand costs \$0.40. How many pounds of sand could Tonya buy with \$3.20? **8**

PART 3 Extended Response

Record your answers on the answer sheet provided by your teacher or on a sheet of paper. Show your work.

10. The distances traveled by cars traveling at 40 miles per hour and at 60 miles per hour are given in the table. **10a–c. See margin.**

Time (hours)	Distance (miles) at 40 mph	Distance (miles) at 60 mph
0	0	0
1	40	60
2	80	120
3	120	180
4	160	240

a. Graph the ordered pairs (time, distance) for 40 miles per hour.

b. Graph the ordered pairs (time, distance) for 60 miles per hour.

c. Predict where the ordered pairs for 50 miles per hour would be graphed. Explain how you know.

NEED EXTRA HELP?										
If You Missed Question...	1	2	3	4	5	6	7	8	9	10
Go to Lesson...	3-7	3-7	1-9	3-1	3-1	3-7	3-7	2-8	1-7	3-7
IN Academic Standards	8.2.4	8.2.4	7.2.1	7.2.1	7.2.1	8.2.4	8.2.4	7.1.7	P.6.6	8.2.4

10c. The line for 50 miles per hour would be between the 40 miles per hour and 60 miles per hour lines, because 50 is between 40 and 60.

Answer Sheet Practice

Have students simulate taking a standardized test by recording their answers on a practice recording sheet.

CRM Student Recording Sheet, p. 53

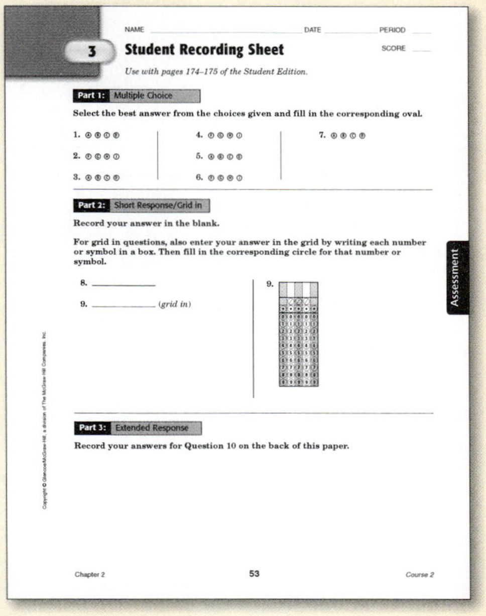
NAME ______ DATE ______ PERIOD ______

3 **Student Recording Sheet** SCORE ______

Use with pages 174–175 of the Student Edition.

Part 1: Multiple Choice

Select the best answer from the choices given and fill in the corresponding oval.

1. 2. 3. 4. 5. 6. 7.

Part 2: Short Response/Grid In

Record your answer in the blank.

For grid in questions, also enter your answer in the grid by writing each number or symbol in a box. Then fill in the corresponding circle for that number or symbol.

8. ______

9. ______ (grid in)

Part 3: Extended Response

Record your answers for Question 10 on the back of this paper.

Chapter 3 53 Course 2

Assessment

Additional Answers

10a.

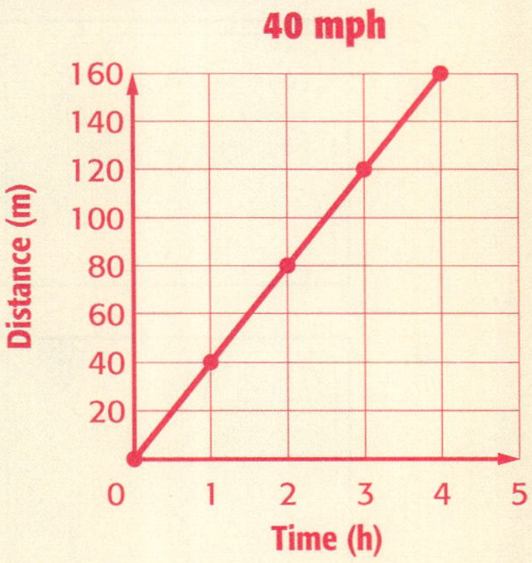

10b.

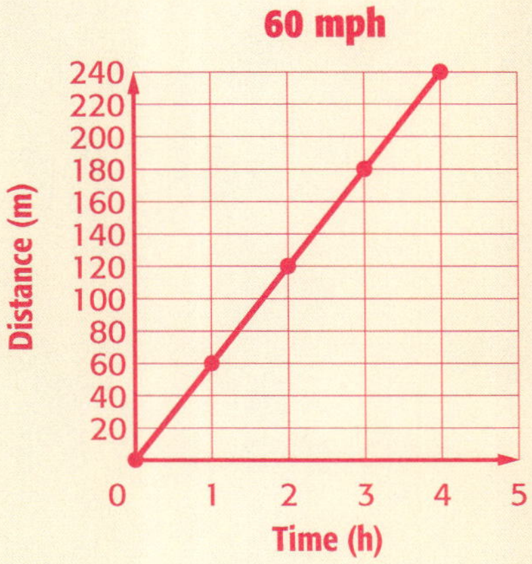

Page 127, Get Ready for Chapter 3

4. 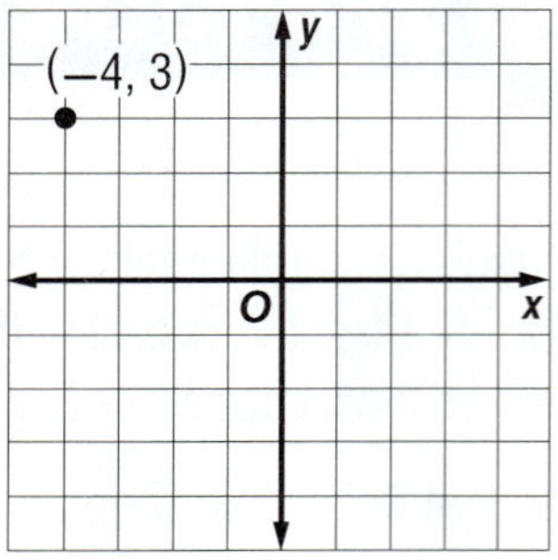

5. 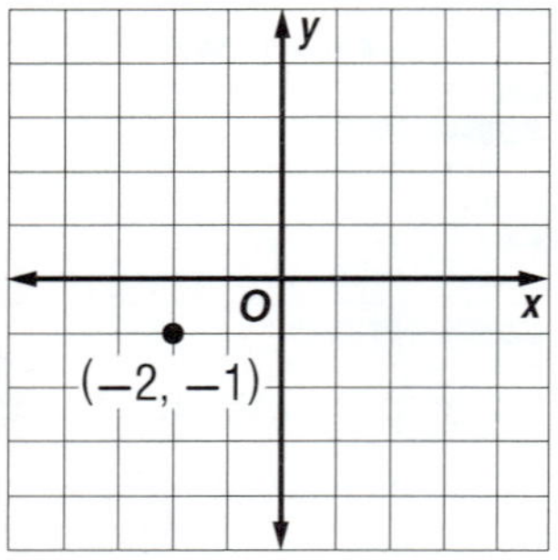

6. 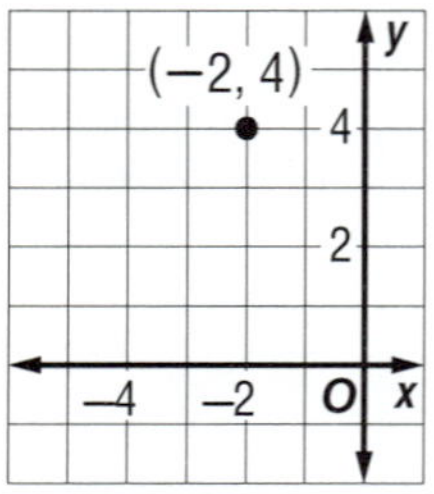

Page 134, Explore 3-2

c. 

d. 

Page 142, Lesson 3-3 (Mini Lab)

1. 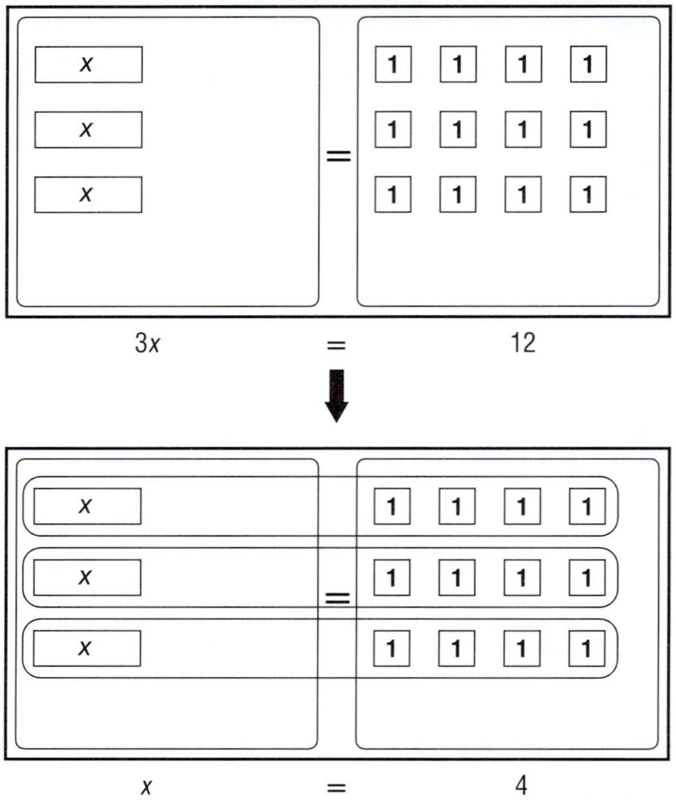

2. 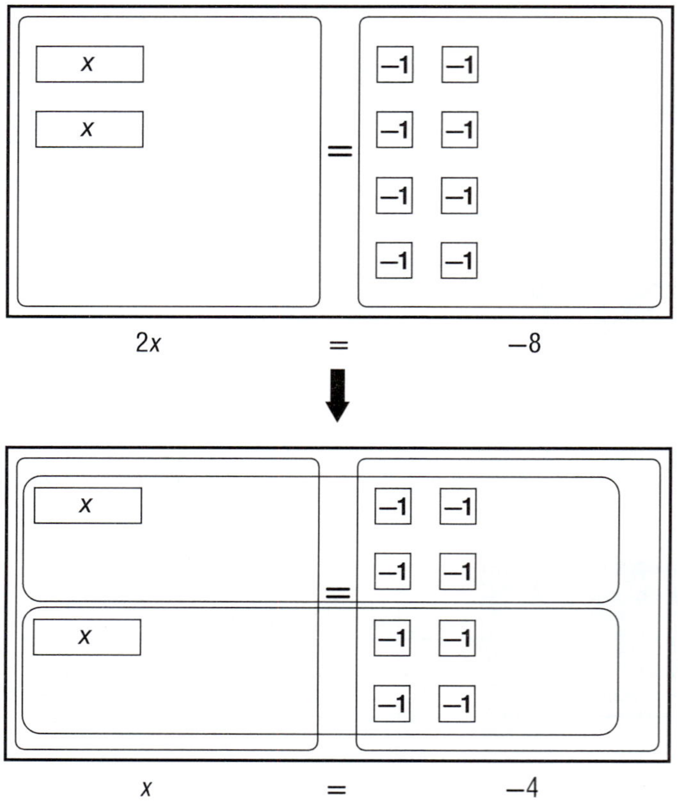

3.

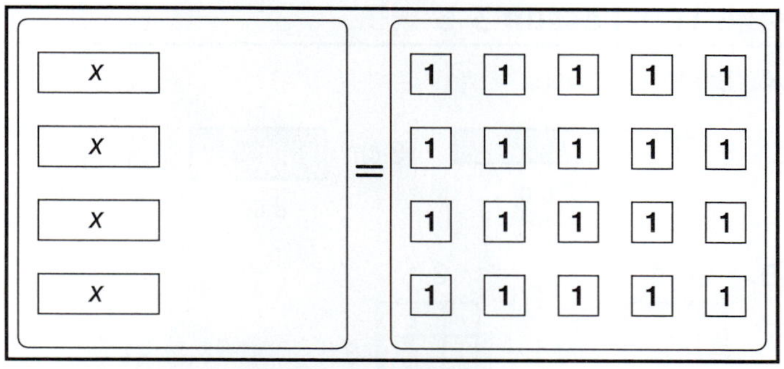

$4x \quad = \quad 20$

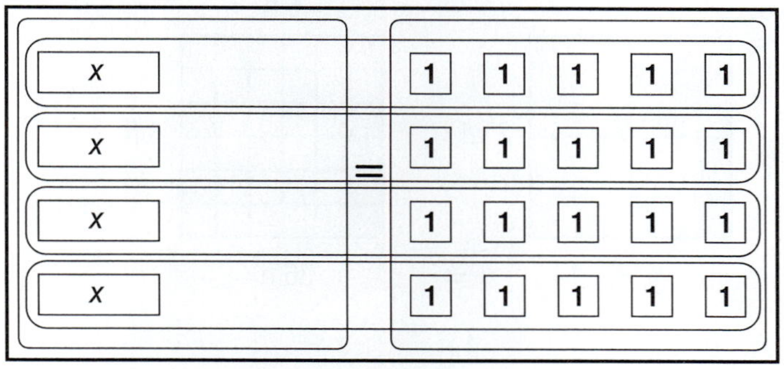

$x \quad = \quad 5$

4.

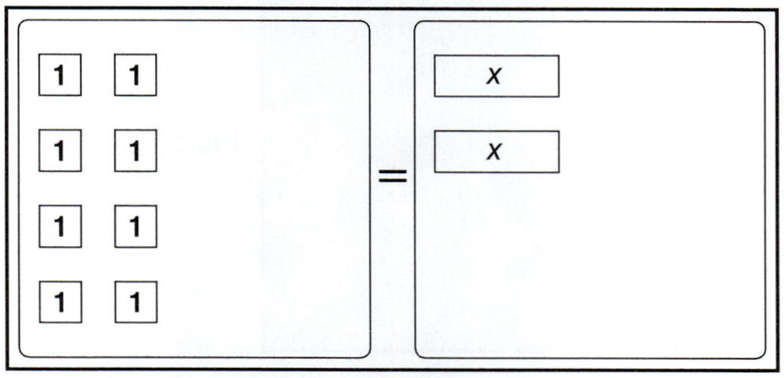

$8 \quad = \quad 2x$

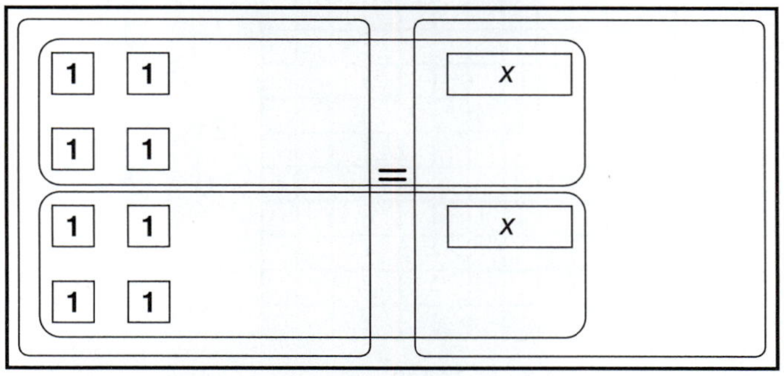

$4 \quad = \quad x$

5.

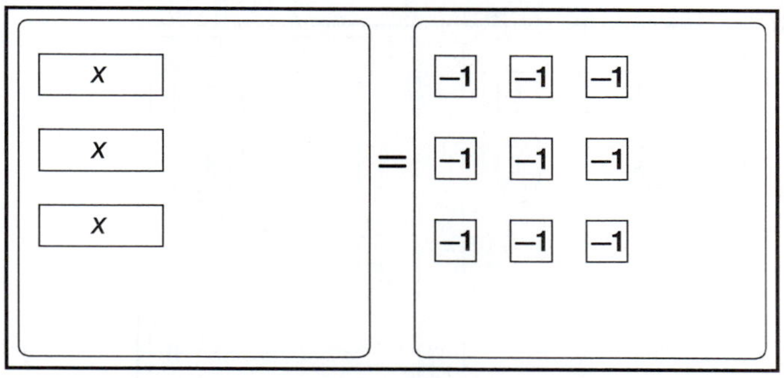

$3x \quad = \quad -9$

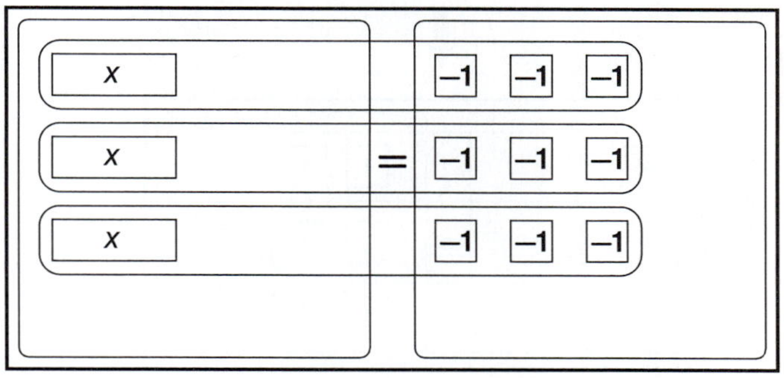

$x \quad = \quad -3$

Page 151, Lesson 3-5 (Mini Lab)

1.

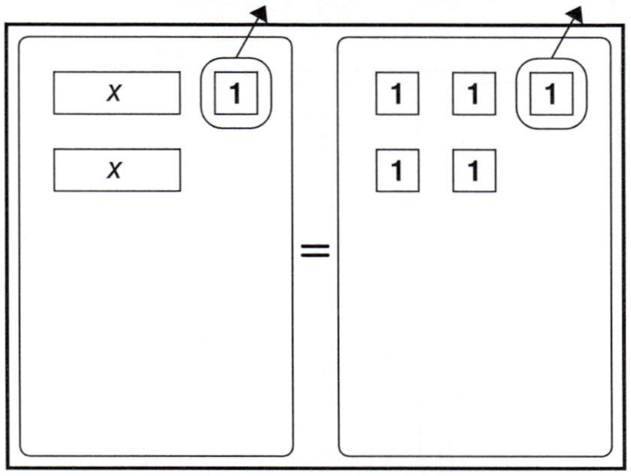

$2x + 1 \quad = \quad 5$

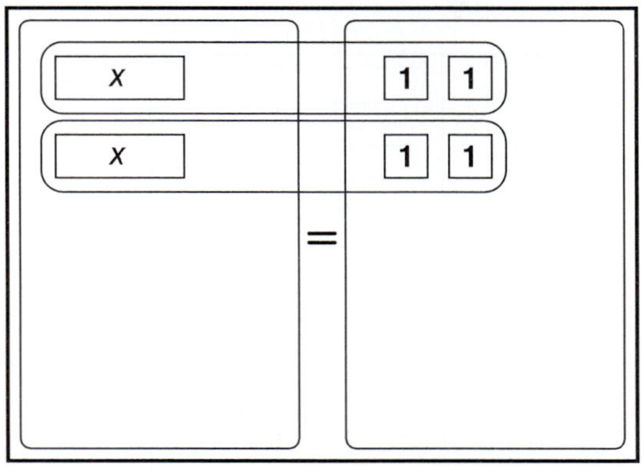

$x \quad = \quad 2$

2.

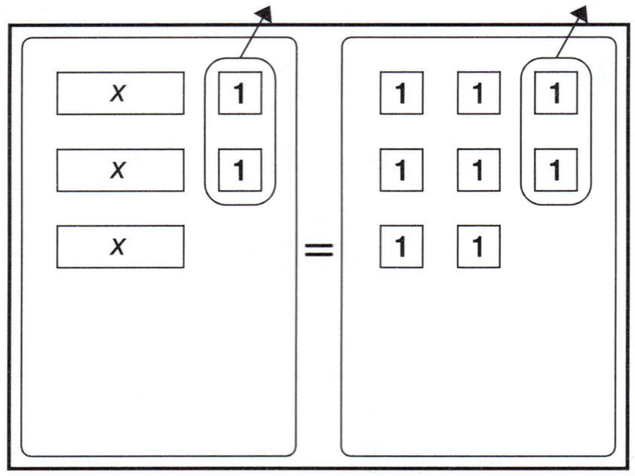

$3x + 2 \quad = \quad 8$

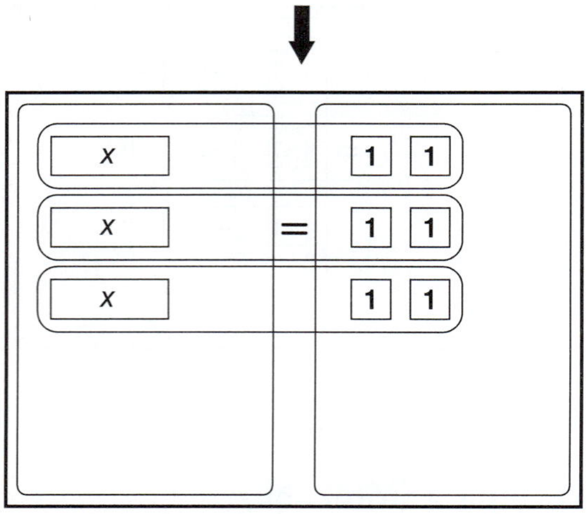

$x \quad = \quad 2$

3.

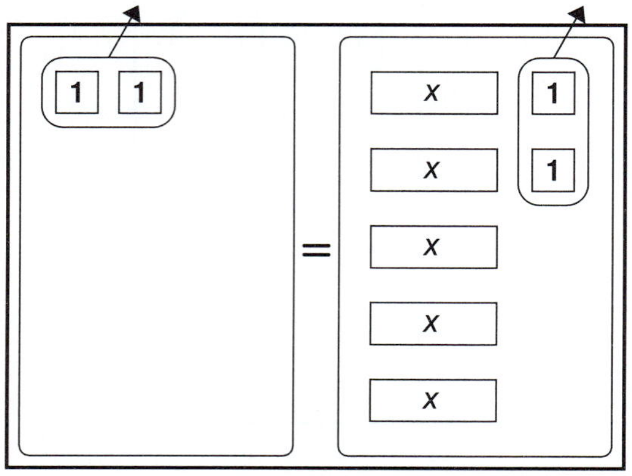

$2 \quad = \quad 5x + 2$

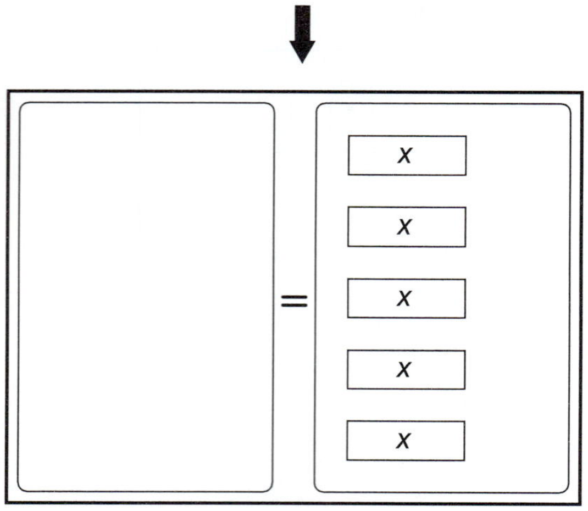

$0 \quad = \quad x$

Page 160, Lesson 3-6

34. Sample answers:

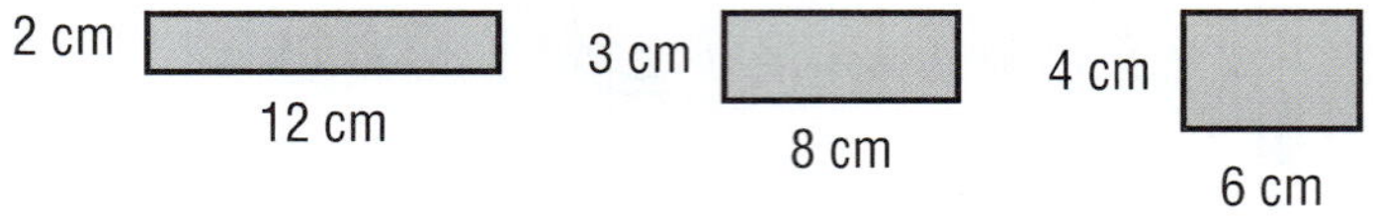

35.

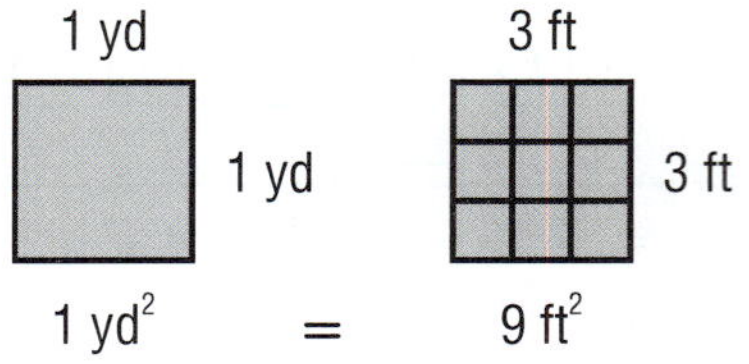

36.

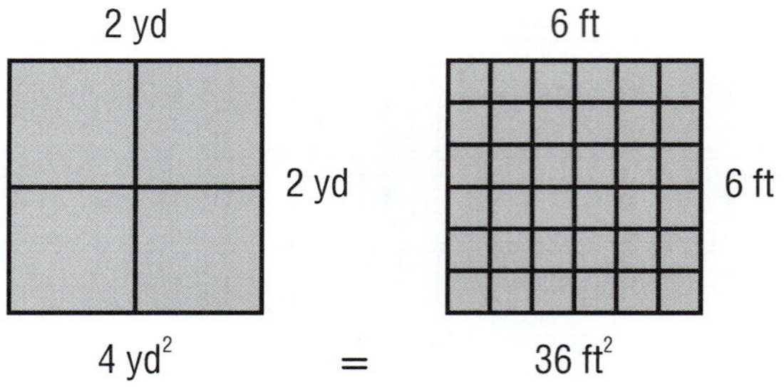

37. 144

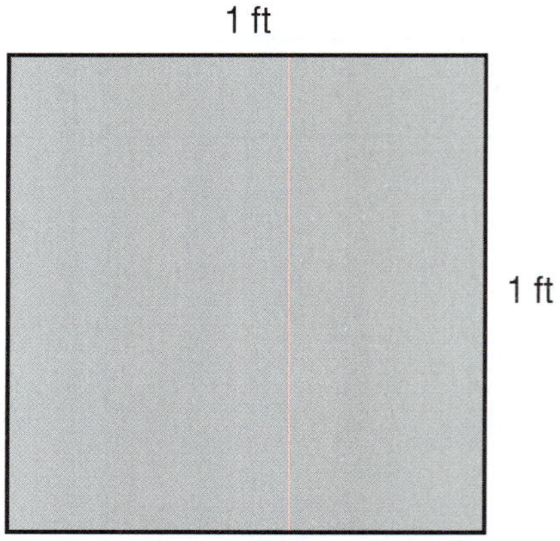

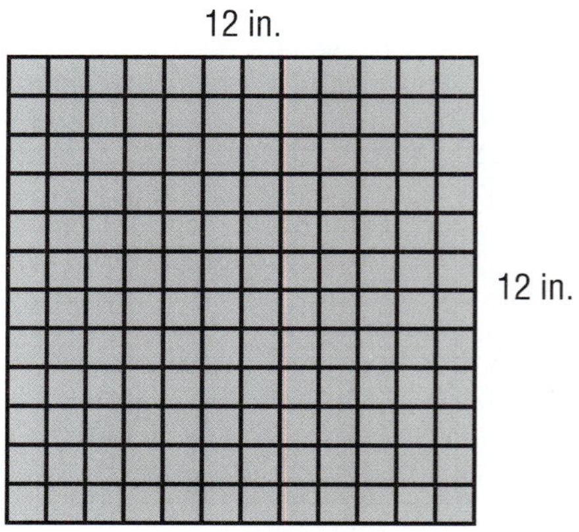

$1\ ft^2 = 144\ in^2$

38. 288

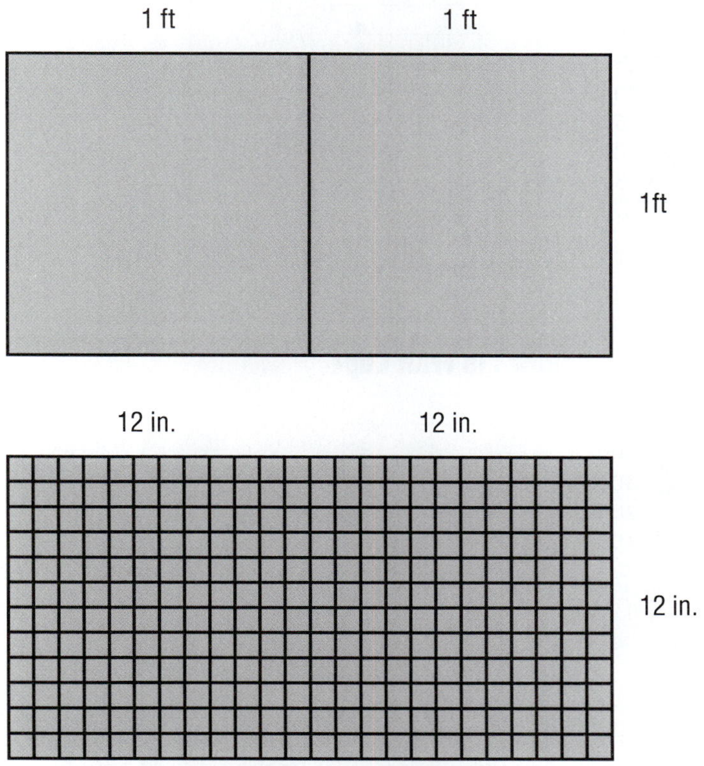

$2\text{ ft}^2 = 288\text{ in}^2$

39. When the width of a rectangle is doubled, the perimeter becomes $2\ell + 4w$ and the area becomes $2\ell w$, or in other words, the area is doubled.

Page 162, Explore 3-7

1. The perimeter of the rectangle is 24 cm.

2. The sum of the length and width of each rectangle is 12; Sample answer: The sum of the length and width of each rectangle is half the length of each stem; $\ell + w = \frac{1}{2}(24)$ or $\ell + w = 12$.

3. 7.5 cm; Sample answer: Since the sum of the two measures must be 12, the length of the rectangle is 12 − 4.5 or 7.5 cm; $w = 12 - \ell$.

4. Sample answer:

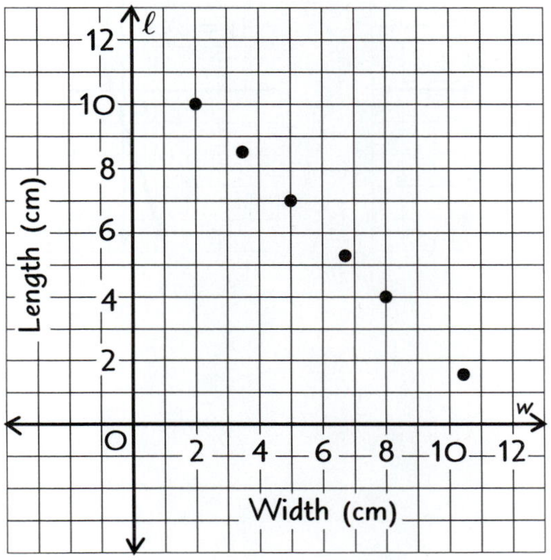

5. The data appear to fall on a line; the width w and length ℓ of a rectangle whose perimeter is 24 cm.

6. Draw the line that goes through the data points. Then find the point on the graph whose ℓ-value is 7. Move down from that point to determine the w-value of the point. The w-value that corresponds to an ℓ-value of 7 is 5.

7. The sum of the data in each row of the table would be 10 centimeters, instead of 12; the rule would become $w = 10 - \ell$; the line on the graph would start at (0, 10) and end at (10, 0).

Page 163, Lesson 3-7 (Get Ready for the Lesson)

2. **Total Cost of Admission**

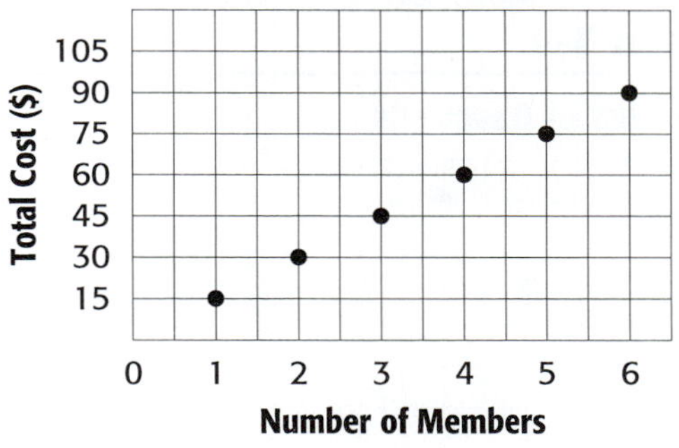

Page 164, Lesson 3-7

a. **$75 Music Gift Certificate**

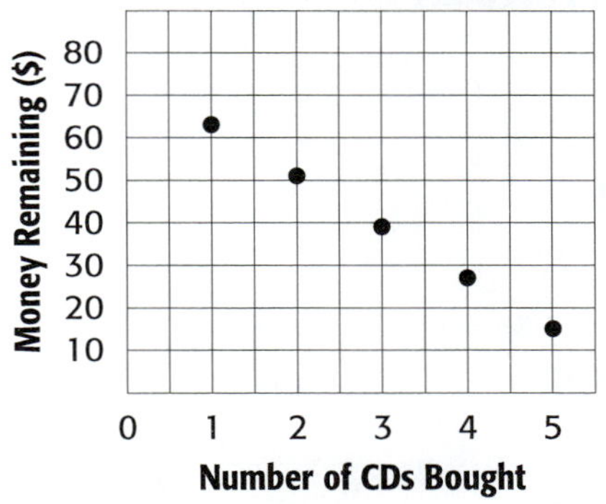

b.

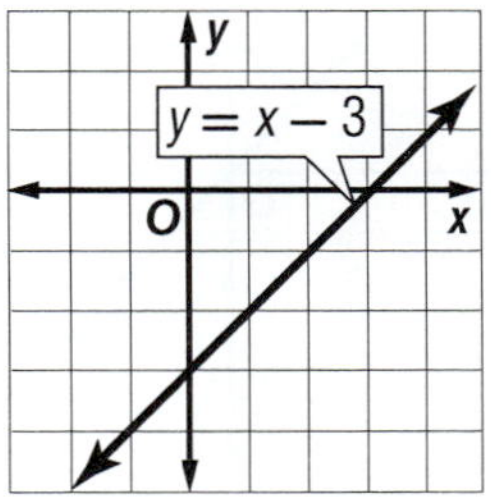

c.

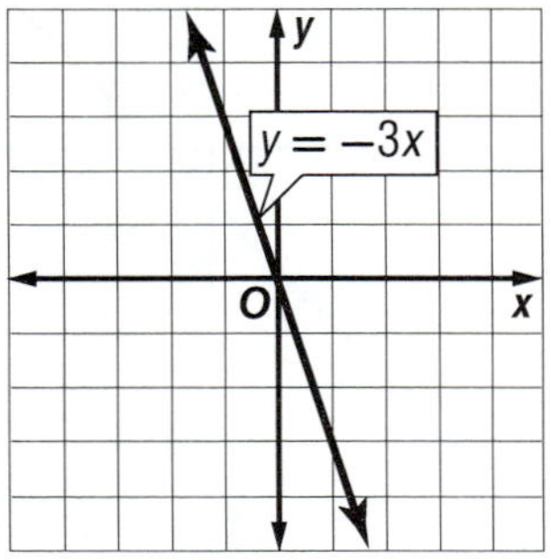

d.

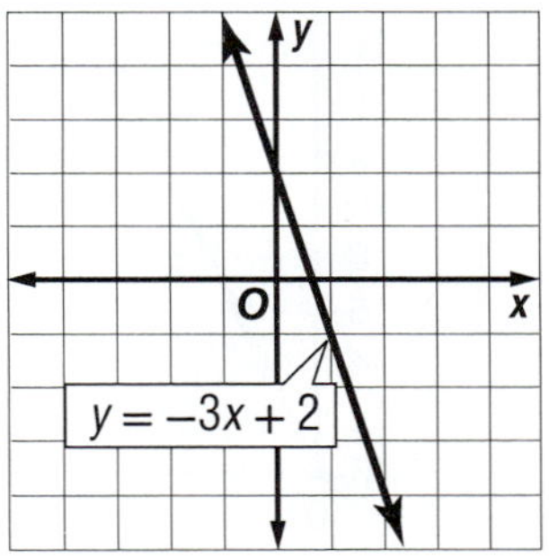

Page 165, Lesson 3-7

e.

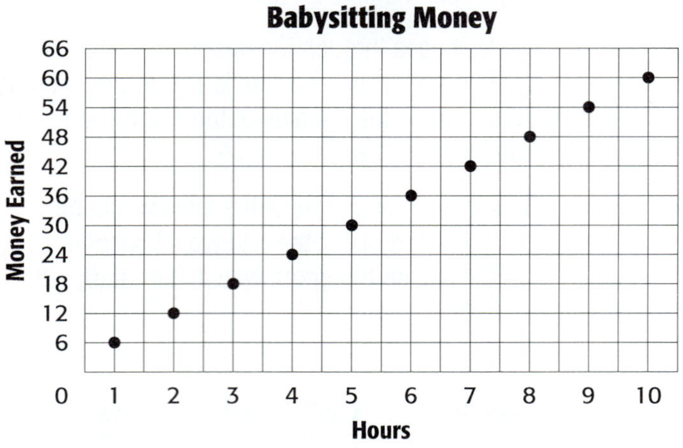

Page 166, Lesson 3-7

1.

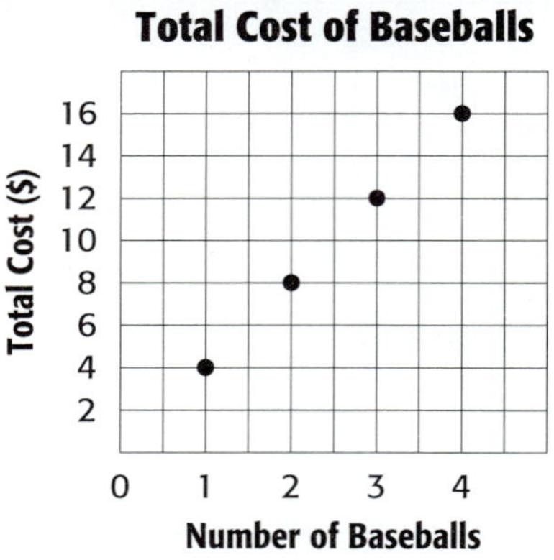

2.

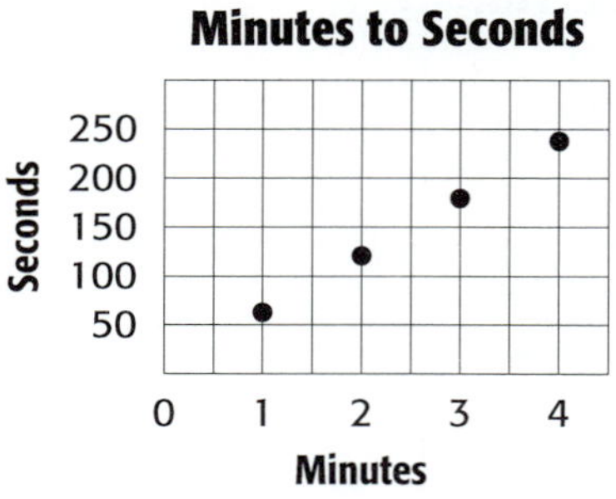

3.

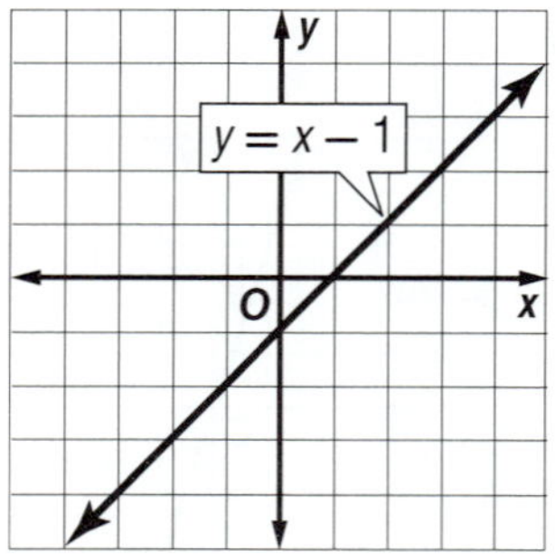

4.

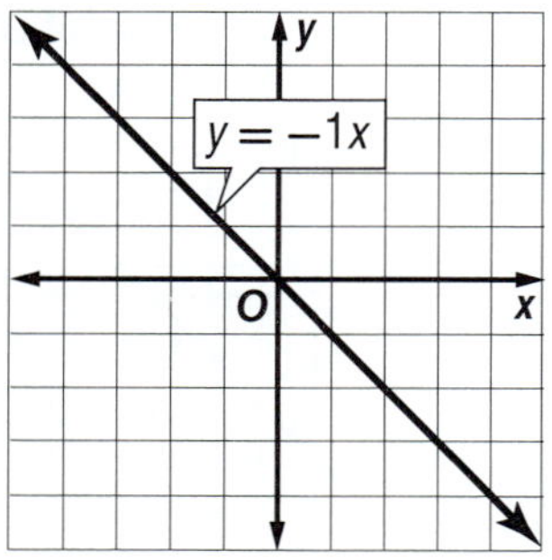

5.

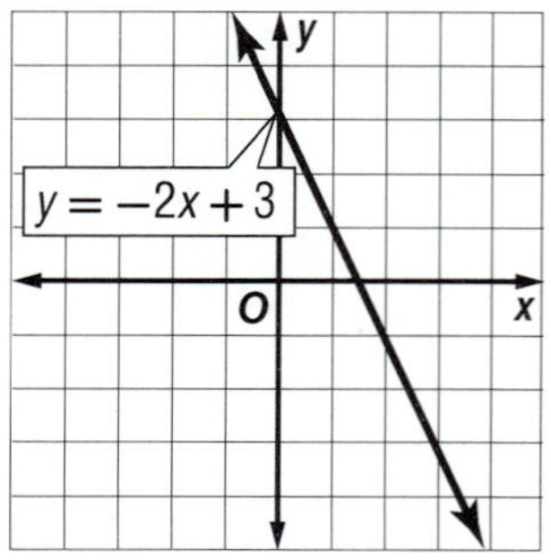

6.

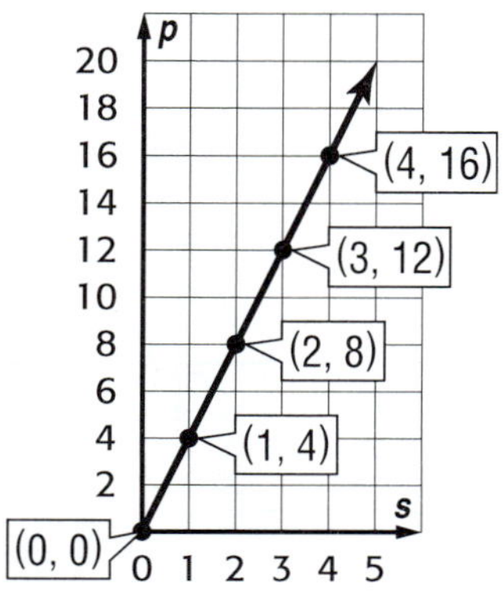

7.

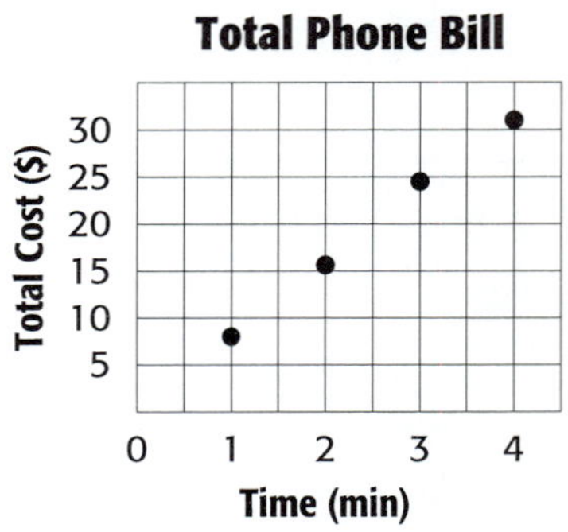

8.

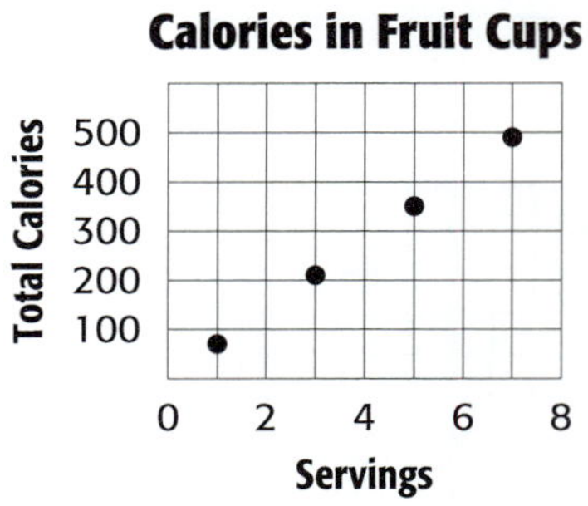

9.

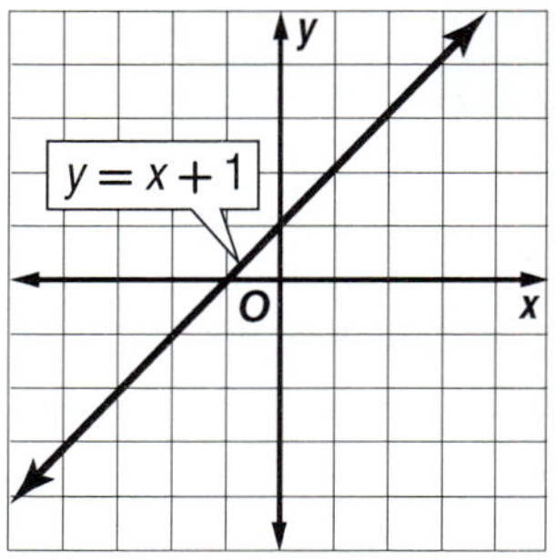

10.

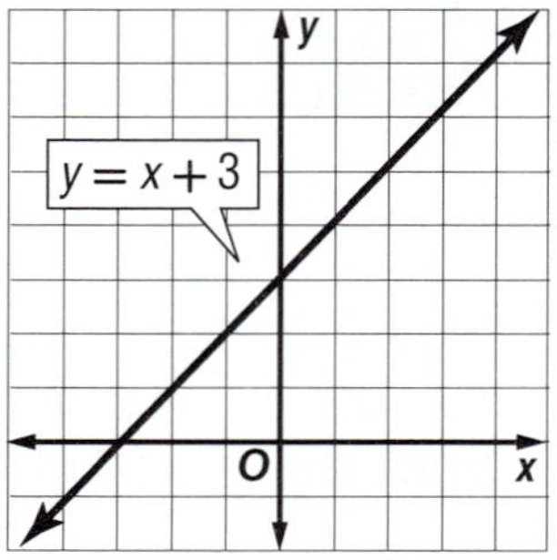

11.

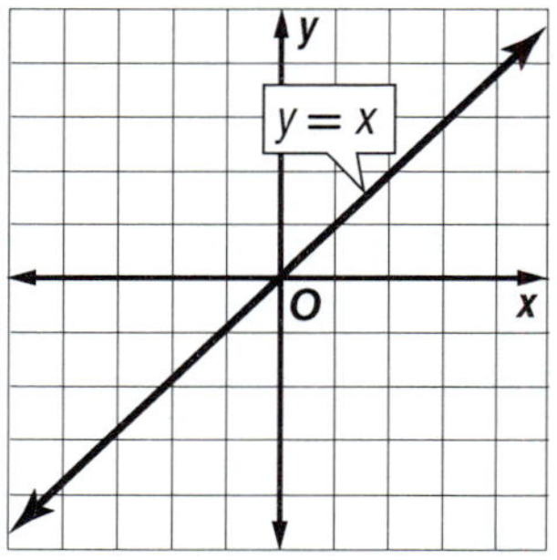

12.

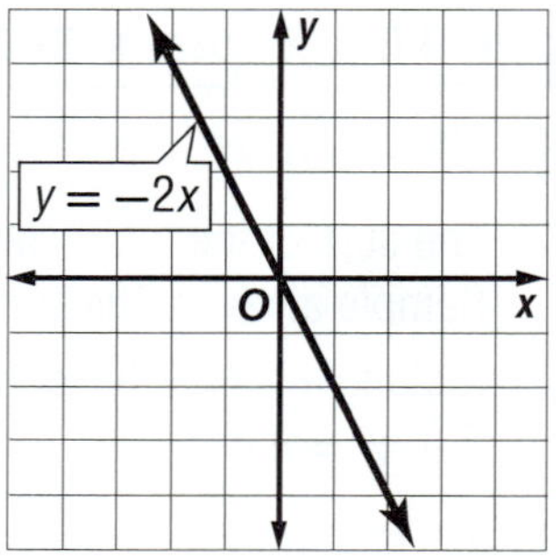

13.

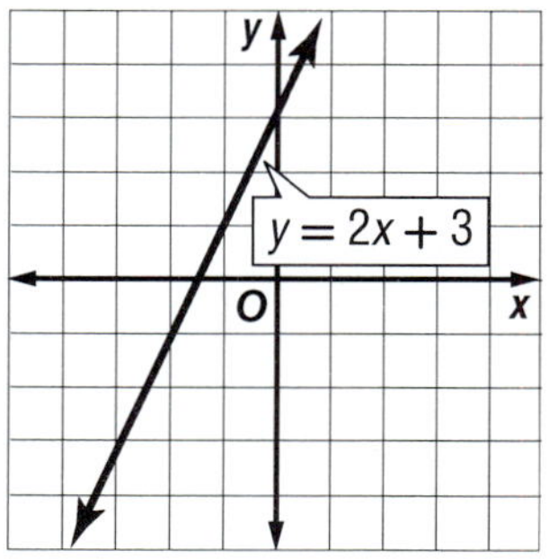

14.

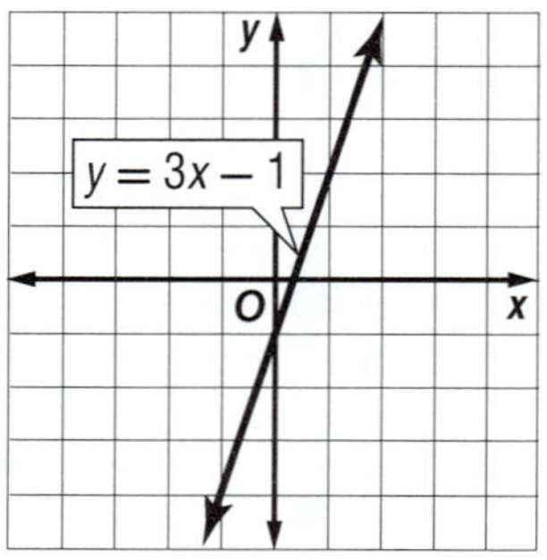

15.

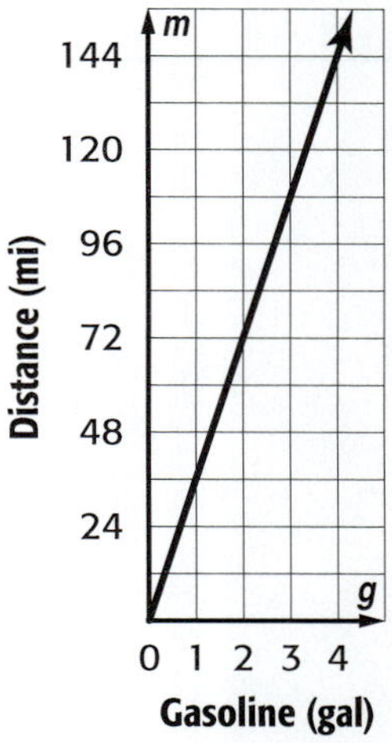

16.

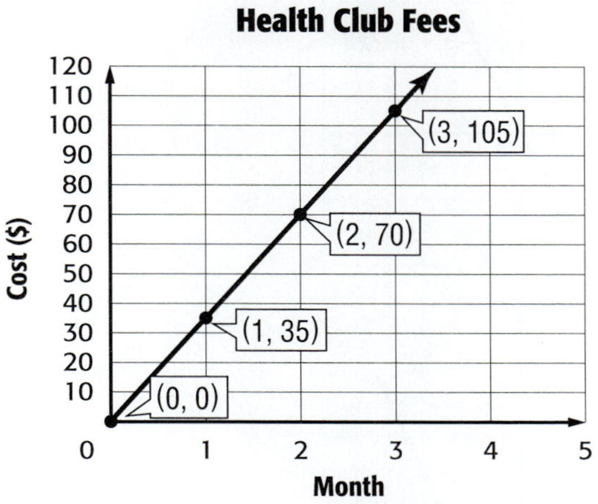

17.

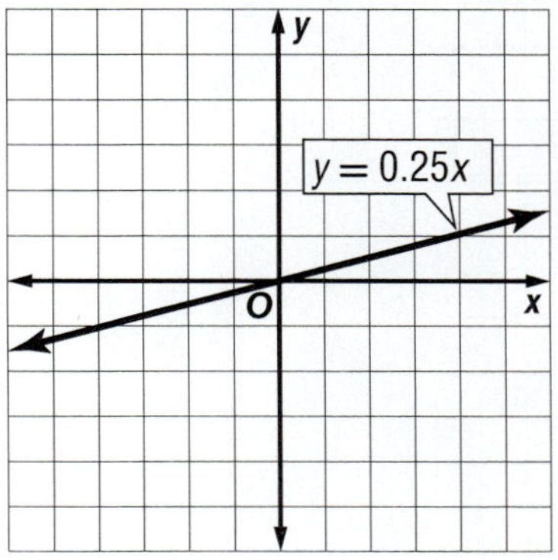

18.

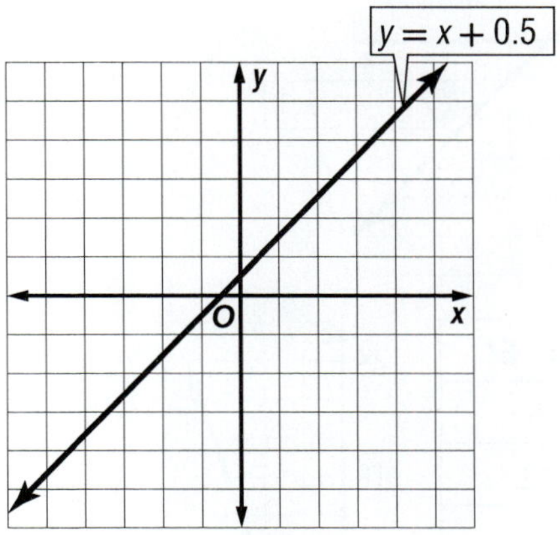

19.

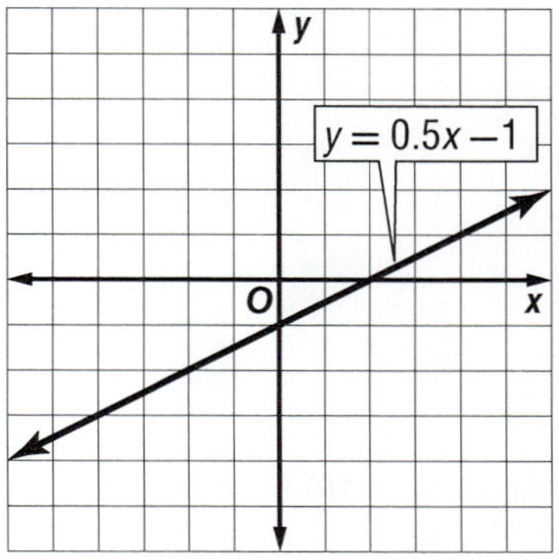

20.

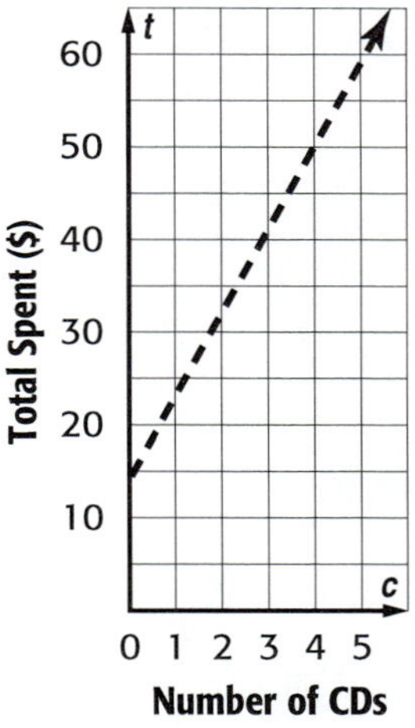

Page 167, Lesson 3-7

24. Sample answer; Once the function table has been completed, plot the coordinates of each point represented in the table. The *x*-coordinate of each point is usually the number in the first column and the *y*-coordinate of each point is usually the number in the second column.

Page 168, Extend 3-7

1. 9; These values represent a conversion of 3 yd to 9 ft and they are represented on the graph by a point on the line with coordinates (3, 9).

2. 21 ft; Use the CALC feature of the calculator to find the *y*-value that corresponds to an *x*-value of 7.

3. $y = \frac{1}{3}x$; Sample answer: Xmin = 0, Xmax = 20, Xscl = 2, Ymin = 0, Ymax = 10, Ysel = 1;

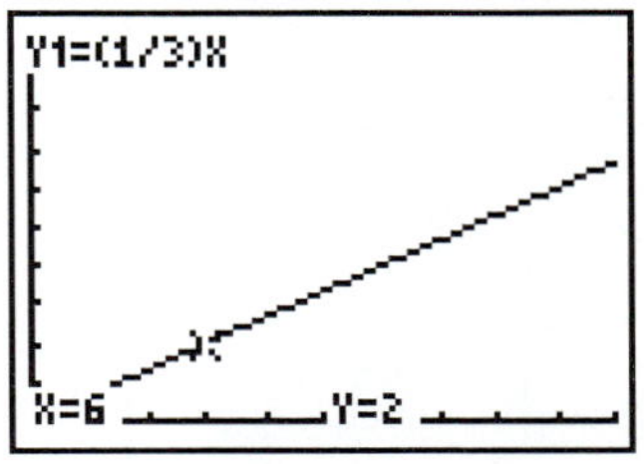

4. 16 ft = $5\frac{1}{3}$ yd;

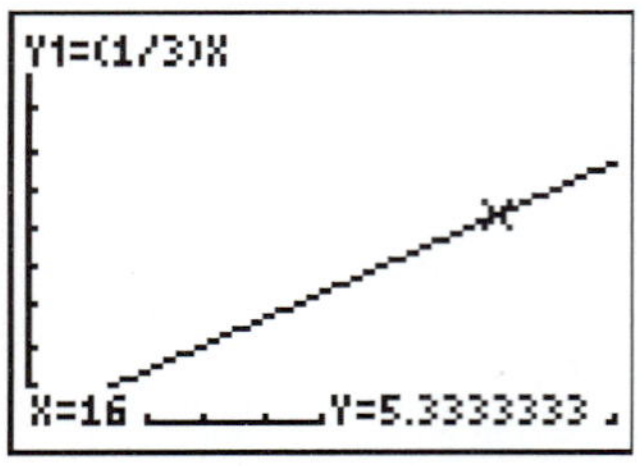

5. $y = \frac{1}{16}x$; Sample answer: Xmin = 0, Xmax = 40, Xscl = 5, Ymin = 0, Ymax = 5, Yscl = 1; 36 oz = 2.25 lbs;

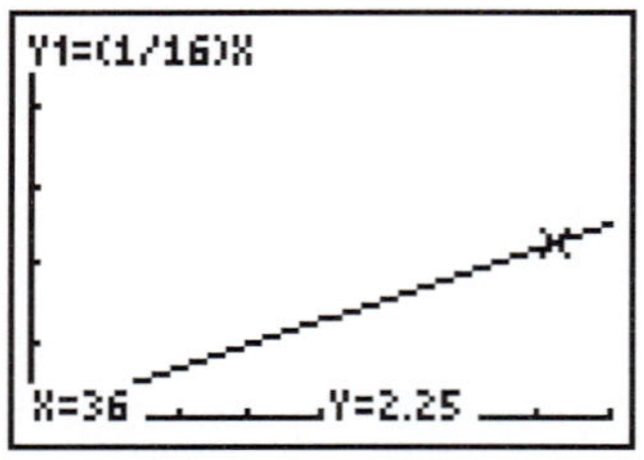

Page 172, Study Guide and Review

52.

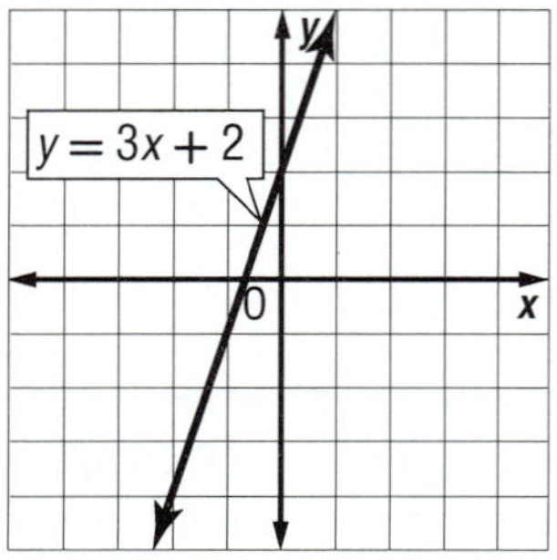

53.

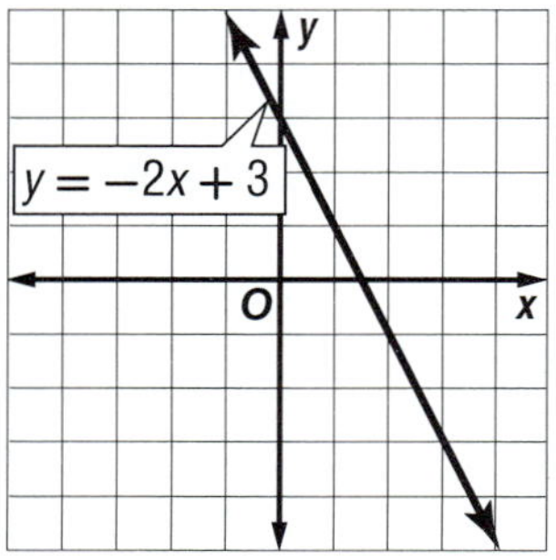

54.

Hours Worked	Dollars Earned
2	$18
4	$36
6	$54
8	$72

56.

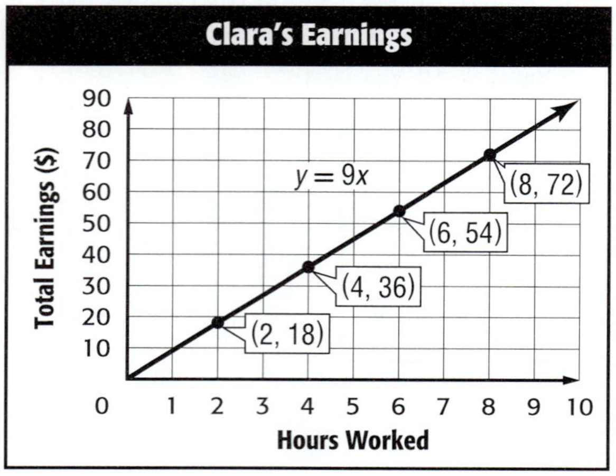

Page 173, Practice Test

21.

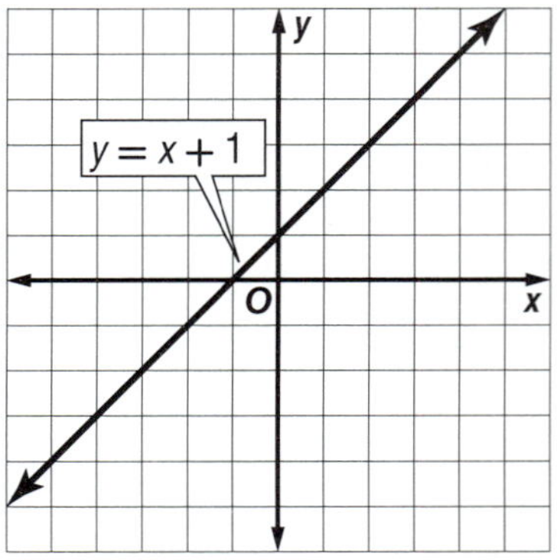

22.

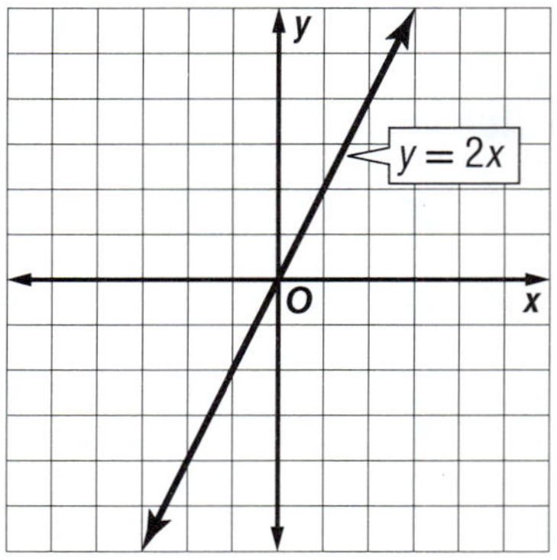

23.

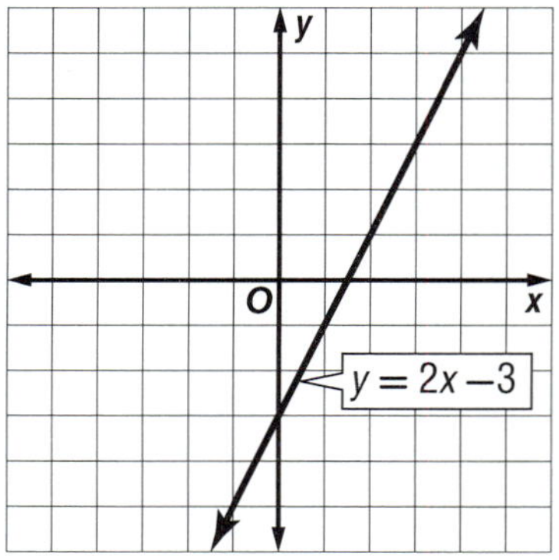

24.

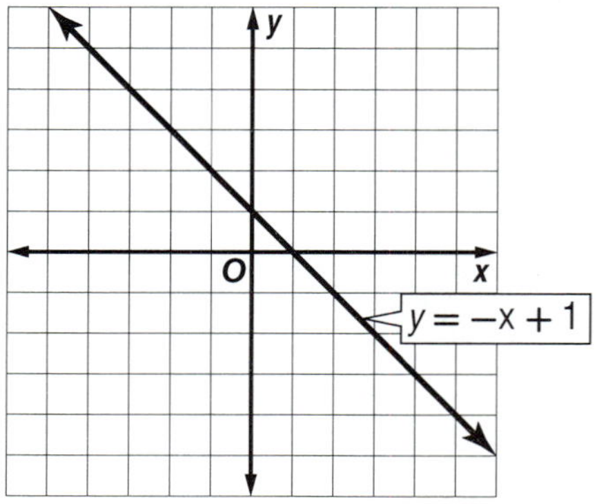

25.

t	$c = 6t$
1	6
2	12
3	18
4	24

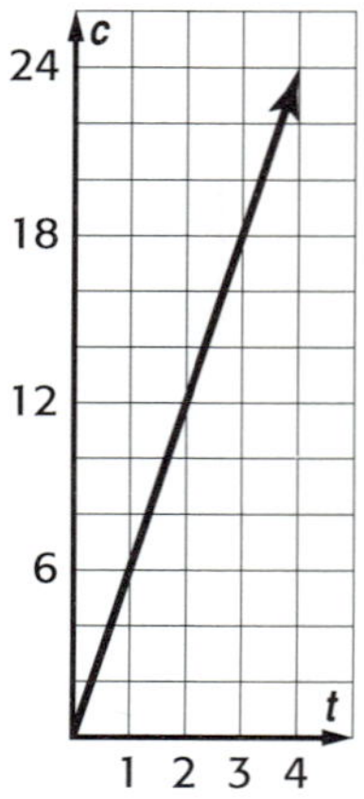

NOTES

Unit 2 Notes

Introduction

In this unit, students will learn to simplify fractions using the greatest common factor (GCF) of the numerator and denominator and by using prime factorization. They will also learn to express fractions as decimals that either terminate or repeat. In addition, students will learn to convert fractions to decimals and percents and vice versa. They then will use the least common denominator (LCD) of a set of fractions to compare and order fractions and other rational numbers.

Students will apply their knowledge of fractions by adding, subtracting, multiplying, and dividing fractions and mixed numbers.

Assessment Options

Unit 2 Test Pages 73–74 of the *Chapter 5 Resource Masters* may be used as a test or a review for Unit 2. This assessment contains both multiple-choice and short-response items.

ExamView Assessment Suite

Create additional customized Unit Tests and review worksheets for differentiated instruction.

Unit 2

Number Sense: Fractions

Focus

Represent and use numbers in a variety of equivalent forms and apply addition, subtraction, multiplication, and division of fractions.

CHAPTER 4
Fractions, Decimals, and Percents

BIG Idea Represent and use numbers in a variety of forms.

CHAPTER 5
Applying Fractions

BIG Idea Extend understandings of operations. Add, subtract, multiply, and divide to solve fraction problems.

What's MATH Got To Do With It? DVD

Real-Life Math Videos engage students, showing them how math is used in everyday situations. Use Video 2 with this unit to discuss how fractions and percents are used in amusement parks and in movie concessions (also available on one Super DVD combined with MindJogger Videoquizzes).

Problem Solving in Geography

Real-World Unit Project

A Traveling We Will Go You're about to embark on a journey to your favorite vacation spot in the United States. In your role as a travel agent, you will plan a vacation for you and your family. You will calculate the total cost including transportation, lodging, and tourist attractions. So bring your sense of adventure and get ready to set off on your trip!

IN Math Online Log on to glencoe.com to begin.

Real-World Unit Project
Problem Solving in Geography

A Traveling We Will Go

This cross-curricular project is an online project in which students do research on the Internet, gather data, and make presentations using word processing, graphing, page-making, or presentation software. In each chapter, students advance to the next step in their project. At the end of Chapter 6, the project culminates with a presentation of their findings.

IN Math Online

glencoe.com Log on for teaching suggestions and sample answers for this project.

Team Teaching You can use this project with your students' geography teacher to make the connection from mathematics to the geography topics your students are studying.

More Cross-Curricular Connections

You may wish to share these suggestions with your students' other teachers.

Math and Life Skills

Imagine that you will be driving a rental car to your favorite vacation spot. Research and find the distance between your home and your destination. If you are able to get 25 miles to the gallon, how many gallons of gas will be used? If gas is $2.50 a gallon, how much will it cost?

Math and Language Arts

Write a paragraph about some of the main attractions found at your favorite vacation spot. Promote your vacation spot to try and attract more tourists. How much does it cost? What makes this location fun? Why would you want to go there?

CHAPTER 4

Chapter Overview

Fractions, Decimals, and Percents

Lesson Plan		Pacing Your Lessons	
LESSONS AND OBJECTIVES	Academic Standards	40–50 Minute Periods	90-Minute Periods
Explore 4-1 Math Lab: Exploring Factors (p. 180) Discover factors of whole numbers. **4-1 Prime Factorization** (pp. 181–184) • Find the prime factorization of a composite number.	7.1.3, 7.1.4 Core Lesson	2	1
4-2 Greatest Common Factor (pp. 186–189) • Find the greatest common factor of two or more numbers.	7.1.3, 7.1.4 Core Lesson	2	1
4-3 Problem-Solving Investigation: Make an Organized List (pp. 190–191) • Solve problems by making an organized list.	P.1.3 Core Lesson	1	0.5
4-4 Simplifying Fractions (pp. 192–195) • Write fractions in simplest form.	7.1.6	2	1
4-5 Fractions and Decimals (pp. 196–200) • Write fractions as terminating or repeating decimals and write decimals as fractions.	7.1.6 Core Lesson	1	0.5
4-6 Fractions and Percents (pp. 202–205) • Write fractions as percents and percents as fractions.	7.1.6 Core Lesson	1	0.5
4-7 Percents and Decimals (pp. 206–210) • Write percents as decimals and decimals as percents.	6.1.4	1	0.5
4-8 Least Common Multiple (pp. 211–214) • Find the least common multiple of two or more numbers.	7.1.3 Core Lesson	2	1
4-9 Comparing and Ordering Rational Numbers (pp. 215–220) • Compare and order fractions, decimals, and percents.	7.1.6 Core Lesson	1	0.5
REVIEW		1	0.5
ASSESSMENT		1	0.5*
	TOTAL	**15**	**7.5**

*The complete **Assessment Planner** for Chapter 4 is provided on page 179.*

** Begin Chapter 5 in the second half of the period.*

Focal Points

G7-FP3 Number and Operations,
G7-FP5C Number and Operations
For the complete wording of the Focal Points for Grade 7, please see page T17.

Professional Development

Vertical Alignment

Before Chapter 4

Related Topics from Grade 6

- determine the prime factors of all numbers through 50 and write the numbers as the product of their prime factors by using exponents to show multiples of a factor
- identify and represent on a number line decimals, fractions, mixed numbers, and positive and negative numbers

Chapter 4

Topics from Grade 7

- determine the least common multiple and the greatest common divisor of whole numbers; use them to solve problems with fractions
- compare and order positive and negative fractions, decimals, and mixed numbers and place them on a number line

After Chapter 4

Preparation for Grade 8

- compare rational numbers
- convert fractions to decimals and percents and use these representations in estimations, computations, and applications
- know that every rational number is either a terminating or repeating decimal and be able to convert terminating decimals into reduced fractions
- add and subtract fractions by using factoring to find common denominators

Backmapping and Vertical Alignment

McGraw-Hill's ***Math Connects*** program was conceived and developed with the final results in mind: student success in Algebra 1 and beyond. The authors, using the **NCTM Focal Points and Focal Connections** as their guide, developed this brand-new series by backmapping from Algebra 1 concepts, and vertically aligning the topics so that they build upon prior skills and concepts and serve as a foundation for future topics.

What the Research Says...

Through twenty years of research, the Rational Number Project has found that the optimum curriculum for learning fractions includes active involvement with multiple concrete models.

- In Lesson 4-4, students use area models to help them simplify fractions.
- In Lesson 4-6, students use decimal models to write fractions as percents.

Professional Development

Targeted professional development has been articulated throughout **McGraw-Hill's *Math Connects*** program. The **McGraw-Hill Professional Development Video Library** provides short videos that support the NCTM Focal Points and Focal Connections. For more information, visit glencoe.com.

Model Lessons

Instructional Strategies

CHAPTER 4

Technology Solutions

Teacher Resources

TeacherWorks™ All-in-One Planner and Resource Center

All of the print materials from the Classroom Resource Masters are available on your TeacherWorks™ CD-ROM.

BL = Below or Approaching Grade Level   OL = On Grade Level   AL = Above or Beyond Grade Level   ELL = English Language Learner

				Chapter Resource Masters	4-1	4-2	4-3	4-4	4-5	4-6	4-7	4-8	4-9
BL	OL		ELL	Lesson Reading Guide	9	16		26	32	39	45	51	58
BL	OL		ELL	Study Guide and Intervention*	10	17	22	27	33	40	46	52	59
BL	OL			Skills Practice*	11	18	23	28	34	41	47	53	60
	OL	AL		Practice*	12	19	24	29	35	42	48	54	61
	OL	AL		Word Problem Practice*	13	20	25	30	36	43	49	55	62
	OL	AL		Enrichment	14	21		31	37	44	50	56	63
	OL	AL		Calculator and Spreadsheet Activities	15				38			57	
	OL	AL		Chapter Assessments*	65–86								
BL	OL	AL		5-Minute Check Transparencies	✓	✓	✓	✓	✓	✓	✓	✓	✓
BL	OL			Teaching Mathematics with Manipulatives	✓					✓			
BL	OL	AL		Real-World Investigations for Differentiated Instruction	39								

**Also available in Spanish.*

Graphing Calculator Easy Files

Timesaving Tech Tools for the TI-Navigator:

- **Quick Checks** to diagnose student progress
- Motivate students with **Concept Launchers**
- Deliver differentiated instruction with **Ready Files**
- **Vocabulary Review**

AssignmentWorks

Differentiated Assignments, Answers, and Solutions

- Print a customized assignment worksheet using the Student Edition exercises along with an answer key or worked-out solutions.
- Use default lesson assignments as outlined in the Differentiated Homework Options in the Teacher Edition.

Interactive Classroom

This CD-ROM is a customizable Microsoft® PowerPoint® presentation that includes:

- In-Class Examples
- Your Turn Exercises*
- 5-Minute Check Transparencies*
- Links to Online Study Tools
- Concepts in Motion

**compatible with response pad technology*

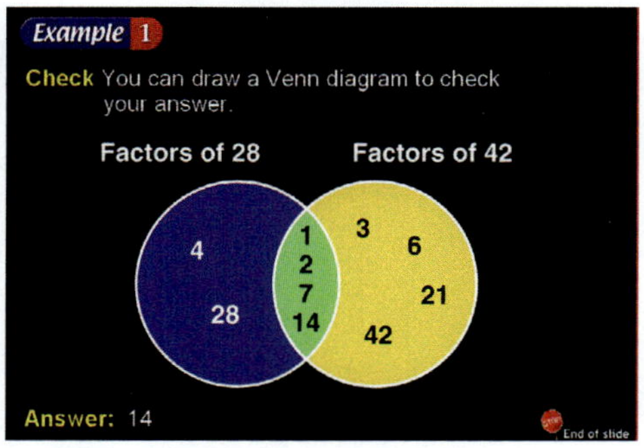

ExamView® Assessment Suite

ExamView® Assessment Suite

- Create, edit, and customize tests and worksheets using QuickTest Wizard.
- Create multiple versions of tests and modify them for a desired level of difficulty.
- Translate from English to Spanish and vice versa.
- Build tests aligned with your state standards.
- Track students' progress using the Teacher Management System.

Student Tools

StudentWorks™ Plus

Textbook, Audio, Workbooks, and more

This CD-ROM is a valuable resource for students to access content online and use online resources to continue learning Chapter 4 concepts. Includes:

- Complete Student Editions in both English and Spanish
- English audio integrated throughout the text
- Links to Concepts in Motion, Personal Tutor, and other online resources
- Access to all student worksheets
- Daily Assignments and Grade Log

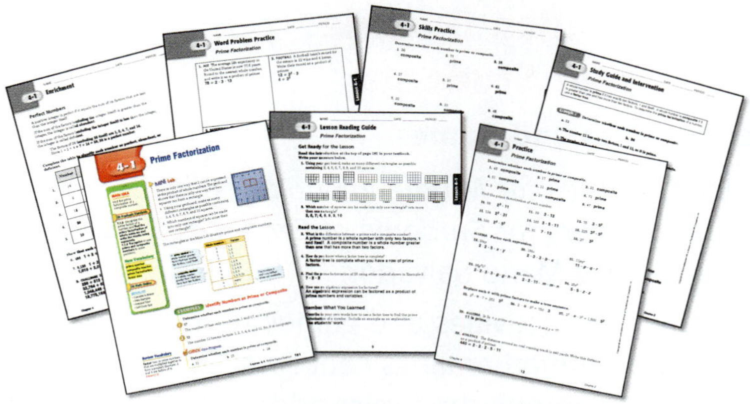

Super DVD

The Super DVD contains two Glencoe multimedia products.

MindJogger Plus An alternative review of concepts in which students work as teams in a game show format to gain points for correct answers.

What's Math Got to Do With It? Real-Life Math Videos
Engaging video that shows students how math is used in everyday situations.

Internet Resources

IN Math Online glencoe.com

TEACHER	STUDENT	PARENT	Online Study Tools
	•	•	Online Student Edition
•	•	•	Multilingual Glossary
			Lesson Resources
	•	•	BrainPOP®
•	•	•	Concepts in Motion
•	•	•	Extra Examples
•			Group Activity Cards
	•	•	Other Calculator Keystrokes
	•	•	Reading in the Content Area
	•	•	Real-World Careers
	•	•	Self-Check Quizzes
			Chapter Resources
	•	•	Chapter Readiness
	•	•	Chapter Test
	•	•	Family Letters and Activities
	•	•	Standardized Test Practice
	•	•	Vocabulary Review/Chapter Review Activities
			Unit Resources
•	•		Cross-Curricular Internet Project
			Other Resources
•			Dinah Zike's Foldables
•	•		Game Zone Games and Recording Sheets
	•	•	Hotmath Homework Help
•			Key Concepts
•	•	•	Math Skills Maintenance
•	•	•	Meet the Authors
•			NAEP Correlations
	•	•	Personal Tutor
•			Project CRISS℠
	•	•	Scavenger Hunts and Answer Sheets
•			Vocabulary PuzzleMakers

CHAPTER 4

Reading and Writing in Mathematics

Noteables™ Interactive Study Notebook with Foldables™

This workbook is a study organizer that provides helpful steps for students to follow to organize their notes for Chapter 4.

- Students use Noteables to record notes and to complete their Foldables as you present the material for each lesson.
- Noteables correspond to the Examples in the *Teacher Edition* and *Interactive Classroom* CD-ROM.

Real-World Problem Solving Graphic Novels

Mathematical problem solving is presented in a motivating, graphic novel format. The novels contain real-world problems for each of the following mathematical strands: Number Sense, Algebraic Thinking, Geometry, Measurement, Statistics and Probability, and Mathematical Reasoning.

READING in the Content Area

This online worksheet provides strategies for reading and analyzing Lesson 4-2, Greatest Common Factor. Students are guided through questions about the main idea, subject matter, supporting details, conclusion, clarifying details, and vocabulary of the lesson.

glencoe.com

Recommended Outside Reading for Students

Mathematics and Games

- *Math Games for Middle School: Challenges and Skill Builders for Students at Every Level* by Joseph Wright and Mario Salvadori ©1998 [nonfiction]

This book uses activities and games to reinforce middle school mathematics concepts. Fractions and decimals are among the topics addressed in the book.

Project CRISS STUDY SKILL

A comparison map can help students understand the differences in two or more similar concepts. Show students the sample map at the right that compares the way prime factorization can be used to find the greatest common factor (GCF) and least common multiple (LCM) of two numbers. While studying Chapter 4, have students work in small cooperative groups to design comparison maps showing how to write fractions as percents, percents as fractions, percents as decimals, and decimals as percents.

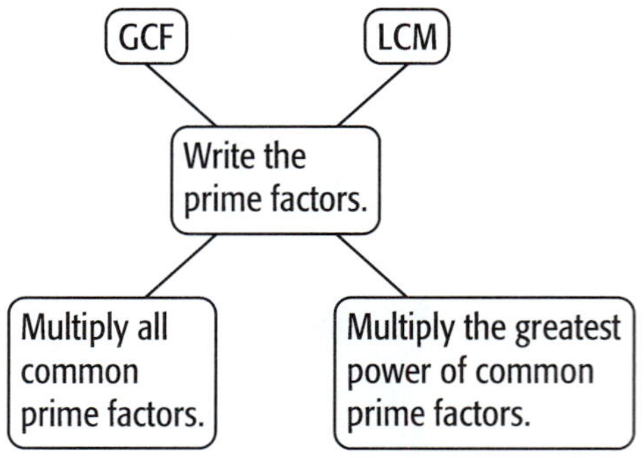

CReating **I**ndependence through **S**tudent-owned **S**trategies

Differentiated Instruction

Investigative Approach

MathScape™

This project was supported, in part, by the
National Science Foundation

MathScape is a mathematics curriculum for grades 6–8 developed by the Seeing and Thinking Mathematically Project at the Education Development Center.

Generalizing About Numbers

Making Mathematical Arguments

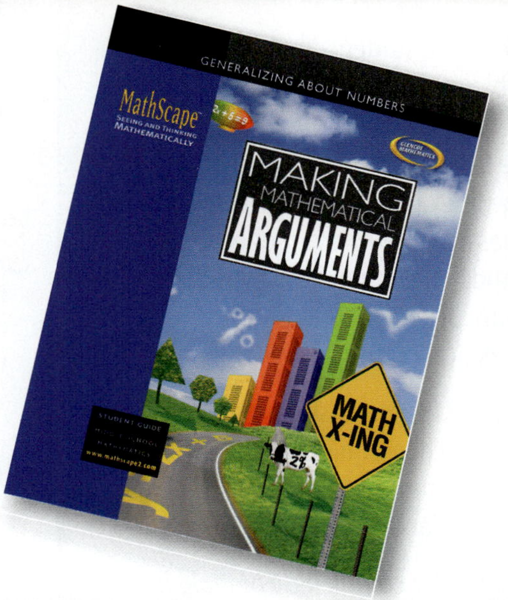

How to Use *MathScape* with Chapter 4

The unit *The Language of Algebra* can be used to enhance Lesson 4-1.

- **Introduce** → Before you begin **Lesson 4-1**, you can introduce prime numbers and prime factorization by using pages 118–119.
- **Enrich** → After you complete **Lesson 4-1**, you can use the activities on pages 120–123 to challenge students to make generalizations about factors of various types of numbers.

RTI (Response to Intervention)

TIER 1 **On-Level Instruction** Use the *Math Connects* program as instruction for your on-level students.

TIER 2 **Strategic Intervention** For options to instruct struggling students, refer to the Diagnostic Assessment table on page 179.

TIER 3 **Intensive Intervention** *Math Triumphs* can provide intensive intervention for students who are at risk of not meeting the objectives addressed in Chapter 4.

Diagnose student readiness with the Quick Check and Quick Review on page 179. Then use *Math Triumphs* to accelerate their achievment.

Fractions, Decimals, and Percents

Prerequisite Skill	*Math Triumphs*
Fractions: Representing, Ordering	Chapter 1
Percentages	Chapter 3

Practice and Review

Quick Review Math Handbook* is Glencoe's mathematical handbook for students and parents.

Hot Words includes a glossary of terms.

Hot Topics consists of two parts:

- explanations of key mathematical concepts
- exercises to check students' understanding.

Lesson	Hot Topics Section	Lesson	Hot Topics Section
4-1	1•4	4-6	2•9
4-2	1•4	4-7	2•9
4-4	2•1	4-8	1•4
4-5	2•5, 2•9	4-9	2•2, 2•5

*Also available in Spanish

CHAPTER 4

Notes

FOLDABLES™ Study Organizer **Dinah Zike's Foldables**

Focus This Foldable is designed to help students organize their notes about fractions, decimals, and percents.

Teach Have students make the Foldable and label the tab for each lesson. Tell students that they should define terms, record key concepts, and write examples under the tab for each lesson. On the front of each tab, students should draw a graph, diagram, or picture that presents the main idea(s) of the lesson.

When to Use It As students work through each lesson, remind them to record notes under the appropriate tab of their Foldables.

A version of a completed Foldable is shown on p. 221.

Differentiated Instruction

CRM Student-Built Glossary, p. 1

Students complete the chart by providing a definition for each term and an example as they progress through Chapter 4.

This study tool can be used to review for the chapter test.

Materials Needed for Chapter 4

- index cards (Explore 4-1)
- geoboard (Lesson 4-1)
- grid paper (Lessons 4-1, 4-4, 4-6)
- colored pencils (Lessons 4-4, 4-6)
- centimeter cubes (Lesson 4-8)

CHAPTER 4

Fractions, Decimals, and Percents

Indiana Academic Standards

7.1.3 Find the prime factorization of whole numbers and write the results using exponents.

7.1.6 Identify, compare and order rational and common irrational numbers and plot them on a number line.

Key Vocabulary

equivalent fractions (p. 192)
percent (p. 202)
ratio (p. 202)
simplest form (p. 192)

Real-World Link

Reptiles North Carolina's state reptile is the Eastern Box Turtle. Adults range in size from $4\frac{1}{2}$ inches to $5\frac{9}{10}$ inches. You can write these fractions as 4.5 and 5.9, respectively.

FOLDABLES® Study Organizer

Fractions, Decimals, and Percents Make this Foldable to help you organize your notes. Begin with five sheets of $8\frac{1}{2}'' \times 11''$ paper.

1. **Stack** five sheets of paper $\frac{3}{4}$ inch apart.

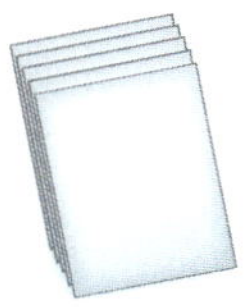

2. **Roll** up bottom edges so that all tabs are the same size.

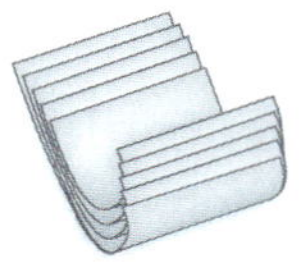

3. **Crease** and staple along the fold.

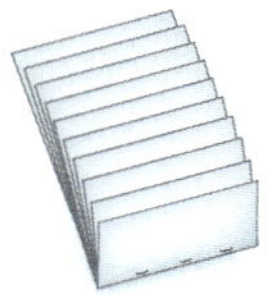

4. **Write** the chapter title on the front. Label each tab with a lesson number and title.

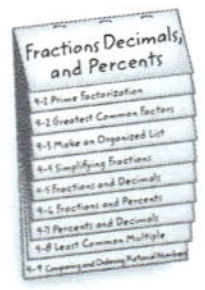

GET READY for Chapter 4

Diagnose Readiness You have two options for checking Prerequisite Skills.

Option 2

IN Math Online Take the Online Readiness Quiz at glencoe.com.

Option 1

Take the Quick Quiz below. Refer to the Quick Review for help.

QUICK Quiz

(Used in Lesson 4-9)

State which decimal is greater. (Prior Grade)

1. 0.6, 0.61 **0.61**
2. 1.25, 1.52 **1.52**
3. 0.33, 0.13 **0.33**
4. 1.08, 10.8 **10.8**
5. **LUNCH** Kirsten spent \$4.21 on lunch while Almanzo spent \$4.12. Who spent the greater amount? (Lesson 3-9) **Kirsten**

(Used in Lessons 4-1 and 4-2)

Use divisibility rules to determine whether each number is divisible by 2, 3, 5, 6, or 10. (Prior Grade)

6. 125 **5**
7. 78 **2, 3, 6**
8. 37 **none**
9. **MUFFINS** Without calculating, determine whether 51 banana nut muffins can be evenly distributed among 3 persons. Explain. (Prior Grade) **Yes; the sum of the digits, 6, is divisible by 3.**

(Used in Lessons 4-4, 4-5, 4-6, and 4-7)

Divide. (Prior Grade)

10. $12 \div 6$ **2**
11. $18 \div 3$ **6**
12. $2 \div 5$ **0.4**
13. $3 \div 4$ **0.75**

(Used in Lesson 4-1)

Write each power as a product of the same factor. (Lesson 1-2)

14. 2^3 **$2 \times 2 \times 2$**
15. 5^5 **$5 \times 5 \times 5 \times 5 \times 5$**
16. 7^2 **7×7**
17. 9^4 **$9 \times 9 \times 9 \times 9$**

QUICK Review

Example 1

State which decimal is greater, 7.4 or 7.04.

7.4
7.04
↑
7.4 is greater.

Line up the decimal points and compare place value. The 4 in the tenths place is greater than the 0 in the tenths place.

Example 2

Use divisibility rules to determine whether 84 is divisible by 2, 3, 5, 6, or 10.

2: Yes, the ones digit, 4, is divisible by 2.
3: Yes, the sum of the digits, 12, is divisible by 3.
5: No, the ones digit is neither 0 nor 5.
6: Yes, the number is divisible by both 2 and 3.
10: No, the ones digit is not 0.

Example 3

Find $1 \div 5$.

$$\begin{array}{r} 0.2 \\ 5\overline{)1.0} \\ \underline{-10} \\ 0 \end{array}$$

Divide 1 by 5 until there is a remainder of 0 or a repeating pattern.

Example 4

Write 4^3 as a product of the same factor.

$4^3 = 4 \times 4 \times 4$

Diagnostic Assessment

Exercises	Academic Standards	Intervention
1–5	**7.1.6**	SE Review Lesson 2-2, pp. 84–87
6–9	**7.1.3**	SE Concepts and Skills Bank, p. 734
10–13	**7.1.6**	*Math Skills Maintenance Masters,* pp. 11–12
14–16	**7.1.6**	SE Review Lesson 1-2, pp. 30–33

ASSESSMENT PLANNER

CHAPTER 4

Formative Assessment

CRM Anticipation Guide, pp. 7–8
Spotting Preconceived Ideas
Students complete this survey to determine prior knowledge about ideas from Chapter 4. Revisit this worksheet after completing the chapter. Also see page 224.

TE Lesson Activities

- Ticket Out the Door, pp. 184, 195, 210
- Crystal Ball, pp. 205, 214
- Name the Math, pp. 191, 220
- Yesterday's News, pp. 189, 200

Chapter Checkpoints

- SE Mid-Chapter Quiz, p. 201
- SE Study Guide and Review, pp. 221–224
- SE Test Practice, pp. 226–227
- CRM Quizzes, pp. 67 and 68
- CRM Standardized Test Practice, pp. 84–86

IN Math Online glencoe.com

- Self-Check Quizzes
- Practice Test
- Test Practice

Summative Assessment

- SE Chapter Practice Test, p. 225
- CRM Mid-Chapter Test, p. 69
- CRM Vocabulary Test, p. 70
- CRM Extended-Response Test, p. 83
- CRM Leveled Chapter Tests, pp. 71–82
- CD-ROM ExamView Pro® Assessment Suite

KEY

- CRM *Chapter 4 Resource Masters*
- SE Student Edition
- TE Teacher Edition
- CD-ROM

Explore 4-1

Lesson Notes

1 Focus

Teaching Tip

You may want to provide students with index cards, representing locker doors, for students to flip as a way of showing whether a locker door is open or closed. You may also want to group students into pairs of varying abilities to complete the activity.

2 Teach

Activity For Step 4, make sure students understand that some lockers (with odd numbers that are multiples of 3) will be closed, while other lockers (with even numbers that are multiples of 3) will be opened. All other lockers will stay the same. Students should realize that as they continue past student 15, only one locker will be opened or shut.

3 Assess

Formative Assessment

Use Exercise 2 to determine whether students understand the effect that the number of factors a number in the exercise had determined the final state of the locker door.

From Concrete to Abstract Use Exercise 3 to bridge the gap between modeling factors and analyzing the difference between prime numbers and composite numbers.

Extending the Concept Ask students to predict numbers greater than 30 that only have two factors, 1 and the number itself.

Explore 4-1

Math Lab
Exploring Factors

MAIN IDEA

Discover factors of whole numbers.

IN Academic Standards

Preparation for 7.1.3 Recognize the prime factors of a number and find the prime factorization of whole numbers and write the results using exponents.

The students in Mrs. Faccinto's homeroom have lockers numbered 1–30, located down a long hallway. One day the class did an experiment.

ACTIVITY

STEP 1 The first student, Student 1, walked down the hall and opened every locker.

STEP 2 Student 2 closed Locker 2 and every second locker after it.

STEP 3 Student 3 closed Locker 3 and changed the state of every third locker after it. This means that if the locker was open, Student 3 closed it; if the locker was closed, Student 3 opened it.

STEP 4 Student 4 changed the state of every fourth locker, starting with Locker 4. The student continued this pattern until all 30 students had a turn.

1, 2. See Ch. 4 Answer Appendix.

Analyze the Results

4. 24 and 30, both were opened or closed 8 times

1. Which lockers were open after Student 30 took a turn? What do the numbers on the open lockers have in common?
2. Explain why the lockers you listed in Exercise 1 were open after Student 30 took a turn.
3. Suppose there were 100 lockers. Which lockers would be open after Student 100 took a turn? 1, 4, 9, 16, 25, 36, 49, 64, 81, 100
4. **CHALLENGE** Which lockers were touched the greatest number of times?
5. What are the fewest lockers and students needed for 31 lockers to be open at the end of the experiment? 961

4-1 Prime Factorization

PACING: **Regular:** 2 periods, **Block:** 1 period

IN Academic Standards **7.1.3 Recognize the prime factors of a number and find the prime factorization of whole numbers and write the results using exponents.** **7.1.4 Recognize** or use **prime and composite numbers** to solve problems.

Options for Differentiated Instruction

ELL = English Language Learner AL = Above or Beyond Grade Level SS = Struggling Students SN = Special Needs

Using Manipulatives SN

Use with the Mini Lab.

Have students use blocks or centimeter cubes to build the rectangles. Examples of rectangles containing 4 "squares" would be a 2×2 rectangle, a 4×1 rectangle, and a 1×4 rectangle.

- Explain to students that each rectangle must use all the blocks. Once students have found the dimensions, have them transfer the rectangles to grid paper.
- Make sure that students understand that a 1×2 rectangle is the same as a 2×1 rectangle.

Kinesthetic Learners ELL SS SN

Use after presenting Examples 1 and 2.

Have students use a 100 chart like the one shown to help them find all the prime numbers that are less than 100:

1. Cross off 1, since a prime number is a whole number greater than 1.
2. Circle the first prime number found in the Mini Lab, 2. Since multiples of 2 are not prime numbers, cross off every even number.
3. Circle the next prime number, 3. Cross off every multiple of 3.
4. Continue the process until every number on the chart is either crossed off or circled.

~~1~~	(2)	(3)	~~4~~	5	~~6~~	7	~~8~~	~~9~~	~~10~~
11	~~12~~	13	~~14~~	~~15~~	~~16~~	17	~~18~~	19	~~20~~
~~21~~	~~22~~	23	~~24~~	25	~~26~~	~~27~~	~~28~~	29	~~30~~
31	~~32~~	~~33~~	~~34~~	35	~~36~~	37	~~38~~	~~39~~	~~40~~
41	~~42~~	43	~~44~~	~~45~~	~~46~~	47	~~48~~	49	~~50~~
~~51~~	~~52~~	53	~~54~~	55	~~56~~	~~57~~	~~58~~	59	~~60~~
61	~~62~~	~~63~~	~~64~~	65	~~66~~	67	~~68~~	~~69~~	~~70~~
71	~~72~~	73	~~74~~	~~75~~	~~76~~	77	~~78~~	79	~~80~~
81	~~82~~	83	~~84~~	85	~~86~~	~~87~~	~~88~~	89	~~90~~
~~91~~	~~92~~	~~93~~	~~94~~	95	~~96~~	97	~~98~~	~~99~~	~~100~~

Ask:

- Do you need to count and cross off the multiples of 4? Explain. Since every other multiple of 2 is a multiple of 4, multiples of 4 are already crossed off.
- Do you need to count and cross off the multiples of 6? Explain. Since all the multiples of 2 and 3 were crossed off, the multiples of 6 are already crossed off.
- What is a quick way to find the multiples of 11? Sample answer: Find every number on the same diagonal as 11.

Once all the prime numbers less than 100 have been circled, post them on the word wall.

Leveled Lesson Resources

Also on TeacherWorks™ Lesson 4-1

Chapter 4 Resource Masters

BL = Below or Approaching Grade Level OL = On Grade Level AL = Above or Beyond Grade Level ELL = English Language Learner

Lesson Reading Guide
p. 9 BL OL ELL

NAME ________ DATE ________ PERIOD ____

4-1 Lesson Reading Guide
Prime Factorization

Get Ready for the Lesson

Read the introduction at the top of page 181 in your textbook. Write your answers below.

1. Using your geo board, make as many different rectangles as possible containing 3, 4, 5, 6, 7, 8, 9, and 10 squares.

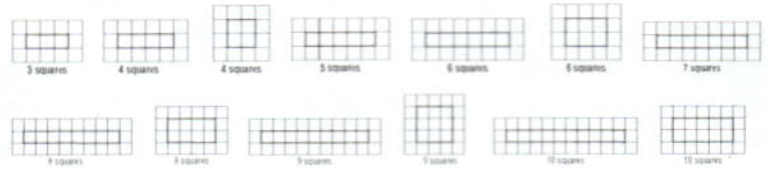

2. Which number of squares can be made into only one rectangle? into more than one rectangle?
3, 5, 7; 4, 6, 8, 9, 10

Read the Lesson

3. What is the difference between a prime and a composite number?
A prime number is a whole number with only two factors, 1 and itself. A composite number is a whole number greater than one that has more than two factors.

4. How do you know when a factor tree is complete?
A factor tree is complete when you have a row of prime factors.

5. Find the prime factorization of 28 using either method shown in Example 3.
7 · 2 · 2

6. How can an algebraic expression be factored?
An algebraic expression can be factored as a product of prime numbers and variables.

Remember What You Learned

7. Describe in your own words how to use a factor tree to find the prime factorization of a number. Include an example as an explanation.
See students' work.

Lesson 4-1

Chapter 4 9 Course 2

*Study Guide and Intervention**
p. 10 BL OL ELL

NAME ________ DATE ________ PERIOD ____

4-1 Study Guide and Intervention
Prime Factorization

A whole number is **prime** if it has exactly two factors, 1 and itself. A whole number is **composite** if it is greater than one and has more than two factors. To determine the **prime factorization** of a number, use a **factor tree**.

Example 1 Determine whether each number is *prime* or *composite*.

a. 11 b. 24

a. The number 11 has only two factors, 1 and 11, so it is prime.

b. The number 24 has 8 factors, 1, 2, 3, 4, 6, 8, 12, and 24. So, it is composite.

Example 2 Determine the prime factorization of 48.

Use a factor tree.

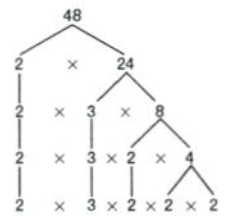

The prime factorization of 48 is 2 × 2 × 2 × 2 × 3 or $2^4 \times 3$

Exercises

Determine whether each number is prime or composite.

1. 27 composite 2. 31 prime 3. 46 composite 4. 53 prime
5. 11 prime 6. 72 composite 7. 17 prime 8. 51 composite

Determine the prime factorization of the following numbers.

9. 64 2^6 10. 100 $2^2 \times 5^2$ 11. 45 $3^2 \times 5$ 12. 81 3^4

Chapter 4 10 Course 2

*Skills Practice**
p. 11 BL OL

NAME ________ DATE ________ PERIOD ____

4-1 Skills Practice
Prime Factorization

Determine whether each number is *prime* or *composite*.

1. 36 composite 2. 71 prime 3. 18 composite
4. 27 composite 5. 37 prime 6. 61 prime
7. 32 composite 8. 21 composite 9. 40 composite

Find the prime factorization of each number.

10. 425 $5^2 \cdot 17$ 11. 82 $41 \cdot 2$ 12. 93 $31 \cdot 3$
13. 142 $71 \cdot 2$ 14. 45 $3^2 \cdot 5$ 15. 56 $2^3 \cdot 7$
16. 63 $3^2 \cdot 7$ 17. 236 $2^2 \cdot 59$ 18. 12 $2^2 \cdot 3$
19. 110 $2 \cdot 11 \cdot 5$ 20. 46 $2 \cdot 23$ 21. 84 $2^2 \cdot 3 \cdot 7$

Lesson 4-1

Chapter 4 11 Course 2

*Practice**
p. 12 OL AL

NAME ________ DATE ________ PERIOD ____

4-1 Practice
Prime Factorization

Determine whether each number is *prime* or *composite*.

1. 45 composite 2. 17 prime 3. 21 composite
4. 51 composite 5. 11 prime 6. 71 prime
7. 3 prime 8. 27 composite 9. 47 prime

Find the prime factorization of each number.

10. 88 $2^3 \cdot 11$ 11. 39 $3 \cdot 13$ 12. 75 $3 \cdot 5^2$
13. 124 $2^2 \cdot 31$ 14. 165 $3 \cdot 5 \cdot 11$ 15. 225 $3^2 \cdot 5^2$
16. 100 $2^2 \cdot 5^2$ 17. 91 $7 \cdot 13$ 18. 27 3^3

ALGEBRA Factor each expression.

19. $20xy$ $2 \cdot 2 \cdot 5 \cdot x \cdot y$ 20. $18bc$ $2 \cdot 3 \cdot 3 \cdot b \cdot c$ 21. $11pqr$ $11 \cdot p \cdot q \cdot r$

22. $36g^2h^2$ $2 \cdot 2 \cdot 3 \cdot 3 \cdot g \cdot g \cdot h \cdot h$ 23. $44m^2n$ $2 \cdot 2 \cdot 11 \cdot m \cdot m \cdot n$ 24. $25z^2$ $5 \cdot 5 \cdot z \cdot z$

Replace each ● with prime factors to make a true sentence.

25. $2^2 \cdot$ ● $\cdot 7 = 252$ 3^2 26. $2 \cdot$ ● $\cdot 5^3 = 750$ 3 27. $2^3 \cdot$ ● $\cdot 3^2 = 1{,}800$ 5^2

28. ALGEBRA Is $2x + y$ *prime or composite* if $x = 2$ and $y = 7$?
11 is prime.

29. ATHLETICS The distance around an oval running track is 440 yards. Write this distance as a product of primes.
$440 = 2 \cdot 2 \cdot 2 \cdot 5 \cdot 11$

Chapter 4 12 Course 2

*Word Problem Practice**
p. 13 OL AL

NAME ________ DATE ________ PERIOD ____

4-1 Word Problem Practice
Prime Factorization

1. AGE The average life expectancy in the United States is now 77.6 years. Round to the nearest whole number, and write it as a product of primes
$78 = 2 \cdot 3 \cdot 13$

2. FOOTBALL A football team's record for the season is 12 wins and 4 losses. Write their record as a product of primes.
$12 = 2^2 \cdot 3$
$4 = 2^2$

3. BASKETBALL The average height of players in the NBA is 6 feet 7 inches. Write this height in inches as a product of primes.
$1 \cdot 79$

4. TRAVELING The distance between Washington, D.C. and Chicago, IL is about 590 miles by air. Write this distance as a product of primes.
$2 \cdot 5 \cdot 59$

5. SCIENCE There are 118 elements in the Periodic Table. List all of the factors of 118. What type of number is this?
1, 2, 59, 118
composite

6. READING A copy of *A Tale of Two Cities*, the classic written by Charles Dickens, has about 530 pages. Write this as a product of primes.
$2 \cdot 5 \cdot 53$

Lesson 4-1

Chapter 4 13 Course 2

Enrichment
p. 14 OL AL

NAME ________ DATE ________ PERIOD ____

4-1 Enrichment

Perfect Numbers

A positive integer is *perfect* if it equals the sum of its factors that are less than the integer itself.

If the sum of the factors (excluding the integer itself) is greater than the integer, the integer is called *abundant*.

If the sum of the factors (excluding the integer itself) is less than the integer, the integer is called *deficient*.

The factors of 28 (excluding 28 itself) are 1, 2, 4, 7, and 14.
Since 1 + 2 + 4 + 7 + 14 = 28, 28 is a perfect number.

Complete the table to classify each number as perfect, abundant, or deficient.

	Number	Divisors (Excluding the Number Itself)	Sum	Classification
1.	14	1, 2, 7	10	deficient
2.	6	1, 2, 3	6	perfect
3.	12	1, 2, 3, 4, 6	16	abundant
4.	20	1, 2, 4, 5, 10	22	abundant
5.	10	1, 2, 5	8	deficient

Show that each number is perfect.

6. 496 1 + 2 + 4 + 8 + 16 + 31 + 62 + 124 + 248 = 496

7. 8,128 1 + 2 + 4 + 8 + 16 + 32 + 64 + 127 + 254 + 508 + 1,016 + 2,032 + 4,064 = 8,128

8. CHALLENGE 33,550,336 1 + 2 + 4 + 8 + 16 + 32 + 64 + 128 + 256 + 512 + 1,024 + 2,048 + 4,096 + 8,191 + 16,382 + 32,764 + 65,528 + 131,056 + 262,112 + 524,224 + 1,048,448 + 2,096,896 + 4,193,792 + 8,387,584 + 16,775,168 = 33,550,336

Chapter 4 14 Course 2

** Also available in Spanish* ELL

Additional Lesson Resources

Transparencies

- *5-Minute Check Transparency*, Lesson 4-1

Other Print Products

- *Teaching Mathematics with Manipulatives*
- *Noteables™ Interactive Study Notebook with Foldables™*

Teacher Tech Tools

- *Interactive Classroom CD-ROM*, Lesson 4-1
- *AssignmentWorks*, Lesson 4-1

Student Tech Tools

glencoe.com

- Extra Examples, Chapter 4, Lesson 1
- Self-Check Quiz, Chapter 4, Lesson 1

4-1 Prime Factorization

MAIN IDEA

Find the prime factorization of a composite number.

IN Academic Standards

7.1.3 Recognize the prime factors of a number and find the prime factorization of whole numbers and write the results using exponents.
7.1.4 Recognize or use **prime and composite numbers** to solve problems.

New Vocabulary

prime number
composite number
prime factorization
factor tree

IN Math Online

glencoe.com

- Concepts In Motion
- Extra Examples
- Personal Tutor
- Self-Check Quiz

MINI Lab

There is only one way that 2 can be expressed as the product of whole numbers. The geoboard shows that there is only one way that two squares can form a rectangle.

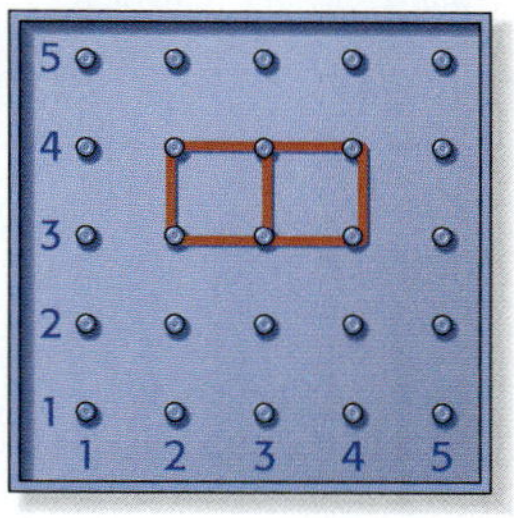

1. Using your geoboard, make as many different rectangles as possible containing 3, 4, 5, 6, 7, 8, 9, and 10 squares.
2. Which numbers of squares can be made into only one rectangle? Into more than one rectangle? **3, 5, 7; 4, 6, 8, 9, 10**

1. See Ch. 4 Answer Appendix.

The rectangles in the Mini Lab illustrate prime and composite numbers.

A **prime number** is a whole number greater than 1 that has exactly two factors, 1 and itself.

A **composite number** is a whole number greater than 1 that has more than two factors.

Whole Numbers	Factors
2	1, 2
3	1, 3
5	1, 5
7	1, 7
4	1, 2, 4
6	1, 2, 3, 6
8	1, 2, 4, 8
9	1, 3, 9
10	1, 2, 5, 10
0	many
1	1

The numbers 0 and 1 are neither prime nor composite.

EXAMPLES Identify Numbers as Prime or Composite

Determine whether each number is *prime* or *composite*.

1 **17**

The number 17 has only two factors, 1 and 17, so it is prime.

2 **12**

The number 12 has six factors: 1, 2, 3, 4, 6, and 12. So, it is composite.

Review Vocabulary

factor two or more numbers that are multiplied together to form a product; *Example*: 2 and 3 are factors of 6.
(Lesson 1-2)

CHECK Your Progress

Determine whether each number is *prime* or *composite*.

a. 11 **prime** b. 15 **composite** c. 24 **composite**

ADDITIONAL EXAMPLES

Determine whether each number is *prime* or *composite*.

1. 63 composite
2. 29 prime

- What are the factors of 18? 1, 2, 3, 6, 9, and 18
- What are some examples of numbers with only two factors? 2, 3, and 7

1 Focus

Vertical Alignment

Before Lesson 4-1

Determine the prime factors of all numbers through 50 and write the numbers as the product of their prime factors by using exponents to show multiples of a factor

Lesson 4-1

Determine the least common multiple and the greatest common divisor of whole numbers; use them to solve problems with fractions

After Lesson 4-1

Add and subtract fractions by using factoring to find common denominators

2 Teach

MINI Lab

You may need to point out that a 1 × 2 rectangle and a 2 × 1 rectangle are considered the same rectangle. They are just drawn differently. Students should realize that with 4 squares they can create multiple rectangles (1 × 4 and 2 × 2), but with 3 squares they can create only one rectangle (1 × 3).

Scaffolding Questions

Remind students that factors are numbers that are multiplied together to get a product.

Ask:

- What are the factors of 6? 1, 2, 3, and 6
- What are the factors of 10? 1, 2, 5, and 10

Formative Assessment

Use the Check Your Progress exercises after the Examples to determine students' understanding of concepts.

ADDITIONAL EXAMPLES

3 Find the prime factorization of 100. $2^2 \cdot 5^2$

4 **ALGEBRA** Factor $21m^2n$. $3 \cdot 7 \cdot m \cdot m \cdot n$

Additional Examples are also in:

- Noteables™ Interactive Study Notebook with Foldables™
- Interactive Classroom PowerPoint® Presentations

Focus on Mathematical Content

The **prime factorization** of a composite number shows the number as a product of prime numbers.

Factor trees are a good way to find the prime factorization of a number.

Every composite number can be written as a product of prime numbers. This product is the **prime factorization** of the number. You can use a **factor tree** to find the prime factorization. The following two factor trees show the prime factorization of 60.

Study Tip

Factors You can also choose any other pair of whole-number factors of 60 such as 3×20 or 4×15.

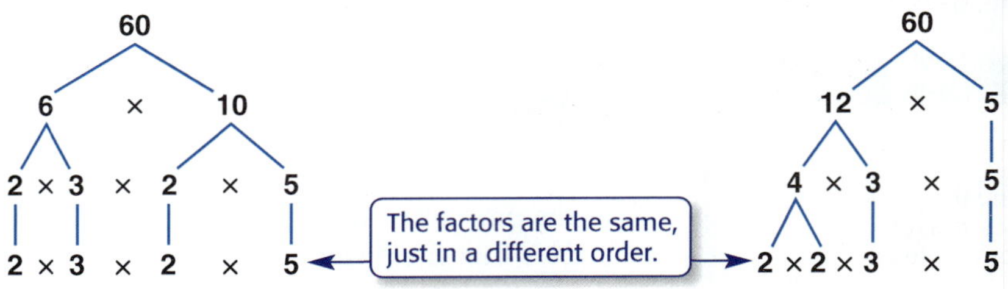

The prime factorization of 60 is $2 \times 2 \times 3 \times 5$, or $2^2 \times 3 \times 5$.

EXAMPLE Find the Prime Factorization

3 **Find the prime factorization of 24.**

METHOD 1

Use a factor tree.

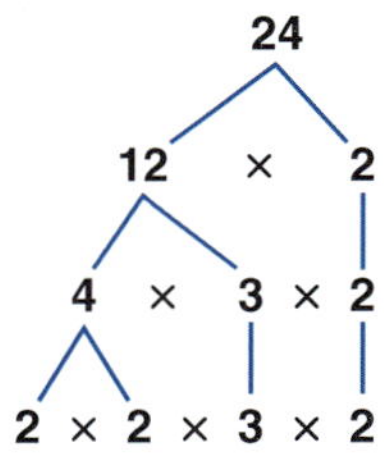

METHOD 2

Divide by prime numbers.

2)24
2)12
2) 6
3

The divisors are 2, 2, 2, and 3.

The prime factorization of 24 is $2 \times 2 \times 3 \times 2$ or $2^3 \times 3$.

CHOOSE Your Method

Find the prime factorization.

d. 18 2×3^2 e. 28 $2^2 \times 7$ f. 16 2^4

Algebraic expressions like $6ab$ can also be factored as the product of prime numbers and variables.

EXAMPLE Factor an Algebraic Expression

4 **ALGEBRA** **Factor $6ab$.**

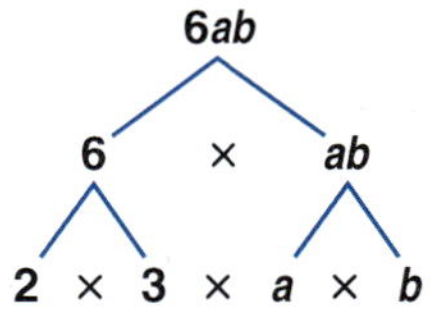

$6ab = 2 \cdot 3 \cdot a \cdot b$

CHECK Your Progress

g. **ALGEBRA** Factor $18xy$. $2 \cdot 3 \cdot 3 \cdot x \cdot y$ or $2 \cdot 3^2 \cdot x \cdot y$

182 Chapter 4 Fractions, Decimals, and Percents

★ indicates multi-step problem

CHECK Your Understanding

Examples 1, 2 (p. 181)

Determine whether each number is *prime* or *composite*.

1. 7 **prime**
2. 50 **composite**
3. 67 **prime**
4. **GARDENING** Louisa has 72 flowers to plant in rows in a flower bed. How many different ways can she plant the flowers? Justify your answer. **See margin.**

Example 3 (p. 182)

Find the prime factorization of each number.

5. 34 2×17
6. 30 $2 \times 3 \times 5$
7. 12 $2^2 \times 3$

Example 4 (p. 182)

ALGEBRA **Factor each expression.**

8. $10ac$ $2 \cdot 5 \cdot a \cdot c$
9. $16x^2$ $2 \cdot 2 \cdot 2 \cdot 2 \cdot x \cdot x$
10. $11g^3$ $11 \cdot g \cdot g \cdot g$

Practice and Problem Solving

HOMEWORK HELP	
For Exercises	See Examples
11–18	1, 2
19–28	3
29–34	4

Exercise Levels
A: 11–34
B: 35–43
C: 44–47

Determine whether each number is *prime* or *composite*.

11. 22 **composite**
12. 44 **composite**
13. 13 **prime**
14. 39 **composite**
15. 81 **composite**
16. 31 **prime**
17. 97 **prime**
18. 43 **prime**

Find the prime factorization of each number.

19. 96 $2^5 \times 3$
20. 42 $2 \times 3 \times 7$
21. 99 $3^2 \times 11$
22. 64 2^6
23. 210 $2 \times 3 \times 5 \times 7$
24. 180 $2^2 \times 3^2 \times 5$
25. 126 $2 \times 3^2 \times 7$
26. 375 3×5^3
27. **LOBSTERS** Lobsters can live up to 50 years. What is this amount expressed as a product of primes? $2 \cdot 5^2$

28. **DOGS** Greyhounds can jump a distance of 27 feet. Write this distance as a product of primes. 3^3

ALGEBRA **Factor each expression.**

29. $15mn$ $3 \cdot 5 \cdot m \cdot n$
30. $20pq$ $2 \cdot 2 \cdot 5 \cdot p \cdot q$
31. $34jkm$ $2 \cdot 17 \cdot j \cdot k \cdot m$
32. $49y^2$ $7 \cdot 7 \cdot y \cdot y$
33. $52gh^2$ $2 \cdot 2 \cdot 13 \cdot g \cdot h \cdot h$
34. $48a^2b^2$ $2 \cdot 2 \cdot 2 \cdot 2 \cdot 3 \cdot a \cdot a \cdot b \cdot b$

Replace each ■ with prime factors to make a true sentence.

35. $2^3 \cdot ■ \cdot 11 = 616$ 7
36. $2 \cdot ■ \cdot 5^2 = 450$ 3^2
37. $3 \cdot 2^4 \cdot ■ = 1{,}200$ 5^2
38. $2^2 \cdot ■ \cdot 3 = 1{,}500$ 5^3
39. **RIVERS** The Colorado River is 1,450 miles long. Write 1,450 as a product of primes. $2 \times 5^2 \times 29$

ALGEBRA **For Exercises 40 and 41, determine whether the value of each expression is *prime* or *composite* if $a = 1$ and $b = 5$.**

40. $3a + 6b$ **composite**
41. $7b - 4a$ **prime**

3 Practice

Formative Assessment

Use Exercises 1–10 to check for understanding.

Then use the chart at the bottom of this page to customize your assignments for students.

Intervention You may wish to use the Study Guide and Intervention Master on page 10 of the *Chapter 4 Resource Masters* for additional reinforcement.

Tips for New Teachers: Factors

Make sure students understand that *factoring* an algebraic expression is like finding the prime factorization of a number–except that the variables may or may not represent prime numbers.

Odd/Even Assignments

Exercises 11–34 are structured so that students practice the same concepts whether they are assigned odd or even problems.

Additional Answer

4. 12 ways; 1 row of 72, 2 rows of 36, 3 rows of 24, 4 rows of 18, 6 rows of 12, 8 rows of 9, 9 rows of 8, 12 rows of 6, 18 rows of 4, 24 rows of 3, 36 rows of 2, and 72 rows of 1

DIFFERENTIATED HOMEWORK OPTIONS

Level	Assignment	Two-Day Option	
BL Basic	11–34, 44, 46, 59	11–33 odd, 48, 49	12–34 even, 44, 46–59
OL Core	11–27 odd, 28, 29–39 odd, 42–46, 47–59	11–34, 48, 49	35–44, 46, 47, 50–59
AL Advanced/Pre-AP	35–55 (optional: 56–59)		

4 Assess

Ticket Out the Door Have students write the prime factorization of 1,000 on a piece of paper. You might want to point out that they already found the prime factorization of 50 (in Exercise 2), and ask: Can this help you find the prime factorization of 1,000?

FOLDABLES Study Organizer **Foldables™ Follow-Up**

Remind students to write—under the tab for this lesson of their Foldable—a question about prime factorization. As students progress through the lesson, encourage them to take notes and record information that answers the question.

Additional Answer

50. 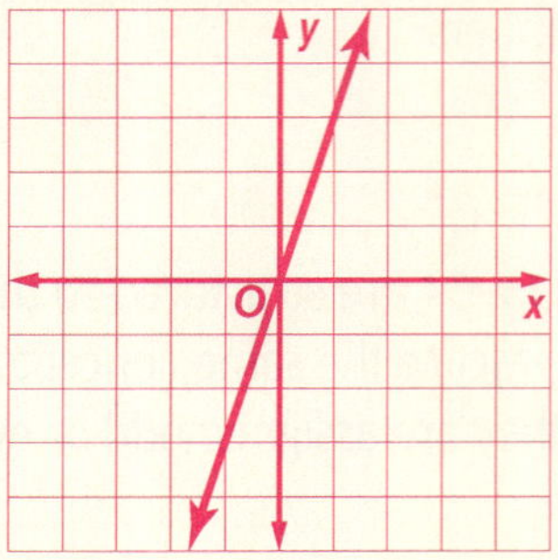

43. Sample answer: 81: 9×9, 3×27; 225: 9×25, 5×45; 441: 9×49; 7×63

Academic Standards • ISTEP+
Extra Practice, pp. 676, 707

CONTESTS **For Exercises 42 and 43, use the following information.**

Sandcastle Day at Cannon Beach, Oregon, is one of the largest sandcastle contests on the west coast. Entrants from each age division are given lots measuring 81 square feet, 225 square feet, or 441 square feet, on which to build their castles.

42. Find the prime factorization of 81, 225, and 441. 3^4, $3^2 \times 5^2$, $3^2 \times 7^2$
43. Use the prime factors to determine two possible dimensions for each plot.

H.O.T. Problems

44. See Ch. 4 Answer Appendix.

47. If $n = 1$, $2n$ is a prime number. If $n > 1$, $2n$ is a composite number with at least three factors.

44. **RESEARCH** Use the Internet or another source to make a Sieve of Eratosthenes to determine the prime numbers up to 100.
45. **CHALLENGE** This whole number is between 30 and 40. It has only two prime factors whose sum is 5. What is the number? 36
46. **OPEN ENDED** Primes that differ by two are called *twin primes*. For example, 59 and 61 are twin primes. Give three examples of twin primes that are less than 50. Sample answer: 5 and 7, 11 and 13, and 17 and 19
47. **WRITING IN MATH** Suppose n represents a whole number. Is $2n$ prime or composite? Explain.

ISTEP+ PRACTICE 7.1.3, 7.1.4

48. Which number is a prime factor of both 63 and 140? D

A 2	C 5
B 3	D 7

49. Which of the following numbers is *not* a prime number? H

F 2	H 16
G 11	J 31

Spiral Review

50. **ALGEBRA** Graph $y = 3x$. (Lesson 3-7) See margin.
51. **MEASUREMENT** Find the perimeter and area of a rectangle with a length of 13 feet and width of 5 feet. (Lesson 3-6) 36 feet; 65 ft^2

Add. (Lesson 2-4)

52. $6 + (-4)$ 2
53. $-13 + 9$ −4
54. $25 + (-26)$ −1
55. $-5 + 5$ 0

GET READY for the Next Lesson

PREREQUISITE SKILL **State whether each number is divisible by 2, 3, 5, 6, 9, or 10.** (Page 668)

56. 24 2, 3, 6
57. 70 2, 5, 10
58. 120 2, 3, 5, 6, 10
59. 99 3, 9

184 **Chapter 4** Fractions, Decimals, and Percents

Pre-AP Activity Use after Exercise 47

Have students answer the following questions: If x represents a whole number, can x^2 be prime? composite? neither? Make sure students explain their reasoning and give examples.

READING to SOLVE PROBLEMS

Everyday Meaning

The key to understanding word problems is to understand the meaning of the mathematical terms in the problem. Many words used in mathematics are also used in everyday language.

For example, you will use the terms *factor* and *multiple* in this chapter. Here are two sentences that show their everyday meanings.

- Weather was a *factor* in their decision to postpone the picnic.
- The star quarterback won *multiple* post-season awards.

The table below shows how the everyday meaning is connected to the mathematical meaning.

Academic Standards **P.3.4 Use the language of mathematics to express mathematical ideas precisely.**

Term	Everyday Meaning	Mathematical Meaning	Connection
factor from the Latin *factor,* meaning doer	something that actively contributes to a decision or result	2 and 3 are *factors* of 6.	A *factor* helps to make a decision, and in mathematics, factors "make up" a product.
multiple from the Latin *multi-*, meaning many, and *plex,* meaning fold	consisting of more than one or shared by many	The *multiples* of 2 are 0, 2, 4, 6, … .	*Multiple* means many, and in mathematics, a number has infinitely many multiples.

PRACTICE

1. Sample answer: *fact-*: fact, faction, factory; *multi-*: multiplex, multimedia, multicultural. The words beginning with *fact-* all refer to parts of something; the words beginning with *multi-* all refer to more than one.

1. Make a list of other words that have the prefixes *fact-* or *multi-*. Determine what the words in each list have in common.
2. **WRITING IN MATH** Write your own rule for remembering the difference between *factor* and *multiple*. **See students' work.**

RESEARCH **Use a dictionary to find the everyday meanings of *least*, *greatest*, and *common*. Then use the definitions to determine how to find each number. Do not solve.**

3. the greatest common factor of 10 and 15
4. the least common multiple of 2 and 3.

3. Greatest: largest in size; common: belonging to or shared by two or more individuals or things; the greatest common factor of 10 and 15 is the largest factor common to both 10 and 15.

4. Least: smallest in size; the least common multiple of 2 and 3 is the smallest multiple common to both 2 and 3.

READING to SOLVE PROBLEMS

1 Focus

Students may sometimes be confused by words that have both a mathematical meaning and an everyday meaning. This activity helps students become aware of the differences (and similarities) of such meanings by examining the mathematical and everyday definitions of two words.

2 Teach

You may want to have students name other words that have both mathematical and everyday meanings. (for example: *remainder*, *difference*, *average*, *area*) Write the words on the chalkboard and ask volunteers to use them in mathematical and everyday sentences.

Before beginning the Exercises, make sure students understand that a *prefix* is a group of letters attached to the beginning of a word (or base) that produces a new word or meaning.

3 Assess

Tell students that tomorrow's lesson is about finding the greatest common factor of two or more numbers. Have them write how they think what they learned today will connect with tomorrow's material.

4-2 Greatest Common Factor

PACING: **Regular:** 2 periods, **Block:** 1 period

IN Academic Standards **7.1.3 Recognize the prime factors of a number and find the prime factorization of whole numbers and write the results using exponents. 7.1.4 Recognize or use prime and composite numbers to solve problems.**
Also addresses 7.1.2.

Options for Differentiated Instruction

ELL = English Language Learner AL = Above or Beyond Grade Level SS = Struggling Students SN = Special Needs

Visual Learners ELL AL SS

Use with Example 1.

Display the Venn diagram at the right, which shows the common factors of 18 and 48.

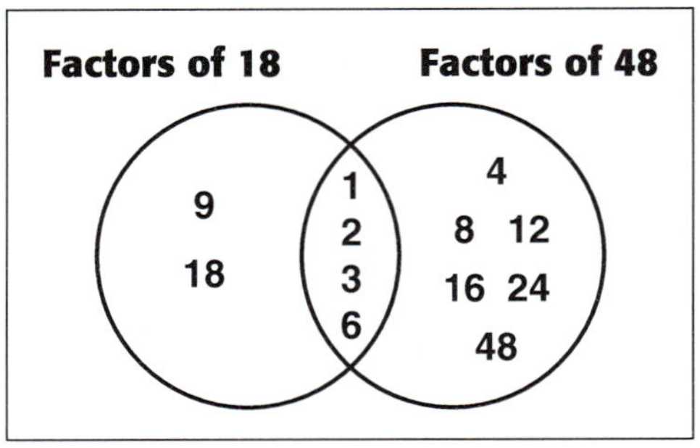

Ask:

- How can you tell from looking at the diagram what the GCF of 18 and 48 is? It is 6, the greatest number in the area where the circles overlap.

If you were to display the common factors of 20 and 24, what would be the numbers in the area where the circles overlap? 1, 2, 4

Alternative Methods AL

Use with the Examples.

Have students solve the Examples using a hundreds chart and colored chips to cover factors of the numbers. Have students mark all factors of the first number with one color and all factors of the second number in another color.

Ask:

- What factors do they have in common?
- What is the GCF?

Organizing Student Work and Thinking ELL SS SN

Use before assigning the Exercises.

Have students use index cards to create a factor card for each of the numbers from 1 to 30. On each card, write the following:

- the number
- a list of all the factors
- a factor tree
- the prime factorization

Have students fasten the cards together by hole-punching the corner of each card and placing a ring through it.

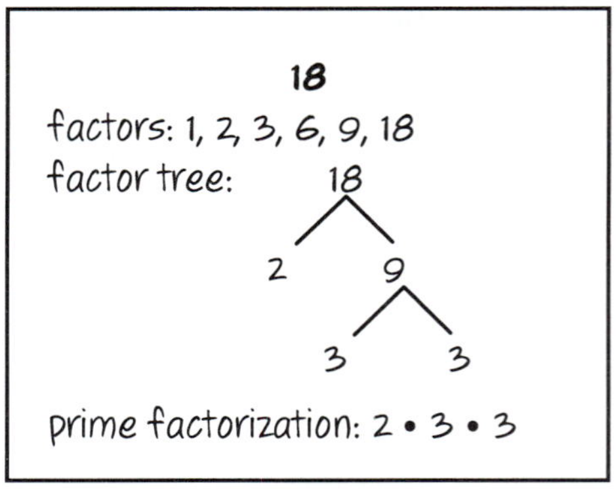

Leveled Lesson Resources

Also on **TeacherWorks™** Lesson 4-2

Chapter 4 Resource Masters

BL = Below or Approaching Grade Level OL = On Grade Level AL = Above or Beyond Grade Level ELL = English Language Learner

Lesson Reading Guide
p. 16 BL OL ELL

NAME ________ DATE ________ PERIOD ____

4-2 Lesson Reading Guide
Greatest Common Factor

Get Ready for the Lesson

Read the introduction at the top of page 186 in your textbook. Write your answers below.

1. Which factors are in the overlapping section? What does this mean? **2, 3; 2 and 3 are prime factors of both 12 and 18.**
2. Is the product of 2 and 3 also a factor of 12 and 18? **Yes; since each prime factor divides the number, the product of factors will also divide the number.**
3. Make a Venn diagram showing the prime factors of 12 and 20. Identify the common factors and find their product. **2, 2; 4**

Read the Lesson

4. What does a Venn diagram show? **how elements among sets of numbers or objects are related**
5. How does a Venn diagram show relationships between elements? **Sample answer: The common elements are within the overlapping part of the circles.**
6. You can find the GCF by using common factors or using common prime factors. What is the difference? **Sample answer: In one method you list all factors of both numbers then find the greatest common factor. In the other method, the prime factorizations are compared, and the GCF is the product of those common factors.**
7. Find the prime factors of 20 and 24. What are the prime factors that are common to both numbers? What is the GCF? $20 = 2^2 \cdot 5$; $24 = 2^3 \cdot 3$; **The common prime factors are 2 and 2; the GCF is 4.**
8. How is the GCF of two numbers found if you know the prime factors common to the numbers? **Multiply the common prime factors to find the GCF.**

Remember What You Learned

9. In your own words, describe what the GCF of two numbers is and explain one way to find it. **Sample answer: The greatest common factor (GCF) of two numbers is the greatest number among the factors common to both numbers; for small numbers you can list the factors easily, and for large numbers find the prime factorization or use division.**

Chapter 4 16 Course 2

Study Guide and Intervention*
p. 17 BL OL ELL

NAME ________ DATE ________ PERIOD ____

4-2 Study Guide and Intervention
Greatest Common Factor

The **greatest common factor (GCF)** of two or more numbers is the largest number that is a factor of each number. The GCF of prime numbers is 1.

Example 1 Find the GCF of 72 and 108 by listing factors.

factors of 72: 1, 2, 3, 4, 6, 8, 9, 12, 18, 24, 36, 72
factors of 108: 1, 2, 3, 4, 6, 9, 12, 18, 27, 36, 54, 108
common factors: 1, 2, 3, 4, 6, 9, 12, 18, 36
The GCF of 72 and 108 is 36.

Example 2 Find the GCF of 42 and 60 using prime factors.

Method 1 Write the prime factorization.
$60 = 2 \times 2 \times 3 \times 5$
$42 = 2 \times 3 \times 7$

Method 2 Divide by prime numbers. Divide both 42 and 60 by 2. Then divide the quotients by 3.
7 10
3)21 30
2)42 60 ← Start here

The common prime factors are 2 and 3. The GCF of 42 and 60 is 2×3, or 6.

Exercises

Find the GCF of each set of numbers.

1. 18, 30 **6**	2. 60, 45 **15**	3. 24, 72 **24**
4. 32, 48 **16**	5. 100, 30 **10**	6. 54, 36 **18**
7. 3, 97, 5 **1**	8. 4, 20, 24 **4**	9. 36, 9, 45 **9**

Lesson 4-2

Chapter 4 17 Course 2

Skills Practice*
p. 18 BL OL

NAME ________ DATE ________ PERIOD ____

4-2 Skills Practice
Greatest Common Factor

Find the GCF of each set of numbers.

1. 14, 20 **2**	2. 16, 42 **2**
3. 8, 18 **2**	4. 24, 36 **12**
5. 72, 22 **2**	6. 77, 15 **1**
7. 32, 80 **16**	8. 90, 120 **30**
9. 45, 30 **15**	10. 12, 62 **2**
11. 15, 27 **3**	12. 21, 28 **7**
13. 12, 20, 26 **2**	14. 15, 20, 25 **5**
15. 60, 72, 36 **12**	16. 32, 48, 64 **16**
17. 36, 48, 30 **6**	18. 28, 56, 42 **14**
19. 80, 110, 90 **10**	20. 9, 25, 49 **1**

Find the GCF of each set of algebraic expressions.

21. $21ab$, $14b$ **$7b$**	22. $20a^2$, $36a$ **$4a$**
23. $15ab$, $5b^2$ **$5b$**	24. $35a^2$, $85ab$ **$5a$**

25. Find the GCF of $2^3 \times 3^2 \times 5$ and $2^2 \times 3 \times 5^2$. **$2^2 \times 3 \times 5$ or 60**

Chapter 4 18 Course 2

Practice*
p. 19 OL AL

NAME ________ DATE ________ PERIOD ____

4-2 Practice
Greatest Common Factor

Find the GCF of each set of numbers.

1. 16, 44 **4**	2. 15, 35 **5**	3. 24, 32 **8**
4. 27, 63 **9**	5. 20, 80 **20**	6. 18, 38 **2**
7. 14, 49 **7**	8. 66, 99 **33**	9. 9, 35 **1**
10. 6, 24, 42 **6**	11. 30, 50, 70 **10**	12. 32, 48, 96 **16**
13. $10w$, $5w$ **$5w$**	14. $16xy$, $24xy$ **$8xy$**	15. $21ab$, $35a$ **$7a$**
16. $10jk$, $15k$ **$5k$**	17. $3mn$, $9mn$, $12mn$ **$3mn$**	18. $6y$, $9x$, $3y$ **3**

19. 4 inches, 1 foot, 6 inches, 2 feet **2 inches**
20. 10 gallons, 55 gallons, 35 gallons, 20 gallons **5 gallons**

Find two numbers whose GCF is the given number.

21. 10 **Sample answer: 20, 50**	22. 8 **Sample answer: 24, 32**	23. 14 **Sample answer: 56, 70**

24. SPORTS CARDS Jason wants to organize his sports cards in packets for each type of sport. Each packet has the same number of cards. If he has 24 baseball cards, 60 hockey cards, and 48 football cards, find the greatest number of cards in each packet. **12 cards**
25. FORESTRY A forest ranger needs to remove three tree trunks by cutting the trunks into equal lengths. If the lengths of the tree trunks are 6 feet, 8 feet, and 12 feet, what is the length of the longest log that can be cut? **2 feet**

Lesson 4-2

Chapter 4 19 Course 2

Word Problem Practice*
p. 20 OL AL

NAME ________ DATE ________ PERIOD ____

4-2 Word Problem Practice
Greatest Common Factor

1. TABLE TENNIS Rebecca has 20 table tennis balls and 16 table tennis paddles. She wants to sell packages of balls and paddles bundled together. What is the greatest number of packages she can sell with no leftover balls or paddles? **4**
2. TUMBLING Mr. Nicolet wants to organize equal-sized groups of boys and girls for tumbling exercises. If there are 12 boys and 18 girls and each group is all boys or all girls, what is the largest size group he can organize? **6**
3. BAKE SALE Volunteers at a bake sale want to sell slices of banana nut bread and raisin bread packaged together. They have 63 slices of banana nut bread and 45 slices of raisin bread, and they plan to use all the bread. What is the greatest number of packages they can put together? How many slices of each type of bread are in a package? **9; 7 slices of banana nut bread and 5 slices of raisin bread**
4. DOG TREATS Krista wants to give her dog a special treat. She has 81 dog bones and 54 pieces of beef jerky. If she wants to give her dog the same number of treats every day, what is the greatest number of days she can feed the dog these treats? How many of each type should she give the dog? **27; 3 dog bones and 2 pieces of beef jerky**
5. FRUIT TREES Mr. Farber has 84 pear trees and 180 apple trees. He wants to plant the trees in rows of equal width. Find the most trees that can be planted in a row if each row has only one type of tree. **12**
6. BOARDS A scouting troop has three boards of lengths 14 feet, 28 feet, and 21 feet. If the boards must be cut to produce equal-sized pieces, what is the longest piece that can be cut with no waste? **7 ft**

Chapter 4 20 Course 2

Enrichment
p. 21 OL AL

NAME ________ DATE ________ PERIOD ____

4-2 Enrichment

Sundaram's Sieve

This arrangement of numbers is called Sundaram's Sieve. Like the Sieve of Eratosthenes, Sundaram's arrangement can be used to find prime numbers.

4	7	10	13	16	19	22	25	28	31
7	12	17	22	27	32	37	42	47	52
10	17	24	31	38	45	52	59	66	73
13	22	31	40	49	58	67	76	85	94
16	27	38	49	60	71	82	93	104	115

Here's how to use Sundaram's Sieve to find prime numbers. If a number, n, is not in the Sieve, then $2n + 1$ is a prime number. If a number, n, is in the Sieve, then $2n + 1$ is not a prime number.

32 is in the sieve. $2 \times 32 + 1 = 65$ 65 is not prime.
35 is not in the sieve. $2 \times 35 + 1 = 71$ 71 is prime.

1. Does the sieve give all primes up to 99? all the composites? **all primes except 2; only 22 of the composites**
2. Sundaram's Sieve is constructed from arithmetic sequences. Describe the pattern used to make the first row. **Start with 4 and add 3 each time.**
3. How is the first column constructed? **It is the same as the first row.**
4. How are the second through fifth rows constructed? **arithmetic sequences using 5, 7, 9, and 11**
5. How would you add a sixth row to the sieve? **Start with 19 and add 13 each time.**
6. Use Sundaram's Sieve to find 5 four-digit prime numbers. You will need to add more numbers to the sieve to do this. **See students' work.**

Lesson 4-2

Chapter 4 21 Course 2

Additional Lesson Resources

** Also available in Spanish* ELL

Transparencies
- *5-Minute Check Transparency*, Lesson 4-2

Other Print Products
- *Noteables™ Interactive Study Notebook with Foldables™*

Teacher Tech Tools
- *Interactive Classroom CD-ROM*, Lesson 4-2
- *AssignmentWorks*, Lesson 4-2

Student Tech Tools
glencoe.com
- Extra Examples, Chapter 4, Lesson 2
- Self-Check Quiz, Chapter 4, Lesson 2

4-2 Lesson Notes

1 Focus

Vertical Alignment

Before Lesson 4-2
Determine the prime factors of all numbers through 50 and write the numbers as the product of their prime factors by using exponents to show multiples of a factor

Lesson 4-2
Determine the greatest common divisor of whole numbers

After Lesson 4-2
Add and subtract fractions by using factoring to find common denominators

2 Teach

Scaffolding Questions

As students answer the questions, write each set of factors on the board.

Ask:

- What are the factors of 18? 1, 2, 3, 6, 9, and 18
- What are the factors of 12? 1, 2, 3, 4, 6, and 12
- What factors do 18 and 12 have in common? 1, 2, 3, and 6

Formative Assessment

Use the Check Your Progress exercises after each Example to determine students' understanding of concepts.

4-2 Greatest Common Factor

MAIN IDEA

Find the greatest common factor of two or more numbers.

IN Academic Standards

7.1.3 Recognize the prime factors of a number and find the prime factorization of whole numbers and write the results using exponents.
7.1.4 Recognize or use prime and composite numbers to solve problems. *Also addresses 7.1.2.*

New Vocabulary

Venn diagram
greatest common factor (GCF)

IN Math Online

glencoe.com

- Extra Examples
- Personal Tutor
- Self-Check Quiz
- Reading in the Content Area

GET READY for the Lesson

VENN DIAGRAM The Venn diagram shows the prime factors of 12 and 18.

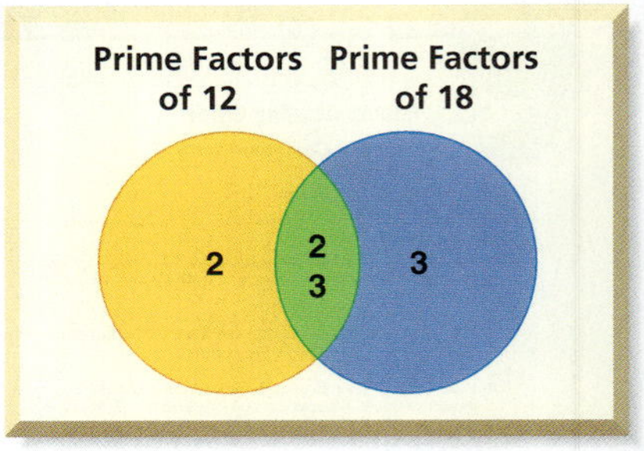

1. Which factors are in the overlapping section? What does this mean?
2. Is the product of 2 and 3 also a factor of 12 and 18?
3. Make a Venn diagram showing the prime factors of 12 and 20. Identify the common factors and find their product. **1–3. See margin.**

As shown above, **Venn diagrams** use overlapping circles to show how common elements among sets of numbers or objects are related. They can also show common factors. The greatest of the common factors of two or more numbers is the **greatest common factor, or GCF**.

EXAMPLE Find the Greatest Common Factor

1 **Find the GCF of 18 and 48.**

METHOD 1 **List the factors of the numbers.**

factors of 18: **1**, **2**, **3**, **6**, 9, 18
factors of 48: **1**, **2**, **3**, 4, **6**, 8, 12, 16, 24, 48

List the factors of 18 and 48.

The common factors of 18 and 48 are 1, 2, 3, and 6.
So, the greatest common factor or GCF is 6.

METHOD 2 **Use prime factorization.**

Write the prime factorization. Circle the common prime factors.

$18 = 2 \times 3 \times 3$
$48 = 2 \times 2 \times 2 \times 2 \times 3$

Write the prime factorizations of 18 and 48.

The greatest common factor or GCF is 2×3 or 6.

CHOOSE Your Method

Find the GCF of each pair of numbers.

a. 8, 10 **2** b. 6, 12 **6** c. 10, 17 **1**

ADDITIONAL EXAMPLE

1 Find the GCF of 28 and 42. 14

Additional Examples are also in:

- Noteables™ Interactive Study Notebook with Foldables™
- Interactive Classroom PowerPoint® Presentations

Additional Answers

1. 2, 3; 2 and 3 are prime factors of both 12 and 18.
2. Yes; Since each prime factor divides the number, the product of factors will also divide the number.

186 Chapter 4 Fractions, Decimals, and Percents

Reading Math

Greatest Common Factor The greatest common factor is also called the *greatest common divisor* because it is the greatest number that divides evenly into the given numbers.

EXAMPLE Find the GCF of Three Numbers

2 **Find the GCF of 12, 24, and 60.**

Write the prime factorization. Circle the common prime factors.

$12 = 2 \times 2 \times 3$

$24 = 2 \times 2 \times 2 \times 3$ — Write the prime factorization of 12, 24, and 60.

$60 = 2 \times 2 \times 3 \times 5$

The common prime factors are 2, 2, and 3. So, the GCF is $2 \times 2 \times 3$, or 12.

CHECK Your Progress

Find the GCF of each set of numbers.

d. 30, 45, 75 **15**

e. 42, 70, 84 **14**

Real-World EXAMPLES

3 **SCHOOL SPIRIT The cheerleaders are making spirit ribbons. Blue ribbon comes in a 24 inch spool, red ribbon comes in a 30 inch spool, and gold ribbon comes in a 36 inch spool. The cheerleaders want to cut strips of equal length and use the entire spool of each ribbon. What is the length of the longest piece of ribbon that can be cut from each spool?**

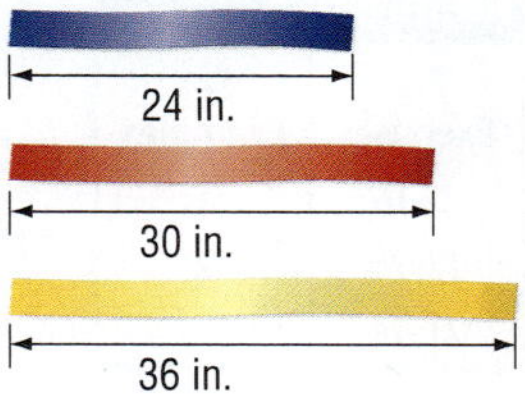

The length of the longest ribbon that can be cut from each spool is the GCF of the three lengths.

$24 = 2 \times 2 \times 2 \times 3$

$30 = 2 \times 3 \times 5$ — Write the prime factorization of 24, 30, and 36.

$36 = 2 \times 2 \times 3 \times 3$

The GCF of 24, 30, and 36 is 2×3 or 6. So, the ribbons should be 6 inches long.

4 **How many spirit ribbons can be made if the ribbons are cut into 6-inch pieces?**

There is a total of 24 + 30 + 36, or 90 inches of ribbon. So, $90 \div 6$, or 15 spirit ribbons can be made.

Study Tip

Prime Numbers The GCF of a group of prime numbers is 1.

CHECK Your Progress

f. **CARPENTRY** Mr. Glover wants to make shelves for his garage using an 18-foot board and a 36-foot board. He will cut the boards to make shelves of the same length and wants to use all of both boards. Find the longest possible length of each shelf. How many shelves can he make? **18 ft, 3**

Additional Answer

3. 2, 2; 4

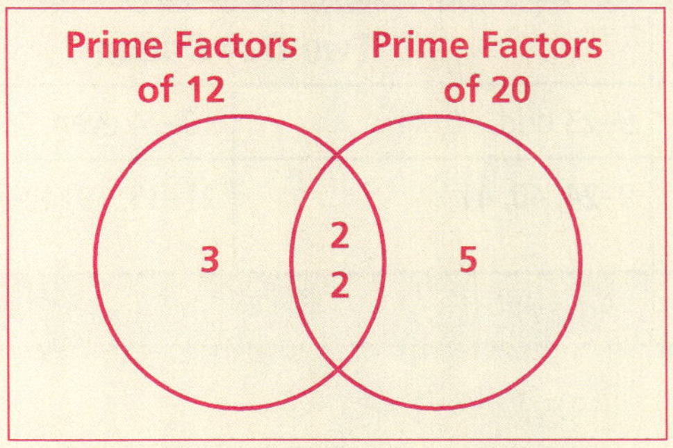

Focus on Mathematical Content

Venn diagrams are a good way to illustrate the intersection of two sets, such as the common factors of two numbers.

One way to find the **greatest common factor**, or GCF, of a set of numbers is to **list the factors of each number.**

Another way to find the greatest common factor of a set of numbers is to **write the prime factorization of each number.** The GCF is the product of the corresponding common factors.

ADDITIONAL EXAMPLES

2 Find the GCF of 21, 42, and 63. 21

3 **ART** Searra wants to cut a 15-centimeter by 25-centimeter piece of tag board into squares for an art project. She does not want to waste any of the tag board and she wants the largest squares possible. What is the length of the side of the squares she should use? 5 cm

4 How many squares can she make if the sides are 5 centimeters? 15

Tips for New Teachers — Prime Numbers

Students may think that the GCF of prime numbers is zero. Reinforce to students that the GCF of prime numbers is 1 by using an example where students list the factors of prime numbers. For example, to find the GCF of 11 and 5, find the factors of both 11 and 5. Since $11 = 11 \times 1$ and $5 = 5 \times 1$, the common factor of both 11 and 5 is 1. Because that is the only common factor, it is also the greatest common factor.

3 Practice

Formative Assessment

Use Exercises 1–8 to check for understanding.

Then use the chart at the bottom of this page to customize your assignments for students.

Intervention You may wish to use the Study Guide and Intervention Master on page 17 of the *Chapter 4 Resource Masters* for additional reinforcement.

Odd/Even Assignments

Exercises 9–24 are structured so that students practice the same concepts whether they are assigned odd or even problems.

Tips for New Teachers: Working in Groups

If students have difficulty finding the GCF of sets of numbers, you may want to separate them into pairs or groups. Let the members of each pair or group discuss the problems and possible solution methods. Each member can find the factors (or prime factorization) of one number, and then all of the members could compare their lists of factors.

Tips for New Teachers: Greatest Common Divisor

Be sure that your students understand that the terms *greatest common factor* (*GCF*) and the *greatest common divisor* can be used interchangeably.

★ indicates multi-step problem

CHECK Your Understanding

Examples 1, 2 (pp. 186–187)

Find the GCF of each set of numbers.

1. 18, 30 **6**
2. 45, 60 **15**
3. 20, 50 **10**
4. 6, 8, 12 **2**
5. 8, 20, 40 **4**
6. 18, 42, 60 **6**

JOBS **For Exercises 7 and 8, use the following information.**
A store manager wants to display the inventory of three styles of bicycle helmets in rows with the same number of each style in each row.

Bike Helmets	
Style	**Inventory**
Sport	36
Road	72
Mountain	45

Examples 3, 4 (p. 187)

7. Find the greatest number of helmets that can be placed in each row. **9**
8. How many rows of each helmet are there? **4, 8, 5**

Practice and Problem Solving

HOMEWORK HELP	
For Exercises	**See Examples**
9–16	1
17–20	2
21–24	3, 4

Exercise Levels
A: 9–24
B: 25–35
C: 36–39

Find the GCF of each set of numbers.

9. 12, 78 **6**
10. 40, 50 **10**
11. 20, 45 **5**
12. 32, 48 **16**
13. 24, 48 **24**
14. 45, 75 **15**
15. 56, 96 **8**
16. 40, 125 **5**
17. 18, 24, 30 **6**
18. 36, 60, 84 **12**
19. 35, 49, 84 **7**
20. 36, 50, 130 **2**

BANDS **For Exercises 21 and 22, use the following information.**
In a marching band, there are 64 woodwinds, 88 brass, and 16 percussion players. When they march in a parade, there is the same number of students in each row.

21. Find the greatest number of students in each row. **8 students**
22. How many rows of each group are there? **8, 11, 2**

COMMUNITY SERVICE **For Exercises 23 and 24, use the following information.**
You want to make care packages for a local shelter. You have 18 toothbrushes, 30 combs, and 12 bars of soap. Each package has the same number of each item.

23. What is the greatest number of care packages you can make using all the items? **6 care packages**
24. How many of each item are in each package? **3 toothbrushes, 5 combs, and 2 bars of soap**

Find the GCF of each set of numbers.

25. 25¢, \$1.50, 75¢, \$3.00 **25¢**
26. 6 feet, 15 feet, 21 feet, 9 feet **3 ft**

ALGEBRA **Find the greatest common divisor of each set of expressions.**

27. $24a$, $6a$ **$6a$**
28. $30mn$, $40mn$ **$10mn$**
29. $15xy$, $55y$ **$5y$**

Find two numbers whose greatest common divisor is the given number.

30. 9
31. 12
32. 15
33. 30

30. Sample answer: 18 and 81
31. Sample answer: 24 and 36
32. Sample answer: 15 and 45
33. Sample answer: 60 and 90

DIFFERENTIATED HOMEWORK OPTIONS

Level	Assignment	Two-Day Option	
BL Basic	9–24, 34–47	9–23 odd, 40, 41	10–24 even, 39, 42–47
OL Core	9–21 odd, 23–25, 27–33 odd, 34–35, 39–47	9–24, 40, 41	21–35, 39, 42–47
AL Advanced/Pre-AP	25–46, (optional: 47)		

35. Sample answer: The first prism is 8 in. high, 3 in. long, and 4 in. wide. The second prism is 8 in. high, 6 in. long, and 5 in. wide. The third prism is 8 in. high, 5 in. long, and 5 in. wide.

GEOMETRY **For Exercises 34 and 35, use the following information.**

Jeremy is building rectangular prisms using one-inch cubes. He is planning to build three prisms, the first with 96 blue cubes, the second with 240 red cubes, and the third with 200 yellow cubes. All of prisms must be the same height, but not necessarily the same length and width.

Academic Standards • ISTEP+

Extra Practice, pp. 676, 707

34. What is the maximum height of each prism Jeremy can build? **8 in.**

35. ★ What are the dimensions of all three prisms?

H.O.T. Problems

CHALLENGE **Determine whether each statement is *sometimes*, *always*, or *never* true.**

36. The GCF of two numbers is greater than both numbers. **never**

37. If two numbers have no common prime factors, the GCF is 1. **always**

38. The GCF of two numbers is one of the numbers. **sometimes**

39. **WRITING IN MATH** Using the words *factor* and *greatest common factor*, explain the relationship between the numbers 4, 12, and 24. **Sample answer: 4 and 12 are factors of 24. The greatest common factor of 4, 12, and 24 is 4.**

ISTEP+ PRACTICE

Reinforcement of 7.1.3

40. Student Council earned \$26 selling bottled water, \$32 selling oranges, and \$28 selling energy bars. If all items cost the same, what is the greatest possible price per item? **A**

A \$2 **C** \$7

B \$4 **D** \$8

41. Which set of numbers has the greatest GCF? **G**

F 4, 5, 20

G 18, 36

H 18, 36, 45

J 23, 29

Spiral Review

42. What is the prime factorization of 75? (Lesson 4-1) **$3 \times 5 \times 5$**

ALGEBRA **Graph each equation.** (Lesson 3-7) **43–45. See margin.**

43. $y = -x$

44. $y = x + 3$

45. $y = 2x - 1$

46. **ALGEBRA** Solve the equation $-7y + 18 = 39$. Check your solution. (Lesson 3-5) **-3**

GET READY for the Next Lesson

47. **PREREQUISITE SKILL** Serena received a gift card to download music from the Internet. She downloaded 3 songs on Monday, 5 songs on Tuesday, and one half of what was left on Wednesday. She has 6 songs left. How many songs were initially on the gift card? Use the *work backward* strategy. (Lesson 3-4) **20 songs**

4 Assess

Yesterday's News Remind students that yesterday's lesson was about finding prime factorizations. Ask them to write how yesterday's concepts helped them with today's material.

Additional Answers

43.

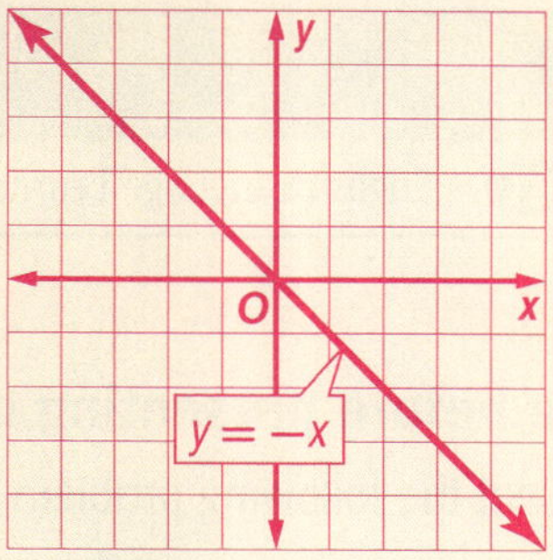

44.

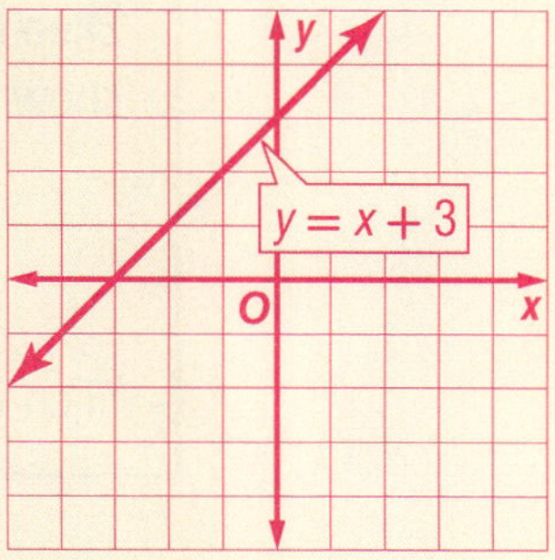

45.

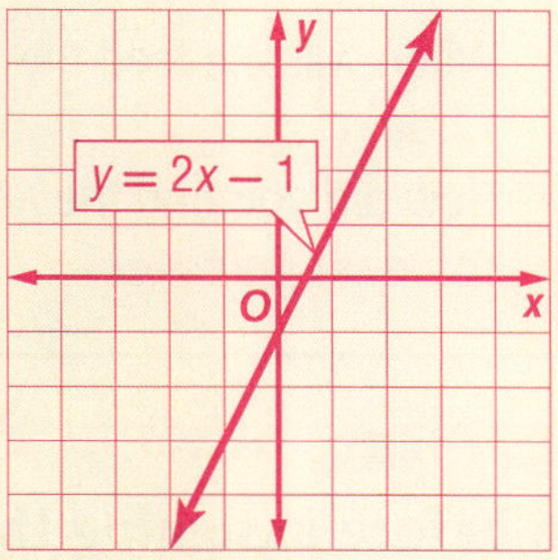

Lesson 4-2 Greatest Common Factor 189

4-3

Problem-Solving Investigation

MAKE AN ORGANIZED LIST

PACING: **Regular:** 1 period, **Block:** 0.5 period

IN Academic Standards **P.1.3 Apply and adapt a variety of appropriate strategies to solve problems.** *Also addresses P.5.1, P.5.2, P.5.3.*

Options for Differentiated Instruction

ELL = English Language Learner AL = Above or Beyond Grade Level SS = Struggling Students SN = Special Needs

Making Real-World Connections ELL SS SN

Use before presenting Lesson 4-3.

Present the following problem to students.

> Ellen has three different fish tanks. The feeding schedule for the fish in each is shown below.
> - The fish in tank A need to be fed every 2 days.
> - The fish in tank B need to be fed every 3 days.
> - The fish in tank C need to be fed every 4 days.
>
> Ellen fed the fish in all three tanks today.

Ask:

- When will she feed the fish in all three tanks on the same day again? How often will that happen? in 12 days; every 12 days
- How did you find the answer? Explain. Sample answer: List the multiples of 2, 3, and 4, and find the first common multiple.

Organizing Student Work and Thinking ELL SS SN

Use before assigning the Exercises.

Have students add the strategy of making an organized list to their problem-solving booklets. They should include the following about the strategy:

- a description of the strategy
- an explanation of the best time to use the strategy
- examples of problems that are solved using the strategy
- advantages and disadvantages of using the strategy

Leveled Lesson Resources

Also on TeacherWorks™ Lesson 4-3

Chapter 4 Resource Masters

BL = Below or Approaching Grade Level

OL = On Grade Level

AL = Above or Beyond Grade Level

ELL = English Language Learner

Study Guide and Intervention*
p. 22 BL OL ELL

NAME ______________________ DATE __________ PERIOD ____

4-3 Study Guide and Intervention

Problem-Solving Investigation: Make an Organized List

When solving problems often times it is useful to make an organized list. By doing so you can see all the possible solutions to the problem being posed.

Example 1 **LUNCH Walnut Hills School has a deli line where students are able to select a meat sandwich, a side, and fruit. Meat choices are ham or turkey. The side choices are pretzels or chips. Fruit options are an apple or a pear. How many different combinations are possible?**

Understand You know that students can choose a sandwich, a side, and fruit. There are 2 meat choices, 2 side choices, and 2 fruit choices. You need to find all possible combinations.

Plan Make an organized list.

Solve

	1	2	3	4	5	6	7	8
Meat	Ham	Ham	Ham	Ham	Turkey	Turkey	Turkey	Turkey
Side	Pretzel	Pretzel	Chips	Chips	Pretzel	Pretzel	Chips	Chips
Fruit	Apple	Pear	Apple	Pear	Apple	Pear	Apple	Pear

There are 8 possibilities.

Check Draw a tree diagram to check the result.

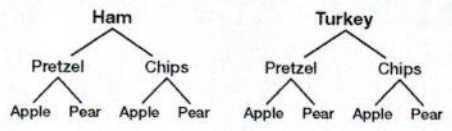

Exercises

1. Susan has 3 shirts; red, blue, and green; 2 pants; jeans and khakis; and 3 shoes; white, black, and tan, to choose from for her school outfit. How many different outfits can she create?
   18 different outfits

2. The Motor Speedway is awarding money to the first two finishers in their annual race. If there are four cars in the race numbered 1 through 4, how many different ways can they come in first and second?
   12 different ways

Skills Practice*
p. 23 BL OL

NAME ______________________ DATE __________ PERIOD ____

4-3 Skills Practice

Problem-Solving Investigation: Make An Organized List

Solve by making an organized list.

1. **BAKING** Virginia and Robert have 1 dozen of each of the following types of cookies: chocolate chip, oatmeal raisin, snickerdoodles, and shortbread. If they want to divide the cookies into packages of two dozen, with one dozen of each of two types of cookie per package, how many different ways can they group the cookies?
   6

2. **NUMBER THEORY** How many different two-digit numbers can be made using the digits 2, 9, 6, and 3?
   12

3. **FOOD** Takanae is ordering lunch at a deli and is trying to decide what she would like on her sandwich. She has her choice of turkey, ham, or roast beef and a choice of cheddar, swiss, or muenster cheese. How many combinations of sandwich could she choose assuming that each sandwich has one type of meat and one type of cheese?
   9

4. **TELEPHONES** How many phone numbers are possible for one area code if the first four numbers are 202-1, in that order, and the last three numbers are 1-7-8 in any order?
   6

5. **CLOTHES** Sheila has four different shirts and two skirts with her on a business trip. How many different outfits can she create?
   8

6. **SPORTS** Juan and Andrew are planning the schedule for a softball tournament. If there are 6 teams, how many different pairings could they make for the first tournament game?
   15

Lesson 4-3

Practice*
p. 24 OL AL

NAME ______________________ DATE __________ PERIOD ____

4-3 Practice

Problem-Solving Investigation: Make An Organized List

Mixed Problem Solving

For Exercises 1 and 2, solve each problem by making an organized list.

1. **VACATION** Kessler, Kacy, and their parents sit in different seats in the car while driving to their grandparents for vacation. If only the parents take turns driving, how many different ways can all four people sit in the car with 2 front and 2 back seats?
   12 different ways

2. **PIZZA** Everyone at the table likes pepperoni, sausage, onions, and black olives on pizza. List the different possibilities of ordering a 2-topping pizza.
   pepperoni and sausage
   pepperoni and onion
   pepperoni and black olives
   sausage and onion
   sausage and black olives
   onion and black olives

Use any strategy to solve Exercises 3–6. Some strategies are shown below.

PROBLEM-SOLVING STRATEGIES
• Guess and check.
• Work backward.
• Make an organized list.

3. **NUMBER SENSE** A number is increased by 12. When this sum is divided by 3, the result is the original number. What is the number?
   The number is 6.

4. **COINS** Three coins are tossed: a quarter, a nickel, and a dime. Complete the table showing the 8 different ways the coins could land by using H for heads and T for tails.

Quarter	H	H	**H**	**H**	**T**	**T**	**T**	**T**
Nickel	H	H	**T**	**T**	**H**	**H**	**T**	**T**
Dime	H	T	**H**	**T**	**H**	**T**	**H**	**T**

5. **MEASUREMENT** Eight furlongs is equal to one mile. If a mile is 5,280 feet, how many feet are in 5 furlongs?
   5 furlongs equal 3,300 feet.

6. **TIME** Greg works at the hardware store on weekends. He worked a total of 53 hours during the month of April. How many hours did Greg work during the last weekend in April, if he worked 14 hours, 12 hours, and 15 hours the other weekends?
   12 hours

Word Problem Practice*
p. 25 OL AL

NAME ______________________ DATE __________ PERIOD ____

4-3 Word Problem Practice

Problem-Solving Investigation: Make an Organized List

Solve using any method.

1. **NUMBER THEORY** How many different 2-digit numbers can be made using the digits 3, 7, 8, 9, 2?
   20

2. **MONEY** Raul is shopping and stops at the drug store, grocery and the mall. He spent $6.99, $12.49, and $16.45 at each respective store, and has $11.20 in his wallet when he returns home. How much money did he have when he began shopping?
   $47.13

3. **BIRTH MONTH** Renee is comparing her birth month to the birth month of the other girls in her class. Sherry was born two months before Renee, and Angela was born 4 months after Sherry. Corrine was born 3 months before Angela but 1 month after Allison. If Allison was born in July, in what month was Renee born?
   September

4. **PATTERNS** The following numbers form a pattern: 1, 2, 4, 8. What is the fifth number in the sequence?
   16

5. **TIME** Juanita is trying to get used to waking up earlier in the morning. She wakes up at 8:30 now, but wants to wake up at 7:15. If she wakes up five minutes earlier each morning, how many mornings will it be until she wakes up at 7:15?
   15

6. **MILEAGE** Julie is making a trip by car. Julie knows that her car gets 32 miles per gallon, and holds ten gallons of gasoline. If Julie has $\frac{1}{4}$ of a tank of gas left, how many more miles can she travel before she needs to refuel?
   80 miles

7. **CLOTHES** Carly is taking a vacation with her family and packs three pairs of shorts and four tops. How many different outfits can she make if she wears each top with each pair of shorts?
   12

8. **FOOD** Carlos is making a fruit salad and wants to use only 2 types of fruit. If he has blueberries, strawberries, grapes, oranges, and bananas on hand, how many combinations could he make?
   10

Lesson 4-3

*** Also available in Spanish** ELL

Additional Lesson Resources

Transparencies

- *5-Minute Check Transparency*, Lesson 4-3

Other Print Products

- *Noteables™ Interactive Study Notebook with Foldables™*

Teacher Tech Tools

- *Interactive Classroom CD-ROM*, Lesson 4-3
- *AssignmentWorks*, Lesson 4-3

Student Tech Tools

glencoe.com

- Extra Examples, Chapter 4, Lesson 3
- Self-Check Quiz, Chapter 4, Lesson 3

4-3 Lesson Notes

1 Focus

Make an Organized List Students used the strategy of making an organized list when they found the prime factorization of composite numbers and when they found the GCF of a set of numbers. This problem-solving strategy will help them when they simplify fractions in Lesson 4-4.

2 Teach

Scaffolding Questions

Write a "menu" of possible pizza toppings on the chalkboard (such as pepperoni, sausage, mushrooms, and olives).

Ask:

- How many different 2-topping pizzas can you order from this menu? Answers will vary depending on selections offered.
- How can you find all of the possible 2-topping pizzas? make a list

ADDITIONAL EXAMPLE

Solve. Use the *make an organized list* strategy.

PASSWORD In order to log on to the computer at school, Miranda must use a password. The password is 2 characters. The first character is the letter A or B followed by a single numeric digit. How many passwords does Miranda have to choose from? 20

Additional Examples are also in:

- Noteables™ Interactive Study Notebook with Foldables™
- Interactive Classroom PowerPoint® Presentations

4-3 Problem-Solving Investigation

MAIN IDEA: Solve problems by making an organized list.

Academic Standards **P.1.3 Apply and adapt a variety of appropriate strategies to solve problems.** *Also addresses P.5.1, P.5.2, P.5.3.*

P.S.I. TEAM +

e-Mail: MAKE AN ORGANIZED LIST

NIKKI: I am ordering a pizza. The crust choices are thin or hand-tossed. The meat choices are pepperoni or sausage. The vegetable choices are olives, mushrooms, or banana peppers.

YOUR MISSION: Nikki chooses from one crust, one meat, and one vegetable choice. Make an organized list to find how many different types of pizza Nikki can order.

Understand	You know the crust, meat, and vegetable options for the pizza. You need to find all the possible pizza combinations that can be made.
Plan	Make an organized list of all the possible combinations. Use T for thin, H for hand-tossed, P for pepperoni, S for sausage, O for olives, M for mushrooms, and B for banana peppers.
Solve	**Choosing thin crust:** TPO, TPM, TPB; TSO, TSM, TSB **Choosing hand-tossed crust:** HPO, HPM, HPB; HSO, HSM, HSB There are 12 different combinations of pizza that can be ordered.
Check	Draw a tree diagram to check the result.

Analyze The Strategy

1. Explain why making an organized list was a useful strategy in solving this problem. **1, 2. See margin.**
2. WRITING IN MATH Write a problem that can be solved by making an organized list. Then explain how to solve the problem using this strategy.

Additional Answers

1. Sample answer: By making an organized list, you can show all the possible pizza combinations. Count the number of pizzas to determine the answer.
2. How many different ways can a woodwind trio be made if the first position needs to be either a bass clarinet or a bassoon? The other two positions should be filled by a clarinet, oboe, or flute. Using an organized list, there will be 6 different possibilities.

Mixed Problem Solving

★ indicates multi-step problem

Academic Standards • ISTEP+
Extra Practice, pp. 676, 707

For Exercises 3–6, solve each problem by making an organized list.

3. **SHOPPING** Charmaine went to the store and bought a yellow shirt, a blue shirt, and a red shirt. She also bought a pair of jeans and a pair of khaki dress pants. How many different outfits can be made using one shirt and one pair of pants? **6 outfits**

4. **WORK** The following four numbers are used for employee identification numbers at a small company: 0, 1, 2, and 3. How many different employee identification numbers can be made using each digit once? **24 numbers**

5. **PHOTOS** Joshua, Diego, and Audri stand side-by-side for a photo. How many different ways can the three friends stand next to each other? **6 ways**

6. **CELL PHONES** How many phone numbers are possible for one area code if the first three numbers are 268, in that order, and the last four numbers are 0, 9, 7, 1 in any order? **24**

Use any strategy to solve Exercises 7–14. Some strategies are shown below.

PROBLEM-SOLVING STRATEGIES
- Guess and check.
- Work backward.
- Make an organized list.

7. **ALGEBRA** Consecutive odd numbers are numbers like 1, 3, 5, and 7. Find two consecutive odd numbers whose sum is 56 and whose product is 783. **27, 29**

8. **FOOD** The table shows the choices for ordering a deli sandwich. How many different subs can be ordered if you choose only one kind of bread and one kind of meat? **9 subs**

The Sandwich Shop	
Bread	White, Wheat, Whole Grain
Meat	Ham, Turkey, Roast Beef
Cheese	American, Swiss
Dressing	Italian, Ranch

9. **DVDS** Paul rented 2 times as many DVDs as Angelina last month. Angelina rented 4 fewer than Bret, but 4 more than Jill. Bret rented 9 DVDs. How many DVDs did each person rent? **Paul: 10; Angelina: 5; Bret: 9; Jill: 1**

10. **CLOTHES** Jeffrey owns 3 shirts, 2 pairs of pants, and 2 pairs of shoes. How many different outfits can he create? **12 outfits**

11. **SNOWFALL** A total of 17 inches of snow fell in a 72-hour period. In the last 24 hours, 6 inches fell, and in the previous 24 hours, 4 inches fell. How many inches fell in the first 24 hours? **7 in.**

12. **GAS MILEAGE** Mrs. Acosta travels 44 miles in her car and uses 2 gallons of gas. If her gas mileage continues at the same rate, how many gallons of gas would she use to travel 528 miles? **24 gallons**

13. **SCIENCE** Hydrothermal vents are similar to geysers, but are found on the ocean floor. A hydrothermal vent chimney can grow at an average rate of 9 meters in 18 months. What is the average rate of growth per month? **0.5 m**

14. **CRAFTS** Paul makes three different sizes of birdhouses. He can paint each style in red, brown, or yellow. How many different birdhouses can Paul make? **9**

3 Practice

Using the Exercises

Exercises 1–2 can be used to check for understanding.

Exercises 3–6 give students an opportunity to practice the make an organized list strategy.

Exercises 7–14 are structured so that students have the opportunity to practice many different problem-solving strategies. You may wish to review some of the strategies they have studied.

- guess and check (p. 43)
- work backward (p. 148)
- make an organized list (p. 190)

4 Assess

Formative Assessment

Check for student understanding of concepts in Lessons 4-1 through 4-3.

CRM Quiz 1, p. 67

Differentiated Instruction

Interpersonal Learners Separate students into groups of 3 or 4 and have each group use the *make an organized list* strategy to solve one of the problems. Then have a volunteer from each group write the group's list on the chalkboard.

Have students compare the lists. Did all of the groups use the same list? If not, did that affect their answers? Why or why not?

Lesson 4-3 Problem-Solving Investigation: Make an Organized List **191**

4-4 Simplifying Fractions

PACING: **Regular:** 2 periods, **Block:** 1 period

IN Academic Standards **7.1.6** Identify, write, **rename,** compare and order **rational** and common irrational **numbers** and plot them on a number line.

Options for Differentiated Instruction

ELL = English Language Learner AL = Above or Beyond Grade Level SS = Struggling Students SN = Special Needs

Connecting to Prior Knowledge SS SN

Use before presenting Lesson 4-4.

Display the following fractions on the board and ask students what is true about them. They are equal.

$\frac{1}{2}$ $\frac{2}{4}$ $\frac{3}{6}$

Have students recall how to find equivalent fractions. Build on what they know about identifying or finding equivalent fractions. Have them use these skills to show that simplifying fractions is working the process backward.

Creating a Checklist SS SN

Use before assigning the Exercises.

Have students create a checklist of the steps they need to follow to simplify a fraction. Have them include an example next to the steps.

Step 1 Find the greatest common factor of the numerator and the denominator.

Step 2 Divide BOTH the numerator and the denominator by the GCF.

Step 3 Check that the new fraction is in simplest form.

Example Simplify $\frac{12}{15}$.

Step 1: The GCF of 12 and 15 is 3.

Step 2: $\frac{12 \div 3}{15 \div 3} = \frac{4}{5}$

Step 3: 4 and 5 have no common factors greater than 1, so $\frac{4}{5}$ is in simplest form.

Find the Error AL

Use after presenting Lesson 4-4.

Present the following statement to students:

> "When a fraction has a prime number in its numerator or denominator, it cannot be simplified since prime numbers have no other factors."

Ask students to explain whether the statement is correct. Have them use examples to reinforce their reasoning.

Sample answer: It is not correct because a fraction like $\frac{3}{12}$ contains the prime number 3, but it can be simplified as $\frac{1}{4}$.

Leveled Lesson Resources

Also on TeacherWorks™ Lesson 4-4

Chapter 4 Resource Masters

BL = Below or Approaching Grade Level   OL = On Grade Level   AL = Above or Beyond Grade Level   ELL = English Language Learner

Lesson Reading Guide
p. 26 BL OL ELL

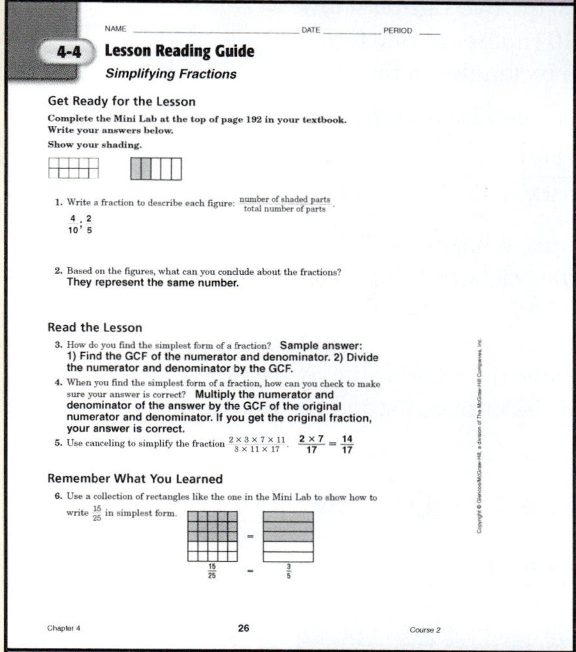
NAME ______ DATE ______ PERIOD ____

4-4 Lesson Reading Guide
Simplifying Fractions

Get Ready for the Lesson

Complete the Mini Lab at the top of page 192 in your textbook. Write your answers below.

Show your shading.

1. Write a fraction to describe each figure: $\frac{\text{number of shaded parts}}{\text{total number of parts}}$.
   $\frac{4}{10}$, $\frac{2}{5}$
2. Based on the figures, what can you conclude about the fractions?
   They represent the same number.

Read the Lesson

3. How do you find the simplest form of a fraction? Sample answer: 1) Find the GCF of the numerator and denominator. 2) Divide the numerator and denominator by the GCF.
4. When you find the simplest form of a fraction, how can you check to make sure your answer is correct? Multiply the numerator and denominator of the answer by the GCF of the original numerator and denominator. If you get the original fraction, your answer is correct.
5. Use canceling to simplify the fraction $\frac{2 \times 3 \times 7 \times 11}{3 \times 11 \times 17}$. $\frac{2 \times 7}{17} = \frac{14}{17}$

Remember What You Learned

6. Use a collection of rectangles like the one in the Mini Lab to show how to write $\frac{15}{25}$ in simplest form.
   $\frac{15}{25} = \frac{3}{5}$

Chapter 4 26 Course 2

*Study Guide and Intervention**
p. 27 BL OL ELL

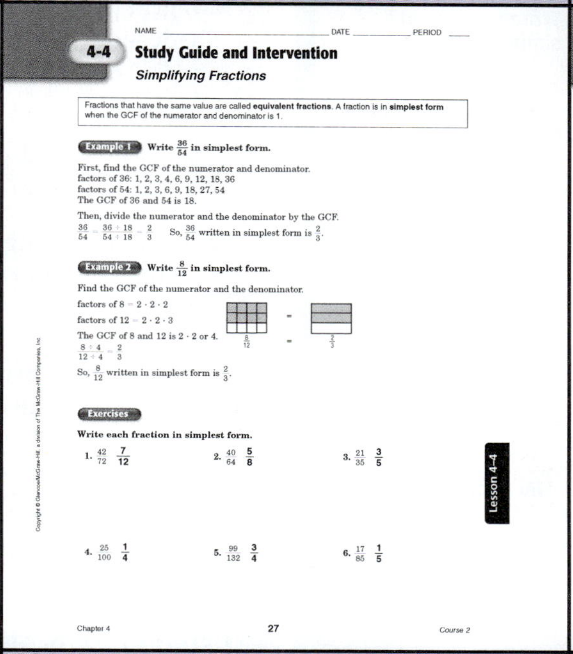
NAME ______ DATE ______ PERIOD ____

4-4 Study Guide and Intervention
Simplifying Fractions

Fractions that have the same value are called **equivalent fractions**. A fraction is in **simplest form** when the GCF of the numerator and denominator is 1.

Example 1 Write $\frac{36}{54}$ in simplest form.

First, find the GCF of the numerator and denominator.
factors of 36: 1, 2, 3, 4, 6, 9, 12, 18, 36
factors of 54: 1, 2, 3, 6, 9, 18, 27, 54
The GCF of 36 and 54 is 18.

Then, divide the numerator and the denominator by the GCF.
$\frac{36}{54} = \frac{36 \div 18}{54 \div 18} = \frac{2}{3}$ So, $\frac{36}{54}$ written in simplest form is $\frac{2}{3}$.

Example 2 Write $\frac{8}{12}$ in simplest form.

Find the GCF of the numerator and the denominator.
factors of 8 = 2 · 2 · 2
factors of 12 = 2 · 2 · 3
The GCF of 8 and 12 is 2 · 2 or 4.
$\frac{8 \div 4}{12 \div 4} = \frac{2}{3}$
So, $\frac{8}{12}$ written in simplest form is $\frac{2}{3}$.

Exercises

Write each fraction in simplest form.

1. $\frac{42}{72}$ $\frac{7}{12}$ 2. $\frac{40}{64}$ $\frac{5}{8}$ 3. $\frac{21}{35}$ $\frac{3}{5}$
4. $\frac{25}{100}$ $\frac{1}{4}$ 5. $\frac{99}{132}$ $\frac{3}{4}$ 6. $\frac{17}{85}$ $\frac{1}{5}$

Lesson 4-4

Chapter 4 27 Course 2

*Skills Practice**
p. 28 BL OL

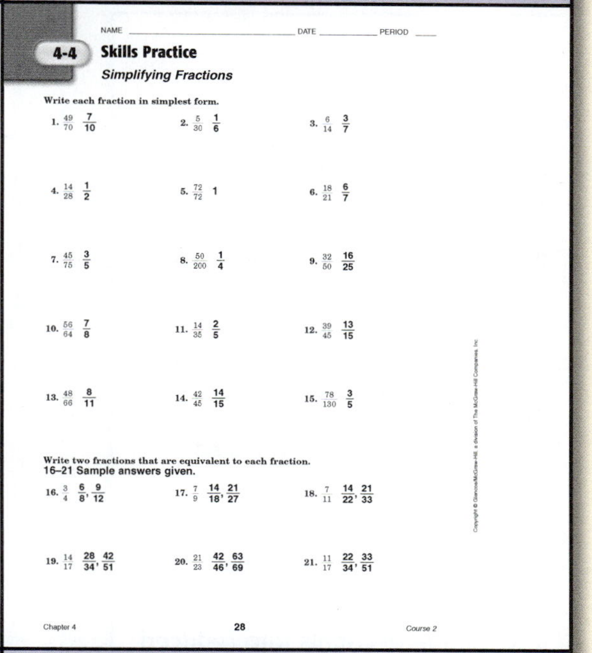
NAME ______ DATE ______ PERIOD ____

4-4 Skills Practice
Simplifying Fractions

Write each fraction in simplest form.

1. $\frac{49}{70}$ $\frac{7}{10}$ 2. $\frac{5}{30}$ $\frac{1}{6}$ 3. $\frac{6}{14}$ $\frac{3}{7}$
4. $\frac{14}{28}$ $\frac{1}{2}$ 5. $\frac{72}{72}$ 1   6. $\frac{18}{21}$ $\frac{6}{7}$
7. $\frac{45}{75}$ $\frac{3}{5}$ 8. $\frac{50}{200}$ $\frac{1}{4}$ 9. $\frac{32}{50}$ $\frac{16}{25}$
10. $\frac{56}{64}$ $\frac{7}{8}$ 11. $\frac{14}{35}$ $\frac{2}{5}$ 12. $\frac{39}{45}$ $\frac{13}{15}$
13. $\frac{48}{66}$ $\frac{8}{11}$ 14. $\frac{42}{45}$ $\frac{14}{15}$ 15. $\frac{78}{130}$ $\frac{3}{5}$

Write two fractions that are equivalent to each fraction. 16–21 Sample answers given.

16. $\frac{3}{4}$ $\frac{6}{8}$, $\frac{9}{12}$ 17. $\frac{7}{9}$ $\frac{14}{18}$, $\frac{21}{27}$ 18. $\frac{7}{11}$ $\frac{14}{22}$, $\frac{21}{33}$
19. $\frac{14}{17}$ $\frac{28}{34}$, $\frac{42}{51}$ 20. $\frac{21}{23}$ $\frac{42}{46}$, $\frac{63}{69}$ 21. $\frac{11}{17}$ $\frac{22}{34}$, $\frac{33}{51}$

Chapter 4 28 Course 2

*Practice**
p. 29 OL AL

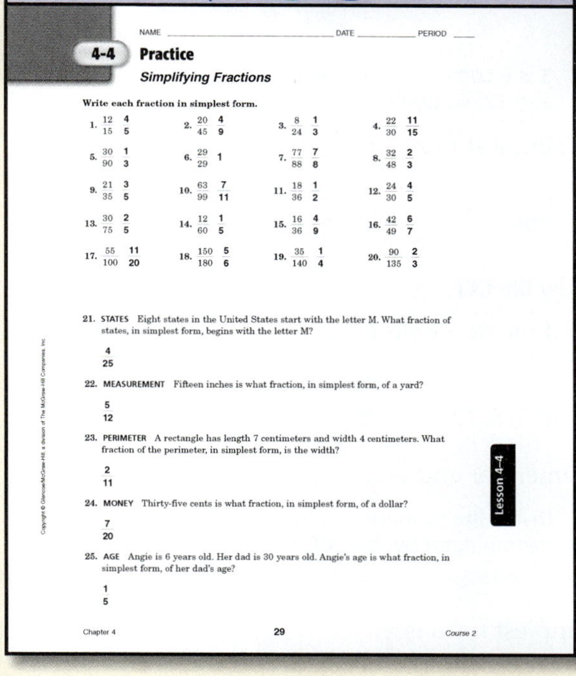
NAME ______ DATE ______ PERIOD ____

4-4 Practice
Simplifying Fractions

Write each fraction in simplest form.

1. $\frac{12}{15}$ $\frac{4}{5}$ 2. $\frac{20}{45}$ $\frac{4}{9}$ 3. $\frac{8}{24}$ $\frac{1}{3}$ 4. $\frac{22}{30}$ $\frac{11}{15}$
5. $\frac{30}{90}$ $\frac{1}{3}$ 6. $\frac{29}{29}$ 1   7. $\frac{77}{88}$ $\frac{7}{8}$ 8. $\frac{32}{48}$ $\frac{2}{3}$
9. $\frac{21}{35}$ $\frac{3}{5}$ 10. $\frac{63}{99}$ $\frac{7}{11}$ 11. $\frac{18}{36}$ $\frac{1}{2}$ 12. $\frac{24}{30}$ $\frac{4}{5}$
13. $\frac{30}{75}$ $\frac{2}{5}$ 14. $\frac{12}{60}$ $\frac{1}{5}$ 15. $\frac{16}{36}$ $\frac{4}{9}$ 16. $\frac{42}{49}$ $\frac{6}{7}$
17. $\frac{55}{100}$ $\frac{11}{20}$ 18. $\frac{150}{180}$ $\frac{5}{6}$ 19. $\frac{35}{140}$ $\frac{1}{4}$ 20. $\frac{90}{135}$ $\frac{2}{3}$

21. STATES Eight states in the United States start with the letter M. What fraction of states, in simplest form, begins with the letter M? $\frac{4}{25}$
22. MEASUREMENT Fifteen inches is what fraction, in simplest form, of a yard? $\frac{5}{12}$
23. PERIMETER A rectangle has length 7 centimeters and width 4 centimeters. What fraction of the perimeter, in simplest form, is the width? $\frac{2}{11}$
24. MONEY Thirty-five cents is what fraction, in simplest form, of a dollar? $\frac{7}{20}$
25. AGE Angie is 6 years old. Her dad is 30 years old. Angie's age is what fraction, in simplest form, of her dad's age? $\frac{1}{5}$

Lesson 4-4

Chapter 4 29 Course 2

*Word Problem Practice**
p. 30 OL AL

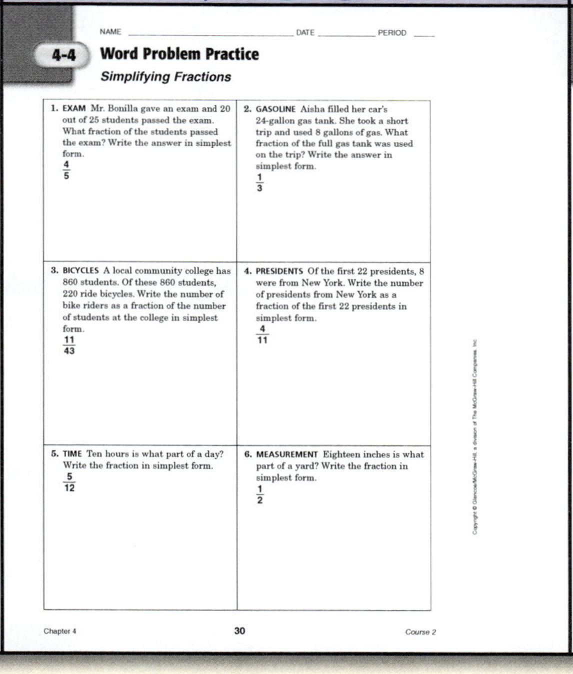
NAME ______ DATE ______ PERIOD ____

4-4 Word Problem Practice
Simplifying Fractions

1. EXAM Mr. Bonilla gave an exam and 20 out of 25 students passed the exam. What fraction of the students passed the exam? Write the answer in simplest form. $\frac{4}{5}$
2. GASOLINE Aisha filled her car's 24-gallon gas tank. She took a short trip and used 8 gallons of gas. What fraction of the full gas tank was used on the trip? Write the answer in simplest form. $\frac{1}{3}$
3. BICYCLES A local community college has 860 students. Of these 860 students, 220 ride bicycles. Write the number of bike riders as a fraction of the number of students at the college in simplest form. $\frac{11}{43}$
4. PRESIDENTS Of the first 22 presidents, 8 were from New York. Write the number of presidents from New York as a fraction of the first 22 presidents in simplest form. $\frac{4}{11}$
5. TIME Ten hours is what part of a day? Write the fraction in simplest form. $\frac{5}{12}$
6. MEASUREMENT Eighteen inches is what part of a yard? Write the fraction in simplest form. $\frac{1}{2}$

Chapter 4 30 Course 2

Enrichment
p. 31 OL AL

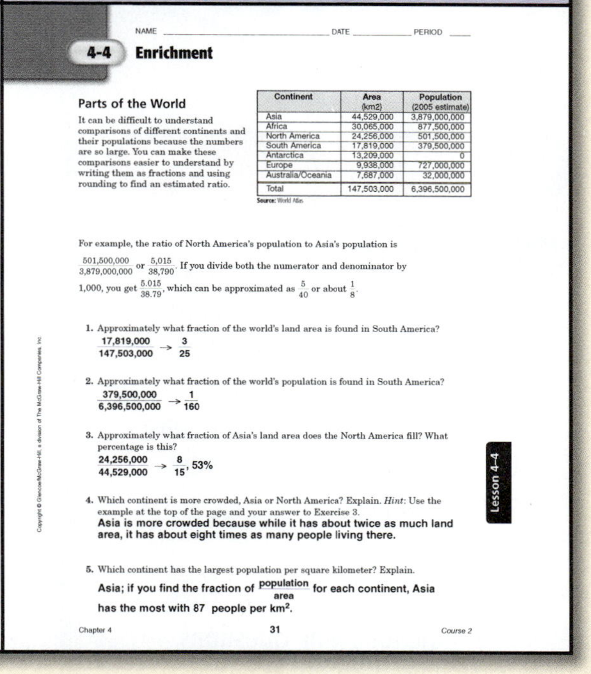
NAME ______ DATE ______ PERIOD ____

4-4 Enrichment

Parts of the World

It can be difficult to understand comparisons of different continents and their populations because the numbers are so large. You can make these comparisons easier to understand by writing them as fractions and using rounding to find an estimated ratio.

Continent	Area (km2)	Population (2005 estimate)
Asia	44,529,000	3,879,000,000
Africa	30,065,000	877,500,000
North America	24,256,000	501,500,000
South America	17,819,000	379,500,000
Antarctica	13,209,000	0
Europe	9,938,000	727,000,000
Australia/Oceania	7,687,000	32,000,000
Total	147,503,000	6,396,500,000

Source: World Atlas

For example, the ratio of North America's population to Asia's population is $\frac{501,500,000}{3,879,000,000}$ or $\frac{5,015}{38,790}$. If you divide both the numerator and denominator by 1,000, you get $\frac{5.015}{38.79}$, which can be approximated as $\frac{5}{40}$ or about $\frac{1}{8}$.

1. Approximately what fraction of the world's land area is found in South America? $\frac{17,819,000}{147,503,000} \rightarrow \frac{3}{25}$
2. Approximately what fraction of the world's population is found in South America? $\frac{379,500,000}{6,396,500,000} \rightarrow \frac{1}{160}$
3. Approximately what fraction of Asia's land area does the North America fill? What percentage is this? $\frac{24,256,000}{44,529,000} \rightarrow \frac{8}{15}$; 53%
4. Which continent is more crowded, Asia or North America? Explain. *Hint:* Use the example at the top of the page and your answer to Exercise 3. Asia is more crowded because while it has about twice as much land area, it has about eight times as many people living there.
5. Which continent has the largest population per square kilometer? Explain. Asia; if you find the fraction of $\frac{\text{population}}{\text{area}}$ for each continent, Asia has the most with 87 people per km².

Lesson 4-4

Chapter 4 31 Course 2

* Also available in Spanish ELL

Additional Lesson Resources

Transparencies
- *5-Minute Check Transparency*, Lesson 4-4

Other Print Products
- *Noteables™ Interactive Study Notebook with Foldables™*

Teacher Tech Tools
- *Interactive Classroom CD-ROM*, Lesson 4-4
- *AssignmentWorks*, Lesson 4-4

Student Tech Tools
glencoe.com
- Extra Examples, Chapter 4, Lesson 4
- Self-Check Quiz, Chapter 4, Lesson 4

4-4 Lesson Notes

1 Focus

Vertical Alignment

Before Lesson 4-4
Determine the prime factors of all numbers through 50 and write the numbers as the product of their prime factors by using exponents to show multiples of a factor

Lesson 4-4
Determine the greatest common divisor of whole numbers; use them to solve problems with fractions or to find the reduced form for a fraction

After Lesson 4-4
Know that every rational number is either a terminating or repeating decimal and be able to convert terminating decimals into reduced fractions

2 Teach

MINI Lab

Make sure students see that the two figures—and their shaded regions—are congruent. The difference is that each figure has been separated into a different number of parts.

Scaffolding Questions

As you ask the following questions, write each pair of numbers on the chalkboard.

Ask:

- What is the greatest common factor of 4 and 6? 2
- What is the greatest common factor of 5 and 10? 5
- What is the greatest common factor of 8 and 9? 1

4-4 Simplifying Fractions

MAIN IDEA

Write fractions in simplest form.

IN Academic Standards

7.1.6 Identify, write, **rename,** compare and order **rational** and common irrational **numbers** and plot them on a number line. *Also addresses P.4.2.*

New Vocabulary

equivalent fractions
simplest form

IN Math Online

glencoe.com

- Extra Examples
- Personal Tutor
- Self-Check Quiz

MINI Lab

On grid paper, draw the two figures shown. Shade 4 out of the 10 squares in one figure. Shade 2 out of the 5 rectangles in the other.

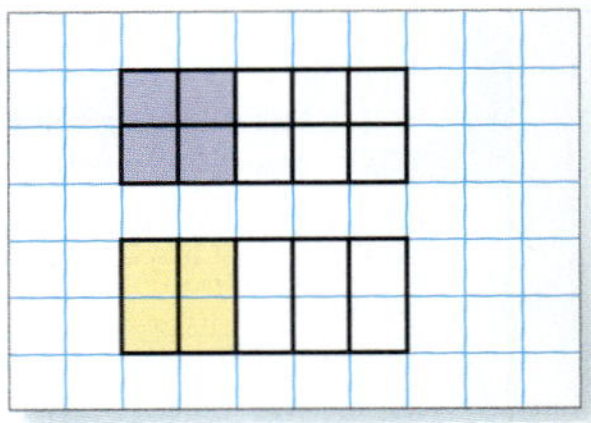

1. Write a fraction to describe each figure: $\frac{\text{number of shaded parts}}{\text{total number of parts}}$ $\frac{4}{10}$; $\frac{2}{5}$
2. Based on the figures, what can you conclude about the fractions? **They represent the same number.**

Equivalent fractions have the same value. A fraction is in **simplest form** when the GCF of the numerator and denominator is 1.

EXAMPLES Write a Fraction in Simplest Form

1 Write $\frac{6}{24}$ in simplest form.

METHOD 1 Divide by common factors.

$\frac{6}{24} = \frac{6 \div 2}{24 \div 2} = \frac{3}{12}$ — 2 is a common factor of 6 and 24, so divide by 2.

$\frac{3}{12} = \frac{3 \div 3}{12 \div 3} = \frac{1}{4}$ — 3 is a common factor of 3 and 12, so divide by 3.

The fraction $\frac{1}{4}$ is in simplest form since 1 and 4 have no common factors greater than 1.

METHOD 2 Divide by the GCF.

First, find the GCF of the numerator and denominator.

factors of 6: 1, 2, 3, 6
factors of 24: 1, 2, 3, 4, 6, 8, 12, 24

The GCF of 6 and 24 is 6.

Then, divide the numerator and denominator by the GCF, 6.

$\frac{6}{24} = \frac{6 \div 6}{24 \div 6} = \frac{1}{4}$ — Divide the numerator and denominator by the GCF, 6.

So, $\frac{6}{24}$ written in simplest form is $\frac{1}{4}$.

192 Chapter 4 Fractions, Decimals, and Percents

2 **Write $\frac{36}{45}$ in simplest form.**

First, find the GCF of the numerator and denominator.

factors of 36: 1, 2, 3, 4, 6, 9, 12, 18, 36

factors of 45: 1, 3, 5, 9, 15, 45

The GCF of 36 and 45 is 9.

Then, divide the numerator and denominator by the GCF, 9.

$\frac{36}{45} = \frac{36 \div 9}{45 \div 9} = \frac{4}{5}$ Divide the numerator and denominator by the GCF, 9.

So, $\frac{36}{45}$ written in simplest form is $\frac{4}{5}$.

Study Tip

More Than One Way
To write in simplest form, you can also divide by common factors.

$\frac{36}{45} = \frac{36 \div 3}{45 \div 3} = \frac{12}{15}$

$\frac{12}{15} = \frac{12 \div 3}{15 \div 3} = \frac{4}{5}$

So, $\frac{36}{45} = \frac{4}{5}$.

CHOOSE Your Method

Write each fraction in simplest form.

a. $\frac{7}{28}$ $\frac{1}{4}$ b. $\frac{8}{20}$ $\frac{2}{5}$ c. $\frac{27}{36}$ $\frac{3}{4}$

Real-World EXAMPLE

3 **SCIENCE** **Lauren measured a grasshopper for her science project. Each line on her ruler represents $\frac{1}{16}$ inch. Find the length of the grasshopper in simplest form.**

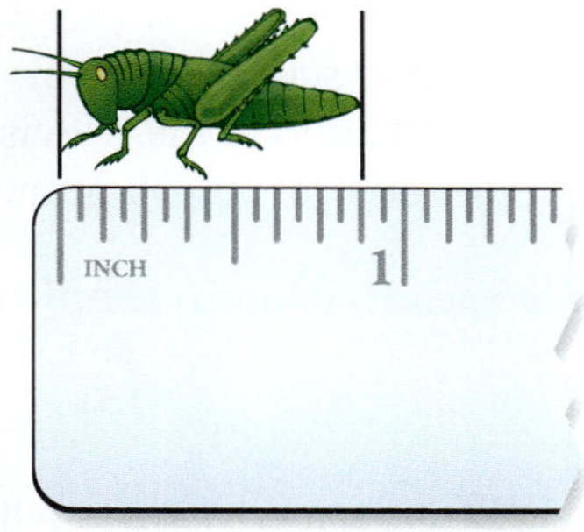

$\frac{14}{16} = \frac{\overset{1}{\cancel{2}} \cdot 7}{\underset{1}{\cancel{2}} \cdot 2 \cdot 2 \cdot 2}$

$= \frac{7}{8}$

The slashes mean that part of the numerator and part of the denominator are both divided by the same number. For example, $2 \div 2 = 1$.

So, $\frac{14}{16}$ written in simplest form is $\frac{7}{8}$.

Real-World Career
How Does a Carpenter Use Math?
Carpenters use fractions when they measure and cut boards.

IN Math Online

For more information visit: glencoe.com

CHECK Your Progress

d. **CARPENTRY** A carpenter measured a shelf and found it to be $\frac{10}{16}$ inch thick. Find the simplified fraction. $\frac{5}{8}$

e. **CARPENTRY** A carpenter measured a board to be $\frac{8}{16}$ inch thick. Find the simplified fraction. $\frac{1}{2}$

Formative Assessment

Use the Check Your Progress exercises after each Example to determine students' understanding of concepts.

ADDITIONAL EXAMPLES

1. Write $\frac{12}{45}$ in simplest form. $\frac{4}{15}$
2. Write $\frac{40}{64}$ in simplest form. $\frac{5}{8}$
3. **MUSIC** Two notes form a *perfect fifth* if the simplified fraction of the frequencies of the notes equals $\frac{3}{4}$. If note D = 294 Hertz and note G = 392 Hertz, do they form a *perfect fifth?* yes

Additional Examples are also in:

- Noteables™ Interactive Study Notebook with Foldables™
- Interactive Classroom PowerPoint® Presentations

Focus on Mathematical Content

One way to write a fraction in simplest form is to **divide the numerator and denominator by common factors.**

Another way to write a fraction in simplest form is to **divide the numerator and denominator by the GCF.**

Lesson 4-4 Simplifying Fractions **193**

3 Practice

Tips for New Teachers: Greatest Common Factor

You may wish to point out to students that the two methods of writing a fraction in simplest form are essentially the same. Dividing the numerator and denominator by common factors may take several steps, but the product of the common factors is the GCF. Have students use both methods to write the fraction $\frac{24}{30}$ in simplest form. What is the GCF? 6 What is the product of the common factors? $2 \times 3 = 6$

Formative Assessment

Use Exercises 1–5 to check for understanding.

Then use the chart at the bottom of this page to customize your assignments for students.

Intervention You may wish to use the Study Guide and Intervention Master on page 27 of the *Chapter 4 Resource Masters* for additional reinforcement.

Odd/Even Assignments

Exercises 6–19 are structured so that students practice the same concepts whether they are assigned odd or even problems.

★ indicates multi-step problem

CHECK Your Understanding

Examples 1, 2 (pp. 192–193)

Write each fraction in simplest form.

1. $\frac{3}{9}$ $\frac{1}{3}$
2. $\frac{4}{18}$ $\frac{2}{9}$
3. $\frac{10}{25}$ $\frac{2}{5}$
4. $\frac{36}{40}$ $\frac{9}{10}$

Example 3 (p. 193)

5. **ALLOWANCE** Mary received $15 for her weekly allowance. She spent $10 at the movie theater with her friends. What fraction of the money, in simplest form, was spent at the theater? $\frac{2}{3}$

Practice and Problem Solving

HOMEWORK HELP	
For Exercises	See Examples
6–17	1,2
18–19	3

Exercise Levels
A: 6–19
B: 20–29
C: 30–33

Write each fraction in simplest form.

6. $\frac{9}{12}$ $\frac{3}{4}$
7. $\frac{25}{35}$ $\frac{5}{7}$
8. $\frac{16}{32}$ $\frac{1}{2}$
9. $\frac{14}{20}$ $\frac{7}{10}$
10. $\frac{10}{20}$ $\frac{1}{2}$
11. $\frac{12}{21}$ $\frac{4}{7}$
12. $\frac{15}{25}$ $\frac{3}{5}$
13. $\frac{24}{28}$ $\frac{6}{7}$
14. $\frac{48}{64}$ $\frac{3}{4}$
15. $\frac{32}{32}$ 1
16. $\frac{20}{80}$ $\frac{1}{4}$
17. $\frac{45}{54}$ $\frac{5}{6}$

18. **PRESIDENTS** Of the 43 U.S. presidents, 15 were elected to serve two terms. What fraction of the U.S. presidents, in simplest form, was elected to serve two terms? $\frac{15}{43}$

19. **TV SHOWS** A television station has 28 new TV shows scheduled to air this week. What fraction of the television shows, in simplest form, are 30-minute programs? $\frac{5}{7}$

WYTB Programming	
30-minute	60-minute
20	8

Write each fraction in simplest form.

20. $\frac{45}{100}$ $\frac{9}{20}$
21. $\frac{60}{150}$ $\frac{2}{5}$
22. $\frac{16}{120}$ $\frac{2}{15}$
23. $\frac{35}{175}$ $\frac{1}{5}$

24. **TIME** Fifteen minutes is what part of one hour? $\frac{1}{4}$

25. **MEASUREMENT** Nine inches is what part of one foot? $\frac{3}{4}$

26. **CALENDAR** Four days is what part of the month of April? $\frac{2}{15}$

27. **SLEEP** Marcel spends 8 hours each day sleeping. What fraction of a week, written in simplest form, does Marcel spend sleeping? $\frac{1}{3}$

28. **MONEY** Each week, Lorenzo receives a $10 allowance. What fraction of his yearly allowance, in simplest form, does he receive each week? $\frac{10}{520}$ or $\frac{1}{52}$

29. **FIND THE DATA** Refer to the Data File on pages 16–19 of your book. Choose some data and write a real-world problem in which you would simplify fractions. See students' work.

Academic Standards • ISTEP+
Extra Practice, pp. 677, 707

30. **OPEN ENDED** Select a fraction in simplest form. Then, write two fractions that are equivalent to it. $\frac{1}{4}, \frac{2}{8}, \frac{4}{16}$

DIFFERENTIATED HOMEWORK OPTIONS

Level	Assignment	Two-Day Option	
BL Basic	6–19, 32–44	7–19 odd, 34, 35	6–18 even, 32, 33, 36–44
OL Core	7–17 odd, 18, 19–23 odd, 24–30, 32–44	6–19, 34, 35	20–30, 32, 33, 36–44
AL Advanced/Pre-AP	20–40, (optional: 41–44)		

H.O.T. Problems

31. No, because both the numerator and denominator can be divided by 2.
32. Nhu; Booker did not divide the numerator and denominator by the GCF.

31. **CHALLENGE** Both the numerator and denominator of a fraction are even. Is the fraction in simplest form? Explain your reasoning.

32. **FIND THE ERROR** Nhu and Booker both wrote $\frac{16}{36}$ in simplest form. Who is correct? Explain.

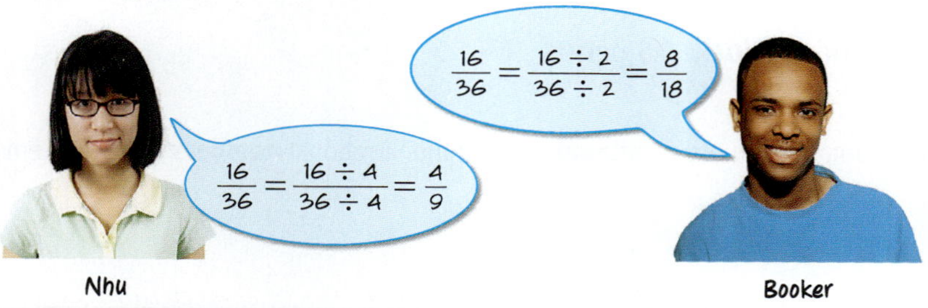

33. **WRITING IN MATH** Explain how to determine whether a fraction is in simplest form. Sample answer: A fraction is in simplest form if the GCF of the numerator and denominator is 1.

ISTEP+ PRACTICE 7.1.6

34. It takes Benito 12 minutes to walk to school. What fraction represents the part of an hour it takes Benito to walk to school? D

A $\frac{12}{1}$ C $\frac{5}{30}$

B $\frac{4}{15}$ D $\frac{1}{5}$

35. What fraction of a foot is 2 inches? F

F $\frac{1}{6}$ H $\frac{1}{3}$

G $\frac{1}{4}$ J $\frac{1}{2}$

Spiral Review

36. **SANDWICHES** A deli offers sandwiches with ham, turkey, or roast beef with American, provolone, Swiss, or mozzarella cheese. How many different types of sandwiches can be made if you choose one meat and one cheese? Use the *make an organized list* strategy. (Lesson 4-3) 12

Find the GCF of each set of numbers. (Lesson 4-2)

37. 27, 36 9
38. 16, 28 4
39. 20, 50, 65 5

★ 40. **ANALYZE GRAPHS** Refer to the graph. At these rates, about how much longer would it take a blue shark to swim 280 miles than it would a sailfish? Use the formula $d = rt$. Justify your answer. (Lesson 3-3) 3 h; See margin for justification.

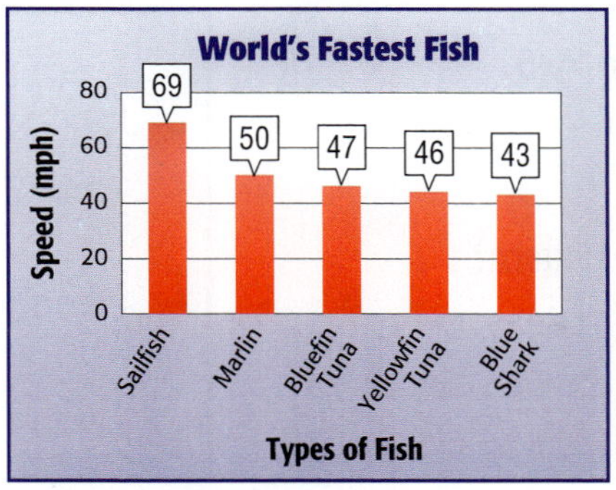

Source: *Top Ten of Everything*

GET READY for the Next Lesson

PREREQUISITE SKILL Divide. (Page 676)

41. $2\overline{)1.0}$ 0.5
42. $4\overline{)1.00}$ 0.25
43. $10\overline{)7.0}$ 0.7
44. $8\overline{)3.000}$ 0.375

⚠ Exercise Alert!

Find the Error In Exercise 32, Nhu is correct. Booker correctly divided the numerator and denominator by a common factor, 2, but then failed to see that he could divide them again by another common factor, 2. Remind students to check whether the GCF of the numerator and denominator of a fraction is 1. If it isn't, then the fraction is not in simplest form.

4 Assess

Ticket Out the Door Write a fraction such as $\frac{125}{1{,}000}$ or $\frac{250}{1{,}000}$ on the chalkboard. Have students write the fraction in simplest form on a piece of paper.

FOLDABLES™ Study Organizer Foldables™ Follow-Up

Remind students to write—under the tab for this lesson of their Foldables—the answer to the question they wrote about the lesson.

Additional Answer

40. Sample answer: A blue shark swims at about 40 mph while a sailfish swims at about 70 mph. To swim 280 miles, a blue shark would take about 280 ÷ 40 or 7 hours while a sailfish would take about 280 ÷ 70 or 4 hours.

Lesson 4-4 Simplifying Fractions **195**

4-5 Fractions and Decimals

PACING: **Regular:** 1 period, **Block:** 0.5 period

IN Academic Standards **7.1.6** Identify, write, **rename,** compare and order **rational** and common irrational **numbers** and plot them on a number line.
Also addresses P.4.2.

Options for Differentiated Instruction

ELL = English Language Learner   AL = Above or Beyond Grade Level   SS = Struggling Students   SN = Special Needs

Creating a Resource Sheet SS SN

Use before presenting the Examples.

Many students would benefit from creating a resource sheet listing some commonly used fraction-decimal equivalencies. Some examples are here.

$\frac{1}{2} = 0.5$	$\frac{1}{3} = 0.\overline{3}$	$\frac{2}{3} = 0.\overline{6}$	$\frac{1}{4} = 0.25$
$\frac{3}{4} = 0.75$	$\frac{1}{5} = 0.2$	$\frac{1}{8} = 0.125$	$\frac{1}{10} = 0.1$

Alternate Examples SS SN

Use with Example 3.

It may be helpful to use a common fraction such as $\frac{3}{4}$ when showing students how to write a fraction as a decimal by long division. Using a fraction whose decimal equivalent they already know will allow students to feel confident with the long division steps and to make connections about where the numbers are coming from.

Also, prevent students from dividing $4 \div 3$ when writing $\frac{3}{4}$ as a decimal. This is a common mistake and students need to think about the fact that $\frac{3}{4}$ is less than 1. Therefore, the decimal should not have a digit in the ones place.

Use Reasoning AL

Use after students complete Lesson 4-5.

Have students examine the pattern at the right.

Ask:

- What should $\frac{9}{9}$ equal according to the pattern? $0.\overline{9}$
- Any number divided by itself equals 1. How can you explain the contradiction? Sample answer: Since the digits of $0.\overline{9}$ repeat forever, the difference between $0.\overline{9}$ and 1 is negligible.

$\frac{1}{9} = 0.\overline{1}$	$\frac{5}{9} = 0.\overline{5}$
$\frac{2}{9} = 0.\overline{2}$	$\frac{6}{9} = 0.\overline{6}$
$\frac{3}{9} = 0.\overline{3}$	$\frac{7}{9} = 0.\overline{7}$
$\frac{4}{9} = 0.\overline{4}$	$\frac{8}{9} = 0.\overline{8}$

Leveled Lesson Resources

Also on TeacherWorks™ Lesson 4-5

Chapter 4 Resource Masters

BL = Below or Approaching Grade Level | OL = On Grade Level | AL = Above or Beyond Grade Level | ELL = English Language Learner

Lesson Reading Guide
p. 32 BL OL ELL

NAME ______ DATE ______ PERIOD ____

4-5 Lesson Reading Guide
Fractions and Decimals

Get Ready for the Lesson

Read the introduction at the top of page 196 in your textbook. Write your answers below.

1. What fraction of the speeds are between 130 and 145 miles per hour? $\frac{4}{10}$
2. Express this fraction using words and then as a decimal. four tenths; 0.4
3. What fraction of the speeds are between 145 and 160 miles per hour? Express this fraction using words and then as a decimal. $\frac{4}{10}$; four tenths; 0.4

Read the Lesson

4. What is meant by the term *place value*? Sample answer: the value of the place of a digit in a numeral
5. In place value, what serves as the divider between ones and tenths? the decimal point
6. What is the difference between a terminating decimal and a repeating decimal? Give an example of each. Sample answer: A terminating decimal has an ending, and a repeating decimal does not; 6.25 is a terminating decimal, and 0.7777... is a repeating decimal.

Remember What You Learned

7. Work with a partner. Use a local newspaper, a favorite magazine, or the Internet. Find real-world situations that use fractions or decimals. Convert the fractions to decimals and the decimals to fractions. Exchange papers with your partner and correct each other's work. See students' work.

Chapter 4 32 Course 2

Study Guide and Intervention*
p. 33 BL OL ELL

NAME ______ DATE ______ PERIOD ____

4-5 Study Guide and Intervention
Fractions and Decimals

To write a decimal as a fraction, divide the numerator of the fraction by the denominator. Use a power of ten to change a decimal to a fraction.

Example 1 Write $\frac{5}{9}$ as a decimal.

Method 1 Use pencil and paper.

$$9\overline{)5.000} = 0.555...$$
45, 50, 45, 50, 45, 5 — The remainder after each step is 5.

Method 2 Use a calculator.
5 ÷ 9 ENTER 0.55555556
You can use bar notation $0.\overline{5}$ to indicate that 5 repeats forever. So, $\frac{5}{9} = 0.\overline{5}$.

Example 2 Write 0.32 as a fraction in simplest form.

$0.32 = \frac{32}{100}$ The 2 is in the hundredths place.
$= \frac{8}{25}$ Simplify.

Exercises

Write each fraction or mixed number as a decimal. Use bar notation if the decimal is a repeating decimal.

1. $\frac{8}{10}$ 0.8
2. $\frac{3}{5}$ 0.6
3. $\frac{7}{11}$ $0.\overline{63}$
4. $4\frac{7}{8}$ 4.875
5. $\frac{13}{15}$ $0.8\overline{6}$
6. $3\frac{47}{99}$ $3.\overline{47}$

Write each decimal as a fraction in simplest form.

7. 0.14 $\frac{7}{50}$
8. 0.3 $\frac{3}{10}$
9. 0.94 $\frac{47}{50}$

Lesson 4-5

Chapter 4 33 Course 2

Skills Practice*
p. 34 BL OL

NAME ______ DATE ______ PERIOD ____

4-5 Skills Practice
Fractions and Decimals

Write each repeating decimal using bar notation.

1. 0.7353535... $0.7\overline{35}$
2. 0.424242... $0.\overline{42}$
3. 5.126126126... $5.\overline{126}$

Write each fraction or mixed number as a decimal. Use bar notation if the decimal is a repeating decimal.

4. $\frac{3}{5}$ 0.6
5. $\frac{19}{20}$ 0.95
6. $3\frac{4}{5}$ 3.8
7. $\frac{23}{50}$ 0.46
8. $1\frac{5}{8}$ 1.625
9. $\frac{19}{25}$ 0.76
10. $4\frac{17}{37}$ $4.\overline{459}$
11. $5\frac{3}{11}$ $5.\overline{27}$
12. $\frac{17}{24}$ $0.708\overline{3}$
13. $6\frac{7}{32}$ 6.21875
14. $7\frac{9}{22}$ $7.4\overline{09}$
15. $1\frac{17}{48}$ $1.3541\overline{6}$

Write each decimal as a fraction in simplest form.

16. 0.8 $\frac{4}{5}$
17. 0.52 $\frac{13}{25}$
18. 0.92 $\frac{23}{25}$
19. 0.48 $\frac{12}{25}$
20. 0.86 $\frac{43}{50}$
21. 0.76 $\frac{19}{25}$

Chapter 4 34 Course 2

Practice*
p. 35 OL AL

NAME ______ DATE ______ PERIOD ____

4-5 Practice
Fractions and Decimals

Write each fraction or mixed number as a decimal. Use bar notation if the decimal is a repeating decimal.

1. $\frac{5}{8}$ 0.625
2. $\frac{2}{9}$ $0.\overline{2}$
3. $\frac{37}{16}$ 2.3125
4. $\frac{3}{4}$ 0.75
5. $\frac{27}{50}$ 0.54
6. $\frac{121}{25}$ 4.84
7. $\frac{5}{6}$ $0.8\overline{3}$
8. $\frac{1}{33}$ $0.\overline{03}$
9. $\frac{62}{11}$ $5.\overline{63}$
10. $\frac{2}{3}$ $0.\overline{6}$
11. $\frac{11}{40}$ 0.275
12. $\frac{13}{20}$ 0.65
13. $\frac{83}{5}$ 16.6
14. $\frac{3}{10}$ 0.3
15. $\frac{1}{9}$ $0.\overline{1}$
16. $\frac{3}{7}$ $0.\overline{428571}$
17. $\frac{111}{24}$ 4.625
18. $\frac{7}{32}$ 0.21875

Write each decimal as a fraction or mixed number in simplest form.

19. 0.4 $\frac{2}{5}$
20. 0.83 $\frac{83}{100}$
21. 3.75 $3\frac{3}{4}$
22. 2.42 $2\frac{21}{50}$
23. 0.16 $\frac{4}{25}$
24. 0.65 $\frac{13}{20}$

25. KILOMETERS One kilometer is approximately 0.62 mile. What fraction represents this length? $\frac{31}{50}$

26. MARATHON Jake completed a marathon race in 3 hours and 12 minutes. Write Jake's running time as a decimal. 3.2

Lesson 4-5

Chapter 4 35 Course 2

Word Problem Practice*
p. 36 OL AL

NAME ______ DATE ______ PERIOD ____

4-5 Word Problem Practice
Fractions and Decimals

1. BOYS AND GIRLS There were 6 girls and 18 boys in Mrs. Johnson's math class. Write the number of girls as a fraction of the number of boys. Then write the fraction as a repeating decimal. $\frac{6}{18}$; $0.\overline{3}$
2. CATS In a neighborhood of 72 families, 18 families own one or more cats. Write the number of families who own one or more cats as a fraction. Then write the fraction as a decimal. $\frac{18}{72}$; 0.25
3. CELLULAR PHONES In Italy, about 74 of every 100 people use cellular telephones. Write the fraction of cellular phone users in Italy. Then write the fraction as a decimal. $\frac{74}{100}$; 0.74
4. FRUITS Ms. Rockwell surveyed her class and found that 12 out of the 30 students chose peaches as their favorite fruit. Write the number of students who chose peaches as a fraction in simplest form. Then write the fraction as a decimal. $\frac{2}{5}$; 0.4
5. TRAVEL Tora took a short trip of 320 miles. He stopped to have lunch after he had driven 120 miles. Write the fraction of the trip he had completed by lunch in simplest form. Then write the fraction as a decimal. $\frac{3}{8}$; 0.375
6. VOTING In a recent school election, 208 of the 325 freshmen voted in their class election. Write the fraction of freshmen who voted. Then write the fraction as a decimal. $\frac{208}{325}$; 0.64

Chapter 4 36 Course 2

Enrichment
p. 37 OL AL

NAME ______ DATE ______ PERIOD ____

4-5 Enrichment

Writing Repeating Decimals as Fractions

All fractions can be written as decimals that either terminate or repeat. You have learned how to use a power of 10 to write a terminating decimal as a fraction. Below, you will study a strategy to write a repeating decimal as a fraction.

For Exercises 1–4, write each fraction as a decimal. Use bar notation if the decimal is a repeating decimal.

1. $\frac{1}{9}$ $0.\overline{1}$
2. $\frac{2}{9}$ $0.\overline{2}$
3. $\frac{3}{9}$ $0.\overline{3}$
4. $\frac{5}{9}$ $0.\overline{5}$

5. Describe the relationship between the numerator of each fraction and its decimal equivalent. The numerator is the same as the repeating part of the decimal.

For Exercises 6–9, write each fraction as a decimal. Use bar notation if the decimal is a repeating decimal.

6. $\frac{7}{99}$ $0.\overline{07}$
7. $\frac{24}{99}$ $0.\overline{24}$
8. $\frac{37}{99}$ $0.\overline{37}$
9. $\frac{82}{99}$ $0.\overline{82}$

10. Describe the relationship between the numerator of each fraction and its decimal equivalent. The repeating part of the decimal is the same as the numerator, with a zero added if the numerator is a single digit.

11. Use the relationship from Exercise 10 to write the decimal $0.\overline{52}$ as a fraction. Check your work using long division. $\frac{52}{99}$

12. Using your observations from Exercises 5 and 11, make a prediction about the decimal equivalent of $\frac{127}{999}$. Check to see if your prediction was correct by using long division. $0.\overline{127}$

13. How are the decimal equivalents of $\frac{4}{9}$, $\frac{4}{99}$ and $\frac{4}{999}$ different? Explain. They differ in the number of digits that repeat. Extra zeros are added in front of the four depending on how many digits repeat.

For Exercises 14–19, write each decimal as a fraction. Check your answers with a calculator.

14. 0.47474747... $\frac{47}{99}$
15. $0.\overline{22}$ $\frac{22}{99} = \frac{2}{9}$
16. $0.\overline{530}$ $\frac{530}{999}$
17. 0.010010010... $\frac{10}{999}$
18. $0.\overline{3266}$ $\frac{3266}{9999}$
19. $0.\overline{00328}$ $\frac{328}{99999}$

Lesson 4-5

Chapter 4 37 Course 2

* Also available in Spanish ELL

Additional Lesson Resources

Transparencies
- *5-Minute Check Transparency*, Lesson 4-5

Other Print Products
- *Noteables™ Interactive Study Notebook with Foldables™*

Teacher Tech Tools
- *Interactive Classroom CD-ROM*, Lesson 4-5
- *AssignmentWorks*, Lesson 4-5

Student Tech Tools
glencoe.com
- Extra Examples, Chapter 4, Lesson 5
- Self-Check Quiz, Chapter 4, Lesson 5

4-5 Lesson Notes

1 Focus

Vertical Alignment

Before Lesson 4-5
Identify and represent on a number line decimals, fractions, mixed numbers, and positive and negative numbers

Lesson 4-5
Compare and order positive and negative fractions, decimals, and mixed numbers and place them on a number line

After Lesson 4-5
Convert fractions to decimals and percents and use these representations in estimations, computations, and applications

2 Teach

Scaffolding Questions

As you ask the following questions, write each money amount on the board.

Ask:

- What fraction of a dollar is ten cents? (Write: $0.10) $\frac{1}{10}$
- What fraction of a dollar is twenty-five cents? (Write: $0.25) $\frac{1}{4}$
- What fraction of a dollar is fifty cents? (Write: $0.50) $\frac{1}{2}$
- What fraction of a dollar is seventy-five cents? (Write: $0.75) $\frac{3}{4}$
- If you are given an amount of money in cents, how can you find the fraction of a dollar it represents in simplest form? Write the amount as the numerator of a fraction with a denominator of 100, and then write the fraction in simplest form.

4-5 Fractions and Decimals

MAIN IDEA

Write fractions as terminating or repeating decimals and write decimals as fractions.

IN Academic Standards

7.1.6 Identify, write, **rename,** compare and order **rational** and common irrational **numbers** and plot them on a number line. *Also addresses P.4.2.*

New Vocabulary

terminating decimals
repeating decimals
bar notation

IN Math Online

glencoe.com

- Extra Examples
- Personal Tutor
- Self-Check Quiz

GET READY for the Lesson

NASCAR The table shows the winning speeds for a 10-year-period at the Daytona 500.

Daytona 500		
Year	**Winner**	**Speed (mph)**
1998	D. Earnhardt	172.712
1999	J. Gordon	148.295
2000	D. Jarrett	155.669
2001	M. Waltrip	161.783
2002	W. Burton	142.971
2003	M. Waltrip	133.870
2004	D. Earnhardt Jr.	156.345
2005	J. Gordon	135.173
2006	J. Johnson	142.667
2007	K. Harvick	149.335

Source: ESPN Sports Almanac

1. What fraction of the speeds are between 130 and 145 miles per hour? $\frac{4}{10}$
2. Express this fraction using words and then as a decimal. four tenths; 0.4
3. What fraction of the speeds are between 145 and 165 miles per hour? Express this fraction using words and then as a decimal.

3. $\frac{5}{10}$; five tenths; 0.5

Our decimal system is based on powers of 10. So, if the denominator of a fraction is a power of 10, you can use place value to write the fraction as a decimal. For example, to write $\frac{7}{10}$ as a decimal, place a 7 in the tenths place.

Words	Fraction	Decimal
seven tenths	$\frac{7}{10}$	0.7

If the denominator of a fraction is a *factor* of 10, 100, 1,000, or any higher power of ten, you can use mental math and place value.

EXAMPLES Use Mental Math

Write each fraction or mixed number as a decimal.

1 $\frac{7}{20}$

THINK $\frac{7}{20} = \frac{35}{100}$ (× 5)

So, $\frac{7}{20} = 0.35$.

2 $5\frac{3}{4}$

$5\frac{3}{4} = 5 + \frac{3}{4}$ Think of it as a sum.

$= 5 + 0.75$ You know that $\frac{3}{4} = 0.75$.

$= 5.75$ Add mentally.

So, $5\frac{3}{4} = 5.75$.

CHECK Your Progress

a. $\frac{3}{10}$ 0.3

b. $\frac{3}{25}$ 0.12

c. $6\frac{1}{2}$ 6.5

Study Tip

Mental Math It will be helpful to memorize the following fraction-decimal equivalencies.

$\frac{1}{2} = 0.5$

$\frac{1}{3} = 0.\overline{3}$ $\frac{2}{3} = 0.\overline{6}$

$\frac{1}{4} = 0.25$ $\frac{3}{4} = 0.75$

$\frac{1}{5} = 0.2$ $\frac{1}{10} = 0.1$

$\frac{1}{8} = 0.125$

Any fraction can be written as a decimal by dividing its numerator by its denominator. Division ends when the remainder is zero.

EXAMPLES Use Division

3 **Write $\frac{3}{8}$ as a decimal.**

$$\begin{array}{r} 0.375 \\ 8\overline{)3.000} \\ -24 \\ 60 \\ -56 \\ 40 \\ -40 \\ 0 \end{array}$$

Divide 3 by 8.

Division ends when the remainder is 0.

So, $\frac{3}{8} = 0.375$.

4 **Write $\frac{1}{40}$ as a decimal.**

$$\begin{array}{r} 0.025 \\ 40\overline{)1.000} \\ -80 \\ 200 \\ -200 \\ 0 \end{array}$$

Divide 1 by 40.

So, $\frac{1}{40} = 0.025$.

CHECK Your Progress

Write each fraction or mixed number as a decimal.

d. $\frac{7}{8}$ **0.875** e. $2\frac{1}{8}$ **2.125** f. $7\frac{9}{20}$ **7.45**

Vocabulary Link

Terminate

Everyday Use coming to an end, as in terminate a game

Math Use a decimal whose digits end

In Examples 1–4, the decimals 0.35, 5.75, 0.375, and 0.025 are called terminating decimals. A **terminating decimal** is a decimal whose digits end.

Repeating decimals have a pattern in their digits that repeats forever. Consider $\frac{1}{3}$.

$$\begin{array}{r} 0.333\ldots \\ 3\overline{)1.000} \\ -9 \\ 10 \\ -9 \\ 10 \\ -9 \\ 1 \end{array}$$

The number 3 repeats. The repetition of 3 is represented by three dots.

You can use **bar notation** to indicate that a number pattern repeats indefinitely. A bar is written only over the digits that repeat.

$0.33333\ldots = 0.\overline{3}$ $0.121212\ldots = 0.\overline{12}$ $11.3858585\ldots = 11.3\overline{85}$

Focus on Mathematical Content

When the denominator of a fraction is a factor or a multiple of 10, the fraction can be written as a decimal by using **mental math** and **place value.**

Formative Assessment

Use the Check Your Progress exercises after the Examples to determine students' understanding of concepts.

ADDITIONAL EXAMPLES

Write each fraction or mixed number as a decimal.

1. $\frac{9}{10}$ 0.9
2. $7\frac{3}{5}$ 7.6
3. $\frac{1}{8}$ 0.125
4. $\frac{1}{25}$ 0.04

Additional Examples are also in:

- Noteables™ Interactive Study Notebook with Foldables™
- Interactive Classroom PowerPoint® Presentations

Tips for New Teachers

Mental Math

Encourage students to use mental math whenever possible when writing fractions as decimals. Have them first ask themselves whether the denominator of a fraction is a factor of 10 (or of 100 or 1,000). If it is, what number can they multiply the denominator by to get a power of ten? Once they multiply the numerator and denominator by that number, they will have an equivalent fraction that can be written as a decimal by using place value.

Lesson 4-5 Fractions and Decimals **197**

ADDITIONAL EXAMPLES

5 Write $\frac{1}{11}$ as a decimal. $0.\overline{09}$

6 **CEREAL** Jorge read that 0.72 of his favorite cereal was whole-grain wheat. Find what fraction of his cereal, in simplest form, is whole-grain wheat. $\frac{18}{25}$

EXAMPLE Write Fractions as Repeating Decimals

5 **Write $\frac{7}{9}$ as a decimal.**

$$\begin{array}{r} 0.777\ldots \\ 9\overline{)7.000} \\ -\underline{63} \\ 70 \\ -\underline{63} \\ 70 \\ -\underline{63} \\ 7 \end{array}$$

Divide 7 by 9.

Notice that the remainder will never be zero. That is, the division never ends.

So, $\frac{7}{9} = 0.777\ldots$ or $0.\overline{7}$.

CHECK Your Progress

Write each fraction or mixed number as a decimal. Use bar notation if the decimal is a repeating decimal.

g. $\frac{2}{3}$ $0.\overline{6}$ h. $\frac{3}{11}$ $0.\overline{27}$ i. $8\frac{1}{3}$ $8.\overline{3}$

Every terminating decimal can be written as a fraction with a denominator of 10, 100, 1,000, or a higher power of ten. Place the digits that come after the decimal point in the numerator. Use the place value of the final digit as the denominator.

numerator

$$0.25 = \frac{25}{100}$$

hundredths place

Real-World Link The recommended water temperature for goldfish is 65–72°F.
Source: Animal-World

Real-World EXAMPLE Use a Power of 10

6 **FISH** **Use the table to find what fraction of the fish in an aquarium are goldfish. Write in simplest form.**

Fish	Amount
Guppy	0.25
Angel Fish	0.4
Goldfish	0.15
Molly	0.2

$0.15 = \frac{15}{100}$ The final digit, 5, is in the hundredths place.

$= \frac{3}{20}$ Simplify.

CHECK Your Progress

Determine the fraction of the aquarium made up by each fish. Write the answer in simplest form.

j. molly $\frac{1}{5}$ k. guppy $\frac{1}{4}$ l. angel fish $\frac{2}{5}$

198 Chapter 4 Fractions, Decimals, and Percents

★ indicates multi-step problem

CHECK Your Understanding

Examples 1–5 (pp. 196–198)

Write each fraction or mixed number as a decimal. Use bar notation if the decimal is a repeating decimal.

1. $\frac{2}{5}$ **0.4**
2. $\frac{9}{10}$ **0.9**
3. $7\frac{1}{2}$ **7.5**
4. $4\frac{3}{20}$ **4.15**
5. $\frac{1}{8}$ **0.125**
6. $3\frac{5}{8}$ **3.625**
7. $\frac{5}{9}$ **$0.\overline{5}$**
8. $1\frac{5}{6}$ **$1.8\overline{3}$**

Example 6 (p. 198)

Write each decimal as a fraction or mixed number in simplest form.

9. 0.22 **$\frac{11}{50}$**
10. 0.1 **$\frac{1}{10}$**
11. 4.6 **$4\frac{3}{5}$**
12. **HOCKEY** During a hockey game, an ice resurfacer travels 0.75 mile during each ice resurfacing. What fraction represents this distance? **$\frac{3}{4}$ mi**

Practice and Problem Solving

HOMEWORK HELP	
For Exercises	See Examples
13–16	1, 2
17–22	3, 4
23–28	5
29–36	6

Exercise Levels
A: 13–36
B: 37–43
C: 44–46

Write each fraction or mixed number as a decimal. Use bar notation if the decimal is a repeating decimal.

13. $\frac{4}{5}$ **0.8**
14. $\frac{1}{2}$ **0.5**
15. $4\frac{4}{25}$ **4.16**
16. $7\frac{1}{20}$ **7.05**
17. $\frac{5}{16}$ **0.3125**
18. $\frac{3}{16}$ **0.1875**
19. $\frac{33}{50}$ **0.66**
20. $\frac{17}{40}$ **0.425**
21. $5\frac{7}{8}$ **5.875**
22. $9\frac{3}{8}$ **9.375**
23. $\frac{4}{9}$ **$0.\overline{4}$**
24. $\frac{8}{9}$ **$0.\overline{8}$**
25. $\frac{1}{6}$ **$0.1\overline{6}$**
26. $\frac{8}{11}$ **$0.\overline{72}$**
27. $5\frac{1}{3}$ **$5.\overline{3}$**
28. $2\frac{6}{11}$ **$2.\overline{54}$**

Write each decimal as a fraction or mixed number in simplest form.

29. 0.2 **$\frac{1}{5}$**
30. 0.9 **$\frac{9}{10}$**
31. 0.55 **$\frac{11}{20}$**
32. 0.34 **$\frac{17}{50}$**
33. 5.96 **$5\frac{24}{25}$**
34. 2.66 **$2\frac{33}{50}$**
35. **INSECTS** The maximum length of a praying mantis is 30.5 centimeters. What mixed number represents this length? **$30\frac{1}{2}$ cm**

36. **GROCERIES** Suppose you buy a 1.25 pound package of ham for $4.99. What fraction of a pound did you buy? **$\frac{5}{4}$**
37. **FIND THE DATA** Refer to the Data File on page 16–19 of your book. Choose some data and write a real-world problem in which you would write a percent as a decimal. **See students' work.**

Write each of the following as an integer over a whole number.

38. −13 **$\frac{-13}{1}$**
39. $7\frac{1}{3}$ **$\frac{22}{3}$**
40. −0.028 **$\frac{-7}{250}$**
41. −3.2 **$\frac{-16}{5}$**
42. **MUSIC** Nicolás practiced playing the cello for 2 hours and 18 minutes. Write the time Nicolás spent practicing as a decimal. **2.3 h**

Academic Standards • ISTEP+
Extra Practice, pp. 677, 707

3 Practice

Formative Assessment

Use Exercises 1–12 to check for understanding.

Then use the chart at the bottom of this page to customize your assignments for students.

Intervention You may wish to use the Study Guide and Intervention Master on page 33 of the *Chapter 4 Resource Masters* for additional reinforcement.

Odd/Even Assignments

Exercises 13–36 are structured so that students practice the same concepts whether they are assigned odd or even problems.

Choose Your Method

Tips for New Teachers

Separate the class into groups of 2–3 students. Have students choose between using mental math, paper and pencil, or a calculator for each exercise in the Check Your Understanding. As they complete each exercise, have them discuss whether or not their method was the most efficient or appropriate. Encourage them to use mental math whenever possible. For example, in Exercise 1, mental math is appropriate because the denominator, 5, is a factor of 10. Since $5 \times 2 = 10$, multiply the numerator by 2 as well. Since $2 \times 2 = 4$, the fraction is equivalent to 4 tenths, or 0.4. In Exercise 7, either paper and pencil or a calculator are appropriate since the denominator, 9, is not a factor of 100.

DIFFERENTIATED HOMEWORK OPTIONS

Level	Assignment	Two-Day Option	
BL Basic	13–36, 44, 46–57	13–35 odd, 47, 48	14–36 even, 44, 46, 49–57
OL Core	13–33 odd, 35–37, 39, 41–44, 46–57	13–36, 47, 48	37–44, 46, 49–57
AL Advanced/Pre-AP	37–53 (optional: 54–57)		

4 Assess

Yesterday's News Remind students that yesterday's lesson was about simplifying fractions, or finding equivalent fractions in simplest form. Ask students to write how yesterday's concepts helped them with today's material.

Formative Assessment

Check for student understanding of concepts in Lessons 4-4 and 4-5.

CRM Quiz 2, p. 67

Foldables™ Follow-Up

FOLDABLES Study Organizer

Remind students to write—under the tab for this lesson of their Foldables—the answer to the question they wrote about the lesson.

Additional Answers

43. Felisa; Sample answer: Felisa's batting average is about 0.286. Harmony's batting average is about 0.263. 0.286 > 0.263, so, Felisa's average is better than Harmony's.

46. Sample answer: The first set of numbers can be factored into primes of 2s. The second set of numbers can be factored into primes of 2s and 3s; the factor of 3 produces the repeating decimal.

★ **43. SOFTBALL** The batting average of a softball player is the number of hits divided by the number of at-bats. If Felisa had 50 hits in 175 at-bats and Harmony had 42 hits in 160 at-bats, who had the better batting average? Justify your answer. **See margin.**

H.O.T. Problems

45. Sample answer: $3\frac{1}{7} \approx 3.14286$ **and** $3\frac{10}{71} \approx 3.14085$; **Since 3.1415927... is between** $3\frac{1}{7}$ **and** $3\frac{10}{71}$, **Archimedes was correct.**

44. OPEN ENDED Write a fraction that is equivalent to a terminating decimal between 0.5 and 0.75. **Sample answer:** $\frac{3}{5}$

45. CHALLENGE The value of pi (π) is 3.1415926… . The mathematician Archimedes believed that π was between $3\frac{1}{7}$ and $3\frac{10}{71}$. Was Archimedes correct? Explain your reasoning.

46. WRITING IN MATH Fractions with denominators of 2, 4, 8, 16, and 32 produce terminating decimals. Fractions with denominators of 6, 12, 18, and 24 produce repeating decimals. What causes the difference? Explain. **See margin.**

ISTEP+ PRACTICE 7.1.6

47. Which decimal represents the shaded region of the model? **B**

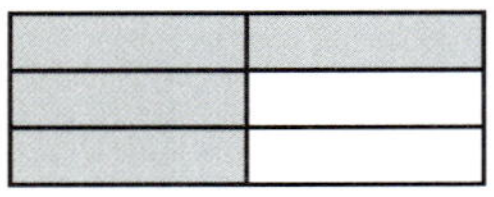

A 0.666 C 0.667

B $0.\overline{6}$ D $0.66\overline{7}$

48. Based on the information given in the table, what fraction represents $0.\overline{8}$? **J**

F $\frac{4}{5}$

G $\frac{80}{99}$

H $\frac{5}{6}$

J $\frac{8}{9}$

Decimal	Fraction
$0.\overline{3}$	$\frac{3}{9}$
$0.\overline{4}$	$\frac{4}{9}$
$0.\overline{5}$	$\frac{5}{9}$
$0.\overline{6}$	$\frac{6}{9}$

Spiral Review

Write each fraction in simplest form. (Lesson 4-4)

49. $\frac{10}{24}$ $\frac{5}{12}$ **50.** $\frac{39}{81}$ $\frac{13}{27}$ **51.** $\frac{28}{98}$ $\frac{2}{7}$ **52.** $\frac{51}{68}$ $\frac{3}{4}$

53. PIZZA How many different pizzas can Alfonso order if he can choose thick, thin, or deep dish crust and one topping from either pepperoni, sausage, or mushrooms? Use the *make an organized list* strategy. (Lesson 4-3) **9 pizzas**

GET READY for the Next Lesson

PREREQUISITE SKILL **Write a fraction for the number of shaded squares to the total number of squares.**

54.  $\frac{2}{3}$

55. 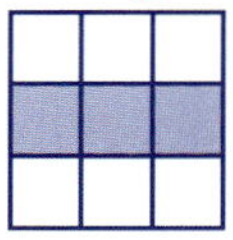 $\frac{3}{9}$ or $\frac{1}{3}$

56. 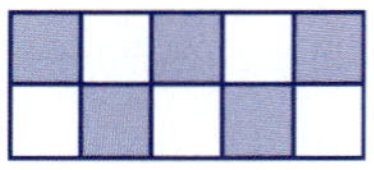 $\frac{5}{10}$ or $\frac{1}{2}$

57. 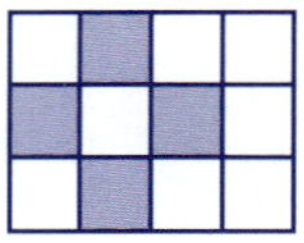 $\frac{4}{12}$ or $\frac{1}{3}$

Pre-AP Activity Use after Exercise 45

The Rhind Papyrus states that the Egyptians used $\frac{256}{81}$ for π. Have students write the fraction as a decimal rounded to the nearest hundred-thousandth. Then ask them which is closer to the actual value of π, Archimedes' value or the Egyptians' value? 3.16049; Archimedes'

CHAPTER 4

Mid-Chapter Quiz

Lessons 4-1 through 4-5

IN Academic Standards
7.1.3, 7.1.6

Determine whether each number is *prime* or *composite*. (Lesson 4-1)

1. 24 **composite**
2. 61 **prime**
3. 2 **prime**

4. **AGE** Kevin just turned 13 years old. How old will he be the next time his age is a prime number? (Lesson 4-1) **17 years old**

Find the prime factorization of each number. (Lesson 4-1)

5. 30 $2 \times 3 \times 5$
6. 120 $2^3 \times 3 \times 5$

Factor each expression. (Lesson 4-1)

7. $14x^2y$ $2 \cdot 7 \cdot x \cdot x \cdot y$
8. $50mn$ $2 \cdot 5 \cdot 5 \cdot m \cdot n$

Find the GCF of each set of numbers. (Lesson 4-2)

9. 16, 40 **8**
10. 65, 100 **5**

11. **MULTIPLE CHOICE** Lakeesha wants to cut a 14-inch by 21-inch poster board into equal-size squares for an art project. She does not want to waste any of the poster board, and she wants the largest squares possible. What is the length of the side of the largest squares she can cut? (Lesson 4-2) **B**

A 14
B 7
C 6
D 2

12. **MULTIPLE CHOICE** Lynne cannot remember her password to check the messages on her cell phone. She knows that it is a three-digit number consisting of the numbers 1, 4, and 7, but she cannot remember the order. Which list shows all the different possibilities for her password? (Lesson 4-3) **G**

F 147, 174, 417, 714, 741
G 147, 174, 417, 471, 714, 741
H 417, 471, 714, 741
J 147, 174, 74, 417, 17, 471, 714, 741

13. **PIANO** Evelina spends 40 minutes practicing the flute each afternoon after school. What part of one hour does she spend practicing? Write as a fraction in simplest form. (Lesson 4-4) $\frac{2}{3}$

Write each fraction in simplest form. (Lesson 4-4)

14. $\frac{20}{36}$ $\frac{5}{9}$
15. $\frac{45}{60}$ $\frac{3}{4}$
16. $\frac{63}{108}$ $\frac{7}{12}$
17. $\frac{60}{72}$ $\frac{5}{6}$

18. **VOTING** In the 2004 presidential election, Kentucky had 8 out of 538 total electoral votes. Write Kentucky's portion of the electoral votes as a fraction in simplest form. (Lesson 4-4) $\frac{4}{269}$

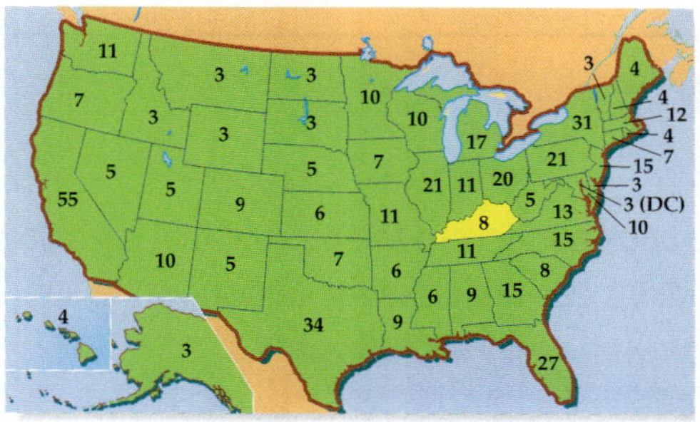

Write each fraction or mixed number as a decimal. Use bar notation if the decimal is a repeating decimal. (Lesson 4-5)

19. $\frac{7}{8}$ **0.875**
20. $\frac{2}{9}$ $0.\overline{2}$
21. $3\frac{13}{20}$ **3.65**

Write each decimal as a fraction in simplest form. (Lesson 4-5)

22. 0.6 $\frac{3}{5}$
23. 0.48 $\frac{12}{25}$
24. 7.02 $7\frac{1}{50}$

25. **ANIMALS** The maximum height of an Asian elephant is 9.8 feet. What mixed number represents this height? (Lesson 4-5) $9\frac{4}{5}$

CHAPTER 4 Mid-Chapter Quiz

Formative Assessment

Use the Mid-Chapter Quiz to assess students' progress in the first half of the chapter.

Have students review the lesson indicated for the problems they answered incorrectly.

Summative Assessment

CRM Mid-Chapter Test, p. 69

ExamView Assessment Suite Customize and create multiple versions of your Mid-Chapter Test and their answer keys.

FOLDABLES Study Organizer Dinah Zike's Foldables

Before students complete the Mid-Chapter Quiz, encourage them to review the questions and answers they recorded on the first five tabs of their Foldables.

Data-Driven Decision Making

Diagnostic Teaching Based on the results of the Chapter 4 Mid-Chapter Quiz, use the following to review concepts that students continue to find challenging.

Exercises	Lesson	Academic Standards
1–8	4–1	7.1.3
9–11	4–2	7.1.3
12	4–3	P.1.3
13–18	4–4	7.1.6
19–25	4–5	6.1.4

Resources for Review

CRM Study Guide and Intervention pp. 10, 17, 22, 27, and 33

IN Math Online glencoe.com
- Extra Examples
- Personal Tutor
- Concepts in Motion

4-6 Fractions and Percents

PACING: **Regular:** 1 period, **Block:** 0.5 period

IN Academic Standards **7.1.6** Identify, **write, rename, compare** and order **rational** and common irrational **numbers** and plot them on a number line.
Also addresses P.4.2.

Options for Differentiated Instruction

ELL = English Language Learner AL = Above or Beyond Grade Level SS = Struggling Students SN = Special Needs

Visual Learners ELL AL SS

Use after presenting the Examples.

Provide students with a 10 × 10 array of dots in which you have drawn a triangle and a square that intersect, like those shown at the right.

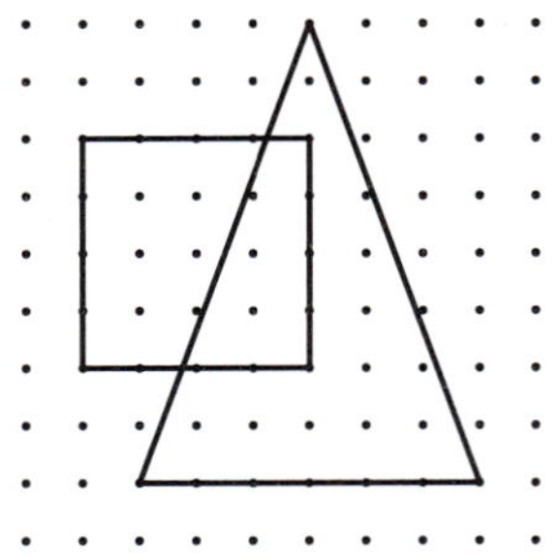

- Ask students to write a percent that expresses the fraction of dots *inside both* the triangle and the square. 3%
- Have students make up similar problems for classmates to solve.

Investigating Literature ELL AL SS

Use after assigning the Exercises.

Have students choose a paragraph in a literature book and record the percent that each vowel is of the total number of vowels. Have students record their findings in a table like the one shown below.

Vowel	Tally	Frequency	Percent
a			
e			
i			
o			
u			
	Total		100%

Have students determine the most common vowel. The most common vowel is "e."

Research AL

Use after presenting Lesson 4-6.

Have students use newspaper or magazines to find real-world examples of fractions and percents. Have them cut out or make a copy of the articles or graphs and make a poster. The posters should include the following:

- a graph or diagram showing the relationship of fractions and percents
- an explanation of what the fractions and percents represent

Have students share their posters with the entire class, demonstrating the usefulness of using fractions or percents in each situation.

Leveled Lesson Resources

Also on **TeacherWorks™**
Lesson 4-6

Chapter 4 Resource Masters

BL = Below or Approaching Grade Level   OL = On Grade Level   AL = Above or Beyond Grade Level   ELL = English Language Learner

Lesson Reading Guide
p. 39 BL OL ELL

NAME ____________ DATE ________ PERIOD ____

4-6 Lesson Reading Guide
Fractions and Percents

Lesson 4-6

Get Ready for the Lesson

Read the introduction at the top of page 202 in your textbook. Write your answers below.

1. For each sport, shade a 10 × 10 grid that represents the number of students that chose the sport.

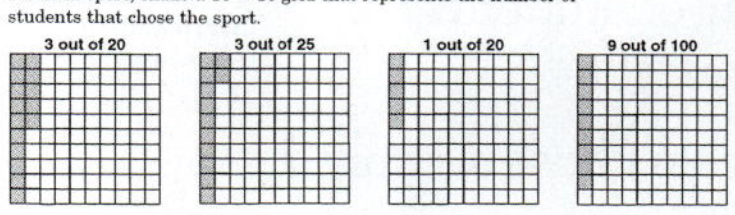

2. What fraction of the students chose swimming?
$\frac{9}{100}$

Read the Lesson

3. There is more than one way to write a ratio. Write the ratio that compares 4 to 25 in three different ways.
Sample answer: 4 out of 25, 4:25, and $\frac{4}{25}$

4. Write the ratio in Exercise 3 as a percent.
16%

5. How does having ratios written as percents make it easier to compare amounts? **Sample answer: Percents have the same denominator (100), so all you need to do to compare ratios is compare the numerators.**

Remember What You Learned

6. Work with a partner. Explain to your partner how to convert a ratio that does *not* compare a number to 100 as a percent. Then have your partner explain to you how to change from a percent to a fraction in simplest form. Both of you should use examples as well as general explanations.
See students' work.

Chapter 4   39   *Course 2*

*Study Guide and Intervention**
p. 40 BL OL ELL

NAME ____________ DATE ________ PERIOD ____

4-6 Study Guide and Intervention
Fractions and Percents

A **ratio** is a comparison of two numbers by division. When a ratio compares a number to 100, it can be written as a **percent**. To write a ratio or fraction as a percent, find an equivalent fraction with a denominator of 100. You can also use the meaning of percent to change percents to fractions.

Example 1 **Write $\frac{19}{20}$ as a percent.**

$\frac{19}{20} \xrightarrow{\times 5} \frac{95}{100} = 95\%$ Since 100 ÷ 20 = 5, multiply the numerator and denominator by 5.

Example 2 **Write 92% as a fraction in simplest form.**

$92\% = \frac{92}{100}$ Definition of percent
$= \frac{23}{25}$ Simplify.

Exercises

Write each ratio as a percent.

1. $\frac{14}{100}$ **14%**   2. $\frac{27}{100}$ **27%**   3. 34.5 per 100 **34.5%**
4. 18 per 100 **18%**   5. 21:100 **21%**   6. 96:100 **96%**

Write each fraction as a percent.

7. $\frac{3}{100}$ **3%**   8. $\frac{14}{100}$ **14%**   9. $\frac{2}{5}$ **40%**
10. $\frac{1}{20}$ **5%**   11. $\frac{13}{25}$ **52%**   12. $\frac{4}{10}$ **40%**

Write each percent as a fraction in simplest form.

13. 35% **$\frac{7}{20}$**   14. 18% **$\frac{9}{50}$**   15. 75% **$\frac{3}{4}$**
16. 80% **$\frac{4}{5}$**   17. 16% **$\frac{4}{25}$**   18. 15% **$\frac{3}{20}$**

Chapter 4   40   *Course 2*

*Skills Practice**
p. 41 BL OL

NAME ____________ DATE ________ PERIOD ____

4-6 Skills Practice
Fractions and Percents

Lesson 4-6

Write each ratio as a percent.

1. 26 out of 100 **26%**   2. 5 per 100 **5%**   3. 13:100 **13%**
4. $\frac{39}{100}$ **39%**   5. 12.5 per 100 **12.5%**   6. 51 out of 100 **51%**

Write each fraction as a percent.

7. $\frac{7}{10}$ **70%**   8. $\frac{6}{50}$ **12%**   9. $\frac{13}{20}$ **65%**
10. $\frac{30}{50}$ **60%**   11. $\frac{7}{20}$ **35%**   12. $\frac{12}{20}$ **60%**
13. $\frac{23}{25}$ **92%**   14. $\frac{3}{10}$ **30%**   15. $\frac{17}{50}$ **34%**

Write each percent as a fraction in simplest form.

16. 15% **$\frac{3}{20}$**   17. 85% **$\frac{17}{20}$**   18. 1% **$\frac{1}{100}$**
19. 70% **$\frac{7}{10}$**   20. 25% **$\frac{1}{4}$**   21. 19% **$\frac{19}{100}$**
22. 33% **$\frac{33}{100}$**   23. 22% **$\frac{11}{50}$**   24. 95% **$\frac{19}{20}$**

Chapter 4   41   *Course 2*

*Practice**
p. 42 OL AL

NAME ____________ DATE ________ PERIOD ____

4-6 Practice
Fractions and Percents

Write each ratio as a percent.

1. 56 out of 100 CDs sold **56%**   2. 75 per 100 adults **75%**
3. 89.2 out of 100 hours worked **89.2%**   4. 26.5:100 Calories **26.5%**
5. $45\frac{7}{8}$ out of 100 meters **45.875%**   6. $33\frac{1}{3}$:100 minutes **33.3%**

Write each fraction as a percent.

7. $\frac{6}{10}$ **60%**   8. $\frac{7}{20}$ **35%**   9. $\frac{21}{25}$ **84%**   10. $\frac{12}{50}$ **24%**
11. $\frac{1}{2}$ **50%**   12. $\frac{4}{5}$ **80%**   13. $\frac{20}{90}$ **22.2%**   14. $\frac{24}{25}$ **96%**

Write each percent as a fraction in simplest form.

15. 40% **$\frac{2}{5}$**   16. 35% **$\frac{7}{20}$**   17. 72% **$\frac{18}{25}$**   18. 44% **$\frac{11}{25}$**
19. 90% **$\frac{9}{10}$**   20. 17% **$\frac{17}{100}$**   21. 5% **$\frac{1}{20}$**   22. 26% **$\frac{13}{50}$**

Replace each ● with >, <, or = to make a true sentence.

23. $\frac{1}{10}$ ● 15% **<**   24. $\frac{3}{4}$ ● 72% **>**   25. 85% ● $\frac{17}{20}$ **=**
26. $\frac{21}{25}$ ● 21% **>**   27. 27% ● $\frac{27}{50}$ **<**   28. $\frac{4}{5}$ ● 60% **>**

29. SPORTS If twenty-seven out of every 50 sports fans attend at least one professional game every year, what percent of sports fans attend at least one professional game every year?
54%

30. WEATHER It rained 18 days during the month of April. What percent of the days during the month of April did it not rain?
40%

Chapter 4   42   *Course 2*

*Word Problem Practice**
p. 43 OL AL

NAME ____________ DATE ________ PERIOD ____

4-6 Word Problem Practice
Fractions and Percents

Lesson 4-6

1. LUNCHES Three out of every 10 students in Mr. Chan's class bring their lunch to school. Write this ratio as a percent. **30%**

2. COMPUTERS In 2007, 57 out of every 100 school age children (ages 6 to 17 years) had access to a computer both at home and at school. Write this ratio as a percent. **57%**

3. SALES TAX In one town, the sales tax is 8%. Write this percent as a fraction in simplest form.
$\frac{2}{25}$

4. HYGIENE Ms. Agosto surveyed her class and found that 15 out of 30 students brushed their teeth more than twice a day. What percent of students brushed more than twice a day? **50%**

5. DISCOUNT A local retail store was having a sale and offered all their merchandise at a 25% discount. Write this percent as a fraction in simplest form.
$\frac{1}{4}$

6. SPACE FLIGHT About 64% of all individuals who have flown in space from 1961 to 2001 are from the United States. Write this percent as a fraction in simplest form.
$\frac{16}{25}$

Chapter 4   43   *Course 2*

Enrichment
p. 44 OL AL

NAME ____________ DATE ________ PERIOD ____

4-6 Enrichment

Margarita Colmenares

Margarita Colmenares is an environmental engineer. She is a native of Los Angeles and a 1981 graduate of Stanford University. In 1989, she became the first woman president of the Society of Hispanic Professional Engineers. Ms. Colmenares was recently appointed to direct an office at the U.S. Department of Education. She has a special interest in education and has traveled extensively to talk to student groups about careers in engineering.

Environmental engineers like Colmenares use mathematics to predict the effect that our actions will have on our environment. They may also recommend ways to protect the environment. On this page, you will consider some data and recommendations concerning water usage.

Daily Water Usage in the United States (Per Person)

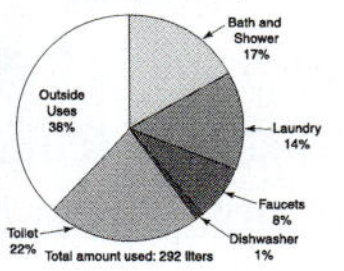

Refer to the graph above.

1. Which one category accounts for more than $\frac{1}{3}$ of the water usage?
outside uses

2. Estimate the fraction of a person's daily water usage that is for bath and shower.
about $\frac{1}{5}$

Use the graph above. Estimate the amount of water used in each category. **Sample answers are given.**

3. outside uses **$\frac{2}{5} \times 300 = 120$ liters**   4. bath and shower **$\frac{1}{5} \times 300 = 60$ liters**
5. toilet **$\frac{1}{5} \times 300 = 60$ liters**   6. laundry **$\frac{3}{20} \times 300 = 45$ liters**
7. dishwasher **$\frac{1}{100} \times 300 = 3$ liters**   8. faucets **$\frac{1}{10} \times 300 = 30$ liters**

In each situation, what percent of the water used can be saved by following the recommendation?

9. Using a water-saving shower head can save 65 liters of water out of the 130 liters normally used in a five-minute shower. **50%**

10. Turning off the water while brushing your teeth can reduce the water used from 20 liters to 2 liters. **90%**

Chapter 4   44   *Course 2*

**** Also available in Spanish*** ELL

Additional Lesson Resources

Transparencies

- *5-Minute Check Transparency*, Lesson 4-6

Other Print Products

- *Teaching Mathematics with Manipulatives*
- *Noteables™ Interactive Study Notebook with Foldables™*

Teacher Tech Tools

- *Interactive Classroom CD-ROM*, Lesson 4-6
- *AssignmentWorks*, Lesson 4-6

Student Tech Tools

glencoe.com

- Extra Examples, Chapter 4, Lesson 6
- Self-Check Quiz, Chapter 4, Lesson 6

4-6 Lesson Notes

1 Focus

Vertical Alignment

Before Lesson 4-6 Identify and represent on a number line decimals, fractions, mixed numbers, and positive and negative numbers

Lesson 4-6
Compare and order positive and negative fractions, decimals, and mixed numbers and place them on a number line

After Lesson 4-6
Convert fractions to decimals and percents and use these representations in estimations, computations, and applications

2 Teach

GET READY

When they shade the grids, students should realize that they need to multiply the number of students who chose each sport by the same number that, when multiplied by the size of the sample, gives a product of 100.

Scaffolding Questions

Tell the class that you have 100 pennies.

Ask:

- If 17 of the pennies are from the 1980s, what fraction of the pennies is that? $\frac{17}{100}$
- If 29 of the pennies are from the 1990s, what fraction of the pennies is that? $\frac{29}{100}$
- If 4 of the pennies are from the 1960s, what fraction of the pennies is that? $\frac{1}{25}$

4-6 Fractions and Percents

MAIN IDEA

Write fractions as percents and percents as fractions.

IN Academic Standards

7.1.6 Identify, **write, rename, compare** and order **rational** and common irrational **numbers** and plot them on a number line. *Also addresses P.4.2.*

New Vocabulary

ratio
equivalent ratios

IN Math Online

glencoe.com

- Extra Examples
- Personal Tutor
- Self-Check Quiz

GET READY for the Lesson

In a recent survey, students were asked to choose their favorite sport to play. The results are shown in the table.

Sport	Number of Students
Basketball	3 out of 20
Football	3 out of 25
Gymnastics	1 out of 20
Swimming	9 out of 100

1. For each sport, shade a 10 × 10 grid that represents the number of students that chose the sport. See margin.
2. What fraction of the students chose swimming? $\frac{9}{100}$

A **ratio** is a comparison of two quantities by division. Ratios like 9 out of 100 can also be written as 9:100 or $\frac{9}{100}$. When a ratio compares a number to 100, it can be written as a **percent**.

Percent — Key Concept

Words A percent is a part to whole ratio that compares a number to 100.

Symbols $\frac{n}{100} = n\%$

Example

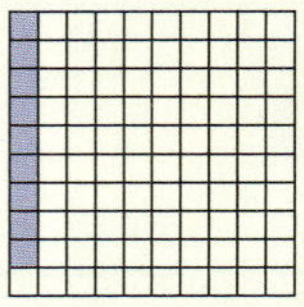

9 out of 100 = 9%

EXAMPLES Write Ratios as Percents

Write each ratio as a percent.

1 **Annie answered 90 out of 100 questions correctly.**

$\frac{90}{100} = 90\%$

Annie answered 90% of the questions correctly.

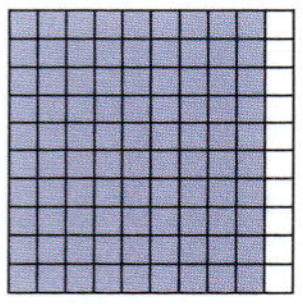

90%

2 **On average, 50.5 out of 100 students own a pet.**

$\frac{50.5}{100} = 50.5\%$

On average, 50.5% of the students own a pet.

Reading Math

Percent *Percent* means *per hundred* or *hundredths*. The symbol % means percent.

CHECK Your Progress

a. 45 out of 100 cars sold **45%**

b. $3.30:$100 spent on soft drinks **3.3%**

Additional Answer

1. 3 out of 20

3 out of 25

1 out of 20

9 out of 100

Study Tip

Percents In Chapter 6 you will learn another way to write percents that does not use equivalent fractions.

Fractions and percents are ratios that can represent the same number. You can write a fraction as a percent by finding an equivalent fraction with a denominator of 100.

EXAMPLE Write a Fraction as a Percent

3 **Write $\frac{3}{20}$ as a percent.**

First, find an equivalent fraction with a denominator of 100.
Then write the fraction as a percent.

$$\frac{3}{20} = \frac{3 \times 5}{20 \times 5} = \frac{15}{100} \text{ or } 15\%$$

So, $\frac{3}{20} = 15\%$.

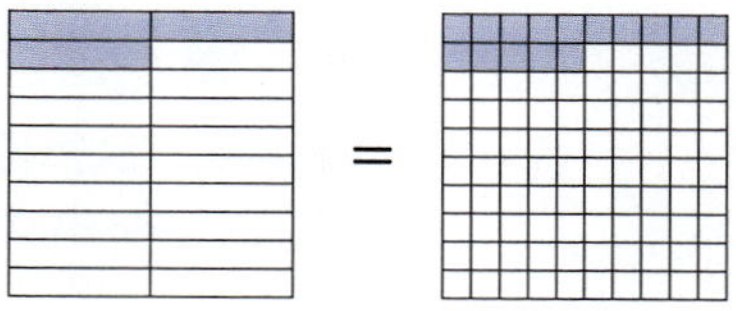

$\frac{3}{20} = \frac{15}{100}$

CHECK Your Progress

Write each fraction as a percent.

c. $\frac{17}{20}$ **85%** d. $\frac{3}{5}$ **60%** e. $\frac{2}{25}$ **8%**

Real-World EXAMPLE

4 **CHEESE In 0.5 ounce of colby cheese, 36 of the 50 Calories are from fat. What percent of the Calories are from fat?**

$\frac{36}{50} = \frac{72}{100}$ Write an equivalent fraction with a denominator of 100.

$= 72\%$ $\frac{72}{100} = 72\%$

About 72% of the Calories are from fat.

Real-World Link Almost 90% of all cheese sold in the United States is cheddar.
Source: Food Reference

CHECK Your Progress

f. **CHEESE** In a small piece of mozzarella cheese, 17 of the 25 Calories come from fat. What percent of the Calories come from fat? **68%**

EXAMPLE Write a Percent as a Fraction

5 **Write 48% as a fraction in simplest form.**

$48\% = \frac{48}{100}$ Definition of percent

$= \frac{12}{25}$ Simplify.

CHECK Your Progress

Write each percent as a fraction in simplest form.

g. 40% $\frac{2}{5}$ h. 6% $\frac{3}{50}$ i. 24% $\frac{6}{25}$

Focus on Mathematical Content

To **convert a percent to a fraction**, rewrite it as a fraction with a denominator of 100 and simplify.

Formative Assessment

Use the Check Your Progress exercises after each Example to determine students' understanding of concepts.

ADDITIONAL EXAMPLES

Write each ratio as a percent.

1. Diana scored 63 goals out of 100 attempts. 63%
2. In a survey, 31.9 out of 100 people preferred crunchy peanut butter. 31.9%
3. Write $\frac{16}{25}$ as a percent. 64%
4. **FISHING** William caught and released 20 trout on his fishing trip. Twelve of them were rainbow trout. What percent of the trout he caught were rainbow trout? 60%
5. Write 22% as a fraction in simplest form. $\frac{11}{50}$

Additional Examples are also in:

- Noteables™ Interactive Study Notebook with Foldables™
- Interactive Classroom PowerPoint® Presentations

Lesson 4-6 Fractions and Percents 203

3 Practice

Formative Assessment

Use Exercises 1–9 to check for understanding.

Then use the chart at the bottom of this page to customize your assignments for students.

Intervention You may wish to use the Study Guide and Intervention Master on page 40 of the *Chapter 4 Resource Masters* for additional reinforcement.

Odd/Even Assignments

Exercises 10–33 are structured so that students practice the same concepts whether they are assigned odd or even problems.

★ indicates multi-step problem

CHECK Your Understanding

Examples 1, 2 (p. 202)

Write each ratio as a percent.

1. 57 : 100 insects are spiders **57%**
2. \$29.20 per \$100 **29.2%**

Example 3 (p. 203)

Write each fraction as a percent.

3. $\frac{1}{4}$ **25%**
4. $\frac{6}{10}$ **60%**
5. $\frac{17}{20}$ **85%**

Example 4 (p. 203)

6. **TECHNOLOGY** Tansy used $\frac{2}{5}$ of the memory available on her flash drive. What percent of the memory did she use? **40%**

Example 5 (p. 203)

Write each percent as a fraction in simplest form.

7. 90% $\frac{9}{10}$
8. 75% $\frac{3}{4}$
9. 22% $\frac{11}{50}$

Practice and Problem Solving

HOMEWORK HELP

For Exercises	See Examples
10–15	1, 2
16–23	3
24–25	4
26–33	5

Exercise Levels
A: 10–33
B: 34–40
C: 41–44

Write each ratio as a percent.

10. 87 out of 100 books read **87%**
11. 42 per 100 teenagers **42%**
12. 12.2 out of 100 points earned **12.2%**
13. 99.9 : 100 miles driven **99.9%**
14. $11\frac{3}{4}$ out of 100 feet **$11\frac{3}{4}$%**
15. $66\frac{2}{3}$: 100 yards run **$66\frac{2}{3}$%**

Write each fraction as a percent.

16. $\frac{7}{10}$ **70%**
17. $\frac{16}{20}$ **80%**
18. $\frac{15}{25}$ **60%**
19. $\frac{13}{50}$ **26%**
20. $\frac{1}{5}$ **20%**
21. $\frac{3}{5}$ **60%**
22. $\frac{19}{20}$ **95%**
23. $\frac{10}{10}$ **100%**

24. **PETS** Twenty out of every 25 households own one dog. What percent of households own one dog? **80%**

25. **SPORTS** If 15 out of every 50 teens like to ski, what percent of teens like to ski? **30%**

Write each percent as a fraction in simplest form.

26. 45% $\frac{9}{20}$
27. 30% $\frac{3}{10}$
28. 62% $\frac{31}{50}$
29. 88% $\frac{22}{25}$
30. 68% $\frac{17}{25}$
31. 13% $\frac{13}{100}$
32. 2% $\frac{1}{50}$
33. 300% **3**

Replace each ● with >, <, or =.

34. $\frac{1}{4}$ ● 25% **=**
35. $\frac{9}{20}$ ● 55% **<**
36. 78% ● $\frac{3}{5}$ **>**
37. 38% ● $\frac{19}{50}$ **=**
38. 12% ● $1\frac{1}{5}$ **<**
39. $2\frac{2}{5}$ ● 24% **>**

40. ★ **VOLUNTEERING** A Girl Scouts event is expecting 40 out of 50 people to volunteer at a charity auction. So far 30 volunteers have arrived at the auction. What percent of the volunteers have not yet arrived? **25%**

Academic Standards • ISTEP+

Extra Practice, pp. 678, 708

DIFFERENTIATED HOMEWORK OPTIONS

Level	Assignment	Two-Day Option	
BL Basic	10–33, 41, 43–57	11–33 odd, 45, 46	10–32 even, 41, 43, 44, 47–57
OL Core	11–23 odd, 24, 25–39 odd, 40, 41, 43–57	10–33, 45, 46	34–41, 43, 44, 47–57
AL Advanced/Pre-AP	34–53, (optional: 54–57)		

H.O.T. Problems

42. You know that $12\frac{1}{2}\% = \frac{12\frac{1}{2}}{100}$ and that $\frac{12\frac{1}{2}}{100} = \frac{12.5}{100}$ or 0.125. Write 0.125 as $\frac{125}{1,000}$ and simplify $\frac{125}{1,000}$ to get $\frac{1}{8}$. So, $12\frac{1}{2}\% = \frac{1}{8}$

43. 5%; the other ratios equal 25%

41. **GEOMETRY** What percent of the larger rectangle shown is *not* shaded? **64%**

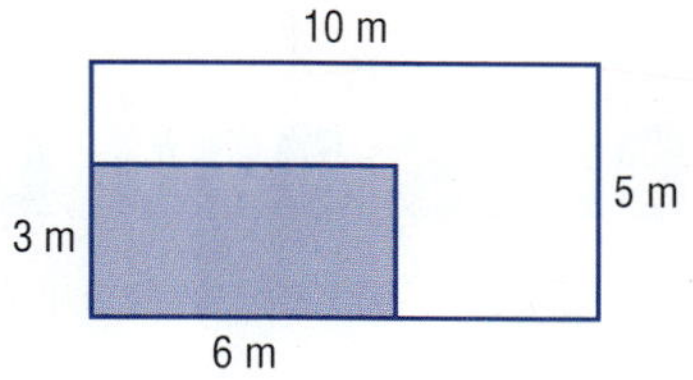

42. **CHALLENGE** Apply what you know about percents, fractions, and decimals to write $12\frac{1}{2}\%$ as a fraction. Justify your answer.

43. **Which One Doesn't Belong?** Identify the ratio that does not have the same value as the other three. Explain your reasoning.

$\frac{5}{20}$	5%	$\frac{1}{4}$	50 out of 200

44. **WRITING IN MATH** Explain how you know which model represents 36%. Then explain why that model also represents $\frac{9}{25}$. **See margin.**

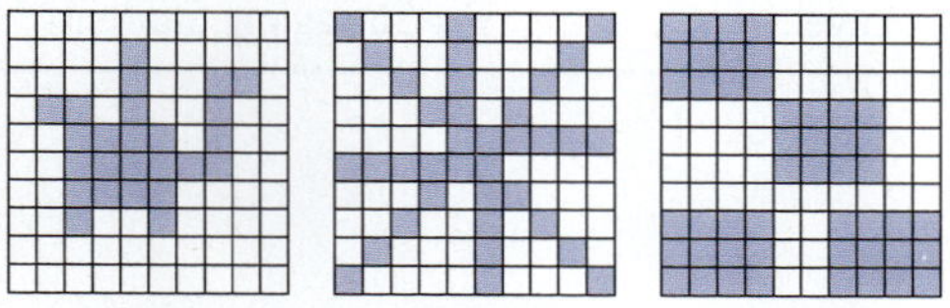

Model 1 Model 2 Model 3

ISTEP+ PRACTICE 7.1.6

45. What percent of the model is shaded? **C**

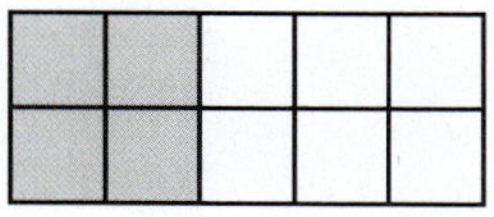

A 25%
B 30%
C 40%
D 60%

46. Cats spend about $\frac{3}{10}$ of their time awake grooming themselves. Which number is equivalent to $\frac{3}{10}$? **G**

F 3%
G 30%
H 33.3%
J 300%

Spiral Review

Write each decimal as a fraction or mixed number in simplest form. (Lesson 4-5)

47. 0.6 $\frac{3}{5}$

48. 0.15 $\frac{3}{20}$

49. 2.8 $2\frac{4}{5}$

50. **TIME** The drive to a football game took 56 minutes. Twenty-four minutes of the time was spent stopped in traffic. What fraction of the drive, in simplest form, was spent in stopped traffic? (Lesson 4-4) $\frac{3}{7}$

Solve each equation. (Lesson 3-2)

51. $x + 7 = 10$ **3**

52. $m - 2 = 8$ **10**

53. $12 + a = 16$ **4**

GET READY for the Next Lesson

PREREQUISITE SKILL **Multiply or divide.** (Pages 675, 676)

54. 16.2×10 **162**

55. 0.71×100 **71**

56. $14.4 \div 100$ **0.144**

57. $791 \div 1,000$ **0.791**

4 Assess

Crystal Ball Tell students that tomorrow's lesson is about writing percents as decimals and writing decimals as percents. Ask them to write how they think what they learned today will connect with tomorrow's material.

Additional Answer

44. Sample answer: To find the percent that is shaded, you can count the number of squares that are shaded. In Model 2, 36 out of 100 or 36% of the squares are shaded. Since $\frac{36}{100} = \frac{9}{25}$, the fraction $\frac{9}{25}$ represents what portion of the model is shaded.

Differentiated Instruction

Verbal/Linguistic Learners Have students work in pairs or groups to choose a section in a novel. Have each pair or group make a tally chart of the first 50 vowels in the section. Then have them write each vowel's fraction of the total vowels. Finally, have them convert the fractions to percents. Have each group present its data. Which vowel is most common?

Lesson 4-6 Fractions and Percents 205

4-7 Percents and Decimals

PACING: **Regular:** 1 period, **Block:** 0.5 period

IN Academic Standards **7.1.6** Identify, write, **rename, compare** and order **rational** and common irrational **numbers** and plot them on a number line. *Also addresses P.4.2.*

Options for Differentiated Instruction

ELL = English Language Learner AL = Above or Beyond Grade Level SS = Struggling Students SN = Special Needs

Clarifying the Concept SS

Use after presenting Example 1.

Students may become confused when percents have a decimal component, such as 55.8%. Remind students that such a percent can be converted to a decimal in the standard way: removing the % symbol, dividing by 100, and moving the decimal two places to the left.

55.8% = 0.558

Kinesthetic Learners ELL AL

Use after presenting the Examples.

Have students find six numbers that are between 0 and 1, of which two are decimals, two are fractions, and two are percents. Examples of six such numbers are shown below.

0.65	0.08	$\frac{3}{8}$	$\frac{1}{2}$	15%	42%

Have them write the numbers in order from least to greatest on a separate sheet of paper. Then have them write each number on a separate index card and shuffle the cards. Students should exchange sets of cards with a classmate, and order each other's set.

Relating to Everyday Concepts ELL AL

Use after presenting Lesson 4-7.

Use the concept that coins are percents of a dollar to reinforce the relationship among decimals, fractions, and percents.

- Have students use combinations of coins to make different money amounts.
- Help students write these amounts in dollar-and-cents notation, as fractions of a dollar, and as percents of a dollar.
- Have them organize their work in a table like the one below.

Coins	Dollars/Cents ($)	Fraction of a Dollar	Percent of a Dollar
2 dimes, 2 pennies	0.22	$\frac{22}{100}$	22%

Leveled Lesson Resources

Also on TeacherWorks™ Lesson 4-7

Chapter 4 Resource Masters

BL = Below or Approaching Grade Level OL = On Grade Level AL = Above or Beyond Grade Level ELL = English Language Learner

Lesson Reading Guide
p. 45 BL OL ELL

NAME ________ DATE ________ PERIOD ____

4-7 Lesson Reading Guide
Percents and Decimals

Get Ready for the Lesson

Read the introduction at the top of page 206 in your textbook. Write your answers below.

1. Write the percent of students who chose black as a fraction. $\frac{36}{100}$ or $\frac{9}{25}$
2. Write the fraction as a decimal. 0.36
3. What do you notice about the percent and decimal forms for students who chose black? Sample answer: They include the same digits.

Read the Lesson

4. Describe each step in changing a percent to a decimal. Sample answer: 1) Write the percent as a fraction with the denominator equal to 100. 2) Write the fraction as a decimal, moving the decimal point two places to the left.
5. Describe each step in changing a percent to a decimal by first writing the percent as a fraction. Sample answer: 1) Write the percent as a fraction with the denominator equal to 100. 2) If necessary, multiply the numerator and denominator by a power of 10 to remove a decimal in the numerator. Then simplify. 3) Write the fraction as a decimal.
6. Describe how to write a percent as a decimal without writing the percent as a fraction. Sample answer: 1) Write any fractions as decimals. 2) Divide by 100 (move the decimal point two places to the left). 3) Remove the % symbol.

Remember What You Learned

7. Work with a partner. Think of a way that will help you remember which way to move the decimal when you go from a percent to a decimal and which way to move it when you go from a decimal to a percent. See students' work.

Lesson 4-7

Chapter 4 45 Course 2

Study Guide and Intervention*
p. 46 BL OL ELL

NAME ________ DATE ________ PERIOD ____

4-7 Study Guide and Intervention
Percents and Decimals

To write a percent as a decimal, divide the percent by 100 and remove the percent symbol. To write a decimal as a percent, multiply the decimal by 100 and add the percent symbol.

Example 1 Write 42.5% as a decimal.

$42.5\% = \frac{42.5}{100}$ Write the percent as a fraction.
$= \frac{42.5 \times 10}{100 \times 10}$ Multiply by 10 to remove the decimal in the numerator.
$= \frac{425}{1{,}000}$ Simplify.
$= 0.425$ Write the fraction as a decimal.

Example 2 Write 0.625 as a percent.

0.625 = 062.5 Multiply by 100.
= 62.5% Add the % symbol.

Exercises

Write each percent as a decimal.

1. 6% 0.06	2. 28% 0.28
3. 81% 0.81	4. 84% 0.84
5. 35.5% 0.355	6. 12.5% 0.125
7. 14.2% 0.142	8. 11.1% 0.111

Write each decimal as a percent.

9. 0.47 47%	10. 0.03 3%
11. 0.075 7.5%	12. 0.914 91.4%

Chapter 4 46 Course 2

Skills Practice*
p. 47 BL OL

NAME ________ DATE ________ PERIOD ____

4-7 Skills Practice
Percents and Decimals

Write each percent as a decimal.

1. 5% 0.05	2. 20% 0.2
3. 21% 0.21	4. 83% 0.83
5. 7% 0.07	6. 56% 0.56
7. 16% 0.16	8. 45% 0.45
9. 27.3% 0.273	10. 14.9% 0.149
11. 91.5% 0.915	12. 29.3% 0.293
13. 14.4% 0.144	14. 80% 0.8
15. 7.5% 0.075	16. $10\frac{1}{2}$% 0.105

Write each decimal as a percent.

17. 0.06 6%	18. 0.13 13%
19. 0.5 50%	20. 0.74 74%
21. 0.14 14%	22. 0.92 92%
23. 0.54 54%	24. 0.66 66%
25. 0.192 19.2%	26. 0.295 29.5%
27. 0.911 91.1%	28. 0.247 24.7%
29. 0.4165 41.65%	30. 0.2199 21.99%
31. 0.7601 76.01%	32. 0.4833 48.33%

Chapter 4 47 Course 2

Practice*
p. 48 OL AL

NAME ________ DATE ________ PERIOD ____

4-7 Practice
Percents and Decimals

Write each percent as a decimal.

1. 35% 0.35	2. 90% 0.90	3. 5% 0.05	4. 1% 0.01
5. 21.8% 0.218	6. 64.8% 0.648	7. 4.1% 0.041	8. 8.5% 0.085
9. $39\frac{21}{50}$% 0.3942	10. $17\frac{2}{5}$% 0.174	11. $40\frac{3}{4}$% 0.4075	12. $88\frac{3}{5}$% 0.886

Write each decimal as a percent.

13. 0.4 40%	14. 0.8 80%	15. 3.7 370%	16. 9.1 910%
17. 0.77 77%	18. 0.03 3%	19. 0.25 25%	20. 0.59 59%
21. 0.375 37.5%	22. 0.123 12.3%	23. 0.005 0.5%	24. 0.6019 60.19%

Replace each ● with >, <, or = to make a true sentence.

25. 1.5 ● 15% >	26. 0.88 ● 8.8% >	27. 33% ● 0.33 =
28. 90% ● 0.09 >	29. 0.26 ● 27% <	30. 65.4% ● 0.645 >

ANALYZE TABLES For Exercises 31–33, use the table and the information given.

The table lists the approximate milk fat content of 5 types of milk products.

31. Which product has the highest milk fat content? heavy cream
32. Find the approximate number of grams of milk fat in a 200-gram serving of whole milk. 7 grams
33. Which milk product will have approximately 15.36 grams of milk fat in an 80-gram serving? light cream

Milk Product	Percent Milk Fat
Heavy Cream	36.7%
Light Cream	19.2%
Whole Milk	3.5%
Low-Fat Milk	1.5%
Skim Milk	0.05%

Chapter 4 48 Course 2

Word Problem Practice*
p. 49 OL AL

NAME ________ DATE ________ PERIOD ____

4-7 Word Problem Practice
Percents and Decimals

1. AREA New Mexico's land area is about 0.03 of the total area of the United States. What percent is New Mexico's land area of the total area of the United States? 3%
2. SCALE MODEL A scale model of a building is 0.25 the actual size. What percent of the actual size of the building is the model? 25%
3. NFL COACHES Don Shula ranks among the most successful coaches in the National Football League. In his career, he won 0.665 of his games. Write the decimal as a percent. 66.5%
4. SOFTBALL Jenny's batting average is 0.346. Write the decimal as a percent. 34.6%
5. VITAMINS A multiple vitamin contains 450 milligrams of calcium. This is 45% of the recommended daily allowance. Write the percent as a decimal. 0.45
6. BASKETBALL Tao makes 74% of his free throws. Write the percent as a decimal. 0.74
7. SALES TAX The sales tax in a town is 7.25%. Write the percent as a decimal. 0.0725
8. FIELD TRIP In Ms. Silver's English class, $20\frac{1}{4}$% of the students signed up to visit a local museum. Write the percent as a decimal. 0.2025

Lesson 4-7

Chapter 4 49 Course 2

Enrichment
p. 50 OL AL

NAME ________ DATE ________ PERIOD ____

4-7 Enrichment

African-American Scientists and Inventors

When you buy a pair of shoes, you usually have a wide variety of styles, sizes, and prices to choose from. It is the work of an African-American inventor, Jan Matzeliger (1852–1889), that makes this possible. In 1882, Matzeliger patented a *lasting machine* that could shape the upper portion of a shoe and attach it to the sole in a fraction of the time it took to do the job by hand. Using this machine, shoe manufacturers were able to increase production and reduce prices dramatically.

African Americans have made many significant contributions to mathematics, science, and invention. By solving the percent problems and matching the problem and the correct solution, you will learn more about just a few of them.

Solutions
A. 20 Benjamin Banneker
B. 21 Majorie Lee Browne
C. 18 Lewis Latimer
D. 17.5 Jane Cooke Wright

1. 35% of 50 is what number? This physician researched and tested chemotherapy as a method of treating cancer. In 1952, she became head of the Cancer Research Foundation at Harlem Hospital. D
2. What percent of 75 is 15? This mathematician was part of the team of surveyors who created the street plan for Washington, D.C. in the late eighteenth century. A
3. 4.5% of 400 is what number? In 1876, this engineer drew up the plans that accompanied Alexander Graham Bell's application for a patent on the telephone. C
4. 120% of what number is 25.2? In 1949, she became one of the first two African-American women to earn a doctorate in mathematics. She was head of the mathematics department at North Carolina Central University from 1951 to 1970. B

Chapter 4 50 Course 2

** Also available in Spanish* ELL

Additional Lesson Resources

Transparencies
- *5-Minute Check Transparency*, Lesson 4-7

Other Print Products
- *Noteables™ Interactive Study Notebook with Foldables™*

Teacher Tech Tools
- *Interactive Classroom CD-ROM*, Lesson 4-7
- *AssignmentWorks*, Lesson 4-7

Student Tech Tools
glencoe.com
- Extra Examples, Chapter 4, Lesson 7
- Self-Check Quiz, Chapter 4, Lesson 7

4-7 Lesson Notes

1 Focus

Vertical Alignment

Before Lesson 4-7
Identify and represent on a number line decimals, fractions, mixed numbers, and positive and negative numbers

Lesson 4-7
Compare and order positive and negative fractions, decimals, and mixed numbers and place them on a number line

After Lesson 4-7
Convert fractions to decimals and percents and use these representations in estimations, computations, and applications

2 Teach

Scaffolding Questions

Ask:

- What fraction, in simplest form, is equivalent to 50%? $\frac{1}{2}$
- What fraction, in simplest form, is equivalent to 25%? $\frac{1}{4}$
- What fraction, in simplest form, is equivalent to 80%? $\frac{4}{5}$

ADDITIONAL EXAMPLE

1 Write 47.8% as a decimal. 0.478

Additional Examples are also in:

- Noteables™ Interactive Study Notebook with Foldables™
- Interactive Classroom PowerPoint® Presentations

4-7 Percents and Decimals

MAIN IDEA

Write percents as decimals and decimals as percents.

IN Academic Standards

7.1.6 Identify, write, **rename, compare** and order **rational** and common irrational **numbers** and plot them on a number line. *Also addresses P.4.2.*

IN Math Online

glencoe.com

- Concepts in Motion
- Extra Examples
- Personal Tutor
- Self-Check Quiz

GET READY for the Lesson

SCHOOL UNIFORMS The graph shows students' favorite school uniform colors.

Favorite School Uniform Colors

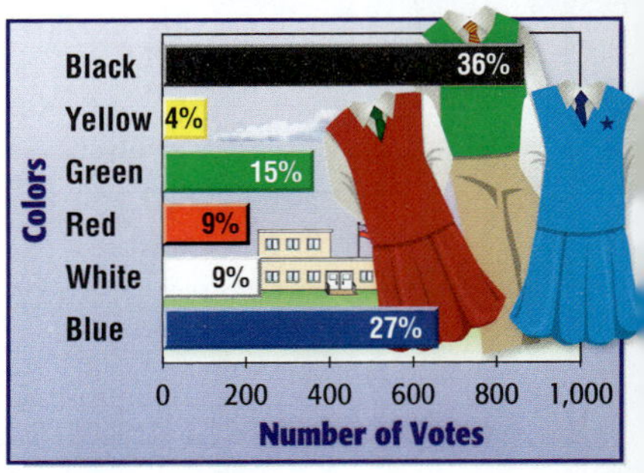

Source: *Kids USA Survey*

1. Write the percent of students who chose black as a fraction. $\frac{36}{100}$ or $\frac{9}{25}$
2. Write the fraction as a decimal. 0.36
3. What do you notice about the percent and decimal form for students who chose black? Sample answer: They include the same digits.

Any percent can be written as a fraction with the percent as the numerator and 100 as the denominator. Use this fact to help write percents as decimals.

EXAMPLE Write Percents as Decimals

1 **Write 7% as a decimal.**

METHOD 1 Write the percent as a fraction.

$7\% = \frac{7}{100}$ Write the percent as a fraction.

$= 0.07$ Write the fraction as a decimal.

METHOD 2 Divide mentally.

The % symbol means to divide by 100. So, remove the % symbol and divide by 100.

$7\% = .07$ Remove the % symbol and divide by 100. Add placeholder zero.

$= 0.07$ Add leading zero.

So, $7\% = 0.07$.

CHOOSE Your Method

Write each percent as a decimal.

a. 8% 0.08 b. 54% 0.54 c. 85.2% 0.852

Formative Assessment

Use the Check Your Progress exercises after each Example to determine students' understanding of concepts.

Real-World EXAMPLE

2 **GEOGRAPHY** **Alaska is the largest state, making up about $16\frac{1}{10}\%$ of the land area of the United States. Write this amount as a decimal.**

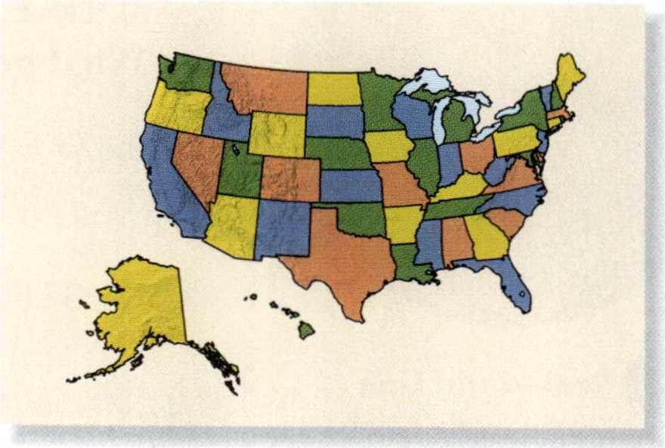

$16\frac{1}{10}\% = 16.1\%$ Write $\frac{1}{10}$ as 0.1.

$= 16.1$ Remove the % symbol and divide by 100.

$= 0.161$ Add leading zero.

So, $16\frac{1}{10}\% = 0.161$.

CHECK Your Progress

d. **GEOGRAPHY** About $6\frac{4}{5}\%$ of the total area of the United States is water. What decimal represents this amount? **0.068**

e. **GEOGRAPHY** The total area of Australia is about $38\frac{11}{20}\%$ of the total area of North America. Write the amount as a decimal. **0.3855**

EXAMPLE Write Decimals as Percents

3 **Write 0.4 as a percent.**

METHOD 1 **Write the decimal as a fraction.**

$0.4 = \frac{4}{10}$ or $\frac{40}{100}$ Write the decimal as a fraction.

$= 40\%$ Write the fraction as a percent.

METHOD 2 **Multiply mentally.**

Multiply by 100 and add the % symbol.

$0.4 = 0.40$ Multiply by 100. Add a placeholder zero.

$= 40\%$ Add the % symbol.

So, $0.4 = 40\%$.

Study Tip

Multiplication When multiplying by 100, the decimal point moves two places right.

CHOOSE Your Method

Write each decimal as a percent.

f. 0.5 **50%**

g. 0.34 **34%**

h. 0.98 **98%**

ADDITIONAL EXAMPLES

2 **POPULATION** According to the Administration on Aging, about $28\frac{1}{5}\%$ of the population of the United States is 19 years of age or younger. Write $28\frac{1}{5}\%$ as a decimal. 0.282

3 Write 0.33 as a percent. 33%

Focus on Mathematical Content

Any **percent** can be written as a fraction, and any fraction can be written as a **decimal**.

To **write a decimal as a percent**, multiply by 100, which is the same as moving the decimal two places to the right.

To **write a percent as a decimal**, divide by 100, which is the same as moving the decimal two places to the left.

Lesson 4-7 Percents and Decimals **207**

ADDITIONAL EXAMPLE

4 **POPULATION** In 1790, about 0.05 of the population of the United States lived in an urban setting. Write 0.05 as a percent. 5%

3 Practice

Formative Assessment

Use Exercises 1–8 to check for understanding.

Then use the chart at the bottom of the next page to customize your assignments for students.

Intervention You may wish to use the Study Guide and Intervention Master on page 46 of the *Chapter 4 Resource Masters* for additional reinforcement.

Tips for New Teachers — Mental Math

Encourage students to use mental math whenever possible when writing percents as decimals and decimals as percents. When writing a percent as a decimal, remind them to remove the percent symbol and divide by 100 by moving the decimal point two places to the left. When writing a decimal as a percent, remind them to add the percent symbol and multiply by 100 by moving the decimal point two places to the right.

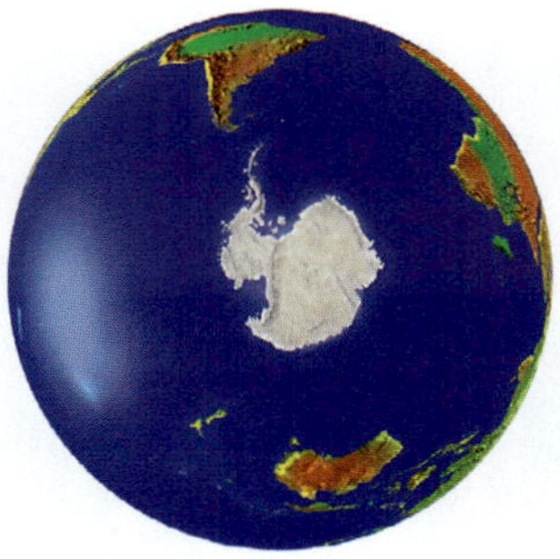

Real-World Link Of the world's icebergs, 93% are found surrounding the Antarctic.
Source: JPL Polar Oceanography Group

Real-World EXAMPLE

4 **SCIENCE** **About 0.875 of an iceberg's mass is underwater. What percent of an iceberg's mass is underwater?**

$0.875 = 0.875$ Multiply by 100.

$= 87.5\%$ Add the % symbol.

So, 87.5% of an iceberg's mass is underwater.

CHECK Your Progress

i. **EXERCISE** Each day, Rico and his dog walk 0.625 mile. What percent of a mile do they walk? 62.5%

Percent as a Decimal — Key Concept

To write a percent as a decimal, divide the percent by 100 and remove the percent symbol.

25% = .25 or 0.25

Decimal as a Percent — Key Concept

To write a decimal as a percent, multiply the percent by 100 and add the percent symbol.

0.58 = 0.58 = 58%

★ indicates multi-step problem

CHECK Your Understanding

Example 1 (p. 206) **Write each percent as a decimal.**

1. 68% 0.68
2. 5% 0.05
3. 27.6% 0.276

Example 2 (p. 207)

4. **SPENDING** A family spends about $33\frac{2}{5}\%$ of their annual income on housing. What decimal represents the amount spent on housing? 0.334

Example 3 (p. 207) **Write each decimal as a percent.**

5. 0.09 9%
6. 0.3 30%
7. 0.73 73%

Example 4 (p. 208)

8. **BASKETBALL** The table shows the top five WNBA players with the highest free throw averages. What percent of the time does Sue Bird make a free throw? 87.8%

Player	Average
Eva Nemcova	0.897
Seimone Augustus	0.897
Elena Tornikidou	0.882
Sue Bird	0.878
Cynthia Cooper	0.871

Source: Women's National Basketball Association

208 Chapter 4 Fractions, Decimals, and Percents

Practice and Problem Solving

HOMEWORK HELP	
For Exercises	See Examples
9–20	1
21–22	2
23–34	3
35–37	4

Exercise Levels
A: 9–37
B: 38–48
C: 49–54

Write each percent as a decimal.

9. 27% **0.27**
10. 70% **0.7**
11. 6% **0.06**
12. 4% **0.04**
13. 18.5% **0.185**
14. 56.4% **0.564**
15. 2.2% **0.022**
16. 3.8% **0.038**
17. $27\frac{7}{10}\%$ **0.277**
18. $15\frac{1}{2}\%$ **0.155**
19. $30\frac{1}{4}\%$ **0.3025**
20. $46\frac{2}{5}\%$ **0.464**
21. **BONES** An adult human body has $68\frac{3}{5}\%$ of the number of bones it had at birth. What decimal represents this amount? **0.686**
22. **VIDEO GAMES** Brian reaches the sixth level of a video game $92\frac{3}{4}\%$ of the time he plays. What decimal represents this percent? **0.9275**

Write each decimal as a percent.

23. 0.7 **70%**
24. 0.6 **60%**
25. 5.8 **580%**
26. 8.2 **820%**
27. 0.95 **95%**
28. 0.08 **8%**
29. 0.17 **17%**
30. 0.78 **78%**
31. 0.675 **67.5%**
32. 0.145 **14.5%**
33. 0.012 **1.2%**
34. 0.7025 **70.25%**

BASEBALL **The table shows the top five Major League Baseball players with the highest batting averages in a recent year. Express each player's batting average as a percent.**

Player	Average
Joe Mauer	0.347
Freddy Sanchez	0.344
Derek Jeter	0.344
Robinson Cano	0.342
Miguel Cabrera	0.339

Source: Major League Baseball

35. Joe Mauer **34.7%**
36. Derek Jeter **34.4%**
37. Miguel Cabrera **33.9%**

Replace each ● with >, <, or = to make a true sentence.

38. 0.25% ● 0.125 **<**
39. 0.76 ● 76.5% **<**
40. 500% ● 50 **<**
41. 99% ● 0.985 **>**
42. 0.325 ● 30% **>**
43. 56% ● 0.5625 **<**

★ 44. **SPORTS** A tennis player won 0.805 of the matches she played. What percent of the matches did she lose? **19.5%**

ANALYZE TABLES **For Exercises 45–48, use the table and the information given.**

Model airplane measurements are based on a scale of the life-size original. For example, a scale of $\frac{1}{72}$ is about 1% of the size of the original. Percents are rounded to the nearest thousandth.

Scale	Percent Equivalent
$\frac{1}{72}$	1.389%
$\frac{1}{24}$	4.167%
$\frac{1}{48}$	2.083%
$\frac{1}{20}$	5%
$\frac{1}{32}$	3.125%

45. Find the decimal equivalents for each scale.
46. Which scale is the smallest? $\frac{1}{72}$
47. About how long is a model of an actual 88.5-foot C-119 boxcar plane using a $\frac{1}{72}$ scale? **1.2 ft**
48. Which scale is used if a model of an 88.5-foot C-119 boxcar plane is about 33.1875 inches long? $\frac{1}{32}$

45. 0.01389, 0.04167, 0.02083, 0.05, 0.03125

Academic Standards • ISTEP+

Extra Practice, pp. 678, 708

Odd/Even Assignments

Exercises 9–37 are structured so that students practice the same concepts whether they are assigned odd or even problems.

Tips for New Teachers — Percents

You may need to remind students that when a percent is written as a mixed number (such as $4\frac{1}{5}\%$), they should first rewrite the fractional part as a decimal (such as 4.2%).

DIFFERENTIATED HOMEWORK OPTIONS

Level	Assignment	Two-Day Option	
BL Basic	9–37, 49–50, 54–66	9–37 odd, 55, 56	10–36 even, 49–50, 54, 57–66
OL Core	9–21 odd, 22, 23–33 odd, 35–37, 39–43 odd, 44–50, 54–66	9–37, 55, 56	38–50, 54, 57–66
AL Advanced /Pre-AP	38–62 (optional: 63–66)		

Exercise Alert!

Find the Error In Exercise 50, Emilio is correct. Janelle incorrectly divided the decimal by 100, thus moving the decimal point two places to the left. Remind students that when writing a decimal as a percent, they need to multiply by 100, moving the decimal two places to the right.

4 Assess

Ticket Out the Door Have students invent a real-world ratio (such as red cars:total cars in a parking lot) and then write the equivalent fraction, decimal, and percent.

Formative Assessment

Check for student understanding of concepts in Lessons 4-6 and 4-7.

CRM Quiz 3, p. 68

FOLDABLES Study Organizer Foldables™ Follow-Up

Remind students to write—under the tab for this lesson of their Foldables—the answer to the question they wrote about the lesson.

Additional Answer

64. $2 \times 2 \times 2 \times 2 \times 2$

H.O.T. Problems

49. OPEN ENDED Write any decimal between 0 and 1. Then write it as a fraction in simplest form and as a percent. **Sample answer: 0.25, $\frac{1}{4}$, 25%**

50. FIND THE ERROR Emilio and Janelle both wrote 0.992 as a percent. Who is correct? Explain.

50. Emilio; Janelle divided by 100 instead of multiplying by 100.

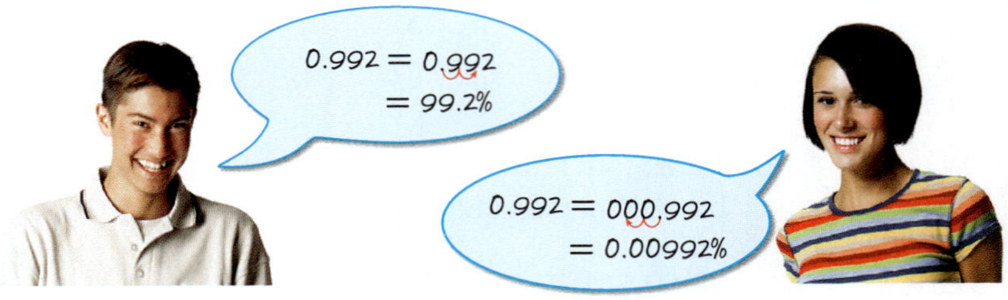

Emilio Janelle

CHALLENGE Write each fraction as a percent.

51. $\frac{3}{8}$ **37.5%** **52.** $\frac{1}{40}$ **2.5%** **53.** $\frac{1}{32}$ **3.125%**

54. WRITING IN MATH Write a word problem about a real-world situation in which you would change a decimal to a percent.

54. Sample answer: Amelia received a 0.95 on her quiz. What percent is this?

ISTEP+ PRACTICE 7.1.6

55. It is estimated that 13.9% of the population of Texas was born outside the United States. Which number is *not* equivalent to 13.9%? **D**

A $\frac{139}{1,000}$ C 0.139

B $\frac{13.9}{100}$ D 1.39

56. Which of the following is ordered from least to greatest? **G**

F 0.42, $\frac{2}{5}$, 50%, $\frac{3}{4}$

G $\frac{2}{5}$, 0.42, 50%, $\frac{3}{4}$

H $\frac{3}{4}$, $\frac{2}{5}$, 0.42%, 50%

J $\frac{3}{4}$, 0.42, $\frac{2}{5}$, 50%

Spiral Review

Write each ratio as a percent. (Lesson 4-6)

57. 72 out of 100 animals **72%** **58.** \$9.90:\$100 **9.9%** **59.** 3.1 out of 100 households **3.1%**

60. Write $9\frac{3}{8}$ as a decimal. (Lesson 4-5) **9.375**

61. AIRPLANES Write an integer that represents an airplane descending 125 feet. (Lesson 2-1) **−125**

★ **62. MONEY** Marina earned \$187.50 by working 30 hours. If she works 35 hours at this rate, how much will she earn? (Lesson 1-1) **\$218.75**

GET READY for the Next Lesson

PREREQUISITE SKILL Write the prime factorization of each number. (Lesson 4-1)

63. 50 **$2 \times 5 \times 5$** **64.** 32 **See margin.** **65.** 76 **$2 \times 2 \times 19$** **66.** 105 **$3 \times 5 \times 7$**

210 Chapter 4 Fractions, Decimals, and Percents

4-8 Least Common Multiple

PACING: **Regular:** 2 periods, **Block:** 1 period

IN Academic Standards **7.1.3 Recognize the prime factors of a number and find the prime factorization of whole numbers and write the results using exponents.** *Also addresses 7.1.2.*

Options for Differentiated Instruction

ELL = English Language Learner AL = Above or Beyond Grade Level SS = Struggling Students SN = Special Needs

Organizing Student Work and Thinking ELL SS SN

Use before assigning the Exercises.

Have students get out the ring of factor cards that they made in Lesson 4-2. On the blank side of each card, have students list the first ten multiples of the number that is written on the front of the card.

Multiples of 8
8, 16, 24, 32, 40, 48, 56, 64, 72, 80

Making Conjectures AL

Use after presenting Lesson 4-8.

Have students find the LCM and GCF for two numbers, the product of the two numbers, and the product of their GCF and LCM.

Ask:

What do you notice? Both products are equal.

Repeat, using other pairs of numbers.

Ask:

What conclusions, if any, can you make? The product of any two numbers equals the product of their GCF and LCM.

Kinesthetic Learners ELL SS

Use after presenting Lesson 4-8.

Write the numbers 3, 5, 10, and 15 on index cards, one number per card. Have students in groups of four each take a card. Looking at a clock with a second hand, have students tap their pencils at 3, 5, 10, or 15 seconds, depending on their card. Stop when all four members tap their pencils at the same time.

Ask:

- How many seconds did this take? 30 s
- What is the LCM of 3, 5, 10, and 15? 30

Leveled Lesson Resources

Also on TeacherWorks™ Lesson 4-8

Chapter 4 Resource Masters

BL = Below or Approaching Grade Level OL = On Grade Level AL = Above or Beyond Grade Level ELL = English Language Learner

Lesson Reading Guide
p. 51 BL OL ELL

NAME ____________ DATE ________ PERIOD ____

4-8 Lesson Reading Guide

Least Common Multiple

Get Ready for the Lesson

Complete the Mini Lab at the top of page 211 in your textbook. Write your answers below.

1. Add a second row to each prism. Record the total number of cubes used in a table like the one shown below.

Number of Rows	1	2	3	4
Cubes in Prism A	4	8	12	16
Cubes in Prism B	6	12	18	24

2. Add rows until each prism has four rows.
3. Describe two prisms that have the same number of cubes. **Both prisms have the same number of cubes when Prism A has 4 rows and Prism B has 3 rows.**
4. If you keep adding rows, will the two prisms have the same number of cubes again? Explain. **Yes; Sample answer: Every fourth row in Prism A will have the same number of cubes as every third row in Prism B.**

Read the Lesson

5. What is a least common multiple of two or more numbers? **It is the least of their common multiples excluding zero.**
6. Describe, in your own words, the first method used to find the LCM in Example 1 at the bottom of page 211. **Method one requires listing several multiples of 6 and 10 and looking for the least common of the multiples.**

Remember What You Learned

7. Explain how to find the LCM of two or more numbers when you know the prime factorization of each number. Give an example. **Sample answer: The LCM is the product of the greatest powers of each of the prime factors; to find the LCM of 16 and 18, first find the prime factorization of each number: $16 = 2 \times 2 \times 2 \times 2 = 2^4$ and $18 = 2 \times 3 \times 3 = 2 \times 3^2$. Then the LCM is the product of the greatest power of 2 and the greatest power of 3, or $2^4 \times 3^2 = 144$.**

Lesson 4–8

Chapter 4 51 Course 2

Study Guide and Intervention*
p. 52 BL OL ELL

NAME ____________ DATE ________ PERIOD ____

4-8 Study Guide and Intervention

Least Common Multiple

A **multiple** of a number is the product of that number and any whole number. The least nonzero multiple of two or more numbers is the **least common multiple (LCM)** of the numbers.

Example 1 **Find the LCM of 15 and 20 by listing multiples.**

List the multiples.

multiples of 15: 15, 30, 45, **60**, 75, 90, 105, **120**, ...

multiples of 20: 20, 40, **60**, 80, 100, **120**, 140, ...

Notice that 60, 120, ..., are common multiples. So, the LCM of 15 and 20 is 60.

Example 2 **Find the LCM of 8 and 12 using prime factors.**

Write the prime factorization.

$8 = 2 \times 2 \times 2 = 2^3$

$12 = 2 \times 2 \times 3 = 2^2 \times 3$

The prime factors of 8 and 12 are 2 and 3.
Multiply the greatest power of both 2 and 3.

The LCM of 8 and 12 is $2^3 \times 3$, or 24.

Exercises

Find the LCM of each set of numbers.

1. 4, 6 **12**
2. 6, 9 **18**
3. 5, 9 **45**
4. 8, 10 **40**
5. 12, 15 **60**
6. 15, 21 **105**
7. 4, 15 **60**
8. 8, 20 **40**
9. 8, 16 **16**
10. 6, 14 **42**
11. 12, 20 **60**
12. 9, 12 **36**
13. 14, 21 **42**
14. 6, 15 **30**
15. 4, 6, 8 **24**
16. 3, 5, 6 **30**

Chapter 4 52 Course 2

Skills Practice*
p. 53 BL OL

NAME ____________ DATE ________ PERIOD ____

4-8 Skills Practice

Least Common Multiple

Find the LCM of each set of numbers.

1. 2, 8 **8**
2. 6, 10 **30**
3. 10, 11 **110**
4. 10, 12 **60**
5. 9, 18 **18**
6. 4, 22 **44**
7. 12, 30 **60**
8. 4, 13 **52**
9. 25, 30 **150**
10. 250, 30 **750**
11. 200, 18 **1,800**
12. 70, 90 **630**
13. 18, 54 **54**
14. 30, 65 **390**
15. 180, 252 **1,260**
16. 20, 55 **220**
17. 21, 60 **420**
18. 3, 5, 10 **30**
19. 3, 4, 13 **156**
20. 4, 10, 12 **60**
21. 6, 15, 20 **60**
22. 48, 16, 3 **48**
23. 66, 55, 44 **660**
24. 29, 58, 4 **116**

Lesson 4–8

Chapter 4 53 Course 2

Practice*
p. 54 OL AL

NAME ____________ DATE ________ PERIOD ____

4-8 Practice

Least Common Multiple

Find the LCM of each set of numbers.

1. 8, 12 **24**
2. 10, 25 **50**
3. 12, 18 **36**
4. 20, 30 **60**
5. 8, 9 **72**
6. 15, 35 **105**
7. 3, 5, 7 **105**
8. 4, 10, 12 **60**
9. 9, 12, 15 **180**
10. 5, 15, 20 **60**
11. 14, 21, 42 **42**
12. 15, 18, 30 **90**
13. 2 feet, 1 yard **2 yards or 6 feet**
14. 6¢, 18¢, 24¢ **72¢**
15. 40 seconds, 1 minute **2 minutes**

Write two numbers whose LCM is the given number.

16. 24 **Sample answer: 3 and 8**
17. 63 **Sample answer: 7 and 9**
18. 50 **Sample answer: 2 and 25**

19. SECURITY In a large industrial complex, three security teams work different types of security checks. The first team makes a complete round in 3 hours, the second team makes a complete round in 2 hours, while the third team makes a complete round in 4 hours. If all three teams start security checks at 7 A.M., when will be the next time all three teams finish a security check at the same time? **7 P.M.**
20. COOKIES A recipe for large oatmeal cookies will make 15 cookies. A recipe for chocolate chip cookies will make 2 dozen cookies. If you want to have the same number of each type of cookie, what is the least number of each that you will need to make using complete recipes? **120 cookies**
21. ICE SKATING Three friends ice skate at different speeds. Parcel skates one lap in 45 seconds. It takes Hansel $1\frac{1}{2}$ minutes to skate one lap and Forrest takes only 30 seconds to skate a lap. If they started out together, in how many minutes will they meet next? **$1\frac{1}{2}$ minutes**

Chapter 4 54 Course 2

Word Problem Practice*
p. 55 OL AL

NAME ____________ DATE ________ PERIOD ____

4-8 Word Problem Practice

Least Common Multiple

1. PROMOTION In a promotion for a local delicatessen, every eighth customer will get a free sandwich and every sixth customer will get a free drink. Which customer will be first to get both a free sandwich and a free drink? **the 24th customer**
2. WORK Alano and Abey both work at night. Alano has every fourth night off and Abey has every sixth night off. If they are both off tonight, how long will it be before they are both off again? **12 nights**
3. RADIO A radio station is giving away a discount coupon to every twelfth caller and a free concert ticket to every twentieth caller. Which caller will be first to win both the coupon and the ticket? **the 60th caller**
4. MUSIC Faith spent the same amount of money on cassette tapes as she did on CDs. If tapes cost $12 and CDs cost $16, what is the least amount of money she could have spent on each? **$48**
5. BIKES Three bike riders ride around a circular path. The first rider circles the path in 12 minutes, the second in 18 minutes, and the third in 24 minutes. If they all start at the same place, at the same time, and go in the same direction, after how many minutes will they meet at the starting point? **72 min**
6. PAPER GOODS At a party store, paper cups come in packages of 15, paper plates come in packages of 30, and napkins come in packages of 20. In order to have the same number of cups, plates, and napkins, what is the least number of each that must be purchased? **60**

Lesson 4–8

Chapter 4 55 Course 2

Enrichment
p. 56 OL AL

NAME ____________ DATE ________ PERIOD ____

4-8 Enrichment

Periodic Cicadas

Cicadas, also commonly known as locusts, are insects that inhabit much of the eastern United States. Some cicadas are called **periodic** because they have life cycles that span periods of several years. The *Magicicada* is a kind of cicada that has an unusually long life cycle of 13 or 17 years. These 13-year and 17-year cicadas spend much of their lives living underground. After 12 or 16 years, the cicadas start to burrow upward. All at once they emerge from the ground, taking flight and eating most of the leaves on nearby plants.

While scientists do not know for sure why the *Magicicada* life cycles last for 13 or 17 years, they do have several theories. One theory is that this life cycle pattern makes it easier for the cicadas to find food. Another theory is that the pattern helps the cicada avoid predators.

For Exercises 1–4, refer to the following information.

Suppose there are many kinds of cicadas. For each of the pair below, find out how many years would pass before each would again emerge at the same time.

1. 11-year and 15-year cicadas **165 yr**
2. 12-year and 16-year cicadas **48 yr**
3. 14-year and 18-year cicadas **126 yr**
4. 13-year and 17-year cicadas **221 yr**
5. In what year will the 13-year and 17-year cicadas that emerged in the summer of 1998 once again emerge at the same time? Explain. **2219; Sample answer: since the LCM of 13 and 17 is 221, they emerge together every 221 years.**

For Exercises 6–8, refer to the following information.

Suppose the cicada has three predators that have life cycles of 2, 3, and 5 years. The population of cicadas was nearly wiped out one summer because all three predators emerged when the cicadas emerged.

6. After how many years will the three predators emerge together again? **30 yr**
7. For each of the cicada populations in Exercises 1-4, find the number of years before the cicada population would again emerge at the same time as all three predators. Record your answers in the table below.

Cicada Type	11-year	12-year	13-year	14-year	15-year	16-year	17-year	18-year
Years	330	60	390	210	30	240	510	90

8. Which two cicada populations have the best chance of survival? Explain. **Sample answer: The 13-year and the 17-year cicadas, because they have the longest period of time before they have to face all three predators at once.**

Chapter 4 56 Course 2

** Also available in Spanish* ELL

Additional Lesson Resources

Transparencies

- *5-Minute Check Transparency*, Lesson 4-8

Other Print Products

- *Noteables™ Interactive Study Notebook with Foldables™*

Teacher Tech Tools

- *Interactive Classroom CD-ROM*, Lesson 4-8
- *AssignmentWorks*, Lesson 4-8

Student Tech Tools

glencoe.com

- Extra Examples, Chapter 4, Lesson 8
- Self-Check Quiz, Chapter 4, Lesson 8

4-8 Least Common Multiple

MAIN IDEA

Find the least common multiple of two or more numbers.

IN Academic Standards

7.1.3 Recognize the prime factors of a number and find the prime factorization of whole numbers and write the results using exponents. *Also addresses 7.1.2.*

New Vocabulary

multiple
least common multiple (LCM)

IN Math Online

glencoe.com
- Extra Examples
- Personal Tutor
- Self-Check Quiz

MINI Lab

Use cubes to build the first row of each prism as shown.

1. Add a second row to each prism. Record the total number of cubes used in a table like the one shown below.

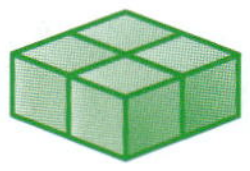

Prism A

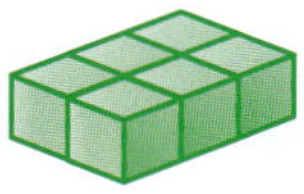

Prism B

Number of Rows	1	2	3	4
Cubes in Prism A	4	■ 8	■12	■16
Cubes in Prism B	6	■12	■18	■24

2. Add rows until each prism has four rows.
3. Describe two prisms that have the same number of cubes. **See margin.**
4. If you keep adding rows, will the two prisms have the same number of cubes again? **See margin.**

A **multiple** is the product of a number and any whole number. The **least common multiple**, or **LCM**, of two or more numbers is the least of their common multiples, excluding zero.

Vocabulary Link

Multiply
Everyday Use to find the product

Multiple
Math Use the product of a number and any whole number

EXAMPLES Find the LCM

1 **Find the LCM of 6 and 10.**

METHOD 1 **List the nonzero multiples.**

List the multiples of 6 until you come to a number that is also a multiple of 10.

multiples of 6: 6, 12, 18, 24, 30, …

multiples of 10: 10, 20, 30, …

Notice that 30 is also a multiple of 10. The LCM of 6 and 10 is 30.

METHOD 2 **Use prime factorization.**

$6 = 2 \cdot 3$

$10 = 2 \cdot 5$

The prime factors of 6 and 10 are 2, 3, and 5.

The LCM is the least product that contains the prime factors of each number. So, the LCM of 6 and 10 is $2 \cdot 3 \cdot 5$ or 30.

Additional Answers

3. Both prisms have the same number of cubes when prism A has 3 rows and prism B has 2 rows.

4. Yes; Sample answer: Every third row in prism A will have the same number of cubes as every second row in prism B.

4-8 Lesson Notes

1 Focus

Vertical Alignment

Before Lesson 4-8
Determine the prime factors of all numbers through 50 and write the numbers as the product of their prime factors by using exponents to show multiples of a factor

Lesson 4-8
Determine the least common multiple of whole numbers

After Lesson 4-8
Add and subtract fractions by using factoring to find common denominators

2 Teach

MINI Lab

Many students will recognize the patterns and thus be able to use multiplication to find the number of cubes in each prism.

Scaffolding Questions

Present the following scenario.
Maria has a collection of quarters, dimes, and nickels. In order to count the coins, she wants to make several piles of each coin that are equal in value.

Ask:
- How many dimes equal 2 quarters? 5
- How many dimes equal 6 quarters? 15
- How many nickels equal 1 dime? 2
- How many nickels equal 4 dimes? 8

Focus on Mathematical Content

The **least common multiple** (LCM) of a set of numbers is the least product that contains the prime factors of each number.

One way to find the LCM of a set of numbers is to list their **nonzero multiples.**

Another way to find the LCM of a set of numbers is to write each number's **prime factorization**, and then multiply the greatest power of each prime factor.

Formative Assessment

Use the Check Your Progress exercises after each Example to determine students' understanding of concepts.

ADDITIONAL EXAMPLES

1. Find the LCM of 4 and 6. 12
2. Find the LCM of 4 and 15. 60
3. **WORK** On an assembly line, machine A must be oiled every 18 minutes, machine B every 24 minutes, and machine C every 48 minutes. If all three machines are turned on at the same time, in how many minutes will all three machines need to be oiled at the same time? 144 minutes

Additional Examples are also in:

- Noteables™ Interactive Study Notebook with Foldables™
- Interactive Classroom PowerPoint® Presentations

Tips for New Teachers

Zero

Make sure students realize that 0 is a multiple of every number but, by definition, is not considered the LCM of any set of numbers.

---

2 **Find the LCM of 45 and 75.**

Use Method 2. Find the prime factorization of each number.

$45 = 3 \cdot 3 \cdot 5$ or $3^2 \cdot 5$

$75 = 3 \cdot 5 \cdot 5$ or $3 \cdot 5^2$

The prime factors of 45 and 75 are 3 and 5. Write the prime factorization using exponents.

The LCM is the product of the prime factors 3 and 5, with each one raised to the *highest* power it occurs in *either* prime factorization. The LCM of 45 and 75 is $3^2 \cdot 5^2$, which is 225.

CHOOSE Your Method

Find the LCM of each set of numbers.

a. 3, 12 **12** b. 10, 12 **60** c. 25, 30 **150**

Real-World EXAMPLE

Real-World Link . . . . Each day, about 700,000 people in the U.S. celebrate their birthday.

3 **PARTY** **Ling needs to buy paper plates, napkins, and cups for a party. Plates come in packages of 12, napkins come in packages of 16, and cups come in packages of 8. What is the least number of packages she will have to buy if she wants to have the same number of plates, napkins, and cups?**

First find the LCM of 8, 12, and 16.

$8 = 2 \cdot 2 \cdot 2$ or 2^3

$12 = 2 \cdot 2 \cdot 3$ or $2^2 \cdot 3$

$16 = 2 \cdot 2 \cdot 2 \cdot 2$ or 2^4

The prime factors of 8, 12, and 16 are 2 and 3. Write the prime factorization using exponents.

The LCM of 8, 12, and 16 is $2^4 \cdot 3$, which is 48.

To find the number of packages of each Ling needs to buy, divide 48 by the amount in each package.

cups: $48 \div 8$ or 6 packages

plates: $48 \div 12$ or 4 packages

napkins: $48 \div 16$ or 3 packages

So, Ling will need to buy 6 packages of cups, 4 packages of plates, and 3 packages of napkins.

CHECK Your Progress

d. **VEHICLES** Mr. Hernandez changes his car's oil every 3 months, rotates the tires every 6 months, and replaces the air filter once a year. If he completed all three tasks in April, what will be the next month he again completes all three tasks? **April**

212 Chapter 4 Fractions, Decimals, and Percents

CHECK Your Understanding

Examples 1–3 (pp. 211–212)

Find the LCM of each set of numbers.

1. 4, 14 **28**
2. 6, 7 **42**
3. 12, 15 **60**
4. 21, 35 **105**
5. 3, 5, 12 **60**
6. 6, 14, 21 **42**

Example 3 (p. 212)

7. **GOVERNMENT** The number of years per term for a U.S. President, senator, and representative is shown. Suppose a senator was elected in the presidential election year 2008. In what year will he or she campaign again during a presidential election year? **2020**

Elected Office	Term (yr)
President	4
Senator	6
Representative	2

Practice and Problem Solving

HOMEWORK HELP

For Exercises	See Examples
8–13, 20	1, 2
14–19, 21	3

Find the LCM for each set of numbers.

8. 6, 8 **24**
9. 8, 18 **72**
10. 12, 16 **48**
11. 24, 36 **72**
12. 11, 12 **132**
13. 45, 63 **315**
14. 2, 3, 5 **30**
15. 6, 8, 9 **72**
16. 8, 12, 16 **48**
17. 12, 15, 28 **420**
18. 22, 33, 44 **132**
19. 12, 16, 36 **144**

Exercise Levels
A: 8–21
B: 22–30
C: 31–34

20. **CHORES** Hernando walks his dog every two days. He gives his dog a bath once a week. Today, Hernando walked his dog and then gave her a bath. How many days will pass before he does both chores on the same day? **14 days**

Friend	Time Interval
Linda	every 30 min
Brandon	every 45 min
Edward	every 60 min

21. **TEXT MESSAGING** Three friends use text messaging to notify their parents of their whereabouts. If all three contact their parents at 3:00 P.M., at what time will all three contact their parents again at the same time? **6:00 P.M.**

Find the LCM of each set.

22. \$3.00, \$14.00 **\$42**
23. 10¢, 25¢, 5¢ **50¢**
24. 9 inches, 2 feet **72 in. or 6 ft**

Write two numbers whose LCM is the given number.

25–28. Sample answers are given.

25. 35 **5, 7**
26. 56 **7, 8**
27. 70 **10, 35**
28. 30 **6, 15**

29. **SNACKS** Alvin's mom needs to buy snacks for soccer practice. Juice boxes come in packages of 10. Oatmeal snack bars come in packages of 8. She wants to have the same number of juice boxes and snack bars, what is the least number of packages of each snack that she will have to buy? **4 packages of juice boxes and 5 packages of oatmeal snack bars**

Academic Standards • ISTEP+

Extra Practice, pp. 678, 707

30. **REASONING** The LCM of two consecutive positive numbers is greater than 200 and is a multiple of 7. What are the least possible numbers? **14 and 15**

3 Practice

Formative Assessment

Use Exercises 1–7 to check for understanding.

Then use the chart at the bottom of this page to customize your assignments for students.

Intervention You may wish to use the Study Guide and Intervention Master on page 52 of the *Chapter 4 Resource Masters* for additional reinforcement.

Odd/Even Assignments

Exercises 8–21 are structured so that students practice the same concepts whether they are assigned odd or even problems.

DIFFERENTIATED HOMEWORK OPTIONS

Level	Assignment	Two-Day Option	
BL Basic	8–21, 32–46	9–21 odd, 35, 36	8–20 even, 32–34, 37–46
OL Core	9–19 odd, 20, 21–29 odd, 30, 32–46	8–21, 35, 36	22–30, 32–34, 37–46
AL Advanced/Pre-AP	22–43, (optional: 44–46)		

4 Assess

Crystal Ball Tell students that tomorrow's lesson is about comparing fractions, decimals, and percents. Ask them to write how they think what they learned today will connect with tomorrow's material.

H.O.T. Problems

31. **CHALLENGE** Two numbers have a GCF of 3 • 5. Their LCM is $2^2 \cdot 3 \cdot 5$. If one of the numbers is 3 • 5, what is the other number? **$2^2 \cdot 3 \cdot 5$, or 60**

32. **SELECT A TECHNIQUE** The schedule for each of three trains is shown. Suppose a train from each line leaves Clark Street at 11:35 A.M. Which of the following technique(s) might you use to determine the next time all three trains will be leaving at the same time? Justify your selection(s). Then use the technique to solve the problem.

Clark Street Train Station

Train	Leaves Station
Red-line	every 14 minutes
Blue-line	every 16 minutes
Brown-line	every 8 minutes

mental math | number sense | estimation

32. Number sense; Sample answer: The LCM of 14, 16, and 8 is 112. So, 112 minutes later, or at 1:27 P.M.

33. **OPEN ENDED** Write three numbers that have an LCM of 30. **Sample answer: 3, 10, 15**

34. **WRITING IN MATH** Describe the relationship between 4, 20, and 5 using the words *factor* and *multiple.* **4 and 5 are factors of 20; 20 is a multiple (and LCM) of 4 and 5.**

ISTEP+ PRACTICE Reinforcement of 7.1.3

35. Which rule describes the common multiples of 12 and 18, where *n* represents the counting numbers? **C**
    - A 12*n*
    - B 18*n*
    - C 36*n*
    - D 216*n*

36. **CONSTRUCTED RESPONSE** Will swims every third day, runs every fourth day, and lifts weights every fifth day. If Will does all three activities today, how many days will pass before he does all three activities on the same day again? **60**

Spiral Review

Write each percent as a decimal. (Lesson 4-7)

37. 55% **0.55**
38. 26.4% **0.264**
39. $\frac{1}{4}$% **0.0025**
40. 2% **0.02**

41. **DIAMONDS** Sixty-eight percent of engagement rings have a diamond that is round in shape. Write this percent as a fraction in simplest form. (Lesson 4-6) $\frac{17}{25}$

42. **ALGEBRA** Solve $3x = 18$. (Lesson 3-3) **6**

43. **ALGEBRA** Rose swam 7 laps more than twice the number of laps her sister swam. Write an algebraic expression to represent this situation. (Lesson 3-1) **$2s + 7$**

GET READY for the Next Lesson

PREREQUISITE SKILL **Replace each ● with <, > or = to make a true sentence.** (Page 670)

44. 6.85 ● 5.68 **>**
45. 2.34 ● 2.43 **<**
46. 6.9 ● 5.99 **>**

Pre-AP Activity Use after Exercise 33

Tell students that the product of two numbers is 324 and that their GCF is 6. Have them find the numbers and their LCM. You may need to provide a hint, suggesting that students first find the prime factorization of 324. 54 and 6; 54

4-9 Comparing and Ordering Rational Numbers

PACING: **Regular:** 1 period, **Block:** 0.5 period

IN Academic Standards **7.1.6 Identify, write,** rename, **compare and order rational** and common irrational **numbers and plot them on a number line.**

Options for Differentiated Instruction

ELL = English Language Learner AL = Above or Beyond Grade Level SS = Struggling Students SN = Special Needs

Vocabulary Development ELL SS SN

Use after presenting the Examples.

Create a word wall with examples of GCF, LCM, and LCD. For sight impaired students, use large type or Braille coding.

Explain what each term is, how it is used, and whether the terms are related in any way. Be sure to give examples of all three.

Working in Pairs ELL SS

Use with the in-class Exercises.

Have students work through a number of problems in pairs. Have one student solve the problem using a calculator and the other using paper and pencil. Partners should switch methods with every problem. Have students compare answers, aiding one another in finding any mistakes in calculations.

Kinesthetic Learners ELL AL SS SN

Use after students complete Lesson 4-9.

Place students in groups of four. Give each group 12 cards, each of which shows a fraction, decimal, or percent. An example of a set of cards is shown below.

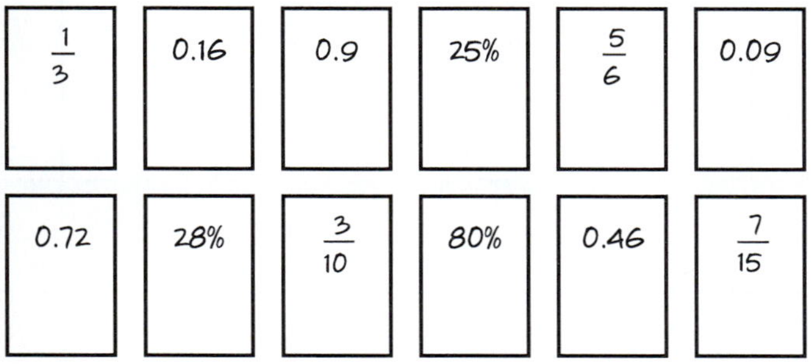

Each member of the group draws one card. Then have students order the cards from least to greatest. Repeat the activity several times.

Leveled Lesson Resources

Also on **TeacherWorks™**
Lesson 4-9

Chapter 4 Resource Masters

BL = Below or Approaching Grade Level **OL** = On Grade Level **AL** = Above or Beyond Grade Level **ELL** = English Language Learner

Lesson Reading Guide
p. 58 BL OL ELL

4-9 Lesson Reading Guide
Comparing and Ordering Rational Numbers

*Study Guide and Intervention**
p. 59 BL OL ELL

4-9 Study Guide and Intervention
Comparing and Ordering Rational Numbers

*Skills Practice**
p. 60 BL OL

4-9 Skills Practice
Comparing and Ordering Rational Numbers

*Practice**
p. 61 OL AL

4-9 Practice
Comparing and Ordering Rational Numbers

*Word Problem Practice**
p. 62 OL AL

4-9 Word Problem Practice
Comparing and Ordering Rational Numbers

Enrichment
p. 63 OL AL

4-9 Enrichment

Also available in Spanish **ELL**

Additional Lesson Resources

Transparencies
- *5-Minute Check Transparency*, Lesson 4-9

Other Print Products
- *Noteables™ Interactive Study Notebook with Foldables™*

Teacher Tech Tools
- *Interactive Classroom CD-ROM*, Lesson 4-9
- *AssignmentWorks*, Lesson 4-9

Student Tech Tools
glencoe.com
- Extra Examples, Chapter 4, Lesson 9
- Self-Check Quiz, Chapter 4, Lesson 9

4-9 Comparing and Ordering Rational Numbers

MAIN IDEA

Compare and order fractions, decimals, and percents.

IN Academic Standards

7.1.6 Identify, write, rename, **compare and order rational** and common irrational **numbers and plot them on a number line.**

New Vocabulary

rational numbers
common denominator
least common denominator (LCD)

IN Math Online

glencoe.com

- Extra Examples
- Personal Tutor
- Self-Check Quiz

MINI Lab

In Chapter 2, you used a number line to compare integers. You can also use a number line to compare positive and negative fractions. The number line shows that $-\frac{1}{8} < \frac{3}{8}$.

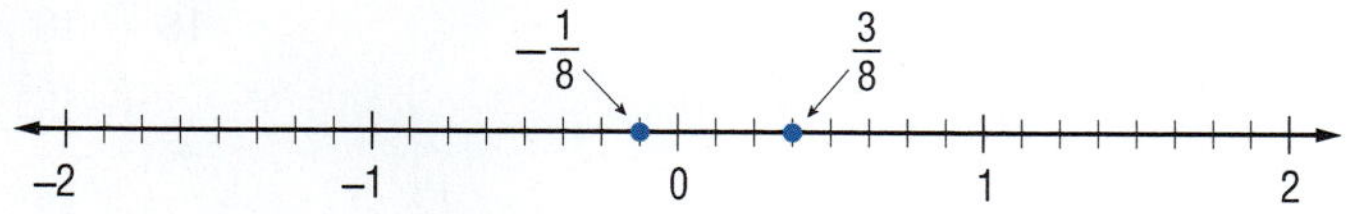

Graph each pair of numbers on a number line. Then determine which number is less.

1. $-\frac{7}{8}, -\frac{3}{8}$
2. $-\frac{5}{8}, -1\frac{1}{8}$
3. $-\frac{13}{8}, -\frac{3}{8}$
4. $-1\frac{7}{8}, -1\frac{5}{8}$
5. $-\frac{1}{2}, -\frac{3}{4}$
6. $1\frac{1}{4}, -1\frac{1}{4}$

The different types of numbers you have been using are all examples of rational numbers. A **rational number** is a number that can be expressed as a fraction. Fractions, terminating and repeating decimals, percents, and integers are all rational numbers. The points corresponding to rational numbers begin to "fill in" the number line.

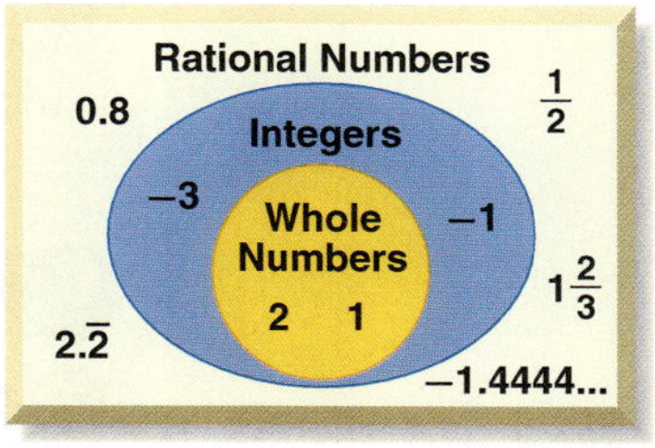

EXAMPLE Compare Rational Numbers

1 **Replace the ● with <, >, or = to make $-1\frac{5}{6}$ ● $-1\frac{1}{6}$ a true sentence.**

Graph each rational number on a number line. Mark off equal size increments of $\frac{1}{6}$ between –2 and –1.

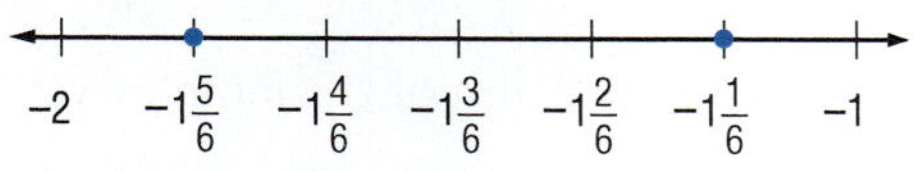

The number line shows that $-1\frac{5}{6} < -1\frac{1}{6}$.

CHECK Your Progress

a. **Replace the ● with <, >, or = to make $-5\frac{5}{9}$ ● $-5\frac{1}{9}$ a true sentence.**

4-9 Lesson Notes

1 Focus

Vertical Alignment

Before Lesson 4-9
Identify and represent on a number line decimals, fractions, mixed numbers, and positive and negative numbers

Lesson 4-9
Compare and order positive and negative fractions, decimals, and mixed numbers and place them on a number line. Determine the least common multiple of whole numbers; use them to solve problems with fractions

After Lesson 4-9
Compare rational numbers

2 Teach

Scaffolding Questions

As you ask the following questions, write each pair of numbers on the board.

Ask:

- Which is a better quiz score, 90% or $\frac{20}{25}$? 90%
- Which is more money, $0.45 or a half-dollar? half-dollar
- Which is a shorter distance, 0.7 meters or $\frac{3}{4}$ meter? 0.7 m
- Which is less sweet, 0.05 sugar or 8% sugar? 0.05 sugar

Lesson 4-9 Comparing and Ordering Rational Numbers **215**

Focus on Mathematical Content

Rational numbers can be written as the ratio of two integers (the second integer cannot be 0).

Decimals that neither terminate nor repeat are **not rational.**

Formative Assessment

Use the Check Your Progress exercises after each Example to determine students' understanding of concepts.

ADDITIONAL EXAMPLES

Replace each ● with <, >, or = to make a true sentence.

1. $-3\frac{3}{8}$ ● $-3\frac{7}{8}$ >
2. $\frac{5}{12}$ ● $\frac{7}{16}$ <
3. **DOGS** According to the Pet Food Manufacturer's Association, 11 out of 25 people own large dogs and 13 out of 50 own medium dogs. Do more people own large or medium dogs? large

Additional Examples are also in:

- Noteables™ Interactive Study Notebook with Foldables™
- Interactive Classroom PowerPoint® Presentations

Tips for New Teachers: Rational Numbers

Help students remember the definition of *rational* numbers by pointing out that they can be written as a *ratio* of integers (provided the second integer isn't 0). You may also wish to remind students that in Lesson 4-5 they learned that terminating and repeating decimals can be written as fractions, or ratios.

A **common denominator** is a common multiple of the denominators of two or more fractions. The **least common denominator** or **LCD** is the LCM of the denominators. You can use the LCD to compare fractions.

EXAMPLE Compare Rational Numbers

2 **Replace the ● with <, >, or = to make $\frac{7}{12}$ ● $\frac{8}{18}$ a true sentence.**

$12 = 2^2 \cdot 3$ and $18 = 2 \cdot 3^2$. So, the LCM is $2^2 \cdot 3^2$ or 36. The LCD of the denominators 12 and 18 is 36.

$\frac{7}{12} = \frac{7 \times 3}{12 \times 3} = \frac{21}{36}$ $\qquad$ $\frac{8}{18} = \frac{8 \times 2}{18 \times 2} = \frac{16}{36}$

Since $\frac{21}{36} > \frac{16}{36}$, then $\frac{7}{12} > \frac{8}{18}$.

CHECK Your Progress

Replace each ● with <, >, or = to make a true sentence.

b. $\frac{5}{6}$ ● $\frac{7}{9}$ > $\qquad$ c. $\frac{1}{5}$ ● $\frac{7}{50}$ > $\qquad$ d. $-\frac{9}{16}$ ● $-\frac{7}{10}$ >

You can also compare fractions by writing each fraction as a decimal and then comparing the decimals.

Real-World EXAMPLE

3 **ROLLER SHOES** **In Mr. Huang's math class, 6 out of 32 students own roller shoes. In Mrs. Trevino's math class, 5 out of 29 students own roller shoes. In which class do a greater fraction of students own roller shoes?**

Since the denominators are large, write $\frac{6}{32}$ and $\frac{5}{29}$ as decimals and then compare.

$6 \div 32 = 0.1875$ $\qquad$ $5 \div 29 \approx 0.1724$ $\qquad$ Divide.

Since $0.1875 > 0.1724$, then $\frac{6}{32} > \frac{5}{29}$.

So, a greater fraction of students in Mr. Huang's class own roller shoes.

Real-World Link The first roller shoe was introduced in 2001.
Source: Associated Content, Inc.

CHECK Your Progress

e. **BOWLING** Twelve out of 32 students in second period class like to bowl. In fifth period class, 12 out of 29 students like to bowl. In which class do a greater fraction of the students like to bowl? fifth period class

These fraction-decimal-percent equivalents are used frequently.

Fractions-Decimals-Percents — Key Concept

$\frac{1}{4} = 0.25 = 25\%$	$\frac{1}{5} = 0.2 = 20\%$	$\frac{1}{8} = 0.125 = 12.5\%$	$\frac{1}{10} = 0.1 = 10\%$
$\frac{1}{2} = 0.5 = 50\%$	$\frac{2}{5} = 0.4 = 40\%$	$\frac{3}{8} = 0.375 = 37.5\%$	$\frac{3}{10} = 0.3 = 30\%$
$\frac{3}{4} = 0.75 = 75\%$	$\frac{3}{5} = 0.6 = 60\%$	$\frac{1}{3} = 0.\overline{3} = 33.\overline{3}\%$	$\frac{7}{10} = 0.7 = 70\%$
$1 = 1.00 = 100\%$	$\frac{4}{5} = 0.8 = 80\%$	$\frac{2}{3} = 0.\overline{6} = 66.\overline{6}\%$	$\frac{9}{10} = 0.9 = 90\%$

The Greek letter π (pi) represents the nonterminating and nonrepeating number whose first few digits are 3.1415926.... This number is not rational. You will learn more about *irrational numbers* in Chapter 12.

ISTEP+ EXAMPLE 7.1.6

4 Which list shows the numbers 3.44, π, 3.14, and $3.\overline{4}$ in order from least to greatest?

A π, 3.14, 3.44, $3.\overline{4}$

B π, 3.14, $3.\overline{4}$, 3.44

C 3.14, π, $3.\overline{4}$, 3.44

D 3.14, π, 3.44, $3.\overline{4}$

Read the Item

Compare the digits using place value.

Solve the Item

Line up the decimal points and compare using place value.

3.140	Annex a zero.	3.440	Annex a zero.
3.1415926...	$\pi \approx 3.1415926...$	3.444...	$3.\overline{4} = 3.444...$
Since $0 < 1$, $3.14 < \pi$.		Since $0 < 4$, $3.44 < 3.\overline{4}$.	

So, the order of the numbers from least to greatest is 3.14, π, 3.44, and $3.\overline{4}$. The answer is D.

CHECK Your Progress

f. The amount of rain received on four consecutive days was 0.3 inch, $\frac{3}{5}$ inch, 0.75 inch, and $\frac{2}{3}$ inch. Which list shows the amounts from least to greatest? G

F 0.3 in., $\frac{2}{3}$ in., $\frac{3}{5}$ in., 0.75 in.

G 0.3 in., $\frac{3}{5}$ in., $\frac{2}{3}$ in., 0.75 in.

H 0.75 in., $\frac{2}{3}$ in., $\frac{3}{5}$ in., 0.3 in.

J $\frac{3}{5}$ in., $\frac{2}{3}$ in., 0.3 in., 0.75 in.

Test-Taking Tip

Reading Choices
Read all answer choices carefully before deciding on the correct answer. Often two choices will look very familiar.

ADDITIONAL EXAMPLE

4 **TEST EXAMPLE** Four frozen dinners had the following amounts of vegetables: $\frac{7}{10}$, 0.6, 72%, and $\frac{16}{25}$. Which list shows the numbers in order from least to greatest? C

A 0.6, $\frac{7}{10}$, $\frac{16}{25}$, 72%

B $\frac{16}{25}$, 0.6, 72%, $\frac{7}{10}$

C 0.6, $\frac{16}{25}$, $\frac{7}{10}$, 72%

D 72%, $\frac{7}{10}$, 0.6, $\frac{16}{25}$

Lesson 4-9 Comparing and Ordering Rational Numbers **217**

3 Practice

Formative Assessment

Use Exercises 1–7 to check for understanding.

Then use the chart at the bottom of this page to customize your assignments for students.

Intervention You may wish to use the Study Guide and Intervention Master on page 59 of the *Chapter 4 Resource Masters* for additional reinforcement.

Odd/Even Assignments

Exercises 8–31 are structured so that students practice the same concepts whether they are assigned odd or even problems.

Additional Answer

5. Elliot; 3 out of 4 has an average of 0.75; 7 out of 11 has an average of 0.64.

★ indicates multi-step problem

CHECK Your Understanding

Examples 1–2 (pp. 215–216)

Replace each ● with <, >, or = to make a true sentence. Use a number line if necessary.

1. $-\frac{4}{9}$ ● $-\frac{7}{9}$ >
2. $-1\frac{3}{4}$ ● $-1\frac{6}{8}$ =
3. $\frac{3}{8}$ ● $\frac{6}{15}$ <
4. $2\frac{4}{5}$ ● $2\frac{7}{8}$ <

Example 3 (p. 216)

5. **SOCCER** The table shows the average saves for two soccer goalies. Who has the better average, Elliot or Shanna? Explain. **See margin.**

Name	Average
Elliot	3 saves out of 4
Shanna	7 saves out of 11

6. **SCHOOL** On her first quiz in social studies, Majorie answered 23 out of 25 questions correctly. On her second quiz, she answered 27 out of 30 questions correctly. On which quiz did Majorie have the greater score? **her first quiz**

Example 4 (p. 217)

7. **MULTIPLE CHOICE** The lengths of four insects are 0.02 inch, $\frac{1}{8}$ inch, 0.1 inch, and $\frac{2}{3}$ inch. Which list shows the lengths in inches from least to greatest? **C**

A $0.1, 0.02, \frac{1}{8}, \frac{2}{3}$

B $\frac{1}{8}, 0.02, 0.1, \frac{2}{3}$

C $0.02, 0.1, \frac{1}{8}, \frac{2}{3}$

D $\frac{2}{3}, 0.02, 0.1, \frac{1}{8}$

Practice and Problem Solving

HOMEWORK HELP

For Exercises	See Examples
8–19	1, 2
20–25, 49	3
26–31, 48	4

Exercise Levels:
A: 8–31
B: 32–44
C: 45–47

Replace each ● with <, >, or = to make a true sentence. Use a number line if necessary.

8. $-\frac{3}{5}$ ● $-\frac{4}{5}$ >
9. $-\frac{5}{7}$ ● $-\frac{2}{7}$ <
10. $-7\frac{5}{8}$ ● $-7\frac{1}{8}$ <
11. $-3\frac{2}{3}$ ● $-3\frac{4}{6}$ =
12. $\frac{7}{10}$ ● $\frac{2}{3}$ >
13. $\frac{4}{7}$ ● $\frac{5}{8}$ <
14. $\frac{2}{3}$ ● $\frac{10}{15}$ =
15. $-\frac{17}{24}$ ● $-\frac{11}{12}$ >
16. $2\frac{3}{4}$ ● $2\frac{2}{3}$ >
17. $6\frac{2}{3}$ ● $6\frac{1}{2}$ >
18. $5\frac{5}{7}$ ● $5\frac{11}{14}$ <
19. $3\frac{11}{16}$ ● $3\frac{7}{8}$ <
20. 40% ● 112 out of 250 <
21. 3 out of 5 ● 59% >
22. 0.82 ● 5 out of 6 <
23. 9 out of 20 ● 0.45 =

24. **MONEY** The table shows how much copper is in each type of coin. Which coin contains the greatest amount of copper? **quarter**

Coin	Amount of Copper
Dime	$\frac{12}{16}$
Nickel	$\frac{3}{4}$
Penny	$\frac{1}{400}$
Quarter	$\frac{23}{25}$

25. **BASKETBALL** Gracia and Jim were shooting free throws. Gracia made 4 out of 15 free throws. Jim *missed* the free throw 6 out of 16 times. Who made the free throw a greater fraction of the time? **Jim; $\frac{10}{16} > \frac{4}{15}$**

DIFFERENTIATED HOMEWORK OPTIONS

Level	Assignment	Two-Day Option	
BL Basic	8–31, 45, 47–62	9–31 odd, 48–50	8–30 even, 45, 47, 51–62
OL Core	9–23 odd, 24, 25–39 odd, 40–45, 47–62	8–31, 48–50	32–45, 47, 51–62
AL Advanced/Pre-AP	32–62		

218 Chapter 4 Fractions, Decimals, and Percents

26. 19%, $\frac{1}{5}$, 0.23
27. $\frac{8}{10}$, 0.805, 81%
28. $-\frac{5}{8}$, −0.62, −0.615
29. −1.4, −1.25, $-1\frac{1}{25}$
30. 7.49, 7.5, $7\frac{49}{50}$
31. 3.47, $3\frac{4}{7}$, $3\frac{3}{5}$

Order each set of numbers from least to greatest.

26. 0.23, 19%, $\frac{1}{5}$
27. $\frac{8}{10}$, 81%, 0.805
28. −0.615, $-\frac{5}{8}$, −0.62
29. −1.4, $-1\frac{1}{25}$, −1.25
30. 7.49, $7\frac{49}{50}$, 7.5
31. $3\frac{4}{7}$, $3\frac{3}{5}$, 3.47

MEASUREMENT **Replace each ● with <, >, or = to make a true sentence.**

32. $\frac{5}{8}$ yard ● $\frac{1}{16}$ yard **>**
33. 0.25 pound ● $\frac{2}{9}$ pound **>**
34. $2\frac{5}{6}$ hours ● 2.8 hours **>**
35. $1\frac{7}{12}$ gallons ● $1\frac{5}{8}$ gallons **<**

MEASUREMENT **Order each of the following from least to greatest.** **36–39. See margin.**

36. 4.4 miles, $4\frac{3}{8}$ miles, $4\frac{5}{12}$ miles
37. 6.5 cups, $6\frac{1}{3}$ cups, 6 cups
38. 1.2 laps, 2 laps, $\frac{1}{2}$ lap
39. $\frac{1}{5}$ gram, 5 grams, 1.5 grams

ANIMALS **For Exercises 40–42, use the table that shows the lengths of the smallest mammals.**

Animal	Length (ft)
Eastern Chipmunk	$\frac{1}{3}$
Kitti's Hog-Nosed Bat	$0.8\overline{3}$
European Mole	$\frac{5}{12}$
Masked Shrew	$\frac{1}{6}$
Spiny Pocket Mouse	0.25

Source: *Scholastic Book of World Records*

Real-World Link
The Olympic gold medals are actually made out of 92.5% silver, with the gold medal covered in 6 grams of pure gold.

40. ★ Which animal is the smallest mammal? **Masked Shrew**
41. ★ Which animal is smaller than the European mole but larger than the spiny pocket mouse? **Eastern Chipmunk**
42. ★ Order the animals from greatest to least size.

42. Kitti's Hog-Nosed Bat, European Mole, Eastern Chipmunk, Spiny Pocket Mouse, Masked Shrew

SOFTBALL **For Exercises 43 and 44, use the following table which shows the at-bats, hits, and home run statistics for four players on the 2004 Olympics U.S. Women's softball team.**

Player	At-Bats	Hits	Home Runs
Crystal Bustos	26	9	5
Kelly Krestschman	21	7	1
Stacey Nuveman	16	5	2
Natasha Watley	30	12	0

Source: Olympic Movement

43. ★ Write the ratio of hits to at-bats as a decimal to the nearest thousandth for each player. Who had the greatest batting average during the Olympic games? **Bustos: 0.346; Krestschman: 0.333; Nuveman: 0.313; Watley: 0.400; Watley**
44. ★ Write the ratio of home runs to at-bats as a decimal for each player. Who had the greatest home run average during the Olympic games? **See margin.**

Academic Standards • ISTEP+
Extra Practice, pp. 679, 707

Additional Answers

36. $4\frac{3}{8}$ mi, 4.4 mi, $4\frac{5}{12}$ mi
37. 6 c, $6\frac{1}{3}$ c, 6.5 c
38. $\frac{1}{2}$ lap, 1.2 laps, 2 laps
39. $\frac{1}{5}$ g, 1.5 g, 5 g
44. Bustos: 0.192; Kretschman: 0.048; Nuveman: 0.125; Watley: 0.0; Bustos

Differentiated Instruction

Bodily/Kinesthetic Learners Before class, write a fraction, decimal, or percent on each of a package of index cards. Separate students into groups of four. Give each group 10 or 12 of the index cards, which should be placed in a pile, face down. Each student picks a card. Have the members of each group work together to order their cards from least to greatest. Have them repeat the activity several times.

Lesson 4-9 Comparing and Ordering Rational Numbers **219**

4 Assess

Name the Math Write the following two pairs of fractions on, the chalkboard: $\frac{3}{8}$ and $\frac{5}{12}$; and $\frac{3}{18}$ and $\frac{5}{22}$. Have students tell what mathematical procedures they would use to compare the fractions in each pair. Have them explain their reasoning.

Formative Assessment

Check for student understanding of concepts in Lessons 4-8 and 4-9.

CRM Quiz 4, p. 68

FOLDABLES Study Organizer Foldables™ Follow-Up

Remind students to write—under the tab for this lesson of their Foldables—the answer to the question they wrote about the lesson.

Additional Answer

45. 0.08; 0.08 equals 8% and the other ratios equal 80%.

H.O.T. Problems

45. Which One Doesn't Belong? Identify the ratio that does not have the same value as the other three. Explain your reasoning. **See margin.**

12 out of 15	0.08	80%	$\frac{4}{5}$

46. CHALLENGE Explain how you know which number, $1\frac{15}{16}$, $\frac{17}{8}$, or $\frac{63}{32}$, is nearest to 2.
Sample answer: $\frac{63}{32}$ is closest to 2 because the difference of $\frac{63}{32}$ and 2 is the least.

47. WRITING IN MATH Write a word problem about a real-world situation in which you would compare rational numbers. Then solve the problem. **Sample answer: Gwen needs $\frac{2}{5}$ yard of fabric and $\frac{3}{8}$ yard of ribbon to make a pillow. Which item does she need more, fabric or ribbon? Answer: fabric**

ISTEP+ PRACTICE 7.1.6

48. Which point shows the location of $\frac{7}{2}$ on the number line? **C**

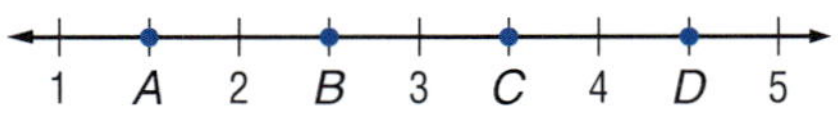

A point *A*
B point *B*
C point *C*
D point *D*

49. Which list of numbers is ordered from least to greatest? **H**

F $\frac{1}{4}$, $4\frac{1}{4}$, 0.4, 0.04

G 0.04, 0.4, $4\frac{1}{4}$, $\frac{1}{4}$

H 0.04, $\frac{1}{4}$, 0.4, $4\frac{1}{4}$

J 0.4, $\frac{1}{4}$, 0.04, $4\frac{1}{4}$

50. Which of the following fractions is closest to 0? **C**

A $-\frac{3}{4}$ **C** $\frac{7}{12}$

B $-\frac{2}{3}$ **D** $\frac{5}{8}$

Spiral Review

Find the LCM of each set of numbers. (Lesson 4-8)

51. 14, 21 **42** **52.** 3, 13 **39** **53.** 12, 16 **48**

SALES TAX **The table shows the sales tax rate for the states shown. Write each sales tax rate as a decimal.** (Lesson 4-7)

54. Kentucky **0.06**
55. Illinois **0.0625**
56. North Carolina **0.0425**

State	Sales Tax
Illinois	6.25%
Kentucky	6%
North Carolina	4.25%
South Carolina	5%

Source: Federation of Tax Administrators

Find the GCF of each set of numbers. (Lesson 4-2)

57. 18, 72 **18** **58.** 40, 12 **4** **59.** 72, 20 **4**

ALGEBRA **Solve each equation.** (Lesson 3-5)

60. $4x + 3 = 15$ **3** **61.** $2n - 5 = 19$ **12** **62.** $-8 = -3d + 1$ **3**

220 Chapter 4 Fractions, Decimals, and Percents

CHAPTER 4

Study Guide and Review

IN Math Online glencoe.com
- STUDY TO GO
- Vocabulary Review

FOLDABLES® Study Organizer

GET READY to Study

Be sure the following Big Ideas are noted in your Foldable.

BIG Ideas

Greatest Common Factor (Lesson 4-2)
- The greatest common factor or GCF is the greatest of the common factors of two or more numbers.

Fractions, Decimals, and Percents (Lessons 4-4 to 4-7)
- A fraction is in simplest form when the GCF of the numerator and denominator is 1.
- A terminating decimal is a decimal whose digits end. Repeating decimals have a pattern in their digits that repeats forever.
- A percent is a part to whole ratio that compares a number to 100.
- To write a percent as a decimal, divide the percent by 100 and remove the percent symbol.
- To write a decimal as a percent, multiply the percent by 100 and add the percent symbol.

Least Common Multiple (Lesson 4-8)
- The least common multiple or LCM of two or more numbers is the least of their common multiples.

Rational Numbers (Lesson 4-9)
- A rational number is one that can be expressed as a fraction.

Key Vocabulary

bar notation (p. 197)
common denominator (p. 216)
composite number (p. 181)
equivalent fractions (p. 192)
factor tree (p. 182)
greatest common factor (GCF) (p. 186)
least common denominator (p. 216)
least common multiple (LCM) (p. 211)
multiple (p. 211)
percent (p. 202)
prime factorization (p. 182)
prime number (p. 181)
ratio (p. 202)
rational number (p. 215)
repeating decimal (p. 197)
simplest form (p. 192)
terminating decimal (p. 197)
Venn diagram (p. 186)

Vocabulary Check

State whether each sentence is *true* or *false*. If *false*, replace the underlined word or number to make a true sentence.

1. A ratio is a comparison of two numbers by <u>multiplication</u>. **false; division**
2. A <u>rational number</u> is a whole number greater than 1 that has exactly two factors, 1 and itself. **false; prime number**
3. 1.875 is an example of a <u>terminating decimal</u>. **true**
4. A common denominator for the fractions $\frac{2}{3}$ and $\frac{1}{4}$ is <u>12</u>. **true**
5. The <u>greatest common factor</u> of 3 and 5 is 15. **false; least common multiple**
6. A ratio that compares a number to <u>100</u> is a percent. **true**
7. The fractions $\frac{9}{21}$ and $\frac{3}{7}$ are <u>equivalent fractions</u>. **true**

CHAPTER 4 Study Guide and Review

FOLDABLES™ Study Organizer

Dinah Zike's Foldables

Have students look through the chapter to make sure they have answered the questions they wrote in their Foldables about each lesson.

Encourage students to refer to their Foldables while completing the Study Guide and Review and while preparing for the Chapter Test.

Formative Assessment

Key Vocabulary The page references after each word in the Key Vocabulary denote where that term was first introduced. If students have difficulty answering Exercises 1–7, remind them that they can use these page references to refresh their memories about the vocabulary terms.

IN Math Online glencoe.com

Vocabulary PuzzleMaker improves students' mathematics vocabulary using four puzzle formats–crossword, scramble, word search using a word list, and word search using clues. Students can work online or from a printed worksheet.

Summative Assessment

CRM Vocabulary Test, p. 70

Lesson-by-Lesson Review

Intervention If the given examples are not sufficient to review the topics covered by the questions, remind students that the page references tell them where to review that topic in their textbooks.

Two-Day Option Have students complete the Lesson-by-Lesson Review on pages 222–224. Then you can use ExamView® Assessment Suite to customize another review worksheet that practices all the objectives of this chapter or only the objectives on which your students need more help.

For more information on ExamView® Assessment Suite, see page 178C.

Differentiated Instruction

Super DVD: MindJogger Plus
Use this DVD as an alternative format of review for the test. For more information on this game show format, see page 178D.

CHAPTER 4 Study Guide and Review

Lesson-by-Lesson Review

4-1 Prime Factorization (pp. 181–184)

7.1.3

Find the prime factorization of each number.

8. 54 2×3^3
9. 128 2^7
10. 68 $2^2 \times 17$
11. 95 5×19
12. **ALGEBRA** Factor $36x^2yz^3$. $2 \cdot 2 \cdot 3 \cdot 3 \cdot x \cdot x \cdot y \cdot z \cdot z \cdot z$
13. **PLANTS** The palm tree *raffia* has leaves up to 65 feet long. Write this length as a product of primes. $65 = 5 \cdot 13$

Example 1 Find the prime factorization of 18.

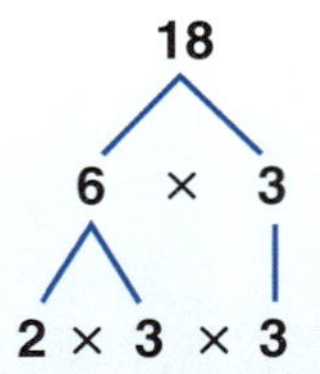

Use a factor tree.

The prime factorization of 18 is 2×3^2.

4-2 Greatest Common Factor (p. 186–189)

7.1.3

Find the GCF of each set of numbers.

14. 18, 27 **9**
15. 30, 72 **6**
16. 28, 70, 98 **14**
17. 42, 63, 105 **21**
18. **ALGEBRA** Find the GCF of $18w$ and $54w^2y$. $18w$
19. **CLOTHING** Maria spent a total of $24 on earrings, $36 on shirts, and $48 on shorts. If each item cost the same amount, what is the greatest possible price per item? **$12**

Example 2 Find the GCF of 24 and 56.

First, make a list of all the factors of 24 and 56.

factors of 24: 1, 2, 3, 4, 6, 8, 12, 24
factors of 56: 1, 2, 4, 7, 8, 14, 28, 56
common factors: 1, 2, 4, 8
The GCF of 24 and 56 is 8.

4-3 PSI: Make an Organized List (pp. 190–191)

P.1.3

Solve by making an organized list.

20. **SEATING** In how many ways can four friends sit in a row at the movies? **24 ways**
21. **TELEPHONES** A phone company offers 5 different types of long-distance plans and 3 different caller features (call waiting, caller ID, and call forward). How many different kinds of plans can be set up that include a long-distance service and a caller feature? **15 different plans**

Example 3 In how many ways can the letters A, B, and C be arranged?

The possible outcomes are written below.

ABC ACB
BAC BCA
CAB CBA

There are 6 different ways to arrange the letters.

Mixed Problem Solving
For mixed problem-solving practice, see page 707.

4-4 Simplifying Fractions (pp. 192–195)

7.1.6

Write each fraction in simplest form.

22. $\frac{12}{15}$ $\frac{4}{5}$ 23. $\frac{35}{60}$ $\frac{7}{12}$ 24. $\frac{11}{121}$ $\frac{1}{11}$
25. $\frac{14}{63}$ $\frac{2}{9}$ 26. $\frac{37}{45}$ $\frac{37}{45}$ 27. $\frac{55}{110}$ $\frac{1}{2}$

28. **CATS** The average household cat sleeps 18 hours a day. Write a fraction in simplest form comparing the number of hours a household cat sleeps to the number of hours in a day. $\frac{3}{4}$

Example 4 Write $\frac{24}{32}$ in simplest form.

Find the GCF of the numerator and denominator.

24 = 1, 2, 3, 4, 6, 8, 12, 24
32 = 1, 2, 4, 8, 16, 32

$\frac{24}{32} = \frac{24 \div 8}{32 \div 8} = \frac{3}{4}$ Divide the numerator and denominator by the GCF.

4-5 Fractions and Decimals (pp. 196–200)

7.1.6

Write each fraction or mixed number as a decimal. Use bar notation if the decimal is a repeating decimal.

29. $\frac{3}{4}$ 0.75 30. $\frac{7}{8}$ 0.875 31. $\frac{5}{9}$ $0.\overline{5}$
32. $4\frac{1}{3}$ $4.\overline{3}$ 33. $6\frac{2}{5}$ 6.4 34. $1\frac{6}{7}$ $1.\overline{857142}$

Write each decimal as a fraction in simplest form.

35. 0.7 $\frac{7}{10}$ 36. 0.44 $\frac{11}{25}$ 37. 0.05 $\frac{1}{20}$
38. 0.18 $\frac{9}{50}$ 39. 0.54 $\frac{27}{50}$ 40. 0.08 $\frac{2}{25}$

41. **RUNNING** Jeremy ran a mile in 5 minutes and 8 seconds. Write this time in minutes as a decimal. $5.1\overline{3}$ min

Example 5 Write $\frac{3}{8}$ as a decimal.

```
  0.375
8)3.000
 - 24
    60
  - 56
    40
  - 40
     0
```

So, $\frac{3}{8} = 0.375$.

Example 6 Write 0.64 as a fraction.

$0.64 = \frac{64}{100}$ Write as a fraction with a denominator of 100.

$= \frac{16}{25}$ Simplify.

4-6 Fractions and Percents (pp. 202–205)

7.1.6

Write each fraction as a percent.

42. $\frac{32}{100}$ 32% 43. $\frac{11}{25}$ 44% 44. $\frac{47}{50}$ 94% 45. $\frac{8}{20}$ 40%

Write each percent as a fraction in simplest form.

46. 68% $\frac{17}{25}$ 47. 95% $\frac{19}{20}$ 48. 42% $\frac{21}{50}$ 49. 16% $\frac{4}{25}$

50. **LUNCH** In Mrs. Soulise's class, 56% of the students buy their lunch. Write this percent as a fraction in simplest form. $\frac{14}{25}$

Example 7 Write $\frac{27}{50}$ as a percent.

$\frac{27}{50} = \frac{54}{100}$ Write an equivalent fraction with a denominator of 100.

$= 54\%$ Definition of percent

Example 8 Write 96% as a fraction.

$96\% = \frac{96}{100}$ Definition of percent

$= \frac{24}{25}$ Simplify.

Chapter 4 Study Guide and Review 223

Chapter 4 Study Guide and Review

Problem Solving Review

For additional practice in problem solving for Chapter 4, see the Mixed Problem Solving Appendix, page 707 in the Student Handbook section.

Anticipation Guide

Have students complete the Chapter 4 Anticipation Guide and discuss how their responses have changed now that they have completed Chapter 4.

CRM Anticipation Guide, p. 7

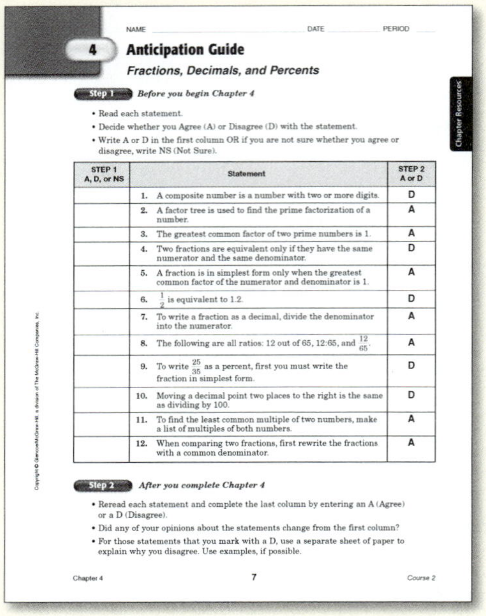

NAME ______ DATE ______ PERIOD ______

4 Anticipation Guide

Fractions, Decimals, and Percents

Chapter Resources

Step 1 *Before you begin Chapter 4*

- Read each statement.
- Decide whether you Agree (A) or Disagree (D) with the statement.
- Write A or D in the first column OR if you are not sure whether you agree or disagree, write NS (Not Sure).

STEP 1 A, D, or NS	Statement	STEP 2 A or D
	1. A composite number is a number with two or more digits.	D
	2. A factor tree is used to find the prime factorization of a number.	A
	3. The greatest common factor of two prime numbers is 1.	A
	4. Two fractions are equivalent only if they have the same numerator and the same denominator.	D
	5. A fraction is in simplest form only when the greatest common factor of the numerator and denominator is 1.	A
	6. $\frac{1}{2}$ is equivalent to 1.2.	D
	7. To write a fraction as a decimal, divide the denominator into the numerator.	A
	8. The following are all ratios: 12 out of 65, 12:65, and $\frac{12}{65}$.	A
	9. To write $\frac{25}{35}$ as a percent, first you must write the fraction in simplest form.	D
	10. Moving a decimal point two places to the right is the same as dividing by 100.	D
	11. To find the least common multiple of two numbers, make a list of multiples of both numbers.	A
	12. When comparing two fractions, first rewrite the fractions with a common denominator.	A

Step 2 *After you complete Chapter 4*

- Reread each statement and complete the last column by entering an A (Agree) or a D (Disagree).
- Did any of your opinions about the statements change from the first column?
- For those statements that you mark with a D, use a separate sheet of paper to explain why you disagree. Use examples, if possible.

Chapter 4 7 Course 2

Additional Answer

66. 2 dozen muffins and 3 packages of orange juice containers

Chapter 4 Study Guide and Review

4-7 Percents and Decimals (pp. 206–210)

7.1.6

Write each percent as a decimal.

51. 48% **0.48**

52. 7% **0.07**

53. 12.5% **0.125**

54. $75\frac{1}{4}\%$ **0.7525**

Write each decimal as a percent.

55. 0.61 **61%**

56. 0.055 **5.5%**

57. 0.19 **19%**

58. 0.999 **99.9%**

59. **FOOD** A serving of oatmeal contains 3 grams of fiber. This is 12% of the recommended daily allowance. Write this percent as a decimal. **0.12**

Example 9 Write 35% as a decimal.

$35\% = \frac{35}{100}$ Write the percent as a fraction.

$= 0.35$ Write the fraction as a decimal.

Example 10 Write 0.625 as a percent.

$0.625 = 0.625$ Multiply by 100.

$= 62.5\%$ Add the % symbol.

4-8 Least Common Multiple (pp. 211–214)

7.1.3

Find the LCM of each set of numbers.

60. 9, 15 **45**

61. 4, 8 **8**

62. 16, 24 **48**

63. 3, 8, 12 **24**

64. 4, 9, 12 **36**

65. 15, 24, 30 **120**

66. **BREAKFAST** At a bakery, muffins come in dozens and individual serving containers of orange juice come in packs of 8. If Avery needs to have the same amount of muffins as orange juice containers, what is the least possible number of sets of each he needs to buy? **See margin.**

Example 11 Find the LCM of 8 and 36.

Write each prime factorization.

$8 = 2 \times 2 \times 2 = 2^3$

$36 = 2 \times 2 \times 3 \times 3 = 2^2 \times 3^2$

LCM: $2^3 \times 3^2 = 72$

The LCM of 8 and 36 is 72.

4-9 Comparing and Ordering Rational Numbers (pp. 215–220)

7.1.6

Replace each ● with <, >, or = to make a true sentence.

67. $\frac{3}{8}$ ● $\frac{2}{3}$ **<**

68. -0.45 ● $-\frac{9}{20}$ **=**

69. $\frac{8}{9}$ ● 85% **>**

70. $-3\frac{3}{4}$ ● $-3\frac{5}{8}$ **<**

71. **SCHOOL** Michael received a $\frac{26}{30}$ on his English quiz and received 81% on his biology test. In which class did he receive the higher score? **English**

Example 12 Replace ● with <, >, or = to make $\frac{3}{5}$ ● $\frac{5}{8}$ a true sentence.

Find equivalent fractions. The LCD is 40.

$\frac{3}{5} = \frac{3 \times 8}{5 \times 8} = \frac{24}{40}$ $\quad \frac{5}{8} = \frac{5 \times 5}{8 \times 5} = \frac{25}{40}$

Since $\frac{24}{40} < \frac{25}{40}$, then $\frac{3}{5} < \frac{5}{8}$.

224 Chapter 4 Fractions, Decimals, and Percents

CHAPTER 4

Practice Test

IN Math Online glencoe.com
• Chapter Test

1. Find the prime factorization of 72. $2^3 \times 3^2$

2. Find the GCF of 24 and 40. 8

3. **SCHEDULES** Farijah registered for French, Pre-Algebra, Life Science, English, and Social Studies. French is only offered first period, Pre-Algebra is only offered fifth period, and she must have lunch fourth period. How many different schedules can she create out of a six period day? Use the *make an organized list* strategy. 6

Write each fraction in simplest form.

4. $\frac{24}{60}$ $\frac{2}{5}$

5. $\frac{64}{72}$ $\frac{8}{9}$

Write each fraction, mixed number, or percent as a decimal. Use bar notation if the decimal is a repeating decimal.

6. $\frac{7}{9}$ $0.\overline{7}$

7. $4\frac{5}{8}$ 4.625

8. 91% 0.91

9. **COINS** The United States Mint released a new quarter every ten weeks from 1999 to 2008 commemorating the 50 states. By the end of 2006, 40 state coins had been released. What percent of the coins is this? 80%

Write each decimal or percent as a fraction in simplest form.

10. 0.84 $\frac{21}{25}$

11. 0.006 $\frac{3}{500}$

12. 42% $\frac{21}{50}$

13. **MULTIPLE CHOICE** Which of the following is equivalent to the decimal 0.087? B

A 0.87%
B 8.7%
C 87%
D 870%

Write each fraction or decimal as a percent.

14. $\frac{15}{25}$ 60%

15. 0.26 26%

16. 0.135 13.5%

17. **FLOORING** Mr. Daniels is putting new floor tiles in his bathroom. He has already tiled 34 square feet of the floor measuring 5 feet by 10 feet. What percent of the floor has he tiled? 68%

18. **MULTIPLE CHOICE** What percent of the figure below is unshaded? H

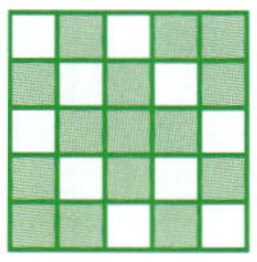

F 15%
G 30%
H 40%
J 60%

Find the LCM of each set of numbers.

19. 18, 42 126

20. 4, 5, 12 60

21. **PRACTICE** Rico has track practice every 3 days. He has saxophone practice every 4 days. If Rico has both track and saxophone practice today, after how many days will Rico have both track and saxophone practice again? 12 days

Replace each ● with <, >, or = to make a true sentence.

22. $-\frac{3}{5}$ ● $-\frac{5}{9}$ <

23. $4\frac{7}{12}$ ● $4\frac{6}{8}$ <

24. $\frac{13}{20}$ ● 65% =

25. **BASKETBALL** To make it past the first round of tryouts for the basketball team, Paul must make at least 35% of his free-throw attempts. During the first round of tryouts he makes 17 out of 40 attempts. Did Paul make it to the next round of tryouts? Explain your reasoning. See margin.

CHAPTER 4 Practice Test

Summative Assessment

CRM Chapter 4 Resource Masters

Leveled Chapter 4 Tests			
Form	**Type**	**Level**	**Pages**
1	MC	BL	71–72
2A	MC	OL	73–74
2B	MC	OL	75–76
2C	FR	OL	77–78
2D	FR	OL	79–80
3	FR	AL	81–82

MC = multiple-choice questions
FR = free-response questions
BL = below or approaching grade level
OL = on grade level
AL = above or beyond grade level

- Vocabulary Test, p. 70
- Extended-Response Test, p. 83

ExamView Assessment Suite Customize and create multiple versions of your chapter test and their answer keys. All of the questions from the leveled chapter tests in the *Chapter 4 Resource Masters* are also available on ExamView® Assessment Suite.

Additional Answer

25. Yes; $\frac{17}{40} = 0.425$ and $0.425 >$ 35% or 0.35.

Data-Driven Decision Making

Diagnostic Teaching Based on the results of the Chapter 4 Practice Test, use the following to review concepts that students continue to find challenging.

Exercises	Lesson	Academic Standards	Resources for Review
1–3	4-1, 4-2, 4-3	7.1.3, P.1.3	CRM Study Guide and Intervention pp. 10, 17, 22, 27, 33, 40, 46, 52, and 59
4–18	4-4, 4-5, 4-6, 4-7	7.1.6, 6.1.4	IN Math Online glencoe.com • Extra Examples • Personal Tutor • Concepts in Motion
19–25	4-8, 4-9	7.1.3, 7.1.6	

CHAPTER 4

ISTEP+ Practice

TEST-TAKING TIP

Exercise 6 Ask students what word (or words) might indicate the operation in the equation (addition). Students should realize that *sum* indicates addition, which should lead them to examine answer choice H.

Formative Assessment

You can use these three pages to benchmark student progress.

Chapter 4 Resource Masters

- Standardized Test Practice, pp. 84–86

ExamView Assessment Suite Create practice worksheets or tests that align to your state's standards, as well as TIMSS and NAEP tests.

CHAPTER 4

ISTEP+ Practice

Cumulative, Chapters 1–4

IN Math Online glencoe.com

- Test Practice

PART 1 Multiple Choice

Read each question. Then fill in the correct answer on the answer sheet provided by your teacher or on a sheet of paper.

1. A large school system estimates that 0.706 of its students will take the bus to school throughout the school year. Which number is greater than 0.706? **C**

   A $\frac{706}{1,000}$

   B $-1\frac{6}{7}$

   C $\frac{76}{100}$

   D -7.06

2. Debra is working on three different art projects. She has completed $\frac{1}{4}$, $\frac{3}{8}$, and $\frac{1}{2}$ of these projects, respectively. Which list shows the percent of work completed on these projects from least to greatest? **H**

   F 37.5%, 50%, 25%

   G 50%, 37.5%, 25%

   H 25%, 37.5%, 50%

   J 25%, 50%, 87.5%

3. Which of the following is the prime factored form of the lowest common denominator of $\frac{1}{6}$ and $\frac{3}{8}$? **D**

   A $2^2 \times 3 \times 5$ C 2×6

   B $2^3 \times 5$ D $2^3 \times 3$

TEST-TAKING TIP

Question 3 Eliminate any answer choices that you know are incorrect. Since the LCD, 24, does not have a factor of 5, you can eliminate answer choices A and B.

4. Solve the equation $x + 7 = -3$. What is the value of x? **J**

   F 4 H -4

   G 3 J -10

5. At a wedding reception, the number of seats s is equal to 8 times the number of tables t. Which equation matches this situation? **C**

   A $s = 8 + t$

   B $t = 8 \cdot s$

   C $s = 8 \cdot t$

   D $t = 8 - t$

6. Which problem situation matches the equation below? **H**

   $$x + 12 = 35$$

   F The difference between two numbers is 35. One of the numbers is 12. What is x, the other number?

   G Laura is 12 years younger than her brother. If Laura is 35 years old, find her brother's age x.

   H The sum of a number, x, and 12 is 35. What is the value of x?

   J Karen had \$35. If she received \$12, what is x, the total amount she now has?

7. Which of the following is true when evaluating the expression $3 \cdot 4^2 - 12 \div 6$? **B**

   A Multiply 3 by 4 first since multiplication comes before subtraction.

   B Evaluate 4^2 first since it is a power.

   C Divide 12 by 6 first since division comes before multiplication.

   D Multiply 3 by 4 first since all operations occur in order from left to right.

Preparing for ISTEP+

For test-taking strategies and practice, see pages 716–733.

8. Which sequence follows the rule $2n + 5$, where n represents the position of a term in the sequence? **H**

F 3, 5, 7, 9, 11, ...
G 6, 8, 10, 12, 14, ...
H 7, 9, 11, 13, 15, ...
J 8, 12, 16, 20, 24, ...

9. Nicholas used the Distributive Property to evaluate the expression $5(12 + 7)$ mentally. Which of the following is a correct use of the Distributive Property to evaluate this expression? **A**

A $5(12 + 7) = 5(12) + 5(7) = 60 + 35$ or 95
B $5(12 + 7) = 5(12) + 7 = 60 + 7$ or 67
C $5(12 + 7) = 12 + 5(7) = 12 + 35$ or 47
D $5(12 + 7) = 5 + 60 + 5 + 7 = 65 + 12$ or 77

10. Which of the following relationships is represented by the data in the table? **F**

x	y
1	5,280
2	10,560
3	15,840
4	21,120
5	26,400

F conversion of miles to feet
G conversion of inches to yards
H conversion of feet to miles
J conversion of yards to inches

11. If $g = 4$, $m = 3$, and $n = 6$, then $\frac{mn + 2}{g} + 1$ is equivalent to which of the following? **A**

A 6
B 5
C 3
D 2

PART 2 Short Response/Grid In

Record your answers on the answer sheet provided by your teacher or on a sheet of paper.

12. Write 7.2% as a decimal. **0.072**

13. Jeremy expects 8 out of the 10 friends he invited to come to his party. What percent of his friends does he expect to come? **80%**

PART 3 Extended Response

Record your answers on the answer sheet provided by your teacher or on a sheet of paper. Show your work.

14. The prime factorization of 24 is $2 \times 2 \times 2 \times 3$. The table lists each unique prime factor and the products of all possible unique combinations of two, three, and four prime factors.

Unique Prime Factors	2, 3
Products of Two Factors	2×2, 2×3
Products of Three Factors	$2 \times 2 \times 2$, $2 \times 2 \times 3$
Product of Four Factors	$2 \times 2 \times 2 \times 3$

a. Find each product. **4, 6, 8, 12, 24**

b. What do the products have in common? **The products are factors of 24.**

c. What other numbers are factors of 24? **the unique factors and 1**

d. Explain how you can use the prime factors of a number to find all of its factors. Test your conjecture by finding the factors of 60. **See margin.**

NEED EXTRA HELP?														
If You Missed Question...	1	2	3	4	5	6	7	8	9	10	11	12	13	14
Go to Lesson...	4-9	4-9	4-2	3-2	3-1	3-1	1-4	1-9	1-8	2-6	1-4	4-7	4-6	4-9
IN Academic Standards	7.1.6	7.1.6	7.1.3	7.2.2	7.2.1	7.2.1	7.2.3	7.2.1	7.2.3	P.1.3	7.2.3	7.1.6	7.1.6	7.1.6

Homework Option

Get Ready for Chapter 5 Assign students the exercises on page 229 as homework to assess whether they possess the prerequisite skills needed for the next chapter.

CHAPTER 4 ISTEP+ Practice

Answer Sheet Practice

Have students simulate taking a standardized test by recording their answers on a practice recording sheet.

CRM Student Recording Sheet, p. 65

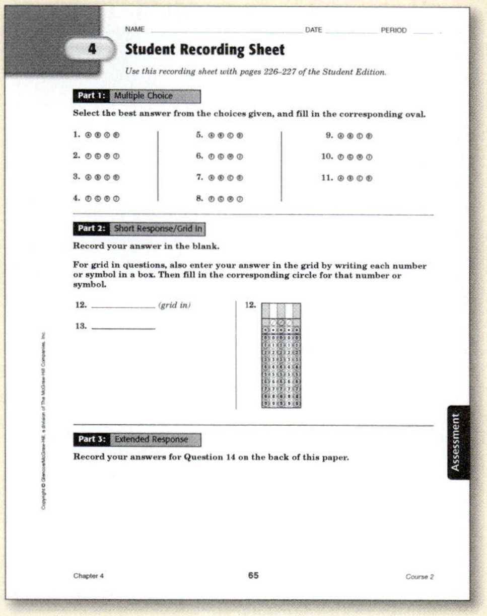

NAME ____ DATE ____ PERIOD ____

4 **Student Recording Sheet**

Use this recording sheet with pages 226–227 of the Student Edition.

Part 1: Multiple Choice

Select the best answer from the choices given, and fill in the corresponding oval.

1. Ⓐ Ⓑ Ⓒ Ⓓ 5. Ⓐ Ⓑ Ⓒ Ⓓ 9. Ⓐ Ⓑ Ⓒ Ⓓ
2. Ⓕ Ⓖ Ⓗ Ⓙ 6. Ⓕ Ⓖ Ⓗ Ⓙ 10. Ⓕ Ⓖ Ⓗ Ⓙ
3. Ⓐ Ⓑ Ⓒ Ⓓ 7. Ⓐ Ⓑ Ⓒ Ⓓ 11. Ⓐ Ⓑ Ⓒ Ⓓ
4. Ⓕ Ⓖ Ⓗ Ⓙ 8. Ⓕ Ⓖ Ⓗ Ⓙ

Part 2: Short Response/Grid In

Record your answer in the blank.

For grid in questions, also enter your answer in the grid by writing each number or symbol in a box. Then fill in the corresponding circle for that number or symbol.

12. ____ *(grid in)*
13. ____

Part 3: Extended Response

Record your answers for Question 14 on the back of this paper.

Assessment

Chapter 4 65 Course 2

Additional Answer

14d. Sample answer: Make a list that includes 1, all of the unique prime factors, plus the products of all possible combinations of two, three, four, ... prime factors; $60 = 2 \times 2 \times 3 \times 5$. The factors are 1, 2, 3, 5, 2×2, 2×3, 2×5, $2 \times 2 \times 3$, $2 \times 2 \times 5$, $2 \times 3 \times 5$, and $2 \times 2 \times 3 \times 5$.

Page 180, Explore 4-1

1. 1, 4, 9, 16, 25; Sample answer: They are equal to a number multiplied by itself. They have an odd number of factors.
2. Sample answer: Each of these numbers has an odd number of factors, so these lockers were touched by an odd number of students. This means the state of the locker was changed an odd number of times. Since a locker starts out closed, changing its state an odd number of times results in an open locker.

Page 181, Lesson 4-1 (Mini Lab)

1. 3 squares

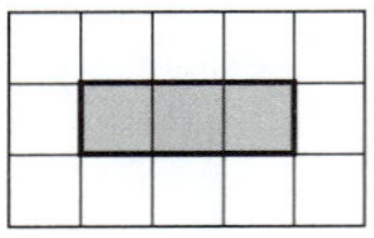

4 squares

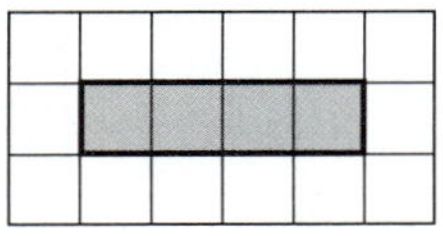

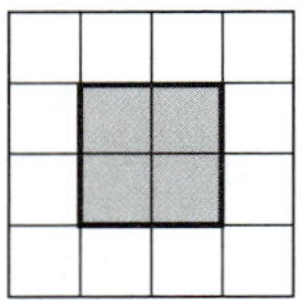

5 squares

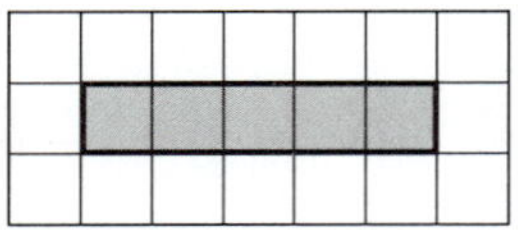

6 squares

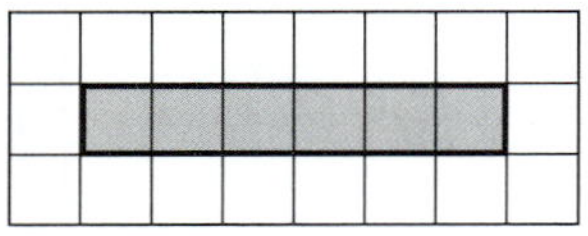

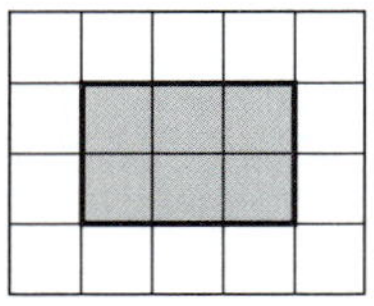

7 squares

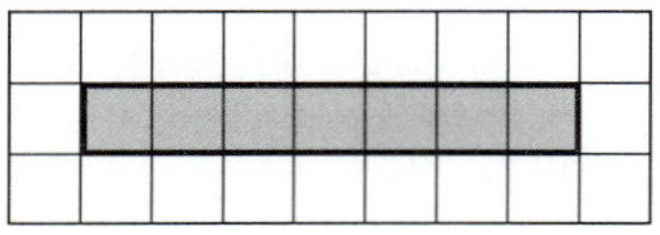

8 squares

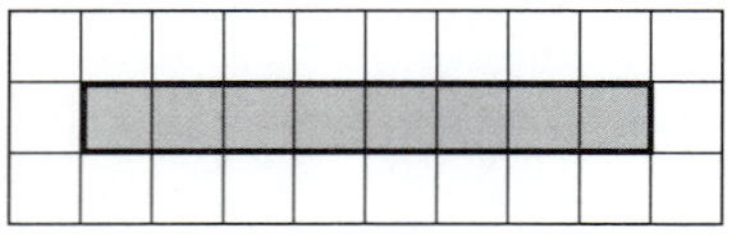

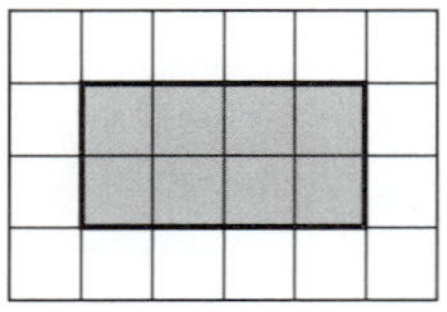

9 squares

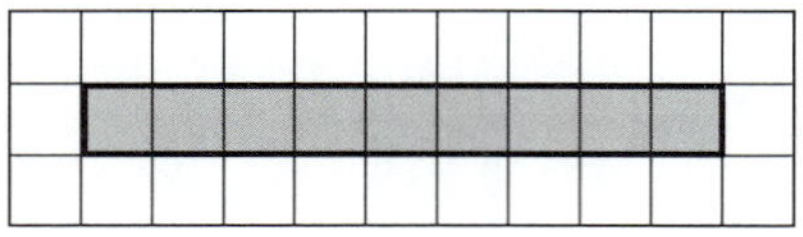

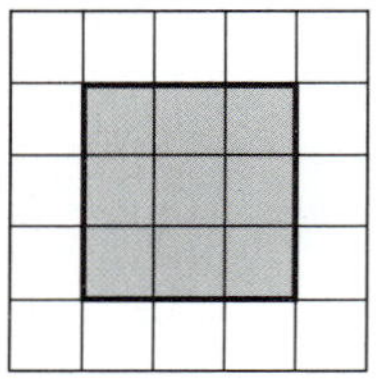

10 squares

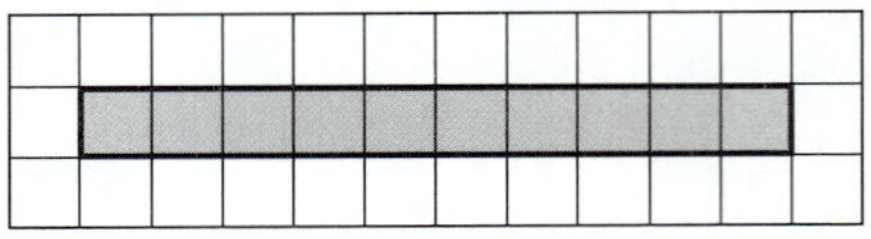

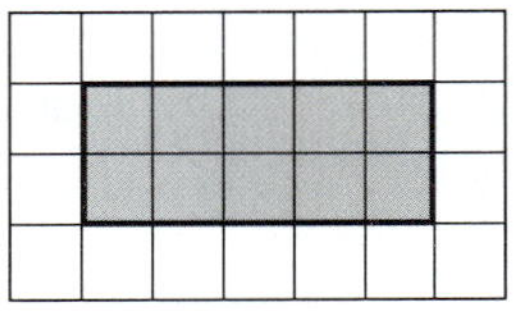

Page 184, Lesson 4-1

44.

1	2	3	~~4~~	5	~~6~~	7	~~8~~	~~9~~	~~10~~
11	~~12~~	13	~~14~~	~~15~~	~~16~~	17	~~18~~	19	~~20~~
~~21~~	~~22~~	23	~~24~~	~~25~~	~~26~~	~~27~~	~~28~~	29	~~30~~
31	~~32~~	~~33~~	~~34~~	~~35~~	~~36~~	37	~~38~~	~~39~~	~~40~~
41	~~42~~	43	~~44~~	~~45~~	~~46~~	47	~~48~~	~~49~~	~~50~~
~~51~~	~~52~~	53	~~54~~	~~55~~	~~56~~	~~57~~	~~58~~	59	~~60~~
61	~~62~~	~~63~~	~~64~~	~~65~~	~~66~~	67	~~68~~	~~69~~	~~70~~
71	~~72~~	73	~~74~~	~~75~~	~~76~~	~~77~~	~~78~~	79	~~80~~
~~81~~	~~82~~	83	~~84~~	~~85~~	~~86~~	~~87~~	~~88~~	89	~~90~~
~~91~~	~~92~~	~~93~~	~~94~~	~~95~~	~~96~~	97	~~98~~	~~99~~	~~100~~;

The prime numbers up to 100 are 2, 3, 5, 7, 11, 13, 17, 19, 23, 29, 31, 37, 41, 43, 47, 53, 59, 61, 67, 71, 73, 79, 83, 89, and 97.

Page 215, Lesson 4-9 (Mini Lab)

1.

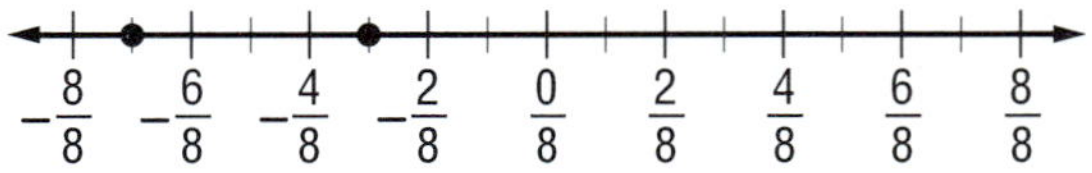

2.

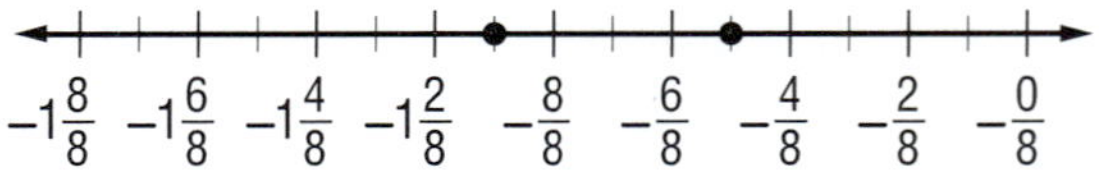

3.

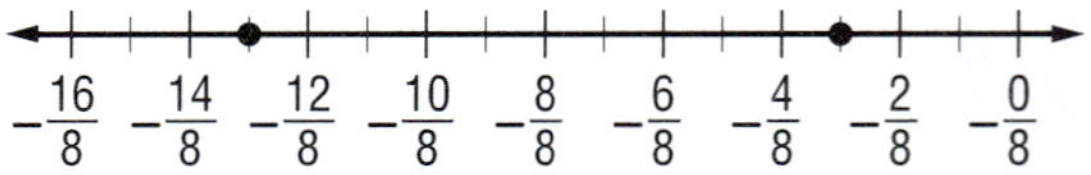

4.

5.

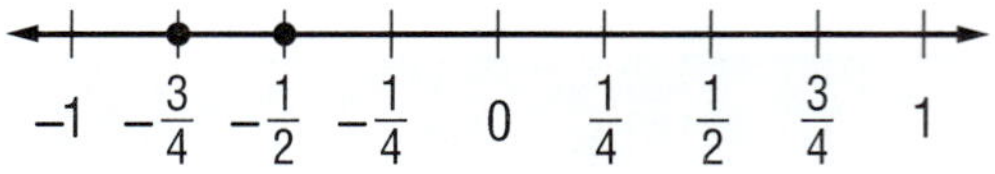

6.

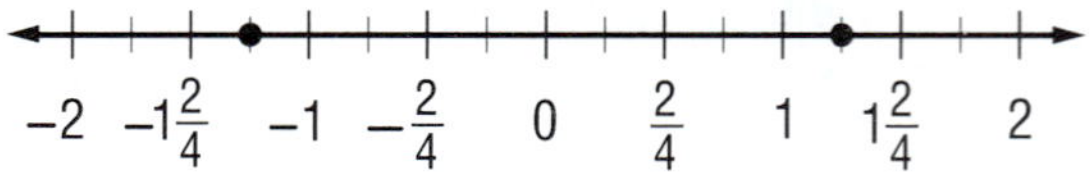

NOTES

CHAPTER 5

Chapter Overview

Applying Fractions

Lesson Plan		Pacing Your Lessons	
LESSONS AND OBJECTIVES	**Academic Standards**	**40–50 Minute Periods**	**90-Minute Periods**
5-1 Estimating with Fractions (pp. 230–235) • Estimate sums, differences, products, and quotients of fractions and mixed numbers.	7.1.7	Core Lesson 1	0.5
5-2 Adding and Subtracting Fractions (pp. 236–241) • Add and subtract fractions.	6.1.6	1	0.5
5-3 Adding and Subtracting Mixed Numbers (pp. 242–246) • Add and subtract mixed numbers.	6.1.6	1	0.5
5-4 Problem-Solving Investigation: Eliminate Possibilities (pp. 248–249) • Solve problems by eliminating possibilities.	P.1.3, P.2.4	Core Lesson 1.5	0.5
Explore 5-5 Math Lab: Multiplying Fractions (p. 250–251) Use area models to multiply fractions and mixed numbers. **5-5 Multiplying Fractions and Mixed Numbers** (pp. 252–257) • Multiply fractions and mixed numbers.	7.1.7	Core Lesson 1.5	0.5
5-6 Algebra: Solving Equations (pp. 258–263) • Solve equations with rational number solutions.	7.2.2	1	0.5
5-7 Dividing Fractions and Mixed Numbers (pp. 265–270) • Divide fractions and mixed numbers.	7.1.7	Core Lesson 1	0.5
REVIEW		1	1
ASSESSMENT		1	0.5*
	TOTAL	**10**	**5**

*The complete **Assessment Planner** for Chapter 5 is provided on page 229.*

** Begin Chapter 6 in the second half of the period.*

Focal Points

G7-FP3 Number and Operations, and Algebra
For the complete wording of the Focal Points for Grade 7, please see page T17.

Professional Development

Vertical Alignment

Before Chapter 5

Related Topics from Grade 6

- identify and represent on a number line fractions and mixed numbers
- solve simple problems, including ones arising in concrete situations, involving the addition and subtraction of fractions and mixed numbers and express answers in the simplest form
- compute and perform simple multiplication and division of fractions and apply these procedures to solving problems
- use a letter to represent an unknown number; write and evaluate simple algebraic expressions in one variable by substitution

Chapter 5

Topics from Grade 7

- solve problems involving addition, subtraction, multiplication, and division of positive fractions
- explain the meaning of multiplication and division of positive fractions and perform the calculations
- determine the least common multiple of whole numbers; use them to solve problems with fractions
- write and solve one-step linear equations in one variable form

After Chapter 5

Preparation for Grade 8

- add, subtract, multiply, and divide rational numbers (integers, fractions, and terminating decimals) and take positive rational numbers to whole-number powers
- add and subtract fractions by using factoring to find common denominators
- multiply, divide, and simplify rational numbers by using the exponent rules

Backmapping and Vertical Alignment

McGraw-Hill's ***Math Connnects*** program was conceived and developed with the final results in mind: student success in Algebra 1 and beyond. The authors, using the **NCTM Focal Points and Focal Connections** as their guide, developed this brand-new series by backmapping from Algebra 1 concepts and vertically aligning the topics so that they build upon prior skills and concepts and serve as a foundation for future topics.

What the Research Says...

According to Marzano, Pickering, and Pollock in *Classroom Instruction that Works: Research Based Strategies for Increasing Student Achievement,* feedback has significant effects on student achievement.

- In each lesson in Chapter 5, Guided Practice exercises present practice problems similar to those in the homework exercises. Students are able to correct any misconceptions about solving problems involving fractions.

Professional Development

Targeted professional development has been articulated throughout **McGraw-Hill's *Math Connects*** program. The **McGraw-Hill Professional Development Video Library** provides short videos that support the NCTM Focal Points and Focal Connections. For more information, visit glencoe.com.

Model Lessons

Instructional Strategies

CHAPTER 5 Technology Solutions

Teacher Resources

TeacherWorks™ All-in-One Planner and Resource Center

All of the print materials from the Classroom Resource Masters are available on your TeacherWorks™ CD-ROM.

BL = Below or Approaching Grade Level   OL = On Grade Level   AL = Above or Beyond Grade Level   ELL = English Language Learner

				Chapter Resource Masters	5-1	5-2	5-3	5-4	5-5	5-6	5-7
BL	OL		ELL	Lesson Reading Guide	9	15	21		31	38	44
BL	OL		ELL	Study Guide and Intervention*	10	16	22	27	32	39	45
BL	OL			Skills Practice*	11	17	23	28	33	40	46
	OL	AL		Practice*	12	18	24	29	34	41	47
	OL	AL		Word Problem Practice*	13	19	25	30	35	42	48
	OL	AL		Enrichment	14	20	26		36	43	49
	OL	AL		Calculator and Spreadsheet Activities					37		
	OL	AL		Chapter Assessments*	53–54, 55, 56, 57–68						
BL	OL	AL		5-Minute Check Transparencies	✓	✓	✓	✓	✓	✓	✓
BL	OL			Teaching Mathematics with Manipulatives					✓		
BL	OL	AL		Real-World Investigations for Differentiated Instruction	19–20, 57						

**Also available in Spanish*

Graphing Calculator Easy Files

- Timesaving Tech Tools for the TI-Navigator
- Quick Checks to diagnose student progress
- Deliver Differentiated Instruction with Ready Files
- Vocabulary Review

AssignmentWorks

Differentiated Assignments, Answers, and Solutions

- Print a customized assignment worksheet using the Student Edition exercises along with an answer key or worked-out solutions.
- Use default lesson assignments as outlined in the Differentiated Homework Options in the Teacher Edition.

Interactive Classroom

This CD-ROM is a customizable Microsoft® PowerPoint® presentation that includes:

- In-Class Examples
- Your Turn Exercises*
- 5-Minute Check Transparencies*
- Links to Online Study Tools
- Concepts in Motion

**compatible with response pad technology*

ExamView® Assessment Suite

ExamView® Assessment Suite

- Create, edit, and customize tests and worksheets using QuickTest Wizard
- Create multiple versions of tests and modify them for a desired level of difficulty
- Translate from English to Spanish and vice versa
- Build tests aligned with your state standards
- Track students' progress using the Teacher Management System

Student Tools

StudentWorks™ Plus

Textbook, Audio, Workbooks, and more

This CD-ROM is a valuable resource for students to access content online and use online resources to continue learning Chapter 5 concepts. Includes:

- Complete Student Edition
- English and Spanish audio
- Links to Concepts in Motion, Interactive Personal Tutor, and other online resources
- Access to all student worksheets
- Daily Assignments and Grade Log

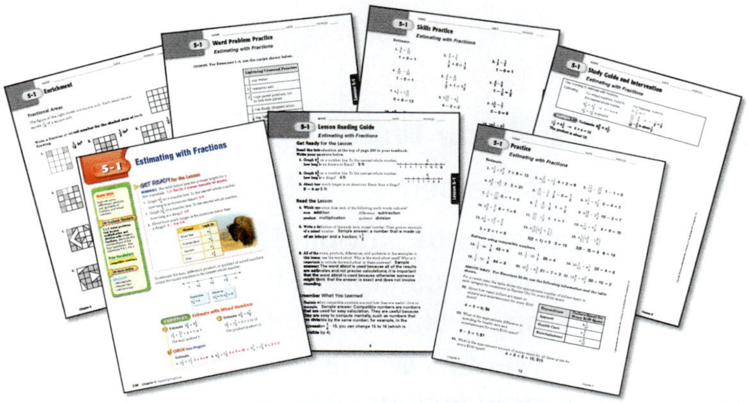

Super DVD

The Super DVD contains two Glencoe multimedia products.

MindJogger Plus An alternative review of concepts in which students work as teams in a game show format to gain points for correct answers.

What's Math Got to Do With It? Real-Life Math Videos
Engaging video that shows students how math is used in everyday situations.

Internet Resources

IN Math Online glencoe.com

TEACHER	STUDENT	PARENT	Online Study Tools
	•	•	Online Student Edition
•	•	•	Multilingual Glossary
			Lesson Resources
	•	•	Extra Examples
	•	•	BrainPOPS
	•	•	Self-Check Quizzes
•	•	•	Concepts in Motion
	•	•	Other Calculator Keystrokes
	•	•	Real-World Careers
	•	•	Reading in the Content Area
•			Group Activity Cards
			Chapter Resources
	•	•	Family Letters and Activities
	•		Chapter Readiness Quiz
	•	•	Vocabulary Review
	•	•	Chapter Test
	•	•	Standardized Test Practice
			Unit Resources
•	•		WebQuest Project
			Other Resources
	•		Personal Tutor
•			NAEP Correlations
•			Key Concepts
•	•	•	Meet the Authors
•	•		Game Zone
•	•	•	Math Skills Maintenance
•			National Resources (Professional Organizations)
•			State Resources
•			Vocabulary PuzzleMakers

CHAPTER 5 Reading and Writing in Mathematics

Noteables™ Interactive Study Notebook with Foldables™

This workbook is a study organizer that provides helpful steps for students to follow to organize their notes for Chapter 5.

- Students use Noteables to record notes and to complete their Foldables as you present the material for each lesson.
- Noteables correspond to the Examples in the *Teacher Edition* and *Interactive Classroom CD-ROM.*

Real-World Problem Solving Graphic Novels

Mathematical problem solving is presented in a motivating, graphic novel format. The novels contain real-world problems for each of the following mathematical strands: Number Sense, Algebraic Thinking, Geometry, Measurement, Statistics and Probability, and Mathematical Reasoning.

READING in the Content Area

This online worksheet provides strategies for reading and analyzing Lesson 5-2, Adding and Subtracting Fractions. Students are guided through questions about the main idea, subject matter, supporting details, conclusion, clarifying details, and vocabulary of the lesson.

glencoe.com

Recommended Outside Reading for Students

Mathematics and Star Wars

- *Dune* by Frank Herbert © 1965 [fiction]

This book is credited with providing ideas for the stories contained in the Star Wars movies. It has a young prince who grows from boy to warrior to ruler. The mathematics is the gift of the Mentats who are versions of human computers. The story includes computations with numbers like those found in Chapter 5.

Project CRISS℠ STUDY SKILL

Taking good notes will help students become actively involved in the learning process. For each lesson, have students read and then write notes about the topic. You may wish to show them the sample notes for Lesson 5-1 at the right to use as a guide. Afterward, allow class time for students to discuss their notes. Encourage students to talk about the procedures used in the lesson for solving the problems and how they addressed those procedures in their notes.

Lesson 5-1

Estimate with mixed numbers

- round to the nearest whole number
- Example: $7\frac{1}{5} + 5\frac{7}{10} \approx 7 + 6$, or 13

Estimate with fractions

- round to 0, $\frac{1}{2}$, or 1
- Example: $\frac{2}{3} + \frac{1}{5} \approx 1 + 0$, or 1

CReating Independence through Student-owned Strategies

Differentiated Instruction

Investigative Approach

MathScape™

This project was supported, in part, by the
National Science Foundation

MathScape is a mathematics curriculum for grades 6–8 developed by the Seeing and Thinking Mathematically Project at the Education Development Center.

Operating with Factors, Multiples, and Fractions
From Wholes to Parts

How to Use *MathScape* with Chapter 5

The unit *From Wholes to Parts* can be used to enhance Lessons 5-5 and 5-7.

- **Introduce** → Before you begin **Lesson 5-5**, introduce multiplying fractions by using pages 130–131.
- **Enrich** → After you complete **Lesson 5-7**, challenge students with fraction division by using pages 138–139.

RTI (Response to Intervention)

TIER 1 **On-Level Instruction** Use the *Math Connects* program as instruction for your on-level students.

TIER 2 **Strategic Intervention** For options to instruct struggling students, refer to the Diagnostic Assessment table on page 229.

TIER 3 **Intensive Intervention** *Math Triumphs* can provide intensive intervention for students who are at risk of not meeting the objectives addressed in Chapter 8.

Diagnose student readiness with the Quick Check and Quick Review on page 229. Then use *Math Triumphs* to accelerate their achievment.

Applying Fractions

Prerequisite Skill	*Math Triumphs*
Fractions	Ch. 1
Operations	Ch. 9

Practice and Review

Quick Review Math Handbook* is Glencoe's mathematical handbook for students and parents.

Hot Words includes a glossary of terms.

Hot Topics consists of two parts:

- explanations of key mathematical concepts
- exercises to check students' understanding.

Lesson	Hot Topics Section	Lesson	Hot Topics Section
5-2	2•3	5-6	2•4, 6•4
5-3	2•3	5-7	2•4
5-5	2•4		

Also available in Spanish

Chapter 5 Notes

FOLDABLES™ Study Organizer — Dinah Zike's Foldables

Focus This Foldable is designed to help students organize their notes about fractions and mixed numbers.

Teach Explain to students that they should record what they learn about fractions and mixed numbers on index cards and sort them into the appropriate pockets of their Foldables.

When to Use It

Pocket	Use with Lesson(s)
Fractions	5-1, 5-2, 5-4, 5-5, 5-6, 5-7
Mixed Numbers	5-1, 5-3, 5-4, 5-5, 5-6, 5-7

A version of a completed Foldable is shown on p. 271.

Differentiated Instruction

CRM Student-Built Glossary, p. 1

Students complete the chart by providing the definition of each term and an example as they progress through Chapter 5.

This study tool can be used to review for the chapter test.

Materials Needed for Chapter 5

- rulers (Lesson 5-2)
- grid paper (Lesson 5-2, Explore 5-5 and Lesson 5-6)
- geoboards (Explore 5-5)
- geobands (Explore 5-5)
- colored pencils (Explore 5-5 and Lesson 5-6)
- paper plates (Lesson 5-7)
- scissors (Lesson 5-7)

Chapter 5 Applying Fractions

Indiana Academic Standards

7.1.7 Solve problems that involve multiplication and division with integers, fractions, decimals and combinations of the four operations.

Key Vocabulary

compatible numbers (p. 232)
like fractions (p. 236)
reciprocal (p. 258)
unlike fractions (p. 237)

Real-World Link

Baking The measurements found on measuring cups and spoons are written as fractions. You will use fractions to find how much of each ingredient is needed when you make part of a whole recipe.

FOLDABLES® Study Organizer

Applying Fractions Make this Foldable to help you organize your notes. Begin with a plain sheet of 11″ by 17″ paper, four index cards, and glue.

1. **Fold** the paper in half widthwise.

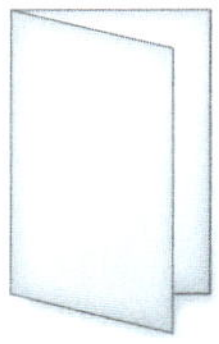

2. **Open** and fold along the length about $2\frac{1}{2}$″ from the bottom.

3. **Glue** the edge on each side to form two pockets.

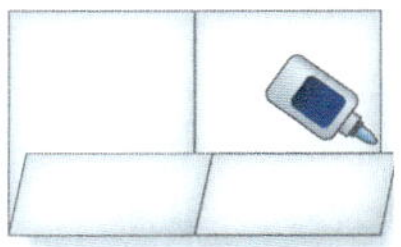

4. **Label** the pockets *Fractions* and *Mixed Numbers*, respectively. Place two index cards in each pocket.

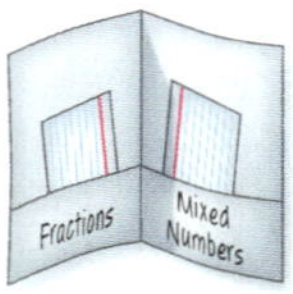

GET READY for Chapter 5

Diagnose Readiness You have two options for checking Prerequisite Skills.

Option 2

IN Math Online Take the Online Readiness Quiz at glencoe.com.

Option 1

Take the Quick Quiz below. Refer to the Quick Review for help.

QUICK Quiz

(Used in Lessons 5-2 and 5-3)

Find the LCD of each pair of fractions. (Lesson 4-8)

1. $\frac{5}{7}, \frac{3}{5}$ **35**
2. $\frac{1}{2}, \frac{4}{9}$ **18**
3. $\frac{8}{15}, \frac{1}{6}$ **30**
4. $\frac{3}{4}, \frac{7}{10}$ **20**

QUICK Review

Example 1

Find the LCD of $\frac{5}{6}$ and $\frac{3}{10}$.

The LCD is the LCM of the denominators, 6 and 10, or 30.

QUICK Quiz

(Used in Lessons 5-5 and 5-7)

Multiply or divide. (Prior Grade)

5. 1.8×12 **21.6**
6. $99 \div 12$ **8.25**
7. $83 \div 100$ **0.83**
8. 4.6×0.3 **1.38**
9. **MEASUREMENT** How many 1.6-meter sections of rope can be cut from a length of rope 6.4 meters? (Prior Grade) **4**
10. **COINS** Manuel owes each of 8 friends \$0.35. How much does he owe in all? (Prior Grade) **\$2.80**

QUICK Review

Example 2

Find $7.8 \div 0.25$.

$$\begin{array}{r} 31.2 \\ 0.25\overline{)7.80\,0} \\ -7\,5 \\ \hline 30 \\ -25 \\ \hline 50 \\ -50 \\ \hline 0 \end{array}$$

Move the decimal point 2 places to the right and divide as with whole numbers.

QUICK Quiz

(Used in Lessons 5-3 and 5-7)

Complete to show equivalent mixed numbers. (Prior Grade)

11. $3\frac{1}{5} = 2\frac{■}{5}$ **$2\frac{6}{5}$**
12. $9\frac{2}{3} = ■\frac{5}{3}$ **$8\frac{5}{3}$**
13. $6\frac{1}{4} = 5\frac{■}{4}$ **$5\frac{5}{4}$**
14. $8\frac{6}{7} = 7\frac{■}{7}$ **$7\frac{13}{7}$**
15. **RECIPES** A recipe calls for $4\frac{2}{3}$ cups of flour. This is equivalent to 3 cups of flour plus an additional how many cups of flour? (Prior Grade) **$\frac{5}{3}$ or $1\frac{2}{3}$ c**

QUICK Review

Example 3

Complete $4\frac{2}{9} = ■\frac{11}{9}$ to show equivalent mixed numbers.

$$\begin{aligned} 4\tfrac{2}{9} &= 3 + 1\tfrac{2}{9} \\ &= 3 + \tfrac{9}{9} + \tfrac{2}{9} \\ &= 3 + \tfrac{11}{9} \\ &= 3\tfrac{11}{9} \end{aligned}$$

Diagnostic Assessment

Exercises	Academic Standards	Intervention
1–4	**6.1.6**	SE Review Lesson 4-9, pp. 215–220
5–10	**7.1.7**	SE Concepts and Skills Bank, pp. 736 and 738
11–15	**7.1.7**	*Math Skills Maintenance Masters,* pp. 63–65

ASSESSMENT PLANNER

CHAPTER 5

Formative Assessment

CRM Anticipation Guide, pp. 7–8

Spotting Preconceived Ideas

Students complete this survey to determine prior knowledge about ideas from Chapter 5. Revisit this worksheet after completing the chapter. Also see page 274.

TE Lesson Activities

- Ticket Out the Door, pp. 249, 257, 270
- Crystal Ball, pp. 235, 241
- Name the Math, p. 246
- Yesterday's News, p. 263

Chapter Checkpoints

- SE Mid-Chapter Quiz, p. 247
- SE Study Guide and Review, pp. 271–274
- SE Test Practice, pp. 276–277
- CRM Quizzes, pp. 53 and 54
- CRM Standardized Test Practice, pp. 70–72

IN Math Online glencoe.com

- Self-Check Quizzes
- Practice Test
- Standardized Test Practice

Summative Assessment

- SE Chapter Practice Test, p. 275
- CRM Mid-Chapter Test, p. 55
- CRM Vocabulary Test, p. 56
- CRM Extended-Response Test, p. 69
- CRM Leveled Chapter Tests, pp. 57–68
- CD-ROM ExamView® Assessment Suite

KEY

- CRM *Chapter 5 Resource Masters*
- SE Student Edition
- TE Teacher Edition
- CD-ROM

5-1 Estimating with Fractions

PACING: **Regular:** 1 period, **Block:** 0.5 period

IN Academic Standards **7.1.7 Solve problems that involve multiplication and division with** integers, **fractions**, decimals and combinations of the four operations. *Also addresses P.6.1, P.6.3.*

Options for Differentiated Instruction

ELL = English Language Learner AL = Above or Beyond Grade Level SS = Struggling Students SN = Special Needs

Extending the Lesson Opener SS

Use after presenting Get Ready for the Lesson.

After completing Get Ready for the Lesson, present the following problem to students.

Estimate how many Opossums would be needed to stand as tall as an American Bison. Explain how you determined your answer.

3: Since an Opossum is approximately 3 feet tall and an American Bison is approximately 9 feet tall it would require three 3 foot tall possums to equal one 9 foot tall American Bison.

Visual Clues SS SN

Use before presenting Examples 1–8.

Have students create an index card with several number lines with benchmark fractions that they can refer to, such as those shown at the right.

This will help them to judge whether to round fractions up or down.

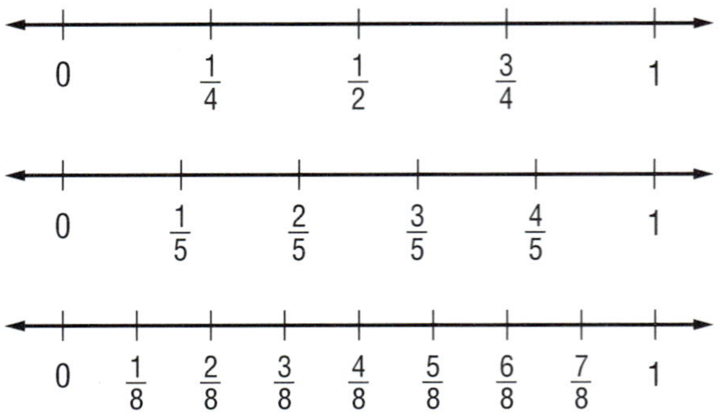

Logical Reasoning ELL AL

Use after presenting Examples 1–8.

Have students create and label a table like the one shown below.

Estimation	
Makes Sense	**Does Not Make Sense**

Have them list situations in which estimating mixed numbers makes sense and situations in which it does not make sense to estimate. For example, when making a loaf of bread, estimating how much flour to buy makes sense; estimating how much flour to use for the dough does not.

Leveled Lesson Resources

Also on TeacherWorks™ Lesson 5-1

Chapter 5 Resource Masters

BL = Below or Approaching Grade Level OL = On Grade Level AL = Above or Beyond Grade Level ELL = English Language Learner

Lesson Reading Guide
p. 9 BL OL ELL

NAME ______ DATE ______ PERIOD ____

5-1 Lesson Reading Guide
Estimating with Fractions

Get Ready for the Lesson

Read the introduction at the top of page 230 in your textbook. Write your answers below.

1. Graph $9\frac{1}{4}$ on a number line. To the nearest whole number, how long is an American Bison? **9 ft**

2. Graph $3\frac{3}{4}$ on a number line. To the nearest whole number, how long is a dingo? **4 ft**

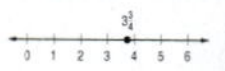

3. About how much longer is an American Bison than a dingo? **9 − 4 or 5 ft**

Read the Lesson

4. Which operation does each of the following math words indicate?
sum **addition** difference **subtraction**
product **multiplication** quotient **division**

5. Write a definition of the math term *mixed number*. Then give an example of a mixed number. **Sample answer: a number that is made up of an integer and a fraction; $1\frac{1}{2}$**

6. All of the sums, products, differences, and quotients in the examples in this lesson use the word *about*. Why is the word *about* used? Why is it important to include the word *about* in these answers? **Sample answer: The word *about* is used because all of the results are estimates and not precise calculations; it is important that the word *about* is used because otherwise someone might think that the answer is exact and does not involve rounding.**

Remember What You Learned

7. Explain what compatible numbers are and how they are useful. Give an example. **Sample answer: Compatible numbers are numbers that are used for easy calculation. They are useful because they are easy to compute mentally, such as numbers that are divisible by the same number; for example, in the expression $\frac{1}{4} \cdot 15$, you can change 15 to 16 (which is divisible by 4).**

Lesson 5-1

Chapter 5 9 Course 2

Study Guide and Intervention*
p. 10 BL OL ELL

NAME ______ DATE ______ PERIOD ____

5-1 Study Guide and Intervention
Estimating with Fractions

Use rounding to estimate with fractions.		
Estimating:	For mixed numbers, round to the nearest whole number. $4\frac{1}{6} + 3\frac{7}{8} \rightarrow 4 + 4 = 8$; $4\frac{1}{6} + 3\frac{7}{8}$ is *about* 8.	For fractions, round to 0, $\frac{1}{2}$, or 1. $\frac{11}{12} - \frac{4}{9} \rightarrow 1 - \frac{1}{2} = \frac{1}{2}$; $\frac{11}{12} - \frac{4}{9}$ is *about* $\frac{1}{2}$.

Example 1 Estimate $2\frac{2}{3} \times 4\frac{1}{4}$.

$2\frac{2}{3} \times 4\frac{1}{4} \rightarrow 3 \times 4 = 12$

The product is *about* 12.

Example 2 Estimate $\frac{6}{7} - \frac{3}{5}$.

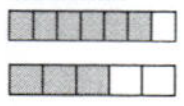

$\frac{6}{7}$ is about 1.

$\frac{3}{5}$ is about $\frac{1}{2}$.

$\frac{6}{7} - \frac{3}{5} \rightarrow 1 - \frac{1}{2} = \frac{1}{2}$ The difference is *about* $\frac{1}{2}$.

Exercises

Estimate.

1. $4\frac{1}{3} + 3\frac{4}{5}$ **4 + 4 = 8**
2. $2\frac{1}{6} \times 3\frac{2}{3}$ **2 × 4 = 8**
3. $\frac{7}{12} - \frac{1}{10}$ **$\frac{1}{2} - 0 = \frac{1}{2}$**
4. $5\frac{1}{4} - 1\frac{1}{2}$ **5 − 2 = 3**
5. $4\frac{3}{4} + 1\frac{1}{5}$ **5 + 1 = 6**
6. $\frac{5}{9} \times \frac{13}{14}$ **$\frac{1}{2} \times 1 = \frac{1}{2}$**
7. $\frac{1}{6} \div \frac{8}{9}$ **0 ÷ 1 = 0**
8. $\frac{6}{7} \div \frac{9}{10}$ **1 ÷ 1 = 1**
9. $13\frac{4}{5} \div 1\frac{7}{8}$ **14 ÷ 2 = 7**
10. $12\frac{1}{4} \div 5\frac{7}{8}$ **12 ÷ 6 = 2**

Chapter 5 10 Course 2

Skills Practice*
p. 11 BL OL

NAME ______ DATE ______ PERIOD ____

5-1 Skills Practice
Estimating with Fractions

Estimate.

1. $\frac{4}{5} + \frac{2}{11}$ **1 + 0 = 1**
2. $\frac{4}{7} + \frac{1}{5}$ **$\frac{1}{2} + 0 = \frac{1}{2}$**
3. $\frac{7}{9} - \frac{1}{5}$ **1 − 0 = 1**
4. $\frac{9}{10} - \frac{1}{23}$ **1 − 0 = 1**
5. $\frac{3}{5} + \frac{9}{11}$ **$\frac{1}{2} + 1 = 1\frac{1}{2}$**
6. $\frac{4}{5} - \frac{4}{9}$ **$1 - \frac{1}{2} = \frac{1}{2}$**
7. $5\frac{1}{7} + 7\frac{9}{11}$ **5 + 8 = 13**
8. $3\frac{10}{11} - 2\frac{1}{6}$ **4 − 2 = 2**
9. $5\frac{1}{4} - \frac{1}{7}$ **5 − 0 = 5**
10. $8\frac{3}{7} - 2\frac{1}{2}$ **8 − 3 = 5**
11. $2\frac{1}{8} + 6\frac{9}{10}$ **2 + 7 = 9**
12. $10\frac{1}{8} - 3\frac{1}{4}$ **10 − 3 = 7**
13. $\frac{4}{5} \times \frac{8}{9}$ **1 × 1 = 1**
14. $\frac{6}{7} \div \frac{10}{11}$ **1 ÷ 1 = 1**
15. $3\frac{6}{7} \times 2\frac{1}{10}$ **4 × 2 = 8**
16. $16\frac{1}{3} \div 3\frac{8}{9}$ **16 ÷ 4 = 4**
17. $31\frac{3}{4} \div 2\frac{1}{8}$ **32 ÷ 2 = 16**
18. $3\frac{4}{5} \cdot 1\frac{1}{4}$ **4 · 1 = 4**
19. $12 \div 2\frac{6}{7}$ **12 ÷ 3 = 4**
20. $44\frac{1}{5} \div 3\frac{7}{8}$ **44 ÷ 4 = 11**
21. $10\frac{1}{7} \cdot 4\frac{1}{3}$ **10 · 4 = 40**
22. $5\frac{1}{8} \cdot 6\frac{9}{11}$ **5 · 7 = 35**
23. $\frac{3}{12} \div 4\frac{4}{5}$ **0 ÷ 5 = 0**
24. $2\frac{1}{2} \div 3\frac{1}{3}$ **3 ÷ 3 = 1**
25. Estimate $36\frac{1}{4}$ divided by 6. **36 ÷ 6 = 6**
26. Estimate the sum of $7\frac{9}{10}$, $2\frac{1}{5}$, and $3\frac{2}{3}$. **8 + 2 + 4 = 14**

Lesson 5-1

Chapter 5 11 Course 2

Practice*
p. 12 OL AL

NAME ______ DATE ______ PERIOD ____

5-1 Practice
Estimating with Fractions

Estimate.

1. $7\frac{1}{6} + 5\frac{8}{9}$ **7 + 6 = 13**
2. $4\frac{2}{10} + 1\frac{1}{2}$ **4 + 2 = 6**
3. $\frac{11}{13} - \frac{15}{16}$ **1 − 1 = 0**
4. $6\frac{4}{5} \cdot 3\frac{2}{7}$ **7 · 3 = 21**
5. $\frac{6}{11} - \frac{1}{5}$ **$\frac{1}{2} - 0 = \frac{1}{2}$**
6. $8\frac{1}{4} \div 3\frac{7}{8}$ **8 ÷ 4 = 2**
7. $\frac{1}{8} \div \frac{17}{20}$ **0 ÷ 1 = 0**
8. $\frac{5}{8} \cdot \frac{9}{10}$ **$\frac{1}{2} \cdot 1 = \frac{1}{2}$**
9. $9\frac{14}{15} - 2\frac{3}{4}$ **10 − 3 = 7**
10. $5\frac{3}{5} \div \frac{5}{6}$ **6 ÷ 1 = 6**
11. $\frac{10}{11} \cdot 1\frac{1}{9}$ **1 · 1 = 1**
12. $4\frac{1}{14} + 5\frac{7}{8}$ **4 + 6 = 10**
13. $5\frac{1}{9} + 1\frac{6}{7} + \frac{5}{6}$ **5 + 2 + 1 = 8**
14. $4\frac{9}{10}\left(2\frac{1}{3} + \frac{7}{8}\right)$ **5(2 + 1) = 5 · 3 = 15**
15. $3\frac{1}{5}\left(7\frac{2}{3} - 1\frac{8}{9}\right)$ **3(8 − 2) = 3 · 6 = 18**

Estimate using compatible numbers.

16. $\frac{1}{5} \cdot 44$ **$\frac{1}{5} \cdot 45 = 9$**
17. $\frac{1}{7} \cdot 29$ **$\frac{1}{7} \cdot 28 = 4$**
18. $33\frac{1}{10} \div 4\frac{1}{3}$ **32 ÷ 4 = 8**
19. $\frac{1}{8} \cdot 62$ **$\frac{1}{8} \cdot 64 = 8$**
20. $20\frac{5}{6} \div 6\frac{2}{5}$ **21 ÷ 7 = 3**
21. $19\frac{4}{5} \div 8\frac{2}{3}$ **20 ÷ 10 = 2**

ANALYZE TABLES **For Exercises 22–24, use the following information and the table shown.**

For a recent year, the table shows the approximate number of dollars spent in each category by consumers in Kansas City for every $100 spent.

Expenditure	Dollars Spent for Every $100 Spent
Apparel	$3\frac{7}{10}$
Health Care	$5\frac{3}{5}$
Entertainment	$5\frac{3}{10}$

22. About how many dollars are spent on apparel and entertainment for every $100 spent? **4 + 5 = 9; $9**

23. What is the approximate difference in spending for health care and entertainment for every $100 spent? **6 − 5 = 1; $1**

24. What is the approximate amount of money spent for all three areas for every $100 spent? **4 + 6 + 5 = 15; $15**

Chapter 5 12 Course 2

Word Problem Practice*
p. 13 OL AL

NAME ______ DATE ______ PERIOD ____

5-1 Word Problem Practice
Estimating with Fractions

COOKING **For Exercises 1–4, use the recipe shown below.**

Lightning Creamed Potatoes
$\frac{1}{3}$ cup water
$1\frac{1}{2}$ teaspoon salt
$3\frac{3}{4}$ cups pared potatoes, cut in bite-size pieces
$\frac{1}{3}$ cup finely chopped onion
$\frac{1}{2}$ cup light cream

serves 6

1. Daniel wants to serve twelve people the Lightning Creamed Potatoes. Estimate how much salt he will need if he doubles the recipe. **2 × 2 or 4 tsp**

2. Rosita wants to triple the recipe above. Estimate how many cups of pared potatoes she will need. **3 × 4 or 12 c**

3. Alvin is going to serve six people. He only has $1\frac{1}{4}$ cups of pared potatoes. About how many cups of potatoes will he have to borrow? **4 − 1 or 3 c**

4. Katrina wants to make half of the recipe. About how many cups of potatoes will she need? **$\frac{1}{2} \times 4$ or 2 c**

5. CARPENTRY A board is $17\frac{3}{4}$ inches long. Carmen wants to shorten the length by about $1\frac{7}{8}$ inches. Estimate the length of the board after the board has been shortened. **18 − 2 or 16 in.**

6. TRACK Akira ran two miles. He ran the first mile in $7\frac{3}{4}$ minutes and the second mile in $8\frac{3}{4}$ minutes. Estimate how long it took Akira to run two miles. **8 + 9 or 17 min**

Lesson 5-1

Chapter 5 13 Course 2

Enrichment
p. 14 OL AL

NAME ______ DATE ______ PERIOD ____

5-1 Enrichment

Fractional Areas

The figure at the right shows one square inch. Each small square equals $\frac{1}{16}$ of a square inch.

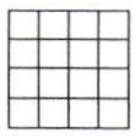

Write a fraction or mixed number for the shaded area of each drawing.

1. 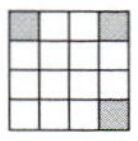 **$\frac{3}{16}$ in²**
2. 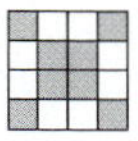 **$\frac{1}{2}$ in²**
3. 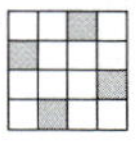 **$\frac{1}{4}$ in²**
4. 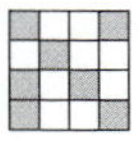 **$\frac{7}{16}$ in²**
5. 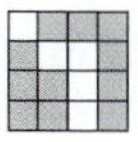 **$\frac{11}{16}$ in²**
6. 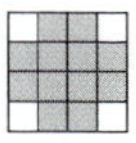 **$\frac{3}{4}$ in²**
7.  **$\frac{13}{32}$ in²**
8. 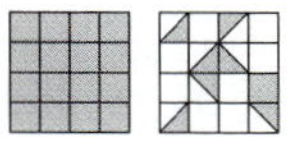 **$1\frac{9}{32}$ in²**
9. 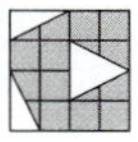 **$\frac{3}{4}$ in²**
10.  **$1\frac{1}{2}$ in²**

Chapter 5 14 Course 2

*** Also available in Spanish** ELL

Additional Lesson Resources

Transparencies

- *5-Minute Check Transparency*, Lesson 5-1

Other Print Products

- *Noteables™ Interactive Study Notebook with Foldables™*

Teacher Tech Tools

- *Interactive Classroom CD-ROM*, Lesson 5-1
- *AssignmentWorks*, Lesson 5-1

Student Tech Tools

glencoe.com

- Extra Examples, Chapter 5, Lesson 1
- Self-Check Quiz, Chapter 5, Lesson 1

5-1 Lesson Notes

1 Focus

Vertical Alignment

Before Lesson 5-1
Identify and represent on a number line fractions and mixed numbers

Lesson 5-1
Solve problems involving addition, subtraction, multiplication, and division of positive fractions

After Lesson 5-1
Add, subtract, multiply, and divide rational numbers (integers, fractions, and terminating decimals) and take positive rational numbers to whole-number powers

2 Teach

Scaffolding Questions

Tell students that a sixth-grade class went to a pizzeria.

Ask:

- If $\frac{1}{2}$ of a mushroom pizza and $\frac{1}{3}$ of a cheese pizza were left over, about how much pizza was left over? about 1 whole pizza, or about $\frac{3}{4}$
- If $1\frac{1}{4}$ pepperoni pizzas and $\frac{5}{6}$ of a sausage pizza were left over, about how much pizza was left over? about 2 pizzas
- If Nick, Lenny, and Miguel each ate $\frac{3}{8}$ of a pizza, about how much pizza did they eat altogether? about 1 pizza

5-1 Estimating with Fractions

MAIN IDEA

Estimate sums, differences, products, and quotients of fractions and mixed numbers.

IN Academic Standards

7.1.7 Solve problems that involve multiplication and division with integers, **fractions,** decimals and combinations of the four operations. *Also addresses P.6.1, P.6.3.*

New Vocabulary

compatible numbers

IN Math Online

glencoe.com
- Extra Examples
- Personal Tutor
- Self-Check Quiz

GET READY for the Lesson

MAMMALS The table below lists the average length for a few mammals. **1, 2. See Ch. 5 Answer Appendix for graphs.**

1. Graph $9\frac{1}{4}$ on a number line. To the nearest whole number, how long is an American Bison? **9 ft**
2. Graph $3\frac{3}{4}$ on a number line. To the nearest whole number, how long is a dingo? **4 ft**
3. About how much longer is the American bison than a dingo? **9 − 4 or 5 ft**

Mammal	Length (ft)
Brown Bear	$6\frac{1}{2}$
American Bison	$9\frac{1}{4}$
Opossum	$2\frac{1}{2}$
Dingo	$3\frac{3}{4}$

To estimate the sum, difference, product, or quotient of mixed numbers, round the mixed numbers to the nearest whole number.

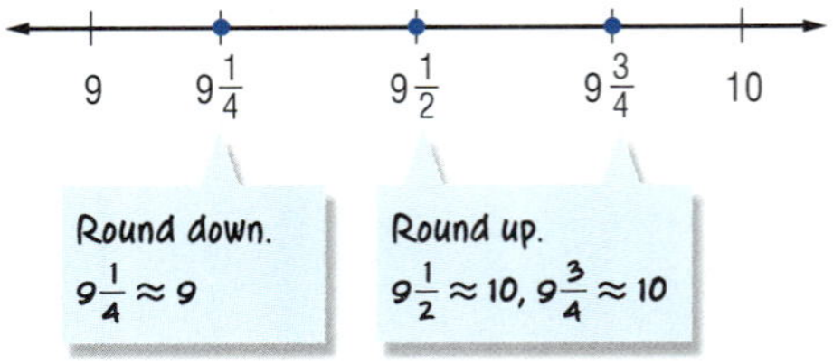

EXAMPLES Estimate with Mixed Numbers

1 Estimate $3\frac{2}{3} + 5\frac{1}{6}$.

$3\frac{2}{3} + \frac{31}{6} \approx 4 + 5$ or 9

The sum is *about* 9.

2 Estimate $6\frac{2}{5} \times 1\frac{7}{8}$.

$6\frac{2}{5} \times 1\frac{7}{8} \approx 6 \times 2$ or 12

The product is *about* 12.

CHECK Your Progress

Estimate.

a. $2\frac{1}{5} + 3\frac{1}{2}$ **$2 + 4 = 6$** b. $4\frac{3}{8} \times 5\frac{1}{4}$ **$4 \times 5 = 20$** c. $8\frac{7}{9} \div 2\frac{3}{4}$ **$9 \div 3 = 3$**

Tips for New Teachers

Estimating with Mixed Numbers

Using front-end estimation, students can add the integers and then estimate the sum of the fractions. For example, to estimate the sum of $3\frac{2}{3}$ and $5\frac{1}{6}$, find 3 + 5, or 8. Then estimate the sum of $\frac{2}{3}$ and $\frac{1}{6}$, which is about 1. An estimate of $3\frac{2}{3} + 5\frac{1}{6}$ is thus about 8 + 1, or 9.

To estimate the sum, difference, product, or quotient of fractions, round each fraction to 0, $\frac{1}{2}$, or 1, whichever is closest. Number lines and fraction models, like the ones shown below, can help you decide how to round.

Fractions Close to 0	Fractions Close to $\frac{1}{2}$	Fractions Close to 1
Number line: 0, $\frac{1}{6}$, 1	Number line: 0, $\frac{1}{2}$, $\frac{5}{8}$, 1	Number line: 0, $\frac{9}{10}$, 1
Fraction model: $\frac{1}{7}$	Fraction model: $\frac{4}{9}$	Fraction model: $\frac{5}{6}$
The numerator is much smaller than the denominator.	The numerator is about half of the denominator.	The numerator is almost as large as the denominator.

EXAMPLES Estimate with Fractions

3 Estimate $\frac{1}{8} + \frac{2}{3}$.

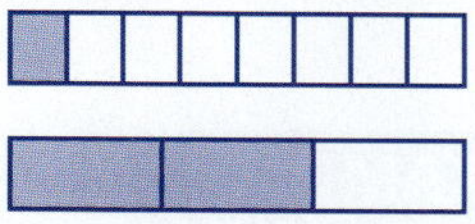

1 is much smaller than 8, so $\frac{1}{8} \approx 0$.

2 is close to half of 3, so $\frac{2}{3} \approx \frac{1}{2}$.

$\frac{1}{8} + \frac{2}{3} \approx 0 + \frac{1}{2} = \frac{1}{2}$ The sum is *about* $\frac{1}{2}$.

Study Tip

Estimating with Fractions If one of the fractions is a mixed number, such as $3\frac{5}{8} + \frac{2}{3}$, round the mixed number to the nearest whole number and the fraction to the nearest half. $3\frac{5}{8} + \frac{2}{3} \approx 4 + \frac{1}{2}$ or about $4\frac{1}{2}$.

4 Estimate $\frac{6}{7} - \frac{7}{10}$.

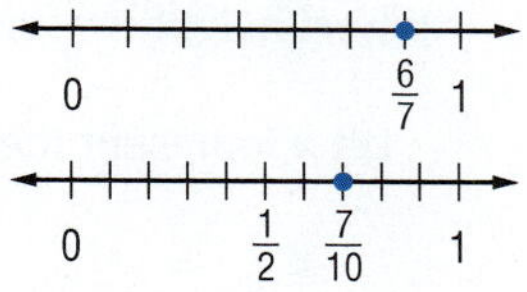

6 is almost as large as 7, so $\frac{6}{7} \approx 1$.

7 is about half of 10, so $\frac{7}{10} \approx \frac{1}{2}$.

$\frac{6}{7} - \frac{7}{10} \approx 1 - \frac{1}{2} = \frac{1}{2}$ The difference is *about* $\frac{1}{2}$.

5 Estimate $\frac{8}{9} \div \frac{5}{6}$.

$\frac{8}{9} \div \frac{5}{6} \approx 1 \div 1 = 1$ $\frac{8}{9} \approx 1$ and $\frac{5}{6} \approx 1$.

The quotient is *about* 1.

CHECK Your Progress

Estimate.

d. $\frac{1}{7} + \frac{3}{5}$ $\frac{1}{2}$ e. $\frac{7}{8} - \frac{5}{9}$ $\frac{1}{2}$ f. $\frac{3}{5} \times \frac{11}{12}$ g. $\frac{7}{8} \div \frac{2}{5}$

f. $\frac{1}{2} \times 1 = \frac{1}{2}$

g. $1 \div \frac{1}{2} = 2$

Focus on Mathematical Content

A good way to estimate the product or quotient of mixed numbers is to adjust them to **compatible numbers**.

Compatible numbers (such as $\frac{1}{3} \cdot 6$, and $8 \div 2$) can be computed mentally.

Formative Assessment

Use the Check Your Progress exercises after the Examples to determine students' understanding of concepts.

ADDITIONAL EXAMPLES

1. Estimate $5\frac{1}{4} + 3\frac{5}{8}$. $5 + 4$, or 9
2. Estimate $7\frac{3}{4} \times 1\frac{7}{8}$. 8×2, or 16
3. Estimate $\frac{1}{3} + \frac{4}{7}$. $\frac{1}{2} + \frac{1}{2}$, or 1
4. Estimate $\frac{5}{8} - \frac{1}{4}$. $\frac{1}{2} - 0$, or $\frac{1}{2}$
5. Estimate $\frac{5}{6} \div \frac{4}{5}$. $1 \div 1$, or 1

Additional Examples are also in:

- Noteables™ Interactive Study Notebook with Foldables™
- Interactive Classroom PowerPoint® Presentations

Tips for New Teachers — Estimating with Fractions

If students round fractions such that they get $\frac{1}{2} \div \frac{1}{2}$, they should recognize that the estimated answer will be 1 since any number divided by itself is 1. If students round fractions such that they get $1 \div 0$, have them round the divisor differently since $1 \div 0$ is undefined. If students round fractions such that they get $\frac{1}{2} \times \frac{1}{2}$, have them round both fractions to zero (0×0) and both to one (1×1). The estimated product is between 0 and 1.

ADDITIONAL EXAMPLES

Estimate using compatible numbers.

6 $\frac{3}{4} \cdot 21$ $\frac{3}{4} \cdot 20$, or 15

7 $15\frac{8}{9} \div 3\frac{2}{5}$ $16 \div 4$, or 4

8 **RUG** Mrs. Loy's front room is $29\frac{1}{4}$ feet long. She wants to find a rug that is about $\frac{4}{5}$ the length of the room. About how long should the rug be? about $30 \times \frac{4}{5}$ or 24 ft long

Tips for New Teachers

Approximations

In Example 8, the equation $x = \frac{2}{3} \times 15\frac{1}{2}$ becomes $x \approx \frac{2}{3} \times 15$ as $15\frac{1}{2}$ is rounded to 15. Because $15\frac{1}{2}$ does not equal 15, the sign *is equal to* must be changed to the sign *approximately equal to*.

Compatible numbers, or numbers that are easy to compute mentally, can also be used to estimate.

EXAMPLES Use Compatible Numbers

Estimate using compatible numbers.

6 $\frac{1}{3} \cdot 14$

THINK What is $\frac{1}{3}$ of 14?

$\frac{1}{3} \cdot 14 \approx \frac{1}{3} \cdot 15$ or 5

Round 14 to 15, since 15 is divisible by 3.

$\frac{1}{3}$ of 15 is $15 \div 3$ or 5.

7 $9\frac{7}{8} \div 4\frac{1}{5}$

$9\frac{7}{8} \div 4\frac{1}{5} \approx 10 \div 4\frac{1}{5}$ Round $9\frac{7}{8}$ to 10.

$\approx 10 \div 5$ or 2 Round $4\frac{1}{5}$ to 5, since 10 is divisible by 5.

Study Tip

Compatible Numbers When dividing mixed numbers, round so that the dividend is a multiple of the divisor.

CHECK Your Progress

Estimate using compatible numbers.

h. $\frac{1}{4} \cdot 21$ $\frac{1}{4} \cdot 20 = 5$ i. $\frac{1}{3} \cdot 17$ $\frac{1}{3} \cdot 18 = 6$ j. $12 \div 6\frac{2}{3}$ $12 \div 6 = 2$

Real-World EXAMPLE

8 **MONSTER TRUCKS** The height of the wheels on the monster truck at the left is about $\frac{2}{3}$ of the total height of the truck. Estimate the height of the wheels.

Words	Wheel height is $\frac{2}{3}$ of the truck height.
Variable	Let x represent the wheel height.
Equation	$x = \frac{2}{3} \cdot 15\frac{1}{2}$

$x \approx \frac{2}{3} \cdot 15$ Round $15\frac{1}{2}$ to 15, since 15 is divisible by 3.

$x \approx 10$ $\frac{1}{3}$ of 15 is 5, so $\frac{2}{3}$ of 15 is $2 \cdot 5$ or 10.

The wheels are about 10 feet high.

Real-World Link. The monster truck shown is $15\frac{1}{2}$ feet tall and weighs 28,000 pounds.

Source: Monster Trucks UK

CHECK Your Progress

k. **MEASUREMENT** The area of a rectangle is $19\frac{3}{4}$ square feet. The width of the rectangle is $5\frac{1}{4}$ feet. What is the approximate length of the rectangle? 4 ft

232 Chapter 5 Applying Fractions

CHECK Your Understanding

★ indicates multi-step problem

Examples 1–5 (p. 230–231)

Estimate. 1. $8 + 2 = 10$ 2. $3 - 1 = 2$ 3. $6 \times 3 = 18$ 4. $9 \div 3 = 3$

1. $8\frac{3}{8} + 1\frac{4}{5}$
2. $2\frac{5}{6} - 1\frac{1}{8}$
3. $5\frac{5}{7} \cdot 2\frac{7}{8}$
4. $9\frac{2}{7} \div 2\frac{2}{3}$
5. $\frac{1}{6} + \frac{2}{5}$ $0 + \frac{1}{2} = \frac{1}{2}$
6. $\frac{6}{7} - \frac{1}{5}$ $1 - 0 = 1$
7. $\frac{5}{8} \cdot \frac{8}{9}$ $\frac{1}{2} \times 1 = \frac{1}{2}$
8. $\frac{4}{5} \div \frac{6}{7}$ $1 \div 1 = 1$

1–10. Sample answers are given.

Examples 6, 7 (p. 232)

Estimate using compatible numbers.

9. $\frac{1}{4} \cdot 15$ 9. $\frac{1}{4} \cdot 16 = 4$
10. $21\frac{5}{6} \div 9\frac{3}{4}$ $22 \div 11 = 2$

Example 8 (p. 232)

11. **BIRDS** A seagull's wingspan is about $\frac{2}{3}$ of a bald eagle's wingspan. The eagle's wingspan is shown at the right. Estimate the wingspan of a seagull. $\frac{2}{3}$ of $6 \approx 4$ ft

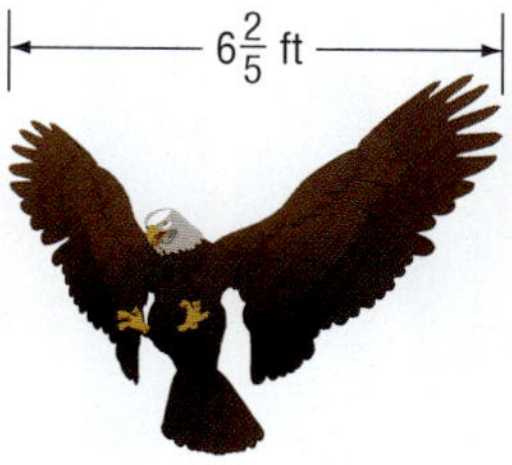

Practice and Problem Solving

HOMEWORK HELP

For Exercises	See Examples
12–19	1, 2
20–29	3–5
30–35	6–8

Exercise Levels
A: 12–35
B: 36–43
C: 44–48

12. $4 + 5 = 9$
13. $1 + 6 = 7$
14. $5 - 3 = 2$
15. $4 - 2 = 2$
16. $3 \cdot 6 = 18$
17. $2 \cdot 3 = 6$
18. $6 \div 2 = 3$
19. $9 \div 3 = 3$
20. $1 + \frac{1}{2} = 1\frac{1}{2}$
21. $\frac{1}{2} + \frac{1}{2} = 1$
22. $\frac{1}{2} - 0 = \frac{1}{2}$
23. $1 - \frac{1}{2} = \frac{1}{2}$

Estimate. 12–27. Sample answers are given.

12. $3\frac{3}{4} + 4\frac{5}{6}$
13. $1\frac{1}{8} + 5\frac{11}{12}$
14. $5\frac{1}{3} - 3\frac{1}{6}$
15. $4\frac{2}{5} - 1\frac{1}{2}$
16. $2\frac{2}{3} \cdot 6\frac{1}{3}$
17. $1\frac{4}{5} \cdot 3\frac{1}{4}$
18. $6\frac{1}{8} \div 1\frac{2}{3}$
19. $8\frac{1}{2} \div 2\frac{5}{8}$
20. $\frac{3}{4} + \frac{3}{8}$
21. $\frac{5}{8} + \frac{3}{7}$
22. $\frac{5}{9} - \frac{1}{6}$
23. $\frac{3}{4} - \frac{3}{5}$
24. $\frac{1}{8} \cdot \frac{3}{4}$ $0 \times 1 = 0$
25. $\frac{4}{9} \cdot \frac{11}{12}$ $\frac{1}{2} \cdot 1 = \frac{1}{2}$
26. $\frac{4}{5} \div \frac{7}{8}$ $1 \div 1 = 1$
27. $\frac{1}{10} \div \frac{5}{6}$ $0 \div 1 = 0$

28. **COOKING** Joaquim wants to make the macaroni and cheese shown at the right, but he has only about $1\frac{3}{4}$ cups of macaroni. About how much more macaroni does he need? $3 - 2$ or 1 c

Macaroni & Cheese
- 3 tbsp butter
- $2\frac{1}{2}$ c uncooked macaroni
- 1 tbsp salt
- $\frac{1}{4}$ tbsp pepper
- 1 qt milk
- $\frac{1}{2}$ lb cheese

29. **MEASUREMENT** Isabella is sewing a trim that is $1\frac{1}{8}$ inches wide on the bottom of a skirt that is $15\frac{7}{8}$ inches long. Approximately how long will the skirt be? $16 + 1$ or 17 in.

Estimate using compatible numbers. 30–33. Sample answers are given.

30. $\frac{1}{4} \cdot 39$ $\frac{1}{4} \times 40 = 10$
31. $\frac{1}{6} \cdot 37$ $\frac{1}{6} \times 36 = 36$
32. $23\frac{2}{9} \div 3$ $24 \div 3 = 8$
33. $25\frac{3}{10} \div 5\frac{2}{3}$ $25 \div 5 = 5$

34. **MONEY** Arleta has \$22. She uses $\frac{1}{3}$ of her money to buy a pair of earrings. About how much money did she spend on the earrings? $\frac{1}{3} \times \$21$ or \$7

35. **SNACKS** A cereal company has 24 pounds of granola to package in bags that contain $1\frac{3}{4}$ pounds of granola. About how many bags will they have? $24 \div 2 = 12$

3 Practice

Formative Assessment

Use Exercises 1–11 to check for understanding.

Then use the chart at the bottom of this page to customize your assignments for students.

Intervention You may wish to use the Study Guide and Intervention Master on page 10 of the *Chapter 5 Resource Masters* for additional reinforcement.

Odd/Even Assignments

Exercises 12–35 are structured so that students practice the same concepts whether they are assigned odd or even problems.

DIFFERENTIATED HOMEWORK OPTIONS

Level	Assignment	Two-Day Option	
BL Basic	12–35, 45–63	13–35 odd, 49, 50	12–34 even, 45–48, 51–63
OL Core	13–35 odd, 37, 39–43, 45–63	12–35, 49, 50	36–43, 45–48, 51–63
AL Advanced/Pre-AP	36–59 (optional: 60–63)		

Tips for New Teachers

Using Manipulatives

If students have difficulty rounding mixed numbers or fractions, you may wish to provide them with strips of paper that they can fold or shade to create fraction strips. Alternatively, students can make number lines on grid paper. Remind students to compare the numerator and denominator. Is the numerator *much less than, about half,* or *almost as great as* the denominator?

Additional Answers

44. It will be smaller than the original quotient. Dividing a smaller dividend by a larger divisor gives you a smaller quotient.

46a. Less than 1; both fractions are less than $\frac{1}{2}$, so the sum is less than 1.

46b. Greater than 1; both fractions are greater than $\frac{1}{2}$, so the sum is greater than 1.

46c. Greater than 1; the sum of $\frac{1}{2}$, and a fraction greater than $\frac{1}{2}$ is greater than 1.

46d. Less than 1; both fractions are less than $\frac{1}{2}$, so the sum is less than 1.

36. FIND THE DATA Refer to the Data File on pages 16–19. Choose some data and write a real-world problem in which you would estimate with fractions. **See students' work.**

★**37. SPORTS** Paquito and Jeff are on a basketball team. The table shows the approximate fraction of the team's points that each of them scored in a game. If the team scored a total of 72 points, about how many did Paquito and Jeff score together? **39**

Player's Names	Fraction of Total Points Scored
Paquito	$\frac{3}{8}$
Jeff	$\frac{1}{6}$

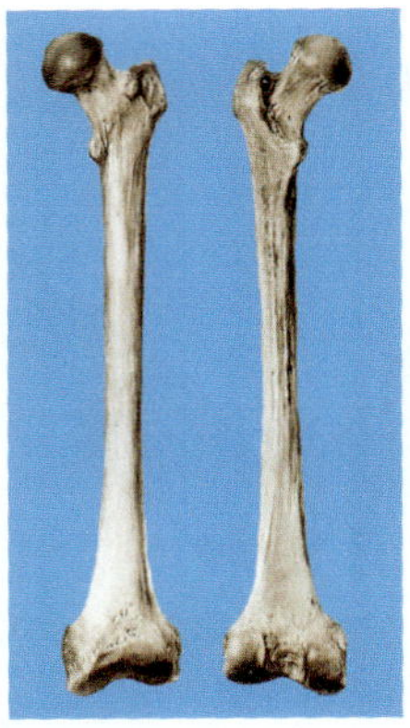

Real-World Link The femur or thigh bone is the longest in length, largest in volume, and strongest bone of the human body.

38. RESEARCH Research the statistics of any basketball team. How can you use fractions to analyze the statistics? **See students' work.**

★**39. COOKING** Kathryn baked the sheet of brownies shown. She wants to cut it into brownies that are about 2 inches square. How many brownies will there be? **24**

ANALYZE TABLES For Exercises 40–43, use the following information and the table shown.

The adult human skeleton is made up of 206 bones. The table shows the approximate fraction of the bones that each body part(s) makes up.

Body Part(s)	Fraction of Total Bones
Feet	$\frac{1}{4}$
Hands & Feet	$\frac{1}{2}$

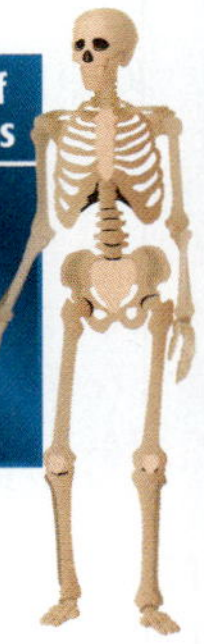

40. About how many bones are in the feet? **40.** $\frac{1}{4} \times 200$ **or 50**

★**41.** About how many bones are in both hands and feet? $\frac{1}{2} \times 200$ **or 100**

42. About how many bones are in one hand? **42. About 100 − 50 or 50; 50 ÷ 2 or 25**

★★**43.** The length of your thighbone is equal to $\frac{1}{4}$ of your height. About how many inches long is your thighbone? **Sample answer:** $\frac{1}{4} \times 60$ **inches or 15 inches**

Academic Standards • ISTEP+
Extra Practice, pp. 679, 708

H.O.T. Problems

44. CHALLENGE In a division expression, the divisor is rounded up and the dividend is rounded down. How does the new quotient compare to the original quotient? Explain. **See margin.**

45. OPEN ENDED Select two fractions whose estimated difference and product is $\frac{1}{2}$. Justify your selection.

45. Sample answer: $\frac{11}{12}$ and $\frac{7}{15}$; $\frac{11}{12} - \frac{7}{15} \approx 1 - \frac{1}{2}$ or $\frac{1}{2}$ and $\frac{11}{12} \cdot \frac{7}{15} \approx 1 \cdot \frac{1}{2}$ or $\frac{1}{2}$

46. NUMBER SENSE Decide which of the following have sums that are less than 1. Explain. **See margin.**

a. $\frac{1}{3} + \frac{2}{5}$

b. $\frac{7}{8} + \frac{1}{2}$

c. $\frac{5}{6} + \frac{2}{3}$

d. $\frac{1}{7} + \frac{3}{9}$

234 Chapter 5 Applying Fractions

47. Estimation; Dion doesn't need an exact answer. Sample answer: $3\frac{1}{4} + 1\frac{2}{3} + 1\frac{2}{3}$ is about halfway between 6 and 7 cups. Since this is more than 6 cups, Dion cannot use this bowl to mix the ingredients.

47. **SELECT A TECHNIQUE** To make the crust for a peach cobbler, Dion needs $3\frac{1}{4}$ cups of flour, $1\frac{2}{3}$ cups of sugar, and $1\frac{2}{3}$ cups of hot water. He needs to mix all of these in a large bowl. The largest bowl he can find holds 6 cups. Which of the following techniques might Dion use to determine whether he can use this bowl to mix the ingredients? Justify your selection(s). Then use the technique(s) to solve the problem.

mental math | number sense | estimation

48. **WRITING IN MATH** Explain when estimation would *not* be the best method for solving a problem. Then give an example. See margin.

ISTEP+ PRACTICE 7.1.7

49. **SHORT RESPONSE** A chef has $15\frac{2}{3}$ cups of penne pasta and $22\frac{1}{4}$ cups of rigatoni pasta. About how much pasta is there altogether? 38 cups

50. On a full tank of gasoline, a certain car can travel 360 miles. The needle on its gasoline gauge is shown. Without refueling, which is the best estimate of how far the car can travel? A

A 150 miles

B 180 miles

C 240 miles

D 329 miles

Spiral Review

Replace each ● with <, >, or = to make a true sentence. (Lesson 4-9)

51. $2\frac{7}{8}$ ● 2.75 >

52. $\frac{-1}{3}$ ● $\frac{-7}{3}$ >

53. $\frac{5}{7}$ ● $\frac{4}{5}$ <

54. $3\frac{6}{11}$ ● $3\frac{9}{14}$ <

55. **SHOPPING** A store sells a 3-pack of beaded necklaces and a 5-pack of beaded bracelets. How many packages of each must you buy so that you have the same number of necklaces and bracelets? (Lesson 4-8) 5 pkg. of necklaces and 3 pkg. of bracelets.

Write each decimal as a percent. (Lesson 4-7)

56. 0.56 56%

57. 0.375 37.5%

58. 0.07 7%

59. 0.019 1.9%

GET READY for the Next Lesson

PREREQUISITE SKILL **Find the LCD of each pair of fractions.** (Lesson 4-9)

60. $\frac{3}{4}, \frac{5}{12}$ 12

61. $\frac{1}{2}, \frac{7}{10}$ 10

62. $\frac{1}{6}, \frac{1}{8}$ 24

63. $\frac{4}{5}, \frac{2}{3}$ 15

4 Assess

Crystal Ball Tell students that tomorrow's lesson will be about adding and subtracting fractions. Have them write how they think what they learned today will connect with tomorrow's material.

FOLDABLES Study Organizer **Foldables™ Follow-Up**

Remind students to record what they learn about estimating with fractions and mixed numbers on index cards, and then to store the cards in their Foldables.

Additional Answer

48. Sample answer: Sometimes you need to know an exact answer. When trying to figure out how much medicine to take, you need an exact answer. You would not want to round a dosage of $1\frac{1}{2}$ tsp of medicine to 2 tsp; you might take too much medicine.

Lesson 5-1 Estimating with Fractions 235

5-2 Adding and Subtracting Fractions

PACING: **Regular:** 1 period, **Block:** 0.5 period

IN Academic Standards **Reinforcement of 6.1.6** Solve problems involving addition, subtraction, multiplication and division of positive fractions and decimals and explain why a particular operation was used for a given situation.

Options for Differentiated Instruction

ELL = English Language Learner AL = Above or Beyond Grade Level SS = Struggling Students SN = Special Needs

Review Vocabulary SS SN

Use before presenting Lesson 5-2.

To help students prepare for Lesson 5-2, provide a short review by presenting the following questions.

Ask:

- What is a least common denominator? How do you find it? the least common multiple of the denominators of two or more fractions; find the LCM of the denominators.
- What is one reason for renaming fractions with the LCD? to compare fractions with unlike denominators
  How do you write a fraction in simplest form? Divide the numerator and denominator by their GCF.
  For students who need additional practice, provide review sheets on these topics.

Using Manipulatives SS SN

Use before presenting Examples 1–6.

Have fractions strips available for students to model problems. Remind students that each strip represents one whole unit.

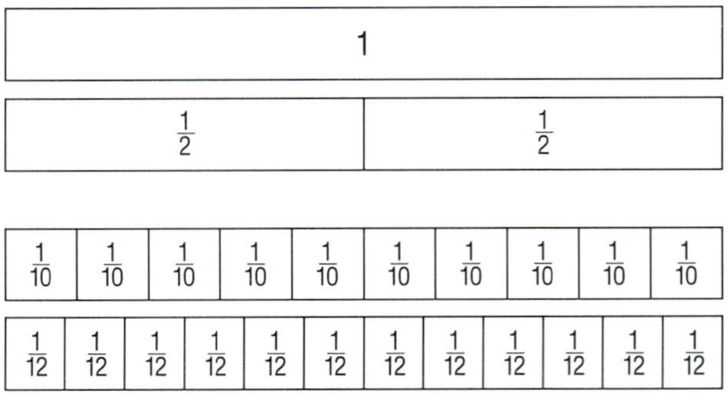

Kinesthetic Learning ELL AL SS SN

Use after presenting Examples 1–6.

Have pairs of students measure each other's vertical jumps in fractions of inches. Have them stand yardsticks on the ground vertically, and mark the highest point reached by each jumper's feet. Have students compare each other's vertical jumps by finding the differences in height. Students can jump multiple times and find their amount of improvement. Some students may not feel comfortable jumping, or may be unable to jump. Either assign these students the task of helping tabulate the class data, or ask for volunteers to help with this task.

Leveled Lesson Resources

Also on TeacherWorks™ Lesson 5-2

Chapter 5 Resource Masters

BL = Below or Approaching Grade Level OL = On Grade Level AL = Above or Beyond Grade Level ELL = English Language Learner

Lesson Reading Guide
p. 15 BL OL ELL

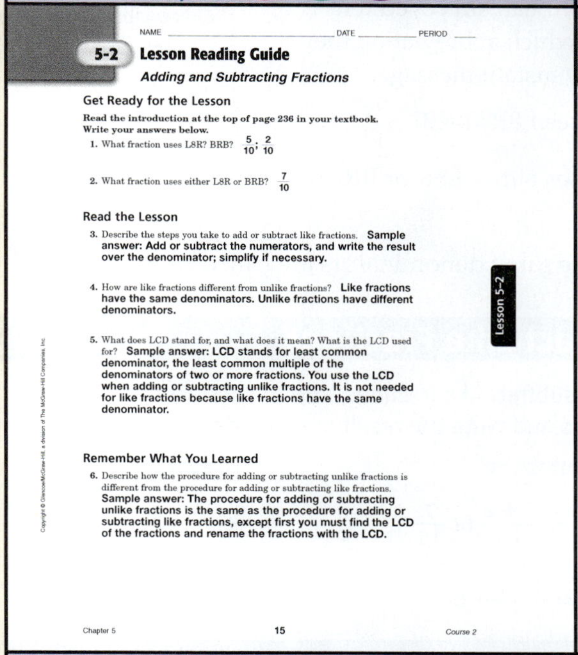

Study Guide and Intervention*
p. 16 BL OL ELL

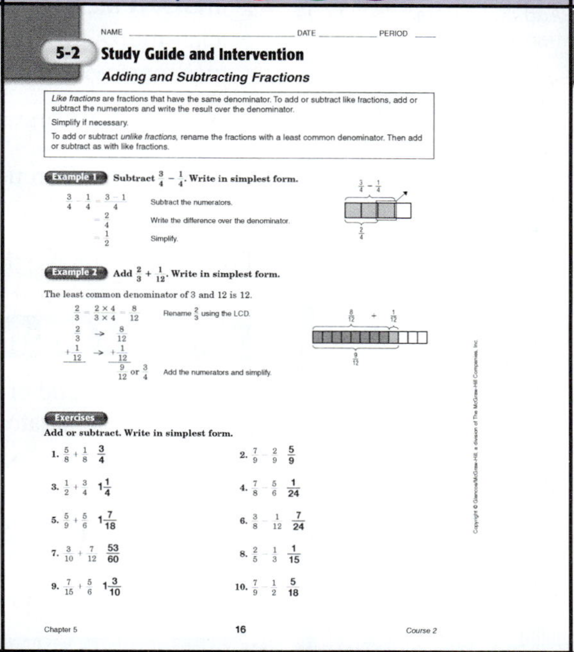

Skills Practice*
p. 17 BL OL

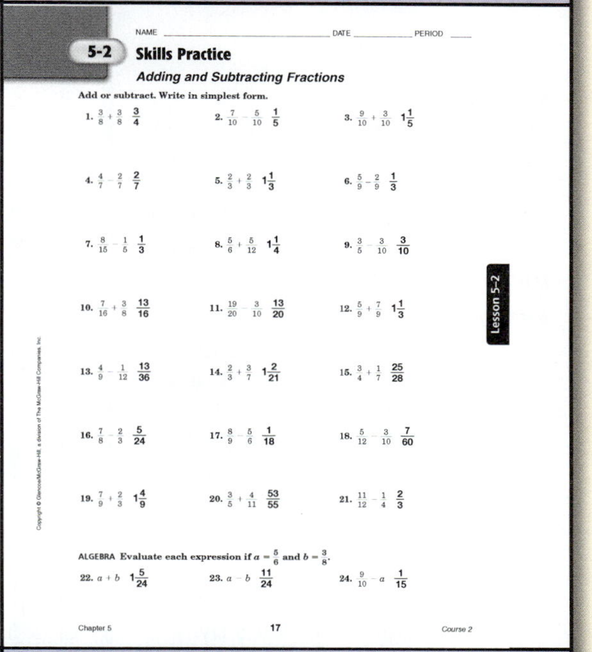

Practice*
p. 18 OL AL

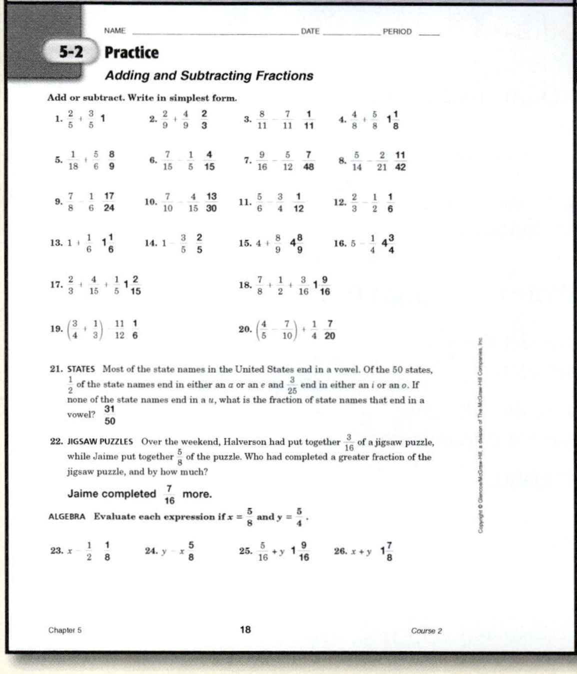

Word Problem Practice*
p. 19 OL AL

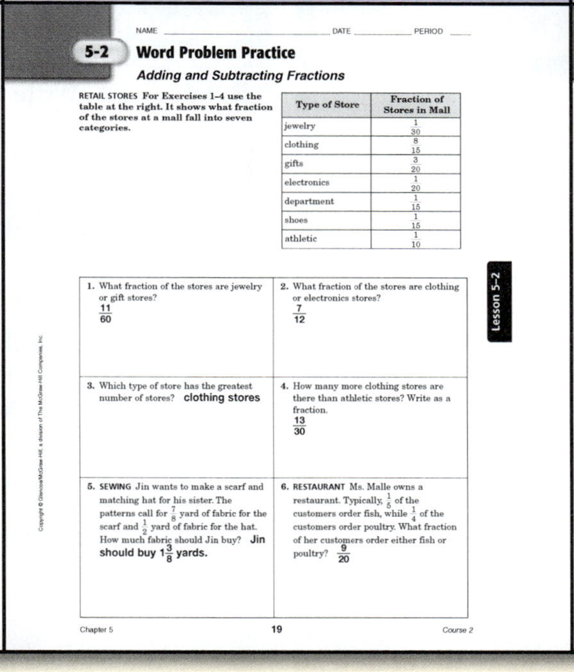

Enrichment
p. 20 OL AL

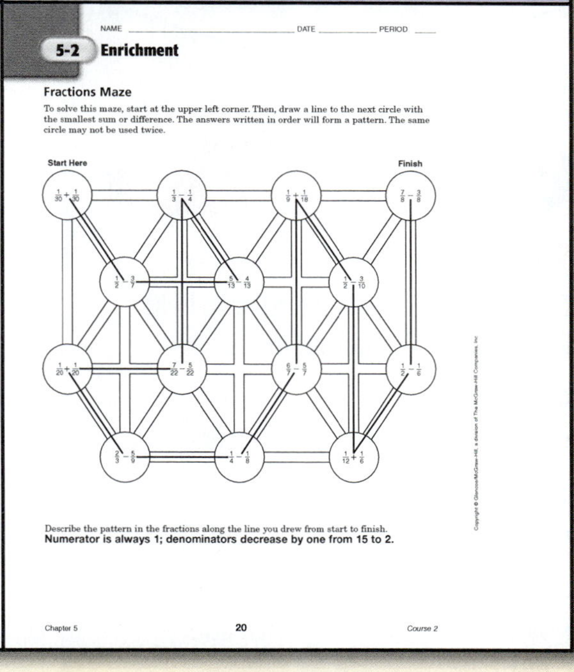

* Also available in Spanish ELL

Additional Lesson Resources

Transparencies
- *5-Minute Check Transparency*, Lesson 5-2

Other Print Products
- *Noteables™ Interactive Study Notebook with Foldables™*

Teacher Tech Tools
- *Interactive Classroom CD-ROM*, Lesson 5-2
- *AssignmentWorks*, Lesson 5-2

Student Tech Tools
glencoe.com
- Extra Examples, Chapter 5, Lesson 2
- Self-Check Quiz, Chapter 5, Lesson 2

5-2 Lesson Notes

1 Focus

Vertical Alignment

Before Lesson 5-2
Solve simple problems, including ones arising in concrete situations, involving the addition and subtraction of fractions and mixed numbers and express answers in the simplest form

Lesson 5-2
Solve problems involving addition, subtraction, of positive fractions and explain why a particular operation was used for a given situation. Determine the least common multiple of whole numbers; use them to solve problems with fractions

After Lesson 5-2
Add and subtract fractions by using factoring to find common denominators

2 Teach

Scaffolding Questions

Tell students to look at a ruler to help them answer the questions.

Ask:

- What is the sum of $\frac{1}{8}$ inch and $\frac{4}{8}$ inch? $\frac{5}{8}$ in.
- What is the sum of $\frac{2}{4}$ inch and $\frac{1}{4}$ inch? $\frac{3}{4}$ in.
- What is the sum of $\frac{3}{16}$ inch and $\frac{5}{16}$ inch? $\frac{8}{16}$ in. or $\frac{1}{2}$ in.

5-2 Adding and Subtracting Fractions

MAIN IDEA

Add and subtract fractions.

IN Academic Standards

Reinforcement of 6.1.6 Solve problems involving addition, subtraction, multiplication and division of positive fractions and decimals and explain why a particular operation was used for a given situation.

New Vocabulary

like fractions
unlike fractions

IN Math Online

glencoe.com

- Extra Examples
- Personal Tutor
- Self-Check Quiz
- Reading in the Content Area

GET READY for the Lesson

INSTANT MESSENGER Sean surveyed ten classmates to find which abbreviation they use most when they instant message.

Abbreviation	Number
L8R	5
LOL	3
BRB	2

1. What fraction uses L8R? BRB? $\frac{5}{10}$; $\frac{2}{10}$
2. What fraction uses either L8R or BRB? $\frac{7}{10}$

Fractions that have the same denominators are called **like fractions**.

Add and Subtract Like Fractions — Key Concept

Words To add or subtract like fractions, add or subtract the numerators and write the result over the denominator.

Examples

Numbers	Algebra
$\frac{5}{10} + \frac{2}{10} = \frac{5+2}{10}$ or $\frac{7}{10}$	$\frac{a}{c} + \frac{b}{c} = \frac{a+b}{c}$, where $c \neq 0$
$\frac{11}{12} - \frac{4}{12} = \frac{11-4}{12}$ or $\frac{7}{12}$	$\frac{a}{c} - \frac{b}{c} = \frac{a-b}{c}$, where $c \neq 0$

EXAMPLES Add and Subtract Like Fractions

1 Add $\frac{5}{9} + \frac{2}{9}$. Write in simplest form.

$\frac{5}{9} + \frac{2}{9} = \frac{5+2}{9}$ Add the numerators.

$= \frac{7}{9}$ Write the sum over the denominator.

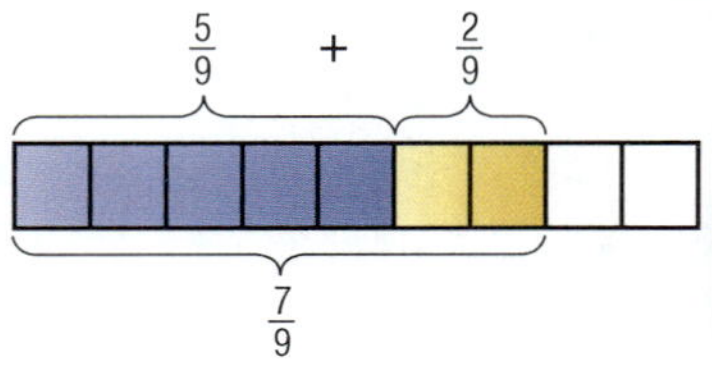

2 Subtract $\frac{9}{10} - \frac{1}{10}$. Write in simplest form.

$\frac{9}{10} - \frac{1}{10} = \frac{9-1}{10}$ Subtract the numerators.

$= \frac{8}{10}$ Write the difference over the denominator.

$= \frac{4}{5}$ Simplify.

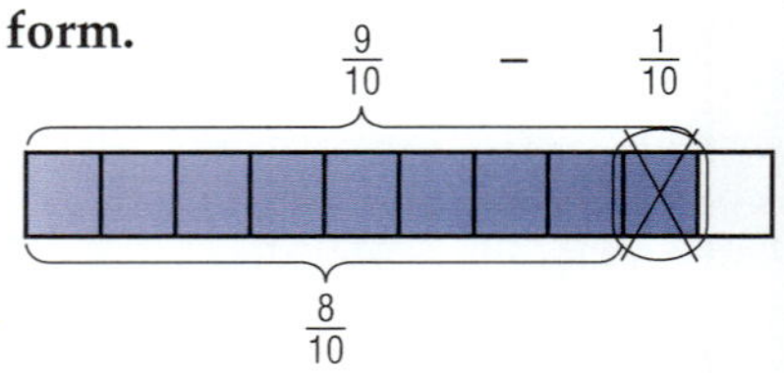

CHECK Your Progress

a. $\frac{1}{6} + \frac{3}{6}$ $\frac{2}{3}$

b. $\frac{3}{7} - \frac{1}{7}$ $\frac{2}{7}$

Tips for New Teachers — Like Fractions

The denominator names the units of what is being added or subtracted. For example, $\frac{1}{5} + \frac{3}{5} = \frac{4}{5}$ can be thought of as 1 fifth + 3 fifths = 4 fifths.

Review Vocabulary

LCD the least common multiple of the denominators of two or more fractions; *Example*: the LCD of $\frac{1}{4}$ and $\frac{2}{3}$ is 12. (Lesson 4-9)

To add or subtract **unlike fractions**, or fractions with different denominators, rename the fractions using the LCD. Then add or subtract as with like fractions.

EXAMPLES Add and Subtract Unlike Fractions

3 Add $\frac{1}{2} + \frac{1}{6}$. Write in simplest form. **Estimate** $\frac{1}{2} + 0 = \frac{1}{2}$

METHOD 1 **Use a model.**

$$\begin{array}{r} \frac{1}{2} \\ +\frac{1}{6} \\ \hline \frac{4}{6} \text{ or } \frac{2}{3} \end{array}$$

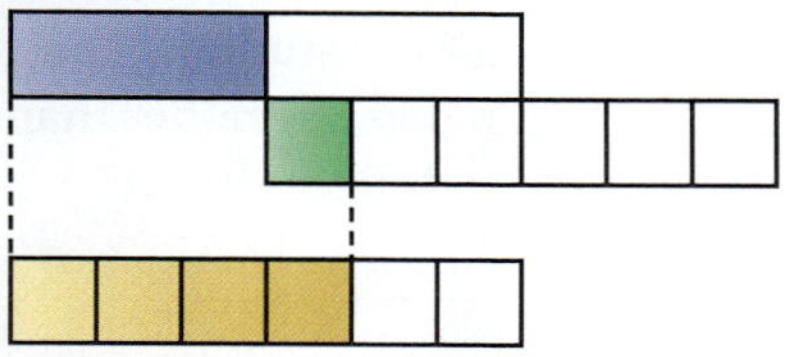

METHOD 2 **Use the LCD.**

The least common denominator (LCD) of $\frac{1}{2}$ and $\frac{1}{6}$ is 6.

Rename using the LCD, 6. — Add.

$$\frac{1}{2} \rightarrow \frac{1 \times 3}{2 \times 3} = \frac{3}{6} \rightarrow \frac{3}{6}$$

$$+\frac{1}{6} \rightarrow \frac{1 \times 1}{6 \times 1} = +\frac{1}{6} \rightarrow +\frac{1}{6}$$

$$\frac{4}{6} \text{ or } \frac{2}{3}$$

So, $\frac{1}{2} + \frac{1}{6} = \frac{2}{3}$. **Check for Reasonableness** $\frac{2}{3} \approx \frac{1}{2}$ ✔

Study Tip

Renaming Fractions To rename a fraction, multiply both the numerator and the denominator of the original fraction by the same number. By doing so, the renamed fraction has the same value as the original fraction.

4 Subtract $\frac{11}{12} - \frac{3}{8}$. Write in simplest form. **Estimate** $1 - \frac{1}{2} = \frac{1}{2}$

Since $12 = 2^2 \cdot 3$ and $8 = 2^3$, the LCM of 12 and 8 is $2^3 \cdot 3$ or 24. Rename each fraction using a denominator of 24. Then subtract.

Think: $12 \times 2 = 24$, so $\frac{11 \times 2}{12 \times 2}$ or $\frac{22}{24}$.

Think: $8 \times 3 = 24$, so $\frac{3}{8} = \frac{3 \times 3}{8 \times 3}$ or $\frac{9}{24}$.

$\frac{11}{12} - \frac{3}{8} = \frac{11 \times 2}{12 \times 2} - \frac{3 \times 3}{8 \times 3}$ — The LCD of $\frac{11}{12}$ and $\frac{3}{8}$ is 24.

$= \frac{22}{24} - \frac{9}{24}$ — Rename the fractions using LCD, 24.

$= \frac{13}{24}$ — Subtract the fractions.

Check for Reasonableness $\frac{13}{24} \approx \frac{1}{2}$ ✔

CHOOSE Your Method

c. $\frac{8}{9} - \frac{2}{3}$ $\frac{2}{9}$

d. $\frac{5}{6} - \frac{3}{8}$ $\frac{11}{24}$

e. $\frac{7}{8} + \frac{3}{4}$ $1\frac{5}{8}$

Focus on Mathematical Content

Estimating a sum or difference is a good way to check a solution.

Formative Assessment

Use the Check Your Progress exercises after the Examples to determine students' understanding of concepts.

ADDITIONAL EXAMPLES

Add or subtract. Write in simplest form.

1. $\frac{7}{12} + \frac{4}{12}$ $\frac{11}{12}$
2. $\frac{5}{6} - \frac{1}{6}$ $\frac{2}{3}$
3. $\frac{1}{3} + \frac{1}{9}$ $\frac{4}{9}$
4. $\frac{3}{4} - \frac{1}{6}$ $\frac{7}{12}$

Additional Examples are also in:

- Noteables™ Interactive Study Notebook with Foldables™
- Interactive Classroom PowerPoint® Presentations

ADDITIONAL EXAMPLES

5 **ART** A picture mounted on art board is $\frac{1}{8}$ inch thick. The frame for the picture is $\frac{1}{2}$ inch thick. How much thicker than the picture is the frame? $\frac{3}{8}$ in.

6 **PIZZA** Jean ate $\frac{5}{12}$ of a pizza. Ambrose ate $\frac{1}{3}$ of the pizza. How much pizza did they eat altogether? $\frac{3}{4}$

3 Practice

Formative Assessment

Use Exercises 1–10 to check for understanding.

Then use the chart at the bottom of the next page to customize your assignments for students.

Intervention You may wish to use the Study Guide and Intervention Master on page 16 of the *Chapter 5 Resource Masters* for additional reinforcement.

Additional Answers

9. addition; Sample answer: To find how much smaller the total height of the photo is now, add $\frac{5}{16}$ and $\frac{3}{8}$.

10. subtraction; Sample answer: To find the part of the water that was used, subtract $\frac{1}{4}$ from $\frac{7}{8}$.

Real-World EXAMPLES

SURVEYS In a recent survey, students were asked what they would choose for a healthy lunch. The results are shown in the graph.

Study Tip

Key Words The phrase *what fraction more* suggests subtraction.

5 What fraction more of the students chose salad bar rather than a deli sandwich?

$\frac{9}{20} - \frac{3}{25} = \frac{9 \times 5}{20 \times 5} - \frac{3 \times 4}{25 \times 4}$ The LCD of $\frac{9}{20}$ and $\frac{3}{25}$ is 100.

$= \frac{45}{100} - \frac{12}{100}$ Rename the fractions using the LCD.

$= \frac{33}{100}$ Subtract the numerators.

So, $\frac{33}{100}$ more students chose salad bar rather than a deli sandwich.

6 What fraction of students chose pizza or chicken nuggets?

$\frac{3}{20} + \frac{1}{10} = \frac{3}{20} + \frac{2}{20}$ Rename.

$= \frac{5}{20}$ Add.

$= \frac{1}{4}$ Simplify.

So, $\frac{1}{4}$ of the students chose pizza or chicken nuggets combined.

CHECK Your Progress

f. **SURVEYS** What fraction more of the students chose a deli sandwich rather than a burger and fries? $\frac{1}{50}$

★ indicates multi-step problem

CHECK Your Understanding

Examples 1–4 (pp. 236–237)

Add or subtract. Write in simplest form.

1. $\frac{4}{9} + \frac{2}{9}$ $\frac{2}{3}$
2. $\frac{5}{6} + \frac{4}{9}$ $1\frac{5}{18}$
3. $\frac{3}{8} - \frac{1}{8}$ $\frac{1}{4}$
4. $\frac{4}{5} - \frac{2}{5}$ $\frac{2}{5}$
5. $\frac{1}{6} + \frac{3}{8}$ $\frac{13}{24}$
6. $\frac{2}{3} + \frac{5}{6}$ $1\frac{1}{2}$
7. $\frac{5}{6} - \frac{7}{12}$ $\frac{1}{4}$
8. $\frac{3}{4} - \frac{1}{3}$ $\frac{5}{12}$

Examples 5, 6 (p. 238)

For Exercises 9 and 10, choose an operation to solve each problem. Explain your reasoning. Then solve the problem. 9, 10. See margin for explanations.

9. **MEASUREMENT** Cassandra cuts $\frac{5}{16}$ inch off the top of a photo and $\frac{3}{8}$ inch off the bottom. How much smaller is the total height of the photo now? $\frac{11}{16}$ in.

10. **CHORES** A bucket was $\frac{7}{8}$ full with soapy water. After washing the car, the bucket was only $\frac{1}{4}$ full. What part of the water was used? $\frac{5}{8}$

238 Chapter 5 Applying Fractions

Practice and Problem Solving

HOMEWORK HELP

For Exercises	See Examples
11–14	1, 2
15–22	3, 4
23–26	5, 6

Exercise Levels
A: 11–26
B: 27–44
C: 45–48

Add or subtract. Write in simplest form.

11. $\frac{3}{7}+\frac{1}{7}$ $\frac{4}{7}$
12. $\frac{5}{8}+\frac{7}{8}$ $1\frac{1}{2}$
13. $\frac{5}{6}-\frac{1}{6}$ $\frac{2}{3}$
14. $\frac{7}{10}-\frac{3}{10}$ $\frac{2}{5}$
15. $\frac{1}{15}+\frac{3}{5}$ $\frac{2}{3}$
16. $\frac{7}{12}+\frac{7}{10}$ $1\frac{17}{60}$
17. $\frac{5}{8}+\frac{11}{12}$ $1\frac{13}{24}$
18. $\frac{7}{9}+\frac{5}{6}$ $1\frac{11}{18}$
19. $\frac{7}{9}-\frac{1}{3}$ $\frac{4}{9}$
20. $\frac{4}{5}-\frac{1}{6}$ $\frac{19}{30}$
21. $\frac{4}{9}-\frac{2}{15}$ $\frac{14}{45}$
22. $\frac{3}{10}-\frac{1}{4}$ $\frac{1}{20}$

For Exercises 23–26, choose an operation to solve each problem. Explain your reasoning. Then solve the problem. 23–26. See margin for explanations.

23. **MEASUREMENT** Ebony is building a shelf to hold the two boxes shown. What is the smallest width she should make the shelf? $1\frac{11}{20}$ ft

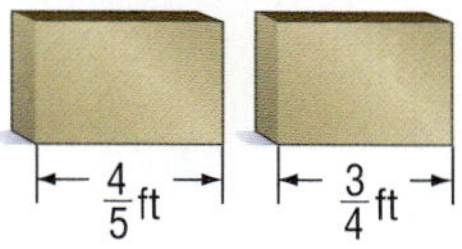

24. **WEATHER** Using the information under the photo, find the difference of the average precipitation for Boise in February and November. $\frac{3}{10}$ in.

25. **MEASUREMENT** Makayla bought $\frac{1}{4}$ pound of ham and $\frac{5}{8}$ pound of turkey. How much more turkey did she buy? $\frac{3}{8}$

26. **ANIMALS** The three-toed sloth can travel $\frac{3}{20}$ miles per hour while a giant tortoise can travel $\frac{17}{100}$ miles per hour. How much faster, in miles per hour, is the giant tortoise? $\frac{1}{50}$ mi/h

Real-World Link The average precipitation for February and November for Boise, Idaho, is $\frac{4}{10}$ and $\frac{7}{10}$ inches, respectively.
Source: The Weather Channel

Simplify.

27. $\frac{1}{7}+\frac{1}{2}+\frac{5}{28}$ $\frac{23}{28}$
28. $\frac{1}{4}+\frac{5}{6}+\frac{7}{12}$ $1\frac{2}{3}$
29. $\frac{1}{6}+\left(\frac{2}{3}-\frac{1}{4}\right)$ $\frac{7}{12}$
30. $\frac{5}{6}-\left(\frac{1}{2}+\frac{1}{3}\right)$ 0
31. $1+\frac{1}{4}$ $1\frac{1}{4}$
32. $1-\frac{5}{8}$ $\frac{3}{8}$
33. $2+\frac{2}{3}$ $2\frac{2}{3}$
34. $3-\frac{1}{6}$ $2\frac{5}{6}$

35. **MONEY** Chellise saves $\frac{1}{5}$ of her allowance and spends $\frac{2}{3}$ of her allowance at the mall. What fraction of her allowance remains? $\frac{2}{15}$

36. **ANALYZE TABLES** Pepita and Francisco each spend an equal amount of time on homework. The table shows the fraction of their time they spend on each subject. Determine the missing fraction for each student.
Pepita: $\frac{1}{6}$ math; Franciso: $\frac{1}{8}$ English

Homework	Fraction of Time	
	Pepita	Francisco
Math	■	$\frac{1}{2}$
English	$\frac{2}{3}$	■
Science	$\frac{1}{6}$	$\frac{3}{8}$

ALGEBRA **Evaluate each expression if $a=\frac{3}{4}$ and $b=\frac{5}{6}$.**

37. $\frac{1}{2}+a$ $1\frac{1}{4}$
38. $b-\frac{7}{10}$ $\frac{2}{15}$
39. $b-a$ $\frac{1}{12}$
40. $a+b$ $1\frac{7}{12}$

Odd/Even Assignments

Exercises 11–26 are structured so that students practice the same concepts whether they are assigned odd or even problems.

Additional Answers

23. addition; Sample answer: To find the smallest width to make the shelf, add $\frac{4}{5}$ and $\frac{3}{4}$.
24. subtraction; Sample answer: To find the difference of the average precipitation for February and November for Boise, subtract $\frac{4}{10}$ from $\frac{7}{10}$.
25. subtraction; Sample answer: To find how much more turkey Makayla bought, subtract $\frac{1}{4}$ from $\frac{5}{8}$.
26. subtraction; Sample answer: To find how much faster the giant tortoise travels, subtract $\frac{3}{20}$ from $\frac{17}{100}$.

DIFFERENTIATED HOMEWORK OPTIONS

Level	Assignment	Two-Day Option	
BL Basic	11–26, 46–64	11–25 odd, 49, 50	12–26 even, 46, 48, 51–64
OL Core	11–35 odd, 36, 37, 39, 41–44, 46–64	11–26, 49, 50	27–44, 46–48, 51–64
AL Advanced/Pre-AP	27–59 (optional: 60–64)		

⚠ Exercise Alert!

Find the Error In Exercise 47, Lourdes is correct. Meagan didn't rename the fractions with the same denominator. Remind students that when adding or subtracting unlike fractions, they first need to rename the fractions by using the LCD, and then they can add or subtract the numerators (not the denominators).

Additional Answers

45. Sample answer: The sum of two unit fractions $\frac{1}{a}$ and $\frac{1}{b}$, where a and b are not 0, is $\frac{a+b}{ab}$.

$\frac{1}{a} + \frac{1}{b} = \frac{1 \cdot b}{a \cdot b} + \frac{1 \cdot a}{b \cdot a}$ Rename each fraction using the LCD, ab.

$= \frac{b}{ab} + \frac{a}{ab}$ Simplify.

$= \frac{b+a}{ab}$ Add the numerators.

$= \frac{a+b}{ab}$ Commutative Property

So, $\frac{1}{99} + \frac{1}{100} = \frac{99+100}{99 \cdot 100}$ or $\frac{199}{9900}$

48. The closest is d.

48a. Filling the $\frac{2}{3}$ measuring cup twice will yield $1\frac{1}{3}$ cups which is $\frac{1}{3}$ cup more than she needs.

48b. Filling the $\frac{2}{3}$ measuring cup once will yield $\frac{1}{3}$ less than she needs.

48c. Filling the $\frac{3}{4}$ cup twice will yield $1\frac{1}{2}$ cups which is $\frac{1}{2}$ cup more than she needs.

48d. Filling the $\frac{3}{4}$ measuring cup once will yield $\frac{1}{4}$ cup less than she needs.

★41. **BOOK REPORTS** Four students were scheduled to give book reports in a 1-hour class period. After the first report, $\frac{2}{3}$ hour remained. If the next two students' reports took $\frac{1}{6}$ hour and $\frac{1}{4}$ hour, respectively, what fraction of the hour remained after the final students' report? Justify your answer.

41. $\frac{2}{3} - \left(\frac{1}{6} + \frac{1}{4}\right) = \frac{1}{4}$

42. **MEASUREMENT** Mrs. Escalante was riding a bicycle on a bike path. After riding $\frac{2}{3}$ of a mile, she discovered that she still needed to travel $\frac{3}{4}$ of a mile to reach the end of the path. How long is the bike path? $1\frac{5}{12}$ mi

43. **CELL PHONES** One hundred sixty cell phone owners were surveyed. What fraction of owners prefers using their cell phone for text messaging or taking pictures? $\frac{3}{4}$

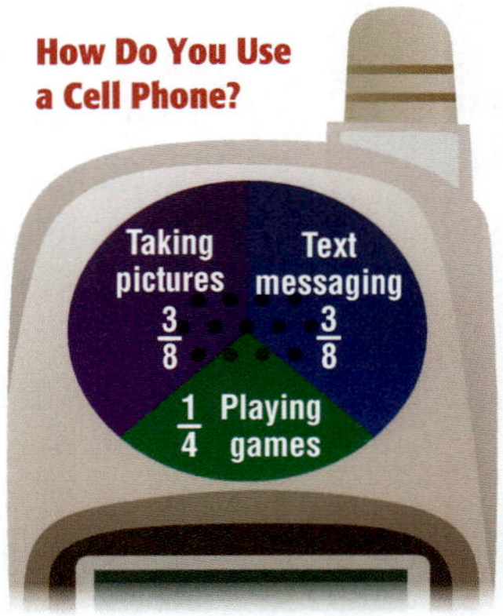

★44. **MEASUREMENT** LaTasha and Eric are jogging on a track. LaTasha jogs $\frac{1}{4}$ of a mile and then stops. Eric jogs $\frac{5}{8}$ of a mile, stops and then turns around and jogs $\frac{1}{2}$ of a mile. Who is farther ahead on the track? How much farther?

44. LaTasha's position on the track is $\frac{1}{4}$ of a mile from the start. Eric's position on the track is $\frac{5}{8} - \frac{1}{2}$, or $\frac{1}{8}$, of a mile from the start. So, LaTasha is farther ahead on the track by $\frac{1}{4} - \frac{1}{8}$ or $\frac{1}{8}$ of a mile.

Academic Standards • ISTEP+
Extra Practice, pp. 679, 708

H.O.T. Problems

45. **CHALLENGE** Fractions, such as $\frac{1}{2}$ or $\frac{1}{3}$, whose numerators are 1, are called *unit fractions*. Describe a method you can use to add two unit fractions mentally. Explain your reasoning and use your method to find $\frac{1}{99} + \frac{1}{100}$. See margin.

46. **OPEN ENDED** Provide a counterexample to the following statement.

The sum of three fractions with odd numerators is never $\frac{1}{2}$. Sample answer: $\frac{1}{4} + \frac{1}{6} + \frac{1}{12}$

47. **FIND THE ERROR** Meagan and Lourdes are finding $\frac{1}{4} + \frac{3}{5}$. Who is correct? Explain.

47. Lourdes; Meagan did not rename the fractions using the LCD.

Meagan

Lourdes

48. **WRITING IN MATH** To make a cake, Felicia needs 1 cup of flour but she only has a $\frac{2}{3}$-measuring cup and a $\frac{3}{4}$-measuring cup. Which method will bring her closest to having the amount of flour she needs? Explain. See margin.

a. Fill the $\frac{2}{3}$-measuring cup twice.
b. Fill the $\frac{2}{3}$-measuring cup once.
c. Fill the $\frac{3}{4}$-measuring cup twice.
d. Fill the $\frac{3}{4}$-measuring cup once.

240 **Chapter 5** Applying Fractions

ISTEP+ PRACTICE Reinforcement of 6.1.6

49. The table gives the number of hours Orlando spent at football practice for one week.

Day	Time (hours)
Monday	$1\frac{1}{2}$
Tuesday	2
Wednesday	$2\frac{1}{3}$
Thursday	$1\frac{5}{6}$
Friday	$2\frac{1}{2}$
Saturday	$1\frac{3}{4}$

How many more hours did he practice over the last three days than he did over the first three days? **A**

A $\frac{1}{4}$ h

B $\frac{1}{2}$ h

C $\frac{2}{3}$ h

D $\frac{3}{4}$ h

50. Which of the following is the prime factored form of the lowest common denominator of $\frac{7}{12} + \frac{11}{18}$? **H**

F 2×3

G 2×3^2

H $2^2 \times 3^2$

J $2^3 \times 3$

51. Find $\frac{5}{6} - \frac{1}{8}$. **D**

A $\frac{4}{7}$

B $\frac{3}{8}$

C $\frac{7}{12}$

D $\frac{17}{24}$

Spiral Review **52–55. Sample answers are given.**

Estimate. (Lesson 5-1) **52.** $1 - \frac{1}{2} = \frac{1}{2}$ **53.** $4 + 4 = 8$ **54.** $16 \div 8 = 2$ **55.** $6 \cdot 3 = 18$

52. $\frac{6}{7} - \frac{5}{12}$ **53.** $4\frac{1}{9} + 3\frac{3}{4}$ **54.** $16\frac{2}{3} \div 8\frac{1}{5}$ **55.** $5\frac{4}{5} \cdot 3\frac{1}{3}$

56. WEATHER The table shows about how much rain falls in Albuquerque and Denver. Which city has the greater fraction of inches of rain per day? Explain. (Lesson 4-9) **Denver;** $\frac{15}{90} > \frac{9}{60}$

City	Amount of Rain (in.)	Number of Days
Albuquerque, NM	9	60
Denver, CO	15	90

Source: The Weather Channel

57. Write 0.248 as a percent. (Lesson 4-7) **24.8%**

ALGEBRA Find each sum if $a = -3$ and $b = 2$. (Lessons 2-4 and 2-5)

58. $a + b$ **−1** **59.** $a - b$ **−5** **60.** $b - a$ **5**

GET READY for the Next Lesson

PREREQUISITE SKILL Complete.

61. $5\frac{2}{3} = 5 + \blacksquare$ $\frac{2}{3}$ **62.** $1 = \frac{\blacksquare}{9}$ **9** **63.** $1 = \frac{\blacksquare}{5}$ **5** **64.** $\blacksquare = 4 + \frac{3}{8}$ $4\frac{3}{8}$

Pre-AP Activity Use as an Extension.

Have students create a function table for $y = \frac{1}{2}x + \frac{2}{3}$ and then graph the function on grid paper.

4 Assess

Crystal Ball Tell students that tomorrow's lesson will be about adding and subtracting mixed numbers. Have them write how they think what they learned today will connect with tomorrow's material.

Formative Assessment

Check for student understanding of concepts in Lessons 5-1 and 5-2.

CRM Quiz 1, p. 53

FOLDABLES Study Organizer Foldables™ Follow-Up

Remind students to record what they learn about adding and subtracting like and unlike fractions on index cards, and then to store the cards in their Foldables.

Lesson 5-2 Adding and Subtracting Fractions 241

5-3 Adding and Subtracting Mixed Numbers

PACING: **Regular:** 1 period, **Block:** 0.5 period

IN Academic Standards **Reinforcement of 6.1.6** Solve problems involving addition, subtraction, multiplication and division of positive fractions and decimals and explain why a particular operation was used for a given situation.

Options for Differentiated Instruction

ELL = English Language Learner AL = Above or Beyond Grade Level SS = Struggling Students SN = Special Needs

Conceptual Understanding SS SN

Use with Example 3.

Explain to students that when adding and subtracting mixed numbers, the way in which whole numbers are renamed depends on the problem. Present the following examples. Include pictures or diagrams like the ones shown below to help explain.

$3 - 1\frac{3}{4} = 2\frac{4}{4} - 1\frac{3}{4}$

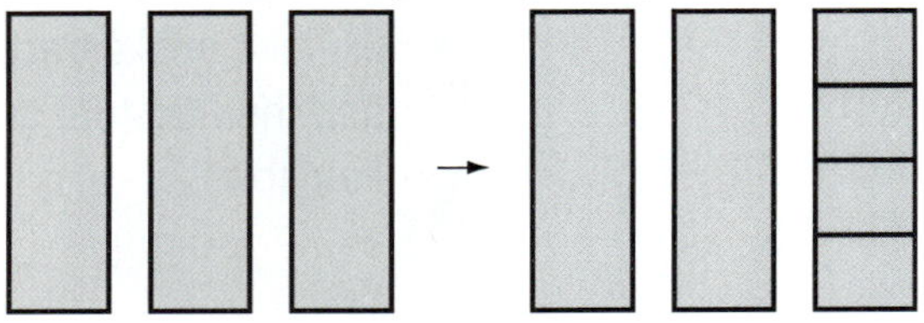

3 is renamed as $2\frac{4}{4}$.

$3 - 1\frac{2}{5} = 2\frac{5}{5} - 1\frac{2}{5}$

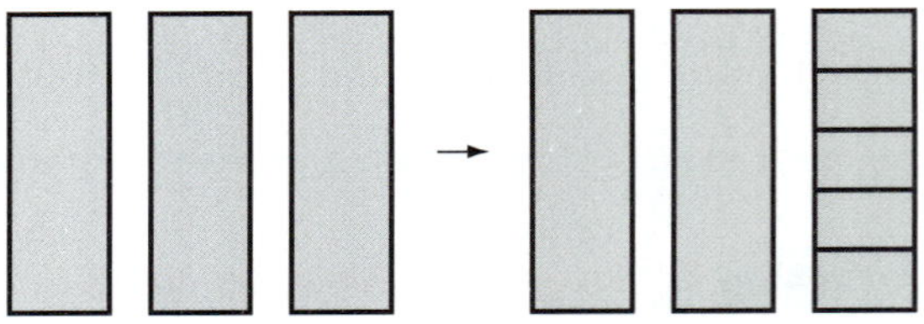

3 is renamed as $2\frac{5}{5}$.

Additional Tips SS

Use before presenting Example 3.

Explain why, when subtracting mixed numbers, it is important to look at the fraction parts first. Use pictures, diagrams, and examples to help explain your reasoning.

Kinesthetic Learning ELL AL

Use after presenting Examples 1–5.

Prepare a set of index cards, with each having a mixed number or fraction written on it. Examples are shown at the right.

$2\frac{1}{3}$	$1\frac{1}{3}$
$5\frac{1}{2}$	$3\frac{5}{8}$

Give each student one card, then call out a sum. Students should mingle, trying to find a student whose number, when added to theirs, equals the sum.

Suggestions:
- Plan well, to be sure that each student finds a match after three or four rounds.
- One possible resource is the Exercises provided in the Extra Practice on page 680.
- You may also wish to extend the activity to include subtraction.

Leveled Lesson Resources

Also on TeacherWorks™ Lesson 5-3

Chapter 5 Resource Masters

BL = Below or Approaching Grade Level   OL = On Grade Level   AL = Above or Beyond Grade Level   ELL = English Language Learner

Lesson Reading Guide
p. 21 BL OL ELL

NAME ______________________ DATE ____________ PERIOD ____

5-3 Lesson Reading Guide

Adding and Subtracting Mixed Numbers

Get Ready for the Lesson

Read the introduction at the top of page 242 in your textbook. Write your answers below.

1. Write an expression to find out how much more Nicolás weighs than Mia. $7\frac{15}{16} - 5\frac{7}{8}$
2. Rename the fractions using the LCD. $7\frac{15}{16} - 5\frac{14}{16}$
3. Find the difference of the fractional parts of the mixed numbers. $\frac{1}{16}$
4. Find the difference of the whole numbers. **2**
5. MAKE A CONJECTURE Explain how to find $7\frac{15}{16} - 5\frac{7}{8}$. Then use your conjecture to find the difference. **Write the fractions with a common denominator. Subtract the fractions and then the whole numbers. $2\frac{1}{16}$**

Read the Lesson

6. In the examples of adding and subtracting mixed numbers, the first step indicated is to estimate the result using whole numbers.
   a. Why do you think it's a good idea to use an estimate? **Sample answer: to have something to compare the actual answer to, so you can check your work**
   b. How do you find the whole numbers used in the estimates? **Sample answer: If the fraction part of the mixed number is $\frac{1}{2}$ or greater, round the whole number part of the mixed number up to the next whole number; if the fraction part is less than $\frac{1}{2}$, round down to the whole number part of the mixed number.**
7. What must you do if the fraction part of a mixed number is greater than the fraction part of the mixed number you are subtracting from? Give an example different from the one used in the example in your textbook. **Sample answer: You must rename the mixed number from which you are subtracting. For example, to subtract $3\frac{3}{4}$ from $4\frac{1}{4}$, first you must rename $4\frac{1}{4}$ as $3\frac{5}{4}$.**

Remember What You Learned

8. Work with a partner. Take turns thinking of a mixed number and having our partner tell you how to rename the mixed number in the way described in this lesson. Repeat until each of you can rename mixed numbers easily. **See students' work.**

Lesson 5-3

Study Guide and Intervention*
p. 22 BL OL ELL

NAME ______________________ DATE ____________ PERIOD ____

5-3 Study Guide and Intervention

Adding and Subtracting Mixed Numbers

To add or subtract mixed numbers:
1. Add or subtract the fractions. Rename using the LCD if necessary.
2. Add or subtract the whole numbers.
3. Simplify if necessary.

Example 1 Find $14\frac{1}{2} + 18\frac{2}{3}$.

$14\frac{1}{2} \rightarrow 14\frac{3}{6}$ Rename the fractions.

$+18\frac{2}{3} \rightarrow +18\frac{4}{6}$ Add the whole numbers and add the fractions.

$32\frac{7}{6}$ or $33\frac{1}{6}$ Simplify.

Example 2 Find $21 - 12\frac{5}{8}$.

$21 \rightarrow 20\frac{8}{8}$ Rename 21 as $20\frac{8}{8}$.

$-12\frac{5}{8} \rightarrow -12\frac{5}{8}$ First subtract the whole numbers and then the fractions.

$8\frac{3}{8}$

Exercises

Add or subtract. Write in simplest form.

1. $7\frac{3}{4} + 2\frac{3}{4}$ **$10\frac{1}{2}$**
2. $14\frac{2}{9} - 6\frac{1}{9}$ **$8\frac{1}{9}$**
3. $9\frac{1}{5} - 4\frac{3}{4}$ **$4\frac{9}{20}$**
4. $7\frac{1}{8} + 5\frac{3}{8}$ **$12\frac{1}{2}$**
5. $7\frac{3}{4} + 2\frac{2}{3}$ **$10\frac{5}{12}$**
6. $5\frac{1}{2} - 5\frac{1}{3}$ **$\frac{1}{6}$**
7. $5\frac{1}{2} - 3\frac{1}{4}$ **$2\frac{1}{4}$**
8. $6\frac{1}{3} + 2\frac{1}{6}$ **$8\frac{1}{2}$**
9. $9 - 3\frac{2}{5}$ **$5\frac{3}{5}$**
10. $2\frac{2}{3} + 7\frac{1}{2}$ **$10\frac{1}{6}$**
11. $6\frac{1}{2} - 6\frac{1}{3}$ **$\frac{1}{6}$**
12. $18\frac{1}{2} + 5\frac{5}{8}$ **$24\frac{1}{8}$**

Skills Practice*
p. 23 BL OL

NAME ______________________ DATE ____________ PERIOD ____

5-3 Skills Practice

Adding and Subtracting Mixed Numbers

Add or subtract. Write in simplest form.

1. $3\frac{2}{7} + 2\frac{1}{7}$ **$5\frac{3}{7}$**
2. $7\frac{1}{3} + 7\frac{1}{3}$ **$14\frac{2}{3}$**
3. $9\frac{3}{5} - 2\frac{1}{5}$ **$7\frac{2}{5}$**
4. $7\frac{3}{4} - 5\frac{1}{4}$ **$2\frac{1}{2}$**
5. $3\frac{1}{4} + 5\frac{1}{4}$ **$8\frac{1}{2}$**
6. $6\frac{3}{4} - 5\frac{3}{4}$ **1**
7. $12\frac{1}{8} + 9\frac{3}{8}$ **$21\frac{1}{2}$**
8. $5\frac{2}{3} - 2\frac{1}{3}$ **$3\frac{1}{3}$**
9. $14\frac{3}{5} - 9\frac{2}{5}$ **$5\frac{1}{5}$**
10. $5\frac{1}{2} + 3\frac{1}{4}$ **$8\frac{3}{4}$**
11. $2\frac{1}{3} + 6\frac{1}{6}$ **$8\frac{1}{2}$**
12. $6\frac{1}{3} - 6\frac{1}{4}$ **$\frac{1}{12}$**
13. $7\frac{5}{6} - 2\frac{2}{3}$ **$5\frac{1}{6}$**
14. $6\frac{7}{10} + 5\frac{1}{4}$ **$11\frac{19}{20}$**
15. $12\frac{3}{8} - 9\frac{1}{3}$ **$3\frac{1}{24}$**
16. $12\frac{13}{15} + 4\frac{1}{9}$ **$16\frac{44}{45}$**
17. $15\frac{2}{3} - 7\frac{1}{5}$ **$8\frac{7}{15}$**
18. $4\frac{7}{12} - 2\frac{3}{16}$ **$2\frac{19}{48}$**
19. $8\frac{3}{4} + 3\frac{2}{5}$ **$12\frac{3}{20}$**
20. $12\frac{1}{3} - 8\frac{5}{9}$ **$3\frac{7}{9}$**
21. $8 - 3\frac{2}{5}$ **$4\frac{3}{5}$**
22. $7\frac{7}{9} + 6\frac{7}{8}$ **$14\frac{47}{72}$**
23. $7\frac{7}{9} - 6\frac{7}{8}$ **$\frac{65}{72}$**
24. $10\frac{3}{8} + 7\frac{11}{12}$ **$18\frac{7}{24}$**

Lesson 5-3

Practice*
p. 24 OL AL

NAME ______________________ DATE ____________ PERIOD ____

5-3 Practice

Adding and Subtracting Mixed Numbers

Add or Subtract. Write in simplest form.

1. $3\frac{1}{8} + 5\frac{3}{8}$ **$8\frac{1}{2}$**
2. $4\frac{1}{6} + 7\frac{1}{6}$ **$11\frac{1}{3}$**
3. $9\frac{3}{4} - 6\frac{1}{4}$ **$3\frac{1}{2}$**
4. $5\frac{5}{9} - 4\frac{2}{9}$ **$1\frac{1}{3}$**
5. $8\frac{2}{3} - 3\frac{1}{6}$ **$5\frac{1}{2}$**
6. $10\frac{3}{4} - 5\frac{3}{8}$ **$5\frac{3}{8}$**
7. $7\frac{3}{10} + 12\frac{2}{5}$ **$19\frac{7}{10}$**
8. $1\frac{1}{6} + 1\frac{1}{8}$ **$2\frac{7}{24}$**
9. $5\frac{1}{3} - 3\frac{2}{3}$ **$1\frac{2}{3}$**
10. $8\frac{4}{7} - 7\frac{5}{7}$ **$\frac{6}{7}$**
11. $11\frac{1}{12} - 6\frac{5}{6}$ **$4\frac{1}{4}$**
12. $3\frac{2}{5} - 1\frac{3}{4}$ **$1\frac{13}{20}$**
13. $5\frac{4}{5} + 6\frac{5}{6}$ **$12\frac{19}{30}$**
14. $8\frac{2}{7} + 6\frac{5}{14}$ **$14\frac{9}{14}$**
15. $9 - 7\frac{3}{8}$ **$1\frac{5}{8}$**
16. $6\frac{4}{5} + 7\frac{1}{5}$ **14**
17. $4\frac{3}{5} + 1\frac{11}{20} + 5\frac{7}{10}$ **$11\frac{17}{20}$**
18. $10 - 9\frac{1}{3}$ **$\frac{2}{3}$**
19. $2\frac{1}{4} + 5\frac{3}{8} + 3\frac{1}{2}$ **$11\frac{1}{8}$**
20. $7 - 6\frac{7}{8}$ **$\frac{1}{8}$**
21. LAND MEASUREMENT Mr. Alfonso owns two adjacent pieces of land totaling $13\frac{3}{8}$ acres. One piece of land is $8\frac{7}{12}$ acres. Find the area of the other piece of land. **$4\frac{19}{24}$ acres**

GEOMETRY **Find the perimeter of each figure.**

22.

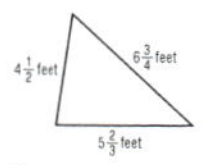

$16\frac{11}{12}$ feet

23.

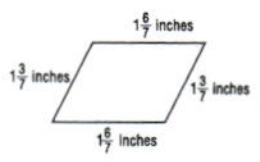

$6\frac{4}{7}$ inches

Word Problem Practice*
p. 25 OL AL

NAME ______________________ DATE ____________ PERIOD ____

5-3 Word Problem Practice

Adding and Subtracting Mixed Numbers

HEIGHT **For Exercises 1–6, use the table below. It shows the heights of five students. Write all answers in simplest form.**

Student	Height (ft)
Karen	$5\frac{1}{6}$
Arturo	6
Felisa	$4\frac{11}{12}$
Max	$5\frac{3}{4}$
Silvia	$5\frac{1}{4}$

1. How much taller is Max than Felisa? **$\frac{5}{6}$ ft**
2. How much shorter is Karen than Arturo? **$\frac{5}{6}$ ft**
3. If Silvia stood on a box that was $1\frac{5}{6}$ feet high, how far would the top of her head be from the floor? **$7\frac{1}{12}$ ft**
4. What is the sum of Felisa and Silvia's heights? **$10\frac{1}{6}$ ft**
5. The distance from the floor to Karen's knee is $1\frac{1}{4}$ feet. What is the distance from her knee to the top of her head? **$3\frac{11}{12}$ ft**
6. Max grew $\frac{1}{3}$ foot last year. How tall was he last year? **$5\frac{5}{12}$ ft**

Lesson 5-3

Enrichment
p. 26 OL AL

NAME ______________________ DATE ____________ PERIOD ____

5-3 Enrichment

Arithmetic Sequences of Fractions

Each term in an *arithmetic* sequence is created by adding or subtracting the same number to the term before. The number added or subtracted is called the *common difference*.

The sequence below is an increasing arithmetic sequence with a common difference of $\frac{1}{4}$.

$$\frac{1}{8}, \frac{3}{8}, \frac{5}{8}, \frac{7}{8}, 1\frac{1}{8}$$

Below is a decreasing arithmetic sequence with a common difference of $1\frac{1}{5}$.

$$7\frac{3}{5}, 6\frac{2}{5}, 5\frac{1}{5}, 4, 2\frac{4}{5}$$

Write the common difference for each arithmetic sequence.

1. $\frac{1}{2}, \frac{5}{8}, \frac{3}{4}, \frac{7}{8}, 1, 1\frac{1}{8}$ **$\frac{1}{8}$**
2. $1\frac{1}{3}, 3\frac{5}{6}, 6\frac{1}{3}, 8\frac{5}{6}$ **$2\frac{1}{2}$**
3. $4\frac{1}{2}, 4\frac{2}{5}, 4\frac{3}{10}, 4\frac{1}{5}$ **$\frac{1}{10}$**
4. $11, 9\frac{2}{3}, 8\frac{1}{3}, 7, 5\frac{2}{3}$ **$1\frac{1}{3}$**

Write the next term in each arithmetic sequence.

5. $\frac{2}{3}, \frac{3}{4}, \frac{5}{6}, \frac{11}{12}, 1$ **$1\frac{1}{12}$**
6. $\frac{13}{20}, \frac{11}{20}, \frac{9}{20}, \frac{7}{20}$ **$\frac{1}{4}$**
7. $5\frac{1}{5}, 5\frac{7}{10}, 6\frac{1}{5}, 6\frac{7}{10}$ **$7\frac{1}{5}$**
8. $4\frac{11}{12}, 3\frac{3}{4}, 2\frac{7}{12}, 1\frac{5}{12}$ **$\frac{1}{4}$**

Write the first five terms in each sequence.

9. This increasing sequence starts with $\frac{1}{6}$ and has a common difference of $1\frac{1}{5}$. **$\frac{1}{6}, 1\frac{11}{30}, 2\frac{17}{30}, 3\frac{23}{30}, 4\frac{29}{30}$**
10. This decreasing sequence starts with $6\frac{1}{3}$ and has a common difference of $\frac{3}{4}$. **$6\frac{1}{3}, 5\frac{7}{12}, 4\frac{5}{6}, 4\frac{1}{12}, 3\frac{1}{3}$**

Additional Lesson Resources

** Also available in Spanish* ELL

Transparencies
- *5-Minute Check Transparency*, Lesson 5-3

Other Print Products
- *Noteables™ Interactive Study Notebook with Foldables™*

Teacher Tech Tools
- *Interactive Classroom CD-ROM*, Lesson 5-3
- *AssignmentWorks*, Lesson 5-3

Student Tech Tools
glencoe.com
- Extra Examples, Chapter 5, Lesson 3
- Self-Check Quiz, Chapter 5, Lesson 3

5-3 Lesson Notes

1 Focus

Vertical Alignment

Before Lesson 5-3
Solve simple problems, including ones arising in concrete situations, involving the addition and subtraction of fractions and mixed numbers and express answers in the simplest form

Lesson 5-3
Solve problems involving addition, subtraction, of positive fractions and explain why a particular operation was used for a given situation. Determine the least common multiple of whole numbers; use them to solve problems with fractions

After Lesson 5-3
Add and subtract fractions by using factoring to find common denominators

2 Teach

Scaffolding Questions

Ask:

- What is $2\frac{1}{2}$ dollars plus $2\frac{1}{2}$ dollars? \$5
- What is $1\frac{1}{4}$ dollars plus $1\frac{1}{2}$ dollars? \$2.75, or $2\frac{3}{4}$ dollars
- What is 10 dollars minus $5\frac{1}{2}$ dollars? \$4.50, or $4\frac{1}{2}$ dollars
- What is 4 dollars minus $1\frac{1}{4}$ dollars? \$2.75, or $2\frac{3}{4}$ dollars

Formative Assessment

Use the Check Your Progress exercises after each Example to determine students' understanding of concepts.

5-3 Adding and Subtracting Mixed Numbers

MAIN IDEA
Add and subtract mixed numbers.

IN Academic Standards

Reinforcement of 6.1.6 Solve problems involving addition, subtraction, multiplication and division of positive fractions and decimals and explain why a particular operation was used for a given situation.

IN Math Online

glencoe.com

- Extra Examples
- Personal Tutor
- Self-Check Quiz

GET READY for the Lesson

BABIES The birth weights of several babies in the hospital nursery are shown.

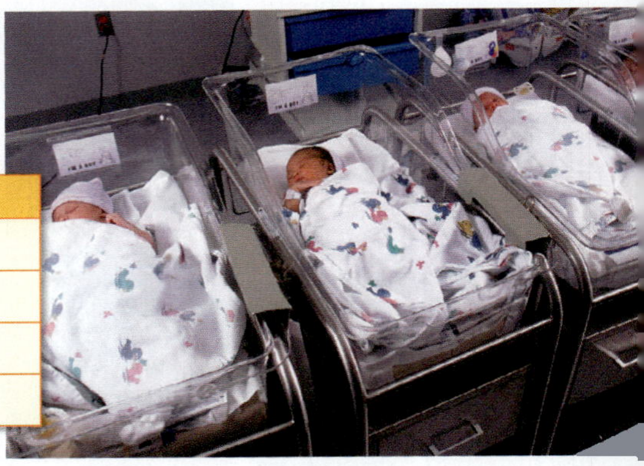

Birth Weight (pounds)	
Jackson	$8\frac{1}{8}$
Nicolás	$7\frac{15}{16}$
Rebekah	$6\frac{13}{16}$
Mia	$5\frac{7}{8}$

1. Write an expression to find how much more Nicolás weighs than Mia. $7\frac{15}{16} - 5\frac{7}{8}$
2. Rename the fractions using the LCD. $7\frac{15}{16} - 5\frac{14}{16}$
3. Find the difference of the fractional parts of the mixed numbers. $\frac{1}{16}$
4. Find the difference of the whole numbers. 2
5. **MAKE A CONJECTURE** Explain how to find $7\frac{15}{16} - 5\frac{7}{8}$. Then use your conjecture to find the difference.

5. Write the fractions with a common denominator. Subtract the fractions and then the whole numbers. $2\frac{1}{16}$

To add or subtract mixed numbers, first add or subtract the fractions. If necessary, rename them using the LCD. Then add or subtract the whole numbers and simplify if necessary.

EXAMPLES Add and Subtract Mixed Numbers

1 **Find $7\frac{4}{9} + 10\frac{2}{9}$. Write in simplest form.**

Estimate $7 + 10 = 17$

$$\begin{array}{r} 7\frac{4}{9} \\ +\ 10\frac{2}{9} \\ \hline 17\frac{6}{9} \text{ or } 17\frac{2}{3} \end{array}$$

Add the whole numbers and fractions separately.

Simplify.

Check for Reasonableness $17\frac{2}{3} \approx 17$ ✔

CHECK Your Progress

a. $6\frac{1}{8} + 2\frac{5}{8}$ $8\frac{3}{4}$

b. $5\frac{1}{5} + 2\frac{3}{10}$ $7\frac{1}{2}$

c. $1\frac{5}{9} + 4\frac{1}{6}$ $5\frac{13}{18}$

ADDITIONAL EXAMPLE

1 Find $3\frac{1}{12} + 14\frac{7}{12}$. Write in simplest form. $17\frac{2}{3}$

Additional Examples are also in:

- Noteables™ Interactive Study Notebook with Foldables™
- Interactive Classroom PowerPoint® Presentations

2 Find $8\frac{5}{6} - 2\frac{1}{3}$. Write in simplest form.

Estimate $9 - 2 = 7$

$$\begin{array}{rcl} 8\frac{5}{6} & \rightarrow & 8\frac{5}{6} \\ \underline{-2\frac{1}{3}} & \rightarrow & \underline{-2\frac{2}{6}} \\ & & 6\frac{3}{6} \text{ or } 6\frac{1}{2} \end{array}$$

Rename the fraction using the LCD. Then subtract.

Simplify.

Check for Reasonableness $6\frac{1}{2} \approx 7$ ✔

CHECK Your Progress

Subtract. Write in simplest form.

d. $5\frac{4}{5} - 1\frac{3}{10}$ $4\frac{1}{2}$
e. $13\frac{7}{8} - 9\frac{3}{4}$ $4\frac{1}{8}$
f. $8\frac{2}{3} - 2\frac{1}{2}$ $6\frac{1}{6}$
g. $7\frac{3}{4} - 4\frac{1}{3}$ $3\frac{5}{12}$
h. $11\frac{5}{6} - 3\frac{1}{8}$ $8\frac{17}{24}$
i. $9\frac{4}{7} - 5\frac{1}{2}$ $4\frac{1}{14}$

Study Tip

Improper Fractions An improper fraction has a numerator that is greater than or equal to the denominator. Examples of improper fractions are $\frac{5}{4}$ and $2\frac{6}{5}$.

Sometimes when you subtract mixed numbers, the fraction in the first mixed number is less than the fraction in the second mixed number. In this case, rename the first fraction as an improper fraction in order to subtract.

EXAMPLES Rename Mixed Numbers to Subtract

3 Find $2\frac{1}{3} - 1\frac{2}{3}$.

Estimate $2 - 1\frac{1}{2} = \frac{1}{2}$

Since $\frac{1}{3}$ is less than $\frac{2}{3}$, rename $2\frac{1}{3}$ before subtracting.

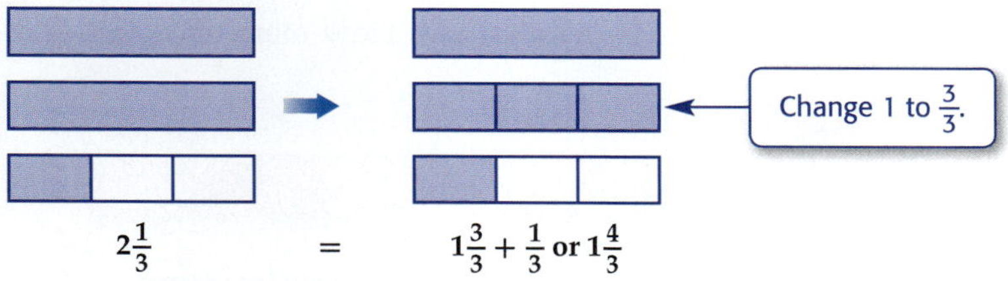

$$\begin{array}{rcl} 2\frac{1}{3} & \rightarrow & 1\frac{4}{3} \\ \underline{-1\frac{2}{3}} & \rightarrow & \underline{-1\frac{2}{3}} \\ & & \frac{2}{3} \end{array}$$

Rename $2\frac{1}{3}$ as $1\frac{4}{3}$.

Subtract the whole numbers and then the fractions.

Check for Reasonableness $\frac{2}{3} \approx \frac{1}{2}$ ✔

Focus on Mathematical Content

If the fractional parts of mixed numbers are **unlike**, use the LCD to rename them before adding or subtracting.

ADDITIONAL EXAMPLES

2 Find $9\frac{7}{10} - 4\frac{3}{5}$. Write in simplest form. $5\frac{1}{10}$

3 Find $8\frac{1}{5} - 3\frac{3}{5}$. $4\frac{3}{5}$

Lesson 5-3 Adding and Subtracting Mixed Numbers **243**

ADDITIONAL EXAMPLES

4 Find $11 - 8\frac{2}{3}$. $2\frac{1}{3}$

5 **COOKING** A quiche recipe calls for $2\frac{3}{4}$ cups of grated cheese. A recipe for quesadillas requires $1\frac{1}{3}$ cups of grated cheese. What is the total amount of grated cheese needed for both recipes? $4\frac{1}{12}$ c

3 Practice

Formative Assessment

Use Exercises 1–9 to check for understanding.

Then use the chart at the bottom of the next page to customize your assignments for students.

Daily Intervention You may wish to use the Study Guide and Intervention Master on page 22 of the *Chapter 5 Resource Masters* for additional reinforcement.

---

4 **Find $8 - 3\frac{3}{4}$.** **Estimate** $8 - 4 = 4$

Using the denominator of the fraction in the subtrahend, $8 = 8\frac{0}{4}$.

Since $\frac{0}{4}$ is less than $\frac{3}{4}$, rename 8 before subtracting.

$$\begin{array}{rcr} 8 & \rightarrow & 7\frac{4}{4} \\ -3\frac{3}{4} & \rightarrow & -3\frac{3}{4} \\ \hline & & 4\frac{1}{4} \end{array}$$

Rename 8 as $7 + \frac{4}{4}$ or $7\frac{4}{4}$.

Subtract.

Check for Reasonableness $4\frac{1}{4} \approx 4$ ✔

CHECK Your Progress

j. $11\frac{2}{5} - 2\frac{3}{5}$ $8\frac{4}{5}$ k. $5\frac{3}{8} - 4\frac{11}{12}$ $\frac{11}{24}$ l. $7 - 1\frac{1}{2}$ $5\frac{1}{2}$

Real-World Career . . .
How Does an Urban Planner Use Math?
An urban planner uses math to measure and draw site plans for future development.

IN Math Online

For more information, go to glencoe.com.

Real-World EXAMPLE

5 **MEASUREMENT** An urban planner is designing a skateboard park. What will be the length of the park and the parking lot combined?

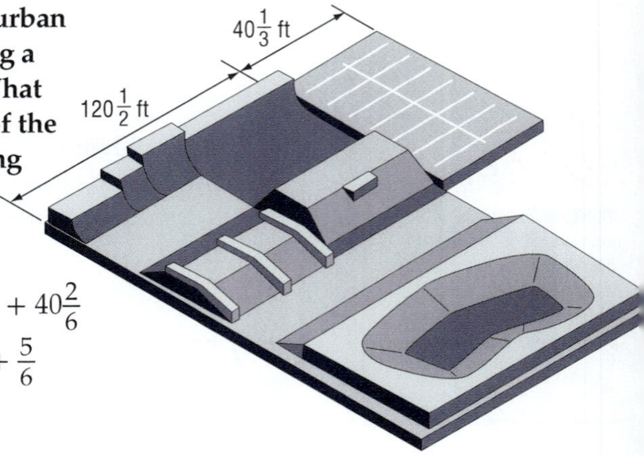

$$120\frac{1}{2} + 40\frac{1}{3} = 120\frac{3}{6} + 40\frac{2}{6}$$
$$= 160 + \frac{5}{6}$$
$$= 160\frac{5}{6}$$

The total length is $160\frac{5}{6}$ feet.

CHECK Your Progress

m. **MEASUREMENT** Jermaine walked $1\frac{5}{8}$ miles on Saturday and $2\frac{1}{2}$ miles on Sunday. How many more miles did he walk on Sunday? $\frac{7}{8}$ mi

★ indicates multi-step problem

CHECK Your Understanding

Examples 1–4 (pp. 242–244)

Add or subtract. Write in simplest form.

1. $1\frac{5}{7} + 8\frac{1}{7}$ $9\frac{6}{7}$
2. $8\frac{1}{2} + 3\frac{4}{5}$ $12\frac{3}{10}$
3. $7\frac{5}{6} - 3\frac{1}{6}$ $4\frac{2}{3}$
4. $9\frac{4}{5} - 2\frac{3}{4}$ $7\frac{1}{20}$
5. $3\frac{1}{4} - 1\frac{3}{4}$ $1\frac{1}{2}$
6. $5\frac{2}{3} - 2\frac{3}{5}$ $3\frac{1}{15}$
7. $11 - 6\frac{3}{8}$ $4\frac{5}{8}$
8. $16 - 5\frac{5}{6}$ $10\frac{1}{6}$

9. $3\frac{3}{20}$ gallons

Example 5 (p. 244)

9. **CARS** A hybrid car's gas tank can hold $11\frac{9}{10}$ gallons of gasoline. It contains $8\frac{3}{4}$ gallons of gasoline. How much more gasoline is needed to fill the tank?

Practice and Problem Solving

HOMEWORK HELP	
For Exercises	See Examples
10–17	1, 2
18–23	3
24–25	4
26–29	5

Exercise Levels
A: 10–29
B: 30–36
C: 37–39

Add or subtract. Write in simplest form.

10. $2\frac{1}{9} + 7\frac{4}{9}$ $9\frac{5}{9}$
11. $3\frac{2}{7} + 4\frac{3}{7}$ $7\frac{5}{7}$
12. $10\frac{4}{5} - 2\frac{1}{5}$ $8\frac{3}{5}$
13. $8\frac{6}{7} - 6\frac{5}{7}$ $2\frac{1}{7}$
14. $9\frac{4}{5} - 2\frac{3}{10}$ $7\frac{1}{2}$
15. $11\frac{3}{4} - 4\frac{1}{3}$ $7\frac{5}{12}$
16. $8\frac{5}{12} + 11\frac{1}{4}$ $19\frac{2}{3}$
17. $8\frac{3}{8} + 10\frac{1}{3}$ $18\frac{17}{24}$
18. $9\frac{1}{5} - 2\frac{3}{5}$ $6\frac{3}{5}$
19. $6\frac{1}{4} - 2\frac{3}{4}$ $3\frac{1}{2}$
20. $6\frac{3}{5} - 1\frac{2}{3}$ $4\frac{14}{15}$
21. $4\frac{3}{10} - 1\frac{3}{4}$ $2\frac{11}{20}$
22. $14\frac{1}{6} - 7\frac{1}{3}$ $6\frac{5}{6}$
23. $12\frac{1}{2} - 6\frac{5}{8}$ $5\frac{7}{8}$
24. $8 - 3\frac{2}{3}$ $4\frac{1}{3}$
25. $13 - 5\frac{5}{6}$ $7\frac{1}{6}$

For Exercises 26–29, choose an operation to solve each problem. Explain your reasoning. Then solve the problem.

26. **HIKING** If Sara and Maggie hiked both of the trails listed in the table, how far did they hike altogether? $6\frac{1}{2}$ mi

26–29. See margin for explanations.

Trail	Length (mi)
Woodland Park	$3\frac{2}{3}$
Mill Creek Way	$2\frac{5}{6}$

27. **JEWELRY** Margarite made the jewelry shown at the right. If the necklace is $10\frac{5}{8}$ inches longer than the bracelet, how long is the necklace that Margarite made? $17\frac{7}{8}$ in.

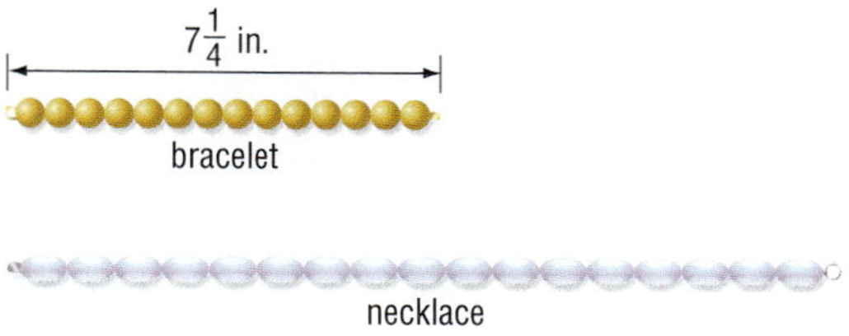

28. **GARDENS** The length of Kasey's garden is $4\frac{5}{8}$ feet. Find the width of Kasey's garden if it is $2\frac{7}{8}$ feet shorter than the length. $1\frac{3}{4}$ ft

29. **HAIRSTYLES** Before Alameda got her haircut, the length of her hair was $9\frac{3}{4}$ inches. After her haircut, the length was $6\frac{1}{2}$ inches. How many inches did she have cut? $3\frac{1}{4}$ in.

Add or subtract. Write in simplest form.

30. $10 - 3\frac{5}{11}$ $6\frac{6}{11}$
31. $24 - 8\frac{3}{4}$ $15\frac{1}{4}$
32. $6\frac{1}{6} + 1\frac{2}{3} + 5\frac{5}{9}$ $13\frac{7}{18}$
33. $3\frac{1}{4} + 2\frac{5}{6} - 4\frac{1}{3}$ $1\frac{3}{4}$

★ 34. **TIME** Karen wakes up at 6:00 A.M. It takes her $1\frac{1}{4}$ hours to shower, get dressed, and comb her hair. It takes her $\frac{1}{2}$ hour to eat breakfast, brush her teeth, and make her bed. At what time will she be ready for school? 7:45 A.M.

MEASUREMENT **Find the perimeter of each figure.**

35. 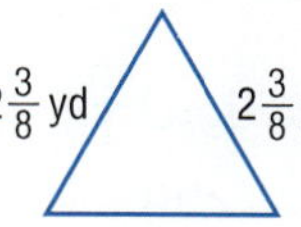

$7\frac{1}{8}$ yd

36. 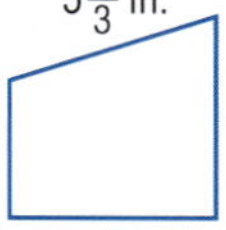

18 in.

Academic Standards • **ISTEP+**
Extra Practice, pp. 680, 708

Odd/Even Assignments

Exercises 10–29 are structured so that students practice the same concepts whether they are assigned odd or even problems.

Tips for New Teachers — Estimation

Encourage students to estimate each sum or difference before computing. The estimate will allow them to check the reasonableness of their solutions.

Additional Answers

26. addition; Sample answer: To find the distance in miles they hiked altogether, add $3\frac{2}{3}$ and $2\frac{5}{6}$.
27. addition; Sample answer: To find the length of the necklace, add $7\frac{1}{4}$ in. and $10\frac{5}{8}$ in.
28. subtraction; Sample answer: To find the width of Kasey's garden, subtract $2\frac{7}{8}$ from $4\frac{5}{8}$.
29. subtraction; Sample answer: To find how many inches Alameda had cut, subtract $6\frac{1}{2}$ from $9\frac{3}{4}$.

DIFFERENTIATED HOMEWORK OPTIONS

Level	Assignment	Two-Day Option	
BL Basic	10–29, 37, 39–48	11–29 odd, 40, 41	10–28 even, 37, 39, 42–48
OL Core	11–33 odd, 34, 35, 37, 39–48	10–29, 40, 41	30–37, 39, 42–48
AL Advanced/Pre-AP	30–47 (optional: 48)		

4 Assess

Name the Math Write a problem such as $9\frac{1}{3} - 6\frac{5}{8}$ on the board. Have students write the mathematical procedures they would use to solve the problem.

FOLDABLES Study Organizer **Foldables™ Follow-Up**

Remind students to record what they learn about adding and subtracting mixed numbers on index cards, and then store the cards in their Foldables.

Differentiated Instruction

Interpersonal Learners Have students work in groups of three or four. Have each group prepare a set of index cards, writing a mixed number between 1 and 21 on each one. Students should shuffle the cards and place them facedown in the middle. Students take turns picking cards and turning them over, two at a time. Everyone estimates the sum and writes his or her estimate on a piece of paper. Then everyone computes the actual sum. The student whose estimate was closest to the actual sum gets a point. In the next round, students find the difference; in the next round, the sum; and so on. The first student with 5 points wins.

Additional Answers

38. 20 ft; If the initial string is 20 feet and cut in half, the two halves would each be 10 feet. Cutting one fifth of one of these 10 foot halves would require splitting the 10 feet into five equal parts. Each part would be 2 feet. So, cutting one fifth of 10 feet would be the same as cutting 2 feet. The remaining portion would be 8 feet long.

39. Sample answer: Since the garden is a rectangle, the length of one side added to the length of the other side would equal half the length of the perimeter. If one side of the garden is $2\frac{5}{12}$ ft long, find 6 ft − $2\frac{5}{12}$ ft, or $3\frac{7}{12}$ ft.

H.O.T. Problems

37. Estimation; You do not need an exact answer; Less than; 7 + 1 < 2 + 7

37. **NUMBER SENSE** Which of the following techniques could be used to determine whether $6\frac{3}{4} + \frac{4}{5}$ is *greater than*, *less than*, or *equal to* $2\frac{1}{9} + 6\frac{7}{8}$? Justify your selection(s). Then use the technique(s) to solve the problem.

number sense | mental math | estimation

38. **CHALLENGE** A string is cut in half. One of the halves is thrown away. One fifth of the remaining half is cut away and the piece left is 8 feet long. How long was the string initially? Justify your answer. **See margin.**

39. **WRITING IN MATH** The fence of a rectangular garden is constructed from 12 feet of fencing wire. Suppose that one side of the garden is $2\frac{5}{12}$ feet long. Explain how to find the length of the other side. **See margin.**

ISTEP+ PRACTICE Reinforcement of 6.1.6

40. The distance from home plate to the pitcher's mound is 60 feet 6 inches and from home plate to second base is 127 feet $3\frac{3}{8}$ inches. Find the distance from the pitcher's mound to second base. **D**

A 68 ft $3\frac{1}{4}$ in.

B 67 ft $8\frac{3}{4}$ in.

C 67 ft $2\frac{5}{8}$ in.

D 66 ft $9\frac{3}{8}$ in.

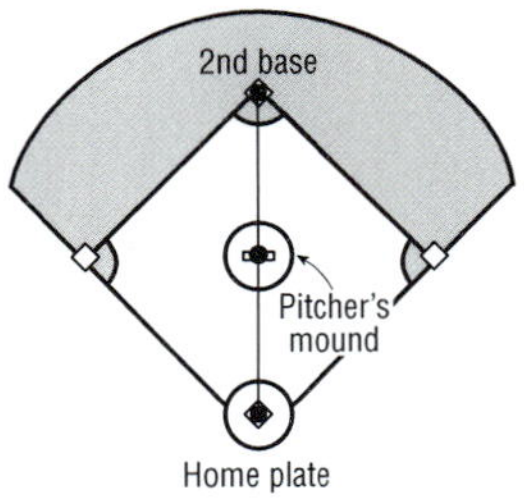

41. A recipe for party mix calls for $4\frac{3}{4}$ cups of cereal. The amount of peanuts needed is $1\frac{2}{3}$ cups less than the amount of cereal needed. How many cups of peanuts and cereal are needed? **H**

F $3\frac{1}{12}$ cups

G $6\frac{1}{2}$ cups

H $7\frac{5}{6}$ cups

J $8\frac{1}{2}$ cups

Spiral Review

42. **SCHOOL** Kai did $\frac{1}{5}$ of her homework in class and $\frac{1}{3}$ more of it on the bus. What fraction of homework does she still need to do? (Lesson 5-2) $\frac{7}{15}$

Estimate. (Lesson 5-1) **43–46. Sample answers are given.**

43. $\frac{8}{9} \div \frac{9}{10}$ $1 \div 1 = 1$ 44. $3\frac{1}{2} + 6\frac{2}{3}$ $4 + 7 = 11$ 45. $8\frac{4}{5} \times 7\frac{1}{9}$ $9 \times 7 = 63$ 46. $4\frac{2}{9} - 1\frac{1}{4}$ $4 - 1 = 3$

47. **MEASUREMENT** To carpet a living room with a length of 17 feet, 255 square feet of carpet is needed. Find the width of the living room. (Lesson 3-6) **15 ft**

GET READY for the Next Lesson

48. **PREREQUISITE SKILL** Andre needs to be at the train station by 5:30 P.M. It takes him $\frac{1}{3}$ hour to pack and $1\frac{1}{4}$ hours to get to the station. Find the latest time he should begin packing. Use the *work backward* strategy. (Lesson 3-4) **3:55 P.M.**

246 Chapter 5 Applying Fractions

CHAPTER 5

Mid-Chapter Quiz

Lessons 5-1 through 5-3

IN Academic Standards
7.1.7, 6.1.6

1. **MONEY** Latisha spends $\frac{3}{4}$ of her money on a birthday present for her brother. If she has \$33, estimate the amount she spends on her brother's present. (Lesson 5-1) **\$24**

Estimate. (Lesson 5-1) **2–7. Sample answers are given.**

2. $5\frac{1}{9} + 1\frac{7}{8}$ **$5 + 2 = 7$**
3. $13\frac{1}{2} \div 7\frac{2}{9}$ **$14 \div 7 = 2$**
4. $\frac{11}{20} - \frac{5}{8}$ **$\frac{1}{2} - \frac{1}{2} = 0$**
5. $4\frac{2}{3} \times 1\frac{3}{4}$ **$5 \times 2 = 10$**
6. $7\frac{3}{4} \div 1\frac{4}{5}$ **$8 \div 2 = 4$**
7. $\frac{8}{9} + 2\frac{13}{15}$ **$1 + 3 = 4$**

8. **MULTIPLE CHOICE** Mrs. Ortega is making 5 batches of muffins for the school bake sale. Each batch uses $2\frac{1}{4}$ cups sugar and $1\frac{1}{2}$ cups milk. Which is the best estimate of the total amount of sugar and milk Mrs. Ortega uses for the muffins? (Lesson 5-1) **B**

   A less than 15 cups
   B between 15 and 20 cups
   C between 20 and 25 cups
   D more than 25 cups

Add or subtract. Write in simplest form.
(Lesson 5-2)

9. $\frac{11}{15} - \frac{1}{15}$ **$\frac{2}{3}$**
10. $\frac{4}{7} - \frac{3}{14}$ **$\frac{5}{14}$**
11. $\frac{1}{2} + \frac{2}{9}$ **$\frac{13}{18}$**
12. $\frac{5}{8} + \frac{3}{4}$ **$1\frac{3}{8}$**

13. **SCIENCE** $\frac{39}{50}$ of Earth's atmosphere is made up of nitrogen while only $\frac{21}{100}$ is made up of oxygen. What fraction of Earth's atmosphere is either nitrogen or oxygen? (Lesson 5-2) **$\frac{99}{100}$**

Add or subtract. Write in simplest form.
(Lesson 5-3)

14. $8\frac{3}{4} - 2\frac{5}{12}$ **$6\frac{1}{3}$**
15. $5\frac{1}{6} - 1\frac{1}{3}$ **$3\frac{5}{6}$**
16. $2\frac{5}{9} + 1\frac{2}{3}$ **$4\frac{2}{9}$**
17. $2\frac{3}{5} + 6\frac{13}{15}$ **$9\frac{7}{15}$**

18. **MULTIPLE CHOICE** The table shows the weight of a newborn infant for the first year. (Lesson 5-3)

Month	Weight (lb)
0	$7\frac{1}{4}$
3	$12\frac{1}{2}$
6	$16\frac{5}{8}$
9	$19\frac{4}{5}$
12	$23\frac{3}{20}$

During which three-month period was the infant's weight gain the greatest? **F**

   F 0–3 months
   H 6–9 months
   G 3–6 months
   J 9–12 months

19. **MEASUREMENT** How much does a $50\frac{1}{4}$-pound suitcase weigh after $3\frac{7}{8}$ pounds is removed? (Lesson 5-3) **$46\frac{3}{8}$ lb**

20. **MULTIPLE CHOICE** The table gives the average annual snowfall for several U.S. cities. (Lesson 5-3)

City	Average Snowfall (in.)
Anchorage, AK	$70\frac{4}{5}$
Mount Washington, NH	$259\frac{9}{10}$
Buffalo, NY	$93\frac{3}{5}$
Birmingham, AL	$1\frac{1}{2}$

Source: Fact Monster

On average, how many more inches of snow does Mount Washington, New Hampshire, receive than Anchorage, Alaska? **B**

   A $330\frac{7}{10}$ in.
   C $166\frac{3}{10}$ in.
   B $189\frac{1}{10}$ in.
   D $92\frac{1}{10}$ in.

CHAPTER 5 Mid-Chapter Quiz

Formative Assessment

Use the Mid-Chapter Quiz to assess students' progress in the first half of the chapter.

Have students review the lesson indicated for the problems they answered incorrectly.

Summative Assessment

CRM Mid-Chapter Test, p. 55

ExamView Assessment Suite Customize and create multiple versions of your Mid-Chapter Test and their answer keys.

FOLDABLES Study Organizer Dinah Zike's Foldables

Before students complete the Mid-Chapter Quiz, encourage them to review the notes they recorded about fractions and mixed numbers on the index cards stored in their Foldables.

Data-Driven Decision Making

Diagnostic Teaching Based on the results of the Chapter 5 Mid-Chapter Quiz, use the following to review concepts that students continue to find challenging.

Exercises	Lesson	Academic Standards	Resources for Review
1–8	5-1	7.1.7	CRM Study Guide and Intervention pp. 10, 16, and 22; IN Math Online glencoe.com • Extra Examples • Personal Tutor • Concepts in Motion
9–13	5-2	6.1.6	
14–20	5-3	6.1.6	

5-4 Problem-Solving Investigation
ELIMINATE POSSIBILITIES

PACING: **Regular:** 1.5 periods, **Block:** 0.5 period

IN Academic Standards **P.1.3 Apply and adapt a variety of appropriate strategies to solve problems. P.2.4 Select and use various types of reasoning** and methods of proof. *Also addresses P.2.1, P.5.2.*

Options for Differentiated Instruction

ELL = English Language Learner AL = Above or Beyond Grade Level SS = Struggling Students SN = Special Needs

Choosing the Strategy ELL SS

Use before assigning the Exercises.

Prior to assigning Exercises 7–14, read each Exercise aloud and discuss with the class which strategy might be best to solve each problem. Possible discussion questions are listed below.

- What is the question asking?
- Have you seen problems like this before?
- What strategy might be helpful to solve the problem?
- How could you check your answer to make sure it is reasonable?

Working in Groups ELL AL SS SN

Use before assigning the Exercises.

Organize students into groups of four or five. Provide each student with a worksheet of multiple-choice problems. An example of a problem is shown below.

Refer to the table at the right. If the trend continues, which is the best estimate for the average movie ticket price in 2008? C

A $6.35 **C** $7.00
B $6.59 **D** $7.89

Average U.S. Movie Ticket Price

Year	Ticket Price ($)
2002	5.80
2003	6.03
2004	6.21
2005	6.40
2006	6.57
2007	6.69

Tell students that they should discuss each problem, eliminate possibilities, and find the solution. Then they are to record the answer on their worksheets. Inform students that you will be collecting only one sheet from each group to determine the group members' scores.

Organizing Student Work and Thinking ELL AL SS SN

Use after completing Lesson 5-4.

Have students add the eliminating possibilities strategy to their problem-solving booklets. They should include the following about the strategy:

- a description of the strategy
- an explanation of the best time to use the strategy
- examples of problems that are solved using the strategy
- advantages and disadvantages of using the strategy

Leveled Lesson Resources

Also on TeacherWorks™
Lesson 5-4

Chapter 5 Resource Masters

BL = Below or Approaching Grade Level

OL = On Grade Level

AL = Above or Beyond Grade Level

ELL = English Language Learner

*Study Guide and Intervention**
p. 27 BL OL ELL

NAME ______________ DATE __________ PERIOD ____

5-4 Study Guide and Intervention

Problem-Solving Investigation: Eliminate Possibilities

By **eliminating possibilities** when problem solving, you can methodically reduce the number of potential answers.

Example

Joan has \$20 to spend on her sister for her birthday. She has already bought her a DVD for \$9.75. There are three shirts that she likes which cost \$8.75, \$10.00, and \$11.00. Which shirt should she buy so that she spends most of her money without going over \$20?

Understand	You know that the total amount of money she has to spend must be \$20 or less.
Plan	Eliminate answers that are not reasonable.
Solve	She couldn't spend \$11.00 because \$9.75 + \$11.00 = \$20.75. So eliminate that choice. Now check \$10.00 \$9.75 + 10.00 = \$19.75 Since this is less than \$20, this is the correct choice. She should buy her sister the \$10.00 shirt.
Check	By buying the \$8.75 shirt, she would only spend a total of \$9.75 + \$8.75 = \$18.50. This is less than the \$20 minimum, but not the most she could possibly spend.

Exercises

Solve the following problems by eliminating possibilities first.

1. **TELEPHONE** Susan talked on her cellular telephone for 120 minutes last month. Her plan charges her a \$15.00 fee per month plus \$0.10 a minute after the first 60 minutes, which are included in the \$15 fee. What was her total bill for last month?
   A. \$12.00 B. \$27.00 C. \$21.00 D. \$6.00
   C
2. **HOME SALES** 450 homes sold in your area in the last year. What number shows a good estimate of the number of homes sold per month?
   A. 38 homes B. 32.5 homes C. 2 homes D. 45 homes
   A
3. **CAR SALES** Derrick sells cars for a living. He sells an average of 22 cars a month. What will his total average car sales be in 5 years?
   A. 110 cars B. 264 cars C. 1320 cars D. 27 cars
   C
4. **TELEVISION** Myra is allowed to watch 6 hours of television on a weekend. She watched $2\frac{1}{2}$ hours this morning. How much television will she be allowed to watch at most this afternoon?
   A. 4 hours B. $4\frac{1}{2}$ hours C. $2\frac{1}{2}$ hours D. $3\frac{1}{2}$ hours
   D

Lesson 5-4

Chapter 5 27 Course 2

*Skills Practice**
p. 28 BL OL

NAME ______________ DATE __________ PERIOD ____

5-4 Skills Practice

Problem-Solving Investigation: Eliminate Possibilities

Eliminate possibilities to solve.

1. **CELL PHONES** Justin has a cell phone plan that costs \$25 per month plus \$0.05 per minute for each minute he talks. How much will it cost Justin for the month of March if he talked for 120 minutes? **C**
   A \$25 C \$31
   B \$25.05 D \$22
2. **PUPPIES** A puppy gains weight at a rate of 1.5 pounds every two weeks for the first 6 months after it is born. If Sam's puppy weighs 6 pounds right now, how much will it weigh six weeks from now? **G**
   F 6 pounds H 15 pounds
   G 10.5 pounds J 13 pounds
3. **RECIPES** Ryan needs $3\frac{1}{4}$ cups of flour for the cookie recipe she is baking. She has already added $2\frac{1}{2}$ cups of flour. How much more flour does she need to add? **D**
   A $2\frac{1}{2}$ cups C $3\frac{1}{4}$ cups
   B 1 cup D $\frac{3}{4}$ cup
4. **HOMEWORK** Jordan does 30 minutes of homework per day. How many hours of homework does she do in one week? **F**
   F $3\frac{1}{2}$ hours H $\frac{1}{2}$ hour
   G 2 hours J 3 hours
5. **FENCING** A rectangular garden is surrounded by a fence. The length of the garden is $3\frac{1}{2}$ feet and the width of the garden is $1\frac{1}{2}$ feet. How much fencing must be used to surround the garden? **C**
   A 5 feet C 10 feet
   B $3\frac{1}{2}$ feet D $1\frac{1}{2}$ feet
6. **PARTIES** The 6th grade class is renting the pool at the recreation center for a holiday party. It costs \$75 plus \$1.50 per person to rent the pool. How much will it cost to rent the pool if 120 people plan on attending ? **H**
   F \$76.50 H \$255
   G \$195 J \$120

Chapter 5 28 Course 2

*Practice**
p. 29 OL AL

NAME ______________ DATE __________ PERIOD ____

5-4 Practice

Problem-Solving Investigation: Eliminate Possibilities

Mixed Problem Solving

Eliminate the possibilities to solve Exercises 1 and 2.

1. **STAIRCASE** A staircase has 14 steps between floors. If the second floor is 10 feet above the first floor, what is the approximate height of each step of the staircase?
   C
   A 2 inches C 9 inches
   B 12 inches D 15 inches
2. **NEWSPAPER** Mr. Kemper delivers the morning newspaper to about 500 customers each day. About how many newspapers does he deliver in a month?
   J
   F 50 H 500
   G 5,000 J 15,000

Use any strategy to solve Exercises 3 and 4. Some strategies are shown below.

PROBLEM-SOLVING STRATEGIES
• Look for a pattern. • Choose the method of computation. • Eliminate possibilities.

3. **PATTERNS** What are the next three fractions in the pattern?
   $\frac{1}{12}, \frac{1}{6}, \frac{1}{4}, \frac{1}{3}, \frac{5}{12}, \ldots$
   $\frac{1}{2}, \frac{7}{12}, \frac{2}{3}$
4. **OFFICE SUPPLIES** Printer ink costs \$23.42 per cartridge if bought separately. If bought by the case of 24 cartridges, the cost per cartridge is only \$19.53. About how much is the difference in cost of buying 4 cases than buying the same number of cartridges separately? **B**
   A \$4 C \$84
   B \$374 D \$1,550

Select the Operation

For Exercises 5 and 6, select the appropriate operation(s) to solve the problem. Justify your selection(s) and solve the problem.

5. **YARDWORK** David mowed $\frac{3}{10}$ of the yard while his brother mowed $\frac{1}{4}$ of it. What fraction of the yard still needs to be mowed? **Addition followed by subtraction;**
   $\frac{3}{10} + \frac{1}{4} = \frac{6}{20} + \frac{5}{20} = \frac{11}{20}$;
   $1 - \frac{11}{20} = \frac{9}{20}$
6. **DOGS** On average, dogs require about 35 Calories per pound of body weight per day. The Parkers own three dogs that weigh 22 pounds, 34 pounds, and 9 pounds. What is the total Calorie requirement for the dogs each day?
   Addition followed by multiplication;
   22 + 34 + 9 = 65;
   65 · 35 = 2,275;
   2,275 Calories

Lesson 5-4

Chapter 5 29 Course 2

*Word Problem Practice**
p. 30 OL AL

NAME ______________ DATE __________ PERIOD ____

5-4 Word Problem Practice

Problem-Solving Investigation: Eliminate Possibilities

Solve each problem using any strategy you have learned.

1. **SHOPPING** Jillian has \$125 to buy school clothes. She bought a sweater for \$45, two pairs of jeans for \$35 each, and 2 headbands that cost \$1.50 each. If socks are \$3.00 per pack, how many packs can she buy?
   2 packs
2. **PATTERNS** List the next three terms in the sequence.
   21, 24, 27,...
   30, 33, 36
3. **CAKE** Libby ate $\frac{1}{4}$ of her birthday cake and Scott ate $\frac{1}{3}$ of her birthday cake. The rest was wrapped up and sent home with the Thomas family. What fraction of the cake was sent home with the Thomas family?
   $\frac{5}{12}$
4. **SNACKS** Jesse eats an apple every day after school. On weekends, he eats 2 apples each day. How many apples does Jesse eat in one week where he goes to school for five days and is at home for two days on the weekend? **D**
   A 7 apples C 14 apples
   B 5 apples D 9 apples
5. **LEMONADE** Amber is making lemonade for her Yearbook Club meeting. She wants to have $4\frac{1}{2}$ gallons and has already made $3\frac{1}{4}$ gallons. How much more does she have to make? **G**
   F $3\frac{1}{4}$ gallons H $4\frac{1}{2}$ gallons
   G $1\frac{1}{4}$ gallons J 2 gallons
6. **GEOMETRY** Draw the next two figures in the pattern.
   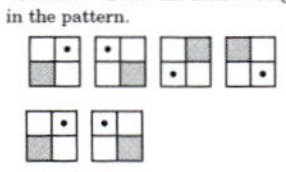
7. **ROLLER COASTERS** A roller coaster has a weight limit of 500 pounds. If a group of teenagers is waiting to ride the roller coaster and the average weight of the teens is 140 pounds, how many can ride the roller coaster?
   3 teens
8. **WORK** The table below shows the number of hours Antoine has worked this week. If he wants to work a total of 25 hours, how many hours does he need to work on Saturday? **5 h**

Day	Hours
Sunday	8
Monday	3
Tuesday	2
Wednesday	3
Thursday	0
Friday	4

Chapter 5 30 Course 2

Additional Lesson Resources

Transparencies

- *5-Minute Check Transparency*, Lesson 5-4

Other Print Products

- *Noteables™ Interactive Study Notebook with Foldables™*

Teacher Tech Tools

- *Interactive Classroom CD-ROM*, Lesson 5-4
- *AssignmentWorks*, Lesson 5-4

Student Tech Tools

glencoe.com

- Extra Examples, Chapter 5, Lesson 4
- Self-Check Quiz, Chapter 5, Lesson 4

5-4 Lesson Notes

1 Focus

Eliminate Possibilities Students can use this strategy to help them solve multiple-choice problems. Estimation is a good way to eliminate answers that are *not* reasonable.

2 Teach

Scaffolding Questions

Write the following problem on the board. Tell students *not* to calculate the difference.

Find $3\frac{3}{7} - 2\frac{1}{2}$.

A 0 **B** $\frac{13}{14}$ **C** $\frac{7}{8}$ **D** 1

Ask:

- Is A a reasonable answer? Why or why not? No; the estimated difference is about 1.
- Is C a reasonable answer? Why or why not? No; 8 is not a common denominator of 7 and 2.
- Is D a reasonable answer? Why or why not? No; $\frac{3}{7} - \frac{1}{2} \neq 1$.

ADDITIONAL EXAMPLE

Solve. Use the *eliminate possibilities* strategy.

GAMES On a television game show, the winning contestant must answer three questions correctly to win the grand prize. Each question is worth twice as many points as the question before it. The third question is worth 1,000 points. How much is the first question worth–250, 500, or 2,000 points? 250 points

5-4 Problem-Solving Investigation

MAIN IDEA: Solve problems by eliminating possibilities.

Academic Standards **P.1.3** Apply and adapt a variety of appropriate strategies to solve problems. **P.2.4** Select and use various types of reasoning and methods of proof. *Also addresses 7.3.4, P.2.1, P.5.2.*

P.S.I. TEAM +

e-Mail: ELIMINATE POSSIBILITIES

MADISON: I am making school pennants to decorate the cafeteria. I use $1\frac{1}{4}$ yards of fabric for each pennant.

YOUR MISSION: Eliminate possibilities to find the greatest number of pennants Madison can make with 12 yards of fabric. Is it 6, 9, or 12?

Understand	You know she has 12 yards of fabric. Each pennant uses $1\frac{1}{4}$ yards of fabric.
Plan	Eliminate the answers that are not reasonable.
Solve	Madison needs more than 1 yard of fabric for each pennant. So, she needs more than 12 yards for 12 pennants. Eliminate this choice. Now check the choice of 9 pennants. • $1\frac{1}{4} + 1\frac{1}{4} + 1\frac{1}{4} + 1\frac{1}{4} = 5$. So, Madison can make 4 pennants with 5 yards of fabric. Therefore, she can make 8 pennants out of 10 yards of fabric. • She can also make 1 more pennant with the remaining 2 yards. So, Madison can make 8 + 1 or 9 pennants.
Check	Making 6 pennants would take $1\frac{1}{4} + 1\frac{1}{4} + 1\frac{1}{4} + 1\frac{1}{4} + 1\frac{1}{4} + 1\frac{1}{4} = 7\frac{1}{2}$ yards. This is not the greatest number she can make. So, making 6 pennants is *not* reasonable.

Analyze The Strategy

1–3. See Ch. 5 Answer Appendix.

1. Describe different ways that you can eliminate possibilities when solving problems.
2. Explain how the strategy of eliminating possibilities is useful for taking multiple-choice tests.
3. **WRITING IN MATH** Write a problem that could be solved by eliminating possibilities.

Additional Examples are also in:

- Noteables™ Interactive Study Notebook with Foldables™
- Interactive Classroom PowerPoint® Presentations

Tips for New Teachers: Multiple-Choice Tests

Make sure students understand that the eliminate possibilities strategy can save them time. Often, students can use mental math or estimation to eliminate one or more answer choices in a multiple-choice problem. Then they can test the remaining answer choices by substituting them in the expression or equation.

Mixed Problem Solving

★ indicates multi-step problem

Academic Standards • ISTEP+

Extra Practice, pp. 679, 681

Eliminate possibilities to solve Exercises 4–6.

4. **TRAINS** A train passes through an intersection at the rate of 3 cars per 30 seconds. Assume that it takes 5 minutes for the train to completely pass through the intersection. How many cars does the train have altogether? **C**

   A 6 cars   C 30 cars

   B 15 cars   D 45 cars

5. **PIZZA** A pizza shop used 100 pounds of pizza dough to make 125 pizzas. If a large pizza requires 1 pound of dough and a medium pizza requires $\frac{1}{2}$ pound, how many large- and medium-sized pizzas were made? **J**

   F 40 large, 85 medium

   G 65 large, 60 medium

   H 55 large, 70 medium

   J 75 large, 50 medium

6. **PILLOWS** Pat is making pillows out of fabric. He uses $\frac{3}{4}$ yard of fabric for each pillow. What is the greatest number of pillows Pat can make with 9 yards of fabric: 9, 12, or 15? **12 pillows**

Use any strategy to solve Exercises 7–14. Some strategies are shown below.

PROBLEM-SOLVING STRATEGIES
- Look for a pattern.
- Work backward.
- Make an organized list.

7. **MEASUREMENT** The diagram shows a shelf ★ that holds CDs. Each shelf is $\frac{1}{8}$ inch thick, and the distance between shelves is as shown. How much space is available on each layer of the shelf for a CD? **$\frac{5}{8}$ in.**

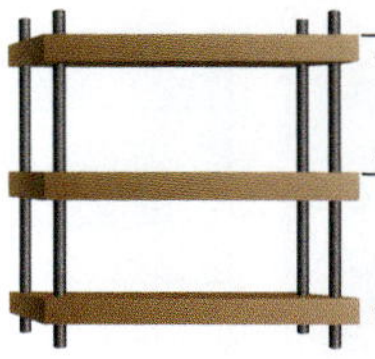

8. **BRIDGES** A covered bridge has a maximum capacity of 48,000 pounds. If an average school bus weighs 10,000 pounds, about how many school buses could a covered bridge hold? **4 buses**

9. **GEOMETRY** Draw the next two figures in the pattern. **See margin.**

10. **SLEEP** A 9-month-old infant needs about ★ 14 hours of sleep each day while a teenager needs about 10 hours of sleep each day. How much more sleep does a 9-month-old need than a teenager? Write as a fraction of a day. **$\frac{1}{6}$ of a day**

11. **PRECIPITATION** In Olympia, Washington, the average annual precipitation is $50\frac{3}{5}$ inches. Is $\frac{1}{49}$ inch, 1 inch, or 14 inches the best estimate for the average precipitation per day? **$\frac{1}{49}$ inch**

12. **MONEY** Kristen has \$15 to go to the movies. ★ Her ticket costs \$7.25, drinks are \$3.50, popcorn is \$5.75, and pretzels are \$4.25. Which two items can Kristen get from the concession stand? **a drink and a pretzel**

13. **PIZZA** Sebastian ate $\frac{2}{5}$ of a pizza while his ★ sister ate $\frac{1}{3}$ of the same pizza. The remainder was stored in the refrigerator. What fraction of the pizza was stored in the refrigerator? **$\frac{4}{15}$**

14. **GRADES** Jerome had an average of 88 on his first three science tests. His score on the second and third tests were 92 and 87. What was his score on the first test? **85**

3 Practice

Using the Exercises

Exercises 1–3 can be used to check students' understanding of the eliminate possibilities strategy.

Exercises 4–6 give students an opportunity to practice the eliminate possibilities strategy.

Exercises 7–14 give students the opportunity to practice many different problem-solving strategies. You may wish to review some of the strategies they have studied.

- use the four-step plan (p. 25)
- look for a pattern (p. 112)
- work backward (p. 148)
- make an organized list (p. 190)

4 Assess

Ticket Out the Door Write the following problem and answer choices on the board.

Find $1\frac{3}{8} + \frac{7}{12}$.

A $1\frac{1}{2}$ **C** $1\frac{15}{16}$

B $1\frac{23}{24}$ **D** $2\frac{23}{24}$

Have students pick one of the answer choices and write why it can be eliminated. Sample answer: D; $1\frac{3}{8} + \frac{7}{12}$ is about $1\frac{1}{2} + \frac{1}{2}$ or 2. Since $2\frac{23}{24}$ is about 3, choice D can be eliminated.

Formative Assessment

Check for student understanding of concepts in Lessons 5-3 and 5-4.

CRM Quiz 2, p. 53

Additional Answer

9. 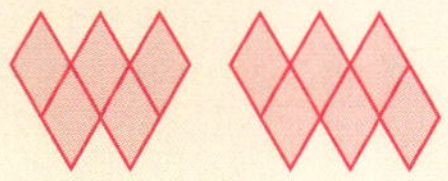

Explore 5-5 Lesson Notes

1 Focus

Materials

- geoboards
- geobands
- grid paper
- blue and yellow pencils

Easy-to-Make Manipulatives

Teaching Mathematics with Manipulatives templates for:

- centimeter grid paper, p. 15

2 Teach

Activity 1 Make sure students realize that the units of the geoboard model are shown by the number of spaces between the pegs on a side (and not by the number of pegs).

Activity 2 Tell students that the actual dimensions of the rectangles don't matter, provided the rectangles are the same size and are divided into fourths.

Differentiated Instruction

Bodily/Kinesthetic Learners

Students can also use geoboards in Activities 2 and 3. In Activity 2, ask students how they could model a whole number multiplied by a fraction, such as $2 \times \frac{1}{4}$ using a geoboard. Then in Activity 3, ask students how they could model a mixed number multiplied by a fraction, such as $1\frac{2}{3} \times \frac{1}{2}$ using a geoboard. Sample answer: For Activity 2, use two geoboards and on each one, use geobands to represent one-fourth of each geoboard. For Activity 3, use two geoboards. On the first geoboard use a geoband to represent half of the geoboard and on the second geoboard, use one geoband to represent $\frac{2}{3}$ and another geoband to represents $\frac{1}{2}$.

Explore 5-5

Math Lab
Multiplying Fractions

MAIN IDEA

Use area models to multiply fractions and mixed numbers.

IN Academic Standards

7.1.7 Solve problems that involve multiplication and division **with** integers, **fractions,** decimals and combinations of the four operations. *Also addresses P.2.2, P.5.1, P.5.2, P.5.3.*

IN Math Online

glencoe.com

- Concepts In Motion

Just as the product of 3×4 is the number of square units in a rectangle, the product of two fractions can be shown using area models.

ACTIVITY

1 Find $\frac{3}{4} \times \frac{2}{3}$ using a geoboard.

The first factor is 3 *fourths* and the second factor is 2 *thirds*.

STEP 1 Use one geoband to show fourths and another to show thirds on the geoboard.

STEP 2 Use geobands to form a rectangle. Place one geoband on the peg to show 3 fourths and another on the peg to show 2 thirds.

STEP 3 Connect the geobands to show a small rectangle.

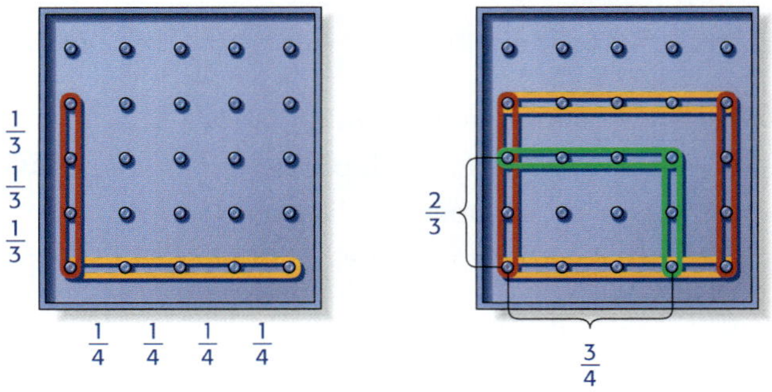

The area of the small square is 6 square units. The area of the large rectangle is 12 square units. So, $\frac{3}{4} \times \frac{2}{3} = \frac{6}{12}$ or $\frac{1}{2}$.

CHECK Your Progress

Find each product using a geoboard.

a. $\frac{1}{4} \times \frac{1}{3}$ $\frac{1}{12}$ b. $\frac{1}{2} \times \frac{1}{2}$ $\frac{1}{4}$ c. $\frac{3}{4} \times \frac{1}{2}$ $\frac{3}{8}$ d. $\frac{2}{3} \times \frac{1}{4}$ $\frac{2}{12}$ or $\frac{1}{6}$

a, b. See margin. c, d. See Ch. 5 Answer Appendix.

ACTIVITY

2 Find $2 \times \frac{1}{4}$ using an area model.

STEP 1 To represent 2 or $\frac{2}{1}$, draw 2 large rectangles, side by side. Divide each rectangle horizontally into fourths. Color both large rectangles blue.

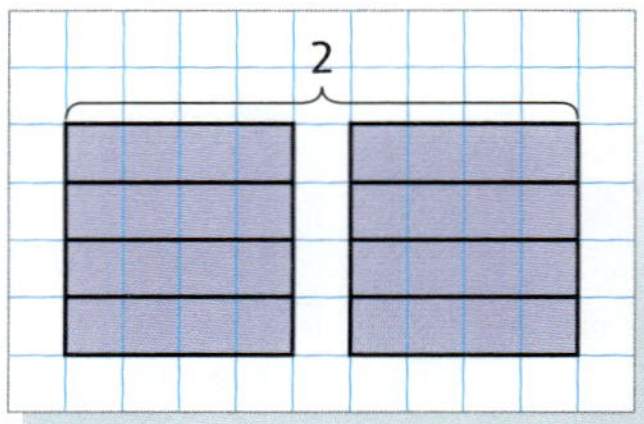

Additional Answers

a.

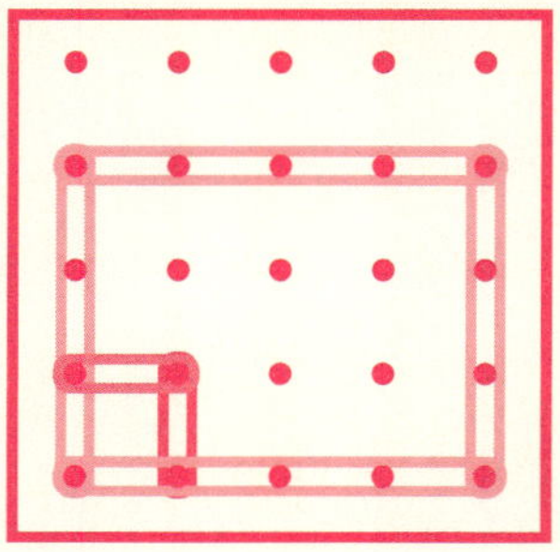

b.

Study Tip

Shading Yellow and blue make green. So, the green sections have been shaded twice and represent the product.

STEP 2 Color 1 fourth of each large rectangle yellow.

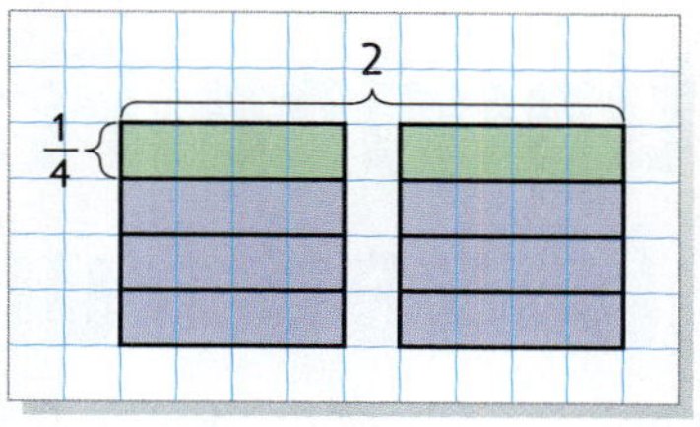

The fraction that compares the number of green sections, 2, to the number of sections in one rectangle, 4, is $\frac{2}{4}$ or $\frac{1}{2}$. So, $2 \times \frac{1}{4} = \frac{1}{2}$.

CHECK Your Progress

Find each product using a model.

e. $3 \times \frac{2}{3}$ $\frac{6}{3}$ or 2 f. $2 \times \frac{2}{5}$ $\frac{4}{5}$ g. $4 \times \frac{1}{2}$ $\frac{4}{2}$ or 2 h. $3 \times \frac{3}{4}$ $\frac{9}{4}$ or $2\frac{1}{4}$

e, f. See margin for models. g, h. See Ch. 5 Answer Appendix for models.

ACTIVITY

3 **Find $1\frac{2}{3} \times \frac{1}{2}$ using a model.**

STEP 1 Draw 2 rectangles divided vertically into thirds and horizontally into halves. Color $1\frac{2}{3}$ of the squares blue.

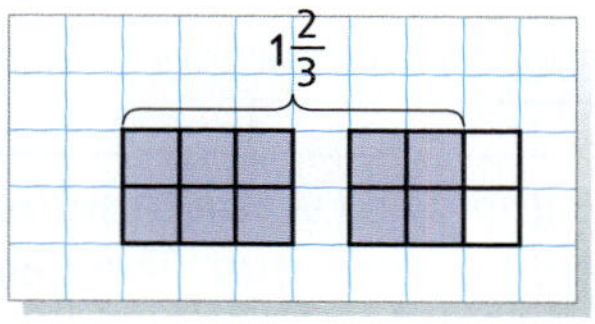

STEP 2 Color $\frac{1}{2}$ of the squares yellow. Then count the small squares that are green.

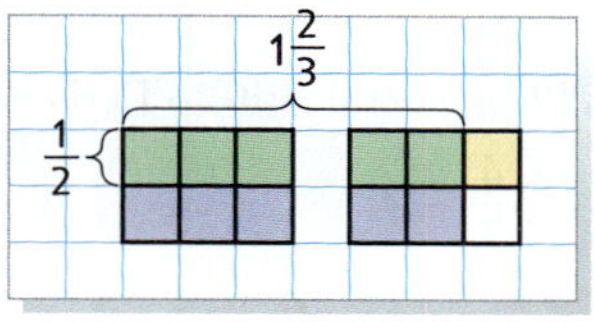

Since the green area is $\frac{3}{6}$ of the first rectangle and $\frac{2}{6}$ of the second rectangle, the total area shaded green is $\frac{3}{6} + \frac{2}{6}$ or $\frac{5}{6}$. So, $1\frac{2}{3} \times \frac{1}{2} = \frac{5}{6}$.

CHECK Your Progress

Find each product using a model.

i. $1\frac{1}{4} \times \frac{1}{5}$ $\frac{5}{20}$ or $\frac{1}{4}$ j. $2\frac{1}{2} \times \frac{3}{4}$ $\frac{15}{8}$ or $1\frac{7}{8}$ k. $1\frac{2}{3} \times \frac{1}{3}$ $\frac{5}{9}$

i–k. See Ch. 5 Answer Appendix for models.

ANALYZE THE RESULTS

1. Analyze Exercises a–k. What is the relationship between the numerators of the factors and of the product? between the denominators of the factors and of the product?

1. The product of the numerators is equal to the numerator of the product. The product of the denominators is equal to the denominator of the product.

2. **MAKE A CONJECTURE** Write a rule you can use to multiply two fractions. **See Ch. 5 Answer Appendix.**

Activity 3 Make sure students realize that each 3 × 2 rectangle represents 1, and that the rectangles have been separated into thirds and halves because the denominators of the factors are 3 and 2.

3 Assess

Formative Assessment

Use Exercise 1 to determine whether students understand how to multiply fractions.

From Concrete to Abstract Use Exercise 2 to bridge the gap between using models to multiply fractions and following the algorithm.

Extending the Concept If students can write the rule for multiplying fractions (Exercise 2), ask them how they might use the rule to multiply mixed numbers and fractions. by first rewriting the mixed number as an improper fraction

Additional Answers

e.

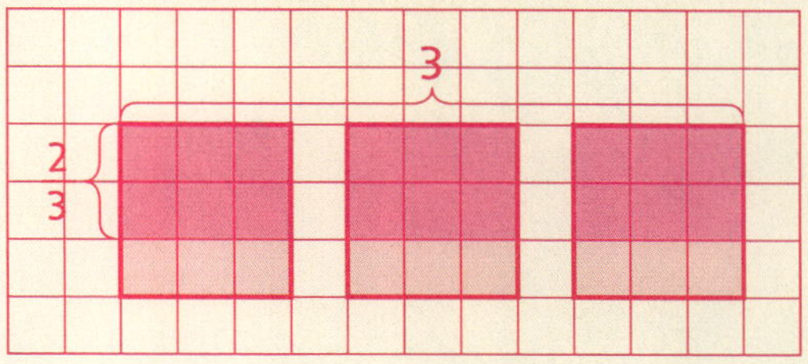

f.

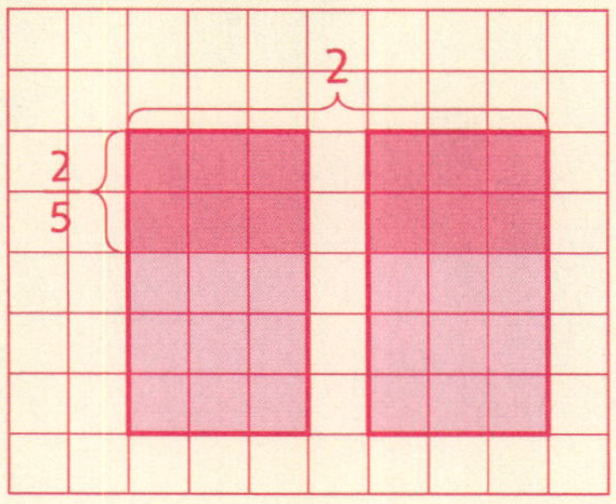

Explore 5-5 Math Lab: Multiplying Fractions **251**

5-5 Multiplying Fractions and Mixed Numbers

PACING: **Regular:** 1.5 periods, **Block:** 0.5 period

IN Academic Standards **7.1.7 Solve problems that involve multiplication** and division **with** integers, **fractions**, decimals and combinations of the four operations. *Also addresses P.5.1, P.5.2, P.5.3, P.6.2.*

Options for Differentiated Instruction

ELL = English Language Learner   AL = Above or Beyond Grade Level   SS = Struggling Students   SN = Special Needs

Reviewing Concepts SS

Use before presenting Lesson 5-5.

Review with students how to write a mixed number as an improper fraction.

$6\frac{1}{2} \rightarrow 6 \times \frac{1}{2} + = \frac{(6 \times 2) + 1}{2} = \frac{13}{2}$

Multiply the whole number and denominator. Then add the numerator.

Have students use this method to write the following mixed numbers as improper fractions.

1. $2\frac{3}{4}$ $\frac{11}{4}$ **2.** $1\frac{7}{8}$ $\frac{15}{8}$ **3.** $3\frac{4}{7}$ $\frac{25}{7}$ **4.** $5\frac{1}{6}$ $\frac{31}{6}$

Using Models SS SN

Use after presenting Example 2.

Remind students that multiplication is repeated addition. This is especially helpful for students to remember when they are multiplying a whole number by a fraction.

$3 \times \frac{2}{5}$ means 3 groups of $\frac{2}{5}$.

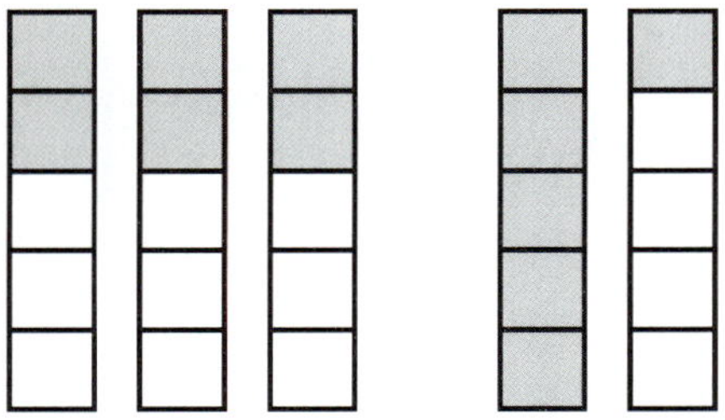

$\frac{2}{5} + \frac{2}{5} + \frac{2}{5} = \frac{6}{5}$ or $1\frac{1}{5}$

Connections to Real-World Activities ELL AL SS SN

Use before assigning the Exercises.

Have students use a cookbook to find a recipe that they would like to make. Ask them to rewrite the recipe, giving the amount of each ingredient that will be needed to serve the entire class.

Leveled Lesson Resources

Also on TeacherWorks™ Lesson 5-5

Chapter 5 Resource Masters

BL = Below or Approaching Grade Level OL = On Grade Level AL = Above or Beyond Grade Level ELL = English Language Learner

Lesson Reading Guide
p. 31 BL OL ELL

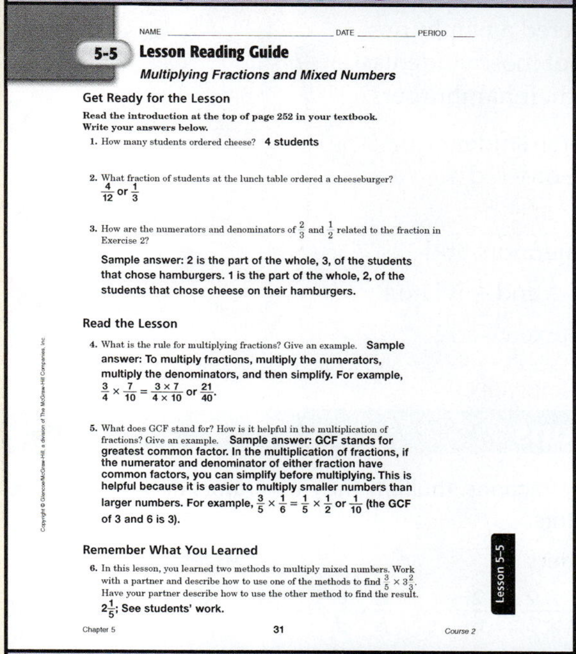

*Study Guide and Intervention**
p. 32 BL OL ELL

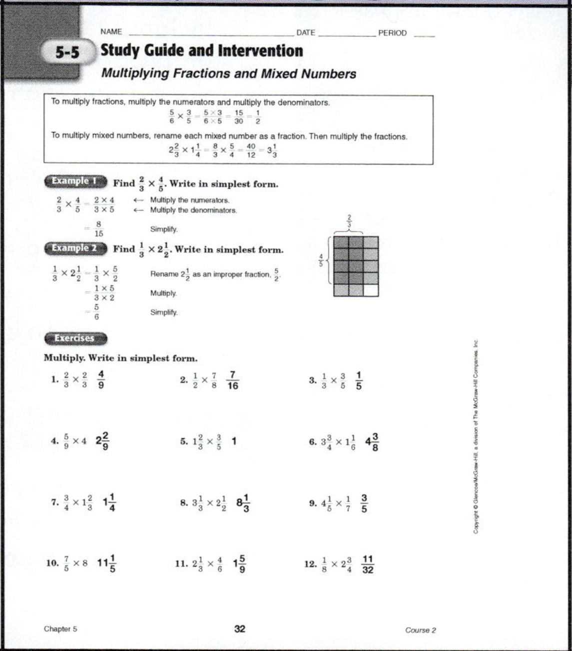

*Skills Practice**
p. 33 BL OL

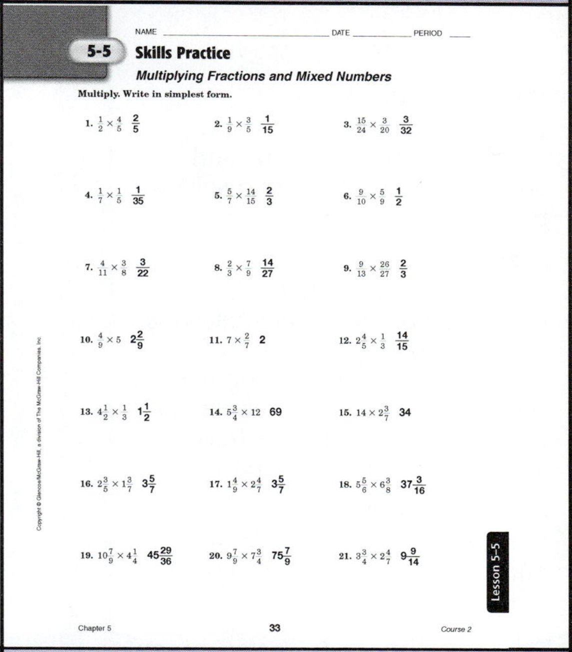

*Practice**
p. 34 OL AL

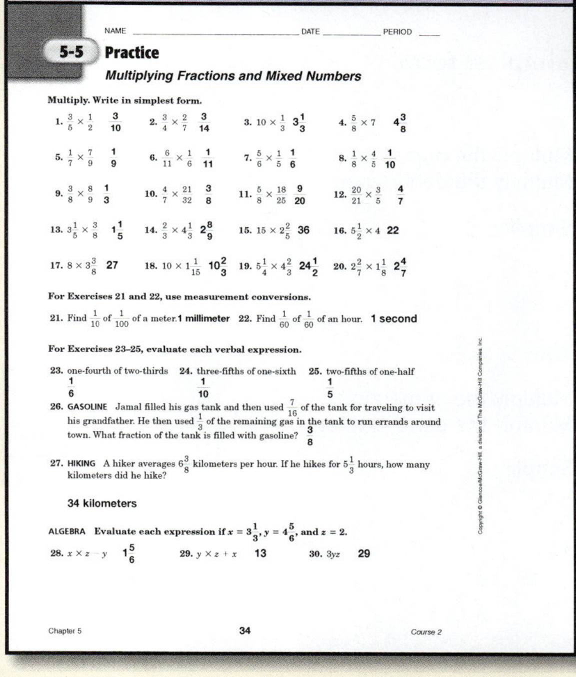

*Word Problem Practice**
p. 35 OL AL

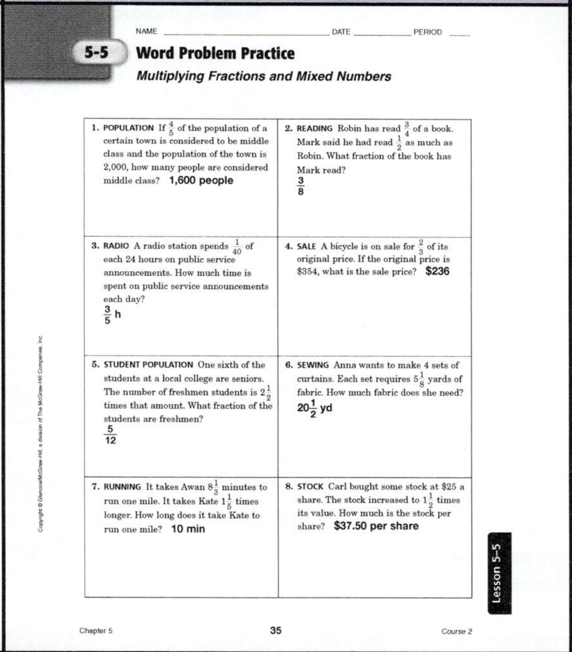

Enrichment
p. 36 OL AL

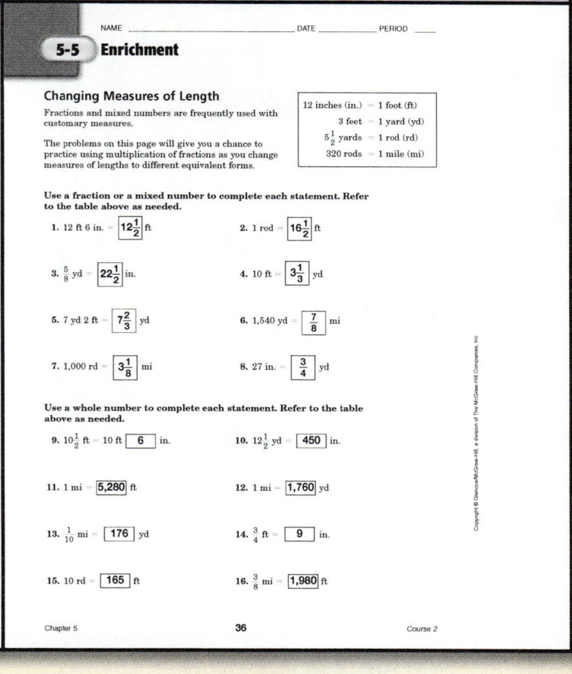

Additional Lesson Resources

** Also available in Spanish* ELL

Transparencies

- *5-Minute Check Transparency*, Lesson 5-5

Other Print Products

- *Teaching Mathematics with Manipulatives*
- *Noteables™ Interactive Study Notebook with Foldables™*

Teacher Tech Tools

- *Interactive Classroom CD-ROM*, Lesson 5-5
- *AssignmentWorks*, Lesson 5-5

Student Tech Tools

glencoe.com

- Extra Examples, Chapter 5, Lesson 5
- Self-Check Quiz, Chapter 5, Lesson 5

5-5 Lesson Notes

1 Focus

Vertical Alignment

Before Lesson 5-5
Compute and perform simple multiplication of fractions and apply these procedures to solving problems

Lesson 5-5
Solve problems involving multiplication of positive fractions and explain why a particular operation was used for a given situation. Explain the meaning of multiplication of positive fractions and perform the calculations

After Lesson 5-5
Multiply and simplify rational numbers by using the exponent rules

2 Teach

Scaffolding Questions

Ask:

- What is half of $\frac{1}{2}$ of a dollar? $\frac{1}{4}$ dollar, or \$0.25
- What is three times $\frac{1}{4}$ of a dollar? $\frac{3}{4}$ dollar, or \$0.75
- What is one third of $1\frac{1}{2}$ dollars? $\frac{1}{2}$ dollar, or \$0.50
- What is one quarter of $\frac{4}{5}$ of a dollar? $\frac{1}{5}$ dollar, or \$0.20

Formative Assessment

Use the Check Your Progress exercises after the Examples to determine students' understanding of concepts.

5-5 Multiplying Fractions and Mixed Numbers

MAIN IDEA

Multiply fractions and mixed numbers.

IN Academic Standards

7.1.7 Solve problems that involve multiplication and division **with** integers, **fractions,** decimals and combinations of the four operations. *Also addresses P.5.1, P.5.2, P.5.3, P.6.2.*

IN Math Online

glencoe.com

- Extra Examples
- Personal Tutor
- Self-Check Quiz

GET READY for the Lesson

LUNCH Two thirds of the students at the lunch table ordered a hamburger for lunch. One half of those students ordered cheese on their hamburgers.

1. What fraction of the students at the lunch table ordered a cheeseburger? $\frac{4}{12}$ or $\frac{1}{3}$
2. How are the numerators and denominators of $\frac{2}{3}$ and $\frac{1}{2}$ related to the fraction in Exercise 1?

See Ch. 5 Answer Appendix.

Multiply Fractions — Key Concept

Words To multiply fractions, multiply the numerators and multiply the denominators.

Examples

Numbers	Algebra
$\frac{1}{2} \times \frac{2}{3} = \frac{1 \times 2}{2 \times 3}$ or $\frac{2}{6}$	$\frac{a}{b} \cdot \frac{c}{d} = \frac{a \cdot c}{b \cdot d}$ or $\frac{ac}{bd}$, where $b, d \neq 0$

EXAMPLES Multiply Fractions

Multiply. Write in simplest form.

1 $\frac{1}{2} \times \frac{1}{3}$

$\frac{1}{2} \times \frac{1}{3} = \frac{1 \times 1}{2 \times 3}$ ← Multiply the numerators. ← Multiply the denominators.

$= \frac{1}{6}$ Simplify.

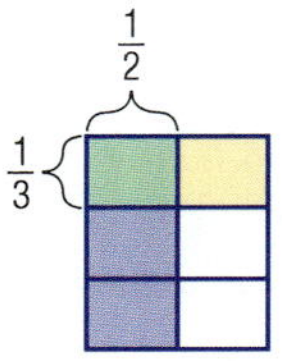

$\frac{1}{6}$ shaded green

2 $2 \times \frac{3}{4}$

$2 \times \frac{3}{4} = \frac{2}{1} \times \frac{3}{4}$ Write 2 as $\frac{2}{1}$.

$= \frac{2 \times 3}{1 \times 4}$ ← Multiply the numerators. ← Multiply the denominators.

$= \frac{6}{4}$ or $1\frac{1}{2}$ Simplify.

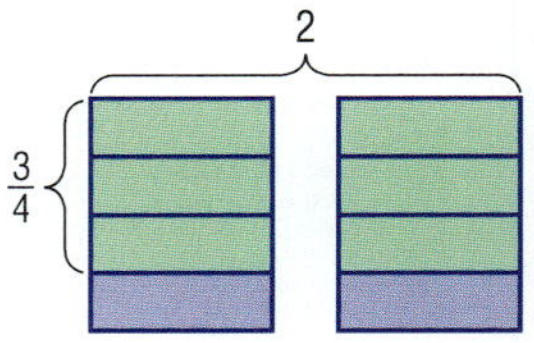

$\frac{6}{4}$ or $1\frac{1}{2}$ shaded green

Study Tip

Whole Numbers When multiplying a fraction by a whole number, write the whole number as a fraction with a denominator of 1.

CHECK Your Progress

a. $\frac{3}{5} \times \frac{1}{2}$ $\frac{3}{10}$

b. $\frac{1}{3} \times \frac{3}{4}$ $\frac{1}{4}$

c. $\frac{2}{3} \times 4$ $2\frac{2}{3}$

Differentiated Instruction

Bodily/Kinesthetic Learners Students can use geoboards in the Get Ready for the Lesson. Ask students how they could model $\frac{1}{3} \times \frac{2}{5}$ using a geoboard. Sample answer: Use a geoband to represent $\frac{1}{3}$ of the geoboard and another geoband to represents $\frac{2}{5}$.

Tips for New Teachers — Models

For the Example in Get Ready for the Lesson, tell students that the hamburgers represent all students at the table. The top two rows are students who ordered hamburgers, or $\frac{2}{3}$. The circled hamburgers are $\frac{1}{2}$ of $\frac{2}{3}$ or $\frac{1}{3}$ of the students at the table who ordered cheese.

If the numerator and denominator of either fraction have common factors, you can simplify before multiplying.

EXAMPLE Simplify Before Multiplying

Review Vocabulary

GCF the greatest of the common factors of two or more numbers; *Example:* the GCF of 8 and 12 is 4. (Lesson 4-2)

3 Find $\frac{2}{7} \times \frac{3}{8}$. Write in simplest form.

$\frac{2}{7} \times \frac{3}{8} = \frac{\overset{1}{\cancel{2}}}{7} \times \frac{3}{\underset{4}{\cancel{8}}}$ Divide 2 and 8 by their GCF, 2.

$= \frac{1 \times 3}{7 \times 4}$ or $\frac{3}{28}$ Multiply.

CHECK Your Progress

Multiply. Write in simplest form.

d. $\frac{1}{3} \times \frac{3}{7}$ $\frac{1}{7}$ e. $\frac{4}{9} \times \frac{1}{8}$ $\frac{1}{18}$ f. $\frac{5}{6} \times \frac{3}{5}$ $\frac{1}{2}$

EXAMPLE Multiply Mixed Numbers

4 Find $\frac{1}{2} \times 4\frac{2}{5}$. Write in simplest form. Estimate $\frac{1}{2} \times 4 = 2$

Study Tip

Simplifying If you forget to simplify before multiplying, you can always simplify the final answer. However, it is usually easier to simplify before multiplying.

METHOD 1 Rename the mixed number.

$\frac{1}{2} \times 4\frac{2}{5} = \frac{1}{\underset{1}{\cancel{2}}} \times \frac{\overset{11}{\cancel{22}}}{5}$ Rename $4\frac{2}{5}$ as an improper fraction, $\frac{22}{5}$. Divide 2 and 22 by their GCF, 2.

$= \frac{1 \times 11}{1 \times 5}$ Multiply.

$= \frac{11}{5}$ or $2\frac{1}{5}$ Simplify.

METHOD 2 Use mental math.

The mixed number $4\frac{2}{5}$ is equal to $4 + \frac{2}{5}$.

So, $\frac{1}{2} \times 4\frac{2}{5} = \frac{1}{2}\left(4 + \frac{2}{5}\right)$. Use the Distributive Property to multiply, then add mentally.

$\frac{1}{2}\left(4 + \frac{2}{5}\right) = 2 + \frac{1}{5}$ **THINK** Half of 4 is 2 and half of 2 fifths is 1 fifth.

$= 2\frac{1}{5}$ Rewrite the sum as a mixed number.

So, $\frac{1}{2} \times 4\frac{2}{5} = 2\frac{1}{5}$. **Check for Reasonableness** $2\frac{1}{5} \approx 2$ ✔

CHOOSE Your Method

Multiply. Write in simplest form.

g. $\frac{1}{4} \times 8\frac{4}{9}$ $2\frac{1}{9}$ h. $5\frac{1}{3} \times 3$ 16 i. $1\frac{7}{8} \times 2\frac{2}{5}$ $4\frac{1}{2}$

Focus on Mathematical Content

To multiply a fraction by a whole number or a mixed number, first **rename the whole number or mixed number** as an improper fraction.

Before multiplying fractions, check whether the numerator and denominator of either fraction have a common factor. If they do, **simplifying** them first will save time.

ADDITIONAL EXAMPLES

Multiply. Write in simplest form.

1 $\frac{1}{8} \times \frac{1}{9}$ $\frac{1}{72}$

2 $6 \times \frac{1}{3}$ 2

3 $\frac{3}{12} \times \frac{4}{5}$ $\frac{1}{5}$

4 $\frac{1}{3} \times 6\frac{6}{7}$ $2\frac{2}{7}$

Additional Examples are also in:

- Noteables™ Interactive Study Notebook with Foldables™
- Interactive Classroom PowerPoint® Presentations

Tips for New Teachers: Unit Fractions

Explain to students that when unit fractions are used in multiplication, division can also be used. Point out that in Example 5, they can use the equation $d = 365\frac{1}{4} \div 3$ to solve the problem.

ADDITIONAL EXAMPLES

5 **BIKING** In a 48-hour bike race, Mel rode $289\frac{1}{3}$ miles. His father rode $\frac{3}{4}$ as far as Mel did. Find the number of miles his father rode. 217 mi

6 **CANNING** Roberta canned 32 quarts of her prize-winning apricot jam. She sold $\frac{5}{8}$ of them at a street fair. Find the number of quarts she sold. 20 qt

Study Tip

Meaning of Multiplication Recall that one meaning of 3×4 is three groups with 4 in each group. In Example 5, there are $365\frac{1}{4}$ groups with $\frac{1}{3}$ in each group.

Real-World EXAMPLES

5 **SLEEP** Humans sleep about $\frac{1}{3}$ of each day. If each year is equal to $365\frac{1}{4}$ days, determine the number of days in a year the average human sleeps.

Words	Humans sleep about $\frac{1}{3}$ of $365\frac{1}{4}$ days.
Variable	Let d represent the number of days a human sleeps.
Equation	$d = \frac{1}{3} \cdot 365\frac{1}{4}$

$d = \frac{1}{3} \cdot 365\frac{1}{4}$ Write the equation.

$d = \frac{1}{3} \cdot \frac{1{,}461}{4}$ Rename the mixed number as an improper fraction.

$d = \frac{1}{\cancel{3}_1} \cdot \frac{\cancel{1{,}461}^{487}}{4}$ Divide 3 and 1,461 by their GCF, 3.

$d = \frac{487}{4}$ or $121\frac{3}{4}$ Multiply. Then rename as a mixed number.

The average human sleeps $121\frac{3}{4}$ days each year.

6 **ANIMALS** The house cat has an average lifespan that is $\frac{4}{5}$ of a lion's. If a lion's lifespan is 15 years, find the average lifespan of a house cat.

Real-World Link The average group of lions, called a pride, consists of about 15 lions with about $\frac{2}{3}$ of the pride being female.
Source: *African Wildlife Foundation*

Words	The lifespan of a house cat is $\frac{4}{5}$ of that of the lion.
Variable	Let c represent the lifespan of a house cat.
Equation	$c = \frac{4}{5} \cdot 15$

$c = \frac{4}{5} \cdot 15$ Write the equation.

$c = \frac{4}{5} \cdot \frac{15}{1}$ Write the whole number 15 as an improper fraction.

$c = \frac{4}{\cancel{5}_1} \cdot \frac{\cancel{15}^{3}}{1}$ Divide 5 and 15 by their GCF, 5.

$c = \frac{12}{1}$ or 12 Multiply, then simplify.

The average lifespan of a house cat is 12 years.

CHECK Your Progress

j. **COOKING** Sofia wishes to make $\frac{1}{2}$ of a recipe. If the original recipe calls for $3\frac{3}{4}$ cups of flour, how many cups should she use? $1\frac{7}{8}$ c

CHECK Your Understanding

★ indicates multi-step problem

Examples 1–4 (pp. 252–253)

Multiply. Write in simplest form.

1. $\frac{2}{3} \times \frac{1}{3}$ $\frac{2}{9}$
2. $2 \times \frac{2}{5}$ $\frac{4}{5}$
3. $\frac{1}{6} \times 4$ $\frac{2}{3}$
4. $\frac{1}{4} \times \frac{8}{9}$ $\frac{2}{9}$
5. $2\frac{1}{4} \times \frac{2}{3}$ $1\frac{1}{2}$
6. $1\frac{5}{6} \times 3\frac{3}{5}$ $6\frac{3}{5}$

Examples 5, 6 (p. 254)

7. **WEIGHT** The weight of an object on Mars is about $\frac{2}{5}$ its weight on Earth. How much would an 80-pound dog weigh on Mars? 32 pounds

Practice and Problem Solving

HOMEWORK HELP	
For Exercises	See Examples
8–11	1, 2
12–19	3, 4
20–23	5, 6

Exercise Levels
A: 8–23
B: 24–52
C: 53–55

Multiply. Write in simplest form.

8. $\frac{3}{4} \times \frac{1}{8}$ $\frac{3}{32}$
9. $\frac{2}{5} \times \frac{2}{3}$ $\frac{4}{15}$
10. $9 \times \frac{1}{2}$ $4\frac{1}{2}$
11. $\frac{4}{5} \times 6$ $4\frac{4}{5}$
12. $\frac{1}{5} \times \frac{5}{6}$ $\frac{1}{6}$
13. $\frac{4}{9} \times \frac{1}{4}$ $\frac{1}{9}$
14. $\frac{2}{3} \times \frac{1}{4}$ $\frac{1}{6}$
15. $\frac{1}{12} \times \frac{3}{5}$ $\frac{1}{20}$
16. $\frac{4}{7} \times \frac{7}{8}$ $\frac{1}{2}$
17. $\frac{2}{5} \times \frac{15}{16}$ $\frac{3}{8}$
18. $\frac{3}{8} \times \frac{10}{27}$ $\frac{5}{36}$
19. $\frac{9}{10} \times \frac{5}{6}$ $\frac{3}{4}$
20. **DVDs** Each DVD storage case is about $\frac{1}{5}$ inch thick. What will be the height of 12 cases sold together in plastic wrapping? $2\frac{2}{5}$ in.
21. **PIZZA** Mark left $\frac{3}{8}$ of a pizza in the refrigerator. On Friday, he ate $\frac{1}{2}$ of what was left of the pizza. What fraction of the entire pizza did he eat on Friday?

21. $\frac{3}{16}$

22. **MEASUREMENT** The width of a vegetable garden is $\frac{1}{3}$ times its length. If the length of the garden is $7\frac{3}{4}$ feet, what is the width? $2\frac{7}{12}$ ft
23. **RECIPES** A recipe to make one batch of blueberry muffins calls for $4\frac{2}{3}$ cups of flour. How many cups of flour are needed to make 3 batches of blueberry muffins? 14 c

Multiply. Write in simplest form.

24. $4\frac{2}{3} \times \frac{4}{7}$ $2\frac{2}{3}$
25. $\frac{5}{8} \times 2\frac{1}{2}$ $1\frac{9}{16}$
26. $14 \times 1\frac{1}{7}$ 16
27. $3\frac{3}{4} \times 8$ 30
28. $9 \times 4\frac{2}{3}$ 42
29. $4 \times 7\frac{5}{6}$ $31\frac{1}{3}$
30. $3\frac{1}{4} \times 2\frac{2}{3}$ $8\frac{2}{3}$
31. $5\frac{1}{3} \times 3\frac{3}{4}$ 20
32. **MEASUREMENT** The width of the fish tank is $\frac{2}{5}$ of its length. What is the width of the fish tank? 12 in.

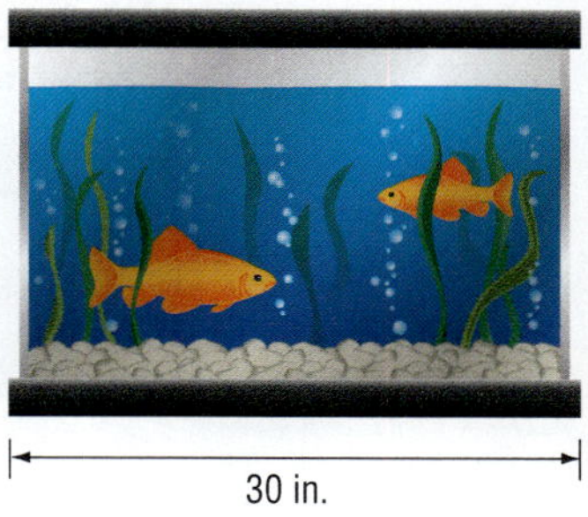

33. **BICYCLING** Philip rode his bicycle at $9\frac{2}{5}$ miles per hour. If he rode for $\frac{3}{4}$ of an hour, how many miles did he cover?

33. $7\frac{1}{20}$ mi

3 Practice

Formative Assessment

Use Exercises 1–7 to check for understanding.

Then use the chart at the bottom of this page to customize your assignments for students.

Intervention You may wish to use the Study Guide and Intervention Master on page 32 of the *Chapter 5 Resource Masters* for additional reinforcement.

Odd/Even Assignments

Exercises 8–23 are structured so that students practice the same concepts whether they are assigned odd or even problems.

DIFFERENTIATED HOMEWORK OPTIONS

Level	Assignment	Two-Day Option	
BL Basic	8–23, 54–66	9–23 odd, 56, 57	8–22 even, 54, 55, 58–66
OL Core	9–31 odd, 32, 33–39 odd, 40, 41–47 odd, 48, 49, 51, 54–66	8–23, 56, 57	24–52, 54, 55, 58–66
AL Advanced/Pre-AP	24–63 (optional: 64–66)		

Additional Answers

40. $1{,}167\frac{1}{5}$ ft; sample answer: Find the perimeter of the pool and then multiply the distance by 4.

49. broccoli: $1\frac{7}{8}$c, pasta: $5\frac{5}{8}$c, salad dressing: 1c, cheese: 2c; Multiply each amount by $1\frac{1}{2}$.

51. $\frac{2}{5} \times \frac{3}{5}$; $\frac{6}{25}$; Sample answer: The model shows that $\frac{3}{5}$ of the rectangle is 15 sections out of 25 sections. Since $\frac{2}{5}$ of 15 sections is six sections, $\frac{2}{5}$ of $\frac{3}{5}$ is $\frac{6}{25}$.

52. $\frac{3}{7} \times \frac{2}{3}$; $\frac{6}{21}$ or $\frac{2}{7}$; Sample answer: The model shows that $\frac{2}{3}$ of the rectangle is 14 sections out of 21 sections. Since $\frac{3}{7}$ of 14 sections is six sections, $\frac{3}{7}$ of $\frac{2}{3}$ is $\frac{6}{21}$, or $\frac{2}{7}$.

Evaluate each verbal expression.

34. one half of five eighths $\frac{5}{16}$
35. four sevenths of two thirds $\frac{8}{21}$
36. nine tenths of one fourth $\frac{9}{40}$
37. one third of eleven sixteenths $\frac{11}{48}$

MEASUREMENT **Find the perimeter and area of each rectangle.**

38. 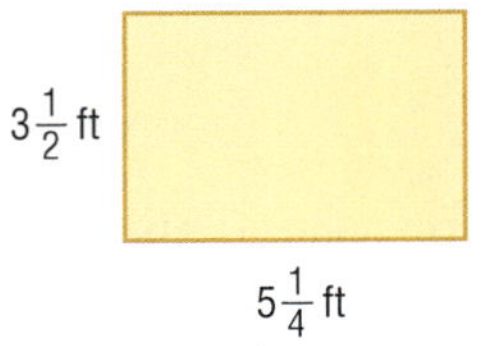

$17\frac{1}{2}$ft; $18\frac{3}{8}$ ft²

39. 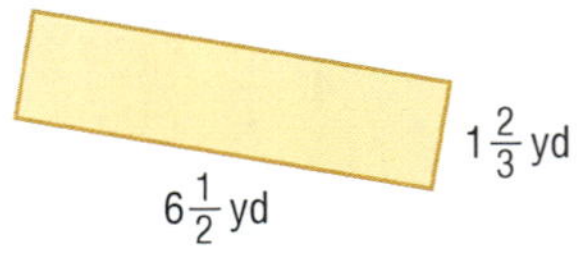

$16\frac{1}{3}$ yd; $10\frac{5}{6}$ yd²

Real-World Link There are an estimated 5 million in-ground swimming pools in the U.S.
Source: *Pool & Spa Service Industry News*

★ 40. **POOLS** A community swimming pool is $90\frac{2}{5}$ feet long and $55\frac{1}{2}$ feet wide. If Natalie swims the perimeter of the pool four times, what is the total number of feet she will swim? Explain how you solved the problem. See margin.

MEASUREMENT **For Exercises 41–44, use measurement conversions.**

41. Find $\frac{1}{2}$ of $\frac{1}{4}$ of a gallon. one pint
42. What is $\frac{1}{60}$ of $\frac{1}{24}$ of a day? one minute
43. Find $\frac{1}{100}$ of $\frac{1}{1{,}000}$ of a kilometer. one centimeter
44. What is $\frac{1}{12}$ of $\frac{1}{3}$ of a yard? one inch

ALGEBRA **Evaluate each expression if $a = 4$, $b = 2\frac{1}{2}$, and $c = 5\frac{3}{4}$.**

45. $a \times b + c$ $15\frac{3}{4}$
46. $b \times c - a$ $10\frac{3}{8}$
47. $2bc$ $28\frac{3}{4}$

★ 48. **TELEVISION** One evening, $\frac{2}{3}$ of the students in Rick's class watched television, and $\frac{3}{8}$ of those students watched a reality show, of which $\frac{1}{4}$ taped the show. What fraction of the students in Rick's class watched and taped a reality TV show? $\frac{1}{16}$

★ 49. **FOOD** Alano wants to make one and a half recipes of the pasta salad recipe shown at the right. How much of each ingredient will Alano need? Explain how you solved the problem. See margin.

Pasta Salad Recipe

Ingredient	Amount
broccoli	$1\frac{1}{4}$ c
cooked pasta	$3\frac{3}{4}$ c
salad dressing	$\frac{2}{3}$ c
cheese	$1\frac{1}{3}$ c

50. **FIND THE DATA** Refer to the Data File on pages 16–19. Choose some data and write a real-world problem in which you would multiply fractions. See students' work.

Write and evaluate a multiplication expression to represent each model. Explain how the models show the multiplication process. 51, 52. See margin.

51. 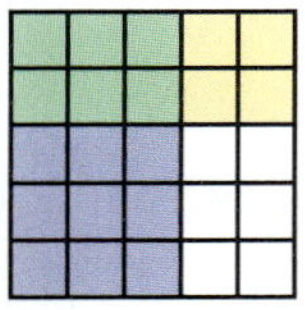

52. 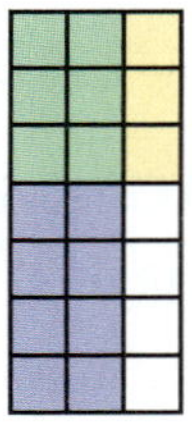

Academic Standards • ISTEP+
Extra Practice, pp. 680, 708

256 Chapter 5 Applying Fractions

H.O.T. Problems

53–55. See margin.

53. **CHALLENGE** Two improper fractions are multiplied. Is the product *sometimes*, *always*, or *never* less than 1? Explain your reasoning.

54. **OPEN ENDED** Write a word problem that involves finding the product of $\frac{3}{4}$ and $\frac{1}{8}$.

55. **WRITING IN MATH** Refer to Example 2. Explain how the model represents the meaning of the multiplication process.

ISTEP+ PRACTICE 7.1.7

56. Of the dolls in Marjorie's doll collection, $\frac{1}{5}$ have red hair. Of these, $\frac{3}{4}$ have green eyes. What fraction of Marjorie's doll collection has both red hair and green eyes? **B**

A $\frac{2}{9}$ C $\frac{4}{9}$

B $\frac{3}{20}$ D $\frac{19}{20}$

57. Which description gives the relationship between a term and n, its position in the sequence? **H**

Position	1	2	3	4	5	n
Value of Term	$\frac{1}{4}$	$\frac{1}{2}$	$\frac{3}{4}$	1	$1\frac{1}{4}$	

F Subtract 4 from n.

G Add $\frac{1}{4}$ to n.

H Multiply n by $\frac{1}{4}$.

J Divide n by $\frac{1}{4}$.

Spiral Review

58. **MEASUREMENT** Find which room dimensions would give an area of $125\frac{3}{8}$ square feet. Use the *eliminate possibilities* strategy. (Lesson 5-4) **D**

A $11\frac{1}{2}$ feet by $10\frac{3}{8}$ feet C $13\frac{5}{8}$ feet by 9 feet

B $10\frac{7}{8}$ feet by $12\frac{1}{4}$ feet D $14\frac{3}{4}$ feet by $8\frac{1}{2}$ feet

59. **MEASUREMENT** How much longer is a $2\frac{1}{2}$-inch-long piece of string than a $\frac{2}{5}$-inch-long piece of string? (Lesson 5-3) **$2\frac{1}{10}$ in.**

Replace each ● with <, >, or = to make a true sentence. (Lesson 4-9)

60. $\frac{5}{12}$ ● $\frac{2}{5}$ **>** 61. $\frac{3}{16}$ ● $\frac{1}{8}$ **>** 62. $3\frac{7}{6}$ ● $3\frac{6}{5}$ **<**

63. **PHONES** A long-distance telephone company charges a flat monthly fee of \$4.95 and \$0.06 per minute on all long-distance calls. Write and solve an equation to find the number of monthly minutes spent talking long-distance if the bill total was \$22.95. (Lesson 3-5) **$4.95 + .06x = 22.95$; 300 min**

GET READY for the Next Lesson

PREREQUISITE SKILL **Solve each equation mentally.** (Lesson 1-7)

64. $x + 2 = 8$ **6** 65. $9 + m = 12$ **3** 66. $7 - w = 2$ **5**

4 Assess

Ticket Out the Door Write a problem such as $\frac{5}{6} \cdot \frac{3}{10} \cdot \frac{4}{9}$ on the board. Have students write the answer to the problem on a small piece of paper.

FOLDABLES Study Organizer

Foldables™ Follow-Up

Remind students to record what they learn about multiplying fractions and mixed numbers on index cards, and then to store the cards in their Foldables.

Additional Answers

53. Always; Sample answer: improper fractions are always greater than 1.

54. Sample answer: $\frac{3}{4}$ of the 200 students at Walnut Middle School were on the honor roll. Of that group, only $\frac{1}{8}$ of them were on the "All A" honor roll. How many students were on the "All A" honor roll?

55. Sample answer: The model shows that $\frac{3}{4}$ of one rectangle is 3 sections out of 4 sections shaded. Since 2 sets of rectangles with 3 sections out of 4 sections shaded is $\frac{6}{4}$, 2 of $\frac{3}{4}$ is $\frac{6}{4}$, or $1\frac{1}{2}$.

Pre-AP Activity **Use as an Extension.**

Write two problems involving multiplication with negative fractions, such as $-\frac{2}{3} \cdot \frac{3}{4}$ and $-\frac{7}{10} \cdot \left(-\frac{5}{6}\right)$, on the board. Have students use what they know about multiplying fractions and multiplying integers to solve both problems, explaining the steps that they take.

5-6 Algebra: Solving Equations

PACING: **Regular:** 1 period, **Block:** 0.5 period

IN Academic Standards **Preparation for 7.2.2** Write and solve two-step linear equations and inequalities in one variable. *Also addresses 7.1.7.*

Options for Differentiated Instruction

ELL = English Language Learner AL = Above or Beyond Grade Level SS = Struggling Students SN = Special Needs

Reviewing Concepts SS SN

Use before beginning Lesson 5-6.

To help students prepare for Lesson 5-6, review the concepts involving inverse operations.

Ask:

- Which operations undo each other? addition and subtraction; multiplication and division
- What are the division facts related to the multiplication problem $3 \times 5 = 15$? $15 \div 3 = 5$ and $15 \div 5 = 3$
- What are the multiplication facts that are related to the division problem $\frac{24}{4} = 6$? $6 \times 4 = 24$ and $4 \times 6 = 24$
- How can you use what you know about inverse operations to solve equations like $3x = 15$ and $\frac{x}{4} = 6$? Sample answer: Use division to undo the multiplication of 3 and x in $3x = 15$; use multiplication to undo the division of x and 4 in $\frac{x}{4} = 6$.

Correcting Common Errors SS SN

Use after presenting Examples 1–6.

Write the following equation on the board.

$-\frac{5}{6}q = 8$

Ask students to write the first step they would use to solve the equation. Students may mistakenly write $(8) \cdot -5q = (6) \cdot 8$ or $(-6q) \cdot -\frac{5}{6}q = (6q) \cdot 8$, assuming that the q is in the denominator. Point out these errors, as well as the correct first step to solve.

$\left(-\frac{6}{5}\right) \cdot \left(-\frac{5}{6}q\right) = \left(-\frac{6}{5}\right) \cdot 8$

Leveled Lesson Resources

Also on TeacherWorks™ Lesson 5-6

Chapter 5 Resource Masters

BL = Below or Approaching Grade Level   OL = On Grade Level   AL = Above or Beyond Grade Level   ELL = English Language Learner

Lesson Reading Guide
p. 38 BL OL ELL

NAME ______ DATE ______ PERIOD ______

5-6 Lesson Reading Guide

Algebra: Solving Equations

Get Ready for the Lesson

Read the introduction at the top of page 258 in your textbook. Write your answers below.

1. Write a multiplication expression to find how much time Shawnda spends doing homework. Then find the product. $2 \times \frac{1}{2}; 1$
2. Complete the table below.
3. What is true about the numerators and denominators in the fractions in Exercise 2? They are switched.

Read the Lesson

4. Write the Multiplication Property of Equality. If you multiply each side of an equation by the same nonzero number, the two sides remain equal.
5. When the coefficient of x in an equation is a fraction, explain how the reciprocal, or multiplicative inverse, of the coefficient is used to solve the equation. Sample answer: Multiply both sides of the equation by the reciprocal.

Remember What You Learned

6. The word *inverse* comes from a Latin verb that means "to turn upside down." How does this definition relate to the content of this lesson? Sample answer: The inverse of a number like 2 is $\frac{2}{1}$ turned upside down, or $\frac{1}{2}$.

Chapter 5 38 Course 2

Study Guide and Intervention*
p. 39 BL OL ELL

NAME ______ DATE ______ PERIOD ______

5-6 Study Guide and Intervention

Algebra: Solving Equations

Multiplicative inverses, or **reciprocals**, are two numbers whose product is 1. To solve an equation in which the coefficient is a fraction, multiply each side of the equation by the reciprocal of the coefficient.

Example 1 Find the multiplicative inverse of $3\frac{1}{4}$.

$3\frac{1}{4} = \frac{13}{4}$ Rename the mixed number as an improper fraction.

$\frac{13}{4} \cdot \frac{4}{13} = 1$ Multiply $\frac{13}{4}$ by $\frac{4}{13}$ to get the product 1.

The multiplicative inverse of $3\frac{1}{4}$ is $\frac{4}{13}$.

Example 2 Solve $\frac{4}{5}x = 8$. Check your solution.

$\frac{4}{5}x = 8$ Write the equation.

$\left(\frac{5}{4}\right)\frac{4}{5}x = \left(\frac{5}{4}\right)8$ Multiply each side by the reciprocal of $\frac{4}{5}$, $\frac{5}{4}$.

$x = 10$ Simplify.

The solution is 10.

Exercises

Find the multiplicative inverse of each number.

1. $\frac{4}{9}$ $\frac{9}{4}$ or $2\frac{1}{4}$
2. $\frac{12}{13}$ $\frac{13}{12}$ or $1\frac{1}{12}$
3. $-\frac{15}{4}$ $-\frac{4}{15}$
4. $6\frac{1}{7}$ $\frac{7}{43}$

Solve each equation. Check your solution.

5. $\frac{3}{5}x = 12$ 20
6. $16 = \frac{10}{3}a$ $4\frac{4}{5}$
7. $\frac{c}{2} = 7$ 14
8. $\frac{15}{7}y = 3$ $1\frac{2}{5}$
9. $\frac{m}{6} = -4$ −24
10. $\frac{14}{3} = \frac{7}{9}b$ −6

Chapter 5 39 Course 2

Skills Practice*
p. 40 BL OL

NAME ______ DATE ______ PERIOD ______

5-6 Skills Practice

Algebra: Solving Equations

Find the multiplicative inverse of each number.

1. $\frac{3}{7}$ $\frac{7}{3}$ or $2\frac{1}{3}$
2. $-\frac{4}{11}$ $-\frac{11}{4}$ or $-2\frac{3}{4}$
3. $\frac{7}{2}$ $\frac{2}{7}$
4. $\frac{9}{5}$ $\frac{5}{9}$
5. -5 $-\frac{1}{5}$
6. $6\frac{1}{3}$ $\frac{3}{19}$
7. $4\frac{1}{9}$ $\frac{9}{37}$
8. $17\frac{1}{2}$ $\frac{2}{35}$
9. $-15\frac{2}{3}$ $-\frac{3}{47}$

Solve each equation. Check your solution.

10. $\frac{x}{10} = 3$ 30
11. $7 = \frac{m}{4}$ 28
12. $\frac{a}{5} = -11$ −55
13. $-8 = \frac{t}{5}$ −40
14. $\frac{3}{4}c = 12$ 16
15. $7 = \frac{w}{6}$ 42
16. $\frac{3}{5}y = 6$ 10
17. $15 = \frac{3}{7}b$ 35
18. $\frac{6}{7}c = 18$ 21
19. $\frac{7}{3}x = \frac{2}{3}$ $\frac{2}{7}$
20. $\frac{11}{12} = \frac{3}{4}h$ $1\frac{2}{9}$
21. $\frac{9}{14}y = \frac{3}{7}$ $\frac{2}{3}$
22. $\frac{m}{2.6} = -5$ −13
23. $0.6 = \frac{n}{5}$ 3
24. $\frac{r}{2.6} = -1.3$ −3.38

Chapter 5 40 Course 2

Practice*
p. 41 OL AL

NAME ______ DATE ______ PERIOD ______

5-6 Practice

Algebra: Solving Equations

Find the multiplicative inverse of each number.

1. $\frac{7}{9}$ $\frac{9}{7}$
2. $\frac{5}{2}$ $\frac{2}{5}$
3. $\frac{1}{9}$ 9
4. $\frac{1}{12}$ 12
5. 4 $\frac{1}{4}$
6. 15 $\frac{1}{15}$
7. $4\frac{1}{3}$ $\frac{3}{13}$
8. $5\frac{4}{5}$ $\frac{5}{29}$

Solve each equation. Check your solution.

9. $\frac{a}{8} = 5$ 40
10. $15 = \frac{y}{2}$ 30
11. $\frac{h}{3.1} = 7$ 21.7
12. $1 = \frac{x}{6.3}$ 6.3
13. $0.9 = \frac{m}{2.5}$ 2.25
14. $\frac{t}{5.4} = 9$ 48.6
15. $\frac{3}{7}g = 9$ 21
16. $28 = \frac{4}{5}d$ 35
17. $\frac{3}{8}n = \frac{1}{4}$ $\frac{2}{3}$
18. $\frac{2}{5} = \frac{4}{5}c$ $\frac{1}{2}$
19. $\frac{2}{3}x = 4\frac{1}{4}$ $6\frac{3}{8}$
20. $\frac{5}{6}b = 1\frac{7}{8}$ $2\frac{1}{4}$
21. $\frac{p}{4} = 7$ −28
22. $-3 = \frac{w}{5}$ 15
23. $27.3 = \frac{3}{4}y$ 36.4
24. $\frac{4}{7}x = -1.6$ −2.8
25. DRAWING An architect needs to make a scale drawing of a home. The width w of the home in the drawing, in inches, is given by the equation $\frac{w}{0.6} = 9.5$. What is the width of the home in the scale drawing? 5.7 inches
26. VOLUNTEERS At a local shelter, 36 people volunteered to help prepare meals for disaster victims. If this represented $\frac{9}{16}$ of the volunteers at the shelter, write and solve an equation to determine how many volunteers helped at the local shelter. $\frac{9}{16}v = 36$; $v = 64$; 64 volunteers

Chapter 5 41 Course 2

Word Problem Practice*
p. 42 OL AL

NAME ______ DATE ______ PERIOD ______

5-6 Word Problem Practice

Algebra: Solving Equations

1. BIKING The speed s that Brandon can ride his bike if he rides $\frac{3}{4}$ of an hour and travels 4 miles is given by the equation $4 = \frac{3}{4}s$. What is Brandon's speed? $6\frac{2}{3}$ mph
2. BAND The woodwind section of the middle school band makes up $\frac{1}{4}$ of the band. There are 9 members in the woodwind section. Use the equation $\frac{1}{4}m = 9$ to find the number of members m in the band. 36 members
3. SALE A coat is selling for $\frac{3}{4}$ of the original price. The sale price is \$180. The original price p can be found using the equation $\frac{3}{4}p = 180$. Find the original price. \$240
4. SALARIES Aaron's annual salary is $\frac{2}{3}$ as much as Juanita's salary. Aaron makes \$46,000. Find Juanita's salary x using the equation $46{,}000 = \frac{2}{3}x$. \$69,000
5. ENDANGERED SPECIES In the U.S., there are $\frac{14}{29}$ as many endangered species of birds as of reptiles. The number of endangered species of birds b can be compared to the 14 endangered species of reptiles using $\frac{14}{29}b = 14$. Find the number of endangered species of birds. 29
6. SALES TAX The sticker price p of a purchase with $\frac{1}{10}$ sales tax and a total price (including tax) of \$5.28 can be found using the equation $\frac{11}{10}p = 5.28$. What is the sticker price? \$4.80
7. SEWING Each costume uses $\frac{3}{4}$ yard of fabric. The number of costumes c that can be made using $11\frac{1}{4}$ yards of fabric can be found using the equation $\frac{3}{4}c = 11\frac{1}{4}$. Find the number of costumes that can be made. 15 costumes
8. SAVINGS Jasmine saves \$46 each month from her part-time job. She saves $\frac{2}{5}$ of her earnings. Her earnings a can be found by using the equation $\frac{2}{5}a = 46$. Find her earnings. \$115

Chapter 5 42 Course 2

Enrichment
p. 43 OL AL

NAME ______ DATE ______ PERIOD ______

5-6 Enrichment

Trail Blazers

Each puzzle on this page is called a **trail blazer**. To solve it, you must find a trail that begins at any one of the small squares and ends at the goal square, following these rules.

1. The sum of all the fractions on the trail must equal the number in the goal square.
2. The trail can only go horizontally or vertically.
3. The trail cannot retrace or cross itself.

When you are solving a trail blazer, try to eliminate possibilities. For instance, in the puzzle at the right, you know that you cannot include $\frac{3}{4}$ using $\frac{3}{4} + \frac{1}{2} = 1\frac{1}{4}$ because you can't reach the goal box. $\frac{3}{4} + \frac{1}{2} = 1\frac{1}{4}$ will not work either as the goal for the entire trail is only 1. Answers may vary.

Chapter 5 43 Course 2

Additional Lesson Resources

* Also available in Spanish ELL

Transparencies

- *5-Minute Check Transparency*, Lesson 5-6

Other Print Products

- *Noteables™ Interactive Study Notebook with Foldables™*

Teacher Tech Tools

- *Interactive Classroom CD-ROM*, Lesson 5-6
- *AssignmentWorks*, Lesson 5-6

Student Tech Tools

glencoe.com

- Extra Examples, Chapter 5, Lesson 6
- Self-Check Quiz, Chapter 5, Lesson 6

5-6 Lesson Notes

1 Focus

Vertical Alignment

Before Lesson 5-6
Use a letter to represent an unknown number; write and evaluate simple algebraic expressions in one variable by substitution

Lesson 5-6
Write and solve one-step linear equations in one variable

After Lesson 5-6
Solve two-step linear equations and inequalities in one variable over the rational numbers, interpret the solution or solutions in the context from which they arose, and verify the reasonableness of the results

2 Teach

GET READY

Some students will recognize the pattern and follow it to complete the table. Other students may need to model each equation on grid paper. Make sure students realize that in order to find the products on grid paper they will have to mentally rearrange some of the shaded regions.

Scaffolding Questions

As you ask the following questions, write each equation on the board.

Ask:

- How can I solve $x + \frac{1}{2} = 5$? subtract $\frac{1}{2}$ from each side
- How can I solve $x - 8.4 = 21$? add 8.4 to each side
- How can I solve $6x = 54$? divide each side by 6

5-6 Algebra: Solving Equations

MAIN IDEA

Solve equations with rational number solutions.

IN Academic Standards

Preparation for 7.2.2 Write and solve two-step linear equations and inequalities in one variable. *Also addresses 7.1.7.*

New Vocabulary

multiplicative inverse
reciprocal

IN Math Online

glencoe.com
- Extra Examples
- Personal Tutor
- Self-Check Quiz

GET READY for the Lesson

HOMEWORK Shawnda spends $\frac{1}{2}$ hour doing homework after school. Then she spends another $\frac{1}{2}$ hour doing homework before bed.

1. Write a multiplication expression to find how much time Shawnda spends doing homework. Then find the product. $2 \cdot \frac{1}{2}$; 1
2. Copy and complete the table below.

$\frac{3}{2} \times \frac{2}{3} =$ ■ 1	$\frac{1}{5} \times$ ■ $= 1$ $\frac{5}{1}$	$\frac{5}{6} \times \frac{6}{5} =$ ■ 1	$\frac{7}{8} \times \frac{8}{7} =$ ■ 1
■ $\times \frac{5}{7} = 1$ $\frac{7}{5}$	$\frac{2}{6} \times \frac{6}{2} =$ ■ 1	$\frac{7}{1} \times$ ■ $= 1$ $\frac{1}{7}$	■ $\times 8 = 1$ $\frac{1}{8}$

3. What is true about the numerators and denominators in the fractions in Exercise 2? They are switched.

Two numbers with a product of 1 are called **multiplicative inverses**, or **reciprocals**.

Inverse Property of Multiplication — Key Concept

Words The product of a number and its multiplicative inverse is 1.

Examples

Numbers	Algebra
$\frac{3}{4} \times \frac{4}{3} = 1$	$\frac{a}{b} \cdot \frac{b}{a} = 1$, for $a, b \neq 0$

EXAMPLES Find Multiplicative Inverses

1 Find the multiplicative inverse of $\frac{2}{5}$.

$\frac{2}{5} \cdot \frac{5}{2} = 1$ Multiply $\frac{2}{5}$ by $\frac{5}{2}$ to get the product 1.

The multiplicative inverse of $\frac{2}{5}$ is $\frac{5}{2}$, or $2\frac{1}{2}$.

2 Find the multiplicative inverse of $2\frac{1}{3}$.

$2\frac{1}{3} = \frac{7}{3}$ Rename the mixed number as an improper fraction.

$\frac{7}{3} \cdot \frac{3}{7} = 1$ Multiply $\frac{7}{3}$ by $\frac{3}{7}$ to get the product 1.

The multiplicative inverse of $2\frac{1}{3}$ is $\frac{3}{7}$.

CHECK Your Progress

a. $\frac{5}{6}$ $\frac{6}{5}$ or $1\frac{1}{5}$
b. $1\frac{1}{2}$ $\frac{2}{3}$
c. 8 $\frac{1}{8}$
d. $\frac{4}{3}$ $\frac{3}{4}$

In Chapter 3, you learned to solve equations using the Addition, Subtraction, and Division Properties of Equality. You can also solve equations by multiplying each side by the same number. This is called the **Multiplication Property of Equality**.

Multiplication Property of Equality

Key Concept

Words If you multiply each side of an equation by the same nonzero number, the two sides remain equal.

Examples

Numbers	Algebra	
$5 = 5$	$\frac{x}{2} = -3$	$\frac{2}{3}x = 4$
$5 \cdot 2 = 5 \cdot 2$	$\frac{x}{2}(2) = -3(2)$	$\frac{3}{2} \cdot \frac{2}{3}x = \frac{3}{2} \cdot 4$
$10 = 10$	$x = -6$	$x = 6$

Study Tip

Fractions The fraction bar indicates division. So, $\frac{x}{2}$ means x divided by 2.

EXAMPLES Solve a Division Equation

3 **Solve $7 = \frac{n}{4}$. Check your solution.**

$7 = \frac{n}{4}$	Write the equation.
$7 \cdot 4 = \frac{n}{4} \cdot 4$	Multiply each side of the equation by 4.
$28 = n$	Simplify.

Check

$7 = \frac{n}{4}$	Write the original equation.
$7 \stackrel{?}{=} \frac{28}{4}$	Replace n with 28.
$7 = 7$ ✔	Is this sentence true?

4 **Solve $\frac{d}{3.5} = 4.2$.**

$\frac{d}{3.5} = 4.2$	Write the equation.
$\frac{d}{3.5} \cdot 3.5 = 4.2 \cdot 3.5$	Multiply each side by 3.5.
$d = 14.7$	Simplify.

The solution is 14.7.

Check

$\frac{d}{3.5} = 4.2$	Write the original equation.
$\frac{14.7}{3.5} \stackrel{?}{=} 4.2$	Replace d with 14.7.
$4.2 = 4.2$ ✔	Is this sentence true?

CHECK Your Progress

Solve each equation. Check your solution.

e. $6 = \frac{m}{8}$ **48** f. $\frac{p}{2.8} = 1.5$ **4.2** g. $\frac{k}{4.7} = 2.3$ **10.81**

Focus on Mathematical Content

The multiplicative inverse of a fraction is a fraction in which the numerator and denominator have **switched positions.**

Multiplying each side of an equation by the same nonzero number maintains the equation.

A fraction such as $\frac{y}{4}$ can be read as **y divided by 4.**

Formative Assessment

Use the Check Your Progress exercises after the Examples to determine students' understanding of concepts.

ADDITIONAL EXAMPLES

Find the multiplicative inverse of each number.

1. $\frac{4}{7}$ $\frac{7}{4}$, or $1\frac{3}{4}$
2. $6\frac{1}{4}$ $\frac{4}{25}$
3. Solve $11 = \frac{p}{6}$. Check your solution. 66
4. Solve $\frac{y}{6.4} = 2.7$. Check your solution. 17.28

Additional Examples are also in:

- Noteables™ Interactive Study Notebook with Foldables™
- Interactive Classroom PowerPoint® Presentations

ADDITIONAL EXAMPLES

5 Solve $\frac{2}{5}x = \frac{6}{15}$. Check your solution. 1

6 **TEST EXAMPLE** Samantha answered $\frac{4}{5}$ of the questions on the science quiz correctly. If she answered 8 questions correctly, how many questions were on the quiz? C

A 2
B 6
C 10
D 14

EXAMPLE Solve a Multiplication Equation

5 Solve $\frac{3}{4}x = \frac{12}{20}$.

$\frac{3}{4}x = \frac{12}{20}$ — Write the equation.

$\left(\frac{4}{3}\right) \cdot \frac{3}{4}x = \left(\frac{4}{3}\right) \cdot \frac{12}{20}$ — Multiply each side by the reciprocal of $\frac{3}{4}$, $\frac{4}{3}$.

$\frac{\overset{1}{\cancel{4}}}{\underset{1}{\cancel{3}}} \cdot \frac{\overset{1}{\cancel{3}}}{\underset{1}{\cancel{4}}}x = \frac{\overset{1}{\cancel{4}}}{\underset{1}{\cancel{3}}} \cdot \frac{\overset{4}{\cancel{12}}}{\underset{5}{\cancel{20}}}$ — Divide by common factors.

$x = \frac{4}{5}$ — Simplify.

Study Tip

Fractions as Coefficients The expression $\frac{3}{4}x$ can be read as $\frac{3}{4}$ of x, $\frac{3}{4}$ multiplied by x, $3x$ divided by 4, or $\frac{x}{4}$ multiplied by 3.

CHECK Your Progress

Solve each equation. Check your solution.

h. $\frac{1}{2}x = 8$ **16** i. $\frac{3}{4}x = 9$ **12** j. $\frac{7}{8}x = \frac{21}{64}$ **$\frac{3}{8}$**

ISTEP+ EXAMPLE Preparation for 7.2.2

6 **Valerie needs $\frac{2}{3}$ yard of fabric to make each hat for the school play. How many hats can she make with 6 yards of fabric?**

A 12 **C** 8
B 9 **D** 4

Read the Item

Each hat needs $\frac{2}{3}$ yard of fabric. Given the number of hats, you would multiply by $\frac{2}{3}$ to find the number of yards of fabric needed.

Solve the Item

Write and solve a multiplication equation.

$\frac{2}{3}n = 6$ — Write the equation.

$\left(\frac{3}{2}\right) \cdot \frac{2}{3}n = \left(\frac{3}{2}\right) \cdot 6$ — Multiply each side by $\frac{3}{2}$.

$n = 9$ — Simplify.

So, the answer is B.

Test-Taking Tip

Verify Your Answer It is a good idea to verify your answer by checking the other answer choices. By doing so, you can greatly reduce your chances of making an error.

CHECK Your Progress

k. Wilson has 9 pounds of trail mix. How many $\frac{3}{4}$-pound bags of trail mix can he make? **J**

F 3 **H** 9
G 6 **J** 12

260 Chapter 5 Applying Fractions

CHECK Your Understanding

★ indicates multi-step problem

Examples 1, 2 (p. 258)

Find the multiplicative inverse of each number.

1. $\frac{8}{5}$ $\frac{5}{8}$
2. $\frac{2}{9}$ $\frac{9}{2}$ or $4\frac{1}{2}$
3. $5\frac{4}{5}$ $\frac{5}{29}$
4. 9 $\frac{1}{9}$

Examples 3–5 (p. 259–260)

Solve each equation. Check your solution.

5. $\frac{k}{16} = 2$ 32
6. $4 = \frac{y}{3}$ 12
7. $\frac{b}{8.2} = 2.5$ 20.5
8. $0.5 = \frac{h}{3.6}$ 1.8
9. $\frac{3}{8}a = \frac{12}{40}$ $\frac{4}{5}$
10. $6 = \frac{4}{7}x$ $10\frac{1}{2}$

Example 5 (p. 260)

11. **FRUIT** Three fourths of the fruit in a refrigerator are apples. There are 24 apples in the refrigerator. The number of pieces of fruit is given by the equation $\frac{3}{4}f = 24$. How many pieces of fruit are in the refrigerator? 32

Example 6 (p. 260)

12. **MULTIPLE CHOICE** Dillon deposited $\frac{3}{4}$ of his paycheck into the bank. The deposit slip shows how much he deposited. What was the amount of his paycheck? C

A $15 C $60
B $33.75 D $75

Practice and Problem Solving

HOMEWORK HELP

For Exercises	See Examples
13–20	1, 2
21–26, 33–34	3, 4
27–32	5
51–52	6

Exercise Levels
A: 13–34
B: 35–46
C: 47–50

Find the multiplicative inverse of each number.

13. $\frac{5}{6}$ $\frac{6}{5}$ or $1\frac{1}{5}$
14. $\frac{11}{2}$ $\frac{2}{11}$
15. $\frac{1}{6}$ $\frac{6}{1}$ or 6
16. $\frac{1}{10}$ $\frac{10}{1}$ or 10
17. 3 $\frac{1}{3}$
18. 14 $\frac{1}{14}$
19. $5\frac{1}{8}$ $\frac{8}{41}$
20. $6\frac{2}{3}$ $\frac{3}{20}$

Solve each equation. Check your solution.

21. $\frac{x}{12} = 3$ 36
22. $28 = \frac{d}{4}$ 112
23. $\frac{b}{2.4} = 6$ 14.4
24. $5 = \frac{w}{4.9}$ 24.5
25. $0.8 = \frac{h}{3.6}$ 2.88
26. $\frac{m}{4.6} = 2.8$ 12.88
27. $\frac{2}{5}t = \frac{12}{25}$ $\frac{6}{5}$
28. $\frac{24}{16} = \frac{3}{4}a$ $\frac{8}{4}$ or 2
29. $\frac{7}{8}k = \frac{5}{6}$ $\frac{20}{21}$
30. $\frac{2}{3} = \frac{8}{3}b$ $\frac{1}{4}$
31. $\frac{1}{2}g = 3\frac{1}{3}$ $6\frac{2}{3}$
32. $\frac{3}{5}c = 6\frac{1}{4}$ $10\frac{5}{12}$

33. **DISTANCE** The distance d Toya travels in her car while driving 60 miles per hour for 3.25 hours is given by the equation $\frac{d}{3.25} = 60$. How far did she travel? 195 mi

34. **ANIMALS** An adult Fitch ferret weighs about 1.8 kilograms. To find its weight in pounds p, you can use the equation $\frac{p}{1.8} = 2.2$. How many pounds does an adult Fitch ferret weigh? 3.96 lb

3 Practice

Formative Assessment

Use Exercises 1–12 to check for understanding.

Then use the chart at the bottom of this page to customize your assignments for students.

Intervention You may wish to use the Study Guide and Intervention Master on page 39 of the *Chapter 5 Resource Masters* for additional reinforcement.

Odd/Even Assignments

Exercises 13–34 are structured so that students practice the same concepts whether they are assigned odd or even problems.

DIFFERENTIATED HOMEWORK OPTIONS

Level	Assignment	Two-Day Option	
BL Basic	13–32, 47, 48, 50–70	13–33 odd, 51, 52	14–34 even, 47, 48, 50, 53–70
OL Core	13–39 odd, 41–48, 50–70	13–34, 51, 52	35–48, 50, 53–70
AL Advanced/Pre-AP	35–66 (optional: 67–70)		

Tips for New Teachers

Whole Numbers

Make sure students know how to find the multiplicative inverse of a whole number such as 5. Ask, How can I rename 5 as an improper fraction? $\frac{5}{1}$

Additional Answer

49. Sample answer: Multiply each side by 2. Then divide each side by $(b_1 + b_2)$. So, $\frac{2A}{b_1 + b_2} = h$.

Solve each equation. Check your solution.

35. $\frac{a}{-5} = 15$ **−75**
36. $-8 = \frac{r}{-2}$ **16**
37. $34.5 = \frac{5}{6}m$ **41.4**
38. $\frac{5}{7}x = -1.5$ **−2.1**
39. $\frac{1}{4}t = \frac{3}{8}$ **$1\frac{1}{2}$**
40. $\frac{3}{8}m = 1\frac{1}{2}$ **4**

For Exercises 41–46, define a variable and write an equation. Then solve.

41. **CAVES** The self-guided Mammoth Cave Discovery Tour includes an elevation change of 140 feet. This is $\frac{7}{15}$ of the elevation change on the Wild Cave Tour. What is the elevation change on the Wild Cave Tour?
x = elevation change on the Wild Cave Tour; $140 = \frac{7}{15}x$; 300 ft

Real-World Link Kentucky's Mammoth Cave is the longest recorded cave system in the world, with more than 360 miles explored and mapped. The Wild Cave Tour requires visitors to crawl through an opening only 9 inches high.
Source: National Park Service

42. **MUSEUMS** Twenty-four students brought their permission slips to attend the class field trip to the local art museum. If this represented $\frac{4}{5}$ of the class, how many students are in the class?
x = number of students; $\frac{4}{5}x = 24$; 30 students

43. **MEASUREMENT** If one serving of cooked rice is $\frac{3}{4}$ cup, how many servings will $16\frac{1}{2}$ cups of rice yield? **x = number of servings; $\frac{3}{4}x = 16\frac{1}{2}$; 22 servings**

44. **HIKING** After Alana hiked $2\frac{5}{8}$ miles along a hiking trail, she realized that she was only $\frac{3}{4}$ of the way to the end of the trail. How long is the trail?
x = length of the trail; $2\frac{5}{8} = \frac{3}{4}x$; $3\frac{1}{2}$ miles

45. **SLEEP** The average person spends $\frac{1}{3}$ of his life asleep. According to this, if a person has spent 26 years asleep, how old is he?
x = the person's age; $\frac{1}{3}x = 26$; 78 years old

★ 46. **ANALYZE TABLES** Tierra recorded the distance she ran each day last week. If she ran $\frac{5}{6}$ of her weekly running goal, what was her running goal? **x = her goal; $\frac{5}{6}x = 7\frac{1}{2}$; 9 mi**

Distance Ran in One Week

Day	Distance (mi)
Monday	$1\frac{3}{4}$
Wednesday	2
Friday	$1\frac{1}{2}$
Saturday	$2\frac{1}{4}$

Academic Standards • ISTEP+
Extra Practice, pp. 681, 708

H.O.T. Problems

47. **REASONING** Complete the statement: If $8 = \frac{m}{4}$, then $m - 12 = $ ■. Explain your reasoning.

48. **Which One Doesn't Belong?** Identify the pair of numbers that does not belong with the other three. Explain.

$\frac{9}{6}, \frac{6}{9}$ | $4, \frac{1}{4}$ | $\frac{3}{5}, 5$ | $\frac{2}{7}, \frac{7}{2}$

49. **CHALLENGE** The formula for the area of a trapezoid is $A = \frac{1}{2}h(b_1 + b_2)$, where b_1 and b_2 are both bases and h is the height. Find the value of h in terms of A, b_1, and b_2. Justify your answer. **See margin.**

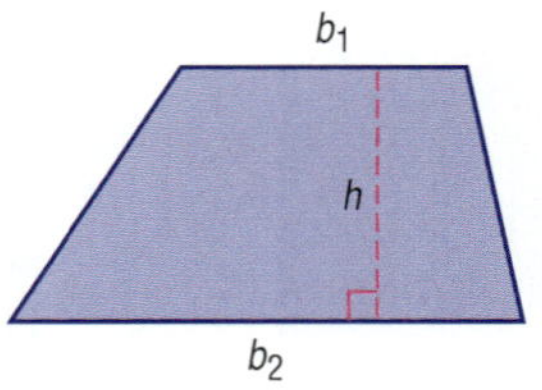

50. **WRITING IN MATH** Explain the Multiplication Property of Equality. Then give an example of an equation in which you would use this property to solve the equation.

47. 20; Sample answer: By solving $8 = \frac{m}{4}$, you find that $m = 32$. So, replace m with 32 to find $32 - 12 = 20$.
48. $\frac{3}{5}$, 5; The other pairs of numbers are reciprocals.
50. Sample answer: If you multiply each side of an equation by the same nonzero number, the two sides remain equal; $\frac{2}{5}x = 7$

Pre-AP Activity — Use after Exercise 46

Write an equation such as $12x = 72$ on the board. Remind students that they know how to solve the equation by using the Division Property of Equality. Ask them whether they can also solve it by using the Multiplication Property of Equality. Have them explain their reasoning. Yes; by multiplying each side of the equation by the multiplicative inverse of 12, or $\frac{1}{12}$.

ISTEP+ PRACTICE Preparation for 7.2.2

51. Audrey drove 200 miles in 3.5 hours. Which equation can you use to find the rate r at which Audrey was traveling? **A**

A $200 = 3.5r$

B $200 \cdot 3.5 = r$

C $\frac{r}{3.5} = 200$

D $200r = 3.5$

52. The table shows the results of a survey.

Music Preference	
Type	**Fraction of Students**
pop	$\frac{5}{8}$
jazz	$\frac{1}{8}$
rap	$\frac{1}{4}$

If there are 420 students surveyed, which equation can be used to find the number of students s who prefer rap? **G**

F $\frac{1}{4}s = 420$ H $s + \frac{1}{4} = 420$

G $s = \frac{1}{4} \cdot 420$ J $420 + s = \frac{1}{4}$

Spiral Review

Multiply. Write in simplest form. (Lesson 5-5)

53. $\frac{3}{8} \times \frac{4}{9}$ $\frac{1}{6}$

54. $1\frac{1}{2} \times 6$ **9**

55. $2\frac{2}{5} \times \frac{1}{6}$ $\frac{2}{5}$

56. $1\frac{1}{2} \times 1\frac{7}{9}$ $2\frac{2}{3}$

57. **COOKING** Lawana had $4\frac{2}{3}$ cups of chopped walnuts. She used $1\frac{1}{4}$ cups in a recipe. How many cups of chopped walnuts are left? (Lesson 5-3) $3\frac{5}{12}$ **c**

Write each percent as a decimal. (Lesson 4-7)

58. 25% **0.25**

59. 8% **0.08**

60. 25.6% **0.256**

61. 123% **1.23**

62. **MEASUREMENT** A farmer has a rectangular pumpkin field with a perimeter of 3,800 feet. If the width of the pumpkin field is 800 feet, what is the length of the field? (Lesson 3-6) **1,100 ft**

ALGEBRA Solve each equation. Check your solution. (Lesson 3-2)

63. $7 = x + 8$ **−1**

64. $k - 3 = -14$ **−11**

65. $-2 = m + 6$ **−8**

66. **ALGEBRA** The table shows the time needed to complete 4 art projects. If the pattern continues, how much time is needed to complete the fifth art project? (Lesson 2-7) **76 min**

Project	1	2	3	4	5
Time (min)	8	25	42	59	■

GET READY for the Next Lesson

PREREQUISITE SKILL Estimate. (Lesson 5-1) **67–70. Sample answers are given.**

67. $18\frac{1}{6} \div 3$

68. $24\frac{3}{8} \div 11\frac{7}{9}$

69. $\frac{2}{11} \div \frac{11}{12}$

70. $\frac{9}{10} \div \frac{6}{7}$

67. $18 \div 3 = 6$
68. $24 \div 12 = 2$
69. $0 \div 1 = 0$
70. $1 \div 1 = 1$

4 Assess

Yesterday's News Remind students that yesterday's lesson was about multiplying fractions and mixed numbers. Have them write how yesterday's lesson helped them with today's material.

Formative Assessment

Check for student understanding of concepts in Lessons 5-5 and 5-6.

CRM Quiz 3, p. 54

FOLDABLES Study Organizer Foldables™ Follow-Up

Remind students to record on index cards what they learn about finding multiplicative inverses and about using the Multiplication Property of Equality to solve equations. Students should then store the cards in their Foldables.

READING to SOLVE PROBLEMS

1 Focus

Students may sometimes be confused by division situations in word problems. Several kinds of situations call for division, though the mathematical operation remains the same. In this Activity, students learn to recognize three different situations that require division.

2 Teach

Make sure students understand that *taking away equal amounts* can also be described as *repeated subtraction*.

Before beginning the exercises, have volunteers pose the kind of questions they should ask themselves to determine which meaning of division is shown by a problem. Is a quantity being shared equally? Could the solution be found by repeated subtraction? Are two quantities being compared?

3 Assess

Tell students that tomorrow's lesson is about dividing fractions and mixed numbers. Have them write how they think what they learned today will connect with tomorrow's material.

READING to SOLVE PROBLEMS

Meaning of Division

You know that one meaning of division is to *put objects into equal groups*. But there are other meanings too. Look for these meanings when you're solving a word problem.

- **To share**

  Zach and his friend are going to share 3 apples equally. How many apples will each boy have?

- **To take away equal amounts**

  Isabel is making bookmarks from a piece of ribbon. Each bookmark is 6.5 centimeters long. How many bookmarks can she make from a piece of ribbon that is 27 centimeters long?

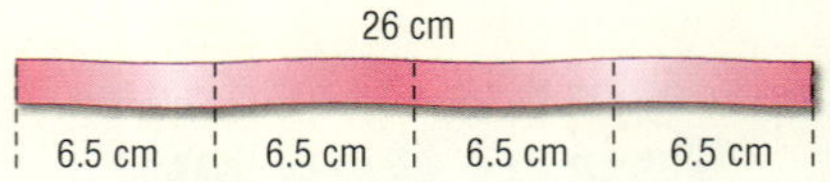

- **To find how many times greater**

  The Nile River, the longest river on Earth, is 4,160 miles long. The Rio Grande River is 1,900 miles long. About how many times longer is the Nile than the Rio Grande?

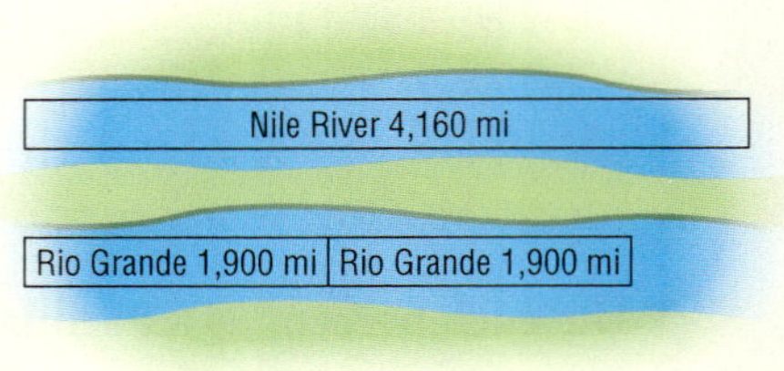

PRACTICE

1. Solve each problem above. **1.5 apples; 4 bookmarks; 2.2 times**

Identify the meaning of division shown in each problem. Then solve the problem.

2. A landscape architect wants to make a border along one side of a garden using bricks that are 0.25 meter long. If the garden is 11.25 meters long, how many bricks does she need? **repeated subtraction; 45 bricks**
3. The Jackson family wants to buy a flat-screen television that costs $1,200. They plan to pay in six equal payments. What will be the amount of each payment? **sharing; $200**
4. A full-grown blue whale can weigh 150 tons. An adult African elephant weighs about 5 tons. How many times greater does a blue whale weigh than an African elephant? **how many times greater; 30 times**
5. Each story in an office building is about 4 meters tall. The Eiffel Tower in Paris, France, is 300 meters tall. How many stories tall is the Eiffel Tower? **repeated subtraction; 75 stories**

5-7 Dividing Fractions and Mixed Numbers

PACING: **Regular:** 1 period, **Block:** 0.5 period

IN Academic Standards **7.1.7 Solve problems that involve** multiplication and **division with** integers, **fractions**, decimals and combinations of the four operations. *Also addresses P.5.1, P.5.2, P.5.3, P.6.2.*

Options for Differentiated Instruction

ELL = English Language Learner AL = Above or Beyond Grade Level SS = Struggling Students SN = Special Needs

Using Patterns ELL AL SS SN

Use after presenting the Mini Lab.

Have students complete the following table and look for a pattern.

Multiply	Divide
$8 \times \frac{1}{2} = 4$	$8 \div 2 = 4$
$24 \times \frac{1}{4} = 6$	$24 \div 4 = 6$
$21 \times \frac{1}{3} = 7$	$21 \div 3 = 7$
$15 \times \frac{1}{5} = 3$	$15 \div 5 = 3$

Ask:

What do you notice about the answers in each column? They are the same.

Use the pattern above to fill in the following blanks.

$\frac{3}{4} \times \frac{1}{3} = \frac{3}{4} \div$? 3 $\frac{3}{4} \times \frac{3}{1} = \frac{3}{4} \div$? $\frac{1}{3}$

$\frac{2}{3} \times \frac{1}{3} = \frac{2}{3} \div$? 3 $\frac{2}{3} \times \frac{3}{1} = \frac{2}{3} \div$? $\frac{1}{3}$

Write a rule for dividing fractions. Dividing by a fraction is the same as multiplying by its inverse.

Enhancing Memory ELL AL SS

Use after presenting Examples 1–3.

Mnemonics utilizes the five principles of learning and memory:

- meaningfulness
- organization
- association
- attention
- visualization

Mnemonics is therefore an effective tool for helping students learn and remember procedures and rules in mathematics. Some methods of doing this include using sentences, phrases, songs, and rhymes. Have students write a simple poem or rhyme that incorporates at least one method or rule for the division of fractions. Rules and methods for other operations on fractions can be included as well. You may wish to have students work in groups and create larger works of poetry or verse.

Leveled Lesson Resources

Also on TeacherWorks™ Lesson 5-7

Chapter 5 Resource Masters

BL = Below or Approaching Grade Level **OL** = On Grade Level **AL** = Above or Beyond Grade Level **ELL** = English Language Learner

Lesson Reading Guide
p. 44 BL OL ELL

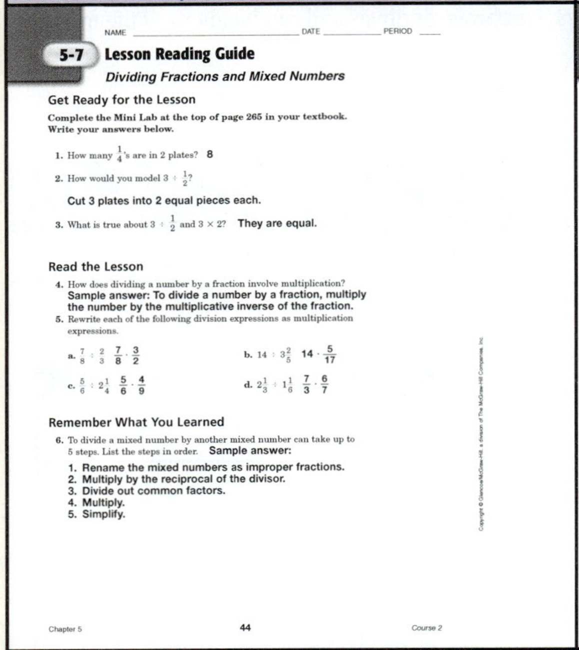
NAME ____ DATE ____ PERIOD ____

5-7 Lesson Reading Guide
Dividing Fractions and Mixed Numbers

Get Ready for the Lesson

Complete the Mini Lab at the top of page 265 in your textbook. Write your answers below.

1. How many $\frac{1}{4}$'s are in 2 plates? 8
2. How would you model $3 \div \frac{1}{2}$? Cut 3 plates into 2 equal pieces each.
3. What is true about $3 \div \frac{1}{2}$ and 3×2? They are equal.

Read the Lesson

4. How does dividing a number by a fraction involve multiplication? Sample answer: To divide a number by a fraction, multiply the number by the multiplicative inverse of the fraction.
5. Rewrite each of the following division expressions as multiplication expressions.

a. $\frac{7}{8} \div \frac{2}{3}$ $\frac{7}{8} \cdot \frac{3}{2}$ b. $14 \div 3\frac{2}{5}$ $14 \cdot \frac{5}{17}$
c. $\frac{5}{6} \div 2\frac{1}{4}$ $\frac{5}{6} \cdot \frac{4}{9}$ d. $2\frac{1}{3} \div 1\frac{1}{6}$ $\frac{7}{3} \cdot \frac{6}{7}$

Remember What You Learned

6. To divide a mixed number by another mixed number can take up to 5 steps. List the steps in order. Sample answer:
1. Rename the mixed numbers as improper fractions.
2. Multiply by the reciprocal of the divisor.
3. Divide out common factors.
4. Multiply.
5. Simplify.

Chapter 5 44 Course 2

Study Guide and Intervention*
p. 45 BL OL ELL

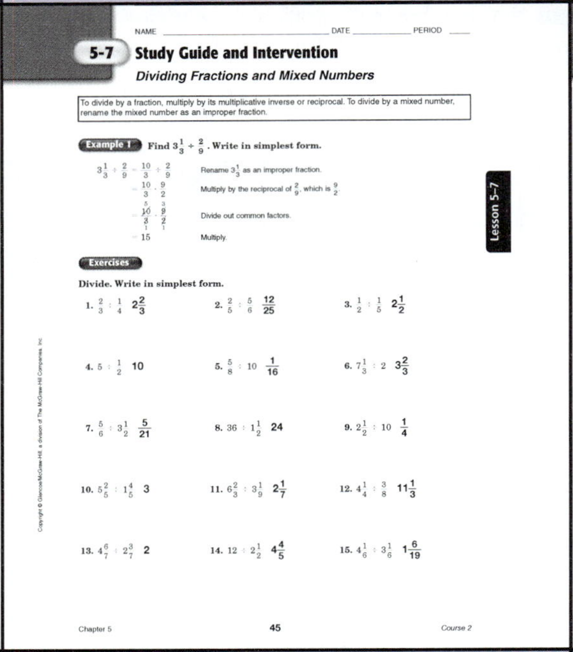
NAME ____ DATE ____ PERIOD ____

5-7 Study Guide and Intervention
Dividing Fractions and Mixed Numbers

To divide by a fraction, multiply by its multiplicative inverse or reciprocal. To divide by a mixed number, rename the mixed number as an improper fraction.

Example 1 Find $3\frac{1}{3} \div \frac{2}{9}$. Write in simplest form.

$3\frac{1}{3} \div \frac{2}{9} = \frac{10}{3} \div \frac{2}{9}$ Rename $3\frac{1}{3}$ as an improper fraction.
$= \frac{10}{3} \cdot \frac{9}{2}$ Multiply by the reciprocal of $\frac{2}{9}$, which is $\frac{9}{2}$.
$= \frac{10}{3} \cdot \frac{9}{2}$ Divide out common factors.
$= 15$ Multiply.

Exercises

Divide. Write in simplest form.

1. $\frac{2}{3} \div \frac{1}{4}$ $2\frac{2}{3}$ 2. $\frac{2}{5} \div \frac{5}{6}$ $\frac{12}{25}$ 3. $\frac{1}{2} \div \frac{1}{5}$ $2\frac{1}{2}$
4. $5 \div \frac{1}{2}$ 10 5. $\frac{5}{8} \div 10$ $\frac{1}{16}$ 6. $7\frac{1}{3} \div 2$ $3\frac{2}{3}$
7. $\frac{5}{6} \div 3\frac{1}{2}$ $\frac{5}{21}$ 8. $36 \div 1\frac{1}{2}$ 24 9. $2\frac{1}{2} \div 10$ $\frac{1}{4}$
10. $5\frac{2}{5} \div 1\frac{4}{5}$ 3 11. $6\frac{2}{3} \div 3\frac{1}{9}$ $2\frac{1}{7}$ 12. $4\frac{1}{4} \div \frac{3}{8}$ $11\frac{1}{3}$
13. $4\frac{6}{7} \div 2\frac{3}{7}$ 2 14. $12 \div 2\frac{1}{2}$ $4\frac{4}{5}$ 15. $4\frac{1}{6} \div 3\frac{1}{6}$ $1\frac{6}{19}$

Lesson 5-7

Chapter 5 45 Course 2

Skills Practice*
p. 46 BL OL

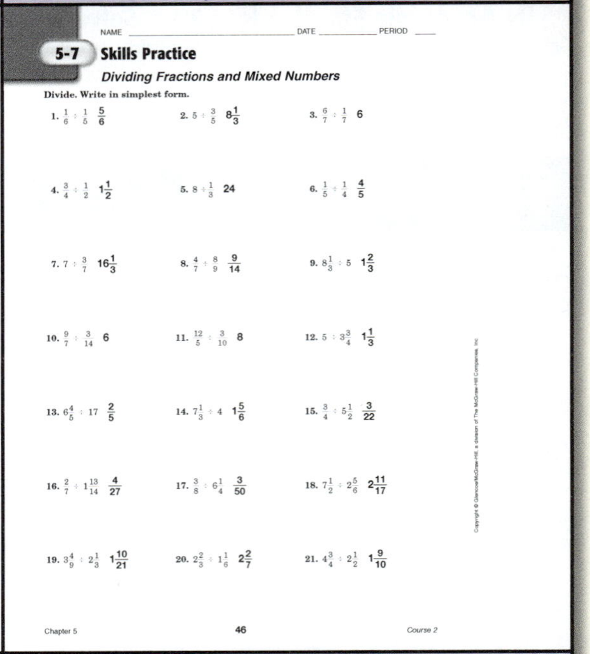
NAME ____ DATE ____ PERIOD ____

5-7 Skills Practice
Dividing Fractions and Mixed Numbers

Divide. Write in simplest form.

1. $\frac{1}{6} \div \frac{1}{5}$ $\frac{5}{6}$ 2. $5 \div \frac{3}{5}$ $8\frac{1}{3}$ 3. $\frac{6}{7} \div \frac{1}{7}$ 6
4. $\frac{3}{4} \div \frac{1}{2}$ $1\frac{1}{2}$ 5. $8 \div \frac{1}{3}$ 24 6. $\frac{1}{5} \div \frac{1}{4}$ $\frac{4}{5}$
7. $7 \div \frac{3}{7}$ $16\frac{1}{3}$ 8. $\frac{4}{7} \div \frac{8}{9}$ $\frac{9}{14}$ 9. $8\frac{1}{3} \div 5$ $1\frac{2}{3}$
10. $\frac{9}{7} \div \frac{3}{14}$ 6 11. $\frac{12}{5} \div \frac{3}{10}$ 8 12. $5 \div 3\frac{3}{4}$ $1\frac{1}{3}$
13. $6\frac{4}{5} \div 17$ $\frac{2}{5}$ 14. $7\frac{1}{3} \div 4$ $1\frac{5}{6}$ 15. $\frac{3}{4} \div 5\frac{1}{2}$ $\frac{3}{22}$
16. $\frac{2}{7} \div 1\frac{13}{14}$ $\frac{4}{27}$ 17. $\frac{3}{8} \div 6\frac{1}{4}$ $\frac{3}{50}$ 18. $7\frac{1}{2} \div 2\frac{5}{8}$ $2\frac{11}{17}$
19. $3\frac{4}{9} \div 2\frac{1}{3}$ $1\frac{10}{21}$ 20. $2\frac{2}{3} \div 1\frac{1}{6}$ $2\frac{2}{7}$ 21. $4\frac{3}{4} \div 2\frac{1}{2}$ $1\frac{9}{10}$

Chapter 5 46 Course 2

Practice*
p. 47 OL AL

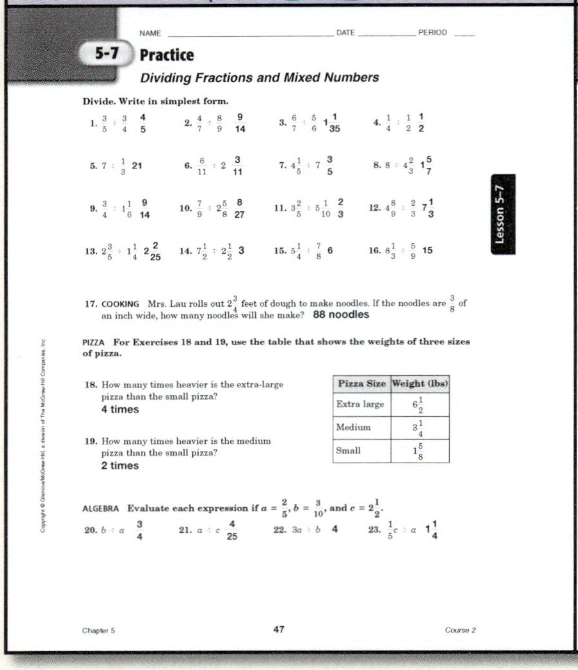
NAME ____ DATE ____ PERIOD ____

5-7 Practice
Dividing Fractions and Mixed Numbers

Divide. Write in simplest form.

1. $\frac{3}{5} \div \frac{3}{4}$ $\frac{4}{5}$ 2. $\frac{4}{7} \div \frac{8}{9}$ $\frac{9}{14}$ 3. $\frac{6}{7} \div \frac{5}{6}$ $1\frac{1}{35}$ 4. $\frac{1}{4} \div \frac{1}{2}$ $\frac{1}{2}$
5. $7 \div \frac{1}{3}$ 21 6. $\frac{6}{11} \div 2$ $\frac{3}{11}$ 7. $4\frac{1}{5} \div 7$ $\frac{3}{5}$ 8. $8 \div 4\frac{2}{5}$ $1\frac{5}{7}$
9. $\frac{3}{4} \div 1\frac{1}{6}$ $\frac{9}{14}$ 10. $\frac{7}{9} \div 2\frac{5}{8}$ $\frac{8}{27}$ 11. $3\frac{2}{5} \div 5\frac{1}{10}$ $\frac{2}{3}$ 12. $4\frac{8}{9} \div \frac{2}{3}$ $7\frac{1}{3}$
13. $2\frac{3}{5} \div 1\frac{1}{5}$ $2\frac{2}{25}$ 14. $7\frac{1}{2} \div 2\frac{1}{2}$ 3 15. $5\frac{1}{4} \div \frac{7}{8}$ 6 16. $8\frac{1}{3} \div \frac{5}{9}$ 15

17. COOKING Mrs. Lau rolls out $2\frac{3}{4}$ feet of dough to make noodles. If the noodles are $\frac{3}{8}$ of an inch wide, how many noodles will she make? 88 noodles

PIZZA For Exercises 18 and 19, use the table that shows the weights of three sizes of pizza.

18. How many times heavier is the extra-large pizza than the small pizza? 4 times
19. How many times heavier is the medium pizza than the small pizza? 2 times

Pizza Size	Weight (lbs)
Extra large	$6\frac{1}{2}$
Medium	$3\frac{1}{4}$
Small	$1\frac{5}{8}$

ALGEBRA Evaluate each expression if $a = \frac{2}{5}$, $b = \frac{3}{10}$, and $c = 2\frac{1}{2}$.

20. $b \div a$ $\frac{3}{4}$ 21. $a \div c$ $\frac{4}{25}$ 22. $3a \div b$ 4 23. $\frac{1}{5}c \div a$ $1\frac{1}{4}$

Lesson 5-7

Chapter 5 47 Course 2

Word Problem Practice*
p. 48 OL AL

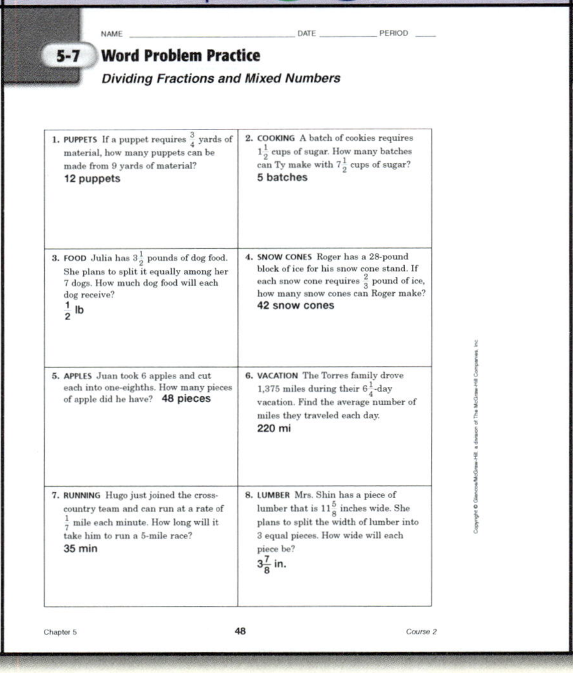
NAME ____ DATE ____ PERIOD ____

5-7 Word Problem Practice
Dividing Fractions and Mixed Numbers

1. PUPPETS If a puppet requires $\frac{3}{4}$ yards of material, how many puppets can be made from 9 yards of material? 12 puppets
2. COOKING A batch of cookies requires $1\frac{1}{2}$ cups of sugar. How many batches can Ty make with $7\frac{1}{2}$ cups of sugar? 5 batches
3. FOOD Julia has $3\frac{1}{2}$ pounds of dog food. She plans to split it equally among her 7 dogs. How much dog food will each dog receive? $\frac{1}{2}$ lb
4. SNOW CONES Roger has a 28-pound block of ice for his snow cone stand. If each snow cone requires $\frac{2}{3}$ pound of ice, how many snow cones can Roger make? 42 snow cones
5. APPLES Juan took 6 apples and cut each into one-eighths. How many pieces of apple did he have? 48 pieces
6. VACATION The Torres family drove 1,375 miles during their $6\frac{1}{4}$-day vacation. Find the average number of miles they traveled each day. 220 mi
7. RUNNING Hugo just joined the cross-country team and can run at a rate of $\frac{1}{7}$ mile each minute. How long will it take him to run a 5-mile race? 35 min
8. LUMBER Mrs. Shin has a piece of lumber that is $11\frac{5}{8}$ inches wide. She plans to split the width of lumber into 3 equal pieces. How wide will each piece be? $3\frac{7}{8}$ in.

Chapter 5 48 Course 2

Enrichment
p. 49 OL AL

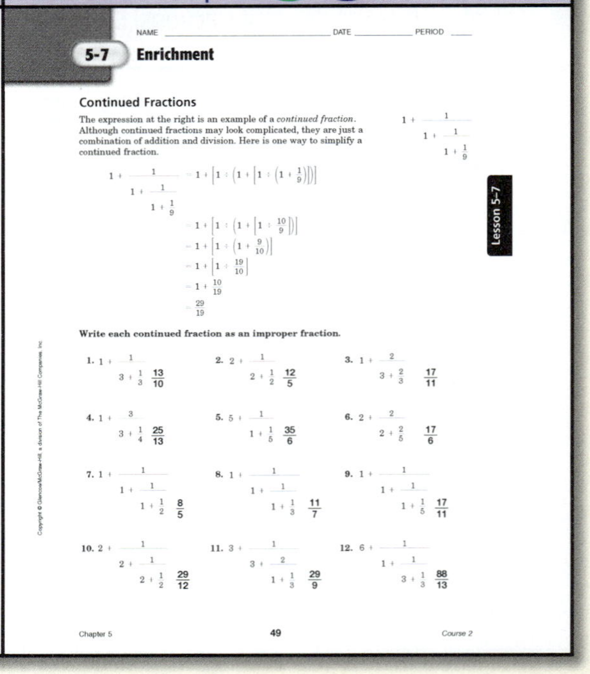
NAME ____ DATE ____ PERIOD ____

5-7 Enrichment

Continued Fractions

The expression at the right is an example of a *continued fraction*. Although continued fractions may look complicated, they are just a combination of addition and division. Here is one way to simplify a continued fraction.

$1 + \cfrac{1}{1 + \cfrac{1}{1 + \cfrac{1}{9}}}$

$= 1 + \left[1 \div \left(1 + \left(1 \div \left(1 + \frac{1}{9}\right)\right)\right)\right]$
$= 1 + \left[1 \div \left(1 + \left(1 \div \frac{10}{9}\right)\right)\right]$
$= 1 + \left[1 \div \left(1 + \frac{9}{10}\right)\right]$
$= 1 + \left[1 \div \frac{19}{10}\right]$
$= 1 + \frac{10}{19}$
$= \frac{29}{19}$

Write each continued fraction as an improper fraction.

1. $1 + \cfrac{1}{3 + \cfrac{1}{3}}$ $\frac{13}{10}$ 2. $2 + \cfrac{1}{2 + \cfrac{1}{2}}$ $\frac{12}{5}$ 3. $1 + \cfrac{2}{3 + \cfrac{2}{3}}$ $\frac{17}{11}$
4. $1 + \cfrac{3}{3 + \cfrac{1}{4}}$ $\frac{25}{13}$ 5. $5 + \cfrac{1}{1 + \cfrac{1}{5}}$ $\frac{35}{6}$ 6. $2 + \cfrac{2}{2 + \cfrac{2}{5}}$ $\frac{17}{6}$
7. $1 + \cfrac{1}{1 + \cfrac{1}{1 + \cfrac{1}{2}}}$ $\frac{8}{5}$ 8. $1 + \cfrac{1}{1 + \cfrac{1}{1 + \cfrac{1}{3}}}$ $\frac{11}{7}$ 9. $1 + \cfrac{1}{1 + \cfrac{1}{1 + \cfrac{1}{5}}}$ $\frac{17}{11}$
10. $2 + \cfrac{1}{2 + \cfrac{1}{2 + \cfrac{1}{2}}}$ $\frac{29}{12}$ 11. $3 + \cfrac{2}{3 + \cfrac{1}{1 + \cfrac{1}{3}}}$ $\frac{29}{9}$ 12. $6 + \cfrac{1}{1 + \cfrac{1}{3 + \cfrac{1}{3}}}$ $\frac{88}{13}$

Lesson 5-7

Chapter 5 49 Course 2

* Also available in Spanish ELL

Additional Lesson Resources

Transparencies
- *5-Minute Check Transparency*, Lesson 5-7

Other Print Products
- *Noteables™ Interactive Study Notebook with Foldables™*

Teacher Tech Tools
- *Interactive Classroom CD-ROM*, Lesson 5-7
- *AssignmentWorks*, Lesson 5-7

Student Tech Tools
glencoe.com
- Extra Examples, Chapter 5, Lesson 7
- Self-Check Quiz, Chapter 5, Lesson 7

5-7 Dividing Fractions and Mixed Numbers

MAIN IDEA

Divide fractions and mixed numbers.

IN Academic Standards

7.1.7 Solve problems that involve multiplication and **division with** integers, **fractions,** decimals and combinations of the four operations. *Also addresses P.5.1, P.5.2, P.5.3, P.6.2.*

IN Math Online

glencoe.com

- Concepts In Motion
- Extra Examples
- Personal Tutor
- Self-Check Quiz

MINI Lab

Cut two paper plates into four equal pieces each to show $2 \div \frac{1}{4}$.

1. How many $\frac{1}{4}$'s are in 2 plates? 8
2. How would you model $3 \div \frac{1}{2}$?
3. What is true about $3 \div \frac{1}{2}$ and 3×2? They are equal.

2. Cut 3 plates into 2 equal pieces each.

Dividing 8 by 2 gives the same result as multiplying 8 by $\frac{1}{2}$, which is the reciprocal of 2. In the same way, dividing 4 by $\frac{1}{3}$ is the same as multiplying 4 by the reciprocal of $\frac{1}{3}$, or 3.

reciprocals

$8 \div 2 = 4 \qquad 8 \cdot \frac{1}{2} = 4$

same result

reciprocals

$4 \div \frac{1}{3} = 12 \qquad 4 \cdot 3 = 12$

same result

Is this pattern true for any division expression?

Consider $\frac{7}{8} \div \frac{3}{4}$, which can be rewritten as $\frac{\frac{7}{8}}{\frac{3}{4}}$.

$$\frac{\frac{7}{8}}{\frac{3}{4}} = \frac{\frac{7}{8} \times \frac{4}{3}}{\frac{3}{4} \times \frac{4}{3}}$$

Multiply the numerator and denominator by the reciprocal of $\frac{3}{4}$, which is $\frac{4}{3}$.

$$= \frac{\frac{7}{8} \times \frac{4}{3}}{1}$$

$\frac{3}{4} \times \frac{4}{3} = 1$

$$= \frac{7}{8} \times \frac{4}{3}$$

So, $\frac{7}{8} \div \frac{3}{4} = \frac{7}{8} \times \frac{4}{3}$. These examples suggest the following rule.

Divide by Fractions — Key Concept

Words To divide by a fraction, multiply by its multiplicative inverse, or reciprocal.

Examples

Numbers	Algebra
$\frac{7}{8} \div \frac{3}{4} = \frac{7}{8} \cdot \frac{4}{3}$	$\frac{a}{b} \div \frac{c}{d} = \frac{a}{b} \cdot \frac{d}{c}$, where $b, c, d \neq 0$

5-7 Lesson Notes

1 Focus

Vertical Alignment

Before Lesson 5-7
Compute and perform simple division of fractions and apply these procedures to solving problems

Lesson 5-7
Solve problems involving division of positive fractions and explain why a particular operation was used for a given situation. Explain the meaning of division of positive fractions and perform the calculations

After Lesson 5-7
Divide and simplify rational numbers by using the exponent rules

2 Teach

MINI Lab

In Exercise 2, you may need to help students model the expression. Return to the original problem, $2 \div \frac{1}{4}$, and compare it with $3 \div \frac{1}{2}$. Students should cut three paper plates into two equal pieces each to model $3 \div \frac{1}{2}$.

Scaffolding Questions

Ask:

- How many quarters are in \$3? 12
- How many dimes are in \$2? 20
- How many half-dollars are in \$2.50? 5

Reinforcing the Concept

To reinforce the Mini Lab, have students cut two paper plates into three equal pieces each to show $2 \div \frac{2}{3}$. Ask students how many groups of $\frac{2}{3}$ there are in 2.

The shading shows that there are 3 groups of $\frac{2}{3}$, therefore $2 \div \frac{2}{3}$ is 3.

Have students make similar models to solve the following division problems: $1\frac{1}{2} \div \frac{1}{4}$, $\frac{3}{4} \div \frac{1}{2}$, $1\frac{1}{8} \div \frac{3}{4}$, $3\frac{1}{2} \div 2$ 6, $1\frac{1}{2}$, $1\frac{1}{2}$, $1\frac{3}{4}$

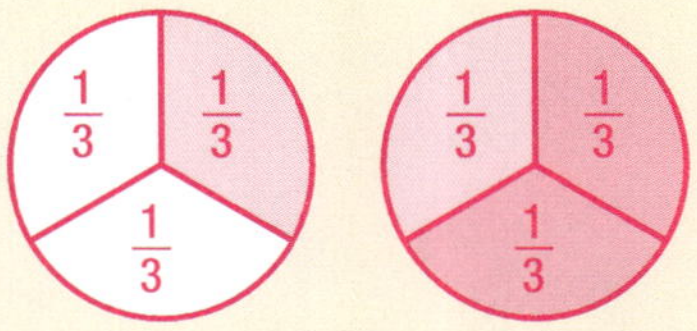

Focus on Mathematical Content

To divide by a mixed number, first **rename it as an improper fraction**.

Estimating a quotient is a good way to check a solution.

Formative Assessment

Use the Check Your Progress exercises after each Example to determine students' understanding of concepts.

ADDITIONAL EXAMPLES

1. Find $\frac{2}{3} \div \frac{4}{9}$. Write in simplest form. $1\frac{1}{2}$
2. Find $\frac{5}{6} \div 2\frac{1}{2}$. Write in simplest form. $\frac{1}{3}$

Additional Examples are also in:

- Noteables™ Interactive Study Notebook with Foldables™
- Interactive Classroom PowerPoint® Presentations

Differentiated Instruction

Bodily/Kinesthetic Learners

Students can use construction paper or other concrete objects to model Example 2.

EXAMPLE Divide by a Fraction

1 Find $\frac{3}{4} \div \frac{1}{2}$. Write in simplest form.

Estimate $1 \div \frac{1}{2} = ■$

Think: How many groups of $\frac{1}{2}$ are in 1? $1 \div \frac{1}{2} = 2$

$\frac{3}{4} \div \frac{1}{2} = \frac{3}{4} \cdot \frac{2}{1}$ Multiply by the reciprocal of $\frac{1}{2}$, which is $\frac{2}{1}$.

$= \frac{3}{\cancel{4}_2} \cdot \frac{\cancel{2}^1}{1}$ Divide 4 and 2 by their GCF, 2.

$= \frac{3}{2}$ or $1\frac{1}{2}$ Multiply.

Check for Reasonableness $1\frac{1}{2} \approx 2$ ✔

CHECK Your Progress

Divide. Write in simplest form.

a. $\frac{3}{4} \div \frac{1}{4}$ **3**

b. $\frac{4}{5} \div \frac{8}{9}$ $\frac{9}{10}$

c. $\frac{5}{6} \div \frac{2}{3}$ $1\frac{1}{4}$

To divide by a mixed number, first rename the mixed number as an improper fraction. Then multiply the first fraction by the reciprocal, or multiplicative inverse, of the second fraction.

EXAMPLE Divide by Mixed Numbers

2 Find $\frac{2}{3} \div 3\frac{1}{3}$. Write in simplest form.

Estimate $\frac{1}{2} \div 3 = \frac{1}{2} \times \frac{1}{3}$ or $\frac{1}{6}$

$\frac{2}{3} \div 3\frac{1}{3} = \frac{2}{3} \div \frac{10}{3}$ Rename $3\frac{1}{3}$ as an improper fraction.

$= \frac{2}{3} \cdot \frac{3}{10}$ Multiply by the reciprocal of $\frac{10}{3}$, which is $\frac{3}{10}$.

$= \frac{\cancel{2}^1}{\cancel{3}_1} \cdot \frac{\cancel{3}^1}{\cancel{10}_5}$ Divide out common factors.

$= \frac{1}{5}$ Multiply.

Check for Reasonableness $\frac{1}{5}$ is close to $\frac{1}{6}$. ✔

Study Tip

Dividing by a Whole Number
Remember that a whole number can be written as a fraction with a 1 in the denominator.

So, $2\frac{1}{3} \div 5$ can be rewritten as $2\frac{1}{3} \div \frac{5}{1}$.

CHECK Your Progress

Divide. Write in simplest form.

d. $5 \div 1\frac{1}{3}$ $3\frac{3}{4}$

e. $-\frac{3}{4} \div 1\frac{1}{2}$ $-\frac{1}{2}$

f. $2\frac{1}{3} \div 5$ $\frac{7}{15}$

g. **NUTS** In planning for a party, $5\frac{1}{4}$ pounds of cashews will be divided into $\frac{3}{4}$-pound bags. How many such bags can be made? **7 bags**

Real-World EXAMPLE

3 WOODWORKING **Students in a woodworking class are making butterfly houses. The side pieces of the house need to be $8\frac{1}{4}$ inches long. How many side pieces can be cut from a board measuring $49\frac{1}{2}$ inches long?**

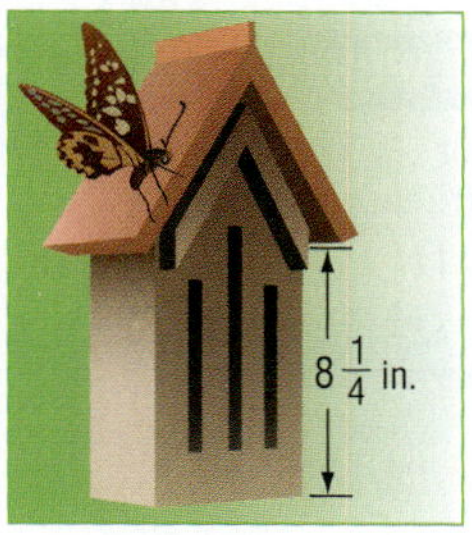

To find how many side pieces can be cut, divide $49\frac{1}{2}$ by $8\frac{1}{4}$.

Estimate Use compatible numbers. $48 \div 8 = 6$

$49\frac{1}{2} \div 8\frac{1}{4} = \frac{99}{2} \div \frac{33}{4}$ Rename the mixed numbers as improper fractions.

$= \frac{99}{2} \cdot \frac{4}{33}$ Multiply by the reciprocal of $\frac{33}{4}$, which is $\frac{4}{33}$.

$= \frac{\overset{3}{\cancel{99}}}{\underset{1}{\cancel{2}}} \cdot \frac{\overset{2}{\cancel{4}}}{\underset{1}{\cancel{33}}}$ Divide out common factors.

$= \frac{6}{1}$ or 6 Multiply.

So, 6 side pieces can be cut.

Check for Reasonableness The answer matches the estimate. ✔

CHECK Your Progress

h. **FOOD** Suppose a small box of cereal contains $12\frac{2}{3}$ cups of cereal. How many $1\frac{1}{3}$-cup servings are in the box? $9\frac{1}{2}$

i. **MEASUREMENT** The area of a rectangular bedroom is $146\frac{7}{8}$ square feet. If the width of the bedroom is $11\frac{3}{4}$ feet, find the length. $12\frac{1}{2}$ feet

★ indicates multi-step problem

CHECK Your Understanding

Examples 1–3 (pp. 266–267)

Divide. Write in simplest form.

1. $\frac{1}{8} \div \frac{1}{3}$ $\frac{3}{8}$
2. $\frac{3}{5} \div \frac{1}{4}$ $2\frac{2}{5}$
3. $3 \div \frac{6}{7}$ $3\frac{1}{2}$
4. $\frac{3}{4} \div 6$ $\frac{1}{8}$
5. $\frac{1}{2} \div 7\frac{1}{2}$ $\frac{1}{15}$
6. $\frac{4}{7} \div 1\frac{2}{7}$ $\frac{4}{9}$
7. $5\frac{3}{5} \div 4\frac{2}{3}$ $1\frac{1}{5}$
8. $6\frac{1}{2} \div 3\frac{5}{7}$ $1\frac{3}{4}$

Example 2 (p. 266)

9. **FOOD** Deandre has 7 apples, and each apple is divided evenly into eighths. How many apple slices does Deandre have? 56 slices

Example 3 (p. 267)

10. **WALKING** On Saturday, Lindsay walked $3\frac{1}{2}$ miles in $1\frac{2}{5}$ hours. What was her walking pace, in miles per hour? $2\frac{1}{2}$ mi/h

ADDITIONAL EXAMPLE

3 FACTORY A bottling machine needs to be restocked with new lids every $2\frac{3}{4}$ hours. If the machine runs $19\frac{1}{4}$ hours, how many times will it have to be restocked with lids? 7 times

3 Practice

Formative Assessment

Use Exercises 1–10 to check for understanding.

Then use the chart on the bottom of the next page to customize your assignments for students.

Intervention You may wish to use the Study Guide and Intervention Master on page 45 of the *Chapter 5 Resource Masters* for additional reinforcement.

Lesson 5-7 Dividing Fractions and Mixed Numbers **267**

Odd/Even Assignments

Exercises 11–32 are structured so that students practice the same concepts whether they are assigned odd or even problems.

Practice and Problem Solving

HOMEWORK HELP	
For Exercises	See Examples
11–14	1
15–32	2, 3

Exercise Levels
A: 11–32
B: 33–47
C: 48–51

Divide. Write in simplest form.

11. $\frac{3}{8} \div \frac{6}{7}$ $\frac{7}{16}$
12. $\frac{5}{9} \div \frac{5}{6}$ $\frac{2}{3}$
13. $\frac{2}{3} \div \frac{1}{2}$ $1\frac{1}{3}$
14. $\frac{7}{8} \div \frac{3}{4}$ $1\frac{1}{6}$
15. $6 \div \frac{1}{2}$ 12
16. $\frac{4}{9} \div 2$ $\frac{2}{9}$
17. $2\frac{2}{3} \div 4$ $\frac{2}{3}$
18. $5 \div 1\frac{1}{3}$ $3\frac{3}{4}$

19. **FOOD** Mason has 8 cups of popcorn kernels to divide into $\frac{2}{3}$-cup portions. How many portions will there be? 12

20. **MOVIES** Cheryl is organizing her movie collection. If each movie case is $\frac{3}{4}$ inch wide, how many movies can fit on a shelf 5 feet wide? 80 movies

Divide. Write in simplest form.

21. $\frac{2}{3} \div 2\frac{1}{2}$ $\frac{4}{15}$
22. $\frac{8}{9} \div 5\frac{1}{3}$ $\frac{1}{6}$
23. $4\frac{1}{2} \div 6\frac{3}{4}$ $\frac{2}{3}$
24. $5\frac{2}{7} \div 2\frac{1}{7}$ $2\frac{7}{15}$
25. $3\frac{4}{5} \div 1\frac{1}{3}$ $2\frac{17}{20}$
26. $9\frac{1}{2} \div 2\frac{5}{6}$ $3\frac{6}{17}$
27. $5\frac{1}{5} \div \frac{2}{3}$ $7\frac{4}{5}$
28. $6\frac{7}{8} \div \frac{3}{4}$ $9\frac{1}{6}$

29. **ICE CREAM** Vinh bought $4\frac{1}{2}$ gallons of ice cream to serve at his birthday party. If a pint is $\frac{1}{8}$ of a gallon, how many pint-sized servings can be made? 36

30. **BEVERAGES** William has $8\frac{1}{4}$ cups of fruit juice. If he divides the juice into $\frac{3}{4}$-cup servings, how many servings will he have? 11

BIRDS For Exercises 31 and 32, use the table that gives information about several types of birds of prey found at the Woodland Park Zoo in Seattle, Washington.

Bird	Maximum Weight (lb)
Golden Eagle	$13\frac{9}{10}$
Northern Bald Eagle	$9\frac{9}{10}$
Red-Tailed Hawk	$3\frac{1}{2}$

Source: Woodland Park Zoo

31. How many times as heavy is the Golden Eagle as the Red-tailed Hawk? $3\frac{34}{35}$

32. How many times as heavy is the Golden Eagle as the Northern Bald Eagle? $1\frac{40}{99}$

Real-World Link Red-tailed hawks are large, stocky birds with long, broad wings and short, broad tails. Females are larger than males and can weigh up to $3\frac{1}{2}$ pounds.
Source: Woodland Park Zoo

Draw a model of each verbal expression and then evaluate the expression. Explain how the model shows the division process.

33–36. See Ch. 5 Answer Appendix for models and explanations.

33. one half divided by two fifths $1\frac{1}{4}$
34. five eighths divided by one fourth $2\frac{1}{2}$
35. one and three eighths divided by one half $2\frac{3}{4}$
36. two and one sixth divided by two thirds $3\frac{1}{4}$

★ 37. **PIZZA** A concession stand sells three types of pizza. The diagram shows how much pizza of each type is left after the concession stand was open for one hour. If the pizza is sold in slices that are $\frac{1}{8}$ of a whole pizza, how many more slices can be sold? 25

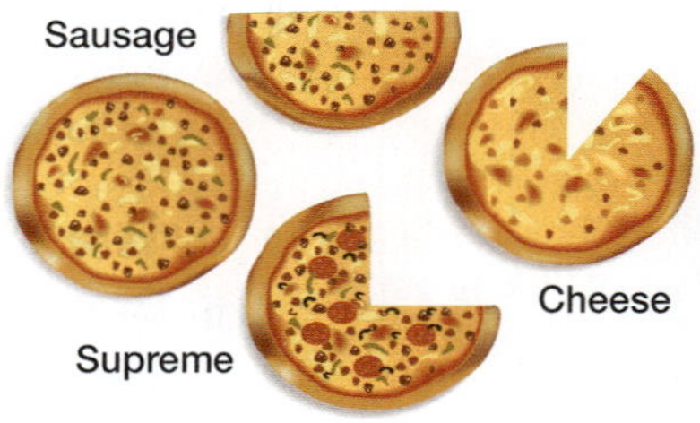

DIFFERENTIATED HOMEWORK OPTIONS

Level	Assignment	Two-Day Option	
BL Basic	11–32, 49–60	11–31 odd, 52, 53	12–32 even, 49–51, 54–60
OL Core	11–41 odd, 42–47, 49–60	11–32, 52, 53	33–47, 49–51, 54–60
AL Advanced/Pre-AP	33–60		

268 Chapter 5 Applying Fractions

ALGEBRA Evaluate each expression if $g = \frac{1}{6}$, $h = \frac{1}{2}$, and $j = 3\frac{2}{3}$.

38. $j \div h$ $7\frac{1}{3}$ 39. $g \div j$ $\frac{1}{22}$ 40. $3g \div h$ 1 41. $h \div \left(\frac{1}{2}j\right)$ $\frac{3}{11}$

42. **SHOPPING** A supermarket sells pretzels in $\frac{3}{4}$-ounce snack-sized bags or $12\frac{1}{2}$-ounce regular-sized bags. How many times larger is the regular-sized bag than the snack-sized bag? $16\frac{2}{3}$ times larger

43. **MEASUREMENT** A recipe calls for $2\frac{2}{3}$ cups of brown sugar and $\frac{2}{3}$ cup of confectioner's sugar. How many times greater is the number of cups of brown sugar in the recipe than of confectioner's sugar? 4

SCHOOL For Exercises 44 and 45, use the table that shows the number of hours students spend studying each week during the school year.

Weekly Study Hours	
Hours	**Fraction of Students**
none	$\frac{1}{50}$
1–2	$\frac{2}{25}$
3–5	$\frac{11}{50}$
6–7	$\frac{17}{100}$
8–10	$\frac{1}{5}$
Over 10	$\frac{1}{5}$
Not sure	$\frac{3}{25}$

Source: *Time Magazine*

44. How many times greater was the number of students who spent over 10 hours each week studying than those who spent only 1–2 hours each week studying? $2\frac{1}{2}$ times as many

45. $7\frac{9}{10}$ times as many

★ 45. How many times greater was the number of students who spent 3 or more hours each week studying than those who spent less than 3 hours each week studying?

★ 46. **SCHOOL SUPPLIES** Tara bought a dozen folders. She took $\frac{1}{3}$ of the dozen and then divided the remaining folders equally among her four friends. What fraction of the dozen did each of her four friends receive and how many folders was this per person? $\frac{1}{6}$ of a dozen or 2 folders

★ 47. **WEATHER** A meteorologist has issued a thunderstorm warning. So far, the storm has traveled 35 miles in $\frac{1}{2}$ hour. If it is currently 5:00 P.M., and the storm is 105 miles away from you, at what time will the storm reach you? Explain how you solved the problem. See margin.

Academic Standards • ISTEP+

Extra Practice, pp. 681, 708

H.O.T. Problems

48. **CHALLENGE** If $\frac{5}{6}$ is divided by a certain fraction $\frac{a}{b}$, the result is $\frac{1}{4}$. What is the fraction $\frac{a}{b}$? $\frac{10}{3}$

49. Sample answer; You could use paper and pencil; $\frac{3}{4}$ of what number is $1\frac{1}{2}$? $1\frac{1}{2}$ feet $\div \frac{3}{4} =$ $\frac{3}{2}$ feet $\cdot \frac{4}{3} = 2$ feet.

49. **SELECT A TOOL** Reynaldo cut a rope to make the running knot shown. The rope used to make the knot was $1\frac{1}{2}$ feet long and was $\frac{3}{4}$ of the original rope length. Which of the following tools could be used to determine the rope's original length? Justify your selection(s). Then use your tool(s) to find the length.

paper and pencil | model | calculator | real object

Additional Answer

47. 6:30 P.M.; Sample answer: $105 \div 35 = 3$, The storm will travel 105 miles in 3 sets of $\frac{1}{2}$ hour, or $1\frac{1}{2}$ hours. Adding $1\frac{1}{2}$ hours to 5:00 P.M. will make it 6:30 P.M.

Differentiated Instruction

Visual/Spatial Learners Separate students into groups of three or four. Write the following expressions on the board: $2 \div \frac{1}{5}$, $3 \div \frac{1}{6}$, $3 \div \frac{3}{4}$, and $5 \div 1\frac{1}{4}$. Have the members of each group predict the quotients and then model the expressions and their solutions. Students might want to use paper plates, as in the Mini Lab draw figures on grid paper, or create their own models.

⚠ Exercise Alert!

Find the Error In Exercise 50, José is correct. When Evan rewrote the division problem as a multiplication problem, he incorrectly changed the first number (the dividend) to its reciprocal. Remind students that when dividing by a fraction, they should multiply by the reciprocal of the second number, or divisor.

4 Assess

Ticket Out the Door Write an equation such as $5\frac{1}{4} \div \frac{3}{4} = ?$ on the chalkboard. Have students write a word problem for the equation.

Formative Assessment

Check for student understanding of concepts in Lesson 5-7.

CRM Quiz 4, p. 54

FOLDABLES Study Organizer Foldables™ Follow-Up

Remind students to record on index cards what they learn about dividing fractions and mixed numbers. Students should then store the cards in their Foldables.

50. José; Evan did not multiply by the reciprocal of $\frac{6}{7}$.
51. Yes; sample answer: If the first proper fraction is larger than the second proper fraction, then the resulting quotient will be a whole number or mixed number.

50. **FIND THE ERROR** Evan and José are finding $\frac{4}{5} \div \frac{6}{7}$. Who is correct? Explain your reasoning.

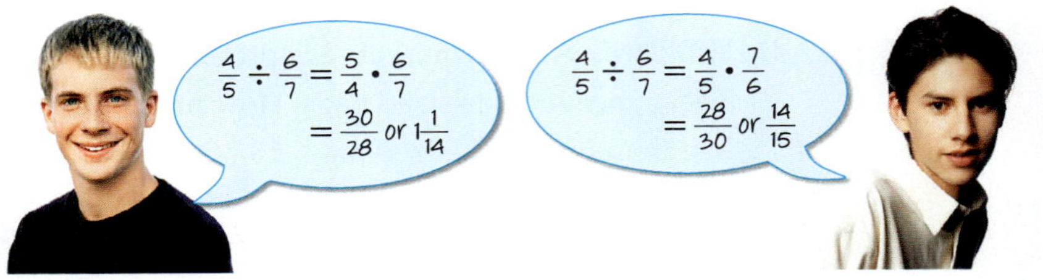

Evan José

51. **WRITING IN MATH** If you divide a proper fraction by another proper fraction, is it possible to get a mixed number as an answer? Explain your reasoning.

ISTEP+ PRACTICE 7.1.7

52. The Corbett family owns 300 acres of land that they plan to rent to people for their horses. How many $7\frac{1}{2}$-acre lots can they make using the 300 acres? **B**

A 21　　C $40\frac{1}{2}$

B 40　　D $292\frac{1}{2}$

53. How many $1\frac{1}{8}$-pound boxes of peanuts can be made using $6\frac{3}{4}$ pounds of peanuts? **H**

F 4　　H 6

G 5　　J 7

Spiral Review

Find the multiplicative inverse of each number. (Lesson 5-6)

54. $\frac{6}{7}$ **$\frac{7}{6}$ or $1\frac{1}{6}$**

55. $\frac{4}{13}$ **$\frac{13}{4}$ or $3\frac{1}{4}$**

56. 8 **$\frac{1}{8}$**

57. $5\frac{1}{4}$ **$\frac{4}{21}$**

58. Find $\frac{1}{10} \times \frac{5}{8}$. Write in simplest form. (Lesson 5-5) **$\frac{1}{16}$**

59. **MEASUREMENT** Find the length of a rectangular flower bed if the perimeter is 12 feet and the width is 1.5 feet. (Lesson 3-6) **4.5 ft**

60. **ANIMALS** An elephant herd can move 50 miles in a day. At this rate, about how many miles can an elephant herd move each hour? (Lesson 1-1) **2**

Problem Solving in Geography

Real-World Unit Project

A Traveling We Will Go It's time to complete your project. Use the data you have gathered about schedules and costs to prepare a travel brochure for your vacation destination. Be sure to include a paragraph describing why you chose your vacation spot.

IN Math Online **Unit Project at** glencoe.com

270 Chapter 5 Applying Fractions

Study Guide and Review

IN Math Online glencoe.com
- STUDY TO GO
- Vocabulary Review

FOLDABLES Study Organizer — GET READY to Study

Be sure the following Big Ideas are noted in your Foldable.

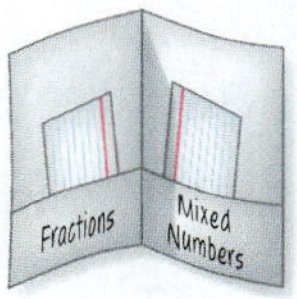

BIG Ideas

Estimating with Fractions (Lesson 5-1)
- When the numerator is much smaller than the denominator, round the fraction to 0.
- When the numerator is about half of the denominator, round the fraction to $\frac{1}{2}$.
- When the numerator is almost as large as the denominator, round the fraction to 1.

Adding and Subtracting Fractions (Lessons 5-2 and 5-3)
- To add or subtract like fractions, add or subtract the numerators and write the result over the denominator.
- To add or subtract unlike fractions, rename the fractions using the LCD. Then add or subtract as with like fractions.
- To add or subtract mixed numbers, first add or subtract the fractions. If necessary, rename them using the LCD. Then add or subtract the whole numbers and simplify if necessary.

Multiplying and Dividing Fractions (Lessons 5-5 and 5-7)
- To multiply fractions, multiply the numerators and multiply the denominators.
- The product of a number and its multiplicative inverse is 1.
- To divide by a fraction, multiply by its multiplicative inverse, or reciprocal.

Solving Equations (Lesson 5-6)
If you multiply each side of an equation by the same nonzero number, the two sides remain equal.

Key Vocabulary

compatible numbers (p. 232)	multiplicative inverse (p. 258)
like fractions (p. 236)	reciprocal (p. 258)
	unlike fractions (p. 237)

Vocabulary Check

Choose the correct term or number to complete each sentence.

1. To add like fractions, add the (numerators, denominators). **numerators**
2. The symbol ≈ means (*approximately*, *exactly*) *equal to*. **approximately**
3. When dividing by a fraction, multiply by its (value, reciprocal). **reciprocal**
4. When estimating, if the numerator of a fraction is much smaller than the denominator, round the fraction to $\left(0, \frac{1}{2}\right)$. **0**
5. Fractions with different denominators are called (like, unlike) fractions. **unlike**
6. The multiplicative inverse of $\frac{5}{6}$ is $\left(\frac{6}{5}, -\frac{5}{6}\right)$. $\frac{6}{5}$
7. The mixed number $2\frac{4}{7}$ can be renamed as $\left(2\frac{7}{7}, 1\frac{11}{7}\right)$. $1\frac{11}{7}$
8. When multiplying fractions, multiply the numerators and (multiply, keep) the denominators. **multiply**
9. The reciprocal of $\frac{1}{3}$ is $(-3, 3)$. **3**
10. The fractions $\frac{4}{16}$ and $\frac{2}{4}$ are (like, unlike) fractions. **unlike**
11. Another word for multiplicative inverse is (reciprocal, denominator). **reciprocal**
12. The fraction $\frac{x}{2}$ can be read *x multiplied by* $\left(2, \frac{1}{2}\right)$. $\frac{1}{2}$

Summative Assessment

CRM Vocabulary Test, p. 56

CHAPTER 5 Study Guide and Review

FOLDABLES Study Organizer — Dinah Zike's Foldables

Have students look through the chapter to make sure they have included study cards in their Foldables for the key concepts of each lesson.

Encourage students to refer to their Foldables while completing the Study Guide and Review and while preparing for the Chapter Test.

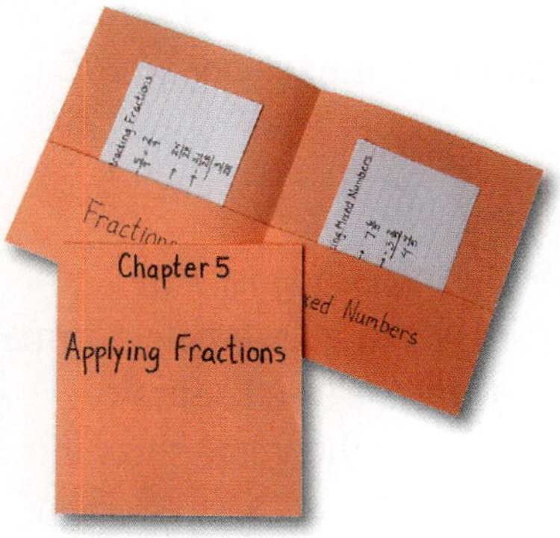

Formative Assessment

Key Vocabulary The page references after each word in the Key Vocabulary denote where that term was first introduced. If students have difficulty answering Exercises 1–12, remind them that they can use these page references to refresh their memories about the vocabulary terms.

IN Math Online glencoe.com

Vocabulary PuzzleMaker improves students' mathematics vocabulary using four puzzle formats–crossword, scramble, word search using a word list, and word search using clues. Students can work online or from a printed worksheet.

Lesson-by-Lesson Review

Intervention If the given examples are not sufficient to review the topics covered by the questions, remind students that the page references tell them where to review that topic in their textbooks.

Two-Day Option Have students complete the Lesson-by-Lesson on pages 272–274. Then you can use ExamView® Assessment Suite to customize another review worksheet that practices all the objectives of this chapter or only the objectives on which your students need more help.

For more information on ExamView® Assessment Suite, see page 228C.

Differentiated Instruction

Super DVD: MindJogger Plus
Use this DVD as an alternative format of review for the test. For more information on this game show format, see page 228D.

Chapter 5 Study Guide and Review

Lesson-by-Lesson Review

5-1 Estimating with Fractions (pp. 230–235)

7.1.7

Estimate. **13–20. Sample answers are given.**

13. $2\frac{9}{10} \div 1\frac{1}{8}$ **$3 \div 1 = 3$**
14. $6\frac{2}{9} - 5\frac{1}{7}$ **$6 - 5 = 1$**
15. $\frac{13}{15} \times \frac{1}{5}$ **$1 \times 0 = 0$**
16. $\frac{1}{2} + \frac{3}{8}$ **$\frac{1}{2} + \frac{1}{2} = 1$**
17. $\frac{1}{2} \cdot 25\frac{1}{2}$ **$\times 26 = 13$**
18. $15\frac{6}{7} \div 7\frac{1}{3}$ **$16 \div 8 = 2$**
19. **MEASUREMENT** Gina wishes to carpet her living room. It has a length of $18\frac{5}{8}$ feet and the width of her living room is $9\frac{1}{2}$ feet. About how many square feet of carpet would be needed for her living room? **19×10 or about 190 ft^2**
20. **FOOTBALL** Jamil practiced football for $1\frac{3}{4}$ hours on Saturday and $2\frac{2}{3}$ hours on Sunday. About how many more hours did he practice on Sunday than on Saturday? **3–2 or about 1 hour**

Example 1 Estimate $5\frac{1}{12} + 2\frac{5}{6}$.

1 is much smaller than 12, so $5\frac{1}{12} \approx 5$.

5 is almost as large as 6, so $2\frac{5}{6} \approx 3$.

$5\frac{1}{12} + 2\frac{5}{6} \approx 5 + 3$ or 8

The sum is *about* 8.

Example 2 Estimate $\frac{7}{8} - \frac{4}{7}$.

7 is almost as large as 8, so $\frac{7}{8} \approx 1$.

4 is about half of 7, so $\frac{4}{7} \approx \frac{1}{2}$.

$\frac{7}{8} - \frac{4}{7} \approx 1 - \frac{1}{2}$ or $\frac{1}{2}$

The difference is *about* $\frac{1}{2}$.

5-2 Adding and Subtracting Fractions (pp. 236–241)

6.1.6

Add or subtract. Write in simplest form.

21. $\frac{2}{6} - \frac{1}{6}$ **$\frac{1}{6}$**
22. $\frac{3}{7} + \frac{9}{14}$ **$1\frac{1}{14}$**
23. $\frac{1}{9} + \frac{5}{9}$ **$\frac{2}{3}$**
24. $\frac{9}{10} - \frac{3}{10}$ **$\frac{3}{5}$**
25. $\frac{5}{8} - \frac{5}{12}$ **$\frac{5}{24}$**
26. $\frac{3}{4} + \frac{7}{20}$ **$1\frac{1}{10}$**
27. **RAIN** At 8 A.M., Della's rain gauge read $\frac{1}{8}$ inch. By 4 P.M., the gauge read $\frac{3}{4}$ inch. How much rain fell between 8 A.M. and 4 P.M.? **$\frac{5}{8}$ in.**
28. **PIZZA** Owen ate $\frac{1}{8}$ of a pizza Tuesday night. The next day, he ate an additional $\frac{1}{2}$ of the pizza. What fraction of the pizza has he eaten? **$\frac{5}{8}$**

Example 3 Find $\frac{1}{6} + \frac{2}{3}$.

Use a model.

$\frac{1}{6}$

$+\frac{2}{3}$

$\frac{5}{6}$

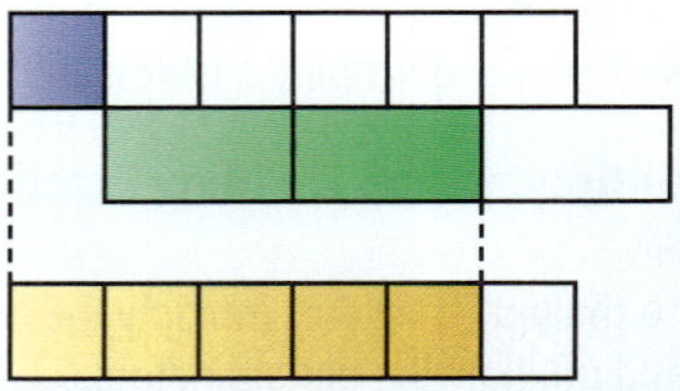

Example 4 Find $\frac{3}{10} - \frac{1}{4}$.

$\frac{3}{10} - \frac{1}{4} = \frac{6}{20} - \frac{5}{20}$ Rename the fractions using the LCD, 20.

$= \frac{1}{20}$ Subtract the numerators.

272 Chapter 5 Applying Fractions

Mixed Problem Solving
For mixed problem-solving practice, see page 708.

5-3 Adding and Subtracting Mixed Numbers (pp. 242–246)

6.1.6

Add or subtract. Write in simplest form.

29. $3\frac{2}{15} + 6\frac{9}{15}$ **$9\frac{11}{15}$**
30. $4\frac{1}{3} - 2\frac{2}{3}$ **$1\frac{2}{3}$**
31. $8\frac{2}{7} + 1\frac{6}{7}$ **$10\frac{1}{7}$**
32. $7\frac{11}{12} - 4\frac{3}{12}$ **$3\frac{2}{3}$**
33. $7\frac{3}{5} - 5\frac{1}{3}$ **$2\frac{4}{15}$**
34. $5\frac{3}{4} + 1\frac{1}{6}$ **$6\frac{11}{12}$**
35. $3\frac{5}{8} + 11\frac{1}{2}$ **$15\frac{1}{8}$**
36. $4\frac{3}{10} - 2\frac{4}{5}$ **$1\frac{1}{2}$**

37. **BABYSITTING** Lucas watched his little sister for $2\frac{1}{2}$ hours on Friday, $3\frac{2}{3}$ hours on Saturday, and $1\frac{3}{4}$ hours on Sunday. How many hours did Lucas watch his little sister? **$7\frac{11}{12}$ h**

Example 5 Find $5\frac{2}{3} + 3\frac{1}{2}$.

$5\frac{2}{3} + 3\frac{1}{2} = 5\frac{4}{6} + 3\frac{3}{6}$ Rename the fractions.

$= 8\frac{7}{6}$ Add the whole numbers and add the fractions.

$= 9\frac{1}{6}$ $8\frac{7}{6} = 8 + 1\frac{1}{6}$ or $9\frac{1}{6}$

Example 6 Find $4\frac{1}{5} - 2\frac{3}{5}$.

$4\frac{1}{5} - 2\frac{3}{5} = 3\frac{6}{5} - 2\frac{3}{5}$ Rename $4\frac{1}{5}$ as $3\frac{6}{5}$.

$= 1\frac{3}{5}$ Subtract the whole numbers and subtract the fractions.

5-4 PSI: Eliminate Possibilities (pp. 248–249)

P.1.3, P.2.4

Solve by eliminating possibilities.

38. **SCHOOL** It takes Beth 15 minutes to walk to school, $\frac{1}{2}$ mile away. What is her walking pace? **A**
 A 2 miles per hour
 B 1 mile per hour
 C 7.5 miles per hour
 D 30 miles per hour

39. **COOKING** Which of the following would yield a larger batch of bagels? **G**
 F Multiply a recipe by $\frac{1}{2}$.
 G Divide a recipe by $\frac{1}{2}$.
 H Multiply a recipe by $\frac{3}{4}$.
 J Divide a recipe by 3.

Example 7 **A group of friends went to a theme park. Six of the friends rode the Ferris wheel. If this was $\frac{2}{3}$ of the group, how many friends were in the group?**

A 3
B 6
C 9
D 12

Since 6 friends rode the Ferris wheel and this was $\frac{2}{3}$ of the total number of friends in the group, the number of friends in the group must be greater than 6. So, eliminate choices A and B.

If there were 12 friends in the group, the 6 that rode the Ferris wheel would represent $\frac{1}{2}$ of the group. So, eliminate choice D.

Choice C is the only remaining possibility. Since 6 out of 9 is $\frac{6}{9}$ or $\frac{2}{3}$, C is correct.

Chapter 5 Study Guide and Review **273**

Problem Solving Review

For additional practice in problem solving for Chapter 5, see the Mixed Problem Solving Appendix, page 708 in the Student Handbook section.

Anticipation Guide

Have students complete the Chapter 5 Anticipation Guide and discuss how their responses have changed now that they have completed Chapter 5.

CRM Anticipation Guide, p. 7

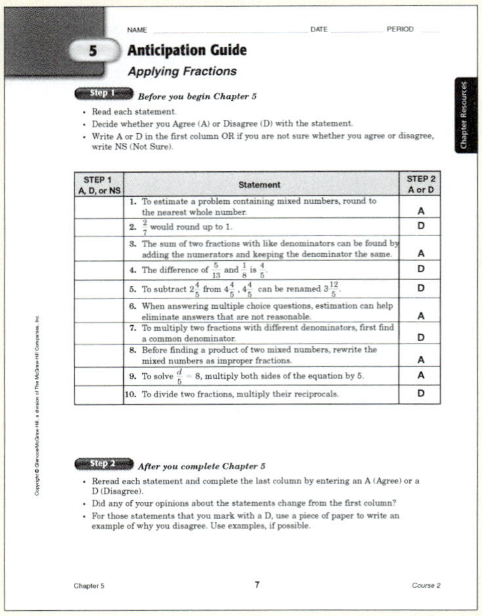
NAME ______ DATE ______ PERIOD ______

5 **Anticipation Guide**

Applying Fractions

Chapter Resources

Step 1 *Before you begin Chapter 5*

- Read each statement.
- Decide whether you Agree (A) or Disagree (D) with the statement.
- Write A or D in the first column OR if you are not sure whether you agree or disagree, write NS (Not Sure).

STEP 1 A, D, or NS	Statement	STEP 2 A or D
	1. To estimate a problem containing mixed numbers, round to the nearest whole number.	A
	2. $\frac{2}{7}$ would round up to 1.	D
	3. The sum of two fractions with like denominators can be found by adding the numerators and keeping the denominator the same.	A
	4. The difference of $\frac{5}{13}$ and $\frac{1}{8}$ is $\frac{4}{5}$.	D
	5. To subtract $2\frac{4}{5}$ from $4\frac{4}{5}$, $4\frac{4}{5}$ can be renamed $3\frac{12}{5}$.	D
	6. When answering multiple choice questions, estimation can help eliminate answers that are not reasonable.	A
	7. To multiply two fractions with different denominators, first find a common denominator.	D
	8. Before finding a product of two mixed numbers, rewrite the mixed numbers as improper fractions.	A
	9. To solve $\frac{d}{5} = 8$, multiply both sides of the equation by 5.	A
	10. To divide two fractions, multiply their reciprocals.	D

Step 2 *After you complete Chapter 5*

- Reread each statement and complete the last column by entering an A (Agree) or a D (Disagree).
- Did any of your opinions about the statements change from the first column?
- For those statements that you mark with a D, use a piece of paper to write an example of why you disagree. Use examples, if possible.

Chapter 5 7 Course 2

Differentiated Instruction

Bodily/Kinesthetic Learners

If students are having difficulty dividing fractions, remind them that they can use geoboards, construction paper, or other concrete objects to model Exercises 55–61.

CHAPTER 5 **Study Guide and Review**

5-5 Multiplying Fractions and Mixed Numbers (pp. 252–257)

7.1.7

Multiply. Write in simplest form.

40. $\frac{3}{5} \times \frac{2}{7}$ **$\frac{6}{35}$**
41. $\frac{5}{12} \times \frac{4}{9}$ **$\frac{5}{27}$**
42. $\frac{3}{5} \times \frac{10}{21}$ **$\frac{2}{7}$**
43. $4 \times \frac{13}{20}$ **$2\frac{3}{5}$**
44. $2\frac{1}{3} \times \frac{3}{4}$ **$1\frac{3}{4}$**
45. $4\frac{1}{2} \times 2\frac{1}{12}$ **$9\frac{3}{8}$**

46. **FOOD** An average slice of American cheese is about $\frac{1}{8}$ inch thick. What is the height of a package containing 20 slices? **$2\frac{1}{2}$ in.**

Example 8 Find $\frac{5}{9} \times \frac{2}{3}$.

$\frac{5}{9} \times \frac{2}{3} = \frac{5 \times 2}{9 \times 3}$ Multiply the numerators and multiply the denominators.

$= \frac{10}{27}$ Simplify.

Example 9 Find $3\frac{1}{2} \times 2\frac{3}{4}$.

$3\frac{1}{2} \times 2\frac{3}{4} = \frac{7}{2} \times \frac{11}{4}$ Rename $3\frac{1}{2}$ and $2\frac{3}{4}$.

$= \frac{7 \times 11}{2 \times 4}$ Multiply the numerators and multiply the denominators.

$= \frac{77}{8}$ or $9\frac{5}{8}$ Simplify.

5-6 Algebra: Solving Equations (pp. 258–263) **47. $\frac{12}{7}$ or $1\frac{5}{7}$**

7.2.2

Find the multiplicative inverse of each number.

47. $\frac{7}{12}$
48. 5 **$\frac{1}{5}$**
49. $3\frac{1}{3}$ **$\frac{3}{10}$**

Solve each equation. Check your solution.

50. $8 = \frac{w}{2}$ **16**
51. $\frac{4}{5}b = 12$ **15**
52. $-7.6 = \frac{n}{3}$ **−22.8**
53. $\frac{x}{0.3} = 2.5$ **0.75**

54. **BOOKS** Of the books on a shelf, $\frac{2}{3}$ are mysteries. If there are 10 mystery books, how many books are on the shelf? **15**

Example 10 Find the multiplicative inverse of $\frac{9}{5}$.

$\frac{9}{5} \cdot \frac{5}{9} = 1$ The product of $\frac{9}{5}$ and $\frac{5}{9}$ is 1.

The multiplicative inverse of $\frac{9}{5}$ is $\frac{5}{9}$.

Example 11 Solve $\frac{3}{4}g = 2$.

$\frac{3}{4}g = 2$ Write the equation.

$\frac{4}{3} \cdot \frac{3}{4}g = \frac{4}{3} \cdot 2$ Multiply each side by the reciprocal of $\frac{3}{4}$.

$g = \frac{8}{3}$ or $2\frac{2}{3}$ Simplify.

5-7 Dividing Fractions and Mixed Numbers (pp. 265–270)

7.1.7

Divide. Write in simplest form.

55. $\frac{3}{5} \div \frac{6}{7}$ **$\frac{7}{10}$**
56. $4 \div \frac{2}{3}$ **6**
57. $2\frac{3}{4} \div \frac{5}{6}$ **$3\frac{3}{10}$**
58. $-\frac{2}{5} \div 3$ **$-\frac{2}{15}$**
59. $4\frac{3}{10} \div 2\frac{1}{5}$ **$1\frac{21}{22}$**
60. $-\frac{2}{7} \div \frac{8}{21}$ **$-\frac{3}{4}$**

61. **MEASUREMENT** How many $\frac{1}{8}$-inch lengths are in $6\frac{3}{4}$ inches? **54**

Example 12 Find $2\frac{4}{5} \div \frac{7}{10}$.

$2\frac{4}{5} \div \frac{7}{10} = \frac{14}{5} \div \frac{7}{10}$ Rename $2\frac{4}{5}$.

$= \frac{\overset{2}{\cancel{14}}}{\underset{1}{\cancel{5}}} \cdot \frac{\overset{2}{\cancel{10}}}{\underset{1}{\cancel{7}}}$ Multiply by the reciprocal of $\frac{7}{10}$.

$= \frac{4}{1}$ or 4 Simplify.

CHAPTER 5

Practice Test

IN Math Online glencoe.com
- Chapter Test

Estimate. Sample answers given.

1. $5\frac{7}{9} - 1\frac{2}{13}$ $6 - 1 = 5$
2. $3\frac{1}{12} + 6\frac{5}{7}$ $3 + 7 = 10$
3. $\frac{3}{7} \times \frac{13}{15}$ $\frac{1}{2} \times 1 = \frac{1}{2}$
4. $5\frac{2}{3} \div 1\frac{4}{5}$ $6 \div 2 = 3$

5. **BAKING** A restaurant uses $2\frac{3}{4}$ pounds of flour to make a batch of dinner rolls. About how many pounds of flour are needed if 3 batches of dinner rolls are to be made? Sample answer: about 3×3 or 9 lb

Add, subtract, multiply, or divide. Write in simplest form.

6. $\frac{4}{15} + \frac{8}{15}$ $\frac{4}{5}$
7. $\frac{7}{10} - \frac{1}{6}$ $\frac{8}{15}$
8. $\frac{5}{8} \times \frac{2}{5}$ $\frac{1}{4}$
9. $6 \times \frac{8}{21}$ $2\frac{2}{7}$
10. $4\frac{5}{12} - 2\frac{1}{12}$ $2\frac{1}{3}$
11. $6\frac{7}{9} + 3\frac{5}{12}$ $10\frac{7}{36}$
12. $8\frac{4}{7} - 1\frac{5}{14}$ $7\frac{3}{14}$
13. $4\frac{5}{6} \times 1\frac{2}{3}$ $8\frac{1}{18}$
14. $\frac{8}{9} \div 5\frac{1}{3}$ $\frac{1}{6}$
15. $\frac{1}{6} \div 5$ $\frac{1}{30}$

16. **MULTIPLE CHOICE** Seth drove $5\frac{3}{4}$ miles to the bank, $6\frac{1}{3}$ miles to the post office, and $4\frac{5}{6}$ miles to the park. What is the total distance Seth drove? D

    A $15\frac{9}{13}$ miles

    B $\frac{7}{12}$ miles

    C $\frac{11}{12}$ miles

    D $16\frac{11}{12}$ miles

17. **SPORTS** Tyler's football practice lasted $2\frac{1}{2}$ hours. If $\frac{1}{4}$ of the time was spent catching passes, how many hours were spent catching passes? $\frac{5}{8}$ h

18. **MEASUREMENT** The floor of a moving van is $11\frac{1}{3}$ feet long and $7\frac{5}{12}$ feet wide. Find the area of the moving van floor. $84\frac{1}{18}$ ft²

19. **MULTIPLE CHOICE** For his birthday, Keith received a check from his grandmother. Of this amount, the table shows how he spent or saved the money.

Fraction of Check	How Spent or Saved
$\frac{2}{5}$	spent on baseball cards
$\frac{1}{4}$	spent on a CD
$\frac{7}{20}$	deposited into savings account

Two weeks later, he withdrew $\frac{2}{3}$ of the amount he had deposited into his savings account. What fraction of the original check did he withdraw from his savings account? H

F $\frac{2}{3}$

G $\frac{9}{23}$

H $\frac{7}{30}$

J $\frac{7}{40}$

20. **MEASUREMENT** An ounce is $\frac{1}{16}$ of a pound. How many ounces are in $8\frac{3}{4}$ pounds? 140 oz

ALGEBRA **Solve each equation. Check your solution.**

21. $\frac{y}{3.7} = 8.1$ 29.97
22. $6 = \frac{2}{5}m$ 15
23. $\frac{3}{4} = \frac{5}{8}x$ $1\frac{1}{5}$
24. $3\frac{1}{6} = \frac{2}{3}p$ $4\frac{3}{4}$

25. **MULTIPLE CHOICE** Maria is making a mural that is $9\frac{2}{3}$ feet long. She wants to divide the mural into sections that are each $\frac{5}{8}$ foot. Which equation can be used to find n, the number of sections in Maria's mural? A

    A $\frac{5}{8}n = 9\frac{2}{3}$

    B $9\frac{2}{3}n = \frac{5}{8}$

    C $\frac{5}{8} + n = 9\frac{2}{3}$

    D $n - \frac{5}{8} = 9\frac{2}{3}$

CHAPTER 5 Practice Test

Summative Assessment

Chapter 5 Resource Masters

Leveled Chapter 5 Tests			
Form	**Type**	**Level**	**Pages**
1	MC	BL	57–58
2A	MC	OL	59–60
2B	MC	OL	61–62
2C	FR	OL	63–64
2D	FR	OL	65–66
3	FR	AL	67–68

MC = multiple-choice questions
FR = free-response questions
BL = below or approaching grade level
OL = on grade level
AL = above or beyond grade level

- Vocabulary Test, p. 56
- Extended-Response Test, p. 69
- Unit 2 Test, pp. 73–74

ExamView Assessment Suite Customize and create multiple versions of your chapter test and their answer keys. All of the questions from the leveled chapter tests in the *Chapter 5 Resource Masters* are also available on ExamView Assessment Suite.

Data-Driven Decision Making

Diagnostic Teaching Based on the results of the Chapter 5 Practice Test, use the following to review concepts that students continue to find challenging.

Exercises	Lesson	Academic Standards	Resources for Review
1–7	5-1, 5-2	7.1.7, 6.1.6	CRM Study Guide and Intervention pp. 10, 16, 22, 27, 32, 39, and 45; IN Math Online glencoe.com • Extra Examples • Personal Tutor • Concepts in Motion
10–12, 16, 19	5-3, 5-4	6.1.6, P.1.3, P.2.4	
8, 9, 13, 17–20	5-5	7.1.7	
14, 15, 21–25	5-6, 5-7	7.2.2, 7.1.7	

CHAPTER 5

ISTEP+ Practice

TEST-TAKING TIP

Exercise 1 Ask students to look for a word or term in the problem that indicates which operation will be used in the equation. Students should realize that *less than* indicates subtraction, which should lead them to examine answer choice A.

Formative Assessment

You can use these two pages to benchmark student progress.

CRM *Chapter 5 Resource Masters*

- Test Practice, pp. 70–72

ExamView Assessment Suite Create practice worksheets or tests that align to your state's standards, as well as TIMSS and NAEP tests.

CHAPTER 5

ISTEP+ Practice

Cumulative, Chapters 1–5

IN Math Online glencoe.com
- Test Practice

PART 1 Multiple Choice

Read each question. Then fill in the correct answer on the answer sheet provided by your teacher or on a sheet of paper.

1. Mrs. Brown needs to make two different desserts for a dinner party. The first recipe requires $2\frac{1}{4}$ cups of flour, and the second recipe requires $\frac{3}{4}$ cup less than the first. Which equation can be used to find n, the number of cups of flour needed for the second recipe? **A**

   A $n = 2\frac{1}{4} - \frac{3}{4}$ C $n = 2\frac{1}{4} + \frac{3}{4}$

   B $n = 2\frac{1}{4} \cdot \frac{3}{4}$ D $n = 2\frac{1}{4} \div \frac{3}{4}$

2. Which of the following is true concerning the least common multiple of 6 and 9? **G**

   F It is greater than the least common multiple of 8 and 12.

   G It is greater than the least common multiple of 5 and 15.

   H It is less than the least common multiple of 4 and 6.

   J It is less than the least common multiple of 3 and 4.

3. Kyle's hockey team has 6 sixth graders, 9 seventh graders, and 5 eighth graders. Which statement below is true? **C**

   A One fourth of the team members are sixth graders.

   B More than half of the team members are seventh graders.

   C 25% of the team members are eighth graders.

   D 30% of the team members are seventh graders.

4. The fraction $\frac{5}{6}$ is found between which pair of fractions on a number line? **J**

   F $\frac{1}{4}$ and $\frac{5}{8}$

   G $\frac{1}{3}$ and $\frac{4}{9}$

   H $\frac{11}{12}$ and $\frac{31}{36}$

   J $\frac{7}{12}$ and $\frac{17}{18}$

5. The table shows the distance Kelly swam over a four-day period. What was the total distance, in miles, Kelly swam? **C**

Kelly's Swimming	
Day	**Distance (miles)**
Monday	1.5
Tuesday	$2\frac{3}{4}$
Wednesday	2.3
Thursday	$3\frac{1}{2}$

   A 10.5 miles C $10\frac{1}{20}$ miles

   B $10\frac{1}{4}$ miles D 9 miles

6. Which of the following gives the correct meaning of the expression $\frac{5}{8} \div \frac{1}{3}$? **G**

   F $\frac{5}{8} \div \frac{1}{3} = \frac{8}{5} \times \frac{3}{1}$

   G $\frac{5}{8} \div \frac{1}{3} = \frac{5}{8} \times \frac{3}{1}$

   H $\frac{5}{8} \div \frac{1}{3} = \frac{5+1}{8+3}$

   J $\frac{5}{8} \div \frac{1}{3} = \frac{5}{8} \times \frac{1}{3}$

276 Chapter 5 Applying Fractions

Preparing for ISTEP+
For test-taking strategies and practice, see pages 716–733.

CHAPTER 5 **ISTEP+ Practice**

7. What is the value of the expression $(3 + 4)^2 \div 7 - 2 \times 6$? **B**

A -9 C 30
B -5 D 1

8. Which line contains the ordered pair $(-1, 2)$? **F**

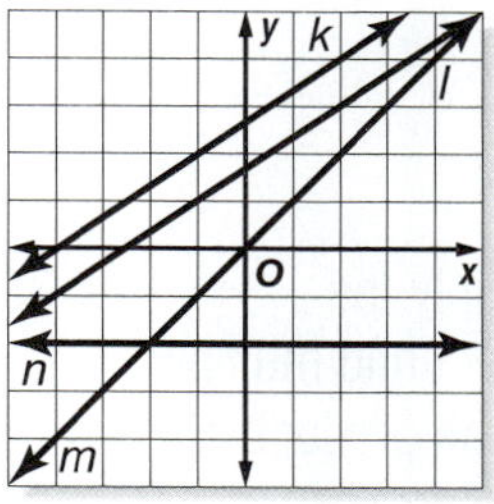

F Line k
G Line l
H Line m
J Line n

9. A pizza shop tried 45 new types of pizza during the past year and 20% of them became popular. Which best represents the fraction of pizzas that did *not* become popular? **D**

A $\frac{1}{5}$ C $\frac{3}{5}$
B $\frac{4}{9}$ D $\frac{4}{5}$

TEST-TAKING TIP

Question 9 Be sure to pay attention to emphasized words, or words that are italicized. In Question 9, you are asked to find which answer is *not* correct.

PART 2 Short Response/Grid In

Record your answers on the answer sheet provided by your teacher or on a sheet of paper.

10. Write an equation using two variables to show the relationship between the position x and the value of a term y. **$4x + 1 = y$**

Position (x)	1	2	3	4	5	n
Value of Term (y)	5	9	13	17	21	

11. Evan runs $2\frac{3}{8}$ miles each week. He runs $\frac{3}{4}$ mile on Mondays and $\frac{3}{4}$ mile on Tuesdays. How far does he run, in miles, if the only other day he runs each week is Thursday? **$\frac{7}{8}$**

12. Find $15 \div (-5)$. **-3**

PART 3 Extended Response

Record your answers on the answer sheet provided by your teacher or on a sheet of paper. Show your work.

13. A box of laundry detergent contains 35 cups. It takes $1\frac{1}{4}$ cups per load of laundry.
   a. Write an equation to represent how many loads ℓ you can wash with one box. **$\ell = 35 \div 1\frac{1}{4}$**
   b. How many loads can you wash with one box? **28 loads**
   c. How many loads can you wash with 3 boxes? **84 loads**

NEED EXTRA HELP?													
If You Missed Question...	1	2	3	4	5	6	7	8	9	10	11	12	13
Go to Lesson...	5-2	4-8	4-6	4-9	4-5	5-7	1-4	3-7	4-6	1-10	5-2	2-8	5-7
IN Academic Standards	6.1.6	7.1.3	6.1.4	7.1.6	6.1.4	7.1.7	7.2.3	8.2.4	6.1.4	7.2.1	6.1.6	7.1.7	7.1.7

Answer Sheet Practice

Have students simulate taking a standardized test by recording their answers on a practice recording sheet.

CRM Student Recording Sheet, p. 51

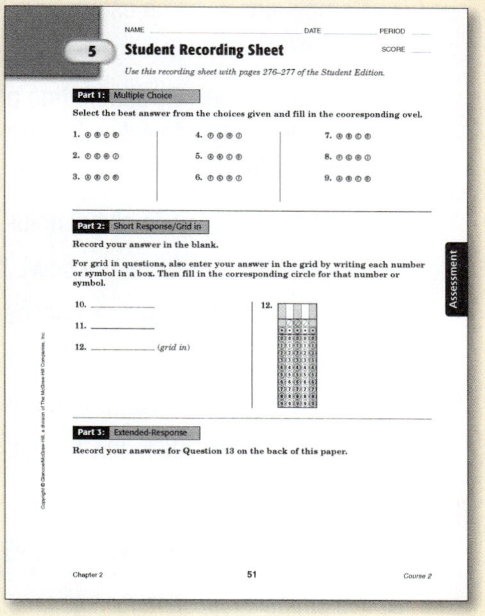

Homework Option

Get Ready for Chapter 6 Assign students the exercises on page 281 as homework to assess whether they possess the prerequisite skills needed for the next chapter.

Chapters 1–5 ISTEP+ Practice **277**

Page 230, Lesson 5-1

1.

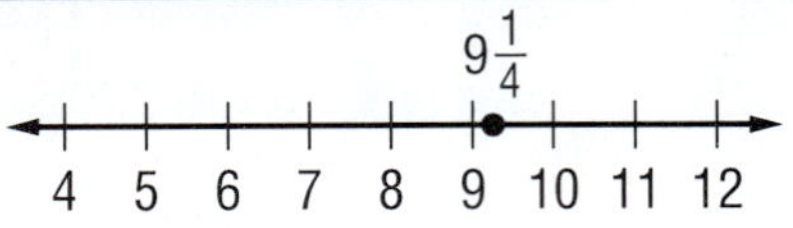

2.

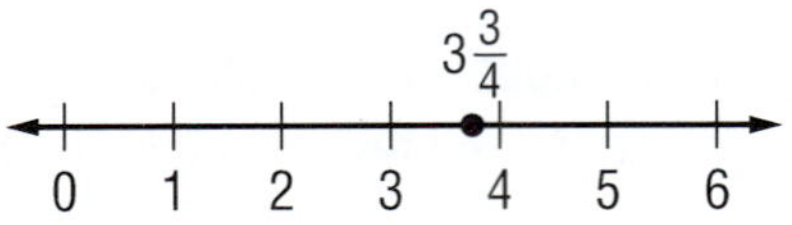

Page 248, Lesson 5-4

1. Sample answer: Use estimation, look for a pattern, work backward.
2. Sample answer: By eliminating possibilities, you can reduce the time it takes to solve the problem since there are fewer answers to consider.
3. Sample answer: A fishbowl holds $1\frac{1}{2}$ gallons of water. If there is $\frac{1}{3}$ gallon of water in the bowl, how many more gallons are needed to fill the bowl; $\frac{2}{3}$ gallons, $1\frac{1}{6}$ gallons, or $2\frac{1}{6}$ gallons. Answer: $\frac{2}{3}$ gallon is not enough because that would make exactly 1 gallon of water in the tank. $2\frac{1}{6}$ gallons is too much, since the tank only holds $1\frac{1}{2}$ gallons. The answer is $1\frac{1}{6}$ gallons.

Pages 250–251, Explore 5-5

c.

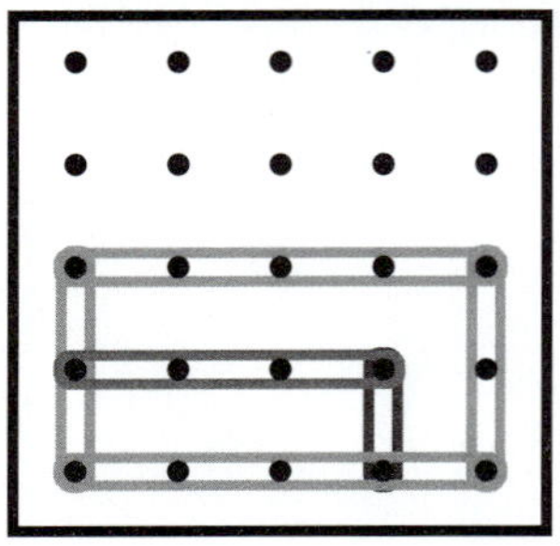

d.

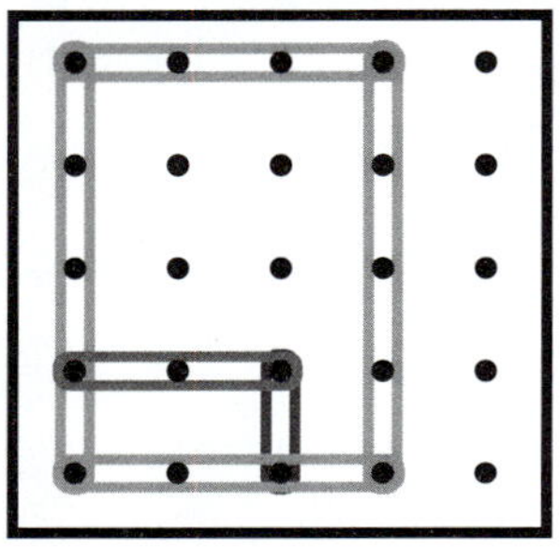

g.

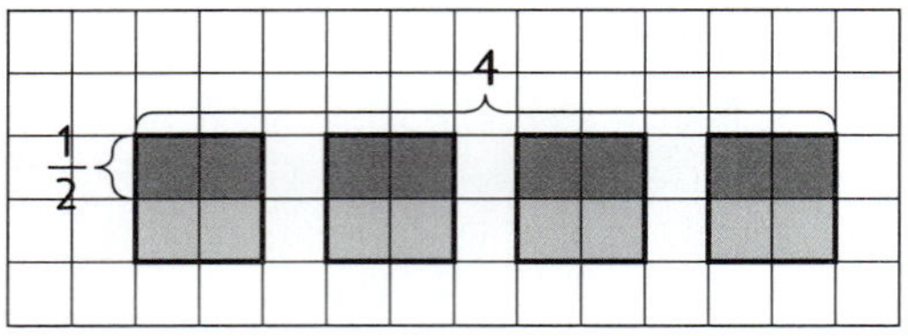

h.

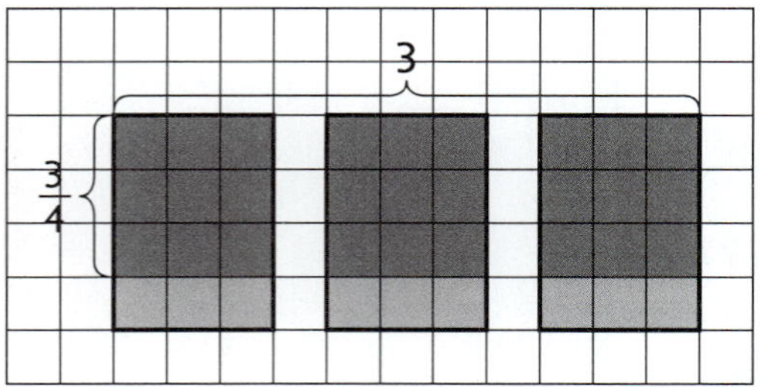

i.

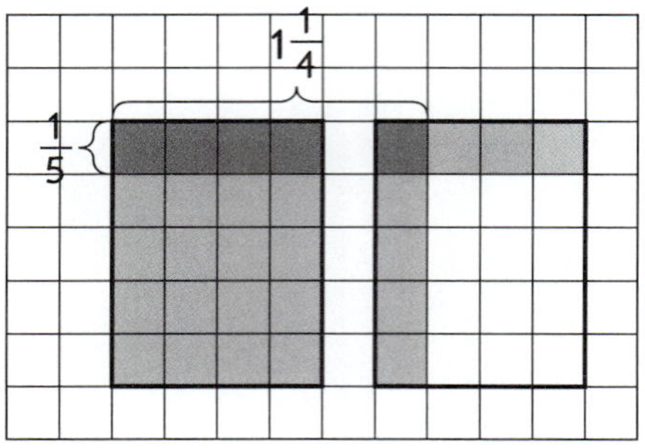

j.

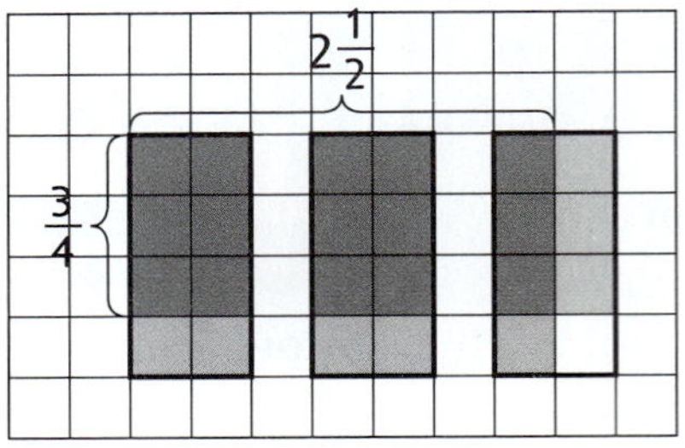

k.

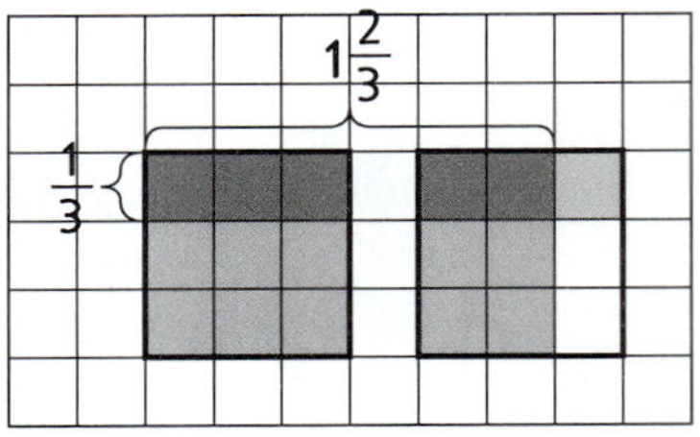

2. Sample answer: To multiply to fractions, multiply the numerators to get the numerator of the product and multiply the denominators to get the denominator of the product.

Page 252, Lesson 5-5 (Get Ready for the Lesson)

2. Sample answer: 2 is the part of the whole, 3, of the students that chose hamburgers. 1 is the part of the whole, 2, of the students that chose cheese on hamburgers.

Page 268, Lesson 5-7

33.

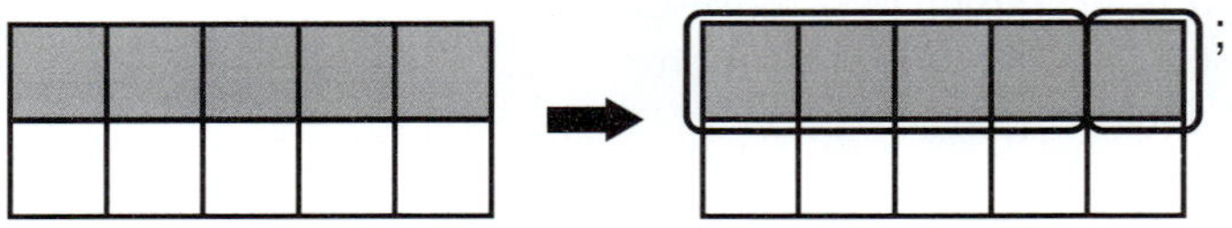

Sample answer: The model on the left shows that one half of a rectangle with ten sections is five sections. Two fifths of ten sections is four sections. The model on the right shows those five sections divided into $1\frac{1}{4}$ groups of four sections.

34.

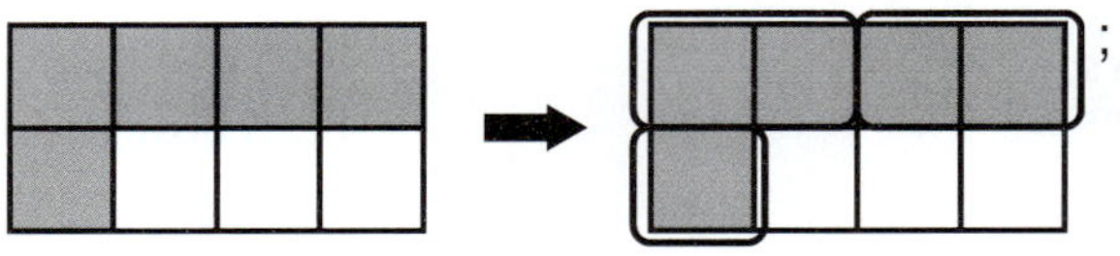

Sample answer: The model on the left shows that five eighths of a rectangle with eight sections is five sections. One fourth of eight sections is two sections. The model on the right shows those five sections divided into $2\frac{1}{2}$ groups of two sections.

35.

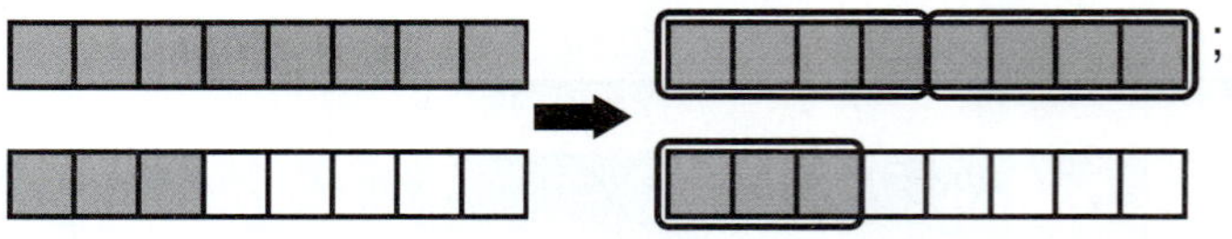

Sample answer: The model on the left shows that one and three eighths of a rectangle with eight sections is eleven sections. One half of eight sections is four sections. The model on the right shows those eleven sections divided into $2\frac{3}{4}$ groups of four sections.

36. 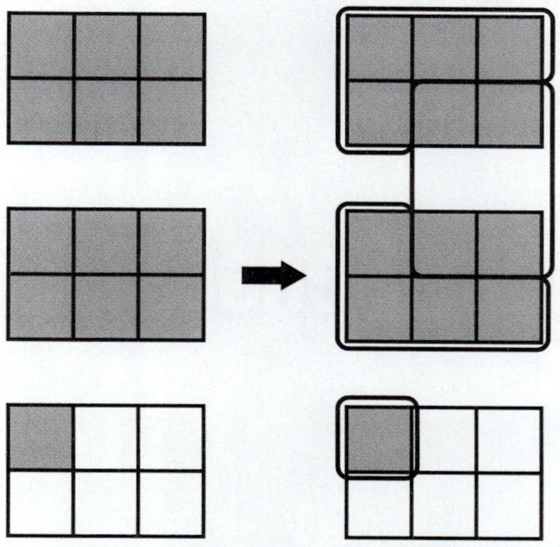

Sample answer: The model on the left shows that two and one sixth of a rectangle with six sections is thirteen sections. Two thirds of six sections is four sections. The model on the right shows those thirteen sections divided into $3\frac{1}{4}$ groups of four sections.

Unit 3 Notes

Introduction

In this unit, students will examine ratios and rates and solve proportions. They will make and interpret scale drawings and convert among fractions, decimals, and percents. In addition, they will use a percent proportion to calculate percent of change, sales tax, discounts, and simple interest, estimate percents, and use statistics to make predictions.

Assessment Options

Unit 3 Test Pages 81–82 of the *Chapter 7 Resource Masters* may be used as a test or a review for Unit 3. This assessment contains both multiple-choice and short-response items.

ExamView® Assessment Suite

Create additional customized Unit Tests and review worksheets for differentiated instruction.

Unit 3

Algebra and Number Sense: Proportions and Percents

Focus

Develop an understanding of and apply proportionality.

CHAPTER 6
Ratios and Proportions

BIG Idea Use ratio and proportionality to solve problems, including those with tables and graphs.

CHAPTER 7
Applying Percents

BIG Idea Solve percent problems using ratios and proportions.

278

What's MATH Got To Do With It? DVD

Real-Life Math Videos engage students, showing them how math is used in everyday situations. Use Video 3 with this unit to discuss how percents and proportions are used in wildlife management and shopping (also available on one Super DVD combined with MindJogger Videoquizzes).

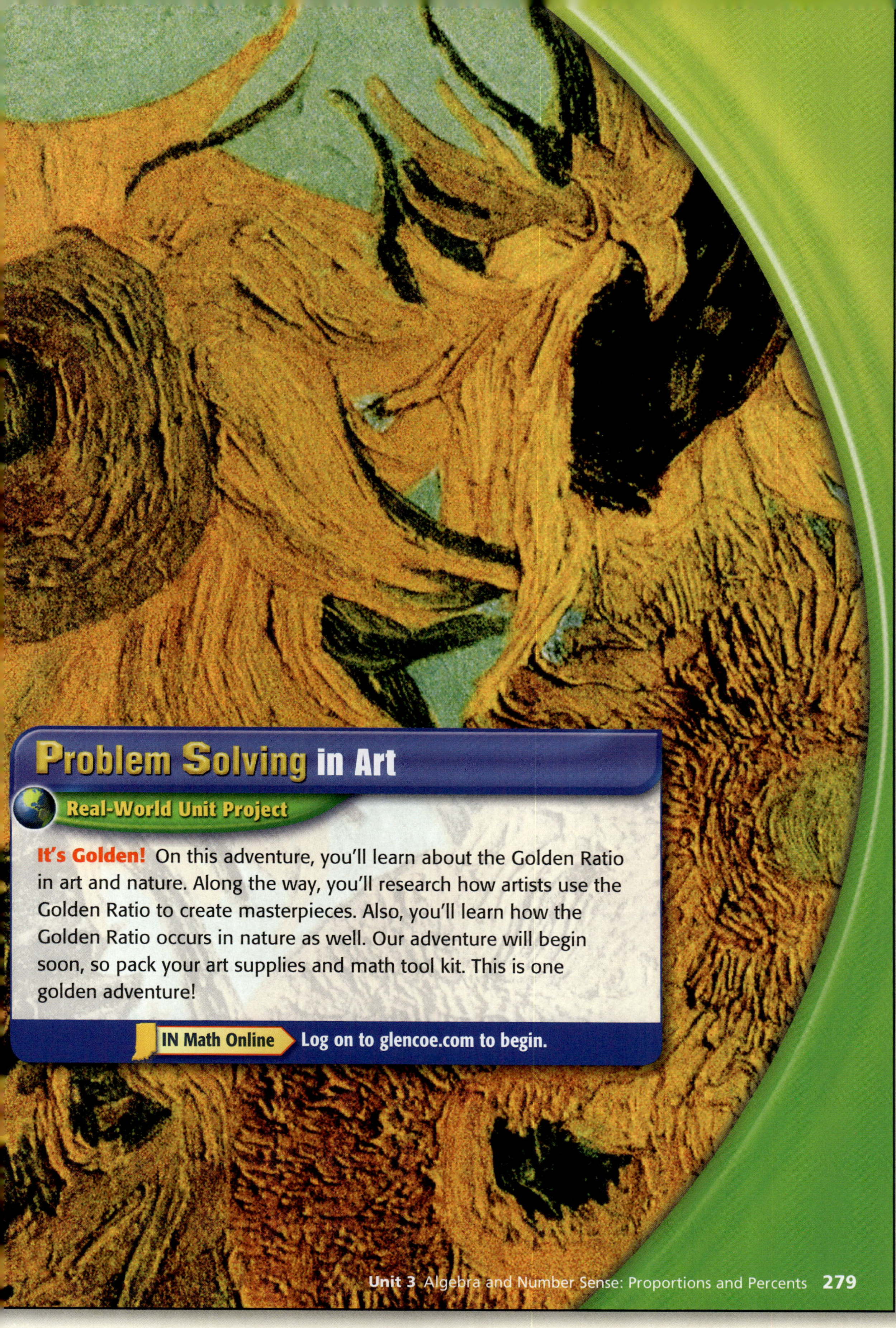

Problem Solving in Art

Real-World Unit Project

It's Golden! On this adventure, you'll learn about the Golden Ratio in art and nature. Along the way, you'll research how artists use the Golden Ratio to create masterpieces. Also, you'll learn how the Golden Ratio occurs in nature as well. Our adventure will begin soon, so pack your art supplies and math tool kit. This is one golden adventure!

IN Math Online Log on to glencoe.com to begin.

Real-World Unit Project
Problem Solving in Art

It's Golden!
This cross-curricular project is an interactive project in which students do research on the Internet or in the library, gather data, and make presentations using word processing, graphing, pagemaking, or presentation software. In each chapter, students advance to the next step in the project. At the end of Chapter 7, the project culminates with a presentation of their findings.

IN Math Online

glencoe.com Log on for teaching suggestions and sample answers for this project.

Team Teaching You can use this project with your students' art teacher to make the connection from mathematics to ideas of the Golden Ratio in art the students are investigating.

More Cross-Curricular Connections

You may wish to share these suggestions with your students' other teachers.

Math and Science

Research the Golden Ratio and where it is found in nature. What effect does the Golden Ratio have on objects in nature?

Math and Art

Create an art project that uses the Golden Ratio. Include an explanation as to where you used it and how it enhanced your artwork.

CHAPTER 6

Chapter Overview

Ratios and Proportions

Lesson Plan		Pacing Your Lessons	
LESSONS AND OBJECTIVES	**Academic Standards**	**45–50 Minute Periods**	**90-Minute Periods**
6-1 Ratios (pp. 282–286) • Write ratios as fractions in simplest form, and determine whether two ratios are equivalent.	7.1.9 (Core Lesson)	1	0.5
6-2 Rates (pp. 287–292) • Determine unit rates.	7.1.9 (Core Lesson)	1.5	1
6-3 Rate of Change and Slope (pp. 293–297) • Identify rate of change and slope using tables and graphs.	7.2.5, 7.2.6 (Core Lesson)	2	1
6-4 Measurement: Changing Customary Units (pp. 298–303) • Change units in the customary system.	8.3.4, 7.3.6 (Core Lesson)	1	0.5
6-5 Measurement: Changing Metric Units (pp. 304–309) • Change units of length, capacity, and mass.	8.3.4, 7.3.6 (Core Lesson)	1	0.5
6-6 Algebra: Solving Proportions (pp. 310–315) • Solve proportions. **Extend 6-6 Math Lab: Inverse Proportionality** (p. 316) • Graph inverse variations.	7.1.9, 7.2.7 (Core Lesson)	2	1
6-7 Problem-Solving Investigation: Draw a Diagram (pp. 318–319) • Solve problems by drawing a diagram.	P.1.3, P.5.1 (Core Lesson)	1	0.5
6-8 Scale Drawings (pp. 320–326) • Solve problems involving scale drawings. **Extend 6-8 Spreadsheet Lab: Scale Drawings** (p. 327) • Use a spreadsheet to calculate measurements for scale drawings.	7.3.5 (Core Lesson)	1.5	1
6-9 Fractions, Decimals, and Percents (pp. 328–332) • Write percents as fractions and decimals, and vice versa.	7.1.6	1	0.5
REVIEW		1	0.5
ASSESSMENT		1	0.5*
	TOTAL	**14**	**7.5**

*The complete **Assessment Planner** for Chapter 6 is provided on page 281.*

** Begin Chapter 7 in the second half of the period.*

Focal Points

G7-FP1 Number and Operations
For the complete wording of the Focal Points for Grade 7, please see page T17.

Professional Development

Vertical Alignment

Before Chapter 6

Related Topics from Grade 6

- compute and perform simple multiplication and division of fractions and apply these procedures to solving problems
- differentiate between and use appropriate units of measures for two- and three-dimensional objects
- interpret percents as a part of a hundred; find decimal and percent equivalents for common fractions and explain why they represent the same value; compute a given percent of a whole number

Chapter 6

Topics from Grade 7

- interpret and use ratios in different contexts to show the relative sizes of two quantities, using appropriate notations
- use proportions to solve problems. Use cross-multiplication as a method for solving such problems, understanding it as the multiplication of both sides of an equation by a multiplicative inverse
- convert one unit of measurement to another
- demonstrate an understanding that rate is a measure of one quantity per unit value of another quantity
- solve problems involving rates

After Chapter 6

Preparation for Grade 8

- solve multistep problems involving rate, average speed, distance, and time or a direct variation
- construct and read drawings and models made to scale

Backmapping and Vertical Alignment

McGraw-Hill's ***Math Connects*** program was conceived and developed with the final results in mind: student success in Algebra I and beyond. The authors, using the **NCTM Focal Points and Focal Connections** as their guide, developed this brand-new series by backmapping from Algebra 1 concepts and vertically aligning the topics so that they build upon prior skills and concepts and serve as a foundation for future topics.

What the Research Says...

According to Lamon in "Ratio and Proportion: Connecting Content and Children's Thinking," which appeared in *Journal for Research in Mathematics Education*, the concept of *unit rate* is useful to students in solving problems involving proportions.

- Lesson 6-2 introduces unit rate. This concept helps students solve problems involving proportions in Lesson 6-6.

Professional Development

Targeted professional development has been articulated throughout **McGraw-Hill's *Math Connects*** program. The **McGraw-Hill Professional Development Video Library** provides short videos that support the NCTM Focal Points and Focal Connections. For more information, visit glencoe.com.

Model Lessons

Instructional Strategies

Technology Solutions

CHAPTER 6

Teacher Resources

TeacherWorks™ All-in-One Planner and Resource Center

All of the print materials from the Classroom Resource Masters are available on your TeacherWorks™ CD-ROM.

BL = Below or Approaching Grade Level OL = On Grade Level AL = Above or Beyond Grade Level ELL = English Language Learner

				Chapter Resource Masters	6-1	6-2	6-3	6-4	6-5	6-6	6-7	6-8	6-9
BL	OL		ELL	Lesson Reading Guide	9	15	21	27	33	39		50	57
BL	OL		ELL	Study Guide and Intervention*	10	16	22	28	34	40	46	51	58
BL	OL			Skills Practice*	11	17	23	29	35	41	47	52	59
	OL	AL		Practice*	12	18	24	30	36	42	48	53	60
	OL	AL		Word Problem Practice*	13	19	25	31	37	43	49	54	61
	OL	AL		Enrichment	14	20	26	32	38	44		55	62
	OL	AL		Calculator and Spreadsheet Activities						45		56	63
	OL	AL		Chapter Assessments*	65–86								
BL	OL	AL		5-Minute Check Transparencies	✓	✓	✓	✓	✓	✓	✓	✓	✓
BL	OL			Teaching Mathematics with Manipulatives	✓	✓			✓		✓		
BL	OL	AL		Real-World Investigations for Differentiated Instruction	pp. 41–38, 49–52								

**Also available in Spanish.*

Graphing Calculator Easy Files

Timesaving Tech Tools for the TI-Navigator:

- **Quick Checks** to diagnose student progress
- Motivate students with **Concept Launchers**
- Deliver differentiated instruction with **Ready Files**
- **Vocabulary Review**

AssignmentWorks

Differentiated Assignments, Answers, and Solutions

- Print a customized assignment worksheet using the Student Edition exercises along with an answer key or worked-out solutions.
- Use default lesson assignments as outlined in the Differentiated Homework Options in the Teacher Edition.

Interactive Classroom

This CD-ROM is a customizable Microsoft® PowerPoint® presentation that includes:

- In-Class Examples
- Your Turn Exercises
- 5-Minute Check Transparencies
- Links to Online Study Tools
- Concepts in Motion
- Compatible with response pad technology

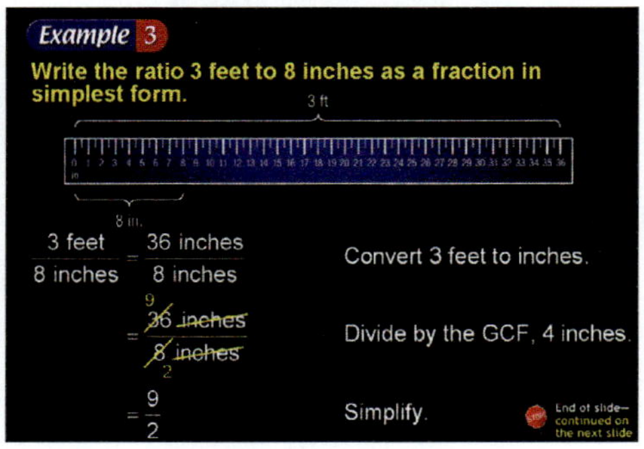

ExamView® Assessment Suite

ExamView® Assessment Suite

- Create, edit, and customize tests and worksheets
- Create multiple versions
- Translate from English to Spanish and vice versa
- Build tests aligned with your state standards

Student Tools

StudentWorks™ Plus

Textbook, Audio, Workbooks, and more

This CD-ROM is a valuable resource for students to access content online and use online resources to continue learning Chapter 6 concepts. Includes:

- Complete Student Editions in both English and Spanish
- English audio integrated throughout the text
- Links to Concepts in Motion, Personal Tutor, and other online resources
- Access to all student worksheets
- Daily Assignments and Grade Log

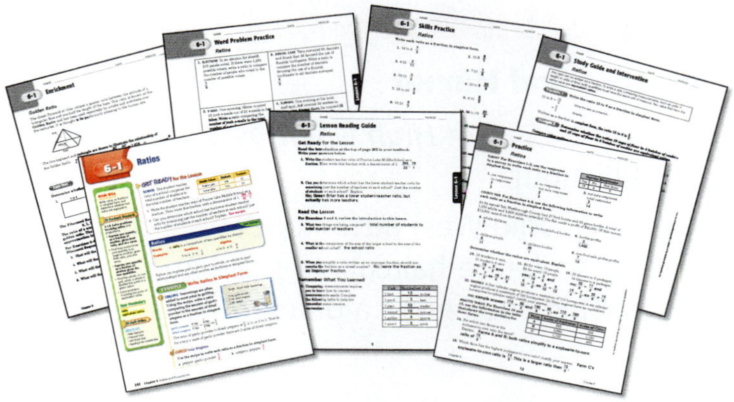

Super DVD

The Super DVD contains two Glencoe multimedia products.

MindJogger Plus An alternative review of concepts in which students work as teams in a game show format to gain points for correct answers.

What's Math Got to Do With It? Real-Life Math Videos
Engaging video that shows students how math is used in everyday situations.

Internet Resources

IN Math Online glencoe.com

TEACHER	STUDENT	PARENT	Online Study Tools
	•	•	Online Student Edition
•	•	•	Multilingual Glossary
			Lesson Resources
	•	•	Extra Examples
	•	•	BrainPOPS
	•	•	Self-Check Quizzes
•	•	•	Concepts in Motion
	•	•	Other Calculator Keystrokes
	•	•	Real-World Careers
	•	•	Reading in the Content Area
•			Group Activity Cards
			Chapter Resources
	•	•	Family Letters and Activities
	•		Chapter Readiness Quiz
	•	•	Vocabulary Review
	•	•	Chapter Test
	•	•	Standardized Test Practice
			Unit Resources
•	•		WebQuest Project
			Other Resources
	•		Personal Tutor
•			NAEP Correlations
•			Key Concepts
•	•	•	Meet the Authors
•	•		Game Zone
•	•	•	Math Skills Maintenance
•			National Resources (Professional Organizations)
•			State Resources
•			Vocabulary PuzzleMakers

CHAPTER 6 Reading and Writing in Mathematics

Noteables™ Interactive Study Notebook with Foldables™

This workbook is a study organizer that provides helpful steps for students to follow to organize their notes for Chapter 6.

- Students use Noteables to record notes and to complete their Foldables as you present the material for each lesson.
- Noteables correspond to the Examples in the *Teacher Edition* and *Interactive Classroom CD-ROM.*

Real-World Problem Solving Graphic Novels

Mathematical problem solving is presented in a motivating, graphic novel format. The novels contain real-world problems for each of the following mathematical strands: Number Sense, Algebraic Thinking, Geometry, Measurement, Statistics and Probability, and Mathematical Reasoning.

READING in the Content Area

This online worksheet provides strategies for reading and analyzing Lesson 6-1, Ratios. Students are guided through questions about the main idea, subject matter, supporting details, conclusion, clarifying details, and vocabulary of the lesson.

glencoe.com

Recommended Outside Reading for Students

Mathematics and Humor

- *Cut Down to Size at High Noon* by Scott Sundby ©2000 [fiction]

This is a funny, Wild West adventure about two barbers who sculpture haircuts to scale in a showdown. This book gives a different look at scale drawings.

Project CRISS STUDY SKILL

A power map can help students organize and display their knowledge of a topic. Show students the sample power map at the right that deals with scale. Explain that the levels of detail in the map are represented by different geometric shapes. As students work through Chapter 6, ask them to think about some ways ratios can be used. Have them design a power map that illustrates what they learn.

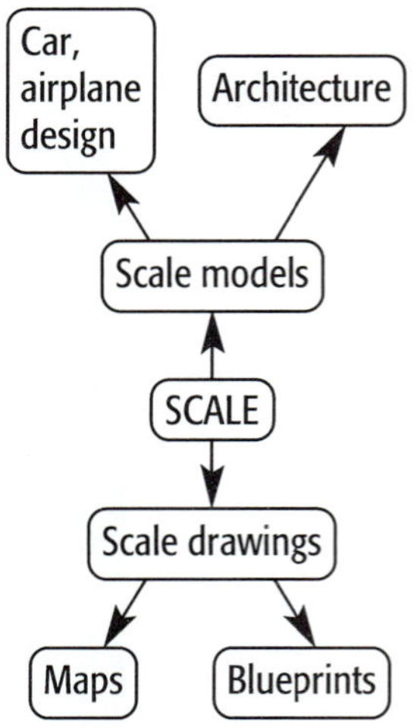

CR**e**ating **I**ndependence through **S**tudent-owned **S**trategies

Differentiated Instruction

Investigative Approach

MathScape™

This project was supported, in part, by the **National Science Foundation**

MathScape is a mathematics curriculum for grades 6–8 developed by the Seeing and Thinking Mathematically Project at the Education Development Center.

Rates, Ratios, Percents, and Proportions
Buyer Beware

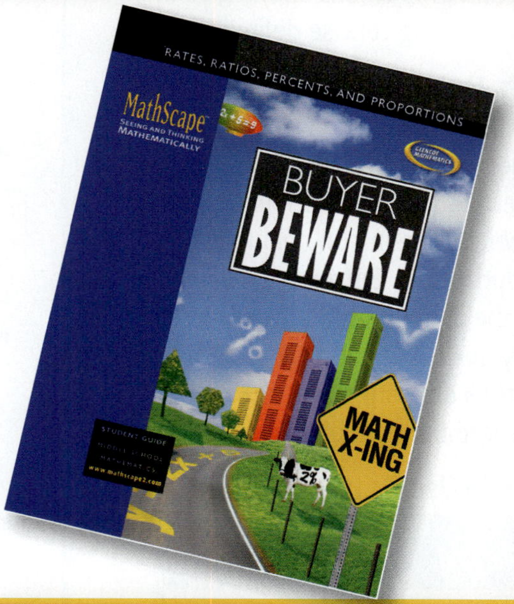

How to Use *MathScape* with Chapter 6

The unit *Buyer Beware* can be used to enhance Lessons 6-2 and 6-6.

- **Reinforce** → Before you complete **Lesson 6-2**, you can use the activities on pages 6–13 to provide additional practice with unit rate and better buys.
- **Introduce** → Before you begin **Lesson 6-6**, you can introduce proportions by using the activities on page 18–19.

RTI (Response to Intervention)

TIER 1 **On-Level Instruction** Use the *Math Connects* program as instruction for your on-level students.

TIER 2 **Strategic Intervention** For options to instruct struggling students, refer to the Diagnostic Assessment table on page 281.

TIER 3 **Intensive Intervention** *Math Triumphs* can provide intensive intervention for students who are two or more grade levels behind.

Diagnose student readiness with the Quick Check and Quick Review on page 281. Then use *Math Triumphs* to accelerate their achievement.

Ratios and Proportions

Prerequisite Skill	*Math Triumphs*
Ratios and Rates	Ch. 2
Customary and Metric Measurement Systems	Ch. 5

Practice and Review

Quick Review Math Handbook* is Glencoe's mathematical handbook for students and parents.

Hot Words includes a glossary of terms.

Hot Topics consists of two parts:

- explanations of key mathematical concepts
- exercises to check students' understanding.

Lesson	Hot Topics Section	Lesson	Hot Topics Section
6-1	6•5	6-5	8•1
6-2	6•5	6-6	6•5
6-3	6•8	6-8	6•5, 8•6
6-4	8•1	6-9	2•7, 2•9

**Also available in Spanish*

Chapter 6 Notes

FOLDABLES Study Organizer — Dinah Zike's Foldables

Focus This Foldable is designed to help students organize their notes about ratios and proportions and to give them practice writing concise definitions.

Teach Have students make their Foldables and label the tabs. Explain to students that they should select one term or concept from each lesson and write its definition behind the appropriate tab. Encourage students to write the definitions in their own words. Finally, have students give an example or draw a diagram of the term or concept to the right of its definition.

When to Use It

Tab	Use with Lesson(s)
Ratios	6-1, 6-6, 6-7
Rates	6-2
Slope and Rate of Change	6-3
Customary/ Metric Units	6-4, 6-5
Proportions	6-6, 6-7
Scale	6-8, Extend 6-8
Fractions, Decimals, and Percents	6-9

Differentiated Instruction

CRM Student-Built Glossary, p. 1

Students complete the chart by providing a definition for each term and an example as they progress through Chapter 6.

This study tool can be used to review for the chapter test.

Chapter 6 Ratios and Proportions

Indiana Academic Standards

7.1.9 Solve problems involving ratios and proportions. **7.2.5** Find the slope of a line from its graph and relate the slope of a line to similar triangles.

Key Vocabulary

rate (p. 287)
ratio (p. 282)
proportional (p. 310)

Real-World Link

Statues A bronze replica of the Statue of Liberty can be found in Paris, France. The replica has the ratio 1 : 4 with the Statue of Liberty that stands in New York Harbor.

FOLDABLES Study Organizer

Ratios and Proportions Make this Foldable to help you organize your notes. Begin with a sheet of notebook paper.

1. **Fold** lengthwise to the holes.

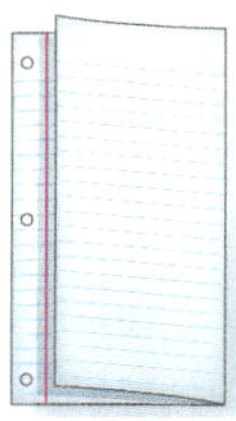

2. **Cut** along the top line and then make equal cuts to form 7 tabs.

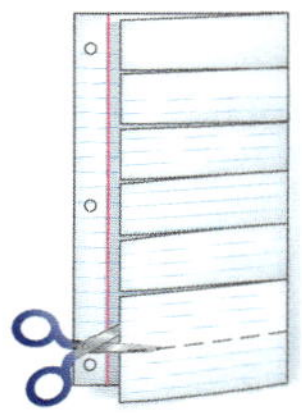

3. **Label** the major topics as shown.

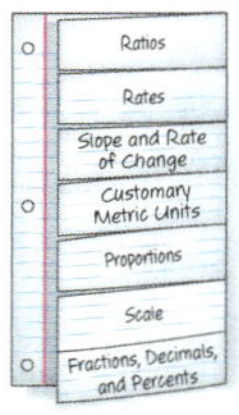

Materials Needed for Chapter 6

- measuring tapes (Lesson 6-8)
- rulers (Lesson 6-8)
- $\frac{1}{4}$-inch grid paper (Lessons 6-4, 6-8, and 6-9)
- colored pencils (Lesson 6-9)
- computer spreadsheet program (Extend 6-8)

GET READY for Chapter 6

Diagnose Readiness You have two options for checking Prerequisite Skills.

Option 2

IN Math Online Take the Online Readiness Quiz at glencoe.com.

Option 1

Take the Quick Quiz below. Refer to the Quick Review for help.

QUICK Quiz

(Used in Lessons 6-2, 6-5, and 6-7)

Evaluate each expression. Round to the nearest tenth if necessary. (Lesson 1-4)

1. $100 \times 25 \div 52$ **48.1**
2. $10 \div 4 \times 31$ **77.5**
3. $\frac{63 \times 4}{34}$ **7.4**
4. $\frac{2 \times 100}{68}$ **2.9**

(Used in Lessons 6-1 through 6-4, 6-7, 6-8)

Write each fraction in simplest form. (Lesson 4-4)

5. $\frac{9}{45}$ **$\frac{1}{5}$**
6. $\frac{16}{24}$ **$\frac{2}{3}$**
7. $\frac{38}{46}$ **$\frac{19}{23}$**
8. **AGES** Mikhail is 14 years old. His father is 49 years old. What fraction, in simplest form, of his father's age is Mikhail? (Lesson 4-4) **$\frac{2}{7}$**

(Used in Lesson 6-8)

Write each decimal as a fraction in simplest form. (Lesson 4-5)

9. 0.78 **$\frac{39}{50}$**
10. 0.320 **$\frac{8}{25}$**
11. 0.06 **$\frac{3}{50}$**
12. **SAVINGS** Belinda has saved 0.92 of the cost of a new bicycle. What fraction, in simplest form, represents her savings? (Lesson 4-5) **$\frac{23}{25}$**

(Used in Lesson 6-4)

Multiply. (Lesson 1-2)

13. 4.5×10^2 **450**
14. 1.78×10^3 **1,780**
15. 0.22×10^4 **2,200**
16. 0.03×10^5 **3,000**

QUICK Review

Example 1 Evaluate $15 \times 32 \div 40$.

$15 \times 32 \div 40 = 480 \div 40$ Multiply 15 by 32.

$= 12$ Divide.

Example 2 Write $\frac{16}{44}$ in simplest form.

$\frac{16}{44} = \frac{4}{11}$ (÷ 4 numerator and denominator) Divide the numerator and denominator by their GCF, 4.

Example 3 Write 0.62 as a fraction in simplest form.

$0.62 = \frac{62}{100}$ 0.62 is sixty-two hundredths.

$= \frac{31}{50}$ Divide the numerator and denominator by their GCF, 2.

Example 4 Find 3.9×10^3.

$3.9 \times 10^3 = 3.900$ Move the decimal point 3 places to the right. Annex two zeros.

$= 3{,}900$

Diagnostic Assessment

Exercises	Academic Standards	Strategic Intervention
1–4	7.1.9	SE Review Lesson 1-4, pp. 38–41
5–8	7.1.9	SE Review Lesson 4-4, pp. 192–195
9–12	7.3.5	SE Review Lesson 4-5, pp. 196–200
13–16	8.3.4	*Math Skill Maintenance Masters*, p. 76

ASSESSMENT PLANNER CHAPTER 6

Formative Assessment

CRM Anticipation Guide, p. 7–8

Spotting Preconceived Ideas

Students complete this survey to determine prior knowledge about ideas from Chapter 6. Revisit this worksheet after completing the chapter. Also see page 336.

TE Lesson Activities

- Ticket Out the Door, p. 303
- Crystal Ball, p. 319
- Name the Math, pp. 286, 309, 326
- Yesterday's News, pp. 292, 315

Chapter Checkpoints

SE Mid-Chapter Quiz, p. 317

SE Study Guide and Review, pp. 333–336

SE Test Practice, pp. 338–339

CRM Quizzes, pp. 67 and 68

CRM Standardized Test Practice, pp. 84–86

IN Math Online glencoe.com

- Self-Check Quizzes
- Practice Test
- Test Practice

Summative Assessment

SE Chapter Practice Test, p. 337

CRM Mid-Chapter Test, p. 69

CRM Vocabulary Test, p. 70

CRM Extended-Response Test, p. 83

CRM Leveled Chapter Tests, pp. 71–82

CD-ROM ExamView® Assessment Suite

KEY

CRM *Chapter 6 Resource Masters*

SE Student Edition

TE Teacher Edition

CD-ROM

6-1 Ratios

PACING: **Regular:** 1 period, **Block:** 0.5 period

IN Academic Standards

7.1.9 Solve problems involving ratios and proportions.
- Express one quantity as a fraction of another, given their ratio, and vice versa.
- Find how many times one quantity is as large as another, given their ratio, and vice versa.
- **Express one quantity as a fraction of another given the two quantities.**
- Find the whole, or one part, when a whole is divided into parts in a given ratio.
- Solve problems involving two pairs of equivalent ratios.

Options for Differentiated Instruction

ELL = English Language Learner   AL = Above or Beyond Grade Level   SS = Struggling Students   SN = Special Needs

Collecting Data ELL SS SN

Use after presenting the Lesson Opener.

Have students collect data to find the student-teacher ratios for their school. Suggest that they compile their data in a table like the one shown at the right.

	Number of Students	Number of Teachers
In the Classroom		
In the School		

Ask:
- What is the student-teacher ratio in the classroom?
- What is the student-teacher ratio in the school?
- Can the ratios be written as whole numbers? If not, what does that mean?

Real-World Applications ELL AL

Use before presenting Example 1.

Arrange students in small groups and have them make lists of how ratios are used in their daily lives. If students have trouble getting started, suggest the following applications:
- paper or photograph sizes
- playing fields
- room dimensions
- data given in news polls

Have them discuss the specific ratios involved, if they know them, as well as the importance of the ratios they mention.

Organizing Student Work and Thinking ELL SN

Use before assigning the Exercises.

Suggest to students that they use tables to organize the data for a given problem. A table for Exercise 38 is shown below.

Total Number of Students	24
Number of Boys	15
Number of Girls	

Using a table like this will help students to see that they need to find the number of girls before finding the ratio of girls to boys.

Leveled Lesson Resources

Also on TeacherWorks™ Lesson 6-1

Chapter 6 Resource Masters

BL = Below or Approaching Grade Level OL = On Grade Level AL = Above or Beyond Grade Level ELL = English Language Learner

Lesson Reading Guide
p. 9 BL OL ELL

NAME ____________ DATE ________ PERIOD ____

6-1 Lesson Reading Guide

Ratios

Get Ready for the Lesson

Read the introduction at the top of page 282 in your textbook. Write your answers below.

1. Write the student-teacher ratio of Prairie Lake Middle School as a fraction. Then write this fraction with a denominator of 1. **$\frac{396}{22}$, $\frac{18}{1}$**

2. Can you determine which school has the lower student-teacher ratio by examining just the number of teachers at each school? Just the number of students at each school? Explain. **No; Green Briar has a lower student-teacher ratio, but actually has more teachers.**

Lesson 6–1

Read the Lesson

For Exercises 3 and 4, review the introduction to this lesson.

3. What two things are being compared? **total number of students to total number of teachers**

4. What is the comparison of the size of the larger school to the size of the smaller school called? **the school ratio**

5. When you simplify a ratio written as an improper fraction, should you rewrite the fraction as a mixed number? **No; leave the fraction as an improper fraction.**

Remember What You Learned

6. Comparing measurements requires you to know how to convert measurements easily. Complete the following table to help you remember some common conversions.

Unit	Equivalent Unit
1 foot	12 inches
1 yard	3 feet
1 year	52 weeks
1 pound	16 ounces
1 gallon	4 quarts
1 quart	2 pints

Chapter 6 9 Course 2

Study Guide and Intervention*
p. 10 BL OL ELL

NAME ____________ DATE ________ PERIOD ____

6-1 Study Guide and Intervention

Ratios

Any ratio can be written as a fraction. To write a ratio comparing measurements, such as units of length or units of time, both quantities must have the same unit of measure. Two ratios that have the same value are **equivalent ratios**.

Example 1 **Write the ratio 15 to 9 as a fraction in simplest form.**

$15 \text{ to } 9 = \frac{15}{9}$ Write the ratio as a fraction.

$= \frac{5}{3}$ Simplify.

Written as a fraction in simplest form, the ratio 15 to 9 is $\frac{5}{3}$.

Example 2 **Determine whether the ratios *10 cups of flour in 4 batches of cookies* and *15 cups of flour in 6 batches of cookies* are equivalent ratios.**

Compare ratios written in simplest form.

10 cups:4 batches $= \frac{10 \div 2}{4 \div 2}$ or $\frac{5}{2}$ Divide the numerator and denominator by the GCF, 2

15 cups:6 batches $= \frac{15 \div 3}{6 \div 3}$ or $\frac{5}{2}$ Divide the numerator and denominator by the GCF, 3

Since the ratios simplify to the same fraction, the ratios of cups to batches are equivalent.

Exercises

Write each ratio as a fraction in simplest form.

1. 30 to 12 **$\frac{5}{2}$**
2. 5:20 **$\frac{1}{4}$**
3. 49:42 **$\frac{7}{6}$**
4. 15 to 13 **$\frac{15}{13}$**
5. 28 feet:35 feet **$\frac{4}{5}$**
6. 24 minutes to 18 minutes **$\frac{4}{3}$**
7. 75 seconds:150 seconds **$\frac{1}{2}$**
8. 12 feet:60 feet **$\frac{1}{5}$**

Determine whether the ratios are equivalent. Explain.

9. $\frac{3}{4}$ and $\frac{12}{16}$ **yes; $\frac{3}{4} = \frac{12}{16}$**
10. 12:17 and 10:15 **no; $12:17 = \frac{12}{17}$, $10:15 = \frac{2}{3}$, and $\frac{12}{17} \neq \frac{2}{3}$**
11. $\frac{25}{35}$ and $\frac{10}{14}$ **yes; $\frac{25}{35} = \frac{5}{7}$ and $\frac{10}{14} = \frac{5}{7}$**
12. 2 lb:36 oz and 3 lb:44 oz **no; 2 lb:36 oz $= \frac{8}{9}$, 3 lb:44 oz $= \frac{12}{11}$, and $\frac{8}{9} \neq \frac{12}{11}$**
13. 1 ft:4 in. and 3 ft:12 in. **yes; 1 ft:4 in. $= \frac{3}{1}$ and 3 ft:12 in. $= \frac{3}{1}$**

Chapter 6 10 Course 2

Skills Practice*
p. 11 BL OL

NAME ____________ DATE ________ PERIOD ____

6-1 Skills Practice

Ratios

Write each ratio as a fraction in simplest form.

1. 14 to 6 **$\frac{7}{3}$**
2. 18:3 **$\frac{6}{1}$**
3. 4:22 **$\frac{2}{11}$**
4. 7:21 **$\frac{1}{3}$**
5. 18:12 **$\frac{3}{2}$**
6. 20 to 9 **$\frac{20}{9}$**
7. 25 to 20 **$\frac{5}{4}$**
8. 4:10 **$\frac{2}{5}$**
9. 18:21 **$\frac{6}{7}$**
10. 84 to 16 **$\frac{21}{4}$**
11. 33 ounces to 11 ounces **$\frac{3}{1}$**
12. 45 minutes:25 minutes **$\frac{9}{5}$**
13. 77 cups:49 cups **$\frac{11}{7}$**
14. 15 pounds to 39 pounds **$\frac{5}{13}$**
15. 40 seconds to 60 seconds **$\frac{2}{3}$**
16. 140 centimeters to 300 centimeters **$\frac{7}{15}$**
17. 9 weeks: 15 weeks **$\frac{3}{5}$**
18. 3 yards to 33 yards **$\frac{1}{11}$**

Lesson 6–1

Determine whether the ratios are equivalent. Explain.

19. $\frac{3}{16}$ and $\frac{9}{48}$ **yes; $\frac{3}{16} = \frac{9}{48}$**
20. $\frac{7}{10}$ and $\frac{8}{11}$ **no; $\frac{7}{10} \neq \frac{8}{11}$**
21. 18 in.:3 ft and 12 in.:2 ft **yes; 18 in.:3 ft $= \frac{1}{2}$ and 12 in.:2 ft $= \frac{1}{2}$**
22. 6 mos:2 yr and 8 mos:3 yr **no; 6 mos:2 yr $= \frac{1}{4}$, 8 mos:3 yr $= \frac{2}{9}$, and $\frac{1}{4} \neq \frac{2}{9}$**

Chapter 6 11 Course 2

Practice*
p. 12 OL AL

NAME ____________ DATE ________ PERIOD ____

6-1 Practice

Ratios

SURVEY **For Exercises 1–3, use the responses to a survey to write each ratio as a fraction in simplest form.**

Survey Responses		
Yes	No	Not Sure
18	4	6

1. *yes* responses: *no* responses **$\frac{9}{2}$**
2. *no* responses: *not sure* responses **$\frac{2}{3}$**
3. *not sure* responses: total responses **$\frac{3}{14}$**

COUNTY FAIR **For Exercises 4–9, use the following information to write each ratio as a fraction in simplest form.**

At its annual fair, Westborough County had 27 food booths and 63 game booths. A total of 1,350 adults and 3,600 children attended. The fair made a profit of $42,000. Of this money, $12,600 came from food sales.

4. adults:children **$\frac{3}{8}$**
5. game booths:food booths **$\frac{7}{3}$**
6. booths:profits **$\frac{3}{1,400}$**
7. children:people **$\frac{8}{11}$**
8. children:booths **$\frac{40}{1}$**
9. non-food sale profits:profits **$\frac{7}{10}$**

Determine whether the ratios are equivalent. Explain.

10. 18 trucks to 4 cars, 21 trucks to 6 cars **no; $\frac{18}{4} = \frac{9}{2}$ and $\frac{21}{6} = \frac{7}{2}$, so $\frac{18}{4} \neq \frac{21}{6}$**
11. $6 for every 10 people, $9 for every 15 people **yes; $\frac{6}{10} = \frac{3}{5}$ and $\frac{9}{15} = \frac{3}{5}$, so $\frac{6}{10} = \frac{9}{15}$**
12. 33 dinners to 6 packages, 14 dinners to 4 packages **no; $\frac{33}{6} = \frac{11}{2}$ and $\frac{14}{4} = \frac{7}{2}$, so $\frac{33}{6} \neq \frac{14}{4}$**

13. ENGINES A four cylinder engine produces a maximum of 110 horsepower. A six cylinder engine produces a maximum of 180 horsepower. Do these engines have an equivalent horsepower-to-cylinder ratio? Justify your answer. **no; sample answer: $\frac{110}{4} = \frac{55}{2}$ and $\frac{180}{6} = \frac{30}{1}$, so $\frac{110}{4} \neq \frac{180}{6}$**

ANALYZE TABLES **For Exercises 14 and 15, use the information in the table that shows the crop statistics for three farms.**

Farm	Acres of Soybeans	Acres of Corn
A	585	225
B	2,990	1,150
C	1,120	400

14. For which two farms is the soybeans-to-corn ratio the same? Explain. **Farms A and B; both ratios simplify to a soybeans-to-corn ratio of $\frac{13}{5}$.**

15. Which farm has the highest soybeans-to-corn ratio? Justify your answer. **Farm C's soybeans-to-corn ratio is $\frac{14}{5}$. This is a larger ratio than $\frac{13}{5}$.**

Chapter 6 12 Course 2

Word Problem Practice*
p. 13 OL AL

NAME ____________ DATE ________ PERIOD ____

6-1 Word Problem Practice

Ratios

1. ELECTIONS In an election for sheriff, 210 people voted. If there were 1,260 possible voters, write a ratio to compare the number of people who voted to the number of possible voters. **$\frac{1}{6}$**

2. DENTAL CARE Taru surveyed 60 dentists and found that 48 favored the use of fluoride toothpaste. Write a ratio to compare the number of dentists favoring the use of a flouride toothpaste to all dentists surveyed. **$\frac{4}{5}$**

3. E-MAIL One morning, Mirna counted 15 junk e-mails out of 21 e-mails in her inbox. Write a ratio comparing the number of junk e-mails to the total number of e-mails. **$\frac{5}{7}$**

4. SURFING One evening at his local surf spot, Jeff counted 28 surfers in the water. Among those, he counted 21 that had hoods on their wetsuits. Write a ratio comparing the number of surfers with hoods to the total number of surfers. **$\frac{3}{4}$**

5. MUSIC A music company signed 12 new artists to its label in 2002. Out of the 12, 10 artists have hit songs. Write a ratio to compare the number of artists with hit songs to the total number of artists signed in 2002. **$\frac{5}{6}$**

6. BASEBALL Nate had 26 hits at 50 times at bat last season. Write a ratio to compare the number of hits to the number of times at bat. **$\frac{13}{25}$**

7. BASEBALL In baseball, David has 10 hits out of 14 at bats. Adam has 15 hits out of 21 at bats. For each player, write a ratio that represents his total number of hits out of times at bat. Are these ratios equivalent? **10:14 and 15:21; yes**

8. DRIVING Sarah can drive 198 miles on 11 gallons of gasoline. On 6 gallons of gasoline, Rachel can travel 138 miles. Write a ratio that compares miles traveled per gallon of gasoline for each car. Do the cars get the same mileage? **198:11 and 138:6; no**

Lesson 6–1

Chapter 6 13 Course 2

Enrichment
p. 14 OL AL

NAME ____________ DATE ________ PERIOD ____

6-1 Enrichment

Golden Ratio

The Great Pyramid at Giza utilizes a special ratio between the altitude of a triangular face and one-half the length of the base. This ratio is known as the **Golden Ratio** and has been used repeatedly by artists and architects over the centuries. It is thought to be particularly pleasing to the human eye.

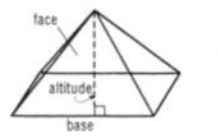

The line segment and rectangle are drawn to illustrate the relationship of the Golden Ratio.

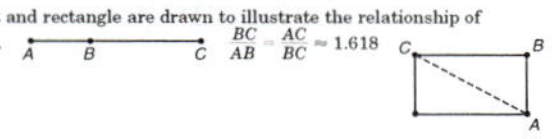

Exercises

Determine whether each rectangle demonstrates the Golden Ratio.

1. **yes**

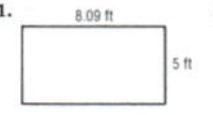

2. **no**

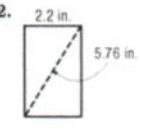

The Fibonacci Sequence, shown below, is related to the Golden Ratio.

0, 1, 1, 2, 3, 5, 8, 13, 21, …

The ratio of a number to the previous number approximates the golden ratio. The greater the numbers in the sequence, the closer the approximation is to the golden ratio.

For Exercises 3–6, use the Golden Ratio to determine numbers in the Fibonacci Sequence. Round each number to the nearest whole number.

3. What will the next five numbers be in the sequence? **34, 55, 89, 144, 233**
4. What will the next number be after 610? **987**
5. What will the next number be after 2,584? **4,181**
6. What will the next number be after 6,765? **10,946**

Chapter 6 14 Course 2

* *Also available in Spanish* ELL

Additional Lesson Resources

Transparencies

- *5-Minute Check Transparency*, Lesson 6-1

Other Print Products

- *Teaching Mathematics with Manipulatives*
- *Noteables™ Interactive Study Notebook with Foldables™*

Teacher Tech Tools

- *Interactive Classroom CD-ROM*, Lesson 6-1
- *AssignmentWorks*, Lesson 6-1

Student Tech Tools

glencoe.com

- Extra Examples, Chapter 6, Lesson 1
- Self-Check Quiz, Chapter 6, Lesson 1

6-1 Lesson Notes

1 Focus

Vertical Alignment

Before Lesson 6-1
Compute and perform simple multiplication and division of fractions and apply these procedures to solving problems

Lesson 6-1
Interpret and use ratios in different contexts to show the relative sizes of two quantities, using appropriate notations

After Lesson 6-1
Graph linear functions, noting that the vertical change per unit of horizontal change is always the same and know that the ratio is called the slope of the graph

2 Teach

Scaffolding Questions

As you ask the following questions, write each fraction or quantity on the board.

Ask:

- What is the fraction $\frac{15}{20}$ written in simplest form? $\frac{3}{4}$
- What is the fraction $\frac{8}{12}$ written in simplest form? $\frac{2}{3}$
- If I have 8 pennies and 12 nickels, what is my ratio of pennies to nickels? $\frac{8}{12}$, or $\frac{2}{3}$
- If my sister has 4 pennies and 6 nickels, what is her ratio of pennies to nickels? $\frac{4}{6}$, or $\frac{2}{3}$

6-1 Ratios

MAIN IDEA

Write ratios as fractions in simplest form and determine whether two ratios are equivalent.

IN Academic Standards

7.1.9 Solve problems involving ratios and proportions.

- **Express one quantity as a fraction of another, given their ratio, and vice versa.**
- Find how many times one quantity is as large as another, given their ratio, and vice versa.
- **Express one quantity as a fraction of another given the two quantities.**
- Find the whole, or one part, when a whole is divided into parts in a given ration.
- Solve problems involving two pairs of equivalent ratios.

New Vocabulary

ratio
equivalent ratios

IN Math Online

glencoe.com

- Extra Examples
- Personal Tutor
- Self-Check Quiz
- Reading in the Content Area

GET READY for the Lesson

SCHOOL The student-teacher ratio of a school compares the total number of students to the total number of teachers.

Middle School	Students	Teachers
Prairie Lake	396	22
Green Brier	510	30

1. Write the student-teacher ratio of Prairie Lake Middle School as a fraction. Then write this fraction with a denominator of 1. $\frac{396}{22}$; $\frac{18}{1}$
2. Can you determine which school has the lower student-teacher ratio by examining just the number of teachers at each school? just the number of students at each school? Explain. **See margin.**

Ratios — Key Concept

Words A **ratio** is a comparison of two quantities by division.

Examples	**Numbers**	**Algebra**
	3 to 4 3:4 $\frac{3}{4}$	a to b $a:b$ $\frac{a}{b}$

Ratios can express part to part, part to whole, or whole to part relationships and are often written as fractions in simplest form.

EXAMPLE Write Ratios in Simplest Form

1 GRILLING Seasonings are often added to meat prior to grilling. Using the recipe, write a ratio comparing the amount of garlic powder to the amount of dried oregano as a fraction in simplest form.

garlic powder / dried oregano $\frac{4 \text{ tsp}}{6 \text{ tsp}} = \frac{\cancel{4 \text{ tsp}}^{2}}{\cancel{6 \text{ tsp}}_{3}}$ or $\frac{2}{3}$

The ratio of garlic powder to dried oregano is $\frac{2}{3}$, 2:3, or 2 to 3. That is, for every 2 units of garlic powder there are 3 units of dried oregano.

CHECK Your Progress

Use the recipe to write each ratio as a fraction in simplest form.

a. pepper:garlic powder $\frac{1}{2}$ b. oregano:pepper $\frac{3}{1}$

Additional Answer

2. No; you need both the number of teachers and the number of students to determine the student-teacher ratio. Once the student-teacher ratio is determined for each school, the school with the lowest student-teacher ratio can be found. Green Brier Middle School has the lower student-teacher ratio with 17 students per teacher.

Ratios that express the same relationship between two quantities are called **equivalent ratios**. Equivalent ratios have the same value.

EXAMPLE Identify Equivalent Ratios

2 **Determine whether the ratios 250 miles in 4 hours and 500 miles in 8 hours are equivalent.**

METHOD 1 **Compare the ratios written in simplest form.**

250 miles : 4 hours $= \frac{250 \div 2}{4 \div 2}$ or $\frac{125}{2}$ Divide the numerator and denominator by the GCF, 2

500 miles : 8 hours $= \frac{500 \div 4}{8 \div 4}$ or $\frac{125}{2}$ Divide the numerator and denominator by the GCF, 4

The ratios simplify to the same fraction.

METHOD 2 **Look for a common multiplier relating the two ratios.**

$$\frac{250}{4} = \frac{500}{8} \quad (\times 2 \text{ numerator and denominator})$$

The numerator and denominator of the ratios are related by the same multiplier, 2.

The ratios are equivalent.

CHOOSE Your Method

Determine whether the ratios are equivalent.

c. 20 nails for every 5 shingles, 12 nails for every 3 shingles

d. 2 cups flour to 8 cups sugar, 8 cups flour to 14 cups sugar

Real-World EXAMPLE

3 **BASEBALL** **Derek Jeter of the New York Yankees had 32 hits out of 93 times at bat. Jorge Posada had 11 hits out of 31 times at bat. Are these ratios equivalent? Justify your answer.**

Derek Jeter	Jorge Posada
$32:93 = \frac{32}{93}$	$11:31 = \frac{11 \times 3}{31 \times 3}$ or $\frac{33}{93}$

Since $\frac{32}{93} \neq \frac{33}{93}$, the ratios are not equivalent.

CHECK Your Progress

e. **SWIMMING** A community pool requires there to be at least 3 lifeguards for every 20 swimmers. There are 60 swimmers and 9 lifeguards at the pool. Is this the correct number of lifeguards based on the above requirement? Justify your answer.

Study Tip

Writing Ratios Ratios greater than 1 are expressed as improper fractions and not as mixed numbers.

c. Yes; $\frac{20}{5} = \frac{4}{1}$ and $\frac{12}{3} = \frac{4}{1}$, so $\frac{20}{5} = \frac{12}{3}$.

d. No; $\frac{2}{8} \neq \frac{8}{14}$ since $2 \cdot 4 = 8$, but $8 \cdot 4 \neq 14$.

e. Yes; sample answer: $3:20 = \frac{3}{20}$ and $9:60 = \frac{9}{60}$ or $\frac{3}{20}$, so the recommended ratio is met.

Real-World Link In 2006, the New York Yankees had a 0.285 batting average as a team.

Source: Major League Baseball

Focus on Mathematical Content

If two ratios (written as fractions) are equivalent, they can be **simplified to the same fraction**.

If two ratios (written as fractions) are equivalent, **multiplying the numerator and denominator of one ratio by the same number** will result in the second ratio.

Formative Assessment

Use the Check Your Progress exercises after each Example to determine students' understanding of concepts.

ADDITIONAL EXAMPLES

1 **APPLES** Mr. Gale bought a basket of apples. Using the table below, write a ratio comparing the Red Delicious apples to the Granny Smith apples as a fraction in simplest form. $\frac{10}{3}$

Mr. Gale's Apples	
12	Fuji
9	Granny Smith
30	Red Delicious

2 Determine whether the ratios 12 onions to 15 potatoes and 32 onions to 40 potatoes are equivalent. yes

3 **POOLS** It is recommended that no more than one person be allowed into the shallow end of an outdoor public pool for every 15 square feet of surface area. If a local pool's shallow end has a surface area of 1,800 square feet, are the lifeguards correct to allow 120 people into that part of the pool? yes

Additional Examples are also in:

- Noteables™ Interactive Study Notebook with Foldables™
- Interactive Classroom PowerPoint® Presentations

Tips for New Teachers

Choose Your Method

After students complete Example 2, have them discuss which method they found most effective or efficient in order to determine whether the ratios were equivalent. Some students may prefer one method over another. Ask students to explain their preferences. Are there any other methods they could have chosen to determine whether the ratios were equivalent? Have them choose a method in which to complete Choose Your Method c and d. Answers will vary.

Lesson 6-1 Ratios 283

3 Practice

Formative Assessment

Use Exercises 1–7 to check for understanding.

Then use the chart at the bottom of this page to customize your assignments for students.

Intervention You may wish to use the Study Guide and Intervention Master on page 10 of the *Chapter 6 Resource Masters* for additional reinforcement.

Odd/Even Assignments

Exercises 8–23 are structured so that students practice the same concepts whether they are assigned odd or even problems.

Additional Answers

5. yes; $\frac{12}{20} = \frac{3}{5}$ and $\frac{6}{10} = \frac{3}{5}$

6. no; $\frac{2}{7} \neq \frac{10}{15}$ or $\frac{2}{3}$

7. no; Sample answer: $\frac{2 \text{ boxes}}{\$5} \neq \frac{6 \text{ boxes}}{\$20}$, since $2 \cdot 3 = 6$, but $5 \cdot 3 \neq 20$

21. no; $\frac{8}{6} = \frac{4}{3}$ and $\frac{12}{10} = \frac{6}{5}$, so $\frac{8}{6} \neq \frac{12}{10}$

22. yes; Sample answer: $\frac{1 \text{ h}}{2 \text{ lb}} = \frac{4.5 \text{ h}}{9 \text{ lb}}$, since $1 \cdot 4.5 = 4.5$ and $2 \cdot 4.5 = 9$

23. no; Sample answer: $\frac{12 \text{ in.}}{3 \text{ in.}} = \frac{4}{1}$ and $\frac{6 \text{ in.}}{1 \text{ in.}} = \frac{6}{1}$, so $\frac{12 \text{ in.}}{3 \text{ in.}} \neq \frac{6 \text{ in.}}{1 \text{ in.}}$

CHECK Your Understanding

Example 1 (p. 282)

FIELD TRIPS Use the information in the table to write each ratio as a fraction in simplest form.

Field Trip Statistics	
Students	180
Adults	24
Buses	4

1. adults : students $\frac{2}{15}$
2. students : buses $\frac{45}{1}$
3. buses : people $\frac{1}{51}$
4. adults : people $\frac{2}{17}$

Example 2 (p. 283)

Determine whether the ratios are equivalent. Explain.

5. 12 out of 20 doctors agree
6 out of 10 doctors agree
See margin.
6. 2 DVDs to 7 CDs
10 DVDs to 15 CDs
See margin.

Example 3 (p. 283)

7. **SHOPPING** A grocery store has a brand-name cereal on sale at 2 boxes for \$5. You buy 6 boxes and are charged \$20. Based on the price ratio indicated, were you charged the correct amount? Justify your answer. See margin.

Practice and Problem Solving

HOMEWORK HELP	
For Exercises	See Examples
8–17	1
18–21	2
22–23	3

Exercise Levels
A: 8–23
B: 24–33
C: 34–36

18. No; $\frac{20}{8} = \frac{5}{2}$ and $\frac{34}{10} = \frac{17}{5}$, so $\frac{20}{8} \neq \frac{34}{10}$.

19. Yes; $\frac{4}{16} = \frac{1}{4}$ and $\frac{10}{40} = \frac{1}{4}$, so $\frac{4}{16} = \frac{10}{40}$.

20. Yes; $\frac{27}{6} = \frac{9}{2}$ and $\frac{18}{4} = \frac{9}{2}$, so $\frac{27}{6} = \frac{18}{4}$.

SOCCER Use the Madison Mavericks team statistics to write each ratio as a fraction in simplest form.

Madison Mavericks Team Statistics	
Wins	10
Losses	12
Ties	8

8. wins : losses $\frac{5}{6}$
9. losses : ties $\frac{3}{2}$
10. losses : games played $\frac{2}{5}$
11. wins : games played $\frac{1}{3}$

CARNIVALS Use the following information to write each ratio as a fraction in simplest form.

At its annual carnival, Brighton Middle School had 6 food booths and 15 games booths. A total of 66 adults and 165 children attended. The carnival raised a total of \$1,600. Of this money, \$550 came from ticket sales.

12. children : adults $\frac{5}{2}$
13. food booths : games booths $\frac{2}{5}$
14. children : games booths $\frac{11}{1}$
15. booths : money raised $\frac{21}{1{,}600}$
16. people : children $\frac{7}{5}$
17. non-ticket sale money : total money $\frac{21}{32}$

Determine whether the ratios are equivalent. Explain.

18. 20 female lions to 8 male lions,
34 female lions to 10 male lions
19. \$4 for every 16 ounces,
\$10 for every 40 ounces
20. 27 students to 6 microscopes,
18 students to 4 microscopes
21. 8 roses to 6 babies breath,
12 roses to 10 babies breath
See margin.
22. **BAKING** It is recommended that a ham be baked 1 hour for every 2 pounds of meat. Latrell baked a 9-pound ham for 4.5 hours. Did he follow the above recommendation? Justify your answer. See margin.
23. **FISHING** Kamala catches two similar looking fish. The larger fish is 12 inches long and 3 inches wide. The smaller fish is 6 inches long and 1 inch wide. Do these fish have an equivalent length to width ratio? Justify your answer. See margin.

284 Chapter 6 Ratios and Proportions

DIFFERENTIATED HOMEWORK OPTIONS

Level	Assignment	Two-Day Option	
BL Basic	8–23, 34, 36–48	9–23 odd, 37, 38	8–22 even, 34, 36, 39–48
OL Core	9–21 odd, 22–34, 36–48	8–23, 37, 38	24–34, 36, 39–48
AL Advanced/Pre-AP	24–44 (optional: 45–48)		

MEASUREMENT The *aspect ratio* of a television is a ratio comparing the width and height. A wide screen television has an aspect ratio of 16:9. Televisions without the same aspect ratio crop the image to fit the screen. Determine which television sizes have a full 16:9 image. Justify your answers.

24. 32″ × 18″ yes; $\frac{32}{18} = \frac{16}{9}$ 25. 71″ × 42″ no; $\frac{71}{42} \neq \frac{16}{9}$ 26. 48″ × 36″ no; $\frac{48}{36} \neq \frac{16}{9}$

MAMMALS For Exercises 27 and 28, use the information below.

Mammal	Average Brain Weight (lb)	Average Body Weight (lb)
Adult Human	3	150
Adult Orca Whale	12	5,500

Real-World Link
An orca whale, also called a killer whale, is not really a whale, but a dolphin. Its average birth weight is 300 pounds.

27. How much greater is the average weight of an adult orca whale's brain than the average weight of an adult human's brain? 9 lb
28. Find the brain-to-body weight ratio for each mammal. Are these ratios equivalent? If not, which mammal has the greater brain-to-body weight ratio? Justify your answer and explain its meaning. See margin.

29. **MUSIC** The pitch of a musical note is measured by the number of sound waves per second, or *hertz*. If the ratio of the frequencies of two notes can be simplified, the two notes are harmonious. Use the information at the right to find if notes E and G are harmonious. Explain. yes; $\frac{330}{396} = \frac{5}{6}$

E : 330 Hertz G : 396 Hertz

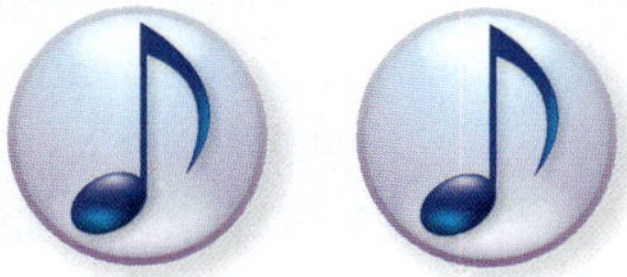

30. **FOOD** The ratio of the number of cups of chopped onion to the number of cups of chopped cilantro in a salsa recipe is 4:3. If the recipe calls for $\frac{2}{3}$ cup chopped onion, how many cups of chopped cilantro are needed? $\frac{1}{2}$ c

ANALYZE TABLES For Exercises 31–33, use the table below that shows the logging statistics for three areas of forest. 31–33. See margin.

Area	Estimated Number of Trees Left to Grow	Estimated Number of Trees Removed for Timber
A	440	1,200
B	1,625	3,750
C	352	960

31. For which two areas was the growth-to-removal ratio the same? Explain.
32. Which area had the greatest growth-to-removal ratio? Justify your answer.
33. Find the additional number of trees that should be planted and left to grow in area A so that its growth-to-removal ratio is the same as area B's. Justify your answer.

Academic Standards • ISTEP+

Extra Practice, pp. 681, 709

Additional Answers

28. human ratio, 3 : 150 or $\frac{1}{50}$; whale ratio, 12 : 5,500 or $\frac{3}{1,375}$; No, the ratios are not equivalent; Since $\frac{1}{50} > \frac{3}{1,375}$, humans have a greater brain to body weight ratio. Our brains account for a larger portion of our total body weight than a whale's brain.
31. Areas A and C; both ratios simplify to a growth-to-removal ratio of $\frac{11}{30}$.
32. Area B's ratio is 13 : 30 = $\frac{13}{30}$. This is a greater ratio than $\frac{11}{30}$.
33. 80; Sample answer: 440 + 80 = 520; $\frac{520}{1,200} = \frac{13}{30}$, which is the same ratio as area B.

Differentiated Instruction

Visual Learners Separate students into groups of two or three. Have each group pick an occupational field such as cooking, business, sports, or science and research and explain how ratios are used in that field. You may wish to have students use a computer with Internet access, or they can consult newspapers or magazines. Have each group write a list of the ratios they find, explaining how they are used. You may wish to have a volunteer from each group present the group's ratios to the class.

Lesson 6-1 Ratios 285

⚠ Exercise Alert!

Find the Error In Exercise 34, Cleveland added—rather than multiplied—the same number to the numerator and denominator of the first ratio. Remind students that two ratios are equivalent if their numerators and denominators are related by a common multiplier.

4 Assess

Name the Math Write the following ratios on the board: 3 tablespoons : 2 gallons, and 27 tablespoons : 24 gallons. Have students determine whether the ratios are equivalent. Then have them write what mathematical procedures they used to solve the problem.

FOLDABLES Study Organizer **Foldables™ Follow-Up**

Remind students to select a term or concept about ratios and to define it in their Foldables. Encourage them to give an example of the term or concept.

H.O.T. Problems

34. **FIND THE ERROR** Cleveland and Luis are determining whether the ratios $\frac{6}{4}$ and $\frac{18}{16}$ are equivalent. Who is correct? Explain. **Luis; Sample answer: to determine equivalent ratios; use multiplication not addition.**

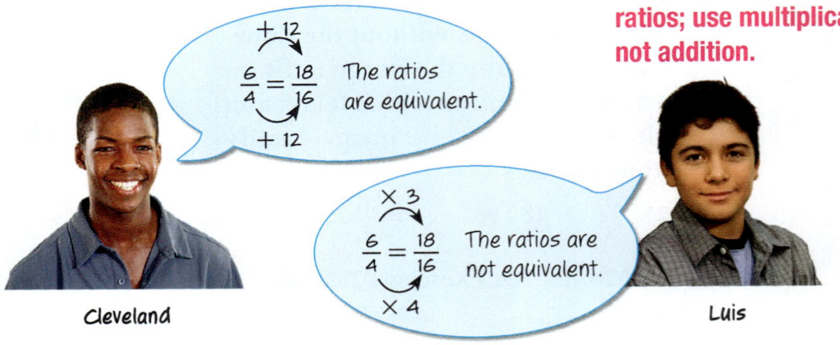

35. 2,400; The denominator of the ratios increases by 1; $\frac{20}{40} = \frac{1}{2}, \frac{40}{120} = \frac{1}{3}, \frac{120}{480} = \frac{1}{4}$

35. **CHALLENGE** Find the missing number in the following pattern. Explain your reasoning. (*Hint*: Look at the ratios of successive numbers.)

20, 40, 120, 480, ■

36. **WRITING IN MATH** Refer to the application in Exercises 31–33. What would a growth-to-removal ratio greater than 1 indicate? **Sample answer: It would mean that a greater portion of the trees in the area were being left to grow when compared to the number of trees that were removed.**

ISTEP+ PRACTICE 7.1.9

37. Which of the following ratios does *not* describe a relationship between the marbles in the jar? **B**

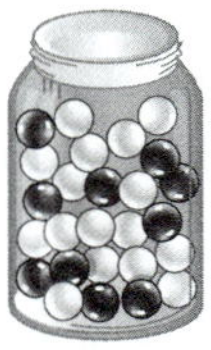

A 8 white : 5 black

B 2 white : 5 black

C 5 black : 13 total

D 8 white : 13 total

38. A class of 24 students has 15 boys. What ratio compares the number of girls to boys in the class? **F**

F 3:5 H 3:8

G 5:3 J 8:3

Spiral Review

39. Find $1\frac{4}{7} \div 1\frac{5}{6}$. Write in simplest form. (Lesson 5-7) **$\frac{6}{7}$**

ALGEBRA **Solve each equation. Check your solution.** (Lesson 5-6)

40. $\frac{y}{4} = 7$ **28**

41. $\frac{1}{3}x = \frac{5}{9}$ **$1\frac{2}{3}$**

42. $4 = \frac{p}{2.7}$ **10.8**

43. $2\frac{5}{6} = \frac{1}{2}a$ **$5\frac{2}{3}$**

44. **MONEY** Grant and his brother put together their money to buy a present for their mom. If they had a total of $18 and Grant contributed $10, how much did his brother contribute? (Lesson 3-2) **$8**

GET READY for the Next Lesson

PREREQUISITE SKILL **Divide.** (p. 676)

45. 9.8 ÷ 2 **4.9**

46. $4.30 ÷ 5 **$0.86**

47. $12.40 ÷ 40 **$0.31**

48. 27.36 ÷ 3.2 **8.55**

286 Chapter 6 Ratios and Proportions

6-2 Rates

PACING: **Regular:** 1.5 periods, **Block:** 1 period

IN Academic Standards

7.1.9 Solve problems involving ratios and proportions.
- Express one quantity as a fraction of another, given their ratio, and vice versa.
- Find how many times one quantity is as large as another, given their ratio, and vice versa.
- Express one quantity as a fraction of another given the two quantities.
- Find the whole, or one part, when a whole is divided into parts in a given ratio.
- Solve problems involving two pairs of equivalent ratios.

Also addresses 7.3.6.

Options for Differentiated Instruction

ELL = English Language Learner AL = Above or Beyond Grade Level SS = Struggling Students SN = Special Needs

Using Modeling ELL SS SN

Use before presenting Example 1.

Have students model a unit rate using counters as the numerator and denominator and a pencil as the fraction bar. For example, show students the model at the right.

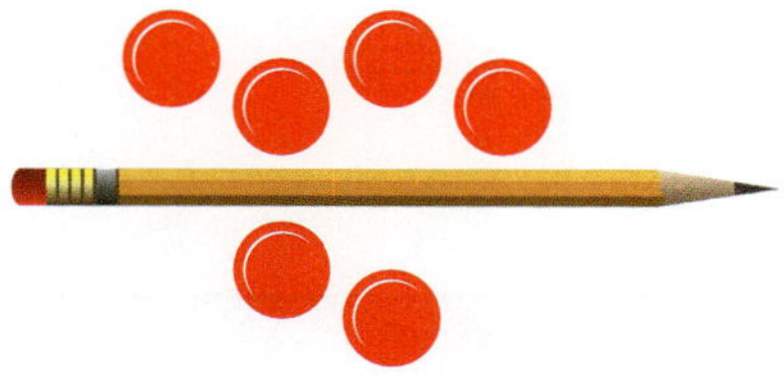

Instruct them to model the unit rate. 2 counters on top, 1 counter on the bottom

Real-Life Applications ELL AL SS SN

Use after presenting Example 3.

Have students collect data from two different grocery stores or advertisements. They should find a product that comes in several sizes, such as cereal, potatoes, or detergent. Have them record the size of the product (in ounces, pounds, liters, and so on) and the total cost of the item. Then have students calculate the unit price of the item for each store. Suggest that they organize their data in a table like the one shown below.

Store	Size of Product	Total Cost ($)	Unit Price ($)
1			
2			

Ask:
- Which store has the better price?
- What is the unit price for each store?

Writing ELL AL

Use after presenting Examples 1–4.

Have students write a problem that uses each type of ratio:
- average speed
- gas mileage
- unit price
- hourly wage

Have students exchange their problems with a classmate and solve each other's problems.

Leveled Lesson Resources

Also on TeacherWorks™ Lesson 6-2

Chapter 6 Resource Masters

BL = Below or Approaching Grade Level   OL = On Grade Level   AL = Above or Beyond Grade Level   ELL = English Language Learner

Lesson Reading Guide
p. 15 BL OL ELL

NAME ____________ DATE ________ PERIOD ____

6-2 Lesson Reading Guide

Rates

Get Ready for the Lesson

Do the Mini Lab at the top of page 287 in your textbook. Write your answers below.

1. Count the number of beats for each of you. See students' work.
2. Write the ratio *beats to minutes* as a fraction. See students' work.

Read the Lesson

3. A rate is a special kind of ratio. What makes it special? A rate is a ratio that compares two quantities with different kinds of units.
4. Describe what makes a rate different from a unit rate. Give an example of a rate and its equivalent unit rate. Sample answer: A unit rate is a rate that has a denominator of 1 unit. For example, $\frac{\$1.98}{6 \text{ cans of soda}} = \frac{\$0.33}{1 \text{ can of soda}}$
5. Write the ratios in words for each unit rate abbreviation.

Abbreviation	Ratio
m/s	number of meters / 1 second
ft/s	number of feet / 1 second
mi/h (mph)	number of miles / 1 hour
mi/gal (mpg)	number of miles / 1 gallon

Remember What You Learned

6. Go to a food store or find several different newspaper food advertisements. Compare prices for several different sizes of the same product, or compare prices for similar sizes of different brands of the same product. Which size or which brand costs the least per unit? Report your results to the class. See students' work.

Chapter 6 15 Course 2

Study Guide and Intervention*
p. 16 BL OL ELL

NAME ____________ DATE ________ PERIOD ____

6-2 Study Guide and Intervention

Rates

A ratio that compares two quantities with different kinds of units is called a **rate**. When a rate is simplified so that it has a denominator of 1 unit, it is called a **unit rate**.

Example 1 DRIVING Alita drove her car 78 miles and used 3 gallons of gas. What is the car's gas mileage in miles per gallon?

Write the rate as a fraction. Then find an equivalent rate with a denominator of 1.

78 miles using 3 gallons $= \frac{78 \text{ mi}}{3 \text{ gal}}$ Write the rate as a fraction.

$= \frac{78 \text{ mi} \div 3}{3 \text{ gal} \div 3}$ Divide the numerator and the denominator by 3.

$= \frac{26 \text{ mi}}{1 \text{ gal}}$ Simplify.

The car's gas mileage, or unit rate, is 26 miles per gallon.

Example 2 SHOPPING Joe has two different sizes of boxes of cereal from which to choose. The 12-ounce box costs $2.54, and the 18-ounce box costs $3.50. Which box costs less per ounce?

Find the unit price, or the cost per ounce, of each box. Divide the price by the number of ounces.

12-ounce box $2.54 ÷ 12 ounces ≈ $0.21 per ounce

18-ounce box $3.50 ÷ 18 ounces ≈ $0.19 per ounce

The 18-ounce box costs less per ounce.

Exercises

Find each unit rate. Round to the nearest hundredth if necessary.

1. 18 people in 3 vans 6 people per van
2. $156 for 3 books $52 per book
3. 115 miles in 2 hours 57.5 mi per h
4. 8 hits in 22 games 0.36 hits per game
5. 65 miles in 2.7 gallons 24.07 mi per gal
6. 2,500 Calories in 24 hours 104.17 C per h

Choose the better unit price.

7. $12.95 for 3 pounds of nuts or $21.45 for 5 pounds of nuts $21.45 for 5 lb
8. A 32-ounce bottle of apple juice for $2.50 or a 48-ounce bottle for $3.84. $2.50 for a 32-oz bottle

Chapter 6 16 Course 2

Skills Practice*
p. 17 BL OL

NAME ____________ DATE ________ PERIOD ____

6-2 Skills Practice

Rates

Find each unit rate. Round to the nearest hundredth if necessary.

1. $112 in 8 hours $14 per h
2. 150 miles in 6 gallons 25 mi per gal
3. 49 points in 7 games 7 points per game
4. 105 students in 3 classes 35 students per class
5. 120 problems in 5 hours 24 problems per h
6. 3 accidents in 12 months 0.25 accident per mo
7. 6 eggs in 7 days 0.86 egg per day
8. 8 batteries in 3 months 2.67 batteries per mo
9. 122 patients in 4 weeks 30.5 patients per wk
10. 51 gallons in 14 minutes 3.64 gal per min
11. $8.43 for 3 pounds $2.81 per lb
12. 357 miles in 6.3 hours 56.67 mi per h
13. 25 letters in 4 days 6.25 letters per day
14. $99 for 12 CDs $8.25 per CD
15. 5 breaks in 8 hours 0.63 break per h
16. 3 trips in 14 months 0.21 trip per mo
17. 2 pay raises in 3 years 0.67 raise per yr
18. 7 errors in 60 minutes 0.12 error per min
19. 15 pounds in 6 weeks 2.5 lb per wk
20. 8 commercials in 15 minutes 0.53 commercial per min
21. 8 glasses every 24 hours 0.33 glass per h
22. 13 feet in 5 steps 2.6 ft per step

Choose the better unit price.

23. $4.99 for 6 cans or $7.99 for 10 cans $7.99 for 10 cans
24. $21.50 for 4 pounds of lunch meat or $15.10 for 3 pounds of lunch meat $15.10 for 3 pounds

Chapter 6 17 Course 2

Practice*
p. 18 OL AL

NAME ____________ DATE ________ PERIOD ____

6-2 Practice

Rates

Find each unit rate. Round to the nearest hundredth if necessary.

1. $11.49 for 3 packages $3.83 per package
2. 2,550 gallons in 30 days 85 gallons per day
3. 88 students for 4 classes 22 students per class
4. 15.6 °F in 13 minutes 1.2 °F per minute
5. 175 Calories in 12 ounces 14.58 C per oz
6. 258.5 miles in 5.5 hours 47 mi per h
7. 549 vehicles on 9 acres 61 vehicles per acre
8. $920 for 40 hours $23 per h
9. 13 apples for 2 pies 6.5 apples per pie
10. SPORTS The results of a track meet are shown. Who ran the fastest? Explain your reasoning. Round to the nearest ten thousandth. Sample answer: Esteban; Theo's rate ≈ 0.3125 km per min, Esteban's rate ≈ 0.3704 km per min, Tetsuo's rate ≈ 0.3135 km per min; 0.3704 km per min > 0.3135 km per min > 0.3125 km per min

Name	Event	Time (min)
Theo	3K Run	9.6
Esteban	5K Run	13.5
Tetsuo	10K Run	31.9

11. MANUFACTURING A machinist can produce 114 parts in 6 minutes. At this rate, how many parts can the machinist produce in 15 minutes? 285 parts
12. RECIPES A recipe that makes 8 jumbo blueberry muffins calls for $1\frac{1}{2}$ teaspoons of baking powder. How much baking powder is needed to make 3 dozen jumbo muffins? $6\frac{3}{4}$ tsp

Estimate the unit price for each item. Justify your answers.

13. $299 for 4 tires $75 per tire; $299 ÷ 4 ≈ $300 ÷ 4 or $75
14. 3 yards of fabric for $13.47 $4.50 per yard; $13.47 ÷ 3 ≈ $13.50 ÷ 3 or $4.50

UTILITIES **For Exercises 15 and 16, use the table that shows the average monthly electricity and water usage.**

Family Name	Family Size	Electricity (kilowatt-hours)	Water (gal)
Melendez	4	1,560	3,500
Barton	6	2,130	6,400
Stiles	2	1,490	2,500

15. Which family uses about twice the amount of electricity per person than the other two families? Explain your reasoning. The Stiles family; The Melendez family uses 390 kwh per person, the Barton family uses 355 kwh per person, and the Stiles family uses 745 kwh per person.
16. Which family uses the least amount of water per person? Explain your reasoning. The Melendez family; The Melendez family uses 875 gal per person, the Barton family uses 1,067 gal per person, and the Stiles family uses 1,250 gal per person.

Chapter 6 18 Course 2

Word Problem Practice*
p. 19 OL AL

NAME ____________ DATE ________ PERIOD ____

6-2 Word Problem Practice

Rates

1. TRAVEL During Sonia's trip across the country, she traveled 2,884 miles. Her trip took 7 days. Find a unit rate to represent the average miles she traveled per day during the trip. 412 mi per day
2. BUDGET Steve was offered $5,025 per year for a weekend lifeguarding job at a local pool. He wants to know how much his monthly income will be at this salary level. What is his rate of pay in dollars per month? $418.75 per mo
3. MUSIC Randall recorded 8 songs on his most recent CD. The total length of the CD is 49 minutes. Find a unit rate to represent the average length per song on the CD. 6.125 min per song
4. CARPETING Hana paid $1,200 for the carpet in her living room. The room has an area of 251.2 square feet. What was her unit cost of carpeting in dollars per square foot? Round to the nearest cent. $4.78 per ft²
5. SHOPPING An 8-ounce can of tomatoes costs $1.14. A 12-ounce can costs $1.75. Which can of tomatoes has the better unit price? 8-oz can
6. PETS Last month, Hao's dog ate 40 cans of dog food in 31 days. How many cans should Hao buy to feed his dog for the next 6 days? 8 cans

Chapter 6 19 Course 2

Enrichment
p. 20 OL AL

NAME ____________ DATE ________ PERIOD ____

6-2 Enrichment

An Educated Consumer

Choosing a checking account is something that most people do at some point in their lives. Because checking accounts vary from institution to institution, and from one type of account to another, you will need to consider the options associated with each account before choosing one of them.

Suppose a bank offers two kinds of checking accounts.

Account A: a $0.20 charge for writing each check and no service charge

Account B: a $0.10 charge for writing each check and a monthly service charge of $1.50

1. Which account would cost less if a person were to write 10 checks in a month? Account A
2. Which account would cost less if a person were to write 20 checks in a month? Account B
3. Using the guess-and-check strategy, find the number of checks that would have to be written for the cost of Account A to equal the cost of Account B. What is that cost? It would take 15 checks; $3.00
4. Which account would cost less if a person were to write 250 checks in a year? By how much? Account B; $7.00
5. Diana Durbin wrote 300 checks in one year. Her total charge for the use of the account that year was $72.00. The bank charges $0.15 for writing one check and charges a fixed amount each month for the use of the account. What is that monthly service charge? $2.25

Chapter 6 20 Course 2

* *Also available in Spanish* ELL

Additional Lesson Resources

Transparencies

- *5-Minute Check Transparency*, Lesson 6-2

Other Print Products

- *Teaching Mathematics with Manipulatives*
- *Noteables™ Interactive Study Notebook with Foldables™*

Teacher Tech Tools

- *Interactive Classroom CD-ROM*, Lesson 6-2
- *AssignmentWorks*, Lesson 6-2

Student Tech Tools

glencoe.com

- Extra Examples, Chapter 6, Lesson 2
- Self-Check Quiz, Chapter 6, Lesson 2

6-2 Rates

MAIN IDEA

Determine unit rates.

IN Academic Standards

7.1.9 Solve problems involving ratios and proportions.

- Express one quantity as a fraction of another, given their ratio, and vice versa.
- Find how many times one quantity is as large as another, given their ratio, and vice versa.
- Express one quantity as a fraction of another given the two quantities.
- Find the whole, or one part, when a whole is divided into parts in a ration.
- Solve problems involving two pairs of equivalent ratios.

Also addresses 7.3.6.

New Vocabulary

rate
unit rate

IN Math Online

glencoe.com

- Extra Examples
- Personal Tutor
- Self-Check Quiz

MINI Lab

Choose a partner and take turns taking each other's pulse for 2 minutes.

1. Count the number of beats for each of you. **See students' work.**
2. Write the ratio *beats* to *minutes* as a fraction. **See students' work.**

A ratio that compares two quantities with different kinds of units is called a **rate**.

$\frac{\text{160 beats}}{\text{2 minutes}}$ — The units *beats* and *minutes* are different.

When a rate is simplified so that it has a denominator of 1 unit, it is called a **unit rate**.

$\frac{\text{80 beats}}{\text{1 minute}}$ — The denominator is 1 unit.

The table below shows some common unit rates.

Rate	Unit Rate	Abbreviation	Name
$\frac{\text{number of miles}}{\text{1 hour}}$	miles per hour	mi/h or mph	average speed
$\frac{\text{number of miles}}{\text{1 gallon}}$	miles per gallon	mi/gal or mpg	gas mileage
$\frac{\text{number of dollars}}{\text{1 pound}}$	price per pound	dollars/lb	unit price
$\frac{\text{number of dollars}}{\text{1 hour}}$	dollars per hour	dollars/h	hourly wage

Real-World EXAMPLE Find a Unit Rate

1 WORKING Desiree earns $280 in 40 hours. What is her hourly pay rate?

$280 in 40 hours $= \frac{\$280}{40\text{ h}}$ — Write the rate as a fraction.

$= \frac{\$280 \div 40}{40\text{ h} \div 40}$ — Divide the numerator and the denominator by 40.

$= \frac{\$7}{1\text{ h}}$ — Simplify.

Desiree's hourly pay rate is $7.

CHECK Your Progress

Find each unit rate. Round to the nearest hundredth if necessary.

a. $300 for 6 hours **$50 per hour**

b. 220 miles on 8 gallons **27.5 miles per gallon**

6-2 Lesson Notes

1 Focus

Vertical Alignment

Before Lesson 6-2
Compute and perform simple multiplication and division of fractions and apply these procedures to solving problems

Lesson 6-2
Interpret and use ratios in different contexts to show the relative sizes of two quantities, using appropriate notations; demonstrate an understanding that rate is a measure of one quantity per unit value of another quantity; solve problems involving rates

After Lesson 6-2
Solve multistep problems involving rate, average speed, distance, and time or a direct variation

2 Teach

MINI Lab

Have students work in pairs. One can take the pulse while the other tells when the 2-minute period begins and ends. Then they can reverse roles.

Scaffolding Questions

Ask:

- What is the speed limit on the highway? 60/65/70 miles per hour
- If you drive at that speed limit, how far will you travel in 1 hour? 60/65/70 miles
- If a student earned $12 in 2 hours, how much would she earn in 1 hour? $6
- If 3 pounds of tomatoes cost $6, how much would 1 pound cost? $2

Focus on Mathematical Content

Students use unit rates in their everyday lives to **measure** and **compare** rates such as speed, price, and wage.

Many real-world problems can be solved by **extending or projecting** a unit rate.

Formative Assessment

Use the Check Your Progress exercises after each Example to determine students' understanding of concepts.

ADDITIONAL EXAMPLES

1. **READING** Julia read 52 pages in 2 hours. What is the average number of pages she read per hour? 26 pages per hour

2. **SODA** Find the unit price per can if it costs $3 for 6 cans of soda. Round to the nearest hundredth if necessary. $0.50 per can

3. **TEST EXAMPLE** The costs of 4 different sizes of orange juice are shown in the table. Which container costs the least per ounce? A

Amount	Total Cost
16 oz	$1.28
32 oz	$1.92
64 oz	$2.56
96 oz	$3.36

A 96-oz container
B 64-oz container
C 32-oz container
D 16-oz container

Additional Examples are also in:

- Noteables™ Interactive Study Notebook with Foldables™
- Interactive Classroom PowerPoint® Presentations

Real-World EXAMPLE — Find a Unit Rate

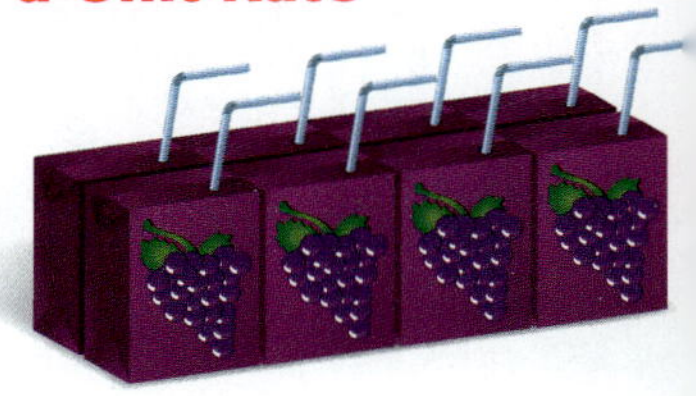

2 **JUICE** Find the unit price if it costs $2 for eight juice boxes. Round to the nearest cent if necessary.

$$\text{\$2 for eight boxes} = \frac{\$2}{8 \text{ boxes}}$$ Write the rate as a fraction.

$$= \frac{\$2 \div 8}{8 \text{ boxes} \div 8}$$ Divide the numerator and the denominator by 8.

$$= \frac{\$0.25}{1 \text{ box}}$$ Simplify.

The unit price is $0.25 per juice box.

CHECK Your Progress

c. **ESTIMATION** Find the unit price if a 4-pack of mixed fruit sells for $2.12. **$0.53**

Unit rates are useful when you want to make comparisons.

ISTEP+ EXAMPLE 7.1.9 Compare Using Unit Rates

3 The prices of 3 different bags of dog food are given in the table. Which size bag has the lowest price per pound?

A the 40-lb bag
B the 20-lb bag
C the 8-lb bag
D All three bag sizes have the same price per pound.

Dog Food Prices	
Bag Size (pounds)	**Price**
40	$49.00
20	$23.44
8	$9.88

Read the Item

To determine the lowest price per pound, find and compare the unit price for each size bag.

Solve the Item

40-pound bag $49.00 ÷ 40 pounds = $1.225 per pound
20-pound bag $23.44 ÷ 20 pounds = $1.172 per pound
8-pound bag $9.88 ÷ 8 pounds = $1.235 per pound

At $1.172 per pound, the 20-pound bag sells for the lowest price per pound.

The answer is B.

Test-Taking Tip

Alternative Method One 40-lb bag is equivalent to two 20-lb bags or five 8-lb bags. The cost for one 40-lb bag is $49, the cost for two 20-lb bags is about 2 × $23 or $46, and the cost for five 8-lb bags is about 5 × $10 or $50. So the 20-lb bag has the lowest price per pound.

Tips for New Teachers

Analyzing Cost

You may wish to point out that the positions of the quantities being compared in a rate can be reversed. For instance, in Example 2, the unit rate per dollar is 4 juice boxes per dollar. Encourage students to analyze a problem to determine which rate is more helpful (e.g., the number of juice boxes per dollar or the cost per juice box). If a person wanted to know how many juice boxes she could buy for $7, the unit rate per dollar would be more helpful. But if a person wanted to compare the cost of juice boxes at different stores, the unit price per juice box would be more helpful.

CHECK Your Progress

d. Tito wants to buy some peanut butter to donate to the local food pantry. If Tito wants to save as much money as possible, which brand should he buy? **G**

Peanut Butter Sales	
Brand	**Sale Price**
Nutty	12 ounces for \$2.19
Grandma's	18 ounces for \$2.79
Bee's	28 ounces for \$4.69
Save-A-Lot	40 ounces for \$6.60

F Nutty, because the quality of the peanut butter is better

G Grandma's, because the price per ounce is about \$0.16

H Bee's, because the price per ounce is about \$0.14

J Save-A-Lot, because he wants to buy 40 ounces

Real-World Link Face paint can be made from 1 teaspoon cornstarch and $\frac{1}{2}$ teaspoon each of water and cold cream.

Real-World EXAMPLE Use a Unit Rate

4 **FACE PAINTING** **Lexi painted 3 faces in 12 minutes at the Crafts Fair. At this rate, how many faces can she paint in 40 minutes?**

Find the unit rate. Then multiply this unit rate by 40 to find the number of faces she can paint in 40 minutes.

$3 \text{ faces in } 12 \text{ minutes} = \frac{3 \text{ faces} \div 12}{12 \text{ min} \div 12} = \frac{0.25 \text{ faces}}{1 \text{ min}}$ Find the unit rate.

$\frac{0.25 \text{ faces}}{1 \cancel{\text{min}}} \cdot 40 \cancel{\text{min}} = 10 \text{ faces}$ Divide out the common units.

Lexi can paint 10 faces in 40 minutes.

CHECK Your Progress

e. \$7.90

e. **SCHOOL SUPPLIES** Kimbel bought 4 notebooks for \$6.32. At this same unit price, how much would he pay for 5 notebooks?

★ indicates multi-step problem

CHECK Your Understanding

Examples 1, 2 (pp. 287–288)

Find each unit rate. Round to the nearest hundredth if necessary.

2. 420 kb per min
4. 9.5 feet per second

1. 90 miles on 15 gallons **6 mi per gal**
2. 1,680 kilobytes in 4 minutes
3. 5 pounds for \$2.49 **\$0.50 per lb**
4. 152 feet in 16 seconds

Example 3 (pp. 288–289)

5. **MULTIPLE CHOICE** Four stores offer customers bulk CD rates. Which store offers the best buy? **C**

A CD Express
B CD Rack
C Music Place
D Music Shop

Bulk CD Offers	
Store	**Offer**
CD Express	4 CDs for \$60
Music Place	6 CDs for \$75
CD Rack	5 CDs for \$70
Music Shop	3 CDs for \$40

Example 4 (p. 289)

6. **TRAVEL** After 3.5 hours, Pasha had traveled 217 miles. At this same speed, how far will she have traveled after 4 hours? **248 mi**

ADDITIONAL EXAMPLE

4 **POTATOES** An assistant cook peeled 18 potatoes in 6 minutes. At this rate, how many potatoes can he peel in 50 minutes? 150 potatoes

3 Practice

Formative Assessment

Use Exercises 1–6 to check for understanding.

Then use the chart at the bottom of the next page to customize your assignments for students.

Intervention You may wish to use the Study Guide and Intervention Master on page 16 of the *Chapter 6 Resource Masters* for additional reinforcement.

Odd/Even Assignments

Exercises 7–24 are structured so that students practice the same concepts whether they are assigned odd or even problems.

Practice and Problem Solving

HOMEWORK HELP

For Exercises	See Examples
7–16	1, 2
17–20	3
21–24	4

Exercise Levels
A: 7–24
B: 25–39
C: 40–44

8. 152 customers per day
9. 30.4 people per class
10. 203.75 Calories per serving
18. 9 bottles for $4.50; $0.50 < $0.57 < $0.63
19. Soft drinks A and B have about 3 grams of sodium per ounce and Soft drink C has about 6 grams per ounce.

Find each unit rate. Round to the nearest hundredth if necessary.

7. 360 miles in 6 hours **60 mi/h**
8. 6,840 customers in 45 days
9. 152 people for 5 classes
10. 815 Calories in 4 servings
11. 45.5 meters in 13 seconds **3.5 m/s**
12. $7.40 for 5 pounds **$1.48/lb**
13. $1.12 for 8.2 ounces **$0.14/oz**
14. 144 miles in 4.5 gallons **32 mi/gal**

15. **ESTIMATION** Estimate the unit rate if 12 pairs of socks sell for $5.79. **about $0.50 per pair**

16. **ESTIMATION** Estimate the unit rate if a 26-mile marathon was completed in 5 hours. **about 5 mi/h**

17. **SPORTS** The results of a swim meet are shown. Who swam the fastest? Explain your reasoning. **Susana; 1.78 m/s > 1.66 m/s > 1.23 m/s**

Name	Event	Time (s)
Tawni	50-m Freestyle	40.8
Pepita	100-m Butterfly	60.2
Susana	200-m Medley	112.4

18. **MONEY** A grocery store sells three different packages of bottled water. Which package costs the least per bottle? Explain your reasoning.

6-pack for $3.79

9-pack for $4.50

12-pack for $6.89

NUTRITION **For Exercises 19 and 20, use the table at the right.**

Soft Drink Nutritional Information

Soft Drink	Serving Size (oz)	Sodium (mg)	Sugar (g)
A	12	40	22
B	8	24	15
C	7	42	30

19. Which soft drink has about twice the amount of sodium per ounce than the other two? Explain.

20. Which soft drink has the least amount of sugar per ounce? Explain. **Soft drink A; 1.83 < 1.88 < 4.29 g/oz**

21. **WORD PROCESSING** Ben can type 153 words in 3 minutes. At this rate, how many words can he type in 10 minutes? **510 words**

22. **FABRIC** Marcus buys 3 yards of fabric for $7.47. Later he realizes that he needs 2 more yards. How much will he pay for the extra fabric? **$4.98**

23. **ESTIMATION** A player scores 87 points in 6 games. At this rate, about how many points would she score in the next 4 games? **Sample answer: about 60**

Real-World Link North Carolina has approximately 8.9 million people living in 48,718 square miles.
Source: U.S. Census Bureau

24. **JOBS** Dalila earns $94.20, for working 15 hours as a holiday helper wrapping gifts. If she works 18 hours the next week, how much money will she earn? **$113.04**

25. **POPULATION** Use the information at the left. What is the *population density* or number of people per square mile in North Carolina? **182.7**

DIFFERENTIATED HOMEWORK OPTIONS

Level	Assignment	Two-Day Option	
BL Basic	7–24, 42–55	7–23, odd, 45, 46	8–24 even, 42–44, 47–55
OL Core	7–23 odd, 25–39, 42–55	7–24, 45, 46	25–39, 42–44, 47–55
AL Advanced/Pre-AP	25–51 (optional: 52–55)		

290 Chapter 6 Ratios and Proportions

26. $1.25 per qt; $2.49 ÷ 2 ≈ $2.50 ÷ 2 or $1.25
27. 38¢ per lb; $1.89 ÷ 5 ≈ $1.90 ÷ 5 or $0.38
28. $0.06 per oz; $1.13 ÷ 20 ≈ $1.20 ÷ 20 or $0.06

ESTIMATION Estimate the unit price for each item. Justify your answers.

26.

$2.49

27.

$1.89

28.

$1.13

29. **RECIPES** A recipe that makes 10 mini-loaves of banana bread calls for $1\frac{1}{4}$ cups flour. How much flour is needed to make 2 dozen mini-loaves using this recipe? 3 c

Real-World Link
The record for the Boston Marathon's wheelchair division is 1 hour, 18 minutes, and 27 seconds.
Source: Boston Athletic Association

SPORTS For Exercises 30 and 31, use the information at the left.

30. ★ The wheelchair division for the Boston Marathon is 26.2 miles long. What was the average speed of the record winner of the wheelchair division? Round to the nearest hundredth. 20.04 mi/h

31. ★ At this rate, about how long would it take this competitor to complete a 30 mile race? about 1 h 29 min 49 s

32. **SPORTS** Mia participated in a race that involved 2 different events. She biked at an average speed of 10 miles per hour for $1\frac{1}{2}$ hours then ran at an average speed of 7 miles per hour for $\frac{3}{4}$ hour. What was her average speed for the entire race? 9 miles per hour

ANIMALS For Exercises 33–37, use the graph that shows the average number of heartbeats for an active adult brown bear and a hibernating brown bear.

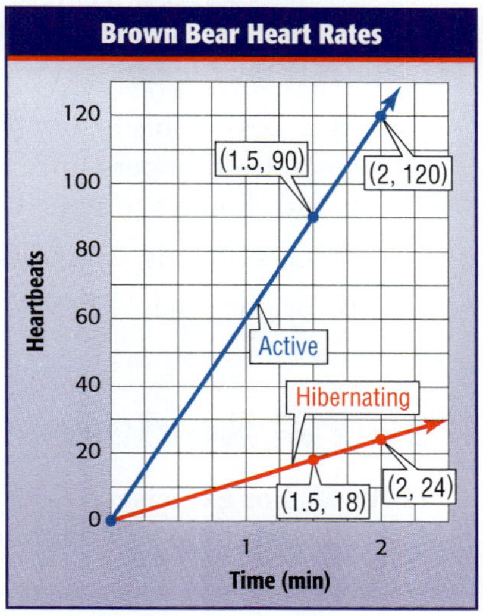

33. What does the point (2, 120) represent on the graph?

34. What does the point (1.5, 18) represent on the graph?

35. What does the ratio of the y-coordinate to the x-coordinate for each pair of points on the graph represent?

36. Use the graph to find the bear's average heart rate when it is active and when it is hibernating.

37. When is the bear's heart rate greater, when it is active or when it is hibernating? How can you tell this from the graph? See margin.

38. **TIRES** At Tire Depot, a pair of new tires sells for $216. The manager's special advertises the same tires selling at a rate of $380 for 4 tires. How much do you save per tire if you purchase the manager's special? $13

39. **FIND THE DATA** Refer to the Data File on pages 16–19. Choose some data and write a real-world problem in which you would compare unit rates or ratios. See students' work.

33. The bear's heart beats 120 times in 2 minutes when it is active.
34. The bear's heart beats 18 times in 1.5 minutes when it is hibernating.
35. the bear's heart rate in beats per minute
36. active: 60 beats per minute; hibernating: 12 beats per minute

Academic Standards • ISTEP+
Extra Practice, pp. 682, 709

Additional Answers

37. when it is active; Sample answer: The active line increases faster than the hibernating line when read from left to right.

Lesson 6-2 Rates 291

4 Assess

Yesterday's News Remind students that yesterday's lesson was about writing ratios in simplest form. Have them write how yesterday's concepts helped them with today's material.

Formative Assessment

Check for student understanding of concepts in Lessons 6-1 and 6-2.

CRM Quiz 1, p. 67

FOLDABLES Study Organizer Foldables™ Follow-Up

Remind students to select a term or concept about unit rates and to define it in their Foldables. Encourage them to give an example of the term or concept.

Additional Answers

40. Sometimes; a ratio that compares two measurements with different units is a rate, such as $\frac{2 \text{ miles}}{10 \text{ minutes}}$. A ratio that compares two numbers or two measurements with like units is not a rate, such as $\frac{2 \text{ cups}}{3 \text{ cups}}$.

44. Sample answer: The rate 55 miles per hour is a measure of the number of miles traveled per unit hour.

H.O.T. Problems

CHALLENGE **Determine whether each statement is *sometimes*, *always*, or *never* true. Give an example or a counterexample.**

40. A ratio is a rate. **See margin.**

41. A rate is a ratio. **Always; every rate is a ratio, because it is a comparison of two quantities by division.**

42. **OPEN ENDED** Create a rate and then convert it to a unit rate. **Sample answer: $\frac{30 \text{ mi}}{2 \text{ h}} = \frac{15 \text{ mi}}{1 \text{ h}}$**

43. **NUMBER SENSE** In which situation will the rate $\frac{x \text{ feet}}{y \text{ minutes}}$ increase? Give an example to explain your reasoning. **a; $\frac{30 \text{ ft}}{2 \text{ min}} = 15$ ft/min, $\frac{40 \text{ ft}}{2 \text{ min}} = 20$ ft/min**

a. x increases, y is unchanged

b. x is unchanged, y increases

44. **WRITING IN MATH** Describe, using an example, how a *rate* is a measure of one quantity per unit of another quantity. **See margin.**

ISTEP+ PRACTICE 7.1.9

45. Mrs. Ross needs to buy dish soap. There are four different size containers at a store.

Dish Soap Prices	
Brand	**Price**
Lots of Suds	$0.98 for 8 ounces
Bright Wash	$1.29 for 12 ounces
Spotless Soap	$3.14 for 30 ounces
Lemon Bright	$3.45 for 32 ounces

Mrs. Ross wants to buy the one that costs the least per ounce. Which brand should she buy? **C**

A Lots of Suds
B Bright Wash
C Spotless Soap
D Lemon Bright

46. The table shows the total distance traveled by a car driving at a constant rate of speed.

Time (h)	Distance (mi)
2	130
3.5	227.5
4	260
7	455

Based on this information, how far will the car have traveled after 10 hours? **H**

F 520 miles
G 585 miles
H 650 miles
J 715 miles

Spiral Review

FLOWERS **For Exercises 47–50, use the information in the table to write each ratio as a fraction in simplest form.** (Lesson 6-1)

Flower Arrangement	
Lilies	4
Roses	18
Snapdragons	6

47. lilies : roses **$\frac{2}{9}$**

48. snapdragons : lilies **$\frac{3}{2}$**

49. roses : flowers **$\frac{9}{14}$**

50. flowers : snapdragons **$\frac{14}{3}$**

51. **SANDWICHES** Lawanda is making subs. She puts $1\frac{1}{2}$ slices of cheese on each sub. If she has 12 slices of cheese, how many subs can she make? (Lesson 5-6) **8 subs**

GET READY for the Next Lesson

PREREQUISITE SKILL **Write each fraction in simplest form.** (Lesson 4-3)

52. $\frac{8}{12}$ **$\frac{2}{3}$**

53. $\frac{9}{18}$ **$\frac{1}{2}$**

54. $\frac{25}{35}$ **$\frac{5}{7}$**

55. $\frac{10}{40}$ **$\frac{1}{4}$**

292 Chapter 6 Ratios and Proportions

6-3 Rate of Change and Slope

PACING: **Regular:** 2 periods, **Block:** 1 period

IN Academic Standards **7.2.5 Find the slope of a line from its graph and relate the slope of a line to** similar **triangles. 7.2.6 Draw the graph of a line given** its slope and one point on the line or **two points on the line.** *Also addresses 7.1.9.*

Options for Differentiated Instruction

ELL = English Language Learner   AL = Above or Beyond Grade Level   SS = Struggling Students   SN = Special Needs

Mathematical Displays ELL AL

Use after Example 3.

Have students create a poster that explains how to find the constant rate of change from a table and from a graph. The poster should include how to find the change in the *y*-value and the change in the *x*-value and how to use them to find the constant rate of change. It should also discuss how to determine whether the rate of change is linear or not.

Real-Life Applications ELL AL SS SN

Use after Example 3.

Have students write down the time traveled and the distance traveled when they go to visit a friend or relative. Have them write down the time and distance they travel each 5 minutes. Have them determine if the relationship between the distance and the time is linear. If it is, have them calculate the constant rate of change.

Writing ELL AL

Use after Example 3.

Have students create a table and a graph that have a constant rate of change. Have students exchange their problems with classmates and solve one another's problems.

Leveled Lesson Resources

Also on TeacherWorks™ Lesson 6-3

Chapter 6 Resource Masters

BL = Below or Approaching Grade Level OL = On Grade Level AL = Above or Beyond Grade Level ELL = English Language Learner

Lesson Reading Guide
p. 21 BL OL ELL

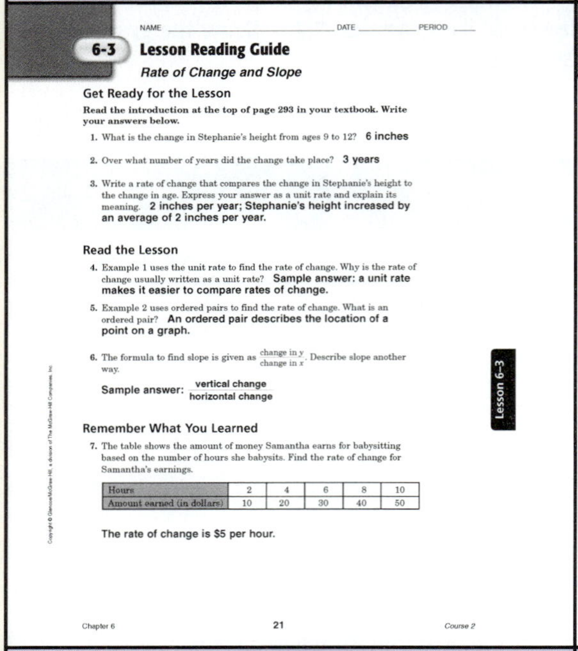

6-3 Lesson Reading Guide
Rate of Change and Slope

Get Ready for the Lesson

Read the introduction at the top of page 293 in your textbook. Write your answers below.

1. What is the change in Stephanie's height from ages 9 to 12? 6 inches
2. Over what number of years did the change take place? 3 years
3. Write a rate of change that compares the change in Stephanie's height to the change in age. Express your answer as a unit rate and explain its meaning. 2 inches per year; Stephanie's height increased by an average of 2 inches per year.

Read the Lesson

4. Example 1 uses the unit rate to find the rate of change. Why is the rate of change usually written as a unit rate? Sample answer: a unit rate makes it easier to compare rates of change.
5. Example 2 uses ordered pairs to find the rate of change. What is an ordered pair? An ordered pair describes the location of a point on a graph.
6. The formula to find slope is given as $\frac{\text{change in } y}{\text{change in } x}$. Describe slope another way. Sample answer: $\frac{\text{vertical change}}{\text{horizontal change}}$

Remember What You Learned

7. The table shows the amount of money Samantha earns for babysitting based on the number of hours she babysits. Find the rate of change for Samantha's earnings.

Hours	2	4	6	8	10
Amount earned (in dollars)	10	20	30	40	50

The rate of change is $5 per hour.

Chapter 6 21 Course 2

Study Guide and Intervention*
p. 22 BL OL ELL

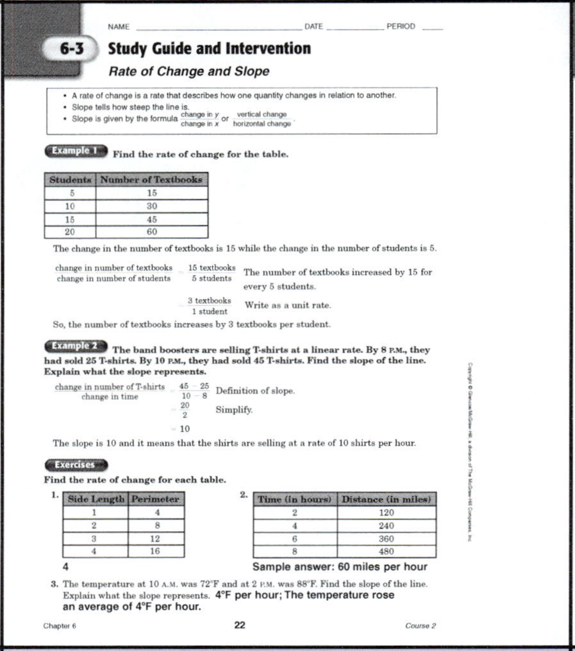

6-3 Study Guide and Intervention
Rate of Change and Slope

- A rate of change is a rate that describes how one quantity changes in relation to another.
- Slope tells how steep the line is.
- Slope is given by the formula $\frac{\text{change in } y}{\text{change in } x}$ or $\frac{\text{vertical change}}{\text{horizontal change}}$.

Example 1 Find the rate of change for the table.

Students	Number of Textbooks
5	15
10	30
15	45
20	60

The change in the number of textbooks is 15 while the change in the number of students is 5.

$\frac{\text{change in number of textbooks}}{\text{change in number of students}} = \frac{15 \text{ textbooks}}{5 \text{ students}}$ The number of textbooks increased by 15 for every 5 students.

$= \frac{3 \text{ textbooks}}{1 \text{ student}}$ Write as a unit rate.

So, the number of textbooks increases by 3 textbooks per student.

Example 2 The band boosters are selling T-shirts at a linear rate. By 8 P.M., they had sold 25 T-shirts. By 10 P.M., they had sold 45 T-shirts. Find the slope of the line. Explain what the slope represents.

$\frac{\text{change in number of T-shirts}}{\text{change in time}} = \frac{45 - 25}{10 - 8}$ Definition of slope.

$= \frac{20}{2}$ Simplify.

$= 10$

The slope is 10 and it means that the shirts are selling at a rate of 10 shirts per hour.

Exercises

Find the rate of change for each table.

1.

Side Length	Perimeter
1	4
2	8
3	12
4	16

4

2.

Time (in hours)	Distance (in miles)
2	120
4	240
6	360
8	480

Sample answer: 60 miles per hour

3. The temperature at 10 A.M. was 72°F and at 2 P.M. was 88°F. Find the slope of the line. Explain what the slope represents. 4°F per hour; The temperature rose an average of 4°F per hour.

Chapter 6 22 Course 2

Skills Practice*
p. 23 BL OL

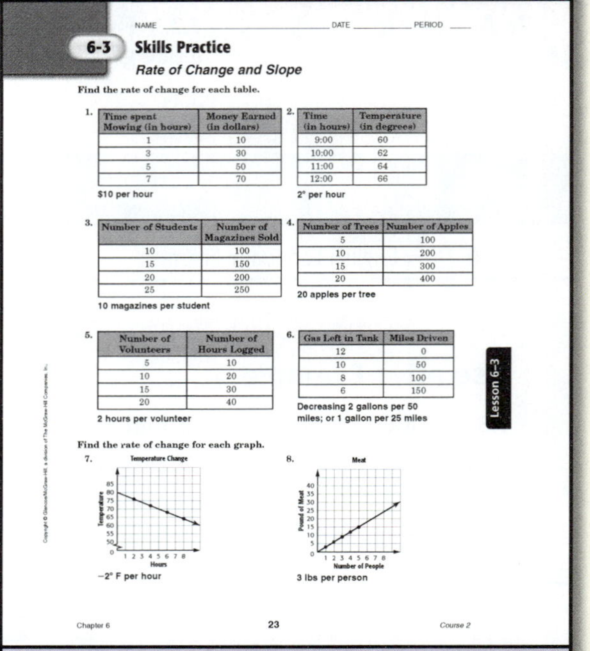

6-3 Skills Practice
Rate of Change and Slope

Find the rate of change for each table.

1.

Time spent Mowing (in hours)	Money Earned (in dollars)
1	10
3	30
5	50
7	70

$10 per hour

2.

Time (in hours)	Temperature (in degrees)
9:00	60
10:00	62
11:00	64
12:00	66

2° per hour

3.

Number of Students	Number of Magazines Sold
10	100
15	150
20	200
25	250

10 magazines per student

4.

Number of Trees	Number of Apples
5	100
10	200
15	300
20	400

20 apples per tree

5.

Number of Volunteers	Number of Hours Logged
5	10
10	20
15	30
20	40

2 hours per volunteer

6.

Gas Left in Tank	Miles Driven
12	0
10	50
8	100
6	150

Decreasing 2 gallons per 50 miles; or 1 gallon per 25 miles

Find the rate of change for each graph.

7. Temperature Change — −2° F per hour
8. Meat — 3 lbs per person

Chapter 6 23 Course 2

Practice*
p. 24 OL AL

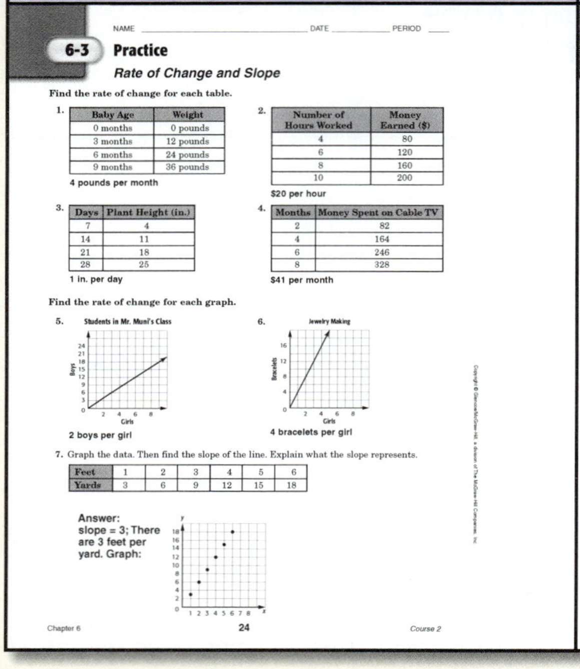

6-3 Practice
Rate of Change and Slope

Find the rate of change for each table.

1.

Baby Age	Weight
0 months	0 pounds
3 months	12 pounds
6 months	24 pounds
9 months	36 pounds

4 pounds per month

2.

Number of Hours Worked	Money Earned ($)
4	80
6	120
8	160
10	200

$20 per hour

3.

Days	Plant Height (in.)
7	4
14	11
21	18
28	25

1 in. per day

4.

Months	Money Spent on Cable TV
2	82
4	164
6	246
8	328

$41 per month

Find the rate of change for each graph.

5. Students in Mr. Muni's Class — 2 boys per girl
6. Jewelry Making — 4 bracelets per girl

7. Graph the data. Then find the slope of the line. Explain what the slope represents.

Feet	1	2	3	4	5	6
Yards	3	6	9	12	15	18

Answer: slope = 3; There are 3 feet per yard. Graph:

Chapter 6 24 Course 2

Word Problem Practice*
p. 25 OL AL

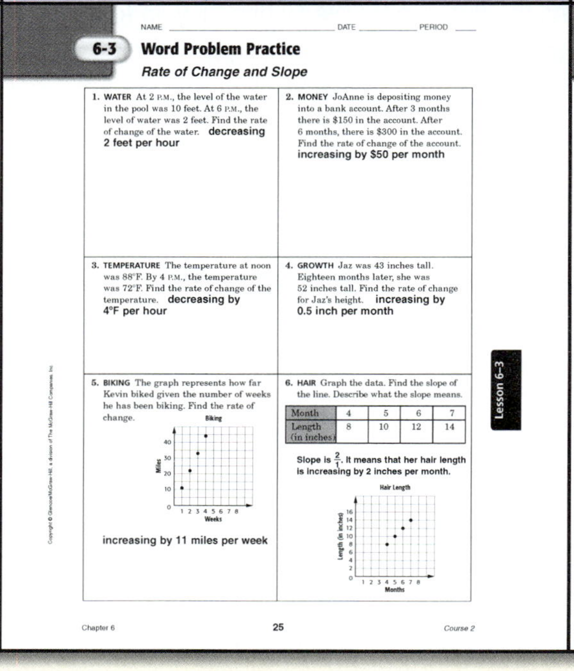

6-3 Word Problem Practice
Rate of Change and Slope

1. WATER At 2 P.M., the level of the water in the pool was 10 feet. At 6 P.M., the level of water was 2 feet. Find the rate of change of the water. decreasing 2 feet per hour
2. MONEY JoAnne is depositing money into a bank account. After 3 months there is $150 in the account. After 6 months, there is $300 in the account. Find the rate of change of the account. increasing by $50 per month
3. TEMPERATURE The temperature at noon was 88°F. By 4 P.M., the temperature was 72°F. Find the rate of change of the temperature. decreasing by 4°F per hour
4. GROWTH Jaz was 43 inches tall. Eighteen months later, she was 52 inches tall. Find the rate of change for Jaz's height. increasing by 0.5 inch per month
5. BIKING The graph represents how far Kevin biked given the number of weeks he has been biking. Find the rate of change. increasing by 11 miles per week
6. HAIR Graph the data. Find the slope of the line. Describe what the slope means.

Month	4	5	6	7
Length (in inches)	8	10	12	14

Slope is $\frac{2}{1}$. It means that her hair length is increasing by 2 inches per month.

Chapter 6 25 Course 2

Enrichment
p. 26 OL AL

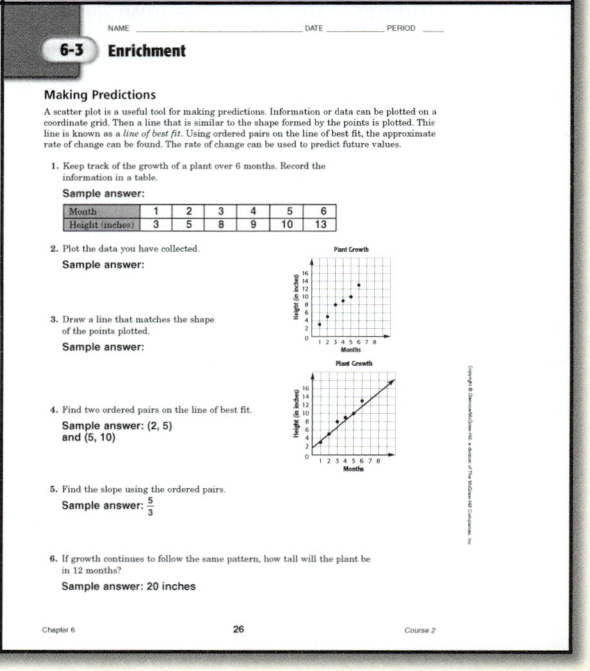

6-3 Enrichment

Making Predictions

A scatter plot is a useful tool for making predictions. Information or data can be plotted on a coordinate grid. Then a line that is similar to the shape formed by the points is plotted. This line is known as a *line of best fit*. Using ordered pairs on the line of best fit, the approximate rate of change can be found. The rate of change can be used to predict future values.

1. Keep track of the growth of a plant over 6 months. Record the information in a table. Sample answer:

Month	1	2	3	4	5	6
Height (inches)	3	5	8	9	10	13

2. Plot the data you have collected. Sample answer:
3. Draw a line that matches the shape of the points plotted. Sample answer:
4. Find two ordered pairs on the line of best fit. Sample answer: (2, 5) and (5, 10)
5. Find the slope using the ordered pairs. Sample answer: $\frac{5}{3}$
6. If growth continues to follow the same pattern, how tall will the plant be in 12 months? Sample answer: 20 inches

Chapter 6 26 Course 2

*Also available in Spanish ELL

Additional Lesson Resources

Transparencies
- *5-Minute Check Transparency,* Lesson 6-3

Other Print Products
- *Teaching Mathematics with Manipulatives*
- *Noteables™ Interactive Study Notebook with Foldables™*

Teacher Tech Tools
- *Interactive Classroom CD-ROM,* Lesson 6-3
- *AssignmentWorks,* Lesson 6-3

Student Tech Tools
glencoe.com
- Extra Examples, Chapter 6, Lesson 3
- Self-Check Quiz, Chapter 6, Lesson 3

6-3 Rate of Change and Slope

MAIN IDEA

Identify rate of change and slope using tables and graphs.

IN Academic Standards

7.2.5 Find the slope of a line from its graph and relate the slope of a line to similar **triangles. 7.2.6 Draw the graph of a line given** its slope and one point on the line or **two points on the line.** *Also addresses 7.1.9.*

New Vocabulary

rate of change
slope

IN Math Online

glencoe.com

- Extra Examples
- Personal Tutor
- Self-Check Quiz

GET READY for the Lesson

HEIGHTS The table shows Stephanie's height at ages 9 and 12.

Age (yr)	9	12
Height (in.)	53	59

1. What is the change in Stephanie's height from ages 9 to 12? **6 inches**
2. Over what number of years did this change take place? **3**
3. Write a rate that compares the change in Stephanie's height to the change in age. Express your answer as a unit rate and explain its meaning. **2 inches per year; Stephanie's height increased by an average of 2 inches per year.**

A **rate of change** is a rate that describes how one quantity changes in relation to another. A rate of change is usually expressed as a unit rate.

EXAMPLE Find Rate of Change from a Table

1 **FUNDRAISING** **The table shows the amount of money a Booster Club made washing cars for a fundraiser. Use the information to find the rate of change in dollars per car.**

Cars Washed	
Number	Money ($)
5	40
10	80
15	120
20	160

(+5 between successive Number values; +40 between successive Money values)

Find the unit rate to determine the rate of change.

$\frac{\text{change in money}}{\text{change in cars}} = \frac{40 \text{ dollars}}{5 \text{ cars}}$ The money earned increases by \$40 for every 5 cars.

$= \frac{8 \text{ dollar}}{1 \text{ car}}$ Write as a unit rate.

So, the number of dollars earned increases by \$8 for every car washed.

CHECK Your Progress

a. **PLANES** The table shows the number of miles a plane traveled while in flight. Use the information to find the approximate rate of change in miles per minute. **about 10 miles per minute**

Time (min)	30	60	90	120
Distance (mi)	290	580	870	1,160

6-3 Lesson Notes

1 Focus

Vertical Alignment

Before Lesson 6-3
Students should be able to simplify fractions

Lesson 6-3
Students will work with rates of change and slopes

After Lesson 6-3
Students will use slopes to graph lines

2 Teach

Scaffolding Questions

Ask:

- What is the rate of change of a plant that grows 0.5 inch per day? $\frac{0.5 \text{ inch}}{1 \text{ day}}$
- What is the rate of change of a pool that is emptying by 25 gallons per minute? $\frac{25 \text{ gallons}}{1 \text{ minute}}$
- What is $\frac{75 \text{ feet}}{3 \text{ days}}$ in simplest form? $\frac{25 \text{ feet}}{1 \text{ day}}$

ADDITIONAL EXAMPLE

1 The table shows the number of miles a car drove on a trip. Use the information to find the approximate rate of change. 65 miles per hour

Distance (miles)	65	130	195	260
Time (hours)	1	2	3	4

Additional Examples also in:

- Noteables™ Interactive Study Notebook with Foldables™
- Interactive Classroom PowerPoint® Presentations

Focus on Mathematical Content

A rate of change describes how one quantity changes in relation to another.

Formative Assessment

Use the Check Your Progress exercises after each Example to determine students' understanding of concepts.

ADDITIONAL EXAMPLES

2 The graph represents the distance traveled flying in a plane. Use the graph to find the rate of change.

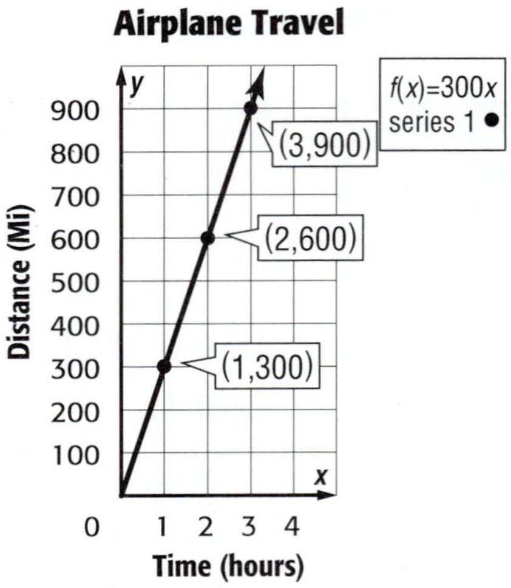

300 miles per hour

3 **GRAPH THE DATA** Find the slope of the line. Explain what the slope represents.

Hours	Amount earned
3	45
6	90
9	135

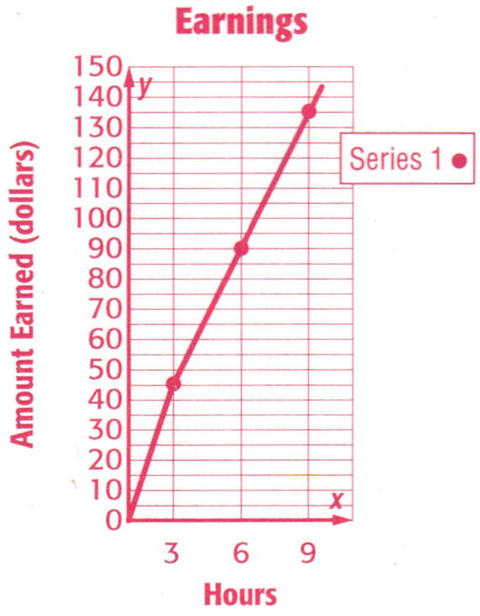

Reading Math

Ordered Pairs The ordered pair (2, 120) represents traveling 120 miles in 2 hours.

EXAMPLE Find Rate of Change from a Graph

2 **DRIVING** The graph represents the distance traveled while driving on a highway. Use the graph to find the rate of change in miles per hour.

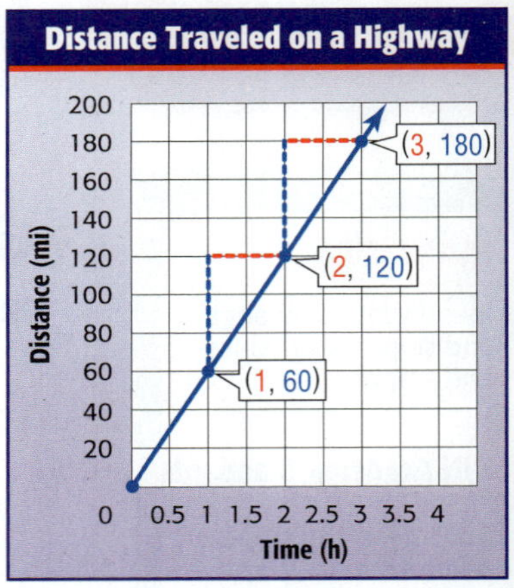

To find the rate of change, pick any two points on the line, such as (1, 60) and (2, 120).

$$\frac{\text{change in miles}}{\text{change in hours}} = \frac{(120 - 60)\text{ miles}}{(2 - 1)\text{ hours}}$$

$$= \frac{60 \text{ miles}}{1 \text{ hour}}$$

The distance increases by 60 miles in 1 hour. So, the rate of traveling on a highway is 60 miles per hour.

CHECK Your Progress

b. **DRIVING** Use the graph to find the rate of change in miles per hour while driving in the city. 30 miles per hour

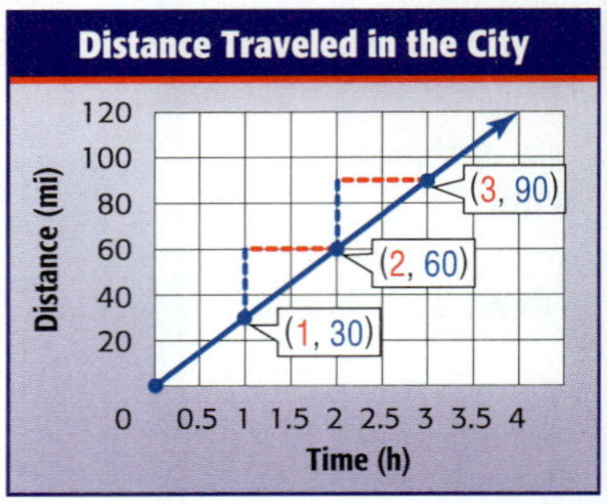

Notice that the graph in Example 2 about driving on a highway represents a rate of change of 60 mph. The graph in Check Your Progress about driving in the city is not as steep. It represents a rate of change of 30 mph.

The constant rate of change in y with respect to the constant change x is also called the slope of a line. Slope is a number that tells how steep the line is. The slope is the same for any two points on a straight line.

Slope

Key Concept

Slope is the rate of change between any two points on a line.

$$\text{slope} = \frac{\text{change in } y}{\text{change in } x} \begin{array}{l} \leftarrow \text{vertical change} \\ \leftarrow \text{horizontal change} \end{array}$$

$$= \frac{2}{1} \text{ or } 2$$

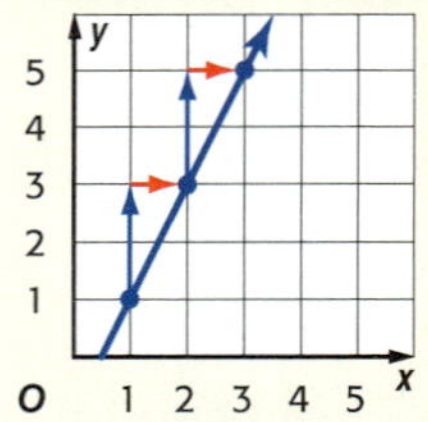

The slope is \$15 and represents the amount earned per hour.

Additional Examples are also in:

- Noteables™ Interactive Study Notebook with Foldables™
- Interactive Classroom PowerPoint® Presentations

Real-World EXAMPLE Find Slope

3 **PHYSICAL SCIENCE** The table below shows the relationship between the number of seconds y it takes to hear the thunder after a lightning strike and the distance x you are from the lightning.

Distance (x)	0	1	2	3	4	5
Seconds (y)	0	5	10	15	20	25

Graph the data. Then find the slope of the line. Explain what the slope represents.

$\text{slope} = \dfrac{\text{change in } y}{\text{change in } x}$ — Definition of slope

$= \dfrac{25 - 10}{5 - 2}$ — Use (2, 10) and (5, 25).

$= \dfrac{15}{3}$ ← seconds / ← miles

$= \dfrac{5}{1}$ — Simplify.

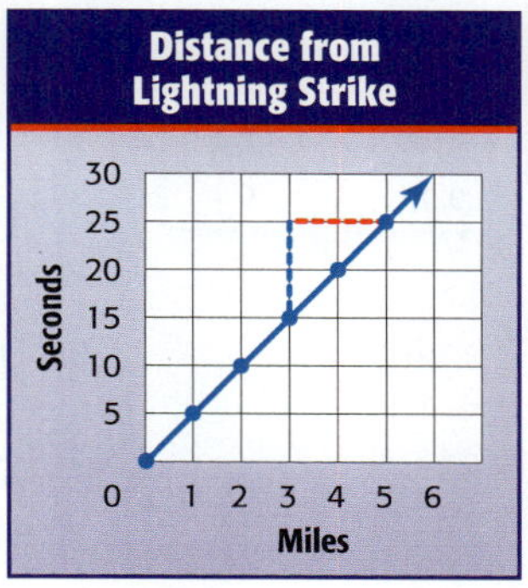

So, for every 5 seconds between a lightning flash and the sound of the thunder, there is 1 mile between you and the lightning strike.

Real-World Link Lightning strikes somewhere on the surface of Earth about 100 times every second.
Source: National Geographic

CHECK Your Progress

c. **WATER** Graph the data. Then find the slope of the line. Explain what the slope represents. **See margin.**

Water Level Loss	
Week	**Water Loss (cm)**
1	1.5
2	3
3	4.5
4	6

★ indicates multi-step problem

CHECK Your Understanding

Example 1 (p. 293)

1. Use the information in the table to find the rate of change in degrees per hour. **1.5°F per h**

Temperature (°F)	54	57	60	63
Time	6 A.M.	8 A.M.	10 A.M.	12 P.M.

Example 2 (p. 294)

★ 2. **DISTANCE** The graph shows Benito's distance from the starting line. Use the graph to find the rate of change. **0.5 m per s**

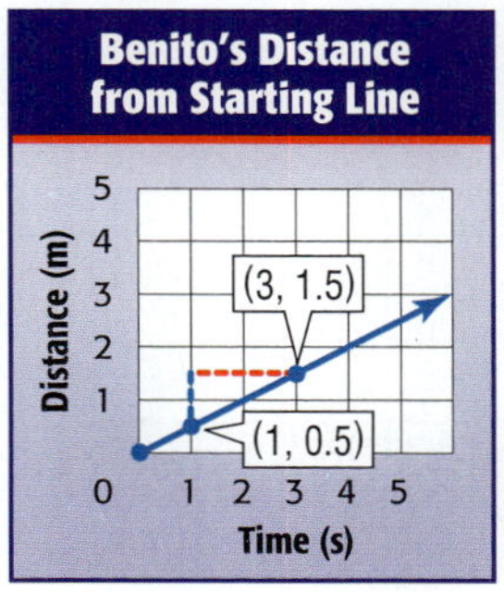

3 Practice

Formative Assessment

Use Exercises 1–3 to check for understanding.

Then use the chart at the bottom of this page to customize your assignments for students.

Intervention You may wish to use the Study Guide and Intervention Master on page 22 of the *Chapter 6 Resource Masters* for additional reinforcement.

Odd/Even Assignments

Exercises 4–10 are structured so that students practice the same concepts whether they are assigned odd or even problems.

Additional Answer

c.

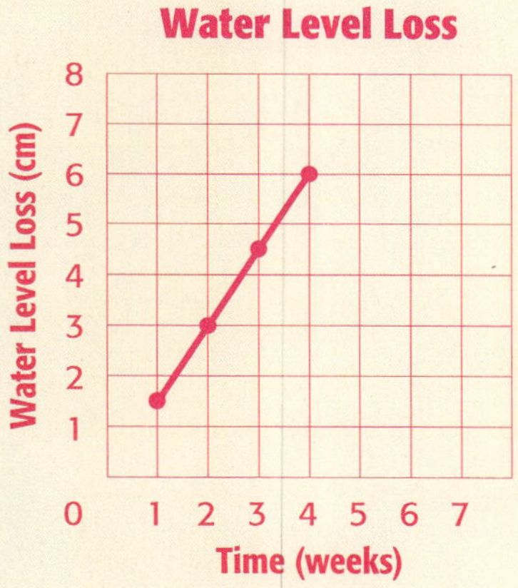

slope: $\frac{3}{2}$; Every two weeks, the water level falls 3 centimeters.

DIFFERENTIATED HOMEWORK OPTIONS			
Level	**Assignment**	**Two-Day Option**	
BL Basic	4–13, 15, 16, 17–24	5–13 odd, 15, 16	4–12 even, 14, 17–24
OL Core	4–8 even, 14–24	4–8, 15, 16	9–14, 17–24
AL Advanced/Pre-AP	9–24 (optional: 21–24)		

4 Assess

Ticket Out the Door Have students create a table of data that has a constant change. Have them find the rate of change for the table. Ask students to show their work as they leave.

FOLDABLES Study Organizer **Foldables™ Follow-Up**

Remind students to select a term or concept about rate of change and slope and to define it in their Foldables. Encourage them to give an example of the term or concept.

Additional Answers

3.

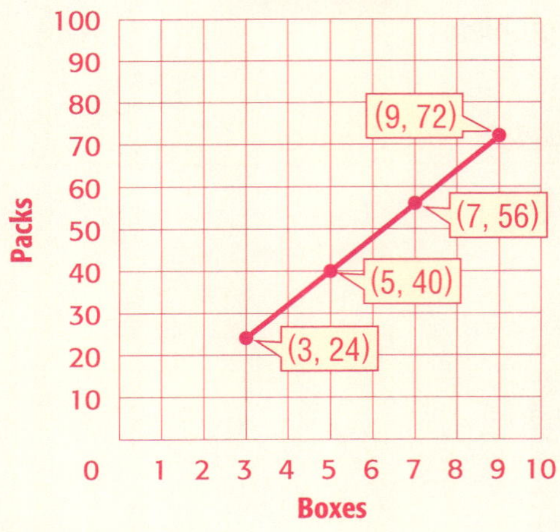

slope: $\frac{8}{1}$ or 8; There are 8 packs of fruit snacks in each box.

9.

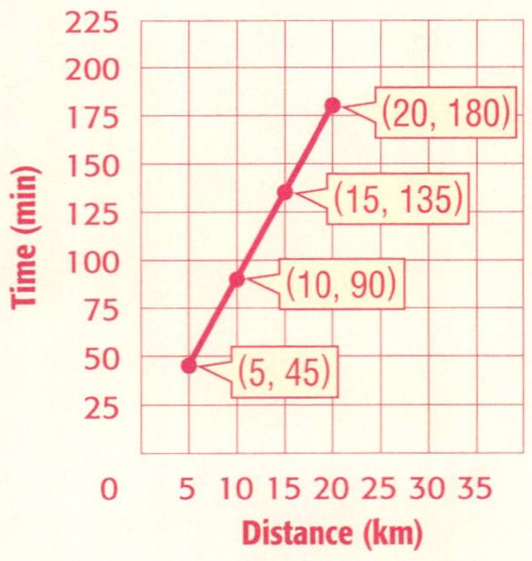

slope: $\frac{9}{1}$ or 9: She ran 1 km every 9 minutes.

Example 3 (p. 295)

3. **SNACKS** The table below shows the number of small packs of fruit snacks y per box x. Graph the data. Then find the slope of the line. Explain what the slope represents. **See margin.**

Boxes (x)	3	5	7	9
Packs (y)	24	40	56	72

Practice and Problem Solving

HOMEWORK HELP

For Exercises	See Examples
4–6	1
7, 8	2
9, 10	3

Exercise Levels
A: 4–10
B: 11–12
C: 13–14

For Exercises 4 and 5, find the rate of change for each table.

4.

Time (s)	Distance (m)
0	6
1	12
2	18
3	24

6 m per s

5.

Time (h)	Wage ($)
0	0
1	9
2	18
3	27

$9 per h

6. The number of minutes included in different cell phone plans and the costs are shown in the table. What is the approximate rate of change in cost per minute? **about $0.02 per minute**

Cost ($)	38	50	62	74	86
Minutes	1,000	1,500	2,000	2,500	3,000

For Exercises 7 and 8, find the rate of change for each graph.

7. $9 per shirt
8. 12 in. of length for every 1 in. of height

7.

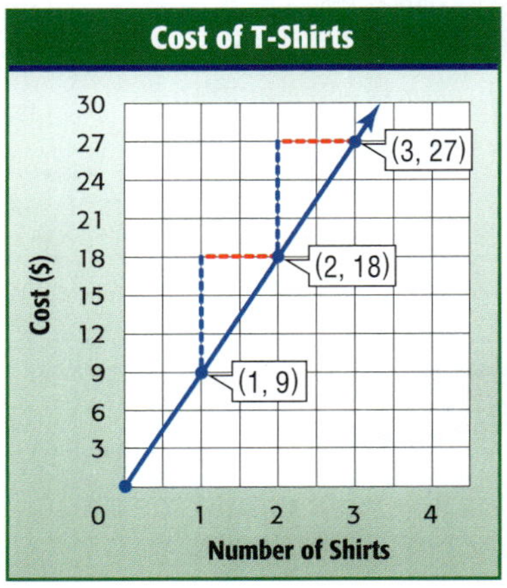

8.

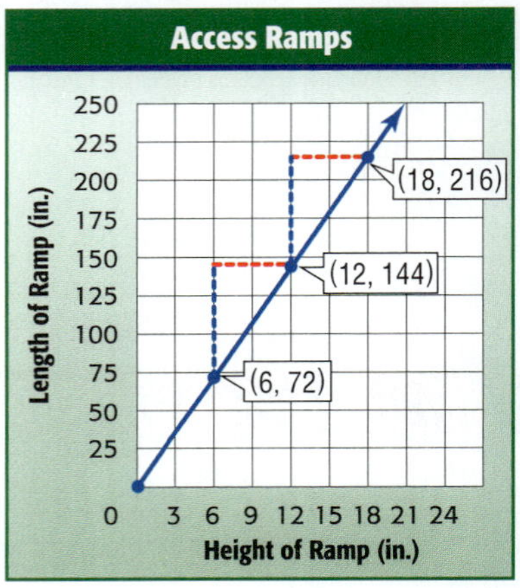

9. **CYCLING** The table shows the distance y Cheryl traveled in x minutes while competing in the cycling portion of a triathlon. Graph the data. Then find the slope of the line. Explain what the slope represents. **See margin.**

Time (min)	45	90	135	180
Distance (km)	5	10	15	20

Academic Standards • ISTEP+
Extra Practice, pp. 682, 709

10. **MAPS** The table shows the key for a map. Graph the data. Then find the slope of the line. **See margin.**

Distance on Map (in.)	2	4	6	8
Actual Distance (mi)	40	80	120	160

11. **WATER** At 1:00, the water level in a pool is 13 inches. At 2:30, the water level is 28 inches. What is the rate of change? **$\frac{1}{6}$ inch per minute**

12. $25 per month for the first 3 months, then $50 per month after that

12. **MONEY** Dwayne opens a savings account with $75. He makes the same deposit every month and makes no withdrawals. After 3 months, he has $150. After 6 months, he has $300. After 9 months, he has $450 dollars. What is the rate of change?

H.O.T. Problems

13. **OPEN ENDED** Make a table where the rate of change is 6 inches for every foot. **See margin.**

14. **WRITING IN MATH** Write a problem to represent a rate of change of $15 per item. **Sample answer: At Sam's Shoes, 2 pairs of sandals cost $30 and 4 pairs cost $60. Find the rate of change.**

ISTEP+ PRACTICE 7.2.5, 7.2.6

15. Use the information in the table to find the rate of change. **A**

Number of Apples	Number of Seeds
3	30
7	70
11	110

A $\frac{10}{1}$ C $\frac{40}{4}$

B $\frac{1}{10}$ D $\frac{4}{40}$

16. **SHORT RESPONSE** Find the slope of the line below that shows the distance Jairo traveled while jogging. **$\frac{4}{1}$**

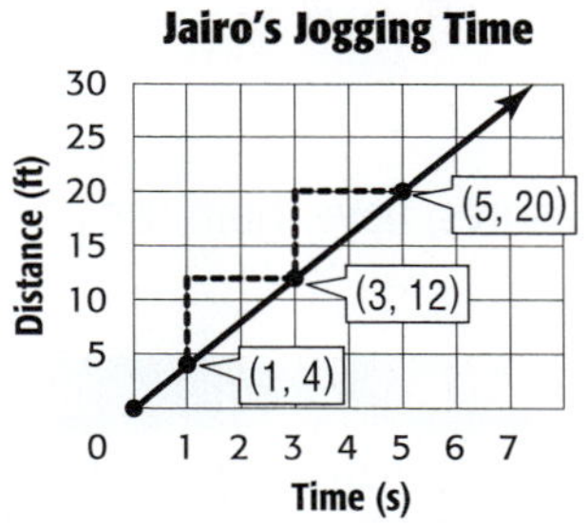

Spiral Review

17. **GROCERIES** Three pounds of pears cost $3.57. At this rate, how much would 10 pounds cost? (Lesson 6-2) **$11.90**

Write each ratio as a fraction in simplest form. (Lesson 6-1)

18. 9 feet in 21 minutes **$\frac{3}{7}$** 19. 36 calls in 2 hours **$\frac{18}{1}$** 20. 14 SUVs out of 56 vehicles **$\frac{1}{4}$**

GET READY for the Next Lesson

PREREQUISITE SKILL Solve. (Page 674)

21. 2.5 × 20 **50** 22. 3.5 × 4 **14** 23. 104 ÷ 16 **6.5** 24. 4,200 ÷ 2,000 **2.1**

Tips for New Teachers: Real-World Comparison

Draw a grid with tape on the floor. Have students stand in a line and have one student move vertically, then horizontally until they meet the next person in line. Explain that this number is the slope.

Additional Answers

10. Distances on a Map

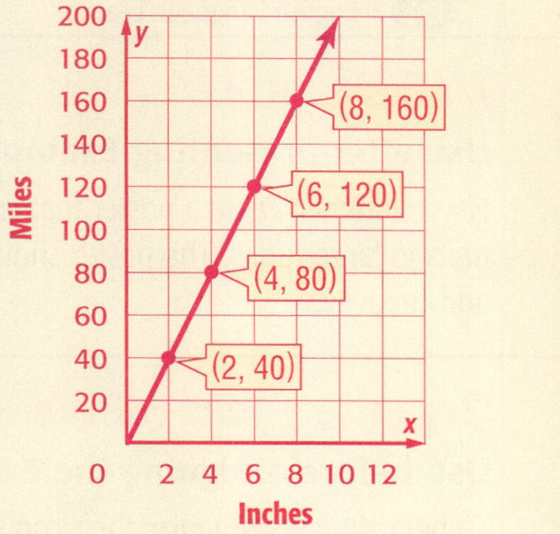

slope: $\frac{20}{1}$ or 20; Every inch on the map represents 20 miles.

13. Sample answer:

Length of Poster (ft)	Ribbon Needed (in.)
3	18
6	36
9	54
12	72

6-4 Measurement: Changing Customary Units

PACING: **Regular:** 1 period, **Block:** 0.5 period

IN Academic Standards **Preparation for 8.3.4** Solve simple problems involving rates and other derived measurements, including problems involving speed, uniform speed, average speed and density, by applying the concept of proportionality to measurement in different contexts. Express measurements in a given unit in terms of other units of the same type. *Also addresses 7.3.6, P.6.4.*

Options for Differentiated Instruction

ELL = English Language Learner AL = Above or Beyond Grade Level SS = Struggling Students SN = Special Needs

Mathematical Displays ELL SS

Use after presenting Examples 1–5.

Have students create a poster that explains how to change from larger units to smaller units and from smaller units to larger units. The poster should include examples from the different types of measure: length, weight, and capacity.

Organizing Student Work and Thinking SS SN

Use before assigning the Exercises.

To help students organize their conversions between measures, have them use a template with the headings shown below. One sample entry is given.

Problem	What I Know	Calculations	Answer
20 ft = ■ in.	1 foot = 12 inches	20 ft × 12 in./ft = 240 in.	20 ft = 240 in.

Research AL

Use after students complete Lesson 6-4.

Have students work in groups to research other customary units of measure that are less common. Examples are shown below.

- bales
- barrels
- bushels
- drams
- gills
- pecks

Students should present their findings accompanied by a conversion table similar to the one on page 298. Assign individual tasks based on students' strengths, such as who will do the research, who will write the report, who will make the table, and who will make a presentation to the class.

Leveled Lesson Resources

Also on TeacherWorks™ Lesson 6-4

Chapter 6 Resource Masters

BL = Below or Approaching Grade Level   OL = On Grade Level   AL = Above or Beyond Grade Level   ELL = English Language Learner

Lesson Reading Guide
p. 27 BL OL ELL

NAME ______ DATE ______ PERIOD ____

6-4 Lesson Reading Guide

Measurement: Changing Customary Units

Get Ready for the Lesson

Read the introduction at the top of page 298 in your textbook. Write your answers below.

1. Complete the ratio table. The first two ratios are done for you.

Tons	1	4	5	8
Pounds	2,000	8,000	10,000	16,000

2. Then graph the ordered pairs (tons, pounds) from the table. Label the horizontal axis *Weight in Tons* and the vertical axis *Weight in Pounds*. Connect the points. What do you notice about the graph of these data? Sample answer: the points lie on a straight line.

Weight of Land Animals

Read the Lesson

3. To the right of each customary unit write its abbreviation.

inch in.	mile mi	ton T	pint pt
foot ft	ounce oz	fluid ounce fl oz	quart qt
yard yd	pound lb	cup c	gallon gal

Complete each sentence.

4. To convert from larger units to smaller units, ______ . multiply
5. To convert from smaller units to larger units, ______ . divide

Remember What You Learned

6. Complete the table.

Customary Units of Length	Customary Units of Weight	Customary Units of Capacity
1 foot = 12 inches	1 pound = 16 ounces	1 cup = 8 fluid ounces
1 yard = 3 feet	1 ton = 2,000 pounds	1 pint = 2 cups
1 mile = 5,280 feet	1 gallon = 4 quarts	1 quart = 2 pints

Lesson 6-4

Chapter 6   27   Course 2

Study Guide and Intervention*
p. 28 BL OL ELL

NAME ______ DATE ______ PERIOD ____

6-4 Study Guide and Intervention

Measurement: Changing Customary Units

Customary Units		
Length	Weight	Capacity
1 foot (ft) = 12 inches (in.)	1 pound (lb) = 16 ounces (oz)	1 cup (c) = 8 fluid ounces (fl oz)
1 yard (yd) = 3 feet	1 ton (T) = 2,000 pounds	1 pint (pt) = 2 cups
1 mile (mi) = 5,280 feet		1 quart (qt) = 2 pints
		1 gallon (gal) = 4 quarts

Example 1 $5\frac{1}{2}$ lb = __?__ oz

To change from larger units to smaller units, multiply.

$5\frac{1}{2} \times 16 = 88$ Since 1 pound is 16 ounces, multiply by 16.

$5\frac{1}{2}$ pounds = 88 ounces

Example 2 28 fl oz = __?__ c

To change from smaller units to larger units, divide.

$28 \div 8 = 3\frac{1}{2}$ Since 8 fluid ounces are in 1 cup, divide by 8.

28 fluid ounces = $3\frac{1}{2}$ cups

Exercises

Complete.

1. 5 lb = ___ oz 80
2. 48 in. = ___ ft 4
3. 6 yd = ___ ft 18
4. 7 qt = ___ pt 14
5. 8,000 lb = ___ T 4
6. $3\frac{1}{4}$ mi = ___ ft 17,160
7. 4 c = ___ fl oz 32
8. 6 c = ___ pt 3
9. $\frac{1}{2}$ gal = ___ qt 2
10. 3 ft = ___ in. 36
11. 9 qt = ___ gal $2\frac{1}{4}$
12. 30 fl oz = ___ c $3\frac{3}{4}$
13. 6,864 ft = ___ mi $1\frac{3}{10}$
14. 40 oz = ___ lb $2\frac{1}{2}$
15. 9 pt = ___ c 18
16. 18 ft = ___ yd 6
17. 11 pt = ___ qt $5\frac{1}{2}$
18. $2\frac{3}{4}$ T = ___ lb 5,500

Chapter 6   28   Course 2

Skills Practice*
p. 29 BL OL

NAME ______ DATE ______ PERIOD ____

6-4 Skills Practice

Measurement: Changing Customary Units

Complete.

1. 3 lb = ___ oz 48
2. 16 qt = ___ gal 4
3. 24 in. = ___ ft 2
4. 12 ft = ___ yd 4
5. 3 mi = ___ ft 15,840
6. 12,000 lb = ___ T 6
7. 64 oz = ___ lb 4
8. 6 pt = ___ qt 3
9. 3 pt = ___ c 6
10. $5\frac{1}{2}$ ft = ___ in. 66
11. 22 yd = ___ ft 66
12. $\frac{1}{4}$ mi = ___ ft 1,320
13. 15 T = ___ lb 30,000
14. 7 lb = ___ oz 112
15. $8\frac{1}{2}$ qt = ___ pt 17
16. 5 gal = ___ qt 20
17. 8 c = ___ pt 4
18. 16 in = ___ ft $1\frac{1}{3}$
19. 24 fl oz = ___ c 3
20. 60 ft = ___ yd 20
21. 6,600 ft = ___ mi $1\frac{1}{4}$
22. 7.5 T = ___ lb 15,000
23. 88 oz = ___ lb $5\frac{1}{2}$
24. 70 qt = ___ gal $17\frac{1}{2}$

Lesson 6-4

Chapter 6   29   Course 2

Practice*
p. 30 OL AL

NAME ______ DATE ______ PERIOD ____

6-4 Practice

Measurement: Changing Customary Units

Complete.

1. 4 c = ___ fl oz 32
2. 5 c = ___ pt $2\frac{1}{2}$
3. 3 lb = ___ oz 48
4. 24 ft = ___ yd 8
5. $1\frac{1}{2}$ pt = ___ c 3
6. 64 oz = ___ lb 4
7. 4 mi = ___ ft 21,120
8. $2\frac{3}{4}$ mi = ___ ft 14,520
9. 3,000 lb = ___ T $1\frac{1}{2}$
10. 5 gal = ___ qt 20
11. $3\frac{1}{4}$ qt = ___ pt $6\frac{1}{2}$
12. $4\frac{5}{8}$ T = ___ lb 9,250
13. $3\frac{1}{2}$ gal = ___ qt 14
14. 7 c = ___ qt $1\frac{3}{4}$
15. 40 fl oz = ___ qt $1\frac{1}{4}$
16. 660 yd = ___ mi $\frac{3}{8}$
17. 1.9 yd = ___ in. 68.4
18. $2\frac{1}{4}$ T = ___ oz 72,000

19. SPORTS The track surrounding a football field is $\frac{1}{4}$ mile long. How many yards long is the track? 440 yd

20. STRAWBERRIES One quart of strawberries weighs about 2 pounds. About how many quarts of strawberries would weigh $\frac{1}{4}$ ton? 250 quarts

ANALYZE GRAPHS For Exercises 21–23, use the graph shown.

21. What does an ordered pair from this graph represent? The *x*-value represents the number of inches, and the *y*-value represents the equivalent number of feet.

22. Write two sentences that describe the graph. Sample answer: The graph is a straight line. For each *x*-value increase of 12, the *y*-value increases by 1.

23. Use the graph to find the length in inches of a 1.5 foot iguana. Explain your reasoning. Sample answer: The *x*-value of the point on the line whose *y*-value is equal to 1.5 is 18, so 1.5 ft = 18 in.

Chapter 6   30   Course 2

Word Problem Practice*
p. 31 OL AL

NAME ______ DATE ______ PERIOD ____

6-4 World Problem Practice

Measurement: Changing Customary Units

1. WEIGHT The average weight of a baby at birth is 7 pounds. How many ounces is this? 112 oz

2. WATERFALLS The height of Niagara Falls is 182 feet. How many yards high is it? $60\frac{2}{3}$ yd

3. GASOLINE The gasoline tank of a minivan holds 18 gallons. How many quarts is this? 72 qt

4. TELEPHONES Portable telephones can weigh as little as 8 ounces. How many pounds is this? $\frac{1}{2}$ lb

5. RECIPE A recipe for ice cream calls for 56 fluid ounces of milk. How many cups of milk is this? 7 c

6. STATUE The Statue of Liberty weighs 450,000 pounds. How many tons is this? 225 T

7. TUNNEL The Ted Williams Tunnel under Boston Harbor is 8,448 feet long. How many yards is this? 2,816 yd

8. COAL The United States exports over 200 billion pounds of coal. How many tons is this? 100 million T

Lesson 6-4

Chapter 6   31   Course 2

Enrichment
p. 32 OL AL

NAME ______ DATE ______ PERIOD ____

6-4 Enrichment

Changing Measurements with Factors of 1

Multiplying an expression by the number 1 does not change its value. This property of multiplication can be used to change measurements.

Let's say you wanted to change 4.5 hours to seconds. Start by multiplying 4.5 by the number 1 written in the form $\frac{60 \text{ minutes}}{1 \text{ hour}}$. This first step changes 4.5 hours to minutes.

$4.5 \text{ hours} \times \frac{60 \text{ minutes}}{1 \text{ hour}}$

Now, multiply by the number 1 again. This time use the fact that $1 = \frac{60 \text{ seconds}}{1 \text{ minute}}$.

$4.5 \text{ hours} \times \frac{60 \text{ minutes}}{1 \text{ hour}} \times \frac{60 \text{ seconds}}{1 \text{ minute}} = 16{,}200 \text{ seconds}$

Complete by writing the last factor and the answer. You may need to use a table of measurements to find the factors.

1. Change 5 pints to fluid ounces.
$5 \text{ pints} \times \frac{2 \text{ cups}}{1 \text{ pint}} \times \frac{8 \text{ fluid ounces}}{1 \text{ cup}} = 80 \text{ fl oz}$

2. Change 0.8 miles to inches.
$0.8 \text{ mile} \times \frac{5{,}280 \text{ feet}}{1 \text{ mile}} \times \frac{12 \text{ inches}}{1 \text{ foot}} = 50{,}688 \text{ in.}$

3. Change 4 square yards to square inches.
$4 \text{ yd}^2 \times \frac{9 \text{ ft}^2}{1 \text{ yd}^2} \times \frac{144 \text{ in}^2}{1 \text{ ft}^2} = 5{,}184 \text{ in}^2$

4. Change 12 bushels to pints.
$12 \text{ bushels} \times \frac{4 \text{ pecks}}{1 \text{ bushel}} \times \frac{8 \text{ quarts}}{1 \text{ peck}} \times \frac{2 \text{ pints}}{1 \text{ quart}} = 768 \text{ pt}$

5. Change one-half of an acre to square inches.
$\frac{1}{2} \text{ acre} \times \frac{4{,}840 \text{ yd}^2}{1 \text{ acre}} \times \frac{9 \text{ ft}^2}{1 \text{ yd}^2} \times \frac{144 \text{ in}^2}{1 \text{ ft}^2} = 3{,}136{,}320 \text{ in}^2$

Chapter 6   32   Course 2

* Also available in Spanish ELL

Additional Lesson Resources

Transparencies

- *5-Minute Check Transparency*, Lesson 6-4

Other Print Products

- *Noteables™ Interactive Study Notebook with Foldables™*

Teacher Tech Tools

- *Interactive Classroom CD-ROM*, Lesson 6-4
- *AssignmentWorks*, Lesson 6-4

Student Tech Tools

glencoe.com

- Extra Examples, Chapter 6, Lesson 4
- Self-Check Quiz, Chapter 6, Lesson 4

6-4 Lesson Notes

1 Focus

Vertical Alignment

Before Lesson 6-4
Differentiate between and use appropriate units of measures for two- and three-dimensional objects

Lesson 6-4
Convert one unit of measurement to another

After Lesson 6-4
Compare weights, capacities, geometric measures, times, and temperatures within and between measurement systems

2 Teach

Scaffolding Questions

Ask:

- How can you find the number of feet in 2 yards? There are 3 feet in 1 yard, and $2 \times 3 = 6$, so there are 6 feet in 2 yards.
- How many feet are in $1\frac{2}{3}$ yards? 5 ft
- How can you find the number of inches in 1 yard? There are 3 feet in 1 yard and 12 inches in one foot, so multiply $3 \times 12 = 36$.
- How many inches are in $\frac{1}{2}$ yard? 18 in.

6-4 Measurement: Changing Customary Units

MAIN IDEA

Change units in the customary system.

IN Academic Standards

Preparation for 8.3.4 Solve simple problems involving rates and other derived measurements, including problems involving speed, uniform speed, average speed and density, by applying the concept of proportionality to measurement in different contexts. Express measurements in a given unit in terms of other units of the same type. *Also addresses 7.3.6, P.6.4.*

New Vocabulary

unit ratio

IN Math Online

glencoe.com

- Extra Examples
- Personal Tutor
- Self-Check Quiz

GET READY for the Lesson

ANIMALS The table shows the approximate weights in tons of several large land animals. One ton is equivalent to 2,000 pounds.

Animal	Weight (T)
Grizzly Bear	1
White Rhinoceros	4
Hippopotamus	5
African Elephant	8

You can use a *ratio table*, which have columns filled with ratios that have the same value, to convert each weight from tons to pounds.

1. Copy and complete the ratio table. The first two ratios are done for you. **See margin.**

×4

Tons	1	4	5	8
Pounds	2,000	8,000		

×4

To produce equivalent ratios, multiply the quantities in each row by the same number.

2. Then graph the ordered pairs (tons, pounds) from the table. Label the horizontal axis *Weight in Tons* and the vertical axis *Weight in Pounds*. Connect the points. What do you notice about the graph of these data?

2. Sample answer: The points lie on a straight line. See margin for graph.

The relationships among the most commonly used customary units of length, weight, and capacity are shown in the table below.

Customary Units — Key Concept

Type of Measure	Larger Unit	→	Smaller Unit
Length	1 foot (ft)	=	12 inches (in.)
	1 yard (yd)	=	3 feet
	1 mile (mi)	=	5,280 feet
Weight	1 pound (lb)	=	16 ounces (oz)
	1 ton (T)	=	2,000 pounds
Capacity	1 cup (c)	=	8 fluid ounces (fl oz)
	1 pint (pt)	=	2 cups
	1 quart (qt)	=	2 pints
	1 gallon (gal)	=	4 quarts

Additional Answers

1.

Tons	5	8
Pounds	10,000	16,000

2.

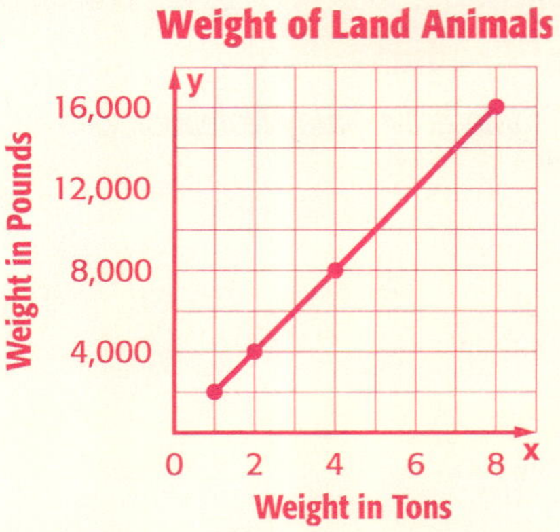

Each of the relationships above can be written as a unit ratio. Like a unit rate, a **unit ratio** is one in which the denominator is 1 unit.

$$\frac{3 \text{ ft}}{1 \text{ yd}} \qquad \frac{2{,}000 \text{ lb}}{1 \text{ T}} \qquad \frac{4 \text{ qt}}{1 \text{ gal}}$$

Notice that the numerator and denominator of each fraction above are equivalent, so the value of each ratio is 1. You can multiply by a unit ratio of this type to *convert* or change from larger units to smaller units.

Study Tip

Multiplying by 1
Although the number and units changed in Example 1, because the measure is multiplied by 1, the value of the converted measure is the same as the original.

EXAMPLES Convert Larger Units to Smaller Units

1 **Convert 20 feet into inches.**

Since 1 foot = 12 inches, the unit ratio is $\frac{12 \text{ in.}}{1 \text{ ft}}$.

$20 \text{ ft} = 20 \text{ ft} \cdot \frac{12 \text{ in.}}{1 \text{ ft}}$ — Multiply by $\frac{12 \text{ in.}}{1 \text{ ft}}$.

$= 20 \cancel{\text{ft}} \cdot \frac{12 \text{ in.}}{1 \cancel{\text{ft}}}$ — Divide out common units, leaving the desired unit, inches.

$= 20 \cdot 12 \text{ in. or } 240 \text{ in.}$ — Multiply.

So, 20 feet = 240 inches.

2 **GARDENING** **Clarence mixes $\frac{1}{4}$ cup of fertilizer with soil before planting each bulb. How many ounces of fertilizer does he use per bulb?**

$\frac{1}{4} \text{ c} = \frac{1}{4} \cancel{\text{c}} \cdot \frac{8 \text{ fl oz}}{1 \cancel{\text{c}}}$ — Since 1 cup = 8 fluid ounces, multiply by $\frac{8 \text{ fl oz}}{1 \text{ c}}$. Then, divide out common units.

$= \frac{1}{4} \cdot 8 \text{ fl oz or } 2 \text{ fl oz}$ — Multiply.

So, 2 fluid ounces of fertilizer are used per bulb.

CHECK Your Progress

Complete.

a. 36 yd = ■ ft **108** b. $\frac{3}{4}$ T = ■ lb **1,500** c. $1\frac{1}{2}$ qt = ■ pt **3**

Review Vocabulary

reciprocal The product of a number and its reciprocal is 1; *Example*: The reciprocal of $\frac{3}{5}$ is $\frac{5}{3}$. (Lesson 5-7)

To convert from smaller units to larger units, multiply by the reciprocal of the appropriate unit ratio.

EXAMPLES Convert Smaller Units to Larger Units

3 **Convert 15 quarts into gallons.**

Since 1 gallon = 4 quarts, the unit ratio is $\frac{4 \text{ qt}}{1 \text{ gal}}$, and its reciprocal is $\frac{1 \text{ gal}}{4 \text{ qt}}$.

$15 \text{ qt} = 15 \text{ qt} \cdot \frac{1 \text{ gal}}{4 \text{ qt}}$ — Multiply by $\frac{1 \text{ gal}}{4 \text{ qt}}$.

$= 15 \cancel{\text{qt}} \cdot \frac{1 \text{ gal}}{4 \cancel{\text{qt}}}$ — Divide out common units, leaving the desired unit, gallons.

$= 15 \cdot \frac{1}{4} \text{ gal or } 3.75 \text{ gal}$ — Multiplying 15 by $\frac{1}{4}$ is the same as dividing 15 by 4.

Focus on Mathematical Content

Unit ratios—and their reciprocals—can be used to **convert measurements to different units**.

To convert a measurement to a smaller unit, **multiply**.

To convert a measurement to a larger unit, **divide**.

Formative Assessment

Use the Check Your Progress exercises after each Example to determine students' understanding of concepts.

ADDITIONAL EXAMPLES

1. Convert 2 miles into feet. 10,560 ft
2. **ELEVATOR** The elevator in an office building has a weight limit posted of one and a half tons. How many pounds can the elevator safely hold? 3,000 lb
3. Convert 11 cups into pints. 5.5 pt

Additional Examples are also in:

- Noteables™ Interactive Study Notebook with Foldables™
- Interactive Classroom PowerPoint® Presentations

ADDITIONAL EXAMPLES

4 **SOCCER** Tracy kicked a soccer ball 1,000 inches. How many feet did she kick the ball? $83\frac{1}{3}$ ft

5 **LEMONADE** Paul made 6 pints of lemonade and poured it into 10 glasses equally. How many cups of lemonade did each glass contain? $1\frac{1}{5}$ c

4 **COSTUMES** **Umeka needs $4\frac{1}{2}$ feet of fabric to make a costume for a play. How many yards of fabric does she need?**

$4\frac{1}{2}\text{ ft} = 4\frac{1}{2}\text{ ft} \cdot \frac{1\text{ yd}}{3\text{ ft}}$ — Since 1 yard = 3 feet, multiply by $\frac{1\text{ yd}}{3\text{ ft}}$. Then, divide out common units.

$= \frac{\overset{3}{\cancel{9}}}{2} \cdot \frac{1}{\underset{1}{\cancel{3}}}\text{ yd}$ — Write $4\frac{1}{2}$ as an improper fraction. Then divide out common factors.

$= \frac{3}{2}\text{ yd or } 1\frac{1}{2}\text{ yd}$ — Multiply.

So Umeka needs $1\frac{1}{2}$ yards of fabric.

CHECK Your Progress

Complete.

d. 2,640 ft = ■ mi $\frac{1}{2}$

e. 5 pt = ■ qt $2\frac{1}{2}$

f. 100 oz = ■ lb $6\frac{1}{4}$

g. 76c = ■ gal $4\frac{3}{4}$

h. 3 c = ■ pt 6

i. 18 in. = ■ ft $1\frac{1}{2}$

j. **FOOD** A 3-pound pork loin can be cut into 10 smaller pork chops of equal weight. How many ounces does each pork chop weigh? **4.8 oz**

You can also convert from one rate to another by multiplying by a unit rate or its reciprocal.

Real-World EXAMPLE — Convert Rates

5 **HELICOPTERS** **A helicopter flies at a rate of 158 miles per hour. How many miles per second is this?**

Since 1 hour = 3,600 seconds, multiply by $\frac{1\text{ h}}{3{,}600\text{ s}}$.

$\frac{158\text{ mi}}{\text{h}} = \frac{158\text{ mi}}{1\text{ h}} \times \frac{1\text{ h}}{3{,}600\text{ s}}$ — Multiply by $\frac{1\text{ h}}{3{,}600\text{ s}}$.

$= \frac{158\text{ mi}}{1\cancel{\text{h}}} \times \frac{1\cancel{\text{h}}}{3{,}600\text{ s}}$ — Divide out common units.

$\approx \frac{0.04\text{ mi}}{1\text{ s}}$ — Simplify.

So, a helicopter flies approximately 0.04 mile per second.

Real-World Link A swordfish reaches a maximum size of 14 feet and almost 1,200 pounds.
Source: Sport Fishing Central

CHECK Your Progress

k. **FISH** A swordfish can swim at a rate of 60 miles per hour. How many feet per hour is this? **316,800 ft/h**

l. **WALKING** Ava walks at a speed of 7 feet per second. How many feet per hour is this? **25,200 ft/h**

300 Chapter 6 Ratios and Proportions

CHECK Your Understanding

★ indicates multi-step problem

Examples 1, 2 (p. 299)

Complete.

1. 3 lb = ■ oz **48**
2. $5\frac{1}{3}$ yd = ■ ft **16**
3. 6.5 c = ■ fl oz **52**
4. **FISH** Grouper are members of the sea bass family. A large grouper can weigh $\frac{1}{3}$ ton. About how much does a large grouper weigh to the nearest pound? **667 lb**

Examples 3, 4 (pp. 299–300)

Complete.

5. 12 qt = ■ gal **3**
6. 28 in. = ■ ft **$2\frac{1}{3}$**
7. 15 pt = ■ qt **$7\frac{1}{2}$**
8. **VEHICLES** The world's narrowest electric vehicle is about 35 inches wide and is designed to move down narrow aisles in warehouses. About how wide is this vehicle to the nearest foot? **3 ft**

Example 5 (p. 300)

9. **RUNNING** The fastest a human has ever run is about 27 miles per hour. How many miles per minute is this? **0.45 mi/min**

Practice and Problem Solving

HOMEWORK HELP

For Exercises	See Examples
10–21	1–4
22–23	2
24–25	4
26–27	5

Exercise Levels
A: 10–27
B: 28–37
C: 38–43

Complete.

10. 18 ft = ■ yd **6**
11. 72 oz = ■ lb **$4\frac{1}{2}$**
12. 2 lb = ■ oz **32**
13. 4 gal = ■ qt **16**
14. $4\frac{1}{2}$ pt = ■ c **9**
15. 3 c = ■ fl oz **24**
16. 2 mi = ■ ft **10,560**
17. $1\frac{1}{4}$ mi = ■ ft **6,600**
18. 5,000 lb = ■ T **$2\frac{1}{2}$**
19. 13 c = ■ pt **$6\frac{1}{2}$**
20. $2\frac{3}{4}$ qt = ■ pt **$5\frac{1}{2}$**
21. $3\frac{3}{8}$ T = ■ lb **6,750**
22. **PUMPKINS** One of the largest pumpkins ever grown weighed about $\frac{1}{2}$ ton. How many pounds did the pumpkin weigh? **1,000 lb**
23. **SKIING** Speed skiing takes place on a course that is $\frac{2}{3}$ mile long. How many feet long is the course? **3,520 ft**
24. **BOATING** A 40-foot power boat is for sale by owner. About how long is this boat to the nearest yard? **13 yd**
25. **BLOOD** A total of 35 pints of blood were collected at a local blood drive. How many quarts of blood is this? **$17\frac{1}{2}$ qt**
26. **GO-KARTS** A go-kart's top speed is 607,200 feet per hour. How many miles per hour is this? **115 mi/h**
27. **BIRDS** A peregrine falcon can fly at over 200 miles per hour. How many feet per hour is this? **1,056,000 ft/h**

3 Practice

Formative Assessment

Use Exercises 1–9 to check for understanding.

Then use the chart at the bottom of this page to customize your assignments for students.

Intervention You may wish to use the Study Guide and Intervention Master on page 28 of the *Chapter 6 Resource Masters* for additional reinforcement.

Odd/Even Assignments

Exercises 10–27 are structured so that students practice the same concepts whether they are assigned odd or even problems.

DIFFERENTIATED HOMEWORK OPTIONS

Level	Assignment	Two-Day Option	
BL Basic	10–29, 38–41, 43–56	11–29 odd, 44, 45	10–28 even, 38–41, 43, 46–56
OL Core	11–33 odd, 34–41, 43–56	10–29, 44, 45	30–41, 43, 46–56
AL Advanced/Pre-AP	30–52 (optional: 53–56)		

Additional Answers

34. The x-value represents the number of quarts and the y-value represents the equivalent number of gallons.

36. Sample answer: The point on the line whose y-value is equal to 2.5 is (10, 2.5), so 2.5 qt = 10 gal.

38. Sample answer: 16 in. is equivalent to 12 in. + 4 in. or 1 ft 4 in., $1\frac{1}{2}$ ft is equivalent to 1 ft 6 in., Since 1 ft 4 in. < 1 ft 6 in., 16 in. < $1\frac{1}{2}$ ft.

39. Sample answer: $8\frac{3}{4}$ gal is equivalent to 35 qt, Since 35 qt > 32 qt, $8\frac{3}{4}$ gal > 32 qt.

40. Sample answer: 2.7 T is equivalent to $2.7\text{ T} \cdot \frac{2{,}000\text{ lb}}{1\text{ T}} \cdot \frac{16\text{ oz}}{1\text{ lb}}$ or 86,400 oz.

41. Yes; 2 quarts = 8 cups, so the ratio of cups of vinegar to water in the recommended mixture is $\frac{\frac{3}{4}\text{ c}}{2\text{ qt}} = \frac{\frac{3}{4}\text{ c}}{8\text{ c}} = \frac{3}{4} \div 8 = \frac{3}{4} \cdot \frac{1}{8}$ or $\frac{3}{32}$. The ratio of the new mixture is $\frac{1.5\text{ oz}}{16\text{ oz}} = \frac{1.5 \cdot 2}{16 \cdot 2}$ or $\frac{3}{32}$. The mixtures have the same ratio of vinegar to water.

42. 720 in^2; Square feet mean a unit of feet × feet. To divide out each unit, you must multiply by two conversion factors that have feet in the denominator and inches in the numerator. $5\text{ ft}^2 \cdot \frac{12\text{ in.}}{1\text{ ft}} \cdot \frac{12\text{ in.}}{1\text{ ft}} = 720\text{ in}^2$

★ 28. **PUNCH** Will a 2-quart pitcher hold the entire recipe of citrus punch given at the right? Explain your reasoning.

28. No; $2 + 2 + \frac{1}{4} + \frac{1}{3} + 4 = 8\frac{7}{12}$ c punch and a 2-qt pitcher holds 2 qt $\cdot \frac{2\text{ pt}}{1\text{ qt}} \cdot \frac{2\text{ c}}{1\text{ pt}} = 2 \cdot 2 \cdot 2$ c or 8 c. Since 8 c < $8\frac{7}{12}$ c, the pitcher will not hold all of the punch.

★ 29. **WEATHER** On Monday, it snowed a total of 15 inches. On Tuesday and Wednesday, it snowed an additional $4\frac{1}{2}$ inches and $6\frac{3}{4}$ inches, respectively. A weather forecaster says that over the last three days, it snowed about $2\frac{1}{2}$ feet. Is this a valid claim? Justify your answer.

29. No; 15 in. + $4\frac{1}{2}$ in. + $6\frac{3}{4}$ in. = $26\frac{1}{4}$ in. and $26\frac{1}{4} \div 12 = 2\frac{3}{16}$. So, it snowed a total of $2\frac{3}{16}$ ft or about 2 ft, not $2\frac{1}{2}$ ft.

MEASUREMENT *Accuracy* **describes how close a measurement is to its actual value. Choose the correct term to determine the degree of accuracy needed in each situation.**

30. The length of a cruise ship would be described in (inches, feet). **feet**

31. Fabric for a jacket would be measured to the nearest (inch, eighth of an inch). **eighth of an inch**

32. A bag of apples would be weighed to the nearest (tenth of a pound, tenth of an ounce). **tenth of a pound**

★ 33. **ESTIMATION** Cristos is a member of the swim team and trains by swimming an average of 3,000 yards a day. About how many miles would he swim by training at this rate for 5 days, to the nearest half-mile? **about $8\frac{1}{2}$ mi**

MEASUREMENT For Exercises 34–37, use the graph at the right.

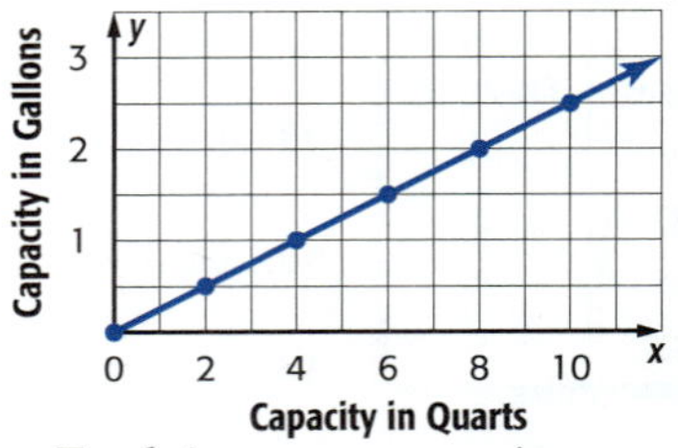

34. What does an ordered pair from this graph represent? **See margin.**

35. Find the slope of the line. $\frac{1}{4}$

36. Use the graph to find the capacity in quarts of a 2.5-gallon container. Explain your reasoning. **See margin.**

37. Use the graph to predict the capacity in gallons of a 12-quart container. Explain your reasoning. **3 gal; Sample answer: the graph increases by 1 gallon for every 4 quarts.**

Academic Standards • ISTEP+

Extra Practice, pp. 682, 709

H.O.T. Problems

REASONING Replace each ● with <, >, or = to make a true sentence. Justify your answers. **39–41. See margin for justification.**

38. 16 in. ● $1\frac{1}{2}$ ft **<**

39. $8\frac{3}{4}$ gal ● 32 qt **>**

40. 2.7 T ● 86,400 oz **=**

41. **CHALLENGE** To whiten fabrics, a certain Web site recommends that you soak them in a mixture of $\frac{3}{4}$ cup vinegar, 2 quarts water, and some salt. Does a mixture that contains 1.5 ounces vinegar and 16 ounces water have the same vinegar-to-water ratio as the recommended mixture? Explain. **See margin.**

42. **WRITING IN MATH** Use multiplication by unit ratios of equivalent measures to convert 5 square feet to square inches. Justify your answer. **See margin.**

Pre-AP Activity **Use after Exercise 37**

Tell students that the average distance of Mars from the Sun is 227,940,000 kilometers. Tell students that astronomers use a unit of length called the astronomical unit (AU), which is equal to the average distance of Earth from the Sun. Have students research the astronomical unit on the Internet (or in an encyclopedia), find its relationship to kilometers, and convert the average distance of Mars from the Sun to astronomical units. 1 AU = 149,597,871 km; The average distance of Mars from the Sun is approximately 1.52 AU.

ISTEP+ PRACTICE Preparation for 8.3.4

43. Which situation is represented by the graph? **D**

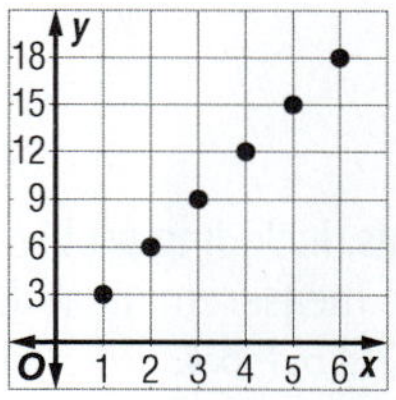

A conversion of inches to yards
B conversion of feet to inches
C conversion of miles to feet
D conversion of yards to feet

44. How many cups of milk are shown below? **G**

F $\frac{3}{4}$ c
H $2\frac{1}{2}$ c
G $1\frac{1}{4}$ c
J 10 c

45. How many ounces are in $7\frac{3}{4}$ pounds? **A**

A 124 oz
C 120 oz
B 122 oz
D 112 oz

Spiral Review

46. Use the information in the table to find the rate of change in dollars per hour. (Lesson 6-3) **$9 per h**

Wage ($)	0	9	18	27
Time (h)	0	1	2	3

47. **GROCERIES** Find the unit price if Anju spent $2 for six oranges. Round to the nearest cent if necessary. (Lesson 6-2) **$0.33 per orange**

48. **MEASUREMENT** By doubling just the length of the rectangular ice skating rink in Will's backyard from 16 to 32 feet, he increased its area from 128 square feet to 256 square feet. Find the width of both rinks. (Lesson 3-6) **8 ft**

ALGEBRA For Exercises 50–52, use the pay stub at the right. (Lesson 3-3)

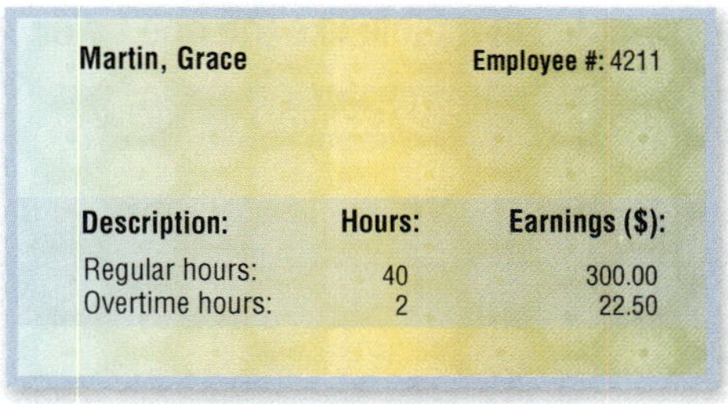

Martin, Grace — Employee #: 4211

Description:	Hours:	Earnings ($):
Regular hours:	40	300.00
Overtime hours:	2	22.50

49. Write and solve an equation to find the regular hourly wage. **$40r = 300$; $7.50/h**

50. Write and solve an equation to find the overtime hourly wage. **$2v = 22.50$; $11.25/h**

51. Write and solve an equation to find how many times greater Grace's overtime hourly wage is than her regular hourly wage. **$7.5t = 11.25$; 1.5**

GET READY for the Next Lesson

PREREQUISITE SKILL Multiply. (p. 674)

52. 14.5×8.2 **118.9**
53. 7.03×4.6 **32.338**
54. 9.29×15.3 **142.137**
55. 1.84×16.7 **30.728**

4 Assess

Ticket Out the Door Tell students that the perimeter of a friend's backyard is 132 feet. Say the friend's dog runs around the backyard 16 times. What part of a mile has the dog run? **0.4 mi**

FOLDABLES Study Organizer Foldables™ Follow-Up

Remind students to select a term or concept about units of measure and to define it in their Foldables. Encourage them to give an example of the term or concept.

6-5 Measurement: Changing Metric Units

PACING: **Regular:** 1 period, **Block:** 0.5 period

IN Academic Standards **Preparation for 8.3.4** Solve simple problems involving rates and other derived measurements, including problems involving speed, uniform speed, average speed and density, by applying the concept of proportionality to measurement in different contexts. Express measurements in a given unit in terms of other units of the same type. *Also addresses 7.3.6, P.6.4.*

Options for Differentiated Instruction

ELL = English Language Learner AL = Above or Beyond Grade Level SS = Struggling Students SN = Special Needs

Visual Learners SS SN

Use before presenting Examples 1–3.

Display the diagram showing metric prefixes on the board or overhead.

Point out the following to students:

- Each place value is 10 times the place value to its right.
- The value of each metric prefix is 10 times the value of the prefix to its right.

1,000	100	10	1	0.1	0.01	0.001
thousands	hundreds	tens	ones	tenths	hundredths	thousandths
kilo	hecto	deka	basic unit	deci	centi	milli

Making Resource Sheet ELL SS SN

Use after presenting Examples 1–3.

Have students write step-by-step directions in their own words for how to convert between different metric units. Have them organize the information and include examples in a table like the one below.

Convert	Steps	Examples
centimeters to meters		
millimeters to meters		
grams to kilograms		
kilometers to centimeters		

Mathematical Displays ELL SS SN

Use after students complete Lesson 6-5.

Have students work in pairs to create a poster about the metric system. Each poster should include the following:

- a drawing or picture of an object
- the metric units for length, mass, and/or capacity labeled on or near the object
- a comparison of that object's measures to the corresponding measures of similar objects

Leveled Lesson Resources

Also on TeacherWorks™ Lesson 6-5

Chapter 6 Resource Masters

BL = Below or Approaching Grade Level OL = On Grade Level AL = Above or Beyond Grade Level ELL = English Language Learner

Lesson Reading Guide
p. 33 BL OL ELL

NAME ________ DATE ________ PERIOD ____

6-5 Lesson Reading Guide

Measurement: Changing Metric Units

Get Ready for the Lesson

Complete the Mini Lab at the top of page 304 in your textbook. Write your answers below.

1. Select three other objects. Find and record the width of all five objects to the nearest millimeter and tenth of a centimeter. **See students' work.**
2. Compare the measurements of the objects, and write a rule that describes how to convert from millimeters to centimeters. **Divide by 10.**
3. Measure the length of your classroom in meters. Make a conjecture about how to convert this measure to centimeters. Explain. **Multiplication; there is a greater number of smaller units than larger units in a measure.**

Read the Lesson

Complete each sentence.

4. To convert from centimeters to kilometers, first divide by ________ to convert to meters, then divide by ________ to convert to kilometers. **100; 1,000**
5. To convert from kiloliters to milliliters, first multiply by ________ to convert to liters, then multiply by ________ to convert to milliliters. **1,000; 1,000**
6. To convert from ________ to centigrams, multiply by 100. **grams**

Remember What You Learned

7. Name an everyday object that you can associate with each base metric unit of measure to help you remember what each unit represents.
   kilogram: **Sample answer: the mass of a one-liter bottle of water**
   meter: **Sample answer: the distance from the floor to a doorknob**
   liter: **Sample answer: the amount of soda in a standard bottle**

Lesson 6-5

Chapter 6 33 Course 2

Study Guide and Intervention*
p. 34 BL OL ELL

NAME ________ DATE ________ PERIOD ____

6-5 Study Guide and Intervention

Measurement: Changing Metric Units

The table below is a summary of how to convert measures in the metric system.

	Larger Units → Smaller Units	Smaller Units → Larger Units
Units of Length (meter)	km to m – multiply by 1,000 m to cm – multiply by 100 m to mm – multiply by 1,000 cm to mm – multiply by 10	mm to cm – divide by 10 mm to m – divide by 1,000 cm to m – divide by 100 m to km – divide by 1,000
Units of Mass (kilogram)	kg to g – multiply by 1,000 g to mg – multiply by 1,000	mg to g – divide by 1,000 g to kg – divide by 1,000
Units of Capacity (liter)	kL to L – multiply by 1,000 L to mL – multiply by 1,000	mL to L – divide by 1,000 L to kL – divide by 1,000

Example 1 Complete. 62 cm = ____ m

To convert from centimeters to meters, divide by 100.
62 ÷ 100 = 0.62
62 cm = 0.62 m

Example 2 Complete. 2.6 kL = ____ L

To convert from kiloliters to liters, multiply by 1,000.
2.6 × 1,000 = 2,600
2.6 kL = 2,600 L

Exercises

Complete.

1. 650 cm = ____ m **6.5**
2. 57 kg = ____ g **57,000**
3. 751 mg = ____ g **0.751**
4. 8.2 L = ____ mL **8,200**
5. 52 L = ____ kL **0.052**
6. 892 mm = ____ m **0.892**
7. 121.4 kL = ____ L **121,400**
8. 0.72 cm = ____ mm **7.2**
9. 67.3 g = ____ kg **0.0673**
10. 5.2 g = ____ mg **5,200**
11. 0.05 m = ____ mm **50**
12. 2,500 mg = ____ g **2.5**
13. 32 mm = ____ cm **3.2**
14. 96 m = ____ cm **9,600**

Chapter 6 34 Course 2

Skills Practice*
p. 35 BL OL

NAME ________ DATE ________ PERIOD ____

6-5 Skills Practice

Measurement: Changing Metric Units

Complete.

1. 660 m = ____ km **0.66**
2. 5.7 m = ____ cm **570**
3. 543 mL = ____ L **0.543**
4. 23.7 g = ____ mg **23,700**
5. 529 mg = ____ g **0.529**
6. 2,640 mL = ____ L **2.640**
7. 4.32 kL = ____ L **4,320**
8. 75.4 mg = ____ g **0.0754**
9. 8,300 mg = ____ g **8.3**
10. 7.3 m = ____ cm **730**
11. 250.3 kL = ____ L **250,300**
12. 799 g = ____ kg **0.799**
13. 8.5 cm = ____ mm **85**
14. 450 kg = ____ g **450,000**
15. 7.3 L = ____ mL **7,300**
16. 6,140 L = ____ kL **6.140**
17. 3,500 m = ____ km **3.5**
18. 89 km = ____ m **89,000**
19. 26.8 mm = ____ cm **2.68**
20. 750 m = ____ km **0.75**
21. 4.8 m = ____ cm **480**
22. 95 g = ____ mg **95,000**
23. 389 mm = ____ m **0.389**
24. 56 L = ____ kL **0.056**
25. 0.32 mm = ____ cm **0.032**
26. 39.1 g = ____ kg **0.0391**

Lesson 6-5

Chapter 6 35 Course 2

Practice*
p. 36 OL AL

NAME ________ DATE ________ PERIOD ____

6-5 Practice

Measurement: Changing Metric Units

Complete.

1. 570 cm = ? m **5.7**
2. 356 mm = ? m **0.356**
3. 4.7 m = ? cm **470**
4. 0.4 m = ? mm **400**
5. 0.63 cm = ? mm **6.3**
6. 0.18 mm = ? cm **0.018**
7. 0.42 km = ? m **420**
8. 0.09 km = ? mm **90,000**
9. 0.13 km = ? cm **13,000**
10. 27 kg = ? g **27,000**
11. 8.3 g = ? mg **8,300**
12. 257 mg = ? g **0.257**
13. 486 g = ? kg **0.486**
14. 55.5 g = ? kg **0.0555**
15. 68,700 mg = ? kg **0.0687**
16. 308 mL = ? L **0.308**
17. 1.7 L = ? mL **1,700**
18. 88 L = ? kL **0.088**
19. 0.059 kL = ? L **59**
20. 64,000 mL = ? L **64**
21. 30,000 mL = ? kL **0.03**

Order each set of measures from least to greatest.

22. 0.06 km, 47 m, 15,800 cm **47 m, 0.06 km, 15,800 cm**
23. 891 g, 7,800 mg, 0.5 kg **7,800 mg, 0.5 kg, 891 g**
24. SPELUNKING The survey length of an underground cave is 0.914 kilometers. How many meters in length is this cave? **914 m**
25. FOOD A 15-ounce box of granola contains 0.425 kilograms of cereal. How many grams of cereal are in the box of granola? **425 g**

Chapter 6 36 Course 2

Word Problem Practice*
p. 37 OL AL

NAME ________ DATE ________ PERIOD ____

6-5 Word Problem Practice

Measurement: Changing Metric Units

1. RUNNING Each morning Carlos runs 1.5 kilometers. How many meters did he run? **1,500 m**
2. AVIATION A helicopter was flying 800 meters above the ground. How many kilometers above the ground was it flying? **0.8 km**
3. SODA A soda can contains 355 milliliters of liquid. How many liters of liquid does it contain? **0.355 L**
4. CONSTRUCTION The ceilings of most classrooms are about 2.5 meters above the floor. How many centimeters high is the ceiling? **250 cm**
5. FENCING Gerri's garden is 1,270 centimeters around the edges. How many meters of fencing material does she need to enclose her garden? **12.7 m**
6. GARDENING Mr. Chou's lawn sprinkler sprays about 150 liters of water each hour. How many kiloliters of water does it spray? **0.15 kL**
7. NUTRITION For 11- to 14-year-olds, the Recommended Dietary Allowance (RDA) for protein is about 60 grams daily. How many milligrams do they need daily? **60,000 mg**
8. MEASUREMENT A measure of one pound is equivalent to about 454 grams. How many kilograms are in one pound? How many milligrams? **0.454 kg; 454,000 mg**

Lesson 6-5

Chapter 6 37 Course 2

Enrichment
p. 38 OL AL

NAME ________ DATE ________ PERIOD ____

6-5 Enrichment

Using a Measurement Conversion Chart

You may sometimes want to convert customary measurements to metric measurements. For example, suppose you are reading about horses and want to know how long 5 furlongs are.

Start by finding a conversion table such as the one shown here. (Dictionaries often include such tables.)

1 mil	= 0.001 inch	= 0.0254 millimeter
1 inch	= 1,000 mil	= 2.54 centimeters
12 inches	= 1 foot	= 0.3048 meter
3 feet	= 1 yard	= 0.9144 meter
$5\frac{1}{2}$ yards, or $16\frac{1}{2}$ feet	= 1 rod	= 5.029 meters
40 rods	= 1 furlong	= 201.168 meters
8 furlongs, 5,280 feet, 1,760 yards	= 1 (statute) mile	= 1.6093 kilometers
3 miles	= 1 (land) league	= 4.828 kilometers

To change from a large unit to a small unit, multiply. To change from a small unit to a large one, divide.

Example 1 Change 5 furlongs to meters.

5 × 201.168 = 1,005.84
So, 5 furlongs is about 1,000 meters, or 1 kilometer.

Change each measurement to a metric measurement. Round each answer to the nearest tenth.

1. 10 yards **9.1 m**
2. 100 leagues **482.8 km**
3. 10 inches **25.4 cm**
4. 100 rods **502.9 m**
5. 1,000 mils **25.4 mm**
6. 10 feet **3.0 m**
7. 50 miles **80.5 km**
8. 50 furlongs **10,058.4 m, or 10.1 km**
9. 50 inches **127.0 cm**
10. 200 feet **61.0 m**
11. 200 miles **321.9 km**
12. 200 yards **182.9 m**

Chapter 6 38 Course 2

*** Also available in Spanish** ELL

Additional Lesson Resources

Transparencies
- *5-Minute Check Transparency,* Lesson 6-5

Other Print Products
- *Noteables™ Interactive Study Notebook with Foldables™*

Teacher Tech Tools
- *Interactive Classroom CD-ROM,* Lesson 6-5
- *AssignmentWorks,* Lesson 6-5

Student Tech Tools
glencoe.com
- Extra Examples, Chapter 6, Lesson 5
- Self-Check Quiz, Chapter 6, Lesson 5

6-5 Lesson Notes

1 Focus

Vertical Alignment

Before Lesson 6-5
Differentiate between and use appropriate units of measures for two- and three-dimensional objects

Lesson 6-5
Convert one unit of measurement to another

After Lesson 6-5
Compare weights, capacities, geometric measures, times, and temperatures within and between measurement systems

2 Teach

MINI Lab

For the first activity, suggest that students measure the width of small, rectangular objects (such as books, erasers, or notebook paper), since measuring to the nearest millimeter can be difficult.

Scaffolding Questions

Write a problem such as 9 × __ = ? on the board. As you ask the following questions, fill in the missing factor and, when students answer, write the product.

Ask:

- What is 9 times 10? 90
- What is 9 times 100? 900
- What is 9 times 1,000? 9,000
- What is 9 times 0.1? 0.9
- What is 9 times 0.01? 0.09
- What is 9 times 0.001? 0.009

6-5 Measurement: Changing Metric Units

MAIN IDEA

Change metric units of length, capacity, and mass.

IN Academic Standards

Preparation for 8.3.4 Solve simple problems involving rates and other derived measurements, including problems involving speed, uniform speed, average speed and density, by applying the concept of proportionality to measurement in different contexts. Express measurements in a given unit in terms of other units of the same type. *Also addresses 7.3.6, P.6.4.*

New Vocabulary

metric system
meter
liter
gram
kilogram

IN Math Online

glencoe.com

- Extra Examples
- Personal Tutor
- Self-Check Quiz

MINI Lab

The lengths of two objects are shown below.

Object	Length (millimeters)	Length (centimeters)
paper clip	45	4.5
CD case	144	14.4

1. Select three other objects. Find and record the width of all five objects to the nearest millimeter and tenth of a centimeter.
2. Compare the measurements of the objects, and write a rule that describes how to convert from millimeters to centimeters.
3. Measure the length of your classroom in meters. Make a conjecture about how to convert this measure to centimeters. Explain. **1–3. See margin.**

The **metric system** is a decimal system of measures. The prefixes commonly used in this system are kilo-, centi-, and milli-.

Prefix	Meaning In Words	Meaning In Numbers
kilo-	thousands	1,000
centi-	hundredths	0.01
milli-	thousandths	0.001

In the metric system, the base unit of *length* is the **meter** (m). Using the prefixes, the names of other units of length are formed. Notice that the prefixes tell you how the units relate to the meter.

Unit	Symbol	Relationship to Meter	
kilometer	km	1 km = 1,000 m	1 m = 0.001 km
meter	m	1 m = 1 m	
centimeter	cm	1 cm = 0.01 m	1 m = 100 cm
millimeter	mm	1 mm = 0.001 m	1 m = 1,000 mm

The **liter** (L) is the base unit of *capacity*, the amount of dry or liquid material an object can hold. The **gram** (g) measures *mass*, the amount of matter in an object. The prefixes can also be applied to these units. Whereas the meter and liter are the base units of length and capacity, the base unit of mass is the **kilogram** (kg).

Real-World Comparison

Tips for New Teachers

A meter is about the distance from the floor to the doorknob on a door. A paper clip has a mass of about one gram. Some soft drinks are sold in two-liter bottles.

Additional Answers

1. See students' work.
2. Divide by 10.
3. Multiply by 100. There are 100 centimeters in 1 meter.

To change a metric measure of length, mass, or capacity from one unit to another, you can use the relationship between the two units and multiplication by a power of 10.

EXAMPLES Convert Units in the Metric System

Study Tip

Metric Conversions When converting from a larger unit to a smaller unit, the power of ten being multiplied will be greater than 1.

When converting from a smaller unit to a larger unit, the power of ten will be less than 1.

1 Convert 4.5 liters to milliliters.

You need to convert liters to milliliters. Use the relationship 1 L = 1,000 mL.

1 L = 1,000 mL	Write the relationship.
4.5 × 1 L = 4.5 × 1,000 mL	Multiply each side by 4.5 since you have 4.5 L.
4.5 L = 4,500 mL	To multiply 4.5 by 1,000, move the decimal point 3 places to the right.

2 Convert 500 millimeters to meters.

You need to convert millimeters to meters. Use the relationship 1 mm = 0.001 m.

1 mm = 0.001 m	Write the relationship.
500 × 1 mm = 500 × 0.001 m	Multiply each side by 500 since you have 500 mm.
500 mm = 0.5 m	To multiply 500 by 0.001, move the decimal point 3 places to the left.

CHECK Your Progress

Complete.

a. 25.4 g = ■ kg **0.0254**

b. 158 mm = ■ m **0.158**

Real-World EXAMPLE

Real-World Link The maximum weight of a grizzly bear is 521.64 kilograms.

Source: North American Bear Center

3 BEARS The California Grizzly Bear was designated the official state animal in 1953. Use the information at the left to find the maximum weight of a grizzly bear in grams.

You are converting kilograms to grams. Since the maximum weight of a grizzly bear is 521.64 kilograms, use the relationship 1 kg = 1,000 g.

1 kg = 1,000 g	Write the relationship.
521.64 × 1 kg = 521.64 × 1,000 g	Multiply each side by 521.64 since you have 521.64 kg.
521.64 kg = 521,640 g	To multiply 521.64 by 1,000, move the decimal point 3 places to the right.

So, the maximum weight of a grizzly bear is 521,640 grams.

CHECK Your Progress

c. **FOOD** A bottle contains 1.75 liters of juice. How many milliliters is this? **1,750 mL**

Focus on Mathematical Content

To convert **from a larger metric unit to a smaller metric unit**, multiply by a power of 10. Move the decimal point to the right the same number of places as the **number of zeros** in the power of 10.

To convert **from a smaller metric unit to a larger metric unit**, multiply by a power of 10 less than 1. Move the decimal point to the left the same number of places as the **number of decimal places** in the power of 10.

Formative Assessment

Use the Check Your Progress exercises after each Example to determine students' understanding of concepts.

ADDITIONAL EXAMPLES

1. Complete 7.2 m = ■ mm. 7,200
2. Complete 40 cm = ■ m. 0.4
3. **FARMS** A bucket holds 12.8 liters of water. Find the capacity of the bucket in milliliters. 12,800 mL

Additional Examples are also in:

- Noteables™ Interactive Study Notebook with Foldables™
- Interactive Classroom PowerPoint® Presentations

Tips for New Teachers: Converting Units

Make sure students understand that when converting from a larger unit to a smaller unit, there will be more of the smaller unit, so they should multiply by a power of 10 *greater than 1*. Similarly, when converting from a smaller unit to a larger unit, there will be fewer of the larger unit, so they should multiply by a power of 10 *less than 1*.

Focus on Mathematical Content

Metric System Students may think that the base unit of mass is the gram. However, in the metric system, the base unit of mass is the kilogram. This is because the mass of many everyday objects, like a textbook, is more easily measured in kilograms, not grams.

ADDITIONAL EXAMPLES

4 Convert 7.13 miles to kilometers. Round to the nearest hundredth if necessary. 11.48 km

5 Convert 925.48 grams to pounds. Round to the nearest hundredth if necessary. 2.04 lb

To convert measures between customary units and metric units, use the relationships below.

Customary and Metric Relationships

Key Concept

Type of Measure	Customary	→	Metric
Length	1 inch (in.)	≈	2.54 centimeters (cm)
	1 foot (ft)	≈	0.30 meter (m)
	1 yard (yd)	≈	0.91 meter (m)
	1 mile (mi)	≈	1.61 kilometers (km)
Weight/Mass	1 pound (lb)	≈	453.6 grams (g)
	1 pound (lb)	≈	0.4536 kilogram (kg)
	1 ton (T)	≈	907.2 kilograms (kg)
Capacity	1 cup (c)	≈	236.59 milliliters (mL)
	1 pint (pt)	≈	473.18 milliliters (mL)
	1 quart (qt)	≈	946.35 milliliters (mL)
	1 gallon (gal)	≈	3.79 liters (L)

EXAMPLES Convert Between Measurement Systems

Study Tip

Alternative Method When converting 17.22 inches to centimeters, you can use the relationship 1 in. ≈ 2.54 cm or the unit ratio $\frac{2.54 \text{ cm}}{1 \text{ in.}}$.

4 Convert 17.22 inches to centimeters. Round to the nearest hundredth if necessary.

Use the relationship 1 inch ≈ 2.54 centimeters.

$1 \text{ inch} \approx 2.54 \text{ cm}$ — Write the relationship.

$17.22 \times 1 \text{ in.} \approx 17.22 \times 2.54 \text{ cm}$ — Multiply each side by 17.22 since you have 17.22 in.

$17.22 \text{ in.} \approx 43.7388 \text{ cm}$ — Simplify.

So, 17.22 inches is approximately 43.74 centimeters.

5 Convert 828.5 milliliters to cups. Round to the nearest hundredth if necessary.

Since 1 cup ≈ 236.59 milliliters, multiply by $\frac{1 \text{ c}}{236.59 \text{ mL}}$.

$828.5 \text{ mL} \approx 828.5 \cancel{\text{mL}} \cdot \frac{1 \text{ c}}{236.59 \cancel{\text{mL}}}$ — Multiply by $\frac{1 \text{ c}}{236.59 \text{ mL}}$.

$\approx \frac{828.5 \text{ c}}{236.59} \text{ or } 3.5 \text{ c}$ — Simplify.

So, 828.5 milliliters is approximately 3.5 cups.

CHECK Your Progress

Complete. Round to the nearest hundredth if necessary.

d. 7.44 c ≈ ■ mL   e. 22.09 lb ≈ ■ kg   f. 35.85 L ≈ ■ gal 9.46

d. 1,760.23
e. 10.02

306 Chapter 6 Ratios and Proportions

Real-World Link Before the seventeenth century, people thought light was transmitted instantly. Now, we know that light is too fast for the delay to be noticeable.

Source: University of California, Riverside

Real-World EXAMPLE Convert with Rates

6 LIGHT **The speed of light is about 186,000 miles per second. Find the approximate speed of light in kilometers per second.**

Since 1 mile ≈ 1.61 kilometers, multiply by $\frac{1.61 \text{ km}}{1 \text{ mi}}$.

$$\frac{186{,}000 \text{ mi}}{\text{s}} \approx \frac{186{,}000 \cancel{\text{mi}}}{1 \text{ s}} \times \frac{1.61 \text{ km}}{1 \cancel{\text{mi}}} \quad \text{Multiply by } \frac{1.61 \text{ km}}{1 \text{ mi}}.$$

$$\approx \frac{299{,}460 \text{ km}}{1 \text{ s}} \quad \text{Simplify.}$$

So, the speed of light is approximately 299,460 kilometers per second.

CHECK Your Progress

g. **RUNNING** Chuck runs at a speed of 3 meters per second. About how many feet per second does Chuck run? **about 9.84 feet per second**

★ indicates multi-step problem

CHECK Your Understanding

Examples 1, 2, 4, 5 (pp. 305–306)

Complete. Round to the nearest hundredth if necessary.

1. 3.7 m = ■ cm **370**
2. 550 m = ■ km **0.55**
3. 1,460 mg = ■ g **1.46**
4. 2.34 kL = ■ L **2,340**
5. 9.36 yd ≈ ■ m **8.52**
6. 11.07 pt ≈ ■ mL **5,238.10**
7. 58.14 kg ≈ ■ lb **128.17**
8. 38.44 cm ≈ ■ in. **15.13**

Examples 3, 6 (pp. 305, 307)

9. **SPORTS** About how many feet does a team of athletes run in a 1,600-meter relay race? **about 5,333.33 ft**

Practice and Problem Solving

HOMEWORK HELP

For Exercises	See Examples
10–23	1, 2, 4, 5
24–27	3, 6

Exercise Levels
A: 10–27
B: 28–36
C: 37–41

Complete. Round to the nearest hundredth if necessary.

10. 720 cm = ■ m **7.2**
11. 983 mm = ■ m **0.98**
12. 3.2 m = ■ cm **320**
13. 0.03 g = ■ mg **30**
14. 997 g = ■ kg **1.00**
15. 82.1 g = ■ kg **0.08**
16. 9.1 L = ■ mL **9,100**
17. 130.5 kL = ■ L **130,500**
18. 3.75 c ≈ ■ mL **887.21**
19. 41.8 in. ≈ ■ cm **106.17**
20. 156.25 lb ≈ ■ kg **70.88**
21. 9.5 gal ≈ ■ L **36.01**
22. 680.4 g ≈ ■ lb **1.5**
23. 4.725 m ≈ ■ ft **15.75**
24. **WATERFALLS** At 979 meters tall, Angel Falls in Venezuela is the highest waterfall in the world. How many kilometers tall is the waterfall? **0.979 km**
25. **FOOD** An 18-ounce jar contains 510 grams of grape jelly. How many kilograms of grape jelly does the jar contain? **0.51 kg**

ADDITIONAL EXAMPLE

6 FARMS Pike's Peak near Colorado Springs, Colorado, rises to a height that is 14,110 feet above sea level. About how many meters high is Pike's Peak? **4,233 m**

3 Practice

Formative Assessment

Use Exercises 1–9 to check for understanding.

Then use the chart at the bottom of this page to customize your assignments for students.

Intervention You may wish to use the Study Guide and Intervention Master on page 34 of the *Chapter 6 Resource Masters* for additional reinforcement.

Odd/Even Assignments

Exercises 10–27 are structured so that students practice the same concepts whether they are assigned odd or even problems.

DIFFERENTIATED HOMEWORK OPTIONS

Level	Assignment	Two-Day Assignment	
BL Basic	10–27, 44, 45, 48–56	11–27 odd, 44, 45	10–26 even, 48–56
OL Core	11–23 odd, 24–27, 29–37 odd, 39, 43–56	10–23, 43–45	24–39, 46–56
AL Advanced/Pre-AP	28–52 (optional: 53–56)		

Lesson 6-5 Measurement: Changing Metric Units 307

⚠ Exercise Alert!

Find the Error In Exercise 39, Gerardo moved the decimal point the wrong direction. Remind students to move the decimal point to the right when converting from a larger unit to a smaller unit, and to the left when converting from a smaller unit to a larger unit.

Additional Answer

34. Since 1 km = 1,000 m, the bridges that are about 1 kilometer long are Mackinac, George Washington, Tacoma Narrows II, and Oakland Bay.

26. **CYCLING** Ramon rides his bike at a rate of 8 kilometers per hour. About how many miles per hour can Ramon ride his bike? **about 4.97 miles per hour**

★ 27. **BIRDS** A gull can fly at a speed of 22 miles per hour. About how many meters per hour can a gull fly? **about 35,420 meters per hour**

Real-World Link The Mackinac Bridge opened on November 1, 1957. It is the longest two-tower suspension bridge between bases in the Western Hemisphere.

Source: *Encyclopaedia Britannica*

Complete. Round to the nearest hundredth if necessary.

28. 8.18 qt ≈ ■ L **7.74**

29. 15.09 km ≈ ■ yd **16,582.42**

30. 72.26 cm ≈ ■ ft **2.37**

31. 0.445 T ≈ ■ g **403,704**

Precision **is the ability of a measurement to be consistently reproduced. Choose the correct term to determine the degree of precision needed in each situation.**

32. length of a line segment (meters, centimeters) **centimeters**

33. mass of a bowl of cereal (kilograms, grams) **grams**

★ 34. **ANALYZE TABLES** The table shows the lengths of bridges in the United States. Which bridges are about 1 kilometer in length? Justify your answer. **See margin.**

Bridge	Length (m)
Mackinac, MI	1,158
George Washington, NY	1,067
Tacoma Narrows II, WA	853
Oakland Bay, CA	704
Pennybacker, TX	345
Sunshine Skyway, FL	8,712
Golden Gate, CA	2,780

★ 35. **CARPENTRY** Jacinta needs a 2.5-meter pole for a birdfeeder that she is building. How many centimeters will she need to cut off a 3-meter pole in order to use it for the birdfeeder? **50 cm**

Academic Standards • ISTEP+
Extra Practice, pp. 683, 709

★ 36. **BAKING** A bakery uses 900 grams of peaches per cobbler. How many cobblers can be made using 10.5 pounds of peaches? **5 cobblers**

H.O.T. Problems

★ 37. **FIND THE ERROR** Jake and Gerardo are converting 3.25 kilograms to grams. Who is correct? Explain your reasoning.

37. Jake; Gerardo divided 3.25 by 1,000. He should have multiplied.

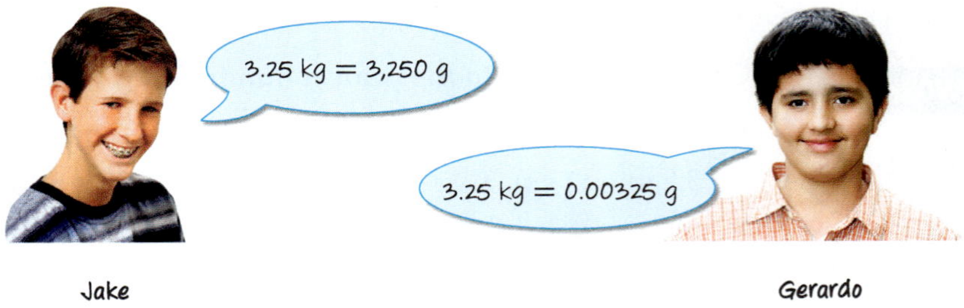

CHALLENGE **For Exercises 38–40, use the following information.**
The metric prefix *giga* refers to something one billion times larger than the base unit.

38. How many meters are in one gigameter? **1,000,000,000 m**

39. About how many miles are in one gigameter? Round to the nearest hundredth. **about 621,118.01 mi**

40. The distance from Earth to the Sun is approximately 93 million miles. About how many gigameters is this? Round to the nearest hundredth.

40. about 149.73 gm

Differentiated Instruction

Verbal/Linguistic Learners Have students whose parents or grandparents immigrated from other countries record a recipe from the other country. What units of mass and capacity are used in the recipe? Have students rewrite the recipe, converting the units to smaller or larger units.

308 Chapter 6 Ratios and Proportions

41. **WRITING IN MATH** Explain why it makes sense to multiply by a power of 10 that is greater than 1 when changing from a larger unit to a smaller unit. **There are a greater number of smaller units.**

ISTEP+ PRACTICE Preparation for 8.3.4

42. The table shows the mass of four wireless telephones. Find the approximate total mass of the telephones in kilograms. **A**

Telephone Owner	Mass (g)
Elena	100.4
Kevin	70.8
Marissa	95.6
Corey	120.4

A 0.39 kilogram

B 3.9 kilograms

C 39.0 kilograms

D 390.0 kilograms

43. Which relationship between the given units of measure is correct? **H**

F One gram is $\frac{1}{100}$ of a centigram.

G One meter is $\frac{1}{100}$ of a centimeter.

H One gram is $\frac{1}{1,000}$ of a kilogram.

J One milliliter is $\frac{1}{100}$ of a liter.

Spiral Review

44. **MEASUREMENT** A certain car weighs 3,200 pounds. What is the weight of the car in tons? (Lesson 6-4) **1.6 T**

45. **MEASUREMENT** The table shows the number of inches per foot. Graph the data. Then find the slope of the line. Explain what slope represents. (Lesson 6-3) **See margin for graph. Slope: $\frac{1}{12}$; there are 12 inches in every foot.**

Feet (x)	1	2	3	4
Inches (y)	12	24	36	48

Add or subtract. Write in simplest form. (Lesson 5-3)

46. $3\frac{4}{7} + 1\frac{1}{7}$ **$4\frac{5}{7}$**

47. $8\frac{3}{5} - 2\frac{2}{5}$ **$6\frac{1}{5}$**

48. $9\frac{1}{6} + 4\frac{3}{8}$ **$13\frac{13}{24}$**

49. $11\frac{7}{10} - 5\frac{3}{4}$ **$5\frac{19}{20}$**

50. **BASKETBALL** Jared made thirty-seven percent of his free-throw attempts during basketball practice. Write this percent as a decimal. (Lesson 4-7) **0.37**

GET READY for the Next Lesson

PREREQUISITE SKILL **Solve each equation.** (Lesson 3-3)

51. $5 \cdot 4 = x \cdot 2$ **10**
52. $9 \cdot 24 = 27 \cdot x$ **8**
53. $x \cdot 15 = 12 \cdot 4$ **3.2**
54. $8\frac{1}{2} \cdot x = 11 \cdot 17$ **22**

4 Assess

Name the Math Have students tell what mathematical procedures they used to solve one of the following exercises: 24, 25, 30, or 31.

Formative Assessment

Check for student understanding of concepts in Lessons 6-3, 6-4, and 6-5.

CRM Quiz 2, p. 67

FOLDABLES Study Organizer Foldables™ Follow-Up

Remind students to take notes about converting from one metric unit to another in their Foldables. Encourage them to include an example of converting from a smaller unit to a larger unit and an example of converting from a larger unit to smaller unit.

Additional Answer

45. **Number of Inches per Foot**

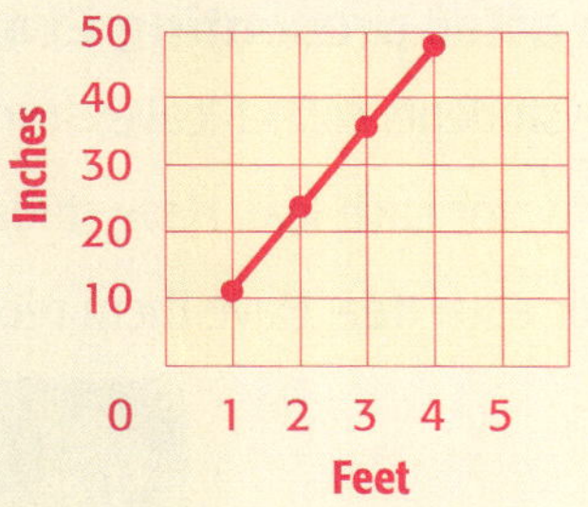

Lesson 6-5 Measurement: Changing Metric Units 309

6-6 Algebra: Solving Proportions

PACING: **Regular:** 2 periods, **Block:** 1 period

IN Academic Standards **7.1.9 Solve problems involving ratios and proportions.**

- **Express one quantity as a fraction of another, given their ratio, and vice versa.**
- Find how many times one quantity is as large as another, given their ratio, and vice versa.
- Express one quantity as a fraction of another given the two quantities.
- Find the whole, or one part, when a whole is divided into parts in a given ratio.
- **Solve problems involving two pairs of equivalent ratios.**

Also addresses 7.2.1, 7.2.2, 7.2.7.

Options for Differentiated Instruction

ELL = English Language Learner   AL = Above or Beyond Grade Level   SS = Struggling Students   SN = Special Needs

Alternative Methods AL

Use after presenting Example 2.

Remind students that they can solve some proportions without using cross products. Encourage them to try using techniques they already know, such as:

- simplifying fractions
- multiplying or dividing both the numerator and the denominator by the same number to find equivalent fractions

For example, in the proportion $\frac{21}{5} = \frac{c}{10}$, it is easy to see that $5 \times 2 = 10$.
Therefore, $21 \times 2 = 42$ is the value for c.

Naturalist Learning ELL AL SS SN

Use after presenting Examples 1–4.

Have students collect leaves from three kinds of trees, measure the length and width of each leaf, and find the ratio $\frac{l}{w}$ for each leaf. Have students measure the widths of the three trees, estimate the heights, and find the ratio $\frac{h}{w}$ for each tree. Have them record their data in a table like the one shown below.

Tree	Leaves			Trees		
	Length	Width	Ratio $\frac{l}{w}$	Height	Width	Ratio $\frac{h}{w}$
1						
2						
3						

Have students compare the ratio of each leaf's length and width to the ratio for the tree's height and width to see if they form a proportion.

Leveled Lesson Resources

Also on TeacherWorks™ Lesson 6-6

Chapter 6 Resource Masters

BL = Below or Approaching Grade Level OL = On Grade Level AL = Above or Beyond Grade Level ELL = English Language Learner

Lesson Reading Guide
p. 39 BL OL ELL

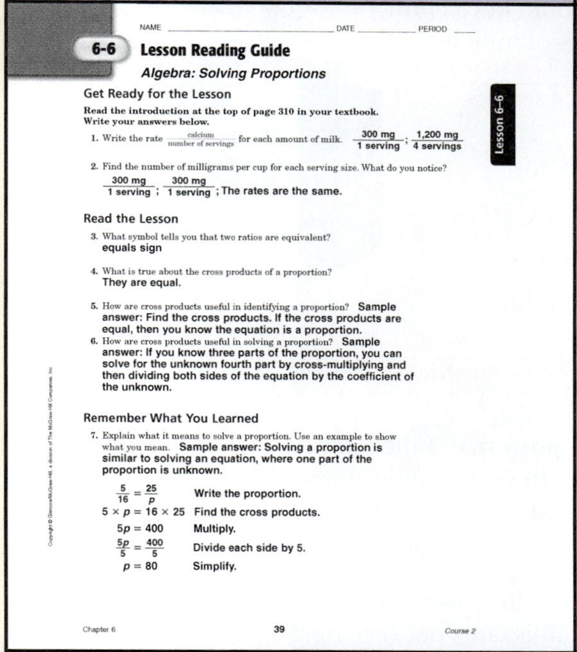
NAME ______ DATE ______ PERIOD ____

6-6 Lesson Reading Guide

Algebra: Solving Proportions

Get Ready for the Lesson

Read the introduction at the top of page 310 in your textbook. Write your answers below.

1. Write the rate $\frac{\text{calcium}}{\text{number of servings}}$ for each amount of milk. $\frac{300 \text{ mg}}{1 \text{ serving}}$; $\frac{1{,}200 \text{ mg}}{4 \text{ servings}}$
2. Find the number of milligrams per cup for each serving size. What do you notice? $\frac{300 \text{ mg}}{1 \text{ serving}}$; $\frac{300 \text{ mg}}{1 \text{ serving}}$; The rates are the same.

Read the Lesson

3. What symbol tells you that two ratios are equivalent? equals sign
4. What is true about the cross products of a proportion? They are equal.
5. How are cross products useful in identifying a proportion? Sample answer: Find the cross products. If the cross products are equal, then you know the equation is a proportion.
6. How are cross products useful in solving a proportion? Sample answer: If you know three parts of the proportion, you can solve for the unknown fourth part by cross-multiplying and then dividing both sides of the equation by the coefficient of the unknown.

Remember What You Learned

7. Explain what it means to solve a proportion. Use an example to show what you mean. Sample answer: Solving a proportion is similar to solving an equation, where one part of the proportion is unknown.

$\frac{5}{16} = \frac{25}{p}$ Write the proportion.
$5 \times p = 16 \times 25$ Find the cross products.
$5p = 400$ Multiply.
$\frac{5p}{5} = \frac{400}{5}$ Divide each side by 5.
$p = 80$ Simplify.

Chapter 6 39 Course 2

*Study Guide and Intervention**
p. 40 BL OL ELL

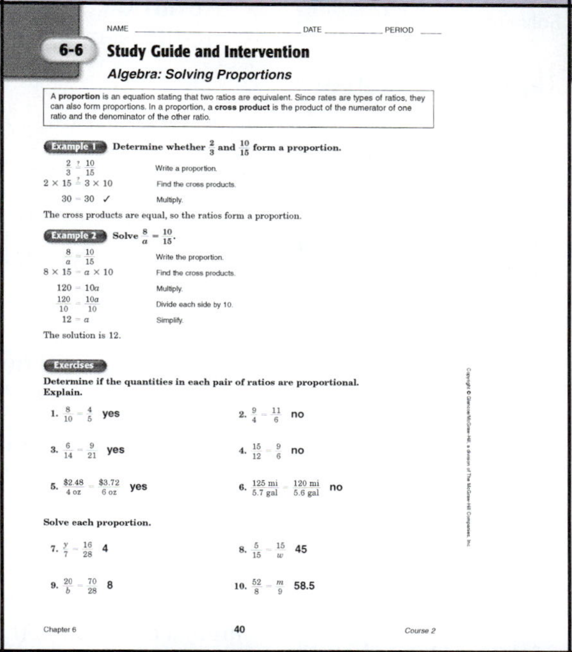
NAME ______ DATE ______ PERIOD ____

6-6 Study Guide and Intervention

Algebra: Solving Proportions

A **proportion** is an equation stating that two ratios are equivalent. Since rates are types of ratios, they can also form proportions. In a proportion, a **cross product** is the product of the numerator of one ratio and the denominator of the other ratio.

Example 1 Determine whether $\frac{2}{3}$ and $\frac{10}{15}$ form a proportion.

$\frac{2}{3} \stackrel{?}{=} \frac{10}{15}$ Write a proportion.
$2 \times 15 \stackrel{?}{=} 3 \times 10$ Find the cross products.
$30 = 30$ ✓ Multiply.

The cross products are equal, so the ratios form a proportion.

Example 2 Solve $\frac{8}{a} = \frac{10}{15}$.

$\frac{8}{a} = \frac{10}{15}$ Write the proportion.
$8 \times 15 = a \times 10$ Find the cross products.
$120 = 10a$ Multiply.
$\frac{120}{10} = \frac{10a}{10}$ Divide each side by 10.
$12 = a$ Simplify.

The solution is 12.

Exercises

Determine if the quantities in each pair of ratios are proportional. Explain.

1. $\frac{8}{10}, \frac{4}{5}$ yes
2. $\frac{9}{4}, \frac{11}{6}$ no
3. $\frac{6}{14}, \frac{9}{21}$ yes
4. $\frac{15}{12}, \frac{9}{6}$ no
5. $\frac{\$2.48}{4 \text{ oz}}, \frac{\$3.72}{6 \text{ oz}}$ yes
6. $\frac{125 \text{ mi}}{5.7 \text{ gal}}, \frac{120 \text{ mi}}{5.6 \text{ gal}}$ no

Solve each proportion.

7. $\frac{y}{7} = \frac{16}{28}$ 4
8. $\frac{5}{15} = \frac{15}{w}$ 45
9. $\frac{20}{b} = \frac{70}{28}$ 8
10. $\frac{52}{8} = \frac{m}{9}$ 58.5

Chapter 6 40 Course 2

*Skills Practice**
p. 41 BL OL

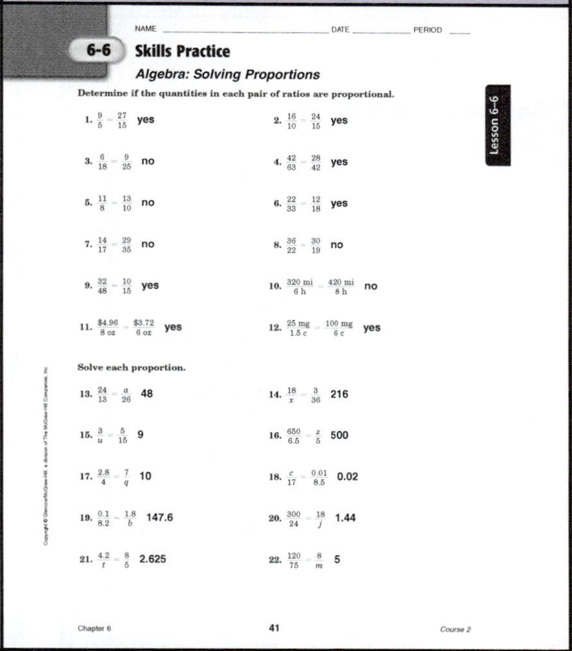
NAME ______ DATE ______ PERIOD ____

6-6 Skills Practice

Algebra: Solving Proportions

Determine if the quantities in each pair of ratios are proportional.

1. $\frac{9}{5}, \frac{27}{15}$ yes
2. $\frac{16}{10}, \frac{24}{15}$ yes
3. $\frac{6}{18}, \frac{9}{25}$ no
4. $\frac{42}{63}, \frac{28}{42}$ yes
5. $\frac{11}{8}, \frac{13}{10}$ no
6. $\frac{22}{33}, \frac{12}{18}$ yes
7. $\frac{14}{17}, \frac{29}{35}$ no
8. $\frac{36}{22}, \frac{30}{19}$ no
9. $\frac{32}{48}, \frac{10}{15}$ yes
10. $\frac{320 \text{ mi}}{6 \text{ h}}, \frac{420 \text{ mi}}{8 \text{ h}}$ no
11. $\frac{\$4.96}{8 \text{ oz}}, \frac{\$3.72}{6 \text{ oz}}$ yes
12. $\frac{25 \text{ mg}}{1.5 \text{ c}}, \frac{100 \text{ mg}}{6 \text{ c}}$ yes

Solve each proportion.

13. $\frac{24}{13} = \frac{a}{26}$ 48
14. $\frac{18}{x} = \frac{3}{36}$ 216
15. $\frac{3}{u} = \frac{5}{15}$ 9
16. $\frac{650}{6.5} = \frac{z}{5}$ 500
17. $\frac{2.8}{4} = \frac{7}{q}$ 10
18. $\frac{c}{17} = \frac{0.01}{8.5}$ 0.02
19. $\frac{0.1}{8.2} = \frac{1.8}{b}$ 147.6
20. $\frac{300}{24} = \frac{18}{j}$ 1.44
21. $\frac{4.2}{t} = \frac{8}{5}$ 2.625
22. $\frac{120}{75} = \frac{8}{m}$ 5

Chapter 6 41 Course 2

*Practice**
p. 42 OL AL

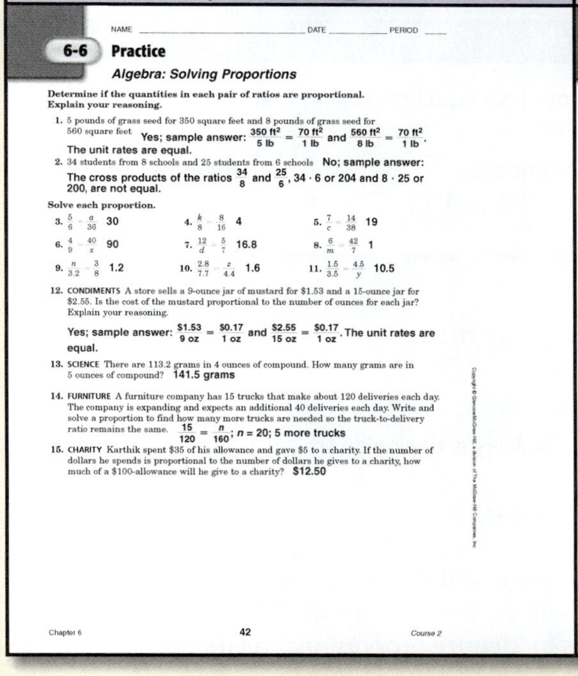
NAME ______ DATE ______ PERIOD ____

6-6 Practice

Algebra: Solving Proportions

Determine if the quantities in each pair of ratios are proportional. Explain your reasoning.

1. 5 pounds of grass seed for 350 square feet and 8 pounds of grass seed for 560 square feet Yes; sample answer: $\frac{350 \text{ ft}^2}{5 \text{ lb}} = \frac{70 \text{ ft}^2}{1 \text{ lb}}$ and $\frac{560 \text{ ft}^2}{8 \text{ lb}} = \frac{70 \text{ ft}^2}{1 \text{ lb}}$. The unit rates are equal.
2. 34 students from 8 schools and 25 students from 6 schools No; sample answer: The cross products of the ratios $\frac{34}{8}$ and $\frac{25}{6}$, 34 · 6 or 204 and 8 · 25 or 200, are not equal.

Solve each proportion.

3. $\frac{5}{6} = \frac{a}{36}$ 30
4. $\frac{k}{8} = \frac{8}{16}$ 4
5. $\frac{7}{c} = \frac{14}{38}$ 19
6. $\frac{4}{9} = \frac{40}{x}$ 90
7. $\frac{12}{d} = \frac{5}{7}$ 16.8
8. $\frac{6}{m} = \frac{42}{7}$ 1
9. $\frac{n}{3.2} = \frac{3}{8}$ 1.2
10. $\frac{2.8}{7.7} = \frac{z}{4.4}$ 1.6
11. $\frac{1.5}{3.5} = \frac{4.5}{y}$ 10.5

12. CONDIMENTS A store sells a 9-ounce jar of mustard for $1.53 and a 15-ounce jar for $2.55. Is the cost of the mustard proportional to the number of ounces for each jar? Explain your reasoning. Yes; sample answer: $\frac{\$1.53}{9 \text{ oz}} = \frac{\$0.17}{1 \text{ oz}}$ and $\frac{\$2.55}{15 \text{ oz}} = \frac{\$0.17}{1 \text{ oz}}$. The unit rates are equal.
13. SCIENCE There are 113.2 grams in 4 ounces of compound. How many grams are in 5 ounces of compound? 141.5 grams
14. FURNITURE A furniture company has 15 trucks that make about 120 deliveries each day. The company is expanding and expects an additional 40 deliveries each day. Write and solve a proportion to find how many more trucks are needed so the truck-to-delivery ratio remains the same. $\frac{15}{120} = \frac{n}{160}$; $n = 20$; 5 more trucks
15. CHARITY Karthik spent $35 of his allowance and gave $5 to a charity. If the number of dollars he spends is proportional to the number of dollars he gives to a charity, how much of a $100-allowance will he give to a charity? $12.50

Chapter 6 42 Course 2

*Word Problem Practice**
p. 43 OL AL

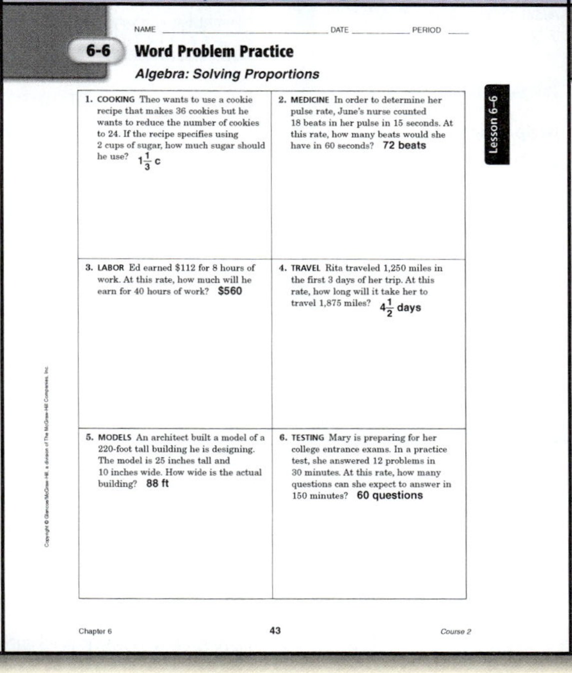
NAME ______ DATE ______ PERIOD ____

6-6 Word Problem Practice

Algebra: Solving Proportions

1. COOKING Theo wants to use a cookie recipe that makes 36 cookies but he wants to reduce the number of cookies to 24. If the recipe specifies using 2 cups of sugar, how much sugar should he use? $1\frac{1}{3}$ c
2. MEDICINE In order to determine her pulse rate, June's nurse counted 18 beats in her pulse in 15 seconds. At this rate, how many beats would she have in 60 seconds? 72 beats
3. LABOR Ed earned $112 for 8 hours of work. At this rate, how much will he earn for 40 hours of work? $560
4. TRAVEL Rita traveled 1,250 miles in the first 3 days of her trip. At this rate, how long will it take her to travel 1,875 miles? $4\frac{1}{2}$ days
5. MODELS An architect built a model of a 220-foot tall building he is designing. The model is 25 inches tall and 10 inches wide. How wide is the actual building? 88 ft
6. TESTING Mary is preparing for her college entrance exams. In a practice test, she answered 12 problems in 30 minutes. At this rate, how many questions can she expect to answer in 150 minutes? 60 questions

Chapter 6 43 Course 2

Enrichment
p. 44 OL AL

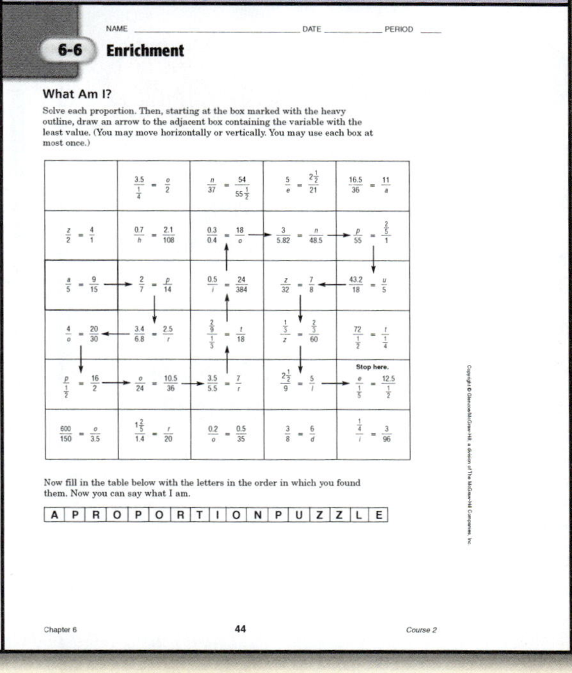
NAME ______ DATE ______ PERIOD ____

6-6 Enrichment

What Am I?

Solve each proportion. Then, starting at the box marked with the heavy outline, draw an arrow to the box containing the variable with the least value. (You may move horizontally or vertically. You may use each box at most once.)

Now fill in the table below with the letters in the order in which you found them. Now you can say what I am.

A	P	R	O	P	O	R	T	I	O	N	P	U	Z	Z	L	E

Chapter 6 44 Course 2

* *Also available in Spanish* ELL

Additional Lesson Resources

Transparencies
- *5-Minute Check Transparency,* Lesson 6-6

Other Print Products
- *Teaching Mathematics with Manipulatives*
- *Noteables™ Interactive Study Notebook with Foldables™*

Teacher Tech Tools
- *Interactive Classroom CD-ROM,* Lesson 6-6
- *AssignmentWorks,* Lesson 6-6

Student Tech Tools
glencoe.com
- Extra Examples, Chapter 6, Lesson 6
- Self-Check Quiz, Chapter 6, Lesson 6

6-6 Lesson Notes

1 Focus

Vertical Alignment

Before Lesson 6-6
Compute and perform simple multiplication and division of fractions and apply these procedures to solving problems

Lesson 6-6
Use proportions to solve problems; use cross-multiplication as a method for solving such problems, understanding it as the multiplication of both sides of an equation by a multiplicative inverse

After Lesson 6-6
Solve multi-step problems involving rate, average speed, distance, and time or a direct variation

2 Teach

Scaffolding Questions

As students answer the following questions, write each rate as a fraction on the board.

Ask:

- If Mark drove 50 miles on 2 gallons of gas, what was his mileage rate? $\frac{50\text{ mi}}{2\text{ gal}}$
- If Alicia drove 75 miles on 3 gallons of gas, what was her mileage rate? $\frac{75\text{ mi}}{3\text{ gal}}$
- If I drove 12.5 miles on half a gallon of gas, what was my mileage rate? $\frac{12.5\text{ mi}}{0.5\text{ gal}}$
- What do you notice about these rates? Sample answers: They are equivalent; each rate can be written as the unit rate $\frac{25\text{ mi}}{1\text{ gal}}$.

6-6 Algebra: Solving Proportions

MAIN IDEA

Solve proportions.

IN Academic Standards

7.1.9 Solve problems involving ratios and proportions.

- **Express one quantity as a fraction of another, given their ratio, and vice versa.**
- Find how many times one quantity is as large as another, given their ratio, and vice versa.
- Express one quantity as a fraction of another given the two quantities.
- Find the whole, or one part, when a whole is divided into parts in a given ration.
- **Solve problems involving two pairs of equivalent ratios.**

Also addresses 7.2.1, 7.2.2, 7.2.7.

New Vocabulary

proportional
proportion
cross product

IN Math Online

glencoe.com

- Extra Examples
- Personal Tutor
- Self-Check Quiz

GET READY for the Lesson

NUTRITION The amount of calcium in different servings of milk is shown. **1.** $\frac{300\text{ mg}}{1\text{ serving}}, \frac{1{,}200\text{ mg}}{4\text{ servings}}$

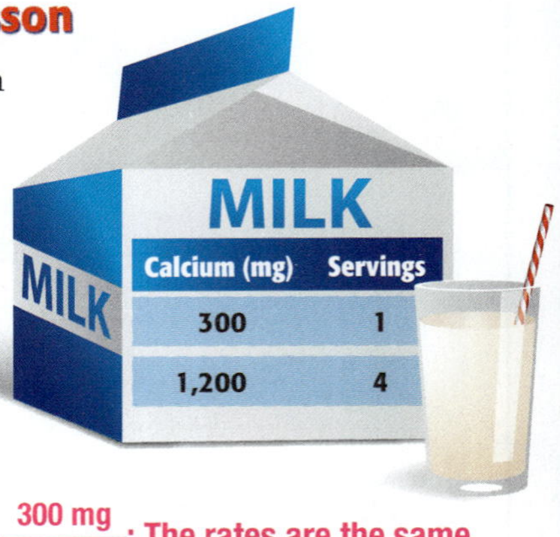

1. Write the rate $\frac{\text{calcium}}{\text{number of servings}}$ for each amount of milk.
2. Find the number of milligrams per cup for each serving size. What do you notice? $\frac{300\text{ mg}}{1\text{ serving}}, \frac{300\text{ mg}}{1\text{ serving}}$; The rates are the same.

Two quantities are **proportional** if they have a constant rate or ratio. In the example above, notice that the number of servings and amount of calcium change or *vary* in the same way.

$$\frac{300\text{ mg}}{1\text{ serving}} = \frac{1{,}200\text{ mg}}{4\text{ servings}} \quad (\times 4)$$

The unit rates for these different-sized servings are the same, a constant 300 milligrams per serving. So, the amount of calcium is proportional to the serving size.

Proportion — Key Concept

Words A **proportion** is an equation stating that two ratios or rates are equivalent.

Symbols

Numbers $\frac{1}{2} = \frac{3}{6}, \frac{8\text{ ft}}{10\text{ s}} = \frac{4\text{ ft}}{5\text{ s}}$

Algebra $\frac{a}{b} = \frac{c}{d}$, where $b, d \neq 0$

Consider the following proportion.

$$\frac{a}{b} = \frac{c}{d}$$

$$\frac{a}{b} \cdot bd = \frac{c}{d} \cdot bd \qquad \text{Multiply each side by } bd.$$

$$ad = bc \qquad \text{Simplify.}$$

The products *ad* and *bc* are called the **cross products** of this proportion. The cross products of any proportion are equal. You can compare unit rates or cross products to identify proportional relationships.

Reading Math

Nonproportional
When ratios do not form a proportion, they are called nonproportional.

EXAMPLE Identify Proportional Relationships

1 **RECREATION** **A carousel makes 4 complete turns after 64 seconds and 5 complete turns after 76 seconds. Based on this information, is the number of turns made by this carousel proportional to the time in seconds? Explain.**

METHOD 1 **Compare unit rates.**

$\frac{\text{seconds}}{\text{complete turns}} \rightarrow \frac{64 \text{ s}}{4 \text{ turns}} = \frac{16 \text{ s}}{1 \text{ turn}} \qquad \frac{76 \text{ s}}{5 \text{ turns}} = \frac{15.2 \text{ s}}{1 \text{ turn}}$

Since the unit rates are not equal, the number of turns is not proportional to the time in seconds.

METHOD 2 **Compare ratios by comparing cross products.**

seconds → / complete turns → $\frac{64}{4} \stackrel{?}{=} \frac{76}{5}$ ← seconds / ← complete turns

$64 \cdot 5 \stackrel{?}{=} 4 \cdot 76$ Find the cross products.

$320 \neq 304$ Multiply.

Since the cross products are not equal, the number of turns is not proportional to the time in seconds.

CHOOSE Your Method

Determine if the quantities in each pair of ratios are proportional. Explain.

a. 60 voted out of 100 registered and 84 voted out of 140 registered

b. \$12 for 16 yards of fabric and \$9 for 24 yards fabric

a. Yes; sample answer: The cross products of the ratios $\frac{60}{100}$ and $\frac{84}{140}$, $60 \cdot 140$ and $100 \cdot 84$, are both equal to 8,400.

b. No; sample answer: $\frac{\$12}{16 \text{ yd}} = \frac{\$0.75}{1 \text{ yd}}$ and $\frac{\$9}{24 \text{ yd}} = \frac{\$0.375}{1 \text{ yd}}$. The unit rates are not equal.

You can also use cross products to find a missing value in a proportion. This is known as *solving the proportion*.

Study Tip

Mental Math
Some proportions can be solved using mental math.

$\frac{2.5}{10} = \frac{x}{30}$

$\frac{2.5}{10} = \frac{7.5}{30}$ (×3 on numerator and denominator)

EXAMPLES Solve a Proportion

2 Solve $\frac{21}{5} = \frac{c}{7}$.

$\frac{21}{5} = \frac{c}{7}$ Write the proportion.

$21 \cdot 7 = 5 \cdot c$ Find the cross products.

$147 = 5c$ Multiply.

$\frac{147}{5} = \frac{5c}{5}$ Divide each side by 5.

$29.4 = c$ Simplify.

Check for Reasonableness Since $\frac{21}{5} \approx \frac{20}{5}$ or $\frac{4}{1}$ and $\frac{29.4}{7} \approx \frac{28}{7}$ or $\frac{4}{1}$, the answer is reasonable. ✓

Focus on Mathematical Content

Rates (or ratios) are proportional if they can be written as **the same unit rate** (or unit ratio).

The quantities in a proportional relationship **vary constantly**. If one quantity in the ratio (or rate) increases by a factor of 3, the other quantity also increases by a factor of 3.

To **solve a proportion**, find the cross products and simplify.

Formative Assessment

Use the Check Your Progress exercises after each Example to determine students' understanding of concepts.

ADDITIONAL EXAMPLES

1 **MATH** Before dinner, Mohammed solved 8 math problems in 12 minutes. After dinner, he solved 2 problems in 3 minutes. Is the number of problems he solved proportional to the time? yes

2 Solve $\frac{5}{8} = \frac{18}{x}$. $x = 28.8$

Additional Examples are also in:

- Noteables™ Interactive Study Notebook with Foldables™
- Interactive Classroom PowerPoint® Presentations

Tips for New Teachers

Proportions Some students may not realize that finding the cross products of a proportion is the same as finding a common denominator for both fractions and then comparing their numerators. You might wish to have students solve Example 2 by finding a common denominator for both fractions. For the proportion to be true, the numerators must then be equal.

$\frac{21}{5} = \frac{c}{7} \rightarrow \frac{21}{5} \cdot \frac{7}{7} = \frac{c}{7} \cdot \frac{5}{5}$

$\rightarrow \frac{147}{35} = \frac{5c}{35}$

Lesson 6-6 Algebra: Solving Proportions 311

ADDITIONAL EXAMPLES

3 Solve $\frac{3.5}{14} = \frac{6}{n}$. $n = 24$

4 **FLAGS** According to specifications, the ratio of the length of the U.S. flag to its width must be 1.9 to 1. How long must a U.S. flag be if it is designed to have a width of 2.5 feet? 4.75 ft

3 Solve $\frac{2.6}{13} = \frac{8}{n}$.

$\frac{2.6}{13} = \frac{8}{n}$	Write the proportion.
$2.6 \cdot n = 13 \cdot 8$	Find the cross products.
$2.6n = 104$	Multiply.
$\frac{2.6n}{2.6} = \frac{104}{2.6}$	Divide each side by 2.6.
$n = 40$	Simplify.

CHECK Your Progress

c. $\frac{16}{k} = \frac{2}{3}$ 24 d. $\frac{2}{6} = \frac{5}{h}$ 15 e. $\frac{10}{k} = \frac{2.5}{4}$ 16

Real-World Career
How Does a Physician's Assistant Use Math?
A physician's assistant uses math when calculating safe dosages of medications.

IN Math Online
For more information visit, glencoe.com.

Real-World EXAMPLE

4 **MEDICINE** **For every 18 people who have a sore throat, there are 2 people who actually have strep throat. If 72 patients have sore throats, how many of these would you expect to have strep throat?**

METHOD 1 **Write and solve a proportion.**

Let s represent strep throat.

$\frac{2 \text{ strep throats}}{18 \text{ sore throats}} = \frac{s}{72 \text{ sore throats}}$	Write a proportion.
$2 \cdot 72 = 18 \cdot s$	Find the cross products.
$144 = 18s$	Multiply.
$8 = s$	Divide each side by 18.

METHOD 2 **Find and use a unit rate or ratio.**

$\frac{2 \text{ strep throats} \div 2}{18 \text{ sore throats} \div 2} = \frac{1}{9}$ The ratio of strep throats to sore throats is 1 : 9.

Words	For every 9 sore throats, there is 1 strep throat.
Variable	Let s represent the number of strep throats.
Equation	$s = \frac{1}{9} \cdot 72$

$s = \frac{1}{9} \cdot 72$ or 8 Multiply.

So, you would expect 8 people to have strep throat.

CHOOSE Your Method

f. **RUNNING** Salvador can run 120 meters in 24 seconds. At this rate, how many seconds will it take him to run a 300-meter race? 60 s

CHECK Your Understanding

Example 1 (p. 311)

1–4. See margin.

Determine if the quantities in each pair of ratios are proportional. Explain.

1. 2 adults for 10 children and 3 adults for 12 children
2. 12 inches by 8 inches and 18 inches by 12 inches
3. 8 feet in 21 seconds and 12 feet in 31.5 seconds
4. $5.60 for 5 pairs of socks and $7.12 for 8 pairs of socks

Examples 2, 3 (pp. 311–312)

Solve each proportion.

5. $\frac{5}{6} = \frac{t}{18}$ **15**
6. $\frac{6}{k} = \frac{24}{28}$ **7**
7. $\frac{21}{5} = \frac{c}{7}$ **29.4**
8. $\frac{15}{w} = \frac{2}{5}$ **37.5**
9. $\frac{3}{n} = \frac{2.7}{18}$ **20**
10. $\frac{0.2}{3} = \frac{3}{d}$ **45**

Example 4 (p. 312)

11. **GROCERIES** Orange juice is on sale at 3 half-gallons for $5. At this rate, find the cost of 5 half-gallons of orange juice to the nearest cent. **$8.33**
12. **TRAVEL** Franco drove 203 miles in 3.5 hours. At this rate, how long will it take him to drive another 29 miles to the next town? **0.5 h**

Practice and Problem Solving

HOMEWORK HELP	
For Exercises	See Examples
13–20	1
21–32	2, 3
33–36	4

Exercise Levels
A: 13–36
B: 37–44
C: 45–48

15–18. See Ch. 6 Answer Appendix.

19. No; $\frac{45 \text{ min}}{25 \text{ pages}} = \frac{1.8 \text{ min}}{1 \text{ page}}$ and $\frac{60 \text{ min}}{30 \text{ pages}} = \frac{2 \text{ min}}{1 \text{ page}}$. These rates are not equivalent.

Determine if the quantities in each pair of ratios are proportional. Explain.

13. 20 children from 6 families to 16 children from 5 families **13, 14. See margin.**
14. 5 pounds of dry ice melts in 30 hours and 4 pounds melts in 24 hours
15. 16 winners out of 200 entries and 28 winners out of 350 entries
16. 5 meters in 7 minutes and 25 meters in 49 minutes
17. 1.4 tons produced every 18 days and 10.5 tons every 60 days
18. 3 inches for every 4 miles and 7.5 inches for every 10 miles
19. **READING** Leslie reads 25 pages in 45 minutes. After 60 minutes, she has read a total of 30 pages. Is her time proportional to the number of pages she reads? Explain.
20. **PETS** A store sells 2 hamsters for $11 and 6 hamsters for $33. Is the cost proportional to the number of hamsters sold? Explain. **See Ch. 6 Answer Appendix.**

Solve each proportion.

21. $\frac{3}{8} = \frac{b}{40}$ **15**
22. $\frac{x}{12} = \frac{12}{4}$ **36**
23. $\frac{c}{7} = \frac{18}{42}$ **3**
24. $\frac{5}{k} = \frac{10}{22}$ **11**
25. $\frac{3}{8} = \frac{n}{4}$ **1.5**
26. $\frac{15}{4} = \frac{3}{g}$ **0.8**
27. $\frac{45}{5} = \frac{d}{7}$ **63**
28. $\frac{30}{a} = \frac{8}{20}$ **75**
29. $\frac{1.6}{m} = \frac{2}{3}$ **2.4**
30. $\frac{4.5}{5} = \frac{t}{7}$ **6.3**
31. $\frac{2.5}{4.5} = \frac{7.5}{x}$ **13.5**
32. $\frac{3.8}{5.2} = \frac{7.6}{z}$ **10.4**
33. **SCHOOL** If 4 notebooks weigh 2.8 pounds, how much do 6 of the same notebooks weigh? **4.2 lb**
34. **COOKING** There are 6 teaspoons in 2 tablespoons. How many teaspoons are in 1.5 tablespoons? **4.5 t**

DIFFERENTIATED HOMEWORK OPTIONS

Level	Assignment	Two-Day Option	
BL Basic	13–36, 45, 49–58	13–35 odd, 49, 50	14–36 even, 45, 51–58
OL Core	13–35 odd, 36–45, 47–58	13–36, 49, 50	35–45, 47, 48, 51–58
AL Advanced/Pre-AP	37–57 (optional: 58)		

3 Practice

Formative Assessment

Use Exercises 1–12 to check for understanding.

Then use the chart at the bottom of this page to customize your assignments for students.

Intervention You may wish to use the Study Guide and Intervention Master on page 40 of the *Chapter 6 Resource Masters* for additional reinforcement.

Odd/Even Assignments

Exercises 13–36 are structured so that students practice the same concepts whether they are assigned odd or even problems.

Additional Answers

1. No; sample answer: $\frac{10 \text{ children}}{2 \text{ adults}} = \frac{5 \text{ children}}{1 \text{ adult}}$ and $\frac{12 \text{ children}}{3 \text{ adults}} = \frac{4 \text{ children}}{1 \text{ adult}}$. The unit rates are not equal.
2. Yes; sample answer: The cross products of the ratios $\frac{12}{8}$ and $\frac{18}{12}$, $8 \cdot 18$ and $12 \cdot 12$, are both equal to 144.
3. Yes; sample answer: The cross products of the ratios $\frac{8}{21}$ and $\frac{12}{31.5}$, $8 \cdot 31.5$ and $21 \cdot 12$, are both equal to 252.
4. No; sample answer: $\frac{\$5.60}{5 \text{ pairs}} = \frac{\$1.12}{1 \text{ pair}}$ and $\frac{\$7.12}{8 \text{ pairs}} = \frac{\$0.89}{1 \text{ pair}}$. The unit rates are not equal.
13. No; sample answer: The cross products of the ratios $\frac{20}{6}$ and $\frac{16}{5}$, $20 \cdot 5$ or 100 and $6 \cdot 16$ or 96, are not equal.
14. Yes; sample answer: $\frac{30 \text{ h}}{5 \text{ lb}} = \frac{6 \text{ h}}{1 \text{ lb}}$ and $\frac{24 \text{ h}}{4 \text{ lb}} = \frac{6 \text{ h}}{1 \text{ lb}}$. The unit rates are equal.

Tips for New Teachers: Proportion Problems

Remind students that they can solve some proportion problems by simplifying the fractions or by multiplying (or dividing) the numerator and denominator of one fraction by the same number.

Additional Answers

37. (3, 15) represents 3 pizzas cost \$15. (5, 25) represents 5 pizzas cost \$25. Yes, as the number of pizzas increases by 1, the cost increases by \$5.

38. (2, 13) represents 2 pizzas cost \$13 with a delivery fee. (4, 23) represents 4 pizzas cost \$23 with a delivery fee. No, the cost of the pizza does not increase by the same amount each time.

39. 5, with delivery fee; 5, no delivery fee; the slope represents the cost per pizza.

40. \$3; the pizzas with the delivery fee always cost \$3 more.

46. 30 c; Sample answer: The ratio of cups of bleach to cups of water is 1:5 which means that the ratio of cups of water to total cups of cleaning solution is 5:6. Set up and solve the proportion $\frac{5}{6} = \frac{x}{36}$, where x represents the number of cups of water.

35. **SCIENCE** The ratio of salt to water in a certain solution is 4 to 15. If the solution contains 6 ounces of water, how many ounces of salt does it contain? **1.6 oz**

36. **CONCERTS** Alethia purchased 7 advanced tickets for herself and her friends to a concert and paid \$164.50. If the total cost of tickets to the concert is proportional to the number purchased, how many tickets to the same concert did Serefina purchase if she paid a total of \$94? **4**

ANALYZE GRAPHS For Exercises 37–40, use the graph. It shows the cost of several pizzas, with and without a delivery fee.

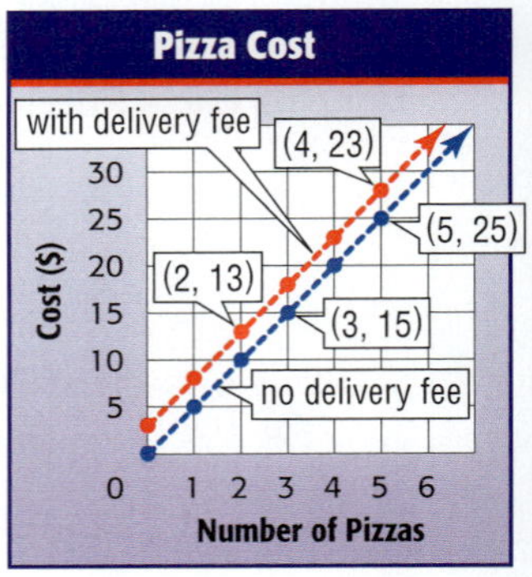

37. What do the points (3, 15) and (5, 25) represent on the graph? Is this situation proportional? Explain. **See margin.**

38. What do the points (2, 13) and (4, 23) represent on the graph? Is this situation proportional? Explain. **See margin.**

39. What is the slope of each line? What does the slope represent? **See margin.**

40. What is the delivery fee? Explain. **See margin.**

Real-World Link . . . Film for an IMAX projection system passes through the projector at the rate of 330 feet per minute or 5.5 feet per second.
Source: IMAX Corporation

41. **SAVINGS** Pao spent \$140 of his paycheck and put the remaining \$20 in his savings account. If the number of dollars he spends is proportional to the number he saves, how much of a \$156-paycheck will he put into savings? **\$19.50**

42. **MOVIES** After 30 seconds, 720 frames of film have passed through a movie projector. At this rate, what is the approximate running time in minutes of a movie made up of 57,000 frames of film? **about 40 min**

43. **SCHOOL** There are 325 students and 13 teachers at a school. Next school year, the enrollment is expected to increase by 100 students. Write and solve a proportion to find the number of teachers that must be hired so the student-teacher ratio remains the same. $\frac{325}{13} = \frac{100}{x}$; **4**

Academic Standards • ISTEP+
Extra Practice, pp. 683, 709

44. **FIND THE DATA** Refer to the Data File on pages 16–19. Choose some data and write a real-world problem in which you would solve a proportion. **See students' work.**

H.O.T. Problems

45. **Which One Doesn't Belong?** Identify the rate that is not proportional to the other three. Explain your reasoning.

\$4.50 for 5 lb	\$2.88 for 3.2 lb	\$5.70 for 6 lb	\$4.86 for 5.4 lb

45. \$5.70 for 6 lb; Sample answer: This ratio has a unit rate of 0.95/lb, while all of the other ratios have a unit rate of \$0.90/lb.

46. **CHALLENGE** In a cleaning solution, the ratio of bleach to water is 1:5. If there are 36 cups of cleaning solution, how many cups of water are needed? Explain your reasoning. **See margin.**

314 Chapter 6 Ratios and Proportions

47. Sample answer: Mental math; $10 is 4 times more than $2.50, so the number of ears is 4 times more than a dozen, which is 4 dozen or 48 ears of corn.

47. **SELECT A TECHNIQUE** Sweet corn is on sale at $2.50 for a dozen at a farmer's market. Select one or more of the following technique(s) to determine how many ears you can buy for $10. Then use this technique to solve the problem.

mental math | estimation | number sense

48. **WRITING IN MATH** Explain why the cross products of a proportion are equal. Use the term *multiplicative inverse* in your explanation. **See margin.**

ISTEP+ PRACTICE 7.1.9, 7.2.7

49. Mirma gives away 84 flyers over a 3-hour period. If the number of flyers she is able to give away per hour remains the same, which proportion can be used to find x, the number of flyers that she would give away over a 5-hour period? **B**

A $\frac{3}{84} = \frac{x}{5}$

B $\frac{84}{3} = \frac{x}{5}$

C $\frac{5}{3} = \frac{84}{x}$

D $\frac{3}{84} = \frac{x}{8}$

50. A recipe that makes 16 muffins calls for $\frac{1}{2}$ cup of flour. How much flour is needed to make 3 dozen muffins using this recipe? **F**

F $1\frac{1}{8}$ c

G 1 c

H $1\frac{1}{4}$ c

J $1\frac{1}{2}$ c

Spiral Review

51. **MEASUREMENT** Felicia bought 5 pounds of onions. About how many kilograms of onions did she buy? (Lesson 6-5) **about 2.27 kg**

MEASUREMENT **Complete.** (Lesson 6-4)

52. 5 qt = ■ pt **10**

53. $3\frac{1}{2}$ lb = ■ oz **56**

54. 28 c = ■ qt **7**

Multiply. Write in simplest form. (Lesson 5-5)

55. $3\frac{1}{2} \times 5\frac{7}{8}$ **$20\frac{9}{16}$**

56. $1\frac{2}{3} \times 5\frac{4}{5}$ **$9\frac{2}{3}$**

57. $2\frac{1}{4} \times 7\frac{5}{8}$ **$17\frac{5}{32}$**

GET READY for the Next Lesson

58. **PREREQUISITE SKILL** Mr. Andres is filling up his car with gas that costs $2.50 per gallon. His car's gas gauge before filling up is shown at the right. If his car's gas tank holds 16 gallons, about how much will Mr. Andres pay to fill up his tank? Use the *eliminate possibilities* strategy. (Lesson 5-4) **B**

A $15.00

B $25.00

C $27.00

D $35.00

4 Assess

Yesterday's News Remind students that yesterday's lesson was about converting from one unit of measure to another in the customary measurement system. Have students write how yesterday's concepts helped them with today's material.

FOLDABLES Study Organizer Foldables™ Follow-Up

Remind students to select a term or concept about proportions and to define it in their Foldables. Encourage them to give an example of the term or concept.

Additional Answer

48. Sample answer: Finding the cross products of a proportion is the same as multiplying both sides of the equation by a multiplicative inverse. For example, the cross products of the proportion $\frac{2}{3} = \frac{4}{6}$ are $2 \cdot 6$ and $4 \cdot 3$. If you rewrite $\frac{2}{3}$ as $2 \cdot \frac{1}{3}$ and $\frac{4}{6}$ as $4 \cdot \frac{1}{6}$ you have the following:

$$2 \cdot \frac{1}{3} = 4 \cdot \frac{1}{6}$$

$$2 \cdot \frac{1}{\cancel{3}} \cdot \cancel{3} \cdot 6 = 4 \cdot \frac{1}{\cancel{6}} \cdot \cancel{6} \cdot 3$$

$$2 \cdot 6 = 4 \cdot 3$$

Notice that $2 \cdot 6$ and $4 \cdot 3$ are the cross products of the original proportion and that they are equal.

Extend 6-6 Lesson Notes

1 Focus

Materials

- graph paper

Teaching Tip

You might want to point out to students that the graph they draw should be decreasing and is not linear. The graph should be curved.

2 Teach

Working in Cooperative Groups

You may wish for students to work in groups of 2 or 3. Students can work together to complete the table and plot the data.

Activity You might want to encourage students to discuss the answers to Exercises 1 and 2. After they have discussed their results, have the students write them down.

3 Assess

Formative Assessment

Use Exercise 2 to determine whether students understand how to recognize inversely proportional relationships.

From Concrete to Abstract Use students' responses to Exercise 2 to understand how inverse proportions can be recognized in any situation.

Extending the Concept Have students discuss other situations that might be inversely proportional. Ask students to graph another relationship that is inversely proportional. How do inverse proportions differ from direct proportions?

Extend 6-6

Math Lab
Inverse Proportionality

MAIN IDEA

Graph inverse variations.

IN Academic Standards

7.2.7 Identify situations that involve proportional relationships, . . ., and recognize that these situations are described by a linear function in the form $y = mx$ where the unit rate m is the slope of the line. *Also addresses P.1.1, P.4.1.*

New Vocabulary

inverse proportion

Jackie walks at an average rate of 4 miles per hour. This situation can be represented by the equation $d = 4t$, where d is the distance in miles, and t is the time in hours. The number of miles is proportional to the number of hours because the ratios are equal.

Let's vary the situation a little. Suppose Jackie wants to walk 12 miles each day, at varying speeds. How long will it take her to walk 12 miles? The answer depends on how fast she walks.

ACTIVITY

STEP 1 Copy and complete the table for the equation $12 = rt$.

t (hours)	12	8	6	■ 4.8	■ 4	■ 3.4	■ 3
r (miles per hour)	1	1.5	2	2.5	3	3.5	4

STEP 2 Copy and complete the graph of the ordered pairs from Step 1. Connect the line with a smooth curve. The first three points are done for you.

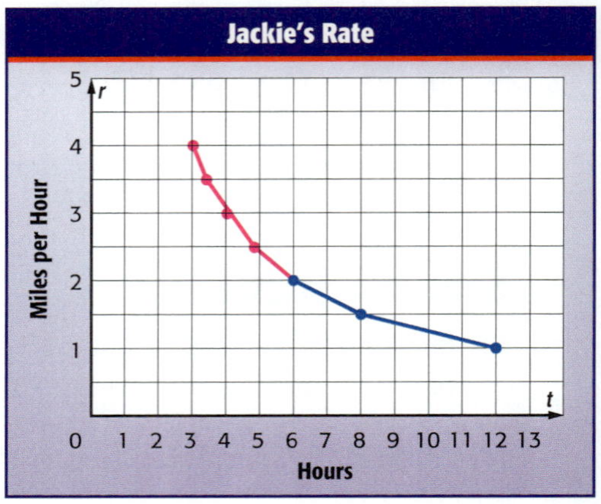

Analyze the Results

1. Is the time proportional to the rate? Explain why or why not. **No; the slower Jackie walks, the more time it takes her to walk each mile.**
2. When the product of two variables is a constant, the relationship forms an **inverse proportion.** Which situation is an inverse proportion: Jackie walking at 4 miles per hour or walking 12 miles at varying rates? Identify the constants in each situation.
3. Mr. Anwar agrees to pay Rob a flat fee of $240 to do some yard work. Mr. Sloan agrees to pay Rob's brother $10 per hour to do some yard work. Make a table of ordered pairs and a graph for each situation. Then decide whether each relationship is a proportion or an inverse proportion. **See Ch. 6 Answer Appendix.**

2. Jackie walks at varying rates is the inverse proportion. Constant: 12 miles. When Jackie walks at 4 miles per hour, the constant is 4 miles per hour.

CHAPTER 6 Mid-Chapter Quiz

Lessons 6-1 through 6-6

IN Academic Standards
7.1.9, 7.2.5

RECIPE For Exercises 1–3, use the information in the table to write each ratio as a fraction in simplest form. (Lesson 6-1)

Cherry Punch Recipe	
Cherry Juice	4 cups
Apple Juice	2 cups
Ginger Ale	16 cups

1. cherry juice : apple juice $\frac{2}{1}$
2. apple juice : ginger ale $\frac{1}{8}$
3. cherry juice : ginger ale $\frac{1}{4}$

Determine whether the ratios are equivalent. Explain. (Lesson 6-1)

4. 6 out of 9 words spelled correctly
   2 out of 3 words spelled correctly yes; $\frac{6}{9} = \frac{2}{3}$
5. 150 athletes to 15 coaches
   3 athletes to 1 coach no; 150:15 = 10:1
6. 24 points in 4 games
   72 points in 8 games
   no; 24:4 = 6:1 and 72:8 = 9:1
7. **MULTIPLE CHOICE** Which amount of chocolate shown in the table has the best unit price? (Lesson 6-2) B

Weight (oz)	Cost ($)
12	2.50
18	3.69
24	4.95
30	6.25

A 12 oz C 24 oz
B 18 oz D 36 oz

8. Use the graph to find the rate of change in cost per magazine. (Lesson 6-3)
   The cost increases by $4 for each magazine purchased.

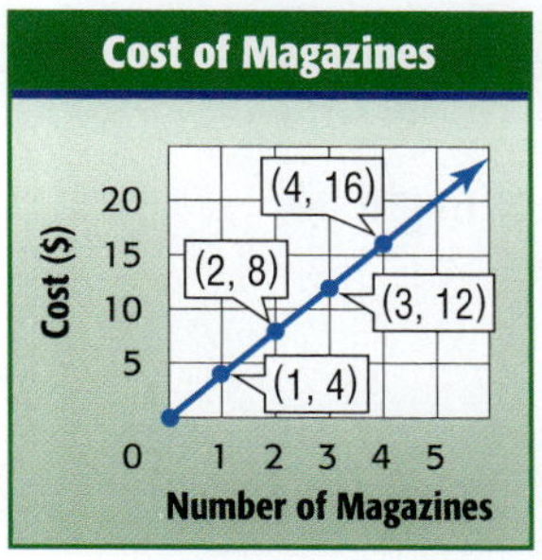

Complete. (Lesson 6-4)

9. 42 ft = ■ yd 14
10. 9 pt = ■ qt $4\frac{1}{2}$
11. 7,600 lb = ■ T 3.8
12. $7\frac{1}{2}$ gal = ■ qt 30
13. **MULTIPLE CHOICE** Which situation is best represented by the graph? (Lesson 6-4) G

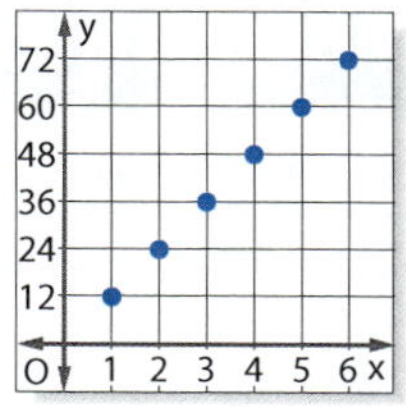

F conversion of inches to yards
G conversion of feet to inches
H conversion of inches to miles
J conversion of yards to feet

Complete. Round to the nearest hundredth if necessary. (Lesson 6-5)

14. 12.5 mi ≈ ■ km 20.13
15. 4.75 gal ≈ ■ L 18.00
16. 76 cm ≈ ■ in. 29.92
17. 31.8 kg ≈ ■ lb 70.11

Determine if the quantities in each pair of ratios are proportional. Explain. (Lesson 6-6)

18. 8 pages in 5 minutes and 40 pages in 25 minutes See margin.
19. 40 blank CDs for $9.60 and 24 blank CDs for $4.80 See margin.

Solve each proportion. (Lesson 6-6)

20. $\frac{3}{d} = \frac{12}{20}$ 5
21. $\frac{7}{8} = \frac{m}{48}$ 42
22. $\frac{w}{8} = \frac{1}{3}$ $2\frac{2}{3}$

23. **MEASUREMENT** It took 45 minutes to fill a circular pool of uniform depth to a level of 18 inches. At this rate, how long will it take to fill the pool to a level of 35 inches? (Lesson 6-6) 87.5 min

CHAPTER 6 Mid-Chapter Quiz

Formative Assessment

Use the Mid-Chapter Quiz to assess students' progress in the first half of the chapter.

Have students review the lesson indicated for the problems they answered incorrectly.

Summative Assessment

CRM Mid-Chapter Test, p. 69

ExamView Assessment Suite Customize and create multiple versions of your Mid-Chapter Quiz and their answer keys.

FOLDABLES Study Organizer Dinah Zike's Foldables

Before students complete the Mid-Chapter Quiz, encourage them to review the definitions and examples they recorded about ratios, rates, units of measure, and proportions in their Foldables table.

Additional Answers

18. Yes; Sample answer: The cross products of the ratios $\frac{8}{5}$ and $\frac{40}{25}$, 40 • 5 and 25 • 8, are both equal to 200.
19. No; Sample answer: $\frac{\$4.80}{24 \text{ CDs}} = \frac{\$0.20}{1 \text{ CD}}$ and $\frac{\$9.60}{40 \text{ CDs}} = \frac{\$0.24}{\text{CD}}$. The unit rates are not equal.

Data-Driven Decision Making

Diagnostic Teaching Based on the results of the Chapter 6 Mid-Chapter Quiz, use the following to review concepts that students continue to find challenging.

Exercises	Lesson	Academic Standards	Resources for Review
1–6	6–1	7.1.9	CRM Study Guide and Intervention pp. 10, 16, 22, 28, 34, and 40
7, 8	6–2, 6–3	7.1.9, 7.2.5, 7.2.6	IN Math Online glencoe.com
9–13	6–4	8.3.4	• Extra Examples • Personal Tutor
14–17	6–5	8.3.4	• Concepts in Motion
18–23	6–6	7.1.9, 7.2.7	

6-7 Problem-Solving Investigation
DRAW A DIAGRAM

PACING: **Regular:** 1 period, **Block:** 0.5 period

IN Academic Standards **P.1.3 Apply and adapt a variety of appropriate strategies to solve problems. P.5.1 Create and use representations to organize, record, and communicate mathematical ideas.**

Options for Differentiated Instruction

ELL = English Language Learner   AL = Above or Beyond Grade Level   SS = Struggling Students   SN = Special Needs

Additional Practice AL

Use after students complete Exercises 1–2.

For students who complete the in-class assignment before the rest of the class is finished, present the following problem and have them draw a diagram to solve.

> Jack's house, the post office, the bank, and the library are on the same road. Jack lives 3.5 miles from the library, which is 2.25 miles farther from his house than the bank. The post office is between the bank and the library and 0.75 mile from the bank. How far is it from Jack's house to the post office?

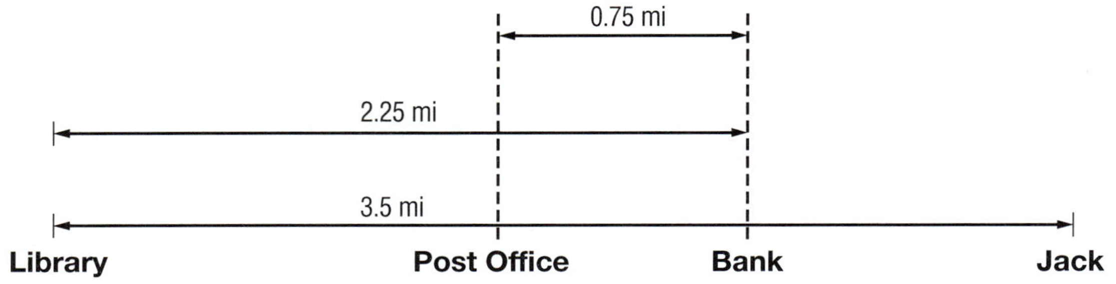

Choosing the Strategy ELL SS SN

Use before assigning the Exercises.

Prior to assigning Exercises 6–10, read each problem aloud and discuss with the group which strategy might be best to solve the problem. Possible discussion questions:

- What question do you need to answer?
- What information is given?
- Is this like any problems you have solved in the past?
- What strategy would be most effective to solve the problem?
- How could you check your answer to make sure it is reasonable?

Make sure that all students have chosen a strategy for each of the problems so they can complete the assignment independently.

Leveled Lesson Resources

Also on TeacherWorks™ Lesson 6-7

Chapter 6 Resource Masters

Study Guide and Intervention*
p. 46 BL OL ELL

NAME ______ DATE ______ PERIOD ______

6-7 Study Guide and Intervention
Problem-Solving Investigation: Draw a Diagram

When solving problems, draw a diagram to show what you have and what you need to find.

Example CARNIVAL **Jim has to reach a target at a carnival game to win a prize. After 3 throws he has gone 75 feet, which is $\frac{3}{4}$ of the way to the target. How far away is the target?**

Understand We know that 75 feet is $\frac{3}{4}$ of the way to the target.

Plan Draw a diagram to show the distance already thrown and the fraction it represents.

Solve

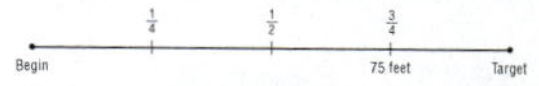

If $\frac{3}{4}$ of the distance is 75 feet, then $\frac{1}{4}$ of the distance is 25 feet. So, the missing $\frac{1}{4}$ must be another 25 feet.

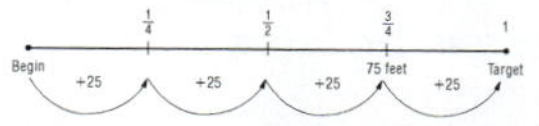

The total distance that Jim must throw to hit the target is 100 feet.

Check Since $\frac{3}{4}$ of the total distance is 75 feet, the equation $\frac{3}{4}x = 75$ represents this problem. Solving, we get $x = 100$ feet. So, the solution checks.

Exercises

1. SALES Sharon wants to buy a new car. She has saved up $ 1,500, which is approximately $\frac{1}{5}$ of the price of the car. How much does she need to save in order to buy the new car? **$7,500**
2. TRAVEL The Jones family has traveled 360 miles. They are $\frac{4}{5}$ of the way to their destination. How far away is their destination from where they started? **450 miles**

Chapter 6 46 Course 2

Skills Practice*
p. 47 BL OL

NAME ______ DATE ______ PERIOD ______

6-7 Skills Practice
Problem-Solving Investigation: Draw a Diagram

Draw a diagram to solve.

1. HOMEWORK Shantel is studying for her history test. After 20 minutes, she is $\frac{1}{4}$ of the way done. How much longer will she study? **60 minutes**
2. RECIPES Damon is making muffins. He has added $\frac{3}{4}$ of the ingredients. If he has added 6 ingredients, how many more does he have to add to be finished? **2**
3. TRAVEL The Smithsons are going to Dallas, TX on vacation. They have traveled $\frac{1}{3}$ of the total distance. If they have traveled 126 miles, how far is it from their house to Dallas? **378 miles**
4. PHYSICS A ball is dropped from 256 feet above the ground. It bounces up $\frac{1}{4}$ as high as it fell. This is true for each successive bounce. What height will the ball reach on the third bounce? **4 feet**
5. SCHOOL Mrs. Wright says that $\frac{2}{3}$ of her class has arrived for the day. If 10 students have arrived, how many students are in her class? **15**
6. TRAVEL Jeremy walked $\frac{1}{4}$ of the way to school, ran $\frac{1}{4}$ of the way to school, then rode with his best friend the rest of the way. If he walked 1.5 miles, how far did he ride with his friend? **3 miles**

Lesson 6-7

Chapter 6 47 Course 2

Practice*
p. 48 OL AL

NAME ______ DATE ______ PERIOD ______

6-7 Practice
Problem-Solving Investigation: Draw a Diagram

Mixed Problem Solving

Use the draw a diagram strategy to solve Exercises 1 and 2.

1. ANTS An ant went 2 meters away from its nest searching for food. The next time, the ant went 3 meters away. Each successive time the ant leaves the nest to search for food, the ant travels the sum of the two previous times. How far will the ant travel on his fifth trip? **13 meters**
2. NECKLACES The center bead of a pearl necklace has a 16 millimeter diameter. Each successive bead in each direction is $\frac{3}{4}$ the diameter of the previous one. Find the diameter of the beads that are three away from the center bead. **$6\frac{3}{4}$ mm**

Use any strategy to solve Exercises 3–6. Some strategies are shown below.

PROBLEM-SOLVING STRATEGIES
• Work backward.
• Make an organized list.
• Eliminate possibilities.
• Draw a diagram.

3. TALENT SHOW At a talent show, 60% of the acts were singing. One-third of the remaining acts were instrumental. If 12 acts were instrumental, how many acts were in the talent show? **90 acts**
4. GEOMETRY Miss Greenwell is adding 4 feet to the length and width of her rectangular garden as shown in the diagram. How much additional area will the garden have? **B**

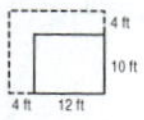

A. 16 ft²
B. 104 ft²
C. 120 ft²
D. 224 ft²

5. YARD SALE Myron has sold $18.50 worth of items at his yard sale. A neighbor bought two items and handed Myron a $10 bill. Myron returned $7.75 in change. How much has Myron now sold? **$20.75**
6. COUNTRIES The table shows the total land area of five countries.

Country	Total Area
Brazil	8.5 million sq km
Canada	10.0 million sq km
China	9.6 million sq km
Russia	17.1 million sq km
United States	9.6 million sq km

Estimate how much more total area Russia has than China. **7.5 million km²**

Chapter 6 48 Course 2

Word Problem Practice*
p. 49 OL AL

NAME ______ DATE ______ PERIOD ______

6-7 Word Problem Practice
Problem-Solving Investigation: Draw a Diagram

Solve each problem using any strategy you have learned.

1. MONEY Chantel has $125 left in her checking account after writing checks for $35, $22.50 and $16. What was her balance before she wrote the checks? **$198.50**
2. GEOMETRY Draw the next three figures in the pattern.

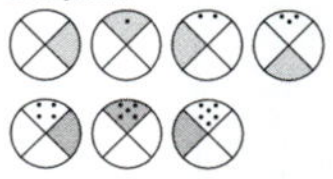

3. PIZZA Olivia has eaten $\frac{1}{3}$ of the pizza. If she has eaten 3 pieces, how many pieces were originally in the pizza? **9**
4. EXERCISE Katlyn runs 2 miles after school each day and 3 miles on Saturday and 4 miles on Sunday. How many miles does she run during one week? **17 miles**
5. WORK Jefferson wants to work at least 25 hours this week. If he has already worked 22 hours, how many hours does he need to work on Saturday? **3 hours**
6. TRAVEL The bus to Washington has traveled $\frac{5}{6}$ of the way there. If it has traveled 80 miles, how much farther does it have to go? **16 miles**
7. MUSEUMS The Art Club is planning on attending a museum. The admission cost is $10 for adults and $7.50 for students. If they plan on having 2 adults attend as chaperones and have $150 saved from a fundraiser, what is the maximum number of students who can attend? **17 students**
8. SPORTS Janean made 50 baskets during the week at practice. The table below shows when she made the baskets. How many baskets did she make on Friday? **10**

Day	Number of Baskets
Monday	5
Tuesday	12
Wednesday	16
Thursday	7
Friday	??

Lesson 6-7

Chapter 6 49 Course 2

* *Also available in Spanish* ELL

BL = Below or Approaching Grade Level
OL = On Grade Level
AL = Above or Beyond Grade Level
ELL = English Language Learner

Additional Lesson Resources

Transparencies
- *5-Minute Check Transparency,* Lesson 6-7

Other Print Products
- *Noteables™ Interactive Study Notebook with Foldables™*

Teacher Tech Tools
- *Interactive Classroom CD-ROM,* Lesson 6-7
- *AssignmentWorks,* Lesson 6-7

Student Tech Tools
glencoe.com
- Extra Examples, Chapter 6, Lesson 7
- Self-Check Quiz, Chapter 6, Lesson 7

6-7 Lesson Notes

1 Focus

Draw a Diagram

Many real-world problems can be solved by drawing a diagram. Diagrams make clear what information is given, what information is needed, and how best to find the missing information. This strategy will be especially useful in Lesson 6-8, in which students solve problems about scale drawings.

2 Teach

Scaffolding Questions

Ask:

- What are some examples of diagrams that you use in everyday life? Sample answers: instructions for assembling a toy, map of a store's layout, instructions for using a DVD player
- What information do these diagrams include? Sample answers: labels of parts, measurements or distances, order or position of parts
- Why are diagrams useful? Sample answer: A diagram helps you visualize a situation.

ADDITIONAL EXAMPLE

Solve. Draw a diagram.

ROCK CLIMBING A rock climber stops to rest at a ledge 90 feet above the ground. If this represents 75% of the total climb, how high above the ground is the top of the rock? 120 ft

Additional Examples are also in:

- Noteables™ Interactive Study Notebook with Foldables™
- Interactive Classroom PowerPoint® Presentations

6-7 Problem-Solving Investigation

MAIN IDEA: Solve problems by drawing a diagram.

Academic Standards **P.1.3** Apply and adapt a variety of appropriate strategies to solve problems. **P.5.1** Create and use representations to organize, record, and communicate mathematical ideas.

P.S.I. TEAM +

e-Mail: DRAW A DIAGRAM

CACEY: I dropped a ball from a height of 12 feet. It hits the ground and bounces up half as high as it fell. This is true for each successive bounce.

YOUR MISSION: Draw a diagram to find the height the ball reaches after the fourth bounce.

Understand	You know the ball is dropped from a height of 12 feet. It bounces up half as high as it falls.
Plan	Draw a diagram to show the height of the ball after each bounce.
Solve	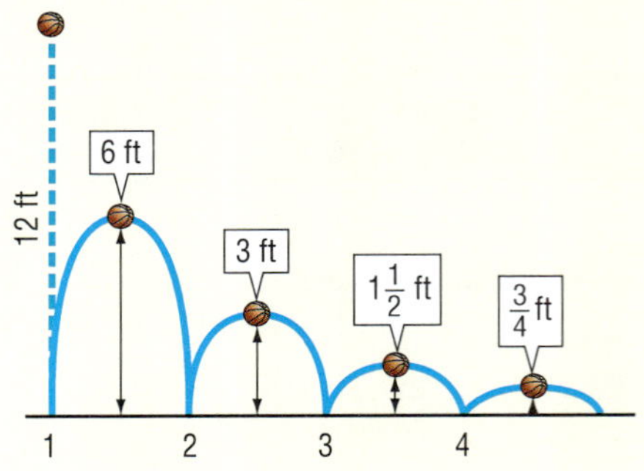 The ball reaches a height of $\frac{3}{4}$ foot after the fourth bounce.
Check	Start at 12 feet. Multiply by $\frac{1}{2}$ for each bounce: $12 \cdot \frac{1}{2} \cdot \frac{1}{2} \cdot \frac{1}{2} \cdot \frac{1}{2} = \frac{12}{16}$ or $\frac{3}{4}$. So, the solution is correct.

Analyze The Strategy

1. Determine what height a ball would reach after the fourth bounce if it is dropped from 12 feet and bounces up $\frac{2}{3}$ as high. Draw a new diagram for this situation. See margin.
2. WRITING IN MATH Write a problem that could be solved by drawing a diagram. Exchange your problem with a classmate and solve. See margin.

Additional Answers

1. $\frac{3}{4}$ foot

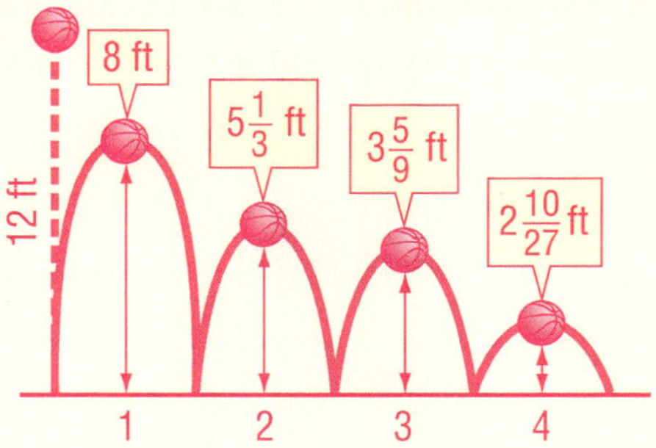

2. There are 4 books in the front window of a book store. How many different ways can you arrange the books in the front window?; 24 ways

Mixed Problem Solving

★ indicates multi-step problem

Academic Standards • ISTEP+

Extra Practice, pp. 683, 709

Solve Exercises 3–5. Use the *draw a diagram* strategy.

3. **TRAVEL** Mr. Garcia has driven 60 miles, which is $\frac{2}{3}$ of the way to his sister's house. How much farther does he have to drive to get to his sister's house? **30 miles**

4. **DISTANCE** Alejandro and Pedro are riding their bikes to school. After 1 mile, they are $\frac{4}{5}$ of the way there. How much farther do they have to go? **$\frac{1}{4}$ mi**

5. **VOLUME** A swimming pool is being filled with water. After 25 minutes, $\frac{1}{6}$ of the swimming pool is filled. How much longer will it take to completely fill the pool, assuming the water rate is constant? **125 minutes**

Use any strategy to solve Exercises 6–10. Some strategies are shown below.

PROBLEM-SOLVING STRATEGIES
- Work backward.
- Make an organized list.
- Eliminate possibilities.
- Draw a diagram.

6. ★ **BASEBALL** Of Lee's baseball cards, $\frac{1}{5}$ show California players. Of these, $\frac{3}{8}$ show San Diego Padres players. Is the fraction of Lee's collection that show Padres players $\frac{23}{40}$, $\frac{4}{13}$, or $\frac{3}{40}$? **$\frac{3}{40}$**

7. **GAMES** Eight members of a chess club are having a tournament. In the first round, every player will play a chess game against every other player. How many games will be in the first round of the tournament? **28 games**

8. **MEASUREMENT** Kiaya is adding a 2-inch border to the length and width of a photograph as shown.

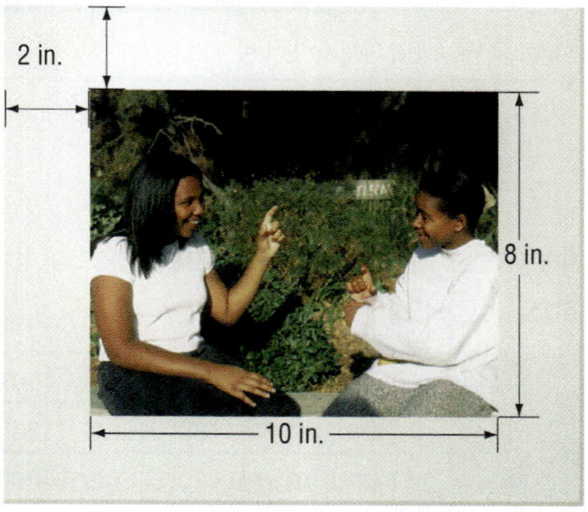

Which expression represents the area of the border to be added to the original photograph? **B**

A $(8 + 4)(10 + 4)$

B $(8 + 4)(10 + 4) - (8)(10)$

C $(8 - 4)(10 - 4)$

D $(8 - 4)(10 - 4) - (8)(10)$

9. **RACES** Anna, Isabela, Mary, and Pilar ran a race. Anna is just ahead of Pilar. Pilar is two places behind Isabela. Isabela is a few seconds behind the leader, Mary. Use the table to place the girls in order from first to last. **Mary, Isabela, Anna, Pilar**

10. **FRACTIONS** Marta ate a quarter of a whole pie. Edwin ate $\frac{1}{4}$ of what was left. Cristina then ate $\frac{1}{3}$ of what was left. What fraction of the pie remains? **$\frac{3}{8}$**

3 Practice

Using the Exercises

Exercises 1 and 2 can be used to check students' understanding of the draw a diagram strategy.

Exercises 3–5 give students an opportunity to practice the draw a diagram strategy.

Exercises 6–10 give students the opportunity to practice many different problem-solving strategies. You may wish to have students review some of the strategies students have studied.

- Work backward (p. 148)
- Make an organized list (p. 190)
- Eliminate possibilities (p. 248)
- Draw a diagram (p. 318)

4 Assess

Crystal Ball Tell students that tomorrow's lesson is about solving problems involving scale drawings. Have them write how they think what they learned today will connect with tomorrow's material.

Differentiated Instruction

Visual Learners Separate students into pairs and distribute number tiles to each pair. Tell them that a contractor is laying new tiles for a kitchen floor. The tiles are 2 feet by 2 feet, and the floor is 16 feet by 12 feet. Have each pair use their number tiles to find the number of floor tiles the contractor needs. 48

Then have each pair draw a diagram of the problem, based on the model they used. Make sure they label the parts and distances in their diagrams. See students' work.

6-8 Scale Drawings

PACING: **Regular:** 1.5 periods, **Block:** 1 period

IN Academic Standards **7.3.5 Identify, describe and construct similarity relationships and solve problems involving similarity** (including similar triangles) and **scale drawings by using proportional reasoning.** *Also addresses P.1.2, P.4.3.*

Options for Differentiated Instruction

ELL = English Language Learner AL = Above or Beyond Grade Level SS = Struggling Students SN = Special Needs

Making Drawings ELL AL SS

Use before presenting Lesson 6-8.

To help students see the effect of using different scales, have them find the dimensions of the classroom and create scale drawings on grid paper using the following scales.

Scale 1	1 unit on grid represents 1 foot.
Scale 2	1 unit on grid represents 2 feet.
Scale 3	1 unit on grid represents 4 feet.

Ask:

- How do the drawings compare?
- What are the similarities and differences?
- Why is it important to label each drawing with the scale you used?
- Would it make sense to use the scale 1 unit represents 3 feet? Why or why not?
- What are the advantages of making a scale drawing?

Research ELL AL

Use after students complete Lesson 6-8.

Have students use the Internet or call a local architecture firm and interview an architect to find answers to the following questions:

- Do architects use the same scale for every blueprint they create?
- What scales are used most often?
- What scales do they use when they create a 3-dimensional model?

Tell students to be prepared to share the information with the class.

Relevant Applications ELL SS SN

Use after presenting the Examples.

Have students make a scale drawing of a room in their home. The drawing should be an overhead view, including furniture that is rectangular in shape. Each student should describe a scale factor that is reasonable for the task.

Leveled Lesson Resources

Also on TeacherWorks™ Lesson 6-8

Chapter 6 Resource Masters

BL = Below or Approaching Grade Level   OL = On Grade Level   AL = Above or Beyond Grade Level   ELL = English Language Learner

Lesson Reading Guide
p. 50 BL OL ELL

NAME ______ DATE ______ PERIOD ____

6-8 Lesson Reading Guide

Scale Drawings

Get Ready for the Lesson

Do the Mini Lab at the top of page 320 in your textbook. Write your answers below.

1. Let 1 unit on the grid paper represent 2 feet. So, 4 units = 8 feet. Convert all your measurements to units. **See students' work.**
2. On grid paper, make a drawing of your gymnasium like the one shown at the top of page 320. **See students' work.**

Read the Lesson

3. Look at the map in the middle of page 320. What is the scale? What does the scale mean? **The scale is 1 centimeter = 20 miles; that means that a distance of 1 centimeter on the map is equal to 20 miles in actual distance.**
4. In Example 1, could you find the actual distance if you did not know the scale? Explain your answer. **Sample answer: No; there can be only one unknown value to solve the proportion. To find the actual distance you need three of the four values of the two cross products.**
5. Give another example of a scale drawing or scale model that is different from the examples of scale drawings and scale models given in this lesson in your textbook. **Sample answer: a scale model of a human heart**

Remember What You Learned

6. How is a scale drawing similar to a scale model? How is it different? **Sample answer: Both a scale drawing and a scale model use a scale and show accurate proportional measures. However, a scale drawing is flat (two-dimensional) and can show measures for any two of three measures (length, width, or height). A scale model can be built to show all three measures because a model is three-dimensional.**

Chapter 6 50 Course 2

Study Guide and Intervention*
p. 51 BL OL ELL

NAME ______ DATE ______ PERIOD ____

6-8 Study Guide and Intervention

Scale Drawings

A **scale drawing** represents something that is too large or too small to be drawn or built at actual size. Similarly, a **scale model** can be used to represent something that is too large or built too small for an actual-size model. The **scale** gives the relationship between the drawing/model measure and the actual measure.

Example On this map, each grid unit represents 50 yards. Find the distance from Patrick's Point to Agate Beach.

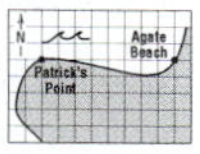

Scale	Patrick's Point to Agate Beach	
map → 1 unit	8 units ←	map
actual → 50 yards	x yards ←	actual
1 × x =	50 × 8	Cross products
x =	400	Simplify.

It is 400 yards from Patrick's Point to Agate Beach.

Exercises

Find the actual distance between each pair of cities. Round to the nearest tenth if necessary.

	Cities	Map Distance	Scale	Actual Distance
1.	Los Angeles and San Diego, California	6.35 cm	1 cm = 20 mi	**127 mi**
2.	Lexington and Louisville, Kentucky	15.6 cm	1 cm = 5 mi	**78 mi**
3.	Des Moines and Cedar Rapids, Iowa	16.27 cm	2 cm = 15 mi	**122.0 mi**
4.	Miami and Jacksonville, Florida	11.73 cm	$\frac{1}{2}$ cm = 20 mi	**469.2 mi**

Suppose you are making a scale drawing. Find the length of each object on the scale drawing with the given scale. Then find the scale factor.

5. an automobile 16 feet long; 1 inch:6 inches **32 in.; $\frac{1}{6}$**
6. a lake 85 feet across; 1 inch = 4 feet **$21\frac{1}{4}$ in.; $\frac{1}{48}$**
7. a parking lot 200 meters wide; 1 centimeter:25 meters **8 cm; $\frac{1}{2{,}500}$**
8. a flag 5 feet wide; 2 inches = 1 foot **10 in.; $\frac{1}{6}$**

Chapter 6 51 Course 2

Skills Practice*
p. 52 BL OL

NAME ______ DATE ______ PERIOD ____

6-8 Skills Practice

Scale Drawings

ARCHITECTURE **The scale on a set of architectural drawings for a house is $\frac{1}{2}$ inch = $1\frac{1}{2}$ feet. Find the length of each part of the house.**

	Room	Drawing Length	Actual Length
1.	Living Room	5 inches	**15 ft**
2.	Dining Room	4 inches	**12 ft**
3.	Kitchen	$5\frac{1}{2}$ inches	**$16\frac{1}{2}$ ft**
4.	Laundry Room	$3\frac{1}{4}$ inches	**$9\frac{3}{4}$ ft**
5.	Basement	10 inches	**30 ft**
6.	Garage	$8\frac{1}{3}$ inches	**25 ft**

ARCHITECTURE **As part of a city building refurbishment project, architects have constructed a scale model of several city buildings to present to the city commission for approval. The scale of the model is 1 inch = 9 feet.**

7. The courthouse is the tallest building in the city. If it is $7\frac{1}{2}$ inches tall in the model, how tall is the actual building? **$67\frac{1}{2}$ ft**
8. The city commission would like to install new flagpoles that are each 45 feet tall. How tall are the flagpoles in the model? **5 in.**
9. In the model, two of the flagpoles are 4 inches apart. How far apart will they be when they are installed? **36 ft**
10. The model includes a new park in the center of the city. If the dimensions of the park in the model are 9 inches by 17 inches, what are the actual dimensions of the park? **81 ft by 153 ft**
11. Find the scale factor. **$\frac{1}{108}$**

Chapter 6 52 Course 2

Practice*
p. 53 OL AL

NAME ______ DATE ______ PERIOD ____

6-8 Practice

Scale Drawings

For Exercises 1–3, use the diagram of a section of the art museum shown. Use a ruler to measure.

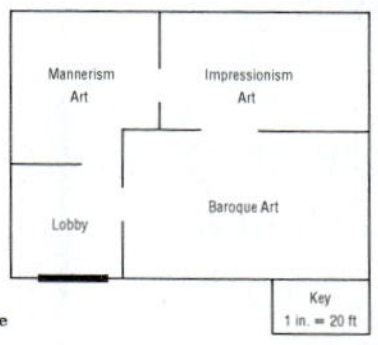

1. What is the actual length of the *Impressionism Art* room? **35 ft**
2. Find the actual dimensions of the *Baroque Art* room. **$41\frac{1}{4}$ ft by 25 ft**
3. Find the scale factor for this blueprint. **$\frac{1}{240}$**

Find the length of each model on the scale drawing with the given scale.

4. 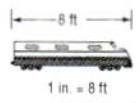 **7.5 in.; $\frac{1}{96}$**
5. 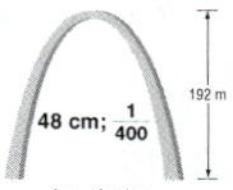 **48 cm; $\frac{1}{400}$**
6. 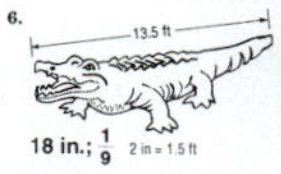 **18 in.; $\frac{1}{9}$**

7. SKYSCRAPER A model of a skyscraper is made using a scale of 1 inch:75 feet. What is the height of the actual building if the height of the model is $19\frac{2}{5}$ inches? **1,455 ft**
8. GEOGRAPHY Salem and Eugene, Oregon, are 64 miles apart. If the distance on the map is $3\frac{1}{4}$ inches, find the scale of the map. **1 in.:19.7 mi**
9. PYRAMIDS The length of a side of the Great Pyramid of Khufu at Giza, Egypt, is 751 feet. If you were to make a model of the pyramid to display on your desk, which would be an appropriate scale: 1 in. = 10 ft or 1 ft = 500 ft? Explain your reasoning. **Sample answer: 1 ft = 500 ft; If using the 1 in. = 10 ft scale, the model would be about 75 inches in length. If using the 1 ft = 500 ft scale, the model would be about 1.5 feet, which would fit on the desk.**

Chapter 6 53 Course 2

Word Problem Practice*
p. 54 OL AL

NAME ______ DATE ______ PERIOD ____

6-8 Word Problem Practice

Scale Drawings

1. CARS A scale drawing of an automobile has a scale of 1 inch = $\frac{1}{2}$ foot. The actual width of the car is 8 feet. What is the width on the scale drawing? **16 in.**
2. MODELS A model ship is built to a scale of 1 centimeter:5 meters. The length of the model is 30 centimeters. What is the length of the actual ship? **150 m**
3. BUILDING Jose wants to build a model of a 180-meter tall building. He will be using a scale of 1.5 centimeters = 3.5 meters. How tall will the model be? Round your answer to the nearest tenth. **77.1 cm**
4. TRAVEL Susan is driving to Mount Shasta. On her map, she is a distance of $7\frac{3}{4}$ inches away. The scale of the map is $\frac{1}{2}$ inch = 50 miles. How far must Susan travel to reach her destination? **775 mi**
5. MAPS A map of Levi's property is being made with a scale of 2 centimeters: 3 meters. What is the scale factor? **$\frac{1}{150}$**
6. LANDSCAPING A pond is being dug according to plans that have a scale of 1 inch = 6.5 feet. The maximum distance across the pond is 9.75 inches on the plans. What will be the actual maximum distance across the pond? **63.375 ft**

Chapter 6 54 Course 2

Enrichment
p. 55 OL AL

NAME ______ DATE ______ PERIOD ____

6-8 Enrichment

Scale Drawings

Use the scale drawings of two different apartments to answer the questions.

1. Which apartment has the greater area? **Apartment B**
2. What is the difference in square feet between Apartment A and Apartment B? **48 ft²**
3. How much more closet space is offered by Apartment B than Apartment A? **74 ft²**
4. How much more bathroom space is offered by Apartment A than Apartment B? **12 ft²**
5. A one-year lease for Apartment A costs $450 per month. A one-year lease for Apartment B costs $525 per month. Which apartment offers the greatest value in terms of the cost per square foot? **Apartment A**

Chapter 6 55 Course 2

Additional Lesson Resources

** Also available in Spanish* ELL

Transparencies
- *5-Minute Check Transparency,* Lesson 6-8

Other Print Products
- *Teaching Mathematics with Manipulatives*
- *Noteables™ Interactive Study Notebook with Foldables™*

Teacher Tech Tools
- *Interactive Classroom CD-ROM,* Lesson 6-8
- *AssignmentWorks,* Lesson 6-8

Student Tech Tools
glencoe.com
- Extra Examples, Chapter 6, Lesson 8
- Self-Check Quiz, Chapter 6, Lesson 8

6-8 Lesson Notes

1 Focus

Vertical Alignment

Before Lesson 6-8
Demonstrate proficiency with division, including division with positive decimals and long division with multidigit divisors

Lesson 6-8
Use proportions to solve problems; use cross-multiplication as a method for solving such problems, understanding it as the multiplication of both sides of an equation by a multiplicative inverse

After Lesson 6-8
Construct and read drawings and models made to scale

2 Teach

MINI Lab

If you don't have enough measuring tapes for each pair of students, have pairs take turns using the tapes. To speed up the process, students can measure items in the gymnasium with yardsticks.

Scaffolding Questions

Tell students that you have a photo that shows a couch, a lamp, a dog, and Uncle Phil. You know that the couch is 8 feet long. In the photo, it is 8 inches long.

Ask:

- If the lamp is 3 feet tall, how tall will it appear in the photo? 3 in.
- If the dog is 2 inches long in the photo, how long is it in real life? 2 ft
- If Uncle Phil is $5\frac{1}{2}$ inches tall in the photo, how tall is he in real life? $5\frac{1}{2}$ ft

6-8 Scale Drawings

MAIN IDEA
Solve problems involving scale drawings.

IN Academic Standards
7.3.5 Identify, describe and construct similarity relationships and solve problems involving similarity (including similar triangles) and **scale drawings by using proportional reasoning.** *Also addresses P.1.2, P.4.3.*

New Vocabulary
scale drawing
scale model
scale
scale factor

IN Math Online
glencoe.com
- Concepts In Motion
- Extra Examples
- Personal Tutor
- Self-Check Quiz

MINI Lab

- Measure the length of each item in a room, such as a gymnasium.
- Record each length to the nearest $\frac{1}{2}$ foot.

1. Let 1 unit on the grid paper represent 2 feet. So, 4 units = 8 feet. Convert all your measurements to units. See students' work.
2. On grid paper, make a drawing of your gymnasium like the one shown at the right. See students' work.

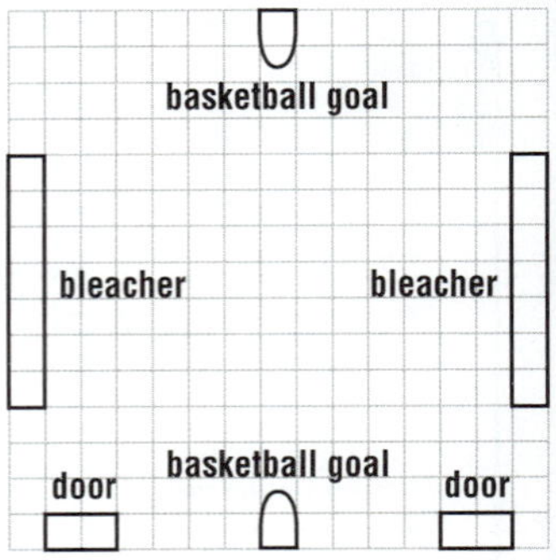

A map is an example of a scale drawing. **Scale drawings** and **scale models** are used to represent objects that are too large or too small to be drawn or built at actual size. The **scale** gives the ratio that compares the measurements of the drawing or model to the measurements of the real object. The measurements on a drawing or model are proportional to measurements of the actual object.

EXAMPLE Use a Map Scale

1 MAPS What is the actual distance between Hagerstown and Annapolis?

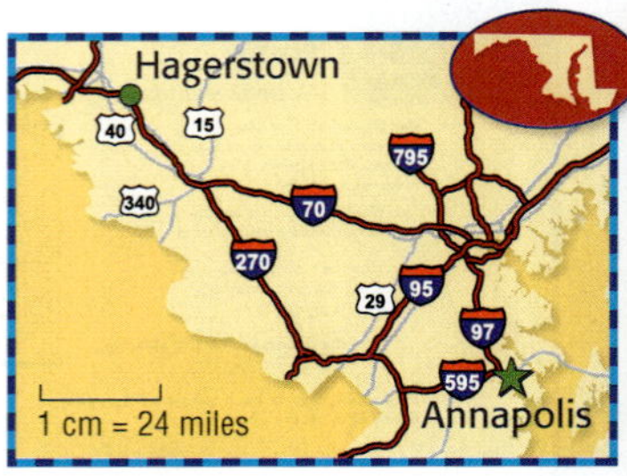

Step 1 Use a centimeter ruler to find the map distance between the two cities. The map distance is about 4 centimeters.

Step 2 Write and solve a proportion using the scale. Let d represent the actual distance between the cities.

	Scale		Length	
map → actual →	$\frac{1 \text{ centimeter}}{24 \text{ miles}}$	=	$\frac{4 \text{ centimeters}}{d \text{ miles}}$	← map ← actual

$1 \times d = 24 \times 4$ Cross products

$d = 96$ Simplify.

The distance between the cities is about 96 miles.

Tips for New Teachers: Scale Drawings

For the Mini Lab, you may wish to give students measurements of your gym yourself, or have them measure the classroom instead.

CHECK Your Progress

a. **MAPS** On the map of Arkansas shown, find the actual distance between Clarksville and Little Rock. Use a ruler to measure. **80 mi**

> **Study Tip**
>
> **Scale** A map scale can be written in different ways, including the following:
>
> 1 cm = 20 mi
>
> 1 cm : 20 mi
>
> $\frac{1 \text{ cm}}{20 \text{ mi}}$

A blueprint is another example of a scale drawing.

EXAMPLE Use a Blueprint Scale

2 DECKS On the blueprint of the deck, each square has a side length of $\frac{1}{2}$ inch. What is the actual width of the deck?

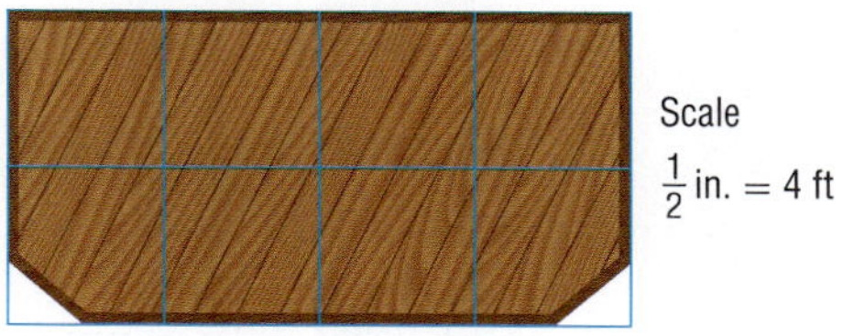

The deck on the blueprint is 2 inches wide. Write and solve a proportion using the scale. Let w represent the actual width of the deck.

	Scale		Width	
blueprint →	$\frac{1}{2}$ inch	=	2 inches	← blueprint
actual →	4 feet		w feet	← actual

$\frac{1}{2} \times w = 4 \times 2$ — Cross products

$\frac{1}{2}w = 8$ — Multiply.

$w = 16$ — Simplify. Multiply each side by 2.

The actual width of the deck is 16 feet.

> **Study Tip**
>
> **Scales** Scales and scale factors are always written so that the drawing length comes first in the ratio.

CHECK Your Progress

b. **INTERIOR DESIGN** On the blueprint of the living room, each square has a side length of $\frac{1}{4}$ inch. What are the actual dimensions of the living room? **12 ft by $10\frac{1}{2}$ ft**

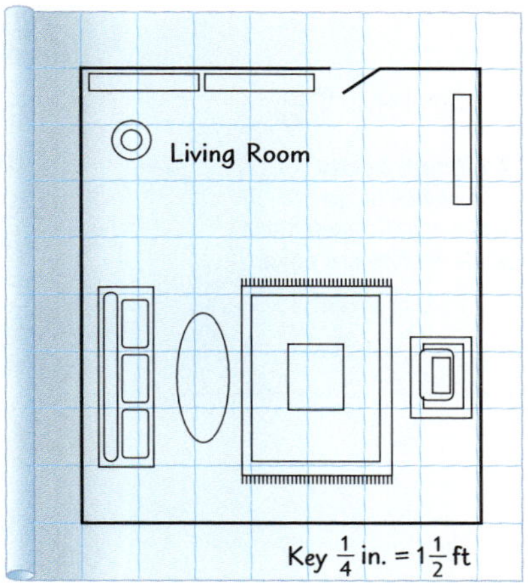

Formative Assessment

Use the Check Your Progress exercises after each Example to determine students' understanding of concepts.

ADDITIONAL EXAMPLES

1 MAPS What is the actual distance between Portland and Olympia? about 103.7 mi

2 ARCHITECTURE On the blueprint of a new house, each square has a side length of $\frac{1}{4}$ inch.

If the length of a bedroom on the blueprint is $1\frac{1}{2}$ inches, what is the actual length of the room? 15 ft

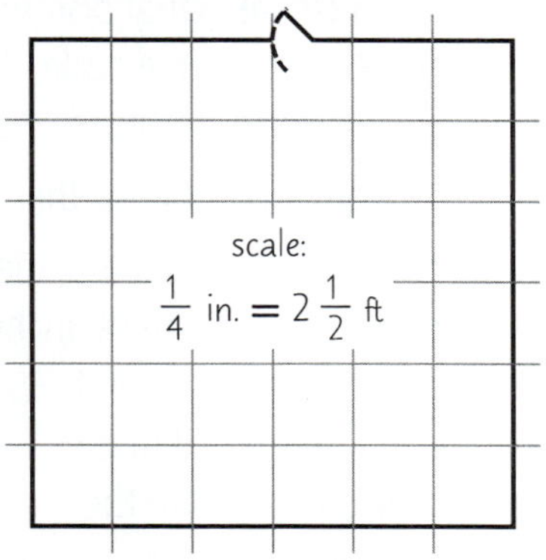

Additional Examples are also in:

- Noteables™ Interactive Study Notebook with Foldables™
- Interactive Classroom PowerPoint® Presentations

ADDITIONAL EXAMPLES

3. **PHOTOGRAPHY** A model is being created from a picture frame which has a length of $4\frac{3}{4}$ inches. If the scale to be used is 8 inches = 1 inch, what is the length of the model? 38 in.

4. Find the scale factor of a blueprint if the scale is $\frac{1}{2}$ inch = 3 feet. $\frac{1}{72}$

Focus on Mathematical Content

The distances shown in scale drawings or models are proportional to the actual distances. So students can calculate the actual distances by **writing and solving proportions.** One ratio of the proportion will be the scale itself.

Another way to calculate actual distance from a scale drawing or model is to **multiply by the reciprocal of the scale factor.**

Tips for New Teachers — Scale Factor

Point out that scale factors can be used to calculate actual distances from the distances shown in a scale drawing or map. If, for example, a drawing has a scale factor of $\frac{1}{96}$, then something that measures 1 inch in the drawing will actually measure 96 inches, or 8 feet. Since scale factors don't include units, the units used in the drawing must also be used in the calculation of actual distances.

Study Tip

Scale The scale is the ratio of the drawing/model measure to the actual measure. It is not always the ratio of a smaller measure to a larger measure.

EXAMPLE 3 Use a Scale Model

PHONES A graphic artist is creating an advertisement for a new cell phone. If she uses a scale of 5 inches = 1 inch, what is the length of the cell phone on the advertisement?

Write a proportion using the scale. Let a represent the length of the advertisement cell phone.

	Scale		Length	
advertisement →	5 inches	=	a inches	← advertisement
actual →	1 inch		4 inches	← actual

$$\frac{5 \text{ inches}}{1 \text{ inch}} = \frac{a \text{ inches}}{4 \text{ inches}}$$

$5 \cdot 4 = 1 \cdot a$ Cross products

$20 = a$ Multiply.

The length of the cell phone on the advertisement is 20 inches long.

CHECK Your Progress

c. **SCOOTERS** A scooter is $3\frac{1}{2}$ feet long. Find the length of a scale model of the scooter if the scale is 1 inch = $\frac{3}{4}$ feet. $4\frac{2}{3}$ in.

In Lesson 6-4, you used ratios to convert units. You can use a similar method to simplify a scale. A scale written as a ratio without units in simplest form is called the **scale factor**.

scale: $\frac{\frac{1}{4}\text{ inch}}{2\text{ feet}} = \frac{\frac{1}{4}\text{ inch}}{24\text{ inches}}$ Convert 2 feet to inches.

$= \frac{4}{4} \cdot \frac{\frac{1}{4}\text{ inch}}{24\text{ inches}}$ Multiply by $\frac{4}{4}$ to eliminate the fraction in the numerator. Divide out the common units.

$= \frac{1}{96}$ scale factor

Study Tip

Equivalent Scales The scales below are equivalent because their scale factors are equal, $\frac{1}{72}$.

- 1 inch = 6 feet
- $\frac{1}{2}$ inch = 3 feet

EXAMPLE 4 Find a Scale Factor

SAILBOATS Find the scale factor of a model sailboat if the scale is 1 inch = 6 feet.

$\frac{1 \text{ inch}}{6 \text{ feet}} = \frac{1 \text{ inch}}{72 \text{ inches}}$ Convert 6 feet to inches.

$= \frac{1}{72}$ Divide out the common units.

The scale factor is $\frac{1}{72}$.

CHECK Your Progress

d. **CARS** What is the scale factor of a model car if the scale is 1 inch = 2 feet? $\frac{1}{24}$

322 Chapter 6 Ratios and Proportions

CHECK Your Understanding

★ indicates multi-step problem

Example 1 (pp. 320–321)

GEOGRAPHY **Find the actual distance between each pair of cities in New Mexico. Use a ruler to measure.**

1. Carlsbad and Artesia **50 km**
2. Hobbs and Eunice **30 km**
3. Artesia and Eunice **130 km**
4. Lovington and Carlsbad **102.5 km**

Example 2 (p. 321)

BLUEPRINTS **For Exercises 5 and 6, use the blueprint. Each square has a side length of $\frac{1}{4}$ inch.**

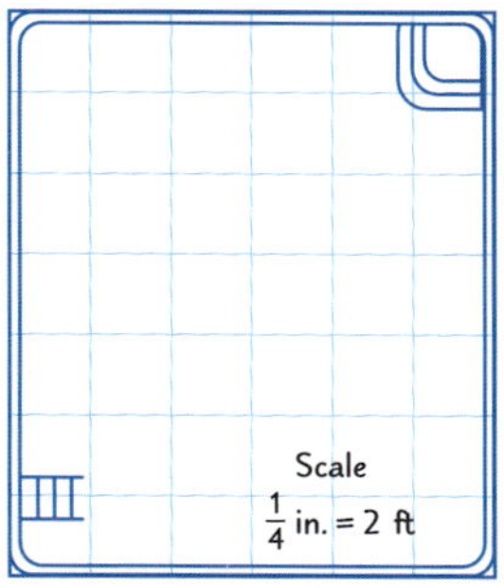

5. What is the actual length of the pool? **14 feet**
6. What is the actual width of the pool? **12 feet**

Example 3 (p. 322)

BRIDGES **For Exercises 7 and 8, use the following information.**

An engineer makes a model of the bridge using a scale of 1 inch = 3 yards.

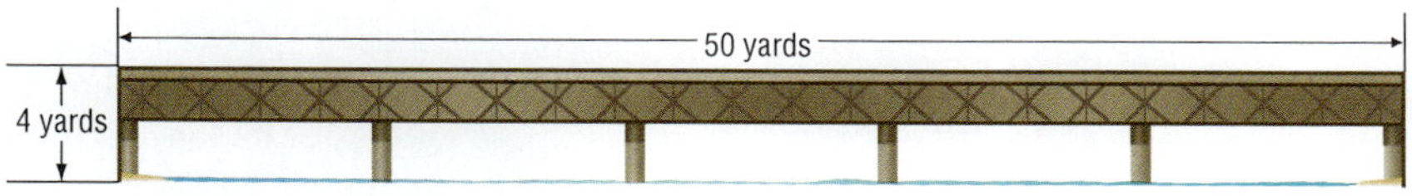

7. What is the length of the model? **$16\frac{2}{3}$ in.**
8. What is the height of the model? **$1\frac{1}{3}$ in.**

Example 4 (p. 322)

Find the scale factor of each scale drawing or model.

9. **$\frac{1}{48}$**

1 inch = 4 feet

10. **$\frac{2}{3}$**

1 centimeter = 15 millimeters

11. **CITY PLANNING** In the aerial view of a city block at the right, the length of Main Street is 2 inches. If Main Street's actual length is 2 miles, find the scale factor of the drawing.

11. **$\frac{1}{63{,}360}$**

3 Practice

Formative Assessment

Use Exercises 1–11 to check for understanding.

Then use the chart at the bottom of the next page to customize your assignments for students.

Intervention You may wish to use the Study Guide and Intervention Master on page 51 of the *Chapter 6 Resource Masters* for additional reinforcement.

Odd/Even Assignments

Exercises 12–24 are structured so that students practice the same concepts whether they are assigned odd or even problems.

Practice and Problem Solving

HOMEWORK HELP	
For Exercises	See Examples
12–15	1
16–17	2
18–24	3, 4

Exercise Levels
A: 12–24
B: 25–29
C: 30–33

GEOGRAPHY Find the actual distance between each pair of locations in South Carolina. Use a ruler to measure.

12. Columbia and Charleston **101 mi**
13. Hollywood and Sumter **81 mi**
14. Congaree Swamp and Charleston **81 mi**
15. Sumter and Columbia **40 mi**

For Exercises 16–18, use the blueprint of an apartment at the right. Each square has a side length of $\frac{1}{4}$ inch.

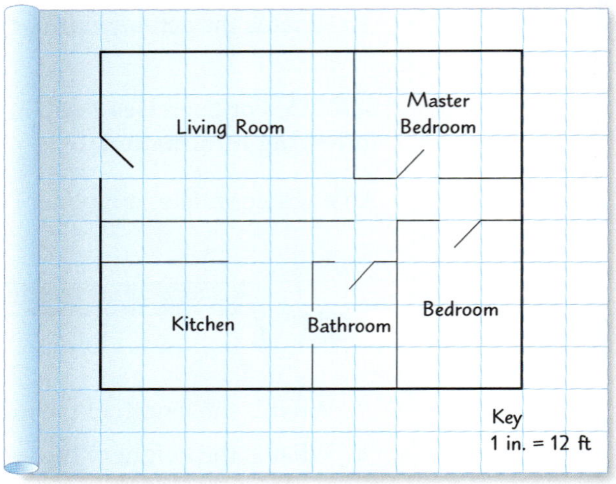

16. What is the actual length of the living room? **18 ft**
17. Find the actual dimensions of the master bedroom.
18. Find the scale factor for this blueprint. $\frac{1}{144}$

17. 12 ft by 9 ft

Find the length of each model. Then find the scale factor.

19. 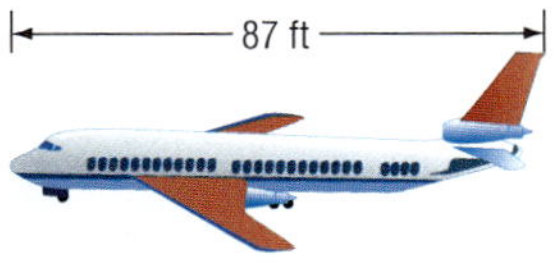

2 in. = 15 ft

19. $11\frac{3}{5}$ in.; $\frac{1}{90}$

20. 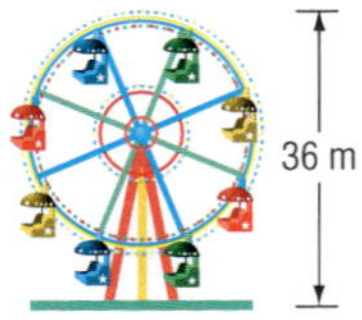

0.5 cm = 1.5 m

12 cm; $\frac{1}{300}$

21. 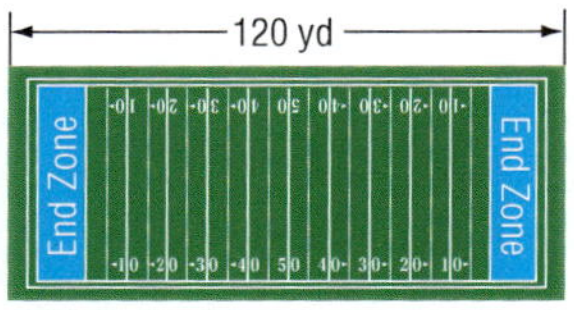

1 in. = 20 yd

21. 6 in.; $\frac{1}{720}$

22. 

1 in. = 0.5 in.

$11\frac{3}{4}$ in.; $\frac{2}{1}$

DIFFERENTIATED HOMEWORK OPTIONS

Level	Assignment	Two-Day Option	
BL Basic	12–24, 30, 32–51	13–23 odd, 34–36	12–24 even, 30, 32, 33, 37–51
OL Core	13–23 odd, 24–30, 32–51	12–24, 34–36	25–30, 32, 33, 37–51
AL Advanced/Pre-AP	25–47 (optional: 48–51)		

Real-World Link

The statue of Thomas Jefferson inside the Jefferson Memorial in Washington, D.C., was made using a scale of 3 feet : 1 foot.

Source: National Register of Historic Places

23. **GEOGRAPHY** A map of Bakersfield, California, has a scale of 1 inch to 5 miles. If the city is $5\frac{1}{5}$ inches across on the map, what is the actual distance across the actual city? Use estimation to check your answer. **26 mi**

24. **TREES** A model of a tree is made using a scale of 1 inch : 25 feet. What is the height of the actual tree if the height of the model is $4\frac{3}{8}$ inches? **$109\frac{3}{8}$ ft**

25. **STATUES** Refer to the information at the left. Find the scale factor and the actual height of Thomas Jefferson if the height of the statue is 19 feet. **$\frac{1}{3}$, about 6.33 feet**

26. **GEOGRAPHY** Lexington and Elizabethtown, Kentucky, are 79 miles apart. If the distance on the map is $2\frac{1}{2}$ inches, find the scale of the map. **1 in : 31.6 mi**

27. **RESEARCH** Find the dimensions of any U.S. presidential monument. Give an appropriate scale that can be used to make a scale model of the monument. State the dimensions of the model using your scale. **See students' work.**

28. **BUILDINGS** If you are making a model of your bedroom, which would be an appropriate scale: 1 inch = 2 feet, or 1 inch = 12 feet? **See margin.**

★ 29. **LIFE SCIENCE** A scale drawing of a red blood cell is shown below. If the blood cell's actual diameter is 0.008 millimeter, use a ruler to find the scale factor of the drawing. **$\frac{5{,}000}{1}$**

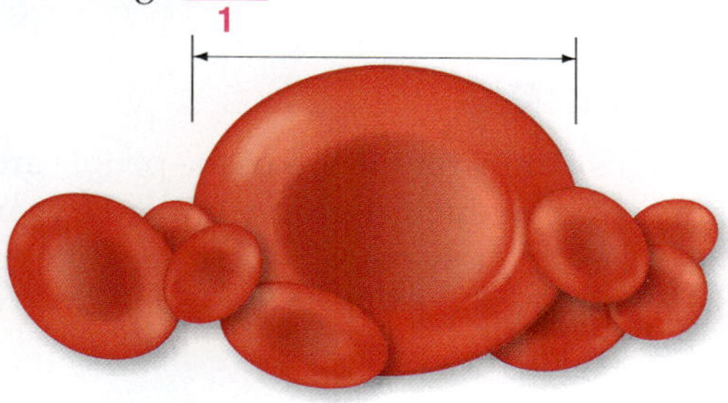

Academic Standards • ISTEP+

Extra Practice, pp. 684, 709

H.O.T. Problems

30. **OPEN ENDED** On grid paper, create a scale drawing of a room in your home. Include the scale that you used. **See students' work.**

31. **CHALLENGE** Montoya constructed three models, A, B, and C, of the same figure, with scales of 0.5 cm = 1 mm, 1.5 mm = 4 cm, and 0.25 cm = 2.5 mm, respectively. **a–c. See margin.**
    a. Which model is larger than the actual figure? Justify your answer.
    b. Which model is smaller than the actual figure? Justify your answer.
    c. Which model is the same size as the actual figure? Justify your answer.

32. **REASONING** Compare and contrast the terms *scale* and *scale factor*. Include an example in your comparison. **See margin.**

33. **WRITING IN MATH** Explain how you could use estimation to find the actual distance between San Diego, California, and Seattle, Washington, on a map. **See margin.**

Pre-AP Activity — Use after Exercise 30

Have students find a map of the United States in an atlas. What is the scale factor? Have them use the scale factor to calculate how many miles are represented by 1 inch on the map. Sample answer: 1:12,000,000; so, 1 inch on the map shows 12,000,000 actual inches, or 1,000,000 feet, or 189.4 mi.

⚠ Exercise Alert!

Use the Internet Exercise 27 requires students to research the dimensions of a presidential monument. You may wish to have students use the Internet or reference material such as an encyclopedia.

Additional Answers

28. 1 in. = 2 ft because it would make the model about 6 to 12 inches in length; the second scale is more appropriate for modeling a much larger object. It would make your room model only 1 or 2 inches in length.

31a. A; 0.5 cm is larger than 1 mm. If 0.5 cm on the model is equal to 1 mm on the actual figure, then model A must be larger than the actual figure.

31b. B; 1.5 mm is smaller than 4 cm. If 1.5 mm on the model is equal to 4 cm on the actual figure, then model B must be smaller than the actual figure.

31c. C; 0.25 cm is equal to 2.5 mm. If 0.25 cm on the model is equal to 2.5 mm on the actual figure, then model C must be the same size as the actual figure.

32. Sample answer: The scale is the ratio comparing the measurements, including the units, on the model to the measurements on the actual figure. Once the units have been converted to the same unit, the scale factor is this ratio written without units as a fraction in simplest form. For example, if the scale of the model to the actual figure is 1 in. = 4.5 ft, then the scale factor would be $\frac{1}{4.5 \times 12}$ or $\frac{1}{54}$.

33. Sample answer: Using the scale given on the map, look at the distance between the two cities on the map and then estimate the actual distance based on the distance given in the scale.

4 Assess

Name the Math Tell students that a map has a scale of 1 inch = 125 miles. Have students write what mathematical procedures they would use to find the actual distance between two points shown on the map.

Formative Assessment

Check for student understanding of concepts in Lessons 6-6, 6-7, and 6-8.

CRM Quiz 3, p. 68

FOLDABLES Study Organizer Foldables™ Follow-Up

Remind students to select a term or concept about scale drawings and to define it in their Foldables. Encourage them to give an example of the term or concept.

ISTEP+ PRACTICE 7.3.5

34. A scale drawing of a doctor's office is shown.

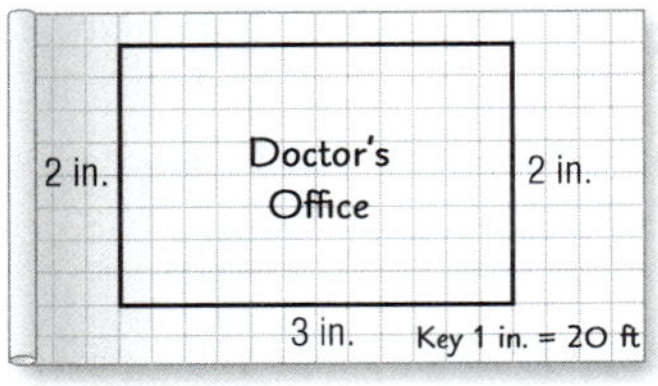

What are the actual dimensions of the doctor's office? **C**

A 24 feet by 48 feet

B 30 feet by 52 feet

C 40 feet by 60 feet

D 37.5 feet by 65 feet

35. A certain map has a scale of $\frac{1}{4}$ inch = 30 miles. How many miles are represented by 4 inches on this map? **F**

F 480 miles

G 120 miles

H 30 miles

J 16 miles

36. Ernesto drew a map of his school. He used a scale of 1 inch : 50 feet. What distance on Ernesto's map should represent the 625 feet between the cafeteria and the science lab? **C**

A 8 in.

B 10.5 in.

C 12.5 in.

D 15 in.

Spiral Review

37. FAMILY At Nelia's family reunion, $\frac{4}{5}$ of the people are 18 years of age or older. Half of the remaining people are under 12 years old. If 20 children are under 12 years old, how many people are at the reunion? Use the *draw a diagram* strategy. (Lesson 6-7) **200 people**

Solve each proportion. (Lesson 6-6)

38. $\frac{5}{7} = \frac{a}{35}$ **25**

39. $\frac{12}{p} = \frac{36}{45}$ **15**

40. $\frac{3}{9} = \frac{21}{k}$ **63**

41. JOGGING The table shows the number of miles Tonya jogged each week for the past several weeks. Estimate the total number of miles she jogged. (Lesson 5-1)
Sample answer: 7 + 9 + 10 + 12 + 7 or 45 mi

Week	Miles
1	$7\frac{1}{6}$
2	$8\frac{3}{4}$
3	10
4	$12\frac{1}{4}$
5	$6\frac{2}{3}$

Find the LCM of each set of numbers. (Lesson 4-8)

42. 2, 4 **4**

43. 4, 8, 12 **24**

44. 3, 7, 5 **105**

45. 5, 10, 15 **30**

46. 2, 6, 9 **18**

47. 3, 15, 20 **60**

GET READY for the Next Lesson

PREREQUISITE SKILL Divide. Write in simplest form. (Lesson 5-7)

48. $2\frac{3}{4} \div 10$ $\frac{11}{40}$

49. $4\frac{1}{3} \div 10$ $\frac{13}{30}$

50. $30\frac{2}{3} \div 100$ $\frac{23}{75}$

51. $87\frac{1}{2} \div 100$ $\frac{7}{8}$

326 Chapter 6 Ratios and Proportions

Extend 6-8

Spreadsheet Lab
Scale Drawings

MAIN IDEA

Use a spreadsheet to calculate measurements for scale drawings.

IN Academic Standards

7.3.5 Identify, describe and construct similarity relationships and solve problems involving similarity (including similar triangles) and **scale drawings by using proportional reasoning.** *Also addresses P.1.2, P.4.3, P.7.1.*

A computer spreadsheet is a useful tool for calculating measures for scale drawings. You can change the scale factors and the dimensions, and the spreadsheet will automatically calculate the new values.

ACTIVITY

Suppose you want to make a scale drawing of your school. Set up a spreadsheet like the one shown below. In this spreadsheet, the actual measures are in feet, and the scale drawing measures are in inches.

Scale Measures.xls

C3 = =(A3*12)/B3

	A	B	C
1	Actual	Scale	Scale Drawing
2	Measure (ft)	Factor	Measure (in.)
3	5	60	1.0
4	30	100	3.6
5	100	250	4.8
6			

Sheet 1

Multiply each actual measure by 12 to convert to inches. Then divide by the scale factor.

The scale factor 100 means that the ratio of drawing measures to actual measures is 1:100.

ANALYZE THE RESULTS

1. The length of one side of the school building is 100 feet. If you use a scale factor of 1:250, what is the length on your scale drawing? **4.8 in.**
2. The length of a classroom is 30 feet. What is the scale factor if the length of the classroom on a scale drawing is 3.6 inches? **1:100**
3. Calculate the length of a 30-foot classroom on a scale drawing if the scale factor is 1:10. **36 in. or 3 ft**
4. The width of a hallway is 20 feet. What is the scale factor if the width of the hallway on a scale drawing is 2.5 inches? **1:96**
5. Suppose the actual measures of your school are given in meters. Describe how you could use a spreadsheet to calculate the scale drawing measures in centimeters using a scale factor of 1:50.
6. Choose three rooms in your home and use a spreadsheet to make scale drawings. First, choose an appropriate scale and calculate the scale factor. Include a sketch of the furniture drawn to scale in each room. **See students' work.**

5. Sample answer: Enter 50 in B3 and enter the formula (A3*100)/B3 in C3. Then enter the actual dimensions in A3.

Extending the Concept Have students use the spreadsheet to calculate measurements for a scale drawing of an object too small to draw as its actual size.

Extend 6-8

Lesson Notes

1 Focus

Materials

- computers
- spreadsheet software

Teaching Tip

Make sure students understand that the spreadsheet screen is a table divided into columns and rows. The columns are labeled with letters, and the rows are labeled with numbers, so the third cell in the first column is A3, the third cell in the second column is B3, and so on.

2 Teach

Activity You may need to remind students that scale factors don't include units, so the spreadsheet program first converts actual measurements (in feet) into inches. Encourage students to experiment with different scale factors for their scale drawings (Exercise 5). If they want to make their drawings on standard notepaper, what is an appropriate scale factor?

3 Assess

Formative Assessment

Use Exercises 1–4 to determine whether students understand how to use a spreadsheet to calculate measurements for a scale drawing.

From Concrete to Abstract Use Exercise 5 to bridge the gap between using a spreadsheet to calculate customary measurements and conceptualizing how to use the spreadsheet to calculate metric measurements.

6-9 Fractions, Decimals, and Percents

PACING: **Regular:** 1 period, **Block:** 0.5 period

IN Academic Standards **7.1.6** Identify, write, **rename**, compare and order **rational** and common irrational **numbers** and plot them on a number line.
Also addresses P.4.2.

Options for Differentiated Instruction

ELL = English Language Learner AL = Above or Beyond Grade Level SS = Struggling Students SN = Special Needs

Reviewing Concepts SS SN

Use before beginning Lesson 6-9.

Before beginning this lesson, review with students the common fraction-decimal-percent equivalencies that they have already used, such as the ones shown in the table below.

Fraction	Decimal	Percent
$\frac{1}{4}$	0.25	25%
$\frac{1}{2}$	0.5	50%
$\frac{3}{4}$	0.75	75%
$\frac{1}{5}$	0.2	20%
$\frac{2}{5}$	0.4	40%
$\frac{3}{5}$	0.6	60%
$\frac{4}{5}$	0.8	80%

Kinesthetic Learning ELL AL SS SN

Use after presenting Examples 1–6.

Create a set of 10 cards, each containing one number, a fraction, a decimal, or percent. An example of a set of cards is shown below. For above grade level students, change the number of cards or the difficulty of the numbers.

35%	0.325	$\frac{1}{3}$	0.4	50%
$\frac{4}{9}$	$\frac{11}{20}$	45%	$\frac{7}{15}$	0.72%

Have students work in pairs and order the numbers from least to greatest. Once students have finished, have them write the strategies they used to determine the order. Have them explain their reasoning.

Leveled Lesson Resources

Also on TeacherWorks™ Lesson 6-9

Chapter 6 Resource Masters

BL = Below or Approaching Grade Level OL = On Grade Level AL = Above or Beyond Grade Level ELL = English Language Learner

Lesson Reading Guide
p. 57 BL OL ELL

NAME ______ DATE ______ PERIOD ____

6-9 Lesson Reading Guide
Fractions, Decimals, and Percents

Get Ready for the Lesson

Read the introduction at the top of page 328 in your textbook. Write your answers below.

1. What percent of the teens chose comedy? **26%**
2. Write this percent as a ratio in simplest form. **13:50 or $\frac{13}{50}$**

Read the Lesson

3. Write $6\frac{1}{2}$% as a fraction in simplest form. **$\frac{13}{200}$**
4. CLOTHING A pair of jeans sells for 180% of its wholesale price. Write this percent as a fraction in simplest form. **$\frac{9}{5}$**
5. How do you write 100 as a fraction? **$\frac{100}{1}$**
6. If the denominator is not a factor of 100, you can write fractions as percents by using a proportion. In Examples 3 and 4, why is the ratio $\frac{n}{100}$ used as part of the proportions? **Sample answer: because you want to write the fraction as a percent, and to convert a fraction to a percent you want the denominator to be 100**

Remember What You Learned

7. Complete the following table of equivalent fractions. Look for patterns in each column. How do the percents increase? How do the fractions increase? Work with a partner. Figure out ways to remember the equivalents.

Common Fraction/Decimal/Percent Equivalents

Fraction	Decimal	Percent	Fraction	Decimal	Percent
$\frac{1}{3}$	$0.\overline{3}$	$33\frac{1}{3}$%	$\frac{3}{8}$	0.375	$37\frac{1}{2}$%
$\frac{2}{3}$	$0.\overline{6}$	$66\frac{2}{3}$%	$\frac{5}{8}$	0.625	$62\frac{1}{2}$%
$\frac{1}{8}$	0.125	$12\frac{1}{2}$%	$\frac{7}{8}$	0.875	$87\frac{1}{2}$%

Lesson 6-9

Chapter 6 57 Course 2

Study Guide and Intervention*
p. 58 BL OL ELL

NAME ______ DATE ______ PERIOD ____

6-9 Study Guide and Intervention
Fractions, Decimals, and Percents

Example Write $4\frac{3}{8}$% as a fraction in simplest form.

$4\frac{3}{8}\% = \frac{4\frac{3}{8}}{100}$ Write a fraction.

$= 4\frac{3}{8} \div 100$ Divide.

$= \frac{35}{8} \div 100$ Write $4\frac{3}{8}$ as an improper fraction.

$= \frac{35}{8} \times \frac{1}{100}$ Multiply by the reciprocal of 100, which is $\frac{1}{100}$.

$= \frac{35}{800}$ or $\frac{7}{160}$ Simplify.

Example 2 Write $\frac{5}{16}$ as a percent.

$\frac{5}{16} = \frac{n}{100}$ Write a proportion using $\frac{n}{100}$.

$500 = 16n$ Find the cross products.

$\frac{500}{16} = \frac{16n}{16}$ Divide each side by 16.

$31\frac{1}{4} = n$ Simplify.

So, $\frac{5}{16} = 31\frac{1}{4}$% or 31.25%.

Exercises

Write each percent as a fraction in simplest form.

1. 60% **$\frac{3}{5}$**
2. $68\frac{3}{4}$% **$\frac{11}{16}$**
3. $27\frac{1}{2}$% **$\frac{11}{40}$**
4. 37.5% **$\frac{3}{8}$**

Write each fraction as a percent. Round to the nearest hundredth if necessary.

5. $\frac{2}{5}$ **40%**
6. $\frac{5}{8}$ **62.5%**
7. $\frac{9}{16}$ **56.25%**
8. $\frac{2}{3}$ **66.67%**

Chapter 6 58 Course 2

Skills Practice*
p. 59 BL OL

NAME ______ DATE ______ PERIOD ____

6-9 Skills Practice
Fractions, Decimals, and Percents

Write each percent as a fraction in simplest form.

1. 18% **$\frac{9}{50}$**
2. 67.5% **$\frac{27}{40}$**
3. 21.25% **$\frac{17}{80}$**
4. 87.5% **$\frac{7}{8}$**
5. $31\frac{1}{4}$% **$\frac{5}{16}$**
6. 17.5% **$\frac{7}{40}$**
7. $18\frac{3}{4}$% **$\frac{3}{16}$**
8. $68\frac{3}{4}$% **$\frac{11}{16}$**
9. 7.5% **$\frac{3}{40}$**
10. 130% **$\frac{13}{10}$**
11. 0.5% **$\frac{1}{200}$**
12. 0.02% **$\frac{1}{5000}$**

Write each fraction as a percent. Round to the nearest hundredth if necessary.

13. $\frac{3}{5}$ **60%**
14. $\frac{3}{8}$ **37.5%**
15. $\frac{2}{18}$ **11.11%**
16. $\frac{3}{16}$ **18.75%**
17. $\frac{7}{9}$ **77.78%**
18. $\frac{21}{50}$ **42%**
19. $\frac{1}{3}$ **33.33%**
20. $\frac{40}{42}$ **95.24%**
21. $\frac{7}{16}$ **43.75%**
22. $\frac{17}{10}$ **170%**
23. $\frac{1}{500}$ **0.2%**
24. $\frac{26}{25}$ **104%**

Lesson 6-9

Chapter 6 59 Course 2

Practice*
p. 60 OL AL

NAME ______ DATE ______ PERIOD ____

6-9 Practice
Fractions, Decimals, and Percents

Write each percent as a fraction in simplest form.

1. 37.5% **$\frac{3}{8}$**
2. 5.8% **$\frac{29}{500}$**
3. 43.75% **$\frac{7}{16}$**
4. 52.5% **$\frac{21}{40}$**
5. $83\frac{1}{3}$% **$\frac{5}{6}$**
6. $66\frac{2}{3}$% **$\frac{2}{3}$**
7. 135% **$\frac{27}{20}$**
8. 0.01% **$\frac{1}{10,000}$**

Write each fraction as a percent. Round to the nearest hundredth if necessary.

9. $\frac{13}{20}$ **65%**
10. $\frac{9}{25}$ **36%**
11. $\frac{7}{8}$ **87.5%**
12. $\frac{39}{40}$ **97.5%**
13. $\frac{5}{9}$ **55.56%**
14. $\frac{6}{7}$ **85.71%**
15. $\frac{2}{1}$ **200%**
16. $\frac{1}{1000}$ **0.1%**

Replace each • with >, < or = to make a true statement.

17. $\frac{3}{16}$ • 24% **<**
18. 0.775 • $\frac{31}{40}$ **=**
19. 16% • 0.016 **>**

Order each set of numbers from least to greatest.

20. 0.6, 23%, 0.07, $\frac{2}{3}$ **0.07, 23%, 0.6, $\frac{2}{3}$**
21. $\frac{4}{5}$%, 0.37, $\frac{1}{4}$, 0.4 **$\frac{4}{5}$%, $\frac{1}{4}$, 0.37, 0.4**

22. SAVINGS Kayla has 14.5% of her salary placed into an Individual Retirement Account. What fraction is this? **$\frac{29}{200}$**
23. INTERNET At home, 2 out of 5 people have access to broadband technology. What percent is this? **40%**
24. SPORTS A golfer made par on 13 of 18 holes. To the nearest tenth, on what percent of the holes did he make par? **72.2%**

ANALYZE TABLES For Exercises 25 and 26, use the table that shows the percent of households with the listed appliance.

Appliance	Percent of Households
Refrigerator	99.3%
Washing Machine	82.0%
Dryer	77.8%
Dishwasher	56.0%

25. What fraction of households have a clothes dryer? **$\frac{389}{500}$**
26. Approximately 34 out of 67 households have a coffeemaker. Is this greater or less than the percent of households with a dishwasher? Explain. **less than; $\frac{34}{67} \approx 50.7$%**

Chapter 6 60 Course 2

Word Problem Practice*
p. 61 OL AL

NAME ______ DATE ______ PERIOD ____

6-9 Word Problem Practice
Fractions, Decimals, and Percents

INTERNET For Exercises 1–4, use the table. It shows the percents of online shopping purchases made by all Internet users and the percents made by Internet users over age 55.

Most Popular Online Purchases

	Internet Users Over 55	All Internet Users
computer software	43%	19%
books	43%	21%
computer hardware	24%	13%
music CDs	29%	22%
clothing	19%	8%

1. What fraction of Internet users over 55 bought clothing online? **$\frac{19}{100}$**
2. What fraction of all Internet users bought clothing online? **$\frac{2}{25}$**
3. What fraction of all Internet users bought music CDs online? **$\frac{11}{50}$**
4. Is the fraction of Internet users over 55 who bought books online greater or less than $\frac{22}{50}$? Explain. **Less than; $\frac{22}{50}$ = 44%, and 43% is less than 44%.**
5. FOOTBALL In 2005, Indianapolis quarterback Peyton Manning completed 305 out of 453 passes. What was his pass completion percentage to the nearest tenth? **67.3%**
6. COMPUTERS In Joan's math class, there are 20 computers and 32 students. What percent of students will be able to use a computer without sharing? **62.5%**
7. VEHICLES In the town of Orick, 5 out of 13 vehicles are trucks. What percent of the vehicles are trucks? Round to the nearest tenth. **38.5%**
8. DENTISTRY Dana has fillings in 4 of her 32 teeth. What percent of her teeth have fillings? **12.5%**

Lesson 6-9

Chapter 6 61 Course 2

Enrichment
p. 62 OL AL

NAME ______ DATE ______ PERIOD ____

6-9 Enrichment

Shaded Regions

The fractions or percents listed below each represent one of the shaded regions.

Match each fraction or percent with the shaded region it represents.

1. $\frac{1}{2}$ **d**
2. $\frac{25}{64}$ **i**
3. $\frac{11}{16}$ **h**
4. 25% **b**
5. $\frac{3}{4}$ **a**
6. $62\frac{1}{2}$% **g**
7. $\frac{29}{64}$ **f**
8. 37.5% **c**
9. $\frac{7}{16}$ **e**

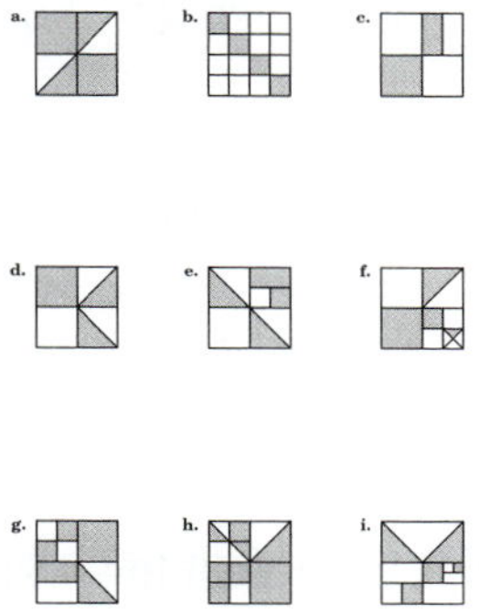

Chapter 6 62 Course 2

*Also available in Spanish ELL

Additional Lesson Resources

Transparencies

- *5-Minute Check Transparency,* Lesson 6-9

Other Print Products

- *Noteables™ Interactive Study Notebook with Foldables™*

Teacher Tech Tools

- *Interactive Classroom CD-ROM,* Lesson 6-9
- *AssignmentWorks,* Lesson 6-9

Student Tech Tools

glencoe.com

- Extra Examples, Chapter 6, Lesson 9
- Self-Check Quiz, Chapter 6, Lesson 9

6-9 Lesson Notes

1 Focus

Vertical Alignment

Before Lesson 6-9
Demonstrate proficiency with division, including division with positive decimals and long division with multi-digit divisors

Lesson 6-9
Find decimal and percent equivalents for common fractions

After Lesson 6-9
Calculate given percentages of quantities and solve problems involving discounts at sales, interest earned, and tips

2 Teach

Scaffolding Questions

Ask:

- What fraction is equivalent to 10%? $\frac{10}{100}$, or $\frac{1}{10}$
- What fraction is equivalent to 25%? $\frac{25}{100}$, or $\frac{1}{4}$
- What decimal is equivalent to 96%? 0.96
- What decimal is equivalent to 96.5%? 0.965

Formative Assessment

Use the Check Your Progress exercises after each Example to determine students' understanding of concepts.

6-9 Fractions, Decimals, and Percents

MAIN IDEA

Write percents as fractions, and decimals and vice versa.

IN Academic Standards

7.1.6 Identify, write, **rename,** compare and order **rational** and common irrational **numbers** and plot them on a number line. *Also addresses P.4.2.*

IN Math Online

glencoe.com

- Extra Examples
- Personal Tutor
- Self-Check Quiz

GET READY for the Lesson

SURVEYS The graph shows the results of a survey about favorite type of TV show.

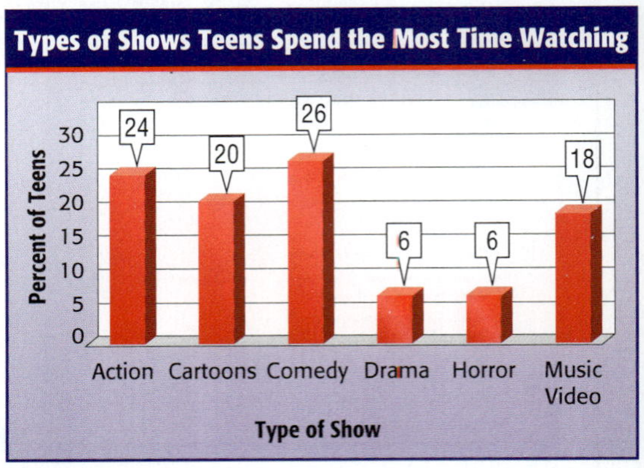

Source: Kids USA Survey

1. What percent of the teens chose comedy? 26%
2. Write this percent as a ratio in simplest form. $13 : 50$ or $\frac{13}{50}$

In Lesson 4-6, you wrote percents like 26% as fractions by writing fractions with denominators of 100 and then simplifying. You can use the same method to write percents like $8\frac{1}{3}\%$ and 190% as fractions.

EXAMPLES Percents as Fractions

1 **Write $8\frac{1}{3}\%$ as a fraction in simplest form.**

$8\frac{1}{3}\% = \frac{8\frac{1}{3}}{100}$ Write a fraction.

$= 8\frac{1}{3} \div 100$ Divide.

$= \frac{25}{3} \div 100$ Write $8\frac{1}{3}$ as an improper fraction.

$= \frac{25}{3} \cdot \frac{1}{100}$ Multiply by the reciprocal of 100, which is $\frac{1}{100}$.

$= \frac{25}{300}$ or $\frac{1}{12}$ Simplify.

2 **TOYS** **A collectible action figure sold for 190% of its original price. Write this percent as a fraction in simplest form.**

$190\% = \frac{190}{100}$ Definition of percent

$= \frac{19}{10}$ or $1\frac{9}{10}$ Simplify.

So, the toy sold for $1\frac{9}{10}$ of its original price.

A percent greater than 100 is equal to a number greater than 1.

Tips for New Teachers

Writing Percents as Fractions

Another way to write $8\frac{1}{3}\%$ as a fraction is to write and solve the proportion: $\frac{25}{3} = \frac{x}{100}$. Solve by finding the cross products.

328 **Chapter 6** Ratios and Proportions

CHECK Your Progress

Write each percent as a fraction in simplest form.

a. 150% $\frac{3}{2}$ b. $17\frac{1}{2}\%$ $\frac{7}{40}$ c. $33\frac{1}{3}\%$ $\frac{1}{3}$

To write a fraction like $\frac{8}{25}$ as a percent, multiply the numerator and the denominator by a number so that the denominator is 100. If the denominator is not a factor of 100, you can write fractions as percents by using a proportion.

EXAMPLES Fractions as Percents

Study Tip

Choose the Method To write a fraction as a percent,

- use multiplication when a fraction has a denominator that is a factor of 100,
- use a proportion for any type of fraction.

3 **Write $\frac{4}{15}$ as a percent. Round to the nearest hundredth.**

Estimate $\frac{4}{15}$ is about $\frac{4}{16}$, which equals $\frac{1}{4}$ or 25%.

$\frac{4}{15} = \frac{n}{100}$ Write a proportion.

$400 = 15n$ Find the cross products.

$\frac{400}{15} = \frac{15n}{15}$ Divide each side by 15.

$26.67 \approx n$ Simplify.

So, $\frac{4}{15}$ is about 26.67%.

Check for Reasonableness 26.67% ≈ 25% ✔

4 **BLOGGING** **In Boston, $\frac{89}{100{,}000}$ residents blog. Write this fraction as a percent.**

$\frac{89}{100{,}000} = \frac{n}{100}$ Write a proportion.

$8{,}900 = 100{,}000n$ Find the cross products.

$\frac{8{,}900}{100{,}000} = \frac{100{,}000n}{100{,}000}$ Divide each side by 100,000.

$0.089 = n$ Simplify.

A percent less than 1% is equal to a number less than 0.01 or $\frac{1}{100}$.

So, 0.089% of Boston's residents blog.

CHECK Your Progress

Write each fraction as a percent. Round to the nearest hundredth if necessary.

d. $\frac{2}{15}$ 13.33% e. $\frac{7}{1{,}600}$ 0.44% f. $\frac{17}{25}$ 68%

Focus on Mathematical Content

Fractions and percents are ratios. So, to find a percent equivalent to a given fraction, students can **set up and solve a proportion.**

Another way to find a percent equivalent to a given fraction is to **divide the fraction's numerator by its denominator;** multiply the resulting decimal by 100, and write the percent symbol (%).

ADDITIONAL EXAMPLES

1 Write $12\frac{1}{2}\%$ as a fraction in simplest form. $\frac{1}{8}$

2 **NUTRITION** In a recent consumer poll, 41.8% of the people surveyed said they gained nutrition knowledge from family and friends. What fraction is this? Write in simplest form. $\frac{209}{500}$

3 Write $\frac{3}{7}$ as a percent. Round to the nearest hundredth. 42.86%

4 **FARMS** A farmer calculated that $\frac{9}{20}$ of her goats were brown. Write this fraction as a percent. 45%

Additional Examples are also in:

- Noteables™ Interactive Study Notebook with Foldables™
- Interactive Classroom PowerPoint® Presentations

ADDITIONAL EXAMPLES

5 Write $\frac{5}{12}$ as a percent. Round to the nearest hundredth. 41.67%

6 **PRODUCE** In one shipment of fruit to a grocery store, 5 out of 8 bananas were still green. Find this amount as a percent. 62.5%

Study Tip

Look Back You can review writing fractions as decimals in lesson 4-3.

In this lesson, you have written percents as fractions and fractions as percents. In Chapter 4, you wrote percents and fractions as decimals. You can also write a fraction as a percent by first writing the fraction as a decimal and then writing the decimal as a percent.

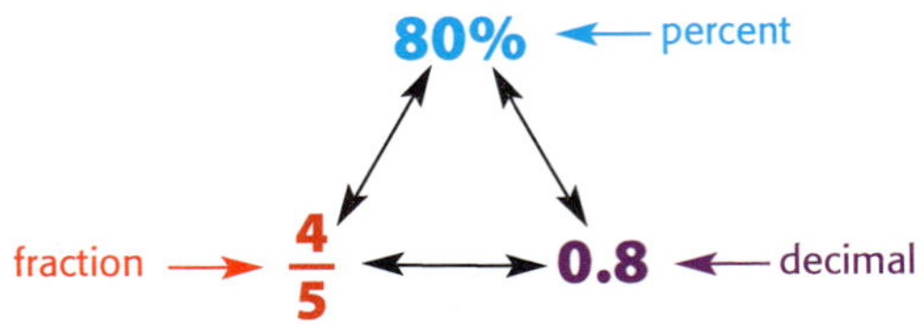

Percents, fractions, and decimals are different names that represent the same number.

EXAMPLES Fractions as Percents

5 **Write $\frac{5}{6}$ as a percent. Round to the nearest hundredth.**

$\frac{5}{6} = 0.833333333...$ Write $\frac{5}{6}$ as a decimal.

$\approx 83.33\%$ Multiply by 100 and add the %.

6 **BOOKS** **Bryce has read $\frac{3}{5}$ of a book. What percent of the book has he read?**

$\frac{3}{5} = 0.6$ Write the fraction as a decimal.

$= 60\%$ Multiply by 100 and add the %.

So, Bryce has read 60% of the book.

CHECK Your Progress

Write each fraction as a percent. Round to the nearest hundredth if necessary.

g. $\frac{5}{16}$ 31.25%

h. $\frac{7}{12}$ 58.33%

i. $\frac{2}{9}$ 22.22%

j. **LAWNS** Mika is mowing lawns to earn extra money. She has mowed 6 out of 13 lawns. What percent of the lawns has she mowed? 46.15%

Some fractions with denominators that are not factors of 100 are used often in everyday situations. It is helpful to memorize these fractions and their equivalent decimals and percents. These common equivalents are shown below.

Common Equivalents (Key Concept)

Fraction	Decimal	Percent	Fraction	Decimal	Percent
$\frac{1}{3}$	$0.\overline{3}$	$33\frac{1}{3}\%$	$\frac{3}{8}$	0.375	$37\frac{1}{2}\%$
$\frac{2}{3}$	$0.\overline{6}$	$66\frac{2}{3}\%$	$\frac{5}{8}$	0.625	$62\frac{1}{2}\%$
$\frac{1}{8}$	0.125	$12\frac{1}{2}\%$	$\frac{7}{8}$	0.875	$87\frac{1}{2}\%$

Differentiated Instruction

Logical Learners Have students study the use of percents and fractions in advertisements in magazines or newspapers. Have students clip or copy several ads and analyze how the percents or fractions are used. Does the advertiser want consumers to think the percent or fraction is a small number or a large number? What does the percent or fraction describe—price, content, consumer satisfaction? Would the ad be less effective if the equivalent fraction or percent were used?

330 Chapter 6 Ratios and Proportions

CHECK Your Understanding

Examples 1, 2 (pp. 328–329)

Write each percent as a fraction in simplest form.

1. 135% $\frac{27}{20}$
2. 18.75% $\frac{3}{16}$
3. $7\frac{1}{2}\%$ $\frac{3}{40}$
4. $66\frac{2}{3}\%$ $\frac{2}{3}$
5. **FOOD** Steven and Rebecca ate 62.5% of a pizza. What fraction of the pizza did they eat? $\frac{5}{8}$

Examples 3–5 (pp. 329–330)

Write each fraction as a percent. Round to the nearest hundredth if necessary.

6. $\frac{3}{4}$ 75%
7. $\frac{4}{2{,}500}$ 0.16%
8. $\frac{4}{11}$ 36.36%
9. $\frac{1}{9}$ 11.11%

Example 6 (p. 330)

10. **SCHOOL** Moses has finished 11 out of 15 homework questions. To the nearest hundredth, what percent of the homework is complete? 73.33%

Practice and Problem Solving

HOMEWORK HELP

For Exercises	See Examples
11–14, 19	1
15–18, 20	2
21–32	3–6
33–34	3

Exercise Levels
A: 11–34
B: 35–43
C: 44–45

Write each percent as a fraction in simplest form.

11. 62.5% $\frac{5}{8}$
12. 6.2% $\frac{31}{500}$
13. 28.75% $\frac{23}{80}$
14. 56.25% $\frac{9}{16}$
15. $33\frac{1}{3}\%$ $\frac{1}{3}$
16. $16\frac{2}{3}\%$ $\frac{1}{6}$
17. $93\frac{3}{4}\%$ $\frac{15}{16}$
18. $78\frac{3}{4}\%$ $\frac{63}{80}$
19. **ENVIRONMENT** Freshwater from lakes only accounts for 0.1% of the world's water supply. Write this percent as a fraction in simplest form. $\frac{1}{1{,}000}$
20. **ATTENDANCE** At last year's spring dance, $78\frac{1}{3}\%$ of the student body attended. What fraction of the student body is this? $\frac{47}{60}$

Write each fraction as a percent. Round to the nearest hundredth if necessary.

21. $\frac{111}{20}$ 555%
22. $\frac{180}{25}$ 720%
23. $\frac{30}{8}$ 375%
24. $\frac{210}{40}$ 525%
25. $\frac{29}{30}$ 96.67%
26. $\frac{8}{9}$ 88.89%
27. $\frac{5}{7}$ 71.43%
28. $\frac{1}{16}$ 6.25%
29. $\frac{1}{800}$ 0.13%
30. $\frac{57}{20{,}000}$ 0.29%
31. $\frac{5}{1{,}200}$ 0.42%
32. $\frac{7}{1{,}500}$ 0.47%
33. **FOOD** The size of a large milkshake is $\frac{7}{5}$ times the size of a medium milkshake. Write $\frac{7}{5}$ as a percent. 140%
34. **PETS** In a class, 28 out of 32 students had a pet. What percent is this? 87.5%

Real-World Link Out of the 50 states, 23 states border an ocean or the Gulf of Mexico.
Source: The US50

Replace each ● with >, <, or = to make a true statement.

35. 0.86 ● $\frac{7}{8}$ <
36. $\frac{9}{20}$ ● 45% =
37. 5% ● 0.004 >

Order each set of numbers from least to greatest.

38. $\frac{1}{4}$, 22%, 0.3, 0.02 0.02, 22%, $\frac{1}{4}$, 0.3
39. 0.48, $\frac{1}{2}\%$, 0.5, $\frac{2}{5}$ $\frac{1}{2}\%$, $\frac{2}{5}$, 0.48, 0.5
40. **GEOGRAPHY** Use the information at the left. What percent of the states in the United States do *not* border an ocean or the Gulf of Mexico? 54%

3 Practice

Formative Assessment

Use Exercises 1–10 to check for understanding.

Then use the chart at the bottom of this page to customize your assignments for students.

Intervention You may wish to use the Study Guide and Intervention Master on page 58 of the *Chapter 6 Resource Masters* for additional reinforcement.

Odd/Even Assignments

Exercises 11–34 are structured so that students practice the same concepts whether they are assigned odd or even problems.

DIFFERENTIATED HOMEWORK OPTIONS

Level	Assignment	Two-Day Option	
BL Basic	11–34, 45–53	11–33 odd, 46, 47	12–34 even, 45, 48–53
OL Core	11–39 odd, 40–43, 45–53	11–34, 46, 47	35–43, 45, 48–53
AL Advanced/Pre-AP	35–49 (optional: 50–53)		

Lesson 6-9 Fractions, Decimals, and Percents **331**

4 Assess

Formative Assessment

Check for student understanding of concepts in Lesson 6-9.

CRM Quiz 4 , p. 68

FOLDABLES Study Organizer Foldables™ Follow-Up

Remind students to select a term or concept about fractions, decimals, or percents and to define it in their Foldables. Encourage them to give an example of the term or concept.

Additional Answer

45. Sample answer: Since a percent is a ratio that compares a number to 100, 80% is the ratio $\frac{80}{100}$. The ratio $\frac{80}{100}$ can be read as *eighty-hundredths* or written as a decimal, 0.80 or 0.8. The ratio $\frac{80}{100}$ also simplifies to $\frac{4}{5}$ if you divide the numerator and denominator by the same number, 20.

---

41. FIND THE DATA Refer to the Data File on pages 16–19. Choose some data and write a real-world problem in which you would write a fraction as a percent. **See students' work.**

CARS For Exercises 42 and 43, use the table, which shows the percent of people in a recent survey who kept the listed items in their car.

Items in Car	Percent of People
Pen/Pencil	73.0%
Cassette Tapes/CDs	66.1%
First-Aid Kit	38.2%
Sports Equipment	28.9%

42. What fraction of people kept a first-aid kit in their car? $\frac{191}{500}$

43. Approximately 26 out of 125 people surveyed kept a hairbrush in their car. Is this greater or less than the percent who kept sports equipment? Explain. **Less than; $\frac{26}{125} = 20.8\%$.**

Academic Standards • ISTEP+
Extra Practice, pp. 684, 709

H.O.T. Problems

44. CHALLENGE For what value of x does $\frac{1}{x} = x\%$? **10**

45. WRITING IN MATH Explain why 80%, 0.8, and $\frac{4}{5}$ all represent the same value. **See margin.**

ISTEP+ PRACTICE 7.1.6

46. Ms. Gallagher made 64 ounces of punch. The punch contained 17 ounces of apple juice. Which equation can be used to find x, the percent of apple juice in the punch? **D**

A $\frac{x}{100} = \frac{64}{17}$

B $\frac{x}{17} = \frac{64}{100}$

C $\frac{x}{64} = \frac{17}{100}$

D $\frac{x}{100} = \frac{17}{64}$

47. A group of 150 students were asked if they own a pet. The results are shown.

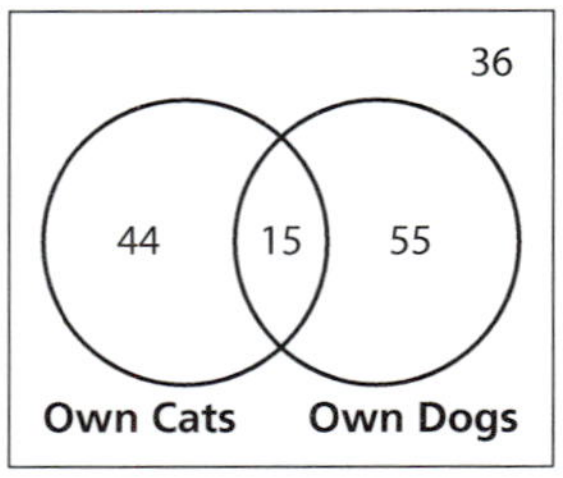

What percent of those surveyed own dogs? **G**

F 50%
G 46.7%
H 36.7%
J 30%

Spiral Review

48. COMPUTERS Designers are creating a larger model of the computer memory board. They use a scale of 20 inches = 1 inch. If the actual board is $5\frac{1}{4}$ inches long, what is the length of the model? (Lesson 6-8) **105 in.**

49. RECIPES Camila is making soup. She has added $\frac{2}{3}$ of the ingredients. If she has added 4 ingredients, how many more does she have to add to be finished? (Lesson 6-7) **2**

GET READY for the Next Lesson

PREREQUISITE SKILL Write each fraction in simplest form. (Lesson 4-4)

50. $\frac{8}{10}$ $\frac{4}{5}$

51. $\frac{45}{100}$ $\frac{9}{20}$

52. $\frac{450}{100}$ $4\frac{1}{2}$

53. $\frac{175}{100}$ $1\frac{3}{4}$

332 Chapter 6 Ratios and Proportions

CHAPTER 6

Study Guide and Review

IN Math Online glencoe.com
- STUDY TO GO
- Vocabulary Review

FOLDABLES Study Organizer — GET READY to Study

Be sure the following Big Ideas are noted in your Foldable.

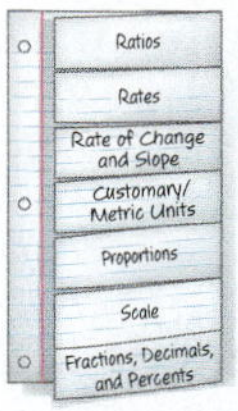

BIG Ideas

Ratios and Rates (Lessons 6-1 and 6-2)
- A ratio is a comparison of two quantities by division.
- A rate is a ratio comparing two quantities with different kinds of units.

Slope and Rate of Change (Lesson 6-3)
- Slope is the rate of change between any two points on a line.

Changing Customary Units (Lesson 6-4)
- To convert from larger units to smaller units, multiply by the appropriate unit ratio.
- To convert from smaller units to larger units, multiply by the reciprocal of the appropriate unit ratio.

Changing Metric Units (Lesson 6-5)
- When converting metric units, multiply by the appropriate power of 10.
- When converting between customary and metric units, use the appropriate unit ratio or relationship.

Proportions (Lesson 6-6)
- Proportions are equations that state two ratios or rates are equivalent.

Scale Drawings (Lesson 6-8)
- Scale drawings represent something that is too large or too small to be drawn at actual size.

Key Vocabulary

cross products (p. 310)	scale (p. 320)
equivalent ratios (p. 283)	scale drawing (p. 320)
inverse proportion (p. 316)	scale factor (p. 322)
proportion (p. 310)	scale model (p. 320)
proportional (p. 310)	slope (p. 294)
rate (p. 287)	unit rate (p. 287)
rate of change (p. 293)	unit ratio (p. 299)
ratio (p. 282)	

Vocabulary Check

Choose the term from the list above that best matches each phrase.

1. a comparison of two quantities by division **ratio**
2. two ratios that have the same value **equivalent ratios**
3. a ratio of two measurements with different units **rate**
4. an equation that shows that two ratios or rates are equivalent **proportion**
5. used to represent something that is too large or too small for an actual-size drawing **scale drawing**
6. the ratio of the distance on a map to the actual distance **scale**
7. a scale written as a ratio in simplest form without units of measurement **scale factor**
8. the constant rate of change in y with respect to the constant change in x **slope**
9. a rate that is simplified so that it has a denominator of 1 **unit rate**
10. two quantities that have a constant rate or ratio **proportional**

CHAPTER 6 Study Guide and Review

FOLDABLES™ Study Organizer — Dinah Zike's Foldables

Have students look through the chapter to make sure they have included definitions and examples about the key concepts of each lesson in their Foldables.

Encourage students to refer to their Foldables while completing the Study Guide and Review and while preparing for the Chapter Test.

Formative Assessment

Key Vocabulary The page references after each word denote where that term was first introduced. If students have difficulty answering Exercises 1–10, remind them that they can use these page references to refresh their memories about the vocabulary terms.

IN Math Online glencoe.com

Vocabulary PuzzleMaker improves students' mathematics vocabulary using four puzzle formats—crossword, scramble, word search using a word list, and word search using clues. Students can work online or from a printed worksheet.

Summative Assessment

CRM Vocabulary Test, p. 70

Chapter 6 Study Guide and Review

Lesson-by-Lesson Review

Intervention If the given examples are not sufficient to review the topics covered by the questions, remind students that the page references tell them where to review that topic in their textbooks.

Two-Day Option Have students complete the Lesson-by-Lesson Review on pages 334–336. Then you can use ExamView® Assessment Suite to customize another review worksheet that practices all the objectives of this chapter or only the objectives on which your students need more help.

For more information on ExamView® Assessment Suite, see page 280C.

Differentiated Instruction

Super DVD: MindJogger Plus
Use this DVD as an alternative format of review for the test. For more information on this game show format, see page 280D.

Additional Answer

19. **José's Savings**

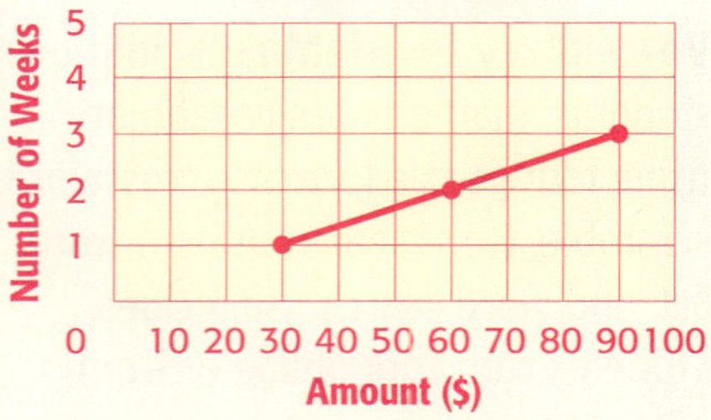

Chapter 6 Study Guide and Review

Lesson-by-Lesson Review

6-1 Ratios (pp. 282–286)

7.1.9

Write each ratio as a fraction in simplest form.

11. 16 dogs : 12 cats $\frac{4}{3}$
12. 5 ft : 25 ft $\frac{1}{5}$
13. 50 boys : 75 girls $\frac{2}{3}$
14. 36 ft : 6 ft. $\frac{6}{1}$

15. Determine whether the ratios 18 out of 24 and 5 out of 20 are equivalent. **no; $\frac{18}{24} = \frac{3}{4}$, $\frac{5}{20} = \frac{1}{4}$, and $\frac{3}{4} \neq \frac{1}{4}$**

Example 1 Write the ratio 32 to 18 as a fraction in simplest form.

32 to 18 $= \frac{32}{18}$ Write the ratio as a fraction.

$= \frac{16}{9}$ Simplify.

Example 2 Determine whether 5 : 6 and 15 : 18 are equivalent.

$5:6 = \frac{5}{6}$ $\quad 15:18 = \frac{15}{18}$ or $\frac{5}{6}$

The ratios in simplest form both equal $\frac{5}{6}$.
So, 5 : 6 and 15 : 18 are equivalent.

6-2 Rates (pp. 287–292)

7.1.9

Find each unit rate.

16. \$23.75 for 5 pounds **\$4.75 per lb**
17. 810 miles in 9 days **90 mi per day**
18. **SHAMPOO** Which bottle of shampoo shown at the right costs the least per ounce? **16 oz**

Bottle	Price
8 oz	\$1.99
12 oz	\$2.59
16 oz	\$3.19

Example 3 Find the unit price of a 16-ounce box of pasta that is on sale for 96 cents.

16-ounce box for 96 cents $= \frac{96 \text{ cents} \div 16}{16 \text{ ounces} \div 16}$

$= \frac{6 \text{ cents}}{1 \text{ ounce}}$

The unit price is 6 cents per ounce.

6-3 Rate of Change and Slope (pp. 293–297)

7.2.5, 7.2.6

Complete.

19. **MONEY** The table shows the amount of money José saved over a period of time. Graph the data. Then find the slope of the line. Explain what the slope represents.

Amount (\$)	30	60	90
Weeks	1	2	3

See margin for graph. slope: $\frac{30}{1}$ or 30; José saved \$30 every week.

Example 4 Find the rate of change in degrees per hour.

Time (h)	0	1	2
Temperature (C°)	50	52	54

(+1, +1 across Time; +2, +2 across Temperature)

$\frac{\text{change in temperature}}{\text{change in time}} = \frac{2^\circ \text{ Celsius}}{1 \text{ hour}}$

So, the temperature increases by 2° Celsius each hour.

334 **Chapter 6** Ratios and Proportions

Mixed Problem Solving
For mixed problem-solving practice, see page 709.

6-4 Measurement: Changing Customary Units (pp. 298–303)

8.3.4

Complete.

20. 4 qt = ■ pt **8**
21. 6 gal = ■ qt **24**
22. 48 oz = ■ lb **3**
23. 9 c = ■ pt **$4\frac{1}{2}$**
24. **RUNNING** Kimi runs at a speed of 30 feet per second. About how many yards per second does Kimi run? **10 yd per s**
25. **ESTIMATION** One bushel of apples weighs about 40 pounds. About how many bushels of apples would weigh 1 ton? **50 bushels**

Example 5 **Complete: 32 qt = ■ gal**

Since 1 gallon = 4 quarts, multiply by $\frac{1 \text{ gal}}{4 \text{ qt}}$.

$32 \text{ qt} = 32 \text{ qt} \cdot \frac{1 \text{ gal}}{4 \text{ qt}}$ Multiply by $\frac{1 \text{ gal}}{4 \text{ qt}}$.

$= \overset{8}{\cancel{32}} \cancel{\text{qt}} \cdot \frac{1 \text{ gal}}{\underset{1}{\cancel{4}} \cancel{\text{qt}}}$ Divide out common factors and units.

$= 8 \text{ gal}$ Multiply.

6-5 Measurement: Changing Metric Units (pp. 304–309)

8.3.4

Complete. Round to the nearest hundredth if necessary. **27. 51,528.96**

26. 18.25 ft ≈ ■ m **5.48**
27. 113.6 lb ≈ ■ g
28. 24 L ≈ ■ gal **6.33**
29. 46.8 cm ≈ ■ in. **18.43**
30. **RUNNING** Justine ran a 5-kilometer race. About how many miles did she run? **about 3.11 mi**
31. **BIRDS** The world's largest bird is the ostrich, whose mass can be as much as 156.5 kilograms. What is the approximate weight in pounds? **about 345 lb**

Example 6 **Complete: 48.8 c ≈ ■ mL**

Use the relationship 1 c ≈ 236.59 mL.

$1 \text{ c} \approx 236.59 \text{ mL}$

$48.8 \times 1 \text{ c} \approx 48.8 \times 236.59 \text{ mL}$

$48.8 \text{ c} \approx 11{,}545.592 \text{ mL}$

So, 48.8 cups is approximately 11,545.59 milliliters.

6-6 Algebra: Solving Proportions (pp. 310–315)

7.1.9, 7.2.7

Solve each proportion.

32. $\frac{x}{10} = \frac{3}{5}$ **6**
33. $\frac{4}{9} = \frac{24}{m}$ **54**
34. $\frac{2}{t} = \frac{8}{50}$ **12.5**
35. $\frac{15}{w} = \frac{35}{21}$ **9**
36. $\frac{12}{8} = \frac{a}{6}$ **9**
37. $\frac{7}{18} = \frac{d}{6}$ **$2\frac{1}{3}$**
38. **WEIGHT** If 3 televisions weigh 240.6 pounds, how much do 9 of the same televisions weigh? **721.8 lb**

Example 7 Solve $\frac{6}{9} = \frac{n}{12}$.

$\frac{6}{9} = \frac{n}{12}$ Write the proportion.

$6 \cdot 12 = 9 \cdot n$ Find the cross products.

$72 = 9n$ Multiply.

$\frac{72}{9} = \frac{9n}{9}$ Divide each side by 9.

$8 = n$ Simplify.

Chapter 6 Study Guide and Review **335**

Chapter 6 Study Guide and Review

Problem Solving Review

For additional practice in problem solving for Chapter 6, see the Mixed Problem Solving Appendix, page 709 in the Student Handbook section.

Anticipation Guide

Have students complete the Chapter 6 Anticipation Guide and discuss how their responses have changed now that they have completed Chapter 6.

CRM Anticipation Guide, pp. 7–8

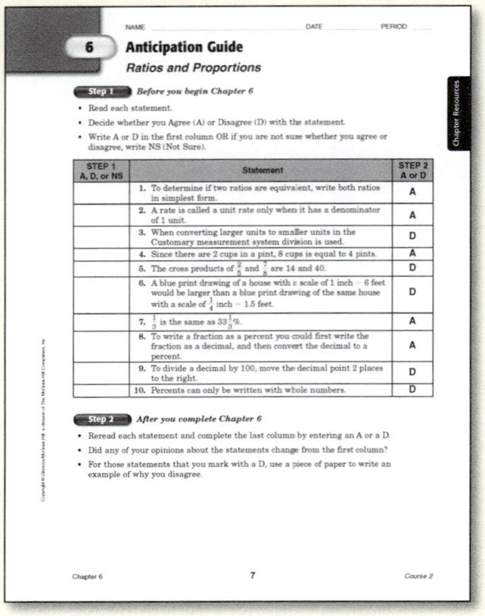

NAME ______ DATE ______ PERIOD ______

6 Anticipation Guide

Ratios and Proportions

Chapter Resources

Step 1 *Before you begin Chapter 6*

- Read each statement.
- Decide whether you Agree (A) or Disagree (D) with the statement.
- Write A or D in the first column OR if you are not sure whether you agree or disagree, write NS (Not Sure).

STEP 1 A, D, or NS	Statement	STEP 2 A or D
	1. To determine if two ratios are equivalent, write both ratios in simplest form.	A
	2. A rate is called a unit rate only when it has a denominator of 1 unit.	A
	3. When converting larger units to smaller units in the Customary measurement system division is used.	D
	4. Since there are 2 cups in a pint, 8 cups is equal to 4 pints.	A
	5. The cross products of $\frac{2}{5}$ and $\frac{7}{8}$ are 14 and 40.	D
	6. A blue print drawing of a house with a scale of 1 inch = 6 feet would be larger than a blue print drawing of the same house with a scale of $\frac{1}{4}$ inch = 1.5 feet.	D
	7. $\frac{1}{3}$ is the same as $33\frac{1}{3}\%$.	A
	8. To write a fraction as a percent you could first write the fraction as a decimal, and then convert the decimal to a percent.	A
	9. To divide a decimal by 100, move the decimal point 2 places to the right.	D
	10. Percents can only be written with whole numbers.	D

Step 2 *After you complete Chapter 6*

- Reread each statement and complete the last column by entering an A or a D.
- Did any of your opinions about the statements change from the first column?
- For those statements that you mark with a D, use a piece of paper to write an example of why you disagree.

Chapter 6 7 Course 2

Chapter 6 Study Guide and Review

6-7 PSI: Draw a Diagram (pp. 318–319)

P.1.3, P.5.1

Solve each problem by drawing a diagram.

39. **PAINTING** Marian is painting a fence that is 72 feet long. She has already painted $\frac{5}{8}$ of the fence. How many feet of fence does she have left to paint? **27 feet**

40. **COOKIES** A cookie jar contains three types of cookies: oatmeal, chocolate chip, and sugar. 60 percent are chocolate chip. Half of the remaining cookies are oatmeal. If there are 9 oatmeal cookies, how many cookies are in the jar? **45**

Example 8 **Ramiro has filled $\frac{1}{3}$ or 50 gallons of his fish tank. Find the total capacity of the fish tank.**

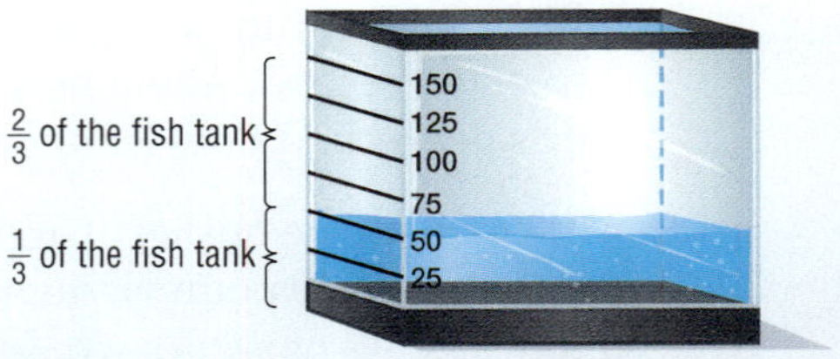

If $\frac{1}{3}$ of the fish tank is 50 gallons, then $\frac{2}{3}$ of the fish tank is 100 gallons. So, the missing two thirds must be 100 gallons. The total capacity of the fish tank is 50 + 100, or 150 gallons.

6-8 Scale Drawings (pp. 320–326)

7.3.5

41. **MAPS** Washington, D.C, and Baltimore, Maryland, are 2 inches apart on a map. If the scale is $\frac{1}{2}$ inch : 6 miles, what is the actual distance between the cities? **24 mi**

42. **MODELS** A Boeing 747 jet is 70.5 meters long and has a wingspan of 60 meters. A model of the 747 has a wingspan of 80 centimeters. What is the length of the model? **94 cm**

Example 9 **On a map, the distance between two cities is 10.9 centimeters. If the scale is 1 centimeter = 250 kilometers, what is the actual distance?**

Scale / Distance

map → / actual →
$$\frac{1 \text{ cm}}{250 \text{ km}} = \frac{10.9 \text{ cm}}{n \text{ km}}$$
← map / ← actual

$$1 \cdot n = 250 \cdot 10.9$$
$$n = 2{,}725$$

The actual distance is 2,725 kilometers.

6-9 Fractions, Decimals, and Percents (pp. 328–332)

7.1.6

Write each percent as a fraction in simplest form.

43. 27.5% $\frac{11}{40}$ 44. 5.40% $\frac{27}{500}$ 45. $45\frac{1}{4}\%$ $\frac{181}{400}$

46. **COINS** A quarter is made of $\frac{1}{12}$ nickel, and the rest is copper. Write the portion of a quarter that is copper as a percent. Round to the nearest hundredth if necessary. **91.67%**

Example 10 **Write 82.5% as a fraction in simplest form.**

$82.5\% = \frac{82.5}{100}$ Write a fraction with a denominator of 100.

$= \frac{825}{1{,}000}$ Multiply 82.5 and 100 by 10 to eliminate the decimal.

$= \frac{33}{40}$ Simplify.

CHAPTER 6 Practice Test

IN Math Online glencoe.com
• Chapter Test

LAWN CARE For Exercises 1 and 2, use the following information to write each ratio as a fraction in simplest form.

A bag of fertilizer nutrients contains 18 pounds of nitrogen, 6 pounds of phosphorus, and 12 pounds of potassium.

1. nitrogen : potassium $\frac{3}{2}$
2. phosphorus : nitrogen $\frac{1}{3}$

Find each unit rate. Round to the nearest hundredth if necessary.

3. 24 greeting cards for $4.80 **$0.20 per card**
4. 330 miles on 15 gallons of gasoline **22 mi per gal**
5. **MULTIPLE CHOICE** The population of bacteria in 4 different-sized lab dishes are given. Which dish has the lowest density of bacteria or bacteria per square inch? **B**

Dish	Bacteria	Dish Area
1	100	205 sq in.
2	50	125 sq in.
3	35	75 sq in.
4	180	300 sq in.

A Dish 1
B Dish 2
C Dish 3
D Dish 4

6. The graph shows the relationship between time and water level of a pool. Find the rate of change. **The water level increases by 1 foot for every 2 hours.**

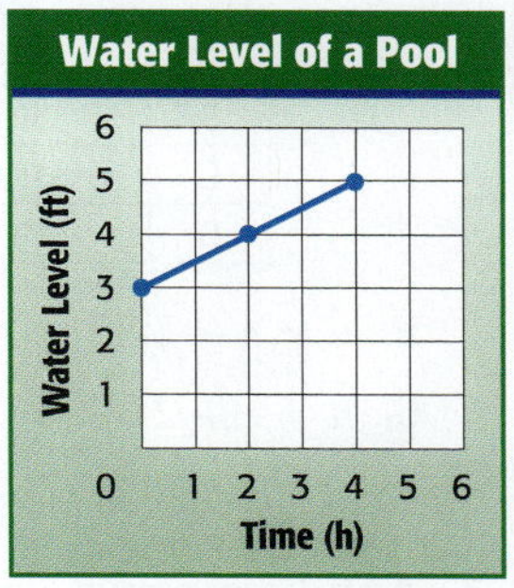

MEASUREMENT Complete. Round to the nearest tenth if necessary.

7. 7.62 yd ≈ ■ m **6.93**
8. 50.8 lb ≈ ■ kg **23.04**
9. 3,600 mL ≈ ■ qt **3.80**
10. 19.25 m ≈ ■ ft **64.17**

ALGEBRA Solve each proportion.

11. $\frac{2}{3} = \frac{x}{42}$ **28**
12. $\frac{t}{21} = \frac{15}{14}$ **22.5**

13. **NUTRITION** If an 8-ounce glass of orange juice has 72 milligrams of vitamin C, how much vitamin C is in a 7-ounce glass? **63 mg**
14. **MAPS** The table shows the key for a map. Graph the data. Then find the slope of the line. **See margin.**

Distance on Map (cm)	1	2	3	4
Actual Distance (km)	20	40	60	80

BLUEPRINTS For Exercises 15 and 16, use the following blueprint of a room.

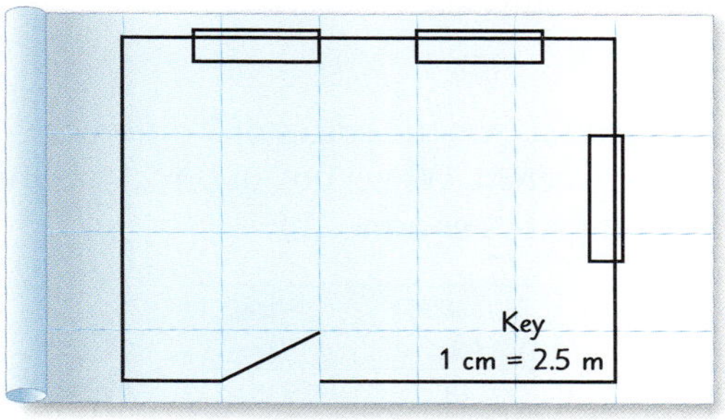

15. Use a centimeter ruler to find the length of the wall with 2 windows. **12.5 m**
16. How wide would a 1.4-meter-wide dresser appear on this drawing? **0.56 cm**

Write each fraction as a percent. Round to the nearest hundredth if necessary.

17. $\frac{5}{8}$ **62.5%**
18. $\frac{7}{15}$ **46.67%**

19. **GUM** A company test-marketed 7 new flavors of gum last year. Only 2 of these received favorable ratings. Which represents the percent of flavors that did *not* receive favorable ratings? **71%**
20. **STOCKS** A company's stock increased 0.83% last month. Write 0.83% as a decimal. **0.0083**

CHAPTER 6 Practice Test

Summative Assessment

Chapter 6 Resource Masters

Leveled Chapter 6 Tests			
Form	**Type**	**Level**	**Pages**
1	MC	BL	71–72
2A	MC	OL	73–74
2B	MC	OL	75–76
2C	FR	OL	77–78
2D	FR	OL	79–80
3	FR	AL	81–82

MC = multiple-choice questions
FR = free-response questions
BL = below or approaching grade level
OL = on grade level
AL = above or beyond grade level

- Vocabulary Test, p. 70
- Extended-Response Test, p. 83

ExamView Assessment Suite Customize and create multiple versions of your chapter test and the answer keys. All of the questions from the leveled chapter tests in the *Chapter 6 Resource Masters* are also available on ExamView® Assessment Suite.

Data-Driven Decision Making	Exercises	Lesson	Academic Standards	Resources for Review
Diagnostic Teaching Based on the results of the Chapter 6 Practice Test, use the following to review concepts that students continue to find challenging.	1–6, 14	6-1, 6-2, 6-3	7.1.8, 7.2.5, 7.2.6	Study Guide and Intervention pp. 10, 16, 22, 28, 34, 40, 46, 51, and 58
	7–13	6-4, 6-5, 6-6	7.1.7, 7.2.7, 8.3.5	IN Math Online glencoe.com • Extra Examples • Personal Tutor • Concepts in Motion
	15–20	6-7, 6-8, 6-9	P.1.3, P.5.1, 7.3.3, 6.1.4	

6 ISTEP+ Practice

TEST-TAKING TIP

Exercise 4 Have students look for a word or term in the problem that indicates which operation will be used in the equation. Students should realize that *more than* indicates addition, which should lead them to examine answer choice G.

Formative Assessment

You can use these two pages to benchmark student progress.

Chapter 6 Resource Masters

- Standardized Test Practice, pp. 84–86

ExamView Assessment Suite Create practice worksheets or tests that align to your state's standards, as well as TIMSS and NAEP tests.

Chapter 6 ISTEP+ Practice

Cumulative, Chapters 1–6

IN Math Online glencoe.com
• Test Practice

PART 1 Multiple Choice

Read each question. Then fill in the correct answer on the answer sheet provided by your teacher or on a sheet of paper.

1. Francesca typed 496 words in 8 minutes. Which of the following is a correct understanding of this rate? **C**

   A On average, it takes 62 minutes for Francesca to type one word.

   B On average, Francesca can type 62 words in 8 minutes.

   C On average, Francesca can type 62 words in one minute.

   D On average, Francesca can type 8 words in one minute.

2. The table shows the prices of 3 different boxes of cereal. Which box of cereal has the highest price per ounce? **F**

Cereal Box Size (ounces)	Price ($)
48	5.45
32	3.95
20	3.10

   F The 20-ounce box

   G The 32-ounce box

   H The 48-ounce box

   J All three boxes have the same price per ounce.

3. A bakery sells 6 bagels for a total of $2.99 and 4 muffins for a total of $3.29. If you bought 4 dozen bagels and 16 muffins, what is the total cost of the bagels and muffins, not including tax? **B**

   A $64.60 **C** $31.10

   B $37.08 **D** $26.50

4. Mrs. Black is making 2 pasta salads for a picnic. The first pasta salad requires $4\frac{2}{3}$ cups of pasta, and the second pasta salad requires $\frac{1}{3}$ cup more than the first. Which of the following equations can be used to find n, the number of cups of pasta needed for the second recipe? **G**

   F $n = 4\frac{2}{3} \div \frac{1}{3}$

   G $n = 4\frac{2}{3} + \frac{1}{3}$

   H $n = 4\frac{2}{3} - \frac{1}{3}$

   J $n = 4\frac{2}{3} \times \frac{1}{3}$

5. Simplify the expression below.

   $$8 + 3(15 - 5) - 3^2$$ **D**

   A 101 **C** 39

   B 44 **D** 29

6. A shoe store had to increase prices. The table shows the regular price r and the new price n of several shoes. Which of the following formulas can be used to calculate the new price? **G**

Shoe	Regular Price (r)	New Price (n)
A	$25.00	$27.80
B	$30.00	$32.80
C	$35.00	$37.80
D	$40.00	$42.80

   F $n = r - 2.80$ **H** $n = r \times 0.1$

   G $n = r + 2.80$ **J** $n = r \div 0.1$

7. Annika can run 2 miles in 15 minutes. At this rate, about how long will it take her to run $3\frac{1}{2}$ miles? **A**

   A 26 minutes **C** 36 minutes

   B 32 minutes **D** 45 minutes

338 **Chapter 6** Ratios and Proportions

Preparing for ISTEP+
For test-taking strategies and practice, see pages 716–733.

8. A building is 55 meters tall. About how tall is the building in feet (ft) and inches (in.)? (1 meter ≈ 39 inches) **G**

F 179 ft 0 in.
G 178 ft 9 in.
H 178 ft 8 in.
J 178 ft 6 in.

9. You can drive your car 21.75 miles with one gallon of gasoline. How many miles can you drive with 13.2 gallons of gasoline? **D**

A 13.2
B 21.75
C 150.2
D 287.1

10. The table shows the number of yards of material Leah used each day last week. What was the total number of yards Leah used last week? **F**

Day	Material (yd)
Monday	2.3
Tuesday	$1\frac{3}{4}$
Wednesday	2.8
Thursday	3.1
Friday	$3\frac{1}{4}$
Saturday	1.7
Sunday	$4\frac{1}{2}$

F 19.4 yd
G 17 yd
H 16.5 yd
J 16 yd

PART 2 Short Response/Grid In

Record your answers on the answer sheet provided by your teacher or on a sheet of paper.

11. Some employees work 40 hours a week. If there are 168 hours in one week, about what part of the week do they work? **25%**

12. During a visit to his favorite bookstore, Kevin bought 3 hardback books priced at \$14.99 each and 4 paperbacks priced at \$7.99 each. Find the total of Kevin's purchase, in dollars, before tax is included. **76.93**

PART 3 Extended Response

Record your answers on the answer sheet provided by your teacher or on a sheet of paper. Show your work.

13 Pistachios cost \$3.99 a pound at the local health food store.

a. Set up a proportion to find the cost of 3 pounds. $\frac{\$3.99}{1\text{ lb}} = \frac{x}{3\text{ lb}}$

b. Solve the proportion. How much do 3 pounds of pistachios cost? **\$11.97**

c. If the pistachios are on sale for \$3.09 a pound, how much money will you save if you buy 3 pounds of pistachios? **\$2.70**

TEST-TAKING TIP

Question 13 When a question involves information from a previous part of a question, make sure to check that information before you move on.

NEED EXTRA HELP?													
If You Missed Question...	1	2	3	4	5	6	7	8	9	10	11	12	13
Go to Lesson...	6-2	6-2	1-1	5-2	1-4	1-10	6-2	6-8	6-6	5-2	6-9	6-7	6-2
IN Academic Standards	7.1.9	7.1.9	7.2.1	6.1.6	7.2.3	7.2.1	7.1.9	7.3.5	7.1.9	6.1.6	7.1.6	P.1.3	7.1.9

Chapter 6 ISTEP+ Practice

Answer Sheet Practice

Have students simulate taking a standardized test by recording their answers on a practice recording sheet.

CRM Student Recording Sheet, p. 65

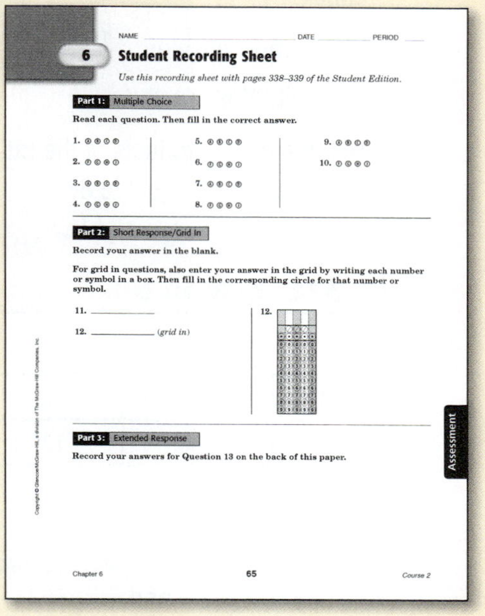
NAME ______ DATE ______ PERIOD ______

6 **Student Recording Sheet**

Use this recording sheet with pages 338–339 of the Student Edition.

Part 1: Multiple Choice

Read each question. Then fill in the correct answer.

1. Ⓐ Ⓑ Ⓒ Ⓓ
2. Ⓕ Ⓖ Ⓗ Ⓙ
3. Ⓐ Ⓑ Ⓒ Ⓓ
4. Ⓕ Ⓖ Ⓗ Ⓙ
5. Ⓐ Ⓑ Ⓒ Ⓓ
6. Ⓕ Ⓖ Ⓗ Ⓙ
7. Ⓐ Ⓑ Ⓒ Ⓓ
8. Ⓕ Ⓖ Ⓗ Ⓙ
9. Ⓐ Ⓑ Ⓒ Ⓓ
10. Ⓕ Ⓖ Ⓗ Ⓙ

Part 2: Short Response/Grid In

Record your answer in the blank.

For grid in questions, also enter your answer in the grid by writing each number or symbol in a box. Then fill in the corresponding circle for that number or symbol.

11. ______

12. ______ *(grid in)*

Part 3: Extended Response

Record your answers for Question 13 on the back of this paper.

Copyright © Glencoe/McGraw-Hill, a division of The McGraw-Hill Companies, Inc.

Assessment

Chapter 6 65 *Course 2*

Homework Option

Get Ready for Chapter 7 Assign students the exercises on page 341 as homework to assess whether they possess the prerequisite skills needed for the next chapter.

Page 313, Lesson 6-6

15. Yes; sample answer: The cross products of the ratios $\frac{16}{200}$ and $\frac{28}{350}$, 16 • 350 and 200 • 28, are both equal to 5,600.

16. No; sample answer: The cross products of the ratios $\frac{5}{7}$ and $\frac{25}{49}$, 5 • 49 or 245 and 7 • 25 or 175, are not equal.

17. No; sample answer: The cross products of the ratios $\frac{1.4\text{ T}}{18\text{ days}}$ and $\frac{10.5\text{ T}}{60\text{ days}}$, 1.4 • 60 or 84 and 18 • 10.5 or 189, are not equal.

18. Yes; sample answer: $\frac{3\text{ in.}}{4\text{ mi}} = \frac{0.75\text{ in.}}{1\text{ mi}}$ and $\frac{7.5\text{ in.}}{10\text{ mi}} = \frac{0.75\text{ in.}}{1\text{ mi}}$; The unit rates are equal.

20. Yes; the cross products of the ratios $\frac{11}{2}$ and $\frac{33}{6}$, 11 • 6 and 2 • 33, are both equal to 66.

Page 316, Extend 6-6

3.

t (hours)	1	2	3	4
r ($)	240	120	80	60

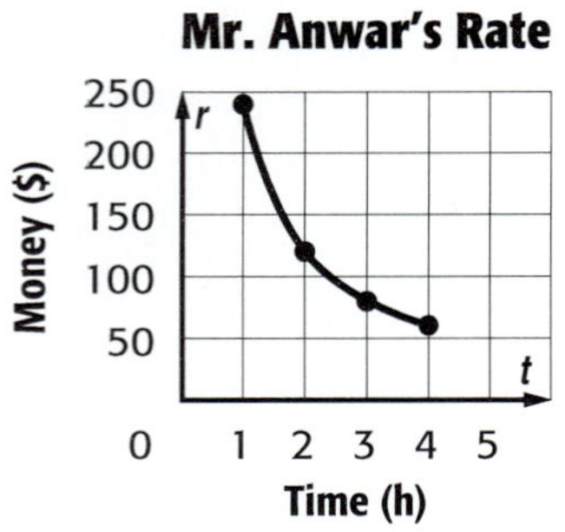

t (hours)	1	2	3	4
r ($)	10	20	30	40

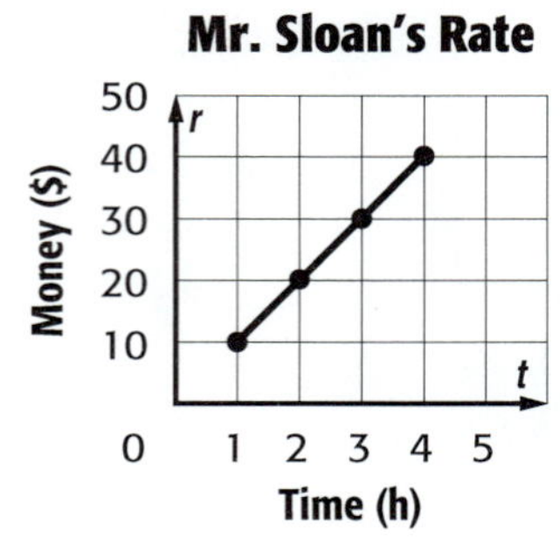

Page 337, Practice Test

14. slope: $\frac{20}{1}$ or 20; Every centimeter on the map represents 20 kilometers.

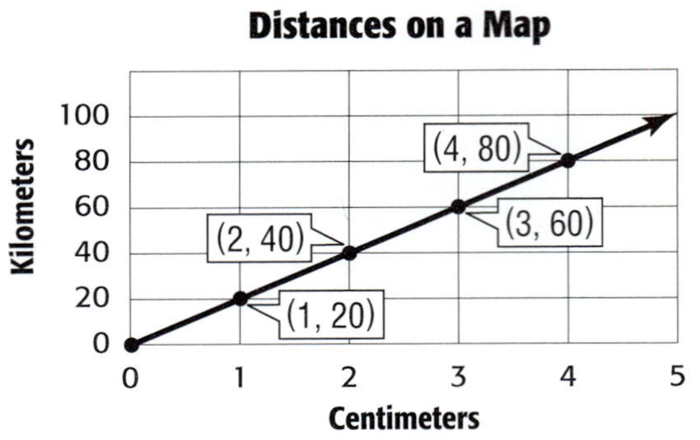

NOTES

CHAPTER 7

Chapter Overview

Applying Percents

Lesson Plan — Pacing Your Lessons

LESSONS AND OBJECTIVES	Academic Standards	45–50 Minute Periods	90-Minute Periods
Explore 7-1 **Math Lab: Percent of a Number** (pp. 342–343) • Use a model to find the percent of a number. **7-1** **Percent of a Number** (pp. 344–348) • Find the percent of a number.	7.1.8 Core Lesson	1.5	1
7-2 **The Percent Proportion** (pp. 350–354) • Solve problems using the percent proportion.	7.1.8 Core Lesson	1	0.5
7-3 **Percent and Estimation** (pp. 355–360) • Estimate percents by using fractions and decimals.	7.1.8 Core Lesson	1	0.5
7-4 **Algebra: The Percent Equation** (pp. 361–365) • Solve problems by using the percent equation.	7.1.8, 7.2.1 Core Lesson	1	0.5
7-5 **Problem-Solving Investigation: Determine Reasonable Answers** (pp. 366–367) • Solve problems by determining reasonable answers.	P.2.1, P.2.2 Core Lesson	1	0.5
7-6 **Percent of Change** (pp. 369–374) • Find the percent of increase or decrease.	7.1.8 Core Lesson	1	0.5
7-7 **Sales Tax and Discount** (pp. 375–378) • Solve problems involving sales tax and discount.	7.1.8 Core Lesson	1	0.5
7-8 **Simple Interest** (pp. 379–382) • Solve problems involving simple interest. **Extend 7-8** **Spreadsheet Lab: Simple Interest** (p. 383) • Use a spreadsheet to calculate simple interest.	8.1.6	1.5	1
REVIEW		1	0.5
ASSESSMENT		1	0.5*
	TOTAL	**11**	**6**

The complete ***Assessment Planner*** *for Chapter 7 is provided on page 341.*

** Begin Chapter 8 in the second half of the period.*

Focal Points

G7-FP1 Algebra
For the complete wording of the Focal Points for Grade 7, please see page T17.

Professional Development

Vertical Alignment

Before Chapter 7

Related Topics from Grade 6

- Interpret percents as a part of a hundred; find decimal and percent equivalents for common fractions and explain why they represent the same value; compute a given percent of a whole number

Chapter 7

Topics from Grade 7

- Interpret and use ratios in different contexts
- Use proportions to solve problems
- Calculate given percents of quantities and solve
- Write and solve one-step linear equations in one variable

After Chapter 7

Preparation for Grade 8

- Convert fractions to decimals and percents and use these representations in estimations, computations, and applications
- Solve problems that involve discounts, markups, commissions, and profit and compute simple and compound interest
- Calculate the percent of increases and decreases of a quantity

Backmapping and Vertical Alignment

McGraw-Hill's ***Math Connects*** was conceived and developed with the final results in mind: student success in Algebra 1 and beyond. The authors, using the **NCTM Focal Points and Focal Connections** as their guide, developed this brand-new series by backmapping from Algebra 1 concepts and vertically aligning the topics so that they build upon prior skills and concepts and serve as a foundation for future topics.

What the Research Says...

According to Sutherland and Rojano in "A Spreadsheet Approach to Solving Algebra Problems," which appeared in *Journal of Mathematical Behavior*, spreadsheets help students understand the meaning of variables and algebraic expressions.

- In the Spreadsheet Investigation on page 383, students use a spreadsheet to calculate simple interest I for different values of principal p, rate r, and time t.

Professional Development

Targeted professional development has been articulated throughout **McGraw-Hill's *Math Connects*** program. The **McGraw-Hill Professional Development Video Library** provides short videos that support the NCTM Focal Points and Focal Connections. For more information, visit glencoe.com.

Model Lessons

Instructional Strategies

CHAPTER 7

Technology Solutions

Teacher Resources

TeacherWorks™ All-in-One Planner and Resource Center

All of the print materials from the Classroom Resource Masters are available on your TeacherWorks™ CD-ROM.

BL = Below or Approaching Grade Level OL = On Grade Level AL = Above or Beyond Grade Level ELL = English Language Learner

				Chapter Resource Masters	7-1	7-2	7-3	7-4	7-5	7-6	7-7	7-8
BL	OL		ELL	Lesson Reading Guide	9	16	23	29		39	46	52
BL	OL		ELL	Study Guide and Intervention*	10	17	24	30	35	40	47	53
BL	OL			Skills Practice*	11	18	25	31	36	41	48	54
	OL	AL		Practice*	12	19	26	32	37	42	49	55
	OL	AL		Word Problem Practice*	13	20	27	33	38	43	50	56
	OL	AL		Enrichment	14	21	28	34		44	51	57
	OL	AL		Calculator and Spreadsheet Activities	15	22				45		
	OL	AL		Chapter Assessments*	59–80							
BL	OL	AL		5-Minute Check Transparencies	✓	✓	✓	✓	✓	✓	✓	✓
BL	OL			Teaching Mathematics with Manipulatives	✓		✓			✓		
BL	OL	AL		Real-World Investigations for Differentiated Instruction	53							

*Also available in Spanish.

Graphing Calculator Easy Files

- Timesaving Tech Tools for the TI-Navigator
- Quick Checks to diagnose student progress
- Deliver Differentiated Instruction with Ready Files
- Vocabulary Review

AssignmentWorks

Differentiated Assignments, Answers, and Solutions

- Print a customized assignment worksheet using the Student Edition exercises along with an answer key or worked-out solutions.
- Use a default lesson assignments as outlined in the Differentiated Homework Options in the Teacher Edition.

Interactive Classroom

This CD-ROM is a customizable Microsoft® PowerPoint® presentation that includes:

- In-Class Examples
- Your Turn Exercises*
- 5-Minute Check Transparencies*
- Links to Online Study Tools
- Concepts in Motion

compatible with response pad technology

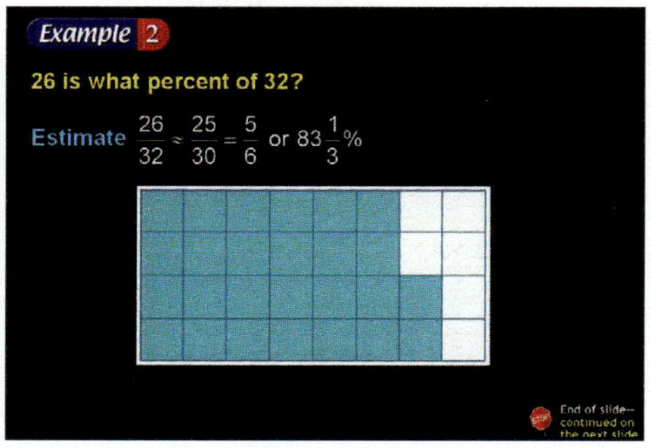

ExamView® Assessment Suite

ExamView® Assessment Suite

- Create, edit, and customize tests and worksheets using QuickTest Wizard
- Create multiple versions of tests and modify them for a desired level of difficulty
- Translate from English to Spanish and vice versa
- Build tests aligned with your state standards
- Track students' progress using the Teacher Management System

Student Tools

StudentWorks™ Plus

Textbook, Audio, Workbooks, and more

This CD-ROM is a valuable resource for students to access content online and use online resources to continue learning Chapter 7 concepts. Includes:

- Complete Student Editions in both English and Spanish
- English audio integrated throughout the text
- Links to Concepts in Motion, Personal Tutor, and other online resources
- Access to all student worksheets
- Daily Assignments and Grade Log

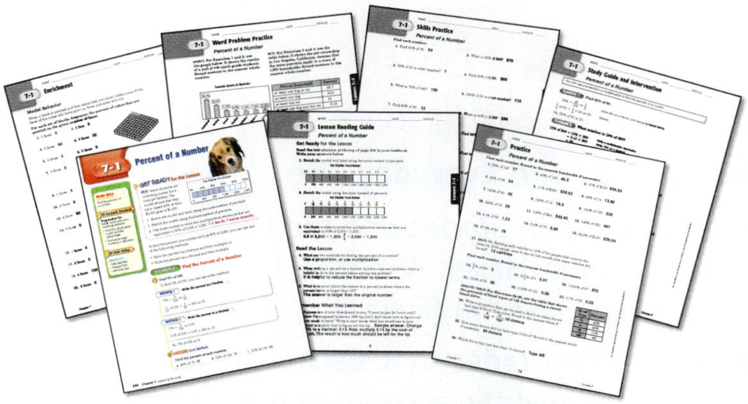

Super DVD

The Super DVD contains two Glencoe multimedia products.

MindJogger Plus An alternative review of concepts in which students work as teams in a game show format to gain points for correct answers.

What's Math Got to Do With It? Real-Life Math Videos
Engaging video that shows students how math is used in everyday situations.

Internet Resources

IN Math Online glencoe.com

TEACHER	STUDENT	PARENT	Online Study Tools
	●	●	Online Student Edition
●	●	●	Multilingual Glossary
			Lesson Resources
	●	●	Extra Examples
	●	●	BrainPOPS®
	●	●	Self-Check Quizzes
●	●	●	Concepts in Motion
	●	●	Other Calculator Keystrokes
	●	●	Real-World Careers
	●	●	Reading in the Content Area
●			Group Activity Cards
			Chapter Resources
	●	●	Family Letters and Activities
	●		Chapter Readiness Quiz
	●	●	Vocabulary Review
	●	●	Chapter Test
	●	●	Standardized Test Practice
			Unit Resources
●	●		WebQuest Project
			Other Resources
	●		Personal Tutor
●			NAEP Correlations
●			Key Concepts
●	●	●	Meet the Authors
●	●		Game Zone
●	●	●	Math Skills Maintenance
●			National Resources (Professional Organizations)
●			State Resources
●			Vocabulary PuzzleMakers

Reading and Writing in Mathematics

Noteables™ Interactive Study Notebook with Foldables™

This workbook is a study organizer that provides helpful steps for students to follow to organize their notes for Chapter 7.

- Students use Noteables to record notes and to complete their Foldables as you present the material for each lesson.
- Noteables correspond to the Examples in the *Teacher Edition* and *Interactive Chalkboard CD-ROM.*

Real-World Problem Solving Graphic Novels

Mathematical problem solving is presented in a motivating, graphic novel format. The novels contain real-world problems for each of the following mathematical strands: Number Sense, Algebraic Thinking, Geometry, Measurement, Statistics and Probability, and Mathematical Reasoning.

READING in the Content Area

This online worksheet provides strategies for reading and analyzing Lesson 7-2, The Percent Proportion. Students are guided through questions about the main idea, subject matter, supporting details, conclusion, clarifying details, and vocabulary of the lesson.

glencoe.com

Recommended Outside Reading for Students

Mathematics and Everyday Life

- *57 Great Math Stories and the Problems They Present* by D. Haver, A. Kozoil, E. Haven, & D. Mulligan ©1998 [fiction]

Appropriate for Grades 5–8. Each story is a humorous yet realistic account of everyday life and the problems life presents. Many stories throughout the book utilize percents. Often the reader must make calculations using the percent equation or proportion to understand the outcome of the story.

Project CRISS℠

STUDY SKILL

Writing out the steps in a mathematical process using a point-by-point format can help students better understand that process. In order to explain a process, they must not only understand how to perform each step, but they must also understand the reasoning behind each step. Provide students with the description at the right as an example of using a point-by-point format to explain how to multiply a fraction and a whole number. After reading Lessons 7-7 and 7-8, have students write a description of how to solve sales tax and simple interest problems. Students may also find two-column notes to be a useful tool in this chapter.

Multiplying a Fraction and a Whole Number

1. Write the whole number as a fraction with a denominator of 1. For example, 8 would be written as $\frac{8}{1}$.
2. Multiply the fractions. The numerators should be multiplied and the denominators should be multiplied.
3. If the numerator is greater than the denominator, write the answer as a mixed number.
4. Be sure the answer is written in simplest form. If not, rename.

CReating Independence through Student-owned Strategies

Differentiated Instruction

Investigative Approach

MathScape™

This project was supported, in part, by the
National Science Foundation

MathScape is a mathematics curriculum for grades 6–8 developed by the Seeing and Thinking Mathematically Project at the Education Development Center.

Rates, Ratios, Percents, and Proportions
Buyer Beware

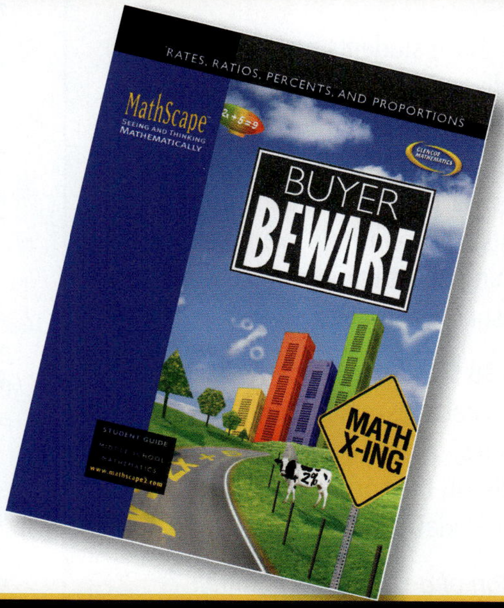

How to Use *MathScape* with Chapter 7

The unit *Buyer Beware* can be used to enhance Lessons 7-2 and 7-3.

- **Introduce** ⟶ Before you start **Lesson 7-2**, you can introduce proportions by using the activities on pages 18–19.
- **Reinforce** ⟶ After you complete **Lesson 7-3**, you can use the activities on pages 26–33 to provide additional practice with percents.

RTI (Response to Intervention)

TIER 1 **On-Level Instruction** Use the *Math Connects* program as instruction for your on-level students.

TIER 2 **Strategic Intervention** For options to instruct struggling students, refer to the Diagnostic Assessment table on page 341.

TIER 3 **Intensive Intervention** *Math Triumphs* can provide intensive intervention for students who are two or more grade levels behind.

Diagnose student readiness with the Quick Check and Quick Review on page 341. Then use *Math Triumphs* to accelerate their achievment.

Applying Percents

Prerequisite Skill	*Math Triumphs*
Percentages	Ch. 3

Practice and Review

Quick Review Math Handbook* is Glencoe's mathematical handbook for students and parents.

Hot Words includes a glossary of terms.

Hot Topics consists of two parts:

- explanations of key mathematical concepts
- exercises to check students' understanding.

Lesson	Hot Topics Section	Lesson	Hot Topics Section
7-1	2•8, 2•9	7-6	2•8, 6•5
7-2	2•8, 6•5	7-7	2•8, 6•5
7-3	2•8	7-8	2•8, 9•4
7-4	2•8, 6•5		

**Also available in Spanish*

Chapter 7 Notes

Foldables™ Study Organizer — Dinah Zike's Foldables

Focus This Foldable is designed to help students organize their notes about percents.

Teach Have students make the Foldable and label the sections. Tell them that they should record the main ideas and key terms of each lesson in the appropriate section. Encourage students also to include examples, explaining how their examples illustrate the lesson's main ideas.

When to Use It As students work through each lesson, remind them to take notes, define terms, and write examples in the corresponding sections of their Foldables.

A version of a completed Foldable is shown on p. 384.

Differentiated Instruction

CRM Student-Built Glossary, p. 1

Students complete the chart by providing the definition of each term and an example as they progress through Chapter 7.

This study tool can be used to review for the chapter test.

Materials Needed for Chapter 7

- grid paper (Explore 7-1)
- colored pencils (Explore 7-1)
- paper strips (Lesson 7-6)
- scissors (Lesson 7-6)
- tape (Lesson 7-6)
- computers with spreadsheet program (Extend 7-8)

Chapter 7 Applying Percents

Indiana Academic Standards

7.1.8 Solve problems involving percents.

- Find the whole given a part and the percentage
- Find percentage increase or decrease.

7.1.9 Solve problems involving ratios and proportions.

Key Vocabulary

percent equation (p. 361)
percent of change (p. 369)
percent proportion (p. 350)

Real-World Link

Boogie Boards You can buy a boogie board in Myrtle Beach, South Carolina, for $25. You will also pay a sales tax of 5%.

Foldables® Study Organizer

Applying Percents Make this Foldable to help you organize your notes. Begin with a piece of 11" by 17" paper.

1. **Fold** the paper in half lengthwise.

2. **Open** and refold the paper into fourths along the opposite axis.

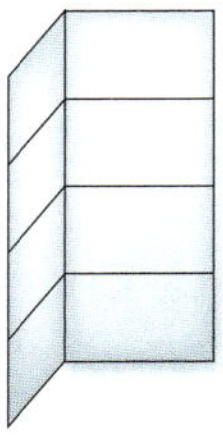

3. **Trace** along the fold lines and label each section with a lesson title or number.

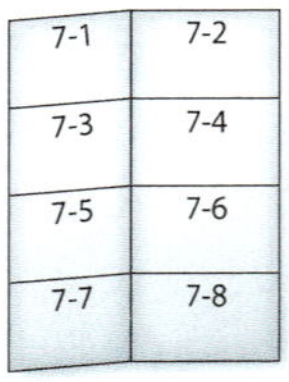

GET READY for Chapter 7

Diagnose Readiness You have two options for checking Prerequisite Skills.

Option 2

IN Math Online Take the Online Readiness Quiz at glencoe.com.

Option 1

Take the Quick Quiz below. Refer to the Quick Review for help.

QUICK Quiz

(Used in Lesson 7-8)

Multiply. (Prior Grade)

1. $300 \times 0.02 \times 8$ **48**
2. $85 \times 0.25 \times 3$ **63.75**
3. $560 \times 0.6 \times 4.5$ **1,512**
4. $154 \times 0.12 \times 5$ **92.4**
5. **MONEY** If Nicole saves $0.05 every day, how much money will she have in 3 years? (Prior Grade) **$54.75**

(Used in Lessons 7-6 and 7-7)

Simplify. Write as a decimal. (Prior Grade)

6. $\frac{22-8}{8}$ **1.75**
7. $\frac{50-33}{50}$ **0.34**
8. $\frac{35-7}{35}$ **0.8**
9. **BASEBALL CARDS** Tim has 56 baseball cards. He gives 14 of them away. What decimal represents the portion he has left? (Prior Grade) **0.75**

(Used in Lessons 7-2 and 7-5)

ALGEBRA Solve. Round to the nearest tenth if necessary. (Lesson 3-3)

10. $0.4m = 52$ **130**
11. $21 = 0.28a$ **75**
12. $13 = 0.06s$ **216.7**
13. $0.95z = 37$ **38.9**

(Used in Lesson 7-5)

Write each percent as a decimal. (Lesson 4-7)

14. 40% **0.4**
15. 17% **0.17**
16. 110% **1.1**
17. 157% **1.57**
18. 3.25% **0.0325**
19. 7.5% **0.075**
20. **FOOD** Approximately 92% of a watermelon is water. What decimal represents this amount? (Lesson 4-7) **0.92**

QUICK Review

Example 1

Evaluate $240 \times 0.03 \times 5$.

$240 \times 0.03 \times 5$
$= 7.2 \times 5$ — Multiply 240 by 0.03.
$= 36$ — Simplify.

Example 2

Simplify $\frac{17-8}{8}$. Write as a decimal.

$\frac{17-8}{8} = \frac{9}{8}$ — Subtract 8 from 17.
$= 1.125$ — Divide 9 by 8.

Example 3

Solve $0.6k = 7.8$

$0.6k = 7.8$ — Write the equation.
$k = 13$ — Divide each side by 0.6.

Example 4

Write 9.8% as a decimal.

$9.8\% = 0.098$ — Move the decimal point two places to the left and remove the percent symbol.

Diagnostic Assessment

Exercises	Academic Standards	Strategic Intervention
1–5	7.1.8	SE Concepts and Skills Bank, p. 736
6–9	7.1.8	SE Review Lesson 4-5, pp. 196–200
10–13	7.1.9	SE Review Lesson 3-3, pp. 142–146
14–20	P.2.1, P.2.2	SE Review Lesson 4-7, pp. 206–210

ASSESSMENT PLANNER — CHAPTER 7

Formative Assessment

CRM Anticipation Guide, pp. 7–8

Spotting Preconceived Ideas
Students complete this survey to determine prior knowledge about ideas from Chapter 7. Revisit this worksheet after completing the chapter. Also see page 388.

TE Lesson Activities

- Ticket Out the Door, pp. 354, 360, 365, 382
- Crystal Ball, p. 374
- Name the Math, pp. 348, 378
- Yesterday's News, p. 367

Chapter Checkpoints

- SE Mid-Chapter Quiz, p. 368
- SE Study Guide and Review, pp. 384–388
- SE Test Practice, pp. 390–391
- CRM Quizzes, pp. 61 and 62
- CRM Standardized Test Practice, pp. 78–80

IN Math Online glencoe.com

- Self-Check Quizzes
- Practice Test
- Test Practice

Summative Assessment

- SE Chapter Practice Test, p. 389
- CRM Mid-Chapter Test, p. 63
- CRM Vocabulary Test, p. 64
- CRM Extended-Response Test, p. 77
- CRM Leveled Chapter Tests, pp. 65–76
- CD ExamView Pro® Assessment Suite

KEY

- CRM *Chapter 7 Resource Masters*
- SE Student Edition
- TE Teacher Edition
- CD-ROM

Explore 7-1 Lesson Notes

1 Focus

Materials

- grid paper
- colored pencils

Easy-to-Use Manipulatives

Teaching Mathematics with Manipulatives, templates for:

- Quarter Inch Grid, p. 14

Teaching Tip

You may need to remind students that percent means *per 100*, so a percent is a ratio comparing a number to 100.

2 Teach

Activity 1 If students have difficulty finding the units for the left side of the scale (Step 2), ask:

- What is the original price of the backpack?
- How many intervals does the scale have?

Make sure students realize that they need to divide the original price by the number of intervals to get the units of the scale ($50 ÷ 10 = $5).

Tips for New Teachers

Percent Models

Teachers may be familiar with percent models that show 0% at the bottom and 100% at the top. We chose to render these models with 0% at the top and 100% at the bottom so that students can make connections with the set up of the proportions more easily.

Explore 7-1

Math Lab
Percent of a Number

MAIN IDEA

Use a model to find the percent of a number.

IN Academic Standards

Preparation for 7.1.8 Solve problems involving percents.

- Find the whole given a part and the percentage
- Find percentage increase or decrease.

Also addresses P.2.2.

Do you enjoy shopping? If so, you may have seen sales or other discounts represented as percents. For example, consider the following situation. A backpack is on sale for 30% off the original price. If the original price of the backpack is $50, how much will you save?

In this situation, you know the percent. You need to find what part of the original price you will save. In this lab, you will use a model to find the percent of a number or *part* of a whole.

ACTIVITY

1 Find 30% of $50 using a model.

STEP 1 Draw a 1-by-10 rectangle as shown on grid paper. Label the units on the right from 0% to 100% as shown.

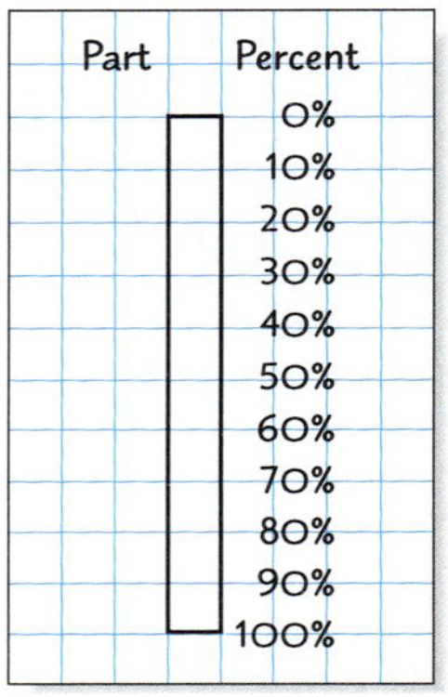

STEP 2 Since $50 represents the original price, mark equal units from $0 to $50 on the left side of the model as shown.

STEP 3 Draw a line from 30% on the right side to the left side of the model as shown and shade the portion of the rectangle above this line.

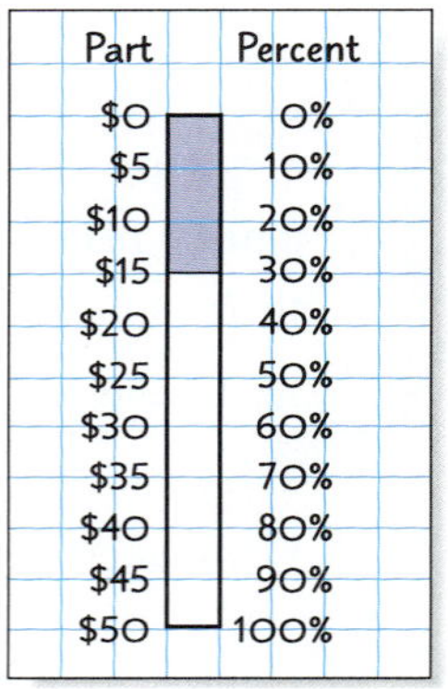

The model shows that 30% of $50 is $15. So, you will save $15.

CHECK Your Progress a–c. See Ch. 7 Answer Appendix for models.

Draw a model to find the percent of each number.

a. 20% of 120 **24** b. 60% of 70 **42** c. 90% of 400 **360**

Tips for New Teachers

Decimal Models

Point out to students that the decimal models used in Activities 1 and 2 use intervals of 10%. If students plan to use a decimal model to find a percent of a number that is not divisible by 10 or 5, they may need to modify the intervals on their decimal model or use their decimal model solely for estimation purposes.

Suppose a bicycle is on sale for 35% off the original price. How much will you save if the original price of the bicycle is $180?

ACTIVITY

2 Find 35% of $180 using a model.

STEP 1 Draw a 1-by-10 rectangle as shown on grid paper. Label the units on the right from 0% to 100% as shown.

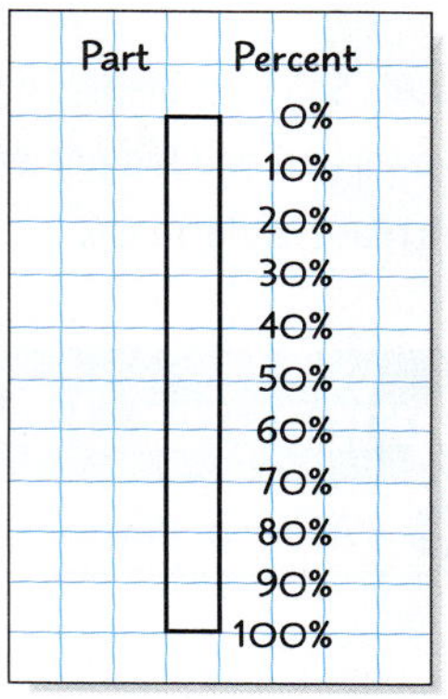

Study Tip

Equal Units
For the model at the right, use an interval of $18 since $180 ÷ 10 = $18.

STEP 2 The original price is $180. So, mark equal units from $0 to $180 on the left side of the model as shown.

STEP 3 Draw a line from 35% on the right side to the left side of the model.

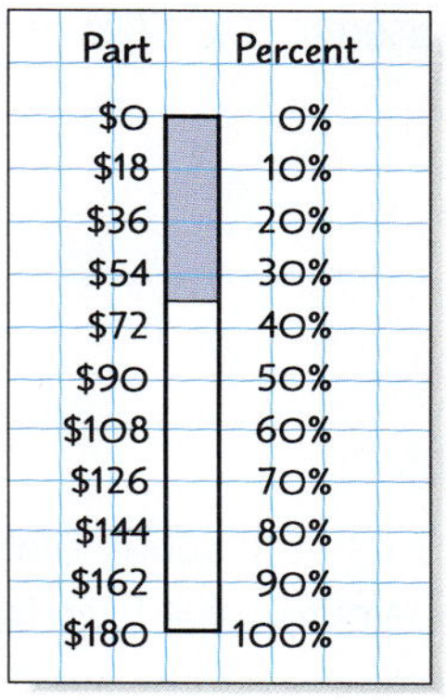

The model shows that 35% of $180 is halfway between $54 and $72, or $63.

So, you will save $63.

CHECK Your Progress d–f. See Ch. 7 Answer Appendix for models.

Draw a model to find the percent of each number. If it is not possible to find an exact answer from the model, estimate.

d. 25% of 140 **35** e. 7% of 50 **about 4** f. 0.5% of 20 **less than 1**

Analyze the Results 1–3. See margin.

1. Tell how to determine the units that get labeled on the left side of a percent model.
2. Explain how to find 40% of 30 using a model.
3. **REASONING** How does knowing 10% of a number help you find the percent of the number when the percent is a multiple of 10%?

Activity 2 If students have mastered the concept, ask them how they can use the model to find the sale price of the bicycle. Some will suggest subtracting the savings from the original price. Others will point out a shortcut: subtracting 35% from 100% to find the sale percent, and then drawing a line across the model at 65% to find the sale price ($117).

3 Assess

Formative Assessment

Use Exercise 2 to determine whether students understand how to use a model to find a percent of a number.

Extending the Concept Remind students that they can write a percent as a fraction or a decimal. Ask them how writing a percent as a fraction or a decimal might help them find the percent of a number. They would be able to multiply the number by the fraction or decimal.

Additional Answers

1. Sample answer: Take the original amount and divide by 10. The result gives the interval of the units that get labeled on the left side of the model.
2. Sample answer: Draw a line from 40% on the right side to the left side and estimate the amount on the left side of the model.
3. Sample answer: When you know 10% of a number and how many times 10% is a multiple of the number, you can multiply 10% of the number by how many times 10% is a multiple of the number to find the percent of the number.

Explore 7-1 Math Lab: Percent of a Number **343**

7-1 Percent of a Number

PACING: **Regular:** 1.5 periods, **Block:** 1 period

IN Academic Standards **Preparation for 7.1.8** Solve problems involving percents.
- Find the whole given a part and the percentage.
- Find percentage increase or decrease.

Options for Differentiated Instruction

ELL = English Language Learner AL = Above or Beyond Grade Level SS = Struggling Students SN = Special Needs

Using Models AL

Use after presenting the Examples.

Have students explain how the model can be used to find 60% of 300.

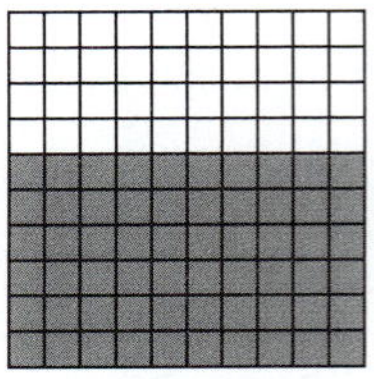

Sample answer: Each square represents 3. Sixty squares are shaded. So, 60% of 300 is 60×3 or 180.

Working in Pairs ELL SS SN

Use with Check Your Understanding.

Students with difficulty applying skills in an academic situation often are successful expressing what they know on an interpersonal level. Have students work in pairs to solve Exercises 1–7. Then have the pairs form groups of four and compare the steps and the strategies that they used to solve the problems.

Extensions and Challenges AL

Use after students complete Lesson 7-1.

Have students think about the percent problems they solved in Lesson 7-1. Ask them to use what they learned to answer the following questions:
- 45 is what percent of 150? 30%
- 240 is what percent of 400? 60%

Be sure they explain how they determined their answers. Then let them know they will learn the steps for solving problems like these in Lesson 7-2.

Leveled Lesson Resources

Also on TeacherWorks™ Lesson 7-1

Chapter 7 Resource Masters

BL = Below or Approaching Grade Level OL = On Grade Level AL = Above or Beyond Grade Level ELL = English Language Learner

Lesson Reading Guide
p. 9 BL OL ELL

NAME ______ DATE ______ PERIOD ____

7-1 Lesson Reading Guide

Percent of a Number

Get Ready for the Lesson

Read the introduction at the top of page 344 in your textbook. Write your answers below.

1. Sketch the model and label using decimals instead of percents.

Pet Shelter Fund-Raiser

0.0 0.1 0.2 0.3 0.4 0.5 0.6 0.7 0.8 0.9 1.0

0 200 400 600 800 1,000 1,200 1,400 1,600 1,800 2,000

2. Sketch the model using fractions instead of percents.

Pet Shelter Fund-Raiser

0 $\frac{1}{10}$ $\frac{2}{10}$ $\frac{3}{10}$ $\frac{4}{10}$ $\frac{5}{10}$ $\frac{6}{10}$ $\frac{7}{10}$ $\frac{8}{10}$ $\frac{9}{10}$ 1

0 200 400 600 800 1,000 1,200 1,400 1,600 1,800 2,000

3. Use these models to write two multiplication sentences that are equivalent to 60% of 2,000 = 1,200. $0.6 \times 2{,}000 = 1{,}200$; $\frac{3}{5} \times 2{,}000 = 1{,}200$

Read the Lesson

4. What are two methods for finding the percent of a number? Use a proportion, or use multiplication.

5. When writing a percent as a fraction to solve a percent problem, what is helpful to do to the percent before solving the problem? It is helpful to reduce the fraction to lowest terms.

6. What is unusual about the answer to a percent problem where the percent taken is larger than 100? The answer is larger than the original number.

Remember What You Learned

7. Suppose one of your friends said to you, "I want to pay for lunch and I know I'm supposed to leave a 15% tip, but I don't know how to figure out how much to leave." Write in your words what you would say to your friend to explain how to figure out the tip. Sample answer: Change 15% to a decimal: 0.15. Now, multiply 0.15 by the cost of lunch. The result is how much should be left for the tip.

Chapter 7 9 Course 2

Study Guide and Intervention*
p. 10 BL OL ELL

NAME ______ DATE ______ PERIOD ____

7-1 Study Guide and Intervention

Percent of a Number

You can use a proportion or multiplication to find the percent of a number.

Example 1 Find 25% of 80.

$25\% = \frac{25}{100}$ or $\frac{1}{4}$ Write 25% as a fraction, and reduce to lowest terms.

$\frac{1}{4}$ of $80 = \frac{1}{4} \times 80$ or 20 Multiply.

So, 25% of 80 is 20.

Example 2 What number is 15% of 200?

15% of $200 = 15\% \times 200$ Write a multiplication expression.

$= 0.15 \times 200$ Write 15% as a decimal.

$= 30$ Multiply.

So, 15% of 200 is 30.

Exercises

Find each number.

1. Find 20% of 50. 10
2. What is 55% of $400? $220
3. 5% of 1,500 is what number? 75
4. Find 190% of 20. 38
5. What is 24% of $500? $120
6. 8% of $300 is how much? $24
7. What is 12.5% of 60? 7.5
8. Find 0.2% of 40. 0.08
9. Find 3% of $800. $24
10. What is 0.5% of 180? 0.9
11. 0.25% of 42 is what number? 0.105
12. What is 0.02% of 280? 0.056

Chapter 7 10 Course 2

Skills Practice*
p. 11 BL OL

NAME ______ DATE ______ PERIOD ____

7-1 Skills Practice

Percent of a Number

Find each number.

1. Find 80% of 80. 64
2. What is 95% of 600? 570
3. 35% of 20 is what number? 7
4. Find 60% of $150. $90
5. What is 75% of 240? 180
6. 380% of 30 is what number? 114
7. Find 40% of 80. 32
8. What is 30% of $320? $96
9. 12% of 150 is what number? 18
10. Find 58% of 200. 116
11. What is 18% of $450? $81
12. What is 70% of 1,760? 1,232
13. Find 92% of 120. 110.4
14. 45% of 156 is what number? 70.2
15. What is 12% of 12? 1.44
16. Find 60% of 264. 158.4
17. 37.5% of 16 is what number? 6
18. What is 82.5% of 400? 330
19. What is 0.25% of 900? 2.25
20. Find 1.5% of 220. 3.3

Chapter 7 11 Course 2

Practice*
p. 12 OL AL

NAME ______ DATE ______ PERIOD ____

7-1 Practice

Percent of a Number

Find each number. Round to the nearest hundredth if necessary.

1. 55% of 140 77
2. 40% of 123 49.2
3. 37% of $150 $55.50
4. 25% of 96 24
5. 11% of $333 $36.63
6. 99% of 14 13.86
7. 140% of 30 42
8. 165% of 10 16.5
9. 150% of 150 225
10. 225% of 16 36
11. 106% of $40 $42.40
12. 126% of 350 441
13. 4.1% of 30 1.23
14. 8.9% of 75 6.68
15. 24.2% of $120 $29.04
16. 97.5% of 80 78

17. SALES Mr. Redding sells vehicles to 20% of the people that come to the sales lot. If 65 people came to the lot last month, how many vehicles did he sell? 13 vehicles

Find each number. Round to the nearest hundredth if necessary.

18. $\frac{5}{8}$% of 600 5
19. $30\frac{1}{3}$% of 3 0.91
20. 1,000% of 87 870
21. 100% of 56 56
22. 0.25% of 150 0.38
23. 0.7% of 50 0.35

ANALYZE TABLES For Exercises 24–26, use the table that shows the percents of blood types of 145 donors during a recent blood drive.

Blood Type	Percent
O	45%
A	40%
B	11%
AB	4%

24. Write a proportion that can be used to find how many donors had type B blood. Then solve. Round to the nearest whole if necessary. $\frac{n}{145} = \frac{11}{100}$; 16 donors

25. How many donors did *not* have type O blood? Round to the nearest whole if necessary. 80 donors

26. Which blood type had less than 10 donors? Type AB

Chapter 7 12 Course 2

Word Problem Practice*
p. 13 OL AL

NAME ______ DATE ______ PERIOD ____

7-1 Word Problem Practice

Percent of a Number

SPORTS For Exercises 1 and 2, use the graph below. It shows the results of a poll of 440 ninth grade students. Round answers to the nearest whole number.

PETS For Exercises 3 and 4, use the table below. It shows the pet ownership in Los Angeles, California. Assume that the same percents apply to a town of 1,650 households. Round answers to the nearest whole number.

Favorite Sports of Students

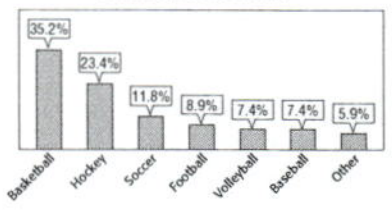

Pets in Household	Percent
at least one dog or cat	26.7
at least one dog	19.9
at least one cat	13
at least one dog and one cat	6.19

1. Write the percent as a fraction to find how many students surveyed chose hockey as their favorite sport. Solve. 103 students

2. How many students surveyed chose basketball as their favorite sport? 155 students

3. Write the percent as a decimal to find how many households have at least one dog. Solve. 328 households

4. How many households have at least one dog or cat? 441 households

5. VOTING Going into a recent election, only about 62% of people old enough to vote were registered. In a community of about 55,200 eligible voters, how many people are registered? 34,224 people

6. COLLEGE A local college recently reported that enrollment increased to 108% percent of last year. If enrollment last year was at 17,113, about how many students enrolled this year? Round to the nearest whole number. 18,482 students

Chapter 7 13 Course 2

Enrichment
p. 14 OL AL

NAME ______ DATE ______ PERIOD ____

7-1 Enrichment

Model Behavior

When a block is painted and then separated into small cubes, some of the faces of the cubes will have paint on them and some will not.

For each set of blocks determine the percent of cubes that are painted on the given number of faces.

1. 0 faces 0
2. 1 face 0
3. 2 faces 64
4. 3 faces 32
5. 4 faces 4
6. 5 faces 0
7. 6 faces 0

8. 0 faces 0
9. 1 face 0
10. 2 faces 0
11. 3 faces 0
12. 4 faces 90
13. 5 faces 10
14. 6 faces 0

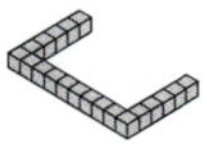

15. 0 faces 0
16. 1 face 0
17. 2 faces 0
18. 3 faces 0
19. 4 faces 100
20. 5 faces 0
21. 6 faces 0

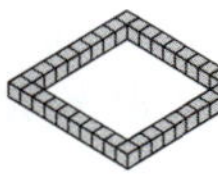

Chapter 7 14 Course 2

* Also available in Spanish ELL

Additional Lesson Resources

Transparencies

- *5-Minute Check Transparency,* Lesson 7-1

Other Print Products

- *Teaching Mathematics with Manipulatives*
- *Noteables™ Interactive Study Notebook with Foldables™*

Teacher Tech Tools

- *Interactive Classroom CD-ROM,* Lesson 7-1
- *AssignmentWorks,* Lesson 7-1

Student Tech Tools

glencoe.com

- Extra Examples, Chapter 7, Lesson 1
- Self-Check Quiz, Chapter 7, Lesson 1

7-1 Lesson Notes

1 Focus

Vertical Alignment

Before Lesson 7-1
Interpret percents as a part of a hundred; find decimal and percent equivalents for common fractions and explain why they represent the same value; compute a given percent of a whole number

Lesson 7-1
Calculate given percentages of quantities and solve problems

After Lesson 7-1
Convert fractions to decimals and percents and use these representations in estimations, computations, and applications; solve problems that involve discounts, markups, commissions, and profit and compute simple and compound interest

2 Teach

Scaffolding Questions

Ask:

- When would a percent be greater than one? When the percent is greater than 100%.
- If you multiplied a number by a percent less than 100%, would the result be less than or greater than the original number? less than
- What would you expect if the number you multiply by is greater than 100%? The result would be greater than the original number.
- What decimal is equivalent to 75%? 0.75
- What decimal is equivalent to 65%? 0.65
- What decimal is equivalent to 140%? 1.40

7-1 Percent of a Number

MAIN IDEA

Find the percent of a number.

IN Academic Standards

Preparation for 7.1.8 Solve problems involving percents.
- Find the whole given a part and the percentage
- Find percentage increase or decrease.

IN Math Online

glencoe.com
- Extra Examples
- Personal Tutor
- Self-Check Quiz

GET READY for the Lesson

PETS Some students are collecting money for a local pet shelter. The model shows that they have raised 60% of their \$2,000 goal or \$1,200.

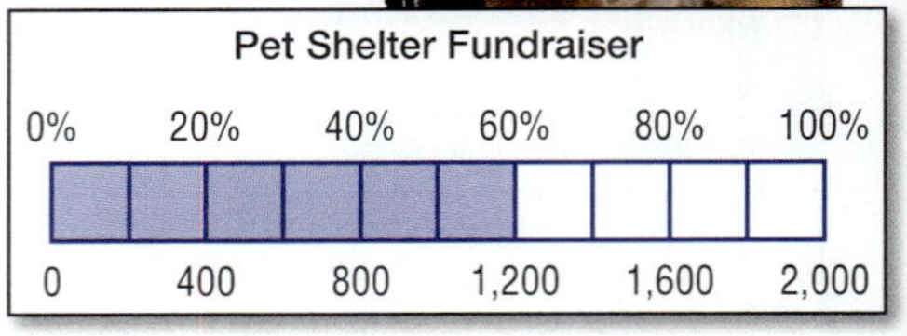

1. Sketch the model and label using decimals instead of percents.
2. Sketch the model using fractions instead of percents.
3. Use these models to write two multiplication sentences that are equivalent to 60% of 2,000 = 1,200. **1–3. See Ch. 7 Answer Appendix.**

To find the percent of a number such as 60% of 2,000, you can use one of the following methods.

- Write the percent as a fraction and then multiply, or
- Write the percent as a decimal and then multiply.

EXAMPLE Find the Percent of a Number

1 **Find 5% of 300.**

To find 5% of 300, you can use either method.

METHOD 1 **Write the percent as a fraction.**

$5\% = \frac{5}{100}$ or $\frac{1}{20}$

$\frac{1}{20}$ of $300 = \frac{1}{20} \times 300$ or 15

METHOD 2 **Write the percent as a decimal.**

$5\% = \frac{5}{100}$ or 0.05

0.05 of 300 = 0.05×300 or 15

So, 5% of 300 is 15.

CHOOSE Your Method

Find the percent of each number.

a. 40% of 70 **28** b. 15% of 100 **15** c. 55% of 160 **88**

Formative Assessment

Use the Check Your Progress exercises after each Example to determine students' understanding of concepts.

EXAMPLE Use Percents Greater Than 100%

2 **Find 120% of 75.**

Study Tip

Check for Reasonableness 120% is a little more than 100%. So, the answer should be a little more than 100% of 75 or a little more than 75.

METHOD 1 **Write the percent as a fraction.**

$120\% = \frac{120}{100} \text{ or } \frac{6}{5}$

$\frac{6}{5} \text{ of } 75 = \frac{6}{5} \times 75$

$= \frac{6}{5} \times \frac{75}{1} \text{ or } 90$

METHOD 2 **Write the percent as a decimal.**

$120\% = \frac{120}{100} \text{ or } 1.2$

$1.2 \text{ of } 75 = 1.2 \times 75 \text{ or } 90$

So, 120% of 75 is 90. Use a model to check the answer.

CHOOSE Your Method

Find each number.

d. 150% of 20 **30**

e. 160% of 35 **56**

Real-World EXAMPLE

3 **ANALYZE GRAPHS** **Refer to the graph. If 275 students took the survey, how many can be expected to have 3 televisions each in their houses?**

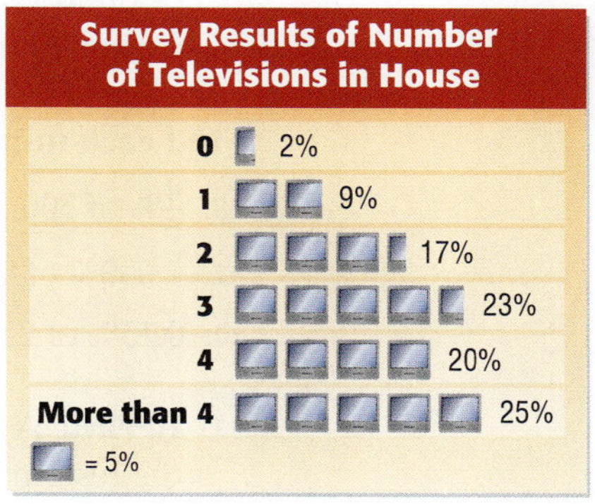

To find 23% of 275, write the percent as a decimal. Then multiply.

$23\% \text{ of } 275 = 23\% \times 275$

$= 0.23 \times 275$

$= 63.25$

So, about 63 students can be expected to have 3 televisions each in their houses.

CHECK Your Progress

f. **ANALYZE GRAPHS** Refer to the graph above. Suppose 455 students took the survey. How many can be expected to have more than 4 televisions each in their houses? **about 114 students**

Focus on Mathematical Content

One way to find the percent of a number is to **write the percent as a fraction** and then multiply.

Another way to find the percent of a number is to **write the percent as a decimal** and then multiply.

ADDITIONAL EXAMPLES

1 Find 8% of 125. 10

2 Find 125% of 64. 80

3 **LANGUAGES** The graph below shows that 30% of the people in a community speak Spanish as their first language. If a community has 800 people, how many people can be expected to speak Spanish as their first language? 240

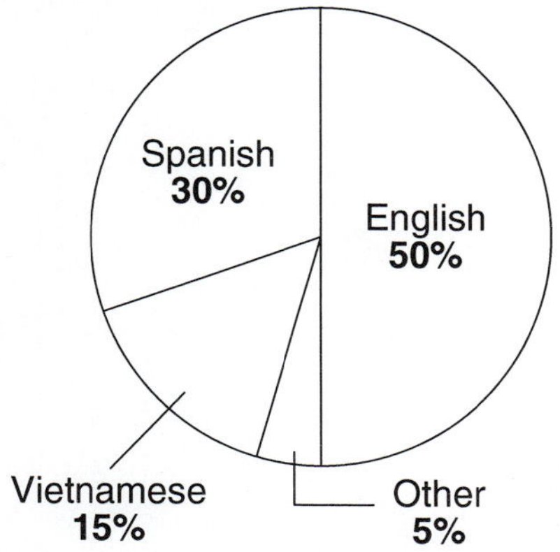

Additional Examples are also in:

- Noteables™ Interactive Study Notebook with Foldables™
- Interactive Classroom PowerPoint® Presentations

Tips for New Teachers

Writing Percents

You may wish to remind students how to write a percent as a decimal (move the decimal point two places to the left and remove the percent sign).

3 Practice

Formative Assessment

Use Exercises 1–7 to check for understanding.

Then use the chart at the bottom of this page to customize your assignments for students.

Intervention

You may wish to use the Study Guide and Intervention Master on page 10 of the *Chapter 7 Resource Masters* for additional reinforcement.

Odd/Even Assignments

Exercises 8–27 are structured so that students practice the same concepts whether they are assigned odd or even problems.

CHECK Your Understanding

★ indicates multi-step problem

Find each number. Round to the nearest tenth if necessary.

Examples 1–2 (pp. 344–345)

1. 8% of 50 **4**
2. 95% of 40 **38**
3. 42% of 263 **110.5**
4. 110% of 70 **77**
5. 115% of 20 **23**
6. 130% of 78 **101.4**

Example 3 (p. 345)

7. **TAXES** Mackenzie wants to buy a new backpack that costs $50. If the tax rate is 6.5%, how much tax will she pay when she buys the backpack? **$3.25**

Practice and Problem Solving

HOMEWORK HELP

For Exercises	See Examples
8–13, 20–25	1
14–19	2
26–27	3

Exercise Levels
A: 8–27
B: 28–52
C: 53–56

Find each number. Round to the nearest tenth if necessary.

8. 65% of 186 **120.9**
9. 45% of $432 **$194.40**
10. 23% of $640 **$147.20**
11. 54% of 85 **45.9**
12. 12% of $230 **$27.60**
13. 98% of 15 **14.7**
14. 130% of 20 **26**
15. 175% of 10 **17.5**
16. 150% of 128 **192**
17. 250% of 25 **62.5**
18. 108% of $50 **$54**
19. 116% of $250 **$290**
20. 3.2% of 40 **1.3**
21. 5.4% of 65 **3.5**
22. 23.5% of 128 **30.1**
23. 75.2% of 130 **97.8**
24. 67.5% of 76 **51.3**
25. 18.5% of 500 **92.5**

26. **BASEBALL** Tomás got on base 60% of the times he was up to bat. If he was up to bat 5 times, how many times did he get on base? **3**

27. **TELEVISION** In a recent year, 17.7% of households watched the finals of a popular reality series. There are 110.2 million television households in the United States. How many households watched the finals? **about 19.5 million**

Find each number. Round to the nearest hundredth if necessary.

28. $\frac{4}{5}$% of 500 **4**
29. $5\frac{1}{2}$% of 60 **3.3**
30. $20\frac{1}{4}$% of 3 **0.61**
31. 1,000% of 99 **990**
32. 100% of 79 **79**
33. 520% of 100 **520**
34. 0.15% of 250 **0.38**
35. 0.3% of 80 **0.24**
36. 0.28% of 50 **0.14**

★ 37. **TIPPING** A customer wants to tip 15% of the restaurant bill. How much change should there be after the tip if the customer pays with a $50 bill? **$9.75**

Sal's Bistro

Herbed Salmon	$16.25
Chicken Pasta	15.25
Iced Tea	1.75
Iced Tea	1.75
Total	$35.00

★ 38. **INTERNET** A family pays $19 each month for Internet access. Next month, the cost will increase 5%. After this increase, what will be the cost for the Internet access? **$19.95**

★ 39. **BUSINESS** A store sells a certain brand of a lawn mower for $275. Next year, the cost of the lawn mower will increase by 8%. What will be the cost of the lawn mower next year? **$297**

DIFFERENTIATED HOMEWORK OPTIONS

Level	Assignment	Two-Day Option	
BL Basic	8–27, 53, 54, 56–67	9–27 odd, 57, 58	8–26 even, 53, 54, 56, 59–67
OL Core	9–35 odd, 37–54, 56–67	8–27, 57, 58	28–54, 56, 59–67
AL Advanced/Pre-AP	28–63 (optional: 64–67)		

346 Chapter 7 Applying Percents

ANALYZE GRAPHS For Exercises 40–42, use the graph below that shows the results of a poll of 2,632 listeners. Round to the nearest whole number.

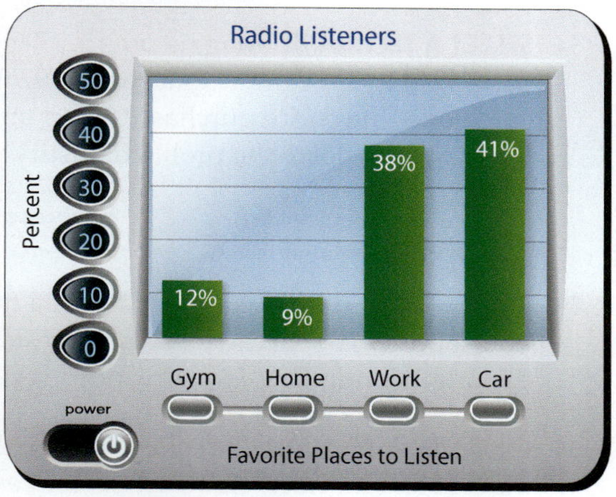

40. How many people listen to the radio during work? **1,000**
41. How many people like to listen to the radio while they are at the gym? **316**
42. Determine how many more people listen to the radio in the car than at home. **842**

Use mental math to find each percent. Justify your answer. **43–45. See margin.**

43. 53% of 60
44. 24% of 48
45. 75% of 19

Real-World Link California, the largest producer of peaches, produces about 60% of all the peaches, grown in the U.S.
Source: California Tree Fruit Agreement

ANALYZE GRAPHS For Exercises 46–49, use the graph that shows the results of a favorite fruit survey.

46. How many people were surveyed? **250**
47. Of those surveyed, how many people prefer peaches? **80**
48. Which type of fruit did more than 100 people prefer? **berries**
49. Of those surveyed, how many people did *not* prefer cherries? Explain how you arrived at the answer. **See margin.**

★ 50. **SHOPPING** The Leather Depot sells a certain leather coat for $179.99. If sales tax is 6.25%, what will be the approximate total cost of the coat? **Sample answer: about $191.24**

★ 51. **SCHOOL** Suppose there are 20 questions on a multiple-choice test. If 25% of the answers are choice B, how many of the answers are *not* choice B? **15**

★ 52. **COMMISSION** In addition to her salary, Ms. Lopez earns a 3% *commission*, or fee paid based on a percent of her sales, on every vacation package that she sells. One day, she sold the three vacation packages shown. What was her total commission? **$241.50**

Package #1	Package #2	Package #3
$2,375	$3,950	$1,725

Academic Standards • ISTEP+
Extra Practice, pp. 684, 710

Additional Answers

43. Sample answer: 53% of 60 → 50% × 60 or $\frac{1}{2} \times 60 = 30$

44. Sample answer: 24% of 48 → 25% × 48 or $\frac{1}{4} \times 48 = 12$

45. Sample answer: 75% of 19 → 75% × 20 or $\frac{3}{4} \times 20 = 15$

49. Sample answer: 24% × 250 or 60 people prefer cherries. So, 250 − 60 or 190 people did not prefer cherries.

Differentiated Instruction

Kinesthetic Learners Separate students into groups of three or four and give several index cards to each group. Have the members of each group write a percent on each index card. Students should then shuffle the cards, place them facedown in the middle, and turn the top card over. Each person uses a pencil and paper, calculator, or mental math to find the equivalent fraction or decimal. The first student to find an equivalent number gets a point. The first student with 10 points wins.

4 Assess

Name the Math Write a problem such as 1.4% of 25 on the board. Have students solve the problem and tell what mathematical procedures they used. Encourage them to use mental math.

FOLDABLES Study Organizer Foldables™ Follow-Up

Remind students to record both methods for finding a percent of a number in their Foldables table. Encourage students to use an original problem and explain how and why they might change a percent to a decimal or a fraction.

Additional Answer

53. Sample answer: Determine the number of questions answered correctly on a test and find how much to tip a restaurant server.

H.O.T. Problems

54. Sample answer: Estimation; $25 + $20 = $45. A 7% sales tax would add $3.15. Since $45 + $3.15 = $48.15, the gift card will cover the entire purchase.

55. Less than the original number; you are subtracting 10% of a greater number.

53. **OPEN ENDED** Give two examples of real-world situations in your life in which you would find the percent of a number. See margin.

54. **SELECT A TECHNIQUE** Maggie uses a $50 gift card to buy a pair of shoes that costs $24.99 and a purse that costs $19.99. If the tax rate is 7%, will the gift card cover the entire purchase? Select and use one or more of the following techniques to solve the problem. Justify your selection(s).

mental math	number sense	estimation

55. **CHALLENGE** Suppose you add 10% of a number to the number, and then you subtract 10% of the total. Is the result *greater than*, *less than*, or *equal to* the original number? Explain your reasoning.

56. **WRITING IN MATH** Explain which method you prefer to use to find the percent of a number: write the percent as a fraction or write the percent as a decimal. Explain your reasoning. See students' work.

ISTEP+ PRACTICE Preparation for 7.1.8

57. Reggie has memorized 60% of the 50 state capitals for a social studies test. How many more capitals does Reggie need to memorize before the test? C

A 35 C 20
B 30 D 18

58. **SHORT RESPONSE** Tanner has 200 baseball cards. Of those, 42% are in mint condition. How many of the cards are *not* in mint condition? 116

Spiral Review

59. **PETS** In Rebecca's class, 17 out of 24 students have pets. What percent of the students have pets? Round to the nearest percent. (Lesson 6-9) 71%

60. **MODELS** On a scale model of a building, 3 in. = 12 ft. If the model is 8 inches tall, how tall is the actual building? (Lesson 6-8) 32 ft

Add or subtract. Write in simplest form. (Lesson 6-2)

61. $\frac{7}{10} - \frac{1}{10}$ $\frac{3}{5}$ 62. $\frac{20}{21} - \frac{3}{7}$ $\frac{11}{21}$ 63. $\frac{5}{6} - \frac{1}{8}$ $\frac{17}{24}$

64. **ALGEBRA** What are the next three numbers in the pattern 3, 10, 17, 24, …? (Lesson 1-9) 31, 38, 45

GET READY for the Next Lesson

PREREQUISITE SKILL Solve each equation. (Lesson 3-3)

65. $12b = 144$ 12 66. $9x = 630$ 70 67. $8,100 = 100k$ 81

READING to SOLVE PROBLEMS

Meaning of Percent

When you solve percent problems, look for three parts: the *part*, the *whole*, and the *percent*. Consider this example.

The table at the right shows the results of a survey about favorite flavor of sugarless gum.

- **Part**

  Ten students chose cinnamon as their favorite.

- **Whole**

  Forty students were surveyed.

- **Percent**

  25% of the students who were surveyed (10 out of 40) chose cinnamon as their favorite.

Using all three parts, 25% of 40 is 10.

Academic Standards **7.1.8 Solve problems involving percents.**
- Find the whole given a part and the percentage
- Find percentage increase or decrease.

Favorite Flavor of Sugarless Gum

Flavor	Number
Cinnamon	10
Peppermint	18
Watermelon	12
Total	40

PRACTICE

Identify each statement as the *part,* the *whole,* or the *percent.* Then write a sentence using all three parts.

1. The table at the right shows the results of a survey about which "bugs" people dislike most.
   a. Fifty people were surveyed.
   b. 60% disliked spiders the most.
   c. Thirty people disliked spiders.

Least Favorite "Bug"

Kind	Number
Centipede	2
Cockroach	18
Spider	30
Total	50

2. Suppose you find a sale at the mall.
   a. Everything was 20% off.
   b. The original price of a jacket was $30.
   c. You saved $6.
3. You and your family are eating at a restaurant.
   a. The meal cost $34.
   b. You want to leave a tip of 15%.
   c. The tip is $5.10.
4. Your sister plays basketball.
   a. She usually makes 75% of her free throws.
   b. In the last game, she made 6 free throws.
   c. She had 8 free throws.

READING to SOLVE PROBLEMS

1 Focus

For students to master percents, they need to understand that a percent is a ratio of one number (or quantity) to another. In this Activity, students learn to identify percents, the numbers that make up the percents' ratios, and their relationship.

2 Teach

Make sure everyone understands the relationship among a percent, a whole, and a part (a percent **of** a whole **is** a part). After students have completed one or two of the exercises, you might want to write sample sentences on the board to make sure everyone understands the relationship. For example:

- *A*% **of** whole *B* **is** part *C*
- Part *C* **is** *A*% **of** whole *B*

3 Assess

Remind students that yesterday's lesson was about finding the percent of a number. Have students write how yesterday's material helped them with this reading activity.

7-2 The Percent Proportion

PACING: **Regular:** 1 period, **Block:** 0.5 period

IN Academic Standards

7.1.8 Solve problems involving percents.

- **Find the whole given a part and the percentage.**
- Find percentage increase or decrease.

Also addresses 7.1.9.

Options for Differentiated Instruction

ELL = English Language Learner | AL = Above or Beyond Grade Level | SS = Struggling Students | SN = Special Needs

Creating a Template ELL SS

Use with the Exercises.

Explain to students that they can use a percent proportion to find a missing part, whole, or percent. Have them create the following template. Provide clear sheet protectors so students can use the template to help them complete the exercises.

Find the percent: $\frac{\text{part} \rightarrow}{\text{whole} \rightarrow} \frac{\square}{\square} = \frac{n}{100} \Big\} \text{percent}$

Find the part: $\frac{\text{part} \rightarrow}{\text{whole} \rightarrow} \frac{n}{\square} = \frac{\square}{100} \Big\} \text{percent}$

Find the whole: $\frac{\text{part} \rightarrow}{\text{whole} \rightarrow} \frac{\square}{n} = \frac{\square}{100} \Big\} \text{percent}$

For students with fine motor skills difficulties, provide a typed version of the template, making sure that the boxes are large enough for students to write in.

Creating a Checklist ELL SS SN

Use before assigning the Exercises.

Have students create a checklist they can use for solving proportions. A sample checklist is shown below.

- Identify what I need to find: *Percent*, *Part*, or *Whole*.
- Fill in the proportion with the given information.
- Find the cross products.
- Solve.

Leveled Lesson Resources

Also on **TeacherWorks™**
Lesson 7-2

Chapter 7 Resource Masters

BL = Below or Approaching Grade Level **OL** = On Grade Level **AL** = Above or Beyond Grade Level **ELL** = English Language Learner

Lesson Reading Guide
p. 16 BL OL ELL

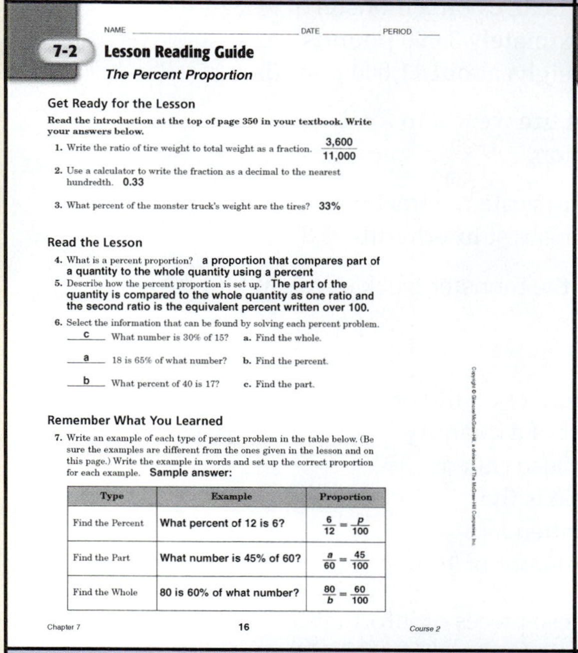
NAME ____ DATE ____ PERIOD ____

7-2 Lesson Reading Guide
The Percent Proportion

Get Ready for the Lesson

Read the introduction at the top of page 350 in your textbook. Write your answers below.

1. Write the ratio of tire weight to total weight as a fraction. 3,600/11,000
2. Use a calculator to write the fraction as a decimal to the nearest hundredth. 0.33
3. What percent of the monster truck's weight are the tires? 33%

Read the Lesson

4. What is a percent proportion? a proportion that compares part of a quantity to the whole quantity using a percent
5. Describe how the percent proportion is set up. The part of the quantity is compared to the whole quantity as one ratio and the second ratio is the equivalent percent written over 100.
6. Select the information that can be found by solving each percent problem.
c What number is 30% of 15? a. Find the whole.
a 18 is 65% of what number? b. Find the percent.
b What percent of 40 is 17? c. Find the part.

Remember What You Learned

7. Write an example of each type of percent problem in the table below. (Be sure the examples are different from the ones given in the lesson and on this page.) Write the example in words and set up the correct proportion for each example. Sample answer:

Type	Example	Proportion
Find the Percent	What percent of 12 is 6?	$\frac{6}{12} = \frac{p}{100}$
Find the Part	What number is 45% of 60?	$\frac{a}{60} = \frac{45}{100}$
Find the Whole	80 is 60% of what number?	$\frac{80}{b} = \frac{60}{100}$

Chapter 7 16 Course 2

*Study Guide and Intervention**
p. 17 BL OL ELL

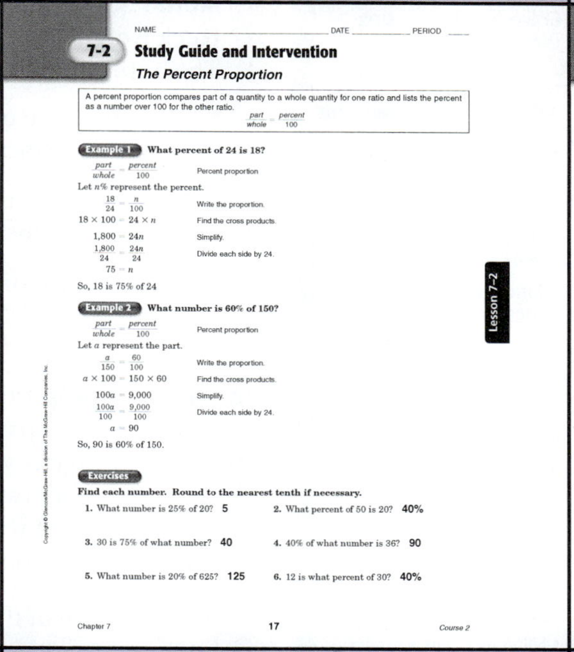
NAME ____ DATE ____ PERIOD ____

7-2 Study Guide and Intervention
The Percent Proportion

A percent proportion compares part of a quantity to a whole quantity for one ratio and lists the percent as a number over 100 for the other ratio. $\frac{part}{whole} = \frac{percent}{100}$

Example 1 What percent of 24 is 18?

$\frac{part}{whole} = \frac{percent}{100}$ Percent proportion
Let n% represent the percent.
$\frac{18}{24} = \frac{n}{100}$ Write the proportion.
$18 \times 100 = 24 \times n$ Find the cross products.
$1{,}800 = 24n$ Simplify.
$\frac{1{,}800}{24} = \frac{24n}{24}$ Divide each side by 24.
$75 = n$
So, 18 is 75% of 24.

Example 2 What number is 60% of 150?

$\frac{part}{whole} = \frac{percent}{100}$ Percent proportion
Let a represent the part.
$\frac{a}{150} = \frac{60}{100}$ Write the proportion.
$a \times 100 = 150 \times 60$ Find the cross products.
$100a = 9{,}000$ Simplify.
$\frac{100a}{100} = \frac{9{,}000}{100}$ Divide each side by 24.
$a = 90$
So, 90 is 60% of 150.

Exercises
Find each number. Round to the nearest tenth if necessary.
1. What number is 25% of 20? 5
2. What percent of 50 is 20? 40%
3. 30 is 75% of what number? 40
4. 40% of what number is 36? 90
5. What number is 20% of 625? 125
6. 12 is what percent of 30? 40%

Chapter 7 17 Course 2

*Skills Practice**
p. 18 BL OL

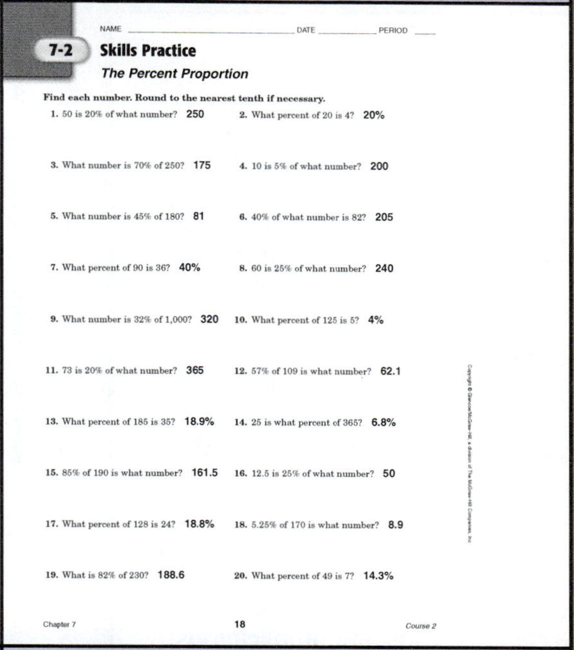
NAME ____ DATE ____ PERIOD ____

7-2 Skills Practice
The Percent Proportion

Find each number. Round to the nearest tenth if necessary.
1. 50 is 20% of what number? 250
2. What percent of 20 is 4? 20%
3. What number is 70% of 250? 175
4. 10 is 5% of what number? 200
5. What number is 45% of 180? 81
6. 40% of what number is 82? 205
7. What percent of 90 is 36? 40%
8. 60 is 25% of what number? 240
9. What number is 32% of 1,000? 320
10. What percent of 125 is 5? 4%
11. 73 is 20% of what number? 365
12. 57% of 109 is what number? 62.1
13. What percent of 185 is 35? 18.9%
14. 25 is what percent of 365? 6.8%
15. 85% of 190 is what number? 161.5
16. 12.5 is 25% of what number? 50
17. What percent of 128 is 24? 18.8%
18. 5.25% of 170 is what number? 8.9
19. What is 82% of 230? 188.6
20. What percent of 49 is 7? 14.3%

Chapter 7 18 Course 2

*Practice**
p. 19 OL AL

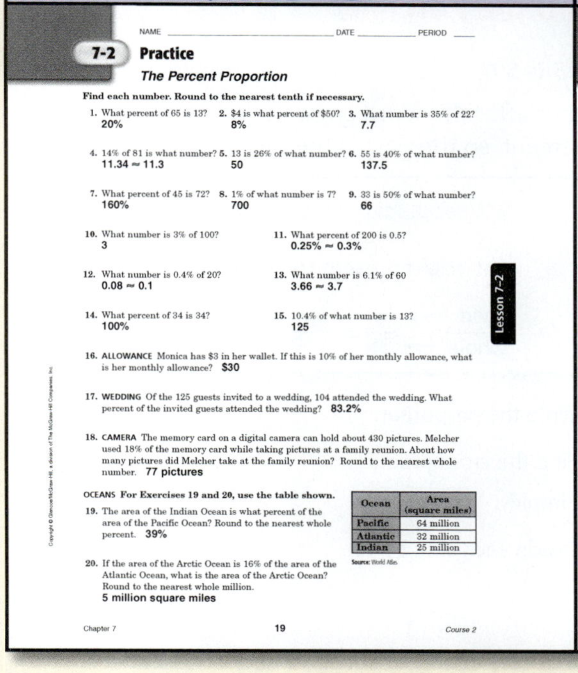
NAME ____ DATE ____ PERIOD ____

7-2 Practice
The Percent Proportion

Find each number. Round to the nearest tenth if necessary.
1. What percent of 65 is 13? 20%
2. $4 is what percent of $50? 8%
3. What number is 35% of 22? 7.7
4. 14% of 81 is what number? 11.34 ≈ 11.3
5. 13 is 26% of what number? 50
6. 55 is 40% of what number? 137.5
7. What percent of 45 is 72? 160%
8. 1% of what number is 7? 700
9. 33 is 50% of what number? 66
10. What number is 3% of 100? 3
11. What percent of 200 is 0.5? 0.25% ≈ 0.3%
12. What number is 0.4% of 20? 0.08 ≈ 0.1
13. What number is 6.1% of 60 3.66 ≈ 3.7
14. What percent of 34 is 34? 100%
15. 10.4% of what number is 13? 125
16. ALLOWANCE Monica has $3 in her wallet. If this is 10% of her monthly allowance, what is her monthly allowance? $30
17. WEDDING Of the 125 guests invited to a wedding, 104 attended the wedding. What percent of the invited guests attended the wedding? 83.2%
18. CAMERA The memory card on a digital camera can hold about 430 pictures. Melcher used 18% of the memory card while taking pictures at a family reunion. About how many pictures did Melcher take at the family reunion? Round to the nearest whole number. 77 pictures

OCEANS For Exercises 19 and 20, use the table shown.

Ocean	Area (square miles)
Pacific	64 million
Atlantic	32 million
Indian	25 million

Source: World Atlas

19. The area of the Indian Ocean is what percent of the area of the Pacific Ocean? Round to the nearest whole percent. 39%
20. If the area of the Arctic Ocean is 16% of the area of the Atlantic Ocean, what is the area of the Arctic Ocean? Round to the nearest whole million. 5 million square miles

Chapter 7 19 Course 2

*Word Problem Practice**
p. 20 OL AL

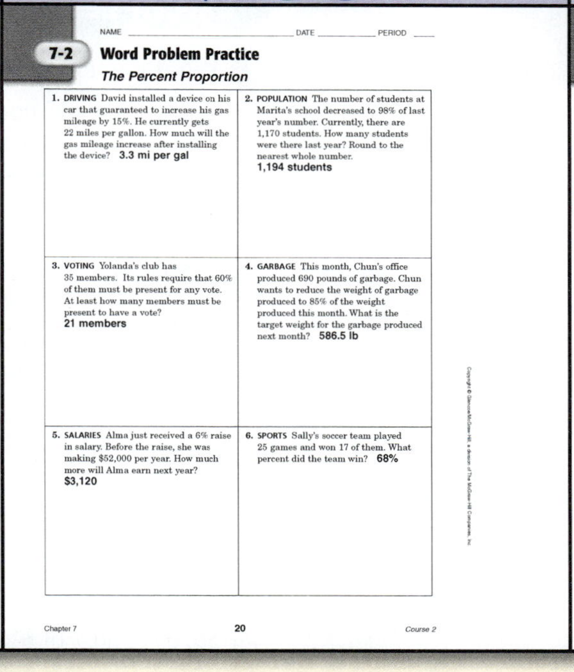
NAME ____ DATE ____ PERIOD ____

7-2 Word Problem Practice
The Percent Proportion

1. DRIVING David installed a device on his car that guaranteed to increase his gas mileage by 15%. He currently gets 22 miles per gallon. How much will the gas mileage increase after installing the device? 3.3 mi per gal
2. POPULATION The number of students at Marita's school decreased to 98% of last year's number. Currently, there are 1,170 students. How many students were there last year? Round to the nearest whole number. 1,194 students
3. VOTING Yolanda's club has 35 members. Its rules require that 60% of them must be present for any vote. At least how many members must be present to have a vote? 21 members
4. GARBAGE This month, Chun's office produced 690 pounds of garbage. Chun wants to reduce the weight of garbage produced to 85% of the weight produced this month. What is the target weight for the garbage produced next month? 586.5 lb
5. SALARIES Alma just received a 6% raise in salary. Before the raise, she was making $52,000 per year. How much more will Alma earn next year? $3,120
6. SPORTS Sally's soccer team played 25 games and won 17 of them. What percent did the team win? 68%

Chapter 7 20 Course 2

Enrichment
p. 21 OL AL

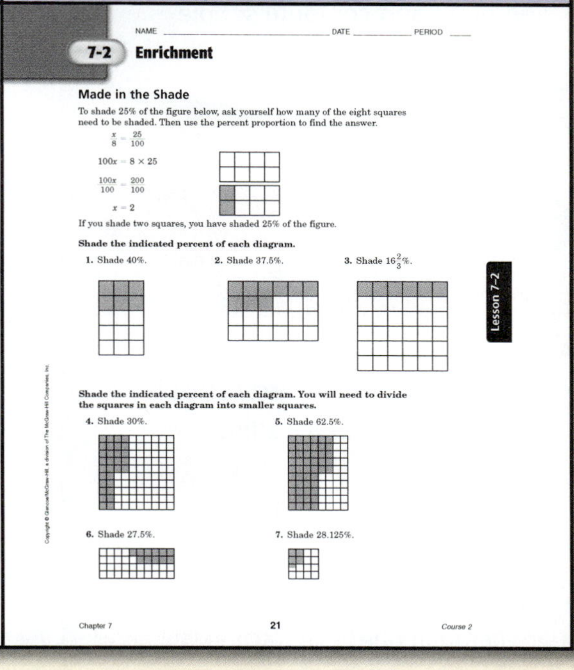
NAME ____ DATE ____ PERIOD ____

7-2 Enrichment

Made in the Shade

To shade 25% of the figure below, ask yourself how many of the eight squares need to be shaded. Then use the percent proportion to find the answer.

$\frac{x}{8} = \frac{25}{100}$
$100x = 8 \times 25$
$\frac{100x}{100} = \frac{200}{100}$
$x = 2$

If you shade two squares, you have shaded 25% of the figure.

Shade the indicated percent of each diagram.
1. Shade 40%.
2. Shade 37.5%.
3. Shade $16\frac{2}{3}$%.

Shade the indicated percent of each diagram. You will need to divide the squares in each diagram into smaller squares.
4. Shade 30%.
5. Shade 62.5%.
6. Shade 27.5%.
7. Shade 28.125%.

Chapter 7 21 Course 2

* *Also available in Spanish* ELL

Additional Lesson Resources

Transparencies
- *5-Minute Check Transparency*, Lesson 7-2

Other Print Products
- *Noteables™ Interactive Study Notebook with Foldables™*

Teacher Tech Tools
- *Interactive Classroom CD-ROM*, Lesson 7-2
- *AssignmentWorks*, Lesson 7-2

Student Tech Tools
glencoe.com
- Extra Examples, Chapter 7, Lesson 2
- Self-Check Quiz, Chapter 7, Lesson 2

7-2 Lesson Notes

1 Focus

Vertical Alignment

Before Lesson 7-2
Interpret percents as a part of a hundred; find decimal and percent equivalents for common fractions and explain why they represent the same value; compute a given percent of a whole number

Lesson 7-2
Use proportions to solve problems; calculate given percentages of quantities and solve problems

After Lesson 7-2
Convert fractions to decimals and percents and use these representations in estimations, computations, and applications; solve problems that involve discounts, markups, commissions, and profit and compute simple and compound interest

2 Teach

Scaffolding Questions

Ask:

- How can you write a percent that is greater than 100 as a fraction? write the percent in the numerator and write one hundred in the denominator
- Will the fraction be less than or greater than one? The fraction will be greater than 1.

Formative Assessment

Use the Check Your Progress exercises after each Example to determine students' understanding of concepts.

7-2 The Percent Proportion

MAIN IDEA

Solve problems using the percent proportion.

IN Academic Standards

7.1.8 Solve problems involving percents.

- **Find the whole given a part and the percentage**
- Find percentage increase or decrease.

Also addresses 7.1.9.

New Vocabulary

percent proportion

IN Math Online

glencoe.com

- Extra Examples
- Personal Tutor
- Self-Check Quiz
- Reading in the Content Area

GET READY for the Lesson

MONSTER TRUCKS The tires on a monster truck weigh approximately 3,600 pounds. The entire truck weighs about 11,000 pounds.

1. Write the ratio of tire weight to total weight as a fraction. $\frac{3,600}{11,000}$
2. Use a calculator to write the fraction as a decimal to the nearest hundredth. 0.33
3. What percent of the monster truck's weight is the tires? 33%

In a **percent proportion**, one ratio or fraction compares part of a quantity to the whole quantity, also called the *base*. The other ratio is the equivalent percent written as a fraction with a denominator of 100.

4 out of **5** is **80%.**

part → $\frac{4}{5} = \frac{80}{100}$ } percent
whole →

When given two of these pieces of information—part, whole, or percent—you can use the proportion to find the missing information.

EXAMPLE Find the Percent

1 **What percent of $15 is $9?**

The number 15 comes after the word *of*, so the whole is 15. You are asked to find the percent, so the part is the remaining number, 9.

Words	What percent of $15 is $9?
Variable	Let n% represent the percent.
Proportion	part → $\frac{9}{15} = \frac{n}{100}$ } percent (whole →)

$\frac{9}{15} = \frac{n}{100}$ Write the proportion.

$9 \cdot 100 = 15 \cdot n$ Find the cross products.

$900 = 15n$ Simplify.

$\frac{900}{15} = \frac{15n}{15}$ Divide each side by 15.

$60 = n$

So, $9 is 60% of $15.

ADDITIONAL EXAMPLE

1 What percent of 24 is 18? 75%

Additional Examples are also in:

- Noteables™ Interactive Study Notebook with Foldables™
- Interactive Classroom PowerPoint® Presentations

CHECK Your Progress

Find each number. Round to the nearest tenth if necessary.

a. What percent of 25 is 20? **80%** b. $12.75 is what percent of $50? **25.5%**

EXAMPLE Find the Part

2 What number is 40% of 120?

The percent is 40%. Since the number 120 comes after the word *of*, the whole is 120. You are asked to find the part.

Words	What number is 40% of 120?
Variable	Let p represent the part.
Proportion	part → whole → $\frac{p}{120} = \frac{40}{100}$ } percent

$\frac{p}{120} = \frac{40}{100}$ Write the proportion.

$p \cdot 100 = 120 \cdot 40$ Find the cross products.

$100p = 4{,}800$ Simplify.

$\frac{100p}{100} = \frac{4{,}800}{100}$ Divide each side by 100.

$p = 48$

So, 48 is 40% of 120.

CHECK Your Progress

Find each number. Round to the nearest tenth if necessary.

c. What number is 5% of 60? **3** d. 12% of 85 is what number? **10.2**

Study Tip

The Percent Proportion The part usually comes before or after the word *is* and the whole usually comes before or after the word *of*.

EXAMPLE Find the Whole

3 18 is 25% of what number?

The percent is 25%. The words *what number* come after the word *of*. So, you are asked to find the whole. Thus, 18 is the part.

Words	18 is 25% of what number?
Variable	Let w represent the whole.
Proportion	part → whole → $\frac{18}{w} = \frac{25}{100}$ } percent

(continued on the next page)

Focus on Mathematical Content

A **percent proportion** shows the equality of two ratios. One ratio compares part of a quantity to the whole quantity; the other ratio shows a percent written as a fraction.

To solve a percent proportion, **find the cross products** and simplify.

ADDITIONAL EXAMPLES

2 What number is 30% of 150? **45**

3 12 is 80% of what number? **15**

Tips for New Teachers: Percent Proportion

To help students remember how the percent proportion is described in word problems, you may wish to write the following version on the board.

$$\frac{\text{is}}{\text{of}} = \frac{\%}{100}$$

ADDITIONAL EXAMPLE

4 **BREAKFAST** Sally read the nutrition facts on a box of her favorite cereal. Each cup of the cereal provides 7% of the recommended daily value of potassium. If a cup of the cereal contains 260 milligrams of potassium, what is the recommended daily value of potassium? 3,714 mg

$$\frac{18}{w} = \frac{25}{100}$$ Write the proportion.

$$18 \cdot 100 = w \cdot 25$$ Find the cross products.

$$1{,}800 = 25w$$ Simplify.

$$\frac{1{,}800}{25} = \frac{25w}{25}$$ Divide each side by 25.

$$72 = w$$

So, 18 is 25% of 72.

CHECK Your Progress

Find each number. Round to the nearest tenth if necessary.

e. 40% of what number is 26? 65

f. 80 is 75% of what number? 106.7

Real-World EXAMPLE

Real-World Link Male Western Lowland gorillas weigh about 350–400 pounds. Females weigh about 160–200 pounds.

Source: Columbus Zoo and Aquarium

4 **ANIMALS The average adult male Western Lowland gorilla eats about 33.5 pounds of fruit each day. How much food does the average adult male gorilla eat each day?**

Western Lowland Gorilla's Diet	
Food	**Percent**
Fruit	67%
Seeds, Leaves, Stems, and Pith	17%
Insects/ Insect Larvae	16%

You know that 33.5 pounds of fruit is 67% of the total amount eaten daily. So, the problem asks 33.5 is 67% of what number. Thus, you need to find the whole.

$$\frac{33.5}{w} = \frac{67}{100}$$ Write the proportion.

$$33.5 \cdot 100 = w \cdot 67$$ Find the cross products.

$$3{,}350 = 67w$$ Simplify.

$$\frac{3{,}350}{67} = \frac{67w}{67}$$ Divide each side by 67.

$$50 = w$$

So, the average adult male gorilla eats 50 pounds of food each day.

CHECK Your Progress

g. **ZOO** If 200 of the 550 reptiles in a zoo are on display, what percent of the reptiles are on display? Round to the nearest whole number. 36%

Types of Percent Problems

Key Concept

Type	Example	Proportion
Find the Percent	What percent of 6 is 3?	$\frac{3}{6} = \frac{n}{100}$
Find the Part	What number is 50% of 6?	$\frac{p}{6} = \frac{50}{100}$
Find the Whole	3 is 50% of what number?	$\frac{3}{w} = \frac{50}{100}$

352 Chapter 7 Applying Percents

★ indicates multi-step problem

CHECK Your Understanding

Examples 1–3 (pp. 350–352)

Find each number. Round to the nearest tenth if necessary.

1. What percent of 50 is 18? **36%**
2. What percent of $90 is $9? **10%**
3. What number is 2% of 35? **0.7**
4. What number is 25% of 180? **45**
5. 9 is 12% of which number? **75**
6. 62 is 90.5% of what number? **68.5**

Example 4 (p. 352)

7. **MEASUREMENT** If a box of Brand A cereal contains 10 cups of cereal, how many more cups of cereal are in a box of Brand B cereal? **3 c**

Practice and Problem Solving

HOMEWORK HELP	
For Exercises	See Examples
8–11	1, 2
12–17	3
18–21	4
22, 23	5

Exercise Levels
A: 8–17
B: 18–29
C: 30–32

Find each number. Round to the nearest tenth if necessary.

8. What percent of 60 is 15? **25%**
9. $3 is what percent of $40? **7.5%**
10. What number is 15% of 60? **9**
11. 12% of 72 is what number? **8.6**
12. 9 is 45% of what number? **20**
13. 75 is 20% of what number? **375**
14. **SCHOOL** Roman has 2 red pencils in his backpack. If this is 25% of the total number of pencils, how many pencils are in his backpack? **8**
15. **BASKETBALL** Lisa and Michelle scored 48% of their team's points. If their team had a total of 50 points, how many points did they score? **24**
16. **SHOES** A pair of sneakers are on sale as shown. This is 75% of the original price. What was the original price of the shoes? **$68**
17. **BOOKS** Of the 60 books on a bookshelf, 24 are nonfiction. What percent of the books are nonfiction? **40%**

Find each number. Round to the nearest hundredth if necessary.

18. What percent of 25 is 30? **120%**
19. What number is 8.2% of 50? **4.1**
20. 40 is 50% of what number? **80**
21. 12.5% of what number is 24? **192**
22. What number is 0.5% of 8? **0.04**
23. What percent of 300 is 0.6? **0.2%**

★ 24. **BUSINESS** The first week of June, there were 404 customers at an ice cream parlor. Eight weeks later, the number of customers was 175% of this amount. How many customers were there eight weeks later? **707 customers**

★ 25. **MONEY** Ajamu saves 40% of his allowance each week. If he saves $16 in 5 weeks, how much allowance does Ajamu receive each week? **$8**

★ 26. **SCHOOL** A class picture includes 95% of the students. Seven students were absent. How many students are in the class? **140**

3 Practice

Formative Assessment

Use Exercises 1–7 to check for understanding.

Then use the chart at the bottom of this page to customize your assignments for students.

Intervention You may wish to use the Study Guide and Intervention Master on page 17 of the *Chapter 7 Resource Masters* for additional reinforcement.

Odd/Even Assignments

Exercises 8–17 are structured so that students practice the same concepts whether they are assigned odd or even problems.

Focus on Mathematical Content

Percent Greater than 100
Point out to students that when the percent is greater than 100, such as in Exercise 24, the part will be greater than the whole. This indicates an increase in the original quantity.

DIFFERENTIATED HOMEWORK OPTIONS

Level	Assignment	Two-Day Option	
BL Basic	8–17, 30, 32–43	9–17 odd, 33, 34	8–16 even, 30, 32, 35–43
OL Core	9–23 odd, 24–30, 32–43	8–17, 33, 34	18–30, 32, 35–43
AL Advanced/Pre-AP	18–40 (optional: 41–43)		

Lesson 7-2 The Percent Proportion 353

4 Assess

Ticket Out the Door Ask students who are wearing red to raise their hands. Have students use the percent proportion to find what percent of the class is wearing red.

Formative Assessment

Check for student understanding of concepts in Lessons 7-1 and 7-2.

CRM Quiz 1, p. 61

FOLDABLES Study Organizer Foldables™ Follow-Up

Remind students to record how to use the percent proportion to find the missing part, whole, or percent in their Foldables tables, along with examples.

Additional Answer

31. 20% of 500, 20% of 100, 5% of 100; If the percent is the same but the base is greater, then the part is greater. If the base is the same but the percent is greater, then the part is greater.

ASTRONOMY For Exercises 27–29, use the table shown.

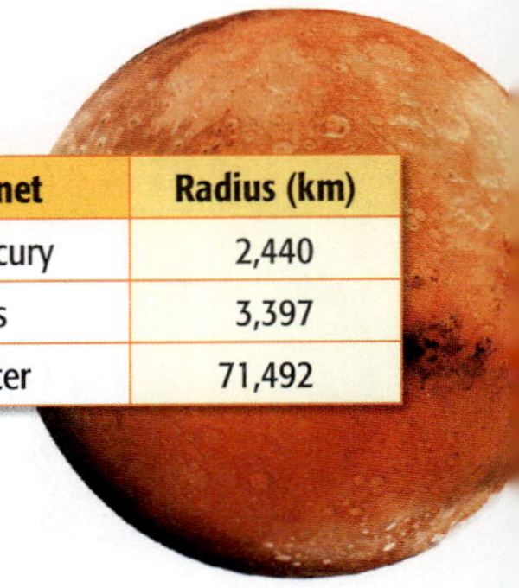

Planet	Radius (km)
Mercury	2,440
Mars	3,397
Jupiter	71,492

27. Mercury's radius is what percent of Jupiter's radius? **about 3.4%**

28. If the radius of Mars is about 13.7% of Neptune's radius, what is the radius of Neptune? **about 24,800 km**

Academic Standards • ISTEP+
Extra Practice, pp. 685, 710

29. Earth's radius is about 261.4% of Mercury's radius. What is the radius of Earth? **about 6,378 km**

H.O.T. Problems

30. **OPEN ENDED** Write a proportion that can be used to find the percent scored on a science quiz that has 10 questions. **Sample answer: $\frac{8}{10} = \frac{x}{100}$**

31. **CHALLENGE** Without calculating, arrange the following from greatest to least value. Justify your reasoning. **See margin.**

20% of 100, 20% of 500, 5% of 100

32. **WRITING IN MATH** Create a problem involving a percent that can be solved by using the proportion $\frac{3}{b} = \frac{15}{100}$.

32. Sample answer: A runner won 15% of the races he ran. If he won 3 races, how many races did he run?

ISTEP+ PRACTICE 7.1.8, 7.1.9

33. Of the 273 students in a school, 95 volunteered to work the book sale. About what percent of the students did *not* volunteer? **B**

A 55%
B 65%
C 70%
D 75%

34. A customer at a restaurant leaves a tip of $2.70. This amount is 15% of the total bill. Which equation can be used to find x, the total amount of the food bill? **G**

F $\frac{2.70}{15} = \frac{15}{100}$
G $\frac{2.70}{x} = \frac{15}{100}$
H $\frac{15}{2.70} = \frac{x}{100}$
J $\frac{x}{2.70} = \frac{15}{100}$

Spiral Review

Find each number. Round to the nearest tenth if necessary. (Lesson 7-1)

35. What is 25% of 120? **30**

36. Find 45% of 70. **31.5**

37. **PLANTS** A plant was 275% taller than the month before. What decimal represents this percent? (Lesson 6-9) **2.75**

MEASUREMENT Complete. (Lesson 6-4)

38. 3,000 lb = ■ T **1.5**

39. 36 in. = ■ ft **3**

40. $4\frac{1}{2}$ lb = ■ oz **72**

GET READY for the Next Lesson

PREREQUISITE SKILL Multiply. (Lesson 5-5)

41. $\frac{1}{2} \cdot 60$ **30**

42. $\frac{3}{4} \cdot 28$ **21**

43. $\frac{2}{5} \cdot 45$ **18**

7-3 Percent and Estimation

PACING: **Regular:** 1 period, **Block:** 0.5 period

IN Academic Standards **Preparation for 7.1.8** Solve problems involving percents.

- Find the whole given a part and the percentage.
- Find percentage increase or decrease.

Also addresses P.6.1, P.6.2, P.6.3.

Options for Differentiated Instruction

ELL = English Language Learner AL = Above or Beyond Grade Level SS = Struggling Students SN = Special Needs

Using Writing ELL SS SN

Use after presenting the Examples.

Have students write a paragraph describing a situation in which estimating with percents would be appropriate. Their paragraphs should both describe the situation and include the numbers used as estimates. They may want to look through newspapers for ideas. Have them present their paragraphs to the class.

Visualizing the Concept SS

Use with the Examples.

Using number lines while presenting the examples may help students understand what it means to estimate percents. A possible use of number lines to represent Example 1 is shown below.

62% of 520 ~ 60% of 520

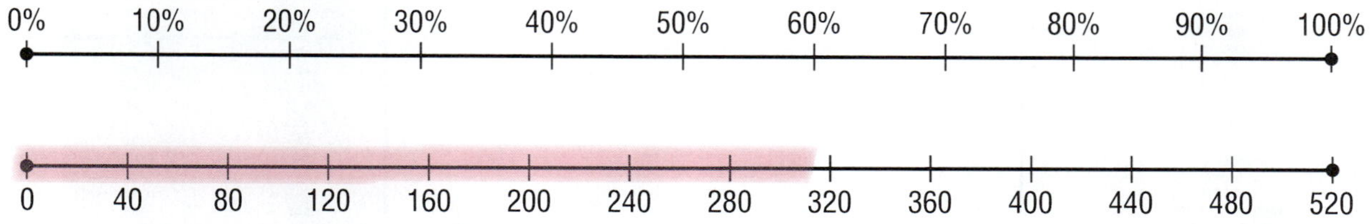

Additional Problems AL

Use after students complete Lesson 7-3.

Present the following problem to students.

> Catherine went shopping during a 20% off sale. She found a pair of jeans for \$60. To figure out the sale price, she did the following multiplication: $8 \times 6 = 48$
> She concluded that the sale price was \$48.

Have students explain why Catherine's method worked. 80% of \$60 $= 0.8 \times 60 = 8 \times 6$ Then have them use the same procedure to determine the sale price for each of the following:

- an item that is \$80 and 30% off $8 \times 7 =$ \$56
- an item that is \$120 and 40% off $12 \times 6 =$ \$72

Leveled Lesson Resources

Also on TeacherWorks™ Lesson 7-3

Chapter 7 Resource Masters

BL = Below or Approaching Grade Level OL = On Grade Level AL = Above or Beyond Grade Level ELL = English Language Learner

Lesson Reading Guide
p. 23 BL OL ELL

NAME ________ DATE ________ PERIOD ____

7-3 Lesson Reading Guide
Percent and Estimation

Get Ready for the Lesson

Read the introduction at the top of page 355 in your textbook. Write your answers below.

1. What fraction of women took lessons at school? How many of the 200 women is this? $\frac{3}{10}$; 60 women
2. Use a fraction to estimate the number of men who took lessons at school. Sample answer: $\frac{1}{4}$ of 200, or about 50

Read the Lesson

3. In Example 1, what does the ≈ sign mean in the sentence 62% of 520 ≈ 60% of 520? Why is it necessary to use this sign? Sample answer: The ≈ sign means *approximately equal to*; this sign is necessary because 48% is not equal to $\frac{1}{2}$. 48% has been rounded up to 50%, so the answer is an estimate.
4. Describe Method 2 of Example 2 on page 356 in your textbook. Method 2 says to first find 10% of $15 which is $1.50 and then multiply $1.50 × 2 = $3 to find the estimate of 20% of $14.72.
5. In Example 5, what is an easy way to find 0.5% of a number? Multiply by 1% and then divide the result by 2.

Remember What You Learned

6. Write fraction equivalents in simplest form for the following percents. Then work with a partner. Take turns asking each other fraction equivalents for any of the percents in the table, or think of others to quiz each other.

20%	$\frac{1}{5}$	40%	$\frac{2}{5}$	60%	$\frac{3}{5}$	80%	$\frac{4}{5}$
25%	$\frac{1}{4}$	50%	$\frac{1}{2}$	75%	$\frac{3}{4}$	100%	1

Lesson 7-3

Study Guide and Intervention*
p. 24 BL OL ELL

NAME ________ DATE ________ PERIOD ____

7-3 Study Guide and Intervention
Percent and Estimation

To estimate the percent of a number, you can use a fraction or a multiple of 10% or 1%.

Example 1 Estimate 77% of 800.

77% is about 75% or $\frac{3}{4}$.

77% of 800 ≈ $\frac{3}{4}$ · 800 Use $\frac{3}{4}$ to estimate.
≈ 600 Multiply.

So, 77% of 800 is about 600.

Example 2 Estimate 137% of 50.

137% is more than 100%, so 137% of 50 is greater than 50.
137% is about 140%.

140% of 50 = (100% of 50) + (40% of 50) 140% = 100% + 40%
= (1 · 50) + ($\frac{2}{5}$ · 50) 100% = 1 and 40% = $\frac{2}{5}$
= 50 + 20 or 70 Simplify.

So, 137% of 50 is about 70.

Example 3 Estimate 0.5% of 692.

0.5% is half of 1%. 692 is about 700.

1% of 700 = 0.01 · 700 To multiply by 1%, move the decimal point two places to the left.
= 7

One half of 7 is $\frac{1}{2}$ · 7 or 3.5.

So, 0.5% of 697 is about 3.5.

Exercises

Estimate. 1–12. Sample answers are given.

1. 24% of 36 $\frac{1}{4}$ · 36 = 9
2. 81% of 25 $\frac{4}{5}$ · 25 = 20
3. 11% of 67 0.1 · 70 = 7
4. 150% of 179 (1 · 180) + ($\frac{1}{2}$ · 180) = 270
5. 67% of 450 $\frac{2}{3}$ · 450 = 300
6. 79% of 590 $\frac{3}{4}$ · 600 = 450
7. 0.4% of 200 0.01 · 200 = 2 and $\frac{1}{2}$ · 2 = 1
8. 42% of 61 0.1 · 60 = 6 and 4 · 6 = 24
9. 19% of 41 0.1 · 40 = 4 and 2 · 4 = 8
10. 129% of 54 (1 · 54) + ($\frac{1}{3}$ · 54) = 72
11. 32% of 66 $\frac{1}{3}$ · 66 = 22
12. 0.2% of 150 0.01 · 150 = 1.5 and $\frac{1}{5}$ · 1.5 = 0.3

Skills Practice*
p. 25 BL OL

NAME ________ DATE ________ PERIOD ____

7-3 Skills Practice
Percent and Estimation

Estimate by using fractions. 1–6. Sample answers are given.

1. 51% of 128 $\frac{1}{2}$ · 128 = 64
2. 76% of 200 $\frac{3}{4}$ · 200 = 150
3. 32.9% of 90 $\frac{1}{3}$ · 90 = 30
4. 23% of 8 $\frac{1}{4}$ · 8 = 2
5. 19% of 45 $\frac{1}{5}$ · 45 = 9
6. 81% of 16 $\frac{4}{5}$ of 15 = 12

Estimate by using 10%. 7–12. Sample answers are given.

7. 12% of 98 0.1 · 100 = 10
8. 89% of 300 0.1 · 300 = 30 and 9 · 30 = 270
9. 31% of 80 0.1 · 80 = 8 and 3 · 8 = 24
10. 28% of 49 0.1 · 50 = 5 and 3 · 5 = 15
11. 62% of 13 0.1 · 10 = 1 and 6 · 1 = 6
12. 77% of 28 0.1 · 30 = 3 and 8 · 3 = 24

Estimate. 13–20. Sample answers are given.

13. 308% of 500 3 · 500 = 1,500
14. 0.5% of 87 0.01 · 90 = 0.9 and $\frac{1}{2}$ · 0.9 = 0.45
15. 153% of 20 (1 · 20) + ($\frac{1}{2}$ · 20) = 30
16. 0.6% of 41 0.01 · 40 = 0.4 and $\frac{1}{2}$ · 0.4 = 0.2
17. 231% of 54 (2 · 54) + ($\frac{1}{3}$ · 54) = 126
18. 0.9% of 116 0.01 · 116 = 1.16
19. 0.26% of 36 0.01 · 36 = 0.36 and $\frac{1}{4}$ · 0.36 = 0.09
20. 425% of 119 (4 · 120) + ($\frac{1}{4}$ · 120) = 510

Practice*
p. 26 OL AL

NAME ________ DATE ________ PERIOD ____

7-3 Practice
Percent and Estimation

Estimate.

1. 39% of 80 $\frac{2}{5}$ · 80 = 32
2. 31% of 40 $\frac{3}{10}$ · 40 = 12
3. 28% of 110 $\frac{3}{10}$ · 110 = 33
4. 74% of 160 $\frac{3}{4}$ · 160 = 120
5. 87% of 19 $\frac{9}{10}$ · 20 = 18
6. 91% of 82 $\frac{9}{10}$ · 80 = 72
7. 34% of 59 $\frac{1}{3}$ · 60 = 20
8. 66% of 148 $\frac{2}{3}$ · 150 = 100
9. 9% of 71 $\frac{1}{10}$ · 70 = 7
10. 73% of 241 $\frac{3}{4}$ · 240 = 180
11. 126% of 80 $\frac{5}{4}$ · 80 = 100
12. 234% of 145 $2\frac{1}{3}$ · 150 = 350
13. $\frac{1}{3}$% of 307 $\frac{1}{300}$ · 300 = 1
14. $\frac{1}{4}$% of 798 $\frac{1}{400}$ · 800 = 2
15. 1.1% of 62 $\frac{1}{100}$ · 60 = 0.6
16. 4.1% of 101 $\frac{4}{100}$ · 100 = 4
17. 67% of 11.9 $\frac{2}{3}$ · 12 = 8
18. 31% of 68.7 $\frac{3}{10}$ · 70 = 21
19. 9.8% of 359 $\frac{1}{10}$ · 360 = 36
20. 97.9% of 39 1 · 40 = 40
21. 52% of 57.9 $\frac{1}{2}$ · 60 = 30
22. 33% of 15.3 $\frac{1}{3}$ · 15 = 5
23. 21.1% of 151 $\frac{1}{5}$ · 150 = 30
24. 2.9% of 61.2 $\frac{3}{100}$ · 60 = 2

25. ELEVATION The highest point in Arizona is Humphreys Peak with an elevation of 12,633 feet. Estimate the elevation of the highest point in Florida, located in Walton County, if it is about 2.7% of the highest point in Arizona. Sample answer: 1% of 12,633 = 0.01 · 12,633 ≈ 125; 2.7 ≈ 3, so 3 · 125 = 375; The elevation of the highest point in Florida is about 375 feet.

26. BRAIN The brain weight of a newborn baby is about 13% of the body weight of the newborn. If a newborn weighs 2,900 grams, about how much does the brain weigh? Sample answer: 2,900 ≈ 3,000; 10% of 3,000 = 0.1 · 3,000 = 300; 1% of 3,000 = 0.01 · 3,000 = 30, 3 · 30 = 90; 300 + 90 = 390; The brain weighs about 390 grams.

27. STOCKS The value of a share of stock in an electronics company increased by $\frac{2}{3}$% during one week. If the value of a share of stock was $141 at the beginning of the week, estimate the increase in value of a share of stock at the end of the week. Sample answer: 141 ≈ 140; 1% of 140 = 0.01 · 140 = 1.4; 2 · 1.4 = 2.8; 2.8 ÷ 3 ≈ 0.9; The increase of a share of stock is about $0.90.

Word Problem Practice*
p. 27 OL AL

NAME ________ DATE ________ PERIOD ____

7-3 Word Problem Practice
Percent and Estimation

1. ORCHESTRA The orchestra at Millard Middle School has 120 members. Of these, 17% are eighth-grade students. Estimate the number of eighth-grade students in the orchestra. Sample answer: $\frac{1}{5}$ · 120 = 24 students

2. RESTAURANTS In one west coast city, 34% of the restaurants are on the river. The city has 178 restaurants. Estimate the number of restaurants that are on the river. Sample answer: $\frac{1}{3}$ · 180 = 60 restaurants

3. FARMING Rhonda planted green beans on 67% of her farm. Rhonda's farm has 598 acres of land. Estimate the number of acres of green beans on Rhonda's farm. Sample answer: $\frac{2}{3}$ · 600 = 400 acres

4. HOTELS At the Eastward Inn hotel, 47% of the rooms face the pool. The hotel has 92 rooms. Estimate the number of rooms that face the pool. Sample answer: $\frac{1}{2}$ · 90 = 45 rooms

5. TREES The students in Leon's seventh grade science class determined that 42% of the trees at a local park are pine trees. If there are 632 trees in the park, about how many of them are pine trees? Sample answer: 0.1 · 600 = 60 and 4 · 60 = 240 trees

6. BOOKS Jenna has read 0.7% of a book. If the book has 431 pages, estimate the number of pages Jenna has read. Sample answer: 0.01 · 420 = 4.2 and $\frac{2}{3}$ · 4.2 = 2.8 pages

7. FITNESS At the office where Mika works, 40% of the 18 employees exercise at least three times a week. Estimate the number of people who exercise at least three times a week. Sample answer: 0.1 · 20 = 2 and 4 · 2 = 8 people

8. PETS Of all seventh grade students at Hart Middle School, 0.3% of the students own a pet iguana. If there are 610 seventh grade students at Hart, about how many own pet iguanas? Sample answer: 0.01 · 600 = 6 and $\frac{1}{3}$ · 6 = 2 students

Lesson 7-3

Enrichment
p. 28 OL AL

NAME ________ DATE ________ PERIOD ____

7-3 Enrichment

The History of %

Math historians believe that the percent symbol, %, may have been developed from the symbol, P c°, that first appeared in an Italian writing dating back to 1425. At that time, percent was commonly written as "per 100", "P cento", and as a circle directly above a number, $\frac{c}{c}$. Roman Numerals were also used to represent a percent. For example, "xx.per.c." meant 20 percent. The symbol continued to develop in mathematical writings as, Per $\frac{c}{c}$, around 1650 to, $\frac{o}{c}$, and eventually to our modern symbol, %.

Find the estimates below to reveal the meaning of a similar symbol, ‰.

R 32% of 123 41
S 90% of 138 126
T 12% of 50 5
O 110% of 20 22
N 25% of 83 20
P $\frac{1}{4}$% of 240 0.6
E 78% of 20 15
U 152% of 41 60
A $\frac{1}{2}$% of 18 0.09
H 0.3% of 62 0.2
D 25.3% of 125 31

P E R   T H O U S A N D
0.6 15 41   5 0.2 22 60 126 0.09 20 31

* *Also available in Spanish* ELL

Additional Lesson Resources

Transparencies

- *5-Minute Check Transparency*, Lesson 7-3

Other Print Products

- *Teaching Mathematics with Manipulatives*
- *Noteables™ Interactive Study Notebook with Foldables™*

Teacher Tech Tools

- *Interactive Classroom CD-ROM*, Lesson 7-3
- *AssignmentWorks*, Lesson 7-3

Student Tech Tools

glencoe.com

- Extra Examples, Chapter 7, Lesson 3
- Self-Check Quiz, Chapter 7, Lesson 3

7-3 Percent and Estimation

MAIN IDEA

Estimate percents by using fractions and decimals.

IN Academic Standards

Preparation for 7.1.8 Solve problems involving percents.
- Find the whole given a part and the percentage
- Find percentage increase or decrease.

Also addresses P.6.1, P.6.2, P.6.3.

IN Math Online

glencoe.com
- Extra Examples
- Personal Tutor
- Self-Check Quiz

GET READY for the Lesson

MUSIC Refer to the graph below.

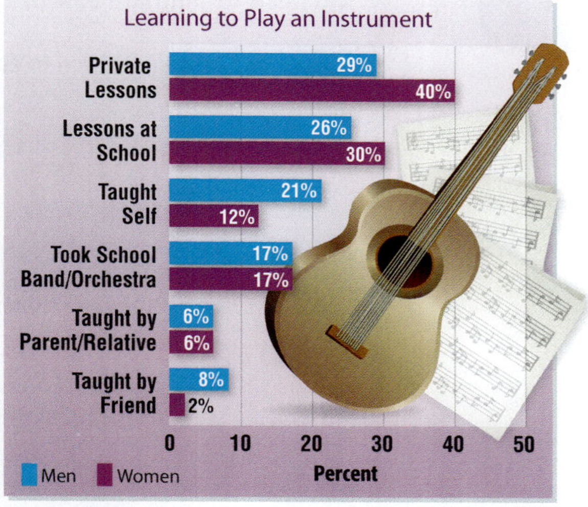

1. What fraction of women took lessons at school? If 200 women were surveyed, how many of them took lessons at school? $\frac{3}{10}$; 60 women
2. Use a fraction to estimate the number of men who took lessons at school. Assume 200 men were surveyed. 2. Sample answer: $\frac{1}{4}$ of 200 or about 50

Sometimes an exact answer is not needed when using percents. One way to estimate the percent of a number is to use a fraction.

Real-World EXAMPLE

1 SPORTS In a recent year, quarterback Carson Palmer completed 62% of his passes. He threw 520 passes. About how many did he complete?

62% of $520 \approx 60\%$ of 520	$62\% \approx 60\%$
$\approx \frac{3}{5} \cdot 520$	$60\% = \frac{6}{10}$ or $\frac{3}{5}$
≈ 312	Multiply.

So, Carson Palmer completed about 312 out of 520 passes.

CHECK Your Progress a. 48 years; $42\% \approx \frac{2}{5}$ and $\frac{2}{5} \cdot 120 = 48$

a. **REPTILES** Box turtles have been known to live for 120 years. American alligators have been known to live 42% as long as box turtles. About how long can an American alligator live?

7-3 Lesson Notes

1 Focus

Vertical Alignment

Before Lesson 7-3
Interpret percents as a part of a hundred; find decimal and percent equivalents for common fractions and explain why they represent the same value; compute a given percent of a whole number

Lesson 7-3
Calculate given percentages of quantities and solve problems involving tips

After Lesson 7-3
Convert fractions to decimals and percents and use these representations in estimations, computations, and applications; solve problems that involve discounts, markups, commissions, and profit and compute simple and compound interest

2 Teach

Scaffolding Questions

Ask:
- When might you need to round to the nearest 100%? Explain and give an example. if the percent is greater than 100%, such as 310%

Formative Assessment

Use the Check Your Progress exercises after each Example to determine students' understanding of concepts.

ADDITIONAL EXAMPLE

1 CONCERTS A town sold 407 tickets to a chamber music concert in the town square. Of the tickets sold, 61% were discounted for senior citizens. About how many senior citizens bought tickets for the concert? about 240

Focus on Mathematical Content

One way to estimate the percent of a number is to **approximate the percent with a fraction** and multiply.

Another way to estimate the percent of a number is to **find 10% of the number** and then multiply by the appropriate factor.

To estimate the percent of a number **when the percent is greater than 100**, use the Distributive Property.

To estimate the percent of a number **when the percent is less than 1**, find or estimate 1% of the number and then multiply by the appropriate fraction.

ADDITIONAL EXAMPLES

2 **COINS** Melinda calculated that 40% of the coins in her coin collection were minted before 1964. If there are 715 coins in her collection, about how many of them were minted before 1964? about 280

3 Estimate 173% of 60. about 105

Additional Examples are also in:

- Noteables™ Interactive Study Notebook with Foldables™
- Interactive Classroom PowerPoint® Presentations

Another method for estimating the percent of a number is to first find 10% of the number and then multiply. For example, 70% = 7 • 10%. So, 70% of a number equals 7 times 10% of the number.

Real-World Link In a recent year, the Internal Revenue Service estimated that Americans paid $15.37 billion in tips.

Real-World EXAMPLE

2 **MONEY** **Marita decides to leave a 20% tip on a restaurant bill of $14.72. About how much money should she tip the restaurant server?**

You need to estimate 20% of $14.72.

METHOD 1 **Use a fraction to estimate.**

20% is $\frac{2}{10}$ or $\frac{1}{5}$.

20% of $14.72 $\approx \frac{1}{5} \cdot$ $15.00 — 20% = $\frac{1}{5}$ and round $14.72 to $15.00.

$\approx$ $3.00 — Multiply.

METHOD 2 **Use 10% of a number to estimate.**

STEP 1 Find 10% of the number.
$14.72 is about $15.00.
10% of $15.00 = 0.1 • $15.00 = $1.50 — To multiply by 10%, move the decimal point one place to the left.

STEP 2 Multiply.
20% of $15.00 is 2 times 10% of $15.00.
2 • $1.50 = $3.00

So, Marita should tip the restaurant server about $3.00.

CHOOSE Your Method

b. **MONEY** Dante plans to put 80% of his paycheck into a savings account. His paycheck this week was $295. About how much money will he put into his savings account? **about $240**

You can also estimate percents of numbers when the percent is greater than 100 or the percent is less than 1.

Study Tip

Check for Reasonableness *When estimating the percent of a number and the percent is greater than 100, the estimate will always be greater than the number.*

EXAMPLES Percents Greater Than 100 or Less Than 1

3 **Estimate 122% of 50.**

122% is about 120%.

120% of 50 = (100% of 50) + (20% of 50) — 120% = 100% + 20%

$= (1 \cdot 50) + \left(\frac{1}{5} \cdot 50\right)$ — 100% = 1 and 20% = $\frac{1}{5}$

= 50 + 10 or 60 — Simplify.

So, 122% of 50 is about 60.

4 Estimate $\frac{1}{4}$% of 589.

$\frac{1}{4}$% is one fourth of 1%. 589 is about 600.

1% of $600 = 0.01 \cdot 600$ — Write 1% as 0.01.

$= 6$ — To multiply by 1%, move the decimal point two places to the left.

One fourth of 6 is $\frac{1}{4} \cdot 6$ or 1.5. So, $\frac{1}{4}$% of 589 is about 1.5.

c. 350; $1\frac{3}{4} \cdot 200 = 350$

d. 150; $3 \cdot 50 = 150$

e. 2; $\frac{1}{4} \cdot 0.01 \cdot 800 = 2$

CHECK Your Progress

Estimate.

c. 174% of 200 d. 298% of 45 e. 0.25% of 789

Real-World EXAMPLE

5 **CELL PHONES In a recent year, there were about 200 million people in the U.S. with cell phones. Of those, about 0.5% used their phone as an MP3 player. Estimate the number of people who used their phone as an MP3 player.**

0.5% is half of 1%.

1% of 200 million $= 0.01 \cdot 200{,}000{,}000$

$= 2{,}000{,}000$

So, 0.5% of 200,000,000 is about $\frac{1}{2}$ of 2,000,000 or 1,000,000.

So, about 1,000,000 people used their phone as an MP3 player.

CHECK Your Progress

f. Sample answer: about $1\% \cdot 600$ or 6 people

f. **ATTENDANCE** Last year, 639 students attended a summer camp. Of those who attended this year, 0.9% also attended last year. About how many people attended the camp two years in a row?

★ indicates multi-step problem

CHECK Your Understanding

Examples 1–4 (pp. 355–357)

Estimate. 1. 5; $\frac{1}{2} \cdot 10 = 5$; $0.1 \cdot 10 = 1$ and $5 \cdot 1 = 5$

1. 52% of 10 2. 7% of 20 3. 38% of 62

3–6. See margin.

4. 79% of 489 5. 151% of 70 6. $\frac{1}{2}$% of 82

2. 2; $\frac{1}{10} \cdot 20 = 2$; $0.1 \cdot 20 = 2$ and $1 \cdot 2 = 2$

Example 1 (p. 355)

7. **BUSINESS** A bicycle store increases its prices by 23%. About how much more will a customer pay for a bicycle that originally costs $200?
about $50; $\frac{1}{4} \cdot \$200 = \$50$; $0.1 \cdot 200 = 20$ and $2.5 \cdot 20 = \$50$

Example 2 (p. 356)

8. **BIRTHDAYS** Of the 78 teenagers at a youth camp, 63% have birthdays in the spring. About how many have birthdays in the spring?
about 48 teenagers; $\frac{3}{5} \cdot 80 = 48$; $0.1 \cdot 80 = 8$ and $6 \cdot 8 = 48$

Example 5 (p. 357)

9. **GEOGRAPHY** About 0.8% of the land in Maine is federally owned. See margin. If Maine is 19,847,680 acres, about how many acres are federally owned?

ADDITIONAL EXAMPLES

4 Estimate $\frac{1}{3}$% of 898. about 3

5 **GAME ATTENDANCE** Last weekend, 96,081 people attended a college football game. About 0.25% of them were reporters from newspapers and television and radio stations. About how many reporters were at the game? about 240 reporters

3 Practice

Formative Assessment

Use Exercises 1–9 to check for understanding.

Then use the chart on the next page to customize your assignments for students.

Intervention You may wish to use the Study Guide and Intervention Master on page 24 of the *Chapter 7 Resource Masters* for additional reinforcement.

Additional Answers

3. 24; $\frac{2}{5} \cdot 60 = 24$; $0.1 \cdot 60 = 6$ and $4 \cdot 6 = 24$

4. 400; $\frac{4}{5} \cdot 500 = 400$; $0.1 \cdot 500 = 50$ and $8 \cdot 50 = 400$

5. 105; $(1 \cdot 70) + \left(\frac{1}{2} \cdot 70\right) = 105$

6. 0.4; $0.01 \cdot 80 = 0.8$ and $\frac{1}{2} \cdot 0.8 = 0.4$

9. about 160,000 acres; $0.01 \cdot 20{,}000{,}000 = 200{,}000$ and $\frac{4}{5}$ of $200{,}000 = 160{,}000$

Odd/Even Assignments

Exercises 10–31 are structured so that students practice the same concepts whether they are assigned odd or even problems.

Tips for New Teachers — Estimation

Explain to students that estimation isn't always done exactly the same way. Depending on the problem, students may find it easier to round the percent, to round the number, or to round both the percent and the number. Similarly, they may find it easier to approximate a percent with a fraction or with a decimal. Encourage students to analyze each problem, asking themselves which estimation method will work best with the given numbers.

Additional Answers

11. $18; \frac{1}{5} \cdot 90 = 18; 0.1 \cdot 90 = 9$ and $2 \cdot 9 = 18$

12. $48; \frac{2}{5} \cdot 120 = 48; 0.1 \cdot 120 = 12$ and $4 \cdot 12 = 48$

13. $135; \frac{3}{4} \cdot 180 = 135; 0.1 \cdot 180 = 18$ and $7.5 \cdot 18 = 135$

14. $18; \frac{3}{5} \cdot 30 = 18; 0.1 \cdot 30 = 3$ and $6 \cdot 3 = 18$

15. $90; \frac{9}{10} \cdot 100 = 90; 0.1 \cdot 100 = 10$ and $9 \cdot 10 = 90$

16. $12.5; \frac{1}{4} \cdot 50 = 12.5; 0.1 \cdot 50 = 5$ and $2.5 \cdot 5 = 12.5$

17. $36; \frac{3}{10} \cdot 120 = 36; 0.1 \cdot 120 = 12$ and $3 \cdot 12 = 36$

18. $180; \frac{9}{10} \cdot 200 = 180; 0.1 \cdot 200 = 20$ and $9 \cdot 20 = 180$

19. $90; \frac{3}{5} \cdot 150 = 90; 0.1 \cdot 150 = 15$ and $6 \cdot 15 = 90$

20. $100; \frac{2}{3} \cdot 150 = 100; 0.1 \cdot 150 = 15$ and $6.6 \cdot 15 \approx 100$

21. $168; \frac{7}{10} \cdot 240 = 168; 0.1 \cdot 240 = 24$ and $7 \cdot 24 = 168$

Practice and Problem Solving

HOMEWORK HELP

For Exercises	See Examples
10–21	1, 3
22–23	2
24–25	3
26–27, 30	4
28–29, 31	5

Exercise Levels
A: 10–31
B: 32–45
C: 46–50

Estimate. 10. $35; \frac{1}{2} \cdot 70 = 35; 0.1 \cdot 70 = 7$ and $5 \cdot 7 = 35$ 11–21. See margin.

10. 47% of 70   **11.** 21% of 90   **12.** 39% of 120

13. 76% of 180   **14.** 57% of 29   **15.** 92% of 104

16. 24% of 48   **17.** 28% of 121   **18.** 88% of 207

19. 62% of 152   **20.** 65% of 152   **21.** 72% of 238

22. **MONEY** Jessica spent $42 at the hair salon. About how much money should she tip the hair stylist if she wants to leave a 15% tip? about $6; $\frac{3}{20} \cdot \$40 = \$6$

23. **HEALTH** You use 43 muscles to frown. When you smile, you use 32% of these same muscles. About how many muscles do you use when you smile? about 12 muscles; $\frac{3}{10} \cdot 40 = 12$

Estimate. 24. $(1 \cdot 50) + \left(\frac{3}{10} \cdot 50\right) = 65$ 25. $(2 \cdot 300) + \left(\frac{1}{4} \cdot 300\right) = 675$

24. 132% of 54   **25.** 224% of 320   **26.** $\frac{1}{2}$% of 412

27. $\frac{3}{4}$% of 168   **28.** 0.4% of 510   **29.** 0.9% of 74 $0.01 \cdot 70 = 0.7$

26. $0.01 \cdot 400 = 4$ and $\frac{1}{2} \cdot 4 = 2$

27. $0.01 \cdot 200 = 2$ and $\frac{3}{4} \cdot 2 = 1.5$

28. $0.01 \cdot 500 = 5$ and $\frac{2}{5} \cdot 5 = 2$

30. **GEOGRAPHY** The United States has 12,383 miles of coastline. If $\frac{4}{5}$% of the U.S. coastline is located in Georgia, about how many miles of coastline are in Georgia? about 96 mi; $0.01 \cdot 12{,}000 = 120$ and $\frac{4}{5} \cdot 120 = 96$

31. **BIRDS** During migration, 450,000 sandhill cranes stop to rest in Nebraska. About 0.6% of these cranes stop to rest in Oregon. About how many sandhill cranes stop in Oregon during migration? about 2,700 birds; $0.01 \cdot 450{,}000 = 4{,}500$ and $\frac{3}{5} \cdot 4{,}500 = 2{,}700$

Real-World Link About 75% of the entire world sandhill crane population stops to rest in Nebraska during migration.
Source: *World Book of Records*

Estimate.

32. 67% of 8.7   **33.** 54% of 76.8   **34.** 32% of 89.9

35. 10.5% of 238   **36.** 22.2% of 114   **37.** 98.5% of 45

32. $\frac{2}{3} \cdot 9 = 6$
33. $\frac{1}{2} \cdot 80 = 40$
34. $\frac{1}{3} \cdot 90 = 30$
35. $\frac{1}{10} \cdot 240 = 24$
36. $\frac{1}{5} \cdot 100 = 20$
37. $1 \cdot 45 = 45$

ANALYZE GRAPHS For Exercises 38–40, use the graph shown.

Amanda's Day

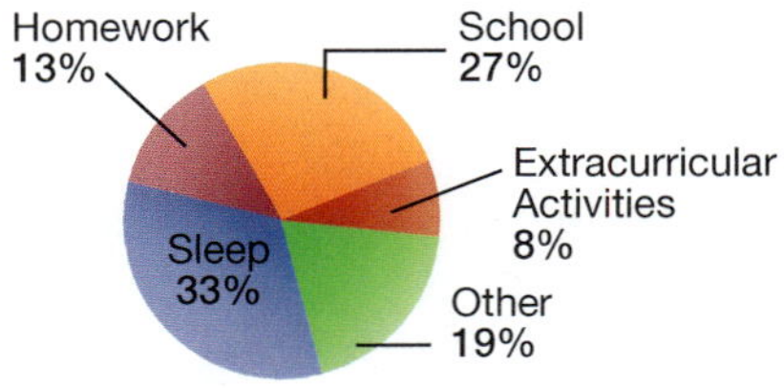

38. About how many hours does Amanda spend doing her homework each day? 38–40. See Ch. 7 Answer Appendix.

★ **39.** About how many more hours does Amanda spend sleeping than doing the activities in the "other" category? Justify your answer.

★ **40.** What is the approximate number of minutes Amanda spends each day on extracurricular activities?

DIFFERENTIATED HOMEWORK OPTIONS

Level	Assignment	Two-Day Option	
BL Basic	10–31, 46, 48–70	11–31 odd, 51–53	10–30 even, 46, 48–50, 54–70
OL Core	11–37 odd, 38–46, 48–70	10–31, 51–53	32–46, 48–50, 54–70
AL Advanced/Pre-AP	32–66 (optional: 67–70)		

41. **ANALYZE GRAPHS** 2,075 tennis fans were asked to name the greatest all time female tennis player. The top five responses are shown. About how many more people chose Martina Navratilova than Steffi Graf? **1,200**

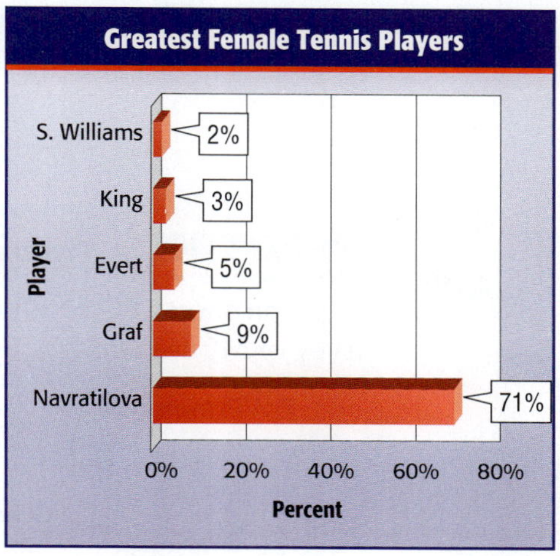

★ 42. **ANIMALS** The average white rhinoceros gives birth to a single calf that weighs about 3.8% as much as its mother. If the mother rhinoceros weighs 3.75 tons, about how many pounds does its calf weigh? **Sample answer: about 320 lb; 0.04 • 4 = 0.16; 0.16 • 2,000 = 320**

43. **POPULATION** According to the 2000 U.S. Census, about 7.8% of the people in Minnesota live in Minneapolis. If the population of Minnesota is about 4,920,000, estimate the population of Minnesota. **Sample answer: about 400,000 people; 0.08 • 5,000,000 = 400,000**

CLEANING For Exercises 44 and 45, use the following information.

A cleaning solution is made up of 0.9% chlorine bleach.

44. About how many ounces of bleach are in 189 ounces of cleaning solution? **1.8 ounces**

45. About how many ounces of bleach would be found in 412 ounces of cleaning solution? **3.6 ounces**

Academic Standards • ISTEP+

Extra Practice, pp. 685, 710

H.O.T. Problems

46. **OPEN ENDED** Write a real-world problem in which the answer can be found by estimating 12% of 50.

47. **CHALLENGE** Explain how you could find $\frac{3}{8}$% of \$800.

48. **FIND THE ERROR** Tom and Elsa are estimating 1.5% of 210. Who is correct? Explain. **Tom; Elsa incorrectly changed 1.5% to 1.5, which is 150%.**

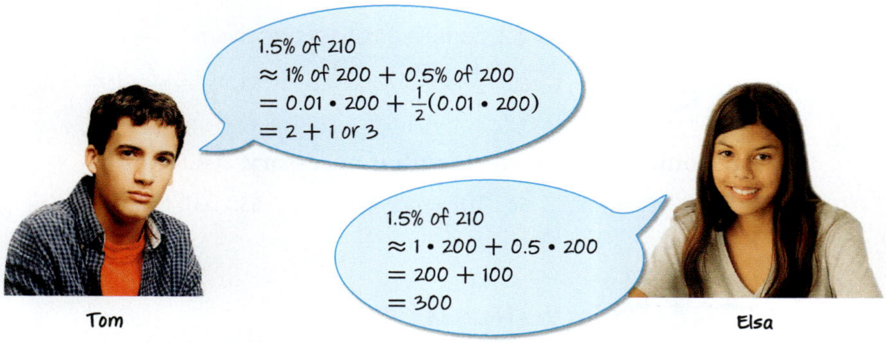

49. **NUMBER SENSE** Is an estimate for the percent of a number *always*, *sometimes*, or *never* greater than the actual percent of the number? Give an example or a counterexample to support your answer. **See margin.**

46. Sample answer: Of the students in a seventh grade class, 12% like to roller blade. If there are 50 students in the class, about how many like to roller blade?

47. Sample answer: Find 1% of \$800, then multiply by $\frac{3}{8}$.

Exercise Alert!

Find the Error In Exercise 48, Elsa didn't follow the steps to write the percent as a decimal. Remind students that in order to write a percent as a decimal, they must move the decimal point two places to the left.

Additional Answer

49. Sometimes; sample answer: one estimate for 37% of 60 is $\frac{2}{5} \cdot 60 = 24$. This is greater than the actual answer because $\frac{2}{5}$ is greater than 37%. Another estimate is $\frac{1}{3} \cdot 60 = 20$. This is less than the actual answer because $\frac{1}{3}$ is less than 37%.

Lesson 7-3 Percent and Estimation **359**

4 Assess

Ticket Out the Door Tell students that another class has about 120% of the number of students in your class. Have them estimate the number of students in the other class and write their estimates on a piece of paper.

FOLDABLES™ Study Organizer **Foldables™ Follow-Up**

Remind students to record what they learn about estimating percents of numbers in their Foldables tables, along with examples.

Additional Answer

50. Sample answer: One way to find 22% of 136 is to find $\frac{1}{5} \cdot 140 = 28$. Another way to find 22% of 136 is to first find $(0.1 \cdot 140)$ and then multiply by 2. The result is 28.

---

50. **WRITING IN MATH** Estimate 22% of 136 using two different methods. Justify the steps used in each method. **See margin.**

ISTEP+ PRACTICE Preparation for 7.1.8

51. The graph shows the results of a survey of 510 students.

Pet Preferences

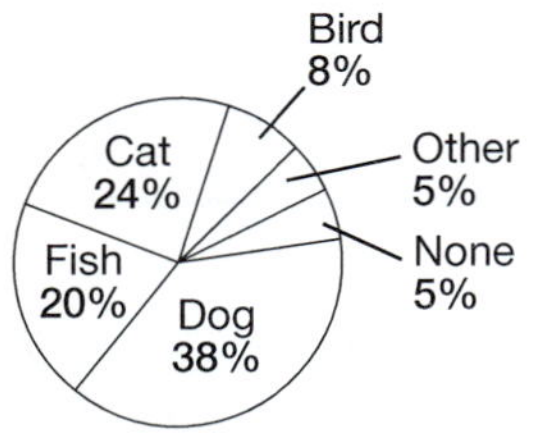

Which is the best estimate for the number of students who prefer cats? **B**

A 75 **C** 225
B 125 **D** 450

52. Megan is buying an entertainment system for $1,789.43. The speakers are 39.7% of the total cost. Which is the best estimate for the cost of the speakers? **H**

F $540 **H** $720
G $630 **J** $810

53. Daniel decides to leave a 20% tip for a restaurant bill of $28.92. About how much money should he tip the restaurant server? **D**

A $2.00 **C** $4.00
B $3.00 **D** $6.00

Spiral Review

Find each number. Round to the nearest tenth if necessary. (Lesson 7-2)

54. 6 is what percent of 15? **40%**
55. Find 72% of 90. **64.8**
56. What number is 120% of 60? **72**
57. 35% of what number is 55? **157.1**

58. **HEALTH** Adults have 32 teeth. Children have 62.5% as many teeth as adults. How many teeth do children have? (Lesson 7-1) **20**

Estimate. (Lesson 5-1) **59–62. Sample answers are given.**

59. $\frac{8}{9} + \frac{1}{12}$ **$1 + 0 = 1$**
60. $\frac{4}{7} + \frac{7}{16}$ **$\frac{1}{2} + \frac{1}{2} = 1$**
61. $\frac{7}{8} - \frac{7}{16}$ **$1 - \frac{1}{2} = \frac{1}{2}$**
62. $\frac{4}{5} - \frac{9}{10}$ **$1 - 1 = 0$**

Solve. Round to the nearest tenth if necessary. (Lesson 3-3)

63. $40 = 0.8x$ **50**
64. $10r = 61$ **6.1**
65. $0.07t = 25$ **357.1**
66. $56 = 0.32n$ **175**

GET READY for the Next Lesson

Solve each equation. Check your solution. (Lesson 3-3)

67. $14 = n \cdot 20$ **0.7**
68. $25 = n \cdot 40$ **0.625**
69. $28.5 = n \cdot 38$ **0.75**
70. $36 = n \cdot 80$ **0.45**

360 Chapter 7 Applying Percents

7-4 Algebra: The Percent Equation

PACING: **Regular:** 1 period, **Block:** 0.5 period

IN Academic Standards

7.1.8 Solve problems involving percents.

- **Find the whole given a part and the percentage.**
- Find percentage increase or decrease.

7.2.1 Use variables and appropriate operations to write an expression, **equation** or inequality **that represents a verbal description.** *Also addresses P.6.1, P.6.2, P.6.3.*

Options for Differentiated Instruction

ELL = English Language Learner AL = Above or Beyond Grade Level SS = Struggling Students SN = Special Needs

Reviewing the Concept SN

Use before beginning Lesson 7-4.

Remind students that to write a decimal as a percent, they need to multiply the decimal by 100, or move the decimal two spaces to the right.

Example:

0.35 as a percent is $0.35 \times 100 \rightarrow 35\%$

0.125 as a percent is $0.125 \times 100 \rightarrow 12.5\%$

Have students add this to their resource sheet if needed.

Using Models ELL AL SS SN

Use before presenting the Examples.

Have students draw an 8×12 rectangle on grid paper. Then have them fold the rectangle into quarters and shade one of the quarters.

Ask:

- How many squares are shaded? 24 squares
- What is 25% of 96? 24

Repeat, using different percents or different rectangles.

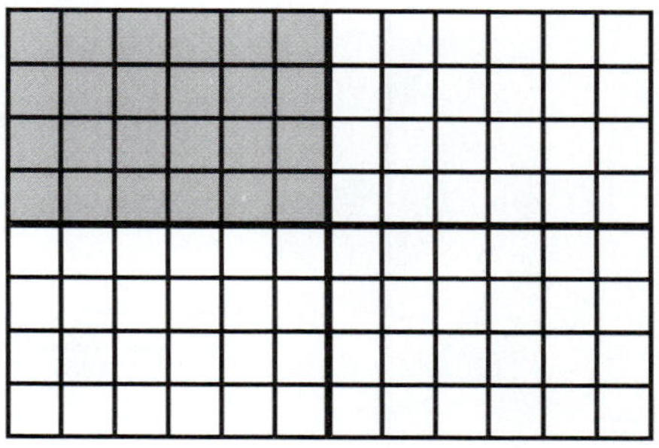

Creating Problems AL

Use after presenting the Examples.

Have students create problems that can be solved using the percent equation. Have them write two of each kind of problem:

- finding the part,
- finding the percent, and
- finding the whole.

Have students exchange their problems with a classmate.

Leveled Lesson Resources

Also on TeacherWorks™ Lesson 7-4

Chapter 7 Resource Masters

BL = Below or Approaching Grade Level   OL = On Grade Level   AL = Above or Beyond Grade Level   ELL = English Language Learner

Lesson Reading Guide
p. 29 BL OL ELL

NAME ______________ DATE ________ PERIOD ____

7-4 Lesson Reading Guide

Algebra: The Percent Equation

Get Ready for the Lesson

Read the introduction at the top of page 361 in your textbook. Write your answers below.

1. Use the percent proportion to find how many species are insects. **751,520**
2. Express the percent of insects as a decimal. Then multiply the decimal by 854,000. **0.88; 751,520; They are the same.**

Read the Lesson

3. The word *percent* is used in both the percent proportion and the percent equation. There is one major difference in the way percent is represented in each. What is the difference? **Sample answer: In the percent proportion, percent is written as the numerator of a fraction whose denominator is 100. In the percent equation, percent is written as a decimal.**
4. Write the following problems as percent proportions and as percent equations.

Problem	Percent Proportion	Percent Equation
9 is 60% of what number?	$\frac{9}{n} = \frac{60}{100}$	$9 = 0.6 \cdot n$
Find 50% of 6.	$\frac{n}{6} = \frac{50}{100}$	$n = 0.5 \cdot 6$
40% of what number is 48?	$\frac{48}{n} = \frac{40}{100}$	$48 = 0.4 \cdot n$
18 is what percent of 72?	$\frac{18}{72} = \frac{n}{100}$	$18 = n \cdot 72$

Remember What You Learned

5. Work with a partner. One person should ask a question like the questions given as examples in the concept summary box. The other person should name the type of percent problem and name the equation that should be used to solve the problem. Do not solve the equation. Then trade roles. Continue until each of you can name the problem type and the related equation easily. **See students' work.**

Lesson 7-4

Chapter 7 29 Course 2

Study Guide and Intervention*
p. 30 BL OL ELL

NAME ______________ DATE ________ PERIOD ____

7-4 Study Guide and Intervention

Algebra: The Percent Equation

To solve any type of percent problem, you can use the **percent equation**, part = percent · base, where the percent is written as a decimal.

Example 1 **600 is what percent of 750?**

600 is the part and 750 is the whole. Let n represent the percent.

part = percent · whole

$600 = n \cdot 750$ Write an equation.

$\frac{600}{750} = \frac{750n}{750}$ Divide each side by 750.

$0.8 = n$ Simplify.

$80\% = n$ Write 0.8 as a percent.

So, 600 is 80% of 750.

Example 2 **45 is 90% of what number?**

45 is the part and 90% or 0.9 is the percent. Let n represent the whole.

part = percent · whole

$45 = 0.9 \cdot n$ Write an equation.

$\frac{45}{0.9} = \frac{0.9n}{0.9}$ Divide each side by 0.9.

$50 = n$ The whole is 50.

So, 45 is 90% of 50.

Exercises

Write an equation for each problem. Then solve. Round to the nearest tenth if necessary.

1. What percent of 56 is 14? **$14 = n \cdot 56$; 25%**
2. 36 is what percent of 40? **$36 = n \cdot 40$; 90%**
3. 80 is 40% of what number? **$80 = 0.4 \cdot n$; 200**
4. 65% of what number is 78? **$78 = 0.65 \cdot n$; 120**
5. What percent of 2,000 is 8? **$8 = n \cdot 2{,}000$; 0.4%**
6. What is 110% of 80? **$n = 1.1 \cdot 80$; 88**
7. 85 is what percent of 170? **$85 = n \cdot 170$; 50%**
8. Find 30% of 70. **$n = 0.3 \cdot 70$; 21**

Chapter 7 30 Course 2

Skills Practice*
p. 31 BL OL

NAME ______________ DATE ________ PERIOD ____

7-4 Skills Practice

Algebra: The Percent Equation

Write an equation for each problem. Then solve. Round to the nearest tenth if necessary.

1. 25% of 176 is what number? **$n = 0.25 \cdot 176$; 44**
2. What is 90% of 20? **$n = 0.9 \cdot 20$; 18**
3. 24 is what percent of 30? **$24 = n \cdot 30$; 80%**
4. 80% of what number is 94? **$94 = 0.8 \cdot n$; 117.5**
5. What is 60% of 45? **$n = 0.6 \cdot 45$; 27**
6. 9 is what percent of 30? **$9 = n \cdot 30$; 30%**
7. What percent of 125 is 25? **$25 = n \cdot 125$; 20%**
8. What is 120% of 20? **$n = 1.2 \cdot 20$; 24**
9. 2% of what number is 5? **$5 = 0.02 \cdot n$; 250**
10. 15% of 290 is what number? **$n = 0.15 \cdot 290$; 43.5**
11. 16 is what percent of 4,000? **$16 = n \cdot 4{,}000$; 0.4%**
12. What is 140% of 60? **$n = 1.4 \cdot 60$; 84**
13. 344.8 is what percent of 862? **$344.8 = n \cdot 862$; 40%**
14. 6% of what number is 21? **$21 = 0.06 \cdot n$; 350**
15. What number is 60% of 605? **$n = 0.6 \cdot 605$; 363**
16. 32% of 250 is what number? **$n = 0.32 \cdot 250$; 80**
17. Find 30% of 70. **$n = 0.3 \cdot 70$; 21**
18. What is 80% of 65? **$n = 0.8 \cdot 65$; 52**

Lesson 7-4

Chapter 7 31 Course 2

Practice*
p. 32 OL AL

NAME ______________ DATE ________ PERIOD ____

7-4 Practice

Algebra: The Percent Equation

Write an equation for each problem. Then solve. Round to the nearest tenth if necessary.

1. What number is 27% of 52? **$n = 0.27 \cdot 52$; $n \approx 14.0$**
2. Find 41% of 48. **$n = 0.41 \cdot 48$; $n \approx 19.7$**
3. What percent of 88 is 33? **$n \cdot 88 = 33$; $n = 37.5\%$**
4. 8 is what percent of 18? **$8 = n \cdot 18$; $n \approx 44.4\%$**
5. What number is 33% of 360? **$n = 0.33 \cdot 360$; $n = 118.8$**
6. What percent of 62 is 58? **$n \cdot 62 = 58$; $n \approx 93.5\%$**
7. 55 is what percent of 100? **$55 = n \cdot 100$; $n = 55\%$**
8. 22% of what number is 24.2? **$0.22 \cdot n = 24.2$; $n = 110$**
9. 19 is 50% of what number? **$19 = 0.50 \cdot n$; $n = 38$**
10. 25 is 32% of what number? **$25 = 0.32 \cdot n$; $n \approx 78.1$**
11. 40% of what number is 28? **$0.40 \cdot n = 28$; $n = 70$**
12. 30 is what percent of 60? **$30 = n \cdot 60$; $n = 50\%$**
13. What percent of 5 is 2? **$n \cdot 5 = 2$; $n = 40\%$**
14. 44% of 10 is what number? **$0.44 \cdot 10 = n$; $n = 4.4$**
15. Find 110% of 88. **$1.10 \cdot 88 = n$; $n = 96.8$**
16. What number is 60% of 21.8? **$n = 0.6 \cdot 21.8$; $n \approx 13.1$**
17. What percent of 180 is 210? **$n \cdot 180 = 210$; $n \approx 116.7\%$**
18. 220 is 95.3% of what number? **$220 = 0.953 \cdot n$; $n \approx 230.8$**
19. BASEBALL A baseball player was at bat 473 times during the regular season. If he made a hit 31.5% of the times he was at bat, how many hits did he make during the regular season? Round to the nearest whole number if necessary. **149 hits**

ANALYZE GRAPHS **For Exercises 20 and 21, use the graph shown. The total enrollment at Central High School is 798 students.**

High School Enrollment

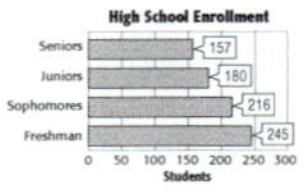

20. About what percent of the students at Central High are freshmen? Round to the nearest tenth if necessary. **30.7%**
21. About what percent of the students at Central High are seniors? Round to the nearest tenth if necessary. **19.7%**

Chapter 7 32 Course 2

Word Problem Practice*
p. 33 OL AL

NAME ______________ DATE ________ PERIOD ____

7-4 Word Problem Practice

Algebra: The Percent Equation

1. DINING Jonas and Linda's restaurant bill comes to $23.40. They are planning to tip the waiter 15% of their bill. How much money should they leave for a tip? **$3.51**
2. CHESS The Briarwood Middle School chess club has 55 members. 22 of the members are in seventh grade. What percent of the members of the chess club are in seventh grade? **40%**
3. TENNIS In the city of Springfield, 75% of the parks have tennis courts. If 15 parks have tennis courts, how many parks does Springfield have altogether? **20 parks**
4. COLLEGE There are 225 students in eighth grade at Jefferson Middle School. A survey shows that 64% of them are planning to attend college. How many Jefferson eighth grade students are planning to attend college? **144 students**
5. BASEBALL In a recent season, the Chicago White Sox won 99 out of 162 games. What percent of games did the White Sox win? Round to the nearest tenth if necessary. **61.1%**
6. HOUSING In the Stoneridge apartment complex, 35% of the apartments have one bedroom. If there are 49 one-bedroom apartments, what is the total number of apartments at Stoneridge? **140 apartments**
7. SPACE On Mars, an object weighs 38% as much as on Earth. How much would a person who weighs 165 pounds on Earth weigh on Mars? **62.7 pounds**
8. FOOTBALL In a recent season, quarterback Jake Plummer of the Denver Broncos had 7 passes intercepted out of 456 attempts. What percent of Jake Plummer's passes were intercepted? Round to the nearest tenth if necessary. **1.5%**

Lesson 7-4

Chapter 7 33 Course 2

Enrichment
p. 34 OL AL

NAME ______________ DATE ________ PERIOD ____

7-4 Enrichment

Inherited Traits

Everyone inherits traits like eye color, hair color, and skin pigmentation from their parents and grandparents, but there are other interesting traits that are also inherited. Right or left handedness is an inherited trait, as are dimples in one's cheeks. The chart below shows some inherited traits and the percentage of the general population that shows the trait.

Trait	Percent of General Population
Right-handedness	87%
Left-handedness	13%
Dimples	75%
Earlobes attached	25%
Able to roll tongue	65%

1. Based on the information presented above, predict how many of your classmates will have each of these traits.

Trait	Number of Students
Right-handedness	See students' work
Left-handedness	See students' work
Dimples	See students' work
Earlobes attached	See students' work
Able to roll tongue	See students' work

2. Survey your classmates to find how many have these traits.

Trait	Number of Students	Percent of Students
Right-handedness	See students' work	See students' work
Left-handedness	See students' work	See students' work
Earlobes attached	See students' work	See students' work
Able to roll tongue	See students' work	See students' work
Dimples	See students' work	See students' work

3. Compare your predictions to your actual results. **See students' work. Sample answer: I predicted that 3 students in my class would be left-handed because that represents 13% of the students in the class. 5 students are left-handed, representing 21% of the students in the class.**
4. How do the class traits compare to the traits of the general population? **Sample answer: The percentage of students with dimples is higher than the percentage in the general population, but the percentage of students who can roll their tongues is lower than that of the general population.**

Chapter 7 34 Course 2

***Also available in Spanish** ELL

Additional Lesson Resources

Transparencies

- *5-Minute Check Transparency*, Lesson 7-4

Other Print Products

- *Noteables™ Interactive Study Notebook with Foldables™*

Teacher Tech Tools

- *Interactive Classroom CD-ROM*, Lesson 7-4
- *AssignmentWorks*, Lesson 7-4

Student Tech Tools

glencoe.com

- Extra Examples, Chapter 7, Lesson 4
- Self-Check Quiz, Chapter 7, Lesson 4

7-4 Algebra: The Percent Equation

MAIN IDEA

Solve problems by using the percent equation.

IN Academic Standards

7.1.8 Solve problems involving percents.
- **Find the whole given a part and the percentage**
- Find percentage increase or decrease.

7.2.1 Use variables and appropriate operations to write an expression, **equation** or inequality **that represents a verbal description.**
Also addresses P.6.1, P.6.2, P.6.3.

New Vocabulary

percent equation

IN Math Online

glencoe.com
- Extra Examples
- Personal Tutor
- Self-Check Quiz

GET READY for the Lesson

ARTHROPODS There are about 854,000 different species of spiders, insects, crustaceans, millipedes, and centipedes on Earth. The graph shows that 88% of the total numbers of species of arthropods are insects.

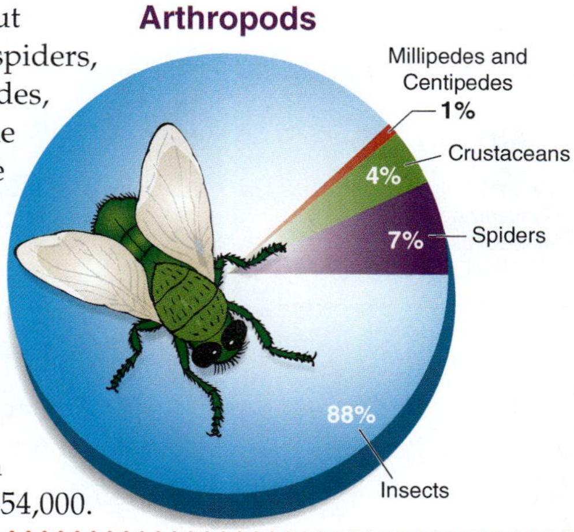

1. Use the percent proportion to find how many species are insects.
2. Express the percent of insects as a decimal. Then multiply the decimal by 854,000.

1. 751,520; 2. 0.88; 751,520; They are the same.

In Lesson 7-2, you used a percent proportion to find the missing part, percent, or whole. You can also use an equation. The percent equation is another form of the percent proportion.

$\frac{\text{part}}{\text{whole}} = \text{percent}$ — The percent must be written as a decimal or fraction.

$\frac{\text{part}}{\text{whole}} \cdot \textbf{whole} = \text{percent} \cdot \textbf{whole}$ — Multiply each side by the whole.

$\text{part} = \text{percent} \cdot \text{whole}$ — This form is called the **percent equation**.

EXAMPLE Find the Part

1 What number is 12% of 150? **Estimate** 12% of 150 ≈ 0.1 • 150 or 15

Write 12% as a decimal, 0.12. The whole is 150. You need to find the part. Let p represent the part.

$\text{part} = \text{percent} \cdot \text{whole}$

$p = 0.12 \cdot 150$ — Write the percent equation.

$p = 18$ — Multiply. The part is 18.

So, 18 is 12% of 150. **Check for Reasonableness** 18 is close to 15. ✔

Study Tip

Percent Equation
A percent must always be converted to a decimal or a fraction when it is used in an equation.

CHECK Your Progress

a. $p = 0.06 \cdot 19$; 1.1
b. $p = 0.72 \cdot 90$; 64.8

Write an equation for each problem. Then solve. Round to the nearest tenth if necessary.

a. What is 6% of 19?

b. Find 72% of 90.

Tips for New Teachers

Percent Equation

Remind students that the *whole* usually comes after the word *of* and the *part* usually comes before or after the word *is*. In Example 1, the *whole* is 150 and the *part* is the unknown.

7-4 Lesson Notes

1 Focus

Vertical Alignment

Before Lesson 7-4
Interpret percents as a part of a hundred; find decimal and percent equivalents for common fractions and explain why they represent the same value; compute a given percent of a whole number

Lesson 7-4
Calculate given percents of quantities and solve problems; write and solve one-step linear equations in one variable

After Lesson 7-4
Convert fractions to decimals and percents and use these representations in estimations, computations, and applications; solve problems that involve discounts, markups, commissions, and profit and compute simple and compound interest

2 Teach

Scaffolding Questions

Tell students that someone scored 90% on a math quiz.

Ask:
- If the quiz had 10 questions, how many questions did the student answer correctly? 9
- If the quiz had 20 questions, how many questions did the student answer correctly? 18
- If the quiz had 50 questions, how many questions did the student answer correctly? 45
- If the student answered 27 questions correctly, how many questions did the quiz have? 30.

Focus on Mathematical Content

The **percent equation** can be used to find a missing part, percent, or whole.

In the percent equation, the percent is written as a **decimal**.

ADDITIONAL EXAMPLES

1. What number is 46% of 200? 92
2. 26 is what percent of 32? 81.25%
3. 12 is 40% of what number? 30

Additional Examples are also in:

- Noteables™ Interactive Study Notebook with Foldables™
- Interactive Classroom PowerPoint® Presentations

Formative Assessment

Use the Check Your Progress exercises after each Example to determine students' understanding of concepts.

EXAMPLE Find the Percent

2 **21 is what percent of 40?** Estimate $\frac{21}{40} \approx \frac{1}{2}$ or 50%

The part is 21. The whole is 40. You need to find the percent. Let n represent the percent.

part = percent • whole

$21 = n \cdot 40$	Write the percent equation.
$\frac{21}{40} = \frac{40n}{40}$	Divide each side by 40.
$0.525 = n$	Since n represents the decimal form, the percent is 52.5%.

So, 21 is 52.5% of 40.

Check for Reasonableness 52.5% ≈ 50% ✔

Study Tip

Percent Remember to write the decimal as a percent in your final answer.

CHECK Your Progress

Write an equation for each problem. Then solve. Round to the nearest tenth if necessary.

c. 35 is what percent of 70?

d. What percent of 125 is 75?

e. What percent of 40 is 9?

f. 27 is what percent of 150?

c. $35 = n \cdot 70$; 50%
d. $75 = n \cdot 125$; 60%
e. $9 = n \cdot 40$; 22.5%
f. $27 = n \cdot 150$; 18%

EXAMPLE Find the Whole

3 **13 is 26% of what number?** Estimate $\frac{1}{4}$ of 48 = 12

The part is 13. The percent is 26, which when written as a decimal, is 0.26. You need to find the whole. Let w represent the whole.

part = percent • whole

$13 = 0.26 \cdot w$	Write the percent equation. 26% = 0.26
$\frac{13}{0.26} = \frac{0.26w}{0.26}$	Divide each side by 0.26.
$50 = w$	The number is 50.

So, 13 is 26% of 50.

Check for Reasonableness 50 is close to 48. ✔

CHECK Your Progress

Write an equation for each problem. Then solve. Round to the nearest tenth if necessary.

g. 39 is 84% of what number?

h. 26% of what number is 45?

i. 14% of what number is 7?

j. 24 is 32% of what number?

g. $39 = 0.84 \cdot w$; 46.4
h. $0.26 \cdot w = 45$; 173.1
i. $0.14 \cdot w = 7$; 50
j. $24 = 0.32 \cdot w$; 75

Real-World Link
In the U.S., Anchorage, Alaska, has the highest percent of cell phone users.
Source: Polk's Research

Real-World EXAMPLE

4 **CELL PHONES** **A survey found that 25% of people age 18–24 gave up their home phone and only use a cell phone. If 3,264 people only use a cell phone, how many people were surveyed?**

Words	3,264 people is 25% of what number of people?
Variable	Let n represent the number of people.
Equation	$3{,}264 = 0.25 \cdot n$

$3{,}264 = 0.25 \cdot n$	Write the percent equation. 25% = 0.25
$\frac{3{,}264}{0.25} = \frac{0.25n}{0.25}$	Divide each side by 0.25. Use a calculator.
$13{,}056 \approx n$	Simplify.

The number of people surveyed is about 13,056.

CHECK Your Progress

k. **POPULATION** The Louisville-Jefferson County metropolitan area contains 17.2% of the population of Kentucky. If the population of Kentucky is about 4,040,000 people, what is the population of the Louisville-Jefferson County metropolitan area? **about 694,880 people**

Types of Percent Problems

Concept Summary

Type	Example	Equation
Find the Part	What number is 50% of 6?	$p = 0.5 \cdot 6$
Find the Percent	3 is what percent of 6?	$3 = n \cdot 6$
Find the Whole	3 is 50% of what number?	$3 = 0.5 \cdot w$

★ indicates multi-step problem

CHECK Your Understanding

Examples 1–3 (pp. 361–362)

Write an equation for each problem. Then solve. Round to the nearest tenth if necessary.

1. What number is 88% of 300? **$p = 0.88 \cdot 300$; 264**
2. What number is 12% of 250? **$p = 0.12 \cdot 250$; 30**
3. 75 is what percent of 150? **$75 = n \cdot 150$; 50%**
4. 24 is what percent of 120? **$24 = n \cdot 120$; 20%**
5. 3 is 12% of what number? **$3 = 0.12 \cdot w$; 25**
6. 84 is 60% of what number? **$84 = 0.6 \cdot w$; 140**

Example 4 (p. 363)

7. **BUSINESS** A local bakery sold 60 loaves of bread in one day. If 65% of these were sold in the afternoon, how many loaves were sold in the afternoon? **39 loaves**

ADDITIONAL EXAMPLE

4 **MOVIES** Of the 1250 people surveyed, 36% preferred comedies over action movies. How many people preferred comedies? 450 people

3 Practice

Formative Assessment

Use Exercises 1–7 to check for understanding.

Then use the chart on the next page to customize your assignments for students.

Intervention You may wish to use the Study Guide and Intervention Master on page 30 of the *Chapter 7 Resource Masters* for additional reinforcement.

Lesson 7-4 Algebra: The Percent Equation **363**

Odd/Even Assignments

Exercises 8–23 are structured so that students practice the same concepts whether they are assigned odd or even problems.

Tips for New Teachers

Estimation

Remind students that a good way to check the reasonableness of their answers is by estimating. Encourage students to use mental math to estimate the unknown value in the percent equation.

Practice and Problem Solving

HOMEWORK HELP

For Exercises	See Examples
8–11	1
12–15	2
16–19	3
20–23	4

Exercise Levels
A: 8–23
B: 24–32
C: 33–35

13. $26 = n \cdot 96$; 27.1%
14. $98 = n \cdot 392$; 25%
15. $30 = n \cdot 64$; 46.9%
16. $1.45 = 0.33 \cdot w$; 4.4
17. $84 = 0.75 \cdot w$; 112

Write an equation for each problem. Then solve. Round to the nearest tenth if necessary. 8. $p = 0.65 \cdot 98$; 63.7 11. $p = 0.53 \cdot 470$; 249.1 12. $9 = n \cdot 45$; 20%

8. What number is 65% of 98?
9. Find 39% of 65. $p = 0.39 \cdot 65$; 25.4
10. Find 24% of 25. $p = 0.24 \cdot 25$; 6
11. What number is 53% of 470?
12. 9 is what percent of 45?
13. What percent of 96 is 26?
14. What percent of 392 is 98?
15. 30 is what percent of 64?
16. 33% of what number is 1.45?
17. 84 is 75% of what number?
18. 17 is 40% of what number? $17 = 0.4 \cdot w$; 42.5
19. 80% of what number is 64? $64 = 0.8 \cdot w$; 80
20. **BOOKS** Emma bought 6 new books for her collection. This increased her collection by 12%. How many books did she have before her purchases? 50 books
21. **VIDEO GAMES** A store sold 550 video games during the month of December. If this made up 12.5% of their yearly video game sales, about how many video games did the store sell all year? 4,400 games
22. **MEASUREMENT** The length of Giselle's arm is 27 inches. The length of her lower arm is 17 inches. About what percent of Giselle's arm is her lower arm? 63%
23. **LOBSTERS** Approximately 0.02% of North Atlantic lobsters are born bright blue in color. Out of 5,000 North Atlantic lobsters, how many would you expect to be blue in color? 1

Write an equation for each problem. Then solve. Round to the nearest tenth if necessary.

24. Find 135% of 64. $p = 1.35 \cdot 64$; 86.4
25. What number is 0.4% of 82.1? $p = 0.004 \cdot 82.1$; 0.3
26. 450 is 75.2% of what number? $450 = 0.752 \cdot w$; 598.4
27. What percent of 200 is 230? $230 = n \cdot 200$; 115%
28. **SALARY** Suppose you earn $6 per hour at your part-time job. What will your new hourly rate be after a 2.5% raise? $6.15

ANALYZE GRAPHS About 672 million metric tons of corn was produced worldwide in 2006. For Exercises 29–31, use the graph at the right.

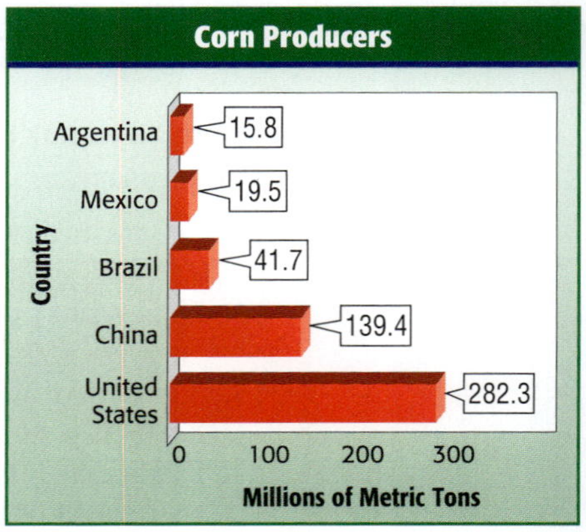

29. about 42%

29. About what percent of corn was produced in the United States?
30. About what percent of corn was produced in Mexico? about 3%
31. What percent of the world's corn production do Brazil and China make together? about 27%

DIFFERENTIATED HOMEWORK OPTIONS

Level	Assignment	Two-Day Option	
BL Basic	8–23, 33, 35–43	9–23 odd, 36–38	8–22 even, 33, 35, 39–43
OL Core	9–27 odd, 28–33, 35–43	8–23, 36–38	24–33, 35, 39–43
AL Advanced/Pre-AP	24–42 (optional: 43)		

364 Chapter 7 Applying Percents

Academic Standards • ISTEP+
Extra Practice, pp. 685, 710

32. **MEASUREMENT** ★ A pool that holds 320 cubic feet of water is 84% filled to capacity. Another pool that holds 400 cubic feet of water is 82.5% filled to capacity. Which pool contains more water? How much more? **400-cubic foot pool; 61.2 cubic feet**

H.O.T. Problems

33. **OPEN ENDED** Write a percent problem for which the percent is greater than 100% and the part is known. Use the percent equation to solve your problem to find the base. **Sample answer: 30 is 125% of what number?; 24**

34. **CHALLENGE** If you need to find the percent of a number, explain how you can predict whether the part will be less than, greater than, or equal to the number. **See margin.**

35. **WRITING IN MATH** Compare the percent equation and the percent proportion. Then explain when it might be easier to use the percent equation rather than the percent proportion. **See margin.**

ISTEP+ PRACTICE 7.1.8, 7.2.1

36. In a survey, 100 students were asked to choose their favorite take-out food. The table shows the results.

Favorite Take-Out Food	
Type of Food	**Percent**
Pizza	40
Sandwiches	32
Fried chicken	28

Based on this data, predict how many out of 1,800 students would choose sandwiches. **B**

A 504 C 680
B 576 D 720

37. If 60% of a number is 18, what is 90% of the number? **H**

F 3 H 27
G 16 J 30

38. Taryn's grandmother took her out to dinner. If the dinner was $34 and she left a 20% tip, how much money did Taryn's grandmother spend? **D**

A $6.80 C $39.50
B $27.20 D $40.80

Spiral Review

39. **RESTAURANT** Mitchell spent $13 on dinner. About how much money should he tip the server if he wants to leave a 15% tip? (Lesson 7-3) **$1.95**

Find each number. Round to the nearest hundredth if necessary. (Lesson 7-2)

40. What percent of 15 is 20? **133.33%**

41. 20.5% of what number is 35? **170.73**

42. What number is 0.5% of 10? **0.05**

GET READY for the Next Lesson

43. **PREREQUISITE SKILL** To estimate the age of a dog in human years, count the first year as 15 human years, the second year as 10 human years, and all of the following years as 3 human years. How old in human years is a 6-year-old dog? (Lesson 1-1) **37 yr**

4 Assess

Ticket Out the Door Have students write a real-world problem involving percent. Make sure they include two of the three elements needed to solve the problem (part, percent, whole).

Formative Assessment

Check for student understanding of concepts in Lessons 7-3 and 7-4.

CRM Quiz 2, p. 61

Additional Answers

34. Sample answer: If the percent is less than 100%, then the part is less than the base; if the percent equals 100%, then the part equals the base; if the percent is greater than 100%, then the part is greater than the base.

35. Sample answer: It may be easier if the percent and the base are known because after writing the percent as a decimal or fraction, the only step is to multiply. When using the percent proportion, you must first find the cross products and then divide.

7-5

Problem-Solving Investigation
DETERMINE REASONABLE ANSWERS

PACING: **Regular:** 1 period, **Block:** 0.5 period

IN Academic Standards **P.2.1 Recognize reasoning and proof as fundamental aspects of mathematics.** **P.2.2 Make and evaluate mathematical conjectures.** *Also addresses P.2.3, P.2.4.*

Options for Differentiated Instruction

ELL = English Language Learner AL = Above or Beyond Grade Level SS = Struggling Students SN = Special Needs

Class Discussions ELL AL SS SN

Use before assigning the Exercises.

Before assigning problems for independent work, read aloud each problem and discuss which problem-solving strategy would be best to use for each problem. Have students write down which strategy to use so they have a place to start for each problem.

Ask:

- How do you decide which problem solving strategy to use?
- Are there particular words that would indicate to use one strategy over another? If so, what are they?
- What is the first step that you take when deciding which strategy to use?
- Are there problems that could be solved by using more than one strategy?

Visual Clues SS SN

Use with Exercise 10.

For students with organizational difficulties, provide a copy of the table below to help them solve Exercise 10.

First Roll	Second Roll	Total

Making Connections ELL SS SN

Use after students complete Lesson 7-5.

Have students develop a strategy for determining reasonable answers in another area of study. For example, if students are taking an Earth Science course, they may need to understand radiocarbon dating. This process is based on the half-life of carbon-14, or 5,730 years. Rounding the half-life of carbon-14 to 6,000 years might help students determine a reasonable, but not exact, answer to a radiocarbon dating problem.

Leveled Lesson Resources

Also on TeacherWorks™
Lesson 7-5

Chapter 7 Resource Masters

BL = Below or Approaching Grade Level

OL = On Grade Level

AL = Above or Beyond Grade Level

ELL = English Language Learner

Study Guide and Intervention*
p. 35 BL OL ELL

NAME ______________ DATE ______ PERIOD ____

7-5 Study Guide and Intervention

Problem-Solving Investigation: Determine Reasonable Answers

When solving problems, often times it is helpful to determine reasonable answers by using rounding and estimation. Checking answers with a calculator is always helpful in determining if the answer found is in fact reasonable.

Example SALES TAX **There is 4.8% sales tax on all clothing items purchased. Danielle wants to buy a shirt, which costs $18.95. Danielle figures that if she has $20 she will have enough to buy the shirt. After adding in sales tax, is $20 a reasonable amount for Danielle to bring?**

Understand The cost of the shirt is $18.95. Sales tax is 4.8%. Danielle has $20.

Plan Round $18.95 to $19.00 and 4.8% to 5%. Then use mental math to find 5% of $19.00.

Solve Round $18.95 to $19.00

Round 4.8% to 5%

10% of $19.00 = 0.1 × 19 or $1.90 — Use mental math. 10% = 0.1

Round $1.90 to $2.00

5% is $\frac{1}{2}$ of 10%

So $\frac{1}{2}$ of $2.00 is $1.00 — $1.00 is the amount of sales tax.

$19.00 + $1.00 = $20.00 — Add $1.00 to $19.00.

So $20 is a reasonable amount of money for Danielle to bring to pay for the shirt.

Check Use a calculator to check.

0.048 × 18.95 = 0.9096

Since 0.9096 is close to 1, the answer is reasonable.

Exercises

1. TIP The total bill at a restaurant for a family of 5 is $64.72. They want to leave a 20% tip. They decide to leave $10.00. Is this estimate reasonable? Explain your reasoning. **No; 20% of $65.00 is $13.00, so a $10.00 tip is too low.**

2. TELEVISION A recent survey shows that 67% of students watch 3 or more hours of television a night. Suppose there are 892 students in your school. What would be a reasonable estimate of the number of students in your school who watch 3 or more hours of television a night? Explain your reasoning. **630 students; 70% of 900 students is 630 students.**

Lesson 7-5

Chapter 7 — 35 — Course 2

Skills Practice*
p. 36 BL OL

NAME ______________ DATE ______ PERIOD ____

7-5 Skills Practice

Problem-Solving Investigation: Determine Reasonable Answers

Determine reasonable answers for each. 1–6 sample answers are given.

1. MONEY Gillian and Roger have lunch at a restaurant and Gillian needs to determine how much tip to leave based on their bill. If their bill was $21.87 and Gillian wants to leave a 15% tip, what is a reasonable estimate for how much she should leave? **$3.00 ($3.28 exactly)**

2. SPORTS Of the 82,000 fans that attended a bowl game between Ohio State and Notre Dame, 60% were Ohio State fans. About how many fans at the game were for Notre Dame? **32,000 (32,800 exactly)**

3. ICE CREAM A survey of 1,950 people found that 39% preferred chocolate ice cream to vanilla. About how many people preferred chocolate ice cream according to the survey? **800 (761 exactly)**

4. EARTH The surface area of Earth is approximately 70% water. If the surface area is about 510,000,000 square kilometers, about how many square kilometers are water? **350,000,000 km^2 (357,000,000 km^2)**

5. COLLEGE Of 7,450 first-year college students interviewed, 72% had changed their major area of study since the beginning of the academic year. About how many students had kept the same major? **2,250 (2,086 exactly)**

6. MONEY While shopping, Hilary spent $149. If the amount she spent was 20% of her savings, how much savings did she have before she shopped? **$750 ($745 exactly)**

Chapter 7 — 36 — Course 2

Practice*
p. 37 OL AL

NAME ______________ DATE ______ PERIOD ____

7-5 Practice

Problem-Solving Investigation: Determine Reasonable Answers

Mixed Problem Solving

For Exercises 1 and 2, determine a reasonable answer.

1. HOMES In a retirement village, 86% of the residents own their home. If the village has 540 homes, how many homes are owned by the residents, about 250, 350, or 450? **450 homes**

2. ANALYZE GRAPHS The graph shows how the Forenzo family spent their money on their summer vacation. Is 25% a reasonable estimate of how much money they spent on dining? Justify your answer. **Yes; 1,100 is about 25% of 4,500.**

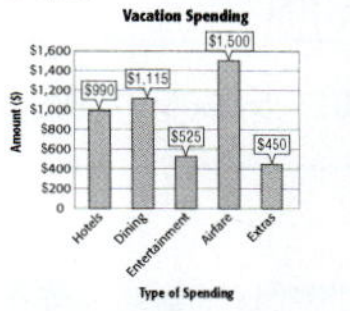

Use any strategy to solve Exercises 3–6. Some strategies are shown below.

PROBLEM-SOLVING STRATEGIES
• Guess and check.
• Make an organized list.
• Determine reasonable answers.

3. NUMBER SENSE 12 is added to 25% of a number. The result is 30. What is the number? **The number is 72.**

4. ANALYZE GRAPHS The graph shows the percent of community attendance during a little league season. Is 90% a reasonable estimate for the percent of community attendance for September? Explain. **No; 82% would be a better estimate since the change would be only 1% to 2% from August to September.**

5. TRAVEL Cecil averages 31 miles per gallon when driving his car on the highway to visit friends 461 miles away. If he filled the 16-gallon gasoline tank before leaving and did not buy any gasoline along the way, about how many gallons of gasoline are left in the tank when he arrives? **divide and subtract; 461 ÷ 31 ≈ 15; 16 − 15 = 1; 1 gallon**

6. FABRIC Mrs. Tillman is making identical dresses for her three granddaughters. She needs $2\frac{1}{8}$ yards of fabric for each dress. If she purchased $8\frac{1}{2}$ yards of fabric, how much fabric will be leftover? **multiply and subtract; $3 \cdot 2\frac{1}{8} = 6\frac{3}{8}$; $8\frac{1}{2} - 6\frac{3}{8} = 2\frac{1}{8}$; $2\frac{1}{8}$ yards remain**

Lesson 7-5

Chapter 7 — 37 — Course 2

Word Problem Practice*
p. 38 OL AL

NAME ______________ DATE ______ PERIOD ____

7-5 Word Problem Practice

Problem-Solving Investigation: Determine Reasonable Answers

Solve using any method.

1. GYM The 6th graders are running the mile in physical education. Jared finishes the mile 2 minutes before Stacey who finished 1 minute 26 seconds behind Kareem. If Joanna completes the mile 1 minute and 42 seconds after Kareem, and her time is 8 minutes 34 seconds, what is Jared's time? **6 minutes, 18 seconds**	2. POLITICS A candidate receives 62% of the vote in an election and there are 1,603 votes recorded. How many votes did the candidate receive? **994 votes**
3. POPULATION The population of the United States is about 296,000,000. Spanish is the primary language for 10.7% of the population, about how many people speak Spanish as their primary language? **about 30,000,000 (exactly 31,672,000)**	4. BAKING Bea has prepared a basic cookie dough to which she will add ingredients to make several types of cookies. She has chocolate chips, raisins, and peanut butter chips. She also has peanuts, pecans, and walnuts. If she wants to put one ingredient from the first group with one type of nut into the dough, how many different types of cookies can she make? **9**
5. COINS Zachary has four different coins that total 41 cents. What coins does he have? **Quarter, nickel, dime, and penny**	6. DECORATING Mr. Chen is planning to wallpaper his family room and dining room. The dining room is 11 feet by 13 feet, while the family room is 20 feet by 10 feet. All of the walls are 8 feet high. How many square feet of wallpaper does he need to wallpaper the two rooms? **864 ft^2**
7. MOVIES Charis is going to the movies with a friend. The price of admission is $5.50, a small popcorn is $2.39, and a small drink is $2.65. If Charis has a ten dollar bill, does she have enough money for admission, popcorn, and a drink? If not, how much more money would she need? **No; she would need $0.54.**	8. TRAVELING Shawn is packing his suitcase for vacation. If he has 2 pairs of shorts, and 5 shirts, how many different outfits can he make? **10**

Chapter 7 — 38 — Course 2

**** Also available in Spanish* ELL**

Additional Lesson Resources

Transparencies

- *5-Minute Check Transparency*, Lesson 7-5

Other Print Products

- *Noteables™ Interactive Study Notebook with Foldables™*

Teacher Tech Tools

- *Interactive Classroom CD-ROM*, Lesson 7-5
- *AssignmentWorks*, Lesson 7-5

Student Tech Tools

glencoe.com

- Extra Examples, Chapter 7, Lesson 5
- Self-Check Quiz, Chapter 7, Lesson 5

7-5 Lesson Notes

1 Focus

Determine Reasonable Answers

By learning to check solutions for reasonableness, students can avoid many common errors. Estimation, a skill that students practiced in Lesson 7-3, is often the best way to determine whether an answer is reasonable.

2 Teach

Scaffolding Questions

Ask:

- What is an estimate of 25% of \$208.99? about \$50
- What is an estimate of 79% of 40? about 32
- What is an estimate of 53% of 180 miles? about 90 miles

ADDITIONAL EXAMPLE

FUNDRAISER A soccer team is having a candy sale to raise funds to buy new shirts. The team gets to keep 25% of the sales. Each candy bar costs \$1.50, and the team has sold 510 bars so far. If the shirts cost a total of \$175, should the team order the shirts yet? Explain. Yes; the team has sold about \$750 (500 • 1.50), so they can keep about \$187 ($\frac{1}{4}$ • 750), which is more than the cost of the shirts.

Additional Examples are also in:

- Noteables™ Interactive Study Notebook with Foldables™
- Interactive Classroom PowerPoint® Presentations

7-5 Problem-Solving Investigation

MAIN IDEA: Solve problems by determining reasonable answers.

Academic Standards **P.2.1 Recognize reasoning and proof as fundamental aspects of mathematics. P.2.2 Make and evaluate mathematical conjectures.** *Also addresses P.2.3, P.2.4.*

P.S.I. TEAM +

e-Mail: DETERMINE REASONABLE ANSWERS

Doug: My dad painted 25% of my bedroom in 28 minutes. I think the whole project will take about 3 hours.

YOUR MISSION: Determine whether it is reasonable for Doug's dad to paint the bedroom in 3 hours.

Understand	Twenty-five percent of the room has been painted in 28 minutes. Doug thinks it will take a total of 3 hours to paint the whole room.
Plan	Since 25% or $\frac{1}{4}$ of the room was painted in about 30 minutes, use a model of 25%.
Solve	Round 28 minutes to 30 minutes 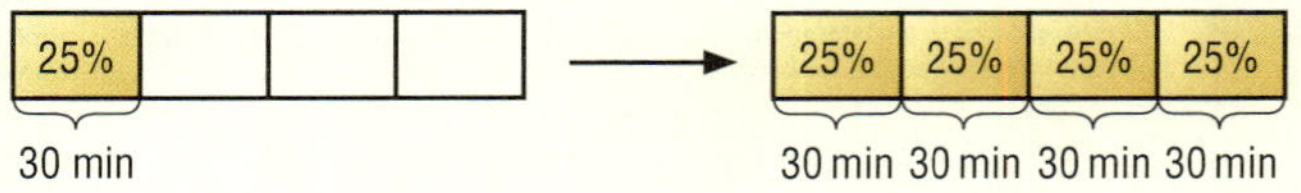 $30 \text{ minutes} \times 4 = 120 \text{ minutes}$ $120 \text{ min} = 2 \text{ h}$ So, 2 hours would be a better estimate than 3 hours.
Check	Thirty minutes is $\frac{1}{2}$ hour. Since $\frac{1}{2} \times 4 = 2$, 2 hours is reasonable answer. ✔

Analyze The Strategy

1, 2. See margin.

1. Describe other problem-solving strategies that you could use to determine whether answers are reasonable.
2. WRITING IN MATH Write two word problems. One should have a reasonable answer and the other should not.

Differentiated Instruction

Verbal/Linguistic Have students create a word problem based on an interest rate of 2.761% and provide two estimated solutions: one being a reasonable answer and the other being an unreasonable answer. Have students exchange questions with a partner whose job is to determine which would be a reasonable answer and why.

Mixed Problem Solving

★ indicates multi-step problem

Academic Standards • ISTEP+

Extra Practice, pp. 686, 710

Determine reasonable answers for Exercises 3–6.

3. **SAVING** Aliayah saves $11 each month for her class trip. What is a reasonable estimate for the amount of money she will have saved after a year: about $100, $120, or $160? Explain. **Sample answer: $10 • 12 = $120**

4. **SCHOOL** Of 423 students, 57.6% live within 5 miles of the school. What is a reasonable estimate for the number of students living within 5 miles of the school? Explain. **Sample answer: 0.6 • 400 or 240 students**

5. **EXERCISE** A survey showed that 61% of middle school students do some kind of physical activity every day. If there are 828 middle school students in your school, would the number of students who exercise be about 300, 400, or 500? Explain. **500; 60% • 830 ≈ 500**

6. **ANALYZE GRAPHS** A travel agency surveyed 140 families about their favorite vacation spots. Is 60, 70, or 80 families a reasonable estimate for the number of families that did *not* choose Hawaii? **70**

Favorite Vacation Spots

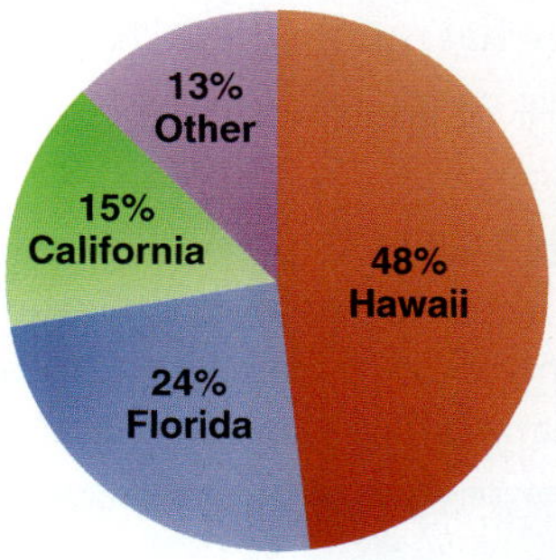

Use any strategy to solve Exercises 7–13. Some strategies are shown below.

PROBLEM-SOLVING STRATEGIES
- Guess and check.
- Make an organized list.
- Look for a pattern.
- Determine Reasonable Answers.

7. **COINS** John has 10 coins that total $0.83. What are the coins? **2 quarters, 1 dime, 4 nickels, 3 pennies**

8. **ANALYZE GRAPHS** Refer to the graph. A pie is set out to cool. Is it reasonable to estimate that the pie will be 90°F after ten minutes of cooling?

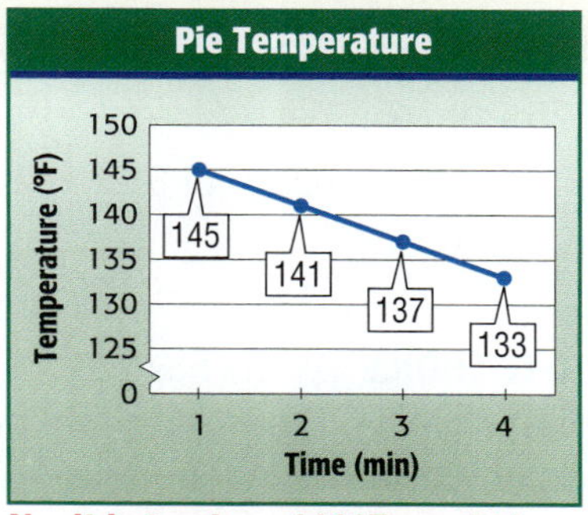

No, it is too low. 110°F would be a more reasonable estimate.

9. **SHOPPING** Deshawn wants to buy a shirt that has a regular price of $41, but is now on sale for 25% off. Is $25, $30, or $35 the best estimate for the cost of the shirt? **$30**

10. **BOWLING** In bowling, you get a spare when you knock down the ten pins in two throws. How many possible ways are there to get a spare? **9**

11. **TIPS** Shawnda decides to leave a 20% tip on a restaurant bill of $17.50. How much should she tip the restaurant server? **$3.50**

12. ★ **FUNDRAISER** During a popcorn sale for a fundraiser, the soccer team gets to keep 25% of the sales. One box of popcorn sells for $1.50, and the team has sold 510 boxes so far. Has the team raised a total of $175? **12, 13. See margin.**

13. ★ **MEASUREMENT** How many square yards of carpet are needed to carpet the two rooms described below? Explain.

Room	Dimensions
living room	15 ft by 18 ft
TV room	18 ft by 20 ft

3 Practice

Using the Exercises

Exercises 1 and 2 can be used to check students' understanding of the determine reasonable answers strategy.

Exercises 3–6 give students an opportunity to practice the determine reasonable answers strategy.

Exercises 7–13 are structured so that students have the opportunity to practice many problem-solving strategies. You may wish to review some of the strategies students have studied.

- guess and check (p. 42)
- make an organized list (p. 190)

4 Assess

Yesterday's News Remind students that yesterday's lesson was about estimating percents of numbers. Have students write how yesterday's concepts helped them with today's material.

Additional Answers

1. Sample answer: Look for a rule or pattern in the data or number facts, estimation, guess and check, make an organized list, or work backward.
2. Sample answer: The cost of Traci's meal was $14.56. She wants to leave a 15% tip, so she left $1.50. (not reasonable) The cost of Traci's meal was $14.56. She wants to leave a 15% tip, so she left $2.20. (reasonable)

12. Yes; They have sold 510 • $1.50 or $765 worth of popcorn. So, they have earned 0.25 • $765 or $191.25, which is more than $175.
13. $15 \cdot 18 + 18 \cdot 20 = 630$ ft^2. Then convert 630 ft^2 to square yards. $630 \div (3 \cdot 3) = 70$ yd^2.

Lesson 7-5 Problem-Solving Investigation: Determine Reasonable Answers **367**

CHAPTER 7 Mid-Chapter Quiz

Formative Assessment

Use the Mid-Chapter Quiz to assess students' progress in the first half of the chapter.

Have students review the lesson indicated for the problems they answered incorrectly.

Summative Assessment

CRM Mid-Chapter Test, p. 63

ExamView Assessment Suite Customize and create multiple versions of your Mid-Chapter Test and their answer keys.

FOLDABLES Study Organizer Dinah Zike's Foldables

Before students complete the Mid-Chapter Quiz, encourage them to review the notes they recorded about percents in their Foldables study tables.

Additional Answers

11. 80; $\frac{1}{5} \cdot 400 = 80$

12. 88; $\frac{4}{5} \cdot 110 = 88$

13. 150; $\frac{1}{2} \cdot 300 = 150$

14. 12; $0.1 \cdot 40 = 4$ and $3 \cdot 4 = 12$

15. 72; $0.1 \cdot 90 = 9$ and $8 \cdot 9 = 72$

16. 84; $0.1 \cdot 210 = 21$ and $4 \cdot 21 = 84$

CHAPTER 7 Mid-Chapter Quiz

Lessons 7-1 through 7-5

IN Academic Standards 7.1.8, 7.2.1

Find each number. Round to the nearest tenth if necessary. (Lesson 7-1)

1. Find 17% of 655. **111.4**
2. What is 235% of 82? **192.7**
3. Find 75% of 160. **120**
4. What number is 162.2% of 55? **89.2**

5. **MULTIPLE CHOICE** Ayana has 220 coins in her piggy bank. Of those, 45% are pennies. How many coins are not pennies? (Lesson 7-1) **A**

   A 121 C 109
   B 116 D 85

Find each number. Round to the nearest tenth if necessary. (Lesson 7-2)

6. What percent of 84 is 12? **14.3%**
7. 15 is 25% of what number? **60**
8. 85% of 252 is what number? **214.2**

ANALYZE GRAPHS For Exercises 9 and 10, refer to the graph that shows the results of a survey of 200 students' favorite DVDs.

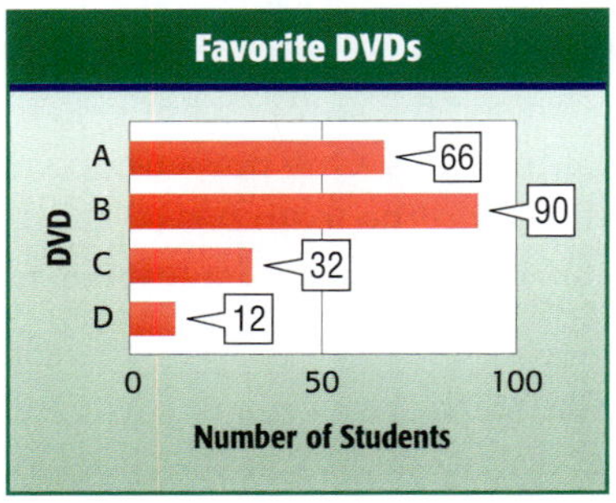

9. What percent of students preferred DVD A? **33%**
10. Which DVD did about 15% of students prefer? **DVD C**

Estimate. (Lesson 7-3) **11–16. See margin for sample answers.**

11. 20% of 392
12. 78% of 112
13. 52% of 295
14. 30% of 42
15. 79% of 88
16. 41.5% of 212

17. **MULTIPLE CHOICE** A football player has made about 75% of the field goals he has attempted in his career. If he attempts 41 field goals in one season, about how many would he be expected to make? **B**

   A 35 C 25
   B 30 D 20

Write an equation for each problem. Then solve. Round to the nearest tenth if necessary. (Lesson 7-4)

18. What number is 35% of 72? **$p = 0.35 \cdot 72$; 25.2**
19. 16.1 is what percent of 70? **$16.1 = n \cdot 70$; 23%**
20. 27.2 is 68% of what number? **$27.2 = 0.68 \cdot w$; 40**
21. 16% of 32 is what number? **$p = 0.16 \cdot 32$; 5.1**
22. 55% of what number is 1.265? **$1.265 = 0.55 \cdot w$; 2.3**
23. 17 is 40% of what number? **$17 = 0.40 \cdot w$; 42.5**
24. **ANALYZE TABLES** The table shows the costs of owning a dog over an average 11-year lifespan. What percent of the total cost is veterinary bills? (Lesson 7-4) **about 26.9%**

Dog Ownership Costs

Item	Cost ($)
Food	4,020
Veterinary Bills	3,930
Grooming, Equipment	2,960
Training	1,220
Other	2,470

Source: American Kennel Club

25. Sample answer: 60% of $850 = $510

25. **SHOPPING** A desktop computer costs $849.75 and the hard drive is 61.3% of the total cost. What is a reasonable estimate for the cost of the hard drive? (Lesson 7-5)

Data-Driven Decision Making

Diagnostic Teaching Based on the results of the Chapter 7 Mid-Chapter Quiz, use the following to review concepts that students continue to find challenging.

Exercises	Lesson	Academic Standards
1–5	7-1	7.1.8
6–10	7-2	7.1.8
11–17	7-3	7.1.8
18–24	7-4	7.1.8, 7.2.1
25	7-5	P.2.1, P.2.2

Resources for Review

CRM Study Guide and Intervention pp. 10, 17, 24, 30, and 35

IN Math Online glencoe.com

- Extra Examples
- Personal Tutor
- Concepts in Motion

368 Chapter 7 Applying Percents

7-6 Percent of Change

PACING: **Regular:** 1 period, **Block:** 0.5 period

IN Academic Standards **7.1.8 Solve problems involving percents.**
- Find the whole given a part and the percentage.
- **Find percentage increase or decrease.**

Options for Differentiated Instruction

ELL = English Language Learner AL = Above or Beyond Grade Level SS = Struggling Students SN = Special Needs

Writing Problems ELL AL SS

Use after presenting Examples 1–3.

Have students write a percent of increase problem and a percent of decrease problem. To help them get started, ask the following questions.
- What information do you need to include for these types of problems?
- What are possible contexts for a percent of change problem?
- Where could you find realistic data for this type of problem?

Have students create an answer key for their problems and exchange them with a classmate to solve.

Preventing Mistakes ELL SS SN

Use with Check Your Understanding.

Some students may mistakenly want to divide the greater number into the lesser number. Encourage them to take the time to identify the amount of change and the original amount and write them as a ratio before calculating.

$$\frac{\text{amount of change}}{\text{original amount}} \begin{array}{l}\longrightarrow \\ \longrightarrow\end{array}$$

Creating a Checklist ELL SS SN

Use before assigning the Exercises.

Have students create a checklist of steps for finding percent of change. A sample checklist is shown below.

- Determine if the problem is a percent increase or percent decrease.
- Subtract the two amounts.
- Divide by the original amount.
- Simplify.
- Write as a percent.
- Write the answer in sentence form.

The percent of increase of ___________ is ___________.
The percent of decrease of ___________ is ___________.

Have students exchange checklists and make suggestions for improving each other's checklist.

Leveled Lesson Resources

Also on TeacherWorks™ Lesson 7-6

Chapter 7 Resource Masters

BL = Below or Approaching Grade Level   OL = On Grade Level   AL = Above or Beyond Grade Level   ELL = English Language Learner

Lesson Reading Guide
p. 39 BL OL ELL

NAME ________ DATE ______ PERIOD ____

7-6 Lesson Reading Guide

Percent of Change

Lesson 7-6

Get Ready for the Lesson

Complete the Mini Lab at the top of page 369 in your textbook. Write your answers below.

Model each percent of change.

1. 25% increase [0% | 100% | 25%]
2. 75% increase [0% | 100% | 75%]
3. 30% increase [0% | 100% | 30%]
4. Describe a model that represents a 100% increase, a 200% increase, and a 300% increase. Sample answer: a straw that is twice as long, 3 times longer, and 4 times longer, respectively
5. Describe how this process would change to show percent of decrease. Subtract the percent of change from the original straw.

Read the Lesson

6. In a percent of change, what are the two numbers that are being compared? the number that represents the amount of change and the number that represents the original amount
7. How can you tell if a percent of change is a percent of increase or a percent of decrease? Sample answer: Compare the new amount to the original amount. If the original quantity is increased, then it is called a percent of increase. If the original quantity is decreased, then it is called a percent of decrease.
8. Tell how to find the amount of increase and the amount of decrease. The amount of increase is the new amount minus the original amount. The amount of decrease is the original amount minus the new amount.

Remember What You Learned

9. Find an example of something in your life that has increased or decreased, such as your height in the past year. Calculate the percent of change and share your results with your class. See students' work.

Study Guide and Intervention*
p. 40 BL OL ELL

NAME ________ DATE ______ PERIOD ____

7-6 Study Guide and Intervention

Percent of Change

A **percent of change** is a ratio that compares the change in quantity to the original amount. If the original quantity is increased, it is a **percent of increase**. If the original quantity is decreased, it is a **percent of decrease**.

Example 1 Last year, 2,376 people attended the rodeo. This year, attendance was 2,950. What was the percent of change in attendance to the nearest whole percent?

Since this year's attendance is greater than last year's attendance, this is a percent of increase.

The amount of increase is 2,950 – 2,376 or 574.

percent of increase = amount of increase / original amount ← new amount – original amount

= 574 / 2,376 Substitution

≈ 0.24 or 24% Simplify.

Rodeo attendance increased by about 24%.

Example 2 John's grade on the first math exam was 94. His grade on the second math exam was 86. What was the percent of change in John's grade to the nearest whole percent?

Since the second grade is less than the first grade, this is a percent of decrease. The amount of decrease is 94 – 86 or 8.

percent of decrease = amount of decrease / original amount ← original amount – new amount

= 8 / 94 Substitution

≈ 0.09 or 9% Simplify.

John's math grade decreased by about 9%.

Exercises

Find each percent of change. Round to the nearest whole percent if necessary. State whether the percent of change is an *increase* or *decrease*.

1. original: 4, new: 5 — 25%; increase
2. original: 1.0, new: 1.3 — 30%; increase
3. original: 15, new: 12 — 20%; decrease
4. original: $30, new: $18 — 40%; decrease
5. original: 60, new: 63 — 5%; increase
6. original: 160, new: 136 — 15%; decrease
7. original: 7.7, new: 10.5 — 36%; increase
8. original: 9.6, new: 5.9 — 39%; decrease

Skills Practice*
p. 41 BL OL

NAME ________ DATE ______ PERIOD ____

7-6 Skills Practice

Percent of Change

Lesson 7-6

Find each percent of change. Round to the nearest whole percent if necessary. State whether the percent of change is an *increase* or *decrease*.

1. original: 35, new: 70 — 100%; inc.
2. original: 8, new: 12 — 50%; inc.
3. original: 45, new: 30 — 33%; dec.
4. original: $350, new: $400 — 14%; inc.
5. original: $75, new: $60 — 20%; dec.
6. original: 250, new: 100 — 60%; dec.
7. original: $30, new: $110 — 267%; inc.
8. original: 35, new: 28 — 20%; dec.
9. original: $12.50, new: $15 — 20%; inc.
10. original: 80, new: 52 — 35%; dec.
11. original: 45, new: 63 — 40%; inc.
12. original: 120, new: 132 — 10%; inc.
13. original: $210, new: $105 — 50%; dec.
14. original: 84, new: 111 — 32%; inc.
15. original: $84, new: $100 — 19%; inc.
16. original: 6.8, new: 8.2 — 21%; inc.
17. original: 1.5, new: 2.5 — 67%; inc.
18. original: 91, new: 77 — 15%; dec.
19. original: $465.50, new: $350 — 25%; dec.
20. original: $87.05, new: $100 — 15%; inc.
21. original: 144, new: 108 — 25%; dec.
22. original: 20.8, new: 12.2 — 41%; dec.
23. original: $75, new: $15 — 80%; dec.
24. original: 8.6, new: 7 — 19%; dec.

Practice*
p. 42 OL AL

NAME ________ DATE ______ PERIOD ____

7-6 Practice

Percent of Change

Find each percent of change. Round to the nearest whole percent if necessary. State whether the percent of change is an *increase* or *decrease*.

1. 8 feet to 10 feet — 25% increase
2. 136 days to 85 days — 38% decrease
3. $0.32 to $0.37 — 16% increase
4. 62 trees to 31 trees — 50% decrease
5. 51 meters to 68 meters — 33% increase
6. 16.5 grams to 24.8 grams — 50% increase
7. 0.55 minutes to 0.1 minutes — 82% decrease
8. $180 to $210 — 17% increase
9. 2.9 months to 4.9 months — 69% increase
10. $\frac{1}{4}$ to $\frac{3}{8}$ — 50% increase
11. $\frac{1}{6}$ to $\frac{1}{3}$ — 100% increase
12. $\frac{4}{3}$ to $\frac{1}{3}$ — 75% decrease
13. SURGERY Recent developments in surgical procedures change the average healing time for some operations from 8 weeks to 3 weeks. 63% decrease
14. ROADS The city added an extra lane in each direction to the 5-lane road. 40% increase

GEOMETRY For Exercises 15 and 16, refer to the rectangle shown. Suppose the width is decreased by 3 inches.

15. Find the percent change in the perimeter. 30% decrease
16. Find the percent change in the area. 50% decrease

[rectangle: 4 in by 6 in]

ANALYZE TABLES For Exercises 17 and 18, refer to the table that shows the average monthly rainfall during the first six months of the year for Singapore.

Month	Average Rainfall (inches/month)
January	9.4
February	6.5
March	6.8
April	6.6
May	6.7
June	6.4

17. Between which two consecutive months is the percent of decrease the greatest? What is the percent change? Round to the nearest whole percent. January to February; 31%
18. Between which two consecutive months is the percent of increase the least? What is the percent change? Round to the nearest whole percent. April to May; 2%

Word Problem Practice*
p. 43 OL AL

NAME ________ DATE ______ PERIOD ____

7-6 Word Problem Practice

Percent of Change

Lesson 7-6

1. SHOES A popular brand of running shoes costs a local store $68 for each pair. If the store sells the shoes for $119, what is the percent of increase in the price? 75%
2. CLUBS Last year the backgammon club had 30 members. This year the club has 24 members. Find the percent of decrease in the number of members. 20%
3. READING In the seventh grade, Rachel read 15 books. In the eighth grade, she read 18 books. Find the percent of increase in the number of books Rachel read. 20%
4. VOTES Last year 762 students voted in the student council election at San Bruno Middle School. This year 721 students voted. To the nearest tenth, what was the percent of change in the number of students that voted? 5.4% decrease
5. HEIGHT When Hugo was 9 years old he was 56 inches tall. Hugo is now 12 years old and he is 62 inches tall. Find the percent of increase in Hugo's height to the nearest tenth. 10.7%
6. PLANTS Alicia planted 45 tulip bulbs last year. This year she plans to plant 65 bulbs. Find the percent of increase in the number of tulip bulbs to the nearest tenth. 44.4%
7. PICTURES The 2008 yearbook at Middleton Middle School had 236 candid pictures of students. The 2007 yearbook had 214 candid pictures of students. To the nearest tenth, what was the percent of change in the number of candid student pictures from 2007 to 2008? 10.3% increase
8. POPULATION In 1990, there were 4,298,000 Mexican immigrants living in the United States. In 2000, this number had increased to 7,858,000. Find the percent of increase to the nearest tenth. 82.8%

Enrichment
p. 44 OL AL

NAME ________ DATE ______ PERIOD ____

7-6 Enrichment

A Taxing Exercise

People who earn income are required by law to pay taxes. The amount of tax a person owes is computed by first subtracting the amount of all *exemptions* and *deductions* from the amount of income, then using a tax table like this.

Schedule X–Use if your filing status is **Single**

If the amount on Form 1040, line 37, is: Over—	But not over—	Enter on Form 1040, line 38	of the amount over—
$0	$20,350	----------------15%	$0
20,350	49,300	$3,052.50 + 28%	20,350
49,300	--------	11,158.50 + 31%	49,300

Compute each person's income. Subtract $5,550 for each person's exemption and deduction. Then use the tax rate schedule to compute the amount of federal tax owed.

1. A cashier works 40 hours each week, earns $7.50 per hour, and works 50 weeks each year. $1,417.50
2. A newspaper carrier works each day, delivers 154 papers daily, and earns $0.12 delivering each paper. $179.28
3. A baby-sitter earns $3.50 per hour per child. During a year, the baby-sitter works with two children every Saturday for 8 hours and with three children every other Sunday for 6 hours. $0.00
4. While home from college for the summer, a painter earns $17.00 per hour, working 45 hours each week for 15 weeks. $888.75
5. Working before and after school in the school bookstore, an employee works 2.5 hours each day for 170 days and earns $4.60 per hour. $0.00
6. After graduating from college, a computer programmer accepts a position earning $2,450 monthly. $4,032.50

*** Also available in Spanish** ELL

Additional Lesson Resources

Transparencies
- *5-Minute Check Transparency*, Lesson 7-6

Other Print Products
- *Teaching Mathematics with Manipulatives*
- *Noteables™ Interactive Study Notebook with Foldables™*

Teacher Tech Tools
- *Interactive Classroom CD-ROM*, Lesson 7-6
- *AssignmentWorks*, Lesson 7-6

Student Tech Tools
glencoe.com
- Extra Examples, Chapter 7, Lesson 6
- Self-Check Quiz, Chapter 7, Lesson 6

7-6 Percent of Change

MAIN IDEA

Find the percent of increase or decrease.

IN Academic Standards

7.1.8 Solve problems involving percents.
- Find the whole given a part and the percentage
- **Find percentage increase or decrease.**

New Vocabulary

percent of change
percent of increase
percent of decrease

IN Math Online

glencoe.com
- Concepts In Motion
- Extra Examples
- Personal Tutor
- Self-Check Quiz

MINI Lab

You can model a 50% increase using straws.

- Begin with two straws. The first straw will represent 100%.
- Cut the second straw in half. One part represents 50%.
- Tape the two straws together. This new straw represents a 50% increase or 150% of the original straw.

Model each percent of change.

1. 25% increase 2. 75% increase 3. 30% increase

1–3. See margin.

4. Describe a model that represents a 100% increase, a 200% increase, and a 300% increase. **See Ch. 7 Answer Appendix.**
5. Describe how this process would change to show percent of decrease. **See Ch. 7 Answer Appendix.**

One way to describe a change in quantities is to use percent of change.

Percent of Change — Key Concept

Words A **percent of change** is a ratio that compares the change in quantity to the original amount.

Equation $\text{percent of change} = \frac{\text{amount of change}}{\text{original amount}}$

The percent of change is based on the original amount. If the original quantity is increased, then it is called a **percent of increase**. If the original quantity is decreased, then it is called a **percent of decrease**.

$$\textbf{percent of increase} = \frac{\text{amount of increase}}{\text{original amount}} \quad \leftarrow \text{new} - \text{original}$$

$$\textbf{percent of decrease} = \frac{\text{amount of decrease}}{\text{original amount}} \quad \leftarrow \text{original} - \text{new}$$

7-6 Lesson Notes

1 Focus

Vertical Alignment

Before Lesson 7-6
Interpret percents as a part of a hundred; find decimal and percent equivalents for common fractions and explain why they represent the same value; compute a given percent of a whole number

Lesson 7-6
Interpret and use ratios in different contexts

After Lesson 7-6
Calculate the percent of increases and decreases of a quantity; solve problems that involve discounts, markups, commissions, and profit and compute simple and compound interest

2 Teach

MINI Lab

Have students compare the lengths of the original straw and the taped straw. Make sure they understand that the taped straw is $1\frac{1}{2}$ times as long as the original straw.

Scaffolding Questions

Ask:
- If a baseball player hit 20 home runs last year and 25 home runs this year, how did his home run production change? increased by 5 home runs
- If a basketball player made 14 points per game last year and 21 points per game this year, how did her points production change? increased by 7 points
- If a football player rushed 83 yards per game last year and 60 yards per game this year, how did his yardage change? decreased by 23 yards

Additional Answers

1. 0% 100% 25%

2. 0% 100% 75%

3. 0% 100% 30%

Focus on Mathematical Content

Percent of change compares a change in a quantity with the original quantity. The change can be an **increase** or a **decrease**.

In the percent of change formula, the percent is calculated as a **decimal**, so it must be rewritten as a percent.

To calculate the percent of change, students can find the difference between the original and new quantities and divide this difference by the original quantity. If positive, the percent of change is a percent of increase. If negative, the percent of change is a percent of decrease.

Formative Assessment

Use the Check Your Progress exercises after each Example to determine students' understanding of concepts.

ADDITIONAL EXAMPLES

1. **SHOPPING** Last year a sweater sold for $56. This year the same sweater sells for $60. Find the percent of change in the cost of the sweater. Round to the nearest percent if necessary. 7% increase
2. **ATTENDANCE** On the first day of school this year, 435 students reported to Howard Middle School. Last year on the first day, 460 students attended. Find the percent of change for the first day's attendance. Round to the nearest whole percent if necessary. 5% decrease

Additional Examples are also in:

- Noteables™ Interactive Study Notebook with Foldables™
- Interactive Classroom PowerPoint® Presentations

EXAMPLE Find Percent of Increase

1 GASOLINE Find the percent of change in the cost of gasoline from 1981 to 2007. Round to the nearest whole percent if necessary.

Since the 2007 price is greater than the 1981 price, this is a percent of increase. The amount of increase is $2.85 – $1.30 or $1.55.

percent of increase $= \dfrac{\text{amount of increase}}{\text{original amount}}$

$= \dfrac{\$1.55}{\$1.30}$ Substitution

≈ 1.19 Simplify.

$\approx 119\%$ Write 1.19 as a percent.

The cost of gasoline increased 119% from 1981 to 2007.

Study Tip

Percents
In the percent of change formula, the decimal representing the percent of change must be written as a percent.

CHECK Your Progress

a. **MEASUREMENT** Find the percent of change from 10 yards to 13 yards. 30% increase

EXAMPLE Find Percent of Decrease

2 DVD RECORDER Yusuf bought a DVD recorder for $280. Now, it is on sale for $220. Find the percent of change in the price. Round to the nearest whole percent if necessary.

Since the new price is less than the original price, this is a percent of decrease. The amount of decrease is $280 – $220 or $60.

percent of decrease $= \dfrac{\text{amount of decrease}}{\text{original amount}}$

$= \dfrac{\$60}{\$280}$ Substitution

≈ 0.21 Simplify.

$\approx 21\%$ Write 0.21 as a percent.

The price of the DVD recorder decreased by about 21 percent.

CHECK Your Progress

b. **MONEY** Find the percent of change from $20 to $15. 25% decrease

Focus on Mathematical Content

Writing Decimals as Percents Point out that the formula for percent of change gives the resultant percent answer written as a decimal. Students must write the decimal answer as a percent by multiplying by 100 or moving the decimal point two places to the right.

370 Chapter 7 Applying Percents

ISTEP+ EXAMPLE 7.1.8

3 **The table shows about how many people attended the home games of a high school football team for five consecutive years. Which statement is supported by the information in the table?**

Attendance of Home Games	
Year	**Total Attendance (thousands)**
2003	16.6
2004	16.4
2005	15.9
2006	17.4
2007	17.6

A The attendance in 2006 was 15% greater than the attendance in 2005.

B The greatest decrease in attendance occurred from 2003 to 2004.

C The attendance in 2005 was 3% less than the attendance in 2004.

D The greatest increase in attendance occurred from 2006 to 2007.

Read the Item

You need to determine which statement is best supported by the information given in the table.

Solve the Item

- Check **A**. The percent of change from 2005 to 2006 was $\frac{17.4 - 15.9}{15.9}$ or about 10%, not 15%.
- Check **B**.
  From 2003 to 2004, the decrease was 16.6 − 16.4 or 0.2.
  From 2004 to 2005, the decrease was 16.4 − 15.9 or 0.5.
  This statement is not supported by the information.
- Check **C**. The percent of change from 2004 to 2005 was $\frac{16.4 - 15.9}{16.4}$ or about 3%. This statement is supported by the information.
- Check **D**.
  From 2005 to 2006, the increase was 17.4 − 15.9 or 1.5.
  From 2006 to 2007, the increase was 17.6 − 17.4 or 0.2.
  This statement is not supported by the information.

The solution is **C**.

CHECK Your Progress

c. Which of the following represents the greatest percent of change? H

F A savings account that had $500 now has $470.

G An MP3 player that stored 15 GB now stores 30 GB.

H A plant grew from 3 inches to 8 inches in one month.

J An airplane ticket that was originally priced at $345 is now $247.

Test-Taking Tip

Check the Results If you have time, check all of the choices given. By doing so, you will verify that your choice is correct.

ADDITIONAL EXAMPLE

3 **TEST EXAMPLE** The table shows the annual city budget of Layton for four years.

Annual Budget City of Layton	
Year	**Budget (millions of $)**
2007	23.1
2008	24.9
2009	26.2
2010	25.5

Which statement is supported by the table? D

A The budget decreased and then increased.

B The greatest budget increase occurred from 2008 to 2009.

C The budget increased 15% from 2007 to 2010.

D The budget decreased about 3% from 2009 to 2010.

Tips for New Teachers: Calculating Change

You may wish to point out that the amount of change—whether an increase or decrease—is always a positive number.

3 Practice

Formative Assessment

Use Exercises 1–5 to check for understanding.

Then use the chart at the bottom of this page to customize your assignments for students.

Intervention You may wish to use the Study Guide and Intervention Master on page 40 of the *Chapter 7 Resource Masters* for additional reinforcement.

Odd/Even Assignments

Exercises 6–19 are structured so that students practice the same concepts whether they are assigned odd or even problems.

★ indicates multi-step problem

CHECK Your Understanding

Find each percent of change. Round to the nearest whole percent if necessary. State whether the percent of change is an *increase* or a *decrease*.

Examples 1, 2 (p. 370)

1. 30 inches to 24 inches **20% decrease**
2. 20.5 meters to 35.5 meters **73% increase**
3. \$126 to \$150 **19% increase**
4. \$75.80 to \$94.75 **25% increase**

Example 3 (p. 371)

5. **MULTIPLE CHOICE** The table shows the number of youth 7 years and older who played soccer from 1998 to 2006. Which statement is supported by the information in the table? **C**

Playing Soccer

Year	Number (millions)
1998	13.2
2000	12.9
2002	13.7
2004	13.3
2006	14.0

Source: National Sporting Goods Association

A The greatest decrease in the number of players occurred from 1998 to 2000.

B There were 7% fewer youth playing soccer in 2004 than in 2002.

C The number of players in 2002 was 6% greater than the number of players in 2000.

D There were 10% more youth playing soccer in 2000 than in 1998.

Practice and Problem Solving

HOMEWORK HELP

For Exercises	See Examples
6–7, 14–15, 18–19	1
8–13, 16–17	2
39, 40	3

Exercise Levels
A: 6–19
B: 20–33
C: 34–38

9. 71% decrease
10. 30% decrease
20. 50% decrease
21. 75% decrease
22. 300% increase
23. 150% increase

For Exercises 6–19, find each percent of change. Round to the nearest whole percent if necessary. State whether the percent of change is an *increase* or a *decrease*.

6. 15 yards to 18 yards **20% increase**
7. 100 acres to 140 acres **40% increase**
8. \$12 to \$6 **50% decrease**
9. 48 notebooks to 14 notebooks
10. 125 centimeters to 87.5 centimeters
11. \$15.60 to \$11.70 **25% decrease**
12. 1.6 hours to 0.95 hour **41% decrease**
13. 132 days to 125.4 days **5% decrease**
14. \$240 to \$320 **33% increase**
15. 624 feet to 702 feet **13% increase**

16. **BOOKS** On Monday, Kenya spent 60 minutes reading her favorite book. Today, she spent 45 minutes reading this book. **25% decrease**

17. **EXERCISE** Three months ago, Ernesto could walk 2 miles in 40 minutes. Today he can walk 2 miles in 25 minutes. **38% decrease**

18. **SCHOOL** Last school year the enrollment of Gilboa Middle School was 465 students. This year the enrollment is 525. **13% increase**

19. **MONEY** Jake had \$782 in his checking account. He now has \$798. **2% increase**

Find each percent of change. Round to the nearest whole percent if necessary. State whether the percent of change is an *increase* or a *decrease*.

20. $\frac{1}{2}$ to $\frac{1}{4}$
21. $\frac{4}{6}$ to $\frac{1}{6}$
22. $\frac{1}{5}$ to $\frac{4}{5}$
23. $\frac{2}{3}$ to $\frac{5}{3}$

DIFFERENTIATED HOMEWORK OPTIONS

Level	Assignment	Two-Day Option	
BL Basic	6–19, 34–36, 38–48	7–19 odd, 39, 40	6–18 even, 34–36, 38, 41–48
OL Core	7–23 odd, 24–36, 38–48	6–19, 39, 40	20–36, 38, 41–48
AL Advanced/Pre-AP	20–44 (optional: 45–48)		

MEASUREMENT **For Exercises 24 and 25, refer to the rectangle at the right. Suppose the side lengths are doubled.**

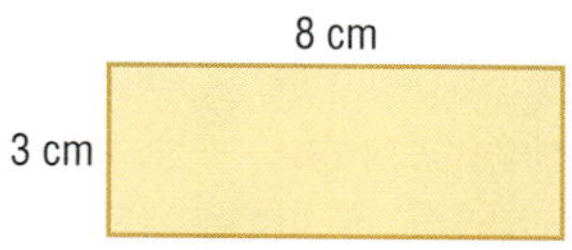

24. Find the percent of change in the perimeter. **100%**
25. Find the percent of change in the area. **400%**
26. **MUSIC PHONES** Between 2006 and 2007, music phone owners increased from 6.8 million to 33 million. Find the percent of increase. Round to the nearest whole percent. **385%**
27. **FIND THE DATA** Refer to the Data File on pages 16–19. Choose some data and write a real-world problem in which you would find the percent of change. **See students' work.**
28. **ANALYZE GRAPHS** Use the graphic shown to find the percent of change in CD sales from 2005 to 2006. **about 4.2%**

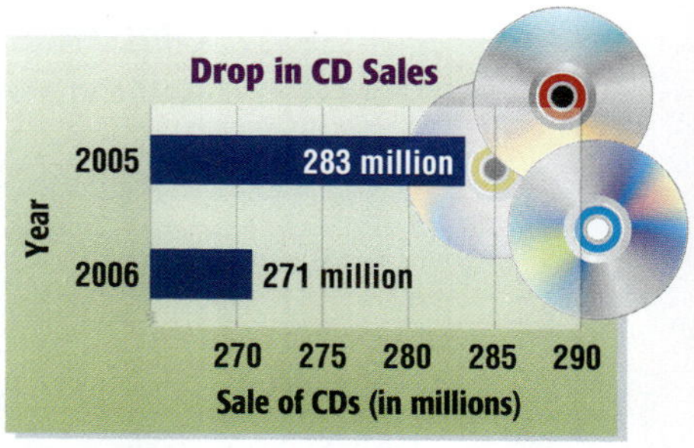

Source: Fox News

29. **SHOES** In 2009, shoe sales for a certain company were $25.9 billion. Sales are expected to increase by about 20% from 2009 to 2010. Find the projected amount of shoe sales in 2010. **about $31 billion**

★ 30. **BABYSITTING** The table shows how many hours Catalina spent babysitting during the months of April and May. If Catalina charges $6.50 per hour, what is the percent of change in the amount of money earned from April to May? **20% decrease**

Month	Hours Worked
April	40
May	32

ANALYZE GRAPHS **For Exercises 31–33, refer to the graph.**

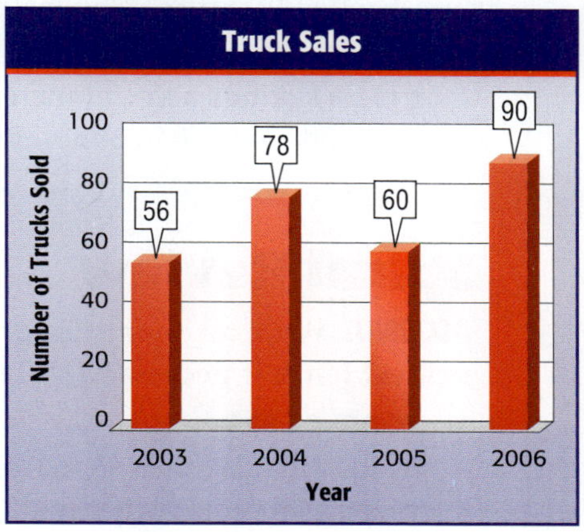

31. Find the percent of decrease of truck sales from 2004 to 2005. Round to the nearest whole percent. **23%**
32. Find the percent of increase of truck sales from 2003 to 2004. Round to the nearest whole percent. **39%**
33. Between which two consecutive years is the percent of increase the greatest? What is the percent of increase? Round to the nearest whole percent. **2005 to 2006; 50%**

34. Sample answer: The sale price of a T-shirt is $14. If the shirt originally cost $25, what is the percent discount? Answer: 44% decrease

Academic Standards • ISTEP+

Extra Practice, pp. 686, 710

H.O.T. Problems

34. **OPEN ENDED** Write a percent of change problem using the quantities 14 and 25, and state whether there is a percent of increase or decrease. Find the percent of change.
35. **NUMBER SENSE** The costs of two different sound systems were decreased by $10. The original costs of the systems were $90 and $60, respectively. Without calculating, which had greater percent of decrease? Explain.

35. The $60 sound system since 10 is a greater part of 60 than of 90.

Differentiated Instruction

Logical Learners Separate students into pairs. Tell them that a tree's height increased 10% from 2007 to 2008, and 5% from 2008 to 2009. Have students discuss whether the tree's height increased by 15% from 2007 to 2009. Then have them use the guess-and-check strategy to test their analyses. The tree's height did not increase by 15% from 2007 to 2009. Each percent of change is calculated separately; the 5% increase is compared to 2008's height, not to 2007's height.

Exercise Alert!

Find the Error In Exercise 36, Trish compared the change in quantity to the new quantity rather than to the original quantity. Remind students that in order to find a percent of change, they must compare the change in quantity to the original quantity.

4 Assess

Crystal Ball Tell students that tomorrow's lesson is about calculating sales tax and discounts on prices. Have students write how they think what they learned today will connect with tomorrow's material.

Formative Assessment

Check for student understanding of concepts in Lessons 7-5 and 7-6.

CRM Quiz 3, p. 62

FOLDABLES Study Organizer Foldables™ Follow-Up

Remind students to record how to find percent of change in their Foldables tables, along with examples.

Additional Answers

37. No; after a 10% increase, the quantity is greater then the original quantity. Decreasing a larger number by the same percent results in a greater change.

38. Sample answer: Compare the change. If the new amount is greater then the original amount, it is a percent of increase. If the new amount is less than the original amount, it is a percent of decrease.

---

36. Sade; Trish did not write a ratio comparing the change to the original amount.

36. **FIND THE ERROR** Sade and Trish are finding the percent of change from $52 to $125. Who is correct? Explain.

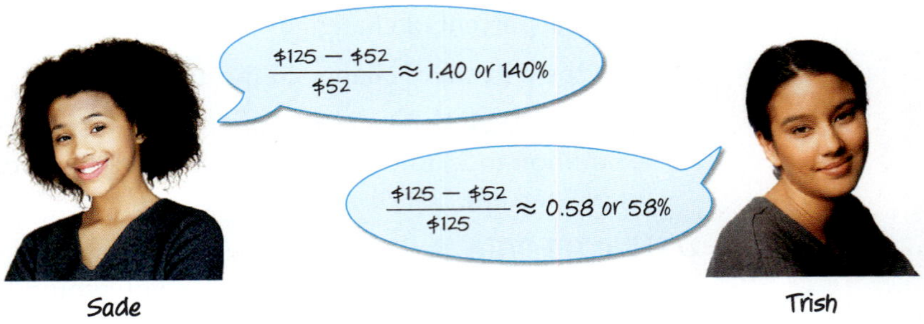

37. **CHALLENGE** If a quantity increases by 10% and then decreases by 10%, will the result be the original quantity? Explain. **See margin.**

38. **WRITING IN MATH** Explain how you know whether a percent of change is a percent of increase or a percent of decrease. **See margin.**

ISTEP+ PRACTICE 7.1.8

39. Which of the following represents the least percent of change? **D**

  A A coat that was originally priced at $90 is now $72.

  B A puppy who weighed 6 ounces at birth now weighs 96 ounces.

  C A child grew from 54 inches to 60 inches in 1 year.

  D A savings account increased from $500 to $550 in 6 months.

40. If each dimension of the rectangle is doubled, what is the percent of increase in the area? **H**

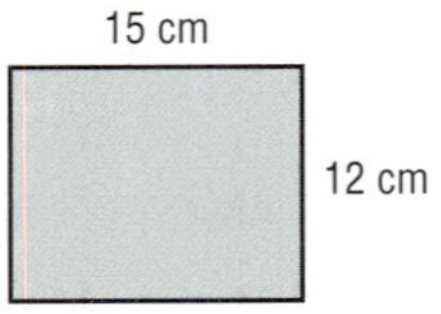

  F 100% H 300%

  G 200% J 400%

Spiral Review

ALGEBRA Write an equation for each problem. Then solve. Round to the nearest tenth if necessary. (Lesson 7-4)

41. **FOOD** Of 823 students 47.2% of the students chose pizza as their favorite food. What is a reasonable estimate for the number of students who chose pizza as their favorite food? Explain. (Lesson 7-5) **Sample answer: 0.5 • 800 or 400 students**

42. 30% of what number is 17? **$0.3w = 17$; 56.7**

43. What is 21% of 62? **$n = 0.21 \cdot 62$; 13.0**

44. **SHOPPING** Four pounds of pecans cost $12.75. How much is this per pound? (Lesson 6-2) **about $3.19/lb**

GET READY for the Next Lesson

PREREQUISITE SKILL Write each percent as a decimal. (Lesson 6-8)

45. 6.5% **0.065** 46. $5\frac{1}{2}$% **0.055** 47. $8\frac{1}{4}$% **0.0825** 48. $6\frac{3}{4}$% **0.0675**

7-7 Sales Tax and Discount

PACING: **Regular:** 1 period, **Block:** 0.5 period

IN Academic Standards

7.1.8 Solve problems involving percents.
- **Find the whole given a part and the percentage.**
- Find percentage increase or decrease.

Also addresses P.1.2, P.4.3.

Options for Differentiated Instruction

ELL = English Language Learner AL = Above or Beyond Grade Level SS = Struggling Students SN = Special Needs

Reviewing Concepts SS SN

Use before presenting Lesson 7-7.

Review with students how to write percents as decimals. Make sure they understand how to work with single digit percents. They often forget to put a zero in the tenths place.

Vocabulary Development ELL SS SN

Use before assigning the Exercises.

Some students may confuse the discount with the discount price. Display the following on the board.

discount price = regular price − discount

Focus on the meaning of the terms by having students write simple descriptions of the terms on an index card.

Term	Description
rate of discount	a percent
discount	the amount of money the price is reduced
discount price	the cost after subtracting the discount

Use Real-World Data ELL AL

Use after students complete Lesson 7-7.

Bring in advertisements from a newspaper or flyer showing sale or discounted items. Then present the following problem.

> Your task is to spend as close to $100 as possible without going over. You have three coupons to use:
>
> 20% off a single item | 35% off a single item | 40% off a single item
>
> You may buy as many items as you need to get close to $100, but you need to use each coupon at least once.

Ask:
- Which coupons did you use with each item?
- How much did you save per item?
- What was your total amount of savings?
- What was the total amount of money you spent?

Have students include calculations to support their work.

Leveled Lesson Resources

Also on TeacherWorks™ Lesson 7-7

Chapter 7 Resource Masters

BL = Below or Approaching Grade Level   OL = On Grade Level   AL = Above or Beyond Grade Level   ELL = English Language Learner

Lesson Reading Guide
p. 46 BL OL ELL

NAME ________ DATE ________ PERIOD ____

7-7 Lesson Reading Guide
Sales Tax and Discount

Get Ready for the Lesson

Read the introduction at the top of page 375 in your textbook. Write your answers below.

1. Calculate the sales tax by finding 4.25% of $1,849. Round to the nearest cent. **$78.58**
2. What will be the total cost including the sales tax? **$1,927.58**
3. Multiply 1.0425 and 1,849. How does the result compare to your answer in Exercise 2? **1,927.58; It is the same.**

Read the Lesson

4. In Example 1, the ≈ is used when the sales tax is found. Why is the value of 0.0575 times 140 rounded? **Sample answer: For dollar amounts, if the decimal has more than two places, the amount is rounded to the nearest cent.**
5. In Method 2 of Example 1, why is the sales tax added to 100%? **Sample answer: 100% represents the cost of the item; the cost of the item plus the sales tax equals 100% plus the percent that is sales tax.**
6. In Examples 2 and 3, the percent equation is used to find discount price and to find the original price. When using the percent equation, how do you represent the percent? **Sample answer: as a decimal**

Remember What You Learned

7. Use the Internet to find the state sales tax in your state, including tax on food, prescription drugs, and nonprescription drugs, if applicable. Then suppose you have a cold and you go to a local pharmacy. You purchase a box of crackers for $2.99 and a bottle of over-the-counter pain reliever for $8.49. Your doctor ordered a prescription for you for your cold and you pay $10 for this prescription. Using the sales tax for your state, what is your total cost at the pharmacy, including taxes? **See students' work.**

Chapter 7 46 Course 2

*Study Guide and Intervention**
p. 47 BL OL ELL

NAME ________ DATE ________ PERIOD ____

7-7 Study Guide and Intervention
Sales Tax and Discount

Sales tax is a percent of the purchase price and is an amount paid in addition to the purchase price. **Discount** is the amount by which the regular price of an item is reduced.

Example 1 SOCCER **Find the total price of a $17.75 soccer ball if the sales tax is 6%.**

Method 1
First, find the sales tax.
6% of $17.75 = 0.06 · 17.75
≈ 1.07
The sales tax is $1.07.
Next, add the sales tax to the regular price.
1.07 + 17.75 = 18.82
The total cost of the soccer ball is $18.82.

Method 2
100% + 6% = 106% Add the percent of tax to 100%.
The total cost is 106% of the regular price.
106% of $17.75 = 1.06 · 17.75
≈ 18.82

Example 2 TENNIS **Find the price of a $69.50 tennis racket that is on sale for 20% off.**

First, find the amount of the discount *d*.
part = percent · whole
d = 0.2 · 69.50 Use the percent equation.
d = 13.90 The discount is $13.90.
So, the sale price of the tennis racket is $69.50 − $13.90 or $55.60.

Exercises
Find the total cost or sale price to the nearest cent.

1. $22.95 shirt; 7% sales tax **$24.56**
2. $39.00 jeans; 25% discount **$29.25**
3. $35 belt; 40% discount **$21**
4. $115.48 watch; 6% sales tax **$122.41**
5. $16.99 book; 5% off **$16.14**
6. $349 television; 6.5% sales tax **$371.69**

Chapter 7 47 Course 2

*Skills Practice**
p. 48 BL OL

NAME ________ DATE ________ PERIOD ____

7-7 Skills Practice
Sales Tax and Discount

Find the total cost or sale price to the nearest cent.

1. $49.95 CD player; 5% discount **$47.45**
2. $69 shoes; 6% sales tax **$73.14**
3. $2.99 socks; 5.5% sales tax **$3.15**
4. $119 coat; 40% discount **$71.40**
5. $299 DVD player; 7% sales tax **$319.93**
6. $49 tie; 15% discount **$41.65**
7. $59 power tool; 5% sales tax **$61.95**
8. $17.99 CD; 10% discount **$16.19**
9. $79 cell phone; 20% discount **$63.20**
10. $65 concert ticket; 7.5% sales tax **$69.88**
11. $459 television; 30% discount **$321.30**
12. $19,995 car; 6.5% sales tax **$21,294.68**

Find the original price to the nearest cent.

13. boots: discount, 30% sale price, $62.50 **$89.29**
14. video game: discount, 15% sale price, $12.64 **$14.87**
15. drum set: discount, 10% sale price, $1,099 **$1,221.11**
16. gloves: discount, 30% sale price, $16.40 **$23.43**
17. sweater: discount, 30% sale price, $34 **$48.57**
18. sunglasses: discount, 20% sale price, $62.95 **$78.69**
19. dinner for two: discount, 5% sale price, $70 **$73.68**
20. bicycle: discount, 25% sale price, $147.85 **$197.13**

Chapter 7 48 Course 2

*Practice**
p. 49 OL AL

NAME ________ DATE ________ PERIOD ____

7-7 Practice
Sales Tax and Discount

Find the total cost or sale price to the nearest cent.

1. $18 haircut; 10% discount **$16.20**
2. $299 lawn mower; 5% tax **$313.95**
3. $9.99 meal; 25% discount **$7.49**
4. $149 guitar; 20% discount **$119.20**
5. $15.75 music CD; 4% tax **$16.38**
6. $24 gym bag; 8% tax **$25.92**
7. $32.88 jacket; 50% discount **$16.44**
8. $3.45 coffee; 33% discount **$2.31**
9. $9.99 chair; $8\frac{1}{2}$% tax **$10.84**

Find the original price to the nearest cent.

10. bracelet: discount, 40% sale price, $13.80 **$23.00**
11. bicycle: discount, 35% sale price, $79 **$121.54**

12. TICKETS State residents get discounts at various theme parks throughout the state. One theme park charges a state resident $51.70. If this price represents a 15% discount from the regular adult admission, find the cost of a regular adult admission to the nearest cent. **$60.82**
13. TRUCKS What is the sales tax on a $17,500 truck if the tax rate is 6%? **$1,050**

COMPUTERS **For Exercises 14–16, use the following information.**
Lionel is buying a computer that normally sells for $890. The state sales tax is 6%.

14. What is the total cost of the computer including tax? **$943.40**
15. If the computer is on sale with a 10% discount, what is the sale price of the computer before adding the sales tax? **$801.00**
16. What is the sales tax on the discounted price? **$48.06**

Chapter 7 49 Course 2

*Word Problem Practice**
p. 50 OL AL

NAME ________ DATE ________ PERIOD ____

7-7 Word Problem Practice
Sales Tax and Discount

1. SKATEBOARDS Ines wants to buy a skateboard but she does not know if she has enough money. The price of the skateboard is $85 and the sales tax is 6%. What will be the total cost of the skateboard? **$90.10**
2. PRETZELS The Spanish club sold hot pretzels as a fund-raiser. The pretzels normally sold for $1.50, but near the end of the sale they wanted to sell as many as possible, so they reduced the price by 30%. What was the new price for a hot pretzel? **$1.05**
3. COMPUTERS Andrea ordered a computer on the Internet. The computer cost $1,499 plus $7\frac{1}{2}$% sales tax. What was the total amount Andrea paid for her computer? **$1,611.43**
4. BOOKS Nate went shopping at a bookstore. The price of the book he selected was $14.95, but it had a sale sticker on it. When he paid for the book, he was charged $12.71 before sales tax was added. What was the percent of discount to the nearest percent? **15%**
5. CELL PHONES Justin is buying a cell phone that has a regular price of $149. The cell phone is on sale for 15% off the regular price. What will be the sale price? **$126.65**
6. MAGAZINES Ivan bought two magazines for $4.95 each. If the sales tax was 6.75%, what was the total amount that he paid for the magazines? **$10.57**
7. MOVIES A video store is having a sale in which DVDs are on sale for 20% off. During this sale, what is the cost of three DVDs that regularly cost $16.99? **$40.78**
8. MODELS The original price of a collectible model airplane is $115. The discounted price is $99. What is the percent of discount to the nearest percent? **14%**

Chapter 7 50 Course 2

Enrichment
p. 51 OL AL

NAME ________ DATE ________ PERIOD ____

7-7 Enrichment

Taxes

Texas is one of the few states that does not impose a state income tax on residents. However, the state does collect sales and use taxes. The Texas state sales tax rate is 6.25%. Local taxing authorities can require additional tax of up to 2%, raising the total possible tax rate to 8.25%.

Use the Sales and Use Tax Chart below to solve the following problems.

Texas City	Total Sales and Use Tax
Abilene	8.25%
Corral City	8%
Sadler	7.25%
Ackerly	7.75%
San Antonio	8.125%
Raccoon Bend	6.75%
Dallas	8.25%

1. Kendra purchases a sweater that costs $24.99 at the Corral City Mall. What is the total cost of the sweater? **$26.99**
2. Brandon agrees to buy a new car for $21,525. As an employee of the company that produces the car, he is entitled to an additional 15% discount. He must pay the Dallas City sales tax. What is the total amount Brandon will pay for his new car? **$19,805.69**
3. While at the Abilene Outlet Store, Barbara purchases an outfit that is regularly priced $113.49 on sale for $99.00. What is the percent of discount? **12.8%**
4. Sara pays a total of $32.43 for an item after a 25% discount and the Ackerly City tax were applied. What is the original amount of Sara's purchase? **$40.13**
5. Davis makes a list of the cost of each item he would like to buy with his $100.00 gift card. Determine if Davis has enough money to purchase everything on his list after the Sadler City tax is applied. If not, how much more money will he need? If so, what is the gift card balance?

Item	Cost of Item
CD	$14.99
DVD	$19.99
Headphones	$59.99

No, Davis will need an additional $1.86 to purchase all of the items on his list.

Chapter 7 51 Course 2

Additional Lesson Resources

** Also available in Spanish* ELL

Transparencies
- *5-Minute Check Transparency,* Lesson 7-7

Other Print Products
- *Teaching Mathematics with Manipulatives*
- *Noteables™ Interactive Study Notebook with Foldables™*

Teacher Tech Tools
- *Interactive Classroom CD-ROM,* Lesson 7-7
- *AssignmentWorks,* Lesson 7-7

Student Tech Tools
glencoe.com
- Extra Examples, Chapter 7, Lesson 7
- Self-Check Quiz, Chapter 7, Lesson 7

7-7 Sales Tax and Discount

MAIN IDEA

Solve problems involving sales tax and discount.

IN Academic Standards

7.1.8 Solve problems involving percents.
- **Find the whole given a part and the percentage**
- Find percentage increase or decrease.

Also addresses P.1.2, P.4.3.

New Vocabulary

sales tax
discount

IN Math Online

glencoe.com
- Extra Examples
- Personal Tutor
- Self-Check Quiz

GET READY for the Lesson

KAYAKS Horatio plans to buy a new kayak that costs $1,849. He lives in North Carolina where there is a 4.25% sales tax.

1. Calculate the sales tax by finding 4.25% of $1,849. Round to the nearest cent. **$78.58**
2. What will be the total cost including the sales tax? **$1,927.58**
3. Multiply 1.0425 and 1,849. How does the result compare to your answer in Exercise 2? **1,927.58; It is the same.**

Sales tax is an additional amount of money charged on items that people buy. The total cost of an item is the regular price plus the sales tax.

EXAMPLE Find the Total Cost

1 **ELECTRONICS** **A DVD player costs $140, and the sales tax is 5.75%. What is the total cost of the DVD player?**

METHOD 1 **Add sales tax to the regular price.**

First, find the sales tax.

5.75% of $140 = 0.0575 × 140 — Write 5.75% as a decimal.
= 8.05 — The sales tax is $8.05.

Next, add the sales tax to the regular price.
$8.05 + $140 = $148.05

METHOD 2 **Add the percent of tax to 100%.**

100% + 5.75% = 105.75% — Add the percent of tax to 100%.

The total cost is 105.75% of the regular price.

105.75% of $140 = 1.0575 × $140 — Write 105.75% as a decimal.
= $148.05 — Multiply.

So, the total cost of the DVD player is $148.05.

CHOOSE Your Method

a. **CLOTHES** What is the total cost of a sweatshirt if the regular price is $42 and the sales tax is $5\frac{1}{2}$%? **$44.31**

Study Tip

Sales Tax and Discount If both are represented as percents, sales tax is a percent of increase, and discount is a percent of decrease.

Discount is the amount by which the regular price of an item is reduced. The sale price is the regular price minus the discount.

7-7 Lesson Notes

1 Focus

Vertical Alignment

Before Lesson 7-7
Interpret percents as a part of a hundred; find decimal and percent equivalents for common fractions and explain why they represent the same value; compute a given percent of a whole number

Lesson 7-7
Calculate given percents of quantities and solve problems

After Lesson 7-7
Solve problems that involve discounts, markups, commissions, and profit and compute simple and compound interest

2 Teach

Scaffolding Questions

Ask:
- If I buy a radio for $100, and the tax is 5%, how much will I pay? $105
- If I buy a chair for $100, and the tax is 3%, how much will I pay? $103
- If a video game normally costs $100, but is on sale at a 10% discount, how much will it cost? $90

Formative Assessment

Use the Check Your Progress exercises after each Example to determine students' understanding of concepts.

Tips for New Teachers

Sales Tax

It may be helpful to point out to students that sales tax varies by states and that some states, like Alaska and Montana, do not have sales tax.

Additional Examples are also in:
- Noteables™ Interactive Study Notebook with Foldables™
- Interactive Classroom PowerPoint® Presentations

ADDITIONAL EXAMPLE

1 **GOLF** A set of golf balls sells for $20, and the sales tax is 5.75%. What is the total cost? $21.15

Focus on Mathematical Content

Sales tax is calculated as a **percent of increase.**

A discount is calculated as a **percent of decrease.**

Total cost can be calculated by **adding the sales tax to the price** of an item. Total cost can also be calculated by **adding the percent of tax to 100%** and then using the percent equation.

Sale price can be calculated by **subtracting the discount from the normal price** of an item. Sale price can also be calculated by **subtracting the percent of discount from 100%** and then using the percent equation.

ADDITIONAL EXAMPLES

2 OUTERWEAR Whitney wants to buy a new coat that has a regular price of $185. This weekend, the coat is on sale at a 33% discount. What is the sale price of the coat? $123.95

3 WATCHES A sports watch is on sale for $60.20 after a 30% discount. What is the original price? $86

Tips for New Teachers — Calculating Tax

Point out that adding the percent of tax to—or subtracting the percent of discount from—100% usually involves simpler computations than adding the sales tax to—or subtracting the discount from—the regular price.

EXAMPLE Find the Sale Price

2 BOOGIE BOARDS A boogie board that has a regular price of $69 is on sale at a 35% discount. What is the sale price of the boogie board?

METHOD 1 Subtract the discount from the regular price.

First, find the amount of the discount.

35% of $69 = 0.35 • $69 — Write 35% as a decimal.
= $24.15 — The discount is $24.15.

Next, subtract the discount from the regular price.
$69 – $24.15 = $44.85

METHOD 2 Subtract the percent of discount from 100%.

100% – 35% = 65% — Subtract the discount from 100%.

The sale price is 65% of the regular price.

65% of $69 = 0.65 • $69 — Write 65% as a decimal.
= 44.85 — Multiply.

So, the sale price of the boogie board is $44.85.

CHOOSE Your Method

b. **MUSIC** A CD that has a regular price of $15.50 is on sale at a 25% discount. What is the sale price of the CD? **$11.63**

Study Tip

Percent Equation
Remember that, in the percent equation, the percent must be written as a decimal. Since the sale price is 70% of the original price, use 0.7 to represent 70% in the percent equation.

EXAMPLE Find the Original Price

3 CELL PHONES A cell phone is on sale for 30% off. If the sale price is $239.89, what is the original price?

The sale price is 100% – 30% or 70% of the original price.

Words	$239.89 is 70% of what price?
Variable	Let p represent the original price.
Equation	$239.89 = 0.7 × p

$239.89 = 0.7p$ — Write the equation.

$\frac{239.89}{0.7} = \frac{0.7p}{0.7}$ — Divide each side by 0.7.

$342.70 = p$ — Simplify.

The original price is $342.70.

CHECK Your Progress **$293.57**

c. Find the original price if the sale price of the cell phone is $205.50.

Tips for New Teachers — Choosing Methods

In Example 2, both methods involve multiplication and subtraction. Method 2 is often preferred over Method 1 because the subtraction is easier in Method 2.

★ indicates multi-step problem

CHECK Your Understanding

Find the total cost or sale price to the nearest cent.

Example 1 (p. 375)
1. \$2.95 notebook; 5% tax **\$3.10**
2. \$46 shoes; 2.9% tax **\$47.33**

Example 2 (p. 376)
3. \$1,575 computer; 15% discount **\$1,338.75**
4. \$119.50 skateboard; 20% off **\$95.60**

Example 3 (p. 376)
5. **IN-LINE SKATES** A pair of in-line skates is on sale for \$90. If this price represents a 9% discount from the original price, what is the original price to the nearest cent? **\$98.90**

Practice and Problem Solving

HOMEWORK HELP

For Exercises	See Examples
6–13	1–2
14–17	3

Exercise Levels
A: 6–17
B: 18–22
C: 23–26

Find the total cost or sale price to the nearest cent. **6. \$46.40**

6. \$58 ski lift ticket; 20% discount
7. \$1,500 computer; 7% tax **\$1,605**
8. \$99 CD player; 5% tax **\$103.95**
9. \$12.25 pen set; 60% discount **\$4.90**
10. \$4.30 makeup; 40% discount **\$2.58**
11. \$7.50 meal; 6.5% tax **\$7.99**
12. \$39.60 sweater; 33% discount **\$26.53**
13. \$89.75 scooter; $7\frac{1}{4}$% tax **\$96.26**
14. **COSMETICS** A bottle of hand lotion is on sale for \$2.25. If this price represents a 50% discount from the original price, what is the original price to the nearest cent? **\$4.50**
15. **TICKETS** At a movie theater, the cost of admission to a matinee is \$5.25. If this price represents a 30% discount from the evening price, find the evening price to the nearest cent. **\$7.50**

Find the original price to the nearest cent.

16. calendar: discount, 75% sale price, \$2.25 **\$9.00**
17. telescope: discount, 30% sale price, \$126 **\$180.00**
18. **VIDEO GAMES** What is the sales tax of a \$178.90 video game system if the tax rate is 5.75%? **\$10.29**

★ 19. **RESTAURANTS** A restaurant bill comes to \$28.35. Find the total cost if the tax is 6.25% and a 20% tip is left on the amount before tax. **\$35.79**

SKATEBOARDS For Exercises 20–22, use the information in the table at the right.

A skateboard costs \$320, not including the sales tax.

State	2007 Sales Tax Rate
Washington	6.5%
Kansas	5.3%
North Carolina	4.25%

Source: Federation of Tax Administrators

20. What is the total cost of the skateboard, including tax in Washington? **\$340.80**
21. What is the total cost of the skateboard, including tax, in North Carolina? **\$333.60**
22. ★ A store in Kansas has the skateboard on sale for 20% off. If the sales tax is calculated after the discount, what is the cost of the skateboard? **\$269.57**

Academic Standards • ISTEP+
Extra Practice, pp. 686, 710

3 Practice

Formative Assessment

Use Exercises 1–5 to check for understanding.

Then use the chart at the bottom of this page to customize your assignments for students.

Intervention You may wish to use the Study Guide and Intervention Master on page 47 of the *Chapter 7 Resource Masters* for additional reinforcement.

Odd/Even Assignments

Exercises 6–17 are structured so that students practice the same concepts whether they are assigned odd or even problems.

DIFFERENTIATED HOMEWORK OPTIONS

Level	Assignment	Two-Day Option	
BL Basic	6–17, 24–36	7–17 odd, 27–29	6–16 even, 24–26, 30–36
OL Core	7–17 odd, 18–22, 24–36	6–17, 27–29	18–22, 24–26, 30–36
AL Advanced/Pre-AP	18–33 (optional: 34–36)		

4 Assess

Name the Math Tell students that a music CD that normally costs $18 is on sale at a 25% discount. If the sales tax is 6.25%, have them write what mathematical procedures they would use to find the actual cost of the CD.

Additional Answer

26. One method is to find 30% of the regular price, then subtract the amount from the regular price. Another method is to find 70% of the regular price. Sample answer: The second method is more efficient because it can be done in one step rather than in two.

H.O.T. Problems

24. Sample answer: The regular price of a CD is $17.95. The total cost is $18.98.

25. $50, $25; The percent of discount is 50%. All of the other pairs have a discount of 25%.

23. **CHALLENGE** A gift store is having a sale in which all items are discounted 20%. Including tax, Colin paid $21 for a picture frame. If the sales tax rate is 5%, what was the original price of the picture frame? **$25**

24. **OPEN ENDED** Give an example of the regular price of an item and the total cost including sales tax if the tax rate is 5.75%.

25. **Which One Doesn't Belong?** In each pair, the first value is the regular price of an item and the second value is the sale price. Identify the pair that does not have the same percent of discount as the other three. Explain.

$24, $18 | $50, $25 | $12, $9 | $80, $60

26. **WRITING IN MATH** Describe two methods for finding the sale price of an item that is discounted 30%. Which method do you prefer? Explain. **See margin.**

ISTEP+ PRACTICE 7.1.8

27. A computer software store is having a sale. The table shows the regular price, r, and the sales price, s, of various items.

Item	Regular Price (r)	Sale Price (s)
A	$5.00	$4.00
B	$8.00	$6.40
C	$10.00	$8.00
D	$15.00	$12.00

Which formula can be used to calculate the sale price? **C**

A $s = r \times 0.2$ **C** $s = r \times 0.8$

B $s = r - 0.2$ **D** $s = r - 0.8$

28. A chair that costs $210 was reduced by 40% for a one day sale. After the sale, the sale price was increased by 40%. What is the price of the chair? **F**

F $176.40 **H** $205.50

G $185.30 **J** $210.00

29. Juanita paid $10.50 for a T-shirt at the mall. It was on sale for 30% off. What was the original price before the discount? **C**

A $3.15 **C** $15.00

B $7.35 **D** $35.00

Spiral Review

Find each percent of change. Round to the nearest whole percent if necessary. State whether the percent of change is an *increase* or *decrease*. (Lesson 7-6)

30. 4 hours to 6 hours **50% increase**

31. $500 to $456 **9% decrease**

32. 20.5 meters to 35.5 meters **73% increase**

33. **TRAVEL** Out of a 511-mile trip, Mya drove about 68% on Monday. Determine a reasonable estimate for the number of miles she drove on Monday. (Lesson 7-5) **about 500 × 0.7 or 350 mi**

GET READY for the Next Lesson

PREREQUISITE SKILL Multiply. Write in simplest form. (Lesson 5-5)

34. $\frac{2}{7} \cdot \frac{4}{5}$ **$\frac{8}{35}$**

35. $\frac{1}{8} \cdot \frac{4}{9}$ **$\frac{1}{18}$**

36. $\frac{6}{11} \cdot \frac{9}{24}$ **$\frac{9}{44}$**

378 Chapter 7 Applying Percents

7-8 Simple Interest

PACING: **Regular:** 1.5 periods, **Block:** 1 period

IN Academic Standards

Preparation for 8.1.6 Solve percent, ratio and proportion problems.

- Find average rates.
- Express one quantity as a percentage.
- Compare two quantities by percentage.
- Use percentages greater than 100%
- Increase or decrease a quantity by a given percentage.
- Find the original amount for a given percentage increase or decrease.
- Solve problems involving percents, ratios and proportions.
- Solve problems involving simple and compound interest.

Also addresses P.1.2, P.4.3.

Options for Differentiated Instruction

ELL = English Language Learner   AL = Above or Beyond Grade Level   SS = Struggling Students   SN = Special Needs

Creating Study Cards ELL SS SN

Use before presenting the Examples.

Have students create a study card for simple interest. It should include the formula, a description of each variable, and a checklist of steps to use to find simple interest.

$I = prt$

I → interest

p → principal, the amount of money deposited or invested

r → rate, written as a decimal

t → time, time invested or borrowed in years

Checklist of steps:

- Write the rate as a decimal.
- Make sure the time is in years.
- Multiply.

Real-World Connections ELL AL SS

Use after presenting Lesson 7-8.

Have students go to several banks in their community or neighborhood and collect information about the interest offered for savings accounts.

Ask:

- Which bank has the best interest on their savings accounts?
- Are there any restrictions about how much money needs to be in the account?
- Are there other types of accounts that offer a higher interest?

Cooperative Learning ELL AL SS SN

Use after students complete Lesson 7-8.

Pair students with different math abilities. Then have partners take turns role-playing banking scenarios similar to those in the lesson. The banker must present options, such as better rates for longer time periods, and provide calculations for interest earned or paid. The customer must verify the calculations and choose an option. Each pair should write a summary of the transactions.

Leveled Lesson Resources

Also on TeacherWorks™ Lesson 7-8

Chapter 7 Resource Masters

BL = Below or Approaching Grade Level OL = On Grade Level AL = Above or Beyond Grade Level ELL = English Language Learner

Lesson Reading Guide
p. 52 BL OL ELL

NAME ______ DATE ______ PERIOD ____

7-8 Lesson Reading Guide
Simple Interest

Get Ready for the Lesson

Read the introduction at the top of page 379 in your textbook. Write your answers below.

1. Calculate 2.50% of $200 to find the amount of money that Suni can earn in one year at Federal Credit Bank. **$5**
2. Calculate 2.75% of $200 to find the amount of money Suni can earn in one year at First Bank. **$5.50**

Read the Lesson

3. In Example 4, why is t replaced with $\frac{1}{12}$? **Sample answer: because the length of time is one month, one-twelfth of a year**
4. Complete the following table that gives the conversion of months to years.

Number of months	2	3	4	6	8	9	10
Ratio of number of months to 12 months	$\frac{2}{12}$	$\frac{3}{12}$	$\frac{4}{12}$	$\frac{6}{12}$	$\frac{8}{12}$	$\frac{9}{12}$	$\frac{10}{12}$
Simplified ratio	$\frac{1}{6}$	$\frac{1}{4}$	$\frac{1}{3}$	$\frac{1}{2}$	$\frac{2}{3}$	$\frac{3}{4}$	$\frac{5}{6}$

Remember What You Learned

5. Write the formula for simple interest and explain what each of the letters in the formula stands for. **$I = prt$: I represents the simple interest; p represents the principal, the amount of money originally deposited, invested, or borrowed; r represents the annual interest rate written as a decimal; t represents the amount of time in years that the principal is invested or borrowed.**
6. Look up the word *interest* in a dictionary. Write the meaning that matches the way the word is used in this lesson. **Sample answer: money paid for the use of money**
7. When do you earn interest? When do you have to pay interest? **You earn interest on money you deposit or invest. You pay interest on money you borrow.**

Chapter 7 52 Course 2

Study Guide and Intervention*
p. 53 BL OL ELL

NAME ______ DATE ______ PERIOD ____

7-8 Study Guide and Intervention
Simple Interest

Simple interest is the amount of money paid or earned for the use of money. To find simple interest I, use the formula $I = prt$. Principal p is the amount of money deposited or invested. Rate r is the annual interest rate written as a decimal. Time t is the amount of time the money is invested in years.

Example 1 **Find the simple interest earned in a savings account where $136 is deposited for 2 years if the interest rate is 7.5% per year.**

$I = prt$ Formula for simple interest
$I = 136 \cdot 0.075 \cdot 2$ Replace p with $136, r with 0.075, and t with 2.
$I = 20.40$ Simplify.

The simple interest earned is $20.40.

Example 2 **Find the simple interest for $600 invested at 8.5% for 6 months.**

6 months $= \frac{6}{12}$ or 0.5 year Write the time as years.
$I = prt$ Formula for simple interest
$I = 600 \cdot 0.085 \cdot 0.5$ $p = \$600$, $r = 0.085$, $t = 0.5$
$I = 25.50$ Simplify.

The simple interest is $25.50.

Exercises

Find the interest earned to the nearest cent for each principal, interest rate, and time.

1. $300, 5%, 2 years **$30**
2. $650, 8%, 3 years **$156**
3. $575, 4.5%, 4 years **$103.50**
4. $735, 7%, $2\frac{1}{2}$ years **$128.63**
5. $1,665, 6.75%, 3 years **$337.16**
6. $2,105, 11%, $1\frac{3}{4}$ years **$405.21**
7. $903, 8.75%, 18 months **$118.52**
8. $4,275, 19%, 3 months **$203.06**

Lesson 7-8

Chapter 7 53 Course 2

Skills Practice*
p. 54 BL OL

NAME ______ DATE ______ PERIOD ____

7-8 Skills Practice
Simple Interest

Find the interest earned to the nearest cent for each principal, interest rate, and time.

1. $500, 4%, 2 years **$40**
2. $350, 6.2%, 3 years **$65.10**
3. $740, 3.25%, 2 years **$48.10**
4. $725, 4.3%, $2\frac{1}{2}$ years **$77.94**
5. $955, 6.75%, $3\frac{1}{4}$ years **$209.50**
6. $1,540, 8.25%, 2 years **$254.10**
7. $3,500, 4.2%, $1\frac{3}{4}$ years **$257.25**
8. $568, 16%, 8 months **$60.59**

Find the interest paid to the nearest cent for each loan balance, interest rate, and time.

9. $800, 9%, 4 years **$288**
10. $280, 5.5%, 4 years **$61.60**
11. $1,150, 7.6%, 5 years **$437**
12. $266, 5.2%, 3 years **$41.50**
13. $450, 22%, 1 year **$99**
14. $2,180, 7.7%, $2\frac{1}{2}$ years **$419.65**
15. $2,650, 3.65%, $4\frac{1}{2}$ years **$435.26**
16. $1,245, 5.4%, 6 months **$33.62**

Chapter 7 54 Course 2

Practice*
p. 55 OL AL

NAME ______ DATE ______ PERIOD ____

7-8 Practice
Simple Interest

Find the simple interest earned to the nearest cent for each principal, interest rate, and time.

1. $750, 7%, 3 years **$157.50**
2. $1,200, 3.5%, 2 years **$84.00**
3. $450, 5%, 4 months **$7.50**
4. $1,000, 2%, 9 months **$15.00**
5. $530, 6%, 1 year **$31.80**
6. $600, 8%, 1 month **$4.00**

Find the simple interest paid to the nearest cent for each loan, interest rate, and time.

7. $668, 5%, 2 years **$66.80**
8. $720, 4.25%, 3 months **$7.65**
9. $2,500, 6.9%, 6 months **$86.25**
10. $500, 12%, 18 months **$90.00**
11. $300, 9%, 3 years **$81.00**
12. $2,000, 20%, 1 year **$400.00**
13. ELECTRONICS Rita charged $126 for a DVD player at an interest rate of 15.9%. How much will Rita have to pay after 2 months if she makes no payments? **$129.34**
14. VACATION The average cost for a vacation is $1,050. If a family borrows money for the vacation at an interest rate of 11.9% for 6 months, what is the total cost of the vacation including the interest on the loan? **$1,112.48**

For Exercises 15–17, use the following information.

Robin has $2,500 to invest in a CD (certificate of deposit).

15. If Robin invests the $2,500 in the CD that yields 4% interest, what will the CD be worth after 2 years? **$2,700**
16. Robin would like to have $3,000 altogether. If the interest rate is 5%, in how many years will she have $3,000? **4 years**
17. Suppose Robin invests the $2,500 for 3 years and earns $255. What was the rate of interest? **3.4%**

Lesson 7-8

Chapter 7 55 Course 2

Word Problem Practice*
p. 56 OL AL

NAME ______ DATE ______ PERIOD ____

7-8 Word Problem Practice
Simple Interest

1. SAVINGS ACCOUNT How much interest will Hannah earn in 4 years if she deposits $630 in a savings account at 6.5% simple interest? **$163.80**
2. INVESTMENTS Terry invested $2,200 in the stock market for 2 years. If the investment earned 12% simple interest, how much money did Terry earn in interest in 2 years? **$528**
3. SAVINGS ACCOUNT Malik deposited $1,050 in a savings account, and it earned $241.50 in simple interest after four years. Find the interest rate on Malik's savings account. **5.75%**
4. INHERITANCE Kelli Rae's inheritance from her great-grandmother was $220,000 after taxes. If Kelli Rae invests this money in a savings account that earns $18,260 in simple interest every year, what is the interest rate on her account? **8.3%**
5. RETIREMENT Mr. Pham has $410,000 in a retirement account that earns 3.85% simple interest each year. Find the amount earned each year by this investment. **$15,785**
6. COLLEGE FUND When Melissa was born, her parents put $8,000 into a college fund account that earned 9% simple interest. Find the total amount in the account after 18 years. **$20,960**
7. LOTTERY Raj won $900,000 in a regional lottery. After paying $350,000 in taxes, he invested the remaining money in a savings account at 4.25% simple interest. How much money is in the account if Raj makes no deposits or withdrawals for two years? **$596,750**
8. SAVINGS Mona opened a savings account with a $500 deposit and a simple interest rate of 5.6%. If there were no deposits or withdrawals, how much money is in the account after $8\frac{1}{2}$ years? **$738**

Chapter 7 56 Course 2

Enrichment
p. 57 OL AL

NAME ______ DATE ______ PERIOD ____

7-8 Enrichment

Taking an Interest

When interest is paid on both the amount of the deposit and any interest already earned, interest is said to be **compounded**. You can use the formula below to find out how much money is in an account for which interest is compounded.

$$A = P(1 + r)^n$$

In the formula, P represents the principal, or amount deposited, r represents the rate applied each time interest is paid, n represents the number of times interest is given, and A represents the amount in the account.

Example **A customer deposited $1,500 in an account that earns 8% per year. If interest is compounded and earned semiannually, how much is in the account after 1 year?**

Use the formula $A = P(1 + r)^n$.
Since interest is earned semiannually, $r = 8 \div 2$ or 4% and $n = 2$.
$A = 1{,}500(1 + 0.04)^2$ Use a calculator.
$= 1{,}622.40$
After 1 year, there is $1,622.40 in the account.

Exercises

Use the compound interest formula and a calculator to find the value of each of these investments. Round each answer to the nearest cent.

1. $2,500 invested for 1 year at 6% interest compounded semiannually **$2,652.25**
2. $3,600 invested for 2 years at 7% interest compounded semiannually **$4,131.08**
3. $1,000 invested for 5 years at 8% interest compounded annually **$1,469.33**
4. $2,000 invested for 6 years at 12% interest compounded quarterly **$4,065.59**
5. $4,800 invested for 10 years at 9% interest compounded annually **$11,363.35**
6. $10,000 invested for 15 years at 7.5% interest compounded semiannually **$30,174.71**

Lesson 7-8

Chapter 7 57 Course 2

*** Also available in Spanish** ELL

Additional Lesson Resources

Transparencies

- *5-Minute Check Transparency*, Lesson 7-8

Other Print Products

- *Noteables™ Interactive Study Notebook with Foldables™*

Teacher Tech Tools

- *Interactive Classroom CD-ROM*, Lesson 7-8
- *AssignmentWorks*, Lesson 7-8

Student Tech Tools

glencoe.com

- Extra Examples, Chapter 7, Lesson 8
- Self-Check Quiz, Chapter 7, Lesson 8

7-8 Simple Interest

MAIN IDEA

Solve problems involving simple interest.

IN Academic Standards

Preparation for 8.1.6 Solve percent, ratio and proportion problems.

- Find average rates.
- Express one quantity as a percentage.
- Compare two quantities by percentage.
- Use percentages greater than 100%
- Increase or decrease a quantity by a given percentage.
- Find the original amount for a given percentage increase or decrease.
- Solve problems involving percents, ratios and proportions.
- Solve problems involving simple and compound interest.

Also addresses P.1.2, P.4.3.

New Vocabulary

principal
simple interest

IN Math Online

glencoe.com

- Extra Examples
- Personal Tutor
- Self-Check Quiz

GET READY for the Lesson

INVESTING Suni plans to save the $200 she received for her birthday. The graphs shows the average yearly rates at three different banks.

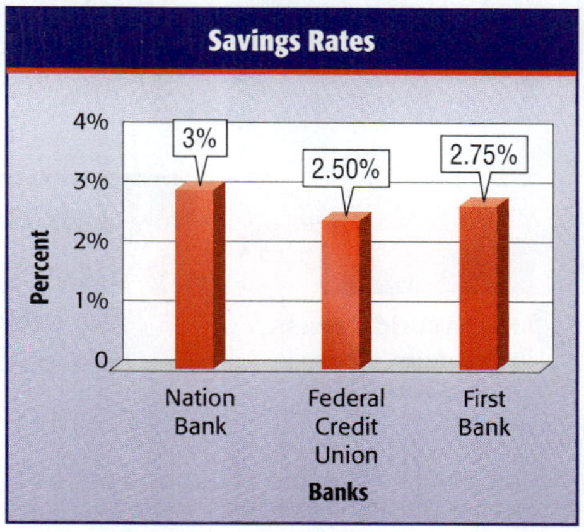

1. Calculate 2.50% of $200 to find the amount of money Suni can earn in one year at Federal Credit Bank. **$5**
2. Calculate 2.75% of $200 to find the amount of money Suni can earn in one year at First Bank. **$5.50**

Principal is the amount of money deposited or borrowed.
Simple interest is the amount paid or earned for the use of money. To find simple interest I, use the following formula.

$$I = prt$$

Interest (I); Principal (p); Annual interest rate, written as a decimal (r); Time, expressed in years (t).

EXAMPLES Find Interest Earned

CHECKING Arnold has $580 in a savings account that pays 3% simple interest. How much interest will he earn in each amount of time?

1 **5 years**

$I = prt$	Formula for simple interest
$I = 580 \cdot 0.03 \cdot 5$	Replace p with \$580, r with 0.03, and t with 5.
$I = 87$	Simplify.

Arnold will earn $87 in interest in 5 years.

2 **6 months**

6 months $= \frac{6}{12}$ or 0.5 year	Write the time as years.
$I = prt$	Formula for simple interest
$I = 580 \cdot 0.03 \cdot 0.5$	$p = \$580, r = 0.03, t = 0.5$
$I \approx 8.7$	Simplify.

Arnold will earn $8.70 in interest in 6 months.

7-8 Lesson Notes

1 Focus

Vertical Alignment

Before Lesson 7-8
Interpret percents as a part of a hundred; find decimal and percent equivalents for common fractions and explain why they represent the same value; compute a given percent of a whole number

Lesson 7-8
Calculate given percents of quantities and solve problems

After Lesson 7-8
Solve problems that involve discounts, markups, commissions, and profit and compute simple and compound interest

2 Teach

Scaffolding Questions

Ask:

- How many of you have savings accounts in a bank?
- What are the advantages of keeping your money in a bank? Security; the bank pays interest.
- What is the rate of interest your bank pays on your account? Answers will vary.

Formative Assessment

Use the Check Your Progress exercises after the Examples to determine students' understanding of concepts.

Tips for New Teachers

Fractions of Years

The amount of time, t, must be expressed in years in order to use the formula $I = prt$. Since 9 months $= \frac{9}{12}$ or 0.75 year, use either $\frac{9}{12}$ or 0.75 for t.

ADDITIONAL EXAMPLES

SAVINGS Brandon found a bank offering a certificate of deposit that pays 4% simple interest. He has $1,500 to invest. How much interest will he earn in each amount of time?

1. 3 years $180
2. 30 months $150

CHECK Your Progress

SAVINGS **Jenny has $1,560 in a savings account that pays 2.5% simple interest. How much interest will she earn in each amount of time?**

a. 3 years **$117**

b. 6 months **$19.50**

The formula $I = prt$ can also be used to find the interest owed when you borrow money. In this case, p is the amount of money borrowed, and t is the amount of time the money is borrowed.

EXAMPLE Find Interest Paid on a Loan

3 **LOANS** **Rondell's parents borrow $6,300 from the bank for a new car. The interest rate is 6% per year. How much simple interest will they pay if they take 2 years to repay the loan?**

$I = prt$	Formula for simple interest
$I = 6{,}300 \cdot 0.06 \cdot 2$	Replace p with \$6,300, r with 0.06, and t with 2.
$I = 756$	Simplify.

Rondell's parents will pay $756 in interest in 2 years.

Real-World Career . . .
How does a Car Salesperson Use Math?
A car salesperson must be able to determine values of cars, calculate interest rates, and determine monthly payments.

IN Math Online
For more information go to glencoe.com.

CHECK Your Progress

c. **LOANS** Mrs. Hanover borrows $1,400 at a rate of 5.5% per year. How much simple interest will she pay if it takes 8 months to repay the loan? **$51.33**

EXAMPLE Find Total Paid on a Credit Card

4 **CREDIT CARDS** **Derrick's dad bought new tires for $900 using a credit card. His card has an interest rate of 19%. If he has no other charges on his card and does not pay off his balance at the end of the month, how much money will he owe after one month?**

$I = prt$	Formula for simple interest
$I = 900 \cdot 0.19 \cdot \frac{1}{12}$	Replace p with \$900, r with 0.19, and t with $\frac{1}{12}$.
$I = 14.25$	Simplify.

The interest owed after one month is $14.25. So, the total amount owed would be $900 + $14.25 or $914.25.

Study Tip
Fractions of Years
Remember to express 1 month as $\frac{1}{12}$ year in the formula.

CHECK Your Progress

d. **CREDIT CARDS** An office manager charged $425 worth of office supplies on a charge card with an interest rate of 9.9%. How much money will he owe if he makes no other charges on the card and does not pay off the balance at the end of the month? **$428.51**

Focus on Mathematical Content

To calculate **simple interest**, multiply the principal, the annual interest rate (written as a decimal), and the amount of time in years.

ADDITIONAL EXAMPLES

3 **LOANS** Laura borrowed $2,000 from her credit union to buy a computer. The interest rate is 9% per year. How much interest will she pay if it takes 8 months to repay the loan? $120

4 **CREDIT CARDS** Alma charged a $30 handbag on her credit card with an interest rate of 8%. How much money will she owe if she has no other charges on the card and she does not pay off the balance at the end of the month? $30.20

Additional Examples are also in:

- Noteables™ Interactive Study Notebook with Foldables™
- Interactive Classroom PowerPoint® Presentations

Tips for New Teachers

Real-World Careers

A car salesperson must be able to determine the value of cars, calculate interest rates, and determine monthly payments.

380 Chapter 7 Applying Percents

CHECK Your Understanding

Examples 1, 2 (pp. 379–380)

Find the simple interest earned to the nearest cent for each principal, interest rate, and time.

1. \$640, 3%, 2 years **\$38.40**
2. \$1,500, 4.25%, 4 years **\$255**
3. \$580, 2%, 6 months **\$5.80**
4. \$1,200, 3.9%, 8 months **\$31.20**

Example 3 (p. 380)

Find the simple interest paid to the nearest cent for each loan, interest rate, and time.

5. \$4,500, 9%, 3.5 years **\$1,417.50**
6. \$290, 12.5%, 6 months **\$18.13**

Example 4 (p. 380)

7. **FINANCES** The Masters family financed a computer that costs \$1,200. If the interest rate is 19%, how much will the family owe after one month if no payments are made? **\$1,219.00**

Practice and Problem Solving

HOMEWORK HELP

For Exercises	See Examples
8–9	1
10–11	2
12–15	3
16–17	4

Exercise Levels
A: 8–17
B: 18–21
C: 22–24

Find the simple interest earned to the nearest cent for each principal, interest rate, and time.

8. \$1,050, 4.6%, 2 years **\$96.60**
9. \$250, 2.85%, 3 years **\$21.38**
10. \$500, 3.75%, 4 months **\$6.25**
11. \$3,000, 5.5%, 9 months **\$123.75**

Find the simple interest paid to the nearest cent for each loan, interest rate, and time.

12. \$1,000, 7%, 2 years **\$140**
13. \$725, 6.25%, 1 year **\$45.31**
14. \$2,700, 8.2%, 3 months **\$55.35**
15. \$175.80, 12%, 8 months **\$14.06**

16. **CREDIT CARDS** Leon charged \$75 at an interest rate of 12.5%. How much will Leon have to pay after one month if he makes no payments? **\$75.78**

17. **TRAVEL** A family charged \$1,345 in travel expenses. If no payments are made, how much will they owe after one month if the interest rate is 7.25%? **\$1,353.13**

BANKING For Exercises 18 and 19, use the table.

Home Savings and Loan	
Time	**Rate**
6 months	2.4%
9 months	2.9%
12 months	3.0%
18 months	3.1%

18. What is the simple interest earned on \$900 for 9 months? **\$19.58**
19. Find the simple interest earned on \$2,500 for 18 months. **\$116.25**

INVESTING For Exercises 20 and 21, use the following information.

Ramon has \$4,200 to invest for college.

20. If Ramon invests \$4,200 for 3 years and earns \$630, what was the simple interest rate? **5%**
21. Ramon's goal is to have \$5,000 after 4 years. Is this possible if he invests with a rate of return of 6%? Explain. **Yes, he would have \$5,208.**

Academic Standards • ISTEP+

Extra Practice, pp. 687, 711

3 Practice

Formative Assessment

Use Exercises 1–7 to check for understanding.

Then use the chart at the bottom of this page to customize your assignments for students.

Intervention You may wish to use the Study Guide and Intervention Master on page 53 of the *Chapter 7 Resource Masters* for additional reinforcement.

Odd/Even Assignments

Exercises 8–17 are structured so that students practice the same concepts whether they are assigned odd or even problems.

Tips for New Teachers

Interest

Some students may be aware that credit card companies normally do not charge interest on a new balance for the first month. Example 4 and Exercise 16 are meant to be illustrative, not necessarily realistic.

DIFFERENTIATED HOMEWORK OPTIONS

Level	Assignment	Two-Day Option	
BL Basic	8–17, 22, 24–33	9–17 odd, 25, 26	8–16 even, 22, 24, 27–33
OL Core	9–17 odd, 18–22, 24–33	8–17, 25, 26	18–22, 24, 27–33
AL Advanced/Pre-AP	18–33		

4 Assess

Ticket Out the Door Have students write whether they would prefer to deposit $1,000 at a simple interest rate of 3% for 5 years, or $1,000 at a simple interest rate of 4% for 4 years. Make sure they explain their reasoning.

Formative Assessment

Check for student understanding of concepts in Lessons 7-7 and 7-8.

CRM Quiz 4, p. 62

FOLDABLES Study Organizer — Foldables™ Follow-Up

Remind students to record how to calculate simple interest in their Foldables tables, along with examples.

Tips for New Teachers — Compound Interest

After students complete Exercise 23, point out that this way of calculating interest and principal is called compound interest. At the end of each time period, the interest is added, or compounded, to the principal. Most banks and financial institutions use this method of compound interest rather than simple interest.

Additional Answer

24. Sample answer: Write the interest rate as a decimal and write the months in years. Then multiply $500 \cdot 0.06 \cdot 1.5 = \$45$.

H.O.T. Problems

22. Sample answer: If the rate is increased by 1%, then the interest earned is $60 more. If the time is increased by 1 year, then the interest earned is $36 more.

22. **OPEN ENDED** Suppose you earn 3% on a $1,200 deposit for 5 years. Explain how the simple interest is affected if the rate is increased by 1%. What happens if the time is increased by 1 year?

23. **CHALLENGE** Mrs. Antil deposits $800 in a savings account that earns 3.2% interest annually. At the end of the year, the interest is added to the principal or original amount. She keeps her money in this account for three years without withdrawing any money. Find the total in her account after each year for three years. **$825.60, $852.02, $879.28**

24. **WRITING IN MATH** List the steps you would use to find the simple interest on a $500 loan at 6% interest rate for 18 months. Then find the simple interest. **See margin.**

ISTEP+ PRACTICE Preparation for 8.1.6

25. Jada invests $590 in a money market account. Her account pays 7.2% simple interest. If she does not add or withdraw any money again, how much interest will Jada's account earn after 4 years of simple interest? **C**

    A $75.80
    B $158.67
    C $169.92
    D $220.67

26. Mr. Sprockett borrows $3,500 from his bank to buy a used car. The loan has a 7.4% annual simple interest rate. If it takes Mr. Sprockett two years to pay back the loan, what is the total amount he will be paying? **G**

    F $3,012
    G $4,018
    H $4,550
    J $3,598

Spiral Review

27. Find the total cost of a $19.99 DVD if the tax rate is 7%. (Lesson 7-7) **$21.39**

Find each percent of change. Round to the nearest whole percent if necessary. State whether the percent of change is an increase or decrease. (Lesson 7-6)

28. 35 birds to 45 birds **29% increase**
29. 60 inches to 38 inches **37% decrease**
30. $2.75 to $1.80 **35% decrease**

Divide. Write in simplest form. (Lesson 5-7)

31. $\frac{3}{5} \div \frac{1}{2}$ **$1\frac{1}{5}$**
32. $\frac{4}{7} \div \frac{5}{8}$ **$\frac{32}{35}$**
33. $2\frac{2}{3} \div 1\frac{1}{4}$ **$2\frac{2}{15}$**

Problem Solving in Art — Real-World Unit Project

It's Golden! It's time to complete your project. Use the information and data you have gathered about the Golden Ratio to prepare a Power Point presentation. Be sure to include your reports and calculations in your presentation.

IN Math Online Unit Project at glencoe.com

382 **Chapter 7** Applying Percents

Extend 7-8

Spreadsheet Lab
Simple Interest

MAIN IDEA

Use a spreadsheet to calculate simple interest.

IN Academic Standards

Preparation for 8.1.6 Solve percent, ratio and proportion problems.

- Find average rates.
- Express one quantity as a percentage.
- Compare two quantities by percentage.
- Use percentages greater than 100%
- Increase or decrease a quantity by a given percentage.
- Find the original amount for a given percentage increase or decrease.
- Solve problems involving percents, ratios and proportions.
- Solve problems involving simple and compound interest.

Also addresses P.1.2, P.7.1.

A computer spreadsheet is a useful tool for quickly calculating simple interest for different values of principal, rate, and time.

ACTIVITY

Max plans on opening a "Young Savers" account at his bank. The current rate on the account is 4%. He wants to see how different starting balances, rates, and times will affect his account balance. To find the balance at the end of 2 years for different principal amounts, he enters the values B2 = 4 and C2 = 2 into the spreadsheet below.

Simple Interest.xls

	A	B	C	D	E
1	Principal (*p*)	Rate (*r*)	Time (*t*)	Interest (*I*)	New Balance
2					
3	500	=B2/100	=C2	=A3*B3*C3	=A3+D3
4	1000	=B2/100	=C2	=A4*B4*C4	=A4+D4
5	1500	=B2/100	=C2	=A5*B5*C5	=A5+D5
6	2000	=B2/100	=C2	=A6*B6*C6	=A6+D6
7	2500	=B2/100	=C2	=A7*B7*C7	=A7+D7

Sheet 1 | Sheet 2 | Sheet 3

For each principal given in column A, simple interest is calculated for any values of rate and time entered in B2 and C2, respectively.

The spreadsheet adds simple interest to the principal.

ANALYZE THE RESULTS

1. Why is the rate in column B divided by 100? **to change the percent to a decimal**
2. What is the balance in Max's account after 2 years if the principal is \$1,500 and the simple interest rate is 4%? **\$1,620**
3. How much interest does Max earn in 2 years if his account has a principal of \$2,000 and a simple interest rate of 4%? **\$160**
4. Is the amount of principal proportional to the interest Max earns if his account earns 4% simple interest over 2 years? Explain.
5. Is the amount of principal proportional to the balance in Max's account if it earns 4% simple interest over 2 years? Explain.
6. What entries for cells B2 and C2 would you use to calculate the simple interest on a principal of \$1,500 at a rate of 7% for a 9-month period? **B2: 7, C2: 0.75**
7. What is the balance of this account at the end of the 9 months? **\$1,578.75**

4, 5. See margin.

Extend 7-8 **Lesson Notes**

1 Focus

Materials

- computers with spreadsheet program

Teaching Tip

If your classroom has computers with a spreadsheet program, you might want to have students use the computers to complete the lab. If so, have students work in pairs or groups of three.

2 Teach

Activity Make sure students realize that the spreadsheet uses the same formula for simple interest that they learned in Lesson 7-8 (see column D).

3 Assess

Formative Assessment

Use Exercise 2 to determine whether students understand how a spreadsheet calculates simple interest.

From Concrete to Abstract Use Exercise 6 to bridge the gap between using a spreadsheet to calculate simple interest and knowing what information the spreadsheet would need.

Additional Answers

4. Yes; Sample answer: As the amount of principle triples from \$500 to \$1,500, the amount of interest triples from \$40 to \$120. This indicates that the principle is proportional to the interest for an account earning 4% interest over 2 years.

5. Yes; Sample answer: As the amount of principal triples from \$500 to \$1,500, the balance in the account triples from \$540 to \$1,620. This indicates that the principle is proportional to the balance in an account earning 4% interest over 2 years.

Chapter 7 Study Guide and Review

FOLDABLES Study Organizer — Dinah Zike's Foldables

Have students look through the chapter to make sure they have included key concepts and examples for each lesson in their Foldable tables.

Encourage students to refer to their Foldables while completing the Study Guide and Review and while preparing for the Chapter Test.

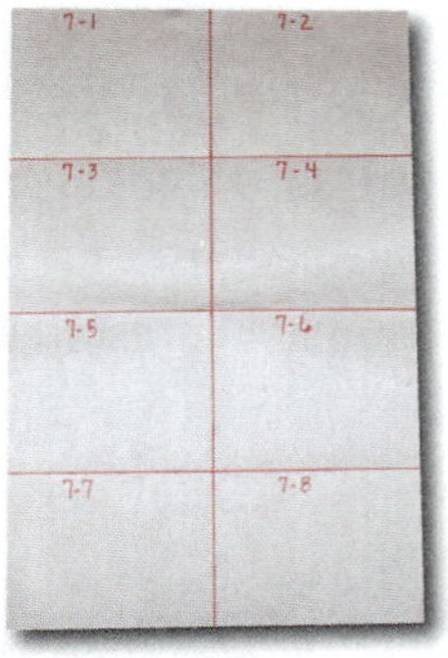

Formative Assessment

Key Vocabulary The page references after each word denote where that term was first introduced. If students have difficulty answering Exercises 1–10, remind them that they can use these page references to refresh their memories about the vocabulary terms.

IN Math Online glencoe.com

Vocabulary PuzzleMaker improves students' mathematics vocabulary using four puzzle formats–crossword, scramble, word search using a word list, and word search using clues. Students can work online or from a printed worksheet.

Summative Assessment

CRM Vocabulary Test, p. 64

Chapter 7 Study Guide and Review

IN Math Online glencoe.com
- STUDY TO GO
- Vocabulary Review

FOLDABLES Study Organizer — GET READY to Study

Be sure the following Big Ideas are noted in your Foldable.

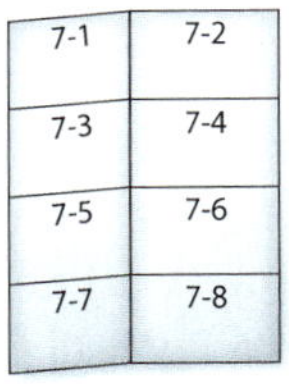

BIG Ideas

Percent of a Number (Lesson 7-1)
- To find the percent of a number, first write the percent as either a fraction or decimal and then multiply.

Percent Proportion (Lesson 7-2)

$$\frac{\text{part}}{\text{whole}} = \frac{n}{100} \Big\} \text{percent}$$

Percent and Estimation (Lesson 7-3)
- One way to estimate the percent of a number is to use a fraction. The other way is to first find 10% of the number and then multiply.

Percent Equation (Lesson 7-4)

$$\text{part} = \text{percent} \cdot \text{whole}$$

Percent of Change (Lesson 7-6)
- A percent of change is a ratio that compares the change in quantity to the original amount.

$$\text{percent of change} = \frac{\text{amount of change}}{\text{original amount}}$$

Sales Tax and Discount (Lesson 7-7)
- Sales tax is an additional amount of money charged on items. The total cost of an item is the regular price plus the sales tax.
- Discount is the amount by which the regular price of an item is reduced. The sale price is the regular price minus the discount.

Simple Interest (Lesson 7-8)
- Simple interest is the amount paid or earned for the use of money.

$$I = prt$$

9. false; original

Key Vocabulary

discount (p. 375)
percent equation (p. 361)
percent of change (p. 369)
percent of decrease (p. 369)
percent of increase (p. 369)
percent proportion (p. 350)
principal (p. 379)
sales tax (p. 375)
simple interest (p. 379)

Vocabulary Check

State whether each sentence is *true* or *false*. If *false*, replace the underlined word or number to make a true sentence.

1. The sale price of a discounted item is the regular price <u>minus</u> the discount. **true**
2. A ratio that compares the change in quantity to the original amount is called the <u>percent of change</u>. **true**
3. A <u>percent proportion</u> compares part of a quantity to the whole quantity using a percent. **true**
4. The formula for simple interest is <u>$I = prt$</u>. **true**
5. A method for estimating the percent of a number is to find <u>21%</u> of the number and then multiply. **false; 10%.**
6. The equation part = percent • whole is known as the <u>principal</u> equation. **false; percent**
7. The <u>principal</u> is the amount of money deposited or borrowed. **true**
8. A <u>tax</u> is the amount by which the regular price of an item is reduced. **false; discount**
9. To find a percent of increase, compare the amount of the increase to the <u>new</u> amount.
10. If the new amount is greater than the original amount, then the percent of change is percent of <u>decrease</u>. **false; increase**

Chapter 7 Study Guide and Review

Lesson-by-Lesson Review

7-1 Percent of a Number (pp. 344–348)

7.1.8

Find each number. Round to the nearest tenth if necessary.

11. Find 78% of 50. 39
12. 45.5% of 75 is what number? 34.1
13. What is 225% of 60? 135
14. 0.75% of 80 is what number? 0.6

Example 1 Find 24% of 200.

24% of 200

$= 24\% \times 200$ Write the expression.

$= 0.24 \times 200$ Write 24% as a decimal.

$= 48$ Multiply.

So, 24% of 200 is 48.

7-2 The Percent Proportion (pp. 350–354)

7.1.8, 7.1.9

Find each number. Round to the nearest tenth if necessary.

15. **SOCCER** A soccer team lost 30% of their games. If they played 20 games, how many did they win? 14 games
16. 6 is what percent of 120? 5%
17. Find 0.8% of 35. 0.3
18. What percent of 375 is 40? 10.7%
19. **PHONE SERVICE** A family pays \$21.99 each month for their long distance phone service. This is 80% of the original price of the phone service. What is the original price of the phone service? Round to the nearest cent if necessary. 19. \$27.49

Example 2 What percent of 90 is 18?

$\frac{18}{90} = \frac{n}{100}$ Write the proportion.

$18 \cdot 100 = 90 \cdot n$ Find the cross products.

$1{,}800 = 90n$ Simplify.

$\frac{1{,}800}{90} = \frac{90n}{90}$ Divide each side by 90.

$20 = n$ So, 18 is 20% of 90.

Example 3 52 is 65% of what number?

$\frac{52}{w} = \frac{65}{100}$ Write the proportion.

$52 \cdot 100 = w \cdot 65$ Find the cross products.

$5{,}200 = 65w$ Simplify.

$\frac{5{,}200}{65} = \frac{65w}{65}$ Divide each side by 65.

$80 = w$ So, 52 is 65% of 80.

7-3 Percent and Estimation (pp. 355–360)

20–25. Sample answers are given. 21. 40; $\frac{1}{3} \cdot 120 = 40$

7.1.8

Estimate. 20. 20; $\frac{1}{4} \cdot 80 = 20$

20. 25% of 81
21. 33% of 122
22. 77% of 38 30; $\frac{3}{4} \cdot 40 = 30$
23. 19.5% of 96 20; $\frac{1}{5} \cdot 100 = 20$

Estimate by using 10%.

24. 12% of 77 8; $0.1 \cdot 80 = 8$
25. 88% of 400 360; $0.1 \cdot 400 = 40$; $9 \cdot 40 = 360$
26. **BOOKS** About 26% of the 208 books in Deja's collection are nonfiction. Estimate how many of Deja's books are nonfiction. See margin.

Example 4 Estimate 52% of 495.

$52\% \approx 50\%$ or $\frac{1}{2}$, and $495 \approx 500$.

52% of $495 \approx \frac{1}{2} \cdot 500$ or 250

So, 52% of 495 is about 250.

Example 5 Estimate 68% of 80.

10% of 80 = $0.1 \cdot 80$ or 8 Find 10% of 80.

68% is about 70%.

$7 \cdot 8 = 56$ 70% of 80 ≈ 7 • (10% of 80)

So, 68% of 80 is about 56.

Chapter 7 Study Guide and Review

Lesson-by-Lesson Review

Intervention If the given examples are not sufficient to review the topics covered by the questions, remind students that the page references tell them where to review that topic in their textbooks.

Two-Day Option Have students complete the Lesson-by-Lesson Review on pages 385–388. Then you can use ExamView® Assessment Suite to customize another review worksheet that practices all the objectives of this chapter or only the objectives on which your students need more help.

For more information on ExamView® Assessment Suite, see page 340C.

Differentiated Instruction

Super DVD: MindJogger Plus
Use this DVD as an alternative format of review for the test. For more information on this game show format, see page 340D.

Additional Answer

26. Sample answer: $\frac{1}{4} \cdot 200 = 50$ books

Chapter 7 Study Guide and Review 385

Chapter 7 Study Guide and Review

7-4 Algebra: The Percent Equation (pp. 361–365)

7.1.8, 7.2.1

Write an equation for each problem. Then solve. Round to the nearest tenth if necessary. 28. $39 = 0.65 \cdot w$; 60

27. 32 is what percent of 50? $32 = p \cdot 50$; 64%
28. 65% of what number is 39?
29. Find 42% of 300. $n = 0.42 \cdot 300$; 126
30. 7% of 92 is what number? 30. $n = 0.07 \cdot 92$; 6.4
31. 12% of what number is 108? $108 = 0.12 \cdot w$; 900
32. **SALONS** A local hair salon increased their sales of hair products by about 12.5% this week. If they sold 48 hair products, how many hair products did they sell last week? 43

Example 6 **27 is what percent of 90?**

27 is the part and 90 is the base.

Let n represent the percent.

part = percent • base

$27 = n \cdot 90$ Write an equation.

$\frac{27}{90} = \frac{90n}{90}$ Divide each side by 90.

$0.3 = n$ The percent is 30%.

So, 27 is 30% of 90.

7-5 PSI: Determine Reasonable Answers (pp. 366–367)

P.2.1, P.2.2

Determine a reasonable answer for each problem.

33. **CABLE TV** In a survey of 1,813 consumers, 18% said that they would be willing to pay more for cable if they got more channels. Is 3.3, 33, or 333 a reasonable estimate for the number of consumers willing to pay more for cable? 333
34. **SCHOOL** There are 880 students at Medina Middle School. If 68% of the students are involved in sports, would the number of students involved in sports be about 510, 630, or 720? 630
35. **VACATION** Suppose you are going on vacation for $689 and the airfare accounts for 43.5% of the total cost. What is a reasonable cost of the airfare?

Example 7 **Mr. Swanson harvested 1,860 pounds of apples from one orchard, 1,149 pounds from another, and 905 pounds from a third. The apples will be placed in crates that hold 42 pounds of apples. Will Mr. Swanson need 100, 200, or 400 crates?**

Since an exact answer is not needed, we can estimate the total of pounds.

1,860	→	1,900
1,149	→	1,100
+ 905	→	+ 900
		3,900

Since 3,900 ÷ 40 is about 100, it is reasonable that 100 crates need to be ordered.

35. Sample answer: $700 × 0.4 = $280

386 Chapter 7 Applying Percents

Mixed Problem Solving
For mixed problem-solving practice, see page 710.

7-6 Percent of Change (pp. 369–374)

7.1.8

Find each percent of change. Round to the nearest whole percent if necessary. State whether the percent of change is an *increase* or *decrease*.

36. original: 172
new: 254

37. original: $200
new: $386

38. original: 75
new: 60
20% decrease

39. original: $49.95
new: $54.95
10% increase

40. Tyree bought a collectible comic book for $49.62 last year. This year, he sold it for $52.10. Find the percent of change of the price of the comic book. Round to the nearest percent. 5% increase

36. 48% increase
37. 93% increase

Example 8 **A magazine that originally cost $2.75 is now $3.55. Find the percent of change. Round to the nearest whole percent.**

The new price is greater than the original price, so this is a percent of increase.

amount of increase $= 3.55 - 2.75$ or 0.80

$$\text{percent of increase} = \frac{\text{amount of increase}}{\text{original amount}}$$

$$= \frac{0.80}{2.75} \quad \text{Substitution}$$

$$\approx 0.29 \quad \text{Simplify.}$$

The percent of increase is about 29%.

7-7 Sales Tax and Discount (pp. 375–378)

7.1.8

Find the total cost or sale price to the nearest cent.

41. $25 backpack; 7% tax $26.75
42. $210 bicycle; 15% discount $178.50
43. $8,000 car; $5\frac{1}{2}$% tax $8,440
44. $40 sweater; 33% discount $26.80

Find the percent of discount to the nearest percent.

45. shirt: regular price: $42
sale price: $36 14%

46. boots: regular price: $78
sale price: $70 10%

47. **MONEY** At the media store a certain DVD normally costs $21.99. This week the DVD is on sale for 25% off. Tara buys the DVD and pays using a $20 bill. Not including tax, how much change will she receive to the nearest cent? $3.51

Example 9 **A new computer system is priced at $2,499. Find the total cost if the sales tax is 6.5%.**

First, find the sales tax.

$6.5\% \text{ of } \$2{,}499 = 0.065 \cdot 2{,}499$

≈ 162.44

Next, add the sales tax. The total cost is $162.44 + 2{,}499$ or $2,661.44.

Example 10 **A pass at a water park is $58. At the end of the season, the same pass costs $46.40. What is the percent of discount?**

$58 - 46.40 = 11.60$ Find the amount of discount.

Next, find what percent of 58 is 11.60.

$11.60 = n \cdot 58$ Write an equation.

$0.2 = n$ Divide each side by 58.

The percent of discount is 20%.

Chapter 7 Study Guide and Review 387

Problem Solving Review

For additional practice in problem solving for Chapter 7, see the Mixed Problem Solving Appendix, page 710 in the Student Handbook section.

Anticipation Guide

Have students complete the Chapter 7 Anticipation Guide and discuss how their responses have changed now that they have completed Chapter 7.

CRM Anticipation Guide, p. 7

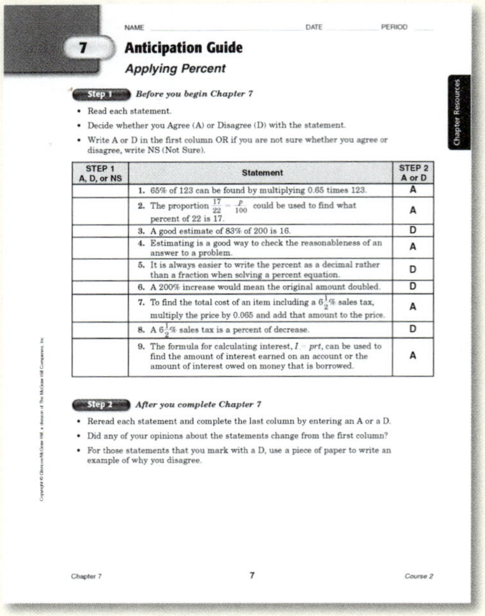

NAME ______ DATE ______ PERIOD ______

7 Anticipation Guide

Applying Percent

Chapter Resources

Step 1 *Before you begin Chapter 7*

- Read each statement.
- Decide whether you Agree (A) or Disagree (D) with the statement.
- Write A or D in the first column OR if you are not sure whether you agree or disagree, write NS (Not Sure).

STEP 1 A, D, or NS	Statement	STEP 2 A or D
	1. 65% of 123 can be found by multiplying 0.65 times 123.	A
	2. The proportion $\frac{17}{22} = \frac{p}{100}$ could be used to find what percent of 22 is 17.	A
	3. A good estimate of 83% of 200 is 16.	D
	4. Estimating is a good way to check the reasonableness of an answer to a problem.	A
	5. It is always easier to write the percent as a decimal rather than a fraction when solving a percent equation.	D
	6. A 200% increase would mean the original amount doubled.	D
	7. To find the total cost of an item including a $6\frac{1}{2}$% sales tax, multiply the price by 0.065 and add that amount to the price.	A
	8. A $6\frac{1}{2}$% sales tax is a percent of decrease.	D
	9. The formula for calculating interest, $I = prt$, can be used to find the amount of interest earned on an account or the amount of interest owed on money that is borrowed.	A

Step 2 *After you complete Chapter 7*

- Reread each statement and complete the last column by entering an A or a D.
- Did any of your opinions about the statements change from the first column?
- For those statements that you mark with a D, use a piece of paper to write an example of why you disagree.

CHAPTER 7 Study Guide and Review

7-8 Simple Interest (pp. 379–382)

8.1.6

Find the interest earned to the nearest cent for each principal, interest rate, and time.

48. \$475, 5%, 2 years **\$47.50**

49. \$5,000, 10%, 3 years **\$1,500**

50. \$2,500, 11%, $1\frac{1}{2}$ years **\$412.50**

51. **SAVINGS** Tonya deposited \$450 into a savings account earning 3.75% annual simple interest. How much interest will she earn in 6 years? **\$101.25**

Find the interest paid to the nearest cent for each loan balance, interest rate, and time.

52. \$3,200, 8%, 4 years **\$1,024**

53. \$1,980, 21%, 9 months **\$311.85**

54. **CREDIT CARDS** David bought a computer for \$600 using his credit card. The interest rate on his credit card is 19%. How much will he pay in all for the computer, if he pays off the balance at the end of 2 years? **\$828**

Example 11 **Find the interest earned on \$400 at 9% for 3 years.**

$I = prt$	Simple interest formula
$I = 400 \cdot 0.09 \cdot 3$	$p = \$400, r = 0.09, t = 3$
$I = 108$	Simplify.

The interest earned is \$108.

Example 12 **Elisa has a loan for \$1,300. The interest rate is 7%. If she pays it off in 6 months, how much interest will she pay?**

$I = prt$	Simple interest formula
$I = 1{,}300 \cdot 0.07 \cdot 0.5$	$p = \$1{,}300, r = 0.07, t = 0.5$
$I = 45.5$	Simplify.

The interest she will pay after 6 months is \$45.50.

CHAPTER 7 Practice Test

IN Math Online glencoe.com
• Chapter Test

Find each number. Round to the nearest tenth if necessary.

1. Find 55% of 164. **90.2**
2. What is 355% of 15? **53.3**
3. Find 25% of 80. **20**

4. **MULTIPLE CHOICE** Of 365 students, 210 bought a hot lunch. About what percent of the students did *not* buy a hot lunch? **B**

   A 35% C 56%
   B 42% D 78%

Estimate. **5–8. See margin.**

5. 18% of 246
6. 145% of 81
7. 71% of 324
8. 56% of 65.4

9. **COMMUNICATION** Theresa makes a long distance phone call and talks for 50 minutes. Of these minutes, 25% were spent talking to her brother. Would the time spent talking with her brother be about 8, 12, or 15 minutes? Explain your reasoning. **12 min; $0.25 \times 48 = 12$**

Write an equation for each problem. Then solve. Round to the nearest tenth if necessary.

10. Find 14% of 65. **$p = 0.14 \cdot 65$; 9.1**
11. What number is 36% of 294?
12. 82% of what number is 73.8? **$73.8 = 0.82 \cdot w$; 90**
13. 75 is what percent of 50? **$75 = n \cdot 50$; 150%**

11. $p = 0.36 \cdot 294$; 105.8

Find each percent of change. Round to the nearest whole percent if necessary. State whether the percent of change is an *increase* or a *decrease*.

14. $60 to $75 **25% increase**
15. 145 meters to 216 meters **49% increase**
16. 48 minutes to 40 minutes **17% decrease**

FOOD For Exercises 17 and 18, use the table below. It shows the results of a survey in which 175 students were asked what type of food they wanted for their class party.

Type of Food	Percent
Subs	32%
Tex-Mex	56%
Italian	12%

17. How many of the 175 students chose Italian food for their class party? **21**
18. How many students chose Tex-Mex food for the party? **98**

Find the total cost or sale price to the nearest cent.

19. $2,200 computer, $6\frac{1}{2}$% sales tax **$2,343**
20. $16 hat, 55% discount **$7.20**
21. $35.49 jeans, 33% discount **$23.78**

Find the simple interest earned to the nearest cent for each principal, interest rate, and time.

22. $750, 3%, 4 years **$90**
23. $1,050, 4.6%, 2 years **$96.60**
24. $2,600, 4%, 3 months **$26**

25. **MULTIPLE CHOICE** Mr. Jackson borrows $3,500 to renovate his home. His loan has an annual simple interest rate of 15%. If he pays off the loan after 6 months, about how much will he pay in all? **F**

    F $3,763
    G $3,500
    H $3,720
    J $4,025

CHAPTER 7 Practice Test

Summative Assessment

Chapter 7 Resource Masters

Leveled Chapter 7 Tests			
Form	**Type**	**Level**	**Pages**
1	MC	BL	65–66
2A	MC	OL	67–68
2B	MC	OL	69–70
2C	FR	OL	71–72
2D	FR	OL	73–74
3	FR	AL	75–76

MC = multiple-choice questions
FR = free-response questions
BL = below or approaching grade level
OL = on grade level
AL = above or beyond grade level

- Vocabulary Test, p. 64
- Extended-Response Test, p. 77
- Unit 3 Test, pp. 81–82

ExamView Assessment Suite Customize and create multiple versions of your chapter tests and the answer keys. All of the questions from the leveled chapter test in the *Chapter 7 Resource Masters* are also available on ExamView® Assessment Suite.

Additional Answers

5. Sample answer: 50; $\frac{1}{5} \cdot 250 = 50$
6. Sample answer: 120; $0.1 \cdot 80 = 8$ and $8 \cdot 15 = 120$
7. Sample answer: 224; $0.1 \cdot 320 = 32$ and $7 \cdot 32 = 224$
8. Sample answer: 33; $\frac{1}{2} \cdot 66 = 33$

Data-Driven Decision Making

Diagnostic Teaching Based on the results of the Chapter 7 Practice Test, use the following to review concepts that students continue to find challenging.

Exercises	Lesson	Academic Standards	Resources for Review
1–8	7-1, 7-2, 7-3	7.1.8	Study Guide and Intervention pp. 10, 17, 24, 30, 35, 40, 47, and 53
9–18	7-4, 7-5, 7-6	7.1.8, 7.2.1, P.2.1, P.2.2, 7.1.8	IN Math Online glencoe.com • Extra Examples • Personal Tutor • Concepts in Motion
19–25	7-7, 7-8	7.1.8	

CHAPTER 7 ISTEP+ Practice

TEST-TAKING TIP

Exercise 6 Have students use mental math to eliminate incorrect answer choices. Since $12 \times 3 = 36$, $12.5 \times 3 > 36$. So, answer choices H and J can be eliminated. Since the product 12.5×3 must end with the digit 5, answer choice F can also be eliminated.

Formative Assessment

You can use these two pages to benchmark student progress.

Chapter 7 Resource Masters

- Standardized Test Practice, pp. 78–80

ExamView Assessment Suite Create practice worksheets or tests that align to your state's standards, as well as TIMSS and NAEP tests.

CHAPTER 7 ISTEP+ Practice
Cumulative, Chapters 1–7

IN Math Online glencoe.com
- Test Practice

PART 1 Multiple Choice

Read each question. Then fill in the correct answer on the answer document provided by your teacher or on a sheet of paper.

1. Sarah wants to buy pillows for her living room. Which store offers the best buy on pillows? **C**

Store	Sale Price
A	3 pillows for $40
B	4 pillows for $50
C	2 pillows for $19
D	1 pillow for $11

A Store A **C** Store C
B Store B **D** Store D

2. The graph below shows the attendance at a summer art festival from 2002 to 2007. If the trend in attendance continues, which is the best prediction of the attendance at the art festival in 2010? **G**

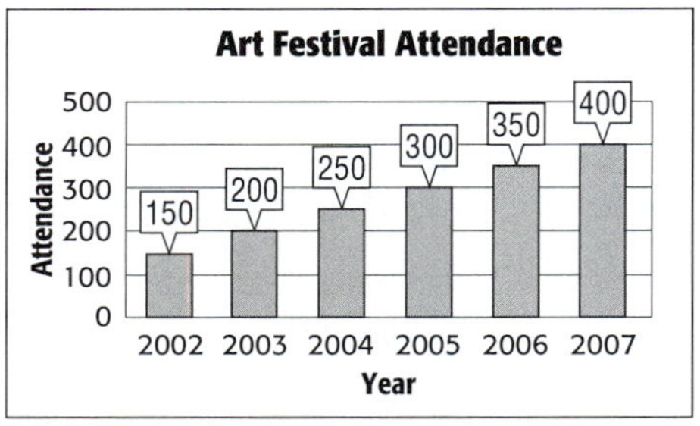

F Fewer than 200
G Between 500 and 600
H Between 700 and 800
J More than 800

3. At their annual car wash, the science club washes 30 cars in 45 minutes. At this rate, how many cars will they wash in 1 hour? **A**

A 40 **C** 50
B 45 **D** 60

4. The cost of Ken's haircut was $23.95. If he wants to give his hair stylist a 15% tip, about how much of a tip should he leave? **G**

F $2.40
G $3.60
H $4.60
J $4.80

5. At a pet store, 38% of the animals are dogs. If there are a total of 88 animals at the pet store, which equation can be used to find x, the number of dogs at the pet store? **C**

A $\frac{x}{88} = \frac{100}{38}$

B $\frac{38}{88} = \frac{100}{x}$

C $\frac{x}{88} = \frac{38}{100}$

D $\frac{100}{88} = \frac{x}{38}$

6. An architect made a model of an office building using a scale of 1 inch equals 3 meters. If the height of the model is 12.5 inches, which of the following represents the actual height of the building? **G**

F 40.0 m
G 37.5 m
H 36.0 m
J 28.4 m

7. Mrs. Stewart painted the door to her deck. The door is a rectangle with length x feet and width y feet. In the middle of the door, there is a rectangular panel of glass that measures 5 feet by 2 feet. Which expression gives the painted area of the door in square feet? **C**

A $x + y - 10$
B $xy + 10$
C $xy - 10$
D $x + y + 10$

390 Chapter 7 Applying Percents

Preparing for ISTEP+
For test-taking strategies and practice, see pages 716–733.

CHAPTER 7 ISTEP+ Practice

8. At a grocery store, half-gallons of milk are on sale 5 for \$4. Find the cost of 7 half-gallons of milk to the nearest cent. **J**

   F \$2.86 H \$5.40
   G \$4.75 J \$5.60

9. If point B is translated 3 units to the left and 2 units up, what will be point B's new coordinates? **D**

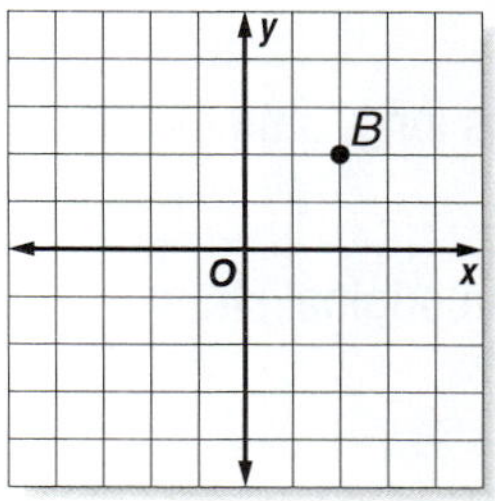

   A $(-3, 2)$ C $(4, -1)$
   B $(5, 0)$ D $(-1, 4)$

10. In Nadia's DVD collection, she has 8 action DVDs, 12 comedy DVDs, 7 romance DVDs, and 3 science fiction DVDs. What percent of Nadia's DVD collection are comedies? **J**

   F 25% H 35%
   G 30% J 40%

11. Cassandra bought 2 dozen juice boxes priced at 6 juice boxes for \$2.29 and 24 snack packages priced at 8 snack packages for \$6.32. What is the total amount, not including tax, she spent on juice boxes and snack packages? **C**

   A \$34.44 C \$28.12
   B \$32.15 D \$25.83

PART 2 Short Response/Grid In

Record your answers on the answer sheet provided by your teacher or on a sheet of paper.

12. The average cost of a 2-bedroom apartment in Grayson was \$625 last year. This year, the average cost is \$650. What is the percent of increase from last year to this year? **4%**

13. A necklace regularly sells for \$18.00. The store advertises a 15% discount. What is the sale price of the necklace in dollars? **15.30**

PART 3 Extended Response

Record your answers on the answer sheet provided by your teacher or on a sheet of paper. Show your work.

TEST-TAKING TIP

Question 14 Remember to show all of your work. You may be able to get partial credit for your answers, even if they are not entirely correct.

14. Cable Company A increases their rates from \$98 a month to \$101.92 a month.

   a. What is the percent of increase? **4%**

   b. Cable Company B offers their cable for \$110 dollars a month, but gives a 10% discount for new customers. Describe two ways to find the cost for new customers. **See margin.**

   c. If you currently use Cable Company A, would it make sense to change to Cable Company B? **See margin.**

NEED EXTRA HELP?														
If You Missed Question...	1	2	3	4	5	6	7	8	9	10	11	12	13	14
Go to Lesson...	6-2	2-6	6-2	7-1	7-2	6-8	3-6	6-6	2-3	7-5	6-1	7-6	7-7	7-6
IN Academic Standards	7.1.9	P.1.3	7.1.9	7.1.8	7.1.9	7.3.5	7.2.4	7.1.9	7.3.6	7.1.9	7.1.9	7.1.8	7.1.8	7.1.8

Answer Sheet Practice

Have students simulate taking a standardized test by recording their answers on a practice recording sheet.

CRM Student Recording Sheet, p. 59

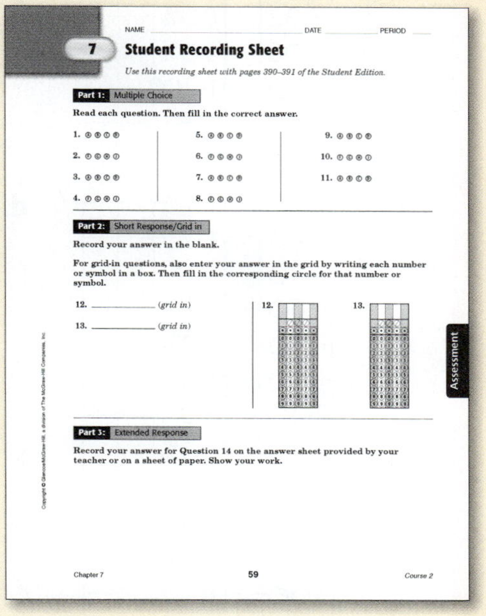

Additional Answer

14b. Sample answer: You can find 10% of \$110 and subtract the amount from \$110; $\$110 - \$11 = \$99$. You can also subtract 10% from 100% and multiply the new percent by \$110; $90\% \times \$110 = \$99$.

14c. Yes, Company B is \$2.92 cheaper a month.

Homework Option

Get Ready for Chapter 8 Assign students the exercises on page 395 as homework to assess whether they possess the prerequisite skills needed for the next chapter.

Pages 342–343, Explore 7-1

a.

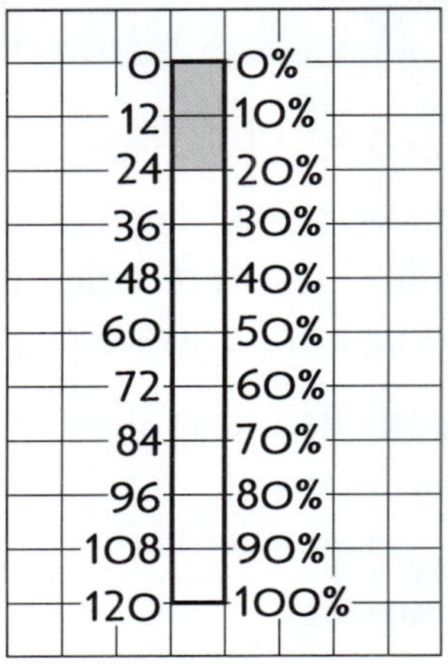

b.

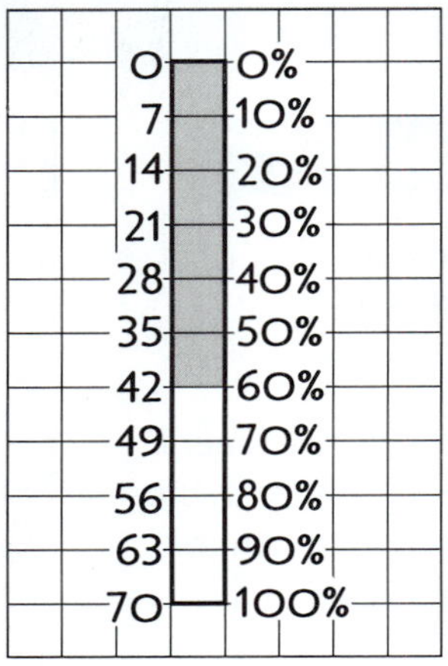

c.

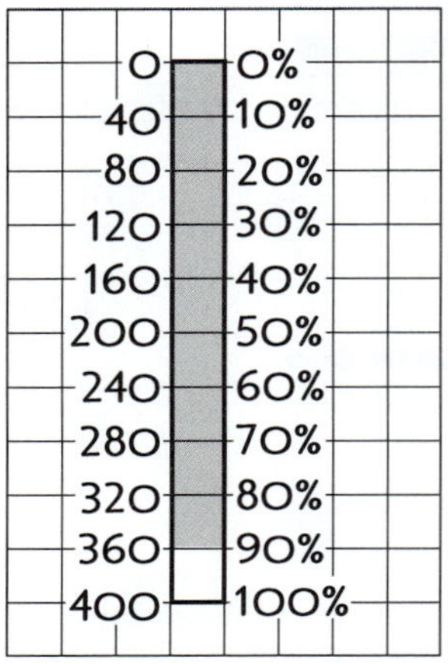

d.

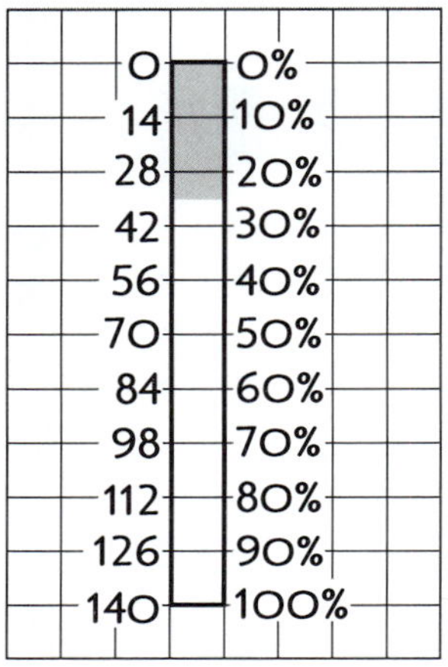

e.

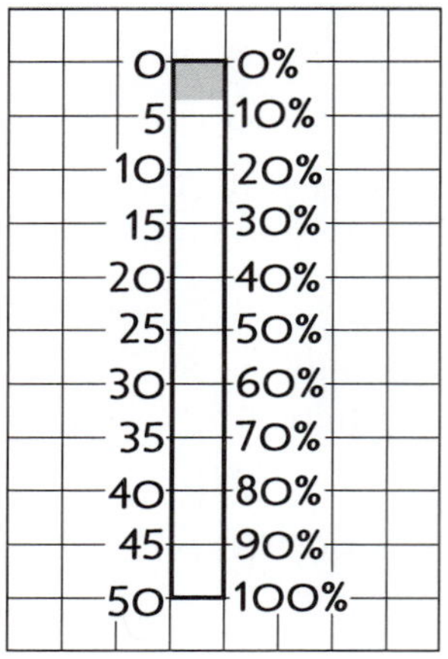

f.

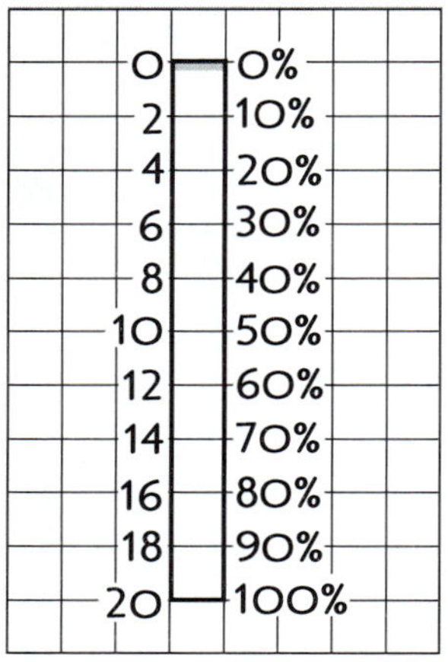

Page 344, Lesson 7-1 (Get Ready for the Lesson)

1. Pet Shelter Fundraiser

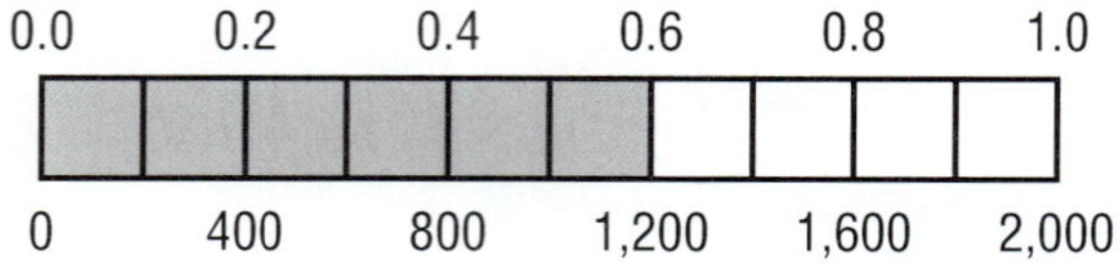

2. Pet Shelter Fundraiser

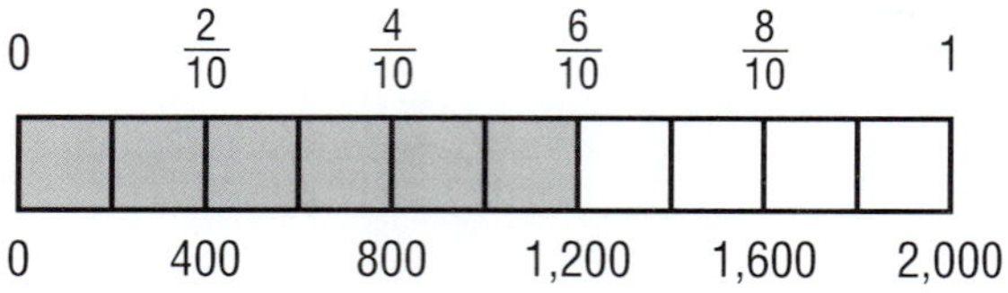

3. $0.6 \times 2{,}000 = 1{,}200$; $\frac{3}{5} \times 2{,}000 = 1{,}200$

Page 358, Lesson 7-3

38. about 2.4 hours; $\frac{1}{10} \cdot 24 = 2.4$

39. about 3 hours; Method 1: $\frac{1}{3} \cdot 24 = 8$ and $\frac{1}{5} \cdot 24 \approx 5$; $8 - 5 = 3$

40. There are $24 \cdot 60$ or 1,440 minutes in one day. So, Amanda spends about $\frac{1}{10}$ of 1,440 or 144 minutes each day on extracurricular activities.

Page 369, Lesson 7-6

4. Sample answer: a straw that is twice as long, 3 times longer, and 4 times longer, respectively.

5. Subtract the percent of change from the original straw.

NOTES

Student Handbook

Built-In Workbooks

Reference

Pages 392–665 can be found in Volume 2.

How to Use the Student Handbook

The Student Handbook is the additional skill and reference material found at the end of books. The Student Handbook can help answer these questions.

What If I Need More Practice?

You, or your teacher, may decide that working through some additional problems would be helpful. The **Extra Practice** section provides these problems for each lesson so you have ample opportunity to practice new skills.

What If I Have Trouble with Word Problems?

The **Mixed Problem Solving** portion of the book provides additional word problems that use the skills presented in each chapter. These problems give you real-world situations where the math can be applied.

What If I Need to Prepare for a Standardized Test?

The **Preparing for Standardized Tests** section provides worked-out examples and practice problems for multiple-choice, gridded response, short-response, and extended-response questions.

What If I Need to Prepare for the ISTEP+?

The **Get Ready for the ISTEP+** section provides practice exercises similar to those found on the ISTEP+.

What If I Forget a Vocabulary Word?

The **English-Spanish Glossary** provides a list of important, or difficult, words used throughout the textbook. It provides a definition in English and Spanish as well as the page number(s) where the word can be found.

What If I Need to Check a Homework Answer?

The answers to the odd-numbered problems are included in **Selected Answers**. Check your answers to make sure you understand how to solve all of the assigned problems.

What If I Need to Find Something Quickly?

The **Index** alphabetically lists the subjects covered throughout the entire textbook and the pages on which each subject can be found.

What If I Forget a Formula?

Inside the back cover of your math book is a list of **Formulas and Symbols** that are used in the book.

Extra Practice

Lesson 1-1

Pages 25–29

Use the four-step plan to solve each problem.

1. The Reyes family rode their bicycles for 9 miles to the park. The ride back was along a different route for 14 miles. How many miles did they ride in all? **23 mi**
2. Four hundred sixty people are scheduled to attend a banquet. If each table seats 8 people, how many tables are needed? **58 tables**
3. A group of 251 people is eating dinner at a school fund-raiser. If each person pays $8.00 for their meal, how much money is raised? **$2,008**
4. Sherita's service charges a monthly fee of $20.00 plus $0.15 per minute. One monthly bill is $31.25. How many minutes did Sherita use during the month? **75 min**
5. ABC Car Rental charges $25 per day to rent a mid-sized car plus $0.20 per mile driven. Mr. Ruiz rents a mid-sized car for 3 days and drives a total of 72 miles. Find the amount of Mr. Ruiz's bill. **$89.40**

Lesson 1-2

Pages 30–33

Write each power as a product of the same factor.

1. 13^4 **13 • 13 • 13 • 13**
2. 9^6 **9 • 9 • 9 • 9 • 9 • 9**
3. 1^7 **1 • 1 • 1 • 1 • 1 • 1 • 1**
4. 12^2 **12 • 12**
5. 5^8 **5 • 5 • 5 • 5 • 5 • 5 • 5 • 5**
6. 15^4 **15 • 15 • 15 • 15**

Evaluate each expression.

7. 5^6 **15,625**
8. 17^3 **4,913**
9. 2^{12} **4,096**
10. 3^5 **243**
11. 1^4 **1**
12. 5^3 **125**
13. 10^2 **100**
14. 2^8 **256**
15. 8^2 **64**
16. 7^4 **2,401**
17. 20^3 **8,000**
18. 42^3 **74,088**

Write each product in exponential form.

19. 2 • 2 • 2 • 2 • 2 **2^5**
20. 3 • 3 **3^2**
21. 1 • 1 • 1 • 1 • 1 • 1 **1^6**
22. 18 • 18 • 18 • 18 **18^4**
23. 9 • 9 • 9 • 9 • 9 • 9 • 9 • 9 **9^8**
24. 10 • 10 • 10 • 10 • 10 • 10 **10^6**

Lesson 1-3

Pages 34–37

Find the square of each number.

1. 4 **16**
2. 19 **361**
3. 13 **169**
4. 25 **625**
5. 9 **81**
6. 2 **4**
7. 14 **196**
8. 24 **576**
9. 40 **1,600**
10. 50 **2,500**
11. 100 **10,000**
12. 250 **62,500**

Find each square root.

13. $\sqrt{324}$ **18**
14. $\sqrt{900}$ **30**
15. $\sqrt{2,500}$ **50**
16. $\sqrt{576}$ **24**
17. $\sqrt{8,100}$ **90**
18. $\sqrt{676}$ **26**
19. $\sqrt{100}$ **10**
20. $\sqrt{784}$ **28**
21. $\sqrt{1,024}$ **32**
22. $\sqrt{841}$ **29**
23. $\sqrt{2,304}$ **48**
24. $\sqrt{3,025}$ **55**

Lesson 1-4

Pages 38–41

Evaluate each expression.

1. $14 - (5 + 7)$ **2**
2. $(32 + 10) - 5 \times 6$ **12**
3. $(50 - 6) + (12 + 4)$ **60**
4. $12 - 2 \cdot 3$ **6**
5. $16 + 4 \times 5$ **36**
6. $(5 + 3) \times 4 - 7$ **25**
7. $2 \times 3 + 9 \times 2$ **24**
8. $6 \cdot (8 + 4) \div 2$ **36**
9. $7 \times 6 - 14$ **28**
10. $8 + (12 \times 4) \div 8$ **14**
11. $13 - 6 \cdot 2 + 1$ **2**
12. $(80 \div 10) \times 8$ **64**
13. $14 - 2 \cdot 7 + 0$ **0**
14. $156 - 6 \times 0$ **156**
15. $30 - 14 \cdot 2 + 8$ **10**
16. $3 \times 4 - 3^2$ **3**
17. $10^2 - 5$ **95**
18. $3 + (10 - 5 + 1)^2$ **39**
19. $(4 + 3)^2 \div 7$ **7**
20. 8×10^3 **8,000**
21. $10^4 \times 6$ **60,000**
22. 4.5×10^3 **4,500**
23. 1.8×10^2 **180**
24. $3 + 5(1.7 + 2.3)$ **23**
25. $4(3.6 + 5.4) - 9$ **27**
26. $10 + 3(6.1 + 3.7)$ **39.4**
27. $6(7.5 + 2.1) - 2.3$ **55.3**

Lesson 1-5

Pages 42–43

Use the *guess and check* strategy to solve each problem.

1. **NUMBERS** A number is divided by 3. Then 8 is added to the quotient. The result is 15. What is the number? **21**
2. **NUMBERS** Benny is thinking of two numbers. Their product is 32 and their difference is 4. Find the numbers. **4 and 8**
3. **MONEY** A theater is charging $5 for children under 12 and $8 for everyone else. If the total for a group of people was $36, how many people under the age of 12 were in the group? **4**
4. **PLACE VALUE** Mindy wrote down a decimal number. The digit in the tenth's place is half the digit in the hundredth's place. If the product of the two digits is 18, what is the number? **0.36**
5. **MONEY** Penny has 14 coins totaling $1.55. She has one more nickel than she has dimes, and three less quarters than nickels. How many quarters, dimes, and nickels does she have if these are the only coin types she has? **3 quarters, 5 dimes, and 6 nickels**
6. **SOUVENIRS** A souvenir shop sells standard-sized postcards in packages of 5 and large-sized postcards in packages of 3. If Juan bought 16 postcards, how many packages of each did he buy? **Juan bought 2 standard size packages and 2 large size packages.**

Lesson 1-6

Pages 44–47

Evaluate each expression if $a = 3$, $b = 4$, $c = 12$, and $d = 1$.

1. $a + b$ **7**
2. $c - d$ **11**
3. $a + b + c$ **19**
4. $b - a$ **1**
5. $c - ab$ **0**
6. $a + 2d$ **5**
7. $b + 2c$ **28**
8. ab **12**
9. $a + 3b$ **15**
10. $6a + c$ **30**
11. $\frac{c}{d}$ **12**
12. abc **144**
13. $2(a + b)$ **14**
14. $\frac{2c}{b}$ **6**
15. $144 - abc$ **0**
16. $2ab$ **24**
17. $\frac{b}{2}$ **2**
18. a^2 **9**
19. $c^2 - 100$ **44**
20. $a^3 + 3$ **30**
21. $2b^2$ **32**
22. $b^3 + c$ **76**
23. $\frac{a^2}{d}$ **9**
24. $5a^2 + 2d^2$ **47**
25. $\frac{4d^2}{b}$ **1**
26. $\frac{15}{a}$ **5**
27. $3a^2$ **27**
28. $10d^3$ **10**
29. $\frac{ab}{c}$ **1**
30. $\frac{(a + b)}{d}$ **7**
31. $2.5b + c$ **22**
32. $\frac{10}{d}$ **10**
33. $\frac{(2c + b)}{b}$ **7**
34. $\frac{(b^2 + 2d)}{a}$ **6**
35. $\frac{(2c + ab)}{c}$ **3**
36. $\frac{(3.5c + 2)}{11}$ **4**

Lesson 1-7

Pages 49–52

Solve each equation mentally.

1. $b + 7 = 12$ **5**
2. $a + 3 = 15$ **12**
3. $s + 10 = 23$ **13**
4. $9 + n = 13$ **4**
5. $20 = 24 - n$ **4**
6. $4x = 36$ **9**
7. $2y = 10$ **5**
8. $15 = 5h$ **3**
9. $j \div 3 = 2$ **6**
10. $14 = w - 4$ **18**
11. $24 \div k = 6$ **4**
12. $b - 3 = 12$ **15**
13. $c \div 10 = 8$ **80**
14. $6 = t \div 5$ **30**
15. $14 + m = 24$ **10**
16. $3y = 39$ **13**
17. $\frac{f}{2} = 12$ **24**
18. $16 = 4v$ **4**
19. $81 = 80 + a$ **1**
20. $9 = \frac{72}{x}$ **8**
21. $66 = 22m$ **3**
22. $77 - 12 = a$ **65**
23. $9k = 81$ **9**
24. $95 + d = 100$ **5**
25. $b = \frac{72}{6}$ **12**
26. $z = 15 + 22$ **37**
27. $15b = 225$ **15**
28. $43 + s = 57$ **14**
29. $4w = 52$ **13**
30. $e - 10 = 0$ **10**
31. $62 - d = 12$ **50**
32. $14f = 14$ **1**
33. $48 \div n = 8$ **6**
34. $a - 82 = 95$ **177**
35. $\frac{x}{2} = 36$ **72**
36. $99 = c \div 2$ **198**

Lesson 1-8 13–24. See Student Handbook Answer Appendix for justification.

Pages 53–56

Use the Distributive Property to evaluate each expression.

1. $3(4 + 5)$ **27**
2. $(2 + 8)6$ **60**
3. $4(9 - 6)$ **12**
4. $8(6 - 3)$ **24**
5. $5(200 - 50)$ **750**
6. $20(3 + 6)$ **180**
7. $(20 - 5)8$ **120**
8. $50(8 + 2)$ **500**
9. $15(1{,}000 - 200)$ **12,000**
10. $3(2{,}000 + 400)$ **7,200**
11. $12(1{,}000 + 10)$ **12,120**
12. $7(1{,}000 - 50)$ **6,650**

Find each expression mentally. Justify each step.

13. $(5 + 17) + 25$ **47**
14. $13 + (22 + 17)$ **52**
15. $(8 + 18) + 92$ **118**
16. $(11 + 32) + 9$ **52**
17. $4 + (15 + 76)$ **95**
18. $(25 + 56) + 75$ **156**
19. $(4 \cdot 21) \cdot 25$ **2,100**
20. $5 \cdot (40 \cdot 8)$ **1,600**
21. $(2 \cdot 38) \cdot 50$ **3,800**
22. $(12 \cdot 7) \cdot 5$ **420**
23. $25 \cdot (12 \cdot 4)$ **1,200**
24. $(15 \cdot 9) \cdot 2$ **270**

Lesson 1-9 1–24. See Student Handbook Answer Appendix.

Pages 57–61

Describe the relationship between the terms in each arithmetic sequence. Then write the next three terms in each sequence.

1. 5, 9, 13, 17, …
2. 3, 5, 7, 9, …
3. 10, 15, 20, 25, …
4. 90, 93, 96, 99, …
5. 8, 14, 20, 26, …
6. 4.5, 5.4, 6.3, 7.2, …
7. 0.3, 0.4, 0.5, …
8. 2.3, 3.4, 4.5, 5.6, …
9. 8.9, 9.1, 9.3, 9.5, …
10. 3, 11, 19, 27, …
11. 350, 375, 400, 425, …
12. 620, 635, 650, 665, …
13. 2, 7, 12, 17, …
14. 10, 17, 24, 31, …
15. 0, 7, 14, 21, …
16. 1, 7, 13, 19, …
17. 95, 101, 107, 113, …
18. 9, 90, 171, 252, …
19. 2.6, 2.8, 3.0, 3.2, …
20. 4.1, 4.6, 5.1, 5.6, …
21. 6.6, 7.7, 8.8, 9.9, …
22. 19.5, 21, 22.5, 24, …
23. 14.5, 14.8, 15.1, 15.4, …
24. 0.1, 0.4, 0.7, 1.0, …

Lesson 1-10

Pages 63–67

Copy and complete each function table. Then identify the domain and range.

1.

x	$2x$	y
0	2(0)	0
1	2(1)	2
2	2(2)	4
3	2(3)	6

domain: {0, 1, 2, 3}
range: {0, 2, 4, 6}

2.

x	$3x + 1$	y
1	3(1) + 1	4
2	3(2) + 1	7
3	3(3) + 1	10
4	3(4) + 1	13

domain: {1, 2, 3, 4}
range: {4, 7, 10, 13}

3.

x	$x - 2$	y
3	3 − 2	1
4	4 − 2	2
5	5 − 2	3
6	6 − 2	4

domain: {3, 4, 5, 6}
range: {1, 2, 3, 4}

4.

x	$x + 0.1$	y
2	2 + 0.1	2.1
3	3 + 0.1	3.1
4	4 + 0.1	4.1
5	5 + 0.1	5.1

domain: {2, 3, 4, 5}
range: {2.1, 3.1, 4.1, 5.1}

Lesson 2-1

Pages 80–83

Write an integer for each situation.

1. seven degrees below zero **−7**
2. a loss of 3 pounds **−3**
3. a loss of 20 yards **−20**
4. a profit of $25 **25**
5. 112°F above 0 **112**
6. 2,830 feet above sea level **2,830**

Graph each set of integers on a number line.

7. $\{-2, 0, 2\}$
8. $\{1, 3, 5\}$
9. $\{-2, -5, 3\}$
10. $\{7, -1, 4\}$

7–10. See Student Handbook Answer Appendix.

Evaluate each expression.

11. $|1|$ **1**
12. $|-8|$ **8**
13. $|0|$ **0**
14. $|-82|$ **82**
15. $|64|$ **64**
16. $|-128|$ **128**
17. $|-22| + 5$ **27**
18. $|-40| - 8$ **32**
19. $|-18| + |10|$ **28**
20. $|-7| + |-1|$ **8**
21. $|98| - |-5|$ **93**
22. $|-49| - |-10|$ **39**

Lesson 2-2

Pages 84–87

Replace each ● with < or > to make a true sentence.

1. 7 ● −7 **>**
2. −8 ● 4 **<**
3. −4 ● −9 **>**
4. −3 ● 0 **<**
5. 8 ● 10 **<**
6. −5 ● −4 **<**
7. 6 ● −7 **>**
8. −12 ● −13 **>**
9. 3 ● 1 **>**
10. −2 ● 2 **<**
11. 7 ● −1 **>**
12. −15 ● −20 **>**
13. −40 ● 30 **<**
14. 0 ● −3 **>**
15. −5 ● 0 **<**
16. 85 ● −17 **>**

Order the integers from least to greatest.

17. −2, −8, 4, 10, −6, −12 **−12, −8, −6, −2, 4, 10**
18. 19, −19, −21, 32, −14, 18 **−21, −19, −14, 18, 19, 32**
19. 18, 23, 95, −95, −18, −23, 2 **−95, −23, −18, 2, 18, 23, 95**
20. 46, −48, −47, −52, −18, 12 **−52, −48, −47, −18, 12, 46**
21. 0, −10, −6, −8, 12 **−10, −8, −6, 0, 12**
22. −15, 18, −1, 0, 14, −20 **−20, −15, −1, 0, 14, 18**

Lesson 2-3
Pages 88–92

Write the ordered pair for each point graphed at the right. Then name the quadrant or axis on which each point is located.

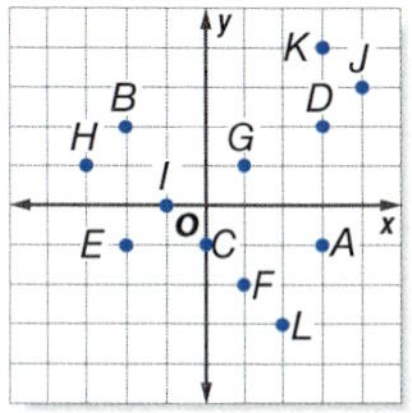

1. A (3, −1), IV
2. B (−2, 2), II
3. C (0, −1), y-axis
4. D (3, 2), I
5. E (−2, −1), III
6. F (1, −2), IV
7. G (1, 1), I
8. H (−3, 1), II
9. I (−1, 0), x-axis
10. J (4, 3), I
11. K (3, 4), I
12. L (2, −3), IV

On graph paper, draw a coordinate plane. Then graph and label each point.

13. $N(-4, 3)$
14. $K(2, 5)$
15. $W(-6, -2)$
16. $X(5, 0)$
17. $Y(4, -4)$
18. $M(0, -3)$
19. $Z(-2, 0.5)$
20. $S(-1, -3)$
21. $A(0, 2)$
22. $C(-2, -2)$
23. $E(0, 1)$
24. $G(1, -1)$

13–24. See Student Handbook Answer Appendix.

Lesson 2-4
Pages 95–99

Add.

1. $-4 + 8$ **4**
2. $14 + 16$ **30**
3. $-7 + (-7)$ **−14**
4. $-9 + (-6)$ **−15**
5. $-18 + 11$ **−7**
6. $-36 + 40$ **4**
7. $42 + (-18)$ **24**
8. $-42 + 29$ **−13**
9. $18 + (-32)$ **−14**
10. $12 + (-9)$ **3**
11. $-24 + 9$ **−15**
12. $-7 + (-1)$ **−8**

Evaluate each expression if $a = 6$, $b = -2$, $c = -6$, and $d = 3$.

13. $-96 + a$ **−90**
14. $b + (-5)$ **−7**
15. $c + (-32)$ **−38**
16. $d + 98$ **101**
17. $-120 + b$ **−122**
18. $-120 + c$ **−126**
19. $5 + b$ **3**
20. $a + d$ **9**
21. $c + a$ **0**
22. $d + (-9)$ **−6**
23. $b + c$ **−8**
24. $d + c$ **−3**

Lesson 2-5
Pages 103–106

Subtract.

1. $3 - 7$ **−4**
2. $-5 - 4$ **−9**
3. $-6 - 2$ **−8**
4. $8 - 13$ **−5**
5. $6 - (-4)$ **10**
6. $12 - 9$ **3**
7. $-2 - 23$ **−25**
8. $63 - 78$ **−15**
9. $0 - (-14)$ **14**
10. $15 - 6$ **9**
11. $18 - 20$ **−2**
12. $-5 - 8$ **−13**
13. $21 - (-37)$ **58**
14. $-60 - 32$ **−92**
15. $57 - 63$ **−6**

Evaluate each expression if $k = -3$, $p = 6$, $n = 1$, and $d = -8$.

16. $55 - k$ **58**
17. $p - 7$ **−1**
18. $d - 15$ **−23**
19. $n - 12$ **−11**
20. $-51 - d$ **−43**
21. $k - 21$ **−24**
22. $n - k$ **4**
23. $-99 - k$ **−96**
24. $p - k$ **9**
25. $d - (-1)$ **−7**
26. $k - d$ **5**
27. $n - d$ **9**

Lesson 2-6
Pages 107–111

Multiply.

1. $5(-2)$ **−10**
2. $6(-4)$ **−24**
3. $4(21)$ **84**
4. $-11(-5)$ **55**
5. $-6(5)$ **−30**
6. $-50(0)$ **0**
7. $-5(-5)$ **25**
8. $-4(8)$ **−32**
9. $3(-13)$ **−39**
10. $12(-5)$ **−60**
11. $-9(-12)$ **108**
12. $15(-8)$ **−120**
13. $(-6)^2$ **36**
14. $(-2)^2$ **4**
15. $(-4)^3$ **−64**
16. $(-5)^3$ **−125**

Evaluate each expression if $a = -5$, $b = 2$, $c = -3$, and $d = 4$.

17. $-2d$ **−8**
18. $6a$ **−30**
19. $3ab$ **−30**
20. $-12d$ **−48**
21. $-4b^2$ **−16**
22. $-5cd$ **60**
23. a^2 **25**
24. $13ab$ **−130**

Lesson 2-7
Pages 112–113

Solve using the *look for a pattern* strategy.

1. **NUMBERS** Determine the next three numbers in the pattern below. **45, 51, 57**
   15, 21, 27, 33, 39, …
2. **TIME** Determine the next two times in the pattern below. **3:50 A.M., 4:10 A.M.**
   2:30 A.M., 2:50 A.M., 3:10 A.M., 3:30 A.M., …
3. **MONEY** The table shows Abigail's savings. If the pattern continues, what will be the total amount in week 6? **$2,400**

Week	Total ($)
1	$400
2	$800
3	$1,200
4	$1,600
5	$2,000
6	■

4. **SCIENCE** A single rotation of Earth takes about 24 hours. Copy and complete the table to determine the number of hours in a week.

Number of Days	Number of Hours
1	24
2	48
3	72
4	■ **96**
5	■ **120**
6	■ **144**
7	■ **168**

Lesson 2-8
Pages 114–118

Divide.

1. $4 \div (-2)$ **−2**
2. $16 \div (-8)$ **−2**
3. $-14 \div (-2)$ **7**
4. $\frac{32}{8}$ **4**
5. $18 \div (-3)$ **−6**
6. $-18 \div 3$ **−6**
7. $8 \div (-8)$ **−1**
8. $0 \div (-1)$ **0**
9. $-25 \div 5$ **−5**
10. $\frac{-14}{-7}$ **2**
11. $-32 \div 8$ **−4**
12. $-56 \div (-8)$ **7**
13. $-81 \div 9$ **−9**
14. $-42 \div (-7)$ **6**
15. $121 \div (-11)$ **−11**
16. $-81 \div (-9)$ **9**
17. $18 \div (-2)$ **−9**
18. $\frac{-55}{11}$ **−5**
19. $\frac{25}{-5}$ **−5**
20. $-21 \div 3$ **−7**

Evaluate each expression if $a = -2$, $b = -7$, $x = 8$, and $y = -4$.

21. $-64 \div x$ **−8**
22. $\frac{16}{y}$ **−4**
23. $x \div 2$ **4**
24. $\frac{a}{2}$ **−1**
25. $ax \div y$ **4**
26. $\frac{bx}{y}$ **14**
27. $2y \div 1$ **−8**
28. $\frac{x}{ay}$ **1**
29. $-y \div a$ **−2**
30. $x^2 \div y$ **−16**
31. $\frac{ab}{1}$ **14**
32. $\frac{xy}{a}$ **16**

Lesson 3-1 1–20. See Student Handbook Answer Appendix.

Pages 128–133

Write each phrase as an algebraic expression.

1. six less than p
2. twenty more than c
3. the quotient of a and b
4. Juana's age plus 6
5. x increased by twelve
6. $1,000 divided by z
7. 3 divided into y
8. the product of 7 and m
9. the difference of f and 9
10. twenty-six less q
11. 19 decreased by z
12. two less than x

Write each sentence as an algebraic equation.

13. Three times a number less four is 17.
14. The sum of a number and 6 is 5.
15. Twenty more than twice a number is −30.
16. The quotient of a number and −2 is −42.
17. Four plus three times a number is 18.
18. Five times a number minus 15 is 92.
19. Eight times a number plus twelve is 36.
20. The difference of a number and 24 is −30.

Lesson 3-2

Pages 136–141

Solve each equation. Check your solution.

1. $r - 3 = 14$ **17**
2. $t + 3 = 21$ **18**
3. $s + 10 = 23$ **13**
4. $7 + a = -10$ **−17**
5. $14 + m = 24$ **10**
6. $-9 + n = 13$ **22**
7. $s - 2 = -6$ **−4**
8. $6 + f = 71$ **65**
9. $x + 27 = 30$ **3**
10. $a - 7 = 23$ **30**
11. $-4 + b = -5$ **−1**
12. $w + 18 = -4$ **−22**
13. $k - 9 = -3$ **6**
14. $j + 12 = 11$ **−1**
15. $-42 + v = -42$ **0**
16. $s + 1.3 = 18$ **16.7**
17. $x + 7.4 = 23.5$ **16.1**
18. $p + 3.1 = 18$ **14.9**
19. $w - 3.7 = 4.63$ **8.33**
20. $m - 4.8 = 7.4$ **12.2**
21. $x - 1.3 = 12$ **13.3**
22. $y + 3.4 = 18$ **14.6**
23. $7.2 + g = 9.1$ **1.9**
24. $z - 12.1 = 14$ **26.1**
25. $v - 18 = 13.7$ **31.7**
26. $w - 0.1 = 0.32$ **0.42**
27. $r + 6.7 = 1.2$ **−5.5**

Lesson 3-3

Pages 142–146

Solve each equation. Check your solution.

1. $2m = 18$ **9**
2. $-42 = 6n$ **−7**
3. $72 = 8k$ **9**
4. $-20r = 20$ **−1**
5. $420 = 5s$ **84**
6. $325 = 25t$ **13**
7. $-14 = -2p$ **7**
8. $18q = 36$ **2**
9. $40 = 10a$ **4**
10. $100 = 20b$ **5**
11. $416 = 4c$ **104**
12. $45 = 9d$ **5**
13. $0.5m = 3.5$ **7**
14. $1.8 = 0.6x$ **3**
15. $0.4y = 2$ **5**
16. $1.86 = 6.2z$ **0.3**
17. $-8x = 24$ **−3**
18. $8.34 = 2r$ **4.17**
19. $1.67t = 10.02$ **6**
20. $243 = 27a$ **9**
21. $0.9x = 4.5$ **5**
22. $4.08 = 1.2y$ **3.4**
23. $8d = 112$ **14**
24. $5f = 180.5$ **36.1**
25. $59.66 = 3.14m$ **19**
26. $98.4 = 8p$ **12.3**
27. $208 = 26k$ **8**

Lesson 3-4

Pages 148–149

Use the *work backward* strategy to solve each problem.

1. **NUMBERS** A number is divided by 2. Then 4 is added to the quotient. Next, the sum of these numbers is multiplied by 3. The result is 21. Find the number. **6**
2. **MONEY** Holly spent $13.76 on a birthday present for her mom. She also spent $3.25 on a snack for herself. If she now has $7.74, how much money did she have initially? **$24.75**
3. ★ **DVDs** Jack rented 2 times as many DVDs as Paloma last month. Paloma rented 4 fewer than Greg, but 4 more than Grace. Greg rented 9 DVDs. How many DVDs did each person rent?
4. ★ **TIME** A portion of a shuttle bus schedule is shown. What is the earliest time after 9 A.M. when the bus departs? **9:43 A.M.**

Departs	Arrives
8:55 A.M.	9:20 A.M.
?	10:08 A.M.
10:31 A.M.	10:56 A.M.
11:19 A.M.	11:44 A.M.

5. **FOOD** After four days, 0.5 pound of lunch meat was left in the refrigerator. If half this amount was eaten on each of the previous four days, how much lunch meat was initially in the refrigerator? **1.5 lb**

Lesson 3-5 3. See Student Handbook Answer Appendix.

Pages 151–155

Solve each equation. Check your solution.

1. $3x + 6 = 6$ **0**
2. $2r - 7 = -1$ **3**
3. $-10 + 2d = 8$ **9**
4. $2b + 4 = -8$ **−6**
5. $5w - 12 = 3$ **3**
6. $5t - 4 = 6$ **2**
7. $2q - 6 = 4$ **5**
8. $2g - 3 = -9$ **−3**
9. $15 = 6y + 3$ **2**
10. $3s - 4 = 8$ **4**
11. $18 - 7f = 4$ **2**
12. $13 + 3p = 7$ **−2**
13. $7.5r + 2 = -28$ **−4**
14. $4.2 + 7z = 2.8$ **−0.2**
15. $-9m - 9 = 9$ **−2**
16. $32 + 0.2c = 1$ **−155**
17. $5t - 14 = -14$ **0**
18. $-0.25x + 0.5 = 4$ **−14**
19. $5w - 4 = 8$ **2.4**
20. $4d - 3 = 9$ **3**
21. $2g - 16 = -9$ **3.5**
22. $4k + 13 = 20$ **1.75**
23. $7 = 5 - 2x$ **−1**
24. $8z + 15 = -1$ **−2**
25. $92 - 16b = 12$ **5**
26. $14e + 14 = 28$ **1**
27. $1.1j + 2 = 7.5$ **5**

Lesson 3-6 6, 8. See Student Handbook Answer Appendix.

Pages 156–161

Find the perimeter and area of each rectangle.

1.
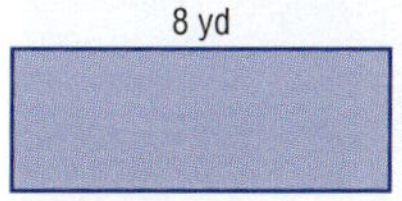

22 yd; 24 yd²

2.

55.4 cm; 189.1 cm²

3.
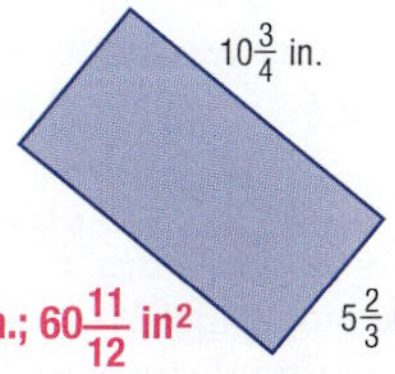

$32\frac{5}{6}$ in.; $60\frac{11}{12}$ in²

4. $\ell = 80$ yd, $w = 20$ yd **200 yd; 1,600 yd²**
5. $\ell = 75$ cm, $w = 25$ cm **200 cm; 1,875 cm²**
6. $\ell = 5.25$ km, $w = 1.5$ km
7. $\ell = 8.6$ cm, $w = 2.5$ cm **22.2 cm; 21.5 cm²**
8. $\ell = 20.25$ m, $w = 4.75$ m
9. $\ell = 12$ ft, $w = 3$ ft **30 ft; 36 ft²**
10. $\ell = 5\frac{1}{4}$ mi, $w = 2\frac{1}{2}$ mi **$15\frac{1}{2}$ mi; $13\frac{1}{8}$ mi²**
11. $\ell = 10\frac{2}{3}$ ft, $w = 5\frac{5}{6}$ ft **33 ft; $62\frac{2}{9}$ ft²**

Lesson 3-7 1–11. See Student Handbook Answer Appendix.

Pages 163–167

Graph the function represented by the table.

1.

Total Cost of Tennis Balls	
Number of Tennis Balls	Total Cost ($)
3	6
4	8
5	10
6	12

2.

Convert Gallons to Quarts	
Gallon	Quarts
1	4
2	8
3	12
4	16

Graph each equation.

3. $y = 3x$
4. $y = 2x + 3$
5. $y = -x$
6. $y = 0.5x + 2$
7. $y = -x + 3$
8. $y = 0.25x + 6$
9. $y = -3x + 6$
10. $y = -x + 1$
11. $y = 5 - 0.5x$

Lesson 4-1

Pages 181–184

Determine whether each number is *prime* or *composite*.

1. 32 **composite**
2. 41 **prime**
3. 52 **composite**
4. 21 **composite**
5. 71 **prime**
6. 102 **composite**
7. 239 **prime**
8. 93 **composite**
9. 123 **composite**

Find the prime factorization of each number.

10. 81 3^4
11. 72 $2^3 \times 3^2$
12. 144 $2^4 \times 3^2$
13. 245 5×7^2
14. 423 $3^2 \times 47$
15. 525 $3 \times 5^2 \times 7$
16. 750 $2 \times 3 \times 5^3$
17. 914 2×457
18. 975 $3 \times 5^2 \times 13$

Factor each expression. **19–24. See Student Handbook Answer Appendix.**

19. $35xy$
20. $14a^2$
21. $30n$
22. $27cd^2$
23. $4s^2t^2$
24. $60p^2qr$

Lesson 4-2

Pages 186–189

Find the GCF of each set of numbers.

1. 12, 16 **4**
2. 63, 81 **9**
3. 225, 500 **25**
4. 37, 100 **1**
5. 32, 240 **16**
6. 412, 640 **4**
7. 36, 81 **9**
8. 140, 350 **70**
9. 72, 170 **2**
10. 12, 18, 42 **6**
11. 24, 56, 120 **8**
12. 48, 60, 84 **12**
13. 32, 80, 96 **16**
14. 14, 49, 70 **7**
15. 8, 10, 20 **2**

Find the GCF of each set of expressions.

16. $18b, 24b$ **$6b$**
17. $2a, 3a$ **a**
18. $5n, 5mn$ **$5n$**
19. $12cd, 24c$ **$12c$**
20. $30x, 50x^2$ **$10x$**
21. $15az, 25az$ **$5az$**
22. $2c, 4ac, 8a$ **2**
23. $d, 6c^2d, 12d$ **d**
24. $10ab, 15bc, 20b^2$ **$5b$**

Lesson 4-3

Pages 190–191

Use the *make a list* strategy to solve each problem.

1. **MEASUREMENT** Gabriel has to make deliveries to three neighbors. He lives at house *b* on the map. Find the shortest route to make the deliveries and return home?

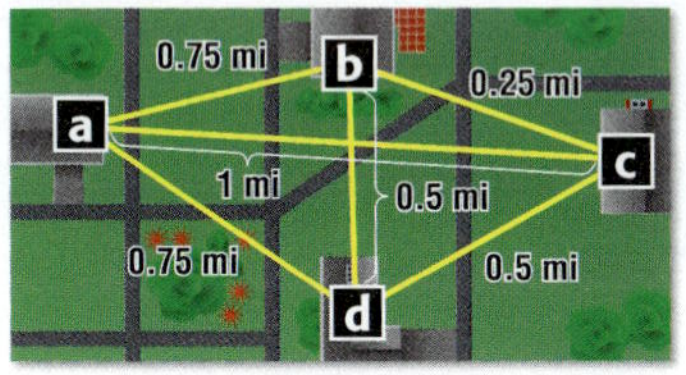

Sample answer: b–a–d–c–b; 2.25 mi

2. **FOOD** Daniel is making a peanut butter and jelly sandwich. His choices are creamy or crunchy peanut butter, white or wheat bread, and grape, apple, or strawberry jelly. How many different types of sandwiches can Daniel make? **12**

3. **GAMES** On the game board, you plan to move two spaces away from square A. You can move horizontally, vertically, or diagonally. How many different moves can you make from square A? List them.

A	B	C
D	E	F
G	H	I

3. 15; A–B–C, A–B–F, A–B–E, A–B–D, A–D–G, A–D–H, A–D–E, A–D–B, A–E–I, A–E–F, A–E–C, A–E–B, A–E–H, A–E–G, A–E–D

Lesson 4-4

Pages 192–195

Write each fraction in simplest form.

1. $\frac{14}{28}$ **$\frac{1}{2}$**
2. $\frac{15}{25}$ **$\frac{3}{5}$**
3. $\frac{100}{130}$ **$\frac{10}{13}$**
4. $\frac{14}{35}$ **$\frac{2}{5}$**
5. $\frac{9}{51}$ **$\frac{3}{17}$**
6. $\frac{54}{56}$ **$\frac{27}{28}$**
7. $\frac{75}{90}$ **$\frac{5}{6}$**
8. $\frac{24}{40}$ **$\frac{3}{5}$**
9. $\frac{180}{270}$ **$\frac{2}{3}$**
10. $\frac{312}{390}$ **$\frac{4}{5}$**
11. $\frac{240}{448}$ **$\frac{15}{28}$**
12. $\frac{71}{82}$ **$\frac{71}{82}$**
13. $\frac{333}{900}$ **$\frac{37}{100}$**
14. $\frac{85}{255}$ **$\frac{1}{3}$**
15. $\frac{84}{128}$ **$\frac{21}{32}$**
16. $\frac{64}{96}$ **$\frac{2}{3}$**
17. $\frac{99}{99}$ **1**
18. $\frac{3}{99}$ **$\frac{1}{33}$**
19. $\frac{44}{55}$ **$\frac{4}{5}$**
20. $\frac{57}{69}$ **$\frac{19}{23}$**
21. $\frac{15}{37}$ **$\frac{15}{37}$**
22. $\frac{204}{408}$ **$\frac{1}{2}$**
23. $\frac{5}{125}$ **$\frac{1}{25}$**
24. $\frac{144}{216}$ **$\frac{2}{3}$**
25. $\frac{15}{75}$ **$\frac{1}{5}$**

Lesson 4-5

Pages 196–200

Write each fraction or mixed number as a decimal. Use bar notation if the decimal is a repeating decimal.

1. $\frac{16}{20}$ **0.8**
2. $\frac{30}{120}$ **0.25**
3. $1\frac{7}{8}$ **1.875**
4. $\frac{1}{6}$ **$0.1\overline{6}$**
5. $\frac{11}{40}$ **0.275**
6. $5\frac{13}{50}$ **5.26**
7. $\frac{55}{300}$ **$0.18\overline{3}$**
8. $1\frac{1}{2}$ **1.5**
9. $\frac{5}{9}$ **$0.\overline{5}$**
10. $2\frac{3}{4}$ **2.75**
11. $\frac{9}{11}$ **$0.\overline{81}$**
12. $4\frac{1}{9}$ **$4.\overline{1}$**

Write each decimal as a fraction or mixed number in simplest form.

13. 0.26 **$\frac{13}{50}$**
14. 0.75 **$\frac{3}{4}$**
15. 0.4 **$\frac{2}{5}$**
16. 0.1 **$\frac{1}{10}$**
17. 4.48 **$4\frac{12}{25}$**
18. 9.8 **$9\frac{4}{5}$**
19. 0.91 **$\frac{91}{100}$**
20. 11.15 **$11\frac{3}{20}$**

Lesson 4-6

Pages 202–205

Write each ratio as a percent.

1. 39 out of 100 **39%**
2. $\frac{23}{100}$ **23%**
3. 17:100 **17%**
4. 72 per 100 **72%**
5. 4 to 100 **4%**
6. 98 in 100 **98%**

Write each fraction as a percent.

7. $\frac{1}{2}$ **50%**
8. $\frac{2}{5}$ **40%**
9. $\frac{60}{100}$ **60%**
10. $\frac{17}{20}$ **85%**
11. $\frac{7}{25}$ **28%**
12. $\frac{1}{20}$ **5%**
13. $\frac{8}{100}$ **8%**
14. $\frac{7}{7}$ **100%**
15. $\frac{9}{10}$ **90%**
16. $\frac{1}{100}$ **1%**
17. $\frac{50}{50}$ **100%**
18. $\frac{49}{50}$ **98%**

Write each percent as a fraction in simplest form.

19. 12% **$\frac{3}{25}$**
20. 23% **$\frac{23}{100}$**
21. 1% **$\frac{1}{100}$**
22. 94% **$\frac{47}{50}$**
23. 36% **$\frac{9}{25}$**
24. 4% **$\frac{1}{25}$**
25. 72% **$\frac{18}{25}$**
26. 100% **1**
27. 65% **$\frac{13}{20}$**
28. 47% **$\frac{47}{100}$**
29. 15% **$\frac{3}{20}$**
30. 48% **$\frac{12}{25}$**

Lesson 4-7

Pages 206–210

Write each percent as a decimal.

1. 42% **0.42**
2. 100% **1.0**
3. 8% **0.08**
4. 20% **0.2**
5. 35% **0.35**
6. 3% **0.03**
7. 62% **0.62**
8. 50% **0.5**
9. 28% **0.28**
10. 87% **0.87**
11. 7.5% **0.075**
12. 87.5% **0.875**
13. 1.8% **0.018**
14. 99.9% **0.999**
15. $85\frac{1}{4}$% **0.8525**
16. $24\frac{1}{2}$% **0.245**
17. $64\frac{4}{5}$% **0.648**
18. $36\frac{3}{4}$% **0.3675**
19. $1\frac{1}{5}$% **0.012**
20. $2\frac{1}{2}$% **0.025**

Write each decimal as a percent.

21. 0.16 **16%**
22. 0.1 **10%**
23. 0.5 **50%**
24. 0.98 **98%**
25. 0.31 **31%**
26. 0.76 **76%**
27. 0.07 **7%**
28. 0.8 **80%**
29. 0.07 **7%**
30. 0.10 **10%**
31. 0.90 **90%**
32. 1.00 **100%**
33. 0.666 **66.6%**
34. 0.725 **72.5%**
35. 0.138 **13.8%**
36. 0.899 **89.9%**
37. 0.256 **25.6%**
38. 0.038 **3.8%**
39. 0.0525 **5.25%**
40. 0.017 **1.7%**

Lesson 4-8

Pages 211–214

Find the LCM of each set of numbers.

1. 4, 9 **36**
2. 6, 16 **48**
3. 24, 36 **72**
4. 48, 84 **336**
5. 8, 9 **72**
6. 49, 56 **392**
7. 42, 66 **462**
8. 15, 39 **195**
9. 56, 64 **448**
10. 24, 42 **168**
11. 80, 250 **2,000**
12. 16, 24 **48**
13. 13, 14 **182**
14. 36, 48 **144**
15. 10, 100 **100**
16. 25, 200 **200**
17. 1, 2, 5 **10**
18. 2, 3, 7 **42**
19. 1, 9, 27 **27**
20. 2, 24, 36 **72**
21. 7, 21, 35 **105**
22. 12, 18, 28 **252**
23. 32, 80, 96 **480**
24. 5, 18, 45 **90**
25. 11, 22, 33 **66**
26. 35, 70, 140 **140**
27. 25, 200, 400 **400**
28. 100, 200, 300 **600**

Lesson 4-9

Pages 215–220

Replace each ● with <, >, or = to make a true sentence.

1. $-\frac{1}{5}$ ● $-\frac{3}{5}$ **>**
2. $-\frac{7}{8}$ ● $-\frac{5}{8}$ **<**
3. $-\frac{1}{6}$ ● $-\frac{5}{6}$ **>**
4. $-\frac{3}{4}$ ● $-\frac{1}{4}$ **<**
5. $-2\frac{1}{4}$ ● $-2\frac{2}{8}$ **=**
6. $-4\frac{3}{7}$ ● $-4\frac{2}{7}$ **<**
7. $-1\frac{4}{9}$ ● $-1\frac{8}{9}$ **>**
8. $-3\frac{4}{5}$ ● $-3\frac{2}{5}$ **<**
9. $\frac{7}{9}$ ● $\frac{3}{5}$ **>**
10. $\frac{14}{25}$ ● $\frac{3}{4}$ **<**
11. $\frac{8}{24}$ ● $\frac{20}{60}$ **=**
12. $\frac{5}{12}$ ● $\frac{4}{9}$ **<**
13. $\frac{18}{24}$ ● $\frac{10}{18}$ **>**
14. $\frac{4}{6}$ ● $\frac{5}{9}$ **>**
15. $\frac{11}{49}$ ● $\frac{12}{42}$ **<**
16. $\frac{5}{14}$ ● $\frac{2}{6}$ **>**

Order each set of numbers from least to greatest.

17. 70%, 0.6, $\frac{2}{3}$ **0.6, $\frac{2}{3}$, 70%**
18. 0.8, $\frac{17}{20}$, 17% **17%, 0.8, $\frac{17}{20}$**
19. $\frac{61}{100}$, 0.65, 61.5% **$\frac{61}{100}$, 61.5%, 0.65**
20. $0.4\overline{2}$, $\frac{3}{7}$, 42% **42%, $0.4\overline{2}$, $\frac{3}{7}$**
21. 2.15, 2.105, $2\frac{7}{50}$ **2.105, $2\frac{7}{50}$, 2.15**
22. $7\frac{1}{8}$, 7.81, 7.18 **$7\frac{1}{8}$, 7.18, 7.81**

Lesson 5-1

Pages 230–235

Estimate. **1–21. Sample answers are given.**

1. $\frac{3}{7}+\frac{6}{8}$ **$\frac{1}{2}+1=1\frac{1}{2}$**
2. $\frac{3}{9}+\frac{7}{8}$ **$\frac{1}{2}+1=1\frac{1}{2}$**
3. $\frac{1}{8}+\frac{8}{9}$ **$0+1=1$**
4. $3\frac{1}{8}+7\frac{6}{7}$ **$3+8=11$**
5. $4\frac{2}{3}+6\frac{7}{8}$ **$5+7=12$**
6. $3\frac{2}{3}\times 2\frac{1}{3}$ **$4\times 2=8$**
7. $\frac{4}{5}\cdot 3$ **$1\cdot 3=3$**
8. $9\frac{7}{8}-6\frac{2}{3}$ **$10-7=3$**
9. $\frac{3}{7}-\frac{1}{15}$ **$\frac{1}{2}-0=\frac{1}{2}$**
10. $\frac{3}{4}\cdot\frac{7}{8}$ **$1\cdot 1=1$**
11. $7\frac{1}{4}\div\frac{2}{3}$ **$7\div 1=7$**
12. $\frac{5}{6}\div\frac{2}{3}$ **$1\div 1=1$**
13. $9\frac{3}{5}+3\frac{1}{8}$ **$10+3=13$**
14. $5\frac{1}{3}-2\frac{3}{4}$ **$5-3=2$**
15. $13\frac{7}{8}-2\frac{1}{3}$ **$14-2=12$**
16. $\frac{13}{15}\cdot\frac{3}{8}$ **$1\cdot\frac{1}{2}=\frac{1}{2}$**
17. $\frac{1}{9}\div 2$ **$0\div 2=0$**
18. $\frac{5}{8}-\frac{1}{16}$ **$\frac{1}{2}-0=\frac{1}{2}$**
19. $9\frac{2}{3}+4\frac{7}{8}$ **$10+5=15$**
20. $\frac{1}{2}\cdot 25$ **$\frac{1}{2}\cdot 26=13$**
21. $35\frac{1}{3}\div 6\frac{3}{4}$ **$35\div 7=5$**

Lesson 5-2

Pages 236–241

Add or subtract. Write in simplest form.

1. $\frac{5}{11}+\frac{9}{11}$ **$1\frac{3}{11}$**
2. $\frac{5}{8}-\frac{1}{8}$ **$\frac{1}{2}$**
3. $\frac{7}{10}+\frac{7}{10}$ **$1\frac{2}{5}$**
4. $\frac{9}{12}-\frac{5}{12}$ **$\frac{1}{3}$**
5. $\frac{2}{9}+\frac{1}{3}$ **$\frac{5}{9}$**
6. $\frac{1}{2}+\frac{3}{4}$ **$1\frac{1}{4}$**
7. $\frac{1}{4}-\frac{3}{12}$ **0**
8. $\frac{3}{7}+\frac{6}{14}$ **$\frac{6}{7}$**
9. $\frac{1}{4}+\frac{3}{5}$ **$\frac{17}{20}$**
10. $\frac{4}{9}+\frac{1}{2}$ **$\frac{17}{18}$**
11. $\frac{5}{7}-\frac{4}{6}$ **$\frac{1}{21}$**
12. $\frac{3}{4}-\frac{1}{6}$ **$\frac{7}{12}$**
13. $\frac{3}{5}+\frac{3}{4}$ **$1\frac{7}{20}$**
14. $\frac{2}{3}-\frac{1}{8}$ **$\frac{13}{24}$**
15. $\frac{9}{10}+\frac{1}{3}$ **$1\frac{7}{30}$**

Evaluate each expression if $a=\frac{2}{3}$ and $b=\frac{7}{12}$.

16. $\frac{1}{5}+a$ **$\frac{13}{15}$**
17. $a-\frac{1}{2}$ **$\frac{1}{6}$**
18. $b+\frac{7}{8}$ **$1\frac{11}{24}$**
19. $\frac{7}{8}-a$ **$\frac{5}{24}$**
20. $a+b$ **$1\frac{1}{4}$**
21. $a-b$ **$\frac{1}{12}$**

Lesson 5-3

Pages 242–246

Add or subtract. Write in simplest form.

1. $2\frac{1}{3} + 1\frac{1}{3}$ $3\frac{2}{3}$
2. $5\frac{2}{7} - 2\frac{3}{7}$ $2\frac{6}{7}$
3. $6\frac{3}{8} + 7\frac{1}{8}$ $13\frac{1}{2}$
4. $2\frac{3}{4} - 1\frac{1}{4}$ $1\frac{1}{2}$
5. $5\frac{1}{2} - 3\frac{1}{4}$ $2\frac{1}{4}$
6. $2\frac{2}{3} + 4\frac{1}{9}$ $6\frac{7}{9}$
7. $7\frac{4}{5} + 9\frac{3}{10}$ $17\frac{1}{10}$
8. $3\frac{3}{4} + 5\frac{5}{8}$ $9\frac{3}{8}$
9. $10\frac{2}{3} + 5\frac{6}{7}$ $16\frac{11}{21}$
10. $17\frac{2}{9} - 12\frac{1}{3}$ $4\frac{8}{9}$
11. $6\frac{5}{12} + 12\frac{5}{12}$ $18\frac{5}{6}$
12. $7\frac{1}{4} + 15\frac{5}{6}$ $23\frac{1}{12}$
13. $6\frac{1}{8} + 4\frac{2}{3}$ $10\frac{19}{24}$
14. $7 - 6\frac{4}{9}$ $\frac{5}{9}$
15. $8\frac{1}{12} + 12\frac{6}{11}$ $20\frac{83}{132}$
16. $7\frac{2}{3} + 8\frac{1}{4}$ $15\frac{11}{12}$
17. $12\frac{3}{11} + 14\frac{3}{13}$ $26\frac{72}{143}$
18. $21\frac{1}{3} + 15\frac{3}{8}$ $36\frac{17}{24}$
19. $19\frac{1}{7} + 6\frac{1}{4}$ $25\frac{11}{28}$
20. $9\frac{2}{5} - 8\frac{1}{3}$ $1\frac{1}{15}$
21. $18\frac{1}{4} - 3\frac{3}{8}$ $14\frac{7}{8}$
22. $1\frac{1}{8} + 2\frac{1}{12}$ $3\frac{5}{24}$
23. $2\frac{1}{12} - 1\frac{1}{8}$ $\frac{23}{24}$
24. $10 - \frac{2}{3}$ $9\frac{1}{3}$

Lesson 5-4

Pages 247–248

Eliminate possibilities to solve each problem.

1. **MEASUREMENT** Guillermo has a 3-gallon cooler with $1\frac{3}{4}$ gallons of juice in it. If he wants the cooler full for his soccer game, how much juice should he add? **C**
   - A 4 gallons
   - B $3\frac{1}{4}$ gallons
   - C $1\frac{1}{4}$ gallons
   - D $\frac{1}{4}$ gallon
2. **ELEPHANTS** An elephant in a zoo eats 58 cabbages in a week. About how many cabbages does an elephant eat in one year? **J**
   - F 7
   - G 700
   - H 1,500
   - J 3,000
3. **TRAVEL** Mr. Rollins drove 780 miles on a 5-day trip. He rented a car for $23 per day plus $0.15 per mile after 500 free miles. About how much did the rental car cost? **C**
   - A $100
   - B $130
   - C $160
   - D $180

Lesson 5-5

Pages 256–257

Multiply. Write in simplest form.

1. $\frac{2}{3} \times \frac{3}{5}$ $\frac{2}{5}$
2. $\frac{1}{6} \times \frac{2}{5}$ $\frac{1}{15}$
3. $\frac{4}{9} \times \frac{3}{7}$ $\frac{4}{21}$
4. $\frac{5}{12} \times \frac{6}{11}$ $\frac{5}{22}$
5. $\frac{3}{8} \times \frac{8}{9}$ $\frac{1}{3}$
6. $\frac{2}{5} \times \frac{5}{8}$ $\frac{1}{4}$
7. $\frac{7}{15} \times \frac{3}{21}$ $\frac{1}{15}$
8. $\frac{5}{6} \times \frac{15}{16}$ $\frac{25}{32}$
9. $\frac{2}{3} \times \frac{3}{13}$ $\frac{2}{13}$
10. $\frac{4}{9} \times \frac{1}{6}$ $\frac{2}{27}$
11. $3 \times \frac{1}{9}$ $\frac{1}{3}$
12. $5 \times \frac{6}{7}$ $4\frac{2}{7}$
13. $\frac{3}{5} \times 15$ 9
14. $3\frac{1}{2} \times 4\frac{1}{3}$ $15\frac{1}{6}$
15. $\frac{4}{5} \times 2\frac{3}{4}$ $2\frac{1}{5}$
16. $6\frac{1}{8} \times 5\frac{1}{7}$ $31\frac{1}{2}$
17. $2\frac{2}{3} \times 2\frac{1}{4}$ 6
18. $\frac{7}{8} \times 16$ 14
19. $5\frac{1}{5} \times 2\frac{1}{2}$ 13
20. $7 \times \frac{1}{14}$ $\frac{1}{2}$
21. $22 \times \frac{3}{11}$ 6
22. $8\frac{2}{3} \times 1\frac{1}{2}$ 13
23. $4 \times 6\frac{1}{2}$ 26
24. $\frac{1}{2} \times 10\frac{2}{3}$ $5\frac{1}{3}$
25. $\frac{2}{3} \times 21\frac{1}{3}$ $14\frac{2}{9}$
26. $\frac{7}{8} \times \frac{8}{7}$ 1
27. $21 \times \frac{1}{2}$ $10\frac{1}{2}$
28. $11 \times \frac{1}{4}$ $2\frac{3}{4}$

Lesson 5-6

Pages 258–263

Find the multiplicative inverse of each number.

1. $\frac{2}{3}$ $\frac{3}{2}$ or $1\frac{1}{2}$
2. $\frac{5}{4}$ $\frac{4}{5}$
3. 1 $\frac{1}{1}$ or 1
4. 10 $\frac{1}{10}$
5. $\frac{1}{7}$ 7
6. $\frac{9}{16}$ $\frac{16}{9}$ or $1\frac{7}{9}$
7. $1\frac{1}{3}$ $\frac{3}{4}$
8. $3\frac{3}{4}$ $\frac{4}{15}$
9. $7\frac{3}{8}$ $\frac{8}{59}$
10. $6\frac{2}{5}$ $\frac{5}{32}$
11. $33\frac{1}{3}$ $\frac{3}{100}$
12. $66\frac{2}{3}$ $\frac{3}{200}$

Solve each equation. Check your solution.

13. $\frac{a}{13} = 2$ 26
14. $\frac{8}{9}x = 24$ 27
15. $\frac{3}{8}r = 36$ 96
16. $\frac{3}{4}t = \frac{1}{2}$ $\frac{2}{3}$
17. $16 = \frac{h}{4}$ 64
18. $\frac{m}{8} = 12$ 96
19. $\frac{5}{8}n = 45$ 72
20. $10 = \frac{b}{10}$ 100
21. $\frac{1}{7}x = 7$ 49
22. $5 = \frac{1}{5}y$ 25
23. $\frac{4}{3}m = 28$ 21
24. $\frac{2}{3}z = 20$ 30
25. $\frac{c}{9} = 81$ 729
26. $\frac{m}{9} = 9$ 81
27. $16 = \frac{4}{9}f$ 36
28. $\frac{15}{8}x = 225$ 120

Lesson 5-7

Pages 265–270

Divide. Write in simplest form.

1. $\frac{2}{3} \div \frac{3}{2}$ $\frac{4}{9}$
2. $\frac{3}{5} \div \frac{2}{5}$ $1\frac{1}{2}$
3. $\frac{7}{10} \div \frac{3}{8}$ $1\frac{13}{15}$
4. $\frac{5}{9} \div \frac{2}{5}$ $1\frac{7}{18}$
5. $4 \div \frac{2}{3}$ 6
6. $8 \div \frac{4}{5}$ 10
7. $9 \div \frac{5}{9}$ $16\frac{1}{5}$
8. $\frac{2}{7} \div 2$ $\frac{1}{7}$
9. $\frac{1}{14} \div 7$ $\frac{1}{98}$
10. $15 \div \frac{3}{5}$ 25
11. $\frac{9}{14} \div \frac{3}{4}$ $\frac{6}{7}$
12. $\frac{7}{8} \div 10$ $\frac{7}{80}$
13. $16 \div \frac{3}{4}$ $21\frac{1}{3}$
14. $\frac{3}{8} \div 2\frac{1}{2}$ $\frac{3}{20}$
15. $5\frac{1}{2} \div 2\frac{1}{2}$ $2\frac{1}{5}$
16. $3\frac{1}{4} \div 5\frac{1}{2}$ $\frac{13}{22}$
17. $12\frac{5}{6} \div 2\frac{1}{6}$ $5\frac{12}{13}$
18. $7\frac{1}{2} \div 3\frac{1}{2}$ $2\frac{1}{7}$

Lesson 6-1

Pages 282–286

LUNCH Use the survey results to write each ratio as a fraction in simplest form.

Favorite School Lunch	Votes
Pizza	64
Hamburger	15
Macaroni and Cheese	14
Fish Sticks	4
Other	3

1. fish sticks:macaroni and cheese $\frac{4}{14} = \frac{2}{7}$
2. pizza:macaroni and cheese $\frac{64}{14} = \frac{32}{7}$
3. all votes:macaroni and cheese $\frac{100}{14} = \frac{50}{7}$
4. pizza:all votes $\frac{64}{100} = \frac{16}{25}$
5. other:hamburger $\frac{3}{15} = \frac{1}{5}$

6, 7. See Student Handbook Answer Appendix.

Determine whether the following ratios are equivalent. Explain.

6. 4 out of 6 balloons popped, 8 out of 12 balloons popped
7. 20 out of 25 students agree, 16 out of 30 students agree

Lesson 6-2

Pages 287–292

Find each unit rate. Round to the nearest hundredth if necessary.

1. \$240 for 4 days **\$60/day**
2. 250 people in 5 buses **50 people/bus**
3. 500 miles in 10 hours **50 mi/h**
4. 18 cups for 24 pounds **$\frac{3}{4}$ cup/pound**
5. 32 people in 8 cars **4 people/car**
6. \$4.50 for 3 dozen **\$1.50/dozen**
7. 245 tickets in 5 days **49 tickets/day**
8. 12 classes in 4 semesters **3 classes/semester**
9. 60 people in 4 rows **15 people/row**
10. 48 ounces in 3 pounds **16 oz/lb**
11. 20 people in 4 groups **5 people/group**
12. 1.5 pounds for \$3.00 **0.5 lb/\$**
13. 45 miles in 60 minutes **0.75 mi/min**
14. \$5.50 for 10 disks **\$0.55/disk**
15. 360 miles for 12 gallons **30 mi/gal**
16. \$8.50 for 5 yards **\$1.70/yd**
17. 24 cups for \$1.20 **20 cups/dollar**
18. 160 words in 4 minutes **40 words/min**
19. \$60 for 5 books **\$12/book**
20. \$24 for 6 hours **\$4/h**

Lesson 6-3

Pages 293–297

For Exercises 1 and 2, find the rate of change for each table.

1. **2 in. per yr**

Age (yr)	Height (in.)
9	54
10	56
11	58
12	60

2. **3°C per 4h**

Time (h)	Temperature (°C)
0	0
4	3
8	6
12	9

3. **MOVIE RENTALS** The graph shows the cost of renting movies. Use the graph to find the rate of change. **cost increases by \$5 for each movie rental**

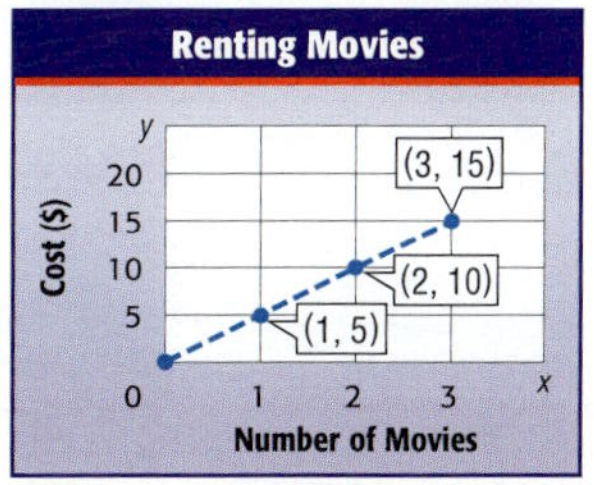

Lesson 6-4

Pages 298–303

Complete.

1. 4,000 lb = ■ T **2**
2. 5 T = ■ lb **10,000**
3. 5 lb = ■ oz **80**
4. 12,000 lb = ■ T **6**
5. $\frac{1}{4}$ lb = ■ oz **4**
6. 12 pt = ■ c **24**
7. 3 gal = ■ pt **24**
8. 24 fl oz = ■ c **3**
9. 8 pt = ■ c **16**
10. 10 pt = ■ qt **5**
11. $2\frac{1}{4}$ c = ■ fl oz **18**
12. 6 lb = ■ oz **96**
13. 10 gal = ■ qt **40**
14. 4 qt = ■ fl oz **128**
15. 4 pt = ■ c **8**
16. 13,200 ft = ■ mi **$2\frac{1}{2}$**
17. 120 oz = ■ lb **$7\frac{1}{2}$**
18. $9\frac{1}{4}$ gal = ■ qt **37**
19. 7,480 yd = ■ mi **$4\frac{1}{4}$**
20. $12\frac{1}{2}$ lb = ■ oz **200**
21. $7\frac{1}{2}$ qt = ■ pt **15**
22. $3\frac{1}{8}$ c = ■ fl oz **25**
23. $2\frac{1}{4}$ mi = ■ ft **11,880**
24. $3\frac{2}{3}$ T = ■ lb **$7{,}333\frac{1}{3}$**

Lesson 6-5

Pages 304–309

Complete. Round to the nearest hundredth if necessary.

1. 400 mm = ■ cm **40**
2. 4 km = ■ m **4,000**
3. 660 cm = ■ m **6.6**
4. 0.3 km = ■ m **300**
5. 30 mm = ■ cm **3**
6. 84.5 m = ■ km **0.0845**
7. ■ m = 54 cm **0.54**
8. 18 km = ■ cm **1,800,000**
9. ■ mm = 45 cm **450**
10. 4 kg = ■ g **4,000**
11. 632 mg = ■ g **0.632**
12. 4,497 g = ■ kg **4.497**
13. ■ mg = 0.51 kg **510,000**
14. 0.63 kg = ■ g **630**
15. ■ kg = 563 g **0.563**
16. 662 m = ■ km **0.662**
17. 5,283 mL = ■ L **5.283**
18. 0.24 cm = ■ mm **2.4**
19. 380 kL = ■ L **380,000**
20. 10.8 g = ■ mg **10,800**
21. 83,000 mL = ■ L **83**
22. 56 in. ≈ ■ cm **142.24**
23. 32.8 ft. ≈ ■ m **9.84**
24. 609 yd ≈ ■ m **554.19**
25. 21.78 mi ≈ ■ km **35.07**
26. 48 lb ≈ ■ g **21,772.8**
27. 2.3 T ≈ ■ kg **2,086.56**
28. 8.5 c ≈ ■ mL **2,011.02**
29. 33 gal ≈ ■ L **125.07**
30. 1.8 qt ≈ ■ mL **1,703.43**

Lesson 6-6

Pages 310–315

Determine if the quantities in each pair of ratios are proportional. Explain. **1–3. See Student Handbook Answer Appendix.**

1. **MONEY** 2 coins for every 3 bills and 6 coins for every 9 bills
2. **SCALE** 3 feet for every 1 in and 15 feet for every 6 in
3. **FAMILY** 2 children for every 1 adult and 8 children for every 3 adults

Solve each proportion.

4. $\frac{u}{72} = \frac{2}{4}$ **36**
5. $\frac{12}{m} = \frac{15}{10}$ **8**
6. $\frac{36}{90} = \frac{16}{t}$ **40**
7. $\frac{g}{32} = \frac{8}{64}$ **4**
8. $\frac{5}{14} = \frac{10}{a}$ **28**
9. $\frac{k}{18} = \frac{5}{3}$ **30**
10. $\frac{15}{w} = \frac{60}{4}$ **1**
11. $\frac{81}{90} = \frac{y}{20}$ **18**
12. $\frac{45}{8} = \frac{36}{d}$ **6.4**
13. $\frac{125}{v} = \frac{20}{5}$ **31.25**
14. $\frac{4}{5} = \frac{x}{3}$ **2.4**
15. $\frac{45}{75} = \frac{j}{3}$ **1.8**

Lesson 6-7

Pages 318–319

Use the *draw a diagram* strategy to solve the following problems.

1. **TESTS** The scores on a test are found by adding or subtracting points as shown below. If Salazar's score on a 15-question test was 86 points, how many of his answers were correct, incorrect, and blank?

Answer	Points
Correct	+8
Incorrect	−4
No answer	−2

See Student Handbook Answer Appendix.

2. **GAMES** Six members of a video game club are having a tournament. In the first round, every player will play a video game against every other player. How many games will be in the first round of the tournament? **15 games**

3. **FAMILY** At Latrice's family reunion, $\frac{4}{5}$ of the people are 18 years of age or older. Half of the remaining people are under 12 years old. If 20 children are under 12 years old, how many people are at the reunion? **200 people**

Lesson 6-8

Pages 320–326

On a map, the scale is 1 inch = 50 miles. For each map distance, find the actual distance.

1. 5 inches **250 mi**
2. 12 inches **600 mi**
3. $2\frac{3}{8}$ inches **$118\frac{3}{4}$ mi**
4. $\frac{4}{5}$ inch **40 mi**
5. $2\frac{5}{6}$ inches **$141\frac{2}{3}$ mi**
6. 3.25 inches **162.5 mi**
7. 4.75 inches **237.5 mi**
8. 5.25 inches **262.5 mi**

On a scale drawing, the scale is $\frac{1}{2}$ inch = 2 feet. Find the dimensions of each room in the scale drawing.

9. 14 feet by 18 feet **$3\frac{1}{2}$ in. by $4\frac{1}{2}$ in.**
10. 32 feet by 6 feet **8 in. by $1\frac{1}{2}$ in.**
11. 3 feet by 5 feet **$\frac{3}{4}$ in. by $1\frac{1}{4}$ in.**
12. 20 feet by 30 feet **5 in. by $7\frac{1}{2}$ in.**

Lesson 6-9

Pages 328–332

Write each percent as a fraction in simplest form.

1. 32% **$\frac{8}{25}$**
2. 89% **$\frac{89}{100}$**
3. 72% **$\frac{18}{25}$**
4. 11% **$\frac{11}{100}$**
5. 1% **$\frac{1}{100}$**
6. 28% **$\frac{7}{25}$**
7. 55% **$\frac{11}{20}$**
8. 18.5% **$\frac{37}{200}$**
9. 22.75% **$\frac{91}{400}$**
10. 25.2% **$\frac{63}{250}$**
11. 75.5% **$\frac{151}{200}$**
12. 48.25% **$\frac{193}{400}$**
13. 6.5% **$\frac{13}{200}$**
14. 1.25% **$\frac{1}{80}$**
15. 88.9% **$\frac{889}{1,000}$**
16. $52\frac{1}{4}$% **$\frac{209}{400}$**
17. 895% **$8\frac{19}{20}$**
18. 480% **$4\frac{4}{5}$**
19. 0.78% **$\frac{39}{5,000}$**
20. 0.3% **$\frac{3}{1,000}$**

Write each fraction as a percent. Round to the nearest hundredth if necessary.

21. $\frac{14}{25}$ **56%**
22. $\frac{28}{50}$ **56%**
23. $\frac{14}{20}$ **70%**
24. $\frac{7}{10}$ **70%**
25. $\frac{17}{17}$ **100%**
26. $\frac{80}{125}$ **64%**
27. $\frac{9}{12}$ **75%**
28. $\frac{4}{6}$ **66.67%**
29. $\frac{11}{12}$ **91.67%**
30. $\frac{9}{16}$ **56.25%**
31. $\frac{8}{9}$ **88.89%**
32. $\frac{3}{16}$ **18.75%**
33. $\frac{5}{32}$ **15.63%**
34. $\frac{1}{16}$ **6.25%**
35. $\frac{8}{15}$ **53.33%**
36. $\frac{9}{11}$ **81.82%**
37. $\frac{1}{250}$ **0.4%**
38. $\frac{1}{500}$ **0.2%**
39. $12\frac{1}{2}$ **1,250%**
40. $18\frac{2}{5}$ **1,840%**

Lesson 7-1

Pages 344–348

Find each number. Round to the nearest tenth if necessary.

1. 5% of 40 **2**
2. 10% of 120 **12**
3. 12% of 150 **18**
4. 12.5% of 40 **5**
5. 75% of 200 **150**
6. 13% of 25.3 **3.3**
7. 250% of 44 **110**
8. 0.5% of 13.7 **0.1**
9. 600% of 7 **42**
10. 1.5% of \$25 **\$0.38**
11. 81% of 134 **108.5**
12. 43% of 110 **47.3**
13. 61% of 524 **319.6**
14. 100% of 3.5 **3.5**
15. 20% of 58.5 **11.7**
16. 45% of 125.5 **56.5**
17. 23% of 500 **115**
18. 80% of 8 **6.4**
19. 90% of 72 **64.8**
20. 32% of 54 **17.3**

Lesson 7-2

Pages 353–354

Find each number. Round to the nearest tenth if necessary.

1. What number is 25% of 280? **70**
2. 38 is what percent of 50? **76%**
3. 54 is 25% of what number? **216**
4. 24.5% of what number is 15? **61.2**
5. What number is 80% of 500? **400**
6. 12% of 120 is what number? **14.4**
7. Find 68% of 50. **34**
8. What percent of 240 is 32? **13.3%**
9. 99 is what percent of 150? **66%**
10. Find 75% of 1. **0.8**
11. What number is $33\frac{1}{3}$% of 66? **22**
12. 50% of 350 is what number? **175**
13. What percent of 450 is 50? **11.1%**
14. What number is $37\frac{1}{2}$% of 32? **12**
15. 95% of 40 is what number? **38**
16. Find 30% of 26. **7.8**
17. 9 is what percent of 30? **30%**
18. 52% of what number is 109.2? **210**
19. What number is 65% of 200? **130**
20. What number is 15.5% of 45? **7.0**

Lesson 7-3

Pages 355–360

Estimate by using fractions. **1–36. Sample answers are given.** **3. $(4 \cdot 20) + \left(\frac{1}{2} \cdot 20\right) = 90$**

1. 28% of 48 **$\frac{1}{4} \cdot 48 = 12$**
2. 99% of 65 **$1 \cdot 65 = 65$**
3. 445% of 20
4. 9% of 81 **$\frac{1}{10} \cdot 80 = 8$**
5. 73% of 240 **$\frac{3}{4} \cdot 240 = 180$**
6. 65.5% of 75 **$\frac{2}{3} \cdot 75 = 50$**
7. 48.2% of 93 **$\frac{1}{2} \cdot 90 = 45$**
8. 39.45% of 51 **$\frac{2}{5} \cdot 50 = 20$**
9. 287% of 122 **$3 \cdot 120 = 360$**
10. 53% of 80 **$\frac{1}{2} \cdot 80 = 40$**
11. 414% of 72 **$4 \cdot 72 = 288$**
12. 59% of 105 **$\frac{3}{5} \cdot 105 = 63$**

Estimate by using 10%. **13–24. See Student Handbook Answer Appendix.**

13. 30% of 42
14. 70% of 104
15. 90% of 152
16. 67% of 70
17. 78% of 92
18. 12% of 183
19. 51% of 221
20. 23% of 504
21. 81% of 390
22. 41% of 60
23. 59% of 178
24. 22% of 450

Estimate.

25. 50% of 37 **$\frac{1}{2} \cdot 40 = 20$**
26. 18% of 90 **$\frac{1}{5} \cdot 100 = 20$**
27. 300% of 245 **$3 \cdot 250 = 750$**
28. 1% of 48 **$\frac{1}{100} \cdot 50 = 0.5$**
29. 70% of 300 **$\frac{7}{10} \cdot 300 = 210$**
30. 35% of 35 **$\frac{7}{20} \cdot 40 = 14$**
31. 60.5% of 60 **$\frac{3}{5} \cdot 60 = 36$**
32. $5\frac{1}{2}$% of 100 **$\frac{3}{50} \cdot 100 = 6$**
33. 40.01% of 16 **$\frac{2}{5} \cdot 15 = 6$**
34. 80% of 62 **$\frac{4}{5} \cdot 60 = 48$**
35. 45% of 119 **$\frac{9}{20} \cdot 120 = 54$**
36. 14.81% of 986 **$\frac{3}{20} \cdot 1,000 = 150$**

Lesson 7-4

Pages 361–365

Write an equation for each problem. Then solve. Round to the nearest tenth if necessary. **1–14. See Student Handbook Answer Appendix for equations.**

1. Find 45% of 50. **22.5**
2. 75 is what percent of 300? **25%**
3. 16% of what number is 2? **12.5**
4. 75% of 80 is what number? **60**
5. 5% of what number is 12? **240**
6. Find 60% of 45. **27**
7. 90 is what percent of 95? **94.7%**
8. $28\frac{1}{2}$% of 64 is what number? **18.2**
9. Find 46.5% of 75. **34.9**
10. What number is 55.5% of 70? **38.9**
11. 80.5% of what number is 80.5? **100**
12. $66\frac{2}{3}$% of what number is 40? **60**
13. Find 122.5% of 80. **98**
14. 250% of what number is 75? **30**

Lesson 7-5
Pages 366–367

Solve each problem using the *reasonable answers* strategy.

1. **SKIING** Benito skied for 13.5 hours and estimated that he spent 30% of his time on the ski lift. Did he spend about 4, 6, or 8 hours on the ski lift? **about 4 h**
2. **CLASS TRIP** The class trip at Wilson Middle School costs $145 per student. A fundraiser earns 38% of this cost. Will each student have to pay about $70, $80, or $90? **$90**
3. **GAS MILEAGE** Miguel's car gets 38 miles per gallon and has 2.5 gallons of gasoline left in the tank. Can he drive for 85, 95, or 105 more miles before he runs out of gas? **95 mi**
4. **DINING** At a restaurant, the total cost of a meal is $87.50. Nadia wants to leave a 20% tip. Should she leave a total of $95, $105, or $115? **$105**

Lesson 7-6
Pages 369–374

Find each percent of change. Round to the nearest whole percent if necessary. State whether the percent of change is an *increase* or *decrease*. **1. 50% increase 2. 160% increase 11. 225% increase 12. 96% decrease**

1. 450 centimeters to 675 centimeters
2. 77 million to 200.2 million
3. 500 albums to 100 albums **80% decrease**
4. 350 yards to 420 yards **20% increase**
5. 3.25 meters to 2.95 meters **9% decrease**
6. $65 to $75 **15% increase**
7. 180 dishes to 160 dishes **11% decrease**
8. 450 pieces to 445.5 pieces **1% decrease**
9. 700 grams 910 grams **30% increase**
10. 55 women to 11 women **80% decrease**
11. 412 children to 1,339 children
12. 464 kilograms to 20 kilograms
13. 24 hours to 86 hours **258% increase**
14. 16 minutes to 24 minutes **50% increase**

Lesson 7-7 **1–12. See Student Handbook Answer Appendix.**
Pages 375–378

Find the total cost or sale price to the nearest cent.

1. $45 sweater; 6% tax
2. $18.99 CD; 15% discount
3. $199 ring; 10% discount
4. $29 shirt; 7% tax
5. $19 purse; 25% discount
6. $145 coat; 6.25% tax
7. $12 meal; 4.5% tax
8. $899 computer; 20% discount
9. $105 skateboard; $7\frac{1}{2}$% tax
10. $599 TV; 12% discount
11. $12,500 car; $3\frac{3}{4}$% tax
12. $49.95 gloves; $5\frac{1}{4}$% tax

Find the percent of discount to the nearest percent.

13. sneakers: regular price, $72; sale price, $60 **17%**
14. dress shirt: regular price, $90; sale price, $22.50 **75%**
15. portable game player: regular price, $125; sale price, $100 **20%**
16. car: regular price, $25,000; sale price, $22,000 **12%**
17. hiking boots: regular price, $139; sale price, $113.98 **18%**
18. airline tickets: regular price, $556; sale price, $500.40 **10%**
19. CD: regular price, $15; sale price, $9 **40%**
20. computer: regular price, $600; sale price, $450 **25%**

Lesson 7-8
Pages 379–382

Find the simple interest earned to the nearest cent for each principal, interest rate, and time. **1–9. See Student Handbook Answer Appendix.**

1. $2,000, 8%, 5 years
2. $500, 10%, 8 months
3. $750, 5%, 1 year
4. $175.50, $6\frac{1}{2}$%, 18 months
5. $236.20, 9%, 16 months
6. $89, $7\frac{1}{2}$%, 6 months
7. $800, 5.75%, 3 years
8. $225, $1\frac{1}{2}$%, 2 years
9. $12,000, $4\frac{1}{2}$%, 40 months

Find the simple interest paid to the nearest cent for each loan, interest rate, and time. **10–18. See Student Handbook Answer Appendix.**

10. $750, 18%, 2 years
11. $1,500, 19%, 16 months
12. $300, 9%, 1 year
13. $4,750, 19.5%, 30 months
14. $2,345, 17%, 9 months
15. $689, 12%, 2 years
16. $390, 18.75%, 15 months
17. $1,250, 22%, 8 months
18. $3,240, 18%, 14 months

Lesson 8-1
Pages 395–400

Display each set of data in a line plot. Identify any clusters, gaps, or outliers. **1–4. See Student Handbook Answer Appendix.**

1. Number of Pets in the Home

0	1	3	4	0
2	1	0	1	1
10	0	1	5	2

2. High Temperatures for 18 Days (°F)

75	81	75	65	76	81
77	80	65	65	80	80
76	85	66	75	80	75

3. Number of Stories for Buildings in Denver

56	43	36	42	29
54	42	32	34	
52	40	32	32	

Source: *The World Almanac and Book of Facts*

4. Ages of Children at Sunny Day Care (years)

4	1	6	4	5	3
4	5	1	2	5	4
3	2	4	1	3	3

Lesson 8-2
Pages 401–407

Find the mean, median, and mode for each set of data.

1. 1, 5, 9, 1, 2, 6, 8, 2 **4.25, 3.5, 1 and 2**
2. 2, 5, 8, 9, 7, 6, 3, 5, 1, 4 **5, 5, 5**
3. 82, 79, 93, 91, 95, 95, 81 **88, 91, 95**
4. 117, 103, 108, 120 **112, 112.5, no mode**
5. 256, 265, 247, 256 **256, 256, 256**
6. 47, 54, 66, 54, 46, 66 **55.5, 54, 54 and 66**
7.

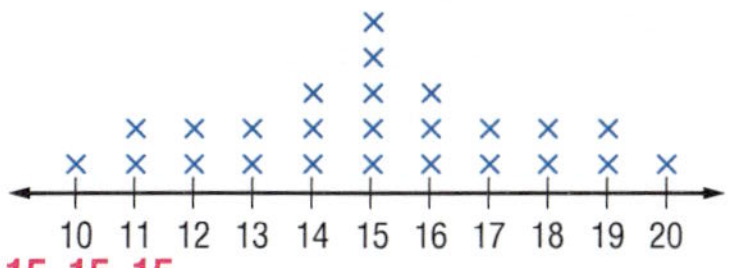

15, 15, 15

8. **1.5, 1, 1**

Number of Absences	Tally	Frequency
0	IIII	4
1	~~IIII~~ IIII	9
2	~~IIII~~ I	6
3	~~IIII~~	5

Lesson 8-3 1–4. See Student Handbook Answer Appendix.

Pages 409–413

Display each set of data in a stem-and-leaf plot.

1. 23, 15, 39, 68, 57, 42, 51, 52, 41, 18, 29
2. 189, 182, 196, 184, 197, 183, 196, 194, 184
3. Average Monthly High Temperatures in Albany, NY (°F)

21	46	72	50
24	58	70	40
34	67	61	27

Source: *The World Almanac and Book of Facts*

4. Super Bowl Winning Scores 1987–2004

39	55	52	27	34	20
42	20	30	35	23	48
20	37	49	31	34	32

Source: *The World Almanac and Book of Facts*

Lesson 8-4 1–4. See Student Handbook Answer Appendix.

Pages 414–420

Select the appropriate graph to display each set of data: bar graph or histogram. Then display the data in the appropriate graph.

1. Longest Snakes

Snake Name	Length (ft)
Royal python	35
Anaconda	28
Indian python	25
Diamond python	21
King cobra	19
Boa constrictor	16

Source: *The Top 10 of Everything*

2. Least Densely Populated States

State	People Per Square Mile
Alaska	1
Wyoming	5
Montana	6
North Dakota	9
South Dakota	10
New Mexico	15

Source: *The Top 10 of Everything*

3. Cost of a Movie Ticket at Selected Theaters

\$5.25	\$6.50	\$3.50	\$3.75
\$7.50	\$9.25	\$10.40	\$4.75
\$10.00	\$4.50	\$8.75	\$7.25
\$3.50	\$6.70	\$4.20	\$7.50

4. Highest Recorded Wind Speeds For Selected U.S. Cities (mph)

52	55	81	46	73	57
75	54	58	76	46	58
60	91	53	53	51	56
80	60	73	46	49	47

Source: *The World Almanac and Book of Facts*

Lesson 8-5

Pages 424–425

WEATHER For Exercises 1–3, solve by using the graph. **3. Sample answer: 88°F, 72°F**

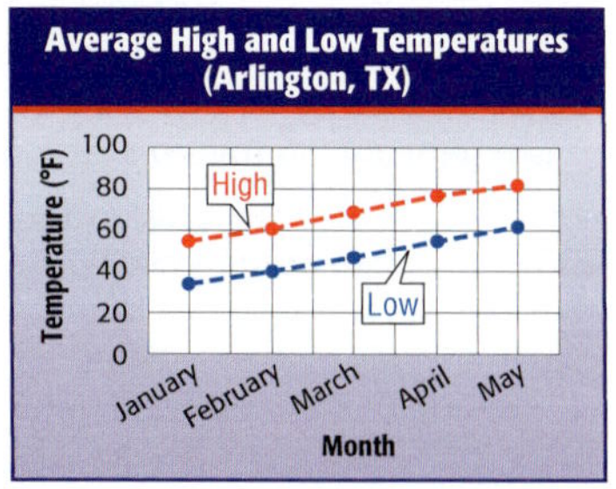

1. In which month is the average high temperature about twice as high as the average low temperature for January? **March**
2. What is the approximate difference between the average high temperature and the average low temperature each month? **about 20°F**
3. Predict the high and low temperatures for June based on the data given on the graph.

Lesson 8-6

Pages 426–431

For Exercises 1–3, refer to the graph at the right which shows Rachel's quiz scores for six quizzes.

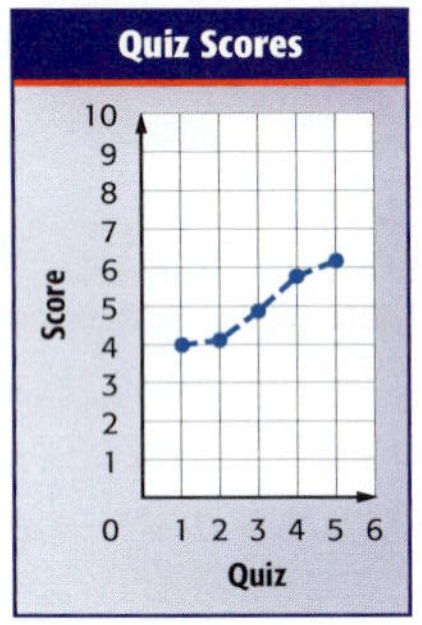

1. Describe the trend in Rachel's quiz scores. **Sample answer: The scores are increasing.**
2. If the trend continues, predict Rachel's score on the seventh quiz. **Sample answer: 7**
3. If the trend continues, predict Rachel's score on the tenth quiz. **Sample answer: 10**

For Exercises 4–6, use the table which shows the average price paid to farmers per 100 pounds of sheep they sold.

Year	Price Per 100 Pounds (\$)
1940	4
1950	12
1960	6
1970	8
1980	21
1990	23
2000	34

Source: *The World Almanac and Book of Facts*

4. Make a scatter plot of the data.
5. Describe the relationship, if any, between the two sets of data.
6. Predict the price per 100 pounds for 2010. Explain. **4–6. See Student Handbook Answer Appendix.**

Lesson 8-7

Pages 435–437

1. **SURVEYS** The table shows the results of a survey of students' favorite cookies. Predict how many of the 424 students at Scobey High School prefer chocolate chip cookies. **about 253 students**

Cookie	Number
chocolate chip	49
peanut butter	12
oatmeal	10
sugar	8
raisin	3

2. **VACATION** The circle graph shows the results of a survey of teens and where they would prefer to spend a family vacation. Predict how many of 4,000 teens would prefer to go to an amusement park. **1,800 teens**

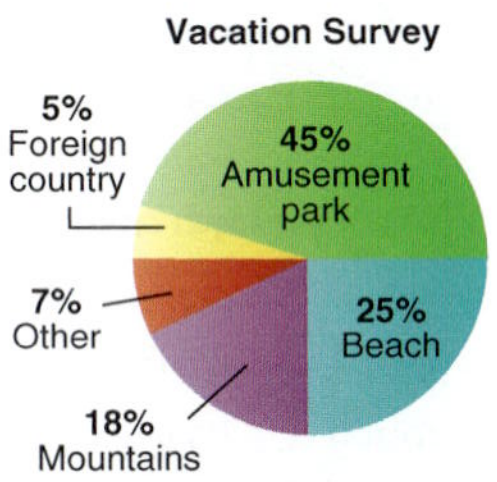

3. **TRAVEL** In 2000, about 29% of the foreign visitors to the U.S. were from Canada. If a particular hotel had 150,000 foreign guests in one year, how many would you predict were from Canada? **43,500 Canadians**

Lesson 8-8 1–3. See Student Handbook Answer Appendix.

Pages 438–443

Determine whether each conclusion is valid. Justify your answer.

1. To determine whether most students participate in after school activities, the principal of Humberson Middle School randomly surveyed 75 students from each grade level. Of these, 34% said they participate in after school activities. The principal concluded that about a third of the students at Humberson Middle School participate in after school activities.
2. To evaluate their product, the manager of an assembly line inspected the first 100 watches produced on Monday. Of these, 2 were defective. The manager concluded that about 2% of all watches produced are defective.
3. A television program asked its viewers to dial one of two phone numbers indicating their preference for one of two brands of shampoo. Of those that responded, 76% said they prefer Brand A. The program concluded that Brand A was the most popular brand of shampoo.

Lesson 8-9 1, 2. See Student Handbook Answer Appendix.

Pages 444–449

Which graph could be misleading? Explain your reasoning.

1. Both graphs show pounds of grapes sold to Westview School in one week.
2. Both graphs show commissions made by Mr. Turner for a four-week pay period.

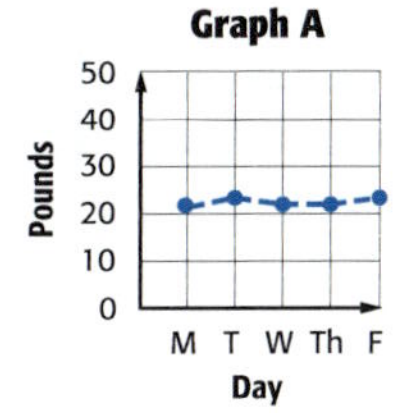

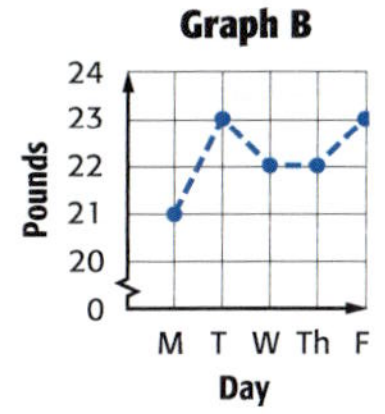

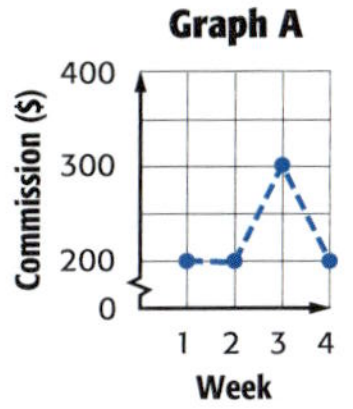

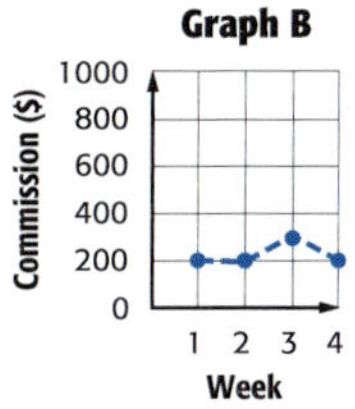

Lesson 9-1

Pages 460–464

Use the spinner at the right to find each probability. Write as a fraction in simplest form.

1. $P(\text{even number})$ $\frac{1}{2}$
2. $P(\text{prime number})$ $\frac{1}{2}$
3. $P(\text{factor of } 12)$ $\frac{5}{8}$
4. $P(\text{composite number})$ $\frac{3}{8}$
5. $P(\text{greater than } 10)$ 0
6. $P(\text{neither prime nor composite})$ $\frac{1}{8}$

A package of balloons contains 5 green, 3 yellow, 4 red, and 8 pink balloons. Suppose you reach in the package and choose one balloon at random. Find the probability of each event. Write as a fraction in simplest form.

7. $P(\text{red balloon})$ $\frac{1}{5}$
8. $P(\text{yellow balloon})$ $\frac{3}{20}$
9. $P(\text{pink balloon})$ $\frac{2}{5}$
10. $P(\text{orange balloon})$ 0
11. $P(\text{red or yellow balloon})$ 11. $\frac{7}{20}$
12. $P(\textit{not}\text{ green balloon})$ $\frac{3}{4}$

Lesson 9-2

Pages 465–470

For each situation, find the sample space using a tree diagram.

1. rolling 2 number cubes 1–5. See Student Handbook Answer Appendix for tree diagrams.
2. choosing an ice cream cone from waffle, plain, or sugar and a flavor of ice cream from chocolate, vanilla, or strawberry
3. making a sandwich from white, wheat, or rye bread, cheddar or Swiss cheese and ham, turkey, or roast beef
4. tossing a penny twice
5. choosing one math class from Algebra and Geometry and one foreign language class from French, Spanish, or Latin

Lesson 9-3

Pages 471–474

Use the Fundamental Counting Principle to find the total number of outcomes in each situation.

1. choosing a local phone number if the exchange is 398 and each of the four remaining digits is different 5,040 outcomes
2. choosing a way to drive from Millville to Westwood if there are 5 roads that lead from Millville to Miamisburg, 3 roads that connect Miamisburg to Hathaway, and 4 highways that connect Hathaway to Westwood 60 outcomes
3. tossing a quarter, rolling a number cube, and tossing a dime 24 outcomes
4. spinning the spinners shown below 96 outcomes

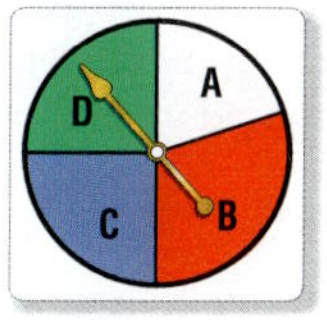

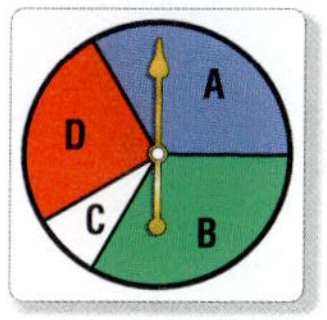

Lesson 9-4

Pages 475–478

1. **RACES** Eight runners are competing in a 100-meter sprint. In how many ways can the gold, silver, and bronze medals be awarded? 336 ways
2. **LOCKERS** Five-digit locker combinations are assigned using the digits 1–9. In how many ways can the combinations be formed if no digit can be repeated? 15,120 ways
3. **SCHEDULES** In how many ways can the classes math, language arts, science, and social studies be ordered on student schedules as the first four classes of their day? 24 ways
4. **TOYS** At a teddy bear workshop, customers can select from black, brown, golden, white, blue, or pink for their bear's color. If a father randomly selects two bear colors, what is the probability that he will select a white bear for his son and a pink bear for his daughter? The father cannot pick the same color for both bears. $\frac{1}{30}$
5. **WRITING** If you randomly select three of your last seven writing assignments to submit to an essay contest, what is the probability that you will select your first, fourth, and sixth essays in that order? $\frac{1}{210}$

Lesson 9-5

Pages 480–483

1. **EXERCISE** How many ways can you choose to exercise three days of a week? **35 ways**
2. **BOOKS** In how many ways can six books be selected from a collection of 12? **924 ways**
3. **REPORTS** In how many ways can you select three report topics from a total of 8 topics? **56 ways**
4. **GROUPS** How many ways can four students be chosen from a class of 26? **14,950 ways**
5. **ROLLER COASTERS** In how many ways can you ride five out of nine roller coasters if you don't care in what order you ride them? **126 ways**

Lesson 9-6

Pages 484–485

Use the *act it out* strategy to solve each problem.

1. **STAIRS** Lynnette lives on a certain floor of her apartment building. She goes up two flights of stairs to put a load of laundry in a washing machine on that floor. Then she goes down five flights to borrow a book from a friend. Next, she goes up 8 flights to visit another friend who is ill. How many flights up or down does Lynette now have to go to take her laundry out of the washing machine? **3 flights up**
2. **LOGIC PUZZLE** Suppose you are on the west side of a river with a fox, a duck, and a bag of corn. You want to take all three to the other side of the river, but…
   - your boat is only large enough to carry you and either the fox, duck, or bag of corn.
   - you cannot leave the fox alone with the duck.
   - you cannot leave the duck alone with the corn.
   - you cannot leave the corn alone on the east side of the river because some wild birds will eat it.
   - the wild birds are afraid of the fox.
   - you cannot leave the fox, duck, and the corn alone.
   - you can bring something across the river more than once.

   If there is no other way to cross the river, how do you get everything to the other side?

   First carry the duck across the river and bring the boat back empty. Then carry the fox across the river and carry the duck back. Then carry the corn across the river and bring the boat back empty. Finally carry the duck across the river.

Lesson 9-7

Pages 486–490

The frequency table shows the results of a fair number cube rolled 40 times.

Face	Frequency
1	5
2	9
3	2
4	8
5	12
6	4

1. Find the experimental probability of rolling a 4. $\frac{1}{5}$
2. Find the theoretical probability of *not* rolling a 4. $\frac{5}{6}$
3. Find the theoretical probability of rolling a 2. $\frac{1}{6}$
4. Find the experimental probability of *not* rolling a 6. $\frac{9}{10}$
5. Suppose the number cube was rolled 500 times. About how many times would it land on 5? **150**

Lesson 9-8

Pages 492–497

1. **COINS** Two evenly balanced nickels are tossed. Find the probability that one head and one tail result. $\frac{1}{4}$
2. **MONEY** A wallet contains four \$5 bills, two \$10 bills, and eight \$1 bills. A bill is randomly selected. Find P(\$5 or \$1). $\frac{6}{7}$
3. **PROBABILITY** Two chips are selected from a box containing 6 blue chips, 4 red chips, and 3 green chips. The first chip selected is replaced before the second is drawn. Find P(red, green). $\frac{12}{169}$
4. **PROBABILITY** A bag contains 7 blue, 4 orange, 8 red, and 5 purple marbles. Suppose one marble is chosen and not replaced. A second marble is then chosen. Find P(purple, red). $\frac{5}{69}$

Lesson 10-1

Pages 510–513

Classify each angle as *acute, right, obtuse,* or *straight.*

1. 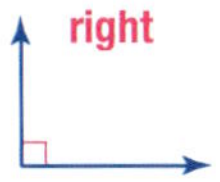 **right**
2.  **obtuse**
3. **straight**
4.  **acute**

5. Identify a pair of vertical angles in the diagram at the right. **∠1 and ∠3**

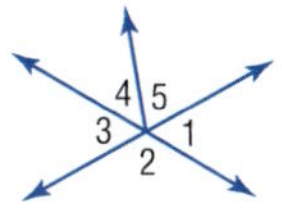

6. Identify a pair of adjacent angles in the diagram at the right. **Sample answer: ∠1 and ∠2**

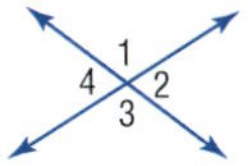

Lesson 10-2

Pages 514–517

Classify each pair of angles as *complementary, supplementary,* or *neither.*

1. 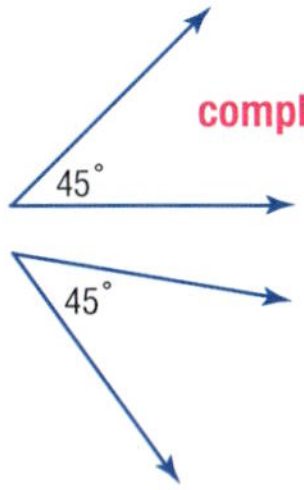

complementary

2. 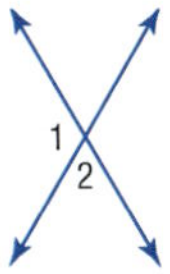

supplementary

3. 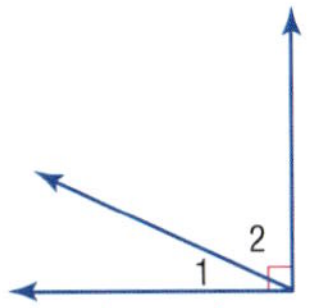

complementary

Find the value of x in each figure.

4. 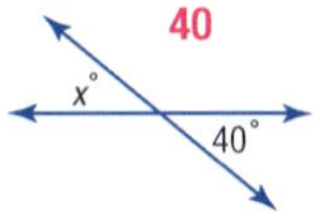

40

5. 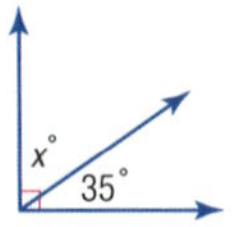

55

6. 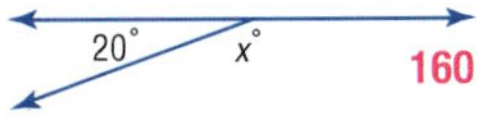

160

Lesson 10-3 1, 2. See Student Handbook Answer Appendix.
Pages 518–523

Display each set of data in a circle graph.

1.

Car Sales	
Style	**Percent**
sedan	45%
SUV	22%
pickup truck	9%
sports car	13%
compact car	11%

2.

Favorite Flavor of Ice Cream	
Flavor	**Number**
vanilla	11
chocolate	15
strawberry	8
mint chip	5
cookie dough	3

Lesson 10-4
Pages 524–529

Find the value of x.

1. 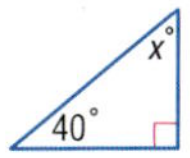

50

2. 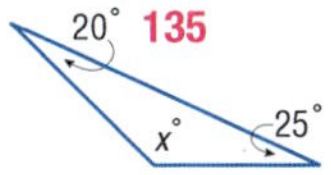

135

3. 

20

Classify each triangle by its angles and by its sides.

4. 
acute, scalene

5. 
right, scalene

6. 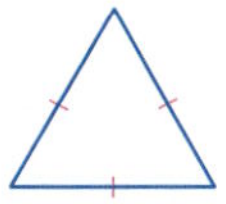
acute, equilateral

Lesson 10-5 1, 2. See Student Handbook Answer Appendix.
Pages 530–531

Use the *logical reasoning* strategy to solve each problem.

1. **GEOMETRY** Draw several isosceles triangles and measure their angles. What do you notice about the measures of the angles of an isosceles triangle.
2. **BASKETBALL** Placido, Dexter, and Scott play guard, forward, and center on a team, but not necessarily in that order. Placido and the center drove Scott to practice on Saturday. Placido does not play guard. Who is the guard?

Lesson 10-6
Pages 533–539

Classify each quadrilateral using the name that *best* describes it.

1. 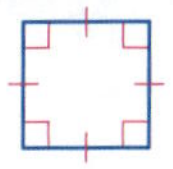
square

2. 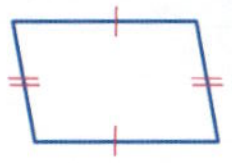
parallelogram

3. 
quadrilateral

Find the missing angle measure in each quadrilateral.

4. 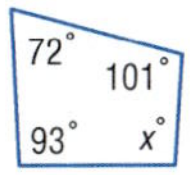

94°

5. 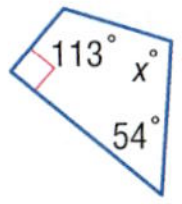

103°

6. 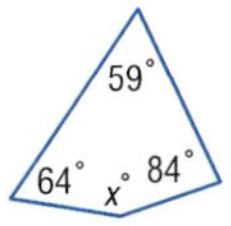

153°

Lesson 10-7
Pages 540–545

Find the value of x in each pair of similar figures.

1. 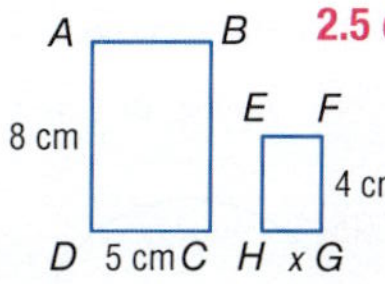

2.5 cm

2. 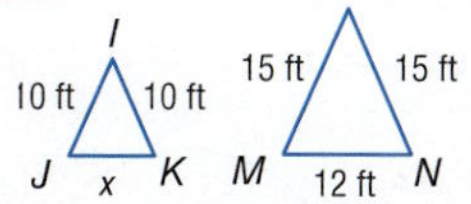

8 ft

3. 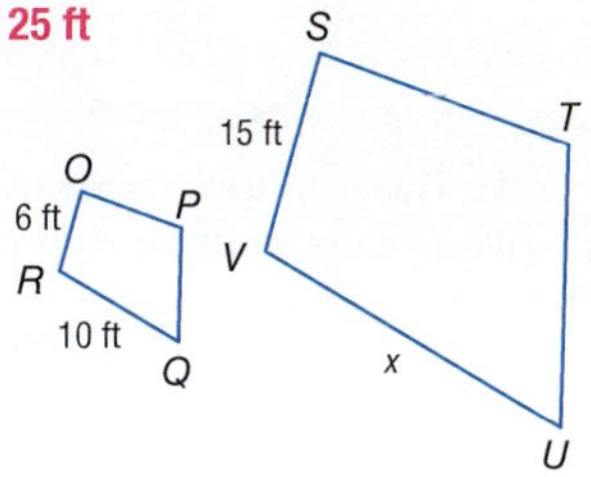

25 ft

4. 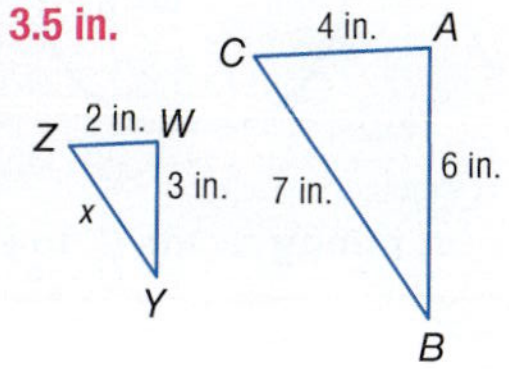

3.5 in.

5. 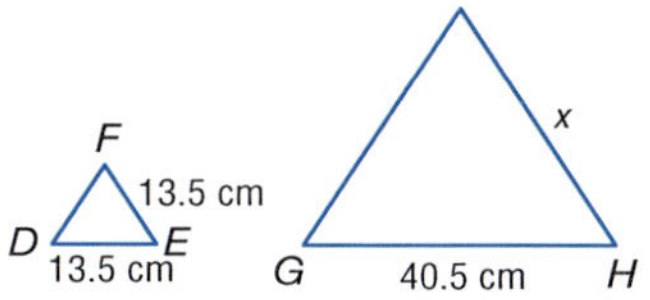

40.5 cm

6. 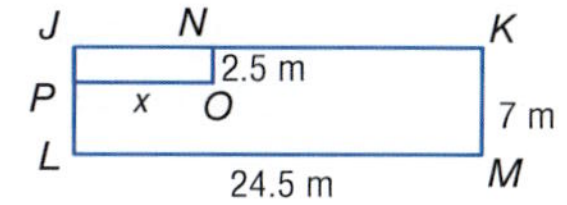

8.75 m

Lesson 10-8
Pages 546–551

Determine whether each figure is a polygon. If it is, classify the polygon and state whether it is regular. If it is *not* a polygon, explain why.

1. 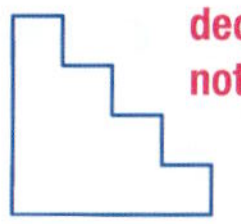
decagon, not regular

2. 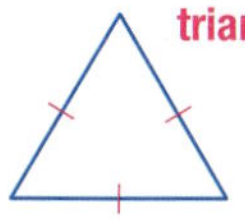
triangle, regular

3. 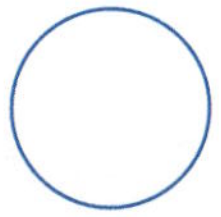
not a polygon, sides are curved

4. 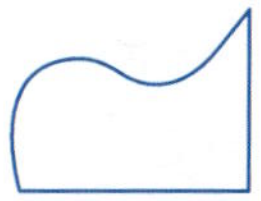
not a polygon, sides are curved

5. 
octagon, not regular

6. 
not a polygon, figure is not closed

Find the measure of an angle in each polygon if polygon is regular. Round to the nearest tenth of a degree if necessary.

7. triangle 60°
8. 30-gon 168°
9. 18-gon 160°
10. 14-gon 154.3°
11. hexagon 120°
12. nonagon 140°
13. 27-gon 166.7°
14. octagon 135°

Lesson 10-9 1, 2. See Student Handbook Answer Appendix.

Pages 553–557

1. Translate $\triangle ABC$ 2 units right and 1 unit down.

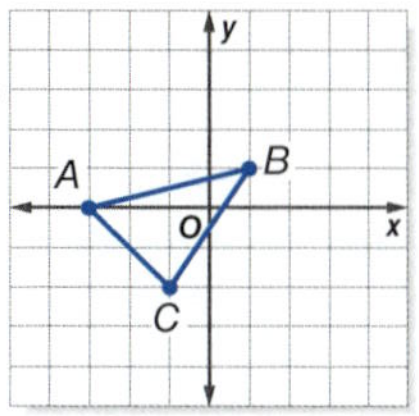

2. Translate quadrilateral $RSTU$ 4 units left and 3 units down.

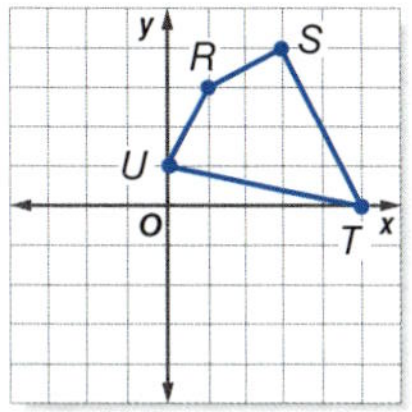

Triangle TRI has vertices $T(1, 1)$, $R(4, -2)$, and $I(-2, -1)$. Find the vertices of $T'R'I'$ after each translation. Then graph the figure and its translated image. **3–6. See Student Handbook Answer Appendix for graphs.**

3. 2 units right, 1 unit down **$T'(3, 0)$, $R'(6, -3)$, $I'(0, -2)$**
4. 5 units left, 1 unit up **$T'(-4, 2)$, $R'(-1, -1)$, $I'(-7, 0)$**
5. 3 units right **$T'(4, 1)$, $R'(7, -2)$, $I'(1, -1)$**
6. 2 units up **$T'(1, 3)$, $R'(4, 0)$ $I'(-2, 1)$**

Lesson 10-10

Pages 558–562

Determine whether each figure has line symmetry. Write *yes* or *no*. If so, copy the figure and draw all lines of symmetry.

1. 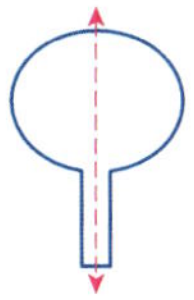 **yes**
2. 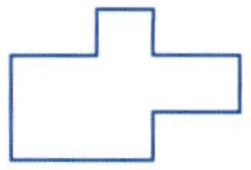 **no**
3. 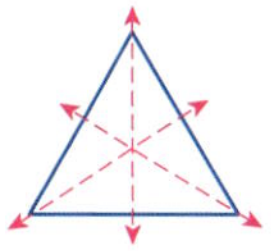 **yes**
4.  **no**
5. 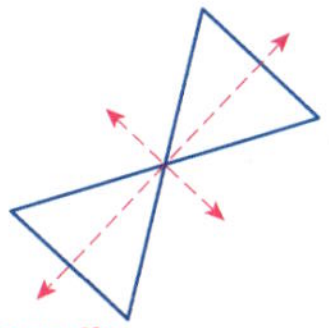 **yes**
6. 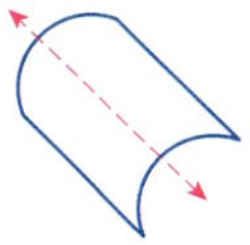 **yes**

7. See Student Handbook Answer Appendix.
8. See Student Handbook Answer Appendix for graph.

Graph each figure and its reflection over the x-axis. Then find the coordinates of the vertices of the reflected image.

7. quadrilateral $QUAD$ with vertices $Q(-1, 4)$, $U(2, 2)$, $A(1, 1)$, and $D(-2, 2)$
8. triangle $\triangle ABC$ with vertices $A(0, -1)$, $B(4, -3)$, and $C(-4, -5)$ **$A'(0, 1)$, $B'(4, 3)$, $C'(-4, 5)$**

9, 10. See Student Handbook Answer Appendix for graphs.

Graph each figure and its reflection over the y-axis. Then find the coordinates of the vertices of the reflected image.

9. parallelogram $PARL$ with vertices $P(3, 5)$, $A(5, 4)$, $R(5, 1)$, and $L(3, 2)$ **$P'(-3, 5)$, $A'(-5, 4)$, $R'(-5, 1)$, $L'(-3, 2)$**
10. pentagon $PENTA$ with vertices $P(-1, 3)$, $E(1, 1)$, $N(0, -2)$, $T(-2, -2)$, and $A(-3, 1)$ **$P'(1, 3)$, $E'(-1, 1)$, $N'(0, -2)$, $T'(2, -2)$, $A'(3, 1)$**

Lesson 11-1

Pages 570–574

Find the area of each parallelogram. Round to the nearest tenth if necessary.

1. 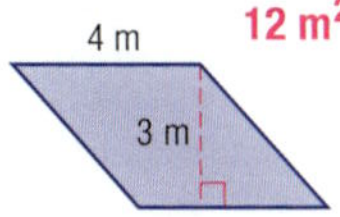

12 m²

2. 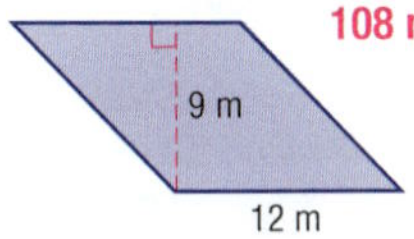

108 m²

3. 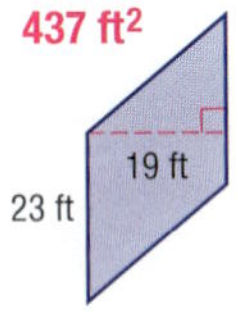

437 ft²

4. base = 19 m, height = 6 m **114 m²**
5. base = 135 in., height = 15 in. **2,025 in²**
6. base = 8.2 cm, height = 5.5 cm **45.1 cm²**
7. base = 29.3 m, height = 10.1 m **295.9 m²**

Lesson 11-2

Pages 576–580

Find the area of each figure. Round to the nearest tenth if necessary.

1. 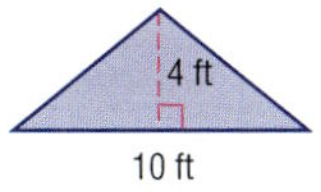

20 ft²

2. 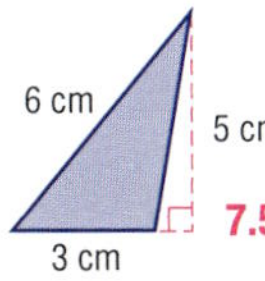

7.5 cm²

3. 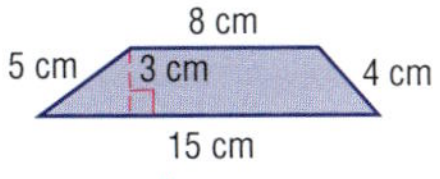

34.5 cm²

4. triangle: base = 5 in., height = 9 in. **22.5 in²**
5. trapezoid: bases = 3 cm and 8 cm, height = 12 cm **66 cm²**
6. trapezoid: bases = 10 ft and 15 ft, height = 12 ft **150 ft²**
7. triangle: base = 12 cm, height = 8 cm **48 cm²**
8. trapezoid: bases = 82.6 cm and 72.2 cm, height = 44.5 cm **3,444.3 cm²**
9. triangle: base = 500.5 ft, height = 254.5 ft **63,688.6 ft²**

Lesson 11-3

Pages 582–586

Find the circumference of each circle. Use 3.14 or $\frac{22}{7}$ for π. Round to the nearest tenth if necessary.

1. 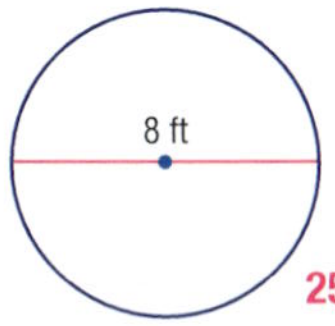

25.1 ft

2. 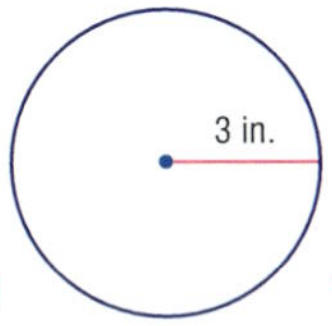

18.8 in.

3. 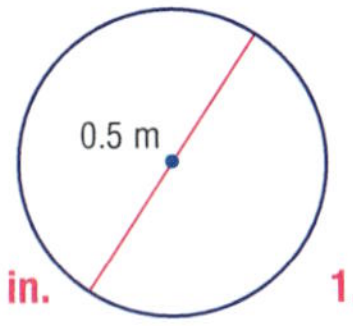

1.6 m

4. 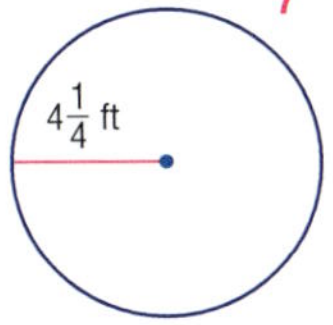

$26\frac{5}{7}$ ft

5. $r = 1$ m **6.3 m**
6. $d = 2$ yd **6.3 yd**
7. $d = 5{,}280$ ft **16,579.2 ft**
8. $r = 0.5$ cm **3.1 cm**
9. $d = 6.4$ m **20.1 m**
10. $r = 10.7$ km **67.2 km**
11. $d = \frac{3}{16}$ in. **$\frac{33}{56}$ in.**
12. $r = 5\frac{1}{2}$ mi **$34\frac{4}{7}$ mi**
13. $d = 42\frac{3}{4}$ ft **$134\frac{5}{14}$ ft**

Lesson 11-4

Pages 587–591

Find the area of each circle. Round to the nearest tenth.

1. 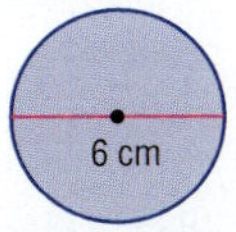

28.3 cm²

2. 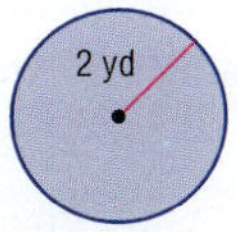

12.6 yd²

3. 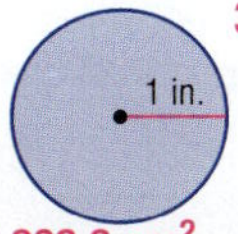

3.1 in²

4. radius = 8 in. **201.0 in²**
5. diameter = 5 ft **19.6 ft²**
6. radius = 24 cm **1,808.6 cm²**
7. diameter = 2.3 m **4.2 m²**
8. diameter = 82 ft **5,278.3 ft²**
9. radius = 68 cm
10. radius = 9.8 mi **301.6 mi²**
11. diameter = 25.6 m
12. diameter = 6.75 in. **35.8 in²**
13. radius = $1\frac{1}{4}$ ft **4.9 ft²**
14. diameter = $5\frac{2}{3}$ yd
15. diameter = $45\frac{1}{2}$ mi

9, 11, 14, 15. See Student Handbook Answer Appendix.

Lesson 11-5

Pages 592–593

Use the *solve a simpler problem* strategy to solve each problem.

1. **EARNINGS** Cedric makes $51,876 each year. If he is paid once every two weeks and actually takes home about 67% of his wages after taxes, how much does he take home each paycheck? Round to the nearest cent if necessary. **$1,336.80**

2. **CARS** Jorge plans to decorate the rims on his tires by putting a strip of shiny metal around the outside edge on each rim. The diameter of each tire is 17 inches, and each rim is 2.75 inches from the outside edge of each tire. If he plans to cut the four individual pieces for each tire from the same strip of metal, how long of a strip should he buy? Round to the nearest tenth. **144.5 in.**

3. **SAVINGS** Erin's aunt invested a total of $1,500 into three different savings accounts. She invested $450 into a savings account with an annual interest rate of 3.25% and $600 into a savings account with an annual interest rate of 4.75%. The third savings account had an annual interest rate of 4.375%. After 3 years, how much money will Erin's aunt have in the three accounts altogether if she made no more additional deposits or withdrawals? Round to the nearest cent. **$1,688.44**

BIOLOGY For Exercises 4–6, use the following information.
About five quarts of blood are pumped through the average human heart in one minute.

4. At this rate, how many quarts of blood are pumped through the average human heart in one year? (Use 365 days = 1 year) **2,628,000 qt**

5. If the average heart beats 72 times per minute, how many quarts of blood are pumped with each beat? Round to the nearest tenth. **0.1 qt**

6. About how many total gallons of blood are pumped through the average human heart in one week? **about 12,600 gal**

7. **LAND** A rectangular plot of land measures 1,450 feet by 850 feet. A contractor wishes to section off a portion of this land to build an apartment complex. If the complex is 425 feet by 550 feet, how many square feet of land will not be sectioned off to build it? **998,750 ft²**

Lesson 11-6

Pages 694–697

Find the area of each figure. Round to the nearest tenth if necessary.

1. 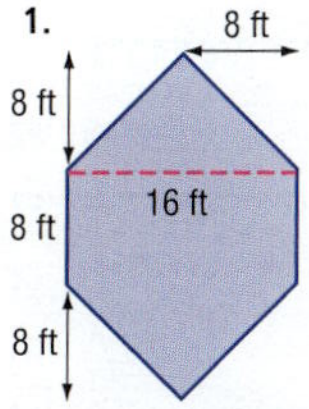

256 ft²

2. 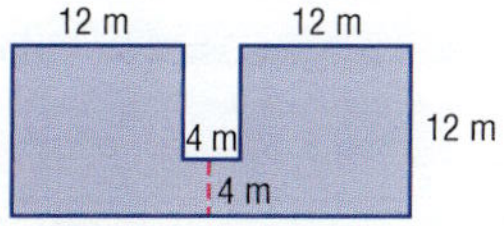

304 m²

3. 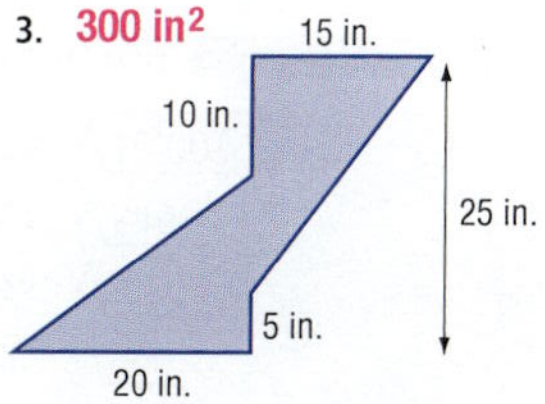

300 in²

4. 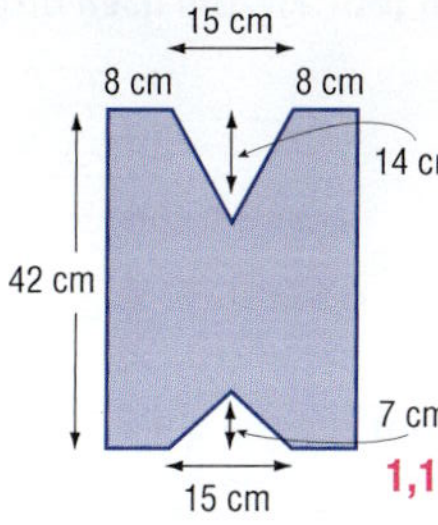

1,144.5 cm²

5. 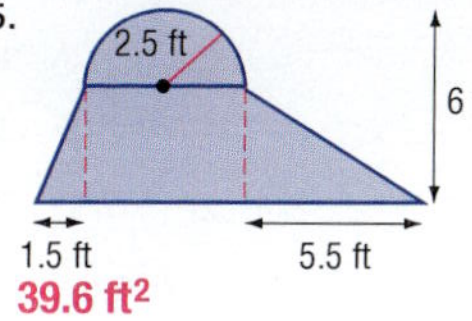

39.6 ft²

6. 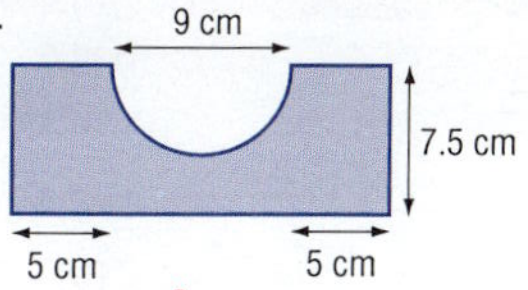

110.7 cm²

7. 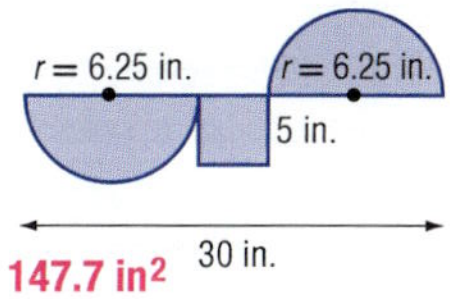

147.7 in²

8. 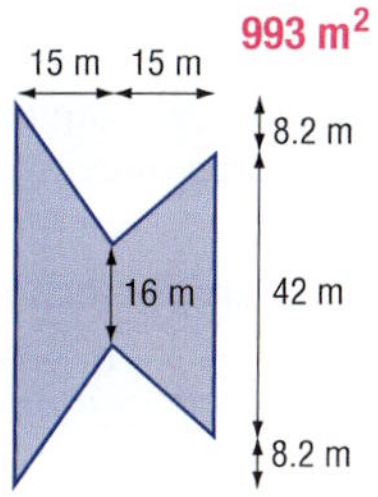

993 m²

9. 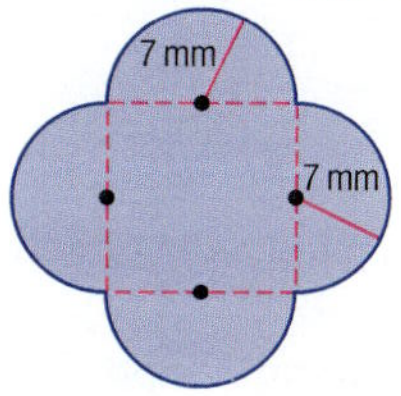

503.9 mm²

Lesson 11-7

Pages 601–604

For each figure, identify the shape of the base(s). Then classify the figure.

1. 
rectangle; rectangular prism

2. 
none; sphere

3. 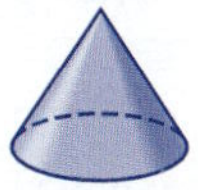
circle; cone

4. 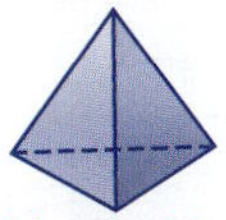
triangle; triangular pyramid

5. 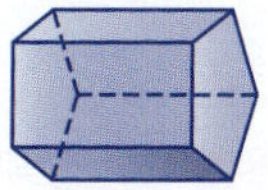
pentagon; pentagonal prism

6. 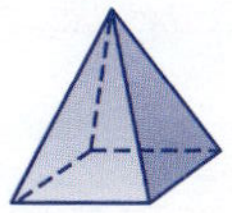
square; square pyramid

7. **SOUP** Classify the shape of a soup can as a three-dimensional figure. **cylinder**

8. **APPLIANCES** Classify the shape of a microwave oven as a three-dimensional figure. **rectangular prism**

Lesson 11-8 1–5. See Student Handbook Answer Appendix.

Pages 606–610

Draw a top, a side, and a front view of each solid.

1. 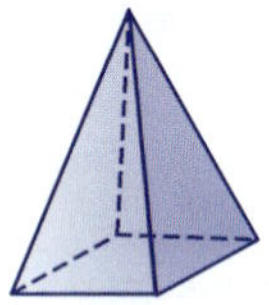

2. 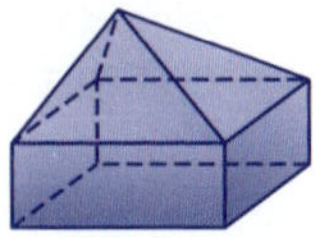

3. 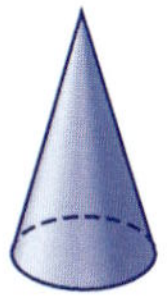

Draw each solid using the top, side, and front views shown. Use isometric dot paper.

4. 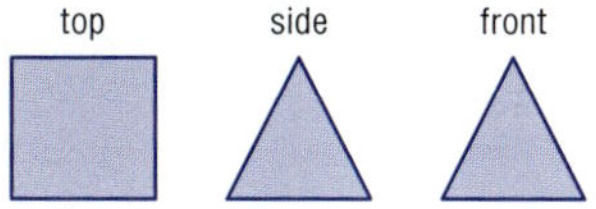

5. 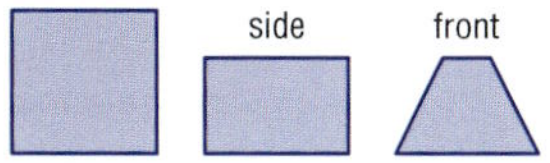

Lesson 11-9

Pages 611–616

Find the volume of each prism. Round to the nearest tenth if necessary.

1. 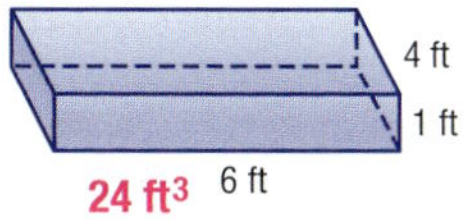

24 ft^3

2. 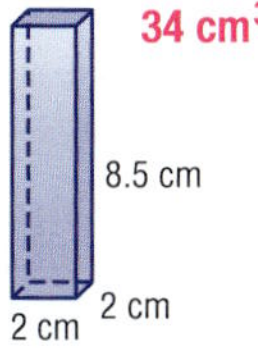

34 cm^3

3. 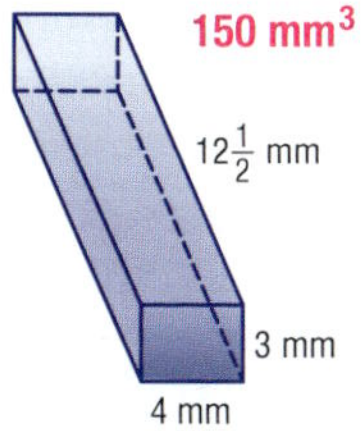

150 mm^3

4. 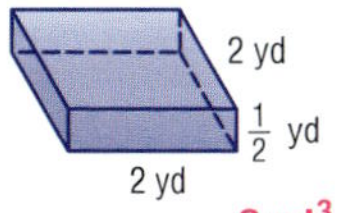

2 yd^3

5. 432 in^3 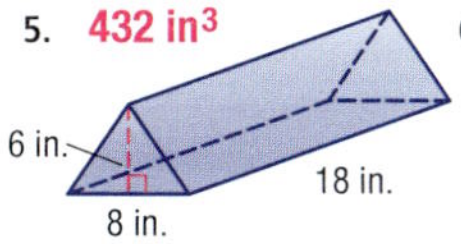

6. 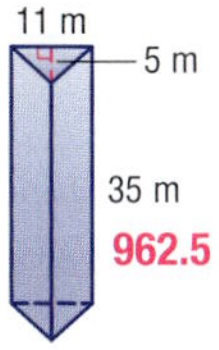

962.5 m^3

7. 240 mm^3 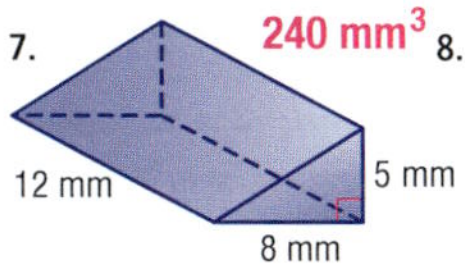

8. 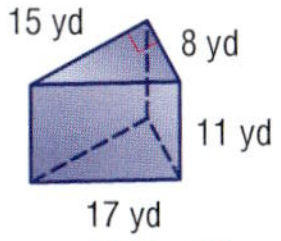

660 yd^3

Find the volume of each rectangular prism. Round to the nearest tenth if necessary.

9. length = 3 ft, width = 10 ft, height = 2 ft **60 ft^3**

10. length = 18 cm, width = 23 cm, height = 15 cm **6,210 cm^3**

11. length = 25 mm, width = 32 mm, height = 10 mm **8,000 mm^3**

12. length = 1.5 in., width = 3 in., height = 6 in. **27 in^3**

13. length = 4.5 cm, width = 6.75 cm, height = 2 cm **60.8 cm^3**

14. length = 16 mm, width = 0.7 mm, height = 12 mm **134.4 mm^3**

15. length = $3\frac{1}{2}$ ft, width = 10 ft, height = 6 ft **210 ft^3**

16. length = $5\frac{1}{2}$ in., width = 12 in., height = $3\frac{3}{8}$ in. **222.8 in^3**

17. Find the volume of a rectangular prism with a length of 3 yards, a width of 5 feet, and a height of 12 feet. **540 ft^3**

18. Find the volume of a triangular prism whose base has an area of 416 square feet and whose height is 22 feet. **9,152 ft^3**

Lesson 11-10

Pages 617–621

Find the volume of each cylinder. Round to the nearest tenth. Use 3.14 for π.

1. 50.2 cm^3 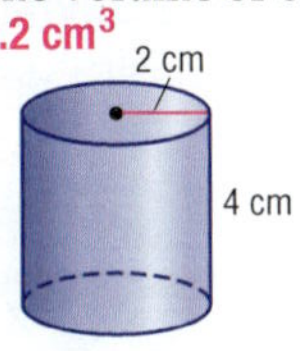

2. 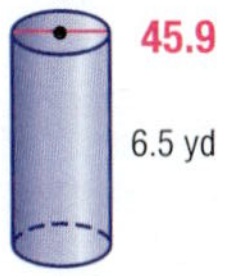

45.9 yd^3

3. 2,826 mm^3 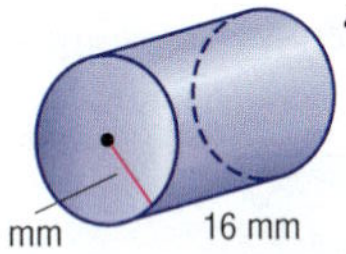

4. 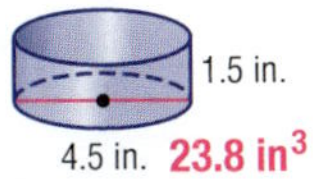

23.8 in^3

5. radius = 6 in., height = 3 in. **339.1 in^3**

6. radius = 8 ft, height = 10 ft **2,009.6 ft^3**

7. radius = 6 km, height = 12 km **1,356.5 km^3**

8. radius = 8.5 cm, height = 3 cm **680.6 cm^3**

9. diameter = 16 yd, height = 4.5 yd **904.3 yd^3**

10. diameter = 3.5 mm, height = 2.5 mm **24.0 mm^3**

11. diameter = 12 m, height = 4.75 m **536.9 m^3**

12. diameter = $\frac{5}{8}$ in., height = 4 in. **1.2 in^3**

13. diameter = 100 ft, height = 35 ft **274,750 ft^3**

14. radius = 40.5 m, height = 65.1 m **335,290.1 m^3**

15. radius = 0.5 cm, height = 1.6 cm **1.3 cm^3**

16. diameter = $8\frac{3}{4}$ in., height = $5\frac{1}{2}$ in. **330.6 in^3**

17. Find the volume of a cylinder whose diameter is 6 inches and height is 2 feet. Round to the nearest tenth. **0.4 ft^3 or 678.2 in^3**

18. How tall is a cylinder that has a volume of 2,123 cubic meters and a radius of 13 meters? Round to the nearest tenth. **4.0 m**

19. A cylinder has a volume of 310.2 cubic yards and a radius of 2.9 yards. What is the height of the cylinder? Round to the nearest tenth. **11.7 yd**

20. Find the height of a cylinder whose diameter is 25 centimeters and volume is 8,838 cubic centimeters. Round to the nearest tenth. **18.0 cm**

Lesson 12-1 16–30. See Student Handbook Answer Appendix.

Pages 634–637

Estimate each square root to the nearest whole number.

1. $\sqrt{27}$ **5**
2. $\sqrt{112}$ **11**
3. $\sqrt{249}$ **16**
4. $\sqrt{88}$ **9**
5. $\sqrt{1,500}$ **39**
6. $\sqrt{612}$ **25**
7. $\sqrt{340}$ **18**
8. $\sqrt{495}$ **22**
9. $\sqrt{264}$ **16**
10. $\sqrt{350}$ **19**
11. $\sqrt{834}$ **29**
12. $\sqrt{3,700}$ **61**
13. $\sqrt{298}$ **17**
14. $\sqrt{101}$ **10**
15. $\sqrt{800}$ **28**

Graph each square root on a number line.

16. $\sqrt{58}$
17. $\sqrt{750}$
18. $\sqrt{1,200}$
19. $\sqrt{1,000}$
20. $\sqrt{5,900}$
21. $\sqrt{999}$
22. $\sqrt{374}$
23. $\sqrt{512}$
24. $\sqrt{3,750}$
25. $\sqrt{255}$
26. $\sqrt{83}$
27. $\sqrt{845}$
28. $\sqrt{200}$
29. $\sqrt{500}$
30. $\sqrt{10,001}$

31. **ALGEBRA** Evaluate $\sqrt{a-b}$ to the nearest tenth if $a = 16$ and $b = 4$. **3.5**

32. **ALGEBRA** Estimate the value of $\sqrt{x+y}$ to the nearest whole number if $x = 64$ and $y = 25$. **9**

Lesson 12-2

Pages 638–643

Find the missing measure of each triangle. Round to the nearest tenth if necessary.

1. 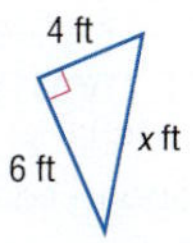

7.2 ft

2. 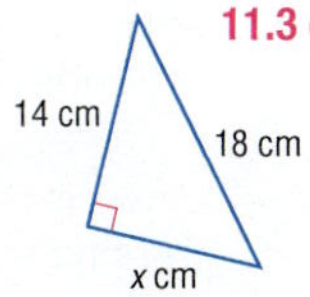

11.3 cm

3. 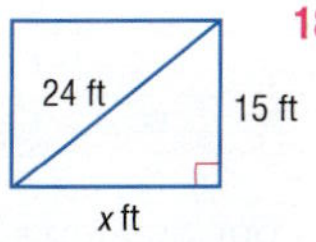

18.7 ft

4. $a = 12$ cm, $b = 25$ cm **27.7 cm**
5. $a = 5$ yd, $c = 10$ yd **8.7 yd**
6. $b = 12$ mi, $c = 20$ mi **16 mi**
7. $a = 15$ yd, $b = 24$ yd **28.3 yd**
8. $a = 4$ m, $c = 12$ m **11.3 m**
9. $a = 8$ mm, $b = 11$ mm **13.6 mm**
10. $a = 1$ mi, $c = 3$ mi **2.8 mi**
11. $a = 5$ yd, $b = 8$ yd **9.4 yd**
12. $b = 7$ in., $c = 19$ in. **17.7 in.**
13. $a = 50$ km, $c = 75$ km **55.9 km**
14. $b = 82$ ft, $c = 100$ ft **57.2 ft**
15. $a = 100$ m, $b = 200$ m **223.6 m**

Lesson 12-3

Pages 644–645

Use the *make a model* strategy to solve each problem.

1. **ARCHITECTURE** An architect is designing a large skyscraper for a local firm. The skyscraper is to be 1,200 feet tall, 500 feet long, and 400 feet wide. If his model has a scale of 80 feet = 1 inch, find the volume of the model. **468.75 in^3**

2. **STACKING BOXES** Box A has twice the volume of Box B. Box B has a height of 10 centimeters and a length of 5 centimeters. Box A has a width of 20 centimeters, a length of 10 centimeters, and a width of 5 centimeters. What is the width of Box B? **10 cm**

3. **TRAVEL** On Monday, Mara drove 400 miles as part of her journey to see her sister. She drove 60% of this distance on Tuesday. If the distance she drove on Tuesday represents one third of her total journey, how many more miles does she still need to drive? **80 mi**

4. **PIZZA** On Monday, there was a whole pizza in the refrigerator. On Tuesday, Enrico ate $\frac{1}{3}$ of the pizza. On Wednesday, he ate $\frac{1}{3}$ of what was left. On Thursday, he ate $\frac{1}{2}$ of what remained. What fractional part of the pizza is left? **$\frac{2}{9}$**

5. **GARDENS** Mr. Blackwell has a circular garden in his backyard. He wants to build a curved brick pathway around the entire garden. The garden has a radius of 18 feet. The distance from the center of the garden to the outside edge of the brick pathway will be 21.5 feet. Find the area of the brick pathway. Round to the nearest tenth. **434.3 ft^2**

Lesson 12-4

Pages 647–651

Find the surface area of each rectangular prism. Round to the nearest tenth if necessary. **8, 11, 12, 14–16. See Student Handbook Answer Appendix.**

1. 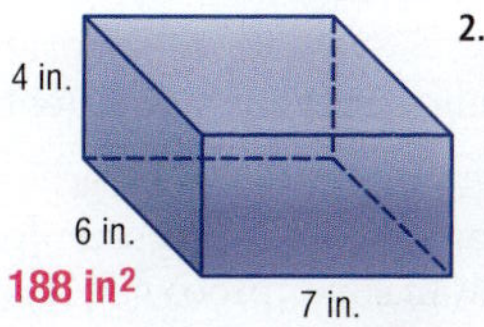

188 in^2

2. 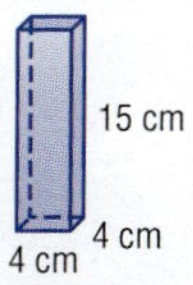

272 cm^2

3. 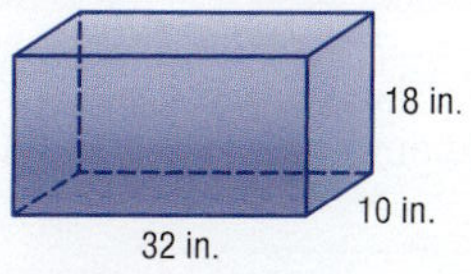

2,152 in^2

4. 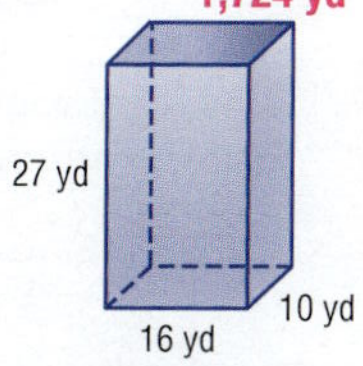

1,724 yd^2

5. length = 10 m, width = 6 m, height = 7 m **344 m^2**
6. length = 20 mm, width = 15 mm, height = 25 mm **2,350 mm^2**
7. length = 16 ft, width = 20 ft, height = 12 ft **1,504 ft^2**
8. length = 52 cm, width = 48 cm, height = 45 cm
9. length = 8 ft, width = 6.5 ft, height = 7 ft **307 ft^2**
10. length = 9.4 m, width = 2 m, height = 5.2 m **156.2 m^2**
11. length = 20.4 cm, width = 15.5 cm, height = 8.8 cm
12. length = 8.5 mi, width = 3 mi, height = 5.8 mi
13. length = $7\frac{1}{4}$ ft, width = 5 ft, height = $6\frac{1}{2}$ ft **231.8 ft^2**
14. length = $15\frac{2}{3}$ yd, width = $7\frac{1}{3}$ yd, height = 9 yd
15. length = $4\frac{1}{2}$ in., width = 10 in., height = $8\frac{3}{4}$ in.
16. length = 12.2 mm, width = 7.4 mm, height = 7.4 mm
17. Find the surface area of an open-top box with a length of 18 yards, a width of 11 yards, and a height of 14 yards. **1,010 yd^2**
18. Find the surface area of a rectangular prism with a length of 1 yard, a width of 7 feet, and a height of 2 yards. **162 ft^2 or 18 yd^2**

Lesson 12-5 **9–12. See Student Handbook Answer Appendix.**

Pages 654–657

Find the surface area of each cylinder. Round to the nearest tenth.

1. 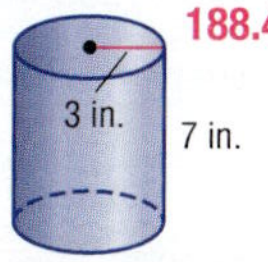

188.4 in^2

2. 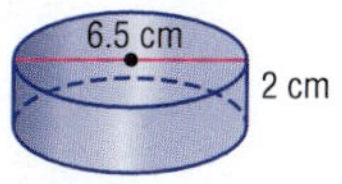

107.2 cm^2

3. 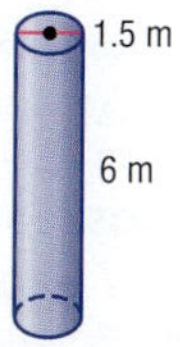

31.8 m^2

4. 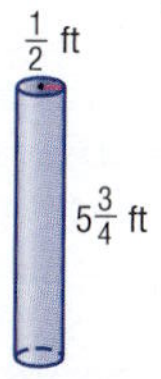

19.6 ft^2

5. height = 6 cm, radius = 3.5 cm **208.8 cm^2**
6. height = 16.5 mm, diameter = 18 mm **1,441.3 mm^2**
7. height = 22 yd, radius = 10.5 yd **2,143.1 yd^2**
8. height = 6 ft, radius = 18.5 ft **2,846.4 ft^2**
9. height = 10.2 mi, diameter = 4 mi
10. height = 8.6 cm, diameter = 8.2 cm
11. height = 5.8 km, diameter = 3.6 km
12. height = 32.7 m, radius = 21.5 m
13. height = $2\frac{2}{3}$ yd, diameter = 6 yd **106.8 yd^2**
14. height = $12\frac{3}{4}$ ft, radius = $7\frac{1}{4}$ ft **910.6 ft^2**
15. height = $5\frac{1}{5}$ mi, radius = $18\frac{1}{3}$ mi **2,709.4 mi^2**
16. height = $5\frac{1}{2}$ in., diameter = 3 in. **65.9 in^2**

Mixed Problem Solving

Chapter 1 Introduction to Algebra and Functions

Pages 22–77

1. **HISTORY** In 1932, Amelia Earhart flew 2,026 miles in 14 hours 56 minutes. To the nearest mile, what was her speed in miles per minute? (Lesson 1-1) **2 mi/min**

2. **LIGHT** The speed of light is about 67^3 kilometers per second. How many kilometers per second is this? (Lesson 1-2) **300,763 km/s**

3. **FARMING** Find the length of one side of a square field with an area of 180,625 square feet. (Lesson 1-3) **425 ft**

4. **SALES** A department store is having a back-to-school sale. The table shows the prices of three popular items.

Item	Price ($)
Jeans	37.99
Sweatshirt	19.88
Polo Shirt	22.50

2(37.99) + 3(19.88) + 1(22.50); $158.12

Latonia wants to buy 2 pairs of jeans, 3 sweatshirts, and 1 polo shirt. Write and evaluate a numerical expression that represents the total cost of all three items. (Lesson 1-4) **5. Sample answer: 7 quarters, 6 dimes, 3 nickels, 8 pennies**

5. **MONEY** Mateo has $2.58 in coins. If he has quarters, dimes, nickels, and pennies, how many of each coin does he have? Use the *guess and check* strategy. (Lesson 1-5)

6. **FITNESS** You can estimate how fast you walk in miles per hour by evaluating the expression $\frac{n}{30}$, where n is the number of steps you take in one minute. Find your speed in miles per hour if you take 96 steps in one minute. (Lesson 1-6) **3.2 mi/h**

7. 11 games

7. **BASEBALL** Last year, Scott attended 13 Minnesota Twins baseball games. This year, he attended 24. Solve $13 + n = 24$ to find how many more games he attended this year than last. (Lesson 1-7)

8. **HOT AIR BALLOONS** Miyoki paid $140 for a four-hour hot air balloon ride over the Bridger Mountains. Solve $4h = 140$ to find the cost per hour of the ride. (Lesson 1-7) **$35**

ENTERTAINMENT For Exercises 9 and 10, use the following information.
The five members of the Wolff family went to an amusement park. They each purchased an all-day ride pass and a water park pass, as shown below. (Lesson 1-8)

Item	Price ($)
All-Day Ride Pass	14.95
Water Park Pass	6.50

5(14.95 + 6.50); 5(14.95) + 5(6.50)

9. Use the Distributive Property to write two different expressions that represent the total cost for the family.

10. Find the total cost of the passes. **$107.25**

11. **NUMBER THEORY** Numbers that can be represented by a square arrangement of dots are called *square numbers*. The first four square numbers are shown below. (Lesson 1-9)

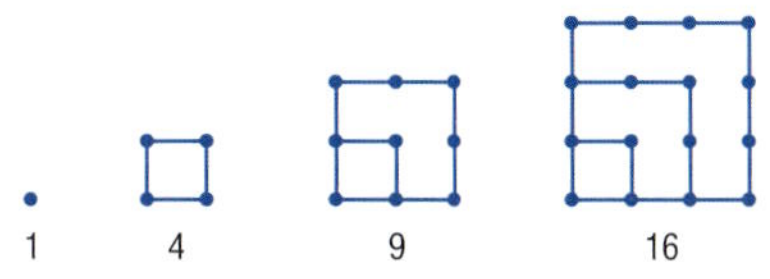

Write a sequence formed by the area of the first eight square numbers. **1, 4, 9, 16, 25, 36, 49, 64**

12. **TIME** Copy and complete the function table showing how many days y there are in various number of weeks x. Then identify the domain and range. (Lesson 1-10)

x	7x	y
1	7(1)	7
2	7(2)	14
3	7(3)	21
4	7(4)	28

Domain: {1, 2, 3, 4} Range: {7, 14, 21, 28}

Chapter 2 Integers

Pages 78–125

1. **AIR CONDITIONING** Jacob turned on the air conditioning and the temperature in his apartment decreased 8 degrees. Write an integer to represent the change in temperature. (Lesson 2-1) **−8**

EARTH SCIENCE For Exercises 2 and 3, use the table below. It describes the deepest land depressions in the world in feet below sea level.
2, 3. See Student Handbook Answer Appendix.

Depth (ft)			
220	436	511	282
383	505	235	230

Source: *The Top 10 Everything*

2. Write an integer to represent each depth. (Lesson 2-1)

3. Order the integers from greatest depth to least depth. (Lesson 2-2)

ENTERTAINMENT For Exercises 4–8, use the diagram below. It shows the locations of several rides at the Outlook Amusement Park. (Lesson 2-3)

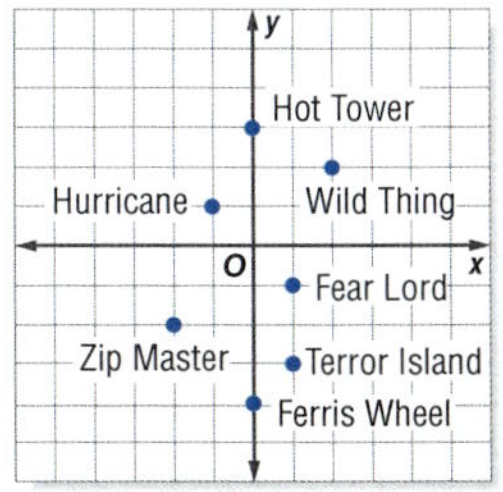

4. Which ride(s) is located in quadrant III? **Zip Master**

5. Which ride(s) is located on the y-axis? Name the coordinates. **See Student Handbook Answer Appendix.**

6. Which ride(s) has coordinates in which the x-coordinates and y-coordinates are equal? **Wild Thing, Zip Master**

7. In which quadrant is the Hurricane located? **Quadrant II**

8. A new ride is built with a location on the x-axis and 5 units left of the origin. Name the coordinates of this point. **(−5, 0)**

9. **CAVERNS** Adriana is 52 feet underground touring the Lewis and Clark Caverns. She climbs a ladder up 15 feet. What is her new location? (Lesson 2-4) **37 ft underground or −37 ft**

10. **RECORDS** The lowest temperature recorded in Verkhoyansk, Russia, was about −90°F. The highest temperature was about 99°F. What is the difference between these temperatures? (Lesson 2-5) **189° F**

11. **EARTH SCIENCE** The highest and lowest points in California are shown in the table. What is the difference in elevations? (Lesson 2-5) **14,776 ft**

Location	Elevation
Mount Whitney	14,494 ft above sea level
Death Valley	282 ft below sea level

Source: *The World Almanac of the U.S.A.*

12. **RIDES** A glider ride over the Crazy Mountains has a maximum altitude of 12,000 feet. It is descending at a rate of about 300 feet per minute. At what altitude will the glider be 20 minutes later? (Lesson 2-6) **6,000 ft**

13. **SPORTS** Every 12 times at bat, Simon hits the ball 3 times. About how many times will he hit the ball after 20 times at bat? 40? 84? Use the *look for a pattern* strategy. (Lesson 2-7)

Times at Bat	Number of Hits
12	3
20	■ 5
40	■ 10
84	■ 21

14. **TEMPERATURE** A temperature of −89°C was recorded in Antarctica. Use the expression $\frac{9C}{5} + 32$, where C is the temperature in degrees Celsius, to find the temperature in degrees Fahrenheit. (Lesson 2-8) **about −128.2°F**

Chapter 3 Algebra: Linear Equations and Functions

1. **TOURISM** The Statue of Liberty in New York, New York, and the Eiffel Tower in Paris, France, were designed by the same person. The Statue of Liberty is 152 feet tall. It is 732 feet shorter than the Eiffel Tower, x. Write an equation that models this situation. (Lesson 3-1) $152 = x - 732$

ELECTIONS For Exercises 2 and 3, use the table below and the following information. New York has one more electoral vote than Texas. Pennsylvania has 9 fewer electoral votes than Texas. (Lesson 3-2)

Number of Electoral Votes 2000	
California	54
New York	33
Texas	■
Florida	25
Pennsylvania	23

$33 = n + 1$; $23 = n - 9$

2. Write two different equations to find the number of electoral votes in Texas, n.
3. Find the number of electoral votes 32 votes
4. **ROLLER COASTERS** The track length of a popular roller coaster is 5,106 feet. The roller coaster has an average speed of about 2,000 feet per minute. At that speed, how long will it take to travel its length of 5,106 feet? Use the formula $d = rt$. (Lesson 3-3) about 2.553 min
5. **NUMBERS** A number is halved. Then three is subtracted from the quotient, and 5 is multiplied by the difference. Finally, 1 is added to the product. If the ending number is 26, what was the beginning number? Use the *work backward* strategy. (Lesson 3-4) 16
6. **BUSINESS** Carla's Catering charges a $25 fee to serve 15 or fewer people. In addition to that fee, they charge $10 per appetizer. You are having a party for 12 people and can spend a total of $85. How many appetizers can you order from Carla's Catering? (Lesson 3-5) 6 appetizers

CHESS For Exercises 7–10, use the chess board below. (Lesson 3-6)

7. What is the perimeter of the chess board? 48 in.
8. What is the area of the chess board? 144 in^2
9. What is the area of each small square? 2.25 in^2
10. A travel chess board has half the length and width of the board shown. What is the perimeter and area? 24 in.; 36 in^2
11. **FENCING** Mr. Hernandez will build a fence to enclose a rectangular yard for his horse. If the area of the yard to be enclosed is 1,944 square feet, and the length of the yard is 54 feet, how much fencing is needed? (Lesson 3-6) 180 ft
12. **GEOMETRY** The formula for the perimeter of a square is $P = 4s$, where P is the perimeter and s is the length of a side. Graph the equation. (Lesson 3-7) See Student Handbook Answer Appendix.

AGES For Exercises 13–16, use the table below. It shows how Jared's age and his sister Emily's age are related. (Lesson 3-7)

Jared's age (yr)	1	2	3	4	5
Emily's age (yr)	7	8	9	10	11

13. Write a verbal expression to describe how the ages are related. Emily is 6 years older than Jared.
14. Write an equation for the verbal expression. Let x represent Jared's age and y represent Emily's age. $y = x + 6$
15. Predict how old Emily will be when Jared is 10 years old. 16 years
16. Graph the equation. 16. See Student Handbook Answer Appendix.

Chapter 4 Fractions, Decimals, and Percents

LAND For Exercises 1–3, use the information below.
A section of land is one mile long and one mile wide. (Lesson 4-1) 1. $2^5 \times 3 \times 5 \times 11$ 2. 27,878,400 ft^2

1. Write the prime factorization of 5,280.
2. Find the area of the section of land in square feet. (*Hint*: 1 mile = 5,280 feet)
3. Write the prime factorization of the area that you found in Exercise 2. $2^{10} \times 3^2 \times 5^2 \times 11^2$

DECORATIONS For Exercises 4 and 5, use the information below.
Benito is cutting streamers from crepe paper for a party. He has a red roll of crepe paper 144 inches long, a white roll 192 inches long, and a blue roll 360 inches long. (Lesson 4-2)

4. If he wants to have all colors of streamers the same length, what is the longest length that he can cut? 24 in.
5. If he cuts the longest possible length, how many streamers can he cut? 29 streamers
6. **PRIZES** By reaching into a bag that has the letters A, B, and C, George will select three winners in order. How many possible combinations are there of the people who could win? Use the *make an organized list* strategy. (Lesson 4-3) 6 combinations; ABC; ACB; BAC; BCA; CAB; CBA

OLYMPICS For Exercises 7 and 8, refer to the table below. It shows the medals won by the top three countries in the 2000 Summer Olympics.

Country	Medals		
	Gold	Silver	Bronze
United States	40	24	33
Russia	32	28	28
China	28	16	15

Source: *The World Almanac*

7. Write the number of gold medals that Russia won as a fraction of the total number that Russia won in simplest form. (Lesson 4-4) $\frac{4}{11}$
8. Write the fraction that you wrote in Exercise 7 as a decimal. (Lesson 4-5) $0.\overline{36}$
9. **SPORTS** At Belgrade Intermediate School, 75 out of every 100 students participate in sports. What percent of students do *not* participate in sports? (Lesson 4-6) 25%

ADVERTISING For Exercises 10–13, use the table below. It shows the results of a survey in which teens were asked which types of advertising they pay attention to.

Type of Advertising	Percent of Teens
Television	80%
Magazine	62%
Product in a Movie	48%
Ad in an E-Mail	24%

Source: *E-Poll*

Write each percent as a fraction in simplest form. (Lesson 4-6) 13. $\frac{6}{25}$

10. television $\frac{4}{5}$
11. magazine $\frac{31}{50}$
12. product in a movie $\frac{12}{25}$
13. ad in an e-mail

GEOMETRY For Exercises 14–16, refer to the grid at the right. (Lesson 4-7)

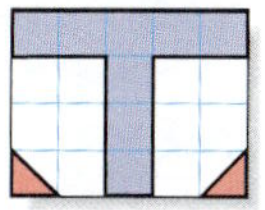

14. Write a decimal and a percent to represent the "T" shaded area. 0.4; 40%
15. Write a decimal and a percent to represent the area shaded pink. 0.05; 5%
16. What percent of the grid is *not* shaded? 55%
17. **FLOWERS** Roses can be ordered in bunches of 6 and carnations in bunches of 15. If Ingrid wants to have the same number of roses as carnations for parent night, what is the least number of each flower that she must order? (Lesson 4-8) 30

18. Alaska, Wisconsin, Michigan

18. **WATER** The table at the right shows the fraction of each state that is water. Order the states from least to greatest fraction of water. (Lesson 4-9)

What Part is Water?	
State	Fraction
Alaska	$\frac{3}{41}$
Michigan	$\frac{40}{97}$
Wisconsin	$\frac{1}{6}$

Source: *The World Almanac of the U.S.A*

Chapter 5 Applying Fractions

Pages 228–277

1. **MEALS** A box of instant potatoes contains 20 cups of flakes. A family-sized bowl of potatoes uses $3\frac{2}{3}$ cups of the flakes. Estimate how many family-sized bowls can be made from one box. (Lesson 5-1) **Sample answer: $20 \div 4$ or 5 bowls**

2. **BAKING** A recipe calls for $2\frac{1}{3}$ cups of flour. Theo wants to make six batches of this recipe. About how much flour should he have available to use? (Lesson 5-1) **about $2 \times 6 + \frac{1}{3} \times 6$ or $12 + 2$ or 14 c**

3. **CRAFTS** Kyle bought $\frac{5}{6}$ yard of fabric to make a craft item. He used $\frac{3}{4}$ yard in making the item. How much fabric was left over? (Lesson 5-2) **$\frac{1}{12}$ yd**

RAINFALL For Exercises 4 and 5, use the table. It shows the average annual precipitation for three of the driest locations on Earth. (Lesson 5-2)

Location	Precipitation (in.)
Arica, Chile	$\frac{3}{100}$
Iquique, Chile	$\frac{1}{5}$
Callao, Peru	$\frac{12}{25}$

Source: *The Top 10 Everything*

4. How much more rain does Iquique get per year than Arica? **$\frac{17}{100}$ in.**

5. How much more annual rain does Callao get than Iquique? **$\frac{7}{25}$ in.**

6. **INTERIOR DESIGN** A living room wall is $16\frac{1}{4}$ feet long. A window runs from the floor to the ceiling and has a length along the floor of $6\frac{3}{8}$ feet. How long is the wall without the window? (Lesson 5-3) **$9\frac{7}{8}$ ft**

7. **HEALTH** The human body is about $\frac{7}{10}$ water. About how much would a person weigh if they had 70 pounds of water weight? Use the *eliminate possibilities* strategy. (Lesson 5-4) **B**

   A 200 pounds C 150 pounds
   B 100 pounds D 70 pounds

8. **FOOD** The table below shows the carry-out menu for a Benito's Restaurant.

Take-out	Price ($)
Main Dish	5.00
Side Dishes	1.00
Dessert	2.00

A family of four spent $24.00 dollars for a take-home meal. What combination is possible for their meal? Use the *eliminate possibilities* strategy. (Lesson 5-4) **H**

   F 3 main dishes and 2 side dishes
   G 4 main dishes and 3 side dishes
   H 3 main dishes, 3 side dishes, and 3 desserts
   J 4 main dishes and 4 desserts

9. **STARS** The star Sirius is about $8\frac{7}{10}$ light years from Earth. Alpha Centauri is half this distance from Earth. How far is Alpha Centauri from Earth? (Lesson 5-5) **$4\frac{7}{20}$ light years**

10. **LIFE SCIENCE** Use the table below. It shows the average growth per month of hair and fingernails. Solve $3 = \frac{1}{2}t$ to find how long it takes hair to grow 3 inches. (Lesson 5-6) **6 mo**

Average Monthly Growth	
Hair	$\frac{1}{2}$ in.
Fingernails	$\frac{2}{25}$ in.

11. **SEWING** Jocelyn has nine yards of fabric to make table napkins for a senior citizens' center. She needs $\frac{3}{8}$ yard for each napkin. Use $\frac{3}{8}c = 9$ to find the number of napkins that she can make with this amount of fabric. (Lesson 5-6) **24 napkins**

12. **WHALES** During the first year, a baby whale gains about $27\frac{3}{5}$ tons. What is the average weight gain per month? (Lesson 5-7) **12. $2\frac{3}{10}$ T/mo**

Chapter 6 Ratios and Proportions

Pages 280–339

1. **SCHOOLS** In a recent year, Oregon had 924 public elementary schools and 264 public high schools. Write a ratio in simplest form comparing the number of public high schools to elementary schools. (Lesson 6-1) **$\frac{2}{7}$**

2. **MONTHS** Write a ratio in simplest form comparing the number of months that begin with the letter J to the total number of months in a year. (Lesson 6-1) **$\frac{1}{4}$**

3. **EXERCISE** A person jumps rope 14 times in 10 seconds. What is the unit rate in jumps per second? (Lesson 6-2) **1.4 jumps per s**

4. **FOOD** A 16-ounce box of cereal costs $3.95. Find the unit price to the nearest cent. (Lesson 6-2) **$0.25 per oz**

5. **MARKERS** The table below shows the number of markers per box. Graph the data. Then find the slope of the line. Explain what the slope represents. (Lesson 6-3) **See Student Handbook Answer Appendix.**

Markers	8	16	24	32
Boxes	1	2	3	4

6. **TEMPERATURE** At 2:00, the temperature is 78°F. At 3:00, the temperature is 81°F. What is the rate of change? (Lesson 6-3) **3° per h**

7. **LIFE SCIENCE** An adult has about 5 quarts of blood. If a person donates 1 pint of blood, how many pints are left? (Lesson 6-4) **9 pt**

8. **COFFEE** In Switzerland, the average amount of coffee consumed per year is 1,089 cups per person. How many pints is this? (Lesson 6-4) **544.5 pt**

9. **BUILDINGS** A skyscraper is 0.484 kilometers tall. What is the height of the skyscraper in meters? (Lesson 6-5) **484 m**

10. **WATER** A bottle contains 1,065 milliliters of water. About how many cups of water does the bottle hold? (Lesson 6-5) **about 4.5 c**

11. **PHOTOGRAPHS** Mandy is enlarging a photograph that is 3 inches wide and 4.5 inches long. If she wants the width of the enlargement to be 10 inches, what will be the length? (Lesson 6-6) **15 in.**

12. **TILES** A kitchen is 10 feet long and 8 feet wide. If kitchen floor tiles are $2\frac{1}{2}$ inches by 3 inches, how many tiles are needed for the kitchen? Use the *draw a diagram* strategy. (Lesson 6-7) **1,536**

13. **MAPS** Washington, D.C., and Baltimore, Maryland, are $2\frac{7}{8}$ inches apart on a map. If the scale is $\frac{1}{2}$ inch : 6 miles, what is the actual distance between the cities? (Lesson 6-8) **$34\frac{1}{2}$ mi**

14. **MODELS** Ian is making a miniature bed for his daughter's doll house. The actual bed is $6\frac{3}{4}$ feet long. If he uses the scale $\frac{1}{2}$ inch $= 1\frac{1}{2}$ feet, what will be the length of the miniature bed? (Lesson 6-8) **$2\frac{1}{4}$ in.**

15. **POPULATION** According to the U.S. Census Bureau, 6.6% of all people living in Florida are 10–14 years old. What fraction is this? Write in simplest form. (Lesson 6-9) **$\frac{33}{500}$**

COINS For Exercises 16 and 17, use the table below. It shows the fraction of a quarter that is made up of the metals nickel and copper. Write each fraction as a percent. Round to the nearest hundredth if necessary. (Lesson 6-9)

Metal	Fraction of Quarter
Nickel	$\frac{1}{12}$
Copper	$\frac{11}{12}$

16. nickel **8.33%**

17. copper **91.67%**

Chapter 7 Applying Percents

Pages 340–391

1. **SEEDS** A packet of beans guarantees that 95% of its 200 seeds will germinate. How many seeds are expected to germinate? (Lesson 7-1) 190 seeds
2. **SKIS** Toshiro spent $520 on new twin-tip skis. This was 40% of the money he earned at his summer job. How much did he earn at his summer job? (Lesson 7-2) $1,300
3. **GEOGRAPHY** In Washington, about 5.7% of the total area is water. If the total area of Washington is 70,637 square miles, estimate the number of square miles of water by using 10%. (Lesson 7-3) See Student Handbook Answer Appendix.
4. **GOVERNMENT** Of the 435 members in the U.S. House of Representatives, 53 are from California and 13 are from North Carolina. To the nearest whole percent, what percent of the representatives are from California? from North Carolina? (Lesson 7-4) 12%; 3%

FOOD For Exercises 5 and 6, use the graph below. It shows the results of a survey in which 1,200 people were asked how they determine how long food has been in their freezer. (Lesson 7-4)

Frozen Foods

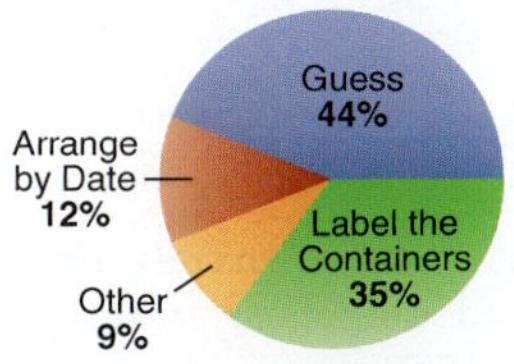

Source: Opinion Research Corporation

5. How many of the 1,200 surveyed guess to determine how long food has been in their freezer? 528 people
6. How many of the 1,200 surveyed label their freezer containers? 420 people

7. **DVDs** A store has 1,504 DVDs in stock. The store sold 19.8% of the DVDs last month. About how many DVDs did they sell last month? Use the *reasonable answers* strategy. (Lesson 7-5) 300

SPORTS For Exercises 8 and 9, use the table below. It shows the number of participants ages 7 to 17 in the sports listed. (Lesson 7-6)

Sport	Number (millions)	
	1990	2000
In-Line Skating	3.6	21.8
Snowboarding	1.5	4.3
Roller Hockey	1.5	2.2
Golf	23.0	26.4

Source: *National Sporting Goods Association*

8. What is the percent of change in in-line skaters 7 to 17 years old from 1990 to 2000? Round to the nearest percent and state whether the percent of change is an *increase* or *decrease*. 506% increase
9. Find the percent of change from 1990 to 2000 in the number of children and teens who played roller hockey. Round to the nearest percent. 47% increase

COMPUTERS For Exercises 10 and 11, use the following information.
The Wares want to buy a new computer with a regular price of $1,049. (Lesson 7-7) 10. $839.20

10. If the store is offering a 20% discount, what will be the sale price of the computer?
11. If the sales tax on the computer is 5.25%, what will be the total cost with the discount? $883.26

BANKING For Exercises 12–15, complete the table below. The interest earned is simple interest. (Lesson 7-8)

	Principal	Rate	Time (yr)	Interest Earned	
12.	$1,525.00	5%	$2\frac{1}{2}$	■	$190.63
13.	$2,250.00	4%	■	$337.50	3.75
14.	■	3.5%	4	$498.40	$3,560
15.	$5,080.00	■	3	$952.50	6.25%

Chapter 8 Statistics: Analyzing Data

Pages 394–457

NUTRITION For Exercises 1–3, use the data below, that gives the grams of carbohydrates in fifteen different energy bars.
24, 16, 16, 16, 2, 20, 26, 14, 20, 20, 16, 16, 16, 15, 20

1. Make a line plot of the data. (Lesson 8-1)
2. What is the range of the data? (Lesson 8-1) 24
3. Identify any clusters, gaps, or outliers and explain what they represent. (Lesson 8-1)

1, 3. See Student Handbook Answer Appendix.

BASKETBALL For Exercises 4–5, refer to the table below. It shows the number of games played by Michael Jordan each year from 1986–1987 to 2001–2002.

Number of Games Played							
82	82	81	82	82	80	78	0
17	82	82	82	0	0	0	60

4. Find the mean, median, and mode of the data. (Lesson 8-2) 55.625; 80.5; 82
5. Make a stem-and-leaf plot of the data. (Lesson 8-3)

5–6. See Student Handbook Answer Appendix.

6. **TOURISTS** The table shows the countries from which the most tourists in the United States came. Make a bar graph of the data. (Lesson 8-4)

Country	Visitors (millions)
Canada	14.6
Mexico	10.3
Japan	5.0
United Kingdom	4.7

7. **LUNCHES** Use the bar graph to determine on what day about twice as many lunches were sold as on Wednesday. (Lesson 8-5) Friday

SWIMMING For Exercises 8 and 9, refer to the table. It shows the winning Olympic times for the Women's 4 × 100-meter Freestyle Relay in swimming. (Lesson 8-6)

Year	Time (s)
1976	225
1980	223
1984	224
1988	221
1992	220
1996	219
2000	217

Source: *ESPN Sports Almanac*

See Student Handbook Answer Appendix.

8. Make a line graph of the data.
9. Predict the winning time in 2008. Sample answer: 215 s
10. **SURVEYS** A survey of randomly selected teens revealed that 68% have a personal cell phone. If there are 1,200 teens at Harrisburg Middle School, about how many have a personal cell phone? (Lesson 8-7) about 816 teens

11, 12. See Student Handbook Answer Appendix.

11. **CATS** To determine what type of cat most customers prefer, the president of a cat food company mailed 250 surveys to cat owners. Of the 185 surveys that were returned, 52% preferred calico cats. The president concluded that about half of cat owners prefer calico cats. Determine whether this conclusion is valid. Justify your answers. (Lesson 8-8)
12. **CELL PHONES** The table shows the number of monthly minutes Mallory used on her cell phone during the past year. She claims that the average number of minutes used is about 324. Explain how this is misleading. (Lesson 8-9)

284	322	286	359	318	294
602	278	292	267	299	285

Chapter 9 Probability

Pages 458–505

1. **DENTISTS** A dental hygienist randomly chooses a toothbrush in a drawer containing 17 white, 12 green, and 5 blue toothbrushes. What is the probability that she chooses a green toothbrush? Write as a fraction in simplest form. (Lesson 9-1) $\frac{6}{17}$

SURVEYS For Exercises 2 and 3, use the table below. It shows the results of a survey in which adults were asked how proud they were to be an American. (Lesson 9-1)

How Proud Are You?	
Response	**Number**
Extremely	650
Very	250
Moderately	60
Little/Not at All	30
No Opinion	10

Source: *Gallup Poll*

2. If one person participating in the survey is chosen at random, what is the probability that the person is extremely patriotic? Write as a fraction in simplest form. $\frac{13}{20}$
3. If one person participating in the survey is chosen at random, what is the probability that he is *not* moderately patriotic? Write as a fraction in simplest form. $\frac{47}{50}$

RANCHING For Exercises 4 and 5, use the following information.
For Roger to reach his cattle pasture, he must pass through three consecutive gates. Any of the three gates can be either *open* or *closed*. (Lesson 9-2)

4. See Student Handbook Answer Appendix.
4. Make a tree diagram to show all of the possible positions of the gates.
5. What is the probability that all three gates will be closed when Roger visits this pasture? Write as a fraction. $\frac{1}{8}$

6. 5 patterns
6. **SKATEBOARDS** World Sports makes skateboards with different deck patterns. You can choose one of four deck lengths and one of six types of wheels. If they have 120 different skateboards, how many deck patterns are there? (Lesson 9-3)

7. **READING** Mr. Steadman plans to read eight children's novels to his second graders during the school year. In how many ways can he arrange the books to be read? (Lesson 9-4) **40,320 ways**
8. **CRAFTS** Marina has print fabric in pink, blue, magenta, green, yellow, and tan. How many different stuffed bears can she make if each bear has only four different fabrics, and the order of the fabrics is not important? (Lesson 9-5)
15 bears
9. **TRAVEL** There are four seats in Pedro's car: two in the front and two in the back. If Benny, Carlita, and Juanita are all in the car with Pedro, how many ways can they be seated in the car if Pedro is driving? Use the *act it out* strategy. (Lesson 9-6)
6 ways
10. **FOOD** The graph shows the results of a survey in which 7th graders at Plentywood Middle School were asked to name their favorite fruit. If a 7th grader at the school is randomly selected, what is the probability that they chose bananas as their favorite? Write as a fraction in simplest form. (Lesson 9-7) $\frac{1}{4}$

Favorite Fruits

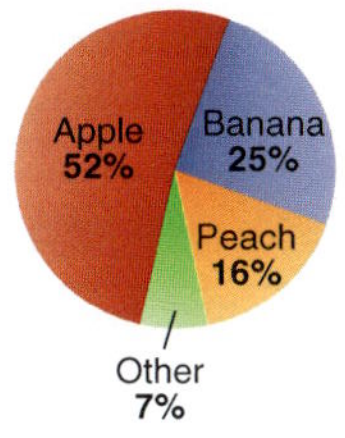

MARBLES For Exercises 11 and 12, refer to the table. (Lesson 9-8)

Color	Number
Red	10
Blue	6
Purple	10
Yellow	4
Green	2

11. What is the probability of randomly selecting one yellow marble and then one purple marble? Assume that the first marble is not replaced. $\frac{5}{128}$
12. What is the probability of randomly selecting two red marbles? Assume that the first marble is replaced. $\frac{25}{256}$

Chapter 10 Geometry: Polygons

Pages 508–569

ART For Exercises 1 and 2, use the diagram of the Native American artifact.

1. Name a right angle and a straight angle. (Lesson 10-1)
2. If $m\angle AOB = 90°$, what is $m\angle DOC$? (Lesson 10-2) **90°**

1. Sample answer: ∠AOB; ∠AOC

TELEVISION For Exercises 3 and 4, use the survey results shown in the table below. (Lesson 10-3)

Channels Families Watch	
Number	**Percent**
5 or fewer	30%
6–12	33%
13–25	19%
26 or more	14%

3. The fifth category in the survey is *no TV or no opinion*. What percent of the people surveyed were in this category? **4%**
4. Make a circle graph of the data.

4, 5. See Student Handbook Answer Appendix.
5. **ART** Victor drew a right triangle so that one of the acute angles measures 55°. Without measuring, describe how Victor can determine the measure of the other acute angle in the triangle. Then find the angle measure. (Lesson 10-4)

6. Mr. Sanchez can increase the width to 11 m.
6. **GARDENING** Mr. Sanchez has a flower bed with a length of 10 meters and a width of 5 meters. If he can only change the width of the flower bed, describe what he can do to increase the perimeter by 12 meters. Use the *logical reasoning* strategy. (Lesson 10-5)

7. Mitchell, Deidre, Carlos, Tramaine
7. **RUNNING** Four friends are entered in a race. Deirdre finishes directly ahead of Carlos. Mitchell finishes three places ahead of Tramaine and directly ahead of Deirdre. If Tramaine finishes fourth, place the runners in order from first to last. Use logical reasoning. (Lesson 10-5)

For Exercises 8 and 9, use the figure below.

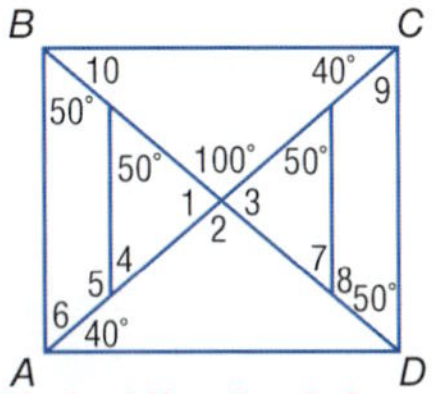

8, 9. See Student Handbook Answer Appendix.
8. Find the measure of each angle numbered from 1–10. (Lesson 10-4)
9. Find the *best* name to classify quadrilateral *ABCD*. Explain your reasoning. (Lesson 10-6)
10. **CRAFTS** Priscilla makes porcelain dolls that are proportional to a real child. If Jody is $4\frac{2}{3}$ feet tall with a 23-inch waist, what should be the waist measure of a doll that is 13 inches tall? Round to the nearest inch. (Lesson 10-7) **5 in.**
11. **ART** Draw a tessellation using two of the polygons listed at the right. Identify the polygons and explain why the tessellation works. (Lesson 10-8)

regular triangles
quadrilaterals
pentagons
hexagons
octagons

11–13. See Student Handbook Answer Appendix.
For Exercises 12 and 13, use the quadrilateral *MOVE* shown below.

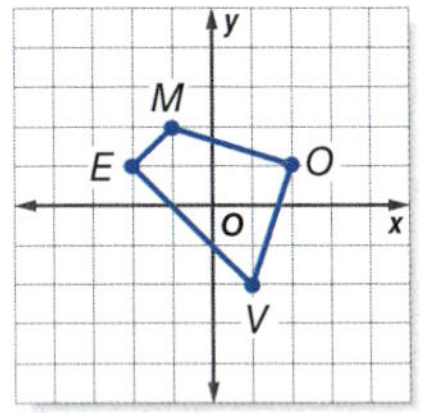

12. Describe the translation that will move *M* to the point at (2, –2). Then graph quadrilateral *M′O′V′E′* using this translation. (Lesson 10-9)
13. Find the coordinates of the vertices of quadrilateral *MOVE* after a reflection over the *y*-axis. Then graph the reflection. (Lesson 10-10)

Chapter 11 Measurement: Two- and Three-Dimensional Figures

Pages 568–631

1. **CRAFTS** A quilt pattern uses 25 parallelogram-shaped pieces of fabric, each with a base of 4 inches and a height of $2\frac{1}{2}$ inches. How much fabric is used to make the 25 pieces? (Lesson 11-1) **250 in^2**

2. **FURNITURE** A corner table is in the shape of a right triangle. If the side lengths of the tabletop are 3.5 feet, 3.5 feet, and 4.9 feet, what is the area? Round to the nearest tenth if necessary. (Lesson 11-2) **6.1 ft^2**

3. **PUZZLES** Find the area of each small and large shaded triangle. Round to the nearest whole. (Lesson 11-2) **small: 13 cm^2, large: 25 cm^2**

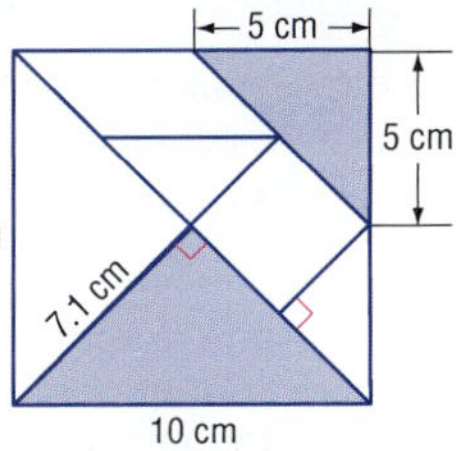

4. **EARTH SCIENCE** Earth has a diameter of 7,926 miles. Use the formula for the circumference of a circle to estimate the circumference of Earth at its equator. (Lesson 11-3) **about 24,900 mi**

5. **COOKIES** In New Zealand, a giant circular chocolate chip cookie was baked with a diameter of 81 feet 8 inches. To the nearest square foot, what was the area of the cookie? (Lesson 11-4) **5,236 ft^2**

6. **SPORTS PROFIT** A stadium seats 1,001,800 people. 22% of the tickets cost \$134.87 each. 45% of the tickets cost \$67.99 each. The remaining 33% cost only \$35.87 each. About how much revenue is made from one game when each seat is sold out? Use the *solve a simpler problem* strategy. (Lesson 11-5) **about \$72,000,000**

3,148 ft^2

7. **LANDSCAPING** Find the area of the flower garden shown in the diagram at the right. Round to the nearest square foot. (Lesson 11-6)

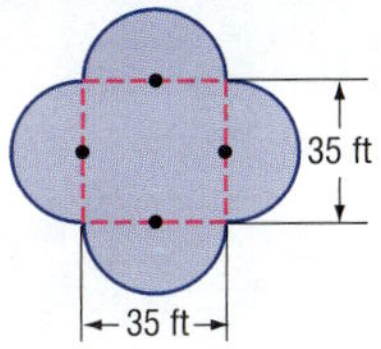

8. **GEOMETRY** A certain three-dimensional figure has four triangular faces and one square face. Classify this figure. (Lesson 11-7) **square pyramid**

9. **RECORDS** According to the *Guinness Book of World Records*, the tallest hotel in the world is the 1,053-foot sail-shaped Burj Al Arab in Dubai, United Arab Emirates.

Draw possible sketches of the top, side, and front views of the hotel. (Lesson 11-8) **See Student Handbook Answer Appendix.**

OCEANS For Exercises 10 and 11, use the following information.

The Atlantic Ocean has an area of about 33,420,000 square miles. Its average depth is 11,730 feet. (Lesson 11-9)

10. To the nearest hundredth, what is the average depth of the Atlantic Ocean in miles? (*Hint*: 1 mi = 5,280 ft) **2.22 mi**

11. What is the approximate volume of the Atlantic Ocean in cubic miles? **74,192,400 mi^3**

WATER For Exercises 12–13, use the cylinder-shaped water tank. (Lesson 11-10)

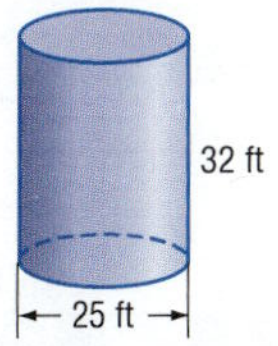

12. Find the volume of the tank. Round to the nearest cubic foot. **15,700 ft^3**

13. 117,436 gal

13. One cubic foot is approximately 7.48 gallons. Find the approximate volume of the water tank to the nearest gallon.

Chapter 12 Extending Geometry and Measurement

Pages 634–663

1. **OMELETS** In Japan, a gigantic omelet was made with an area of 1,383 square feet. If the omelet was a square, what would be its side lengths? Round to the nearest tenth. (Lesson 12-1) **37.2 ft**

2. **SOFTBALL** A softball diamond is a square measuring 60 feet on each side.

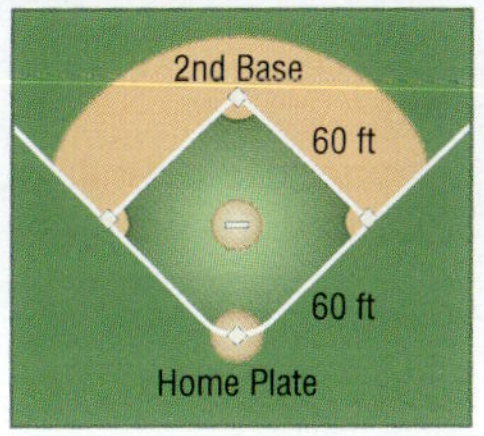

How far does a player on second base throw when she throws from second base to home? Round to the nearest tenth. (Lesson 12-2) **84.9 ft**

3. **BANDS** Mr. Garcia is planning a band formation at a football game. The diagram shows the dimensions of the field.

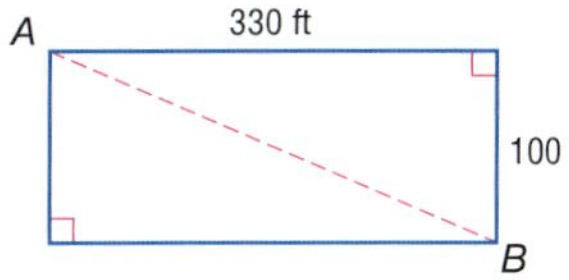

To the nearest foot, what is the distance from *A* to *B*? (Lesson 12-2) **345 ft**

4. **GEOMETRY** Two right triangles are side by side such that they form a larger isosceles triangle. If the two right triangles are congruent and each have angle measures of 90°, 45°, and 45°, what type of triangle will the new isosceles triangle be? Use the *make a model* strategy. (Lesson 12-3) **right triangle**

5. **CUBES** A rectangular prism is formed from 48 centimeter cubes such that the height of the prism is one half of the width and one third of the length of the prism. Find the dimensions of the rectangular prism. Use the *make a model* strategy. (Lesson 12-3) **6 cm by 4 cm by 2 cm**

For Exercises 6 and 7, use the following information.

Liz is designing some gift boxes. The small box is 6 inches long, 4 inches wide, and 2.5 inches high. The medium box has dimensions that are each 3 times the dimensions of the small box. (Lesson 12-4)

6. 98 in^2

6. Find the surface area of the small box.

7. What are the dimensions of the medium box? Then find the surface area of the medium box. **18 in. by 12 in. by 7.5 in.; 882 in^2**

STORAGE For Exercises 8–10, use the following information.

The two canisters shown below each have a volume of about 628.3 cubic inches. (Lesson 12-5)

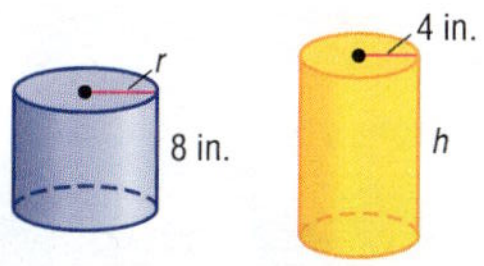

8. What is the radius of the blue canister? Round to the nearest tenth. **5.0 in.**

9. What is the height of the yellow canister? Round to the nearest tenth. **12.5 in.**

10. What is the difference between the surface areas of the two canisters? **6.3 in^2**

HATS For Exercises 11–13, use the following information. (Lesson 12-5)

A certain cylinder-shaped hat box has a height of 9 inches and a radius of 5.5 inches. Its lid is also shaped as a cylinder, with a slightly larger diameter so that the lid fits over the box.

11. How many square inches of material are needed to make the hat box, not including the lid? Round to the nearest tenth. **405.8 in^2**

12. If the lid has a height of 3.5 inches and a diameter of 11.8 inches, how many square inches of material are needed to make the lid? Round to the nearest tenth. **239.0 in^2**

13. How many times more material is needed to make the hat box than the lid? Round to the nearest tenth. **1.7**

Preparing for Standardized Tests

Throughout the school year, you may be required to take several standardized tests, and you may have many questions about them. Here are some answers to help you get ready.

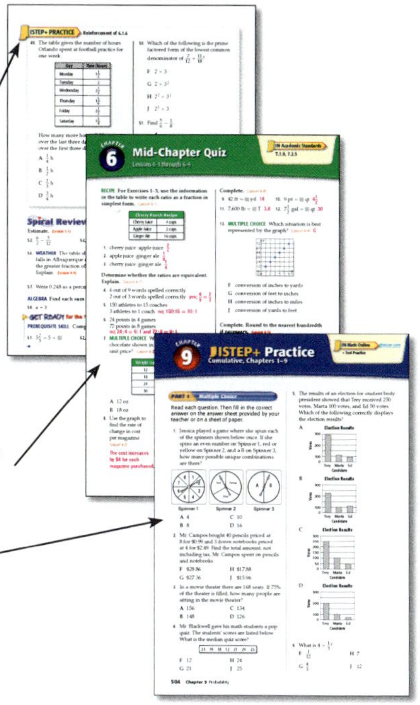

How Should I Study?

The good news is that you've been studying all along—a little bit every day. Here are some of the ways your textbook has been preparing you.

- **Every Day** Each lesson had multiple-choice practice questions.
- **Every Week** The Mid-Chapter Quiz and Practice Test also had several practice questions.
- **Every Month** The Test Practice pages at the end of each chapter had even more questions, including short-response/grid-in and extended-response questions.

Are There Other Ways to Review?

Absolutely! The following pages contain even more practice for standardized tests.

Tips for SUCCESS

Prepare

- Go to bed early the night before the test. You will think more clearly after a good night's rest.
- Become familiar with common formulas and when they should be used.
- Think positively.

During the Test

- Read each problem carefully. Underline key words and think about different ways to solve the problem.
- Watch for key words like *not*. Also look for order words like *least, greatest, first,* and *last*.
- Answer questions you are sure about first. If you do not know the answer to a question, skip it and go back to that question later.
- Check your answer to make sure it is reasonable.
- Make sure that the number of the question on the answer sheet matches the number of the question on which you are working in your test booklet.

Whatever you do...

- Don't try to do it all in your head. If no figure is provided, draw one.
- Don't rush. Try to work at a steady pace.
- Don't give up. Some problems may seem hard to you, but you may be able to figure out what to do if you read each question carefully or try another strategy.

Multiple-Choice Questions

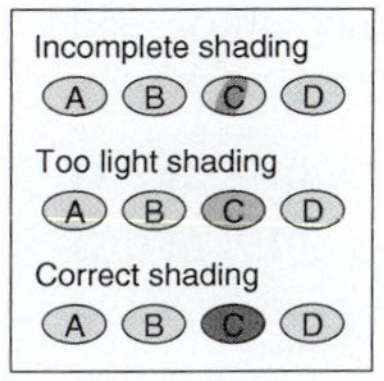

Multiple-choice questions are the most common type of question on standardized tests. These questions are sometimes called *selected-response questions*. You are asked to choose the best answer from four or five possible answers.

To record a multiple-choice answer, you may be asked to shade in a bubble that is a circle or an oval or just to write the letter of your choice. Always make sure that your shading is dark enough and completely covers the bubble.

The answer to a multiple-choice question may not stand out from the choices. However, you may be able to eliminate some of the choices. Another answer choice might be that the correct answer is not given.

Notice that the problem asks for the expression that *cannot* represent the situation.

TEST EXAMPLE

1 Mrs. Hon's seventh grade students are purchasing stuffed animals to donate to a charity. They bought 3 boxes containing eight animals each and 2 boxes containing twelve animals each. Which expression *cannot* be used to find the total number of animals they bought to give to the charity?

A $8 + 8 + 8 + 12 + 12$ **C** $3(8) + 2(12)$
B $3 \times 8 + 2 \times 12$ **D** $5 \times (8 + 12)$

Read the problem carefully and locate the important information. There are 3 boxes that have eight animals, so that is 3×8, or 24 animals. There are 2 boxes of twelve animals, so that is 2×12, or 24 animals. The total number of animals is $24 + 24$, or 48.

You know from reading the problem that you are looking for the expression that *does not* simplify to 48. Simplify each expression to find the answer.

A $8 + 8 + 8 + 12 + 12 = (8 + 8 + 8) + (12 + 12)$
$= 24 + 24$
$= 48$

B $3 \times 8 + 2 \times 12 = 24 + 24$
$= 48$

C $3(8) + 2(12) = 24 + 24$
$= 48$

D $5 \times (8 + 12) = 5 \times 20$
$= 100$

The only expression that *does not* simplify to 48 is D. The correct choice is D.

Some problems are easier to solve if you draw a diagram. If you cannot write in the test booklet, draw a diagram on scratch paper.

STRATEGY
Diagrams
Draw a diagram for the situation.

TEST EXAMPLE

2 On a hiking trip, Grace and Alicia traveled 10 miles south and 4 miles west. If they take the shortest return route, how far will the hike be back to their starting point? Round to the nearest tenth of a mile.

A 6.0 mi **B** 9.2 mi **C** 10.8 mi **D** 14.0 mi

To solve this problem, you need to draw a diagram of the situation. Label the directions and the important information from the problem.

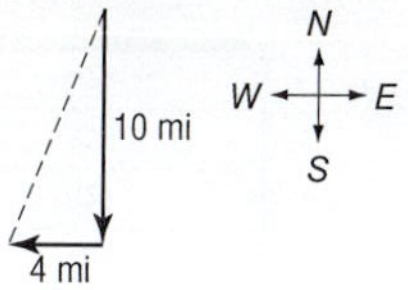

Use the Pythagorean Theorem to find the distance that they will hike back to their starting point.

$c^2 = a^2 + b^2$ — Pythagorean Theorem
$c^2 = 4^2 + 10^2$ — Replace *a* with 4 and *b* with 10.
$c^2 = 16 + 100$ — Simplify.
$c^2 = 116$ — Add.
$\sqrt{c^2} = \sqrt{116}$ — Take the square root of each side.
$c \approx 10.8$ — Use a calculator to simplify.

Round the answer to the correct decimal place.

The hike back will be about 10.8 miles. The correct choice is C.

Some problems give you more information than you need to solve the problem. Read the question carefully to determine the information you need.

STRATEGY
Formulas
Use the reference sheet to find the correct formula.

TEST EXAMPLE

3 One of the biggest pieces of cheese ever produced was made in 1866 in Ingersoll, Canada. It weighed 7,300 pounds. It was shaped as a cylinder with a diameter of 7 feet and a height of 3 feet. To the nearest cubic foot, what was the volume of the cheese? Use 3.14 for π.

A $462\ ft^3$ **B** $143\ ft^3$ **C** $115\ ft^3$ **D** $63\ ft^3$

You need to use the formula for the volume of a cylinder. The diameter is 7 feet, so the radius is $\frac{7}{2}$ or 3.5 feet. The height is 3 feet.

$V = \pi r^2 h$ — Volume of a cylinder
$V \approx (3.14)(3.5)^2(3)$ — Replace π with 3.14, *r* with 3.5, and *h* with 3.
$V \approx 115.395$ — Simplify.

The volume of the cheese is about 115 cubic feet. The correct choice is C.

Multiple-Choice Practice

Choose the best answer.

Number and Operations

1. The world's smallest fruit is the fruit of a wolffia plant, which measures about 0.01 inch in length. Another small fruit is the eye of a sewing needle, with a length of 0.20 inch. How many times longer is the eye of a sewing needle fruit than a wolffia fruit? D

   A 0.002 C 2
   B 0.005 D 20

2. The table shows what types of trash fill landfills in the United States. What fraction of the trash in landfills is plastic? J

Type of Trash	Percent in Landfills
metal	8%
plastic	24%
food, yard waste	11%
rubber, leather	6%
paper	21%
other trash	30%

Source: *The World Almanac for Kids*

   F $\frac{1}{100}$ H $\frac{1}{6}$
   G $\frac{1}{24}$ J $\frac{6}{25}$

3. A recent movie earned 317 million dollars in ticket sales. What is this value in scientific notation? C

   A 3.17
   B 317×10^6
   C 3.17×10^8
   D 3.17×10^{11}

4. Mercury orbits the sun at 29.75 miles per second. Earth orbits the sun at 18.51 miles per second. How many more miles does Mercury travel in one minute than Earth? H

   F 11.24 mi H 674.4 mi
   G 269.76 mi J 40,464 mi

Algebra

5. The table shows the population growth of a certain bacteria. How many bacteria will there be after 5 hours? C

Hours	0	1	2	3	4	5
Number of Bacteria	32	48	72	104	144	?

   A 243 B 200 C 192 D 178

6. Which function rule describes the relationship between distance from home y and hours traveled x? J

Time (h)	Distance from Home (mi)
x	y
0	0
1	65
2	130
3	195

   F $65y = x$ H $y = x + 65$
   G $y = 65 \div x$ J $y = 65x$

7. For a family portrait, a photographer charges a sitting fee and an amount of money per portrait ordered. Which function rule describes the relationship between the total cost y and number of portraits x? C

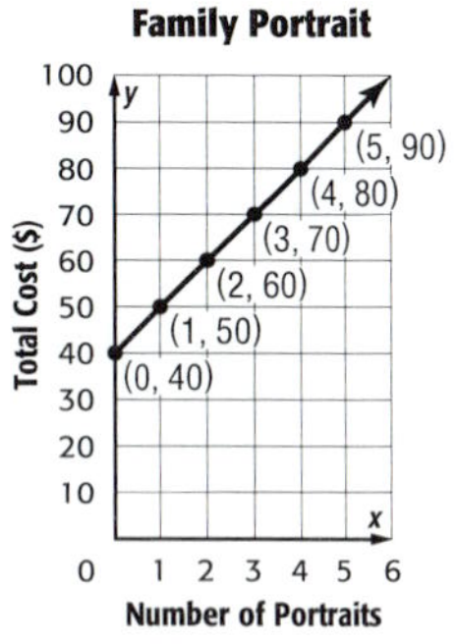

   A $y = 10 + 40x$ C $y = 40 + 10x$
   B $y = 40x + 10x$ D $y = 10x$

Geometry

8. The three towns on the map form a triangle. Which term *best* describes the angle with vertex at Worthington? F

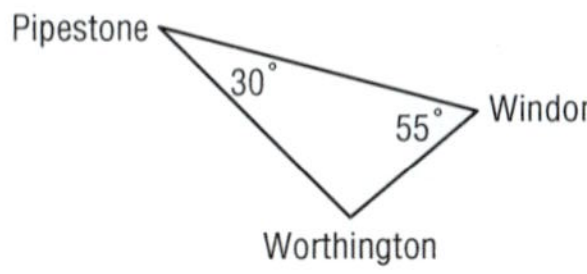

   F obtuse H acute
   G right J straight

9. Pedro is using a triangle in a computer graphics design. On a coordinate plane, the vertices of the triangle are $A(-1, 1)$, $B(0, 2)$, and $C(5, -1)$. If Pedro translates the triangle 4 units left and 3 units down, what will be the coordinates of B'? D

   A $(-1, -4)$ C $(4, 5)$
   B $(4, -1)$ D $(-4, -1)$

10. Jasmine is using this polygon on a poster she is making for the basketball team. Which term *best* describes the polygon? J

   F quadrilateral H hexagon
   G decagon J heptagon

Measurement

11. Crispy Crackers are packaged in a box that measures 6 inches by 2.5 inches by 10 inches. Which dimensions are of a prism that has the same volume as the Crispy Crackers box? B

   A 6.5 in. by 2 in. by 10 in.
   B 6.25 in. by 3 in. by 8 in.
   C 7.25 in. by 2 in. by 9.5 in.
   D 4 in. by 7.5 in. by 6 in.

TEST-TAKING TIP

Question 11 Most standardized tests will include any commonly used formulas at the front of the test booklet. Quickly review the list before you begin so that you know what formulas are available.

12. The Crab nebula is a cloud of gas and dust particles in space that is expanding at a rate of 930 miles per second. What is its rate of expansion in miles per hour? J

   F 22,320 mph H 1,339,200 mph
   G 55,800 mph J 3,348,000 mph

13. Super Toys makes two sizes of building blocks shaped as cubes. The large block has side length four times the length of the small block. What is the ratio of the surface area of the small block to the surface area of the large block? C

   A 1 to 4 C 1 to 16
   B 1 to 6 D 1 to 32

Data Analysis and Probability

14. The table shows the number of students playing each sport at Wilson Junior High. Find the mean of the data. H

Sport	Number of Students
baseball/softball	49
basketball	74
soccer	82
swimming	21
track and field	115
volleyball	25

   F 23 G 49 H 61 J 94

15. The spinner is divided into four equal-sized sections. If you spin the spinner 62 times, which is the *best* estimate for the number of times you will land on 2? A

   A 15 B 30 C 40 D 50

Gridded-Response Questions

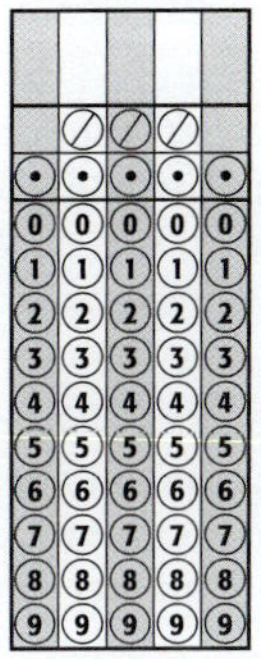

Gridded-response questions are another type of question on standardized tests. These questions are sometimes called *student-produced response* or *grid in*.

For gridded response, you must mark your answer on a grid printed on an answer sheet. The grid contains a row of four or five boxes at the top, two rows of ovals or circles with decimal and fraction symbols, and four or five columns of ovals, numbered 0–9. An example of a grid from an answer sheet is shown.

STRATEGY
Formulas
Use the reference sheet to find the formula you need.

TEST EXAMPLE

1 **Mr. Byrd builds and sells storage buildings. The dimensions of his most popular model are shown in the diagram. What is the volume of the building in cubic feet?**

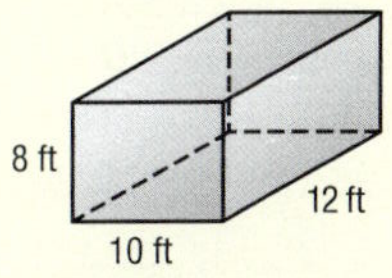

What do you need to find?

You need to find the volume of a rectangular prism. Use the formula and the dimensions given in the diagram.

$V = \ell wh$ — Volume of a rectangular prism

$V = 12 \cdot 10 \cdot 8$ — Replace ℓ with 12, w with 10, and h with 8.

$V = 960$ — Multiply.

The volume is 960 cubic feet.

How do you fill in the grid for the answer?

- Write your answer in the answer boxes.
- Write only one digit or symbol in each answer box.
- Do not write any digits or symbols outside the answer boxes.
- You may write your answer with the first digit in the left answer box, or with the last digit in the right answer box. You may leave blank any boxes you do not need on the right or the left side of your answer.
- Fill in only one bubble for every answer box that you have written in. Be sure not to fill in a bubble under a blank answer box.

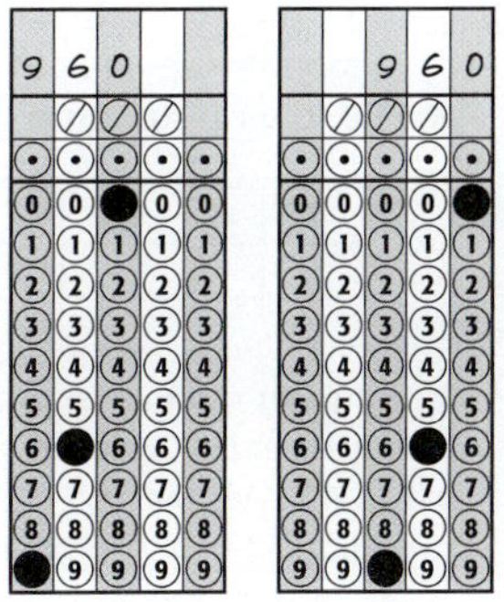

Many gridded-response questions result in an answer that is a fraction or a decimal. These values can also be filled in on the grid.

TEST EXAMPLE

2 **A prize box contains 12 glitter pencils, 5 fluorescent pens, and 13 mechanical pencils. If Alex randomly selects a prize, what is the probability that he will choose a glitter pencil?**

$$P(\text{glitter pencil}) = \frac{\text{number of favorable outcomes}}{\text{number of possible outcomes}}$$

$$= \frac{12}{12 + 5 + 13} = \frac{12}{30} \text{ or } \frac{2}{5}$$

You can either grid the fraction $\frac{12}{30}$ or $\frac{2}{5}$. You also can rewrite the fraction as a decimal and grid 0.4. Be sure to write the decimal point or fraction bar in the answer box. The following are acceptable answers.

Any equivalent fraction that fits the grid will be counted as correct.

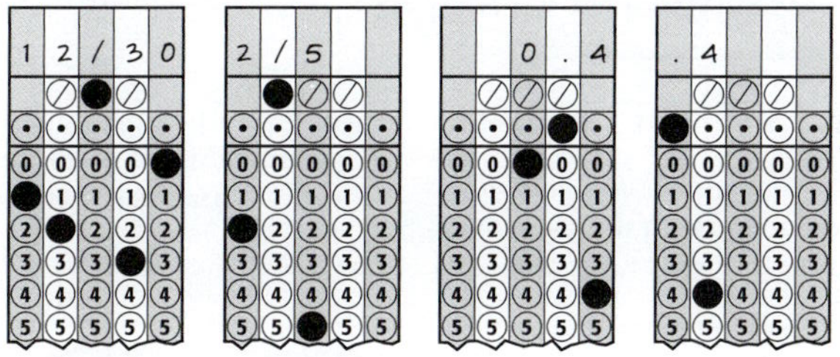

Do not leave a blank answer box in the middle of an answer.

If the answer is a mixed number, change it to an equivalent improper fraction or decimal.

TEST EXAMPLE

3 **A hummingbird measures $2\frac{1}{2}$ inches in length. A sandpiper, measures $4\frac{1}{2}$ inches in length. How many times as long is the sandpiper as the hummingbird?**

Divide the length of the sandpiper by the length of the hummingbird.

$4\frac{1}{2} \div 2\frac{1}{2} = \frac{9}{2} \div \frac{5}{2}$ — Rename $2\frac{1}{2}$ as $\frac{5}{2}$.

$= \frac{9}{2} \cdot \frac{2}{5}$ — Multiply by the reciprocal of $\frac{5}{2}$, which is $\frac{2}{5}$.

$= \frac{9}{5}$

You can either grid the improper fraction $\frac{9}{5}$, or rewrite it as 1.8 and grid the decimal. Do not enter 14/5, as this will be interpreted as $\frac{14}{5}$.

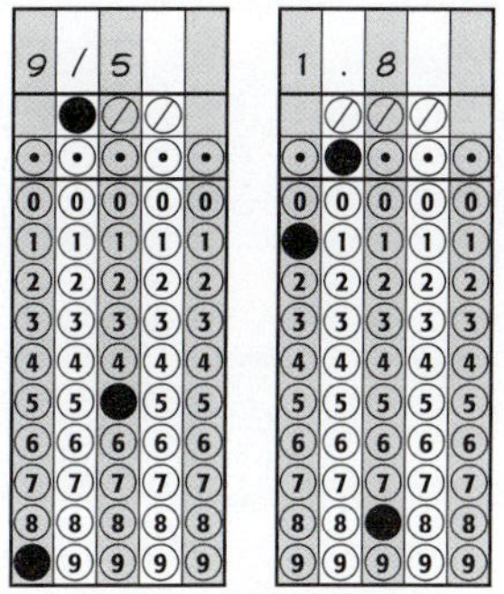

Gridded-Response Practice

Solve each problem. Then copy and complete a grid like the one shown on page 722.

Number and Operations

1. The seventh-grade class at Willow Creek Middle School is planning a class trip. Each student will need to pay $4.50 for the bus ride, $8.00 for a ticket to the museum, and $5.25 for lunch. If there are 52 students in the class, what will be the total cost in dollars of the trip? **923**

2. The highest point in Louisiana is Driskill Mountain at 585 feet. The lowest point is −8 feet in New Orleans. What is the difference in feet between the highest and lowest elevation points? **593**

3. People in the United States own about 204 million cars. If the number of cars is written in scientific notation, what is the exponent of the 10 in the expression? **8**

4. Ashlee has $5\frac{1}{4}$ cups of cocoa powder. If each batch of chocolate cookies uses $\frac{1}{2}$ cup of cocoa powder, how many batches could she make? **$2\frac{1}{2}$ or 10.5**

Algebra

5. The number of televisions per 1,000 people in France is 598. The number of televisions per 1,000 people in the United States is 208 greater than the number in France. How many televisions are there in the United States per 1,000 people? **806**

6. The table shows the number of white beads that Carmen uses in each row for a particular pattern in a necklace that she designed. How many white beads will there be in the sixth row? **32**

Row	1	2	3	4	5
Beads	1	2	4	8	16

7. The table shows the cost of renting a booth at the week-long Fall Festival. There is an initial charge for reserving a booth and a fee per day. What is the cost in dollars of renting a booth for the 7 days of the festival? **330**

Days	0	1	2	3
Cost ($)	50	90	130	170

8. The graph shows the cost to rent a power paint sprayer. Let x be the number of hours the sprayer is rented and y be the total cost of the rental. Suppose an equation of the form $y = ax$ represents the data in the graph. What is the value of a? **2.5 or 2.50**

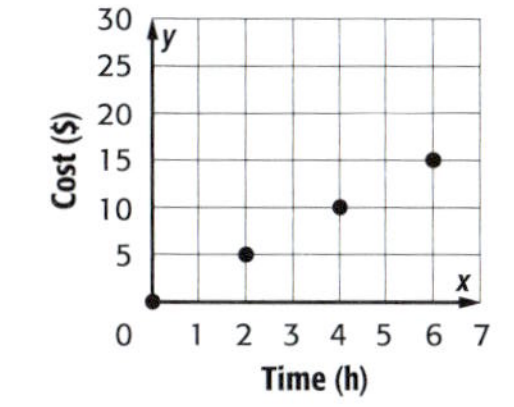

9. The temperature on a January morning is −18°F. The temperature is expected to rise at a rate of 5° each hour for the next several hours. In how many hours will the temperature be 7°F? **5**

Geometry

10. Triangle ABC is similar to triangle XYZ. What is the measure of $\angle Z$ in degrees? **75**

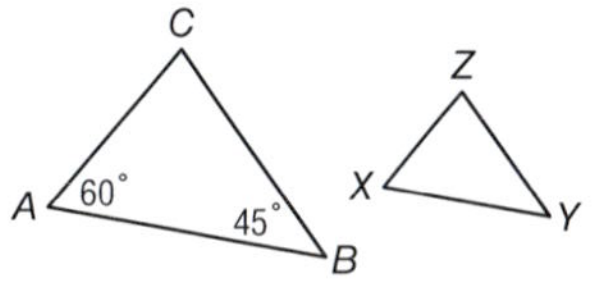

11. Triangle DEF has vertices $D(1, 1)$, $E(4, -2)$, and $F(0, -3)$. Find the y-coordinate of point E after the triangle is reflected over the x-axis. **2**

12. In the diagram, $\angle 1$ and $\angle 2$ are supplementary. Find the measure of $\angle 3$ in degrees. **62**

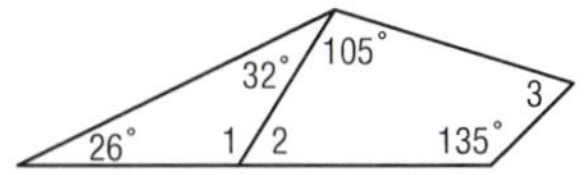

13. Rectangle B has width and length 3 times the width and length of Rectangle A. As a fraction, what is the ratio of the area of Rectangle A to the area of Rectangle B? **1/9**

Measurement

14. In the United States, the average amount of meat eaten per person is 261 pounds per year. If there are 365 days in a year, what is the average number of ounces of meat eaten per day? Round to the nearest ounce. **11**

TEST-TAKING TIP

Question 14 The units of measure given in a question may not be the same as the units of measure asked for in the answer. Check that your solution is in the correct unit.

15. A rectangle has an area of 318 square centimeters and a width of 12 centimeters. What is the length of the rectangle in centimeters? **26.5**

16. The circle graph shows the results of a survey in Ms. Chen's fifth period math class. What is the exact degree measure of the section of the circle graph representing soccer? **162**

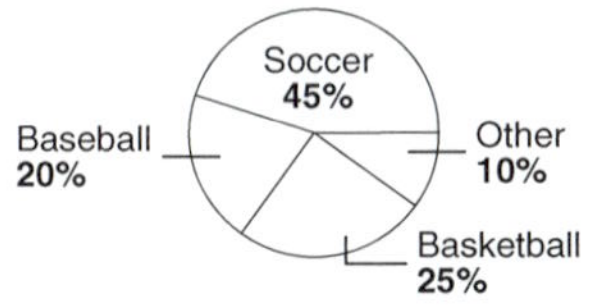

17. One acre of land is 43,560 square feet. How many square yards are in one acre? **4840**

18. The Browns plan to paint the top, bottom, and sides of the cylinder-shaped barrel with a waterproof coating. What is the surface area in square feet of the barrel? Round to the nearest square foot. **113**

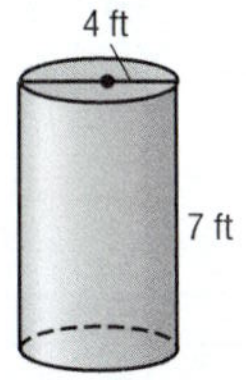

Data Analysis and Probability

19. The table shows the world's highest dams and the countries in which they are located. Find the range of the data. **128**

Country	Height (ft)
Tajikistan	984
Switzerland	935
Georgia	892
Italy	859
Mexico	856

Source: *Scholastic Book of World Records*

20. The table shows the prices in dollars that Mike spent on his college textbooks. What is the mean of the data? **53.50**

66.00	51.25	50.00	63.00
56.25	9.00	82.00	50.50

21. Kaya has the following scores for the first four tests in her science class: 82%, 95%, 100%, and 90%. She wants the mean of her first five tests to be 93%. What score as a percent must she earn on the fifth test? **98**

22. In a carnival game, the probability of winning is 0.005. As a percent, what is the probability of losing? **99.5**

23. A beverage cooler contains 6 regular colas, 5 orange drinks, 7 iced teas, and 7 diet colas. James reaches into the cooler and randomly takes two drinks, one after the other. Find the probability that he will choose a regular cola and then an orange drink. **1/20 or 0.05**

Short-Response Questions

Short-response questions require you to provide a solution to the problem as well as any method, explanation, and/or justification you used to arrive at the solution. These are sometimes called *constructed-response, open-response, open-ended, free-response,* or *student-produced questions.*

The following is a sample **rubric**, or scoring guide.

Credit	Score	Criteria
Full	2	Full credit: The answer is correct and a full explanation is provided that shows each step in arriving at the final answer.
Partial	1	Partial credit: There are two different ways to receive partial credit. • The answer is correct, but the explanation provided is incomplete or incorrect. • The answer is incorrect, but the explanation and method of solving the problem is correct.
None	0	No credit: Either an answer is not provided or the answer does not make sense.

On some standardized tests, no credit is given for a correct answer if your work is not shown.

STRATEGY

Reread the Problem
Look for the important information in the problem.

TEST EXAMPLE

1 **Hanna is deciding between a desktop and a laptop that are on sale. The desktop costs $609.00 with a 10% discount. The laptop costs $725.00 with a 25% discount. There is also a 6.75% sales tax on all purchases. Which computer is less expensive? What will be the total cost of the computer including discount and sales tax?**

Full Credit Solution

Since there are two computers to compare, I will first find the discounted price of each computer. I will change each percent to a decimal to make the calculations.

desktop	laptop
$609.00 \times 0.10 = 60.90$	$725.00 \times 0.25 = 181.25$
$609.00 - 60.90 = 548.10$	$725.00 - 181.25 = 543.75$

The laptop is less expensive after the discount.

I still need to find the cost of the laptop computer with tax.

543.75×0.0675 $\quad$ $6.75\% = 0.0675$

$= 36.703125$ $\quad$ Use a calculator.

≈ 36.70

Now I will add the sales tax to the cost of the laptop.

$543.75 + 36.70 = 580.45$

The laptop will cost Hanna $580.45, including sales tax.

The steps, calculations, and reasoning are clearly stated.

Partial Credit Solution

In this sample solution, the calculations are correct and the answer is correct. However, there is no explanation for any of the calculations.

$609.00 \times 0.10 = 60.90$

$609.00 - 60.90 = 548.10$

$548.10 \times 1.0675 = 585.09675$

$725.00 \times 0.25 = 181.25$

$725.00 - 181.25 = 543.75$

$543.75 \times 1.0675 = 580.453125$

The laptop is cheaper for $580.45.

Notice that the student multiplies the discounted price by 1.0675 since the cost is 1 and the tax is 0.0675. So, the total is then 1.0675.

Partial Credit Solution

In this sample solution, the answer is partially incorrect because the student does not add the sales tax.

I will find the discount price for each set.

Desktop: Since the current price is 100% and the discount is 10%, the sale price will be

$100 - 10 = 90\%$ or 0.9.

$609.00 \times 0.9 = 548.10$

Laptop: Since the current price is 100% and the discount is 25%, the sale price will be

$100 - 25 = 75\%$ or 0.75.

$725.00 \times 0.75 = 543.75$

Hanna should get the laptop for $543.75.

The student does not add the cost of the tax.

No Credit Solution

In this sample solution, the student does not understand how to find discounted prices and the sales tax. There are just some calculations using the numbers in the problem.

$609.00 - 10\% = 602.91$

$725.00 - 25\% = 625.00$

$602.91 + 6.75\% = 609.66$

$625.00 + 6.75 = 631.75$

I think Hanna should buy the desktop for $609.66.

Preparing for Standardized Tests

Short-Response Practice

Solve each problem. Show all your work.

Number and Operations

1. A main unit of currency in Egypt is the pound. One U.S. dollar is equal to $3\frac{4}{5}$ pounds. How many pounds are equivalent to \$10.00 in the U.S.? **38 pounds**

2. The average daytime temperature on Venus is 870°F. The average temperature on Jupiter is −160°F. What is the difference between the average temperatures on Venus and Jupiter? **1,030°F**

3. A bag of chocolate candies has a nutrition label stating that each serving contains 20% of the recommended daily amount of fat. A serving has 13 grams of fat. Using this information, what is the total recommended daily amount of fat in grams? **65 g**

4. The Montana Department of Fish, Wildlife, and Parks raised the price of a tag to catch a paddlefish from \$2.50 to \$5.00 for residents and from \$7.50 to \$15.00 for nonresidents. Which percent of increase is greater, the increase for residents or for nonresidents? **They are the same with both being a 100% increase.**

5. A recent article in the newspaper said that there were 75 cell phones for every 100 people in Finland. The number of cell phones in Finland was given to be 3,893,000. Estimate the population of Finland using this information. **about 5,000,000 people**

Algebra

6. Florida has 8,426 miles of shoreline. Alaska has 25,478 more miles of shoreline than Florida. Write and solve an equation to find the number of miles of shoreline for Alaska. **$a = 8{,}426 + 25{,}478$; $a = 33{,}904$ mi**

7. Juana is saving money to buy a skateboard that costs \$95. She has \$25 and plans to save \$5 per week. In how many weeks will she have enough money for the skateboard? **14 weeks**

8. Tyler delivers televisions for Electronics Depot. The graph shows the amount Tyler charges for delivery based on distance. Name the slope and y-intercept of the graph and describe what they mean in this situation. **See Student Handbook Answer Appendix.**

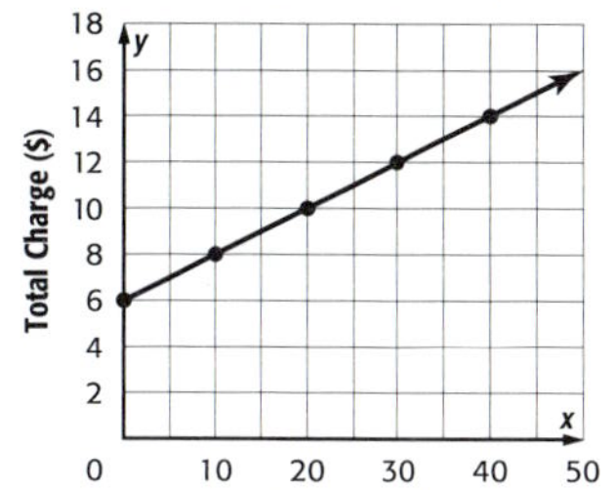

9. Solve $\frac{2}{3}b = \frac{8}{7}$. **$\frac{12}{7}$**

Geometry

10. The formula for the area of a trapezoid is $A = \frac{1}{2}h(b_1 + b_2)$. Find the area of the trapezoid. **70 ft²**

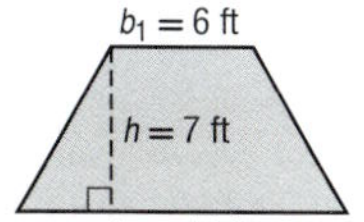

11. Angles MNP and PNO are supplementary. Find $m\angle PNO$. **155°**

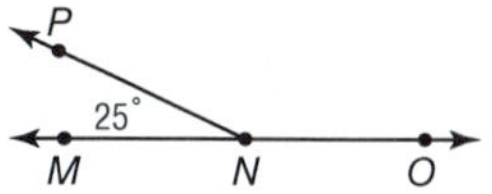

12. What is the value of x? **62**

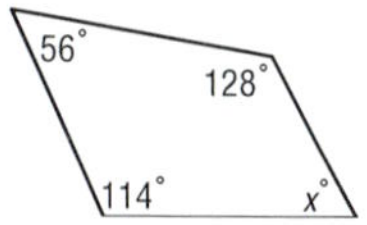

13. Colby is planning to use $\triangle CDE$ for a design by using transformations. He plans to reflect it over the y-axis. Find the coordinates of $\triangle CDE$ after this reflection. Graph the reflected image of the triangle. **See Student Handbook Answer Appendix.**

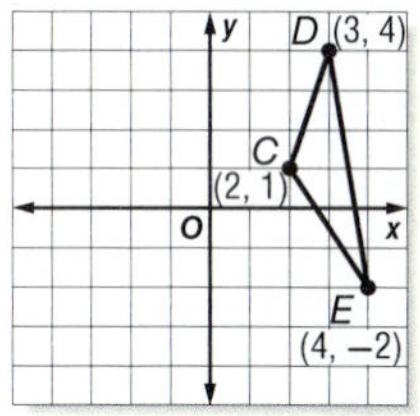

Measurement

14. Diego ran in a 10-kilometer race. What is the distance of this race in meters? **10,000 m**

15. What is the surface area of the box? **2,656 in²**

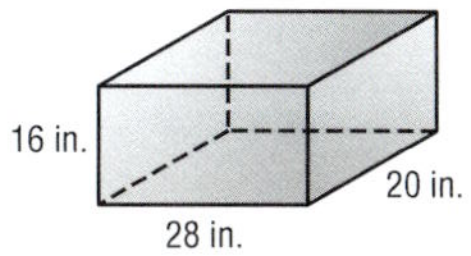

16. A certain aircraft uses 350 gallons of fuel per hour. If the plane used 1,925 gallons of fuel on a flight between two cities, how many hours long was the flight? **5.5 h**

17. Curtis is painting the four columns for the set of a school play. What is the surface area that needs to be painted? Assume that the tops and bottoms of the columns do *not* need to be painted. **251.3 ft²**

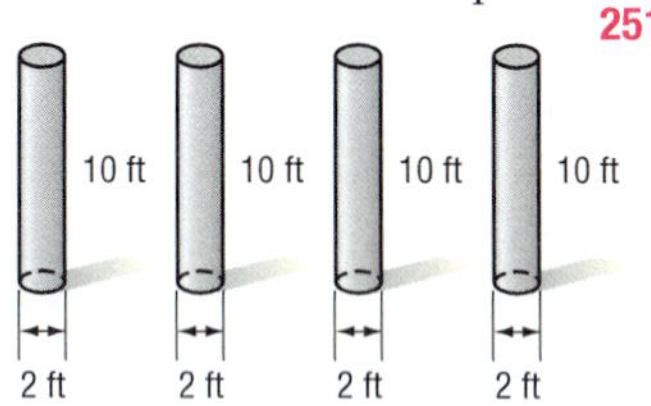

18. The record for women running the Boston Marathon was set in 2002 when Margaret Okayo of Kenya ran the 26.2-mile course in approximately 2 hours and 21 minutes. What was her average speed in miles per hour? **about 11.15 mph**

TEST-TAKING TIP

Questions 17 and 18 After finding the solution, always go back and read the problem again to make sure your solution answers what the problem is asking.

Data Analysis and Probability

19. The stem-and-leaf plot shows the scores on the last math test in Mr. Hill's class. What is the range of the data? **39**

Stem	Leaf
9	1 2 3 5 6 9
8	0 2 5 6 6 7 8 8
7	1 2 3 5 7 9 9
6	0 5 8 9 9 8|2 = 82 points

20. The table shows the heights of the world's largest flightless birds. Make a bar graph of the data. **See Student Handbook Answer Appendix.**

Bird	Height (in.)
Ostrich	96
Emu	60
Cassowary	60
Rhea	54
Emperor Penguin	45

21. The table shows the average precipitation in inches for each month in Syracuse, New York. Make a scatter plot of the data. Use the months on the horizontal axis and the precipitation on the vertical axis. Describe the graph. **See Student Handbook Answer Appendix.**

Month	Precipitation (in.)	Month	Precipitation (in.)
Jan	2.34	July	3.81
Feb	2.15	Aug	3.51
Mar	2.77	Sep	3.79
Apr	3.33	Oct	3.24
May	3.28	Nov	3.72
June	3.79	Dec	3.2

22. Two number cubes each marked with 1, 2, 3, 4, 5, 6 on their faces are rolled. List all the possible outcomes. **There are 36 possible outcomes: 1, 1; 1, 2; 1, 3; ... 6, 6.**

Extended-Response Questions

Extended-response questions are often called *open-ended* or *constructed-response questions*. Most extended-response questions have multiple parts. You must answer all parts to receive full credit.

Extended-response questions are similar to short-response questions in that you must show all of your work in solving the problem and a rubric is used to determine whether you receive full, partial, or no credit. The following is a sample rubric for scoring extended-response questions.

On some standardized tests, no credit is given for a correct answer if your work is not shown.

Credit	Score	Criteria
Full	4	Full credit: A correct solution is given that is supported by well-developed, accurate explanations.
Partial	3, 2, 1	Partial credit: A generally correct solution is given that may contain minor flaws in reasoning or computation, or an incomplete solution is given. The more correct the solution, the greater the score.
None	0	No credit: An incorrect solution is given indicating no mathematical understanding of the concept, or no solution is given.

Make sure that when the problem says to *Show your work*, you show every aspect of your solution including figures, sketches of graphing calculator screens, or the reasoning behind computations.

TEST EXAMPLE

1 Each fall, the community pool is drained. The pool contains 100,000 gallons of water. The pool has two drains that together drain the pool at a rate of 10,000 gallons per hour.

a. Make a function table for this situation. Let x represent the time in hours the pool drains. Let y represent the gallons of water left in the pool.

b. Make a graph of the data in the function table.

c. Predict how many hours it will take for the pool to drain.

Full Credit Solution

Part a A complete table includes labeled columns.

Every 2 hours there will be 20,000 gallons less water.

Hours (x)	Water Left (y)	(x, y)
2	80,000	(2, 80,000)
4	60,000	(4, 60,000)
6	40,000	(6, 40,000)
8	20,000	(8, 20,000)
10	0	(10, 0)

Part b A complete graph includes a title for the graph, appropriate scales and labels for the axes, and correctly graphed points.

The student gives reasoning in graphing the ordered pairs.

To make a graph, I graphed the ordered pairs from my table and decided to connect them with a line.

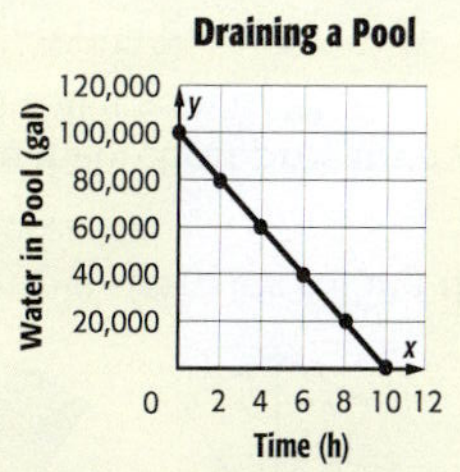

Part c

The pool is drained when the y-value is 0. That is at 10 hours. It will take 10 hours to drain the pool.

Partial Credit Solution

Part a This sample answer has an incomplete table.

1	90,000
2	80,000
3	70,000

Part b Partial credit is given because the points are graphed correctly, but the scale on the y-axis jumps from 0 to 70,000 with no break.

Partial credit can be given if parts of the table and graph are missing.

Water in the Pool

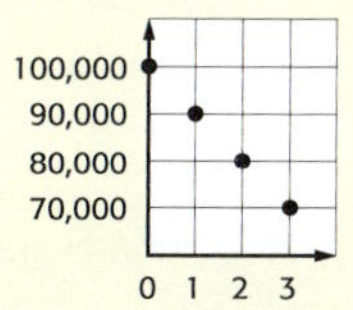

Part c

Full credit is given for Part c.

I wrote a function rule to find how long it will take to drain the pool. I let $y = 0$ to find the number of hours.

$$y = 100{,}000 - 10{,}000x$$
$$0 = 100{,}000 - 10{,}000x$$
$$10{,}000x = 100{,}000$$
$$x = 10$$

It will take 10 hours to drain the pool.

No Credit Solution

If the student demonstrates no understanding of making a table or graph or making a prediction, then no credit is given.

Extended-Response Practice

Solve each problem. Show all your work.

Number and Operations

1. The table shows the land area and water area of five states.
a–c. See Student Handbook Answer Appendix.

Land and Water Area of Five States		
State	Land Area (mi^2)	Water Area (mi^2)
Florida	53,937	5991
Colorado	103,729	371
Alaska	570,374	44,856
Iowa	55,875	401
Rhode Island	1,045	186

a. Find the percent of each state that is water. The entire state area is the sum of the land and water areas.

b. Order the states from the state with the least percent water to the greatest percent water.

c. Suppose a state had land and water areas such that the water area was 20% of the total area. Give a possible land and water area, with land area greater than 1,000 square miles, such that this is true.

Algebra

2. The table shows the rental rates for a crane rental service. There is an initial fee to reserve the crane and a daily fee.
a–c. See Student Handbook Answer Appendix.

Days	Cost	Days	Cost
0	$100	4	$280
1	$145	5	$325
2	$190	6	$370
3	$235		

a. Graph the data. Let x = number of days and y = cost. Connect the points.

b. What is the slope of the line? What does the slope represent?

c. What would be the charge for renting the crane for 10 days?

3. A long-distance phone company charges 40¢ per call plus 4¢ per minute.

a. Write and solve an equation to find the number of minutes used for a call that costs $2.80.

b. Another long-distance company charges 6¢ per minute and no connection fee. What is the cost of a 60-minute call?

c. Which service would charge less for a 90-minute call?
a–c. See Student Handbook Answer Appendix.

Geometry

4. Ava and Bryn are making rectangular fleece blankets. Ava is making her blanket 40 inches by 60 inches. Bryn says she wants to make her blanket "twice as big."

a. What is the area of Ava's blanket?

b. Bryn makes her blanket such that both the length and width are each twice the length and width of Ava's blanket. What will be the area of Bryn's blanket?

c. What is the ratio of the area of Bryn's blanket in Part b to the area of Ava's blanket in Part a?

d. Ava tells Bryn that a blanket is "twice as big" if the area is twice the area of the other. Give a possible length and width for a blanket twice as big as Ava's using this idea of "twice as big."
a–d. See Student Handbook Answer Appendix.

5. The map shows five towns and the angle measures for roads connecting them.

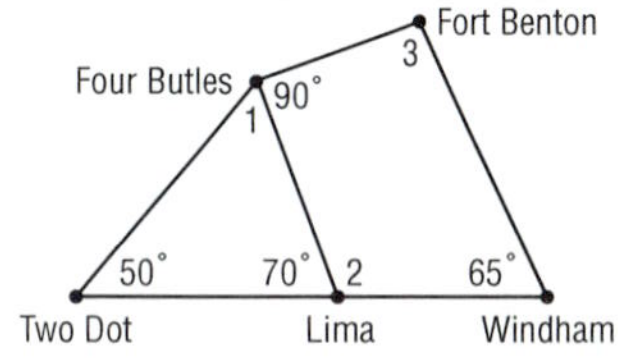

a. Find the measure of $\angle 1$. Explain.

b. Find the measures of $\angle 2$ and $\angle 3$. Explain.

Measurement

6. City planners are considering enlarging the circular manholes in their streets. Currently, the diameter of a manhole cover is 24 inches. The new size being considered is 2 inches greater all the way around.
a–c. See Student Handbook Answer Appendix.

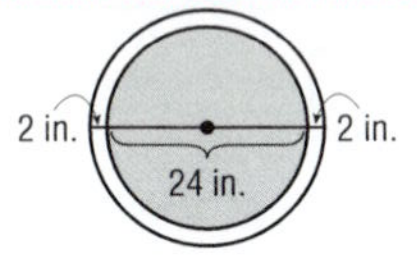

a. Find the area of a current manhole cover with diameter of 24 inches. Round to the nearest square inch.

b. Find the area of a new manhole cover. Round to the nearest square inch.

c. What would be the percent increase in the area of a manhole cover if the new covers are made?

TEST-TAKING TIP

Question 6 Be sure to completely and carefully read the problem before beginning any calculations. If you read too quickly, you may miss a key piece of information.

7. A company that sells beads for craft projects has the two containers shown for packaging the beads.
a–c. See Student Handbook Answer Appendix.

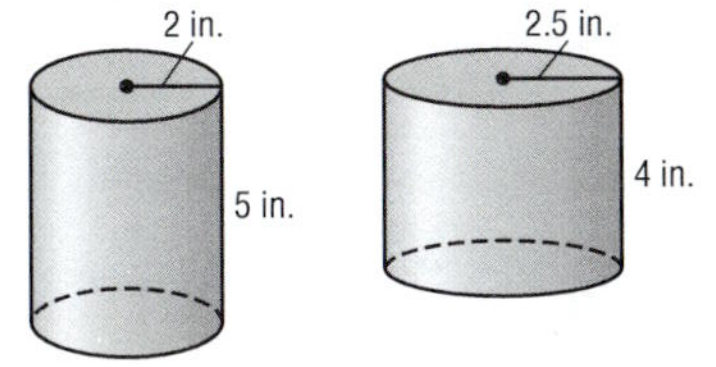

a. Find the volume of each container. Round to the nearest tenth of a cubic inch.

b. Find the ratio of the volume of container A to the volume of container B.

c. The company wants to make a container shaped as a rectangular prism. Find a possible length, width, and height for the container such that its volume is twice the volume of container B.

Data Analysis and Probability

8. The table shows the normal monthly temperatures in degrees Fahrenheit for Honolulu, Hawaii, and Minneapolis, Minnesota.
a–c. See Student Handbook Answer Appendix.

Month	Honolulu	Minneapolis
Jan	73	13
Feb	73	20
Mar	74	32
Apr	76	47
May	77	59
Jun	80	68
Jul	81	73
Aug	82	71
Sep	82	61
Oct	80	49
Nov	78	33
Dec	75	19

Source: *The World Almanac*

a. Make a scatter plot of the data for Honolulu. Place the months on the x-axis and the temperatures on the y-axis. Describe the graph.

b. Make a scatter plot of the data for Minneapolis. Place the months on the x-axis and the temperatures on the y-axis. Describe the graph.

c. Compare the range for each city's temperature data. Explain a possible reason for the difference in the data.

9. Two 4-sided number cubes are rolled for a game, one white and one black. Each number cube has faces numbered 1 through 4.
a–c. See Student Handbook Answer Appendix.

a. List the sample space for rolling the two number pieces.

b. What is the theoretical probability that a player will roll a sum of 8?

c. If you played this game 50 times, how many times would you expect to get a sum of 4?

Extra Practice

Page 670, Extra Practice, (Lesson 1-8)

13. Distributive
14. Commutative (×)
15. Associative (+)
16. Commutative (+)
17. Distributive
18. Identity (×)
19. Associative (×)
20. Associative (+)
21. Associative (×)
22. Identity (+)
23. Commutative (×)
24. Commutative (+)

Page 670, Extra Practice, (Lesson 1-9)

1. 4 is added to each term; 21, 25, 29
2. 2 is added to each term; 11, 13, 15
3. 5 is added to each term; 30, 35, 40
4. 3 is added to each term; 102, 105, 108
5. 6 is added to each term; 32, 38, 44
6. 0.9 is added to each term; 8.1, 9.0, 9.9
7. 0.1 is added to each term; 0.6, 0.7, 0.8
8. 1.1 is added to each term; 6.7, 7.8, 8.9
9. 0.2 is added to each term; 9.7, 9.9, 10.1
10. 8 is added to each term; 35, 43, 51
11. 25 is added to each term; 450, 475, 500
12. 15 is added to each term; 680, 695, 710
13. 5 is added to each term; 22, 27, 32
14. 7 is added to each term; 38, 45, 52
15. 7 is added to each term; 28, 35, 42
16. 6 is added to each term; 25, 31, 37
17. 6 is added to each term; 119, 125, 131
18. 81 is added to each term; 333, 414, 495
19. 0.2 is added to each term; 3.4, 3.6, 3.8
20. 0.5 is added to each term; 6.1, 6.6, 7.1
21. 1.1 is added to each term; 11.0, 12.1, 13.2
22. 1.5 is added to each term; 25.5, 27, 28.5
23. 0.3 is added to each term; 15.7, 16.0, 16.3
24. 0.3 is added to each term; 1.3, 1.6, 1.9

Page 671, Extra Practice, (Lesson 2-1)

7. 

8. 

9. 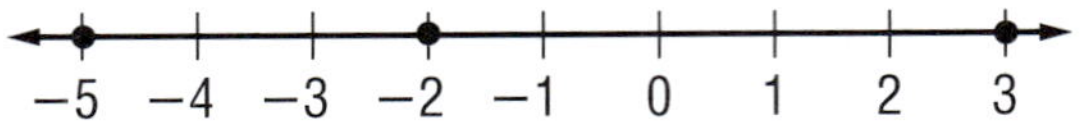

10. 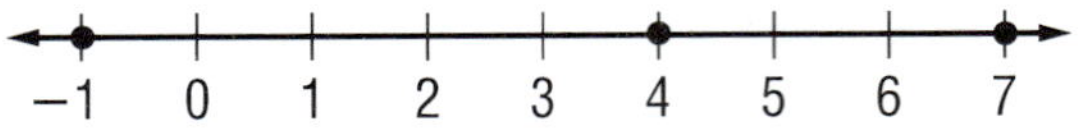

Page 672, Extra Practice, (Lesson 2-3)

13–24. 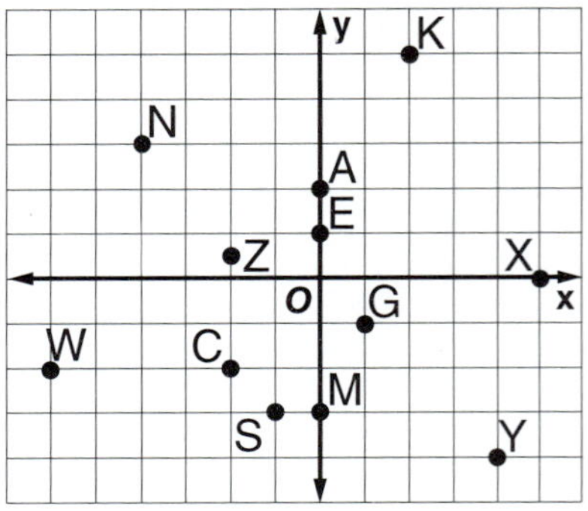

Page 674, Extra Practice, (Lesson 3-1)

1. $p - 6$
2. $20 + c$
3. $\frac{a}{b}$
4. $a + 6$
5. $x + 12$
6. $\frac{\$1{,}000}{z}$
7. $\frac{y}{3}$
8. $7m$
9. $f - 9$
10. $26 - q$
11. $19 - z$
12. $x - 2$
13. $3x - 4 = 17$
14. $n + 6 = 5$
15. $20 + 2n = -30$
16. $\frac{n}{-2} = -42$
17. $4 + 3n = 18$
18. $5n - 15 = 92$
19. $8n + 12 = 36$
20. $n - 24 = -30$

Page 675, Extra Practice, (Lesson 3-4)

3. Greg rented 9 videos, Paloma rented 5, Grace rented 1, and Jack rented 10.

Page 675, Extra Practice, (Lesson 3-6)

6. 13.5 km; 7.875 km^2
8. 50 m; 96.1875 m^2

Page 676, Extra Practice, (Lesson 3-7)

1.
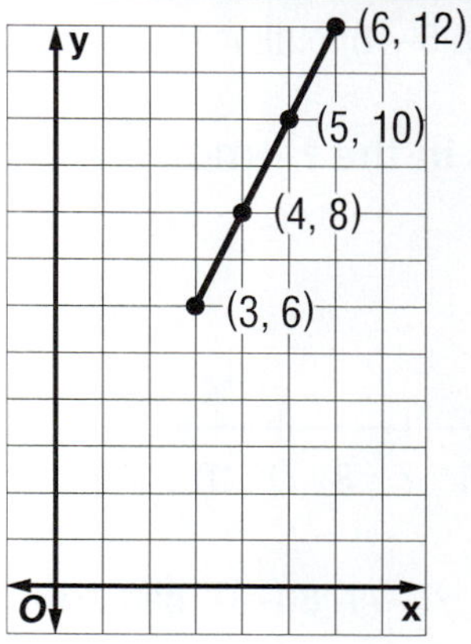

2.
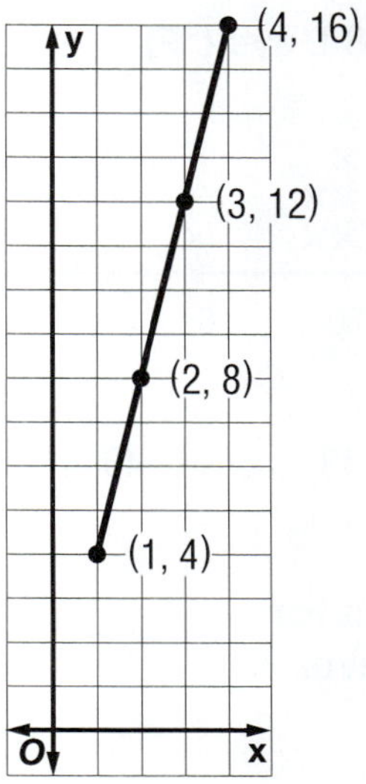

3.
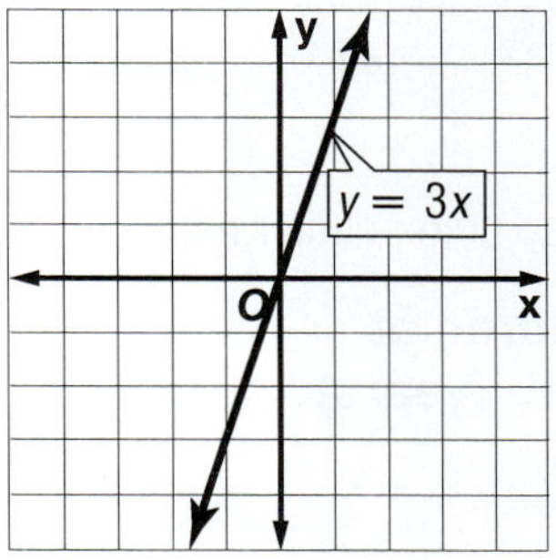

4.
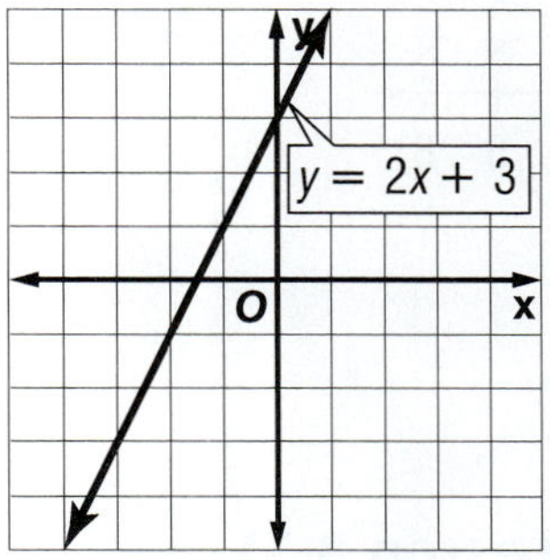

5.
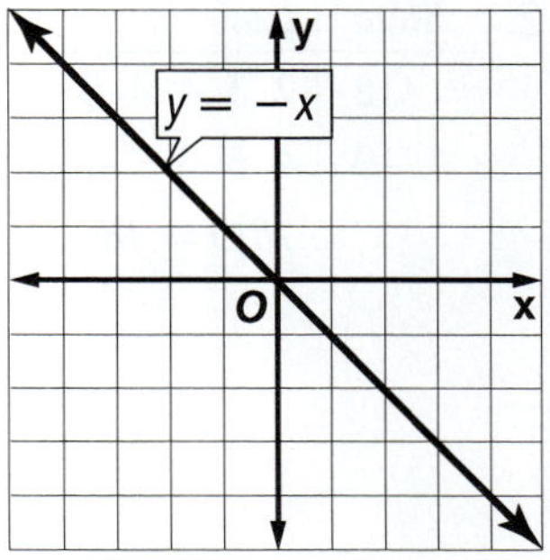

6.
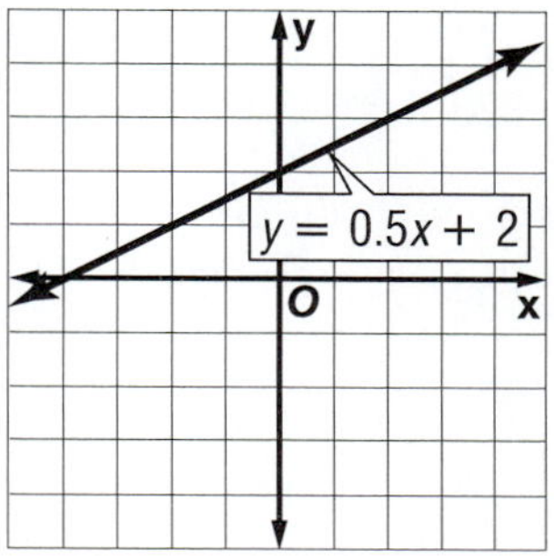

7.
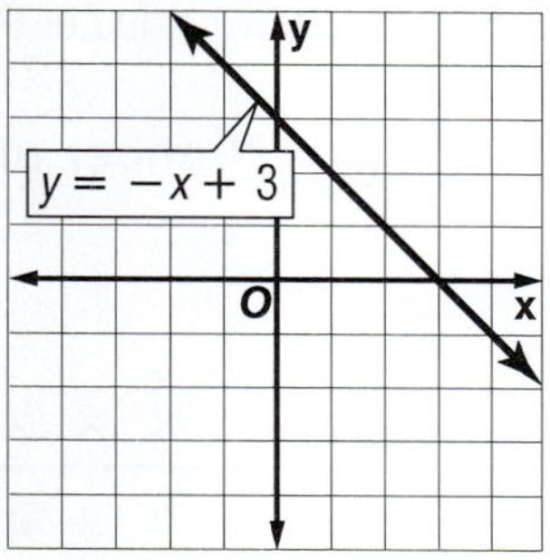

8.
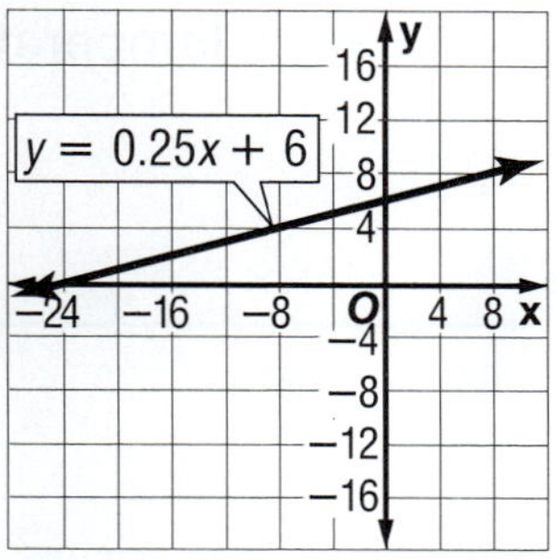

9.
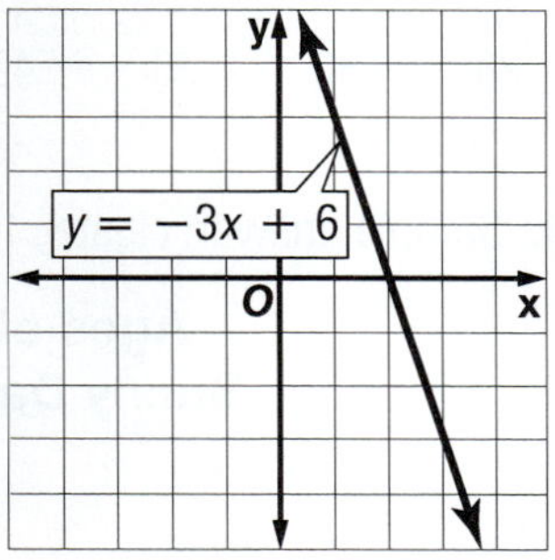

10.
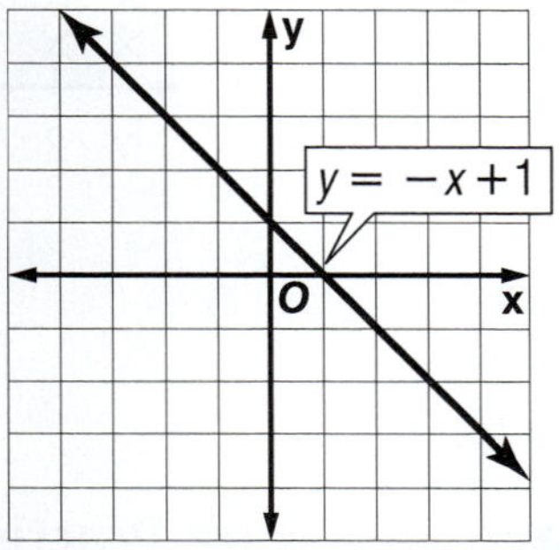

11.
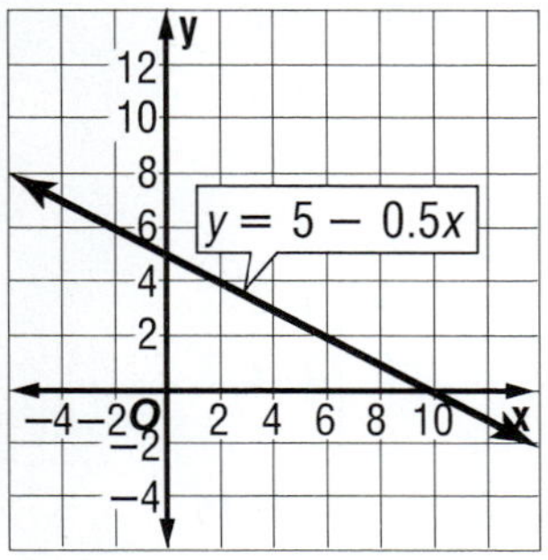

Page 676, Extra Practice, (Lesson 4-1)

19. $5 \times 7 \times x \times y$

20. $2 \times 7 \times a \times a$

21. $2 \times 3 \times 5 \times n$

22. $3 \times 3 \times 3 \times c \times d \times d$

23. $2 \times 2 \times s \times s \times t \times t$

24. $2 \times 2 \times 3 \times 5 \times p \times p \times q \times r$

Page 681, Extra Practice, (Lesson 6-1)

7. yes; $\frac{4}{6} = \frac{2}{3}$ and $\frac{8}{12} = \frac{2}{3}$, so $\frac{4}{6} = \frac{8}{12}$

8. no; $\frac{20}{25} \neq \frac{16}{30}$ since $\frac{20}{25} = \frac{4}{5}$ and $\frac{16}{30} = \frac{8}{15}$

9. no; $\frac{20}{15} \neq \frac{30}{25}$ since $\frac{20}{15} = \frac{4}{3}$ and $\frac{30}{25} = \frac{6}{5}$

10. yes; $\frac{36}{63} = \frac{4}{7}$ since $\frac{28}{49} = \frac{4}{7}$, so $\frac{36}{63} = \frac{28}{49}$

Page 682, Extra Practice, (Lesson 6-2)

8. 3 classes/semester

Page 683, Extra Practice, (Lesson 6-6)

1. yes; $\frac{2}{3} = \frac{6}{9}$ since $2 \times 9 = 18$ and $3 \times 6 = 18$

2. no; $\frac{3}{1} \neq \frac{15}{6}$ since $3 \times 6 = 18$ but $1 \times 15 \neq 18$

3. no; $\frac{2}{1} \neq \frac{8}{3}$ since $2 \times 3 = 6$, but $1 \times 8 \neq 6$

Page 683, Extra Practice, (Lesson 6-7)

1. Multiplication followed by subtraction; $12 \times 8 = 96$, $96 - 8 = 88$, $88 - 2 = 86$, 12 correct, 2 incorrect, 1 no answer

Page 685, Extra Practice, (Lesson 7-3)

13. $0.1 \times 40 = 4$ and $3 \times 4 = 12$

14. $0.1 \times 100 = 10$ and $7 \times 10 = 70$

15. $0.1 \times 150 = 15$ and $9 \times 15 = 135$

16. $0.1 \times 70 = 7$ and $7 \times 7 = 49$

17. $0.1 \times 90 = 9$ and $8 \times 9 = 72$

18. $0.1 \times 180 = 18$

19. $0.1 \times 220 = 22$ and $5 \times 22 = 110$

20. $0.1 \times 500 = 50$ and $2 \times 50 = 100$

21. $0.1 \times 400 = 40$ and $8 \times 40 = 320$

22. $0.1 \times 60 = 6$ and $4 \times 6 = 24$

23. $0.1 \times 180 = 18$ and $6 \times 18 = 108$

24. $0.1 \times 450 = 45$ and $2 \times 45 = 90$

Page 685, Extra Practice, (Lesson 7-4)

1. $n = 0.45 \times 50$; 22.5

2. $75 = p \times 300$; 25%

3. $2 = 0.16 \times w$; 12.5

4. $n = 0.75 \times 80$; 60

5. $12 = 0.05 \times w$; 240

6. $n = 0.60 \times 45$; 27

7. $90 = p \times 95$; 94.7%

8. $n = 0.285 \times 64$; 18.2

9. $n = 0.465 \times 75$; 34.9

10. $n = 0.555 \times 70$; 38.9

11. $80.5 = 0.805 \times w$; 100

12. $40 = \frac{2}{3} \times w$; 60

13. $n = 1.225 \times 80$; 98

14. $75 = 2.5 \times w$; 30

Page 686, Extra Practice, (Lesson 7-7)

1. $47.70

2. $16.14

3. $179.10

4. $31.03

5. $14.25

6. $154.06

7. $12.54

8. $719.20

9. $112.88

10. $527.12

11. $12,968.75

12. $52.57

Page 687, Extra Practice, (Lesson 7-8)

1. $800

2. $33.33

3. $37.50

4. $17.11

5. $28.34

6. $3.34

7. $138

8. $6.75

9. $1,800

10. $270

11. $380

12. $27

13. $2,315.63

14. $298.99

15. $165.36

16. $91.41

17. $183.33

18. $680.40

Page 687, Extra Practice, (Lesson 8-1)

1. Sample answer: cluster 0–2; gap 5–10; outlier 10

Number of Pets in the Home

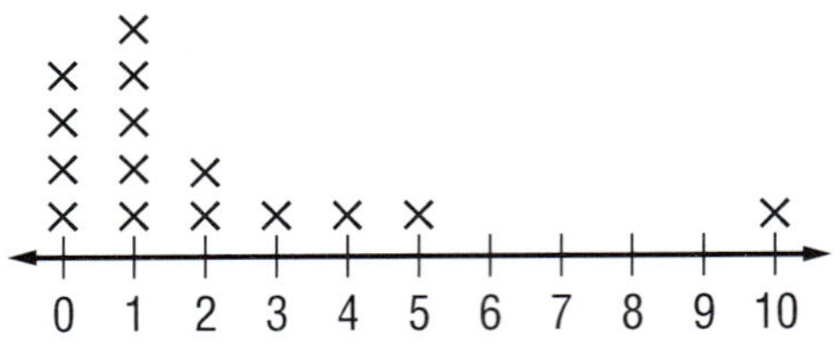

2. Sample answer: clusters 65–66, 75–77, 80–81; gaps 66–75, 77–80, 81–85; outlier 85

High Temperature for 18 Days (°F)

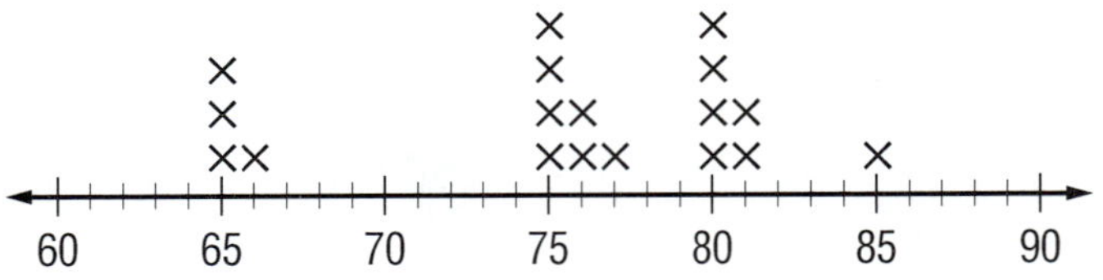

3. Sample answer: clusters 32–36, 40–43; gaps 36–40, 44–52; outlier none

Number of Stories for Buildings in Denver

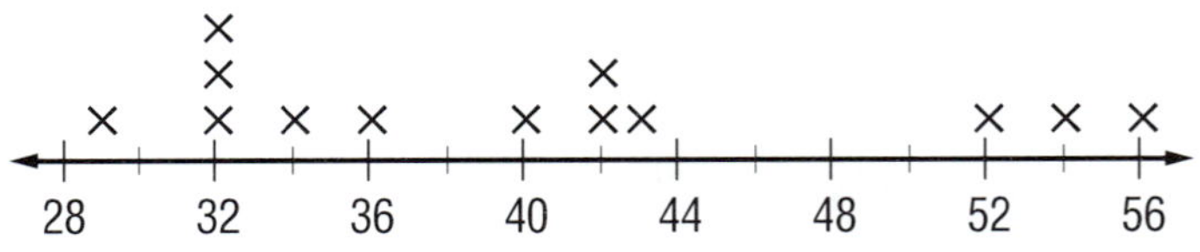

4. Sample answer: cluster 1–9; gap none; outlier none

Ages of Children at Sunny Day Care (years)

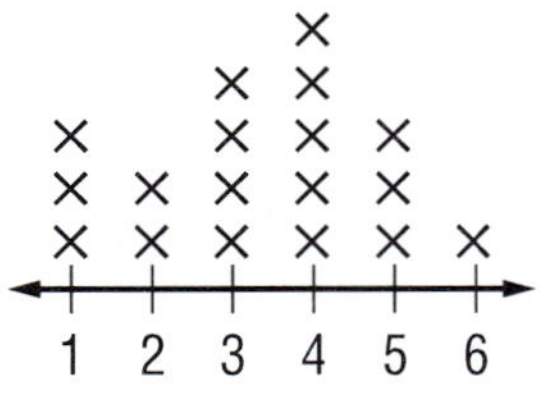

Page 688, Extra Practice, (Lesson 8-3)

1.

Stem	Leaf
1	5 8
2	3 9
3	9
4	1 2
5	1 2 7
6	8

1|5 = 15

2.

Stem	Leaf
18	2 3 4 4 9
19	4 6 6 7

18|9 = 189

3.

Stem	Leaf
2	1 4 7
3	4
4	0 6
5	0 8
6	1 7
7	0 2

$3|4 = 34$

4.

Stem	Leaf
2	0 0 0 3 7
3	0 1 2 4 4 5 7 9
4	2 8 9
5	2 5

$2|0 = 20$

Page 688, Extra Practice, (Lesson 8-4)

1. **Longest Snakes**

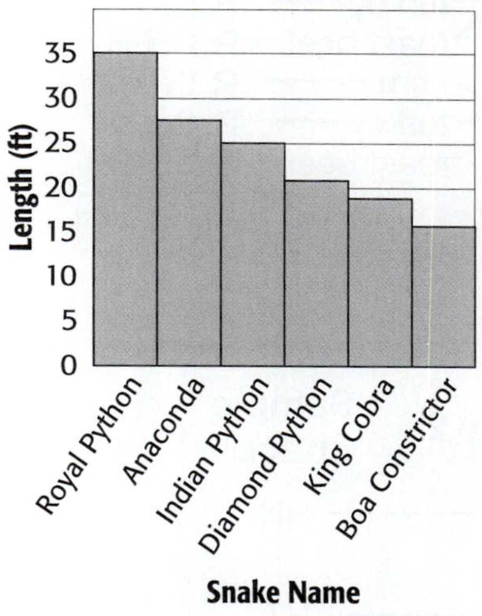

2. **Least Densely Populated States**

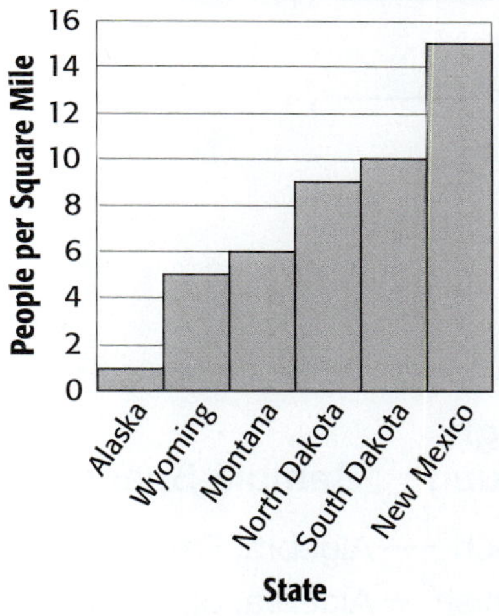

3. Histogram

Cost of a Movie Ticket

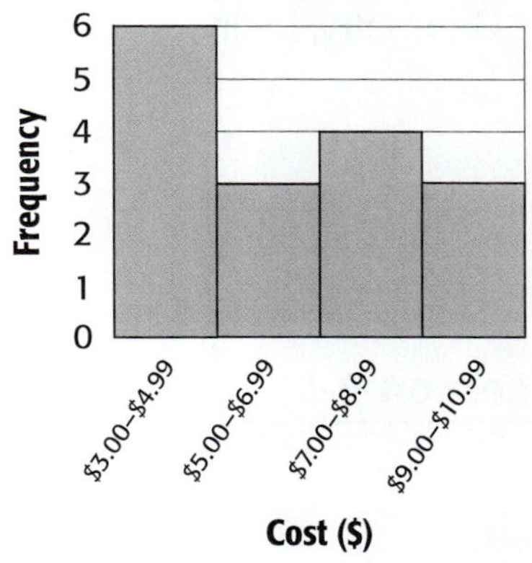

4. Histogram

Highest Recorded Wind Speeds

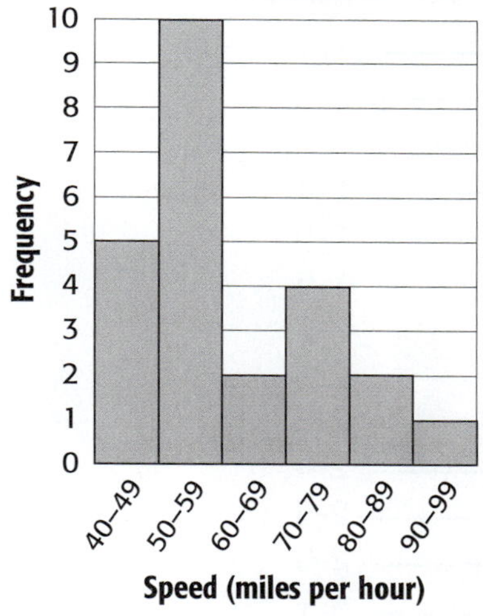

Page 689, Extra Practice, (Lesson 8-6)

4. **Price for Sheep**

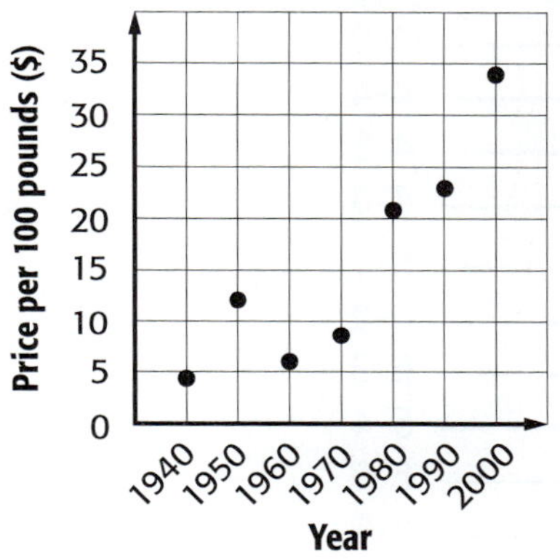

5. Sample answer: Except for the interval from 1950 to 1960, the price increases during each ten-year period.

6. Sample answer: about $40; if you draw a line lying close to the points from 1960 to 2000, 40 lies at 2010.

Page 690, Extra Practice, (Lesson 8-8)

1. The conclusion is valid; Sample answer: The sample is a simple random sample.

2. The conclusion is not valid; Sample answer: The sample is a convenience sample.

3. The conclusion is not valid; Sample answer: The sample is a voluntary response sample.

Page 690, Extra Practice, (Lesson 8-9)

1. Graph B is misleading. The change is the vertical scale makes it seem as if the pounds of grapes sold made drastric changes over the course of the week.

2. Graph A is misleading. The change in the vertical scale makes it seem as if Mr. Turner made a lot more money in the third week.

Page 691, Extra Practice, (Lesson 9-2)

1.

Number Cube 1	Number Cube 2	Sample Space
1	1	1-1
	2	1-2
	3	1-3
	4	1-4
	5	1-5
	6	1-6
2	1	2-1
	2	2-2
	3	2-3
	4	2-4
	5	2-5
	6	2-6
3	1	3-1
	2	3-2
	3	3-3
	4	3-4
	5	3-5
	6	3-6
4	1	4-1
	2	4-2
	3	4-3
	4	4-4
	5	4-5
	6	4-6
5	1	5-1
	2	5-2
	3	5-3
	4	5-4
	5	5-5
	6	5-6
6	1	6-1
	2	6-2
	3	6-3
	4	6-4
	5	6-5
	6	6-6

2.

Ice Cream Cone	Ice Cream Flavor	Sample Space
waffle	chocolate	waffle, chocolate
	vanilla	waffle, vanilla
	strawberry	waffle, strawberry
plain	chocolate	plain, chocolate
	vanilla	plain, vanilla
	strawberry	plain, strawberry
sugar	chocolate	sugar, chocolate
	vanilla	sugar, vanilla
	strawberry	sugar, strawberry

3.

Bread	Cheese	Meat	Sample Space
white	cheddar	ham	W, C, H
		turkey	W, C, T
		roast beef	W, C, RB
	Swiss	ham	W, S, H
		turkey	W, S, T
		roast beef	W, S, RB
wheat	cheddar	ham	WH, C, H
		turkey	WH, C, T
		roast beef	WH, C, RB
	Swiss	ham	WH, S, H
		turkey	WH, S, T
		roast beef	WH, S, RB
rye	cheddar	ham	R, C, H
		turkey	R, C, T
		roast beef	R, C, RB
	Swiss	ham	R, S, H
		turkey	R, S, T
		roast beef	R, S, RB

4.

Penny 1	Penny 2	Sample Space
H	H	HH
	T	HT
T	H	TH
	T	TT

5.

Math	Foreign Language	Sample Space
Algebra	French	Algebra, French
	Spanish	Algebra, Spanish
	Latin	Algebra, Latin
Geometry	French	Geometry, French
	Spanish	Geometry, Spanish
	Latin	Geometry, Latin

Page 692, Extra Practice, (Lesson 9-5)

2. 924 ways
3. 56 ways

Page 694, Extra Practice, (Lesson 10-3)

1. **Car Sales**

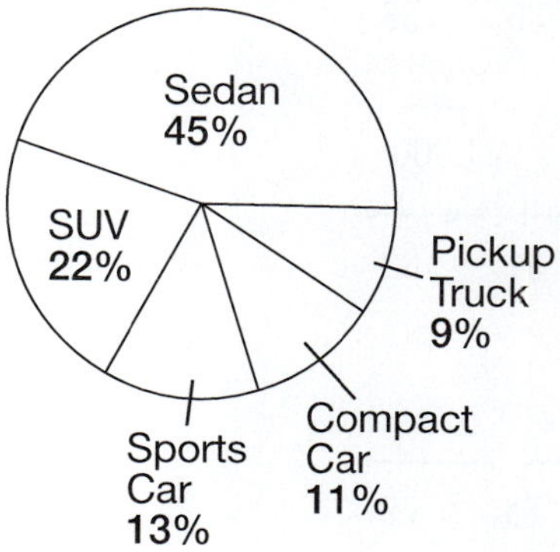

2. **Favorite Flavor of Ice Cream**

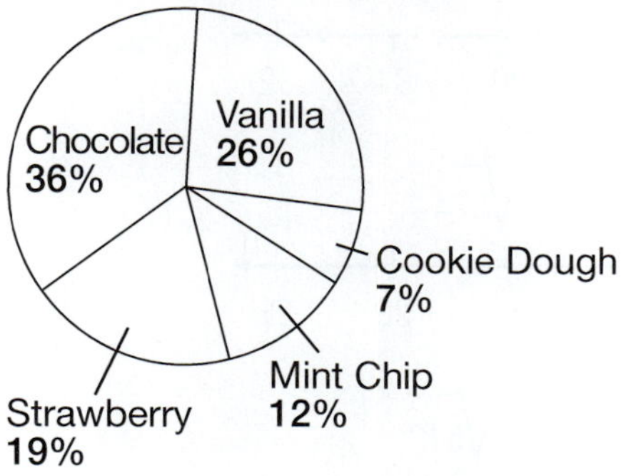

Page 694, Extra Practice, (Lesson 10-5)

1. See students' drawings; Sample answer: Two of the angles in an isosceles triangle are congruent.
2. Scott

Page 696, Extra Practice, (Lesson 10-9)

1.

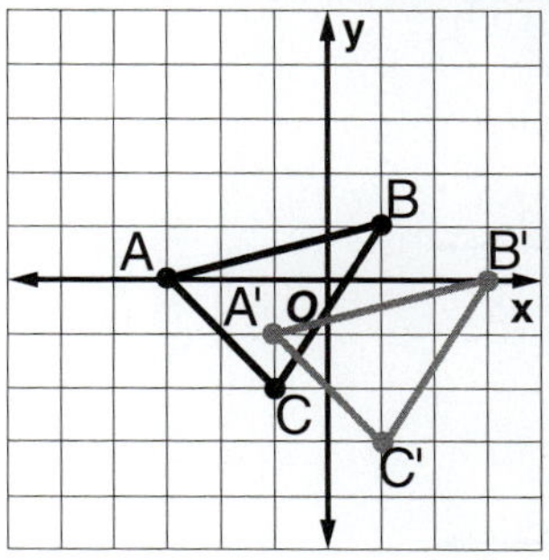

2.

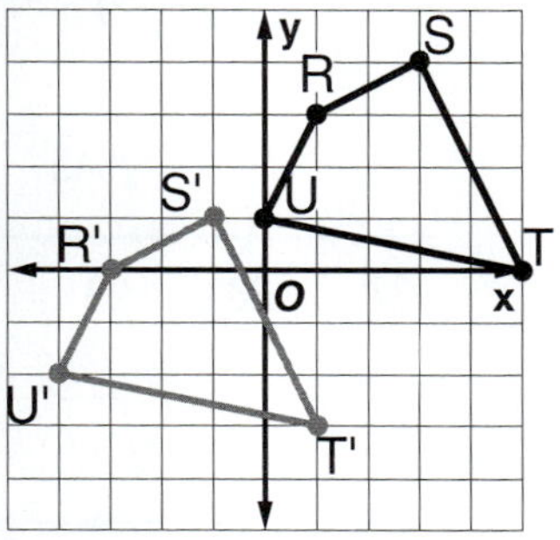

3.

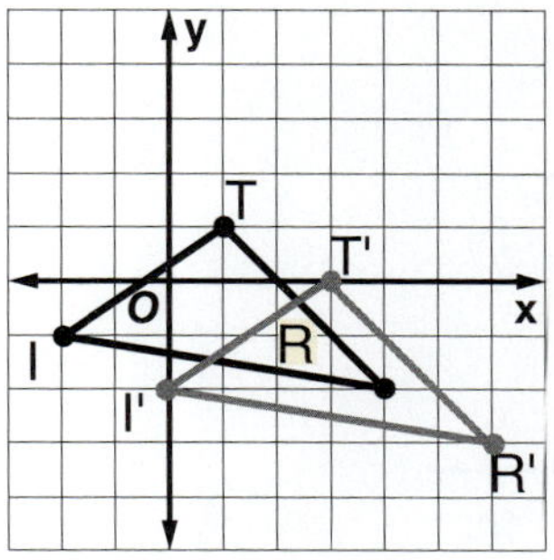

4.

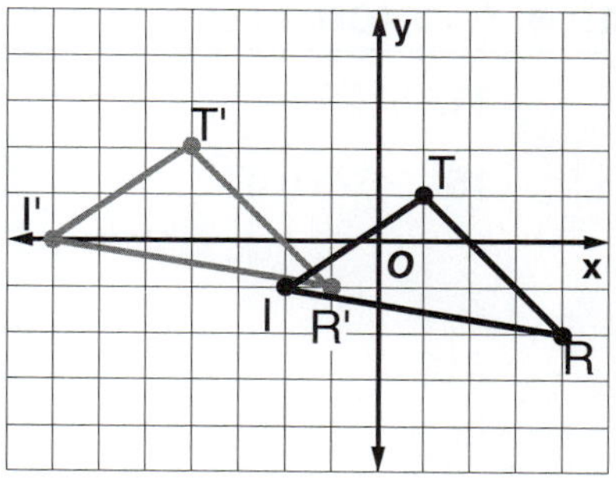

5.

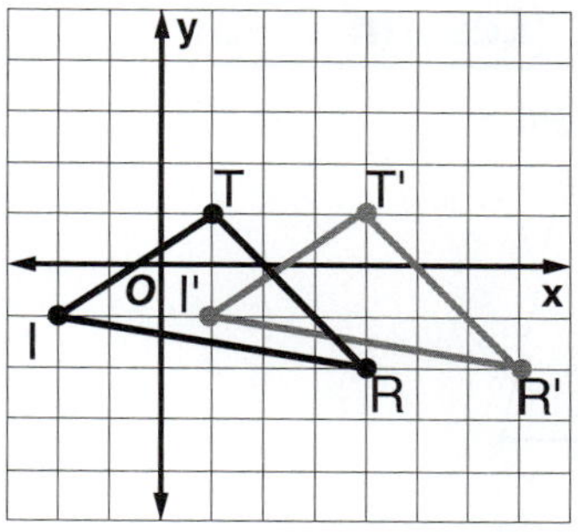

6.

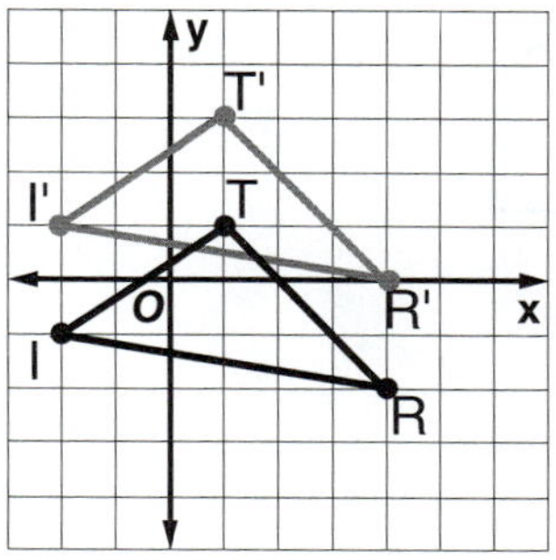

Page 696, Extra Practice, (Lesson 10-10)

7. $Q'(-1, -4)$, $U'(2, -2)$, $A'(1, -1)$, $D'(-2, -2)$

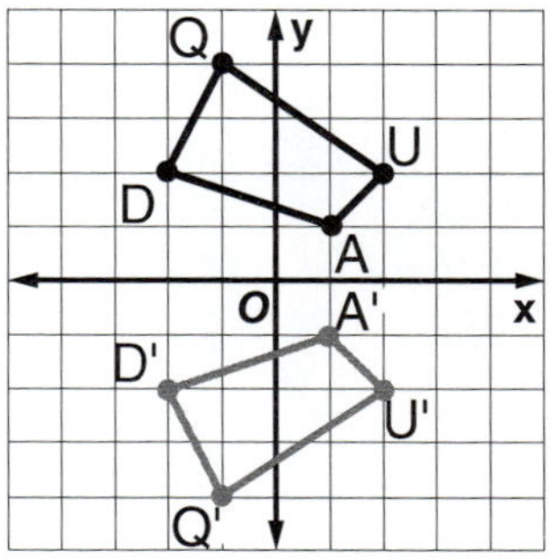

9.

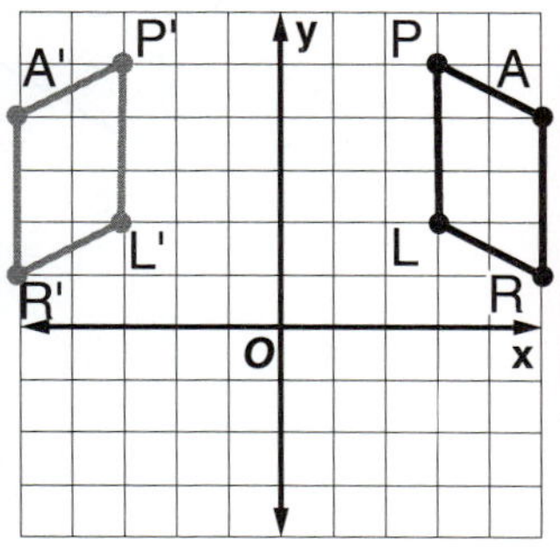

8.

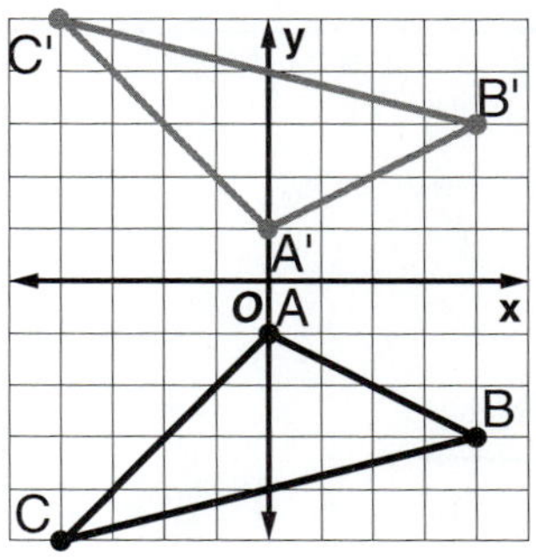

10.

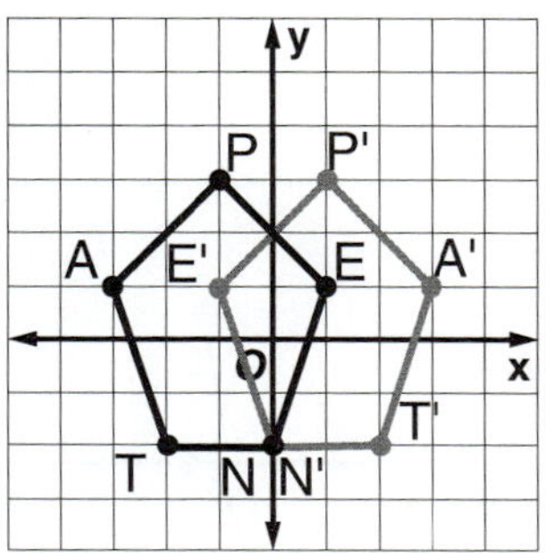

Page 698, Extra Practice, (Lesson 11-4)

9. 14,526.7 cm^2 **11.** 514.7 m^2

14. 25.2 yd^2 **15.** 1,626.0 mi^2

Page 700, Extra Practice, (Lesson 11-8)

1.
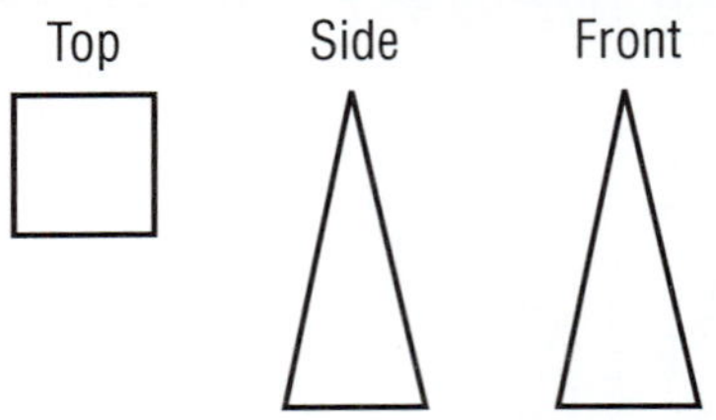

2.
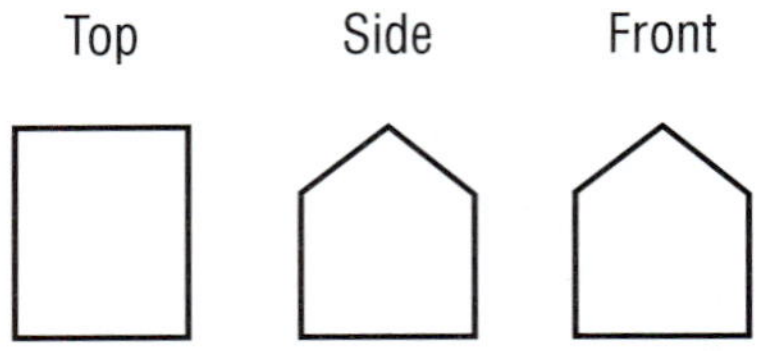

3.
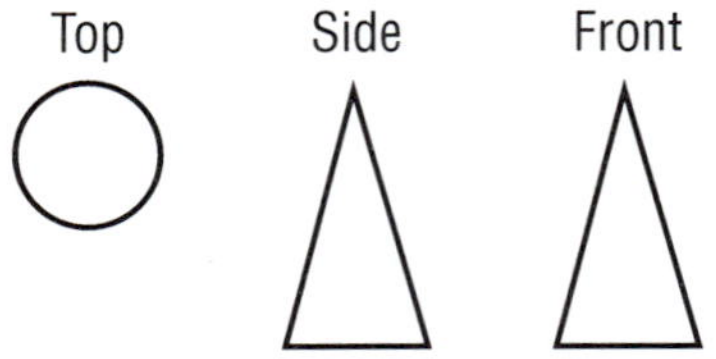

4.
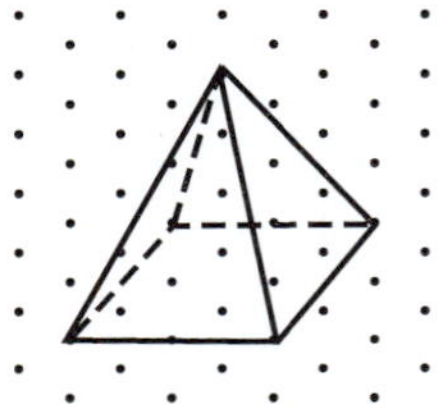

5.
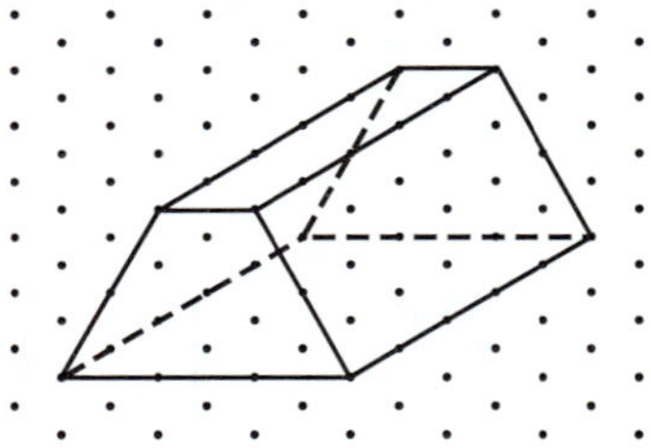

Page 701, Extra Practice, (Lesson 12-1)

16.
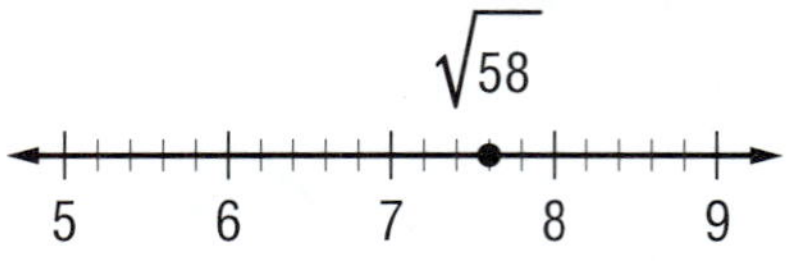

17.
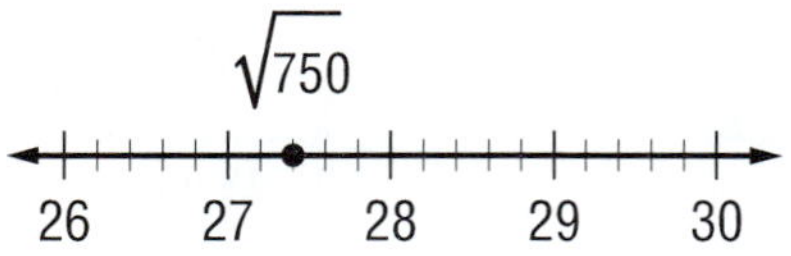

18.
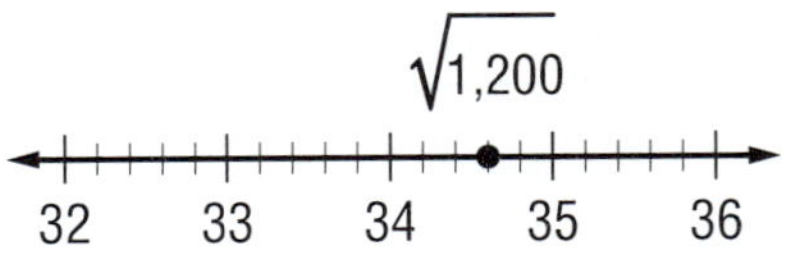

19.
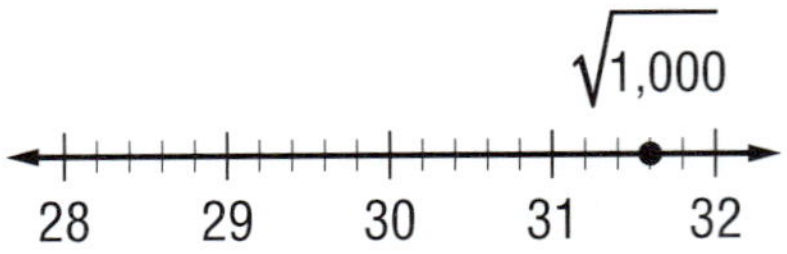

20.
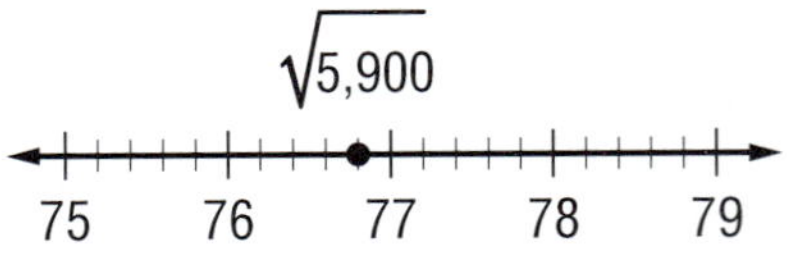

21.
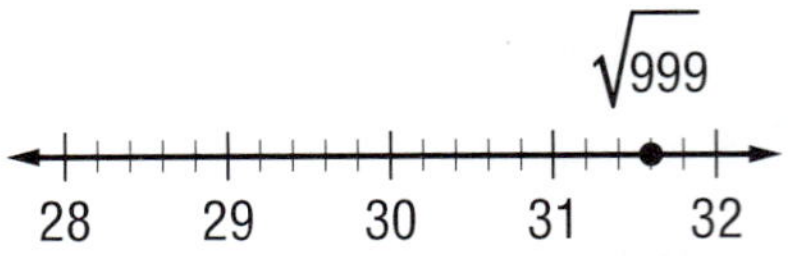

22.
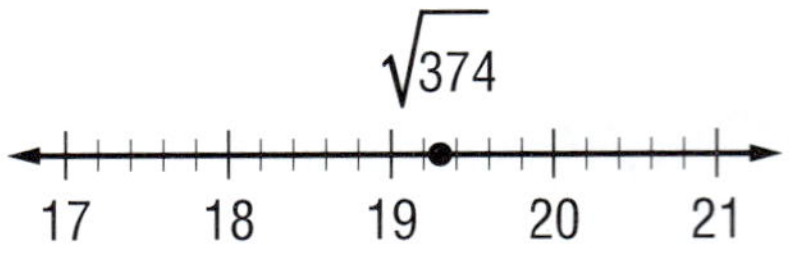

23.
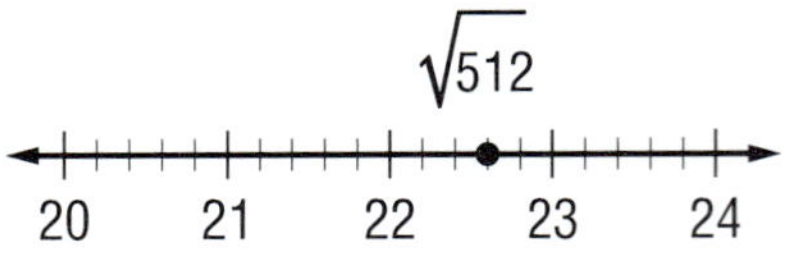

24.
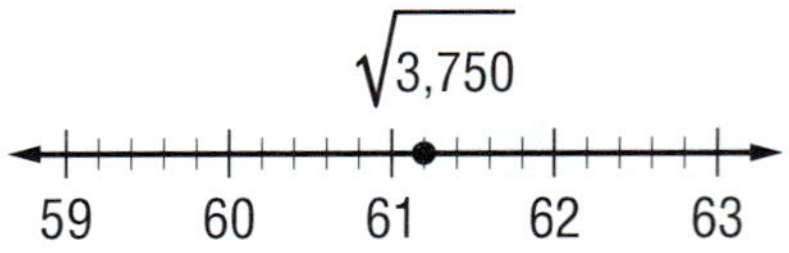

25.
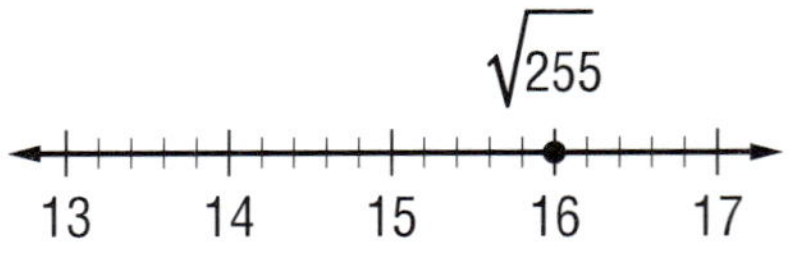

26.
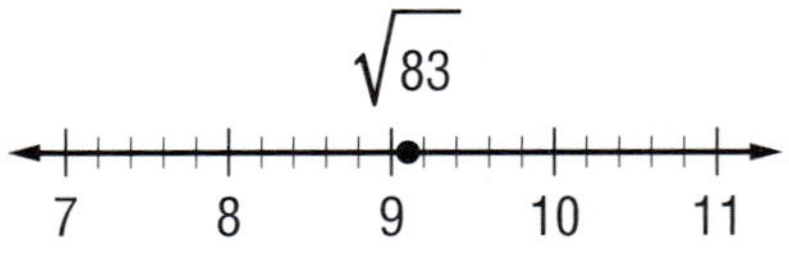

27.
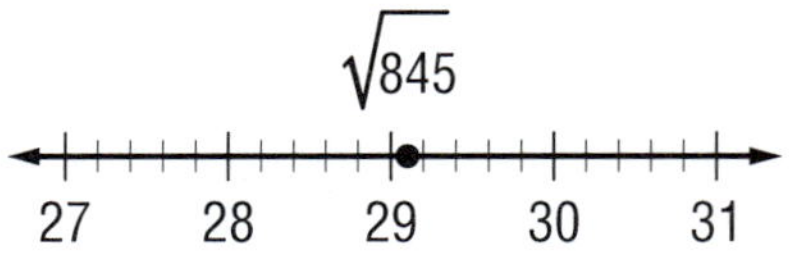

28.
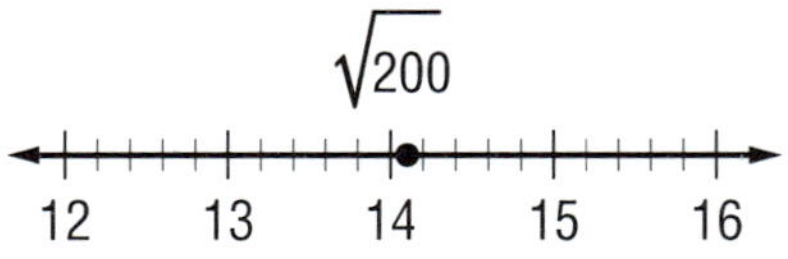

29.
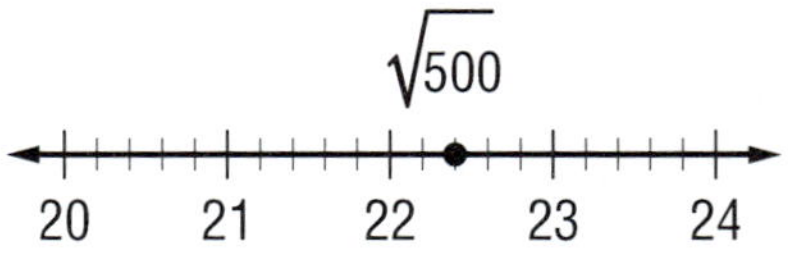

30.
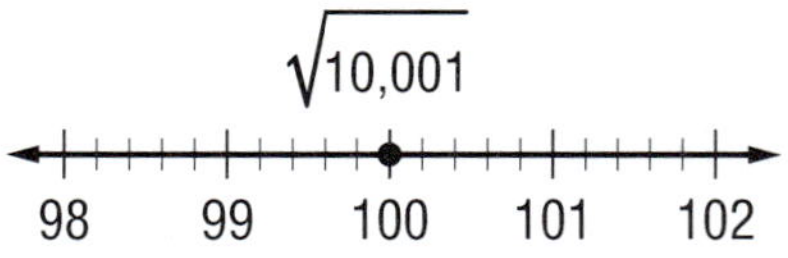

Page 703, Extra Practice, (Lesson 12-4)

8. 13,992 cm^2
11. 1,264.2 cm^2
12. 184.4 mi^2
14. 643.8 yd^2
15. 343.8 in^2
16. 470.6 mm^2

Page 703, Extra Practice, (Lesson 12-5)

9. 153.3 mi^2
10. 327.2 cm^2
11. 86.0 km^2
12. 7,321.8 m^2

Mixed Problem Solving

Page 705, Mixed Problem Solving, (Chapter 2)

2. –220, –436, –511, –282, –383, –505, –235, –230

3. –511, –505, –436, –383, –282, –235, –230, –220

5. Hot Tower (0, 3); Ferris Wheel (0, –4)

Page 706, Mixed Problem Solving, (Chapter 3)

12.

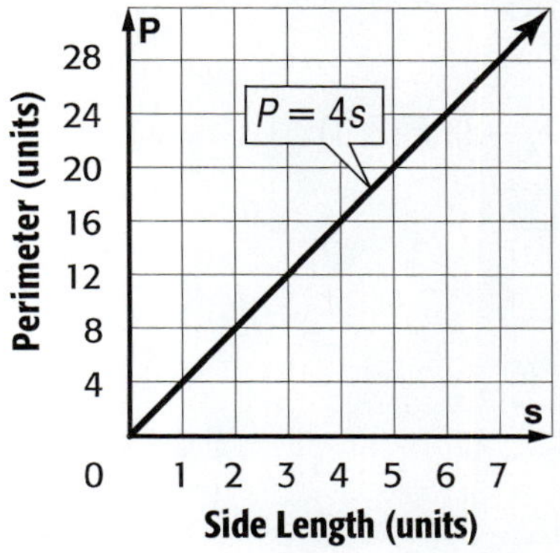

16.

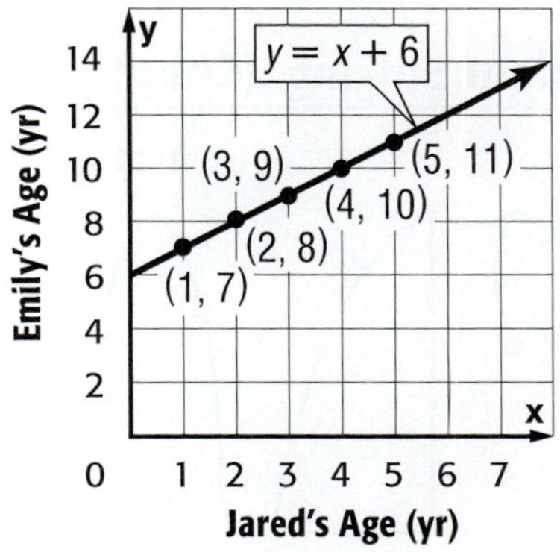

Page 709, Mixed Problem Solving, (Chapter 6)

5.

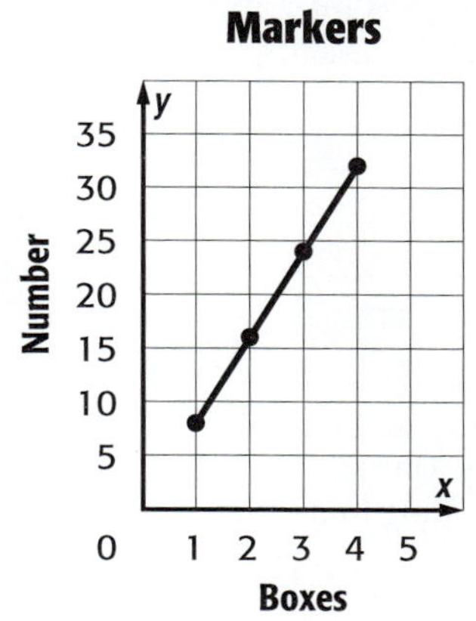

Page 710, Mixed Problem Solving, (Chapter 7)

3. Sample answer: $0.1 \times 70{,}000 = 7{,}000$ and $\frac{1}{2} \times 7{,}000 = 3{,}500$ mi^2

Page 711, Mixed Problem Solving, (Chapter 8)

1.

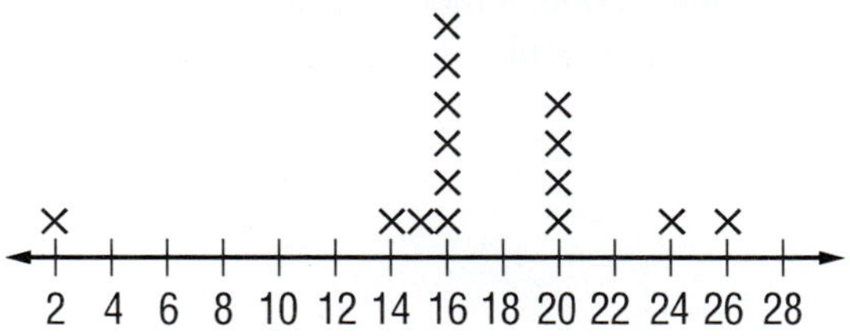

3. Sample answer: cluster 14–16: most of the energy bars have 14–16 grams of carbohydrates; gaps 2–14 and 16–20: outlier 2: one bar has 2 grams which is much less than the rest of the bars.

5.

Stem	Leaf
0	0 0 0 0
1	7
2	
3	
4	
5	
6	0
7	8
8	0 1 2 2 2 2 2 2 2

7|8 = 78 games

6.

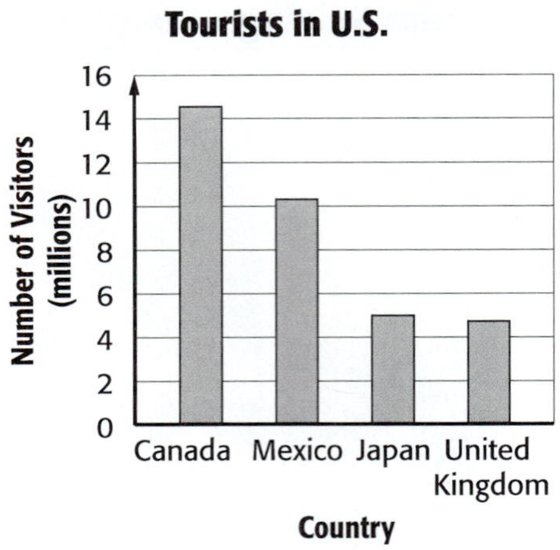

8.

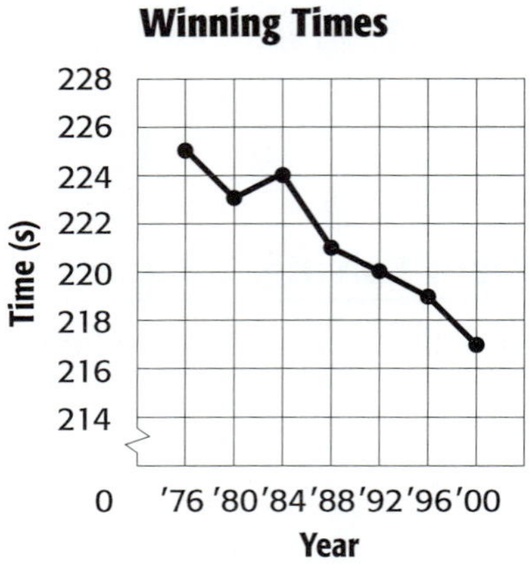

11. The conclusion is not valid; Sample answer: The sample is a voluntary response sample.

12. Sample answer: Mallory used the mean to calculate her average number number of monthly minutes. This is misleading because of the outliner, 602. A more appropriate measure to use to describe the data would be the median.

Page 712, Mixed Problem Solving, (Chapter 9)

4.

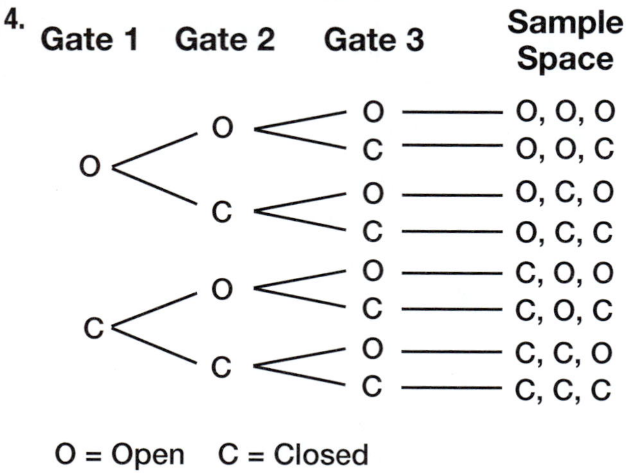

Page 713, Mixed Problem Solving, (Chapter 10)

4.

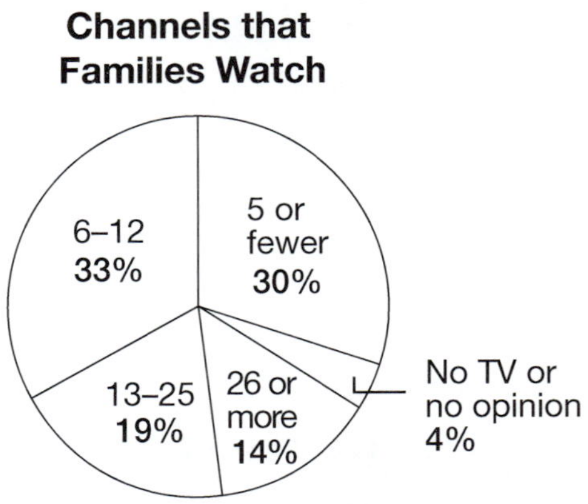

5. Sample answer: Victor could subtract 90° and 55° from 180°, leaving 35°. Thus, the measure of the third angle is 35°.

8. $m\angle 1 = 80°$, $m\angle 2 = 100°$, $m\angle 3 = 80°$, $m\angle 4 = 50°$, $m\angle 5 = 130°$, $m\angle 6 = 50°$, $m\angle 7 = 50°$, $m\angle 8 = 130°$, $m\angle 9 = 50°$, $m\angle 10 = 40°$.

9. Rectangle; sample answer: it was four right angles, but the four sides may not be congruent.

11. Sample answer: triangles and quadrilaterials; the sum of the angles where the vertices meet is 360°.

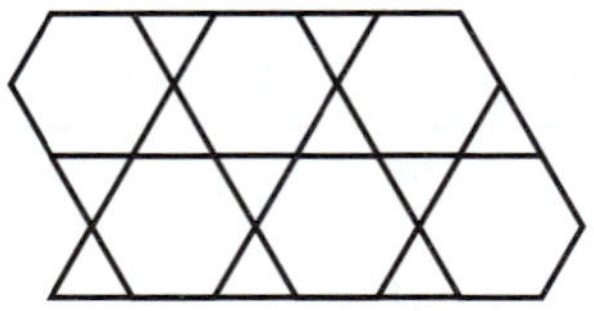

12. 3 units right, 4 units down

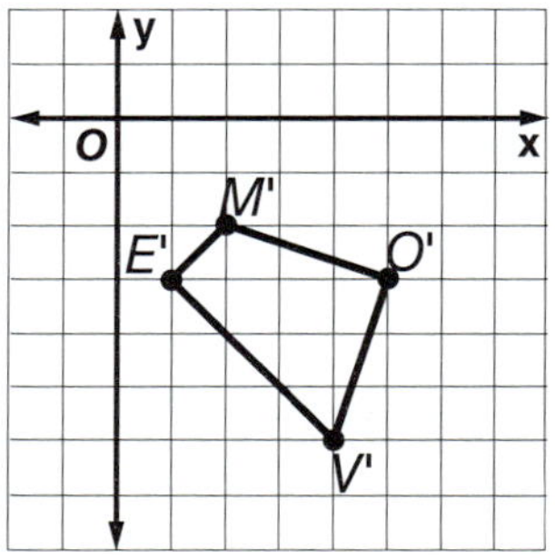

13. $M'(1, 2)$, $O'(-2, 1)$, $V'(-1, -2)$, $E'(2, 1)$

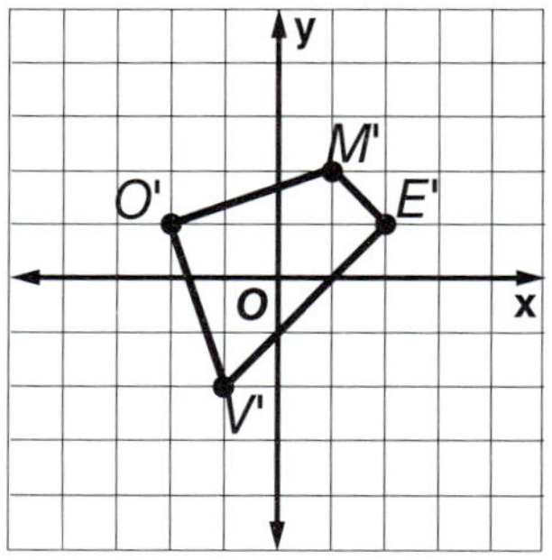

Page 714, Mixed Problem Solving, (Chapter 11)

9. Sample answer:

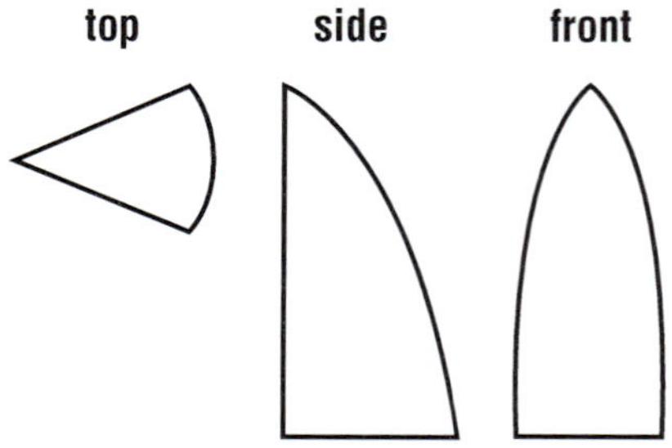

Preparing for Standardized Tests

Page 728, Short-Response Practice

8. The slope is 0.2. It means that Tyler charges \$0.20 per mile. The y-intercept is \$6. It means that there is an initial charge of \$6 for any delivery in addition to the miles driven.

13. $C'(-2, 1)$, $D'(-3, 4)$, $E'(-4, -2)$

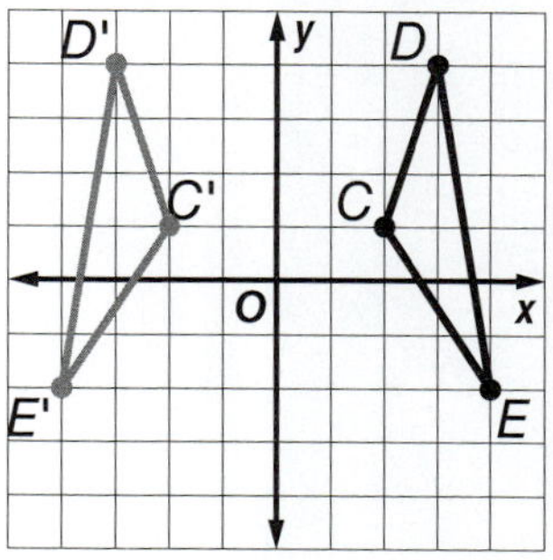

20. **World's Largest Flightless Birds**

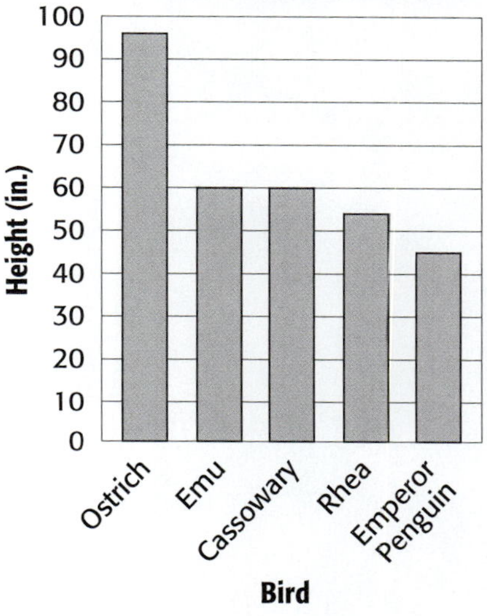

21. **Precipitation in Syracuse**

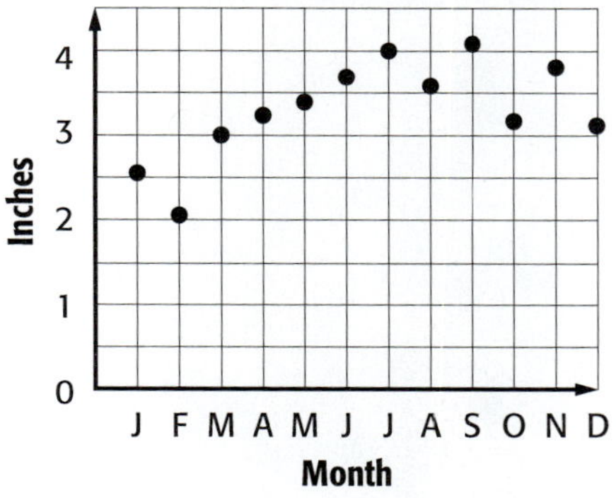

Sample answer: The amount of precipitation is lowest in February and then increases until July.

Page 732, Extended Response Practice

1a. Florida: about 10.0%; Colorado: about 0.4%; Alaska: about 7.3%; Iowa: about 0.7%; Rhode Island: about 15.1%

1b. Colorado, Iowa, Alaska, Florida, Rhode Island

1c. Sample answer: land area of 2,000 square miles, water area of 500 square miles, percent comparing water to total $= 500 \div 2{,}500 \times 100 = 20\%$

2a. **Cost to Rent a Crane**

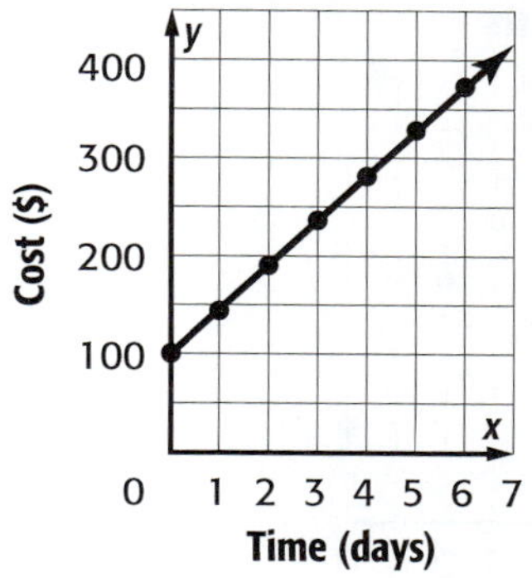

2b. The slope of the line is 45. That is the rental fee per day.

2c. \$550

3a. $2.80 = 0.40 + 0.04x$; 60 minutes.

3b. \$3.60

3c. Use the service that charges 40 cents per connection and 4 cents per minute.

4a. The area is 2,400 square inches.

4b. The dimensions are 80 inches by 120 inches. The area is 9,600 square inches.

4c. The ratio of the areas is 4 to 1.

4d. Sample answer: 60 inches by 80 inches

5a. The measure of $\angle 1$ is 60° since the sum of the measures of the angles of any triangle is 180°.

5b. The measure of $\angle 2$ is 110° because the two angles are supplementary. The measure of $\angle 3$ is 95° since the sum of the measures of the angles of a quadrilateral is always 360°.

6a. The area is about 452 square inches.

6b. The area is about 616 square inches.

6c. The percent increase in area is about 36%.

7a. A: 62.8 in^3; B: 78.5 in^3

7b. 0.8

7c. Sample answer: 5 in. by 4 in. by 7.85 in.

8a. **Normal Temperatures for Honolulu**

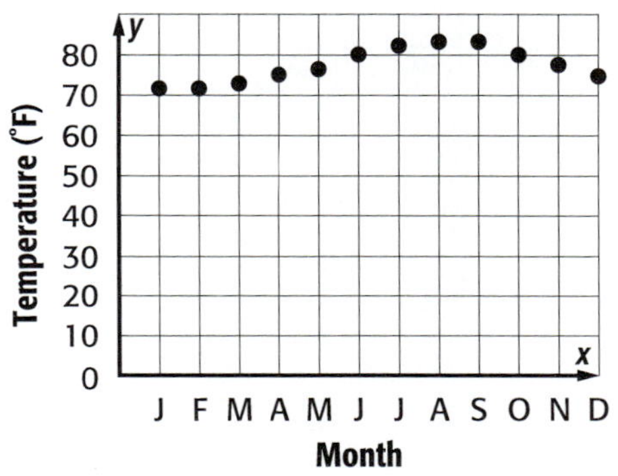

Sample answer: The points suggest a curve if connected. The curve is very slight but goes to its highest point during August and September and then curves downward again.

8b.

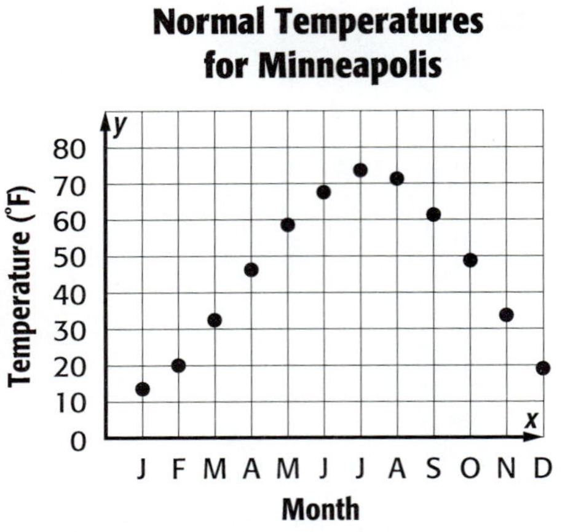

Sample answer: The points suggest a curve if connected. The curve is fairly steep as it goes up from January to July and then goes back downward to December.

8c. The range for Honolulu is 9, while the range for Minneapolis is 60. Sample reasons: Honolulu is close to the equator and is also an island, which affects the climate. Minneapolis is in the northern portion of the continental United States, so will have more varied temperatures.

9a.

	1	**2**	**3**	**4**
1	1, 1	1, 2	1, 3	1, 4
2	2, 1	2, 2	2, 3	2, 4
3	3, 1	3, 2	3, 3	3, 4
4	4, 1	4, 2	4, 3	4, 4

9b. $\frac{1}{16}$

9c. Using theoretical probability, you would get a sum of 4 threes out of sixteen times. So, $50 \cdot \frac{3}{16} \approx 9$ times

ISTEP+

Mastering the ISTEP+, Grade 7

This workbook combines ***Mastering the ISTEP+, Grade 7*** with the *Math Connects, Course 2 Study Guide and Intervention and Practice Workbook.*

Mastering the ISTEP+ contains a Prerequisite Skills Check to assess student retention of the previous grade's standards, a Diagnostic Test to evaluate the Grade 7 standards, a Problem Solving practice section, Practice by Standard with at least one page per indicator, and Practice Test with problems similar to those that might appear on the ISTEP+.

Flip the workbook over to find the *Math Connects, Course 2 Study Guide and Intervention and Practice Workbook.* This workbook contains at least two pages of instruction and practice for each lesson in *Indiana Math Connects, course 2.*

GET READY FOR THE ISTEP+

This spring, you will take your Grade 7 ISTEP+ test. ISTEP+ stands for Indiana Statewide Testing for Educational Progress-Plus. You will apply the concepts and skills that you have learned throughout the year in order to answer multiple-choice, gridded-response, constructed-response, and extended-response questions. The test will be given in two parts.

Part One

Part One contains constructed-response and extended-response questions. You will write answers to open-ended questions. You are required to show your work to receive full credit. In some cases, you will be required to explain, in words, how you arrived at your response.

Part Two

Part Two contains multiple-choice questions in which you will select the correct response from four answer choices. Your teacher will provide you with an answer sheet to fill in your answer choices. Part Two also contains gridded-response questions.

How Can I Get Ready?

The ISTEP+ covers the Indiana Academic Standards for Mathematics, Grade 7. The following pages give you practice questions similar to those found on the test. You can use these practice pages in the weeks before the test to determine if you are ready. If you are struggling with any of the items, lesson references are provided so you can go back and review from the pages in your textbook.

Number Sense and Computation

1. Which of the following statements BEST describes how to write 1.35×10^5 in standard notation? **(Lesson 1-2)** **(7.1.1)** **C**

A. Move the decimal point five places to the left and annex four zeros.

B. Move the decimal point five places to the left and annex five zeros.

C. Move the decimal point five places to the right and annex three zeros.

D. Multiply 1.35 by 5. Then annex five zeros.

2. Which of the following statements is TRUE? **(Lesson 12-1)** **(7.1.5)** **B**

A. $3^3 = \sqrt{3}$

B. $(\sqrt{3})^2 = 3$

C. $(\sqrt{3})^3 = 3$

D. $3^2 = \sqrt{3}$

3. A certain substance weighs 0.000531 gram. Which of the following expressions shows 0.000531 in scientific notation? **(Lesson 1-2)** **(7.1.1)** **A**

A. 5.31×10^{-4}

B. 5.31×10^{-3}

C. 5.31×10^{3}

D. 5.31×10^{4}

4. Jackson needs to show the relationship between 25% and $\frac{1}{3}$. Which statement should he write? **(Lesson 4-9)** **(7.1.5)** **A**

A. $25\% < \frac{1}{3}$

B. $25\% > \frac{1}{3}$

C. $\frac{1}{3} < 25\%$

D. $\frac{1}{3} = 25\%$

5. A square dog pen has an area of 16 square feet. The length of each side can be found by evaluating $\sqrt{16}$. Which of the following points shows the location of $\sqrt{16}$ on the number line? **(Lesson 1-3)** **(7.1.5)** **A**

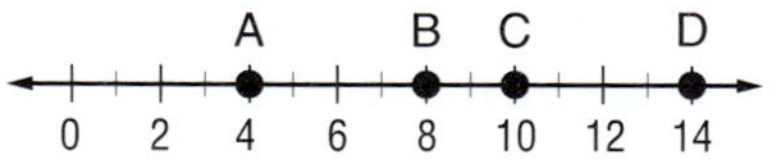

A. point A

B. point B

C. point C

D. point D

6. Which of the following expressions has the same value as $7^2 \cdot 8^3$? **(Lesson 1-2)** **(7.1.2)** **B**

A. $7 \cdot 2 \cdot 8 \cdot 3$

B. $7 \cdot 7 \cdot 8 \cdot 8 \cdot 8$

C. $7 \cdot 2 + 8 \cdot 3$

D. 56^6

7. How many square feet are in a square yard? **(Lesson 6-3)** **(7.1.9)** **C**

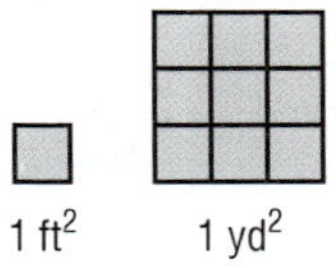

A. 3

B. 6

C. 9

D. 12

NEED EXTRA HELP?							
If You Missed Question...	1	2	3	4	5	6	7
Go to Lesson...	1-2	12-1	1-2	4-9	1-3	1-2	6-3
Academic Standards	7.1.1	7.1.5	7.1.1	7.1.5	7.1.5	7.1.2	7.1.9

ISTEP+ 1

The following rubric should be used to evaluate student answers to the constructed-response questions.

Rubric for Extended-Response Content Questions

Score Point 2

A score of two indicates a thorough understanding of the mathematical concepts embodied in the task.
The response
- shows algorithms, computations, and other content related work executed correctly and completely.

Score Point 1

A score of one indicates a partial understanding of the mathematical concepts embodied in the task.
The response
- contains errors in the execution of algorithms, computations, and/or other content related work.

Score Point 0

A score of zero indicates limited or no understanding of the mathematical concepts embodied in the task.

8. Jeremy wrote the following expression in his notebook.

$$m = n \cdot p$$

If m is a negative number, which of the following statements must be true? **(Lesson 2-6)** **(7.1.7)** **C**

A. Both of the variables n and p are positive numbers.
B. Both of the variables n and p are negative numbers.
C. The variables n and p represent numbers that have different signs.
D. Either of the variables n or p must be equal to zero.

9. GRIDDED RESPONSE Refer to the can of peas below. What is the cost in dollars per ounce of peas? **(Lesson 6-2)** **(7.1.9)**

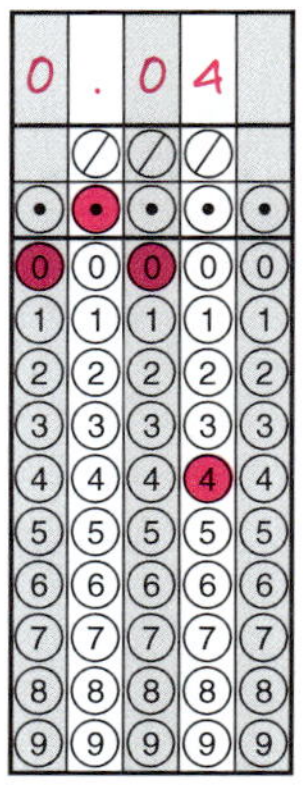

10. Shenequa forgot the rule for dividing integers. The table below gives several division expressions and their quotients.

Division Expression	Quotient
$8 \div 2$	4
$8 \div (-2)$	-4
$-8 \div 2$	-4
$-8 \div (-2)$	4

Which rule should she use for dividing integers? **(Lesson 2-8)** **(7.1.7)** **D**

A. The quotient of two integers has the same sign as the larger integer.
B. The quotient of two integers has the same sign as the divisor.
C. The quotient of two integers has the same sign as the dividend.
D. The quotient of two integers with the same sign is positive and the quotient of two integers with different signs is negative.

11. Which of the following statements is true? **(Lesson 4-9)** **(7.1.6)** **A**

A. $\sqrt{9} < 4$
B. $\sqrt{9} > 4$
C. $\sqrt{9} = 4$
D. $\sqrt{9} \geq 4$

EXTENDED RESPONSE

The number line models the equation $|x| = 8$.

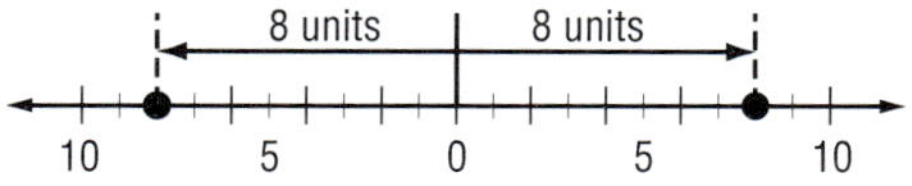

12. If $|x| = 8$, what are the possible values of x? Explain your answer. **(Lesson 2-1)** **(7.1.6, P.5.2)**

13. Refer to your answer above. If $|y| = y$ and $y = x$, what is the only possible value of y? Explain your answer. **(Lesson 2-1)** **(7.1.6, P.5.2)**

12. -8 or 8; Sample answer: If x is 8 units from zero, it could be either -8 or 8.
13. 8; Sample answer: From part a, x could be either 8 or -8. However, if y is the same value as x and the absolute value of y is the same value as y, then y can only be positive 8. $|-8| \neq -8$ but $|8| = 8$

NEED EXTRA HELP?						
If You Missed Question...	8	9	10	11	12	13
Go to Lesson...	2-6	6-2	2-8	4-9	2-1	2-1
Academic Standards	7.1.7	7.1.9	7.1.7	7.1.6	7.1.6, P.5.2	7.1.6, P.5.2

14. Randall's mom drove him 100 miles to his soccer playoffs. It took them 2 hours. Jessie's dad drove her 300 miles to an amusement park. It took them 6 hours. Which statement is TRUE? **(Lesson 6-2)** **(7.1.9)** C

A. Jessie's dad drove at a faster average rate than Randall's mom.

B. Randall's mom drove at a faster average rate than Jessie's dad.

C. They drove at the same average rate.

D. Jessie's dad drove a shorter distance than Randall's mom.

15. GRIDDED RESPONSE The number 4.75 is divided by 2. Then 1.17 is added to the quotient. what is the result? **(Lesson IN 4)** **(7.1.7)**

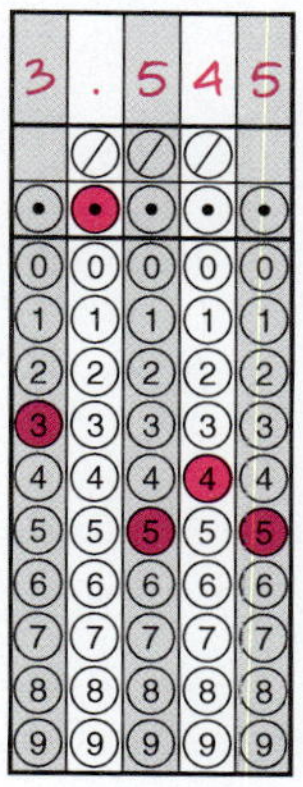

16. Which of the following shows 3,000,000 in scientific notation? **(Lesson IN 1)** **(7.1.1)** C

A. 3×10^4

B. 3×10

C. 3×10^6

D. 3×10^7

17. Which of the following shows the approximate location of $\sqrt{17} + (-4.1)$? **(Lesson 4-9)** **(7.1.6)** B

A.

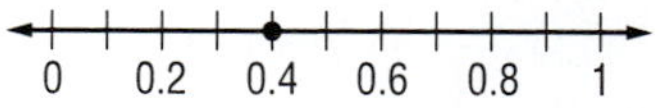

B.

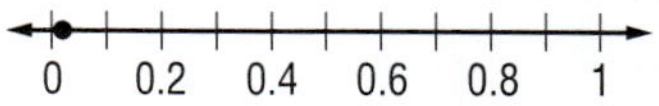

C.

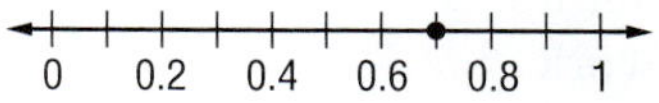

D.

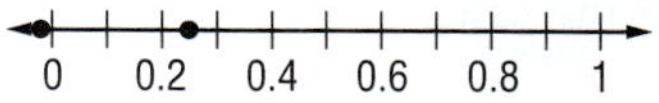

18. A number is squared. The result is 100. Which operation would you perform to find the original number? **(Lesson 12-1)** **(7.1.5)** D

A. $100 \div 2$

B. $100 - 50$

C. 100×100

D. $\sqrt{100}$

19. Which problem can be solved using the model shown? **(Lesson 5-5)** **(7.1.7)** C

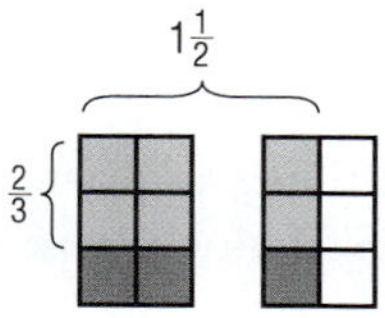

A. $1\frac{1}{2} + \frac{2}{3}$

B. $1\frac{1}{2} - \frac{2}{3}$

C. $1\frac{1}{2} \times \frac{2}{3}$

D. $1\frac{1}{2} \div \frac{2}{3}$

20. Canned soup is on sale at the grocery store at a price of $5 for 4 cans of soup. How much will it cost to buy 10 cans of soup at this price? **(Lesson 6-6)** **(7.1.9)** B

A. $10.00

B. $12.50

C. $17.50

D. $20.00

21. Which of the following represents *six hundred thousand* in scientific notation? **(Lesson IN 1)** **(7.1.1)** D

A. 6×10^8

B. 6×10^7

C. 6×10^6

D. 6×10^5

Rubric for Constructed-Response Problem-Solving Questions

Score Point 2

A score of two indicates a thorough understanding of the problem-solving concepts embodied in the task.

The response

- shows an appropriate strategy to solve the problem, and the strategy is executed correctly and completely.
- identifies all important elements of the problem and shows a complete understanding of the relationships among them.
- provides clear and complete explanations and/or interpretations when required.

Score Point 1

A score of one indicates a partial understanding of the problem-solving concepts embodied in the task. The response contains one or more of the following errors.

The response

- shows an appropriate strategy to solve the problem. However, the execution of the strategy contains errors and/or is incomplete.
- identifies some of the important elements of the problem and shows a general understanding of the relationships among them.
- provides incomplete, partial, or unclear explanations and/or interpretations when required.

Score Point 0

A score of zero indicates limited or no understanding of the problem-solving concepts embodied in the task.

NEED EXTRA HELP?								
If You Missed Question...	14	15	16	17	18	19	20	21
Go to Lesson...	6-2	IN 4	IN 1	4-9	12-1	5-5	6-6	IN 1
Academic Standards	7.1.9	7.1.7	7.1.1	7.1.6	7.1.5	7.1.7	7.1.9	7.1.1

The following rubric should be used to evaluate student answers to the extended-response questions.

Rubric for Extended-Response Content Questions

Score Point 3

A score of three indicates a thorough understanding of the mathematical concepts embodied in the task.

The response

- shows algorithms, computations, and other content related work executed correctly and completely.

Score Point 2

A score of two indicates a partial understanding of the mathematical concepts embodied in the task.

The response

- shows an attempt to execute algorithms, computations, and other content related work correctly and completely; computation errors may be present.

Score Point 1

A score of one indicates a limited understanding of the mathematical concepts embodied in the task.

The response

- contains major errors, or only a partial process.
- contains algorithms, computations, and other content related work which may only be partially correct.

Score Point 0

A score of zero indicates no understanding of the mathematical concepts embodied in the task.

Get Ready for the ISTEP+

22. Refer to the table below. Compare Statement A with Statement B in each row. Choose the missing statement. **(Lesson 12-1) (7.1.5) D**

Statement A	Statement B
$3 + 7 = 10$	$10 - 7 = 3$
$5 \times 6 = 30$	$30 \div 6 = 5$
$8^2 = 64$	■

A. $64 \div 2 = 32$
B. $64 \div 2 = 8$
C. $8 \times 8 = 64$
D. $\sqrt{64} = 8$

23. Which of these numbers has the GREATEST value? **(Lesson IN 1) (7.1.1) C**

A. 9.62×10^7
B. -3.22×10^9
C. 8.0×10^8
D. 7.35×10^{-9}

24. Simplify the expression $6^8 \times 6^4$. **(Lesson 1-2) (7.1.2) B**

A. 6^4
B. 6^{12}
C. 6^{32}
D. 36^{12}

25. Which response describes ALL the members of the set below? **(Lesson 4-9) (7.1.6) B**

$\{-77, \frac{5}{\sqrt{81}}, 8.266597, 0.52\overline{3}, 56\}$

A. irrational numbers
B. rational numbers
C. natural numbers
D. whole numbers

26. What is the prime factorization of 180 written in exponential form? **(Lesson 4-1) (7.1.3) A**

A. $2^2 \times 3^2 \times 5$
B. $2^2 \times 3 \times 5^2$
C. $2^3 \times 3 \times 2^2$
D. $2^3 \times 3^2 \times 5$

27. The Jeffers family went to a restaurant fo lunch. The bill came to \$27. If they want to leave a 15% tip, which is the BEST estimate for how much tip money they should leave? **(Lesson 7-2) (7.1.8) C**

A. \$6.00
B. \$5.00
C. \$4.00
D. \$3.00

CONSTRUCTED RESPONSE

Kirima is buying a new coat. The original price of the coat she would like to buy is \$53.00. The sign at the right is displayed in the store window. **(Lesson 7-7) (7.1.8, P.1.2)**

28. Find the amount of the discount. Show all work. **\$15.90**

29. Find the sale price of the coat after the discount is applied. Show all work. **\$37.10**

30. If the tax rate is 8%, find the amount of tax on the coat after the discount is applied. Round to the nearest cent. Show all work. **\$2.97**

31. Find the final cost of the coat, after both the discount and the sales tax are applied. Show all work. **\$40.07**

NEED EXTRA HELP?										
If You Missed Question...	22	23	24	25	26	27	28	29	30	31
Go to Lesson...	12-1	IN 1	1-2	4-9	4-1	7-2	7-7	7-7	7-7	7-7
Academic Standards	7.1.5	7.1.1	7.1.2	7.1.6	7.1.3	7.1.8	7.1.8, P.1.2	7.1.8, P.1.2	7.1.8, P.1.2	7.1.8, P.1.2

32. Which of the numbers below is an irrational number? **(Lesson 4-9)** **(7.1.6)** C

A. −2.7 **C.** $\sqrt{18}$

B. $\frac{5}{93}$ **D.** $\sqrt{49}$

33. **GRIDDED RESPONSE** Jordan ran the 400-yard dash in 52.78 seconds on Tuesday. On Thursday, he ran the 400-yard dash in 49.83 seconds. By how many seconds was his time faster on Thursday than Tuesday? **(Lesson IN 4)** **(7.1.7)**

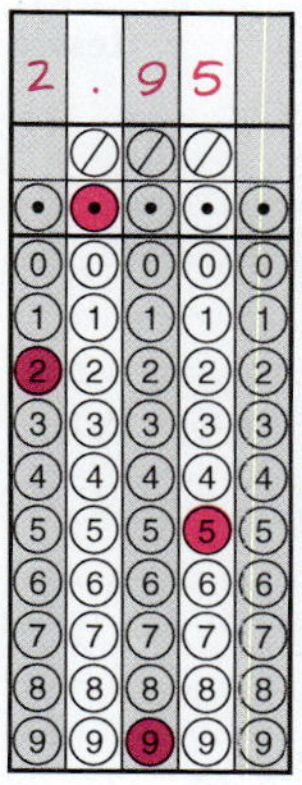

34. Keisha found the prime factorization of 24 and 36 using factor trees as shown below. What is the greatest common factor of 24 and 36? **(Lesson 4-1)** **(7.1.3)** D

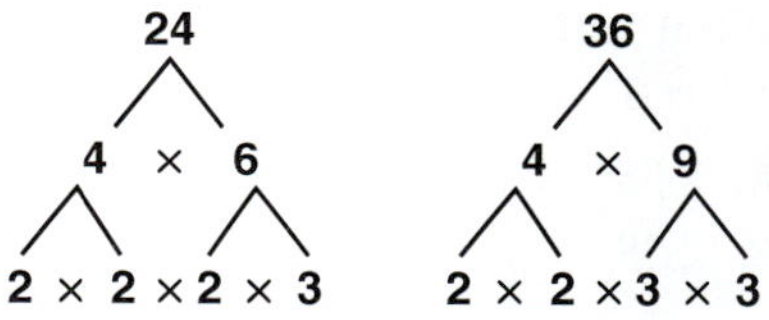

A. 2 **C.** 6

B. 3 **D.** 12

35. Wallace ran more than 12 miles in 3 hours. If he ran at a constant rate, what is the SLOWEST he could have run? **(Lesson 6-2)** **(7.1.9)** B

A. 3 miles per hour

B. 4 miles per hour

C. 12 miles per hour

D. 36 miles per hour

36. The distance from Earth to the Sun is about 150,000,000 kilometers. What is this number written in scientific notation? **(Lesson IN 1)** **(7.1.1)** C

A. 1.5×10^7 kilometers

B. 15×10^7 kilometers

C. 1.5×10^8 kilometers

D. 1.5×10^9 kilometers

37. Brent wants to compare the two numbers below. Which symbol makes the statement true? **(Lesson IN 1)** **(7.1.1)** A

5×10^5 ● 5,000,000

A. $<$

B. $>$

C. $=$

D. $\geq$

38. Find the prime factorization of the perimeter of the quadrilateral below. **(Lesson 4-1)** **(7.1.3)** B

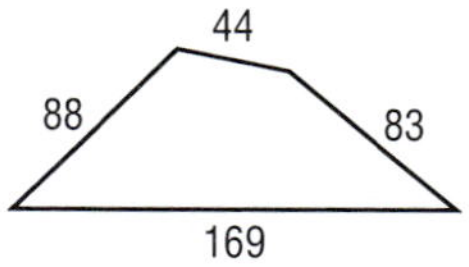

A. $2^6 \times 3$

B. $2^7 \times 3$

C. $2^8 \times 3$

D. $2^9 \times 3$

39. If the area of a square is 196 square inches, what is the length in inches of the side of the square? **(Lesson 12-1)** **(7.1.5)** D

A. 11 **C.** 13

B. 12 **D.** 14

Rubric for Extended-Response Problem-Solving Questions

Score Point 3

A score of three indicates a thorough understanding of the problem-solving concepts embodied in the task. The response

- shows an appropriate strategy to solve the problem, and the strategy is executed correctly and completely.
- identifies all important elements of the problem and shows a complete understanding of the relationships among them.
- provides clear and complete explanations and/or interpretations when required.

Score Point 2

A score of two indicates a partial understanding of the problem-solving concepts embodied in the task. The response contains one or more of the following errors. The response

- shows an appropriate strategy to solve the problem. However, the execution of the strategy contains computation errors or lacks an essential element.
- identifies some of the important elements of the problem and shows a general understanding of the relationships among them.
- provides incomplete or unclear explanations and/or interpretations when required.

Score Point 1

A score of one indicates a limited understanding of the problem-solving concepts embodied in the task. The response contains one or more of the following errors. The response

- shows an appropriate strategy to solve the problem. However, the execution of the strategy is applied incorrectly and/or is incomplete.
- shows a limited understanding of the relationships among the elements of the problem.
- provides incomplete, unclear, or omitted explanations and/or interpretations when required.

Score Point 0

A score of zero indicates limited or no understanding of the problem-solving concepts embodied in the task.

NEED EXTRA HELP?

If You Missed Question...	32	33	34	35	36	37	38	39
Go to Lesson...	4-9	IN 4	4-1	6-2	IN 1	IN 1	4-1	12-1
Academic Standards	7.1.6	7.1.7	7.1.3	7.1.9	7.1.1	7.1.1	7.1.3	7.1.5

40. Which of the following is the prime factorization of 42? **(Lesson 4-1)** **(7.1.3)** **B**

A. 2×3^2 **C.** $2^2 \times 7$
B. $2 \times 3 \times 7$ **D.** $3^2 \times 7$

41. If each dimension of the rectangle is doubled, what is the percent of increase in the area? **(Lesson 7-6)** **(7.1.8)** **C**

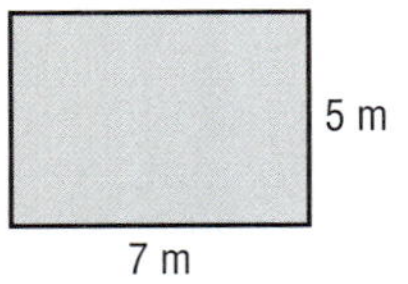

A. 100% **C.** 300%
B. 200% **D.** 400%

42. Hannah spent \$11.75 at the bakery. She bought 3 donuts at \$0.75 each and 6 bagels for \$1.25 each. How much money did she leave for a tip? **(Lesson IN 4)** **(7.1.7)** **D**

A. \$1.25 **C.** \$1.75
B. \$1.50 **D.** \$2.00

43. Simplify the expression below. **(Lesson 1-4)** **(7.1.2)** **C**

$$(4^2 - 2^3) + (3 \times 4 + 8)$$

A. 44 **C.** 28
B. 38 **D.** 22

44. **GRIDDED RESPONSE** Wesley invests \$260 in a savings account. His account pays 2.25% simple interest. If he does not add or withdraw any money again, how much interest in dollars will Wesley's account earn after 4 years of simple interest? **(Lesson 7-8)** **(7.1.8)**

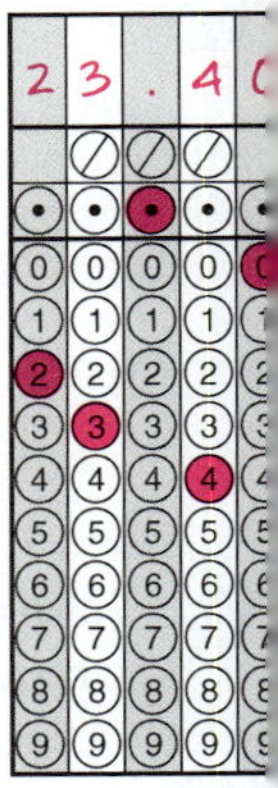

45. Which model represents the square of 3? **(Lesson 1-3)** **(7.1.5)** **A**

A. 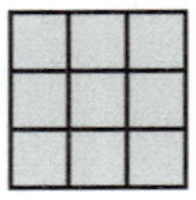

C. 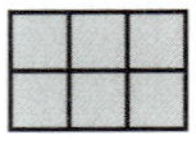

B. 

D. 

46. What is the value of $-3.4 \times \frac{3}{4}$? **(Lesson 5-5)** **(7.1.7)** **D**

A. 2.55
B. 2.38
C. -2.38
D. -2.55

CONSTRUCTED RESPONSE

For homework, Mrs. Lee required her students to find the prime factorization of several four-digit numbers, such as 1,176. **(Lesson 4-1)** **(7.1.3, P.1.1)**

47. What is the prime factorization of 1,176? **$1{,}176 = 2 \times 2 \times 2 \times 3 \times 7 \times 7$**

48. How is the prime factorization of 1,176 written in exponential form? **$1{,}176 = 2^3 \times 3 \times 7^2$**

49. Without multiplying 1,176 times 3, find the prime factorization of the product of 1,176 and 3. Write using exponential form. **$2^3 \times 3^2 \times 7^2$**

NEED EXTRA HELP?										
If You Missed Question...	40	41	42	43	44	45	46	47	48	49
Go to Lesson...	4-1	7-6	IN 4	1-4	7-8	1-3	5-5	4-1	4-1	4-1
Academic Standards	7.1.3	7.1.8	7.1.7	7.1.2	7.1.8	7.1.5	7.1.7	7.1.3, P.1.1	7.1.3, P.1.1	7.1.3, P.1.1

ISTEP+ 6

Algebra and Functions

1. The expression below represents the total cost in dollars, including postage p of a number of theater tickets n.

$$15n + p$$

Based on the expression above, what is the total cost of 5 tickets when postage is $4? **(Lesson 1-6)** **(7.2.1)** D

A. $19 **C.** $64
B. $34 **D.** $79

2. Solve the inequality below for x.
(Lesson IN 2) **(7.2.2)** A

$$5x \geq 30$$

A. $x \geq 6$
B. $x \leq 6$
C. $x \geq 150$
D. $x \leq 150$

3. Simplify $4^2 + 6 \div 2 + 4$. **(Lesson 1-4)** **(7.2.3)** C

A. 15 **C.** 23
B. 17 **D.** 28

4. Which of the following tables shows a proportional relationship between the variables x and y? **(Lesson 6-6)** **(7.2.7)** A

A.

x	1	2	3	4
y	3	6	9	12

B.

x	1	2	3	4
y	3	4	5	6

C.

x	1	2	3	4
y	1	4	9	16

D.

x	1	2	3	4
y	3	6	9	10

5. Which expression can be written as $4(5 + 9)$? **(Lesson 1-8)** **(7.2.3)** B

A. $5 \cdot 4 + 5 \cdot 9$
B. $4 \cdot 5 + 4 \cdot 9$
C. $9 \cdot 5 + 9 \cdot 4$
D. $4 + 5 \cdot 4 + 9$

6. **GRIDDED RESPONSE** What value of x makes the following equation TRUE? **(Lesson 3-5)** **(7.2.2)**

$$\frac{x}{3} + 8 = 16$$

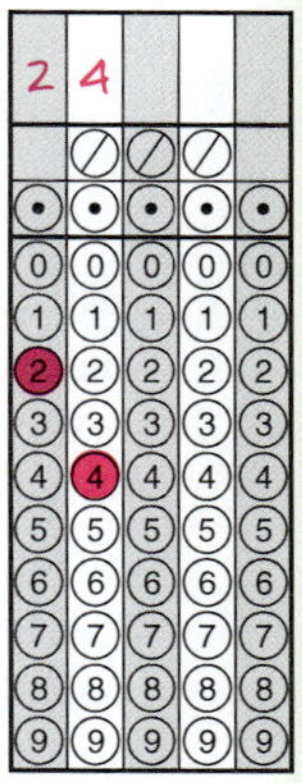

7. The formula for the density of a solid is $D = \frac{M}{V}$ where M represents mass and V represents volume. What is the density of a block with a mass of 10 kilograms with a volume of 5 cubic meters? **(Lesson 1-6)** **(7.2.1)** C

A. $15\ kg/m^3$
B. $10.5\ kg/m^3$
C. $2\ kg/m^3$
D. $0.5\ kg/m^3$

8. Find $-a + b - c$ if $a = 5$, $b = -2$, and $c = -6$. **(Lesson 1-8)** **(7.2.3)** B

A. -13
B. -1
C. 1
D. 9

NEED EXTRA HELP?

If You Missed Question...	1	2	3	4	5	6	7	8
Go to Lesson...	1-6	IN 2	1-4	6-6	1-8	3-5	1-6	1-8
Academic Standards	7.2.1	7.2.2	7.2.3	7.2.7	7.2.3	7.2.2	7.2.1	7.2.3

ISTEP+ 7

Get Ready for the ISTEP+

9. GRIDDED RESPONSE What is the value of the expression $3x^2 + 2y + 5$ when $x = 4$ and $y = 1$? **(Lesson 1-6)** **(7.2.3)**

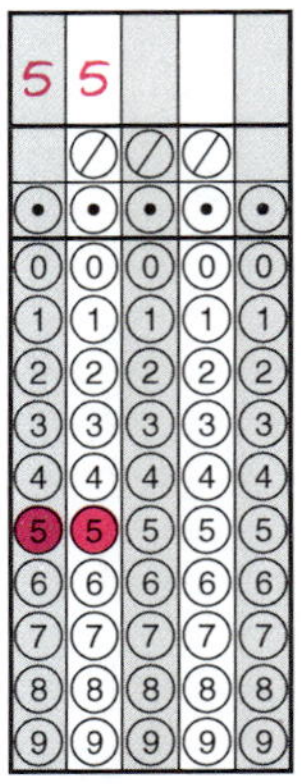

10. Brittany needs \$35 to go to the water park. She has \$11. She earns \$6 per hour working at her job. The equation $6h + 11 = 35$ shows this relationship. How many hours does Brittany need to work to earn enough money to go to the park? **(Lesson 3-5)** **(7.2.4)** D

A. 7 **C.** 5
B. 6 **D.** 4

11. The expression $4n + 3$ represents the total cost in dollars of renting a certain number of movies. If n represents the number of movies, what is the total cost to rent 3 movies? **(Lesson 1-6)** **(7.2.3)** C

A. \$9 **C.** \$15
B. \$12 **D.** \$46

12. Find the slope of the line below that shows the cost of T-shirts and the number of T-shirts sold. **(Lesson 6-3)** **(7.2.5)** B

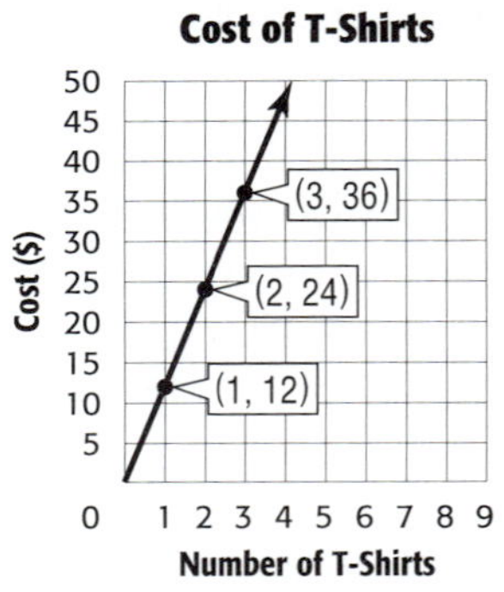

A. 6 **C.** 18
B. 12 **D.** 24

13. Which of the following is a direct variation? **(Lesson IN 7)** **(7.2.7)** C

A. $y = 2x + 1$
B. $y = 2$
C. $y = 2x$
D. $y = \frac{1}{2}x - 3$

14. Kareem has already read 94 pages of a novel. If he reads 25 more pages every day, which expression shows how many pages total he will have completed after x days? **(Lesson 3-1)** **(7.2.1)** A

A. $25x + 94$
B. $25(x + 94)$
C. $25 - 94$
D. $94x + 25$

CONSTRUCTED RESPONSE

The equation $C = 29.95 + 0.1n$ gives the monthly cost C of a cell phone plan with n number of text messages sent. **(Lesson IN 3)** **(7.2.4, P.5.3)**

15. Solve the equation for n. Show all work. $n = \frac{C - 29.95}{0.1}$

16. Find the number of text messages that can be sent if the total cost is \$31.45. Show all work. 15

NEED EXTRA HELP?								
If You Missed Question...	9	10	11	12	13	14	15	16
Go to Lesson...	1-6	3-5	1-6	6-3	IN 7	3-1	IN 3	IN 3
Academic Standards	7.2.3	7.2.4	7.2.3	7.2.5	7.2.7	7.2.1	7.2.4, P.5.3	7.2.4, P.5.3

17. Use the formula $A = bh$ to find the base length of a rhombus with an area of 40 in^2 and a height of 5 inches. **(Lesson 3-6) (7.2.4) C**

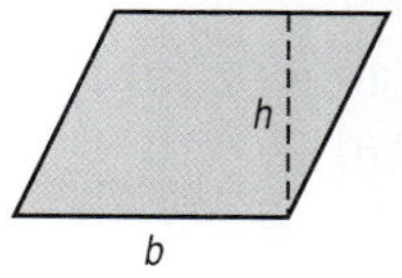

A. 15 in. **C.** 8 in.
B. 10 in. **D.** 6 in.

18. What is the value of b if $-5b - 6 = -21$? **(Lesson 6-6) (7.2.2) C**

A. -3
B. -2
C. 3
D. 4

19. Which line graphed below shows a direct variation with a constant of variation of 2? **(Lesson IN 7) (7.2.7) D**

A.
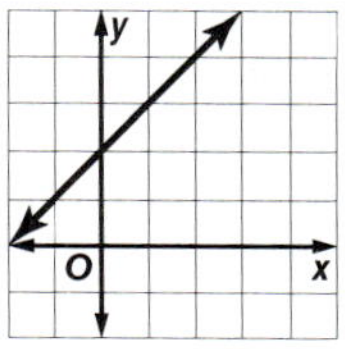

C.
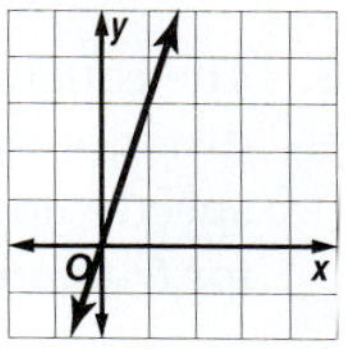

B.
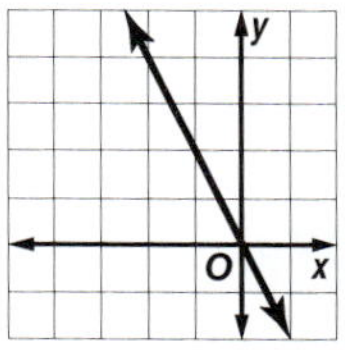

D.
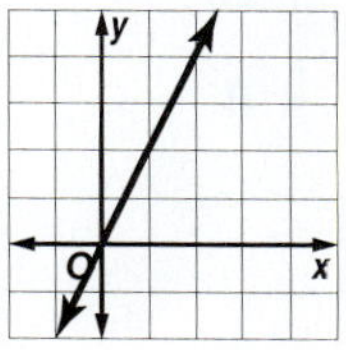

20. Simplify $-62 - 6 \div (2 + 4)$. **(Lesson 1-4) (7.2.3) D**

A. 5
B. 35
C. -5
D. -63

21. Anna withdrew $40 from her savings account and the new balance is $176. Which equation could be used to find the starting balance? **(Lesson 3-2) (7.2.4) A**

A. $s - 40 = 176$
B. $s + 40 = 176$
C. $s = 176 - 40$
D. $s + 176 = 40$

22. Which of the following tables does NOT show a proportional relationship between the variables x and y? **(Lesson 6-6) (7.2.7) C**

A.

x	1	2	3	4
y	5	10	15	20

B.

x	1	2	3	4
y	10	20	30	40

C.

x	1	2	3	4
y	3	4	5	6

D.

x	1	2	3	4
y	4	8	12	16

23. Which of the following graphs passes through the point (0, 3) and has a slope of -2? **(Lesson IN 6) (7.2.6) A**

A.
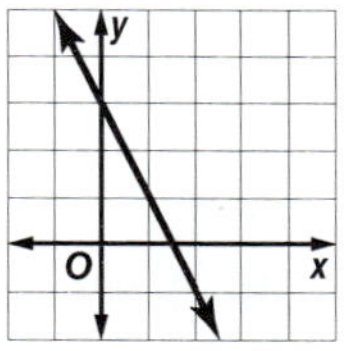

C.
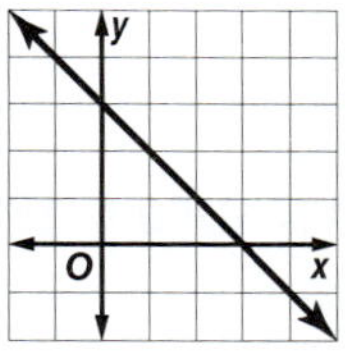

B.
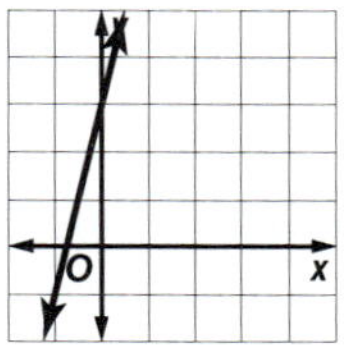

D.
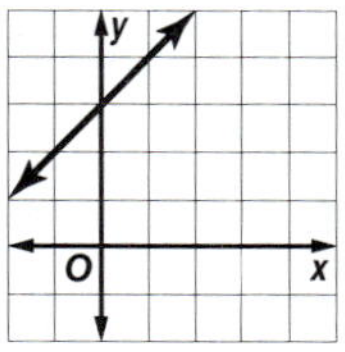

NEED EXTRA HELP?							
If You Missed Question...	17	18	19	20	21	22	23
Go to Lesson...	3-6	6-6	IN 7	1-4	3-2	6-6	IN 6
Academic Standards	7.2.4	7.2.2	7.2.7	7.2.3	7.2.4	7.2.7	7.2.6

24. Matthew has 3 boxes with 24 apples each and 4 boxes with 15 oranges each. Which expression CANNOT be used to find the total number of items he has? **(Lesson 1-4)** **(7.2.3)** **C**

A. $3(24) + 4(15)$

B. $4 \times 15 + 3 \times 24$

C. $5 \times (24 + 15)$

D. $15 + 15 + 15 + 15 + 24 + 24 + 24$

25. Solve the inequality below for k. **(Lesson IN 2)** **(7.2.2)** **C**

$$3k + 7 \geq 16$$

A. $k \leq 3$

B. $k \leq 2$

C. $k \geq 3$

D. $k \geq 2$

26. What is the value of g if $7g + 8 = -13$? **(Lesson 6-6)** **(7.2.2)** **A**

A. $g = -3$

B. $g = \frac{-5}{7}$

C. $g = \frac{5}{7}$

D. $g = 3$

27. Carla spent \$32.10 for jeans and a shirt. The total included \$2.10 for sales tax. Which equation could be used to find the cost of the two items before taxes? **(Lesson 3-2)** **(7.2.1)** **B**

A. $x - 2.10 = 32.10$

B. $x + 2.10 = 32.10$

C. $x + 32.10 = 2.10$

D. $x - 32.10 = 2.10$

28. Party House charges \$35 plus \$6.50 per person for a birthday party. Mrs. Lutz wants to spend no more than \$120 on he party. Which of the following inequalitie could be used to solve this problem? **(Lesson 6-6)** **(7.2.2)** **C**

A. $6.5x + 35 \geq 120$

B. $6.5 + 35x \geq 120$

C. $6.5x + 35 \leq 120$

D. $6.5 + 35x \leq 120$

29. The equation $d = rt$ is used to find the distance traveled d, given the rate of speed r and the time t. Solve the equatio for t. **(Lesson IN 3)** **(7.2.4)** **A**

A. $t = \frac{d}{r}$

B. $r = \frac{d}{t}$

C. $r = \frac{t}{d}$

D. $t = \frac{t}{d}$

EXTENDED RESPONSE

The steps Lori took to evaluate the expression $6b + 6 \div 6$ when $b = 7$ are shown at the right. **(Lesson 1-4)** **(7.2.3, P.4.1)**

$6b + 6 \div 6 = 6 \times 7 + 6 \div 6$
$= 42 + 6 \div 6$
$= 48 \div 6$ or 8

30. Explain what Lori did on Line 1. Identify and correct any mistakes. **She replaced *b* with 7. She did not make any mistakes.**

31. Explain what Lori did on Line 2. Identify and correct any mistakes. **She multiplied 6 by 7. She did not make any mistakes**

32. Explain what Lori did on Line 3. Identify and correct any mistakes. **She added 42 and 6. Then she divided 48 by 6. She should have divided 6 by 6 to get 1, before adding 42. The correct answer is 43.**

NEED EXTRA HELP?									
If You Missed Question...	24	25	26	27	28	29	30	31	32
Go to Lesson...	1-4	IN 2	6-6	3-2	6-6	IN 3	1-4	1-4	1-4
Academic Standards	7.2.3	7.2.2	7.2.2	7.2.1	7.2.2	7.2.4	7.2.3, P.4.1	7.2.3, P.4.1	7.2.3, P.4.1

33. Use the formula $A = \frac{1}{2}bh$ to find the height of a triangle with a base of 10 centimeters and an area of 35 square centimeters. **(Lesson 3-3)** **(7.2.4)** **B**

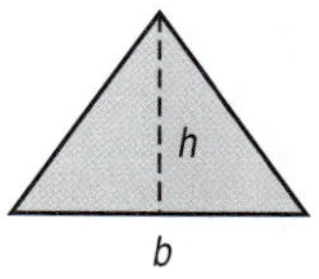

A. 14 cm **C.** 175 cm
B. 7 cm **D.** 350 cm

34. Which of the following represents the graph of a line with a slope of 1 that passes through the point (0, 4)? **(Lesson IN 5)** **(7.2.6)** **A**

A.
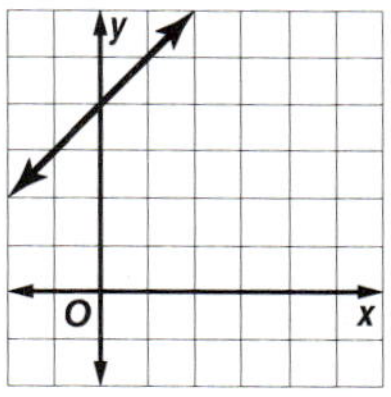

B.
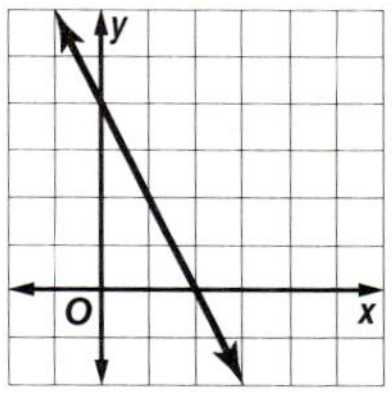

C.
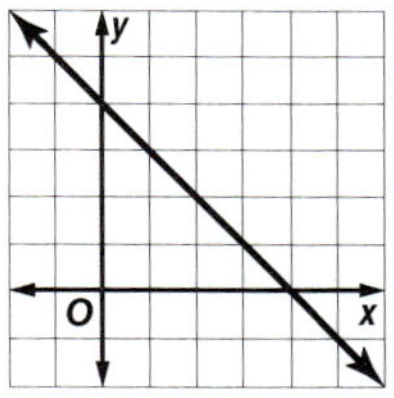

D.
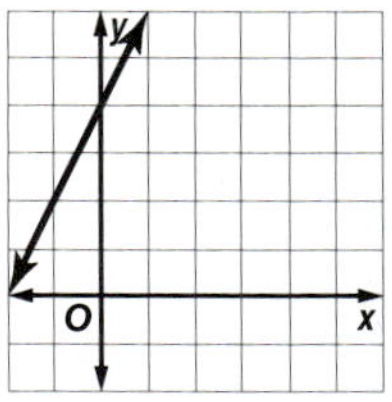

35. Find the slope of the line in the graph below. **(Lesson IN 5)** **(7.2.5)** **D**

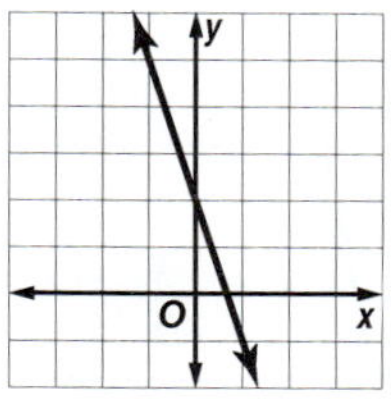

A. 3 **C.** −2
B. 2 **D.** −3

36. Determine whether the set of numbers in the table is a direct variation. **(Lesson IN 7)** **(7.2.7)** **A**

Shaded circles	1	2	3	4
Total circles	8	15	30	42

A. No; the ratios are not equal.

B. Yes; each ratio is equal to $\frac{2}{3}$.

C. Yes; each ratio is equal to $\frac{1}{3}$.

D. Yes; each ratio is equal to $\frac{1}{8}$.

37. Aida is 4 years older than Brad. Together their ages total 22 years. Which of the following equations could be used to find Brad's age b? **(Lesson 6-6)** **(7.2.2)** **D**

A. $4b = 22$ **C.** $b + 4 = 22$
B. $4b + b = 22$ **D.** $2b + 4 = 22$

38. GRIDDED RESPONSE Use the formula $A = \ell w$ to find the length in yards of a rectangle with a width of 8 yards and an area of 104 square yards. **(Lesson 3-3)** **(7.2.4)**

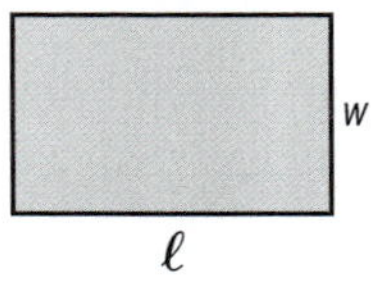

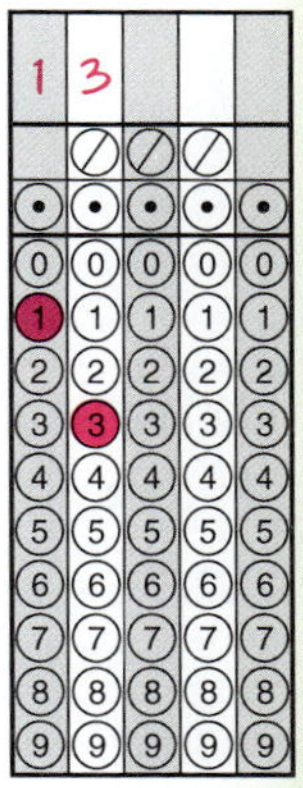

NEED EXTRA HELP?						
If You Missed Question...	33	34	35	36	37	38
Go to Lesson...	3-3	IN 5	IN 5	IN 7	6-6	3-3
Academic Standards	7.2.4	7.2.6	7.2.5	7.2.7	7.2.2	7.2.4

ISTEP+ 11

Additional Answer

42. Sample answer: Use a proportion to determine the number of left-handed students in the group. Then subtract this number from 40 to find the number of right-handed students. Finally, subtract the number of left-handed students from the number of right-handed students.

39. Which of the following graphs represents a slope of 3 and y-intercept of -1?
(Lesson IN 6) (7.2.6) **D**

A.

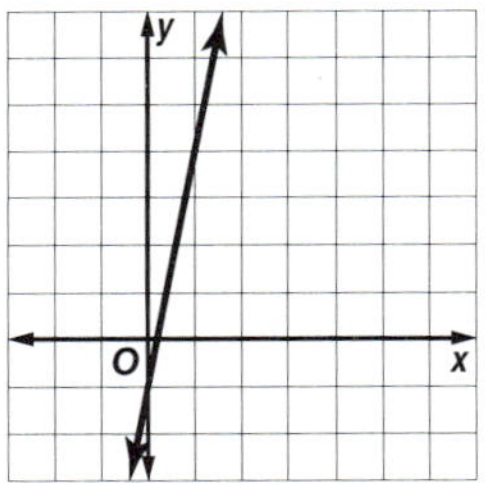

B.

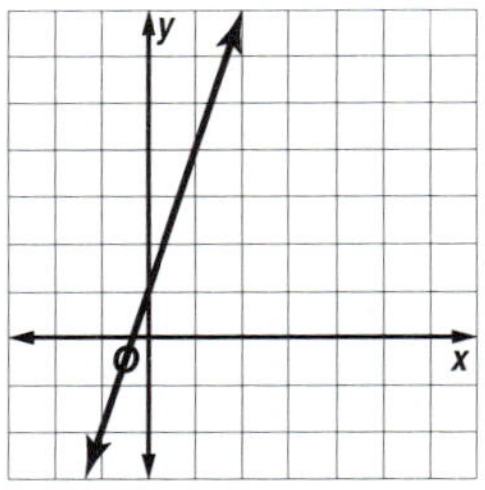

C.

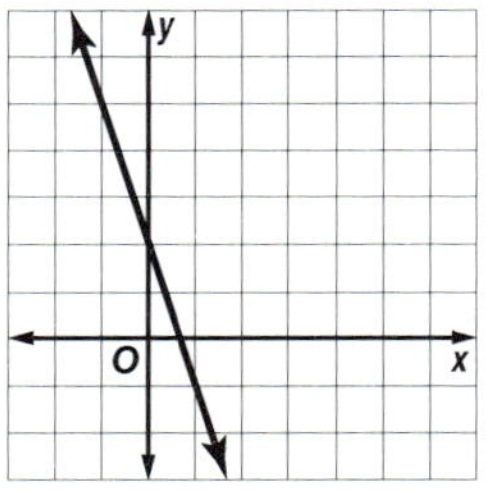

D.

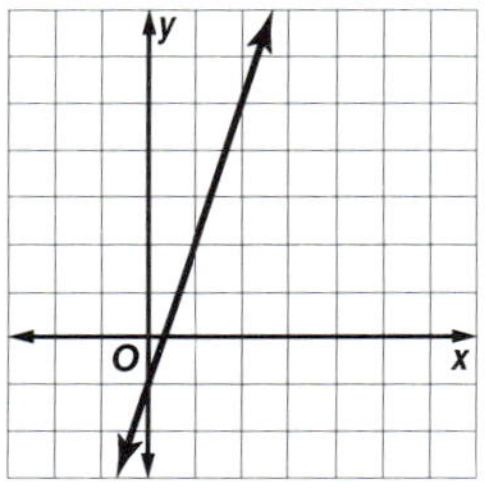

40. The table shows the number of pizzas th Pizza Barn can make every hour.

Number of Hours, x	Total Number of Pizzas, y
1	24
2	48
3	72
4	96

Which function rule represents the data? **(Lesson 1-10)** (7.2.1) **C**

A. $y = 12x$ **C.** $y = 24x$
B. $y = 18x$ **D.** $y = 36x$

41. Refer to the graph below.
(Lesson IN 5) (7.2.5)

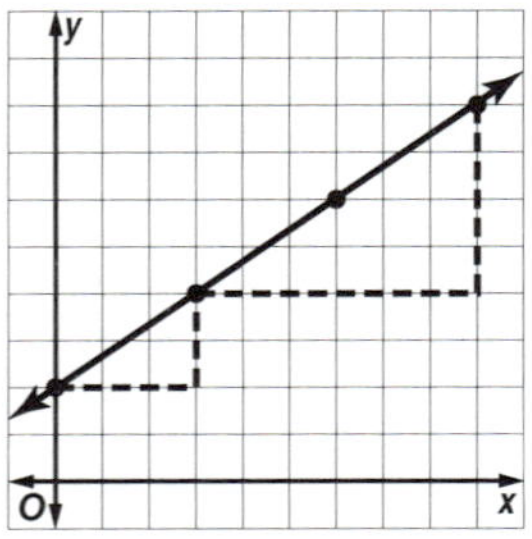

Which of the following is NOT true? **B**

A. The triangles formed are similar.

B. The triangles formed are congruent.

C. The ratio of the side lengths of the smaller triangle to the larger triangle is $\frac{2}{3}$.

D. The slope of the line is $\frac{2}{3}$.

EXTENDED RESPONSE

In a group of 40 students, 3 out of 8 students are left-handed. **(Lesson 6-6)** (7.2.7, P.2.4)

42. Describe how you would determine how many more students are right-handed in this group than are left-handed. **See margin.**

43. Use your method to solve the problem. Show all work. **10 students**

NEED EXTRA HELP?					
If You Missed Question...	39	40	41	42	43
Go to Lesson...	IN 6	1-10	IN 5	6-6	6-6
Academic Standards	7.2.6	7.2.1	7.2.5	7.2.7, P.2.4	7.2.7, P.2.4

Geometry and Measurement

1. Tara drove at a speed of 55 miles per hour for 3 hours. She then drove at a speed of 60 miles per hour for 2 hours. Find her average speed. **(Lesson 6-2)** **(7.3.6)** **C**

A. 55 miles per hour
B. 56 miles per hour
C. 57 miles per hour
D. 58 miles per hour

2. Find the value of x in the similar triangles below. **(Lesson 10-7)** **(7.3.5)** **A**

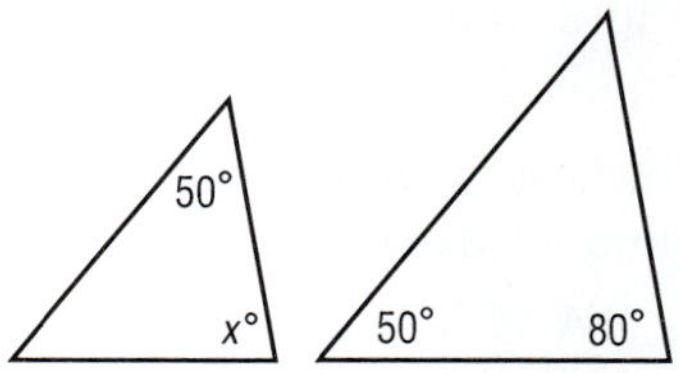

A. 80
B. 50
C. 30
D. 15

3. Find the value of x in the figure below. Lines m and n are parallel. **(Lesson IN 10)** **(7.3.1)** **D**

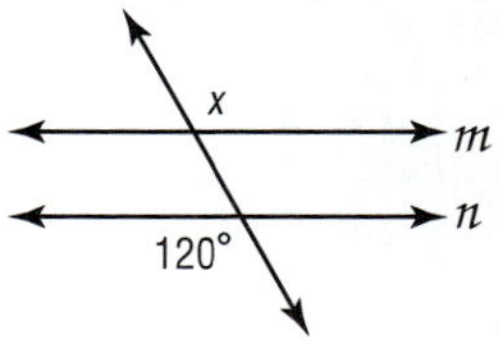

A. 40°
B. 60°
C. 100°
D. 120°

4. Which graph shows triangle ABC with vertices at $A(3, 6)$, $B(4, 9)$, and $C(7, 6)$ after a translation of 3 units left? **(Lesson 10-9)** **(7.3.2)** **C**

A.

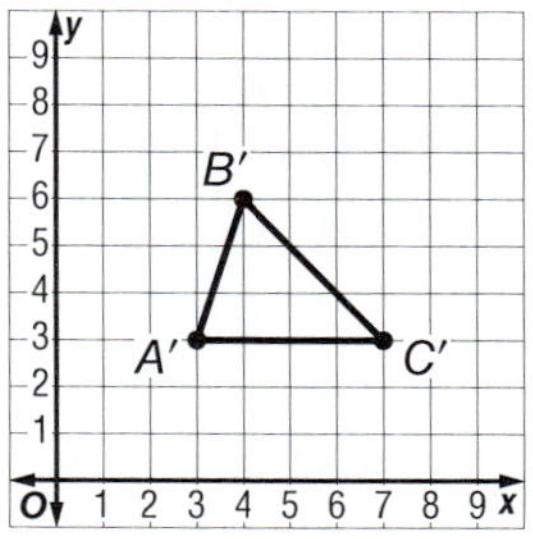

B.

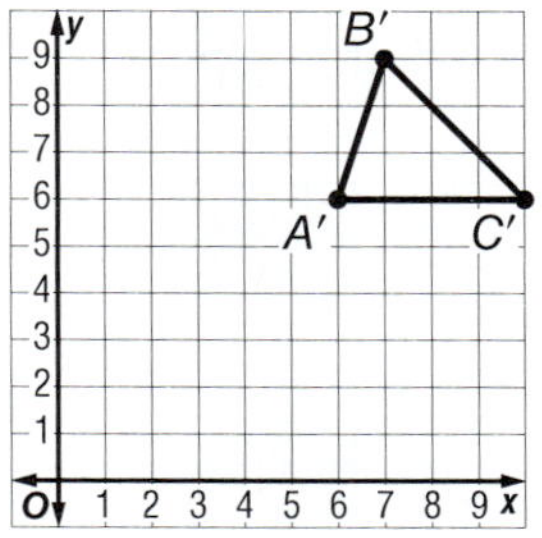

C.

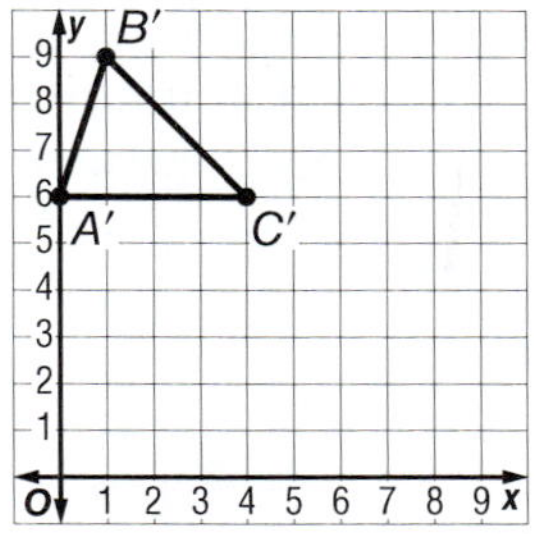

D.

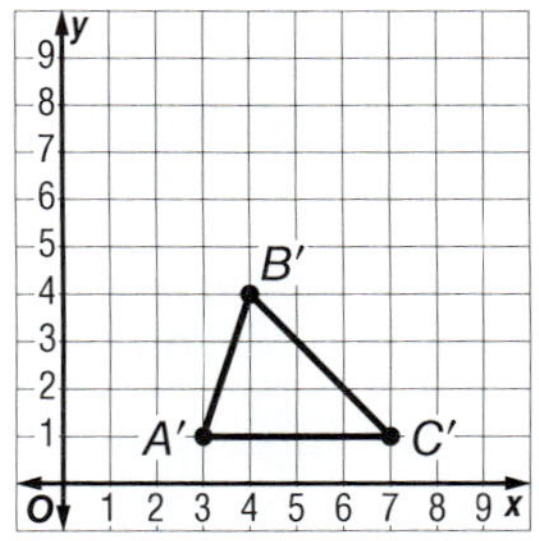

NEED EXTRA HELP?				
If You Missed Question...	1	2	3	4
Go to Lesson...	6-2	10-7	IN 10	10-9
Academic Standards	7.3.6	7.3.5	7.3.1	7.3.2

5. A scale drawing of a room is shown.

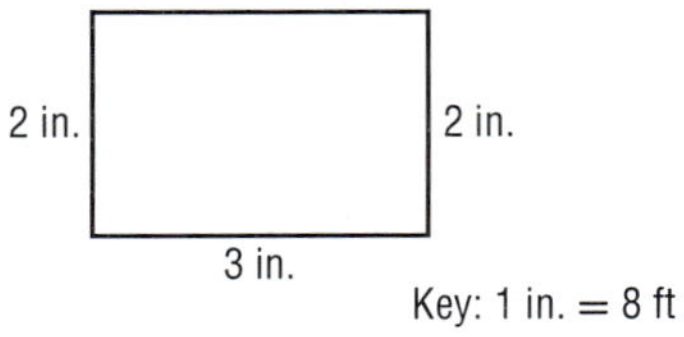

What are the actual dimensions of the room? **(Lesson 6-8)** **(7.3.5)** **C**

A. 8 feet by 24 feet
B. 8 feet by 16 feet
C. 16 feet by 24 feet
D. 16 feet by 32 feet

6. The shaded part of the grid represents the plans for a swimming pool.

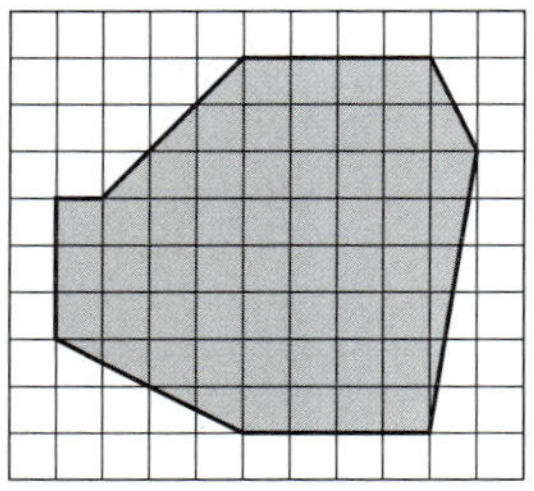

If each square on the grid represents 6 square feet, what is the approximate area of the swimming pool? **(Lesson 11-6)** **(7.3.5)** **A**

A. 330 ft^2
B. 275 ft^2
C. 240 ft^2
D. 56 ft^2

7. Which transformation is shown below? **(Lesson 10-9)** **(7.3.2)** **C**

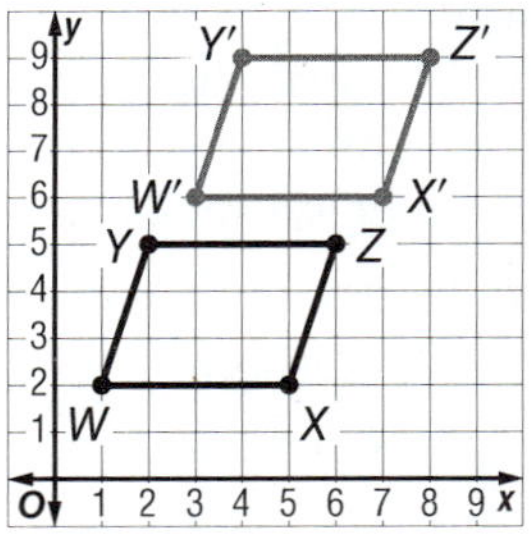

A. rotation
B. reflection across the y-axis
C. translation up four units and right two units
D. translation up two units and right four units

8. Which of the following is a net of a cylinder? **(Lesson IN 12)** **(7.3.3)** **B**

A.

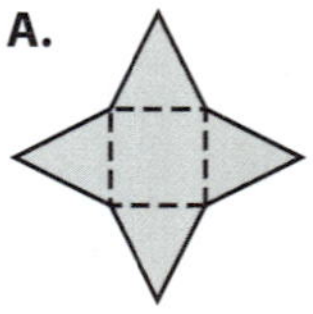

C.

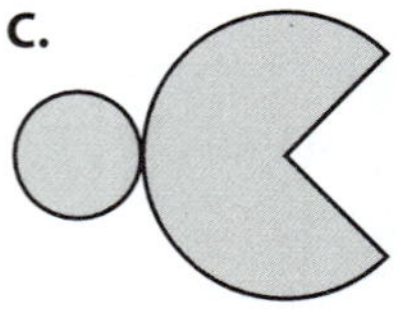

B.

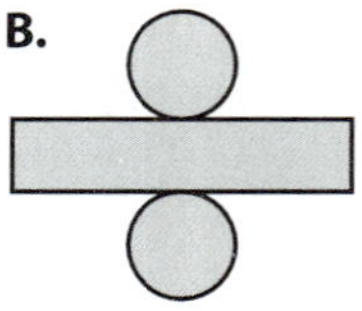

D.

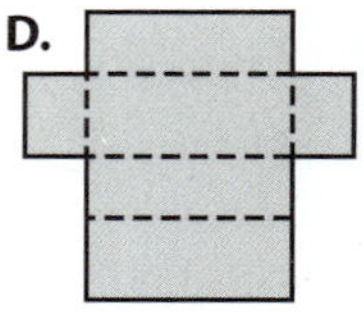

EXTENDED RESPONSE

9. Sample answer: Each successive figure has two more total squares than the previo figure. Each successive figure has one more shaded square than the previous figure.

Refer to the pattern of figures at the right. **(Lesson 2-7)** **(7.3.4)**

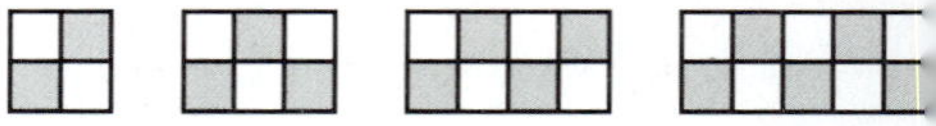

Figure 1 Figure 2 Figure 3 Figure 4

9. Write a few sentences describing the pattern of total squares and the pattern of shaded squares.

10. If the pattern continues, how many total squares will there be in Figure 8? Explain how you determined your response. **18; Sample answer: Continue adding tw more squares until you get to Figure 8.**

11. If the pattern continues, how many shaded squares will there be in Figure 8? Explain how you determined your response. **9; Sample answer: Continue adding one more square until you get to Figure 8.**

NEED EXTRA HELP?							
If You Missed Question...	5	6	7	8	9	10	11
Go to Lesson...	6-8	11-6	10-9	IN 12	2-7	2-7	2-7
Academic Standards	7.3.5	7.3.5	7.3.2	7.3.3	7.3.4, P.1.1	7.3.4, P.1.1	7.3.4, P.1.1

12. The point (9, −4) was translated n units up and m units to the right. Then it was reflected across the y-axis. The resulting coordinates were (−12, −2). Which of the following is TRUE regarding the values of m and n? **(Lesson 10-10)** **(7.3.2)** **B**

A. The value of m is positive and the value of n is negative.
B. The value of m is negative and the value of n is positive.
C. They are both positive.
D. They are both negative.

13. Which of the following is a net of a pyramid? **(Extend 11-6)** **(7.3.3)** **A**

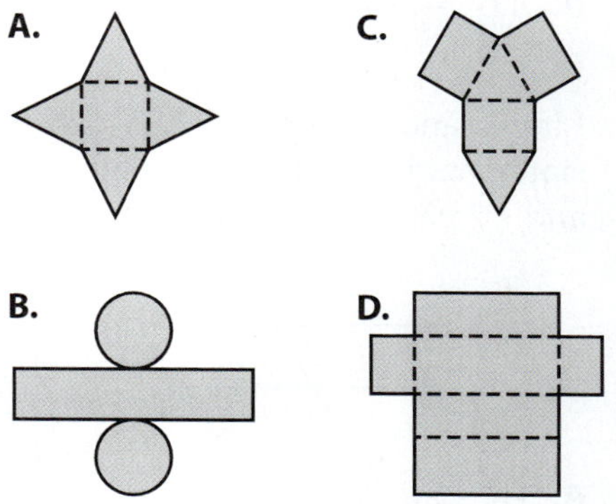

14. Felisa ran at a speed of 6 miles per hour for 40 minutes. She then ran at a speed of 5 miles per hour for 20 minutes. Find her average speed. **(Lesson 6-2)** **(7.3.6)** **C**

A. 5 miles per hour
B. $5\frac{1}{2}$ miles per hour
C. $5\frac{2}{3}$ miles per hour
D. $5\frac{3}{4}$ miles per hour

15. Triangle ABC and $\triangle DEF$ are similar. The scale factor comparing $\triangle ABC$ to $\triangle DEF$ is $\frac{2}{3}$. What MUST be true about their perimeters? **(Lesson 10-7)** **(7.3.5)** **A**

A. The perimeter of $\triangle ABC <$ the perimeter of $\triangle DEF$.
B. The perimeter of $\triangle ABC >$ the perimeter of $\triangle DEF$.
C. The perimeter of $\triangle ABC =$ the perimeter of $\triangle DEF$.
D. There is no relationship between the perimeter of $\triangle ABC$ and the perimeter of $\triangle DEF$.

16. Find the value of y in the figure below. Lines g and h are parallel. **(Lesson IN 10)** **(7.3.1)** **B**

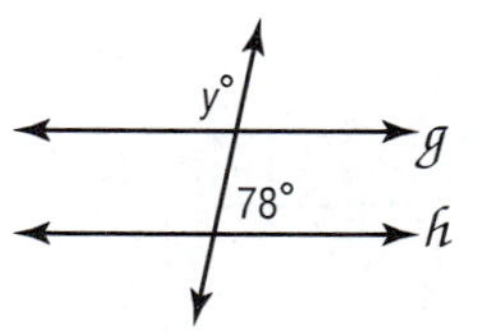

A. 78　　**C.** 110
B. 102　　**D.** 180

17. Which transformation is represented by the figure and its image? **(Lesson 10-10)** **(7.3.2)** **B**

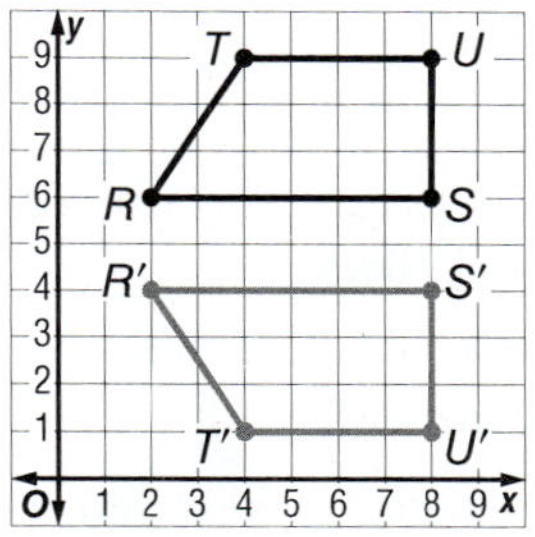

A. rotation of 180° about the origin
B. reflection across a horizontal line
C. translation up two units
D. translation up nine units

ISTEP+ 15

NEED EXTRA HELP?						
If You Missed Question...	12	13	14	15	16	17
Go to Lesson...	10-10	Extend 11-6	6-2	10-7	IN 10	10-10
Academic Standards	7.3.2	7.3.3	7.3.6	7.3.5	7.3.1	7.3.2

18. Which of the following statements is TRUE concerning the relationship between distance d, rate r, and time t given by the equation $d = rt$? **(Lesson 3-3)** **(7.3.6)** A

A. The rate r is equal to the quotient of the distance d and the time t.

B. The rate r is equal to the sum of the distance d and the time t.

C. The rate r is equal to the difference of the distance d and the time t.

D. The rate r is equal to the product of the distance d and the time t.

19. Which of the following is a net of a cone? **(Extend 11-6)** **(7.3.3)** B

A.

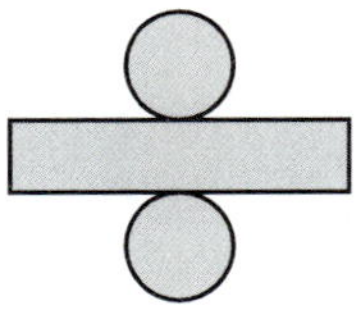

C.

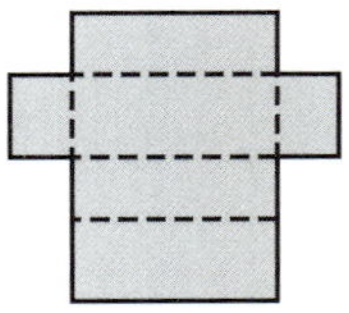

B.

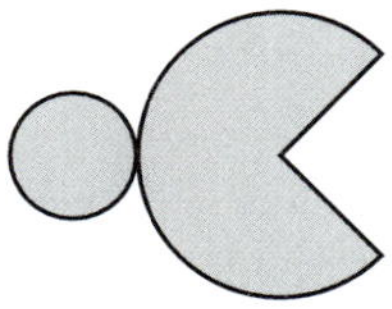

D.

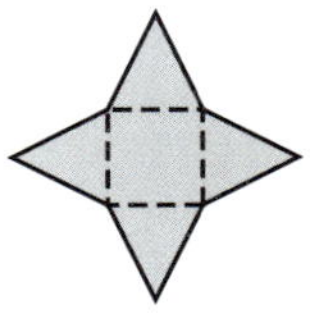

20. A triangle with vertices $A(3, 4)$, $B(2, -5)$ and $C(-1, 6)$ is reflected across the x-axis. Then it is translated up three units and to the right four units. What are the resulting coordinates of the triangle after both transformations? **(Lesson 10-10)** **(7.3.2)**

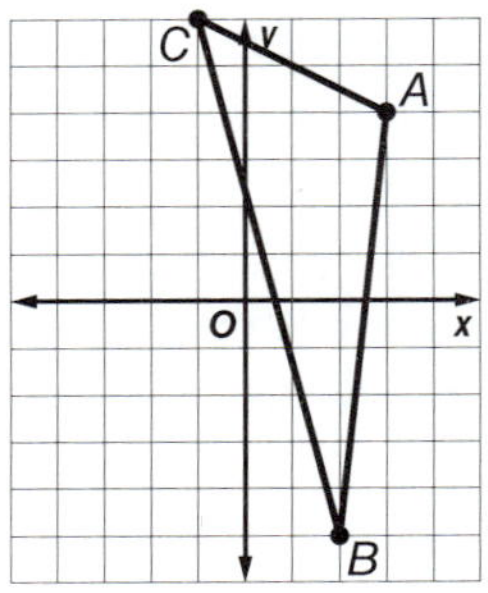

A. $A'(3, -1)$, $B'(2, 8)$ and $C'(-1, -3)$

B. $A'(3, -4)$, $B'(2, 5)$ and $C'(-1, -6)$

C. $A'(7, 7)$, $B'(6, -2)$ and $C'(3, 9)$

D. $A'(7, -1)$, $B'(6, 8)$ and $C'(3, -3)$

21. Lines p and q are parallel. Which statement is TRUE concerning $\angle 1$ and $\angle 2$ below? **(Lesson IN 10)** **(7.3.1)** B

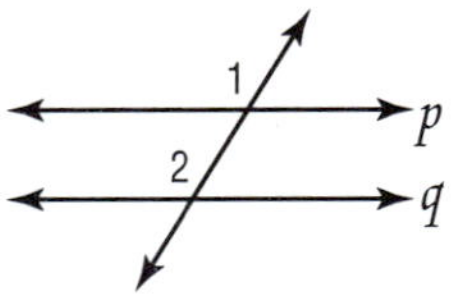

A. They are complementary.

B. They are congruent.

C. They are supplementary.

D. They are vertical.

22. no; Sample answer: The corresponding side lengths do not have the same ratio.

EXTENDED RESPONSE

The dimensions of Kendra's yard are shown in the drawing at the right. **(Lesson 10-7)** **(7.3.5, P.5.3)**

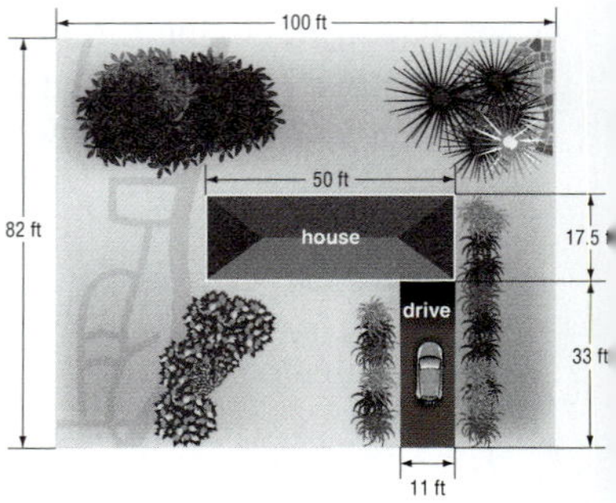

22. Are the rectangles represented by the house and the driveway similar figures? Justify your response.

23. Determine the dimensions of a driveway that would be similar to the house. Justify your response. Sample answer: The dimensions of the house are in the ratio 20:7. So, a driveway with dimensions 40 feet and 14 feet would be similar to the house.

NEED EXTRA HELP?						
If You Missed Question...	18	19	20	21	22	23
Go to Lesson...	3-3	Extend 11-6	10-10	IN 10	10-7	10-7
Academic Standards	7.3.6	7.3.3	7.3.2	7.3.1	7.3.5, P.5.3	7.3.5, P.5.3

24. Which graph shows only a rotation of the figure? **(Lesson IN 11)** **(7.3.2)** A

A.

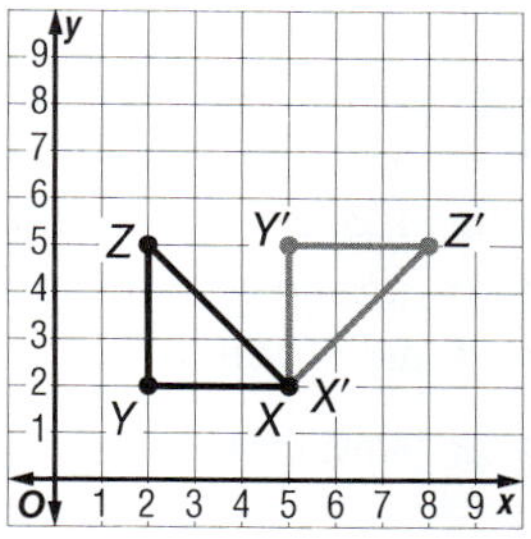

B.

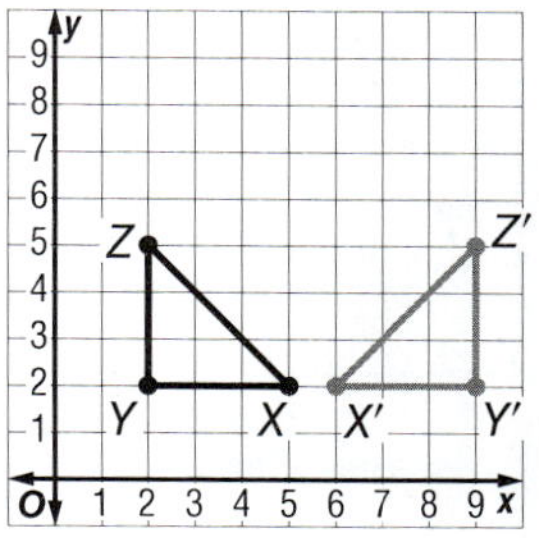

C.

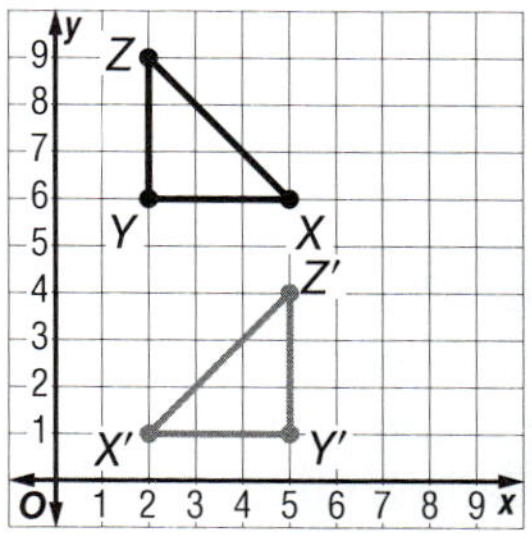

D.

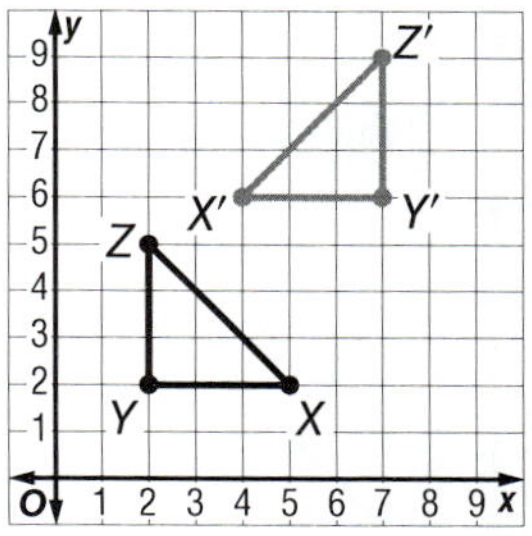

25. The point (−3, 5) is translated down 2 units and to the right 4 units. What are the resulting coordinates? **(Lesson 10-9)** **(7.3.2)** B

A. (−5, 9)
B. (1, 3)
C. (−1, 9)
D. (−5, 1)

26. Refer to the figures below. If the pattern continues, which of the following statements is TRUE? **(Lesson 2-7)** **(7.3.4)** C

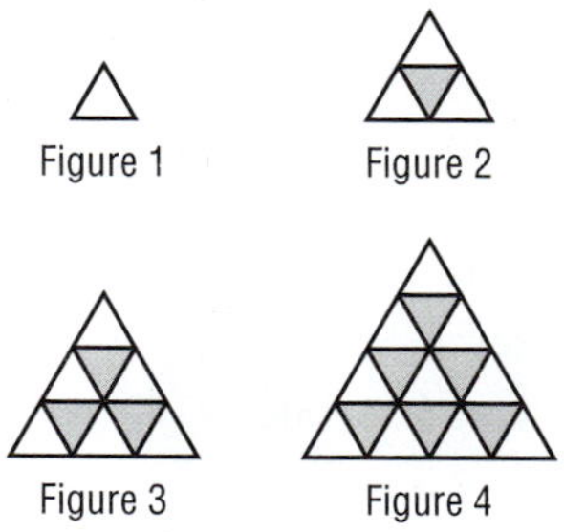

A. There will be sixteen triangles in the sixth figure.
B. There will be nine shaded triangles in the sixth figure.
C. There will be fifteen shaded triangles in the sixth figure.
D. There will be thirty triangles in the sixth figure.

27. A statue is 4.5 feet tall and casts a shadow of 15 inches. What is the height of a nearby tower if it casts a shadow 60 inches long at the same time? **(Lesson 10-7)** **(7.3.5)** D

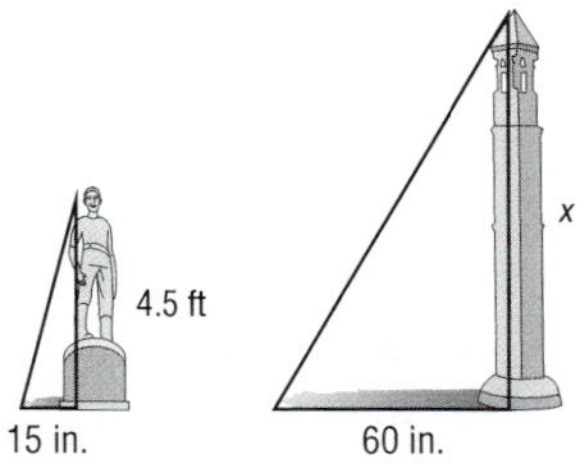

A. 200 ft
B. 30 ft
C. 27 ft
D. 18 ft

NEED EXTRA HELP?				
If You Missed Question...	24	25	26	27
Go to Lesson...	IN 11	10-9	2-7	10-7
Academic Standards	7.3.2	7.3.2	7.3.4	7.3.5

Data Analysis and Probability

1. Irene planted a bamboo shoot that grows at the rate of 11 inches a day. It will grow at this rate for 60 days. After 11 days, how tall will the bamboo plant be? **(Lesson 8-6) (7.4.2) D**

A. 12 feet
B. 11 feet 6 inches
C. 10 feet 8 inches
D. 10 feet 1 inch

2. GRIDDED RESPONSE Sabino randomly selects one letter from the word *piano*. What is the probability that he selects a vowel? **(Lesson 9-8) (7.4.5)**

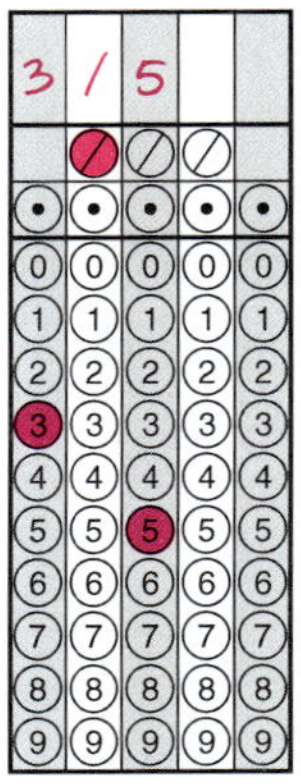

3. Hannah has 16 music CDs. What is the probability she will randomly pull out one particular CD? **(Lesson 9-1) (7.4.5) A**

A. $\frac{1}{16}$ **C.** $\frac{1}{4}$
B. $\frac{1}{8}$ **D.** $\frac{1}{2}$

4. Jenifer volunteers at a day care center. She collected data about the months children at the center were born. Which data display would be the MOST appropriate to use to compare that data? **(Lesson 8-4) (7.4.1) D**

A. line graph **C.** circle graph
B. histogram **D.** bar graph

5. Ernesto is playing basketball. The graph shows how many total points he has afte each basket made. For each two baskets that he makes, by how many points doe his score increase? **(Lesson 8-6) (7.4.2) C**

Total Points Ernesto Made

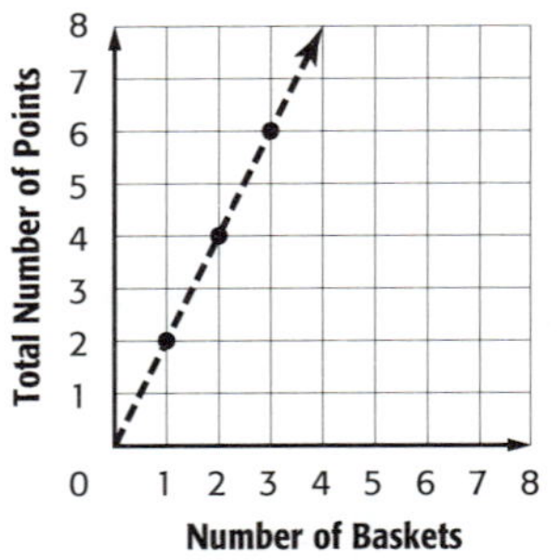

A. 1 **C.** 4
B. 2 **D.** 8

6. John makes $5 for every hour of work. Below is a graph that shows how much he gets paid compared to how long he works. If Fatima makes $8 each hour, how would her graph compare to John's **(Lesson 8-6) (7.4.2) A**

John's Earnings

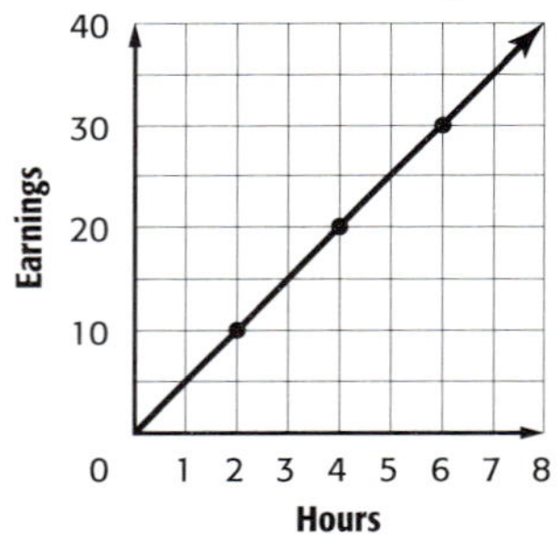

A. It would be steeper.
B. It would be less steep.
C. The lines would have the same slope.
D. They would have different *y*-intercept

NEED EXTRA HELP?						
If You Missed Question...	1	2	3	4	5	6
Go to Lesson...	8-6	9-8	9-1	8-4	8-6	8-6
Academic Standards	7.4.2	7.4.5	7.4.5	7.4.1	7.4.1	7.4.2

ISTEP+ 18

7. GRIDDED RESPONSE Myron tosses a coin 10 times and it comes up heads 7 times. Based on these results, if he tosses a coin 100 times, how many times can he expect to toss tails? **(Lesson 9-7)** **(7.4.2)**

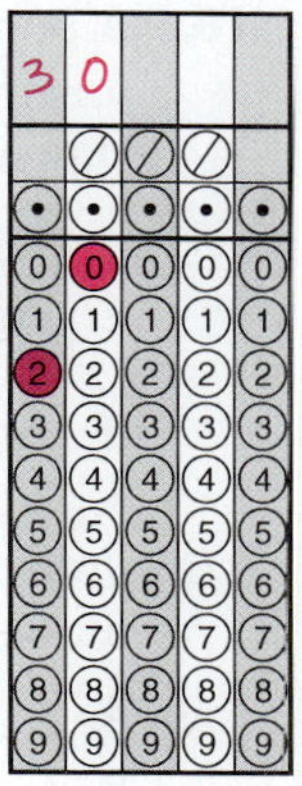

8. Wakim saw the graph shown below in a magazine article about dog ownership. He spends about $240 a year on dog food. Which of the following represents the approximate annual cost to own his dog? **(Lesson 8-7)** **(7.4.2)** **C**

Cost of Owning a Dog

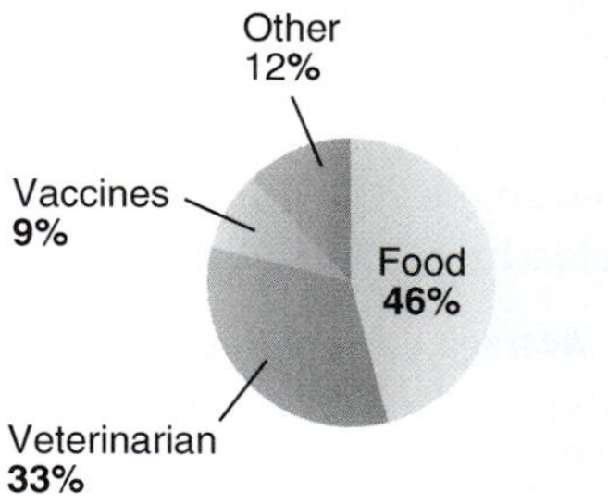

A. $110
B. $260
C. $520
D. $680

9. If Danielle spins a spinner like the one shown below 400 times, how many times should she expect the spinner to land on the circle? **(Lesson 9-7)** **(7.4.5)** **C**

A. 400
B. 200
C. 100
D. 75

10. Which statement is TRUE concerning the data set below? **(Lesson 8-2)** **(7.4.3)** **A**

{100, 110, 109, 25, 105, 107, 100}

A. The mean is most affected by the outlier.
B. The median is most affected by the outlier.
C. The mode is most affected by the outlier.
D. None of the measures of central tendency are affected by the outlier.

EXTENDED RESPONSE

Refer to the graph at the right. **(Lesson 8-9)** **(7.4.4, P.5.2)**

11. How many times taller is the bar corresponding to Tyra's score than the bar corresponding to James' score? **2**

12. What is the actual difference between Tyra's score and James' score? **4**

13. Explain why the graph of the test scores is misleading. **See margin.**

Test Scores

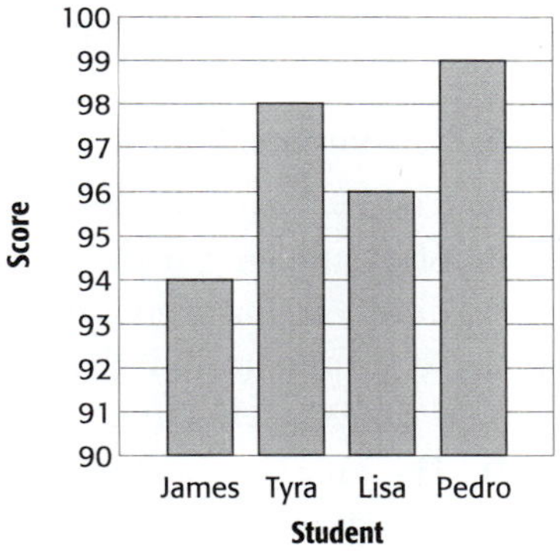

Additional Answer

13. Sample answer: The scale on the *y*-axis only shows part of the possible range, so it appears there are large differences in scores. They are actually all close together.

NEED EXTRA HELP?							
If You Missed Question...	7	8	9	10	11	12	13
Go to Lesson...	9-7	8-7	9-7	8-2	8-9	8-9	8-9
Academic Standards	7.4.2	7.4.2	7.4.5	7.4.3	7.4.4, P.5.2	7.4.4, P.5.2	7.4.4, P.5.2

14. The graph shows the number of people who attended Rochester's Fourth of July celebration each year. How many people should be expected to attend the celebration in 2010? **(Lesson 8-6)** **(7.4.2)** D

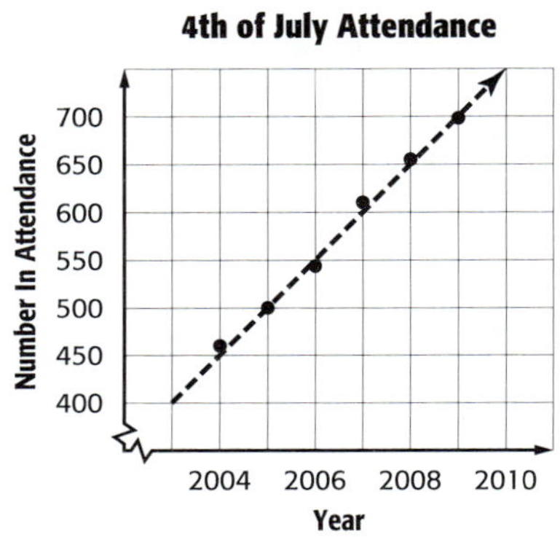

A. 600
B. 650
C. 700
D. 750

15. What is the BEST reason for why the following graph is misleading? **(Lesson 8-9)** **(7.4.4)** C

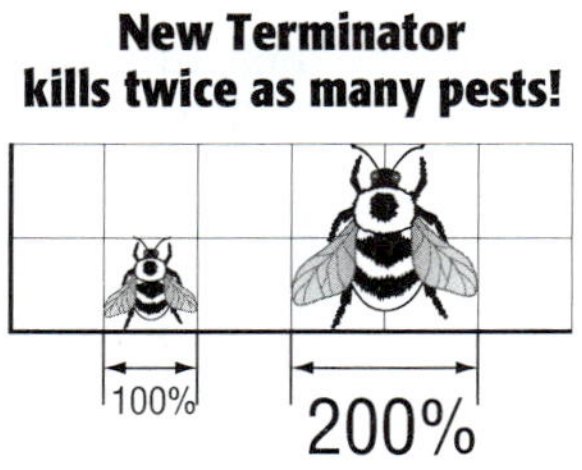

A. The vertical axis is not labeled.
B. The vertical axis has no scale.
C. Since the length and width are both doubled, the area is 4 times as large, so it appears as if the new pesticide is 4 times as effective.
D. The graph only compares two types of pesticides.

16. A popular board game uses letter tiles to form words. The vowel distribution is shown in the table below.

Letter	A	E	I	O	U
Number of Tiles	9	12	9	8	4

If Anna randomly chooses a tile and replaces it 50 times, about how many times should she expect to choose a tile that is NOT "O"? **(Lesson 9-7)** **(7.4.5)** D

A. 4
B. 6
C. 15
D. 41

17. The number of siblings each student on the tennis team has are below. What is the mean number of siblings? **(Lesson 8-2)** **(7.4.2)** C

0, 3, 0, 1, 2, 7, 0, 1, 3, 2

A. 0
B. 1.5
C. 1.9
D. 7

18. What makes the following graph misleading? **(Lesson 8-9)** **(7.4.4)** A

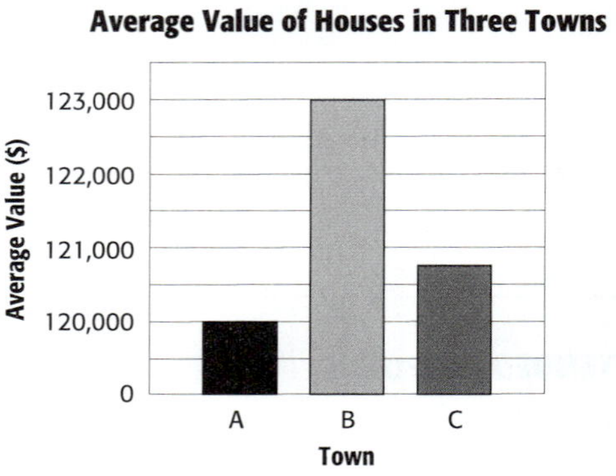

A. The intervals on the vertical axis make it appear that the averages are far apart when they are fairly close.
B. The average house value should be listed on the horizontal axis.
C. The graph compares only three towns.
D. A bar graph is not an appropriate type of display for this information.

NEED EXTRA HELP?					
If You Missed Question...	14	15	16	17	18
Go to Lesson...	8-6	8-9	9-7	8-2	8-9
Academic Standards	7.4.2	7.4.4	7.4.5	7.4.2	7.4.4

19. The circle graph shows the results of a poll to which 500 students at Rosalinda's school responded.

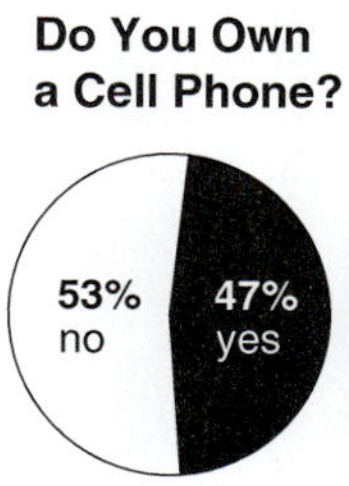

If there are 25 students in Rosalinda's homeroom, how many would you predict own cell phones? **(Lesson 8-6)** **(7.4.2)** **A**

A. 12 **C.** 47
B. 13 **D.** 53

20. Rochelle's French test scores are shown below.

86, 84, 80, 65, 90, 75, 88

Her teacher will drop the lowest score. By how much will Rochelle's average change? **(Lesson 8-2)** **(7.4.3)** **B**

A. −3 points
B. +3 points
C. +5 points
D. +7 points

21. Which of the following types of displays is MOST appropriate to show how Jaclyn's height has changed over time? **(Lesson IN 8)** **(7.4.1)** **C**

A. histogram **C.** line graph
B. stem-and-leaf plot **D.** line plot

22. The manager of a fast food restaurant made the graph below showing what percent of the daily sales were from each type of food. If he expects 250 customers today, how many hot dogs should he prepare? **(Lesson 8-6)** **(7.4.2)** **B**

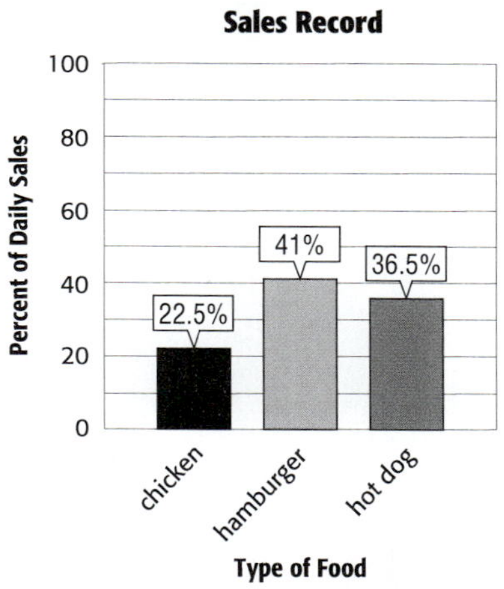

A. 56 **C.** 103
B. 91 **D.** 250

CONSTRUCTED RESPONSE

A movie theater in Elkhart wants to increase attendance at its evening shows. The manager decides to conduct a survey to see what movies people like. Decide whether each of the following survey questions would produce valid results. If it would not, change the wording so that it is a valid survey question. **(Lesson IN 9)** **(7.4.4, P.4.1)**

23. "Which movie would you prefer seeing: an exciting action film or a boring love story?" **not valid; "what kind of movie do you prefer: action or romance?"**

24. "Will you vote yes or no on Issue 12?" **valid**

25. "Don't you think all students should wear uniforms to school?" **not valid; "Should students wear uniforms to school?"**

NEED EXTRA HELP?

If You Missed Question...	19	20	21	22	23	24	25
Go to Lesson...	8-6	8-2	IN 8	8-6	IN 9	IN 9	IN 9
Academic Standards	7.4.2	7.4.3	7.4.1	7.4.2	7.4.4, P.4.1	7.4.4, P.4.1	7.4.4, P.4.1

Photo Credits

Cover Richard Hutchings/Digital Light Source, shot on location courtesy of Busch Gardens/Adventure Island, Tampa Florida; **iv** File Photo; **v** Digital Vision/Getty Images; **vi** Aaron Haupt; **vi-vii** Bryan Mullennix/Getty Images; **x-xi** David Frazier/CORBIS; **xii-xiii** Robert Glusic/Photodisc/Getty Images; **xiv-xv** Brand X Pictures/PunchStock; **xvi-xvii** Eastcott Momatiuk/Photodisc/Getty Images; **xviii-xix** Michael Ventura/Alamy Images; **xx-xxi** Kim Karpeles/Alamy Images; **xxii-xxiii** W.A.Hamilton/Alamy; **IN0-IN1** Ilene MacDonald/Alamy Images; **IN2** Charles O'Rear/CORBIS; **IN3** Chris A Crumley/Alamy Images; **IN4** Hugh Lansdown/Alamy; **IN8** Greg Ceo/Getty Images; **IN10** Jim Reed/Photo Researchers; **IN12** Photodisc/Getty Images; **IN14** Mark Steinmetz; **IN16** Stockdisc/PunchStock; **IN17** Microzoa/The Image Bank/Getty Images; **IN29** G.K. Vikki Hart/Getty Images; **IN39** (t)G.K. Vikki Hart/Getty Images, (b)PhotoDisc, Inc./Getty Images; **001** Digital Vision/PunchStock; **003** Reuters/CORBIS; **004** David Frazier/CORBIS; **005** curved-light/Alamy Images; **006** Jonathan Ferrey/Getty Images; **007** Robert Laberge/Getty Images; **008** William Manning/www.williammanning.com/CORBIS; **009** Krista Kennell/ZUMA/CORBIS; **010** Arcaid/CORBIS; **011** Momatiuk-Eastcott/CORBIS; **012** Royalty-Free/CORBIS; **013** PhotoLink/Photodisc/Getty Images; **014** Joe McDonald/Animals Animals; **015** Masterfile; **016** (t)Joel A. Rogers/www.CoasterGallery.com, (b)Daniel Dempster Photography/Alamy Images; **017** (t)Chuck Pefley/Alamy images, (c)Penny Boyd/Alamy Images, (bl)Goodshoot/ CORBIS, (br)Marie Read/Animals Animals; **018** (t)Marian Bacon/Animals Animals, (c)Scott Smith/CORBIS, (b)kansastravel.org; **019** (t)Volkmar Wentzel/Getty Images, (cl)John December, (cr)M. Timothy O'Keefe/Alamy Images, (b)Steve Hamblin/Alamy Images; **020-021** JG Photography/Alamy Images; **022** Andre Jenny/Alamy Images; **026** Jose Luis Pelaez, Inc./Blend Images/Getty Images; **032** Stefano Bianchetti/CORBIS; **035** Lawrence Manning/CORBIS; **039** The McGraw-Hill Companies Inc.; **041** (l)Michael Newman/PhotoEdit, (r)David Young-Wolff/PhotoEdit; **042** Kevin Peterson/Photodisc/Getty Images; **045** SW Productions/Photodisc/Getty Images; **049** Photo courtesy of BGSU Photo Services; **052** (l)David Young-Wolff/PhotoEdit, (r)Tony Freeman/PhotoEdit; **054** Tim de Waele/CORBIS; **064** (l)Noel Hendrickson/Digital Vision/Getty Images, (r)Eric and David Hosking/CORBIS; **066** Herbert Kehrer/zefa/CORBIS; **078** SW Productions/Brand X/CORBIS; **080** Chase Jarvis/CORBIS; **090** Kevin Schafer/Photographer's Choice RF/Getty Images; **099** (l)Myrleen Ferguson Cate/PhotoEdit, (r)David Young-Wolff/PhotoEdit; **104** NASA/Photodisc/Getty Images; **106** (l)Cleve Bryant/PhotoEdit, (r)David Young-Wolff/PhotoEdit; **109** Ralph White/CORBIS; **112** John Evans; **116** Lothar Lenz/zefa/CORBIS; **126** Sarah Hadley/Alamy Images; **128** JPL/NASA; **129** Photo by Brad Kuntz; **132** (t)David Siccardi/CORBIS, (bl)Comstock/CORBIS, (br)Dann Tardif/LWA/Blend Images/Getty Images; **137** Stephen Frink/zefa/CORBIS; **139** Eddie Adams/Sygma/CORBIS; **140** Streeter Lecka/Stringer/Getty Images; **143** Jose Luis Pelaez, Inc./Blend Images/Getty Images; **146** (l)Ryan McVay/Photodisc/Getty Images, (r)Comstock/CORBIS; **148** John Evans; **153** John Eder/Stone/Getty Images; **154** Robert Glusic/Photodisc/Getty Images; **160** David Young-Wolff/PhotoEdit; **176-177** Brand X Pictures/PunchStock; **178** Robert Marien/CORBIS; **183** Zigmund Leszcynski/Animals Animals; **184** Mark Duffy/Alamy Images; **185** Raymond K Gehman/National Geographic/Getty Images; **190** Matt Meadows; **193** Jose Luis Pelaez Inc/Blend Images/Getty Images; **195** (l)Seth Kushner/Taxi/Getty Images, (r)Image Source/SuperStock; **198** Comstock/SuperStock; **203** Bäumle Studios/Alamy Images; **208** Steve Bloom/Taxi/Getty Images; **210** (l)RubberBall/SuperStock, (r)RubberBall/SuperStock; **212** Roy Ooms/Masterfile; **216** John Wilkes/SuperStock; **218** United States coin images from the United States Mint; **219** Yiorgos Karahalis/Reuters/CORBIS; **228** Eclipse Studios; **230** Eastcott Momatiuk/Photodisc/Getty Images; **232** Michael Newman/PhotoEdit; **234** Russell Kightley/Photo Researchers; **239** David R. Frazier Photolibrary, Inc./Alamy Images; **240** (l)George Doyle/Stockbyte/Getty Images, (r)Michael Newman/PhotoEdit; **242** Diane Macdonald/Stockbyte/Getty Images; **244** Stockbyte/Getty Images; **248** Getty Images; **254** Garry Black/Masterfile; **256** Rob Lewine/CORBIS; **262** Jeff Greenberg/Alamy Images; **268** Phyllis Greenberg/Animals Animals; **270** (l)Jack Hollingsworth/CORBIS, (r)Barbara Penoyar/Photodisc/Getty Images; **278-279** Christie's Images/CORBIS; **280** Alan Schein/zefa/CORBIS; **283** Brian Snyder/Reuters/CORBIS; **285** (l)Tom Brakefield/CORBIS, (r)Judith Collins/Alamy Images; **286** (l)Donna Day/ImageState, (r)JupiterImages/Thinkstock/Alamy Images; **287** David Young-Wolff/PhotoEdit; **289** Doug Menuez/Photodisc/Getty Images; **290** Ryan McVay/Stone+/Getty Images; **291** Don Emmert/AFP/Getty Images; **295** Thomas Allen/Digital Vision/Getty Images; **298** John Lambert/Brand X/CORBIS; **300** Norbert Wu/Minden Pictures; **305** age fotostock / SuperStock; **307** Lawrence Lawry/Photodisc/Getty Images; **308** (t)Bruce Edwards/America 24-7/Getty Images, (bl)Jonathan Nourok/PhotoEdit, (br)Michael Newman/PhotoEdit; **312** CORBIS; **314** Alley Cat Productions/Brand X/CORBIS; **318** KS Studios; **319** Michael Newman/PhotoEdit; **325** Bilderbuch/Design Pics/CORBIS; **331** Franz Marc Frei/CORBIS; **340** Masterfile; **344** DLILLC/CORBIS; **347** G. Biss/Masterfile; **350** Ingemar Edfalk/Pixonnet.com/Alamy Images; **352** Donna Ikenberry/Animals Animals; **354** Digital Vision/Getty Images; **356** Big Cheese Photo/SuperStock; **358** D. Robert & Lorri Franz/CORBIS; **359** (l)FIRST LIGHT ASSOCIATED PHOTOGRAPHERS, (r)Flying Colours Ltd/Digital Vision/Getty Images; **363** Alaskastock; **366** Adrian Peacock/Digital Vision/Getty Images; **374** (l)RubberBall/ImageState, (r)Barbara Penoyar/Photodisc/Getty Images; **376** Gregor Schuster/Photographer's Choice RF/Getty Images; **380** Don Mason/Blend Images/Getty Images; **392-393** Matthias Kulka/zefa/CORBIS; **394** Michael Ventura/Alamy Images; **399** Harald Sund/Photographer's Choice/Getty Images; **400** (l)MedioImages/Alamy Images, (r)Tony Freeman/PhotoEdit; **406** CORBIS; **410** Barbara Peacock/Taxi/Getty Images; **411** JUPITERIMAGES/Liquid Library Value/Alamy; **413** Brandon D. Cole/CORBIS; **419** Daryl Balfour/The Image Bank/Getty Images; **424** Gabe Palmer/Alamy Images; **431** Bob Daemmrich/Stock Boston; **438** Paul Costello/Getty Images; **441** photocuisine/CORBIS; **446** Andrew J.G. Bell; Eye Ubiquitous/CORBIS; **458** Robert Michael/ CORBIS; **461** Bettmann/ CORBIS; **468** Ariel Skelley/CORBIS; **469** Tom Hauck/Getty Images; **473** O'Brien Productions/CORBIS; **476** Shenval/Alamy Images; **477** Tetra Images/Alamy Images; **481** Mitchell Layton/NewSport/CORBIS; **483** (l)George Doyle/Stockbyte Platinum/Alamy Images, (r)Jose Luis Pelaez Inc/Blend Images/Getty Images; **484** Laura Sifferlin; **488** Zefa RF/Alamy Images; **492** United States coin images from the United States Mint; **506-507** Oberto Gill/Beateworks/CORBIS; **508** Dennis MacDonald/Alamy Images; **510** Kelly-Mooney Photography/CORBIS; **519** Stephen Dalton/Animals Animals; **526** Jeff Greenberg/PhotoEdit; **528** Damir Frkovic/Masterfile; **530** Ryan McVay/Photodisc/Getty Images; **537** (l)Michael Newman/PhotoEdit, (r)Michelle Pedone/zefa/CORBIS; **544** Martin Shields/Alamy Images; **548** (t)Andriy Doriy Textures/Alamy Images, (b)Somos/Veer/Getty Images; **550** (l)Jeff Greenberg/PhotoEdit, (r)Todd Gipstein/National Geographic/Getty Images; **556** Artwork courtesy of Marjorie Rice; **560** Robert Spoenlein/zefa/CORBIS; **561** (t)Jose Fuste Raga/CORBIS, (b)Allen Wallace/Photonica/Getty Images; **570** Kim Karpeles/Alamy Images; **573** Don Farrall/Photodisc/Getty Images; **575** Jules Frazier/Photodisc/ Getty Images; **580** Byron Schumaker/Alamy; **583** Getty Images; **584** Iconotec/Alamy Images; **587** (l)BananaStock/PictureQuest/Jupiter Images, (t)Studio Wartenberg/zefa/CORBIS, (cr)Klaus Leidorf/zefa/CORBIS, (r)BananaStock/PunchStock; **590** United States coin images from the United States Mint; **592** (l)MedioImages/CORBIS, (r)Michael Newman/PhotoEdit; **594** Jim Esposito Photography LLC/Photodisc/Getty Images; **604** Judith Collins/Alamy images; **605** (t)C Squared Studios/Photodisc/Getty Images, (c)Glencoe, (b)PhotoLink/Photodisc/Getty Images; **608** Phil Degginger/Alamy Images; **610** Chris Bell/Taxi/Getty Images; **611** (tl)Mark Karrass/CORBIS, (t)Ryan McVay/Photodisc/Getty Images, (b)Lew Robertson/CORBIS; **614** Charles Gupton/CORBIS; **617** Keate/Masterfile; **620** Tony Freeman/PhotoEdit; **621** Duncan Usher/Foto Natura/Minden Pictures; **629** Gregor Schuster/zefa/CORBIS; **634** Horizons Companies; **638** Myrleen Ferguson Cate/PhotoEdit; **641** Steve Bly/Alamy Images; **645** (l)Comstock/SuperStock, (r)Stockbyte/SuperStock; **646** Michael Newman/PhotoEdit; **652** Daly & Newton/Getty Images; **657** W.A.Hamilton/Alamy; **666** Eclipse Studios; **ISTEP+0** (bl)Charles Gupton

Photo Credits

Cover (t)Created by Michael Trott with Mathematica. From "Graphica 1", Copyright ©1999 Wolfram Media, Inc.; **T3** Corbis; **T6–T7** Medioimages/Photodisc/Getty Images; **T8** Bloom Works Inc./Alamy; **T12** Digital Vision/Getty Images; **T13** BananaStock/PictureQuest; **T14** Jose Luis Pelaez, Inc./CORBIS; **v** S. Solum/PhotoLink/Getty Images; **xi** Jeff Osborne/Getty Images; **xiv-xv** Kitt Cooper-Smith/Alamy Images.

Glossary/Glosario

IN Math Online A mathematics multilingual glossary is available at glencoe.com.
The glossary includes the following languages.

Arabic	Cantonese	Korean	Tagalog
Bengali	English	Russian	Urdu
Brazilian Portuguese	Haitian Creole	Spanish	Vietnamese
	Hmong		

Cómo usar el glosario en español:
1. Busca el término en inglés que desees encontrar.
2. El término en español, junto con la definición, se encuentran en la columna de la derecha.

English / Español

A

absolute value (p. 81) The distance the number is from zero on a number line.

valor absoluto Distancia a la que se encuentra un número de cero en la recta numérica.

acute angle (p. 511) An angle with a measure greater than 0° and less than 90°.

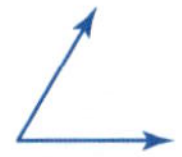

ángulo agudo Ángulo que mide más de 0° y menos de 90°.

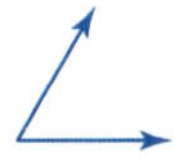

acute triangle (p. 525) A triangle having three acute angles.

triángulo acutángulo Triángulo con tres ángulos agudos.

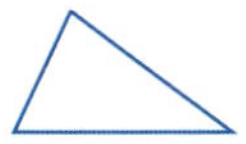

Addition Property of Equality (p. 138) If you add the same number to each side of an equation, the two sides remain equal.

propiedad de adición de la igualdad Si sumas el mismo número a ambos lados de una ecuación, los dos lados permanecen iguales.

additive inverse (p. 96) The opposite of an integer. The sum of an integer and its additive inverse is zero.

inverso aditivo El opuesto de un entero. La suma de un entero y su inverso aditivo es cero.

adjacent angles (p. 511) Angles that have the same vertex, share a common side, and do not overlap.

ángulos adyacentes Ángulos que comparten el mismo vértice y un común lado, pero no se sobreponen.

algebra (p. 44) The branch of mathematics that involves expressions with variables.

álgebra Rama de las matemáticas que involucra expresiones con variables.

algebraic expression (p. 44) A combination of variables, numbers, and at least one operation.

expresión algebraica Combinación de variables, números y por lo menos una operación.

analyze (p. 397) To describe, summarize, and compare data.

analizar Describir, resumir o comparar datos.

angle (p. 510) Two rays with a common endpoint form an angle. The rays and vertex are used to name the angle.

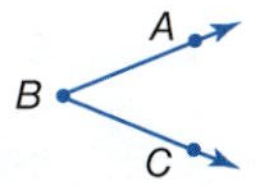

$\angle ABC$, $\angle CBA$, or $\angle B$

ángulo Dos rayos con un extremo común forman un ángulo. Los rayos y el vértice se usan para nombrar el ángulo.

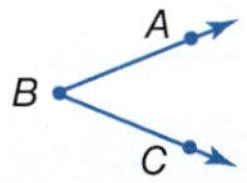

$\angle ABC$, $\angle CBA$ o $\angle B$

area (p. 157) The number of square units needed to cover a surface enclosed by a geometric figure.

área El número de unidades cuadradas necesarias para cubrir una superficie cerrada por una figura geométrica.

arithmetic sequence (p. 57) A sequence in which each term is found by adding the same number to the previous term.

sucesión aritmética Sucesión en que cada término se encuentra sumando el mismo número al término anterior.

Associative Property (p. 54) The way in which three numbers are grouped when they are added or multiplied does not change their sum or product.

propiedad asociativa La manera de agrupar tres números al sumarlos o multiplicarlos no cambia su suma o producto.

average (p. 402) The mean of a set of data.

promedio La media de un conjunto de datos.

B

bar graph (p. 415) A graphic form using bars to make comparisons of statistics.

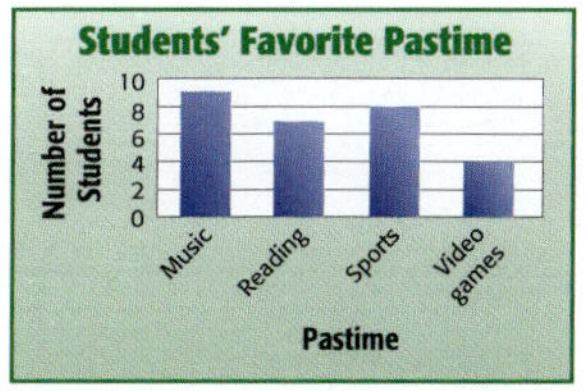

gráfica de barras Forma gráfica que usa barras para hacer comparaciones estadísticas.

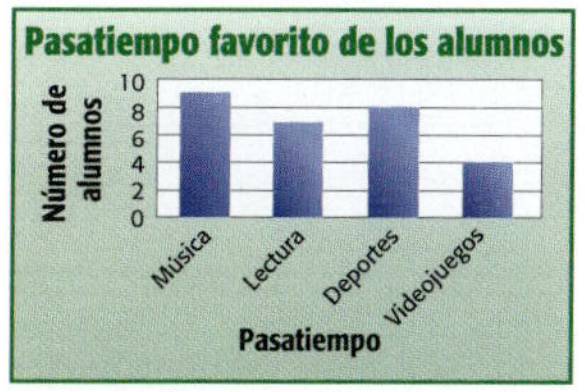

bar notation (p. 197) In repeating decimals, the line or bar placed over the digits that repeat. For example, $2.\overline{63}$ indicates that the digits 63 repeat.

notación de barra Línea o barra que se coloca sobre los dígitos que se repiten en decimales periódicos. Por ejemplo, $2.\overline{63}$ indica que los dígitos 63 se repiten.

base (p. 30) In a power, the number used as a factor. In 10^3, the base is 10. That is, $10^3 = 10 \times 10 \times 10$.

base En una potencia, el número usado como factor. En 10^3, la base es 10. Es decir, $10^3 = 10 \times 10 \times 10$.

base (p. 572) The base of a parallelogram or triangle is any side of the figure. The bases of a trapezoid are the parallel sides.

base La base de un paralelogramo o triángulo es el lado de la figura. Las bases de un trapecio son los lados paralelos.

base (p. 603) The top or bottom face of a three-dimensional figure.

base La cara inferior o superior de una figura tridimensional.

biased sample (p. 439) A sample drawn in such a way that one or more parts of the population are favored over others.

muestra sesgada Muestra en que se favorece una o más partes de una población.

C

center (p. 584) The given point from which all points on a circle or sphere are the same distance.

circle (p. 584) The set of all points in a plane that are the same distance from a given point called the center.

circle graph (p. 518) A type of statistical graph used to compare parts of a whole.

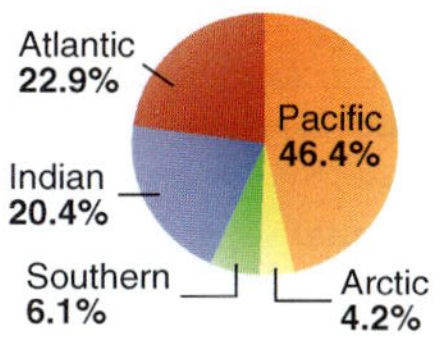

circumference (p. 584) The distance around a circle.

cluster (p. 397) Data that are grouped closely together.

coefficient (p. 45) The numerical factor of a term that contains a variable.

combination (p. 480) An arrangement, or listing, of objects in which order is not important.

common denominator (p. 215) A common multiple of the denominators of two or more fractions. 24 is a common denominator for $\frac{1}{3}$, $\frac{5}{8}$, and $\frac{3}{4}$ because 24 is the LCM of 3, 8, and 4.

Commutative Property (p. 54) The order in which two numbers are added or multiplied does not change their sum or product.

complementary angles (p. 514) Two angles are complementary if the sum of their measures is 90°.

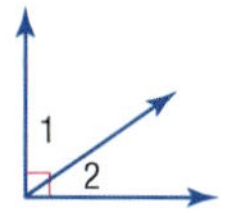

∠1 and ∠2 are complementary angles.

centro Un punto dado del cual equidistan todos los puntos de un círculo o de una esfera.

círculo Conjunto de todos los puntos en un plano que equidistan de un punto dado llamado centro.

gráfica circular Tipo de gráfica estadística que se usa para comparar las partes de un todo.

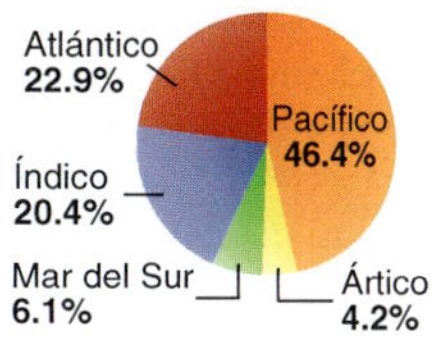

circunferencia La distancia alrededor de un círculo.

agrupamiento Datos estrechamente agrupados.

coeficiente El factor numérico de un término que contiene una variable.

combinación Arreglo o lista de objetos donde el orden no es importante.

común denominador El múltiplo común de los denominadores de dos o más fracciones. 24 es un denominador común para $\frac{1}{3}$, $\frac{5}{8}$ y $\frac{3}{4}$ porque 24 es el mcm de 3, 8 y 4.

propiedad conmutativa El orden en que se suman o multiplican dos números no afecta su suma o producto.

ángulos complementarios Dos ángulos son complementarios si la suma de sus medidas es 90°.

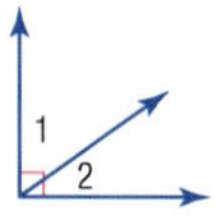

∠1 y ∠2 son complementarios.

complementary events (p. 462) The events of one outcome happening and that outcome not happening are complementary events. The sum of the probabilities of complementary events is 1.

complex figure (p. 596) A figure made of circles, rectangles, squares, and other two-dimensional figures.

composite number (p. 181) A whole number greater than 1 that has more than two factors.

compound event (p. 492) An event consisting of two or more simple events.

cone (p. 604) A three-dimensional figure with a curved surface and a circular base.

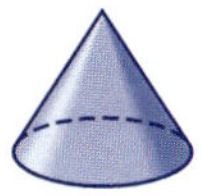

congruent angles (p. 511) Angles that have the same measure.

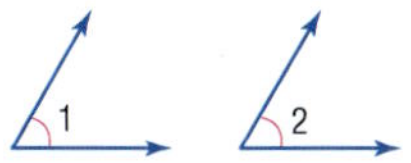

∠1 and ∠2 are congruent angles.

congruent figures (p. 554) Figures with equal corresponding sides of equal length and corresponding angles of equal measure.

congruent segments (p. 525) Segments having the same measure.

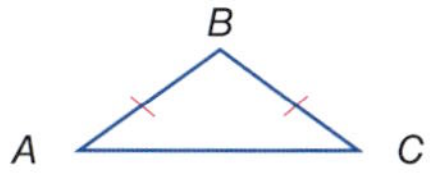

Side $\overline{AB}$ is congruent to side $\overline{BC}$.

convenience sample (p. 439) A sample which includes members of the population that are easily accessed.

coordinate plane (p. 88) A plane in which a horizontal number line and a vertical number line intersect at their zero points. Also called a coordinate grid.

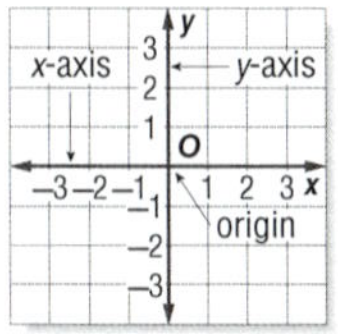

eventos complementarios Se dice de los eventos de un resultado que ocurren y el resultado que no ocurre. La suma de las probabilidades de eventos complementarios es 1.

figura compleja Una figura compuesta por círculos, rectángulos, cuadrados y otras dos figuras bidimencionales.

número compuesto Un número entero mayor que 1 que tiene más de dos factores.

evento compuesto Un evento que consiste en dos o más eventos simples.

cono Figura tridimensional con una superficie curva y una base circular.

ángulos congruentes Ángulos que tienen la misma medida.

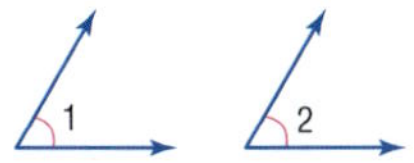

∠1 y ∠2 son congruentes.

figuras congruentes Figuras cuyos lados y ángulos correspondientes son iguales.

segmentos congruentes Segmentos que tienen la misma medida.

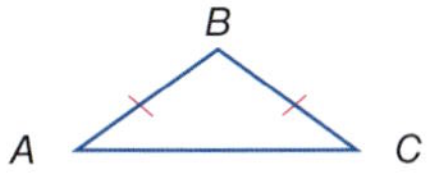

$\overline{AB}$ es congruente a $\overline{BC}$.

muestra de conveniencia Muestra que incluye miembros de una población fácilmente accesibles.

plano de coordenadas Plano en el cual se han trazado dos rectas numéricas, una horizontal y una vertical, que se intersecan en sus puntos cero. También conocido como sistema de coordenadas.

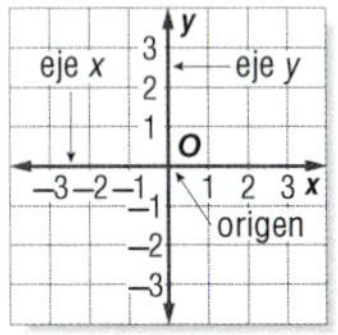

corresponding angles (p. 540) Congruent angles of similar figures.

corresponding sides (p. 540) Congruent or proportional sides of similar figures.

counterexample (p. 56) An example showing that a statement is not true.

cross product (p. 310) In a proportion, a cross product is the product of the numerator of one ratio and the denominator of the other ratio.

cubed (p. 30) The product in which a number is a factor three times. Two cubed is 8 because $2 \times 2 \times 2 = 8$.

cylinder (p. 604) A three-dimensional figure with two parallel congruent circular bases.

ángulos correspondientes Ángulos iguales de figuras semejantes.

lados correspondientes Lados iguales o proporcionales de figuras semejantes.

contraejemplo Ejemplo que demuestra que un enunciado no es verdadero.

productos cruzados En una proporción, un producto cruzado es el producto del numerador de una razón y el denominador de la otra razón.

al cubo El producto de un número por sí mismo, tres veces. Dos al cubo es 8 porque $2 \times 2 \times 2 = 8$.

cilindro Figura tridimensional que tiene dos bases circulares congruentes y paralelas.

D

data (p. 376) Pieces of information, which are often numerical.

decagon (p. 546) A polygon having ten sides.

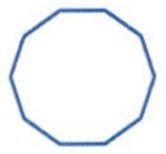

defining the variable (p. 50) Choosing a variable to represent an unknown value in a problem, and using it to write an expression or equation to solve the problem.

degrees (p. 510) The most common unit of measure for angles. If a circle were divided into 360 equal-sized parts, each part would have an angle measure of 1 degree.

dependent events (p. 493) Two or more events in which the outcome of one event affects the outcome of the other event(s).

diameter (p. 584) The distance across a circle through its center.

disjoint events (p. 494) Events that cannot happen at the same time.

datos Información, la cual a menudo se presenta de manera numérica.

decágono Un polígono con diez lados.

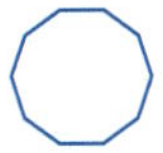

definir una variable El elegir una variable para representar un valor desconocido en un problema y usarla para escribir una expresión o ecuación para resolver el problema.

grados La unidad más común para medir ángulos. Si un círculo se divide en 360 partes iguales, cada parte tiene una medida angular de 1 grado.

eventos dependientes Dos o más eventos en que el resultado de un evento afecta el resultado de otro u otros eventos.

diámetro La distancia a través de un círculo pasando por el centro.

eventos disjuntos Eventos que no pueden ocurrir al mismo tiempo.

Distributive Property (p. 53) To multiply a sum by a number, multiply each addend of the sum by the number outside the parentheses.

Division Property of Equality (p. 142) If you divide each side of an equation by the same nonzero number, the two sides remain equal.

domain (p. 63) The set of input values for a function.

propiedad distributiva Para multiplicar una suma por un número, multiplica cada sumando de la suma por el número fuera del paréntesis.

propiedad de igualdad de la división Si divides ambos lados de una ecuación entre el mismo número no nulo, los lados permanecen iguales.

dominio El conjunto de valores de entrada de una función.

E

edge (p. 603) The segment formed by intersecting faces of a three-dimensional figure.

equation (p. 49) A mathematical sentence that contains an equals sign, =.

equilateral triangle (p. 525) A triangle having three congruent sides.

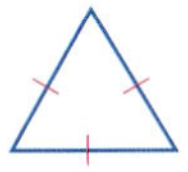

equivalent expressions (p. 53) Expressions that have the same value.

equivalent fractions (p. 192) Fractions that have the same value. $\frac{2}{3}$ and $\frac{4}{6}$ are equivalent fractions.

equivalent ratios (p. 288) Two ratios that have the same value.

evaluate (p. 31) To find the value of an expression.

experimental probability (p. 486) An estimated probability based on the relative frequency of positive outcomes occurring during an experiment.

exponent (p. 30) In a power, the number that tells how many times the base is used as a factor. In 5^3, the exponent is 3. That is, $5^3 = 5 \times 5 \times 5$.

exponential form (p. 31) Numbers written with exponents.

arista Segmento de recta formado por la intersección de las caras en una figura tridimensional.

ecuación Enunciado matemático que contiene un signo de igualdad, =.

triángulo equilátero Triángulo con tres lados congruentes.

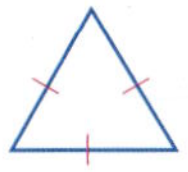

expresiones equivalentes Expresiones que tienen el mismo valor.

fracciones equivalentes Fracciones que tienen el mismo valor. $\frac{2}{3}$ y $\frac{4}{6}$ son fracciones equivalentes.

razones equivalentes Dos razones que tienen el mismo valor.

evaluar Calcular el valor de una expresión. probabilidad experimental

probabilidad experimental Estimado de una probabilidad que se basa en la frecuencia relativa de los resultados positivos que ocurren durante un experimento.

exponente En una potencia, el número que indica las veces que la base se usa como factor. En 5^3, el exponente es 3. Es decir, $5^3 = 5 \times 5 \times 5$.

forma exponencial Números escritos usando exponentes.

F

face (p. 603) The flat surface of a three-dimensional figure.

cara Superficies planas de una figura tridimensional.

factors (p. 30) Two or more numbers that are multiplied together to form a product.

factores Dos o más números que se multiplican entre sí para formar un producto.

factor tree (p. 182) A diagram showing the prime factorization of a number. The factors branch out from the previous factors until all of the factors are prime numbers.

diagrama de árbol Diagrama que muestra la factorización prima de un número. Los factores se ramifican a partir de los factores previos hasta que todos los factores son números primos.

formula (p. 144) An equation that shows the relationship among certain quantities.

fórmula Ecuación que muestra la relación entre ciertas cantidades.

function (p. 63) A relation in which each element of the input is paired with exactly one element of the output according to a specified rule.

función Relación en que cada elemento de entrada es apareado con un único elemento de salida, según una regla específica.

function rule (p. 63) The operation performed on the input of a function.

regla de función Operación que se efectúa en el valor de entrada.

function table (p. 63) A table used to organize the input numbers, output numbers, and the function rule.

tabla de funciones Tabla que organiza las entradas, la regla y las salidas de una función.

Fundamental Counting Principle (p. 471) Uses multiplication of the number of ways each event in an experiment can occur to find the number of possible outcomes in a sample space.

Principio Fundamental de Contar Este principio usa la multiplicación del número de veces que puede ocurrir cada evento en un experimento para calcular el número de posibles resultados en un espacio muestral.

G

gram (p. 304) A unit of mass in the metric system equivalent to 0.001 kilogram.

gramo Unidad de masa del sistema métrico. Un gramo equivale a 0.001 de kilogramo.

graph (p. 80) The process of placing a point on a number line at its proper location.

graficar Proceso de dibujar o trazar un punto en una recta numérica en su ubicación correcta.

greatest common factor (GCF) (p. 186) The greatest of the common factors of two or more numbers. The GCF of 18 and 24 is 6.

máximo común divisor (MCD) El mayor factor común de dos o más números. El MCD de 18 y 24 es 6.

H

height (p. 572) The length of the segment perpendicular to the base with endpoints on opposite sides. In a triangle, the distance from a base to the opposite vertex.

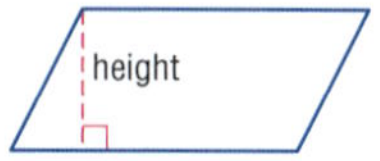

altura Longitud del segmento perpendicular a la base y con extremos en lados opuestos. En un triángulo, es la distancia desde una base al vértice opuesto.

heptagon (p. 546) A polygon having seven sides.

heptágono Polígono con siete lados.

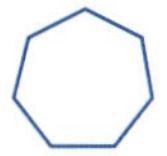

hexagon (p. 546) A polygon having six sides.

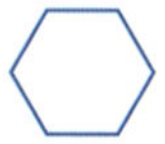

hexágono Polígono con seis lados.

histogram (p. 416) A special kind of bar graph in which the bars are used to represent the frequency of numerical data that have been organized in intervals.

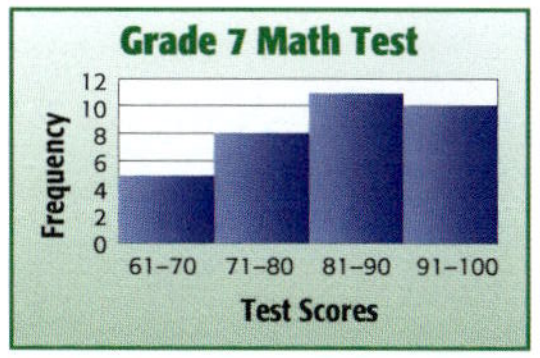

histograma Tipo especial de gráfica de barras que usa barras para representar la frecuencia de los datos numéricos, los cuales han sido organizados en intervalos iguales.

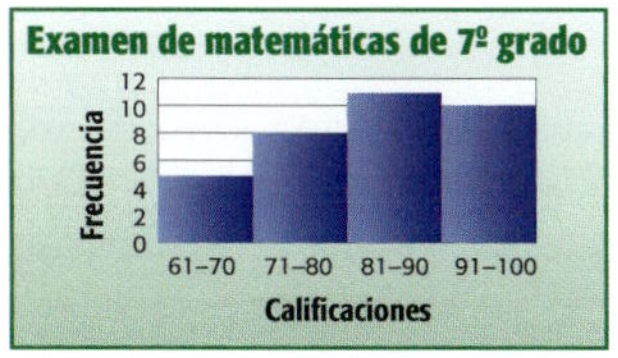

hypotenuse (p. 640) The side opposite the right angle in a right triangle.

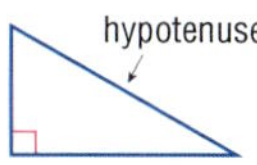

hipotenusa El lado opuesto al ángulo recto en un triángulo rectángulo.

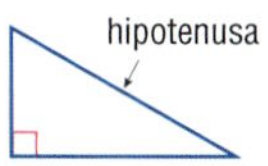

I

Identity Property (p. 54) The sum of an addend and 0 is the addend. The product of a factor and 1 is the factor.

propiedad de identidad La suma de un sumando y 0 es el sumando mismo. El producto de un factor y 1 es el factor mismo.

independent events (p. 492) Two or more events in which the outcome of one event does not affect the outcome of the other event(s).

eventos independientes Dos o más eventos en los cuales el resultado de uno de ellos no afecta el resultado de los otros eventos.

indirect measurement (p. 542) Finding a measurement by using similar triangles and writing a proportion.

medida indirecta Técnica que se usa para calcular una medida a partir de triángulos semejantes y proporciones.

integer (p. 80) Any number from the set {..., −4, −3, −2, −1, 0, 1, 2, 3, 4, ...}

entero Todo número del conjunto {..., −4, −3, −2, −1, 0, 1, 2, 3, 4, ...}

inverse operations (p. 136) Operations that "undo" each other. Addition and subtraction are inverse operations.

operaciones inversas Operaciones que se "anulan" mutuamente. La adición y la sustracción son operaciones inversas.

irrational number (p. 637) A number that cannot be expressed as the quotient of two integers.

número irracional Número que no se puede expresar como el cociente de dos enteros.

isosceles triangle (p. 525) A triangle having at least two congruent sides.

K

kilogram (p. 304) The base unit of mass in the metric system equivalent to 1,000 grams.

L

lateral face (p. 603) One side of a three-dimesional figure.

leaf (p. 410) The second greatest place value of data in a stem-and-leaf plot.

least common denominator (LCD) (p. 215) The least common multiple of the denominators of two or more fractions.

least common multiple (LCM) (p. 211) The least of the common multiples of two or more numbers. The LCM of 2 and 3 is 6.

leg (p. 640) Either of the two sides that form the right angle of a right triangle.

like fractions (p. 236) Fractions that have the same denominator.

line graph (p. 426) A type of statistical graph using lines to show how values change over a period of time.

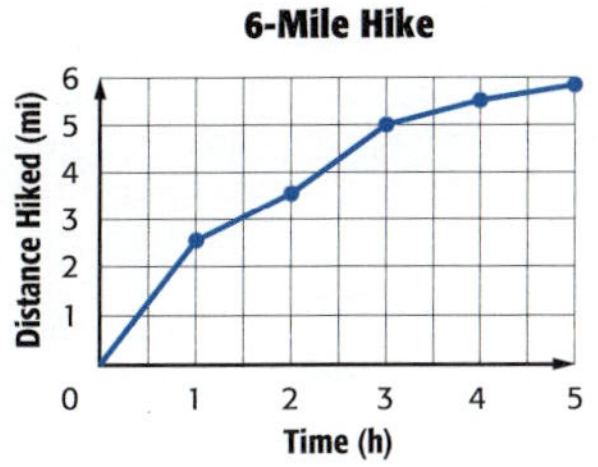

line of reflection (p. 559) The line over which a figure is reflected.

triángulo isósceles Triángulo que tiene por lo menos dos lados congruentes.

kilogramo Unidad fundamental de masa del sistema métrico. Un kilogramo equivale a mil gramos.

cara lateral Lado de una figura tridimensional.

hoja El segundo valor de posición mayor en un diagrama de tallo y hojas.

mínimo común denominador (mcd) El menor múltiplo común de los denominadores de dos o más fracciones.

mínimo común múltiplo (mcm) El menor múltiplo común de dos o más números. El mcm de 2 y 3 es 6.

cateto Cualquiera de los lados que forman el ángulo recto de un triángulo rectángulo.

fracciones semejantes Fracciones con el mismo denominador.

gráfica lineal Tipo de gráfica estadística que usa segmentos de recta para mostrar cómo cambian los valores durante un período de tiempo.

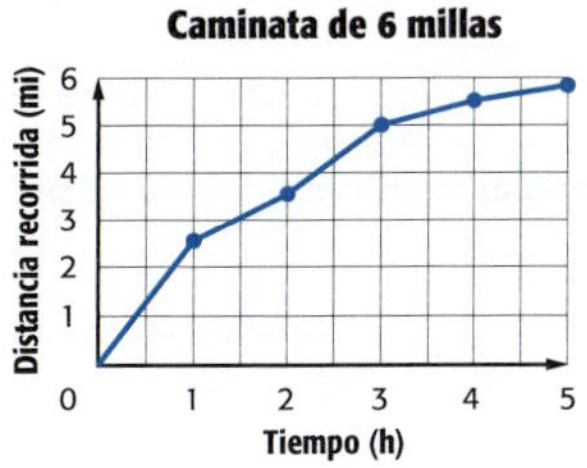

eje de reflexión La línea sobre la cual se refleja una figura.

line of symmetry (p. 558) A line that divides a figure into two halves that are reflections of each other.

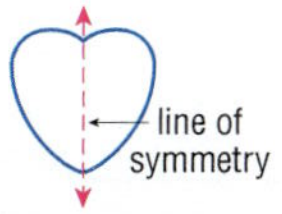

line plot (p. 396) A diagram that shows the frequency of data. An × is placed above a number on a number line each time that number occurs in a set of data.

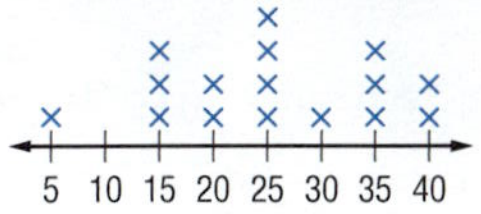

line symmetry (p. 558) Figures that match exactly when folded in half have line symmetry.

linear equation (p. 164) An equation for which the graph is a straight line.

liter (p. 304) The base unit of capacity in the metric system. A liter is a little more than a quart.

M

mean (p. 402) The sum of the data divided by the number of items in the data set.

measures of central tendency (p. 402) Numbers that are used to describe the center of a set of data. These measures include the mean, median, and mode.

median (p. 403) The middle number in a set of data when the data are ordered from least to greatest. If the data has an even number of items, the median is the mean of the two numbers closer to the middle.

meter (p. 304) The base unit of length in the metric system.

metric system (p. 304) A base-ten system of measurement using the base units: meter for length, kilogram for mass, and liter for capacity.

eje de simetría Recta que divide una figura en dos mitades que son reflexiones entre sí.

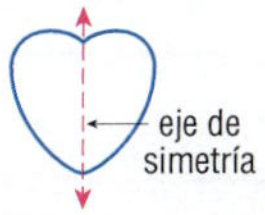

esquema lineal Grafica que muestra la frecuencia de datos. Se coloca una × sobre la recta numérica, cada vez que el número aparece en un conjunto de datos.

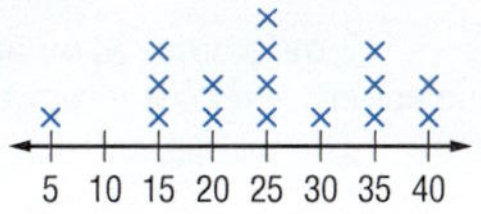

simetría lineal Exhiben simetría lineal las figuras que coinciden exactamente al doblarse una sobre otra.

ecuación lineal Ecuación cuya gráfica es una recta.

litro Unidad básica de capacidad del sistema métrico. Un litro es un poco más de un cuarto de galón.

media La suma de los datos dividida entre el número total de artículos en el conjunto de datos.

medidas de tendencia central Números que se usan para describir el centro de un conjunto de datos. Estas medidas incluyen la media, la mediana y la moda.

mediana El número del medio en un conjunto de datos cuando los datos se ordenan de menor a mayor. Si los datos tienen un número par de artículos, la mediana es la media de los dos números más cercanos al medio.

metro Unidad fundamental de longitud del sistema métrico.

sistema métrico Sistema de medidas de base diez que usa las unidades fundamentales: metro para longitud, kilogramo para masa y litro para capacidad.

mode (p. 403) The number or numbers that appear most often in a set of data. If there are two or more numbers that occur most often, all of them are modes.

moda El número o números que aparece con más frecuencia en un conjunto de datos. Si hay dos o más números que ocurren con más frecuencia, todosellos son modas.

multiple (p. 211) The product of a number and any whole number.

múltiplo El producto de un número y cualquier número entero.

Multiplication Property of Equality (p. 259) If you multiply each side of an equation by the same nonzero number, the two sides remain equal.

propiedad de multiplicación de la igualdad Si multiplicas ambos lados de una ecuación por el mismo número no nulo, lo lados permanecen iguales.

multiplicative inverse (p. 258) The product of a number and its multiplicative inverse is 1.

The multiplicative inverse of $\frac{2}{3}$ is $\frac{3}{2}$.

inverso multiplicativo El producto de un número y su inverso multiplicativo es 1.

El inverso multiplicativo de $\frac{2}{3}$ es $\frac{3}{2}$.

N

negative integer (p. 80) An integer that is less than zero.

entero negativo Un entero menor que cero.

net (p. 600) A two-dimensional figure that can be used to build a three-dimensional figure.

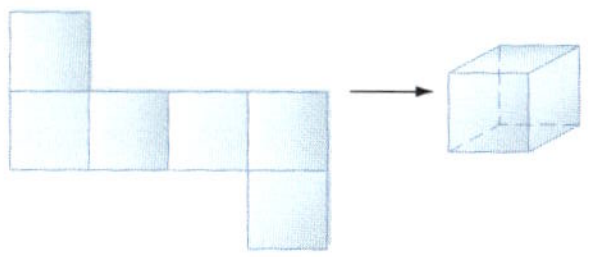

red Figura bidimensional que sirve para hacer una figura tridimensional.

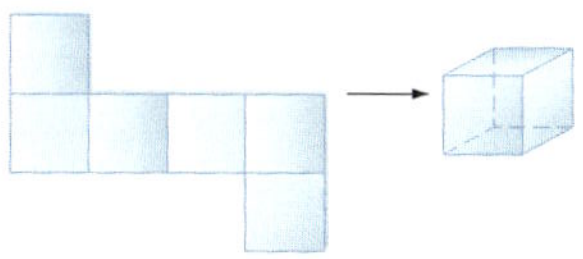

nonagon (p. 546) A polygon having nine sides.

enágono Polígono que tiene nueve lados.

numerical expression (p. 38) A combination of numbers and operations.

expresión numérica Combinación de números y operaciones.

O

obtuse angle (p. 511) Any angle that measures greater than 90° but less than 180°.

ángulo obtuso Cualquier ángulo que mide más de 90° pero menos de 180°.

obtuse triangle (p. 525) A triangle having one obtuse angle.

triángulo obtusángulo Triángulo que tiene un ángulo obtuso.

octagon (p. 546) A polygon having eight sides.

octágono Polígono que tiene ocho lados.

opposites (p. 96) Two integers are opposites if they are represented on the number line by points that are the same distance from zero, but on opposite sides of zero. The sum of two opposites is zero.

opuestos Dos enteros son opuestos si, en la recta numérica, están representados por puntos que equidistan de cero, pero en direcciones opuestas. La suma de dos opuestos es cero.

order of operations (p. 38) The rules to follow when more than one operation is used in a numerical expression.

1. Evaluate the expressions inside grouping symbols
2. Evaluate all powers
3. Multiply and divide in order from left to right.
4. Add and subtract in order from left to right.

orden de operaciones Reglas a seguir cuando se usa más de una operación en una expresión numérica.

1. Primero ejecuta todas las operaciones dentro de los símbolos de agrupamiento
2. Evalúa todas las potencias antes que las otras operaciones.
3. Multiplica y divide en orden de izquierda a derecha.
4. Suma y resta en orden de izquierda a derecha.

ordered pair (p. 88) A pair of numbers used to locate a point in the coordinate plane. An ordered pair is written in the form (x-coordinate, y-coordinate).

par ordenado Par de números que se utiliza para ubicar un punto en un plano de coordenadas. Se escribe de la siguiente forma: (coordenada x, coordenada y).

origin (p. 88) The point at which the x-axis and the y-axis intersect in a coordinate plane.

origen Punto en que el eje x y el eje y se intersecan en un plano de coordenadas.

outcome (p. 460) One possible result of a probability event. For example, 4 is an outcome when a number cube is rolled.

resultado Uno de los resultados posibles de un evento probabilístico. Por ejemplo, 4 es un resultado posible cuando se lanza un dado.

outlier (p. 397) A piece of data that is quite separated from the rest of the data.

valor atípico Dato que se encuentra muy separado del resto de los datos.

P

parallel lines (p. 533) Lines in a plane that do not intersect.

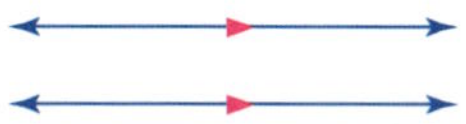

líneas paralelas Rectas situadas en un mismo plano y que no se intersecan.

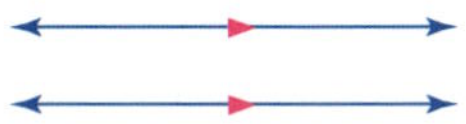

parallelogram (p. 533) A quadrilateral with opposite sides parallel and opposite sides congruent.

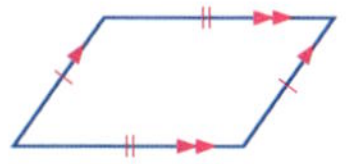

paralelogramo Cuadrilátero cuyos lados opuestos son paralelos y congruentes.

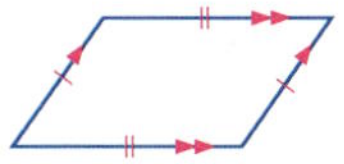

part (p. 350) In a percent proportion, the number that is compared to the whole quantity.

parte En una proporción porcentual, el número que se compara con la cantidad total.

pentagon (p. 546) A polygon having five sides.

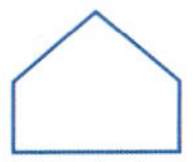

percent (p. 202) A ratio that compares a number to 100.

percent equation (p. 361) An equation that describes the relationship between the part, whole, and percent.
part = percent • whole

percent of change (p. 369) A ratio that compares the change in a quantity to the original amount.

percent of decrease (p. 369) A percent of change when the original quantity decreased.

percent of increase (p. 369) A percent of change when the original quantity increased.

percent proportion (p. 350) Compares part of a quantity to the whole quantity using a percent.

$$\frac{\text{part}}{\text{whole}} = \frac{\text{percent}}{100}$$

perfect squares (p. 34) Numbers with square roots that are whole numbers. 25 is a perfect square because the square root of 25 is 5.

perimeter (p. 156) The distance around a closed geometric figure.

permutation (p. 475) An arrangement, or listing, of objects in which order is important.

perpendicular lines (p. 512) Lines that meet to form right angles.

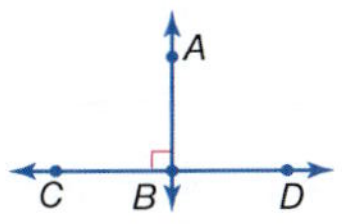

pi (π) (p. 584) The ratio of the circumference of a circle to its diameter. An approximation often used for π is 3.14.

polygon (p. 546) A simple closed figure in a plane formed by three or more line segments.

pentágono Polígono que tiene cinco lados.

por ciento Razón que compara un número con 100.

ecuación porcentual Ecuación que describe la relación entre la parte, el todo y el por ciento.
parte = por ciento • todo.

porcentaje de cambio Razón que compara el cambio en una cantidad, con la cantidad original.

porcentaje de disminución Porcentaje de cambio cuando disminuye la cantidad original.

porcentaje de aumento Porcentaje de cambio cuando aumenta la cantidad original.

proporción porcentual Comparar partes de una cantidad, a la cantidad entera, usando un porcentaje.

$$\frac{\text{parte}}{\text{todo}} = \frac{\text{porcentaje}}{100}$$

cuadrados perfectos Números cuya raíz cuadrada es un número entero. 25 es un cuadrado perfecto porque la raíz cuadrada de 25 es 5.

perímetro La distancia alrededor de una figura geométrica cerrada.

permutación Arreglo o lista en que el orden es importante.

rectas perpendiculares Rectas que al encontrarse forman ángulos rectos.

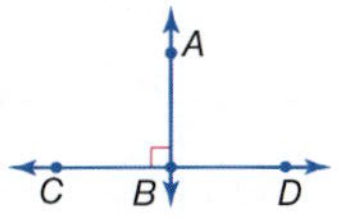

pi (π) Razón entre la circunferencia de un círculo y su diámetro. A menudo, se usa 3.14 como aproximación del valor de π.

polígono Figura simple cerrada en un plano, formada por tres o más segmentos de recta.

population (p. 434) The entire group of items or individuals from which the samples under consideration are taken.

positive integer (p. 80) An integer that is greater than zero.

powers (p. 30) Numbers expressed using exponents. The power 3^2 is read *three to the second power, or three squared.*

prime factorization (p. 182) Expressing a composite number as a product of prime numbers. For example, the prime factorization of 63 is $3 \times 3 \times 7$.

prime number (p. 181) A whole number greater than 1 that has exactly two factors, 1 and itself.

principal (p. 379) The amount of money deposited or invested.

prism (p. 601) A three-dimensional figure with at least three rectangular lateral faces and top and bottom faces parallel.

probability (p. 460) The chance that some event will happen. It is the ratio of the number of ways a certain event can occur to the number of possible outcomes.

properties (p. 54) Statements that are true for any number or variable.

proportion (p. 310) An equation that shows that two ratios are equivalent.

proportional (p. 310) The relationship between two ratios with a constant rate or ratio.

protractor (p. 680) An instrument used to measure angles.

pyramid (p. 603) A three-dimensional figure with at least three lateral faces that are triangles and only one base.

Pythagorean Theorem (p. 640) In a right triangle, the square of the length of the hypotenuse is equal to the sum of the squares of the lengths of the legs. $c^2 = a^2 + b^2$

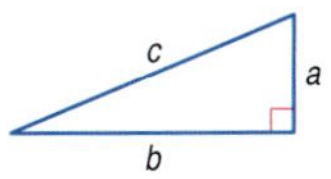

población El grupo total de individuos o de artículos del cual se toman las muestras bajo estudio.

entero positivo Un entero mayor que cero.

potencias Números que se expresan usando exponentes. La potencia 3^2 se lee *tres a la segunda potencia o tres al cuadrado.*

factorización prima Escritura de un número compuesto como el producto de números primos. La factorización prima de 63 es $3 \times 3 \times 7$.

número primo Número entero mayor que 1 que sólo tiene dos factores, 1 y sí mismo.

capital La cantidad de dinero depositada o invertida.

prisma Figura tridimensional que tiene por lo menos tres caras laterales rectangulares y caras paralelas superior e inferior.

probabilidad La posibilidad de que suceda un evento. Es la razón del número de maneras en que puede ocurrir un evento al número total de resultados posibles.

propiedades Enunciados que se cumplen para cualquier número o variable.

proporción Ecuación que muestra que dos razones son equivalentes.

proporcional Relación entre dos razones con una tasa o razón constante.

transportador Instrumento que sirve para medir ángulos.

pirámide Figura tridimensional que tiene por lo menos tres caras laterales triangulares que son triángulos y una sola base.

Teorema de Pitágoras En un triángulo rectángulo, el cuadrado de la longitud de la hipotenusa es igual a la suma de los cuadrados de las longitudes de los catetos. $c^2 = a^2 + b^2$

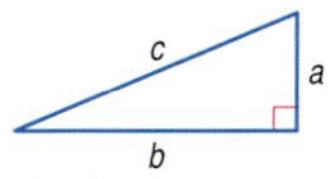

Q

quadrant (p. 88) One of the four regions into which the two perpendicular number lines of the coordinate plane separate the plane.

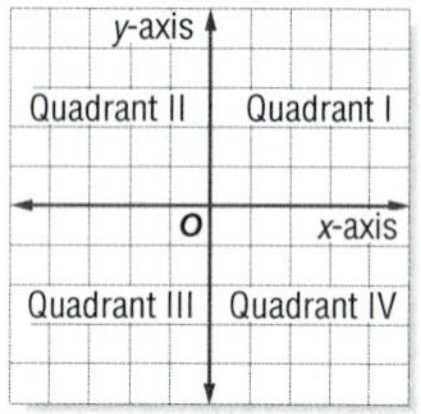

quadrilateral (p. 533) A closed figure having four sides and four angles.

cuadrante Una de las cuatro regiones en que dos rectas numéricas perpendiculares dividen el plano de coordenadas.

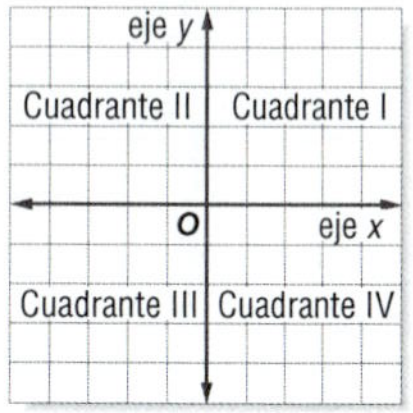

cuadrilátero Figura cerrada que tiene cuatro lados y cuatro ángulos.

R

radical sign (p. 35) The symbol used to indicate a nonnegative square root, $\sqrt{\ }$.

radius (p. 584) The distance from the center of a circle to any point on the circle.

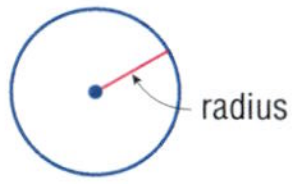

random (p. 461) Outcomes occur at random if each outcome is equally likely to occur.

range (p. 63) The set of output values for a function.

range (p. 397) The difference between the greatest and least numbers in a data set.

rate (p. 287) A ratio that compares two quantities with different kinds of units.

rate of change (p. 293) A ratio that shows a change in one quantity with respect to a change in another quantity.

ratio (p. 202) A comparison of two numbers by division. The ratio of 2 to 3 can be written as 2 out of 3, 2 to 3, 2 : 3, or $\frac{2}{3}$.

signo radical Símbolo que se usa para indicar una raíz cuadrada no negativa, $\sqrt{\ }$.

radio Distancia desde el centro de un círculo hasta cualquier punto del mismo.

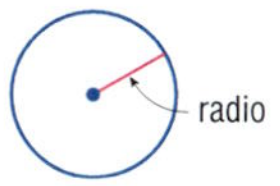

aleatorio Un resultado ocurre al azar si la posibilidad de ocurrir de cada resultado es equiprobable.

rango Conjunto de los valores de salida de una función.

rango La diferencia entre el número mayor y el menor en un conjunto de datos.

tasa Razón que compara dos cantidades que tienen distintas unidades de medida.

tasa de cambio Razón que representa el cambio en una cantidad con respecto al cambio en otra cantidad.

razón Comparación de dos números mediante división. La razón de 2 a 3 puede escribirse como 2 de cada 3, 2 a 3, 2:3 ó $\frac{2}{3}$.

rational number (p. 216) A number that can be expressed as a fraction.

reciprocal (p. 258) The multiplicative inverse of a number.

rectangle (p. 533) A parallelogram having four right angles.

rectangular prism (p. 611) A solid figure that has two parallel and congruent bases that are rectangles.

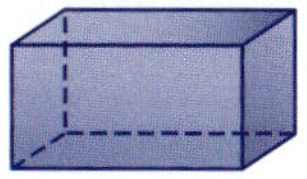

reflection (p. 559) A type of transformation in which a figure is flipped over a line of symmetry.

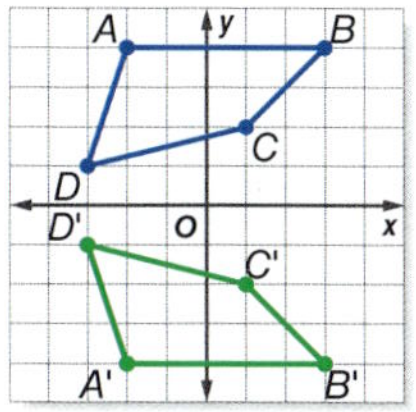

regular polygon (p. 546) A polygon that has all sides congruent and all angles congruent.

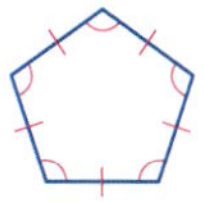

repeating decimals (p. 197) A decimal whose digits repeat in groups of one or more. Examples are 0.181818... and 0.83333... .

rhombus (p. 533) A parallelogram having four congruent sides.

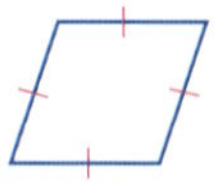

right angle (p. 511) An angle that measures 90°.

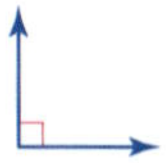

número racional Número que puede expresarse como fracción.

recíproco El inverso multiplicativo de un número.

rectángulo Paralelogramo con cuatro ángulos rectos.

prisma rectangular Figura sólida con dos bases paralelas y congruentes que son rectángulos.

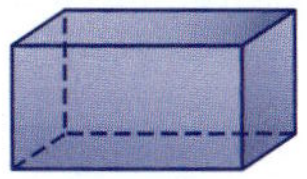

reflexión Tipo de transformación en el que se da vuelta a una figura sobre un eje de simetría.

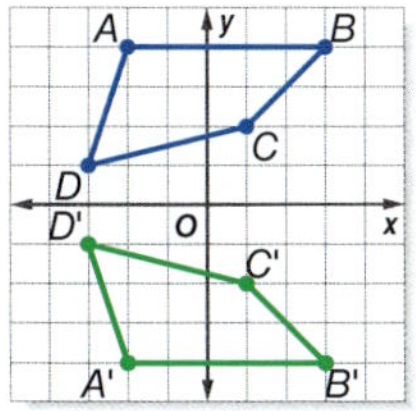

polígono regular Polígono con todos los lados y todos los ángulos congruentes.

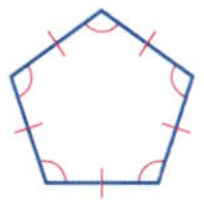

decimales periódicos Decimal cuyos dígitos se repiten en grupos de uno o más. Por ejemplo: 0.181818... y 0.83333... .

rombo Paralelogramo que tiene cuatro lados congruentes.

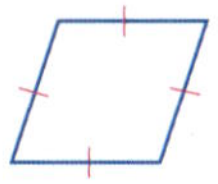

ángulo rect Ángulo que mide exactamente 90°.

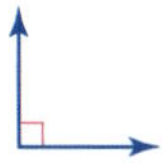

right triangle (p. 525) A triangle having one right angle.

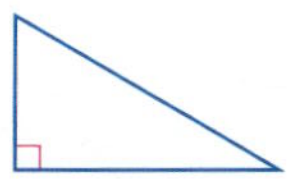

S

sample (p. 438) A randomly selected group chosen for the purpose of collecting data.

sample space (p. 465) The set of all possible outcomes of a probability experiment.

sampling (p. 312) A practical method used to survey a representative group.

scale (p. 320) On a map, intervals used representing the ratio of distance on the map to the actual distance.

scale drawing (p. 320) A drawing that is similar but either larger or smaller than the actual object.

scale factor (p. 322) A scale written as a ratio in simplest form.

scale model (p. 320) A model used to represent something that is too large or too small for an actual-size model.

scalene triangle (p. 525) A triangle having no congruent sides.

scatter plot (p. 427) In a scatter plot, two sets of related data are plotted as ordered pairs on the same graph.

School Commute

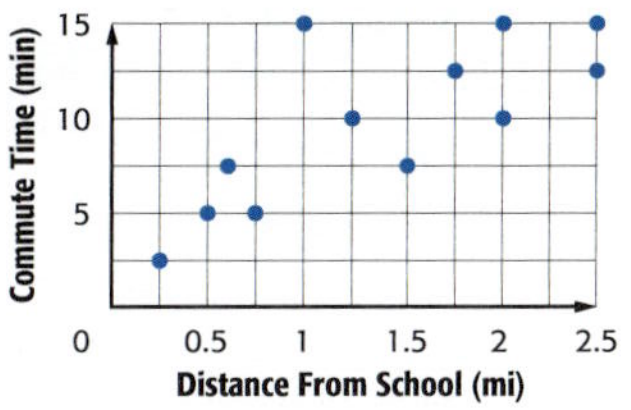

triángulo rectángulo Triángulo que tiene un ángulo recto.

muestra Grupo escogido al azar o aleatoriamente que se usa con el propósito de recoger datos.

espacio muestral Conjunto de todos los resultados posibles de un experimento probabilístico.

muestreo Método conveniente que facilita la elección y el estudio de un grupo representativo.

escala En un mapa, los intervalos que se usan para representar la razón de las distancias en el mapa a las distancias verdaderas.

dibujo a escala Dibujo que es semejante, pero más grande o más pequeño que el objeto real.

factor de escala Escala escrita como una tasa en forma reducida.

modelo a escala Réplica de un objeto real, el cual es demasiado grande o demasiado pequeño como para construirlo de tamaño natural.

triángulo escaleno Triángulo sin lados congruentes.

diagrama de dispersión Diagrama en que dos conjuntos de datos relacionados aparecen graficados como pares ordenados en la misma gráfica.

Tiempo para llegar a la escuela

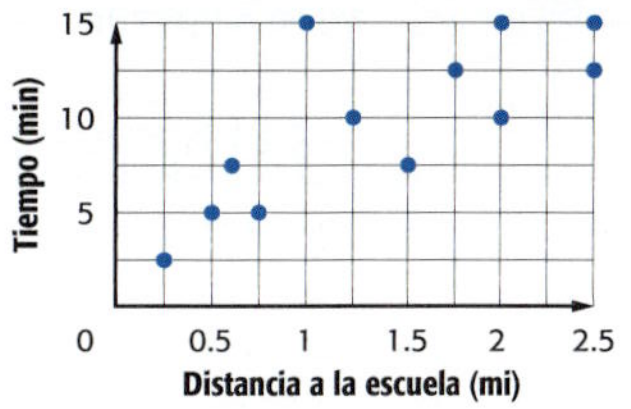

semicircle (p. 696) Half of a circle.

sequence (p. 57) A list of numbers in a certain order, such as 0, 1, 2, 3, or 2, 4, 6, 8.

similar figures (p. 540) Figures that have the same shape but not necessarily the same size.

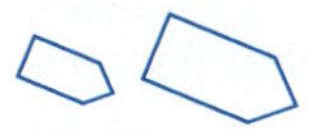

simple event (p. 460) One outcome or a collection of outcomes.

simple interest (p. 425) The amount paid or earned for the use of money. The formula for simple interest is $I = prt$.

simple random sample (p. 438) A sample where each item or person in the population is as likely to be chosen as any other.

simplest form (p. 192) A fraction is in simplest form when the GCF of the numerator and the denominator is 1.

simulate (p. 491) A way of acting out or modeling a problem situation.

slope (p. 293) The rate of change between any two points on a line. The ratio of vertical change to horizontal change.

solution (p. 49) A value for the variable that makes an equation true. The solution of $12 = x + 7$ is 5.

solving an equation (p. 49) The process of finding a solution to an equation.

sphere (p. 604) A three-dimensional figure in which all points are equal distance from the center.

square (p. 34) The product of a number and itself. 36 is the square of 6.

square (p. 533) A parallelogram having four right angles and four congruent sides.

square root (p. 35) One of the two equal factors of a number. The square root of 9 is 3.

standard form (p. 31) Numbers written without exponents.

semicírculo Mitad de un círculo con el mismo diámetro.

sucesión Lista de números en cierto orden, tales como 0, 1, 2, 3 ó 2, 4, 6, 8.

figuras semejantes Figuras que tienen la misma forma, pero no necesariamente el mismo tamaño.

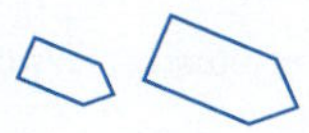

eventos simples Un resultado o una colección de resultados.

interés simple Cantidad que se paga o que se gana por el uso del dinero. La fórmula para calcular el interés simple es $I = prt$.

muestra aleatoria simple Muestra de una población que tiene la misma probabilidad de escogerse que cualquier otra.

forma reducida Una fracción está escrita en forma reducida si el MCD de su numerador y denominador es 1.

simulación Manera de modelar o representar un problema.

pendiente Razón de cambio entre cualquier par de puntos en una recta. La razón del cambio vertical al cambio horizontal.

solución Valor de la variable de una ecuación que hace verdadera la ecuación. La solución de $12 = x + 7$ es 5.

resolver una ecuación Proceso de encontrar el número o números que satisfagan una ecuación.

esfera Figura tridimensional en que todos los puntos están equidistantes del centro.

cuadrado El producto de un número por sí mismo. 36 es el cuadrado de 6.

cuadrado Paralelogramo con cuatro ángulos rectos y cuatro lados congruentes.

raíz cuadrada Uno de dos factores iguales de un número. La raíz cuadrada de 9 es 3.

forma estándar Números escritos sin exponentes.

statistics (p. 396) The branch of mathematics that deals with collecting, organizing, and interpreting data.

stem (p. 410) The greatest place value common to all the data values is used for the stem of a stem-and-leaf plot.

stem-and-leaf plot (p. 410) A system used to condense a set of data where the greatest place value of the data forms the stem and the next greatest place value forms the leaves.

straight angle (p. 511) An angle that measures exactly 180°.

Subtraction Property of Equality (p. 136) If you subtract the same number from each side of an equation, the two sides remain equal.

supplementary angles (p. 514) Two angles are supplementary if the sum of their measures is 180°.

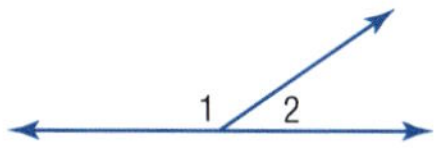

∠1 and ∠2 are supplementary angles.

surface area (p. 649) The sum of the areas of all the surfaces (faces) of a three-dimensional figure.

survey (p. 434) A question or set of questions designed to collect data about a specific group of people.

T

term (p. 57) Each number in a sequence.

terminating decimals (p. 197) A decimal whose digits end. Every terminating decimal can be written as a fraction with a denominator of 10, 100, 1,000, and so on.

tessellation (p. 548) A repetitive pattern of polygons that fit together with no holes or gaps.

estadística Rama de las matemáticas cuyo objetivo primordial es la recopilación, organización e interpretación de datos.

tallo El mayor valor de posición común a todos los datos es el que se usa como tallo en un diagrama de tallo y hojas.

diagrama de tallo y hojas Sistema que se usa para condensar un conjunto de datos y en el cual el mayor valor de posición de los datos forma el tallo y el segundo mayor valor de posición de los datos forma las hojas.

ángulo llano Ángulo que mide exactamente 180°.

propiedad de sustracción de la igualdad Si restas el mismo número de ambos lados de una ecuación, los dos lados permanecen iguales.

ángulos suplementarios Dos ángulos son suplementarios si la suma de sus medidas es 180°.

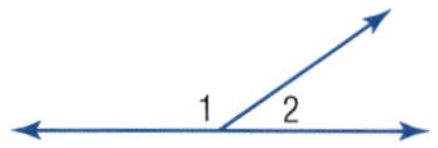

∠1 y ∠2 son suplementarios.

área de superficie La suma de las áreas de todas las superficies (caras) de una figura tridimensional.

encuesta Pregunta o conjunto de preguntas diseñadas para recoger datos sobre un grupo específico de peronas.

término Cada número en una sucesión.

decimales terminales Decimal cuyos dígitos terminan. Todo decimal terminal puede escribirse como una fracción con un denominador de 10, 100, 1,000, etc.

teselado Un patrón repetitivo de polígonos que coinciden perfectamente, sin dejar huecos o espacios.

theoretical probability (p. 486) The ratio of the number of ways an event can occur to the number of possible outcomes.

three-dimensional figures (p. 603) A figure with length, width, and depth (or height).

transformation (p. 553) A movement of a geometric figure.

translation (p. 553) One type of transformation where a geometric figure is slid horizontally, vertically, or both.

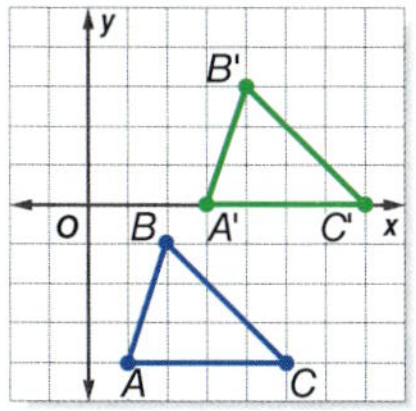

trapezoid (p. 533) A quadrilateral with one pair of parallel sides.

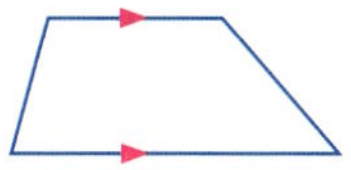

tree diagram (p. 466) A diagram used to show the total number of possible outcomes in a probability experiment.

triangle (p. 524) A polygon that has three sides and three angles.

triangular prism (p. 615) A prism that has bases that are triangles.

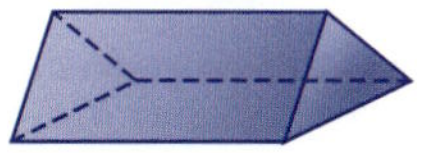

two-step equation (p. 151) An equation having two different operations.

probabilidad teórica La razón del número de maneras en que puede ocurrir un evento al número total de resultados posibles.

figuras tridimensionales Figuras que poseen largo, ancho y profundidad (o altura).

transformación Movimientos de figuras geométricas.

traslación Tipo de transformación en que una figura se desliza horizontal o verticalmente o de ambas maneras.

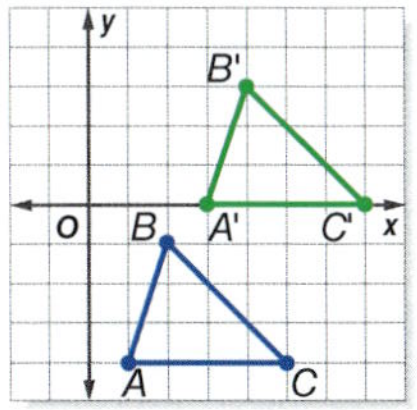

trapecio Cuadrilátero con un único par de lados paralelos.

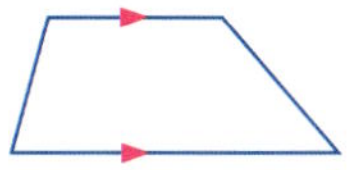

diagrama de árbol Diagrama que se usa para mostrar el número total de resultados posibles en experimento probabilístico.

triángulo Polígono que posee tres lados y tres ángulos.

prisma triangular Prisma cuyas bases son triángulos.

ecuación de dos pasos Ecuación que contiene dos operaciones distintas.

U

unbiased sample (p. 438) A sample representative of the entire population.

muestra no sesgada Muestra que se selecciona de modo que se representativa de la población entera.

unit rate (p. 287) A rate with denominator of 1.

tasa unitaria Una tasa con un denominador de 1.

unit ratio (p. 298) A unit rate where the denominator is one unit.

razón unitaria Tasa unitaria en que el denominador es la unidad.

unlike fractions (p. 237) Fractions with different denominators.

fracciones con distinto denominador Fracciones cuyos denominadores son diferentes.

V

variable (p. 44) A placeholder, usually a letter, used to represent an unspecified value in mathematical expressions or sentences. In $3 + a = 6$, a is a variable.

variable Marcador de posición, por lo general, una letra, que se usa para representar un valor desconocido en expresiones o enunciados matemáticos. En $3 + a = 6$, a es una variable.

Venn diagram (p. 186) A diagram that uses overlapping circles to show how elements among sets of numbers or objects are related.

diagrama de Venn Diagrama que usa círculos para mostrar la relación entre los elementos en un conjunto de números u objetos

vertex (p. 510) A vertex of an angle is the common endpoint of the rays forming the angle.

vértice El vértice de un ángulo es el extremo común de los rayos que lo forman.

vertex (p. 603) The point where the edges of a three dimensional figure intersect.

vértice Punto donde se intersecan las aristas de una figura tridimensional.

vertical angles (p. 511) Opposite angles formed by the intersection of two lines.

∠1 and ∠2 are vertical angles.

ángulos opuestos por el vértice Ángulos opuestos que se forman de la intersección de dos rectas.

∠1 y ∠2 son ángulos opuestos por el vértice.

volume (p. 613) The number of cubic units needed to fill the space occupied by a solid.

volumen Número de unidades cúbicas que se requieren para llenar el espacio que ocupa un sólido.

voluntary response sample (p. 439) A sample which involves only those who want to participate in the sampling.

muestra de respuesta voluntaria Muestra que involucra sólo aquellos que quieren participar en el muestreo.

W

whole (p. 350) In a percent proportion, the number to which the part is being compared.

todo En una proporción porcentual, el número con que se compara la parte.

X

x-axis (p. 88) The horizontal number line in a coordinate plane.

eje x La recta numérica horizontal en el plano de coordenadas.

x-coordinate (p. 88) The first number of an ordered pair. It corresponds to a number on the x-axis.

coordenada x El primer número de un par ordenado. Corresponde a un número en el eje x.

Y

y-axis (p. 88) The vertical number line in a coordinate plane.

eje y La recta numérica vertical en el plano de coordenadas.

y-coordinate (p. 88) The second number of an ordered pair. It corresponds to a number on the y-axis.

coordenada y El segundo número de un par ordenado. Corresponde a un número en el eje y.

Z

zero pair (p. 93) The result when one positive counter is paired with one negative counter.

par nulo Resultado que se obtiene cuando una ficha positiva se aparea con una ficha negativa.

Selected Answers

For Homework Help, go to Hotmath.com
Complete, step-by-step solutions of most odd-numbered exercises are provided free of charge.

Chapter 1 Introduction to Algebra and Functions

Page 23 **Chapter 1** **Getting Ready**

1. 105.8 **3.** 60.64 **5.** \$72.94 **7.** 2.5 **9.** 6.2 **11.** 29.4 **13.** 10.2 **15.** 5.3 **17.** 4.46

Pages 27–29 **Lesson 1-1**

1. Sample answer: 4 times; 16,000 ÷ 4,000 = 4 **3.** 3,000 **5.** \$763.75

7. 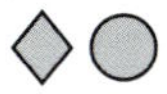

9. every 45 minutes **11.** 5:10 P.M. **15.** 13 wk **17.** Sample answer: For the school bake sale, Samantha bakes 79 cookies and 42 brownies. If two other students baked the same amount of cookies and brownies, how many items did they bake altogether? **19.** C **21.** 100 **23.** 625

Pages 31–33 **Lesson 1-2**

1. 9 • 9 • 9 **3.** 8 • 8 • 8 • 8 • 8 **5.** 49 **7.** Sample answer: 9,765,625 people **9.** 1^4 **11.** 1 • 1 • 1 • 1 • 1 **13.** 3 • 3 • 3 • 3 • 3 • 3 • 3 • 3 **15.** 9 • 9 • 9 **17.** 64 **19.** 2,401 **21.** 1 **23.** 1,000,000 **25.** 3^2 **27.** 1^8 **29.** 4 • 4 • 4 • 4 • 4 **31.** 1,296 **33.** 3^3 **35.** $5^4 \cdot 4^3$ **37.** $1^{14}, 17^3, 6^5, 4^{10}$ **39.** $7^2, 5^3, 2^{11}, 4^6$ **41.** $8^2 = 64$ and $4^3 = 64$ **43.** Sample answer: The pattern is that each successive term is $\frac{1}{2}$ of the previous one, so $2^0 = 1$ and $2^{-1} = \frac{1}{2}$. **45.** 7 wins **47.** 4 **49.** 25

Pages 36–37 **Lesson 1-3**

1. 36 **3.** 289 **5.** 3 **7.** 11 **9.** 24 in. by 24 in. **11.** 1 **13.** 121 **15.** 400 **17.** 1,156 **19.** 4 **21.** 10 **23.** 16 **25.** 25 **27.** 40 ft **29.** 361 **31.** 53,824 mi^2

33. 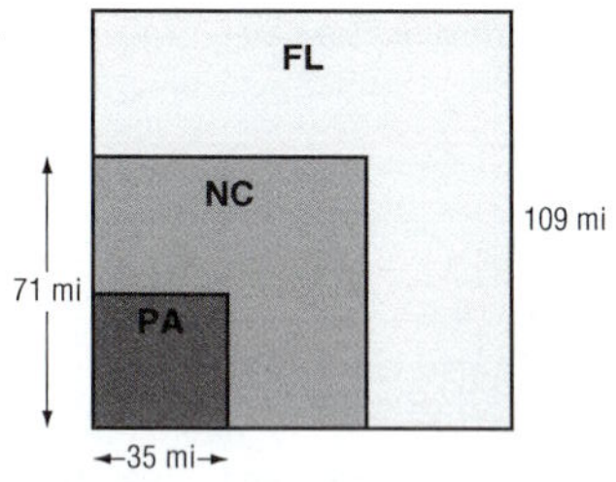

35. $41 m^2$ greater; The area of a 7 by 7 square has an area of 49 m^2. **37.** Yes; for example, a pen that measures 10 feet by 10 feet has the same perimeter, but its area is 100 square feet, which is greater than 84 square feet. **39.** Sample answer: It is called squaring the number because the area of a square is found by multiplying the two side lengths together. **41.** J **43.** 8 • 8 • 8 • 8 • 8 **45.** 2 • 2 • 2 • 2 • 2 • 2 **47.** 21 **49.** 30

Pages 40–41 **Lesson 1-4**

1. 11; Sample answer: Subtract first since 5 − 2 is in parentheses. Then add 8. **3.** 11; Sample answer: Multiply 2 by 6 first since multiplication comes before addition or subtraction. Then subtract and add in order from left to right. **5.** 400; Sample answer: Evaluate 10^2 first since it is a power. Then multiply by 4. **7.** 11; Sample answer: Subtract first since 6 − 3 is in parentheses. Then multiply the difference by 2 and multiply 3 by 4 since multiplication comes before addition or subtraction. Finally, add 17 + 6 and subtract 12 in order from left to right. **9.** 3(0.05) + 2(0.25) + 2(0.10) + 7(0.01); \$0.92 **11.** 3; Sample answer: Add first since 3 + 4 is in parentheses. Then subtract. **13.** 1; Sample answer: Subtract first since 11 − 2 is in parentheses. Then divide. **15.** 8; Sample answer: Divide first since division comes before addition or subtraction. Then subtract 1 and add 7 in order from left to right. **17.** 5; Sample answer: Multiply first since multiplication comes before addition or subtraction. Then subtract the product from 118 and add 5. **19.** 30,000; Sample answer: Evaluate 10^4 first since it is a power. Then multiply by 3. **21.** 386; Sample answer: Evaluate 7^2 first since it is a power. Then multiply by 8 since multiplication comes before subtraction. Finally, subtract. **23.** 75; Sample answer: Evaluate 9^2 since it is a power. Then divide 14 by 7 and multiply the quotient by 3 since multiplication and division occur from left to right. Finally, subtract. **25.** 22; Sample answer: Add first since 6 + 5 is in parentheses. Then subtract 6 from 8 since 8 – 6 is in parentheses. Finally, multiply. **27.** 23; Sample answer: Add first since 4 + 7 is in parentheses. Then multiply the sum by 3. Next, multiply 5 by 4 and divide the product by 2 since multiplication and division occur in order from left to right. Finally, subtract. **29.** \$3.25 **31.** 19; Sample answer: Evaluate 3^3 first since it is a power. Then add 8. Next subtract 6 from 10 since 10 – 6 is in parentheses. Then square the difference since the power is 2. Finally subtract 16 from 35. **33.** 64; Sample answer: Subtract first since 4 − 3.2 is in parentheses. Multiply 7 by 9 next since multiplication occurs from left to right. Then subtract 0.8 from the product, 63, and add 1.8 since addition and subtraction occur from left to right. **35.** Peggy; the first step is to do the division 24 ÷ 6. Phoung incorrectly multiplied 6 and 2 first. **37.** Yes; For example, a pen that measures 10 feet by 10 feet has the same perimeter, but its area is 100 square feet, which is greater than 84 square feet. **39.** H **41.** 8 **43.** 28 **45.** 968

Pages 42–43 **Lesson 1-5**

1. Sample answer: You need to keep track of what numbers you have already guessed, so that you do not make the same guess twice. You also need to know what numbers produce answers that are too large or too small, so you can make better guesses. **3.** 125 adult tickets and 250 student tickets **5.** birthday, holiday, vacation **7.** The circumference of Earth is 24,900 miles long at the Equator. **9.** 512 and 1,024 **11.** 324.8 in. of snow. **13.** 2, 3, 6

Pages 46–47 ***Lesson 1-6***

1. 10 **3.** 2 **5.** 32 **7.** 22 **9.** 7 **11.** 3 **13.** 4 **15.** 7 **17.** 5 **19.** 12 **21.** 48 **23.** 4 **25.** 18 **27.** 36 **29.** 5 **31.** 4 quarts **33.** 5.1 **35.** $19.99d + 0.17m$ **37.** 64 ft **39.** Sample answer: $5x - 37$ if $x = 8$ **41.** Sample answer: Sometimes; $x - 3$ and $y - 3$ represent the same value only when $x = y$ **43.** G **45.** 28 **47.** 56 **49.** 19 **51.** false

Pages 51–52 ***Lesson 1-7***

1. 3 **3.** 54 **5.** $2.25 **7.** 7 **9.** 28 **11.** 46 **13.** 33 **15.** 64 **17.** 7 **19.** 11 **21.** m = the number of miles Derrick walked on Monday; $m + 2.5 = 6.3$; 3.8 mi **23.** 5.4 **25.** 4.4 **27.** 1.2 **29.** $1.75 + c = $6.25; c = $4.50 **31.** Antonio; 105 – 35 = 70 is a true statement. 35 – 35 ≠ 70 **33.** A **35.** J **37.** 31 **39.** 19 **41.** 28 **43.** 150

Pages 55–56 ***Lesson 1-8***

1. 7(4) + 7(3); 49 **3.** 3(9 + 6); 45 **5.** 4(12 + 5); $68; Sample answer: The expression 12 + 5 represents the cost of one ticket and one hot dog. The expression 4(12 + 5) represents the cost of four tickets and four hot dogs. Since 4 × 12 = 48 and 4 × 5 = 20, find 48 + 20, or 68, to find the total cost of four tickets and four hot dogs. **7.** Sample answer: Rewrite 44 + (23 + 16) as 44 + (16 + 23) using the Commutative Property of Addition. Rewrite 44 + (16 + 23) as (44 + 16) + 23 using the Associative Property of Addition. Find 44 + 16, or 60, mentally. Then find 60 + 23, or 83, mentally. **9.** 2(6) + 2(7); 26 **11.** 4(3 + 8); 44 **13.** Sample answer: Rewrite (8 + 27) + 52 as (27 + 8) + 52 using the Commutative Property of Addition. Rewrite (27 + 8) + 52 as 27 + (8 + 52) using the Associative Property of Addition. Find 8 + 52, or 60, mentally. Then find 60 + 27, or 87, mentally. **15.** Sample answer: Rewrite 91 + (15 + 9) as 91 + (9 + 15) using the Commutative Property of Addition. Rewrite 91 + (9 + 15) as (91 + 9) + 15 using the Associative Property of Addition. Find 91 + 9, or 100, mentally. Then find 100 + 15, or 115, mentally. **17.** Sample answer: Rewrite (4 • 18) • 25 as (18 • 4) • 25 using the Commutative Property of Multiplication. Rewrite (18 • 4) • 25 as 18 • (4 • 25) using the Associative Property of Multiplication. Find 4 • 25, or 100, mentally. Then find 100 • 18, or 1,800, mentally. **19.** Sample answer: Rewrite 15 • (8 • 2) as 15 • (2 • 8) using the Commutative Property of Multiplication. Rewrite 15 • (2 • 8) as (15 • 2) • 8 using the Associative Property of Multiplication. Find 15 • 2, or 30, mentally. Then find 30 • 8, or 240, mentally. **21.** Sample answer: Rewrite 5 • (30 • 12) as 5 • (12 • 30) using the Commutative Property of Multiplication. Rewrite 5 • (12 • 30) as (5 • 12) • 30 using the Associative Property of Multiplication. Find 5 • 12, or 60, mentally. Then find 60 • 30, or 1,800, mentally. **23.** 5(20 + 7); 135 million **25.** 7(9 – 3); 42 **27.** 9(7 – 3); 36 **29.** $y + 5$ **31.** $32b$ **33.** $2x + 6$ **35.** $6c + 6$ **37.** 55 + 184 = 184 + 55 **39.** Sample answer: $(5 + z) + 9 = 5 + (z + 9)$ **41.** Sample answer: Since 24 ÷ (12 ÷ 2) = 4 and (24 ÷ 12) ÷ 2 = 1, 24 ÷ (12 ÷ 2) ≠ (24 ÷ 12) ÷ 2. **43.** B **45.** 11.3 **47.** 75 yr **49.** 10 **51.** 4.6

Pages 59–61 ***Lesson 1-9***

1. 9 is added to each term; 36, 45, 54 **3.** 0.1 is added to each term; 1.4, 1.5, 1.6 **5.** $3n$; 36 in. **7.** 6 is added to each term; 25, 31, 37 **9.** 12 is added to each term; 67, 79, 91 **11.** 5 is added to each term; 53, 58, 63 **13.** 0.8 is added to each term; 5.6, 6.4, 7.2 **15.** 1.5 is added to each term; 10.5, 12.0, 13.5 **17.** 4 is added to each term; 20.6, 24.6, 28.6 **19.** $7n$; 42 laps **21.** 25 is added to each term; 120, 145, 170 **23.** 256, 1,024, 4,096 **25.** 324, 972, 2,916 **27.** 1,200 **29.** 4,950 **31.** The Fibonacci sequence is 1, 1, 2, 3, 5, 8, 13, ... In this sequence, each term after the second term is the sum of the two terms before it. Fibonacci numbers occur in many areas of nature, including pine cones, shell spirals, and branching plants. **33.** + 2, + 4, + 6, + 8, ...; 30, 42, 56 **35.** Sample answer: paper/pencil; Write the equation that represents this situation, $15n$. Since 2 years = 24 months, evaluate the expression when n is 24. 15(24) = 360. So, after 2 years, $360 will be saved. **37.** D **39.** 48; Sample answer: Rewrite (23 + 18) + 7 as (18 + 23) + 7 using the Communicative Property of Addition. Rewrite (18 + 23) + 7 as 18 + (23 + 7) using the Associative Property of Addition. Find 23 + 7, or 30, mentally. Then find 18 + 30, or 48, mentally. **41.** 29 **43.** 20 **45.** 8 **47.** 3

Pages 65–67 ***Lesson 1-10***

1.

x	3x	y
1	3 • 1	3
2	3 • 2	6
3	3 • 3	9
4	3 • 4	12

; domain: {1, 2, 3, 4}; range: {3, 6, 9, 12}

3.

x	8x	y
1	8 • 1	8
2	8 • 2	16
3	8 • 3	24
4	8 • 4	32

; domain: {1, 2, 3, 4}; range: {8, 16, 24, 32}

5. 693 mi; Sample answer: Replace h with 3 in the equation $m = 231h$ to find the distance in miles the race car travels in 3 hours.

7.

x	6x	y
1	6 • 1	6
2	6 • 2	12
3	6 • 3	18
4	6 • 4	24

; domain: {1, 2, 3, 4}; range: {6, 12, 18, 24}

9.

x	25x	y
1	25 • 1	25
2	25 • 2	50
3	25 • 3	75
4	25 • 4	100

; domain: {1, 2, 3, 4}; range: {25, 50, 75, 100}

11. $c = 40m$ **13.** $t = 35m$

15.

x	x – 1	y
1	1 – 1	0
2	2 – 1	1
3	3 – 1	2
4	4 – 1	3

; domain: {1, 2, 3, 4}; range: {0, 1, 2, 3}

17.

x	x + 0.25	y
0	0 + 0.25	0.25
1	1 + 0.25	1.25
2	2 + 0.25	2.25
3	3 + 0.25	3.25

; domain: {0, 1, 2, 3}; range: {0.25, 1.25, 2.25, 3.25}

19.

Width (units)	6w	Area (sq units)
2	6 • 2	12
3	6 • 3	18
4	6 • 4	24
5	6 • 5	30

21. $m = 8s$ **23.** 480 mi; 1,140 mi; Sample answer: Replace s with 60 in the equation $m = 8s$ and in the equation $m = 19s$ to find the number of miles Jupiter travels in 1 minute the number of miles Earth travels in 1 minute, respectively. **25.** $y = 3x$ **27.** Sample answer: Sam charges $3 for each dog that he walks. In the equation $y = 3x$, x represents the number of dogs and y represents the total amount of money earned. **29.** C **31.** 63, 72, 81 **33.** (12)4 +(4)4; 64 **35.** 10(6 – 5); 10 **37.** 7 **39.** 7

Pages 70–74 ***Chapter 1*** ***Study Guide and Review***

1. false, equivalent expressions **3.** false, domain **5.** true **7.** false, square **9.** 60 ft **11.** 3 • 3 • 3 • 3 **13.** 5 **15.** 5 • 5 • 5 • 5 **17.** 40,353,607 **19.** 324 **21.** 100 **23.** 8 **25.** 169 **27.** 18 **29.** 25 **31.** 33 **33.** 36 ÷ 4 + 12 ÷ 3; 13 **35.** 22 **37.** 5 **39.** 48 **41.** 8 **43.** 108 **45.** $9 + x = 15$; 6 tickets **47.** 68; Sample answer: Rewrite 14 + (38 + 16) as 14 + (16 + 38) using the Commutative Property of Addition. Rewrite 14 + (16 + 38) as (14 + 16) + 38 using the Associative Property of Addition. Find 14 + 16, or 30, mentally. Then find 30 + 38, or 68, mentally. **49.** $2(15 + 12); $54; Sample answer: The expression 15 + 12 represents the total number of roses Wesley sold. The expression $2(15 + 12) represents the total amount of money Wesley earned. Since $2 × 15 = $30 and $2 × 12 = $24, find $30 + $24, or $54, to find the total amount Wesley earned. **51.** Each term is found by adding 0.8 to the previous term; 6.6, 7.4, 8.2 **53.** $4.50n

55.

x	4x	y
5	4(5)	20
6	4(6)	24
7	4(7)	28
8	4(8)	32

; domain: {5, 6, 7, 8}; range: {20, 24, 28, 32}

Chapter 2 Integers

Page 79 ***Chapter 2*** ***Getting Ready***

1. < **3.** < **5.** Garrett **7.** 20 **9.** 9 **11.** 216 **13.** 29 **15.** 1,900 mi

Pages 82–83 ***Lesson 2-1***

1. –11 **3.** 16 **5.** –15

7.

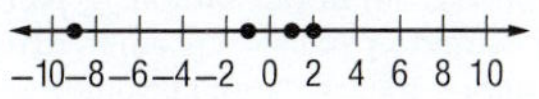

9. 8 **11.** 9 **13.** –53 **15.** –2 **17.** 12 **19.** –7

21.

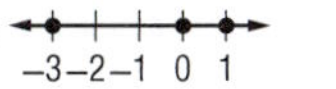

23.

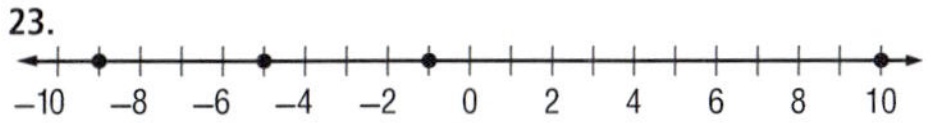

25. 10 **27.** 2 **29.** 14 **31.** 25 **33.** 5 **35.** 17 positive charges: 17; 25 negative charges: –25 **37.** false; 0 **39.** C

41.

x	x – 4	y
4	4 – 4	0
5	5 – 4	1
6	6 – 4	2
7	7 – 4	3

; domain: {4, 5, 6, 7}; range: {0, 1, 2, 3}.

43.

x	5x + 1	y
1	5 • 1 + 1	6
2	5 • 2 + 1	11
3	5 • 3 + 1	16
4	5 • 4 + 1	21

; domain: {1, 2, 3, 4}; range: {6, 11, 16, 21}

45. > **47.** >

Pages 85–87 ***Lesson 2-2***

1. > **3.** > **5.** {–18, –16, –10, 12, 19} **7.** < **9.** > **11.** > **13.** < **15.** {–8, –5, –3, 6, 11} **17.** {–7, –6, –4, 1, 3, 5} **19.** Sunlight, Twilight, Midnight, Abyssal, Hadal **21.** < **23.** < **25.** –5, –2, 5, 10, 20 **27.** 5° with a 10-mile-per-hour wind **29.** true **31.** true **33.** –1 **35.** C **37.** –9 **39.** $r = 6t$

41–44.

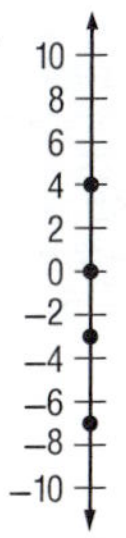

Pages 90–92 **Lesson 2-3**

1. (−2, −4), III **3.** (0, 3), y-axis

5–8.

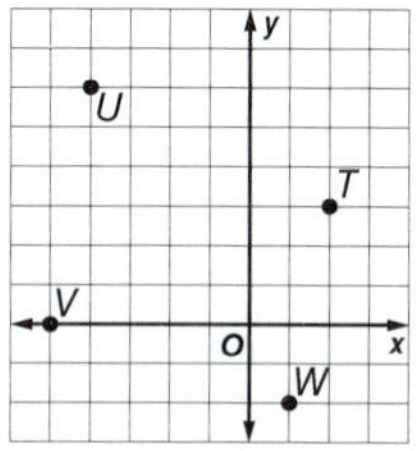

9. Sea Cliffs
11. (−2, 2), II
13. (−5, 0), x-axis
15. (2, −2), IV
17. (−4, −1), III
19. (2, 2), I
21. (0, 4); y-axis

23–34.

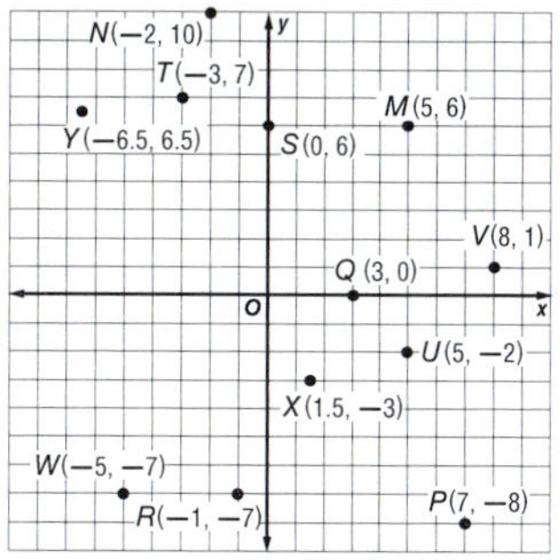

35. Africa **37.** South America

39–41.

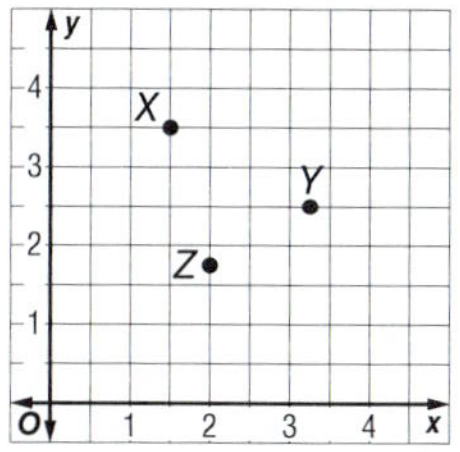

43. Sample answer: Rene Descarte is often credited with inventing the coordinate plane and so the coordinate plane is sometimes called the Cartesian plane, in his honor. The myth is that while a child, Descarte lay in bed one day watching a fly crawling around on the ceiling. In wondering how to tell someone else where the fly was, he realized that he could describe its position by its distance from the walls of the room. **45.** Sample answer: Sometimes; both (0, −2) and (0, 2) lie on the y-axis.

47. Sample answer: Using the graphic, you can see that an ordered pair such as (−5, −4) is in Quadrant III.

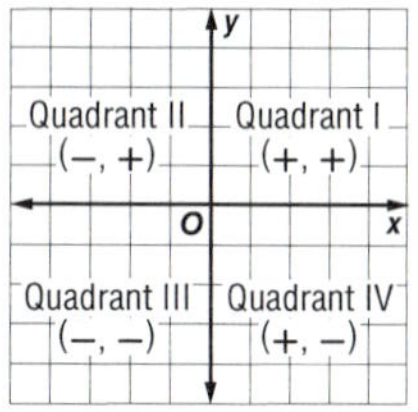

49. Sample answer: Point A is 1 unit to the right and 2 units down from the origin, in quadrant IV. Point B is 2 units to the left and 1 unit up from the origin, in quadrant II. **51.** G **53.** > **55.** < **57.** 41 mi **59.** 1,326 **61.** 11,737

Pages 98–99 **Lesson 2-4**

1. −14 **3.** 7 **5.** −4 **7.** 0 **9.** −\$25 + \$18; −\$7; Camilia still owes her brother \$7. **11.** −25 **13.** 28 **15.** −6 **17.** −13 **19.** −2 **21.** 2 **23.** 0 **25.** 22 **27.** −19 **29.** 60 + (−60); 0; The pelican is now at sea level. **31.** −5 + (−15) + 12; The team has lost a total of 8 yards. **33.** 4 **35.** −3 **39.** a **41.** m + (−15) **43.** Sample answer: Look at the signs. If the numbers being added are both positive, the sum is positive. If the numbers being added are both negative, the sum is negative. If the numbers being added have different signs, subtract their absolute values and give the sum the sign of the number with the greatest absolute value. If the numbers being added are opposites, the sum is zero. **45.** B **47.** (−2, 4); 11 **49.** (−3, −1); 111 **51.** −8, −4, −3, 0, 1, 4, 6 **53.** 103 **55.** 3,109

Pages 105–106 **Lesson 2-5**

1. −3 **3.** −12 **5.** 24 **7.** −2 **9.** −21 **11.** 22 **13.** −10 **15.** −14 **17.** 23 **19.** 31 **21.** −14 **23.** −30 **25.** 104 **27.** 6 **29.** 0 **31.** 0 **33.** 15 **35.** 11 **37.** 8,757 ft **39.** 5,066 ft **41.** −31 **43.** 23 **45.** Mei; Alicia did not add the additive inverse of −18. **47.** Sample answer: To subtract an integer, add its additive inverse. **49.** J **51.** −11 **53.** −14 **55.** 8 **57.** −33 **59.** −24

Pages 109–111 **Lesson 2-6**

1. −60 **3.** −28 **5.** 45 **7.** 64 **9.** −12 **11.** 100(−3) = −300; Tamera's investment is now worth \$300 less than it was before the price of the stock dropped. **13.** 70 **15.** −220 **17.** −70 **19.** −50 **21.** 80 **23.** −125 **25.** 81 **27.** −45 **29.** 49 **31.** −24 **33.** 24 **35.** 64 **37.** −160 **39.** 5(−650) = −3,250; Ethan burns 3,250 Calories each week. **41.** −243 **43.** 88

47.

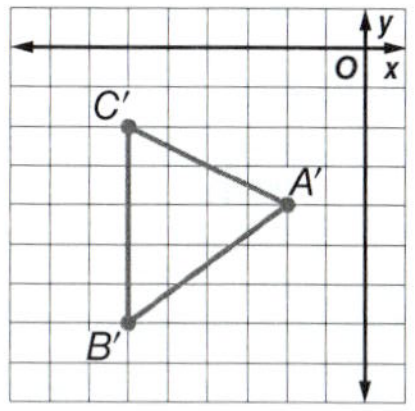

Sample answer: new triangle $A'B'C'$ is on the other side of the origin (in quadrant III) from original triangle ABC (which is in Quadrant I).

49. Sample answer: −6 × 3 = −18 **51.** Sample answer: 1; (−1)(−1) = 1. Since there are 50 ÷ 2 = 25 pairs of (−1) factors, $(-1)^{50} = 1^{25}$. One raised to any power is still 1. **53.** Sample answer: The product of three integers is positive when exactly two integers are negative or all three integers are positive. **55.** J **57.** 8 **59.** −21 **61.** −6 **63.** −9 **65.** 18 + x = 51; x = 33

Pages 112–113 **Lesson 2-7**

1. Sample answer: Use the look for a pattern strategy when there is a data table, a series of numbers, or a geometric pattern as part of the problem. **3.** Sample answer: Amanda has \$2 in change in her bank. If she adds \$0.50 each week for 7 weeks, how much money will be in her bank? \$5.50 **5.** 8 months **7.** Sample answer: 3 quarters, 2 nickels, and 1 penny **9.** 2 letters and 10 postcards **11.** 8,914,113 **13.** 84 cm

Pages 116–118 **Lesson 2-8**

1. −4 **3.** −6 **5.** 5 **7.** −3 **9.** −48.3°C **11.** −7 **13.** −9 **15.** 10 **17.** −7 **19.** −9 **21.** 9 **23.** 5 **25.** −12 **27.** −3 **29.** 2 **31.** −1 **33.** −10°F **35.** 8 **37.** 1 **39.** −53 ft **41.** −32 ÷ (−4) has a positive quotient; the others have negative quotients **43.** −20, −10, −5, −4, −2, −1, 1, 2, 4, 5, 10, 20 **45.** A

47.

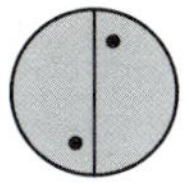

49. 60 **51.** 81 **53.** −10 **55.** 30

Pages 119–122 **Chapter 2** **Study Guide and Review**

1. false, negative **3.** false, opposite **5.** false, y-coordinate **7.** true **9.** false, positive **11.** 350 ft **13.** −12° **15.** 32 **17.** −48 mL **19.** > **21.** < **23.** < **25.** {−32, −23, −21, 14, 19, 25} **27.** −10, −6, −5, 0, 2, 5, 10, 12, 20, 25

28–31.

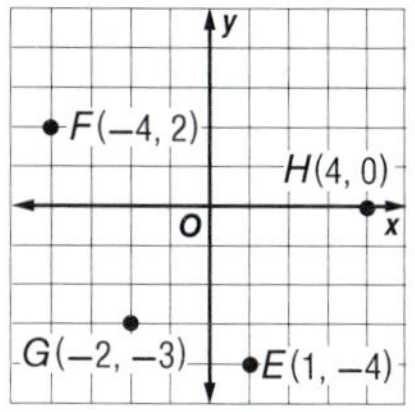

33. 2 **35.** −5 **37.** 123 ft **39.** −3 **41.** 4 **43.** −12 **45.** 35 **47.** 28 **49.** −35 **51.** 17,280 **53.** 576 ft **55.** −3 **57.** 9

Chapter 3 Algebra: Linear Equations and Functions

Page 127 **Chapter 3** **Getting Ready**

1. 4 **3.** −11

5.

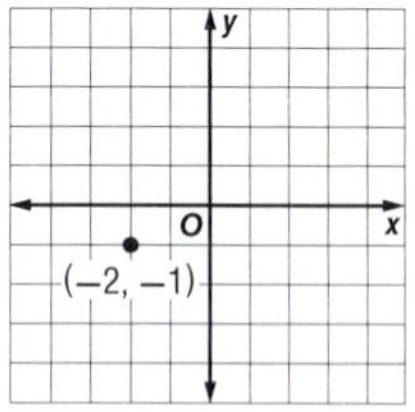

7. −8 **9.** 4 **11.** −11 **13.** 14 **15.** 2 **17.** −2

Pages 131–133 **Lesson 3-1**

1. $n + 8$ **3.** $n - 9 = 24$ **5.** $2m = 18$ **7.** $x - 1 = 34.3$ **9.** $15 + t$ **11.** $n - 10$ **13.** $8r$ **15.** $\frac{a}{3}$ **17.** $n + 4 = -8$ **19.** $5d = -20$ **21.** $h - 10 = 26$ **23.** $c + 3.5 = 5.5$ **25.** the length is 4 times the width **27.** the width is 5 less than the length **29.** $2b + 2$ **31.** $3(a - 43)$ **33.** $13k^2$ **35.** American toad **37.** 3 less than a number is 6. **39.** $x + 2$; $x - 2$ **41.** C **43.** −7 **45.** 15 **47.** 25 **49.** 49 **51.** Plan A **53.** −11 **55.** −8

Pages 139–141 **Lesson 3-2**

1. 2 **3.** −2 **5.** $d + 120 = 364$; 244 ft **7.** 5 **9.** 7 **11.** 7 **13.** −3 **15.** −9 **17.** 17 **19.** 7 **21.** $7 = w + 2$; 5 **23.** $15 = t - 3$; 18 years old **25.** 61 **27.** −5 **29.** −12 **31.** 18.4 **33.** 6.4 **35.** −0.68 **37.** $d - 5 = 18$; \$23 **39.** $35 + 45 + x = 180$; 100° **41.** $1 - 1 + s = -5$; −5 **43.** $s - 65 = 13$; 78 mph **45.** $n - 13 = 163$; 176 ft **47.** The value of y decreases by 2. **49.** C **51.** $p + 180$ **53.** 46 pages **55.** 2.6 **57.** 1.52

Pages 144–146 **Lesson 3-3**

1. 3 **3.** −3 **5.** 8 h **7.** 7 **9.** −3 **11.** 7 **13.** −9 **15.** 4 **17.** −8 **19.** $15w = 300$; 20 weeks **21.** $3h$ **23.** 23 **25.** 18 **27.** 4.7 **29.** Sample answer: Evelyn Ashford has the faster average speed. Her race is half the distance as Sanya Richards, and it took her less than half the time as Sanya Richards to complete the race. **31.** $20.88h = 145$; $h \approx 6.94$ **33.** Steve; the variable is multiplied by −6. To solve for x, you need to divide each side of the equation by the entire coefficient, −6. **35.** Sample answer: Billie has twice as many cards as Tyree. If Billie has 16 cards, how many does Tyree have? **37.** Sample answer: If it takes a scuba diver 4 seconds to swim 8 meters below the surface of the water, what is the rate of descent? **39.** 8 **41.** 5 **43.** $-3y$

45.

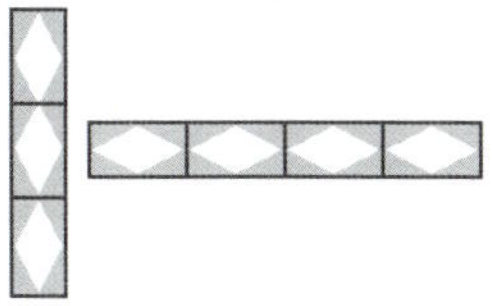

Pages 148–149 **Lesson 3-4**

1. When you are given the final result and asked to find an earlier amount. **3.** Sample answer: In the first four games, Hannah scored a total of 83 points. In the fourth game she scored 19 points. In game three, she scored 27 points and in the second game she scored 22 points. How many points did she score in the first game? To solve, first subtract 19 from 83, which is 64. Then subtract 27 from 64 to get 37. Finally, subtract 22 from 37. So, Hannah scored 15 points in her first game. **5.** 4 **7.** 19,200 tennis balls **9.** Brie is 14 years old.

11.

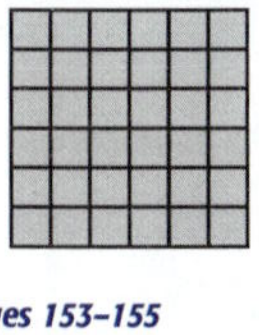

13. Raquels's car gets 1,774,074 more inches per gallon than an aircraft carrier. **15.** 1-\$10 bill, 2-\$5 bills, and 7-\$1 bills

Pages 153–155 **Lesson 3-5**

1. 2 **3.** 3 **5.** 3 **7.** $14c + 23 = 65$; 3 CDs **9.** 3 **11.** −4 **13.** 4 **15.** 9 **17.** 8 **19.** 11 **21.** $2c + 10 = 14$;

2 cups **23.** 2.25 **25.** 2.1 **27.** 28 **29.** $8 + 47.6d = 960$; 20 days **31.** 92.2°F **33.** $\frac{1}{2}(20x) - 18 = 200$; $x = 21.8$; They must sell at least 22 subscriptions. **35.** Sample answer: A flower shop charges $2 for each flower in a vase and $5 for the vase. How many flowers can you place in a vase if you have $15 to spend? **37.** G **39.** 7 **41.** 41 **43.** 213 ft **45.** 14 **47.** 16

Pages 158–161 ***Lesson 3-6***

1. 18 yd **3.** 7 in. **5.** 26.25 ft^2 **7.** 36 ft **9.** 14.8 mm **11.** 11 ft **13.** 18 in. **15.** 78 ft^2 **17.** 183.6 m^2 **19.** 6.5 in^2 **21.** 5 squares **23.** $\ell = 33$ ft **25.** 3,200 yd^2 **27.** perimeter; 4 mi **29.** area; 13 ft **31.** 270 m^2

35. 9;

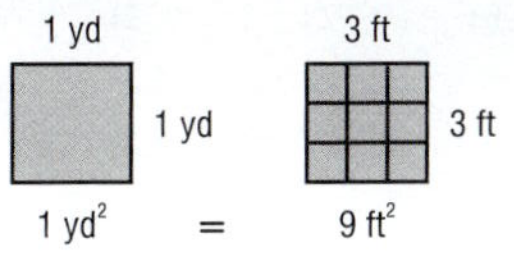

37. 144;

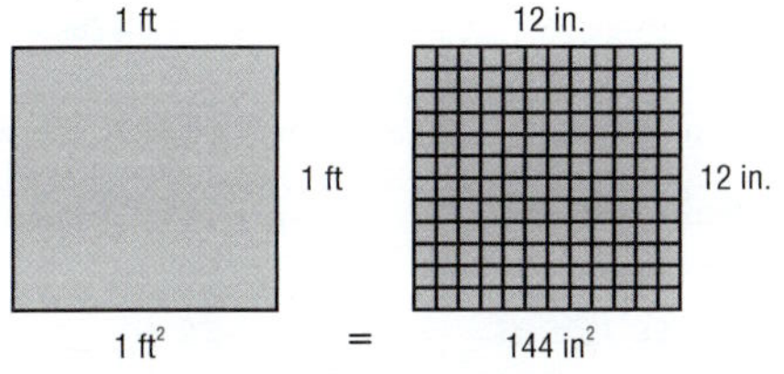

39. When the width of a rectangle is doubled, the perimeter becomes $2\ell + 4w$ and the area becomes $2\ell w$, or in other words, the area is doubled. **41.** $P = 2(3w + 1) + 2w$ or $P = 8w + 2$ **43.** A **45.** −2 **47.** 3.5 **49.** $5x = 11.25$; $2.25 **51.** −27 **53.** 11 years old

55.

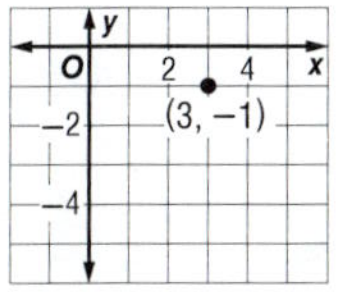

57.

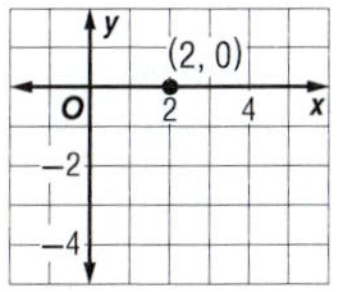

Pages 166–167 ***Lesson 3-7***

1.

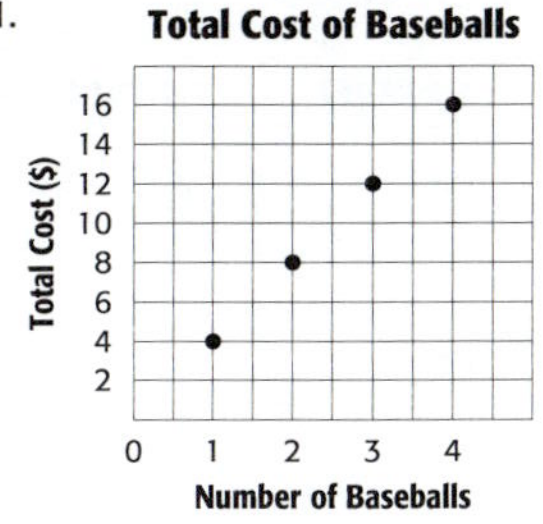

3.

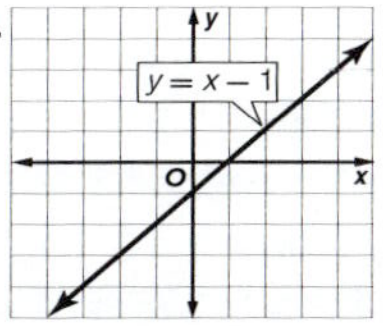

5.

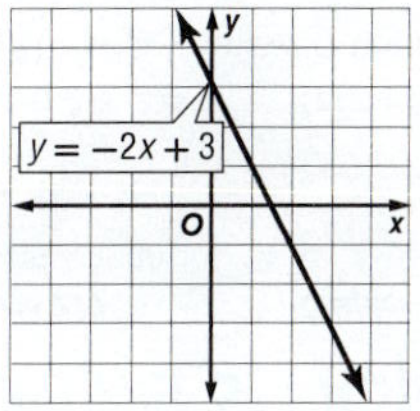

7.

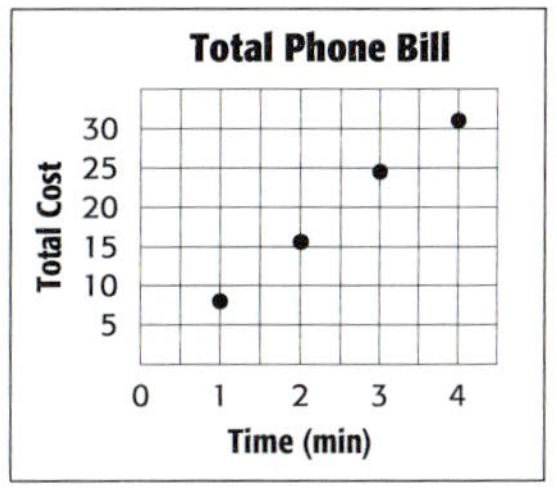

9.

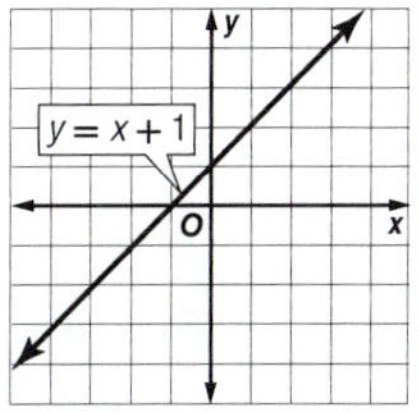

11.

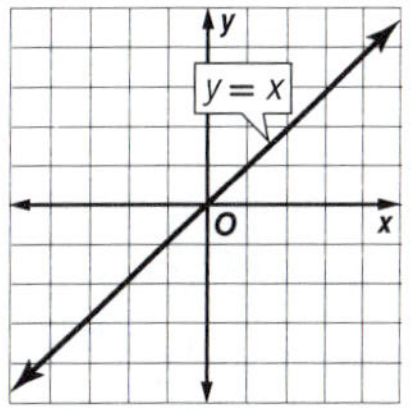

13.

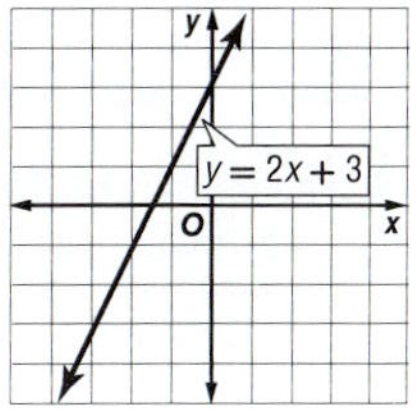

15.

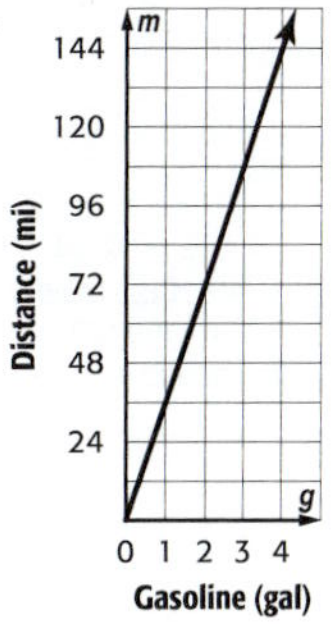

17.

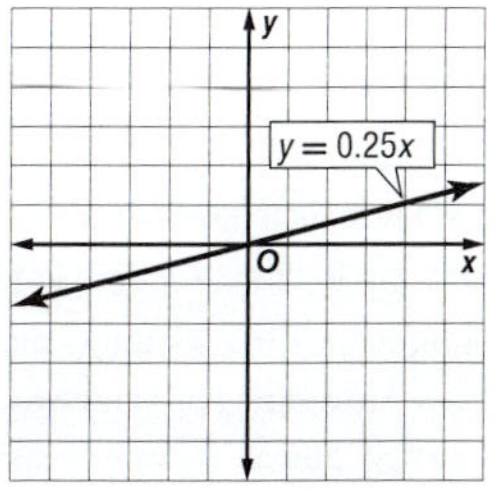

19.

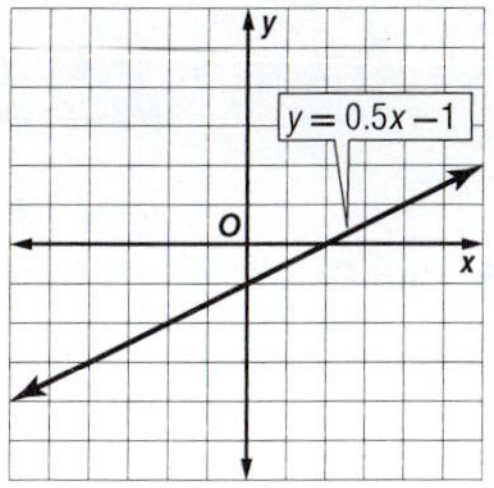

23.

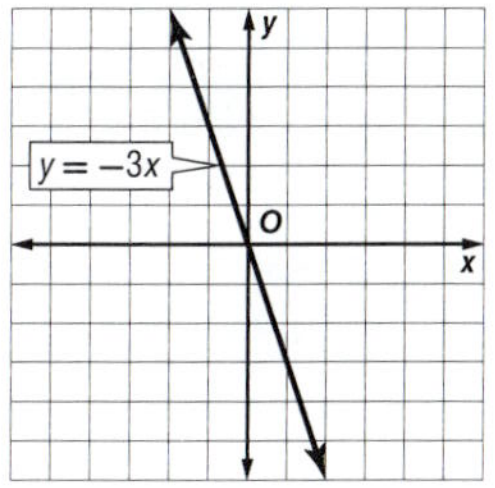

25. C **27.** −3 **29.** 4 **31.** 15

Pages 169–172 ***Chapter 3*** ***Study Guide and Review***

1. true **3.** true **5.** true **7.** False; subtract 3 from each. **9.** true **11.** false; perimeter **13.** $x + 5$ **15.** $2a$ **17.** $n - 4 = 19$ **19.** $f + \$8.75$ **21.** −6 **23.** 23 **25.** 37 **27.** 4 **29.** −9 **31.** $14w = 98$; 7 weeks **33.** $146.70 **35.** 4 **37.** −2 **39.** 5 **41.** 53.4 in.; 142.82 in^2 **43.** 7 mi **45.** 16 yd **47.** 12 ft

49.

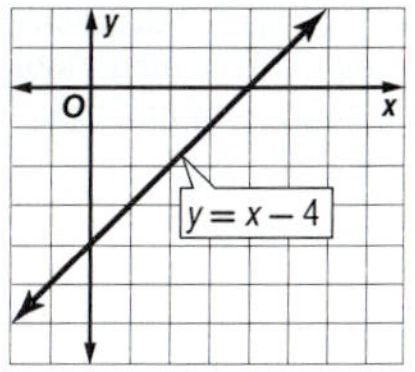

51.

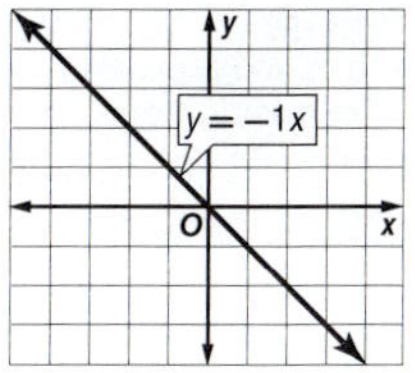

53.

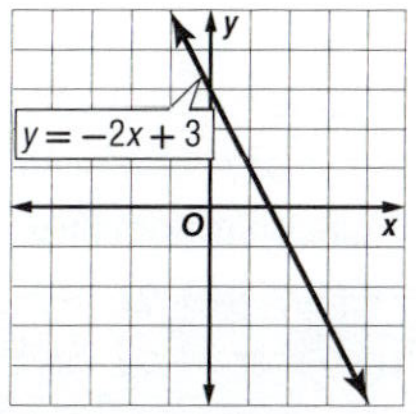

55. $y = 9x$

Chapter 4 Fractions, Decimals, and Percents

Page 179 ***Chapter 4*** ***Getting Ready***

1. 0.61 **3.** 0.33 **5.** Kirsten **7.** 2, 3, 6 **9.** Yes; the sum of the digits, 6, is divisible by 3. **11.** 6 **13.** 0.75 **15.** $5 \times 5 \times 5 \times 5 \times 5$ **17.** $9 \times 9 \times 9 \times 9$

Pages 183–184 ***Lesson 4-1***

1. prime **3.** prime **5.** 2×17 **7.** $2^2 \times 3$ **9.** $2 \cdot 2 \cdot 2 \cdot 2 \cdot x \cdot x$ **11.** composite **13.** prime **15.** composite **17.** prime **19.** $2^5 \times 3$ **21.** $3^2 \times 11$ **23.** $2 \times 3 \times 5 \times 7$ **25.** $2 \times 3^2 \times 7$ **27.** $2 \cdot 5^2$ **29.** $3 \cdot 5 \cdot m \cdot n$ **31.** $2 \cdot 17 \cdot j \cdot k \cdot m$ **33.** $2 \cdot 2 \cdot 13 \cdot g \cdot h \cdot h$ **35.** 7 **37.** 5^2 **39.** $2 \times 5^2 \times 29$ **41.** prime **43.** 81: 9×9, 3×27; 225: 9×25, 5×45; 441: 9×49; 7×63 **45.** 36 **47.** If $n = 1$, $2n$ is a prime number. If $n > 1$, $2n$ is a composite number with at least three factors. **49.** H **51.** 36 ft; 65 ft^2 **53.** −4 **55.** 0 **57.** 2, 5, 10 **59.** 3, 9

Pages 188–189 ***Lesson 4-2***

1. 6 **3.** 10 **5.** 4 **7.** 9 **9.** 6 **11.** 5 **13.** 24 **15.** 8 **17.** 6 **19.** 7 **21.** 8 students **23.** 6 care packages **25.** 25¢ **27.** $6a$ **29.** $5y$ **31.** Sample answer: 24 and 36 **33.** Sample answer: 60 and 90 **35.** Sample answer: The first prism is 8 in. high, 3 in. long, and 4 in. wide. The second prism is 8 in. high, 6 in. long, and 5 in. wide. The third prism is 8 in. high, 5 in. long, and 5 in. wide. **37.** always **39.** Sample answer: 4 and 12 are factors of 24. The greatest common factor of 4, 12, and 24 is 4. **41.** G

43.

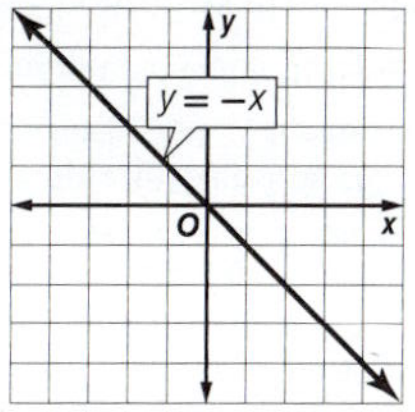

45. 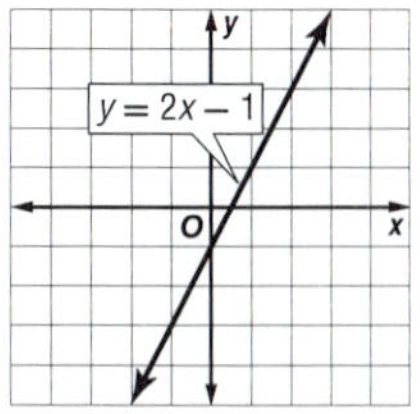

47. 20 songs

Pages 190–191 ***Lesson 4-3***

1. Sample answer: By making an organized list, you can show all the possible pizza combinations. Count the number of pizzas to determine the answer. **3.** 6 outfits **5.** 6 ways **7.** 27, 29 **9.** Paul: 9; Angelina: 5; Bret: 9; Jill: 1 **11.** 7 in. **13.** 0.5m

Pages 194–195 ***Lesson 4-4***

1. $\frac{1}{3}$ **3.** $\frac{2}{5}$ **5.** $\frac{2}{3}$ **7.** $\frac{5}{7}$ **9.** $\frac{7}{10}$ **11.** $\frac{4}{7}$ **13.** $\frac{6}{7}$ **15.** 1 **17.** $\frac{5}{6}$ **19.** $\frac{5}{7}$ **21.** $\frac{2}{5}$ **23.** $\frac{1}{5}$ **25.** $\frac{3}{4}$ **27.** $\frac{1}{3}$ **31.** No, because both the numerator and denominator can be divided by 2. **33.** Sample answer: A fraction is in simplest form if the GCF of the numerator and denominator is 1. **35.** F **37.** 9 **39.** 5 **41.** 0.5 **43.** 0.7

Pages 199–200 ***Lesson 4-5***

1. 0.4 **3.** 7.5 **5.** 0.125 **7.** $0.\overline{5}$ **9.** $\frac{11}{50}$ **11.** $4\frac{3}{5}$ **13.** 0.8 **15.** 4.16 **17.** 0.3125 **19.** 0.66 **21.** 5.875 **23.** $0.\overline{4}$ **25.** $0.\overline{16}$ **27.** $5.\overline{3}$ **29.** $\frac{1}{5}$ **31.** $\frac{11}{20}$ **33.** $5\frac{24}{25}$ **35.** $30\frac{1}{2}$ cm **39.** $\frac{22}{3}$ **41.** $\frac{-16}{5}$ **43.** Felisa; Sample answer: Felisa's batting average is about 0.286. Harmony's batting average is about 0.263. 0.286 > 0.263, so Felisa's average is better than Harmony's. **45.** Sample answer: $3\frac{1}{7} \approx 3.14286\ldots$ and $3\frac{10}{71} \approx 3.14085$; Since 3.1415927… is between $3\frac{1}{7}$ and $3\frac{10}{71}$, Archimedes was correct. **47.** B **49.** $\frac{5}{12}$ **51.** $\frac{2}{7}$ **53.** 9 pizzas **55.** $\frac{3}{9}$ or $\frac{1}{3}$ **57.** $\frac{4}{12}$ or $\frac{1}{3}$

Pages 204–205 ***Lesson 4-6***

1. 57% **3.** 25% **5.** 85% **7.** $\frac{9}{10}$ **9.** $\frac{11}{50}$ **11.** 42% **13.** 99.9% **15.** $66\frac{2}{3}$% **17.** 80% **19.** 26% **21.** 60% **23.** 100% **25.** 30% **27.** $\frac{3}{10}$ **29.** $\frac{22}{25}$ **31.** $\frac{13}{100}$ **33.** 3 **35.** < **37.** = **39.** > **41.** 64% **43.** 5%; the other ratios equal 25% **45.** C **47.** $\frac{3}{5}$ **49.** $2\frac{4}{5}$ **51.** 3 **53.** 4 **55.** 71 **57.** 0.791

Pages 208–210 ***Lesson 4-7***

1. 0.68 **3.** 0.276 **5.** 9% **7.** 73% **9.** 0.27 **11.** 0.06 **13.** 0.185 **15.** 0.022 **17.** 0.277 **19.** 0.3025 **21.** 0.686 **23.** 70% **25.** 580% **27.** 95% **29.** 17% **31.** 67.5% **33.** 1.2% **35.** 34.7% **37.** 33.9% **39.** < **41.** > **43.** < **45.** 0.01389; 0.04167; 0.02083; 0.05; 0.03125 **47.** 1.2 ft **49.** Sample answer: 0.25, $\frac{1}{4}$, 25%

51. 37.5% **53.** 3.125% **55.** D **57.** 72% **59.** 3.1% **61.** −125 **63.** 2 × 5 × 5 **65.** 2 × 2 × 19

Pages 213–214 ***Lesson 4-8***

1. 28 **3.** 60 **5.** 60 **7.** 2020 **9.** 72 **11.** 72 **13.** 315 **15.** 72 **17.** 420 **19.** 144 **21.** 6:00 P.M. **23.** 50¢ **25.** Sample answer: 5, 7 **27.** Sample answer: 10, 35 **29.** 4 packages of juice boxes and 5 packages of oatmeal snack bars **31.** $2^2 \cdot 3 \cdot 5$, or 60 **33.** Sample answer: 3, 10, 15 **35.** C **37.** 0.55 **39.** 0.0025 **41.** $\frac{17}{25}$ **43.** $2s + 7$ **45.** <

Pages 218–220 ***Lesson 4-9***

1. > **3.** < **5.** Eliot; 3 out of 4 has an average of 0.75; 7 out of 11 has an average of 0.64 **7.** C **9.** < **11.** = **13.** < **15.** > **17.** > **19.** < **21.** > **23.** = **25.** Jim; $\frac{10}{16} > \frac{4}{15}$ **27.** $\frac{8}{10}$, 0.805, 81% **29.** −1.4, −1.25, $-1\frac{1}{25}$ **31.** 3.47, $3\frac{4}{7}$, $3\frac{3}{5}$ **33.** > **35.** < **37.** 6c, $6\frac{1}{3}$c, 6.5c **39.** $\frac{1}{5}$g, 1.5g, 5g **41.** Eastern Chipmunk **43.** Bustos: 0.346; Kretschman: 0.333; Nuveman: 0.313; Watley: 0.400; Watley **45.** 0.08; 0.08 equals 8% and the other ratios equal 80%. **47.** Sample answer: Gwen needs $\frac{2}{5}$ yard of fabric and $\frac{3}{8}$ yard of ribbon to make a pillow. Which item does she need more, fabric or ribbon? Answer: fabric **49.** H **51.** 42 **53.** 48 **55.** 0.0625 **57.** 18 **59.** 4 **61.** 12

Pages 221–224 ***Chapter 4*** ***Study Guide and Review***

1. false; division **3.** true **5.** false; least common multiple **7.** true **9.** 2^7 **11.** 5 × 19 **13.** 65 = 5 • 13 **15.** 6 **17.** 21 **19.** $12 **21.** 15 different plans **23.** $\frac{7}{12}$ **25.** $\frac{2}{9}$ **27.** $\frac{1}{2}$ **29.** 0.75 **31.** $0.\overline{5}$ **33.** 6.4 **35.** $\frac{7}{10}$ **37.** $\frac{1}{20}$ **39.** $\frac{27}{50}$ **41.** $5.1\overline{3}$ min **43.** 44% **45.** 40% **47.** $\frac{19}{20}$ **49.** $\frac{4}{25}$ **51.** 0.48 **53.** 0.125 **55.** 61% **57.** 19% **59.** 0.12 **61.** 8 **63.** 24 **65.** 120 **67.** < **69.** > **71.** English

Chapter 5 Applying Fractions

Page 229 ***Chapter 5*** ***Getting Ready***

1. 35 **3.** 30 **5.** 21.6 **7.** 0.83 **9.** 4 **11.** $2\frac{6}{5}$ **13.** $5\frac{5}{4}$ **15.** $\frac{5}{3}$ or $1\frac{2}{3}$ c

Pages 233–235 ***Lesson 5-1***

1–41. Sample answers are given. **1.** 8 + 2 = 10 **3.** 6 × 3 = 18 **5.** $0 + \frac{1}{2} = \frac{1}{2}$ **7.** $\frac{1}{2} \times 1 = \frac{1}{2}$ **9.** $\frac{1}{4} \cdot 16 = 4$ **11.** $\frac{2}{3}$ of 6 ≈ 4ft **13.** 1 + 6 = 7 **15.** 4 − 2 = 2 **17.** 2 • 3 = 6 **19.** 9 ÷ 3 = 3 **21.** $\frac{1}{2} + \frac{1}{2} = 1$ **23.** $1 - \frac{1}{2} = \frac{1}{2}$ **25.** $\frac{1}{2} \cdot 1 = \frac{1}{2}$ **27.** 0 ÷ 1 = 0 **29.** 16 + 1 or 17 in. **31.** $\frac{1}{6} \times 36 = 6$ **33.** 25 ÷ 5 = 5 **35.** 24 ÷ 2 = 12 **37.** 39 **39.** 24 **41.** $\frac{1}{2} \times 200$ or 100

43. Sample answer: $\frac{1}{4} \times 60$ inches or 15 inches **45.** Sample answer: $\frac{11}{12}$ and $\frac{7}{15}$; $\frac{11}{12} - \frac{7}{15} \approx 1 - \frac{1}{2}$ or $\frac{1}{2}$ and $\frac{11}{12} \cdot \frac{7}{15} \approx 1 \cdot \frac{1}{2}$ or $\frac{1}{2}$ **47.** Estimation; Dion doesn't need an exact answer. Sample answer: $3\frac{1}{4} + 1\frac{2}{3} + 1\frac{2}{3}$ is about halfway between 6 and 7 cups. Since this is more than 6 cups, Dion cannot use this bowl to mix the ingredients. **49.** 38 cups **51.** > **53.** < **55.** 5 pkg. of necklaces and 3 pkg. of bracelets **57.** 37.5% **59.** 1.9% **61.** 10 **63.** 15

Pages 238–241 ***Lesson 5-2***

1. $\frac{2}{3}$ **3.** $\frac{1}{4}$ **5.** $\frac{13}{24}$ **7.** $\frac{1}{4}$ **9.** addition; Sample answer: To find how much smaller the total height of the photo is now, add $\frac{5}{16}$ and $\frac{3}{8}$; $\frac{11}{16}$ in. **11.** $\frac{4}{7}$ **13.** $\frac{2}{3}$ **15.** $\frac{2}{3}$ **17.** $1\frac{13}{24}$ **19.** $\frac{4}{9}$ **21.** $\frac{14}{45}$ **23.** addition; Sample answer: To find the smallest width to make the shelf, add $\frac{4}{5}$ and $\frac{3}{4}$; $1\frac{11}{20}$ ft **25.** subtraction; Sample answer: To find how much more turkey Makayla bought, subtract $\frac{1}{4}$ from $\frac{5}{8}$; $\frac{3}{8}$ **27.** $\frac{23}{28}$ **29.** $\frac{7}{12}$ **31.** $1\frac{1}{4}$ **33.** $2\frac{2}{3}$ **35.** $\frac{2}{15}$ **37.** $1\frac{1}{4}$ **39.** $\frac{1}{12}$ **41.** $\frac{2}{3} - \left(\frac{1}{6} + \frac{1}{4}\right) = \frac{1}{4}$ **43.** $\frac{3}{4}$ **45.** Sample answer: The sum of two unit fractions $\frac{1}{a}$ and $\frac{1}{b}$, where a and b are not 0, is $\frac{a+b}{ab}$.

$\frac{1}{a} + \frac{1}{b} = \frac{1 \cdot b}{a \cdot b} + \frac{1 \cdot a}{b \cdot a}$ Rename each fraction using the LCD, ab.

$= \frac{b}{ab} + \frac{a}{ab}$ Simplify.

$= \frac{b+a}{ab}$ Add the numerators.

$= \frac{a+b}{ab}$ Commutative Property

So, $\frac{1}{99} + \frac{1}{100} = \frac{99 + 100}{99 \cdot 100}$ or $\frac{199}{9{,}900}$ **47.** Lourdes; Meagan did not rename the fractions using the LCD. **49.** A **51.** D **53.** Sample answer: 4 + 4 = 8 **55.** Sample answer: 6 • 3 = 18 **57.** 24.8% **59.** −5 **61.** $\frac{2}{3}$ **63.** 5

Pages 244–246 ***Lesson 5-3***

1. $9\frac{6}{7}$ **3.** $4\frac{2}{3}$ **5.** $1\frac{1}{2}$ **7.** $4\frac{5}{8}$ **9.** $3\frac{3}{20}$ gal **11.** $7\frac{5}{7}$ **13.** $2\frac{1}{7}$ **15.** $7\frac{5}{12}$ **17.** $18\frac{17}{24}$ **19.** $3\frac{1}{2}$ **21.** $2\frac{11}{20}$ **23.** $5\frac{7}{8}$ **25.** $7\frac{1}{6}$ **27.** addition; Sample answer: To find the length of the necklace, add $7\frac{1}{4}$ in. and $10\frac{5}{8}$ in.; $17\frac{7}{8}$ in. **29.** subtraction; Sample answer: To find how many inches Alameda had cut, subtract $6\frac{1}{2}$ from $9\frac{3}{4}$; $3\frac{1}{4}$ in. **31.** $15\frac{1}{4}$ **33.** $1\frac{3}{4}$ **35.** $7\frac{1}{8}$ yd **37.** Estimation; You do not need an exact answer; Less than; 7 + 1 < 2 + 7 **39.** Sample answer: Since the garden is a rectangle, the length of one side added to the length of the other side would equal half the length of the perimeter. If one side of the garden is $2\frac{5}{12}$ ft long, find 6 ft − $2\frac{5}{12}$ ft, or $3\frac{7}{12}$ ft. **41.** H **43.** Sample answer: 1 ÷ 1 = 1 **45.** Sample answer: 9 × 7 = 63 **47.** 15 ft

Pages 248–249 ***Lesson 5-4***

1. Sample answer: Use estimation, look for a pattern, work backward. **3.** Sample answer: A fishbowl holds $1\frac{1}{2}$ gallons of water. If there is $\frac{1}{3}$ gallon of water in the bowl, how many more gallons are needed to fill the bowl; $\frac{2}{3}$ gallons, $1\frac{1}{6}$ gallons, or $2\frac{1}{6}$ gallons. Answer: $\frac{2}{3}$ gallon is not enough because that would make exactly 1 gallon of water in the tank. $2\frac{1}{6}$ gallons is too much, since the tank only holds $1\frac{1}{2}$ gallons. The answer is $1\frac{1}{6}$ gallons. **5.** J **7.** $\frac{5}{8}$ in.

9. 

11. $\frac{1}{49}$ inch **13.** $\frac{4}{15}$

Pages 255–257 ***Lesson 5-5***

1. $\frac{2}{9}$ **3.** $\frac{2}{3}$ **5.** $1\frac{1}{2}$ **7.** 32 pounds **9.** $\frac{4}{15}$ **11.** $4\frac{4}{5}$ **13.** $\frac{1}{9}$ **15.** $\frac{1}{20}$ **17.** $\frac{3}{8}$ **19.** $\frac{3}{4}$ **21.** $\frac{3}{16}$ **23.** 14 c **25.** $1\frac{9}{16}$ **27.** 30 **29.** $31\frac{1}{3}$ **31.** 20 **33.** $7\frac{1}{20}$ mi **35.** $\frac{8}{21}$ **37.** $\frac{11}{48}$ **39.** $16\frac{1}{3}$ yd; $10\frac{5}{6}$ yd^2 **41.** one pint **43.** one centimeter **45.** $15\frac{3}{4}$ **47.** $28\frac{3}{4}$ **49.** broccoli: $1\frac{7}{8}$ c, pasta: $5\frac{5}{8}$ c, salad dressing: 1 c, cheese: 2 c; Multiply each amount by $1\frac{1}{2}$. **51.** $\frac{2}{5} \times \frac{3}{5}$; $\frac{6}{25}$; Sample answer: The model shows that $\frac{3}{5}$ of the rectangle is 15 sections out of 25 sections. Since $\frac{2}{5}$ of 15 sections is six sections, $\frac{2}{5}$ of $\frac{3}{5}$ is $\frac{6}{25}$. **53.** Always; Sample answer: Improper fractions are always greater than 1. **55.** Sample answer: The model shows that $\frac{3}{4}$ of one rectangle is 3 sections out of 4 sections shaded since 2 sets of rectangles with 3 sections out of 4 sections is $\frac{6}{4}$, 2 of $\frac{3}{4}$ is $\frac{6}{4}$, or $1\frac{1}{2}$. **57.** H **59.** $2\frac{1}{10}$ in. **61.** > **63.** $4.95 + 0.6x = 22.95$; 300 min **65.** 3

Pages 261–263 ***Lesson 5-6***

1. $\frac{5}{8}$ **3.** $\frac{5}{29}$ **5.** 32 **7.** 20.5 **9.** $\frac{4}{5}$ **11.** 32 **13.** $\frac{6}{5}$ or $1\frac{1}{5}$ **15.** $\frac{6}{1}$ or 6 **17.** $\frac{1}{3}$ **19.** $\frac{8}{41}$ **21.** 36 **23.** 14.4 **25.** 2.88 **27.** $\frac{6}{5}$ **29.** $\frac{20}{21}$ **31.** $6\frac{2}{3}$ **33.** 195 mi **35.** −75 **37.** 41.4 **39.** $1\frac{1}{2}$ **41.** x = elevation change of the Wild Cave Tour; $140 = \frac{7}{15}x$; 300ft **43.** x = number of servings; $\frac{3}{4}x = 16\frac{1}{2}$; 22 servings **45.** x = the person's age; $\frac{1}{3}x = 26$; 78 years old

For Homework Help, go to Hotmath.com

47. 20; Sample answer: By solving $8 = \frac{m}{4}$, you find that $m = 32$. So, replace m with 32 to find $32 - 12 = 20$. **49.** Sample answer: Multiply each side by 2. Then divide each side by $(b_1 + b_2)$. So, $\frac{2A}{b_1 + b_2} = h$. **51.** A

53. $\frac{1}{6}$ **55.** $\frac{2}{5}$ **57.** $3\frac{5}{12}$ c **59.** 0.08 **61.** 1.23

63. −1 **65.** −8 **67.** Sample answer: $18 \div 3 = 6$ **69.** Sample answer: $0 \div 1 = 0$

Pages 267–270 ***Lesson 5-7***

1. $\frac{3}{8}$ **3.** $3\frac{1}{2}$ **5.** $\frac{1}{15}$ **7.** $1\frac{1}{5}$ **9.** 56 segments **11.** $\frac{7}{16}$ **13.** $1\frac{1}{3}$ **15.** 12 **17.** $\frac{2}{3}$ **19.** 12 **21.** $\frac{4}{15}$ **23.** $\frac{2}{3}$ **25.** $2\frac{17}{20}$ **27.** $7\frac{4}{5}$ **29.** 36 **31.** $3\frac{34}{35}$

33. $1\frac{1}{4}$;  ;

35. $2\frac{3}{4}$;

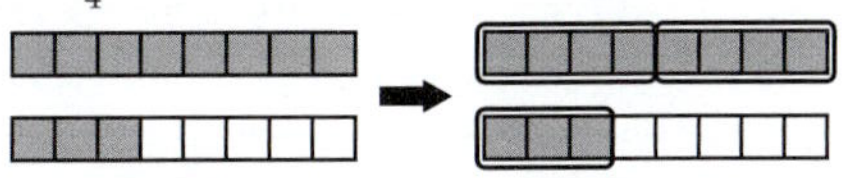

37. 25 **39.** $\frac{1}{22}$ **41.** $\frac{3}{11}$ **43.** 4 **45.** $7\frac{9}{10}$ times as many **47.** 6:30 P.M.; Sample answer: $105 \div 35 = 3$, The storm will travel 105 miles in 3 sets of $\frac{1}{2}$ hour, or $1\frac{1}{2}$ hours. Adding $1\frac{1}{2}$ hours to 5:00 P.M. will make it 6:30 P.M. **49.** Sample answer; You could use paper and pencil; $\frac{3}{4}$ of what number is $1\frac{1}{2}$? $1\frac{1}{2}$ feet $\div \frac{3}{4} = \frac{3}{2}$ feet $\cdot \frac{4}{3} = 2$ feet. **51.** Yes. If the first proper fraction is larger than the second proper fraction then the resulting quotient will be a whole number or mixed number. **53.** H **55.** $\frac{13}{4}$ or $3\frac{1}{4}$ **57.** $\frac{4}{21}$ **59.** 4.5 ft

Pages 271–274 ***Chapter 5 Study Guide and Review***

1. numerators **3.** reciprocal **5.** unlike **7.** $1\frac{11}{7}$ **9.** 3 **11.** reciprocal **13.** Sample answer: $3 \div 1 = 3$ **15.** Sample answer: $1 \times 0 = 0$ **17.** Sample answer: $\frac{1}{2} \times 26 = 13$ **19.** Sample answer: 19×10 or about 190 ft² **21.** $\frac{1}{6}$ **23.** $\frac{2}{3}$ **25.** $\frac{5}{24}$ **27.** $\frac{5}{8}$ in. **29.** $9\frac{11}{15}$ **31.** $10\frac{1}{7}$ **33.** $2\frac{4}{15}$ **35.** $15\frac{1}{8}$ **37.** $7\frac{11}{12}\,h$ **39.** G **41.** $\frac{5}{27}$ **43.** $2\frac{3}{5}$ **45.** $9\frac{3}{8}$ **47.** $\frac{12}{7}$ or $1\frac{5}{7}$ **49.** $\frac{3}{10}$ **51.** 15 **53.** 0.75 **55.** $\frac{7}{10}$ **57.** $3\frac{3}{10}$ **59.** $1\frac{21}{22}$ **61.** 54

Chapter 6 Ratios and Proportions

Page 281 ***Chapter 6 Getting Ready***

1. 48.1 **3.** 7.4 **5.** $\frac{1}{5}$ **7.** $\frac{19}{23}$ **9.** $\frac{39}{50}$ **11.** $\frac{3}{50}$ **13.** 450 **15.** 2,200

Pages 284–286 ***Lesson 6-1***

1. $\frac{2}{15}$ **3.** $\frac{1}{51}$ **5.** yes. $\frac{12}{20} = \frac{3}{5}$ and $\frac{6}{10} = \frac{3}{5}$ **7.** no; Sample answer: $\frac{2\text{ boxes}}{\$5} \neq \frac{6\text{ boxes}}{\$20}$, since $2 \cdot 3 = 6$, but $5 \cdot 3 \neq 20$ **9.** $\frac{3}{2}$ **11.** $\frac{1}{3}$ **13.** $\frac{2}{5}$ **15.** $\frac{21}{1{,}600}$ **17.** $\frac{21}{32}$ **19.** yes; $\frac{4}{16} = \frac{1}{4}$ and $\frac{10}{40} = \frac{1}{4}$, so $\frac{4}{16} = \frac{10}{40}$ **21.** no; $\frac{8}{6} = \frac{4}{3}$ and $\frac{12}{10} = \frac{6}{5}$, so $\frac{8}{6} \neq \frac{12}{10}$ **23.** no; Sample answer: $\frac{12\text{ in.}}{3\text{ in.}} = \frac{4}{1}$ and $\frac{6\text{ in.}}{1\text{ in.}} = \frac{6}{1}$, so $\frac{12\text{ in.}}{3\text{ in.}} \neq \frac{6\text{ in.}}{1\text{ in.}}$ **25.** no; $\frac{71}{42} \neq \frac{16}{9}$ **27.** 9 lb **29.** yes; $\frac{330}{396} = \frac{5}{6}$; **31.** Areas A and C; both ratios simplify to a growth-to-removal ratio of $\frac{11}{30}$. **33.** 80; Sample answer: $440 + 80 = 520$; $\frac{520}{1{,}200} = \frac{13}{30}$ which is the same ratio as area B **35.** 2,400; The denominator of the ratios increases by 1. $\frac{20}{40} = \frac{1}{2}$, $\frac{40}{120} = \frac{1}{3}$, $\frac{120}{480} = \frac{1}{4}$ **37.** B **39.** $\frac{6}{7}$ **41.** $1\frac{2}{3}$ **43.** $5\frac{2}{3}$ **45.** 4.9 **47.** $0.31

Pages 289–292 ***Lesson 6-2***

1. 6 mi per gal **3.** $0.50 per lb **5.** C **7.** 60 mi/h **9.** 30.4 people per class **11.** 3.5 m/s **13.** $0.14/oz **15.** about $0.50 per pair **17.** Susanna; 1.78 m/s > 1.66 m/s > 1.23 m/s **19.** Soft drinks A and B have about 3 grams of sodium per ounce and Soft drink C has about 6 grams per ounce. **21.** 510 words **23.** Sample answer: about 60 **25.** 182.7 **27.** 38¢ per lb; $1.89 ÷ 5 ≈ $1.90 ÷ 5 or $0.38 **29.** 3 c **31.** about 1 h 29 min 49 s **33.** The bear's heart beats 120 times in 2 minutes when it is active. **35.** the bear's heart rate in beats per minute **37.** when it is active; Sample answer: The active line increases faster than the hibernating line when read from left to right. **41.** Always; every rate is a ratio, because it is a comparison of two quantities by division. **43.** Sample answer: a; $\frac{30\text{ ft}}{2\text{ min}} = 15$ ft/min, $\frac{40\text{ ft}}{2\text{ min}} = 20$ ft/min **45.** C **47.** $\frac{2}{9}$ **49.** $\frac{9}{14}$ **51.** 8 subs **53.** $\frac{1}{2}$ **55.** $\frac{1}{4}$

Pages 295–297 ***Lesson 6-3***

1. 1.5°F every hour **3.** slope: $\frac{8}{1}$ or 8; There are 8 packs of fruit snacks in each box.

Fruit Snacks

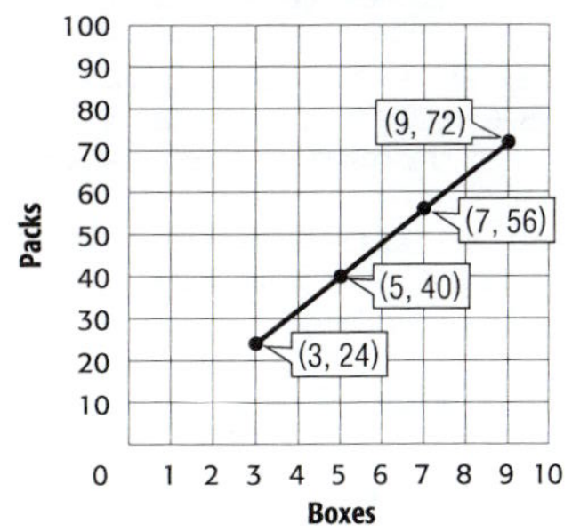

5. $9 per h **7.** $9 per shirt **9.** 0.45mi/min

Cycling

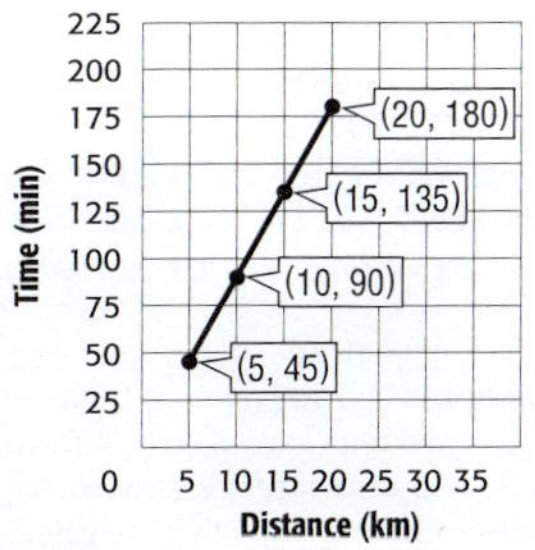

11. $\frac{1}{6}$ inch per minute

13.

Length of Poster (ft)	Ribbon Needed (in.)
3	18
6	36
9	54
12	72

15. A **17.** $11.90 **19.** $\frac{18}{1}$ **21.** 50 **23.** 6.5

Pages 301–303 ***Lesson 6-4***

1. 48 **3.** 52 **5.** 3 **7.** $7\frac{1}{2}$ **9.** 0.0075 mi/s **11.** $4\frac{1}{2}$ **13.** 16 **15.** 24 **17.** 6,600 **19.** $6\frac{1}{2}$ **21.** 6,750 **23.** 3,520 ft **25.** $17\frac{1}{2}$ qt **27.** 1,056,000 ft/h **29.** No; 15 in. + $4\frac{1}{2}$ in. + $6\frac{3}{4}$ in. = $26\frac{1}{4}$ in. and $26\frac{1}{4} \div 12 = 2\frac{3}{16}$. So, it snowed a total of $2\frac{3}{16}$ ft or about 2 ft, not $2\frac{1}{2}$ ft. **31.** eighth of an inch **33.** about $8\frac{1}{2}$ mi **35.** $\frac{1}{4}$ **37.** 3 gal; Sample answer: the graph increases by 1 gallon for every 4 quarts. **39.** < **41.** = **43.** 720 in²; Square feet mean a unit of feet × feet. To divide out each unit, you must multiply by two conversion factors that have feet in the denominator and inches in the numerator. 5 ft² $\cdot \frac{12\text{ in.}}{1\text{ ft}} \cdot \frac{12\text{ in.}}{1\text{ ft}} = 720$ in² **45.** G **47.** $9 per h **49.** 8 ft **51.** $2v$ **53.** 118.9 **55.** 142.127

Pages 307–309 ***Lesson 6-5***

1. 370 **3.** 1.46 **5.** 8.52 **7.** 128.17 **9.** about 5,333.33 ft **11.** 0.98 **13.** 3.0 **15.** 0.08 **17.** 130,500 **19.** 106.17 **21.** 36.01 **23.** 15.75 **25.** 0.51 kg **27.** about 35,420 meters per hour **29.** 16,582.42 **31.** 403,704 **33.** grams **35.** 50 cm **37.** Jake; Gerardo divided 3.25 by 1,000; he should have multiplied. **39.** about 621,118.01 mi **41.** There are a greater number of smaller units. **43.** H

45. slope: $\frac{12}{1}$ or 12; There are 12 inches in 1 foot.

Number of Inches per Foot

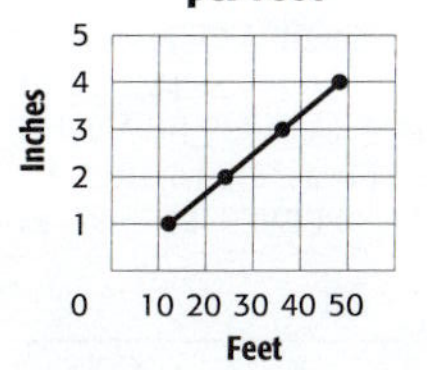

47. $6\frac{1}{5}$ **49.** $5\frac{19}{20}$ **51.** 10 **53.** 3.2

Pages 313–315 ***Lesson 6-6***

1. No; sample answer: $\frac{10\text{ children}}{2\text{ adults}} = \frac{5\text{ children}}{1\text{ adult}}$ and $\frac{12\text{ children}}{3\text{ adults}} = \frac{4\text{ children}}{1\text{ adult}}$. The unit rates are not equal. **3.** Yes; sample answer: The cross products of the ratios $\frac{8}{21}$ and $\frac{12}{31.5}$, 8 × 31.5 and 21 × 12, are both equal to 252. **5.** 15 **7.** 29.4 **9.** 20 **11.** $8.33 **13.** No; sample answer: The cross products of the ratios $\frac{20}{6}$ and $\frac{16}{5}$, 20 × 5 or 100 and 6 × 16 or 96, are not equal. **15.** Yes; sample answer: The cross products of the ratios $\frac{16}{200}$ and $\frac{28}{350}$, 16 × 350 and 200 × 28, are both equal to 5,600. **17.** No; sample answer: The cross products of the ratios $\frac{1.4\text{ T}}{18\text{ days}}$ and $\frac{10.5\text{ T}}{60\text{ days}}$, 1.4 × 60 or 84 and 18 × 10.5 or 189, are not equal. **19.** No; $\frac{45\text{ min}}{25\text{ pages}} = \frac{1.8\text{ min}}{1\text{ page}}$ and $\frac{60\text{ min}}{30\text{ pages}} = \frac{2\text{ min}}{1\text{ page}}$. These rates are not equivalent. **21.** 15 **23.** 3 **25.** 1.5 **27.** 63 **29.** 2.4 **31.** 13.5 **33.** 4.2 lb **35.** 1.6 oz **37.** (3, 15) represents 3 pizzas cost $15. (5, 25) represents 5 pizzas cost $25. Yes, as the number of pizzas increases by 1, the cost increases by $5. **39.** 5, with delivery fee; 5 no delivery fee; the slope represents the cost per pizza **41.** $19.50 **43.** $\frac{325}{13} = \frac{100}{x}$; 4 **45.** $5.70 for 6 lb; Sample answer: This ratio has a unit rate of 0.95/lb, while all of the other ratios have a unit rate of $0.90/lb. **47.** Sample answer: Mental math; $10 is 4 times more than $2.50, so the number of ears is 4 times more than a dozen, which is 4 dozen or 48 ears of corn. **49.** B **51.** about 2.27 kg **53.** 56 **55.** $20\frac{9}{16}$ **57.** $17\frac{5}{32}$

Pages 318–319 ***Lesson 6-7***

1. $\frac{3}{4}$ feet

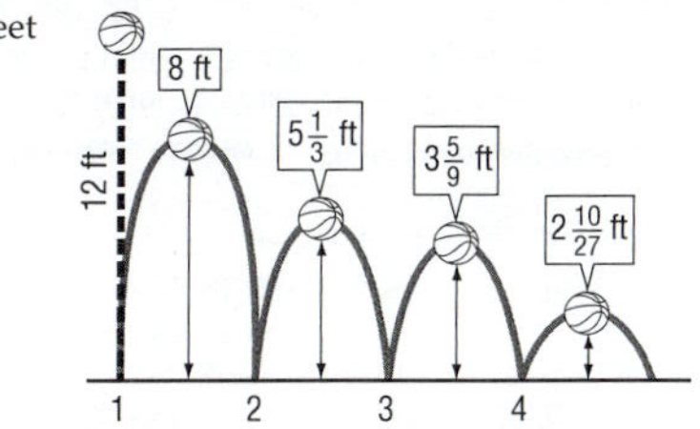

3. 30 miles **5.** 125 minutes **7.** 28 games
9. Mary, Isabela, Anna, Pilar

Pages 323–326 ***Lesson 6-8***

1. 50 km **3.** 130 km **5.** 14 feet **7.** $16\frac{2}{3}$ in. **9.** $\frac{1}{48}$ **11.** $\frac{1}{63,360}$ **13.** 81 mi **15.** 40 mi **17.** 12 ft by 9 ft **19.** $11\frac{3}{5}$ in.; $\frac{1}{90}$ **21.** 6 in.; $\frac{1}{720}$ **23.** 26 mi **25.** $\frac{1}{3}$; about 6.33 feet **29.** $\frac{5,000}{1}$ **31a.** A; 0.5 cm is larger than 1 mm. If 0.5 cm on the model is equal to 1 mm on the actual figure, then model A must be larger than the actual figure. **31b.** B; 1.5 mm is smaller than 4 cm. If 1.5 mm on the model is equal to 4 cm on the actual figure, then model B must be smaller than the actual figure. **31c.** C; 0.25 cm is equal to 2.5 mm. If 0.25 cm is equal to 2.5 mm on the actual figure, then model C must be the same size as the actual figure. **33.** Sample answer: Using the scale given on the map, look at the distance between the two cities on the map and then estimate the actual distance based on the distance given in the scale. **35.** F **37.** 200 people **39.** 15 **41.** Sample answer: 7 + 9 + 10 + 12 + 7 or 45 mi **43.** 24 **45.** 30 **47.** 60 **49.** $\frac{13}{30}$ **51.** $\frac{7}{8}$

Pages 331–332 ***Lesson 6-9***

1. $\frac{27}{100}$ **3.** $\frac{3}{40}$ **5.** $\frac{5}{8}$ **7.** 0.16% **9.** 11.11% **11.** $\frac{5}{8}$ **13.** 0.13% **15.** $\frac{1}{3}$ **17.** $\frac{15}{16}$ **19.** $\frac{1}{1000}$ **21.** 555% **23.** 375% **25.** 96.67% **27.** 71.43% **29.** 0.13% **31.** 0.42% **33.** 140% **35.** < **37.** > **39.** $\frac{1}{2}$%, $\frac{2}{5}$, 0.48, 0.5 **43.** Less than; $\frac{26}{125}$ = 20.8% **45.** Sample answer: Since a percent is a ratio that compares a number to 100, 80% is the ratio $\frac{80}{100}$. The ratio $\frac{80}{100}$ can be read as eighty-hundredths or written as a decimal, 0.80 or 0.8. The ratio $\frac{80}{100}$ also simplifies to $\frac{4}{5}$ if you divide the numerator and denominator by the same number, 20. **47.** G **49.** 2 **51.** $\frac{9}{20}$ **53.** $1\frac{3}{4}$

Pages 333–336 ***Chapter 6*** ***Study Guide and Review***

1. ratio **3.** rate **5.** scale drawing **7.** scale factor **9.** unit rate **11.** $\frac{4}{3}$ **13.** $\frac{2}{3}$ **15.** no; $\frac{18}{24} = \frac{3}{4}$, $\frac{5}{20} = \frac{1}{4}$, and $\frac{3}{4} \neq \frac{1}{4}$ **17.** 90 mi per day

19.

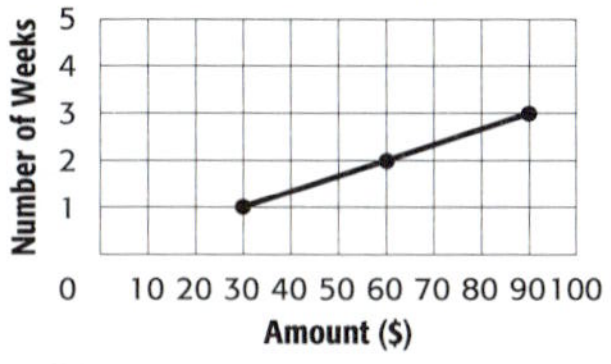

slope: $\frac{30}{1}$ or 30; José saved $30 every week. **21.** 24 **23.** $4\frac{1}{2}$ **25.** 50 bushels **27.** 51,528.96

29. 18.43 **31.** about 345 lb **33.** 54 **35.** 9 **37.** $2\frac{1}{3}$ **39.** 27 feet **41.** 24 mi **43.** $\frac{11}{40}$ **45.** $\frac{181}{400}$ **47.** 91.67%

Chapter 7 Applying Percents

Page 341 ***Chapter 7*** ***Getting Ready***

1. 48 **3.** 1,512 **5.** $54.75 **7.** 0.34 **9.** 0.75 **11.** 75 **13.** 38.9 **15.** 0.17 **17.** 1.57 **19.** 0.075

Pages 346–348 ***Lesson 7-1***

1. 4 **3.** 110.5 **5.** 23 **7.** $3.25 **9.** $194.40 **11.** 45.9 **13.** 14.7 **15.** 17.5 **17.** 62.5 **19.** $290 **21.** 3.5 **23.** 97.8 **25.** 92.5 **27.** about 19.5 million **29.** 3.3 **31.** 990 **33.** 520 **35.** 0.24 **37.** $9.75 **39.** $297 **41.** about 316 **43.** Sample answer: 53% of 60 → 50% × 60 or $\frac{1}{2}$ × 60 = 30 **45.** Sample answer: 75% of 19 → 75% × 20 or $\frac{3}{4}$ × 20 = 15 **47.** 80 **49.** Sample answer: 24% × 250 or 60 people prefer cherries. So, 250 – 60 or 190 people did not prefer cherries. **51.** 15 **53.** Sample answer: Determine the number of questions answered correctly on a test and find how much to tip a restaurant server. **55.** Less than the original number; you are subtracting 10% of a greater number. **57.** C **59.** 71% **61.** $\frac{3}{5}$ **63.** $\frac{17}{24}$ **65.** 1267.81

Pages 353–354 ***Lesson 7-2***

1. 36% **3.** 0.7 **5.** 75 **7.** 3 c **9.** 7.5% **11.** 8.6 **13.** 375 **15.** 24 **17.** 40% **19.** 4.1 **21.** 192 **23.** 0.2% **25.** $8 **27.** about 3.4% **29.** about 6,378 km **31.** 20% of 500, 20% of 100, 5% of 100; If the percent is the same but the base is greater, then the part is greater. If the base is the same but the percent is greater, then the part is greater. **33.** B **35.** 30 **37.** 2.75 **39.** 3 **41.** 30 **43.** 18

Pages 357–360 ***Lesson 7-3***

1. 5; $\frac{1}{2}$ • 10 = 5; 0.1 • 10 = 1 and 5 • 1 = 5 **3.** 24; $\frac{2}{5}$ • 60 = 24; 0.1 • 60 = 6 and 4 • 6 = 24 **5.** (1 • 70) + $\left(\frac{1}{2} \cdot 70\right)$ = 105 **7.** about $50; $\frac{1}{4}$ • $200 = $50; 0.1 • 200 = 20 and 2.5 • 20 = $50 **9.** about 160,000 acres; 0.1 • 20,000,000 = 200,000 and $\frac{4}{5}$ of 200,000 = 160,000 **11.** 18; $\frac{1}{5}$ • 90 = 18; 0.1 • 90 = 9 and 2 • 9 = 18 **13.** 135; $\frac{3}{4}$ • 180 = 135; 0.1 • 180 = 18 and 7.5 • 18 = 135 **15.** 90; $\frac{9}{10}$ • 100 = 90; 0.1 • 100 = 10 and 9 • 10 = 90 **17.** 36; $\frac{3}{10}$ • 120 = 36; 0.1 • 120 = 12 and 3 • 12 = 36 **19.** 90; $\frac{3}{5}$ • 150 = 90; 0.1 • 150 = 15 and 6 • 15 = 90 **21.** 168; $\frac{7}{10}$ • 240 = 168; 0.1 • 240 = 24 and 7 • 24 = 168 **23.** about 12 muscles; $\frac{3}{10}$ • 40 = 12 **25.** (2 • 300) + $\left(\frac{1}{4} \cdot 300\right)$ = 675 **27.** 0.01 • 200 = 2 and $\frac{3}{4}$ • 2 = 1.5 **29.** 0.01 • 70 = 0.7 **31.** about 2,700 birds; 0.01 • 450,000 = 4,500 and $\frac{3}{5}$ • 4,500 = 2,700 **33.** $\frac{1}{2}$ • 80 = 40 **35.** $\frac{1}{10}$ • 240 = 24 **37.** 1 • 45 = 45 **39.** about 3 hours; Method 1: $\frac{1}{3}$ • 24 = 8 and $\frac{1}{5}$ • 24 ≈ 5; 8 – 5 = 3 **41.** 1,200 **43.** Sample answer: about 400,000 people; .08 • 5,000,000 = 400,000 **45.** 3.6 ounces **47.** Sample answer: Find 1% of $800, then multiply by $\frac{3}{8}$. **49.** Sometimes; sample answer: one estimate for 37% of 60 is $\frac{2}{5}$ × 60 = 24. This is greater than the actual answer because $\frac{2}{5}$ is greater than 37%. Another estimate is $\frac{1}{3}$ × 60 = 20. This is less than the actual answer because $\frac{1}{3}$ is less than 37%. **51.** B **53.** D **55.** 64.8 **57.** 157.1 **59.** Sample answer: 1 + 0 = 1 **61.** Sample answer: $1 - \frac{1}{2} = \frac{1}{2}$ **63.** 50 **65.** 357.1 **67.** 0.7 **69.** 0.75

Pages 363–365 ***Lesson 7-4***

1. p = 88 • 300; 264 **3.** 75 = n • 150; 50% **5.** 3 = 0.12 • w; 25 **7.** 39 loaves **9.** p = 0.39 • 65; 25.4 **11.** p = 0.53 • 470; 249.1 **13.** 26 = n • 96; 27.1% **15.** 30 = n • 64; 46.9% **17.** 84 = 0.75 • w; 112 **19.** 64 = 0.8 • w; 80 **21.** 4,400 games **23.** 1 **25.** p = 0.004 • 82.1; 0.3 **27.** 230 = n • 200; 115% **29.** about 42% **31.** about 27% **33.** Sample answer: 30 is 125% of what number?; 24 **35.** Sample answer: It may be easier if the percent and the base are known because after writing the percent as a decimal or fraction, the only step is to multiply. When using the percent proportion, you must first find the cross products and then divide. **37.** H **39.** $1.95 **41.** 170.73% **43.** 37 yr

Pages 366–367 ***Lesson 7-5***

1. Sample answer: Look for a rule or pattern in the data or number facts, estimation, guess and check, make an organized list, or work backward. **3.** Sample answer; $10 • 12 = $120 **5.** 500; 60% • 830 ≈ 500 **7.** 2 quarters, 1 dime, 4 nickels, and 3 pennies **9.** $30 **11.** $3.50 **13.** 15 • 18 + 18 • 20 = 630 ft^3. Then convert 630 ft^3 to square yards; 630 ÷ (3 • 3) = 70 yd^2

Pages 372–374 ***Lesson 7-6***

1. 20% decrease **3.** 19% increase **5.** C **7.** 40% increase **9.** 71% decrease **11.** 25% decrease **13.** 5% decrease **15.** 13% increase **17.** 38% decrease **19.** 2% increase **21.** 75% decrease **23.** 150% increase **25.** 400% **29.** about $31 billion **31.** 23% **33.** 2005 to 2006; 50% **35.** The $60 sound system since 10 is a greater part of 60 than of 90. **37.** No; after a 10% increase, the quantity is greater then the original quantity. Decreasing a larger number by the same percent results in a greater change. **39.** D **41.** Sample answer: 0.5 • 800 or 400 students **43.** n = 0.21 • 62; 13.0 **45.** 0.065 **47.** 0.0825

Pages 377–378 ***Lesson 7-7***

1. $3.10 **3.** $1,338.75 **5.** $98.90 **7.** $1,605 **9.** $4.90 **11.** $7.99 **13.** $96.26 **15.** $7.50 **17.** $180.00 **19.** $35.79 **21.** $333.60 **23.** $25 **25.** $50, $25; The percent of discount is 50%. All of the other pairs have a discount of 25%. **27.** C **29.** C **31.** 9% decrease **33.** about 500 × 0.7 or 350 mi **35.** $\frac{1}{18}$

Pages 381–382 ***Lesson 7-8***

1. $38.40 **3.** $5.80 **5.** $1,417.50 **7.** $1,219.00 **9.** $21.38 **11.** $123.75 **13.** $45.31 **15.** $14.06 **17.** $1,353.13 **19.** $116.25 **21.** Yes, he would have $5.208. **23.** $825.60, $852.02, $879.28 **25.** C **27.** $21.39 **29.** 37% decrease **31.** $1\frac{1}{5}$ **33.** $2\frac{2}{15}$

Pages 384–388 ***Chapter 7*** ***Study Guide and Review***

1. true **3.** true **5.** false; 10% **7.** true **9.** false; original **11.** 39 **13.** 135 **15.** 14 games **17.** 0.3 **19.** $27.49 **21.** Sample answer: 40; $\frac{1}{3}$ • 120 = 40 **23.** Sample answer: 20; $\frac{1}{5}$ • 100 = 20 **25.** Sample answer: 360; 0.1 • 400 = 40; 9 • 40 = 360 **27.** 32 = p • 50; 64% **29.** n = 42 • 300; 126 **31.** 108 = 0.12 • w; 900 **33.** 333 **35.** Sample answer: $700 × 0.4 = $280 **37.** 93% increase **39.** 10% increase **41.** $26.75 **43.** $8,440 **45.** 14% **47.** $3.51 **49.** $1,500 **51.** $101.25 **53.** $311.85

Chapter 8 Statistics: Analyzing Data

Page 395 ***Chapter 8*** ***Getting Ready***

1. 95.89, 96.02, 96.2 **3.** 22, 22.012, 22.02 **5.** 74.7, 74.67, 74.65 **7.** 3.340, 3.304, 3.04 **9.** 2.32

Pages 398–401 ***Lesson 8-1***

1.

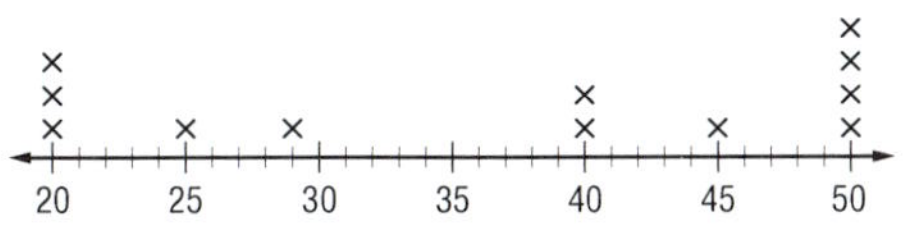

3. clusters: 6–12; gaps: 12–20; outlier: 20; range: 20 – 4, or 16 **5.** 1 or 2 glasses per day **7.** 5 glasses

9.

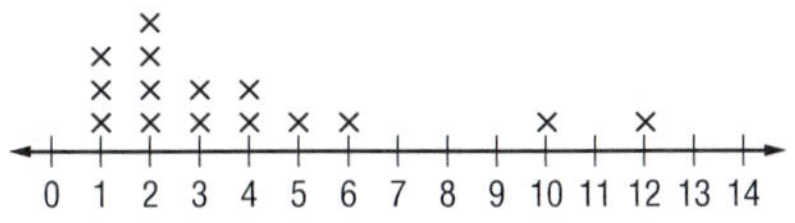

11.

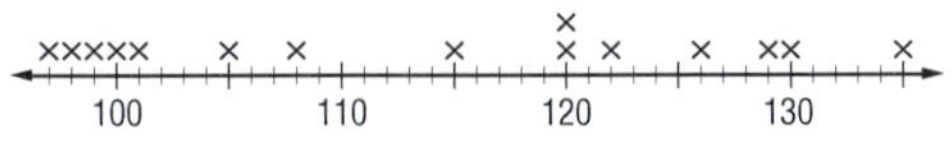

13. 34° **15.** Sample answer: cluster 104°F–122°F; gaps 100°F–104°F, 122°F–125°F, 125°F–128°F, and 128°F–134°F; outliers 100°F and 134°F **17.** 36 – 10 or 26 **19.** 15 **21.** Sometimes; the range will only change if the new data value lies above or below the greatest and least points, respectively, of the original data set. **23.** 10 **25.** about 72% **27.** Sample answer: range 28; cluster 1–19; gap 19–29; outlier 29

For Homework Help, go to Hotmath.com

29. **The House of Representatives, Southwestern States**

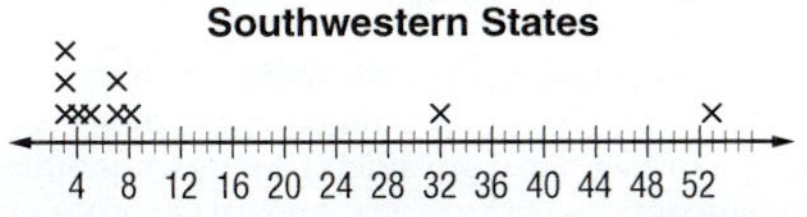

Sample answer: The data are more clustered between 4 and 25 with a range of 35 and a gap from 25 to 39. Most frequently occurring is 7, 8, and 9. 39 is an outlier. **31.** Sample answer: The range of a data set excluding the outlier(s) is a lesser value than the range of the same data set including the outlier(s). This is because any outliers will lie below and above the least and greatest values, respectively, of the data set and the range will change to include these values. **33.** Sample answer: A frequency table shows the number of times data occur by using tally marks. A line plot shows the number of times data occur by using ×s. A frequency table usually shows intervals of data and is useful when a summary is needed. A line plot shows individual data points and is useful when you need to see how all the data points are spread out. **35.** C **37.** $60 **39.** $4.46 **41.** 47 **43.** 12.6

Pages 405–408 *Lesson 8-2*

1. 52.3; 57; 59 **3.** 26.5, 25.5, 23, and 25 **5.** Sample answer: Either the mean, median, or mode could be used to represent the data. The mean is slightly less than most of the data items, and therefore is a less accurate description of the data. **7.** 87; 90; 80 and 93 **9.** $12; $9; $6 **11.** 46, 45, 44 **13.** Sample answer: The mean, 15.6, is higher than most of the data. The median, 1, or mode, 1, best represents the data. **15.** $3.50, $3.50, $3.50 **17.** Always; Sample answer: Any value that is added which is greater than the maximum value, 23, will increase the average, or mean, of the values. **19.** Sometimes; Sample answer: The mean of the data set is currently 14.5. If a value that is greater than 14.5 is added, the mean will increase. If a value that is less than 14.5 is added, the mean will decrease. If a value that is exactly 14.5 is added, the mean will remain unchanged. **21.** Sample answer: A length of 960 inches is much greater than the other pieces of data. So, if this piece of data is added, the mean will increase. **23.** 10 points; Sample answer: The sum of the points for the first thirteen games is 158. In order for the average number of points to be 12, the total number of points for fourteen games would need to be 12 × 14 or 168. So, 168 – 158 or 10 points need to be scored during the last game. **25.** Sample answer: 4, 5, 2, 2, 3, 3, 1, 0, 1, 2, 4, 68, 5; the mean, 7.7, is not the best representation since it is greater than all the data items except one. **27.** Sometimes; if there is an odd number of items, the median is the middle number. If there is an even number of items, the median is the mean of the two middle numbers. **29.** Mean; a mode must be a member of the data set, and it is impossible to have 2.59 family members. **31.** H

33. **High Temperatures for July in Kentucky**

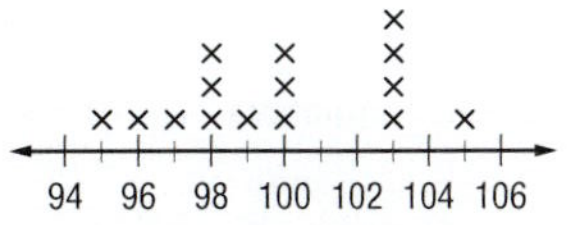

35. $10.43 **37.** Commutative (×) **39.** ones **41.** tenths

Pages 412–414 *Lesson 8-3*

1. **Height of Trees(ft)**

Stem	Leaf
0	8 8
1	0 2 5 5 6 8
2	0 5

2|0 = 20 ft

3. 5 **5.** mean

7. **Low Temperatures (°F)**

Stem	Leaf
1	3 3 5
2	0 4 8
3	0 1 2 2 5 6 8 8 8

1|3 = 13°F

9. **School Play Attendance**

Stem	Leaf
22	5 7 9
23	0
24	3 6
25	
26	7 9 9
27	8 8 8

26|7 = 267 people

11. 4; 1 **13.** $45 **15.** mean **17.** 26 **19.** Sample answer: Yes; Thirty-six of the 56 signers were 30–49 years. Since 36 out of 56 is greater than half, you can say that the majority of the signers were 30–49 years old.

21. **Average Length (ft) of Crocodiles**

Stem	Leaf
6	3
7	
8	1
9	8 8
10	
11	4
12	
13	6
14	
15	
16	0 3 3 3 3
17	
18	
19	5

13|6 = 13.6 ft

Sample answer: A reasonable length for an average crocodile is about 16 feet.

23. Diana; three out of the six or 50% of the pieces of ribbon are 20–30 inches in length.

25. **Fiber in Cereal (g)**

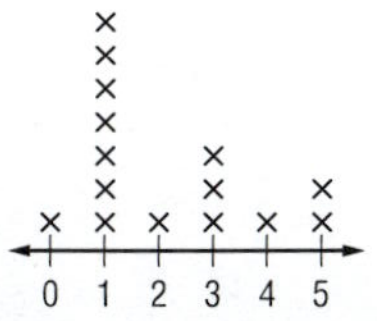

Stem	Leaf
0	0 1 1 1 1 1 1 1
	2 3 3 3 4 5 5

0|1 = 1 gram

Both representations show the frequency of data occurring. The line plot gives a good picture of the spread of the data. The stem-and-leaf plot shows individual grams of fiber as in the line plot, as well as intervals. See students' favorites and reasons. **27.** C **29.** 48.7; 50; 55

31. **Test Scores**

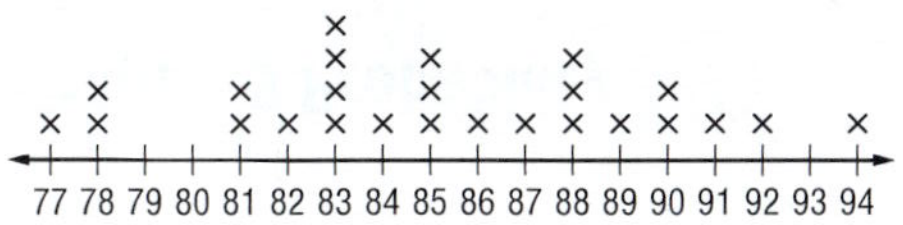

33. $\frac{3}{8}$ **35.** Sample answer: 20; 20–120

Pages 418–421 *Lesson 8-4*

1. histogram

State Sales Tax Rates

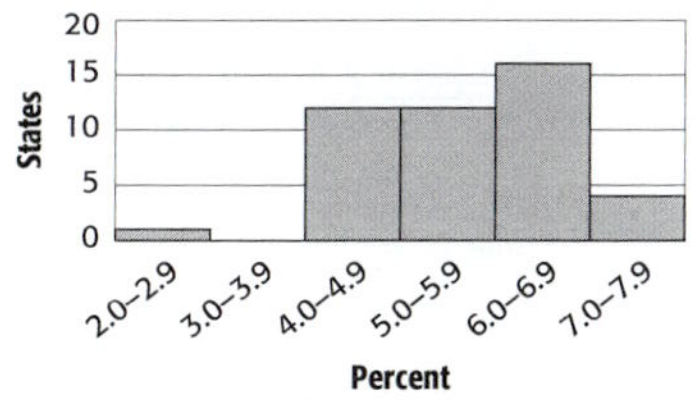

3. health

5. bar graph

Most Threatened Reptiles

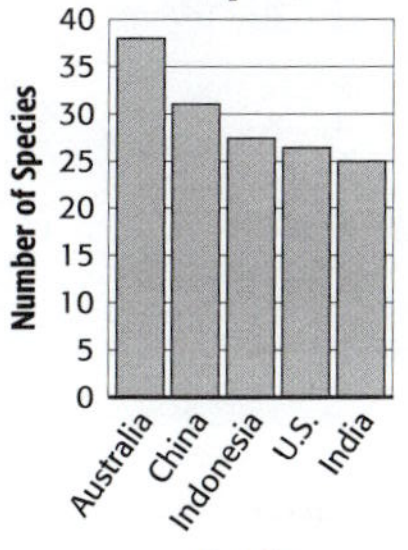

For Homework Help, go to Hotmath.com

7. histogram

Major U.S. Rivers

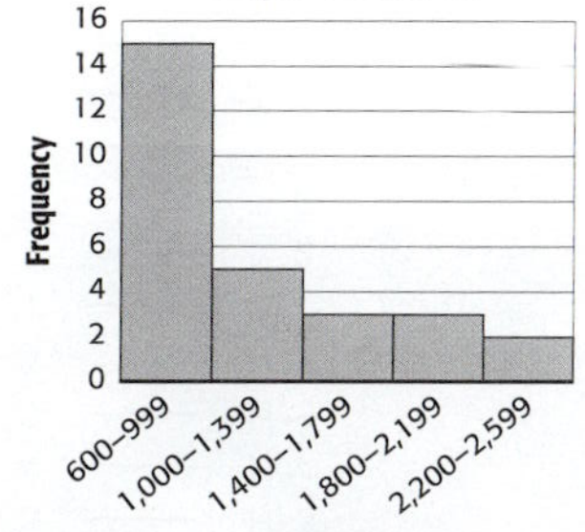

9. 13 students **11.** The 60–69 interval is three times larger than the 70–79 interval. **13.** 43 **15.** Sample answer: The number of zoos with 0.0–0.9 million visitors is about 4 times the number of zoos with 3.0–3.9 million visitors. **17.** a **19.** b **21.** about 15.8% **23.** Sample answer: It is easier to compare two sets of data. **25.** tennis **27.** Yes, 20% of girls prefer basketball and 35% of boys prefer basketball. **29.** Sample answer: Each interval represents a portion of the data set. The number of items in each interval is indicated by the frequency, typically shown along the vertical scale. By adding the frequencies for each interval, you can determine the number of values in the data set. **31.** C

33. **Number of Wins**

Stem	Leaf
1	5 7 9
2	3 5 6
3	0 1 2 6
4	0 0 1 3 4 5 6 7 7
5	0 0 0 1 2 3 3 5 6 6

5|3 = 53 wins

35. Mental math; the numbers are easy to computer mentally. Sample answer: $\frac{1}{5}$ of $50 is $10 and $50 – $10 = $40. So, he will need an additional $40.

Pages 424–425 *Lesson 8-5*

1. Sample answer: Graphs provide a visual representation of a situation involving comparisons. A graphical model can sometimes show conclusively what is often difficult to interpret from looking at lists alone.

3. **Temperature Conversions**

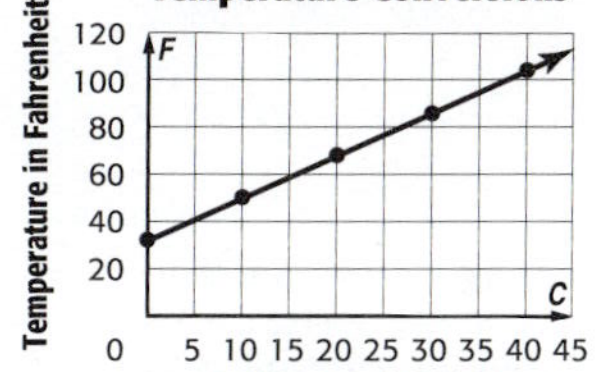

5. Taylor 7. Wednesday 9. 27, 29 11. 2

Pages 428–431 *Lesson 8-6*

1. Sample answer: The graph shows a positive relationship. That is, as the years pass, the population increases. 3. about 155–160 people 5. about 400 7. about 95 min 9. Sample answer: As sleep decreases, the math test score decreases.

11. **Free Throws Made out of Attempts**

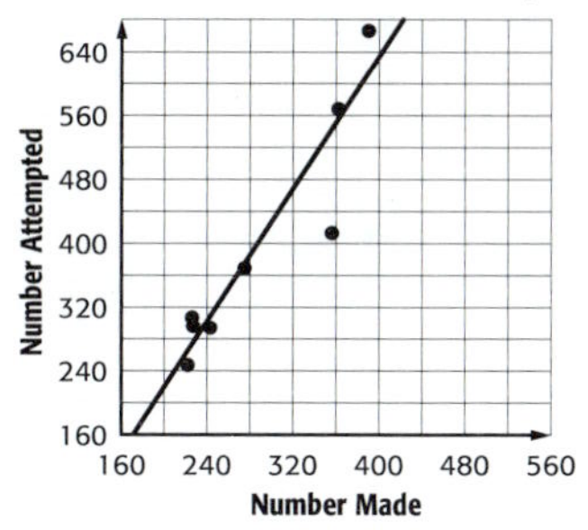

13. There is a positive relationship. That is, as the number of attempts increases, the number of free throws made increases. 15. about $55,000 17. Sample answer: Both lines have a positive trend. The population of Phoenix, Arizona, is now more than San Diego, California. 19. mode; the other three are ways to display data. 21. Graphs often show trends over time. If you continue the pattern, you can use it to make a prediction. 23. J

25. **Favorite Color**

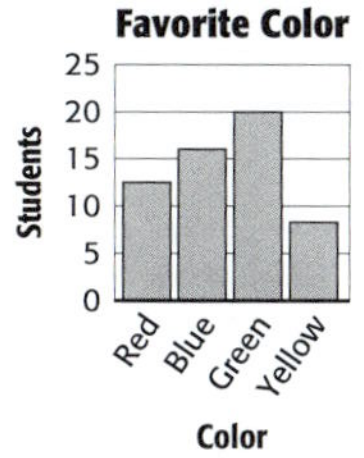

27. 83°; 83°

Pages 435–437 *Lesson 8-7*

1. 19,800 3. about 59 5. 1,419 people 7. 62,280 teens 9. b. 11. a. 13. about 38 people 15. about 1,040 19. D 21. B 23. It takes Dale a little bit longer to run each successive mile of the 5-mile run. 25. −24 27. 54 29. $\frac{3}{10}$ or 0.3 31. $\frac{9}{2}$ or 4.5

Pages 440–443 *Lesson 8-8*

1. The conclusion is invalid. This is a biased sample, since people in other states might have more umbrellas than those in Arizona. The sample is a convenience sample since all the people are from the same state. 3. This is an unbiased random survey, so the sample is valid; about 102 students. 5. The conclusion is invalid. This is a biased, convenience sample. 7. The conclusion is valid. This is an unbiased random sample. 9. The conclusion is invalid. This is a biased, convenience sample. 11. This is an unbiased random sample, so the results are valid; about 132 boxes. 13. This sample is a voluntary response sample. Therefore, no valid conclusion can be made. 15. about 443 17. Sample answer: This is an unbiased random sample. The time a student spends on the Internet during this week may not be typical of other weeks. 19. Sample answer: This is a convenience sample. The softball team may not represent the entire student population. 21. Not necessarily; Sample answer: Because you may be surveying different people in each sample, you may get different results. 23. Sample answer: If the entire population is too large to survey, it will be less time-consuming and easier to use a sample. 25. Yes; Sample answer: Every 10th person at a basketball game is asked whether they prefer basketball or baseball. This survey is a convenience sample because people attending a basketball game probably prefer basketball. 27. C 29. about 292 students 31. $58.44 33. $\frac{5}{8}$ 35. true

Pages 447–449 *Lesson 8-9*

1. Graph B; From the length of the bars, it appears that it appears that Cy Young had about 3 times as many wins as Jim Galvin. However, Jim Galvin had 365 wins and Cy Young had 511 wins. So, the conclusion is not valid. 3. Sample answer: The mean is 8,638 and the median is 8,941. Since the median is greater than the mean, use the median to emphasize the average length. 5. The sample is a biased convenience sample. Mr. Kessler's first period class may not be representative of all his students. The display is biased because the data used to create the display came from a biased sample. 7. The median or the mode because they are much closer in value to most of the pieces of data. 9. The sample is a biased convenience sample. The first 100 batteries produced may not be representative of all the batteries produced. The display is biased because the data used to create the display came from a biased sample.

11. **Monthly Cost to Rent an Apartment**

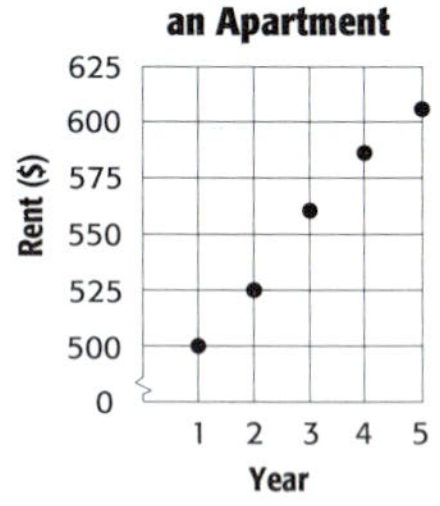

13. Sample answer: Outliers may distort measures of central tendency; data shown in graphs may be exaggerated or minimized by manipulating scales and intervals. 15. G 17. about 391 teens

Pages 450–454 *Chapter 8* *Study Guide and Review*

1. true 3. true 5. false; outlier 7. true

9. **Temperatures**

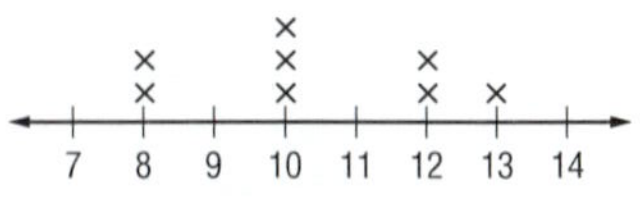

Sample answer: no significant clusters, gaps, or outliers.

11. **Number of Calories**

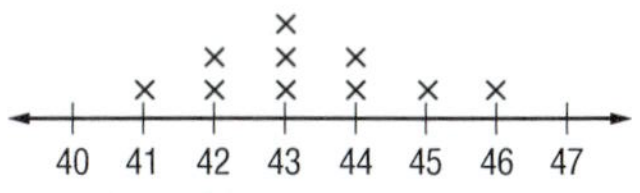

Sample answer: cluster 42–44; no gaps or outliers.

13. 84.3°; 86°; none

15. **Hours Worked**

Stem	Leaf
2	1 3 6 9
3	1 2 7 8
4	6
5	4

3|2 = 32 hours

17. **Birthdates**

Stem	Leaf
0	3 5 7 9
1	0 1 2 4 6 8
2	1 4

1|2 = 12

19. 10.75 million 21. *Crazy Horse* 23. Sample answer: The graph shows a positive relationship. That is, as the number of people in a family increases, the number of telephone calls per week increases. 25. about 208 27. 162 teens 29. The conclusion is valid. This is an unbiased random sample. 31. The graph does not include the hot summer months or the cold winter months, which could have higher electricity bills.

Chapter 9 Probability

Page 459 *Chapter 9* *Getting Ready*

1. 105 3. 52 5. 160 7. 210 9. 360 11. 5,040 13. $315 15. $\frac{1}{6}$ 17. $\frac{1}{3}$ 19. 5 21. 4

Pages 462–464 *Lesson 9-1*

1. $\frac{1}{8}$ 3. $\frac{1}{8}$ 5. $\frac{3}{5}$ 7. $\frac{23}{30}$ 9. 1 11. $\frac{1}{20}$ 13. $\frac{3}{10}$ 15. $\frac{19}{20}$ 17. $\frac{5}{8}$ 19. $\frac{7}{20}$ 21. 1 23. $\frac{3}{4}$ 25. 60% 27. $\frac{14}{33}$

29. Sample answer: The complementary event is the chance of no rain. Its probability is 63% 31a. 1; Sample answer: Since 2032 is a leap year, there will be 29 days in February, making this event certain to happen; 31b. 0; Sample answer: Since 2058 is not a leap year, there will only be 28 days in February, making this event impossible to happen. 33. 0.33, 0.44 are probabilities that are not complementary because 0.33 + 0.44 ≠ 1. The other sets of probability are complementary. 35. C 37. There are no labels on the vertical scale. 39. $\frac{1}{3}$ 41. $\frac{1}{2}$ 43. $\frac{9}{16}$

Pages 467–470 *Lesson 9-2*

1. Sample answer:

	Outcomes					
	1	**2**	**3**	**4**	**5**	**6**
1	1, 1	1, 2	1, 3	1, 4	1, 5	1, 6
2	2, 1	2, 2	2, 3	2, 4	2, 5	2, 6
3	3, 1	3, 2	3, 3	3, 4	3, 5	3, 6
4	4, 1	4, 2	4, 3	4, 4	4, 5	4, 6
5	5, 1	5, 2	5, 3	5, 4	5, 5	5, 6
6	6, 1	6, 2	6, 3	6, 4	6, 5	6, 6

3. C 5. Sample answer:

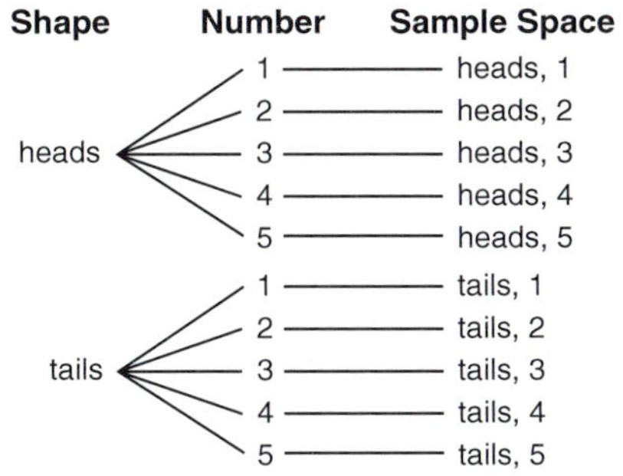

7. Sample answer:

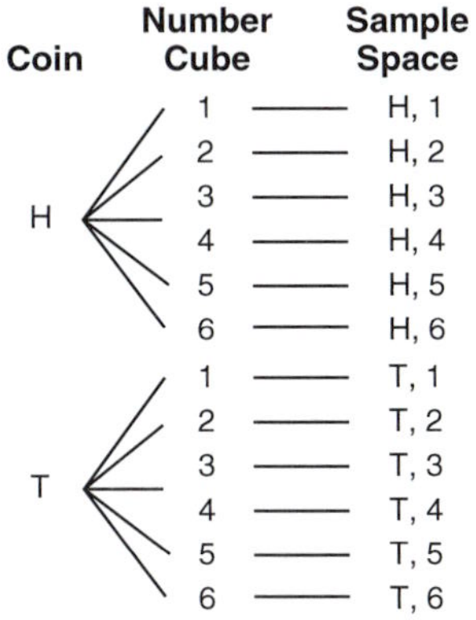

9. Sample answer:

Color	Speeds	Sample Space
purple	10	purple, 10-speed
	18	purple, 18-speed
	21	purple, 21-speed
	24	purple, 24-speed
green	10	green, 10-speed
	18	green, 18-speed
	21	green, 21-speed
	24	green, 24-speed
black	10	black, 10-speed
	18	black, 18-speed
	21	black, 21-speed
	24	black, 24-speed
silver	10	silver, 10-speed
	18	silver, 18-speed
	21	silver, 21-speed
	24	silver, 24-speed

11. Sample answer:

Outcomes		
Short Sleeve	Gray	Small
Short Sleeve	Gray	Medium
Short Sleeve	Gray	Large
Short Sleeve	White	Small
Short Sleeve	White	Medium
Short Sleeve	White	Large
Long Sleeve	Gray	Small
Long Sleeve	Gray	Medium
Long Sleeve	Gray	Large
Long Sleeve	White	Small
Long Sleeve	White	Medium
Long Sleeve	White	Large

13. Sample answer:

Quarter	Dime	Nickel	Sample Space	
H	H	H	H, H, H	Elba wins
		T	H, H, T	Elba wins
	T	H	H, T, H	Elba wins
		T	H, T, T	Steve wins
T	H	H	T, H, H	Elba wins
		T	T, H, T	Steve wins
	T	H	T, T, H	Steve wins
		T	T, T, T	Steve wins

There are 8 equally likely outcomes with 4 favoring Elba. So, the probability that Elba wins is $\frac{1}{2}$. **15.** $\frac{1}{8}$ **17.** $\frac{3}{8}$ **19.** $\frac{1}{8}$ **21.** 16 **25.** Sample answer: Mei can draw a model of the situation using a tree diagram to show the sample space. Then she can determine the probability. The probability of guessing correctly is $\frac{1}{4}$.

Right/Wrong	Right/Wrong	Sample Space
R	R	R, R
	W	R, W
W	R	W, R
	W	W, W

27. Sample game: Each player tosses a coin 10 times. If it comes up heads, player 1 receives 1 point. If it comes up tails, player 2 receives 1 point. The player with the most points at the end of 20 tosses wins. **29.** $\frac{2}{5}$ **31.** $\frac{13}{20}$ **33.** $\frac{3}{10}$ **35.** The cost is increasing over time. In about a year's time, the cost has more than tripled. **37.** $3,876 **39.** 15.6 **41.** 154 **43.** 460

Pages 472–474 Lesson 9-3

1. 8 **3.** 24 **5.** 12 **7.** 84 **9.** 24 **11.** 6 possible routes; $\frac{1}{6}$ **13.** 7,776 **15.** No; the number of selections is 32 • 11 or 352, which is less than 365. **17.** 2; 4; 8; 2^n; Sample answer: I used a pattern to determine the number of outcomes for n coins. One coin: 2^1 outcomes, two coins: 2 • 2 or 2^2 outcomes, three coins: 2 • 2 • 2 or 2^3 outcomes, n coins: 2^n outcomes.
19. Sample answer: When there are multiple events, the Fundamental Counting Principle is a much faster method of obtaining the total number of outcomes than drawing a tree diagram. The Fundamental Counting Principle also saves paper space and can often be done mentally. When you need to see what the specific outcomes are, make a tree diagram since the Fundamental Counting Principle only gives the number of outcomes. **21.** 6 **23.** $\frac{1}{2}$ **25.** $\frac{1}{5}$, 0.22, 27%, 20.1 **27.** 6 **29.** 120

Pages 476–478 Lesson 9-4

1. 5,040 **3.** $\frac{1}{20}$ **5.** 24 **7.** 720 **9.** $\frac{1}{90}$ **11.** $\frac{1}{12}$
13. Sample answer: Calculator; An exact answer is required. 24 × 23 × 22 × 21 = 255,024 **15.** $\frac{1}{4}$
17. Sample answer: The number of ways you can order 3 books on a shelf is 3 • 2 • 1 or 6. **19.** H

21.

Meat	Cheese	Outcomes
turkey	cheddar	turkey, cheddar
	Swiss	turkey, Swiss
ham	cheddar	ham, cheddar
	Swiss	ham, Swiss
salami	cheddar	salami, cheddar
	Swiss	salami, Swiss

23. $1\frac{13}{15}$ **25.** $4\frac{11}{48}$ **27.** 56 **29.** 3

Pages 482–483 Lesson 9-5

1. 21 ways **3.** 6 **5.** 210 **7.** 924 **9.** $\frac{1}{20}$ **11.** 10; $\frac{1}{10}$
13. permutation; 90 **15.** 15 **17.** The number of ways you can choose three CDs from a collection of ten CDs is 120 ways. **19.** H **21.** 72 **23.** Sample answer: $\frac{1}{2} - 0 = \frac{1}{2}$ **25.** $\frac{1}{5}$

Pages 484–485 Lesson 9-6

1. Sample answer: Results would vary slightly.
3. No; Sample answer: the experiment produces about 1–2 correct answers, so using a spinner with 4 sections is not a good way to answer a 5-question multiple-choice quiz. **5.** 30 **7.** 65 is a reasonable answer because 40% of 160 is 64. **9.** No, the 6th row should have the numbers 1, 5, 10, 10, 5, 1. **11.** No; Sample answer: the experiment produces about 2–3 correct answers, so using a number cube is not a good way to answer a 5-question true-false quiz. **13.** $195

Pages 488–490 Lesson 9-7

1. $\frac{14}{25}$ **3.** The experimental probability, $\frac{14}{25}$ or 56%, is close to its theoretical probability of $\frac{1}{2}$ or 50%.
5. 22 people **7.** $\frac{9}{10}$; the experimental probability, $\frac{9}{10}$ or 90%, is close to its theoretical probability of $\frac{5}{6}$, or about 83% **9.** $\frac{3}{35}$ **11.** 134 **13.** $\frac{6}{25}$; $\frac{13}{50}$ **15.** $\frac{13}{25}$ **17.** No; The experimental probability that a mother will receive jewelry is $\frac{17}{100}$. Out of 750 mothers that receive gifts, only about 128 can expect to receive jewelry not 250. **19.** Yes; Sample answer: If there are 40 unsharpened pencils in the box, then there are twice as many unsharpened pencils as there are sharpened pencils. If there are five sharpened pencils in the sample that was taken out, then there should be ten unsharpened pencils which would give a total of 15 pencils in the sample, which was the size of the sample. It is important to note that this was only one sample. To be sure that the sample represents the population, other samples should be taken and compared to the first sample. **21.** B **23.** 6 **25.** 60% **27.** 55% **29.** 78%

Pages 495–497 Lesson 9-8

1. $\frac{1}{30}$ **3.** $\frac{1}{10}$ **5.** $\frac{2}{9}$ **7.** $\frac{1}{90}$ **9.** $\frac{2}{3}$ **11.** $\frac{1}{2}$ **13.** $\frac{1}{6}$ **15.** $\frac{3}{25}$
17. 0 **19.** $\frac{3}{16}$ **21.** $\frac{15}{92}$ **23.** $\frac{3}{7}$ **25.** $\frac{4}{7}$ **27.** $\frac{3}{20}$ **29.** $\frac{1}{10}$
31. $\frac{1}{1{,}024}$ **33.** 21%

35.

1st Spin	2nd Spin	3rd Spin	Sample Space
B	B	B	B, B, B
		R	B, B, R
		G	B, B, G
	R	B	B, R, B
		R	B, R, R
		G	B, R, G
	G	B	B, G, B
		R	B, G, R
		G	B, G, G
R	B	B	R, B, B
		R	R, B, R
		G	R, B, G
	R	B	R, R, B
		R	R, R, R
		G	R, R, G
	G	B	R, G, B
		R	R, G, R
		G	R, G, G
G	B	B	G, B, B
		R	G, B, R
		G	G, B, G
	R	B	G, R, B
		R	G, R, R
		G	G, R, G
	G	B	G, G, B
		R	G, G, R
		G	G, G, G

37. These events are dependent, not independent. Selecting one book and not returning it to the shelf limits your choices for the next pick to 2 books, not 3, as on the first pick. **39.** G **41.** 6 **43.** –48 **45.** 80

Pages 498–502 Chapter 9 Study Guide and Review

1. true **3.** false; probability **5.** false; independent events **7.** false; disjoint **9.** $\frac{1}{6}$ **11.** $\frac{13}{18}$ **13.** 8%

15.

Outcomes	
Pepperoni	Water
Pepperoni	Milk
Pepperoni	Juice
Mushroom	Water
Mushroom	Milk
Mushroom	Juice
Cheese	Water
Cheese	Milk
Cheese	Juice

17. 36 **19.** $\frac{1}{12}$ **21.** 40,320 **23.** 105 **25.** 364 **27.** No; Sample answer: the experiment produces about 3 correct answers, so tossing a coin is not a good way to answer a 6-question true-false quiz. **29.** 8 **31.** $\frac{5}{16}$ **33.** $\frac{9}{32}$ **35.** $\frac{23}{32}$ **37.** $\frac{3}{64}$; $\frac{1}{20}$ **39.** $\frac{1}{16}$; $\frac{7}{120}$ **41.** $\frac{1}{3}$

Chapter 10 Geometry: Polygons

Page 509 Chapter 10 Getting Ready

1. 306 **3.** 0.15 **5.** 0.11 **7.** 44 **9.** 105 **11.** 14 **13.** 36

Pages 512–513 Lesson 10-1

1. ∠*MNP*, ∠*PNM*, ∠*N*, ∠1; obtuse **3.** ∠1 and ∠3; Sample answer: Since ∠1 and ∠3 are opposite angles formed by the intersection of two lines, they are vertical angles. **5.** ∠*DEF*, ∠*FED*, ∠*E*, ∠5; right **7.** ∠*MNP*, ∠*PNM*, ∠*N*, ∠7; straight **9.** ∠*RTS*, ∠*STR*, ∠*T*, ∠9; acute **11.** neither **13.** adjacent **15.** vertical **17.** ∠1 and ∠2; Sample answer: Since ∠1 and ∠2 share a common vertex, a common side, and do not overlap, they are adjacent angles.
19. True; Sample answer:

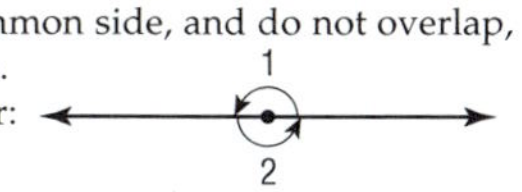

21. A **23.** $\frac{1}{24}$ **25.** $\frac{5}{24}$ **27.** 46 **29.** 54

Pages 516–517 Lesson 10-2

1. supplementary **3.** 135 **5.** supplementary **7.** supplementary **9.** neither **11.** 65° **13.** 137° **15.** Sample answer: ∠*CGK*, ∠*KGJ* **17.** adjacent; adjacent; vertical **19.** $m\angle 1 = 180° - m\angle 2$; $m\angle 3 = 180° - m\angle 2$; Sample answer: $m\angle 1$ and $m\angle 3$ both equal the same expression. **21.** $m\angle E = 39°$, $m\angle F = 51°$ **23.** B **25.** ∠*P*, ∠*I*, ∠*RPQ*, ∠*QPR*; acute **27.** 223.2 **29.** 0.12

Pages 520–523 Lesson 10-3

1. Blood Types in U.S.

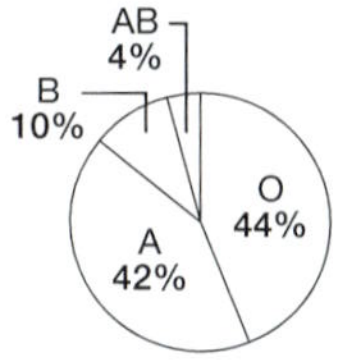

3. blue

5. U.S. Steel Roller Coasters

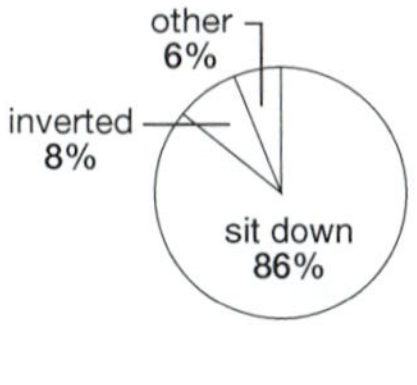

7. Endangered Species in U.S.

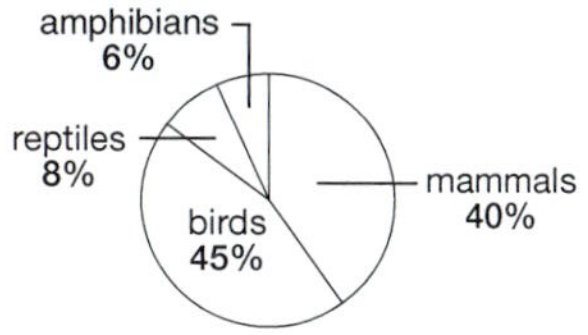

9. paper **11.** 48 million tons **13.** about 12 million **15.** 15
17. bar graph

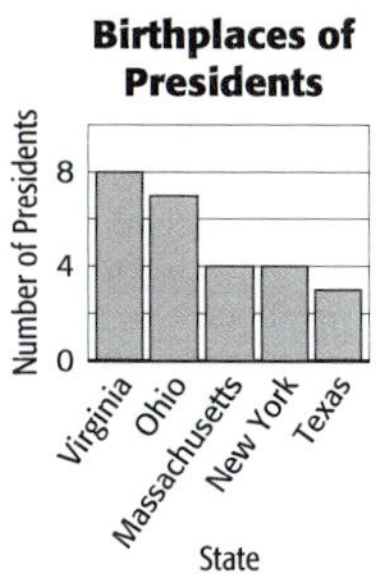

19.

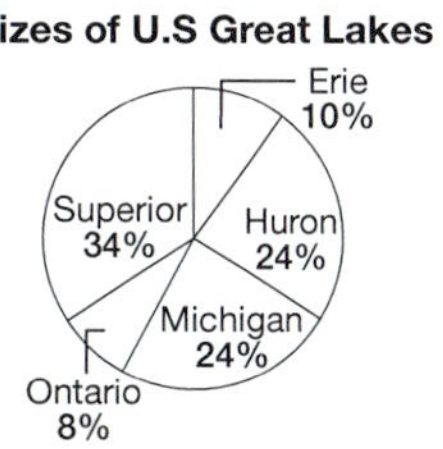

21. Lake Ontario is one third the size of Lake Michigan. **23.** No; a 50% increase in 126 students is 189, and 189 is not equal to 366. So, it is not reasonable to say that 50% more students said they could make a difference. Since 300% of 126 is 378, it is reasonable to say that 300% more students said they could make a difference than those who said they cannot make a difference. **25.** 12.5%; English is half of the circle. Since Science is half of English, Science is half of 50% or 25%. Math is half of Science, which is half of 25% or 12.5%. **27.** Sample answer: No; the sum of the percents is greater than 100. The people surveyed must have been able to choose more than one fruit juice. **29.** Sample answer: ∠1 and ∠3 **31.** 68 **33.** 101

Pages 527–529 Lesson 10-4

1. 44 **3.** 45 **5.** C **7.** right, scalene
9.

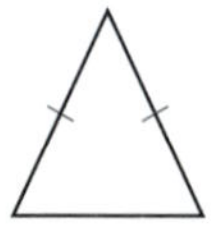

11. 118 **13.** 27 **15.** 90 **17.** 53° **19.** acute, equilateral **21.** obtuse, isosceles **23.** obtuse, isosceles **25.** right
27.

29.

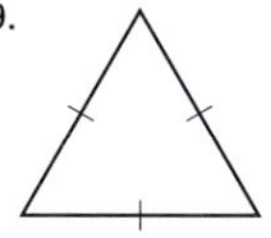

31. 79.5 **33.** 79.2 **35.** 21.3 **37.** 80° **39.** 60 **41.** 77.5
43.

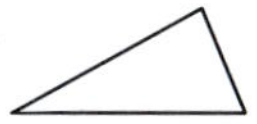

Sample answer: All of the angles are acute and there are no congruent sides. **45.** Never; Sample answer: The sum of the three angles in a triangle is 180°. If a triangle has two obtuse angles, the sum of these two angles, not including the third angle, would already be greater than 180°. **47.** B **49.** about 101° **51.** supplementary **53.** about $9

Pages 530–531 Lesson 10-5

1. Sample answer: They used inductive reasoning because they made a rule after seeing four examples. **3.** See students' work; none of the angles are congruent. **5.** Julio: mango, Rashanda: banana, Perry: orange. **7.** $3.75 **9.** 196 sq units **11.** 3 packs **13.** Sample answer: addition and division; Find the score that when added to the others, the total sum divided by the number of scores, 5, is equal to 82. The answer is 79.

Pages 535–538 Lesson 10-6

1. rectangle **3.** parallelogram **5.** 120° **7.** 64° **9.** square **11.** quadrilateral **13.** trapezoid **15.** 56° **17.** 67° **19.** 90° **21.** 116° **23.** Bricks A, B, and D are rectangles and brick C is a square. **25.** 129.1° **27.** 131.8° **29.** trapezoids, squares, scalene triangles, equilateral triangles **31.** right isosceles triangles, squares, trapezoids **33.** No; a quadrilateral with three right angles will have both pairs of opposite sides parallel. So, it cannot be a trapezoid. **35.** 45 **37.** 80 **39.** Property B states that there are 4 right angles; Sample answer: A rectangle has 4 right angles in addition to property A. So, property B must state that there are 4 right angles. **41.** Never; Sample answer: A trapezoid has only one pair of parallel sides. A parallelogram has 2 pairs of parallel sides. **43.** Sometimes; Sample answer; A rhombus is only a square if all 4 angles are right angles. **45.** Since a square has all the properties of a rectangle and a rhombus, the diagonals of a square must be congruent and perpendicular. Nothing can be concluded about the diagonals of a parallelogram unless more information is provided. If a quadrilateral is a parallelogram, it is not necessarily a rectangle or a rhombus. So, it would not necessarily have the properties of a rectangle or a rhombus. **47.** J **49.** Neva: hamster, Sophie: turtle, Seth: dog **51.** right, scalene **53.** 720 **55.** $3.45 **57.** 3 **59.** 7

Pages 543–545 Lesson 10-7

1. rectangle *PQRS* **3.** 45 mm **5.** triangle *CAB* **7.** 25 mi **9.** 7.2 in. **11.** 6 ft **13.** 12 m **15.** 1,207 feet **17.** 120 m **19.** 1:16 **21.** B **23.** C **25.** trapezoid **27.** 69° **29.** 90 **31.** 120

Pages 549–551 Lesson 10-8

1. decagon; not regular **3.** hexagon; regular **5.** 128.6° **7.** not a polygon; the figure is not simple **9.** isosceles right triangle; not regular **11.** hexagon; not regular **13.** 144° **15.** 90° **17.** No; the figure is a decagon. Each angle of a decagon measures 144°; since 144° does not divided evenly into 360°, a decagon cannot make a tessellation. **19.** hexagon and triangle **21.** octagon and square **23.** $36\frac{1}{4}$ yd **25.** No; the stop sign is an octagon in shape. An octagon cannot make a tessellation. So, there will be some steel that is wasted after the nine signs are cut from the sheet.
27. trapezoid
29. square **31.** pentagon hexagon

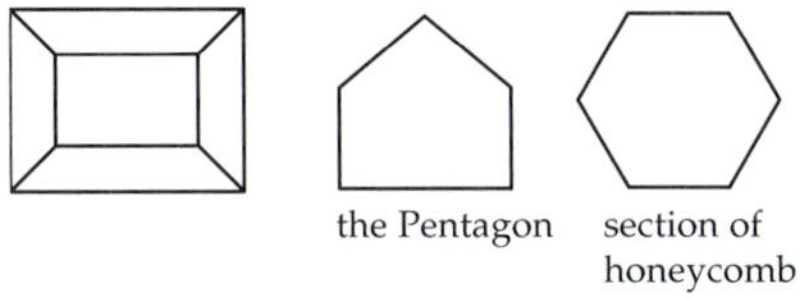

33. Sample answer; A copy of the parallelogram can fit next to it since 45° + 135° = 180° and above or below it since 135° + 45° = 180°. **35.** B **37.** trapezoid **39.** 1.5 m per s **41.** $3\frac{1}{6}$ **43.** $4\frac{37}{40}$
44–47.

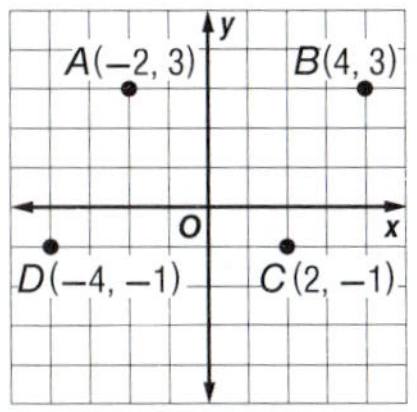

For Homework Help, go to Hotmath.com

Pages 555–557 **Lesson 10-9**

1.

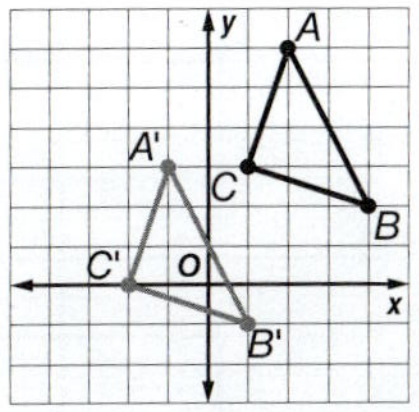

3. $D'(7, 0)$, $E'(4, -2)$, $F'(8, 4)$, $G'(12, -3)$

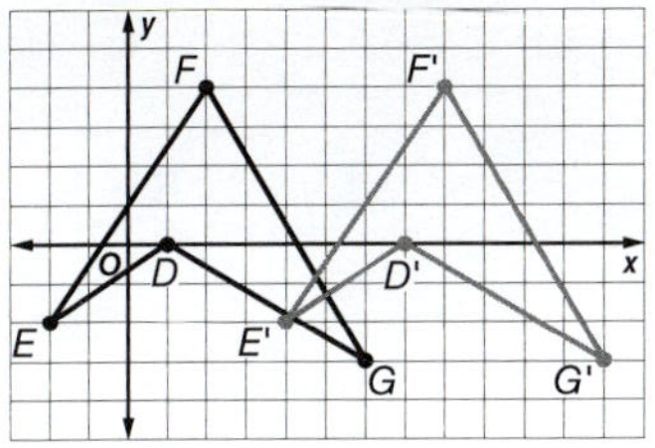

5.

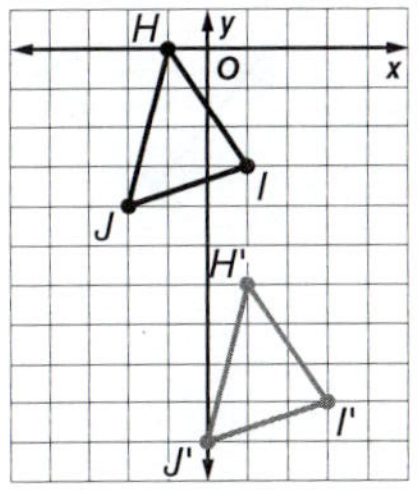

7. $P'(6, 5)$, $Q'(11, 3)$, $R'(3, 11)$

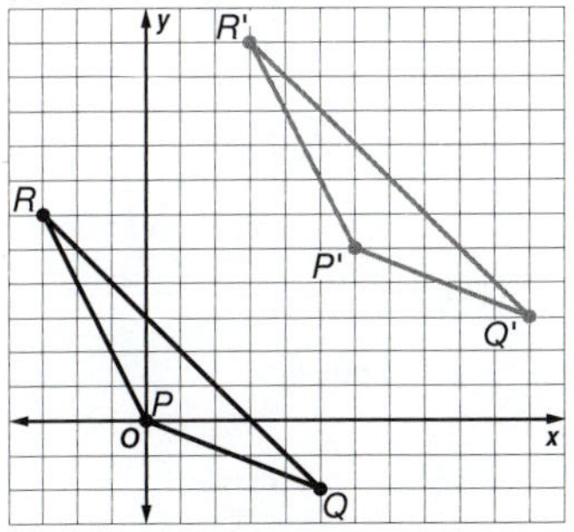

9. $P'(-3, 0)$, $Q'(2, -2)$, $R'(-6, 6)$

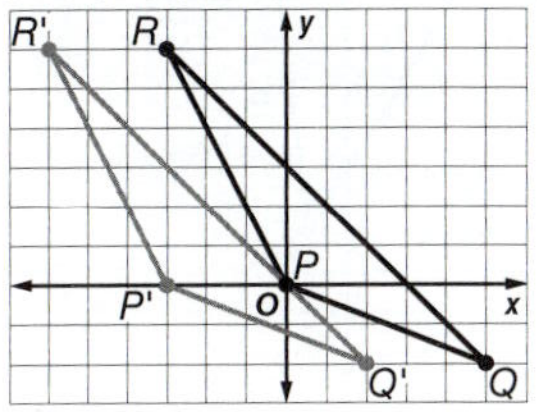

11. 3 units right and 1 unit up; (3, 1)

13.

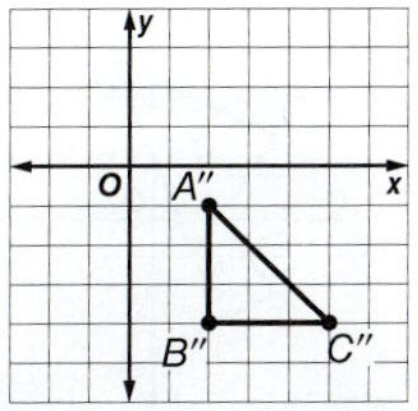

15. Sample answer: There are two main images, the small fish and the large fish. The fish are translated to different parts of the picture. These translations allow for the tessellation of the fish.

17. $F'\left(8\frac{1}{2}, 2\frac{1}{2}\right)$, $G'\left(4\frac{1}{2}, \frac{1}{2}\right)$, $H'\left(2\frac{1}{2}, 1\frac{1}{2}\right)$

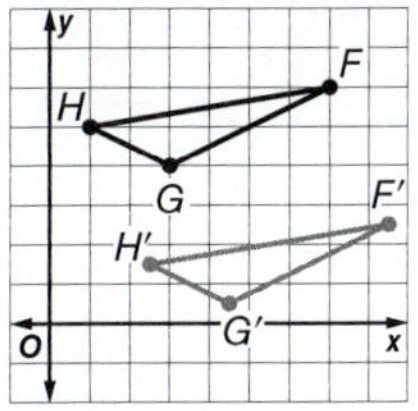

19. 5 units left and 3 units down; (−5, −3) **21.** 5 units right and 4 units up; (5, 4) **23.** Transformation A is not a translation; the others are translations. **25.** B **27.** octagon **29.** 2 × 4 × 3 or 24 dinners **31.** The range would be 62 instead of 55. **33.** The range would be 8 instead of 6. **35.** Sample answer: 0.567 **37.** Sample answer: 1.026 **39.** no **41.** yes

Pages 560–562 **Lesson 10-10**

1. no **3.** yes **5.** $A'(5, -8)$, $B'(1, -2)$, and $C'(6, -4)$

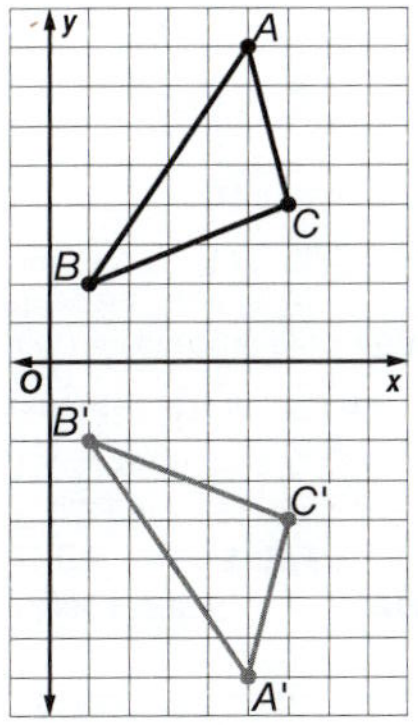

7. $Q'(-2, -5)$, $R'(-4, -5)$, and $S'(-2, 3)$

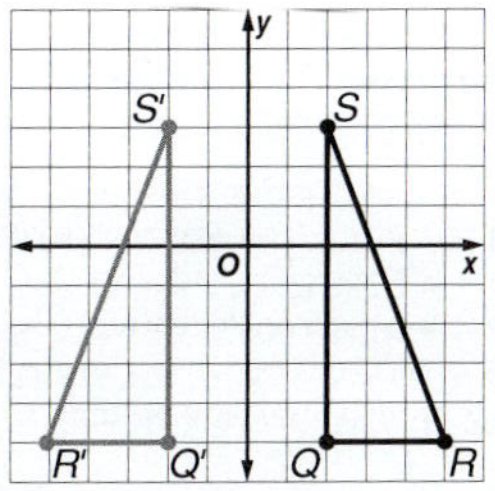

9. yes

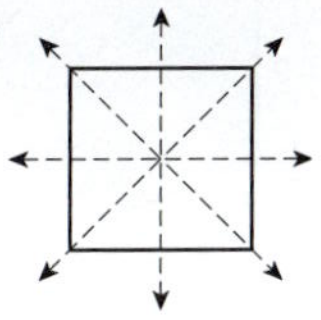

11. yes

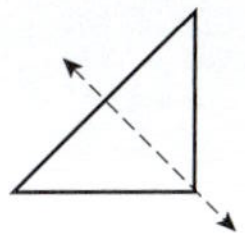

13. yes

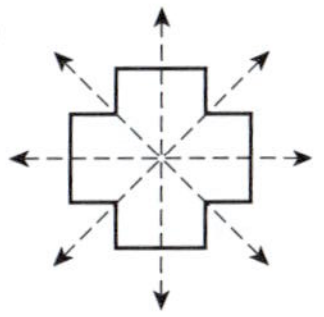

15. $T'(-6, 1)$, $U'(-2, 3)$, and $V'(5, 4)$

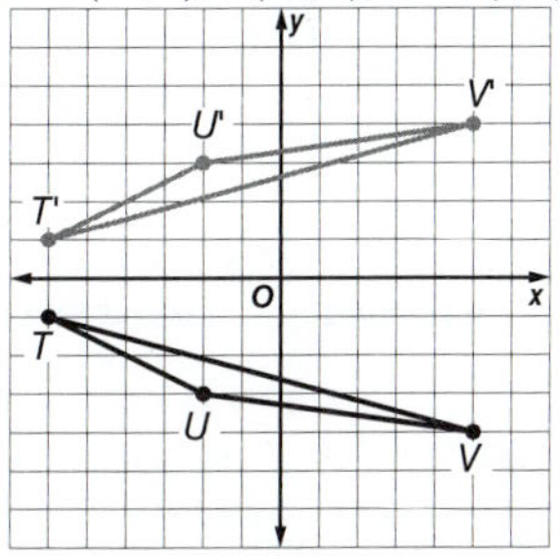

17. $A'(2, -4)$, $B'(-2, -4)$, $C'(2, -8)$, $D'(-2, -8)$

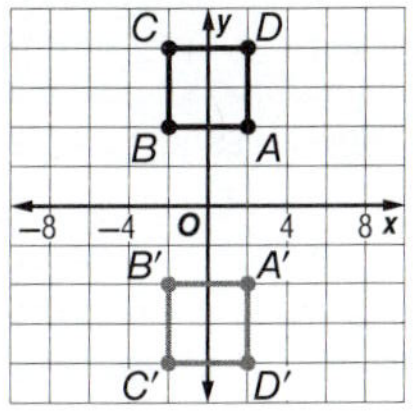

19. $R'(5, 3)$, $S'(4, -2)$, $T'(2, 3)$

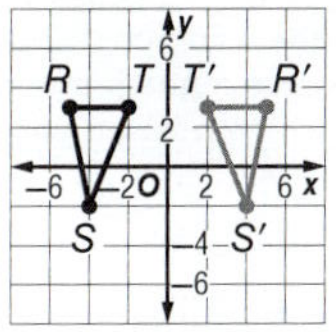

21. $H'(1, 3)$, $I'(1, -1)$, $J'(-2, -2)$, and $K'(-2, 2)$

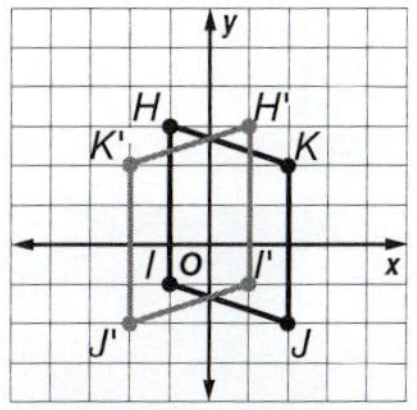

23. There is a line of symmetry vertically down the center of the picture. **25.** 1 **27.** figures *A* and *C* **29.** Sample answer; A reflection over the *y*-axis followed by a reflection over the *x*-axis.

31.

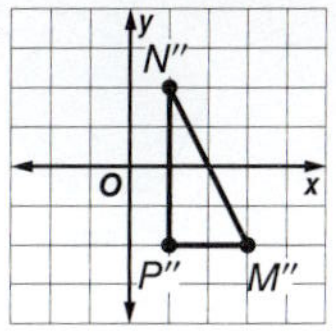

33. *x*-axis **35.** *y*-axis **37.** $J''(7, -4)$, $K''(-7, -1)$, and $L''(-2, 2)$ **39.** C

41. $F'(1, 6)$, $G'(3, 4)$, $H'(2, 1)$

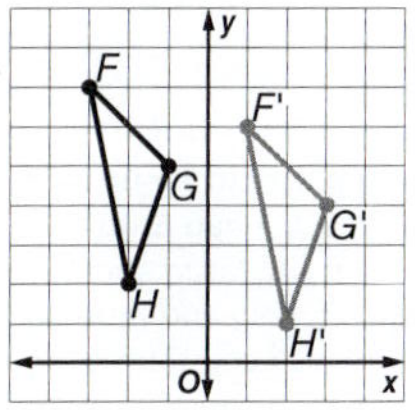

43. Sample answer: $\frac{1}{2} + 8 = 8\frac{1}{2}$ **45.** Sample answer: $12 \div 6 = 2$

Pages 563–566 **Chapter 10** **Study Guide and Review**

1. false; supplementary angles **3.** false; acute angle **5.** false; (−2, 1) **7.** ∠1 and ∠4; Sample answer: Since ∠1 and ∠4 are opposite angles formed by the intersection of two lines, they are vertical **9.** neither

11.

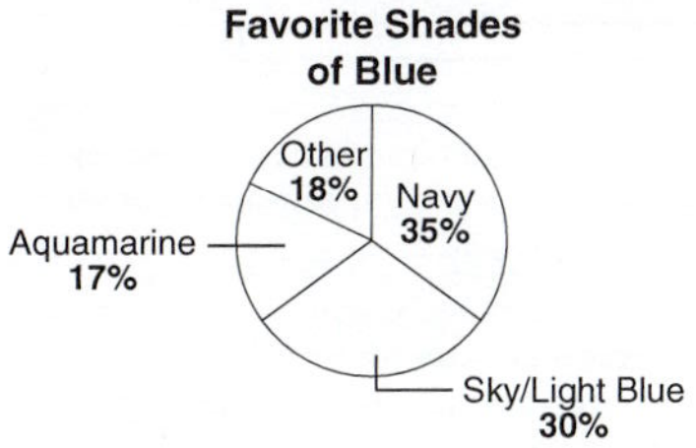

13. 45 **15.** right, isosceles **17.** parallelogram **19.** 10 cm **21.** 8m **23.** nonagon; regular

25. $P'(-2, 1)$, $Q'(-8, 0)$, and $R'(-7, 9)$

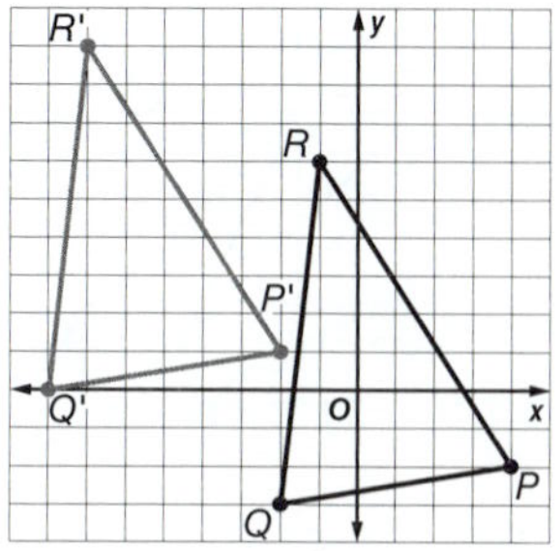

27. $P'(1, -2)$, $Q'(-5, -3)$, and $R'(-4, 6)$

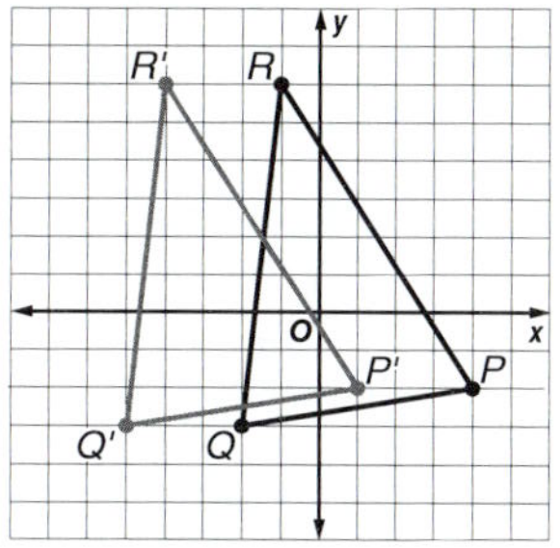

29. $R'(-1, -3)$, $S'(2, -6)$, and $T'(6, -1)$

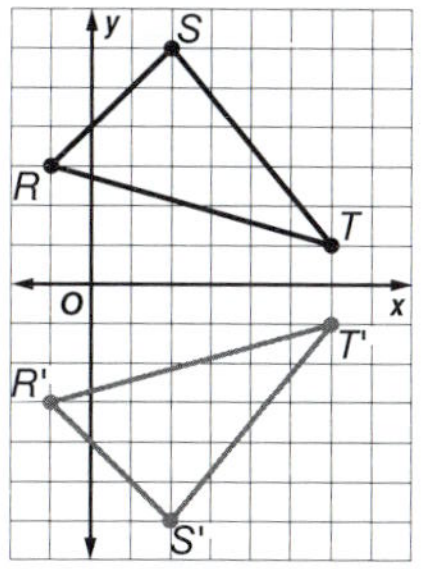

31. $E'(4, -2)$, $F'(-2, -2)$, $G'(-2, 5)$, $H'(4, -5)$

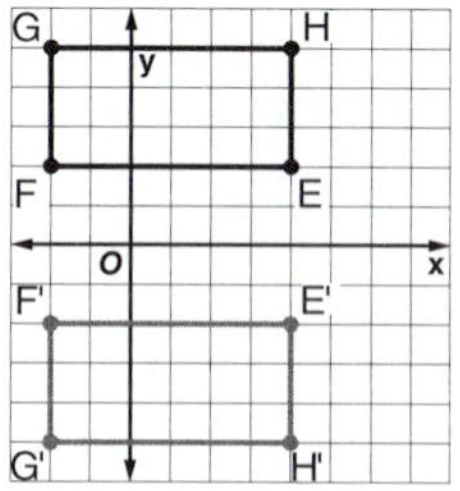

Chapter 11 Measurement: Two- and Three-Dimensional Figures

Page 571 Chapter 11 Getting Ready

1. 136 **3.** 1,248 **5.** 77 **7.** \$41.67 **9.** 121 **11.** 36 **13.** 12.6 **15.** 31.4 **17.** 254.5

Pages 574–576 Lesson 11-1

1. 135 cm² **3.** 17.5 in² **5.** 32 in² **7.** 60 cm² **9.** 0.2 cm² **11.** 49.5 yd² **13.** 190.625 m² **15.** 525 mm² **17.** 216 in² or 1.5 ft² **19.** 972 in² or 0.8 yd² **21.** 42,000 mi² **23.** 15 in. **25.** $11\frac{2}{3}$ ft²

27. False; if the base and height are each doubled, then the area is $2b \cdot 2h = 4bh$, or 4 times greater. **29.** D **31.** $A'(2, 5)$, $B'(1, 2)$, $C'(4, 1)$

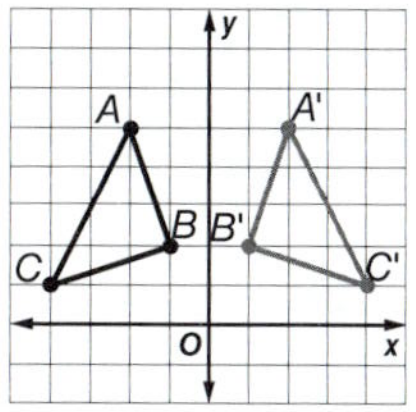

33. Sample answer: The sum of the measures of an octagon is 1,080°. Each angle measure is 1,080° ÷ 8 or 135°. Since 135 does not go into 360 evenly, an octagon does not tessellate the plane. **35.** 84 **37.** 19.5

Pages 580–582 Lesson 11-2

1. 6 in² **3.** 90.4 ft² **5.** 147 in² **7.** 4.5 cm² **9.** 183.7 in² **11.** about 95,000 mi² **13.** 125 ft **15.** Sample answer: 10 cm² **17.** Sample answer: 7 ft²

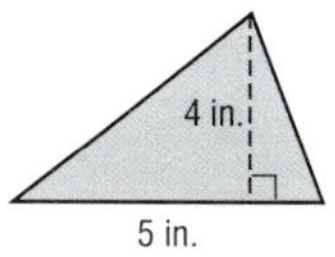

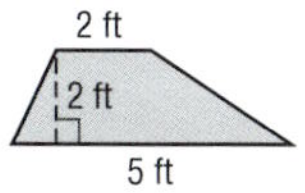

19. 6,500 ft² **21.** Sample answer: the ratio of the area is the square of the ratio of the bases. **23.** The area of a triangle is half the area of a parallelogram with the same base and height, because two of these triangles make up the parallelogram. **25.** 11,000 ft² **27.** $J'(-1, 4)$, $K'(1, -1)$, $L'(3, 2)$

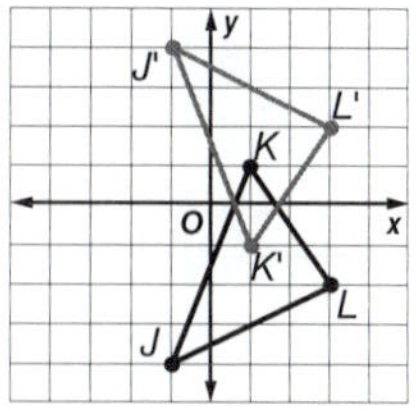

29. 25% **31.** 156.3 **33.** 91.1 **35.** 72.4

Pages 586–588 Lesson 11-3

1. 31.4 ft **3.** 44 m **5.** 67.2 cm **7.** 50.2 ft **9.** 22.6 cm **11.** 66 ft **13.** 33 in. **15.** 33.9 km **17.** $38\frac{1}{2}$ mi **19.** $28\frac{2}{7}$ in. **21.** 94.2 ft **23.** 11.0 in. **29.** 8.0 ft

31. 4.8 yd **33.** Sample answer: Using the circumference formula, you find that the unicycle travels 3.14 • 10 • 2 or 62.8 inches on one revolution. So, in 5 revolutions, it will travel 62.8 • 5 or 314 inches. To change into feet, divide 314 by 12. So, the unicycle will travel $26\frac{1}{6}$ feet in 5 revolutions. **37.** Elsa; Logan incorrectly applied the formula that uses the diameter. **39.** Both will be doubled. If the value of x is doubled, the diameter will be $2x$ instead of x. The circumference will increase from $2\pi x$ to $2\pi(2x)$ to $4\pi x$. **41.** C **43.** B **45.** 3.7 ft² **47.** $\frac{15}{27}$ or $\frac{5}{9}$ **49.** 153.9 **51.** 63.6

Pages 591–593 Lesson 11-4

1. 78.5 cm² **3.** 201.1 m² **5.** B **7.** 28.3 in² **9.** 227.0 cm² **11.** 32.2 mm² **13.** 124.7 cm² **15.** 44.2 ft² **17.** 338.2 yd² **19.** 2,827.4 ft² **21.** Sample answer: $3 \cdot 6^2 = 108$ ft² **23.** 32; 60 **25.** about 50.3 cm² **27.** 29.0 m² **29.** 52,276.1 km² • 0.1 = 1,582.9 yd² **31.** 62.8 m² **33.** 103.5 cm² **35.** Sample answer: If the radius of a circular garden is 6 feet, how much room is there for gardening? about 113.1 ft² **37.** J **39.** 50.2 yd **41.** 120 in² **43.** 100.1 m² **45.** 113.04 **47.** 150.5

Pages 594–595 Lesson 11-5

1. Sample answer: Finding the areas of the separate geometric figures and then adding is easier than trying to find the area of the irregular figure as a whole. **3.** Sample answer: Find the area of the wall below to determine how much paint to buy. To solve, find the area of the triangle and the area of the rectangle, then add. The answer is 77 ft².

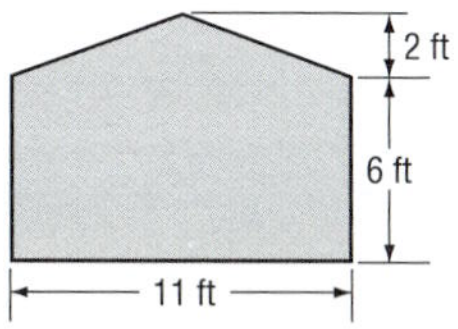

5. Sample answer: Asia, 17,251,712.4 mi²; Africa, 11,616,153.02; N. America, 9,488,441.82 mi²; S. America, 6,900,684.96 m²; Antarctica, 5,118,008.012 mi²; Europe, 3,852,882.436 mi²; Australia/Oceania, 3,047,802,524 mi² **7.** B **9.** 175.84 ft²

Pages 597–599 Lesson 11-6

1. 112 m² **3.** 145 m² **5.** 195 ft² **7.** 58.6 in²

9. 257.1 mm² **11.** 66.2 yd² **13.** approximately 847.2 ft² **15.** 196.1 in² **17.** $x^2 + \frac{1}{2}(6x)$ or $x^2 + 3x$ **19.** 467.4 ÷ 350 ≈ 1.34; Since only whole gallons of paint can be purchased, you will need 2 gallons of paint. At \$20 each, the cost will be 2 • \$20 or \$40. **21.** Sample answer: Add the areas of a small rectangle and a trapezoid. Area of a rectangle: 3 × 1 = 3; Area of trapezoid: $\left(\frac{1}{2} \times 6.5\,(4 + 5)\right) = 29.25$; 3 + 29.25 = 32.25. So, an approximate area is 32.25 = 2,400 or 77,400 mi². **23.** B **25.** Sample answer: about 30% of \$500 or \$150 **27.** 452.2 in²

29.  **31.** 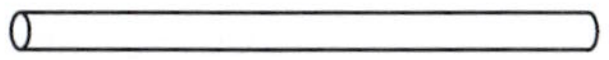

Pages 605–606 Lesson 11-7

1. square; square pyramid **3.** circle; cylinder **5.** triangle; triangular pyramid **7.** rectangle; rectangular pyramid **9.** cone **11.** trapezoid; trapezoidal prism **13.** octagon; octagonal prism **15.** triangular prism and rectangular prism **17.** rectangular prism **19.** Sample answer: A cone has only one base that is a circle. A pyramid also has only one base, but its base is a polygon. They both have only one vertex. A cone does not have any lateral faces and a pyramid has at least three lateral faces. **21.** F **23.** 102.0 m² **25.** 53° **27.** square **29.** circle

Pages 610–612 Lesson 11-8

1.

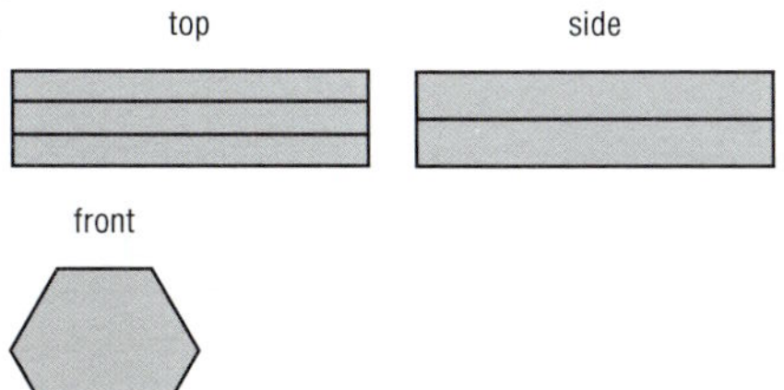

3.

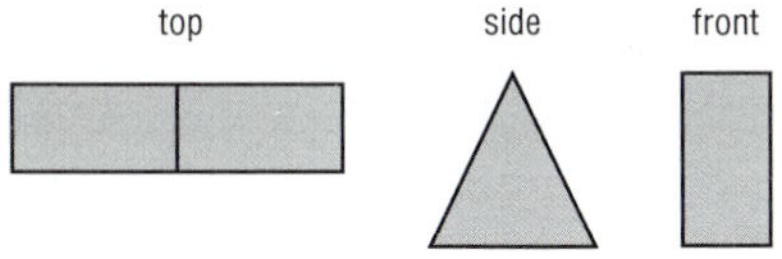

5.

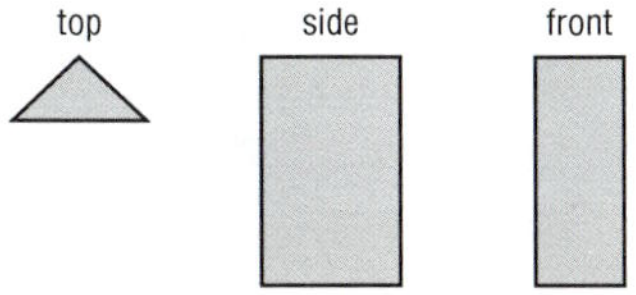

7. 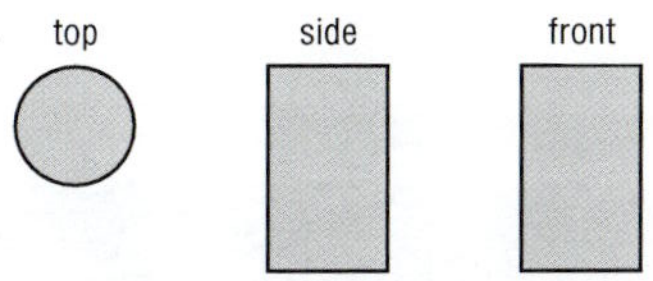

9. 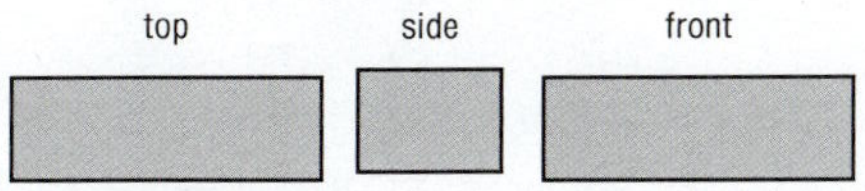

11. 

13. 

15. 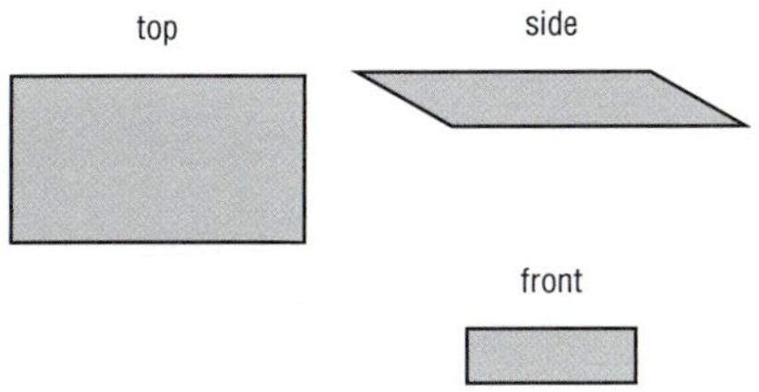

17. 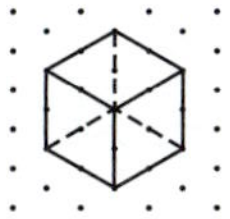

19. Sample answer:

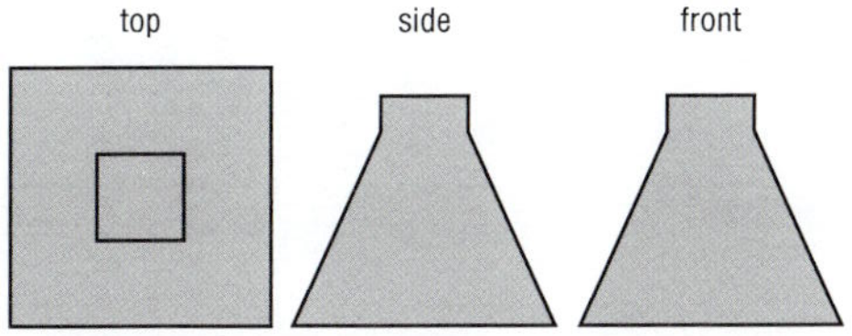

21. 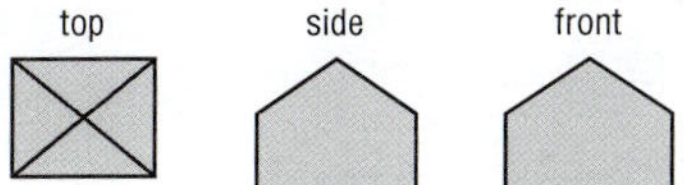

23. 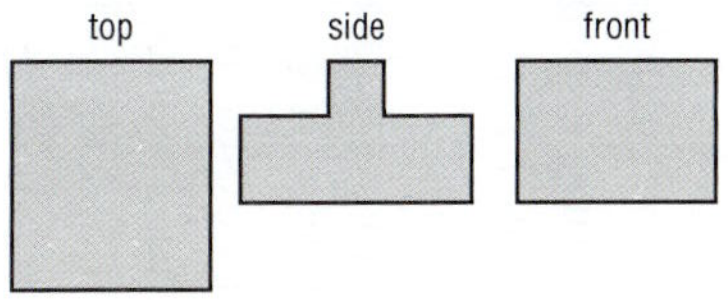

25. Sample answer:

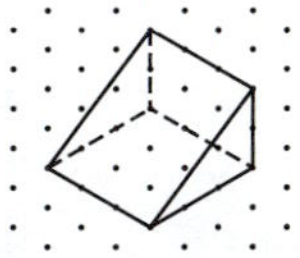

29. B **31.** sphere **33.** 96 ft^2 **35.** 112.8 in^2 **37.** \$77.39 **39.** 22 **41.** 68

Pages 616–618 ***Lesson 11-9***

1. 220 in^3 **3.** 63 yd^3 **5.** 37.5 ft^3 < 63 ft^3; second cabinet **7.** 90 ft^3 **9.** 236.3 cm^3 **11.** 108 m^3 **13.** 20.4 mm^3 **15.** 40 ft^3 > 36 ft^3, so too much was bought **17.** $166\frac{1}{4}$ yd^3 **19.** 2,157,165 ft^3 **21.** 306.52 = $19.4h$; 15.8 m **23.** Sample answer: 5 × 4 × 2 or 40 ft^3 **25.** 6 ft **27.** No; the area of Prism A is 80 in^2, and the area of Prism B is 640 in^2, which is eight times greater. **29.** D

31. 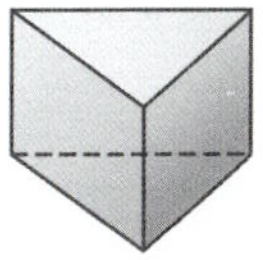

33. rectangle; rectangular prism
35. 50 mph
37. Sample answer: $5 \cdot 3^2$ or 45
39. Sample answer: $3 \cdot 2^2 \cdot 2$ or 24

Pages 620–623 ***Lesson 11-10***

1. 141.4 in^3 **3.** 617.7 ft^3 **5.** about 603.2 cm^3 **7.** 4,071.5 ft^3 **9.** 2,770.9 yd^3 **11.** 35.6 m^3 **13.** 103.4 m^3 **15.** 288.6 in^3 **17.** about 226.2 in^3 **19.** 124,642.7 m^3 **21.** d. **23.** a. **25.** 2,375 cm^3 **27.** 8 in. **29.** The volume is 8 times greater than the previous cylinder. **31.** Sample answer:

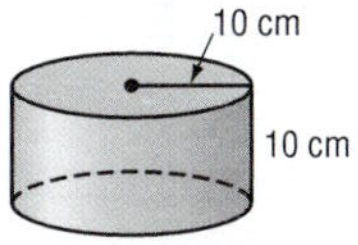

33. 1 to 4 **35.** D **37.** 152.9 m^3 **39.** Sample answer:

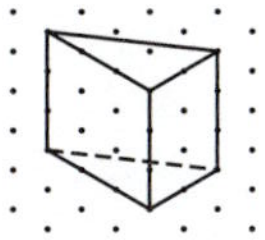

41. $\frac{1}{4}$ **43.** $\frac{5}{12}$

Pages 626–630 ***Chapter 11*** ***Study Guide and Review***

1. rectangular prism **3.** trapezoid **5.** cylinder **7.** circle **9.** 2,520 in^2 **11.** 36 ft^2 **13.** 527.3 yd^2 **15.** 75.4 in. **17.** $26\frac{2}{5}$ ft **19.** 29.8 ft **21.** 1,520.5 cm^2 **23.** 800 cakes **25.** \$105 **27.** 67.8 yd^2 **29.** triangle; triangular prism **31.** cylinder **33.** rectangular pyramid

35. 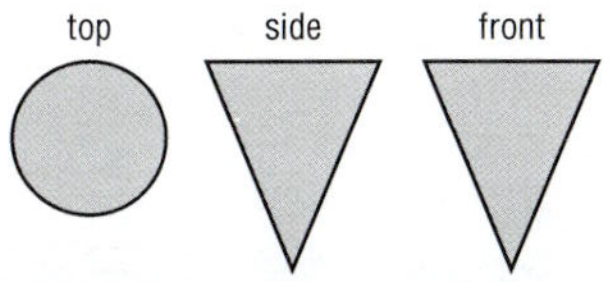

37. 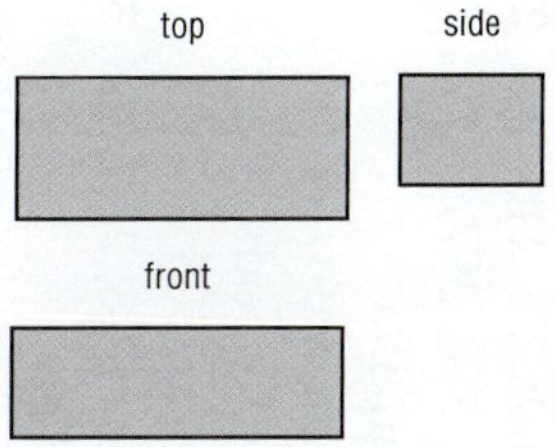

39. 639.6 in^3 **41.** 1,330 ft^3 **43.** 3,728.7 mm^3 **45.** 942 $in.^3$

Chapter 12 Geometry and Measurement

Page 635 ***Chapter 12*** ***Getting Ready***

1. 16 **3.** 169 **5.** 89 **7.** 225 **9.** 130 yr **11.** 226 **13.** 42.1 **15.** 527.8

Pages 637–639 ***Lesson 12-1***

1. 6 **3.** 9 **5.** 2.6 **7.** 7.1 **9.** 10 ft **11.** 4 **13.** 8 **15.** 11 **17.** 20 **19.** 2.8 **21.** 9.4 **23.** 23.9 **25.** 52.9 **27.** 6 **29.** 50 **31.** 81 **33.** 0.7 **35.** 1.7 **37.** 3.8 **39.** 3.17 cm **43.** Sample answer: 17, 18, 19 **45.** 2 **47.** 5 **49.** It cannot be written as a fraction. **51.** G **53.** 28.3 in^3 **55.** acute **57.** obtuse **59.** 74 **61.** 16

Pages 643–645 ***Lesson 12-2***

1. 26 mm **3.** 18.5 cm **5.** 4.0 ft **7.** 16.1 m **9.** 14.1 m **11.** 5.4 ft **13.** 2.8 yd **15.** 25 in. **17.** 5.6 mi **19.** 72.1 in. **21.** Sample answer: The plank will not fit horizontally or vertically. However, the diagonal of the doorway measures about 18 feet. So, the plank will fit through the doorway if you tilt it diagonally. **23.** about 10.4 in. **27.** G **29.** 1,413 in^3 **31.** 0.08 **33.** 2.65

Pages 646–647 ***Lesson 12-3***

1. Sample answer: making a model helps you see what is happening in the problem to help solve it. **3.** 8 cars and 4 motorcycles **5.** 47 in. **7.** $5\frac{1}{3}$ min **9.** Sample answer: The boxes could be arranged on the shelf 4 boxes wide and 5 boxes deep. **11.** $125\frac{7}{16}$ ft^2 **13.** 6 DVDs

Pages 651–653 ***Lesson 12-4***

1. 108 ft^2 **3.** Yes; the surface area of the box is 252 in^2. The surface area of the paper is 288 in^2. Since 252 in^2 < 288 in^2, she has enough paper. **5.** 314 cm^2 **7.** 833.1 mm^2 **9.** 125.4 in^2 or $124\frac{3}{8}$ in^2 **11.** 234 in^2 **13.** 243.8 ft^2 **15.** 64.5 in^2 **17.** $s = 6x^2$ **19.** Sample answer: Not all sides of the rectangular prism will be painted. The top will not be painted. The number of square feet to be painted is (18)(12) + 2(18)(6) + 2(12)(6). **21.** Surface area measures the area of the faces, and area is measured in square units. **23.** G **25.** 12.4 ft **27.** 804.2 ft^2 **29.** 145.3 yd^2

Pages 657–659 ***Lesson 12-5***

1. 88.0 mm^2 **3.** about 471.2 m^2 **5.** 1,215.8 m^2 **7.** 272.0 mm^2 **9.** 1,120.0 in^2 or $1{,}119\frac{44}{45}$ in^2 **11.** 61.3 cm^2 **13.** Sample answer: $2 \cdot 3 \cdot 4^2 + 2 \cdot 3 \cdot 4 \cdot 4$ or 192 m^2 **15.** 205.0 in^2 **17.** No; the surface area of the side of the cylinder will double, but the area of the bases will not. **19.** A cylinder with radius 6 cm and height 3 cm has a greater surface area than a cylinder with height 6 cm and radius 3 cm; Sample answer: The first cylinder has a surface area of 339.3 cm^2 while the second cylinder has a surface area of 169.6 cm^2. **21.** G **23.** 112 cm^2 **25.** 12.8 in. **27.** 7.2 cm

Pages 660–662 ***Chapter 12*** ***Study Guide and Review***

1. false; right triangle **3.** true **5.** true **7.** false; positive and negative **9.** false; cylinder **11.** 2 **13.** 7 **15.** 4 **17.** 7.8 **19.** 21.1 **21.** 11 ft **23.** 26.7 in. **25.** 29.8 ft **27.** 875 in^2 **29.** 202 yd^2 **31.** 43 ft^2 **33.** 2,261.9 in^2

Index

A

B

C

D

E

Index

K

L

M

Index

Index

Index

S

Index

U

V

W

X

Y

Index

Symbols

Number and Operations

$+$	plus or positive
$-$	minus or negative
$a \cdot b$, $a \times b$, ab or $a(b)$	a times b
$\div$	divided by
$\pm$	plus or minus
$=$	is equal to
$\neq$	is not equal to
$>$	is greater than
$<$	is less than
$\geq$	is greater than or equal to
$\leq$	is less than or equal to
$\approx$	is approximately equal to
%	percent
$a:b$	the ratio of a to b, or $\frac{a}{b}$
$0.7\overline{5}$	repeating decimal 0.75555…

Algebra and Functions

$-a$	opposite or additive inverse of a
a^n	a to the nth power
a^{-n}	$\frac{1}{a^n}$
$\lvert x \rvert$	absolute value of x
$\sqrt{x}$	principal (positive) square root of x
$f(n)$	function, f of n

Geometry and Measurement

$\cong$	is congruent to
$\sim$	is similar to
$^\circ$	degree(s)
$\overleftrightarrow{AB}$	line AB
$\overrightarrow{AB}$	ray AB
$\overline{AB}$	line segment AB
AB	length of $\overline{AB}$
⊾	right angle
$\perp$	is perpendicular to
$\parallel$	is parallel to
$\angle A$	angle A
$m\angle A$	measure of angle A
$\triangle ABC$	triangle ABC
(a, b)	ordered pair with x-coordinate a and y-coordinate b
O	origin
π	pi $\left(\text{approximately } 3.14 \text{ or } \frac{22}{7}\right)$

Probability and Statistics

$P(A)$	probability of event A

Formulas

Perimeter	square	$P = 4s$
	rectangle	$P = 2\ell + 2w$ or $P = 2(\ell + w)$
Circumference	circle	$C = 2\pi r$ or $C = \pi d$
Area	square	$A = s^2$
	rectangle	$A = \ell w$
	parallelogram	$A = bh$
	triangle	$A = \frac{1}{2}bh$
	trapezoid	$A = \frac{1}{2}h(b_1 + b_2)$
	circle	$A = \pi r^2$
Surface Area	cube	$S = 6s^2$
	rectangular prism	$S = 2\ell w + 2\ell h + 2wh$
	cylinder	$S = 2\pi rh + 2\pi r^2$
Volume	cube	$V = s^3$
	prism	$V = \ell wh$ or Bh
	cylinder	$V = \pi r^2 h$ or Bh
	pyramid	$V = \frac{1}{3}Bh$
	cone	$V = \frac{1}{3}\pi r^2 h$ or $\frac{1}{3}Bh$
Pythagorean Theorem	right triangle	$a^2 + b^2 = c^2$
Temperature	Fahrenheit to Celsius	$C = \frac{5}{9}(F - 32)$
	Celsius to Fahrenheit	$F = \frac{9}{5}C + 32$

Measurement Conversions

Length	1 kilometer (km) = 1,000 meters (m) 1 meter = 100 centimeters (cm) 1 centimeter = 10 millimeters (mm)	1 foot (ft) = 12 inches (in.) 1 yard (yd) = 3 feet or 36 inches 1 mile (mi) = 1,760 yards or 5,280 feet
Volume and Capacity	1 liter (L) = 1,000 milliliters (mL) 1 kiloliter (kL) = 1,000 liters	1 cup (c) = 8 fluid ounces (fl oz) 1 pint (pt) = 2 cups 1 quart (qt) = 2 pints 1 gallon (gal) = 4 quarts
Weight and Mass	1 kilogram (kg) = 1,000 grams (g) 1 gram = 1,000 milligrams (mg) 1 metric ton = 1,000 kilograms	1 pound (lb) = 16 ounces (oz) 1 ton (T) = 2,000 pounds
Time	1 minute (min) = 60 seconds (s) 1 hour (h) = 60 minutes 1 day (d) = 24 hours	1 week (wk) = 7 days 1 year (yr) = 12 months (mo) or 52 weeks or 365 days 1 leap year = 366 days
Metric to Customary	1 meter ≈ 39.37 inches 1 kilometer ≈ 0.62 mile 1 centimeter ≈ 0.39 inch	1 kilogram ≈ 2.2 pounds 1 gram ≈ 0.035 ounce 1 liter ≈ 1.057 quarts